THE
INTERNATIONAL ENCYCLOPEDIA
OF
CURRICULUM

Advances in Education

This is an internationally acclaimed series of Pergamon education reference works. Each volume in the series is thematically organized and aims to provide comprehensive and up-to-date coverage of its own specialist subject area. The series is being developed primarily from the well-received *International Encyclopedia of Education* using the latest electronic publishing technology for data capture, manipulation and storage of text in a form which allows fast and easy modification and updating of copy. Where appropriate a number of other volumes have been specially commissioned for the series. Volumes that are not derived from *The International Encyclopedia of Education* are indicated by an asterisk.

DUNKIN (ed.)
The International Encyclopedia of Teaching and Teacher Education

ERAUT (ed.)
The International Encyclopedia of Educational Technology

KEEVES (ed.)
Educational Research, Methodology, and Measurement: An International Handbook

POSTLETHWAITE (ed.)
The Encyclopedia of Comparative Education and National Systems of Education

PSACHAROPOULOS (ed.)
Economics of Education: Research and Studies

REYNOLDS (ed.)*
Knowledge Base for the Beginning Teacher

THOMAS (ed.)
The Encyclopedia of Human Development and Education: Theory, Research, and Studies

TITMUS (ed.)
Lifelong Education for Adults: An International Handbook

WALBERG & HAERTEL (eds.)
The International Encyclopedia of Educational Evaluation

WANG, REYNOLDS & WALBERG (eds.)* (3 volumes)
Handbook of Special Education: Research and Practice

A Related Pergamon Journal[†]
International Journal of Educational Research

Editor: Herbert J Walberg, University of Illinois, Chicago, Illinois, USA

[†]Free Specimen copy available on request.

THE

INTERNATIONAL ENCYCLOPEDIA

OF

CURRICULUM

Edited by

ARIEH LEWY

Tel Aviv University, Tel Aviv, Israel

PERGAMON PRESS

Member of Maxwell Macmillan Pergamon Publishing Corporation

OXFORD · NEW YORK · BEIJING · FRANKFURT
SÃO PAULO · SYDNEY · TOKYO · TORONTO

U.K.	Pergamon Press plc, Headington Hill Hall, Oxford OX3 0BW, England
U.S.A.	Pergamon Press, Inc., Maxwell House, Fairview Park, Elmsford, New York 10523, U.S.A.
PEOPLE'S REPUBLIC OF CHINA	Pergamon Press, Room 4037, Qianmen Hotel, Beijing, People's Republic of China
FEDERAL REPUBLIC OF GERMANY	Pergamon Press GmbH, Hammerweg 6, D-6242 Kronberg, Federal Republic of Germany
BRAZIL	Pergamon Editoria Ltda, Rua Eça de Queiros, 346, CEP 04011, Paraiso, São Paulo, Brazil
AUSTRALIA	Pergamon Press Australia Pty Ltd., P.O. Box 544, Potts Point, N.S.W. 2011, Australia
JAPAN	Pergamon Press, 5th Floor, Matsuoka Central Building, 1-7-1 Nishishinjuku, Shinjuku-ku, Tokyo 160, Japan
CANADA	Pergamon Press Canada Ltd., Suite No 271, 253 College Street, Toronto, Ontario, Canada M5T 1R5

Library of Congress Cataloging-in-Publication Data
The international encyclopedia of curriculum/edited by A. Lewy.—1st ed.
p.   cm.—(Advances in education)
1. Education—Curricula. I. Lewy, Arieh, 1923–. II. Series.
LB1570.I5676 1991
375'.0003—dc20 90-29143

British Library Cataloguing in Publication Data
The international encyclopedia of curriculum.—(Advances in education).
1. Curriculum
I. Lewy, Arieh II. Series
375.03

ISBN 0-08-041379 X

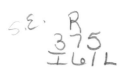

⊗ ™ The paper used in this publication meets the minimum requirements of the American National Standard for Information Sciences—Permanence of Paper for Printed Library Materials, ANSI Z39.48-1984.

Computer data file designed and computer typeset by Page Bros, Norwich

Printed in Great Britain by BPCC Wheatons Ltd, Exeter

Contents

SECTION 2 **CURRICULUM APPROACHES AND METHODS**

SECTION 3 CURRICULUM PROCESSES

SECTION 10 MATHEMATICS EDUCATION

(b) Innovative Topics

(c) Issues in Mathematics Education

Preface

Educational processes of any type cannot be fully described without referring to their curricular components. Irrespective of whether education is defined in terms of transmitting the cultural heritage of a particular society, creating favorable conditions for the growth of the individual, guiding the individual's behavior in a desired direction, or preparing the individual adequately to fulfill socially endorsed roles and tasks, the educational process itself implies dealing, both in formal and nonformal education systems, with specific items of information and knowledge, feelings, values, and skills, or in more technical terms with *curricular contents*. Problems related to selecting such content units and organizing them in a way which facilitates their meaningful treatment within the framework of the educational process in general, and in school programs in particular, constitute the subject of curriculum studies.

In this sense curriculum is as age-old as education itself. Nevertheless, curriculum studies as a domain of scholarly inquiry emerged only at the beginning of the twentieth century. As Goodlad (1985 p. 1141) noted: "Curriculum praxis is, then, an old endeavor. Curriculum praxeology—the study of curriculum-building activity—appears to be a relatively new endeavor."

It is true that references to curricular problems can be found in scholarly books about education published long ago. Thus, for example, Schubert (1980) describes Fleury's book, *The History of Choice and Method of Studies*, published in French in 1686 and then translated and published in English in 1695, as the first attempt to approach problems of curriculum in a scholarly manner. However, only from the beginning of the twentieth century has there developed an incessant stream of analytical and empirical studies examining numerous aspects of the school curriculum and attempting to systematize relevant knowledge.

The early curriculum books, such as those authored by Bobbitt (1918) and by Charters (1923), contain only relatively small sections dealing with general principles of producing school curriculum, while a substantial proportion of the space is devoted, in both cases, to demonstrating and describing the applicability of these principles to individual subjects taught in the school. The theoretical core of these early books is meager and the concern of the authors is to suggest procedures for determining the relative weight of individual subjects within the overall framework of the school program, and to select topics to be included in the syllabus of each particular subject. The scope of curriculum theory has gradually expanded to include issues such as using curricula and evaluating their adequacy and worth. Nevertheless, as Goodlad (1985) noted, the field of curriculum studies has remained amorphous and epistemologically ill-defined. There is little agreement about what pertains to its domain. In practice, the content covered in one textbook differs widely from that of another textbook, and most conceptual frameworks, which are labelled as curriculum theory, address only pieces of the whole and are far from being comprehensive.

Notwithstanding the lack of a commonly accepted comprehensive curriculum theory, it is possible to identify a common core of issues, topics, and problems, which recur in curriculum literature. Approaches to these core components of curriculum research and studies became diversified, but some of them, such as the selection and definition of educational objectives, reappear again and again, and a continually growing variety of arguments are brought up by those who support or oppose one or another way of treating this issue. Other core elements of this field, like curriculum implementation and the measurement and evaluation of implementation, have a shorter history, but over the past two decades quite an extensive literature has been generated around these topics, in which different views and approaches have been expounded, and the bearing of theories from fields like communication, innovation, and social psychology on these views and approaches has been meticulously examined. A third group of core elements of the field, like the concept of *core curriculum*, were completely redefined and gained an entirely different denotation in debates about curriculum reform in England and Wales (see Skilbeck 1984) from that which it had approximately 50 years earlier, when it was used in the context of examining the merits of another curricular innovation in the United States (see Chamberlin et al. 1942) in the context of the Eight Year Study of the Progressive Education Association (1932–1940). An encyclopedic summary of core elements sporadically appearing in the literature of the past 80 years, and of novel ideas and conceptions related to curriculum, which emerged in the wake of, and as a reaction to, the curriculum movement of the 1960s, will serve the information needs both of the practitioner and the theorist. For the practitioner it will serve as an inventory of issues and alternatives which should be taken into consideration in the process of decision making, and for the theorist it may serve as a catalyst for developing comprehensive curriculum theories on the basis of pulling together and integrating the extant part-theories.

Owing to the lack of commonly endorsed comprehensive curriculum theory at the time of creating this *Encyclopedia* it was necessary to use an empirical basis for mapping the entries to be dealt with in this book. This was done using the ERIC information base, a selected set of 14 basic textbooks and encyclopedic summaries of curriculum studies, and several well-read volumes of curriculum journals. As the first step of this mapping procedure, the Thesaurus (1982) of the ERIC system was examined and all entries dealing with issues which pertain to the domain of curriculum were marked and listed. This list was then checked and a few items which appeared in major chapter headings and indices of curriculum textbooks were added, though the survey of the curriculum journals did not generate new entries. While the compilation of the list was based on a systematic survey of relevant sources, it is not claimed that it represents an objective approach to establishing the list of the entries, since in many cases the decision as to whether an entry pertains to the domain of curriculum or not has been made on the basis of the judgment exercized by the person conducting the survey. In the case of the ERIC database, it was cross-checked to see if the Major and Minor Area designation of a particular keyword contained the curriculum category, and thus there was a possibility of obtaining an external validation for the editorial decision. Nevertheless, in numerous cases decisions reflect the views of the Editor.

At a later phase, more than 300 entries listed were clustered on the basis of analytic considerations. As a first step in this phase the entries were divided into two major groups: (a) those dealing with curriculum in general and representing theories, principles, and generalizations which cut across the boundaries of individual subjects and topics taught in schools; and (b) those which examined curricular considerations pertaining to a particular study area. As already indicated, the curriculum textbooks published during the first quarter of the twentieth century followed this pattern of division; the first section of these books presented general principles of curriculum construction, and the second section dealt with individual subjects and basic skills. With the growth in scope of curriculum theories and the diversification of views and approaches, the curriculum textbooks became devoted totally to general principles and theories and dropped the sections dealing with the application of general curricular ideas to individual subjects.

This does not mean that the field of curriculum research and study was redefined in such a way that its boundaries excluded problems related to individual study areas. In educational practice, curricular generalizations have been intensively used in making decisions concerning dilemmas related to teaching individual subjects and the curriculum literature systematically treated this topic accordingly. Moreover, from the outset of the Curriculum Movement of the 1960s subject-specific curricular theories have emerged and they have gradually constituted the major topic of single-subject related books such as Fenton (1967) in Social Studies, Harlen (1983) in Science Teaching, Freudenthal (1973) in Mathematics, and Stern (1967) in Teaching Foreign Languages. In the wake of such diversification of curriculum studies, universities in many countries established separate departments for the teaching of Science, Mathematics, Social Studies, Language, Arts, and so on in the framework of which the subject-specific curricular topics received great attention and have developed into a systematically structured body of knowledge.

The growth of subject-specific curriculum research and studies, which coincided with the establishment of university departments specifically for dealing with these topics and the launching of scholarly journals devoted mainly to curricular developments in numerous subject fields, justifies the fact that a volume summarizing the knowledge accumulated in the field of curriculum should contain a section which summarizes developments in subject-specific areas too.

The subsequent sections of this Preface describe the structure of the two main parts of the volume: Curriculum as a Domain of Scholarly Inquiry, which deals with research and studies cutting across boundaries of subjects and topics of the school program, and Specific Study Areas, which deals with subject- and topic-specific research and studies.

1. Part 1: Curriculum as a Domain of Scholarly Inquiry

Entries representing scholarly inquiry which cut across the boundaries of school subjects and topics of the school program are divided into four Sections: Conceptual Framework; Approaches and Methods; Curriculum Processes; and Curriculum Evaluation. It should be remembered that these Sections have not been identified a priori, but rather were derived from the results of an empirical attempt to classify topics dealt with in curriculum literature. In other words, the starting point of this scheme is not a theory of curriculum, but rather a survey aiming to find out what are the concerns of scholars writing about curriculum. In this respect, the approach to determining the scheme of this *Encyclopedia* was affected by the view of Schwab (1969) who urged that curriculum specialists should systematically study everyday practice and should derive generalizations of a theoretical nature from findings of empirical studies. Schwab calls attention to the dangers of "tunnel vision" which occurs when scholars view practical phenomena in the light of a single theory, disregarding the parameters of other competing theories. However, Schwab was concerned with generating curriculum knowledge, and accordingly his references to empirical studies meant observing curriculum procedures of various types, while the aim of this volume is to summarize available knowledge and not to generate new knowledge; therefore, the empirical approach of this *Encyclopedia* consists of surveying published curriculum literature.

The Sections of Part 1 also reflect Schwab's views with regard to ways of organizing knowledge. Schwab (1964) argues that domains of scholarly inquiry are characterized by certain relationships between the elements of the domain, and he refers to these relationships as *structures*. A highly structured domain of inquiry constitutes a *discipline* and the nature of a particular discipline is described by responses to three *structural* question types. The first question type is: What are the boundaries of the *domain*? By which criteria can it be decided whether a certain phenomenon, issue, problem, or dilemma belongs to a particular domain of inquiry, or is contained within the boundaries of a specified discipline? In more general terms, these questions may be referred to as definition of boundaries. The second type of question concerns itself with ways of providing evidence and proving the veracity of certain statements or generalizations. What kind of methodology is recognized as legitimate within the specific domain of inquiry? Clearly enough the method of generating knowledge in history and proving the veracity of a thesis is different from that in physics or anthropology. This group consists of questions of syntax. Finally, the third group of questions relates to the identification of basic concepts, constructs, ideas, and so on, which guide the process of inquiry and give rise to generalizations of different types. Schwab refers to them as *substantive structures*.

The major Sections of Part 1 of this *Encyclopedia* do not fully represent the three groups of structural questions suggested by Schwab, but they are strongly related to them. Section 1, Conceptual Framework, is related to what Schwab termed the *boundaries*. Section 2, Approaches and Methods, is not fully identical with what Schwab called the *syntax*; the *Methods* in the Section title refer to methods of organizing school curricula and the articles representing *Approaches* describe different attitudes to dealing with problems of curriculum inquiry. Section 3, Curriculum Processes, consists of an inventory of substantive issues to be dealt with in curriculum research and studies. These three Sections describe the unique disciplinary characteristics of curriculum inquiry and the place of curriculum inquiry within the broader context of educational research and studies. Section 4, Curriculum Evaluation, represents a bidisciplinary domain of inquiry located at the interface area of the disciplines of Curriculum and Evaluation. Some practitioners and curriculum-evaluation theorists are inclined to view the field of Curriculum Evaluation as an emerging discipline which has already established its well-defined boundaries, specified the methods of inquiry which can be effectively used for evaluating school curricula, and also defined the substantive structures or major concepts and constructs which guide the process of inquiry within this domain. Indeed, it is easier to respond to the three structural questions of boundaries, syntax, and substantive constructs as referring to Curriculum Evaluation as a field of study than as referring to Curriculum Studies in general.

A more detailed characterization of Curriculum as a Domain of Scholarly Inquiry appears in the Introduction to the first part of the book as well as in the separate introductions to each of the four Sections in Part 1.

2. Part 2: Specific Study Areas

Research and studies dealing with curricular issues related to Specific Study Areas such as scientific disciplines and vocation or daily-life oriented skills constitute a substantial proportion of the curriculum literature. Although the majority of research is of an applicative nature, in most sections of this area, as in the field of science teaching and teaching foreign languages, attempts to develop theories and models that are uniquely applicable to a single subject have been made. Therefore, a summary of curriculum literature which does not contain information about ideas and findings generated in the field of Specific Study Areas would present only a partial picture of the domain of curriculum studies.

Findings and ideas related to Specific Study Areas are of interest not only to those who are directly involved in dealing with curricular issues of the respective study areas, but also to curriculum practitioners and theorists in general. Those who provide professional services in the field of curriculum have to make decisions about allocating time and resources to programs in various study areas. Educational management staff as well as district and school-level curriculum coordinators have to make decisions about course offerings within the school and course requirements for graduation. To be able to deal with such problems effectively, it is necessary to acquire knowledge about the unique characteristics of each study area and become familiar with a broad variety of innovative curricular topics which have gained a legitimate status as study areas in various educational systems. Additionally, practitioners who are specialists in a certain discipline have to acquire basic knowledge about curricula in other subjects in order to be able to participate in decisions which affect the whole school program or cut across the boundaries of several study areas. Finally, curriculum theorists may use findings of subject-specific studies for systematizing knowledge and developing general or subject-specific curricular theories. To respond to these needs, Part 2 of this *Encyclopedia* is devoted to a summary of knowledge generated in special study areas.

The decision was taken to structure Part 2 according to the traditionally accepted division of scholarly disciplines in schools and institutions of higher education. Although attempts have been made in the past to use various innovative models and schemes for classifying school programs, it seemed more appropriate to use the traditional subject classification schemes in this *Encyclopedia*. There are three reasons for this. First, the innovative schemes, in most cases, have not been successful in educational contexts. Thus, for example, the Assessment of Performance Unit in England and Wales tried to use a scheme of six general lines of development for examining students' achievements in schools. They decided to carry out assessment projects in the following areas: language, mathematics, science, personal and social development, aesthetic development, and physical development. Eventually it turned out that it was not possible to develop assessment programs in these areas, and it was decided to assess achievements in areas which are not substantially different from those which characterize the traditional division of the school program (Gipps and Goldstein 1983). Second, the relevant knowledge is generated and organized so that it is easy to prepare summaries according to groups of traditional school subjects. Finally, in a substantial proportion of educational systems, teaching is organized according to the traditional grouping of subjects and therefore users will perceive subject-specific information as more relevant to their needs than information structured in any other form. Part 2 of this *Encyclopedia* comprises the following eight Sections: Language Arts; Foreign Language Studies; Humanities Curricula; Arts Curricula; Social Studies; Mathematics Education; Science Education Programs; and Physical Education. A more detailed introduction to the Specific Study Areas appears at the beginning of Part 2 and a special introduction to each Section spells out the unique structure of the respective Sections. Beyond the traditional subjects contained in each Section there also appears a list of special topics which represent new study areas. The majority of them do not have the status of a scholarly discipline, but nevertheless they do appear in the course offerings of numerous educational systems. Thus, for example, in the Section on Social Studies, aside from coverage of traditional subjects such as history, geography, and psychology which are well-defined disciplines of scholarly inquiry, study areas such as peace studies, human rights education, daily living skills, and so on which are not considered to be scholarly disciplines are also covered. In the Section covering Science Education Programs study areas such as scientific literacy and energy education which are not scholarly disciplines, but have become popular areas of study, are also covered.

3. Acknowledgements

Many people have given invaluable assistance and encouragement in the production of this *Encyclopedia*. *The International Encyclopedia of Education: Research and Studies* and, ultimately, this Volume, owe their birth to the imagination of Robert Maxwell. Torsten Husén and Neville Postlethwaite, the Editors-in-Chief of the parent encyclopedia, together with the Editorial Board and Barbara Barrett, the Editorial Director at Pergamon Press, were largely responsible for overseeing the development of that remarkable work.

For their assistance on this encyclopedia, I wish to thank W. H. Schubert of the University of Illinois, J. Kilpatrick of the University of Georgia, and S. Eden, the former Director of the Israel Curriculum Center. I am also profoundly grateful to Pergamon Press for the excellent work done on this *Encyclopedia*. In particular, I would like to thank Joan Burks, Senior Publishing Editor, for her editorial management of this project and Alison Dunnett, Editorial Assistant, who did the more detailed editorial work at Pergamon.

I received help from many friends and colleagues around the world who were always available for encouragement and advice and am grateful for the cooperation which I received from Tel Aviv University. In particular, I wish to express my gratitude to E. C. Short of Pennsylvania State University, who encouraged me to proceed with the preparation of this *Encyclopedia*.

Finally, I should like to thank the Authors, without whose commitment, expertise, and enthusiasm, this *Encyclopedia* could not have been produced.

Bibliography

Beauchamp G A 1961 *Curriculum Theory*. Kagg Press, Wilmette, Illinois
Bobbitt F 1918 *The Curriculum*. Houghton Mifflin, Boston, Massachusetts
Brubacher J S 1947 *History of Problems of Education*. McGraw-Hill, New York
Chamberlin C D, Chamberlin E, Drought N E, Scott W E 1942 *Did they Succeed in College? The Follow-up Study of Graduates of Thirty High Schools*, Adventures in American Education, Vol. 4. Harper, New York
Charters W W 1923 *Curriculum Construction*. Macmillan, New York
Davis O L (ed.) 1976 *Perspectives on Curriculum Development*. Association for Supervision and Curriculum Development, Washington, DC
ERIC Clearinghouse on Higher Education 1982 *Thesaurus of ERIC Descriptors*, 9th edn. Oryx Press, Phoenix, Arizona
Fenton E 1967 *The New Social Studies*. Holt, Rinehart, and Winston, New York
Fleury C 1965 *The History of Choice and Methods of Studies*. Keble, London
Freudenthal H 1973 *Mathematics as an Educational Task*. Reidel, Dordrecht
Frey K, Achtenhagen F, Haft H 1975 *Curriculum-Handbuch*. Piper, Munich
Gipps C, Goldstein H 1983 *Monitoring Children: An Evaluation of the Assessment Performance Unit*. Heinemann, London
Goodlad J I 1979 *Curriculum Inquiry: The Study of Curriculum Practice*. McGraw-Hill, New York
Goodlad J I 1985 Curriculum as a field of study. In: Husén T, Postlethwaite T N (eds.) 1985 *The International Encyclopedia of Education*. Pergamon, Oxford, pp. 1141–44
Harlen W (ed.) 1983 *New Trends in Primary School Science Teaching*, Vol. 1. UNESCO, Paris
Pratt D 1980 *Curriculum, Design and Development*. Harcourt, Brace, and Janovich, New York
Robinson S B 1971 *Bildungsreform als Revision des Curriculum*, 3rd edn. Luchterhand, Neuwied
Saylor J G, Alexander W M 1954 *Curriculum Planning for Better Learning and Teaching*. Holt, Rinehart, and Winston, New York
Schubert W H 1980 *Curriculum Books: The First Eighty Years*. University Press of America, Lanham, Maryland

Schwab J J 1964 Structure of the disciplines: Meanings and significances. In: Ford G W, Pugno L (eds.) 1964 *The Structure of Knowledge and Curriculum.* Rand McNally, Chicago

Schwab J J 1969 The practical: A language for curriculum. *Sch. Rev.* 78:1–23

Skilbeck M 1984 *School Based Curriculum Development.* Harper and Row, London

Smith B O, Stanley W O, Shores J H 1950 *Fundamentals of Curriculum Development.* Harcourt, Brace, and World, New York

Stenhouse L 1975 *An Introduction to Curriculum Research and Development.* Heinemann, London

Stern H H 1967 *Foreign Languages in Primary School: The Teaching of Foreign or Second Languages to Young Children.* Oxford University Press, Oxford

Taba H 1962 *Curriculum Development: Theory and Practice.* Harcourt, Brace, and World, New York

Tanner D, Tanner L N 1975 *Curriculum Development: Theory and Practice.* Macmillan, New York

Tyler R 1949 *Basic Principles of Curriculum and Instruction.* University of Chicago Press, Chicago, Illinois

February 1991

ARIEH LEWY
Tel Aviv, Israel

Part 1

Curriculum as a Domain
of
Scholarly Inquiry

Part 1

Curriculum as a Domain
of
Scholarly Inquiry

Introduction

Curriculum as a Field of Study

1. Curriculum Praxis and Praxeology

Human beings have created curricula—that is, schedules of work and courses of study—down through the ages. These have ranged from specified rites of circumcision to prescribed programs for a nation's schools. Curriculum praxis is, then, an old endeavor.

Curriculum praxeology—the study of curriculum-building activity—appears to be a relatively new endeavor. The emergence of curriculum as a field of study sufficient to attract generations of devotees and stimulate a formal literature is a twentieth-century development. This does not mean, however, that there were not previous attempts to be self-conscious about the curriculum development process to the point of passing along whatever legacies might be useful for those to follow. Schubert (1980) identified Fleury's *The History of Choice and Methods of Studies* (1695) as the earliest curriculum book.

The advancement of industrialization during the late 1800s and into the twentieth century brought with it a decline in the role of the home and increased attention to the role of the school. Consequently, the nature of the subject matter to be taught and the values to be represented became matters of particular attention. There emerged a sustained concern with the nature of curricula and, accompanying it, a literature of curriculum making sufficient to mark a distinct field of study (Cremin 1971). Its legitimacy was established in the United States with the appearance in 1927 of a yearbook prepared by a committee of the National Society for the Study of Education which sought to pull together the extant ideas about constructing curricula (Rugg 1927). Although the volume of writings produced in subsequent years appears to have been greater in the United States than in other countries, there were parallel developments elsewhere, particularly in the Western countries. Ultimately, interest among governments and educators in understanding as well as improving curriculum planning processes became virtually worldwide, as demonstrated by the International Seminar for Advanced Training and Curriculum Development and Innovation, which brought together in Gränna, Sweden, during the summer of 1971, teams of curriculum workers representing more than 20 countries (Bloom 1971).

This is not, however, an essay on the history of curriculum as a field of study. Preceding paragraphs are intended, rather, to make the point that curriculum praxis is very old while curriculum praxeology, at a level of intensity at least, is very new. The balance of the article is directed almost exclusively to sorting out the nature and status of this field.

2. Problems in Curriculum Definition

Even though the field presumably exists (or else why are there departments and professors of curriculum in so many schools and colleges of education?), it remains elusive and its epistemology is ill-defined. One explanation for these shortcomings is that ongoing processes of curriculum development consume an extraordinary amount of time and energy. Professors of curriculum and specialists in curriculum development inevitably are drawn into these processes; they have little time for and, often, interest in systematically contemplating them. Further, there is little agreement on where curriculum matters leave off and all the rest of educating begins; some who call themselves curriculum theorists maintain that the distinction is specious. Not surprisingly, then, there are many different definitions of what a curriculum is and, therefore, what curriculum as a field of study is. Obviously, it is necessary to study different and many more things when curriculum is defined as "all the experiences one has under the jurisdiction of a school" rather than "a course of study."

3. Curriculum Literature

The amorphous character of the field is reflected in the literature. First, very few books carry the word "theory" in the title. One of the best known has straightforwardly carried the title *Curriculum Theory* through four editions (Beauchamp 1981). But it is a book primarily about the processes and issues of theory building. It neither systematically critiques extant theories nor builds one. Perhaps this is because, on one hand, there is so little of a theoretical nature available and what is available addresses only pieces of the whole, and, on the other hand, constructing a theory is so difficult that prescriptions have to be substituted. Indeed, people have chosen to prescribe even while lacking descriptions of the phenomena, a necessary but not sufficient first step in developing the understanding on which sound prescription, practice, and theory depend (Walker 1973). It was Schwab (1970) who brought the "theorists" up short with his admonition that they talked about theory instead of engaging in the studies of everyday practice upon which theoretical understanding ultimately might be built.

Theory is only part of a field of study, however. The central ingredient is a set of topics that students of the field must address almost inescapably in common. These are "commonplaces." Specialists in the field of human learning, for example, address such commonplaces as motivation, retention, and transfer and include them in their theories. Data from *A Study of Schooling* (Goodlad et al. 1979b) addressed 16 commonplaces of schools which might very well constitute the ingredients of schooling as a field of study: teaching practices, content or subject matter, instructional materials, physical environment, activities, human resources, evaluation, time, organization, communications, decision making, leadership, goals, issues and problems, implicit (or "hidden") curriculum, and controls or restraints. Schools possess these elements in common. The ways these elements manifest themselves and might alternatively manifest themselves in schools constitute appropriate inquiry for the field of schooling. Some of these are curricular commonplaces and, therefore, subject matter for the field of curriculum.

There is substantial lack of agreement on these curricular commonplaces. They are not to be found laid out in a curriculum textbook. In fact, the subject matter differs so much from textbook to textbook that one wonders whether the authors are addressing a common field, let alone commonplaces within a single field. Consequently, there is a disturbingly noncumulative character to curriculum as a field of study. Recent proponents of behavioral objectives as a basis for engineering curricula, such as Mager (1962), seem unaware of the almost identical enthusiasm of Bobbitt (1924) and Charters (1924) several decades earlier. This noncumulative characteristic is in part a product, too, of the degree to which curriculum making, the subject of curriculum praxeology, is a political process. To get their ideas into the political arena, specialists in the field become advocates of their views on some timely element, thereby tending to obscure the fact that balanced curriculum inquiry and balanced curriculum practice encompass many elements. As a result, there are today practitioners worldwide who firmly believe that setting precise objectives is not only the necessary first step in all curriculum planning but also that it provides the criteria for every other curricular decision. They seem not to understand that there are commonplaces other than goals and objectives with which it is possible to begin, and that ends are insufficient criteria for justifying means.

In the United States, several publications appearing between 1949 and 1962 serve collectively to provide a reasonably comprehensive set of curricular commonplaces and, therefore, to define the nature and scope of curriculum as a field of study. These are: *Basic Principles of Curriculum and Instruction* (Tyler 1949), *Toward Improved Curriculum Theory* (Herrick and Tyler 1950), *Fundamentals of Curriculum Development* (Smith et al. 1950), *Collected Papers and Source Materials on Curriculum Operations and Structure* (Herrick 1962), and *Curriculum Development: Theory and Practice* (Taba 1962). Explicitly or implicitly, all of these address four macrocurricular commonplaces: goals, learning activities, organization, and evaluation. Tyler's formulation of these into four basic questions to be answered in developing curricula has influenced curriculum specialists around the world. Not all of them would agree with the way Tyler structures questions and subquestions in the so-called "Tyler rationale" but it is almost impossible to deal with curricular issues comprehensively, whatever a person's philosophical perspective, without discussing the four commonplaces.

They are dealt with more implicitly than explicitly in the work of Smith et al. (1950). Their added contribution introduces the significance of the philosophical, political, and social context within which curricular decisions are made. Reading their book, the reader comes to the inevitable conclusion that, although a school's curriculum, for example, contains the results of decisions, the study of curricula must embrace the perspectives and processes contributing to these decisions. The proceedings of the 1950 conference edited by Herrick and Tyler effectively add to the substantive dimensions of curriculum inquiry the importance of human elements in the process of planning curricula.

Herrick's particular contribution was to the more microcurricular commonplaces of curriculum study. He focused on the problems of fusing organized subject matter, knowledge of the learning process, and the special characteristics of learners so as to create what he called "organizing centers"—focal points for drawing students into the learning. This was to be done sequentially, with each successive organizing center building around a theme, skill, concept, or value serving as an organizing element. Herrick made visible and helped clarify curricular commonplaces such as continuity, sequence, and scope.

Taba's work successfully addresses and juxtaposes domains of inquiry not commonly covered by the others. Goodlad identified three kinds of phenomena embraced by curriculum as a field of study:

> The first is *substantive* and has to do with goals, subject matter, materials, and the like—the commonplaces of any curriculum. Inquiry is into their nature and worth. The second is *political–social*. Inquiry involves the study of all those human processes through which some interests come to prevail over others so that these ends and means rather than others emerge. The third is *technical–professional*. Curriculum inquiry examines those processes of group or individual engineering, logistics, and evaluation through which curricular are improved, installed, or replaced. (Goodlad 1979)

The substantive commonplaces appear to persist and hence to warrant the designation, "common," whether it is curricula for a nation's schools or for the children of a given school that are being addressed. But the actors change, as do the political–social processes and the technical–professional requirements and demands. Consequently, if these two types of domain constitute part of curriculum as a field of study, then a single definition of curriculum will not suffice. There are curricula for entire educational systems, institutions, and classes (Goodlad and Richter 1966). There are curricula experienced by individual students (Tyler and Klein 1973). They require differing definitions but inquiry into them constitutes part of what curriculum as a field of study is.

The perceptions and conceptions characterizing the study of a field should both mirror and project beyond practice. Above all, they should guide the study of practice. In endeavoring to study the curricula of elementary and secondary schools in the United States, Goodlad and his colleagues reported that they received relatively little help from the literature. They found no convenient list of commonplaces. Tyler's questions proved useful, once the verbs, "should" or "should be" were changed to "are" or "does." For example, "does" was substituted for "should" in the question: "What educational purposes *does* the educational institution seek to attain?" It is necessary to be very precise about what is chosen for use as evidence regarding the condition or state of curricular commonplaces. Earlier conceptions of curriculum as a field were modified as a result of this process of inquiry (Goodlad et al. 1979a).

This observation leads back full circle to the paucity of even the descriptive research needed to validate much of the speculation that passes for theory in this field. Huebner (1966) has argued eloquently that the study of curriculum is the heart and soul of the study of education. There are growing signs that curricular phenomena are increasingly becoming the focus of disciplined analysis from different perspectives, especially the sociological (Eggleston 1977). By the turn of the century, given sustained interest in such inquiry, curriculum as a field of study might well have come of age.

Bibliography

Beauchamp G A 1981 *Curriculum Theory*. 4th edn. Peacock, Itasca, Illinois
Bloom B S 1971 *The Report of the International Seminar for Advanced Training in Curriculum Development and*

Innovation, Gränna, Sweden, July 5–August 14. International Association for the Evaluation of Educational Achievement, Stockholm

Bobbitt J F 1924 *How to Make a Curriculum*. Houghton Mifflin, Boston, Massachusetts

Charters W W 1924 *Curriculum Construction*. Macmillan, New York

Cremin L A 1971 Curriculum-making in the United States. *Teach. Coll. Rec.* 73: 207–12

Eggleston J 1977 *The Sociology of the School Curriculum*. Routledge and Kegan Paul, London

Goodlad J I 1979 The scope of the curriculum field. In: Goodlad J I et al. 1979 *Curriculum Inquiry: The Study of Curriculum Practice*. McGraw-Hill, New York, pp. 17–41

Goodlad J I, Richter M N Jr. 1966 *The Development of a Conceptual System for Dealing with Problems of Curriculum and Instruction*. Cooperative Research Program, United States Office of Education, Project No. 454, University of California, Los Angeles, California

Goodlad J I, Klein M F, Tye K A 1979a The domains of curriculum and their study. In: Goodlad J I et al. 1979 *Curriculum Inquiry: The Study of Curriculum Practice*. McGraw-Hill, New York, pp. 43–76

Goodlad J I, Sirotnik A, Overman B C 1979b An overview of "A Study of Schooling." *Phi Delta Kappan* 61 (3): 174–78

Herrick V E 1962 *Collected Papers and Source Materials on Curriculum Operations and Structure*. College Printing and Typing, Madison, Wisconsin

Herrick V E, Tyler R W (eds.) 1950 *Toward Improved Curriculum Theory*. University of Chicago Press, Chicago, Illinois

Huebner D 1966 Curriculum as a field of study. In: Robison H F (ed.) 1966 *Precedents and Promise in the Curriculum Field*. Teachers College Press, New York

Mager R F 1962 *Preparing Instructional Objectives*. Fearon, Palo Alto, California

Rugg H O 1927 *The Foundations of Curriculum Making*. Twenty-sixth Yearbook of the National Society for the Study of Education, Part II. Public School Publishing, Bloomington, Illinois

Schubert W H 1980 *Curriculum Books: The First Eighty Years: Context, Commentary and Bibliography*. University Press of America, Lanham, Maryland

Schwab J J 1970 *The Practical: A Language for Curriculum*. National Education Association, Washington, DC

Smith B O, Stanley W O, Shores J H 1950 (rev. edn. 1957) *Fundamentals of Curriculum Development*. World Book, Yonkers-on-Hudson, New York

Taba H 1962 *Curriculum Development: Theory and Practice*. Harcourt, Brace and World, New York

Tyler L L, Klein M F 1973 *Not Either–Or*. Paper delivered at the Annual Meeting of the American Educational Research Association, New Orleans

Tyler R W 1949 *Basic Principles of Curriculum and Instruction*. University of Chicago Press, Chicago, Illinois

Walker D F 1973 What curriculum research? *J. Curric. Stud.* 5: 58–72

J. I. Goodlad

Section 1

Conceptual Framework

Overview

Curriculum is a massive, comprehensive, ill-defined field. Any effort to conceptualize it is necessarily arbitrary. This Section attempts to do so through the identification and development of three subsections: (a) The Domain of Curriculum Studies, (b) Curriculum Components, and (c) Factors Affecting Curriculum.

1. The Domain of Curriculum Studies

Section 1(a), The Domain of Curriculum Studies, provides the reader with some understanding of the broad terrain covered by those who seek to define the curriculum field and conduct curriculum inquiry. There is no single definition and so there is no single line of inquiry.

In the first article in Section 1(a), Goodlad provides a largely historical perspective on the emergence of *Curriculum as a Field of Study*. He addresses the difficulty of agreeing on commonplaces demarcating the field and concludes with the phenomena generally embraced by those who study the curriculum domain.

The next article, *Definitions of Curriculum*, identifies nine rather discrete definitions of the term *curriculum*, and bears out the diversity in its use as a concept. Connelly and Lantz suggest two major dimensions for classifying curriculum definitions appearing in the professional literature: (a) the "means and ends" dimension which focuses on learning experiences and its relationship to outcomes, and (b) the "existential–personal" dimension which distinguishes between systems of knowledge organized according to subject matter and the involvement of the learner in the studies.

Differing conceptions of curriculum inescapably lead to differing theoretical approaches, especially when these are derived from well-established disciplines rather than from direct observation of curricular phenomena. In his article *Curriculum Theory*, Hameyer refers to these as referential theories—theories derived from disciplines in the behavioral sciences such as organizational, sociological, and political theories. He identifies the major topics in curriculum theories, namely, how curricula are developed and how people interact within the framework of curriculum systems. His article gives special attention to theories of curriculum legitimation.

Hameyer's article is followed by four articles which examine the meaning of curriculum from differing philosophical perspectives. Von Glasersfeld highlights two principles of constructivism which have bearings on curriculum: (a) that knowledge is not passively received but is created and built upon by the learner, and (b) that cognition is adaptive, serving to organize the experienced, not merely already-discovered ontological realities. Next, Watkins describes the implications of the social reconstructionist movement which emerged in the United States in the 1930s. The movement advocated a *collectivist* society, claiming that the capitalist system was the source of human misery, unemployment, and divisiveness. It claimed that schools should participate in the reshaping of society to realize education's true mission. To achieve this goal, schools must adopt a curriculum sufficiently critical of the old social order, while supportive of new collectivism.

Finally, Pinar provides a summary of the ideas characterizing the reconceptualist movement in curriculum that challenged, in particular, the so-called rational, linear approach. Reconceptualism enjoyed a lineage with Neo-Marxism. Gordon describes the Neo-Marxist view of knowledge as cultural capital. Through middle-class language and middle-class biased subjects, the dominant social strata enjoy the privilege of determining who will be denied and who will have access to this knowledge capital.

Curriculum theorists have argued that there is an implicit curriculum of built-in values, norms, and expectations which is at least equal in importance to the explicit curriculum of topics for study. Vallance addresses this as the *Hidden Curriculum*, namely practices and outcomes of schooling which are not stated in curriculum guides but which are nonetheless part of the school experience.

As stated at the beginning of this Introduction, the breadth of the curriculum field spawns a wide range of research activity, some of which barely overlaps. Jenkins attempts a classification of types from the descriptive to action research accompanying efforts to change or revise curricula. There are studies in the policy realm ranging from those describing what exists to those seeking to guide the formation of new policies. Schubert distinguishes between empirical–analytical students and the critical approach. The former deal with the rational aspects of social reality, employing the hermeneutic paradigm of interpreting phenomena. The alternative critical paradigm assumes the necessity of critiquing the economic, political, and cultural context and its impact on the school curriculum, particularly in regard to discrimination on the basis of gender, social class, or race.

2. Curriculum Components

To the layperson, the term *curriculum* means a course of studies and the materials accompanying it. Not surprisingly, there is considerable research activity around this definition. It is to educational materials used in schools that special interest groups look in seeking to determine whose interests are dominant or neglected. Curriculum materials embody values, decisions regarding what to teach, and often, a conception of how learning proceeds.

Section 1(b), Curriculum Components, deals with studies of the tangible components of prescribed curricula. These components are the end products of curricular intentions prescribed for school and other programs such as syllabi, textbooks, workbooks, teachers' guides, and manipulables such as blocks, flash cards, and so on. These materials have been enriched but not replaced by films, filmstrips, videotapes and cassettes, television programs, and computerized learning systems.

In this Section, research related to objects which are the major components of curricula is dealt with in a cluster of articles, each one summarizing studies related to one particular component. Pratt describes the nature and the role of the *Curriculum Rationale*. A detailed statement of the rationale usually appears in the syllabus booklet and it refers to principles which justify the curriculum. Eash views the *Syllabus* as a means of controlling the content of the curriculum and as a way of communicating a message from the authorities to the textbook writers.

Textbooks are usually viewed as the most influential components of the curriculum. Researchers claim that 80 percent of classroom activities are determined by what is contained in the textbook. Articles in this Section by Westbury and by Armbruster and Anderson deal with a variety of problems related to the approval, diffusion, and utilization of textbooks and with evaluating their quality. McNeil differentiates between *Teachers' Guides* which are highly prescriptive and those which adopt a choice strategy. Teachers want guides but research is needed, he claims, on how guides influence teacher behavior and pupil achievement.

Quite frequently, materials are arranged in packages containing a great variety of curriculum artifacts. Some curriculum packages disseminated in the United States advertize as many as 200 curriculum items. Baker describes *Curriculum Packages* as having a self-instructional flavor and, consequently, as somewhat "teacher free." Frequently, curriculum packages contain resources for study, such as historical documents or materials for experimentation. Thomas, in his article on *Enrichment and Supplementary Materials*, deals with those curriculum components which come to serve learners with special needs (like the gifted and the slow learner), or to extend the scope of studies by adding information of local flavor, or specifying cross-disciplinary links for certain issues and topics.

Among the electronic communication devices, computers and television are dealt with in separate articles. The unique functions of computers in education are examined by Salomon. He points out the capability of computers to use a variety of symbol systems, ranging from printed words to dynamic schemes, from graphs to musical notation. Computers can be used for the delivery of prepackaged programs or in an interactive mode. Rockman then describes a variety of approaches to using television for transmitting the school curriculum. Television may be highly coordinated with requirements specified in the syllabus, but it may also be used as an enrichment component of the program. High expectations that the utilization of educational television programs will alleviate the problem of teacher shortage have caused much disappointment. Television cannot be used as a teacher surrogate. It can be used effectively in the class with the supervision and guidance of classroom teachers.

3. Factors Affecting Curriculum

Section 1(c), Factors Affecting Curriculum, makes the point that there is much more to curriculum as a field of study than the end products of the process that produces curriculum materials. There are competing ideologies, legal considerations, and processes, bureaucratic regulations, monetary restraints, and other factors that impinge on and to a considerable degree determine what is taught. The articles appearing in this Section can be grouped around themes such as the knowledge to be acquired, the societal context and the values that dominate it, and the behavioral processes of acquiring knowledge.

Two articles focus on the nature of knowledge. First, Elkana examines the implications of the *Explosion of Knowledge* on the school curriculum. He distinguishes between two meanings of this term. On one hand, a rapid growth of encyclopedic information takes place, which raises questions of how to organize, select, and communicate knowledge. On the other hand, in a democratic society each person needs to have a basic knowledge about a broad variety of issues, such as labor relations, international finance, political ideologies, nuclear disarmament, energy, water desalination, epidemics, and so on in order to form an opinion and to participate in social decision-making processes. Clandinin and Connelly's article, *Personal Knowledge*, approaches the issue of knowledge from the point of view of examining the preconceptions, and frequently misconceptions, of persons (i.e., students and teachers) participating in the teaching–learning process. These preconceptions and misconceptions redirect the curricular intentions of those outside of school who prescribe curricula.

Society as a factor affecting curriculum is dealt with in several articles. Skilbeck examines economic and sociocultural factors. Economic commentators and analysts approach curriculum in two different ways: first, the deterministic way—minimizing or even disregarding the impact of pedagogical and ideological factors on the curriculum, and emphasizing the impact of underlying economic values; and second, the critical way, in which the central theme is lack of efficiency of the schools according to economic criteria.

Lamm's article addresses *Educational Ideologies*. Lamm defines ideologies as cognitive structures containing interdependent beliefs, views, principles, and myths which reflect the preferences and interests of a particular group in the political, social, moral, and religious spheres of society. Ideologies may act as forcing factors which impinge on the activities of educators. Democracy, liberalism, nationalism, socialism, and so on which hold sway in society are, in the final analysis, powerful determinants of the goals, content, and even methods of education and schooling.

The legal system, another manifestation of prevailing social values, and its impact on curriculum are examined by Van Geel. Finally, the educational policies which regulate the distribution of decision-making power between central administrative bodies and local and school authorities are addressed by Hughes.

Factors dealing with the process of acquiring knowledge constitute the third set of topics in this Section. The articles are on educational psychology, cognitive psychology, and information technology. Tanner examines the impact of learning and developmental theories on the curriculum. Haertel argues that psychological models must be specific for school subjects, in order to take account of the distinct structure of knowledge in different disciplines. The mind should be understood as processing various types of content in different ways. The processes of language and its syntax may be quite different from those of spatial images or of the aromas of flowers. Chen and Oren examine the impact of innovation in informational technology on learning. Townsend highlights the impact of four institutions that bring together political authorities and managers, namely courts, budgets, commissions, and political parties.

To sum up, these articles reveal the scope of the field of curriculum, the definitional problems arising out of the breadth and diversity of the field, and the futility of searching for a single theory of curriculum.

A. Lewy and J. I. Goodlad

Conceptual Framework

Definitions of Curriculum: An Introduction

F. M. Connelly and O. C. Lantz

This introduction reviews the origin and definition of the term "curriculum". A wide variety of definitions exists in the literature. Basically, the definition of curriculum varies depending on how a particular author conducts his or her work. A selected list of definitions is presented to illustrate the diversity. It is shown that the diversity of definitions may be understood as falling along two dimensions: means–ends and existential–personal. A series of rules for the recovery of curriculum meaning is presented, based on the topics, targets, and perspectives of curriculum writers and speakers. Finally, the discrepancy between the prescribed and actual curriculum is discussed and limitations to the use of curricula in school reform are considered.

1. Definitions of Curriculum

The Latin root for the word "curriculum" means "race-course". Following this origin, the most common definition of curriculum is a course of subject matter studies (see *Subject Matter*). However, this notion has been widely criticized and frequently modified and replaced in the modern curriculum literature. Currently, there is no widely accepted definition of the term. Its definition varies with the concepts that a researcher or practitioner uses in his or her curricular thinking and work. There is, therefore, no way of specifically defining curriculum outside of the context of a particular study, paper, presentation, or policy document under discussion. Some writers stipulate their working definition while others define the term by implication in what they say and do. Definition flows from the concept in use.

2. A Diversity of Uses of the Term "Curriculum"

The following list of quoted definitions is presented to illustrate different emphases in the definition of curriculum. The list is not complete, nor does it reflect the range of definitions. The purpose of the list is to demonstrate the existing diversity of uses of the term and to create a backdrop to subsequent sections of this paper. Nine definitions follow:

(a) A sequence of potential experiences is set up in the school for the purpose of disciplining children and youth in group ways of thinking and acting. This set of experiences is referred to as the curriculum (Smith et al. 1957).

(b) All the experiences a learner has under the guidance of the school (Foshay 1969).

(c) A general over-all plan of the content or specific materials of instruction that the school should offer the student by way of qualifying him for graduation or certification or for entrance into a professional or vocational field (Good 1959).

(d) We hold that curriculum is a methodological inquiry exploring the range of ways in which the subject matter elements of teacher, student, subject, and milieu can be seen (Westbury and Steimer 1971).

(e) Curriculum is the life and program of the school . . . an enterprise in guided living; the curriculum becomes the very stream of dynamic activities that constitute the life of your people and their elders (Rugg 1947).

(f) A curriculum is a plan for learning (Taba 1962).

(g) The planned and guided learning experiences and intended learning- outcomes, formulated through the systematic reconstruction of knowledge and experience, under the auspices of the school, for the learner's continuous and wilful growth in personal–social competence (Tanner and Tanner 1975).

(h) Curriculum must consist essentially of disciplined study in five great areas: (i) command of the mother tongue and the systematic study of grammar, literature, and writing; (ii) mathematics; (iii) sciences; (iv) history; (v) foreign language (Bestor 1955).

(i) The curriculum is considered to be the increasingly wide range of possible modes of thinking about men's experiences—not the conclusions, but the models from which conclusions derive, and in context of which these conclusions, so-called truths, are grounded and validated (Belth 1965).

3. Dimensions of the Definition of Curriculum

There are two major dimensions along which curricular definitions fall; "means–ends" and "existential–personal".

3.1 Ends and Means

Curriculum ends are often defined in terms of intended learning outcomes (ILOs). Intended learning outcomes may be expressed in terms of goals, aims, and objectives. When curriculum is defined this way, the form of its content may be behavioral, that is "to be able to do something"; expressive, that is "to have rich but undefined potential"; or substantive, that is "to know this or that".

The definition of curriculum in terms of intended learning outcomes implies that subject matter be chosen to reflect those outcomes. Subject matter is variously defined (see *Subject Matter*). Subject matter as a means to achieve curricular ends may be defined as planned experiences for learners; the knowledge needed to achieve the ILOs; or the beliefs, understandings, and habits required. Knowledge is frequently divided into cultural, cognitive, and affective dimensions.

Curriculum may, instead, be defined as the means to achieving ends. It is necessary, therefore, to read curriculum research and curriculum policy documents carefully since curriculum content for some is the means to achieve certain ends rather than the ends themselves which require a content to be achieved (see *Curriculum Content*).

Those who define content in terms of means may represent only a semantic issue. That is, intended learning outcomes and means to achieve them may simply be switched in the definition. However, conceptual issues may be at stake, for example, when content is taken as given and the outcomes are seen as expressions of, rather than predeterminers of, the means. Consider, for example, a means-defined biology curriculum where the outcomes of studying biology are expressions of the learning of it. In this case, the ends issue becomes a matter of outcomes and achievement rather than one of intention. Overall, this shifts the discussion of curriculum and its content from one of planning to one of evaluation. Planning issues are central to the notion of curriculum defined in terms of intended learning outcomes while evaluation issues are central to the notion of curriculum defined as means.

3.2 Existential–Personal

Here, the definition of content varies depending on whether the emphasis is on the things studied or the student studying. When curriculum is defined existentially, it will refer to textbooks and materials of instruction and to their content such as concepts, theories, and facts. This kind of definition highlights the issue of teaching methodology and instruction since the problem of the students' interaction with the content is the main instructional concern.

Curriculum may, instead, refer to the students' experience rather than to the things in the students' instructional environment. This kind of definitional emphasis raises the issue of "meaning". The curricular content becomes the meaning which the instructional situation has for the student. For example, if Quantum theory were part of the curriculum for a 6-year-old, an existential definition would simply label Quantum theory as the curriculum content. Extraordinary instructional methods would, of course, be developed for the 6-year-old's interaction with the theory. For a personal experiential definition of curriculum, Quantum theory would not be considered to be the content since this theory could have little meaning for the student. Rather, whatever the student made out of his or her instructional interaction with Quantum theory, that is, the meaning the Quantum theory had for the student, would be defined as the curriculum content.

This dimension has consequences for policy making and research. According to the existential definition of curriculum, content is defined and outlined according to knowledge categories, whereas, when curriculum is defined in personal terms, it is necessary to understand the student's level of experience and to study in detail the curriculum's meaning for the student.

4. Recovering an Author's Meaning of Curriculum

The fact that there are numerous definitions of curriculum and that the only proper way to deal with the problem of definition is to determine how an author uses the term in his or her work implies the use of reading and listening tools for the recovery of meaning. One such possibility was presented in the previous section where the use of the two dimensions would aid in understanding an author's meaning. Still another process is outlined by Connelly and Elbaz (1980) and is presented in summary form below. This reading device is based on the classification of the substance of curricular arguments: their "main topics", their "target", and their "point of view".

There are four main topics treated in the curriculum: (a) curriculum making, frequently referred to as curriculum development (see *Curriculum Development*); (b) curriculum managing, frequently seen as an administrative and implementation problem (see *Curriculum Implementation*); (c) the study of the curriculum, which is essentially the rules and methods for curriculum research; and (d) the nature of the curriculum, in which views of subject matter, content, disciplines, children, and the like are presented. The bulk of the literature is on the topic of "the nature of the curriculum" but, in recent years, curriculum making and curriculum managing have received a great deal of attention. Implementation topics are currently most prevalent.

When articles on the topic of "the nature of the curriculum" are identified, they may be targeted on general curriculum considerations or to specific content concerns. General considerations are those that refer to a wide variety of areas in the curriculum, for example, an article or speech on the formulation of objectives. Specific content refers to areas in the curriculum of interest only to a selected audience, for example, articles on secondary-school English.

All articles, regardless of their topic and target, adopt one of three general points of view. An author may be writing from the point of view of foundation fields and, therefore, give a psychological, philosophical, sociological, or other account; from the point of view of the subject matter disciplines and, therefore, give an account in terms of disciplinary knowledge; or from the point of view of personal experience, and, therefore, give a point of view based on practical experience.

A particular topic may, accordingly, be treated very differently within any one point of view, for example, a psychological versus a philosophical approach to the teaching of science. These differences are magnified when a personal experience perspective is used since a variety of experiences are possible.

The significance of these topics, targets, and points of view is that they may aid a reader in the classification of the kind of article read. They function as a kind of skeleton key to the curriculum literature permitting the reader to recover an author's curricular meaning. The three areas discussed may be summarized in the form of three reading rules.

(a) The article or speech should be classified according to the main "topics" in the curriculum.

(b) It should be decided whether the article is about general curriculum concerns or about more specific subject matter concerns (the "target" of the article).

(c) The "point of view" adopted by the author should be determined. It should then be decided whether the author is writing from the perspective of social science foundation fields, subject matter disciplines, or personal experience.

These three reading rules do not, of course, exhaust the devices of possible use to a reader in recovering meaning. Many articles, for example, are practically oriented and may be treated as prescriptive, whereas others are intended as theoretical accounts aimed at informing, but not governing the actions of, a reader. The language and tone of such curriculum articles is considerably different and needs to be read differently.

Since the definition of curriculum, and the various assumptions associated with the writing of curricula are personal, it is necessary for an author to adopt a critical attitude when reading the curriculum literature. Authors need to decide for themselves whether they agree with the curricular assumptions and whether what the curriculum is proposing is a "good thing".

These latter points may also be summarized in the form of a set of rules.

(d) Is the article practical and prescriptive, or primarily oriented to theory and knowledge?

(e) Do I, (the reader), agree with what the author is saying?

(f) Is what the author proposes a "good" thing?

Readers will, of course, develop their own methods for recovering meaning from curriculum literature. The key point is not so much that the rules presented here are followed but that readers and listeners of curricula actively seek ways of sorting out an author's meaning for themselves. There are no theoretically established principles to allow a reader to abdicate responsibility for the personal search for meaning.

5. Research and Actual Uses of Curriculum

Ultimately, the actual uses of curricula are more important than the prescriptions obtained in the theoretical definition, conceptualization, selection, and organization of content since classroom practices define what actually occurs. Just as the meaning of curriculum is best seen in what an author does, so too, the meaning of any particular curriculum is best seen in how it is used in practice.

The discrepancy between the planning and use of curriculum, often referred to as the difference between intentions and outcomes in the implementation literature, has been of worldwide concern (see *Curriculum Implementation*). The curriculum-in-action is primarily a function of the teachers and students in the situation. Their experience and personal knowledge brought to instructional situations are the key determiners of how the curriculum is used. There have been worldwide efforts to reduce the discrepancy, but much of this effort has been of little avail. Accordingly, the view that the prescribed and actual curriculum should "match", continues to create one of education's most difficult policy problems.

There are sound theoretical and ethical reasons for the alternative view that "curriculum", however defined and presented, should be seen as a "potential" (Ben-Peretz 1975) to be expressed in different ways in classroom situations. Research focused on "curriculum potential" does not view the discrepancy as an inadequacy, as implementation research is inclined to do, but, rather, is concerned to credit the legitimately different uses to which the curriculum is actually put. This view encourages the attitude that curricular adaptations in practice are reflections of local ability to accommodate to the community, the teacher, and to student needs (see *Curriculum Adaptation*).

Practically speaking, whether the "matching" view or the "adaptation" view is adopted, there will never be ultimate control over ends. Diversity of use will occur according to the personal knowledge of individual students, the orientation of particular classrooms, especially as a function of particular teacher perspectives, and other local factors of intellectual importance such as the orientation of the board of education, its schools, and their departments.

6. *Curriculum and School Reform*

The school curriculum has always been used by school reformers as a means to bring about their reforms. Governments with literacy policies, agrarian policies, cultural policies, and so on turn to curriculum reform (see *Curriculum Reform*). There is good reason for using the curriculum in this way since school children are in the process of developing intellectual and attitudinal outlooks. But the hopes of reformers are rarely met by the curriculum.

Partly because of the above considerations, current thinking on the relationship between the curriculum and school reform downplays the likely effectiveness of, and possible control by, school reformers over curriculum ends. Practical considerations, especially those associated with the personal knowledge of teachers and students, as well as political considerations, have considerable legitimate influence on school reforms. Thus, while the issues of definition and conceptualization of curriculum and its content are critical in curriculum planning, they are not, as often imagined in rational plans for curriculum development, the ultimate determiners of school reform. The personal practical knowledge of participants in schooling performs this function.

Bibliography

Belth M 1965 *Education as a Discipline: A Study of the Role Models in Thinking.* Allyn and Bacon, Boston, Massachusetts, p. 317

Ben-Peretz M 1975 The concept of curriculum potential. *Curric. Theory Network* 151–59

Bestor A E 1955 *The Restoration of Learning: A Program for Redeeming the Unfulfilled Promise of American Education.* Knopf, New York

Connelly F M, Elbaz F 1980 Conceptual bases for curriculum thought: A teacher's perspective. In: Foshay A W (ed.) 1980 *Considered Action for Curriculum Improvement.* Association for Supervision and Curriculum Development, Washington, DC, pp. 95–119

Foshay A W 1969 Curriculum. In: Ebel R I (ed.) 1969 *Encyclopedia of Educational Research: A Project of the American Educational Research Association*, 4th edn. Macmillan, New York

Good C V (ed.) 1959 *Dictionary of Education*, 2nd edn. McGraw-Hill, New York

Rugg H O 1947 *Foundations for American Education*, 1st edn. World Book Company, Yonkers-on-Hudson, New York

Smith B O, Stanley W O, Shores J H 1957 *Fundamentals of Curriculum Development*, rev. edn. Harcourt, Brace and World, New York

Taba H 1962 *Curriculum Development: Theory and Practice.* Harcourt, Brace and World, New York

Tanner D, Tanner L N 1975 *Curriculum Development: Theory into Practice.* Macmillan, New York

Westbury I, Steimer W 1971 Curriculum: A discipline in search of its problems. *Sch. Rev.* 79: 243–67

The Domain of Curriculum Studies

Curriculum Theory

U. Hameyer

The study of curriculum theory is a complex project. Firstly, the field of curriculum research is extremely broad in scope and scale whereas curriculum theories are mostly limited to a particular segment (Tanner and Tanner 1980, Hameyer et al. 1983). At the same time, efforts to integrate theoretical knowledge as with Herrick and Tyler (1950) or Frey (1971) have not been continued effectively. Secondly, there are very few comparative and cross-cultural curriculum studies (see, however, Goodson 1986 and Hameyer et al. 1986). For example, in most cases, the Mediterranean, African, Asian, and Japanese approaches have not sufficiently been brought to international attention. Thirdly, the question of how to define the purpose, criteria, and scientific quality of curriculum theories is a matter of continuous scientific dispute. Scholars such as Beauchamp (1968), Frey (1971), Hameyer (1983), and Tyler (1988) have debated the principles of theory construction, whereas Klafki (1963), Dahllöf (1974) and Walker (1976) among various other theorists have addressed the issue of aim setting and content selection in particular.

The purpose of this article is to describe major groups of curriculum theories. All have a concern to unify phenomena within a set of events encompassed by the theory and to contribute to continuous reflection (Schubert 1986) in common. However, theories differ in terms of how they unify phenomena, how they define sets of events, and to what extent they try to define, explain, hypothesize, predict, or create action. This kind of differentiation indicates a methodological and metatheoretical concern.

Curriculum theories can also be specified in view of a substantive–structural concern. This approach leads to grouping theories in terms of what they are about. This method is preferred here because it will better serve to describe the theoretical diversity.

Numerous conceptions of what a curriculum theory should be about are available. Phenix (1968) and Tykociner (1966) refer to disciplinary knowledge as a major reference resource for curriculum theorizing (Hirst 1974). Several German-speaking *Didaktiken* also emphasize this point (an excellent overview is given by Diederich 1988).

Beauchamp (1968) first considers a curriculum as a document describing content, aims, and the learning situations; second, as a curriculum system which deals with the context of human action and curriculum decisions, and third, as an area of activity. A curriculum theory, as defined by Beauchamp, is a set of related statements that gives meaning to a school's curriculum by pointing out the relationships among its elements and by directing its development, its use, and its evaluation (see *Curriculum Development*; *Curriculum Evaluation*).

Other authors circumscribe a curriculum theory as a set of norms and rules. It provides a rationale for reasoning about curricular decisions and learning (Frey 1971, 1980, Künzli 1975, 1983, Reid 1978, Robinsohn 1971). Norms and rules of interactions are to be elaborated and shared by everybody involved in the curriculum process. The creation of rules for interaction appears to be generally valuable for a curriculum process and thus it is a subject of curriculum theory.

Lundgren (1972) defines curriculum theory in terms of a systematic link between curriculum and instruction. Instructional process research is taken as an important resource for curriculum theory. A curriculum has to explain the relevance of content in connection with methods of learning (Walker and Schaffarzick 1974).

In his study on *The Child and the Curriculum* (1902), Dewey formulated basic fundamental ideas for American curriculum theory. Fundamental resources (learner, society, organized subject matter) were said to be the theoretical criteria for curriculum decisions. Taba (1945) worked on the resources (Herrick and Tyler 1950).

Tyler (1971) proposed a rationale which tries to answer the following questions: (a) What educational purposes should the school seek to attain? (b) How can learning experiences be selected which are likely to be useful in attaining these objectives? (c) How can learning experiences be organized for effective instruction? (d) How can the effectiveness of learning experiences be evaluated?

Schwab (1978) criticizes exaggerated hopes invested in theory in general and differentiates between arts of the practical, arts of the quasipractical, and arts of the eclectic. Results of practical operations are decisions or proposals for actions. They do not claim to meet criteria of truth or validity whereas a theory pursues validity beyond a practical situation or application context. Theoretical problems are states of mind. Practical problems arise from states of affairs in relation to ourselves. Quasipractical operations deal with practical problems which affect several cases, individuals, and units of operations. Eclectic operations take the achievement of theories into account. Practical problems give orientation guidelines on how to work with theories, how to apply them, and how to benefit from them. Schwab proposes that curriculum development and deliberation should combine the above-mentioned arts of acting and reasoning.

Another differentiation of curriculum theories is provided by the process–product issue (Hameyer 1978). A "process" refers to a series of interactions during instruction or curriculum processes whereas "product" refers to a document or medium. According to Frey (1980) the basic question of curriculum theory addresses issues related to product and process, including evaluation and legitimation:

> How can learning situations be created which are legitimated in the context of their social–cultural environment as well as in the individual's self-interpretation, being conceived as promoting the autonomous development of those involved before, during, and after the learning process?

This question suggests what curriculum theory should be about. The subsequent sections refer to elements of the above-stated question.

1. Conceptual Models of Curriculum

Conceptual models of curriculum are known from the United States, Canada, and selected European countries. Theorists here consider curriculum as an interaction process. They deal with the structure of a curriculum system, its context and setting, and with the dynamics of self-renewal. Generally speaking, a conceptual model is a referential system for curriculum planning. Additionally, a conceptual model provides rules for deliberate interaction and activities, criteria for intervention, and guidelines for evaluation.

Thus, most conceptual models of curriculum refer to the question of how to develop learning situations which guarantee autonomous development of the individual involved in the curriculum process. Frey and Aregger (1975) suggest a model called *Generatives Leitsystem*. The system organizes processes of research, theory building, problem solving, curriculum development, and implementation of a curriculum. These processes are conceived as a social system wherein individuals mutually interact, learn, cooperate, and decide on common tasks. They activate norms, attitudes, meanings, modes of collaboration, and negotiation. This framework has been reformulated in terms of a curriculum conference model (Frey 1981, Frei et al. 1989). The

model has been used practically in adult education, Swiss in-service teacher training, syllabus work, and renewing the vocational curriculum in various parts of West Germany and Switzerland (see also Malliou 1990).

How people interact and learn in the context of a curriculum system is a key question which still lacks substantial research and conceptual clarification. The theory of elementary discourse is applied in Frey's works in order to create a nonpersuasive pattern of deliberative interaction. The conceptual origin stems from German practical philosophy. In conceptual models, nonpersuasive communication is considered an important aspect of the development process.

The conceptual model is composed of analytical, developmental, evaluative, and diverse practical activities. These cannot strictly be divided or sequenced, but reappear intermittently during the process. The *Generatives Leitsystem* is not a phase model; rather, it conceptualizes human interaction aiming at autonomous development in view of a common aim.

Issues for research and problems to be solved cannot be identified by planning experts in advance. Nor can major decisions be made in advance by scientists or decision makers. Decisions, problems, and issues for research are gradually elaborated and cooperatively revised.

Subjectivity and individual concerns are paramount. They can be articulated from four points of view: aims of the project; underlying assumptions; principles of the process; conditions of the project work. These dimensions constitute one component of the conceptual model. Another component articulates the relationships among these dimensions and demonstrates how they should or might be transformed during the curriculum process. A third component reorganizes these four dimensions in terms of sequencing activities by means of differentiating between short- and long-term systems.

Planning and executing the activities is, above all, a matter of everyone being involved in the process. There is an interplay between systematic, analytical activities, the development of consensus, and deliberation (*verständigte Aufklärung*).

Several curriculum projects start with institutional premises or the contexts under which a project is envisaged to work. Referential theories from other disciplines are borrowed for this purpose. They are applied in a way that allows the substantial analysis of a setting where a curriculum is created.

The use and reinvention of a curriculum (program) can be partially explained by referential theories. Organizational theory, educational sociology, theories of schooling, social psychology, political theory, and others are considered.

Another conceptual system for curriculum research and practice has been developed by Goodlad et al. (1979). This approach focuses on decisions at the societal, institutional, instructional, and individual levels. Studying the constraints of decision making is considered a major task in curriculum planning or, as

Goodlad puts it, making "the best possible appraisals of what exists".

2. Theories of Curriculum Legitimization

This branch of curriculum theory has been systematized by Künzli (1975), reviewed by Hameyer in *Handbuch der Curriculumforschung* (1983), and further elaborated by Künzli (1983). In Switzerland, West Germany, and the USA, key concepts from educational philosophy have been adopted to explain the factors that constitute the school curriculum. In other words, how to identify what is worthwhile to be taught in schools? How to reveal the rationale behind a curriculum in action (Reid 1986)?

Meyer (1972) identifies three types of legitimization: (a) normative legitimization, (b) procedural approaches, and (c) legitimization by discourse. Normative legitimization, the logic of which has been carefully unfolded by Zedler (1976), looks at what should or must be taught (e.g., by means of "deducing" educational aims from a peculiar concept of God). Procedural approaches create legitimization from rules for decision-making and interaction processes. Frey developed a theoretically grounded process model of curriculum development which has been repeatedly applied in Western Europe. It is qualified on a high level of practicality, interactivity, and reflectiveness which goes far beyond procedural formalism. Legitimization by discourse requires the art of criticism, connoisseurship (Eisner), and deliberative understanding.

With regard to the question of what is to be taught in schools, the liberal arts debate in the Eighty-seventh Yearbook of the National Society for the Study of Education (Westbury and Purves 1988) is paramount. The contributors reiterate the idea of general education and the core curriculum (see also Jozefzoon and Gorter 1985). The renaissance of humanistic ideals for the general curriculum is clearly expressed, for instance in the contribution of Kliebard (1988b), who traces back this point to Spencer's famous essay "What knowledge is of most worth?" (1859). The liberal arts seek for utility which lies "in the development of rationality and the freedom that rationality provides to discover why I should believe and act as I do" (Kliebard 1988b p. 49).

The increasing need for justifying a curriculum has repeatedly been stated in view of the growth of knowledge in society and the increasing dissatisfaction with schooling. Reid (1978) differentiates between "the forced (or arbitrary) move", the "move having 'relative' justification", and "the move having 'general' justification" (p. 51). He associates these moves with questions about what "must" be done, what "should" be done, and what "ought" to be done.

Theories of curriculum legitimization emphasize the educational impact of basic human rights such as autonomy, self-expression, or independence on curriculum and instruction. This requires guaranteed access to a core curriculum for everyone who is affected, either directly or indirectly, by the process of implementation within the established fields of study in the public school. Frey et al. (1979) exemplified how such a model can be applied to curriculum renewal.

Legitimization can be distinguished according to at least the following aspects: (a) reflecting upon a given curriculum, and (b) giving reasons for new ideas, activities, and programs to be added to the public curriculum. Both the limits to and the prerequisites for change have to be studied. Some theorists conceptualize such constraints to curriculum renewal (Kliebard 1986, 1988b), whereas others restrict their efforts to the "shoulds" and "musts".

In the 1980s in particular, curriculum history contributed substantially to answering the questions of why something was taught and why other aims were excluded from general education (Franklin 1986, Goodson 1986, Kliebard 1986, Schubert 1986, Haft and Hopmann 1990). These scholars show by case studies and comparative reasoning that the social construction of society is a powerful force defining the limits of curriculum renewal. The curriculum is considered an important social artefact (Goodson 1986), and "a socially constructed practice" which is politically bound (Popkewitz 1988 p. 69).

Apple (1986) specified the political dimension in his study on *Teachers and Texts*. The interactions between the school curriculum and economic, cultural, and political power are the core concern in this book. Apple found a growing move towards centralized control over the curriculum and the teacher in the United States. State-mandated competency testing in the United States and other countries is given as one example of many to illustrate the impact of control mechanisms on the school curriculum and, associated with this movement, a growing standardization of public education.

Reconceptualists analyse the legitimizing rationale behind a curriculum by looking at factors of schooling, such as the ideological background and functions of the school (Huber 1981). They criticize schooling and curricula in view of normative assumptions, side effects, and the hidden mechanisms that reduce educational quality.

3. Process Theories of Curriculum

Theories which are referred to in this section conceptualize the curriculum as a process of reflective interaction and development. A curriculum process, in its broadest sense, is considered a multi-level cycle of mutual learning and sustained improvement which occurs stepwise and cooperatively.

A new curriculum document itself does not guarantee successful implementation even if it emerges from convincing insights (see *Curriculum Implementation*). Replacing an old textbook or the prevailing rationale of a syllabus does not necessarily induce any real instructional change. A reflective system of interlinked steps towards effective curriculum renewal increases the likelihood that lasting change will occur (see Fullan 1985; Miles et al. 1987). Therefore, process theories accentuate the role of interaction as constituent for curriculum design. A curriculum document is one particular aspect of the curriculum process which encompasses adaptive changes on individual, social, and institutional levels. Adaptation in this context signifies assimilative and accommodative aspects of learning and development between the innovation, the context, and the individual (see *Curriculum Adoption*).

The adaptation process has been investigated by several researchers (e.g., Fullan 1983, Lütgert and Stephan 1983). Leithwood investigated adaptation processes in Canada; van den Berg and Vandenberghe (1981) in Belgium and the Netherlands, and Dahllöf et al. (1971) and Wallin (1981) in Sweden (see *Curriculum Adaptation*).

Rassekh and Vaideanu (1987) emphasize another process aspect closely related to the social dimension of curriculum renewal. They state that the theory of curriculum planning and process design as carried out in several states "attaches particular importance to the study of the interactions between the components of this process—objectives, content, learning methods, teaching resources, forms of organization of instruction, evaluation methods and techniques" (p. 130).

The process involves comprehending the innovation, communicating it, valuing its pedagogical quality and relevance, and then weighting the impact on one's own practice, and examining its adaptability to local conditions. Hameyer (1978) has explored the factors of social innovation development on the basis of 42 *Modellversuche* (school experiments) in Austria, Switzerland, and the Federal Republic of Germany focusing on interviews from the 42 school improvement projects. A follow-up study, Implementing Activity-Based Learning in Elementary Science Teaching (IMPACT), investigates the processes of lasting curriculum renewal in elementary science teaching. The study encompasses case studies from the Netherlands, Sweden, United States, and West Germany (Hameyer et al. 1990).

Van Manen (1977) emphasizes, from a phenomenological point of view, the need for a theoretical conceptualization of communication patterns and mutual understanding during curriculum renewal. He draws special attention to the relevance of educational activities because innovations will be adopted and implemented only if they fit into the thinking and action patterns of the individuals who are affected by the innovation planned. He particularly proposes taking the changing perceptions and preconceptions of teachers, learners, and other participants in the curriculum process into account and investigating them. Curriculum is a matter of interpersonal relations and interactions which should be guided by the common criteria of discourse or deliberative understanding.

Expanding this idea, it is possible to ask: How can conditions for creating and improving learning situations be identified? Which configurations of context characteristics can be used or restructured so that curriculum improvements will be more likely to occur? Under which circumstances are adaptation and communicative requirements favored? By which patterns of action do people interact, communicate, comprehend, learn, come to an understanding, and decide within a curriculum system? Which standards of deliberative understanding and interaction are appropriate in view of a theory of social action and change?

Process-oriented curriculum research discovered a set of key factors which affect the curriculum process. First, the need and relevance of curriculum renewal as interpreted by individuals, groups, and institutions affects the curriculum process. Fullan (1982) complains that many innovations are attempted without a careful examination of whether or not they address what are perceived to be priority needs. The importance of a curriculum should be assessed in the face of the current situation (see *Needs Assessment Studies*). How significant individuals interpret the proposed innovation should be examined, and in this context the following key factors should also be considered: former experiences of innovative attempts, readiness for change, existing norms and value systems, and ability and readiness to search creatively for new solutions and to participate in elaborating curriculum renewal.

Second, capacity for change in terms of time available, willingness to take risks, and the ability to consider alternatives to the present situation and practice will affect the curriculum process. Capacity as a concept refers not only to the microlevel, it refers to social groups and cultures or subcultures as well (Sarason 1982). Subcultures or certain groups may not have sufficient resources (time, people, competencies, and self-renewal systems) to join certain improvement activities. Additionally, the curriculum innovation proposed may raise too many unanswered questions or even induce anxiety. Furthermore, there is no success without the ability to learn and communicate with others within a common frame of rules. Thus, deliberative understanding and cooperation should meet criteria such as nonpersuasiveness, noncoercive attitudes, unprejudiced views, and seriousness of the arguments.

A third factor affecting the curriculum process is the quality and adaptability of the curriculum programme. These factors ellucidate characteristics of the programme, which will depend on the programme's association with the way people interpret the quality and adaptability factors. Issues such as the complexity of the programme or process, clarity of aims and components, accessibility, probable impact, and others can be mentioned here. Thus, for example, Gross et al. (1971) found that the majority of teachers were unable to identify the essentials of the innovation they were using (Lehming and Kane 1981). Finally, adaptability includes the possibility of using a curriculum economically and trying it out (trialability). Adaptability also demands a sound innovation in terms of being based upon recent research and practical experience.

Finally, the quality of decision will affect the curriculum process. Criteria for curricular decision processes may be: legitimacy, competency of the decision maker, transparency of procedures of decision making, and efficiency of decisions in terms of communicability, practicability, and accessibility for evaluation (Flechsig and Haller 1973). Other decision-oriented curriculum theories are summarized by Frey (1971 pp. 160–65), Kirst and Walker (1971), and Haller (1973).

4. Structural Curriculum Theories

Structural theories of curriculum deal with two basic questions: (a) how to select and justify worthwhile educational knowledge, and (b) how to organize educational knowledge within a curriculum.

A core task of a structural curriculum theory is to identify and transform knowledge which is considered educationally meaningful into a subject matter proposal or into learning activities as part of the curriculum.

4.1 Structural Theories that Draw Upon Principles of Education, Utilizing Theories From the Field of Educational Philosophy, Anthropological Disciplines, Sociology and History of Education, or Others

The majority of approaches differentiate among three levels of competency to be acquired: (a) subject and interdisciplinary knowledge, (b) human/social learning demands, and (c) development of personality. Such principles serve as a guide for selecting educational aims, contents, and learning activities.

Structural theories, however, differ as to the criteria of cogency and justification. Some clearly state that any decision about contents is bound to democratic processes of deliberation, whereas others derive content legitimacy from a presupposed inner logic of their theory which is not exposed to reflective criticism.

Some educational philosophers structure the body of educational knowledge in accordance with the functions of the school (Whitty 1985). Examples of school functions are as follows: economic–technical function in order to qualify for vocational or prevocational tasks; religious function in order to provide orientation concerning ethics and metaphysics; social–political function; and others. Künzli differentiates in his works between four functions: qualifying for life and work, developing common sense, teaching how to learn and think, and preparing to cope with current and future problems of life.

Classical German didactics concentrated upon justification of educational knowledge (content to be taught, *Bildungsinhalte*). They justify content in view of basic educational values which can be ascribed to a contest (among others see Klafki 1963). Others add that educational theory should clarify, analyse, and conceptualize ideas and/or principles inherent in school programs. They should identify the meaning of "regulative ideas" or hidden intentions in educational documents or materials. By doing this, basic educational decisions become accessible to reconstruction and criticism.

Loch (1979) suggests an anthropological theory of education which makes use of analyses of biographies of individuals to be educated. The life histories of the environments of each individual learner are referential categories in Loch's theory. The overall purpose of education in this theory is the development of human abilities and the provision of aids for coping with cultural environments (*Enkulturationshilfe*) immediately and later in life. Therefore, the learner has to achieve certain curricular competencies which enable him or her to achieve these aims.

4.2 Structural Theories which Conceptualize Life Situations, Areas of Human Activities, and a Praxeology of Human Actions

This subgroup deals with problems of how to identify curriculum content in view of its value for mastering conditions and challenges in (later) life. Note, however, that most theorists focus on the public school. It is more desirable to refer to demands of lifelong learning or recurrent education (Hameyer 1979; Rassekh and Vaideanu 1987) and their impact on the school curriculum.

The praxeological theory of Derbolav (1975) is a representative example for structural approaches. Derbolav considers his work a *practical* theory which draws educationally relevant knowledge from an historical analysis of basic human practices, such as technology, economy, medicine, pedagogy, politics, journalism, and so on. These are used as a reference system for the school curriculum. Each practice is conceptualized according to three categories: (a) original state, (b) rationality, and (c) regulative ideas. An example of the original state is the use of magic to conceptualize nature, whereas rationality corresponds to scientific understanding and technological knowledge. Social welfare would be a regulative idea in "economy".

Another group of structural curriculum theories stems from Robinsohn (1971). By means of situational analyses of societal and cultural environments, situations are identified which serve as reference units for creating relevant curriculum content and goals. In the Federal Republic of Germany a curriculum for the kindergarten and preschools, using Robinsohn's situational theory, was developed, which contains curriculum units such as children in hospitals, shelter, and so on. Life and the environments of learners are taken as reference frames for curriculum development and theory.

Bernstein (1977) deals with structuring knowledge by means of cultural transmission. He asks how experience, identity, and relation are evoked, maintained, and changed by formal transmission of educational knowledge. He introduces the terms "classification" and "framing" of educational knowledge. Classification refers to the relationships between content and to the degree of boundary maintenance between contents.

Classification, here, refers to the extent of insulation of contents whereas framing is used to determine the structure of the pedagogical message system. "Frame" refers to the form of the *context* in which knowledge is transmitted and received, and to the specific pedagogical relationship of teacher and taught. If framing is strong, there is sharp boundary between what may and may not be transmitted. Thus frame refers "to the degree of control teacher and pupils possess over the selection, organization, pacing, and timing of the knowledge transmitted and received" (p. 89).

European syllabi are structured according to subject-oriented knowledge which is rather classified. Bernstein goes beyond the approach of Blankertz (1971) insofar as he systematically includes the dimension of knowledge use (framing). Thereby he is able to provide sensitivity to the context and its impact on the control of knowledge selection and use. Blankertz focuses on the justification of scientific knowledge for educational purposes. Thus, both theories serve different aims and functions.

The situation-oriented approach has also been applied in mathematics teaching, in the geography curriculum, and so on. In programs of this type, the reference point is the ability to perform real-life tasks such as reading a newspaper, writing a letter for employment, reading maps and timetables, locating a library book, making change, computing interest rates, learning to swim, or completing a simple income tax form.

Probably the best-known subgroup of curriculum theory deals with an idea called the "structures of disciplines" (see *The Structure of Discipline*). Some of them represent scientific knowledge as "realms of meaning" (Phenix 1968), as a "zetetics" (Tykociner 1966), or as a topological system (Künzli 1983). Bruner (1960) restructures scientific knowledge for educational purposes by means of unifying ideas and basic concepts. Conceptual, logical, and methodological features of knowledge are taken as being the core of curriculum theory. Disciplines provide the knowledge requested because they constitute the range of the unique ways there are of understanding experience.

Blankertz (1971) has contributed to the development of structural curriculum theory. He takes basic concepts from particular sciences and transforms them by means of educational criteria into a curriculum.

Epistemological curriculum theory differentiates four kinds of knowledge use: replicative use of knowledge, associative use of knowledge, applicative use of knowledge, and interpretive use of knowledge. As Broudy (1976) specifies:

> By the associative use of knowledge I mean the retrieval from experience of the images, concepts, and words that for some reason or cause (which often we cannot identify) seem to be relevant to the issue at hand. What is called richness in experience is largely a function of the scope of the imagic-conceptional store and its availability. Part of the justification for the study of the sciences, arts, and the humanities is the stocking of this associative store. Uneducated

persons often betray their lack of schooling by a poverty of concepts and images rather than by a lack of intelligence.

5. Theories of Curriculum Implementation

Implementation theories address the conditions under which curriculum change will be more likely to happen and be substained both on the individual and the institutional level. A guiding question here is: Who works with a new curriculum and in what way so that patterns of instruction and learning are improved?

It is evident that such inquiries are closely interconnected with evelation theory (Lewy 1977) and methods to certify impeding and supporting factors of curriculum renewal.

Fullan (1982) proposed incorporating the issue of continuation into theory-building. This aspect of lasting curriculum renewal has been substantially conceptualized by Miles et al. (1987). Ten years ago, this aspect was totally neglected in favor of adoption studies which looked at the user of something new without explaining the processes of initiation not the institutional context wherein changes undergo a metamorphosis according to prevailing rules, needs, routines, priorities, and mechanisms of social interaction (see Hameyer et al. 1990).

Checking recent volumes of the *Journal of Curriculum Studies*, such aspects have been given clear priority (e.g., Akker 1988). Strong attention is given for instance to the link between the teacher's personal knowledge and the curriculum (among others see Clandinin and Connelly 1987; Clark and Peterson 1986; Elbaz 1983; Halkes and Olson 1984).

What does this subgroup of curriculum theories finally aim at? Are there any new directions to be observed? Some argue that there is an explicit need for better criteria of implementation validity. Many former approaches studied implementation only in terms of fidelity according to aims of a new curriculum or program. Frey goes far beyond this model proposing that implementation be considered as a reflective reconstruction of the curriculum process. This understanding goes beyond that of assessing implementation as only being a phenomenon of accepting or rejecting something (see *Curriculum Implementation*). The definition given by Frey includes the consideration of how to work with the results of a curriculum process and how to learn from implementation during the curriculum process itself. Therefore implementation cannot be a final activity but rather is a formative and intermediate effort that lasts for a long time (Hameyer 1983).

6. Interim Summary

The methodology of curriculum theory construction has not made substantial progress since the early 1970s. Most theorists did not examine complementary theories for the purpose of integration, nor did they include research from related academic fields. Thus, comparative studies of curriculum theories are urgently needed.

Yet there have been other advancements. Process-oriented curriculum theories enlighten the circumstances under which curriculum renewal is more likely to be sustained in institutional settings. Additionally, there is an articulate need to better understand the conditions of mutual learning among adults who are involved in curriculum innovation—be it teachers, administrators, principals, stakeholders in the community, parents, or others. Conceptualizing curriculum innovation as a reflective learning cycle would be a promising task for future research and theorizing.

In 1977 Tyler complained about an insufficient number of "comprehensive explanatory systems" in the field of curriculum. He expressed hope to "build a sound architectural theory, one that periodically re-examined, continually tested, and was able to deal intelligently and comprehensively with changes in society and in knowledge".

Goodlad similarly found that a curriculum theory with "predictive power is virtually non-existent". In view of curriculum theories referred to in this article his assessment has to be revised. Walker, however, goes one step further. Curriculum research "may also have to create new curricular possibilities if it and public education are to survive. Comprehension is a good first step toward improvement. But it is not enough" (Walker 1976 p. 304).

In the 1980s curriculum theorists laid emphasis on the contextual impact on the public curriculum, on epistemological processes of knowledge acquisition, and experimental models of learning.

7. Issues for Future Research

Future theorizing in the field of curriculum is likely to pursue some elements of the following question: What is known about the public curriculum as it is constituted in view of the learner's biography, the instructional context and content, the historical background and changes in the curriculum, and the way it is enacted or institutionalized?

The curriculum for public education can be viewed from four interconnected perspectives which, being elaborated with the help of Rudolf Künzli, might serve as a starting point for future reviews:

(a) the institutional curriculum

(b) the biographical curriculum

(c) the instructional curriculum

(d) the subject-matter curriculum.

7.1 The Institutional Curriculum

Public education can almost never be satisfactorily understood by its formal functions only. What is to be taught and how to teach it in a public school is effected by politics and powerful rules, rituals, and routines at the school level itself (see Sarason 1982; Fullan 1985; Heckman 1987). The real nature of curriculum for public education is multifaceted according to whether the *conceived*, the *perceived* or the *performed curriculum* (Goodlad) is in question. The embedding culture of the school is a major condition determining the extent to which a curriculum is actually varied. Four institutional levels of influence can be discerned here:

(a) policy guidelines of/for the school

(b) profile of educational essentials

(c) patterns of instructional practice

(d) procedures of interaction.

A curriculum is born into or out of the life of an organization called school. It is contaminated with the structures and brought up by school life. Its aims follow expectations, avoid risks, and are confined by various contextual limits. For example, it makes a difference whether the supreme criterion for public education and its school curriculum is primarily striving for excellence, emphasizing happiness of the students, aiming at a core curriculum for all, or serving the ultimate aim to teach the students how to become citizens.

7.2 The Biographical Curriculum

Every curriculum is based upon an implicit or explicit anthropological view of the pupil, i.e. the learner. How does she/he acquire knowledge both inside and outside school? Which model serves best the aim to enrich learning opportunities in view of each individual's needs? At what stage of development more than another does the student meaningfully learn in what ways? More simply stated: When does she/he learn what is best, and why? Are there life cycle rhythms or sequences to follow?

Topics related to such issues are as follows: Sequential organization of subject matter knowledge in the curriculum, integrating learning experiences both in terms of instruction and the individual, discrepancy between formal and informal knowledge, common knowledge and its function in the learning process, what is conceived as meaningful knowledge by the student, and so on.

7.3 The Instructional Curriculum

In public education every curriculum has to pass through four major stages: first, from its originator to other people; second, from policy to school; third from inside the school into the classroom; and fourth, from instructor to learner. Curriculum theory has to explain what happens to the curriculum during the journey. The instructional curriculum is primarily about what remains after the progress of the curriculum into the classroom and how it is actually taught.

How can the rationale of an instructional curriculum be identified and explained? To what extent does the classroom level allow for variation and additional curriculum elements? What impact does the teacher exert on it according to what we currently know from research? In what way is the instructional curriculum affected by the teacher's thinking and preconception of the student?

7.4 The Subject Matter Curriculum

How can the rules for subject matter selection be identified? What constitutes the core curriculum and the additional parts? What are the educational essentials that represent the effective resources of a curriculum? What are the constituents of the curriculum (a) as stated in documents, (b) as perceived by the teacher, (c) as transformed by the student? Are there any new patterns for recognizing subject matter knowledge according to different learning environments? Are there any changes in curriculum design, and why? What function is given to design principles such as the spiral, sequential, situational, paradigmatic, problem-oriented design, or others?

At least some of these questions may gain increased attention in future theorizing to extend and ameliorate current explanatory knowledge about the curriculum, to integrate what is known from related academic fields, and to provide reflective insights into conditions under which the quality of our schools will be improved.

Bibliography

Adams H 1988 The faith of knowledge. In: Westbury I, Purves A C (eds.) 1988 *Cultural Literacy and the Idea of General Education*. National Society for the Study of Education, University of Chicago Press, Chicago, Illinois, pp. 52–68

Apple M W 1986 *Teachers and Texts: The Political Economy of Class and Gender Relations in Education*. Routledge and Kegan Paul, New York

Beauchamp G A 1968 *Curriculum Theory*, 2nd edn. Kagg, Wilmette, Illinois

Berg R, Hameyer U, Stokking K 1989 *Dissemination Reconsidered: The Demands of Implementation*. OECD Publication, Acco, Leuven

Bernstein B B 1977 On the classification and framing of educational knowledge. In: Bernstein B B (ed.) 1977 *Class, Codes and Control*, Vol. 3, 2nd edn. Routledge and Kegan Paul, London

Blankertz H (ed.) 1971 *Curriculumforschung: Strategien, Strukturierung, Konstruktion*. Neue Pädagogische Bemühungen, Bd. 46. Neue Deutsche Schule, Essen

Broudy H S 1976 Needs assessment and the curriculum. *Curric. Inq.* 6(2): 101-10

Bruner J S 1960 *The Process of Education*. Harvard University Press, Cambridge, Massachusetts

Brunner J, Eigenmann J, Mayer B, Schmid K 1979 *Die Leitideen: Ziele für die Primarstufe auf anthropologischer und didaktischer Grundlage*. Klett and Balmer, Zug

Clandinin D J, Connelly F M 1987 Teacher's personal knowledge: What counts as "personal" in studies of the personal. *J. Curric. Stud.* 19(6): 487–500

Clark C, Peterson P 1986 Teacher's thought processes. In:

Wittrock M C (ed.) 1986 *Handbook of Research on Teaching*, 3rd edn. Macmillan, New York

Corbett H D, Dawson J A, Firestone W A 1984 *School Context and School Change*. Teachers College Press, New York

Cornbleth C, Gottlieb E E 1988 Reform discourse and curriculum reform. Papers Presented at the Annual Meeting of the AERA, New Orleans, Louisiana

Dahllöf U 1974 Trends in process-related research on curriculum and teaching at different problem levels in educational sciences. *Scand. J. Educ. Res.* 18: 55–77

Dahllöf U, Lundgren U P, Siöö M 1971 Reform implementation studies as a basis for curriculum theory. *Curric. Theory Network* 99: 117

Derbolav J 1975 *Pädagogik und Politik: Eine systematische-kritische Analyse ihrer Bezichungen*. Kohlhammer, Stuttgart

Dewey J 1902 *The Child and the Curriculum*. University of Chicago Press, Chicago, Illinois

Diederich J 1988 *Didaktisches Denken*. Juventa, Münich

Eisner E W 1976 Educational connoisseurship and criticism: Their form and functions in educational evaluation. *J. Aesthetic Educ.* 10: 3–4, 135–50

Eisner E W 1979 *The Educational Imagination: On the Design and Evaluation of School Programs*. Macmillan, New York

Elbaz F 1983 *Teacher Thinking: A Study of Practical Knowledge*. Croom Helm, London

Feinberg P R 1985 Four curriculum theorists: A critique in light of Martin Buber's philosophy of education. *J. Curric. Theorizing* 6(1): 5–164

Flechsig K-H, Haller H D 1973 *Entscheidungsprozesse in der Curriculumentwicklung*. (Gutachten und Studien der Bildungskommission des Deutschen Bildungsrates, Band 24) Klett, Stuttgart

Franklin B M 1986 *Building the American Community: The School Curriculum and the Search for Social Control*. Falmer, London

Frei A, Frey K Lang, Malliou K 1989 *The Curriculum Conference as a New Approach to the Development of a Mathematics Curriculum in Technical Training*. Institute for Science Education, Kiel

Frey K 1971 *Theorien des Curriculums*. Beltz, Weinheim

Frey K 1980 Curriculum—lehrplan. In: Roth L (ed.) 1980 *Handlexikon zur Didaktik der Schulfächer*. Ehrenwirth, Munchen, pp. 44–51

Frey K (ed.) 1981 *Curriculum-Konferenz: Gebiet Mikroprozessor*. Institute for Science Education, Kiel

Frey K, Aregger K 1975 Ein modell zur integration von theorie und praxis in curriculumprojekten: Das generative leitsystem. In: Haft H, Hameyer U (eds.) 1975 *Curriculumplanung, Theorie und Praxis*. Kösel, München, pp. 133–56

Frey K, Bossart K, Niedermann A, Santini B 1979 Developmental strategy and evaluation of a new school in Switzerland. In: Centre for Educational Research and Innovation (CERI) 1979 *School-based Curriculum Development*. Organisation for Economic Co-operation and Development, Paris, pp. 129–53

Fullan M 1982 *The Meaning of Educational Change*. Teachers College Press, New York

Fullan M 1983 Implementation und evaluation von curricula: USA und Kanada. In: Hameyer U, Frey K, Haft H (eds.) 1983 *Handbuch der Curriculumforschung*. Beltz, Weinheim, pp. 489–500

Fullan M 1985 Change processes and strategies at the school level. *Elem. Sch. J.* 85(3): 391–421

Goodlad J I 1969 Curriculum: State of the field. *Rev. Educ. Res.* 39: 367–75

Goodlad J I (ed.) 1987 The ecology of school renewal. *Eighty-sixth Yearbook of the Society for the Study of Education*, Part 1. University of Chicago Press, Chicago, Illinois

Goodlad J I et al. 1979 *Curriculum Inquiry: The Study of Curriculum Practice*. McGraw-Hill, New York

Goodson I (ed.) 1986 *International Perspective in Curriculum History*. Croom Helm, London

Goodson I 1987 *School Subjects and Curriculum Change*. Falmer Press, London

Gross N C, Giacquinta J B, Bernstein M 1971 *Implementing Organizational Innovations: A Sociological Analysis of Planned Educational Change*. Harper and Row, London

Haft H, Hopmann S (eds.) 1990 *Case Studies in Curriculum Administration History*. Falmer Press, London

Halkes R, Olson J (eds.) 1984 *Teaching Thinking: A New Perspective on Persisting Problems in Education*. Swets and Zeitlinger, Amsterdam

Haller H-D 1973 *Prozeßanalyse der Lehrplanentwicklung in der Bundesrepublik Deutschland*. Universität Konstanz, Konstanz

Hameyer U 1978 *Innovationsprozesse: Analysemodell und Fallstudien zum sozialen Konflikt in der Curriculum-revision*. Beltz, Weinheim

Hameyer U 1979 *School Curriculum in the Context of Lifelong Learning*. UNESCO Institute for Education, Hamburg

Hameyer U 1982 Understanding social processes of innovation development. *J Curric. Stud.* 14: 362–66

Hameyer U 1983 Systematisierung von Curriculum-theorien. In: Hameyer U, Frey K, Haft H (eds.) 1983 *Handbuch der Curriculumforschung*, Vol. 1. *Ausgabe*. Beltz, Weinheim, pp. 53–100

Hameyer U 1987 Planning to institutionalize a new science curriculum. In: Miles M B, Ekholm M, Vandenberghe R 1987 (eds.) *Lasting School Improvement: Exploring the Process of Institutionalization*. OECD Publication. Acco, Leuven, pp. 221–39

Hameyer U, Frey K, Haft H (eds.) 1983 *Handbuch der Curriculumforschung*, Vol. 1. *Ausgabe*. Beltz, Weinheim

Hameyer U, Frey K, Haft H, Kuebart F (eds.) 1986 *Curriculum Research in Europe*. Swets and Zeitlinger, Amsterdam

Hameyer U, Ekholm M, Anderson R, Akker J van den 1990 IMPACT–*Implementing Activity-based Learning in Elementary Science Teaching. A Comparative Study of Lasting School Renewal*. Institute for Science Education, Kiel

Heckman P 1987 Understanding school culture. In: Goodlad J I (ed.) 1987 *The Ecology of School Renewal*. University of Chicago Press, Chicago, Illinois, pp. 63–78

Herrick V E, Tyler R W (eds.) 1950 *Toward Improved Curriculum Theory*. Conf. on Curriculum Theory, University of Chicago, Oct 16–17, 1947. Supplementary Educational Monograph No. 71. University of Chicago Press, Chicago, Illinois

Hirst P H 1974 Liberal education and the nature of knowledge. In: Hirst P H 1974 *Knowledge and the Curriculum: A Collection of Philosophical Papers*. Routledge and Kegan Paul, London

Holmes M 1988 The fortress monastery: The future of the common core. In: Westbury I, Purves A C (eds.) 1988 *Cultural Literacy and the Idea of General Education*. National Society for the Study of Education, University of Chicago Press, Chicago, Illinois, pp. 231–58

Hopmann S 1988 *Lehrplanarbeit als Verwaltungshandeln*. Institute for Science Education, Kiel

Huber M A 1981 The renewal of curriculum theory in the 1970s: An historical study. *J. Curric. Theorizing* 3: 14–84

Jozefzoon E O, Gorter R J (eds.) 1985 *Core Curriculum: A Comparative Analysis*. National Institute for Curriculum Development, Enschede

Kirst M W, Walker D F 1971 An analysis of curriculum policy-making. *Rev. Educ. Res.* 41: 479–509

Klafki W 1963 *Studien zur Bildungstheorie und Didaktik*. Beltz, Weinheim

Kliebard H M 1986 *The Struggle for the American Curriculum*. Routledge and Kegan Paul, London

Kliebard H M 1988(a) Fads, fashions, and rituals: The instability of curriculum change. In: Tanner L N (ed.) 1988 *Critical Issues in Curriculum. Eighty-seventh Yearbook of the National Society for the Study of Education*. University of Chicago Press, Chicago, Illinois, pp. 16–34

Kliebard H M 1988(b) The liberal arts curriculum and its enemies: The effort to redefine general education. In: Westbury I, Purves A C (eds.) 1988 *Cultural Literacy and the Idea of General Education*. National Society for the Study of Education, University of Chicago Press, Chicago, Illinois, pp. 29–51

Künzli R 1975 Begründung und rechtfertigung als anspruch curricularer planung. In: Künzli R (ed.) 1975 *Curriculumentwicklung: Begründung und Legitimation*. Beltz, Weinheim, pp. 9–28

Künzli R 1983 *Topik des Lehrplandenkens: Habilitationsschrift*. Institute for Science Education, Kiel

Lehming R, Kane M (eds.) 1981 *Improving Schools: Using What We Know*. Sage, Beverly Hills, California

Leithwood K A in press *A Strategy for Managing the Implementation of Curriculum Innovations*.

Lewy A (ed.) 1977 *Handbook of Curriculum Evaluation*. UNESCO, Paris

Lieberman A, Rosenholtz S 1987 The road to school improvement: Barriers and bridges. In: Goodlad J I (ed.) 1987 *The Ecology of School Renewal*. University of Chicago Press, Chicago, Illinois, pp. 79–98

Loch W 1979 Curriculare kompetenzen und pädagogische paradigmen. *Bildung und Erziehung* 32: 241–66

Lundgren U P 1972 *Frame Factors and the Teaching Process: A Contribution to Curriculum Theory and Theory on Teaching*. Almqvist and Wiksell, Stockholm

Lütgert W, Stephan H-U 1983 Implementation und evaluation von curricula: Deutschsprachiger raum. In: Hameyer U, Frey K, Haft H (eds.) 1983 *Handbuch der Curriculumforschung*, Vol. 1. *Ausgabe*. Beltz, Weinheim, pp. 501–20

Malliou K 1990 *Die Qualität der Handlungen in der Curriculum-Konferenz*. Institute for Science Education, Kiel

Manen M van 1977 Linking ways of knowing with ways of being practical. *Curric. Inq.* 7: 205–28

Meyer H-L 1972 *Einführung in die Curriculum-Methodologie*. Kösel, München

Miles M B, Ekholm M, Vandenberghe R (eds.) 1987 *Lasting School Improvement: Exploring the Process of Institutionalization*. OECD Publication, Acco, Leuven, pp. 221–39

Phenix P H 1968 The disciplines as curriculum content. In: Short E C, Marconnit G D (eds.) 1968 *Contemporary Thought on Public School Curriculum: Readings*. Brown, Dubuque, Iowa, pp. 133–37

Popkewitz T S 1988 Knowledge, power, and a general curriculum. In: Westbury I, Purves A C (eds.) 1988 *Cultural Literacy and the Idea of General Education*. National Society for the Study of Education, University of Chicago Press, Chicago, Illinois, pp. 69–93

Rassekh S, Vaideanu G 1987 *The Contents of Education: A*

Worldwide View of Their Development From the Present to the Year 2000. UNESCO, Paris

Reid W A 1978 *Thinking About the Curriculum: The Nature and Treatment of Curriculum Problems.* Routledge and Kegan Paul, London

Reid W A 1986 Curriculum theory and curriculum change: What can we learn from history? *J. Curric. Stud.* 18(2): 159–66

Robinsohn S B 1971 *Bildungsreform als Revision des Curriculum,* 3rd edn. Luchterhand, Neuwied

Sarason S B 1982 *The Culture of the School and the Problem of Change,* 2nd edn. Allyn and Bacon, Boston, Massachusetts

Schubert W H 1986 *Curriculum Perspective, Design, and Possibility.* Macmillan, New York

Schwab J J 1978 *Science, Curriculum and Liberal Education: Selected Essays.* University of Chicago Press, Chicago, Illinois

Taba H 1945 *General Techniques of Curriculum Planning. American Education in the Postwar Period: Curriculum Reconstruction,* 44th Yearbook, Part 1. National Society for the Study of Education. University of Chicago, Chicago, Illinois

Tanner D 1988 The textbook controversies. In: Tanner L N (ed.) 1988 *Critical Issues in Curriculum. Eighty-seventh Yearbook of the National Society for the Study of Education.* University of Chicago Press, Chicago, Illinois, pp. 122–47

Tanner D, Tanner L N 1980 *Curriculum Development. Theory into Practice,* 2nd edn. Macmillan, New York

Tykociner J T 1966 *Outline of Zetetics.* Dorrance, Philadelphia, Pennsylvania

Tyler R W 1971 *Basic Principles of Curriculum and Instruction.* University of Chicago Press, Chicago, Illinois

Tyler R W 1977 Toward improved curriculum theory: The inside story. *Curric. Inq.* 6: 251–56

Tyler R W 1988 Progress in dealing with curriculum problems. In: Tanner L N (ed.) 1988 *Critical Issues in Curriculum. Eighty-seventh Yearbook of the National Society for the Study of Education.* University of Chicago Press, Chicago, Illinois, pp. 267–76

van den Akker J 1988 The teacher as learner in curriculum implementation. *J. Curric. Stud.* 20(1): 47–55

van den Berg R, Vandenberghe R 1981 *Onderwijsinnovatie in verschuivend perspectief.* Uitgeverij, Zwijsen

Walker D F 1976 Toward comprehension of curricular realities. In: Shulman L S (ed.) 1976 *Review of Research in Education,* Vol. 4. Peacock, Itasca, Illinois, pp. 268–308

Walker D F, Schaffarzick J 1974 Comparing curricula. *Rev. Educ. Res.* 44: 83–111

Walker D F, Soltis J F 1986 *Curriculum and Aims.* Teachers College Press, New York

Wallin E 1981 *To Change a School: Experiences From Local Development Work.* Department of Education, University of Uppsala, Uppsala

Westbury I 1988 Who can be taught what? General education in the secondary school. In: Westbury I, Purves A C (eds.) 1988 *Cultural Literacy and the Idea of General Education.* National Society for the Study of Education, University of Chicago Press, Chicago, Illinois, pp. 171–97

Westbury I, Purves A C (eds.) 1988 *Cultural Literacy and the Idea of General Education.* National Society for the Study of Education, University of Chicago Press, Chicago, Illinois

Whitty G 1985 *Sociology and School Knowledge: Curriculum Theory, Research, and Politics.* Methuen, London

Zedler H P 1976 *Zur Logik von Legitimationsproblemen: Möglichkeiten der Begründung von Normen.* Kösel, München

Neo-Marxist Approach

D. Gordon

The neo-Marxist approach to education is concerned first and foremost with education's contribution to the reproduction of the means and the relations of production in society (particularly capitalist society). In other words neo-Marxists are concerned with the process of reproduction of class structure. They are also interested in the possibilities of contesting this reproductive process, and thus in education's potential for radical political change. The neo-Marxists' concerns have led them to stress the prime importance of skills taught, knowledge and ideologies transmitted, and also of the centrality of the reproduction of consciousness in the general reproduction process. Inevitably this has led them to investigate the school's overt and hidden curricula, and in general to stress the significance of curriculum as a mechanism for reproduction.

1. Reconceptualism and the "New" Sociology

The first-generation neo-Marxist group flourished in the mid-1970s and was in fact a part and, to an extent, an extension of the reconceptualist approach to curriculum in the United States (Giroux et al. 1981), and the "new" sociology of education in Great Britain. It is the group's relationship to the latter which best demonstrates the contribution and limitations of their particular neo-Marxist theory to curriculum research, and to educational thought in general.

The new sociology of education (Young 1971) arose as a reaction to the dominant paradigm in sociology of education in the late 1960s, that is, the functionalist, educational input–output approach. The "new" sociologists of education rejected functionalism and charged sociologists with having ignored the process of schooling itself, and in particular condemned their ignoring of what goes on in classrooms. A central aspect of classroom life is the way knowledge is transmitted, and thus the "new" sociologists developed a sociology of education which was largely a sociology of curriculum, using ideas from the sociology of knowledge. They tended to eschew a grand theory and a macrolevel of analysis. The reproduction theorists' contribution was to fill this gap by linking the sociology of curriculum to macrosocietal processes, within the framework of

Marxism, that is, one of the major grand themes in the sociological tradition. Their paradigm rapidly became perhaps the most influential and flourishing paradigm of the 1970s in educational sociology and in curriculum studies.

2. The Reproduction Theory

The classic statement of the neo-Marxist position vis-à-vis school and curriculum is Althusser's *Ideology and Ideological State Apparatuses* (1971). Althusser distinguishes between (a) repressive state apparatuses (police, military, etc.) which ensure the political conditions of the reproduction of relations of production primarily through the use of force, and (b) ideological state apparatuses (church, mass media, family, schools, etc.) which work more covertly through ideology, or as Bourdieu has put it—through symbolic violence (Bourdieu and Passeron 1977). Of these, the most important for Althusser is the school:

> One ideological State apparatus certainly has the dominant role, although hardly anyone lends an ear to its music: it is so silent! This is the school. It takes children from every class at infant-school age, and then for years, the years in which the child is most "vulnerable" . . . it drums into them, whether it uses new or old methods, a certain amount of "know-how" wrapped in the ruling ideology (French, arithmetic, natural history . . .) . . . or simply the ruling ideology in its pure state (ethics, civic instruction . . .). . . . Each mass [of children] ejected en route is practically provided with the ideology which suits the role it has to fulfill in class society. . . . [It] is by [this] apprenticeship that the relations of production in a capitalist social formation, i.e., the relations of exploited to exploiter are largely reproduced. The mechanisms which produce this vital result . . . are . . . concealed by a universally reigning ideology of the school . . . which represents the school as a neutral environment purged of ideology (Althusser 1971 pp. 155–56)

This quote encapsulates three of the central ideas characteristic of the writings of a first generation of neo-Marxist thinkers concerned with curriculum, who became known as reproduction theorists. These ideas are outlined below.

2.1 Knowledge as a Form of Capital

Knowledge is viewed as part of what has been called cultural capital (Bourdieu and Passeron 1977). Thus the knowledge (procedural and substantive) that a person "owns", like all capital, determines, at least in part, his or her position within the class structure. One of the mechanisms whereby societies reproduce the class structure is through control of access to cultural capital. That is, children of different social classes are given access to different forms of knowledge, the status of the various sorts of knowledge reflecting the social status of those who "own" them. This is accomplished in at least three ways:

(a) *Different curricula*. Children from different social backgrounds who attend different sorts of schools (e.g., vocational vs. academic high schools) will study different subjects.

(b) *Middle-class subject bias*. The content of high-status subjects, studied in school by all students, will be easier for middle-class students to master because they have already acquired at home a familiarity with the language of school and the content of the high-status subject (Bourdieu and Passeron 1977, Bernstein 1977). This is not to say that the contents of one school subject are intrinsically superior to another, but that the kinds of knowledge with which the working-class students would be more likely to be familiar are not included in the common curriculum. Thus Vulliamy (1976) has argued, for example, that school music generally means "serious", that is, classical music in the Western tradition, and that a "culture clash" exists between school music and working-class pupils' non-classical musical interests outside school.

(c) *Middle-class language*. The presentation of information in school is often couched in a language and/or style with which middle-class students are more familiar (Bourdieu and Passeron 1977, Bernstein 1977). Again, what is being claimed is that this language and or style is not intrinsically superior to that of the working class, but rather acts to maintain class structure.

2.2 The Ideological Nature of the School Curriculum

The ostensibly ideologically neutral content of the school curriculum is, in fact, highly ideological in nature and reflects the need to reproduce class structure. Take, for example, natural science. The study of physics, chemistry, and biology would appear as far from being ideological in content as one could imagine. Yet Apple (1979) has argued that science is taught in such a way as to play down the role of scientific revolutions in research. This results in a general deemphasis of revolution, encourages political acquiescence, and thus helps maintain the status quo.

2.3 The Hidden Curriculum

The hidden curriculum, consisting of unacknowledged but highly consistent messages transmitted to the students (Bloom 1972, Gordon 1982), is assumed to be the most powerful and effective means available in schools to help reproduce class structure. These unacknowledged messages derive both from implicit aspects of the manifest curriculum and also from structural properties of the school. The latter, and in particular the hierarchical structure of social relations in the school, have been seen as exhibiting a correspondence with the hierarchical division of labor [this is known as the correspondence principle analysed by the Marxist economists Bowles and Gintis (1976)].

The interests of the reproduction theorists in the "hidden curriculum" follow from their interest in the theory of "working class false consciousness", a theory developed by Lukács (1968). The notion that schools silently and covertly transmit concealed but powerful messages to the students also links closely with the concept of class hegemony, developed by the Italian Marxist Gramsci (Gramsci 1971). Hegemony, which refers to "the successful attempt of a dominant class to utilize its control over the resources of state and civil society . . . to establish its view of the world as all-inclusive and universal" (Giroux 1981b p. 23) in fact became a central concept of neo-Marxist educational thought.

3. Criticisms of Reproduction Theory

Naturally the reproduction approach came in for a considerable amount of criticism from thinkers who rejected the entire Marxist framework. However by the late 1970s the reproduction approach was also being criticized by neo-Marxists and even by some of the original reproduction theorists themselves (e.g., Apple 1982). These criticisms centered particularly on the assertion that in arguing that the reproduction process in general, and in schools especially, is so powerful that it seems to be an almost inevitable and inescapable result of the way societies and schools work, Althusser and his fellow reproduction theorists seemed to be adopting a deterministic stance to societal processes. Thinkers like Anyon (1981), Apple (1982), and Giroux (1981a) saw this stance as overly pessimistic, and as denying the possibilities of political and social change. These criticisms of the second generation group of neo-Marxist educators led them to an interest in the phenomenon of resistance.

4. Resistance Theory

The trigger for the work around resistance theory was Paul Willis' (1977) classic study *Learning to Labour: How Working Class Kids Get Working Class Jobs*. This is an ethnographic study of a group of working-class teenagers both in school and, after they leave school, in the work place. This group—known as "the lads"—simply wrought havoc in their school. Willis shows that their behavior stemmed in fact from a sophisticated awareness of the hegemonic function of the school, and in particular of its hidden curriculum. Their rebellion derived from their refusal to "buy" the school's ideology and is, for Willis, a form of political resistance. Ironically however, this resistance was self-defeating. The "lads" ended up with an official education of so low a standard that it led them inevitably to getting menial, low-status jobs when they left school. Thus their sort of resistance in fact helps perpetuate the existing class structure.

Willis' study has invited the resistance theorists to set themselves the following tasks:

(a) To identify and document (mainly through ethnographic studies) examples of student resistance to schooling and to the hidden curriculum in particular.

(b) To differentiate between self-defeating and productive examples of resistance (i.e., resistance which can lead to political change).

(c) To suggest ways of mobilizing the resistance phenomenon for political change.

5. Recent Trends

Resistance theory gave the neo-Marxist approach to curriculum a new direction, and in the late 1970s and early 1980s this was once again probably the dominant school of thought in curriculum studies. However it is an approach that has had to try to counter some telling criticisms. Hargreaves (1982) has published a powerful attack on resistance theorists. In his view, their assumptions and activist political stance has led them to the absurd position of reading "resistance" into every conceivable sign of disaffection, boredom, or passivity on the part of pupils in school. Thus, in his opinion, their empirical work is loose and methodologically weak.

From the vantage point of the late 1980s, resistance theory, and, in fact, neo-Marxist approaches to curriculum in general, seem to be at the crossroads. It may be that their paradigm has exhausted the interesting questions it is capable of asking and answering. On the other hand, there have been attempts to link the approach to modern work in discourse analysis and to the work of Foucault (Whitty 1985). These may once again encourage a further development of the neo-Marxist paradigm in curricular work.

Bibliography

Althusser L 1971 Ideology and ideological state apparatuses: Notes towards an investigation. In: Althusser L (ed.) 1971 *Lenin and Philosophy and Other Essays*. New Left Books, New York, pp. 121–73

Anyon J 1981 Elementary schooling and distinctions of social class. *Interchange* 12(2/3): 118–32

Apple M W 1979 *Ideology and Curriculum*. Routledge and Kegan Paul, London

Apple M W 1982 *Education and Power*. Routledge and Kegan Paul, London

Bernstein B 1977 *Class Codes and Control*, Vol 3. *Towards a Theory of Educational Transmissions*. Routledge and Kegan Paul, London

Bloom B S 1972 Innocence in education. *School Review* 80(3): 333–52

Bourdieu P, Passeron J-C 1977 *Reproduction in Education and Society*. Sage, London

Bowles S, Gintis H 1976 *Schooling in Capitalist America: Educational Reform and the Contradictions of Economic Life*. Basic Books, New York

Giroux H A 1981a Hegemony, resistance and the paradox of educational reform. *Interchange* 12(2/3): 3–26

Giroux H A 1981b *Ideology, Culture and the Process of Schooling*. Temple University Press, Philadelphia

Giroux H A, Penna A N, Pinar W F (eds.) 1981 *Curriculum and Instruction: Alternatives in Education*. McCutchan, Berkeley, California

Gordon D 1982 The concept of the hidden curriculum *J. Philos. Educ.* 16(2): 187–98

Gramsci A 1971 *Selections from the Prison Notebooks.* International Publishers, New York

Hargreaves A 1982 Resistance and relative autonomy theories: Problems of distortion and incoherence in recent Marxist analyses of education. *Br. J. Sociol. Educ.* 3(2): 107–26

Lukács G 1968 *History and Class Consciousness: Studies in Marxist Dialectics.* MIT Press, Cambridge, Massachusetts

Vulliamy G 1976 What counts as school music? In: Whitty G. Young M F D (eds.) 1976 *Explorations in the Politics of School Knowledge.* Nafferton Books, Nafferton, pp. 19–34

Whitty G 1985 *Sociology and School Knowledge: Curriculum Theory, Research and Politics.* Methuen, London

Willis P E 1977 *Learning to Labour: How Working Class Kids Get Working Class Jobs.* Saxon House, Farnborough

Young M F D (ed.) 1971 *Knowledge and Control: New Directions for the Sociology of Education.* Collier-Macmillan, London

Constructivism in Education

E. von Glasersfeld

Constructivism is a theory of knowledge with roots in philosophy, psychology, and cybernetics. It asserts two main principles whose application has far-reaching consequences for the study of cognitive development and learning as well as for the practice of teaching, psychotherapy, and interpersonal management in general. The two principles are: (a) knowledge is not passively received but actively built up by the cognizing subject; (b) the function of cognition is adaptive and serves the organization of the experiential world, not the discovery of ontological reality.

To accept only the first principle is considered *trivial constructivism* by those who accept both, because that principle has been known since Socrates and, without the help of the second, runs into all the perennial problems of Western epistemology.

The present flourishing of constructivism owes much to the doubts about the accessibility of an *objective* reality in modern physics and philosophy of science (Hanson, Kuhn, Lakatos, Barnes) and the concomitant interest in the sceptical core of eighteenth-century empiricism. Constructivism has as yet only an implicit relation with the constructivist approach to the foundations of mathematics (Lorenzen, Brouwer, Heyting).

The first explicit formulation of a constructivist theory of knowledge was proposed by Giambattista Vico in his little-known Latin treatise *De antiquissima Italorum sapientia* (1710). He coined the phrase "verum est ipsum factum" and explained that to *know* something means to know what parts it is made of and how they have been put together. Objective, ontological reality, therefore, may be known to God, who constructed it, but not to a human being who has access only to subjective experience. "God", Vico wrote, "is the artificer of nature, man the god of artifacts" (p. 122).

In modern psychology, the notion of cognitive construction was first forged into a major component of developmental theory by Baldwin and Piaget. Almost certainly unaware of Vico's treatise, they set out from a Kantian position and endeavored to map the procedures and operations by means of which the human subject, having access only to sensation and to the operations of the mind, constructs a relatively stable experiential world. "L'intelligence organise le monde en s'organisant elle-même" (Piaget 1937 p. 311).

Both Baldwin and Piaget could draw on a source that had not been available to Kant and Vico; the theory of evolution. Already William James (1880) and Georg Simmel (1895) had forcefully suggested that the function of the cognitive capability was *adaptive*, that is, it was not to produce a "true" picture of the "real" world, but rather to enhance the organism's management of experience. This enabled them to avoid Kant's assumption of a priori categories: "... also the forms of thought, that create our conception of the world, result from the practical consequences and reactions which shape our mental constitution, just like our physical one, according to evolutionary requirements" (Simmel 1895 p. 45).

The revolutionary aspect of constructivism lies in the assertion that knowledge cannot and need not be "true" in the sense that it *matches* ontological reality; it only has to be "viable" in the sense that it *fits* within the experiential constraints that limit the cognizing organism's possibilities of acting and thinking.

Cybernetics and control theory, being concerned with self-regulating systems, have developed a similar approach to cognition, according to which adaptation to the environment and a viable conception of the world must and can be constructed from data generated internally by "trial and error" and require no input of "information" (Maturana and Varela 1980, Foerster 1985).

Another source of constructivism was the analysis of communication and language stimulated by computer science. Shannon's mathematical theory (1948) confirmed that only directives of choice and combination could travel between communicators, but not the *meanings* that have to be selected and combined to interpret a message. Language users, therefore, build up their meanings on the basis of their individual experience, and the meanings remain subjective, no matter how much they become modified and homogenized through the subject's interactions with other language users. From the constructivist point of view, meanings are conceptual structures and, as such, to a large extent influence the individual's construction and organization of his or her experiential reality.

At present the constructivist approach has had most impact on psychotherapy and the empirical study of literature. Among family therapists, for instance, the notion that every individual constructs his or her own experiential reality has led to the realization that, in order to eliminate interactional conflicts, subjective constructs must be modified, rather than elements of an "objective" situation (Elkaim 1984, Keeney 1983).

In literary studies, the realization that *meanings* are not materially inherent in words or texts, but have to be supplied by readers from their individual stores of experiential abstractions, has drawn attention to the fact that interpretations are necessarily subjective and that the source of interpersonal agreement concerning an author's intentions must be found in the social construction of a consensual domain (Schmidt 1983).

The students' subjective interpretation of texts and teachers' discourse, and thus the subjective view of linguistically presented problems, is increasingly being taken into account in educational practice and research. Such a constructivist perspective has noteworthy consequences (von Glasersfeld 1983). There will be a radical separation between educational procedures that aim at generating *understanding* ("teaching") and those that merely aim at the repetition of behaviors ("training"). The researcher's and to some extent also the educator's interest will be focused on what can be inferred to be going on inside the student's head, rather than on overt "responses."

The teacher will realize that knowledge cannot be *transferred* to the student by linguistic communication but that language can be used as a tool in a process of guiding the student's construction. The teacher will try to maintain the view that students are attempting to *make sense* in their experiential world. Hence he or she will be interested in students' "errors" and, indeed, in every instance where students deviate from the teacher's expected path; because it is these deviations that throw light on *how* the students, at that point in their development, are organizing their experiential world. This last point is crucial also for educational research and

has led to the development of the Teaching Experiment (Steffe 1983), an extension of Piaget's clinical method, that aims not only at inferring the student's conceptual structures and operations but also at finding ways and means of modifying them.

Bibliography

Baldwin J M 1902 *Development and Evolution*. Macmillan, London

Baldwin J M 1906–1911 *Thought and Things or Genetic Logic: A Study of the Development and Meaning of Thought*, Vols. 1–3. Macmillan, New York

Elkaim M 1984 *Psychothérapie et reconstruction du réel: Epistémologie et thérapie familiale*. Editions Universitaires, Brussels

Foerster H von 1985 Entdecken oder erfinden—wie lässt sich Verstehen verstehen? In: Gumin H, Mohler A (eds.) 1985 *Einführung in den Konstruktivismus*. Oldenbourg, Munich, pp. 27–68

Glasersfeld E von 1983 Learning as a constructive activity. In: Janvier C (ed.) 1986 *Problems of Representation in the Teaching and Learning of Mathematics*. Lawrence Erlbaum, Hillsdale, New Jersey, pp. 3–17

Gumin H, Mohler A (eds.) 1985 *Einführung in den Konstruktivismus*. Oldenbourg, Munich

James W 1880 Great men, great thoughts, and the environment. *Atlantic Monthly* 46: 441–59

Keeney B P 1983 *Aesthetics of Change*. Guilford Press, New York

Maturana H R, Varela F J 1980 *Autopoiesis and Cognition*. Reidel, Dordrecht, The Netherlands

Piaget J 1937 *La Construction du réel chez l'enfant*. Delachaux et Niestlé. Neuchâtel [Cook M (trans.) 1954 *The Construction of Reality in the Child*. Basic Books, New York]

Schmidt S J 1983 The empirical science of literature: A new paradigm. *Poetics* 12: 19–34

Shannon C E 1948 A mathematical theory of communication. *Bell Syst. Tech. J.* 27: 379–423, 623–56

Simmel G 1895 Ueber eine Beziehung der Selectionslehre zur Erkenntnistheorie. *Arch. Systematische Phil.* 1: 34–45

Steffe L P 1983 The teaching experiment methodology in a constructivist research program. In: Zweng M, Green T, Kilpatrick J, Pollack H, Suydam M (eds.) *Proc. 4th Int. Congr. Math. Educ.* Birkhäuser, Boston, Massachusetts

Vico G 1710 *De antiquissima Italorum sapientia*. Felice Mosca, Naples

Social Reconstructionist Approach

W. H. Watkins

By the turn of the twentieth century a new criticism was emerging in the United States's social science community. Concern was being expressed about the inequities and impersonal nature of the then emergent corporate industrial organization of society. Veblen's *Theory of the Leisure Class* (1899), along with essays by muckraking journalists, dramatized social and economic problems in the midst of plenty. The emerging progressive movement with its themes of democracy,

humanism, and social reform was to profoundly affect the educational community.

1. Origins

With Dewey as its principal theoretician, progressive education criticized mechanization, the efficiency movement, and the impersonal nature of education (Tanner and Tanner 1975). It offered new approaches to understanding the child, curriculum, and the processes of education. Progressive education gave us the cult of the child. Through its organizational arm, the Progressive Education Association (PEA), progressive educators promoted child-centered education. They championed the rights of children and insisted that the fundamental interests of the learner be recognized. Dewey posited that the experience of the community should be the subject matter of education and that school ought to be the community in embryo. Progressive rhetoric talked of the whole child and worked to create fully humanized individuals.

While progressive education made its influence felt in the post-First World War period, the PEA was never a strong centralized organization. It had no single voice (Bowers 1969) and was always numerically inferior to the larger National Education Association. By the mid-1930s the intellectual climate of the country took a noticeable turn to the left. The social criticism of the early 1900s was now expanded. A significant section of the intelligentsia and politically conscious populace began to question the moral worth of the capitalist system, while insisting that human rights take priority over property rights. The educational community could not remain outside this discourse.

A discernably dissident group began to make their voices heard from within the PEA. One rallying point for this group was the report of the Commission on the Social Studies within the American Historical Association. The report, funded by the Carnegie Foundation, was presented in 17 volumes between the years 1932 and 1937. Among those who contributed to the project were well-known educators and social theorists like Beard, Curti, Counts, and Newlon.

The year 1932 became eventful for this dissident group, which was to become known as Social Reconstructionists or Social Frontiersmen. While the PEA remained committed to child-centered education, the Reconstructionists wanted more of progressivism than the exaltation of the child. They wanted education to feature a social point of view, that is, a descriptive and prescriptive examination of social problems.

When Counts of the University of Chicago delivered his disturbing lecture "Dare Progressive Education Be Progressive?" to the PEA in April 1932, the new movement took on identity. Counts criticized the progressive education movement as one of middle-class dilettantes. He stated:

> The great weakness of Progressive Education lies in the fact that it has elaborated no theory of social welfare, unless it be that of anarchy or extreme individualism. In this, of course, it is but reflecting the viewpoint of the members of the liberal-minded upper middle class. (Counts 1932a p. 258)

Further in this lecture, which was to be greeted by a stunned silence that sent shockwaves through the Progressive education community, he suggested that these progressives were romantic sentimentalists not interested in addressing the economic and social crises.

He called on Progressive educators to:

> face squarely and courageously every social issue, come to grips with life in all of its stark reality, establish an organic relation with the community, develop a realistic and comprehensive theory of welfare, fashion a compelling and challenging vision of human destiny, and become somewhat less frightened than it is today at the bogeys of imposition and indoctrination. (Counts 1932a p. 259)

Counts continued to speak about how our competitive capitalist society "must be replaced by cooperation" and "some form of socialized economy." This blockbuster lecture along with two others, "Freedom, Culture, Social Planning, and Leadership" and "Education Through Indoctrination" were issued in what Butts (1978 p. 385) called "perhaps the most widely discussed pamphlet in the history of American education," *Dare the School Build a New Social Order?* (Counts 1932b). In this work, which became the blueprint for Social Reconstructionism, Counts challenged the educational community to bridge the gap between school and society where schools create a vision of a new world based on the principles of collectivism.

The works of Counts in 1932, combined with the publication of the Commission on the Social Studies in the Schools' *A Charter for the Social Sciences in the Schools* (1932) drafted by Beard, served as a unifying framework to bring together such individuals as Kilpatrick, Childs, Raup, and Rugg. Additionally, other well-known progressives like Dewey and Bode were attracted to the call of the reconstructionists.

2. Social Reconstructionism: An Educational and Political Program

While the dissident Social Reconstructionists remained within the PEA and enjoyed a measure of support, it became clear that they had a different focus. In an effort to respond to the insurgents, particularly Counts, the PEA in 1932 established the Committee on Social and Economic Problems. This committee at once served to rally the reconstructionists and further split the ranks of the PEA. Between 1932 and 1934 the reconstructionist position became more clearly defined and more radical. Two more books joined the essays of Counts to advance their cause. One, *A Call to the Teachers of the Nation* (1933) written by the PEA's Committee on Social and Economic Problems, summoned teachers to act; while the second, *The Educational Frontier* (1933), edited and partially written by the respected Kilpatrick, called for the politicization of education. The Social Reconstructionists now had their own identity.

As the Reconstructionists more forcefully affirmed their position, the larger sentiment within the PEA began to assert itself. Though still not tightly administered, the PEA focused its commitment and its journal, *Progressive Education*, on child-centered classroom techniques. The Reconstructionists, experiencing increased difficulties in getting published (Bowers 1969), founded their own journal, *The Social Frontier*, which first appeared in October 1934. They could thus continue to develop their distinctive position. The hard core of the Reconstructionists, that is, Hook, Counts, Rugg, Newlon, Watson, and Childs best articulated their view. Three sociopolitical and educational propositions formed the foundation of Social Reconstructionism.

First, the advocacy of a collectivist society. The evil capitalist system was seen as the source of human misery, unemployment, and divisiveness. Capitalism was to be replaced by economic collectivism. Though Hook was a Marxist and Counts spoke of his serious study of Karl Marx, the beliefs and language of the Reconstructionists seldom suggested a violent proletarian revolution as Marx had called for. The Reconstructionists instead spoke of evolutionary change. They in fact suggested that, given New Deal politics and the intellectual climate, the country had already evolved into an era of economic collectivism. For them, a benevolent and democratic socialist collectivism represented desirable social development. A redistribution of wealth and resources would allow public morality and cooperation to reshape society.

Second, the Reconstructionists called for linking education with (collectivist) political ideology. The attainment of a truly progressive society required an expanded role for education. Treating children humanistically was fine but education must take on a major role in the plan to transform society. Education must be utilized to transform social institutions, and should be viewed as a form of social action. Schools must take an active role in determining the new social order.

Third, schools should participate in reshaping society to realize education's true mission. Kilpatrick argued that the worn socioeconomic system was making it difficult for schools to produce worthy citizens. Schools should foster a broader social responsibility and work for the common good. By helping to transform laissez-faire capitalism, education could help make society more humane. Education should be at the cutting edge of civilization. In short, the process of schooling should be inextricably linked to social progress.

3. The Role of the Teacher

Among the most intriguing formulations presented by the Reconstructionists were their views on the role of the teacher. If education was to play a key role in changing the old social and economic order, as well as an expanded role in the new collectivist order, educators could not remain neutral. Dewey wrote in the pages of the *Social Frontier* of teachers as active and militant participants in a new social order. Counts exhorted teachers to mobilize themselves into a militant force and take sides in the struggle to forge a new collectivist society.

Interestingly, the hard core Reconstructionists clung to an optimistic yet unfounded hope that teachers would quickly adopt the Reconstructionist program as their

own. As it would turn out, this was to be a gross miscalculation emanating from an exaggerated reading of the political climate and a misreading of the social consciousness of the 10,000 teachers who were to serve as a core and the one million teachers they hoped to inspire.

Counts hoped that every teacher would be an agent for change. He suggested that teachers continue to unionize themselves and join ranks with the disaffected, radical labor movement at large. Teachers should fight for social progress and reform both in the street as well as the classroom. In the January 1935 (Vol. 1 (4) p. 31) issue of *Social Frontier*, the editorial board articulated this position statement:

> The Social Frontier consequently proposes to the teachers of the country that they ally themselves with that conception of social welfare which may be expected to serve the many rather than the few—that they strive to substitute human for property rights, a democratic collectivism for an oligarchic individualism in economy, social planning and security for anarchy and chaos. Positively and consistently they should seek to develop in the population those values, attitudes, ideals, and loyalties consonant with the new way of life, as well as habits of thought and action calculated to bring that way of life into being.

4. Remaking the Curriculum

If education was going to significantly contribute to social change, schools must necessarily adopt a curriculum sufficiently critical of the old social order while supportive of the new collectivism. The Social Reconstructionists called on the curriculum community to support wholesale change in curriculum materials, activities, and outlooks.

A leading curriculum theoretician among the Reconstructionists was Prof. Rugg of Teachers College, Columbia University. Long committed to change, Rugg in *The Scientific Method in the Reconstruction of Elementary and Secondary School Subjects* (1921), argued for a curriculum that would combine critical sociopolitical inquiry with the life's experience of the learner. Above all, Rugg wanted to guarantee that any new curriculum was pedagogically sound. In the early 1920s Rugg began to publish his own social studies pamphlets. In his series, entitled *Man and His Changing Society*, Rugg offered a comprehensive social science curriculum based on democratic and humanistic values.

In the October 1936 (Vol. 3 (19), p. 15) issue of *Social Frontier*, Rugg challenged "commissioners, presidents, deans, superintendents, principals, supervisors, teachers . . . to stir the mass into action!" Rugg went on to blast "professional Directors of Curriculum and a powerful behind-the-scenes body of textbook writers and publishers who have controlled the program of American education . . . primarily in the interest of the status quo."

In his blueprint for a new curriculum Rugg suggests that schools focus on the "Social Scene," a "new psychology," and a "syllabi of activities and materials directly out of the crucial conditions, problems and issues of our changing social order." He goes on to advocate confronting controversial issues, exploring alternative decision making, and teaching the basic issues of civilization in the classrooms.

5. Dissension to Collapse: The End of an Era

The years 1934–35 were a peak period for these Social Frontiersmen. However, by 1936 their unresolved internal contradictions could no longer be ignored. A shifting national and international mood revealed fissures in the movement. Although the Social Frontier had between 5,000 and 10,000 subscribers at varying times and claimed among its editorial board and spokespeople some of the most influential educational theorists in the country, its leaders could never agree on a single platform that could bind the movement. By 1936 the difficulties became glaring.

First, the issue of indoctrination would not die. Counts, all along, had held that the dominant elite groups exerted a monopoly on indoctrination in the schools and perhaps it was time that another voice was heard. Eventually detractors asserted that Counts wanted to brainwash students.

Second, and more important, by 1936 Dewey and Bode, never fully in the radical camp, reaffirmed their commitment to experimentalism and progressivism. Bode argued that schools were not the proper place to evolve public policy. Dewey, now no longer interested in radical Reconstructionist initiatives, turned his attention to a critical analysis of the pedagogy of Hutchins.

As the war years approached, radicalism gave way to patriotism. The fascist menace was so threatening it became the priority for conservatives and socialists alike. The resignation of Counts from the *Social Frontiers* editorial board in 1937 signaled the end of this energetic, yet short-lived movement.

As the Reconstructionists began to lose momentum, the newly formed John Dewey Society began to attract many of the old forces and actually absorbed the Social Frontier. During the war years a few half-hearted efforts

were undertaken, particularly by Rugg, to rekindle the old vigor but without much success. By the mid-1950s even the PEA was in mortal decline.

It can be concluded that the Social Reconstruction movement was very much a product of its time. While it attracted the attention of significant educational and curriculum thinkers, it never became the hoped-for mass movement of teachers. Energetic though short-lived, this body of thought left its indelible imprint on educational theorizing and curriculum reform.

Since the Second World War, scattered efforts, such as the work of Brameld, the Society for Educational Reconstruction, and other individuals have kept this once lively movement in memory.

Bibliography

Bowers C A 1969 *The Progressive Educator and the Depression: The Radical Years.* Random House, New York

Bullough R V 1981 *Democracy in Education—Boyd H. Bode.* General Hall, Bayside, New York

Butts R F 1978 *Public Education in the United States: From Revolution to Reform.* Holt, Rinehart and Winston, New York

Counts G S 1932a Dare the progressives be progressive? *Prog. Educ.* 9: 257–63

Counts G S 1932b *Dare the School build a New Social Order?* John Day, New York

Cremin L A 1961 *The Transformation of the School: Progressivism in American Education 1876–1957.* Alfred A. Knopf, New York

Kilpatrick W H 1932 *Education and the Social Crises.* Liveright, New York

Kilpatrick W H (ed.) 1933 *The Educational Frontier.* Appleton-Century-Crofts, New York

Kliebard H M 1986 *The Struggle for the American Curriculum 1893–1958.* Routledge and Kegan Paul, Boston, Massachusetts

Progressive Education Association's Committee on Social and Economic Problems 1933 *A Call to the Teachers of the Nation.* John Day, New York

Rugg H O 1932 Social reconstruction through education. *Prog. Educ.* 9(8): 11–18

Tanner D, Tanner L N 1975 *Curriculum Development: Theory into Practice.* Macmillan, New York

The Reconceptualist Approach

W. F. Pinar

Reconceptualization refers to a paradigm shift in United States curriculum studies. Schwab's *The Practical: A Language for Curriculum* initiated a decade of critiques of the traditional field (Schwab 1970, Jackson 1981). Reconceptualization is an umbrella term referring to a diverse group whose common bond was opposition to the Tyler rationale, to behaviorism in curriculum conceptualization (including behavioral or performance objectives, quantitative evaluation, mastery learning, time on task), and to the ahistorical and atheoretical

character of the field. Reconceptualism is a misnomer which overstates the degree of thematic and methodological unity among so-called reconceptualists.

One emphasis during the early stages of reconceptualization was upon so-called reproduction theory, the reproduction of society via school curriculum (Apple 1975). A central concept in this scholarship was the hidden curriculum. Other major scholars who viewed curriculum preeminently as a political text included Giroux (1981) and Anyon (1988). Reproduction theory (also known as correspondence theory, a theory of the correspondence between curriculum and ideology) shifted to resistance theory in the early 1980s.

The second emphasis of the reconceptualization is *currere* or autobiographical curriculum research (Pinar 1988a). This emphasis upon individual experience of school curriculum spawned and was accompanied by scholarship on various aspects of experience (Aoki 1988) and gender (Grumet 1988). Biographic function, lived experience, autobiographical curriculum research, poor curriculum, personal–practical knowledge are among the central concepts in the study of curriculum as autobiographical/biographical and phenomenological texts.

1. Major Ideas

According to Pinar (1988b), reconceptualization is said to have occurred. Theory and other forms of qualitative research have displaced the traditional emphasis upon curriculum development. Scholars study curriculum as (a) a gender text, (b) a political text, (c) a phenomenological text (Aoki 1988), (d) an aesthetic text, (e) an autobiographical/biographical text, (f) an institutionalized text, including curriculum development, implementation, and evaluation, (g) a racial text, (h) a religious text, (i) a historical text, and (j) as a deconstructed text, that is, studies informed by so-called poststructuralism (Pinar 1988a). Curriculum is understood as a multidimensional text in which the major currents of the culture are expressed, denied, distorted, or reconstituted in complex ways.

2. Implications

Curriculum studies represents the one major specialization within education (in the United States) wherein mainstream social science, typified by educational psychology and educational administration, has been defeated. The major informing traditions of curriculum studies are literary theory, feminist theory, Marxian social theory, French poststructuralism, phenomenology, aesthetic theory, and theology. Epistemological struggles will continue less within the field than at its borders with competing specializations, such as educational psychology, via scholarship and bureaucratic politics within departments, schools, and colleges of education.

Public and private primary and secondary schools represent a second site of reconceptualization (Pinar 1988b). The implications of contemporary curriculum theory include:

(a) an enlarged knowledge base, to include non-European knowledge of literature and culture, and to include history and sociology of science as well as mainstream science (see *Science, Technology, and Society as a Curricular Topic***) curriculum movement in American science education;

(b) a reformulated curriculum center away from traditional science and mathematics and a strengthened curricular position for social studies, literature, and the arts;

(c) inclusion of feminist and gender understanding of specific disciplines;

(d) decreasing emphasis upon standardized examinations;

(e) increasing emphasis upon an individualization of teaching and learning informed by rigorous phenomenological and autobiographical/biographical research;

(f) increasing emphasis upon the lived experience of students from phenomenological, gender, and political perspectives; and

(g) reorganization of school structure and size to support altered social relations within schools, namely, smaller size, less centralized administration, empowered teacher authority, increased student involvement in curricular and organizational matters.

3. The Future of Reconceptualization

Just as theory was the site of movement in the 1970s, history is predicted to be a major site of scholarship in the 1990s as the field moves to incorporate the reconceptualization into a reformulated and more complex identity, including a revised conception of its history and its structure (central concepts, research methodologies, institutionalized functions). Synoptic texts reflect this movement of incorporation and reformulation. In addition to historical studies, ethnographic and other forms of qualitative research will examine functions of curriculum in schools informed by curriculum theory. Finally, a systematic effort to reconceptualize primary and secondary schools as well as related areas (for instance, teacher preparation, see Pinar 1989, Shaker and Kridel 1989) is predicted.

Bibliography

Anyon J 1988 Schools as agencies of social legitimation. In: Pinar W F (ed.) 1988 *Contemporary Curriculum Discourses*. Gorsuch Scarisbrick, Scottsdale, Arizona, pp. 175–200

Aoki T 1988 Toward a dialectic between the conceptual world and the lived world: Transcending instrumentalism in curriculum orientation. In: Pinar W F (ed.) 1988 *Contemporary Curriculum Discourses*. Gorsuch Scarisbrick, Scottsdale, Arizona, pp. 402–16

Apple M W 1975 The hidden curriculum and the nature of conflict. In: Pinar W F (ed.) 1975 *Curriculum Theorizing: The Reconceptualists*. McCutchan, Berkeley, California, pp. 95–119

Giroux H 1981 Hegemony, resistance, and the paradox of educational reform. In: Giroux H, Penna A, Pinar W F (eds.) 1981 *Curriculum and Instruction: Alternatives in Education*. McCutchan, Berkeley, California, pp. 400–32

Grumet M 1988 Women and teaching: Homeless at home. In: Pinar W F (ed.) 1988 *Contemporary Curriculum Discourses*. Gorsuch Scarisbrick, Scottsdale, Arizona, pp. 531–40

Jackson P 1981 Curriculum and its discontents. In: Giroux H, Penna A, Pinar W F (eds.) 1981 *Curriculum and Instruction: Alternatives in Education*. McCutchan, Berkeley, California, pp. 367–81

Pinar W F 1980 The voyage out: Curriculum as the relation between the knower and the known. *J. Curric. Theor.* 2(1): 72–91

Pinar W F 1988a Autobiography and the architecture of self. *J. Curric. Theory.* 8(1): 7–36

Pinar W F 1988b Introduction. In: Pinar W F (ed.) 1988 *Contemporary Curriculum Discourses*. Gorsuch Scarisbrick, Scottsdale, Arizona, pp. 1–8

Pinar W F 1989 A reconceptualization of teacher education. *J. Teach. Educ.* 40(1): 9–12

Schwab J 1970 *The Practical: A Language for Curriculum*. National Education Association, Washington, DC

Shaker P, Kridel C 1989 The return to experience: A reconceptualist call. *J. Teach. Educ.* 40(1): 2–8

Curriculum as Ethics

M. Holmes

Curriculum is defined as the formal program of the school. It includes extraclass activities such as morning prayer, assemblies, and class visits outside the school. It does not include either spontaneous, informal interaction among peers or unplanned, spontaneous interaction, unrelated to the formal program, between pupils and teachers.

Ethics is defined as a formal or informal code of approved conduct. The code is normally applicable to people occupying a specific role, for example, parents, employers, and teachers. Ethics has strong connections with morality. It is both immoral and unethical for elementary teachers to have sexual relations with pupils in their classes; immoral because it is wrong to take sexual advantage of young people, unethical because it contravenes teachers' professional obligations. Although both ethical and moral codes prescribe and proscribe conduct, ethics and morality are not coterminous. It may be considered unethical for a teacher to criticize another teacher to a member of the public, even though such action may be a moral act intended, for instance, to prevent a principal's private relationship with a pedagogically incompetent person from further damaging the lives of those taught. However, the distinction becomes blurred both because professionals do not confine their ethical judgments to their formal code and because the absence of such a code does not mean that all behavior is thereby considered ethical. Indeed, professionals would typically not accept that their codes of professional ethics may be immoral, even if others may sometimes find them so.

The development of formal programs in moral or ethical education is not considered here. The focus is on ethical generalities involved in curriculum development, implementation, and interpretation. The article is subdivided into three sections. They concern ethical issues in: (a) the establishment of curriculum, (b) the implementation of curriculum and curricular change, and (c) the delivery and interpretation of curriculum. The three sections are developed in the context of elementary and secondary schooling.

1. Selection of Curricular Context

Ethical aspects of curriculum have generally been neglected by standard texts on the topic, for example, Tyler (1949), Taba (1962), and Pratt (1980). Eisner (1979), in an avowedly "normative" study, while avoiding the technocratic, value-free approaches of Tyler, Taba, and Pratt, considers different approaches to education but does not directly address the ethical issue. Phenix (1964) gives ethics a prominent place within curricular content. For him, it is a central component of curriculum. He attempts to help educators arrive at an appropriate set of ethics with which curriculum should be suffused. That concern, important as it is, leaves aside the important question of the ethics of developing a curriculum for young people whose parents may be opposed to the ethical and moral basis on which the curriculum has been developed. It is one thing to develop an ideal curriculum that can be justified on the basis of established criteria; it is another to deliver it to a varied group of young people. It is not a question of the teacher's interpretation, which is considered later; it is not a question of relevance to students or even community; it is a question of the ethics of presenting something repugnant to even one parent and, by extension, to one learner. Parents who are willing to defer to educators' expertise in history are often unwilling to do so in the moral arena. Is it ethical in a modern democracy where freedom of thought, belief, and religion is valued to teach moral ideas and assumptions, directly or indirectly, formally or informally, to which a parent is opposed? If the answer is negative, then education itself becomes a questionable enterprise in many schools enrolling a diversity of young people. If the answer is positive, it becomes important for the legitimate educational authority to specify most precisely the officially approved, moral foundations which it deems to be ethical to teach.

In practice, an ethical statement defining a specific moral framework is unlikely to be found within public policy precisely because the clearer the policy, the easier dissent becomes. Political and administrative inaction is reinforced, on the one hand by fear of public reaction, and on the other by mainstream, liberal, pedagogical discourse that "de-ethicizes" human relationships and personal understandings (Apple 1979 p. 111). Apple identifies the problem of supposedly "value-free" systems and the accompanying manipulation by educators. Earlier, as the moral crisis of democratic freedom began to become evident, Counts (1964) had advocated a school program whose ethics would be open and accountable; it would be the school's job to create a new social order. In contrast, Maritain (1943) advocated a "Christian" ethic based on traditional "fundamental dispositions" to be fostered; truth, love of the good, openness to existence, sense of a job well done, cooperation.

The openness and relative clarity of the left-wing agenda of, among others, Counts and Apple and of the traditional agenda of Maritain contrasts with the ethically vacuous, technocratic approaches more generally adopted in socially diverse Western democracies in recent times. A central problem of contemporary curriculum development is the lack of ethical awareness, both in terms of the implicit underpinnings and in terms of the ethical implications for delivery to individuals.

A school program to which parents and students may be expected to give emotional and ideological, as well as or instead of, contractual commitment will be characterized by clear, unambiguous underlying values and by clear understanding on the part of teachers as to what it is ethical to teach and to whom. Continued failure to meet those criteria is leading to the substitution of the influence of the school by that of such competing social institutions as the peer group, youth culture, and the media, with their enlistment in the cause of collective criteria of dress and comportment, genres of popular music, and teams represented in a professional sport.

2. The Implementation of Curriculum and Curricular Change

The "de-ethicizing" of curriculum is nowhere more apparent than in the process of program implementation. Traditionally, curriculum has been based on goals and objectives, explicit or implicit, which receive ongoing consensual support from the community they serve. As populations become more culturally diverse, the ethical applicability of program to individuals and groups becomes increasingly problematic. Ironically, it is possible that the very lack of consensus has been one of the forces leading to emphasis on curricular implementation. In the absence of consensual commitment, administrators deliver, with difficulty, anemic programs they believe to be value-free. Implementation is therefore sometimes hardly at all concerned with announced goals (which are obscure, to avoid public dissent) or even with content, but, increasingly, with methodology and with changing teachers' beliefs and attitudes. Programs are being implemented whose emphasis is almost entirely on process, teachers' behavior and beliefs, for example child-centered programs in primary education, and writing skills through personal development. The ethics of changing teachers' beliefs and behavior is not considered in the mainstream implementation literature, for example, Sarason (1982) and Fullan (1982). Teachers' "inappropriate" beliefs and behavior are seen as problems to be overcome by careful use of inservice training, peer counseling, and reward systems.

Changing teachers' beliefs and behavior in the area of curriculum may be approached in three ways; persuasion, command, and manipulation. Of the three, persuasion is the least problematic ethically. Indeed, it would normally be unethical not to try to persuade colleagues to do the right or best thing. Two essential criteria of persuasion, as the term is used in this context, are openness and the right of rejection by the person being persuaded. A fundamental ethical principle in education is that those who are being persuaded (learners capable of moral and ethical reasoning, teachers, and administrators) should understand the object of persuasion and have the option to listen but to reject.

A command that teachers must change their beliefs and/or behavior is ethically acceptable in some circumstances. It is generally accepted that the goals of an educational institution are determined by the legitimate authority; a teacher may not ethically ignore or subvert curricular goals, assuming they have been put in place clearly, openly, consensually, and legitimately. As a corollary, the cumulative and purposeful education of children requires sequence of content; it is unethical for teachers to change the sequence or content in a substantial way. However, teachers' professionalism depends on their having some discretionary control over the method by which the legitimate goals are achieved. It is therefore generally unethical to demand that teachers change their methodology in the absence of clear, empirical evidence of the unsatisfactory nature of their current methodology and the almost certain superiority of an alternative.

Manipulation is becoming more evident in curricular implementation because persuasion frequently fails and commands, like clear goals, are apt to be challenged. Manipulation, by definition, is unethical. It refers to the treatment of fellow professionals as objects, in such a way that they feel constrained to change without necessarily being morally or intellectually convinced, and without even fully appreciating the influences that are being brought to bear on them.

The mainstream approach to curricular implementation has not gone uncriticized. Apple sees the entire curriculum development and implementation process as being an unexamined political process in the exercise of hegemony. However, the acceptance of neo-Marxists' quasi-conspiratorial explanations requires that one accept that virtually everyone in the "capitalist" West has been enculturated with the exception of those who have come to hold neo-Marxist viewpoints. Barrow (1984) is a vigorous critic of mainstream implementation. His grounds are utilitarian rather than ethical or political. He argues from the empirical research that the consequences of forcing all teachers into a uniform pattern of instruction are unlikely to be positive in terms of educational outcomes.

Curricular change of goals and content should take place after a prolonged period of consensus building within an open, political process. In that way, it becomes ethically legitimate to demand that teachers adhere to what represents an informal public will. Curricular changes in methodology, in contrast, should normally be introduced by persuasion, never by manipulation. Commands should be used only in the most unusual, possibly nonexistent, situation where it can be demonstrated by clear, large-scale empirical research that failure to change would be substantially detrimental to the achievement of the school's legitimate purposes. Apple and Barrow identify the hidden hand of the curriculum mainstream, but fail to clarify the overriding ethical issue.

3. The Delivery and Interpretation of Curriculum

The concern here is with the application of curriculum within the microcosm of the school and classroom. Many of the important ethical issues at the level of school and classroom lie outside curriculum, particularly with respect to the behavior of administrators and teachers beyond the confines of the intended program. Such issues are a major concern of teachers' codes of ethics, of which curriculum is but one component. The American National Education Association Code of Ethics (Strike and Solitis 1985 pp. xiii–xv), for example, limits its concern with curriculum to the suppression or distortion of subject matter and to educational inclusion, irrespective of, for example, race, sex, and religion. It does not make reference to rights to exclusion from the teacher's moral or amoral framework.

Even after goals, content, and methodology have been determined, ethical problems may remain for the teacher who delivers the program and for administrators who supervise it. Individual educators may not share the consensual goals of the program. At an extreme, it is unethical for educators to participate in the realization of important goals with which they fundamentally disagree. Most would agree that an atheist should not teach in a Christian fundamentalist school, although an argument might be made for the teaching of a purely technical skill from which consensual values can perhaps be excluded. A more frequent but less recognized problem is for the relativist educator who is expected but typically neglects to inculcate a set of absolute values. Also important are such issues as: educators acceptance of abortion and birth control working in Roman Catholic or Orthodox Jewish schools; educators who

deliberately choose "deviant" sexual and social arrangements for their private lives working in schools that promote the traditional family and sex within marriage; teachers using role play, thereby encouraging pupils to loosen their commitment to culturally derived values and beliefs; and educators selecting works of literature that reflect their own more modern and secular values rather than the predominantly traditional values within the school community. Such issues are not easily resolved in cultures that value both individual freedom and elaborate codes of human rights, where the rights of educators conflict with the legitimate expectations of parents. Strike and Soltis (1985), in an ethical handbook for teachers, address some of the problems in this area. However, the mainstream educator will not unreasonably infer that the correct, ethical behavior lies in some moderate compromise. That approach does not help address the questions raised by the parents and students who do not assume a moderate, contemporary, relativist stance.

Although this is an area of increasing sensitivity, a few ethical precepts can be established. It is unethical for teachers to teach or pretend to support ideas they believe to be morally wrong. It is unethical for teachers to subvert goals and objectives that have been legitimately established. It will be noted that educational goals are frequently not established in a manner considered legitimate in the context described here. Only in very clear, publicly defensible cases is it ethical for an educator to subvert a learner's moral code reflecting carefully chosen parental values.

Thus one may argue that it is ethical to inculcate a fundamental virtue such as truthfulness, even when that virtue is not held by parents, when the goal has been legitimately established and the educator shares the belief. Even that fairly clear case raises the problem of individual rights of the parent, if it cannot be shown that the home environment provides overall harm to the child. A more likely situation is the failure on the part of educators, who do not believe in absolute values, to inculcate virtues that are mandated by law; the ethical solution seems clear but the practical execution difficult.

4. Ethics of Curriculum: The Future

The topic of ethics and curriculum has not received major attention in the literature; this can be illustrated by reference to an educational index such as the Educational Resources Information Center (ERIC) or to established popular texts on curriculum. Historically, there are grounds for the omission. When education reflects consensual, public will, its ethics are inherent in the established school program. In contemporary totalitarian regimes, where consensus may not exist at all or where it may have been generated by methods that Western observers might consider unethical in themselves, a single, comprehensive curriculum is developed whose ethics, or behavioral principles, are inherent in and drawn from the overriding conspectus.

In the absence of consensus and legislation, ethics require public discussion, resolution, and definition.

The decline of consensus in the democratic West has been accompanied by technocratic approaches in educational psychology, administration, and curriculum which de-ethicize their study and application. These fields of study have moved from an environment of consensual tradition to one of value-free, pseudo-science. The justification of educational policies, practices, procedures, and innovations on the grounds that they are technically superior or are based on the objective needs of young people is under attack from both left, where the school system is seen to be legitimating capitalist inequality, and right, where it is seen to be subverting traditional morality and belief. Thus central ethical issues in curriculum studies of the future are likely to be: the moral content of the curriculum, for example, the selection of literature used in schools; the ethics of imposing curricular methodology on professional educators; and the context of curriculum delivery in terms of the moral life of the teacher and the moral framework desired for the learner. The question arises as to whether monopolistic, mass, public education is compatible with professional ethics in a free, multicultural, individualistic society.

Bibliography

Apple M W 1979 *Ideology and Curriculum*. Routledge and Kegan Paul, London
Barrow R 1984 *Giving Teaching Back to Teachers*. Wheatsheaf Books, Brighton
Counts G S 1964 Dare the school build a new social order? In: Gross C H, Chandler C C (eds.) 1964 *The History of American Education Through Readings*. Heath, Boston, Massachusetts, pp. 370–77
Eisner E W 1979 *The Educational Imagination: On the Design and Evaluation of School Programs*. Macmillan, New York
Fullan M 1982 *The Meaning of Educational Change*. Ontario Institute of Studies in Education, Toronto
Maritain J 1943 *Education at the Cross Roads*. Yale University Press, New Haven, Connecticut
Phenix P H 1964 *Realms of Meaning: A Philosophy of the Curriculum for General Education*. McGraw-Hill, New York
Pratt D 1980 *Curriculum, Design, and Development*. Harcourt, Brace, Jovanovich, New York
Sarason S P 1982 *The Culture of the School and the Problem of Change*, 2nd edn. Allyn and Bacon, Boston, Massachusetts
Strike K A, Soltis J F 1985 *The Ethics of Teaching*. Teachers College Press, New York
Taba H 1962 *Curriculum Development: Theory and Practice*. Harcourt, Brace and World, New York
Tyler R W 1949 *Basic Principles of Curriculum and Instruction*. University of Chicago Press, Chicago, Illinois

Hidden Curriculum

E. Vallance

The hidden curriculum refers to those practices and outcomes of schooling which, while not explicit in curriculum guides or school policy, nevertheless seem to be a regular and effective part of the school experience. The hidden curriculum may be viewed as covert, unintended, implicit, or simply unacknowledged; the intentionality and depth of the "hiddenness" vary according to each writer's conception of the phenomenon, but generally the term describes those forces shaping the nonacademic and unmeasured learnings of students. The term remains imprecise.

Educational practices treated as part of the hidden curriculum include ability grouping, teacher–pupil relationships, classroom rules and procedures, implicit textbook content, sex-role differentiation of pupils, and classroom reward structures. Outcomes typically considered to be products of a hidden curriculum include political socialization, obedience, docility, the learning of values and cultural mores, the development of attitudes toward authority, and the reinforcement of class distinctions. Researchers on the hidden curriculum have approached the phenomenon as both process and outcome, though it is noteworthy that educators whose work contributes most to an understanding of the hidden curriculum do not necessarily use the term themselves. Many, in fact, do not. The concept invites the synthesis of a diverse body of research, not all of which is explicitly focused on the hidden curriculum. The hidden curriculum concept allows the acknowledgement that something systematic happens in schools that educators control only slightly and can predict but faultily; it also provides some guidelines as to how best to understand it.

That a concept as imprecise as "the hidden curriculum" should prove so useful suggests the paucity of more confident explanations available to account for what is not known about schooling. The concept of a hidden curriculum, first treated as such by Overly (1970), has not been greatly refined in its brief life span, though it has been widely accepted; the term has been applied to specific classroom practices and used as a generic term referring to nearly everything that goes on in school. It is one of the few concepts in education which by its very name acknowledges the limits of understanding. It has been called various things, including the "latent" or "covert" curriculum, the "non-academic outcomes of schooling", the "by-products" or "residue" of schooling, or the "unstudied curriculum" (Overly 1970), though it has been progressively more "studied" in recent years. And it is a kind of aberration in the recent history of educational research, in at least two senses. First, it is curious that a concept so fraught with multiple meanings should find such currency in education, a discipline struggling to establish itself as a science by reducing its problems to manageable sets of variables and controls. The hidden curriculum by definition defies easy experimental treatment and clear cause–effect relationships, and is a kind of anomaly within the research tradition. It is even more curious that the hidden-curriculum concept emerged at approximately the same time that behavioral objectives, "measurable" outcomes, and accountability were gaining currency in the United States, in the early 1970s, when evaluations of publicly funded education programs demanded data that were replicable and valid. It is noteworthy that a single era should breed both scholars hopeful that educational change could be quantified and scholars eager to acknowledge that schools operate in mysterious ways. Both attitudes survive today; the appeal of the hidden curriculum seems undiminished.

The imprecision of the concept accounts in part for its enduring appeal, since it encourages new lines of research and the refinement of new methodologies. Generally answers are sought through research that seeks to identify the regular, the replicable, and the predictable in educational practice, so that a better understanding can be gained of how schooling works (or fails). Experimental educational research, as a result, is necessarily focused and fragmented: the phenomenon of schooling is broken into manageable bits in order to master them, little by little. But to acknowledge a "hidden curriculum" requires a broader view and acknowledges that researchers are not quite certain what the variables are, much less which are independent and which dependent. The concept gives some clues— depending on whether this hidden "curriculum" is conceived to be cause or effect—as to where to begin the search anew. The investigation seems typically to focus on one of these two meanings of the term.

1. Hidden Curriculum as Educational Practice

The hidden curriculum may be construed as a set of practices whose ultimate effects, while still unknown, are suspected. Under this conception, researchers identify observable practices which, by teaching things other than what the explicit curriculum claims as goals, may operate as a hidden curriculum. The puzzle is to identify what this "curriculum" ultimately teaches. This causal approach to the hidden curriculum is typified best by such writers as Dreeben (1967, 1968), who focuses on the identifiable social structure of the classroom and argues that classroom structure teaches children about authority. Researchers doing content analysis of textbooks (FitzGerald 1979, Stacey et al. 1974) hypothesize that the tacit content of textbooks conveys messages about cultural stereotypes that may conflict with overt statements in the same books. The strong criticisms of American schooling by teachers during the 1960s cited case after case of classroom practices which, they claimed, were damaging children far more than the formal curriculum could possibly help them (see for

example Holt 1965, Kozol 1967, Kohl 1968, Goodman 1960, 1964). Rosenthal and Jacobson uncovered the "self-fulfilling prophecy" of teacher expectations which, they said, doomed some children to failure early in their school careers (1968). Martin (1976), in asking what should be done with a hidden curriculum once found, implies that the hidden curriculum is a set of practices susceptible to change. While few of these writers use the term "hidden curriculum", all essentially argue that existing practices may be doing far more (or less) to children than our official curricula claim they do.

2. Hidden Curriculum as Educational Outcome

The opposite approach is taken by those who criticize schools less for what they specifically do day-to-day than for the outcomes they seem to foster. This group of writers generally takes a broader view of schooling, placing the school in a societal context and critiquing it from the viewpoint of the sociopolitical learnings imparted to children. This view of the hidden curriculum, even more than the other, is usually cast in a critical mode: schools are faulted for what they unwittingly do so well. Most educators working on the hidden curriculum from this perspective criticize the schools for reinforcing a social structure that they see as inequitable and unjust. It is, of course, equally possible to take a more positive view of the same phenomenon and to applaud the schools for maintaining tradition. Conservatives in the United States arguing that the schools should maintain traditional sex-role stereotypes, for example, effectively argue in the same terms as the more liberal critics but from the opposite perspective.

Educators describing the hidden curriculum of schools in terms of its outcome include Henry's (1955) identification of "docility" as a covert outcome of schooling, Illich (1971), Reimer (1971), and Bowles and Gintis (1976), who criticize the schools for maintaining social-class distinctions of capitalistic society, Apple and King (1977) and Anyon (1980) who argue that the different concepts of "work" held by different social classes are partly a function of the school environment, and Vallance (1973/74) who argues that the hidden curriculum became "hidden" when its goals of creating a relatively homogeneous American culture had been reached.

3. Importance to Educators

Both approaches to the hidden curriculum have been fruitful in their fashions. Studies of classroom practice as a tacit curriculum have generated detailed documentations of what really goes on in classrooms. The research methodologies used to study classroom practice include most of the methodologies used by traditional educational research, plus a renewed emphasis on classroom ethnography and other naturalistic modes of research. Critics of the covert results of schooling tend more often to produce complex analyses and to raise subtle policy and value questions transcending individual classrooms.

As an aspect of schooling, the hidden curriculum can include any or all of the various qualities of schooling not overtly governed by the formal curriculum, and these may be studied by educational researchers in such combinations as may seem appropriate. As a concept, the hidden curriculum acknowledges the nonacademic but salient qualities of schooling and describes a large but acceptable area of unknowns in standard descriptive systems of the cause-and-effect dynamics of schooling; it frees educators to conceive of possibilities other than those susceptible to study by traditional means.

Most importantly, the concept of the hidden curriculum provides a framework within which to interpret a wide variety of seemingly unrelated research. Its greatest value to the educational profession may be that the questions raised by the concept of a hidden curriculum demand a synthesis of the knowledge and hypotheses that this still-fledgling "science" has produced. The hidden-curriculum concept functions best as one of many "sources" of a science of education (Dewey 1929): its broad perspective allows interpretations and insights that narrower questions necessarily forgo.

Bibliography

Anyon J 1980 Social class and the hidden curriculum of work. *J. Educ.* 162(1): 67–92

Apple M W, King N 1977 What do schools teach? *Curric. Inq.* 6(4): 341–58

Bowles S, Gintis H 1976 *Schooling in Capitalist America: Educational Reform and the Contradictions of Economic Life*. Basic Books, New York

Dewey J 1929 *The Sources of a Science of Education*. Liveright, New York

Dreeben R 1967 The contribution of schooling to the learning of norms. *Harvard Educ. Rev.* 37: 211–37

Dreeben R 1968 *On What is Learned in School*. Addison-Wesley, Reading, Massachusetts

FitzGerald F 1979 *America Revised: History Schoolbooks in the Twentieth Century*. Little-Brown, Boston, Massachusetts

Giroux H A (ed.) 1980 Education, ideology and the hidden curriculum: A symposium. *J. Educ.* 162: 1–151

Goodman P 1960 *Growing Up Absurd: Problems of Youth in the Organized System*. Random House, New York

Goodman P 1964 *Compulsory Mis-education*. Horizon, New York

Gordon D 1988 Education as text: The varieties of educational hiddenness. *Curric. Inq.* 18: 425–49

Henry J 1955 Docility, or giving teacher what she wants. *J. Soc. Issues* 11: 33–41

Hess R D, Torney J V 1967 *The Development of Political Attitudes in Children*. Aldine, Chicago, Illinois

Holt J C 1965 *How Children Fail*. Dell, New York

Illich I 1971 *De-schooling Society*. Harper and Row, New York

Kohl H 1968 *36 Children*. New American Library, New York

Kozol J 1967 *Death at an Early Age: The Destruction of the Hearts and Minds of Negro Children in the Boston Public Schools*. Houghton-Mifflin, Boston, Massachusetts

Martin J 1976 What should we do with a hidden curriculum? *Curric. Inq.* 6(2): 35–152

Overly N V (ed.) 1970 *The Unstudied Curriculum: Its Impact on Children*. Association for Supervision and Curriculum Development, Washington, DC

Reimer E W 1971 *School is Dead: An Essay on Alternatives in Education*. Doubleday, Garden City, New York

Rist R C 1970 Student social class and teacher expectations: The self-fulfilling prophecy in ghetto education. *Harvard Educ. Rev.* 40: 411–51

Rosenthal R, Jacobson L 1968 *Pygmalion in the Classroom: Teacher Expectation and Pupils' Intellectual Development*. Holt, Rinehart and Winston, New York

Stacey J, Béreaud S, Daniels J (eds.) 1974 *And Jill Came Tumbling After: Sexism in American Education*. Dell, New York

Vallance E 1973/74 Hiding the hidden curriculum: An interpretation of the language of justification in nineteenth-century educational reform. *Curric. Theory Network* 4(1): 5–21

Cybernetics and Curriculum

D. Pratt

Cybernetics, the science of self-regulation in systems, studies the ways in which open systems maintain a state of dynamic equilibrium. Systems can be constructed using cybernetic principles to maintain stable output by monitoring and correcting error. It is instructive to examine the principles of cybernetics to discover which of them can be applied to the planning of educational systems in general, and curriculum in particular.

1. Development of Cybernetics

The modern use of the term cybernetics owes its origin to Wiener (1950), although the term was originally used by the French physicist Ampère more than a century earlier. In developing aiming systems for antiaircraft guns during the Second World War, Wiener noted the critical role of feedback, "a method of controlling a system by reinserting into it the results of its past performance" (1950 p. 61). He extended the concept to such areas as cognitive, motor, and organic functions, arguing that these could also be considered controlled processes based on the management of information.

Several contemporary scientific movements accelerated the development of cybernetic theory. One was the work of such scholars as the United States biologist Cannon on homeostasis, which had defined the physiological operations by which organisms maintained equilibrium as an essentially cybernetic process. Another was the development of information theory, notably by Shannon, which explicated many principles of communication in mathematical terms. There was also fruitful exchange between cyberneticians and workers in the new fields of systems engineering and operational research. Most important was the development of system theory.

System theory, a field which developed rapidly in the 1950s, argued that open systems drew energy from their environment and used it to grow and develop in opposition to the forces of entropy. Open systems maintained their equilibrium by monitoring their own internal states and making adjustments to adapt to destabilizing perturbations. Cybernetics fitted precisely into this part of the theory. Exaggerated early hopes for cybernetics as a general explanatory paradigm in science were not realized, although cybernetics did provide a model and a language for description of many biological and ecological processes. The practical value of cybernetics lay in the progress it stimulated in the design of complex controlled systems, a process accelerated by the development of computers. With time, cybernetic terminology began to lose some of its definition. In part, this was due to its increasing application, notably in the Soviet Union, to all aspects of computing, and in part to indiscriminate use in popular parlance of such cybernetic terms as feedback. The formal study of cybernetics, however, continues to be pursued by scholars in many different disciplines, particularly in Eastern and Western Europe, while fields such as biocybernetics have emerged as distinct subdisciplines.

2. The Cybernetic System

The basic cybernetic model is of two linked or nested systems: a controlled system producing an output, and a control system that monitors the output and feeds back corrective information to the controlled system.

A system (organic, organizational, or ideational) exists within an environment. The system has a boundary limiting the amount of environmental noise or variety allowed to enter and impact on the system. The system monitors its output and that of its subsystems, comparing the information from the monitors to a set point representing the desirable state of the system. In the event of a discrepancy, an error signal prompts a controller to activate effectors which cancel the error and restore the system or its output to equilibrium. Human thermoregulation may be used as an example. A series of boundaries—buildings, clothes, skin—protect the human body from extremes of heat and cold. The hypothalamus receives information from heat sensors in the skin and body core, and if body temperature begins to deviate from the set point of 37 degrees, a series of changes are initiated, including changes in vasodilation, respiration, blood pressure, perspiration, erection of skin papillae, and shivering. The system maintains a temperature equilibrium in the body, and particularly in the brain, the temperature of which rarely varies more than one hundredth of a degree.

An understanding of cybernetics has enabled designers to build self-regulating systems. These vary in complexity from the fuse in a domestic electrical supply which breaks the circuit in the event of a power surge, to complex systems such as those for landing an aircraft on autopilot or for simultaneous control of the thousands of processes operating in a steel rolling mill. The construction of cybernetic machines predates development of the theory. A well-known early example was James Watt's flyball governor for his steam engine, a simple device which used centrifugal force to open and close a steam valve to compensate for changes in load.

The flow of information in a system to correct its values is known as negative feedback. Negative feedback cancels an error and drives a system back to equilibrium. Positive feedback magnifies a deviation and drives the system away from equilibrium. This may result in a runaway to destruction of the system, as in a forest fire or an explosion, or to a new equilibrium outside the original limits, as in bacterial growth, crowd behavior, feuds, and romantic love.

Curriculum and instruction can be conceptualized as open systems interacting with the environment and maintaining equilibrium by transformation of energy and exchange of information among component subsystems. The issue for curriculum planners is less one of the exactness of the analogy between curriculum and cybernetic systems found in nature, than one of how planning can best take advantage of the principles of cybernetics to design curricula that produce desired kinds of stable output. These principles may be addressed in terms of five main characteristics of cybernetic systems: set point, boundary, sensors, controller, and effectors.

3. The Five Main Characteristics of Cybernetic Systems

3.1 The Set Point

All cybernetic systems have a set point which is the optimal state or normal value that they seek or are designed to attain. In informational terms, the set point is a message of extremely low variability. Often it is a constant, as in the case of the homeostatic set point of 37 degrees for human temperature. Systems do not so much remain at rest at a set point as equilibrate around it. The temperature in a controlled chamber would be plotted not as a straight line, but as a symmetrical oscillation between an upper and a lower limit. The set point is not invariable; for example, the set point for human thermoregulation is higher than normal during fever. Strong perturbations may have the effect of changing the set point. Le Chatelier's Principle postulates that following a perturbation, the system will return to equilibrium with the set point moved slightly in the direction of the perturbation. This phenomenon is frequently evident in the process of social change.

In human behavior, the set point is represented by the goals, norms, and values of an individual or an organization. The goals may be conscious or unconscious, and they may be the ultimate intent of instrumental behavior, or inherent in the activity itself, as in playful activities or intrinsically valued experiences.

In curricula, the set point is represented by the goals, aims, objectives, and performance criteria of the curriculum, that is, by the expectations of the system. Cybernetic theory would predict that the stability of curriculum outputs, for example student learning, will be a function of the degree to which curriculum goals are clear, explicit, realistic, and accepted by teachers and learners. Ideally, at any point both teachers and learners understand and support the purposes of the instruction. The significance of the set point appears to be borne out by the effective school's research, which consistently indicates a climate of high expectations as a key factor in school effectiveness. The hierarchical nature of open systems also implies consistency of goals at different levels of a system; thus in curriculum, goals enunciated at the national level would be reflected in the more detailed curriculum plans which guide specific instructional decisions. The pursuit by subsystems of goals which differ from, and are in competition with, goals of superordinate systems is known as suboptimization, a phenomenon not infrequent in educational organizations.

While most school systems engage in some systematic collection of data about student learning, others endeavor to control schooling solely through management of input variables such as curricula, funding, and certification of teachers. Cybernetic principles would suggest that it is impossible to obtain system stability through manipulation of input factors alone.

Specification of a clear set point does not ensure stability of the total system, only of the values stipulated. The issue is one of the adequacy of sampling of the outputs of a complex system. The imposition of explicit instructional objectives may result in schools which produce quantities of learning but are otherwise unattractive institutions. Educational systems require set points not only for learning outcomes, but also for programs as a whole, and for the quality of the educational experiences of their students.

3.2 The Boundary

A system's boundary maintains the identity and integrity of the system by separating it from its environment and limiting the variety to which it must adapt. The feathers and nests of birds provide a barrier against the thermal environment, as the pupil of the human eye provides a barrier against intensity of light in the environment. Social organizations, whether families, clubs, schools, businesses, churches, gangs, or nations, have rules of eligibility and membership which seek to limit the variability which has to be managed within the system.

Instructional contexts invariably have entry qualifications. These may be formal (academic prerequisites for medical school) or informal (gender bias in engineering or nursing schools). Frequently these qualifications have little to do with human learning, but are related to extraneous considerations such as social class. For the past century, student entry into instructional groups has been primarily in terms of age. As student age is at best weakly associated with learning, this produces stability of age but contributes little to stability of achievement.

A major task of the curriculum planner is to identify the kinds of variety that need to be restricted at the entry point to any unit of instruction. This involves an understanding of logical and developmental learning sequences, and specification of instructional prerequisites and the means by which they are to be taught, assessed, and if necessary remediated. Not surprisingly, identification and prompt remediation early in an instructional unit of learners who lack cognitive prerequisites has been found to contribute significantly to the mean quality of learning output (Bloom 1984). Tolerance of high levels of variety in critical areas such as reading competence, results in a situation in which the system cannot manage the variety it contains and hence produces unstable output.

3.3 The Sensors

All cybernetic systems monitor their performance or output. The stability of the system depends on the sensitivity of the sensors and the frequency with which they operate. The driver of an automobile monitors speed both continuously and intermittently by various visual and auditory means. A servomechanism installed and set for a certain speed would be more sensitive and continuous and hence produce less variability of speed. The sensitivity required of the sensors depends on the magnitude, duration, and frequency of errors, and the seriousness of their consequences. Monitoring which is inaccurate, infrequent, or the results of which are ignored by the system, contributes little to system stability and may in fact make the system more unstable. When monitoring is conducted too late for the effectors to control the instability, a crisis results as the system breaks through the boundaries of stable performance. Government monitoring of economic factors such as supply and demand of workers in particular occupations quite frequently follows this pattern.

Teachers monitor student response formatively and continuously by such informal means as observation and interaction, and summatively and intermittently by such formal means as tests and examinations. Monitoring can identify not only underachievers, but also those learners for whom the instruction is redundant or the pace too slow. In cybernetic terms, what is being done is not to depress the amplitude of oscillation, because there is no attempt to reduce the upper level of achievement; rather, it is to minimize the oscillation at the lower end of the wave—somewhat like a house which has a heating system but no cooling system. The more frequent and sensitive the monitoring, the smaller the errors which will be detected. In critical curriculum areas, teachers may need the equivalent of amplifiers to magnify error signals. A brief formal quiz written by all learners may identify critical misconceptions with an exactness not discernible by informal observation. Rapid identification and correction of errors has implications not only for student achievement, but also for student self-image, which will be less affected by frequent minor corrections than by periodic major failure.

Often such evaluation is too restricted to identify more than a narrow range of error. Formative evaluation that attends only to preordinate outcomes may fail to notice unanticipated events, positive or negative. Unpredicted events may be detected by such non-preordinate measures as observation, interviews, discussion, surveys, suggestion boxes, anecdotes, document analysis, thick description, journals, and monitoring of such phenomena as absenteeism and dropout, disruptive behavior, graffiti and vandalism. The ideal is that positive qualities are recognized and negative experiences are diagnosed and remediated before their cumulative effects result in major failure or alienation.

3.4 The Controller

Signals from the sensors are received by the controller, which compares the information about the present state of the system with the set point for the system. The controller may act continuously, like the brain responding to signals from the body's heat sensors, or it may act intermittently, like the on–off switch for a domestic furnace. A system's threshold is the amount of deviation from the set point that the system will tolerate. The stability of the system is a function of the height of the threshold and the rapidity of response of the controller.

Ashby's Law, also known as the Law of Requisite Variety, is considered the most basic principle of cybernetics. It rules that only variety can absorb variety. In other words, the amount of variety entering a system can be managed only by an equally varied set of management states. In instructional contexts, a case in point might be the variety of students' learning styles. Students who learn effectively through auditory or visual means are generally accommodated in schools. But few instructional systems are sufficiently varied to be able to respond appropriately to those students whose preferred learning style is spatial, tactile, or kinesthetic; such learners are frequently mislabeled as academically incapable.

In instructional contexts the main consideration is to narrow the time between the occurrence of error and its detection and correction. Programmed learning and computer-based instruction are designed to optimize this feature, but typically within narrow definitions of output. The full complexity of instructional contexts requires monitoring by teachers sensitive to multiple qualities of the educational environment. Such teachers require an array of preplanned remedial strategies, as well as the ability to respond creatively to unanticipated events and outcomes.

3.5 The Effectors

The task of the controller is to ascertain error; the task of the effectors is to correct it. A furnace may do this in a house; in the mammalian body the thermoregulatory effectors are the thyroid, adrenal, and sweat glands; the heart; the vasodilator and vasoconstrictor centers; the arrector pili muscles attached to the hair follicles; and the small muscles involved in shivering. A nuclear reaction may be maintained in a steady state by the insertion of boron rods into the reactor core to absorb neutrons and prevent the reaction from proceeding exponentially. The relaxation time of a system is the amount of time required for the system to resume stability following a perturbation. Generally, the faster the response of the effectors, the more stable the system.

The effectors in a curriculum are those actions taken by the instructor to restore the system and its output to its desired state. Ideally, the information yielded by formative evaluation is diagnostic, indicating the exact nature of learning problems. The appropriate response may be to change some instructional variable, such as pacing, difficulty, or motivational value for all or for specific students. The response needs to be prompt enough to remediate underachieving students before the class as a whole moves much further ahead. While individual attention is ideal, it can be onerous and time-consuming for teachers and students, and some self-instructional form of remediation may be preferable. Interesting print or audio materials, remedial computer-based instruction, cooperative group work and peer tutoring are often appropriate vehicles for remediation.

4. The Cybernetic Perspective

Cybernetics provides a model and a set of terms to describe significant elements of curriculum. The ideas themselves are not new. As is often the case with educational concepts, the intuitive grasp and application of cybernetic principles by creative teachers long antedate formulation of the theory. But according to the Russian cybernetician Landa, "The principal shortcoming of instruction at present is the fact that it is a process with poor feedback" (1976 p. 21). Dissemination of the instructional implications of cybernetics illuminates some of the dimensions of curriculum structures, and makes accessible to the educational community principles that it can use to examine the quality of its instructional systems.

Bibliography

Ashby W R 1956 *Introduction to Cybernetics*. Wiley, New York
Block J H, Efthim H E, Burns R B 1989 *Building Effective Mastery Learning Schools*. Longman, New York

Bloom B S 1984 The 2 sigma problem: The search for methods of group instruction as effective as one-to-one tutoring. *Educ. Res.* AERA 13(6): 4–16

Landa L N 1976 *Instructional Regulation and Control: Cybernetics, Algorithmization and Heuristics in Education.* Educational Technology Publications, Englewood Cliffs, New Jersey

Mortimore P 1988 *School Matters: The Elementary Years.* Open Books, London

Pekelis V D 1974 *Malen'kaia entsiklopediia o bol'shoi kibernetike* (*Cybernetics A to Z* Tr. M Samokhvalov). Mir Publishers, Moscow

Schmeck R R (ed.) 1988 *Learning Strategies and Learning Styles.* Plenum, New York

Sutherland J W 1975 System theoretic limits on the cybernetic paradigm. *Behav. Sci.* 20: 191–200

Trappl R (ed.) 1983 *Cybernetics: Theory and Applications.* Hemisphere, Washington, DC

Wiener N 1950 *The Human Use of Human Beings: Cybernetics and Society.* Houghton Mifflin, Boston, Massachusetts

Curriculum Research

D. Jenkins

Simplistically, curriculum research is an umbrella term for the application of research techniques to problems of understanding posed by curriculum proposals, activities, or consequences. It is necessary to centralize the contribution of research to understanding because curriculum research is a practical rather than a theoretic art, typically concerned with defensible judgments rather than warrantable conclusions. Most established traditions of educational research lend themselves to curriculum problems, and both quantitative and qualitative methods offer strong contributions.

Nevertheless, there are daunting problems in attempting to map the terrain covered by the term "curriculum research". It is clear from the most superficial reading in the field that there is no firm agreement on the precise usage of either term, and in consequence definitions tend either to be stipulative (attempts by various writers to legislate for the field) or else programmatic (carrying implicit recommendations for action). Historically, some of the stipulative definitions canvassed for the term curriculum have been overly and overtly narrow. For example, a researcher conceptualizing curriculum as a statement about changes in behaviour that a course of study intends to bring about is arguably already predisposed towards a particular research focus (student achievement under described conditions) and a particular methodology (comparative studies on a behaviourist base). Similarly, an ideological commitment to praxis might easily dispose a researcher to view curriculum, not only as a legitimate object of cultural inquiry, but also as a potential arena for reconstructionist intervention. Thus the choice of a theory or a research perspective might be considered directly analogous to the adoption of a political stance. But there are methodological consequences of particular orientations; the cultural analysis of a curriculum, by viewing it as socially embedded, reverberates with the concern of naturalistic research (i.e., close-up studies in natural settings) and might easily see case study as its appropriate product. Similarly, if an intervention is "reconstructionist" (viewing teachers as cultural change agents and perceiving curriculum at the

growing edge of cultural adaptivity to changing social conditions) a curriculum initiative might also be a systematic quest for a certain kind of understanding, and therefore, prima facie, research. This line of argument is used to lend legitimacy to the concept of curriculum action research.

1. Historical Background

Some comment is required on the relatively recent emergence of curriculum research. The conventional historical truism is no doubt correct, that the revival of curriculum theorizing, and of systematic enquiry into curriculum matters, resulted from the impetus given to these activities by the "curriculum reform movement" particularly in North America, Australasia, and Western Europe (see *Curriculum Reform*). The movement itself has been characterized by a number of dominant themes, each of which has posed problems of conceptual understanding and of what is to count as justified practice, as well as suggesting possible research agendas. These themes have included attempts to update the knowledge component in teaching, to reappraise the "knowledge maps" against which organizing categories of the curriculum might be selected, and to understand the processes of planned change by which innovations might be encouraged to take root in schools. Not unexpectedly, there has been some interpenetration between the emerging research agendas and what has been going on more broadly in the field. The general tension in curriculum theory between positivistic and naturalistic paradigms is echoed in curriculum research by the tensions between a truth-orientated empiricism and a judgment-orientated ethnography. Again not unexpectedly, the selection of research methodologies has tended to vary situationally via a pleasing attentiveness to the needs of particular topics.

Although no particular formulation can be pressed into service as defining the agreed "topics of curriculum research", in the interests of convenient analysis the following clusters are offered: quasifundamental research; policy-related descriptive data; the analysis of curriculum proposals; studies in curriculum design, implementation, or action research (see *Curriculum Design*; *Curriculum Implementation*); and finally curriculum evaluation, whether descriptive or judgmental. The scope and methodologies of curriculum research will be viewed within these topic areas, although some of the commonalities will be discussed in a subsequent section on trends.

2. *Quasifundamental Research*

Although central to curriculum research must be investigation taking curriculum as its object of study, interesting marginal cases can be cited. All curricula are premised on explicit or implicit models, notably of learners, knowledge domains, and appropriate pedagogies. The question is this: at what point might any number of studies carrying "implications" for designing, analysing, or evaluating curricula be treated as quasifundamental research in the curriculum domain? It is probably wise to be undogmatic, and treat the boundaries as permeable, but some distinctions carry at least the force of common sense. Straight developmental psychology, Piagetian or otherwise, scarcely qualifies, although studies undertaken for the purpose of generating curriculum models, or exhuming their assumptions, might [e.g., Goldman's (1964) developmental model for the teaching of religious studies].

Similarly, although general epistemology is only tangentially related to curriculum research, there are clear cases where attempts to chart knowledge domains have been undertaken from a curriculum perspective. One might cite as marginal the willingness of Hirst and Peters (1970) to take their "forms of knowledge" argument to a consideration of curriculum integration. Recently, too, the curriculum problems posed by the inadequacy of existing canonical forms for representing knowledge have been sharpened by computer-assisted and computer-managed learning. Computer-assisted and computer-managed learning in some versions require some representation of the knowledge component to be held "in the machine". The journal *Instructional Science* has consistently addressed some of the issues. Yet the boundaries remain. Are the ubiquitous taxonomies, with their hierarchical classification of possible objectives, themselves nonempirical curriculum research? Or the work of people like Gagné (1970) on learning hierarchies? Or the attempt by Pask and Lewis (1972) to articulate an iconography of knowledge structures in terms of relational nets? One point at which investigation of these matters clearly qualifies as curriculum research is when they are studied empirically with regard to their incarnation in particular educational programmes. Thus Walker (1976) in a plea for more empirical research into curricula, was able to pinpoint as underexplored three areas which might be considered somewhere near the boundary between instructional research and curriculum research: the relationship between general goals and the specific objectives that guide teaching; the educational potential of different fields of study at each level of instruction; and questions of subject matter sequencing.

Another tradition of educational enquiry shading across into curriculum research is the observational study of classrooms. Classroom research is wide ranging and eclectic, neither having a single overarching theory, nor an agreed package of research techniques. Broadly there have been two strands, category-based schemes looking to quantified description with high interobserver reliability, and ethnographic techniques interpreting events and disclosing meanings. For some writers this is associated with a willingness to treat curricula as legitimate objects of aesthetic analysis, most sharply within a "literary–critical" style. Although there is a school of thought that sees teaching studies as "curriculum problems in miniature" and objective classroom descriptions as de facto accounts of curriculum implementation, the balance of the judgment must be elsewhere. Attempts to categorize and mirror classroom behaviour are necessarily filtered through perceptions of what is problematic, and historically most category-based interaction studies have sought to establish a descriptive rubric for charting styles of teaching, particularly within instructional modes, with half-an-eye to an eventual contribution towards teacher effectiveness studies. Contrariwise, ethnographic or microethnographic studies of classrooms will under the pressure of certain kinds of question become indistinguishable from curriculum evaluation or naturalistic curriculum research.

3. *Policy-related Curriculum Research*

The kind of curriculum research seen as legitimate policy-related study varies from country to country in a way reflecting the locus of authority in education systems at large. Countries having centrally determined curricula are more likely to collect data concerning performance characteristics; what is eligible for teaching, give or take the ability of teachers to add their personal signatures to educational programmes, is treated as known. Under the press of economic hardship, most advanced industrial countries have espoused fashionable notions of accountability and the related tendency to see schooling as a delivery system. Thus education has attracted the kind of hard-edged social scientific research that goes in for the measurement of indicators. The indicators themselves are constructs representing those facets of a policy by which its implementation might be managed.

Other educational systems demonstrate a more dispersed distribution of responsibility. In such systems policy processes move back and forth between levels of organizational hierarchies, between concreteness and abstractness, and between central and peripheral locations. In such settings policy-related curriculum research is characterized by the needs of its particular audiences, and the metatheoretical assumptions of its sponsors and practitioners. It might aspire to value neutrality, a mere information service to a "rational actor"; it might become so embedded bureaucratically that it becomes politicized as a contribution to the resolution of conflicting interests; or it might take an interactive stance, being part of the ongoing dialogue of policy deliberation. But there is some evidence that the research community may be overaggrandizing its role. An investigation placed policy-related studies bottom of the list of factors influencing federal education legislators in America, well behind "the strong views of respected and trusted friends".

Where there is some on-site flexibility, policy-related curriculum research might be employed to increase the capacity for local adaptiveness. In his book *Beyond the Stable State*, Donald Schon argued for "institutions that learn". But the kind of learning he had in mind is one relying on the experiences, judgments, and tacit knowledge of the local policy maker. Thus, over recent years, case studies of individual schools, approached naturalistically, and often light on formal generalization, have been offered to policy makers as authentic curriculum research. Such research does not perceive the policy maker as a "rational actor"; neither does it simply respond to an agenda of questions capable of quantified presentation. Rather it attempts to widen the experiential base on which the "reasonable guesses" that underlie deliberative action might be "checked against experience".

A few countries, particularly the United Kingdom, are so lacking in central curriculum direction that some confusion surrounds what the curriculum in aggregate, or in particular schools, actually entails. Basic research is required merely to establish base-line data concerning what actually is being taught and learned in schools. In the United Kingdom the curriculum has become an arena for conflicting versions of where responsibility should lie, a conflict between broad views that might be characterized respectively as professional (stressing the judgment of teachers) and bureaucratic (stressing top-down accountability). The Department of Education and Science, and the local education authorities, are both conducting in-house research into curriculum provision. The ends of this activity are to acquire greater control. The *Green Paper* of July 1977 talked of a "need to investigate" what part might be played by a "core or protected element" in any projected common curriculum. Two years later, Department of Education and Science (DES) Circular 14/77 required local authorities to detail their arrangements for the school curriculum. Alongside this, the Schools Council has published a number of research studies analysing more focused needs appearing to require a curriculum solution.

Countries attempting to institutionalize the processes of curriculum reform have with various degrees of conviction employed a research and development (R & D) rhetoric for the activity. The OECD (1974) assessed the current position of R & D and its relation to educational policy, with regard to its European member states (fol-

lowing a comprehensive analysis of the United States). Although the general picture remains confusing, the trend has been for the curriculum reform movement to encourage decision-orientated, commissioned, policy-related research. The sequence of pilot investigation, trials in "experimental schools", and executive dissemination was broadly followed in Sweden, Finland, and Norway followed by the United Kingdom, the Netherlands, and Yugoslavia. The "research" element related principally to the establishment of observed experimental classrooms, which at best fostered an issues-centred ethnography. Nevertheless, most curriculum change was inspired by social, economic, or political factors, and has been research monitored rather than research based.

4. Curriculum Analysis

One important focus of curriculum research concerns the analysis of existing curricula or of curriculum proposals. The methods employed vary considerably, not least due to the intrusion of an overtly political agenda in the kind of macroanalysis associated with a strong neo-Marxist tradition. Although there seems to be little possibility of dialogue existing between the "deliberative theorists" and the "system-opposing a priorists", there is no doubt an authentic "research" orientation in the best of the Marxists' writings, by which is meant that there is a serious interest in explicating the mechanisms they describe and even chastening some middle-level theory, even if the larger insights are held dogmatically.

Although the canonical text is Bowles and Gintis (1976), most of the interesting research concerns explicating the processes at work in schools, particularly the "symbolic violence" perpetrated by the so-called "hidden curriculum". Microethnography grounding in a macroperspective is notoriously hard to achieve in curriculum or classroom research, which is why the few good examples are extravagently lauded, especially by their political friends. Overall, however, the saga demonstrates the dependence of research on general orientation, in this case the view that curriculum in capitalist societies is a bourgeois artifact reproducing from generation to generation the myths of supremacy of the dominant classes. The trick is to turn "inequalities of power" into "inequalities of culture".

Alongside the neo-Marxist analysis of the hidden curriculum has lain another research tradition, its roots in the work of symbolic interactionists. This strand in curriculum research treats the hidden curriculum as the amalgam of adaptive learnings by individual pupils learning to survive culturally in a hostile milieu. It contrasts the hidden curriculum with the espoused curriculum, seeing the world of schools, as of children, having "real" as well as "pretend" elements.

Another facet of analytical curriculum research deals with logical or empirical studies of curriculum proposals. Fraser (1977) has reviewed a number of styles of enquiry addressing fundamental problems of the intrinsic worth of curriculum goals. He sees a place for empirical analysis in determining whether a programme might responsibly claim validation by expert opinion. Thus the Australian Science Education Project had its stated goals checked against a literature survey. As with consistency studies of curriculum plans, there is some suspicion of a cop-out, as the researcher avoids having his or her own values flushed into the open. Anderson (1980), although not going all the way towards the methodologies of textual analysis, seeks to arm the reader with a basis for appraising written proposals in the curriculum domain. Although his highly literate armchair scepticism dismayed some, his critique of the claims of several examined curriculum proposals to be "research based" is undeniably sharp. Curriculum research, in the sense of a claimed research justification for action, is more suspect than was realized.

5. Curriculum Design, Implementation, and Action Research

Matters of curriculum design or development most clearly press research agendas towards a practitioners' perspective. Occasionally this appears to embrace no more than the view that accumulated well-described "tips" might build unsteadily towards a compendium of good practice, perhaps on the analogy of medicine. More frequently the research task is conceived explicitly within some overarching model, as when models of, say, "rational planning" or "deliberation" are used heuristically to generate models for curriculum design, so that the fit between the prescriptive model and actual planning becomes a research issue. Examples of this kind of research into planning processes include Taylor's (1970) *How Teachers Plan their Courses* and Walker's (1975) account of the particular incarnation of "deliberative theory".

Although there is no compelling reason to disagree with Walker (1976) that curriculum development and ordinary teaching are not in typical circumstances forms of research, it is not unusual for large-scale curriculum projects to represent the "developments" they recommend as having a "research" base, although there is no logical requirement that the research of the research, development, and diffusion model should itself be curriculum research. In general, the curriculum reform movement has perhaps been too prone to claim a quasi-scientific research legitimacy for its activity, either generatively or per se (e.g., both Goldsmiths' College in London and Educational Services Incorporated in the United States set up in the 1960s what they chose to call curriculum or educational "laboratories").

Although theories of planned change are pretty untidy and ill-ordered, research into planned curriculum change (see *Curriculum Change*) has tended to fall under tribute to one of the two dominant paradigms (and supportive ideologies) available. System-building or managerial approaches, often premised on mech-

anistic models, have tended to imply that stable underlying regularities are waiting to be exhumed. This lies behind the techniques of regression analysis used by Tisher and Power (1978) to chart the effect of learning environment on an Australian curriculum innovation. At its quaintest, such positivist preconceptions led Tebbutt and Atherton (1979), possibly beguiled by the metaphorical reverberation of the term "catalyst", to propose a "reaction kinetics" model for the growth of curriculum projects, based on the behaviour of catalystic molecules in chemistry.

Studies of curriculum implementation have tended to cluster according to the perspectives brought to bear, say from management theory, the sociology of innovation, or even a Tavistock-based social psychology. Increasingly, implementation studies have been case studies of individual schools, with a quite recent trend towards ethnographic research in multisite settings, with some interest in cross-site generalizations (Stake and Easley 1978). At times, research in these conditions appears less like traditional ethnography and more like "the bureaucratization of fieldwork". Alongside this trend can be found survey-based "impact and take up" studies, and more broadly based policy studies.

Finally, a more-than-fashionable lively interest has developed recently in action research. Commonsensically this involves the style of participant observation in which a natural participant engages in self-monitoring observation in order to learn from the experience. Clearly it requires a curious, exploratory, and even speculative cast of mind towards one's own performance. It may or may not involve "outside" as well as "inside" perspectives (as when a university researcher works with a teacher). But it is the teacher who is the "curriculum researcher", usually going beyond intelligent description to some considerable analysis of curriculum propositions being tested in context. In one version, these propositions are seen as "pedagogical hypotheses". The work of the Ford Teaching Project (see Elliott and Adelman 1973) has done much to establish the research style, although there would be some disagreement with their view that the outsider should be valued less for this truth-telling than his or her ability to foster self-reflection in participants.

6. Curriculum Evaluation

The activity of curriculum evaluation has both reflected and contributed towards the contemporary debates surrounding research methodology in education. Some writers have been tempted to distinguish evaluation from research, for example by citing its incapacity to generate its own research problems due to a functional "responsiveness" to the problems posed by others, be they sponsors, curriculum developers, or user groups. But given that curriculum necessitates "practitioners' knowledge" and "deliberative theory" this just isn't good enough. A more interactive view of the relationship between curriculum evaluation and educational research would stress the emergence of common trends, research paradigms, and methodological practices.

Curriculum evaluation, arguably, is a logical requirement of responsible curriculum development (see *Curriculum Development*). Stenhouse (1981) has suggested that the curriculum reform movement represented a redistribution of financial resources in education and that early attempts to generate "research" paradigms for evaluation can be read as attempts by the research establishment to corner some of the money. Thus evaluation methodology was first postulated as essentially isomorphic with nomothetic research methodology in education. Curriculum development became a "treatment" sufficiently "frozen" for its effects to be monitored in the manner of crop–yield studies in agricultural botany. These effects, to meet the requirements of the methodology, needed to be measurable, and a psychometric approach to desired knowledge, skills, and attitudes resulted. But soon the poverty of iterative or comparative studies became clear and the techniques swung behind before-and-after designs. At best, such evaluation studies catalogued what had been learned in particular educational programmes, and in areas of the curriculum characterized by describable skills or well-analysed tasks the approach has much to recommend it.

The difficulties, however, lay elsewhere. Curriculum development proved too volatile to be treated in these ways; the technology of "varying the treatment" required multiple iteration of a kind of mismatching with the available time scales; the differences between alleged "treatment" and "control" groups too frequently appeared trivial; the basic assumption that the experimental approach would generate law-like generalizations for the slippery domain of curriculum practice proved unrealistic; and, finally, a settled realization emerged that the truths at stake are peculiarly embedded. This led Cronbach (1975) to argue, for educational research in general, as well as for curriculum evaluation, that priorities should be reversed, and that generalization should not be made a ruling consideration but that a proposition should be appraised in a setting and effects observed in context.

Nonetheless, as Lewy (1973) pointed out, it would be reasonable to characterize the current state of curriculum evaluation as burdened with an overproliferation of theoretical models and an overdichotomized stance on research methodology. The dichotomies are variously posed: between psychometric and "illuminative"; between positivism and naturalism; between nomothetic and idiographic. Only recently have the somewhat obvious advantages of triangulation via mixed methodology been canvassed. A glance at Fraser's *Annotated Bibliography of Curriculum Evaluation Literature* (1982) reveals how widely cast is the methodological net. On the one hand, writers like Bernstein et al. (1975) concern themselves primarily with "hard" research issues like threats to external validity, and hope to disentangle "confounded treatment

effects" and "situational effects". On the other hand, the interest of writers like Guba (1978) and Smith (1978) in naturalistic styles of enquiry has taken the curriculum ethnographer towards interpretative studies of curriculum-in-action based on participant observation, the collection of testimony and judgments, and quasi-historical documentation. Even so, evaluation studies will be closer to their "research" roots when they emphasize systematically acquired understandings rather than simply relay a "surrogate experience", although even on this wing there are affinities with phenomenological research and with Pinar's (1975) somewhat over-self-conscious "reconceptualization" of the curriculum domain.

One final point is perhaps worth making, given the recent emergence of "reflective" counters to the dominant model of bureaucratic accountability. Self-study and self-evaluation inside curricula milieux have become quite fashionable. This ties in quite neatly both with curriculum action research and with Stenhouse's (1975) view that curriculum practitioners can be trained to take a view of their own endeavours sufficiently detached to qualify them as "curriculum researchers".

7. Trends

In spite of the wide range of methodological styles employed in curriculum research, the general tendency recently has been towards qualitative, ethnographic, or interpretive studies. Law-establishing nomothetic studies (based on the model of *naturwissenschaften*) have to some extent given way to hermeneutic or idiographic studies (based on the model of *geisteswissenschaften*). As Walker (1976) has pointed out, this is in part because the complexities of curriculum do not readily generate "a rich store of plausible and interesting hypotheses to test". The verification-and-proof research model as applied to curriculum problems has also come under indirect attack from Glass (1972) who deemed "the laws of the social and behavioural sciences as of extremely limited generality", and Cronbach (1975) who depicted generalizations as unstable and subject to "decay".

Attempts to understand the curriculum through case studies, have varied between descriptive studies ("story telling"), analytical studies ("the innovation obstacle race"), and process studies ("problems, proposals, arguments, clarifications"). The worst of the studies have been sloppy, the best rigorous, combining rich earthy data with freedom from retrospective distortion and allowing serendipitous findings to emerge. But, there are some tensions between grounded theory and a supportive framework, between techniques of data collection and writing-up. Naturalistic research is also very demanding, its validity depending on the amount of on-site observation.

As curriculum problems are perceived as moral rather than technical, they combine the two "knowledge–

constitutive interests" that Habermas (1972) called "practical" and "emancipatory", and their "science" is consequently "interpretive–hermeneutic", or critical, arising from reflection. Because of the nature of the curriculum domain itself the trend has been, much more than in educational research in general, a flight from the technologization of reason.

Curriculum research, in short, is increasingly in keeping with a wider observation, made by Cronbach (1975):

> Systematic inquiry can reasonably hope to make two contributions. One reasonable aspiration is to assess local events accurately, to improve short-run control. The other reasonable aspiration is to develop explanatory concepts, concepts that will help people to use their heads.

Bibliography

Anderson D C 1980 *Evaluating Curriculum Proposals: A Critical Guide*. Wiley, New York

Bernstein I, Bohrnstedt G, Borgatta E 1975 External validity and evaluation research: A codification of problems. *Soc. Methods Res.* 4

Bowles S, Gintis H 1976 *Schooling in Capitalist America: Educational Reform and the Contradictions of Economic Life*. Routledge and Kegan Paul, London

Cronbach L J 1975 Beyond the two disciplines of scientific psychology. *Am. Psychol.* 30: 116–27

Eisner E W 1981 On the differences between scientific and artistic approaches to qualitative research. *Educ. Res. AERA* 10(5): 5–9

Elliott J, Adelman C 1973 Reflecting where the action is: The design of the Ford teaching project. *Educ. Teach.* 92: 8–20

Fraser B J 1977 Evaluating the intrinsic worth of curricular goals: A discussion and an example. *J. Curric. Stud.* 9: 125–32

Fraser B J 1982 *Annotated Bibliography of Curriculum Evaluation Literature*. Curriculum Center, Ministry of Education, Jerusalem

Gagné R M 1970 *The Conditions of Learning*, 2nd edn. Holt, Rinehart and Winston, New York

Glass G 1972 The wisdom of scientific inquiry on education. *J. Res. Sci. Teach.* 9: 3–18

Goldman R J 1964 *Religious Thinking from Childhood to Adolescence*. Routledge and Kegan Paul, London

Guba E 1978 Towards a methodology of naturalistic enquiry in educational evaluation. *CSE Monograph 8* University of California, Los Angeles, California

Habermas J 1972 *Knowledge and Human Interests*. Heinemann, London

Hirst P H, Peters R S 1970 *The Logic of Education*. Routledge and Kegan Paul, London

Lewy A 1973 The practice of curriculum evaluation. *Curric. Theory Network* 11: 6–33

Organisation for Economic Co-operation and Development (OECD) 1971 *Reviews of National Policies for Education: The United States*. OECD, Paris

Organisation for Economic Co-operation and Development (OECD) 1974 *Research and Development in Education: A Survey*. OECD, Paris

Pask G, Lewis B 1972 *Teaching Strategies: A Systems Approach*. Open University Press, Milton Keynes

Pinar W (ed.) 1975 *Curriculum Theorizing: The Reconceptualists*. McCutchan, Berkeley, California

Robinson A 1982 *The Schools Cultural Studies Project: A Contribution to Peace: Directors' Report*. New University of Ulster, Northern Ireland

Schon D A 1971 *Beyond the Stable State: Public and Private Learning in a Changing Society*. Norton, New York

Smith L 1978 An evolving logic of participant observation, educational ethnography, and other case studies. In: Schulman L S (ed.) 1979 *Review of Research in Education*, Vol. 6, Peacock, Itasca, Illinois, pp. 316–77

Stake R E, Easley J 1978 *Case Studies in Science Education*, Vol. 1: *The Case Reports*; Vol. 2: *Design, Overview, and General Findings*. Center for Instructional Research and Curriculum Evaluation, University of Illinois, Urbana-Champaign, Illinois

Stenhouse L 1975 *An Introduction to Curriculum Research and Development*. Heinemann, London

Stenhouse L 1981 *Case Study in Educational Research and Evaluation*. Centre for Applied Research in Education (CARE), University of East Anglia, Norwich

Taylor P H 1970 *How Teachers Plan Their Courses: Studies in Curriculum Planning*. National Foundation for Educational Research (NFER), Slough

Tebbutt M J, Atherton M A 1979 A "reaction kinetics" model for the growth of curriculum projects. *J. Curric. Stud.* 11: 159–66

Tisher R P, Power C N 1978 The learning environment associated with an Australian curriculum innovation. *J. Curric. Stud.* 10: 169–84

Walker D F 1975 Curriculum development in an art project. In: Reid W A, Walker D F (eds.) 1975 *Case Studies in Curriculum Change: Great Britain and the United States*. Routledge and Kegan Paul, London

Walker D F 1976 What curriculum research? *J. Curric. Stud.* 5: 58–72

Curriculum Inquiry: Alternative Paradigms

W. H. Schubert and A. L. Schubert

Since the late 1960s the topic of paradigms of inquiry has steadily emerged as a principal issue in curriculum discourse (Schubert 1986). In fact, the educational research community itself has witnessed a surge of interest in clarifying the conceptual assumptions or paradigms that guide inquiry. It can be argued that apart from philosophy of education, which takes as a primary responsibility the clarification of modes of inquiry or epistemological bases, curriculum studies is the subfield of education that provided the earliest in the question of paradigms. Deeply concerned with the nature of inquiry, curriculum scholars in the late

1960s and early 1970s shared with the larger community of scholars in social sciences and humanities an interest in questions that Thomas Kuhn elicited in his landmark book, *The Structure of Scientific Revolutions* (Kuhn 1962). During the next two decades, philosophers began to sketch underlying assumptions and values behind alternative positions on inquiry, noting empirical, analytic, phenomenological, and critical categories (see Bernstein 1976, Bredo and Feinberg 1982). Moreover, concrete approaches to research methodology appeared using pragmatic, phenomenological, and critical orientations under the label "human sciences" (Polkinghorne 1983), a term which has more currency in European circles than American.

The issue of paradigms of inquiry is discussed overtly in the curriculum literature. In 1976 the journal *Curriculum Inquiry* was founded, after beginning under the title *Curriculum Theory Network* in 1968 at the Ontario Institute for Studies in Education, Toronto. Other journals have since emerged to further discourse on matters of curriculum inquiry.

Despite the increasingly widespread interest in the topic of paradigms of curriculum inquiry, the way the term paradigm is used is quite diverse. This diversity is not unique to curriculum, for after Kuhn initiated the discussion in his 1962 classic, Lakatos and Musgrave (1970) identified more than 20 meanings attributed to Kuhn's own treatment of the topic. In curriculum, at least three dominant uses can be found: (a) classification systems; (b) assumptions about inquiry; and (c) dimensions that define curriculum.

1. Paradigm as Classification Systems

A number of attempts to categorize existing positions on curriculum theory and practice have emerged since the late 1960s. Each is an attempt to illustrate prevailing differences and contending views, but none is offered with the intent that the categories represent invariant divisions. It must be understood that overlap does exist, often productively, and that differing categories illustrate a richness in diversity rather than contending parties immobilized by a lack of common purpose. Curriculum scholars and practitioners share the common aim of trying to determine that which is worthwhile for learners to know and experience.

Thelen (1960) identified four models for education and sketched a broad portrayal of curriculum elicited by each: (a) personal inquiry, (b) group investigation, (c) reflective action, and (d) skill development. While each of these positions can be used along with the others, it is possible for one to dominate, and the consequences of domination and/or collaboration need to be anticipated carefully in a spirit of action inquiry (Thelen 1960 pp. 208–09).

Eisner (1985) portrays five basic orientations to curriculum, including: (a) development of cognitive processes, which focuses on learning and the intellect; (b) academic rationalism, which emphasizes intellectual attainment through disciplines of knowledge; (c) personal relevance, which involves the centrality of personal meaning derived from teacher–student collaboration in creating curricular experiences; (d) social adaptation and social reconstruction, which focus curriculum on ends that meet social needs; and (e) curriculum as technology, which views curriculum design as a procedural enterprise having the potential to facilitate any substantive purpose.

Pinar (1975) identifies three categories of curriculum developers and theorists: (a) traditionalists, (b) conceptual empiricists, and (c) reconceptualists. Each is illustrated by sets of articles vis-à-vis curriculum, instruction, and evaluation in Giroux et al. (1981). Traditionalists evolved from immersion in school settings where the job had to be done to meet technocratic needs of the system, and thus had difficulty developing new images of what curriculum might be. Conceptual empiricists emerged with post-Sputnik curriculum reform which involved social and behavioral scientists who espoused neopositivist orientations to curriculum inquiry and design. Reconceptualists were born through a configuration of interests in literary sources, post-Marxist political theory, existentialism, phenomenology, and radical psychoanalysis. Curriculum scholars of this category brought matters of personal meaning and social justice to the fore.

Schubert (1986) derived three categories from historical studies of curriculum literature: (a) intellectual traditionalist; (b) social behaviorist, and (c) experientalist. The intellectual traditionalist values the liberal arts, great books, or disciplines and knowledge approach to curriculum. The social behaviorist sees curriculum as a scientifically warranted technique or formula for curriculum design that causes learning of behaviors valued by society. The experientalist values experience that begins with personal interest, moves to pursuit of common human interests, and continuously monitors consequences of such pursuit in terms of the social justice and personal meaning that accrue.

Kliebard (1986) identifies four historical categories: (a) humanists, (b) social effiency advocates, (c) developmentalists, and (d) social meliorists. While social meliorists develop curriculum to make society better, social efficiency experts try to more productively perpetuate status quo bureaucracies. While humanists tie curricular quality to benefit of the intellect through the time-honored liberal arts and sciences, developmentalists argue that intellectual attainment best obtains from curriculum based on study of human growth processes. Earlier, Kliebard (1972) argued that curriculum policy and proposals can be interpreted through three guiding metaphors: travel, production, and growth. Clearly one can see distinctly the travel metaphor in the humanist, the production metaphor in social efficiency, and the growth metaphor in both the developmentalist and the social meliorist.

The above category schemes are illustrative; they are not intended to be all-inclusive, Schiro (1978), for instance, identifies four curricular "ideologies": academic, social efficiency, child-study, and social reconstruction. Orlosky and Smith (1978) offer a four-part classification of curriculum theory styles: humanistic, disciplines of knowledge, technical or analytic, and futuristic, while Huenecke (1982) classifies curriculum theory in three quite different domains: structural, generic, and substantive. As one continues to identify systems it is possible to perceive similarity among them. For instance, McNeil's (1985) use of humanistic, social reconstructionist, technology, and academic subjects bear relationship to the classification language of Eisner, Kliebard, and others. Similarly, one can see many of the above systems reflected by Miller (1983) who introduces a spectrum of seven orientations to curriculum (behavioral, subject/disciplines, social, developmental, cognitive processes, humanistic, and transpersonal) as well as potential "meta-orientations."

From the foregoing it can be argued that one image of paradigm in curriculum literature pertains to classification systems that attempt to differentiate alternative positions on curriculum theory and practice. Some scholars believe that classification systems impair the complexity of curricular inquiry by oversimplification, and others at the opposite end of the continuum hold that the systems of classification rightly differentiate alternatives within curricular discourse.

2. Paradigm as Assumptions about Inquiry

The existence of classification systems directly speaks to substantive positions on curriculum matters, and indirectly implies the need to investigate alternative forms of curriculum inquiry. The issue of forms of inquiry clearly relates to Kuhn's (1962) treatment of paradigm. His analysis addresses revolutionary conceptual changes in natural sciences, for example from geocentric to heliocentric universe, from Newtonian to Einsteinian physics, from pre- to post-Darwinian biology. When any given system dominates, the rules of scientific inquiry are governed by certain presumptions, but as anomalies increase that cannot be explained by the prevailing system, a reconceptualization is required. Thus, a new paradigm is wrought and the system continues.

Habermas (1971) in philosophy, and Bernstein (1976) in social and political theory have elaborated paradigms that pertain to inquiry in the social sciences and to a lesser extent the humanities. The work of Habermas has aided in discussions of paradigmatic reconceptualization of curriculum paradigms. Building upon Habermas (1971), and Bernstein (1976), Schubert (1986) depicts three paradigms of curriculum inquiry: (a) empirical–analytic, (b) hermeneutic, and (c) critical. Each can be interpreted relative to interests served, kinds of organization used to serve those interests, and modes of rationality manifest in each paradigm. It must be noted

that considerable variation exists within each paradigm or type of science (inquiry). Moreover, those selected as illustrative of a given paradigm may not perceive themselves as operating within that conceptual orientation to inquiry. This further exemplifies the problematic character of curriculum inquiry.

The empirical–analytic paradigm draws upon research traditions that stem back to E. L. Thorndike, and Willhelm Wundt before him. The interest served is technical, reflecting a positivist vision of science, and the social organization that facilitates empirical–analytic inquiry is that of hierarchies in the work-place. This mode of rationality accepts social reality as it is, values parsimony, assumes knowledge to be objective and value free, seeks to discover empirically testable lawlike propositions, and assumes principles of control and certainty. The canons of replication, validity, and reliability are central to this paradigm. Schwab (1970) argued that the dominance of this paradigm made the curriculum field moribund, preoccupied with easily managed research that finds problems in the minds of researchers rather than in states of affairs, that operates exclusively by inductive and hypothetical–deductive methods of inquiry, that seeks laws of curricular behavior rather than situationally specific insights, and that sees knowledge qua knowledge and publication as the end of inquiry. Schwab called this empirical–analytic orientation "theoretic," drawing upon Aristotelian roots.

The hermeneutic paradigm focuses on interpretation. Literally and historically, hermeneutics refers to the interpretation of religious texts; metaphorically applied to curriculum, the text becomes curriculum, context, practice, and discourse. The interest served by hermeneutic inquiry is practical. Schwab contrasts practical inquiry with theoretic and argues that a move from the theoretic to the practical, quasipractical, and eclectic is the only way to revive curriculum from its moribund state. This would include a problem source for inquiry found in actual states of affairs rather than in conceptualizations of researchers who abstract and combine similarities from situations, disregarding the vast amount of idiosyncrasy left behind. Practical inquiry also values direct and sustained interaction with phenomena under investigation, seeks situationally specific insights, and foresees meaningful and morally defensible decision and action as its end. Such inquiry is clearly in the pragmatic tradition of John Dewey (1938).

The hermeneutic emphasis on serving practical interests through interactive social organization, however, is as relevant to phenomenonology as to pragmatism. At times the two seem to blend in the hermeneutic mode of rationality which sees human beings as active creators of knowledge, emphasizes understanding and communication, views reality as intersubjectively constituted and grounded within a historical and political context, looks for meaning beneath the texture of everyday life, and focuses sensitively on meaning through language.

While Schwab addresses practical and theoretic languages of curriculum discourse, Huebner (1966) calls for languages of a moral and aesthetic character to move beyond the predominantly technical, scientific, and political language of curriculum in use by scholars and practitioners today. Moral language is well-illustrated in work by Macdonald (1977), while aesthetic language is quite evident in work by Eisner (1985).

The journals *Phenomenology and Pedagogy* and *The Journal of Curriculum Theorizing* contain a considerable variety of writing of hermeneutic or interpretive character. The interpretive has found several quite different variations. Willis (1978), for example, provides an array of both concepts and cases of the interpretive study of curriculum evaluation. The debate over quantitative and qualitative inquiry seems to have begun in the evaluation literature and proceeded to embrace the whole of educational research (Smith and Heshusius 1986). Eisner, in particular, challenges scholars in education to realize the great potential for educational insight and understanding through artistic inquiry and study of the arts.

Critical inquiry in curriculum forms a paradigm of praxis that serves the interest of emancipation and proceeds under the social organization of power. Its mode of rationality assumes the necessity of ideological critique, that is, of interrogating the economic, political, and cultural contexts and assumptions of curriculum as influenced by such factors as gender, class, and race (Apple and Weis 1983).

The works of Apple (1982) and Giroux (1983) have done a great deal to focus attention upon key critical issues. These authors encourage educators to ask such questions as the following, which were outlined in Schubert (1986 p. 315).

(a) How is knowledge reproduced by schools?

(b) What are the sources of knowledge that students acquire in schools?

(c) How do students and teachers resist or contest that which is conveyed through lived experience in schools?

(d) What do students and teachers realize from their school experiences? In other words, what impact does school have on their outlooks?

(e) Whose interests are served by outlooks and skills fostered by schooling?

(f) When served, do these interests move more in the direction of emancipation, equity, and social justice, or do they move in the opposite direction?

(g) How can students be empowered to attain greater liberation, equity, and social justice through schooling?

Encouraging practitioners to engage in critical praxis that attends to such questions is furthered by recent developments in action research. Stenhouse (Rudduck and Hopkins 1985) encouraged this sort of reflection among teachers in England, and Carr and Kemmis (1986), in Australia, built upon Stenhouse's work to develop critical mindedness in practitioners.

3. Paradigm as Dimensions that Define Curriculum

Tyler (1949) developed a set of constructs that constitute a paradigm for curriculum work. Moreover, Tyler's guidelines or rationale, as it is called, is the most widely used set of principles in curriculum today. One can hardly find a curriculum guide, a teacher's manual, a lesson or unit plan, or a curriculum and instructional methods book that does not contain Tyler's four main topics: purpose, learning experiences or content, organization, and evaluation. These topics may be used descriptively as categories deemed necessary for analyzing a curriculum, or they may be used prescriptively as the starting point for determining purposes, learning experiences, organization, and evaluation for a given curriculum. Tyler further advocates that it is necessary to "filter" responses to these topics through carefully clarified philosophical and psychological "screens," that is, basic positions or underlying assumptions. Finally, Tyler calls for balance among three knowledge sources for developing purposes: students, subject matter, and society.

Taba and Goodlad have made influential variations on the Tyler rationale. Although Tyler did not intend his four topics (purposes, learning experiences, organization, and evaluation) to be used predominantly as a recipe, they were often followed as a stepwise formula for making curriculum. Taba (1962) expanded the stepwise interpretation into seven phases: (a) diagnosis of needs, (b) formulation of objectives, (c) selection of content, (d) organization of content, (e) selection of learning experiences, (f) organization of learning experiences, and (g) determination of what and how to evaluate. Goodlad (1979) introduced the notion "learning opportunities" to replace Tyler's "learning experiences" as a more tangible category, and set Tyler's categories in a larger content, suggesting that each of these categories can be treated at instructional, institutional, societal, ideological, and individual levels.

The Tyler rationale, in its several incarnations, has received criticism from a number of sources. Walker (1971) provides a conceptual alternative, drawing upon naturalistic study of curriculum decision-making committees. He argues that curriculum committees rarely follow the Tylerian model. Instead, they operate much more politically. They begin with a platform, or set of beliefs, background knowledge, prejudices, hidden agendas, images of what might be, and so on. These all became a formidable part of deliberation or discussion and negotiation, the second phase. The final phase, design, is realized when time constraints mandate that proposed practices be implemented, often regardless of logical closure.

Schwab (1973) argues that a conception of curriculum consistent with practical inquiry invokes four fundamental commonplaces: teachers, learners, subject matter, and milieu or environment (psychosocial, as well as physical and institutional). The curriculum that has impact on the outlook of students is derived from the composite of interactions among the commonplaces.

Berman (1968) offers a set of curricular priorities as alternatives to the conventional subject matter areas. She argues that the curriculum should focus directly on processes such as perceiving, communicating, loving, knowing, decision making, patterning, creating, and valuing. She also suggests that it is possible to integrate these processes with each of the conventional content areas.

Schubert (1986 p. 411) describes curriculum inquiry as increasingly perceived as the process of asking fundamental questions such as: "What is worth knowing and experiencing? What kind of life does such knowing and experiencing assume is good for both individuals and the society? How can worthwhile knowledge and experience be provided by educators? How can we know if it is provided?" To respond fully to such questions requires a sense of perspective (the historical, philosophical, sociological, economic, cultural, psychological, and political contexts of curriculum), paradigm (the empirical–analytic, the practical and hermeneutic, and critical praxis), and possibility (understanding of ways to conceptualize and deal with curriculum problems, ways to provide for the ongoing education of educators, and reflective capabilities to imagine alternative futures, the means to realize them, and the consequences of doing so). To pursue this kind of inquiry requires that all concerned with curriculum, educators and students, address these topics; thus, in many respects one can find that curriculum itself deals with fundamental concerns of curriculum inquiry.

4. Conclusion

Three kinds of conceptualizations of paradigm have been described, along with examples of each. Each, of course, has limitations that should be acknowledged, along with potential.

4.1 Paradigm as Classification System

Paradigm can be viewed as classification system, that is, as categories of major viewpoints or lines of thinking in the field. To acknowledge prevailing diversity can lead to unwarranted relativism and it can encourage the use of oversimplified lines of demarcation. Moreover, it can give the impression that confusion reigns if the most notable scholars differ extensively. Walker (1980), however, sees this as a sign of robustness, calling it a "rich confusion." To admit uncertainty can be seen as a symbol of maturity that acknowledges a pluralistic universe, rather than immaturity that expresses itself in the false security of clutching to the one idea known well.

4.2 Paradigm as Assumptions about Inquiry

Viewing paradigms of curriculum inquiry as assumptions about inquiry has greatest kinship with the treatment of paradigms in the social sciences and humanities. The question has been raised, however, as to whether any of the scholarly alternatives (empirical, analytic, hermeneutic, critical) represent a fundamental departure from one another. Because the result of each is usually rendered available in written form, each can be seen as susceptible to commodification. It is taken from the world of lived experience, and by scholarly rendition in writing ceases to grow as if it remained embedded in action. While scholars must heed such cricitism, their world of scholarship is part of lived experience; thus, their analyses and advocacies of paradigms can be seen as clarification of alternative sources of meaning, knowing, valuing, and expressing that which they study. It remains to be asked whether current attention to paradigms of inquiry is indeed a novel contribution to scholarship or whether it is a renewal of concern that philosophers have long exhibited for fundamental principles in metaphysical, epistemological, axiological, ethical, political, and other realms. For example, is contemporary concern for paradigms of curriculum inquiry significantly different from, say, Phenix's (1964) inquiry into realms of meaning? Nevertheless, today's inquiry into curriculum paradigms enables more persons to question basic assumptions, whether or not the inquiry is of a new variety.

4.3 Paradigm as Defining Dimensions

Paradigms viewed as dimensions that define curriculum in turn guide conceptualizations of curriculum development. The disadvantage of this interpretation of paradigm is that one set of categories may be perceived as incompatible with the others. The idea that Tyler's (1949) categories are mutually exclusive from Schwab's (1973) or that either of these is incompatible with those advanced by Walker (1971) may have some validity, but extends little appreciation to an eclectic stance. When exercised reflectively and with careful deliberation, the art of being eclectic (see Schwab 1971) reveals the potential complementarity of sets of dimensions of curriculum heretofore deemed alternative or contradictory.

Finally, any of the three images of paradigm discussed in the article have great potential for enabling a form of internal critique which enriches inquiry in curriculum studies. Simultaneously, if taken as final answers, the idea of paradigms can stultify curriculum inquiry by making categories rigid and causing scholars to take sides. Perhaps the best response to the interest in paradigms is for educators at all levels to take seriously the spirit of questioning exhibited in the literature on paradigms, and to eschew the doctrinaire in exchange for continuous striving to develop through deeper understanding of curricular phenomena.

Bibliography

Apple M W 1982 *Education and Power*. Routledge and Kegan Paul, Boston, Massachusetts

Apple M W, Weis L 1983 *Ideology and Practice in Schooling*. Temple University Press, Philadelphia, Pennsylvania

Berman L 1968 *New Priorities in the Curriculum*. Merrill, Columbus, Ohio

Bernstein R J 1976 *The Restructuring of Social and Political Thought*. University of Pennsylvania Press, Philadelphia, Pennsylvania

Bredo E, Feinberg W (eds.) 1982 *Knowledge and Values in Social and Educational Research*. Temple University Press, Philadelphia, Pennsylvania

Carr W, Kemmis S 1986 *Becoming Critical: Education, Knowledge and Action Research*. Taylor and Francis, Philadelphia, Pennsylvania

Dewey J 1938 *Logic, the Theory of Inquiry*. Henry Holt, New York

Eisner E W 1985 *The Educational Imagination: On the Design and Evaluation of School Programs*. Macmillan, New York

Giroux H A 1983 *Theory and Resistance in Education: A Pedagogy for the Opposition*. Bergin and Garvey, South Hadley, Massachusetts

Giroux H A, Penna A N, Pinar W F (eds.) 1981 *Curriculum and Instruction: Alternatives in Education*. McCutchan, Berkeley, California

Goodlad J I 1979 *Curriculum Inquiry: The Study of Curriculum Practice*. McGraw-Hill, New York

Habermas J 1971 *Knowledge and Human Interests*. Beacon, Boston, Massachusetts

Huebner D 1966 Curricular language and classroom meanings. In: Macdonald J B, Leeper R R (eds.) 1966 *Language and Meaning*. Association for Supervision and Curriculum Development, Washington, DC, pp. 8–26

Huenecke D 1982 What is curriculum theorizing? What are its implications for practice? *Educ. Leadership* 39: 290–94

Kliebard H M 1972 Metaphorical roots of curriculum design. *Teachers College Record* 72(3): 403–04

Kliebard H M 1986 *The Struggle for the American Curriculum, 1893–1958*. Routledge and Kegan Paul, Boston, Massachusetts

Kuhn T S 1962 *The Structure of Scientific Revolutions*. University of Chicago Press, Chicago, Illinois

Lakatos I, Musgrave A (eds.) 1970 *Criticism and the Growth of Knowledge*. Cambridge University Press, Cambridge

Macdonald J B 1977 Value bases and issues for curriculum. In: Molnar A, Zahorik J A (eds.) 1977 *Curriculum Theory*. Association for Supervision and Curriculum Development, Washington, DC, pp. 10–21

McNeil J D 1985 *Curriculum: A Comprehensive Introduction*. Little, Brown, Boston, Massachusetts

Miller J P 1983 *The Educational Spectrum: Orientations to Curriculum*. Longman, New York

Orlosky D E, Smith B O 1978 *Curriculum Development: Issues and Insights*. Rand McNally, Chicago, Illinois

Phenix P 1964 *Realms of Meaning: A Philosophy of the Curriculum for General Education*. McGraw-Hill, New York

Pinar W F (ed.) 1975 *Curriculum Theorizing: The Reconceptualists*. McCutchan, Berkeley, California

Polkinghorne D 1983 *Methodology for the Human Sciences: Systems of Inquiry*. State University of New York Press, Albany, New York

Rudduck J, Hopkins D (eds.) 1985 *Research as a Basis for Teaching: Readings from the Work of Lawrence Stenhouse*. Heinemann, London

Schiro M 1978 *Curriculum for Better Schools: The Great Ideological Debate*. Educational Technology Publications, Englewood Cliffs, New Jersey

Schubert W H 1986 *Curriculum: Perspective, Paradigm, and Possibility*. Macmillan, New York

Schwab J J 1970 *The Practical: A Language for Curriculum*. National Education Association, Washington, DC

Schwab J J 1971 The practical: Arts of eclectic. *Sch. Rev.* 79: 493–542

Schwab J J 1973 The practical 3: Translation into curriculum. *Sch. Rev.* 81: 501–22

Smith J K, Heshusius L 1986 Closing down the conversation: The end of the quantitative–qualitative debate among educational inquirers. *Educ. Res.* 15(1): 4–12

Taba H 1962 *Curriculum Development: Theory and Practice*. Harcourt, Brace, and World, New York

Thelen H A 1960 *Education and the Human Quest*. Harper and Brothers, New York

Tyler R W 1949 *Basic Principles of Curriculum and Instruction*. University of Chicago Press, Chicago, Illinois

Walker D F 1971 A naturalistic model for curriculum development. *Sch. Rev.* 80(1): 51–65

Walker D F 1980 A barnstorming tour of writing on curriculum. In: Foshay A W 1980 *Considered Action for Curriculum Improvement*. Association for Supervision and Curriculum Development, Washington, DC, pp. 71–81

Willis G (ed.) 1978 *Qualitative Evaluation: Concepts and Cases in Curriculum Criticism*. McCutchan, Berkeley, California

Curriculum Inquiry: Commonplace Topics

M. Ben-Peretz

The term "commonplaces" was introduced into the language of curriculum by Schwab (1964). By "topics" or "commonplaces" Schwab meant

... those foci of attention within an area of interest which fulfill two conditions:

(a) they demand the attention of serious investigators;

(b) their scrutiny generates diverse investigations and conse-

quent diversities of definitions, doctrines, and emphases. (Schwab 1964 pp. 5–6)

"Commonplaces" are conceived as foci of researchers' attention in any discipline or field of study. Commonplaces viewed as a set of common elements, "enable us to map a field and to compare different theories in one discipline" (Fox 1985 p. 67). According to Herron (1971) "the 'commonplaces' constitute, in effect, a checklist of aspects or topics at issue which reasonably complete accounts of scientific enquiry should be expected to treat" (Herron 1971 p. 172).

The four commonplaces of education identified and investigated by Schwab (1964) are: the learner, the teacher, the milieu of teaching and learning, and the subject matter. Treatment of all these commonplaces is deemed essential for any defensible process of curriculum development. The commonplaces are interlinked as conceptions of one invade the others. Scholars of curriculum have suggested different topics, or "commonplaces" of curriculum enquiry. Tyler (1949) mentioned three sources of information for the process of curriculum development: learner, society, and subject matter. Enquiry into each of these domains provides the basis for the constructed curriculum. Teachers are described by Tyler (1984) as curriculum planners and do not constitute an equal "commonplace" to be investigated in the course of curriculum development.

A different set of foci for curricular enquiry was suggested by Robinsohn (1969). Robinsohn's analysis of the field of curriculum development yielded the following three common topics or commonplaces: life situations, qualifications of individuals, and content elements. While these topics could be seen as similar in their meaning to 'society', 'learners', and 'subject matter', Robinsohn rejects a sharp distinction between these topics. He prefers to speak about the identification of situations and functions of individuals *in* society. According to Robinsohn teachers have to become partners in curriculum development and their advice and active involvement in curriculum revisions is considered essential. The role of teacher is deemed important but teachers do not figure as the principal agents in curriculum development, as they do in Tyler's view, nor are "teachers" viewed by Robinsohn as one of the "commonplaces" of curriculum, namely, a focus of curricular studies.

Whatever the exact wording used by writers on curriculum, whether they include the "teacher" as one of the commonplaces or not, the treatment of "commonplaces" is an inherent part of the process of curriculum development.

1. The Commonplaces in Curriculum Deliberations

The commonplaces of education are conceived as standard features of the curriculum process, which is characterized by "flexible rationality" and a deliberative, eclectic mode of transaction carried out in the curriculum group (Eisner 1984). According to Schwab (1970) curriculum is a practical domain seeking defensible solutions to practical problems in education. Commonplaces play a double role in this process. The commonplaces of education—that is, learner, teacher, milieu, and subject matter, have to be considered in the search for curricular solutions. Unexamined reliance on theories pertaining to these foci of curriculum decision

making may lead to unsatisfactory results, and may be the cause for "bandwagons" which tend to dominate education (Schwab 1970). Schwab claims that theories are partial, incomplete, and abstract and their application to concrete educational situations is highly problematic. Theories have to be prepared for practice and commonplaces serve as a tool for helping to solve the problem of the incomplete nature of theories (Fox 1985). The comparison of theories makes use of the notion of commonplaces "to discriminate and relate the bias of each theory" (Schwab 1970 p. 13). The arts of the eclectic, the systematic comparison of the principles, premises, and methods used in each enquiry, serve to combine partial theories and to generate decisions for practice (Schwab 1971). The role of commonplaces in the analysis of social theories transforms theories into materials for curriculum deliberation (Garver 1984). Through the deliberative process educational problems are identified and formulated, possible solutions are considered, and consequences are weighed. Theoretical principles are selected and adapted to each other and to the concrete and particular case. The arts of the eclectic and the arts of deliberation are thus linked together (Schwab 1971).

2. Representatives of the Commonplaces in the Curriculum Group

Consideration of the complexity and richness of the four commonplaces of education requires a group setting which will provide opportunities for bringing a range of perspectives to bear on a curricular problem. Schwab (1973) proposes a group consisting of representatives of five bodies of experience, the four commonplaces and the experience of curriculum development. A group is required because of the dependence of curriculum decision making on consideration of the commonplaces and because no one person may adequately represent all the commonplaces. The group may consist of more or less than five participants. A commonplace may be represented by more than one member or, conversely, one member may represent more than one commonplace. The experience of curriculum making is represented, according to Schwab, by the curriculum chairperson whose task is to guide the whole process. Reid (1984) interprets Schwab's proposal for curriculum groups as "the reflection of and the means of sustaining a vision of 'community'" (Reid 1984 p. 105). Schulman (1984) presents various reasons for the importance of the social setting which provides the broad range of perspectives required for an adequate understanding of the curricular problem and its potential solution. The group setting is perceived to be important because it enlists a sense of commitment and may enable participants to act more wisely and justly.

Representatives of the commonplaces are not necessarily scholars and theorists. Schwab (1983) suggests teachers, who possess personal knowledge about educational situations, as the most important members of the curriculum group. Teachers are best informed about the characteristics and behaviours of members of their profession in concrete and specific classroom situations. Teachers are also able to represent the "learner" commonplace because of their knowledge of particular students. Principals are considered by Schwab to be indispensable members of the group because of their administrative functions, and because they have fullest knowledge of the milieu of the school itself. Thus, principals are conceived as representatives of the "milieu" commonplace. Members of the community, such as school board members, are additional representatives of the "milieu". In the same line of reasoning the "student" commonplace is to be represented by students themselves, who are aware of their own particular needs in specific localities. Schwab suggests that representatives of the "subject matter" and the larger "milieu" commonplaces act as advisors and consultants to the curriculum group. These representatives are academics in the various disciplines and social scientists, whose function is to ensure that the group will consider "a range of legitimated bodies of knowledge and skills" (Schwab 1983 p. 250), and provide the group with useful advice on psychological and sociological issues.

Schwab (1983) tends to transfer the role of representatives in the realms of the commonplaces from theoretic experts to practitioners, suggesting that theorists act as consultants. Fox (1985) proposes to maintain the role of experts as representatives of the commonplaces and as members in the curriculum group, side by side with practitioners. The composition of the curriculum group reflects curricular orientations. An orientation towards local curriculum planning, in response to diverse needs and resources of a school or a district, leads to greater emphasis on the contribution of practitioners who possess personal knowledge about the local situation. Another mode of dealing with diversity is that a local group deals with modification of curricula that are prepared by a central curriculum agency (Fox 1985). In that case the central group would tend to rely on the contribution of experts with more generalized knowledge about the commonplaces.

3. The Relationship Between the Commonplaces

The commonplaces of education constitute the foci of attention which have to be treated in the process of curriculum deliberations. According to Schwab (1983) the commonplaces are of intrinsically equal importance.

Two kinds of relationships between the commonplaces may be envisioned:

(a) coordinacy, namely, equal weight given to each of the commonplaces in every curricular situation; and

(b) ranking, namely, creating a hierarchy of the commonplaces according to changing local needs in specific times.

The tendency to base curriculum decisions on considerations stemming from one of the commonplaces, yielding child-centred, society-centred, or subject-matter-centred curricula, may lead to distortions and curricular errors. According to Schwab (1983), pressures of practical situations may create situations in which preference to one of the commonplaces has to be given. Yet, it is essential that such a decision be justified on the basis of careful consideration of the state of curriculum and the surrounding circumstances, all in the light of all the commonplaces.

Bibliography

Eisner E 1984 No easy answers: Joseph Schwab's contributions to curriculum. *Curric. Inq.* 14 (2): 201–10

Fox S 1985 The vitality of theory in Schwab's conception of the practical. *Curric. Inq.* 15 (1): 63–89

Garver E 1984 The arts of the practical: Variations on a theme of Prometheus. *Curric. Inq.* 14 (2): 165–82

Herron M D 1971 The nature of scientific inquiry. *School Rev.* 79: 171–212

Reid W A 1984 Curriculum, community, and liberal education: A response to The Practical 4. *Curric. Inq.* 14 (1): 103–11

Robinsohn S B 1969 A conceptual structure of curriculum development. *Comp. Educ.* 5 (3): 221–34

Schwab J J 1964 Problem, topics and issues. In: Elam S (ed.) 1964 *Education and the Structure of Knowledge.* Rand, McNally, Chicago, Illinois, pp. 4–47

Schwab J J 1970 *The Practical: A Language for Curriculum.* National Education Association, Washington, DC

Schwab J J 1971 The practical: Arts of the eclectic. *School Rev.* 79: 493–542

Schwab J J 1973 The practical 3: Translation into curriculum. *School Rev.* 81: 501–22

Schwab J J 1983 The practical 4: Something for curriculum professors to do. *Curric. Inq.* 13 (3): 239–65

Shulman L S 1984 The practical and the eclectic: A deliberation on teaching and educational research. *Curric. Inq.* 14 (2): 183–200

Tyler R W 1949 *Basic Principles of Curriculum and Instruction.* University of Chicago, Chicago, Illinois

Tyler R W 1984 Personal reflections on *The Practical 4. Curric. Inq.* 14 (1): 97–102

Social History of Curriculum Subjects

I. Goodson

The school curriculum is a social artefact, conceived of and made for deliberate human purposes. However, in many accounts of schooling, the written curriculum, this most manifest of social constructions, has been treated as a given. Moreover, the problem has been compounded by the fact that it has often been treated as a neutral given, embedded in an otherwise meaningful and complex situation. Yet in anyone's own schooling, it is known very well that while some subjects, topics, or lessons were loved, others were hated. Some were learnt easily and willingly, others were rejected whole-heartedly. Sometimes the variable was the teacher, or the time, or the room, or the people, but often if was the form or content of the curriculum itself.

Beyond such individualistic responses, there are of course significant collective responses to curriculum, and when patterns are discerned it suggests that the school curriculum is far from a neutral factor. There is a social construction which sits at the heart of the process by which children are educated. Yet, in spite of the patchy exhortations of sociologists—sociologists of knowledge in particular—there has been little in the way of serious study of the process of social history of the curriculum.

1. Why Study School Subjects?

Once it is accepted that the curriculum itself is an important source for historical study, a number of further problems surface. The curriculum is a perennially elusive and multifaceted concept. The curriculum is a difficult concept because it is defined, redefined, and negotiated at a number of levels and in a number of arenas. It would be impossible to arbitrate over which points in the ongoing negotiations were critical. Furthermore, the terrain differs substantially according to local or national structures and patterns. In such a shifting and unfocused terrain, it is plainly problematic to try to define common ground for this study. After all, if there is a lacuna in the study, it is likely to be for good reasons.

In fact a good deal of the most important scholarship on curriculum, certainly on curriculum as a social construction, took place in the 1960s and early 1970s. This was, however, a period of change and flux everywhere in the Western world, and nowhere more so than in the world of schooling in general, and curriculum in particular. For this burgeoning of critical curriculum scholarship to happen during such times was both encouraging and, in a sense, symptomatic. The emergence of a field of study of curriculum as social construction was an important new direction. However, while itself symptomatic of a period of social questioning and criticism, this burgeoning of critical scholarship was not without its negative side. This negative side has two important aspects. Firstly, influential scholars in the field often took a value position which assumed that schooling should be reformed, root and branch, revolutionized, the maps of learning being redrawn. Secondly, this scholarship took place at a time when a wide range of curriculum reform movements were seeking to do precisely this—to revolutionize school curricula on both grounds. Therefore, it was unlikely that such scholars would wish to focus upon, let alone concede,

the areas of stability that may have existed within the school curriculum.

Standing out more clearly is the school subject, the basic or traditional subjects. Throughout the Western world, there is not only exhortation, but also evidence about a return to basic, a readoption of traditional subjects. In England, for instance, the National Curriculum defines a range of subjects to be taught as a core curriculum in all schools. The subjects thereby instated bear an uncanny resemblance to the list generally defined as secondary school subjects in the 1904 Regulations. The *Times Educational Supplement* of 31 July 1987 p. 2 commented about this reassertion of traditional subject dominance: "The first thing to say about this whole exercise is that it unwinds 80 years of English (and Welsh) educational history. It is a case of go back to go." In the early years of the nineteenth century the first state secondary schools were organized. Their curriculum was presented by the National Board of Education under the detailed guidance of Sir Robert Morant:

> The course should provide for instruction in the English Language and Literature, at least one Language other than English, Geography, History, Mathematics, Science and Drawing, with due provision for Manual Work and Physical Exercises, and in a girls' school for Housewifery. Not less than $4\frac{1}{2}$ hours per week must be allotted to English, Geography and History; not less $3\frac{1}{2}$ hours to the Language where one is taken or less than 6 hours where two are taken; and not less than $7\frac{1}{2}$ hours to Science and Mathematics, of which at least 3 must be for Science.

However, in looking at the new 1987 National Curriculum, it can be seen that: "The 8–10 Subject timetable which the discussion paper draws up has as academic a look to it as anything Sir Robert Morant could have dreamed up."

Likewise, in scrutinizing curriculum history in the United States high school, Kliebard (1986) has pointed to the saliency of the traditional school subjects in the face of waves of curriculum reform initiatives from earlier decades. He characterizes the school subject within the United States high school curriculum as "The Impregnable Fortress" in the period of American history from 1893 to 1958.

The conceptualization of curriculum as a source for study remains elusive and slippery, even in times of centrality and tradition where there is a return to basics. In the 1960s and 1970s, critical studies of curriculum as social construction pointed to the school classroom as the site wherein the curriculum was negotiated and realized. The classroom was the centre of action, the arena of resistance. By this view what went on in the classroom was the curriculum. The definition of preactive, written curriculum—the view from the high ground—was, it was thought, not just subject to redefinition at classroom level but quite simply irrelevant.

Such a view, and such a standpoint from which to begin to study curriculum, is now unsustainable. Certainly the high ground of the written curriculum is subject to renegotiation at lower levels, notably the classroom. However, the view, common in the 1960s, that it is therefore irrelevant is less common. Once again, the view is gaining currency that the high ground is of importance. In the high ground what is to be basic and traditional is reconstituted and reinvented. The given status of school subject knowledge is therein reinvented and reasserted. However this is more than political manoeuvring or rhetoric: such reassertion affects the discourse about schooling and relates to the parameters to practice. In the 1990s it would be folly to ignore the central importance of the control and definition of the written curriculum. In a significant sense, the written curriculum is the visible and public testimony of selected rationales and legitimating rhetoric for schooling. It has been argued that the written curriculum in England and Wales:

> both promulgates and underpins certain basic intentions of schooling as they are operationalized in structures and institutions. To take a common convention in preactive curriculum, the school subject: while the written curriculum defines the rationales and rhetoric of the subject, this is the only tangible aspect of a patterning of resources, finances and examinations and associated material and career interests. In this symbiosis, it is as though the written curriculum provides a guide to the legitimating rhetoric of schooling as they are promoted through patterns of resource allocation, status attribution and career distribution. In short, the written curriculum provides us with a testimony, a documentary source, a changing map of the terrain: it is also one of the best official guide books to the institutionalized structure of schooling. (Goodson 1988 p. 16)

What is most important to stress is that the written curriculum, notably the school subject syllabus, guidelines, or textbook has, in this instance, both symbolic but also practical significance: symbolic, in that certain intentions for schooling are thereby publicly signified and legitimated; practical, in that these written conventions are rewarded with finance and resource allocation and thereby with associated work and career benefits.

A study of the written curriculum should afford a range of insights into schooling. However, it is important to stress that such inquiry must be allied to other kinds of study: in particular studies of school process, of school texts, and of the history of pedagogy. Schooling is composed of the interlinked matrix of these, and indeed, other vital ingredients. With regard to schooling and to curriculum in particular, the final question is Who gets what and what do they do with it?

The definition of curriculum is part of this story. That is not the same as asserting a direct or easily discernable relationship between the preactive definition of written curriculum and its interactive realization in classrooms. It is, however, to assert that the written curriculum most often sets important parameters for classroom practice (not always, not at all times, not in all classrooms, but most often). The study of written curriculum will firstly increase understanding of the influences and interests active at the preactive level. Secondly, this understanding will further knowledge of the values and purposes represented in schooling and the manner in which preactive definition, notwithstanding individual and local variations, may set parameters for interactive realization and negotiation in the classroom and school.

2. Programmes for Studying School Subjects

With the growth of the state systems of education, the school subject became the major focus of schooling for increasing numbers of pupils. As a result, scholarship began into the origins of school subjects. Watson (1909), a pioneer in this field, was clear that:

> Owing to the rapid development of a system of County and Municipal Secondary Schools in England and Wales, at the present time, a special interest is centred on the place and function of the "modern" subjects in the secondary schools. (p. vii)

This rationale anticipates in some manner the later exhortations of sociologists of knowledge, for he argued that:

> It is high time that the historical facts with regard to the beginnings of the teaching of modern subjects in England were known, and known in connection with the history of the social forces which brought them into the educational curriculum. (Watson 1909 p. viii)

In the 50-year period following 1909 few scholars followed Watson and sought to relate school subjects to the social forces which brought them into the educational curriculum in any general way.

In the 1960s, however, a new impetus to scholarship on school subjects came from sociologists and specifically from sociologists of knowledge. Musgrove (1968) exhorted educational researchers to "examine subjects both within the school and the nation at large as social systems sustained by communication networks, material endowments, and ideologies" (p. 101). In the communication networks, Esland later argued that research should focus in part, on the subject perspective of the teacher.

> The knowledge which a teacher thinks "fills up" his subject is held in common with members of a supporting community who collectively approach its paradigms and utility criteria, as they are legitimated in training courses and "official" statements. It would seem that teachers, because of the dispersed nature of their epistemic communities, experience the conceptual precariousness which comes from the lack of significant others who can confirm plausibility. They are, therefore, heavily dependent on journals, and, to a lesser extent, conferences, for their reality confirmation. (Esland 1971 p. 79)

Esland and Dale later developed this focus on teachers within subject communities:

> Teachers, as spokesmen for subject communities are involved in an elaborate organization of knowledge. The community has a history, and, through it, a body of respected knowledge. It has rules for recognizing "unwelcome" or "spurious" matter, and ways of avoiding cognitive con-

tamination. It will have a philosophy and a set of authorities, all of which give strong legitimation to the activities which are acceptable to the community. Some members are accredited with the power to make "official statements"—for instance, editors of journals, presidents, chief examiners and inspectors. These are important as "significant others" who provide models to new or wavering members of appropriate belief and conduct. (Esland and Dale 1973 pp. 70–71)

In particular, Esland was concerned that scholarship which illuminates the role of professional groups in the social construction of school subjects be developed. These groups can be seen as mediators of the social forces to which Watson (1909) had alluded:

The subject associations of the teaching profession may be theoretically represented as segments and social movements involved in the negotiation of new alliances and rationales, as collectively held reality constructions became transformed. Thus, applied to the professional identities of teachers within a school, it would be possible to reveal the conceptual regularities and changes which are generated through membership of particular subject communities, as they were manifested in textbooks, syllabi, journals, conference reports, etc.

In the light of the importance of historical perspectives Esland added that "Subjects can be shown to have 'careers' which are dependent on the social-structural and social-psychological correlates of membership of epistemic communities. (Esland 1971 p. 107)

The relationship between what counts as education and issues of power and control had been elucidated in 1961 by Williams in the *Long Revolution*:

It is not only that the way in which education is organized can be seen to express consciously and unconsciously, the wider organization of a culture and a society so that what has been thought of a single distribution is in fact an actual shaping to particular social ends. It is also that the content of education which is subject to great historical variation, again expresses, again both consciously and unconsciously, certain basic elements in the culture. What is thought of as "an education" being in fact a particular set of emphases and omissions. (Williams 1975 p. 146)

One might add to Williams notion of "the content of education". Goodson (1987b) notes that "the battle over the *content* of the curriculum while often more visible is in many senses less important than the control over the underlying *forms*."

Young (1971) sought to follow up the relationship between school knowledge and social control, and to do so in a manner which focused on content and form. He argued, following Bernstein, that:

Those in positions of power will attempt to define what is to be taken as knowledge, how accessible to different groups any knowledge is, and what are the accepted relationships between different knowledge areas, and between those who have access to them and make them available. (p. 52)

His concern with the form of high status school subjects focused on the "organizing principles" which he discerned as underlying the academic curriculum:

These are literacy, or an emphasis on written as opposed to oral presentation, individualism (or avoidance of group work or cooperativeness) which focused on how academic work is assessed and is a characteristic of both the "process" of learning and the way the "product" is presented; abstractness of the knowledge and its structuring and compartmentalizing independently of the knowledge of the learner; finally and linked to the former is what I have called the unrelatedness of academic curricula, which refers to the extent to which they are "at odds" with daily life and experience. (Young 1971 p. 38)

This emphasis on the form of school knowledge should not exclude concerns like that of Williams with the social construction of particular contents. The crucial point to grasp is that it is the interrelated force of form and content which should be at the centre of any study of school subjects. The study of subject form and content should moreover be placed in an historical perspective.

In fact, Young later came to acknowledge the somewhat static determinism of his earlier writing and to argue that historical work should be an essential ingredient of the study of school knowledge. He wrote of the need to understand the historical emergence and persistence of particular conventions (school subjects for example). When people are limited from being able to situate the problems of contemporary education historically they are again limited from understanding issues of politics and control. He concluded that: "one crucial way of reformulating and transcending the limits within which we work is to see . . . how such limits are not given or fixed but produced through the conflicting actions and interests of men in history" (Young 1977 pp. 248–49).

3. Studying the Social History of School Subjects

The important work by sociologists of knowledge in defining research programmes for studies of school knowledge led on to an acknowledgement by some of them that historical study might complement and extend their project. In studying school subjects the inquiry has arrived at a new stage. Initial work in the early twentieth century has provided some important precursors to this work; the sociologists of knowledge have subsequently played a vital role in rescuing and reasserting the validity of this intellectual project; in the process however, some of the necessary focus on historical and empirical circumstances has been lost. The task being undertaken is to reexamine the role of historical methods in the study of curriculum and to rearticulate a mode of study for extending an understanding of the social history of the school curriculum and, in this work, particularly school subjects.

Goodson (1983) looks at the history of three subjects: geography, biology, and environmental studies. Each of the subjects followed a similar evolutionary profile, and this initial work allowed a series of hypotheses to be developed about the way that status and resources, the structuralization of school subjects, push school subject knowledge in particular directions—towards the embrace of the academic tradition. Following this work a new series *Studies in Curriculum History* was launched. In the first volume, *Social Histories of the Secondary Curriculum* (Goodson 1985), work is collected together on a wide range of subjects: classics, science, domestic subjects, religious education, social studies, and modern languages. These studies reflect a growing interest in the history of curriculum and, besides elucidating symbolic drift of school knowledge towards the academic tradition, raise central questions about explanations of school subjects whether they be sociological or philosophical. Other work in the series *Studies in Curriculum History* has looked in detail at particular subjects. McCulloch et al. (1985) examines the politics of school science and technology curriculum in England and Wales since the Second World War. Subsequent work by Woolenough (1988) has looked at the history of physics teaching in schools in the period 1960 to 1985. Another area of emerging work is the history of school mathematics: Cooper (1985) looks at the fate of a number of traditions within mathematics and articulates a model for the redefinition of school subject knowledge; Moon (1986) meanwhile examines the relationship between maths in England and the United States and includes some very interesting work on the dissemination of textbooks.

Emerging work in the United States has also begun to focus on the evolution of the school curriculum studied in historical manner. Kliebard (1986), writing on the curriculum in the United States from 1893 to 1958 discerns a number of the dominant traditions within the school curriculum, and comes to the intriguing conclusion that by the end of the period covered the traditional school subject remained an impregnable fortress. However, Kliebard's work does not go into the detail of school life. In this respect Franklin (1986) provides some valuable insights in a case study of Minneapolis. Here the vital negotiation from curriculum ideas, the terrain of Kliebard's work, towards implementation as school practice is seen. In addition, a collection of papers put together by Popkewitz (1987) examines the historical aspects of a range of subjects: early education, art, reading and writing, biology, mathematics, social studies, special education, socialist curriculum, and a study of Rugg's work.

In Canada, curriculum history has been launched as a field most notably by Tomkins' seminal work *A Common Countenance* (1986). This work examines the patterns of curriculum stability and change in a range of school subjects in the nineteenth and twentieth centuries throughout Canada. The book has stimulated a wide range of important new work of curriculum history, and another volume (Goodson 1987a) which seeks to bring together some of the more important work emerging in different countries on curriculum history. Besides some of the work already noted, there are important articles on the history of school physics, on Victorian school science, on science education, English, the Norwegian common school, and the development of senior school geography in West Australia.

Other work has begun to look beyond traditional school subjects to study broader topics. For example, Cunningham (1988) has examined the curriculum change in the primary school in Britain since 1945. Musgrave (1988) is a case study of the Victorian University Examinations Board 1964 to 1979. Here historical work begins to elucidate the change from curriculum content to examinable content which is such an important part of understanding the way that status and resources are apportioned within the school.

4. Future Directions

Future directions for the study of school subjects and curriculum will require a broadened approach. The base line of work reported above is only a precursor to more elaborate work. In particular this work will have to move into examining the relationship between school subject content and form, and issues of school practice and process. In addition, more broadly conceived notions of curriculum will have to be explored: the hidden curriculum, the curriculum conceived of as topics and activities, and most important of all, the primary and preschool curriculum. As work begins to explore the way in which school subject content relates to the parameters of practice we shall begin to see in a more grounded way how the world of schooling is structured. In addition more work must be undertaken on comparative studies of the school curriculum. However, enough work has been completed on the history of school subjects to assure us that this is a promising entry point from which to reconstitute studies of curriculum and schooling.

Bibliography

Cooper B 1985 *Renegotiating Secondary School Mathematics.* Falmer Press, Philadelphia, Pennsylvania

Cunningham P 1988 *Curriculum Change in the Primary School Since 1945.* Falmer Press, Philadelphia, Pennsylvania

Esland G M 1971 Teaching and learning as the organization of knowledge. In: Young M F D 1971 *Knowledge and Control: New Directions for the Sociology of Education.* Collier Macmillan, London, p. 79

Esland G M, Dale R (eds.) 1973 *School and Society,* Course E282, Unit 2. Open University, Milton Keynes

Franklin B 1986 *Building the American Community.* Falmer Press, Philadelphia, Pennsylvania

Goodson I F 1983 *School Subjects and Curriculum Change.* Falmer Press, Philadelphia, Pennsylvania

Goodson I F 1985 *Social Histories of the Secondary Curriculum.* Falmer Press, Philadelphia, Pennsylvania

Goodson I F (ed.) 1987a *International Perspectives in Curriculum History.* Croom Helm, London

Goodson I F 1978b On curriculum form. Mimeograph. University of Western Ontario, London, Ontario

Goodson I F 1988 *The Making of Curriculum: Collected Essays.* Falmer Press, Philadelphia, Pennsylvania

Kliebard H 1986 *The Struggle for the American Curriculum 1893–1958.* Routledge and Kegan Paul, Boston, Massachusetts

McCulloch G, Jenkins E, Layton D 1985 *Technological Revolution?* Falmer Press, Philadelphia, Pennsylvania

Moon B 1986 *The 'New Maths' Curriculum Controversy.* Falmer Press, Philadelphia, Pennsylvania

Musgrave P W 1988 *Whose Knowledge.* Falmer Press, Philadelphia, Pennsylvania

Musgrove F 1968 The contribution of sociology to the study of the curriculum. In: Kerr J F (ed.) 1968 *Changing the Curriculum.* University of London Press, London

Popkewitz T S 1987 *The Formation of School Subjects: The Struggle for Creating an American.* Falmer Press, Philadelphia, Pennsylvania

Tomkins G S 1986 *A Common Countenance: Stability and Change in the Canadian Curriculum.* Prentice-Hall, Scarborough, Ontario

Watson F 1909 *The Beginnings of the Teaching of Modern Subjects in England.* Pitman, London

Williams R 1975 *The Long Revolution.* Penguin, London

Woolenough B E 1988 *Physics Teaching in Schools 1960–85: Of People and Power.* Falmer Press, Philadelphia, Pennsylvania

Young M F D (ed.) 1971 *Knowledge and Control: New Directions for the Sociology of Education.* Collier Macmillan, London

Young M F D 1977 Curriculum change: Limits and possibilities. In: Young M F D, Whitty G (eds.) 1977 *Society, State, and Schooling.* Falmer Press, Philadelphia, Pennsylvania, pp. 248–49

Historical Research on Curriculum

B. M. Franklin

Efforts to chronicle the development of the school curriculum are not of recent origin. During the first three decades of the twentieth century, several United States scholars, including Inglis, Rugg, and Stout, undertook studies of the history of the curriculum (Kliebard and Franklin 1983 p. 141). At about the same time, Watson published his study of the history of school subjects in England (Goodson 1988 p. 49), and Durkheim delivered his lectures on the history of French secondary education (Durkheim 1977). Yet it has only been since the 1970s and 1980s that curriculum history has appeared on the scene as a distinct area of specialization within the field of curriculum studies. It has in fact been during this period that scholars, primarily in the United Kingdom and the United States, have begun to engage in those kinds of historiographical debates concerning the subject matter, purpose, methodology, and future research agenda of curriculum history, that has provided identity to this area of inquiry. It is these historiographical debates, specifically as they have occurred among United Kingdom and United States researchers that constitute the subject of this article.

1. The Subject Matter of Curriculum History

The principal concern of United Kingdom researchers interested in curriculum history has been the development of school subjects (Goodson 1985 pp. 9–17, 343–67). On the other hand, United States researchers have taken a broader view of the subject matter of this area of study. In 1969, Bellack identified several topics that United States scholars interested in the history of curriculum were then investigating. Bellack noted that like their counterparts in the United Kingdom, these scholars had been examining the curricular and instructional practices of schools. In addition, however, they had also undertaken studies of the early years of the curriculum field, the careers of significant curriculum theorists, and the recommendations over time of national committees (Bellack 1969 pp. 284–90).

Goodson (1986) has explained this difference in subject matter between United Kingdom and United States curriculum historians by contrasting how curriculum decisions are made in the two countries. In England and Wales, with its centralized state system of schooling, curriculum decisions arise out of the debates among numerous and often nameless bureaucrats and educators concerning what should be taught. The data for the English curriculum historian, according to Goodson, are the official pronouncements concerning what should be taught that appear in the form of examination syllabi and the reports of school inspectors and other members of the Department of Education and Science. On the other hand, Goodson maintains that in the United States a decentralized system of schooling has created a multitude of sites where curriculum decisions are made. As in England, local and state school officials make curriculum pronouncements. In addition, however, curriculum recommendations that may ultimately appear in practice are made by educational theorists who inhabit university schools of education and educators, politicians, and influential citizens who serve on numerous government and private committees. It is, Goodson concludes, this difference in the sites where curriculum decisions are made that explains why United States curriculum historians take a broader view of their subject than do their United Kingdom counterparts (Goodson 1986 pp. vii–ix).

There was, as it turned out, a short-lived debate during the 1970s between United States researchers concerning the subject matter of curriculum history. In his review of a collection of essays on the history of the United States curriculum published by the Association for Supervision and Curriculum Development as its 1976 Yearbook, Franklin (1977) criticized the editor (Davis 1976) for failing to distinguish the content of curriculum history from the subject matter that belonged to the field of educational history. The problem, according to Franklin, was that Davis and his colleagues included the development of the course of study as part of the subject matter of curriculum history. Franklin argued that issues of content were so inextricably linked to other aspects of schooling that the course of study could not stand by itself as the subject matter of curriculum history. Instead, he suggested that the subject matter of curriculum history should be the development of curriculum as a field of study and as an occupational role. He went on to argue that curriculum history ought to be seen as analogous in scope and concern to such subjects as the history of medicine, psychology, and sociology, studies that focus their attention on the history of certain professional groups (Franklin 1977 pp. 68–74). In a reply, Davis (1977) noted that Franklin's focus was too narrow and missed much of what was most important to an understanding of the curriculum. He suggested that both the course of study and the curriculum field as an occupational role were equally legitimate subjects for the curriculum historian (Davis 1977 pp. 162–64).

Seeking a resolution to this conflict, Kliebard and Franklin (1983) defined three areas of study for the curriculum historian. Most investigations of the history of the curriculum, they argued, involved studies of significant curriculum movements, such as the social efficiency movement, that have over time transformed the entire school program.

Less popular among curriculum historians have been investigations of the emergence of certain curriculum areas within the school program, such as vocational education and special education, and studies of the changes over time within the traditional school subjects that make up the curriculum. Existing research in these three areas, Kliebard and Franklin note, has almost exclusively involved studies of proposals for curriculum change advanced by university professors and national curriculum committees. Little attention, however, has been paid to examining the introduction of these programs over time in actual school settings (Kliebard and Franklin 1983 pp. 140, 147–48).

In defining the subject matter of their field, curriculum historians have also sought to define their relationship to the larger field of educational history. Bellack (1969) has argued that curriculum history is one element of the study of educational history. "The history of curriculum thought and practice cannot be separated from the general history of American education, which, in turn, cannot be divorced from the broader stream of cultural and intellectual history" (Bellack 1969 p. 291). Franklin, however, has advocated the establishment of curriculum history as a specialized field of inquiry apart from educational history. Educational historians, he argues, lack training in curriculum and as a result often overlook or misinterpret issues that are of most importance to the curriculum field (Franklin 1977 pp. 73–74).

Other curriculum historians, while agreeing with Franklin that specialists in curriculum are better prepared to examine issues of curriculum history, have parted company with him in his call for an independent field of study. They have insisted that there should not be any hard and fast distinctions between the two enterprises (Davis 1977 pp. 164–66, Tanner 1982 pp. 407–09). Goodson (1988), for example, criticizes United Kingdom educational historians for treating the school as a "black box" whose internal workings are not considered or examined. Educational historians, he notes, have devoted their attention to looking at schools as bureaucratic agencies, paying particular attention to their organization and administration. They rarely consider issues, such as curriculum, that involve what goes on within the schools. Goodson, however, disagrees with Franklin about the need to create a specialty of curriculum history distinct from that of educational history. There is, he believes, sufficient room within the discipline of educational history for considering both the internal and external aspects of the history of schooling. What is called for is a productive "dialogue" between educational historians and curriculum specialists (Goodson 1988 pp. 41–58).

2. Why Curriculum History?

There is, it appears, no clear agreement among researchers concerning why curriculum history should be studied. Curriculum historians routinely offer one or more of the following justifications for this area of study. Examining the history of the curriculum will, according to some researchers, aid a better understanding of why the school curriculum and the profession of curriculum work developed in the direction that they did (Davis 1977 pp. 159–60, Goodson 1983 pp. 6–7, Kliebard and Franklin 1983 pp. 150–51). Kliebard and Franklin believe that such an understanding is valuable for two reasons. First, such studies particularly when they are carried out by those who have specialized training in curriculum, can provide insights into the development of the school program that are often ignored in the research of many educational historians. Second, the curriculum as it has appeared over time is an important artifact of culture. It is, in effect, a statement of what a society at a given period of time wishes to preserve and to pass on to future generations. Studying the history of the curriculum, reveals what a society over time values and seeks to perpetuate (Kliebard and Franklin 1983 pp. 150–52).

Investigating the history of the curriculum can, in the opinion of some researchers, enhance current attempts at curriculum change (Goodson 1983 p. 7, Tanner 1982 pp. 406–07). Tanner maintains that the study of curriculum history can identify past problems that have interfered with curriculum reform, which may provide lessons to help contemporary curriculum workers. Curriculum specialists can, she suggests, overcome immediate difficulties by searching for similar problems in the past. "Studying the steps taken to resolve similar problems can only enhance the decision-making process by making available a set of solutions and consequent results against which to compare current proposals" (Dewey and Tyler revisited 1988).

Finally, some curriculum historians believe that this area of study can serve a critical role. Goodson has maintained that studying the development of school subjects leads to an examination of the political interests and motivations of those individuals and groups who have championed these curricular elements. He argues that the historical practice of English educational reformers of organizing school knowledge around the traditional disciplines of knowledge, a pattern of organization that is often remote from the lives of ordinary youth, has placed the schools in the service of elite groups. An academic curriculum, according to Goodson, has worked well to prepare the children of privileged classes for high status careers in society while at the same time channeling children of the working class to subordinate positions in the nation's industrial work force (Goodson 1983 p. 203, 1988 p. 162). In the United States, Popkewitz (1987 p. 2) has expressed a similar understanding of the history of school subjects, arguing that they emerged on the scene as "social inventions of people struggling in a world of competing interests and contradictions". Like Goodson, Popkewitz believes that school subjects were the creations of the middle and upper classes to bring the school into the service of their children while socially controlling the children of lesser status. Taking a less deterministic view than Goodson, Popkewitz argues that it is not inevitable that the schools serve the interests of those of power and privilege. Understanding the history of school subjects, he believes, can help educators design school programs that serve the interests of all children (Popkewitz 1987 pp. 1–24).

3. The Methodology of Curriculum History

Curriculum historians have traditionally seen their subject as a form of intellectual history. Their favorite subjects were the careers and contributions of important curriculum thinkers, such as Dewey and Tyler, and the recommendations for what the schools should teach that have been advanced by committees of one sort or another, government bureaucrats, and various interest groups. The most recently published histories by American researchers have clearly followed this pattern (Franklin 1986, Kliebard 1986, Popkewitz 1987). While there is much merit in attempting to examine and interpret curriculum ideas and policies, such a focus has led researchers to pay little attention to what has happened over time as these curricular recommendations have been introduced into actual school settings.

Some researchers have, however, begun to undertake case studies of the history of curriculum reform in actual schools. In the United States during the 1970s and 1980s, case studies of curriculum reform have been conducted in Atlanta, Georgia (Urban 1981); Gary, Indiana (McKinney and Westbury 1975); and Minneapolis, Minnesota (Franklin 1982). Goodson has edited two volumes of case studies of the histories of school subjects, one that examines the development of English, mathematics, social studies, science, and foreign languages in England and the other that provides similar case studies of events in Australia, Canada, England, New Zealand, Norway, Sweden, and the United States (Goodson 1985, 1987).

4. A Research Program for Curriculum History

Examining the most recent work of United Kingdom and United States curriculum historians indicates that they are following a two-pronged research program. Some are seeking to find more interesting and conceptually richer ways of studying the history of curriculum ideas. Kliebard, for example, has been looking at the symbolic role that proposals for introducing vocational education have played in the development of twentieth-century schooling. Although these proposals did have the effect of rendering the curriculum more directly functional, this was not their most important impact. More important, Kliebard argues, was the symbolic role that these proposals played in providing an emerging group of curriculum specialists with the status and professional expertise which they needed to legitimate their role in defining the nature and purpose of the school program (Kliebard 1989). Similarly, Popkewitz is employing the methods of the Annales school of French history along with the insights of such poststructuralist thinkers as Michel Foucault to better understand the linkage between the development of curriculum theory and larger historical transformations in social thought (Popkewitz 1989).

Other researchers are attempting to enhance the ability to understand curriculum practice. Although case studies offer particular value in explaining changes in curriculum practice, they present a significant problem for the curriculum historian. The most important sources for these studies are often not Board of Education minutes, school reports, and other official documents that are preserved in archives. Rather, the best source for obtaining information about curriculum practice are the correspondence of school curriculum specialists and other middle level bureaucrats, minutes of the meetings of teachers, school principals or heads, and staff bulletins. Such materials, however, are rarely preserved and, if available, are more likely to be found in the back files of school systems than in libraries (Kliebard and Franklin 1983 p. 149). To deal with the absence of these sources, several researchers are employing the quantitative methods characteristic of contemporary social history. In his history of Philadelphia's Central High School, Labaree (1988) used census manuscripts and student records to link changes in the class background of the school's students to changes over time in curriculum offerings. In addition,

Labaree used an increasingly popular statistical procedure among social historians, multiple classification analysis, to relate student graduation rates over time with such factors as class background, achievement, ethnicity, and family structure. Mirel and Angus (1986) have constructed maps of Detroit's ethnic composition and compared them with high school attendance boundaries to identify the relationship between curriculum offerings and the ethnic and racial composition of the city's high schools during the 1930s.

Other researchers have advocated the use of ethnographic techniques, particularly participant observation and life history, to get around the problem posed by the limited availability of appropriate primary source documents (Goodson 1988 pp. 71–92, Hammersley 1984 pp. 15–24). Smith, for example, has coupled participant observation of actual classrooms with the more traditional historical method of examining school records to relate the appearance of a new science curriculum in the pseudonymous Alte Schools with the district's history of curriculum change (Smith 1988 pp. 107–38). Goodson has used the life history of a teacher, Patrick Johnson, to explain the transformation of rural studies into environmental studies in England between 1947 and 1979 (Goodson 1988 pp. 93–116). It remains, however, to be seen whether the majority of curriculum historians will be willing to embrace these new methods as they pursue their future research.

Bibliography

Bellack A A 1969 History of curriculum thought and practice. *Rev. Educ. Res.* 39: 283–92

Davis O L 1976 Perspectives on curriculum development, 1776–1976. In: Davis O L (ed.) *Perspectives on Curriculum Development 1776–1976.* 1976 Yearbook of the Association for Supervision and Curriculum Development. Association for Supervision and Curriculum Development, Washington, DC

Davis O L 1977 The nature and boundaries of curriculum history: A contribution to dialogue over a yearbook and its review. *Curric. Inq.* 7: 157–68

Dewey and Tyler revisited: An interview with Laurel Tanner 1988 *Report from the Center.* Benton Center for Curriculum and Instruction. 1: 1–2

Durkheim E 1977 *The Evolution of Educational Thought: Lectures on the Formation and Development of Secondary Education in France.* Routledge and Kegan Paul, Boston, Massachusetts

Franklin B M 1977 Curriculum history: Its nature and boundaries. *Curric. Inq.* 7: 67–79

Franklin B M 1982 The social efficiency movement reconsidered: Curriculum change in Minneapolis, 1917–1950. *Curric. Inq.* 12: 9–33

Franklin B M 1986 *Building the American Community: The School Curriculum and the Search for Social Control.* Falmer Press, Philadelphia

Goodson I 1983 *School Subjects and Curriculum Change.* Croom Helm, London

Goodson I F (ed.) 1985 *Social Histories of the Secondary Curriculum: Subjects for Study.* Falmer Press, Philadelphia

Goodson I F 1986 Forward. In: Franklin B M 1986 *Building the American Community: The School Curriculum and the Search for Social Control.* Falmer Press, Philadelphia, pp. vii–ix

Goodson I F (ed.) 1987 *International Perspectives in Curriculum History.* Croom Helm, London

Goodson I F 1988 *The Making of Curriculum: Collected Essays.* Falmer Press, Philadelphia

Hammersley M 1984 Making a vice of our virtues: Some notes on theory in ethnography and history. In: Goodson I F, Ball S J (eds.) 1984 *Defining the Curriculum: Histories and Ethnographies.* Falmer Press, Philadelphia, pp. 15–24

Kliebard H M 1986 *The Struggle for the American Curriculum, 1893–1958.* Routledge and Kegan Paul, Boston, Massachusetts

Kliebard H M 1989 Curriculum policy as symbolic action: Connecting education with the workplace. Paper presented at the annual meeting of the American Educational Research Association, San Francisco, California

Kliebard H M, Franklin B M 1983 The course of the course of study: History of curriculum. In: Best J H (ed.) 1983 *Historical Inquiry in Education: A Research Agenda.* American Educational Research Association, Washington, DC, pp. 138–57

Labaree D F 1988 *The Making of an American High School: The Credentials Market and the Central High School of Philadelphia, 1838—1939.* Yale University Press, New Haven

McKinney W L, Westbury I 1975 Stability and change: The public schools of Gary, Indiana, 1940–1970. In: Reid W, Walker D (eds.) 1975 *Case Studies in Curriculum Change.* Routledge and Kegan Paul, London, pp. 1–53

Mirel J E, Angus D L 1986 The rising tide of custodialism: Enrollment increases and curriculum reform in Detroit, 1928–1940. *Issues Educ.* 4: 101–20

Popkewitz T S (ed.) 1987 *The Formation of School Subjects: The Struggle for Creating an American Institution.* Falmer Press, Philadelphia

Popkewitz T S 1989 A political sociology of educational reform and change: Power, knowledge, and the state. Paper presented at the annual meeting of the American Educational Research Association, San Francisco, California

Smith L M 1987 Process of curriculum change: An historical sketch of science education in the Alte schools. In: Goodson I F (ed.) 1987 *International Perspectives in Curriculum History.* Croom Helm, London, pp. 107–38

Tanner L N 1982 Curriculum history as usable knowledge. *Curric. Inq.* 12: 405–11

Urban W J 1981 Educational reform in a new south city: Atlanta, 1890–1925. In: Goodenow R K, White A O (eds.) 1981 *Education and the Rise of the New South.* G K Hall, Boston, Massachusetts pp. 114–30

Curriculum Components

Curriculum Components

M. J. Eash

Curricula consist of five widely agreed upon dimensions or components: (a) a framework of assumptions about the learner and society; (b) aims and objectives; (c) content or subject matter with its selection, scope, and sequence; (d) modes of transaction, for example, methodology and learning environments; and (e) evaluation. [Since the appearance of Tyler's (1949) "rationale" (see Madaus and Stufflebeam 1989), synoptic curriculum books have included distinct variations on the topics of purposes (aims and objectives), learning experiences (content and subject matter), organization (environment and methodology), and evaluation. Schubert (1982) discusses this at some length. Important synoptic texts that have dominated the curriculum field from 1950 onwards, evidence the continued use of variations on these components of curriculum, for example, Smith et al. (1957), Taba (1962), McNeil (1981), Tanner and Tanner (1989).] Each of these components gives form and substance to syllabi, teachers' guides, textbooks, workbooks, and supplementary materials. These documents exemplify instrumentalities that embody the curriculum components. The components are interdependent in a manner analagous to the systems (muscular, respiratory, circulatory) of the human body. Any alteration in one system (component) affects the structure and functioning of the others. They must all be well-coordinated for the organism to live and develop; yet, they may be separated for purposes of description, study, and research. When separated for study, curriculum components also serve a productive analytic function. This is illustrated in the following sections which discuss research and practice in component areas, and thereby allow for specialized inquiry into each.

The fluid character of the component in a functioning curriculum must be understood alongside of the separation for analytic purposes. As any given curriculum component functions with teachers and learners, decisions are reconstructed on other components which determine what teachers may teach and what students have an opportunity to learn. Just as the effective functioning of the human body is a product of the interactive orchestration of component systems, the holistic effect of a curriculum derives from the integration of its components.

Differences in curricula reside largely in choices made among alternatives for the design of components. This choice making can be referred to as provisioning. Each component is multioptioned; thus, the way in which it is provisioned in a functioning curriculum reflects assumptions that are cultural and political as well as individualistic determinations by schools, teachers, and learners (Kliebard 1987). All curricula take form through the provisioning of these components and they may differ in their emphasis. The assumptions underlying teaching and learning may remain in the unspoken and unwritten realm. Because of the requirements of the society in which the learning takes place and the unique demands of human learning, all curriculum components are provisioned in some form in a total curriculum. Provisioning may be conscious, overt, and planned on the part of curriculum authorities and teachers, or it may accrue from ritualistic, mindless practices and unexamined assumptions. Combinations of these two extremes are often observed side by side in the same school. Holistic investigation on the results of integrated but differential provisioning of components and on the learning products which are produced as a result is not an arena of active empirical research. Yet, it is of great interest to policy makers in government and is viewed as a vital index of schools' contributions to advancing national policy (Eash and Fitzgerald 1987). Characteristically, curriculum research is done on more specific elements of a component rather than on the integrated relationship of all five components. Researchers investigate comparative methodology, the advantage of one organization of subject matter over another, the degree of accomplishment of certain aims, or the function of evaluation in assisting teachers and learners. However, few studies try to assess the total impact of a curriculum on learners where the components are viewed as working in concert to produce a broad-gauged outcome such as democratic citizens, as exemplified by the Eight-year Study (Aikin 1942). The five curriculum components and examples of their provisioning are provided below.

1. The Individual and the Society as a Framework

All curriculum organization begins with assumptions concerning the learner and the society in which he or she lives. A first guiding construct among curriculum planners is the determination of the learner's ability, needs, interest, motivation, and potential for learning certain cultural content. The learner's ability to assimilate and shape experience is the focus of major studies in psychology, anthropology, and sociology as well as the basis for much of educational research. What the learner can assimilate, under what conditions, and with what results are among the telling questions that have historically guided these investigations. Society—its orientation to nurturing or using the individual—is the second guiding construct in selecting the options within curriculum components. How the schools select individuals for various curricula (e.g., vocational, liberal arts, sciences) reflects an orientation to the society in which the individual will be a functioning member. The purposes of the society, its need for trained personnel, and the pre-eminence given to society's needs over the individual purposes of the learner are telling areas for curriculum makers. In some curricula, these two constructs are reconciled to the end that both the individual and the society are served and in other societies one or the other is given greater priority. The reconciliation or the pre-eminence of society or the individual can be determined by inspection of statements of national aims and objectives for education. The assumptions guiding the choices in provisioning components of the curriculum largely emerge in the answer to the questions of whether a curriculum is to be based on (a) the needs of the learner, (b) the needs of the society, or (c) a position that is a reconciliation of the two (Dewey 1948).

2. Aims and Objectives

As the first component to be provisioned in the development of a curriculum, aims and objectives and their choices become significant for they assume a directing relationship to the provisioning of the subsequent components (see *Selecting Educational Objectives*). This article is concerned with a broader use of aims and objectives as they reflect a construct provisioned for a sequence of study conducted over a year or several years in a major discipline such as the sciences. Of primary concern to selection of subject matter and to student experiences, aims and objectives also map out the arena for a teacher's directed effort. There is no standardization among statements of aims and objectives; thus, in their various forms they reflect philosophical assumptions and positions on the pre-eminence of the learner or society and how these are to be played out in the curriculum. They may be global or specific in aim, they may be directed towards developing specific learner behaviors and common or discrete behavioral patterns. Aims and objectives evolve and change as cultures and their participants change. Curricula lag in reflecting these changes—a common problem worldwide is how to maintain currency in curriculum (Tanner 1988).

3. Form of Subject Matter (Scope and Sequence)

Subject matter is selected, organized, cultural content which is packaged for use by teachers and learners. Student experiences are largely shaped from cultural content, derived from the major areas of human learning, and organized along subject matter discipline lines for purposes of formal curriculum implementation (see *Curriculum Implementation*). As the article on textbook demonstrates, the form of subject matter and its packaging comes in many shapes but the textbook has been the standard work for use by teachers and students in the study of subject matter in the curriculum. However, electronics promises to add new dimensions through computers and word processors which increase the range of subject matter and the power of manipulation by the teacher and learner for combinatory and recombinatory forms of learning of the subject matter (Brandt 1988).

Guided by a knowledge of learners' abilities and a position on society's requirements of learners' knowledge of subject matter, the curriculum planner exercises selection in the choice of subject matter and develops a scope, the range of the subject matter to be studied, and sequence or order in which the subject matter is to be studied (Talmage 1985). These selections are translated through textbooks, curriculum guides, syllabi, electronic data banks, and other directives to teachers and learners.

Subject matter may be selected on the basis of the general education of all students or the specialized development of a selected group of students. Concern over the proliferation of subject matter in disciplines, especially science, brings new urgency to the form of subject matter and its organization. Analysis of conceptual networks and their accessing by computer seem to be promising ways of inducing savings in learning and more rapid advancement of the learner in the complexities of the discipline (Hathway 1989).

4. Modes of Transactions

Modes of transactions, as a curriculum component, have by convention been provisioned as recommended teacher methodology to inculcate subject matter. They have a rich base in research and practice and are a chief concern in teacher guides that are designed to accompany the subject matter presentation. Modes of transaction figure heavily also in syllabi as authorities attempt to guide teacher behavior and influence learner outcomes chiefly for national purposes. Modes of transaction are viewed as major determinants in learner outcomes especially as they affect attitudes of students as well as content mastery.

Influences on modes of transaction have swung between teacher-centric and pupil-centric emphases, but current developments in electronic presentation of subject matter and replacement of the standard textbook have induced changes in the role of the teacher as a mediator of subject matter and repository of a bank of methodologies for transmitting the required learnings as set forth in the aims and objectives and presented in the subject matter. Modes of transaction may be further classified as direct or indirect. These classifications stem from the role of the teacher and the role of the learner in the transaction of learning and their respective degree of choice in determining the modes of learning, for example, learner active/learner passive, verbal mode/symbolic mode (Joyce and Weil 1980). As a field of research inquiry, modes of transactions are probably the most heavily studied of the curriculum constructs (Wittrock 1986).

5. Evaluation

Evaluation as a curriculum component may be provisioned in several dimensions. As an integral element to a curriculum, evaluation may give emphasis to providing the individual with information on performance to guide the learner to the next steps in the sequence of the subject matter. Thus, as provisioned for maximum individual guidance, the evaluation is related as a guide to modes of transaction and sequencing. Another form of provisioning the construct evaluation is to obtain information on students' learning that can be directed to screening and selecting students or providing data on how well schools are serving national policy (Walker 1976). In these choices of evaluation data, the evaluation components reflect assumptions and decisions about the role of the individual learner and roles of society. Evaluation provisioning then, can be directed toward providing information directly to the learner for guidance, directly to the teacher for orientation of the next instructional activities, and directly to external agencies for their assessment of schools functioning in the light of national purpose. The speed of collecting, processing, and analyzing data has been transformed by electronic data processing. Evaluation and its function as a guide and feedback to the learner and teacher is an important part of curriculum syllabi (Eash 1974). Evaluation as a way of measuring educational systems' contributions to national welfare becomes more important as industrial and military strength hinge ever more increasingly on the human resources capital available to these efforts. Provisioning of curriculum components moves from becoming a private individual matter to one of national policy and engages government at several levels (Symposium 1987). It is probably a safe prediction that curriculum components provisioning will become a more technically sophisticated field of study with advances anticipated in knowledge of specific ways to improve organization of learning and a closer monitoring of product outcomes from a national level.

Bibliography

Aikin W 1942 *The Story of the Eight-year Study with Conclusions and Recommendations.* Harper, New York

Brandt R S 1988 *Content of the Curriculum* (1988 Yearbook of the Association for Supervision and Curriculum Development). Association for Supervision and Curriculum Development, Alexandria, Virginia

Dewey J 1948 *Reconstruction in Philosophy.* Beacon, Boston, Massachusetts, pp. 187–213

Eash M 1974 Intructional materials. In: Walberg H J (ed.) 1974 *Evaluating Educational Performance.* McCutchan, Berkeley, California, pp. 125–52

Eash M, Fitzgerald R 1987 *Occupational Education and Industrial Policy: Revitalizing the United States Economy.* Center for Industrial Policy and Occupational Education, University of Massachusetts, Boston, Massachusetts

Eash M, Waxman H 1983 *Our Class and Its Work (OCIW) User Manual.* University of Illinois at Chicago, Chicago, Illinois

Hathway W E 1989 A network-based curriculum: The basis for the design of a new learning system. *Educ. Technol.* 29: 23–8

Joyce B R, Weil M 1986 *Models of Teaching*, 3rd edn. Prentice Hall, Englewood Cliffs, New Jersey

Kliebard H M 1987 *Struggle for the American Curriculum 1893–1958.* Routledge, Chapman and Hall, New York

McNeil J D 1981 *Curriculum: A Comprehensive Introduction.* Little, Brown, Boston, Massachusetts

Madaus G F, Stufflebeam D 1989 *Educational Evaluation: Classic Works of Ralph Tyler.* Kluwer Academic Publishers, Norwell, Maine

National Assessment of Educational Progress 1981 *Has Title I Improved Education for Disadvantage Students?* ERIC Document No. ED 201 995

Posner G J, Strike K A 1976 A categorization scheme for principles of sequencing content. *Rev. Educ. Res.* 46: 665–90

Schubert W H 1982 Curriculum research. In: Mitzel H (ed.) 1982 *Encyclopedia of Educational Research.* Macmillan, New York

Smith B O, Stanley W O, Shores J H 1957 *Fundamentals of Curriculum Development*, rev. edn. Harcourt, Brace, and World, New York

Symposium 1987 Curriculum development in the United States and the world. *Educ. Leadership* 44: 3–16

Taba H 1962 *Curriculum Development: Theory and Practice.* Harcourt, Brace, and World, New York

Talmage H 1985 Evaluating the curriculum: What, why and how. *National Association of Secondary School Principals Bulletin* 69: 1–8

Tanner D, Tanner L N (eds.) 1989 *History of the School Curriculum.* Macmillan, New York

Tanner L N (ed.) 1988 *Critical Issues in Curriculum* (National Society for the Study of Education, Eighty-Seventh Yearbook: Part I). University of Chicago Press, Chicago, Illinois

Tyler R W 1949 *Basic Principles of Curriculum and Instruction.* University of Chicago Press, Chicago, Illinois

Tyler R W 1977 Desirable content for a curriculum syllabus today. In: Molnar A, Zahorik J A (eds.) 1977 *Curriculum Theory.* Milwaukee Curriculum Theory Conf., University of Wisconsin–Milwaukee Nov. 11–14, 1976. Association for Supervision and Curriculum Development, Washington, DC, pp. 36–44

Walker D A 1976 *The IEA Six Subjects Survey: An Empirical Study of Education in Twenty-one Countries.* Almqvist and Wiksell, Stockholm

Wittrock M C (ed.) 1986 *Handbook of Research on Teaching*, 3rd edn. Macmillan, New York

Curriculum Rationale

D. Pratt

A rationale is a reasoned exposition or explanation of principles. The term is also used to mean the logical basis or fundamental reason for something. In brief, a rationale is a reason or statement of reasons. Unlike physical phenomena, which are understood mainly by reference to causes, human behavior is understood principally by reference to reasons. Reasons are the essence of purposive explanations, which illuminate the meaning of actions by linking them to ends or intentions. Justification of actions requires an exposition of reasons; the function of a rationale is to demonstrate that a course of action is justified by explicating its reasons, principles, and intents.

1. The Rationale in Education

In the arena of public policy, programs and decisions are usually expected to be supported by an explicit rationale. In education, a rationale commonly accompanies a proposal for research, administrative policy, or curriculum change. In recent years, political and economic pressures have obliged educators to account for both new decisions and existing structures. The demand for educational accountability, however, has generally focused on the effectiveness of schools in meeting their goals, rather than on the more significant question of the worth of the goals themselves. It is the latter question which educational rationales primarily address.

The cultural and philosophical diversity within many societies is a deterrent to the development of explicit educational rationales which open the value basis of decisions to public scrutiny and debate. But in the absence of a rationale, it is difficult to justify the commitment of human and material resources to a particular educational program. Responsibility, which implies actions guided by their anticipated consequences, would seem to require open examination of policies in terms of their principles, intentions, and results; that is, in terms of their rationales.

2. Curriculum Rationales

In educational discourse, it is in the context of curriculum that the term rationale is most commonly used. The first elaborated curriculum rationale could be said to be that outlined in Plato's *Republic*. But it was not until the nineteenth century that the demand was widely heard for explicit justification of curricula. Nineteenth-century curriculum rationales were commonly *ex post facto*, developed to defend existing practice rather than as explications of purposes which curricula were deliberately designed to attain.

In the twentieth century, curriculum rationales have tended to fall into one of two broad classes. One class justifies a curriculum in terms of its value in initiating learners into cultural traditions and established forms of knowledge by means of the academic disciplines. Sometimes termed "academic rationalism," this mode of justification has a pedigree going back at least to the curriculum of the medieval European universities. It received impetus from mid-twentieth-century research into the structure of the disciplines, and was the basis of many of the large-scale science curricula of the 1960s. The other main approach to curriculum justification is based on the concept of significant human needs. This approach owes much to the thought of such writers as Herbart, Spencer, Dewey, and Maslow. Although academic rationalism is the implicit justification for much curriculum practice, the needs approach is more widely accepted within the field of curriculum study. Needs assessment, a set of procedures originating in the 1960s for collecting and analyzing data on needs, encouraged designers to document curriculum rationales with empirical evidence as well as logical argument (see *Needs Assessment Studies*).

Recent scholarship has pointed to the problematic nature of curriculum decisions, including curriculum rationales. Such decisions, scholars have argued, are made within a social context in which rational justification is often subordinate to political considerations. Analysts of teacher behavior, meanwhile, have shown that curriculum innovation is rarely successful unless the rationale for the change is endorsed by the teachers who are expected to implement it.

The primary function of a curriculum rationale is to justify the purposes of the curriculum as worthwhile ends towards which to direct learners and expend resources. This involves clear statement of the curriculum goals and justification of these goals in relation to superordinate goals or values. Not only must the goals have tenable value, they must also be shown to be relatively more valuable than alternative possible goals which the curriculum designers choose not to pursue. A secondary function is to justify the means proposed to achieve the curriculum ends, in terms of effectiveness and efficiency, and in terms of their compatibility with the basic values underlying the curriculum. While there is widespread agreement among educators concerning their importance, it is an intriguing educational phenomenon that adequate curriculum rationales are the exception rather than the rule.

3. Formulation of a Curriculum Rationale

A curriculum document is written primarily to guide teachers. It may also serve to inform other interested parties, such as students, parents, and administrators. Most of its content is prescriptive and descriptive, and hence written with a view to precision, conciseness, and clarity. The curriculum rationale, on the other hand, is written both to inform and to persuade. Consequently, the style of a rationale is appropriately less technical and more eloquent than other parts of a curriculum document. The rationale must pass the scrutiny of specialists in the field of study, but must also be comprehensible and convincing to nonspecialist readers, who may need to be persuaded of the value of the superordinate as well as the immediate purposes of the curriculum. The rationale is best placed early in a curriculum document. In this position, it serves the additional function of an introduction, touching on the significant issues, topics, and generalizations of the curriculum, and showing the place of the curriculum in the wider educational program.

Economic pressures limit the ends which education can pursue or attain, while the expansion of knowledge constantly increases the available curriculum content.

These pressures exacerbate political and ideological conflicts in education. Explicit rationales function to broaden the political basis of educational decision making and to safeguard an element of rationality and responsibility in an educational system.

Bibliography

Eisner E W 1982 *Cognition and Curriculum: A Basis for Deciding What to Teach.* Longman, New York

Giroux H A 1981 *Ideology, Culture, and the Process of Schooling.* Falmer Press, London

Goodson I F 1988 *The Making of Curriculum: Collected Essays.* Falmer Press, London

Hargreaves A 1989 *Curriculum and Assessment Reform.* OISE Press, Toronto, Ontario

Schubert W H 1986 *Curriculum: Perspective, Paradigm, and Possibility.* Macmillan, New York

Walker D F, Soltis J F 1986 *Curriculum and Aims.* Teachers College Press, New York

Syllabus

M. J. Eash

Syllabi are undoubtedly one of the oldest teaching tools in formal education. They are vehicles by which organization and structure of intended learnings are communicated from teacher to teacher and teacher to learner. As frameworks, syllabi by definition are the organizing documents in areas of instruction (Chandler 1985). Under some systems of instruction they become highly formalized, authority-oriented instruments which control the amount of decision making that teacher and learner take. In other systems they are more informal documents operating only as a general guide (Buchanan 1988).

Syllabi take many forms and shapes and are of varying lengths. They may be simple one-page course descriptions; they may describe a course that runs for a given period of time, such as one semester or one year; they may be lengthy documents covering the full range and organization of subject matter and suggested ways of implementing it in classrooms over several years such as a syllabi on a science or mathematics program in grades kindergarten through to eighth grade. Despite the apparent difference in the documents which could range from one page to 300 pages they do have a common concern, that is, transmission of knowledge on how to formulate and organize an instructional area. In some countries the organization and issuing of syllabi are invested in a central authority. In other decentralized systems of education the building of syllabi and their use is left almost exclusively to the teacher who is directly concerned with the transmitting of subject matter in the classroom. Between these two extremes there are a number of positions on how to develop syllabi, for they are frequently the chief products of curriculum

development activity in instructional departments of a school or school system (see *Curriculum Development*).

As organizers of instruction, syllabi have a long tradition in formal education. In a sense, textbooks were an outgrowth of and an attempt to organize the instructional area conceptually so that it could be transmitted in a more efficient, consistent manner by many teachers. Syllabi gave educational authorities some confidence that there was a body of knowledge being consistently transmitted to a number of learners by different teachers. Control of syllabi has been seen as a way of controlling curriculum, and attempts to shape curriculum rely heavily upon syllabi as the vehicles.

Most syllabi come in written form: course outlines, units of work, guides, lists of materials to be taught, suggested or prescribed methodology for the teacher. A new development is the electronic storage and production of subject matter whereby control of subject matter and the way students can interact with it are largely within the programmed computer, whereupon the traditional role of the syllabus is as a code book to the computer program. The building of syllabi constitutes, in most educational systems, the major curriculum development efforts. There are different philosophical positions on how best to develop a syllabus in order to guarantee its implementation in the educational system and this is the subject of curriculum development literature (Molnar 1985). The common framework of a syllabus includes the provisioning of curriculum constructs.

Not all of the curriculum components are provisioned in every syllabus but there are implicit assumptions as decisions are made on the way subject matter and learning activities are organized in a unit of instruction (Bailey 1988). The first step in organization of the syllabus is to establish a rationale for the unit of instruction being planned. Within this rationale, ordinarily, curriculum developers will assume a position on why subject matter should be taught. Usually the rationale involves the society in which the learner will live or the learners need for the subject matter. Decisions in the area of rationale are quite crucial because they predicate many other following decisions on provisioning of other constructs within the syllabus. There are positions on needs of society and needs of the learner which reconcile and bring them together as well as advocate the preeminence of one or the other in the decision-making process (Dewey 1948). Once the rationale is explicated, the other constructs of aims and objectives, organization of specific subject matter (scope and sequence), modes of transaction (methodology of instruction), and evaluation are usually provisioned for the user of the syllabus. Syllabi can be developed for learners as well as for teachers and in the following discussion attention will be given to how construction of syllabi gives consideration to both as clients.

1. Aims and Objectives

Aims and objectives define the conceptual map on which a syllabus will be based. There is a wide range of formats for statements of aims and objectives—they may be quite vague and considered implicit in the provisions made for the other curriculum constructs. If a syllabus is developed by a central authority, careful attention will usually be given to aims and objectives for they are seen as guides to classroom activity and to shaping and directing a curriculum from a central authority. Whether aims and objectives will be fixed or evolving from activities of students, subject matter is another continuum for curriculum writers of a syllabus. Whether aims and objectives are prescribed or discretionary for the teacher/learner will also shape the framework and the use of the syllabus. Moreover, it is not uncommon for there to be a priority listing of aims and objectives for ordering them within the unit of instruction, across several units of instruction, or within the total scope of subject matter across grades of school or systems of education. Most syllabus writers assume some hierarchy of instruction as they write aims and objectives. For example, a student who is not going to become a mathematician or pursue activities that require in-depth knowledge of advanced mathematics has different goals in the study of mathematics courses than one who is going to pursue it as a major life activity or be involved in a profession where it is required for success.

Objectives in a syllabus may be macro, that is global and over-arching that tie together large elements of subject matter, or they may be micro, as they specify intended learning outcomes for a student and even categorize them according to the type of learning involved. An example of this difference would be the macro objective, "the student will understand the importance of being a contributing citizen to his country through his work, his participation in the support of government and his willingness to defend his country." An example of a micro objective, which would be contributory towards this macro objective would be: "the student will be able to do basic addition in day-to-day activities in which he encounters the use of numbers in buying products or necessities of life."

The organization of subject matter, particularly the scope (what is taught) and sequence (the order in which it is taught), has occupied a major place in syllabi. The organization of subject matter may provide a list of intended learning outcomes as stated within the subject matter framework. Syllabi usually limit the scope, since subject matter in most instructional areas has increased to a level whereby a major curriculum development activity involves choosing what should be taught or ignored. Setting the scope of subject matter is often undertaken by a central authority, especially where political goals are pursued through the educational system. Examination of curricula for bias is often done through review of the scope for inclusion or exclusion of subject matters.

The sequence of a curriculum may be organized through several approaches making assumptions about whether the logical organization of subject matter, or the psychological approach of the learner ought to be of primary consideration. The organization of the conceptual map of a syllabus is the reconciliation of logical relationships in subject matter with a sequence, consistent with the individuals' learning process. The quality of scope and sequence is critical to the ease with which students absorb the critical learnings of the instructional area and to the development of longer term learner interest in material.

Another form used in syllabi along with conceptual maps is flow charts depicting the relationships between the complex skills to be taught. Much of the controversy on syllabi revolves around scope and sequence activities and reflects different assumptions about the way subject matter is organized and the way learning proceeds.

2. Modes of Transaction (Methodology)

Syllabi directed at teachers are often exclusively oriented to specification of the modes of transaction that are to be used in the curriculum. These teacher prescriptions are featured where the methodological approach is viewed as a major learning outcome for students and critical to their advancement in the subject matter. Where there is an abundance of pedagogical resources, syllabi assist teachers in selecting among them for greater efficiency in student learning. The learner verification of materials, a new development in the creation of instructional materials, helps teachers to know what types of learner outcome to expect. Frequently, the syllabus will contain a listing of essential materials that must be purchased and incorporated in the curriculum if the syllabus is to be implemented as written. In some newer approaches where syllabi are becoming part of an electronics instructional system, formed around computers and word processors, the modes of transactions are specified by the way the subject matter is controlled and presented to students (Smith and Sherwood 1976). If there is a highly structured approach to the modes of transaction, authorities are moving to the position that learner verification of the prescribed mode should be done in advance of their commitment to a syllabus which then becomes the authorized course of study. Some syllabi provide the modes of transaction as an instructional plan which presents in sequence: (a) what each unit is about; (b) what the desired aim or learning outcomes of each unit are; and (c) prescribed general teaching strategies in order to accomplish intended learning outcomes.

3. Evaluation in Syllabi

Evaluation tools for use by teachers and learners are frequently a part of the syllabus framework. They may come in the form of written tests or other types of measurement instruments which are placed within the instructional process either to give the student immediate feedback, or to inform the teacher or other educational authorities whether the student is achieving those aims and objectives which are set forth. Syllabi will, at times, give attention to the main effects of learning outcomes as products that are idiosyncratic to the interaction of teacher, learner, and subject matter. Consequently, syllabi may provide suggestions on ways of gathering data on side-effects of instruction as well as main effects of instruction. Where evaluation is directed toward controlling effects of curriculum and teaching, procedures of evaluation may become separated from the syllabus with only the information to the teacher and learner that there will be an evaluation component from an outside source which will check upon the syllabus, its use, and learning outcomes. This form of outside examination is used where the curriculum is determined by a central authority and there is concern that learnings will have uniformity across the diversity of contexts where it is implemented.

4. Evaluation of Syllabi

There has been relatively little systematic evaluation of syllabi, although the way the constructs are provisioned, the attention given to the paradoxes and contradictions are a rich source of information for the evaluation of the effectiveness of a curriculum framework which comes in syllabus form (Eash 1970, 1972, 1974). The future of curriculum syllabi is guaranteed by the need for increased formal education in larger and larger sectors of populations. However, the form of future

curriculum syllabi is not as clear (Donald 1987). With increased knowledge about the individual's ability to process information, and the further knowledge of the way subject matter can be conceptually organized so that the network of concepts becomes more readily available in less time to a greater number of learners, it might be expected that frameworks and forms of syllabi will rapidly change from the traditional written statements that have been characteristic of the syllabi of the past.

Bibliography

Bailey G D 1988 Guidelines for improving the textbook/materials selection process. *National Association Secondary School Principals Bulletin* 72: 87–92

Buchanan B, Eash M J, Kelley S, MacCormack J 1988 *Caring for Children in the Commonwealth*. Center for Industrial Policy and Occupational Education, University of Massachusetts at Boston, Boston, Massachusetts

Chandler C 1985 Curriculum and syllabus design. ELT Journal 39: 101–8

Dewey J 1948 *Reconstruction in Philosophy*, enlarged edn. Beacon, Boston, Massachusetts, pp. 187–213

Donald J 1987 Learning schemata: Methods of representing cognitive content and curricular structures in higher education. *Instr. Sci.* 16(2): 87–211

Eash M 1970 Evaluation of instructional materials for exceptional children and youth: A preliminary instrument. *Resources in Education*. Educational Resources Information Center (ERIC), Document No. ED 040 540. National Institute of Education, Educational Resources Information Center, Washington, DC

Eash M 1972 Developing an instrument for assessing instructional materials. In: Eash M (ed.) 1972 *Curriculum Theory Network*. Ontario Institute for Studies in Education, Toronto, Ontario, pp. 193–220

Eash M 1974 Evaluating instructional materials. In: Eash M (ed.) 1974 *Selecting Media for Learning*. Association for Education Communications and Technology, Washington, DC, pp. 38–39

Godwin D 1970 The structure of knowledge. *Educ. Theory* 20(4): 319–28

Molnar A (ed.) 1985 *Current Thought on Curriculum* (1985 Association for Supervision and Curriculum Development Yearbook). Association for Supervision and Curriculum Development, Alexandria, Virginia

Popham W J, Baker E L 1970 *Systematic Instruction*. Prentice-Hall, Englewood Cliffs, New Jersey

Posner G J, Rudnitsky A N 1982 *Course Design: A Guide to Curriculum Development for Teachers*, 2nd edn. Longman, New York

Posner G, Strike K 1976 A categorization scheme for principles of sequencing content. *Rev. Educ. Res.* 46: 665–90

Smith S G, Sherwood B A 1976 Educational uses of the PLATO computer system. *Science* 192: 344–52

Tyler R W 1977 Desirable content for a curriculum syllabus today. In: Molnak A, Zahorik J A (eds.) 1977 *Curriculum Theory*. Milwaukee Curriculum Conference, University of Wisconsin–Milwaukee Nov. 11–14, 1976. Association for Supervision and Curriculum Development, Washington, DC, pp. 36–44

Wittrock M C (ed.) 1986 *Handbook of Research on Teaching*, 3rd edn. Macmillan, New York

Textbooks

I. Westbury

The books which surround and support teaching of all kinds at all levels of instruction are the central tools and objects of attention in all schooling. The information carried within books defines, for many, the tasks of education; books are the most important resources which teachers and schools have as they do their work of educating. Indeed, it may be that the core work of all schooling consists in developing the skills and attitudes associated with the mastery of the ideas and information carried by books without regard to their "ultimate" quality and social significance. Certainly, as given in particular situations (as a result of prescription or availability), the books which a teacher has are often the most significant limitation on the capacity of a school or teacher to work out his or her own purposes. Educational development and curriculum development thus go hand-in-hand with textbook selection and writing. Yet, in spite of the centrality of the book to education, and in spite of the attention that has been given to aspects of the book (design, readability, bias in text, etc.), the textbook itself and its use, seen in holistic terms, is an elusive component of schooling, at least from the viewpoint of conventional educational research and theory.

1. The Book as an Educational "Tool"

Any treatment of the book in the context of education must distinguish the book as a general repository of information and ideas and a general medium of thought and communication from the book (or textbook) as a tool used within situations of formal education. While there is no necessary difference in the character or form of the book when used in general (i.e. recreational or information seeking) or educational settings, the ways in which the book is used do differ. Gowin (1981), for example, stipulates that the defining condition of an educational event is a teacher teaching meaningful materials (typically book-based information or expressions) to a student who grasps the meaning of the materials. He suggests that the prerequisite of such teaching is an awareness on the part of the teacher of the meanings embedded in his/her materials which can be shared within teacher–pupil interactions. Such interaction may use books in any of the following roles:

(a) as vehicles of criteria of excellence of thought or sensibility;

(b) as records of prior events which have the potential for making new events happen;

(c) as authoritative records of ideas or procedures;

(d) as organizers of bodies of concepts or information;

(e) as stimuli for the multiplication of meaning and the enhancement of experience—through reorganization of what is already known, for thinking or feeling, or as invitations to explore new patterns of relationship.

Different educational tasks are, following Gowin, associated with different kinds of text materials. In each there is a body of critical questions to be asked about potential and actual meanings, and the materials which can carry those meanings, to make them suitable for recovery within educational contexts. Thus, a teacher or text author must ask which Greek tragedy, or which speech within a given tragedy, has the most potential for illuminating these ideas for these students; he or she must ask how a topic like mathematical modeling or correlation can be most appropriately simplified for this or that instructional purpose.

Less expository roles are also very common. For example, within examination-based traditions of schooling the textbook may be a "crib" which outlines a body of standardized information to be learned for representation in examination format and under examination conditions. Within mathematics, the textbook's primary function may be to provide a convenient collection of problems. For the teacher who emphasizes ideational fluency as a basis for writing, the optimal textbook may be one that contains many competing sources of ideas presented in many ways. It is difficult, if not impossible in these circumstances, to offer any generalizable considerations which might apply to all types of textbook.

2. The Textbook in Educational Theory and Research

Given such a conception of the role of texts within education, it might be assumed that the discussion of the book as an educational medium, and the ways books might be used, would be major themes within educational research and theory. This is not the case; in the main, the research and the associated expository literature within education, is acceptance of the educational and pedagogical assumptions embedded in the materials conventionally used within schools, and is indifferent to the educational, institutional, and rhetorical issues and developments associated with various traditions of textbook development and use.

The textbook is an integral part of all "modern" technologies and systems of schooling. Looked at from the perspective of history, these systems (a) assume that the book is the repository of the knowledge that schools communicate, (b) are built around the existence of the textbook as a basic instrument for organizing curricula and as a basic tool for teaching and learning. For most of its history, teacher education has focused on the preparation of personnel for work within the existing system and not on the questioning, and recovery, of the assumptions that lie behind those systems. Animation of teachers rather than reformation has been the socially sanctioned core undertaking of teacher education and its related research and theory building.

All systems of organized education presume social understanding of the goals and means of education. In many school systems these social understandings are incorporated into curriculum control structures which use the textbook as a vehicle for making such expectations explicit. The concern of such systems centers on the enactment of conventional educational interactions rather than the self-conscious search for materials which can support educating as an abstract goal. Of course, the effects of such forces differ depending on the firmness and directionality of the norms associated with given kinds of education; in graduate education, the books which might be used, how they might be used, and the adequacy of the given set of texts vis-à-vis ends and varying definitions of subjects and fields are typically more open issues than they are for teachers in elementary schools.

Given these constraints on the ways in which educational research has defined its problems, fundamental research on textbooks has more often been undertaken by scholars in other fields. Training, advertising, trade publishing, and elite higher education have offered better contexts than "education" as such for the consideration of the ways in which text materials might be used and conceived. And the contributions which have been made to the understanding of textbooks as social, institutional, and cultural forms have more often come from sociologists of knowledge, science, and culture, intellectual historians, psychologists working in industry and military training, and typographers and designers working in "trade publishing" rather than "educational research." Bridge building from these areas of professional concern into educational research has emerged as a self-conscious scholarly preoccupation only since the early 1970s and only in a small number of centers.

Further attention here is confined to issues of textbook content and textbook bias.

3. Textbook Content

A school or university subject is, most typically, a body of information about a field that is thought appropriate for the education of students, and, implicitly at least, an organization of that field that defines what the field is and what should be emphasized within it. Successful textbooks typically offer both an effective rhetoric and a widely accepted treatment of the scope of their fields. And there are many "important" textbooks [for example, the Physical Sciences Study Commission (PSSC) (1960) *Physics*] which have not been successful in the marketplace over the long run but have derived their significance from their impact on the definition of the content of the "subjects." In the topics they treat and the ways in which they are discussed, such textbooks create a norm which other textbooks follow.

This quality of many "classical" school and university textbooks illustrates one of the most important continuing tasks of textbook writing and development within an educational system. Thus, while in one sense the textbook is a medium of presentation of a subject, it is also an ordering of a subject for purposes of teaching and, as such, operationalizes the social construct that is represented by such words as "sixth-grade arithmetic" or "sixth-form British history." And, typically, it is the appearance of an appropriate textbook which creates a subject or a new definition of a subject as its presentation penetrates the consciousness of teachers. Later textbooks tend to follow the patterns offered by such innovative textbooks. And the "subjects" which follow often develop a life of their own in the schools as they become the object of attention in teacher education and define for the public at large what the content of schooling is—and, often, should be. And in such subjects it is often the framework which was created by the first textbooks which creates the terms of all subsequent teaching. Thus, as Hodgetts (1968) has pointed out, it was the concerns of Canadian historians of the 1920s which were still dominating the teaching of Canadian history in the schools in the late 1960s by way of a textbook tradition—despite the fact that the issues which concerned Canadians and Canadian historians were far distant from issues which created the interpretation of Canada's history in the 1920s.

This issue becomes especially difficult analytically if it is posited, as it must be, that no-one can know a discipline or a subject at first hand, but must instead rely on secondary sources to develop even a tentative synthesis of the kind required to know or teach a subject. From this perspective any "original" development of a textbook must be a work of scholarly synthesis—as it often was and is in the case of first textbooks in a field or in the case of fundamental revisions of previous textbook content and knowledge. But such concerns are characteristically far different from the concerns of both teachers who are interested in the here-and-now problems of teaching their subjects as they are conventionally understood and textbook writers who are seeking to meet the needs of those teachers. As a consequence there are many instances in which the seeming facts and interpretations of subjects presented in textbooks are, from the viewpoint of the research worker and the "advanced" scholar in a field, egregiously incorrect. Their status as facts and canonical interpretations comes from repetition in the textbook tradition rather than from disciplinary-embedded understanding.

Awareness of these kinds of issues about textbook content has been extended in a number of different directions by researchers. Sociologists of science have suggested that from the viewpoint of the socialization of students who work in routine scientific research, such issues are of little consequence. It is the task of students to learn the traditional content whatever it may be, with the implication that the social structures of such sciences only grant the freedom to question such interpretations to those who have passed the test of mastery of such interpretations. Schwab (1978), on the other hand, has suggested that the tentativeness of all knowledge must be communicated to students from the beginning of their study of a subject by means of treatments that convey firmly the revisionary character of all subjects.

Howson and Westbury (1980) have suggested that if it is assumed that most subjects are textbook based, there is a body of important research on the ways in which "new" understandings of what content should be treated in textbooks, and how that content should be treated, that emerges. Drawing on examples from mathematics they suggest that two different processes can be seen lying behind content revision or content invention within mathematics education; the translation of ideas from advanced mathematics into ideas which are amenable to treatment within schools by a process of "making accessible" (Kirsch 1976), and the development of embodiments by which mathematical ideas and classroom experiences are given form appropriate to classroom work. They suggest further that in all such processes of content invention there are important questions about the processes which determine the propensity of both individuals and groups to engage in authentic inventive activity.

Educational research has given little attention to the social processes which are associated with either content development and invention or the reception of content developments by teachers and schools. Both school systems and historical periods vary in their inventive capability, or, in other words, in their capacity to engage in content revision and content development and in the receptivity of schools or subsystems of schools to such content revision and development, but little research has been done on such issues. There are suggestions that, in some fields at least, the content found in the dominant school textbooks changes very slowly, but most such perceptions are speculative rather than firmly grounded in the analysis of actual textbook content.

4. Textbook Bias

The values and attitudes that are taught in schools are of obvious and central interest to the parents of schoolchildren, and to those who are concerned with the social futures that the patterns of schooling seem to foreshadow or with the world view that the schools seem to reflect at a given time. When the values that the schools reflect become inconsistent with the values that groups or individuals hold as important or critical to their futures, bias is often claimed. This charge reflects, however, the perspective of the person or persons making the charge; it can be made when schooling seems to threaten to reject or denigrate traditional values of religion and morality, nationality, race or ethnicity, sex roles and sexuality, and the like, or it can be made *because* schooling reflects these values.

The study of education finds its most typical starting points in the values represented by the idea of education itself and, as a result, the sustained study of the biases represented in schooling reflects liberal and cosmopolitan values and value systems.

This article will describe some of the basic characteristics and dimensions of studies of textbook bias that have been undertaken within a broadly liberal framework. It should be remembered, of course, that perhaps the majority of those concerned with the forms of bias found within schooling would be indifferent to, and may even actively reject the assumptions of the work that will be discussed here. One 1972 opinion poll of United States school administrators found, for example, that 84 percent of the respondents did not think that a significant sex bias existed in elementary-school textbooks (Pottker and Fishel 1977). And in some countries at least, textbooks and other school materials are regularly removed from the schools because of their advocacy of "liberal" and "modern" values.

4.1 Textbook Bias and Textbook Revision: History

Beginning in the nineteenth century, European scholars have shown a continuing preoccupation with the extent to which school textbooks nurture and reflect crude nationalist and ethnocentric attitudes in their presentation of national histories and nationally oriented geographies. This has created a sustained concern for the specification of particular biases and distortions that might be found in texts, the revision of these texts, and the development of recommendations for future texts which might avoid the problems that had been identified. Research and dissemination activity within this tradition has been undertaken by national, bilateral, and multilateral working parties and has been given substantial institutional support by many national, regional, and international agencies, for example, UNESCO and the Council of Europe (Schüddekopf 1967).

Although an increasing variety of analytic methods are to be found in this work, the principal method is critical interpretation of the manifest content of texts, from the points of view both of omission and commission. The most distinctive characteristics are the strong normative concern and the concern for determining what an appropriate treatment of a particular topic should contain. The checklists of sources of distortion that have been developed within the tradition of possible sources of bias are one of the distinctive achievements of this field of study. Billington (1966), for example, in his discussion of the nationalistic biases of Anglo-American history textbooks identified the following sources of such distortion:

(a) The bias of inertia—the perpetuation of legends and half truths and the failure to keep abreast of scholarship.
(b) Bias by omission—the selection of information that reflects credit only on the writer's nation.

(c) Bias in use of language—the use of words with favorable connotations to describe one group and those with unfavorable connotations to describe another.

(d) Bias by cumulative implication—the tendency to give all credit to one nation or group.

4.2 Content Analysis of Textbooks

A parallel tradition of analysis of bias in textbooks has emerged in the years since the Second World War which draws on the methodologies of "content" and "propaganda analysis." This work builds on the assumption that the manifest and latent "messages" contained within texts and other communicative media penetrate the consciousness of readers as a result of their cumulative effect; research seeks to expose the character of this accumulation by measuring the frequency of given kinds of messages.

Content analysis proceeds by positing a universe of concerns and seeking indices which can be used to measure how a concern is treated in a particular set of messages. The universe can be defined in terms of the frequency with which a given attitude object appears in a text, the form of representation given the attitude object by its referential context (i.e. the quality of the activity in which different actors figure), and the strength or intensity of the term that links an attitude object with its referential context. All of the qualities that might be found associated with these components of a message system can be reliably measured.

In the recent past, many studies using one or another method of content analysis and one or another focus of analysis have been undertaken to explore gender and ethnic stereotyping with textbooks. The common outcome is the discovery of profound and pervasive stereotyping and bias in the textbooks used in many subjects and many nations.

5. Textbook Development and Distribution

In many nations, textbook development is the task of commercial textbook publishing companies. As such, the major factor that affects development practices is the marketability of the resulting textbook. While different traditions of textbook use within schools, different textbook adoption practices, and different curricular and instructional traditions open a variety of commercial possibilities for profitable textbook publishing, marketability and profitability are always the principal goals of commercial publishing (Broudy 1975, Goldstein 1978).

The other common mode of textbook development is through government or ministry-based centers or projects. These may have a monopoly over textbook production or there may be some form of mixed economy. In either case the cost of textbook development, production and distribution is a formidable barrier to wide content coverage, experiments with new approaches and regular updating. Not surprisingly, therefore, the influence of a Western commercial publishing industry is still strong in many nations.

The distribution of textbooks has been shown to be a critical factor affecting successful learning in many less industrialized societies. Surveys have been conducted in 10 countries which included data on pupil achievement and access to reading materials in schools, and 15 of these studies, in areas as diverse as mathematics, science, reading, and language, have reported positive correlations between the availability of textbook materials and pupil achievement. This finding can be compared to parallel findings about the effects of variables like teacher training on academic achievement where the results of studies indicate more ambiguous effects. Heyneman et al. (1981) have concluded on the basis of such studies that the availability of a textbook to a student should be one of the central concerns of planners and administrators in such school systems; the provision of textbooks to students is a significant focus for efforts at school improvement on a systemwide basis. It also seems that textbook provision to lower social status students has significant effects in assisting the learning of such students.

Bibliography

Billington R A 1966 *The Historian's Contribution to Anglo-American Misunderstanding.* Hobbs, Dorman, New York

Broudy E 1975 The trouble with textbooks. *Teach. Coll. Rec.* 77(1): 13–34

Council of Europe 1974 *Religion in School History Textbooks in Europe.* Council of Europe, Strasbourg

Goldstein P 1978 *Changing the American Schoolbook.* Lexington Books, Lexington, Massachusetts

Gowin D B 1981 *Educating.* Cornell University Press, Ithaca, New York

Heyneman S P, Farrell J P, Sepulveda-Stuardo M A 1981 Textbooks and achievement in developing countries: What we know. *J. Curric. Stud.* 13(3): 227–46

Hodgetts A B 1968 *What Culture: What Heritage?* OISE Curriculum Series, No. 5. Ontario Institute for Studies in Education, Toronto, Ontario

Howson A G, Westbury I 1980 Creative activity in mathematics education: A first attempt at definition and problem-identification. *Comparative Studies of Mathematics Curricula: Stability and Change 1960–80.* Materialien und Studien Band 19. Institut für Didaktik der Mathematik, Universität Bielefeld, Bielefeld

Kirsch A 1976 Aspects of simplification in mathematics teaching. *Proceedings of the Third International Congress on Mathematics Education.* International Congress on Mathematics Education, Karlsruhe

Lorimer R, Long M 1979 Sex-role stereotyping in elementary readers. *Interchange* 19(2): 25–45

McDiarmid G, Pratt D 1971 *Teaching Prejudice.* Ontario Institute for Studies in Education, Toronto

Pottker J, Fishel A (ed.) 1977 *Sex Bias in Schools.* Associated University Press, Cranbury, New Jersey

Schüddekopf O-E 1967 *History Teaching and History Textbook Revision.* Council of Europe, Strasbourg

Schwab J J 1978 *Science, Curriculum and Liberal Education.* University of Chicago Press, Chicago, Illinois

Textbook Analysis

B. B. Armbruster and T. H. Anderson

Procedures for analyzing textbooks have been dominated by the use of readability formulas (Klare 1982). These formulas yield an index which supposedly makes it possible to match the reading demands of a textbook with the reading capabilities of the reader as determined by reading achievement scores. Two of the more well-known readability formulas, Dale and Chall (1948) and Fry (1977) use measures of word difficulty and sentence complexity to determine the appropriate reading level of the text.

In addition to readability formulas, an array of checklist instruments has been advocated as a potentially helpful way of analyzing textbooks. A sample of these checklists (Ball 1976, Jevitz and Meints 1979, Krause 1976) shows that they direct the textbook analyst to potentially important aspects of the textbook that are not necessarily measured by readability formulas. Checklist items direct the reader to consider such aspects of the textbook as the use of visual aids, cultural and sex biases, teacher's manuals or supplements, the quality of workmanship, the quality of materials, the costs, and the quality of writing. One checklist (Jevitz and Meints 1979) has 72 such items. In addition to the sheer magnitude of items to consider, many of them are stated so vaguely that the analyst may find it difficult to make the judgments required by them.

In this article some theoretical ideas and research findings are presented about how students read, understand, and remember ideas that can contribute to the process of analyzing textbooks. These ideas will enable the textbook analyst to set rational priorities on the potentially large set of criteria (such as those referenced above) and also help clear up the vagueness associated with some of the items.

Current theories suggest that learning from textbooks is a function of characteristics of the text itself and cognitive strategies used by the reader during reading.

1. The Text

One factor affecting learning from text is structure. Structure refers to the way ideas are connected together in logical organizational patterns. A few basic rhetorical structures appear to reflect fundamental patterns of human thought: (a) simple listing—a listing of items or ideas where the order of presentation of the item is not significant; (b) conclusion/evidence—a special case of simple listing, consisting of a proposition and a list of reasons serving as evidence for that fact; (c) comparison/contrast—a description of similarities and differences between two or more things; (d) temporal sequence—a sequential relationship between items or events considered in terms of the passage of time; (e) cause–effect—an interaction between at least two ideas or events, one considered a cause or reason and the other an effect or result; and (f) problem–solution—similar to the cause–effect pattern in that two factors interact, one citing a problem and the other a solution to that problem. These basic structures can be subsumed in higher order structures that underlie particular text genres (e.g., narratives, newspaper articles) and content areas (e.g., biology, history) (Anderson and Armbruster 1984).

The structure of text can be conveyed in many ways: (a) words denoting relationships (because, before, for example, in comparison); (b) explicit statements of the structure; (c) previews or introductory statements, including titles; and (d) summary statements. Information in the text that points out aspects of structure has been called "signaling" (Meyer 1975). Research has shown that better organized text, and text that makes the organization clear to the reader (for example, through the use of signaling), increases the likelihood of the reader's understanding, remembering, and applying information learned from the text (Meyer 1979).

Another characteristic of text that influences learning outcomes is local coherence, also called cohesion by linguists (Halliday and Hasan 1976). Local coherence is achieved by several kinds of simple linguistic links or ties that connect ideas together within and between sentences. Among the most common links are various forms of reference (e.g., pronoun, anaphora, etc.) and conjunctions or connectives (e.g., and, or, but, because, however). Research has established the importance of cohesive ties in understanding and remembering text. For example, repeated references that help to carry meaning across sentence boundaries can decrease reading time and increase recall of text as an integrated unit (deVilliers 1974, Haviland and Clark 1974, Kintsch et al. 1975, Manelis and Yekovich 1976, Miller and Kintsch 1980). Also, children prefer to read, read faster, and have better memory for sentences connected by explicit conjunctions, particularly causal connectives, than sentences in which the conjunction is left to be inferred (Katz and Brent 1968, Marshall and Glock 1978–79, Pearson 1974–75).

Characteristics of the content itself also affect learning from reading. Kintsch and his colleagues have shown that one of these characteristics—idea density—contributes to reading difficulty. For example, Kintsch and Keenan (1973) kept text length constant while varying the number of propositions (ideas) in text. They found that reading time was more a function of the number of propositions than the number of words. Kintsch et al. (1975) showed that reading times were longer and recall less for texts with many different word concepts than for texts with fewer word concepts. In other words, it is easier for readers to process and retain in memory a proposition built from old, familiar elements than to process propositions which introduce new concepts into the text. In sum, the denser the text (the greater the number of new ideas per unit of text), the longer it takes to read and the less the likelihood of remembering it.

Another aspect of content that affects learning outcomes is the proportion of important to unimportant information, or main ideas to details. In a series of experiments by Reder and Anderson (1980), college students who read summaries one-fifth the length of original texts were better able to recognize important facts and learn new, related material than students who read the full version. Reder and Anderson (1980) conclude that text that helps students focus attention and avoid having to time-share between main points and details is an effective way to aid learning.

Another finding from research is that learning and memory are improved when people are given information clarifying the significance of facts that might otherwise seem arbitrary, particularly causal elaborations that establish a causal relationship between ideas (Bransford and Johnson 1973, Bransford et al. 1980). For example, in research on narratives, provision of information about the character's goal and events leading up to the goal has a significant effect on comprehension and memory (Kintsch and van Dijk 1978, Rumelhart 1977, Thorndyke 1977). Presumably, knowledge of the goal and the events leading up to the goal helps readers understand the significance of the character's actions and the consequences of those actions.

In sum, various features of the text itself—structure, local coherence, content—influence learning from reading. Characteristics of the reader, however, probably play an even more crucial role in learning from textbooks. Of particular importance are the cognitive strategies used during reading.

2. Cognitive Strategies

Cognitive strategies are what the students use to get the information from the text page into their heads. These information-processing strategies include not only the initial focusing of attention and the subsequent encoding of the information attended to but also an "executive level" aspect of these processes called metacognition. Metacognition refers to both the awareness and control that readers have over their own thinking and learning (Baker and Brown 1983). Research has demonstrated that several cognitive strategies (including the metacognition component) are associated with learning from text. Some of these strategies are discussed below. (For additional strategies of effective learners, see Baker and Brown 1983).

One beneficial strategy in learning from text is selective attention to, and processing of, the most important information in text as defined by the criterion task (that is, what students must do to demonstrate that learning

has occurred; for example, answer questions at the end of the chapter or take a test). Numerous studies have shown a clear relationship between learning outcomes and readers' knowledge of or expectations about criterion tasks. For example, one line of research has examined the effect on learning of questions inserted periodically in the text. These studies have shown that questions inserted in the text have a striking focusing effect on studying behaviors and learning outcomes. Students tend to spend more time studying the text that is relevant to the types of inserted questions they receive and they tend to perform better on posttest items testing the type of information tapped by the inserted questions they receive (Reynolds et al. 1979). The inserted questions establish expectations about the criterion task, which then guides cognitive processing.

A second strategy associated with effective learning from text is selective attention to, and processing of, the most important information in text as defined by the author's structure. Mature readers, at least, are able to detect the most important information from text and remember it. The ability to do this seems to develop gradually; immature or less competent readers are less likely to identify and process important information than more mature readers (Brown and Smiley 1977, 1978, Meyer et al. 1980). However, an encouraging line of research indicates that less mature students can be taught to identify and use text structure to facilitate learning. For example, Bartlett (1978) taught ninth graders (14-year-olds) to identify and use four common expository text structures as an aid to learning. Likewise, Dansereau (1983) has successfully trained college students to identify and use the inherent structure of text as an aid to learning.

Another strategy that can help students learn from text is to make use of their own prior knowledge to interpret and remember new information. Research has confirmed that what readers know already greatly influences what they learn and remember from text (Anderson et al. 1977, Spilich et al. 1979). One must not only have the relevant knowledge but also activate it at the appropriate time. In other words, readers must be able to "call up" appropriate prior knowledge when it is needed to understand new information. Research indicates that children often fail to spontaneously activate relevant prior knowledge when it could help them in learning from text, but that they can be trained to do so (Bransford et al. 1980, Bransford 1984).

Another important cognitive strategy is to encode information in such a way that it can be remembered. Research shows that some kinds of studying strategies or learning activities are particularly helpful. Studying strategies that involve the identification and manipulation of the author's structure (structuring strategies) appear to be especially helpful in learning, given that students know how to use the strategy. For example, students taught to outline can use outlining as a learning aid (Barton 1930), and students instructed in semantic mapping techniques (diagrammatic representations of text structure) can improve their memory for text (Armbruster and Anderson 1980, Dansereau 1983). Another studying technique that appears to promote processing is causal elaboration. Bransford and his colleagues (Bransford 1979, Bransford et al. 1980) have shown that people remember ideas better if they can establish a meaningful causal relationship between them. That is, in causal elaboration, readers use prior knowledge (information from the text or from their heads) to construct a significant connection between ideas that might otherwise seem unrelated. For example, readers might use prior knowledge of the function of an object to help them understand and remember the object's structure.

Selectively attending to and processing "important" information, engaging prior knowledge, and using high pay-off studying techniques are some of the cognitive strategies that research has shown to facilitate learning from text. Research has also shown that instruction in strategies can have a positive effect on learning outcomes. Research has already been mentioned in which instruction in identifying the author's structure and in using studying strategies has resulted in improved learning. Research has not only shown that instruction can be effective but has also suggested how teachers can best help students learn to learn from reading. The major practical implication from the research is that students should be taught to use cognitive strategies with awareness. That is, students should be informed about why, when, where, and how they should use particular strategies (Brown et al. 1981).

3. Implications for Practice

A prime reason for analyzing textbooks is to enable educators to make wise decisions when selecting textbooks for classroom use. As mentioned in the introduction, two techniques are rather widely used in analysis-for-selection. One is the use of readability formulas to index the general language complexity of the textbook prose. The other is checklist instruments which direct the analyst to various aspects of textbooks that are not indexed by the readability formulas. Both of these techniques can be helpful in deciding which textbooks are generally appropriate for classroom use.

In addition to these techniques, some questions are proposed that respond to the interpretation of what research on reading has to suggest about textbook evaluation. Answering these questions should add important information to the textbook selection decision. The first series of questions relate to the text:

(a) Does the textbook make a systematic effort to help the reader connect new ideas with ideas already learned? Does the author include well-written introductions, summaries to chapters, and questions that encourage students to use relevant prior knowledge?

(b) Are the texts coherent at a global level? Are they well-structured and is that structure readily apparent to the reader as evidenced by chapter titles, headings, outlines, introductions, conclusions, and topic sentences?

(c) Are the texts coherent at a local level? Do pronouns have clear referents and are the relationships between ideas explicit or obvious?

(d) Do the texts work toward some important purpose at an appropriate rate by introducing new, main ideas when they are needed? Are the intervening ideas between main ones the type that extend, elaborate, and make explicit the relationship between the main ones, or do the intervening ones simply introduce irrelevant detail?

The following questions concern student exercises.

(a) Do the student exercises at the end of chapters and in workbooks help students learn to locate and process important information from the text? If the students were to learn well the answers to questions at the end of the chapters, would they have an important body of knowledge to help them read and understand the next chapter, or next year's textbook?

(b) Do the student exercises at the end of chapters and in workbooks help students learn a variety of studying techniques? Are the when's, where's, how's, and why's of the studying techniques explained?

The final questions concern the teacher's materials.

(a) Do the teacher's manuals which accompany some textbooks explain to teachers the when's, where's, how's, and why's to teach students about some of the difficult studying aspects, such as text structure and what-to-do-when-something-is-not-well-understood?

(b) Do the teacher's manuals which accompany some textbooks explain to teachers the when's, where's, how's and why's students should be taught to become aware of and monitor their own cognitive processes while studying?

Bibliography

Anderson R C, Reynolds R E, Schallert D L, Goetz E T 1977 Frameworks for comprehending discourse. *Am. Educ. Res. J.* 14: 367–82

Anderson T H, Armbruster B B 1984 Content area textbooks. In: Anderson R C, Osborn J, Tierney R J (eds.) 1984 *Learning to Read in American Schools: Basal Readers and Content Texts.* Erlbaum, Hillsdale, New Jersey

Armbruster B B, Anderson T H 1980 *The Effect of Mapping on the Free Recall of Expository Text.* (Tech. Rep. No. 160). Center for the Study of Reading, University of Illinois, Urbana, Illinois

Baker L, Brown A L 1983 Cognitive monitoring in reading. In:

Flood J (ed.) 1983 *Understanding Reading Comprehension*. International Reading Association, Newark, Delaware

Ball H G 1976 Standards for material selection. *J. Read.* 20: 208–11

Bartlett B J 1978 Top-level structure as an organizational strategy for recall of classroom text. Unpublished doctoral dissertation, Arizona State University

Barton W A 1930 *Outlining as a Study Procedure*. Teachers College, Columbia University, New York

Bransford J D 1979 *Human Cognition: Learning, Understanding, and Remembering*. Wadsworth Belmont, California

Bransford J D 1984 Schema activation and schema acquisition: Comments on Richard C. Anderson's remarks. In: Anderson R C, Osborn J, Tierney R J (eds.) 1983 *Learning to Read in American Schools: Basal Readers and Content Texts*. Erlbaum, Hillsdale, New Jersey

Bransford J D, Johnson M K 1973 Considerations of some problems of comprehension. In: Chase W (ed.) 1973 *Visual Information Processing*. 8th Symposium on Cognition, Carnegie-Mellon University, 1972. Academic Press, New York

Bransford J D, Stein B S, Shelton T S, Owings R 1980 Cognition and adaptation: The importance of learning to learn. In: Harvey J L (ed.) 1980 *Cognition, Social Behavior, and the Environment*. Erlbaum, Hillsdale, New Jersey

Brown A L, Smiley S S 1977 Rating the importance of structural units of prose passages: A problem of metacognitive development. *Child Dev.* 48: 1–8

Brown A L, Smiley S S 1978 The development of strategies for studying texts. *Child Dev.* 49: 1076–88

Brown A L, Campione J C, Day J D 1981 Learning to learn: On training students to learn from texts. *Educ. Res. AERA.* 10: 14–21

Dale E, Chall J S 1948 A formula for predicting readability. *Educ. Res. Bull.* 27: 11–20, 37–54

Dansereau D F 1983 Learning strategy research. In: Segal J, Chipman S, Glaser R (eds.) 1983 *Thinking and Learning Skills: Relating Instruction to Basic Research*, Vol. 1. Erlbaum, Hillsdale, New Jersey

de Villiers P A 1974 Imagery and theme in recall of connected discourse. *J. Exp. Psychol.* 103: 263–68

Fry E B 1977 Fry's readability graph: Clarification, validity, and extension to level 17. *J. Read.* 21: 242–52

Halliday M A K, Hasan R 1976 *Cohesion in English*. Longman, London

Haviland S E, Clark H H 1974 What's new? Acquiring new information as a process in comprehension. *J. Verb. Behav.* 13: 512–21

Jevitz L, Meints D W 1979 Be a better book buyer: Guidelines for textbook evaluation. *J. Read.* 22: 734–38

Katz E, Brent S 1968 Understanding connections. *J. Verb. Learn. Verb. Behav.* 1: 501–9

Kintsch W, Keenan J M 1973 Reading rate as a function of the number of propositions in the base structure of sentences. *Cognit. Psychol.* 5: 257–74

Kintsch W, van Dijk T 1978 Toward a model of text comprehension and production. *Psychol. Rev.* 85: 363–94

Kintsch W, Kozminsky E, Streby W J, McKoon G, Keenan J M 1975 Comprehension and recall of text as a function of content variables. *J. Verb. Learn. Verb. Behav.* 14: 196–214

Klare G R 1982 Readability. In: Pearson P D (ed.) 1982 *Handbook of Reading Research* Longman, New York

Krause K C 1976 Do's and don'ts in evaluating textbooks. *J. Read.* 20: 212–14

Manelis L, Yekovich F R 1976 Repetitions of propositional arguments in sentences. *J. Verb. Learn. Verb. Behav.* 15: 301–12

Marshall N, Glock M D 1978–79 Comprehension of connected discourse: A study into the relationship between the structure of text and information recalled. *Read. Res. Q.* 16: 10–56

Meyer B J F 1975 *The Organization of Prose and its Effects on Memory*. North Holland, Amsterdam

Meyer B J F 1979 Organizational patterns in prose and their use in reading. In: Kamil M L, Moe A J (eds.) 1979 *Reading Research: Studies and Applications*. 28th Yearbook of the National Reading Conference

Meyer B J F, Brandt D M, Bluth G J 1980 Use of top-level structure in text: Key for reading comprehension of ninth-grade students. *Read. Res. Q.* 16: 72–103

Miller J R, Kintsch W 1980 Readability and recall of short prose passages: A theoretical analysis. *J. Exp. Psychol: Human Learning and Memory* 6: 335–54

Pearson P D 1974–75 The effects of grammatical complexity on children's comprehension, recall, and conception of certain semantic relations. *Read. Res. Q.* 10: 155–92

Reder L M, Anderson J R 1980 A comparison of texts and their summaries: Memorial consequences. *J. Verb. Learn. Verb. Behav.* 19: 121–34

Rumelhart D E 1977 Understanding and summarizing brief stories. In: LaBerge D, Samuels J (eds.) 1977 *Basic Processes in Reading: Perception and Comprehension*. Erlbaum, Hillsdale, New Jersey

Spilich G J, Vesonder G T, Chiesi H L, Voss J F 1979 Text processing of domain-related information for individuals with high and low domain knowledge. *J. Verb. Learn. Verb. Behav.* 18: 275–90

Thorndyke P W 1977 Cognitive structures in comprehension and memory of narrative discourse. *Cognit. Psychol.* 9: 77–110

Teacher's Guide

J. McNeil

The teacher's guide is a tool for helping the teacher present the curriculum. Usually a guide is designed for use with a specific textbook. Sometimes, however, guides are independent from the text material and contain sufficient background information, activities, questions, and lesson plans for teaching a limited topic such as soccer, ocean awareness, paints, or dental health. A teacher's guide is not a textbook for students. Synonyms are the teacher's manual, teacher's handbook, teacher's guidebook, and teacher's edition.

1. Status of the Teacher's Guide

Around the early 1940s the teacher's guide was chiefly for elementary-school teachers and limited to the presentation and treatment of a particular student textbook. Guides for secondary-school and college teachers were brief, primarily containing keys to exercises and solutions to problems. Two trends emerged simultaneously in 1940. The elementary teacher's guide was expanded to include general theory of instruction and child growth and development, and a demand arose for a more elaborate guide for secondary-school teachers (Deighton 1971). Publishers at that time created extensive manuals to provide basic instruction for teachers who lacked the formal education in subject matter that most teachers have today.

The expanded guides of the 1940s were subsequently criticized for giving teachers more assistance than they could use. Consequently, innovative simpler formats appeared. The teacher annotated edition of the pupil text is a case in point. An annotated edition includes suggestions in overprint on a duplicate copy of the pupil's page, insert pages to aid the teachers in analyzing the material to be taught, and suggestions for motivating and evaluating a pupil's preparation for the lesson. A separate section of the teacher's edition usually includes a rationale for the instructional textbook(s) along with an outline of the scope and sequence and a description of other supplementary material. Clear statements of objectives at the beginning of lessons and related follow-up activities are recent features of the teacher's guide.

Analyses of changes in guides for the teaching of reading show that publishers are responding to both research findings and the concerns of teachers. For example, these guides now offer more suggestions for teaching reading as a total language concept, display greater care in familiarizing the teacher with the goals and objectives of the program, show an increase in the number of questions demanding an inference, and have fewer questions on trivia.

A few publishers have aimed at presenting an instructional sequence that is both effective and reproducible. Accordingly, their guides support the idea of a "teacher proof" text by which the teacher is relegated to making an initial presentation of material using prespecified scripts and to monitoring pupil responses with a list of answers to accept.

The use of the teacher's guide as a political instrument is a new development. Countries undergoing political transformation have expanded the teacher's guide to include the teaching of ideological views. The *Teacher's Guide for Literacy Volunteers* used in Nicaragua, for example, provides step-by-step instruction on the use of a literacy methodology as well as social, political, and economic information necessary for conducting discussions aimed at developing political criteria (Cardenal and Miller 1981). The guide also outlines a systematic set of study activities for the teachers themselves. Questions in the guide are designed to develop analytic skills and a sense of social responsibility. The literacy campaign in Cuba had previously shown the value of a teacher's guide in helping to heighten the political awareness of teachers. Cuban guides such as *Let's Teach Literacy* and *Orientation for the Brigadista* helped volunteers understand how to initiate informal conversation and how to establish the essential sense of equals working toward a common cause.

2. Evaluative Studies of Guides

Three kinds of evaluative approaches have been undertaken: those where the evaluator applies particular criteria such as one calling for determining the levels of questions given in the guide; those comparing what teachers want in their guides with what the guides actually offer; and those assessing how guides are utilized and with what effect.

There is no single criterion for judging a guide. Stanton says a guide can best be evaluated in terms of those to whom it is directed—teachers (Stanton 1980). He believes that a good guide helps teachers organize experiences without dictating precisely what those experiences should be. On the other hand, some believe that guides should describe in detail the kinds of behavior which the teachers should exhibit. A central problem is to offer a uniform presentation of curriculum and at the same time help teachers respond to their own diverse needs and to the uniqueness of their pupils.

A summary of evaluative studies of teacher's guides accompanying basal reading series in the United States shows a lack of consensus concerning what constitutes the pertinent parts of a reading lesson (Pieronek 1979). Guides present either a mere skeleton that gives teachers little assistance or they present such a myriad of suggestions that confusion results. Criticisms of the teacher's guide are as follows: too detailed guidance, insufficient suggestions for individualizing strategies, lack of differing levels of questions, and lack of broadening experience.

Guides are also criticized for offering questions that stress memory and the direct recall of information. Content analyses of teacher editions for reading programs typically fault the guides because well-based instructional strategies such as the giving of explicit cues, practice opportunities for pupils, and feedback in independent practice are offered much less frequently than expected. Guides are also faulted for not providing known rules, definitions, and strategies which can be explained and used in developing abilities such as decoding, deriving word meanings, and inferring meaning. Some guides provide cues for phonic analysis but fail to offer the teacher help in teaching other skills. Guides are faulted for failing to emphasize understanding as the purpose of lessons and for stressing mechanistic behavior.

A study of what Israeli teachers want in the way of curriculum materials indicates that teachers give less priority to guides that prescribe strategies than to guides that offer opportunity to choose strategies (Ben-Peretz and Tamir 1981). Teachers put foremost the subject matter principles and concepts to be featured. They also value provisions for adapting material to students of different ability level and provisions for individualizing active involvement of pupils. Specification of the target population and detailed objectives are of little importance to these teachers.

On the other hand, a study of the preferences of elementary science teachers revealed they preferred manuals with statements specifying: (a) desired pupil outcomes in clear terms, (b) points where the teacher should give particular directions to pupils, (c) the beginning and ending of each activity, (d) question forms in heading, rather than topic forms, and (e) a list form for directions for conducting activities over using a paragraph form (Divesta and Reber 1988).

Comparison of 20 published English handbooks with the characteristics desired by college English teachers indicated that none of the handbooks fulfilled all characteristics (Pickett 1977). Regarding physical characteristics, teachers want an inexpensive concise handbook with exercises and an instructional manual. Regarding textual characteristics, the teachers order their preferences as follows: emphatic spacing, boxes for the most important concepts, two or more colors, many headings, and a variety of type style. In their ranking of characteristics concerning accessibility of information, teachers rank items in this order: detailed index, quick reference chart, detailed table of contents, guide words on each page, chapter tabs, and color key.

3. Utilization of Guides

Although the implementation of the teacher's guide varies with individual teachers, there is evidence that the instructional strategies found in guides heavily influence the teacher's classroom behavior. Many teachers rely on the content sequence and instructional strategies specified in the manual. Further, there is some evidence that achievement of pupils with respect to a specific skill is greater when teachers are given suggestions for teaching the skill.

Many teachers reply to the question of why they engage in a practice of doubtful merit by saying, "The manual said to do it." Teachers do what the guide says because it is an easy way to conduct school. Elementary-school teachers faced with complex decisions appear to discount the usefulness of research and turn their attention to guides for answers to their problems. In her observations of the consistency of teacher use of the procedures given in guides for the teaching of mathematics, Folsom found that one-half of the teachers used the procedures as given; 40 percent felt the guides helped them understand maths better; all agreed that the procedures were easy to follow but only 22 percent used the supplementary activities because they were too time consuming (Folsom 1960). Most teachers find guides helpful in planning but they find the suggestions

for individualizing too general. Further, teachers do not read the introduction section and overview seriously. Teachers who request a teacher's handbook to accompany an educational television series have been found to make better use of the televised program.

4. Opportunities for Research

There is a paucity of research on the teacher's guide. Most of the little research there is, has been restricted to small-scale studies of teacher preference. More attention should be given to guides inasmuch as the multiple resources of the text and the guide is likely to have more effect on student achievement than any other refinement of the curriculum or medium of instruction. Further, the teacher's guide can be a means for introducing more effective teaching methods without revising the textbook. What kinds of research are needed? Experimental studies should be undertaken to throw light on the way guides influence both teaching behavior and the achievement of pupils. There is need for study of the effects of guides used in teacher education programs for helping beginning teachers learn to think pedagogically (Ball and Feiman-Neimser 1986). One possibility is to study the effects of a particular methodology featured in guides. Study of the characteristics that identify what a guide will accomplish when used by teachers of different backgrounds and experience is another.

A related area of needed inquiry is the manipulation of specifiable variables in the designing of guides. Variables identified in discourse analysis might be considered in planning inquiries aimed at finding out the mental activities of teachers as they try to learn and apply the content of their guides. Several kinds of variables have been suggested (McConkie 1977). Firstly, variables in the staging of information alert the teacher to what is important and present a viewpoint to what is being said. The order of presentations for topics, comments, and examples is an example of a staging variable. Secondly, variables in content structure, such as the value of image-arousing statements, the amount of information presented, and the relations among propositions could also be important in the communication of meaning and information to the teacher. And thirdly, variables in cohesive structure can be manipulated so that it is possible to learn what is most effective in getting teachers to apply the methodology suggested by the guides.

Bibliography

Ball D, Feiman-Neimser S 1986 *Using Textbooks and Teachers' Guides: What Beginning Elementary Teachers Learn and What They Need to Know.* Institute for Research on Teaching, Michigan State University, East Lansing, Michigan
Ben-Peretz M, Tamir P 1981 What teachers want to know about curriculum materials. *J. Curric. Stud.* 13: 45–53
Cardenal F, Miller V 1981 Nicaragua 1980: The battle of the ABCs. *Harvard Educ. Rev.* 51: 1–26

Deighton L C 1971 Textbooks: Role in education. In: Deighton L C (ed.) 1971 *The Encyclopedia of Education*, Vol. 9. Macmillan, New York, pp. 211–14

Divesta F, Rieber L 1988 *Characteristics of Cognitive Instructional Design: The Next Generation Resources in Education.* Educational Resources Information Center (ERIC), Alexandria, VA (ERIC Document 295636)

Folsom M 1960 Teachers look at arithmetic manuals. *Arithmetic Teach.* 7: 13–18

McConkie G W 1977 Learning from text. In: McConkie G W (ed.) 1977 *Review of Research in Education*, Vol. 5. Peacock, Itasca, Illinois, pp. 3–48

Morales A F 1981 The literacy campaign in Cuba. *Harvard Educ. Rev.* 51: 31–39

Pieronek F T 1979 Using basal guidebooks—the ideal integrated reading lesson plan. *Read. Teach.* 33: 167–72

Pickett N A 1977 *A Comparison of Characteristics Desired by College English Teachers in a Composition Handbook with Characteristics of Recent Composition Handbooks.* Hinds College, Raymond, Mississippi. ERIC Document No. ED 013 371

Stanton M 1980 Staff manuals in secondary schools. *Educ. Stud.* 6: 147–56

Enrichment and Supplementary Materials

R. M. Thomas

Curriculum enrichment can be divided into two interrelated types. The first may be called extended planning, for it consists of activities the teacher devises to go beyond the basic curriculum prescribed in the course of study furnished to direct the school's instructional program. The second type may be called individualized enrichment, for it consists of the teacher's providing additional learning activities for the faster learners or for ones with special needs and interests.

The following article inspects both of these varieties in terms of their purposes, sources, and criteria for judging their effectiveness.

1. Extended Planning

The purpose of this form of enrichment is to offer an entire classroom of learners opportunities to study topics in addition to those contained in the basic curriculum guidebook or textbook. One reason for such planning can be to teach material of local importance that has not been included in the nationwide or regional curriculum. Among the varieties of such locally important learning goals are ones treating religious beliefs, local history and geography, arts and crafts, forms of drama and dance, regional languages and literature, biographies of notable people in the area, local laws and customs, and social and scientific affairs of the district (Mogil 1979, Schamess 1978).

Another reason for extended planning is to bring the material in the basic curriculum guidebook up to date. Recent scientific, historical, or literary events can be added by the teacher to supplement outdated textbook accounts.

A third form of extended planning integrates other subject fields into the study of a particular subject-matter area, such as showing the societal aspects of science in a science class (Solomon 1980) or relating humanities to occupational programs (Beckwith 1981).

A fourth form is intended neither to localize nor to update the curriculum but rather to add topics which the teacher believes are desirable for students but are not in the basic curriculum. Often such topics are ones in which the teacher has particular interest or skill. For example, a teacher may be an expert in puppetry, in mathematical puzzles, in foreign languages, or in the history of warfare and may thus add such a topic to the curriculum.

The sources of material for extended planning are nearly unlimited. For information about regional or community affairs, teachers can turn to the local historical society, newspapers, libraries, regional industries, residents who have participated in the affairs, and government publications (LaHurd 1978). To update the curriculum, an instructor can use news magazines, newspapers, almanacs, yearbooks, professional journals, television and radio programs, and such resource persons as local scientists, craftspersons, artists, political figures, journalists, and scholars.

As criteria for judging the effectiveness of extended planning, educators can pose the following questions. (a) Educational importance—how will such enrichment activities profit the learners or the community or nation? (b) Replacement importance—when new topics are added, they typically replace existing ones or reduce the time spent on topics already in the program. So which original topics will be replaced or their time reduced by the enrichment activities, and why are the new activities more valuable than those displaced? (c) Adequacy of sources—were the sources of the enrichment activities the most suitable ones available?

2. Individualized Enrichment

As already noted, individual enrichment is not intended for an entire class of students but only for those with special needs. The most prominent types of students requiring enrichment are the faster learners, for they have extra time available after completing the regular study assignments sooner than their classmates.

Another type of student profiting from enrichment is the one with a special talent or interest which the teacher is willing to nurture with individualized or small-group activities. A student with a bent for writing can be assigned to create stories and poems, one with interest in science can devise experiments and exhibits, and ones with interest in acting can develop dramatic skits of historical events.

When searching for individualized activities, teachers can recognize that such activities vary greatly in their nature. For example, an activity can either be closely allied to the topic studied by the rest of the class or can be far removed from it. In a geometry class a closely allied activity could be that of assigning a pair of the faster learners the task of using newly learned geometry theorems in drawing a map of a park adjacent to the school grounds. A far-removed activity for this same class could be that of permitting the faster learners to read literary works they would not otherwise meet in school.

Enrichment activities may also vary in the length of time they require. It is useful for teachers to devise experiences that take only a few minutes as well as ones that require an hour or more, so that the type of activity can be suited to the amount of time a given student will have available after completing the basic curriculum assignments. Examples of experiences requiring only a few minutes are: assign a pupil to read a single passage in a story and answer one question about the passage, or to create three questions to test classmates' understanding of the science topic just studied, or to draw a pencil sketch of the imagined appearance of the hero from a story the class has been reading. Examples of longer term activities are: assign a student to construct a model of a village from an historical event just studied, or to read the biographies of famous scientists, or to write descriptions of a local historical incident on the basis of interviews the student has carried out with three elderly members of the community.

The same sources of activities described earlier for extended planning are useful for individual enrichment.

In addition, teachers' guidebooks and student workbooks that accompany textbooks often include suggestions for enrichment activities, as do books and journal articles intended for improving teachers' instructional skills (Colon and Treffinger 1980, Martinson 1968, Muessig 1978, Thomas and Thomas 1965).

Criteria for judging the suitability of individualized enrichment activities are suggested by such questions as: (a) worthwhile objectives—did the activity teach the student something of real value or merely provide trivial information or worthless skills? (b) New knowledge and heightened skills—did the activity enable the student to learn something new and achieve higher levels of skills, or did it merely repeat something the student had already mastered? (c) Classroom-management efficiency—did the activity require an undue amount of teacher time, so that the learning of the rest of the class members suffered? Did the activity distract other students from their studies?

Bibliography

Beckwith M M 1981 An ERIC review: Integrating the humanities and occupational programs: An inventory of current practices. *Comm. Coll. Rev.* 9: 57–64
Colon P T, Treffinger D J 1980 Providing for the gifted in the regular classroom. *Roeper Rev.* 3(2): 18–21
LaHurd C S 1978 Don't overlook the government depositories. *Today's Educ.* 67(4): 66–67
Martinson R A 1968 *Curriculum Enrichment for the Gifted in the Primary Grades*. Prentice-Hall, Englewood Cliffs, New Jersey
Mogil H M 1979 Bringing weather into your classroom. *Science and Children* 16(5): 14–16
Muessig R H (ed.) 1978 *Social Studies Curriculum Improvement*. National Council for the Social Studies, Washington, DC
Schamess S 1978 Ceremony, celebration, and culture. *Elem. Sch. J.* 79(1): 1–5
Solomon J 1980 Science and society studies in the school curriculum. *Sch. Sci. Rev.* 62: 213–19
Thomas R M, Thomas S M 1965 *Individual Differences in the Classroom*. McKay, New York

Curriculum Packages

E. L. Baker

A curriculum package is a set of coordinated instructional materials designed to achieve particular goals. These materials may either provide for extended instructional time, for example, two weeks or a year, or be limited to a brief period. Often these materials consist of multiple activities, perhaps in different media. They consist at least of materials for the direct use by students, and adjunct materials to assist the teacher, or another instructor, such as the parent.

1. Two Types of Curriculum Packages

What distinguishes the curriculum "package" from curricula of the unpackaged type? The answer depends upon which type of curriculum package one means. The emergence of the idea of curriculum package came from two very distinct sources. One source was based on the revision of curriculum movements that occcurred in the United States in the late 1950s and early 1960s, which strived to change both the content and the method of instruction. The focus of this effort was to improve and to update the content presented in public education. Courses were developed in social science, laboratory science, English language, and mathematics, and these courses were designed to present the most accurate view of the discipline in terms that children could understand. In addition to the reformation of content, the "new" curricula emphasized inquiry approaches. Students were encouraged to inquire about the nature of the discipline, to use discovery methods based largely on their autonomous application of the processes of the discipline, in contrast to earlier pedagogical styles that emphasized memory, drill, and practice. Curriculum packages answering the demands for changes of these types provided multiple options for students and teachers and emphasized outcomes focused on skill in using particular procedures, for example, observation and verification. Typically, such packages were designed to provide resources for a year, or even longer.

Almost concurrently, a second source of today's curriculum package was developing in the work of behavioral psychology. In this framework, instruction was conceived as the process of controlling learning through cues and feedback, and "programmed instruction" was the earliest school-oriented product of this line of research. Critical features of such packages were operationally stated objectives, criterion tasks, self-paced learning, gradually increasing difficulty, active participation, and feedback. Curriculum packages evolving from this line of development might be course length or as short as a 15 minute, single concept program.

2. Characteristics of Curriculum Packages

Despite having origins in the content reform movement and the operant learning movement, there are at least some common elements that define today's curriculum package, and while other curricula may share some of the features in combination they seem to circumscribe the universe of curriculum packages. First, a package is directed to a set of goals. These goals may be broadly focused on learning a process, for example, judgment, or directly tied to particular skills and content, for example, computational skills. Often, these goals are translated into behavioral skills, and component tasks (Gagné 1973) may be specified. A common set of goals may be specified for all learners, or differentiation of goals may occur as a function of individual differences, task complexity, or creativity. In many cases, particular activities and resources, or units of instruction, may be keyed to particular goals.

A second feature of curriculum packages is that they are self-contained, that is, they provide sufficient resources for instruction. In some cases, they may be used without extensive modification, improvisation, or instructional planning by the user. Materials presented to children directly may have a self-instructional flavor.

They may offer a sequenced set of self-paced instruction to students. This sort of instruction derives from behavioral psychology and programmed instruction, especially the idea that learners should be given relevant practice on specified objectives. Other packages may be organized to present coordinated tasks for students using a variety of methods, cued, for example, by color-coded materials. For instance, in a set of materials designed to teach "main idea" in reading comprehension, students might be given the opportunity to read various paragraphs and to select the main idea from a list of choices. Additional tasks on the same general skill might include asking the student to provide the "best" title for a story, to write a brief story when given a title, or to draw a picture when given a particular topic. From a learning perspective, all these tasks might be considered relevant, particularly if a student's view of reading comprehension is atheoretical. Under specific learning theories, certain of the above tasks would be deleted. Other learning or curriculum packages, with stronger ties, perhaps, to the content reformation lineage, would not consist of particular instruction for students, but might present a wide range of resources, including simulated drafts of important historical documents, materials to conduct scientific experiments, and other manipulatives. These materials provide a library of resources for the learners that may be used in infinite ways.

In addition to the variety of particular activities provided for the student, the teacher may be provided with a set of coordinated, or at least compatible, options to use in teaching. These options may include directions for rearranging the group into teams for auxiliary games, providing information for students prior to their individual or team activity, suggestions for discussion, media presentations, or posters or drawings for display during the instructional unit. A wide range is found in the amount, type, and specificity of these instructions to teachers. In certain packages, they may be included in a teacher's edition of the major text. They may be provided as a separate volume or as a teacher's manual or leader's guide. In part, these decisions relate to the number of options suggested and the specificity of the suggestions. At the most general end of the continuum, the teacher may be merely presented with a list of references on the topic, with the assumption that the teacher will obtain the appropriate materials and extract from them ideas to augment the provided materials. At the other end of the continuum, certain manuals are provided with complete scripts for the teacher to use, with the assumption that compliance will lead to effective implementation of the package. Underlying this assumption was the general idea that materials can and should be made "teacher-proof," a notion which regards teacher contribution as a "noise" or interference in the system. Less severe versions of that notion result in the inclusion of lesson plans for the teacher to use. In either case, however, the intent is to provide instruction to the student with the teacher as adjunct mediator rather than using the teacher's own experience, knowledge of setting, and intelligence as a principal organizing element. The choice of teachers' role may depend upon estimates of their familiarity with curriculum content, the quality of the teachers, and the evidence, or strength of belief, that instructional cues provided to the teacher result, in fact, in desired student performance.

Curricula need to be "packaged" when more than one artifact is provided. As implied above, a minimum package contains something for the student and something for the teacher. More frequently, however, a range of materials is provided. These materials may provide different instructional methods, different particular tasks, and may use different formats and media for instruction. For instance, one would have a package when the student is provided with a text, a workbook, or set of worksheets coordinated with the text, and a teacher's guide. More elaborate multimedia packages may contain games (with all necessary paraphernalia, such as board, tokens, scoring procedures), records, audiotapes, discs for the microcomputer, films, videotapes, or videodiscs.

In addition, other components may be included, particularly procedures for assessing student progress. Such procedures may be as simple as a tracking mechanism to monitor where the student is in a set of hierarchically structured materials, perhaps presented on a wall chart. Special grade books, or student-managed record sheets may provide the teacher and student with a clear sense of accomplishment.

More direct estimates of student accomplishment, that is, their actual performance, can be made from assessment materials that may be found in such packages. These procedures may include general ideas for testing, a list of suggestions for questions, or projects presented in the teachers' guide. In some cases, actual tests to be used for pretesting, progress assessment, and grading are included, either as prototypes, ready for local duplication and distribution, or in numbers appropriate for class administration. Quizzes, for either group or self-administration, may also be available, some with answer keys for the student.

The quality and care with which these assessment instruments are developed represents another feature which varies greatly from package to package. Tests may cover only the information or the content provided and ignore the complex cognitive processes the student has learned. The tests may favor a particular format, for example, multiple-choice tests, without particular reference to the validity of the procedure or to the objectives as stated in the curriculum. If essay or project-based assessments are suggested, criteria are very rarely provided for the reliable scoring of student performance. By and large, these assessment devices are presented *de novo* with no technical information related to reliability and validity of the devices. This lack of information is unlikely to be an oversight and more probably results because no technical base exists for the assessment instruments.

3. Trends in Using Curriculum Packages

A critical question surrounding the use of these curriculum packages relates to their effectiveness. Although it was before the 1960s that standards for the assessment of curriculum packages were first provided (see Lumsdaine 1963 for a description), most curriculum packages distributed for school use do not receive any systematic validation, particularly extended trials with teachers and learners where student achievement is the principal criterion. In fact, these recommendations had more effect on the field of achievement measurement, leading to the field of criterion-referenced measurement (Glaser 1963) than on the field of curriculum (see *Criterion-referenced Measurement*). Even though a network of educational laboratories in the United States was specifically created to provide a model for the systematic design and revision of such packages based on their effects on student achievement, most curriculum packages do not go through this research and development process. The reason commonly provided is that the costs of such trials are too high. Another valid reason relates to the differential goals of some curriculum packages, particularly those designed to serve as general resources or as a cache of activities for the teacher to use. The different processes of implementation, idiosyncratic to the teacher, make the use of a standard assessment difficult. However, the quality of projects or other "creative" work could be judged and evaluation of practicality, content accuracy, and satisfaction could provide sufficient information for an informed adoption to be made. At the present time, however, few curricula come with estimates of their effectiveness.

In view of the lack of information available about the quality of most curriculum packages, under what conditions should they be used? Packages of the highly structured sort requiring minimal contribution by teachers may be most appropriate when the content area is likely to be unfamiliar to the teacher or when the pool of teachers or the available teacher training is marginal, or when there is a need to differentiate instruction so that a subset of students can proceed, or review, with relative independence. For those curricular materials that provide resources for the teaching of processes or inquiry, it is important to ensure settings that include teachers and students with sufficient background, for example, in terms of reading comprehension for students, and subject matter familiarity for teachers. In either case, local educational agencies can make their own contribution to the utility of curriculum packages by documenting, in relatively simple terms, their usefulness and other performance information teachers can make available. At least, others in the same school system would have some basis for choice.

The future of curriculum packages will undoubtedly be linked with emerging technologies, particularly the personal computer. Curriculum packages must still be directed to educational goals and be based on sound pedagogy. Maintaining such concerns in the light of rapidly growing courseware markets and astounding advances in the visual technologies will require vigilance by those concerned with student learning.

Bibliography

Baker E L 1973 The technology of instructional development. In: Travers R M W (ed.) 1973 *Second Handbook of Research on Teaching: A Project of the American Educational Research Association*. Rand McNally, Chicago, Illinois, pp. 245–85

Gagné R M 1973 *The Conditions of Learning*. Holt, Rinehart and Winston, New York

Glaser R 1963 Instructional technology and the measurement of learning outcomes: Some questions. *Am. Psychol.* 18(8): 519–21

Lange P C (ed.) 1967 *Programmed Instruction*. The Sixty-sixth Yearbook of the National Society for the Study of Education, Part 2. National Society for the Study of Education, Chicago, Illinois, pp. 104–38

Lumsdaine A A 1963 Instruments and media of instruction. In: Gage N L (ed.) 1963 *Handbook of Research on Teaching: A Project of the American Educational Research Association*. Rand McNally, Chicago, Illinois

Computers in Curriculum

G. Salomon

With the decrease in computer costs and the development of more, better, and more diversified learning materials designed for personal computers (courseware), there has been an impressive growth in the use of computers in schools all over the world. The early years of unqualified enthusiasm accompanied by naive explorations of computer usages have given way to a more thoughtful examination and development of the uses of computers in the curriculum. This process is guided by two major questions: What *unique* functions can computers serve in education? How can the use of computers be *integrated* into curricula and daily school activities? The first question stems from the growing impression and from research findings which indicate that computers can profoundly contribute to the educational process only under particular conditions and only when some unique attributes of theirs are capitalized upon. The second question is raised as an anti-thesis to the widespread usage of computers as a technology and curriculum that have become independent of all other school curricula and activities; a computer, it is felt, ought to be an integrated part of the ongoing life in school much like the pencil and the book. This article is devoted to these two questions.

1. Unique Attributes of Computers in Curricular Use

Computers must be seen as part of the wider category of instructional technologies. Each technology—whether books, television, pocket calculators, or microscopes, has some unique attributes which, given appropriate modes of usage, might "make a difference" in learning. However, the unique attributes of technologies ought to be integrated into some more general, multidimensional map, so that each technology and each technological use in instruction could be placed vis-à-vis that of other technologies.

Such a map would entail at least four dimensions along which one could align various technologies and point out their unique attributes. The first dimension of such a map would be *information*, that is, the particular content that a technology can present to or elicit from the learner. The second dimension concerns the *symbolic modality*, or symbol system of information presentation: word, picture, number, space, tone, and so on. There is a close link between the informational dimension and the symbol-system: certain contents are better suited to certain modes of symbolic representation and certain symbol systems are better suited to represent certain contents. As there is a strong link between technologies and symbol systems (television is better suited to deal with concrete spatial and figural Gestalts, whereas print is better suited to deal with abstract, linear, and discrete symbols), there is also a link between technology and content; television is well-suited to represent ongoing dynamic but concrete events, whereas print is better suited to represent abstract and formal knowledge.

The third dimension pertains to the kinds of *activities* a technology requires or affords: viewing, reading, measuring, testing hypotheses, reconstructing, and the like. The fourth dimension pertains to the *relations* that become possible between the student user and the technology. This dimension entails such issues as whether the technology and its use place the student at the receiving end or whether the student participates in the process of information generation; whether the communication with the student is one-sided or interactive; whether the information and activity are individually tailored, and the like.

All other instructional technologies are restricted to particular kinds of symbol systems and hence to a limited range of contents. Computers, on the other hand, are not limited to either one. They are tools that allow a large variety of contents and symbolic modes—ranging from printed word to dynamic scheme, from graph to musical notation, and from realistic picture to dance-notation. Their uniqueness lies in their informational capacity to present the learner with a whole dynamic simulated world in a capsule ("microworld"), enabling the learner to interact directly with a domain of knowledge hitherto inaccessible.

Another kind of uniqueness is the variety of alternative symbolic modes of representation that computers allow, whereby the same information can be represented in different modes. Even more importantly, computers differ from other technologies in the variety and kinds of activities that they afford—ranging from responses to questions as in drill and practice programs, to autonomous hypothesis testing in simulations; from discovery-like activities via game playing to rigorous, logical planning as in programming; and from writing and revising to categorizing and calculating. No other technology known to us allows such a wide variety of contents, symbolic modes, and learning activities.

Last, computers allow the development of partner-like interactive and individualized relations with the user which no other technology (save a human teacher) can. The most impressive distinctiveness of computers is manifested in the *combination of attributes*, as when learners are given the opportunity to interact with computerized microworlds by means of, say, a discovery-like activity based on a science simulation where information—both computer and student generated—can be represented in a variety of symbolic modes. Add such features as immediate and informative feedback, the explicit "mirroring" of students' own underlying logic, and the personally tailored guidance that is now possible, and a unique combination becomes evident.

Computers differ from most other technologies in still another sense. They are not only interactive instructional devices but also useful tools that extend in many important ways our mental capacities (see, for example, Bolter 1984). As such, they amplify learners' capacities, allowing them to carry out tasks like hypothesis generation and testing, using expert logic that no other device or method affords. Furthermore, they serve as possible models for certain kinds of thinking that learners could use to discover powerful ideas with, as well as emulate, internalize, and use as newly acquired mental tools (Papert 1980).

This raises the more general question of whether computers could serve not only as superb instructional devices but also as unique cultivators of mental skills and strategies. Scholars have often suggested that such activities as programming could, potentially, develop in students procedural logic, planning ability, clarity of thinking, and self-regulation. Unfortunately, most research to date has not succeeded in providing persuasive evidence that such effects are forthcoming (see, for instance, Pea and Kurland 1984). One possibility is that despite the uniqueness described above, no computer-afforded activity can, under normal conditions of usage, cultivate mental abilities. The computer is thus to be seen as an important *amplifier* of cognitive, communicational, and instructional functions, but not as a technology capable of affecting the functions it ampli-

fies. An alternative possibility is that the cultivation of mental abilities is possible and that computers could accomplish, in this respect, a rather unique function, provided that certain—as yet unknown—conditions are met. Much current research and thoughtful consideration are devoted to the study of such conditions (see, for example, Perkins 1985).

Given computers' diversity, it becomes evident that neither the computer itself, nor even a particular kind of software in and of itself, are likely to affect learning in any profound way. Research clearly shows that while software and activities that realize computers' unique attributes are a necessary condition, much still depends on the particular way computers come to be used. For example, learning to use word processing has not been found to affect the quality of essays written nor students' ability to write, unless accompanied by a whole writing curriculum. If computers are to accomplish unique instructional functions, let alone to cultivate abilities, they must become fully integrated into school curricula. It is to this that the article turns next.

2. The Integration of Computers into the Curriculum

Computers, as Taylor (1980) has pointed out, can serve as tutors, tutees, and as tools. Until recently most usages of computers in the schools were relatively limited to their functions as tutors in computer-assisted instruction (CAI). They served also, although to a lesser extent, as tutees, as when students learned to program in mainly the languages of BASIC or LOGO. Serving in these capacities, computers were treated as separate and independent tutors and tutees, segregated from all other school activities. Such modes of computer use have led to disappointments as no profound changes in either students' achievements or in curricular design and teaching have been witnessed. Presently, there is a growing desire to capitalize on computers' unique attributes and to fully integrate them into regular learning activities in the three capacities described by Taylor. The difference now is that these three capacities become part and parcel of various curricula.

What is the nature of this integration and how is it accomplished? The integration of computers into a curriculum means that these two components affect each other reciprocally. The designers of a curriculum take into consideration computers' unique possibilities, whereas the use of computers comes to serve the curriculum rather than its own purposes. More specifically, this reciprocal relationship takes place on at least three levels: the level of goals and objectives, the level of pedagogical thought, and the level of instructional contents and activities.

Concerning the first level, there is a change in the goals towards which computers come to be used. While in the initial days of computer use activities such as programming were self-serving, increasingly more computer activities are now designed to serve curricular goals. For example, LOGO is now often taught as part of a mathematics curriculum and comes to serve the attainment of that curriculum's goals. Similarly, curricula are now designed taking into consideration that computers are not just new means to old goals, but can serve rather novel ones as well. Perhaps the best manifestation of integration on this level is in the design of new curricula which were impossible in the past and for which the computer is best suited, for example, ecological programs that afford, for the first time, first-hand experience in the manipulation of complex and interrelated ecological variables. The world of ecology can now be symbolically recreated in all its complexity, enabling the design of a suitable curriculum.

Such changes need to be accompanied by a change in pedagogical thought manifested by a growing acceptance of the computer as a technology that allows more independent exploration, more personally tailored activities, more team work, and significantly less didactic instruction (see, for example, Wilkinson 1983). This implies a gradual change in the perception of the teacher's role—from information delivery to learning management, and from an authoritative source of information to a guide of self-propelled exploration. Similar changes take place with respect to the computer; it is gradually perceived as a tool to be placed in the hands of active students rather than as a tutor that instructs a relatively passive student-responder.

Reciprocal changes of goals and of educational thought are reflected in instructional contents and activities, the level at which the integration of computers and curricula is actually realized. Here, the integration appears as the incorporation of computer microworlds into the curriculum: the student encounters new contents in ways that simulate the world outside (e.g., exploratory simulations of outer space). The integration is also reflected in the introduction of novel, often unique kinds of student activities with computer tools such as intelligent electronic spread-sheets that allow new modes of interaction with academic materials. Rather than have a drill-and-practice program accompany a curriculum as an independent add-on, we begin to see exciting instructional games, intelligent tools, and problem-solving programs that are central parts of a curriculum. The result of this integration is that computers become used all the time, by all students, for a variety of purposes, and in a variety of capacities. Computers, much like microscopes in the study of biology, affect what is taught and how.

It ought to be emphasized that the role of computers in curriculum, based on the realization of their unique attributes, is still in its infancy. Organizational, psychological, philosophical, and financial hurdles are still to be overcome. Moreover, wholesale and hasty integration of computers into well designed and tried curricula may in some cases be more harmful than helpful. Not everything possible is necessarily also desirable. The research and the accumulation of experiences may ultimately show us how best to reap the potential advantages of computers in education.

Bibliography

Bolter J D 1984 *Turing's Man: Western Culture in the Computer Age*. University of North Carolina, Chapel Hill, North Carolina

Papert S 1980 *Mindstorms: Children, Computers and Powerful Ideas*. Basic Books, New York

Pea R D, Kurland D M 1984 On the cognitive effects of learning computer programming. *New Ideas in Psychology* 2: 137–68

Perkins D N 1985 The fingertip effect: How information-processing technology shapes thinking. *Educ. Res.* 14(7): 11–17

Taylor R P (ed.) 1980 *The Computer in the School: Tutor, Tool, Tutee*. Teachers College, New York

Wilkinson C A (ed.) 1983 *Classroom Computers and Cognitive Science*. Academic Press, New York

Computer Software for Curriculum

M. L. Kamil

Instructional computer systems consist of hardware—the physical aspects of a computer—and software—the sets of instructions that tell the machine what to do. A given computer can act in any number of different manners, depending on the software. Consequently, software is viewed as the most important and critical element of computer-assisted instruction (CAI). However, hardware limitations can often be reflected in software implementations. In the last decade, microcomputers have become commonplace, decreasing reliance on large mainframe computers. The proliferation of computer resources has made it possible for more individuals to gain access to computers for more different purposes than ever before. Reductions in cost have made the use of computers more attractive as an instructional alternative. Niemiec et al. (1986) suggest that CAI may be an extremely cost-effective instructional intervention.

However, smaller microcomputers have limitations that can be problematic for instructional uses. They cannot process as quickly as mainframe computers, often making for long delays between elements in an instructional sequence. They cannot access as much memory directly. This often places limitations on the complexity of software that can be used. A similar limitation occurs with storage media. Diskettes limit the size of programs that can be stored on them. This can limit the size of programs (or the number) that can be run at any given time. Advances in storage technology seem to be mitigating most of these problems. CD-ROM devices can store up to one thousand times the data on a floppy diskette and have it all accessible to the computer.

Although they have disadvantages, microcomputers do have the advantage of being independent from each other so that users are not dependent on a single machine. Microcomputers can easily be linked with each other to communicate information or share programs. They can also be more readily programmed, making local production of instructional software a viable alternative to commercial materials.

In using computers for instruction, a recurrent problem is that computers generally do not have the capabilities of teachers; however, recent technological advances may overcome some of these difficulties. For example, while computers are not, at present, adaptable to unique student responses, artificial intelligence concepts may enable future software to respond to students more like a teacher would (Wilson and Bates 1981).

For many instructional applications (beginning reading instruction, for example), speech is an important component. Computer speech can be generated by synthesizers or from digital representations stored with the software. Synthesized speech is preferred to digital speech because of the extensive storage requirements of digital representation. While present-day computers can generate rudimentary speech synthesis, the general quality often leaves much to be desired. Speech recognition is also available in rudimentary forms for restricted vocabularies; it has yet to find extended applications in instruction.

1. Software Across the Curriculum

Six types of software for instructions can be distinguished by their use in the curriculum:

(a) software for management of instruction;

(b) software for delivery of instruction;

(c) computer literacy software;

(d) authoring languages;

(e) programming languages;

(f) applications programs to be used in instruction.

1.1 Software for Managing Instruction

Software designed for management of instruction is used for tracking student performance, planning individualized student lessons, assigning grades, and generating assessment instruments. The generic term given to this use of computer software is computer-managed instruction (CMI). Not all software is designed to accomplish all of the tasks. CMI can be either internal to instructional software or designed to be used with

instructional materials of conventional format. In addition, software for CMI is classified as either program-dependent or program-independent. That is, the software is either designed to manage a specific set of materials or it can be tailored to manage any materials.

1.2 Instructional Software

Several types of computer software for delivering instruction can be distinguished as follows:

(a) *Drill and practice.* This software presents repetitive tasks for practice. There is usually little or no explanatory instruction, even though there is reinforcement and/or at least minimal corrective feedback. Most often the learning units are narrowly defined skills. Game formats are often used in this type of software to take advantage of motivational aspects of competition to promote learning.

(b) *Tutorial CAI.* This is software that attempts to explain concepts as well as convey information. Software in this category attempts to "teach" rather than simply allow practice. Good software will attempt to "branch," or alter instructions, dependent on the user's performance. Software that does not "branch" is often referred to as linear CAI since all learners receive the same sequence of instruction. Branching can be in the form of expanded explanations, more detailed background knowledge instruction, or remedial or advance instruction on any concept part of a lesson. The branching feature of CAI is its most apparent advantage—the ability to create individualized instruction for any user, instantaneously, dependent on performance.

(c) *Simulations.* Simulations software create environments that allow students to apply the results of learning in a nearly realistic situation. High-quality simulations provide opportunities for integration of prior instruction. They allow students to manipulate variables and observe the results. Computer simulations can present students with "control" over situations that could not be created in any other manner.

1.3 Computer Literacy Software

Computer literacy software is a special type of CAI in which the main goal is to acquaint students with uses and structure of computers. Computer literacy does not have to be taught by CAI. It is often accomplished by conventional technology. A major debate is whether computer literacy software should teach students about technical skills like programming, or whether it should focus on using the computer for applications like word processing. Some computer literacy efforts (e.g. Johnson et al. 1980) have focused on programming and knowledge of machine architecture as an integral component. More recent computer literacy efforts stress the need to use computers as tools to accomplish other tasks, minimizing the need to know about programming, and so forth. As computers become more "user friendly" there is less need for most computer users to be sophisticated programmers.

1.4 Authoring Languages

Authoring languages are computer languages designed specifically to allow nonsophisticated computer users to produce high quality computer-assisted instructional lessons. They are important in that CAI materials can be designed by content experts who have only minimal working knowledge of computers. Most of the work of arranging the content into acceptable formats for computer presentation is accomplished by the authoring language itself. The most common of these languages for microcomputers is PILOT. For mainframe computers using the PLATO system, an authoring language called TUTOR is used.

1.5 Programming Languages

Students who learn to program must be instructed in one of a large number of computer languages. Some of the more common languages are LOGO, BASIC, PASCAL, and FORTRAN. There is currently a debate over the value of learning programming. Papert (1980) has claimed that the ability to program computers can produce in children a sense of mastery over powerful technology. Linn (1985) suggests that outcomes of actual programming instruction do not often reach those sort of goals. However she does suggest that programming may have beneficial results for problem-solving behaviors.

1.6 Applications Programs

Three sorts of common applications software are used as tools in instruction: *word processing software, database software,* and *spreadsheet software.* Each of these types of software has the potential to produce qualitatively different experiences for users in a computer environment. Word processing seems to produce a qualitatively different editing experience: revising and editing can be done without effort spent in copying text; students also are encouraged to consider the text as a changeable entity until a printed copy is produced.

Databases offer efficient information organization, retrieval and use: computer searches through databases are faster and more extensive than any other form of search; appropriate use of databases can encourage students to view information in different ways from conventional information. Spreadsheets can be used in applications where variables need to be modeled and changed, and hypothetical results examined. While spreadsheets are often thought of as a tool of accountants or financial planners, science and mathematics instruction can make extensive use of them.

Applications programs do not represent software that is used for direct instruction (like CAI). These programs can be incorporated into the curriculum, where appropriate, to produce learning that is different, and presumably better, than that produced by conventional methods.

2. Research on the Effectiveness of Computer-based Instruction

One important limitation to the effectiveness of computer-based instruction is that there is usually a difference between reading from a computer terminal and reading from printed copy (Gould and Grischkowsky 1984, Haas and Hayes 1985a, Haas and Hayes 1985b). If amount of time for reading is held constant, comprehension is usually poorer when material is read at a computer terminal, than when it is read from hard copy. If comprehension is the criterion, reading at a computer display is slower than from hard copy, often by as much as 25 percent. These effects can be largely mitigated by improvements in the resolution of the computer display and by increasing the amount of information on the screen at a given time.

Research over the last two decades has demonstrated that at least some forms of instruction can be delivered by computer. Vinsonhaler and Bass (1972) reported an advantage of 0.1 to 0.4 school years for students who were given computer drill and practice instruction. Edwards et al. (1975) showed similar effects for instruction that went beyond drill and practice. Jamison et al. (1974) suggested that even when there were no differences in achievement, CAI did produce some savings of time. They also found that CAI yielded the most improvement when used in small amounts with slower students.

A recent meta-analysis of 48 studies of computer instruction in elementary schools (Niemiec and Walberg 1985) revealed that the effect size for drill and practice was 0.47 while it was only 0.34 for tutorial CAI and only 0.12 for problem-solving instruction. In general, the improvement was about one-third of a standard deviation, suggesting that a student at the 50th percentile could move to approximately the 65th percentile by being placed in computer-assisted instruction. There were variations in the effect sizes, with the lowest for reading comprehension (0.11) and the highest for mathematics problem solving (0.61). One important finding was that CMI was relatively ineffective, having an effect size of only 0.03. This finding is interesting in that CMI is one of the more common uses of computers in instruction. Instruction delivered by microcomputer showed an extremely large effect (1.26) compared with only a moderate effect for mainframe computers (0.33). Although this is based on only a few studies, it may be indicative of future potential successes for CAI.

A final set of data on the effectiveness of CAI relates to the effects that student control of lessons has on learning. Students are often required to determine how long lessons will last, whether the content will be hard or easy and how many problems or questions they will try. This has often been cited as a major advantage of CAI. It has been shown that there is little relation between performance on tests and self-assessed learning of CAI lesson content (Garhart and Hanafin 1986). Carrier (1984) and Tennyson (1980) have pointed out the disadvantages of CAI when there are too many options for students. This can be alleviated with potentially beneficial effects by restricting student options in certain situations (Reinking 1986).

Bibliography

Carrier C 1984 Do learners make good choices? *Instr. Innovator* 29: 15–17

Edwards J, Norton S, Taylor S, Weiss M, Dusseldorp R 1975 How effective is CAI? A review of the research. *Educ. Leadership* 33: 147–53

Garhart C, Hanafin M 1986 The accuracy of cognitive monitoring during computer-based instruction. *J. Comp. Based Instruction* 13: 88–95

Gould J D, Grischkowsky N 1984 Doing the same work with hard copy and with cathode-ray tube (CRT) computer terminals. *Hum. Factors* 26: 323–37

Haas C, Hayes J 1985a *Effects of Text Display Variables on Reading Tasks: Computer Screen vs. Hard Copy*, CDC Technical Report No. 3. Carnegie-Mellon University, Communications Design Center, Pittsburgh, Pennsylvania

Haas C, Hayes J 1985b *Reading on the Computer: A Comparison of Standard and Advanced Computer Display and Hard Copy*, CDC Technical Report No. 7. Carnegie-Mellon University, Communications Design Center, Pittsburgh, Pennsylvania

Jamison D, Suppes P, Wells S 1974 The effectiveness of alternative instructional media: A survey. *Rev. Educ. Res.* 44: 1–67

Johnson D, Anderson R, Hansen T, Klassen D 1980 Computer literacy—what is it? *Math. Teacher* 73: 91–96

Linn M C 1985 The cognitive consequences of programming instruction in classrooms. *Educ. Res.* 14 (5): 14–29

Niemiec R P, Walberg H 1985 Computers and achievement in the elementary schools. *J. Educ. Comput. Res.* 1 (14): 435–40

Niemiec R P, Blackwell M, Walberg H J 1986 CAI can be doubly effective. *Phi Delta Kappan* 67 (10): 750–51

Papert S 1980 *Mindstorms: Children, Computers and Powerful Ideas*. Basic Books, New York

Reinking D 1986 Six advantages of computer-mediated text. *Read. Instruct. J.* 29: 8–16

Tennyson R D 1980 Instructional control strategies and content structure as design variables in concept acquisition using computer-based instruction. *J. Educ. Psychol.* 72: 525–32

Vinsonhaler J F, Bass R K 1972 A summary of ten major studies on CAI drill and practice. *Educ. Technol.* 12: 29–32

Wilson K, Bates M 1981 Artificial intelligence in computer-based language instruction. *Volta Rev.* 83: 336–49

Television: Classroom Use

S. Rockman and R. Burke

This article deals mainly with the systematic use of instructional television programs in elementary and secondary classrooms. Other uses are treated elsewhere. A historical introduction leads to a discussion of roles for classroom television and hence to patterns of use. The presentation of some specific examples is then followed by a brief concluding section.

1. Introduction

Many countries that adopted classroom television in the late 1950s and early 1960s had already had some experience with classroom radio. Educators had seen the benefits of using electronic mass media to bring stimulating materials from the world at large into the classroom. Television broadcasters, like their radio predecessors, saw school programming as a good opportunity to render an important and necessary public service. Yet what seemed to be a mutually satisfactory relationship was in many instances an uneasy alliance. Educators were concerned mainly with pedagogical values, whereas broadcasters, focusing on the medium, were concerned mainly with entertainment and audience appeal.

The pattern of development was markedly different in North America and Europe. North American initiatives were primarily local and usually ambitious. Encouraged by the extravagant claims of proponents of new media, school administrators looked on television as a means of improving curricula, of upgrading teachers, and of bringing about significant changes in educational practice. Teachers, on the other hand, often looked on classroom television as an imposition from above and as a threat to their long-cherished sense of autonomy. They resented the implication that their teaching was somehow deficient, and they found repugnant such terms as "follow-up teacher" or "receiving teacher." They further resented the inflexible broadcasting schedules, which made little allowance for individual needs.

Many teachers, along with administrators, were appalled by the quality of most of the early programs. Television had been promoted as a "window on the world," a "magic box," and so forth, but in fact it offered too many programs of "talking heads"—teachers standing in front of chalkboards, giving conventional lectures in a conventionally didactic manner.

By the late 1960s, however, educators and broadcasters started moving in more productive directions. Each group made greater efforts to understand the other's point of view, with the result that classroom television became, often, a product of cooperation and integration, built from creative tension rather than from antagonism and mistrust.

The quality problem was less marked in Europe, where production was in the hands of national broadcasting agencies. But the development of classroom television was nevertheless quite slow. There was little pressure on teachers to use the television programs available; and many education authorities were apprehensive of the cost of progressively equipping all their schools. Although a minority of teachers were enthusiastic from the outset, many were unwilling to adapt their teaching to accommodate the new medium. They felt unsure of themselves in handling it, and scheduling was a major source of difficulty in most secondary schools.

The producers, meanwhile, had been experimenting with pilot schemes and were learning what television could most usefully and effectively provide for the classroom. In the United Kingdom, where the term used was always educational rather than instructional broadcasting, the first television programs were almost exclusively directed to the enrichment both of children's experiences and of their teachers' resources. In the secondary schools, which were their first target, both the British Broadcasting Corporation (BBC) and the independent television companies endeavored by means of a varied output in such subjects as geography, science, current affairs, and drama to add a dimension of their own to the teacher's work. In spite of the difficulties of timetabling and the priority generally given by teachers to their own basic courses, television often being referred to as a frill, these enrichment programs acquired a faithful and appreciative clientele sometimes of considerable size. Talking heads were an infrequent source of complaint, and programs were valued for the skilful application of studio techniques, a wide ranging use of film, and a generally high standard of performance.

In the primary schools the flexibility of the curriculum made it easier for teachers to adopt television as a stimulus to their work and as a springboard for interesting new projects. The visual element soon became immensely popular, making conspicuous contributions over a wide field of general knowledge, in music and in remedial work. Eventually some series attracted audiences in 70 or even 80 percent of junior and infant schools.

In contrast to developed countries, developing countries have seen the emergence of different problems as they have attempted to use television in classrooms. Since the early 1970s, developing countries have devoted enormous resources to education. Because of the expense of developing a traditional Western school system, administrators turned to technology in an effort to do more with fewer teachers and at the same time to take advantage of the economies of scale associated with broadcasting.

Although more planning has been done in recent years, at first many groups rushed in too quickly. Weaknesses in curriculum and instructional planning became widely evident in short order. Plans to provide universal quality education through television in a few years were unrealistic, and the several attempts to do so were unsuccessful. What took a century in Europe and North America could not be done in a year or two.

The belief that television would reduce educational costs was also mistaken. Television still required the presence of a teacher for its most advantageous use. It was an addition to the system and often improved neither the quality nor the quantity of classroom instruction.

Problems similar to those in developed nations also emerged. The teachers who had training, especially at the high-school level, found television programs to be inconsistent with their teaching values and styles. Administrative mandates were not sufficient justifications for the use of television; poorly developed curricula led to teachers' rejection of materials. Television was superimposed on the educational system without respect for the nature of the system.

Television should not be blamed for the failures. A medium that promised everything—a solution to all of education's problems, a cure for an ailing society, economical and political benefits—was not capable of living up to expectations. It is less productive to blame the medium than to change the expectations.

Classroom television can be highly beneficial to education and society in nations with widely diverse political, economic, and educational systems. But to succeed, television must do only what it does best.

2. Roles

Educators who have chosen to adopt classroom television have usually done so for one or more of the following reasons:

2.1 Improvement of Quality

Ideally, the television programs represent the best educational efforts of curriculum specialists, program designers, audiovisual artists, and broadcasting specialists; the programs incorporate the best, most up-to-date thinking in the field; and the content is presented in an attractive and stimulating format.

2.2 Television as a Catalyst

Classroom television can also stimulate educators to reconsider curricular options, to evaluate methods of pedagogy now in practice, and to see new relationships among discrete curricular areas. It provides a source of ideas for teachers and can catalyze their development of more varied, more motivating, and more contemporary practices. Classroom television has helped to facilitate the rapid dissemination of new curricular ideas, many of which remain long after their parent projects or programs have been abandoned.

2.3 Television as a Means of Extending Children's Experience

Television in the classroom is truly what UNESCO has often called it: "a window on the world." The programs allow students to transcend the boundaries of space and time, and to see society in new and diverse ways.

The rural child sees life in the city, and the urban child sees life in the country; various patterns of consumption and economic structure, alternative religious forms, cultural patterns, and sexual role models become available.

2.4 Television as a Means of Introducing Affective Education

Television has been instrumental in introducing affective education into elementary classrooms. Television programs that provide shared, relatively universal experiences have given teachers and students the opportunity to examine their feelings about themselves and their environment. Similar opportunities arise in secondary social studies and humanities. Developing a national identity is an important goal of television in newly independent countries; and television can also be used to encourage and strengthen diverse cultural and religious traditions.

2.5 Television as a Means of Equalizing Educational Opportunity

Educational inequality is a persistent problem in most countries, from both economic and sociocultural viewpoints. A broadcast signal, however, is not limited to wealthy school districts or to new schools. For young children, in particular, the impact of programs developing basic skills has been encouraging, and similar programs for older students are now being created.

Presenting black faces in all-white schools and white faces in all-black schools provides useful role models of all races to facilitate interracial acceptance and understanding. But what school television can do best in equalizing educational opportunity is to provide instructional presentations so universal that they become specific to every viewer and are effective regardless of sex, race, ethnic background, or economic condition.

2.6 Television as a Means of Improving Efficiency and Productivity

Productivity in education means significantly more than the ability of fewer teachers to teach more students. It means better preparing students to be effective and fulfilled members of the community at large. When school television adds to the number of possible approaches to instruction, stimulates improved class interactions, initiates and reinforces cognitive learning, or motivates better classroom behavior, it is providing better, more efficient education.

To increase productivity requires finding the right mixture of school television and classroom teaching. By using school television economically—that is, by examining the variety of available utilization and programming options and by choosing wisely—educators can effect improvements in the patterns and results of instruction with minimal increases in cost. Television is not seeking to replace teachers, only to assist them in reaching their desired goals.

2.7 Television-based Instructional Systems

In several countries, the main vehicle for achieving some of these goals has been a television-based instructional system. Such systems are distinguished not by their format or purpose but by their mode of development. The program designers are committed to a method of development that incorporates a student needs assessment (see *Needs Assessment Studies*), a lesson design, formative evaluation, product revision, summative evaluation (see *Formative and Summative Evaluation*), and the revision of objectives and strategies. Their product may include not only television programs but also any printed supplementary materials, such as teacher's guides or student workbooks, designed to complement the curriculum directly. The programs are viewed in the classroom on a regular, long-term basis, and should then result either in a measurable difference between the students who receive instruction by television and those who do not, or in some attributable change over time in learning gain, attitude, or behavior. Otherwise further revision is needed.

3. Patterns of Use

Classroom television must be seen as more than a television program. Complex interactions between the program, people, and their environment all contribute to instruction. To describe the process, it is perhaps easiest to begin with utilization.

3.1 Viewing Conditions

In some cases, the unit of instruction is the television program alone. Individual viewers learn by themselves. But in most cases, the instructional unit is the television lesson. A teacher spends a few minutes preparing the class, with a series of questions for discussion or independent thought, or a review of previously taught concepts, vocabulary words, or other advance organizers. Then the class attends to the television set and views the program with the teacher. Teachers viewing prerecorded tapes on classroom playback equipment are able to stop and start the tapes, illustrating and reinforcing teaching points throughout the viewing period.

After the viewing, teachers use a variety of techniques—structured discussions, the teaching of related content, written exercises and tests—to continue the lesson. Any activity that reinforces and extends the content will be valuable to students. Sometimes homework, testing, or a long-term project is part of the lesson.

The classroom environment influences the use and the effectiveness of school television. The television receiver must be visible to all students and in good working order; the conditions for transmission and reception or playback must provide a usable signal. The time of day may also be important. Television is a change of pace in a lecture-and-workbook classroom; it may be especially welcome in the late morning before lunch, just after lunch, or in the late afternoon.

Accumulated research evidence suggests that the degree to which the television program becomes part of the traditional classroom process and the degree to which it is treated like other instructional materials, can significantly effect learning. Conversely, the degree to which teachers diminish the perceived value of the program—for example, by leaving the room when it is on or by ignoring its content after viewing—will determine how credible students find the program.

To use classroom television successfully, one must take into account the nature of the interacting variables: the personal characteristics of teachers and students, the interpersonal relationships within the school and the class, the program itself as designed and produced, and the environmental conditions under which it is viewed.

3.2 Teacher

Teachers vary greatly in their ability (and willingness) to develop comprehensive lessons for a television program; often they depend on a teacher's guide for the program. Often they take cues from their students and form opinions about the program based on students' reactions to it; a program that holds the attention of the students may be seen as successsful even if its content is weak.

Teachers vary also in their attitudes towards television and other technologies in the classroom. If television is presented to them as a means of replacing them or reducing their autonomy, they will use it with great reluctance. But if television lessons are designed to help meet the learning goals of the classroom, teachers will be quick to adopt and use them. The attitude of administrators also greatly affects the willingness of teachers to use television and the degree of emphasis they place on it. The support system for teachers—administrative, technical, student, and parent attitudes—also contributes to successful school television utilization.

Students take cues from their teachers and treat television as they do. But even if the students bring a positive attitude to the viewing, the program may change their attitude. The program must be at the appropiate developmental level, must treat the content and the viewer with intelligence, and must appeal to the viewer.

Attention to the television program is a serious concern. While distractions to the viewer at home are common and inconsequential, attention to the program at school is a neccessary, though insufficient, condition for learning. Moreover, inattention by a few students can easily escalate if they do something that distracts the teacher and other students.

3.3 Instructional Design

Research into the nature of viewing and of the viewing audience has led to some understanding of how tele-

vision works best. The attributes of television programs that contribute to their appeal, salience, interest, and educational value must be insured in the design and production of the programs. The technical resources on command include music, movement, sequencing, format, and character appeal. To make the most of these, researchers may often cooperate with designers and producers to create successful programs.

The instructional design of school television programs must also take viewing conditions into account. If the program is to require no follow-up from the teacher, it should include factors that promote immediate student learning, for example, advance organizers, repetition, and so on. However, if the teacher is to be an integral part of the lesson, the role of the program can be:

(a) to introduce the content for the teacher to elaborate later and to drill the students on;

(b) to provide background material for a lesson the teacher will deliver;

(c) to reinforce and review ideas already covered in class;

(d) to provide salient illustrations that will stimulate class discussion and discovery.

These pedagogical functions should be taken into account in the design and production of school television programs.

4. Examples

4.1 United States: ThinkAbout

One well-documented classroom television project is the "ThinkAbout" series developed by a consortium of American states and Canadian provinces. The state and provincial education and television agencies received unlimited and unrestricted use of the materials for seven or more years in return for their financial and intellectual support. This series was initiated, developed, and produced over a six-year period by the Agency for Instructional Television and consists of sixty 15-minute programs for students 10 to 12 years of age.

The project's initial focus was presenting various general problem-solving skills in realistic settings as a means of improving the way students learned and studied. Over the course of the project's development period, the focus shifted towards the reinforcement of already-taught skills in language arts, social studies, and mathematics. The programs illustrated the application of these subject matter skills in out-of-school situations. The general problem-solving theme remained in many of the programs but with less emphasis than originally planned. The curriculum was developed in conjunction with teachers and subject matter specialists and extensively verified with classroom teachers.

The design of the programs moved along this path as a result of the influence of the consortium of states and provinces funding the project. The representatives of these funding agencies were, for the most part, middle level administrators of their state or provincial education or television agency who met regularly during the development and production phases to review programs and reflect on the project's activities. The problem-solving curriculum appeared to them as a drastic departure from the traditional emphasis on subject matter skills and as possibly too advanced for teachers to easily adapt and use in the classroom. The political pressure from the funders resulted in a modification of the curriculum, in a change meant to make the instructional materials more accessible to and usable by fifth- and sixth-grade teachers.

The television programs themselves are short, realistic dramas that set up a plausible problem for students but end before the problem has been resolved. This approach gains the attention of students by the appeal of the "real-life" drama, and motivates them to finish solving the problem in the classroom. Extensive formative evaluation helped instructional designers identify appealing dramatic segments and salient teaching points. Programs were revised during production based on the feedback provided by representative teachers and classrooms.

The pattern of classroom use is as follows: the teachers focus students' attention on the topic or theme of the program and often relate the theme to ongoing classwork in a specific curriculum. The class and the teacher then view the program together. Following the viewing the teacher directs a discussion of the program, its theme, and the application of ideas presented in the program to activities in school and out. The discussion often takes a spiraling route, at first a recapitulation of the events in the program to be sure everyone understands what has been seen, followed by a generation of alternative hypotheses or solutions to the problem. This is followed, in turn, by relating the problem and its theme to classwork currently underway. Seatwork assignments and long-term class activities are included in the teacher guide but do not seem to be used frequently.

In use, many teachers find 60 programs to be more than they can comfortably fit into their schedule, especially since they commonly use more than one television series. Thus, alternative utilization patterns have emerged. Rather than using the series at a two-per-week rate over the course of a school year, some teachers, with the cooperation of their broadcasting agencies or with access to videocassette recorders, use the first 30 programs for the fifth grade and the second 30 for the sixth grade. A more common pattern, especially in areas where the use of videocassette machines is the norm, is the selection and viewing of individual programs or groups of programs on a common theme when convenient. In this manner the correlation of the programs with course material is more precise and, because of the foresight and planning required, the television program is very likely to be well-integrated into the lesson.

Evidence from research associated with the "ThinkAbout" project shows very modest changes in problem-solving abilities, a result due to several factors. First, measurement of problem-solving skills is an emerging and exploratory effort with few valid and reliable measures; second, the research design desired by the consortium militated against finding strong experimental-control group differences; and third, the modification of the curriculum placed less emphasis on problem-solving skills, which remained the overall goal of the series. Nevertheless, research evidence indicates the widespread appeal and use of the material. The modified curriculum in problem solving—an organized curriculum heretofore not present in more than a handful of classrooms—was adopted and used successfully by a wide variety of teachers who differed greatly in background, teaching style, and subject matter emphasis. The series continues to be in wide use as of its fourth year.

4.2 Canada: Eureka!

Television Ontario (TVO) has taken a different approach to the development and use of a school television series. TVO is a provincial organization responsible for many aspects of intraprovince communications including elementary and secondary classroom television. In contrast to the curriculum development efforts of the Agency for Instructional Television (AIT), which had to find common agreement across state, provincial, and national borders, TVO starts with a centrally adopted curriculum statement and a relatively homogenous population.

To help define educational needs that can best be served by television, discipline-specific advisory committees were formed. These committees periodically commission needs ascertainment surveys of the membership of professional organizations and other teachers of a subject. These surveys explore what is taught (both core and optional topics within the established curriculum) and what is difficult to teach (especially among the core topics). In exploring the themes that seemed especially difficult to teach, survey results often point to the lack of curriculum support materials for those topics.

The discipline advisory committee and TVO staff review the material that is perceived as difficult to teach and partition out those concepts that television would find difficult to do (or that a teacher could do better), and those concepts that are undergoing a change in curricular emphasis and should not be tackled at present. The remaining concepts become a ranked list of priorities.

Two or three practicing teachers who teach the subject well work with a TVO producer and writer to develop program materials that can engage teachers and students, remediate the curriculum deficiency, and match the established provincial curriculum.

The "Eureka!" series was developed to meet the needs of seventh- and eighth-grade science teachers, usually science generalists, who were having difficulty teaching certain physics topics. The high priority curriculum needs identified by the needs ascertainment survey were all central to the students' understanding of physics and could be directly taught as independent single concepts. The content for short models developed by the TVO team was then validated by university faculty and made into single-concept, 5-minute units in full cell-animation. Within this 5-minute unit there were several potential stopping points built in, so that a teacher could have discussion with the class on one aspect of the content, clarify the material, and raise issues for continued focus before continuing the program. This design practically demands the use of videocassettes and about 90–95 percent of the use is with the teacher-controlled tape unit. This design also permits the teacher to use the single concept program, follow it with an experiment or book work exercise, and then the class (or individuals within the class) can view the program again.

While the material is designed for in-school use, its highly appealing animation format makes it useful in other contexts. TVO presently uses the programs as fillers between science programs during the evening broadcasts. The material is widely used and evaluation data are currently being collected to explore its impact.

4.3 United States: Freestyle

The "Freestyle" series is a well-documented project initiated from a strong federal perspective. These 13 half-hour-long programs were designed to aid children's career development and reduce restrictions on career selection based on sex and social stereotyping. These programs are "prosocial" in their goals and are directed more towards attitude change than towards classroom-related knowledge or behavior. Nevertheless, these materials found their widest use and greatest impact in the classroom.

This television project was conceived as a major federal initiative to meet broad social goals and its creation was undertaken by a consortium of independent television education, university, and research organizations. Much background research and formative evaluation led to the selection of themes included in the project's curriculum. The mix of educators and "Hollywood" production personnel led initially to great confusion over the amount of instructional content and the degree to which it would be emphasized. A strong executive producer was able to get the production process under control, striking a balance between education and entertainment, with a tilt toward the latter.

The programs were designed with a strong dramatic format. The programs were structured to balance the highly entertaining material with the social modeling needed to meet educational goals. While initially scripted as half-hour programs, the design called for a dramatic high-point about half-way through the program. In this format, a single program could be divided in two in order to fit classroom time periods more easily. Thus, a half-hour program useful in the broadcast schedule for at-home viewing, could be seen in two parts within the same week in a classroom.

As the project was being developed, the influence of the funders and the conflicting demands placed on the producer led to a modification of the project's goals. Rather than give equal focus to racial and gender stereotyping, the emphasis was placed on sexual bias and stereotyping. It was thought that a single major issue could be more easily handled through the format selected.

During its first year of availability, a major study of the series impact was conducted on its use at home and in school. Using a best-case model in the schools, the researchers noted impressive changes in attitudes towards nontraditional sex-role behavior. This best-case model studies the programs under ideal rather than normal conditions of use. Little flexibility is permitted in the manner and amount of viewing and postviewing activities. Teachers used a warm-up activity to introduce the viewing of the lesson, followed the class viewing with extensive discussion, and used prepared printed materials for short- and long-term follow up.

The impact of the series was reduced under at-home conditions and when the emphasis in classrooms was reduced. The setting in which the programs were used and the importance attributed to the instructional nature of the programs seem to have greatly influenced the impact of the series.

The series was widely broadcast to homes and schools during its first year, but its availability diminished rapidly over the next two. It is no longer available since, under the commercially based system of production, the rights to the material were obtained only for three years.

4.4 United Kingdom: "Scene"

For the 15-year-old school student in the United Kingdom there are some 15 to 20 broadcasts available in any week of the school year. Over half of these will be concerned with the main curricular subjects—mathematics, the sciences, English, history, geography, modern languages. The remainder cover such areas as career guidance, the arts, and social studies. In the latter class the most popular and successful is "Scene," a weekly transmission of documentary or dramatized programs for teenagers, providing material for discussion, investigation, and written work.

The introduction and early development of this series is described in some detail by Kenneth Fawdry (1974) who was Head of the British Broadcasting Corporation (BBC) Schools Television at that time, and an account by the producer, Ronald Smedley, has also been published (Marland 1972). Some of the broadcasts are on hotly controversial topics, and several were specially commissioned scripts from well-known contemporary playwrights. Most are presented from the teenager's angle, with a special thought for the nonintellectual student who is impatient to leave school at 16.

The two descriptions which follow cannot represent the diversity of themes encompassed by "Scene," but they can give some indication of the producer's approach to the audience and of the reactions at the viewing end.

"The Last Bus" tells in dramatized form how a group of high-spirited, irresponsible teenage boys board the last bus home, pick a quarrel with the bus conductor, beat him up and, as an afterthought, steal his purse. There were a few fellow passengers and, though mildly protesting, none of them came to the victim's aid. The driver, a West Indian, froze to his seat, fearing the consequences to himself and to his family's precarious existence if he should intervene and himself be mugged in consequence.

A BBC schools' liaison officer reported, after watching the broadcast with a large class of 45 adolescents: "I am convinced they really lived through the whole incident: they had been caught up in those feelings of devilment, arrogance and hatred that presumably account for many acts of teenage aggression."

Then the scene abruptly changed. The presenter of the program turned investigator and cross-examined each of the passengers as they made excuses for their inaction. Finally the bus conductor himself showed more magnanimity than the youths deserved, saying that he understood these pranks that got out of hand; he had helped in youth clubs etc.

Not all the viewing classes appear to have understood this inquisitorial ploy; but, by the crude measuring rod of excited comments and questions afterwards, the program was a spectacular success. Another visiting BBC officer wrote: "This . . . arresting, provocative but simple story line is a certain way of getting through to this kind of child, who has little reading ability, is bored with traditional teaching . . . . It may be the nearest they will get to any depth of thought on current social issues."

The following week's broadcast, "The Sentence of the Court," told what happened to the boys and showed the ringleader, very much deflated, in a Borstal prison, while a probation officer and a Borstal governor were interviewed about their work and spoke frankly about the difficulties and shortcomings of the system of punishment and rehabilitation of which they were a part. This well-devised program did not have the impact of "The Last Bus," but enabled the thoughtful viewer to ponder further the problems of teenage violence and its consequences.

The second recent broadcast which also made a considerable impression, "James is our Brother," is a study of a mentally handicapped boy. The program starts with his first unassisted journey home from school—catching the right bus, paying his fare, changing buses, getting off at the right stop—a landmark of achievement in James' struggle to cope with the outside world. Then his brothers and sisters describe life at home with James, and through copious film inserts he is seen gradually surmounting his difficulties, establishing a modus vivendi among his peers, and finally entering for the Olym-

pics for the Disabled and receiving a bronze medal from the Duke of Edinburgh. By now he is articulate enough to speak for himself and describes his conquest of the problems of everyday life ("They don't take the mickey any more; they don't laugh"), and he proudly shows the press photograph of himself with the Duke.

The audience reaction may be judged from a selection of the postcard reports sent by viewing teachers to the producer of the series:

Very good because it portrays life from the point of view of the mentally handicapped person, particularly the last conversation with James. They greatly admired the interviewer's sympathetic handling of James . . . .

The programme was excellent . . . . Many of the class were very moved. They had been able to appreciate James' gallant attitude to life and his philosophical acceptance of being "different." They noted the maturity of his brothers' attitude, and this led on to discussion led by two pupils who had mongol chlidren in the family . . . .

This outstanding programme . . . ought to be a part of every school's compulsory studies . . . .

In one school, a class composed a letter to the local council asking for a hostel to be built in the area, and in another school a group of girls decided to offer to help at a nearby school for severely subnormal children.

A BBC schools liaison officer visited a class of 35 boys and girls of good intelligence and watched the taped programme with them. "The atmosphere was electric . . . . Everyone laughed a lot with James and some of the girls and Hazel (their teacher) were close to tears several times . . . ." Immediately afterwards the teacher got everyone to write down their instant reactions. "Feelings of anger, sadness over the whole situation predominated . . . . The boys were very articulate in expressing their anger at those who laugh at mongols . . . . A group of girls said they didn't realize how human the mentally handicapped feel." They then built up a character study of James and were surprised to find that his qualities and his attitudes were very much like their own. The officer's report goes on to commend the teacher's versatile and imaginative handling of "this superbly moving programme."

4.5 Comparisons   ⊃⊃⊃⊃⊃⊃⊃⊃

Of these four projects, the first three were all developed from carefully researched bases of information and direction. They differed in the way they related to the educational mission of the schools. "Eureka!" illustrates the closest fit with the existing curricula of schools and was designed to be integrated closely with existing instruction. "ThinkAbout" attempted to extend the curriculum slightly by introducing and organizing problem-solving skills (many of which were being haphazardly taught in the classroom). This infusion of new curriculum material succeeded because it built on the familiar, and on the related skills in basic subject areas taught universally in the schools.

"Freestyle," in contrast, attempted to deal with a social problem through instruction. Its initiative was from a federal source in a nation where state and local agencies have the responsibility for education. While the focus of this series is certainly important to the United States (and other nations), it is not seen as important to schools.

These three projects also used an instructional design process through which the programs and related print materials could be developed, evaluated, and revised. In some cases the political process imposed itself, but with the best intention—that of getting the series used.

All three had the highest of production values, and the expectations for the projects were supported with large budgets. As a result, all were seen as highly appealing to students and teachers and obtained, at a minimum, an initial use in large numbers of classrooms. The continued use, however, was based on the programs' perceived utility in assisting teachers to reach their stated instructional goals.

The fourth example, "Scene," differs somewhat from the other three, being a continuing miscellany of programs not necessarily related to any special syllabus or project. Replacing a current affairs series, "Spotlight," of some years' standing, "Scene" was easily integrated into the nationwide service of broadcasts to schools whose general policy is laid down by an Educational Broadcasting Council representative of the whole educational spectrum. Within these policy lines, program proposals are examined and accepted, modified or rejected by committees of educationists appointed by the Council. They are normally subject to no other political pressures.

School producers have access to the whole resources of the BBC and, subject to a modest but not illiberal budget, can go where they please for scriptwriters, presenters, actors, and production facilities. There are periodical postal surveys of audience size, and reactions to the programs are communicated by panels of reporting teachers and by visiting BBC liaison officers (called Education Officers), extracts from whose reports have been given above.

Teachers receive printed notes indicating the aim and content of each program and the proposed treatment of the topic, together with some follow-up suggestions. Broadcasts may be fitted into an existing scheme of work but are often used as a starting point for discussion and to prompt initiatives like those described in the forgoing account of "James is our Brother."

In 1981, the "Scene" broadcasts were seen off air or on videotape, regularly or selectively in 48 percent of British secondary schools. A number of the broadcasts have been repeated in the BBC's evening schedules for the general audiences by virtue of their human interest and the excellence of their production.

5. Concluding Observations

It is clear from previous experience that classroom television is not simply another audiovisual teaching device. It is too powerful and pervasive for that. The technology that supports it can, if desired, be used to support distance learning systems, adult education programs, the promotion of national identity, and the fostering of national culture. It can also be used, and in some countries has been used, for political purposes that do not always benefit education. Undoubtedly, classroom television serves education best when planners, curriculum specialists, teachers, and television programmers work together to capitalize on the strengths of the medium and to diminish its weaknesses.

Classroom television is often thought of in the context of conventional broadcasting, but surely, within this century, it will benefit from such new technologies as cable television, direct broadcast satellite, videodiscs, and videocassette recorders. These will compensate for the inflexibility of broadcast program scheduling, which educators have sometimes found inconvenient.

Television is an expensive medium; in few instances has it reduced the cost of instruction. As Wilbur Schramm (1977) has noted in *Big Media, Little Media: Tools and Technologies*:

> One conclusion that emerges strongly is that systems, built around the broadcast media in particular, can be used with favorable economic results to extend and expand learning opportunities. In this case the media cost is not merely an add-on to the normal cost of instruction, as supplementary media instruction might be, but can be compared directly with the cost of doing the same thing by conventional means . . . . If we can assume then, that favorable cost ratios can be expected from using media to do something that would otherwise have to be done by conventional means, what can we expect of the costs of simply adding media to ongoing class instruction? This is clearly an add-on cost, to be justified, if at all, by its contribution to quality of instruction, unless it makes possible a reduction of some kind in present costs.

Many would argue that several television programs in this supplementary category do indeed contribute a significant additional quality, but the extra cost is difficult to justify unless it is distributed over a large number of classrooms.

As educators and broadcasters feel increasing economic pressures, they are increasingly likely to look for less expensive methods of obtaining classroom television programs. One method is coproduction, either among the states or provinces of one or two countries or among several countries. This can reduce the cost of the programs to each coproducer, and at the same time generate large enough audiences to justify the investment. Another method is the structured instructional use of entertainment programs—to increase students' motivation to read, to improve their foreign language comprehension, to complement social studies activities, and so on. Such use must involve assignments and interventions, either by teachers or teacher surrogates (e.g., aides or parents). Both the viewing of the program and some follow-up activity must be required, and the focus must remain on education rather than entertainment.

Finally, some promising directions for future research must be mentioned.

The effectiveness of television as a teaching device is no longer in doubt. Indeed, it has been verified so thoroughly that comparisons between the television classroom and the so-called traditional classroom are no longer interesting. Yet much remains to be learned about some elements of the learning situation.

While little research has been done in diversifying formats and production techniques, those of the Children's Television Workshop and other groups in the United States, Canada, Western Europe, and Japan have shown how differences in those elements, differently combined, variously affect students' learning and attitudes. In addition, developmental studies have shown how comprehension and learning vary with age. As children pass from one stage of cognitive development to another (see *Cognitive Development*), their ability to perceive and use the content and organization of television programs grows more sophisticated.

Instructional design is now more important than ever in the production of classroom television. This greater importance has led to an increase in formative research, designed to improve the programs as they are being developed. More time and money are being spent to determine the needs and abilities of audiences before production and to test-run scripts, parts of programs, and whole programs in classrooms throughout produc-tion. Thus it is possible to revise one or a few programs in a series, if necessary, rather than the entire number.

Bibliography

Arnove R F (ed.) 1975 *Educational Television: A Policy Critique and Guide for Developing Countries.* Praeger, New York

Bates T, Robinson J (eds.) 1977 *Evaluating Educational Television and Radio.* Proc. of the Int. Conf. on Evaluation and Research in Educational Television, Milton Keynes, 9–13 April 1976. Open University Press, Milton Keynes

Carlisle D (ed.) 1978 *Patterns of Performance: Public Broadcasting and Education 1974–1976.* Corporation for Public Broadcasting, Washington, DC

Fawdry K 1974 *Everything but Alf Garnett: A Personal View of BBC School Broadcasting.* British Broadcasting Corporation (BBC), London

Johnston J, Ettema J 1982 *Positive Images.* Sage, Beverly Hills, California

Marland M (ed.) 1972 *"Scene" Scripts: Seven Television Plays from the BBC School TV Series, "Scene", by Michael Cahill, Keith Dewhurst, Rex Edwards, Donald Eyre, Bill Lyons, Alan Plater, Fay Weldon.* Longman, London

Schramm W L 1977 *Big Media, Little Media: Tools and Technologies for Instruction.* Sage, Beverly Hills, California

Sloan K R 1980 *Thinking Through Television: The First Six Years of the Skills Essential to Learning Project.* Agency for Instructional Television, Bloomington, Indiana

Wood D N, Wylie D G 1977 *Educational Telecommunications.* Wadsworth, Belmont, California

Factors Affecting Curriculum

Educational Ideologies

Z. Lamm

The connection between social and cultural factors and the content of knowledge transmitted by education to young people operates through specific cognitive structures known as ideologies. The planning of curricula was, in the past, principally guided by questions such as the one articulated by Herbert Spencer: "What knowledge is of most worth?" This outlook has been regarded as naive ever since the opinions of what ought to be taught were classified as ideologies. The new question which has been asked is "What causes people to believe that a certain selection of knowledge is the most worthwhile?"

1. Ideologies

Ideologies are cognitive structures containing the interdependent beliefs, views, principles, and myths prevailing in a given social group and reflecting the preferences and interests of that group in the political, social, moral, and religious spheres. These preferences are accepted by the members of the group as articles of faith and are supported by their strong emotional attitude towards them. Despite this, such people are generally convinced that they have reached their ideological beliefs through rational assessment (Mannheim 1936, Plamenatz 1970, Berger and Luckman 1966).

2. Educational Ideologies

Ideologies of education (like all other ideologies) are devices of social control. The function of ideologies as control devices is twofold: (a) they mobilize the people's will to implement a certain socially required activity—in this case a particular way favored by society of caring for children, and (b) they determine who will learn and what and how much will be learnt—this too being according to the needs of society (Young 1971).

There are two lines of approach to assessing the effect of educational ideologies on the activities of education. First, there are those who regard the ideologies as forcing factors which interfere with the activities of educators; activities which were previous to their arrival, comprised of a relatively autonomous system, and were propelled by professional rules and principles of education itself. Secondly, there are those who view such ideologies as the deep structure of all types of thought concerning education which appear on the surface as a philosophy, a theory, or a tradition which has proven itself in action in the course of generations.

According to the first, the interference approach, educational ideologies derive from social or political ideologies prevalent in society. Democracy, liberalism, nationalism, socialism, and so on, which hold sway in a given society are liable to dictate to education (a) its structure, such as elitism or egalitarism, coeducation or sexual segregation; (b) its methods, such as authoritarianism or permissiveness; (c) its goals, such as the transmission of culture and preparation for life; and (d) its contents such as choice of books and courses on the national culture, science, and technology, and classical studies.

According to the second, the deep structure approach, it is not external ideological ideas which affect decisions in education—thought about education is ideology by its very nature, and it is this which determines which scientific findings, philosophical generalizations, techniques, and activities are accepted and endorsed therein and which are rejected and ruled out. All the conceptions of education, that is progressivism, essentialism, humanism, naturalism, and so on, are merely ideologies reflecting the needs and interests of various groups in society (Bourdieu 1975, Pratte 1977).

An attempt to classify the ideologies of education prevalent in contemporary societies demonstrates that they may be presented in three groups: (a) the ideologies of socialization, whose premise is that the socially accepted must serve as the norm of educational activity; (b) the ideologies of acculturation, whose premise is that there are certain cultural values, perenially valid, which must be accepted as norms of education; and (c) the ideologies of individuation, whose premise is that the developmental needs of the child are the decisive starting point in the determination of the needs and the contents of education (Lamm 1976).

3. Ideologies of Education and Curriculum

Ideologies of education fulfill three functions in determining curriculum: (a) they lend legitimation to certain fields of knowledge (such as literature, sciences, religion, premilitary training, driving); (b) they rule out, in accordance with the same principles upon which the legitimation was based, other such fields of knowledge (in accordance with various ideologies, each of the aforementioned contents is liable to be prohibited from being taught); and (c) they participate in the choice of the specific content to be covered in each of the subject areas which attained legitimation (e.g., Which aspects of literature or history—only national, or general as well? Which aspects of the sciences—only findings, or methods and values implied in the sciences as well? The articles of religion alone, or training in the worship activities as well?). Since the ideologies reflect the preferences and the interests of different groups in society, today's pluralistic and differentiated societies contain at one and the same time differing ideologies and thus differing curricula. The dominant groups dictate to the schools, by means of their ideologies, curricula intended to justify the continuation of their rule, whereas the assertive groups attempt, through their ideologies, to question the validity of those curricula in their general effort to eliminate the rule of the dominant groups (Vaughan and Archer 1971).

Eggleston (1974) presented these two ideological models as different perspectives: the received and the reflexive perspectives on curriculum. The received perspective, characterizing the curricula of dominant groups, is based upon the premise that bodies of knowledge exist whose structures are independent of humans and their desires, and that it is desirable for youngsters growing up in society to internalize these structures of knowledge. Those whose point of reference is the reflexive perspective contend, to the contrary, that the esteem attained by the curricula accepted in society owes its origin to the fact that by means of them the ruling groups maintain their rule; these contents are learned not because they increase the chances for a better life for the new generation, but only because they ensure, by means of the control of knowledge, the continuance of the existing regime. It is the received perspective which defines chosen types of knowledge as disciplines, and in so doing gives them a privileged status in the schools, and gives to those who aquire a command of them a privileged status in society. The reflexive perspective, on the other hand, questions the social relevance of the curricula, (Is the curriculum relevant economically and employment-wise?) as well as questioning the curricula's compatibility to the psychological needs of the pupils, in accordance with their age and social and cultural groups. The received perspective strengthens the traditional foundations of the curricula, whereas the reflexive perspective supports their change and renewal. Together they determine that curriculum is an ideological selection (Apple 1979).

4. Theoretical Frameworks

What is implied by the consensus of the scholars in this field that curriculum is an ideological selection taught by the schools? The answer to this question depends upon the philosophical–epistemological outlook adopted by the scholar. A selection of approaches on this issue was presented in a collection of articles edited by M. F. D. Young (1971). Lawton (1975) analyzed these articles and classified them into five groups according to approach:

(a) Curricula (together with other components of education) are intended to preserve the status quo in an unjust society through the social distribution of knowledge. This approach has its origin in the theory of Karl Marx, according to which education is a part of the "superstructure" whose function is to protect the "basis," that is, the capitalist regime and the privileges of the capitalist class. Knowledge is power and the existing educational system distributes knowledge in accordance with class considerations.

(b) Knowledge itself, and not merely the means of its distribution [as in (a)], is a matter requiring examination, that is, what is considered as knowledge in a society and how knowledge is stratified or differentially valued. Why, for example, is the prestige of the dead languages Latin and Greek greater in certain societies than the prestige of living languages, or why is carpentry lower in prestige than pottery?

(c) What causes the division of knowledge into subjects and fields? It is possible that there is no reason for this save an interest of those in control of education. Subject barriers are arbitrary and artificial. There is no certainty that the accepted division of knowledge into subjects and fields answers the needs of students.

(d) All knowledge is socially constructed. It is not merely those in control who distribute knowledge according to their interests. Knowledge itself is a social product. In this approach the influence of phenomenology is strongly felt.

(e) Rationality itself, not only knowledge, is merely a convention. This is a development of the idea that all knowledge is socially constructed. The criteria by which it is determined what is truth and what is falsehood are also socially constructed, and thus their status is not absolute and eternal but is subject to change.

All of these approaches serve as theoretical frameworks for curriculum research as well as recommendations for planning of new curricula. On the overt level of curriculum, it is possible to distinguish between three types according to their relationship to the ideologies of education: (a) discipline-centered curriculum, influenced mainly by the ideologies of acculturation;

(b) sociocentered curriculum, influenced mainly by the ideologies of socialization; and (c) child-centered curriculum influenced by ideologies of individuation (see *Student-centered Curriculum*). However, the distinction according to the overt level is not sufficient for the comprehension of the social function of curriculum. Many highly important social functions of curriculum are hidden functions. Research into hidden curriculum teaches how the school acts as a psychological agent of the existing society in fields of which both the teachers and the pupils are liable to be unaware and which are guided by unarticulated ideological objectives. Research into the hidden dimensions of curriculum explains how children learn in school among other things to accept assessment by others, to tolerate passivity, to compete, to please both teachers and fellow students, to live in a hierarchical society, and so on (Jackson 1968).

In summary, research into the effects of the ideologies of education upon curriculum, which is still in its early stages, is searching for a way of deepening understanding of the complex ties which exist between society and education by means of human knowledge and human emotions.

Bibliography

Apple M W 1979 *Ideology and Curriculum.* Routledge and Kegan Paul, London

Berger P L, Luckman T 1966 *The Social Construction of a Treatise on the Sociology of Knowledge.* Doubleday, Garden City, New York

Blackburn R (ed.) 1972 *Ideology in Social Science: Readings in Critical Social Theory.* Collins, London

Bourdieu P 1975 The school as a conservative force: Scholastic and cultural inequalities. In: Eggleston J (ed.) 1974 *Contemporary Research in the Sociology of Education.* Methuen, London

Eggleston J (ed.) 1974 *Contemporary Research in the Sociology of Education.* Methuen, London

Jackson P W 1968 *Life in Classrooms.* Holt, Rinehart and Winston, New York

Lamm Z 1976 *Conflicting Theories of Instruction: Conceptual Dimensions.* McCutchan, Berkeley, California

Lawton D 1975 *Class, Culture and the Curriculum.* Routledge and Kegan Paul, London

Mannheim K 1936 *Ideology and Utopia: An Introduction to the Sociology of Knowledge.* Routledge and Kegan Paul, London

Plamenatz J P 1970 *Ideology.* Macmillan, London

Pratte R 1977 *Ideology and Education.* McKay, New York

Thompson J B 1984 *Studies in the Theory of Ideology.* Polity Press, Cambridge

Thompson K 1986 *Beliefs and Ideology.* E. Hotwood, Chichester and Tavistock, London

Vaughan M, Archer M S 1971 *Social Conflict and Educational Change in England and France 1789–1848.* Cambridge University Press, London

Young M F D 1971 *Knowledge and Control: New Directions for the Sociology of Education.* Macmillan, London

Legal Factors

T. van Geel

Three categories of law affect the prescribed and actual curriculum. In the first category are those legal provisions (i.e., constitutional provisions, statutes, judicial decrees, regulations, directives, syllabi, plans, guidelines, policy statements, authoritative agreements) which allocate the roles and authority that parents, legislatures, public officials, and public and private institutions are to have in shaping the school program or curriculum, as well as prescribing the procedures by which curricular decisions are to be made. The second category includes those laws and other mandates which specifically prescribe what shall, may, or may not be part of the curriculum to which children are exposed. In the third category are those other laws which may have an indirect yet important effect on the curriculum—laws such as teacher certification requirements. These different categories of law in turn are related to three different kinds of studies of the legal factors affecting the curriculum, studies which may be undertaken separately or in combination with each other.

1. Three Types of Studies

Those studies directed toward examining the laws which prescribe role relationships and procedures may be termed "system studies." System studies may examine civil rights and liberties as a device for structuring role relationships and allocating authority between individuals such as parents and the government. System studies may also concentrate upon examining the relationship between different parts of the government at the same level of government, for example, the relationship between a legislature and a ministry of education. Systems studies, however, more typically undertake to examine the relationships between and among the parts of a federal system including the judiciary, and perhaps also including teachers, their unions, and parents. System studies may be undertaken simply to inform, but also to raise questions regarding the efficiency and effectiveness of the system in yielding a quality education for the young; to raise questions regarding the extent to which the system is designed to preserve and protect individual liberty and freedom; and to raise questions regarding the degree to which the system promotes equal educational opportunity or protects and realizes the notion of a right to an education.

A second type of study, which may be termed "content studies," examines those legal mandates which specify what it is that children may or must or must not study and learn and how this may or must or must not be accomplished. These studies may be undertaken for a number of purposes including describing the culture of a particular country as revealed in the authoritatively adopted prescriptions controlling the kind of education to which students are, must or may be exposed; the raising of questions regarding the proper content, methods, and goals of the curriculum; and simply informing people of a particular country of the law of which they should be cognizant as they go about the business of educating children.

A third type of study which examines the indirect effects on the curriculum of laws not specifically intended to control the curriculum may be termed "impact studies." Such studies may be undertaken to uncover what might otherwise be hidden barriers to curriculum reform and change, and to reveal the unintended consequences, and opportunity costs associated with these laws (see *Curriculum Reform*; *Curriculum Change*).

2. Systems Studies

Systems studies may be usefully further subdivided into descriptive studies, predictive studies, and normative studies, each of which reveals something different about the legal factors affecting curriculum.

2.1 Descriptive Studies

Historical and other closely related analytical studies typically involve descriptions of the changing legal relationships among those concerned with controlling the curriculum to which children are or may be exposed (van Geel 1976, Cronin 1973). Such studies may reveal something about tendencies toward increased centralization within an educational system or efforts to shift control of education from one political group to another with implications for the kind of educational program to which children are to be exposed. Political studies involve a description of the operations of a particular curriculum system at a particular historical moment and how the participants use and are affected by their legally defined authority to influence the decisions that shape the curriculum to which children are exposed and the educational opportunities afforded or denied to them (Glatter 1977, Zeigler and Jennings 1974). Such studies may be useful in the effort to specify an answer to the question of who controls the curriculum and what difference it makes (Boyd 1976). Comparative studies tend toward providing formal descriptions of the different legal relationships of participants in a cur-

riculum system that exist in various countries of the world with a view to providing those benefits to be gained from learning how different countries arrange the sharing of control over the curriculum (MONBUSHO 1979, Beauchamp and Beauchamp 1972, King 1979).

2.2 Predictive Studies

These studies, of which there are very few, assume the existence of a particular set of legally established rights, then, employing certain basic postulates or "as if" models of human behavior, first, predict what will or will not be done regarding the education of children and, second, test those predictions empirically. For example, a widely agreed upon conclusion among economists is that under widely prevailing notions of property rights the phenomenon of externalities occurs. When these externalities take the form of a collective good or collective bad, certain behavior will follow. Therefore, because education involves the production of collective goods (and perhaps collective bads), it follows that the behavior associated with the collective good phenomenon will plague the supply of education in certain ways and to specified degrees. Such studies can have great relevance for prescribing how a federal system of education ought to be organized and financed (Weisbrod 1964). Other studies using an economic perspective, assuming certain legally defined roles, explain and predict the behavior of people holding those roles in light of the incentives and disincentives the law has created (Michaelsen 1977, 1981)

2.3 Normative Studies

Normative studies are those studies directed toward choosing among alternative legally defined arrangements for sharing control over the curriculum to which children are to be exposed (van Geel 1976). A useful if perhaps "unrealistic" basic premise for such studies with which they may begin is that all roles parents, institutions, and officials play in controlling the education of children have been or may be consciously and purposefully designed and constructed through an authoritative legal process. That is, these roles are not the product of evolution, chance, or natural law, but the product of conscious and purposeful human choice and subject to purposefully designed change (Mill 1854). In addition to adopting this premise, these studies may also employ a method for systematically describing the alternative arrangements for sharing authority and criteria for ranking these alternatives.

One useful scheme for systematically describing alternative arrangements for sharing control is that offered by Wesley Hohfeld (Hohfeld 1923). Hohfeld identified four basic entitlements: rights, privileges, powers, and immunities. A "right" or "claim-right" is a claim a person has to require or prevent, with the state's assistance if needed, a certain act or set of acts of another, while a "privilege" just refers to certain acts or classes of acts which a person can do (or not do) without anyone else's being able to summon governmental force in opposition. A "power" is the legal relation of A to B when A's own voluntary act will cause new legal relations between A and B or between B and a third person, while a person's "immunity" is the absence of power in another to alter the person's relations. Hohfeld also stipulated a term for the negation, or "opposite," of each of the four positive relations for a total of eight terms with which to construct his table of "jural opposites" and "jural correlatives." That is, for example, each pair of correlatives always exists together so that if one person has a right another person necessarily has a duty. As for the jural opposites, if a person has a right he or she cannot have a no-right with respect to the same subject matter and the same person (see Table 1). An important lesson Hohfeld drew from his tables was that there is no logically necessary relationship between a claim-right over some act and a privilege over that same act, no logical reason why having the right means having the privilege or vice versa. It is also worth noting that what Hohfeld called "privileges" may also be called liberties or civil rights, such as the right of freedom of belief, and the right of freedom of speech, and that a claim-right entails the liberty to claim it or not.

Using this scheme it is possible to describe alternative arrangements for controlling the curriculum. For example, under one arrangement it may be the case that parents enjoy a Hohfeldian privilege to be free of governmental efforts to control how they choose to educate their children, whereas under another arrangement such a privilege may be nonexistent or extremely narrow, for example, it includes only a privilege to be free of governmental interference regarding the religious education of the child. For another example, under one arrangement the legislature may have a certain "power" to define the relationship between parent and child, but not under another arrangement.

Having described two or more of these arrangements for sharing control over the curriculum, the analyst then may use his or her preferred criteria for assessing those arrangements with a view to rejecting one or all or choosing one among them. The criteria to be used can be those which stress the value of efficiency, liberty, equality, or some preferred mixture of these values (West 1970, van Geel 1976).

Table 1
Hohfeld's four basic control entitlements

Jural opposites			
Right	Privilege	Power	Immunity
No-right	Duty	Disability	Liability

Jural correlatives			
Right	Privilege	Power	Immunity
Duty	No-right	Liability	Disability

3. Content Studies

Studies of the content of the statutes, regulations, directives, plans, and syllabi, and judicial decrees which constrain and confine the discretion of individuals and officials can range to the mere cataloging of these legal mandates to the in-depth analysis, often employing techniques of legal reasoning, of their content and meaning (Shelton 1979, Edelman 1976, National Institution of Education 1978). These studies may trace changes over time in the mandates, or concentrate on describing the requirements at a particular point in time.

Mandates which can be studied for their content include compulsory education mandates; those laws which prescribe the basic and special courses to which students must be exposed; the laws which prescribe ceremonies to be performed (flag salutes) and the national and other holidays expected to be observed and how they are to be observed in schools; those which establish the basic grade structure of the public school system; those laws which classify pupils according to educational needs and prescribe special services and programs for them; the laws which control the selection of textbooks; the laws and mandates which exclude from the curriculum certain subjects and topics, or which require the inculcation of certain values and perspectives and attitudes; and the mandates which prescribe graduation requirements. In addition, there are those laws which mandate the provision and taking of certain standardized tests as well as establishing who shall control the writing of those tests. Governmental grant-in-aid programs may also be examined insofar as they exert an influence on the content of the school program (Jacobs 1981, van Geel 1976). Similarly antidiscrimination laws can shape what is to be offered to which students, and constitutionally based rights may also significantly affect the content of the schools' programs (van Geel 1976).

Legal mandates may be issued by a national or state ministry of education but it remains an open question whether local schools and their teachers obey those mandates, and to what other unanticipated consequences those mandates may lead. Thus, there remains the need to study the effect of curriculum mandates and their unintended consequences (Weatherley 1979). These studies can range from simple case studies to more sophisticated studies which attempt to analyze the contribution of a whole range of determinants, including legal mandates of the content of the school curriculum (Henning et al. 1979).

4. Impact Studies

Impact studies, less commonly undertaken than other studies, can employ a variety of theoretical frameworks and methodologies. For example, the research may employ the perspective of organizational behavior and theory to understand the contribution of legal requirements to organizational rigidity and resistance to curriculum innovation (Hawley 1975, 1978). Alternatively, the research may not rely on any particular theoretical framework, but simply inquire of participants in the educational system their perceptions regarding the effects of certain laws on their ability to innovate or change the curriculum (Henning et al. 1979).

Bibliography

Beauchamp G A, Beauchamp K E 1972 *Comparative Analysis of Curriculum Systems*, 2nd edn. Kagg Press, Wilmette, Illinois

Boyd W L 1976 The public, the professionals and educational policy-making: Who governs? *Teach. Coll. Rec.* 48: 539–77

Cronin J M 1973 *The Control of Urban Schools: Perspective on the Power of Educational Reformers*. Free Press, New York

Edelman L 1976 Basic American. *NOLPE Sch. Law J.* 6: 83–122

Glatter R (ed.) 1977 *Control of the Curriculum: Issues and Trends in Britain and Europe*. Proc. of 5th Annual Conf., British Educational Administration Society, London, Sept. 1976. University of London Institute of Education, London

Hawley W D 1975 Dealing with organizational rigidity in public schools. In: Wirt F M (ed.) 1975 *The Polity of the School*. Heath, Lexington, Massachusetts

Hawley W D 1978 Horses before carts: Developing adaptive schools and the limits of innovation. In: Mann D (ed.) 1978 *Making Changes Happen?* Teachers College Press, New York

Henning J F, White C, Sorgen M, Stelzer L 1979 *Mandate for Change: The Impact of Law on Educational Innovation*. American Bar Association, Chicago, Illinois

Hohfeld W 1923 *Fundamental Legal Conceptions as Applied in Judicial Reasoning, and Other Legal Essays*. Yale University Press, New Haven, Connecticut

Jacobs B 1981 *The Political Economy of Organizational Change: Urban Institutional Response to the War on Poverty*. Academic Press, New York

King E J 1979 *Other Schools and Ours: Comparative Studies for Today*, 5th edn. Holt, Rinehart and Winston, Eastbourne

Michaelsen J B 1977 Revision, bureaucracy, and school reform: A critique of Katz. *Sch. Rev.* 85: 229–46

Michaelsen J B 1981 The political economy of school district administration. *Educ. Admin. Q.* 17: 98–113

Mill J S 1854 On liberty. *Utilitarianism, Liberty, Representative Government*. Dent, London

National Institute of Education 1978 *State Legal Standards for the Provision of Public Education: An Overview*. National Institute of Education, Washington, DC

Science and International Affairs Bureau Ministry of Education, Science and Culture (MONBUSHO) 1979 *Outline of Education in Japan*. MONBUSHO, Japan

Shelton D 1979 Legislative control over public school curriculum. *Willamette Law Rev.* 15: 473–505

van Geel T 1976 *Authority to Control the School Program*. Heath, Lexington, Massachusetts

van Geel T 1987 *The Courts and American Education Law*. Prometheus Books, Buffalo, New York

Weatherley R A 1979 *Reforming Special Education: Policy Implementation from State Level to Street Level*. MIT Press, Cambridge, Massachusetts

Weisbrod B A 1964 *External Benefits of Public Education: An Economic Analysis*. Industrial Relations Section, Department of Economics, Princeton University, Princeton, New Jersey

West E G 1970 *Education and the State: A Study in Political Economy*, 2nd edn. Institute of Economic Affairs, London

Zeigler L H, Jennings M K 1974 *Governing American Schools: Political Interaction in Local School Districts*. Duxbury Press, North Scituate, Massachusetts

Educational Psychology

L. N. Tanner

Major streams of psychological thought in the twentieth century have profoundly influenced educational theory and practice. In fact, psychology has become the basic educational science. "Learning" and "development" which are central concepts in psychology are central concepts in education. The importance of learning theories and developmental theories to curriculum development is indisputable. Theories of learning imply theories of teaching. Yet there is more to an educational program than teaching methods. The content of the curriculum deserves at least equal attention. Some curriculum theorists contend that the domination of educational thinking by psychology has led to an overemphasis on method and a neglect of content. The history of the curriculum certainly testifies to this conclusion. Most curriculum reforms are simply rearrangements of content in accord with the principles of child development or theories of learning (see *Curriculum Reform*).

1. Conflicting Conceptions of the Learner

Psychology is not a unitary system. Psychology is comprised of competing camps with differing views about the nature of humans, their learning processes, and thus their education. The curriculum of today reflects the influence of many different theories of learning and development, even theories which have long been discredited. Latin, for example, is still regarded by many as a trainer of the mind. They may not recognize it, but this is the theory of mental discipline which had great power in the educational world of the nineteenth century, but was demolished by Thorndike before the First World War.

Psychologically speaking, there is confusion in the curriculum. In the same educational program practices can be found based on two conflicting views of the learner: (a) the learner as a thinking individual who is capable of intelligent action and controlling his or her destiny, and (b) the learner as an organism to be conditioned so as to respond automatically in an externally controlled way. The former conception is based on gestalt and cognitive developmental theories of learning, and the latter is derived from behaviorist theory. There is no coherent theory embracing all aspects of learning and development to apply in shaping the curriculum. This is not the fault of psychologists. Psychology is in search of its own theoretical knowledge and does not set out to answer curriculum questions (Huebner 1968). Nor should this be a problem if educators draw upon psychology and other fields as needed to provide insight into educational problems. As Dewey pointed out more than half a century ago, educators must understand that no single discipline can illumine, much less govern the curriculum questions asked. Such questions must emerge from the educational situation itself, not be supplied (along with the answers) by any particular science (Dewey 1929 p. 74).

2. Child Development and Curriculum Development

As early as 1899, William James cautioned teachers that psychological ideas are not curriculum guides for immediate use in schoolrooms. But a persistent problem in education has been the confusion of developmental theories with curriculum theories. The confusion can be traced to G. Stanley Hall, a pioneer in child development who urged that the curriculum be determined by the data of child development, and that educators stay out of the child's way so as not to interfere with nature's processes (Cremin 1961). Although the roots of the child-centered school go back to Rousseau, Hall brought the idea to educators' attention as a psychological theory. More importantly, unlike James, who was his contemporary, Hall proffered psychology as a complete curriculum theory. However, while developmental psychology may have seemed to Hall and his followers to offer a simple scientific solution for curriculum development, it is nothing more or less than an attempt to explain the course of human development. Hall's idea of a curriculum based on child growth was a failure.

3. Psychology and a Science of Education

Reinventions of failed curriculum reforms with all of their original theoretical difficulties are all too common in education. Recent curriculum literature reflects a concern with the atheoretical character of curriculum reform (Tanner and Tanner 1980). Although many shopworn reforms are based on psychological theories, psychology is not to blame. Educators do have a paradigm or model for curriculum development if they care to use it. The "Tyler rationale" takes into account the interaction of key elements in curriculum development:

(a) the nature of the learner, (b) codified knowledge, and (c) society. Every curriculum reform that has failed has done so because it did not take into account the vital interaction of these three sources. Thus the curriculum must be influenced by ideas from psychology, but any reform that derives from psychological knowledge in isolation is bound to fail (Tanner and Tanner 1988).

Unquestionably, the most influential educational psychologist of all time was John Dewey who put forward as a psychological problem the individual's need to participate in his or her own destiny. Intelligent action was a major psychological conception in Dewey's psychology of learning. Mind is the ability of the person to solve personal and social problems. Desirable self-development can only take place in a social environment. There has been no viable substitute for Dewey's psychological theory. This is not surprising, for it is consistent with democratic social philosophy in a way that Skinnerian conditioning theories are not. Most notably here, Dewey saw the problem of the curriculum whole. Dewey insisted that the child, society, and knowledge be viewed interactively (Dewey 1902). Curricula reflecting Dewey's psychological principles were developed and tested in the 1930s, in the Progressive Education Association's Eight-year Study (Cronbach 1977).

An educator's view of humans will determine how he or she uses psychology. Those who believe in human intelligence, for example, will stress problem-solving processes (Tanner and Tanner 1987). Psychology can help to answer curriculum questions, but the questions must be asked by curricularists. A science of education depends on nothing less.

Bibliography

Central Advisory Council for Education (England) 1967 *Children and Their Primary Schools.* Her Majesty's Stationery Office, London
Cremin L A 1961 *The Transformation of the School: Progressivism in American Education.* Knopf, New York
Cronbach L J 1977 *Educational Psychology.* Holt, Rinehart and Winston, New York
Dewey J 1902 *The Child and the Curriculum.* University of Chicago, Chicago, Illinois
Dewey J 1929 *The Sources of a Science of Education.* Liveright, New York
Huebner D 1968 Implications of psychological thought for the curriculum. In: Unruh G G, Leeper R R (eds.) 1968 *Influences on Curriculum Change.* Association for Supervision and Curriculum Development, Washington, DC
James W 1929 *Talks to Teachers on Psychology: And to Students on some of Life's Ideals.* Holt, New York
Tanner D, Tanner L N 1980 *Curriculum Development: Theory Into Practice,* 2nd edn. Macmillan, New York
Tanner D, Tanner L N 1987 *Supervision in Education: Problems and Practices.* Macmillan, New York
Tanner D, Tanner L N 1988 The emergence of a paradigm in the curriculum field—A reply to Jickling. *Interchange* 19: 50–58

Cognitive Psychology and Curriculum

G. D. Haertel

Cognitive psychology refers to a set of paradigms that have emerged since the 1950s, largely supplanting the earlier paradigms of behaviorism. It is characterized by explicit consideration, and usually modeling, of internal mental states and events. This article addresses the implications of cognitive psychology for curriculum, conceived both as a range of intended learning outcomes and as a program of planned activities intended to bring those outcomes about. In the first section, the emergence of cognitive psychology is described and a working definition is presented. In the second section of the article, the term *curriculum* is defined for present purposes. The question of whether cognitive psychology can inform educational practice is considered in the third section. The final section describes implications for curriculum of research in cognitive psychology.

1. Cognitive Psychology: Its Emergence and a Brief Description

Since the 1950s there has been a revolution in the study of the mind. As behaviorism's influence declined, there occurred a fruitful alliance among scientists from the disciplines of psychology, artifical intelligence, linguistics, philosophy, anthropology, and neuropsychology (Gardner 1985). The exchanges among these separate disciplines revealed a common episteme: they demonstrated the importance of employing a level of mental representation in understanding complex linguistic and conceptual activities. They also used new methods, often employing computers to investigate these phenomena. In each discipline, it became acceptable to talk of what was going on inside the "black box" of the mind.

Calfee (1981) chronicles the cognitive revolution through the appearance of such important works as Miller's paper on processing information (Miller 1956), Newell and Simon's classic work on the "logic theory machine" (Newell and Simon 1956), Bruner et al.'s volume on thinking (Bruner et al. 1956), and Chomsky's *Syntactic Structures* (Chomsky 1957). Miller et al. (1960) made it fashionable to talk of "plans," "TOTE (Test-Operate-Test-Exit) Units," and "goals." Finally, as the rising tide of the cognitive revolution coursed through graduate schools of psychology, Neisser's landmark textbook *Cognitive Psychology* appeared (Neisser 1967).

With the appearance of these and other significant works, psychologists' use of constructs such as short- and long-term memory, frames, organizing schemas, and story grammars increased. The work of cognitive psychologists was to study the activity of knowing: how knowledge was acquired; how it was organized; and finally, how it was used. Some cognitive psychologists chose to emphasize not the activity of knowing but

rather the structural plan, or architecture of the mind (Calfee 1981).

2. Curriculum: A Brief Description

The term *curriculum* may be defined more broadly than the term *cognitive psychology*. Schubert (1986) distinguishes eight different images of curriculum. He uses the term *image* in preference to *definition,* in order to urge the reader toward conceptualizing curriculum broadly. Schubert's eight images represent major conceptions of curriculum such as: curriculum as content or subject matter, curriculum as cultural reproduction, curriculum as experience. Three of the eight images are of special interest in understanding the contribution of cognitive psychology to curriculum. These are: (a) curriculum as a program of planned activities; (b) curriculum as intended learning outcomes; and (c) curriculum as discrete tasks and concepts. The first of these images regards curriculum as ranging from a teacher's detailed planning for specific instructional activities all the way to the curriculum guides which set forth an entire course of study. The second image of curriculum, curriculum as intended learning outcome, encompasses the knowledge and skills students are expected to acquire, as well as the attitudes and values collectively referred to as "affective" learning outcomes. Finally, the third image, curriculum as discrete tasks and concepts, is most easily understood as task analysis, or the use of highly detailed sequences of learning tasks. The contribution of cognitive psychology to each of these three images of curriculum will be considered.

Curriculum makes eclectic use of theories of different kinds (Schwab 1969), and it is through this eclectic use of theory that cognitive psychology can best contribute. There is no simple formula that cognitive psychology can offer curriculum, but there are numerous points at which cognitive psychology can inform deliberations about the imparting of complex, formal knowledge to students.

3. Can Cognitive Psychology Inform Educational Practice?

Psychologists and educators alike have warned against the naive application of psychological studies and theories to educational practice and curriculum (Schwab 1969, Shulman 1974). Schwab (1969) cautioned educators against attacking educational problems from a purely psychological perspective. He advised educators to employ theories appropriately in solving educational problems, warning that theories contribute only partial truths and not whole truths. A psychological theory of learning is not a theory of schooling. In the light of

Schwab's admonitions, what material from cognitive psychology contributes most to solving problems in curriculum?

3.1 The Psychology of School Subjects: A Renaissance

Schulman (1974) offers some incisive observations about the ways in which cognitive psychology can contribute to educational practice. Shulman calls for a renaissance of the psychology of school subjects. He asks that it be a "modern" psychology, presumably benefiting from the fruits of cognitive studies of the knowledge base. Shulman warns against researchers and educators seeking a unitary psychology explaining all of teaching and learning. Rather, psychological constructs such as retention and transfer must be understood within each school subject. Psychological models must be specific to school subjects in order to take account of the distinct structure of knowledge in different disciplines. Not only does knowledge in each school subject have a distinct structure, but as time passes and the knowledge base of a content area evolves, so will the psychology of the corresponding school subject.

In contrast to the idea of distinct psychological theories of different school subjects, there is a long tradition within psychology arguing that the specific content of information can safely be ignored (Gardner 1985). Early researchers in cognitive psychology sought to locate and describe a general cognitive system. Cognitive understandings were thought to be content-blind. Two psychologists conforming to this approach were Piaget, who exemplified the idea of a general system of cognitive processes, and more recently, Anderson (1983), whose ACT (Adaptive Control of Thought) system is regarded as a general model for the architecture of cognition. Nevertheless, Fodor (1983) has argued persuasively that the mind is best understood as a set of separate information-processing devices which process various types of content in different ways. The processing of language and its syntax may be quite different from that of spatial images or of the aromas of flowers.

3.2 Theories: Eclectic, Middle-range, and Grounded in Practice

Shulman (1974) advocates the use of middle-range theories to inform educational practice, including the use of the empirical research such theories can stimulate. Even though Shulman's discussion is not limited to contributions from cognitive psychology alone, nor addressed solely to the practical pursuits of curriculum, his recommendations are germane. Middle-range theories generate theoretical propositions that can guide further inquiry. These theories are not intended to represent general "laws of nature," and they seldom lead directly to prediction or control of the phenomena under study. They can, however, contribute critically in the practical deliberations of curriculum development.

Even though they are limited in scope and longevity, middle-range theories can lend coherence and increase understanding of observed phenomena. Theories at this level of specificity are appropriate for Schwab's (1969) "eclectic use of theory." Characterized by "specifications of ignorance" (Merton 1967), the middle-range theory is not presented as a solution to all pressing educational problems.

Of what particular concern are middle-range theories to curriculum experts? Curriculum planning involves the written statement of instructional activities and events through which knowledge is imparted. Curriculum planning, by its nature, must be theory-laden. The middle-range theories of most use to curriculum planners are those grounded in practice, theories emerging out of the study of schooling: the schools' organizations, their learners, their teachers, and the psychology of their subject matters. Middle-range theories can aid in the description, interpretation, and understanding of actual occurrences in educational practice.

3.3 Theories of Learning versus Theories of Instruction

The previous section described the kinds of theories likely to inform educational practice. In the light of that analysis, this section addresses the kinds of cognitive theories most likely to contribute to curriculum. It is useful first to distinguish two broad types of psychological theories: learning theories and instructional theories.

Learning theories are concerned with relationships among variables that account for learning, represented by changes in a person's behavior. They comprise the kinds of variables and processes amenable to study by the methods of experimental psychology, more often in the laboratory than in the classroom. Early learning theories were almost exclusively concerned with changes in manifest behaviors, as opposed to internal mental states. They conceived of internal changes as the simple accretion of associations, discriminations, concepts, and other units of information. Newer theories of learning, reflecting the principles of cognitive psychology, are concerned more with the integration of new knowledge and skills with old, and with their assembly into functional systems for use in thought and action. School subjects have provided a range of meaningful learning tasks of suitable complexity for cognitive research, and the emergence of cognitive psychologies of school subjects has brought a revival of stronger connections between psychology and school learning (Greeno 1980).

Even though cognitive psychologists have developed a substantial number of models representing knowledge acquisition in specific school subjects, these models in themselves are generally limited in their direct implications for educational practice. Like the earlier learning theories, cognitive models of knowledge in school subjects largely ignore such aspects of the school setting as the teacher's behavior; students' attitudes, motivation, and background characteristics; classroom organization and the social context of schooling; alternative instructional media; and the global structure of the curriculum. In contrast, instructional theories are broader and more complex than theories of learning. They incorporate learning theories, but by definition address the range of instructional processes necessary to bring about intended learning outcomes in actual school settings. The importance for education of transcending learning theories has long been recognized. During the 1960s, there were several well-documented arguments explicating the limitations of "laws of learning" and learning theories, and calling for the development of instructional theories, in contast to learning theories. The seminal work of Taba (1967), grounded in Piaget's psychological theories, began to suggest the potential of such an instructional theory.

The distinction between theories of learning and of instruction is still critically important. Cognitive psychologists working with a variety of school subjects have recognized that substantial theoretical development and empirical research will still be required to discover the direct implications of their theories for classroom practice (Glaser and Takanishi 1986). In their present stage of development, cognitive psychologies of school subjects can serve the needs of curriculum development, but are more likely to be useful as middle-range theories, suggesting useful working hypotheses, than as complete and developed models of instruction.

3.4 True Functionalism

During the 1970–80s, there has been an increased press among the psychological community for an "ecologically valid" cognitive psychology. Neisser (1967) had anticipated a fruitful cognitive psychology. By the mid-1970s, however, many of his hopes had dimmed. in 1976 Neisser expressed his disenchantment with mechanistic information-processing models, an overuse of the computer metaphor, and the almost exclusive use of laboratory settings for experiments. Neisser (1976) lamented that cognitive psychology had little relevance to solving problems in complex real-world settings. The same sentiment was graphically expressed by Glass et al. (1979) who described cognitive psychology as a "fast race on a short round track." Jenkins (1980) likewise called upon cognitivists to study meaningful, real problems, not presupposed theories, and to cease conducting "experiments about experiments."

In fact, much of the initial enthusiasm recommending cognitive psychology as a key to unlock the mysteries of the human mind has dwindled. Too many experiments were conducted exclusively in laboratory settings; too many experiments examined simple cognitive processes; the more complex, but realistic problems remained unexamined and too many findings lacked generalizability (Gardner 1985). With these criticisms in mind, the educational community needs to be cautious in the expectations it holds for the cognitive sciences.

However, as the final section of this article points out, there are new lines of cognitive research conducted in instructional settings, with increased generalizability and robustness, that may inform educational practice.

4. Applications of Cognitive Psychology to Curriculum

In this section, a few examples are presented of middle-range theories, or working hypotheses from such theories, that bear upon some of Schubert's (1986) images of curriculum. These examples were chosen to suggest the range and power of the cognitive psychology of school subjects; numerous other examples would have served as well.

4.1 Curriculum as a Program of Planned Activities

One powerful instructional method that is finding increased use in reading instruction is the method of reciprocal teaching (Brown and Palincsar 1982). This method, in which the teacher and students take turns leading discussions of the meaning of text segments, is grounded in psychological models that suggest comprehension skills should be enhanced by having students observe and then practice the activities of questioning, clarifying, summarizing, and predicting. Brown and Campione (1986) discuss the use of reciprocal teaching with learning-disabled students, and cite additional planned instructional approaches, including the provision of supportive contexts and of expert guidance, and the provision of individually tailored instruction.

In another content area, cognitive psychologists have studied the naive theories of motion many students hold prior to formal instruction in physics. These models, which have been characterized as "Aristotelian" or "pre-Newtonian," typically embody various ideas reflecting natural but inappropriate inferences from everyday observations, including for example the ideas that uniform motion requires a constant application of force, that objects can sometimes follow curved paths in the absence of any external force, and that heavier bodies fall more rapidly than lighter ones. In his review of these naive theories, McCloskey (1983) summarizes the observations of several researchers that if physics teachers do not discuss students' naive notions explicitly, or use other instructional activities that force students to confront these ideas, the result is often a poorly integrated conception in which ideas from Newtonian mechanics are maintained side by side with earlier, incompatible notions. Thus, this line of work offers an additional middle-range theory that can inform the planning of instructional activities in a particular content area.

4.2 Curriculum as Intended Learning Outcomes

The cognitive psychology of school subjects can inform curriculum more directly by offering rich models of learning outcomes. Egan and Greeno (1973) have studied the cognitive learning outcomes resulting from alternative instructional approaches, contrasting discovery and rule-based learning. They have reported that the former results in a better-integrated cognitive structure which permits students to solve problems requiring them to relate what they knew previously to what they have just learned. Rule-based instruction results primarily in the addition of new components to the previously existing cognitive structure, but poorer integration. This is shown by somewhat better performance on routine problems, but poorer transfer to situations where ideas must be applied in novel ways.

Perhaps the most intensively studied school subject has been reading. One contribution of cognitive psychology to the conception of learning outcomes in this area has been the idea of comprehension monitoring, which is a learned activity carried out automatically by skilled readers (Brown and Campione 1986). Poor readers for whom this faculty is weak or absent may fail to detect blatant inconsistencies in what they are reading, and do not stop to take corrective action when they encounter an unknown word or when they lose track of the structure of the material being read. The inclusion of comprehension monitoring and other so-called metacognitive activities among the intended outcomes of reading instruction has powerful implications for curriculum.

4.3 Curriculum as Discrete Tasks and Concepts

Cognitive psychologists have developed highly detailed models of specific tasks and skills in the school curriculum, especially in mathematics. In beginning to learn addition, for example, Nesher (1986) reviews studies showing that most children progress spontaneously through a sequence of several distinct counting algorithms of increasing sophistication. At first, they count out the magnitudes of each addend using objects or fingers, then recount the entire set. Later, they learn to bypass the recounting of the subset representing the first addend, and still later they gain efficiency by recounting only the subset representing the smaller addend, regardless of the sequence in which the two addends are presented. This kind of detailed understanding of tasks or concepts can help to inform curriculum deliberations about the amount of practice children should be given, the kinds of instructional activities that may be most helpful, and the indicators by which teachers can decide when children are ready to progress.

In separate lines of work, other cognitive psychologists have formulated detailed models of children's computation using paper and pencil. Brown and Burton (1978) developed detailed models for subtraction, and implemented these models in computer programs that could simulate and predict children's errors as well as their correct performances. Later, Brown and Van Lehn (1980) extended these models to account for some of the mechanisms by which errors, or "bugs," come into existence and are incorporated into children's sub-

traction algorithms. This work has made it clear that even the learning of procedural skills like subtraction involves processes of active construction and sometimes invention on the part of the learner. Models of this kind can enrich the curriculum theorist's understanding of the nature of the teaching and learning process.

5. Summary

The renaissance of a cognitive psychology of school subjects has produced a wealth of theories and models. The examples presented here, and other examples that could have been chosen, possess a kind of ecological validity that comes only with the study of real tasks of practical importance. It bears repeating that none of these models or findings is derived from a complete theory of instruction. Rather, they have value as middle-range theories, to be applied in the eclectic, practical arts of curriculum theory and construction.

Bibliography

Anderson J R 1983 *The Architecture of Cognition.* Harvard University Press, Cambridge, Massachusetts

Brown J S, Burton R R 1978 Diagnostic models for procedural bugs in basic mathematics. *Cognit. Sci.* 2: 155–92

Brown A L, Campione J C 1986 Psychological theory and the study of learning disabilities. *Am. Psychol.* 41: 1059–68

Brown A L, Palincsar A S 1982 Inducing strategic learning from texts by means of informed, self-control training. *Topics Learn. Learn. Disabil.* 2(1): 1–17

Brown J S, Van Lehn K 1980 Repair theory: A generative theory of bugs in procedural skills. *Cognit. Sci.* 4: 379–426

Bruner J S, Goodnow J J, Austin G A 1956 *A Study of Thinking.* Wiley, New York

Calfee R 1981 Cognitive psychology and educational practice. *Rev. Res. Educ.* 9: 3–73

Chomsky N 1957 *Syntactic Structures.* Mouton, The Hague

Egan D E, Greeno J G 1973 Acquiring cognitive structure by discovery and rule learning. *J. Educ. Psychol.* 64: 85–97

Fodor J A 1983 *The Modularity of Mind.* MIT/Bradford Press, Cambridge, Massachusetts

Gardner H 1985 *The Mind's New Science: A History of the Cognitive Revolution.* Basic Books, New York

Glaser R, Takanishi R (eds.) 1986 Special issue: Psychological science and education. *Am. Psychol.* 41: 1025–77

Glass A L, Holyoak K J, Santa J L 1979 *Cognition.* Addison-Wesley, Reading, Massachusetts

Greeno J G 1980 Psychology of learning, 1960–1980: One participant's observations. *Am. Psychol.* 35: 713–28

Jenkins J J 1980 Can we have a fruitful cognitive psychology? In: Howe H E, Flowers J H (eds.) 1980 *Cognitive Processes*, 1980 Nebraska Symposium on Motivation. University of Nebraska, Lincoln, Nebraska, pp. 211–38

McCloskey M 1983 Naive theories of motion. In: Gentner D, Stevens A L (eds.) 1983 *Mental Models.* Lawrence Erlbaum Associates, Hillsdale, New Jersey, pp. 299–324

Merton R K 1967 *On Theoretical Sociology.* Free Press, New York

Miller G A 1956 The magical number seven, plus or minus two: Some limits on our capacity for processing information. *Psychol. Rev.* 63: 81–97

Miller G A, Galanter E, Pribram K H 1960 *Plans and the Structure of Behavior.* Holt, Rinehart, and Winston, New York

Neisser U 1967 *Cognitive Psychology.* Appleton-Century-Crafts, New York

Neisser U 1976 *Cognition and Reality* W. H. Freeman, San Francisco, California

Nesher P 1986 Learning mathematics: A cognitive perspective. *Am. Psychol.* 41: 1114–22

Newell A, Simon H A 1956 The logical theory machine.

Institute of Radio Engineers (IRE) *Transactions Inform. Theory.* 2(3): 61–79

Schubert W H 1986 *Curriculum: Perspective, Paradigm, and Possibility.* Macmillan, New York

Schwab J J 1969 The practical: A language for curriculum. *Sch. Rev.* 78: 1–23

Shulman L 1974 The psychology of school subjects: A premature obituary? *J. Res. Sci. Teach.* 11: 319–39

Taba H 1967 *Teacher's Handbook for Elementary Social Studies.* Addison-Wesley, Palo Alto, California

U-shaped Behavioral Growth: Implications for Curriculum Development

S. Strauss

Some behaviors appear, then disappear, only to reappear at a later age. A variant of this is that young children produce a correct answer for a particular problem, older children produce incorrect answers for the same problem, while still older children produce correct answers once again for the same problem. Were we to plot the percentage of correct answers across age on a graph, we would produce a U-shaped behavioral growth curve.

Numerous cases of this phenomenon have been documented, and they have been found across a wide range of cognitive content: language acquisition, artistic expression, metaphor production, number conservation, face and voice representation, physical concepts such as temperature and sweetness, proportional reasoning, gender identity, motor development, and many other areas of human development. In short, the finding of U-shaped behavioral growth has been documented in many domains and by many different investigators. For a review of these findings see Bever (1982), Strauss (1982a, 1982b) and Strauss and Stavy (1982).

This phenomenon has raised no small amount of controversy, in part because it does not seem to fit an implicit assumption in many models of development that development is always upwards and onwards towards a more competent understanding of the world. Adherents of this position look only at the behavior. In contrast, adherents of structuralist and information-processing approaches separate behaviors from the underlying mental organizations that give rise to these behaviors. They interpret the U-shaped behavioral growth phenomenon as indicating that the correct initial understanding of the problem at hand is the result of primitive reasoning; the subsequent drop in performance indicates cognitive advance because underlying the incorrect answer is a more advanced mental organization, and the reappearance of the correct answer is seen as yet another cognitive advance over the incorrect answer. It is not understood as a reinstatement of the former correct answer.

1. Implications for Curriculum Development and Implementation

A number of curriculum areas are affected by what has been sketched above about the phenomenon of U-shaped behavioral growth. These areas are informed by what has been termed a developmental model of instruction that includes curriculum development and implementation in its purview (Strauss 1986, 1987). This model consciously works with middle-level mental organizations that have two properties: (a) they can be changed, as opposed to deep mental organizations that are too deep to be changed and (b) they are moderately general so that when change does take place it has effects beyond itself, as opposed to surface-level mental organizations where change can occur, but is extremely limited.

Two curricular implications that flow from some conclusions about U-shaped behavioral growth are presented: assessing children's achievements and phases in curriculum development.

1.1 Assessing Children's Achievements

U-shaped behavioral growth makes it quite clear that one must separate children's performances from the competence that underlies them. Were one to look only at children's performances when attempting to describe and explain U-shaped behavioral growth, the assumption would have been that children, for some reason, became confused when there was a drop in performance. One would have probably remained at the performance level in attempting to help them overcome their misunderstandings. Instead, an analysis of the competencies underlying the different performances led to the understanding that the changing competence was monotonically progressive, and gave rise to nonmonotonic behavioral change.

The conclusion arising from this is that the same performance on a test item by two different children or by the same child at two different times does not necessarily indicate the same level of reasoning. Children producing the same performances, such as the youngest and oldest children in U-shaped behavioral growth, may be at different levels of reasoning. Similarly, when two performances are not the same in that one is incorrect and the other is correct, the incorrect performance may be the result of more advanced reasoning, as in the case of the youngest versus the intermediate-age children. All of this is to say that when assessing children's achievements, it is not sufficient only to describe the behaviors themselves. One must also determine the nature of the competences that gave rise to the performances because they give the performances meaning and imbue them with interpretative material.

1.2 Phases in Curriculum Development

It has been argued (Strauss 1987) that a curriculum, no matter how widely or narrowly one wants to define it, must include at least two psychological components. First, it must be informed by what it is that children understand about the subject matter to be taught (sometimes indicating that children have misconceptions). Without knowing how children's knowledge is organized about subject matter content, attempts to teach that subject matter will be like firing into the fog. Second, curricula must be informed by a model of learning and cognitive development. Curriculum activities are intended to change children's knowledge about subject matter content. Without a model (or models) of how knowledge organizations change, what could be the basis for building curriculum activities? Curriculum should be viewed as the physical embodiment of principles of middle-level knowledge organization and middle-level knowledge organization change.

Five phases of curriculum development are informed by the psychological components of curriculum development. The first is to construct assessment tasks and test children over a wide age range in order to obtain information about the normative development trajectory of children's understanding of the subject matter content that is to be taught. This may be a monotonically ascending curve, a U-shaped curve, or any other shaped curve. The shape is less important than the mental organizations underlying the performances that produce the curves.

In the second phase, the training phase, one attempts to teach children at different ages and with different mental organizations the subject matter content that appears to be particularly difficult for them. The basis for teaching should be deeply imbedded in a theoretical approach to how knowledge changes. The training studies should be conducted over a wide age range in order to determine the nature and timing of that intervention. If, for example, training is successful for many children at age 12 and is less successful for 10-year-olds, clearly one would attempt to introduce the curriculum activities to 12-year-olds.

The third phase of curriculum development involves the translation of the research results into curriculum

activities. This phase combines the normative development of the concepts to be taught, as garnered in the first phase, and the results of training studies obtained in the second phase of curriculum development. This has been done for two concepts: (a) heat and temperature (Strauss 1987) where the method of inducing progressive cognitive change was to take advantage of children's conflicting notions about these concepts, and (b) the arithmetic average (Strauss and Bichler 1988) where the method of inducing cognitive change was through analogy reasoning.

The fourth phase is curriculum implementation in which the curriculum is introduced into regular classrooms. This phase also includes teacher training where teachers must be helped to understand the psychological principles that imbue the curriculum activities. Teachers are then better informed about what to expect about children's understanding of the concepts to be taught and the learning principles that energize the activities.

The fifth phase involves the assessment of the effects of the curriculum on children's understanding of the subject matter they have been taught. Tests for assessing children's understanding were developed in the first phase of curriculum development, and are informed by the issues raised in section 1.1.

2. Future Trends

Although there was initial reluctance on the part of many developmental psychologists to accept the U-shaped behavioral growth phenomenon, it has now been accepted as part of the developmental literature. It has also been accepted as a phenomenon worthy of attention by educational researchers. Both groups see the phenomenon as signifying a peeling-off of performance from competence, thus making the developmental and educational implications clearer.

There are initial signs that the assessment implications of the phenomenon are being taken into account by curriculum developers, and the five phases of curriculum development sketched above have the potential to influence ways in which curriculum developers conceptualize and practice their field.

Bibliography

Bever T G (ed.) 1982 *Regressions in Mental Development.* Erlbaum, Hillsdale, New Jersey
Bower T G R 1974 Repetition in human development. *Merrill-Palmer Q.* 20: 303–18
Bower T G R 1978 Concepts of development. In: *Proc. 21st Int. Congress Psychology.* Presses Universitaires de France, Paris, pp. 79–98
Bowerman M 1978 Systematizing semantic knowledge: Changes over time in the child's organization of word meaning. *Child Dev.* 49: 977–87
Carey S, Diamond R, Woods B 1980 The development of face perception: A maturational basis? *Dev. Psych.* 16: 257–69
Emmerich W, Goldman K S, Kirsch B, Sharabany R 1977

Evidence for a transitional phase in the development of gender constancy. *Child Dev.* 48: 930–36

Gardner H, Kircher M, Winner E, Perkins D 1975 Children's metaphoric productions and preferences. *J. Child Lang.* 2: 125–41

Strauss S 1982a Ancestral and descendant behaviors: The case of U-shaped behavioral growth. In: Bever T G (ed.) 1982 pp. 191–220

Strauss S (ed.) 1982b *U-shaped Behavioral Growth.* Academic Press, New York

Strauss S 1986 Three sources of differences between educational and developmental psychology: Resolution through educational–developmental psychology. *Instruct. Sci.* 15: 275–86

Strauss S 1987 Educational–developmental psychology and school learning. In: Liben L (ed.) 1987 *Development and Learning: Conflict or Congruence?* Erlbaum, Hillsdale, New Jersey, pp. 133–57

Strauss S, Bichler E 1988 The development of children's concept of the arithmetic average. *J. Res. Math. Educ.* 19: 64–80

Strauss S, Stavy R 1982 U-shaped behavioral growth: Implications for theories of development. In: Hartup W W (ed.) 1982 *Review of Child Development Research* University of Chicago Press, Chicago, Illinois, pp. 547–99

Turiel E 1974 Conflict and transition in adolescent moral development. *Child Dev.* 45: 14–29

Curriculum Politics

K. Frey

Curriculum politics characterizes all those actions consciously aimed at influencing a planned learning situation. Examples of such actions are declarations made by teachers' associations demanding more hours for their subject in the curriculum, or statements made by a political group interested in having a certain theme treated in a particular way. Such actions are not necessarily qualified as curriculum specific. They do not always have an educational quality. Curriculum research does, however, take these actions into account in order to better understand the influences on the curriculum process, that is, on the development of planned learning situations (e.g., for the United States: Boyd 1978, for Sweden, the Federal Republic of Germany, the United Kingdom, the Soviet Union: Hörner and Waterkamp 1981). Analysis of such conscious influences on curricula is referred to by researchers as curriculum politics.

Curriculum politics and curriculum policy are sometimes used interchangeably. The term curriculum policy making, is also often encountered, referring to the process of decision making; for example, setting curricular goals or selecting a particular type of curriculum. Whenever a distinction is made between the terms, curriculum policy refers more to the systematic principles which are the basis for making decisions on teacher's autonomy, learning freedom, or the importance of scientific discipline for example. There is, however, no internationally recognized definition of the terms. Most authors define their terms ad hoc, and there is no homogeneous set of questions or methods which represent a normal scientific operation for the terms curriculum politics and curriculum policy.

1. Historical Background

The term curriculum politics is relatively new. The expression was rarely used before 1950. This is surprising since managerial points of view were used as early as 1890 in the planning of school systems (e.g., Rice 1912). Nevertheless the managerial points of departure have not been used as a basis for analyzing curriculum policy processes. Bobbitt (1924), and others since have emphasized the scientific construction of curricula and disregarded policy factors.

Examining the international literature, another interesting fact becomes apparent. Although the term curriculum exists in Spanish, French, Italian, German, and many other languages and is used in a scientific context, there are hardly any publications about curriculum politics or curriculum policy. Curriculum studies using the terms curriculum politics or curriculum policy have apparently become the speciality of British and American experts. Mainly in their work, studies are encountered which examine the process of decision making, the use of experts and expertise in the process of curriculum development, or the use of models for curriculum legitimation (e.g., Hameyer et al. 1983, Laporta et al. 1978, Frey et al. 1979).

The term "curriculum policy" is not usually found in socialist countries as policy processes are generally decided upon by the governing bodies of the party, and it is not a research topic of great interest. The majority of studies dealing with curriculum policy and politics address themselves to the school program, while in the context of studies about the mass media educational programs or about educational programs of large cultural or religious groups, these terms are seldom encountered. An exception is the lifelong education program of UNESCO and the Organisation for Economic Co-operation and Development (OECD).

2. Organization of Curriculum Processes

Organization of curriculum processes is a main theme in the literature on curriculum politics and curriculum policy. The basic question is whether curricular decisions should be made by the central (national) authorities or at the local level, or more precisely, what should be the responsibility of central and of local authorities in decision making (Lawton 1980, Boyd 1978).

A series of case studies documents the functions of centralized and decentralized curriculum decisions and provides information about their effects (Bass and Berman 1979, van Geel 1976). Internationally, the most important studies have been carried out by the Centre for Educational Research and Innovation (CERI) of OECD with the program title *School-based Curriculum Reform* (OECD 1979). Numerous conceptual studies have originated in developing countries as well as in highly industrialized countries. In these studies the question of organization of curricula at the regional and local level has been treated (Furter 1980, Debeauvais 1976). Most conceptual studies recommend stronger centralization (in comparison to existing state school systems) in order to meet regional and local requirements and to increase the chances of adequate program implementation. These studies present various models and paradigms of decentralization; however, there is no evidence that these programmatic models will be implemented. On the contrary, the national studies of the World Bank and UNESCO report an increase in school enrollment, and suggest that this may lead towards a higher level of curriculum centralization.

3. Power and (Cultural) Reproduction

This theme also runs through the studies about curriculum politics and curriculum policy that have been carried out since the early 1960s. Here the question is, how does the present culture and civilization fit into the curriculum? How is the present social structure reinforced by the school curriculum? What are the mechanisms built into the curriculum which contribute to maintaining the social structure, the economic order of the society, the dominant religious and cultural values, and the general living conditions?

Several studies attempted to answer these questions. Thus, for example, Bourdieu and Passeron (1964) demonstrate how the knowledge and attitudes of various social classes are reflected in the school curriculum in France, and how, independent of the school selection system, the school curriculum helps to perpetuate the existing social order. Bernstein (1974) presented the thesis that the curricula are, to a great extent, determined by the classification system of existing knowledge, and by the framework within which it is offered. A Swedish group of researchers headed by Lundgren (1981) investigated the mechanisms used in revising primary-school curricula and identified communication

forms and organizational structures as central factors in curriculum processes.

Worldwide there are more than a dozen studies of this type. Unfortunately, there are no comparative presentations and synopses. The reason for this is, on the one hand, the differing conditions in the various language areas, nations, or educational systems, and, on the other hand, the lack of a uniform formulation of questions and methods of analysis. To produce such a platform it would be necessary to agree upon systematic and standard methods for studying curriculum politics.

Bibliography

Bass G V, Berman P 1979 *Federal Aid to Rural Schools: Current Patterns and Unmet Needs*. Rand, Santa Monica, California

Bernstein B 1974 On the classification and framing of educational knowledge. In: Bernstein B 1974 *Class, Codes and Control*, 2nd edn., Vol. 1: *Theoretical Studies Towards a Sociology of Language*. Routledge and Kegan Paul, London, pp. 202–30

Bobbitt J F 1924 *How to Make a Curriculum*. Houghton Mifflin, Boston, Massachusetts

Bourdieu P, Passeron J-C 1964 *Les Héritiers, les étudiants et la culture*, Vol. 1. Editions de Minuit, Paris

Boyd W L 1978 The changing politics of curriculum policymaking for American schools. *Rev. Educ. Res.* 48: 577–628

Debeauvais M 1976 *L'Université ouverte: Les dossiers de Vincennes*. Presses Universitaires de Grenoble, Grenoble

Frey K et al. 1979 *Developmental Strategy and Evaluation of a New School in Switzerland*. Organisation for Economic Co-operation and Development (OECD), pp. 129–53

Furter P 1980 *Les Systèmes de formation dans leurs contextes*. Lang, Bern

Hameyer et al. (eds.) 1983 *Handbuch der Curriculumforschung*. Beltz, Weinheim

Hörner W, Waterkamp D (eds.) 1981 *Curriculumentwicklung im internationalen Vergleich*. Beltz, Weinheim

Laporta R et al. 1978 *Curricolo e scuola. Innovazione educativa e sviluppo sociale*. Istituto della Enciclopedia Italiana fondata da G. Treccani, Roma

Lawton D 1980 *The Politics of the School Curriculum*. Routledge and Kegan Paul, London

Lundgren U P, Svingby G, Wallin E 1981 *Från Lgr 69 till Lgr 80. Erfarenheter från läroplansarbete*. Högsskolan för lärarutbildning i Stockholm 2 Stockholm

Organisation for Economic Co-operation and Development (OECD) 1979 *School-based Curriculum Development*. OECD, Paris

Rice J M 1912 *Scientific Management in Education*. Hinds, Noble and Eldredge, New York

van Geel T 1976 *Authority to Control the School Program*. Heath, Lexington, Massachusetts

Curriculum Policy Management

R. G. Townsend

By way of sketching a portion of the interplay that helps shape curriculum, this article highlights four institutions that bring together political authorities and managers.

Also mapped are two dichotomies within that interplay: morality and prudentiality, incrementalism, and comprehensiveness. Brief mention is also made of research at school and district levels on the crucial part that teachers and principals play in policy management for curriculum.

Strictly speaking, curriculum policy making is the determination of who gets taught what in schools; management is the enactment of that determination. In the past, elected officials—the presumed political authorities—sometimes have been seen as mere rubber stamps of managerial enactments about the pace, substance, and method of instruction. However, certain politicians have voiced a deep interest not only in issues of finance, personnel, school plant, and district organization, but also in curriculum policies that would develop the personal capacities of individuals, impart skills useful to society, induce conformity to community values, and generally promote socialization (Townsend 1988). As a result, in some jurisdictions, the political and managerial facets of curriculum policy are so difficult to disentangle that career administrators, with their multifaceted analyses (Creighton 1983) and their preferences that politicians often honor, can be regarded as professional policy makers. Meantime, because politicians come to their overseer role by election or appointment rather than by training, and because they may be as much concerned with how their curricular purpose is achieved as with their purpose itself, politicians can be regarded as amateur administrators (Hodgkinson 1978, Allison 1983). This suggestion, which underlies the treatment below, extends the political science commonplace that senior managers, if they are to have impact, must become amateur politicians.

1. A Typology at the Societal Level

Gauthier (1963) has argued that practical judgments involve both prudential and moral reasoning. Prudential reasoning is restricted to the wants, desires, needs, and aims of the agent; moral reasoning, however, takes account of the wants of others. That distinction between "I want, so I act" (prudential reasoning) and "you want, so you act, so I assist you" (moral reasoning) can be a starting point for sorting out interactions around curriculum.

Another dimension of policy management can revolve around the two dominant approaches towards collective problem solving (Lindblom 1977, Boyd 1978). The first is the rationality of incrementalism. There, authorities react to issues in a highly disjointed and decentralized manner. Interactive processes such as debate and bargaining are tapped to find policies that prove acceptable to participants. A second approach to collective problem solving is the nonincremental rationality of comprehensiveness. In this mode, political and managerial actors try to analyze extensively problem situations, determine clear objectives, and search widely for reasonable options. The comprehensive style of policy making also might be described as anticipatory (Richardson et al. 1982), as decision makers try to anticipate and resolve potential policy problems before they become crises.

With only one allusion to education, Manzer (1984) has fused those four elements into a typology of public policy making in general. Manzer's two dichotomies can be understood as variables in a societal field wherein different institutions of policy management can be systematically located for curriculum. Decidedly, exceptions will always exist to the distinctions made below. Certainly too, other depictions are possible, for example, of cosmopolitan professional reformers who tend toward comprehensiveness, and of local officials who, in avoiding the controversial, tend toward incrementalism (Boyd 1978). All the same, with a focus (not treated by Manzer) on the interaction between policy makers and managers, four other examples of curriculum policy management can be presented as fitting reasonably well into each of the four corners of that societal field (see Table 1). Note that along with the Author's use of the term "policy management" instead of "policy making," the emphasis on political parties departs from Manzer's (1984) suggestion of "ministry policy making."

2. The Courts as Incremental Institutions

Judicial policy management for curriculum, still fairly rare in most nations, involves the incremental reactions of judges who necessarily deal with cases one at a time. Moral reasoning comes into play as judges ensure that adversarial lawyers adhere to principles of procedural justice. The law—taking into account concern for others and interested in resolving possible disruptions of relationships—constitutes an important constraining or structuring influence on policy choices made by courts. For as judges sort through the evidence and ponder the

Table 1
A typology with societal examples of curriculum policy management

Predominant approach to problem solving	Predominant type of practical reasoning	
	Moral	Prudential
Incremental, reactive	Judicial	Budgetary
Comprehensive, anticipatory	Commission	Political party

statutes they are expected to implement, considerations of fairness are expected to prevail over partisanship. To reinforce that moral press for nonpartisanship, on appeal the courts' measured responses can be overturned.

The place of religion in the public curriculum has been a common matter for judicial review. Thus, in Australia, a state court upheld general religious teaching for public schools (Birch 1983), while—to take another Commonwealth example—certain Canadian judges have decreed that, at least in their multicultural society, the saying of the Lord's Prayer unfairly promotes one religion over others. A United States court's moral reasoning about the teaching of creation science necessarily relied on that different culture's norm: sacred in-school teachings were held to violate constitutional provisions for church and state separation. Among other aspects of United States curricula affected, on a case-by-case basis, by judges' reactions are bilingual education (Lau vs. Nichols), minimum competency (Robinson vs. Cahill), and the notion that outcomes should be achieved in a thorough and efficient system of public education (Pauley vs. Kelly).

For school managers—charged with mobilizing resources, overseeing tasks, and monitoring programs—courts carry considerable but not invincible authority (Baum 1985). Hence, after the United States Supreme Court's decisions in the early 1960s prohibiting certain school religious practices, some school managers felt an obligation to eliminate those practices even prior to threats of direct court orders. In effect, these managers realized that failure to implement a policy faithfully could lead to costly legal challenges, adverse judicial rulings, and losses of their organizations' autonomy should court-appointed officials take over their school districts. When, however, courts are somewhat vague (failing to identify precisely who is responsible for action, the timing required for rectifying policy defects, or the specific manner in which justice is to be achieved), managers can delay action and pass the buck. Thus, when the United States Supreme Court maintained an ambiguous position on the timing of school desegregation for more than a decade, the all deliberate speed formula maximized managerial discretion, thereby promoting evasion and delaying the introduction of new curricula for blacks and whites as colearners (Peltason 1971).

3. Budgets as Incremental Institutions

Typically, budgetary policy management involves prudential reasoning and a mode of problem solving that, like the judicial institutions, is reactive and incremental. Because of the sheer complexity of any district's budget, generally only incremental problem solving is attempted from budget year to budget year, and through low-profile adjustments at that. Allocations are made to facilitate new approaches, but politicians and educators usually are constrained by such accepted norms as fair

shares of the total budget, to which all of a district's programs have historical claim. Proponents of various systems-analysis tools (such as zero-based budgeting, program evaluation review techniques, and teaching as a series of technologies) have attempted to introduce more comprehensive rationality into the process of resource allocation for curricula. Yet these approaches have met with little widespread success (Hoos 1983).

In budgeting for education, prudentialism is evident as authorities take on the colorations of their policy roles. Agency leaders self-interestedly vie for more funds for programs; treasury officials just as self-interestedly seek to save taxpayers' money. Hence, as Minister of Education, Margaret Thatcher could boast at one point that "In my monthly battles with the Treasury, I managed to get another £76 million" (Jordan and Richardson 1987 p. 204). Later, as Prime Minister of a government elected on a promise to cut public spending, Thatcher acted as more of a guardian of the state's purse: money saved in education (and in other areas) was diverted to pay for increases in defense. Similarly, school administrators also fight their corner, that is, a curriculum manager will look for infusions of money, a business manager will push for across-the-board economies.

Budgetary determinations can reflect particular sets of values, so much so that both politicians and managers prudentially interact around the details. Consider, for example, a set of possible funding schemes in classifying United States students for programs of special education (Hartman 1980). A policy actor self-interested in discouraging both the over-classification of students as handicapped and the reintegration of children with disabilities into regular classrooms (mainstreaming) will favor a resource-based formula. A policy actor wanting, on the other hand, to encourage more students to be served (including more mildly handicapped children), while encouraging the retention of children there, thereby netting higher reimbursements from treasuries, will support a child-based formula. Thirdly, a policy actor would opt for a cost-based formula if he or she wants to discourage overclassification while encouraging appropriate placement. Much as a budget's intricacies help to shape a policy, funding levels also reflect a policy, as, for example, when cuts in allocations for certain text books would enable United States policy makers and managers to defuse the charge that their texts teach predominantly militaristic, male, and white history at the expense of attention to blacks, Hispanics, Native Americans, women, and the working class.

Managers may indicate to policy makers that their budgets are efficient, but managers have not especially exploited research on the most cost-effective techniques for delivering curriculum policy (Levin 1988). For instance, cross-age tutoring in reading and mathematics achievement at elementary levels is highly cost-effective, especially for students from low and medium socio-economic backgrounds. Yet this technique, and others, await extensive adaptation.

4. *Commissions as Comprehensive Institutions*

With its attention to societal needs and characteristics, commission policy management offers the possibility of a more comprehensive and anticipatory approach in defining instructional objectives and means. To be sure, the prominent laypersons and experts on some commissions take more of an investigatory than a long-range policy or planning tack, perhaps exaggerating the problem while wallowing in strong rhetoric and very selective uses of evidence. Others, however, such as the Federal Republic of Germany's Education Commission, Quebec's Parent Commission, and Sweden's Royal Commissions have probed comprehensive education over several years in truly rationalist and synoptic ways. So too have study groups in United States state capitals who have advocated curricular alignment, where the same content is emphasized and covered across a state— via lessons, tests, textbook adoption criteria, university entrance content expectations, and criteria for teacher evaluation (Kirst 1987). As they morally reason, such blue-ribbon bodies propose any number of curricular ideas to assist selected others, for example, the disadvantaged deserve equal opportunity, immigrants should be socialized by the host society's schools.

Commissions often have expressed their ideas in so abstract a manner that managers have been able to maintain that their programs already meet commission standards. Regretfully too, some commissions have seemed to overlook problems of curriculum implementation, failing to reconcile their policies with the resources that managers actually can mobilize. Even so, managers can respond to certain commissions as useful ideamongers for bruiting about curricular ideas at national or state/provincial levels. Over time, a number of those ideas filter down through layers of government, provoking discussion and eventually becoming cast into language that leads to managerial monitoring and enforcement (Ginsberg and Wimpelberg 1987).

Certain commissions do go beyond simply studying a problem and generating discussion about recommendations. Given a broad mandate over a narrow domain, not only to devise guidelines but also to prepare, produce, and distribute free textbooks and work books to all children in the first six grades of school, Mexico's National Commission for Free Textbooks was an ongoing enterprise. In its duration and managerialism, Mexico's Commission can be contrasted, say, to Britain's solution-proposing, synoptic, and short-lived, advisory Plowden Commission for child-centered education.

5. *Political Parties as Comprehensive Institutions*

A second mode with comprehensive reasoning, political party policy management, also has strong elements of self-regarding prudential thinking. Political parties are guided in many of their actions by a calculation of electoral effect (Sartori 1973). Subject to some constraints, they develop platforms which can aggregate assorted interests. To maximize votes, they anticipate what constituents will want next year and they work on aspects of the future that they can influence. Parties also may enhance their vote-capturing positions by responding to public and professional malaise, as when the Haby reforms in France in 1975 enabled social studies teachers to choose among alternative topics, a departure from the schools' previous encyclopedic approach (Hough 1984). Similarly, certain United States Republicans in the 1980s fastened on the idea of a revitalized core, and an Australian ruling party banned textbooks, a course of study, and a set of materials for a controversial culturally relative subject, "Man: A Course of Study" (Smith and Knight 1978).

Curriculum reforms often are just one of a party's agenda items. Thus in Vancouver, two municipal parties have championed contrasting and well-thought-out alternatives for school curricula, one socialistic and the other conservative (Morgan and Robinson 1976). Those platforms respectively reflect the parties' orientations towards overcoming class inequities, on one side, and towards favoring social continuity and free enterprise, on the other side. In the same vein, in those regions of the Federal Republic of Germany with a Prussian tradition and controlled by Social Democrats, the ruling party advocates curricula that value such qualities as creativity and an inquiring attitude to society and the state. In contradiction, within those regions controlled by the Christian Democrats and with a long Roman Catholic tradition, the ruling party espouses curricula with the old school subjects that tend to support an emotional identification with nation and home (Schwark and Wolf 1984). Again, both parties' curriculum thrusts reflect their general dispositions towards change.

Professionals in the managerial ranks of education often interact heatedly with—or try to talk past—partisan politicians. Commonly, educators hold that curriculum represents the very essence of their expert judgment and so, the standards of their particular profession ought to carry greater weight in policy-setting than those which do not. These educators point to mistakes made by politicians who would ensure, for instance, that all students encounter the same information in the same way, demonstrating the same skills within a given course or grade level. Educators see this as a process which is detrimental to education, not allowing either for student differences or teacher judgment (Darling-Hammond 1987). For their part, political-party activists counter that while educators might be the right people to decide whether and how a certain kind of instructional policy can be delivered, the educators' standards might not be appropriate to deciding, rightly or wrongly, if a particular curriculum should be delivered. In any event, curriculum-setting increasingly is regarded as a shared responsibility (Short 1983), one that involves contributions from political parties.

6. Deliberations at the District and School Levels

Stimulated by a call from Schwab (1973) for knowledge about what practitioners actually do, a number of scholars have developed a body of literature on teachers' instructional and organizational arrangements for curriculum construction. These writings, far smaller and less empirical than the spate of works about implementation, explore the spiral discovery of meanings among teachers putting together their understandings of content, resources, and activities (see Roby 1985, Atkins 1986, Bonser and Grundy 1988). Scholars have noted how teachers argue over curriculum alternatives, the types of reasons they entertain for preferring one option over another, and the bases on which they ultimately accept and reject proposals.

The distinctions in this field are not yet settled. They range from Pereira's (1984) interpretation of Schwab's arts of the practical (with attention to students, teachers, subject matter, and milieu) to Harris' (1986) suggestion of persuasive, descriptive, and theoretical discourses. Roby (1985) emphasizes critical reflection, review, and revision while Walker and Soltis (1986) highlight a democratic approach to debating the merits of competing policies, programs, and practices.

Finally, after years of de-emphasis, the principal as manager of curriculum policy is being appreciated (see Leithwood and Montgomery 1985), sometimes as one who helps to shape the policy through the implementation process, perhaps by enacting changes or by referring problems with the new policy back to superordinates. It is thought that the principal can bring pressure on the curriculum by conducting personnel and program evaluation, by specifying subjects to be taught with different materials, by inspecting lesson plans for their appropriateness and coherence, by valuing detailed record-keeping on student's progress, by ascertaining that policies regarding use of time on task are being fulfilled, and by ensuring that differential resources go to deserving students.

Bibliography

Allison D 1983 Policy and the practice of educational administration. *Canad. Admin.* 23(1): 1–8

Atkins E 1986 The deliberative process: An analysis from three perspectives. *J. Curric. Superv.* 1(4): 265–93

Baum L 1985 Legislatures, courts, and the disposition of policy implementors. In: Edwards G C (ed.) 1985 *Public Policy Implementation.* JAI Press, Greenwich, Connecticut, pp. 29–58

Birch I K F 1983 Non-public education in the US and Australia: The courts in educational policymaking. In: Hancock G, Kirst M W, Grossman D L (eds.) 1983 *Contemporary Issues in Educational Policy: Perspectives from Australia and USA.* ACT Schools Authority and Curriculum Development Centre, Canberra, pp. 203–22

Bonser S A, Grundy S J 1988 Reflective deliberation in the formulation of a school curriculum policy. *J. Curric. Stud.* 20(1): 35–45

Boyd W L 1978 The changing politics of curriculum policy-making for American schools. *Rev. Educ. Res.* 48: 577–628

Creighton H 1983 Analysing policy development in curriculum innovation: A suggested approach. *J. Educ. Adm.* 21(2): 121–36

Darling-Hammond L 1987 The over-regulated curriculum and the press for teacher professionalism. *NASSP Bull.* 71(498): 22–29

Gauthier D P 1963 *Practical Reasoning.* Clarendon Press, Oxford

Ginsberg R, Wimpelberg R K 1987 Educational change by commission: Attempting "trickle down" reform. *Educ. Eval. Pol. Anal.* 9(4): 344–60

Harris I B 1986 Communicating the character of 'deliberation'. *J. Curr. Stud.* 18(2): 115–32

Hartman W T 1980 Policy effects of special education funding formulas. *J. Educ. Finance* 6: 135–59

Hodgkinson C 1978 *Towards a Philosophy of Administration.* Blackwell, Oxford

Hoos I R 1983 *Systems Analysis in Public Policy: A Critique.* University of California, Berkeley, California

Hough J R 1984 France. In: Hough J R (ed.) 1984 *Educational Policy: An International Survey.* Croom Helm, London, pp. 71–99

Jordan A G, Richardson J J 1987 *British Politics and the Policy Process.* Allen and Unwin, London

Kirst M W 1987 Curricular leadership at the state level: What is the new focus? *NASSP Bull.* 71(498): 8–14

Leithwood K A, Montgomery D J 1985 The role of the principal in school improvement. In: Austin G R, Garber H (eds.) 1985 *Research on Exemplary Schools.* Academic, Orlando, Florida, pp. 155–77

Levin H M 1988 Cost-effectiveness and educational policy. *Educ. Eval. Pol. Anal.* 10(1): 51–69

Lindblom C E 1977 *Politics and Markets: The World's Political-Economic Systems.* Basic Books, New York

Manzer R 1984 Public policy-making as practical reasoning. *Canad. J. Pol. Sci.* 17(3): 377–93

Morgan M T, Robinson N 1976 The "back to the basics" movement in education. *Canad. J. Educ.* 1(2): 1–11

Peltason J W 1971 *Fifty-eight Lonely Men: Southern Federal Judges and School Desegregation.* University of Illinois Press, Urbana, Illinois

Pereira P 1984 Deliberation and the arts of perception. *J. Curric. Stud.* 16(4): 347–66

Richardson J, Gustafsson G, Jordan A G 1982 The concept of policy style. In: Richardson J (ed.) 1982 *Policy Styles in Western Europe.* Allen and Unwin, London, pp. 1–16

Roby T W 1985 Habits impeding deliberation. *J. Curric. Stud.* 17: 17–35

Sartori G 1973 *Democratic Theory.* Greenwood, Westport, Connecticut

Schwab J 1973 The practical 3: Translation into curriculum. *Sch. Rev.* 81: 501–22

Schwark W, Wolf A 1984 West Germany. In: Hough J R (ed.) 1984 *Educational Policy: An International Survey.* Croom Helm, London, pp. 257–92

Short E C 1983 Authority and governance in curriculum development: A policy analysis in the United States context. *Educ. Eval. Pol. Anal.* 5(2): 195–205

Smith R A, Knight J 1978 MACOS in Queensland: The politics of educational knowledge. *Aust. J. Educ.* 22(5): 225–48

Townsend R G 1988 *They Politick For Schools.* OISE Press, Toronto

Walker D F, Soltis J F 1986 *Curriculum and Aims.* Teachers College, New York

Economic, Social, and Cultural Factors

M. Skilbeck

The curriculum may be thought of as a map or chart of experiences through which the student is expected to learn efficiently and to apply those learnings in life situations. From a social standpoint, that map or chart of experiences is, or ought to be, a systematic introduction to the culture, a means whereby the student is drawn into the major forms and modes of thought and experience and learns to use them—in however limited a fashion—creatively and practically as well as cognitively. These are, of course, idealized notions of the curriculum since, in practice, the chart of students' experience and the map of the culture are subject to pressures and forces which both impart imbalances and distortions and sharpen up or place in focus particular themes, issues, or areas of contemporary experience.

How these sociocultural pressures and forces affect the curriculum has been the subject of intensive investigation in many countries. Insight has been gained into the manner in which the curriculum does change in its social context, and experience has been gained in ways of organizing large-scale curriculum change aimed at keeping it topical and relevant. Yet there are still large gaps in our understanding, and little agreement over certain key issues. Educational theorists are divided on the question of whether the school curriculum is, or can be, other than a social artifact, a rather flat image, or a reflection of prevailing social values and dominant interest groups, or whether, as some radical commentators aver, it is capable of sponsoring and fostering significant social and cultural change. There is little disagreement, however, over the extent and complexity of sociocultural factors that need to be taken into account if how the curriculum relates to the sociocultural context is to be explained, and ways are to be sought to change its direction and its effect on learning. It is no longer possible to treat the curriculum of any educational institution as if it exists in isolation from a wider community, or separate from the society from which it draws its students, teachers, and the resources needed to sustain it.

1. Curriculum Exposed to Economic Forces

A common assumption amongst several schools of social theorists, ranging from Marxists and neo-Marxists to advocates of a market approach, is that the curriculum either is, or can be made to be, directly responsive to forces and trends in the economy. Sometimes this point is generalized, from the economy to a wider set of features of social structure, notably the interests of particular social classes or occupational groups, or specific value sets such as those associated with religious beliefs.

There has been a strong move by governments, in recent years, to use the curriculum as part of a wider strategy of economic restructuring and development. This goes beyond the by now common prevocational and work experience programs in secondary schools, as utilitarian values and language feature increasingly in policies and priorities for the whole of education.

From an analytic standpoint, the workings of the economy have come into greater prominence in curriculum affairs since the early 1960s and especially in the mid- to late 1980s than at any previous time in history. This is true of both the so-called developed Western economies and the so-called developing world, where the uses of education for economic advancement have been actively explored by national governments and aid and development agencies, as well as by educational interest groups.

The key factor in explaining curriculum trends, for all of these schools of thought, lies in the dynamics of the economy in interaction with traditional beliefs, prevailing values, and customary practices in schooling. On the one hand, these dynamics and interactions are believed to determine what schools teach and what they give priority to, who attends school, for how long, and with what measure of success: curriculum equates with economic substructure by responding mechanically to its demands. This is an extreme form of economic determinism, which minimizes or discounts the significance either of pedagogically inspired reform or of broadly based national policies which attempt to determine the curriculum according to the needs and interests of a wide array of social groups. Such extreme opinions are seldom supported by empirical data but do represent a fashionable intellectual theory. On the other hand there are those who, adopting an essentially economic efficiency stance, criticize the school curriculum for its traditionalism, inflexibility, and irrelevance in the face of changes in investment, consumption, and employment. This is not a deterministic position but rather one which argues for curriculum to show responsiveness to one of several sets of forces which are changing the world.

The first of the above positions is, typically in Western society, that adopted by Marxist and neo-Marxist economic determinists. The second position is favored by politicians, officials, applied economists, and employer groups, especially in those societies which have succumbed to economic recession and high youth unemployment, for example England and Wales, the United States, and Australia. In these societies—and indeed more widely—disbelief has grown in the returns from investment in formal education and in expanded schooling as a generator of economic growth. This reaction is partly a natural consequence of exaggerated and poorly formulated claims advanced by economists and taken up by international agencies and national governments during the period of worldwide economic expansion in the 1950s and 1960s. In part, it reflects a shift in social policy and in resource allocation towards other sectors, such as health and social welfare. It is significant that where population growth and hence the proportion of young people in the population has eased or declined, these shifts are most noticeable.

These economic changes and their educational reverberations suggest that the salience of a particular social factor in the political arena will affect curriculum policy, whether or not that factor has been shown through analysis to have an underlying structural significance. The influence of a social factor on the curriculum is discernible in media interest in education and political response to public interest in issues. It would be a mistake to suppose that the influence of such factors is determined either by rational policy analysis, or by specifically educational concerns.

Whether the position of economic commentators is deterministic in the sense that the curriculum is treated as a function of underlying economic values and trends, or voluntaristic, in the sense that educationalists are being urged to restructure the curriculum to meet changing economic goals and conditions, it is still economic processes that are proposed as primary. The curriculum is, accordingly, perceived instrumentally rather than in terms that suggest either intrinsic educational or broadly cultural considerations. The inadequacy of this view is its inattention to the diversity of sociocultural forces and their interactions, and the reluctance to consider philosophical and cultural analyses which treat education and the curriculum as themselves actually or potentially being key factors in the society. The economic approaches of both the Marxist and market schools are essentially reductionist in their treatment of culture and curriculum.

Given the scale and upward trends of public investment in education, it is to be expected that an economic critique of the curriculum would give rise to political concern followed by action. There is evidence of this in many parts of the world but perhaps most obviously in those societies where there are highly developed and competitive media industries and a high degree of literacy. In developing countries, belief in the economic as well as the wider social returns of educational investment has remained strong, if not uniformly so. However, in many developed societies, literacy is very largely taken for granted outside the education profession itself and the function of schooling as an agency of social mobility has been increasingly questioned, by empirical investigators, and, more recently, through the impact of growing unemployment amongst youth who have completed several years of secondary schooling. The political response has been to call for accountability measures, to encourage a more utilitarian approach to the curriculum, to reduce the rate of increase of

educational expenditure, and to give support to those educational innovations which appear to point the way towards enhanced practical and recreational skills at the expense of a more broadly based general education. These responses are not, of course, independent of community concerns but are indeed an accurate reflection of growing public scepticism about the quality of education and those innovations in curriculum that have called into question many traditional practices. A further consequence for the curriculum has been a strengthening, in some countries, of public examinations and formal assessment procedures.

A striking example is the 1988 Education Act in England and Wales, through which central control of the curriculum and a comprehensive age-related assessment system have been introduced (or reintroduced).

2. Responses to Population Shifts

The effect of demographic movements combines with the economic trends and critiques in several different ways. Where rates of population increase are declining or stable, governments experiencing economic difficulties are inclined to reduce the flow of resources into education, or to shift resources to what are regarded as more dynamic processes such as research and development or technical/vocational programs, thus disregarding teacher union pressure for improved staffing ratios and better facilities. Major imbalances and uncertainties are created for the curriculum: declining enrolments in secondary schools, and higher retention rates, accompanied by cuts in staffing, make the delivery of certain kinds of curricula impossible; reductions in funds for materials and texts prevent schools from updating their learning resources. Where population continues to increase in developing countries, governments struggle, as they have done for decades, to provide a basic minimum curriculum for those in schools, and are unable to prevent overall increases in the number of illiterates even where they effect percentage improvements. The problem for developing countries has been intensified by oil price fluctuations, heavy loan debts, and recession in major Western markets. Another demographic consideration, in developed and developing countries alike, is that improvements in health care, nutrition, working conditions, and so forth, combined with birth rate trends, are resulting in massive increases in numbers of older people: the need for curricula for lifelong education is not a distant dream but a rapidly emerging reality.

A factor in population movements which is having a profound influence on the curricula of many countries is the movement of ethnic and cultural groups across national boundaries. Immigrant workers in Europe and the Americas, sponsored immigration in Australia and Israel, refugees in Southeast Asia, cultural regrouping in Africa are but examples of a massive, worldwide change in the ethnic and cultural components of the populations of nation states. They give rise to the teaching of mother tongue and national languages and multiculturalism across the curriculum, inequalities imposed by dominant group influence in the curriculum, and sheer pressure of space and resources. Nationalism has resurfaced throughout Central and Eastern Europe and, as national boundaries come under challenge, changes are occurring in the hegemonic curriculum regimes that emerged in the aftermath of World War Two.

3. Traditional Education and Changing Sociocultural Values

The most powerful of all curriculum traditions is the persistence of textbook-structured learning in curriculum areas where cognitive skills are essential, a method attractive to parents and teachers, if not always to pupils. Mastery of the text is the single most important goal in education and the means of achieving upward social mobility. This tradition derives from ancient religious practices and values in both Eastern and Western societies: all the major world religions lay emphasis on sacred texts and on knowledge of them.

Strengthened by the impact of professionalization in society and the consequent interest of the commercial and manufacturing bourgeoisie in formal schooling, and by its attractiveness as a low-cost tool for effective mass learning, the text has gained the consent of all occupational groups and social classes. The text symbolizes a received and bookish character in learning and, even where the curriculum has been castigated for its irrelevance, exclusiveness, and neglect of the practical and the everyday that character has persisted. In the minds of many, the text is the curriculum.

Two sociocultural factors offer an increasing challenge to the book domination of learning or, more generally, to the dominance of the academic curriculum: electric media and the drive towards vocational, trade, and practical skills training. The challenge is directed towards the assumptions that subject matter derived from a small set of cognitive subjects, such as language, mathematics, history, and science, and from their codification within texts of received knowledge, are the principal base and means of learning. The social changes underlying the challenges include the widespread displacement of labor and structural unemployment, technological revolutions, the growth of leisure industries, and the emergence of mass society on a world scale.

In the Western societies, in parts of the developing world and increasingly in the older communist societies, there is growing dissatisfaction with the performance and potential of the academic curriculum as a means for mass education. Television, where it is well-established, offers a challenge to the classroom as a focus of attention and a source of information; family and peer group experience are more basic sources of social and moral values than the school. Increasingly it is suggested that formal schooling is less the means of upward social mobility in the mass than in the elitist society and, for the older age group, work experience, travel, television, and leisure pursuits vie with formal education as a means of learning through experience.

4. A Sociocultural Critique of the Curriculum

Essentially, the critique of school curricula takes this form: education in schools and colleges is, in aggregate, a high-cost activity and a heavy charge on public funds. To be justified, this cost must lead to substantial returns including a high level of public satisfaction with the results of schooling and a visible responsiveness of curricula to changes in the wider sociocultural environment. Yet the educational service, in practice, seems to give high status to certain kinds of academic knowledge and ways of learning and to confer relative advantage on the minority who perform well in this curriculum, and thus it reinforces the social and economic advantage enjoyed by the more prosperous and socially powerful sections of the population. Access to knowledge via the academic curriculum is not in practice equally available to all. At the same time, this emphasis and status, by spreading over into the curriculum of all students, creates a mismatch between social need, personal opportunity, and learning tasks.

The curriculum, according to this view, is in its basic configuration overloaded with information and dominated by mental processes which correspond poorly with the large social and cultural transformations that the world is undergoing. In order to train groups of specialists to operate the modern economy and provide citizens with the rudiments of general social education and personal life skills, an elaborate and expensive system has to be maintained. Yet, it is said, such indicators as illiteracy rates in developing countries, and levels of practical social efficiency (and a concealed problem of adult illiteracy in many developed societies), suggest that schooling is making little progress relative to factors like population growth, structural changes in the economy, and the growth of communications media and leisure opportunities. It is social change itself that has rendered invalid the structuring of knowledge and experience through the academic curriculum and its delivery via the formal agency of schooling.

This school of thought is using its analysis of modern culture as a critique of curriculum and of schooling. Yet this critique is but one interpretation and assessment and although it has gained some ground, it has by no means displaced confidence in the conventional curriculum, as modified through updating of content and adjustments within the component subjects. The impact of this critique, and of the sociocultural factors in which it is grounded, is to be observed in research studies, in developments in curriculum theory, and in such practical changes as, in the developed countries, the upsurge of instrumentalist, practical, and skills-based courses and, in the developing world, in the growth of administrative and political interest in recurrent or lifelong education, adult learning by informal means, distance education, and mass applications of communications technology.

5. Curriculum for Development

From the perspective of most developing countries, where exceptional population pressures combine with poverty to make even universal primary schooling an unattainable goal, the issue is the relationship of curriculum to declared targets of nation building. Inheritance from colonial powers of curriculum assumptions has been a major influence even where new national goals and development targets call into question the continuing relevance of the inheritance. Development is seen as dynamic and open-ended, and new curricula for development are needed to replace those which derive from another kind of past.

From the perspective of developed countries, the impact of social, economic, and technological change upon the curriculum has meant that there have been attempts to transform content in existing subject areas (the curriculum project movement centering on the United States and the United Kingdom in the 1960s and spreading to many countries in the 1970s) and more radical schemes for rebuilding the whole curriculum in order to respond to the kinds of criticisms already noted. Despite the criticism and research evidence (sometimes contradictory) on the perceived value and performance of school curricula, the changes in most of these countries have been slow and evolutionary, rather than dramatic.

The curriculum of the school has a remarkable resistance to those social and cultural factors which seem to call for or imply substantial institutional adjustments, and a receptivity towards those factors which seem to reinforce existing values and practices. It is for this reason that many who accept that the school curriculum is a significant determiner of learning and of life chances, are doubtful about the reconstructionist argument that the curriculum itself should be a major force for social and cultural change. Despite this scepticism, and the intellectual popularity of neo-Marxist claims that the essential social function of the school curriculum is to reproduce the cultural order of the dominant classes in society and to ensure mass acquiescence in this state of affairs, the reconstructionist position has not been abandoned. It first gained prominence in the early-twentieth-century writings of John Dewey and amongst his American followers, in the depression of the 1930s, and was also an early dimension of communist educational theory in the Soviet Union in the 1920s. Reconstructionism has re-emerged in the context of postcolonial education for nation building.

Reversing the usual sociological interpretation of the curriculum as the mediator and transmitter of existing culture, the reconstructionist claim is that a radically transformed curriculum may be our major means of transforming that culture both by encouraging in students a critique of it and providing them with intellectual and practical resources for the recreation of culture. These are dramatic claims which have not been conceded by many educationists and are strongly resisted by some politicians and administrators.

The continuing impact on the curriculum of technological change, of shifts of populations across national boundaries, and hence the multiculturalism of schooling, of reduced rates of spending on education, and other social and cultural factors is seen by some as evidence of the adaptability of schooling and the capacity of educators to adjust curricula adequately. This is the view that schooling is able to continue to be socially responsive through curriculum evolution. For others, these movements have pointed out major structural weaknesses in curriculum content and design (see *Curriculum Content*; *Curriculum Design*). They constitute a challenge to show how curriculum may in fact serve as an agency of sociocultural development in an era when the competition for resources is greater than ever.

Bibliography

Apple M W (ed.) 1982 *Cultural and Economic Reproduction in Education: Essays on Class, Ideology and the State*. Routledge and Kegan Paul, Boston, Massachusetts

Bowles S, Gintis H 1976 *Schooling in Capitalist America: Educational Reform and the Contradictions of Economic Life*. Routledge and Kegan Paul, Boston, Massachusetts

Dawkins J S 1988 *Strengthening Australia's Schools*. Department of Employment and Training, Canberra, Australian National Capital

Dewey J 1916 *Democracy and Education: An Introduction to the Philosophy of Education*. Macmillan, New York

Gorter R (ed.) 1986 *Views on Core Curriculum*. National Institute for Curriculum Developments, Enschede, Netherlands

Hamilton D 1989 *Towards a Theory of Schooling*. Falmer Press, London

Hargreaves D II 1982 *The Challenge for the Comprehensive School*. Routledge and Kegan Paul, London

Husén T 1979 *The School in Question: A Comparative Study of the School and its Future in Western Society*. Oxford University Press, London

Kliebard H M 1986 *The Struggle for the American Curriculum*. Routledge and Kegan Paul, London

Lawton D 1983 *Curriculum Studies and Educational Planning*. Hodder and Stoughton, London

Musgrove F 1980 *School and the Social Order*. Wiley, London

OECD 1989. *Schools and Quality*. OECD, Paris

Rizvi F 1985. *Multiculturalism as an Educational Policy*. Deakin University Press, Geelong, Victoria

Rutter M, Maughan B, Mortimore P, Ouston J, Smith A 1979 *Fifteen Thousand Hours: Secondary Schools and their Effects on Children*. Open Books, London

Skilbeck M 1984 *School-based Curriculum Development*. Harper and Row, London

Explosion of Knowledge

Y. Elkana

Knowledge explosion refers to two well-known aspects of contemporary culture. First to the rapid growth of encyclopedic knowledge. The direct result of this phenomenon is that the "library" of all accumulated knowledge is rapidly growing, and serious technical problems are posed for information storing which, in turn, pose interesting theoretical problems for the communication and information sciences (Kochen 1974). Secondly it refers to the fact that with the globally spreading literacy and organization of society on the model of one of the great civilizations (Western, Chinese, Japanese, or Indian), more and more individuals belong to that stratum of society that reads daily newspapers and must be knowledgeable enough to understand what is read, and form an opinion about the issues. This is what may be called the social explosion of knowledge.

The present article deals with the educational consequences of the rapidly growing accumulated knowledge.

1. The Individual's Store of Knowledge

The growth of accumulated knowledge does not imply that parallel to it, it is desirable that the quantity of the individual's knowledge should equally increase or should increase at all. That the individual's store of knowledge need not, and does not in fact change drastically can be supported by two arguments:

(a) A change occurs in the individual's store of commonsense knowledge;

(b) A cultural amnesia may be observed inside the disciplines.

1.1 The Changing Content of Knowledge

In literate cultures the average "person-in-the-street" today must have sufficient knowledge to understand, and take a stand on, all issues brought by daily newspapers. This means some level of understanding for labour relations, international finance, political ideologies, nuclear disarmament and nuclear reactors for peaceful purposes, problems of energy, water desalination, cultural policy, state support for the arts and higher education, water-borne diseases, epidemics, public health, and so on. This haphazard list was compiled after looking at one issue of a daily paper. No doubt, even if the stand taken on each and every issue here is ill-founded or wrong, and even if the understanding underlying the position taken is partial or faulty, much more knowledge is involved than an average literate person would have had a few hundred years ago. However, there is also a huge store of information and even knowledge that today's person-in-the-street does not possess which his or her lucky or unlucky forebears had to have if they wanted to lead a normal life. A few hundred years ago a person would have had to know as much as today's rare expert astronomers know, about the movements of the stars, about the tides and the climate, the names of the Saints and the days of the year dedicated to them, the hierarchy of the clergy and of the aristocracy by status and name, the vicissitudes of the supply of grain and other commodities in detail in neighbouring areas, the numberless regulations (superstitious or not, according to our standards) about avoiding epidemics and diseases. Some of this is true for illiterate peasants, too. To gain insight into this issue, it is enough to read with this in mind one of the weighty local studies stemming from the Annales School of writing history, like for example, Emmanuel Le Roy Laudrie's '*Montaillou*' (1978), and see how a modern person would find his or her way in that society. He or she would not, mainly because of a lack of knowledge.

1.2 Cultural Amnesia

Cultural amnesia is also active inside disciplines. Students of physics study classical mechanics for a term or two in their first or second year at university. They will spend one week or so learning one chapter on the physics of the "top". Not so long ago, at the turn of the century, two leading physicists, Felix Klein and Arnold Sommerfeld, collaborated on a 1,000-page treatise *Über die Theorie des Kreisels* (1897–1911)—the theory of the top—which was taught for a whole year at German Universities. Now practically all that was contained in that heavy tome is included in principle in one chapter of the modern textbooks. This, however, does not mean that today's physics students, having studied that one chapter, have actually "mastered" the contents of the 1,000-page work by Klein and Sommerfeld. They have not, nor do they need to. The culture of contemporary science has made all that information superfluous. One more example: before the mechanical theory of heat was developed, namely the conviction and proof that heat was actually motion of particles—a realization that emerged together with Joule's (1818–1889) calculation of the mechanical equivalent of heat and Helmholtz's (1821–94) formulation of the general principle of conservation of energy—heat was considered an imponderable fluid called caloric, and before that a material substance called phlogiston. In the early stages of the modern theory of energy, fewer phenomena could be explained in terms of the new theory than in terms of caloric or even phlogiston. All that superseded knowledge, of explaining numerous thermal phenomena in caloric or phlogiston terms, was forgotten and is no longer available. This is cultural amnesia inside disciplines.

"Cultural amnesia" works in two directions: while it is true that much of what was forgotten can be unearthed or revived today—this is one of the main tasks of the historian of science—it is also true that predecessors, if they had set their minds to it or if the problem had been put to them, would have gained or developed knowledge about much of what was not known to them. The reason why this is rarely stated is that most cultural analysts tend to believe in a deterministic, more or less linear growth of knowledge. It is widely held that not only did the laws of mechanics develop before the laws of electromagnetism; taxonomy of plants before the genetic code; chemistry of affinities before the theory of atomic valence; "tabula rasa" cognitive psychology before Piagetian theory; mercantilism before Keynesian theory, and so on, but that the development had to proceed in this order. This view, however, is highly questionable and methodologically its status is no better than that of the other. The deterministic view of the growth of knowledge that A. N. Whitehead called the dramatic view is an epistemological presupposition of the same level as its opposite, namely that whatever had happened could have happened differently—the epic view as it was called by the German–Jewish thinker Walter Benjamin, in his book on Brecht (1966).

2. *Implications for What to Teach in School*

The view that there is a "genuine explosion" of knowledge as well as the opposite view, as explicated above, if accepted, is normative for curriculum planning.

The view that demands are posed by society on the individual's store of knowledge encourages a goal-oriented, specialized curriculum at all levels of schooling, a de-emphasizing of intellectual exploration because it may lead to "waste of time" and not to the acquisition of desired knowledge. It also may result in the discouragement of intellectual risk taking. The goal-oriented curriculum eliminates "unnecessary" literary skills, the burden of memorizing prose and poetry, of memorizing historical dates, of memorizing grammatical rules; it eliminates the learning of "dead" languages and with it the norm-setting immersion into the daily lives of long-extinct societies. Since it is allegedly necessary to know much more about present-day physics, present-day economics, present-day languages, present-day mathematics, and present-day international relations, the "unnecessary" information of the past and the historical modes of thought are de-emphasized. In addition to the wish "not to burden the memory", research in cognitive psychology until a few years ago also supported the view that learning by rote is unnecessary since it does not contribute to the cognitive skill of acquisition of knowledge beyond the memorized material. Not only does this approach constitute a serious loss, since many areas of life need and presuppose a well-trained memory—not in every situation is it feasible, advisable, or convenient to have to look up a reference book—but in the last few years cognitive psychologists started to rediscover the cognitive role of memory.

Goal-oriented specialized teaching strongly urges the teaching and learning communities to try to cover a specialized set of materials, the "material" to be "transmitted" by the teacher to the student. The language of "emitting" and "receiving", or rather the image of the funnel through which material to be studied is poured from the teacher's supposedly full bottle into the student's supposedly empty one, has become dominant. As a result, rarely is a textbook so taught that the teacher discusses with his or her students every other chapter, while those in-between are left to the students to be worked through on their own. Even the new science-teaching models like PSSC (the Physical Science Study Committee), BSCS, and the CHEMstudies, which all stress the student's independent thinking powers by introducing the teaching-by-enquiry method and its related approaches, insist on leading the students, albeit by "enquiry", towards every law of science they have to "master". One negative by-product of this approach is the rigid methodological framework set up to enable the student to make his or her own discovery, and thus teaching him or her a "method of discovery" which does not exist or, if at all, at best applies to the one and only discovery for which it was set up.

The goal-oriented specialized curriculum puts an ever-growing emphasis on textbooks: these are intellectually very economical formulations of established knowledge with little or no room for open questions and detailed exposition of communal ignorance.

The rapidly growing professionalization, and specialization, and the kind of curriculum and teaching aimed at these, have de-emphasized intellectual risk taking to a dangerous minimum. Intellectual risk taking involves inquiry into areas that do not promise quick results and immediate contributions to knowledge, the chances of failure are great, and above all it involves problem choice of a kind that the teachers, supervisors, and leaders of the profession cannot easily prescribe, predict, and reward or promote by moulding, supporting, or obstructing the risk taker's career. Yet what history of science teaches is that most important discoveries were unpredictable and even opposed by the established leaders of the relevant field; sociology of science teaches that many innovators were marginal to their area of exploration and had to fight for recognition by their professional peers.

Though some critical views were made clear in the above argument, the educational implications still need to be formulated in positive terms too.

It is the role of education to promote knowledge and the fruitful labours of those engaged in its generation. Past mistakes can be corrected by education—with all its drawbacks still the only peaceful means of introducing change into our lives.

Since explosion of knowledge with respect to the individual has not been validly demonstrated, a golden mean has to be found between goal-oriented teaching and a risk-encouraging curriculum. To some extent, the new science-teaching models, at least in theory, adopted this approach to selecting learning activities. They stress the importance of the student's independent thinking power by introducing the teaching-by-enquiry method and its related approaches, insisting on leading the students, by "enquiry", towards laws of science they have to "master". This approach adequately implemented in the classroom may create a proper balance between goal-oriented studies and intellectual risk taking. Textbooks should start with and emphasize the open problem in each discipline. Intermittent chapters in any textbook should be left to the student, so that he or she can come to grips with them on his or her own. Intelligent exploration should be valued and systematically supported, even if it does not lead to positive results. Finally, the learning theory which, nowadays at any rate, is not in good shape, ought to heed Bacon's dictum:

> On waxen tablets you cannot write anything new until you rub out the old. With the mind it is not so; there you cannot rub out the old till you have written in the new. (Bacon 1970)

Bibliography

Agassi J 1963 Towards an historiography of science. *History and Theory: Studies in the Philosophy of History*, Beiheft 2. Mouton, s'Gravenhage

Bacon F 1970 Temporis partus masculus. In: Farrington B (ed.) 1970 *The Philosophy of Francis Bacon*. Liverpool University Press, pp. 61–72

Benjamin W 1966 *Versuche über Brecht*. Suhrkamp, Frankfurt/Main

Elkana Y 1981 A programmatic attempt at an anthropology of knowledge. In: Mendelsohn E, Elkana Y (eds.) 1981 *Sciences and Cultures: Anthropological and Historical Studies of the Sciences*. Reidel, Dordrecht, pp. 1–77

Klein F, Sommerfeld A 1897–1911 *Über die Theorie des Kreisels*. Teubner, Leipzig. Reprint 1965 Johnson, New York

Kochen M 1974 *Integrative Mechanisms in Literature Growth*. Greenwood, Westport, Connecticut

Lakatos J 1970 Falsification and the methodology of scientific research programmes. In: Lakatos I, Musgrave A (eds.) 1970 *Criticism and the Growth of Knowledge: Proceedings of the International Colloquium in the Philosophy of Science, London, 1965*. Vol. 4. Cambridge University Press, London, pp. 91–195

Laudrie E le Roy 1978 *Montaillou: Cathars and Catholics in a French Village, 1294–1324*. Scolar Press, London

Personal Knowledge

D. J. Clandinin and F. M. Connelly

Personal knowledge in curriculum is relatively new as a field of study. Its particular distinctive focus is on the person, that is, the teacher and the learner in curricular situations. Much has been written and said about teacher and learner as curriculum common-places. However, few inquiries have focused on the person in curriculum situations. There have been inquiries into such areas as: conditions under which teachers teach and learners learn, teacher and learner cognitive structures, and the social and political contexts in which teachers and learners function. Only recently has research focused on teachers and learners from the point of view of person, that is, from an examination of how new experience integrates with the more general life knowledge of the teacher or learner as person.

This new field of inquiry, personal knowledge in curriculum, examines, from a knowledge perspective, teacher and learner as personal agents. While many researchers have examined the organization of knowledge in curriculum, little work has been done on personal knowledge in curriculum. For example, research into the organization of knowledge, such as that of Bruner (1966) and Ausubel (1968), examines the knowledge structures of learners and teachers. Work of this sort, however, does not focus on understanding the personal knowledge of a learner or teacher but focuses on generalized knowledge structures. These and other similar lines of research have focused on how learners or teachers relate to things formally introduced into teaching/learning situations. The focus has not been from the point of view of the involved persons, the personal agents in the situations.

Understanding personal knowledge in curriculum requires the examination of curriculum from the point of view of the persons involved. For teachers, such a view requires that we understand curriculum development and curriculum planning as questions of teacher thinking and teacher doing. It is the personal knowledge of teachers that determines all matters of significance relative to the planned conduct of classrooms. In this way, the two questions: "What is curriculum?" and "How do we do curriculum?", are brought together within the person, the teacher. The "what is" and the "doing" are intimately connected through the personal knowledge of the individual teacher.

For learners, such a view requires an understanding of curriculum from the point of view of the experience of the learner. It is the learner's experience that must be understood in order to understand the learner's personal knowledge in curriculum. Some studies are beginning to focus on the learner's personal knowledge in curriculum.

The field of personal knowledge in curriculum is a developing field of inquiry. Most research has focused on the teacher's personal knowledge in curriculum and it is this work that is summarized below.

1. Defining the "Personal" in Personal Knowledge in Curriculum

In research on teaching, several studies purport to study the personal, that is, the what, why, and wherefore of individual pedagogical action. Some illustrative studies of the personal focus deal with: "teachers' conceptions" (Duffy 1977), "teacher perspectives," "teachers' understandings" (Bussis et al. 1976), "teacher constructs" (Olson 1981), "teacher principles of practice" (Marland 1977), "teacher beliefs and principles" (Munby 1983), "teacher practical knowledge" (Elbaz 1981), "teachers' conceptions" (Larsson 1984), "teachers' thinking criteria" (Halkes and Deijkers 1984), "personal constructs" (Pope and Scott 1984), "personal knowledge" (Lampert 1985) and "teachers' personal practical knowledge" (Connelly and Clandinin 1984).

An extensive analysis and description of inquiries into the nature of the personal in teacher personal knowledge (Clandinin and Connelly 1987) suggested a degree of commonality in how researchers conceive of the personal in these inquiries. An underlying commonality exists in problems undertaken in the research on the personal. Several focus directly on teacher thought by "identifying," "exploring," "describing," and "examining" some particular content aspect of knowledge. The work of Olson (1981) and Munby (1983) examines the problem of accounting for action in terms of teacher thought, and, more specifically, of determining why curricula are differentially implemented by teachers. Research methods are, for many of the studies, very similar. In a review of 12 studies (Clandinin and Connelly 1987) 9 were aimed at discovering the content of teacher thought and 3, while also concerned with content, were primarily focused on the form of, and/or the language of, discourse about personal knowledge. There is commonality in the patterns of inquiry into the study of teacher personal knowledge despite apparent discrepancies in the researchers' language and intentions. Researchers using different terms such as "construct," "criteria," "beliefs and principles" appear to mean much the same thing. A variety of theoretical resources are used to enrich inquiry into the field.

However, there are significant differences in how the composition of teacher personal knowledge is conceptualized. Three general components noted in the review are practical actions, biographical history, and thoughts in isolation of these two. Most research focuses on the third, but various combinations are possible as seen, for example, in biographical studies (Pinar 1981) and in narratively oriented studies of all three components in combination (Connelly and Clandinin 1985).

Most studies of the personal conceive of teacher personal knowledge in cognitive terms. Some researchers, however, now conceive of personal knowledge simultaneously in cognitive and affective terms. This allows for a cognitive and affective understanding of the personal knowledge of teachers in curriculum.

2. A Narrative Understanding of Curriculum

Understanding personal knowledge in curriculum involves looking at all teaching and learning questions, all curriculum matters, from the point of view of the persons involved. This personal knowledge focus stresses an understanding of curriculum as something experienced in situations made up of people and their surrounding environments. A concept of curriculum, summarized below, emerges from such a view.

A situation is composed of persons in an immediate environment of things, interacting according to certain processes. In this view, curriculum is seen as something in which person, things, and processes are in dynamic interaction. Every classroom situation grows out of some preceding classroom situation, that is, all situations are historical. From this perspective comes the understanding that situations, persons, things, and processes, have a history. Situations have a future, that is, each situation leads to another situation with a sense of the situation moving forward and reaching into the future. These two sides of the time dimension of a situation, its history and its future, contribute to a dynamic, temporal sense of situation in this notion of curriculum. Situations are directional, that is, they are pointed into the future towards certain ends. Directionality acts upon situations in the way that the history of situations does, that is, it shapes and reconstructs the situation.

Curriculum from a personal knowledge perspective means thinking in terms of experience and situation. The teacher and the learners are the most important agents in a curriculum situation and it is their personal knowledge that is particularly important in our understanding of personal knowledge in curriculum.

3. Personal Knowledge in Curriculum

As already noted, little research has focused on learners' personal knowledge in curriculum. In this section the research on teachers' personal knowledge in curriculum is discussed.

Teachers' personal knowledge in curriculum is composed of both theoretical knowledge in the sense of theories of learning, teaching, and curriculum and practical knowledge in the sense of knowing children. Personal knowledge is blended by the personal background and characteristics of the particular teacher and is expressed in particular situations. It is knowledge which involves aesthetic, moral, emotional, and cognitive dimensions. It is the personal and the situational which confers on teachers a special claim to personal knowledge in curriculum.

The term *personal knowledge in curriculum* puts the emphasis on the teacher's knowing of the classroom. Some researchers refer to the teacher's personal knowledge in curricular situations as *personal practical knowledge*. Personal practical knowledge is a term designed to capture the idea of experience in a way that allows us to talk about teachers as knowledgeable and knowing persons. Personal practical knowledge is in the teacher's past experience, in the teacher's present mind and body, and in the teacher's future plans and actions. Personal practical knowledge is found in the teacher's practices. It is, for any one teacher, a particular way of reconstructing the past and the intentions of the future to deal with the exigencies of a present situation.

A narrative curricular understanding of the person is an understanding which is flexible and fluid and which, therefore, recognizes that people say and do different things under different circumstances and, conversely, that different circumstances bring forward different aspects of their experience to bear on the situation. According to this view, a person's personal practical knowledge depends in important measure upon the situation.

Personal practical knowledge emerges from our experience. Experiences have emotional, moral, and aesthetic dimensions. Our personal practical knowledge which makes up our narratives of experience is an emotional, moral, and aesthetic knowledge.

A narrative understanding of curriculum is conceived with the personal histories of individuals embedded within the social history of schools and schooling. Central constructs within the narrative perspective are the notions of image, narrative unity, personal philosophy, and rhythms in individual lives. *Image* (Clandinin 1986) is defined as something within our experience, embodied in us as persons and expressed and enacted in our practices and actions. Situations call forth our images from our narratives of experience and these images are available to us as guides to future action. An image reaches into the past, gathering up experiential threads meaningfully connected to the present. And it reaches intentionally into the future and creates new meaningfully connected threads as situations are anticipated from the perspective of the image. Thus, images are part of our past, called forth by situations in which we act in the present, and are guides to our futures. Images as they are embodied in us entail emotion, morality, and aesthetics. *Narrative unity* (Connelly and Clandinin 1985) is defined as a continuum within a person's experience; experiences are made meaningful through the unity they achieve for the person. Unity means the union in a particular person in a particular time and place of all that he or she has been and undergone and of the tradition which helped shape him or her. Johnson (1984) remarks that:

> This focus would involve examining the images and metaphors that structure, not just teachers' classroom knowledge, but also the personal knowledge and human affairs, personal past history, and so forth that any teacher brings into the classroom experience. That is, we need to begin looking at the dominant images and metaphors of the teacher's entire world, in and out of the classroom. (p. 486)

Personal philosophy is the way one thinks about oneself in teaching situations. Personal philosophy has within it a notion of beliefs and values. Personal philosophy goes beneath the surface manifestations of values and beliefs to their experiential narrative origins and refers to a reconstruction of meaning contained in a teacher's actions and her or his explorations of them expressed in the form of a narrative of experience. To understand rhythm in the narrative of teaching is to understand something of the way in which a person conforms to the cyclic temporal structure of schooling and the social life and becomes what we call a "teacher" while at the same time stamping his or her own particular cultural and personal mark on the teaching process via the rhythms she or he develops.

These notions and their entailments express a narrative personal knowledge perspective on curriculum. They provide a way of understanding the personal knowledge of persons in curriculum.

4. *Practical Significance*

There are a number of practical entailments resulting from an understanding of personal knowledge in curriculum. Such a focus does not provide knowledge of how things work in general or criteria for effective teaching. Personal knowledge in curriculum is knowledge of the individual, of what things are and how they work in particular cases. Thus, in understanding curriculum from a personal knowledge perspective, we turn our attention to the knowledge individual teachers and students construct in curricular situations. We focus not on the general but on the unique and particular understandings developed by teachers and students in the situation. The focus is experiential rather than conceptual. Adopting such a perspective requires new ways of conceptualizing what happens in curricular situations.

Connelly and Clandinin (1985) offer an account of how one might understand teaching and learning situations using the notion of unity in personal knowledge. The focus is on experience, in particular teacher and student narrative unities in curricular situations. In drawing upon, developing, remaking, and introducing narratives, the richness of past experience was seen as bringing forward and crediting teachers' and learners' personal knowledge of their teaching and learning situations. Teaching and learning situations need, from this perspective, continually to "give back" a learner's narrative experience so that it may be reflected upon, valued, and enriched. In this way, knowing comes alive in classrooms as the multifaceted, embodied, biographical and historical experience that it is.

The focus on personal knowledge in curriculum also provides a way to account for what policy makers, curriculum developers, and implementors know; that is, that their plans and intentions for change in practice do not work out as intended. When we examine curricular situations from a personal knowledge perspective, there are consequences for how we might imagine school improvement. Well-intentioned notions about the tactics and strategies of implementation do not adequately account for our understanding of personal knowledge in curriculum. We need new ways of conceptualizing the relations between theory and practice (Connelly and Clandinin 1986).

Understanding personal knowledge in curriculum highlights the limitations of all general rules, principles, and prescriptions for practice. It draws our attention to the importance of reflection as a process through which practitioners can use general rules and principles as heuristics from which to reflect on their practice. The inappropriateness of a one-way logistic relationship between theory and practice is highlighted.

The focus on personal knowledge in curriculum has significance for how teacher education, both at the level of preservice and inservice, is conceived. In adopting a personal knowledge perspective, reflection will gain importance as a critical element in teacher education. By making reflection an integral part of three kinds of teacher education experience, observation, student teaching, and other courses, an intellectual experience is set up. Student teachers have not yet worked out a dynamic relationship between their imagery and other dimensions of their personal knowledge and their practices. The significance of the personal knowledge in curriculum perspective in teacher education is it attempts to go beyond theoretical principles and rules of teaching and beyond the practical description of action found in statements of strategies and routines, and to focus on ways of thinking and plans and programs by which teachers and student teachers may reflect on themselves as knowing, teaching beings. Examining research knowledge, participating in applied research, observing other teachers teaching, trying out ideas developed elsewhere, can all be valuable if they are part of a process of professional interaction, action, and reflection.

There are, no doubt, other areas where a personal knowledge in curriculum perspective would have practical significance, such as in curriculum development, policy development, and curriculum evaluation.

Bibliography

Ausubel D P 1968 *Educational Psychology: A Cognitive View.* Rinehart and Winston, New York

Bruner J S 1966 *Toward a Theory of Instruction.* Harvard University Press, Cambridge, Massachusetts

Bussis A M, Chittenden E A, Amarel M 1976 *Beyond Surface Curriculum: An Interview of Teachers' Understandings.* Westview, Boulder, Colorado

Clandinin D J 1986 *Classroom Practice: Teacher Images in Action.* Falmer Press, Barcombe, Lewes

Clandinin D J, Connelly F M 1987 Teachers' personal knowledge: What counts as "personal" in studies of the personal. *J. Curr. Stud.* 19(6): 487–500

Connelly F M, Clandinin D J 1984 Personal practical knowledge at Bay St School: Ritual, personal philosophy and image. In: Halkes R, Olsen J (eds.) 1984 *Teacher Thinking: A New Perspective on Persisting Problems in Education.* Swets and Zeitlinger, Lisse

Connelly F M, Clandinin D J 1985 Personal practical knowledge and the modes of knowing: Relevance for teaching and learning. In: Eisner E (ed.) 1985 *Learning and Teaching the Ways of Knowing,* Eighty-fourth yearbook of the National Society for the Study of Education, Part 2. University of Chicago Press, Chicago, Illinois, pp. 174–98

Connelly F M, Clandinin D J 1986 The reflective practitioner and practitioners' narrative unities. *Can. J. Educ.* 11(2): 184–99

Duffy G 1977 A study of teacher conceptions of reading. Paper presented at the National Reading Conference, New Orleans

Elbaz F 1981 The teacher's "practical" knowledge: Report of a case study. *Curr. Inq.* 11(1): 43–71

Halkes R, Deijkers R 1984 Teachers' thinking criteria. In: Halkes R, Olson J (eds.) 1984 *Teacher Thinking: A New Perspective on Persisting Problems in Education.* Swets and Zeitlinger, Lisse, pp. 149–62

Johnson M 1984 Review of Elbaz, Freema, Teacher thinking: A study of practical knowledge. *Curr. Inq.* 14(4): 465–68

Lampert M 1985 How do teachers manage to teach? Perspectives on problems in practice. *Harvard Educ. Res.* 55(2): 178–94

Larsson S 1984 Describing teachers' conceptions of their professional world. In: Halkes R, Olson J (eds.) 1984 *Teacher Thinking: A New Perspective on Persisting Problems in Education.* Swets and Zeitlinger, Lisse, pp. 123–33

Marland P 1977 A study of teachers' interactive thoughts. Unpublished doctoral dissertation, University of Alberta

Munby H 1983 A qualitative study of teachers' beliefs and principles. Paper presented at the annual meeting of the American Educational Research Association, Montreal, Canada

Olson J 1981 Teacher influence in the classroom. *Instr. Sci.* 10: 259–75

Pinar W 1981 Life history and educational experience. *J. Curr. Theor.* 31(1): 259–86

Pope M L, Scott E M 1984 Teachers' epistemology and practice. In: Halkes R, Olson J (eds.) 1984 *Teacher Thinking: A New Perspective on Persisting Problems in Education.* Swets and Zeitlinger, Lisse, pp. 112–22

Knowledge Technology and Curriculum Theory

D. Chen and A. Oren

Technology forms an integral part of the history of humankind and of culture. Technologies enabling people to cope with material and energy transformation have always played a major role in civilization. However, it is knowledge technology that dominates social change at the end of the twentieth century, to the extent that scientists call this era the "knowledge era" or the "information revolution" (Simon 1981).

The terms *knowledge* and *information* are widely used as synonyms. However, this article distinguishes between the two terms. The term *information* will be used in its restricted definition, confined to quantitative and syntactic aspects. The term *knowledge* will be used in its epistemological, broad meaning to include the semantic dimension. Therefore, knowledge includes information as a subclass.

This article concentrates on the impact of knowledge technology on the nature of the curriculum. Knowledge technology refers to the way information of public interest is accumulated, stored, continuously updated, processed, and communicated to the users. While until the nineteenth century the major technology was print, disseminated in the form of the printed book, since the beginning of the twentieth century new technologies have been introduced. The movie, radio, telephone, television and, later, the computer and telecommunications, are the new technologies that have broadened the scope of sources used in contemporary life for the moulding and dissemination of human knowledge. Dissemination of human knowledge is what education is about, and the curriculum is one of its major vehicles. This is a good reason to examine the effects of the changing technologies on curriculum theory.

In this article, the main features of knowledge technology and concepts defined in some of the fields related to knowledge will be presented. The impact of these issues on curriculum theory and practice will be discussed.

1. The Nature of the Curriculum

Hundreds of books have been written on curriculum theory and practice (Schubert 1984). The curriculum movement has encompassed west and east, trying to cope with the scope and magnitude of the growing scientific body of knowledge. However, most of the research concerning curricular issues has dealt with the practice of curriculum development and implementation, and relatively very little has focused on the theoretical aspects of the curricular issues related to knowledge.

The prevailing classical models of curriculum are best represented by the Tyler paradigm which relates the curriculum to three major variables: the student, the discipline, and society (Tyler 1949). While Bloom's much acclaimed taxonomy has operationally defined student parameters (Bloom 1956), the social criteria for structuring curricula remained the subject for ideological and political discussions, debates, and personal preferences. The "discipline" component, namely the knowledge of the subject matter, is usually analyzed with regard to the contemporary scientific paradigm but with regard neither to the theory of knowledge nor

to knowledge technology. Thus, the epistemological virtues of knowledge are not usually considered as part of the curriculum model.

The era of the information age is the result of the interaction of information technology with contemporary society. Theoretical knowledge has become the prime mover in our own culture and knowledge technology is driving the change. Computers are gradually being implemented in the schools and at home.

It is expected that the convergence of ideas emerging in the fields of knowledge theory, information theory, and knowledge technology with learning systems is going to change the very nature and definitions of curriculum. This change calls for a new conceptual framework of contemporary theories.

In principle, the contemporary curriculum is the mediating interface between knowledge and student. Until the 1970s most public knowledge was accumulated and kept in printed format. Only in the 1980s, developments in information technology introduced the electronic media as a major carrier of public knowledge. It is the question of how this knowledge is represented by the different technologies that is of concern with regard to the curricular issue. Likewise, the emerging knowledge technology implies new issues concerning the mediating interface and should be studied with regard to modes of knowledge presentation.

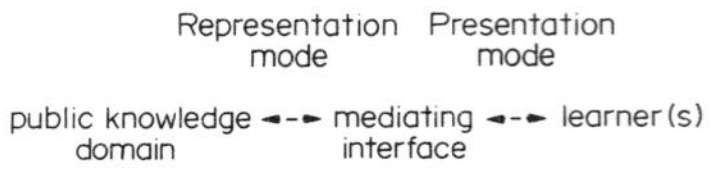

Figure 1
The Relationships between Knowledge, Curriculum, and Learner

Figure 1 describes the relationships between curriculum and public knowledge domain on the one hand and between the curriculum and the learner on the other. All knowledge produced and accumulated by civilization belongs to the public knowledge domain. The way knowledge is represented, both logically and physically, is determined by technology and is crucial to its relationships with humankind. In principle, the notion of curriculum refers to a concerted effort of education to sample public knowledge in a way convenient for use in individual learning. The mode of knowledge presented to the learner is determined to a large extent by the nature of the prevalent technology. The relationships described in Figure 1 should serve as a conceptual framework for this analysis.

2. Issues Related to Knowledge

Curriculum theory and practice are affected both by characteristic features of knowledge technology and by concepts related to epistemology of knowledge.

2.1 Features of Knowledge Technology

Late twentieth century curriculum theory has been moulded mainly by print technology. It is expected that the introduction of highly developed new knowledge technology will enforce a very different kind of curriculum, based on the interaction between knowledge and the learner. If one conceptualizes technology as an extention of the human being, one may say that writing and print technologies have extended humankind's ability to represent knowledge exogenously or outside the human brain.

By and large, print technology operated as an extention of the memory by storing knowledge, as indicated in Table 1. Once printed, knowledge is frozen physically. Knowledge is represented in a linear format, and its main feature is being static. No changes can be made by the user. In contrast, the new technology has extended the whole range of human capacities.

Table 1
Extension of human qualities by technology

Human capacities	Technology-extended human capacities	
	Print	Knowledge Technology
Perception	—	Input devices
Memory	Printed text	Storage devices
Mental processes	—	Information processing
Behavior	—	Output devices

Knowledge technologies can extend perception by telesensing and utilizing input devices. Storage capacity has increased immensely. It has become possible to search and incorporate new knowledge into the already existing body of knowledge. The processing capacity of the new technologies has introduced a dynamic dimension aimed at intensifying mental processes. Artificial intelligence methods strive to refine intelligent processing by machines, and while there is still a very long way to go in order to achieve human-like cognition, much has been already done in that direction.

It is the dynamic nature of knowledge representation that is the main feature of the new technology. Quantitative and qualitative changes become an ongoing process in handling exogenous knowledge.

2.2 Concepts Related to Epistemology of Knowledge

In some fields related to knowledge, ideas emerge concerning the essence of knowledge. It is relevant to examine the major concepts emanating from knowledge theory, information theory and cognitive science which may provide a foundation for a new curricular approach.

The notion of scientific knowledge as a growing entity is based on the quantitative measurements introduced by the scientometric approach (Price De Solla 1979). By measuring the increase in the number of scientific

publications in time, it was demonstrated that the body of public knowledge is growing in a logarithmic fashion. The growth of knowledge is based on both accumulation and decay of knowledge, and the present rate of growth has a doubling time of 5–15 years depending on the scientific discipline. The scientometric observations imply that public knowledge must be seen as a dynamic, everchanging body. The amount of net knowledge not only grows to the point of "explosion," but the actual content is constantly changing.

In his famous paper on the mathematical basis of communication, Shannon (Shannon and Weaver 1963) defined information through a quantitative approach. A unit of information was defined as the amount of information necessary to choose between two alternatives. This unit was called BIT (Binary Digit). Shannon provided a way to quantify information regardless of semantics. The definition of information in terms of mechanical statistics (entropy equation) can be given in a nonmathematical simplified statement: the transition from a state of chaos (no order) to an increased orderly state is followed by a decrease in the amount of information in the system. Therefore, any act of curriculum planning can be considered as an act of decreasing information load in the knowledge space, as it is an act of increasing order.

Cognitive science, and artificial intelligence in particular, has introduced new methodologies of knowledge representation based on computational models. Here the semantic aspects of natural language are being taken into consideration in addition to its syntactic aspects. Notions such as "semantic networks," "frames," and "slots" represent in fact knowledge patterns which define not only structural aspects, but also dynamic and logical relationships within the knowledge space emanating from semantics. Thus, introduction of the semantic aspects of natural language enables coping with knowledge in its full meaning. It is this kind of formal knowledge representation that is of interest with regard to curriculum and learning.

3. The Impact of Knowledge Technology and Epistemology on Curriculum

Three aspects of the above-mentioned concepts are likely to contribute to changes in curriculum theory and practice: the dynamic dimension, the quantitative dimension, and the structural dimension of knowledge.

3.1 The Dynamic Dimension of Knowledge

In the traditional curriculum, knowledge flows in one direction only: from the book to the learner. The interaction between the learner and the knowledge represented in the book could hardly change the structure of the printed knowledge. In contrast, knowledge technology enables interaction with knowledge stored in databases. This interaction between the learner and knowledge is based on the dynamic representation of knowledge. If an appropriate feedback mechanism is utilized, adaptive instruction can emerge whereby the mediated knowledge flow is changing during, and as a result of, the learning process, producing an individualized curriculum.

3.2 The Quantitative Dimension of Knowledge

The quantitative approach provides the curriculum designer with new perspectives in regard to the growing body of public knowledge and the formal knowledge representation. With reference to the relationships between the growing body of public knowledge and the cognitive load of the individual learner, new questions concerning curriculum planning arise. Does the curriculum represent the knowledge context of the discipline? What is the quantitative extent of the representation? Does print technology enable a sound representation or does it merely impose its constraints on quantity of knowledge conveyed? It has already been estimated that the magnitude of an average school curriculum is currently somewhere between 100–200 megabite. Likewise, the relationship between curriculum and the learner in the formal knowledge representation aspect, will have to be defined in quantitative units such as "frames," "slots," "nodes," and "bits," regardless of content. The careful definition of "knowledge units" and their internal relationships implies far more defined, accurate, and realistic curriculum planning and design. The curriculum designer will be required to conduct a rigorous and coherent examination of the content components in the knowledge space. The effect of "quantitative" scaling of the curriculum would have a far-reaching impact on school management, standardization, testing, evaluation of achievements, and educational policies.

3.3 The Structural Dimension of Knowledge

The order and structure of knowledge as defined in information theory introduces a new point of view to the act of curriculum planning. The curriculum can be defined in terms of introducing planned order into a section of the vast public knowledge domain, resulting in a reduced information load on the learner. By the same token, order as highly structured learning materials can be diminished to increase the amount of information to be studied. Scope, sequence, and spatial relationships become amenable to change, both by the curriculum developer and by the user.

The scheme in Figure 2 describes the structural relationships between public knowledge domain and the curriculum:

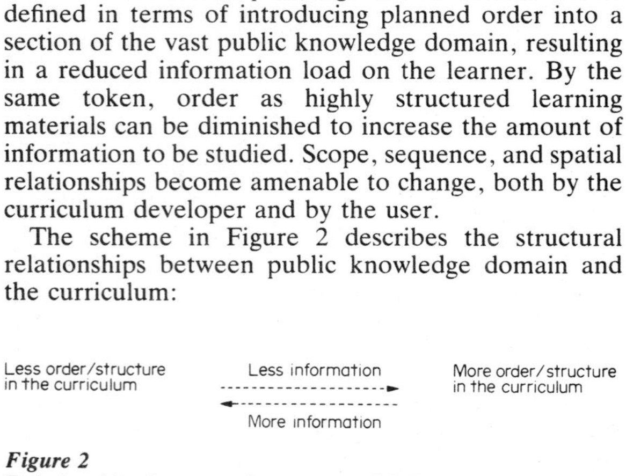

Less order/structure in the curriculum   Less information   More order/structure in the curriculum

More information

Figure 2
Relationships between Structure and Information

In a dynamic knowledge environment provided by technology, curriculum planning becomes an ongoing process of finding an equilibrium between the degree of cognitive load the learner can stand, and the degree of increased order that reduces information to the point of still being comprehensible to the learner. Different "degrees" of order can be introduced by changing content, tasks, and schemes within the knowledge space.

4. Knowledge Technology Driven Curriculum (KTDC)

The nature of changes in the curriculum can be best understood by an overview of knowledge technology's current development in two directions: first, knowledge environments and second, intelligent tutoring systems. Professional descriptions of systems operating in both directions use the term *knowledge based* systems. According to these descriptions, two levels of knowledge base can be distinguished: low-level and high-level bases. Knowledge environment is defined as low-level knowledge based and intelligent tutoring systems as high-level knowledge based.

4.1 Rich Knowledge Environments (RKE)

The new technologies greatly advance the development of rich knowledge environments. There are several types of rich knowledge environment, the main ones being the following:

(a) Database management systems (DBMS) which store and retrieve indexed data elements, and process exactly matched queries.

(b) Information retrieval systems (IRS) which store and retrieve indexed documents and process approximate queries.

(c) Hypertext/hypermedia systems which store linked information items in various modes of representation and process various knowledge units using browsing as a retrieval strategy.

These systems create a new type of learning environment that requires the curriculum developer to handle the content component and the instructional component of the curriculum (learning objectives and learning activities) in new ways. In developing rich knowledge environment (RKE), concepts mentioned in previous sections have to be taken into account, distinguishing the RKE as a learning environment from the printed environment.

Computer technology provides an immense capacity for storage of knowledge. Integrated electro-optical techniques and sophisticated software engineering enable the storage of the raw information necessary for learning assignments in the form of information items, data lists, and sets of production skills. Moreover, hypermedia technology extends storage and retrieval to all forms of knowledge representation that may be digitally encoded (text, maps, numbers, graphs, video, and sound), thus creating a multimedia knowledge system. Current knowledge technology allows realization of an expanding knowledge system. Electronic communication makes it easier to reach new knowledge items stored in public databases and integrate them into the educational knowledge base in real time, thus bridging the gap between the growing body of public knowledge and the knowledge embedded in the curriculum. New functions of curriculum maintenance operations such as adding, deleting, changing, and rearranging learning materials and learning activities will ensure an ongoing readjustment of curriculum knowledge to public knowledge.

The design of a knowledge base becomes a process of knowledge engineering. Within this process a detailed content analysis specifies knowledge particles on the one hand, and relationships between the various components on the other, promoting a coherent body of knowledge. Ideas concerning the relationships between quantity and structure of information are well represented by the structural multimedia organization of the knowledge system. This mode of organization is based on nonlinear relationships between information items provided by the hypertext/hypermedia technology (Weyer 1988). Such a mode of organization supplies the foundation for alternative access to knowledge and user-adjustable environment. The design of the access to knowledge is characterized by the ability to reach the knowledge components in alternative ways through menus, indexes, content maps, logical differentiation, and so on. The magnitude of knowledge in the system, and its divergent structure, call for alternative access procedures (Weyer 1988, Cook 1988). Operating within the knowledge system is related to the process by which the learner browses through the knowledge space he or she accessed. Browsing is available through the paths designed in accordance with the links defined in the knowledge system.

The new type of RKE was implemented in several educational systems: in the 1990s databases are in common use in schools. This might be concluded from articles and reports that also indicate the new potential of the technology for education (Hannah 1987, Monterosso 1988). Information retrieval systems are beginning to interest teachers as a way to reach bibliographic items through electronic catalogs (Malsam 1984, Kallmeier and Stoudt 1987) or as a main information source in the classroom (Degl'Innocenti and Ferraris 1988, Savoy 1989, Weyer 1982). Applications of hypertext/hypermedia technology are being developed and tested as learning environment. The *Groliers Encyclopedia* on CD ROM is an example of an informal learning environment which is based on the storage and retrieval capacities of the technology. Courses designed through the Intermedia system manifest the capabilities of the new knowledge environment by storage of an amount and variety of items enhancing learning activities. They are supported by video disk technology storing photos,

documentary films, maps, reports, experiments, and so forth. Such courses realize the potential of the technology by allowing direct access to the knowledge base, as well as access through structured learning activities.

All the systems mentioned above have the following advantages over the printed type:

(a) access to large quantities of information;

(b) ability to store multimedia;

(c) ability to readjust knowledge in real time;

(d) a nonlinear mode of knowledge search.

These features of the new environment open ways of accessing, selecting and relating knowledge elements that never existed in the printed environment. Terms emanating from a technological origin, such as "microworlds" (Papert 1980) and "artificial realities" (Foley 1987) indicate the possible role of the knowledge system in mediating the public domain of knowledge to the individual learner.

4.2 Intelligent Tutoring Systems (ITS)

All artificial intelligence systems like expert systems, decision support systems, medical diagnosis systems, and so on, belong to the group of high-level knowledge bases. In contrast to the low-level knowledge bases which only contain knowledge, the high-level knowledge base includes features that allow the generation of new knowledge. Intelligent tutoring systems (ITS) are an application of artificial intelligence which utilizes a high-level knowledge base while focusing on instruction.

The major objective of a computerized instructional system is to utilize technology for effective and optimal learning. The theoretical framework for "instructional technology" is best provided by the adaptive instruction approach (Glaser 1977). This theory aspires to optimize the learning process via individualized instruction. Individualized instruction can be obtained via a three-stage operation: diagnosis of students' variables (cognitive style, developmental stage, aptitude learning, history, and so on), tutoring based on feedback mechanism, and generation of an individualized curriculum. The computer-assisted instruction (CAI) format so widely used in education was limited in diagnostic procedures; feedback was rigid and related to structured learning activities (multiple choice, yes–no questions, etc.). Therefore, a real individualized curriculum could not be generated in the CAI format.

ITS research and development is moving fast to provide us with operating models of intelligent (adaptive) instruction. The capacity of ITS to overcome the limitations of CAI is clearly manifested in its structure. An ITS consists usually of three modules interacting with each other: first, an expert module in which the expertise related to subject matter is represented; second, a diagnostic module which identifies students' knowledge and errors and creates a student model; and third, an instructional module which provides, according to the input from the diagnostic module, feedback and tutoring advice on the basis of content expertise. Though supported by the concept of high-level knowledge bases, ITS fails to utilize features of low-level knowledge bases that are concerned with the richness of the environment as described in the previous section. Developments in the field of ITS do not exploit all the features developed in the low-level knowledge system for the following reasons:

(a) development of a theoretical framework for an ITS focuses on a psychological framework (Anderson et al. 1984) or on an instructional one (Lesgold 1988);

(b) the knowledge base of an ITS is limited in its knowledge space, and is centered around specific themes;

(c) most of the systems were based on one module. Some systems are based on diagnostic elements (Brown and Burton 1978), others on instructional units (Woolf and McDonald 1984).

At the start of the 1990s there is a tendency, though it is not yet common, to integrate expertise, student modelling, and tutorial capabilities in a real-life supporting system. *Sherlock*, a coaching system developed by Lesgold aimed at training technicians to perform electronic troubleshooting, manifests this approach. The prospects of developing an adaptive instructional system depend entirely on the ITS approach. A host of tools is being developed from expert systems, computerized testing, and decision support systems to simulators, interactive interfaces, and authoring systems. A variety of instructional strategies is being explored, ranging from fully automated to a mixed bag of human-machine approaches. Nevertheless, without a rich knowledge environment even an intelligent instructional system will remain a local episode instead of a pointer to changing curricular concepts. Supporting Environment For Teaching Algebra (SEFTA) is an example of the new approach to KTDC, manifesting an integration of the knowledge concepts derived from both levels. There are attempts to develop ITS systems with a hypertext notion. They are based on artificial intelligence mechanisms that create the knowledge needed to solve a linear equation and the feedback to the user. Likewise, learning assignments and instructional items are linked and create a hypertext environment in which various paths of sequence may be chosen by the learner.

The concepts presented here of a knowledge technology driven curriculum (KTDC) demonstrate the fact that the curriculum becomes gradually linked to technology, and therefore to the concepts underlying the technology.

5. Summary

Analysis of knowledge technology integrated within the curriculum suggests that both the theory and practice of curriculum development wil have to change substantially. Contemporary curriculum development, which was based on print technology, will have to turn to knowledge engineering and its underlying principles. New technology driven curriculum (KTDC) will have two major qualities: (a) the dynamic nature of knowledge representation; and (b) the adaptability of knowledge presentation (instruction).

Curriculum, as a dynamic mediating interface between public knowledge and the learner, would, as a result, represent knowledge in a nonlinear mode. Knowledge representation would become flexible and the cognitive load amenable to change during the learning process. Knowledge would be conveyed via multimedia devices, organization would be modular and defined by bits, frames, and slots, while instruction could be constantly monitored.

Adaptive instruction hence becomes part and parcel of the curriculum, in the effort to achieve effective learning. The adaptation cycle, emanating from the dynamic nature of knowledge representation in the KTDC, will be based on intelligent interface, diagnostic procedures, and generating individualized curriculum frames tailored to individual need in real time. The scope and magnitude of the content, the nature of instructional strategy, the nature of media, and the relationships with the rest of the knowledge system will not be predetermined as in the case of textbooks. Each of the aforementioned dimensions of the curriculum will have a degree of freedom determined by the interaction between the individual learner and knowledge to be studied. Thus the convergence of the technology and the curriculum would yield an entirely different relationship between human beings and knowledge, which new curriculum theory will have to take into account.

Bibliography

Anderson J R, Boyle C F, Farrell R, Reiser B J 1984 *Cognitive Principles in the Design of Computer Tutors, Advanced Computer Tutoring Project.* Carnegie-Mellon University, Pittsburgh, Pennsylvania

Bloom B S (ed.) 1956 *Taxonomy of Educational Objectives; The Classification of Educational Goals.* McKay, New York

Brown J S, Burton R R 1978 Diagnostic models for procedural bugs in basic mathematical skills. *Cog. Sci.* 2: 155–92

Cook P 1988 Multimedia technology. In Ambron S, Hooper K (eds.) 1988 *Interactive Multimedia.* Microsoft Press

Degl'Innocenti R, Ferraris M 1988 Database as a tool for promoting research activities in the classroom: An example in teaching the humanities. *Comput. Educ.* 12(1): 157–62

Foley J D 1987 Interfaces for advanced computing. *Sci. Am.*

Glaser R 1977 *Adaptive Education: Individual Diversity and Learning.* Holt, Rinehart and Winston, New York

Hannah L 1987 The database: Getting to know you. *Comput. Teach.* 15(1): 20–27

Kallmeier H H, Stoudt K H 1987 Composition student online database search in the undergraduate research paper course. *Comput. Humanities* 21(3): 147–55

Lesgold A 1988 Towards a theory of curriculum for use in designing intelligent instructional systems. In: Mandl H, Lesgold A (eds.) 1988 *Learning Issues for Intelligent Tutoring Systems.* Springer Verlag, New York, pp 114–37

Malsam M 1984 The computer replaces the card catalog in one Colorado elementary school. In: Paterson D (ed.) 1984 *Readings in Computer and Learning.* Reston, Virginia, pp. 144–46

Monterosso G 1988 Micro climates. *Comput. Teach.* 15(8): 17–18

Papert S 1980 *Mindstorms.* Basic Books, New York

Price De Solla D 1979 The citation cycle. American Society for Information Science, paper presented at the 8th Mid-Year Meeting, pp. 195–209

Savoy J 1989 The electronic book EBook3, *Int. J. Man-Machine Stud.* 30: 505–23

Schubert W H 1984 *The First Eighty Years.* University Press of America

Shannon E C, Weaver W 1963 *The Mathematical Theory of Communication.* University of Chicago Press; Illinois

Simon H A 1981 What computer means for man and society. In: Forester T (ed.) 1981 *The Microelectronics Revolution.* Basil Blackwell, Oxford

Tyler R W 1949 *Basic Principles of Curriculum and Instruction.* University of Chicago Press, Chicago, Illinois

Weyer S A 1982 The design of a dynamic book for information search. *Int. J. Man-Machine Stud.* 17(1): 87–107

Weyer S A 1988 As we may learn. In: Ambron S, Hooper K (eds.) 1988 *Interactive Multimedia.* Microsoft Press, pp. 89–103

Woolf B P, McDonald D D 1984 Building a computer tutor: Design issues. *IEEE Comput.* 17(9): 61–73

Curriculum Policies

A. S. Hughes

There are two major types of policy that have bearing on the school curriculum primarily. One is policy that prescribes the procedures to be followed in formulating the curriculum, whether in its broad outline or in detail. Often, such policy will specify who is to be involved and will establish the limits of their authority. This can be referred to as policy on curriculum policy making. The other type of policy is the product of the curriculum policy-making process and can be viewed as curriculum policy per se. This policy establishes the character of the curriculum, often specifying what must, should, or may be taught. Both types of policy are subject to considerable international variation and, indeed, even within nations there can be significant fluctuation over relatively short time periods.

The distinction between policy on curriculum policy making and curriculum policy itself can be a helpful one in confronting current curricular issues, for, in recent years, it has seemed that concern for who will make curricular decisions has often taken precedence over what will be taught (Schaffarzick 1979).

1. Curriculum Policy Making

One way of viewing the curriculum policy-making process is in terms of the distribution of decision-making authority. On the one hand there are systems that stress centralized curriculum prescription; on the other, systems that emphasize local or school autonomy. The essence of the difference is often to be found in the weight given to the teacher in the curriculum development equation (Goodlad 1981). The issue is whether the teacher will be an active participant in curriculum policy and program formulation or the consumer and executor of previously taken decisions.

Evidence accumulated since the early 1970s has tended to suggest that many large-scale, centralized curriculum projects with minimal teacher participation have experienced only limited success. This view has been confirmed by MacDonald and Walker (1976) on the work of the Schools Council in Great Britain, and by House (1974) and the Rand Corporation (1975–78) in the United States, with House referring to the "debris of federal programs."

An important point here is that the lack of success is attributed not so much to the curriculum projects themselves but to the concomitant center-periphery model of dissemination. As an alternative to the center-periphery approach, considerable emphasis has recently been advocated for school-based approaches and periphery–periphery approaches referred to as metapolicy (Atkin and House 1981). Here the values of localism such as diversity, reliance on local knowledge, and acceptance of local control are pitted against efficiency and equity.

In spite of the difficulties experienced with highly centralized projects, the trend in the late 1970s and early 1980s in many jurisdictions is toward ever-increasing centralization (Hughes 1982). Recently, there have been instances of governments stressing their legal responsibilities and asserting increasing degrees of control over the decision-making process, often by means of a complex array of "advisory boards." Control is moved closer and closer to the politicians with the losers being the local schools, and particularly parents and teachers.

2. Curriculum Policy

The trend toward establishing greater central control over the curriculum policy-making process is associated with the belief that this will result in greater control over the product, that is, the basic nature of curriculum policy itself; the blueprint from which detailed objectives, teaching strategies, evaluation procedures, or whatever, are to be derived. Expressions of curriculum policy may range from vague advice and general guidelines to official directives established as public policy through government legislation, and from detailed prescriptions of the competencies to be achieved by each learner to lists of subjects from which students may select with greater or lesser degrees of freedom.

Much recent curriculum policy has tended toward increased prescription and a restriction of student choice though, paradoxically, often for the purpose of ensuring for the student a broader and more balanced curricular experience. For example, in the United States the debate is currently focusing upon "general education" and in the United Kingdom upon the "common curriculum." While the details of the pattern vary, the experience is currently similar in many countries, developed and underdeveloped, East and West, where the classic curriculum question of "what knowledge is of most worth?" is confronted. Nevertheless, there seems to be considerable diversity in whether the appropriate response should focus on the form or substance of the curriculum, the objectives or the content, what children have access to or what they take away with them.

3. Curriculum Policy Impact

As yet, there has been little detailed analysis of the impact of emerging curriculum policies, or indeed, of their predecessors. What is becoming clear is that the relationship between curriculum policy and curriculum practice can be tenuous. Curriculum policy is a blunt instrument and, as has always been the case, local schools and teachers will find ways of circumventing curricular policies which are not compatible with local preferences. In an age of conservatism and in an atmosphere of increasing centralization, such noncompliance may evoke a reaction toward an ever-narrowing and centralizing of authority as political authorities seek greater control over the child's curricular experience.

Bibliography

Atkin J M, House E R 1981 The federal role in curriculum development, 1950–80. *Educ. Eval. Policy Anal.* 3(5): 5–36
Goodlad J I 1981 Curriculum development beyond 1980. *Educ. Eval. Policy Anal.* 3(5): 49–54
House E R 1974 *The Politics of Educational Innovation.* McCutchan, Berkeley, California
Hughes A S 1982 Which way general education? *Educ. Leadership* 39: 585–87
MacDonald B, Walker R 1976 *Changing the Curriculum.* Open Books, London
Rand Corporation 1975–78 *Federal Programs Supporting Educational Change*, Vols. 1–8. Rand Corporation, Santa Monica, California
Schaffarzick J 1979 Federal curriculum reform: A crucible for value conflict. In: Schaffarzick J, Sykes G (eds.) 1979 *Value Conflicts and Curriculum Issues: Lessons from Research and Experience.* McCutchan, Berkeley, California

The Impact of Textbooks

E. Ballér

From the numerous definitions of the term *curriculum*, this article focuses on two approaches: firstly, the curriculum is viewed as the content of instruction in a subject area within the school system which is selected on the basis of educational considerations and organized into topics and structures according to special principles; secondly, the curriculum is viewed as an overall plan of goals, subjects, timetables, materials, and intended learning outcomes of institutionalized teaching and learning as expressed in official, more-or-less standard, syllabi, usually adopted by educational authorities. The textbook, on the other hand, serving as an educational medium or manual of instruction in a certain subject area, is the product of a "technological process", which specifies and interprets the content of the curriculum and structures it in a way that is suitable for teaching and learning.

The relationship between curriculum and textbook is determined by several factors. It is affected—among other things—by the national traditions, the overall political, cultural, and educational aims of the school system, the curricular policy and the procedures employed for approving the syllabus and authorizing textbooks in a particular country. Thus, even if the content of a particular subject is uniform across countries, the textbooks used for teaching vary considerably.

1. Centralized and Decentralized Systems

In exploring this complex issue, a distinction should be made between centralized and decentralized educational systems and their curriculum development practices. The differentiation between centralized and decentralized educational systems emerged in the second half of the nineteenth century, and it usually coincided with the introduction of compulsory education. In some countries the pursuit of cultural homogeneity, which was supposed to be attainable through the acquisition of a common and standardized body of knowledge, resulted in centralistic tendencies. For centuries, especially after the invention of printing, textbooks represented and shaped the school curriculum. Famous authors and eminent educators such as Erasmus (1469–1536), Comenius (1592–1670), Pestalozzi (1746–1827), and Ushinsky (1824–1870) developed school textbooks that profoundly influenced the content of instruction as well as its processes and methods, not only within a single country but even across frontiers (Michel 1973).

When, in a number of countries, centrally produced, mandatory syllabi were introduced, they incorporated this textbook-based and information-loaded knowledge. When this notion of formally legitimized syllabi gained prominence in centralized systems, then curriculum development and textbooks played a secondary role only. Textbooks were evaluated and approved on the basis of their fidelity to the regulations laid down in the official documents, that is, faithfulness to their spirit and sometimes even to their content and structure. This was the major instrument by which centralized administrations could exercise control over teaching–learning processes in the school. This was true not only in most socialist countries, but also in some of the Western types of social systems (Hacker 1983).

Even under such circumstances, however, textbooks have not lost their influence. They have remained the major instructional medium, the most important resource for teaching and learning, the most prominent means for improving pupils' achievement, and indeed they have enjoyed the kudos of official legitimation and support. At the same time they affected the central syllabi, since experience derived from using a particular textbook in the schools has often had an impact upon the centrally initiated curriculum reforms.

In countries with decentralized education systems, the original unity or "symbiosis" between curricula and textbooks prevailed. In the English-speaking world, for example, the improvement and production of instructional materials was regarded as actual curriculum development. Due to the lack of centrally prescribed curricula, schools had a decisive say in selecting textbooks from the range of available choices offered by the publishing companies. In turn, textbook publishing became a commercial enterprise, where profitability and the demand of the market dominated.

2. Trends

Since the 1950s, significant changes have influenced the curriculum–textbook relationship in both centralized and decentralized systems. Centralized systems have moved away from merely prescribing curricular content and have begun to emphasize outcome-based and process-oriented management of instruction. Consequently, central planning assumed the role of an infrastructure, facilitating alternative approaches and instructional innovations which required decision-making at local levels. This, in turn, has had consequences for the selection of the content of instruction and for its organization both in central documents and in textbooks (Báthory 1986). At the same time, textbooks today constitute only one component of instructional media kits, which comprise a variety of teaching aids.

In decentralized systems of education, on the other hand, one can observe a struggle for controlling the curriculum by prescribing standards and achievement requirements, which in turn influences curriculum and textbook development (Lawton 1983). The effect of widely publicized and successful centrally developed textbooks and curriculum packages has also imposed a certain uniformity on the curricula used by the schools. This tendency has been precipitated by the requirements of external examinations. These trends have resulted in increasing the similarity of curriculum and textbook development and administration in the two main types of educational systems.

Bibliography

Báthory Z 1986 Decentralization issues in the introduction of new curriculum: The case of Hungary. *Prospects* 16: 33–47

Hacker H (ed.) 1980 *Das Schulbuch. Funktion und Verwendung im Unterricht.* Klinkhardt, Bad Heilbrunn

Hacker H 1983 Kodifizierte Bestimmungsfaktoren Curricularer Lernereignisse: Schulbücher. In: Hameyer U, Fray K, Haft E (eds.) 1983 *Handbuch der Curriculumforschung.* Beltz, Weinheim, pp. 351–60

Lawton D 1983 *Curriculum Studies and Educational Planning.* Hodder and Stoughton, London

Michel G 1973 *Schulbuch und Curriculum. Comenius im 18 Jahrhundert.* Henn, Ratingen, Düsseldorf

Schulbuchgestaltung in der DDR 1984. Von einem Autorenkollektiv. Volk und Wissen Volkseigener, Berlin

Gender Studies: Impact on Curriculum

J. L. Miller

The studies of gender that have most influenced school curriculum are those which are conceptualized within frameworks provided by women's studies programs at the university and, to a lesser degree, at secondary school levels. However, the highly developed and conceptually refined body of scholarship about women that has emerged since the early 1970s has yet to influence teacher preparation programs or elementary school curricula to any great extent. In the United States, current pressures for teacher and student performance and accountability have diminished possibilities for nontraditional curricula; gender studies are still categorized as such by many even though a plethora of curriculum materials and resources has been produced under the auspices of organized research centers and the Women's Educational Equity Act (WEEA) of 1974, among others. Thus, relevant curricular innovation and pedagogical approaches emerging from new paradigms of gender research and knowledge production are in danger of being submerged beneath the press for academic excellence and mastery of basic skills.

Further, sex equity issues at the national level are in flux, given, for example, the recent US Supreme Court decision in *Grove City College vs. Bell* (1984) and *Fire-Fighters Local Union vs. Stotts* (1984). Such resistance to sex equity and affirmative action positions has the potential to negate, to a great extent, the impact of the recent explosion of gender-related knowledge creation and utilization within educational settings. Awareness of the variety and depth of these gender studies is a necessary component in assuring the continuance and growth of educational opportunities and understandings for all students. The following descriptions of gender studies and their impact on school curriculum at various educational levels may illuminate the curricular and research goals of those who are committed to "an understanding of the history and function of education as support and codifier of sex segregation as well as education as an agent for change in the past and present" (*Women's Studies Newsletter* 1980 p. 2).

1. Women's Studies and Feminist Scholarship in Higher Education

In the United States, over 500 women's studies programs at the university level, 60 faculty and curriculum development projects, and 40 research centers actively engage in gender studies. Most women's studies programs are interdisciplinary; that is, they combine courses in literature, language, or art, for example, with work in sociology, anthropology, economics, political science, history, philosophy, psychology, biology, and related fields. Some programs offer minors, graduate minors, or certificates; others offer A.A., B.A., M.A., Ph.D., or Ed.D. degrees in women's studies. Some B.A.-granting programs offer an interdisciplinary autonomous degree. Other programs may offer the B.A. with a concentration in women's studies through another departmental unit of the college or university. A complete list of women's studies programs in the United States is maintained and published as an educational service of the *Women's Studies Quarterly*, Feminist Press, City University of New York, 311 E. 94th St., New York, NY 10128, USA.

While the intention of early women's studies programs was to develop a body of scholarship and a new curriculum about women and issues of gender, the more recent emphasis is upon integration of this new knowledge into existing curricula and general education (Schuster and Van Dyne 1984). These varied emphases have provoked an "autonomy/integration" debate. Many women's studies scholars fear that integrationist efforts will be too accepting of existing structures and definitions of knowledge (McIntosh and Minnich 1984), and will ignore the emerging paradigms being created by conceptualizations of feminist epistemology (Du Bois

et al. 1985), and pedagogy and research (Bunch and Pollack 1983).

Acknowledging that the danger of integration includes the possible assumption that there is nothing wrong with existing canons of knowledge that inclusion and minor revision will not correct, many feminist scholars now favor the concept of many streams of knowledge and culture (McIntosh and Minnich 1984). Such a concept enables women's studies to continue expanding its multifaceted nature. Areas of emphasis and development in the 1980s include Black women's studies, feminist science, and feminism as it relates to war and peace (Cheatham and Powell 1986).

Another major research focus is the "hidden curriculum," that is, what is subtly taught through the many ways in which both male and female teachers discriminate against female students in the classroom. Many argue that the "autonomy/integration" debate will remain a moot point as long as women students and teachers alike do not enjoy full equality of educational opportunity. A national report prepared by the Project on the Status and Education of Women in 1981 and its 1986 update ("The campus climate revisited: Chilly for women faculty, administrators, and graduate students"), addresses the subtle ways in which academic women are treated differently from men, including the classroom's silent language and subtle messages in class participation pattern, and makes recommendations for policy, faculty, and curricular change.

In the field of education, new scholarship on women in education is emerging (Burstyn 1986). The American Educational Research Association sponsored the preparation of a book on women researchers in education which will be an attempt to fill the gap in the history of educational research, which, until now, has virtually ignored the contributions of women who helped to shape the research foundations of modern educational thought (Shakeshaft 1986).

2. The Influence of Curriculum Theory

The work of curriculum theorists includes the examination of the relationships between schooling and social change as one way of transforming the production and dissemination of knowledge. What has emerged from such examinations is a vigorous inquiry by some into feminist perspectives as one analytic tool that may be used in the creation of new curriculum theory and transformative knowledge.

Feminist studies within the curriculum field focus upon the transformative possibilities inherent within the nature of such studies as well as upon the necessary reconstruction of women's lives and their roles within the educational realm.

Some curricularists utilize the autobiographical mode to examine the effects as well as implications of their own schooling experience upon their conceptions of themselves as educators and as curriculum specialists. By concentrating upon themselves as subjects and knowers in their worlds, these curriculum theorists are also creating a radical critique of the cultural and epistemological underpinnings of school curriculum (Grumet 1981).

Other curriculum theorists concentrate upon the possibilities of expanding the conceptual bases of critical theory to include the counter-hegemonic possibilities and practices of gender studies among its transformative potentials (Lather 1984). Such a focus has the potential to enlarge the theoretical formulations regarding the school's role in social reproduction that inform curriculum exclusions and bias as well as to identify curriculum as a site of ideological struggle (Anyon 1983, Apple 1982, Giroux 1983).

Another area of critique and analysis for some curriculum theorists includes reform efforts in education which encompass issues of curriculum inequality. Some argue that the press for academic excellence obscures ways in which that definition of excellence, for example, contributes to reification of patriarchal control (Grumet 1986).

These perspectives, critiques, and new theoretical constructions have raised consciousness about the influences of gender and the accompanying contexts of race and social class on the production of knowledge and quality of experience in schools.

3. Secondary and Elementary School Curricula

Given the tremendous outpouring of scholarship and the educational applications of gender studies since the late 1960s, these applications and implications are moving very slowly into kindergarten through secondary classrooms. As previously noted, the combination of accountability measures and emphasis on basic skills has resulted in rigid public school curricula and reluctance on the part of educators to deviate from mandated norms. However, the need to expand into this crucial area is not being ignored by those committed to the ultimate goal of an "inclusive curriculum" that acknowledges all women of all races, all ages, all classes. An entire day's programming at the 1984 National Women's Studies Association Conference focused upon the curriculum from kindergarten to the end of secondary school, and various national organizations in a variety of the disciplines are considering gender issues within the context of their specific knowledge areas (Ferguson 1981). By the mid-1980s particular attention was being directed toward issues of gender in mathematics and the sciences (Scheuneman 1986). Further, a number of college and university programs to integrate scholarship by and about women into elementary and secondary curricula were in progress.

At the high school level, many curriculum materials and resource guides have been developed, not only under the auspices of WEEA but also through regional and independent curriculum projects. Such resources often include course syllabi, suggestions for faculty development, assessment approaches, and annotated bibliographies; and emphasize reading, discussion skills, role playing, career education, decision making, and problem solving (Schmitz 1985).

Curriculum changes in response to gender studies at the elementary level perhaps are most apparent in the areas of language, children's literature, and creation of sex equitable classroom environments.

Studies have pointed to the need to help children make the transition between their naturally learned language and the language of standard formal English; such transitions may highlight the masculine orientation of the language itself as well as the ways in which the standard formal language often minimizes the experiences of females, special classes (women of handicapped status, lesbians, and so forth), and ethnic minorities.

Analyses of sexual stereotypes and cultural and sexual selection/exclusion in children's literature contributed to heightened awareness of these issues in the late 1970s and 1980s. Some argue that the gender of the characters in literature is subordinate to the social/gender relations portrayed. Thus, even though female characters may be more apparent in children's literature than was previously the case, the extent to which these characters assume roles of active agency determines the extent to which children might internalize nonsexist role expectations (Council on Interracial Books for Children 1981). Further, because human liberation is the goal of most gender studies, many wish to consider the treatment of males in children's books, as males also have been victimized by stereotypic expectations. Suggestions for young readers include observing how male characters are treated and expected to act, noting the literary role of the father, and watching for the imposition of a competitive system in which males are required to win.

Observational studies of classroom interactions show that teachers tend to give boys both more negative and more positive feedback about their actions than they give girls. Although girls volunteer significantly more often than boys, they are called upon less often (Sadker and Sadker 1982). Thus, girls become somewhat invisible not only in the curricular materials that they are studying but also in the classroom interactions that constitute, along with textbooks, test materials, and educational resources, the total curriculum.

4. Teacher Preparation and Development

In light of such findings as noted above, one would expect teacher preparation and staff development programs in the 1980s to highlight issues of gender as reflected in all areas of the overt as well as hidden curriculum. However, the programs in this period actually reflect the conservative nature of educational endeavors in general; further, males continue to dominate in school administration and in departments of education, the ranks of tenured female faculty remain relatively small, and thus forms of bias and discrimination continue to emerge.

Further, the teacher education curriculum in general does not exemplify a commitment to educational equity. Analysis of 24 widely used teacher education texts found that 23 gave less than 1 percent of space to issues of sexism and not a single text provided future teachers with curricular awareness and instructional strategies to counteract sexism in the classroom and its harmful impact on children (Sadker and Sadker 1982).

Although researchers continue to point to the necessity of sex equity practices in classrooms (Klein and Bogart 1986), it is perhaps in the work of curriculum theorists in the 1980s that educators might find personal exemplifications as well as commitment to the uncovering of bias and revealing of embedded pre-understandings of gender roles and expectations.

Focus upon the historical role of women in the teaching profession as well as upon contemporary enactments of this historical role (Miller 1986) enables teachers to understand their conceptions of themselves as teachers, to illuminate ways in which such conceptions may or may not contribute to reification of gender-specific expectations for their students, and to move into creation of new and transformative curricula that acknowledge the potential in all humans.

Bibliography

Anyon J 1983 Accommodation, resistance, and female gender. In: Walker S, Burton L (eds.) 1983 *Gender and Education*. Falmer, Barcombe, Sussex, pp. 19–38

Apple M W 1982 *Education and Power*. Routledge and Kegan Paul, Boston, Massachusetts

Bunch C, Pollack S. (eds.) 1983 *Learning Our Way: Essays in Feminist Education*. The Crossing Press, Trumansburg, New York

Burstyn J N 1986 Integrating the new scholarship on women into required courses in schools of education: The case of history. *Educ. Res.* 15 (6): 11–13

Cheatham A, Powell M C 1986 *This Way Daybreak Comes: Women's Values and the Future*. New Society Publishers, Philadelphia, Pennsylvania

Council on Interracial Books for Children (CIBC) 1981 *Interracial Books for Children Bulletin* 12 (4–5). CIBC, New York

Du Bois E C, Kelly G, Kennedy E, Korsmeyer C, Robinson L 1985 *Feminist Scholarship: Kindling in the Groves of Academe*. University of Illinois Press, Urbana, Illinois

Ferguson M A (ed.) 1981 *Images of Women in Literature*, 3rd edn. Houghton-Mifflin, Boston, Massachusetts

Freebody P, Baker C D 1985 Children's first schoolbooks: Introduction to the culture of literacy. *Harvard Educ. Rev.* 55: 381–98

Giroux H 1983 *Theory and Resistance in Education: Pedagogy for the Opposition*. Bergin and Garvey, South Hadley, Massachusetts

Grumet M R 1981 Conception, contradiction and curriculum. *J. Curric. Theor.* 3 (1): 287–98

Grumet M R 1986 The Paideia Proposal: A thankless child replies. *Curric. Inq.* 16 (3): 335–44

Klein S S, Bogart K 1986 Implications for increasing sex equity at all educational levels. *Educ. Res.* 15 (6): 20–21

Lather P 1984 Critical theory, curricular transformation, and feminist mainstreaming. *J. Educ.* 166 (1): 49–62

McIntosh P, Minnich E 1984 Varieties of women's studies. *Women's Stud. Int. Forum.* 7 (3): 138–44

Miller J L 1986 Women as teachers: Enlarging conversations on issues of gender and self-control. *J. Curric. Supervis.* 1 (2): 111–21

Sadker M P, Sadker D M 1982 *Sex Equity Handbook for Schools*. Longman, New York

Scheuneman J D 1986 The female perspective on methodology and statistics. *Educ. Res.* 15 (6): 22–23

Schmitz B (ed.) 1985 *Integrating Women's Studies into the Curriculum*. Feminist Press, Old Westbury, New York

Schuster M R, Van Dyne S (eds.) 1984 *Selected Bibliography for Integrating Research on Women's Experience in the Liberal Arts Curriculum*. Smith College, Northampton, Massachusetts

Shakeshaft C 1986 Methodological issues in researching. Women in education research: The legacy of a century. *Educ. Res.* 15 (6): 13–14

Section 2

Approaches and Methods

Overview

This Section contains articles on approaches to defining the content of curriculum, organizing the knowledge for transmission to the learner, and determining the sequence of activities and methods of teaching which have direct implications for curriculum construction. The decision to include articles which deal with methods of teaching reflects the view emphasized by the originators of the New Curriculum Movement in the 1950s that adopting a method of teaching may have implications for devising learning activities for the curriculum. Nevertheless, only those teaching methods which have had direct influence on selecting or devising learning experiences are dealt with in this *Encyclopedia*. Thus, for example, topics such as discovery learning and experience-based learning are dealt with, whereas topics such as team teaching or open education, which have not been associated with innovative curricula, are not covered.

Approaches to curriculum have changed during the course of history, they differ from each other across national educational systems and across broader frameworks of cultural and religious communities, and also as a result of the epistemological and pedagogical views adopted by their originators. These characteristics of curricula have served as a basis for clustering entries contained in this Section. The classification scheme used here does not constitute a rigid model. The dimensions employed are neither fully mutually exclusive, nor are they fully exhaustive. They represent a variety of causes, circumstances, ideas, and considerations, which lead curriculum experts to produce a curriculum of a certain type.

1. Historical Perspectives

The two articles contained under this heading are related to the modern school curriculum. The omission of early educational programs, such as the Trivia and Quadrivia, is in line with the purpose of this *Encyclopedia* to expound issues directly related to contemporary education. Tanner's article reviews the impact of the Enlightenment movement and of Dewey's ideas on the nineteenth and early twentieth century curriculum, and Kliebard compares two twentieth century curriculum movements in the United States. The first of these is the functional efficiency or Life-adjustment Movement which emerged in the 1950s, and the second, which emerged in the 1960s, is known as the New Curriculum Movement, which precipitated the renewal of the discipline-oriented curricula.

2. Methods of Organizing Knowledge

Section 2(b) reviews differences in ways of organizing knowledge for the purpose of teaching. Three approaches are represented in this Section: the subject-matter approach, the integrated approach, and the short-units approach.

Ben-Peretz and Connelly define the term *subject-matter* as it is used in the context of curriculum, and distinguish between subject-matters of different types, such as disciplinary and nondisciplinary knowledge. Another article in this Section focuses on the most common type of subject-matter, namely discipline-oriented subject-matter.

Glatthorn and Foshay review approaches to organizing knowledge, and examine ways to ensure that separate divisions of the curriculum should be properly related to each other. They distinguish between two ways of striving to attain this goal. One is the correlated curriculum, which strictly preserves the separateness of each discipline and considers the simultaneous teaching of related topics across different disciplines as a satisfactory solution to the issue of relationship between disciplines. The other approach weakens the disciplinary boundaries of knowledge taught in the school, or fully ignores them.

Special examples of weakening the disciplinary boundaries of curricular knowledge are presented in the articles on *Integrated Science Studies*, by Blum and *Interdisciplinary Approach*, by Batts. In the first of these articles, integration is restricted to a relatively narrow range of disciplines, namely those dealing with science, and in the second article a particular topic is examined through the prisms of all relevant disciplines, using the disciplinary structures and methodologies of each particular discipline. A third approach is to use small curricular units, such as modules or minicourses which free the educator to determine the sequence of study units, thus facilitating correlation between related topics.

3. Focus on Basics

A group of articles examines the implications of the back to basics idea in the field of curriculum studies. This idea emerged in the United States as a reaction to the pedagogical trend of the 1960s, which put high emphasis on studies at an advanced level. In contrast, the back to basics movement strived to restore the central place of the 'three Rs'— reading, writing, and arithmetic—in the curriculum. At the same time, in European countries the idea of core curriculum gained popularity.

The leading article in this section, written by Tyler, describes the circumstances which contributed to the spread of the *Core Curriculum* idea in numerous educational systems and specifies its main components. One of the manifestations of this trend was the spread of competency testing across most school districts of the United States. Emphasis on basics is implied by the term *key concept*, however, the *key concept* approach to determining the curriculum content is strongly linked to the discipline-oriented curriculum, while the concepts of back to basics and core curriculum are more concerned with the functional outcomes of the curriculum and they are biased towards the life-adjustment trend.

Klafki's article on the *Exemplar Approach* also contains arguments for reducing the scope of curricular content taught in schools, with the aim of enabling in-depth study within a narrow range of examplary topics. This argument is probably one of the most important contributions of a German scholar to the New Curriculum Movement.

4. Focus on the Individual

A variety of program types have been generated with the aim of meeting the needs of the individual learner. Typical classroom teaching is carried out in groups of 20–40 learners, and in numerous educational systems the class size reaches even higher averages. As reducing class size is very costly, educators have strived to identify ways of meeting the needs of the individual without undue increase in the educational budget.

Each article contained in Section 2(d) describes a particular method for individualizing instruction. The methods described differ from each other in respect of the aim of individualization, its scope, and so on. Some of the approaches described employ only individualized pacing of the instructional materials, without offering differential contents of instruction, Other approaches are in favor of adjusting the level of difficulty of the assignments to the ability level of the students, but the topic taught in the class remains identical for all learners. Approaches differ also in respect of justifying the process of individualization. Some approaches view individualization as an effective means of imparting knowledge, others view it as a means of responding to a broad range of individual needs, such as needs of the affective, social, and self-realization type. Finally, some approaches view individualization as a way to enhance independent learning, which may lead towards the realization of the ideal of lifelong learning.

The leading article in this Section is Bolvin's article on *Individualized School Programs*. It provides an overall picture of the varieties of programs geared towards meeting the needs of the individual learner. Some of the articles in this Section discuss satisfying the needs of special subpopulations. Thus, the articles on *Accelerated Programs* and *Honors Courses* deal with satisfying the needs of the gifted learner, and the article on *Diversified Curriculum* deals with teaching vocational knowledge to those who have a nonacademic orientation.

The article on *Elective Courses*, describes the attempts of schools to offer a wide range of curricular topics beyond the relatively narrow range of compulsory subjects. The curricula for elective subjects is similar to those for the compulsory subjects. They are structured and uniform for all those who opt to enroll for them.

Finally, two articles in this Section, *Curriculum Contracts* and *Independent Studies*, deal with educational programs which imply changes in the role of the teacher. Using these programs, the teacher has to fulfill the role of guiding, facilitating, and monitoring, rather than selecting, informing, and organizing.

5. *Focus on Learning Activities*

Three articles contained in Section 2(e) describe different approaches to structuring learning experiences. The article by Weiss and Regan on *Process-oriented and Product-oriented Programs* describes the differences between traditional school curricula which emphasize knowledge outcomes, and the innovative curricula which favor the teaching of problem solving, information gathering skills, and social skills with the aim of fostering readiness towards lifelong education. Highly structured methods of teaching process skills are the *Discovery and Inquiry Methods* which have been employed in numerous innovative curricula. In the article on *Experience-based Studies* learners are expected to interact directly with real-life situations. The program prescribes assignments which require students to explore reality (such as studying consumer habits or finding out details about people's career patterns), but it also takes advantage of extra-school experiences gained by the learners.

6. *Focus on Environment*

Numerous curricula are geared to meet the needs of a particular social stratum of the total population such as the socioeconomically disadvantaged, minority groups, rural groups, and so on. Three articles deal with school programs of this type. Banks' article on *Multicultural Education* deals with the educational needs of ethnic minorities. The author points out that the term may also apply to programs which are designed to teach the majority group pupils about the cultural values of the minority group with the aim of promoting cultural pluralism. *Urban Education* programs cater for the needs of disadvantaged population strata dwelling in the central areas of large cities, which have been vacated by the more prosperous middle classes for the suburbs. These areas are characterized by chronic dropout, discipline problems, violations of law, and a high unemployment rate of the adult population. Bude's article on *Rural Education* analyzes recent trends in this field. Traditionally, rural education programs put high emphasis on knowledge which may serve the aim of increasing agricultural production. This approach favored the rural establishment, rather than the masses and the small tenants. Subsequent rural education programs put greater emphasis on the needs of the disadvantaged rural population, striving to bridge the gap between rural masses and the rural elite groups.

Finally, the practice of *Nongraded Curriculum* is also related to the idea of meeting the needs of the individual learner. Originally, nongraded schools were maintained in rural areas in response to economic necessity. Graded schools could not be maintained in locations with few children, so it was necessary to have all children, or at least several grade levels, in a single class with a single teacher. The idea of nongraded schools emerged as an innovative approach to schooling, which may contribute to the improvement of instruction.

7. *National Systems of Education*

Section 2(g) contains 14 articles describing the curriculum history of a number of national systems of education. This Section contains articles on an illustrative sample of English-speaking countries, Western Europe, socialist countries, the Third World, Japan and the People's Republic of China. In the overview to this group of articles, Schubert discusses their contribution to the knowledge of the general history of curriculum theory and practice, to the comparative perspective of curriculum across countries and cultures, and to the improvement of curriculum practice across the world.

8. *Cultural Approaches*

The articles included in Section 2(h) discuss the curriculum-related ideas and practices that have emerged in four religions across the world, with the aim of transmitting the moral and cultural heritage of the religion to followers of its creed.

Guruge examines ideas about education and educational practices which contributed to the spread of the Buddhist creed and specifies the content and the method of teaching in the traditional schools. Nanavaty discusses the roots of Hindu education as they are embodied in the *Vedas, Upanishads*, and the *Bhagavad Gita*, and the contribution of modern thinkers like Gandhi, Tagore, and Sri Aurobindo to the evolution of traditional education in India. Wagner describes the curriculum and the teaching methods used in traditional Koranic schools, the impact of these traditional institutions on the modern world, and problems related to the coexistence of modern and Koranic schools in the Moslem world. Finally, Reshef examines the forms of education which emerged in Jewish communities across the world for developing Jewish identity and preserving Jewish life.

A. Lewy

Curriculum Approaches and Methods

Introduction

M. Ben-Peretz

Approaches to, and methods employed in the curriculum field reflect views about the portrayal of knowledge in the curriculum, learning activities, and the relationship between curriculum and the social environment. Different educational ideologies generate different types of curriculum theory which guide curricular practice. Giroux et al. (1981) propose three perspectives on curriculum: traditionalist, conceptual–empirical, and reconceptual. These perspectives differ in relation to the kinds of questions that are raised, or ignored, by each framework. According to Giroux et al. the traditionalist framework concerns itself with questions about the best and most efficient ways to learn specific kinds of knowledge—the *cultural heritage*. Outside of this framework there are issues concerning the role of the school as an agent involved in the reproduction of a class-divided society, as well as questions relating to the generation of a personal meaning of knowledge.

The conceptual–empirical perspective is bound to a model of logic and investigation based on science. Its concerns include control and prediction in the realm of curriculum development, viewed separately from sociopolitical issues and class conflicts. The reconceptualist perspective is associated with the hermeneutical tradition, emphasizing subjectivity, existential experience, and the importance of intentionality in human actions. The political character of culture and transmission of knowledge is central to this approach. These different orientations may be viewed as ideal forms, in the sense that they are not necessarily to be found in their pure form in any approach to curriculum practice.

Some dominant innovative approaches to curriculum have their roots in the ideals and educational practices of the past. Thus, for example, when explaining the legitimacy of the academic freedom bestowed upon the German universities at the beginning of the eighteenth century, Paulsen (1919) emphasized the changing nature of knowledge. He contrasted the assumptions underlying university instruction in previous epochs with those present in the climate of academic freedom, and claimed that

> in the past university instruction was based on the assumption that the truth has already been given, that instruction had to do with transmission only, and that it was the duty

of the controlling authorities to see to it that no false doctrines were taught. The new university instruction began with the assumption that the truth must be discovered and that it was the duty of instruction to qualify and guide the student in this task. (Cubberley 1948 p. 554)

There is no doubt that this idea greatly affected the science curricula developed in the era of the New Curriculum Movement.

Ideas about the advantages of learning by doing, rather than by merely reciting words, and the importance of observation and investigation in learning, are emphasized by Pestalozzi (1746–1827) (Downs 1975). Rousseau's (1963) ideas about the child's natural curiosity and its inborn capacities contain the basic tenets of the child-centered approach to curriculum.

While history of education abounds in approaches to curriculum, it is only since the 1970s that systematic efforts have been made to identify factors associated with these differences. Schwab (1973) describes four groups of factors, referring to them as *curriculum commonplaces*: the subject-matter, the learner, the teacher, and the milieu. Ben-Peretz (1989) added a fifth dimension: time. The commonplaces may provide a framework for curriculum scholarship and curriculum practice.

Treatment of all commonplaces is deemed a prerequisite for a defensible and valid process of curriculum development. Curriculum deliberations aim at the identification of the nature of educational problems. Possible solutions are considered and their consequences weighed. Considerations of the commonplaces is important in this process. Subject-matter specialists contribute their understanding of the nature of the disciplines. Their function is to ensure that a range of bodies of knowledge and skills is considered by curriculum developers. Knowledge about, and experience with, learners is crucial if curriculum deliberations are to be sensitive to the needs of diverse student populations. Teaching and learning take place in specific physical and social environments—the milieu. Insights into the specific features of different environments are valuable for developing appropriate curriculum materials. These materials, the products of curriculum development, are used by teachers and are transformed into learning experiences. Therefore, teachers' knowledge is a crucial component of curriculum deliberations.

Time plays an important role in schools and is another factor to be weighed carefully by curriculum developers and implementors. On the one hand, allocation of appropriate amounts of time to different curriculum themes may be considered essential for successful curriculum development. On the other hand, educational philosophers like Rousseau and Schleiermacher (1826–1951) view the experience of time differently and argue that schools must be ready to "lose time", and that it is unethical to sacrifice the present moment for a future one. Different approaches to time in schools have to be considered and may have far-reaching implications for curriculum development and use.

The curriculum commonplaces mentioned above may be treated differently in the framework of the three curricular perspectives proposed by Giroux et al. (1981), namely, the traditionalist, the conceptual–empirical, and the reconceptualist perspectives. In the consideration of the commonplaces developers may tend to give equal weight to each, or alternatively, may decide to create a hierarchy of commonplaces according to changing local needs in specific times. It seems appropriate to conclude this introduction with a quote from Connelly and Lantz (1985 p. 1162): "Ultimately, the actual uses of curricula are more important than the prescriptions obtained in the theoretical definition, conceptualization, selection, and organization of content since classroom practices define what actually occurs".

Bibliography

Ben-Peretz M 1989 Perspectives on time in education. In: Ben-Peretz M, Bromme R (eds.) 1990 *The Nature of Time in Schools: Theoretical Concepts, Practitioner Perceptions.* Teachers College Press, New York

Connelly F M, Lantz O 1985 Definitions of curriculum. In: Husen T, Postlethwaite T N (eds.) 1985. *The International Encyclopedia of Education.* Pergamon, Oxford, pp. 1160–63

Cubberley E P 1948 *The History of Education.* Houghton Mifflin, Cambridge, Massachusetts, p. 554

Downs R B 1975 *Heinrich Pestalozzi: Father of Modern Pedagogy.* Twayne Publishers, Boston, Massachusetts

Giroux H A, Penna A N, Pinar W F (eds.) 1981 *Curriculum and Instruction.* McCutchan, Berkeley, California

Rousseau J J 1963 *Emile Uber die Erziehung.* Reclam, Stuttgart

Schleiermacher F D E 1826, 1957 Padagogische schriften. In: Weniger V E (ed.) 1957 *Die Vorlesungen aus dem Jahre 1826.* Duesseldorf-Muenchen

Schwab J J 1973 The practical 3: Translation into curriculum. *Sch. Rev.* 81: 501–22

Historical Perspectives

Curriculum History: Nineteenth and Early Twentieth Century

L. Tanner

It is said that all historical events are part of a chain of human development; in any era one can find the influences of the past and the beginnings of the future. This is particularly true of the school curriculum. Nineteenth and early twentieth century developments still affect our own thinking about what should be included in today's schools. These developments, in turn, are inseparable from the history of the entire world. This article attempts to present the significant events and actors in the history of the school curriculum from the early nineteenth century until the end of the Second World War.

Section 1 presents the ideas and theories about the curriculum that influenced what happened in this period, while Section 2 is concerned with characteristic curriculum practices. Curriculum history, like the history of any professional field, is a matter of people—people with ideas and people who put ideas into practice. Sometimes these are the same people.

1. Curriculum Theories

Nineteenth century curriculum thought was profoundly influenced by the intellectual currents and reform ideals of the Enlightenment. Based on the idea that the intelligent mind can lead humankind to goodness, the Enlightenment movement gained many adherents in Europe and colonial America in the seventeenth and eighteenth centuries. The idea that the social order was a matter of divine invention and depended on supernatural authority gradually gave way to a belief in natural rights, whether from God or some natural source, and the principle that people should play a part in developing the policies under which they should be governed. In addition to shifts in political theory, there were changes in psychological and social theory. John Locke, who had a background in medicine and philosophy, argued that human nature was shaped in part, at least, by the environment. Locke's *Essay Concerning Human Understanding* (1690) was a crucial link in the chain of human development. If people could just know more they could reason properly, and they could improve themselves and their society. The proposals of Enlightenment writers in England, France, and the American colonies led not only to demands for more and better education but to a curriculum that was more secular in content.

Enlightenment thinkers believed that, given the proper environment and education, humankind was endlessly perfectible. Based on this view of humankind, a new philosophy of education emerged in Europe. According to this philosophy, which was expounded by Rousseau in *Emile* (1762), and developed further and actually applied by Pestalozzi in Switzerland, education is a pleasant process through which children develop naturally in a healthy and sound environment. Furthermore, these philosophers adopted the idea of sense realism namely that the human mind is a blank tablet at birth, ready to receive perceptions of the world through the senses—seeing, hearing, smelling, tasting, feeling, and doing. Clearly, from this concept, education involved far more than dealing with ideas and books. It was a rich variety of experiences, aimed to draw out the individual's possibilities.

These ideas did not remain in Europe but crossed the Atlantic, and in the early nineteenth century were found with increasing frequency in United States educational thinking. In the early twentieth century, realism in education would cross the Atlantic once again, this time in an easterly direction. For example, German educators expressed enormous enthusiasm for the project method of instruction developed by William Kilpatrick (1918) and it became a new instructional method in the German school system (Knoll 1989).

A theory about the way people acquire knowledge is nothing more or less than a philosophy of learning. Realism in education was the result of the formulation of a new method of thinking and arriving at truth: the scientific method. The old view had been that the human is born with a faculty of reason which was best developed by disciplined study of the classical languages, philosophy, and mathematics. The new view, which would always be battling against the old, was that truth and knowledge develop from observation and experience rather than from the manipulation of given ideas or a playing with words with no consideration of actuality. Sense experience was an important beginning of progressivism in education, as was the idea that education is a pleasurable process by which children develop naturally in a beneficial environment. The result of these two ideas was the gradual building up of a theory of curriculum development. The learner was one source of curriculum objectives and knowledge was another. A third was the usefulness of knowledge—how it contributes to the needs of society and the business of living. However, it was not until the middle of the twentieth century that these rudimentary ideas developed into a full-bodied theory of curriculum.

1.1 The Curriculum as a Field of Study

Although curriculum thought and innovation have always been present in Western education, the curriculum did not actually become a professional field of study until the 1920s. The first general book on the curriculum was published in 1918 by Franklin Bobbitt, a professor of educational administration at the University of Chicago. In 1920, in Los Angeles, he led the first city system-wide curriculum revision program. Whereas curriculum revision had been approached earlier on a piecemeal, course-by-course basis, Bobbitt took a new step forward, dealing with the curriculum in all grades and subjects on a unified basis. Other system-wide revision programs followed in Denver and St. Louis.

A second book of major importance in the early years of the curriculum field was an analysis on the subject by W W Charters of The Ohio State University. In 1926, the first curriculum laboratory was established at Teachers College, Columbia University. By 1940, it contained thousands of courses of study and ideas from all over the world. The coming of age of curriculum as a distinct field of study also happened at Teachers College, when the first curriculum department was founded there in 1938. The department was headed by Hollis L Caswell, a leader in state curriculum programs in the 1930s.

1.2 The Main Curriculum Problem

The problem of the curriculum is and always has been to select what is best, namely what should be selected and taught from the wider world of knowledge. Herbert Spencer posed this question in 1860 in his article entitled "What knowledge is of most worth?" For Spencer, science was of most worth. As a result of his work, science was more rapidly introduced into all levels of the curriculum. In the 1920s, the problem of determining what was of most worth was of particular concern because of the large-scale curriculum revision programs being conducted in city school systems. The Twenty-sixth Yearbook of the National Society for the Study of Education (NSSE 1926) was a special effort to bring together and unify the varying and antagonistic philosophies of the curriculum that were being espoused by curriculum leaders.

The hero in the effort was Harold Rugg, chairman of the NSSE's Committee on Curriculum-Making and a professor at Columbia's Teachers College. The members of the committee were all curriculum leaders and their philosophical orientations ranged from child-centeredness (no curriculum planned in advance) to intellectual discipline (the acquisition of knowledge) as chief goal of the curriculum, with the assumption that education was likely to be hard and unpleasant. They sent a questionnaire to superintendents of selected United States cities to ascertain their involvement in curriculum revision and found that what was going on was "partial, superficial, and timorous 'revision' rather than general, fundamental, and courageous reconstruction" (Rugg and Counts 1926 p. 427). Why did the curriculum need reconstruction? The committee had found "definite evidence" that a gap existed "between the curriculum and the capacities, interests, and development of the child" (p. 426).

1.3 The Search for Consensus

Both volumes of the Twenty-sixth Yearbook identify problems that are still critical in the development of the curriculum and instructional program. The Yearbook is a landmark because of the composite statement of the leaders of the field that stressed the importance of thoroughly systematized, codified knowledge "developed through a long social evolution," but concluded that the curriculum should be developed "from the starting point of the needs of the learner" (NSSE, Committee on Curriculum-Making, 1926 pp. 21–22).

It was in actual fact, Dewey (1902) who identified the fundamental factors in the educational process as: (a) the learner ("the immature, undeveloped being"), (b) society ("certain social aims, meanings, values incarnate with the matured experience of the adult"), and (c) organized subject matter ("the specialization and divisions of the curriculum"). Dewey warned that if we treat these factors in isolation or we focus on one at the expense of the others, we end up with an unsurmountable problem of antagonisms, such as the child versus the curriculum, individual nature versus social culture, and so on (Dewey 1902 pp. 4–8). Dewey stressed how the curriculum must be constructed so as to be in harmonic interaction with the nature and needed growth of the learner and with the goals and ideals of a democratic society.

Through a continuous process of evolution (Tanner and Tanner 1988) culminating with what is often referred to as the "Tyler rationale," where Ralph W Tyler (1949) identified the same three factors as did his predecessors and contemporaries, there developed a model for curriculum development. According to Tanner and Tanner (1988) "the paradigm (model) provides a compass for treating the fundamental factors in vital interaction rather than in opposition" (p. 57). The curriculum field is a professional community of scholars who search for solutions to the persistent and new problems in curriculum development. The sense of community is reflected through such organizations as the Association for Supervision and Curriculum Development, Division B (Curriculum Studies) of the

American Educational Research Association and many national and international journals focused on the curriculum field.

2. Curriculum Practices

2.1 Object Teaching and Curriculum Expansion

Pestalozzi's ideas about ways to teach children were actually put into practice in his own schools. More important here is that his conceptions of how learning takes place influenced what should be learned, namely the subjects to be included in the curriculum. Pestalozzi thought up a series of "object lessons" in order to develop the child's senses of sight, touch, and sound. Animals, plants, drawing, geography, and music were important in Pestalozzi's curriculum for fostering the development of the perceptive powers.

The use of Pestalozzian methods in Europe began to influence the United States curriculum in the middle of the nineteenth century. The Pestalozzian form of instruction called "object teaching" required children to use their senses and their minds and be able to answer questions because they had observed and reasoned carefully. This showed the importance of oral language in the curriculum and a new subject, oral language work, entered the primary grades in United States public schools. In the upper elementary grades, oral and written language replaced to some extent the narrow emphasis on drill in English grammar. Object teaching was very important in introducing science as a school subject. (Herbert Spencer favored object teaching.) Arithmetic, too, underwent changes from words about numbers to actual number ideas. The introduction of drawing and music into the elementary school was also based on Pestalozzian ideas.

Just as Pestalozzian instructional principles resulted in expansion of the curriculum, so did the ushering in of a new technological era. The development of machines that improved farming, mining, manufacturing, and the means of transportation and communication led to demands for a more utilitarian education. The 1820s were a peak period in the development of the academy, which was the immediate ancestor of the United States high school. During this period the academies offered a multiplicity of courses dealing with such studies as book-keeping, astronomy, navigation, and surveying as well as the classical curriculum required for college entrance.

2.2 Mental Discipline and the Curriculum

Curriculum expansion was not without opposition. Many conservatives sought to retain classical languages and studies as the core of the secondary school curriculum. Even those conservatives who admitted the need to expand the secondary studies somewhat, argued that the study of Greek and Latin would discipline the youthful mind. Once trained in logic and reason, that mind would experience little difficulty mastering skills and knowledge in more practical fields.

In 1901, Thorndike and Woodworth published their monumental studies refuting this justification for offering subjects in the school curriculum. As a result of this research, academic subjects could no longer be justified in terms of discredited formal discipline theory. Thorndike concluded from his studies that there must be identical elements in what is learned in school and the opportunities for their use by the learner. Tyler (1949), Taba (1962), Tanner and Tanner (1980, 1987), and other curriculum theorists stress the necessity of making curriculum decisions that are consistent with what is known about learning. Certainly Thorndike's studies profoundly influenced thought about the curriculum. Nevertheless, in the late 1980s many lay citizens and educators still assert belief in theories of learning that derive from the disciplinary theories and faculty psychology of the nineteenth century.

Dewey also criticized faculty psychology and mental discipline, and his work, *Interest in Relation to Training of the Will* (1896), later published as *Interest and Effort in Education* (1913), did much to overturn curriculum thinking about these doctrines. He argued that "It is absurd to suppose that a child gets more intellectual or mental discipline when he goes at a matter unwillingly than when he goes at it with complete interest and out of the fullness of his heart" (Dewey 1896 p. 6). Among Dewey's many important contributions that were influential upon the curriculum was the idea that tasks or projects should interest the student and require real effort, but the difficulties should not be such that frustration results. One result of Dewey's ideas on interest and effort was that long, child-frightening words (which were never in most people's vocabularies anyhow) began to disappear from spelling lists.

2.3 Dewey's Conception of the Thinking Process

One of Dewey's most important and revolutionary ideas was his conception of thinking as a problem-solving method. Thinking was applying the scientific method to all sorts of problems. Dewey developed a problem-solving method for use in schools that corresponded to the method of experimental inquiry. Dewey's book *How We Think* (1933) was intended to help teachers understand what thinking (problem solving) is and how to develop habits of reflective thinking in pupils. In defining and solving a real problem which concerned them students would learn to think. "Here," wrote Butts and Cremin (1953), "was a great lever to pry loose the encrusted regime of formal subjects and logically organized subject matters that characterized most of the schools of the nineteenth and early twentieth centuries" (p. 347).

Dewey's idea of thinking as the scientific method applied to problems was misconstrued by many of his interpreters, most notably his student William H Kilpatrick. In 1918, Kilpatrick published an article, "The Project Method," which denied that thinking was a necessary condition for an activity to be labeled a project. Anything could be a project as long as child interest was present. Kilpatrick's project method caught on like wildfire in various parts of the world, causing Dewey to warn sharply that "interest is not enough" (1933 p. 218). A project must involve thought, which excludes merely trivial activities, and it must awaken curiosity and lead students' minds into new fields.

Dewey was practitioner as well as theorist. From 1896 to 1904 he conducted a laboratory school at the University of Chicago where he developed and tested many of his ideas about the curriculum. More than any other theorist or practitioner, Dewey influenced the world of practice. He influenced such innovations as projects in agricultural education, curriculum synthesis, the inquiry–discovery method, science laboratories, home economics, industrial arts, and field trips. Dewey's call for a curriculum that dealt with the real world of everyday life was very influential. "He more than any one person is responsible for changing the tone and temper of American education within the past three decades," wrote William Kilpatrick in 1939 (p. 464). However, Dewey's influence was, and continues to be, worldwide.

Problems that plagued the curriculum field should not be left out of the picture. For example, at the close of the Second World War, the need to prevent "thoughtless, trivial, and hasty responses to pressures and fads" was identified as a critical problem by Taba (1945 p. 82). This still remains a persistent problem in the early 1990s.

Bibliography

Bobbitt F 1918 *The Curriculum*. Houghton Mifflin, Boston, Massachusetts
Butts R F, Cremin L A 1953 *A History of Education in American Culture*. Holt, Rinehart, and Winston, New York
Charters W W 1923 *Curriculum Construction*. Macmillan, New York
Dewey J 1896 Interest as related to will. In: *Second Supplement to the National Herbart Year Book for 1895*. National Herbart Society, Bloomington, Illinois, pp. 209–55
Dewey J 1902 *The Child and the Curriculum*. University of Chicago, Chicago, Illinois
Dewey J 1933 *How We Think*, 2nd ed. (1st ed. published in 1910). D C Heath, Lexington, Massachusetts
Kilpatrick W H 1918 The project method. *Teach. Coll. Rec.* 19(3): 319–35
Kilpatrick W H 1939 Dewey's influence on education. In: Schilpp P A (ed.) 1939 *The Philosophy of John Dewey*. Northwestern University, Evanston, Illinois, pp. 445–73
Knoll M 1989 Transatlantic influences: The project method between the USA and Germany. In: Kridel C (ed.) 1989 *Curriculum History: Conference Presentations from the Society for the Study of Curriculum History*. University Press of America, Lanham, Maryland
National Society for the Study of Education (NSSE), Committee on Curriculum-Making 1926. The foundations of curriculum-making. In: *The Foundations of Curriculum-Making*, Twenty-sixth Yearbook, NSSE, Part II. Public School Publishing, Bloomington, Illinois
Rugg H, Counts G S 1926 A critical appraisal of current methods of curriculum-making. In: *Curriculum-Making: Past and Present*, Twenty-sixth Yearbook, NSSE, Part I. Public School Publishing, Bloomington, Illinois, pp. 425–47
Spencer H 1860 What knowledge is of most worth? *Education: Intellectual, Moral, and Physical*. Appleton, New York, pp. 1–55
Taba H 1945 General techniques of curriculum planning. In: Tyler R W (ed.) 1945 *American Education in the Postwar Period*, Forty-fourth Yearbook, NSSE, Part I. University of Chicago, Chicago, Illinois, pp. 85–92
Taba H 1962 *Curriculum Development: Theory and Practice*. Harcourt Brace and World, New York
Tanner D, Tanner L N 1980 *Curriculum Development: Theory into Practice*, 2nd edn. Macmillan, New York
Tanner D, Tanner L N 1987 *Supervision in Education: Problems and Practices*. Macmillan, New York
Tanner D, Tanner L N 1988 The emergence of a paradigm in the curriculum field: A reply to Jickling. *Interchange* 19(2): 50–58
Thorndike E L, Woodworth R S 1901 The influence of improvement in one mental function upon efficiency of other functions. *Psychol. Rev.* 8: 247–61, 384–95, 553–64
Tyler R W 1949 *Basic Principles of Curriculum and Instruction*. University of Chicago, Chicago, Illinois

Curriculum Movements in the United States

H. M. Kliebard

One of the most dramatic confrontations between two curriculum movements representing almost diametrically opposing positions on the American course of study began to take shape in the period following the Second World War. During the war, professional educators had sought to demonstrate how a directly functional course of study could be constructed in terms of the immediate national interest. To a large extent, this drive had its inception earlier in the century when the professionalization of the field of curriculum in the United States was taking place. In many respects, that drive involved attacks on the conventional academic course of study as being largely nonfunctional and irrelevant to the needs of the majority of the students in American schools. Typical of this approach was the Educational Policies Commission's *Education for All American Youth* (1944) which envisioned a radically new form of secondary education in the postwar period. A central feature of the report was the "Ten Imperative Needs of Youth" covering a wide variety of nonacademic as well as academic needs, needs which, it was assumed, the school had to fulfill and around which a curriculum should be organized. There was attention to what were called "common learnings," but also to differentiated programs depending on classifications of the student population, such as those who expected to complete high school and those who did not. To some extent this drive for a more functionally efficient curriculum was tied to the effort to obtain broad federal aid to education which, heretofore, had been provided in the main only for such specialized areas within the curriculum as vocational education.

Life-adjustment education had its formal inception at a White House conference sponsored by the vocational division of the United States Office of Education in June of 1945. At that time, Charles A. Prosser, who had since the early part of the century been a major figure in the movement to install vocational education in American schools, offered a resolution which indicated that although 20 percent of the high-school population was being prepared adequately for college and 20 percent for an occupation, there remained 60 percent who were not receiving the life-adjustment training they needed to become fully functioning citizens of the United States. This (somewhat dubious) division of the American secondary-school population was later de-emphasized and, in time, professional educators were prescribing life-adjustment education for all. Because life-adjustment education remained largely on the slogan level during much of its existence, it is difficult to establish either the specific nature of its program of studies or the extent to which it actually made headway in changing the American school curriculum.

In broad outline, life-adjustment education seemed to be a revival of the social efficiency programs which had their inception in about the second decade of the twentieth century, although critics often erroneously contributed these proposals to the educational ideas of John Dewey. Life-adjustment education became associated with such nonacademic activities as social dancing and peer-group relationships. As to its impact, there were reports by proponents and critics alike that the American curriculum was being or actually had been transformed by the kind of directly functional programs that life-adjustment education promoted. While it is true that the movement received the wholehearted endorsement of the United States Office of Education, especially John W. Studebaker, the commissioner of education, the federal government was not in a position at that time to influence school programs directly. For the most part, support took the form of sponsoring two life-adjustment conferences and publishing and disseminating documents favoring the program. The best evidence available indicates that the actual impact on the school was isolated and fragmentary (Broder 1977).

Probably the most significant impact of the movement was the unusually harsh and sometimes potent criticism that life-adjustment education generated. By and large, the critics were drawn from the faculties of colleges and universities who for years had regarded the American educational establishment as excessively utilitarian in outlook and even anti-intellectual (Lynd 1953). Life-adjustment education provided an easy target for these critics to aim at. By the 1950s, charges by academic critics began to reach a larger audience, and their criticism was being echoed by politicians concerned with the cold war and with America's alleged technological inferiority to the Soviet Union. As early as 1951, the University of Illinois Committee on School Mathematics began to consider the effectiveness of mathematics teaching in elementary and secondary schools and, a few years later, Jerrold Zacharias, a physicist at the Massachusetts Institute of Technology organized an effort to reconstruct secondary-school physical sciences. Momentum in curriculum matters began to shift from professional educators to academic mathematicians and scientists and from curricula that emphasized direct utility in everyday affairs to rigorously academic and highly structured programs of study.

When the Soviet Union launched its Sputnik I in the fall of 1957, the fate of life-adjustment education was sealed. To the mass media and to the American public generally, the Soviet technological achievement provided vindication of the charge of "soft pedagogy" in American schools. Within a year, in 1958, the National Defense Education Act was passed providing massive amounts of money for curriculum reform, particularly in the areas of mathematics, science, and foreign languages, with some provisions as well to train guidance counselors. To a large extent, money was provided through the National Science Foundation which encouraged new programs such as those developed by the School Mathematics Study Group (SMSG), the Physical Sciences Study Committee (PSSC), the Chemical Bond Approach (CBA), and the Biological Sciences Curriculum Study (BSCS). In time, the focus of the structure of the disciplines movement was broadened to include such other curricular areas as English and social studies. Implementation of these programs was enhanced by provision of federal support, not simply for the development of the programs of study themselves, but for the training of teachers in their use.

The structure of the disciplines movement represented a shift in three important curriculum policy areas. First, there was the rejection of directly functional criteria in curriculum planning in favor of discipline-centered, academic criteria. A good mathematics program was one that emphasized key concepts in mathematics rather than one emphasizing every day mathematical operations, such as balancing a checkbook. Secondly, there was a shift in the power structure that made curriculum policy from educationists, like Prosser, who had promoted life-adjustment education to university-based academic scholars in the various disciplines. By and large, it was to these academicians that the large federal grants were awarded. While some educationists later became associated with the structure of the disciplines movement, they rarely held leadership positions in federally sponsored programs of curriculum reform. Thirdly, there was a shift from the longstanding emphasis on local curriculum change with teachers participating directly in the change process to centrally controlled curriculum change with teachers seen primarily as consumers of federally sponsored initiatives. Partly as a consequence, suspicions arose as to whether the teachers responsible for implementing the new curricula actually shared the theoretical perspectives of the academicians who created them.

Beginning in the mid-1960s (Holt 1964) and intensifying toward the end of that decade, new criticisms of American schools began to appear attacking what was believed to be a repressive and dehumanized school system (Kozol 1967, Dennison 1969). Attention began to shift from sheer academic rigor to the plight of the poor and of minority groups in the school population. In addition, the youth rebellion of the late 1960s and early 1970s, while mainly political in character and focusing on United States participation in the Vietnam War, also contained elements of a drive for personal freedom. "Relevance" became the new watchword, and this, in a sense, marked the demise of the structure of the disciplines movement.

While wide swings in curriculum fashion have often been noted, little by way of explanation exists for this phenomenon. The virtual demolition of the life-adjustment movement by the structure of the disciplines movement suggests that there are certain basic ideologies in the curriculum field which lie beneath the surface and which spring to life when propitious political, social, or economic conditions are present. Life-adjustment educators found fertile ground in the immediate postwar era with their promise of order and stability, through a curriculum geared to individual adjustment to existing social conditions. The popular perception of an external threat, the Soviet Union, shattered that vision and lent credence to the idea that academic rigor, particularly in the sciences and mathematics, could be turned to meet that external threat. It appears that neither the curriculum ideology alone nor broader social and political events alone can account for radical shifts in the popularity of curriculum ideas. Rather, the success or failure of curriculum movements appears to be a function of the interaction between existing curriculum ideologies and popular interpretations of social and political conditions.

Bibliography

Broder D E 1977 Life adjustment education: An historical study of a program of the United States Office of Education, 1945–1954. Unpublished Ed.D. dissertation, Teachers College, Columbia University, New York

Dennison G 1969 *The Lives of Children: The Story of the First Street School*. Random House, New York

Educational Policies Commission 1944 *Education for ALL American Youth*. National Education Association of the United States, Washington, DC

Elam S M (ed.) 1964 *Education and the Structure of Knowledge*. 1st Curriculum Conf., San Jose State College, California, June 1963. Rand McNally, Chicago, Illinois

Ford G W, Pugno L (eds.) 1964 *The Structure of Knowledge and the Curriculum*. Rand McNally, Chicago, Illinois

Heath R W (ed.) 1964 *New Curricula*. Harper and Row, New York

Holt J C 1964 *How Children Fail*. Pitman, New York

Keppel F 1966 *The Necessary Revolution in American Education*. Harper and Row, New York

Kozol J 1967 *Death at an Early Age: The Destruction of the Hearts and Minds of Negro Children in the Boston Public Schools*. Houghton Mifflin, Boston, Massachusetts

Lynd A 1953 *Quackery in the Public Schools*. Little, Brown, Boston, Massachusetts

Methods of Organizing Knowledge

Structure of Disciplines in Education

M. Finegold and F. M. Connelly

In curriculum practice, the term "structure" refers both to logical and psychological relationships between content elements. Logical structure establishes relations in terms of properties assumed to adhere to the content itself, for example, necessary relations between addition and subtraction. Psychological structure assigns relations in terms of properties assumed to adhere to the learner, for example, concept requirements based on Piagetian notions of cognitive development. There is a tendency to adopt logically structured content in the senior grades and psychologically structured content in the primary grades.

1. The Significance of Structure of the Disciplines in Education

The educational significance of the notion of the structure of the disciplines resides in the direct and practical effect it has upon planning and structuring curricula. Content sequence and integration, teaching method, and learning style are all related to the concept of structure adopted. Bruner (1963), has argued for the organization of curricula around the fundamental concepts and relationships which constitute, in his view, the structure of any given discipline. Every subject, he suggests, has a structure that provides the underlying simplicity of things, and it is by learning the nature of this structure that the intrinsic meaning of the subject can be appreciated. Such structure-based understanding aids comprehension by stressing fundamentals, makes knowledge gained usable beyond the learning situation, improves memory by organizing facts in terms of principles and ideas from which they may be inferred, and narrows the gap between elementary and advanced knowledge.

Any way of structuring a discipline reflects a theory of knowledge. Accordingly, the study of any curriculum carries with it implications for the learner's understanding of the nature of the world. Thus, for example, curriculum content structured in terms of a principle of induction implies a fixed phenomenal world with corresponding theories and facts. A curriculum structured in deductive terms may have the same implications for phenomena and knowledge. But the two have radically different implications for disciplinary enquiry and for the place of the human agent in enquiry. Another curriculum structure, based on the historical dynamics of enquiry, has other implications for enquiry, knowledge, and phenomena. Such a view would stress the interpretive act in enquiry, implying that all knowledge and, therefore, all phenomena are functions of mental acts. Such a view is usually labeled as a constructionist view.

2. Problems in the Structure of the Disciplines

2.1 Diversity in the Disciplines

Since disciplines, and terms for their structuring, are many, there are numerous plausible structures. Schwab (1964) has developed a typology of three kinds of structural questions that may be asked of the disciplines. The first type of question is one of classification: "What are the disciplines and how do they relate to one another?" For the curriculum designer this question becomes a problem in determining which of the disciplines are to be included in the school curriculum, and in what order. The second kind of question is one of syntax: "What methods are used to obtain warranted knowledge?" The curricular problem becomes one of determining how to reconstruct the history of enquiry in particular topics and of balancing instruction in method with instruction in content. The third type of question is one of substance, posing questions on the conceptual terms which define and bound the subject matter: "What conceptions of the discipline guide enquiry and how do they give rise to different structures?" For the teacher this question becomes one of determining which kinds of questions should be dealt with in the class.

2.2 Metastructure

A very generalized metastructure, which is at once interdisciplinary (see *Interdisciplinary Studies*) and intradisciplinary, has been identified independently by Kuhn (1970) and by Schwab (1964). Kuhn uses the terms paradigm and paradigm shift, with paradigmatic science generated by and succeeded by revolutionary science. Schwab uses the terms stable science and fluid science. The former identifies a series of discrete, relatively short, research programs, each of which is seen in terms of a definitive end and in each of which accuracy and thoroughness are considered a mark of excellence. The latter identifies an examination of principles carried out in research programs in which processes and ends are indeterminate and uncertainty is conspicuous. Both views present a definitive intradisciplinary structure, and a tool for the examination of structures common to the disciplines. Both describe the means by which established disciplines are extended and new disciplines developed. It is of interest that, despite the compatibility between the two views and despite their similarities, comparative discussion of the studies of Schwab and Kuhn has been limited, possibly because Kuhn addresses philosophers of science, whereas Schwab addresses philosophers of education.

2.3 Unification

The notion of unified knowledge, in which each of the disciplines is seen as part of a whole and in which all-embracing general statements are seen to apply to each of the disciplines, provides one way of answering Schwab's first kind of question on the organization of the disciplines. Some unified views are based upon broad themes such as "conservation of mass–energy," "generalized inquiry methods," and "unified field theory." Other unified views focus on topics at the interface of existing disciplines which have led to the creation of interrelated areas of research such as biophysics and biochemistry, or upon topics at the boundaries of established disciplines which have led to the development of new areas of research such as solid state physics.

There are curricular gains, or losses, in adopting either a unified or a categorized view of knowledge. For instance, curriculum developers, wishing to present a unified world view, have generated integrated courses, such as "unified science," "general science," and "social studies." Some of these courses carry with them the risk that in stressing interconnectivity and unity they may omit knowledge derived from within the separate disciplines.

3. Curriculum Decisions and the Structure of the Disciplines

Considerations of the nature of knowledge, of the structures of the disciplines, and of structural differences apparent between one discipline and another are theoretical issues. They become practical when they are used to support decisions related to content selection, to curriculum organization, to the logical and practical relationship between content and experience, and so on. At the practical level, and within the framework of curriculum deliberation, the decision maker has to integrate considerations related to the concept "structure of the discipline" with those related to societal and to learners' needs, to views about the process of learning, and to the idiosyncrasies of the educational system.

Bibliography

Bruner J S 1963 Structures in learning. *Today's Educ.: J. Nat. Educ. Assoc.* 52 (3)

Hirst P H 1970 Liberal education and the nature of knowledge. In: Martin J R (ed.) 1970 *Readings in the Philosophy of Education: A Study of Curriculum.* Allyn and Bacon, Boston, Massachusetts

Kuhn T S 1970 The structure of scientific revolutions. *Encyclopedia of Unified Science*, Vol. 2, No. 2. University of Chicago Press, Chicago, Illinois

Schwab J J 1964 Structure of the disciplines: Meanings and significances. In: Ford G W, Pugno L (eds.) 1964 *The Structure of Knowledge and the Curriculum.* 1st curriculum conf. San Jose, California, June 1963. Rand McNally, Chicago, Illinois

Steeves F L 1968 *The Subjects in the Curriculum: Selected Readings.* Odyssey Press, New York

Zais R S 1976 *Curriculum: Principles and Foundations.* Harper and Row, New York

Subject Matter

M. Ben-Peretz and F. M. Connelly

Traditionally school programs consist of several loosely coordinated macrocomponents or elements. Thus, for example, medieval education contained the trivium (grammar, logic, rhetoric) and the quadrivium (arithmetic, geometry, astronomy, music) reflecting the actual division of scholarly knowledge into separate domains of studies. In contemporary schools, the program consists of macrounits such as mother tongue, mathematics, arts, physical education, and so on. These separate components of the school programs are usually referred to as curricular subjects or subject matter. Typically, subjects being taught in a particular school are distinctly listed in its time-table. They have separate specifications as to the objectives, contents, and methods of teaching, quite frequently also unique sets of instructional materials, textbooks, and so on and in the higher grade levels of primary and secondary school they are taught by teachers who received special professional training for teaching that particular subject.

1. Types of Subject Matter

Martin (1970) distinguishes between subject matter of various types. The great majority of school subjects correspond to scholarly disciplines. It should be noted however that school programs frequently break down a single scholarly discipline into two subjects or alternatively link together several disciplines into a single subject. Thus, for example, in numerous school systems geometry is treated as a separate subject despite the fact that it is only a particular area of mathematics, while geology, astronomy, and meteorology, which constitute independent scientific disciplines, are absorbed into the school program under the subject geography. Subjects of this type normally place emphasis on key concepts, theories, and modes of enquiry of a discipline.

An alternate principle for organizing school subjects relates to student needs and to particular life skills, such as family living, social action, civics or health education. Subjects based on this principle place emphasis on realms of personal and social life such as social action, conservation, vocational pursuits, and family living. Disciplinary knowledge and modes of enquiry have only a supportive function in a curriculum designed on these terms. They become resources for curricular problem solving.

Still another principle for defining school subjects holds that ultimately knowledge is unified. Therefore various issues and problems from the point of view of all relevant disciplines are examined simultaneously, rather than studied as fragments of subject matter representing the unique disciplines. Subject matters of this type emphasize grand themes, theories, processes, and focus on the elements of various disciplines which have bearing on the topic being studied. The disciplines, while they are the source of curricular subject matter of this type, are transformed to strengthen their relevance for the specific context of the subject taught.

A fourth group of school subjects deals with nondisciplinary knowledge such as art, practical wisdom, or specific skills. Peters' (1965) view of education as initiation into worthwhile activities constitutes justification for structuring such subject matters as components of the curriculum. The "worthwhile activities principle" allows for subject matter which does not stem from a discipline to be included in the curriculum. According to this principle, nondisciplinary knowledge about subjects such as home repair, music listening, conversation skills, and so on becomes part of the curriculum.

2. Knowledge, Inquiry, and Norm-oriented Subject Matter

Knowledge-oriented subject matter presents learners with facts and principles regarding significant phenomena and teaches the application of these principles for problem solving. Some current curricula emphasize the importance of acquainting learners with an "insiders" view of the field of study. This is accomplished by treating the patterns of enquiry within the field as the subject matter for curricular study. Such curricula emphasize the methods of enquiry and conceptual outlooks of researchers. Normative subject matter consists of the norms and standards by which individuals make moral and aesthetic choices (Smith et al. 1957). Values become an important curricular consideration in such programs. Subjects of this type are moral education, civics, value clarification studies, though usually such subjects contain a varying number of knowledge elements too. Values curricula have been developed where the subject matter is the personal values held by students. (More frequently, the place of disciplinary subject matter in society is stressed as, for example, in the topic of genetic engineering.) Frequently normative elements are included in specific knowledge-oriented subject areas. Thus, for example, experimentation with live organisms and the discussion of environmental problems are intrinsically related to value issues and decisions. It may also be that the normative components of such subjects are not made explicit. They constitute a part of the "hidden curriculum" and are not made explicit in the stated intentions of the program (see *Hidden Curriculum*).

3. Subject Matter Selection

For curricular purposes it is useful to distinguish between general and specialized subject matter. General subject matter constitutes the body of knowledge considered appropriate for all members of a society. Specialized subject matter is the knowledge needed for those who specialize themselves in a certain occupational area (Smith et al. 1957). General subject matter is the basis for a liberal education. Special subject matter yields vocational, professional, and technical competencies.

According to Phenix (1964), the general education curriculum has to be balanced among six realms: language, science, art, personal knowledge, ethics, and synoptics. To cope with the problems of knowledge explosion, Phenix suggests the following criteria for selecting curriculum content:

(a) content for instruction should be drawn from the organized scholarly disciplines;

(b) content should be chosen so as to exemplify the representative ideas of the disciplines;

(c) content should be selected so as to exemplify the methods of inquiry in the disciplines;

(d) content selected for instruction should appeal to the imagination of students.

These principles may be considered appropriate when school subjects correspond to scholarly disciplines.

Selection of subject matter takes place at the level of the whole educational system and also at the school and the individual level.

Most educational systems, formally or informally, legitimize a series of subjects for being taught in school. The legitimation is justified by views about the organization of the knowledge, by perceptions of societal needs, available resources, and so on. In some school systems, distinction has been made between major subjects such as language and mathematics, and minor subjects such as singing, crafts, and physical education.

A particular school includes a more restricted set of subjects in its program. Local needs and resources play a major role in selecting subject at the school level. Finally, the individual learner may select subjects for studies according to personal interest, vocational aspiration, ability level, convenience, and so on.

Bibliography

Broudy H S 1977 Can curriculum escape the disciplines? In: Rubin L J (ed.) 1977 *Curriculum Handbook: The Disciplines, Current Movements, Instructional Methodology, Administration, and Theory*. Allyn and Bacon, Boston, Massachusetts

Martin J R 1970 The disciplines and the curriculum. In: Martin J R (ed.) 1970 *Readings in the Philosophy of Education: A Study of Curriculum*. Allyn and Bacon, Boston, Massachusetts

Peters R S 1965 Education as initiation. In: Archambault R D (ed.) 1965 *Philosophical Analysis and Education*. Routledge and Kegan Paul, London, pp. 87–111

Phenix P H 1964 *Realms of Meaning: A Philosophy of the Curriculum for General Education*. McGraw Hill, New York

Smith B O, Stanley W O, Shores J H 1957 *Fundamentals of Curriculum Development*, rev. edn. Harcourt, Brace and World, Yonkers-on-Hudson, New York

Integrated Curriculum

A. A. Glatthorn and A. W. Foshay

One of the perennial questions confronting curriculum planners is the twofold issue of how to divide the program of studies and then how to ensure that those divisions are closely related to each other. This attempt to relate more closely the separate divisions of the program of studies, usually referred to as curriculum integration, takes several different forms. This article will review the types of curriculum integration usually advocated and practiced, cite some examples of each, and examine briefly the arguments and evidence for curriculum integration.

Curriculum integration can customarily take one of four different forms: correlation of two or more fields of study; integration within a broad field of study; interdisciplinary studies; and transdisciplinary programs. While there are numerous variations of these four types, with the terminology varying from period to period and from nation to nation, these four approaches in general represent the essential ways by which integration can be achieved.

1. Correlated Curriculum

Correlation is the attempt to relate two or more fields of study so that what is learned in one field reinforces and builds upon what is studied in another. Correlation seems to take two common forms. The first attempts to correlate content in the natural sciences with concepts in mathematics. Thus, curriculum planners will ensure that the student studying physics is at the same time learning the advanced mathematics required for solving the problems posed in the science class. The other common type of correlation usually involves the study of one's native language and the study of history. In the United States, for example, American literature and American history are frequently taught in the same

year. Both types of correlation may take a loose or close form. Subjects may be seen as loosely correlated only when they are brought into general alignment: study algebra during the same year that you study chemistry. Or they may be closely correlated when given units of study are temporally aligned: study the literature of the Elizabethan period when you study the history of Elizabethan England.

2. Broad Field and Emerging Curriculum

Following the first attempts at correlating school subjects, various changes were made to correct for the inadequacies of the early plans. One of these was the broad field curriculum, in which several subjects were combined into one. The best known remaining example of this plan is the social studies. This subject began by combining history and geography into a single offering. More recently, other disciplines have been added: economics, sociology, political science, law, and anthropology. This has so far been a very difficult combination to achieve, though it allows for at least a touch upon subjects that would otherwise be excluded for lack of time. Some schools, using an organizing topic as a center, claim success.

One version of the broad fields curriculum currently stimulating much interest is the "whole language" approach to teaching and learning the native language. While the term is often used as a vague honorific, it seems to denote approaches to native language instruction that include the following features: focusing on general themes and relating reading, writing, speaking, and listening to those themes; using whole texts, rather than anthologies; emphasizing the use of oral language in the classroom; using the student's own language for analysis, rather than contrived textbook exercises; and emphasizing reading as meaning-making, not as the use of specific skills.

One of the forms the integrated curriculum takes is called the emerging curriculum. In the emerging curriculum one topic grows out of another. It is intended to correct the original correlated curriculum's lack of logic. In the course of studying the history of a town on a river, for example, the economics of the town arises. Economics having emerged, it is studied next. Perhaps the study of economics leads to the study of geography. If so, geography is next. Thus the artificial separation of school subjects is avoided.

At the elementary-school level, the emerging curriculum has led to the integrated day, in which the connections between school subjects are stressed, and there is frequent reference back to portions of the school day already studied. For example, some of the mathematics problems might have been designed around the workings of the water system in a town. Later in the day, when the students are involved in social studies and are studying a town, the maths problems and their solutions might be recalled. School subjects become not subjects, but emphases. The student proceeds from an emphasis on reading to an emphasis on mathematics to an emphasis on writing to an emphasis on social studies, and so on. At all times, however, the school day is treated as a whole.

3. *Interdisciplinary and Transdisciplinary Studies*

While correlation maintains the separate identities of the several broad fields or disciplines, interdisciplinary studies combine two or more disciplines into a single field of study. The United Nations Educational, Scientific, and Cultural Organization (UNESCO), for example, has been sponsoring curriculum work which integrates population education and literacy programs. Several attempts have been made to integrate the aesthetic arts into innovative curricula in which students study how general aesthetic principles inform music, dance, the visual arts, and literature. And in the United States, many schools and colleges offer courses called "American Studies," which essentially integrate social studies and English language arts.

The final approach to curriculum integration may perhaps be seen as the most radical of all. While interdisciplinary courses really seem to combine or fuse two or more disciplines, transdisciplinary programs transcend or ignore the disciplines. Those advocating transdisciplinary programs believe that the curriculum should be built upon broad learning experiences or pervasive social problems. An experience-centered curriculum would begin by identifying some experiential project, such as developing a utopian community or constructing a play yard. The students would then be taught whatever skills they needed to accomplish that experience. A problem-centered curriculum would begin by identifying some social problem, such as conflict and violence, and then draw content from several disciplines in the examination of that problem. Thus, students would analyze conflict and violence from the perspectives of the artist, the sociologist, the psychologist, the biologist, and the philosopher.

4. *Arguments For and Against Curriculum Integration*

What are the arguments for these several approaches to integration? Four are usually cited by proponents, who usually attack "curricular fragmentation" in the process of advocating curricular integration. First, they argue, curriculum integration increases learner motivation: students are more interested in learning content that seems related and meaningful. Second, curriculum integration results in more inclusive learning: integrated programs of several sorts enable the learner to confront problems that are ignored or slighted by the separate disciplines. Third, integration is more effective: learning is improved when skills and concepts are reinforced in a systematic fashion. Finally, curriculum integration is more efficient: time is saved when carefully integrated curricula eliminate redundancy.

Those questioning the value of curriculum integration admit the reasonableness of loose correlation but doubt the more extravagant claims of those advocating integration. The defenders of the disciplines contend that a skillful teacher can make any discipline seem interesting, that the separate disciplines can in their own way deal with any important personal or social problem, and that the claims for effectiveness and efficiency are not supported by empirical evidence. They further assert that each discipline has its own structure, its own "syntax of inquiry," which innovative curricula unwisely ignore.

Two general findings seem to emerge from decades of research on curriculum integration. The first is that, for the most part, students who have studied in several sorts of "integrated curricula" learn to read, write, and compute about as well as students who have experienced the more conventional programs. The second is that in general, curricula achieve what they are designed to achieve. Thus, students who study a course called "Problems of Democracy" seem to be more competent in analyzing broad social problems than students who take a course in political science. But those studying political science understand in greater depth the concepts of that discipline than those learning about "the problems of democracy." These findings have led most curriculum experts to recommend that the program of studies should pay appropriate attention both to the separate disciplines and to the integration of those disciplines.

Bibliography

Abbey D 1976 *Designing Interdisciplinary Studies Programs: A Project Search Development.* John D. Rockefeller, 3d Fund, New York

Foshay A W (ed.) 1963 *The Rand-McNally Handbook of Education.* Rand-McNally, Chicago, Illinois

Goodman K S 1986 *What's Whole in Whole Language?* Heinemann, Portsmouth, New Hampshire

Kersh M E 1987 Integrative curriculum for gifted learners. Paper presented at annual meeting of American Educational Research Association, Washington, DC. ERIC Document Reproduction Service ED 288 306

Posner G J 1974 The extensiveness of curriculum structure: A conceptual scheme. *Rev. Educ. Res.* 44: 401–07

Seguel M L 1966 *The Curriculum Field: Its Formative Years.* Teachers College Press, New York

Singh P 1975 *Centralized Workshops in Singapore: Education and Work 1.* UNESCO, Bangkok

UNESCO 1980 *Population Education in Literacy Programmes: 2—A Collection of Curriculum Materials.* UNESCO, Bangkok

Walker D F, Schaffarzik J 1974 Comparing curricula. *Rev. Educ. Res.* 44: 83–112

Interdisciplinary Approach

D. G. Batts

Interdisciplinary studies organize learning in a way that leads to a relatedness of the disciplines and their distinct methods of enquiry and verification. It is a prudential mode of curriculum "integration" conserving some of the advantages of subject structures.

The argument for subject-based or discipline-based studies rests on the view that reliable knowledge is yielded through structured systems; that the settled conceptual apparatus of a discipline of knowledge, its developed syntax of enquiry, and the truth conditions of its characteristic propositions, offer a secure basis both for digesting its conclusions and for induction into the relevant forms of enquiry.

But counter arguments might be pressed against this view. Considerable interest in general education, and the place within it of studies of humans and society, has necessarily resulted in programmes transcending discipline boundaries. Whenever knowledge is to be used interpretively or applicatively, curriculum content will tend to be determined by real-life situations, and the network of ideas, concepts, patterns, or relationships pursued largely determined pragmatically. This approach was articulated persuasively in Broudy et al. (1964), who envisaged the generation of "cognitive and evaluative maps", of interpretive usefulness to nonspecialists.

Cross-discipline collaboration has sometimes arisen from a general epistemological position held by venturing subject teachers; for example, that the sciences or social sciences exhibit "family relationships". Contributing subjects might be taught as part of an overarching synthesis, as context for each other, or as routes into particular topics. Although by no means standard practice, each of these are discernible subthemes in the Stake and Easley (1978) review of practice in the United States.

Yet integrated units of study are interdisciplinary only if they use the disciplines self-consciously as exploratory tools. Ruled out are styles of integration based on common sense, on opportunistic exploration, or on subjective or expressive modes of internal model making.

Interdisciplinary courses employ the disciplines as intellectual structures offering some guarantee of methodological and conceptual clarity; they deploy their approaches through unified subject matter, or around themes, topics, or problems admitting of planned multiple exploration.

It is possible to justify interdisciplinary topics within their own terms, for example, themes of social living premised on the kind of cultural analysis that underpins *Man: A Course of Study*, or the kind of subcultural lifestyle analysis that has yielded black studies in the United States or Aboriginal studies in Australia, or as exemplary arrangement, for example, *Exploration Man* in the Keele Integrated Studies Project which arranged relatively arbitrary or opportunistic areas of study to demonstrate the interrelationship of enquiry modes. Exemplary models of interdisciplinary study have crossed the subject boundary at different points. James (1968) suggested that enquiry itself naturally disrespects discipline boundaries. Her IDE (interdisciplinary enquiry) is a form of supported curiosity. Other concerted attempts to establish interdisciplinary structures have evolved in relation to the introduction into schools of practical domains like social work, child care, regional development, or integrated craft/design. Environmental schooling often exhibits an interdisciplinary organization (a kind of simultaneous field-tripping) as in the Schools Council's Environmental Studies Project and aspects of its Science 5-13 Project. Trant (1978) and the Curriculum Development Unit, Dublin (1979) studied cross-Europe environmental education for the European Commission. They saw upper-primary interdisciplinary work in sequential terms as a preparation for the strongly subject-centred secondary schools, but point to the entrenched subject structures permeating downwards.

Interdisciplinary organization appears to be judged more appropriate for older pupils in developed countries. Its rise and fall has mirrored the curriculum reform movement itself, and to some extent has been university led. Since the early 1960s, innovators at all levels have had an increased sensitivity to the structural constraints on radical change and are wary of the daunting tasks posed by a redrawing of the knowledge maps. Reformist interest has shifted towards exploring and permeating institutional boundaries.

162

Bibliography

Broudy H O, Smith B O, Burnett J R 1964 *Democracy and Excellence in American Secondary Education: A Study in Curriculum Theory.* Rand McNally, Chicago, Illinois

Curriculum Development Unit, Dublin 1979 *Life and Environment: A Report Prepared for the Consumer and Environment Protection Service of the Commission of the European Communities.* O'Brien Educational, Dublin

James C 1968 *Young Lives at Stake: A Reappraisal of Secondary Schools.* Collins, London

Stake R E, Easley J A 1978 *Case Studies in Science Education.* Center for Instructional Research and Curriculum Evaluation (CIRCE), University of Illinois at Urbana-Champaign, Urbana, Illinois

Trant A 1978 *Environmental Education 9–14 Years in the European Communities.* Commission of the European Communities, Luxembourg

Integrated Science Studies

A. Blum

Integrated science education or teaching can mean two things: (a) that all science is seen as a unity of knowledge with universal laws, common conceptual structures, and enquiry processes, in which the unifying elements are stronger than the differences between distinct scientific disciplines; or (b) that for teaching purposes the various disciplines of science are taught in an integrated way. In the first case the emphasis is on integrated science education, based on epistemological and methodological arguments; in the second it is on integrated science teaching, for pedagogical and didactic reasons.

The term integrated science is often used as a synonym for interdisciplinary and unified science, although some writers distinguish nuances between these terms. Even protagonists of integrated science teaching disagree on the optimal scope of integration—how far it should contain concepts from mathematics or the social sciences, and elements from the humanities and other areas of knowledge. The choice of integrative principles also depends on the philosophical outlook of curriculum developers. The varying interpretations of integrated science can be seen in the integrated science curricula which were developed since the 1960s. Although they are still looked upon with some suspicion by many examination boards, the influence of integrated science in elementary and high schools grew since the early 1960s. Because integrated science curricula are often local products which deal with the implications of science for a variety of environmental issues, it is sometimes difficult to identify the most suitable programs for possible adaptation.

1. The Rationale for Integration

Basically two clusters of arguments are used to advocate integrated science teaching. On the one hand are epistemological and methodological arguments which see science as a unity with distinct substantive and syntactic structures (Schwab 1964). On the other hand are those who emphasize the need to integrate the teaching of science for psychological, pedagogical, societal, and practical reasons.

1.1 The Search for Unity of Knowledge

The search for unifying principles is as old as humankind. Ancient natural philosophers such as Aristotle, and many scientists including Einstein, believed in the unity of the universe and tried to discover the unifying laws of nature. Such a view would see the present system of describing the universe in relation to a number of different disciplines as indicative of the limitations of present knowledge and procedures, rather than as evidence of any inherent disunity in knowledge. The appeal of this holistic view of knowledge frequently stems from an emotional attachment to unity or from metaphysical arguments.

The view of knowledge as a unity is sometimes based on reductionist theory. Thus, in Comte's hierarchy of disciplines, the findings of each discipline can be described in terms of the discipline which is seen as a level more basic (Comte 1877). At the base is mathematics as a kind of natural logic, in terms of which all the findings of physics can be described and put into mathematical formulas. Findings of chemistry can then be reduced to physical principles; the characteristics of biological organisms can be seen as complex physicochemical systems; psychological characteristics can be expressed in biological terms; and even sociological phenomena can be conceptualized as aggregates of psychological systems, and so on.

If this view is accepted it must be assumed that no study of biology is complete without some study of chemistry, and to understand chemistry it is necessary to study physical phenomena and laws (Schwab 1964). But since the study of biology cannot be postponed until the student has mastered chemistry (and before that, physics and mathematics), elements from one science have to be used whenever they are needed to understand a problem arising from the study of another science.

The reductionist view is opposed by those who attribute to the disciplines distinct ways of enquiry. Yet, in the development of science, the frontiers of various disciplines are in constant and continuous movement. New boundary disciplines arise and are gradually established as disciplines in their own right, for example, biochemistry, biophysics, physical chemistry, and bioengineering. Koestler (1969) suggested solving the conflict between the holistic and the atomistic views by looking concurrently at both aspects. He coined the term *holon*, a combination of holos (the whole) and proton (particle).

1.2 Unity of Conceptual Structures and Enquiry Procedures

Science can be viewed as having a structure of common basic concepts which make up a unified framework, the elements of which can be identified in various disciplines. Basic units such as matter, energy, and interaction, combine to form higher structures (electrons, atoms, molecules, cells, organisms, societies, planets, etc.). The conceptual framework of science is assumed to be experimentally verifiable and therefore was termed "empirics" (Phenix 1964). Thus, all sciences are assumed to have two structures: a conceptual (substantive) and a methodological (syntactic) structure—empirical enquiry. The details of the enquiry process may be somewhat different in various disciplines, but the basic method is common to all sciences and distinguishes science from other areas of knowledge.

Often, breakthroughs in research occur when creative scientists begin to use the way of thinking and methods of one discipline to investigate problems in another field. Specialization has often been a hindrance by leading the enquirer into a narrow approach, which did not produce a satisfactory solution. In many of these situations a team of scientists from different disciplines could have overcome the difficulty. After all, their basic approach of empirical verification of hypotheses based on theory is common to all scientific disciplines. A quick glance through some of the major scientific journals shows that today most research is done by teams which are more often than not made up of scientists with special knowledge and skills in their respective, narrow fields, but who can communicate and interact creatively with members of other disciplines. Integrated science teaching can help to educate students to look at a field of study not only from within, but also from the viewpoint of links between disciplines.

1.3 Psychological and Pedagogical Arguments

Many of the arguments for integration in science education are based on its assumed value in fulfilling learners' needs. Support for teaching science as a whole comes from the psychology of learning. In particular, followers of Gagné's (1965) and Bruner's (1960) theories of learning have argued that integrated science teaching can augment the transfer of training, because learners perceive the similarities of concepts, principles, and strategies better than those who study separate disciplines with little emphasis on the interrelationships. In integrated science teaching, students have occasion to use concepts learned in one situation in different fields, such as applied science. For example, students might use biological principles to solve nutritional, agricultural, or environmental problems.

Piaget's work also has supplied arguments for integrated science education. Since most students at the elementary level are in the concrete operations stage of development, science teaching at this level should be based on identifiable objects and not abstract ideas. The study of what happens with such objects cannot be confined to the realm of a single discipline. Developers of the Australian Science Education Program (ASEP) and Science 5–13 curricula used this argument when they chose an integrated approach.

Further arguments for integrated science teaching are that children do not learn in the same logical order in which a scientific discipline is organized, and that the structures of acquiring, assimilating, and retaining knowledge are the same for physical and biological knowledge.

Where science teaching objectives emphasize the fostering of critical thinking and the use of scientific scrutiny in everyday life, applied and integrated science is advantageous, because in a narrow, disciplinary approach students could get the impression that scientific attitudes are valid only in the laboratory.

Since integrated science curricula are more free to select familiar objects and topics which students find interesting, it was considered in various cases to augment motivation, especially in students who have little interest in classical science.

In many cases biology, chemistry, and physics are taught concurrently by separate teachers (especially in European schools). These teachers meet their students usually only once a week, while teachers of integrated science do so more often and therefore have a better opportunity to build up a substantial relationship. This argument is strongest at the stage when pupils transfer from the protected one-teacher-per-class elementary school to middle and high schools with their specialized teachers. Brown et al. (1976) found this argument to be the strongest among Scottish Integrated Science teachers. According to the same study, when teachers meet to plan and teach cooperatively an integrated science course, they become more relaxed and interdepartmental cooperation grows. On the other hand, teachers have to yield some of their idiosyncrasies in teaching, and this can be threatening to those who do not accept the basic rationale.

1.4 Societal and Practical Arguments

"Industrial democracy has made science the foundation of national power and productivity" (Schwab 1964). Therefore it is not only the scientist who should understand the relationship between science in its widest sense and society, but also the political leadership and the general public, who will have to decide major issues involving science and society.

Science is a central factor in the development of nations. It becomes relevant to development when people realize its importance to their lives and develop positive attitudes towards science as a developmental tool. Major conferences on rural development in the

Third World have stressed that integrated science teaching which relates to development problems can make a major contribution towards development itself. Integrated science curricula treat interactions between scientific research and the agricultural, technological, and social problems which arise in the developing village, the growing city, and the emerging nation. Unfortunately, science education is not a significant element in nonformal education and it has little interaction with development agencies.

The view that science education should include the study of the interactions between science and society was expressed also in technologically well-developed countries. It led to the development of science curricula which integrated humanistic elements (e.g., Harvard University's Project Physics) or applied aspects (Agriculture as Environmental Science in Israel) and sociopolitical issues (e.g., Science and Society in the United Kingdom). Recently, the Science-Technology-Society (STS) movement in science education has gained ground, and there is also a trend to integrate mathematics and science into technology education (e.g., Maley 1987).

The increasing technological culture magnifies environmental problems which demand interdisciplinary solutions. It is, therefore, only natural that environmental problems are dealt with more often and in a wider context in integrated science programs than in disciplinary science courses.

In addition there are political reasons for integration. Where school reforms were enacted, the main purpose was usually to integrate students with different backgrounds and abilities, and to postpone selection. Therefore integrated science is sometimes chosen as the common course preceding the classical science disciplines in high school. Bernstein (1971) argued that introduction of an integrated curriculum will break down the traditional authority structure, because interdepartmental team teaching, or at least common planning, helps to create a less rigid hierarchical structure.

Finally, practical reasons have often been behind the creation of integrated science courses. In many countries the examination system has a strong influence on what is taught in school, and three separate science courses would take too big a share of the time table. As a result, integrated science was found to be a better solution than forcing the student to choose one or two of these courses, thereby forfeiting the possibility of studying, at least to some extent, the whole range of science. Also, where there is a shortage or imbalance of staff across the classical science subjects, integrated science is sometimes seen as an advantage. On the other hand, teachers with training in only one of these subjects are often reluctant to teach in an area new to them.

In conclusion it can be said that many and very different arguments are advanced in favor of integrated science education; but since only a few evaluation studies were published, there is no empirical proof that integrated science yields better results than teaching separate subjects. The growth number of integrated science projects shows that an integrated approach to science education is popular with curriculum developers, but apparently for a wide range of different reasons.

2. Integrating Principles

The belief in the unity of all knowledge may have influenced integrated science curriculum developers, but it did not prove fruitful in suggesting integrating principles around which curricula could be built. Many integrated science curricula are organized around the idea of common concepts; for example, the Conceptually Oriented Program in Elementary Science (COPES) in the United States has four conceptual schemes: the structural unity of the universe; interaction and change; degradation of energy; and the statistical view of nature. The Schools Council Integrated Science Project (SCISP) in the United Kingdom calls its central concepts building blocks, interactions, and energy.

Other curricula use scientific processes and methodology as integrating principles. One of the first was Science—A Process Approach (SAPA) in the United States. In this project the emphasis is on "what scientists do"—observation, classifying, measuring, hypothesizing, experimenting, and so on. In the United Kingdom the Scottish Integrated Science course is a typical case of the process approach.

Piaget's psychological studies strongly influenced the Science 5–13 project in the United Kingdom and the Australian Science Education Project (ASEP). Gagné's learning hierarchy had its impact on the Schools Council Integrated Science Project and other concept-oriented courses. Those curriculum developers who were mainly concerned with low student motivation or ability often choose as integrating principles themes from the students' close environment which have a direct meaning for the students and in the investigation of which they can actively take part. Examples are Nuffield's Working with Science, in the United Kingdom, and the Biological Science Curriculum Study (BSCS) course for mildly mentally handicapped students called Me Now.

Curricula with a strong societal approach can be divided into various groups, according to their organizing principles. Some emphasize the interactions between science and culture (e.g., Harvard's Project Physics) or science and society (e.g., SATIS in the United Kingdom).

In developing countries, where efforts are made to move from examination science to everyday science, often health, food production, nutrition, technology, and other development issues are favored as central topics. Good examples are the Science Education Program for Africa (SEPA), the Brazilian Primary Science Program, Foundational Approach to Science Teaching (FAST) in Hawaii and in the Marshall Islands. Some of these programs and the materials of the Science Education Center in the Philippines tried to bridge the gap between Western science and indigenous knowledge. Agricultural and technological problems of a more sophisticated character have been made the pivot in the Agriculture as Environmental Science project in Israel, in Project Technology in the United Kingdom, and in the Engineering Concepts Curriculum Project (ECCP) in the United States.

Societal concerns are central to practically all curricula which have the adjective "environmental" in their name. These curricula usually favor a problem-centered approach and often treat social, legal, political, cultural, and aesthetic aspects as well as science. Because of the problem-centered approach, systems analysis and decision-making techniques are considered to be important, but only relatively few relevant units have been developed to teach these two topics.

3. The Dimensions of Integration

Integrated science programs have three dimensions (Blum 1973): scope, intensity and environmental involvement. Scope refers to the range of disciplines and fields of study from which content has been used in an integrated science curriculum. The scope of integration gives an indication of whether the integration was made between similar disciplines or between traditionally removed ones. By intensity is meant the degree to which the subject matter has been truly integrated.

3.1 Scope

Differentiation can be made between widening scopes of integration:

(a) within one of the classical natural sciences, for example botany and zoology in biology;

(b) between two close natural sciences, for example chemistry and physics as physical science;

(c) between the natural sciences (with or without mathematics);

(d) between basic and applied sciences and technology;

(e) between natural and social science; and

(f) between science and humanities or arts.

A maximal scope of integration is not always the best. It is most appropriate where children are left to investigate their own environment freely, according to their own interest. A wide scope will also be used where a program or unit is built round a complex problem, taken out of contemporary life. But as the students' investigations reach a higher level of sophistication, the scope will usually narrow.

The customary division of human knowledge into disciplines does not imply that in the integration process one tries to produce a coherent whole from bits taken on purpose from different disciplines. This might be done in many cases (and some good "synthetic" programs have been created in this way). A better approach would be to decide first what educational aims should be reached, and then choose, together with the subject matter specialists, the best way to achieve this aim. More probably than not the planners will then come to the same conclusion as the group of scientists who planned the successful introductory science course for the Open University in the United Kingdom. They started out as discipline specialists who bargained for a fair share for their respective disciplines. But as the deliberations went on, the boundaries fell, and they came up, as a group, with a fully integrated program, covering a wide scope of the sciences and focusing on science-related aspects from both the technologies and the humanities.

The place of mathematics in integrated science is not always clearly defined. Its unique character is often overlooked. Mathematics derives from the invention of logical forms which are outside our power of observation, and it is based on axioms. In spite of its special place among the empirical sciences, mathematics can play an important role in integrated science: it is the discipline which abstracts and codifies the structures which other disciplines have invented and tested. It enables the creation of models, with the help of which scientists in other disciplines search for new structures and insights. Mathematics is a language and as such serves to organize thought and to express generalizations in numerical, symbolic, and graphical form in all natural and most social sciences. Examples of this approach are Science Uses Mathematics, and the Continuing Mathematics Project (with topics like systems, critical path analysis, information, and coding) in the United Kingdom.

3.2 Intensity

Integrated science curricula differ in the degree to which they are integrated. Blum (1973) distinguishes between coordination, combination, and amalgamation (full integration). Coordination would usually apply to independent programs taught simultaneously, which were influenced to a varying degree by a common agency, for example, an educational authority or planning committee. A combined science program would have chapters or other major units organized round headings taken from the various disciplines, whereas in a truly amalgamated program an interdisciplinary topic or issue would form the unifying principle at the chapter level.

In reality programs are not separated into three clear-cut classes of intensity; they range from being more or less coordinated to more or less combined or amalgamated. The trend seems to be a movement from the former to the latter.

Various factors affect the degree of intensity in the integration of science teaching. Differentiation between the school subjects increases with the age of the student. Technical and comprehensive schools tend to integrate subjects more easily than grammar schools. But above all, local traditions and administrative structures have a strong bearing on the integration process. Often integration starts with the coordination and combination of programs and moves gradually towards the introduction of full integration.

In some countries, formerly separated courses are combined, for example, general science and hygiene-physiology in Nepal. In other cases existing materials of separate science courses are used in more combined and amalgamated projects—as in some of the later Nuffield and Schools Council projects. Even in a country with a strong tradition of discipline-based syllabi like the Federal Republic of Germany, new projects widen their scope and intensify their integration effort. The biology group of the *Institut für die Pädagogik der Naturwissenschaften* in Kiel, for instance, stressed the need for more coordination between school subjects and produced a motivating unit on "Swimming in Biology and Technology," which integrated elements from sport, biology, physics, and technical crafts.

3.3 Environmental Involvement

Integrated science teaching is not complete without environmental involvement. Most definitions of integrated science teaching contain the educational aim of "helping students to gain an understanding of the role and function of science in their everyday lives and the world in which they live." While environmental involvement is a typical constituent of integrated science programs, they are not restricted to it. Some "segregated" courses have gone in the same direction, but wherever they did so, they widened their scope and came nearer to an integrated approach.

Integrated science curricula, and especially STS programs, can be classified into three levels of environmental involvement:

(a) *Description* of environmental issues, with the objective of bringing students to the level of (cognitive) understanding and (affective) responding.

(b) *Search for a solution* to an environmental problem by applying the knowledge gained in a simulated situation and working on alternative suggestions for a solution to the problem. This level demands higher intellectual skills and aims at a higher degree of internalization.

(c) *Action* taken by students to actually improve the environmental quality in a realistic project. This level goes beyond the cognitive and affective domains into the world of hands-on action.

Environmental involvement makes integrated science more meaningful, but also more difficult for teachers, who are expected to master a wide range of subjects, strengthen the intensity, bring out clearly the integrative principles, and apply them meaningfully to the students' environment.

3.4 An Integration Matrix

The extent to which a particular program is integrated can be shown on a matrix, the dimensions of which are

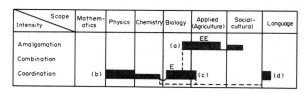

Figure 1[e]
Integration matrix for junior-high-school science courses in Israel

[a] Agriculture as Environmental Science; [b] Physical Sciences; [c] Biology; [d] "The World of Science".
[e] Source: Blum (1973) revised.

scope, intensity, and environmental involvement. This matrix can be useful in describing and comparing integrated science programs. Integrated science curricula emphasize their constituent content fields differently. These can be demonstrated in the integration matrix by using a thick line for the main content field and a thinner line for the subjects which are treated less intensively. The length of the line can give an idea of how much the different disciplines contribute to the program. The matrix can also be used to show, by a broken connecting line, the coordination between partially integrated programs. For example, the junior-high-school science course in Israel consists of parallel courses in physical and biological sciences, which are coordinated in a national curriculum center among themselves, and the amalgamated Agriculture as Environmental Science course which includes a good deal of biology as basic science, and treats some societal and cultural problems. The science courses are also coordinated with a unit in the language arts, called "The World of Science." Since it is difficult to show a third dimension on a matrix, the degree of environmental involvement is indicated by the number of E's: one for description, two for search of solution and three for students taking action. The relations between these courses are shown in Fig. 1.

4. Information Sources

Integrated science curricula were listed with other science projects in the reports of the International Clearinghouse on Science and Mathematics Curricular Developments. The ninth and last report (1974) which covers the 18-year period 1956–74 showed a growing trend with 53 percent of the 392 curricula listed considered by their developers to be integrated or interdisciplinary. UNESCO (1971–80) has published a series of *New Trends in Integrated Science Teaching*, and also *Innovations in Science and Technology Education*.

An International Network of Centers for Integrated Science Education that uses a uniform information system (Blum 1981) to describe the programs, thus enabling better retrieval, has not yet materialized. The best source of information on integrated science programs, though focusing mainly on programs in the United States, is the ERIC Clearinghouse on Science, Mathematics, and Environmental Education, in Columbus, Ohio. The International Organization for Science and Technology Education (IOSTE) organizes biannual symposia.

5. Synonymous Terms

Although strictly speaking the term interdisciplinary refers to those areas between scientific disciplines which often gradually become disciplines in their own right, such as biochemistry or bioengineering, in practice the terms integrated, interdisciplinary, transdisciplinary, crossdisciplinary, and unified science are used synonymously. In the United States the term interdisciplinary is popular with curriculum developers while in Europe integrated is preferred.

Bibliography

Bernstein B 1971 On the classification and framing of educational knowledge. In: Young M F D (ed.) 1971 *Knowledge and Control: New Directions for the Sociology of Education.* Collier-Macmillan, London, pp. 47–69

Bloch J R 1977 The analysis of integrated science curriculum materials. In: Cohen D (ed.) 1977 *New Trends in Integrated Science Teaching*, Vol. 4. UNESCO, Paris, pp. 37–52

Blum A 1973 Towards a rationale for integrated science teaching. In: Richmond P (ed.) 1973 *New Trends in Integrated Science Teaching*, Vol. 2. UNESCO, Paris, pp. 29–51

Blum A 1980 Environmental science education programs in and outside the United States. *Int. Rev. Educ.* 26: 76–79

Blum A 1981 The development of an integrated science curriculum information scheme. *Eur. J. Sci. Educ.* 3: 1–15

Brown S A, McIntyre D I, Drever E, Davies J K 1976 *Innovation in Integrated Science in Scottish Secondary Schools.* Stirling Educational Monographs No. 2. University of Stirling, Stirling

Brown S 1977 A review of the meaning of, and arguments for, integrated science. *Stud. Sci. Educ.* 4: 31–66

Bruner J S 1960 *The Process of Education.* Harvard University Press, Cambridge, Massachusetts

Comte A 1877 *Cours de philosophie positive*, 4th edn. Bailliere, Paris

Gagné R M 1965 *The Conditions of Learning.* Holt, Rinehart and Winston, New York

Haggis S, Adey P 1980 A review of integrated science education worldwide. *Stud. Sci. Educ.* 6: 69–89

Koestler A 1969 Beyond atomism and holism—the concept of the holon. In: Koestler A, Smithies J R (eds.) 1969 *Beyond Reductionism—New Perspectives in the Life Sciences.* Hutchinson, London, pp. 192–232

Lockard D (ed.) 1977 International Clearinghouse on Science and Mathematics Curricular Activities. *Tenth Report.* University of Maryland Science Teaching Center, College Park, Maryland

Maley D 1987 Integrating math and science into technology education. *Technology Teacher* 46(8): 9–12

Phenix P H 1964 *Realms of Meaning: A Philosophy of the Curriculum for General Education.* McGraw-Hill, New York

Schwab J J 1964 The teaching of science as enquiry. In: Schwab J J, Brandwein P F (eds.) 1964 *The Teaching of Science.* Harvard University Press, Cambridge, Massachusetts

Showalter V (ed.) 1975 *Survey of Unified Science Programs.* Center for Unified Science Education, Columbus, Ohio

UNESCO 1971–80 *New Trends in Integrated Science Teaching*, 5 Vols. UNESCO, Paris

UNESCO 1968–88 *Innovations in Science and Technology Education*, 2 Vols. UNESCO, Paris

Module Approach

S. N. Postlethwait

What is a module? Stated simply, a module is a self-contained and independent unit of instruction with the primary focus on a few well-defined objectives. The substance of a module consists of materials and instructions needed to accomplish these objectives. The boundaries of a module are definable only in terms of stated objectives. A module consists of the following components: (a) statement of purpose; (b) desirable prerequisite skills; (c) instructional objectives; (d) diagnostic pretest; (e) implementers for the module; (f) the modular program; (g) related experiences; (h) evaluative post-test; (i) assessment of module. (Creager and Murray 1971)

This definition was the result of a meeting of several biologists under the sponsorship of the American Institute of Biological Sciences. While this meeting was not the origin of the concept, it did much to promote the idea of modules. No definition of a module has been acceptable to everyone, and as a consequence, the term has been applied variously to include all sorts of units,

materials, and the combination. However, in each case a module seems to represent a self-contained instructional package covering a single conceptual unit of subject matter. The idea did not have its inception in any one individual or individual groups, but was generated spontaneously by many people interested in improving education and instructional design. The use of modules grew rapidly through the 1960s and 1970s, and currently the modular approach is well-entrenched as a means of tailoring instruction to individual needs. Nearly all individualized instruction is based on the use of modules, minicourses, concept-o-packs, or otherwise defined components of a whole.

1. Programmed Instruction (1950s)

The development of a module dates from the early days of programmed instruction in the 1950s. Most of the early paper-and-pencil programs were designed to teach small units of subject matter—operating a slide rule, playing chess, writing a declarative sentence, using a Pythagorean theorem, and so on. The research of B. F. Skinner at Harvard University in the middle and late 1950s and others during this period led to the formulation of several teaching principles which became characteristic of programmed instruction: small steps, active student involvement, immediate confirmation, reinforcement, and self-pacing. These same principles are used in making modules.

2. Audiotutorial and Personalized System Approaches (1960s)

Two approaches to individualized instruction in the 1960s helped to further clarify and implement the modular concept. In 1961, S. N. Postlethwait began using audiotaped presentations to supplement the instruction in his botany course at Purdue University (Postlethwait et al. 1972). During the next decade, he developed the audiotutorial approach which is structured around a self-instructional learning carrel. The system he developed incorporated objectives, a programmed audio-tape, printed study guides, visual aids, and actual botanical specimens. The subject matter was divided into units he called "minicourses" which permitted variable credit, self-pacing, and so on. As used in his courses, the system also provides for teaching assistants to aid students in understanding complex concepts. The audiotutorial approach has proven to be an effective and successful learning experience for many students.

In 1963, Fred Keller and Gilbert Sherman developed the personalized system of instruction (Keller 1968). This approach involved primarily written materials and the use of tutors to interact and test the student's progress. Progress was measured by tests over individual subject matter units taken in connection with tutors. Structure for a course was provided by the use of written guidelines which directed the student's reading and other associated activities. Motivational activities such as lectures and films were used as the teacher felt desirable and depending on the subject matter. The personalized system of instruction, sometimes called the Keller Plan, has been widely adopted by many teachers and in many different subject areas. Research data indicate significant improvement of learning when this approach is properly implemented.

3. Advantages and Disadvantages

The following list contains some of the advantages offered to a teacher who uses the modular approach.

(a) The use of modules provides an opportunity for organizing numerous sequences of experience to reflect special interests of the teacher or the student.

(b) Self-instructional units allow the teacher to focus on student deficiencies in subject matter that must

be corrected and also serve to eliminate the necessity of covering subject matter already known by the student.

(c) The modular approach provides a way of assessing the student's progress in learning.

(d) Modules reduce the routine aspects of instruction, leaving the teacher free to engage in personal contact with the student.

(e) The independent nature of self-instructional units facilitates the updating of study materials without major revisions.

(f) Modules can serve as models for teachers who wish to develop their own materials and insert their own individuality.

(g) Self-instructional units potentially can be exchanged between institutions.

In the same context, the modular approach offers avenues for individualized study on the part of the student. The following is a list of some of the possibilities inherent in such a scheme of study for the student.

(a) The student must be involved in the learning process so his or her commitment to the task is likely to be enhanced.

(b) A large pool of modules will permit students to explore portions of subjects of particular interest without having to enroll in a full course containing topics not relevant to their needs.

(c) The students have full control of the rate of study; thus, they can progress at their own pace.

(d) Students are not forced to cover materials which are already familiar to them.

(e) The consequences of failure are reduced. Each student can master each module completely before proceeding to the next.

(f) Each student can participate in the decision as to whether he or she has learned the subject matter adequately.

(g) It may be practical for some modules to be checked out and studied at home, resulting in a saving for both the student and the university.

(h) Each student has the opportunity to develop a sense of responsibility for his or her own learning.

And, finally, there are advantages to the institutions which must not be overlooked. Some of these follow.

(a) Modules make it possible to define the content of a course so that inadvertent duplications or omissions can be avoided and members of other departments can determine what portions of courses might be useful to their students.

(b) Modules can provide for dividing the responsibilities of course preparation among members of a team, thus achieving the main advantage of team teaching without many of the disadvantages of team teaching.

(c) Modules are exportable from one campus to another so that the expense of preparation can be shared among institutions. Many can benefit from the modules prepared at any one institution.

(d) In the evaluation of the productivity of teachers, an institution could treat the preparation of modules in the same light as publications are now treated.

The modular approach has been proven to be an effective and efficient tool to help students learn. Most subjects can be taught with this approach. The production of instructional materials is time consuming, but modular effectiveness can be evaluated and thus revisions can be done in a positive way. For some teachers and for some subject matter this creates problems; however, the use of modules is slowly being more widely accepted.

4. Research on Modules

A computer literature search in May 1982 on "Modules—Effectiveness" recorded 4,594 entries. Clearly, a tremendous amount of research has been conducted attempting to document the value of modules to instructional design. Unfortunately, since no specific definition of module is universally accepted by all researchers, it is not possible to generalize about the use of modules despite the widespread investigation. Much of the literature refers to a specific situation involving a local interpretation of the nature of a module and locally produced materials. These materials can range in construction from excellent to poor and can incorporate good learning principles or almost none at all.

One of the leading efforts to evaluate modules in a systematic way has been done by James A. Kulik and his co-workers at the University of Michigan. Their work has focused primarily on the personalized system of instruction. A paper by Kulik et al. (1976), for example, states:

> The effectiveness of PSI has been measured with several criteria: end-of-course performance, retention, transfer, and student attitudes. By any of these measures, PSI is more effective than conventional methods of college teaching. Recent research also suggests that PSI is an efficient method of learning for students. PSI and conventional courses apparently make equal demands on student time, even though students in PSI courses generally outperform students in conventional courses.

Besides making a case for the effectiveness and efficiency of PSI, researchers have also begun to discover the reasons for its effectiveness. The key features of the system appear to be three: small steps, immediate feedback, and a unit-mastery requirement. While mastery models of instruction suggest that these instructional features will be of most benefit to the lower aptitude student, empirical results suggest that the picture is more complex. In some courses, higher aptitude students benefit most from the introduction of these instructional features, but in other courses, PSI procedures have their strongest impact on lower aptitude students.

Bibliography

Creager J G, Murray D L (eds.) 1971 *The Use of Modules in College Biology Teaching*. The Commission on Undergraduate Education in the Biological Sciences, Washington, DC

Keller F S 1968 Good-bye, teacher . . . . *J. Appl. Behav. Anal.* 1: 79–89

Kulik J A, Kulik C C, Smith B B 1976 Research on the personalized system of instruction. *Program. Learn. Educ. Technol.* 13: 3–30

Postlethwait S N, Novak J, Murray H T 1972 *The Audiotutorial Approach to Learning, Through Independent Study and Integrated Experiences*, 3rd edn. Burgess, Minneapolis, Minnesota

Minicourses

A. I. Oliver

Although the term "mini" is a diminutive, experiences in the United States since the early 1960s shows a "maxi" potential in the development of a curriculum arrangement known as the minicourse. The term appears chiefly in educational literature in the United States with Carlsen (1972) asserting that this form of an ungraded elective system "was pioneered back in 1960 at the University School at the University of Iowa." Since that time the idea has spread extensively in various formats and at school levels from the elementary school into collegiate offerings.

Minicourses are generally characterized by being short term (at least less than a semester), elective, capitalizing upon interests of both students and teachers, with emphasis upon depth rather than breadth. There are two basic types: noncredit (often referred to as "free form") and credit. They may also be academic or nonacademic in nature. The free form offerings may appear only one day in a semester or year, appear systematically once or twice a month, or take up an entire week while the regular school program is suspended. Credit minicourses, on the other hand, tend to coincide in length with the school system's marking period; thus, the quarter is a common span. A student could take four quarters of minis in a school year to fulfill the customary year's credit in a secondary school. Instead of English I, II, III, IV (corresponding to the four grades of high school), the department develops 40 to 50 quarter electives based upon teacher topics or areas of interest and student selection.

The variety of offerings is noted in the following list taken from actual school programs (some are free form, others for credit): raising praying mantis for fun and profit; math and domes; the think tank; horror literature; a psychological approach to drug usage; lawn care clinic; astronomy for beginners; life space (for grade two); Socrates to Sartre; the mini-world (microbiology); jet-age reading; German for commerce and business.

Not only is interest a prime consideration but attention is also paid to ability. For this purpose, courses are "phased" or "leveled" usually on a scale of 1 to 5 indicating the relative difficulty of the offering—with 1 for the student with limited skills or background and 5 aimed at challenging the more able.

From a nationwide survey by Oliver (1978), a variety of 50 purposes are found to be in use. Most common are these:

(a) provide greater variety in the course offerings;

(b) utilize the interests and strengths of individual teachers;

(c) enhance opportunities for curriculum experimentation ("pilot" some ideas);

(d) provide alternatives for student choices as well as input from students;

(e) provide for a change of pace in the school year (a free form week to combat the common "spring slump");

(f) extend community involvement (members often serve as resource persons or even teach courses in the free form set-up).

Since the 1960s the minicourse movement has spread widely with free form common in elementary schools, a mixture of credit and nocredit in middle/junior high schools, and credit courses in upper/senior high schools. Leadership has come in offerings by English and social studies departments. Mathematics teachers are more reluctant since they feel that the highly sequential nature of their discipline does not lend itself to the free choice/ elective system.

Reports from the field indicate several guidelines and cautions. To be effective, the course must be carefully planned with the objectives clearly stated and the content appropriately selected. Students should be advised of these points—a consideration not often carried out in the conventional long-term courses. To insure development of basic skills and foundational knowledges, plans have to be worked out so that these necessary elements become threads in all relevant offerings. Evaluation must be built into the entire program (Oliver 1978).

Although many schools have carried out poststudies on the effectiveness of their minicourses, there has been little substantive research. Studies in Pennsylvania and New Jersey indicate that student attitude is improved toward the subject field in particular and school in general (Heitzmann 1977). Questionnaires and interviews on the local level generally find strong support from students, teachers, and parents. Concern over the basics and lowered College Board scores has lead some to fault the elective system, nevertheless Myers' (1971) study of the graduates of a prestigious high school found that those who chose the minicourse route did well in college (see *Elective Subjects*). As one of his respondents stated, "Electives may not be perfect for preparing students for college, but they are better than regular English!"

Some schools have tried credit minicourses and have dropped them—chiefly because of scheduling difficulties or because insufficient planning has brought about a feeling of a "fragmented curriculum." Other schools see this as a pilot venture into curriculum change and have taken precautions to shore up the difficulties associated with innovation. The development of minicourses is one way to look at alternatives in education, to try out the cooperative approach to curriculum development, and to build courses on teacher strengths and student interests.

Bibliography

Boespflug L R 1980 *Dickinson High School. Career Awareness: Nine-week Miniunit.* ERIC Document No. ED 183–920

Carlsen G R 1972 Some random observations: About the English curriculum. *Engl. J.* 61: 1004–09

Heitzmann W R 1977 *Minicourses.* National Education Association, Washington, DC

Hillocks G 1972 *Alternatives in English: A Critical Appraisal of Elective Programs.* National Council of Teachers of English, Urbana, Illinois

Myers F G 1971 English electives passes a test: An abstract of an evaluation of the electives program at Scarsdale High School. *Engl. Rec.* 21: 52–60

Oliver A I 1978 *Maximizing Minicourses: A Practical Guide to a Curriculum Innovation.* Teachers College Press, New York

Patterson J 1973 *Why Doesn't an Igloo Melt Inside? A Handbook for Teachers of the Academically Gifted and Talented.* ERIC Document No. ED 083 760

Spiral Curriculum

A. W. Foshay

The spiral curriculum is a way of arranging complex subject matter such that each time it is re-entered during the course of study, the student goes deeper into the subject or studies a different aspect of it. The spiral system of determining the sequence of learning experience introduces children to certain aspects of the subjects as soon as they enter the elementary school and makes provision for revisiting them in more complex form in the subsequent years. (Ragan and Shepherd 1977).

Spiral curriculum was devised in order to permit the student to go into depth in his or her studies, at the same time taking advantage of increasing maturity. A year's work in a subject might be spread over several years.

Science as offered at some schools is a good example of spiraling. The following is a spiral plan for science showing topics for study:

Grade 1: Study of the needs of a pet animal, such as a rabbit or a guinea pig

Grade 2: Study of the needs of a plant

Grade 3: Beginning study of ecosystems involving plants and animals

Grade 4: Ecosystems involving humans

Grade 5: Animals and plants as systems

Grade 6: The Physical system—the Earth as a system

Grade 7: The chemistry of the household

Grade 8: The physics of a town

Grade 9: Biology

Grade 10: Chemistry

Grade 11: Physics

Ideally, each grade includes all that has gone before, at least schematically. A variation on the spiral curriculum originated by Chas Keller in the United States during the 1960s is called "post-holing." A subject was completely covered two or three times in the course of 12 years of schooling, but each time a different portion of it was treated in depth. Since American history is often covered three times in the 12 years of United States elementary and secondary education, this was the subject first treated by "post-holing."

The first time United States history was covered, the "post-hole" was "dug" into the Colonial and Revolutionary periods, and the intervening and remaining material was merely touched upon. The next time the material was studied, another period—perhaps the Civil War—might be "post-holed." The third time, the era since Roosevelt might be studied in depth, the remainder being sketched.

The intent was that the student should have some of the experience of an historian, while digging the "post-hole," as well as an acquaintance with United States history as a whole. "Post-holing" required the students to consult primary documents and to construct their own interpretation, then to compare their work with that of a professional historian.

The intent of both the spiral curriculum and "post-holing" was to give the student an experience in depth. It is hoped that in both approaches the student would taste the flavor of scholarship. The basic approach was to use methods of inquiry appropriate to the discipline under study.

The two approaches are similar. They differ only in that the successive spirals in the spiral curriculum are presumed to be inclusive of what has gone before and to make use of it, while the "post-holes" need not be organically interconnected.

Innovative curricula of the 1960s revealed a tendency to utilize the spiral organizational pattern for dealing with various topics. This tendency reflected the ideas of Bruner (1960) who claimed that "a curriculum as it develops should revisit the basic ideas building upon them until the student has grasped the full formal apparatus that goes with them."

Bibliography

Bruner J 1960 *The Process of Evaluation*. Harvard University Press, Cambridge, Massachusetts

Ragan W B, Shepherd G D 1977 *Modern Elementary Curriculum*, 5th edn. Holt, Rinehart and Winston, New York

Tanner D, Tanner L N 1980 *Curriculum Development: Theory into Practice*, 2nd edn. Macmillan, New York

Flexible Scheduling

J. M. Cooper

Flexible, or modular, scheduling is an organization for instruction which provides classes of varying size, varying lengths, and varying frequency. Through the use of computers, school schedules are generated that provide for instruction of various sizes, including large groups, small inquiry groups, laboratory periods, and extensive independent study. Class lengths are determined by a variety of combinations of time units called "modules," usually 15 to 30 minutes each. Class frequency also varies, with some classes meeting for longer periods once a week and others for shorter periods several times

a week. The major goal of flexible scheduling is to individualize teaching and learning by matching class size, length, and frequency of meeting with the activities taking place in the classroom.

Flexible scheduling was a product of the 1960s, a decade of educational innovations. Initiated by five American secondary schools in 1963, computer-generated flexible scheduling caught the imagination of innovative secondary-school educators and grew to the point where in 1970 it was estimated that some 5 to 10 percent of the high schools in the United States had adopted flexible scheduling. Among the reasons so many secondary schools accepted flexible scheduling were:

(a) The limitations of the traditional 45–55 minute class, five days a week.

(b) The desire to individualize instruction by arranging for variable time blocks for different classes and on separate days, and by creating variable instructional patterns such as large groups, laboratories, regular classes, small groups, and independent study.

(c) The need to allow students a greater selection of courses.

(d) The desire to engage in more team teaching (see *Team Teaching*).

(e) The need for students to make decisions pertaining to their education.

(f) The need to increase the unstructured time in the school day for a student to engage in independent study (see *Independent Study*).

(g) The hope of breaking the monotony of the traditional schedule.

Constructing a school's master schedule consists of arranging several variables, including teaching talent, content, student learning needs, time, and facilities. How these variables are brought together has a profound effect on the quality of both teaching and learning in a given school. For each course the school offers, the faculty must determine the size of each learning group, the frequency of learning-group meetings, and the duration of each learning activity. A history teacher, for example, might decide to have two modules twice a week for large group lectures, a small group discussion for three modules once a week, and independent study for two modules twice a week. The teacher makes these decisions on the basis of the course objectives, the students, and appropriate learning activities. A biology teacher, on the other hand, might want to schedule a laboratory session twice a week for three modules, large group lecture for two modules twice a week, and independent study once a week for two modules. Each teacher has designed the course structure according to the way he or she thinks most appropriate. In some schools teams of teachers plan courses to use more effectively the skills and expertise of individual team members.

Those administrators who are responsible for creating the school's schedule must take the requests of the individual teacher or team, along with the school's physical facilities, and work with computer programmers to try to generate a schedule for students that is free from conflicts. The ideal schedule is one that honors all the students' choices of courses and satisfies every recommendation of the staff for group membership. This ideal is rarely attainable and some compromises in the schedule are usually necessary. Several runs

of the computer may be necessary to attain an adequate schedule.

Several computerized scheduling systems were developed during the 1960s and used widely by high schools seeking assistance in establishing flexible scheduling. Most notable among these scheduling programs were the Stanford School Scheduling System, developed at Stanford University (USA); Generalized Academic Simulation Programs (GASP), developed at the Massachusetts Institute of Technology (USA); and the Indiana Flexible Schedule (IndiFlexS), developed at Indiana University (USA). Consultant assistance, as well as the programs themselves, were available to secondary-schools administrators who required help in constructing the master schedule.

The most visible difference between a school with flexible scheduling and one with traditional scheduling patterns arises from a system that places students at various times in independent study for approximately one-third of the school week, in laboratory periods lasting for 80 minutes or longer, in seminar classes of 15 students, and in open laboratories and mediated self-taught units. Other differences are evident in the personally initiated projects of many students, and the continual flow of students from area to area throughout the day.

One of the hoped-for benefits of flexible scheduling is the opportunity for personal growth and the development of special interests available to students through independent study. For many students this indeed was the case. Several research studies (Nicholson 1973) suggest that the better and more mature students, that is, students with self-motivation, self-control, and self-direction, were able to use the unscheduled time to work independently in the library or specialized resource centers. Less mature and less motivated students, however, tended to use their unscheduled time for socializing with friends. For these latter students a more traditional, structured schedule is probably more beneficial in terms of learning outcomes.

Student achievement scores in schools using flexible scheduling appeared to be equal to or slightly better than achievement scores for students in traditionally scheduled schools. Most research studies that examined student and teacher attitudes toward flexible scheduling found them to be positive, preferring the flexible scheduling system to the traditional one that had previously operated (Dieterich 1971).

Despite its hoped for and actual successes, flexible scheduling did experience problems and difficulties. As has already been mentioned, many students were not mature enough or not sufficiently motivated to use the scheduled independent study time appropriately. As a result, these students earned lower grades than they had under the traditional scheduling system, which created parental discontentment with flexible scheduling.

While most teachers supported and preferred the flexible scheduling to the traditional one, some teachers experienced difficulties with new teaching methods demanded by the schedule. Instead of teaching a class of 30 students, teachers now were expected to work with large groups, small groups, and in tutorial settings. Furthermore, they were expected to direct the independent activities of their students. Some teachers experienced problems lecturing to large groups, others did not know how to lead and conduct small discussion groups, while still others lacked either the skill or motivation to develop self-learning packages or independent study programs for their students. Consequently, rather than adapting their teaching style and techniques as the different situations demanded, many teachers continued teaching in the same way they had always taught to groups of 30 students. In addition, many flexibly scheduled schools employed team teaching, a form of teaching that requires considerable time for the joint planning and implementing of instruction. Because of the open schedule, more students sought out teachers for individual help, thus adding to the teachers' workload. The planning necessary to create new and more appropriate curricula and teaching approaches sapped a dwindling supply of teacher time and energy. Any attempt to personalize instruction, to deal with students as individuals, results in increased pressure on the teaching staff, and, ultimately, a need for more staff.

Some schools faced the problem of inadequate physical facilities created by the demand for learning resource centers, library facilities, large group meeting rooms, small group seminar rooms, media materials, and independent study facilities. Schools that had been designed to house students in groups of 30 or so now had to find the space for groups of varying size. Some schedules were constrained severely as a result of deficiencies in physical facilities.

Flexible scheduling also suffered from overselling and inflated claims for its capabilities. Implementation of flexible scheduling did not lead to an educational Shangri-la where all achievement scores were higher and students, freed from the shackles of an unnaturally confining environment, pursued learning with love and curiosity. Indeed, while addressing some problems, flexible scheduling created others. Because of excessive claims regarding what flexible scheduling could do, it was natural for parents to assume that it also was responsible for the school's failures and those of their children.

Today there are relatively few schools still using computer-generated flexible schedules. Flexible scheduling appears to have been an educational innovation of the 1960s and 1970s that had an impact on the secondary schools of the United States for a period of 10 years or so, and then faded from the educational spotlight. For the average high school the outcomes did not seem to justify the additional effort and money required to generate and implement a flexible modular schedule.

Bibliography

Bush R N, Allen D W 1964 *A New Design for High School Education*. McGraw-Hill, New York

Dieterich D J 1971 NCTE/ERIC Report: Summaries and Sources: The mod mod world of flexible modular scheduling. *Engl. J.* 60: 1264–71

Lawrie N, Veitch H 1975 *Timetabling and Organization in Secondary Schools*. National Foundation for Educational Research, Slough

Manlove D C, Beggs D W 1965 *Flexible Scheduling*. Indiana University Press, Bloomington, Indiana

Nicholson E W 1973 Comments on research: Student use of unscheduled time. *NASSP Bull.* 57 (372): 105–8, 111–12

Petrequin G 1968 *Individualizing Learning Through Modular–Flexible Programming*. McGraw-Hill, New York

Yelland R 1987 Time for a change? Conclusions of a seminar on the organization of school time and its implications for buildings. OECD, Paris, ED 297–471

Focus on Basics

Core Curriculum

R. Tyler

Every school and college has developed a curriculum: a plan for teaching and for student learning. Typically, this plan includes what subjects are to be taught, and what the students are expected to learn. Most of these curricula also list the topics within each subject that are included in the plan.

In an earlier period, this plan included what the developers considered essential for the education of all students, but as new subjects arose which had produced organized bodies of knowledge, their proponents sought to have them included in the school and college curriculum. More subjects were being proposed for inclusion than could be accommodated in practice within the time and with the resources available. As this constraint was recognized the basic question was shifted to: What is the common core of knowledge that all students should be expected to learn? The curriculum has come to be viewed as composed of two parts: common core, and peripheral subjects that provide instructions for differences in student populations, environmental contexts and purposes. Throughout the twentieth century the debate over the composition of the core curriculum has continued.

1. Factors Influencing the Debate

It might appear to some educators that this debate should have been settled once and for all time. Why is it continuing? By examining the ongoing discussions one can recognize several factors that account for this. One is the continuing development of new subjects or new divisions within subjects. Eventually, some of these subjects are recognized as potentially appropriate for teaching and student learning. For example, science, based on empirical studies began to develop organized knowledge nearly 500 years ago. By the early nineteenth century it was recognized as a subject for the college curriculum and 50 years later was given a place in the secondary school curriculum.

As another example, sociology, based on empirical studies, began to develop a body of knowledge around 1900, but it has not become part of the core curriculum of the secondary school. Examples of other new subjects or new subdivisions of subjects that are not part of the core curriculum include linguistics, molecular biology, genetics, and political science.

A second factor in maintaining a continuing debate over the core curriculum is the recognition by educators that a subject title does not define the things being taught. For example, modern European history is often taught as a series of wars and battles and a succession of kings and political parties which students are to memorize, or alternatively, it may be taught as lessons in the development of nations from feudal fiefdoms. Again it may be taught as examples of economic production growing from rural farms to industrial factories and the resulting changes in occupations and lifestyles of the common people. There are various other ways in which the content of modern European history is defined. As educators discovered these different courses all listed as the same subject, they sought more appropriate ways to define the content of the core curriculum. The one most commonly used is to define a curriculum in terms of the subject, the topics to be included and the aims or objectives to be attained. As teachers are finding new possibilities for student learning in different subjects, these discoveries stimulate debates over the potential value of teaching the subject with these new purposes to guide the teacher and learner. Such debates have been continuing for many years.

A third factor influencing the continuing debate has been the changing interests of students. When the students believe that the curriculum enables them to learn what they consider important to learn, they will try to learn what the teachers are teaching. When they see no connection between their own concerns and interests and the content of the curriculum, they may try to do the school assignments and pass the school tests but will quickly forget what they have been taught because they see no way to use what they are taught except to pass school tests. John Dewey wrote in 1913 of his experience with the Chicago Experimental School, reporting that when students were interested in the school work they made much more effort to learn. In the early 1990s, a large number of students come from homes where the parents have had little or no education. Many of these families think of schooling only as a means to get better jobs for their children. When they see no connection between the school tasks and good jobs, the students lose interest in doing their school assignments. The solution to this problem is seen by some educators to be a core curriculum of vocational education for these students and a core curriculum of academic subjects for those who are interested in academic activities. Other educators see the solution to the problem to be the development of a core curriculum which emphasizes academic work carried on in the activities of interest to the students, including occupational interests. There are other variants, like cooperative education in which students alternate between periods in the work force and periods in the school, aided by a coordinator to help them see how the school assignments assist one in carrying out the work effectively.

A fourth factor influencing the continuing debate is the implicit belief of the public that most social problems can be solved by education in the schools. Some aspects of contemporary social problems can be successfully treated by education of school children and youth. Racial attitudes of students, for example, have been and can be strongly influenced by what students learn in school, both in courses and in the way in which the school community is operated. Sometimes the attitudes developed by children in the school influences their parents and other adults in the community, but the beliefs and practices of adults are usually affected very little by school programs that present positions in contrast to their own. In most cases, adults themselves must be involved in study and action programs to accept ideas in conflict with the beliefs they have held for many years.

2. Pressures for Inclusion in Core Curriculum

In spite of the 200 years experience many nations have had in dealing with serious social problems, in which schools have had few successes and many failures, when asked to solve these problems, leaders of the public still place responsibility upon the schools for dealing with unexpected crises. Pressure groups, for example, are trying to get their agenda into the core curriculum. Among the current proposals are courses in AIDS prevention, in the prevention of smoking, in the battle against teenage pregnancy, in the prevention of war, and so on. This pressure for the inclusion of ad hoc subjects creates serious debates among educators regarding the proper criteria for the identification of bodies of knowledge to include in the core curriculum.

Pressures for inclusion in the core curriculum come not only from individuals and groups seeking effective attacks on serious social problems but also from selfish interests seeking to promote their products or services. For example, organizations of milk producers distribute a syllabus for a course in nutrition which emphasizes the importance of milk in the diet of children and adults. The producers of mason jars used in canning fruits and vegetables distribute a syllabus for a course in food preservation for use in home economics programs that are being recommended for the core curriculum. Some

computer companies seek to influence the sale of computers to schools and families by offering to furnish some leading schools with computers together with course work for a basic computer course to be part of the core curriculum. This kind of marketing seeks to circumvent the selection of curriculum content on the basis of experience and experiment, the results of which are verified and judged by educators making the decisions.

3. Essential Components of Core Curriculum

As educators have participated in the debates, their leaders have identified certain subjects to be included in the core curriculum and have also recognized the need for each generation to redefine the content of these subjects for different age levels of students and to include consideration of new knowledge and new demands for knowledge arising from societal changes.

The study of language has continued over the years to be one component of the core curriculum. Language includes developing understanding and skill in the use of language in speech, in listening, in reading, and in writing and for the many purposes in which each age group can effectively utilize language.

Closely associated with language in the core curriculum is the study of literature. Literature has many functions in the lives of modern people. It serves much more than providing amusement to fill one's leisure time. It can furnish exploration into many aspects of the human condition, providing vicarious experience of matters not readily obtained through direct experience. This enables the reader not only to perceive and understand these situations but also to sense their emotional appeals and pains.

Mathematics is a third subject which continues to be an essential component of the core curriculum. To guide one's life as well as to understand the society in which we live requires answers to questions such as: When did this happen? How long was it? When will I do these things? Where do I go? How far is it? How heavy is it?

As one gains understanding of the environment and of one's self, conceptual maps are developed which serve as guides to action and to clearer understanding. These maps involve mathematical relations expressed by answers to such questions as those listed above. One uses some form of mathematical thinking in developing answers to such questions. The process may be crude or it may be more refined as one studies mathematics, including actual and possible quantitative relations.

History is the fourth subject which continues to be a component of the core curriculum. To understand most complex issues, to appreciate the current situation of peoples and of nations, requires knowledge of the developments over long periods of time. Not only is it necessary to understand the successful steps that have been taken but also the tragic ones. Without an understanding of historical experiences, nations and individuals are likely to make the same mistakes that were made in the past.

Science is now generally accepted as a major component of the core curriculum. It is the subject most recently accepted by educators as appropriate. By the middle of the nineteenth century, bodies of knowledge had been developed and organized by scientists using the methods of empirical inquiry and experimentation. It was then clear that science provided a means of exploring and understanding the world of nature that could be of great importance in the education of children, youth, and adults. In the early 1990s the core curriculum includes five major subjects: language, literature, mathematics, history, and science. The inclusion of other subjects in the core curriculum is still being debated.

4. Other Issues

The problem of the organization of the core curriculum is another subject of debate. Should the educational program be organized into five separate subjects, or in one large aggregation or into some two or three separate subjects? All of these possible organizations can be found in the programs of schools and colleges. The organization into five separate subjects is most common; next most common are organizations in which two of the subjects are fused into one, such as science and mathematics, history and literature, and language and literature. The chief constraint preventing organizations of several subjects into one is the belief of teachers that they are unable to master several fields of knowledge in sufficient depth to teach them.

The educational objectives of the core curriculum are also matters of debate. To what extent should the focus of teaching be on memorizing the relevant knowledge, on understanding it, on using it to solve problems of importance, especially of importance to the students? Although educational leaders are stressing the focus on problem solving, in practice memorization is still the dominant teaching and learning emphasis.

Finally, the teaching arrangements for the core curriculum are in debate. Several educational groups are urging the use of team teaching, that is, several teachers working together as a team to carry out the instructional program rather than the dominant practice, in which a separate teacher is responsible for the teaching of each subject. Clearly, the development and implementation of the core curriculum is a lively and controversial operation.

Bibliography

Brandt R S (ed.) 1988 *Association for Supervision and Curriculum Development 1988 Yearbook: Content of the Curriculum.* Association for Supervision and Curriculum Development, Alexandria, Virginia

Department of Education and Science (England and Wales) 1989 *National Curriculum: From Policy to Practice.* DES, London

Faunce R C, Bossing N L 1958 *Developing the Core Curriculum*, 2nd edn. Prentice-Hall, Englewood Cliffs, New Jersey

Foshay A W (ed.) 1963 *The Rand McNally Handbook of Education.* Rand McNally, Chicago, Illinois

Goodlad J I 1987 A new look at an old idea: Core Curriculum. *Educ. Leadership* 44(4): 8–16

Jozefzoon E O J, Gorter R J 1985 *Core Curriculum: A Comparative Analysis.* National Institute for Curriculum Development, Enschede

Parkinson K J, Broderick J S 1988 *An Evaluation of the Implementation of National Core Curricula in Australia.* TAFE National Centre for Research and Development, Payneham (ERIC No. ED 292 954)

Rachal J, Pontheiux J 1988 *A National Study of High School Graduation Requirements and Multiple Curricula Offerings in the Secondary Schools across the United States.* Louisiana State Department of Education, Office of Research and Development, Baton Rouge, Louisiana (ERIC No. ED 297 005)

Skilbeck M 1982 *A Core Curriculum for the Common School,* University of London, Institute of Education, London

Tyler R W 1953 The core curriculum. *Nat. Educ. Ass. J.* 42: 563–65

Back to Basics Movement

L. Berk

The so-called "Back to Basics Movement" was the educational expression of that rightward shift which characterized American politics in the 1970s. The movement, largely unorganized, was a popular reaction against both the pedagogical trends of the late 1960s and the professional authority of the educators who followed them. Its most distinctive manifestations were the advent of fundamental schools and the spread of minimum competency testing.

Fundamental schools, which began to appear in 1973, offered programs of limited scope—the 3Rs (reading, writing, and arithmetic), American history, geography, and government—together with didactic instruction in morals and patriotism. They were instituted, often in

affluent communities, as an alternative within the public school system. Their pedagogy, which sometimes smacked of authoritarianism, appealed to parents of conservative bent: teachers resorted unapologetically to rote methods, and deliberately fostered a spirit of competition among pupils; principals employed corporal punishment.

Minimum competency testing was a plan to use uniform examinations as a means of certifying that a pupil who had passed a given grade could perform certain rudimentary tasks requiring elementary literacy and numeracy. Such tasks were, for example, reading a clock, balancing a checkbook, completing a job application.

1. Proponents, Charges, and Issues

The Back to Basics Movement was, at the national level, unorganized. Its most vigorous and effective promoters were local and state politicians. It received no endorsement from any organization of professional educators, although many school people lent it support as individuals. Its only national proponent, the Council for Basic Education, was an advocacy group publicly opposed to the paddling, dress codes, and moral indoctrination that so gratified the ideologues of the fundamental schools. The movement had been constituted through its proclamation by the media (Crisis in the schools 1975) rather than through the collaboration of its adherents, who shared mainly the rhetoric of reaction.

"Back to basics" was first employed as a slogan in the mid-1970s, in the United States, to signal opposition to the libertarian forms of school practice then epitomized by open or progressive education (see *Open Versus Formal Instruction*). The charges against open education were that its child-centered pedagogy was "permissive" and ineffective; it was believed to foster disorder and immorality, and to slight the teaching of literacy and numeracy. Schools of the past were thought to have done far better. These claims were much debated by educators and educational researchers.

But had there been issues behind the charges, perhaps more important than the charges themselves though less conspicuously debated? Educators were quick to note that this very case against progressive pedagogy, which was being brought at the same time in the United Kingdom (Cox and Dyson 1971), had recurred in the United States for nearly a century. Why a recrudescence in the 1970s? The economy was weakening in the early 1970s, especially in the wake of the Arab oil embargo of 1973. Rates of violent crime in the schools were rising, as was absenteeism. Public feelings of alienation from government were growing, especially in the case of forced bussing of school children. The cultural climate was heavy with nostalgia. Educators frequently pointed at such conditions as the breeding ground of the Back to Basics Movement.

2. What has Research Taught?

Though educators have often speculated in print on the causes and conditions of the Back to Basics Movement, educational research has not yet pursued an explanation. It has been preoccupied with the charges.

Educational researchers have attempted, principally through opinion polling, testing, and data analysis to determine where the public stood and whether the claims of the disputants were warranted. Were the schools in the 1970s less effective than formerly? In 1975 the media turned to the reports of test results routinely collected by the Educational Testing Service and the National Assessment of Educational Progress, finding there a general decline in test scores. Whereupon the College Entrance Examination Board (1977) convened a panel of experts, who commissioned several studies, which found that the decline could not be ascribed solely to the schools. There had been profound changes in cultural and societal conditions from which the effect of the schools was inextricable.

Educational researchers have also attempted to criticize the policies of the disputants, thus stepping onto the field of battle. Bennett et al. (1976) supplied the most celebrated example when they ventured to resolve the dispute between the progressives and traditionalists by comparing the effectiveness of various teaching styles (see *Open Versus Formal Instruction*). Also noteworthy was a study by Resnick and Resnick (1977), who cast doubt on the efficacy of reviving rote methods of teaching reading; they demonstrated historically that standards of literacy have changed since rote methods were last used widely. Jaeger and Tittle (1980) sampled the researchers' critique of minimum competency testing.

Bibliography

Bennett N, Jordan J, Long G, Wade B 1976 *Teaching Styles and Pupil Progress.* Harvard University Press, Cambridge, Massachusetts

College Entrance Examination Board 1977 *On Further Examination: Report of the Advisory Panel on the Scholastic Aptitude Test Score Decline.* College Entrance Examination Board, New York

Cox C B, Dyson A D (eds.) 1971 *The Black Papers on Education.* Davis-Poynter, London

Crisis in the schools 1975 *US News and World Report* 79: 42–59

Jaeger R M, Tittle C K (eds.) 1980 *Minimum Competency Achievement Testing: Motives, Models, Measures, and Consequences.* McCutchan, Berkeley, California

Resnick D P, Resnick L B 1977 The nature of literacy: An historical exploration. *Harvard Educ. Rev.* 47: 370–85

Shaw J S 1975 The new conservative alternative. *Nation's Schools and Colleges* 2: 31–34, 39

Weber G 1975 Back to the basics in schools: Here's a case for pushing the current trend into a landslide. *Am. Sch. Board J.* 162: 45–46

Minimum Competency Testing

E. L. Baker and B. H. Choppin

When students are expected to pass a test in order to progress through an educational system, some judgment of their competency is made. Minimum competency

testing has more explicit connotations. On the one hand, the emphasis on competency rather than achievement suggests that some practical application is expected as a consequence of mastery of the test, that is, transfer to some real life or later school experience. On the other hand, the term "minimum" communicates that the performance level is adequate rather than excellent. But the minimum competence movement goes well beyond its consequences to individuals, for it may very well be used to convey to the school system the public's requirements for accountability.

Although the possibility of such testing has been widely discussed in other countries, it is only in the United States that it has been implemented to any serious extent. During the 1970s, many states enacted laws that obliged high-school students to pass competency tests, usually in basic skill areas, before they could receive a high-school diploma—the sign that they had completed secondary education.

> . . . critics of the schools, believers in basic education as the first business of the schools, observers of the decline of scores registered by the National Assessment of Educational Progress, and people aware that textbooks are often written to the ability of students several grade levels below the level of intended use have joined in a public revolt against school failures and have become advocates of minimum competency testing. The news media have strengthened the minimum competency testing movement by giving it national publicity and by spotlighting dismaying news about test scores. The movement gains added force from the general disaffection of the public with many traditional institutions that were formerly above reproach, and citizens are not reluctant to confront educators with their dissatisfaction. (Gray 1980 p. 5)

In clear ways, the entire movement can be traced to the common uses and public reporting of test scores, the credibility that these scores carry, and the judgment of the American public that education must be improved. Implicit in minimum competency rhetoric, and explicit in practice, is the requirement to provide remedial instruction for learners until they can satisfactorily perform on the test itself. Seen in its most generous light, the minimum competency test effort is a benign, but enormously enlarged, version of mastery learning as described by Bloom (1969). However, controversy grows over the appropriateness of the entire practice, the development of the specific measures, and the effects on the ordinary activity of teachers.

1. Competency Testing Programs

Minimum competency tests are almost always referenced to objectives that describe the general type of skill the student should be able to demonstrate. Items are assembled to constitute a test of such competency, and a cutoff score or band is set, below which students do not pass. The consequences for individuals who fail vary with the sanctions imposed by the authorities. In some cases (mainly in primary school), failing children are required to repeat a grade. In other cases, failure

on the test places the student in a special remedial strand of instruction where he/she receives extra practice in test-taking skills and/or in the content and skills measured on the test. Often students are permitted an unlimited number of trials until they are successful. In other cases, the high-school diploma is withheld and students receive merely a certificate of completion. The management of these sanctions varies from region to region. In some states in the United States, for example, a student must pass the regulation test or he/she will be denied the diploma, whereas in other states individual school districts are permitted to use their own tests, or no tests at all.

2. The Tests

The characteristics of the tests actually used naturally vary but some common elements can be discerned. First, the test is almost always a criterion-referenced measure (see *Criterion-referenced Measurement*). This means that some form of objective, or outcome statement, has been promulgated about the skills to be measured and some attempt to provide items corresponding to the general objectives has been made. Often, the statement of the objectives follows from the recommendations of a policy group in the school district or state. The policy group may be an elected board of education, or may be an ad hoc task force consisting of parents, teachers, administrators, and other public officials.

In practice, the care devoted to test construction varies greatly. Often, the development of the test items is left to a contractor who provides the test, a technical manual, and sometimes a scoring service to the school authority. In other cases, the test is designed directly by school personnel, with the assistance or review of a technical expert.

A major issue in the development of these tests is the matter of test security, that is, a way to safeguard the test from being seen by teachers or students in advance. The matter of security influences the strategy for developing comparable test forms, and in some cases, only one form of the test is developed. (In light of the repeated opportunities to attempt the test, practice and memory effects are likely to contribute to students' scores when they make multiple attempts.) Security also influences the extent to which the specifications for the test are fully disseminated to interested parties. For example, if test specifications are vague, such as the ability to read prose, teachers and students are not much advanced by having the specifications available. Seeing sample or actual test items is the only way to ensure that instruction, remedial or otherwise, is properly directed towards what is to be tested. Where the specifications are well-defined and strong cues are presented to the teacher and student about appropriate tasks (for instance: "to paraphrase literal facts in consumer awareness information"), then the security of individual tests is less necessary because the specifications facilitate the generation of comparable items, and hence new test forms.

3. Criteria

To have confidence in the practical, as opposed to motivational, value of competency tests, certain criteria for test development and implementation need to be observed. First, the specifications for the test must be clear and public, affording all interested parties the opportunity to prepare for the test. Secondly, the test should assess cognitive skills involving transfer, to warrant the emphasis on the test and the belief that a pass has some meaning. Third, standards should be set that provide meaning in terms of the school curriculum rather than only in relation to the competency test itself. Fourth, the competencies and items should attend to issues of cultural bias to promote the fairness of the test. Fifth, because any test is imperfect, decisions about students should be based on broader data than test performance alone. Performance on school work, teachers' judgments, and other information should be considered in making a decision, particularly when denial of certification is the consequence of failure. Last, the test should be used as an opportunity to improve the quality of education. The *minimum* in "minimum competency tests" should have meaning only if the aim of the test is to stratify and track students. In successive revisions, higher standards of performance should be expected. Unless attempts are made to focus on the instructional implications of poor test performance, the result of minimum competency testing may be a restricted curriculum for students from poorer or culturally different backgrounds.

Test formats have tended to emphasize responses that permit rapid and efficient scoring and, therefore, items which require the selection of responses from a fixed list have been most frequently adopted. However, these test formats give rise to criticism related to the basic issue of validity. For example, many competency tests with objectives related to student writing use multiple choice proxies of writing, such as editing ability. In some cases, the competency notion has been translated to mean practical, life skills, such as filling out a job application or balancing a check book, but the multiple choice format may not be well suited for this.

4. Standards

Another issue concerns the standards used in minimum competency testing (MCT), and the meaning such standards have for the community and for the schools and students. For instance, it appears that the "pass" levels for many tests in the United States have been set at around the normal performance for eighth or ninth grade students (i.e. 14-year olds). The meaning that that particular level has for establishing competency for secondary school graduation, for 18-years olds, is blurred. None of the statistical or arithmetic methods used for establishing standards have escaped without criticism. As with most performance measurement, the number of trials (items) interacts with the reliability of the measure, and in MCT, reliability is especially influenced by where the cut, or dividing, score between pass and fail is placed. Reliability becomes a central issue when one considers the numbers of students taking the test. Because the consequences of passing and failing apply to individuals rather than to groups, it is desirable to minimize the chances of classifying a student incorrectly. However, to raise the reliability of a test to an acceptable level, the number of items necessary for each competency would be impractical and lead to fatigue and other errors.

A related issue is the type of error the school is prepared to make in setting standards. Schools may wish their errors to be symmetrical, or they may wish to minimize the probability of holding back students who in truth should be passed. Since retention is a direct cost to schools, and passing a student who deserved to fail is an indirect cost to society, the judgment needs to be made carefully.

5. Minimum Competency Testing as Educational Policy

Minimum competency testing was developed in the United States more as a result of political pressures than strictly educational considerations. As such it has often been introduced "hastily, chaotically, haphazardly, and ill-advisedly" (Gray 1980). By 1982, MCT programs were in operation, or at an advanced stage of planning, in 42 of the 50 United States.

A number of those authorities who jumped on the bandwagon when it first began to roll are now having to face courtroom challenges from the families of students who failed the test and who feel that the MCT was unfair (biased, discriminatory, unreliable, irrelevant, etc.). Beckham (1980) provides a detailed analysis of the legal situation.

Many experts in the educational field, including a number who have endorsed other testing programs, have expressed considerable unease at the way in which MCT has developed—and the controversy surrounding the topic was aired on nationwide television as a result of a major "clarification hearing" sponsored by the National Institute of Education in 1981.

On the other hand, Bloom (1979) states, in modest terms, the good that MCT might achieve.

> The recent interest in setting academic standards in terms of minimum competency requirements for graduation is a development which may be the basis for insuring that most students reach particular standards of learning at various earlier grade points in the school system. If such standards can be achieved at each target point, this can be one of the more effective methods of insuring that (all the children) do learn more effectively. If such minimum standards can be related to the optimal standards as well as optimal learning conditions, then most children can be brought up to the best that the public educational system can offer.

If MCT is to succeed in these terms, then it needs to be better thought out than many of the schemes currently in operation. Brickell (1978) proposed a key set of questions to be asked and answered as a prerequisite to establishing a coherent policy on minimum competency testing. Even when satisfactory answers to these questions are available, much remains to be done before the positive results described by Bloom can be achieved. The current American emphasis on the legal implications of MCT, and other forms of testing, serve to distract attention from the serious educational issues that MCT has raised.

Bibliography

Beckham J 1980 *Legal Implications of Minimum Competency Testing.* Phi Delta Kappa, Bloomington, Indiana

Bloom B S 1969 Learning for mastery. *Evaluation Comment* 1: (2)

Bloom B S 1979 *Prejudice and Pride: The Brown Decision after Twenty-five Years.* US Government Printing Office, Washington, DC

Brickell H M 1978 *Let's Talk about Minimum Competency Testing.* Education Commission of the States, Denver, Colorado

Gray D 1980 *Minimum Competency Testing: Guidelines for Policymakers and Citizens.* Council for Basic Education, Washington, DC

Jaeger R M, Tittle C K (eds.) 1980 *Minimum Competency Achievement Testing, Motives, Models, Measures, and Consequences.* McCutchan, Berkeley, California

Koffler S L 1987 Assessing the impact of a state's decision to move from minimum competency testing toward higher level testing for graduation. *Educ. Eval. and Policy Analysis,* 9: 325–36

Exemplar Approach

W. Klafki

The application of examples in the teaching–learning process as a tool for imparting knowledge is one of the major characteristics of the exemplar approach.

The basic ideas underlying the exemplar approach can be formulated as follows. Formative learning which encourages the independence of the learner and thus contributes to the development of understanding, abilities, and attitudes does not take place by a reproductive mastery of single items or of disjointed units of knowledge. Only by actively working on several selected representative or exemplary instances of a particular body of knowledge can learning lead to such outcomes. It is necessary to identify those characteristics of a particular concept which are essential, fundamental, typical and structural, and utilize these concepts for dealing with concrete problems. It is possible to deal with structurally identical or similar problems, and even solve them with the help of general ("categorical") insights and abilities derived from thoroughly examining characteristic examples (Klafki 1964, 1975).

1. Historical View

Historical precedents of the "principle of example" can be found in the *Encyklios Paideia* of Hellenism and in the *Studia Humanitalis* of Cicero (Derbolav 1957). It also appears in the pedagogical and philosophical writings of Comenius, Wolff, Kant, and Husserl and above all in Pestalozzi's theory of elementary education and in its offshoot, the reform pedagogy (Buck 1971). As a systematic approach to the teaching–learning process it was developed and first put to test between the years 1950 to 1970 in the Federal Republic of Germany. Martin Wagenschein adapted this idea to teaching mathematics and natural sciences (Wagenschein 1977, 1980).

Bruner's conception of "generic learning" and "discovery learning" and his suggestion of concentrating curricula on "the structure of the disciplines" and developing spiral curricula are also associated with the notion of the exemplar approach (Bruner 1960). Outside the realm of the school, Oskar Negt, in his critical blueprint for the social–political education of workers represents an original variant of this principle (Negt 1975). Since the 1970s, interest in the exemplar approach has diminished.

2. Definitions and Problems

The exemplar approach is based on the conception that learning within and outside the school should enhance both independent thinking and critically justified action and should impart the ability of continued independent learning. The teaching process is not regarded as a mere transmission of accumulated knowledge and predetermined sets of contents, but rather as a support to the pupil's active learning or as a "Socratic teaching" (Wagenschein 1977). In this respect, the exemplar approach opposes the traditional curricula of past and present, which are overloaded with materials to be mastered by the learners.

Independent learning is, however, possible only if the teaching–learning process is clearly related to the cognitive, aesthetic, motivational, and moral stages of the learner, and if it is suitable to the learner's interest, style of thinking, and learning habits. Additionally, the learning must not focus on readily provided sets of rules, principles, or structures to be memorized, but it should rather lead the learner to discover rules and afterwards, step by step, through logical analysis of changing situations, the learner should be able to extend the applicability of these rules. Wagenschein thus speaks of "generic teaching and learning," whilst Bruner demands "learning by discovery." Both support a kind of spiral curriculum which takes into consideration the intellectual capabilities of the learner and his/her ability to process information of a certain type.

The exemplar approach also resists the erroneous interpretation of the academic orientation toward learning. It rejects attempts to build the school curriculum in a way which constitutes a watered-down reflection of the entire systematic structure of a particular discipline. Rather it supports a curriculum which helps the learner to become familiar, step by step, with the nature of scientific questions, methods, and hypotheses through selected examples, and through knowledge of and competence in everyday matters.

The central curricular problem consists of classifying which fundamental questions, basic ideas, or concepts, and which rudimentary methods should be mastered by pupils at various ages and stages of development, in order to develop and appropriate critical understanding of themselves and of the world, and in order to acquire skills needed to deal with situations within the scope of their experience and practice.

The solution of this problem necessitates "categorical" research in the field of general and disciplinary didactics, since the concrete manifestations of the exemplar approach vary from discipline to discipline.

Thus, for example, the application of the example principle to the study of natural sciences differs from its application to the study of sociohistorical studies. Moreover, even within the context of a single discipline the principles may change as various sections of that particular discipline are dealt with.

Bibliography

Bruner J S 1960 *The Process of Education*. Harvard University Press, Cambridge, Massachusetts

Buck G 1971 Beispiel, Exempel, exemplarisch. In: Ritter J (ed.) 1971 *Historisches Wörterbuch der Philosophie*, Vol. 1. Schwabelo, Stuttgart, pp. 818–23

Derbolav J 1957 Das "Exemplarische" im Bildungsraum des Gymnasiums: *Versuch einer Pädagogischen Ortbestimmung des exemplarischen Lehrens*. Schwann, Düsseldorf

Klafki W 1964 *Das pädagogische Problem des Elementaren und die Theorie der Kategorialen Bildung*. Beltz, Weinheim

Klafki W 1975 Kategoriale Bildung. In: Klafki W (ed.) 1975 *Studien zur Bildungstheorie und Didaktik*, 2nd edn. Beltz, Weinheim, pp. 25–45

Negt O 1975 *Soziologische Phantasie und exemplarisches Lernen. Zur Theorie und Praxis der Arbeiterbildung*, 6th edn. Eurpäischera, Frankfurt

Wagenschein M 1977 *Verstehen Lehren: Genetisch, sokratisch, exemplarisch*, 6th edn. Beltz, Weinheim

Wagenschein M 1980 *Naturphänomene sehen und verstehen: Genetische Lehrgänge*. Klett, Stuttgart

Key Concepts: Humanities

A. C. Purves

The humanities derive in part from the Western medieval curriculum, which was divided into the quadrivium (arithmetic, geometry, astronomy, and music) and the trivium (grammar, logic, and rhetoric). More recently, the humanities have been seen as language (including literature and composition), arts, history, and philosophy. These have come to be separated from mathematics and sciences, and from the newer fields of the social sciences, so that in contemporary thinking, the humanities tend to include literature, composition or rhetoric, art, music, philosophy, and history. The study of the humanities has tended to focus on criticism and appreciation rather than performance and has as its aim the acculturation of the populace (Said 1983).

Accepting the common definition of the humanities, their focus tends to be seen as being the critical appreciation of various arts and modes of expression and training in discourse about those arts. Given that restriction, perhaps one of the best models of their study is that devised by Abrams (1953), who viewed the study of literature from the model shown in Fig. 1.

The study of the humanities, Abrams argues, focuses on one of the four main vertices of the diagram:

(a) Mimetic theories based on the relation of the work to the universe;

(b) Pragmatic theories based on the relation of the work to the audience;

(c) Expressive theories based on the relation of the work to the artist;

(d) Objective theories based on the work seen in isolation from the other factors.

Curricula in the humanities have tended to follow one of the four theoretical bases, and history and philosophy as humanities have tended to provide background information and organizing concepts.

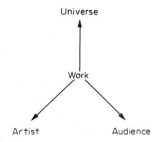

Figure 1
The study of humanities

As a result of this division, the concepts most frequently referred to in discussion of the curriculum in the humanities, have included the following:

(a) The text or the artwork: content; form or structure; medium; point-of-view or perspective.

(b) The producer (writer, artist, composer): point-of-view; purpose (intention).

(c) The universe: culture; intellectual or emotional background.

(d) The audience (viewer, reader, listener): critical appreciation; feeling; comprehension; preconception; effect.

Curricula in different societies have focused on one of the four vertices and have tended to emphasize one of the four sets of concepts. Running across all of these approaches, however, have been certain concepts that have shaped the curriculum:

(a) Genre or form, which has focused on the persistent structures of literary, artistic, or historical works.

(b) Content or ideas, which has focused on the message conveyed through the artistic or literary expression.

More often than not, a curriculum in the humanities has taken one of these two as its central object of study and examined it from one of the four perspectives. If the object has been the content, the curriculum has generally been designated as having a "humanities" perspective. If the object has been the form, the curriculum has generally been designated as having an aesthetic focus. At times, curricula have sought a wedding of the two.

Another way of considering curricula in the humanities is to see them as basically chronological or historical or as essentially analytical. Historical curricula have generally focused on the producer and the universe represented in the art works; analytical curricula have generally focused on the text, or more recently on the reader. Both approaches have dealt with genre and content, although the historical curriculum has been more content based and has resulted in the history of ideas, and the analytical curriculum has been more form based and has resulted in critical theory and appreciation. As far as course organization is concerned, the historical curricula have produced the following:

(a) Cultural organization based on a national, supranational, or subnational group.

(b) Thematic organization based on a concept that pervades a number of works and transcends a single culture.

The analytic curriculum has produced the following:

(a) Generic organization based on a series of structural types.

(b) Analytic concept organization based on a number of discrete subaspects of a work (e.g., line, shade, color, balance).

Finally, the curriculum in the humanities has tended to be dominated by one or two major objectives: the instrumental, which seeks to develop skills and abilities on the part of the student and which concentrates on modes of discourse; and the cultural–humanistic which seeks to develop the background and attitudes of the student, to impart a heritage, and enhance and enrich the experience of the student. These objectives have been used to promote each of the types of curriculum cited above.

Bibliography

Abrams M H 1953 *The Mirror and the Lamp: Romantic Theory and the Critical Tradition.* Oxford University Press, London
Said E 1983 *The World, The Text and the Critic.* Harvard University Press, Cambridge, Massachusetts

Key Concepts: Social Studies

I. Morrissett

At the precollege level, educators have felt the need to be selective in identifying social science concepts, in view of the limited time that could be devoted to individual disciplines and the practice of cutting across disciplinary lines to a greater extent than is customary in universities. Consequently, precollege educators have produced many lists of selected concepts drawn from the social sciences, adding some that seemed especially appropriate for the purposes of the social studies as taught in the elementary and secondary grades.

While an emphasis on concepts as representing the essence of knowledge has recurred throughout the history of social studies (Hertzberg 1981), the "conceptual approach" received particular emphasis as a part of the "new social studies" in the United States in the 1960s and 1970s. The conceptual approach usually pointed not only to concepts but also to the entire body of generalizations and the structure of each discipline (Morrissett 1971).

Concepts typically listed for the seven disciplines commonly considered as constituting the social sciences follow (Michaelis 1976, Pennsylvania Department of Education 1979, Morrissett 1967, California State Board of Education 1981).

(a) Anthropology: culture, tradition, role, society, customs, technology, values, change, community, beliefs, social organization, civilization.

(b) Economics: scarcity, services, money, specialization, production, saving, interdependence, market, trade, goods, prices, opportunity cost.

(c) Geography: location, scale, population, maps, habitat, settlements, globe, urbanization, mountains, lakes, region, resources, deserts, and so on.

(d) History: chronology, periods, revolution, causation, facts, civilization, continuity, interpretation, ancient, change, institutions, modern.

(e) Political science: authority, laws, citizenship, state, sovereignty, revolution, power, politics, democracy, government, bureaucracy.

(f) Psychology: learning, personality, individual, perceptions, memory, differences, senses, behavior, group processes, motivation, attitudes, intelligence.

(g) Sociology: society, group, norms, socialization, status, social control, institutions, role, values, family, class.

Lists of this kind point toward the individual nature of each discipline. For purposes of integrating or cutting across disciplines, as well as adding concepts and emphases more characteristic of social studies in the elementary and secondary grades, another approach has been taken. The following is a well-known example of this alternative approach, taken from the early days of the "new social studies" (Price et al. 1965).

(a) Substantive concepts: sovereignty, power, habitat, conflict, morality and choice, culture, industrialization/urbanization, scarcity, institution, input and output, social control, secularization, saving, social change, compromise and adjustment, modified market economy, interaction, comparative advantage.

(b) Value concepts: dignity of man, loyalty, freedom and empathy, government by consent, equality.

(c) Method concepts: historical method, analysis and synthesis, interpretation, geographical approach, questions and answers, evaluation, causation, objectivity, evidence, observation, classification, measurement, skepticism.

Efforts to relate, integrate, or synthesize the social sciences are rare among academicians, in contrast with the precollege educators who find it inconvenient or undesirable to treat social science disciplines in isolation. A rare exception is found in the work of Alfred Kuhn (1974, 1975), in which a beginning is made in constructing a unified social science, not a selection or combination of the existing disciplines. The organizing structure is systems analysis, which includes the concepts of acting, pattern, controlled (cybernetic), open and closed systems, and intrasystem and intersystem analysis. Key concepts that cut across many of the social sciences—particularly economics, political science, and sociology—are communication, transaction, and organization.

Bibliography

California State Board of Education 1981 *History–Social Science Framework for California Public Schools Kindergarten Through Grade Twelve*. California State Department of Education, Sacramento, California

Hertzberg H 1981 *Social Studies Reform: 1880–1980*. Social Science Education Consortium, Boulder, Colorado

Kuhn A 1974 *The Logic of Social Systems: A Unified, Deductive, Systems-based Approach to Social Science*. Jossey-Bass, San Francisco, California

Kuhn A 1975 *Unified Social Science: A System-based Introduction*. Dorsey Press, Homewood, Illinois

Michaelis J U 1976 *Social Studies for Children in a Democracy: Recent Trends and Developments*. Prentice-Hall, Englewood Cliffs, New Jersey

Morrissett I (ed.) 1967 *Concepts and Structure in the New Social Science Curricula*. Holt, Rinehart and Winston, New York

Morrissett I 1971 Social studies education: Conceptual approaches. *The Encyclopedia of Education*, Vol. 8. Macmillan, pp.270–77

Pennsylvania Department of Education 1979 *The Use of Social Studies Concepts in Curriculum Development*. Pennsylvania Department of Education, Harrisburg, Pennsylvania

Price R, Hickman W, Smith G 1965 *Major Concepts for the Social Studies*. Social Studies Curriculum Center, Syracuse University, Syracuse, New York

Key Concepts: Mathematics

R. A. Garden

The key concepts of mathematics from a curricular point of view are those which have wide and powerful application in the development of mathematical knowledge and understanding. In the development of a curriculum for school mathematics, the nature of mathematics as a discipline and psychological theories of learning must be considered. Thus the substantial changes to school mathematics curricula throughout the world since the early 1960s, motivated by a need for greater numbers of mathematically proficient persons in increasingly technological societies, have been shaped by a rapidly increasing rate of development and use of mathematics and by new knowledge of how children learn mathematical ideas. Developments in mathematics have resulted in the introduction of new content, and research into the process of learning has led to new approaches to the teaching of mathematics. Careful attention to the development of conceptual understanding is evidenced in the adoption of spiral curricula in which important concepts are extended and refined periodically throughout schooling and in the introduction of such unifying and clarifying concepts as set, relation, and function at elementary-school level.

Those who have been prominent in research into mathematics learning include Jean Piaget, Robert M. Gagné, Zoltan P. Dienes, R. R. Skemp, Jerome S. Bruner, K. Lovell, John F. Travers, V. A. Krutetskii, J. B. Biggs, and K. F. Collis. Studies have shown that, in general, concept acquisition is orderly, sequential, integrative, and hierarchical (Piaget and Inhelder 1969). Thus for efficient learning, the curricular sequence of the conceptual building blocks of mathematics should reflect the students' changing cognitive status.

Concepts which begin to be developed in the preschool years and have a general currency in cognitive growth, but which are of special significance in underpinning the class of concepts regarded as mathematical concepts, include classification, conservation, correspondence, seriation, reversibility, and qualitative similarity. Key concepts in mathematics include:

(a) *Set*. The concept of a set provides a basis for the effective and efficient further development of ideas such as inclusion, cardinality, equivalence, and correspondence which are, in turn, prerequisite to the understanding of number.

(b) *Number*. This concept, critical to mathematical understanding, is one of the most difficult (Lovell 1961) and much research has been focused on the process by which children acquire it. Understanding of cardinality requires previous conceptualization of conservation and correspondence, and the notion of seriation is prerequisite to understanding ordinality. Cardinality and ordinality provide the intellectual base for the concept of equality.

For the fundamental operations of arithmetic, the concept of place value has great significance, while extension of the number system through integers and rational numbers to real numbers introduces the need for further concepts such as directionality of number and ratio.

(c) *Variable*. The notion of a variable which may be replaced by any element of a prescribed set is central to the understanding and communication of generalized mathematical arguments and to the formulation of mathematical models.

(d) *Relations and functions*. The concept of a function, a special class of relations, pervades mathematics. Students must have become familiar with the various points of view from which relations and functions can be considered—correspondence, sets of ordered pairs, sets of points, tables, mappings, the generation of a set of ordered pairs by rule—in order to comprehend the general concept.

(e) *Measurement*. Few students are ready for the concept of measurement of length before age 7 to 8 years and concepts of measurement of area and volume are acquired still later. An appreciation of the invariance of length and angle measure under isometric transformations is fundamental to the understanding of many school geometry concepts.

(f) *Space and spatial relationships*. The concept of perceptual space developed during the early years is built on to give the concept of representational space needed to demonstrate and mentally manipulate relationships between points, lines, planes, and figures. Initially these manipulations can be tied to motor acts but eventually the concept must be internalized to the extent that complex combinations of transformations can be comprehended. At this level algebraic description of spatial relationships is possible and the concept of locus is introduced.

(g) *Proof*. Deductive proof is at the heart of mathematical thinking but the concept of a mathematical proof requires many years to develop in students' minds. A long-term spiral approach beginning with very simple deductive arguments is necessary (Bell 1978).

(h) *Structure*. Familiarity with such properties of mathematical systems as closure, commutativity, associativity, identity, and inverse aid students to appreciate the concept of structure in mathematics. This unifies a number of other concepts in each of number theory, algebra, geometry, and analysis.

(i) *Probability*. The concept of probability is basic to statistical thinking which enables decisions to be made in the face of uncertainties. Although probability is not fundamental to mathematics as a discipline as the above concepts are, it must be regarded as one of the most important branches of mathematics in terms of its application to a wide range of other disciplines.

Bibliography

Bell F H 1978 *Teaching and Learning Mathematics in Secondary Schools*. Brown, Dubuque, Iowa

Copeland R W 1984 *How Children Learn Mathematics*, 4th Ed. Macmillan Publishing Company, New York

Davis R B 1984 *Learning Mathematics: The Cognitive Science Approach to Mathematics Education*. Ablex Publishing Corporation, New Jersey

Gelman, R, Gallistel C R 1978 *The Child's Understanding of Number*. Harvard University Press, Cambridge, Massachusetts

Groen G, Kieran C 1983 The many faces of Piaget. In: Ginsburg H P (ed.) *The Development of Mathematical Thinking*. Academic Press, London

Hughes E R, Rogers J 1979 *Conceptual Powers of Children: An Approach Through Mathematics and Science*. Schools Council Research Studies, Macmillan Education, London

Hughes M 1986 *Children and Number*. Basil Blackwell, Oxford

Lovell K 1961 *The Growth of Basic Mathematical and Scientific Concepts in Children*. University of London Press, London

National Council of Teachers of Mathematics 1959 *The Growth of Mathematical Ideas, Grades K–12*, 24th Yearbook. National Council of Teachers of Mathematics, Washington, DC

Piaget J, Inhelder B 1969 *The Psychology of the Child*. Basic Books, New York

Travers J F 1972 *Learning: Analysis and Applications*, 2nd edn. McKay, New York

Key Concepts: Science

A. Hofstein

The major problem in developing modern science courses is to decide how to communicate to the student an expanding and comprehensive body of scientific knowledge (Hurd 1970). The "new," post-Sputnik, science curricula such as Physical Science Study Committee (PSCS), Biological Science Curriculum Study (BSCS) and CHEMstudy tackled this problem by selecting the more important and significant concepts and organizing them in the conceptual structure of the scientific discipline (for detailed descriptions of these curricula see Lockard 1975).

These concepts then become the key concepts of a particular discipline. Shamos (1960) argues that the best way to help students attain a level of understanding and appreciation of the scientific enterprise is to teach the so-called "big ideas"—key concepts in science.

According to Hurd (1970), key concepts are selected for use in teaching and learning science if they:

(a) represent the basic ideas of the structure of the discipline;

(b) have the greatest capacity for explaining scientific phenomena;

(c) have the greatest potential for interpretation and generalization;

(d) can be developed from experimental evidence;

(e) provide many opportunities for the development of cognitive skills;

(f) convey the role of science in the human being's intellectual achievement.

On the bases of these and similar ideas the following key concepts were selected to be used in the "new" science curricula:

(a) Biology (Biological Science Curriculum Study): evolution, genetic continuity, biological behavior, homeostasis.

(b) Chemistry (CHEMstudy): conservation of mass, equilibrium, energetics, bonding and structure.

(c) Physics (Physical Science Study committee): time, space, matter.

Most of the "new" science curricula adapted the inquiry–investigatory learning schemes to teaching key concepts. It was hypothesized that this scheme would convey to the student both the scientific method and scientific thinking.

Different science curricula used different approaches in adapting the inquiry scheme to a particular science discipline. In the CHEMstudy curriculum each of the key concepts is developed on the basis of a key experiment conducted by the student. In these experiments the students collect observations and experimental evidence upon which the key concepts are based and developed. In the various biology curricula several different inquiry techniques were implemented. The most popular inquiry method involves the class or laboratory designed "Invitations to inquiry." Each of the invitations allows the student to consider key concepts in biology in an inquiry process which demonstrates the fact that science is an open ended intellectual activity. This approach (based on Hurd 1970) has great capacity for explaining scientific phenomena and could provide for development of cognitive skills.

Science is regarded by some scientists and philosophers to be unified both in substance and in knowledge (Rutherford and Gardner 1970). On the basis of this philosophy, in recent years several integrated science curricula were developed and implemented.

Key concepts in science can serve as organizers for an integrated learning scheme. It is suggested that the integrated approach allows the teaching of certain concepts without the traditional boundaries (Trowbridge et al. 1981). For example, the teaching of "energy" in an integrated approach could involve the student in activities that have personal significance and relevance for the student, e.g. decision making, critical thinking, and problem solving (see Fig. 1). This approach could con-

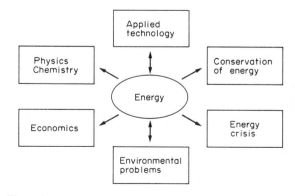

Figure 1

Integrated approach to teaching of energy concept

vey to the student the role of science in human beings' intellectual development. Within this integrated approach the student might be involved in many important discussions concerning scientific, technological, and societal issues.

Bibliography

Hurd D H P 1970 *New Directions in Teaching Secondary School Science*. Rand McNally, Chicago, Illinois

Lockard D (ed.) 1975 *Science and Mathematics Curricular Developments Internationally 1956–1974*. University of Maryland, Center for Science Teaching, College Park, Maryland

Rutherford J, Gardner M 1970 Integrated science teaching. *New Trends in Integrated Science Teaching*, Vol. 1. UNESCO, Paris

Shamos M H 1960 Science and the humanities. In: Henry N B (ed.) 1960 *Rethinking Science Education*, 59th Yearbook of the National Society for the Study of Education. Chicago University Press, Chicago, Illinois

Trowbridge L W, Bybee R W, Sund R B 1981 *Becoming a Secondary School Science Teacher*, 3rd edn. Columbus, Ohio

Focus on the Individual

Individualized School Programs

J. O. Bolvin

For years educators have attempted to find means to individualize instruction. Grouping practices, tracking schemes, project work, independent study, nongraded systems, dual progress plans, continuous progress plans, and remedial systems have all been attempts to adapt to student differences. Cronbach (1967) has identified five patterns for describing education systems and their adaptability to the individual. His fifth pattern, establishing sets of goals and learning outcomes with a variety of instructional techniques and resources with time to reach the desired competencies varying from student to student, most closely represents the intent of most individualized programs currently in use. Most programs seem to have the following assumptions in common: (a) they can be adaptive to the abilities, interests, backgrounds, and needs of the student; (b) they can provide optional means for different students to achieve the same goals; (c) they can provide the opportunity for different students to pursue different goals and to differing degrees of attainment; and (d) the goals to be attained by the student are individually planned.

Among the many programs currently in use to adapt to the individual differences of students there are wide variations in their adherence to the assumptions stated above, as well as in their approaches in providing for them. There are programs for individualizing single school subjects, such as maths or reading, while there are others that include most, if not all, of the subjects offered by the school. There are programs that provide, as a part of their system, a core of instructional materials developed for a specific set of objectives while others provide suggested objectives and materials but leave the selection up to the user. There are programs that suggest adherence to mastery criteria while others do not. As a final example, there are individualized programs that suggest that new units begin with group instruction branching into individualized plans while there are others that begin all units with individualized plans.

In spite of these differences there are components of the various individualized systems which seem to be common to most (Bolvin and Glaser 1971, Glaser 1977). These are:

(a) A redefinition of school time to provide the opportunity to vary instructional time in order that students may complete tasks and reach planned outcomes.

(b) Well-defined and well-structured curricula which provide for necessary sequencing and multiple options for learning to facilitate student progress. For most subject areas there are a variety of ways of expressing the structure and even the most highly structured scope and sequence statements of a curriculum provide optional paths for the learner.

(c) Procedures for assessing student readiness, needs, characteristics, and accomplishments to assist in student and teacher decision making. Since the major focus of assessment instruments to meet these purposes is to provide information about "how much" or "how well" a student can perform a given task or set of tasks the instruments must provide criterion-referenced or performance-referenced scores.

(d) The availability of instructional materials and other resources to facilitate learning which are open and accessible to students and which can provide a variety of means to attaining the desired mastery. There is considerable variation among individualized instruction programs as to the number of alternative learning aides which are available to the learner.

(e) Individual lesson plans for each student that address the tasks to be accomplished, estimated time for accomplishment, materials and resources appropriate, and the criterion of accomplishments expected. Such plans are essential not only for communicating with the student but also for planning for the operation and management of the classroom(s).

(f) Strategies for information feedback to permit periodic monitoring of progress and to facilitate decision making. Programs vary from having to rely entirely on the student to compile the information on some predetermined form, to having clerks generate the information, or to computer storage of information.

(g) The reorganization of the school environment to permit greater flexibility in assignments of staff, utilization of facilities, and reallocation of time. Many individualized systems have moved to a "planning and instructional team" for organizing the staff since many decisions must now be shared ones.

The more closely a school begins to provide for the seven components outlined above, the more difficult it becomes for a teacher to provide the desired learning options needed for any one group of students. Instructional systems such as Individually Prescribed Instruction (Lindvall and Bolvin 1967), Primary Education Project (Resnick et al. 1975), Program for Learning in Accordance with Needs (Flanagan et al. 1975), Mastery Learning Plan (Block 1980), the Elementary and Middle School Program of the Korean Education Development Institute (Kim et al. 1973), and Individually Guided Instruction (Klausmeier 1976) have necessitated role changes for principals, teachers, and other staff. The one system that has gone the furthest in specifying organizational changes necessary is the Individually Guided Instruction System of the University of Wisconsin's Research and Development Center for Cognitive Learning (Klausmeier 1976). Each school is organized into multiage "units" responsible for the education of 100–500 students, coordinated by a unit leader and staffed by teachers, paraprofessionals, student teachers, or interns. The unit leader serves with the other unit leaders and the principal on building an Instructional Improvement Committee. This committee, working with the principal, is responsible for coordinating, planning, and managing the instructional program of the school. Although functions of all professionals change, the only new position within the structure is the unit leader. This individual is a teacher and an instructional leader of the unit (Sorenson et al. 1976).

The teacher's role in Individually Guided Instruction, as in most individualized instruction or adaptive education systems, changes from one who spends considerable amounts of time conveying and explaining information and ideas to a large group to one who guides and directs the learning which has been adapted to the needs of the learners. Teachers must spend time in organizing instruction (planning) for each student, assessing the student when she or he is ready, providing a variety of learning strategies in an attempt to relate specific strategies to specific students, establishing small groups for instruction as the need arises, and in planning with others for space, time, and instructional resources necessary to meet the short-term needs of a group of students.

Evaluation of the outcomes of individualized instructional programs is inconclusive whether conducted by the sponsors or by independent evaluators (Block et al. 1977, Resnick et al. 1975, Rosenshine 1976, Soar 1973, Stallings and Kaskowitz 1974). Generally, the results show no real differences in student achievement when different organizational patterns are compared. They indicate some improvement in students' attitudes toward school but no difference in attitude toward the teacher.

Due to the complex nature of most of the systems developed to adapt to learner differences, program developers have turned their attention to improving: learning materials; strategies for teaching; environments for learning; procedures to involve students in their own goal planning; and organizational arrangements to facilitate shared planning, decision making, and instruction. At the same time evaluators have turned their attention to developing better conceptual schemes for instructional evaluation including the study of factors related to student outcomes (Cooley and Leinhardt 1975, Rosenshine 1976).

Bibliography

Block G, Stebbs L, Proper E 1977 *Effects of Follow Through Models*, Vol. 4B. Abt Associates, Cambridge, Massachusetts

Block J H 1980 Promoting excellence through mastery learning. *Theory Pract.* 19: 66–74

Bolvin J O, Glaser R 1971 Individualizing instruction. In: Allen D W, Seifman E (eds.) 1971 *The Teacher's Handbook.* Scott, Foresman, Glenview, Illinois, pp. 270–79

Cooley W W, Leinhardt G 1975 *Application of a Model for Investigating Classroom Processes.* University of Pittsburgh, Learning Research and Development Center, Pittsburgh, Pennsylvania

Cronbach L J 1967 How can instruction be adapted to individual differences? In: Gagné R M (ed.) 1967 *Learning and Individual Differences: A Symposium at the Learning Research and Development Center, University of Pittsburgh.* Merrill, Columbus, Ohio, pp. 23–39

Flanagan J C, Shanner W M, Brudner H J, Market R W 1975 An individualized instructional system: Program learning in accordance with needs. In: Talmage H (ed.) 1975 *Systems of Individualized Education.* McCutchan, Berkeley, California

Glaser R 1977 *Adaptive Education: Individual Diversity and Learning.* Holt, Rinehart and Winston, New York

Kim Y, Kwac S B, Park J, Park M, Song Y 1973 *Toward a New Instructional System: Summary Report of the First Small-scale Tryout.* Research Report No. 1. Korean Educational Development Institute, Seoul

Klausmeier H J 1976 Individually guided education. *J. Teach. Educ.* 27: 199–207

Lindvall C M, Bolvin J O 1967 Programmed instruction in the schools: An application of programming principles in "Individually Prescribed Instruction." In: Lange P C (ed.) 1967 *Programmed Instruction.* Sixty-sixth Yearbook of the National Society for the Study of Education. University of Chicago Press, Chicago, Illinois

Resnick L B, Wang M C, Rosner J 1975 *Adaptive Education for Young Children: The Primary Education Project.* University of Pittsburgh, Learning Research and Development Center, Pittsburgh, Pennsylvania

Rosenshine B 1976 Classroom instruction. In: Gage N L (ed.) 1976 *The Psychology of Teaching Methods.* Seventy-fifth Yearbook of the National Society for the Study of Education. University of Chicago Press, Chicago, Illinois, pp. 335–71

Soar R 1973 Final report. *Follow-through Classroom Process Measurement and Pupil Growth (1970–1971).* University of Florida, College of Education, Gainesville, Florida

Sorenson J, Rossman P A, Barnes D 1976 The unit leader and educational decision making. *J. Teach. Educ.* 27: 224–25

Stallings J A, Kaskowitz D H 1974 *Follow-through Classroom Observation Evaluation 1972–1973*. Stanford Research Institute, Menlo Park, California. ERIC Document No. ED 104 969

Whitley T W 1979 The effects of individualized instruction on the attitudes of middle school pupils. *J. Educ. Res.* 72: 188–93

Interest-based Programs

L. W. Anderson

An interest-based curriculum is one in which the selection and inclusion of content, objectives, materials, and/or activities is based primarily on students' wants or desires. Interest-based curricula frequently are contrasted with needs-based curricula: curricula based on what is desirable for students rather than what is desired by them.

In some ways the distinction between interest-based and needs-based curricula is one of emphasis. The importance of considering students' interests in the design of curricula for effective learning has long been recognized (Dewey 1913). Citing Dewey, Tyler writes, "learning is relatively inefficient, if effective at all, when it is stimulated by coercion rather than by genuine interest of the learners" (Tyler 1973 p. 2). Perhaps Smith and his colleagues state the relationship of interest-based and needs-based curricula most succinctly when they write, "Interests of the individual learner are not a sufficient criterion of curriculum content, they are a necessary criterion" (Smith et al. 1957 p. 603).

Student interests can be (and have been) considered at many phases of the curriculum development process (see *Curriculum Development*). The following is a brief description of five phases in the process during which student interests can be incorporated.

Firstly, student interest is incorporated into the identification of content or objectives when students are given a choice as to the particular content or objectives they wish to learn. Elective courses, common to American secondary schools, permit such a choice. At the elementary level the Learning Research and Development Center (LRDC) individualized instructional program incorporates both required ("prescriptive") and elective ("exploratory") components (Wang and Stiles 1976 pp. 172–74).

Secondly, even when the content and objectives are specified, students can be permitted to choose when they will study what. The Self-Schedule System incorporates this aspect of an interest-based curriculum (Wang and Stiles 1976).

Thirdly, when student interest is considered in curricular sequencing, content and objectives which are more likely to evoke student interest are included before topically related, but less interesting, content and objectives. For example, students can be taught how to pick a lock before they are taught how the lock works (Mager and Beach 1967).

Fourthly, independent of the content or objectives included in the curriculum, it may be possible to use materials related to the learning of the content or objectives that evoke the interest of students. Such high interest materials have been incorporated into several commercially developed curricula. There is some evidence to suggest that the use of high interest materials is related to increased reading comprehension (Asher 1979).

Finally, students have to "do something" in order to learn. From an interest-based curriculum perspective, students should be interested in what they do in order to learn. The use of games and simulations is congruent with this latter principle (Coleman et al. 1973). Similarly, choosing writing activities of interest to students seems promising in light of the recent evidence that different writing activities have different interest levels (e.g., letters, stories, reports).

While an entire focus on student interests in designing curricula would most likely be detrimental, the incorporation of such interests in the development of certain aspects of curricula seems worthwhile.

Bibliography

Asher S R 1979 Influence on topic interest on black children's and white children's reading comprehension. *Child Dev.* 50: 686–90

Coleman J S, Livingston S A, Fennessey G M, Edwards K J, Kidder S J 1973 The Hopkins games program: Conclusions from seven years of research. *Educ. Res.* 2(8): 3–7

Dewey J 1913 *Interest and Effort in Education*. Houghton Mifflin, Boston, Massachusetts

Hogan T P 1980 Students' interests in writing activities. *Res. Teach. English* 14: 119–26

Mager R F, Beach K M 1967 *Developing Vocational Instruction*. Fearon, Palo Alto, California

Posner G J, Strike K A 1976 A categorization scheme for principles of sequencing content. *Rev. Educ. Res.* 46: 665–90

Pratt D 1980 *Curriculum: Design and Development*. Harcourt, Brace, Jovanovich, New York

Smith B O, Stanley W O, Shores J H 1957 *Fundamentals of Curriculum Development*. World Book Company, Yonkers-on-Hudson, New York

Tyler R W 1973 Assessing educational achievement in the affective domain. *Meas. Educ.* 4(3): 1–8

Wang M C, Stiles B 1976 An investigation of children's concept of self-responsibility for their school learning. *Am. Educ. Res. J.* 13: 159–79

Student-centered Curriculum

K. Strickland

Student-centered curricula organize instruction around the individual needs and interests of pupils, rather than around predetermined units of subject matter. Proponents of this philosophy view the traditional content-oriented curricula as narrow, boring, and irrelevant, and believe that the immediate concerns expressed by students are central to successful learning and provide a valid basis for the curriculum. They reject the notion that the study of the structure and content of a discipline is the best training for the mind, and see organized knowledge simply as a resource upon which to draw to solve problems and obtain skills. They are particularly aware of the need to respond to individual differences and to adapt instruction to the developmental stage of the learner, and believe that the student-centered curriculum performs these tasks most successfully. Advocates of the student-centered curriculum also view the school as needing to attend to all aspects of the individual—physical, emotional, social, and mental. They wish to produce an independent, creative, self-directed learner, and find the organization of instruction around the interests of students most compatible with these goals (Saylor and Alexander 1974).

Student-centered curricula differ from subject-centered curricula not only in philosophy, but also in the curriculum planning process, the role of the students and teacher, the resources and facilities required, and the instructional techniques employed. Planning in student-centered curricula proceeds as a cooperative venture, with the emerging curriculum composed of a series of activities or projects selected by the pupils. The projects generally cut across subject lines, and depending on the age of the student, may range from "how to grow sunflowers" to "things which make life worth living." Activities may involve individuals, small groups, or the entire class, with the basic procedure being the identification, planning, execution, and evaluation of the project. The teacher's role is not to select, organize, and present information, but rather to guide, facilitate, and monitor the activities. Lectures and drills are replaced by investigation and problem solving, with the student viewed as an active rather than a passive participant in the learning process. The classroom, too, generally undergoes modification, with textbooks and desks replaced by working areas and a variety of resources (King et al. 1974).

Student-centered curricula first appeared in discernible numbers during the 1920s and 1930s primarily in the United Kingdom and the United States. Drawing on the works of Pestalozzi, Rousseau, Froebel, and Dewey, as well as the findings of the emerging field of psychology, these early child-centered or activity schools, as they were often called, operated under a loosely defined philosophy which emphasized learning by doing and responding to the child's natural instincts. They varied greatly in their adherence to the ideals of a student-centered curriculum, with some resorting to teachers "suggesting" projects, and others allowing students total freedom with virtually no guidance or accountability. Defining goals or clearly stating a philosophy was not generally a priority of these educators, nor was the careful evaluation or recording of their work (Tanner and Tanner 1975). One notable exception was the rural elementary school operated by Ellsworth Collings in the United States during the 1920s (Collings 1926). Working with children aged 6 to 14, Collings' teachers carefully guided the selection, planning, execution, and evaluation of play, excursion, story, and handwork projects. By matching students from the project curriculum with their counterparts in a traditional subject curriculum, Collings was able to show over a five year period that the student-centered curriculum actually produced better achievement in the standard academic areas, and resulted in more positive attitudes on the part of both parents and students (Hines 1972).

In the Federal Republic of Germany, the student-centered approach to curriculum is related to the educational reform movement. The book *The Century of Children* written in 1900 by the Swedish author Ellen Key expressed the hopes that in the twentieth-century children's rights will gain universal recognition and this will lead toward changes in the school programs too. The German educator Berthold Otto established a student-centered school in Berlin in 1906 which continued to operate until his death in 1933. Otto claimed that even the greatest psychologist cannot predict which topics or issues may be of interest for a 12-year-old child at a particular week of the school year. Therefore he argued for a great flexibility of the school program, and in his school he considered the interest of the children as a major determinant of the content of the studies (Scheibe 1969).

The open classrooms of the 1960s and 1970s are the most recent examples of student-centered curricula, and they share many of the same characteristics, as well as the weaknesses, exhibited in the earlier movement. Like the activity curricula of the 1920s and 1930s, open classrooms are found primarily in the United Kingdom and the United States and most often at the elementary level. They, too, are referred to by various names, including open education, informal education, and the integrated day, and the resulting confusion makes evaluation of the open classroom movement difficult. Proponents of the open classroom movement also seem to have difficulty in enunciating a clear philosophy, although references to the works of John Dewey, Jean Piaget and Susan Isaacs are frequent (Rathbone 1971).

Like their predecessors, they are more interested in developing open classrooms than in assessing the effectiveness of their work, and despite many colorful descriptions of various experiments (Barth 1972), ultimately much of what is claimed about the open classroom must be taken on faith. The research which has been done on the open classroom seems to indicate that academic achievement has not suffered, but the quality and quantity of studies leaves much to be desired.

Schools adopting a student-centered curriculum, whether it is termed an open classroom, an activity curriculum, or informal education, seem destined to remain in the minority at least for the immediate future. For in addition to a lack of research, and a failure to define a philosophy which presents a real alternative to the subject curriculum, proponents of the student-centered curriculum have yet to deal adequately with the questions of teacher quality and training and student achievement. There can be little doubt that the lack of a set curriculum makes increased demands on teacher competency, and that few teacher-training institutes are preparing individuals who are able to adequately guide students in their selection, execution, and evaluation of projects. Even more significant, however, is the question of whether individuals will develop the skills, attitudes, and knowledge needed by society in a curriculum based only on the immediate needs and interests of students. The fear that essential subject matter may not

be covered has led most schools to integrate practices such as the concept of student projects into the traditional subject curriculum, rather than adopting the student-centered curriculum for the total educational program (Saylor and Alexander 1974).

Bibliography

Barth R S 1972 *Open Education and the American School.* Agathon Press, New York
Collings E 1926 *An Experiment with a Project Curriculum.* MacMillan, New York
Hines V A 1972 Progressivism in practice. In: Squire J R 1972 *A New Look at Progressive Education.* Association for Supervision and Curriculum Development, Washington, DC
King M L, Dunn S, McKenzie M 1974 Individuality is inherent in the informal classroom. *Theory Pract.* 13: 107–16
Rathbone C H (ed.) 1971 *Open Education: The Informal Classroom: A Selection of Readings that Examine the Practices and Principles of the British Infant Schools and their Ameican Counterparts.* Citation Press, New York
Saylor J G, Alexander W M 1974 *Planning Curriculum For Schools.* Holt, Rinehart and Winston, New York
Saylor J G, Alexander W M, Lewis A J 1981 *Curriculum Planning For Better Teaching and Learning.* Holt, Rinehart and Winston, New York
Scheibe W 1969 *Die Reformpädagogische Bewegung 1902–1932: Eine Einführende Darstellung.* Beltz, Weinheim
Tanner D, Tanner L N 1975 *Curriculum Development; Theory into Practice.* MacMillan, New York

Independent Study

F. M. Klein

Independent study is a term used to describe a variety of educational practices. Some terms used in the literature seem to have the same approximate meaning: independent learning and self-directed learning, for example. Other terms have slightly different meanings or characteristics which suggest that they are similar to, but not the same as independent study. Some of these terms are: computer-assisted instruction, self-instruction, and individualized study. Still other terms suggest forms of independent study: homework, contracts, study halls, and learning modules. As these terms are examined, general patterns begin to emerge which clarify the concept of independent study. This article describes two sets of definitions and essential characteristics of independent study, each of which appears extensively in the literature; discusses the potential benefits of independent study to students; cites barriers to practices; and summarizes the research conducted on the two sets of definitions. It concludes with a brief discussion of the potential role of each definition in a comprehensive, balanced curriculum. The discussion of the concept is limited to those practices conducted under the auspices of a school or institution of higher learning.

1. Definitions and Characteristics

Within the literature, there are two distinct sets of definitions, each of which is labeled as independent study. One meaning of the concept refers to a goal or a desired outcome of schooling (Alexander and Hines 1967, Dressel and Thompson 1973). This set of definitions does not assume any standardized body of content to be learned by students, rather it is defined as a process by which students develop important skills which enable them to be independent learners. It is a very personalized process by which the student helps to make the essential decisions about what is to be learned and how it will be done. Inherent in this definition are the following characteristics: the student is motivated by his or her own goals; the reward of learning is intrinsic to the student and not dependent upon some external system of rewards; and the teacher is a resource in, but not the controller of, the learning process. Although conducted under the auspices of a school, the practices exist independently of regularly scheduled classes. It does not necessarily mean, however, the student is isolated from others in the learning process.

This type of independent study is not widespread, in spite of the desired attributes it possesses. It has been proposed that students at all levels of schooling have the opportunity to engage in independent study, but surveys of schools and colleges indicate that it remains more a concept than a practice (Thompson and Dressel 1970). Few students at the high-school, and even at the college, level have the opportunity to engage in this type of independent study. Perhaps the best known example of practice of this form is the tutorial program at Oxford University in England (Holtzman 1969).

A second set of definitions in the literature reflects a methodology of teaching which is commonly called the audiotutorial method (Postlethwait et al. 1969). These are characterized by a body of content which is defined by the developer for the student to learn and an efficient and effective methodology which is developed to help the student learn it. The technology of instruction is brought to bear extensively upon what is to be taught. The audiotutorial method usually involves several different media for instruction with which the student interacts on an individual basis. The content is determined well before the student becomes involved in the curriculum because effective and efficient instructional materials must be developed. The student decides when to study the materials, often placed in a special laboratory or study room, and at what pace to proceed through the sequence of instructional modules. In some programs the student can also decide whether all the materials must be studied or whether, because of prior learnings, certain modules can be deleted from the sequence. The audiotutorial method assumes that content can be organized meaningfully for the student rather than assuming that the organization of content by the student is an essential learning task.

This type of independent study is most frequently found at the college level and has been used in a wide variety of content areas. The practice, however, is not a common feature in most institutions of higher learning (Bonthius et al. 1957).

2. Potential Benefits of Independent Study

Independent study is viewed by proponents as having highly desirable educational consequences. The benefits to the learner cited by those who define independent study as a goal are: better academic achievement, greater choice in what is learned, important process skills and abilities, and significant personal attitudes. Better academic achievement is fostered in several ways. Because of the active involvement of the student required by the process, academic achievement is greater (Alexander and Hines 1967). Higher cognitive behaviors are also more often emphasized in independent study than in other forms of instruction (Henney 1978). Not only do students learn more, they retain what they have learned for a longer period of time (Alexander and Hines 1967). Students can see greater

applicability of what they learn in school to their lives outside of school and thus the undesirable distinction often made between home life and school is broken down (Henney 1978).

Independent study offers opportunities to broaden the curriculum by allowing students to choose topics which might not be included in the regular curriculum. By providing a choice of topics, learning becomes more personalized and thus, more meaningful and relevant.

Students also gain important process skills and abilities. Skills in learning how to learn which enable students to become self-directed learners are fostered through independent study. Students learn personal decision-making skills, how to deal with the consequences of decisions, and to persevere in spite of obstacles. Students also learn to relate more effectively to a wide range of people since independent study often takes them out of the particular age group usually found in a single class (Brown 1968).

Significant personal attitudes can be learned also. Willingness to take risks, a sense of personal worth, accomplishment, self-reliance, and personal adequacy are fostered through independent study (Alexander and Hines 1967).

The advantages of the audiotutorial methodology include instructional benefits, the adaptability of the method, and the process skills learned. The instructional benefits are varied. The student gains from the expertise of senior staff members since they are the ones involved in developing the learning materials. Better attention is paid to the learning task since students interact with the materials and are not easily distracted by others in the learning environment. The teacher is better able to give individual attention since the audiotutorial methodology provides specific information about any difficulty a student may be experiencing. Responsibility for learning is placed upon the student and not upon the teacher.

Benefits are also attributed to the flexibility of the audiotutorial method. It is adaptable to the needs of the student. It allows the student to set his or her own pace and allows for individual preferences for learning times to be met. Use of institutional resources can be made available whenever the student needs them since instruction is not dependent upon a teacher's schedule (Postlethwait et al. 1969, Fischer and MacWhinney 1976, Sturges and Grobe 1976).

The audiotutorial method fosters important process skills. The advantage of self-pacing emphasizes personal inquiry in the learning process. Students also learn to manage their time which allows them to adequately plan for completing work for other courses.

3. Barriers to Independent Study

Students, teachers, and the institution can be sources of barriers which limit the benefits of independent study. The view of learning held by students can be a barrier if it is different from the process of learning as defined by independent study. A preference for the traditional methodology which encourages a passive reaction can interfere with the benefits of the more active and demanding involvement in independent study. A combination of regular course work and the requirements and procedures necessary for independent study can be disconcerting and frustrating to students (Thompson and Dressel 1970). It is recognized that some students will not be prepared for independent study and a few authors suggest that not all students should engage in the process (Brown 1968).

Teachers note problems with scheduling, finding adequate planning time, lack of effective evaluation procedures, and difficulties with having one person in charge of the program. Departmental autonomy, unclear goals and objectives by the faculty, concerns for maintaining high standards, and resistance to the increased work are also named. A new role must be learned by the teacher and often some frustration and decreased initial satisfaction with this role are experienced. Confidence in a student's ability to engage in independent study is essential. If teachers believe students cannot engage successfully in the process, a significant barrier is encountered.

The institution also can present barriers to independent study. Adequate resources and facilities, general administrative support for the process, and any additional costs of the program (most likely to occur at the outset) must be provided by the institution if the benefits of independent study are to be gained by students (Dressel and Thompson 1973, Thompson and Dressel 1970).

4. Research on Effectiveness of Independent Study

Although independent study as a goal has very limited experimental research to document its effectiveness, several extensive survey studies on this definition have been conducted. The authors of these surveys conclude that this form of independent study is equal to, if not better than, other forms of learning for increasing student achievement. They also conclude that independent study produces positive student attitudes toward learning (Dressel and Thompson 1973).

Much experimental research has been conducted on the audiotutorial definition of independent study although the studies differ greatly in the purpose of the research, the variables studied, and the adequacy of the overall research design. Most of the research has been conducted on the effectiveness of the audiotutorial method compared to the traditional lecture–discussion mode of teaching and learning. Variables studied relate to student achievement, student attitudes toward the method and toward the content of the course, personality and motivational factors of students who select the audiotutorial method, and economic factors.

Overall, the research on the audiotutorial methodology clearly indicates that it is at least equal to the more traditional approaches to instruction in increasing student achievement and in many cases it is superior. Further, the studies indicate that students develop positive attitudes towards the methodology even when attitudes toward the course content do not change (Dawson 1977). A profile of students who choose to engage in some variation of the audiotutorial method is being developed through some research. Intelligence and a complex set of motivational personality variables correlate to the choice made (Devitt 1979).

Although initial costs are higher for developing the audiotutorial materials than for other forms of instruction, research suggests that these costs are recovered over a period of a few years. The programmed materials developed save time as well as money for students and teachers (Moore 1976).

5. Independent Study in the Curriculum

Two different types of independent study exist, each of which has important strengths and offers significant potential benefits to students. Both have a body of research which documents their effectiveness in relation to other teaching and learning methods. Which type is selected will depend, in part, on how the goals of the curriculum have been defined. The audiotutorial method of independent study can assist students to learn effectively and efficiently a body of content which must be learned. This is a traditional, and sometimes the exclusive, outcome of many curricula. Some curricula, however, go beyond this outcome and include goals such as acquiring skills in learning how to learn, fostering growth in decision-making skills, and developing unique abilities and interests. Independent study defined as a goal becomes one of these significant outcomes. Comprehensive and broad curricula which combine the goals of learning essential content, fostering growth in process skills, and developing areas of unique abilities and interests will need to include both types of independent study. The curricular question here is not which form of independent study is better, but rather how to assist students in receiving the benefits of both forms. The benefits will be made available to students only when necessary materials and adequate facilities are available, and when administrators, teachers, and students understand and are committed to independent study.

Bibliography

Alexander W M, Burke W I 1972 Independent study in secondary schools. *Interchange* 3: 101–13

Alexander W M, Hines V A 1967 *Independent Study in Secondary Schools*. Holt, Rinehart and Winston, New York

Beggs D W, Buffie E G (eds.) 1965 *Independent Study: Bold New Venture*. Indiana University Press, Bloomington, Indiana

Bonthius R H, Davis F J, Drushol J G 1957 *The Independent Study Program in the United States: A Report on an Undergraduate Instructional Method.* Columbia University Press, New York

Brown B F 1968 *Education By Appointment: New Approaches to Independent Study.* Parker, West Nyack, New York

Dawson G G 1977 *A Summary of Research in Personalized, Individualized, and Self Paced Instruction in College Economics.* New York Council on Economics Education, State University of New York, Old Westbury, New York. ERIC Document No. ED 144 859

Devitt T O 1979 Personality and motivational factors in student choice of independent study. *Educ. Technol.* 19(4): 52–56

Dressel P L, Thompson M M 1973 *Independent Study.* Jossey-Bass, San Francisco, California

Fischer K M, MacWhinney B 1976 A V autotutorial instruction: A review of evaluative research *Audio-Vis. Commun. Rev.* 24: 229–61

Henney M 1978 Facilitating self-directed learning. *Imp. Coll. Univ. Teach.* 26: 128–30

Holtzman W H 1969 Study. *Encyclopedia of Educational Research*, 4th edn. Macmillan, London

Klein M F 1982 Independent study. *Encyclopedia of Educational Research*, 5th edn. Free Press Macmillan, New York

Moore G A 1976 The evaluation of a media resource-based learning project and its modification of traditional classroom procedures. *Audiotutorial Instruction* 21(2): 36–40

Postlethwait S N, Novak J, Murray H T Jr 1969 *The Audiotutorial Approach to Learning Through Independent Study and Integrated Experiences*, 2nd edn. Burgess, Minneapolis, Minnesota

Sturges A W, Grobe C H 1976 Audio-tutorial instruction: An evaluation. *Improving College and University Teaching* 24(2): 81

Thompson M M, Dressel P L 1970 A survey of independent study practices. *Educ. Record* 51: 392–95

Curriculum Contract

D. Cohen

A curriculum contract is a negotiated agreement about learning between a teacher and one or more learners. The curriculum contract provides the learner with a plan, and both teacher and learner with learning expectations, guidelines, or dimensions of activities. It also provides the teacher with an organizational device to accommodate the elements of learning common to two or more of a group or class of learners, whilst still accommodating unique elements for any one learner.

Many schemes which purportedly individualize curriculum in fact allow solely for variations in rates of learning. However, there are many possible variations in strategies for individualization, and these can be built into the curriculum contract. Provisions can be made for individual and stylistic learning preferences, including differential needs for structure. From a series of suggested alternative experiences or others which they substitute, students may elect whether they wish to engage in breadth or depth studies, or in some intermediate blends. Students also help to decide upon the number, duration, and sequence of experiences, upon their learning environment and time structure, group or subgroup structure, media, due dates for assignments or reporting, and evaluation method.

Gibbons (1971) has listed 15 different dimensions for individualizing learning, and each of these can be incorporated to provide variations in curriculum contracts. Most dimensions range from prescription to individual choice or nonstructure. Important examples of the Gibbons dimensions are materials, pace, selection of activity, time structure, and evaluation.

Some writers (e.g., Bockman and Bockman 1973) have emphasized that it is the processes of negotiation which are more important than the decisions reached

and the documents produced. Students may be asked what they wish to learn, and why, how, when, with whom, and how they prefer to be evaluated. Their responses can then be built into the contract.

The curriculum contract has been successfully used in tertiary, secondary, and primary (elementary) classes (Berte 1975). It was basic to the Dalton plan devised in 1920 by Parkhurst (see Bockman and Bockman 1973). It is used in many "open" and "progressive" classrooms and schools, in which students participate in making such decisions as what to learn, when, and how.

The use of the curriculum contract is based largely upon the acceptance of a number of premises. These include:

(a) Motivation is a crucial key to effective learning, and since contracts require participatory decision making, they are an aid to motivation.

(b) The commonest teaching approaches reported are teacher domination of classrooms via autocratic, imposed, and often didactic strategies. These are not the most effective techniques for motivating a majority of learners, although they may be effective sometimes for some aspects of learning. The curriculum contract provides an effective alternative.

(c) The learner is the singly most important source of information about what are the most effective conditions, including the interests and needs, for that learner. By participation in the negotiation of a contract, the learner can build these conditions into the contract.

(d) The teacher will have a reservoir of teaching strategies which can be matched in the contract to a learner's participation.

(e) The use of the curriculum contract is part of the process of "learning to learn" which helps to educate for independent learning.

Some of the advantages of curriculum contracts are as follows:

(a) The curriculum contract provides each learner with a personalized curriculum tailored to the abilities, interests, and needs of the learner. It accommodates individual differences between learners. Such differences may stem from such factors as the varying backgrounds, experiences and maturity, learning styles and rates, interests, and expertise of learners.

(b) Higher levels of motivation, relevance, understanding, and performance may result where learners participate in formulating their own curriculum.

(c) The use of the contract "helps to give both security and responsibility within an atmosphere of freedom" (Rogers 1969).

(d) The curriculum contract provides the student with purpose and a basic structure with fewer imposed constraints, and these are negotiable. This assists in weaning the teacher-dependent student to a stage of independence and participation in active decision making.

(e) The negotiations between teachers and learners of a curriculum contract bring the teacher into a one-to-one dialogue with each learner.

Curriculum contracts also have some disadvantages:

(a) The contract perceived as an inflexible type of legalistic instrument could result in rigidity, leading to depersonalization of learning.

(b) The teacher could misuse the curriculum contract to convey a working plan via a printed sheet, and this could have the reverse effect of reducing teacher–learner interactions, thereby dehumanizing the learning process.

(c) If used regularly and for large proportions of time, the curriculum contract could itself become an instrument of monotony.

(d) Effective use of the curriculum contract requires learner self-direction, and some students may lack the necessary initiative or skills.

(e) The role of the teacher is degenerated, since written specifications and feedback and other clerical tasks will occupy an increased proportion of the teacher's time.

Bibliography

Berte N R (ed.) 1975 *Individualizing Education by Learning Contracts.* University of Alabama Press, Alabama

Bockman J F, Bockman V M 1973 Contracting for learning outcomes: Potentialities and limitations. *National Association of Secondary School Principals* NASSP *Bull.* 57: 17–26

Gibbons M 1971 *Individualized Instruction: A Descriptive Analysis.* Teachers College Press, Columbia University, New York

Rogers C 1969 *Freedom to Learn: A View of What Education Might Become.* Merrill, Columbus, Ohio

Accelerated Programs

A. H. Passow

"Accelerated program" is a term which refers to any form of educational program which is begun at an earlier age than is normal or is completed in less time than is usual.

Acceleration may be accomplished through a variety of procedures, some of which are basically instructional and others which are primarily administrative in nature although they affect instruction as well. For example, if a foreign language course is designed to take three years to complete and, by speeding up the instructional pace and the time spent on units and modules some students finish the course in two years or less, then acceleration is achieved through instructional means, increasing the tempo or pace of instruction. If a child is permitted to enter first grade a year earlier than usual or is promoted from third grade to the fifth grade thus skipping the fourth grade, then acceleration is achieved administratively. Administrative acceleration does affect curriculum and instruction in that the student is engaged with more advanced content.

Early admittance to kindergarten or first grade or early entrance to college represent acceleration. Moving a course to an earlier grade or making it available to younger children—for example, if algebra is generally taught in the ninth grade and, for a class of rapid learners, it is begun in the seventh grade—represents another form of an accelerated program. Condensing or compacting a program, such as a three-year junior-high-school program into a two-year program constitutes still another form of acceleration. Rapid promotion or grade skipping are still other forms of accelerated programs. Credit-by-examination, a procedure by which a student receives credit for a program by passing a test without actually taking the course is considered to be another variety of acceleration. Thus, any modification of a program which provides for rapid progress through or early completion of a course of study or program can be considered a form of acceleration.

There are many reasons advanced for providing accelerated programs. Enabling the student to complete a program more quickly may then make it possible to provide the individual with curriculum and instructional activities more commensurate with his/her potential and ability to progress. Providing for curricular or instructional acceleration breaks the "academic lockstep" and implements the concept that the student should take the least time required to attain the desired level of achievement. Making it possible for the individual to complete secondary and tertiary programs at a younger age puts an earlier end to full-time schooling and enables an earlier entry into productive careers. Students kept in classes and programs in which they are not sufficiently challenged contributes to the development of negative attitudes and poor habits. Accelerated programs make enriched educational opportunities possible by using the time saved for exploring areas of major interest and talent or to delve in fields unfamiliar to the student.

The practice of acceleration is, however, not without its critics and opponents. One of the major arguments against accelerated programs is the differential between cognitive and affective development: a child may be intellectually advanced but socially and emotionally less mature or immature and acceleration may aggravate these differences. Because not all curricula are logically, sequentially organized, accelerated programs may result in discontinuities and gaps in the development of the student. Comparability of mental age does not necessarily mean similarity in intellectual functioning; rapid promotion or skipping may provide more difficult academic work but may not result in more appropriate educational experiences. Because individuals have different maturation rates, development is often quite uneven. While a student may profit from acceleration in one area, such pacing may be inappropriate in other areas.

The weight of experimental evidence on acceleration is generally supportive with respect to both the cognitive and affective consequences.

Accelerated programs may involve single students or groups of students. For instance, an entire class may be involved in an accelerated program such as the "SP-2: Special Progress-2" classes in New York City which complete a three-year junior-high-school program in two years. On the other hand, rapid progress may be provided for a single student through curricular or administrative adjustments.

Acceleration requires curricular adjustments in all elements of curriculum—content, instructional strategies, material resources, timing or pacing, evaluation, assignments, and so on. Such adjustments are partially planned by the teacher and partially emerge from the interaction of the students with the curricular content.

While accelerated programs are most often associated with provisions for the intellectually or academically gifted student, acceleration is now being thought of in connection with disadvantaged/at risk students as well. Rather than rely on the traditional approaches involving remediation and compensatory programs, some educators argue that the achievement gap can only be closed when such students are provided with accelerated/faster paced learning opportunities. As applied by Levin (1987) in the Accelerated Schools Program, "the instructional pace must be adequate to keep students attentive and learning at a rate that is productive in contrast to the deliberate slowdown usually associated with remedial instruction" (pp. 35–36). Thus, the basic concept of acceleration/faster paced instruction is now being extended beyond the gifted to other students as being equally appropriate to achieve academic goals for them.

Bibliography

George W C, Cohen S J, Stanley J C 1979 *Educating the Gifted: Acceleration and Enrichment.* 9th Annual Hyman Blumberg Symp. on Research in Early Childhood Education, New York, 1977. Johns Hopkins University Press, Baltimore, Maryland

Levin H M 1987 *New Schools for the Disadvantaged.* Mid-Continent Regional Educational Laboratory, Stanford, California

Passow A H 1958 Enrichment of education for the gifted. In:Henry N B (ed.) 1958 *Education for the Gifted.* 57th Yearbook of the National Society for the Study of Education, Pt. 2. University of Chicago Press, Chicago, Illinois, pp. 193–221

Pressey S L 1949 *Educational Acceleration: Appraisals and Basic Problems.* The Ohio State University Press, Columbus, Ohio

Honors Courses

A. I. Oliver

Honors courses, as the name implies, are conceived as attempts to differentiate the curriculum in order to challenge students with "high academic potential" and, in a sense, to honor them. To study this topic it is necessary to be aware of related terminology. At the secondary educational level the terms honors classes, seminars, advance placement, and International Baccalaureate are found referring to this concept. At the higher education level the terms honors curriculum and honors courses are the most commonly used ones.

1. Secondary Education Level

In the secondary school, honors courses are usually limited to selected juniors and seniors. Secondary education in the United States is indebted to Oxford University in England and to Swarthmore College, Pennsylvania in the United States. In 1921, President Frank Aydelotte introduced to Swarthmore the "pass–honors" concept which he had encountered while studying as a Rhodes Scholar at Oxford University. Secondary schools have picked up the idea as one answer to relate to the needs of gifted adolescents. As Fink noted (1969), here was a reaction against "the undifferentiated and unstimulating repetition that characterized the successive cycles of American history in schools and colleges."

Objectives include: to develop habits of inquisitiveness, of questioning, research skills, understanding of self and others; improved communication skills; growing cultural insights; an antidote to anti-intellectualism; and above all, a perspective to confront and explore ideas.

In order to achieve such goals it is important to emphasize quality rather than quantity. The classroom should become a learning center in which there is a feeling of freedom and mutual respect. The establishment of an "honors browsing room" will enhance the investigative activities. To select teachers who will be both stimulants and reference sources, search must be made for superior teacher–scholars who will be adequate for superior students.

Although restricted by the program requirements, the International Baccalaureate (IB) may be considered a form of honors offerings. Begun in the early 1960s by a group of concerned teachers at the International School of Geneva, by 1979 there were 111 International Baccalaureate schools from 35 countries. This seems to carry out the intent of "an international entrance examination which could be taken in any country" (Peterson 1972). To "pass", a candidate must be examined in six subjects. The examination has two levels, higher and subsidiary, and appropriate combinations are necessary for the full diploma. Syllabi for guided course work are provided in the courses to be offered; thus, while the direction of classes depends on the individual instructor, the work is controlled by the anticipated examinations.

For students engaged in a serious academic program, the IB offers limited study of selected topics in depth; yet the requirement of six examinations, including one in "the theory of knowledge," provides range and hopes to ensure a base of general education. Evidence of the honors direction can be gained by noting aims such as "the development of an understanding of the nature of historical evidence" (in history) and "to develop the ability to analyze the work of others critically" (in physics). Not surprisingly the emphasis in participating schools is on international and humanistic education.

Whereas the International Baccalaureate is used chiefly outside the United States, advanced placement (AP) is basically found in the United States. Both are designed to certify competency to undertake university study. When AP was started in 1954–55 by the College Board as a cooperative venture between 104 secondary schools and 130 colleges and universities, there were 1,229 students taking a total of 2,199 examinations. By 1980–81 there were 5,253 schools and 1,995 cooperating colleges with 133,702 students taking 178,159 examinations. The purpose is to provide highly motivated and academically able students with an opportunity to pursue college-level courses while still in secondary school. The College Board contracts with Educational Testing Services—an independent, nonprofit agency with headquarters in Princeton, New Jersey—for technical and operational services. Participating schools offer their better students courses which the program has planned and for which it has established examinations.

The examinations are graded from 1 to 5 by a group of several hundred college and school teachers. College credit is recommended for scores of 3 and above, but decisions about credit awards are made independently by the participating colleges. Advanced placement allows the student to avoid work already done, thus comparable first year courses need not be taken. This permits the student to start college with advance courses in that AP subject, explore other subjects that interest them, and/or join honors and other special programs. By 1981 many institutions reported to the College Board that they were ready to award immediate sophomore (second year) standing, or its local equivalent, to students presenting qualifying grades in enough AP examinations. Currently AP courses are offered in 14 disciplines; each course has a description booklet on the course's essential content along with some sample examination questions.

Studies by Dr. Carl H. Haag, Director of the College Board Placement Testing Program at Educational Testing Service, show that as a group AP students perform as well as, and often better than, other college students. When placed in advanced courses in college, they do very well with 98 percent passing the courses and generally getting higher grades than do other students. One important by-product noted is an enthusiasm for learning which is kindled by involvement in AP. Such enthusiasm is a capstone for honors courses.

2. Higher Education Level

Honors courses in colleges and universities have European antecedents in the Socratic dialogue, the Oxford tutorial, and the German seminars. However, as Cohen (1966) pointed out, it was chiefly the small private Eastern colleges that "took the initiative in providing special treatment for superior students in the early decades of the century." Cohen spearheaded the founding, in 1957, of the Inter-university Committee on the Superior Student (ICSS) as a "systematic, coordinated effort" to extend honors programs to the large private and state universities. The ICSS was superseded in 1966 by the National Collegiate Honors Council which provides a variety of services to interested colleges and universities.

There seems to be some tendency, especially in larger institutions to differentiate between (a) general honors—alternatives to the regular general education offerings (it is common for these to be interdisciplinary in nature), and (b) departmental honors—within a discipline (such as English) differing from "regular courses" in depth and scope. For instance, instead of a course in Shakespeare it might be possible to take an honors course in Shakespeare and Renaissance Thought.

Although individual institutions may note different goals for their honors offerings, most include, in one wording or another, the following:

(a) to provide challenges and support beyond the ordinary;

(b) to provide in-depth background to high quality pre-professional students;

(c) to provide the most gifted undergraduate students with special access to the academic resources of a distinguished university;

(d) to explore the foundation of a discipline in depth;

(e) to "liberate men and women to realize their potentialities, to encourage and foster their search for identity, purpose, and meaning . . ." Austin (1975);

(f) to give "faculty members the psychic reward that derives from working with students . . ." Austin (1975);

(g) to assist in attracting both students and faculty of outstanding academic ability.

From an organizational point of view there are several common factors:

(a) a director with an advisory committee. Often students provide input, possibly a student executive council;

(b) statement of a selection policy;

(c) provisions for interdisciplinary cooperation;

(d) an introductory honors seminar;

(e) the identification of honors classes by nomenclature such as G H History 19, Program in History and Critical Thinking, or HO NR 110C, Introduction to Compleat Wisdom;

(f) small classes to facilitate a highly participatory process;

(g) seminar approach and/or independent study, especially in senior year;

(h) competent staff advisors.

As in any valid curriculum endeavor, a clear statement of objectives must be followed by systematic ongoing evaluation. Heist, in his chapter "Evaluating honors programs" for Cohen's *The Superior Student in Ameri-can Higher Education*, found evaluation plans scattered and disappointing. Efforts have improved since then.

Most attention is given to evaluation or appraisal of the efforts of individual students. In some places no grades are given but suitable descriptive notations are placed on the student's record. Some programs, especially departmental, require a thesis. An oral examination before a special committee is common in the senior year. At graduation a general honors citation may be given with appropriate designation of Cum Laude, Magna Cum Laude, or Summa Cum Laude.

As for evaluation of the honors program, one method is to obtain interview or written feedback from participants. While there is merit in getting this student reaction at the completion of a program, follow-up at a later period is valuable to see how the experience did or did not raise educational aspirations and influence later productivity. Limited work has been done on comparing honors and nonhonors students in a college or university in terms of: holding positions of scholarship, holding positions of leadership, development of critical thinking, broadening of scholarly interests, acceptance by peers, continuation into graduate and professional schools, self-concept, fostering creativity.

Good evaluation is a cyclical process. It not only gives the institution a "reading" on what has or has not been done but also calls for a new look at objectives, student selection, management matters and, above all, what kind of scholarly climate has been created.

3. Honors Courses as a Means for Developing High Potential

From secondary school through undergraduate work the honors concept provides a viable approach to locating and developing high potential. Parents, teachers, and counselors are often concerned and baffled by the mediocre performance of the very able—hence a body of literature on the underachiever. A common finding is boredom based on nonchallenging programs. Honors is one antidote. Perhaps the advice attributed to Goethe is the message here, "Treat people as if they were what they ought to be, and you help them to become what they are capable of being."

Bibliography

Austin C G 1975 Honors learning in the seventies. *Educ. Rec.* 56: 160–69

Bancroft G W (ed.) 1978 *Guidelines for Conducting Intercultural Seminars.* Ministry of Culture and Recreation, Toronto, Ontario

Cohen J W (ed.) 1966 *The Superior Student in American Higher Education.* McGraw-Hill, New York

Fink L A 1969 *Honors Teaching in American History.* Teachers College Press, New York

Peterson A D C 1972 *The International Baccalaureate: An Experiment in International Education.* Harrap, London

Swarthmore College Faculty 1941 *An Adventure in Education: Swarthmore College under Frank Aydelotte.* Macmillan, New York

Diversified Curriculum

J. Lauglo

Diversification of the curriculum refers to the introduction of more practical or vocational content into schools or stages of schooling which previously have been dominated by general education of an academic kind. In practice, the term refers to lower- and upper-secondary education and to schools in developing countries. There has, however, also been a strong interest in many industrialized countries in the 1970s and early 1980s in strengthening school-based vocational and prevocational education.

Curriculum diversification includes such changes as the introduction of "prevocational" subjects or streams, programmes aiming at complete vocational preparation, or work experience introduced as part of the general education that schools organize for all pupils. To establish or strengthen vocational schooling parallel to other schools is also to diversify provisions. But usually diversification policies aim at vocationalizing curricula in existing general education schools. A diversified curriculum is implied in the concepts of the comprehensive school and the multilateral school.

1. Aims

In its most radical form, curriculum diversification reflects a concept of general education that rejects the traditional Western academic idea of the educated person, also for those preparing for university entry, and which instead gives pride of place to vocational knowledge and skills, solidarity with manual workers, and ideological commitment. Socialist ideology, with its concepts of polytechnical education and of unity between theory and practice in education, provides strong support for radical curriculum diversification. It is those developing countries which have strongly pursued socialist policies in general, such as the People's Republic of China, Cuba, and Tanzania, which have tried to vocationalize secondary schooling most thoroughly, not only by stressing vocational education, but also participation in manual work as part of general education.

Curriculum diversification policies have often been pursued in order to enhance the economic value of schooling. In less developed countries and Western industrialized countries alike, vocationalization of general education to varying degrees was a typical policy response in the late 1970s and early 1980s to the employment problems facing school leavers. These problems have been especially severe in many developing countries where the growth in school enrolments has far outstripped the growth in opportunities for wage employment in the modern sector. By adapting curricula more directly to particular occupations, it was hoped to promote economic development and mitigate unemployment among school leavers. In some developing

countries, vocationalization has also been accompanied by a shift in official development priorities away from the modern sector and towards improvement of peasant productivity. This idea of "adapting school curricula to rural development needs" and to the traditional local economy is not novel. It was promoted in many colonial territories in the 1920s and 1930s by influential administrators, notably in Sub-Saharan Africa. Such curricula failed to take hold then, because parents and pupils did not look to schools for useful skills in their traditional occupations, but for social promotion. "Adapted curricula" were also resented by leaders in the struggle for independence as a type of education that would bar indigenous people from ascent to position of influence.

2. A Sri Lankan Example

Events in Sri Lanka illustrate recent diversification policies and early unsuccessful attempts by the colonizers to vocationalize the curriculum. Recent attempts have been influenced by a blend of motives: socialist educational ideals, concerns about school leaver unemployment, and a "broadly based" development strategy (Wijemanne 1978). Developments there also illustrate another common experience: controversy about whether more vocationally biased curricula in fact serve their purpose. In Sri Lanka, the Handessa Rural Education Scheme in the 1930s sought to develop a curriculum to meet the needs of rural dwellers, but "it had to be abandoned as it came to be viewed as a ruse designed to keep the under-privileged away from the prestigious academic curriculum". In 1971, following political unrest among unemployed school leavers, prevocational studies were introduced for all pupils in junior secondary schools, geared towards agriculture and traditional crafts. Development-related projects were to be an important part of the senior secondary curricula. These policies were rooted in a development strategy that was both influenced by socialist ideals and stressed gradual improvement of productivity in the traditional rural economy. A new government came to power in 1977. It reaffirmed the importance of the modern sector and of a market economy. It reversed the policy of prevocational education, giving instead priority to general education on the grounds that it makes the school leaver more economically adaptable, and stressing the need for modern technical schools.

3. Critics and Advocates

There is a continuing controversy about vocationalization of general education. Critics, such as Foster (1965) and Blaug (1973), argue that vocational curricula will not be taken seriously by pupils and parents as long as the associated economic opportunities remain very inferior compared to those provided by a general education. They also maintain that "academic" general education usually *is* a vocationally relevant training because of its adaptability, and that curriculum change would have negligible effects on school leaver unemployment, the drift to towns, or the superior esteem in which white-collar work is held. The cost per pupil is liable to be higher in vocational education. The most ambitious form of diversified secondary education—multilateral schools that provide vocational education in earnest for a range of occupations—is especially costly. Critics also question the effectiveness of school-based vocational education: competent teachers are scarce and hard to recruit and keep, and equipment is liable to be obsolete or too advanced for the local economy. Therefore, they argue, vocational education is generally better provided for on the job than in the school. Reportedly, employers often have a sceptical view of youth coming from the school-based vocational courses even in generously financed multilateral schools.

Compared to the critics, the advocates of diversified curriculum tend to have greater faith in manpower planning and in the role that schools can play in shaping attitudes, and in teaching needed occupational skills. President Nyerere of Tanzania stands out as an advocate (1967, 1977) for a vocational orientation, centred on community development problems, throughout the curriculum. His influential concept of *Education for Self-reliance* is, it should be noted, part of a socialist programme of societal transformation. This is increasingly stressed by advocates of diversified curricula in the face of the arguments of critics. They then concede that the prospects for successful curriculum diversification are bleak in the context of gradualist development strategies (Bacchus 1981). However, it is possible to speculate that school-based vocational education is more viable when "vocational" employment opportunities are already expanding in the modern sector of the economy.

4. Shifting World Bank Policy

In spite of the great many curriculum diversification projects which have been undertaken around the world, there is very little publicly available evaluation of such projects. Existing material is largely in the form of reports internal to ministries of education and international aid agencies, and the impression is that systematic evaluation of the effectiveness of projects is rare even in such internal documents. The World Bank has been a major source of finance for such projects: 79 in the 1963 to 1978 period. Curriculum diversification accorded well with the Bank's 1974 policy paper on education in which (1974 p. 21) it was claimed that school curricula were excessively theoretical and abstract, insufficiently orientated to local conditions, and insufficiently concerned with attitudes and with manual, social, and leadership skills. It was suggested (p. 22) that the content of education must be reorientated to relate skills taught to jobs, and vocationalization of the curricula of academic schools was mentioned approvingly along with separately provided vocational and technical schools.

The 1980 World Bank Sector Policy Paper on Education, on the other hand, written after an initial internal review of the Bank's experience with such projects, concludes that diversified secondary schools are in general inappropriate for "training large numbers in specific vocational skills", (1980 p. 45) and that there is no consistent empirical support for the hope that prevocational curricula would instil in students more favourable attitudes towards manual labour. However, it may be appropriate on a limited scale, as a basis for the training of technicians or as a preparation for higher education, especially in technical fields.

As of 1982, diversified curriculum remains a controversial concept. There appears to be mounting disillusionment in international aid agencies and some governments with that version of it which involves vocationalization of general secondary education. Comparative and more systematic evaluation of diversified curriculum projects is needed to illuminate the conditions which make different types of vocational education viable. Such research is now underway in Tanzania and Colombia in collaboration with the World Bank, and in Kenya with sponsorship from the Swedish International Development Authority.

Bibliography

Bacchus M K 1981 Education for development in underdeveloped countries. *Comp. Educ.* 17: 215–27
Blaug M 1973 *Education and the Employment Problem in Developing Countries.* International Labour Organization, Geneva
Foster P 1965 The vocational school fallacy in development planning. In: Anderson C A, Bowman M J (eds.) 1965 *Education and Economic Development.* Aldine, Chicago, Illinois
Lillis K, Hogan D 1983 Dilemmas of diversification: Problems associated with vocational education in developing countries. *Comp. Educ.* 19: 89–108
Nyerere J K 1967 *Education for Self-reliance.* Government Printer, Dar es Salaam
Nyerere J K 1977 *The Arusha Declaration Ten Years After.* Government Printer, Dar es Salaam
Wijemanne E L 1978 *Educational Reforms in Sri Lanka.* Report Studies C 70. Division of Educational Policy and Planning, UNESCO, Paris
World Bank 1974 *Education.* Sector Working Paper. World Bank, Washington, DC
World Bank 1981 *Education.* Sector Policy Paper. World Bank, Washington, DC

Elective Subjects

W. H. Schubert and T. Miklos

Elective subjects is a term that designates those courses that students may select themselves or with the guidance of a professional educator. Electives, as they are often called, are distinguished from required courses: together elective subjects and required subjects constitute most of the course offerings that an educational institution provides. The purposes and varieties of elective subjects can best be understood through reference to their origins.

A primary contribution to the idea of elective subjects is the growth and diversification of knowledge; as knowledge grows it becomes analyzed, creating new categories or subjects. The rise and expansion of scientific knowledge in the German universities of the eighteenth-century Enlightenment "made the elective system virtually a necessity and directly affected the rise of the elective system in American colleges in the nineteenth century" (Butts 1947). Experimentation with electives could be found in the private "English" schools and within the academy movement initiated by Benjamin Franklin in the United States, both schools of the secondary level. One principal force behind the elective movement of this period was the pressure to include practical subjects of a commercial and vocational kind.

At the elementary-school level, the philosophy of naturalism that stemmed from Rousseau and Pestalozzi was coupled with notions of democracy and capitalistic individualism in nineteenth-century American educational systems; however, the idea was dominated by other emphases in most sectors. Seguel (1966) notes that it is more than a coincidence that elective subjects in the university and in the secondary school emerged at the same time as learned societies were established, during the second half of the nineteenth century. The vast increase in the number of possible subjects made the elective system a necessity. It was temporally and economically impossible to offer all subjects to each student.

Much of the work of the curriculum field, which evolved as a twentieth-century phenomenon (Schubert 1980) was devoted to the problem of dealing with the proliferation of courses. A number of different proposals emerged to deal with the problem and each carried a somewhat different notion of what was meant by elective subjects. Many curriculum theorists saw the need to be that of preventing both myopic specialization and haphazard selection of disconnected electives. One response to these problems is to specify a core of courses that are basic to a particular major area of study, to recommend sets of courses within which students may select areas of specialization, and also to provide a certain percentage of the program for students to be allowed to select freely from all courses available. This is a dominant form of curriculum design in the colleges and secondary schools of many nations today (see *Curriculum Design*).

Other curriculum theorists sought to resolve the course proliferation problem by departing from a subject orientation in varying degrees. Some advocated the joining of courses by combining subjects into broad fields. Another approach saw social problems as central themes that cut across disciplinary lines, enabling depth and breadth that had been missed in both required courses and free electives. In the 1950s, this style of curriculum was further refined and called a "core curriculum" (Faunce and Bossing 1958). At the elementary level, certain activities or projects became a central focus around which the curriculum was built, although these two examples represent opposite poles in terms of their curricular philosophy. An even greater deviation from the subject curriculum took experience of students (rather than activities, projects, texts, or course content) as the organizing center of the curriculum. This approach enabled learners, facilitated by teachers, to eclectically choose and create knowledge that added meaning and direction to their lives.

The point here is that the very idea of elective subjects is transformed away from one of taking course offerings imposed by an educational institution. It becomes, instead, centered in the student and community of learners who elect to study subjects that they decide will add meaning and direction to their lives (Schubert and Schubert 1981). This focus on reflection and choice is evident in the work of some curriculum writers known as reconceptualists (Pinar 1975).

While the above bear directly upon alternative interpretations of elective subjects in principle, recent curriculum practice has leaned toward increasing the variety and flexibility of course offerings, leading to minicourses, community-based learning experiences, alternative schools and paths within schools, free schools, and a vast array of elective offerings too numerous to mention here (Fantini 1976, Glatthorn 1975). It is also necessary to turn to literature on extracurricular offerings, for these too are electives that play an important role in the education of learners especially at the secondary-school level.

The literature on both alternatives and extracurricular activities provides a rich field of offerings that broadens the character of elective subjects. Conceptions range from an expanding array of courses, to methods of organizing them centered upon topics or student experiences, and to radically altered learning environments. The interest in providing a more productive repertoire of electives continues to be important today, as are new dimensions of the problem invoked by technological advance, the expansion of knowledge, and new conceptions of psychological and social development.

Bibliography

Butts R F 1947 *A Cultural History of Education: Reassessing our Educational Traditions*. McGraw-Hill, New York

Centro de Estudios Educativos (CEE) 1979 *El curriculo flexible*. CEE, Mexico

Fantini M D (ed.) 1976 *Alternative Education: A Source Book for Parents, Teachers, Students and Administrators*. Doubleday, Garden City, New York

Faunce R C, Bossing N L 1958 *Developing the Core Curriculum*, 2nd edn. Prentice Hall, Englewood Cliffs, New Jersey

Glatthorn A A 1975 *Alternatives in Education: Schools and Programs*. Dodd, Mead, New York

Pinar W F (ed.) 1975 *Curriculum Theorizing: The Reconceptualists*. McCutchan, Berkeley, California

Schubert W H 1980 *Curriculum Books: The First Eighty Years*. University Press of America, Lanham, Maryland

Schubert W H, Schubert A L 1981 Toward curricula that are of, by, and therefore for students. *J. Curric. Theorizing* 3: 239–51

Seguel M L 1966 *The Curriculum Field: Its Formative Years*. Teachers College Press, New York

Focus on Learning Activities

Experience-based Studies

A. Bank

Experiential learning is usually defined as "learning in which the learner is directly in touch with the realities being studied. Experiential learning typically involves not merely observing the phenomenon being studied but also doing something with it, such as testing the dynamics of the reality to learn more about it, or applying the theory learned to deliver some desired result" (Keeton and Tate 1978a).

However, others define it more broadly as the living through of events and assert that, at least for the purposes of building an experiential taxonomy, "There is no taxonomic difference between an experience in which one is physically involved or one in which there is vicarious involvement" (Steinaker and Bell 1979 p. 9). Steinaker and Bell's generic experiential taxonomy includes five levels: exposure, participation, identification, internalization, and dissemination.

The concept of experiential learning is related to other older terms in education such as discovery learning, lifelong learning, fieldwork, school–community education, and clinical experience. There has been a recent resurgence of interest in experience-based learning by educational institutions, although learning by doing, master–protégé, as well as other types of apprenticeship arrangements, are of ancient and historic vintage. A modern counterpart for this historic orientation occurs in the lifelong learning movement encouraged by UNESCO for both developed and developing countries. In their view, lifelong learning "includes formal, nonformal, and informal learning extended throughout the life span of an individual and . . . includes learning that occurs in the home, school, community and workplace and through mass media [becoming] a continuous quest for a higher and better quality of life" (Dave 1975 p. 42).

Today, experience-based curricula or programs exist at the elementary, secondary, collegiate, and graduate levels. They may be either alternatives to formal instruction, supplementary to or integrated with classroom instruction.

At the elementary level, experiential learning is often encouraged in classrooms taught by teachers familiar either with the cognitive development theories of Jean Piaget or with John Dewey's emphasis on discovery of the "backward and forward connection between what we do to things and what we suffer from things in consequence" (Dewey 1964 p. 140). In those classrooms, the role of the teacher is "to provide a variety of concrete materials for the children to manipulate, to allow and encourage them to work with and learn from one another, and to assist them in their efforts to assimilate information from their environment by asking them questions which will help them to think about and interpret their experiences" (Bank et al. 1981 p. 133). Mathematics and science materials for such classrooms have been developed by the Nuffield Foundation (1967), among others, and are used in infant schools in England and Wales.

At the secondary level, experiential learning programs have focused on a number of subject areas. Foremost among them are work experience and training programs, career exploration programs, and community service programs. During the 1970s, at least four different models for experience-based career education programs were developed for use in United States high schools. Additional areas in which local experiential learning programs have been created are writing, outdoor education, consumer education, and health care (see *Consumer Education*; *Health Education*). Special secondary-school populations served by experiential programs include the handicapped, the gifted, and migrant children.

James Coleman's contrast between an information assimilation instructional pattern whose medium is symbolic language—written, spoken, visual, or graphic—and an experiential learning pattern whose medium is the reality of natural, constructed, social, and cultural environments encouraged reform-minded educators in the 1970s to assert that the two interactional patterns are not conflicting but complementary (Coleman 1976). However, some educators resist experiential education partly because of unresolved issues of how to maintain academic quality, how to assess achievement of outcomes, and how to plan relationships among purposes, procedures, and outcomes without adequate research-based knowledge.

Evaluation studies, rather than research studies, have been the dominant mode of inquiry about secondary schools' experience-based programs. Shortcomings of those studies include lack of an adequate conceptual framework, an absence of a comparison group to identify program effects, and they focus on short-term rather than long-term impacts.

A coordinated approach to research on experiential education at the secondary level has been suggested by Owens et al. (1979). Among their suggestions are:

(a) derive specific postulates that could help explain existing findings about experiential programs and direct future research and planning from theories about social learning, attribution, maturation, personal/social development;

(b) identify instruments that can detect significant gains for particular populations and for particular outcomes; develop new instruments to fill the gaps;

(c) synthesize study findings, differentiating by relevant participants' characteristics such as age, sex, achievement level, socioeconomic status.

In higher education, two areas of paramount concern related to experiential education are: (a) how to assess students' previously acquired life or work experiences, and (b) how to organize sponsored work experience or clinical programs within collegiate or graduate studies.

Both of these concerns have been stimulated by an increasingly heterogeneous student population of older adults. Some are returning to undergraduate or graduate work with extensive experience. Others are seeking professional advancement, credentials, or skills for career shifts.

Colleges and universities therefore have had to develop standardized procedures for placing such students in appropriate courses, for modifying existing programs to fit the special needs of skilled students, and for granting course credit for work or life experience. This has become an especially pressing need for those higher-education institutions which grant external or professional degrees or operate continuing education programs. Among the procedures they use to assess prior work experience are portfolio evaluations, testimony and references, structured interviews, and oral examinations.

The justification of experiential learning programs within the university setting has been traced by Maehl (1982) to scholarly empirical inquiries into archeology and history emanating from nineteenth-century German universities.

The tools of this new knowledge were essentially experiential. Rhetoric was replaced by research. Direct experiences with original artifacts and documentary sources, field and laboratory methods were reserved for those elite students who were permitted to participate in original research, whose "home" in the German university was the graduate seminar. (p. 33)

Among the experiential courses currently offered at the graduate level and integrated with regular degree programs are internships, practica, directed field work, supervised clinical work, practice teaching, and studio art. In assessing these offerings, some argue that generic characteristics for experiential courses should be the same as those for didactic courses: rigor, that is, possessing academic quality controls and standards; appropriateness, that is, integral to overall program goals; and balance, that is, only one of several approaches to the study of the discipline or profession (Jacobs 1982).

Theory development, research on the effects of crediting prior experience, and the systematic development of experiential formats has lagged behind the practical needs of educational institutions to respond quickly to student needs. Kolb (1976) has described a four-stage learning cycle which uses (a) concrete experience as the basis for (b) observation and reflection, which in turn assist in the (c) formulation of concepts and generalizations, they, in turn, leading to (d) testing of concepts in new situations, which is then followed by additional concrete experience. Other work on styles of learning and teaching suggest that experiential learning programs may have special benefits for certain students, for specific disciplines, for particular types of learning outcomes, and under particular conditions. "Given the utility of experiential methods in classroom as well as nonclassroom learning, in independent study as well as in group endeavors, the outcomes of a research effort in this field are likely to enrich and be applicable to the whole of higher education" (Keeton and Tate 1978b p. 99).

Bibliography

Bank A, Henerson M, Eu L 1981 *A Practical Guide to Program Planning: A Teaching Models Approach.* Teachers College Press, New York

Coleman J S 1976 Differences between experiential and classroom learning In: Keeton M T (eds.) 1976 *Experiential Learning: Rationale, Characteristics and Assessment.* Jossey-Bass, San Francisco, California

Dave R H (ed.) 1975 *Reflections on Lifelong Education and the Schools.* UIE Monograph 3. UNESCO Institute for Education, Hamburg

Dewey J 1964 *Democracy and Education: An Introduction to the Philosophy of Education,* Macmillan. New York

Jacobs F 1982 Experiential programs in practice: Lessons to be learned. In: Jacobs F, Allen R J (eds.) 1982 *Expanding the Missions of Graduate and Professional Education.* Jossey-Bass, San Francisco, California

Keeton M T, Tate P J 1978a The boom in experiential learning. In: Keeton M T, Tate P J (eds.) 1978 *Learning by Experience: What, Why, How.* Jossey-Bass, San Francisco, California

Keeton M T, Tate P J 1978b What next in experiential learning? In: Keeton M T, Tate P J (eds.) 1978 *Learning by Experience: What, Why, How.* Jossey-Bass, San Francisco, California

Kolb D A 1976 *Learning Style Inventory: Self-scoring Test and Interpretation Booklet.* McBer, New York

Maehl W H Jr 1982 The graduate tradition and experiential learning. In: Jacobs F, Allen R J (eds.) 1982 *Expanding the Missions of Graduate and Professional Education.* Jossey-Bass, San Francisco, California

Nuffield Foundation 1967 *I Do and I Understand; Beginnings; The Duck Pond; Apparatus; Animals and Plants and Others.* Wiley, New York

Owens T R, Owen S K, Druian G 1979 *Experiential Learning Programs: Synthesis of Findings and Proposed Framework*

for Future Evaluations. Northwest Regional Laboratory Education and Work Program, Portland, Oregon

Steinaker N A, Bell M R 1979 *The Experiential Taxonomy: A New Approach to Teaching and Learning.* Academic Press, New York

Process-oriented and Product-oriented Programs

E. M. Weiss and J. Regan

In the language of curriculum, the terms process oriented and product oriented are familiar and seemingly established descriptors. Both appear in the literature with two meanings. For both meanings, each term is either explicitly paired with the other, or a dichotomy can be inferred from the meanings associated with one term or the other. Because an understanding of one without the other is difficult, it seems advisable to consider them together rather than offer separate treatments.

Perhaps the widest interpretation of these terms involves the notion of curriculum as product and those activities associated with instruction (the delivery of the product) as process. If the curriculum (product) is what teachers work with then instruction (process) is how they implement the curriculum. A conception of curriculum and instruction as two distinct entities is a commonly held view within the field of curriculum. A number of curriculum theorists have conceptualized the curriculum as distinct from instructional activity. According to this view the development of curriculum materials, including the determination of objectives, choice of content, and plans for learning activities might also include the delineation of instructional strategies. However, the culmination of these endeavors is a product, be it text, module, or package. How these curriculum materials are used by teachers refers to the process of instruction. To the extent that instruction and implementation can be viewed as similar processes, a clear notion of the distinction between curriculum development and instruction is offered by Ben-Peretz (1975). She suggests that any curriculum product has curriculum potential; regardless of the intentions of curriculum developers, the materials can be implemented in numerous ways. What matters is *how* the materials are used, so that instruction may become divorced from the developer's original curricular intentions.

A more concrete way of expressing the product/process dualism is revealed in ideas surrounding the design and substance of curriculum, as embodied in differing views of the specification of learner outcomes. One view sees subject matter content as the important facet, that is, what students learn as particular products. These products may take several forms including specific competencies and knowledge of subject matter content. Most curriculum designs and developed curricular materials either advocate or include content within a subject matter context. The large-scale National Science Foundation sponsored curriculum projects in the United States during the 1950s and 1960s and the materials developed through the Nuffield Foundation in England are examples of product-oriented curricula.

By contrast, several curriculum writers have developed curriculum designs which have deliberately focused on process skills (e.g., Parker and Rubin 1966, Berman 1968). The major thesis of this approach is that there are skills that students should learn that are not only useful in learning specific competencies within the school curriculum but will be useful in nonschool related contexts, and helpful in future learning situations.

Among the types of processes that have served as organizers for curricula are problem solving, social processes, and valuing processes. Advocates of process-oriented curricula have argued the following to support their view:

(a) since the most significant goal of schooling is the development of lifelong learning skills and interests, curriculum plans should make these skills and interests central;

(b) the curriculum should be planned and organized so as to have maximum carry-over into life processes and skills; greater carry-over is likely when the curriculum design directly reflects these processes and skills;

(c) the process of valuing and other processes having a high affective element can be taught as well as essentially cognitive skills; the former should be as well represented in the curriculum as the latter. (Saylor and Alexander 1974 p. 227)

The focus on process skills has been the major organizing principle in several curriculum programs, for example, Science—A Process Approach, sponsored by the American Association for the Advancement of Science, and the values clarification materials of Raths et al. (1966). However, this number is quite small by comparison with the amount of product-oriented curricula. Process-oriented curriculum has had many adherents among those espousing progressive education and the more contemporary open-education movement. Some observers have argued that the latter stages of the progressive-education movement in the United States represented deterioration to an emphasis on process to the detriment of content, which led to the movement to reform curriculum through subject matter. Similarly, a back-to-basics emphasis appears to be a reaction to the open-education movement of the 1970s.

1. Process/Product as Means/Ends

For both levels of meaning, the process–product dualism can be viewed within the debates surrounding the distinction between means and ends. It is interesting to note that the term (and seemingly the concept) "process" has the greater holding power. It is frequently used to identify or describe "means" whereas "content," "substance," and similar terms are used as frequently as "product" in denoting "ends." It may be that the term product is more descriptive of particular ends than its sometimes global reference suggests. The usual way of viewing the dualism may be offered in the form of an analogy: process is to means as product is to ends (process: means = product: ends). With process-oriented curricula, however, there is an interesting reversal of the analogy: the means become the ends with content serving as the vehicle for bringing them about (i.e., process: ends = product: means). As has been suggested earlier, when there appears to be an imbalance in favor of process-oriented curricula, a reaction seems to be triggered which leads to more of an emphasis on product-oriented curricula, thus bringing into balance the usual means/ends distinction.

2. Criticism of Dualism

Regardless of the terms employed, the notion that product and process can be separated is criticized by those who find such dualism conceptually unsound and of little practical value. With respect to both classroom learning and curriculum design, it is argued that content (product) and process interact rather than exist as separate, self-sustaining phenomena. Efforts to operate in the context of a content–process dualism is described as analogous to attempting to separate ". . . the act of swimming from water" (Tanner and Tanner 1975 p. 3).

The fallacy of the dualism perspective has been argued for over 50 years. Although progressive education was viewed by many as almost totally concerned with process, Dewey (1938) himself criticized the idea of an activity–subject matter dichotomy, stating that it reflected an "either/or" philosophy of education. He saw as equally unproductive the promotion of knowledge to the neglect of experience, and concern with experience to the neglect of knowledge. In his view the notion of activity as an appropriate end in itself was unsound; further he saw this as a misinterpretation of his philosophy. The crux of Dewey's argument was that learning through activity depends on the interaction between the activity and content or subject matter. Additionally, he saw activity and subject matter interacting in a continuing and spiralling process in which ideas (knowledge) became the foundation for experience which leads to other ideas and experience and so

on. This process has been described as also involving interaction between and among teachers, pupils, subject matter, and environment (Tanner and Tanner 1975).

The interactive relationship of product and process is used to refute the claim that it is only possible to be concerned with, or interested in, only one or the other (Miel 1946, Smith and Keith 1971). The argument, again, is that means and ends interact in a continuing process in which means become ends and ends become means. A somewhat related concept of means–ends functioning is advanced by Joyce (1969) who claims that ends (objectives) cannot be identified in a meaningful way until the means for achieving them have been identified. Eisner (1974) sets forth a similar argument in claiming that process shapes product just as product shapes process. He views as "wrong headed" the idea of separating process from product and vice versa.

3. The Perpetuation of Process/Product Dichotomy

The view that there is a process/product dichotomy has been a pervasive part of educational thought. Among the possibilities that might account for this state of affairs are the ways that individuals view the world (both cognitively and philosophically), the temporal nature of educational activity, the influence of a certain type of evaluation, the location of individuals within the educational system, and certain properties of the educational system itself.

3.1 How Individuals View the World

One explanation of the dualism perspective seems to be found in the fact that, like beauty, process and product are "in the eye of the beholder." One's concept of person and one's personality are seen as influencing what will attract the individual's interest, and what will be emphasized in the classroom or in curriculum design. The concept of person as discussed by Hunt and Sullivan (1974) refers to how one views the learner. These authors argue that content is emphasized when learning and development are viewed from the behaviorist perspective; process is emphasized when the cognitive–developmental view is held. A different but related view of the influence of personal beliefs and preferences is offered by Smith and Keith (1971) who see process interests and concerns reflected in the preferences of individuals who want to talk about schools and curriculum in either general terms or in a global way. In contrast, an emphasis on substance is associated with those concerned with the specifics of school and of concrete classroom operations. Smith and Keith contend that neither emphasis ". . . leads to 'better' solutions," and that, in fact, ". . . each ultimately digresses into the other . . ." (Smith and Keith 1971 p. 95). What is suggested is that, regardless of mind set or preference, neither process nor product emphasis can be maintained exclusively without the other.

A person's educational philosophy is another feature of an individual's orientation that may help in understanding the dichotomy. Educational philosophy is ". . . a formulation of theoretical ideas derived from systematic consideration of the educational condition" (Tanner and Tanner 1975 p. 100). These ideas influence the way values, the ends of education, and the achievement of such ends are approached and judged. Although individuals may not be conscious of their educational philosophy, it is nonetheless present and serves to mediate decisions surrounding alternative educational conditions. Because educational philosophies differ on a number of dimensions which conflict one with another, these differences may be reflected in one's view of content, method, and their interaction. Some philosophies, for example, perennialism and essentialism, might be construed as placing major emphasis on content, while others, for example, romantic naturalism, and existentialism, place a heavy accent on the means for self-awareness and self-meaning. It would not be surprising if an extreme interpretation of a particular philosophy influenced the ways that educators approach curricular decision making.

3.2 The Temporality of Educational Activity

The temporal nature of the activities surrounding curriculum making might also influence thinking on the process/product dualism. Most people distinguish between planning and doing, between thinking and acting. A teacher plans for the next week's curriculum, and then implements those plans at the appropriate time. Similarly curriculum makers develop a curricular package as a product, which teachers then implement through an instructional process. The very clearly developed sense of temporal difference between the two activities does not allow for considering product and process in an interactive way.

3.3 Objectives-based Evaluation

The influence of the curriculum approach posited by Ralph Tyler and which found its expression as evaluation in the *Taxonomies of Educational Objectives* (Bloom et al. 1956, Krathwohl et al. 1964) cannot be discounted in a consideration of different views of curriculum. With this approach, student testing is used to determine the extent to which program objectives are being met. Clearly, the important consideration is the delineation of educational objectives. In order to determine what to test, a two-way grid is developed, representing content specifications along one dimension, and objectives formulated as behavioral processes, on the other dimension. This matrix is used as a set of specifications for developing test items. The net effect of this procedure may be the development of a mind set toward separating process from subject matter content. The process/content distinction that underlies the Taxonomies has been criticized by many, and these are summarized in Furst's (1981) review of philosophical and educational issues arising from Bloom's Taxonomy.

In spite of this major conceptual problem it is also conceded that the approach has outpaced alternative views of the curricular-making enterprise. As De Landsheere (1977) has written: "The enormous influence exercised by their (Bloom and associates) imperfect tool proves that it answered a deep and urgently felt need" (p. 105).

3.4 The Location of Individuals Within the Educational System

As previously mentioned, the concept of a dualism receives some of its thrust from the concerns and ideas about change held by individuals located in different positions within the educational enterprise. However, underlying individual perceptions of change may be a shared notion (i.e., regardless of a person's role) that change involves the implementation of "ideas" or "things" as these terms are differentiated by Shutz (1979). Change is frequently introduced to teachers in the form of new objectives, materials, and the like. As a result, it is likely that they see curriculum as involving "things" or "products." A product view of curriculum was encouraged by the externally based curriculum projects of the 1960s which lead to an emphasis on subject matter and the production of program materials. Even when teachers themselves participate in the development of objectives or guidelines, their involvement is sometimes described as focusing on the product (Smith and Keith 1971). In teachers' minds, process may be more associated with the learning processes of students, both affective and cognitive. In other words, teachers' ideas of process may be tied to so-called process skills needed by students for intellectual and social problem solving.

Hemphill's (1969) conceptualizations of the "change support process" and the "product development process," and the distinction between the two, may reflect the dualism notion as found in beliefs about change held by curriculum theorists and researchers. Shutz (1979) discusses this dualism in terms of the difference between change that focuses on people and that which focuses on product. Product and process as conceptual and practical anchors are even further separated when product is seen as rooted in educational technology. Baker (1973) argues, for example, that considering the "process of curriculum development" is inappropriate in a discussion of "technology of development" which is concerned with ". . . the production of replicable materials through relatively codified means" (p. 249). Through the eyes of educational technology, product takes on a particular meaning or designation. Shutz (1979), for example, argues that programmatic research and development (product) rooted in educational technologies is not the same as product in other curriculum design efforts, that is, efforts such as those of the large-scale subject matter-based curriculum projects. Product in the form of an instrumental product system is first and foremost a "thing" to be implemented in the view of its developer.

3.5 Characteristics of the Educational System

Finally, it is being suggested that there are characteristics of the educational system that induce feelings and actions surrounding the process/product dichotomy in curriculum work. The more centralized the system, the more likely that curriculum materials and instructional activities will be separated in terms of responsibility for deliberations regarding the delineation of objectives and the choice of materials. Although highly centralized curriculum choice making might have a net effect of moving toward teacher-proof curricula, it is likely that many teachers use materials in a personal way, that is not always following the curriculum developer's prescriptions. Where a system allows schools and teachers within schools to develop their own objectives and to choose curriculum materials, there is likely to be more opportunity for the interaction of process/product. The most favorable context for interaction occurs when teachers take responsibility for developing their own materials within an open programmatic situation; but this situation rarely occurs.

4. A Matter of Emphasis

In addition to being conceptually unsound, a strict dualism is unlikely to be revealed in practice. It has already been suggested that the notion of interaction is conceptually more viable. Further, any distinction in practice between process and product becomes one of relative emphasis in the learning situation (Hunt and Sullivan 1974) or in designing curriculum innovation (Smith and Keith 1971). An example of relative emphasis in learning situations may be found in the use of the Taxonomies for generating educational objectives. As mentioned previously, this approach leads to educational objectives that contain both subject matter and behavioral referents. However, the structures of the conceptual system (i.e., the Taxonomies) suggest an increasing emphasis on process as one moves toward higher levels of behavior. Similarly, there is more emphasis on content at the lower levels of the process dimension.

With respect to process and product distinctions in curriculum terms, perhaps Taba's (1962) observation is the most useful. She suggests that the distinction to be made is not between content and process, per se, but between process and content as concerns of curriculum design, and process and content that are the province of teaching. Educators have to consider both process and product, but realistically must either start with one,

or give relative emphasis to one over the other as they engage in their curricula-making activities.

Bibliography

Baker E L 1973 The technology of instructional development. In: Travers R M W (ed.) 1973 *Second Handbook of Research on Teaching: A Project of the American Educational Research Association.* Rand McNally, Chicago, Illinois, pp. 245–85

Ben-Peretz M 1975 The concept of curriculum potential. *Curric. Theory Network* 5: 151–59

Berman L M 1968 *New Priorities in the Curriculum.* Merrill, Columbus, Ohio

Bloom B S, Englehart M D, Furst E J, Hill W H, Krathwohl D R (eds.) 1956 *Taxonomy of Educational Objectives: The Classification of Educational Goals,* Handbook 1: *Cognitive Domain.* McKay, New York

De Landsheere V 1977 On defining educational objectives. *Eval. Educ.* 1: 73–150

Dewey J 1938 *Experience and Education.* Macmillan, New York

Eisner E W 1974 The mythology of art education. *Curric. Theory Network* 4: 2–3

Furst E J 1981 Bloom's taxonomy of educational objectives for the cognitive domain: Philosophical and educational issues. *Rev. Educ. Res.* 51: 441–53

Hemphill J K 1969 Educational development. *Urban Rev.* (Center for Urban Education) 4: 23–27

Hunt D E, Sullivan E V 1974 *Between Psychology and Education.* Dryden Press, Hinsdale, Illinois

Joyce B R 1969 *Alternative Models of Elementary Education.* Blaisdell, Waltham, Massachusetts

Krathwohl D R, Bloom B S, Masia B B 1964 *Taxonomy of Educational Objectives,* Handbook 2: *Affective Domain.* McKay, New York

Miel A 1946 *Changing the Curriculum: A Social Process.* Appleton-Century, New York

Parker J C, Rubin L J 1966 *Process as Content: Curriculum Design and the Application of Knowledge.* Rand McNally, Chicago, Illinois

Raths L E, Harmin M, Simon S B 1966 *Values and Teaching: Working with Values in the Classroom.* Merrill, Columbus, Ohio

Saylor J G, Alexander W M 1974 *Planning Curriculum for Schools.* Holt, Rinehart and Winston, New York

Shutz R E 1979 Learning about the costs and instruction about the benefits of research and development in education. *Educ. Res. AERA* 8(4): 3–7

Smith L M, Keith P M 1971 *Anatomy of Educational Innovation: An Organizational Analysis of an Elementary School.* Wiley, New York

Taba H 1962 *Curriculum Development: Theory and Practice.* Harcourt, Brace and World, New York

Tanner D, Tanner L N 1975 *Curriculum Development: Theory into Practice.* Macmillan, New York

Discovery and Inquiry Methods

B. G. Massialas

Discovery and inquiry processes can be described as methods of teaching and learning. This article will relate them to recent curriculum efforts, and specific models

and classroom applications will be presented to further illustrate the dominant characteristics of the methods. Discovery refers to a process of self-learning whereby learners generate concepts and ideas with very little teacher intervention. Inquiry refers to stages beyond discovery where learners become systematically acquainted with scientific and logical rules used to verify those ideas. In a larger framework, discovery may be thought of as a psychological construct which is based on the concern to provide necessary motivation for students to participate in the generation of new ideas related to the subject of instruction. Inquiry, on the other hand, can be thought of primarily as an intellectual construct (or a construct dealing with Bruner's "analytic thinking") which is based on the concern of enabling students to move, step by step, from hypothesis, to data collection, verification, generalization, and so on. In the complete act of thought, discovery processes are used in the initial perplexing phases of thinking whereas inquiry processes are used in the more advanced formal verification phases. In this context, some may argue that discovery as contrasted to inquiry is more process oriented rather than product oriented.

1. What is Discovery?

Studies conducted by Bruner (1960), Thelen (1960), Massialas and Zevin (1967), and others have shown that children, regardless of their age, can fruitfully engage in discovering solutions to psychological or intellectual problems. Engaging in discovery involves the opportunity (a) to make a leap into that part of the world which is unknown to them personally; (b) to project and speculate intelligently, on the basis of limited clues, on underlying principles or generalizations explaining human interactions or physical phenomena; and (c) to develop and refine heuristic devices (conceptual schemes, documentary clues, measuring devices) which can then be used in future investigations. According to Bruner, the highest state of human autonomy and perfection is achieved when children begin to find out for themselves regularities or irregularities in their physical and sociopolitical environments (Bruner 1960).

Discovery-based programs focus on powerful classroom environments using springboards that prompt children and youth to participate in their own learning. These programs assume that children need to be highly motivated through an initial psychological perplexity to engage in meaningful (not memoriter) learning.

2. Applications of Discovery Processes

Bruner tried to recapture the kind of intellectual adventure 10-year-old students experienced when asked to locate Chicago on a physical map of the central states. The map contained all the conventional geographic information—rivers and other large bodies of water, mountains, natural resources, agricultural products—but it did not include place names. A variety of suggestions and arguments were offered by the students in support of certain desirable locations for Chicago. One associated "big city" with waterways, transportation,

and accessibility; another pointed to the fact that cities are large aggregates of people who require "lots of food." The discovery of each principle of urban location served as a clue which induced further learning.

In another situation, reported by Massialas and Zevin (1967), a group of students were asked to identify the country and the approximate year that the population count had been taken on the basis of an "age pyramid," which indicated the age structure in that country. The country's name was not given. A simple pyramid was drawn with five-year intervals (beginning with 0–5 up to 80+) marked on the vertical axis and the percentage of the total population in each group on the horizontal axis. In their search to find a justifiable answer the students explored a number of hunches dealing with birth and infant mortality rates, longevity rates, distribution of sexes, and the like. Virtually all class members participated in drawing further conjectures with regard to relationships between the composition of a population and personnel resources channeled to military, industrial, agricultural, or nonproductive activities. Had the experiences been extended, the students might have been given the opportunity to speculate intelligently and to anticipate the pattern of international politics and the complicated system of alliances in the years to come. Such speculation would have been based on the assumption that population growth, pressure, and structure are factors in estimating national power. Thus learning becomes a continuous interplay of intuitive and counter intuitive or analytic processes.

3. What is Inquiry?

One of the most important treatises on inquiry or "reflective thinking" is the work of John Dewey, published around the turn of the century. Although various authors since that time have referred to inquiry by using such terms as problem solving, inductive method, critical or reflective thinking, scientific method, or conceptual learning, the essential elements of the process in many studies or school programs are those identified and elaborated on by Dewey.

According to Dewey, inquiry is the "active, persistent, and careful consideration of any belief or supposed form of knowledge in the light of the grounds that support it and the further conclusions to which it tends" (Dewey 1933 p. 9). Inquiry generally aims at the grounding of belief through the use of reason, evidence, inference, and generalization. A person is prompted to engage in reflective inquiry when faced with a "forked-road situation" or a perplexing problem that causes some discomfiture. Thus thinking moves from a state of doubt or confusion (the prereflective state) to a situation characterized by satisfaction and mastery over the initial conditions that gave rise to doubt and perplexity (the postreflective thought) which may be distinguished as follows: (a) suggestion, (b) intellectualization, (c) hypothesis, (d) reasoning, and (e) testing the hypothesis (Dewey 1933).

During the first phase (while the person is still under the immediate and direct influence of the felt difficulty) spontaneous suggestions (or wild guesses) are offered which may or may not lead to the solution of the problem. During this phase the mind leaps to possible solutions, and this may be thought of being the phase of discovery. The second phase, which entails a more systematic and rational examination of the problem at hand, results in its location and definition. At this point the person begins to grasp the various aspects of the problem. A working hypothesis is formulated during the third phase of the thinking process (which may or may not derive from the original suggestion) that places subsequent intellectual operations under control and leads to the collection and selection of additional data. The working hypothesis, in other words, serves as a search model that guides the mind towards the solution of the problem. In the fourth phase the mind relates ideas to one another and traces the logical implications of hypotheses. Here the person tries to reason out what might happen if the proposed solution were acted on. The final phase brings about a confirmation, verification, or rejection of the idea or hypothesis based on direct observation or experimentation. If the hypothesis is confirmed, the individual may generalize about its applicability to a category of problems, one of which is the problem that initiated the thought process to begin with; if the hypothesis is not confirmed the individual may proceed to modify it in the light of the newly acquired experience. In sum, in inquiry, intellectual activity is always purposeful, moves from problem to solution, and entails a series of related but operationally distinguishable cognitive tasks (e.g., hypothesizing and testing the hypotheses).

4. Applications of Inquiry Processes

Several authors of programs of instruction have used or related to Dewey's framework in the development of their own instructional model based on inquiry. Joyce and Weil (1980) have identified six such models, all related closely to each other, based on John Dewey's initial conceptualization. These models are: "group investigation" (Thelen 1960, Dewey 1933); "social inquiry" (Massialas and Cox 1966); "laboratory method" (National Training Laboratory, NTL); "jurisprudential" (Oliver and Shaver 1966); and "social simulation" (Boocock and Schild 1968). An example of these models applied to social studies inquiry is offered by Massialas and Cox and is presented in Fig. 1.

The classroom in which the model in Fig. 1 is applied is psychologically open and there is a definite sense of purpose to the discussion. Either the teacher or the student presents the problem or issue in the form of a "springboard." The goal of instruction is to clarify the problem or issue and to offer different hypotheses or positions related to it, and then to resolve conflicts that arise and to determine defensible solutions to them. The overall role of the teacher is to create conditions

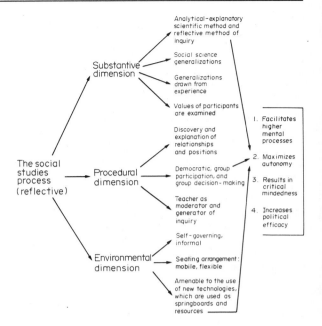

Figure 1
Social inquiry model

from which a problem may develop; to have materials and resources available that the students may tap to research the issue; and to encourage students through questions to identify additional issues, state hypotheses, and then clarify, probe, and resolve conflicting ideas and positions.

5. Summary

Discovery–inquiry learning processes, as illustrated by the forgoing examples, have been the basis for textbooks and materials developed in the United States and in many other parts of the world since the 1960s and 1970s. Due to this, the core subjects in the curriculum were radically transformed to what has become known as "new math," "new science," "new social studies," and "new English." Many of these programs were known by their initials: ISCS, Intermediate Science Curriculum Study; BSCS, Biological Science Curriculum Study; and so on. Beyond these subjects discovery–inquiry processes were used in the teaching of reading, art, home economics, music, and archeology, among others. Discovery–inquiry methods were also used with gifted students, adults, urban youth, handicapped, and preschool children, among others. The main characteristics of these programs were:

(a) a focus on ideas and concepts, rather than on conceptually unrelated pieces of information;

(b) a strong activity–participation component where students were motivated to "learn by doing";

(c) an emphasis on learning the methods of verifying and testing hypotheses in each field; and

(d) the idea that content and process are inseparable components of learning.

Unlike previously designed school programs, the major orientations of these programs were to explain the world rather than to merely describe it.

Bibliography

Boocock S S, Schild E O (eds.) 1968 *Simulation Games in Learning.* Sage, Beverly Hills, California

Bruner J S 1960 *The Process of Education.* Harvard University Press, Cambridge, Massachusetts

Dewey J 1933 *How We Think: A Restatement of the Relation of Reflective Thinking to the Education Process.* Heath, Boston, Massachusetts

Joyce B R, Weil M 1980 *Models of Teaching,* 2nd edn. Prentice-Hall, Englewood Cliffs, New Jersey

Massialas B G, Cox C B 1966 *Inquiry in Social Studies.* McGraw-Hill, New York

Massialas B G, Hurst J B 1978 *Social Studies in a New Era: The Elementary School as a Laboratory.* Longman, New York

Massialas B G, Zevin J 1967 *Creative Encounters in the Classroom: Teaching and Learning through Discovery.* Wiley, New York

Oliver D W, Shaver J P 1966 *Teaching Public Issues in the High School.* Houghton Mifflin, Boston, Massachusetts

Thelen H A 1960 *Education and the Human Quest.* Harper and Row, New York

Focus on Environment

Multicultural Education

J. A. Banks

Programs and practices designed to help improve the academic achievement of ethnic and immigrant populations and/or teach majority group students about the cultures and experiences of the ethnic minority groups within their nations are referred to as multicultural education.

Western nations, such as the United States, the United Kingdom, Canada, and Australia, are inhabited by diverse immigrant and ethnic groups, many of whom are not totally integrated into their societies. These nations have democratic ideologies that affirm the rights of all of their citizens to experience economic, political, and educational equality. However, these public ideologies and creeds are often inconsistent with the institutionalized discrimination and exclusion that ethnic and immigrant groups experience in these nations. Democratic political ideologies, rising expectations, and institutionalized discrimination led to the emergence of civil rights and ethnic revitalization movements in various Western democracies in the 1960s and 1970s.

School reform became one of the major goals of civil rights and ethnic revitalization movements in the 1960s and 1970s. Ethnic groups such as Afro–Americans in the United States, Asians in the United Kingdom, and Indians in Canada demanded that the schools teach more about their cultures and histories, eliminate racial and ethnic bias from textbooks, and implement language programs that positively reflect the language heritages and characteristics of ethnic minority groups.

In nations such as the United States (Banks 1981), the United Kingdom (Lynch 1981), Canada (Wood 1978), and Australia (Bullivant 1981) educators responded to these demands by ethnic and immigrant groups to reform the school by implementing a wide variety of programs, courses, and activities. These diverse programs and practices often have different assumptions and goals and are known by various names, including ethnic studies, multiethnic education, cross-cultural education, and bilingual–bicultural education.

The diverse programs and practices related to the education of and about ethnic groups, which are known by various names, are sometimes referred to collectively as multicultural education. However, this usage is more popular in the United States and Canada than in other nations. In the United States, multicultural education is often used in a more general way to describe educational reforms related to ethnic groups, handicapped persons, religious groups, and lower socioeconomic populations. When used in this more comprehensive way, ethnic studies and multiethnic education are distinguished from multicultural education (Banks 1981). Ethnic studies describes the humanistic and scientific study of ethnic groups; multiethnic education describes educational programs designed to provide ethnic groups with equal educational opportunities (Banks 1979).

The field of multicultural education is not only characterized by diverse concepts with vague boundaries, but also by ideological disagreements about its major assumptions and goals. Consequently, conflicting policy recommendations are often made, and research findings—related to such issues as busing to achieve racial desegregation, and the intellectual aptitude of black students—are frequently undergirded by ideological assumptions and conclusions. Research on the effects of bilingual education on student achievement is also replete with ideological conflicts and arguments.

Multicultural education theorists agree that the school should help to increase the academic achievement of ethnic minority students and to help majority-group students learn more about the cultures of ethnic minorities. However, there is little agreement about how these goals can best be achieved. Views on ethnicity and schooling range from the belief held by some that ethnicity should be an integral and salient part of the school curriculum (Novak 1977), to the belief of those who caution that too much emphasis on ethnicity in the schools might be harmful to the national culture and promote ethnic polarization (Glazer 1977). Various views on ethnicity and schooling can be described using a Weberian-type of typology. At least three major ideologies can be identified: the cultural pluralist, the assimilationist, and the multiethnic.

The cultural pluralist argues that ethnicity and ethnic identities are very important in modernized societies and that ethnicity strongly influences the behavior of ethnic group members (Sizemore 1973). The pluralist argues that modernized nations are made up of competing ethnic groups, each of which champions its economic and political interests. It is therefore essential that individuals develop commitments to their ethnic groups and the skills and attitudes needed to engage in reflective social and political reform. The pluralist believes that the curriculum should be substantially revised to that it will reflect the cognitive styles, cultures, and political and social aspirations of ethnic groups.

The assimilationist maintains that the pluralist exaggerates the cogency of ethnicity in modernized nation-states. The assimilationist believes that ethnic attachments are fleeting and temporary in an increasingly modernized world (Patterson 1977). Ethnicity, argues the assimilationist, wanes or disappears under the impact of modernization and industrialization. The primary attachments of individuals within a postindustrial society are to class, not ethnic group. The assimilationist sees the modernized nation-state as universalistic rather than as being characterized by pluralism and particularism. The assimilationist believes that the best way to promote the goals of the nation-state is to promote the full socialization of all individuals and groups into the common national and civic culture. The primary goal of the school, like other publicly supported institutions, should be to socialize individuals into the common civic culture and help them to function more successfully within it.

The multiethnic theorist believes that the cultural pluralist exaggerates the extent and cogency of ethnicity in modernized nation-states and gives insufficient consideration to the extent to which ethnic groups in modernized societies share their universal national cultures. The multiethnic theorist feels that the assimilationist underestimates the importance of ethnicity and ethnic attachments in modernized nation-states; that individuals within modernized societies are bicultural and have important commitments and attachments both to their ethnic subsocieties and to the nation-states of which they are citizens. Consequently, argues the mul-

tiethnic theorist, a primary goal of the school should be to help ethnic students develop the attitudes and skills needed to function successfully within their ethnic subsocieties and within their universal national cultures, as well as within other ethnic subsocieties.

The conceptual and ideological conflicts that characterize multicultural education are characteristic of emerging educational movements and social science disciplines. The concepts within multicultural education will acquire tighter boundaries, and the ideological conflicts within the field will lessen as it matures and becomes more institutionalized within schools.

Bibliography

Banks J A 1981 *Multiethnic Education: Theory and Practice.* Allyn and Bacon, Boston, Massachusetts

Banks J A 1984 *Teaching Strategies for Ethnic Studies*, 3rd edn. Allyn and Bacon, Boston, Massachusetts

Bullivant B M 1981 *The Pluralist Dilemma in Education: Six Case Studies.* Allen and Unwin, Sydney

Glazer N 1977 Cultural pluralism: The social aspect. In: Tumin M M, Plotch W (eds.) 1977 *Pluralism in a Democratic Society.* Praeger, New York, pp. 3–24

Husén T, Opper S (eds) 1983 *Multicultural and Multilingual Education in Immigrant Countries.* Pergamon, Oxford

Lynch J (ed.) 1981 *Teaching in the Multi-cultural School.* Ward Lock Educational, London

Novak M 1976 Cultural pluralism for individuals: A social vision. In: Tumin M M, Plotch W (eds.) 1977 *Pluralism in a Democratic Society.* Praeger, New York, pp. 25–57

Patterson O 1977 *Ethnic Chauvinism: The Reactionary Impulse.* Stein and Day, New York

Sizemore B A 1973 Shattering the melting pot myth. In: Banks J A (ed.) 1973 *Teaching Ethnic Studies: Concepts and Strategies.* National Council for the Social Studies, Washington, DC, pp. 72–101

Verma G K, Bagley C (eds.) 1979 *Race, Education, and Identity.* Macmillan, London

Wood D 1978 *Multicultural Canada: A Teachers' Guide to Ethnic Studies.* Ontario Institute for Studies in Education, Toronto, Ontario

Rural Education

U. Bude

Educational programmes for people in rural areas are generally seen as a means of compensating for and counteracting the dominance of powerful urban centres over the weaker rural community. Compared with people living in urban areas, country dwellers are in many respects at a disadvantage with regard to essential services, including access to educational institutions and quality of education. This is particularly true for the poor rural masses in developing countries. This article concentrates on their problems and the educational programmes designed to overcome this imbalance.

The term "rural education" is normally linked with

development, that is, educational programmes are meant to help people to improve their standard of living and enable them to be more self-reliant and productive. Therefore, "rural education" is defined as a structured learning facility designed with and for the population in rural areas. Learning facilities may be provided either as part of a national formal school system or they can be organized in nonformal settings.

The less centralized and formalized such programmes are, the more opportunity there is for those concerned to ensure a greater local "feel" according to their own perception of educational and training needs in rural communities.

1. The Limited Role of Education in Rural Development

The need to promote rural education stems mainly from the fact that the majority of programmes for the improvement of rural areas gave a disproportionately high emphasis to an increase in agricultural production. Such approaches favoured the members of the rural "establishment", rather than the masses of small peasants and tenant farmers who were producing at subsistence level. The role of education in this context was either overemphasized or neglected.

A critical glance at the typical learning opportunities available to an average rural community in developing countries shows that the various ways of providing basic education rarely suit the development needs of rural communities. To achieve social and economic change in rural areas, education is normally provided via the existing formal educational system, mainly the primary school, or by nonformal education programmes.

The efforts of such educational programmes have produced only limited results. Most formal educational systems in Third World countries have rarely been adapted to the rural environment, with the result that school has become counterproductive to rural development. Rural development takes place largely without the intervention of formalized schooling. Where farmers have had access to markets and have benefited from extension services they have increased their income from agriculture considerably, without any education programmes. More important than formal schooling is the experience a farmer has outside his village, for example, as a migrant worker or soldier.

The most recent comparative studies indicate that a certain amount of general education is needed in order to produce higher yields of agricultural crops. Whatever kind of education is provided in rural areas, it is said to help promote development, making people more receptive to innovations and new ideas (Lockheed et al. 1980). Nevertheless, education is only one of the ingredients of rural development. Applied in isolation, education can even show negative effects, in particular by adding to the problems of the rural exodus.

Mosher has convincingly shown that education plays an important but minor role in the development process (Mosher 1971). He distinguishes between essentials for development and accelerators of this process. The five essentials include:

(a) incentives, via favourable prices for agricultural products;

(b) access to markets and establishments of marketing organizations;

(c) availability of transport facilities;

(d) supply of agricultural inputs and extension services;

(e) agricultural research.

Only if these essentials are available to stimulate rural development do other factors, the so-called accel-erators, gain in importance; and amongst these accelerators is education. In this model, education clearly has a complementary function. Even illiterate peasants will obtain higher yields if the essential factors for development are available. As farming becomes more sophisticated and involves a higher level of investment, literacy skills and knowledge of more complicated transactions are increasingly important and the educational component gains in value. Withdrawal from a subsistence economy and integration into a national or international market has to be accompanied by provision of relevant educational programmes so that people can handle their own affairs independently, without domination from outside institutions or people.

In the following section some of the attempts to provide a relevant education for rural communities beyond a mere increase in productivity are analysed as well as the reasons for their comparative failure.

2. Rural Primary Schools

Primary schools provide education for children and young persons within the framework of a national curriculum, sometimes allowing for local or regional variations and modifications. They are by far the most widespread educational institution catering for the rural population, and can be found even in isolated or remote areas. Although the general situation in most of these schools in developing countries is more frustrating than stimulating, the school as an institution for learning the basic skills of reading, writing, and arithmetic seems to have established its place in society, only questioned or shunned by those groups in rural areas who are virtually cut off from communication with the outside world or where indigenous educational institutions, such as the koranic school, are still very much valued.

Whereas primary school is seen by the great majority of its rural clientele as the first step on the educational ladder leading to the qualifications and certificates necessary to secure a higher income—earning position in society, preferably outside agriculture, educational planners would like to see the school providing a more relevant education that enables rural people to improve their daily life. The primary school is regarded as an important starting point for laying the foundations for future learning capacities encouraging self-reliant rural development. Not only should children in rural areas receive a general education based on the experience and opportunities offered by their environment, but they should also be exposed to basic modes of scientific thinking. Such an expanded general education includes agricultural and manual activities. However, this is less for purposes of productivity than for pedagogical reasons. Learning in an applied way emphasizes such skills as observation, measuring, drawing conclusions, and so on. These learning experiences can be enriched and guided if centres at the regional or divisional level can be established for feedback purposes (see Fig. 1).

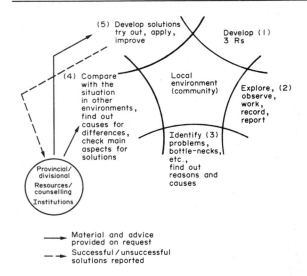

(5) Develop solutions try out, apply, improve

Develop (1) 3 Rs

(4) Compare with the situation in other environments, find out causes for differences, check main aspects for solutions

Local environment (community)

Explore, (2) observe, work, record, report

Provincial/ divisional Resources/ counselling Institutions

Identify (3) problems, bottle-necks, etc., find out reasons and causes

——→ Material and advice provided on request

- - → Successful / unsuccessful solutions reported

Figure 1
Education for rural development

The training of practical vocational skills is normally not part of the primary school curriculum.

In most countries the objectives of rural education programmes pursued in primary schools can be identified as follows:

(a) development of the "3 Rs" (reading, writing, and arithmetic) to help children to cope more effectively with their environment;

(b) development of the intellectual capacity of children and their self-confidence;

(c) development of the skills and knowledge that lead children to become productive and useful members of society;

(d) providing a sound educational foundation to ensure the continuation of learning after school;

(e) reinforcement of the culture and ideology of the particular country;

(f) improving the chances of children from rural areas with regard to equality of opportunity within the national educational system.

In order to make primary education more relevant and to counteract rural–urban migration (seen partly as a result of previous primary school systems based on those of industrialized countries), some developing countries have tried to reform their imported educational systems by creating new curriculum content and structures based on the problems and needs of their own rural population. "Ruralization" and "vocationalization" have been the slogans characterizing such reform attempts.

Ruralization was meant to provide that kind of formal education that would result in immediate improvements for rural areas, by:

(a) creating or reawakening a sense of identity amongst the population;

(b) bridging the social and economic gap between the rural masses and the small group of urban-oriented elites;

(c) increasing the practical and economic relevance of schooling (Fremerey 1981).

The curriculum for primary schools in rural areas was heavily infused with references to agriculture, since it was hoped that the emphasis on rural problems in a predominantly agricultural environment would help to keep young people in the countryside.

Unfortunately, the ruralized school was not in a position to provide job opportunities after school, and possibilities for self-employment proved to be marginal. The monetary reward of farming, rather than the ruralized school curriculum, determines the future development of rural areas, as does the capacity of farming to absorb qualified labour. Ruralized primary schools soon developed into second-choice programmes for the underprivileged majority, whereas at the same time the selective academically oriented formal primary school system continued at the national level. Under such circumstances the existing socioeconomic disparities tend to deepen further, with the result that parents in rural areas strenuously reject such reforms (see the example of Upper Volta, Ahmed and Coombs 1975).

Since colonial days there have been attempts to include agriculture into the curriculum of primary schools throughout the developing world. After political independence, rural science gained in importance as a primary school subject, and was very often seen as the panacea for all educational problems, or at least as a means of fostering the development of rural areas. Agricultural education was regarded as part of general education, although very closely related to the life of the local community. Again, the results of teaching agriculture in primary schools are hardly convincing and cannot be said to have contributed substantially to the solution of the main problems of rural areas. Recent research shows that rural science at primary school level is ill suited to contribute to the agricultural development of local communities. The less a rural community is equipped with infrastructure, the worse is the performance of a school in the realm of agriculture, since the school is not in a position to provide sufficient impetus for reform. In better developed rural areas, the school adapts itself to the higher standards of agriculture prevailing in the locality (Bude 1981). There are always exceptions, and it is still possible to find schools with stimulating school farms, devoted teachers, and pupils who benefit from rural science instruction. The more typical situation, however, is one which can be characterized in the following ways:

(a) although rural science has had a place in primary schools in rural areas since colonial days, it is primarily based on the concepts of "modern" farming which is mainly oriented towards maximizing yields;

(b) rural science is rarely relevant enough to the specific local agricultural conditions;

(c) the modern farming methods taught in school are applied for ideological rather than pragmatic reasons ("what is modern must be good");

(d) the knowledge and skills imparted in rural science at school are still considered to be in contrast to traditional farming methods used by the local farmer which must be abolished.

Rural science teaching in primary schools may enable rural communities in part to meet their basic learning needs. It is theoretically possible to deal with agricultural problems in school and devise solutions, but in practice such attempts are seldom to be found, since the circumstantial factors which ultimately permit effective teaching and training do not prevail.

3. Nonformal Education Programmes

Even if rural primary education becomes more relevant to rural life, it must be borne in mind that the great majority of the children of the most deprived rural families are the last to enter a school and normally the first to drop out. Learning facilities outside the formal school system for people in rural areas have tried to bring the relevant skills and knowledge to rural dwellers to improve their living conditions. Initiatives in rural development (whether their focus is on agricultural productivity, rural industry, health, women's programmes, etc.) always have some educational component, whereby different kinds of knowledge, information, and skills must be provided to different groups to ensure the success of such programmes.

Nonformal education programmes for rural areas have been implemented over the last few decades throughout Third World countries. The variety of activities include literacy campaigns, training programmes for farmers, community development activities, vocational training for young persons, and so on. Foreign donors have usually provided the finance and the conceptual ideas. An intensive stocktaking of nonformal programmes in rural areas over recent years has shown that " . . . taken as a whole, these activities have served useful efficacy and impact and, like formal schools, have frequently fallen far short of initial hopes and expectations" (Coombs 1975 p. 14).

Nonformal educational programmes and projects have had a certain degree of impact on the overall educational system in many countries. Despite the fact that most of these programmes are small in size and only a few have a nationwide coverage, they must be

regarded as useful experiments provoking further reflection on the role of education for rural areas.

4. Future Directions for Rural Education

The main characteristics of rural education programmes are insufficient resources and a low position on national lists of priorities. Limited success has been achieved only where programmes were supported at the political level, for example, in India in Ghandhi's time and in Cuba. Although the formal school system in rural areas has serious limitations with respect to rural development, parents still prefer even an irrelevant academic schooling for their children as long as it allows the hope of a statistical chance of gaining a secure and well-paid job in the modern sector of society, whereas more development-oriented curricula in primary schools are seen only as an attempt to improve marginally what children already know or to make them aware of problems they cannot solve alone. On the other hand nonformal educational programmes cannot substitute for the lack of opportunity to gain access to upper-level schooling and future elite positions.

Education in the broadest sense is an essential prerequisite for meeting the most pressing needs of the rural poor in Third World countries. Any programme that intends to improve the living conditions of rural families is an educational programme. What is needed is a flexible network of diverse learning facilities for different rural population groups according to local requirements. But education is only one important ingredient in rural development. In the absence of other essential inputs, the most relevant rural education programmes are doomed to failure.

Bibliography

Ahmed M, Coombs P H 1975 *Education for Rural Development: Case Studies for Planners.* Praeger, New York
Bude U 1985 *Primary Schools, Local Community and Development in Africa.* Nomos, Baden-Baden
Coombs P H 1975 *Education for Rural Development: Some Implications for Planning. A Contribution to the IIEP Seminar on the Planning Problems in Rural Education, 13–17 Oct 1975.* IIEP/S36/9A. UNESCO, Paris
Foster P, Sheffield J 1973 *The World Year Book of Education 1974: Education and Rural Development.* Evans, London
Fremerey M 1981 *The Motivator Concept. Thoughts on a "Small Strategy" for Rural Development in the Third World.* Deutsches Institut für Internationale Pädagogische Forschung, Frankfurt/Main
Higgs J, Mbithi P 1977 *Learning and Living. Education for Rural Families in Developing Countries.* Food and Agricultural Organization (FAO), Rome
Lockheed M, Jamison D, Lau L 1980 Farmer education and farm efficiency: A survey. *Econ. Dev. Cult. Change* 28
Mosher A 1971 *To Create a Modern Agriculture: Organization and Planning.* The Agriculture Development Council, New York
Nash R 1980 *Schooling in Rural Societies.* Methuen, London

Urban Education: Educational Programs

J. A. Banks

Geographers use the term "urban" to describe the central city, its suburbs, satellite cities, and the entire metropolitan region. However, in the educational literature, urban education refers to the issues and problems related to schooling in central cities. Schools that are located in central cities have a number of problems and characteristics that are associated with their inner-city locations and with the unique characteristics of their students and teachers.

A disproportionate number of poor and minority-group children attend inner-city urban schools. In the United States, poor youths and ethnic minority youths make up the majority of the student populations in a number of large cities, including Chicago, Detroit, and Washington, DC. As central city residents attain middle- and upper-class status, they tend to move from the central city to the surrounding suburban areas. This dispersal pattern has several negative effects on inner-city schools. As middle-class groups leave the city and move to the suburbs, the taxes available for the support of local schools become increasingly smaller. Also, when middle-class populations desert inner-city schools, cultural conflict between teachers and students intensifies. Most teachers identify with middle-class values and attitudes; many poor city students do not.

The desertion of inner-city schools by middle-class populations also intensifies racial and ethnic segregation. Majority ethnic groups are usually over-represented in the middle and upper classes. Consequently, urban schools become disproportionately populated by minority groups when middle-class populations move from the city to the suburbs. Many middle-class parents who remain in the city send their children to independent, privately financed schools rather than to schools that are publicly funded. This is true for both minority and majority group parents.

Inner-city urban schools also experience other complex problems. Because they are populated disproportionately by poor youths, many of the problems of inner-city communities are mirrored in the schools. Inner-city urban schools are characterized by chronic dropout rates of students, acute discipline problems, funds inadequate to support many educational innovations, teachers who have less experience than suburban teachers, and strong teachers' unions that make it difficult to increase the professionalism of teachers. In recent years in the United States, inner-city schools have been involved in political issues and problems related to school desegregation mandated by the courts. Inner-city schools are usually located in areas of high unemployment. Consequently, the students often see few incentives for staying in school. The problems of inner-city urban schools, such as discipline and strong unionism, also exist in suburban schools, but these problems are usually more pronounced in inner-city schools.

Students who attend inner-city urban schools do not achieve nearly as well as suburban students in basic subjects such as reading, mathematics, and writing. There is consensus among educational researchers on this point; however, they disagree about the reason that this is the case. Discussions about the reasons for the lower academic achievement of inner-city students has focused on ways to bring about educational equity for all students. There is little consensus among educational theorists and researchers about how educational equity should be defined or how it can best be attained.

When educational equity is defined in terms of input variables, equity is attained when input variables such as expenditure per pupil, teachers' salaries, and supplies are equal for different social class and ethnic populations. However, Coleman (1969) popularized the output concept of equality. When educational equity is defined in terms of output rather than input variables, equity is attained only when the leading indicators of educational achievement are roughly equal for students from different social classes and ethnic groups.

Since the 1960s, several theories have emerged that are designed to explain the limited achievement of minority youths and to help them achieve at higher levels, including the genetic theory, popularized by Jensen (1969), and the revisionist theory (Bowles and Gintis 1976, Katz 1975). Jensen maintains that heredity severely limits the ability of black youths to think conceptually. The revisionists and researchers such as Jencks et al. (1972) point out that the school is only one of the important educational institutions in society and that it is limited in what it can achieve. The genetic and revisionist theories have probably had less impact on school reform than the cultural deprivation, cultural difference, and integrationist theories.

Cultural deprivation was one of the first theories concerned with the education of lower-class students to emerge in the 1960s. Bernstein (1964) and Reissman (1962) were two of its major architects. Cultural deprivation theorists assume that lower-class youths do not achieve highly academically because of the debilitating effects of poverty and the intellectual and cultural deficits that these students experience during their first years of life. These theorists maintain that a major goal of school programs for "culturally deprived" students is to provide them with cultural and other experiences that will compensate for their cognitive and intellectual deficits.

The cultural difference theorists, notably Valentine (1968) and Baratz and Baratz (1970), reject the arguments of the cultural deprivationists. They maintain that ethnic minority and poor youths have strong, rich, and diverse cultures. These cultures, argue the cultural difference theorists, consist of languages and dialects that are rich and elaborate, and of values, behavioral styles, and perspectives that can enrich the lives of all students. Minority youths, argue these theorists, fail to achieve highly in school not because they have deprived or deficit cultures but because they have cultures that are different from the school's middle-class culture. To help poor and minority youths achieve at higher levels, the school must respect, legitimize, and use the cultures of these students in the schooling process.

Another group of social scientists (Green 1977) argues that the most effective way to help poor and minority youths to achieve academically is to place them in higher status, racially integrated schools. The integrationists maintain that the social class and racial composition of the schools are the most important correlates of academic achievement for poor and minority-group students. The integrationists' strategy for improving the education of urban youths has evoked acid controversy. Coleman et al. (1975) strongly challenged the integrationists' theory by arguing that school desegregation drives whites from the cities, resulting in the resegregation of city schools. Evidence has been presented which suggests that desegregated schools often have negative effects on minority youths.

In nations such as the United Kingdom (Lynch 1981, Stone 1981), the United States, Canada (Wolfgang 1975), and Australia (Bullivant 1981), immigrant groups often settle in inner-city areas. Consequently, the problems of educating students in urban areas are often highly related to those of educating students who are culturally different. Immigrant students often speak languages that differ from those spoken by the majority groups in their new nations and frequently have values that conflict, sometimes strikingly, with those of the peoples in their host societies. Language and value conflicts often result in confrontations, discrimination, and misunderstandings in urban schools. Different nations have used myriad approaches to solve the educational problems of immigrant youths who are highly concentrated in inner-city areas. The cultural deprivation, cultural difference, and integrationist theories are often reflected in the educational policies shaped in different nations.

Different models and educational experiments must continue before an effective solution to the problems of educating inner-city populations will be developed. The problems of inner-city urban schools bespeak the problems of schools in the suburbs. Thus, if educators are successful in solving the problems of inner-city students, they will contribute greatly to the improvement of the education of all youths.

Bibliography

Baratz S S, Baratz J C 1970 Early childhood intervention: The social science base of institutional racism. *Harvard Educ. Rev.* 40: 29–50

Bernstein B 1964 Elaborated and restricted codes: Their social origins and some consequences. *Am. Anthrop.* 66(6,2): 55–70

Bowles S, Gintis H 1976 *Schooling in Capitalist America: Educational Reform and the Contradictions of Economic Life.* Basic Books, New York

Bullivant B M 1981 *The Pluralist Dilemma in Education: Six Case Studies.* Allen and Unwin, Sydney

Coleman J S 1969 The concept of equality in educational opportunity. *Equal Educational Opportunity.* Harvard University Press, Cambridge, Massachusetts

Coleman J S, Kelley S D, Moore J A 1975 Recent trends in school integration. Paper presented at the annual meeting of the American Educational Research Association, Washington, DC, April, 1975

Green R L 1977 *The Urban Challenge: Poverty and Race.* Follett, Chicago, Illinois

Jencks C et al. 1972 *Inequality: A Reassessment of the Effect of Family and Schooling in America.* Basic Books, New York

Jensen A R 1969 How much can we boost IQ and scholastic achievement? *Harvard Educ. Rev.* 39: 1–123

Katz M B 1975 *Class, Bureaucracy, and Schools: The Illusion of Educational Change in America,* expanded edn. Praeger, New York

Lynch J (ed.) 1981 *Teaching in the Multi-cultural School.* Ward Lock Educational, London

Reissman F 1962 *The Culturally Deprived Child.* Harper, New York

Stone M 1981 *The Education of the Black Child in Britain: The Myth of Multiracial Education.* Collins, Glasgow

Valentine C A 1968 *Culture and Poverty: Critique and Counterproposals.* University of Chicago Press, Chicago, Illinois

Wolfgang A (ed.) 1975 *Education of Immigrant Students: Issues and Answers.* Ontario Institute for Studies in Education, Toronto, Ontario

Nongraded Curriculum

D. M. Purdom

A nongraded approach to the curriculum refers to the removal of grade level barriers in order that individuals can experience continuous progress through the school's program and develop their abilities to the maximum. The approach is part of a concept and philosophy of schooling which is based upon knowledge about individual differences and a value for individuality. In attempting to implement nongradedness, much confusion has resulted about the nature of a nongraded curriculum and nongraded education. An examination of the development of the concept and its theoretical bases helps to illuminate differences in approaches and to understand problems with research findings.

1. The Nongraded Movement

The term "nongraded" was created by educators in the United States to describe a plan of schooling proposed as an alternative to the graded system of education. The nongraded plan has roots in the Jenaplan found in the Federal Republic of Germany and the Netherlands and can be traced to the ideas expressed by the German educator, Peter Petersen, in the early 1900s (Horney et al. 1970 pp. 580–83).

Nongrading emerged in the United States as a response to a number of developments occurring at the turn of the twentieth century. Humanistic thinking prevalent in Europe during the late 1800s influenced American educators to accept a broader range of purposes than those served by the graded schools. Research into human growth and development provided new insights into the nature and extent of individual differences. Empirical evidence revealed negative effects of refusing to promote students who failed to meet grade-level standards of the graded system. These developments led American educators to challenge the graded plan of schooling they had established in the mid-1800s (Goodlad and Anderson 1987 pp. 49–52).

An innovative nongraded plan on schooling was first attempted in the United States in 1934; but the acceptance of a plan which involved doing away with grade levels was slow. Not until the mid- and late-1950s did many school systems in the United States begin to change. Nongrading was mostly implemented in elementary schools, with a nongraded primary unit replacing the first three grades of schooling. Some elementary schools also decided not to grade their intermediate levels (grades 4, 5, and 6) but only a few secondary schools attempted to establish nongraded programs (National Education Association 1965). During the 1960s there were increased efforts to implement nongraded plans, but since the 1970s interest in nongrading has waned in the United States. At present, the concept is kept alive through its application in models of individualized instruction for special education students, materials designed for individualized instruction, and such plans as Individually Guided Education (IGE). An assessment of the current status of nongrading is presented in the introduction of the 1987 edition of *The Nongraded Elementary School* (Goodlad and Anderson 1987 pp. ix–xLviii).

Educators in other countries of the world have also sought to implement the concept of nongrading. Pockets of interests can be found in the Netherlands, the Federal Republic of Germany, and Italy. A strong commitment to nongrading is especially evident in those British primary schools utilizing an open education approach with multiage family grouping patterns (Rogers 1970). In Canada, Australia, and New Zealand instances can be found of nongraded primary education.

2. Theoretical Bases of Nongradedness

The primary aim of a nongraded plan is to provide for the maximum development of each student's talents and abilities. Inherent in this aim are the basic values of respect for the worth and dignity of every individual, equality of opportunity, encouragement of variability among humans, and the development of self-actualizing individuals. These values in combination with certain assumptions regarding learners, the process of learning, individual differences, and the nature of knowledge provide the theoretical framework for nongraded schools and a nongraded approach to the curriculum (Goodlad 1970).

Learning is assumed to be personal and relative to the individual learner, with regard to what is to be learned as well as when it is learned. A substantial body of knowledge documents the variability among human beings. Another assumption is that humans best develop their potentialities when they experience success and are provided with a secure and supportive environment. A readiness to learn and successful learning experiences are basic principles of nongraded education.

Since knowledge is socially constructed and because sections of knowledge can be related, major organizing elements can be identified. Acquisition of the key concepts, skills, and values which form the basic structure of content areas is a goal of nongraded schools that requires years to achieve; nongraded schools must be organized to facilitate continual and cumulative acquisition of major curricular elements over many years of schooling.

Since the assumptions and values underlying nongradedness are very general and only suggestive, translating them into practice often results in schools which are quite different in specific operational procedures.

3. Approaches to Nongrading

Early attempts to put the concept and philosophy of nongrading into operation were aimed at changing the vertical pattern of school organization. Progression through school was changed from a system based on grade levels to one in which students could move in a continuous unbroken manner over several years of schooling. Once grade levels were removed, the common tendency was for practitioners to identify a series of specific topics or skills and group them into levels. The levels were sequentially arranged and served as standards which students were to master at their own rates of learning. Individually assessing students in relation to these levels of achievements and then prescribing in terms of diagnostic results characterizes the nongraded plan implemented in most American schools (Institute for Development of Educational Activities 1970 pp. 8–22).

However, the levels approach is rejected by leading theoreticians on nongraded education. According to these theorists, a truly nongraded school is characterized by a longitudinal view of curriculum (Goodlad and Anderson 1987 pp. 79–89). Over a span of years, the curriculum provides opportunities for exploring fundamental ideas within content areas in more complex ways. Particular topics and specific skills serve only as vehicles through which broad concepts, skills, relationships, and values are developed. Specifying the broad bases of the curriculum permits flexibility in dealing with diverse student interests and maturity levels. Not only is curriculum viewed as the development of basic ideas from separate content areas, but as an integration of knowledge and skill from different content areas as well. A spiral curriculum that broadens and deepens the structure of knowledge, and enables learners to acquire comprehensive insights, is the essence of a nongraded curriculum.

4. Research and Nongrading

Most studies related to nongrading were conducted in the United States and Canada during the 1960s and 1970s. From a review of these studies, three major areas of inquiry can be discerned: inquiry aimed at understanding the concept; investigations focused on implementing nongrading; and research designed to determine the effectiveness of nongraded programs.

A variety of conceptual models of the nongraded school have been produced in an attempt to clarify the concept. The models usually consist of statements of principles which describe various aspects of schooling, for example goals, curriculum, instruction, organization, and evaluation (Institute for Development of Educational Activities 1970).

Descriptive studies of schools which have implemented nongraded plans reveal practices so diverse that it is difficult to know what exists in schools labeled as nongraded. Frequently nongraded schools have been found to be very similar to graded schools in their instructional methods (McLoughlin 1972 p. 203). When practices of nongraded schools are compared to conceptual models and principles of nongrading, most researchers and theoreticians conclude that few if any truly nongraded schools exist.

Numerous experimental studies have been conducted to determine whether nongraded programs are more effective than graded schools in promoting the academic, social, and emotional development of students. Findings from such studies are so mixed that no clear cut conclusions can be drawn (McLoughlin 1972). Failure to define clearly the nature of the nongraded program being evaluated and to describe and control other variables of a school's operation, in addition to the organizational plan are common methodological problems. However, the major problem with the research that has been conducted is the use of criteria and procedures based on assumptions of the graded school to measure the success of nongraded programs (Goodlad and Anderson 1987 pp. 213–19). For example, students in nongraded schools are usually evaluated with tests designed to assess the mastery of content designated for particular grade levels, although in a nongraded classroom the teacher uses content from many grades. What is needed are studies which determine the success of nongraded schools on the basis of the theoretical assumptions upon which they are founded.

Bibliography

Brown B F 1965 *The Appropriate Placement School: A Sophisticated Nongraded Curriculum.* Parker, New York

Goodlad J I 1970 The nongraded school. *Nat. Elem. Prin.* 50(1): 24–29

Goodlad J I, Anderson R H 1987 *The Nongraded Elementary School,* rev. edn. Teachers College Press, New York

Horney W, Ruppert J P, Schultze W (eds.) 1970 *Pädagogisches Lexikon,* Vol. 2. Bertelsmann Verlag, Gütersloh

Institute for Development of Educational Activities (IDEA) 1970 *Models for Nongrading Schools.* IDEA, Dayton, Ohio

McLoughlin W P 1972 The effectiveness of the nongraded school. *Int. Rev. Educ.* 18: 194–211

National Education Association 1965 Nongraded school organization. *NEA Res. Bull.* 43(3): 93–95

Rogers V R (ed.) 1970 *Teaching in the British Primary School.* Macmillan, New York

National Systems of Education

National Curriculum Histories: An Overview

W. H. Schubert

Curriculum history is a relatively new scholarly enterprise or topic of inquiry throughout the world. Clearly, the general history of education has been part of scholarly discourse for a century or so, and within it one finds documented aspects of curriculum policy, practice, and theory of the past. However, the systematic construction of curriculum history is largely a development that began in the late 1970s and continues to evolve. While a few earlier works are acknowledged as curriculum history (e.g., Cremin 1961, Seguel 1966), the writings on the topic of curriculum history in the 1970s were usually calls to overcome "ahistoricism." Ahistoricism, or the tendency to construct curricular policies and practices without recourse to precedent, was seen by numerous curriculum scholars in the United States as a major contributor to inadequate innovation, bandwagonism, adherence to tradition for its own sake, and the use of curriculum to serve political and economic ends having dubious educational value. In 1977, the Society for the Study of Curriculum History (SSCH) was founded in the United States. Its founders hoped that such a society might in some small way contribute to greater historical awareness among all who engage in curriculum work. The variety of papers of the SSCH (see Kridel 1989) symbolizes increased awareness of the value of curriculum history among curriculum scholars throughout the world.

The fact that curriculum history has emerged in a more full-blown way in the United States and United Kingdom is probably due to the fact that curriculum studies first emerged as a specialized subfield of education in these two locations (see Schubert 1980, Tanner and Tanner 1980, Connell 1980, Kliebard 1986, Kridel 1989, Goodson 1985). While it can be argued quite defensibly that curriculum matters have been part of the long record of discourse on philosophy, politics, education, and family life since time immemorial, curriculum history as a subdivision of curriculum studies is a much more specialized and recent area. It pertains (as borne out in the articles that follow) to the systematic and interpretive study of that which is taught and learned in schools, to the analysis of the policy documents designed to influence that which is taught in schools,

and to a lesser extent to the debates about theory and research that lie behind policy and practice.

Through the articles presented here it is evident that curriculum history is, in its beginnings, a subset of educational history that focuses on the subject matter or content that is designed for, taught in, and/or learned in schools. Treatments provided give rise to certain topical concerns: (a) similarities and differences among patterns of national curriculum histories; (b) characteristics of curriculum histories by groupings of educational systems; (c) factors affecting curriculum history; and (d) similarities and differences in the structure of the articles describing history in individual countries. Each of these topics is examined briefly below, with the realization that in an embryonic field such as curriculum history such examination yields more questions than answers.

1. Patterns of National Curriculum Histories

It would be a mistake to suggest a set of developmental stages for curriculum history, even though parallel episodes seem to exist among certain countries. Clearly, one can perceive parallels in Western European countries (e.g., Federal Republic of Germany, France, Spain, Sweden) that appear to exhibit stage-wise development; nevertheless, these similarities are more likely due to the common political, cultural, and economic history faced during the growth of these countries. Influenced by similarities in religious history, feudal organization, striving for nationhood, and so on, educational systems reflected these historical developments. An important question deals with the tendency of many countries to favor a highly centralized curriculum and others to become more decentralized. This phenomenon is explored in the United States context by several authors (see Klein 1991). It remains for future analysis to determine why centralized control of schools pervades many capitalist countries, socialist countries, and developing countries of the Third World alike. Is control of the growth of future generations a common value held by differing ideological orientations?

2. Characteristics of Groups of Countries

One wonders about the common characteristics of groups of countries often classified together (e.g., the capitalistic West, socialist or communist countries, and developing nations). Surely, one can see the formative impact of different phases of communist revolutions (cultural and/or militaristic) on the Soviet Union, the People's Republic of China, Hungary, and so on, but other factors of history, geography, economics, and politics give idiosyncratic character to each country. Moreover, regions and specific locations within nations further an ideographic or situational character to curriculum history.

A question emerges about the appropriateness of a country-oriented organization of curriculum history. Such an organization may mask insights about regions that cut across borders, it may prevent perception of a global image of curriculum history, and it may prevent realization of local differences within nations that exceed differences between nations. No easy alternative, however, is available for the organization of worldwide perspective on curriculum history. It is certain that the collection presented here of histories of 12 individual nations and two constellations of nations (socialist and Third World) is a greater step than ever before made toward a globally comprehensive presentation of curriculum history.

3. Factors Affecting Curriculum History

The several histories presented here each corroborate the vast influence of social, political, economic, and cultural factors on curriculum that emerges in a given historical period and/or geographic locale. It is increasingly clear, too, that recent years have brought an international, even global, set of influences. Third World countries, for example, are not only influenced by internal matters and post-colonial strivings for identity, survival, and acceptance, they are pressured from outside by larger economic and political alliances that transcend national boundaries. Thus, a question emerges about how the influence of such forces affects curriculum in all countries. The growing power of economic and political alliances alters the character of other factors of influence that have long been part of curriculum literature, such as government policy, political parties, interest groups, religious groups, universities, other centers of learning and knowledge production, unions, teachers, administrators, students, legislatures, courts, and publishers.

4. The Structure of Articles on Curriculum History

It is, of course, difficult to determine whether the main differences among articles on curriculum history depend more on the nature of the country or region written about or on the perspective and perception of the historian who authored an article. What is quite obvious in the articles that follow is that attention is given to three aspects of curriculum history: policy, practice, and foundational ideas. Ideas and theoretical discourse that relate to policy and practice are treated rather extensively in articles on the United States, the United Kingdom, and the Federal Republic of Germany. The remainder of articles focus mainly on key policy initiatives and transformations of practice. Such policy and practice presumably were influenced by some level of debate on curriculum alternatives and assumptions behind them. To what extent were policies and practices of the past influenced by defensible debate and informed by scholarship? What makes curriculum debate defensible? A next major phase of historical curriculum scholarship should be to develop a structure of discourse that addresses the ideas and level of theory and research that informs the debate resulting in policy and practice. This is no mean task, indeed, but it is a laudable goal for future work in curriculum history. The articles that follow make significant progress toward this end.

Bibliography

Connell W F 1980 *A History of Education in the Twentieth Century World.* Teachers College Press and the Curriculum Development Center of Australia, New York and Canberra

Cremin L A 1961 *The Transformation of the School.* Knopf, New York

Goodson I (ed.) 1985 *Social Histories of the Secondary Curriculum.* Falmer, London

Klein M F (ed.) 1991 *Curriculum Issues in Legislating and Centralizing the Curriculum.* State University of New York Press, Albany, New York

Kliebard H M 1986 *The Struggle for the American Curriculum: 1893–1958.* Routledge and Kegan Paul, Boston, Massachusetts

Kridel C (ed.) 1989 *Curriculum History.* University Press of America and the Society for the Study of Curriculum History, Lanham, Maryland

Schubert W H 1980 *Curriculum Books: The First Eighty Years.* University Press of America, Lanham, Maryland

Seguel M L 1966 *The Curriculum Field: Its Formative Years.* Teachers College Press, New York

Tanner D, Tanner L N 1980 *Curriculum Development: Theory into Practice.* Macmillan, New York

Australia

D. Cohen

Upon federation in 1901, the Australian Constitution reserved education—and therefore curriculum—as a state responsibility. Previously, the six colonial parliaments had each adopted Education Acts requiring free and compulsory education.

To provide equality of opportunity and access to

schooling for all children (compulsory in general from ages 6 to 16), each of the six states and two territories established a centralized education department.

1. Procedures for Curriculum Development

The education departments have always played crucial roles in curriculum activities. The procedures for curriculum development differ markedly at primary (elementary) from those at secondary (high) school levels. Likewise, there are pronounced interstate differences. However, a generalized Australian perspective must be presented here.

Historically, at primary-school level, senior administrators within the departments established state curriculum committees on an ad hoc basis. Membership generally included school principals, teachers, and inspectors. Until at least the mid-1960s, these committees produced bound copies of new syllabi intended to last a decade or more. These provided the homogenized content, sequences, and duration of statewide curriculum prescriptions. Since the early 1970s, committee membership has been widened to include representatives of college lecturers, teacher federations, subject associations, and parents.

At secondary-school level, state curriculum committees are usually expanded to include academics from subject disciplines, representatives of nongovernment schools and sometimes of business or industry. Especially through the backwash effects of their entry requirements, universities have continued to dominate secondary curricula.

Following the Second World War, each state and territory education department established some form of curriculum branch, and their roles have been strengthened since the mid-1960s. The establishment of these branches heralded professional recognition of specialist curriculum personnel and the replacement of one-person or part-time curriculum committees by tenured full-time personnel. These branches have developed curriculum documents which specify state requirements or guidelines and indicate whatever flexibility there might be for implementation. Branches have also administered the curriculum committees. The nature, composition, and functions of these committees vary widely from state to state. In addition to their curriculum branches, each state has one or more statutory board whose responsibility it is both to oversee curricula for secondary schools, and (in nearly all states) to administer statewide examinations at the completion of year 12 for both government and nongovernment schools. (In 1980, about 20 percent of Australian students attended nongovernment schools. In practice, these schools largely follow the curriculum patterns of the respective state departments of education.) Once curriculum documents have been finalized, they generally require sanction of the minister, after which they become mandatory throughout the state.

At both primary and secondary levels, curriculum development usually proceeds in a compartmentalized way within the traditional subject areas, and largely in isolation from both the work of other subject committees and the committees at the other (primary or secondary) level.

2. Curricula as Products

As to the content of curricula, a legacy from prefederation was specific time allocations for specific subjects. For example, in 1855 Wilkins in New South Wales introduced a "table" designating requirements in primary classes in reading, writing, arithmetic, grammar, geography, scripture, and object lessons (Turney 1969 p.212). Reading, writing and arithmetic have generally continued to occupy more than half the time, and remain as mandatory subjects.

Diversification of talents and interests of secondary students (as 88 percent of 15 year olds were still at school in 1980 compared with 56 percent in 1960) has resulted in a wider range of subjects, more relevant to more students (e.g., "general studies" to introduce current affairs; "personal development" to provide socioemotional education).

3. Influences on Curriculum Decision Making

The variety of factors influencing curricula has likewise widened, as international, national, regional, and local influences now complement central influences. At the international level, Australian curricula experienced some flow-on effects from the science projects both of the United Kingdom (Nuffield) and the United States (National Science Foundation-sponsored), and also from the humanities and modern languages materials. These effects varied widely, with some direct adoptions of overseas materials, as well as exerting an influence in generating a wider range of materials, going beyond textbooks to curriculum kits and technologies (including the language laboratory). Following adoptions, there were also adaptations (e.g., the Australian "Web of Life" from the United States "Biological Science Curriculum Study"). Perhaps the greatest impact was the stimulus for national level activities. Thus, in 1968 was launched the first Australian government-sponsored activity, the Australian Science Education Project, which terminated in 1972. Soon after was established (in 1976) the Curriculum Development Centre (CDC), a Commonwealth-funded national statutory body. The CDC was intended to identify national curriculum priorities, support local initiatives, and maintain state activities. The CDC has supported a diversity of ideas and materials, including core curricula, environmental education, Japanese, multicultural education, legal, religious, consumer and electoral education, Aboriginal education, expressive arts, drug education, agricultural science, the Social Education Materials Project, as well as mathematics and science. However, government cutbacks in 1982 heavily reduced its activities.

During the 1970s, decentralization of curriculum decision making was escalated as a result of improvements in administrations, teacher education, and support services (e.g. consultants, inservice programs), as well as abolition or modification of external examinations, increased concerns for relevance, and greater commitment to participatory decision making. Devolution has provided opportunities for autonomy. Since the 1970s, many schools have developed curricula and provided their own accreditation. The Australian Schools Commission encouraged 4,400 local initiatives in 3,000 schools from 1973 through the Innovations Programme abolished by the Commonwealth Government in 1982. However, some teacher opposition to school-based decisions, coupled with external examinations, have constrained more widespread practice of autonomy.

4. Recent Trends in Curricula in Australia

Australian trends are characterized by "diversification" of curriculum products and processes. A wider participant range is involved in decision-making processes. A conservative trend in decision making has been epitomized since 1976 by New South Wales through its "three-tier" policy for primary schools which allocates specific responsibilities to the "centre" (head office), 11 regions and schools. This policy provides a balance between autonomy and ministerial accountability. Curriculum products are being extended beyond purely academic products to embrace socioemotional, physical, and cultural subjects, materials beyond textbooks, and teaching methods beyond didactic are being adopted, with less concern for examination preparation and more concern for student motivation.

Bibliography

Cohen D 1985 *Curriculum in Australia: Intentions and Realities.* Prentice-Hall of Australia, Sydney
Cohen D, Harrison M 1982 *The Curriculum Action Project: A Report of Curriculum Decision-making in Australian Secondary Schools.* School of Education, Macquarie University, Sydney
Turney C (ed.) 1969 *Pioneers of Australian Education: A Study of the Development of Education in New South Wales in the Nineteenth Century.* Sydney University Press, Sydney

People's Republic of China

W. F. Connell and Zhang Lizhong

After the Long March of 1934–35 the communists settled in Shaanxi province in north-west China, making their headquarters at Yan'an until they assumed control of China in 1949. In that 14-year period the basic direction and the future characteristics of Chinese education were worked out. The Yan'an experience produced three distinctive and abiding views on the development of curricula appropriate for a communist society: (a) the curriculum should serve the needs of a mass society; (b) it should be saturated with political education committed to Marxist-Leninist-Maoist thought; and (c) it should emphasize the connection between education and productive work. In general also, it should be simple and utilitarian, and teach mutual cooperation rather than competitiveness.

1. Curriculum Reorganization in the 1950s and 1960s

With respect to the school curriculum, the period from 1949 to 1966 was experimental and somewhat confused. The schools' curriculum had to be developed to cope with three fundamental tasks. First it had to try to produce a literate mass society committed to Chinese communism; second it had to produce committed leaders throughout that society; and third it had to assist the modernization of China.

It is probable that in 1949 more than 80 percent of the population over the age of 10 years was illiterate. Spare-time schooling for adults which concentrated on literacy programmes was enormously expanded in villages, factories, and community centres. In primary schools a large proportion of the curriculum had always been spent on language learning, and in the 1950s a similar proportion was allotted. Considerable efforts were made, however, to simplify, and at the same time to politicize, the reading material used in primary and in spare-time schools, and to introduce a simplified system of characters, and a simpler phonetic system. At the same time, the whole school curriculum was gradually pruned of some traditional elements to make room for programmes of productive work which ran from the kindergarten through to tertiary level education, and to enable the gradual introduction of more mathematics and science. In 1954 an agreement on scientific and cultural cooperation was signed with the Soviet Union. For the following six years until the break in 1960, Soviet ideas spread in teacher education, Soviet teachers and textbooks helped in the modernization of secondary and tertiary education, the Russian language vied with English as the most popular foreign language taught in secondary schools and universities, and higher education was remodelled along more specialized lines according to Soviet practice.

During that period the concerted effort to expand production, known as the Great Leap Forward, took place from 1958 to 1960. Its effect on the school curriculum was to highlight the need to produce persons who were "red and expert". A larger proportion of the school curriculum was given over to productive work, and small factories were established in an increasing number of schools. Half-work half-study programmes for young adults also continued to spread. The impact, however, though noticeable, was not deep. During the decade and a half following the Liberation of 1949 the general principles of Mao Zedong's thought could be seen at work in the schools both in the content and the spirit with which the curriculum was implemented, but in many schools there was evidence of the continuation of traditional practices by many teachers whom the reconstruction had not greatly touched. It was the ensuing Cultural Revolution which was to stir the educational establishment to its very core.

2. The Cultural Revolution 1966–1976

During the Cultural Revolution the interdependence of intellectuals, workers, and peasants working together in the service of the whole people became a central feature in the task of educational remodelling. As a result, many office and intellectual workers were sent to work with peasants in the countryside to increase their understanding of life in a rural community. At the same time, strenuous efforts were made to raise the educational level of the peasants and workers and provide them with easier access to higher levels of education. Formal entrance examinations were eliminated, courses were shortened, and in many institutions it was not possible to maintain some courses and previous levels of work.

The other major change in this period was that political education took first place in the school curriculum. Politics came to infiltrate each subject and also to be a subject in its own right, often taught by members of the school's revolutionary committee. The schools became a much more integral part of the political and social revolution, and the pupils under the pressure of strenuous political teaching, developed a strong sense of purpose. All subjects of the curriculum became saturated with the teaching of revolutionary politics in a vigorous effort to bring about the cultural transformation of the Chinese people into a firm acceptance of Mao Zedong's approach to communism. History was reexamined and reinterpreted to raise the general consciousness of the part played by peasants and workers in the development of Chinese civilization. The necessity for constant struggle and the importance of mastering the techniques of problem solving not only in mathematics and science, but also in the social sciences were continually emphasized throughout the curriculum. Research was undertaken in teacher education institutions into the nature of problem solving and its applications in various subjects and in individual and cooperative situations in the schools.

The school programme at both primary and secondary level was a balanced general education consisting of language, mathematics, science, social science (usually called common knowledge), art, physical education, and productive work. The object of general education was to produce the new socialist who would be loyal to the people and the party and without personal ambition, conscious of class and ready to engage in class struggle, and imbued with an industrious and scientific attitude (Mao Zedong 1967). The connection between education and productive work was stressed even more than in previous years. It was usually related to the local community. For example, the making by primary and secondary school children of transformer parts or transistor tubes supplemented that of the local industry. Similarly, the cultivation in schools of vegetables, rice, or wheat would benefit the local community. The programmes were an exercise in applied science which culminated, in the curriculum of tertiary institutions, in the manufacture of substantial products such as metal lathes and automobiles. In effect the whole curriculum was an intensification and speeding up of the objectives and aspirations of the revolutionaries of 1949: to provide an education relevant to a mass society and to China in the modern age; to circumvent the development of a minority bourgeois social and intellectual elite; and to ensure that socialist consciousness should pervade the thoughts and activities of all who were growing up in the new People's Republic of China.

3. Post Cultural Revolution 1977–1988

After the death of Mao Zedong and the overthrow of the "gang of four" much of the pressure was released and some of the practices of the Cultural Revolution were repudiated. Formal examinations, particularly for entry to higher education were immediately restored, and the emphasis on the practice of linking the curriculum with productive factory work in the school was lessened. Selective "key" primary and secondary schools were established, leading to "key" universities and technological colleges. Secondary education was further diversified by the development of specialized technical schools.

In 1978 Deng Xiaoping (1979 pp. 5–7) enunciated the principles of the coming educational change. It was necessary, he said, "to improve the quality of education by insisting on higher standards of knowledge by raising our science and culture to a higher level", and it was essential to strengthen school discipline, and to ensure that education kept pace with the modernization of China and "with the requirements of national economic development" (p. 10). His speech was the beginning of a continuing discussion on the economics of education similar to that in developed countries.

Science and mathematics assumed greater importance in the curriculum of the 1980s. The change was brought about by the issuing from the central authorities of new primary and secondary school syllabuses and new textbooks in science and mathematics in 1978–79. Some of the traditional material in mathematics that was of little use in production, science, and technology was omitted, and new elements such as computing, elementary calculus, probability statistics, and logical algebra were introduced into the upper secondary school. In chemistry and physics, emphasis was to be placed on the development of problem-solving and experimental skills, ability to calculate, and knowledge of modern concepts and theories. In the preceding decades, the curriculum from kindergarten to university had been related to productive work by associating school projects with modern techniques used by workers in factories and on the land. For the 1980s, education was identified even more with production and economic development, but the objective was approached by an emphasis on the need to develop scientific and technological understanding, and on the necessity to produce intellectual cadres who could apply their knowledge to the advancement of the nation's technology. Hence the development of "key" schools with preferential treatment and a new emphasis on a search for talent and the specific cultivation of intellectuals.

Primary and secondary schooling are provided for 10 to 12 years. Attendance for nine years was made compulsory in 1986, but in the early 1990s many districts cannot implement full compulsory education. The curriculum of the 5- or 6-year primary school consists of politics, Chinese language, English or Russian, arithmetic, general knowledge, physical education, music, and fine arts. The 3-year junior and the 2-year senior secondary school provide courses in politics, Chinese language, English or Russian, mathematics, physics, chemistry, biology, elementary agriculture, history, geography, physical education, health, music, and fine arts. The range of the curriculum is very similar to that available in schools during the previous two decades, however, the approach has become more academic and examination oriented.

The school system is centrally planned but leeway is given to local authorities to vary the content of the curriculum. Differences are therefore to be found between economically developed and underdeveloped areas, between urban and rural districts, and in the areas inhabited by minority nationalities such as the Mongolian, Uighur, Tibetan, and Kazahk, as well as between "key" and other schools. There has been much discussion about the nature of these differences. In particular there have been questions about the nature of "key" schools, and about possible adjustments to the

curriculum and methods of teaching for them, and about the effects of such schools on the work of the ordinary schools (*Chinese Education* 1984, Guo Hanye 1987–88). To assist teachers and curriculum developers and to promote research on these and other curricular questions a journal dealing with curriculum, teaching material, and method, was started in 1981.

School discipline has also been tightened. In 1979, and again in 1988, the Ministry of Education issued codes of conduct for primary and secondary schools "that every student must observe in his or her daily study and life" (pp. 3–4). Students were bidden, among other things, to "cherish the motherland, the people, and support the Chinese Communist Party" (pp. 3–4), to study hard, work and think diligently, abide by school discipline, observe public order and the law, and respect their teachers.

The curriculum retains a lively interest in political education which still remained an important ingredient of Chinese schooling in the 1980s. The four cardinal principles: keeping to the socialist road, upholding the people's democratic dictatorship, leadership by the Communist Party, and guidance by Marxist-Leninist-Maoist thought are firmly observed in the process of developing curricula and in teaching and learning in the schools. Students are to become both red and expert, but, in the interests of national development, the political dimension of education is no longer to outdistance the economic.

Bibliography

Chinese Education 1984. Issue devoted to China's keypoint school controversy 1978–1982. 17(2), Summer 1984

Deng Xiaoping 1979 Speech at the national educational work conference. *Chinese Educ.* 12(1): 5–10

Guo Hanye 1987–88 Viewing key middle school education from all sides (trans.). *Chinese Educ.* 20(4): 31–40

Löfstedt J-I 1980 *Chinese Educational Policy.* Almqvist and Wiksell, Stockholm

Löfstedt J-I 1990 Human Resources in Chinese Development. IIEP-UNESCO, Paris

Mao Zedong 1967 In memory of Norman Bethune (trans.) In: Mao Zedong 1967 *Selected Works.* Foreign Language Press, Peking 2: 337–38

Mao Zedong 1968 *On the Correct Handling of Contradictions among the People.* Foreign Language Press, Peking

Ministry of Education 1979 Code of conduct. *Chinese Educ.* 13: 3–4, 102–03

Federal Republic of Germany

C. Wulf

Since the publication of Saul B. Robinson's programmatic work (1967), the concept of curriculum and its accompanying subconcepts of curriculum theory, research, development, evaluation, and implementation have come to be widely accepted in the Federal Republic of Germany (see *Curriculum Theory*; *Curriculum Research*; *Curriculum Development*; *Curriculum Implementation*). The introduction of this concept was furthered by the influence of Anglo-Saxon terminology and international usage. Even though the concept of curriculum had already been used in connection with education, it was not until 1967 that it began to play more than a minor role. In the German-speaking countries from the seventeenth to the middle of the twentieth century, questions concerning aims, content, methods, and materials for education in general, and the classroom in particular, were mostly subsumed under the concept of didactics. This concept is derived from the Greek word *didaskein* and means the theory of teaching, instruction, or, more specifically, education and content. Thus, an historical analysis of the concept of curriculum in the German-speaking countries has first to be examined in the light of the various approaches to the theory of didactics. In contrast to the concept "curriculum," "didactics" is mainly concerned with problems of curriculum theory, and does not include the aspects of thorough planning and evaluation through the use of systematically developed learning aids. Only with the introduction of the concept of curriculum was attention focused on these aspects. This article deals with some of the important didactic–curricular theories which, to a certain extent, still influence curricular and didactic planning. Although the terms "curriculum" and "didactics" are used interchangeably, the difference in emphasis should be kept in mind.

1. Early Ideas about Curriculum

Detailed reflections can be found concerning curricula in the writings of seventeenth-century authors such as Wolfgang Ratke (1571–1635), and, more importantly, Johan Amos Comenius (1592–1670) (*Didactica Magna* 1657). Comenius maintained, much as do the proponents of mastery learning today, that it was possible to teach anyone anything thoroughly. Comenius' point of departure was the conviction that content and goals could be derived from a preordained divine plan (*ordo rerum*). Consequently, usage of the *didactica magna* (curriculum and teaching strategy) was supposed to mirror the fundamentals of the divine plan. This process was to be realized by all human beings in their role as God's dutiful servants. According to Comenius, learning proceeds in steps, and at a pace concordant with the learner's ability. This approach shifted the pedagogical focus onto the individual for the first time (Schaller 1962).

2. The Eighteenth and Nineteenth Century in Curriculum History

The Age of Enlightenment brought about a new way of looking at the world, which in turn affected educational and curricular theory. The content in the curriculum could no longer be based on, nor justified by, a preordained divine plan. Jean-Jacques Rousseau (1712–1778), the great French philosopher and educational thinker, whose influence on curriculum theory is still felt today, focused attention on the young person's natural "needs" as exemplified in his book *Emile*. Education should be oriented to the needs of the learner. Rousseau assumed the existence of a previously established harmony between the requirements of society, on the one hand, and the needs of the young person on the other, something which the philanthropists had already expressed doubt about. Their criticism of his concepts of a given equilibrium between society's and the individual's needs is still a moot point in modern curriculum development. Johann Heinrich Pestalozzi (1746–1827), the Swiss educational reformer, who laid the foundation for modern elementary education, modified Rousseau's ideas and carried them a step further. According to Pestalozzi, the pivotal point of educational and curricular philosophy should be the individual child in his or her social milieu. The individual child has to be helped to gradually come to terms with, and exert a positive effect on, his or her environment. Friedrich Daniel Schleiermacher (1768–1834) continued this line of reasoning by postulating the following: education, and consequently curriculum theory, should only comprise those goals and subjects which directly bear on the future of the child and which satisfy his or her needs of the moment. More clearly than any of his predecessors, Schleiermacher recognized the powerful influence that the church, state, and centers of learning have on the determination of educational goals and subject matter. Schleiermacher's understanding brought educational goals, subject matter, and methods into historical perspective for the first time (Rang 1959, Delekat 1968, Rang 1967, Schurr 1975).

In the nineteenth century, the German philosophers and educators Johann Friedrich Herbart (1776–1841) and Wilhelm von Humboldt (1767–1835) dominated the thinking in the field of curriculum theory. Humboldt, the great educational reformer and founder of the Berlin University, felt that a general education would enable the individual to become as independent as possible of the constraints of his or her limited social situation. This could be achieved through the study of the classics and the humanities through which one could at the same time acquire a critical understanding of the present. The central tenet of Herbart's education and curriculum theory is the concept of "instruction as education" (*Erziehender Unterricht*) in connection with morality. Here, the aim is to introduce young people to ethical principles exemplified by the moral conduct of great people of the past. Herbart's followers, Tuiscon Ziller (1817–1882) and Wilhelm Rein (1847–1929), expanded upon the "Herbartian" formal stages of analysis, synthesis, association, system, and method. This revised model became widely accepted in the nineteenth century. Its principles were used as mandatory criteria for the organization of curriculum units and the execution of classroom teaching. In modified form, these criteria still have an influence on the development of modern curriculum units (Asmus 1968/1970, Paulsen 1919, 1921).

3. *The Twentieth Century in Curriculum History*

At the beginning of the twentieth century, the more child-centered European Educational Reform Movement or *Reformpädagogik*, which was based, to a certain extent, on Rousseau's and Pestalozzi's philosophy, began to turn against the Herbart School, and its attempts to implement rigid "Herbartian" principles in curriculum development and in classroom teaching. The most important branches of the reform movement were the work-oriented education movement (*Arbeitsschulbewegung*), the experience-oriented education (*Erlebnispädagogik*), and group and project-oriented education (*Gruppen- und Projektpädagogik*). They developed criteria for the organization of curricula which are today being rediscovered in connection with the controversy surrounding open curricula. In general, the various branches of the European Educational Reform Movement were interested in putting a stronger emphasis on the child and his or her needs in curriculum and classroom planning (Röhrs 1980).

During the period of National Socialism, curriculum development and classroom methods largely served as tools for indoctrination into the National Socialist ideology. After the war, educational and curricular theory returned to the lines of thinking which had previously been established in the Weimar Republic.

4. *Contemporary Ideas about Curriculum*

In the middle of the 1960s—before Germany adapted the concept of curriculum and developed its own curriculum research program—three main streams of curricular thought could be distinguished in the Federal Republic of Germany (Blankertz 1973).

The information theory position (*informationstheoretische Position*) emerged in the 1960s. It concerns itself with planning curricula in such a way that learning is treated as a process of regulation and control. The target to be reached is first determined; then, with the aid of a curriculum developer, the optimal strategy for reaching the target is worked out; the media for best guiding the learner are chosen; the particular situation of the learner is taken into consideration; and, finally, the learning process is evaluated as to whether or not the learner has reached the target. In this context, the learning process is seen as input, storage, processing, and retrieval of information. Although this approach has been useful in the development of materials for programmed instruction, it has only had a small impact on the educational system in the Federal Republic of Germany (Cube 1965).

The learning theory position (*lerntheoretische Position*) focuses attention on classroom instruction. The problem is to determine which elements in curricular structure and in planning teaching procedures are important for classroom teaching. The following variables must be taken into account: (a) situation variables—(i) anthropological conditions (individual situation, school situation, and the make-up of the student's class), and (ii) sociocultural conditions (societal forces which influence classroom teaching); (b) decision variables—(i) goal (deciding on the goal of the lesson), (ii) theme (content of the lesson), (iii) method (organization of the lesson), (iv) choice of media. These aspects should be taken into consideration when developing curriculum units and when carrying out the lesson (Heimann et al. 1972).

The educational theory position (*bildungstheoretische Position*), which was formulated and elaborated by Herman Nohl (1879–1960), Erich Weniger (1894–1961), and especially Wolfgang Klafki, comprises two aspects: a more specific sense which means the theory of educational content and topical relevance and a broader sense which also includes theory concerning methods and teaching procedures. Overall, the "educational theory" position has had a great impact on the organization of teaching materials for particular subjects. It was necessary to adapt the "general educational theory" (*Allgemeine Bildungstheoretische Didaktik*) to fit specific subjects which resulted in specialized educational theories (*Fachdidaktiken*). Much as Schleiermacher had done in the past, the supporters of the "educational theory" realized the importance of the role of social forces, government administration, political parties, denominational groups, unions, and centers of learning in determining syllabi. They felt, consequently, that there were definite constraints on the freedom of the teacher to teach and the student to learn according to his or her individual needs. Decisions regarding curricula should be concerned with reconciling the differences between society's demands and individual needs. The important thing is to determine the educational value (*Bildungswert*) of the goal or teaching procedure. For this purpose the following categories were developed:

(a) representativeness of the topic to be learned;

(b) relevance to the child of the knowledge and experience gained from learning about this topic;

(c) relevance for the future;

(d) structure of the content.

Klafki's position rejects all solely content-oriented educational theories (*materiale Bildungstheorien*) which maintain that education is chiefly a process of imparting certain kinds of knowledge extracted from a universal body of knowledge; his position also rejects solely process-oriented educational theories (*formale Bildungstheorien*) which maintain that learning takes place mainly through the acquisition of techniques and skills. Instead, Klafki and the adherents of his position use the term *Kategoriale Bildung*, an approach to curriculum development which emphasizes the integration of criteria for the specification of goals, content, and processes in learning. According to them, the goal of all curricular and classroom planning should aim at the following: to create environmental reality open to the individual, and an individual open to the reality of his or her environment (Klafki 1964).

Bibliography

Asmus W 1968/1970 *Johann Friedrich Herbart: Eine Pädagogische Biographie*. Quelle und Meyer, Heidelberg

Blankertz H 1973 *Theorien und Modelle der Didaktik*. Juventa, München

Cube F von 1965 *Kybernetische Grundlagen des Lernens und Lehrens*. Klett-Cotta, Stuttgart

Delekat F 1968 *Pestalozzi*. Quelle und Meyer, Heidelberg

Frey K, Achtenhagen F, Haft H, Haller M D, Hameyer U, Hesse H A, Hiller G G, Gotthilf G, Klafki W, Teschner W P, Trotsenburg E A, Wulf C 1975 *Curriculum-Handbuch*. Piper, München

Heimann P, Otto G, Schulz W 1972 *Unterricht: Analyse und Planung*. Schrödel, Hannover

Klafki W 1964 *Das Pädagogische Problem des Elementaren und die Theorie der Kategorialen Bildung*. Beltz, Weinheim

Klafki W 1971 Didaktik. In: Groothoof H-H, Stallmann M (eds.) 1971 *Neues Pädagogisches Lexikon*. Kreutz, Stuttgart

Paulsen F 1919, 1921 *Geschichte des gelehrten Unterrichts auf den Deutschen Schulen und Universitäten von Ausgang des Mittelalters bis zur Gegenwart*. Veit, Leipzig

Rang A 1967 *Der politische Pestalozzi* Europäische Verlagsanstalt, Frankfurt

Rang M 1959 *Rousseaus Lehre vom Menschen*. Vandenhueck und Ruprecht, Göttingen

Robinson S B 1967 *Bildungsreform als Revision des Curriculum und: Ein Strukturkonzept für Curriculumentwicklung*. Neuwied, Berlin

Röhrs H 1980 *Die Reformpädagogik: Ursprung und Verlauf in Europa*. Schrödel Hermann, Hannover

Schaller K 1962 *Die Pädagogik des Johan Amos Comenius und der Anfang des pädagogischen Realismus im 17. Jahrhundert*. Quelle und Meyer, Heidelberg

Schurr J 1975 *Schleiermachers Theorie der Erziehung: Interpretationen zur Pädagogik Vorlesung von 1826*. Pädagogischer Verlag, Schwann, Düsseldorf

Willmann O 1957 *Didaktik als Bildungslehre nach ihren Beziehungen zur Sozialforschung und zur Geschichte der Bildung*. Herder, Freiburg

Wulf C (ed.) 1984 *Wörterbuch der Erziehung*. Piper, München

Hungary

E. Ballér

The history of the curriculum in Hungary is inseparable from that of the economic, social, political, and cultural development of the country and from the changes in the school system. However, here the discussion will be restricted to the curriculum itself. The term is used both in a general and in a formal sense. In the first case we are dealing with the real, actual content or subject matter of instruction in the institutes of public education. The second approach regards the curriculum as a set of centrally issued documents that define the overall goals and aims of instruction, specify the range of school subjects and the time to be allocated to them for different types of school, and determine the specific tasks, content, structure, objectives, and methodological principles for each subject.

1. Christian Influence in the Curriculum

After the foundation of the independent Hungarian State (from about AD 1000), the first schools were established by the Catholic Church, especially by religious orders around monasteries, parish churches, and cathedrals, mainly for the purpose of training priests. In most cases the content of instruction consisted of the "trivium" but in some schools elements of the "quadrivium" were also offered. The catechism, the psalms, and the teachings of the early Church fathers served the purposes of this all-pervading religious and moral education. The language of instruction was Latin.

With the emergence of the Renaissance the curriculum became more humanistic, with special emphasis on classical literature and even on some basic natural sciences. At the same time urban and village schools came into existence, which also taught practical subjects, and relied more on the mother tongue.

The great upsurge of the Reformation brought about a new phase. The protestant schools—especially in Transylvania, where the Princes succeeded by delicate manoeuvering between the Ottoman and the Hapsburg Empires in preserving independence for almost 150 years—introduced new curricula for their elementary and secondary institutions and their so-called academies. Under the influence of famous foreign universities, where a great number of Hungarian scholars were educated, they paid more attention to the vernacular (first of all for reading and writing), but Latin maintained its dominance. An important chapter in the history of the curriculum in Hungary was opened by the teaching of Comenius (Komenšky) in Sárospatak between 1650 and 1654. He wrote and introduced several of his well-known textbooks here and tried to put into practice his concept of "pansophism" (teaching all things to everyone). In his footsteps Apáczai Csere János (1625–1659)—who had graduated in the Netherlands—elaborated in his Hungarian Encyclopedia (1653) an amazingly comprehensive body of knowledge for instruction.

During the seventeenth and eighteenth centuries the Hungarian school system and the curriculum slowly took shape. On the lower level, in the village or parish schools, children learned religion, reading, singing and in some cases writing and arithmetic in their mother tongue. In the field of secondary education it was principally the Catholic and Protestant Churches that established and maintained the grammar schools and colleges. Latin and the humanities preserved their salience, but in several institutions mathematics, science, and even productive work were also introduced, together with improved teaching methods, often under the influence of important foreign educational movements such as pietism and philanthropism, and the influence of educators such as Francke (1663–1727), Basedow (1724–90), Campe (1746–1818), Salzmann (1744–1811), and above all Pestalozzi (1746–1827).

2. *The Rise of Central Curriculum Planning*

The first official, centrally issued regulation concerning the Hungarian school system and its curriculum was published in 1777 under the title "Ratio Educationis". It laid down the content of instruction and specified the time-table and the subject matter for every type of elementary and secondary school and even for "academies" and universities.

Though in the first half of the nineteenth century— during the tempestuous social and political struggles and upheavals, such as the Age of Reform and the Revolution and War of Independence of 1848–49— schools and the content of instruction often proved to be hotly debated political issues and teaching practice itself developed rather slowly. Elementary and vocational education was backward and obsolete. The curriculum of the secondary schools—which usually provided six-year and later eight-year courses—remained unbalanced, as, in most cases, science and practical subjects were overshadowed. The Catholic Church exercised tight control and overwhelming influence over the materials taught in schools, and teaching conditions were unfavourable.

After the fall of the Revolution and especially after the Accord of 1867, which ended direct Hapsburg oppression and laid the foundation of the Austro-Hungarian Monarchy, several important measures were taken. The Education Act of 1868 can be regarded as a milestone in the development of basic education. It reshaped the system of popular education by establishing the six-year elementary school (plus three years for remedial education), attendance at which was made compulsory from the age of 6 up to 15. From that time on, central, official, mandatory documents—plans of instruction—issued by the State and the Church, and periodically reformed, defined the curriculum for every level of public education. The comprehensive curriculum reform of the grammar school (1884), led by Kármán Mór (1843–1913), the first eminent exponent of curriculum theory in Hungary, creatively adopted Herbartian principles in selecting and organizing subject matter into a coherent structure concentrated around the national cultural heritage. Towards the end of the century secondary vocational schools were established with a practical, often over-specialized, curriculum.

A survey of this period would not be complete without at least a mention of Nagy László (1857–1931). Though

he believed in the concept of child-centered, interest-based teaching, in contrast to the representatives of "reform pedagogy" and the "new school" movement, he worked out a practical curriculum theory for an eight-year experimental elementary-school course in his *Didactics on the Basis of Child Development* (1921).

3. *Curricula Between the Two World Wars*

The curricula of the period between the two World Wars played an important role in creating a strong class orientation and sharp contrasts in the contemporary school system. Though curriculum reforms made some progress in streamlining the content of instruction (e.g., the reforms for the elementary schools in 1925 and 1941 and for the grammar schools in 1924 and 1938), the subject matter studied in the schools attended by the mass of the population remained inferior to that of the schools for the minority elite. For example, the curriculum for the upper elementary classes did not include a foreign language or world history, whereas that for the lower grades of the grammar school did (pupils between the ages of 10 and 14 were taught in both). Such curricular "blind alleys" made it extremely difficult, if not impossible, for the children of workers and peasants to struggle upwards through the various levels of the school system. As for the eight-year grammar schools—which offered the "royal road" to universities and catered for the small minority—their first-year group represented only 7 percent of 10-year-olds. After several attempts at curricular differentiation between "the humanities" and "the sciences" (also known as the "humane" and the "real" branches of study in many European countries), the curriculum became unified in the curriculum reform of 1938.

4. *Curriculum Changes from 1945*

After the second World War, curriculum reform contributed to, followed, or sometimes even preceded—in the midst of revolutionary changes in society—the complete reorganization of the school system, the switch of orientation from selective to mass education, and the dissemination of socialist ideology.

The newly created eight-year general school provided the foundation of the educational system. In the course of successive curricular changes its subject matter became more up-to-date, with greater emphasis on the basic skills, the mother tongue, science, and poly-technical education as part of general culture. Practical training—later technology—became an independent subject of an industrial or agricultural character. Special classes were organized in several fields, with higher level curricula in selected subjects (e.g., foreign languages, mathematics, singing, and physical training). The content of mathematics was transformed on the basis of the "new maths".

Significant changes took place in the four-year grammar school, as the upper section of the general school absorbed its four lower classes. School subjects were restructured, the time devoted to the sciences being increased at the expense of Latin. To cater for pupils' individual interests special classes were introduced. In the spirit of the Education Act of 1961, a short-lived, unsuccessful attempt was made to introduce a more practical grammar-school curriculum. The new timetable made provision for academic education for five days a week, while one day was devoted to practical work in school workshops or factories. Owing to the shortage of material and personnel this so-called "5 + 1 system" failed and was abolished.

The secondary vocational school curriculum has been subjected to several alterations as a result of the frequent restructuring of this type of school. They are organized according to professional branches including industry, agriculture, economics, health, commerce, and the arts.

The curriculum of the two- to three-year trade schools (the fourth main type of schooling) is designed to provide practical vocational training for skilled workers. The general culture and professional theory content is limited. This is one of the reasons why trade schools do not provide direct access to the institutes of higher learning.

It is at least worth mentioning that there are several schools with special functions and curricula. These include institutes for the education of handicapped children, correspondence and evening courses for adults, schools for national minorities (where most of the subjects are taught in the minority language, or the mother tongue of the nationalities is kept in the foreground), schools run by the churches, and special foreign language grammar schools.

The latest ambitious, comprehensive curriculum reform which was introduced gradually from 1978 onwards, aimed at modernizing the content, methods, and media of education and instruction. It introduced modern scientific achievement, widened the horizon of general culture, put stress on the objectives and the requirements of minimum competence, subdivided the

materials into a common core and supplementary parts, and expanded the fields of optional and elective courses. New textbooks and other media of instruction were also issued.

At the same time new problems and difficulties have emerged. The overloading of pupils has increased; pupils' achievements have become more polarized, and in certain cases even deteriorated; fragmentation and narrow vocationalism have led to disintegration and rigidity in pupils' knowledge. As a result, the ambitious central curricula of the 1970s have run the gauntlet of adverse criticism.

A new strategy of curriculum development and implementation is being worked out to cope with these problems and to keep abreast of the rapid changes. This strategy emphasizes a profound transformation of central curriculum planning, giving more motivation, impetus, alternatives, and freedom for local initiative, research, and innovation. The ongoing process of continual change is being brought into prominence, instead of periodic, all-embracing, centrally administered curriculum reforms. Work has been going on to define a national basic curriculum for a common culture at elementary, basic, and secondary levels which would serve as a compulsory basis for local curricula in every type of school.

Bibliography

Báthory 1986 Decentralization issues in the introduction of new curriculum: The case of Hungary. *Prospects.* 16(1): 34–47

Grant N 1970 Curriculum change in Eastern Europe. In; Hooper R (ed.) 1970 *The Curriculum. Context, Design and Development.* Oliver and Boyd, Edinburgh, pp. 76–89

Ministry of Education 1973 *Public Education in Hungary.* Ministry of Education, Athenaeum, Nyomda, Budapest

Nagy L 1921 *Didactics on the Basis of Child Development: Curriculum for the Eight-class General Public Elementary School,* Library of Child Study No. 8. Hungarian Society of Child Study, Badapest

Tóth L (ed.) 1976 *Hungarian Education.* Tanköny vkiadó, Budapest

Japan

K. Kihara

By the feudal period of Japanese history there were already popular educational institutions for commoners, the so-called writing schools, or *terakoya* (literally: temple school), which by the seventeenth century were purely secular institutions. There were 34 *terakoya* by the mid-eighteenth century and 4,293 by the mid-nineteenth century. In addition to the *terakoya*, most feudal territories also had clan schools (*hanko*), which were mainly for children of the samurai class. Toward the end of the feudal regime, Western studies such as medicine,

foreign language (particularly Dutch and English), and military science were widespread.

In 1867, feudalism disappeared with the establishment of the new Meiji government. Japan became a modern state. In 1871 the Ministry of Education was established, and in 1872 the Code of School Education (*Gakusei*) was promulgated. It divided Japan into eight university districts. Each district was to have one university and 32 middle-school districts. The plan thus called for a total of 256 middle schools and 53,760 elementary schools. The ideas of G. F. Verbeck and Marion M. Scott were fundamental to Japanese schools. Scott, a California school teacher, introduced such equipment as the blackboard and the desk and brought the idea of a timetable. After some modifications to adapt them to the Japanese school system, these novelties became widespread in the 1870s.

The Educational Ordinance of 1879 was issued by the Ministry of Education on the basis of a plan suggested by Dr. David Murray, a professor of mathematics at Rutgers College in New Jersey. A few months before the 1872 movement for establishing new schools was launched, the Japanese Government dispatched to the West a high-level mission under Prince Tomomi Iwakura. In 1878, the Ministry of Education published a book entitled *The US School Law*.

Influenced by Western practice, the Elementary School Order established four years of compulsory schooling in 1886. In 1900, the Elementary School Order Regulation prescribed a curriculum which contained studies in morals, Japanese language, physical training, and other required subjects. This syllabus did not change until 1941.

In 1901, the curriculum of the middle school was enacted, and in 1907 the compulsory elementary school was extended from four years to six years.

In the twentieth century, the school curriculum has been influenced by John Dewey, William H. Kilpatrick,

and other representatives of American pragmatism. Influenced by American pedagogy, liberal and comprehensive education was established in some elementary schools affiliated with national universities.

After the Second World War, under the influence of the American occupation, the entire system was reorganized, and changes were introduced into both the school structure and the curriculum. Compulsory education was increased to nine years of schooling, and a further three years of upper-secondary school (corresponding to American high school) was adopted throughout Japan. Social studies were introduced into the curriculum in elementary and lower-secondary school. The current curriculum for elementary and secondary school is based on the publication *Course of Study* issued by the Ministry of Education and revised about once every 10 years.

Bibliography

Education in Japan – Journal for Overseas 1968 Vol. 3 (Special issue devoted to curriculum development in elementary education)

Education in Japan – Journal for Overseas 1969 Vol. 4 (Special issue devoted to curriculum development in elementary education)

Ministry of Education, Japan 1960 *Revised Curriculum in Japan for Elementary and Lower Secondary Schools*. Ministry of Education, Tokyo

Nigeria

W. H. Watkins and Y. Byo

Nigeria's curriculum history is inextricably linked to its social and political history. Her disparate peoples existed for centuries during the great West African empires as independent ethnic groups with no common national community. European colonial policy thrust divergent people into an artificially created political state. Over 250 ethnic tongues are spoken in present-day Nigeria. Traditional territorial divisions between the largely Islamic north and the largely Christian south combined with other indigenous peoples and systems have contributed to Nigeria's complex educational and curriculum history.

1. The Traditional Curriculum

Prior to the sixteenth century, West African education was guided by the principles of functionalism. Though informal, education aimed to prepare individuals for adulthood and social interaction. The curriculum of old Africa was a verbal transmission of culture through ceremonies, rituals, imitation, recitation, and demonstration. Subject matter included practical farming, fishing, weaving, cooking, carving, knitting, dance, acrobatic display, and so on. Intellectual training

included the study of local history, legends, the environment, poetry, reasoning, riddles, proverbs, and storytelling. The curriculum was an integrated one aimed at socialization and character building.

The territory, later to be called Nigeria, consisted of many ethnic groups, each with its own culture and tradition. Fafunwa (1974) identified seven common educational objectives around which the traditional curriculum was organized:

(a) to develop the child's latent physical skills;

(b) to develop character;

(c) to inculcate respect for elders and those in positions of authority;

(d) to develop intellectual skills;

(e) to acquire specific vocational training and to develop a healthy attitude towards honest labor;

(f) to develop a sense of belonging and to participate actively in family and community affairs;

(g) to understand, appreciate, and promote the cultural heritage of the community at large.

2. The Islamic Curriculum

Islam reached the savannah of West Africa in the eighth century AD. Koranic schools helped to spread the Islamic tradition: the Holy Koran and the Arabic language anchored the new curriculum. Courses of study in syntax, logic, arithmetic, algebra, rhetoric, jurisprudence, and scholastic theology were all designed around the principles and rules of interpretation of the laws of Islam. Islamic education, particularly in the north, strongly influenced and perhaps dominated the Nigerian curriculum until the arrival of the colonialists.

3. The Curriculum of Colonialism

During the late fifteenth and early sixteenth centuries, Portuguese merchant traders became the first Europeans to visit Nigeria. Primarily interested in commerce, they nevertheless established the foundations for a Christian (Catholic) education and conforming curricular system.

For 300 years missionaries established outposts of Christian education in Nigeria. Their curriculum was aimed at the training of teachers who would propagate Christianity.

Devastated by the slave trade, raw material extraction, poverty, and fossilized social relations, Nigeria was ravaged by European colonialism. During this period, educative systems stagnated at the feet of commercial plunder.

By the mid-nineteenth century the British, already commercially active, began to encourage the establishment of Christian mission schools, mostly in southern Nigeria. Though Christian training was the objective of the curriculum, some basic education was undertaken. This daily class curriculum was sent to head-teachers in 1848 by Rev Thomas Birch Freeman, superintendent of the Methodist Mission:

9:00 a.m.	Singing, rehearsals of scripture passages, reading one chapter of scripture, prayers
9:15–12:00 noon	Grammar, reading, spelling, writing, geography, tables [except Wednesday, when there was catechism in place of grammar]
2:00–4:00 p.m.	Ciphering (i.e., arithmetic), reading, spelling, meaning of words
4:00 p.m.	Closing prayers

By 1900, the colonial government in Nigeria existed almost exclusively to guarantee the repatriation of profits from commercial ventures to England. Education, including the curriculum, was left to the missionary societies. The "Tuskegee Philosophy" developed by Booker T Washington and popularized by Thomas Jesse Jones and J H Oldham was exported to Nigeria. A curriculum was to be designed for vocational training, agricultural education, and character development. The curriculum was designed to foster a differentiated educational system, that is, one to train African leaders, the other for the masses. This curriculum model was based on the premise that the African would be forever doomed to the backwardness of rural servitude while a privileged few would be trained to administrate and conduct the business of the colonists.

In 1929 the education departments of Northern and Southern Nigeria were merged and the government moved centrally into the spheres of education and curriculum. Still under colonial rule, the Nigerian government began to redirect certain aspects of the curriculum. Various commissions on education, for example Phelps-Stokes (1925), recommended that education be expanded largely through the establishment of more institutions of higher learning. Additionally, "indigenizing" the curriculum came to be viewed as both a practical and inevitable measure. Starting with higher education, the curriculum turned to "creating professionals." Utilizing British models, curriculum programs in medicine, agriculture, engineering, and teacher training were established.

4. Political Independence and New Curriculum Directions

With the achievement of independence from Great Britain in 1960, the "indigenization" or "Nigerianization" of the curriculum gained momentum. Under the watchword of modernization, Nigeria set about making its curriculum serve technological advancement. The following subjects were taught throughout the young nation: arithmetic, physical training, history, religious instruction, geography, nature study, domestic science, needlework and cookery for girls, music and singing, art and handiwork, English, and indigenous languages.

In the mid-1960s, Nigeria too was affected by the movement for curriculum reform sweeping the Western world, especially the United States. A new enthusiasm for science and technology emerged. Inspired and funded, in part, by American universities, philanthropic foundations, and international agencies, innovative programs were started. Curriculum projects such as the well-known "Entebbe Mathematics" launched by the Education Development Center, the Nuffield Mathematics project developed in the United Kingdom, and the new "Integrated Social Studies" project funded largely by Western agencies were but a few examples of this movement at the lower levels of public schooling. At higher levels, technical education and teacher-training programs received increased attention.

In 1969 the landmark National Curriculum Conference was convened. The Conference brought curriculum reformers and school people together with businessmen, trade unionists, professionals, farmers, military men, theologians, youth leaders, and a substantial cross-section of Nigerian society. The Conference, without recommending specific course content, identified overarching national goals for curriculum and education as a part of the larger program of nation-building, national reconstruction, and economic progress. Among the goals later articulated by the federal government's National Policy on Education (1977) were:

(a) a free and democratic society;

(b) a just and egalitarian society;

(c) a united, strong, and self-reliant nation;

(d) a great and dynamic economy; and

(e) a land of bright and full opportunities for all citizens.

5. Problems and Prospects

In Nigeria's federal system, each state has authority over education and curriculum programs; however, the national government is the central authority. Among the main goals of both the federal and state governments in recent years has been the full implementation of the Universal Primary Education (UPE) Act enacted in 1976. The Federal Ministry of Education has embarked on a protracted campaign of persuasion to centralize the curriculum or, at minimum, to bring the states within acceptable bounds of conformity. Nigeria's recent economic difficulties combined with continued social and ethnic divisiveness render this task one of monumental proportions

Bibliography

African Curriculum Organization (ACO) 1983 *Aspects of Education and Curriculum Development in Nigeria*. Institute of Education, Ibadan
Fafunwa A B 1974 *History of Education in Nigeria*. Allen and Unwin, London
Federal Republic of Nigeria 1977, 1981 *National Policy on Education*. Federal Government Press, Lagos
Graham S F 1966 *Government and Mission Education in Northern Nigeria, 1900–1919, with Special Reference to the Work of Haans Vischer*. University Press, Ibadan
Ikejiani O (ed.) 1964 *Nigerian Education*. Longmans of Nigeria, Ikeja, Nigeria
Lewis L J 1965 *Society, Schools and Progress in Nigeria*. Pergamon, Oxford
Nduka O 1964 *Western Education and the Nigerian Cultural Background*. Oxford University Press, Ibadan
Rodney W 1972 *How Europe Underdeveloped Africa*. Bogle-L'Ouverture, London
Taiwo C O 1981 *The Nigerian Educational System: Past, Present, and Future*. Thomas Nelson, Lagos
Watkins W H 1986 The political sociology of postcolonial social studies curriculum development: The case of Nigeria, 1960–1980. Unpublished doctoral thesis, University of Illinois, Chicago, Illinois
Yoloye E A 1981 *Problems of Curriculum Development in Africa*. African Curriculum Organization (ACO), Ikeja, Nigeria

Socialist Countries

E. Ballér

Curriculum history in the socialist countries has two interrelated aspects. The first one is set forth in the official, mostly centrally devised documents, which provide guidelines for selecting and organizing the subject matters to be taught in different types of schools and at different grade levels. The second aspect is reflected in the theory related to the processes of developing, structuring, and administrating new curricula. These two aspects are interrelated insofar as experiences from school curricula usually provide the empirical basis for theory construction, and theory, in turn, offers the scientific basis for curriculum reform.

Curricula in the socialist countries consist of an official, centrally designed set of documents which establish the structure of each school subject and the time allocated for its study. Those documents also define both the general and the specific aims of each subject; they outline the objectives that shall be covered each term and the performance that is to be expected of the students; and they address the basic methodological principles to be considered in the instruction.

In most socialist countries, the school curriculum is as old as the system of public education itself. The first programs and syllabi appeared in the second half of the nineteenth century at the time when the first education acts were establishing general and compulsory public education. Subsequent reforms have made the curriculum more and more organic, and based mostly on the national cultural heritage.

The socialist revolution in Soviet Russia in 1917 and the subsequent social transition of the East European countries in the second half of the 1940s transformed the curricula so that they were more in line with the radical changes in the goals, function, content, and structure of the school systems. In Soviet Russia, polytechnical work schools were established, in which the curriculum was organized on psychological principles that encouraged students to do creative manual work in laboratories and where workshops and school activities were integrated with community life. Dewey, who paid a visit to the Soviet Union in 1928, was highly appreciative of community-related work experiences which he observed in schools. Nevertheless, after the criticism in the 1930s of the "pedagogical aberrations" in both the theory and the practice of education, the curriculum became more scientific and systematic, with more emphasis placed on formal education. This change coincided with the gradual extension and build-up of compulsory general and secondary schooling. The process continued after the Second World War, with the

Education Act of 1958 giving a new impetus to curriculum reform.

The curricula of the 1980s in the socialist countries consist of a variety of elements. They contain, first of all, a rather detailed and structured system of goals and aims, which intend to regulate the educational and instructional processes as well as the selection of subject matters. This system emphasizes the development of socialist personality which is characterized by strong ideological convictions combined with efficiently functioning knowledge, adequate aptitude and abilities, and a self-conscious and highly motivated behavior. Modern polytechnical, scientific, and social knowledge is imparted, and productive work and permanent learning skills are encouraged. The contents of the curricula provide a balanced general education and impart a solid collection of transferable knowledge and skills for a vocational life. In general education, 40 percent of the school time is devoted to languages and social studies, 30 to 35 percent to mathematics and science, 10 to 15 percent to arts, 10 percent to productive work, and 7 to 10 percent to physical training.

School programs are diversified either through tracking (e.g., classical and modern languages, mathematics, science) and/or by compulsory and/or optional, "elective" subjects. The list of objectives contains the specification of the desired educational outcomes for various grade levels and study groups. Usually it includes—directly or indirectly—some guidelines for the recommended teaching–learning strategies and methods. Recently, centrally devised and published textbooks, working papers, tests, selected reading materials, school radio and television programs, handbooks for teachers, and so on have become an integral part of the school curricula. Curriculum reforms—either general or partial—are carefully prepared and gradually introduced. Thus, for example, the implementation of a curriculum reform in the Soviet Union lasted from 1967 to 1975, while a reform in the Democratic Republic of Germany lasted from 1970 to 1978. In Hungary, implementation of a reform started in 1978, and according to official plans it will not be completed until the middle of the 1980s.

The first studies in the field of curriculum theory were published in the last decades of the nineteenth century by Friedrich Adolf Diesterweg (1790–1866) and Friedrich Wilhelm Dörpfeld (1824–1893) in Germany, Konstantyin Dimitrijevits Ushinsky (1824–1870) in Russia, and later Mór Kármán (1843–1915) in Hungary and Bogdan Nawroczynski (1882–1974) in Poland. After the socialist revolution the first minister of culture of Soviet Russia was Lunacharsky, whose 1918 analysis of the curriculum of the polytechnical work school might well be considered one of the first contributions to curriculum theory in a socialist country. Since the middle of the twentieth century, significant development has taken place. The development of curriculum theory has come to be officially encouraged, and has gained financial support (see *Curriculum Theory*). It has been carried out at the Academy of Pedagogical Sciences, at other national institutes for education, and in university and college departments. In most countries, researchers have applied methods of comparative and historical studies to deal with the structure of aims and objectives of curricula, and with problems of selecting and organizing the content for the entire school system. In most countries, systematic preparatory work is carried out to help prepare plans for new curricula for the new millennium. The empirical basis for this work is provided by the continuous evaluation of ongoing curricula and by periodical and continuous restricted reforms (see *Curriculum Reform*). Curriculum theory has achieved relative independence, though it still has strong ties to other fields of study both within and outside pedagogy. It is frequently treated as a part of didactic studies, with an attempt to revise some theories of this field or alternatively subdividing its major areas into more specifically defined subareas.

Bibliography

Connell W F 1980 *A History of Education in the Twentieth Century World.* Teachers College Press, New York, pp. 196–225, 228–41, 426–56

Mader O 1979 *Fragen der Lehrplantheorie: Beitrage zur Pädagogik,* Vol. 16. Volk und Wissen, Berlin

Spain

A. de la Orden

The history and cultural traditions of each country determine its curriculum, which in turn constitutes the translation of the general aims of the educational system into school programmes.

In Spain, the school curriculum, interpreted as a "formal course of studies", is the consequence of the prevailing centralized educational system, itself a reflection of the political centralization. The history of the curriculum in Spain, and research taking place on the curriculum, are very much conditioned by this fact. Only very recently has a change begun towards decentralization, which may bring with it a greater diversification in educational options and flexibility in the curriculum.

The long tradition of regulating education began at the beginning of the nineteenth century. Although some previous steps had been taken, without doubt the 1813 "Quintana Report" (Guerrero 1979) was the first major step in the line of study programmes and plans which were to guide Spanish education during the nineteenth and twentieth centuries. López del Castillo (1982) presented in a recent study an analysis of these plans for primary education, and Utande (1964) produced an analysis for secondary education.

The specificity of these plans varies considerably, but mostly they prescribe the subjects to be taught, their arrangement in cycles, stages, or grades, calendars and timetables, teaching methods and norms, and occasionally codes of discipline. Only late in the twentieth century do the so-called questionnaires or programmes appear as additional norms, presenting in detail the content of each subject and lists of the topics to be covered. For secondary education the first detailed syllabus was established in the Plan of 1953 and for primary education in the National Questionnaires of 1953, which included orientations and educational viewpoints claiming to be based on subject structures and on the developmental characteristics of the student.

During the 1960s, significant changes took place in the curriculum of the Spanish primary school, namely the formulation of acceptable levels of attainment by subject and grade level in order to evaluate and pass students (CEDODEP 1964), and the establishment of new questionnaires (CEDODEP 1965). Accent on the development of learning habits, intellectual aptitudes and attitudes, and emphasis on projects involving different traditional subjects are important characteristics of these questionnaires.

From 1970 onwards, and as a result of a new education act, Spanish education (primary, secondary, and vocational) began a process of reform and modernization guided by national pedagogical orientations of 1970. New objectives, contents, methods, evaluation, and organization patterns of learning were suggested as a basis for the development of the curriculum (see *Curriculum Reform*).

The new syllabus for secondary education introduced in 1974 brought a change of direction in the traditional orientation of the Spanish Bachillerato. Important innovations were the introduction of electives, particularly technical–vocational, and a noticeable reduction of classical studies (Latin and Greek).

Although curriculum studies have existed independently in education faculties and institutes since the 1920s, significant systematic research in this field did not reach a critical volume in Spain until the 1970s, as a result of the educational reform and the concomitant creation of the university institutes of education (the *Centro Nacional de Investigación y Desarrollo en Educación-Instituto de Ciencias de la Educación* or CENIDE-ICEs) (INCIE 1975). Research has centred fundamentally on curriculum design and its fit to the subject structure, interrelation of subjects, and the interests and needs of students (see *Curriculum Research*). The most relevant aspects of the curriculum which have been studied have been:

(a) sequence of content in different subjects;
(b) continuity between different educational levels;
(c) curriculum and genetic epistemology;
(d) adequacy of curriculum objectives and content;
(e) globalization of content;
(f) curriculum interpretation of textbooks.

Although these studies identified several flaws in the new programmes, they have contributed to creating a climate of concern about curriculum problems, and their first perceptible effects are a new attempt at producing a national syllabus for primary education, trying to correct previous deficiencies brought to light. In effect, the introduction of the so-called "renovated programmes for preschool education and general basic education" establishes the minimum competencies for Spanish children aged 5 to 14. The characteristics of these programmes, which structure the education in comprehensive cycles of two or more conventional grades, facilitate vertical streaming and group teaching.

As a result of the government proposal for a global reform of the school system (Ministerio de Educación y Ciencia 1987) a new curricular conception is emerging. The new curriculum will again be a national norm regulating the contents and processes of preschool, elementary, and secondary education in Spain; but each region, and, eventually, each school, will be obliged to specify its own study program by adapting and complementing the national basic curricular guidelines (Ministerio de Educación y Ciencia 1989). Decentralization is an innovation in Spanish curriculum history, and this will generate a second wave of research work on curriculum design, development, and evaluation.

Bibliography

Castillejo J L 1977 *Secuencialidad de los programas de EGB*. Instituto de Ciencias de la Educación, Universidad Politécnica de Valencia

Centro de Documentación y Orientación de Enseñanza Primaria (CEDODEP) 1964 Niveles de adquisiciones por cursos. *Rev. Vida Escolar* 55–56: 1–64

Centro de Documentación y Orientación de Enseñanza Primaria (CEDODEP) 1965 Cuestionarios Nacionales para la Enseñanza Primaria. *Rev. Vida Escolar* 70–71: 1–96

Guerrero E 1979 *Historia de la Educación en España*. Textos y Documentos, Ministerio de Educación y Ciencia, Madrid

Instituto Nacional de Ciencias de la Educación (INCIE) 1975 *Investigaciones educativas de la Red INCIE-ICEs*. Ministerio de Educación y Ciencia, Madrid

López del Castillo Mª–T 1982 Planes y programas escolares en la legislación española. *Rev. Bordón*. 34: 242–43

Ministerio de Educación y Ciencia 1987 *Proyecto Para la Reforma de Enseñanza*. Centro de Publicaciones del Ministerio de Educación y Ciencia, Madrid

Ministerio de Educación y Ciencia 1989 *Diseno Curricular Base*. Centro de Publicaciónes del Ministerio de Educación y Ciencia, Madrid

Utande Igualada M 1964 *Planes de estudio de Enseñanza Media*. Dirección General de Enseñanza Media, Ministerio de Educación Nacional, Madrid

Sweden

S. Marklund

The term curriculum is restricted here to three principal aspects: the goals, content, and methods of teaching. The goals seem to have been self-evident in Sweden to begin with. Universal schooling was to serve the Church and its doctrine. It was not until the nineteenth and twentieth centuries that goals of civic and democratic education became widespread. By contrast, the content of education has been defined in what are frequently detailed syllabi and timetables. Historically speaking, these have constituted the nucleus of the school curriculum.

1. The Old Grammar Schools

The goals, content, and methods of schooling have acquired legal form in the laws and education ordinances applying to schools at various times. When schools were first set up in Sweden, in the thirteenth century, most of them were entirely controlled by the Church. They were organized by bishops and cathedral chapters as cathedral schools. Their pupils were destined to enter the priesthood or to serve the Church in other capacities. In addition, there were small monastic and town schools which taught their pupils to read and write.

The Reformation in the sixteenth century put the Church under the authority of the State, and schools came under the control of the State as constituted by the king and the estates. Then in 1571 came the first Schools Ordinance, which was part of the Ecclesiastical Law from that same year. School subjects were now defined as Latin, religious knowledge, and liturgical singing. Rhetoric and dialectics were also included. Mathematics and science subjects were not. This type of school had three or four classes, all of them apparently of two years' duration.

The next education ordinance, promulgated in 1611, extended cathedral schooling to six two-year classes, added to which certain towns and cities could have shorter "provincial schools". Greek was now added to the timetable. Schooling gradually came to be divided into three levels, that is, a four-year trivial school, a four-year gymnasium and, after that, academies for higher studies. In addition to classes in the previous theological subjects, the trivial school acquired special writing and arithmetic classes in which pupils could train for secular occupations. The subject repertoire of trivial schools and gymnasiums under the next school ordinance, from 1649, can be deduced from the stipulated teaching strength: two theology teachers, one teacher of logic and physics, one teacher of rhetoric and Latin eloquence, one teacher of history and poetry, and one teacher of Greek and mathematics. Despite the new elements of humanities and natural science, the school system remained what in Sweden was later to be known as a Latin high school.

Two short-lived attempts were made to maintain secular "academies of chivalry" for the sons of the nobility, on the same lines as in England and other Western European countries. In addition to military exercises, the curriculum here included subjects like politics, surveying, fortification, mathematics, and languages. Sweden's two universities, Uppsala and Lund, also introduced appointments for "language and exercise masters" (Landquist 1965).

Hebrew, the language of the Bible, was introduced into the grammar schools in 1693. A new school ordinance, in 1724, introduced geography in the form of cartographical studies. Instruction in commerce, industry, and book-keeping was also introduced during the eighteenth century, under the influence of the mercantilist ideas of the time. Elements of science were also added, through the inspiration of scientists like Carl Linnaeus.

The French Revolution and attendant world events in the closing years of the eighteenth century also generated demands for civic education. Latin had virtually played out its part as an international *lingua franca*. New school ordinances in 1807 and 1820 retained the subject on a reduced scale, mostly on account of its alleged usefulness in formal and aesthetic education.

2. Differentiation of the School Curriculum

The development of the non-Latin writing and arithmetic class, described above, led in 1849 to the division of schools into two lines—science and Latin—both of which qualified students for university entrance.

This bifurcated secondary school was gradually combined with commercial schools and technical schools on the same level. The commercial schools were taken over by the State in 1913, the technical schools in 1919. Special girls' high schools had long existed, offering "curricula particularly suited to the female sex". They began to receive State grants in 1874, and from 1905 onwards they were also established on a public-sector basis (Marklund 1968).

3. Compulsory Education

The Reformation in the sixteenth century made compulsory education an ecclesiastical responsibility. The Ecclesiastical Law of 1686 clearly stipulated that the clergy were required to teach everyone—children and adults, men and women—to read. Thus long before the passing of the Elementary Schools Act in 1842 the Swedish population had become literate through confirmation instruction, literacy teaching, and catechetical examination.

The Elementary Schools Act of 1842 introduced a compulsory elementary school, the curriculum for which was initially defined in terms of "skills", not subjects. Children were to learn to read, write, and count (using the four rules of arithmetic), added to which they were to learn the elements of religion and liturgical singing. Over and above this "minimum course", they could be taught geography, history, and general science (Fredriksson 1940–1971, Sjöstrand 1953–65).

Throughout the nineteenth century, in most schools, the curriculum stopped short at the "minimum course". Subject designations were not introduced until the 1882 Elementary Schools Statute. This division into subjects was completed in the 1919 curriculum, but at the same time directions were issued concerning methods of interdisciplinary, integrated teaching in keeping with the activity learning theories of the time.

Subsequent curricula for compulsory schools, in their design and application and also as regards the kind of teaching materials used, came to reflect the debate between two different approaches, with respect to courses based on scientific disciplines, or courses organized on an interdisciplinary basis to suit the pupils' experience, needs, and aptitudes. This debate is also increasingly characteristic of postcompulsory education.

4. Making and Application of Curricula

It is typical of postwar official curricula that questions concerning the nature and content of study programmes have tended more and more to be viewed in relation to the overriding goals of education, as regards education for democracy, equality, and peace. And in addition to rules as to *what* teaching is to include, the curricula now also include rules and recommendations concerning *how* this is to be done.

This is clearly apparent from the latest curricula for compulsory and postcompulsory education (1980 Basic School Curriculum, 1970 Upper Secondary School Curriculum).

Curricula in Sweden have always been adopted by the Government or by the National Board of Education. The goals of the school system and the goals for individual subjects are nationally uniform. So too are time schedules and syllabi, although these are written in such a way that local variations both can and should occur. Textbooks and other teaching materials are chosen by the schools themselves, though teaching materials were subject to inspection by national authorities between 1937 and 1973. All that remains today is the "objectivity scrutiny" of materials for social subjects. The National Board of Education supplies centrally compiled achievement tests for a limited number of subjects. These are only compulsory for the secondary school level; on the postsecondary level they can be replaced with tests constructed by the individual school.

Bibliography

Fredriksson V (ed.) 1940–71 *Svenska folkskolans historia I–VI* [History of Swedish elementary schools I–VI]. Bonnier, Stockholm

Landquist J 1956 *Pedagogikens historia* [History of education]. Gleerup, Lund

Läroplaner för grundskolan 1962, 1969 and 1980 [Curriculum for Swedish basic school 1962, 1969 and 1980]. Skolöverstyrelsen, Stockholm

Läroplan för gymnasieskolan 1970 [Curriculum for upper-secondary school 1970]. Skolöverstyrelsen, Stockholm

Marklund S 1968 *Gymnasiet—skola i förvandling* [Upper-secondary school in transition]. Bonniers, Stockholm

Marklund S 1985 *Skolsverige 1950–1975. Del 4: Differentieringsfrågan* [School in Sweden 1950–1975. Part 4: The differentiation question]. Liber-Utbildningsförlaget, Stockholm

Marklund S, Söderberg P 1967 *The Swedish Comprehensive School*. Longmans, London

Sjöstrand W 1953–65 *Pedagogikens historia I–III:2* [History of education I–III:2]. Gleerup, Lund

Undervisningsplan för rikets folkskolar 1919 [Curriculum for elementary education]. Skolöverstyrelsen, Stockholm

Third World Countries

H. W. R. Hawes

Current curricula in schools in Third World countries derive historically from a number of sources. Traditional and religious education have influenced methodologies and approaches used in teaching, accounting for the high importance placed, in many systems, on the authority of the teacher and of the spoken and written word. Colonial policies often emphasized the production of middle level clerical and administrative grades, hence emphasis on correct language, sound numeracy, and an adequate fund of general knowledge—as distinct from scientific, aesthetic, or vocational subjects. However in British African colonies a conflicting set of traditions also existed deriving in part from principles of indirect

rule and emphasizing adaption to environment as expressed, for instance, in the Colonial Office Memoranda 1925, "Education Policy in British Tropical Africa". Metropolitan practices also influenced all countries, and most particularly French and Portuguese territories. Often such practices continued long after they were abandoned in their countries of origin. The British "revised code" of 1862 was exported with only slight modifications to Caribbean and West African countries and was still in use in the early 1900s, 20 years after its abandonment in the United Kingdom. The term "standards" still widely used in primary schools derives from it.

Curricula in French Territories were highly centralized. In English and Dutch dependencies despite attempts by governments to devise syllabi of instruction, curricula tended to be less centrally prescribed and moderated than they are today, particularly at intermediate and secondary levels. There were some examples of highly innovative and community-based curricula for example, at Omu in Nigeria and Bakht er Ruda in the Sudan.

The concept of systematic planning of curricula either of subjects or levels was hardly in evidence until the 1960s and major changes postwar in Asia and Africa centred around the languages of instruction (except in Francophone countries), rather than content, one preoccupation being the unification of large heterogeneous societies, thus emphasis on Bahasa in Indonesia, on the "three language formula" in India, and on English in Nigeria.

In the 1960s however, pressures to change curricula built up from both inside and outside the countries. Nationally there were pressures to indigenize content particularly in social sciences; in Africa resolutions of the Tananarive Conference in 1962 reinforced this: to modernize content, emphasis being placed particularly on mathematics and science in secondary and higher education, but significant attention also directed towards the primary level in the influential New Primary Approach in Kenya which subsequently influenced developments in a number of other countries such as Zambia, Swaziland, and Northern Nigeria. Finally, and in some distinction to these, there were pressures to vocationalize curricula, particularly evident in diversification of secondary-school curricula in Latin America, strongly supported by World Bank loans, and in attempts in Africa to provide vocational content for young school leavers at primary or junior secondary levels (see UNESCO/OAU Conference of Ministers of Education, Nairobi 1968). In certain countries, particularly those whose governments turned towards socialism, political ideologies gave a strong additional impetus towards ruralization as in Tanzania and Cuba.

From outside, and under the influence of developments in Western Europe and the United States—came pressures, first to revolutionize content and approaches, particularly in mathematics and science, and also, increasingly, pressures to systematize and institutionalize curriculum reform.

In mathematics and science, international initiatives were derived from UNESCO, as in the UNESCO Biology project, and also from the African Education Programme of Educational Services Incorporated, later the Education Development Center (EDC), which had played a leading role in launching major curriculum projects in the United States. The latter organized and funded, with USAID support, two major programmes directed at Anglophone Africa but with considerable spinoffs worldwide. These were the African Mathematics Programme (the Entebbe Mathematics) and the African Primary Science Programme, using a more flexible, unit-based approach with national centres developing, adapting, and comparing materials.

At the same time at the national level there was much borrowing and adaption of programmes which originated in, for the most part, the United Kingdom and North America—for example, the Nuffield Science Programmes in Southeast Asia and Africa, the EDC devised programmes such as the Physical Sciences Study Commission (PSSC), *Physics* in Latin America and the Schools Mathematics Project in East Africa.

Publishers, often taking relatively independent initiatives also had a major influence on change, particularly in language. Writers such as French (Oxford English Course) and West (New Method Courses) fundamentally affected curricula in English-speaking countries in Asia, Africa, and the Caribbean during the 1950s. Later revisions of such standard language courses often took place with university or ministry collaboration.

The move to systematize and institutionalize the curriculum process which evolved after many of the major subject initiatives had been launched, has led to the establishment of national research and development councils; to units attached to planning divisions of ministries as in most countries in Francophone Africa, and also to the initiation of curriculum development centres in many Anglophone countries. Many of these institutions have had influence internationally as well as nationally—for example, the National Council of Educational Research and Training (NCERT) in India (1961), Office of Educational and Cultural Research and Development (BP3K) in Indonesia (1969), Kenya Institute of Education (KIE) (1968), Malaysian Curriculum Development Centre (1973), and many more. There have been programmes in nearly all systems to evolve more systematic processes of preparation, presentation, and subsequently evaluation of curriculum programmes.

International conferences, workshops, and training programmes have been organized, largely under the influence of UNESCO and its affiliated bodies—IIEP (Paris), UIE (Hamburg), Regional Offices in Dakar and Bangkok, particularly through the Asian Programme of Educational Innovation for Development (APEID). An African Curriculum Organization has been set up (1976) based in Ibadan, Nigeria, which organizes its own training courses through correspondence and contact sessions in Nairobi.

Attempts to clarify and talk through national aims and goals as fundamental determinants of curriculum policy tended to emerge somewhat later either initiated by national statements as in the Pancesilla Philosophy in Indonesia or the Arusha Declaration in Tanzania (1967), by development plans, by national surveys of opinion as in Upper Volta (1973) or Zambia (1976), or by national curriculum conferences as in Nigeria (1969). In some systems such national consensus is still to emerge or has become outdated with the emergence of new structures, as with UPE, new political movements or new economic circumstances.

Consequent on the pressures outlined above, attempts to evolve new programmes have proceeded with vigour nearly all centrally inspired and commonly designed in the "objectives–content–evaluation" pattern of systematic curriculum design with considerable variation in the extent to which the more rigid patterns of behaviouralism are applied.

Although programmes and projects still continue to be mounted in the 1980s to meet new demands, there is heightened concern that the nature, speed, and extent of changes mounted in the 1960s and 1970s may have caused unacceptable gaps between official curricula and actual practice; also that the nature of changes proposed may not be entirely appropriate to national and local needs. In particular, the following areas of concern presently affect curriculum planning and policies worldwide:

(a) concern over the gap between the expectations of programmes, particularly in maths and science, and the realities of classroom practice, teacher competence, and student achievement, particularly in poorer and rural areas. This has led in some cases to political intervention, the cancelling of New Maths Programmes as in Nigeria (1977), Kenya (1981), or the promulgation of "back to basics" curricula in Malaysia (1980);

(b) concern over the means by which the wide degree of local and individual differences can be managed within the framework of a curriculum which is planned centrally. This has led to increasing attempts to evolve patterns of locally based curriculum and materials development, as in Sri Lanka or Botswana (1975 to 1980), and to experiments with modular learning, as in Indonesia and the Philippines;

(c) concern over the way in which individual subject initiatives, particularly at secondary level, can be coordinated within a unified curriculum to serve needs and emphasize priorities of local and national development;

(d) concern over the adaption of techniques of curriculum development—developed initially for schools (and in certain subjects) to a new pattern of lifelong education which links formal with nonformal education and school learning with community learning. Thus conferences and training courses, for example, those mounted by UNESCO Institute for Education Hamburg, now include both formal and nonformal educators;

(e) concern over the means by which systematic, formative evaluation can be integrated into the management of all curriculum projects from the very outset and the evaluation of outcomes through to examinations, and how this evaluation should be designed so that it feeds back positively and not negatively into the process of curriculum design. The establishment of the International Centre for Educational Evaluation, Ibadan, 1972 is an example of such concern.

Bibliography

Asian Programme of Educational Innovation for Development (APEID) 1980 *National Strategies for Curriculum Design and Development*. UNESCO Regional Seminar, Canberra. UNESCO/APEID, Bangkok

Dove L A (ed.) 1980 *Curriculum Reforms in Secondary Schools: A Commonwealth Survey*. Commonwealth Secretariat, London

Hawes H W R 1979 *Curriculum and Reality in African Primary Schools*. Longman, Harlow, Essex

United Kingdom

D. Lawton

Although Scotland and Northern Ireland have separate systems of education, the general pattern of curriculum development has been similar for all of the United Kingdom. This article however deals mainly with the history of curriculum development in England and Wales.

Curriculum studies did not really exist as a separate field of enquiry in the nineteenth century, but there were important discussions about the content of the curriculum. Educational debate tended to be dominated by a combination of two related social theories—economic laissez faire and the political philosophy of the utilitarians. There were religious arguments in favour of compulsory education, but these tended not to have any lasting influence on the curriculum as a whole,

except that for many years religious instruction retained its high priority.

Laissez-faire doctrine discouraged government interference so that the "hidden hand" of the market could operate to maximum advantage. For some, education was an exception to this rule. Utilitarianism was based on the premise that any government policy could only be justified in terms of increasing human happiness and diminishing pain. Utilitarians argued that the benefits of education could not be judged by the amount of immediate gratification produced, but only in terms of long-term benefit to society as a whole. Jeremy Bentham (1748–1832) produced a collection of papers on education in *Chrestomathia* (1815). The most complete account of the utilitarian approach to education, however, was given by James Mill (1773–1836) in an article on "Education" in the 1818 edition of the *Encyclopaedia Britannica*. The qualities which should be produced by a utilitarian curriculum were sagacity, temperance, justice, and generosity. Mill brought together a theory of knowledge and a psychological theory of learning. He made the assumption that the human mind begins as a "clean slate" and the origin of all knowledge is sense experience; knowledge is built up by "association".

The credit for applying, or perhaps misapplying, this kind of curriculum theory to practice must go to Robert Lowe (1811–92). In 1833 the government had taken the decision to put public funds into "elementary" education. This "interference" was very small and intended to supplement the funds of two voluntary (that is, religious) bodies. But by the middle of the nineteenth century, expenditure had escalated and questions were being asked about efficiency and "value for money". Lowe's theoretical views on curriculum can best be seen in *Primary and Classical Education* which was published a few years later (1867). He made it clear that the kind of useful knowledge which he thought appropriate for the upper classes was not the same as "sound and cheap elementary instruction" for the poor.

The 1862 Revised Code prescribed for the lower orders a curriculum consisting of reading, writing, and arithmetic (plus plain needlework for girls). It was a deliberately narrow curriculum which could be tested quickly by visiting inspectors. Objectives were prespecified in terms of six standards and the grant payable to a school was adjusted according to the number of pupils passing—"payment by results".

The 1862 Revised Code was attacked by an inspector who might legitimately be cited as an early curriculum theorist—Matthew Arnold (1822–88). The narrow 1862 Code was modified over the following 20 years, partly as a result of action by teachers who in 1871 formed the National Union of Elementary Teachers which later became the National Union of Teachers (NUT). The early history of the NUT was largely concerned with the struggle against a centrally controlled narrow curriculum.

A "progressive" antiutilitarian influence on the curriculum had already been felt in the official codes and circulars of the 1890s, but was intensified after the 1902 Education Act. The New Education Fellowship was founded in 1920 representing many points of view. Some like Edmond Holmes condemned bad practice: in his book *What Is and What Might Be* (1911) he contrasted the training for "mechanical obedience" he saw in so many elementary schools with "education for self-realisation". The movement was also part of an international trend towards a less authoritarian, more child-centred approach to education based on the writings of Rousseau, Pestalozzi, Froebel, Freud Homer Lane, and John Dewey. But throughout the 1920s and 1930s, most elementary schools retained traditional curricula and formal teaching methods despite the abolition of regu-

lations in 1926. In the case of secondary schools, regulations prescribed the curriculum from 1904 until the 1944 Act, and this formal curriculum was backed up by an examination system controlled, to some extent, by the universities.

Until the 1950s, most of the writing which could be classified as curriculum studies was contained in official government reports. Three notable examples are Hadow (1926), Spens (1938), and Norwood (1943). The theory reflected in such reports was often out of date and inaccurate. The Spens Report of 1938, for example, illustrates the influence of pseudo-psychological theory on curriculum studies.

The tradition of curriculum theory taking the form of official reports written by civil servants continued after the 1944 Education Act with such reports as Crowther (1959), Newsom (1963), and Plowden (1967). But from about 1960, curriculum studies as a university subject emerged. Even this development came about partly as a reaction to official policy. In 1960, the Minister of Education, Sir David Eccles, announced a proposal to set up a Curriculum Study Group. This was seen by local education authorities and teachers as a sinister move in the direction of central control of the curriculum; the government was persuaded to abolish the Curriculum Study Group and replace it by the Schools Council for Curriculum and Examinations (1964) on which teachers would have much stronger representation.

The typical early Schools Council Curriculum project was based on the centre–periphery model with a university subject "expert" at the centre. Much of the academic study of curriculum emerged out of a development from, or opposition to, that model.

The development of curriculum studies may also have resulted in a change of attitude by the Department of Education and Science (DES). Since the mid-1970s there have been clear indications that many civil servants and politicians wanted more central influence on curriculum. This has resulted in two official (DES) documents, *Framework for the School Curriculum* (1980) and the *School Curriculum* (1981), both of which were badly argued and lacked any clear theoretical basis.

The influence of academic curriculum theory on official (i.e., DES) policy is negligible, but can be detected—faintly—in some of the advisory documents produced by Her Majesty's Inspectors. An example of this atheoretical approach may be seen in the kind of subject-based approach to the National Curriculum proposed in the Education Reform Act (1988) (Lawton 1989).

Bibliography

Board of Education 1926 *Report of the Consultative Committee on the Education of the Adolescent.* (The Hadow Report.) Her Majesty's Stationery Office, London

Board of Education 1938 *Report, with Special Reference to Grammar Schools, and Technical High Schools.* (The Spens

Report, report of the Consultative Committee on Secondary Education.) Her Majesty's Stationery Office, London

Department of Education and Science 1967 *Children and their Primary Schools*. (The Plowden Report, report of the Central Advisory Council for Education.) Her Majesty's Stationery Office, London

Lawton D 1989 *Education, Culture and the National Curriculum*. Hodder and Stoughton Educational, London

Ministry of Education 1959 *15 to 18*. Report of the Central Advisory Council for Education. (The Crowther Report.) Her Majesty's Stationery Office, London

Ministry of Education 1963 *Half our Future*. A Report of the Central Advisory Council for Education. (The Newsom Report.) Her Majesty's Stationery Office, London

Secondary School Examinations Council 1943 *Curriculum and Examinations in Secondary Education*. (The Norwood Report.) Her Majesty's Stationery Office, London

United States

H. M. Kliebard

The course of study is always in a process of evolution. Curriculum history attempts to trace that evolution with special reference to the social and intellectual forces which affect the question of what gets taught in schools. Periods of perceived social change, real or imagined, are usually associated with conflict about the nature and scope of the curriculum. In the United States, a drive for curriculum change became especially intense in the 1890s with different reform groups arguing for a course of study that would be more scientifically determined and more in tune with the nature of a modern industrial society. By about 1918, a field of specialization had emerged within the general field of education that focused directly on curriculum issues.

1. Early American Curricula

The earliest American curricula were drawn largely from European antecedents, particularly from English secondary schools and colleges. Latin, Greek, and mathematics, for example were the standard fare in the earliest Latin Grammar Schools in colonial Massachusetts. To a large extent, subjects were not distinguishable from the works studied, and, in many cases the curriculum consisted simply of a list of the books themselves. Thus, in colonial times, a typical Latin curriculum would be recorded as *Cheever's Accidence*, the *Colloquies of Corderius*, *Aesop's Fables*, *Caesar*, *Ovid's Metamorphoses*, and so on (Meriwether 1907). During the national period, particular books continued to be the basis of the curriculum, but, increasingly, they tended to be the work of American authors, the most famous being the McGuffey series of readers. Early in the nineteenth century, as the academy replaced the Latin Grammar School as the predominant form of secondary education, the curriculum tended to be broadened to include practical subjects such as surveying and navigation (Sizer 1964). As the United States became increasingly urbanized, there was also a tendency toward greater uniformity in the course of study and correspondingly less attention to the individual teacher as the source of what was taught. In Chicago, for example, between 1856 and 1864, the superintendent

of schools divided all students in the city into grades and established a distinct curriculum for each subject at every grade level (Tyack 1974 pp. 45–46).

2. Early Reform

As the nineteenth century drew to a close, interest in curriculum intensified. By 1880, William Torrey Harris, the powerful and articulate United States Commissioner of Education, had declared, "The question of the course of study is the most important the educator can have before him" (National Education Association p. 174). The strong intensification of attention to curriculum matters seems to have been associated with a recognition that the industrialization that had been going on in the country for some time was having important consequences for such institutions as the family and the church. Many educational leaders saw in such changes a need to reconstruct the course of study in order to bring the school in line with a changing social order. By the 1890s, concern about the course of study had reached the point where several interest groups were emerging each with its own agenda for restructuring the curriculum. Coincidental with these social changes, or perhaps as a consequence of them, the fundamental rationale for the American curriculum, mental discipline, began to unravel. For years, the study of the classical languages, mathematics, and traditional academic subjects had been buttressed by the idea that certain subjects had the power to strengthen the intellectual faculties and to develop good habits of thought. According to mental discipline theory, for example, mathematics was believed to strengthen the power of reasoning. To a large extent, that rationale served for a time to sustain certain traditional subjects against the onslaught of such newer subjects as the modern foreign languages, social science, and manual training. One of the most significant of the challenges to mental discipline came in 1890 when the great American psychologist and philosopher, William James, reported an experiment which he had conducted with his students at Harvard University designed to test the proposition that memory could be improved through practice. James reported in

1890 that, contrary to the assumptions of mental discipline, his ability to memorize poetry along with that of his students had actually deteriorated slightly after a period of practice. Although, by modern standards, James's experiment would hardly be considered conclusive, it did help initiate a series of experimental and other challenges to the efficacy of mental discipline as a way to justify the continuance of certain subjects in the school curriculum (Thorndike and Woodworth 1901, Thorndike 1924).

3. Reform Through National Committees

At the same time that attention to the consequences of social change was intensifying and mental discipline was being challenged as a curriculum theory, enrollments in American secondary schools began to increase dramatically. By about 1880, the public high school had surpassed academies in terms of enrollments. In 1890, only 6.7 percent of the population of youth, 14 to 17 years old, was attending secondary school. By 1900, it had already reached 11.4 percent, and in 1920, about one-third of that age group was enrolled in secondary schools. By 1930, the number had reached almost 4.5 million, over 51 percent of that population. These increases in the secondary-school population implied, for many educational leaders, a corresponding change in the curriculum. One of the most significant events of the period just before the turn of the century was the appointment by the National Education Association of the Committee of Ten in 1892, with Charles W. Eliot, the president of Harvard University, as chairman. Ostensibly, the committee was appointed to deal with a question involving the relationship between the secondary school and the college. The immediate problem, essentially, was that different colleges were prescribing different requirements for admission, and this put the high schools in the untenable position of trying to prepare small segments of their student populations differently depending on what colleges they were seeking to attend. The overall charge of the committee, therefore, was to achieve some sort of uniformity in the high-school curriculum. Inevitably, however, the committee found itself dealing with a wide range of theoretical and practical curriculum issues.

Eliot, himself, was a mental disciplinarian, and, to some extent, the report of the committee reflected that orientation. Eliot was also, however, a reformer, albeit a moderate one, and some of the recommendations of the committee reflected modest changes that he sought to institute in the curriculum of secondary schools. The heart of the report was a set of four courses of study— Classical, Latin–Scientific, Modern Languages, and English—each of which, according to the committee, represented an appropriate course of study in the high school and also appropriate as a basis for admission to college. The decline of Greek as a major element in a college-entrance program, for example, was reflected in the fact that Greek appeared in only one of the

recommended courses of study, the Classical one, and, even there, the period of study was reduced from the more customary three years to two. Eliot was trying to avoid early "bifurcation" of the high-school population into college going and noncollege going, and the reduction in Greek in the Classical curriculum gave students one more year to make that decision. Even Latin appeared only in the Classical and the Latin–Scientific courses of study so that, according to the committee's recommendation, students could be admitted to college with only one modern foreign language. Unlike most mental disciplinarians, Eliot believed that prolonged study of a modern language such as French or German would have as much disciplinary value as Greek or Latin.

One of the most significant questions that the committee considered was whether there ought to be a curricular distinction between students who were preparing for college and students who were preparing for "life." The committee unanimously endorsed Eliot's view that such a distinction was undesirable since the school's function to develop good habits of thought ought to remain the same for all students regardless of probable destination. Although the committee saw some advantage in the Classical and the Latin–Scientific courses of study over the Modern Language and English, this was probably because the former two had the more experienced teachers and the more proven methods of study. Much contemporary interpretation of the work of the Committee of Ten involves the charge that the committee through its recommendations succeeded in imposing college domination over the high-school curriculum thereby inhibiting innovation and change for decades to come. Actually, however, when seen within the context of its time, the Committee of Ten's recommendations represented a moderate step in the direction of what were then regarded as modern subjects (National Education Association 1893).

The chief critic of the committee's recommendations was Granville Stanley Hall, one of the leading psychologists of the time. Shortly after he had returned in 1880 from a period of study in Germany, Hall assumed leadership of the child-study movement in American education. For the most part, those associated with that movement believed that a proper course of study could be constructed around the child's true nature and that a scientifically based curriculum could emerge from gathering a massive amount of data on the child. The child-study movement was part of a growing challenge to the humanist curriculum, a challenge which claimed the authority of science. Hall saw the new population of high-school students essentially as a "vast army of incapables" (Hall 1902 p. 510), making the curriculum that the Committee of Ten had endorsed unworkable. The range of ability in schools, according to Hall, was so vast, that it required sharp differentiation in the curriculum, and not only in terms of ability, but in terms of such other significant factors as gender. Hall was also deeply suspicious of the emphasis on intellectual development in the school arguing that children were, by and large, not ready for it and that intellectual activity represented something of a danger to a child's health and vitality.

When the Committee of Fifteen reported to the National Education Association in 1895, the leading spokesman for the traditional humanist curriculum was Harris. Unlike Eliot, Harris was not a mental disciplinarian, but much of his long career as Commissioner of Education was devoted to articulating a rationale for the traditional course of study, earning for him the reputation as "the great conservator" in American education. Harris had for years advocated a curriculum based on what he liked to think of as "five coordinate groups of study," arithmetic and mathematics, geography, history, grammar, and literature and art. Each of these studies, Harris felt, were ways by which the "five windows of the soul" could be opened, and, together, they represented a coherent representation of the Western cultural heritage. In the main, the section on curriculum in the Committee of Fifteen Report was the work of Harris and reflected his justification for a humanist course of study (National Education Association 1895).

A major attack against Harris's report was mounted by a group of reform-minded educators who thought of themselves as the disciples of the German philosopher, Johann Friedrich Herbart. The National Herbart Society had been formed in 1892, with John Dewey as one of its members, and for about a decade that group served as a focal point for what they believed to be a scientifically valid attack on the traditional curriculum. Although their interpretations of such key Herbartian concepts as concentration, correlation, and apperception are open to some question, their attack on the traditional curriculum of the nineteenth century provided an opening wedge for reformers with quite different conceptions of what the curriculum should be like.

4. John Dewey's Laboratory School

In 1896, John Dewey left the University of Michigan to assume the position of head of the combined department of philosophy, psychology, and pedagogy at the University of Chicago. Within about a year, he formed a plan for what became the Laboratory School (commonly known as the Dewey School), and in 1896, the school opened its doors. Initially, Dewey seemed intrigued with the Herbartian concept of culture epochs as a basis for the curriculum. The basic idea was that there existed a correspondence between the historic stages through which the human race had passed and the individual stages in human development, and that this correspondence could be used as a basis for constructing a course of study. Dewey objected, however, to the tendency of the Herbartians to draw inferences from historical development to individual development with-

out any verification that such a corresponding stage existed in the child. He also felt that the Herbartian emphasis on the products of various historical epochs as the materials of instruction was misguided. It was quite common, for example, for Herbartian schools to teach myths and fairy tales to children who were presumed to be undergoing their "savage" stage of development. In many cases, literary works such as Longfellow's *Hiawatha* were also used for that purpose. Dewey felt that, if there were any point to the question of correspondence, it should involve the children's engaging in the same sorts of social activities which were characteristic of a particular historical epoch. Thus, when children were presumed to be in a stage in their individual development which corresponded to the agricultural stage in human history, they would not read literary works on the subject, but engage in those basic activities that were characteristic of the agricultural way of life.

After about a two-year period of experimentation with the curriculum of the Laboratory School, Dewey evolved what may be considered his own theory of curriculum. In certain superficial respects, it resembled Herbartian culture epochs, but in certain very fundamental respects it had been completely transformed. Critical to the curriculum of the Laboratory School was what Dewey called "occupations." The term was sometimes erroneously construed to be related to vocational education or an emphasis on sheer overt activity. Actually, Dewey used the term to mean the fundamental social activities in which the human race had engaged and from which, he assumed, human intelligence evolved. Through the concept of occupations, Dewey hoped, first, to coordinate the various elements in the curriculum around a common center, and, secondly, to create a basis for building a relationship between knowledge and human affairs—a relationship that had become obscured in a technological society. It was for this reason that the children in the Dewey School engaged in such fundamental activities as growing food, cooking, building a clubhouse, raising a pair of sheep, and weaving (Mayhew and Edwards 1936). By recapitulating the kinds of activities that were fundamental to an earlier time, Dewey was hoping not only to restore a vital connection between intelligence and human purposes but to recapitulate the evolution of human knowledge in the curriculum. Thus, as children advanced chronologically, they proceeded from experiences that were more direct and immediate to activities and experiences that were more abstract and differentiated, experiences that more closely resembled the experience of the human race as embodied in the disciplines of knowledge (Dewey 1902). Dewey left the University of Chicago in 1904 to join the faculty at Columbia University, and, although many reforms were later proposed and even implemented in his name, the curriculum of the Dewey School had no substantial impact on the direction that the American curriculum took in the twentieth century.

5. *The Era of the Scientific Curriculum Makers*

Of the various forces for reform of the curriculum in the early twentieth century was the group that often referred to themselves as scientific-curriculum makers, although their version of science was substantially different from the science of the child-study group who sought to discover a natural order of studies and Dewey's effort to transform the methods of science into what he called a "complete act of thought." Led by such figures as John Franklin Bobbitt (1918, 1924), and W. W. Charters (1923), the scientific curriculum makers drew their inspiration mainly from the efficiency techniques of industry and particularly from the work of Frederick Winslow Taylor, the father of the scientific management movement. From that movement, they drew inferences to curriculum development that included such now-familiar principles as the careful prespecification of objectives in concrete terms, the precise measurement of student progress toward the achievement of established standards, and the differentiation of the curriculum in line with what was considered to be the wide variation in student abilities. In general, the curriculum was seen as a preparation for a particular social and occupational role, and the curriculum was to be adjusted as far as possible in the light of what was considered to be the probable destination of the students. Part of the appeal of this doctrine was its promise of social improvement almost exclusively through efficiency techniques thus insuring a measure of social stability.

One of the major events of the period was the Report of the Commission on the Reorganization of Secondary Education, the Cardinal Principles of Secondary Education (National Education Association 1918). Coming a quarter of a century after the Report of the Committee of Ten, it reflected the great changes that had occurred in that period in educational doctrine. The most famous feature of the report was the seven aims enunciating educational goals that covered almost every facet of human life reflecting the notion that the curriculum should be extended beyond the aim of intellectual development into the full range of human activity. Referring to what he called "profound changes in American life," (p. 7), Clarence Kingsley, the chief architect of the report, called for correspondingly major changes in the American secondary-school curriculum. These changes, by and large, were designed to be much more directly utilitarian in character than had previously been the case, a change believed to be consistent with the needs of the new student population and democratic values generally. Although the conventional subjects were not dismissed entirely, the basic recommendation was that they transform themselves so as to bear directly on the future lives of students. Considering the time in which it was issued, the Cardinal Principles Report was actually a moderate statement of social efficiency doctrine, arguing, for example, for the retention of the comprehensive high school against the wishes of those

reformers who saw the European system of secondary education with its different types of secondary institutions as more efficiently serving the needs of a highly variable student population.

One reason for the relative success of the scientific curriculum movement was the active involvement of many of their leaders in schools surveys. By the 1920s hundreds of school systems across the country had invited prominent educators to review their programs of study and to make recommendations for improvement. Almost invariably, those recommendations embodied the principles of scientific curriculum making. Among the surveys that Bobbitt himself directed were those in Cleveland, Ohio (1915b), San Antonio, Texas (1915a), and Los Angeles, California (1922).

6. *Curriculum Change in the 1930s*

In the wake of the great economic depression of the 1930s there rose to prominence a new group of educators who tried to rally American school teachers under the banner of social reconstruction. Such educational leaders as George S. Counts (1932) and Harold Rugg (1947) foresaw the possibility that the schools could be used to correct deficiencies in the American social order and to build attitudes of social cooperation rather than around such allegedly outmoded American values as "rugged individualism." In curriculum terms, this was frequently interpreted as a program of studies that focused directly on major social problems, such as unemployment, and on creating not only a consciousness of those problems on the part of the students, but a certain sophistication in dealing with them. The idea of education creating a new social order fired the imagination of an important group of educational leaders, but the movement reached only a small segment of schools. Perhaps the most visible manifestation of the social reconstructionist movement was the adoption by many school systems of a series of textbooks written by Rugg which incorporated many of the basic ideas of the movement. By the 1940s, however, a concerted effort had already been mounted to remove those textbooks from American schools on the grounds that they were basically socialistic in character and contrary to American ideals (Rugg 1941).

With the entry of the United States into the Second World War in December 1941, the effects of the economic depression were mitigated and attention was turned away from matters of educational doctrine. To a large extent, American educational leaders sought to demonstrate that education was, in fact, in the direct national interest and could contribute substantially to the war effort.

Bibliography

Bobbitt J F 1915a *The San Antonio Public School System: A Survey.* San Antonio School Board, San Antonio, Texas
Bobbitt J F 1915b *What the Schools Teach and Might Teach.* Survey Committee of the Cleveland Foundation, Cleveland, Ohio

Bobbitt J F 1918 *The Curriculum*. Houghton Mifflin, Boston, Massachusetts

Bobbitt J F 1922 *Curriculum-making in Los Angeles* Supplementary Educational Monographs No. 20. University of Chicago Press, Chicago, Illinois

Bobbitt J F 1924 *How to Make a Curriculum*. Houghton Mifflin, Boston, Massachusetts

Charters W W 1923 *Curriculum Construction*. Macmillan, New York

Counts G S 1932 *Dare the School Build a New Social Order?* Day, New York

Dewey J 1902 *The Child and the Curriculum, Contributions to Education*, No. 5. University of Chicago Press, Chicago, Illinois

Hall G S 1902 *Adolescence: Its Psychology and its Relations to Physiology, Anthropology, Sociology, Sex, Crime, Religion and Education*, Vol. 2. Appleton, New York, p. 510

Mayhew K C, Edwards A C 1936 *The Dewey School: The Laboratory School of the University of Chicago, 1896–1903*. Appleton-Century, New York

Meriwether C 1907 *Our Colonial Curriculum, 1607–1776*. Capital, Washington, DC

National Education Association of the United States 1880 *Addresses and Proceedings*. National Education Association of the United States, Salem, Ohio, p. 174

National Education Association of the United States 1893 *Report of the Committee of Ten on Secondary Studies*. Government Printing Office, Washington, DC

National Education Association of the United States 1895 *Report of the Committee of Fifteen on Elementary Education, with the reports of the Sub-committees*. American Book Company, New York

National Education Association of the United States 1918 *Report of the Commission on the Reorganization of Secondary Education*, Bureau of Education Bulletin, No. 35. Bureau of Education, Washington, DC

Rugg H O 1941 *That Men May Understand: An American in the Long Armistice*. Doubleday, Doran, New York

Rugg H O 1947 *Foundations for American Education*. World Book Company, Yonkers-on-Hudson, New York

Sizer T R (ed.) 1964 *The Age of the Academies*. Teachers College Press, New York

Thorndike E L 1924 Mental discipline in high school studies. *J. Educ. Psychol.* 15: 1–22, 83–98

Thorndike E L, Woodworth R S 1901 The influence of improvement in one mental function upon the efficiency of other functions. *Psychol. Rev.* 8: 247–61, 384–95, 553–64

Tyack D B 1974 *The One Best System: A History of American Urban Education*. Harvard University Press, Cambridge, Massachusetts

Soviet Union

W. F. Connell and A. Tulikova

Following the revolution of 1917, there was a 10-year period of luxuriant and immensely interesting experimentation in education which was brought to a close by the economic constraints of the first Five Year Plan. In the 1930s the basic structure of education was stabilized and an enduring curriculum pattern was established. Based on a return to a more systematic academic programme, it was designed to increase the level of literacy throughout the Soviet Union, to provide a wider and more thorough general education, to raise the political consciousness of the population, and to develop greater technological competence. The Second World War had a devastating effect on the schools and it took more than a decade of reconstruction to build up something like a universal 8-year education. From that point a considerable expansion took place, particularly at the secondary and tertiary levels of education. From the mid-1960s through to the mid-1980s school curricula were adjusted and remodelled to cope with the expanded school population and the economic and political requirements of the Soviet Union.

1. Curriculum Development in the 1960s and 1970s

The curriculum of the early 1960s was still much as it had been in the 1930s, although modified by the Khrushchev reforms of 1958 which had given a greater emphasis to work experience and polytechnical programmes. It was still basically designed for an 8-year school; the work in its early grades was thought to be too elementary for the children of the Sputnik age of the 1960s, and its subjects were in need of better sequencing in both content and teaching procedures. Many educators also thought that there was too much emphasis on formal instruction. From 1957 and during the 1960s a team sponsored by the Academy of Pedagogical Sciences and led by Zankov undertook important large-scale research and experimentation in schools throughout the Soviet Union into the school curriculum and methods of teaching. The research, following the line of thought put forward by Vygotsky in the 1930s, demonstrated ways in which appropriately stimulating methods of teaching could promote a student's cognitive development, and suggested that complex subject matter could be introduced into the curriculum at an earlier stage than had hitherto been thought feasible.

Following the extensive period of research and consultation among teachers, researchers, and government agencies, a revised curriculum was put into operation in the late 1960s and the 1970s. It was an enhancement of the all-age, comprehensive school at just the time when the movement for comprehensive secondary education was at its height in western Europe.

Four principal changes were introduced. Firstly, the primary school years were reduced from four to three and secondary subject specialization began at the fourth year.

Secondly, the curriculum was designed as a 10-year school programme with entry at 7 years of age, and was properly sequenced from year 1 at primary to year 10 at secondary level. It was more sophisticated and of a higher standard than the curriculum it replaced both in its arrangement of content and in the kind and level of intellectual development at which it aimed. The curriculum reforms made use of appropriate research findings and gave particular attention to the matching of cognitive tasks to levels of cognitive development in pupils.

Thirdly, scientific and mathematical studies were strengthened, and the polytechnical elements in the curriculum were made both more scientific and more practical.

Finally, the curriculum was designed to provide a solid general education in language, science, social science and politics, physical education, and productive labour. But, in addition, students from the seventh grade on were able to choose to study several optional subjects according to their interests. The commonest options that were offered appear to have been in the engineering field (general, electrical, and radio), in automobile driving, in computer programming, and in typewriting, but it was possible in some schools to choose to study subjects such as physiology, logic, and psychology.

2. Reform in the 1980s

Since the 1960s there has been a considerable amount of research, reflection, and discussion on curriculum theory and the bases of curriculum construction. Curriculum objectives—their formulation, their interrelationships, and their use in the selection of materials and in the evaluation of learning—have received much attention. The general structure of the curriculum with its vertical and horizontal continuity has been researched. The structure of subject disciplines and their relationship, modified by pedagogical considerations, to the ideas and concepts of the subjects taught in schools have been carefully analysed. The problems and organization of polytechnical education have been continually investigated. The criteria for selection of curriculum material and the relationship between curriculum and various teaching methods have been explored. In particular, developmental teaching in the Vygotsky tradition, various activity methods, and problem-oriented teaching have been experimented with. New textbooks in most of the subjects have been designed and produced by scholars and professional educators to meet the requirements of modern levels of knowledge and recent psychological research.

The weight of all that discussion, writing, and research was applied in the recasting of the curriculum that took place in the mid-1980s. By making six years of age, instead of the traditional seven, the age of entry, the period of schooling was extended from 10 to 11 years (Central Committee of the CPSU and the Council of Ministers of the USSR 1984). The primary level again covered grades 1 to 4 and the full secondary level grades 5 to 11, with the possibility of transfer after grade 9 into a technical school. Within the 11-year school the curriculum was considerably modified.

The general purposes of the curriculum changes were to widen and strengthen the scientific outlook of the students, to develop an integrated general education building the leading ideas of the various disciplines into a meaningful whole, to enhance the ideological level of the students' understanding, and to upgrade the polytechnical approach and content of both primary and secondary education. In addition to the general objectives, there was some fine tuning required throughout the organization and content of the curriculum:

> The [1984] reform documents formulated the critical requirements that were to provide a basis for the improvement of educational content: to refine the roster and coverage of school subjects to be studied; to eliminate pupil overload; to lay out fundamental concepts and leading ideas clearly; to reflect recent achievements in science and practical activity; to strengthen the polytechnical bent; and to define the optimum corpus of mandatory knowledge, skills, and habits that pupils must assimilate. (Zverev 1985 p. 24)

The curriculum was changed in several substantial ways. In language teaching there was more emphasis on its social function, and, in the case of Russian, on its use as an intermediary language throughout the Soviet Union. Encouragement was given also to a more thorough understanding of ethnic literature and culture. In areas where Russian was not the native language, additional time was built into the school timetable to allow for the learning of the mother tongue. A foreign language was begun in grade 5 and continued through to year 11.

The new science and mathematics curricula operating from 1987 were described as "streamlined" and were intended to "reflect the basic directions in scientific and technological progress and the contemporary achievements of science, technology, and culture. They exhibit a more pronounced practical bent" (Mathematics Curriculum 1987 p. 57). In the sciences some material was regraded or discarded, and new and appropriate material introduced. In particular, there was an emphasis on intellectual training in dialectical scientific method, and on the applications of science in the economic and technological worlds. A new short course of basic information science and computer technology has been added for grades 10 and 11. Linked with mathematics and physics it was designed to provide an understanding of the technological aspects of computing and to make all students literate in machine language.

The social sciences were seen as a significant basis through which to nurture in students a sense of social responsibility and communist solidarity, and to provide for them a more profound understanding of Marxist-Leninism and its place in shaping the politics and culture of their life. Restructuring (*perestroika*) and openness (*glasnost*) were to characterize the teaching of history and its textbooks which were to be authentic and accurate. The history of the Soviet Union was made the core of an effort to teach world history so as to provide a knowledge of the background of the main regions of the world and provide students with a Marxist-Leninist world view. Geography, similarly, was to deal with regions, environments, and social systems throughout the world; it also provided opportunity for the study of aspects of each of the 15 union republics and selected districts. The study of natural resources and their economic and social management became one of the central features of the course. There were also three short courses provided for the senior years. Fundamentals of the Soviet State and Law for grade 9 is a study of the constitution; Psychology and Ethics of Family Life, a new course developed out of a previously optional one, is for grades 9 and 10 and is designed to examine the relationships between personal life and society; and the course called Social Science for grades 10 and 11 is an integral study of Soviet society.

The upgrading and extension of polytechnical education was a major task of the school reform of the mid-1980s. Ever since the 1917 Revolution, Soviet educators have thought about, experimented with, and constantly sought for the best means of relating education to socially useful labour. The changing needs of the economy, the diversity and growth of technology, and the limited facilities of schools have made it difficult to produce a satisfactory form of polytechnical education. There is a vast and interesting literature on the topic in the Soviet Union. The reforms in the 1980s aimed to strengthen the students' orientation to and understanding of productive and socially useful labour, and to improve their vocational guidance and training. The time allocation in the curriculum for polytechnical edu-

Table 1
General 11-year school timetable, 1985[a]

Subjects	Grades	1	2	3	4	5	6	7	8	9	10	11
1. Language												
Russian (Language and Literature)		7	9	11	11	11	9	6	5	5	3	3
Russian and mother tongue (where Russian is not native)		7	12	14	14	14	12	9	8	8	6	6
Foreign language						4	3	2	2	1	1	1
2. Science and Mathematics												
Nature study				1	1	1						
Biology							2	2	2	2	1	1
Physics								2	2	3	4	4
Astronomy												1
Chemistry									3	3	2	2
Mathematics		4	6	6	6	6	6	6	6	6	5	4
Basic information science and computer technology											1	2
3. Social Sciences												
Learning the world around you		1	1									
History						2	2	2	2	3	4	3
Geography							2	3	2	2	2	
Fundamentals of the Soviet state and law										1		
Social science											2	2
Psychology and ethics of family life										1	1	
Technical Drawing								1	1			
Art		2	1	1	1	1	1	1				
Music		2	1	1	1	1	1	1				
Physical education		2	2	2	2	2	2	2	2	2	2	2
4. Work Education												
Education for work and fundamentals of production:												
Choosing an occupation		2	2	2	2	2	2	2	3	3	4	4
Public productive work		1	1	1	1	2	2	2	3	3	4	4
Work practice (in total days)							3	3	3	4	4	6
							(10)	(10)	(10)	(16)	(16)	(20)
5. Optional studies								2	2	2	4	4

a Source: adapted from the Bulletin of Standard Acts, USSR Ministry of Education 1985 No. 6, pp. 25–32 cation was increased, practical vocational training was improved and extended in the later years of secondary education, and a new subject was introduced, Fundamentals of Production: Choosing an Occupation, to be studied in grades 10 and 11. By the time students had completed their 11th year they were expected to have developed a consciousness of the need to engage in socially useful work, to have acquired a basic knowledge of technical procedures and production of use in many occupational areas, and to have mastered a specific occupation.

The above subjects, together with art and music in grades 1 to 7, and physical education in all grades, formed the compulsory curriculum for all students throughout the Soviet Union. In addition there were a number of optional subjects offered from grade 7 to grade 11. These were often special interdisciplinary science subjects such as Health and the Environment, Basics of Ecology and Natural Conservation, Technology and the Environment, and The Biosphere and Man. Table 1 shows the 1985 11-year timetable overview.

3. The Search for Balance in Curriculum Development

Curriculum development in the Soviet Union, as in Western countries also, has to take account judiciously of the decisions and contributions of a number of differing authorities and interests. Academicians, educational researchers and administrators, teachers, local and national representatives of the Communist party, and the legislative bodies in the union republics and the central government have views and findings that have to be considered and reconciled. In formulating educational policies and curriculum objectives there is a balance to be struck between economic demand, political education, cultural requirements, and personal and social development. Flexibility, humanity and mature judgment are necessary. The Soviet Ministry of Education, State Committee for Public Education, through its various agencies, is at the centre of this rich and complicated tissue of opinion, advice, experiment, and decision, which it must bring into productive operation in the form of published curricula, texts, materials, equipment, and, where necessary, courses of reeducation for teachers.

Bibliography

Averichev I P 1984 Bol'shaia zadacha shkol'noi reformy. *Shkola i Proizvodstvo* 8: 3–8 trans. in *Sov. Educ.* 28(3): 7–24

Central Committee of the CPSU and the Council of Ministers of the USSR 1984 *Concerning the Further Optimization of General Secondary Education for Young People and the Improvement of Conditions of Work in the General Education School*

Mathematics Curriculum for Secondary General Education Schools (Grades Five through Eleven) 1987 trans. in *Sov. Educ.* 29(3): 56–108

Zverev I D 1985 Preemstvennost v sovershenstvovanii shkol'nykh programm. *Sov. Pedag.* 10: 22–29, trans. (Continuity in the improvement of school curricula) in *Sov. Educ.* 29(3): 21–40

Cultural Approaches

Buddhist Education

A. W. P. Gurugé

Buddhist Education consists primarily of the formal system of monastic training and the informal efforts in lay education, developed by various schools and sects of Buddhism in Asia. In this article are discussed: the foundations of Buddhist education, its historical development, and some of its significant distinctive features. In view of the acute paucity of information on the subject, the need for research is emphasized.

1. Foundations of Buddhist Education

Northern India of the sixth century BC was in a veritable religious and philosophical ferment. Prominent among the many religious teachers of the time was Siddhārtha Gautama, better known by the honorific, "Buddha" (meaning "enlightened" or "awakened"). His 45-year mission as a wandering teacher was to proclaim a path of deliverance. Moral discipline, concentration of mind, and realization of the nature of life were its essential steps. It enjoined a life of study and meditation aimed at training and "taming" the mind. Four factors relating to the Buddha's educational effort have influenced the evolution of a Buddhist system of education and constitute its foundations.

1.1 Model Teacher

The first among them was the Buddha's own technique of teaching. He was a skilful teacher and held instruction to be the most effective of all miracles. He chose to teach in the language of the masses. His discourses were organized with meticulous care. Beginning with an attention-catching statement, he analysed a concept into its constituent elements. He elaborated them with one or more lists of enumerations serving both as a framework for orderly presentation of ideas and as an aid to memory. In dialogues and debates, the Buddha posed a battery of questions aimed at convincing the discussants of the fallacies of their arguments and leading them gradually to his point of view. Often, he set tasks which made people come, by their own efforts, to conclusions which he could have simply, but much less effectively, preached. Strings of synonyms were used to ensure the comprehension of difficult or important

terms. Similes and analogies, usually drawn from the day-to-day life of the people, made his discourses picturesque. He delved into legend and history for anecdotes and illustrations. He made apt use of dramatization and visual aids drawn from the environment. Metrical compositions—usually a quatrain of 32 syllables—were employed to summarize a doctrinal point. Being a poet himself, the use of poetry to reinforce learning was consistently pursued. The Buddha has been held as a model teacher and his techniques of teaching continue to be emulated.

1.2 Learning Society

The second factor was the founding of the Order of Monks and Nuns (i.e., the Buddhist Sangha) with a specific mandate to pursue the missionary function of wandering far and wide to teach the doctrine. The Sangha developed into a learning society with two paramount educational objectives among others: namely, (a) evolving ways and means of preserving the teachings of the Buddha through systematic codification and transmission through oral tradition; and (b) propagating them through exegetical, commentarial, and scholastic literary efforts as well as formal and informal teaching. The first objective led to the eventual formulation of the Buddhist Canon, called Tripiṭaka (literally, three baskets, signifying its major division into discipline, doctrine, and metaphysics). The latter, in turn, resulted in a voluminous literature of commentaries, subcommentaries, and learned treatises, including abstracts and indexes. Together, the canonical and noncanonical literature has provided the basic content for Buddhist education.

1.3 Institutional Base

The third factor influencing the development of Buddhist education was the encouragement, given by the rise of Buddhism as a religion, to the foundation of permanent residences for large communities of monks and nuns. Settled life within monasteries (i.e., *Vihāra*) promoted the pursuit of study, discussion, debate, teaching, and research. Monasteries performed three principal functions: (a) initial and continuing education of monks

255

and nuns, specially devoting the compulsory stay-in retreat of the rainy season for refresher and retraining activities; (b) backstopping the missionary work of the itinerant Buddhist teacher through scholastic and literary pursuits; and (c) instructing the laity in the basic principles of the religion and its moral code both through regular and occasional sermons and by means of more formal programmes of study for those who sought deeper knowledge either as a preparation to join the Sangha or for their edification. At the early stage, the monasteries were served by specialist reciters of canonical texts (called *bhānaka*) who transmitted the canon from generation to generation. When writing was adopted, monasteries became not only repositories of books and documents but also centres where texts were copied and, later on, printed. Thus the Buddhist monastery evolved into an educational institution and several attained the level of a university in terms of the standards of study and the diversity of curricula.

1.4 Intellectual Liberalism

An overriding factor which conditioned the Buddhist attitude to teaching, learning, and research has been the intellectual liberalism which the Buddha expounded: his injunction to his disciples was to eschew tradition and dogmatism and to submit even his own teachings to critical examination. From a social point of view, he upheld the capacity of every individual irrespective of caste, class, creed, or sex, to attain the highest intellectual and spiritual goals of his path of deliverance by means of application and perseverance. From an intellectual standpoint, he denounced both conservatism and the tacit acceptance of an idea on someone else's authority. In the rules of discipline for monks, it is laid down that the student "should combat by discussion any false doctrine the teacher might hold or get others to hold". The emphasis was on analysis and investigation—hence the description of Buddhism as *Vibhajjavāda* (doctrine of analysis). These principles gave Buddhist education a significant openness as regards both clientele and content. Monasteries have been open to all classes of people and, specially, have catered for the socially and economically disadvantaged. The freedom of analysis and investigation, while subjecting the Buddha's teachings to dissent, innovation, reinterpretation, and even misinterpretation, promoted a spirit of tolerance which permeated the Buddhist educational system. Not only have the curricula included the study of rival religious and philosophical systems, besides subjects not related to religious purposes, but the scholastic activity in the monasteries resulted in the rise of many Buddhist sects and schools (Gurugé 1982).

As Buddhism spread to various parts of Asia, principles and practices of education emerging from these foundations evolved in response to needs and challenges of the intellectual and spiritual life of the host country.

2. Historical Development

The historical development of Buddhist education has been largely determined by the position which Buddhism held in a given society. Where rival religious and philosophical systems were strong and the Buddhist Sangha had to explain and defend its doctrines, in order to retain and augment adherents, the thrust of the monastic training was directed to debate, discussion, logic, and apologia. But, where Buddhism was unchallenged and enjoyed popular or state patronage, the emphasis was on the preservation of the word of the Buddha through reliable modes of transmission, with special attention to exegesis. In both instances, the education of the laity was pursued by means of informal sermons, which combined doctrinal expositions with illustrative storytelling. Knowledge, thus conveyed to the community, was reinforced through visual aids in the form of temple paintings and sculptures.

2.1 India

In India itself, Buddhism encountered opposition from not only Vedic Brahmanism, but also other religious and philosophical systems, notably Jainism and classical schools of Hindu philosophy. In the process of "explaining and defending", Buddhism itself underwent a major change, bringing into existence the Mahāyāna school. Essential to its growth in popularity was the effectiveness with which debates and discussions were conducted with both the exponents of traditional Buddhism and others. Influenced by this need, Buddhist education concentrated on the training of the disputant, resulting in three developments: (a) the curriculum grew rapidly to consist of a wide variety of subjects including secular studies such as medicine, astronomy, and mathematics, since a successful missionary had to be a well-informed and socially useful person; (b) dialectics, logic, and epistemology received the utmost attention both in instruction and in the production of scholarly literature; and (c) Sanskrit, the language of the intellectual elite, and, therefore, the medium of debates, was adopted for instruction and literary purposes.

Such an expanding system of monastic education favoured large institutions where scholars from various parts of India as well as from neighbouring countries could meet and pursue study and research. Three Chinese pilgrims, who visited some of these institutions between the fifth and the seventh century AD, describe them as centres of educational and literary activity, maintained and supported through royal grants and endowments from the laity. Nalanda and Valabhi in eastern and western India respectively were the most important among them. Hiuen-Tsang's account of Nalanda, where he was a student for over five years, shows that it was a full-fledged university with schools of studies, admission and examination procedures, a complex system of academic administration, and requisite facilities such as libraries and lecture halls. There were 1,500 teachers catering for 10,000 students (both religious and lay, Indian and foreign), who studied 100 different subjects, including philosophy, grammar, astronomy, and medicine. "Learning and discussing, they find the day too short", was Hiuen-Tsang's observation (Dutt 1956). While the educational efficacy of Nalanda is borne out by the quality of its teachers and students, who had left a lasting imprint on Buddhist history through their writings and missionary activities, the vast campus which has been excavated and conserved testifies to its grandeur.

2.2 *Mahāyāna Buddhist Countries*

As Mahāyāna Buddhism spread through Central Asia to China, Tibet, Mongolia, Korea, and Japan, it faced opposition from popular beliefs as well as established religious and philosophical systems. Interactions with Confucianism and Taoism, in particular, re-emphasized the training of the debater, while the need to gain popular support underscored ethical and moral values, on the one hand, and public service including lay education, on the other. Formal logic dominated the curriculum and, as exemplified for instance, by the prevailing Tibetan system, learning was achieved by teachers and students engaging themselves in a debate where, through strict application of logic, they aimed at reaching an unassailable conclusion. The vast literature in defence of Buddhism against Confucianism and Taoism bears further testimony to this aspect of Buddhist education.

As new schools—particularly those which sought to Sinosize or Japanize Buddhism—arose, various unconventional methods of teaching were developed. Particularly in the meditational schools of Ch'an/Zen, the control of mind and body was taught not only through practice in quiet meditation, but also (as specially in Lin-chi/Rinzai school) through beatings and verbal paradoxes (namely, *kung-an/kōan*) (Buchanon 1979). In Japan, the Zen approach to education influenced the training of the samurai (warrior statesmen).

The monastic system supplemented the state-sponsored lay education in two significant ways: first, it provided popular elementary education, mainly to boys, and, in particular, for commoners and poor sections of the population to whom state schools were not accessible. Schools attached to temples (e.g., Terakoya in Japan), provided them with basic instruction in reading, writing, and arithmetic. Second, the monastic system founded specialized schools for the liberal student to engage in study and speculation, as in Shu-yüan in China. These efforts in lay education gave a further impetus to printing and in all these countries Buddhist texts were the first to be printed (Anesaki 1964, Dutt 1956, Prip-Møller 1968).

2.3 *Theravāda Buddhist Countries*

In Sri Lanka, where Theravāda Buddhism flourished with an unbroken history from the third century BC, with no serious rivalry from any other religious or philosophical system, monastic education concentrated on transmission of the teachings and their explanation, with special emphasis on preserving the word of the Buddha in the language in which he preached. The Buddhist Canon which the missionaries of Emperor Asoka brought to Sri Lanka was in Pāli (literally meaning "the text")—most probably a formalized version of the vernacular of Magadha, the region where the Buddha was most active. Until it was reduced to writing in circa 80 BC, at Aluvihara in central Sri Lanka, a principal goal of monastic education was its oral transmission through memorization and regular rehearsal. While the text was thus preserved in Pāli, the commentaries and exegetical works were produced in Sinhala, the national language. This vast commentarial literature was translated, in the fifth century AD, into Pāli, the lingua franca of the Theravāda Buddhist communities in India and Sri Lanka. With this movement, Pāli superseded Sinhala as the language of literary expression.

From time to time, Maāyāna schools, with Sanskrit as their medium of expression, gained ground in Sri Lanka. Sanskrit opened the door to a rapidly developing secular literature ranging from ornate court poetry and drama to scientific treatises on medicine, astronomy, mathematics, and architecture. The education imparted in the monasteries—some of which, like the Mahāvihāra of Anuradhapura and Ālāhana Pirivena of Polonnaruwa, had become veritable universities—expanded its scope from traditional monastic training for monks and nuns to include a wide range of linguistic, literary, and secular studies. Among them a very important element was the study of ecclesiastical history which brought into existence a copious literature of chronicles. Education in these monasteries was not restricted to monks and nuns. They catered for the laity too. At a particular stage, a concern was expressed over the growing secular content of monastic education and a royal decree of the twelfth century actually banned the study as well as the teaching of "poetry, drama, and such other base subjects". In spite of this concern, the monastic educational institutions, which came to be known as *pirivenas*, continued to provide an all-round education as conceivable at the time. Several contemporary accounts of the fifteenth-century pirivenas testify to this fact.

When Theravāda Buddhism spread to Burma, Thailand, Cambodia, and Laos, the Sri Lankan model of Buddhist education went with it. Pāli (with special emphasis on grammar), as a necessary preliminary to the study of the Buddhist Canon, became so widespread that a history of Buddhism, written in Burma in the thirteenth century, says that grammar was popular even among women and young girls. Another contemporary chronicle describes King Kyaswa to have "read and become a master of every book, held public disputations and seven times a day instructed his household" (Kaung 1963 p. 16). National languages received equal attention although Pāli, as the ecclesiastical language common to all Theravāda countries, was used in the production of learned treatises. An impetus was given to the art of writing and alphabets were evolved with kings taking the initiative as in Thailand where King Rama Kamhaeng invented Thai writing in 1283. Monasteries, attracting students from far and wide and engaging in a wide range of literary activity and research, existed in or near all major cities of the region. A similar pattern of Buddhist learning appears to have been prevalent in earstwhile Buddhist lands constituting Malaysia, Indonesia, and the Maldive Islands. A very significant innovation in Burma, Thailand, Cambodia, and Laos was "temporary ordination" which encouraged, if not demanded, every young man to spend at least a few months as a monk in a monastery. Persisting still as an important socioreligious institution, this practice ensures that at least the male population is exposed to a period of formal learning (Dharmapala 1965, Gurugé 1982, 1984, Mookerji 1947).

2.4 Decline and Regeneration

With the expansion of Islamic influences in Asia between the twelfth and fifteenth centuries, Buddhist education along with Buddhism itself, declined in the Indian subcontinent as well as Malaysia, Indonesia, and the Maldive Islands. Elsewhere, it persisted in varying degrees of vigour and effectiveness until the advent of modern education, whether through colonial or national policy. The colonial policy of encouraging Christian missionaries to take over public education, on the one hand, and the incentives provided for study in the language of administration, on the other, deprived monastic educational institutions of lay participation and support. Similarly, under the impact of modernization, secular school systems sprang up in China, Japan, Korea, and Thailand. Paradoxically, in almost all countries under reference it is the Buddhist monastery that helped the modern system of education to become widespread in that the modern school owes its ubiquity even in very remote areas to the Buddhist monk who provided it with the first base. The Japanese Terakoya reformed itself under the Meiji Restoration in 1873 to be a base for universalizing primary education and their Buddhist character disappeared with the new education scheme of 1886 (Anesaki 1964). In Burma, the British policy of developing secular primary education was achieved in 1868–1870 by grants of specified modern books and the appointment of a qualified teacher to each of the existing 3,500 temple schools (Kaung 1963). In Thailand, 71.3 percent of all schools and 85.6 percent of primary schools in 1931 were conducted in monastic grounds and about one-third of the schools in the kingdom are yet in temple lands (Wells 1975). The situation has been identical in Sri Lanka, even though the traditional temple schools were ordered to be closed in 1865. But the two systems did not blend even where they coexisted in the same premises. Thus, reverting to a strictly monastic role, Buddhist education, in its formal mode, could hardly survive. But the informal, social

educational function of the Buddhist monastery was not affected.

Where Buddhism remained the popular religion, a part of the strategy for nationalistic revival or struggle for independence was to promote the regeneration of Buddhist education. Revival and modernization characterized these efforts, which were twofold: (a) to streamline monastic education through curricular reforms to incorporate not only advances in knowledge in general, but also the broadening range of Buddhist studies developed by worldwide research; and (b) to develop a system of Buddhist schools for children, based on the model of Christian missionary schools, but paying due attention to Buddhist learning and practices. Several new types of monastic educational institutions have come into existence since the 1880s. Sri Lanka saw the revival of pirivenas which cater for both monks and lay students. Burma and Thailand developed Pāli schools. Japan, China, and Korea set up Buddhist colleges. Some of these institutions have been elevated to the level of universities and provide the Sangha with facilities for higher education in a wide range of subjects. Their main objectives are to train Buddhist monks for missionary, scholarly, and social service functions and to facilitate scholars to pursue research into Buddhist philosophy, literature, and civilization.

Schools and colleges which the Buddhists established for children provide, in general, a secular education according to respective national policies. At the early stages of national movements for cultural identity and independence, these institutions played a significant role. But they are gradually being absorbed in objectives, contents, and methods (if not in management) into the growing systems of national schools, which have adopted, to a major extent, the cultural function of the Buddhist schools. The impact of the Buddhist intervention in secular education in a number of Asian countries is to be observed in the emphasis on national languages, history, and civilization, on the one hand, and, quite interestingly, on agriculture, traditional crafts, and vocational education, on the other. Thus it paved the way for a transition from the narrow civil service-oriented school systems to those reflecting wider national needs.

3. Some Significant Distinctive Features

On an examination of concepts, modalities, methods, and practical approaches in Buddhist education, as known from both historical accounts and the existing institutions in Asia, a number of significant distinctive features could be identified.

3.1 Goals and Objectives

The ultimate objective of Buddhist education and its process of mental development is the liberation of the individual from all types of bondages. This liberation is to be achieved by each individual at his own pace and at his own initiative. The teacher is a facilitator, a guide and, more than that, a skill model to be emulated. Example rather than precept is emphasized as the true medium of communication between the teacher and the pupil. The teacher takes note of individual differences among students and designs each one's courses of training (especially the subjects of meditation) to suit those particular traits. Learning is not an end in itself, but a process leading to self-realization, which is equated in Buddhism to deliverance or liberation—the ultimate aim of the religious life. What leads a particular person to self-realization is a series of strictly personal experiences which cannot be reproduced at random to apply to any other individual. Time involved in the process is as variable as the techniques. This same principle, which has been in operation with regard to spiritual training, has been applied to all learning experiences in the Buddhist monastic system. In Buddhism, there is no book or set quantum of literary material to be studied or mastered or to be held as authority. To know just enough to set one's self on the path of mental training has been the primary objective. That is to say that knowledge itself was not an objective of learning. The Buddha consistently discouraged those who wanted to be "masters of the books". While recognizing the importance of scholastic achievement and rewarding scholarship with both honours and material benefits, the monastic system maintained that learning had to be accompanied by ethical sensitivity and moral principles. Learning was valuable only up to the point it made the individual a better person morally and spiritually.

3.2 Individual-centred Learning

In the monastic system, a class being taught collectively by a teacher is a relatively late development. A teacher, ordinarily, met each student individually to ensure whether the assigned tasks were correctly accomplished and to set new tasks. Teaching in the sense of lecturing or explaining a lesson to a group of students was rare and was strictly confined to matters which students had either misunderstood or failed to comprehend. The students spent almost all their time in self-learning using commentaries, subcommentaries, glossaries, indexes, and lexicons. The method of evaluating learning outcomes was twofold: the students were required either to show their capacity to draw from the self-learning materials and present their own commentary or explanations of a given text, or to enter into a debate with their teachers and peers and defend a particular point of view. An original composition by the student usually marked the culmination of studies.

3.3 Operational Aspects of Concept Formation

The maieutic method of questioning and leading the disciple to realize the limitations of his premises or conclusions made a contribution both to the evolution of a distinct Buddhist system of logic and to the fashioning, through interaction, of the growth of the Indian theory of epistemology. In the process, the Buddhists played a pioneering role in delving into the mechanics of concept formation. Developed in greater detail in the *Abhidhamma Pitaka* and subsequent commentaries and treatises, this particular branch of Buddhist scholarship moves away from a pure theory of cognition and consciousness to operational aspects which are later exemplified by the methods of training and meditational observances, particularly of Zen and Tibetan Buddhism.

3.4 Committed Change Agents

The role of the Sangha as a band of self-renewing change agents has been a significant feature of Buddhist education. The constitution of the Sangha as a decentralized democratic organization of peers enabled it to evolve according to the genius and needs of different peoples at different places and times. The motivation came from an ideal which bordered simultaneously on both personal benefit and altruism. The Buddhist monk has, primarily, left the householder's life for his own spiritual advancement and salvation. Yet, he is involved in many activities aimed at perpetuating the organization and repaying in service those that support it. As one of the most resilient organizations with a proven capacity for self-regeneration, the Sangha had been an effective change agent not only preaching change but adjusting to it.

3.5 Teacher–Pupil Relations

The Buddhist concept of the teacher is a very wide one: anyone from whom one learns something, even a single syllable, is one's teacher. The parents are designated the first teachers (*pubbuācariya*). Buddhist education promotes the development of an emotional and moral bond between the teacher and the taught. While no obligation is cast on the student to agree with the teacher or to take him or her as an undisputed authority, the Buddhist tradition requires the teacher to be held in respect. Irrespective of the age of the parties concerned, the relationship engendered is that between parent and child. As such, the teacher is required not only to protect the pupil from all kinds of danger, but also to introduce the pupil to friends and spread his or her reputation. A significant corollary to this is that the teacher is never a rival of the pupil. Instead, the pupil's accomplishments and success add to the reputation of the teacher. It is considered bad form, however, for pupils to presume to compete with their teachers. The interpersonal relations so promoted between the teacher and the pupil generated a wholesome atmosphere for study and search for knowledge. A salient feature of monastic education is that learning is expected to take place without tension.

3.6 Medium of the Spoken Word

The spoken word was the only medium which the Buddha and his early disciples used. Its use as a means of instruction in the formal monastic education was limited. But in the informal education of the masses, the Buddhist Sangha down the ages has produced masterly users of the rhythmic charm, the convincing power and the image-conjuring versatility of the spoken word. Buddhists have been among the earliest to use drama as a medium of religious propagation. The oldest Indian drama hitherto discovered is on a Buddhist theme. The religious drama and wandering drama troupes in all Buddhist countries preserve a very old tradition.

3.7 Medium of the Written Word

Starting from the edicts of Asoka, wherein the spirit of Buddhism was conveyed to the people in the vast Mauryan empire of the third century BC, Buddhists have pressed the written word into service in a variety of ways. Commencing from the first century BC, when the Canon was written down, the monastic educational system relied on the book as the primary tool of self-learning. The written word became very early an important medium of the Buddhist informal education. The earliest books imitated the style of the preachers and produced what could be called written sermons. Community reading has remained until very recent times a regular pastime of the rural folk, both in temples and in their homes. In two sites in Mandalay, Burma, are hundreds of marble slabs on which is neatly engraved the whole of the Tripitaka. This open-air "library" by itself, is an invitation to people to read. The display of religious writings in flags, banners, wall-hangings as in Japan, Korea, Mongolia, and Tibet serves a similar purpose. A purely religious motive keeps on adding to the popular Buddhist literature. Both writing and publishing religious books is considered a form of *Dhammadāna* (gift of dhamma) and an aphorism of the Buddha rates the gift of dhamma to be superior to all other gifts.

3.8 Visual Aids

More than for aesthetic reasons, the Buddhists employed sculpture and painting as a means of communication. The temple wall evolved to be another medium of informal education. Themes were drawn from the entire narrative literature comprising the present and past lives of the Buddha, biographies of his disciples, and the history of Buddhism, as well as figurative accounts of hells and heavens. A pilgrimage, often, is a study tour to temples which are famous for their paintings and sculptures.

3.9 Methods of Formal Learning

To train scholars and specialists, writers and preachers, organizers and administrators, Buddhists developed and maintained a formal system of education with special emphasis on three aspects: namely, memorization, calligraphy, and clear and faultless diction. Memorization of large volumes of textual and commentarial material

is resorted to mainly as a means of training and exercising the mind. With the reliance on the book, the widespread establishment of libraries and the regular exercise of copying manuscripts (or in Tibet, Korea, Japan, and elsewhere of printing from wood blocks), the memorization is not an effort to store information in one's head. The ability to repeat long texts from memory may still be admired as a feat but is not, by itself, reckoned to be a sign of learning. Learning is assessed on the ability to correlate and synthesize what has been acquired through different media. No Buddhist educators would uphold rote learning; but they would argue in favour of a very strict regime of memory training. Good handwriting has been regarded as more than an asset. In the monastic system, it is the very sign of scholarship. As such, students spend a major part of their time perfecting their script. In Tibetan monasteries, that is about the main activity, because memory training accompanies writing and a student produces volumes of "copy books" as a proof of studying. With the importance attached to oral communication, the student has to acquire the ability to read and speak clearly and correctly, articulating each syllable. It is a training needed for group chanting of scriptures (both as a daily monastic ritual and as a service to the laity) and for the delivery of sermons. Graduated texts, starting with simple words and progressing systematically to very complex words, have been in use for this purpose alone. Thus a good memory, legible and well-rounded handwriting, and clear speech are associated with learning. The disciplined drill, which is required to achieve them over years of application, is regarded as worthwhile and strongly upheld by some scholars to be the very essence of learning.

3.10 Work Experience

In Buddhist monastic education, learning is not divorced from work. The student, whether religious or lay, has to perform a variety of tasks relating to the maintenance and upkeep of the monastery. Frequent ceremonials entail special types of work. A fair amount of woodwork, masonry, and metalwork has to be picked up by students to be useful on these occasions. Skills pertaining to painting, paper and butter sculpture, and other artistic creations have opportunities for development. The average alumnus of the Buddhist monastic system of education is a versatile worker, with a wide range of manual and technical skills. In the Tibetan system, monks actually studied carpentry, masonry, sewing, and embroidery, besides their examination subjects.

3.11 Social Services

A monastery has obligations to fulfil to its lay supporters in the community. A student monk usually participates in household ceremonials, which bring him into contact with community life. A common task is to teach young children, as, in most Buddhist countries, the parents still try to supplement the children's school education with an exposure to the traditional literacy and literary training of the temple. They participate in community activities whether they be for development or for relief and rehabilitation. The unstructured programme of studies, usually with no time-bound requirements like examinations or promotions, enables the student monks to combine study, work experience, and social service and extend their period of studentship as long as circumstances permit.

4. Need for Research

The information available on Buddhist education—both past and present—is extremely limited. A few attempts have been made to unravel a Buddhist philosophy of education with modest results as a comprehensive analysis of the literature has not been undertaken. Histories of Buddhist education confine themselves to vignettes of Indian education, as narrated in Buddhist stories, or to accounts of institutions visited by Chinese pilgrims. The ouster of the temple school, the attempts to revive Buddhist education, and the sociocultural impact of these developments in each of the Buddhist countries of Asia remain to be documented and critically studied. Of equal significance is to examine whether concepts, modalities, methods, and practical approaches developed by Buddhist education are, in any way, relevant to current efforts in educational development.

Bibliography

Anagarika Dharmapala 1965 *Return to Righteousness: A Collection of Speeches, Essays and Letters.* Ministry of Cultural Affairs, Colombo
Anesaki M 1964 *History of Japanese Religion.* Tuttle, Tokyo
Bell A 1928 *The People of Tibet.* Clarendon Press, Oxford
Buchanan F R 1979 Living the life of a Zen monk. *Soc. Educ.* 43: 522–26
Dutt S 1956 *Buddhist Education: 2500 Years of Buddism.* Ministry of Information, Delhi
Gurugé A W P 1982 *The Miracle of Instruction.* Lake House Investments, Colombo
Gurugé A W P 1984 *From the Living Fountains of Buddhism.* Department of National Archives, Colombo
Kaung U 1963 A survey of the history of education in Burma before the British Conquest and after. *J. Burma Res. Soc.* 46(2): 9–124
Mookerji R K 1947 *Ancient Indian Education: Brahmanical and Buddhist.* Macmillan, London
National Institute for Educational Research 1981 *Moral Education in Asia: Report of a Joint Study on Moral Education in Asian Countries.* National Institute for Educational Research, Tokyo
Prip-Møller J 1968 *Chinese Buddhist Monasteries: Their Plan and its Function as a Setting for Buddhist Monastic Life.* Hong Kong University Press, Hong Kong
Tambiah S J 1970 *Buddhism and the Spirit Cults in North-east Thailand.* Cambridge University Press, Cambridge
Watson J K P 1973 The monastic tradition of education in Thailand. *Paedag. Hist.* 13: 515–29
Wells K E 1975 *Thai Buddhism: Its Rites and Activities.* Suriyabarn, Bangkok

Hindu Education

J. J. Nanavaty

Hinduism is not an organized religion. It is a philosophy which, in the final analysis, exalts action over contemplation. All social and religious movements of India, including those which originated there as well as those which were imported from outside, bear the stamp of Hinduism. It covers the wide expanse of thought embodied in the Vedas, the Upanishads, and the Bhagavad Gita. Buddhism, which is an offshoot of Hinduism as well as the Sufi movement in Islam also came under its influence.

Education is the active side of the Hindu philosophy. Even in India today, the majority of people argue about the same questions of karma (life in previous birth) and maya (illusion), believe in the same doctrines, and act in the same way as they did thousands of years ago.

In their quest for truth, ancient Hindu teachers taught the rising generations of their age that the link between the actual and the ideal world should never be broken. The ideal was sought to be accomplished not by running away from the jars and buffets of life, but by facing them. This is the essence of ancient Hindu educational philosophy.

1. Ancient Hindu Educational Philosophy

In the history of human civilization, human achievements have always fallen short of human aspirations. It has, therefore, been a difficult task for teachers in all ages to reconcile the "ideal" with the "real." Nevertheless, educational thinkers in ancient India have always tried to solve this problem by endeavoring to bridge the gulf between the two polarities.

Ancient Hindu philosophy, as such, is basically interested in the problems of the infinite. It does not attach much importance to the superficialities of life.

The Vedas, the Upanishads, and the Bhagavad Gita endeavor to reach "the one beyond the categories of human thought," which is the "primary cause of all," the ultimate reality. This preoccupation on the part of Ancient Indian *rishis* (seers) to go in search of the unchanging and eternal essence permeating the universe is, according to some thinkers, a manifestation of speculative regression (Graves 1938).

This view was not supported by more enlightened thinkers. In their estimation, preoccupied as they were with their quest for the "primary cause of all," Ancient Hindu teachers did not underrate the importance of human beings, their duties and social obligations, as well as the part they were expected to play in creating a society based on justice, equality, freedom, and even material progress. They stressed the importance of selflessness, and assigned selfhood to a lower category of existence. Human beings, they said, should try to efface their egos and aspire to realize those desires in life which do not lead merely to the blind acquisition of wealth and power.

Ancient Hindu educational philosophy encouraged human beings to attain perfection at all levels of day-to-day life. True, the ideal would be beyond their grasp. But their untiring efforts to reach it would, in itself, be a great achievement. In that sense, ancient Hindu educational philosophy is not submissive and negative.

In Ancient India, the Vedas, the Upanishads, and other schools of philosophy influenced educational thinking to a considerable extent. But in the absence of a fully articulated and monolithic structure of thought, which would have been regarded as a consistent system of educational philosophy, a constraint is felt when selecting those ideals which have intrinsic educational values (Kabir 1949).

The discovery of the spiritual at the heart of life was the aim of ancient Hindu education. It was its bedrock. At the same time, teachers in Ancient India did not underestimate empirical knowledge of things. It is true that they stressed the importance of developing the inner self. Nevertheless, education in Ancient India had dynamic and even pragmatic overtones. It was an instrument which enabled the individual to alleviate human misery and suffering, and attain the heights of truth, beauty, and goodness. Indeed, it was the key to human fulfillment.

2. The Vedas

Ancient Hindu educational thought was considerably moulded by the Vedas. The latter are the earliest scriptures of Hinduism. The dates assigned to them lack exact historical support. They are conjectural, and vary by as much as 2,500 years. The period between 1,300 BC and 1,000 BC seems to have been accepted by a large number of historians.

There are four Vedas. Of these the Rig Veda is the earliest and most speculative. It consists of hymns of praise which rise to transcendental heights. The principle of Rta, embodied in these hymns, is of great ethical, aesthetical, and educational value. Rta signifies order. Varuna (God of Cosmic law) is the upholder of this order. The operation of this law is not confined to the material field of life. It extends itself to the moral, spiritual, and intellectual aspects of life.

Besides the concept of Rta, the Rig Vedic hymns embody two more concepts: those of *monism* and *samsara*. These underline the existence of a great spiritual power, which always strives towards righteousness.

Monism says that all existing things and activities are manifestations of "the one ultimate principle." *Samsara*, on the other hand, recognizes the existence of a creative force, whose continuous operation transcends all notions of finiteness. Although basically philosophical, both these concepts have some educational significance. *Monism* is a soul-elevating doctrine. It makes the seeker of truth realize the true reality represented by God. *Samsara* denies the existence of inertia at all levels of life. It stresses the endless continuity of life. Its dynamism made the student in Ancient India conscious of the worthwhileness of life. At the same time, it proclaimed that those who do not endeavor to gain true knowledge and are afraid to face life and run away from it are mere cyphers. They achieve nothing worthwhile. *Samsara* therefore encouraged people in those early days to face life as it came.

Although the Yajur Veda and the Sama Veda are mainly liturgical, and were useful for conducting religious ceremonies, they shed light on a variety of interesting topics. The Yajur Veda, in particular, is full of illuminating comments on colonization, astronomy, and other sciences. It explains the basic principle of *Vimen Vidya* (navigation of the air). Ancient Hindus, it is believed, had complete mastery of this science. The development of this science implied a knowledge of mechanics and meteorology. The Yajur Veda also encouraged human beings who were righteous to cross the seas in fast-moving sailing ships and traverse the skies in scientifically built airships.

In the Sama Veda, a number of passages can be found in which the ancient system of music has been explained. This system of music, as a written science, is the oldest in the world, and its principal features were discussed long ago in Vedic writings.

In ancient India, music played an important part in spiritualizing the nature of human beings. It was therefore regarded as one of the most indispensable adjuncts of education. The Sama Veda, better known as the Veda of Music, reveals the divine harmony of music.

The Atharva Veda has an importance of its own. It illustrates the capacity of the Aryans to assimilate culture patterns of other nations. This wonderful capacity to absorb some of the elements of other people is one of the most admirable features of Indian culture and education.

In modern India, it is manifesting itself through the innumerable ways in which science and technology are transforming a traditional society into a scientific one, without losing the basic values of Aryan culture.

3. The Upanishads

The Upanishads embody the speculations of sages about whose lives very little is known. These speculations are interpretations of the Vedas from an original angle. The Vedic hymns tended to rise to monistic heights of thinking. But the Upanishads, by probing from the external world of physical forces to the internal world of experience and soul force actually reach the summit of monistic thought. (Monism negates the ideal of a God who lives in seclusion from the world of human beings. It is a doctrine of unity which treats all reality as an individual whole.)

The Upanishads also encourage the mastery of secular knowledge. They divide knowledge into two broad categories, namely, *Para Vidya* (true knowledge) and *Apara Vidya* (secular knowledge). Although *Para Vidya* alone is recognized as the highest type of knowledge, it is clear that both are necessary for self-realization.

It was, therefore, as necessary to study the Vedas and the Upanishads as it was to study mathematics, geography, and economics. In fact, a proper study of secular subjects, it was held, would enable an individual to acquire a considerable amount of secular knowledge, and, at the same time, enable him or her to cultivate a pragmatic attitude in life.

According to the Upanishads, when atman (the individual self) merges with brahman (the universal or infinite self) such a fusion results in self-realization. Ancient India had a rich heritage of spiritual culture. Some of the most important questions pertaining to humans and their inner nature, their lives, spiritual as well as material, were discussed with their pupils by great ancient Hindu teachers and seers, like Vashishtha and Vishwamitra. This tradition of search for the truth, and for the essential significance of the universe and one's existence in it has continued over the centuries. There is one common current running through all of them, and that is of the supreme value of self-realization.

4. Mnemonic Devices

The principle of Conservation is a great educational force. In order to preserve this precious heritage, a few teachers took upon themselves the task of memorizing the entire Vedic literature. As they lacked the ability to explain and interpret the texts, they were opprobriously called "parrot-like reciters." Various mnemonic devices were employed to prevent corruption of Vedic texts and to perpetuate their purity and accuracy. The *Pada Path* device (memorizing each word divorced from its context) presented to the learners a formidable ideal. All the devices taxed the memory of the learners.

5. The "Rishis" of Vedic Times and the Forest Schools ("Ashrams")

In Vedic times, the *rishis* (seers/teachers) had the reputation of being holy people, who had dedicated themselves to the service of God and Humanity. As teachers, one of their duties was not only to owe allegiance to the Gods and Rta, the great cosmic law, but also to interpret its significance to their disciples, and make them deeply conscious of its purpose and design.

In the Forest Schools (*Ashrams*), situated in the heart of forests of great scenic beauty, the *rishis* and their disciples led a life of contemplation and meditation. The *Ashram* was an institution in which moral and spiritual discipline was learned and practiced. It was neither a prison house nor a house of correction. "It was a little university—not a service station supported by people for utilitarian ends . . . It helped in uplifting individual and collective life through *Yajna* (sacrifice), *diksha* (consecration), *brahmacharya* (disciplined studentship), and *brohman* (prayer)" (Munshi 1965). Rigid rules were laid down for the conduct of pupils. The *rishis* fervently believed that by translating the precepts of Rta into action, an indestructible link can be established between human beings and God.

6. Influence of Buddhism

The Buddhist system of education, which was monastic in character, was based on the concept of a well-ordered organization. It is interesting to note that although it was nonselective, it did not encourage mass teaching.

The *Bhikshus* (monks) led a corporate life in the *Viharas* (monasteries). These *Viharas* were situated in rural areas, far from the "madding crowd." They were educational-cum-religious centers, and their atmosphere was conducive to the growth of an intimate teacher–pupil relationship, which was one of the greatest educational innovations of Ancient Hindu education. Buddhist educational ideals and practices, it should be noted, did not differ very much from Vedic and Upanishadic ideals of education.

One of the most redeeming features of the Buddhist system of education was that it emphasized the importance of primary education. In fact, primary education was widespread. Monks and teachers who were interested in children were entrusted with the work of educating them.

A Buddhist tract called the *Silas*, which dates from about 400 BC, gives a list of children's games. One of these, called *Akkharika* (lettering), which consisted in guessing the letters traced in the air, must have been one of the organized games played in the *Viharas* in which young pupils were admitted, and received preliminary training and education. It must have been one of the "play-way" media for teaching the alphabet.

7. The Principle of Interiorization in the Vedas and Upanishads Upheld and Reinterpreted

In modern India, Dayanand, Vivekananda, Gandhi, Tagore, and Sri Aurobindo highlighted the principle of interiorization which manifested itself to a remarkable degree in ancient Hindu education. Their educational ideals derived much of their inspiration from the Vedas and the Upanishads. Basically, all these educational thinkers were unorthodox. None of them wanted a complete breach with Europe. Their educational thoughts were not locked up in "a small house with all its windows shut."

Although these educational thinkers achieved continuity with the past by recognizing to a certain extent the hard, irrevocable facts of material progress, their emphasis was on the moral, spiritual, and cultural development of India. Towards the end of the nineteenth century, Vivekananda said significantly that education must solve the problem of life. Even the West, he said, was beginning to realize that this could not be done effectively by ignoring the claims of the spirit of men and women.

The principle of interiorization prompted Swami Dayanand to revive and reinterpret the Vedas in the context of modern times. His was not a totally atavistic attitude.

In 1875, Dayanand founded the Arya Samaj. A reformed Hindu society free from prejudice and superstition was one of the greatest objectives of his educational mission. The Arya Samaj, an organization devoted to the reformation of Hindu religion, was first established in Bombay in 1875. In 1877, it took final shape in Lahore (now in Pakistan). In 1885, two years after the death of Dayanand, the Dayanand Anglo Vedic College was established in Lahore. Its primary object was to weld together the educated and uneducated classes by encouraging the study of the national language and the vernaculars; to spread a knowledge of moral and spiritual truths by insisting on the study of classical Sanskrit, to encourage sound acquaintance with English literature; and to afford a stimulus to the material progress of the country by a knowledge of the physical and applied sciences. Thus, the glorious past as well as the progressive trends of modern times lived in Dayanand. Like all great educationists, he believed that the entire educational system should, on the one hand, be inspired by the great traditional culture of the country and, on the other, be forward looking and oriented to modern science and technology.

Vivekananda's spiritual and educational approach was more broad based than that of Dayanand. The monistic idealism of the Vedas was more deep rooted in him than in Dayanand. One of the greatest achievements of Vivekananda was the introduction of compulsory social service.

Mahatma Gandhi gave a fresh and realistic lease of life to the prevailing lifeless educational ideology of India. His theory of basic education sought to exalt the dignity of productive work by making the educands feel that they were giving expression to their creative impulses, not by consciously projecting their "selves" but by effacing them through an inner experience, which identified them with an important nation-building activity. Basic education is a "soul-lifting," productive, work-centered experiment. Its main objective is to achieve a correlation of basic crafts with knowledge. Prayer is one of its most essential features. During the course of daily prayers, in basic schools, children are taught and, occasionally, have explained to them in their mother tongue some of the wise precepts of the Vedas. (Basic schools as originally conceived by Gandhi are no longer in existence. As "work experience" has taken the place of the basic crafts of spinning, weaving,

agriculture, and carpentry, these schools have become "basic oriented.")

Rabindranath Tagore's naturalism, which seeks to exalt the concepts of joy and beauty, surpasses Rousseau's naturalism, which tends to ignore a person's spirit. His *Ananda Yoga* (realization of joy in life) in the sphere of "artistic" education and Gandhi's *Karma Yoga* (realization of selflessness through work) in the sphere of basic education are very meaningful educational experiments of our times. They reflect the fundamental values of the Vedas. Both the experiments are the emanations of the personalities of their originators.

Sri Aurobindo's concept of integral education has an intimate bearing on his concept of integral yoga. The latter signifies a movement towards perfection. Integral education is based on the concept of the evolutionary nature of men and women. It implies a movement towards perfection by recognizing psychologically and educationally the different levels of human consciousness—the physical, the vital, the mental, and the psychic. Like the Upanishadic thinkers, Sri Aurobindo believed that in one and the same individual there was "an inherited portion of divinity."

On the other hand, Sri Aurobindo's theory of integral education has scientific overtones. Sri Aurobindo is greatly influenced by the Western positive attitude towards the material world. Education, according to him, will transform humanity. Its impact on the human race will have global implications.

8. Hindu Education in Contemporary Society

From ancient records and inscriptions it has been found that there were in existence some colleges which were attached to temples. These temple colleges flourished mainly in South India in the Middle Ages. Their close proximity to temples was symbolic of the traditional affinity between religion and education. There is hardly any evidence of temples undertaking educational work earlier than the tenth century. But from the tenth century onwards, some Hindu temples became centers of higher education. The main emphasis, as far as the curricula of these institutions were concerned, was on the study of the Vedas. But grammar and other ancillary subjects were also taught in nearly all these temple colleges.

Old South Indian inscriptions say that these temple colleges were grant-in-aid institutions, and down to the eighteenth century, many religious centers in South India maintained the tradition of teaching Sanskrit. There were perhaps similar educational institutions in North India, whose aim was to achieve a harmonious blend between religious and secular instruction. There are, however, no records to testify to their existence.

Even today, there are a number of Sanskrit schools in the Kutch-Saurashtra region of the present Gujarat State which impart Vedic knowledge. Many of them receive meagre government grants. There is a tendency to look upon them as relics of a bygone age. In West Bengal and Bihar, also, there are a few schools exclusively devoted to the teaching of the Vedas and the Upanishads. In Maharashtra and in a few other states of India, there are some special centers for the learning of Sanskrit. These centers also impart Vedic knowledge. Modern Sanskritists and Vedantists want such institutions to be revived and vitalized. Government by and large seems to be responsive to their legitimate demands.

Bibliography

Altekar A S 1948 *Education in Ancient India*, 3rd edn. Kishore, Benares

Cenkner W 1976 *The Hindu Personality in Education: Tagore, Gandhi, Aurobindo.* Manohar Book Service, New Delhi

Graves F P 1938 *A Student's History of Education: Our Education Today in the Light of its Development*, rev. edn. Macmillan, New York

Kabir H 1949 *Indian Philosophy of Education.* Asia Publishing House, London

Munshi K N 1965 *Foundations of Indian Culture.* Bharatiya Vidya Bhavan, Bombay

Nanavaty J J 1973 *Educational Thought: A Critical Study (in the Perspective of History) of Ideas and Concepts Which Shaped the Pattern and Determined the Content of Education in Ancient and Medieval India*, Vol. 1. Joshi and Lokhande, Poona

Rawat P L 1970 *History of Indian Education*, 6th edn. Ram Prasad, Agra

Islamic Education

D. A. Wagner

Though often ignored by contemporary education specialists, Islamic education remains one of the most important types of education in the world today. Millions of children in dozens of countries attend Islamic or Koranic schools for either part or all of their formal education. Despite its single origin in seventh-century Arabia, Islamic schooling may vary significantly across Moslem communities and societies. In addition, recent socioeconomic, demographic, and political changes have led to further diversity in Islamic schooling. This article considers contemporary trends in Islamic education, with a special focus on traditional pedagogy and children's learning processes.

1. Historical Background

With the death of the prophet Muhammad in AD 632, the prophet's followers began to propagate the revelations of the holy Koran in order to expand the faith. Koranic schooling began, as with most traditional religious schools, as a way of exposing more and more people to the teachings of the Koran. Although an "official" (*uthmanic*) version of the Koran had been agreed upon within several decades following Muhammad's death, the Arabic text in these early manuscript Korans lacked complete vocalization and punctuation. Thus, proper prayer, pronunciation, and recitation of the Koran, required a learned person who was capable of teaching Islam to new believers. The Koranic teacher (*faqih*) became a central part of Islamic education. Although his primary function was to be a teacher, the *faqih* was also a moral guide, and a resource person for the Moslem community; and across the Islamic world, he began to take on functions ranging from legal arbiter to political leader. While the first teachers taught individuals or small groups of students, over the course of several centuries, Islamic schools became diversified and highly specialized institutions for young children,

adolescents, and adults, while at the same time retaining the basic elements of traditional curriculum and pedagogy.

2. Koranic Pedagogy

One meaning of the word Koran is "recitation," and for Moslems, prayer is usually interpreted to mean the recitation of the Koran. Thus, the teaching of proper recitation through the memorization of the Koran has been a central feature of Islamic education. As noted earlier, Koranic texts were not sufficiently explicit to allow completely accurate recitation, thereby necessitating orally transmitted versions of the Koran. An additional explanation for the importance of oral recitation lies in the historical significance of the oral tradition itself, which was carried on by the Greeks, Jews, and Christians long after the written tradition was established and manuscripts became widely available. Although aesthetic value and religious duty were invoked as rationales for the maintenance of oral recitation despite the presence of written text, a lineage of oral recitation (and reciters) was also a way of limiting the number of acceptable Koranic recitation styles and religious interpretations.

By the thirteenth century AD, great Islamic universities had been established in Cairo, Tunis, Fes, and elsewhere, drawing advanced students and teachers from the ever-expanding Islamic community (*umma*). These high-level institutions could accept only the very top students from a vast, pyramid-shaped school structure, while the overwhelming majority of schools (often called *kuttabs*) were reserved for young beginning students.

As in most traditional religious schools, the Islamic *kuttab* was generally limited to male teachers and male students. Children would attend the schools—which might consist of a room in the teacher's house, or even a tent—beginning at about age 4 or 5. Depending on a variety of personal, family, and social constraints, the child might attend *kuttab* for up to six or eight years, about the time it takes to completely memorize the Koran for recitation. Many, of course, would drop out before achieving this goal, while a few would go on for subsequent study with an especially learned *faqih* (or *shaykh*) or to an Islamic university.

Regardless of the host culture, *kuttab* instruction was considered not only to be sacred, but also as a rite of passage for the child. Teachers were often revered as social models, and were given almost complete authority over the child on a master–disciple basis. Since the text was holy, "rote" memorization, rather than comprehension or interpretation (which might come much later on), was stressed. While teachers were cognizant of outstanding students, little or no effort was made to require children to achieve a certain standard of performance; there were no grades, though completion of a given task (say, memorization) could lead to more advanced study of, for example, Koranic exegesis (*tafsir*) or law (*sharia*).

The teaching method most often used in Africa and the Middle East involved copying a Koranic verse onto a wooden slate (*luha*) so that the child would be able to memorize and recite it before moving on to the next verse. The memorized verse was then washed off, and new verses were copied onto the *luha*. Each child would spend four to eight hours a day in the *kuttab*, perhaps learning a craft or farming while not in school.

Since the Koran is written in classical Arabic (Islam does not permit the study of the Koran through translation), many non-Arabic-speaking children have to learn the Arabic alphabet in order to recite from the *luha*. In these societies, and in those where Arabic dialects were spoken, children were often unable to comprehend what they were required to read. However, since memorization was an acceptable manner of "knowing" the Koran, traditional teachers did not consider lack of comprehension to be a problem. (It should be noted that the same phenomenon was, and is, typical in many Jewish and Catholic schools where Hebrew and Latin are used but often not understood.)

Within and particularly beyond the societies of the Arab Middle East, the effects of not knowing the language of the Koran are several. Since the Koran is not age graded, and simplified primers with pictures were generally unavailable until recently, children often had difficulty in learning to read with comprehension. In addition, Koranic teachers had little incentive to break away from time-honored method of memorization without comprehension. Given very low Arabic literacy at the societal level, the literate Islamic teacher in non-Arab societies acquired more power and prestige than in Arab societies, since he was one of the few individuals competent in the sacred Arabic script. In Indonesia, for example, traditional Islamic teachers were thought to be able to make magic through derivations from the Arabic script. In West Africa, Arabic text is still worn

as an amulet to protect against evil spirits. These examples illustrate ways in which Arabic religious literacy has come to play a significant role in the social fabric of Moslem societies.

3. Contemporary Change

Many areas of the Moslem world—especially in Africa and Asia—were under European colonial domination for several centuries, up until the mid-twentieth century. An important aspect of most colonial administrations was the attempt to impose European modern educational systems which used the colonial language. Since precolonial schools were most often Islamic ones, the colonial regimes tried to diminish their strength through means of confrontation, competition, or cooptation. The latter occurred in several French-dominated societies (e.g., Senegal and Algeria), where Franco–Arab schools retained a semblance of Islamic teaching, but were ultimately designed by colonial authorities to replace the traditional *kuttab* system.

Ironically, in many cases such as Morocco, Nigeria, and Indonesia, pressure from colonial regimes seemed to strengthen the importance of traditional education as an institution which could resist the foreign intrusion. By contrast, in Middle Eastern countries such as Syria, Egypt, and Iraq, which were much less affected by European influence, Islamic education did not serve as the guarantor of indigenous culture, and thus was more easily displaced when post Second World War governments decided to adopt European systems of education. In these countries, the *kuttab* seems to have decreased in importance.

While the *luha* is still used in sub-Saharan Africa, it is rapidly disappearing from the *kuttab* in other parts of the Moslem world. The chalkboard and machine printed Korans, as well as secular Arabic primers, are beginning to replace the time-worn manuscripts of earlier centuries. Perhaps even more significant is the change in the type of person who becomes a *faqih*. Until recently, this teacher was trained in the traditional Islamic schools, usually through a lengthy apprenticeship to a learned *faqih*. As the *kuttab* becomes more of a stepping stone to the modern school establishment—as is the case in Morocco, Yemen, and Indonesia—the teacher is likely to have less traditional and more secular training. For example, in some urban centers of Morocco, in contrast to earlier times, secular high-school graduates may be sought as *faqihs*, since they are thought to provide better Arabic training, and a more modern "mentality," than the traditionally trained teachers.

Thus, while many of the older teachers cling to the traditional methods of teaching and learning, important demographic and ideological changes seem to be inexorably producing change in the traditional pedagogy of Islam. This is not to say that the traditional Koranic pedagogy is universally seen as less valued than modern pedagogy. It is probably more accurate to say that the dearth of traditionally trained teachers is a principal component of a changing assessment of what is "best" for children who attend Islamic schools.

4. Future Considerations

In recent years, writers and specialists concerned with Moslem society have promoted the concept of an Islamic "revival." With respect to Islamic education, such a term may be rather indicative of the contemporary situation. A number of national governments have issued decrees to strengthen traditional Koranic education. Most often, this action primarily appears to include a movement toward the secularization of the traditional curriculum, and an increase in government control and economic subsidies for the teachers and for new buildings. It is not yet clear whether this form of support will lead to a real revitalization of the traditional school system, or rather to more cooptation and internal dissention similar to that of the colonial period described earlier. It seems too early to make a reasonable prediction, particularly with the wide variety of traditional Islamic schools still operating in today's world. Nonetheless, the traditional school system is embedded in the cultural fabric of Islamic societies to such a degree that it is likely to endure and be influential for decades to come.

Bibliography

Al-Attas S M N (ed.) 1979 *Aims and Objectives of Islamic Education.* Hodder and Stoughton, London

al-Sa'id L 1975 *The Recited Koran: A History of the First Recorded Version.* Darwin, Princeton, New Jersey

Belarbri A 1988 *Bibliographie Systematique sur l'Education Islamique.* International Institute of Educational Planning, Paris

Dodge B 1962 *Muslim Education in Medieval Times.* Middle East Institute, Washington, DC

Goldziher I 1927 Education (Muslim). *Encyclopedia of Religion and Ethics*, Vol. 5. Clark, Edinburgh, pp. 198–207

Husain S S, Ashraf S A 1979 *Crisis in Muslim Education.* Hodder and Stoughton, London

Kane C H 1961 *L'Aventure ambiguë.* Juillard, Paris [1969 *Ambiguous Adventure.* Macmillan, New York]

Marty P 1917 *Etudes sur l'Islam au Sénégal.* Leroux, Paris

Nakosteen M 1978 Religious influences in higher education (Islam). In: Knowles A S (ed.) 1978 *International Encyclopedia of Higher Education*, Vol. 8. Jossey-Bass, San Francisco, California

Sanneh L D 1975 The Islamic education of an African child: Stresses and tensions. In: Brown G N, Hiskett M (eds.) 1975 *Conflict and Harmony in Tropical Africa.* Papers presented at a 3-day interdisciplinary conf. on conflict and harmony between traditional and western education in tropical Africa, March 1973. Allen and Unwin, London

Santerre F 1973 *Pedagogie musulmane d'Afrique noire.* Presses de l'Université de Montreal, Montreal

Tibawi A L 1972 *Islamic Education: Its Traditions and Modernization into the Arab National Systems.* Luzac, London

Trimingham J S 1962 *A History of Islam in West Africa.* Oxford University Press, London

Tritton A S 1957 *Materials on Muslim Education in the Middle Ages.* Luzac, London

Wagner D A 1989 In support of primary schooling in developing countries: A new look at traditional indigenous schools. World Bank Paper Series, Doc. No. PHREE/89/23, World Bank, Washington, DC

Wagner D A, Lotfi A 1980 Traditional Islamic education in Morocco: Sociohistorical and psychological perspectives. *Comp. Ed. Rev.* 24: 238–51

Jewish Education

S. Reshef

Jewish education relates to all forms of education whose goal is to develop and foster Jewish identity. For the most part the term relates to Jewry living outside the State of Israel, which comprises the majority of the Jewish people.

Because Judaism is both a religion and a nationality, the sources of Jewish identity are diverse: religious, cultural, and universal–humanistic. The survival of the national and religious identity of the Jewish people, who since the destruction of their country have been dispersed among various societies and regimes around the world, is a unique historical phenomenon. Throughout the centuries, faith, religious ceremony, and education have served as the principal means of preserving Jewish identity based upon the eternal connection to the land of Israel and the hopes for the revival of political and national life there.

The Jewish Diaspora made its way between two extremes—a full Jewish life on the one hand and total involvement in the surrounding society on the other. It is this polarity that accounts for the variations in patterns of Jewish education under various regimes and during different periods. The ideological basis and shared contents of this education in its sundry manifestations were and remain religious ceremony, the Bible, the Hebrew language, Jewish literature and thought, universal studies, and above all the attachment to the land of Israel. The relation between these components and the structure of the Jewish school were determined under the influence of internal and external conditions differing from society to society and from period to period.

1. Jewish Education in Historical Perspective

1.1 Ancient Times

Jewish education began in the biblical period. Its purpose was to shape a "kingdom of priests and a holy nation" through the study of the history of Israel and the worship of God. Education took place within the family as the father taught his children the biblical laws, religious ceremony, and precepts, in addition to providing training in a craft or agriculture. Education was incidental, as the father explained when necessary how to act in daily life according to religious values. The girls were taught domestic duties by their mothers. Only writers, priests, and prophets were trained within a formal framework.

After the destruction of the Temple and the exile of the Jewish people to Babylonia, Jewish education focused on the study of Torah and the fulfillment of the precepts in order to ensure national religious and moral life.

The period of the second Temple and the period after the destruction of the Temple by the Romans at the close of the first century AD were important stages in the spiritual life of the Jewish people in which the canonization of the Oral Law took place. The Oral Law comprises the commandments, rulings, and judgments that do not appear in the Written Law, but are interpretations making its application possible. The interpretations given to the Mishna to find solutions to contemporary questions were called the Gemara. The Talmud, which includes both the Mishna and Gemara, became the most important foundation of education for generations. The Law (Torah) in its entirety served three purposes: (a) study, deliberation, and meditation; (b) proposals for legislation; and (c) the worship of God.

At the end of the first century, study houses were established in synagogues in Babylonia, in every city in which Jews lived. The course of study was set: 5-year-olds would study the Torah, 10-year-olds Mishna, and 15-year-olds the Talmud. The study of the Torah and the Mishna was structured on three levels: the order of the subjects, the connection between them, and knowledge of the principles. It was in this period that the yeshiva evolved, a framework of study for adolescents and adults which became the basis for Jewish higher education.

1.2 Middle Ages

As the Talmud in Babylonia was completed, alongside the Talmud prepared in Jerusalem, Babylonian Jewry gained the spiritual leadership of the Jewish people. The concept "Babylonia and Jerusalem" testified to the symmetry between the two spiritual centers of the Jewish nation. The Babylonian yeshivas determined the "Jewish ways of life" (Halacha) whose foundations are in the Torah, and the Gaonim who headed the yeshivas were the supreme spiritual authority. The form of education established in Babylonia served for generations as the model system for preserving Jewish life in a foreign environment. The child began at home with the study of religious precepts. Lessons commenced at school at the age of 6: reading, Torah, and prayer. In the beginning, the Prophets and the writings were also studied, and even arithmetic and the vernacular, but afterwards the study of Talmud took the place of these. The "melamed" of the children—the teacher— received his pay from public funds and his economic and social status was low. At the next stage, boys would study Midrash Mishna and/or Midrash Talmud and thereafter could study independently. The girls were educated only in their homes.

The spiritual influence of Babylonian Jewry extended to the western Mediterranean with the Arab conquest, and eventually leadership passed to Spanish Jewry. A common pattern of education was established in Spain, Italy, and southern France. Added to the study of Halacha in these countries was the study of the Hebrew language and grammar, Hebrew poetry—which flowered in medieval Spain—as well as the Prophets and the Writings. Secular studies and Arabic were also taught in Spain. In Germany and northern France however, Jewish education was limited to the study of the Torah, adherence to religion, and devotion to God and the Jewish people. During this period, Torah passages that were unclear were interpreted by commentators, among them the celebrated "Rashi" (Rabbi Shmuel Yitzhaki). The curriculum included the alphabet, words, the Torah in Aramaic, and the local language, after which gifted students would be sent on to famous yeshivas where they studied Talmud for seven years. It was customary in France to set aside a room in the synagogue for beginners' classes, and toward the end of the Middle Ages the term *heder* (room) began to denote a Jewish elementary school. In Russia, Poland, and Lithuania where small Jewish communities were established, education followed the German example.

1.3 The Renaissance

Political and economic conditions had considerable influence on the structure of Jewish life and the form of Jewish education between the sixteenth to eighteenth centuries. In Eastern Europe the Jews lived in ghettos, in economic distress, and without political influence. Education was designed to ensure a full Jewish life hermetically sealed against outside influences. Secular studies were absolutely forbidden as were Jewish studies not directly connected with daily life. The curriculum included reading, Torah and its translation in Yiddish, and Gemara; while at the higher level, in the yeshiva, emphasis was placed on the commentaries and what was termed *pilpul*, casuistic intellectual exercises for their own sake, not aimed at clarifying rulings.

What were the merits of education in the *heder*? The curriculum was not divided into separate courses, but studies were connected with the life of the community and were based on the pedagogical principle of education for life through life itself. Religion tied together the family, school, and life. Education aspired to cultivate awareness of the world-to-come, and the keeping of the precepts on man's relation to his fellow man, and to God, all within a social structure in which the individual's dependence on the religious hierarchy was absolute.

In contrast, the Jewish community in Italy, which was the most important in the Mediterranean area, aspired to a Jewish education merged into Italian life. Schools were provided for all children and a uniform program instituted which included more extensive Jewish studies than were customary in Eastern Europe, and the sciences as well.

In the nineteenth century a clear struggle developed between two trends: (a) the preservation of the integrity of Jewish life by resisting all external influence, and (b) the acceptance of various forms of accommodation to the society surrounding the Jewish community. The conflict led to the form of Jewish education usual in the modern world which includes general studies along with Jewish studies. Integration between these two components is almost nonexistent, to the present day.

The tendency to offer a general education increased as Jews took their place in economic life under the influence of the Enlightenment movement. In France and Italy, Jewish schools recognized by the authorities were founded where mainly general subjects were taught, and Jewish subjects only on a reduced scale. Two types of schools evolved in Germany: in one, Jewish studies were limited to the Bible in German, some Jewish history, religion, and ethics. The second type of school included Jewish studies on a wider scale and was designed to prevent assimilation. When children increasingly attended public schools, the Jewish supplementary school was developed, with sessions in the afternoon. This form also developed in England. The Austrian emperor, Josef II, encouraged the establishment of schools for Jews in which they would be trained in various crafts, agriculture, and the liberal professions. This approach was supported by prominent Jews who maintained that Jewish education should include the "law of man" as well as the "law of God" and that education took precedence over Torah. The strong opposition to this approach failed to prevent assimilationist tendencies which eventually led to the closing of Jewish schools. Similar trends developed in Eastern Europe and, despite the substantial opposition of community heads and religious leaders, the approach combining general and Jewish studies prevailed.

Beginning in the mid-nineteenth century, a number of Jewish philanthropic societies were founded in Western Europe for the purpose of assisting Jewish education in the Middle East and thus advancing their own countries' political interests in that region: the Alliance (*Alliance Israélite Universelle*) was founded in France in order to advance the education of children that had previously studied in the *kutab*, the oriental version of the *heder*. These schools stressed French culture, and also taught Hebrew, Bible, and Jewish subjects. In 1901 the Ezra (*Hilfsverein der deutschen Juden*) was established in Germany and founded in the Middle East and Palestine dozens of schools based on the German language and culture.

1.4 The Twentieth Century

At the close of the First World War, European Jewry, except in the Soviet Union, was generally recognized as a national minority with cultural and educational rights. The rise of nationalism in the different societies in which Jews lived affected the Jews as well and brought about the establishment of politically oriented Jewish educational systems—which included kindergartens, schools, and teachers' seminaries. The establishment of the Zionist movement which aspired to Jewish national and political revival in Eretz Israel led to the creation of Zionist-oriented schools, both religious and secular. Outstanding among these were the *Tarbut* schools, mainly in Poland, which prepared their students for immigration to Eretz Israel. In them, Hebrew was the language of instruction, and teachers were receptive to progressive educational thought. Under the Nazi occupation, Jewish education was forbidden in most parts of Europe, but continued to exist underground in several of the ghettos. The holocaust which overtook European Jewry also brought about the destruction of Jewish education. After the war, the day schools and supplementary schools established by Jewish war refugees in Central and Western Europe were for the most part Orthodox religious. In Eastern Europe, Jewish education was almost completely prohibited. In South America, where Jews had begun to immigrate to early in the century, the Jewish schools established were for the most part secular. The establishment of the State of Israel created new motivation for Jewish education and for the study of the Hebrew language.

2. Jewish Education in the United States

Jewish education in the United States, which has considerable influence on Jewry as a whole, is important because it serves the largest Jewish community in the world, a community which developed its educational models according to the conditions created by American immigrant society. All the educational institutions existing in Eastern Europe were brought by immigrants from there to the United States: the *heder*, the yeshiva, and the study house (Bet Midrash) which was utilized as an informal public place of study for young and old, singly and in groups.

The first schools, founded by Jewish immigrants of Spanish and Portuguese and afterwards German background, were private. However, the development of the American public school as the accepted educational vehicle, and the emergence of Reform Judaism as the dominant way of life, brought about the decline of the private school. From the mid-nineteenth century on, Reform Jews interpreted Judaism as a universal moral code and moral education as the goal of Judaism. For them the public school symbolized the equality of the Jews in America. The teaching of Jewish material took place in Reform Jewish schools on Saturday (Sabbath) or Sunday morning, and was not usually pursued beyond the age of 13 when the Bar Mitzvah ceremony takes place.

The approximately 280,000 Jews in North America in 1880 grew to almost 4½ million by 1925, in the wake of the great immigration from Eastern Europe. These Jews wanted to integrate into the new society while preserving Jewish tradition and at the beginning the salient tendency was the preservation of the old religious ways of the Orthodox. The afternoon Jewish *heder* supplementary to public school taught Hebrew, and sometimes Midrash, Torah, laws, and customs. In the mid-twentieth century, the American public school declined somewhat and cultural and pedagogical outlooks developed that emphasized pluralism. American Jewry added to Orthodox and Reform Judaism a new religious trend, Conservative Judaism, whose moderate approach strove to integrate the past and present, while emphasizing the centrality of the Torah and the connection between religion and nationality. Fostering a strong attachment to Israel and to American democracy, this movement expanded as did the number of schools affiliated with its synagogues. Jewish education developed a world view applied to everyday life. It no longer favored assimilation of existing forms but rather an Americanism based upon a blend of cultures in the "melting pot." This educational view did not change even when cultural pluralism became the more generally accepted American ideal. At the time, the Jewish educational system came to comprise all levels of education from kindergarten to Jewish universities, and at the same time Jewish studies have expanded at American universities. The more common pattern of Jewish education in the United States has been, however, that of supplementary classes in afternoon schools.

3. Jewish Education at Present

In the present, as in the past, the goal of Jewish education is the maintenance of Jewish life through institutional means, among them education. Most Jewish education today has a religious character even though the home is not generally religious and this fact influences the child's attitude toward education. The connection with the State of Israel and the attempt to find a way between full Jewish identity and integration into the surrounding society are the deciding factors in determining the direction of Jewish education.

Jewish education does not constitute an educational system as this term is commonly understood. Every country has an independent educational authority or authorities. The link between any one school and the national authority is also a tenuous one. The school is under the jurisdiction of whoever "owns" it: a local community, a synagogue, or a private body. The World Zionist Organization, through its Departments of Education and of Religious Education, supplies services and assistance in the field of Jewish education (except to extremely religious institutions), but has no authority over, or formal affiliation with, Jewish schools and school systems. Jewish education thus has a distinctly federalistic, decentralized character. As opposed to other educational systems, the Jewish educational sys-

tem does not benefit from the research that all educational systems coping with social goals enjoy, nor from the contributions of scholars, as the consideration given to research findings is virtually nil. In any case, the number of empirical studies written on Jewish education since the 1930s is not more than 250, and these are almost entirely in the United States. Most of these studies deal with fund raising and budgeting, teacher training, the educational staff, informal education, educational achievements, and attachment to Israel. In recent years there has been a growing trend among sociologists to study Jewish education as an area dealing in national identity and the connection between Jews, as a minority, to their social environment (Himmelfarb 1977).

The number of Jewish children (outside of Israel) between the ages of 6 and 17 was estimated at the end of the 1970s to be about 1,325,000. Of these, 37 percent received some Jewish education, 13 percent in Jewish day schools and 24 percent in supplementary classes. Studies show a decline in the number of children registered in Jewish schools, explained by the decline in the number of Jewish children in the world. A relative stability has, however, been preserved in the percentage of children receiving a Jewish education. The gap between the various countries is great: from none in the Soviet Union up to two-thirds of all Jewish children in South Africa, and in a number of small countries as high as 90 percent. The salient trends point to an increase in the number of children registered in preschool educational frameworks, to a decline in the number receiving supplementary Jewish education, and to a concurrent expansion of the number of day schools and the pupils enrolled in them.

A breakdown for several countries shows that in the United States during the 1970s 37 percent of the Jewish children received a Jewish education, in France 22 percent, in the United Kingdom 55 percent, in Canada 39 percent, in Argentina 52 percent, in South Africa 67 percent, and in Brazil 53 percent (Himmelfarb and Dellapergola 1982).

The relative stability in the percentage of those enrolling for a Jewish education and the increase in the number of Jewish day schools reinforces the demand that the principal effort be directed at the improvement in the quality of this education, and thus highlights the importance of research on the subject of Jewish education. The view that contact between the Jewish child and Jewish (educational) content creates an individual instilled with a Jewish consciousness and that educational achievements can be measured in simple statistical terms has been refuted by relevant research. Without relating to the nature of the Jewish content, these studies state that a minimum number of hours of study are necessary to ensure the influence of the school on the involvement of its graduates in institutional Jewish life. Most of the children receiving a Jewish education do not attain this minimum, perhaps because most supplementary classes meet in the afternoons and on Sundays, and perhaps because the majority of pupils in all types of Jewish education leave the Jewish school upon reaching high-school age, that is, after the Bar Mitzvah ceremony. Research findings point out that the professional qualifications of the teachers are the key to the problem of the standard of Jewish education, and unfortunately a large proportion of teachers of Jewish subjects lack proper training. Although there are approximately 50 institutions training teachers for Jewish schools, they are unable to meet the needs of Jewish schools and their level is often considerably different from that of many colleges training teachers for public schools. The professional qualifications required by the authorities employing these teachers do not augur a drastic improvement in the level of the teachers. The teaching of Jewish subjects is not valued as a profession, due in part to low salaries, and to other conditions such as the necessity of teaching in the afternoons, the lack of motivation on the part of the pupils, and so forth. Another difficulty is the lack of integration between Jewish studies and general studies in the Jewish school. Whereas the latter are based on accepted criteria of modern education, Jewish studies in many cases have an extracurricular character without clear academic standards. Added to this is the great difficulty in learning the Hebrew language which is the basis for Jewish studies.

Two basic problems emerge from the current state of Jewish education, one a value question, the other professional: (a) Good Jewish education means the continuity of Jewish life in the Diaspora and of the Jewish community and its institutions which serve as a framework for that life. However, since the crux of this education is the connection to Israel, the effectiveness of this education will normally be expressed in the identification with Israel and the willingness to immigrate there. Because of this contradiction between immigration to Israel and the perpetuation of Jewish life in the Diaspora, the school has difficulty taking a clear ideological stance, and is subject to inertia. (b) Jewish education lacking a central educational and administrative authority seeks to aid the Jewish community to preserve its patterns and continue its existence without the proper means available to all other modern educational systems: suitable curriculum, teaching and learning methods, teacher training, assessment of achievements, and school organization.

In recent years, several universities in Israel and in other parts of the world have taken an interest in Jewish education and have assisted various communities to develop educational vehicles, evaluate results, and conduct research. Many universities with no Jewish affiliation have developed departments of Judaic studies of academic quality.

The absence of research and evaluation is glaringly evident, however, and that situation excuses the policy makers in Jewish education, and the Jewish community as a whole, from embarking upon any systematic consideration of educational needs. Consequently, the Jewish school fails to receive help of the sort available to teachers in any modern school system. Yet in view of the diminishing influence of the family and the synagogue—the other two institutions charged with the socialization of the younger Jewish generation—the Jewish school could fulfill an increasingly vital function as a framework in which patterns of Jewish life are formulated and created within a changing society. That function could best be carried out in comprehensive Jewish day schools based on modern pedagogical principles in which Jewish and general subjects are totally integrated curricularly and extracurricularly, from nursery school to the end of secondary school, with classes provided for parents as well. Schools of this type would be able to evolve a life-style appealing to youngsters because it copes with the problems of how to live as Jews within a non-Jewish society. Such a change in the structure and practices of Jewish schools will naturally involve a need for research on education and for a national clarification of its means and end.

Bibliography

Ackerman W 1980 Jewish education today. *American Jewish Yearbook* 70: 130–49

Dushkin A M 1970 *Comparative Study of the Jewish Teacher Training Schools in the Diaspora.* Hebrew University, Jerusalem

Encyclopedia Judaica, Vol. 6, 1972 Jewish education. Keter, Jerusalem, pp. 382–446

Gartner L P (ed.) 1969 *Jewish Education in the United States: A Documentary History.* Teachers College Press, New York

Himmelfarb H S 1977 The non-linear impact of Jewish schooling: Comparing different types and amounts of Jewish education. *Sociol. Educ.* 50: 114–32

Himmelfarb H S, Dellapergola S 1982 *Enrollment in Jewish Schools in the Diaspora.* Hebrew University, Jerusalem

Scharfstein Z 1960 *Toldoth haHinuch beYisrael beDoroth haAhronim* [History of Jewish Education in Modern Times], rev. edn. Mass, Tel Aviv

Schiff A I 1977 The Jewish day school in America 1962–1977. *The Pedagogic Reporter* 29: 2–7

Sklare M, Greenblum J 1979 *Jewish Identity on the Suburban Frontier*, 2nd edn. University of Chicago Press, Chicago, Illinois

Section 3

Curriculum Processes

Overview

This Section, Curriculum Processes, is divided into four subsections. It begins with a general description of The Nature of Curriculum Innovation and continues with a series of articles on The Process of Curriculum Development. The Section concludes with a group of articles dealing with problems faced when using the curriculum in the educational system in general and, in the classroom in particular.

Section 3(a) begins with Fullan's article defining *Curriculum Change* as a generic concept which applies to any alteration of instruction or educationally arranged conditions of instruction. Rulcker examines the features of *Curriculum Reform* which are defined as an innovation of a particular type which establishes the aim and content of education in so far as it leads to change in other social areas as well.

Section 3(b) deals with The Process of Curriculum Development. Tyler reviews the resources available to assist curriculum developers in answering important questions arising in the course of their work. Gay examines the dynamics of decision-making in *Curriculum Development*. She describes this process as an interpersonal and collaborative enterprise of which interests, values, ideologies, priorities, roles, functions, and differentiated responsibilities form the contours. In his article on *Curriculum Deliberation*, Beyer analyzes the process of deliberation taking place among persons involved in decision-making.

The articles by Eraut and De Landsheere deal with educational objectives and the part they play in the school curriculum. They provide an historical overview of definition and a taxonomic classification of educational objectives. They also deal with problems in selecting objectives, and criteria for setting priorities.

Clandinin and Connelly provide two definitions of *Curriculum Content*: (a) the problem areas, subjects, or disciplines included in the school program, and (b) the topics included in a single course of study. Louise Tyler summarizes research on *Learning Experiences*—one of the four components of the Tyler curriculum model—and calls attention to promising directions.

The organizational pattern of the curriculum is dealt with in two articles. In the first, Klein refers to this organization as *Curriculum Design* and examines the criteria for preferring a design of a particular type. Skilbeck examines elements or components of the curriculum such as study plans, instructional materials, equipment, expertise of the teaching force, and examination requirements and he finds that it is in bringing these elements together into a coherent whole, that the organization of the curriculum is achieved.

Section 3(c) Participants in the Curriculum Process, deals with the involvement of various persons or groups of people in curriculum planning. The first article deals with the activities of *Curriculum Development Centers* and the last one deals with *School-based Curriculum Development*. These two articles describe two dominant patterns of curriculum development during the period from 1960 to 1990. At the beginning of this period it was possible to observe a strong bias towards a centralistic pattern of curriculum development and towards the end of this period these two patterns were given equal weight within a framework of joint responsibility for schools' curricular needs.

In the wake of the New Curriculum Movement, curriculum experts gained professional status and in a number of countries Curriculum Development Centers were established. Eden describes the differences in operation patterns of these centers in terms of their source of legitimacy, their responsibility, the freedom of schools in curricular matters, and the professional freedom of the institution. A comparative analysis of system-level decisions in three different countries appears in Lewy's article on this subject.

The professional status of *Curriculum Personnel* is examined by Haller and Lewy. Maxwell distinguishes between the types of *Curriculum Consultants*, namely, those who act as experts and recommend solutions for their client's problems on the basis of personal experience, and those who act as facilitators and help the client to diagnose and find a solution to their problems. May discusses various approaches to the supervisor's role in curricular matters.

The participation of lay people in curriculum development is discussed in the articles by Steffy on *Involving Parents* and *Community Participation*. She distinguishes between the role of parents as clients, producers, consumers, and governors and views community participation as an effective method of ensuring both responsiveness to local needs and utilization of local resources.

The articles by Elbaz on *Teachers' Participation in Curriculum Development* and Sabar on *School-based Curriculum Development* have strong links with each other. While teachers may actively participate in the work of curriculum development centers, school-based curriculum development, by definition, emphasizes the desirability of cooperation between teachers and curriculum centers and implies teacher involvement. Elbaz elaborates on the desirability of cooperation between teachers and curriculum centers whereas Sabar focuses on the participation of teachers in the work of local teams producing curriculum materials, selecting them, and adapting them to local needs.

Using the Curriculum is dealt with in Section 3(d). The use of a new curriculum in schools implies its diffusion and adoption. Leithwood concentrates on curricular innovation and examines the generalizability of diffusion research to educational settings. In her article on *Curriculum Adoption*, Loucks indicates that in the 1960s adoption was viewed as the end point of diffusion efforts, however, in the 1970s adoption was shown not necessarily to lead to the systematic use of the innovation. As a result, Loucks examines factors which may pave the way from adoption to the full innovation and defines terms which have become basic concepts in implementation research. Adapting a curriculum that was developed for a particular target population to another target group, or adapting a centrally developed curriculum to the needs of a particular class, are examined in the articles by Blum and Grobman, and Smylie. The range of curriculum alternatives offered to the student is the subject of Schubert's article. Lundgren and Colliander discuss *Curriculum Pacing*. Finally, Silberstein reviews the trend of including curriculum studies in programs of teachers' education and examines the reasons for and the expected consequences of this practice.

S. Eden and A. Lewy

Curriculum Processes

Introduction

A. Lewy and S. Eden

The meaning of the term *curriculum processes* largely depends on the meaning attached to the term *curriculum*. In his Introduction to Section 1, Connelly, illustrating differences in emphasis, lists nine definitions of the term *curriculum* and indicates that they only constitute a sample of the many definitions of the term appearing in the educational literature. This diversity in definition imparts an amorphous character to the field of study. In his Introduction to Part 1, Goodlad notes that very few books on curriculum carry the word *theory* in their title and he conjectures that this is the case simply because there is so little theory and when it is found, it only applies to parts of the whole. The difficulty of constructing theory about an ill-defined concept is even more emphatically indicated by the Soviet educator Tsetlin, who questions the Western concept of *curriculum* (using the Latin word) and confesses that he is unable to see exactly what the word means to a Western educator. Tsetlin believes that the term *curriculum* is different from the Russian term *soderzhanie obrazovaniya* (content of education) and that curriculum theory should be seen as a theory of programs of instruction for Westerners (Muckle 1988).

It is interesting to note that although the term *curriculum* has been used in English language literature since the beginning of the seventeenth century and in the last one hundred years has become central to educational thinking, there is no exact translation of the term in most European languages. The German term *lehrplan* and the French term *programme scholaire* have a meaning which more resembles the concept of syllabus than of curriculum.

Goodlad tried to reduce the ambiguity of the term *curriculum* by distinguishing between curriculum as schedules of work and courses of study, and curriculum praxeology, that is curriculum building activity. He indicated, by implication, that curriculum studies are mainly devoted to the term in the latter connotation. By adopting Goodlad's distinction, one focus of curriculum studies is the process of making curriculum, including decisions about what to teach and the preparation of instructional materials. This focus of curriculum studies examines the principles which guide these decisions and also the actual work of those who are involved in the decision-making.

One dimension of differences between patterns of curriculum development is the locus of decision-making. In some educational systems decisions about curriculum are made at national level, or at the level of major political units of the nation such as state, province, or territory. In other systems decisions about curricula are considered to be the prerogative of the school. An example of the former pattern is to be found in France, where a well-defined and fully detailed school program was produced between 1821 and 1840. In Prussia, the first steps to develop a detailed study-plan for all schools including a complete timetable for each subject, stipulations on the aims, content, methods of teaching, and a list of compulsory reading assignments were taken in the eighteenth century and completed by the beginning of the nineteenth century. By contrast, in the United States, no specific directives about curriculum, beyond general recommendations of ad-hoc committees, have ever been issued at national level. In England and Wales between 1944 to 1988, the only nationally prescribed curriculum directive dealt with the school's obligation to provide religious education.

As a reaction to the highly centralized curriculum projects initiated during the 1960s, strong support has been expressed in favor of school-based curriculum development. Indeed, during the 1970s and 1980s this was one of the major topics of interest in the field of curriculum research and studies. It should, however, be noted that the scope of school-based curriculum development has, in practice, remained limited and even in countries where a favorable attitude towards this approach was held, there are estimates that less than 10 percent of the actual school program has been developed at the school level. Reid (1987) views the support for school-based curriculum development as a reversal of an historical trend which has characterized educational systems in Europe and North America since the end of the nineteenth century. This was achieved by the creation of hierarchically organized bureaucratic agencies linked to a stable apparatus of power and control.

It is important to note that the centralistic pattern of

curriculum development is not necessarily related to the existence of centralistic prescriptions of the educational authorities. Thus, for example, in the United States in the 1950s and 1960s, large curriculum programs were initiated at a time when more than 20,000 school boards enjoyed full autonomy in taking decisions about curricular matters in the districts of their jurisdiction. Nevertheless, large scale curriculum projects attracted wide public attention and had an impact, if not on what happened, at least on what has been considered to be a desirable pattern of curriculum-development activity.

By the end of the 1980s more were in favor of a partnership between the nation's central authorities and the schools, than in favor of either one of these two competing patterns of curriculum-decision making. The Education Reform Act of England and Wales constitutes an example of implementing partnership between grass-root school level and centralistic national level curriculum-decision making. Skilbeck (1990 p. 74) characterizes the governmental curriculum frameworks of the 1980s as being at the same time centralistic directives and an invitation to teachers and school communities to exercise more responsibility in developing curricula. He claims that this illustrates

> a pervasive paradox in curriculum reform. Freedom is, in a sense, being enjoined. At the same time it is being constrained or at least highly structured, most obviously by grade-related criteria, examinations or other assessment

criteria now in vogue. Close attention will need to be paid to the multiple and potentially contradictory effects of these various strategies and processes of curriculum development.

Connelly (1972) approaches the debate about the locus of curriculum decisions quite differently. He denies the existence of two alternative patterns and claims that in practice, teachers use instructional materials produced by external developers as well as materials prepared by themselves. Thus, the question is not who should make decisions about the curriculum, but what decisions should be made by the user or the implementer of the curriculum at school or class level. Nevertheless, despite its convincing argument, such conceptualization of the curriculum development process still leaves open the question about the scope of the school's autonomy in curricular matters.

Bibliography

Connelly M 1972 Functions of curriculum development. *Interchange* 3: 161–77
Muckle J 1988 *A Guide to Soviet Curriculum*. Croom Helm, London
Reid W 1987 The functions of SBCD: A cautionary note. In: Sabar N, Rudduck J, Reid W (eds.) 1987 *Partnership and Autonomy in School Based Curriculum Development*. University of Sheffield, Sheffield, pp. 115–24
Skilbeck M 1990 *Curriculum Reform: Overview of Trends*. Centre for Educational Research and Innovation, OECD, Paris

The Nature of Curriculum Innovations

Curriculum Change

M. Fullan

The term "curriculum" is used very broadly in the literature to refer to instructionally related educational experiences of students. It encompasses educational philosophy, values, objectives, organizational structures, materials, teaching strategies, student experiences, assessment, and learning outcomes (Leithwood 1981). Curriculum change can be defined as any alteration in the aspects of curriculum just mentioned. It should be noted that nearly all references define change as something which is new to the people affected by the change. It is not defined in terms of its intrinsic newness—the latter being called invention.

The number of concepts related to curriculum change are numerous and the different ones are not used with any degree of consistency. It is possible, however, to identify the main terms and to describe some of their characteristics. They can be grouped into two categories—those pertaining to the nature of change; and those related to the process or phases of change. The former includes change, innovation, reform, and movement (see *Curriculum Movements in the United States*); the latter covers the following: development, diffusion, dissemination, planning, adoption, implementation, (including fidelity and adaptation), and evaluation (including institutionalization). Each of these two sets of terms will be discussed in turn.

1. The Nature of Curriculum Change

The nature of alterations in curriculum is usually talked about as a change, an innovation, a reform, or a movement. While these terms are frequently used interchangeably, it is helpful to make some distinctions between them. Curriculum change is used most frequently and most generally. It is the most generic concept which applies to any alterations in instruction or in the educationally arranged conditions surrounding instruction. As a generic term it is sometimes used very vaguely to refer to general changes and directions in the curriculum, and sometimes very specifically to describe a particular change.

While curriculum change is sometimes used in reference to a particular change, the term "innovation" is most frequently used to refer to specific curricular changes. Innovations can range from single subject changes (e.g., a new reading program) to more comprehensive changes (e.g., an integrated approach to teaching children of a certain age level). In either case, innovations are characterized by their relatively clear boundaries and by specific labels attached to them, although this is not to claim that all innovations are clear in their goals and means of achievement. Innovations can be analyzed according to their different characteristics such as cost, complexity, clarity, and so on.

The concept "reform" also relates to particular changes, but it usually concerns more comprehensive and fundamental curriculum change. Reforms involve restructuring of the school system, wholesale revision of the curriculum, and the like. They are based on major value changes or redirections, and are often initiated in the political system. Parenthetically, curriculum change in North America tends to focus on innovations (specific relatively narrow curricular products) while reforms (more major fundamental changes), tend to dominate the field of curriculum change and research in Europe.

Reforms, although fundamental in nature, concern particular changes or areas of change in the educational system—for example, the development of comprehensive secondary schools. The term "curriculum movement" has more of an historical connotation and is used to characterize periods of change by their main common themes. For example, Kliebard, identifies three broad themes in the United States from 1945 to 1975—life adjustment education, the structure of the disciplines movement, and the minority groups and relevance period. Similarly, Atkin and House (1981) trace the different themes in the history of the federal role in curriculum development in the United States from 1950 to 1980. The dominance of certain themes in certain periods of time can be described as curriculum movements.

In summary, the nature of change in education is normally addressed through the use of one of four concepts—change, innovation, reform, and movement. These concepts differ in their scope, specificity, radicalness, and historical orientation. Some of the attributes of each of the four concepts have been outlined, with the main qualification being that curriculum writers do not always use these concepts carefully and consistently.

2. *Processes of Curriculum Change*

Most researchers describe the processes of curriculum change in three broad phases which can be labelled most generally as initiation, use, and assessment. The change process is, of course, much more complex than these three phases imply, depending on whether the focus is on a particular innovation, a large-scale reform, the entire system of innovation, a group of local educators, national authorities, and so on. The phases, however, can be used to give a brief introduction to the concepts most frequently used in analyzing curriculum change. At the initiation phase, the terms development, diffusion, dissemination, planning, and adoption can be used. In reference to actual use, implementation is the main concept with important distinctions between fidelity and adaptation. At the assessment phase, institutionalization and evaluation are most prominent. Most researchers caution that the change process is not quite so linear, and that the phases are overlapping.

There are at least two broad schools of thought about the process of educational change. One closely aligned to the research–development–diffusion paradigm views the production and subsequent implementation of quality innovations as the main goal. This is sometimes called the fidelity perspective in that the criterion for success is the faithful use of an innovation as intended by its developer. The other change process perspective is more open ended, and views development and use as a continuous process with many decisions taken by users about the nature of change. This approach is variously called mutual adaptation, evolutionary adaptation, and inquiry-based adaptation. Depending on which of the two orientations are taken, the definition of the main concepts take on different meanings. With this caution in mind the main concepts mentioned above can be discussed.

Development consists of the decisions taken in the construction of a new or revised curriculum involving its goals, materials, instructional activities, assessment, and the like. For specific innovations, these decisions might be taken by developers (the fidelity perspective) or by a combination of users and external personnel (the adaptation perspective). For more comprehensive changes, development may consist of policy formation, general directions, and frameworks within which any number of curricular innovations may occur.

Diffusion and dissemination are used interchangeably. They involve the spread of information about curricular changes. Technically, diffusion refers to the natural spread of information, while dissemination consists of planned activities to bring new information to people's attention for potential use, but the terms are used so inconsistently that they may be considered as one and the same. Depending on the level and the specificity, diffusion or dissemination are sometimes used in reference to single innovations, and sometimes to analyze or plan entire curricular information systems. Similarly, the concept planning is used at both the specific level (i.e., how to plan for changes in one subject area), and the general level (i.e., how to plan to set up a system for considering and introducing any changes).

Adoption takes the process one step closer to use in that it refers to the process which leads up to and includes the decision to proceed with a new curriculum or curricular direction. Not much is known about how such decisions are taken.

Up to this point, actual use has not been considered. Much of the research in the late 1960s and the 1970s documented that development, diffusion, dissemination, planning, and adoption frequently did not result in actual change in practice (Fullan 1982). It was during the 1970s that curriculum researchers became preoccupied with implementation studies in an attempt to discover what, if anything, was really changing in the classroom, and what factors influenced the extent of change. Some researchers concentrated on the degree of implementation in relation to the intentions of developers, while others were interested in exploring whatever changes happened regardless of the intentions of developers or policy makers. Both were concerned with what was happening at the level of practice in the first few years of a curriculum change effort.

In the third and final phase in the process of change, questions are raised about the extent to which innovations, reforms, and so on, become embedded in the system and with what consequences. The degree of embeddedness or institutionalization is indicated when a change becomes routinized in the system by becoming a regular part of the budget and staffing decisions. The impact of change stresses evaluation issues. It is the case that curriculum evaluation as a field of study has expanded dramatically since the early 1970s. Moreover, it encompasses all phases of change in attempting to determine what factors are related to development and diffusion, how to measure the extent of implementation, and how to assess the intended and unintended consequences of curriculum changes. Obviously, specific innovations are easier to evaluate than large reforms, but models of evaluation have been developed to assess all aspects of curricular change (House 1980).

Bibliography

Atkin J M, House E 1981 The federal role in curriculum development, 1950–1980. *Educ. Eval. Policy Anal.* 3(5): 5–36

Fullan M 1982 *The Meaning of Educational Change.* Teachers College Press, New York

House E 1980 *Evaluating with Validity.* Sage, Beverly Hills, California

Leithwood K A 1981 The dimensions of curriculum innovation. *J. Curric. Stud.* 13: 25–36

Curriculum Reform

T. Rülcker

Curricula in one form or another have existed for a long time already. Accordingly, procedures for the inspection and amendment of curricula have also always been employed (Dolch 1965). The question that must be asked, therefore, is what has been so new in the developments since the 1950s that was perceived by professional people as a fundamental, or even a revolutionary change?

In addressing this question, it is best to begin with the observation that curriculum reform, until the middle of this century, took place in a diffuse form within the framework of other structures, such as school administration, schoolbook production, teaching, and so on. Fundamental arguments for new and further developments were at that time principally pedagogic, didactic, and ideological considerations, that is to say considerations which arose from the framework of an interpretation of the currently prevalent understanding of education. It is only since the 1950s that a unique and specialized reform system in the field of curriculum can be separately identified; this reform system has advanced to a position where it interacts with other social systems—especially with occupational systems, but also with political and educational systems. Consequently, the relationships which had always existed between curriculum and other areas of society, but previously only implicitly, have become a topic of major interest, since the development of curricula is seen as an educational–political reaction to events in other areas. Facts related to those other areas must therefore be systematically analysed, in order to make decisions about the functionally appropriate curricular goals and contents in each subject.

The reform system known as "curriculum" may be described in quite general terms as innovation in the educational system with regard to its content. Thus it is not merely a matter of adapting the education system to new and urgent requirements arising from changes in other social systems. In other words, it is not simply an attempt to fill in some "cultural lag". This may be necessary today as it was in the past. The essentially new, however, is to be found in the field of autonomous innovations, which means that the newly defined aims and contents of education are apt to initiate changes in other social areas too. Curriculum reform as innovation comes to the fore with a claim that it is in essence ideological, and is deliberately, purposefully, and methodically carried out. If it is borne in mind that the influence of the education system on other social areas is always effective only through the people educated by it, then the relationship between the two functions, adaptation and autonomous innovation, becomes clear. On the one hand, people must be prepared to deal with the demands of emerging social situations in order to be able to fulfil their roles adequately; they must, however, also have criteria and objectives in order to be able creatively to develop these roles further. For without the ability to adapt, people sink; without the power to adapt roles, they lose their identity.

The explicit thematization of the relationships between the "curriculum" reform system and other social component areas leads to a second fundamental distinction between the earlier forms of curriculum reforms and those since the 1950s. In the place of a craftsperson-like approach guided by experience, a theoretically based approach was introduced. Stenhouse specifies two functions of theory: "It serves to organize the data, the facts we have, in such a way as to provide an understanding. The second function of theory in a policy science is to provide a basis for action" (Stenhouse 1975). The development of the "curriculum" reform system is thus accompanied from the very outset by efforts to develop a sound theory. This task, however, has not yet been by any means satisfactorily accomplished. What is lacking above all, is the binding together of the accumulated data and theoretical fragments with the practical conditions in various national, regional, and local areas of practice. Consequently, actual curriculum reform is effected contrary to requirements—that is to say, either not at all guided by theory, or else having only a coincidental relationship to some theoretical fragment or other.

1. The Social Requirement of Curriculum Reform

The relation of the "curriculum" reform to society as a whole or to particular aspects of society can be analysed using two criteria. On the one hand, society may be interpreted as the sum of all conditions, and inquiries may be made into the general conditions under which curriculum reform takes place. On the other hand, society may be viewed as the totality of standards for which education has to prepare people, and inquiries may be made into the manner in which curriculum projects may identify these standards and draw from them new goals and new contents for education and training. Both questions are equally fundamental to an understanding of curriculum reform. The next section will deal with the first criterion; the second one will be dealt with in subsequent sections.

1.1 Widespread Problems

Recent discussions about curriculum reform concerned themselves with widespread economic problems in the Western industrial states. Changes in the production pattern necessitated changes in production resources, too, so that science and technology became important resources of production. This development led to radical changes in occupational patterns. Consequently direct demands were made on the education system to provide a highly qualified labour force. In response to these demands made on the education system, two significantly different tendencies emerged: in the first decade of the curriculum reform movement in the United States, the main concern was to qualify a scholastic elite to a higher standard (see *Curriculum Movements in the United States*). Later, greater prominence was accorded to the aim of raising the greatest possible number of pupils to a higher academic level.

Closely linked with these changes in the production resources, there arose in the Western industrial societies a fundamental crisis of values and ways of thinking. From Goodlad's assertion that "Values which had long guided American life where shifting and crumbling, a process sharply accelerated by World War II" (Goodlad 1966) through to the Cassandra cries of the German movement "Towards a Brave Education" [*Mut zur Erziehung*], complaints against lacking value consciousness and consequent instability have been constantly and widely voiced. The educational system in general, and curriculum reform in particular, have suffered acutely through these crises of values, insofar as schooling is always concerned with the transmission of cultural traditions. Consequently, these cultural crises also resulted in heated and prolonged disputes on the schools, their aims, the content of teaching, textbooks, and so on. The resolution of this tension may only be achieved if pedagogy—and, in particular, the curriculum reform system—can provide a convincing definition of the culture of the school. It is for this reason that the question of the authority to prescribe curricular innovations acquired central significance.

1.2 The Authority of Curricular Reform

In the face of the crisis of values and thought, curriculum reform as an innovation in the content of the educational system calls for a convincing basis of authority. It must be clearly explained why the aims and contents of a new curriculum should be included in the school programme, and thus why it is justifiable to demand that pupils should get involved with them. This justification not only supports the reform, but appeals also to the attitudes and motivations of those who, in practice, will be the users of the curricula. It is, therefore, instructive to examine thoroughly what kind of explicit or implicit arrangements are made to procure authority in the modern curriculum development.

Before the emergence of the new curriculum reform system, curricula relied upon a broad public consensus about social and cultural goals in general, and about the goals of the education system in particular. This relationship by no means precluded change. Social ideologies do change in the wake of social change, and on each stage of the process a consensus has to be attained about the goals of education. Nevertheless,

curriculum planners in the past could always rely on a certain prior consensus among the parties involved in education. The newness of the situation since the beginning of the 1950s lies in the fact that such a consensus is no more to be taken for granted. In the crises, for example, of the "new education" in the United States and of the *Geisteswissenschaftliche* pedagogy in the Federal Republic of Germany, a generation factor has come into play: "Part of what we must confront is the fact that many of the young are rejecting values, goals, and identities we have always taken for granted" (Silberman 1970). Thus the task of curriculum reform takes on a substantially new aspect: it is no longer a matter merely of transforming a social consensus on the content of education into curricula, but rather of bringing about this consensus in the process of creating new curricula. For this reason, the question of the authoritative foundation of new curricula emerges as a key problem in curriculum reform.

If an eye is cast backwards over the time since the beginning of the new curriculum reform movement, it can be ascertained that the earliest strategy of justification was the linking of the movement to academic work. As is shown by the findings of the Woods Hole Conference of 1959 (Bruner 1960), the hope of securing support for academically orientated projects relied not only on a promise of reasonableness, but above all on the publicized consequences. Academia offers itself as a way out of the supposed national crisis. The early curriculum projects in the United States, as too in England and Wales, were accordingly marked by close association with academic disciplines, leading to a close interconnection between curriculum reform and science. In accordance with this dominance of the sciences, scientific subjects and their specialist branches became the almost exclusive source of curriculum content. The consequence was that curriculum reforms over a period of almost two decades were dominated by a puristic structure-of-a-discipline doctrine. Admittedly this concept was soon to become the subject of revisions—but that alters nothing.

In the Federal Republic of Germany, too, the first phase of curriculum reform—albeit delayed in relation to the United States, and taking place only in the second half of the 1960s—displays a certain orientation towards academia. That is, however, only partly in the form of modelling the school curricula on the structure of the discipline, as is the case with a number of curricula in the natural sciences. Very influential in the Federal Republic of Germany is a piece of research which takes as its starting point a criticism of the curriculum reform movement in the United States on account of the lack of academic research into its aims (Huhse 1968). In contrast, the research group led by Robinsohn stresses the primary necessity of accurate research into these aims. The principle of scientific orientation dominates here, too, the application of scientific method which is supposed to guarantee the soundness of proposed educational aims. A high level of research expenditure is devoted to the working out of scientifically based methods of curriculum development. The underlying assumption of authority may, then, be formulated as follows: scientifically produced curricula determine which elements of content are the most appropriate in a given situation. And since no-one can deny the persuasiveness of scientific objectivity, the questions of a consensus and of acceptance are simultaneously solved. For science has basically only highlighted those necessary areas with which individuals must concern themselves in their activities.

The academic orientation of curricula is prominent also at another juncture: in the formulation of objectives. The general criticism of earlier forms of syllabi raised by the initiators of curriculum reform is on the level that their formulation of aims was unclear and confused. Thus they could neither show precisely the direction in which one ought to be aiming, nor could they form any basis on which to monitor the effectiveness of teaching. Redress is therefore sought in the adoption of conceptions and methods developed in behavioural psychology. "A statement of objectives should describe both the kind of behaviour expected and the content or the context to which that behaviour applies" (Taba 1962). Clearly defined objectives certainly have more than one function. Taba discusses a whole series of possible assignments. She draws particular attention to the consensus-producing function of study goals specified with scientific exactitude.

In the further progress of the curriculum reform movement, it very soon became clear, however, that scientific method was obviously not a sufficient, justifying basis for innovation. In particular, it was not, apparently, sufficient to guarantee the inclination of all concerned to accept the curricula. This was the case with teachers, but most crucially also with pupils. Thus Silberman, who in 1966 had still welcomed scientifically orientated reforms, claimed in 1970 that the reformers of the 1950s and 1960s "opted for adult dictation. They knew that they wanted children to learn; they did not think to ask what children wanted to learn. Because the reformers were university scholars with little contact with public schools or schools of education, they also tended to ignore the harsh realities of classroom and school organization" (Silberman 1970). In the later phases of curriculum reform, therefore, justification through some form of participation seems of increasing importance. Those concerned with the curriculum—that is to say, those who must work with it—should be in some way or other involved in its development. This participation extends from cooperation in adapting curricula to regional and local requirements, to the conception that "teachers make their own curricula", as in the school-linked curriculum development in the Federal Republic of Germany (Gerbaulet et al. 1972). The belief underlying this may be reduced to the formula of consensus through communication with equal rights.

1.3 Curriculum Reform and Educational Policy

Curriculum development is interwoven with attempts to answer the question: what is education? Curriculum reform therefore has a significant political component. The authors of the earlier projects remained largely unaware of this. Previous reforms were overshadowed by attempts to improve the academic content of curricula. So long as curriculum reform was seen only as a process on the fringe of learning and didacticism, the interest of state authorities in it remained limited. This situation changed with the advance of the reform movement. On the one hand, the political component became exploited with increasing significance by curriculum researchers, by showing that curricula can, and should, be employed in the service of purposeful social change. On the other hand, it is noticeable that, in all countries, state authorities discovered the value of curriculum reform as a lever in educational policy. A few examples here will be helpful. In the United States, the National Defense Education Act (1958) has expanded the budget and the tasks of the United States Office of Education. Since 1963, research and development centres have been financed with federal funds, and since 1965, public funds have been used to finance regional educational laboratories, whose task is also the provision of certain curriculum projects. "Financial support has come from the National Science Foundation, the United States Office of Education, and private foundations. This flow of funds from the first two sources has placed the government squarely in the mainstream of educational affairs" (Goodlad et al. 1966). With regard to England and Wales, MacDonald and Walker (1978) have ascertained that during the 1970s a marked politicization of curricular reform occurred, in the sense of a shift of emphasis in educational discussion from the problem of what should be done to improve the education system, to the question of who should make those decisions about it. In the Federal Republic of Germany, in particular, since the beginning of the 1970s, state institutes of curriculum development have been founded in several of the Länder: the Centre for Pedagogy in Berlin, founded in 1964, which has served increasingly through the 1970s as an instrument of state policy on curricula in Berlin; the Institute for Educational Technology in Wiesbaden (founded in 1970); the Institute for Educational Planning and Course Information in Stuttgart (founded in 1970); the Institute for Theory and Practice of Schooling in Kiel (founded in 1971); and the State Institute for School Pedagogy in Munich (founded in 1966). In view of the political significance which curriculum reform has acquired, this interest on the part of state authorities is neither deplorable, nor is it illegitimate. The decisive factor, however, is that the principle of state responsibility should not be transformed into total control. "There is a political need for some kind of central system of accountability which will *not* amount to central control of the curriculum" (Lawton 1978). Just how great this danger is, it is at present still hard to estimate in overall terms, since it is heavily dependent on different national contexts. The scope, tendencies, and prospects for the success of reform depend on national traditions governing school organization, political culture, and political structure.

1.4 Various National Contexts

Within the scope of the present article, it is possible to illustrate the significance of national context only with a few examples. In the United States curricular reform in its newer form emerged at the end of the era of "progressive education", which was criticized above all for its excessive orientation toward the child and for its low academic standards. Curriculum reform began, then, with the aim of enforcing academic standards. The large-scale curriculum projects of the 1950s and 1960s with a specialist academic orientation (as, for example, Biological Science Curriculum Study—BSCS, the Physical Science Curriculum Study Committee— PSSC, Science-A Process Approach) adhered to the "structure of discipline" principle. The projects were executed by groups of academics, some of them at institutes founded especially for the purpose of curriculum development. This academically orientated beginning exerted a substantial influence on the first phase of curriculum reform in the Federal Republic of Germany.

Curriculum reform in England and Wales, likewise, was set into motion by a concern for the training of specialized academic personnel. There was, however, neither the same massive criticism of schools and of the teaching profession as in the United States, nor the consistent claim from academics, that they alone could develop the new curricula. Therefore the academically oriented curriculum development in the early 1960s took place in a national context where the "autonomy of the teacher in matters of curriculum" was prominent. Thus, for example, the pioneering work of the Nuffield Foundation, in total contrast to the first projects in the United States, was guided principally by teachers' initiative. And in the charter of the Schools Council, set up in 1964 as the "major curriculum body in England and Wales", the general principle is explicitly stated, "that each school should have the greatest possible share of responsibility for its own work, with an individual curriculum and individual teaching methods, developed by its own teachers in accordance with the needs of its own pupils" (MacDonald and Walker 1978). In keeping with this, the training and further training of teachers, as a support measure to curriculum reform, should be undertaken by local teachers' centres. This teacher-centred contribution has had a substantial influence above all on the second phase of the curriculum reform movement in the Federal Republic of Germany, which took as its slogan the idea of "participation".

Curriculum reform in the Federal Republic of Germany arose in a strongly restorative school system, the educational substance of which was neither relevant to, nor commensurate with, social development. Schools administration, which embraces within the scope of its duties the planning and the control of syllabi, proved inadequate to the newly arisen needs for decision making, precisely because of the crumbling of the consensus on education. Curriculum reform in the Federal Republic of Germany thus began with the problem of evolving criteria and procedures suitable for providing schools administration with a rational basis for decision making. As Robinsohn (1967) stated: "In place of official ad hoc arrangements there is a need for academically founded and systematically constructed apparatuses. It is a matter of removing decisions on the content of curricula from sheer decisionism, and founding them on positive and acceptable criteria". This aspect of its activity demonstrates that curriculum reform in the Federal Republic of Germany begins not with the production of curricula, but with discussions about methods, and that the conception of curriculum development models continues to play a major role also in the later stages of development.

2. Models of Organizing the Processes of Curriculum Development

Contemporary curriculum reform strives to strengthen the links between education and society. This is realized not only through the analysis of the social conditions of curricular reform, but also by viewing society as the totality of standards for which schools must prepare young people. Curriculum reform, thus, has to deal not only with abstract questions related to the interface between culture and education, but it also has to carry out pragmatic tasks such as translating social standards into teaching and learning goals, into specific contents of instruction, and so on. The development process itself is very complex, because elements of various kinds must be moulded to one another. Decisions at various levels must be integrated, and cooperation between various bearers of the decision-making powers must be established. Consensus must be reached between academics, teachers, administrators, and so on.

In all curriculum projects, therefore, the organization of the work routine plays a central role. The success of the project largely depends on the organization of the production process. To a certain extent, of course, each project is unique: its course depends on the nature of the subjects and of schools, on the people responsible for decision making, and on national and regional conditions. Nevertheless, since the early 1950s, a limited number of clearly distinguishable basic models have emerged, which may be used as points of orientation in the planning and development of curriculum projects. Here, the term "model" is used not in the strictly experimental, mathematical sense, but rather in accordance with its commonly accepted usage in social sciences. It means that a model should be conceived as a simplifying and illustrative presentation of structures and connections, achieved through reduction and the accentuation of individual factors.

2.1 The Research–Development–Diffusion (R–D–D) Model as a Model of Phases

In the early stages of the modern curriculum reform movement, experts believed in the possibility of producing scientifically validated curricula which were considered to be readily implementable in school. To that end they proposed the so-called research–development–diffusion (R–D–D) model. Saylor and Alexander estimate that more than 100 projects were developed on the basis of this model in the United States (Saylor and Alexander 1974); and according to the judgment of a UNESCO study group in 1975, most innovative projects in the Federal Republic of Germany followed this pattern of development (Classen-Bauer et al. 1975).

The essential characteristics of this widely popularized model may be outlined in the following points: the existence of a rationally based and clearly divisible sequence of stages of work is assumed. Since in most American projects the evaluation activities were fully integrated with the development activities, a three-phase model seemed to be perfectly satisfactory. Where evaluation was brought in as an additional and independent factor, a four-phase model is obtained. This description contains details about the three-phase model only:

(a) *The research phase: establishment of goals.* In curriculum development of the 1960s in the United States, the formulation of goals was considered to be of great importance. Nevertheless, relatively little research was done in this phase. Research concerning programme objectives appeared less necessary, for it was assumed that they may be easily deduced from the readily available classification schemes of such objectives.

(b) *The development phase: the construction of instructional materials.* This phase constituted the central task in the development of American curriculum projects. This is demonstrated by the cases of the Physical Science Curriculum Study Committee (PSSC) and of the Biological Science Curriculum Study (BSCS), where packages of learning materials consisting of textbooks, laboratory equipment, films, teachers' handbooks, and so on, were produced (see *Curriculum Packages*).

(c) *The diffusion phase: utilizing the new programme.* The utilization of the new programme by the teacher and its successful implementation in the class constituted the third phase of the R–D–D model. Nevertheless, the question of how curricular reforms are successfully implemented, at least as a research problem, was not viewed as an important issue.

The second crucial characteristic of this model is the fact that responsibility for decision making in the various phases is shared between various authorities.

(a) The establishment of goals and the development of materials are performed principally by academics. The teachers who are occasionally drawn into the development phase, and who try out the com-ponents of the curricula, have significantly less responsibility for decision making.

(b) The teaching profession, as a whole, is first addressed in the implementation phase, when the curricula are ready to be used in school—by which time all essential decisions have already been made.

(c) The final dissemination of the new materials is carried out largely through publishing companies; in this phase, however, scarcely any contact remains between users and producers.

The validity of the curricula produced according to this model depends on the functionality of its rationale. This presupposes that all concerned, including the users, act on the basis of rational judgment and, so to speak, of curricular logic. What happens, though, when teachers and/or pupils refute this rationale?

In practice, a number of variants have been developed within the framework of this basic model, which are distinguished chiefly with regard to their points of departure. The projects which drew their point of departure from one or more scientific disciplines have been the most influential of these variants. They tried to focus on the structure of the discipline as the basic theme of teaching, assuming that the scientifically organized disciplines embrace all knowledge necessary for society. The advantage of this approach is the absence of ambiguity in the process of development, while the disadvantage is the impossibility of taking into account the needs of the learners.

A second variant is a model based on situation analysis, and was formulated in particular by the Berlin research group led by Robinsohn. In contrast to the structure-of-the-discipline curricula, Robinsohn takes as his thesis the argument that school should be a preparation to handle the tasks set by life (Robinsohn 1967). Thus the analysis of life situations in terms of capabilities needed to cope with them became the starting point of all curricular decisions.

In a differentiated working procedure, in which empirical, hermeneutic, and ideologically critical methods are to be combined, learning objectives and contents are coordinated. The crucial innovation of this variant depends on the fact that it conceives of curricula not as a reduced image of specialized disciplines of science, but rather as answers to problem areas in society. The organizational structure proposed by the Berlin group retains, however, the principal features of an engineering model, with its strict separation of the development done by academics and educational experts from the activity of teachers, who are expected to incorporate the results into their teaching. The problem of all the models constructed after the R–D–D Model is manifested in the implementation phase.

The models accept with great confidence the assumption that a well-developed curriculum which was scrutinized and approved by academic people will automatically work when put into practice. By accepting these assumptions uncritically, they overlook the conditions of practical teaching and disregard the sensitivity of those working in schools. Rational curriculum planning must take account of the realities of the classroom. It is not enough to be logical. Berman and McLaughlin (1978) in particular develop the mechanistic thought that underlies this model: "In a very real sense, school districts were thought of as 'black boxes'. Federal 'inputs' would be supplied to change and control district behaviour so that a desirable educational 'output' could be achieved." The inhabitants of the "black boxes" put up their own form of resistance: by ignoring them. Indeed many observers have pointed out that in some cases, expensively produced projects have had only relatively little influence on the practice of teaching.

Consequently, it was not long before attempts began to be made to improve on the R–D–D Model. The "linkage model" developed by Havelock provides for feedback between users and developers of curricula (Havelock 1970). Niederer (1971) advocates a "strategy of iterative process", which should make possible interaction between the project group and the teachers actively practising it. The branch of research known as "organization development" (which, indeed, arose not only in connection with curriculum reform), develops a strategy for innovation which allows innovative intentions to be allied to the requirements of schools and their teachers (Schmuck et al. 1977).

2.2 The Democratic Model as a Model of Interaction

All the variants of the democratic model (Rülcker 1982) are agreed on the fact that curricula should be formed by those who will work with them in teaching, in other words, by the teachers. Demands are also made for the participation of parents and pupils, but nowhere has much progress been made in this direction. The demand for the participation of teachers in curriculum development arises on various grounds. The argument of democratic theory operates on the political thesis "that the school in a democratic society is also, above all, the school of those involved, of the teachers, the pupils, and parents" (Gerbaulet et al. 1972). The notion of simply adopting prescribed curricula results in the loss of independence of this group of people. Conversely, the prominent participation of teachers in the process of curriculum development can contribute to their growing self-determination becoming an established constitutive part of the didactic process.

The argument of innovatory theory follows upon that of democratic theory. Curriculum development is only significant if it takes into account the social organization of schools and the way that those who uphold it view themselves. "Only if the most important representatives of the reform become the subject of their activity, if they are motivated and engaged as reformers in the everyday functioning of schools, is successful curriculum reform possible" (Gerbaulet et al. 1972).

In the final analysis, more strictly pedagogic considerations are entailed in both arguments. Thus it is established, for example, that only democratic models

can respond to the interests and requirements of those teaching and learning. It is, however, pedagogically necessary to increase the persuasiveness of the content of school work, without which instruction is reduced to something externally imposed.

It must, of course, also be pointed out and stressed that the simple fact of teachers' participation in the process of curriculum reform development does not alone guarantee that a democratic model will succeed. Specialist commissions composed of teacher specialists can stand out in just as sharp a contrast to the foundation as can groups of academics. Democratic models must, therefore, fulfil at least three conditions:

(a) The development of curricula should be effected in schools or in direct collaboration with them. Examples of this are, in the Federal Republic of Germany for example, the "teacher study groups in regional cooperation" which operate within the framework of the Hessian pilot scheme for "regional further training of teachers". In England and Wales, many teachers' centres are working along these lines.

(b) Curriculum reform should set out from the concrete problems of teaching and learning. The teaching process and the teacher's role in it are thus placed at the centre of the development work.

(c) Curriculum reform should take place in the form of the interaction of all parties concerned. "The course of innovations within a pragmatic strategy is conceived as the interaction of practice, academia, and policy" (Gerbaulet et al. 1972). Thus the crucial point in democratic models is not that there is no functional differentiation, but rather that those who fulfil various functions are not arranged hierarchically in separate phases, but cooperate with one another in each phase.

If these three conditions of the democratic model are fulfilled, then there is a tendency for the strict separation from one another of the phases of work to cease to exist. The discussion of goals and content as well as the evaluation of results assumes a status secondary to that of teaching; that is to say, the research and development phase glides smoothly into the implementation phase.

There has not been, to date, any comprehensive, systematic critique of the democratic model and its numerous variants. Therefore it is not possible to do more than specify a few points for discussion. One question with democratic projects concerns the contribution of academics. It is doubtful whether teachers' study groups alone are competent to analyse the relationship between society and the education system, and to draw conclusions for the development of curricula. Even when work on curricula is limited to adapting the structures of specialized academic disciplines for use in schools, local teachers' groups can hardly claim to be equipped to keep pace with the expansion of knowledge in the majority of the sciences. The problem to be solved is how to place academic skills at the disposal of local teachers' groups, without academics dominating the teachers.

A second difficulty of democratic models is created by the fact that they must operate against a backdrop of growing recognition of the economic significance of educational investments, and of a corresponding tendency towards the bureaucratization of the education system. On the one hand, large investments in the field of education are being made, whilst on the other hand, demands are also made for demonstrable results which may then be further employed as diversely as possible. Thus, for example, MacDonald and Walker (1978) point out that, since the 1970s, the concept of "accountability" has played a major role in discussions in England and Wales. Democratic projects are likely to run into embarrassment, however, when transferable results are demanded of them, for their work is too distinctly tailored to local and unique situations.

Inquiries carried out in the Federal Republic of Germany, complementary to the work of the teachers' groups, have drawn attention to a third difficulty. They show that teachers' motivation to carry out development work may not at all be taken for granted. In the regions studied, only 15–20 percent of the teaching profession took part in (voluntary) projects. A significant factor for the participation of teachers is the framework of conditions determined by educational policy. If greater participation is wanted from the teaching profession, then a "political culture that supports reform" is called for. If this is lacking, the majority of teachers will remain on the sidelines.

3. Making Reform Effective: Curricula and their Implementation

3.1 The Products of Curriculum Development

Curriculum research has, without doubt, a legitimate goal in the formulation of theory. Its central task, however, consists in real production, that is, in the preparation of innovative curricula which can be used in schools. Whether an innovation does succeed, depends certainly on the quality of the curricula.

Unfortunately, it is difficult to give an unambiguous answer to the question about the desired qualities of a curriculum innovation. Curriculum experts of the 1950s naively believed that the effectiveness of a curriculum is maximized when it is developed and organized as perfectly as possible. At the same time, the teacher appeared rather as a disruptive factor, which could distort the intentions of the curriculum if too influential a role were accorded to him or her. Therefore, efforts were made to produce "closed curriculum packages" which contained everything that was considered to be important, including the specification of the objectives and tests for monitoring their attainment. The essential characteristics of these packages can be summarized as follows:

(a) Objectives are stated in the form of precise behavioural descriptions.

(b) The objectives are related to one another in a hierarchical structure, so that general objectives may be realized by means of whole series of subsidiary objectives.

(c) Curriculum materials are produced through which these objectives ought to be obtained.

(d) Instructions are provided as to the organization of teaching, the sequence of learning activities, and the time devoted to each topic in order to facilitate the attainment of the objectives.

If one adds to this the fact that such packages usually contain all necessary instructional materials, then "closed" curricula emerge as a virtually perfect anticipation of instruction: everything is regulated in advance, nothing is left to chance; even the results are predicted.

Quite contrary to all expectations, these curricula have not only contributed little to innovation in teaching, but they are blamed by their critics for the failure of the reform. Severe criticism has been directed against the "behavioural objectives". The principal objections are as follows: they make teachers into the submissive agents of interested parties from outside the school, and bind pupils to results calculated in advance, thus rendering creativity and individual discernment impossible. Critics emphasize in particular the fact that closed curricula allow for no more detailed excursuses into the specific situations of the class or school, or into the interests of the teachers and pupils. Their polished perfection offers no such point of departure: users cannot, so to speak, take up any interaction with them which might allow them to introduce their points of view concerning problems, or their ideas. Closed curricula thus lead instead to anxieties and defence mechanisms.

It has, therefore, become more and more clearly recognized that the innovative quality of a curriculum depends partly on its openness. Curriculum theory was confronted with the question of how curricula can channel learning activities toward an expected direction, and at the same time challenge their users to introduce their own formulations of questions. Finally, Stenhouse (1975) conceives of a "process model" of the curriculum. It is characterized by its abandonment of the formulation of behavioural objectives, which stipulates the behaviour to be demonstrated by the pupil. In their place, according to Stenhouse, should be the specification of content, which is to be worked on, and the statement of procedural principles, which say what the teacher is to do. The result of the learning process thus remains open. It arises from the pupil's occupation with content, and is, in the last analysis, dependent upon personal conditions and those dictated by situations.

All these conceptions of products, however, work on the common assumption that the curriculum is, so to speak, developed outside the school and introduced from without. Only a radical suspension of this relationship produces the "research model" as presented by Stenhouse. This model views the curriculum developer as an investigator of problems which arise in schools in the pursuit of specific goals: Stenhouse cites as an example instruction on racial problems. In this, however, "teacher participation in research" is necessary, because the teacher alone can identify the problems arising in teaching. The result is not a specification of goals set from outside, but rather a listing of problems which arise from "inside", from instruction itself. "What is needed is a grasp of the range of problems and effects with enough contextual data to allow schools embarking on teaching about race relations to anticipate what sorts of things are likely to happen and to know how other teachers have handled the potential and problems of these situations. Accordingly, the research must aspire to situational verifiability. That is, the findings must be so presented that a teacher is invited not to accept them but to test them by mounting a verification procedure in his own situation."

3.2 Basic Models of Implementation

Curriculum reform is only effective if its products are really implemented in practice. Otherwise, the innovation remains lurking in libraries. In more recent discussions on innovation, a distinction is made between their simple adoption and their implementation. Adoption means the simple, formal taking over of an innovation; that is, in the case of curricula, the purchase of the packages of materials and their introduction onto the shelves of the school library. Their efficacy in practice is in such cases altogether uncertain and uncontrollable. Implementation, on the contrary, means the institutional adaptation of an innovative strategy, that is, the incorporation of an innovation into the institution, which must then change, in however slight a measure. Implementation is defined as the change process that occurs when an innovative project impinges upon an organization.

Taking this distinction as a basis, the inherent difficulties of the adoption perspectives prevalent in the R–D–D model may easily be comprehended. Preprepared curricula were offered for sale to schools or local educational authorities by commercial publishing houses or semicommercial agencies. This form of distribution, along with the polished perfection of the products themselves, has undoubtedly contributed more than a little to the fact that the reform has reached the schools to such a limited extent. As Silberman (1970) writes: "One need only sit in the classroom, in fact, and examine the texts and reading lists to know that, with the possible exception of mathematics, the curriculum reform movement has made a pitifully small impact on classroom practice."

Efforts to improve the implementation procedure are concentrated at first principally on the teachers. Thus various forms of further training for teachers are devel-

oped, in the interests of spreading the new curricula; proposals for the foundation of local or regional centres, where teachers may obtain advice and learn the techniques of new curricula, are formulated and, in part, effected in practice (United States: regional educational laboratories; England and Wales: teachers' centres; Federal Republic of Germany: regional pedagogic institutes; Sweden: pedagogic development blocks). Important though these efforts to win over teachers are, they lead, nevertheless, to a new problem: a one-sided orientation towards the teacher and his or her teaching, whilst variables in the school system are not adequately taken into consideration. The underlying assumption is that teachers are free agents, whose consent alone decides on the acceptance of a curriculum, whereas they are, in fact bound by an institution. Reports already point out the difficulties that arise in institutions, and show that individual teachers who had been won over by innovations encountered major opposition when they sought to introduce these into their own schools.

The curriculum reform movement has, therefore, found itself obliged recently to include in its considerations its relationship to the school as an institution.

The investigations make clear, above all, the fact that an innovation is not an additional process by means of which a portion is appended to an existing system, but rather that a modification is demanded of the system itself. From this recognition in principle, three important lessons may be learned, which can be presented here as conclusions:

(a) Curriculum reforms—however revolutionary they may appear to be—may be kept out of schools if the school, on whatever grounds and in whatever manner, is refused the necessary adjustments.

(b) Curriculum reforms cannot complacently limit themselves to the development of curricula, but must, rather, develop procedures for modifying the school system. Since quite specific skills are clearly required for this, a new group of change agents, curriculum advisers and moderators, and so on must be formed.

(c) The curriculum reform movement thereby acquires a further, and hitherto little heeded, political dimension: that of the confrontation with local, regional, and national school authorities.

Bibliography

Berman P, McLaughlin M W 1978 *Federal Programs Supporting Educational Change*, Vol. 8: *Implementing and Sustaining Innovations*. Rand, Santa Monica, California

Bruner J S 1960 *The Process of Education*. Harvard University Press, Cambridge, Massachusetts

Classen-Bauer I, Hausmann G, In K K 1975 *Curriculum-Entwicklung in der Bundesrepublik Deutschland: Studie einer Arbeitsgruppe beim UNESCO-Institut für Pädagogik in Hamburg*. Bundesministerium für Bildung und Wissenschaft, Bonn

Dolch J 1965 *Lehrplan des Abendlandes Zweieinhalb Jahrtausende seiner Geschichte*, 2nd edn. Henn, Ratingen

Gerbaulet S et al. 1972 *Schulnahe Curriculumentwicklung: Ein Vorschlag zur Errichtung Regionaler Pädagogischer Zentren mit Analysen über Innovationsprobleme in den USA, England und Schweden: Eine Denkschrift*. Klett, Stuttgart

Goodlad J I, von Stoephasios R, Klein M F 1966 *The Changing School Curriculum*. Fund for the Advancement of Education, New York

Havelock R G 1970 *A Guide to Innovation in Education*. Institute for Social Research, Ann Arbor, Michigan

Huhse K 1968 *Theorie und Praxis der Curriculum-Entwicklung: Ein Bericht über Wege der Curriculum Reform in den USA mit Ausblicken auf Schweden und England*. Max-Planck-Gesellschaft, Berlin

Lawton D 1978 *Theory and Practice of Curriculum Studies*. Routledge and Kegan Paul, London

MacDonald B, Walker R 1978 Die Curriculumreform-Bewegung in England: Eine kritische Bilanz. *Zs. f. Päd*. 24: 581–600

Niederer H J 1971 Die erprobungsorientierte Strategie bei der Entwicklung des IPN Curriculum Physik. *Bild. Erz*. 24: 424–31

Robinsohn S B 1967 *Bildungsreform als Revision des Curriculum und Ein Strukturkonzept für Curriculumentwicklung*. Luchterhand, Neuwied

Rülcker T 1982 Modelle zur Planung und Organisation von Curriculumprozessen. In: Hameyer U, Frey K, Haft H (eds.) 1982 *Handbuch der Curriculumforschung*. Beltz, Weinheim

Saylor J G, Alexander W M 1974 *Planning Curriculum for Schools*. Holt, Rinehart and Winston, New York

Schmuck R A, Runkel P, Arends J, Arends R J 1977 *The Second Handbook of Organization Development in Schools*. Mayfield, Palo Alto, California

Silberman C E 1970 *Crisis in the Classroom: The Remaking of American Education*. Random House, New York

Stenhouse L 1975 *An Introduction to Curriculum Research and Development*. Heinemann, London

Taba H 1962 *Curriculum Development: Theory and Practice*. Harcourt Brace and Ward, New York

The Process of Curriculum Development

Curriculum Resources

R. W. Tyler

Those who develop a curriculum and a plan of instruction must find suitable answers to three questions. What should the students be helped to learn? What learning experiences can be provided to enable the students to learn? How can these learning experiences be organized to maximize their cumulative effects? Furthermore, if the curriculum is to be continuously monitored and, where necessary, improved, a plan for continuing evaluation must be developed. In seeking answers to these questions and in devising a plan for evaluation, a variety of resources are helpful.

1. Resources for Objectives

Selecting educational objectives for the curriculum (that is, identifying what students should be helped to learn) requires thoughtful judgment informed by several kinds of information. The reasons for the complexity of this task include the fact that there are many desirable things that students could learn, far more than the time available in the school permits. Hence, selecting objectives involves assigning priorities among possible ones. Another consideration derives from the responsibility of the school to serve in the socialization of young people, that is, in helping them to learn those things that will enable them to participate constructively in their society. This requires information about the knowledge, skills, and dispositions required for effective participation in that society, and those opportunities the society offers for the employment of individual talents (Husén and Dahllöf 1965).

Since schools are particularly responsible for helping students gain access to the heritage represented by the work of scholars, scientists, and artists, a careful examination of these subject matters is necessary. This review should be in terms of their values as resources on which students can draw throughout life.

The curriculum must be planned for particular students and not for the "typical" or "average" student. Hence, the objectives appropriate for particular students or groups of students should avoid focusing on what these students have already learned but should build on the backgrounds of knowledge, skills, and dispositions they have already developed.

With these considerations in mind, the resources for educational objectives are: (a) investigations of the contemporary society that identify or suggest the knowledge, skills, and dispositions required to participate effectively in that society, and to take advantage of the opportunities it offers; (b) reviews and examinations of the various subject matters that suggest resources on which students can helpfully draw in carrying on their daily activities and in achieving their own goals; (c) studies of children and youth in general, and of the particular students for which the curriculum is being developed to identify relevant knowledge, skills, and dispositions already possessed and those lacking that these students need to learn, and to suggest the supporting background on which their educational program can be built (Warren 1978, Torney et al. 1975).

2. Resources for Learning Experiences

Conscious, complex, human learning, the kind of learning for which schools are responsible, involves more than the learner merely responding to the presentation of information. Although there are variations in the terms used by different psychologists, a fairly common description of this kind of learning is as follows: The student makes an effort to learn (motivation). He or she gains a notion of what is to be learned (perceives objective). The learning task requires the student to carry on the behavior to be learned and also requires real exertion to go beyond present knowledge, skill, or disposition, but the task is not impossible (suitable learning task). The student has enough confidence in his or her ability that he or she seriously tries to perform the learning activity (attempts learning task). If successful in performing the task, the student obtains satisfaction (reward). If unsuccessful, he or she is informed about what went wrong and is encouraged to try again, either the same task or one that appears to be more suitable (feedback and encouragement). The student practices what is being learned on tasks in which each subsequent practice goes beyond the previous one, thus requiring continuing attention and improved performance (sequential practice). The learner finds opportunities to apply what is being learned in school and to those situations outside the classroom where the knowledge, skill, or disposition is appropriate (transfer) (Tyler 1977).

Resources which can be drawn upon when planning learning experiences are those that can help in establishing the conditions for learning outlined above. With regard to motivation, studies of the activities and interests of children and youth in general, and investigations of the interests and activities of the particular learners for which the curriculum is being planned are useful. These sources furnish suggestions about the activities, projects, problems, assignments, seat work, and other possible learning tasks that are likely to arouse in the students strong motives for learning what the curriculum emphasizes.

In clarifying objectives, the teacher can often serve as an excellent example for the students by demonstrating the knowledge and its use, the skill and its use, and the disposition and its value. There are other resources which can help the students to perceive the objectives clearly—field trips in which students observe the objectives in the context of their significant employment, and television programs, video tapes, movies, and audio tapes in which skills of performance and of speech, acts of unselfishness, and other observable learning outcomes are shown. Guests who are proficient with reference to the objective can be invited to the classroom to show and discuss the desired objectives in terms of their own experience.

The selection of appropriate learning tasks requires not only information about the present knowledge, skills, and dispositions of the particular students for whom the selections are being made, but also the development of a reservoir of projects, activities, and materials that are suitable for the range of individual differences among these students. Hence, the resources helpful in selecting appropriate learning tasks are: information about the present knowledge, skills, and dispositions of these students that are necessary to carry out different learning tasks, and a collection of possible activities and materials that require a range of skill and knowledge levels for their use. Thus, for example, reading laboratories, or other collections of multilevel reading materials dealing with the same subjects can provide suitable reading tasks for students whose present levels of reading skills are varied. Similar collections of projects and other activities demanding different levels of knowledge and skill are helpful resources on which to draw when developing suitable assignments for groups of students (Williams 1975).

The primary resource for helping students gain the confidence to attempt a learning task seriously is the encouragement of persons who are viewed by the student as wanting him or her to be successful, persons who really care. The teacher should be able to instill this confidence, but when this is not possible, a parent, an aide, or a friend can do so. Another source is the successful performance of the task by someone the student views as a peer. A student in the class may demonstrate successful performance, or descriptions of the success of other peers may be useful.

Insofar as is possible, the reward the student obtains from successful performance of the learning task should be intrinsic, that is, the student should discover the satisfaction that comes from learning what one sets out to learn. In addition, the learner can be rewarded by being able to use what has been learned in situations he or she considers significant, such as: reading a story to the class, working out the daily food expenditures for the family, writing a letter to the airport official to obtain permission for a class visit. Furthermore, the approval of other students is satisfying to many learners, often more so than commendations by the teacher, but both are helpful. Studies of the interests and satisfying activities of children and youth can furnish a reservoir of suggestions for rewards and to them can be added the suggestions that arise from experience with particular students that are recorded by the teachers (Tyler 1973).

Feedback, identifying unsuccessful performance of learning tasks, and explaining what went wrong, is a common teaching practice. The identification can be aided by diagnostic tests that are designed to discover the particular errors in the performance of students. Computer programs are now available for the administration and recording of such tests, thus furnishing a convenient source of feedback information for both students and teachers. Check lists of common errors have been published for various skills and areas of knowledge. These lists provide a helpful guide for the observation and evaluation of student work in order to identify the learner's difficulties. As another resource, teachers can build up lists of errors and develop their own check lists. The identification of the errors made by a particular student may suggest a more suitable learning task or indicate how the student should proceed in trying the previous learning task again. Feedback of this sort should be accompanied by words of encouragement to help the student gain confidence in trying again.

Instructional materials in elementary-school reading and mathematics (textbooks, workbooks, and the like), are usually designed to provide sequential practice of skills but there are few such resources readily obtainable in other subjects, and for other objectives. Sources mentioned earlier for learning tasks are helpful in furnishing suggestions for practice activities of many sorts but generally those developing the curriculum will need to select and arrange the learning tasks in appropriate sequences. Sequence is important. Repetitive practice quickly becomes boring to the learner and he or she ceases to give attention to it. This often results in a lowered performance. Each new task should require something more of the learner so that attention is required and greater understanding, greater skills, and more appropriate dispositions are developed (Tyler 1960).

Opportunities for the learner to apply what he or she has learned in those situations outside the classroom where the knowledge, skill, or disposition is relevant are largely determined by the environment in which the student lives. Teachers will generally know the environment of the school and something of the neighborhood, and the students themselves act as an important resource when they tell their teachers about their normal extracurricular activities and other opportunities that they have to use what they are learning. When little attention is given to transfer, some students forget what they have learned because they do not use it outside the classroom. That transfer is a serious problem is shown by the results of the United States National Assessment of Educational Progress. In 1977–78, for example, more than 90 percent of 13-year-old students could add, subtract, multiply, and divide with whole numbers but less than 45 percent could apply their computational skills to common quantitative problems such as computing the per unit cost of articles displayed in food markets (National Assessment of Educational Progress 1979). For this reason, providing for practice outside the classroom is an essential part of the curriculum (see *Curriculum Components*).

3. Resources for Organizing Learning Experiences

The purpose of organizing learning experiences is to maximize their cumulative effect in helping the student attain the curriculum objectives. If each lesson or each unit of instruction has little relation to those that went before or those that follow, what is learned is relatively superficial. Furthermore, the student needs to perceive the relation of what he or she is learning in one subject to his or her learning in other subjects and to the situations outside the classroom, so that he or she can draw upon learning in the various subjects wherever they are appropriate rather than being restricted to narrow compartmentalization of his or her knowledge, skills, and dispositions.

Organization involves identifying the basic concepts, skills, and values that can be arranged like threads throughout the fabric of the learning activities. These are called the organizing elements of the curriculum. Studies of the structure of subjects furnish resources for concepts. For example, the Physical Science Study Committee of the United States developed a high-school physics course organized around 34 concepts that furnish the basis for explaining many of the natural phenomena encountered in the environment.

Investigations of generalizable skills like those in mathematics and in reading, provide lists of skills that are useful in many subjects and many situations outside the classroom. There are, however, very few studies of generalizable attitudes, interests, and appreciations that could furnish helpful lists of generalizable dispositions. The lack of these lists places upon those developing the curriculum the task of identifying and selecting the dispositions to serve as organizing elements for the curriculum.

4. Resources for Developing a Plan for Evaluation

Curriculum evaluation, commonly called program evaluation, has become a major field of study and is treated elsewhere in this Encyclopedia.

Bibliography

Torney J V, Oppenheim A N, Farnen R F 1975 *Civic Education in Ten Countries: An Empirical Study*. Almqvist and Wiksell, Stockholm

Husén T, Dahllöf U 1965 An empirical approach to the problem of curriculum content. *Int. Rev. Educ.* 11: 51–76

National Assessment of Educational Progress 1979 *Mathematical Applications: Selected Results from the Second Assessment of Mathematics*. National Assessment of Educational Progress, Denver, Colorado

Tyler R W 1960 The importance of sequence in teaching reading. In: Robinson H M (ed.) 1960 *Sequential Development of Reading Abilities*. Proceedings of the Annual Conference on Reading held at the University of Chicago, Vol. 22. University of Chicago Press, Chicago, Illinois, pp. 3–8

Tyler R W 1973 Assessing educational achievement in the affective domain. Special Report of the National Council. *Meas. Educ.* 4(3): 4–5

Tyler R W 1977 What have we learned about learning? Overview and update. In: Hansen K H (ed.) 1977. *Learning: An Overview and Update*. Report of the Chief State School Officers 1976 Summer Institute. United States Office of Education, Washington, DC, pp. 1–6

Warren D R et al. 1978 Part one: From youth to adulthood: Problems in socialization. In: Tyler R W (ed.) 1978 *From Youth to Constructive Adult Life: The Role of the Public School*. McCutchan, Berkeley, California, pp. 1–89

Williams C M 1975 *The Community as Textbook*. Phi Delta Kappa Educational Foundation, Bloomington, India

Curriculum Development

G. Gay

Professional literature and discourse are filled with examples of curriculum development being equated only with the technology of writing instructional objectives, content, activities, and evaluation procedures. Little or no systematic attention is given to the processes or dynamics which undergird this technology. This mistaken conception or oversight should be corrected. More attention needs to be given to the complex inter-actions, negotiations, and compromises surrounding questions of who makes curriculum decisions and how these decisions are made, in order to better understand the organization and emphases of given curriculum designs or plans.

Zais (1976) attempts to provide some clarity and precision in the various dimensions of the curriculum enterprise by distinguishing curriculum design or con-struction from curriculum development. According to him, "curriculum" is used typically by specialists to refer either to a plan for educating youth or as a field of study. When the intent is to identify the collective components of the substantive entity, that is, a plan for instruction, curriculum is being considered as "design." When the focus of attention is the people and operative procedures out of which the design or plan for instruc-tion emerges, the reference ordinarily is to "curriculum development." Lawton (1975) makes a similar dis-tinction between "the curriculum" and "curriculum planning." According to him, curricula are made up of those particular aspects of life, knowledge, attitudes, and values selected from the total culture of a society for transmission to future generations within the struc-ture of educational systems. The ways in which edu-cators make these selections and put them into practice is curriculum planning. Thus, curriculum development is the process, the syntactical structure, the inter-personal dynamics of decision making about instruc-tional planning. By comparison, curriculum design is the product, the substantive entity, the end result of the decision-making processes. Curriculum development does not necessarily precede curriculum design or con-struction in a linear fashion. Instead, the two enterprises overlap and occur conjunctively.

Although helpful as a point of departure, a mere definitional distinction between curriculum develop-ment and curriculum design is not sufficient to capture the essence of the two dynamic enterprises. Rather, a detailed descriptive analysis of the two is required. The focus of attention in this discussion is curriculum development.

The purpose of this discussion is to explore some of the major dimensions of the interactive dynamics of the processes which produce curriculum plans. The issues discussed include: (a) the distinguishing characteristics of the curriculum development process; (b) who par-ticipates in curriculum decision making; and (c) the forces and factors that influence curriculum dev-elopment and how. General principles related to each of these are discussed, as well as some specific examples of curriculum development dynamics in different coun-tries. The purpose of these examples is twofold—to illustrate that some elements of the process of cur-riculum development are universal, and to demonstrate how the dynamics of the process are configured dif-ferently as a result of the particular cultural and political contexts in which they occur.

1. Nature of Curriculum Development

The essential elements of the curriculum development process involve issues of power, people, procedures, and participation. The critical questions are: Who makes decisions about curricular issues? What choices or decisions are to be made? and How are these decisions made and implemented? Invariably, these concerns lead to curriculum development being charac-terized as an interactional process that is political, social, collaborative, and incremental in nature.

First, curriculum development is an interpersonal process or system of operations for making decisions about where curriculum planning will take place (e.g. the political zone of influence according to legal stature), who will be involved in the planning, the selection and execution of working procedures, and how curriculum documents will be implemented, appraised, and revised (Beauchamp and Beauchamp 1972). It is a dynamic, vital complex network of interactions among people and forces, all of which occur in fluid settings or contexts that are in perpetual states of emergence. The particular contours of the process are shaped as much by the legal arenas in which curriculum decision making takes place as by the particular compilation of actors included, and by the substantive demands of the instructional issues under consideration. For example, while curriculum development at local and central governmental levels will encompass some of the same procedural dynamics, the people involved and the decisions to be made vary according to the societal and cultural contexts. Whereas in France education is a national function mandated by constitutional provisions, in the United States and Can-ada legal responsibility for curriculum belongs to regional governments (states and provinces respect-ively). Though England and Wales now have a national curriculum framework, considerable responsibility still remains with individual schools.

Second, curriculum development is a political process. Local, regional, and national governmental agencies regularly engage in policy making about instructional programming. In the United States, edu-cation is the province of state governments since it was not specifically delegated to the national government by the Constitution. Typically, states exert control over what schools teach by outlining general requirements of the curriculum. Illustrative of these are specifications about time allocations for the daily instruction of read-ing in the elementary grades, the number of credits required in particular subjects for students to graduate from high school, and the grade level intervals when minimum competency tests will be administered. Other mechanisms through which national governments become involved in curriculum decision making include: inspectors' reports in England and Wales, curriculum commissions appointed by the state Ministries of Edu-cation in the Federal Republic of Germany, policy regulations of the National Ministry of Education in Sweden, and the examination systems in Japan.

In Sweden, for instance, any one of three different national agencies—the Ministry of Education and Cultural Affairs, Parliament, and the National Board of Education—can initiate curriculum development. Generally, though,

> the Minister of Education and Parliament act in concert, i.e., Parliament may ask the Minister of Education and Cultural Affairs to come up with a needed curriculum proposal, or the minister may initiate a proposal for consideration by Parliament . . . most of the detail of curriculum planning work is done under the authority and direction of the National Board of Education. . . . In many cases curriculum decisions made at very high levels . . . include only decisions about overall objectives, range of subjects, and weekly time schedules for the subjects. The development of content into sequential organization in harmony with the objectives and the organizational plan of the school in question . . . is done under the direct supervision of the National Board of Education. (Beauchamp and Beauchamp 1972 pp. 99–100)

As is true with other political processes, curriculum development also involves various constituent groups in power negotiations. These negotiations concern "a series of choices, often based upon values" (Saylor et al. 1981 p. 27), the "allocation of resources towards certain ends" (Pratt 1980 p. 111), and "the creation and distribution of benefits" (Hunkins 1980 p. 140). Moreover, "pressure groups of all kinds are always proposing competing values about what to teach" (McNeil 1977 p. 260). Simon (1980) contends that the political character of curriculum decisions becomes most apparent when the focus of attention is content about school customs and values, and when one interest group attempts to define the social character of society for others.

Obviously, then, the selection of curriculum objectives, content, activities, and evaluation are influenced as much by values and politics as by pedagogy. As Eggleston (1977 p. 23) suggests, these selections are essentially

> processes of conflict that give rise to a range of compromises, adjustments, and points of equilibrium of varying degrees of stability. In all of these negotiations an underlying concept is that of power . . . the power to make decisions that influence the work of students and teachers and . . . the control over the power that can be achieved by students or withheld from them by determining access to high or low status curriculum components and the evaluation and opportunities associated with them. Unquestionably curriculum determination is centrally concerned with both the use and the allocation of power.

Third, curriculum development is a social enterprise. It is a "people process" with all the attending potentialities and obstacles associated with humans engaged in social interactions. The interests, values, ideologies, priorities, role functions, and differentiated responsibilities form the contours of the interactional and dynamic contexts in which curriculum decisions are made. The personalities of curriculum developers, the structures of school systems, and the different patterns of group relations among members of school communities are significant determinants of power negotiations, resource allocations, and valuative conflict resolutions, which permeate curriculum determination.

Curriculum development implies the need for some kind of modifications in existing instructional systems. These modifications result from the interactional processes which occur among the people who have the power and authority to make these decisions. As Miel (1946 p. 10) suggests, curriculum development is

> something much more subtle than revising statements written down on paper. To change the curriculum of the school is to change the factors interacting to shape that curriculum. In each instance this means bringing about changes in people—in their desires, beliefs, and attitudes, in their knowledge and skill. . . . In short, the nature of curriculum change should be seen for what it really is—a type of social change in people. . . .

Zais (1976 p. 448) endorses Miel's analysis of the social character of curriculum development in his observation that "curriculum change is people change and cannot be brought about merely by fate or by organizational manipulation."

Furthermore, any kind of educational change always involves human, emotional, and valuative factors (Taba 1962). For this reason, Smith et al. (1957) equate changing the curriculum with social engineering. The school curriculum is inextricably interwoven into the patterns of relationships, social positions, expectations, and values of the different individuals, groups, and cultural ecologies that make up school communities. It cannot be separated from its social contexts and treated as if it were a totally independent entity existing in a vacuum. Rather, effective curriculum development requires concomitant change in the established normative structures of school communities, in existing patterns of interpersonal relationships, in people's attitudes towards what is most worthy of knowing, and in the perceptions of individuals and groups about educational roles, purposes, power, and procedures. In other words, "in order to change the curriculum, the social fabric must be changed. . . . Broadly conceived, then, the problem of curriculum change is a problem in social engineering" (Smith et al. 1957 p. 440).

Fourth, curriculum development, at any level, is a collaborative and cooperative enterprise. The fact that instructional planning involves a variety of technical and human relations skills, and must attend to many different priorities, perceptions, vested interests, and value commitments makes it virtually impossible for individuals, operating alone, to complete the task efficiently and effectively. Cooperation is essential in curriculum development. This does not mean that everyone involved in the process should participate indiscriminately in all aspects of curriculum determination. The technical complexities of curriculum construction, as well as its social and political character, require many kinds of competencies in different combinations at different points in the developmental process. Decisions about who participates when and how must be based upon the distinct function to be served, and the competencies of the participants. Thus, effective curriculum development must operate on the principles of cooperation, collaboration, and shared responsibility within the contextual framework of complementary and differentiated levels of involvement (Taba 1962).

Usually, curriculum decisions are made at three different levels of influence simultaneously. These are (a) the instructional level, or by classroom teachers; (b) the institutional level, or by school building and/or system personnel; and (c) the societal level, or by boards of education, governmental officials, and a plethora of interest groups (Kirst and Walker 1971). These decisions vary somewhat by zone or level of influence and according to the position, power, and expectations of the participants, but all of them contribute significantly to shaping the overall character of the curriculum development process. Therefore, collaboration and cooperation are essential to ensure that all vested interests are sufficiently represented, that the various technical skills needed for qualitative curriculum planning are included, and that coherency and cohesion exist throughout the entire development process, from conception to completion.

Fifth, curriculum development is, according to Kirst and Walker (1971) a "disjointed incremental" system of decision making. It is neither a purely rational and scientifically objective, nor a neatly sequentialized and systematic process. Rarely are the various sets of decisions necessary in curriculum planning systematically coordinated throughout the entire cycle. Instead, "multiple starts are made and these efforts are scattered in several directions. A rule-of-thumb method still dominates, and often the persons involved do not know why they succeeded or why they failed" (Taba 1962 p. 454). Curriculum decisions are frequently made "through small or incremental moves on particular problems rather than through a comprehensive reform program" (Braybrooke and Lindblom 1963 p. 71). Macdonald (1971) describes curriculum development as an "historical accident" instead of a completely rational–technical process. By this he means that historically, curriculum planning has been "the outcome of a very long and dynamically complex process of social involvement and interaction. It is not something that has been deliberately chosen and rationally developed for a specific purpose it is intended to serve" (Macdonald 1971 p. 95).

These descriptions of curriculum development led Walker (1976 p. 299) to recommend a change in the image and ideal of the process. Rather than viewing it as a carefully planned and rational system of operations, he advises

> we recognize that curriculum changes are necessarily subject to the operation of enormously powerful social forces that cannot possibly be brought under the control of any technical procedures or systematically designed process. The action of these powerful forces is influenceable at times and in some

ways, and professional educators charged with responsibility for curricular maintenance and change need to learn how to cope with those forces as well as they can. The image of the technician at the control panel directing the entire operation needs to be replaced by a more realizable one, perhaps that of the mountaineer using all the tricks of modern science, together with personal skill and courage and an intimate study of the particular terrain, to scale a peak.

2. Participants in the Process

A key question to understanding the dynamics of curriculum development is, Who controls the decision making process, and how is this control exerted? Phillips and Hawthorne (1978 p. 365) answer these questions by saying "nearly any organization, at any level, that has a concern" determines school curriculum. According to Saylor et al. (1981 p. 47), curriculum development involves "a cast of thousands." This cast of thousands can be grouped into two major categories—participants in the planning process (e.g. clients, critics, professionals, legislative groups, courts) and resources for the planners (e.g. authors, publishers, testers, accreditors, pollsters, lobbyists, media). Typically, "planners" make policy and determine the substantive details of curriculum designs while "resources" monitor the processes of planners, serve as quality controllers, and suggest alternative realities for consideration in curriculum planning.

From these observations and the preceding discussions it can be deduced that those who participate in curriculum development comprise a diversified and numerous lot. This is true irrespective of whether the societal context is the United Kingdom, the Soviet Union, United States, Israel, Japan, or Nigeria. However, the degree and kind of involvement vary according to the role functions and relationships of the actors and influences to the official structure of the school system, and the intensity of commitment and regularity of participation. For example, while some kind of specifically designated governmental agencies are involved directly and regularly in curriculum decision making in all countries, the authority for and extent of their involvement vary by the legal regulations governing control of education, and the political zone of influence in which curriculum development occurs. Conversely, the involvement of community-based pressure groups is indirect and sporadic. The extent and nature of their involvement is determined by the level of interest in particular issues and power of persuasion.

For purposes of analysis in this discussion the major actors and influences shaping curriculum decisions are classified as internal and external forces. The internal and formal determinants of curricula are those forces that are legally responsible for curriculum policy making and planning, and whose involvement is channeled through some regularized, structured arrangements. The external and informal forces exist outside governmental structures and the administrative bureaucracy of school systems. They influence curriculum planning

Table 1
The web of forces influencing the curriculum development process[a]

	External		Internal	
	Formal	Informal	Formal	Informal
Forces influencing the process	(a) Testing bureaus and boards (b) Professional associations (c) Accrediting associations (d) Public opinion polls (e) Lobbyists (f) Student/parent/business (g) Labor organizations (h) Regulatory agencies of governments	(a) Special interest groups (b) Publishers of instructional materials (c) Mass media (d) Individual critics (e) Sociocivic crises (f) Customs and traditions (g) Philanthropic foundations (h) Pressure politics	(a) Governmental authorities (b) Advisory and administrative agencies (c) The law (legislative acts, court decisions, funding patterns) (d) School governance structures (e) District and building administrators and teachers (f) Bureaucratic style of school system (g) Resources and facilities (h) Decision-making system (i) Subjects taught	(a) Staff views of curriculum and instruction (b) Politics of the working of the formal structure (c) Customs and traditions (d) Sociology of group dynamics (e) Personalities and competencies of participants (f) Human relations skills (g) Arena of curriculum planning

Curriculum decision

Clients		
Society Parents Employers Institutions of higher learning		The curriculum plan Teachers Students School systems

a Adapted from Nicholas E J 1980 A comparative view of curriculum development. In: Kelly A V (ed.) 1980 *Curriculum Context*. Harper and Row, London, pp. 150–72 through irregular patterns of pressure politics and powers of persuasion. These categories and relationships are summarized in Table 1. They prevail internationally; however, specific individuals and groups, as well as the particulars of their influence vary by country and culture. Invariably, though, in the actual operations of curriculum planning the two categories of participants and influences overlap significantly.

In acknowledging the diversity of internal and external, formal and informal, legal and extralegal forces involved in curriculum decision making, Kirst and Walker (1971 p. 488) assert that

> a mapping of the leverage points for curriculum policy making . . . would involve three levels of government, and numerous private organization foundations, accrediting associations, national testing agencies, textbook–software companies, and interest groups. . . . Moreover, there would be a configuration of leverage points within a particular local school system including teachers, department heads, the assistant superintendent for instruction, the superintendent and the school board. Cutting across all levels of government would be the pervasive influence of various celebrities, commentators, interest groups, and the journalists who use the mass media to disseminate their views on curriculum.

Nicholas (1980) attributes this plethora of participants involved in curriculum development to the normative features of the process. By nature of its existence and functions curriculum development invariably concerns questions of values, politics, control, and power. Even what appear to be consensus issues (such as teaching basic literacy skills)

> raise several possible answers which are in turn contradictory or irreconcilable . . . some preferred answers are offered and canvassed by a variety of groups or individuals for a variety of motives from the ulterior to the altruistic. Examples of such groups abound, i.e., elected representatives of the central, regional, or local political structure, all perhaps in disagreement; employers' associations; trade unions; university authorities; groups of teachers and their associations; professional bodies; parent or community groups—and this list is by no means exhaustive. (Nicholas 1980 p. 153)

3. Perspectives on the Operations of the Process

Various levels of civic government, along with the governance structures of school systems, are the major determinants of formal curriculum policy and planning processes. Generally, governmental agencies establish general educational policies and curriculum guidelines. Specification of operational details is the responsibility of school system bureaucracies. The relative distribution of authority among governmental agencies and school system officials varies from nation to nation, as do the nature and extent of the external pressures which impinge upon the internal system of curriculum decision making. This is expected, given that schools and their programs are designed to perpetuate the cultures of which they are a part. They are, therefore, unavoidably culturally relativistic. Several examples of curriculum development in different countries are provided to illus-

trate how the dynamics of the process operate on different legal levels of decision making, and to demonstrate their similarities across nations irrespective of the official arenas of decision making.

3.1 Canada

In Canada the legal arena of curriculum decision making is regional. All official curriculum planning, as well as other education decisions, are the domain of provincial legislatures. In fact, "Canada has the distinction of being the only advanced nation in the world without a federal office of education" (Katz 1974 p. 7). This does not mean, however, that there are no national or local factors and forces operating which exert significant power and influence over educational matters. Other provincial departments of state often sponsor certain education programs. For example, the Department of Health and Welfare frequently initiates and sponsors athletic and physical activities; the Canadian Broadcasting Corporation helps prepare educational radio and television programs; and the Departments of Mining and Natural Resources, Trade and Commerce prepare information brochures on the Canadian economy for use in schools. In 1969 the central government announced plans to make funds available to those provinces willing to plan and implement bilingual education programs (Katz 1974).

The provincial ministries of education, official directors of Canadian education, are also susceptible to other internal and external, formal and informal forces which influence curriculum decisions. Typically, curriculum committees that are created to develop guidelines for curriculum planning are made up of representatives from schools, universities, business, industry, labor, and the community at large. Professional organizations, such as the Canadian Teachers' Federation and the Canadian Education Association, may create their own commissions to study different educational concerns and make recommendations pertinent to curriculum. Ethnic groups lobby for inclusion of their cultures and language in curricula and/or for the right to operate their own cultural studies schools. Mass media serves as a public forum for the debate of educational issues. Therefore, while the Canadian legal mechanisms of curriculum development may differ somewhat from those of other advanced nations, the pragmatic and operative dimensions of the process, in terms of individuals, groups, and circumstances that exert directional pressures upon it, are quite similar.

3.2 United States

The legal arena of curriculum decision making in the United States is similar to that of Canada. State governments are constitutionally responsible for education. They establish minimum requirements and general guidelines, but boards of education within local school districts make "the ultimate legal decisions about what shall be taught in the schools of that district" (Beauchamp and Beauchamp 1972 p. 137). The administrative personnel of the local school systems are responsible for executing board policy.

More often than not, a system of development committees and advisory councils is used to translate school board policies and state government guidelines into operational plans for instruction. A combination of political realities, educational practices, economic exigencies, legal mandates, and pressure politics determine the dynamics of how these committees address the task of curriculum planning. For instance, if a curriculum committee is operating in a local school system within a region which uses state-adopted textbooks, its functions may be restricted to selecting a textbook for use in the community schools. Frequently, this selection is made from a list that has already gone through preliminary screening at the state level. The textbook adoption process is highly susceptible to the influence of publishers' advertising campaigns, mass media, and other various special interest pressure groups (e.g. parental, religious, ethnic, feminist, etc.). Public hearings on the books being considered for adoption are held at both the state and local level. These hearings provide opportunity for any interested person or group to publicly state its opinions on the suggested books. Also, all textbooks are examined by various sets of sociopolitical criteria (such as sexism, racism, classism, ageism, handicapism, and regionalism) to determine their levels of acceptability.

The task of local curriculum committees might be to write lists of minimum competencies, or performance criteria objectives, for a given grade level or subject area to bring the local school system in line with state mandates on minimum competency testing. Or, the composition and functions of local curriculum committees may be dictated by a school board's decision to solicit national government funds earmarked for specifically designated programs and populations, such as sex equality, desegregation, educating the handicapped, vocational education, bilingualism, and the gifted. Often, for these specially targeted programs, the national government stipulates, in the regulations governing the distribution of monies, who should participate in curriculum planning, and how these plans are to be structured. A case in point is the Education of the Handicapped Act of 1974. Commonly known as Public Law 94–142, this legislative act specifies that any school system, state or local, receiving national funds for educating handicapped youth must develop Individual Education Programs (IEP) for each student being served by the program. The IEP must use a minimum competency or performance criteria format in writing objectives, and must be developed collaboratively with different experts within the school who are familiar with the child's needs, and in consultation with the parents.

Periodically, the national government creates commissions to study specific education problems, and funds national curriculum development projects. Examples of the former are presidential commissions appointed to study functional literacy, drug abuse, employment trends, and violence and vandalism among high-school-age youth. The members of these commissions are reputable experts in different political, social, economic, and educational fields. Invariably, their official reports include recommendations of how school programs should be modified to help alleviate these social ills. The current emphasis on vocational education in the United States is a direct outgrowth of prestigious commission reports. The national government also, on occasion, gives financial support to national curriculum projects. The decade of the 1960s witnessed an unprecedented level of central government involvement in curriculum development through this mechanism. What began initially as governmental support of curriculum development efforts, directed by scholars, to improve the quality of mathematics, science, and foreign language instruction spread to the entirety of the high-school curricula before the trend ebbed. A plethora of inquiry science curriculum projects, conceptual-based mathematics, and new social studies curriculum projects emerged. Who directed these projects is another major force to be reckoned with in the process of curriculum development. In almost every instance, the project directors were scholars and academicians, not professional educators. United States schools, especially at the secondary level, have a long history of scholars dominating curriculum development. This tradition was exemplified in the curriculum reform movement of the 1960s.

In effect, then, state and local authorities in the United States still retain de jure responsibility for curriculum development, but more and more this function is being eroded by national influences. During the 1970s it seemed that national policy regulations and funding patterns were making curriculum development a de facto function of the central government (Della-Dora 1976, Sturges 1976). Then central government funding diminished, only to be succeeded by other centralizing tendencies.

Alarmist outcries from all segments of society about declining test scores, increasing rates of illiteracy, and deficiencies in basic intellectual skills have been instrumental in popularizing and institutionalizing demands for returning to "the basics," vocational skill development, and minimum competencies. Commercial publishers of instructional materials spend millions of dollars each year to produce, package, and publicize their products. Electronic media, through the use of advertisements, public announcements, and prime time programs are conveying convincing messages about such social issues as substance abuse, sex, teenage suicide, power of reading, and crimes against human nature. Some of these programs are even accompanied by study guides for teachers and students. Fundamentalist groups accuse schools of teaching "secular humanism," of destroying the sanctity of the family, and of using instructional materials and techniques that are anti-God and anti-country. Liberationists appeal to curriculum designers for the inclusion of more broadly based conceptions of humanity, sexuality, individual realizations, and life options. Private foundations and philanthropic organizations provide funds for the development of curriculum programs in certain subjects. Scholars and academicians continue to dominate teams assembled by commercial publishers to write textbooks and other instructional materials. Professional organizations of classroom teachers, school supervisors, counselors, and administrators sponsor conferences, resolutions, and study groups, and publish books and journals which suggest directions and priorities for educational programs. A case in point is the 1981 interorganizational statement on *Essentials of Education*, which carries the endorsement of 19 different professional associations.

Censorship of instructional materials continues to plague the processes of curriculum development. The challenges of censors tend to focus on sex and sexuality, unchristian attitudes and beliefs, objectionable language, unpatriotic sentiments, and criticism of United States history, and the more recent attacks of secular humanism, creationism versus evolution, values clarification, antiestablishment viewpoints, and moral relativism of situational ethics. A recent study on censorship (*Limiting What Students Shall Read* 1981) reports that challenges to textbooks increases as the school grade level increases, that a sizeable percentage of censors have not read or viewed in entirety the materials they are challenging, and that, consistently, the intent of censors is to limit or restrict the information and viewpoints made available to youth through instructional materials.

The magnitude of the pressures effecting curriculum development in the United States and other countries with respect to "who makes demands" and "what kinds of demands they make" gives validity to the observations of Saylor et al. (1981) that this enterprise includes "a cast of thousands," as well as to Phillips and Hawthorne's (1978) assessment that "any organization at any level that has a concern" can become involved in curriculum decision making. It also lends credence to Taba's caveats about extending the base of participation in curriculum development without a corresponding specification of the appropriate roles of different participants. She adds further that

> Perhaps "being concerned" is too broad a criterion for participation in curriculum development. Some delineation is needed regarding the nature of that participation. Much grief has come from an indiscriminate participation of everyone in everything. . . . Clearly, there is a distinct function that all these groups can serve in the total job of curriculum development, and the decisions on participation must rest on who can best do what, and not on a sentimental concept of democratic participation. (Taba 1962 p. 252)

3.3 England

Until recently the English education system was based on considerable devolution of curriculum planning to individual schools. However, schools still worked within the framework of a national system of examinations at 16 and 18, strong curriculum traditions, parental expectations and a range of national government influences (Skilbeck 1984). Throughout the 1980s, however, the influence of national government was growing. The number of examination boards was reduced, national criteria were introduced for examinations at 16 and a series of reports from the Department of Education and Science and Her Majesty's Inspectors were published which were wide ranging in content and quite prescriptive in tone. Increasing politicization of education in general and the curriculum in particular came to a head with a new Education Act in 1988. This set up a National Curriculum Council for England and a curriculum Council for Wales to keep the curriculum under review and advise the Secretary of State, who was given powers to establish a complete national curriculum. This curriculum is defined in terms of core subjects (English, Mathematics, Science), foundation subjects (specified) and other subjects (not specified). Programs of study will be specified but not the time to be allocated to them. It is being assumed that there will be more local discretion outside the core and foundation subjects, at least in theory. But in practice national assessment targets at 7, 11, 14 and 16 are to be stipulated in core and foundation subjects, so there will be pressure to maximize the time accorded to the prescribed curriculum.

Within this framework, the new Act aims to place considerable responsibility on individual schools by giving them a great deal of financial autonomy and putting them into open competition for pupils with their neighbouring schools. This is intended both to improve school effectiveness and to subject schools to further local pressure. The government appears to be trying to channel this pressure into the arena of performance on national tests and examinations by requiring publication of these results. If successful, this would divert attention away from curriculum policy and have a powerfully conservative effect. Local groups who disagree with national curriculum policy will have to mobilize political pressure at national level and contend with a National Curriculum Council entirely appointed by the Secretary of State. Whether there will be a residual role for local education authorities in curriculum planning is not at all clear.

There is considerable concern that the long British tradition of school-based curriculum innovation will be stifled, and that teachers will be deprofessionalized. On the other hand, proponents of the new system argue that teachers have had too much influence on the curriculum and too little accountability. Even they remain worried that the new system will prove insensitive to local needs until new patterns of consultation have been properly developed.

Observers should not disregard, however, the extent to which national influences have already had a major impact on the British curriculum during the 1980s. The

Science curriculum is undergoing a major transformation as a result of pressures from Her Majesty's Inspectors, centrally funded In-Service Training, changing examinations, and a major national curriculum project, the Secondary Science Curriculum Review. Ironically, the Review was predominantly led by teachers. Prevocational education has also rapidly developed during this period, though in this case there is doubt whether the trend will be confirmed by the new national curriculum.

An important side-effect of this strong local tradition, whether or not it survives in England, is the experience of school-based curriculum development which has been gained and to some extent embodied in publications. Given the increasing evidence of the role of local factors in curriculum implementation (see the final article of this section) much of this accumulated experience is likely to be relevant in the future.

3.4 National Curriculum Planning

The legal responsibility for curriculum development is a function of the central government in many nations. For instance, the national constitutions of Italy, Sweden, Spain, and France make explicit provisions for education. Agencies of the national government play very substantial roles in determining curriculum policy and plans. These curricula are expected to be the points of departure for instruction in all schools; however, opportunities are provided, in most instances, for them to be adapted to accommodate local needs. Consistent with these centralized systems of curriculum planning, the groups involved in the legal process are constituted by the national government. They include inspectors, standing committees that are subsidiaries of ministries of education, appointed committees of experts, and advisory committees of lay people (Beauchamp and Beauchamp 1972).

The observations made earlier that curriculum development does not occur in a vacuum, that it is a complex sociopolitical enterprise wherein conflicting interests compete for recognition, and that external, informal, and extralegal forces frequently penetrate the internal boundaries of legal decision-making structures are as valid for nationally based curriculum development as for planning at regional and local levels. A barrage of politicians, publishers, professionals, parents, interest groups, and socioecological elements participate informally, but nonetheless very significantly, in determining school curricula in Italy, France, Spain, and Sweden. Illustrative of these dynamics is Beauchamp's and Beauchamp's (1972 pp. 100–01) description of how curriculum development proceeds in Sweden:

> Although major curriculum change must be initiated or approved by Parliament, most of the detail of curriculum planning work is done under the authority and direction of the National Board of Education . . . [and] commissions.

> . . . The composition of high-level commissions reflects the social and political dedication of the Swedes to integrate education and the realities of social life, and to democratically involve representatives of organized groups in their society in the decision making processes about public education. Commissions with large-scale curriculum assignments may be composed of representatives of the creating body (Parliament or the National Board of Education), specialists in education, and representatives of social groups such as labor, business, and professional organizations . . . the preliminary draft of a major curriculum proposal is sent to major outside organizations for their comment and support approval. Among the organizations are; national labor groups, business organizations, other professional organizations, parent organizations, student organizations, religious organizations . . .

Similarly, in Singapore and Malaysia where curriculum planning is also the responsibility of national ministries of education, the opinions and suggestions of heads of schools, parents, scholars, employment agencies, and various civic and special interest groups are solicited. In these countries the curriculum development process is also susceptible to influences which are particularly prominent in recently independent countries. These arise from the need to establish a stable government and a sense of national unity among very diversified populations, while developing a literate citizenry. The challenge is to build a nation out of people whose traditional allegiances have been to regional and/or tribal groups, and to imperialistic powers. Part of this challenge for the curriculum developer is to create a system of education that provides a common set of experiences for all youth. The same concerns are paramount in developing nations in Africa, South America, the Caribbean, and Southeast Asia as well. Establishing a viable education system is a natural extension of the political structures of these countries. Hence, general education aims and directions, as well as specific subject syllabi, textbook lists, and national examinations are produced or administered by agencies and subcommittees under the auspices of national ministries of education (Hoy Kee and Yee Hean 1971, Thomas et al. 1968).

4. Conclusion

While the level and purpose of political participation in curriculum development in developing nations may be manifested somewhat differently than in advanced nations, the underlying operative principle is the same. That is, curriculum decision making, in any social or cultural context, has very strong political and valuative elements since it involves power negotiations about the allocation of resources and benefits toward the advancement of certain ends. In developing nations, the formal and legal structures regulating curriculum development are more directly determined and controlled by national governments, and the influences of extralegal, informal, and externally organized groups are not as diversified or powerful as in more developed nations. Still, the forces and the viewpoints they symbolize must be considered when curriculum decisions are made.

It therefore becomes patently clear that the dynamics of the curriculum development process are similar in most nations, regardless of whether curriculum planning is the legal responsibility of local, regional, or national governments. Curriculum decision making is inundated with social, political, and human factors. These stem from both formally constituted bodies with legal obligations for curriculum development, and community-based informal, often loosely structured, interest groups who claim the right and authority to participate in curriculum development by virtue of their representative voices and powers of persuasion. There also appears to be a growing erosion of the distinction between formal–informal, legal–extralegal, and internal–external determinants of curriculum policies and plans. Developments are underway in most nations which are expanding the roles and functions of everyone concerned about and involved with curriculum development. As the public becomes more actively involved in making its own decisions, and as economic conditions make governmental involvement in education an increasing and unavoidable reality, curriculum development cannot help but become more politicized. Similarly, as the educational enterprise becomes more complex, the need for cooperation and collaboration among different constituencies and professionals within a society, as well as among societies, is essential. It is evident, then, that curriculum development is indeed a dynamic process of political, social, and personal negotiations that must occur in a cooperative and collaborative context if it is to produce viable education plans. These characteristics of the planning process are likely to become even more prominent in the future than they are today.

Bibliography

Association for Supervision and Curriculum Development 1981 *Limiting What Students Shall Read*. Association for Supervision and Curriculum Development, Alexandria, Virginia

Beauchamp G A, Beauchamp K E 1972 *Comparative Analysis of Curriculum Systems*, 2nd edn. Kagg, Wilmette, Illinois

Braybrooke D, Lindblom C E 1963 *A Strategy of Decision: Policy Evaluation as a Social Process*. Free Press, New York

Della-Dora D 1976 Democracy and education: Who owns the curriculum? *Educ. Leadership* 34: 51–57

Eggleston J 1977 *The Sociology of the School Curriculum*. Routledge and Kegan Paul, London

Hoy Kee F W, Yee Hean G 1971 *Perspectives: The Development of Education in Malaysia and Singapore*. Heinemann Educational (Asia), Kuala Lumpur

Hunkins F P 1980 *Curriculum Development: Program Planning and Improvement*. Merrill, Columbus, Ohio

Katz J 1974 *Education in Canada*. David and Charles, Newton Abbot

Kirst M W, Walker D F 1971 An analysis of curriculum policy making. *Rev. Educ. Res.* 41: 479–509

Lawton D 1975 *Class, Culture and the Curriculum*. Routledge and Kegan Paul, London

Lawton D 1980 *The Politics of the School Curriculum*. Routledge and Kegan Paul, London

Macdonald J B 1971 Curriculum development in relation to social and intellectual systems. In: McClure R M (ed.) 1971 *The Curriculum: Retrospect and Prospect*, 70th Yearbook of the Society for the Study of Education, Part 2. University of Chicago Press, Chicago, Illinois, pp. 95–113

McNeil J D 1977 *Curriculum: A Comprehensive Introduction*. Little, Brown, Boston, Massachusetts

Miel A 1946 *Changing the Curriculum: A Social Process*. Appleton-Century-Croft, New York

National Council for Social Studies 1981 *Essentials of Education*. National Council for Social Studies, Washington, DC

Nicholas E J 1980 A comparative view of curriculum development. In: Kelly A V (ed.) 1980 *Curriculum Context*. Harper and Row, London, pp. 150–72

Phillips J A, Hawthorne R 1978 Political dimensions of curriculum decision making. *Educ. Leadership* 35: 362–66

Pratt D 1980 *Curriculum, Design and Development*. Harcourt Brace Jovanovich, New York

Saylor J G, Alexander W M, Lewis A J 1981 *Curriculum Planning for Better Teaching and Learning*, 4th edn. Holt, Rinehart and Winston, New York

Simon R I 1980 Editorial. *Curric. Inq.* 10: 1–2

Skilbeck M 1984 *School-Based Curriculum Development*. Harper and Row, London

Smith B O, Stanley W O, Shores J H 1957 *Fundamentals of Curriculum Development*. World Book, Yonkers-on-Harcourt, Brace and World, New York

Sturges A W 1976 Forces influencing the curriculum. *Educ. Leadership* 34: 40–43

Taba H 1962 *Curriculum Development: Theory and Practice*. Harcourt, Brace and World, New York

Thomas R M, Sands L B, Brubaker D L (eds.) 1968 *Strategies for Curriculum Change: Cases From 13 Nations*. International Textbook, Scranton, Pennsylvania

Walker D F 1976 Toward comprehension of curricular realities. In: Shulman L S (ed.) 1976 *Review of Research in Education*, Vol 4. Peacock, Itasca, Illinois, pp. 268–308

Zais R S 1976 *Curriculum: Principles and Foundations*. Crowell, New York

Curriculum Decisions

A. A. Oberg

The term, "curriculum decision" belongs to the intellectual tradition called in curriculum studies "conceptual-empirical" (as distinct from the "reconcep-

ist" tradition which was rooted in the work of Pinar and Grumet in the 1970s and has blossomed since the 1980s). In the rational, analytic terms of the conceptual-empirical paradigm, a curriculum decision is a judgment about the ends or means of education or socialization, usually taken in an institutional (schooling) context, and usually focused on programmes (rather than on personnel, budget, etc.). The judgment is the result of some conscious deliberation and represents an intention to act either in a particular manner or so as to effect a desired outcome.

Decisions about the ends and means of education are often grouped into five major types, each with an array of related or alternative terms: (a) "Curriculum goals", the generic term for the first decision type, are the ends or ends-in-view toward which educational activities are directed. They are usually classed as cognitive, affective, or psychomotor. "Aims" are broad statements of life learnings. "Goals" refer to intermediate-range school learnings with immediate observable indicators. "Behavioural objectives" are detailed specifications of desired learner behaviours, which include the criterion level of the performance and the context for the behaviour. (b) "Curriculum content" consists in the subject matter, often but not always discipline based, which is used as the vehicle for achieving curriculum goals. (c) "Learning experiences", "student activities", or "teacher–learner interactions" indicate decisions focused on what learners are intended to do as a means of moving toward curriculum goals; while "teaching or instructional strategies", "methods", or "organization of instruction" focus on what teachers are intended to do to help learners move toward the goals. "Time" is sometimes considered a separate type of decision, as is "organization". In fact, organizational decisions are implied in each of the five types of curriculum decisions. (d) "Resources" are the means through which content is displayed to learners. Resources may be print, nonprint, realia, or human. As a decision type, "resources" may be subsumed under "learning experiences". Together these two categories may be referred to as the "learning environment". (e) "Evaluation" is a judgment about the value of the degree and type of learning that has taken place. The result is used for either formative or summative purposes. Alternate terms include "diagnosis" and "needs assessment", which occur before a learning experience; "assessment" and "feedback", which occur after a learning experience.

The sequence in which curriculum decisions are logically made is that implied in the preceding list of types of curriculum decisions. However, the descriptive literature is not consistent with this prescription, but suggests instead that the order varies irregularly, and often involves repeated cycling back for reconsideration to decisions taken earlier in the deliberation (Peterson et al. 1978, Zahorik 1975).

The databases for curriculum decisions are both theoretical and situational. The theoretical bases for curriculum decisions come from the disciplines of history and philosophy of education, sociology, anthropology, economics, political science, and psychology, and from the applied fields of curriculum and instruction. Situational data arise from the characteristics and interactions of particular teachers, learners, subject matter, and learning environments. Information from these databases functions as an influence on curriculum decisions (Borko et al. 1979).

The scope and bases for curriculum decisions vary depending on the level at which the decision is made within the institution. At the level most remote from learners are policy decisions which define primarily, but not only, the ends of education or schooling. These societal-level decisions are based ideally on theoretical data and are influenced by norms and pressure groups current in the society. Intermediate between policy and learners are decisions which serve to translate policy statements into specific terms. The scope and bases of these institutional-level decisions vary widely depending on the specificity of societal-level decisions and on the political and organizational characteristics of the institution. At the level of learners, the most important curriculum decisions are considered to be those made by teachers. While the curriculum decisions most often officially delegated to teachers are usually limited to contributory decisions about learning experiences, resources, and evaluation (means, as opposed to ends), the actual power of teachers to impact all curriculum decisions is acknowledged to be significant. The database on which teachers draw for his or her curriculum decisions is always situationally unique. The primary influence on the teachers' curriculum decisions are their perceptions of student needs, characteristics, and responses; and the teacher's own background, preferences, and skills. There are multiple and diverse descriptions of how teachers manage in the complex decision environment of the classroom. (See, for example, Halkes and Olson 1984; Ben-Peretz, Bromme, and Halkes 1986.)

Bibliography

Ben-Peretz M, Bromme R, Halkes R (eds.) 1986 *Advances of Research on Teacher Thinking.* Swets and Zeitlinger, Lisse

Borko H, Cone R, Russo N A, Shavelson R J 1979 Teachers' decision making. In: Peterson P L, Walberg H J (eds.) 1979 *Research on Teaching: Concepts, Findings, and Implications.* McCutchan, Berkeley, California

Halkes R, Olsen J K (eds.) 1984 Teacher Thinking: A New Perspective on Persisting Problems in Education. Swets and Zeitling, Lisse

Peterson P, Marx R, Clark C 1978 Teacher planning, teacher behavior, and student achievement. *Am. Educ. Res. J.* 15: 417-32

Zahorik J A 1975 Teachers' planning models. *Educ. Leadership* 33: 134-39

Curriculum Deliberation

L. E. Beyer

The curriculum contains two primary components. The formal or overt curriculum refers to the forms of knowledge, areas of study, and skills that are explicitly intended to be taught. The hidden or tacit curriculum (Jackson 1968) refers to the values, dispositions, and attitudes that students acquire as the result of spending large amounts of time within educational institutions; it includes the effects of socialization on students as they develop habits, forms of demeanor, and other personal attributes interacting with others in the classroom. As the "message system" of the school, the curriculum conveys important facts, skills, values, and dispositions to students, which have both short- and long-term consequences.

1. The Necessity for Deliberation

Given the complexity of the decisions that confront teachers as they implement curricular choices, it is imperative that they reflect critically on the effect of the curriculum on their students. As the curriculum helps shape students' consciousness of themselves, their relations with others, and their view of larger social concerns and values, the teacher's role is one of developing individuals and creating larger realities. Recent studies of both the formal and hidden curricula of schools have documented the complex relationships that exist between school practice and a host of social, economic, political, and ideological issues (Apple and Weis 1983, Apple 1979, Feinberg 1983, Bowles and Gintis 1976). Since the curriculum has larger cultural and political consequences for our students, and for the future of society, it is imperative that deliberation over curriculum issues include their linkages to such questions.

This emphasis on broad-based deliberation contrasts with a view of curriculum development and design that has been influential in the field since its inception as a formal area of inquiry. Some previous writers have taken a technical or managerial approach to the development of curricula. This tendency to regard curriculum deliberation as essentially concerned with "how to" questions—for example, centered on how to develop, organize, and evaluate curricula and teaching—sees curricular decisions as technical problems to be resolved through the adoption and implementation of the correct procedures and processes. It treats curriculum deliberation as an engineering-like phenomenon, with identifiable, sequential steps and phases of development (Tyler 1949). The history of this approach to curriculum deliberation is rather long, going back as far as some of the founders of the modern curriculum field (Bobbitt 1918, Bobbitt 1924, Charters 1927). It is an approach which has resulted in a "factory model" of curriculum making with elaborate systems designed to foster efficiency and standardized, uniform results.

When curriculum deliberation becomes reduced to deciding among "how to" options that are valued for their efficiency in accomplishing prestated outcomes, other questions and issues get pushed aside or dismissed as extraneous. For example, complex ethical and political questions are thereby ignored: questions such as what content is most legitimate or valuable within the formal curriculum, whose knowledge ought to be included in school subjects and individual lessons, what kinds of social relationships ought to be furthered in the way we organize and develop teaching activities, what values ought to guide curriculum evaluation, and the like. Adopting technical procedures for resolving complex and difficult issues about the curriculum results in substituting procedural resolutions for more substantive interchange.

2. Critical Inquiry and the Curriculum

Curricular decisions have consequences that extend far beyond the scope of individual students, teachers, and classrooms. For example, educators frequently suggest that education in the social studies ought to prepare students to be "good citizens," and business and governmental leaders are currently urging schools to develop programs to ensure more qualified workers who can rekindle a sense of competitiveness. There is an important relationship between school activities and social realities. In accentuating the development of specific skills, habits, and forms of knowledge in students through the dissemination of overt and hidden curricula, we help build the future of our world.

Critical inquiry in curriculum in the last quarter century has emphasized several things. First, the language that we use to discuss and debate curriculum questions must go beyond the technical, individualistic, and psychological discourse that has dominated much curriculum discussion (Huebner 1975). The languages and values of the arts, ethics, and politics can be used to clarify and deal more adequately with the complex issues that confront those engaged in curriculum deliberation. Curricular questions involve "why" and "what" questions at least as much as procedural ones. And since the latter depend on responses to such normative interrogatives, a system of language is required that is sufficiently comprehensive and sensitive to capture the intricacies of those questions. The adoption of a particular form of language does more than just give a name to events, people, and objects. It also has the potential to reveal or conceal alternative perspectives and values, thus changing the nature of what is named through the language form adopted.

Second, curricular issues must be seen together with the social context that constitutes an organic whole. Curriculum deliberation must be concerned not only with questions such as, "is this skill area being adequately developed?" or "are students scoring at or above the median on achievement tests?" but with broader issues as well. Recent studies of the formal content of the curriculum have documented the extent to which social inequalities are reflected in the treatment of women, minority groups, the working class, and so forth, in schools' curricula. The exclusion or marginalization of such groups, while hardly itself responsible for the appearance of social and political disparities, carries important ideological messages in reinforcing unequal roles in the wider society; at the same time, such exclusions are intellectually dishonest, since they deny the important contributions that oppressed groups have made, and continue to make. To understand the dynamics involved here requires thinking about schools relationally, as woven into the economic, cultural, and political institutions and practices of the social fabric generally. Moreover, the assumption that education should, or must, be supportive of current social arrangements must be challenged as a part of critical inquiry in curriculum. Instead, as practitioners sensitive to a range of normative issues, those engaged in curriculum decisions must be prepared to interrogate the moral, social, and political assumptions and consequences of the decisions they make (Beyer and Apple 1988).

To proceed in this way requires, third, that curriculum decision makers be prepared to raise a number of complex, difficult sorts of questions. Among the kinds of questions are those that are

(a) epistemological: what is to serve as genuine knowledge and ways of knowing? Are the ways knowledge is conceived of in schools broad enough to cover the range of possibilities for genuine knowledge?

(b) ideological: what (and whose) knowledge is of most worth? Who benefits from the inclusion and exclusion of particular bodies of knowledge?

(c) aesthetic: in what ways is curriculum an art form and how can teachers' interactions with students be "artfully" conducted? What effect would this have on how they see themselves, their students, and their interactions with them?

(d) ethical: how can relationships between teachers and students be based on a notion of moral conduct and community? What should be the operant moral principles in deciding these questions?

(e) political: what sort of political order is it desirable to promote and work toward? More specifically, what is the meaning of democracy and how can greater participation be fostered for those people, and in those areas, not now given sufficient consideration?

(f) historical: what can be learnt from past ways of responding to curricular questions and how is it possible to go beyond those?

3. Deliberation and Social Possibilities

The curriculum either supports current social and institutional arrangements and values or resists them in the creation of alternative possibilities. Educators cannot escape the moral responsibility of deciding what kind of world they want to work toward in designing curriculum and encouraging some form of socialization.

Since curriculum decisions are related to social and political questions in a variety of ways, it is important to have both an understanding of current social realities and a view of what alternative possibilities might be generated and worked toward. The unconscious furtherance of extant social realities through an uncritical adoption of current overt and hidden curricula is rejected in favor of the recognition that curriculum questions are moral and social problems. Deliberation over them can commence only when social reality is regarded as created rather than discovered, constructed by people rather than given by "experts" or existing simply "in the nature of things" (Berger and Luckmann 1967).

In responding to the relational aspects of curriculum deliberation, efforts should be coordinated around what Raskin (1986) has called "the common good." This program of criticism and renewal asserts the political and ethical principle that, "no human act should be used as a short cut to a better day," and that any social program "will be judged against the likelihood that it will result in linking equity, sharing, personal dignity, security, freedom, and caring." Those involved in curriculum deliberation must ensure that "the course they follow, inquire into, [and] analyze . . . will dignify human life, recognize the playful and creative aspects of people," and see others not as objects but as "co-responsible" subjects involved in the process of democratically deliberating over the ends and means of all of their actions and involvements (Raskin 1986 p. 8).

It would, of course, make the life of the curriculum worker much easier and less complicated if curricular deliberations did not involve those complicated and difficult social and political questions. Yet the vitality of the field and of its practitioners is in no small measure due to the synthetic, multifaceted nature of the issues and problems that are an inevitable part of curriculum deliberation. To settle for a neater, more isolated, and socially removed view of the field would be a regression from what has already been accomplished, and would have serious implications for future generations of students.

Bibliography

Apple M W 1979 *Ideology and Curriculum.* Routledge and Kegan Paul, Boston, Massachusetts

Apple M W, Weis L 1983 *Ideology and Practice in Schooling.* Temple University Press, Philadelphia, Pennsylvania

Berger P L, Luckmann T 1967 *The Social Construction of Reality: A Treatise in the Sociology of Knowledge.* Doubleday, Garden City, New Jersey

Beyer L E, Apple M W 1988 *The Curriculum: Problems, Politics, and Possibilities.* State University of New York, Albany, New York

Bobbitt F 1918 *The Curriculum.* Houghton Mifflin, Boston, Masachusetts

Bobbit F 1924 *How to Make a Curriculum.* Houghton Mifflin, Boston, Massachusetts

Bowles S, Gintis H 1976 *Schooling in Capitalist America: Educational Reform and the Contradictions of Economic Life.* Basic Books, New York

Charters W W 1923 *Curriculum Construction.* Macmillan, New York

Feinberg W 1983 *Understanding Education: Towards a Reconstruction of Educational Enquiry.* Cambridge University Press, Cambridge

Huebner D 1975 Curricular language and classroom meanings. In: Pinar W F (ed.) 1975 *Curriculum Theorizing: The Reconceptualists.* McCutchan, Berkeley, California, pp. 217–36

Jackson P W 1968 *Life in Classrooms.* Holt, Rinehart and Winston, New York

Raskin M G 1986 *The Common Good.* Routledge and Kegan Paul, New York

Tyler R W 1949 *Basic Principles of Curriculum and Instruction.* University of Chicago, Chicago, Illinois

Defining Educational Objectives

M. R. Eraut

The term "objective" is frequently used by educators and laymen as a synonym for "goal". Sometimes it can be replaced by the word "aim" or "intention" without appreciable loss of meaning. However, the term "objective" has also come to acquire a more technical meaning, the significance of which is not so readily apparent to those unfamiliar with its use in the education literature. In this more specialized sense, the term "objective" normally refers to an intended and prespecified outcome of a planned programme of teaching and it is expressed in terms of what it is hoped the student will have learned. The two usages are often distinguished by referring either to general objectives (goals) or to specific objectives (intended learning outcomes).

This more technical use of the term "objectives", with its associated demand for lengthy detailed statements of intended learning outcomes, is criticized by a number of writers on both practical and theoretical grounds. Thus to help the reader understand some of the controversies, as well as the development among some educators of a specialized terminology for communicating objectives, the article begins with a brief historical survey. This introduces different recommendations for the specification of objectives, with special attention to the notion of levels of specification and to various formulations of the concept of behavioural objectives. The ensuing discussion of problems associated with the status of objectives examines structural relationships between objectives, the logic of intentions expressed by an objective, and the political status of statements of objectives. The next section examines approaches to the differentiation and classification of objectives, but without going deeply into taxonomies of objectives. Then finally the uses and usefulness of objectives are examined in five contexts: curriculum development, lesson planning, instructional design, evaluation, and communication with students.

1. Historical Development

The origin of thinking about objectives in a more technical manner is usually attributed to Bobbitt (1918) whose book *The Curriculum* was probably the earliest systematic treatise on curriculum theory. The circumstances were significant. Only five years previously, Bobbitt had been the first to expound principles of educational administration directly based on Taylor's (1912) theory of scientific management. Industrial language suffused the book while Bobbitt readily accepted Spencer's utilitarian approach to knowledge selection. Where Spencer (1860) had merely asserted that "the first step must be to classify, in order of importance, the leading kinds of activity which constitute human life", Bobbitt proposed to use Taylor's time and motion study techniques to make this a reality.

A similar position was advocated by Charters (1924) whose notes for curriculum construction began as follows:

First, determine the major objectives of education by a study of the life of man in its social setting. Second, analyse these objectives into ideals and activities, and continue the analysis to the level of working units.

Following this advice led Pendleton to list 1,581 objectives for English and Billings to find 888 important generalizations for social studies teachers. Hence the objectives movement was already collapsing under its own weight when its prevailing utilitarian ideology was eclipsed by the progressivism of the 1930s. Its revival by Ralph Tyler, a former student of Charters, was in a different context—that of diagnostic testing and evaluation—and with a differerent philosophy—one of individual development rather than utilitarian efficiency (Smith and Tyler 1942). Tyler's Eight-year Study was a cooperative venture with a group of progressive schools; one of its main purposes was to formulate educational objectives which involved pupils in thinking for themselves and applying their knowledge rather than merely memorizing it or performing routine exercises. This aspect of the work was further developed by Tyler's former student, Benjamin Bloom, and a group of college examiners who eventually published two taxonomies of objectives, one for a cognitive domain and one for an effective domain.

Tyler's approach to curriculum development was based on reciprocal interaction between the formulation of objectives and the evaluation of their attainment (Tyler 1949). Evaluation was important for the improvement of educational programmes and proper evaluation required knowledge of what objectives the programmes were aiming to achieve. Thus objectives needed to be formulated with sufficient specificity to guide evaluation and subsequent attempts at course improvement in which the objectives themselves might be altered, both to include new possibilities and to remove that which was no longer considered feasible or of sufficiently high priority. For this purpose Tyler recommended that curriculum planners use behavioural objectives, in which both the content and the intended type of student behaviour are specified, and that course objectives be summarized in a two-dimensional matrix with content categories along one dimension and behavioural categories along the other.

It is sometimes forgotten that Tyler and the taxonomists defined objectives at a relatively general level, and it was Mager's (1962) influential book on preparing objectives for programmed instruction which more fully recaptured the spirit of Bobbitt. Moreover, like Bobbit before him, Mager derived his position from the behavioural technology approaches of trainers in military and industrial settings.

First Mager (1962) argued that behaviour should be specified only in observable terms and outlawed the use of verbs like "know", "understand", "feel", or "appreciate" that were indicative only of unobservable internal states of mind. Second, he insisted that the standard of performance should be specified in minute detail and with a built-in assumption of mastery or near-mastery, for example 90 percent of the students should get 90 percent of the questions correct on a test covering addition and subtraction of two digit numbers. Then, third, to avoid any ambiguity he asked for the conditions of performance to be clearly identified. Given the emphasis on the nature of the terminal performance itself, objectives which satisfy Mager's criteria are sometimes referred to as performance objectives, though the term behavioural objective is still more usual.

Gagné (1965) was among many psychologists who welcomed Mager's operational definition because it would help to determine the particular type of learning required. Unlike Tyler who was concerned with providing general guidance to teachers and curriculum planners, Mager and Gagné were interested in instructional design, which at that time was seen in terms of the detailed planning of instructional events in accordance with the principles of behaviourist psychology. If the design did not always lead to programmed learning, it was still expected to yield something very like it.

Several authors took up Mager's guidelines on specifying observable behaviours and gave special attention to the action verbs whose incorporation into the statement of an objective was said to meet this requirement. More recently, however, Gagné and Briggs (1974), realizing that operational definitions of performance often conveyed little information about the kind of learning that had taken place, recommended the addition of a "learned capability" component to the specification of an objective. There would seem to be some contradiction between the focus on performance and the abandonment of operationalism implicit in the addition of the learned capability component.

Finally, it should be noted that it is possible for a planning group formulating objectives to pursue each of the four main dimensions noted in this discussion—content, behaviour, conditions, and standards—to varying degrees of specificity, and this issue is further discussed below.

2. Levels of Specificity and the Limits of Specification

Krathwohl (1965) has distinguished three levels of specificity and suggests that each is appropriate for a different purpose:

> At the first and most abstract level are the quite broad and general statements most helpful in the development of programs of instruction, for the laying out of types of courses and areas to be covered, and for the general goals towards which several years of education might be aimed or for which an entire unit such as an elementary, junior, or senior high school might strive.
>
> At a second and more concrete level, a behavioural objectives orientation helps to analyse broad goals into more specific ones which are useful as the building blocks for curricular instruction. These behaviourally stated objectives are helpful in specifying the goals of an instructional unit, a course, or a sequence of courses.
>
> Third and finally. there is the level needed to create instructional materials—materials which are the operational embodiment of one particular route (rarely are multiple routes included) to the achievement of a curriculum planned at the second and more abstract level, the level of detailed analysis involved in the programmed instruction movement.

The first level corresponds to what Taba has called a "platform of general objectives" though it may also apply to a specific programme within a school (Taba 1962). The second level corresponds to Tyler's and Taba's version of the term "behavioural objective", and is also the level at which the taxonomies were developed. Davies (1976) calls these "general objectives", a term which Taba reserves for Level 1.

While it is customary to describe levels of specificity in terms of language and purpose, the addition of a quantitative density dimension can also sometimes be helpful. Since objectives are usually formulated in groups or clusters, an index of density can be simply defined as

$$\frac{\text{Number of objectives in list}}{\text{Hours of learning which list is intended to cover}}$$

Thus, when working at Krathwohl's Level 1, a ministry of education lists eight objectives for primary mathematics over the 5–9 age range, and about 600 hours of learning are involved, so the density is 8/600 or 1/75. Teachers planning a course of 100 hours using a Tyler matrix at Level 2 might well arrive at a list of about 20 objectives that would mean a density of 20/100 or 1/5. Then at Level 3 the objectives for an individual lesson, a self-instructional unit or a chapter in a book are likely to number between about 1 and 10 for a learning period of between 30 minutes and 2 hours, giving a density index that is usually greater than 1. The position is summarised in Table 1 below.

Another writer to identify three levels of objectives was Scriven (1967), though his perspective was primarily epistemological. His first level, entitled a "conceptual description of educational objectives", gives priority to conceptual structure and to student motivation. Then his second level, "manifestation dimensions of criterial variables", is concerned with the various ways in which a student's conceptual knowledge and understanding and his or her attitudes and nonmental abilities may be manifest or made observable. The third level provides an operational description of an objective in terms of how it is to be assessed. Thus Scriven's second and third levels correspond fairly closely to those of Krathwohl, but the first level has quite a different character, being based on curriculum content rather than general goals.

Both Krathwohl and Scriven state that Level 1 statements of objectives can guide the development of Level 2 objectives and that Level 2 statements can guide Level 3. But this process is much more complicated than simple logical deduction. There is no defensible set of rules or procedures for deriving specific objectives from general objectives because (a) selection decisions are made which involve judgments about appropriateness and priority; and (b) the kind of analysis required goes beyond the existing state of philosophical and psychological knowledge (Hirst 1973).

Gronlund (1970) makes a useful distinction between *minimum essentials* and *developmental objectives*. While minimum essentials can be handled as Level 3 objectives, developmental objectives are so complex that:

(a) Only a sample of representative behaviours can be tested.

(b) Teaching is directed towards the general class of behaviour that the objective represents rather than towards the sample that is specifically tested.

(c) Standards of performance are extremely difficult, if not impossible to define; so it is more meaningful to talk of encouraging and directing each student towards the maximum level of development he or she is capable of achieving.

A more radical distinction is made by Eisner (1969) who argues for separate treatment for instructional and expressive objectives. While instructional objectives can be prespecified and mastered, expressive objectives are concerned with outcomes that cannot and should not be prespecified because some form of original response is being sought. An expressive objective may specify an educational encounter, situation, problem, or task but it cannot predict what will be learned from what is intended to be an idiosyncratic response. While more usually associated with art and literature, the term is equally applicable to essays and projects in which students are encouraged to develop personal perspectives and insights.

3. The Status of Objectives

3.1 Structural Status

An educational objective cannot be considered in isolation, either from its companion objectives or from objectives which are intended to come before or after it in some planned sequence. It is necessarily embedded in some structure of intentions, whether this is described explicitly in some plan or document or left implicit in

Table 1
Levels of specificity

Krathwohl Terms	Davies Terms	Level of application	Density[a]
1 General Goals	Aims	Institution Programme	less than 1/50
2 Behavioural Objectives (as in Tyler, Taba, Bloom)	General Objectives	Course Module Topic	$\frac{1}{2}$ to 1/20
3 Instructional Objectives (as in Mager, Gagné and Briggs)	Specific Objectives	Lesson Assignment	1 to 10

a Density = number of objectives/hours of learning

the way the curriculum is organized. The list format which is commonly used to communicate sets of objectives is particularly ill-suited to conveying structural information. So quite different assumptions may inform the selection of a set of objectives from those which later guide the grouping and sequencing of those objectives for teaching purposes. There may also be considerable differences between the structure embedded in course materials, the structure in the mind of the teacher, and the structures developing in the mind of each student.

When compilers of objectives do give attention to structural assumptions, they frequently turn to the concept of a learning hierarchy. A group of objectives is said to constitute a learning hierarchy when it can be represented by a structure rather like a family tree, in which the achievement of each objective is dependent on the achievement of all the objectives connected to it on the level below. A hierarchy is usually developed by logical analysis, breaking down an objective into subobjectives until each step constitutes a clearly distinguishable learning task. Both the dependency claims of the hierarchy and the concomitant assumption that the level of analysis is appropriate may need to be empirically verified.

This notion of learning hierarchies, when combined with Carroll's (1963) suggestion that individual differences might be more appropriately attributed to rate of learning than to quality of learning, leads naturally to the type of individualized instruction that is commonly referred to as mastery learning. All knowledge within a mastery learning system is assumed to be essentially hierarchical in nature; instruction is individualized so each student can proceed at his or her own rate; and there is a built-in requirement for every student to master each unit before proceeding to the next. Hence the formulation and sequencing of objectives and the development of assessment instruments to indicate their mastery are an essential part of the strategy (Bloom et al. 1981).

The terms "terminal objective" and "enabling objective" are also associated with sequencing. A terminal objective represents the end of a learning sequence and needs to be justified in its own right; while an enabling objective situated in the middle of a sequence need only be justified in terms of its role in facilitating the achievement of one or more terminal objective(s). The distinction, though useful, is still an oversimplification because many objectives can be justified on both grounds and their description as "terminal" or "enabling" depends mainly on the time-scale adopted: the terminal objective of a lesson becomes an enabling objective in the context of a topic or course; and the terminal objective of a course becomes an enabling objective in the context of a student's subsequent life.

From the student's point of view, what probably matters most is an objective's position on the immediacy–remoteness continuum (Dressel 1976). Many objectives will appear to students both as conceptually remote, because they are far from what seems to be relevant in the community outside school, and as temporally remote because their utility lies far in the future. Perceiving links between their immediate objectives and possible ultimate goals can be crucial for some students' motivation. It has been suggested that objectives being communicated to students should be accompanied by individual rationales or justifications which relate them to more distant and more valued goals.

3.2 Logical Status

The logical status of an objective also deserves attention as it greatly affects the part it might play in planning and teaching. First, there is the distinction made by White who noted that the phrase "behavioural objective" can mean one of two things:

(a) objectives which themselves *consist in* pupils behaving in certain ways;

(b) objectives whose attainment is *tested by* observing pupils behaving in certain ways. (White 1971).

To state that no cognitive activity other than the repetition of memorized responses can be behavioural in sense (a) is not to claim that greater clarity cannot be achieved by giving close attention to the formulation of an objective; but it does imply that most educational objectives can be behavioural only in sense (b). Such objectives cannot wholly specify the ways in which they might be assessed, and no form of assessment can provide unambiguous evidence of their achievement. In practice, some forms of assessment are widely accepted as providing adequate evidence of the attainment of certain objectives, some have their adequacy disputed, and some are clearly unsatisfactory. If this were not the case, assessment would not be such a complex and elaborate field of study.

A second problem arises if one questions more carefully the notion of an objective being an intended outcome. In what sense is it intended? Is it expected to happen? Is its achievement specifically planned? Is it always explicit? Much of the writing about objectives seems to imply affirmative answers to all these questions, but observations of practice suggest a more cautious approach. Lists of objectives are often used to express aspirations rather than expectations and course documents often include a mixture of the two. More significantly, perhaps, an objective which is an expectation for one student may be an aspiration for another.

The term "emergent objectives" has been used to refer to objectives which may not even have been formulated in advance, but which, when the opportunity arises, are seen to contribute to important educational aims which tend to get neglected under the pressures of institutional expectations.

3.3 Political Status

The status of an objective is also affected by political factors. Who specifies them and with what authority?

Who uses them and how strongly do they feel obliged to keep within the specifications? There are a large number of possible situations. For example, influences on objectives from outside school may be of any of the following kinds:

(a) external specification as part of a pattern of curriculum control;

(b) an external requirement for the school to formulate its own objectives, which may or may not be accompanied by a further requirement to have them formally approved;

(c) external specification as part of a system of external examinations;

(d) external specification as part of a package of curriculum materials which the school may choose or be obliged to adopt or adapt;

(e) external comments by district officers, advisers, or inspectors.

Only in the first two uses will objectives necessarily be formally specified. However, evidence from curriculum implementation studies suggests that external specification of objectives alone has relatively little impact unless accompanied by sanctions or by other forms of specification such as textbook approval or external examinations. Congruence between externally specified objectives and classroom practice may be more readily explained by their sharing a common tradition than by hypotheses of cause and effect. Even when objectives have been internally specified, it must remain an empirical question whether they play a significant role in classroom practice. Accounts in the literature would seem to indicate that sometimes they do not.

4. Differentiation and Classification of Objectives

Advocates of using objectives in curriculum planning have been concerned not only with specificity and status but also with differentiation and classification. The connection between the two is clear: the more one specifies outcomes, the more responsible one becomes for seeing that an appropriate range of outcomes is considered. Otherwise the process of specification is likely to restrict the scope of the curriculum beyond the intentions of the specifiers. While reductions in curriculum scope are

deliberately sought by followers of the "back to basics" movement, this was certainly not the intention of post-war curriculum theorists like Tyler and Taba, but quite the opposite. They perceived current practice as unduly narrow and used planning by objectives as a technique for broadening it.

Schemes for distinguishing between different kinds of objectives range from simple typologies to classifications involving two or three levels of differentiation. Table 2 compares Bloom's first level separation into three *domains* with the typologies of Taba and Gagné and Briggs.

Even at this first level, there is considerable interaction between separate categories of objective because all learning entails cognition of some kind and all human transitions involve values and attitudes. But this does not prevent simple typologies from being of assistance in the formulation and selection of a balanced set of objectives, provided that the structural status of the objectives and the delicate interplay between reasons and emotions are not forgotten. These considerations are equally important at the second level, that of taxonomies of educational objectives.

The scope and assumptions of taxonomies will be given some attention in the sections below. Here, the purpose is to compare and contrast the taxonomies with other approaches to the classification of objectives. While, for convenience, the discussion is divided according to Bloom's three domains, the domain distinction is not taken for granted; and a fourth section is devoted to objectives such as social skills which have no obvious place in the Bloom classifications.

The main focus of this discussion is on general rather than subject-specific classifications, because there are so many subject-specific schemes in use. Several of these more specialised schemes can be found in the Bloom et al. (1971) handbook and the publications of groups, such as the International Association for the Evaluation of Educational Attainment (IEA), and the British Assessment of Performance Unit (APU) who are concerned with monitoring educational achievement at national level.

4.1 Classification of Cognitive Objectives

The traditional distinction in the *cognitive domain* has been between knowledge and skills, content and process, conceptual structure and critical thinking. Tyler

Table 2
First level differentiation of objectives

Bloom (1956)	Gagné and Briggs (1974)	Taba (1962)
Cognitive domain	Verbal information	Knowledge
Affective domain	Intellectual skills	Reflective thinking
Psychomotor domain	Cognitive strategies	Skills (basic, inquiry, social)
	Attitudes	Values and attitudes
	Motor skills	Sensitivities and feelings

called it content and behaviour. However, since terms like behaviour, process, and skill have multiple meanings, many of which lie outside the cognitive domain, we prefer to use the terms *knowledge* and *cognitive operations* and to emphasize their interdependence. Thus knowledge is acquired, interpreted, transformed, used and even created by cognitive operations in such a manner that it is misleading to regard it as static or fixed.

Descriptions of knowledge are usually couched in such terms as facts, conventions, concepts, procedures, principles, and theories; and these features may be depicted as loosely or tightly linked by some kind of network or conceptual structure. The loosest kind of link would be a metaphoric association of ideas while the tightest would be a learning hierarchy of the type discussed above. There are many gradations in between as when several concepts are linked by their relevance to some common problem. Bloom's *taxonomy* is based on cognitive operations and more readily understood if we adopt Alles's (1967) suggestion that the lowest level be renamed "recall and recognition" to avoid the semantic confusion caused by Bloom's idosyncratic use of the term "knowledge". Research suggests that there is some justification for treating Bloom's lower four levels—recall and recognition, comprehension, application, and analysis—as taxonomic, but not for including synthesis and evaluation in the same category (Madaus et al. 1973). Eraut (1975) has suggested a distinction between the lower three levels which concern cognitive operations with clearly delineated pieces of content and the upper levels where more generalized thinking skills are involved and selection of facts, concepts, theories, and criteria is part of the desired behaviour. This draws attention to the possible substitution of Bloom's upper three levels of some alternative breakdown of generalized *thinking skills*, a procedure which was in fact followed by several contributors to Bloom et al.'s (1971) handbook. Klopfer, for example, substituted four categories under the general heading "Processes of scientific inquiry": observing and measuring; seeing a problem and seeking ways to solve it; interpreting data and formulating generalizations; building, testing and revising a theoretical model.

Ormell (1974) argues that "patching up" the taxonomy in this way will not prove satisfactory:

A much more radical reconstruction seems to be needed; which, (i) will relate to conceptual levels in subject areas, (ii) will not imply a single linear hierarchy of objectives and (iii) will include the ingredient of imaginative development from the beginning.

His first two criticisms would seem to be supported by the wide range of subject-specific classification schemes put forward by Bloom's own collaborators and other authors; and by their frequent abandonment of the single linear hierarchy principle. But it must also be recognized that much of this rethinking has been stimulated by the enormous impact of the taxonomy itself. Without it we might well not have the range of classification schemes available today.

Ormell's third criticism, however, would also apply to most of these newer subject-specific schemes. He argues that the taxonomy is implicitly based on materialist values: knowledge is treated as a commodity and imagination and personal meaning seem to have no place. Though not originally designed for classifying objectives, a model teaching-learning sequence suggested by Parker and Rubin (1966) provides an interesting example of a much more interactive approach.

1. Processes which expose the student to a particular body of knowledge: formulating questions, reading, observing, listening, collecting evidence, discovering principles.

2. Processes which allow the student to extract meaning from the body of knowledge: analyzing, experimenting, reorganizing, consolidating, integrating.

3. Processes which enable the learner to affix significance to the knowledge: inferring generalizations, reconstructing, relating to other situations, testing for usability.

4. Processes which cause the learner to put his or her knowledge to functional use—to operate with it in different situations and to manipulate it through intellectual activity: solving a problem, creating a problem, clarifying a problem.

4.2 Classification of Objectives in the Affective Domain

Cazden (1971), writing about early language development, likens the relationships between the cognitive and affective domain to the linguistic distinction between competence and performance. Educators want students to be interested in what they are taught, to value it and to use it; and this major concern is identified with what many see as "the problem of motivation". Thus, many objectives in the affective domain can be appropriately described as socialization into the norms and values of educators. The terms most commonly used are "interest" and "appreciation", and the three lower levels of Krathwohl et al.'s (1964) *taxonomy*—receiving, responding, and valuing—provide a useful analysis of the successive stages in the achievement of these aims. Though formal statements tend to confine their attention to socialization into school subjects, the hidden curriculum emphasizes socialization into the norms and values of schooling in general. Educators seek not just good conduct but participation.

A second strand of the affective domain concerns the areas of moral education and social education. Here there is a delicate balance to be found between socialization of students into the norms and values of the local community and the nation and the development of the student's own personal value system. In any society, some values are broadly accepted, some are only accepted within certain subcultures, and others are regarded as deviant. This potential for conflict is ignored by the Krathwohl taxonomy which focuses only on the progressive internalization and development of students' personal value systems without paying attention to what might be considered as good and bad or right or wrong (Gribble 1970). Thus there is an inherent danger that sophistication and coherence will be valued for their own sakes. While it may reasonably be argued that cognitive excellence is necessarily based on the higher levels of the cognitive domain (at least within the academic arena), it is highly debatable whether a moral person needs to have a moral philosopher's understanding of value systems.

A third strand in the affective domain concerns feelings and sensitivities. While Kamii's (1971) use of the term "socio-emotional development" is clearly derived from the aim of socialization into schooling, other writers have talked about the education of the emotions. This discussion is most prominent in the context of the arts, but also becomes relevant in social studies, where the aim of developing empathy is likely to have a strong emotional component. Many psychologists, however, have argued that emotion is important in all types of learning and that it is particularly important in fostering creativity. There have been few attempts to analyze this aspect of education in terms of objectives, and most authors have argued that the language of objectives is inappropriate.

In conclusion, the interconnection between the cognitive and affective domains should be reemphasized. All cognitive operations both require and engender some form of affective response. The kind of valuing described in the socialization and personal development aims above, is strongly cognitive in many respects, at least as dependent on cognitive arguments about relevance as upon immediate emotional impact. It has been argued that feelings and emotions have a substantial cognitive component (Yarlott 1972); and many of the objectives discussed in section 4.4 below have strong affective components. Thus, the justification for the domain concept appears to be decidedly thin.

4.3 Classification in the Psychomotor Domain

Classification work in the psychomotor domain has been based more on physiology than on recognizable learning objectives. Thus Kibler et al.'s (1970) and Harrow's (1972) taxonomies set out different types of bodily movement and a range of perceptual and physical abilities. Even communication is classified physiologically into facial expressions, gestures, bodily movement, speech behaviour and the like. Since these movements serve such different purposes, one wonders how useful such general classifications can be. Eye-hand coordination in playing tennis is so radically different from eye-hand coordination in playing the piano that it is difficult to see what is gained from putting them in the same category.

The main exception to this physiological emphasis is the group of classification schemes based on the development of a physical skill. Seymour (1966), for example, distinguishes four stages:

1. Acquiring knowledge.
2. Executing the task in a step-by-step manner, with conscious watching and thinking-out of each step.
3. Transfer of control to the kinaesthetic sense, with consequent increase in the fluidity and rapidity of action, and freeing the eye for perceptual control.
4. Automatization of the skill.

A further stage involving the adaptation of a skill to new circumstances has also been suggested (Simpson 1966, Wellens 1974). The analysis is clearly relevant to such skills as driving a car or playing a simple tune on the piano, but cannot be applied to riding a bicycle or pole vaulting because the steps cannot be separately rehearsed. Again, subject-specific or even task-specific classifications are possibly more useful than general ones. The work of Harrow and Simpson seems primitive in comparison with Laban's analysis of dance or Flesch's analysis of violin playing. Moreover, the performing arts in general involve such a complex interplay between cognition, feeling, and motor skill that thinking in terms of separate domains will often be quite inappropriate.

4.4 Social Skills and Other Objectives Outside the Bloom Domains

Taba (1962) included social skills in her typology of objectives but they do not seem to fit into any of Bloom's domains. The same would probably be true of sculpture, but since that already has a subject identity and a potential place in the timetable, the omission is less serious. Romiszowski (1981) suggests a fourth domain to include social, personal, and interactive skills but this seems to be giving the domain concept rather more significance than it perhaps deserves. However, the skills he mentions are interesting because they go beyond the usual aim of getting on with people and include entrepreneurial skills such as leadership, persuasion, discussion, and salesmanship.

The most elaborate exploration of the territory that lies outside school subjects is probably that of Raven (1977) whose approach to the concept of competence is refreshingly broad. He argues that the self-motivated competencies he advocates involve a major values component and are best thought of as motivational dispositions. They may also be regarded as personal skills. A few typical examples are: tendency to seek feedback, ability to recognize it and tendency to utilize it; ability to learn without instruction; and willingness to tolerate frustrations. Raven does not offer a classification scheme, but by drawing attention to objectives which are suggested neither by subject structures nor by classification schemes, he draws attention to important values and skills which might otherwise escape notice.

5. Arguments For and Against Using Objectives

When discussing the advantages and limitations of planning and working with objectives, it is important to specify the user, the context, and the type of use envisaged. Five main types of use will be distinguished—curriculum development, lesson planning, instructional design, evaluation, and communication to students. These different uses are often confused in the literature, with arguments for and against one type of use being frequently applied to another. Moreover, it has not been unusual for authors to set up "straw-man" images of their opponents in order to demolish extreme statements while avoiding entanglements with more moderate positions [see, for example, the often quoted papers by Popham (1969) and Macdonald-Ross (1973)].

5.1 Using Objectives in Curriculum Development

Attention will be confined here to the use of objectives at Krathwohl's second level, leaving discussion of the use of highly specific objectives for the next section. In doing so, however, it must be remembered that most advocates of instructional objectives at the third level are agreed that prior specification at the second level is essential. But the converse is not true. Objectives may be used in curriculum development without any assumption that more detailed specification by teachers or by instructional designers will necessarily follow.

The principal arguments for using objectives for curriculum development purposes alone would appear to be (a) that they clarify the intentions of the developers and (b) that they focus attention upon the learner as well as the teacher. What the use of objectives cannot do is resolve disputes over what should be taught, though sometimes they may help to map out the issues. Objectives at the second level will never be devoid of ambiguity, and some educators are more skilful than others in using the language of objectives, so the question of whether or not objectives do indeed clarify intentions can only be answered in terms of individual cases.

Many authors have stressed that the clarification of teaching intentions is a difficult exercise involving considerable insight and delicacy of phrasing, and that it is incapable of totally satisfactory resolution. People who prepare curriculum specifications at district, regional, or national level need to understand these problems, if their use of objectives is not to do more harm than good. In particular, there is a tendency to issue lists of objectives which are specified at a mixture of different levels. This causes confusion for teachers seeking to translate curriculum documents into lesson plans and often leads to selective neglect of the more general, and seemingly more rhetorical objectives. A similar problem occurs when developmental or expressive objectives are treated as if they are competencies to be mastered, for this neglects the whole issue of quality performance.

At institutional level, however, the context of curriculum specifications is quite different because formal curriculum documents are only a small part of the communication between the teachers concerned. A statement of objectives then has a strong indexical character in which its meaning is enriched by and partly dependent upon other communications which occurred before, during, and after its preparation. The advantages of using objectives will depend on whether the curriculum developers want to use them or merely feel obliged to use them; on whether they are genuinely seeking agreement as opposed to finding a form of words which maximizes the independence of individual teachers; and on whether intentions are easily communicated by other means, such as a common textbook or examination.

Above the institutional level, the political status of an objective is often critical. While some teachers are used to being told what to teach, others regard the formulation of objectives as the teachers' own responsibility. Normal practice varies greatly between one country and another, but in any country, attempts to alter the balance of power by changing either the locus or the extent of specification of objectives are likely to meet resistance. In practice, however, whether politically welcome or not, objectives may be misunderstood or even ignored by teachers. Even when the process of formulating objectives clarifies the intentions of a curriculum team or committee (and it is not unknown for it to lead to a deliberately vague compromise), the document that results does not necessarily convey those intentions adequately to teachers. This is not an argument against using objectives but rather one against placing too much reliance on them as a form of curriculum communication. The literature on curriculum implementation is replete with examples where misunderstanding or lack of sanctions or infeasibility have prevented externally specified curricula from being implemented as intended.

An important criticism from a theoretical rather than a practical perspective concerns not the use of objectives per se but approaches to curriculum development which assume that statements of objectives are adequate on their own in the first stage of curriculum planning. Several authors (see, for example, Stenhouse 1970/71), have argued for prime attention to content; others for an early consideration of assessment, which often counteracts the impact of objectives; and yet others for the early specification of certain crucial and often nontraditional learning experiences such as project work, community service, work experience, or artistic performance. Many of these other curriculum elements can be so important for a course that they need discussion prior to any detailed formulation of objectives. Moreover, when curriculum development is viewed as a problem-solving activity with a premium on creative imagination, an early emphasis on objectives may lead only to the reformulation of traditional practice at a time when more radical change is what is really needed

(Eraut 1976). Thus, when the emphasis is on curriculum innovation, objectives may not be a starting point but a "late development of the curriculum maker's platform" (Walker 1971).

The argument against using objectives which has probably received the greatest support is that they are only appropriate for some areas of the curriculum. Eisner (1969) has eloquently argued against behavioural objectives in the arts, and their usefulness for describing higher level learning in the humanities (Stenhouse 1970/71) and social sciences (Eraut et al. 1975) has also been questioned. In all these cases it is the individuality and complexity of students' work which is said to limit the applicability of the language of objectives. Two major issues are at stake—the nature of the subject and the autonomy of the learner. Both have been and will long continue to be matters for debate among educators, though many would now agree that objectives are more helpful in some situations than in others. The principal problem lies in recognizing those situations in which the use of objectives is appropriate.

Given the problems of deriving, formulating, and justifying objectives, it is much safer if in the context of the education system as a whole objectives are regarded as means rather than ends. The courses and curricula that are planned constitute the means whereby students have to be guided towards a variety of ends; and the language of objectives provides one means of clarifying intentions during the planning process.

5.2 Using Objectives in Lesson Planning

The claim that highly specific objectives at Krathwohl's third level improve the quality of lesson plans and subsequent pupil performance is usually argued by asserting that good lesson planning is logically dependent on knowing what one is seeking to achieve; and that this necessarily entails having learning objectives. Both parts of this assertion have been challenged. To begin with the second—one counterargument is that teachers know what they are doing because they are working in a recognized teaching tradition. Provided that they can relate the content of their lessons to a topic on a syllabus, a chapter in a textbook, or a possible question in an examination, they do not need any separate list of course objectives. Once a tradition is clearly established, objectives become redundant. The use of objectives in such a context is less likely to be one of defining the course than one of inspiring teachers to move their students beyond the level of routine completion of textbook exercises or memorization of content, a purpose for which specifying beyond the second level is clearly inappropriate.

When more informal approaches to teaching are adopted, objectives are less likely to be implicit in textbooks, syllabi, and examinations. But then the first part of the assertion becomes more of an issue. Is good lesson planning logically dependent on knowing what objectives one is seeking to achieve? Sockett (1976) argues that objectives are totally inadequate as a description of a teacher's ends, because a teacher always has other equally important ends, to which his or her actions are directed: being fair to groups, getting students to ask questions, building up weaker children's confidence, developing interpupil discussion, and so on. Though one can argue that these "procedural aims" should be included as general course objectives, they need to be pursued over a long period. Such aims have a justifiably important influence on teaching, but cannot be converted into specific objectives for individual lessons.

Another criticism comes from Jackson (1968) whose interviews with teachers who were judged as "outstanding" revealed that both their planning and their classroom responding were aimed not directly at the achievement of objectives but at creating productive learning conditions and securing student involvement. Since involvement in learning activities is logically necessary for learning, one might be permitted to modify the original assertion to argue that good lesson planning is dependent on having appropriate activities and strategies to achieve a high degree of student involvement. If that primary goal can be achieved then surely productive learning will follow. Where there is no established tradition, course objectives may be helpful in choosing between possible activities and in alerting a teacher to special opportunities. However, it is unreasonable to expect the teacher to be able to sustain a detailed knowledge of how each of 30 or more students is progressing towards each of a dozen or so objectives in every single lesson. Worse still is the possibility that it might distract the teacher from the primary task of securing involvement in learning.

A further argument against using highly specific objectives in lesson planning is that they overconstrain the teacher. Both Jackson and Sockett characterize good teaching as being strong on opportunism. Atkin (1968) suggests that higher order objectives are best pursued whenever the opportunity arises rather than according to preplanned schedules. For example, when students' questions lead to the discussion of some significant moral problem or issue, the teacher may see the opportunity for pursuing objectives whose introduction might have seemed artificial or nonproductive if the teacher had initiated them. Eisner's expressive objectives also resist very precise planning. In general, support for the use of specific objectives at Krathwohl's third level is now largely confined to situations where the teaching is highly directive and objectives are limited to the lower cognitive levels. Using general course objectives to guide lesson planning is quite a different procedure from allowing lesson planning to be dominated by the detailed specification of behavioural objectives; and there is little conclusive empirical evidence to support either practice. Until there is good evidence of how people who work with objectives plan or teach differently and of how this benefits their students, the use or nonuse of objectives should remain a matter of personal preference.

5.3 Using Objectives in Instructional Design

The term "instructional design" commonly refers to the design of teaching and learning materials by a specially designated team, who may or may not include teachers who will be responsible for their implementation. Although some writers on instructional design appear to address ordinary teachers, there is little evidence that their recommendations get used by individual teachers who are not members of a design team.

The claim that using highly specific objectives at Krathwohl's third level improves the quality of instructional design is prominent in the literature. Indeed it is often taken for granted. Yet there is little empirical evidence to support this claim for learning systems other than those based on individualized learning. The detailed specification of objectives is an extremely time-consuming operation, which requires considerable skill if common pitfalls are to be avoided; and it is, perhaps, unlikely to be a good use of scarce personnel when there is an urgent need to create and try out new teaching ideas.

The more restricted claim that highly specific objectives are needed for individualized learning programmes based on mastery learning receives much stronger theoretical and practical backing. The advocates of highly specific objectives adopt a similar theoretical position to advocates of mastery learning; and designers of mastery-learning-based instructional systems consistently use highly specific objectives. It can be argued that designers could proceed directly from second level objectives to criterion tests, but this would ignore the detailed mapping of hierarchies of learning objectives which most designers working in this tradition recommend.

5.4 Using Objectives in Evaluation

It is in the context of evaluation that the concept of objectives has been most continuously used and most elaborately evolved. Tyler's primary concern was with evaluation and the taxonomies were also developed for evaluation purposes. Arguments for and against using objectives in evaluation are treated at greater length elsewhere, so the discussion here will be brief.

One of the purposes of an evaluation, sometimes the main purpose, is to examine the realization of intention. To what extent have various people's intentions been realized in practice? People have many kinds of intentions but these usually include at least some that relate to student outcomes. Whether or not they are documented or made explicit, intended student outcomes can often be expressed either as objectives or in terms of performance on some task or in some anticipated situation. Thus an evaluation concerned with the realization of intention will usually need either to collect existing evidence of student performance (folders of work, test papers, etc.) or to devise some means of assessing what students have learned. If some differentiated comment on student performance is required, then this can be achieved by separate reports on each performance task or by using a list of objectives and commenting on the achievement of each. Classification schemes may be used to help set out the range of objectives, either at the data analysis stage or as an aid to constructing assessment instruments where these are deemed necessary (see *Criterion-referenced Measurement*).

The convenience of collecting student achievement data in this way and using them for improving the course by what is now called formative evaluation is what led to Tyler's model of curriculum development and it helps to explain the continuing popularity of that model with many evaluators (Bloom et al. 1981). However, formative evaluation normally requires more than just student performance data. Moreover, as recent disputes about performance contracting (Stake 1973) and careful studies of test performance (Cicourel et al. 1974) have revealed, the kind of cognitive behaviour which leads to a particular performance is not necessarily the same as that which was intended. Students interpret tasks differently and get tested in many different contexts. Even assigning an examination question to a particular level in Bloom's cognitive domain may depend on the assumptions made about the teaching prior to that examination. Thus the usefulness of information about objectives and their achievement is dependent on additional information about transactions and conditions which can assist in their interpretation. Even statements of objectives have to be seen in context because they are not absolute criteria but indications of people's attempts to express their intentions.

In case studies and small-scale evaluations, collecting qualitative contextual evidence to assist with the interpretation of achievement data is a feasible proposition. But the larger the scale of evaluation, the more diverse will be the programme being evaluated, until it becomes extremely difficult to collect sufficient contextual information to provide useful guidance for decision making. A further problem in evaluating large-scale educational programmes is that their objectives are usually negotiated as part of some political compromise, and are therefore ill-suited for bearing the brunt of a programme evaluation based on educational objectives (Cronbach et al. 1980).

Closely related to the use of objectives in evaluation is their use in the monitoring of student achievement and in accountability. In both cases objectives may be used as a guide to test construction or as an aid to data analysis. Their use, however, will not obviate the need for a careful demonstration of the validity of any assessment instruments. It will always need to be argued that an objective is an adequate statement of an intention and that a test item is an adequate indication of the achievement of an objective.

5.5 Using Objectives to Communicate to Students

There is much more empirical evidence on this issue than on other uses of objectives, presumably because it lends itself to short simple experiments. Several reviews of this research have been published (Hartley and Davies 1976, Faw and Waller 1976, Lewis 1981). The analysis is complicated by the existence of alternative methods for drawing learners' attention to what is expected of them. Hartley and Davies discuss pretests, overviews, and advance organizers as alternative attention directors; while Faw and Waller also included inserted questions. Most of the evidence reported is based on work with college students, some on work with high-school students and very little with other populations; and it has usually stemmed from situations where students learned from textual material rather than a teacher.

While several studies have shown that providing objectives enhances student achievement, an equal number have reported no significant difference (Lewis 1981). Some of the more favourable results can be "explained" in terms of increased learning time (Faw and Waller 1976). Alternative methods of guidance appear to have a similar impact—sometimes there are positive effects, sometimes there are none, but there are no reports of negative effects. On the whole the evidence for inserted questions seems to be the strongest, especially when applied to long passages of prose. However, the research is beset with methodological difficulties: when, for example, does an introduction become an implicit statement of objectives; and when does a statement of objectives become a form of coaching for a test? The general conclusion of reviews is that giving a student clearer directions normally enhances his or her learning, but a statement of objectives is only one of several ways of doing it. Such additional guidance may only be necessary when the instruction was not well-designed in the first place.

Bibliography

Alles J et al. 1967 *Theoretical Constructs in Curriculum Development and Evaluation*. Ministry of Education, Sri Lanka

Atkin J M 1968 Behavioral objectives in curriculum design: A cautionary note. *Sci. Teach.* 35: 27–30

Bloom B S (ed.) 1956 *Taxonomy of Educational Objectives*. Handbook 1: *Cognitive Domain*. McKay, New York

Bloom B S, Hastings J T, Madaus G F 1971 *Handbook on Formative and Summative Evaluation of Student Learning*. McGraw-Hill, New York

Bloom B S, Madaus G F, Hastings J T 1981 *Evaluation to Improve Learning*. McGraw-Hill, New York

Bobbitt F 1918 *The Curriculum*. Houghton Mifflin, Boston, Massachusetts

Carroll J B 1963 A model of school learning. *Teach. Coll. Rec.* 64: 723–33

Cazden C B 1971 Evaluation of learning in preschool education: Early language development. In: Bloom B S et al. 1971 *Handbook on Formative and Summative Evaluation of Student Learning*. McGraw-Hill, New York, pp. 345–98

Charters W W 1924 *Curriculum Construction*. Macmillan, New York

Cicourel A V et al. 1974 *Language Use and School Performance*. Academic Press, New York

Cronbach L J et al. 1980 *Toward Reform of Program Evaluations*. Jossey-Bass, San Francisco, California

Davies I K 1976 *Objectives in Curriculum Design*. McGraw-Hill, Maidenhead

Dressel P L 1976 *Handbook of Academic Achievement*. Jossey-Bass, San Francisco, California

Eisner E W 1960 Instructional and expressive educational objectives: Their formulation and use in curriculum. In: Popham W J, Eisner E W, Sullivan H J, Tyler L L (eds.) 1969 *Instructional Objectives*. (AERA Curriculum Evaluation Monograph 3.) Rand McNally, Chicago, Illinois, pp. 1–18

Eraut M R 1976 Some perspectives on curriculum development in teacher education. *Educ. Teach.* 99: 11–21

Eraut M R, MacKenzie N, Papps I 1975 The mythology of educational development: Reflections on a three-year study of economics teaching. *Br. J. Educ. Technol.* 6(3): 20–34

Faw H W, Waller T G 1976 Mathemagenic behaviours and efficiency in learning from prose materials: Review, critique and recommendations. *Rev. Educ. Res.* 46: 691–720

Gagné R M 1965 The analysis of instructional objectives for the design of instructions. In: Glaser R (ed.) 1965 *Teaching Machines and Programmed Learning*, Vol 2: *Data and Directions*. Department of Audio-visual Instruction, National Education Association (NEA), Washington, DC, pp. 21–65

Gagné R M, Briggs L J 1974 *Principles of Instructional Design*. Holt, Rinehart and Winston, New York

Gribble J 1970 Pandora's box: The affective domain of educational objectives. *J. Curric. Stud.* 2(1): 9–24

Gronlund N E 1970 *Stating Behavioral Objectives for Classroom Instruction*. Macmillan, New York

Harrow A 1972 *A Taxonomy of the Psychomotor Domain*. McKay, New York

Hartley J, Davies I K 1976 Preinstructional strategies: The role of pretests, behavioral objectives, overviews and advance organizers. *Rev. Educ. Res.* 46: 239–65

Hirst P H 1973 Towards a logic of curriculum development. In: Taylor P H, Walton J (eds.) 1973 *The Curriculum: Research Innovation and Change*. Ward Lock Educational, London

Jackson P W 1968 *Life in Classrooms*. Holt, Rinehart and Winston, New York

Kamii C K 1971 Evaluation of learning in preschool education: Socio-emotional, perceptual-motor, cognitive development. In: Bloom B S et al. 1971 *Handbook on Formative and Summative Evaluation of Student Learning*. McGraw-Hill, New York

Kibler R J, Barker L L, Miles D T 1970 *Behavioral Objectives and Instruction*. Allyn and Bacon, Boston, Massachusetts

Krathwohl D, Bloom B S, Masia B 1964 *Taxonomy of Educational Objectives*. Handbook 2: *Affective Domain*. McKay, New York

Krathwohl D 1965 Stating objectives appropriately for program, for curriculum and for instructional materials. *J. Teach. Educ.* 17: 83–92

Laban R 1963 *Modern Educational Dance*, 2nd edn. MacDonald and Evans, London

Lewis J M 1981 Answers to twenty questions on behavioral objectives. *Educ. Technol.* 21: 27–31

Macdonald-Ross M 1973 Behavioral objectives: A critical review. *Instr. Sci.* 2(1): 1–52

Madaus G F, Woods E M, Nuttall R L 1973 A causal model analysis of Bloom's taxonomy. *Am. Educ. Res. J.* 10(14): 353–62

Mager R F 1962 *Preparing Instructional Objectives*. Fearon, Palo Alto, California

Ormell C 1974 Educational objectives: Bloom's taxonomy and the problem of classification. *Educ. Res.* 17(1): 3–18

Parker J C, Rubin L J 1966 *Process as Content: Curriculum Design and the Application of Knowledge.* Rand McNally, Chicago, Illinois

Popham W J 1969 Objectives and instruction. In: Popham W J et al. (eds.) 1969 *Instructional Objectives.* (AERA Curriculum Evaluation Monograph 3.) Rand McNally, Chicago, Illinois

Raven J 1977 *Education, Values and Society: The Objectives of Education and the Nature and Development of Competence.* H K Lewis, London

Romiszowski A J 1981 *Designing Instructional Systems.* Kogan Page, London

Scriven M 1967 The methodology of evaluation. In: Tyler R W, Gagné R M, Scriven M (eds.) 1967 *Perspectives of Curriculum Evaluation.* (AERA Curriculum Evaluation Monograph 1.) Rand McNally, Chicago, Illinois

Seymour W D 1966 *Industrial Skills.* Pitman, London

Simpson E J 1966 The classification of educational objectives: Psychomotor domain. *Illinois J. Teach. Home Econ.* 10: 110–44

Smith E R, Tyler R W 1942 *Appraising and Recording Student Progress.* Harper, New York

Sockett H 1976 *Designing the Curriculum.* Open Books, London

Spencer H 1860 What knowledge is of most worth? In: Spencer H (ed.) 1910 *Education: Intellectual, Moral and Physical.* Appleton, New York, pp. 1–66

Stake R E 1973 Measuring what learners learn. In: House E R (ed.) 1973 *School Evaluation: The Politics and Process.* McCutchan, Berkeley, California

Stenhouse L 1970/71 Some limitations on the use of objectives in curriculum research and planning. *Paedag. Eur.* 6: 73–83

Taba H 1962 *Curriculum Development: Theory and Practice.* Harcourt, Brace and World, New York

Taylor F W 1912 *Scientific Management.* Harper, New York

Tyler R W 1949 *Basic Principles of Curriculum and Instruction.* University of Chicago Press, Illinois

Tyler R W 1964 Some persistent questions on the defining of objectives. In: Lindvall C M (ed.) 1964 *Defining Educational Objectives.* University of Pittsburgh Press, Pittsburgh, Pennsylvania

Walker D F 1971 A naturalistic model for curriculum development. *Sch. Rev.* 80: 51–65

Wellens J 1974 *Training in Physical Skills.* Business Books, London

White J P 1971 The concept of curriculum evaluation. *J. Curric. Stud.* 3: 101–12

Yarlott G 1972 *Education and Children's Emotions.* Weidenfeld and Nicolson, London

Taxonomies of Educational Objectives

V. De Landsheere

Originally, the term taxonomy (or systematics) was understood as the science of the classification laws of life forms. By extension, the word taxonomy means the science of classification in general and any specific classification respecting its rules, that is, the taxonomy of educational objectives.

A taxonomy related to the social sciences cannot have the rigour or the perfect branching structure of taxonomies in the natural sciences. In education, a taxonomy is a classification constructed according to one or several explicit principles.

The term "taxonomy of educational objectives" is closely associated with the name of B. S. Bloom. This is explained by the extraordinary worldwide impact of the *Taxonomy of Educational Objectives* first edited by Bloom in 1956. This taxonomy was enthusiastically received by teachers, educationists, and test developers because it offered easily understandable guidelines for systematic evaluation covering the whole range of cognitive processes (and not only the lower mental processes, as was too often the case in the past). This taxonomy had also a definite influence on curriculum development and teaching methods for the same reason: it emphasized processes rather than content matter, and helped determine a proper balance between lower and higher cognitive processes.

Bloom's taxonomy of cognitive objectives was soon followed by taxonomies for the affective and psychomotor domains. Within two decades, several taxonomies were developed by other authors and a great number of philosophical and empirical studies appeared on this topic.

A presentation of the main taxonomies so far published follows.

1. The Cognitive Domain

1.1 Bloom's Taxonomy

This taxonomy, which has inspired the majority of the other taxonomies, uses four basic principles: (a) the major distinction should reflect the ways teachers state educational objectives (methodological principle); (b) the taxonomy should be consistent with our present understanding of psychological phenomena (psychological principle); (c) the taxonomy should be logically developed and internally consistent (logical principle); and (d) the hierarchy of objectives does not correspond to a hierarchy of values (objective principle).

The taxonomy itself comprises six cognitive levels:

(a) Knowledge: recall or recognition of specific elements in a subject area. The information possessed by the individual consists of specifics (terminology, facts), ways and means of dealing with specifics (conventions, trends, sequences, classifications, categories, criteria, universals), and abstractions in a field (principles, generalizations, theories, and structures).

(b) Comprehension:
  (i) Translation: the known concept or message is put in different words or changed from one kind of symbol to another.
  (ii) Interpretation: a student can go beyond recognizing the separate parts of a communication and see the interrelations among the parts.
  (iii) Extrapolation: the receiver of a communication is expected to go beyond the literal communication itself and make inferences about consequences or perceptibly extend the time dimensions, the sample, or the topic.

(c) Application: use of abstractions in particular and concrete situations. The abstractions may be in the form of general ideas, rules of procedure, or generalized methods. The abstractions may also be technical principles, ideas, and theories which must be remembered and applied.

(d) Analysis: breakdown of a communication into its constituent elements or parts such that the relative hierarchy of ideas is made clear and/or the relations between the ideas expressed are made explicit. One can analyse elements, relationships, organizational principles.

(e) Synthesis: the putting together of elements and parts so as to form a whole. This involves arranging and combining in such a way as to constitute a pattern of structure not clearly there before.

(f) Evaluation: evaluation is defined as the making of judgments about the value of ideas, works, solutions, methods, material, and so on. Judgments can be in terms of internal evidence (logical accuracy and consistency) or external criteria (comparison with standards, rules . . .).

The content validity of the taxonomy is not considered as perfect by any author but, in general, they are satisfied with it: taken as a whole, it allows nearly all the cognitive objectives of education to be classified. Nevertheless, the taxonomical hierarchy is questionable and the category system is heterogeneous. De Corte (1973) has pointed out that the subcategories used are not always based on the same classification principle. He writes: "For knowledge, analysis and synthesis, the subcategories correspond to a difficulty scale of products resulting from cognitive operations. For comprehension, the subdivisions are specifications of operations and not of their products. For evaluation, the subcategories depend on the nature of the criteria chosen to formulate a judgment."

Gagné (1964) has also pointed out that some categories or subcategories only differ in their content and not by formal characteristics which affect their conditions of learning.

According to Cox (De Corte 1973), the agreement on classification among the users of the taxonomy ranges from 0.63 to 0.85. The lack of reliability must come from the vagueness of the concepts for which the authors of the taxonomy propose essential rather than operational definitions.

The taxonomy has been elaborated for evaluation purposes. It has also been very useful in developing blueprints for curriculum development. It helped in identifying and formulating objectives, and, as a consequence, in structuring the material and specifying assessment procedures.

When developing a test for a particular curriculum, the curriculum often only presents a theme (Bacher 1973). No indication is given about which behaviours of the theme are to be tested. The test constructor is left to guess about which behaviours are to be tested. Furthermore, the taxonomy of objectives movement could signal a renaissance of nineteenth-century faculty psychology. Instead of training separate mental faculties such as memory, imagination, etc., one could artificially cultivate memory (knowledge in Bloom), application, analysis, synthesis, judgment, aptitudes.

Several authors are of the opinion that the taxonomy pays too much attention to knowledge, and not enough to higher mental processes.

It is not possible to use the taxonomy without reference to the behavioural background of the individual. There is an obvious difference between the individual who solves a specific problem for the first time and the individual who has met the same problem before. In both cases, however, the answer can be the same.

To test the validity of the hierarchical structure of the taxonomy, Madaus and his associates developed a quantitative causal model (see Fig. 1) to reveal not only the proportion of variance at each level explained directly by the preceding adjacent level, but also any proportion of variance explained indirectly by nonadjacent levels. The statistical techniques used were principal components analysis to identify the role of a factor of general ability g, and multiple regression analysis to measure the links between taxonomic levels. Hill (1984) has employed maximum likelihood estimation procedures, using LISREL, to list the hierarchical assumptions of the

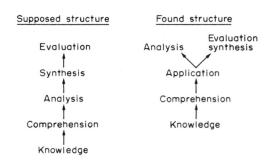

Figure 1
Schematic representation of an hypothesized perfect hierarchy and of the hierarchical structure found by Madaus et al. 1973

Bloom taxonomy, and has provided important evidence to support a hierarchical structure between the five higher-order categories.

In a pure hierarchy, there must be a direct link between adjacent levels and only between these two. As one proceeds from the lower to the higher levels in Bloom's taxonomy, the strength of the direct links between adjacent levels decreases and many links between nonadjacent levels appear. Knowledge, comprehension, and application are well-hierarchized. Higher up in the hierarchy, a branching takes place. On one side, analysis is found (even if the *g* factor is taken into account, analysis entertains an indirect link with comprehension). It is what Ebel (1973) calls the stage of content mastery. On the other side, synthesis and evaluation are found; they are differentiated clearly from the rest in that they are highly saturated in the *g* factor. This dependence increases if the material is not well-known to the students, or is very difficult, or if the lower processes have not been sufficiently mastered to contribute significantly to the production of higher level behaviours.

Horn (1972) suggested an algorithm to classify objectives along Bloom's taxonomy. He notes that in lower mental processes, objectives content and problem cannot be separated. For instance, for the objective: "The student will be able to list the parts of a plant", there is no problem. The answer will be possible only if the student has it "ready made" in his or her memory. For higher mental processes, the problem is general, and can be formulated without reference to a specific content.

To quasioperationalize Bloom's taxonomy, Horn takes the level of complexity of the problem posed as a classification criterion. At each level, he considers the formal aspect and the content. Figure 2 presents Horn's algorithm.

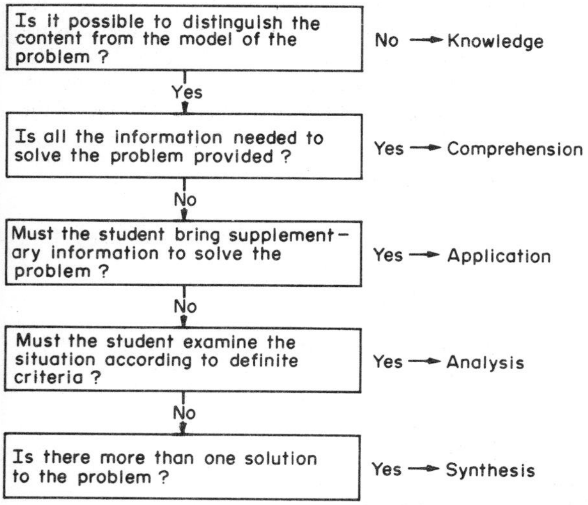

Using Horn's algorithm, well-trained judges can reach a high interreliability in their classification of objectives.

Bloom's taxonomy is formulated in an abstract way. To help the users apply the taxonomy properly, Metfessel et al. (1970) suggested a list of verbs and a list of objects which, appropriately combined, give the framework for an operational objective at the different taxonomic levels.

Bloom is aware of the limits of the instrument to whose development he has contributed. What really matters to Bloom is that educators question as often as possible whether they have varied the cognitive level of the tasks, exercises, and examinations they propose, whether they stimulate their students sufficiently, and whether they really help them develop.

1.2 Guilford's Structure of Intellect Model

To organize intellectual factors, identified by factor analysis or simply hypothesized, Guilford (1967) designed a structure of intellect (SI) model (see Fig. 3). This model was essentially conceived to serve the heuristic function of generating hypotheses regarding new factors of intelligence. The placement of any intellectual factor within this nonhierarchical model is determined by its three unique properties: its operation, its content, and its product.

Content categories are:

(a) Figural: figural information covers visual, auditive, and kinesthesic sense.

(b) Symbolic: signs that can be used to stand for something else.

(c) Semantic: the verbal factor.

(d) Behavioural: behavioural content is defined as information, essentially nonverbal, involved in

Figure 2
Horn's algorithm

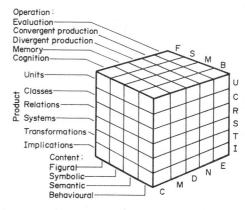

Figure 3
Guilford's Structure of Intellect Model

human interactions, where awareness or attention, perceptions, thoughts, desires, feelings, moods, emotions, intentions, and actions of other persons and of ourselves are important.

Operation categories are:

(a) Cognition: awareness, immediate discovery or rediscovery, or recognition of information in various forms; comprehension or understanding.

(b) Memory: retention or storage, with some degree of availability, of information in the same form in which it was committed to storage, and in connection with the same cues with which it was learned.

(c) Divergent production: the generation of information from given information where the emphasis is upon variety and quantity of output from the same source; this category is likely to involve transfer.

(d) Convergent production: the area of logical productions or at least the area of compelling inferences. The input information is sufficient to determine a unique answer.

(e) Evaluation: the process of comparing a product of information with known information according to logical criteria, and reaching a decision concerning criterion satisfaction.

Product categories are:

(a) Units: relatively segregated or circumscribed items of information having "thing" character.

(b) Classes: recognized sets of items grouped by virtue of their common properties.

(c) Relations: recognized connections between two items of information based upon variables or upon points of contact that apply to them.

(d) Systems: organized or structured aggregates of items of information, a complex of interrelated or interacting parts.

(e) Transformations: changes of various kinds, of existing or known information in its attributes, meaning, role, or use.

(f) Implications: expectancies, anticipations, and predictions, the fact that one item of information leads naturally to another.

Each cell of Guilford's model represents a factor that is a unique combination of operation, content, and product. For instance, cell 1 (see Fig. 3) represents cognition of figural units.

Can Guilford's model be utilized to formulate or at least to generate objectives? First of all, it can be noted that the three dimensions of the model are hierarchical at least to a certain extent. Furthermore, Guilford has discussed the implications of his model for education. He thinks that it indicates clearly the kinds of exercises

that must be applied to develop intellectual abilities. He remarks, in particular, that school, in general, over-emphasizes cognition and the memorization of semantic units. It is important, says Guilford, to apply oneself much more to the exercise of the other products: classes, relations, systems, transformations, and implications.

The fact that Guilford compares his model to Bloom's taxonomy and acknowledges important similarities between both of them seems to confirm that Guilford does not exclude the possibility that his model may be used to generate and classify objectives.

Guilford's model can absorb Bloom's whole cognitive taxonomy (see Fig. 4). By its greater precision, the SI model may allow easier operationalization and, more generally, may offer greater taxonomic possibilities.

De Corte (1973) has adapted and transformed Guilford's model. The four dimensions of De Corte's general model of classification are: (a) the subject matter of specific content of a given universe of objectives; (b) the domain of information to which the subject matter belongs (content in Guilford's model); (c) the product: the objectives are classified with respect to the formal aspect of the information they produce (products in Guilford's model); (d) the operation is defined as in Guilford's model.

De Corte focuses on this fourth category and develops Guilford's five operations into a seven category system.

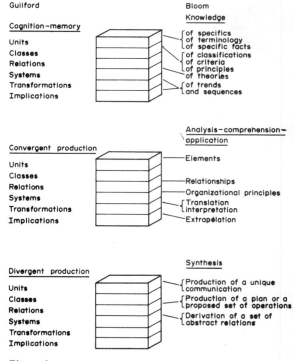

Figure 4
Parallelism between Guilford's model and Bloom's cognitive taxonomy

Cognition comprises receiving–reproducing operations: (a) perception of information; (b) recall of information; (c) reproduction of information and productive operations; (d) interpretative production of information; (e) convergent production of information; (f) evaluative production of information; (g) divergent production of information.

De Corte's system is of interest in that it develops Guilford's model in such a manner that it becomes a practical tool for the definition of the cognitive objectives of education. It seems to indicate how Bloom and Guilford's contributions could be integrated and be of use to education.

1.3 The Gagné–Merrill Taxonomy

Gagné proposes a hierarchy of processes needed to achieve the learning tasks assigned by objectives. Merrill designates the behaviour and psychological condition under which learning can be observed.

With Gagné's learning conditions, the push-down principle constitutes the basis of the Gagné–Merrill taxonomy. In the process of development, a person acquires behaviour at the lower levels before acquiring behaviour at the higher levels. Later, the conscious cognitive demand on the learner increases. Learners have an innate tendency to reduce the cognitive load as much as possible; consequently, a learner will attempt to perform a given response at the lowest possible level. The push-down principle states that a behaviour acquired at one level will be pushed down to a lower level as soon as conditions have changed sufficiently so that the learner is able to respond to the stimulus using lower level behaviour. It is rather surprising that this important principle is often neglected or even ignored in the literature related to the taxonomies of educational objectives.

The Gagné–Merrill taxonomy is an original formulation, integrating the affective, psychomotor, and cognitive domains.

The following is a condensed version of Merrill's presentation:

(a) *Emotional behaviour (signal learning)*. In the presence of every stimulus situation, students involuntarily react with physiological changes which they perceive as feelings. The direction (positive or negative) and the relative magnitude of this emotional behaviour can be inferred by observing the students' approach/avoidance responses in unrestrained choice situations.

(b) *Psychomotor behaviour*. A student is able to execute rapidly, without external prompting, a specified neuromuscular reaction in the presence of a specific stimulus situation. The observable behaviour is an overt skeletal–muscular response which occurs in entirety without hesitation. Psychological conditions of importance are the presence of a specific cue and the absence of prompts. Psychomotor behaviour may be further broken down into three constituent behaviours.

First, topographic behaviour (stimulus response) is where a student is able to execute rapidly without external prompting, a single new neuromuscular reaction in the presence of a particular stimulus cue. This can be observed as a muscular movement or combination of movements not previously in the student's repertoire. The important psychological conditions are the presence of a specific cue and the absence of prompts.

Second, chaining behaviour, where a student is able to execute, without external prompting, a coordinated series of reactions which occur in rapid succession in the presence of a particular stimulus cue, is observed as a series of responses, and occurs in the presence of a specified cue and in the absence of prompts.

Third, skilled behaviour is where a student is able to execute sequentially, without external prompting, complex combinations of coordinated psychomotor chains, each initiated in the presence of a particular cue when a large set of such cues are presented. In some skills, cue presentation is externally paced while in other skills cue presentation is self-paced. This is seen as a set of coordinated chains, and occurs when there is a paced or unpaced presentation of a set of cues and an absence of prompts prior to or during the performance.

(c) *Memorization behaviour*. A student immediately reproduces or recognizes, without prompting, a specific symbolic response when presented with a specific stimulus situation. The observable behaviour always involves either reproduction or recognition of a symbolic response, and occurs under psychological conditions similar to those of psychomotor behaviour. Memorization behaviour can be broken into naming behaviour where a student reproduces or recognizes, without prompts, a single symbolic response in the presence of a particular stimulus cue; serial memorization behaviour (verbal association) which occurs in the presence of a particular stimulus cue, so that a student reproduces, without prompting, a series of symbolic responses in a prespecified sequence; and discrete element memorization behaviour (multiple discrimination) where a student reproduces or recognizes, without prompting, a unique symbolic response to each of a set of stimulus cues.

(d) *Complex cognitive behaviour*. The student makes an appropriate response to a previously unencountered instance of some class of stimulus objects, events, or situations. This can further be broken into classification behaviour, analysis behaviour, and problem-solving behaviour.

Classification behaviour (concept learning) is where a student is able to identify correctly the class membership of a previously unencountered object or event, or a previously unencountered representation of some object or event. It occurs when the student must make some kind of class identification, the important psychological conditions being the presentation of unencountered instances or non-instances.

Analysis behaviour (principle learning) is when a student is able to show the relationship between the component concepts of an unencountered situation in which a given principle is specified as relevant. The student must first identify the instances of the several classes involved in the situation and then show the relationship between these classes. The psychological condition of importance is presentation of a situation which the student has not previously analysed or seen analysed.

Problem-solving behaviour is when a student is able to select relevant principles and sequence them into an effective solution strategy when presented with an unencountered problem situation for which the relevant principles are not specified. Creativity and/or divergent thinking occurs when some of the relevant principles are unknown to the student and the strategy developed represents a new higher order principle. It can be observed when the student must synthesize a product which results from analysing several principles in some appropriate sequence and generalize new relationships not previously learned or analysed. The psychological conditions of importance are: an unencountered problem for which the relevant principles are not specified, and which in some cases may require principles not previously analysed by the student or perhaps even by the instructor.

Without any doubt, Gagné–Merrill's taxonomy provides some order in the field of fundamental learning processes. However, it does not claim exhaustivity, and certain categories such as "process learning" and "problem solving" are rather vague.

D'Hainaut (1970) believes that Gagné does not give enough emphasis to the creative processes. Divergent thinking can be categorized under the heading "problem solving", but this category is perhaps too large.

Merrill and Gagné have made two important contributions to the definition of objectives. Their categories are expressed in terms of definite behaviour and the psychological conditions are considered, although these conditions are still to be integrated into an operational definition of objectives.

1.4 Gerlach and Sullivan's Taxonomy

Sullivan in association with Gerlach (1967) attempted to replace a description of mental processes in general terms (as in Bloom's taxonomy) by classes of observable learner behaviours which could be used in task description and analysis. Their model is empirical. After listing hundreds of learning behaviours, Sullivan has progressively grouped them into six categories, each headed by a typical verb. The six categories are ordered according to the increasing complexity of behaviours they represent, but the whole does not constitute a rigorous hierarchy and, for that reason, cannot be considered as a true taxonomy.

(a) Identify: the learner indicates membership or non-membership of specified objects or events in a class when the name of the class is given.

(b) Name: the learner supplies the correct verbal label (in speech or writing) for a referent or set of referents when the name of the referent is not given.

(c) Describe: the learner reports the necessary categories of object properties, events, event properties, and/or relationships relevant to a designated referent.

(d) Construct: the learner produces a product which meets specifications given either in class or in the test item itself.

(e) Order: the learner arranges two or more referents in a specified order.

(f) Demonstrate: the learner performs the behaviours essential to the accomplishment of a designated task according to pre-established or given specifications.

Gerlach and Sullivan consider their "taxonomy" as a check list helping to ensure that no important behaviour is forgotten when planning school activities. This may succeed, as long as "mastery objectives" (i.e., objectives concerning a fully defined behaviour universe) are kept in sight. However, the six categories suggested do not cover creative productions and do not even make a clear place for transfer.

1.5 De Block's Taxonomy

De Block (1975) suggests a model of teaching objectives (see Fig. 5). He thinks that teaching pursues objectives in three directions: (a) from partial to more integral learning. Comprehension seems more desirable than rote learning (knowledge); in this perspective, mastery and integration are final objectives; (b) from limited to fundamental learning. Facts gradually become background data; concepts and methods come to the fore; (c) from special to general learning. The objective is thinking in a productive rather than in a reproductive way, taking initiatives, and being able to adapt oneself to a great variety of situations.

The combination of all subcategories yields 72 classes of objectives. De Block's system does not deal suf-

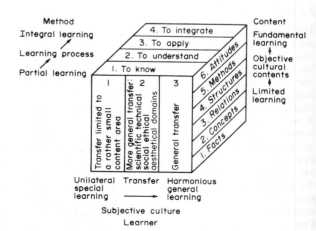

Figure 5
De Block's model of instruction

iciently with the criteria by which it is recognized whether an objective has been achieved or not. However, it can certainly help teachers to reconsider their activities, and to make their students work at higher cognitive or affective levels.

1.6 Conclusion to the Cognitive Domain

Not one of these taxonomies can be considered as entirely satisfying. Looking at highly nuanced classifications, only moderate reliability can be hoped for. If the system is reduced to a few operationalized categories, content validity decreases.

The taxonomy of Bloom and his associates has already been used successfully by hundreds of curriculum and test developers throughout the world. Furthermore, it has stimulated fruitful discussion and reflection on the problem of objectives. The several taxonomies that appeared after Bloom are useful to curriculum developers, to test constructors, and to teachers planning their next lesson and preparing mastery tests for their pupils.

2. The Affective Domain

According to Bloom, the affective domain includes objectives which describe changes in interest, attitudes, and values, and the development of appreciations and adequate adjustment.

What are the main difficulties in the pursuit of affective objectives? Imprecision of concepts, overlap of the affective and the cognitive domains, cultural bias (Western culture still tends to consider feelings as the most secret part of personality), ignorance about affective learning processes, and poor evaluation instruments.

So far, the only significant taxonomy for the affective domain is the one published by Krathwohl et al. (1964), hence the brevity of this section when compared to the first.

2.1 Krathwohl's Taxonomy

The main organizing principles for the cognitive domain were "from simple to complex" and "from concrete to abstract". It soon appeared that these could not be used for the affective domain which dealt with attitudes, interests, values, and so on. After a long search, the authors discovered an ordering principle that was precisely characteristic of affective development: the degree of internalization, that is, the degree of incorporation of the affects within the personality. When the process of internalization is completed, the person feels as if the interests, values, attitudes, etc. were his or her own and lives by them. In Krathwohl's taxonomic terms, the continuum goes from merely being aware that a given phenomenon exists, and giving it a minimum attention, to its becoming one's basic outlook on life. The main organizing principles in Krathwohl's taxonomy are receiving, responding, valuing, organization, and characteristics.

(a) Receiving: "Sensitivity to the existence of certain phenomena and stimuli, that is, the willingness to receive or attend to them." Receiving consists of three subcategories that represent a continuum: (i) awareness; (ii) willingness to receive; and (iii) controlled or selected attention.

(b) Responding: "Behaviour which goes beyond merely attending to the phenomena; it implies active attending, doing something with or about the phenomena, and not merely perceiving them." Subcategories of responding are: (i) acquiescence in responding; (ii) willingness to respond; and (iii) satisfaction in response.

(c) Valuing: "It implies perceiving phenomena as having worth and consequently revealing consistency in behaviour related to these phenomena." The individual is motivated to behave in the line of definite values. Subcategories are: (i) acceptance of a value; (ii) preference for a value; and (iii) commitment.

(d) Organization: "For situations where more than one value is relevant, the necessity arises for (i) the organization of the values into a system; (ii) the determination of the interrelationships among them; and (iii) the establishment of the dominant and pervasive one." Subcategories are: (i) conceptualization of a value and (ii) organization of a value system.

(e) Characteristics by a value or value complex: "The values already have a place in the individual's value hierarchy, are organized into some kind of internally consistent system, have controlled the behaviour of the individual for a sufficient time that he has adapted to behaving in this way." Subcategories are: (i) generalized set and (ii) characterization.

The most striking feature of this taxonomy is its abstract, general character. Krathwohl is aware of the problem. The taxonomy deals with objectives at the curriculum construction level. This means that objectives as defined in the taxonomy are approximately midway between very broad and very general objectives of education and the specific ones which provide guidance for the development of step-by-step learning experiences.

For a short presentation of Krathwohl's taxonomy, G. De Landsheere (1982) tried to find a classification principle that would be easier to formulate in behavioural terms than internalization. He suggested a continuum of activity, or of personal engagement. De Landsheere's frame of reference was developmental psychology. He wrote: "An individual has really reached the adult stage if his behaviour has found its coherence, its logic and stability; he has developed at the same time a sound tolerance to change, contradiction, frustration; he is cognitively and affectively independent; he is, at the same time, able to abide by his engagement and feelings." Education is a long process leading to this ultimate balance.

De Landsheere suggests the following taxonomy:

(a) *The individual responds to external stimulation.*

(i) The individual receives: this is a rather amorphous stage. The individual encounters, for instance, beauty or ugliness without any reaction, like a mirror that would not reflect any image. This behaviour is hard to distinguish from the cognition (in Guilford's sense) that takes place before memorization. Only some manifestation of attention is observable.

(ii) The individual receives and responds to the stimulus: an observable reaction takes place. The individual obeys, manifests pleasure by his or her words or attitudes. At this stage, there is not yet explicit acceptance or rejection that would reflect a deliberate choice.

(iii) The individual receives and reacts by accepting or refusing: now the individual knows what he or she wants or likes, provided things or events are presented.

(b) *The individual takes initiatives.* The individual tries spontaneously to understand, to feel, and then act according to the options available. Here the adult stage is reached. For instance, the individual lives a life in accordance with his or her values, feelings, beliefs, likings, but is also able to change his or her mind if convincing proofs or arguments are offered. This stage is parallel to evaluation in the cognitive domain.

The classification suggested by De Landsheere seems clearer than Krathwohl's taxonomy, but more limited. Objectives can be more easily operationalized, but the criticism of Krathwohl's work also applies here.

2.2 Conclusion to the Affective Domain

The situation in the affective domain remains unsatisfactory. Why does it appear that so much work is still to be undertaken in the field? Krathwohl has not succeeded in filling completely the gap in the theoretical framework and the methodology of educational evaluation in the affective domain. A more systematic attack on the problem of affective objectives is required, and, in particular, an inventory of existing studies, experiments, and evaluation instruments in the field should be undertaken. Indubitably, the affective domain will constitute a priority area in the field of educational research in the decades to come.

3. The Psychomotor Domain

Why is the psychomotor domain important? First of all, motion is a necessary condition of survival and of independence. Life sometimes depends on physical strength correctly applied, on agility, and on rapidity. Locomotor behaviour is needed to explore the environment and sensory-motor activities are essential for the development of intelligence. Some psychomotor behaviours such as walking and grasping, are also necessary for physical and mental health to be maintained. Dexterity is crucial for the worker, and also in civilizations giving a lot of time to leisure, corporal ability plays a considerable role in artistic and athletic activities.

Numerous taxonomies have been developed for the psychomotor domain. Some of them tend to be comprehensive, in strict parallelism with the taxonomies inspired by Bloom and Krathwohl for the cognitive and affective domains. Others have been developed for specialized fields and have, in many cases, a very technical character. Only six taxonomies which fall in the first category are presented in this article.

Ragsdale, Guilford, Dave, and Kibler's taxonomies are summarized very briefly for they are mainly of historical interest.

3.1 Ragsdale's Taxonomy

As early as in 1950, Ragsdale published a classification for "motor types of activities" learned by children. He worked with three categories only: (a) object motor activities (speed, precision): manipulation or acting with direct reference to an object; (b) language motor activities: movement of speech, sight, handwriting; (c) feeling motor activities: movements communicating feelings and attitudes.

These categories are so general that they are of little help in the definition of educational objectives.

3.2 Guilford's Taxonomy

Guilford (1958) suggested a simple classification in seven categories that is not hierarchical, and also does not seem of great utility for generating objectives. The seven categories are: power, pressure, speed, static precision, dynamic precision, coordination, and flexibility.

3.3 Dave's Taxonomy

Dave's classification (1969), although also rather schematic, can be considered as an embryo of a taxonomy. The categories are: initiation, manipulation, precision, articulation, naturalization (mechanization and internalization). The meaning of the first three categories is clear. Articulation emphasizes the coordination of a series of acts which are performed with appropriate articulation in terms of time, speed, and other relevant variables. As for naturalization, it refers to the highest level of proficiency of an act that has become routine.

3.4 Kibler's Classification

Kibler and his associates suggest a classification (1970) more developed than that of previous authors. The main frame of reference is developmental child psychology.

(a) Gross bodily movements: movements of entire limbs in isolation or in conjunction with other parts of the body (movements involving the upper limbs, the lower limbs, two or more bodily units).

(b) Finely coordinated movements: coordinated movements of the extremities, used in conjunction with the eye or ear (hand–finger movements, hand–eye coordination, hand–ear coordination, hand–eye–foot coordination, other combinations of hand–foot–eye–ear movements).

(c) Nonverbal communication behaviours: facial expression, gestures (use of hands and arms to communicate specific messages), bodily movements (total bodily movements whose primary purposes are the communication of a message or series of messages).

(d) Speech behaviours: sound production (ability to produce meaningful sounds), sound–word formation (ability to coordinate sounds in meaningful words and messages), sound projection (ability to project sounds across the air waves at a level adequate for reception and decoding by the listener), sound–gesture coordination (ability to coordinate facial expression, movement, and gestures with verbal messages).

3.5 *Simpson's Taxonomy (1966)*

Simpson's taxonomy can be divided into five main categories.
(a) *Perception*. This is the process of becoming aware of objects, qualities, or relations by way of the sense organs.

(i) Sensory stimulation: impingement of a stimulus upon one or more of the sense organs (auditory, visual, tactile, taste, smell, kinesthesic).

(ii) Cue-selection: deciding to what cues one must respond in order to satisfy the particular requirements of task performance, for example, recognition of operating difficulties with machinery through the sound of the machine in operation.

(iii) Translation: relation of perception of action in performing a motor act. This is the mental process of determining the meaning of the cues received for action, for example, the ability to relate music to dance form.

(b) *Set*. Preparatory adjustment of readiness for a particular kind of action or experience.

(i) Mental set: readiness, in the mental sense, to perform a certain motor act.

(ii) Physical set: readiness in the sense of having made the anatomical adjustments necessary for a motor act to be performed.

(iii) Emotional set: readiness in terms of attitudes favourable to the motor act's taking place.

(c) *Guided response*. Overt behavioural act of an individual under the guidance of the instructor (imitation, trial and error).

(d) *Mechanism*. Learned response became habitual.

(e) *Complex overt response*. The individual can perform a motor act that is considered complex because of the movement pattern required. A high degree of skill has been attained. The act can be carried out smoothly and efficiently.

(i) Resolution of uncertainty: the act is performed without hesitation.

(ii) Automatic performance: the individual can perform a finely coordinated motor skill with a great deal of ease and muscle control.

Simpson suggests that there is perhaps a sixth major category: adapting and originating. "At this level, the individual might originate new patterns of actions in solving a specific problem."

The weakness of this taxonomy is to be found again in its very abstract and general formulation.

3.6 *Harrow's Taxonomy*

As operationally defined by Harrow (1972), the term "psychomotor" covers any human voluntary observable movement that belongs to the domain of learning. Harrow's taxonomy is the best available for the psychomotor domain, although some of the category descriptives are unsatisfactory:

(a) Reflex movements: segmental, intersegmental, suprasegmental reflexes.

(b) Basic–fundamental movements: locomotor, non-locomotor, manipulative movements.

(c) Perceptual abilities:
Kinesthetic discrimination: body awareness (bilaterality, laterality, sidedness, balance), body image, body relationship of surrounding objects in space.
Visual discrimination: visual acuity, visual tracking, visual memory, figure–ground differentiation, perceptual consistency.
Auditory discrimination: auditory acuity, tracking, memory.
Tactile discrimination.
Coordinated abilities: eye–hand and eye–foot coordination.

(d) Physical abilities: endurance (muscular and cardiovascular endurance), strength, flexibility, agility (change direction, stops and starts, reaction–response time, dexterity).

(e) Skilled movements: simple adaptive skill (beginner, intermediate, advanced, highly skilled), compound adaptive skill (beginner, intermediate, advanced, highly skilled), complex adaptive skill (beginner, intermediate, advanced, highly skilled).

(f) Nondiscursive communication: expressive movement (posture and carriage, gestures, facial expression), interpretative movement (aesthetic movement, creative movement).

In fact, Harrow does not describe her model in relation to a general, unique criterion (i.e. co-ordination), but simply looks for a critical order; mastery at an inferior level is absolutely necessary to achieve the immediate higher level in the hierarchy of movements.

This taxonomy has great qualities. First, it seems complete, not only it its description of the major categories of psychomotor behaviour, but also in terms of the subcategories within the different taxonomic levels. Furthermore, the author defines the different levels clearly. For each subcategory, she proposes a clear definition of the concept and indicates, where necessary, the differences from other authors who have written in this field. She also presents concrete examples.

Harrow's taxonomy seems to be of direct use to teachers in physical education. Level (c) is specially interesting for preschool and for elementary-school teachers. It contains a good example of a battery for testing the perceptive abilities of pupils, diagnosing difficulties, and proposing appropriate remedial exercises. The author underlines the dependence between the cognitive and psychomotor domains at the level of perceptual abilities. Several examples also show the great interrelation between the three domains. However, Harrow's hierarchy is not governed by a specified criterion, such as internalization or coordination. Moreover, the subcategories are not mutually exclusive.

3.7 Conclusion to the Psychomotor Domain

It seems that taxonomies in the psychomotor domain have not yet been given the attention they deserve. They should be tried in many varied situations and their relations with the other two domains should be carefully investigated.

4. Conclusion

The cognitive domain is the best developed. First, it is by nature favourable to the construction of logical models. Second, schools have traditionally been interested in cognitive learning, especially in the acquisition of factual knowledge which in turn leads to easy evaluation.

Compared with the cognitive domain, the affective domain is less developed. Only since about 1970 has the educational world been trying to change the situation (in the past, affectivity has sometimes been intensively cultivated, but nearly always in terms of indoctrination processes). Affects seem less observable than cognitive activities and in most cases are less susceptible to rigorous measurement.

One would think that the psychomotor domain would present fewer difficulties, but little systematic work has been undertaken. In most Western educational systems,

physical and artistic education is comparatively neglected in the curriculum.

Despite certain weaknesses, the two taxonomies with which Bloom is associated, and Harrow's taxonomy dominate the field. The others should, however, not be neglected, since they supply further clarifications and suggestions.

At present, the taxonomy movement in education is of great value. Even though the instruments are so far imperfect, they stimulate educators to fruitful reflection. Half-way between the great ideological options and the micro-objectives, the taxonomies seem to relate philosophy and educational technology and practice. It is one of their great merits.

Bibliography

Bacher F 1973 La docimologie. In: Reuchlin M (ed.) 1973 *Traité de psychologie appliquée*. Presses Universitaires de France (PUF), Paris

Bloom B S (ed.) 1956 *Taxonomy of Educational Objectives: The Classification of Educational Goals*, Handbook 1: *Cognitive Domain*. McKay, New York

Dave R H 1969 *Taxonomy of Educational Objectives and Achievement Testing. Developments in Educational Testing*, Vol. 1. University of London Press, London

De Block A 1975 *Taxonomie van Leerdoelen*. Standard Wetenschappelijke Uitgererij, Amsterdam

De Corte E 1973 *Onderwijsdoelstellingen*. Universitaire Pers, Louvain

De Landsheere G 1982 *Introduction à la recherche en éducation*. Thone, Liège; Armand Colin, Paris

De Landsheere V, De Landsheere G 1984 *Définir les objectifs de l'éducation*. Presses Universitaires de France (PUF), Paris

D'Hainaut L 1970 Un modèle pour la détermination et la sélection des objectifs pédagogiques du domaine cognitif. *Enseignement Programmé* 11: 21–38

Ebel R L 1973 Evaluation and educational objectives. *J. Educ. Meas.* 10: 273–79

Gagné R M 1964 The implications of instructional objectives for learning. In: Lindvall C M (ed.) 1964 *Defining Educational Objectives*. University of Pittsburgh Press, Pittsburgh, Pennsylvania

Gerlach V, Sullivan A 1967 *Constructing Statements of Outcomes*. Southwest Regional Laboratory for Educational Research and Development, Inglewood, California

Guilford J P 1958 A system of psychomotor abilities. *Am. J. Psychol.* 71: 164–74

Guilford J P 1967 *The Nature of Human Intelligence*. McKay, New York

Harrow A J 1972 *A Taxonomy of the Psychomotor Domain: A Guide for Developing Behavioral Objectives*. McKay, New York

Hill P W 1984 Testing hierarchy in educational taxonomies: A theoretical and empirical investigation. *Eval. Educ.* 8: 181–278

Horn R 1972 *Lernziele und Schülerleistung: Die Evaluation von den Lernzielen im kognitiven Bereich*, 2nd edn. Beltz, Weinheim

Kibler R J, Barker L L, Miles D T 1970 *Behavioral Objectives and Instruction*. Allyn and Bacon, Boston, Massachusetts

Krathwohl D R, Bloom B S, Masia B B 1964 *Taxonomy of Educational Objectives: The Classification of Educational Goals*, Handbook 2: *Affective Domain*. McKay, New York

Madaus G F, Woods E N, Nuttal R L 1973 A causal model analysis of Bloom's taxonomy. *Am. Educ. Res. J.* 10: 253–62

Merrill M D 1971 Necessary psychological conditions for defining instructional outcomes. In: M D Merrill (ed.) 1971 *Instructional Design: Readings.* Prentice-Hall, Englewood Cliffs, New Jersey

Metfessel N S, Michael W B, Kirsner D A 1970 Instrumentation of Bloom's and Krathwohl's taxonomies for the writing of educational objectives. In: Kibler R J, Barker L L, Miles D J (eds.) 1970 *Behavioural Objectives and Instruction.* Allyn and Bacon, Boston, Massachusetts

Ragsdale C E 1950 How children learn motor types of activities. *Learning and Instruction.* 49th Yearbook of the National Society for the Study of Education, Washington, DC

Simpson E J 1966 *The Classification of Educational Objectives, Psychomotor Domain.* University of Illinois, Urbana, Illinois

Selecting Educational Objectives

M. R. Eraut

It is not uncommon for the problem of selecting and justifying objectives to be concealed by the simple declaration that objectives are derived from aims. Since statements of aims and statements of objectives are usually produced for different purposes and different audiences, it would be naive to expect total consistency between the two. Moreover, the claim that objectives are simply derived from aims diverts attention from three critical issues with which curriculum developers have to contend. First, aims are not the only possible source of objective. In theory there is no limit to the number of places where people may find ideas for objectives. In practice, existing curriculum traditions probably serve as the major source. Second, there are no generally agreed or universally applicable procedures for deducing objectives from aims (Hirst 1973). Third, while aims may be used to justify the educational value of a particular objective, they often cannot determine the relative value of two alternative or competing sets of objectives, each of which appear consistent with the aims.

This article confines itself to three questions:

(a) What are the sources of objectives? From where can people get ideas for objectives they wish to consider for inclusion?

(b) How might the inclusion of an objective be justified?

(c) What guidance is available for tackling the problem of priorities?

1. Sources of Objectives

Hirst (1973) criticizes Tyler and others for failing to distinguish the sources of curriculum objectives from the grounds for their justification. The most frequently used sources are not Tyler's (1949) primary sources—the learners, contemporary life, subject specialisms, or even the philosophy of education—but secondary sources such as current practices and well-known curriculum traditions. So the process of formulating objectives is likely to be one of selecting goals from these practices and traditions and translating them into an appropriate linguistic form. Consultations with educators, parents, students, and the local community often provide useful information on preferences but seldom suggest any newer types of objective. However, there are occasional deliberate attempts to look beyond current practice and traditions; and some of these have had considerable impact. The curriculum reform movement of the 1960s sought to bring the curriculum into line with new views of academic knowledge by enlisting the support of eminent scholars. The planning of vocational courses seeks to reflect the changing structure of the job market. Social education is altered to include new conceptions of adult roles—that of women, for example. Even the curriculum traditions themselves get reconstructed and reconceptualized by great thinkers like Bruner and Freire. These occasions for fundamental curriculum change are fewer than many would like; and the rethinking of the curriculum is a worthy candidate for financial support. But it is also important to recognize when such rethinking is not taking place, so that tradition-based curriculum development is not hampered by the mistaken idea that all objectives have to be derived from primary sources—a task whose difficulty and complexity will be apparent from the ensuing discussion.

Many curriculum practices and traditions leave their objectives unstated and implicit, but there have also been many attempts to translate them into the language of objectives or to develop new courses with an objective-based approach. Hence there are many well-documented lists of objectives that can be used as secondary sources. Short subject-specific lists may be found in official curriculum documents, in textbooks, in examination syllabi, and in books on subject teaching. Longer lists may be found in the teaching manuals of individualized programmes, in the massive compilations of objectives prepared under the auspices of the Russell Sage Foundation (Kearney 1953, French et al. 1957) and in the Instructional Objectives Exchange (Popham 1974). Using such secondary sources has three problems. They are variable in quality, their contextual or cultural specificity may not be immediately apparent, and selection from lists is likely to lead to a fragmented curriculum. These problems would be significantly reduced if such lists were used not as main sources but as supplementary sources after the first attempt at objective formulation had already been completed.

2. The Justification of Objectives

Leaving aside technical considerations such as clarity, the justification of an objective is based on two kinds of argument—feasibility and desirability (Bloom et al. 1981). Both are necessary. Feasibility arguments are normally based on evidence from practice, and they are often dependent on there being sufficient similarity of student population and interest for the transfer of experience to be valid. The criteria will be much tighter when mastery is being sought than when the objectives are of a more expressive variety; but even in the latter case it will still have to be argued that something of value is likely to occur. While feasibility arguments should not be used to prevent intelligent experiments, there is an equal danger that experiments will be treated as if they were bound to succeed.

Desirability arguments are of two main kinds: evidence of expressed preferences and arguments from basic values—the former concerns who thinks an objective is desirable, the latter concerns why it should be thought desirable. Techniques for collecting expressed preferences have been reviewed by Stake (1970), and their usefulness for selection is discussed below. The procedure is commonly referred to as needs assessment, but this designation is misleading because it takes an argument from basic values to establish that a preference is also a need. Pratt (1980) provides a useful summary of the issues involved in justification.

What, then, are the basic values on which arguments for the desirability or worthwhileness of an objective can rest? Combining a number of authors' suggestions gives four major categories in which such values may be said to reside—occupational practice, roles in society, cultural and academic knowledge, and the interests of the learners. Objectives relating to occupational practice can be justified in terms of national manpower needs, in terms of local needs for particular kinds of knowledge and skills, or an individual's need to be able to work with application. Sometimes these needs come into conflict as when doctors get sucked away from rural to urban areas or a subsistence farmer's education is based on the occupational requirements of industry. Often the technical problems of establishing occupational needs are greater than is commonly assumed. Job analysis techniques are well-developed only for lower level skills and tend to ignore important aspects of human relations. Manpower forecasting is a notoriously chancy activity. Thus arguments from occupational practice are likely to meet five major problems: (a) the large number of different occupations; (b) variations within the same occupation between different work contexts; (c) the changing nature of occupations; (d) the limitations of job analysis; and (e) uncertainty as to whether the student will spend any time in the occupation for which he or she is being prepared.

Roles in society include citizenship, membership of a local community, family life, and so on in addition to the occupational roles already discussed. This is controversial territory. First, there is considerable argument about what would be an appropriate role model. Second, there is evidence that most educational systems prepare students differentially according to their socioeconomic and cultural status—this is often a latent rather than an intended function of schooling. Then third, it is argued that many objectives in this area should not be taught in schools because they are the responsibility of the home, the church, or the local community.

Much that is found in the "role in society" category can also be subsumed under the heading of "cultural knowledge", a term to which curriculum thinkers are often attracted but whose implications have yet to be fully worked out. Thus it has been used both in the context of justifying attention to the arts and humanities and in the context of preparing students to live in a multicultural society. When one also considers many students' strong interest in youth culture, the potential for conflicting interpretations and priorities becomes even greater. Within the sphere of academic knowledge, arguments are better articulated but still not resolved. For example, there is considerable dispute as to whether generalizable and transferable thinking skills exist across disciplines; and even as to whether it is feasible to separate thinking processes from conceptual content within a discipline in the manner claimed by some curriculum theorists. Arguments from within a subject are likely to be based on notions of key concepts, on the position of an objective in some important learning hierarchy, or on induction into the ways of thinking in the discipline. Thus an objective's utility is defined in terms of its contribution to the further study of the subject. Otherwise some other form of justification would be invoked.

Arguments based on the learners' interests are of two main types. The motivational argument rests on what students are claimed to be interested in, while the needs argument rests on what is claimed to be in the children's interests. The two are combined if it is asserted that it is basic value for children to enjoy themselves or to have a wide range of interests. Otherwise the motivational argument is merely a means to ends which have to be justified on other grounds. Many authors have suggested lists of children's needs that can serve as basic values for curriculum justification. Pateman (1978) for example suggests eight: "to be able to survive; to get or stay healthy; to be able to work with application; to enjoy themselves; to have a sense of their own worth; to be able to relate to others; to understand the world in which they live; and to be able to participate in its major institutions." While some of these would be catered for under the other headings—occupational practice, roles in society, academic and cultural knowledge—they might receive a radically different emphasis in that other justificatory context. Moreover, Pateman suggests that some of these basic needs are virtually ignored in formal schooling. In spite of their prominence in educators' discussions about the aims of education, personal development objectives tend to get overwhelmed by more academic and vocational considerations.

Another area of need in the learners' interests category is the need to make the most of the educational process itself. This involves developing such skills as note taking, learning from books, working with others, preparing for and taking examinations, and so on. Even in higher education it is increasingly acknowledged that these skills should no longer be taken for granted but need to be incorporated into the formal curriculum.

3. Selecting Objectives: The Problem of Priorities

The wider the range of possible objectives considered—and many argue that it should be very wide indeed—the greater becomes the problem of selection. There are so many forms of justification that the value judgments involved in selection can never be resolved by reference to some single underlying principle. This does not prevent an appropriately designated group of experts or representatives from arriving at a compromise plan and gaining sufficient political support to get it adopted; but it does limit the degree to which issues can be settled by rational argument. Moreover, the technical problems of collecting evidence of people's preferences in order to guide such a debate are considerable. Stake and Gooler (1971) present a three-dimensional design for a study of people's educational priorities based on:

(a) the audiences whose preferences are being sought;

(b) different indicators of priority, namely—importance, time allocation, cash allocation, and vigour of efforts to remediate;

(c) a dichotomy between the "real"—what they think are the current priorities—and the "ideal"—what they would like the priorities to be.

This last dimension is particularly important in view of evidence that parents can be greatly mistaken about the "real", especially at the elementary level (Becher et al. 1981), and may therefore argue from premises that are demonstrably false. In practice, however, Stake and Gooler encountered three major obstacles. First, they found that teachers and citizens had a great deal of difficulty in thinking about the curriculum as a whole:

> They appear to be devoid of the information needed to make judgments about the importance of the work of even a major subdivision of the curriculum, such as the science department or the athletic department. They do not know what the total effort to teach social responsibility is, and they feel most uncomfortable making even the crudest estimate of resources that might best be allocated to it.

Second, they found it impossible to give absolute priority information that was meaningful. It does not make sense to argue about the ideal allocation of time to mathematics without continual reference back to the status quo. Then, third, there is so much redundancy in the total education system that things are taught many times and in many ways. How can one assign a teaching time to an objective, when other objectives are also being taught at the same time?

These difuculties explain why planning a whole curriculum *ab initio* is rarely attempted. Instead piecemeal reform is found whenever someone can justify some change and mobilize the necessary support. Perhaps the most that can be expected is a series of attempts to narrow what Goodlad (1974) has called the "education gap" between the human race's noblest view of what it might become and the conventional wisdom that motivates current practice. But this is to assume that agreement can be reached on the nature of the gap, and that Goodlad's aspirational perspective can still command political support when the emphasis is shifting towards efficiency and effectiveness.

Within a single subject, the problem of selecting objectives becomes more manageable because people can at least conceptualize the task. However, rival forms of justifications still exist. "A" may be more feasible, "B" more enjoyable, "C" more immediately useful, and "D" more important for the development of advanced thinking in the subject. Moreover, it is not uncommon for a subject to be included because it is argued to be useful, but then planned as if utility were no longer an important criterion. The introduction of classification schemes for objectives has probably helped people to examine the emphasis and level of teaching in addition to the content balance. Though such schemes cannot create new principles for choosing priorities, they can at least make it easier to recognize those that are already there; and they may even suggest some interesting alternatives. All this, of course, depends on the schemes being judiciously chosen and their limitations being recognized.

Bibliography

Becher T, Eraut M, Knight J 1981 *Policies for Educational Accountability*. Heinemann, London
Bloom B S, Madaus G F, Hastings J T 1981 *Evaluation to Improve Learning*. McGraw-Hill, New York
French W et al. 1957 *Behavioral Goals of General Education in High School*. Russell Sage Foundation, New York
Goodlad J 1974 Program development: Identification and formulation of desirable educational goals. In: Blaney J et al. (eds.) 1974 *Program Development in Education*. Education–Extension Centre for Continuing Education, University of British Columbia, Vancouver, British Columbia
Hirst P H 1973 Towards a logic of curriculum development. In: Taylor P H, Walton J (eds.) 1973 *The Curriculum: Research Innovation and Change*. Ward Lock, London, pp. 9–26
Kearney N C 1953 *Elementary School Objectives: A Report Prepared for the Mid-century Committee on Outcomes in Elementary Education*. Russell Sage Foundation, New York
Pateman T 1978 Accountability, values and schooling. In:

Becher T, Maclure S (eds.) 1978 *Accountability in Education*. National Foundation for Educational Research, Slough, pp. 61–94

Popham W J 1974 Curriculum design: The problem of specifying intended learning outcomes. In: Blaney J et al. (eds.) 1974 *Program Development in Education*. Education–Extension Centre for Continuing Education, University of British Columbia, Vancouver, British Columbia

Pratt D 1980 *Curriculum: Design and Development*. Harcourt Brace Jovanovich, New York

Stake R E 1970 Objectives, priorities and other judgment data. *Rev. Educ. Res.* 40: 181–212

Stake R E, Gooler D D 1971 Measuring educational priorities. *Educ. Technol.* 11: 44–48

Tyler R W 1949 *Basic Principles of Curriculum and Instruction*. University of Chicago Press, Chicago, Illinois

Curriculum Content

F. M. Connelly and D. J. Clandinin

The term curriculum content refers to particular facts, ideas, principles, problems, and so on, included in a course of studies. Any specific content items may serve different instructional goals, and, conversely, any given goal may be served by different content items. The conceptualization of the content of a particular course, the selection of content items, and their organization into a coherent course of study are the major content-related problems in developing curricular materials.

It should be noted, however, that some curriculum theorists use the term "curriculum content" in the sense of problem areas, subjects, or disciplines included in a course of studies. Nevertheless, an increasing trend may be observed in contemporary curriculum literature to use this term in the context of dealing with a single course of study.

1. Conceptualization of Content

Researchers, policy makers, and curriculum planners will conceptualize content differently depending on their definitions of the term curriculum. Conceptualization, like selection, treated below, is both a theoretical and practical problem. Some believe that conceptualization is essentially a logical and theoretical problem and it is true that the concept of content may be enhanced by such considerations. For example, the application of ideas in a theory of knowledge to the conceptualization of content will enhance definitions of content specified in knowledge terms. Likewise, the application of ideas from experiential philosophy will enhance definitions of content specified in personal terms. But the ultimate choice over which of these definitions to adopt, whatever their theoretical support, rests both upon personal preference and upon political considerations associated with the curriculum in question.

Personal preferences constitute, in effect, a value base for choosing a definition. Political considerations refer to the dynamics of complex curriculum situations where different stakeholders have different, legitimate claims upon the curriculum. In the development of a history curriculum, for example, a group of parents may define history in terms of the meaning it has for their children; trustees may define it in terms of its social significance; and local university professors may define it in terms of the discipline of history. The political resolution of these competing claims will be an important factor in how history is conceptualized for this curriculum.

2. Selection of Content

As with the problem of conceptualization, the selection of content is both a theoretical and practical problem. If the problem of conceptualization has not been thought through prior to the actual selection process, then selection will be confounded by the issue of conceptualization. If the conceptualization problem has been treated, there remains the problem of choice of detail. For instance, if the content of a history curriculum is defined in terms of historical knowledge, there remains the problem of what view of knowledge and what specific knowledge to include. "Chronological" accounts of history, "epoch" accounts of history, "great people" accounts of history, and the like are all possible. Likewise, the cultural perspective on history will remain as an element of choice. For example, many critics at present believe that history curricula give a biased representation to certain cultural groups. The apparently simple choice of photographic and diagrammatic material reflects views which effectively modify the understanding to be obtained about a certain cultural group and its place in history.

The choices are theoretical in that they may appeal to historical fact and to theory of knowledge but they are also political and personal. It may be shown that the historical research on which the curriculum is based was conducted with a certain political orientation and bias towards a particular cultural group. Or, it may be that in an effort to enhance or downgrade the status of a cultural group, local government, the press, and other groups may have "shaped" the historical record. Accordingly, a certain event interpreted negatively in one decade may be interpreted positively in another.

Choices are also personal in that, when a selection is finally made, it reflects the views of the person or committee making the choice. For this reason, membership on curriculum writing teams is usually seen as a position of influence.

In general, selection is a deliberative process in which ends and means are debated in their practical and theoretical contexts. The process is a reasoned one and reasons in support of selections made may be given. These reasons are laden with personal, political, and theoretical considerations which modify the actual content entering a curriculum and, in consequence, the actual ends to be achieved.

3. Organization of Content

Selected content is organized for curricular purposes both vertically and horizontally. The vertical organization of content refers to its sequencing throughout the curriculum. In the most general sense this refers to sequence across grades. In its more detailed sense, vertical organization refers to the development of an idea within a particular lesson.

The vertical organization of curriculum is most easily rationalized in centralized educational systems where planning occurs centrally for all schools. In decentralized systems, where local choice predominates, sequencing may occur differently from school to school. This characteristic emerges since there is no one fixed sequence for any subject. A centralized system may give the appearance of a theoretically sound sequence but the sequence is "correct" only by virtue of the political control exerted. Alternative sequences are theoretically and practically possible. The principal reasons for justifying any particular vertical organ-

ization of content are that students build a coherent learning structure and that students may transfer from school to school or community to community with minimal interruption in their learning.

Horizontal organization refers to the integration and balance of one part of the curriculum's content with another. The introduction of new curriculum content, such as environmental studies, highlights the horizontal organization problem. Questions having to do with age–grade level, instructional time, and effects on other subjects come to the fore. In addition, matters such as the possibility of overlap, redundancy, and support for the new content in other parts of the curriculum are at issue.

Curriculum planners are required, therefore, to concern themselves with a harmonious balance within the curriculum at any one time as well as its short- and long-term sequencing.

Bibliography

Beauchamp G A 1975 *Curriculum Theory*, 3rd edn. Kagg Press, Wilmette, Illinois

Connelly F M, Clandinin D J 1988 *Teachers as Curriculum Planners: Narratives of Experience*. Teachers College Press, New York

Hooper R 1971 *The Curriculum: Context, Design and Development: Readings*. Oliver and Boyd, Edinburgh

Neagley R L, Evans N 1967 *Handbook for Effective Curriculum Development*. Prentice-Hall, Englewood Cliffs, New Jersey

Schubert W H 1986 *Curriculum: Perspectives, Paradigm and Possibility*. Macmillan, New York

Zais R S 1976 *Curriculum: Principles and Foundations*. Cromell, New York

Learning Experiences

L. L. Tyler

The term "learning experiences" refers to the personal meaning and significance derived by an individual from being engaged in a particular learning activity. Its widespread use among curriculum theorists and writers is due to the general realization that while several students may engage in a particular activity, such as viewing a film, or reading a report, and so on, each of them may respond to it differently, and thus have different "experiences" and therefore may learn different things. Nevertheless, and unfortunately, the term "learning experiences" is still used interchangeably with "learning activities" and recently also with the terms "learning opportunities" and "curriculum experiences."

1. Formal Definitions

Good's *Dictionary of Education* defines learning experience as "a purposeful activity that has meaning to students at their developmental level, carried through to

completion and evaluation." John Dewey (1938) clarified the concept of a learning experience by setting forth the idea that experience involves the interaction of the individual (internal conditions) with the objective conditions (external). Equal importance is assigned to both factors of experience: internal and external conditions. As he stated: "Any normal experience is an interplay of these two sets of conditions."

In dealing with the concept of interaction as a criterion of experience, Dewey said that traditional education violated the principle of interaction by paying little attention to the internal factors, and the new education (progressive education) would violate the principle if it overemphasized the internal conditions. While Dewey clarified his concept of experience, the difficulty of implementing it for planning instruction led to the formation of the term "learning opportunities." The reasoning went somewhat as follows: educators can make available an environment; however, it is the student actively interacting with the means (external conditions) who experiences; consequently the educator should concentrate on providing opportunities which may lead toward certain experiences.

Learning opportunities, as a term, appears for the first time in the 1973 edition of Good's Dictionary:

> . . . the means available in the school curriculum through which the students learn; examples are experiences, such as individualized instruction, small group instruction, team teaching, interaction processes between teacher and learner, and background referents which include knowledge, society, and the learner himself.

Accordingly, educators can only make available an environment in which learners can interact and therefore experience. Although the definition of learning opportunities makes reference to the interaction process between teacher and learner, the emphasis is on a wide variety of external conditions, whereas internal conditions of the learner are overlooked or glaringly minimized.

2. Differing Conceptualizations, Theoretical Stances, and Methodological Approaches

Curriculum studies emerge from differing conceptualizations, theoretical stances, and methodological approaches all of which are predicated upon assumptions about human nature, the relationship between people and society, schooling, and the like.

Probably the most well-known and widely used conception of curriculum is the Tyler rationale (Tyler 1950) which posits four questions for viewing and analyzing curriculum: objectives, learning experiences, organization, and evaluation. These terms have been abbreviated into a triangle model: objectives, learning experiences (activities), and evaluation. Other conceptualizations are set forth by the group of the "reconceptualists" (MacDonald 1975). In much of their writings terms such as objectives, learning experiences, and evaluation are either not encountered or if used, are used differently. Widely used terms by the "reconceptualists" are meaning, subjectivity, autobiography, self-knowledge, transcendence. Psychology and sociology are the most frequently used theoretical stances in curriculum studies, explicitly or implicitly. Although a recent investigation has been characterized by the authors as atheoretical, nevertheless, the authors indicate their interest in a systemic view of schooling. Recently, there has been a growing interest in and use of phenomenology, sociolinguistics, and psychoanalysis (Mehan 1978, Mishler 1979). Most widely used methodological approaches are still experimental and survey designs. Inadequacies of experimental design have been receiving much attention. Because of dissatisfaction with experimental and survey approaches, other approaches, variously labeled as "naturalistic," "simulated recall," "constitutive ethnography," and "clinical method" are being used.

3. Emerging Promising Directions

Using the term learning experience as defined requires attention to ideas about purpose, meaning, developmental level, activity, and evaluation. Two promising thrusts are emerging in the educational literature. The first is in a return to studying meaning, but not limiting studies to comprehension. The second is the ready acceptance of methodological approaches more appropriate to the study of human meaning and action.

While scholars have been writing about meaning (Phenix 1964), their work has not been heavily drawn upon in curriculum studies. Recently, Tyler (1977) has examined why learning opportunities are perceived differently and are responded to in differing ways by various learners. Mishler (1979) outlines the importance of context for understanding language and behavior as well as for setting forth the inadequacy of the traditional approaches of the social and behavioral sciences as applied to education, and finally for proposing some alternative approaches to the study of meaning in context, derived from phenomenology, sociolinguistics, and ethnomethodology. Mehan's (1978) constitutive ethnography approach examines the processes of interaction between participants in schools. He advocates equal attention to the processes as well as the outcomes of structuring activities. Constitutive studies of educational testing with regard to item meaning, the influence of the testing situation, the role of the tester, and so on, all raise doubts about some commonly held assumptions in evaluation, namely, that a common culture exists between adult testers and student respondents, that testers passively observe and record students' answers, and that the interaction process between tester and student is inconsequential.

Bibliography

Apple M W 1975 Commonsense categories and curriculum thought. In: MacDonald J B, Zaret E (eds.) 1975 *Schools in Search of Meaning.* Association for Supervision and Curriculum Development, Washington, DC

Dewey J 1938 *Experience and Education.* Collier-Macmillan, London

Good C V (ed.) 1973 *Dictionary of Education,* 3rd edn. McGraw-Hill, New York

MacDonald J B 1975 The quality of everyday life in school. In: MacDonald J B, Zaret E (eds.) 1975 *Schools in Search of Meaning.* Association for Supervision and Curriculum Development, Washington, DC

Mehan H 1978 Structuring school structure. *Harvard Educ. Rev.* 48: 32–64

Mishler E G 1979 Meaning in context: Is there any other kind? *Harvard Educ. Rev.* 49: 1–19

Phenix P H 1964 *Realms of Meaning: A Philosophy of the Curriculum for General Education.* McGraw-Hill, New York

Tyler R W 1950 *Basic Principles of Curriculum and Instruction.* University of Chicago Press, Chicago, Illinois

Tyler L L 1977 Materials in persons. *Theory Pract.* 16: 231–37

Concept Mapping

P. Tamir

A *concept map* has been defined by Novak and Gowin (1984) as "a schematic device for representing a set of concept meanings embedded in a framework of propositions" (p. 15). Novak and Gowin define *concept* as "a regularity in events or objects designated by some label" (such as "whale" or "mammal") (p. 4), while "*propositions* are two or more concept labels linked by words in a semantic unit" (for example "whales are mammals") (p. 15). The regularity represented by the concept label is given additional meaning through propositional statements that include the concept (e.g., "whales are sea animals"; "whales live on plant food" etc.).

Howard (1987 p. 4) defines *concept* as "a mental representation of a category, something in a person's head that allows him to place stimuli in or out of the category." For example, the category "mammal" includes all real and imaginary mammals in the world while people's own concept of mammal allows them to class various animals as mammals, or nonmammals. Novak and his colleagues developed concept mapping as a tool for describing the framework of relevant concepts or propositions that the individual possesses about a particular subject matter. As reported by Novak et al. (1983), concept mapping was at first the investigator's construction of the concepts and propositions evidenced by the learner, either in a clinical interview or in a work sample, and only later concept maps have been constructed to represent the propositional meaning in a lecture or other unit of instructional material.

In this way concept maps have become a tool which can represent the cognitive structure of a person as well as the structure of a given subject matter.

1. The Structure of Concept Maps

According to Novak et al. (1983) a concept map is constructed by arranging the labels of selected concepts in such a way that the most inclusive most general concept is placed at the top and then successively less inclusive concepts are shown at lower positions in the hierarchy. Students must decide not only how best to present the concepts hierarchically but also the words to put on the lines which meaningfully link the concepts together.

Figure 1 presents an example of a concept map. It is interesting to note that although Novak and Gowin (1984) justify the hierarchical structure by asserting that according to Ausubel's theory, meaningful learning proceeds most easily when new concepts or concept meanings are subsumed under broader, more inclusive concepts, concept maps fit quite well the hierarchical structure proposed by Gagné for learning skills. This follows the opposite direction, namely, starting at the bottom with the least inclusive and moving up the ladder until finally the top has been reached. Another relevant

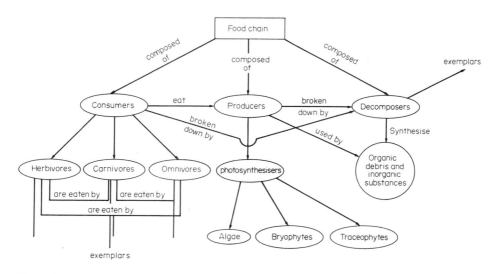

Figure 1
A sample concept map[a]

a Source: Novak and Gowin (1984 p. 122)

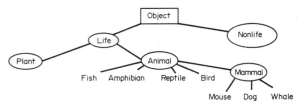

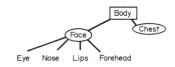

Figure 2
Examples of taxonomy and partonomy.

observation is the similarity between the hierarchical structure of concept maps and the taxonomies and partonomies traditionally used to represent concept map relationships (see Howard 1987 Chap. 1 as well as Fig. 2).

2. Uses of Concept Maps

Concept maps have been used in a variety of ways. The following sections briefly describe the possible uses of the technique for learning, teaching, curriculum development, evaluation, and research.

2.1 Learning

Basically maps are expected to enhance meaningful rather than rote learning. This can be accomplished in many ways and through various mechanisms, such as:

(a) Providing a visual representation of a particular domain (e.g., text material), which helps the student make better sense of the material, especially when the domain is rather complex.

(b) Providing a schema to relate course material to.

(c) Providing a basis and framework for writing essays.

(d) Summarizing material when preparing for examinations.

(e) Forcing students to think and engage in active learning as they try to construct the most plausible relationships.

(f) Helping students identify gaps in their knowledge.

(g) Helping students develop new relationships among concepts in a particular domain, thereby creating new meanings.

(h) Making students aware of the explicit role language plays in the exchange of information.

(i) Promoting reflective thinking associated with pushing and pulling of concepts, putting them together, and separating them again.

(j) Allowing learners to exchange views, thereby achieving shared meaning, which is possible because concept maps are explicit, overt representation of the concepts and propositions a person holds.

Construction of maps may be provided as an activity prior to a lesson to reveal prior knowledge, as homework, for consolidation, for summarizing and review, in a group discussion during a lesson, or as an individual assignment.

2.2 Teaching and Curriculum Development

Concept mapping may serve the teachers in several ways, such as:

(a) Helping in planning a lesson by identifying key concepts, their prerequisites and relevant examples.

(b) Serving as a means for providing an overview of some domain.

(c) Providing an operational definition of an instructional goal by indicating specific understandings which are to be attained.

(d) Serving as a remarkably effective tool for showing students' alternative frameworks.

(e) Helping in planning a unit or course in a certain discipline.

(f) Helping in planning interdisciplinary instruction.

2.3 Evaluation

Concept maps have proved to serve as useful tests for assessing the attainment of certain objectives. They may be scored objectively and reliably. Students may be provided with a set of unlinked concepts with which they have to construct a map, or they may be asked to construct a concept map for a certain important concept such as "a food chain" or "force". Scoring is based on several criteria such as the validity of the propositions connecting the concepts, the correctness of the hierarchical levels, the validity of cross-links, the examples provided, and the richness of the map. Concept maps are remarkably effective in identifying idiosyncratic conceptions and, hence, they are useful tools for revealing and diagnosing misconceptions.

2.4 Research

As already mentioned, concept maps were first initiated as research tools for describing the cognitive structure of learners. To date their use in research has expanded. The following are two examples which illustrate the use of concept mapping in research.

Champagne and Klopfer (1981) studied the relationship between structuring process skills and the solution of verbal problems involving science concepts. The student's structuring process skills were assessed by means of two tasks employing the Concept Structuring Analysis Technique (Con SAT). In doing a Con SAT task the student is asked to construct a concept map. The student receives a set of cards, each with one concept written on it and is asked to arrange the cards in a way that will show "how you think about the words". After the arrangement has been made, the student is asked to explain why he or she did what they did. By the use of Con SAT the researchers found that structuring process skills contribute more to the successful solution of set-membership problems than to the solution of analogy problems.

Harty et al. (1985) defined a new construct designated as Concept Structure Interrelatedness Competence (Con SIC). This competence has been measured by comparing student-constructed concept maps to expert-designed criterion maps. Significant positive correlations were found between Con SIC and science achievement course grades as well as other attributes related to science learning.

3. Dangers and Limitations in Using Concept Maps

Although concept maps are expected to represent meaningful learning, special care must be taken to make sure that students really understand the concept maps and the relations among the concepts rather than rote learn the material and thus produce a list-like map. In general, although concept mapping may be useful, employing additional techniques as well will provide greater insight.

While concept maps provide information on the cognitive structure of a given person, a one-to-one correspondence between a concept map drawn by a person and his or her structure of semantic memory may not necessarily be implied.

4. Effectiveness of Concept Mapping

There is some evidence which shows that for certain students and for certain teachers the use of concept mapping is less effective and less attractive than for others.

For example Armandin et al. (1984) found that some college students enjoyed mapping and found it helpful while others did not. The students were especially cautious about the place of concept mapping in evaluation. As a result, it was concluded that concept mapping may be a valuable adjunct to conventional evaluation approaches, rather than a substitute.

Okebukola and Jegede (1988) found that students who had relatively high preference for general principles benefited more than others from using concept mapping in their learning.

Several studies have compared the achievement of students using concept mapping to that of students who had not used concept maps (e.g., Lehman et al. 1985). As observed by Rogan (1988), so far no significant differences could be detected on the average, and the expectation that concept mapping can improve learning directly remains an intriguing possibility.

Bibliography

Armandin M W, Mintzes J I, Dunn C S, Shafer T H 1984 Concept mapping in college science teaching. *J. Coll. Sci. Teach.* 13: 117–21
Champagne A B, Klopfer L E 1981 Structuring process skills and the solution of verbal problems involving science concept maps. *Sci. Educ.* 65: 493–511
Harty H, Hamrick L, Samuel K V 1985 Relationships between middle school students' science concept structure interrelatedness competence and selected cognitive and affective tendencies. *J. Res. Sci. Teach.* 22: 179–91
Howard R W 1987 *Concepts and Schemata: An Introduction.* Cassell, Eastbourne
Lehman J D, Carter C, Kahle J B 1985 Concept mapping, vee mapping, and achievement: Results of a field study with black high school students. *J. Res. Sci. Teach.* 22: 663–73
Novak J D, Gowin D B, Johansen G T 1983 The use of concept mapping and knowledge vee mapping with junior high school science students. *Sci. Educ.* 67: 625–45
Novak J D, Gowin D B 1984 *Learning How to Learn.* Cambridge University Press, Cambridge
Okebukola P A, Jegede O J 1988 Cognitive preference and learning mode as determinants of meaningful learning through concept mapping. *Sci. Educ.* 72: 489–500
Rogan J M 1988 Conceptual mapping as a diagnostic aid. *Sch. Sci. Math.* 88: 50–59

Curriculum Design

F. M. Klein

Curriculum design is the organizational pattern or structure of a curriculum. It is determined by decisions made at two different levels of development: a broad level which involves basic value choices and a specific level which involves the technical planning and implementation of curricular elements. At the broader level of decision making, curriculum design is influenced by the choice of the data source or sources which the developer chooses to emphasize. Three primary data sources his-

torically have been used as bases for choices in making curricular decisions: organized subject matter, the students who are to experience the curriculum, and society (Tyler 1950). Although most scholars in curriculum advocate using a combination of all three data sources in order to insure a balanced curriculum, in practice one usually has a dominance over the other two. Even more often in practice, one data source is used to the exclusion of the other two. Which data source is chosen to be the primary or exclusive basis for making curricular decisions depends largely upon the values of the developer about what the curriculum ought to do for or contribute to the growth of students.

The pattern or structure of the curriculum is also influenced at a more specific technical level when decisions are made in relation to the curricular elements. There is variation regarding the curricular elements which different scholars advocate for designing curriculum. The curricular elements usually referred to in a discussion of a design are objectives, content, learning activities, and evaluation procedures (Zais 1976). Beauchamp (1983) identifies four: statement of goals or purposes, statement of document intent and use, evaluation plan, and the selected and organized culture content. Eisner (1985) specifies seven: goals, content, types of learning opportunities, organization of learning opportunities, organization of content areas, mode of presentation and mode of response, and evaluation. Other authors include nine: goals and purposes, content, materials and resources, activities, teaching strategies, evaluation, grouping, time, and space (Goodlad 1979, Klein in press). These nine elements can be treated in different ways when developing curricula and through these different treatments, a variety of designs can be created. Thus, at this technical level of development, a specific curriculum design is created by the ways in which the elements are treated and the interrelationships which occur among them.

Any preplanned or student-initiated curriculum has an inherent design whether the developer has dealt explicitly with the component parts and their interrelationships or merely made decisions about some of them on an unexamined basis. The challenge to curriculum developers is to make the necessary decisions so that the curriculum which is created has a high degree of internal consistency (Hunkins 1980). This results from a careful consideration of the elements involved in curriculum design. If the decisions made about each of the data sources and curricular elements are compatible, the curriculum will have internal consistency. When the curriculum possesses high internal consistency, it will have a greater potential for having the desired impact upon the students. If the data sources and curricular elements are not treated in a consistent manner and have no clearly defined relationships to each other, the design of the curriculum will be confused and the potential impact upon students will be lessened.

This article discusses how a curriculum design is created by devoting major or exclusive emphasis to each of the three primary data sources for decision making: organized subject matter, the student, and the society. Within the discussion of each primary data source, a description is included of how the nine curricular elements should be, and often are treated so that maximum internal consistency can be achieved within the design. Each section on a primary data source concludes with the identification of the strengths and weaknesses of that design. A brief discussion then follows of two

curriculum designs which combine some aspects of those based on the three primary data sources: specific competencies and process skills. Two others are also included in the discussion: a newly emerging humanistic design and the core curriculum. The article concludes with an identification of general characteristics of design needed in any curriculum.

Decisions about curriculum design are, in part, value choices which should be made as a result of rational and logical deliberation. Each design will achieve different goals and meet different purposes for learning. Designs created on a theoretical level rarely exist in practice in a pure form (Zais 1976). The realities of schooling force changes and require compromises. Thus, conducting research to determine the best curriculum design to use is not feasible. Evaluative studies can be, and have been conducted to determine the impact of a particular curriculum upon the students. These studies, however, are not intended to help make decisions about other curricular designs which are created for different learning goals and purposes. This article, therefore, contains no research section, but does attempt to make clear the value positions involved and the deliberations to be conducted for each of the major designs.

1. Organized Subject Matter as a Data Source

Organized subject matter is the most commonly used data source for decisions to be made about curriculum design (Beauchamp 1983, Ornstein and Hunkins 1988). It is used because it reflects humankind's collective wisdom and represents the cultural heritage of people. A study of the disciplines as an organized body of knowledge is thought to be essential to the continued progress of civilizations. Also, such a body of knowledge is considered to be a significant characteristic of an educated person.

A particular period of curriculum history in the United States illustrates the type of curriculum which results when organized subject matter becomes the dominant or exclusive source for curriculum design (Klein 1978). From approximately 1960 to 1970, large amounts of private and federal funds were made available for curriculum reform. Because of rather widespread dissatisfaction with the public schools, it was generally agreed that the curriculum of the public schools needed considerable revision and updating. One group contributing to the criticisms of the curriculum was scholars at the university level who taught the disciplines included in the public-school curriculum. As the new funding became available, the university scholars in these disciplines were looked to for leadership in developing the new curriculum. These scholars, of course, turned to their disciplines as the basis for revising the school curriculum.

Most of the curriculum projects from this era defined the content to be learned in terms of the structure of the discipline. The structure of the discipline is those concepts and processes which are necessary to an understanding of the discipline and essential to the study of it. Content not considered a part of the structure was eliminated, even though traditionally it had been included in the curriculum. The intent of the new curricula from this era was to assist students in learning to become, for example, young scientists and mathematicians. Students would engage in the processes central to the discipline and inquire into it using the basis concepts. Although the structure of the disciplines is not emphasized in current curricula, the emphasis is still upon organized subject matter. The subject matter design is reflected in such publications as *Content of the Curriculum* (Brandt 1988) and *Toward the Thinking Curriculum: Current Cognitive Research* (Resnick and Klopfer 1989).

In using subject matter as the major data source, a logical organization of the content is emphasized. The selection and organization of the content, however that may be defined, is a major task in developing the design (Taba 1962).

Curricula are planned in advance for the students so that a logically organized body of content can be taught to them efficiently and effectively. Learning, however, can become a mechanistic process which emphasizes covering the desired content rather than developing understanding of it by the students (Taba 1962).

Four variations in this curriculum design which uses organized subject matter as the primary data source have been developed. They are separate subjects, multidisciplinary, interdisciplinary, and broad fields. When the separate subjects are used, each one is treated as a discrete area of the curriculum. Thus, geography, history, and economics become offerings in the social science curriculum; geology, biology, physics, and chemistry are offered in the science curriculum and spelling, handwriting, and reading are offered at different times in the elementary-school curriculum. This variation of the design emphasizes the logical organization of each subject and no deliberate attempt is made to interrelate them (Hunkins 1980).

The multidisciplinary or correlated variation occurs when several subject areas are coordinated for study, but are still taught as separate subjects (Hunkins 1980, Ragan and Shepherd 1977, Smith et al. 1957). For example, in a multidisciplinary variation, the literature of a country would be taught in conjunction with its history and geography. Students may be asked to write themes for composition classes on some aspect of that period of time. Through this approach, it is hoped that students will experience a greater degree of unity in their knowledge (Hunkins 1980, Zais 1976).

A third variation is the unterdisciplinary approach. In this approach, a topic or concept is selected to which several separate subjects are related. Each separate subject is brought to bear upon the concept as an aspect of study. For example, the concept of energy might be studied from a physical science, economic, and historical perspective. Each discipline is seen as contributing an important, separate, but discrete part of the student's

learning. It is thought that a comprehensive understanding of the concept can be gained only by studying the contributions of any discipline which relates to it. In this design the student has the opportunity to experience even greater integration of humankind's store of knowledge.

The fourth variation in the subject area is the broad fields (Hunkins 1980, Ragan and Shepherd 1977, Smith et al. 1957, Taba 1962, Zais 1976). In this one, the distinctions among the separate subjects are more blurred than in the previous three. Spelling, handwriting, and reading come together to form a language arts approach to help students become proficient in their native language. History, geography, economics, and sociology are combined in a social studies program to help students understand their social world. No attempt is made to emphasize the separate contributions of economics, history, or sociology to the study of the family, for example. It is hoped that this broad fields design assists the student in achieving a high degree of integration of the separate subjects and through integration, the content becomes more functional. A commonly recognized limitation of this approach, however, is a more superficial encounter with content (Hunkins 1980).

Within the separate subject design, decisions are made about the curricular elements to assure that the student learns the desired body of content. Objectives may be stated explicitly or they may be implicit within the selection and organization of other curricular elements such as content and activities. The objectives provide the direction for learning and the achievement for the learning process. They are often stated in behavioral terms (Tyler 1950) in relation to the content to be learned and they are usually in the cognitive domain. Although in practice, most of the objectives are lower cognitive behaviors (often emphasizing recall of the content), behavioral objectives clearly can be written for the higher cognitive behaviors such as application, analysis, and evaluation. Objectives in the affective domain emphasizing values, beliefs, and attitudes can also be written within the separate subject design, but they are usually neglected in practice.

Content to be taught is selected and organized by scholars or the curriculum developer for the student and this is done prior to instruction. Two concepts are particularly important to the organization of content: scope and sequence. Sequence refers to the vertical organization of the content. Careful consideration is paid to the sequencing of the content so that the student progresses continuously in learning tasks throgh hierarchical or logical steps. Scope refers to the horizontal arrangement of content. The scope is carefully defined so content will be as meaningful and integrated as possible for the student and manageable within the length of time allocated (Zais 1976). Content may be concepts, generalization, ideas, processes, or skills within the subject area.

Materials are selected or developed which present the content to the student in a carefully organized form. The text is the most commonly used piece of learning material and it presents the content to be learned in a carefully designed sequential, logical order. The student has little or no role in selecting the materials to be used.

Learning activities are designed to relate directly to the explicit or implicit objectives or directions for learning. Activities are to foster the change in the behavior of the student as stated in the objectives or to keep the student focused on the intended directions for the learning process (usually learning a body of content or skills). They are often of the traditional verbal type: reading, writing, and listening. Activities are planned so that students will be motivated to learn.

Teaching strategies are planned, often as an inherent part of the activities, with the same intent. The teacher uses appropriate methods to assist the student in learning the stated behavior and content in the behavioral objective, if used, or the defined body of content. One commonly used strategy is the diagnostic-prescriptive-evaluative one. In this strategy, the teacher diagnoses where the student is in his or her progress and what difficulties are being encountered, prescribes the next step in the learning sequence, and after the student has experienced the prescription, the teacher evaluates to determine if the student has learned what was expected. Lecture and discussion is another commonly used strategy. The teacher as an expert in the subject area uses methodologies designed to impart his or her knowledge to the students.

Evaluation procedures are planned and developed to determine the extent to which the student has achieved the behavioral objectives or learned the body of content. Periodic determinations are often made. Emphasis is usually placed on a quantitative measurement and some curriculum scholars advocate measuring only observable behavior. Progress is often reported in terms of letter grades such as A, B, C, or F which presumably indicate some degree of achievement. A particularly close, direct relationship should exist among the behavioral objectives, content, learning activities, and evaluation procedures.

Much instruction occurs in a total group setting. When small groups are used, they are formed on the basis of where the students are in their learning and what the next sequential or logical steps are. A student is placed in a group with other students who are at a similar place in their progress toward some objective and an activity is planned or selected for them in relation to the next step in learning. Instructional groups are usually formulated by the teacher on the basis of his or her diagnosis of the students. The student stays in the group until he or she is ready for the next learning task. Often the group is kept together for some period of time since students of similar learning abilities are normally grouped together.

This type of grouping provides for some individualization to occur so that each student's needs can be better met. Another way in which individualization occurs is through the use of programmed materials and learning modules, through printed materials or the computer. These materials are designed for use by a single student so that a high degree of individualization occurs in the amount of time used and the pacing for each student. Each student progresses through the materials at his or her own pace. It is important to note that individualization primarily occurs in relation to time in this instance. In some cases students have options among materials, activities, and strategies. Individualization for objectives, content, and evaluation does not usually occur.

Time is viewed as a limited resource and students and teachers are expected to make maximum use of it. Teachers keep students actively engaged in the learning task and hold disruptions to routines, and socializing among students to a minimum. Time spent in classrooms is viewed as most valuable, although homework is often assigned at the older ages so that learning can continue beyond the confines of the school. Time is divided into blocks so that each subject area receives some special allocation.

The boundaries of space are usually those of the classroom, although special rooms may be used such as libraries, instructional materials centers, music or art rooms, and maths or science laboratories. The classroom space is organized so that large group instruction and small group work can occur.

Clearly, variations within the above description of curricular elements can occur within the organized subject matter design, and do so in practice. If the elements are to be internally consistent within the design, however, they all must be used to assist the student in learning the important content whether that has been defined from the separate subjects or broad fields.

The advantages often cited for using organized subject areas as a data source for curriculum design emphasize the logical organization of content and the fact that this is the traditional way of designing curriculum (Hunkins 1980, Saylor and Alexander 1974, Taba 1962, Zais 1976). Subject areas represent a systematic and efficient way to help students learn their cultural heritage. Knowledge of the subjects and the intellectual processes inherent within them form an essential foundation of schooling. Also, there is a long historical tradition of designing curricula upon this foundation. Teachers are educated in this way and the most prevalent materials and resources for schooling are developed on this basis. Additionally, it is a convenient and easy way to administer curricula and schools.

The weaknesses of this design center upon six points. First, it compartmentalizes and fragments the knowledge to be presented to the student. This leads to rapid forgetting of the content and does not make it very functional for students. Second, it is removed from the real world of the students. The problems, events, and concerns they face on a daily basis are not adequately included in the curriculum. Third, it pays inadequate attention to the abilities, needs, interests, and past experiences of the students. This may cause a lack of fit for the content with the students and thereby reduce motivation for learning. Fourth, it is an inefficient arrangement for the students; one which is alien to the way students learn in a more natural setting. Fifth, it encourages a passive and somewhat superficial approach to learning. Coverage of content becomes more important than depth of understanding by students. It may include a narrow range of goals and neglect higher cognitive skills. Sixth, as the knowledge of humankind accumulates, new subjects must be created. They are added to the curriculum and this causes a proliferation of subjects in an already crowded curriculum. The curriculum is expected to be responsive, however, to some degree at least, to the problems encountered by the society and the students. This requires that new subjects be created such as driver education, drug education, and sex education. These are then treated as a body of organized subject matter for the curriculum.

2. The Student as a Data Source

A different curriculum design is created when the dominant or exclusive data source for decision making is the student. In this approach, the needs, interests, abilities, and past experiences of the students are chosen as the basis for making decisions about the curricular elements. Students are consulted, observed, and studied for cues to selecting and organizing the direction or purposes of learning as well as the content, materials, and activities. The subject areas become a means by which students pursue problems or topics derived from their interests. Although the curriculum cannot be preplanned in the logically organized way of the subject area design, there is advance preparation by the teacher so that the necessary resources are available and the necessary arrangements are made to enable the students to become and remain actively involved in the learning process. The student is consulted whenever choices must be made. Problem solving and other processes are prime emphases, not a body of predetermined content. This design involves much cooperation among the students and the teacher and is a highly flexible, personalized one. It is valued because students learn to direct their own education, an essential ability for lifelong learning (Saylor and Alexander 1974, Smith et al. 1957).

When the student is emphasized as the primary source for designing the curriculum, it is often called the emerging, activity, or experience-based curriculum. Free schools, alternative schools, open education, and the British infant schools use this curriculum design. In all of these examples, the student is valued as the dominant source to look to in making decisions.

To achieve this design, a different way of utilizing the curricular elements must occur. The concept of predetermined objectives, either explicitly or implicitly stated, is rejected and the purposes of the student or a

group of students are used to direct the learning process. The purposes may develop out of a cooperative planning endeavor between the teacher and the student, however. There are no predetermined outcomes for the curriculum intended for all students (Macdonald et al. 1973).

Content is selected on the basis of interests, and by active involvement of the students themselves. Advocates of this design believe real learning occurs only when the student organizes the content for himself or herself and attaches some personal meaning to it. It is to be organized *by* the student; not by others *for* the student. The concepts of scope and sequence are minimized in curriculum planning, but the concept of integration is an overarching one. The student experiences a wholeness and unity in the learning process which is not possible in the subject area design.

Materials are defined broadly as whatever the student requires for learning. Texts are not highly valued since they organize content for students. Rather, a wide variety of materials is needed since the student must explore and organize for himself or herself.

Activities are planned and selected by the students, or students are consulted frequently by the teacher for any necessary prior planning of activities. The activities are likely to be ones in which students are very actively involved such as constructing, interviewing, locating their own materials, and organizing resources for learning. Activities are not designed to achieve specified predetermined outcomes, although they should help the student achieve his or her purposes for learning.

The teacher is expected to be a colearner with the student and be a guide in the learning process. There are no essential methods or strategies for a teacher to use in order to facilitate learning. The teacher helps the students in the learning process in any way possible as needed by the student.

Evaluation becomes a joint endeavor between the teacher and the student. Self-evaluation is also an important process. Evaluation of the process students engage in is as important, if not more so than evaluation of any product.

Grouping practices are highly flexible and groups are formed only as needed or desired. Instructional groups are based on common interests of students rather than on diagnosis of their abilities. Groups when formed are flexible, short term, and somewhat spontaneous.

Time is kept flexible and unstructured by the teacher. It is a resource which students are responsible for using for their own purposes. A fixed schedule is not kept or desired (Taba 1962). Time for learning is not viewed as restricted to the classroom and homework; learning what is important to the student occurs whenever time is available. Space is equally unstructured and undefined. The classroom is a central meeting place, but the learning process will require the use of many other places and resources within the school and community.

The advantages of a curriculum design based primarily upon the student are several. Learning is personalized, relevant, and meaningful when student needs, interests, abilities, and experiences direct it. Students are intrinsically motivated and do not depend upon an external system of rewards. It is an active process for students. Emphasis is upon development of individual potential and interests and individual differences are fully met. Process skills are developed which enable students to cope more adequately with the demands of life (Hunkins 1980, Zais 1976).

A design based primarily upon the student has several disadvantages. First, some critics charge that such a design does not prepare adequately for life since it neglects social goals of education and the cultural heritage of humankind. Students experience a curriculum which does not assure learning outcomes common to all students. Second, the activities are often inadequately organized and do not assure that the curriculum will provide any defined scope or sequence to learning. A series of unexamined experiences may not produce intellectual abilities or any organized body of knowledge. Third, commonly available learning materials are not organized in this way and to accumulate the necessary resources can be very expensive. Fourth, the teacher is not prepared to teach in this spontaneous process. It makes heavy demands upon the most skillful teachers to stay abreast of the students' needs. Finally, this design contradicts the academic structure of schools and colleges and entrance to new institutions is made more difficult and complex.

The interrelationships among the curricular elements in the above design are looser and less strong than in the organized subject area design. In the design using the student as the data source, students are the prime decision makers, and control at least to some degree, the elements in the design. This is the essential point regarding this design. If the design is to be used with any validity, the student as a prime decision maker must be assured.

3. Society as a Data Source

Society is a third source which may be used as a dominant or exclusive basis for curriculum decision making. It produces a unique curriculum design which is valued as a way of understanding and improving society. It is called the societal design and is also sometimes referred to as the problem-solving design (Ornstein and Hunkins 1988). Community schools often use this approach. Social-studies programs also sometimes use society as a primary data source.

Although explicit objectives may be used, they do not play as major a role in this design as when subject areas are used as a basis for decision making. There is usually a definite focus for the learning process for all students but definite outcomes are not prescribed in advance.

Content is derived from life in a society or societies. It may emphasize the functions of a society, the major activities of social life, or the persistent problems of

students and humankind (Stratemeyer et al. 1957). Any subject area is used as it relates to the topic or problem under study. Problem-solving processes and human relations and social skills are major emphases rather than possession of a body of content.

Materials of great diversity are needed with community resources and original documents preferred rather than texts. Evaluation is likely to be a cooperative endeavor between students and teachers. It focuses upon resolutions of, or actions related to, the problems being studied and the processes engaged in during the study.

Activities would be a result of student and teacher planning. They would require the active participation of students in all phases of study. The teacher plays a more active role, however, in determining these than when the student is the primary data source. Teaching strategies would be those which have the teacher as a guide in the learning process more than as the authority and expert as in the subject area design. The teacher, again, would play a more direct role than in the student design, however.

Space would be broadly defined to include all the resources of the school and community which relate to the problem or topic under study. Time would be defined also as a general resource which students use as the study dictates. Artificial allocations of time would be minimized as much as possible. Grouping would be determined on the basis of student needs and desires as the study progresses and much use of committee work would be made.

The interrelationships among the curricular elements in this design are broadly defined. They are stronger and more direct than in the student design, but less strongly related when separate subjects are used as the primary basis for design.

The advantages of this type of curriculum design emphasize the unity and utility of content and the relevance to the student and society (Taba 1962). The subject areas are integrated and play a subordinate role to the topic being studied. Problem solving is emphasized and the content studied is in a functional form for the student. Thus, content is relevant and meaningful for the student. The student is actively involved in all phases of the study so there is considerable intrinsic motivation to sustain the study. In addition, the design contributes in a significant way to the improvement of society.

The weaknesses cited are several. The scope and sequence of the curriculum are not clearly defined. This can contribute to superficial treatment of content. Also, the units of study can be fragmented for students. This would reduce the unity of content that students might achieve. Another weakness is a fear that the focus of study can indoctrinate students to existing conditions and thus prepare them for the status quo rather than improvement of society. It can also provide inadequate exposure to a cultural heritage through the lack of organized content used in the approach. Finally, it is criticized because of tradition. Teachers are not prepared to teach in this manner nor are the usual resources available to schools prepared for this type of study. It is also different from what parents and colleges normally expect.

4. Other Curriculum Designs

Two curriculum designs being advocated appear to be a departure from, or perhaps a combination of the traditional ones in that they cut across the three bases of decision making discussed above. They are specific competencies and process skills. A third one is being advocated which is similar to the student as a basis for a design but it is less clearly defined. A fourth design, the core curriculum, has been advocated in the past, but it is less clearly a unique design. These four are discussed briefly below.

The competency approach emphasizes specific behavioral objectives as defining what students need to learn. These are derived from any data source. Skills are usually emphasized and growth in the affective domain is neglected or underemphasized. An example of this is the recurrent theme of "back to basics" which curricula seem to emphasize periodically. In this, behavioral objectives spell out the specific competencies the student must possess to function adequately in the society. They also reflect the separate subjects. The specific curricular elements are likely to be treated as in the separate subjects design.

The second approach that cuts across traditional designs emphasizes processes which are not subject specific. The content of the curriculum is the processes which are considered to have maximum transfer to real life, not those basic to inquiry within a discipline. The affective domain of human behavior and personal development are highly emphasized. Values clarification, skills basic to the learning process (essential for lifelong learning), and problem-solving skills are examples of processes as content. Decisions made about the specific curricular elements are likely to be similar to the student as a primary source for curriculum design.

A new source for curriculum design has also been identified: the humanistic view of the person. This is, in part, a reaction against schooling based on the industrial, technological model as represented best in the separate subjects design. It is a search for new ways to conceptualize curriculum. Those who pursue this approach are referred to as the reconceptualists (Pinar 1988, Sears and Marshall in press). Although limited progress has been made in the specifics of the design, it undoubtedly will be closer to the student as a source for design than the separate subjects and society.

A fourth and final design referred to often in the literature is the core curriculum. The most essential characteristics of this approach are the common learnings which all students are expected to achieve and the administrative arrangements for larger blocks of time than are customarily found. Beyond these two basic characteristics, the core curriculum can take on elements of the organized subject matter or society centered designs described in the preceding sections.

5. Essential Characteristics of Curriculum Design

The preceding discussion identifies the importance of questions concerning design in the curriculum development process and highlights the fundamental nature of it. The design achieved must be the result of deliberate and enlightened decision making and should not occur as a result of omission and neglect. The design selected must match the intent or function of the curriculum. Curricula differ in their purposes or functions; the design should follow from this as a result of enlightened deliberations. Once the design has been decided upon, the curricular elements must be handled with considerable consistency. Decisions made about objectives and evaluation must be compatible with decisions made, for example, about materials and activities. Unless this consistency is present, the design will have gaps in it and the impact of the curriculum upon students will be lessened. This has important implications for the kinds of resources needed for schooling, the types of programs needed in teacher education, and the ways in which finances and personnel in school districts must be utilized.

The designs available for use in curriculum development must evolve as new demands are placed upon the schools. Older patterns of curriculum design must be improved and new ones must be developed as knowledge, societies, and students change. Curriculum design must not be perceived as, nor allowed to become, static and unchanging. Creativity and adaptability must be essential characteristics of existing and evolving patterns of curriculum design.

Within a given school, it becomes apparent that a balance is needed among curriculum designs. No single pattern is adequate for the entire curriculum of a school. Each design discussed in this article has particular strengths which can contribute in very significant ways to the education of students. Each also has weaknesses which can be compensated for by providing students with experiences in others. Most schools have goals toward which each of the designs could contribute in a unique way. It would be unnecessarily limiting to restrict the design of the total curriculum to only one. And yet, this is what usually occurs in practice. The challenge to each school is to make thoughtful and deliberate decisions regarding how each curriculum design can be used to make the best contribution to the diverse aims of education.

Bibliography

Beauchamp G A 1983 Curriculum design. In: English F W (ed.) *Fundamental Curriculum Decisions*, 1983 Yearbook of The Association of Supervision and Curriculum Development (ASCD). Alexandria, Virginia, pp. 90–98

Brandt R S (ed.) 1988 *Content of the Curriculum.* 1988 Year-book of the Association for Supervision and Curriculum Development. ASCD, Alexandria, Virginia

Eisner E W 1985 *The Educational Imagination: On the Design and Evaluation of School Programs.* Macmillan, New York, pp. 127–155

Goodlad J I 1979 *Curriculum Inquiry: The Study of Curriculum Practice.* McGraw-Hill, New York

Herrick V E 1950 The concept of curriculum design. In: *Toward Improved Curriculum Theory.* University of Chicago Press, Chicago, Illinois, pp. 37–50

Hunkins F P 1980 *Curriculum Development Program Planning and Improvement.* Merrill, Columbus, Ohio

Klein M F 1978 *About Learning Materials.* Association for Supervision and Curriculum Development, Washington, DC, No. 8, pp. 1–45

Klein F M in press A framework for curriculum decision making In: Klein F M in press *The Politics of Curriculum Decision Making: Issues in Legislating and Centralizing Curriculum.* State University of New York Press, Albany, New York

Macdonald J B, Wolfson B J, Zaret E 1973 *Reschooling Society: A Conceptual Model.* Association for Supervision and Curriculum Development, Washington, DC

Ornstein A C, Hunkins F P 1988 *Curriculum: Foundations, Principles and Issues.* Prentice Hall, Englewood Cliffs, New Jersey

Pinar W (ed.) 1975 *Curriculum Theorizing: The Reconceptualists.* McCuthan, Berkeley, California

Pinar W F (ed.) 1988 *Contemporary Curriculum Discourses.* Gorsuch Scarisbrick, Scottsdale, Arizona

Kagan W B, Shepherd G D 1977 *Modern Elementary Curriculum.* Holt, Rinecuthan and Winston, New York

Resnick L B, Klopfer L E (eds.) 1989 *Toward the Thinking Curriculum: Current Cognitive Research.* Association for Supervision and Curriculum Development, Alexandria, Virginia

Saylor J G, Alexander W M 1974 *Planning Curriculum for Schools.* Holt, Rinehart and Winston, New York

Sears J T, Marshall J D (eds.) in press *Teaching and Thinking About Curriculum: Empowering Educators through Curriculum Studies.* Teachers College Press, New York

Smith B O, Stanley W O, Shores J H 1957 *Fundamentals of Curriculum Development.* Harcourt, Brace and World, New York

Stratemeyer F B, Hamden L F, McKim M G, Passow A H 1957 *Developing a Curriculum for Modern Living,* 2nd edn. Teachers College Press, New York

Taba H 1962 *Curriculum Development: Theory and Practice.* Harcourt, Brace and World, New York

Tyler R W 1950 *Basic Principles of Curriculum and Instruction.* University of Chicago Press, Chicago, Illinois

Zais R S 1976 *Curriculum: Principles and Foundations.* Crowell, New York

Curriculum Organization

M. Skilbeck

Curriculum organization refers to the manner in which the elements that constitute the curriculum of an educational system or institution are arranged, inter-related, and sequenced. These elements comprise such general factors as teaching plans and schemes, learning materials, equipment and plant, the professional expertise of the teaching force, and the requirements of assessment and examinations bodies. Less obvious but equally important are the atmosphere of the school or college, the support given to education by society, community and home, the capabilities and interests of the students, and the styles and strategies of the teachers. The curriculum that is to be organized is more than the syllabus content in different subjects or areas: it is the learning environment, the goals and values of the teachers, and the learning experiences of the students. Organizing the curriculum is a complex and crucial undertaking upon which the overall performance of the educational system rests.

1. The Scope of the Curriculum and of Organizational Considerations

Given the breadth of curriculum defined as the totality of learning experiences in and through schooling, its organization cannot be reduced to a few simple rules and precepts. It is clear, however, that educational institutions and providing authorities must give curriculum organization a high priority in their planning and resource allocation. Significant changes or developments in curriculum organization, such as the introduction of integrated studies in primary schools, or the updating of the content of secondary-school science, or experimentation with new instructional technologies resulting in a more active mode of student learning, require a reconsideration of the whole mode of operation of a school or school system. Neglect of this principle has been one of the main reasons for the inadequate implementation of curriculum change and hence dissatisfaction with the limited success of many curriculum innovations around the world. Thus, different forms of curriculum organization, proposed or introduced through pedagogical innovations, require changes in both material resources and staffing and staff expertise. The organization, and in a period of rapid social change the necessary reorganization, of the curriculum call into play a wide range of factors whose neglect will ensure a failure in the curriculum itself.

Assumptions about educational values and objectives, the content and structure of subject matter (see *Subject Matter*), and the requirements of learners and learning situations all enter into curriculum organization, as do the pattern of schooling and the kinds of services available to support the work of teachers. In organizing the curriculum, curriculum designs must be used and an effort made to implement them in the practical situations of schooling.

How the curriculum is and might be organized are questions whose answers depend on clarity about just what the curriculum encompasses. Modern conceptions and definitions of curriculum, for example in Western Europe and the United States, go well beyond the older and more limited idea that the curriculum is an assemblage of subjects and topics within and across subjects (syllabus-based approach). Included now are the numerous and varied learning experiences of students under the overall guidance of the school or college.

The curriculum is a social artifact—an expression and an outcome of social life—as well as a pedagogical device—a means of directing learning. Organizing the curriculum necessitates attention to wider social factors and forces as well as to the internal workings of the educational institution. Conversely, social forces impinge upon the curriculum and affect the manner in which it is organized, a fact which is evident in many countries, such as communist regimes or Third World nations, where the organization of the curriculum is in direct response to stated policy goals or, in others, where widespread public dissatisfaction with schooling has led to a reformation of priorities towards more utilitarian goals and resulted in greater prominence in the curriculum of literacy and numeracy skills.

An approach to curriculum organization which identifies key or basic learnings and articulates them into a core of skills, concepts and factual learnings to be taught to all students has become popular with governments particularly in English speaking countries during the past decade. A key document in this movement is the American Report, *A Nation at Risk*. In Britain, this approach is embodied in legislation (1988 Education Act).

Organization of the curriculum is more than the arrangement and interrelationship of areas of knowledge and experience, their structuring and sequencing for student learning. Nevertheless, it is essentially the pedagogical task which is of direct importance for curriculum makers, teachers, and administrators. What is it that is being structured and sequenced? According to the wider definition of curriculum, the learning experiences of the student must be the centre of attention. As a consequence (a) the characteristics and qualities of learners and their needs must be posited; (b) it is necessary to specify and know how to establish appropriate learning situations and environments; (c) it is necessary to decide upon appropriate strategies and methodologies of teaching; (d) it is necessary to specify and select from the areas of knowledge and experience from which learning tasks are to be drawn; and (e) it is necessary to determine procedures for monitoring and assessing both the curriculum and individual student learnings. Research and development work in all of these have helped to improve the capacity of educational

systems to reorganize curricula when expansion of student places has put enormous pressure on resources.

A strong revival of interest in systematic pedagogy is occurring as a result of theoretical and empirical work in psychology under the rubric of cognitive science. This is leading to such attempts to organize the curriculum according to student oriented learning strategies, including problem solving, creative thinking, and cognitive mapping.

It is in bringing the foregoing elements together into a coherent whole, that the organization of the curriculum is achieved. A programme of learning is thereby constructed, which is justifiable in the light of our theoretical knowledge and capable of being delivered effectively in specific learning environments and situations. Complex relationships and processes characterize effective curriculum organization, calling for skill and sensitivity on the part of the personnel involved. The tendency to reduce this complexity to slogans such as "back to the basics" or "inquiry learning" has contributed in recent years to the raising of false expectations about how the curriculum might be restructured (see *Back to Basics Movement*). Comprehensive changes in practice require thoroughgoing review and modification of every aspect of the curriculum system, and recognition that the implementation of change is dependent on organization no less than inspiration.

2. Three Levels of Curriculum Organization in the Educational System

The point about the complexity of organization may be better appreciated if it is related to the educational system. In most countries, regardless of regime, the system operates through structures and procedures at three levels: national; state, regional, or local; and the school level. Within these there are further distinctions which do not affect the main point that there are tasks and responsibilities for curriculum organization at each level, and their performance has implications for what is done at the other levels.

At the school level, in all systems, the teacher as much as any system administrator is faced with the challenge of articulating diverse elements in such a way that student learning does in fact take place: the ultimate objective of curriculum organization. However, this challenge cannot be met by individual teacher action alone. There are questions of scope, breadth, and balance, and of the orderly sequencing of learning, which require collaborative effort. School-level managers and administrators have a dual responsibility here, to ensure that there are satisfactory procedures for maintaining continuity and interrelatedness of learning and to distribute the scarce resources of teacher expertise and time for learning in such a way that the goals of the curriculum are achieved. They have varying degrees of freedom with which to exercise these responsibilities.

At the levels of local, regional, and state or prefecture administration within a national system, a different set of curriculum organization tasks has to be performed. As with the national-level tasks, the only justification for their performance is that they should contribute to effective organization at the school level, where teachers and students meet. These tasks vary in scope and significance according to the nature of the educational system as a whole, and there are considerable variations reflecting both national traditions of government and administration, and ideological shifts. In countries like the United Kingdom, the United States, the Federal Republic of Germany, Canada, Australia, and Japan, and in all federal and decentralized systems, very considerable responsibilities are exercised at this "intermediate" level. Some states or provinces in federal systems have virtually sovereign powers. In highly centralized systems and in many developing countries, there is less scope for initiative in curriculum organization at the local or regional level since the major task is ensuring that national policies are carried out and that nationally determined curriculum structures are implemented. Where there is considerable autonomy at this level, it is likely that curriculum advisers and consultants, local resource or development centres, and consortia of schools will play a significant role in curriculum review and analysis. Variations are frequently found in curriculum organization that reflect their interventions even where the basic pattern of the curriculum may be much the same across the country. Wherever regional differences have a long historical tradition or are expressed in differences in language and culture, the organization of the curriculum will, at the local level, exhibit strong ideological features.

At the national level, curriculum organization will—at least in centralized systems or wherever there is a politically strong national ministry—embody overall educational policy goals and be subject to political influence. Such influence on the organization of the curriculum may be observed in countries as diverse as France, Sweden, Nigeria, and Tanzania and throughout the communist world. In recent years, a similar phenomenon has emerged in traditionally decentralized systems such as England and Wales and New Zealand and in the federal systems of Australia and the United States of America.

There is frequently an interplay between professional associations, such as subject associations and teachers' unions, and the politicians and officials whereby the curriculum plan or policy is a compromise between competing interests. Thus questions like whether science should be taught in primary schools, or primary children be grouped by ability and attainment, or whether social subjects in the secondary school should be integrated, or the languages of minority groups made available in school time, are likely to be tested against political and bureaucratic as much as educational criteria. How such questions are answered will, naturally, affect the manner in which, at both local or state and school levels, educators and administrators are able to address their organizational questions.

Except in some federal systems, it is also at the national level, ultimately, that crucial decisions are taken about overall quantitative matters, such as budget levels, teacher–pupil ratios, and the qualifications teachers are required to possess. Increasingly, as international ties between countries become closer, policies of international bodies such as UNESCO, the Organisation for Economic Co-operation and Development (OECD), the European Economic Community (EEC), World Bank, etc. influence these financial and personnel items. Such considerations, frequently glossed over by curriculum theorists and designers, impact directly upon the organization of the curriculum in practice and qualify the roles of those seeking to modify the curriculum or to introduce innovations. This point is particularly apposite to the rapid growth—and in many cases the subsequent decline or demise—of national and local or state specialist curriculum research and development agencies, for example in the United States, Australia, and England and Wales. These bodies have an overriding interest in the reorganization of the curriculum, yet nowhere, even when located firmly within national ministries as in many parts of Southeast Asia and Africa, do they occupy a central position in policy making and resource allocation at the national level. Curriculum organization at the national level is unlikely to be significantly affected by such agencies which, as a consequence, generally seek to influence and relate to local, state, and school groups, working within the national policy framework.

3. Patterns of Organization: Pedagogical and Managerial

Given the interrelationships of curriculum policies and structures with many other parts of the social order, it is not to be expected that purely pedagogical approaches to curriculum organization can be adopted. Economic, political, and other sociocultural factors function at every point to impact upon the curriculum. Tradition, values, and ideologies operate within as well as upon the curriculum and its organization in practice reflects these concerns. This is true no less of the Western mixed economies with their diverse ideologies than of the communist world where curriculum is avowedly ideological and its organization inevitably a matter of political interest.

The recent cataclysmic political changes throughout Eastern Europe are bound to have repercussions in curriculum organization as previously monolithic ideologies are replaced by more plural values and interests.

Thus principles of curriculum organization cannot be formulated entirely from within the context of formal education. They must embody a cultural component that will vary across societies and over time. It cannot be assumed, however, that there is a definite set of relationships between particular value and belief systems and forms of social life on the one hand, and specific patterns of curriculum organization on the other. The relationship is not as clear or simple as that and perhaps is best thought of as a constant tendency for discussions about and decisions on curriculum organization to draw in these wider sociocultural concerns and to apply them in support—or criticism—of forms of organization that are preferred on other grounds which are not always made explicit. Nowhere is this more apparent than in the worldwide debate about the place in the curriculum of personal and social skills: literacy, numeracy, interpersonal relationships, decision making, application to practical tasks, and so on.

Notwithstanding the different ideologies and social–political–economic systems that occupy the world stage, a relatively small number of fundamental patterns of curriculum organization may be observed. As indicated above, what cannot be determined is an invariant set of relationships between these patterns and particular educational ideologies and systems.

The patterns may be classified into two main types, and further internally classified:

(a) Those patterns which are concerned with how content and experiences are articulated for learning and teaching (patterns of content and pedagogy).

(b) Those patterns which refer to procedures, methodologies, and techniques for organizing (managerial and process patterns).

It would be a mistake to suppose that one kind of pattern (content and pedagogy) can be equated with what school people do and the other (management and process) with what bureaucrats and administrators do.

In the practice of schooling, patterns of both types are to be observed, and are seen to combine in the unitary processes of decision making and implementation.

Taking, first, the content and pedagogical patterns, historically three major types have emerged:

(a) Curriculum organization may be seen as: the selection and classification of the content of learning according to subjects or subject areas, forms or fields of knowledge, ways of knowing, understanding and experiencing, and dominant cultural motifs (e.g., the literary classics in Confucianism). The central organizing principles here are embedded in the logic of the forms or fields of knowledge and in the lived culture of subjects and ways of life, and at the level of theory are of special interest to philosophers, philosophical anthropologists, curriculum theorists, cognitive scientists, social critics, and more academically minded teachers.

(b) Curriculum organization is derived from a theory of human development through activity: the learners' construction and reconstruction of reality through active engagement with specially marked out (by educators) features of their environment. The central organizing principles here are a combination drawn from dynamic and developmental

psychology, constructivist theories of knowledge and social action, and the practice of experimental pedagogy associated with the international progressive education movement. Names such as Dewey and Piaget, and bodies like the New (now World) Education Fellowship and the erstwhile Progressive Education Association in the United States are associated with these patterns of curriculum.

(c) Curriculum organization is identified with social priorities which have high salience in the governmental and industrial sectors. Emphasis is placed upon declared socially useful knowledge and skills, regardless of whether the curriculum is, broadly speaking, subject or activity based. A common catchword here is relevance, based on firm views about social need as defined not by teachers and pupils but by governmental and industrial representatives and some economic, social, and political theorists. In the history of education Herbert Spencer in England, Calvin Woodward in the U.S.A., and Georg Kerschensteiner in Germany have provided theoretical justification for these approaches. They are undergoing a strong revival as a consequence of governmental interest in achieving an "economic return" from educational investment.

These three patterns lend themselves to many variations in practice and are not, of course, mutually exclusive. It is common for the whole curriculum of a school to display aspects of all three, although closer analysis will usually disclose the prevalence of one or the other.

As for management or process patterns of curriculum organization, various approaches are favoured, reflecting not only surface differences about "best methods" but deeper differences over the nature of human action. Thus one of the most significant of contemporary debates about processes of organizing the curriculum is over management-by-objectives, and what is essentially at issue is the status of behaviourism as an adequate account of human action. Curriculum correlates of this approach include programmed learning and curriculum process models in which learning outcomes are structured through detailed objectives and specified as discrete student behaviours.

The organization of the curriculum, into whatever form is sought, may be achieved by many different processes and these may be grouped into three main types:

(a) Curriculum organization especially in well-established institutions, can grow or emerge, evolving and being modified progressively over time through everyday working relations amongst a teaching team, the interaction of their assumptions and values, and their felt need for corporate activity. The pattern here is tacit, the structures adaptive, and curriculum organization is less the goal of planning or the outcome of reflective analysis than the result of natural encounters in characteristic professional environments. This is sometimes described as an "ecological" approach.

(b) The management-by-objectives movement has set as one of its principal targets in education the planning of the curriculum as a set of internally consistent and explicitly rational activities. Organization here is both a goal and a dominant element in whatever curriculum design is undertaken. Educational behaviours are defined, to express specified objectives and become, in turn, the object of clearcut assessment procedures. This procedural approach to organization of the curriculum has had its widest following in parts of the United States and in the vocational and technical sectors.

(c) Curriculum organization is achieved through a wide repertoire of techniques and planning processes, involving aims and goals statements which are proposed not as behavioural outcomes but as growth points through which new possibilities and ideas may emerge. This approach has experimental elements, inasmuch as review and monitoring procedures are built in and it has an open-ended character. The approach is eclectic since it incorporates elements from both of the approaches already mentioned. 'Negotiation" is a key concept, as is the "process" curriculum.

4. Curriculum Organization and the Core Curriculum

After a period of review and rebuilding of individual components of the curriculum (subjects, topics, areas of study) in the early to mid-1970s, several countries began to reconsider the whole curriculum, by asking which areas of study might be regarded as essential for all students. Part of the inspiration for this came from public and political criticism of an alleged (but seldom demonstrated) decline in overall standards of pupil performance. The idea emerged of a "core curriculum", comprising a limited set of postulated basic and essential learnings, and assessment procedures were developed to concentrate attention on the core. England and Wales, the United States, Canada, and Australia all provide examples (see *Core Curriculum*).

More critical and fundamental analyses followed this first attempt to define basic and essential learnings, such as work in Australia through the national Curriculum Development Centre which outlined a broad core of general education, and indicated major roles for schools in selecting from this core and building up specific programmes of study.

Core has thus become a crucial theme in policy, theory building, research, and national assessment procedures and is now achieving in school practice the status of a major new movement. It is probable that, as more pressure is laid upon schools to review and redesign their curricula and to maintain general monitoring programmes, interest is likely to grow in the idea that the curriculum as a whole may be organized and interrelated through a central core of studies. It will be in the determination of this core that schools and educational institutions will be able to demonstrate their capacity to reorganize curricula in response to wider trends of social and cultural change, as well as to the changing characteristics of the school population.

Bibliography

Connell W F 1980 *A History of Education in the Twentieth Century World.* Curriculum Development Centre, Canberra

Lawton D, Chitty C (eds.) 1988 *The National Curriculum.* University of London Institute of Education, London

Lee V, Zeldin D (eds.) 1982 *Planning in the Curriculum.* Hodder and Stoughton, London

National Commission on Excellence 1983 *A Nation at Risk.* US Department of Education, Washington, DC

Organisation for Economic Co-operation and Development (OECD) 1975 *Handbook on Curriculum Development.* OECD, Paris

Skilbeck M 1984 *School-based Curriculum Development.* Harper and Row, London

Skilbeck M 1989 Revitalizing the core curriculum. *Journal of Curriculum and Supervision* 4(3): 197–210

Smith B O, Stanley W O, Shores J H 1957 *Fundamentals of Curriculum Development.* Harcourt, Brace and World, New York

Stenhouse L 1975 *An Introduction to Curriculum Research and Development.* Heinemann, London

Participants in the Curriculum Process

Curriculum Development Centers

S. Eden

Since the early 1950s, significant changes have occurred in the organizational structure of curriculum development activities. Before the emergence of the curriculum movement in the 1950s this work was performed by ad hoc committees of teachers and subject matter specialists. The curriculum movement granted professional status to curriculum development activities. Consequently curriculum development centers were established in various countries around the world in which experts specializing in curriculum development have been employed on a permanent basis in full-time jobs. Some curriculum development centers gained the status of independent institutes and others have operated as departments in their ministries of education, as departments or projects of universities, or as special research units (Taylor and Johnson 1974).

1. The Link with Educational Authorities

The structure of curriculum development centers and their function is one affected by context factors such as the characteristics of the educational system, its articulation, the resources available, and the educational philosophy dominant in a particular area or country. History and tradition also leave their imprints on the structure of the centers. A distinction may be made between development units of two types. Those of the first type were established by governmental or municipal bodies, and are entrusted with the responsibility of providing curricula for the entire educational system or for a particular section of it. The other type of development units were organized by universities or private foundations. These units produce curricula and market them without assuming responsibility for satisfying all the needs of the educational system, and operate without establishing an obligatory link between the production system and the users system. Most of the development units of the first type are known as "curriculum centers," although some use the terms "institute," "department," "council," and so on. The development units of the second type are normally known as "study groups" or "projects" (CERI 1975). It must nevertheless be noted that the variation within each of the two types is greater than the differences between the two.

Some distinctive features of curriculum development centers follow.

1.1 Legitimacy

The source of the legitimacy of curriculum development centers may stem from the authorities endowed by law with the duty to administer the educational system in a specific area (Klein and Goodlad 1978). Frequently a single development center is requested to produce curricula for the entire system, or, alternatively, the administrative body may set up several curriculum development centers with a clear division of labor among them. A curriculum project may also operate as a voluntary enterprise of a group of experts, the work of which is then submitted for approval to the educational authorities. There are also countries with a number of centers that produce alternative programs and compete for the patronage of the users.

1.2 Responsibility

Linked to the issue of legitimacy is the scope of responsibility of a curriculum development center. It may assume responsibility for the curriculum of an entire system or for that of a smaller administrative unit; it may limit itself to one or several stages of education (such as primary or secondary); to one or more types of schools (such as academic or vocational); to one or more school subjects (language, arts, mathematics, science, etc.); or to one or more areas of education (e.g., enrichment programs, exceptional children, etc.).

1.3 Mandatory Status of Curricula

One of the major variables in regard to curriculum development centers is the extent to which the schools are obliged to use the products of the center. In some educational systems the products of the center are mandatory, in others only the rationale of the curriculum and a very general outline must be used. The development of learning materials is performed by the teacher or by private authors and publishers. In some educational systems there is no mandatory curriculum and the teachers and the principal make decisions about the curriculum. In most such cases the main responsibility of centers is to develop model curricula, that is, to produce examples of learning materials and to give advice to interested teachers.

1.4 Professional Freedom

The extent of professional freedom of development teams differs from one center to another. The highest degree of freedom characterizes "projects" or "study groups" at the universities. Scholars in such a setting approach topics and subjects in a way which, according to their view, is most appropriate, without obtaining any directives or guidelines from superior authorities. They may prepare learning materials for a particular subject area or they may develop interdisciplinary programs and invite experts according to their choice. Professional freedom is more limited in those centers which constitute a part of the bureaucratic hierarchy of the educational system. In such centers, the principal decisions are made by committees of officials. The constraint on professional freedom is even greater in cases where the approval of the curriculum is the prerogative of a political body. Between these two extremes one may find a variety of compromises. Some possible arrangements are as follows (Klein and Goodlad 1978):

(a) The governing body delegates power to an appointed committee, and does not control its work.

(b) An expert from a university is invited to serve as chairperson of the development team, and is authorized to make necessary decisions.

(c) The center develops alternative programs, and schools may choose a particular one, and may supplement it with teacher-made materials, or may adapt the chosen program to local needs.

(d) The center only develops examples of curriculum materials to serve as a model for teachers developing curricula for their schools or classes.

2. Activities Performed by Curriculum Development Centers

Curriculum developments perform a variety of activities:

(a) Data gathering—curriculum centers conduct needs assessment studies (see *Needs Assessment Studies*); they collect data about and from teachers, learners, parents, scholars, and the general public, with the aim of finding out whether there is a need for revising the existing curricula or producing new ones.

(b) Planning—the centers determine priorities, define educational objectives, interpret formal documents, prepare program outlines, and compile inventories of learning activities.

(c) Development—they develop learning materials, models, and examples of learning packages for

learners and teachers. They carry out the trial of new materials, perform formative evaluation activities, and monitor the process of mass production of materials.

(d) Implementation—some of the curriculum development centers assume responsibility for implementing the curricula produced by their teams. They take care to disseminate the new programs through organizing conferences, delivering lectures, preparing information bulletins, and so on.

As well as the above activities, the centers also organize inservice training activities for teachers who intend to use the new programs. They provide help in adapting the learning materials to local needs and provide continuous services, including providing equipment and supplies to schools using the program (Eden 1979, Lewy 1977).

3. Approaches and Orientations to the Process of Curriculum Development

The major differences in approaches and orientations to the process of development between curriculum development centers are as follows.

Most centers operate on the assumption that the preparation of new curricula and the production of learning materials requires a reasonable amount of time and should be done by specially trained professionals. Thus such work cannot be considered as part of the daily activities of the teacher. An opposing approach refuses to view the teacher as a passive "consumer" of programs developed by others. The supporters of this approach claim that the curriculum prepared by the teachers themselves may suit the needs of the pupils and their own capabilities best. Accordingly, a distinction is made between the "center" and "periphery" orientation to curriculum development. The supporters of the "center" approach claim that the curriculum prepared by professional teams should fit the needs of the typical teacher and learner of the target population. The main criticism of this approach is that any curriculum developed under conditions detached from the real teaching–learning situation does not fit the needs of a particular teacher or learner. The supporters of the "periphery" approach claim that the teacher knows best what fits the needs of the learner, and the preparation of the curriculum therefore must be a regular element of the teacher's responsibility. The main criticism of this approach is that it discourages innovation and produces poor learning materials. Some teachers tend to use existing learning materials repeatedly.

Most centers produce only part of the materials, leaving some responsibility of curriculum production to the teachers.

Lately there have been a growing number of teachers' centers of local character that supply services and advice to teachers in the development of their own learning materials. Curriculum development centers which produce mainly model curricula and examples of learning units as well as supporting curriculum development activities of the teachers try to create a sound balance between the "center" and "periphery" activities in the field of curriculum development.

The growing inclination toward interaction between "center" and "periphery" points to a possible compromise between the two approaches.

4. The Role of Curriculum Development Centers

Originally, curriculum development centers were established as instruments for implementing reforms conceptualized at higher hierarchical levels of the educational bureaucracy. They were requested to produce learning materials which reflected recent advancements in various subject areas, excelled in relevance to extant social needs, and fitted the interest and the ability level of the learners (Fullan and Pomfret 1977). Gradually, however, the roles of the centers were broadened and they became instrumental in disseminating new programs, facilitating their absorption in the schools, generating interest in curriculum innovations, establishing local resource centers, motivating teams of

teachers to work cooperatively in developing programs of local interest, and monitoring local activities in the field of curriculum production.

Bibliography

Center for Educational Research and Innovation (CERI) 1975 *Handbook on Curriculum Development*. Organisation for Economic Co-operation and Development, Paris

Eden S 1979 *Implementation of Innovations in Education: A Case Study in Curriculum Planning*. Studies in Educational Evaluation, monograph No. 2. University of California, Los Angeles, California

Eden S, Moses S, Amiad R 1987 Multi-track curriculum planning. In: Sabar N, Ruddick J, Reid W (eds.) *Partnership and Autonomy in School-based Curriculum Development*. University of Sheffield, Sheffield

Fullan M, Pomfret A 1977 Research on curriculum and instruction implementation. *Rev. Educ. Res.* 47: 335–97

Klein M F, Goodlad, I J 1978 *A Study of Curriculum Decision Making in Eighteen Selected Countries*. University of California, Los Angeles, California

Lewy A 1977 *Handbook of Curriculum Evaluation*. Longman, New York

Taylor P H, Johnson M (eds.) 1974 *Curriculum Development: A Comparative Study*. National Foundation for Educational Research, Slough

Decisions at Educational System Level

A. Lewy

This article describes the operational modes of decision-making bodies in various countries which review and examine the adequacy of school curricula, make decisions about the content of educational programs and about time allocated to subject areas, and provide legitimation for introducing new subjects into the framework of school studies. The differences in study time schedules across countries and overt and covert aspects of the time schedule are also discussed.

In the examination of school curricula in educational systems across the world one may detect striking similarities as well as differences. Some core elements are taught in almost all educational systems. Tyler has specified five such core elements: the study of language, literature, mathematics, history, and science (see *Core Curriculum*). In their first attempt to set up the Assessment of Performance Unit, British educators devised a national project aimed at providing data about the achievement level of schoolchildren in six specified areas of school studies or lines of development which should be pursued in schools. These include: mathematics, language, sciences, physical development, aesthetics, and personal and social development (Pring 1981). A team of experts of the Hungarian Academy of Science identified the following seven areas of erudition: language and communication, mathematics, sciences, history and socio-political knowledge, aesthetics, physical

education, and technology (Rét 1978). No matter whether one prefers to specify a narrower or broader range of such core elements, it is possible to detect all of these elements in the educational programs of primary schools in nearly all educational systems across the world. These core elements become more articulated as one moves towards higher grades in school. In the highest grades of secondary schools most educational systems permit some specialization and students may drop one or several core topics from their individual scheme of studies.

At the same time one may observe substantial differences across educational systems with regard to the amount of time devoted to the study of these core elements, the continuity of teaching them across the whole range of grade levels, and their particular content components.

The Second Mathematics Study of the International Association for the Evaluation of Educational Achievement (IEA) revealed that the number of mathematics study periods per week, for students who take mathematics classes, varies from 3 to 10, and the percentage of mathematics periods of all study periods varies from 12 to 30 percent. Differences are also found in the topics taught in classes and in the conditions under which mathematics may be dropped from individual study programs (McKnight et al. 1987).

Table 1
Curriculum time schedule (in periods) in five countries[a]

Subjects	Turkey	Morocco	German Democratic Republic	Thailand Compulsory	Optional	Colombia
Religion	1*					3
Moral education	1					
Mother tongue	5	7	6	4		6
Mathematics	4	5	6	4		5
History, Social Studies	4	3	4	5		5
Science	4		5	4		5
Foreign Language	3	9	5		6	
Art	2		2	2	2	3
Physical education	2		3	3	2	3
Work			2	4	6	
Electives	4			3	2	
Total	30	24	33	35		30

a Adapted from Holmes (1983) and Kienitz (1985)   * Optional

Table 1 contains information about the time allocated to various subjects for children of age 13 in five different countries. The information contained in Table 1 reveals that there is a high level of uniformity across countries in time allocation to mathematics and physical education, while there are considerable differences in the time allocation to other subjects.

More striking differences can be observed with regard to the inclusion in the educational program of subjects which do not pertain to the core study areas, like moral education, religion, art, and so on. In the domain of Social Studies more than 30 innovative subjects are listed in curriculum catalogs and educational systems differ from each other with regard to the status given to these areas of study.

The comparison of study timetables appearing in Table 1 provides only partial information about similarities and differences across systems. Quite frequently, under the label of a single subject in various systems, or even in various schools in the same system, different content is taught in the classes, and conversely it may happen that the same topic is dealt with under other subject labels. Thus, for example, within the framework of the mother tongue, rudimentary elements of science or history are frequently taught in schools. The connotative significance of subject labels should not be disregarded but this does not always tell the whole truth.

1. The Management of Curriculum Change

In most educational systems there are some formal provisions for adapting the curriculum to changing conditions. Most frequently the Minister of Education assumes formal responsiblity for approving changes and modifications in the program following the recommendations of advisory bodies of different types. Advisory bodies across educational systems differ from each other in terms of their legal status, the permanency of their operation, and the scope of persons involved in formulating changes. In some systems the operational mode of the advisory bodies is determined through legislation, and they act as a standing committee on a continuous basis for a certain period of time. In other systems the advisory bodies are ad hoc committees appointed to deal with a single issue, and the term of their service expires after formulating recommendations.

The operation of the advisory bodies is characterized both by elitist and democratic patterns of decision making, that is, considering the views of highly reputed experts and also of popular votes of all parties affected by the decision. The actual changes reflect "top down" ideas, namely, suggestions of educational leaders, and also "bottom up" ideas, or grass-root innovations, which were tried out by teachers and found to be effective. The weight of these two sources, nevertheless, widely differs across systems. To illustrate these differences details of national decision-making bodies in three countries are presented.

1.1 Republic of Korea

The ideological parameters of the school curriculum are determined by the 1968 Charter of National Education which promulgates commitment to continuous improvement in learning and arts, to the development of the innate faculties of each person and to overcoming the existing difficulties of the rapid progress of the nation (Ministry of Education 1986). According to the law, the Minister of Education is empowered to determine what actual curricular arrangements are conducive to the attainment of the above-mentioned ideals. Practically however, the Minister acts on the basis of the recommendations issued by the Curriculum Department of the Ministry. This department has a staff of 40 pro-

Table 2
Curriculum decision procedures in the Republic of Korea

Procedure	Decision maker	Nature of decision
Planning R and D[a]	MoE[b] Unit KEDI Team	Administrative Professional
	Discussions with teachers, subject experts, MoE unit staff, educational psychologists, school administrators, and so on.	
Deliberation	Committee of MoE	Semiprofessional Semipolitical
Finalization	MoE Unit and KEDI team	Fine-tuning
Authorizing	Minister of Education	Administrative

a Research and Development b Ministry of Education

fessionals, who establish ad hoc committees every 5 to 7 years to examine the sustained adequacy of the school programs. These Curriculum Committees of the Ministry operate in an advisory and reviewing capacity. On the basis of their recommendations, the Ministry instructs the Korean Educational Development Institute (KEDI) to suggest revised curricula for the schools. In order to carry out this task KEDI establishes its own curriculum committees which contain subject specialists, teachers, curriculum experts, and representatives of the community and the parents.

A schematic representation of the curriculum revision process appears in Table 2. The KEDI committees, after a series of meetings and after a process of thorough deliberation and negotiation with the committee of the Ministry of Education, prepare proposals for revising the curriculum. The proposals contain the specifications for the content components of the new program, suggestions for teaching strategies, and suggestions for time allocation to various programs. These proposals, having been approved by the committee of the Ministry and the Curriculum Department itself, are signed by the Minister of Education, and thus obtain legal validity.

In practice, the committees of the Ministry of Education exhibit a very cautious approach to curriculum changes, and so fulfill the role of stabilizing the system, as well as supporting changes.

1.2 Australia

The dominant factor in the field of curriculum development in Australia is the Curriculum Development Centre (CDC) of the Commonwealth School Commission. The statutory power of making decisions about curricular issues is delegated to the Federal Minister and the State Ministers of Education.

The Curriculum Development Centre was established according to the Act of Parliament in 1975, but following the report of the Committee of the Review of Commonwealth Functions in April 1981 it was abolished, and

was replaced by the Curriculum Development Branch within the Commonwealth Department of Education. The 1984 law reestablished the Federal Curriculum Development Centre, and also established the Council of the Curriculum Development Centre. The members of the Council include representatives from the Commonwealth School Commission, the Commonwealth Department of Education, the Australian Educational Council (a body comprising the State Ministers of Education and the Federal Minister of Education), and also highly reputed educational professionals, including subject specialists and school teachers appointed the Minister.

The Council is obliged to consult formally and cooperate with representatives of the States and Territories and with persons, bodies, and authorities conducting nongovernmental schools in Australia. It has to consult, on a less formal basis, a wider range of interest groups in the education community in the course of activities related to curriculum development. The regulations published by the Commonwealth School Commission represent a highly balanced division of power between the central and local education authorities.

The CDC is expected to fulfill a dual role. First, it is requested to promote national curriculum objectives, such as initiating positive steps to ensure that everyone should have access to the best curriculum, and that those who are seen as somehow disadvantaged should be adequately catered for. Second, it implies encouraging and promoting attitudes and understandings in young people that lead to an acceptance of, and enthusiasm for, a diverse yet peaceful and cohesive Australian society.

These common educational goals should guide curriculum development activities across all States and Territories. At the same time it should support the States/Territories and wider community of teachers, students, and parents in terms of a capacity to coordinate and facilitate joint activities, marshal resources across a number of sectors, provide educational and curriculum information, and as necessary, provide publishing and distribution services.

The operational guidelines specify that the Council should adopt a cooperational and collaborative approach to the performance of its functions. It should consult and be prepared to work with groups and individuals in all the major types of educational settings.

The 1984 Bill obliges the CDC to contribute to curriculum renewal. To attain this goal it is expected to conduct regular reviews in all subject areas, including the traditional study areas such as English, mathematics, and science. The modification of courses of studies should take account of new knowledge and understanding, and changes in the society that are organized in ways which arouse and maintain student interest. The Bill does not specify how often the curriculum content should be modified or revised. Nevertheless, it requires that the Council should furnish the Minister with a report containing recommendations with respect to matters of curriculum, at least once a year.

1.3 Hungary

Four major curriculum reforms carried out in Hungary during the post-Second World War period were the initiatives of the central educational authorities, that is, the Ministry of Education. The first, in 1945, occurred in the wake of the political changes. Its aim was to replace the previously used nationalistic and quasi-Fascist materials by new programs, which were expected to promote the democratization of life in the country. The reform of 1948 was promulgated and designed to transform Hungarian society along socialist lines. The 1961 Education Act and the consequent changes in the curricula were undertaken in a period of political consolidation, and reflected pedagogical rather than political considerations (Báthory 1986). A major curriculum reform was introduced in 1978. To prepare this reform adequately the National Institute of Education carried out a meticulously planned Needs Assessment Study. Also, at the request of the Hungarian Socialist Workers' Party and the Ministry of Education, the Hungarian Academy of Science established a Public Education Committee to provide high-level scientific assistance "for preparing the modernization of subjects in the long-range school reform and for performing a partial school reform (relating only to the curriculum) at medium range" (Rét 1978 p. 229). The work of the Committee culminated in publishing a model of erudition, which had been approved by the presidium of the Hungarian Academy of Sciences (Statement and Recommendation 1976), and recommending to the Ministry of Education the use of this model in determining the contents of new curricula. The Committee emphasized that the ideal of erudition should not necessarily be realized in a single person, but rather in an entire generation.

While the 1978 reform was initiated by the central educational authorities, its major feature was the recommendation to share the responsibility for curriculum development with local school authorities. According to this reform, the compulsory core curriculum occupies only 70 percent of the whole program, and the rest is determined by the local authorities and schools themselves.

During the period from 1945 to 1978 four educational reforms were carried out in Hungary, and it can be observed that the time lag between a particular reform and the subsequent one has continuously increased. Seemingly, the consolidation of political and economic life in the country lead towards a greater stability in school programs, and instigated the emergence of locally initiated incremental changes in school programs, without necessarily relying on national legislation.

In Hungary, as in other socialist countries, educational planning is fully integrated with economic and cultural planning among all government institutions. National plans are made for various periods of time. Long-range planning is instituted for a period of up to 15 to 20 years, and medium-range 5-year plans specify concrete tasks (Rét 1978).

2. Across-country Differences in the Emphasis of Various Subjects

Differences across countries in the emphasis of various subjects are to a large extent explained by differences in social conditions, occupational stratification, national culture, and the like. However, both the similarities and differences across educational systems suggest that the freedom of educational authorities in determining what should be taught in the schools is quite limited. The decision makers are bound by international trends and national traditions. This is true for curriculum development centers as well as for ad hoc committees in charge of educational reforms.

In the first place, it is necessary to consider the constraints of time. The regular weekly time-schedule for children of the age of 10 to 15 is between 24 to 35 study periods. Both financial and mental health reasons do not permit further extension of the study time in school. Any further extension of time spent in school would mean an increment in leisure and social activities rather than in demanding intellectual studies.

Countries differ widely from each other from the point of view of time needed to study language arts. The complexity of the mother tongue, the similarity of the spoken language to the written one, the need to acquire knowledge in a foreign language, the richness of the written cultural treasures of a nation, and the value attributed to the cultural heritage are important considerations in determining what proportion of the time should be devoted to the study of languages.

Thus, for example, in Morocco in the seventh-grade (age 12 to 13) children spend seven weekly periods studying the national language, and they also spend nine hours per week studying French. Arabic is a diglotic language, that is, the formal written language is greatly different from the spoken one, and consequently first-grade children coming to school have to start to use a language which is quite new to them. If one adds to this the fact that both for cultural and for economic reasons there is a great demand for the knowledge of the French language, then it becomes clear that in order to keep the study time constant, relatively little scheduled time remains for studying other subjects in the school. Also in countries in which various population groups use different languages, the acquisition of a foreign language may be a personal and a national necessity for enabling communication among people living in the country. When a country with such language needs faces the challenge of industrialization, it may wish to increase the scope of teaching science and mathematics in the school. Frequently this can be done only by reducing the study periods for the language arts. Such situations of conflicting demands can be resolved only through deliberations which lead to compromises, and this does not provide full satisfaction to all interested parties. Under such conditions the life span of a school program may be relatively short and it may be necessary to carry out curriculum reviews and modifications quite frequently.

Another source of demand for study time is the expansion of knowledge and the emergence of new study areas, such environmental studies or computer sciences, and so on (see *Knowledge Explosion**). School systems which are interested in incorporating such studies in their school program unavoidably have to reduce time available for studying basic skills and the core component of major school subjects. Conflicting demands between placing emphasis on a limited set of core elements versus dealing with continuously increasing expansion of knowledge was the underlying motive for several curriculum modifications in the 1980s. The solutions observed represent a broad variety of balance patterns between these conflicting demands.

3. Overt and Covert Aspects of System Level Curriculum Decisions

The procedural aspects of introducing curriculum changes within an educational system are quite clearly specified and sufficiently well-documented. The researcher may encounter difficulties in obtaining information about procedures of curriculum changes in several countries, but with great tenacity and perseverance such information can be gathered. It is, however, almost impossible to obtain information about the extent to which these formal changes affect the actual curriculum of the schools.

The problem is more complex than merely measuring curriculum implementation. Since extant proposals of curriculum changes tend to favor the participation of all stake-holders in the process of program planning (and they are not fully prescriptive, but rather tend to offer a range of electives from which schools and individuals

are supposed to select courses of studies), different measures for assessing success are needed from those which have been used hitherto in implementation-evaluation studies. Measures are needed which assess both quantitative and qualitative aspects of participation. What kind of participation seems to be desirable? What should be the scope of participation and its intensity? Would it be considered a success if in 10 percent of schools some kind of community participation occurred, or do the educational planners aim to attain the participation of much broader strata of the population?

There is also a need to establish standards and criteria for assessing the effectiveness of alternative course offerings. What constitutes an effective procedure of selecting from alternative offerings? Surveys of curriculum utilization patterns suggest that 80 to 90 percent of the schools align themselves according to the mainstream, and do not take advantage of the freedom given them to initiate curriculum changes or modifications (Stake and Easley 1978, Squire 1985). In several countries, parents have been granted the right to determine a substantial proportion of the curriculum for the their children (20 percent of study time in Indonesia and in Israel). Nevertheless, in these countries the involvement of parents is quite limited, and in most cases, when asked, they tend to vote for adding more time to the teaching of the core components of the program, rather than suggesting broadening the scope of the curriculum areas.

Surprisingly enough no comprehensive reports are available about the actual school programs in countries which traditionally have not had centrally prescribed school curricula. Details are not available about the degree of diversification of the actual school programs in these educational systems. Nevertheless, it seems that the right to make decisions about the curriculum does not, of itself, lead towards diversification in practice. In the early 1990s there is a lack of not only descriptive information about the success of curriculum changes, but also lack of an inventory of relevant questions. Under such circumstances it may be preposterous to ask the question "what works?" in the context of curriculum reviews and renewals.

Bibliography

Báthory Z 1986 Decentralization issues in the introduction of new curriculum: The case of Hungary. *Prospects* 16: 33–47

Commonwealth Schools Commission 1985, *Role and Operations.* Curriculum Development Centre, Canberra

Holmes B (ed.) 1983 *International Handbook of Education Systems.* Wiley, New York

Kienitz W 1985 German Democratic Republic: System of education. In: Husén T, Postlethwaite T N (eds.) 1985 *International Encyclopedia of Education.* Pergamon Press, Oxford, pp. 2024–31

Ministry of Education 1986 *Education in Korea 1985–86.* Ministry of Education, Seoul

McKnight C C, Crosswhite F J, Dossey J A, Kifer E, Swafford

J O, Travers K J, Cooney T J 1987 *The Underachieving Curriculum: Assessing US School Mathematics from an International Perspective*. Stipes, Champaign, Illinois

Pring R 1981 Monitoring performance: Reflections on the Assessment of Performance Unit. In: Lacey C, Lawton D (eds.) 1981 *Issues in Evaluation and Accountability*. Methuen, London, pp. 156–71

Rét R 1978 The Hungarian plan for the school of tomorrow. *Prospects* 8: 228–37

Squire J 1985 Basal readers. In: Husén T, Postlethwaite T N (eds.) 1985 *International Encyclopedia of Education*. Pergamon, Oxford, pp. 409–11

Stake R, Easley J 1978 *Case Studies in Science Education*. University of Illinois College of Education, Urbana, Illinois

Curriculum Personnel

H.-D. Haller and A. Lewy

Curriculum personnel are those who, on the basis of their professional competence, prepare or assist in preparing curriculum materials, or make decisions concerning adoption and adaptation of curriculum materials prepared by others.

The central concerns related to curriculum personnel are the professional status and the role of professionals and nonprofessionals, in the process of curriculum development. While curriculum theory (see *Curriculum Theory*) and curriculum research (see *Curriculum Research*) gained a recognized academic status within the framework of educational studies and several schools of education maintain curriculum departments of high academic prestige, still in the domain of educational practice the status of curriculum professionals and their role remains unclear. Curriculum departments of educational systems as well as curriculum development projects are frequently headed by administrators or subject experts, who view their work in that particular job as a transitory one.

Attempts to professionalize the process of curriculum development had been made by the 1920s by the leaders of the scientific curriculum movement (Bobbitt 1918, Charters 1923). Later in the 1960s and 1970s a renewed and more effficient effort was made to strengthen the scientific basis of curriculum development, which led to an increased professionalization of the curriculum personnel. Nevertheless, curriculum development has remained a team effort in which curriculum experts work together with experts from other fields and with nonprofessional people. Thus laypersons, together with professionals from fields such as sociology, philosophy, and so on, participate in making decisions relating to educational goals and curricular objectives; subject experts have a say in selecting curricular contents; and teachers together with experts in subject didactics assume a leading role in devising learning experiences and in trying out curricular materials (see *Curriculum Tryout*).

All in all, a great variation can be observed in the composition of curricular development teams and in the pattern of dividing responsibilities among team members having expertise in various fields (Great Britain Schools Council 1973).

1. Two Bodies of Knowledge Related to Curriculum Development

Curriculum development entails knowledge of a particular subject and also of curriculum theory. Specific curriculum-oriented knowledge is a necessary precondition for adequately dealing with curriculum issues. Subject matter experts must acquire knowledge about curriculum theory in addition to expertise in their particular discipline.

Nonprofessionals participating in the process of curriculum development must overcome their lay status and acquire the technical knowledge needed for their work. To quote a theory on the sociology of knowledge: "the problem with the subject matter professionals is the development of a *Deutungswissen* (explanation knowledge); the problem with nonprofessionals, laymen, is the development of a *Problemlosungswissen* (problem-solving knowledge)" (Berger and Luckmann 1970).

Numerous attempts have been made to identify and define the elements of the two bodies of knowledge needed for curriculum work. Analytical studies by curriculum theorists list required competencies for curriculum workers. Doll (1978) emphasizes the importance of leadership traits such as empathy, interest in assuming leadership, emotional control, ability to interact with fellow staff, facilitating communication within the organization. Leithwood (1982) presents a two-dimensional grid in which one dimension consists of four management functions: planning, organizing, supervising, communicating. The other dimension consists of four types of curriculum decisions: establishing a conceptual framework, development, implementation, evaluation. By using this two-dimensional grid he defines 16 specific skills needed in the process of curriculum development.

2. Service- and Development-oriented Curriculum Work

Curriculum work which has bearings on school practice is carried out in two distinct settings, differing from each other with regard to the definition of the term curriculum, the kind of materials being produced, and the type of professionals being employed. One such setting is the service-oriented curriculum department, affiliated to administrative bodies or constituting a part of them, and the other one is the curriculum project or the curriculum development center which produces instructional materials of an innovative nature.

Most frequently, service-oriented curriculum departments conceive curricula as the specification of the objectives and academic contents of courses to be taught in schools. Accordingly, such departments content themselves with producing orientation materials for guiding teachers in their work. Typical products of such departments are guidelines, syllabi, *programmes et instructions*, *Lehrpläne*, or *Rahmenrichtlinien*. Such departments also assume responsibility for convoking ad hoc curriculum committees, monitoring their work, and examining and approving textbooks used in school. Service-oriented curriculum departments recruit their staff members from the ranks of educational professionals of various types. The prerequisite for being employed in such a department is experience rather than formal training or expertise in curriculum-related domains. The head of such a department is usually a person who previously worked as an inspector and frequently continues in this capacity, while at the same time being engaged in curriculum matters. The majority of the personnel are school teachers and principals who excelled in their work, and were promoted to the position of staff members in the department. Many of them work on a part-time basis and consider their work at the department as a transitory phase in their professional careers. Occasionally professionals from related fields, such as educational psychology, sociology, and so on are co-opted to the staff, mostly on a part-time basis.

The second type of setting which concerns itself with problems of school curricula is a variety of curriculum development projects or centers. They may differ from each other from the point of view of their organizational affiliation. Some of them are affiliated to universities, others operate as a body of academic or semiacademic status within the framework of the national or local educational bureaucracy. Still others are fully independent institutes financed by special grants. The common feature of such institutes is their involvement in the production of detailed course outlines of an innovative type, and also instructional materials to be used by the learners. According to the conceptions dominating these institutes, the term curriculum means more than the specification of course objectives and contents. As stated by Oliver (1965), the term curriculum includes all the experiences of children for which the school should accept responsibility. In contrast with the bureaucratic climate of the service-oriented curriculum departments, the development-oriented projects or centers are characterized by an academic climate.

The development work is carried out according to scientifically legitimized procedures. The team members also prepare articles and monographs of academic interest, explaining various aspects of their curriculum work, and aid in selecting staff members with serious consideration being given to their academic qualifications. It is mainly the status of curriculum personnel in this setting which was dealt with in research and studies of the 1960s and 1970s and accordingly it constitutes the topic of the subsequent sections.

3. Curriculum Development Teams

Rülcker (1983) reviews a variety of curriculum development patterns and distinguishes between hierarchically structured linear models, according to which the development activities are broken down into sequential phases, and multidimensional interactive models.

Among the linear models, the best known one is the research–development–diffusion model (briefly the R–D–D model) described by Havelock (1971). Each of its three distinct phases is characterized by activities of a unique nature and accordingly the staff composition also varies from phase to phase. At the research phase, researchers are at work. Postlethwaite (1977) describes a variety of research activities which should be carried out at this phase of curriculum development. Demographic trend studies, shifts in occupational structure, changes in values, health-related habits, perception of students regarding their learning needs, and so on may provide relevant information to be used during this phase of the process. Suarez (1981) describes models of needs assessment studies, which may assist the project teams in setting curricular goals (see *Needs Assessment Studies*). Researchers employed at this phase should be recruited from the fields of sociology, educational and social psychology, management sciences, demography, educational measurement, and so on. It should be noted however, that those who carry out such studies do not constitute a part of the curriculum personnel. They are commissioned researchers, or teams, who work to satisfy the information needs of the curriculum project, but they continue to maintain their professional identity as experts in their own field. The genuine curricular work to be carried out at this phase is the identification of information needs and the utilization of research findings for facilitating decision making about curricular issues. This work is usually done by the project director or by curriculum experts working in close contact with him or her.

The greatest involvement of the project team in the development activities occurs at the development phase. While at the other two phases many activities are commissioned out to extraneous agents, at the development phase the project team assumes responsibilities for all activities, and for doing this efficiently, it has to employ staff members possessing expertise and experiences of various types. Three distinct tasks are carried out at this phase: constructing the program outline, preparing instructional materials, and trying out the new programs. The work at this phase requires continuous cooperation among educational psychologists, sociologists, subject experts, educational evaluators, teachers, school administrators, and so on. Chew (1977) specifies the differential roles of experts of various types in the process of examining the adequacy of objectives, contents, and learning strategies suggested by the writing teams. Some examples of this list are presented here. Curriculum specialists are expected to judge the internal consistency of the curriculum plan. They have to determine whether the course objectives are related to the broader educational goals, and whether they provide sufficient cues for devising learning experiences. Sociologists should judge whether course objectives are related to changing social and occupational needs, and whether topics appearing in educational programs bear relevance to learners' environments. Subject matter specialists have to check the up-to-dateness of curricular materials and their importance for further studies in the field of the specific subject or in related fields. The educational psychologist has to examine the topic's appeal, the learning strategies that will gain the interest of the learner, and also their adequacy to the cognitive and emotional developmental level of the learner. Teachers, too, are expected to serve as judges of the quality of the suggested materials. Blankertz (1971) discusses the nature of cooperation between subject didactics experts and sociologists in the process of curriculum legitimization and suggests the construction of a two-dimensional content grid in which one dimension represents categories of social significance of the content and the other dimension represents categories derived from the subject field.

Grobman (1970) describes working procedures related to the production of instructional materials. She indicates that many curriculum projects have used writing conferences as a technique for materials preparation. Some of these writing conferences are staffed by subject matter experts only, particularly if the materials are to be used in high schools. Others use various mixtures of subject matter experts and educators. Some projects bring in special kinds of writers, such as programmers or film script writers. During the program tryout (see *Curriculum Tryout*), subject experts, psychologists, teachers, and supervisors are called in to assist the curriculum team (Bloom 1977).

The diffusion phase is frequently carried out by change agents who are not members of the curriculum project. Experts participating in these activities are recruited from the field of educational administration who are aided by communication experts, organizational psychologists, and school teachers.

In contrast to the linear phase models, the multidimensional interactive models create a greater integration of activities of various types from the very start of the project work. Teachers participate in the team activities not only as subject or educational experts, but also as persons who are affected by the curricula and who are expected to implement them in the classroom.

The interactive model does not attempt to improve teaching through clearly formulated educational objectives or through rationally delineated production procedures. The major concern of the team is "what the teacher is to do" (Stenhouse 1975). Consequently during the whole process of preparing the curriculum various activities related to the curriculum production are closely related to each other.

4. Training Curriculum Personnel

Empirical studies on curriculum personnel followed one of two paradigms. Some examined the process of the curriculum development, others examined the relationship between the development activities and the quality of the materials produced. Studies of both types have implications for the composition of the curriculum personnel and for training. Shield (1965) examined how curriculum councils are organized, what activities they carry out, what are the criteria for selecting council members, and what is the status of members of various types. McClure (1965) compared procedures, processes, and products of three curriculum councils at the laboratory school of the University of California, Los Angeles. He related flaws in the products (more specifically in the quality of the objectives listed in the program) to flaws in the working procedures of the staff members. A similar trend is observed by Ammons (1964). These findings have implications for the training of curriculum personnel.

It seems that training in communication and interaction procedures is no less important than training in the subject field and in educational theory. Talmage (1967) found that knowledge in educational psychology affects the quality of the curriculum materials.

The 1970s were marked by a demand, in many countries, for better trained curriculum personnel. This led to special curricula for curriculum developers such as correspondence courses offered by the Open University in the United Kingdom. Another course, Flechsig's (1977) simulation game, *Planning of Curriculum Units*, was developed for African Curriculum Councils.

Bibliography

Ammons M 1964 An empirical study of process and product in curriculum development. *J. Educ. Res.* 57: 451–57

Berger P L, Luckmann T 1970 *Die Gesellschaftliche Konstruktion der Wirklichkeit: Eine Theorie der Wissen-soziologie.* Fischer, Frankfurt/Main

Blankertz H (ed.) 1971 *Curriculumforschung: Strategien, Strukturierung, Konstruktion.* Neue Deutsche Schule, Essen

Bloom B S 1977 Tryout and revision of educational materials and methods. In: Lewy A (ed.) 1977 *Handbook of Curriculum Evaluation.* Longman, New York, pp. 84–103

Bobbitt J F 1918 *The Curriculum.* Houghton Mifflin, Boston, Massachusetts

Charters W W 1923 *Curriculum Construction.* Macmillan, New York

Chew T Y 1977 Evaluation at the planning stage. In: Lewy A

(ed.) 1977 *Handbook of Curriculum Evaluation*. Longman, New York, pp. 62–83

Doll R C 1978 *Curriculum Improvement: Decision Making and Process*, 4th edn. Allyn and Bacon, Boston, Massachusetts

Flechsig K H 1977 *Planning of Curriculum Units: A Simulation Game*. Zentrum für didaktische Studien, Göttingen

Great Britain Schools Council 1973 *Pattern and Variation in Curriculum Development Projects*. Macmillan, London

Grobman H G 1970 *Developmental Curriculum Projects: Decision Points and Processes: A Study of Similarities and Differences in Methods of Producing Developmental Curricula*. Peacock, New York

Havelock R G 1971 *Planning for Innovation: A Comparative Study of the Literature on the Dissemination and Utilization of Scientific Knowledge*. University of Michigan Press, Ann Arbor, Michigan

Leithwood K A 1982 *Studies in Curriculum Decision Making*. Ontario Institute for Studies in Education (OISE) Press, Toronto, Ontario

McClure R M 1965 Procedures, processes and products in curriculum development (Doctoral dissertation, University of California, Los Angeles, California) *Dissertation Abstracts International* 1966 26: 3784 (University Microfilms No. 65–12, 649)

Oliver A I 1965 *Curriculum Improvement: A Guide to Problems, Principles, and Procedures*. Dodd, Mead, New York

Postlethwaite T N 1977 Determination of general educational aims and specification of major objectives. In: Lewy A (ed.) 1977 *Handbook of Curriculum Evaluation*. Longmans, New York, pp. 37–61

Rülcker T 1983 Modelle zur Planung und Organisation von Curriculum Prozessen. In: Hameyer U (ed.) 1983 *Handbuch der Curriculumforschung*. Beltz, Weinheim

Shield E A 1965 The Curriculum Council: Its purposes, functions, organization and activities (Doctoral dissertation, Columbia University) *Dissertation Abstracts International* 1966 26: 5833–5834 (University Microfilms No. 65–14, 993)

Stenhouse L 1975 *An Introduction to Curriculum Research and Development*. Heinemann, London

Suarez T 1981 Needs assessment. In: Lewy A, Nevo D (eds.) 1981 *Evaluation Roles in Education*. Gordon and Breach, New York

Talmage H 1967 An experimental study in curriculum engineering (Doctoral Dissertation, Northwestern University) *Dissertation Abstracts International* 1967 28: 2150A–2151A (University Microfilms No. 67–15, 350)

Curriculum Consultants

T. W. Maxwell

A curriculum consultant is a person who has accessible skills, and/or knowledge, and/or resources for a client who has curriculum concern. A curriculum consultant provides assistance to clients on knowledge, its organization, implementation, and evaluation as well as on decision-making processes and other curriculum-related activities. The task for the consultant is to assist clients to solve curriculum problems or to cope better with any aspect of the client's curriculum. A client may be a person, group, institution, or system, for example, an individual teacher, a school or prison, a syllabus committee, a project team, or a government department.

1. Approaches of a Curriculum Consultant

Approaches of curriculum consultants vary. Although this variation may result from a variety of factors or combination of factors, for example, the nature of the problem, the client, the time the consultant has available, the differences in approach to the consultancy itself reflect different assumptions. It is useful for the consultant, and the client, to be aware of these different assumptions and Habermas has proposed a scheme whereby these differences can be explicated (see Grundy 1987, pp. 12–19). Firstly, a consultant with a technical interest will tend to emphasize control and management of clients and their concerns, based upon the consultant's experience and observation. Such a consultant would diagnose and provide solutions for clients. The consultant as "expert" would generally fall within the technical interest. Secondly, a consultant

whose approach could be termed practical in its orientation (Habermas, in Grundy 1987 p. 14) would tend to be more concerned with understanding of the the curriculum concern in context and helping those with the concern toward its greater understanding. Action would follow from concensus. A process consultant (Schein 1969) would be informed by the practical interest. Finally, the consultant with an emancipatory interest supports the autonomy and responsibility of the client by promoting self-reflection and professional development related to the curriculum concern. Thus clients would become empowered to act out of their own critical insights of their context (see e.g. Dawes 1987). The experienced consultant may need to be able to draw upon all three basic approaches across consultancies or within one consultancy since the variety of factors which are present when a consultant addresses a client's curriculum concern can be so large. However, it is likely that individual consultants will tend to favour one of the three approaches.

2. Curriculum Consultant Attributes

The need for the curriculum consultant to exercise different approaches to consultancy, depending upon the circumstances and the way these change, indicates that flexibility is one desirable personal attribute. The Australian Marsh (1988 pp. 145–6) lists effective consultants' attributes and highlights the following: "tolerance for ambiguity"; ability to cope with multiple roles often within the one day; and the consultant's drive, commitment, and high energy reserves. In North America, Miles et al.'s (1988) two-year study of 17 persons (change agents) doing work very similar to that of curriculum consultants identified six general skills and 12 specific skills necessary for effective consultancy to take place. General skills included high levels of communication; interpersonal ease; training/workshops; educational; administrative/organizational; and group functioning. The 12 specific skills were arranged in four areas: (a) personal (in which initiative taking was seen as crucial), (b) socio-emotional process (e.g. rapport building and collaboration), (c) task (e.g. diagnosis and managing) and (d) educational content (e.g. demonstration). Fullan et al. (1986 p. 36) identified similar attributes but added a well-developed philosophy, credibility, and tolerance of frustration as characteristics of effective curriculum consultants. Fullan et al. (1986 p. 85) observe that administrators and consultants placed more value on the consultants' all-round teaching expertise than on subject area expertise.

3. Selection of Consultants

Miles et al. 1988 assert that it is likely that the six general skills are those that would be found upon entry to the position of consultant. Certainly these and the personality attributes could form the basis of a selection checklist together with other local criteria, for example, knowledge of the educational system and a driving licence. The specific skills identified by Miles et al. may be desirable attributes.

Prospective curriculum consultants might also note that, while the position can be extremely rewarding, it can also place considerable demands on the consultant's resources, particularly time (Maxwell in press). Consultants should also be aware that their positions are often considered marginal by administrators and may be subject to the effects of political or economic changes (Cohen 1987).

4. Curriculum Consultant Training

Training to achieve the array of skills identified above, especially the specific skills identified by Miles et al. (1988), is not currently well developed. It is most likely that training is on-the-job and experiential although some education systems do have forms of in-house induction and ongoing inservice (Maxwell 1987). Few instances have been reported where consultant training is part of university study. McGreevy (1978) does describe a course in which were developed the concepts and skills he saw as central to the task of an effective process consultant. Miles et al. (1988) report the production of six training modules that were developed out of their research on change agent skills. These, they assert, are highly flexible materials and have been successfully tested. The materials were developed following a review of available materials to see what was required and the six modules covered the topics: (a) trust/rapport

building, (b) organizational diagnosis, (c) dealing with the process, (d) resource utilization, (e) managing the work, and (f) building skill and confidence in people to continue.

5. Impact of Curriculum Consultants

More than one observer of curriculum consultants' work has noted that no consultant is better than a poor one. An analysis of the research on the impact of consultants suggests that effective consultants are those who have the necessary attributes and who consider the client's total context. Despite their best endeavours some effective consultants will be nullified by the difficulty of the context. Some consultants' effectiveness will not show because their length of time in the client's context will have been too short. Ultimately the effectiveness of a curriculum consultant depends upon the effects made upon the clients in context (personal, social, political, administrative, etc.) over time, in addition to other more structural changes that may take place. Personal and organizational needs will usually both need to be met. Fullan et al. (1986 pp. 303–306) were able to cite a number of research studies on curriculum projects in which curriculum consultants were seen as initiators of, indirect facilitators for, and critical to, successful implementation.

Although the work of curriculum consultants will be considerably varied, an effective consultant is one who leaves clients more able to cope with their own concerns. Thus, in accepting the initial dependence of clients, the effective curriculum consultant will work toward transferring the dependency back to clients themselves. This might be achieved in a variety of ways, for example, by client acceptance of consultant advice, development of client problem solving skills, or formation of a curriculum team to carry through particular decisions and/or tackle new issues. The ultimate success or otherwise of the consultant's performance might be assessed in terms of client perceptions of problem reduction, together with other positive outcomes such as increased confidence and more effective curriculum decision making.

Bibliography

Cohen D 1987 Curriculum consultancy in Australia: The national context. *Curric. Perspec.* 7(2): 51–55

Dawes L 1987 *Getting past the brick wall: The consultant's role in working for gender equity. A new paradigm for controversial curriculum change?* Paper presented at the Australian Curriculum Studies Association Conference, Sydney, July 16–19

Fullan M, Anderson S E, Newton E 1986 *Support Systems for Implementing Curriculum in School Boards.* Ontario Institute for Studies in Education, Toronto

Grundy S 1987 *Curriculum: Product or Praxis?* Falmer Press, London

McGreevy C P 1978 Training consultants: Issues and approaches. *Personnel Guid. J.* 56(7): 432–35

Marsh C 1988 *Spotlight on School Improvement.* Allen and Unwin, Sydney

Maxwell T W 1987 Curriculum consultancy: Inservice and other issues. *Curric. Perspec.* 7(2): 49–51

Maxwell T W in press One thousand days as a consultant: Estimates of ex-office work. *J. Educ. Admin.*

Miles M, Saxl E R, Lieberman A 1988 What skills do educational "change agents" need? An empirical view. *Curric. Inq.* 18(2): 157–193

Schein E H 1969 *Process Consultancy: Its Role in Organizational Development.* Addison Wesley, Reading, Massachusetts

Curriculum and Supervision

W. T. May

Curriculum and supervision involve practical activities that occur within the organizational, institutional, and contextual realms and constraints of educational settings. "Doing" curriculum involves the creation, articulation, and continuous conceptualization of educational goals. It requires educators to articulate the teaching and learning experiences that will best enhance the achievement of these goals.

Supervision involves supporting beginning and experienced teachers in curriculum and instructional endeavors. However, the nature of this support is likely to vary because supervision, like curriculum, is defined in a variety of ways and is open to interpretation. The array of possible definitions of supervision suggests different relationships among supervisors and teachers and how knowledge, people, and practice are defined and approached (May and Zimpher 1986). Drawing from Habermas (1971) and Sergiovanni (1982), the numerous definitions and models can be clustered into three categories or approaches to supervision: (a) applied science or the technical; (b) interpretative or the practical; and (c) critical or emancipatory. Humans possess all three of these interests; however, some of these interests may be emphasized to the detriment of others.

1. The Applied Science Approach

The applied science approach to supervision relies on the empirical-analytical sciences and incorporates a technical interest in work, instrumental action, and rational choice. In its most narrow and conservative sense, supervision implies that some persons are overseers of other persons; they critically watch and direct others' actions, or they are in a better position to "see" what is to be done and how, than are those observed. This conception suggests that supervisors are experts, and teachers are not. Teachers are often assisted in conforming to mandated curriculum policies and instructional practices. This view of teaching and/or supervision carries several labels which embody a theme of control: directive; executive (Fenstermacher and Soltis 1986); behavioristic or positivistic; and clinical, when some of the basic tenets of this model are misinterpreted or overused (Cogan 1973, Goldhammer et al. 1980).

This technical theme is recognized in curriculum improvement efforts in several ways. In the supervisor–practitioner relationship, both supervision and teaching are viewed as an applied science. The supervisor diagnoses problems while observing the teacher, prescribes a more efficient or effective course of action with reinforcement, and evaluates to see if these objectives are mastered. Teachers are expected to modify their behavior toward these prescribed ends. These prescribed ends frequently emerge from research based upon effective teaching, which some would argue has been narrowly defined. Some of the concerns of the technical supervisor are the improvement of classroom management skills, student time on task, or training teachers to carefully diagnose, prescribe, and monitor student performance in the basic skills.

Organizationally, the technical approach is illustrated when expertise in curricular and pedagogical knowledge is imported into classrooms in a top-down hierarchical fashion with policy mandates, required inservice, or teacher-proof curricular designs (Schubert 1986). The supervisor is concerned with quality control, cost efficiency, and standardization in the improvement effort. Teachers are "inserviced" in the curriculum innovation and expected to adopt and use it with as little deviation as possible.

2. The Interpretative–Practical Approach

The historical–hermeneutical approach to supervision incorporates a practical interest related to phenomenology, communication, interaction, and shared understandings. This approach is reflected in person-centered supervision. Uniform answers to educational problems are viewed as impossible to apply because practical problems are seen to be context bound, situationally determined, and complex. Rather than assume the role of trainer, the supervisor acts as counselor, mentor, facilitator, or confidante in an attempt to understand, participate with, and assist teachers in their professional development (Garman 1982, Gitlin et al. 1984, Sergiovanni 1985, Schön 1983, van Manen 1984). Research interests and/or supervision models that illustrate this practical theme are: cognitive–developmental, teachers' practical knowledge/reasoning, action research, clinical (when the interpersonal and collegial aspects of this model are emphasized over externally prescribed methods), indirect/nondirective, horizontal, differentiated, or collaborative.

In the practical framework, the supervisor is concerned with the personal and cultural lifeworld of teachers; what teachers value, feel, and describe; the practical dilemmas presented in the classroom; how teachers make sense of their work; and the practical knowledge that teachers have personally developed and share as a group. To enhance curriculum improvement, the supervisor is most interested in assisting teachers with what they have identified as problematic or worthy of attention. Such a supervisor is likely to act in ways that enhance interpersonal skills, establish trust, nurture teacher reflectivity, and assist teachers in developing collegial relationships. Each teacher and his/her situation is viewed as unique and worthy of personal attention.

Practically oriented supervisors regard the constraints and uncertainties with which teachers work as legitimate and problematic in any curriculum improvement effort. They are sensitive to the concerns of teachers, facilitate discussion and activities that encourage teachers to modify and create curriculum, encourage personal/professional development, and provide psychological support in teachers' self-defined endeavors. A primary interest is to help teachers build supportive networks among themselves so that the more alienating or isolating features of teaching can be replaced with shared dialogue and action.

3. The Critical–Emancipatory Approach

The last approach to supervision involves an emancipatory interest related to critique of the sociopolitical contexts of schools and the empowerment of teachers through rflection and collective action. This approach is illustrated in models that are concerned primarily with reflective action (Dewey 1933) and critical inquiry (Apple 1979, Freire 1985, Smyth 1985, Zeichner and Teitlebaum 1982). This focus calls into question what we take for granted and encourages both supervisors and teachers to examine the moral, ethical, and political dimensions embedded in everyday thinking and practice. "The notion of reflection involves not only reflection about one's own beliefs and choices in practice, but also relates to consciousness-raising about the sociopolitical contexts in which one must act and even transform" (May and Zimpher 1986 p. 95).

The emancipatory supervisor helps teachers develop a reflective and critical stance toward their own practice, particularly with regard to educational goals and purposes and the potential negative effects of the implicit or hidden curriculum on students. The supervisor is interested in learners and teachers having equal access to knowledge and their becoming empowered to construct and critique knowledge. There is an effort to raise teachers' consciousness, to illuminate their tactit understanding, and to assist teachers in becoming more aware and critical of the sociopolitical contexts in which they work. Ultimately, the supervisor acts in ways that would empower teachers to assume a greater role in shaping the direction of educational environments according to purposes which they have deliberated and justified in moral and ethical terms.

In the emancipatory framework, the supervisor assumes the role of change agent in order to facilitate a transformative role among practitioners. Without reflection and critique, teachers risk being oppressed and deskilled as a group, particularly if they work in a rationalistic or technically oriented environment that emphasizes applied science rather than practical knowledge or practitioners' ability to make informed, professional decisions. Emancipatory supervisors use tenets from both the practical and emancipatory approaches to help teachers collectively clarify and act upon beliefs and practice that foster equity. Thus, the supervisor generates attention to existing and potential social inequities in the institutional workplace called school where larger, societal inequities may be perpetuated through its structures.

4. The Need for Balance

To act effectively in a supervisory role, a balance of all three approaches is necessary because teachers face problems that are technical, practical, and political. Each framework suggests a legitimate human interest; each interest poses a particular set of questions unique to its framework. With regard to supervision, Sergiovanni (1982) suggests that we must ask three questions: What *is* going on in this classroom? What do these events, activities, and aspirations *mean*? And, what *ought* to be going on? All three conceptual lenses are necessary if we are to see supervision in its complexity and adequately understand its relationship to curriculum work.

Numerous models of supervision already exist, and new models continue to be developed. Thus, educators must tease out the underlying assumptions of such proposals, determine what primary interests are represented in these models, and consider the moral and ethical implications of choosing any one approach to supervision over another. After critical analysis, decisions can be made about the desired relationship of supervision to curriculum creation, implementation, and evaluation.

Bibliography

Apple M W 1979 *Ideology and Curriculum*. Routledge and Kegan Paul, Boston, Masachusetts
Cogan M L 1973 *Clinical Supervision*. Houghton Mifflin, Boston, Massachusetts
Dewey J 1933 *How We Think: A Restatement of the Relation of Reflective Thinking to the Educative Process*. D.C. Heath, Boston, Massachusetts
Fenstermacher G D, Soltis J 1986 *Approaches to Teaching*. Teachers College, Columbia University, New York
Freire P 1985 *The Politics of Education, Culture, Power, and*

Liberation. Bergin and Garvey, South Hadley, Massachusetts

Garman N 1982 The clinical approach to supervision. In: Sergiovanni T (ed.) 1982 *Supervision of Teaching*. Association for Supervision and Curriculum Development, Alexandria, Virginia, pp. 35–52

Gitlin A, Ogawa R, Rose E 1984 Supervision, reflection, and understanding: A case for horizontal evaluation. *J. Teach. Educ.* 35: 46–52

Goldhammer R, Anderson R, Krajewski R 1980 *Clinical Supervision: Special Methods for the Supervision of Teachers*, 2nd edn. Holt, Rinehart and Winston, New York

Habermas J 1971 *Knowledge and Human Interests*. Beacon Press, Boston, Massachusetts

Manen M van 1984 Reflections on teacher experience and pedagogic competence. In: Short E C (ed.) 1984 *Competence*. University Press of America, Lanham, Maryland, pp. 141–60

May W, Zimpher N 1986 An examination of three theoretical perspectives on supervision: Perceptions of preservice field supervision. *J. Curric. Super.* 1(2): 83–99

Schön D A 1983 *The Reflective Practitioner: How Professionals Think in Action*. Basic Books, New York

Schubert W H 1986 *Curriculum: Perspective, Paradigm, and Possibility*. Macmillan, New York

Sergiovanni T 1982 Toward a theory of supervisory practice: Integrating scientific, clinical, and artistic views. In: Sergiovanni T (ed.) 1982 *Supervision of Teaching*. Association for Supervision and Curriculum Development, Alexandria, Virginia

Sergiovanni T 1985 Landscapes, mindscapes, and reflective practice in supervision. *J. Curric. Super.* 1(1): 5–17

Smyth W J 1985 Developing a critical practice of clinical supervision. *J. Curric. Stud.* 17(1): 1–15

Zeichner K, Teitelbaum K 1982 Personalized and inquiry-oriented teacher education: An analysis of two approaches to the development of curriculum for field-based experiences. *J. Educ. Teach.* 8: 95–117

Involving Parents

B. E. Steffy

While parental involvement is generally seen as an important factor in fostering positive support for schools internationally, researchers in the United States have attempted to classify the various roles parents play in education and identify those which are most effective in fostering cognitive growth. This article will address these roles and their relationship to student achievement. In addition, parental involvement prior to formal schooling, teacher and administrator attitudes toward parental involvement, and program development for parental involvement will be discussed.

1. Typologies for Parental Involvement

Typologies used to describe parental involvement have included descriptors such as inactives, noters, parents, activists; expressive–supportive and instrumental–purposive; and audience, volunteers, employees, policy makers, and teachers. Generally these typologies distinguish between parental involvement in actual instruction and parental involvement in the administration and policy-making functions of the school.

Mario Fantini has developed a typology which attempts to distinguish between the various types of parental participation in actual instruction and relate the typology to effects on student achievement (Sinclair 1980). Fantini has classified parental involvement into four categories: parents as clients, parents as producers, parents as consumers, and parents as governors. When parents are seen as clients they are serving a public relations role for the school. Membership in the Parent Teacher's Association (PTA) is seen as an example of this role. Within the United States there has been a major trend toward expanded involvement of parents in curriculum decision making through advisory boards.

This has been fostered by the United States Congress and the Department of Education by including mandates for advisory boards in many laws and regulations adopted since the early 1970s. It has been estimated that over 1,250,000 persons are serving on over 100,000 advisory councils in the United States. However, there is little evidence that this involvement has gone beyond serving as a public relations tool for schools. Some research evidence suggests that a child's self-concept is improved by parent involvement in a client role (Watson 1977), however there appears to be little relationship between the parent in the client role and improved student achievement.

When parents serve in the role of producers, they are viewed as offering support to the instructional program. This support can take the form of school volunteers, paraprofessionals, aides, hall monitors, tutors, or advisors. These groups offer assistance in monitoring student work, providing information, helping teachers, and supplying technical assistance. While research is extremely limited, evidence suggests that parents serving in the role of producers can effect student achievement. The key factor seems to be how closely the involvement is related to actual instructional activities. When parental involvement supports instruction there is evidence of increased student achievement. This is generally related to the parent serving in the role of tutor.

Parents as consumers are usually participants in adult education classes offered at the local school facility. One popular definition of community involvement in education is exemplified by this model. While parent use of the school facility for continuing education purposes is often economically sound, the impact of such involvement on instructional decision making is often minimal to the point of being nonexistent. Theoretically, the community school could serve as an integrating force for the school and community. However, in reality the student-oriented day school and the adult-oriented night school remain separate and distinct.

The role of parents as governors is exemplified by parent involvement in the governance of the school. This type of participation is grounded in three widely accepted ideas: first, public officials should be held accountable; second, parents have granted schools the right to serve on their behalf (in loco parentis), and finally parents have the right and the responsibility to organize and express their ideas regarding education. In this area too, there appears to be minimal support from research for the efficacy of parental participation to enhance student achievement (Sinclair 1980).

2. Parental Involvement Prior to Formal Schooling

Studies focusing on the involvement of parents prior to the formal school experience have generally shown positive results (Bronfenbrenner 1974). These programs, labeled early intervention programs, call for training parents in specific educational techniques. The application of these techniques along with other family factors tend to enhance student achievement. These factors include student and parent expectations for success, belief in the work ethic, and out-of-school activities which support and supplement classroom experiences.

Miriam Stearns has developed a schema which depicts the positive effects of parental involvement. When parents learn how to teach their own children, they tend to give more individual attention to their children. The children see that their parents value education and are motivated to achieve by that perception. The parent gains more confidence in his or her ability to help the child, and the children achieve.

3. Teacher and Administrative Attitudes Toward Parental Involvement

Studies conducted by the Institute for Responsive Education indicate that the attitude of school administrators regarding parental involvement in the educational process is crucial for the effectiveness of the cooperative effort. Parents want to be involved. The Eighth Annual Gallup Poll revealed that 90 percent of those responding indicated a desire to be involved in advisory councils. However, studies have shown that few councils truly share decision-making responsibilities with parents in three policy areas: budget, personnel, and program. Developing an effective partnership requires an analysis by both parties of their philosophical orientation toward such cooperative efforts, an exploration of how communication should progress, and an analysis of appropriate action.

Teachers tend to fall into two categories regarding parent involvement in the educational process. Some view parental participation as a valuable underutilized resource while others believe parents lack the skills necessary to support instruction. There is very little research to support or rebut either position which focuses directly on teachers' attitudes toward parental involvement in home learning. Those teachers who foster parental involvement in home learning generally use techniques which fall into five categories: those which involve reading and use of books, those which encourage communication between parent and child, those which stimulate informal learning activities, those which involve the parent in a structured learning activity, and activities which develop parent teaching skills.

Results of a survey conducted by Johns Hopkins University, Baltimore, suggest that the most effective form of parental participation may be the supervision of learning activities at home although the role of parents in this regard is not well-defined. Whether teachers encourage this type of parental involvement appears to be dependent on the teacher's attitude.

Many parents in the United States are reassuming their critical role in schooling. The trend toward linking school effectiveness and parental support is strong. In schools deemed effective, a comprehensive viable program of parent involvement is generally found. In schools where administrators feel parents lack interest, knowledge, time, or the right to be involved, the school system suffers. Parental involvement in schools fosters student motivation and a positive attitude toward learning.

4. Developing Programs

Developing programs for parental involvement requires careful administrative planning. Duties and purposes for the involvement need to be clear; the parents' authority in a given situation needs to be specified; the goals and objectives of the program need to be stated; and capable leadership must be identified and an appropriate training and monitoring process implemented.

Properly managed, parental involvement in schools in the role of client, producer, consumer, or governor can contribute to building a sound, dynamic, effective educational program.

Bibliography

Barth R 1979 Home-based reinforcement of school behavior: A review and analysis. *Rev. Educ. Res.* 49: 436–58

Brandt R S (ed.) 1979 *Partners, Parents and Schools.* Association for Supervision and Curriculum Development, Alexandria, Virginia

Bronfenbrenner U 1974 *A Report on Longitudinal Evaluations of Preschool Programs,* Vol. 2: *Is Early Intervention Effective?* Department of Health, Education and Welfare (DHEW) Publication no. (Office of Child Development, OCD) 75–240. DHEW, Washington, DC

Salisbury R H 1980 *Citizen Participation in the Public Schools.* Heath, Lexington, Massachusetts

Sinclair R (ed.) 1980 *A Two-way Street—Home–School Coop-*

eration in Curriculum Decisionmaking. Institute for Responsive Education, Boston, Massachusetts

Watson K J 1977 *The "Going Places" Classroom: A Community Involvement Program of Action Learning for Elementary*

Students, Research Monograph no. 23. University of Florida, Gainesville, Florida

Williams G L 1976 Revolution in Italian education. *The Clearing House* 50: 168-71

Community Participation

B. E. Steffy

Current trends in community participation in curriculum planning reflect efforts by schools and communities, internationally, to work cooperatively together. These efforts, in Third World countries and industrialized nations, are directed toward improving the quality of instruction, enhancing the relevance of the curriculum in meeting community needs, and the utilization of the total community as an environment for learning.

Internationally, there is a great need for additional research in this area. At the present time, most of the literature dealing with community participation in curriculum planning is descriptive. To compound the problem, there is little consensus among researchers on the definition of the word "community." A 1972 study in the United States revealed 292 definitions for the term. However, definite trends can be identified.

1. Community Participation in Developing Nations

These trends can be classified into two general categories: trends in community participation in developing Third World nations, and trends in community participation in industrialized nations. In Third World countries like Peru, India, Tanzania, the People's Republic of China, and others, a number of innovative programs are being developed to integrate the school and the community into a mutually supportive, cooperative, and effective vehicle to develop centers for productive work, foster community support, and perpetuate the political ideology of the country.

In the past, education in developing nations has persisted as a sophisticated method for the recruitment of elites. The majority of new innovative programs are designed to reduce the elitist bias of education and integrate education with rural life. Education for self-reliance, initiated in Tanzania, is an example of such a program (Maliyamkono 1980). The curriculum is designed to meet the local needs of the community. School committees are elected by parents to facilitate the development of school and community education, to assist teachers, oversee the use of school-produced products, and provide technical assistance, as well as to insure the acquisition of academic skills.

The Center of Integrated Popular Education in Guinea-Bissau, and the Community Education Nucleus (NEC) initiated in Peru, are additional examples of educational reform in developing nations. The Community Education Nucleus system can be traced to the Warisata School and the concept of nuclearization (Malpica 1980). Nuclearization is a social process to insure the progressive integration of the former school system into a new educational system. This concept has influenced educational reform in a number of Latin American countries in the 1970s.

These programs are seen as a social reform rather than as an economic or administrative one. They are based on the concept of education in the community—the school serving the community, and the community serving the school. Theoretically, education is seen as a community responsibility involving all citizens.

A 1974 study of education in rural India showed that in order to increase student attendance it would be necessary to make the school more relevant to village life through teaching methods and curriculum adapted to the environment, to involve the community in program planning, and to adapt a flexible school calendar compatible with family needs (Roy 1980).

These programs generally demand a radically different methodology. The textbook often becomes supplemental reading, while the environment provides the main resources for the teacher. While program design is quite different, most of these innovative programs attempt to achieve the same academic goals as the more traditional programs. Parental support for these programs is often increased because of the emphasis on agriculture in the curriculum.

In the People's Republic of China there is a close relationship between rural schools and communes (Kexia 1980). By combining education with productive labor, the schools foster the students' appreciation for manual labor. The communes provide the schools with financial support and the environment for work and study.

The innovative educational programs developing in many Third World nations share the goal of improving the quality of life for the population. While this cannot be accomplished through educational reform alone, it is a powerful tool when combined with economic and political reform. Problems arising in these Third World programs include articulation and coordination of the experimental programs with the rest of the educational system, and recruitment of teachers proficient in teaching strategies applicable to classroom learning and community learning. Benefits include the creation of area community councils which have a major responsibility in the design of educational programs, the use of the community as a classroom, financial support for education partially supplied through the sale of student-produced products, and the involvement of students in meaningful work situations. To help train educational leaders for community-based schools, Western Michigan University sponsors a program for doctoral students from around the world.

2. Community Participation in Industrialized Nations

Traditionally schools in industrialized nations use community involvement to foster good public relations, to give tacit approval for administrative decisions, and to extend and enrich the traditional educational program.

Citizen involvement in education and the idea of the school as an extension of the family is deep rooted in the United States. Lay boards of education act as school trustees. Schools, in the role of parent (in loco parentis) in districts throughout the United States, have taken on increasing numbers of parental tasks.

School community cooperation in the United States was considered vital by the progressivists, John Dewey, Joseph Hart, and Ellsworth Collins, who believed the school should work with and through the resources of the community. The National Congress of Parents and Teachers (PTA) has historically been the primary vehicle used by school administrators to communicate with parents. In recent years community involvement in the schools has expanded to include citizen advisory councils, volunteer aids, and expanded use of community resources.

In many industrialized countries there is a trend toward sharing school facilities with the community. However, real community involvement in curriculum decision making is often superficial and politically motivated. While there is much talk concerning increased community involvement in policy formation and implementation, there is little evidence that teachers or local education agencies are willing to share decision making, since true participation involves power sharing.

Community involvement and participation beyond the use of school facilities is largely a myth. The need to integrate the school and the community has been supported in the United Kingdom since the 1920s, when Henry Morris argued for a community institution involving day care centers, community colleges, and the schools (Watson 1980). Morris adhered to the philosophy of work and culture in one institution. This trend was continued with the Plowden Report in 1967, followed by the creation of education priority areas with schools seen as an integral part of community renewal and catalysts for social change. The curriculum was seen as a link with the local community. Students were encouraged to use the total community as part of the learning environment, and parents became involved in educational decision making through representation on governing and advisory bodies. However, a 1972 study showed that only 40 percent of secondary schools had modified their curriculum toward the community in any way.

3. Future Trends

Pressures for community involvement in curricular decisions will probably increase during the 1980s as a result of financial pressures, limited resources, demands for practical and vocationally oriented curricula, greater accountability, and demands for lifelong learning. In North America, community involvement in the form of pressure groups tends not to be broadly based, but to focus on specific issues, such as sex education, school prayer, and so on. There is also a trend in the United States toward community censorship, particularly in the acquisition of new textbooks: the advent of scientific creationism has once again prompted a strong desire to mix religion and education.

Currently there appears to be a major shift in the way education is conceptualized. There is greater interest in education as a broad concept and the schools as only one arena for its delivery. The idea of lifelong learning with a variety of community organizations and agencies delivering educational services is widely accepted. Research on out-of-school learning is underway at Stanford, Harvard, and other major universities in order to gain insights into the nature of a broadened definition of education.

Barriers to community involvement exist in both Third World countries and industrialized nations. In Third World countries these barriers include lack of parental knowledge regarding the operation of schools, the generally low educational level of the population, and the lack of appropriate vehicles to foster and formalize that involvement. In industrialized nations, lack of community involvement can often be attributed to general apathy on the part of the citizenry toward education, the growing percentage of citizens without children in school, and school administrators who give only tacit approval to such involvement.

Still, trends operating in both Third World and industrialized nations point dramatically to the emergence of a new paradigm for school–community relations which will reflect the integration of the community and the school in decision-making processes to provide lifelong learning for all members of the community.

Bibliography

Centro de Investigacion y Promocion Educative (CIPE) 1979 *The Educational Reform and the Nuclear System in Peru.* International Institute for Educational Planning, Paris

Kexia L 1980 The relations between the school and the commune in New China. *Int. Rev. Educ.* 26: 379–84

Maliyamkono T L 1977 *The Unproductive School.* University of Dar es Salaam, Dar es Salaam

Maliyamkono T L 1980 The schools as a force for community change in Tanzania. *Int. Rev. Educ.* 26: 335–47
Malpica C 1980 Education and the community in the Peruvian educational reform. *Int. Rev. Educ.* 26: 357–67
Roy A 1980 Schools and communities: An experience in rural India. *Int. Rev. Educ.* 26: 369–78

Watson J K P 1979 Community schooling: The rhetoric and the reality of community involvement in English education. *Educ. Rev.* 31(3)
Watson J K P 1980 The growth of community education in the United Kingdom. *Int. Rev. Educ.* 26: 273–87

Teachers' Participation in Curriculum Development

F. Elbaz

The participation of teachers in curriculum development varies both in its extent and in its nature: in some school systems the teacher is given a detailed curriculum plan to be followed down to the attainment of precisely specified objectives; in other instances, teachers receive only general guidelines which are to be elaborated on and adapted to their individual classrooms. These arrangements are mandated by the school system in accordance with a conception of the teaching–learning process and of the nature of the knowledge it treats. In recent years teacher involvement in curriculum development has increased significantly, and teachers have taken part in a wide range of activities which enhance their professional status and their control over their working lives.

1. Conceptions Underlying Teacher Participation

Two views of teacher participation in curriculum development can be derived from historical models of teaching. One is the Socratic model, in which no distinction can be made between the teacher and the curriculum developer; in his teaching, Socrates was simultaneously developing knowledge, finding ways of presenting that knowledge to his audience, and helping students to attain knowledge themselves. As a dialogue such as the Meno makes apparent, the teacher's own understanding is furthered by the student's efforts (Hamilton and Cairns 1963). A second model is the scholastic one where the teacher is part of a hierarchically organized scheme in which knowledge, divinely inspired, is handed down to students in precisely the same manner and form that it was acquired by the teacher; here the teacher's task is sharply distinguished from that of the curriculum developer. A set of terms that captures the distinction between these two models is offered by Barnes who speaks of a "transmission" view of teaching and learning, versus an "interpretation" view. "The transmission teacher sees it as his or her task to transmit knowledge and to test whether the pupils have received it", and the knowledge in question is a coherent, public body of knowledge to which the teacher, but not the student, has access. The "interpretation" approach, on the other hand, is concerned mainly with the "knower's ability to organize thought and action", and sees the task of the teacher as

primarily "the setting up of a dialogue in which the learner can reshape his knowledge through interaction with others" (Barnes 1976, pp. 142–44). In practice these two approaches represent opposite ends of a wide spectrum of ways of conceiving the teaching–learning process.

If the decision makers in a given school system adopt an "interpretation" view, teachers—whose role it is to interact with students—will necessarily be involved in the choice of materials, methods, and contexts most suitable for their students. Where a "transmission" view is held, it is the role of experts in the various academic disciplines taught in schools to select and elaborate the knowledge which students are expected to acquire, as well as correct sequencing and teaching methods; teachers, on such a view, are expected to be the faithful implementers of the intentions of curriculum developers, but their participation in development may be seen as necessary to ensure that programmes will be carried out as intended.

2. Developments in Teacher Participation in Curriculum

The recent history of the curriculum field bears witness to a series of changes in the involvement of teachers in curriculum development. In the United States, for example, teacher participation in state- and district-wide curriculum development teams had been common practice until the 1960s, when the shock of Sputnik brought about a wave of academically oriented curriculum revision. This massive devaluation of teacher's curriculum knowledge in favour of expert knowledge was noted by Bruner (1960). Even then, however, some continued to argue for the importance of teacher participation in development activities at the local level (see, for example, Verduin [1967]). Only a few years later, evaluation of the new programmes made it apparent that real implementation was a rarity: in practice, teachers who had not been consulted, who sometimes did not understand the new materials or simply did not identify with them, continued to teach the way they had before, despite the new materials (Sarason 1971). This revelation was met in the curriculum field by promoting various forms of teacher involvement in new programmes as follows.

(a) No participation, or the move toward "teacher-proof" curricula—programmes that are given directly to pupils, in sufficient detail so that the teacher's intervention is not required;

(b) Participation of teachers in ways, and to the extent needed, to ensure that they understand, and are committed to and equipped to teach the programme as intended by developers (inservice training, materials try-out);

(c) Active involvement of teachers in development of materials that account for their needs and capabilities and take advantage of their particular contribution to development;

(d) School-based curriculum development, or giving up the attempt to control curriculum by a central authority.

In practice it may be difficult to distinguish among the different forms of teacher participation; in a given school authority, all forms of participation may be found, and even within a single project developers may solicit active involvement of teachers for some aspects of their materials and insist on faithful implementation for other aspects. It is, however, fair to say that teacher participation has been accepted as a necessary and positive feature of development; teacher-training programmes now see preparation for development work as part of their task, and books on curriculum intended for teachers have appeared with increasing frequency (Lawton et al. 1978, Kelly 1977).

3. Curriculum Development Activities of Teachers

Teachers have always been involved in planning for teaching (Taylor 1970), occasionally writing their own materials but more often choosing from existing materials. They may select among entire programmes or among sections from various programmes, make changes in the order of topics and activities, in the depth of coverage and level of difficulty, in the type and nature of the message. Such participation is essential to any programme for it ensures the "match" among the school, pupils, teacher, and materials without which no programme can be effectively implemented. Sometimes developers take such participation of teachers into account and encourage it by writing materials that invite teachers to examine their own views and reflect on the suitability for themselves and their classes of the developer's materials (Connelly et al. 1977). The importance of teacher analysis of curriculum materials is argued convincingly by Ben-Peretz (1975).

A further degree of participation by teachers occurs when they fill the role of consultant to a central curriculum team. Here the teacher may participate in the team's discussions, serve as a reader of first and subsequent drafts of the materials, try out materials in the classroom and report back, allow the team to observe the materials being taught, and test pupils' performance. All these activities are essential in allowing the developers to anticipate consequences and difficulties and make necessary corrections.

Some projects involve teachers in a central way in the development process, in one version or another of the partnership conceptualized by Connelly (1972) between the academically based central developer and the "user–developer" whose concerns are more immediately practical. For example Shipman (1974) gives an account of an integrated humanities project which aimed to involve teachers in developing new roles for themselves as they explored new ways and means of integrating the study of the humanities. The many difficulties encountered by teachers in such a process (stemming primarily from lack of time, lack of supporting conditions in the schools, conflicting responsibilities, and lack of clarity as to tasks) perhaps explains why such projects tend to have been unique, limited efforts rather than permanent features of a school system.

Some curriculum projects shift the centre of gravity of the development process almost entirely onto the teacher. One example is the Ford Teaching Project (Elliott and Adelman 1975), which aimed to develop in teachers an orientation to, and skills needed for, classroom action research around a focus of enquiry teaching.

The final development in teacher participation in curriculum is school-based development, done at the school level by teams of teachers (Eggleston 1980). The starting point for such work is in the school itself and in issues raised by the staff, rather than in ideas or theories brought to the school by outsiders. School-based development has the potential to avoid some of the problems of other forms of teacher participation, since the entire school staff is involved and presumably able to make whatever organizational changes are required to support its planning. The main weakness of development at this level is the risk of inferior quality programmes given the schools' limited access to professional skills and academic knowledge.

4. Limits to Teacher Participation in Curriculum Development

There is no doubt that increased teacher participation in curriculum work has been a positive development in many respects, leading to enhanced professionalism, more effective implementation of programmes, curricula that are more appropriate to local needs, and more control by teachers of their work situations. However, it is important to realize that there will always be limitations on the partipation of teachers in curriculum development, of which the principal ones are listed below.

(a) *Limited training*. Training for curriculum development has become an accepted part of both preservice and inservice programmes, but it is one of many topics to be covered, and only a minority of teachers are likely to obtain extensive professional training in curriculum development.

(b) *Limited time*. The working week of teachers is finite, and time spent in interaction with students will always take priority. It is important that in the limited time available for planning, teachers avoid spreading their resources too thin; fortunately teachers seem to learn quickly not to be over-ambitious in this area.

(c) *Mandated curriculum*. Syllabi and guidelines of some sort will always be with us. Of necessity, pressures for a common or core curriculum, and the desire to offer equal educational provision for all, limit the degree of input that will be allowed teachers at the local level.

(d) *Rationalization and bureaucratization of schooling*. The development of increasingly rationalized school systems (performance by objectives, school accountability systems) and curriculum materials (mastery learning programmes, competency-based programmes in language or mathematics, widely distributed commercial programmes in all subjects) constitute a countervailing force to increased teacher participation in curriculum development. Apple and Teitelbaum (1986) see such developments as bringing about a "deskilling" of teaching which may operate even in situations where teachers appear to retain a high degree of participation in development.

Bibliography

Apple M W, Teitelbaum K 1986 Are teachers losing control of their skills and curriculum? *J. Curric. Stud.* 18(2): 177–84

Barnes D 1976 *From Communication to Curriculum*. Penguin, Harmondsworth

Ben-Peretz M 1975 The concept of curriculum potential. *Curr. Theory Network* 5(2): 151–59

Bruner J S 1960 *The Process of Education*. Harvard University Press, Cambridge, Massachusetts

Connelly F M 1972 The functions of curriculum development. *Interchange* 3: 161–77

Connelly F M, Wahlstrom M W, Finegold M, Elbaz F 1977 *Enquiry Teaching in Science: A Handbook for Secondary School Teachers*. Ontario Institute for Studies in Education (OISE), Toronto, Ontario

Eggleston J (ed.) 1980 *School-based Curriculum Development in Britain: A Collection of Case Studies*. Routledge and Kegan Paul, Boston, Massachusetts

Elliott J, Adelman C 1975 Teacher education for curriculum reform: An interim report on the Ford Teaching Project. *Br. J. Teacher Educ.* 1: 105–14

Hamilton E, Cairns H (ed.) 1963 *The Collected Dialogues of Plato*. Pantheon, New York

Kelly A V 1977 *The Curriculum: Theory and Practice*. Harper and Row, London

Lawton D, Gordon P, Ing M, Gibby B, Pring R, Moore T 1978 *Theory and Practice of Curriculum Studies*. Routledge and Kegan Paul, London

Sarason S B 1971 *The Culture of the School and the Problem of Change*. Allyn and Bacon, Boston, Massachusetts

Shipman M D 1974 *Inside a Curriculum Project: A Case Study in the Process of Curriculum Change*. Methuen, London

Taylor P H 1970 *How Teachers Plan their Courses*. National Foundation for Educational Research (NFER), Slough

Verduin J R Jr 1967 *Cooperative Curriculum Improvement*. Prentice-Hall, Englewood Cliffs, New Jersey

School-based Curriculum Development

N. Sabar

School-based curriculum development (SBCD) implies that decisions related to planning, designing, implementing, and evaluating curriculum take place within the school and its community, rather than being imposed from the outside. This decision making and its execution, therefore, comprise a locus of curricular authority and action (Skilbeck 1985).

Instances of SBCD differ from each other with regard to the degree and the focus of the variables involved. In a narrow sense, one can view SBCD as a series of autonomous decisions to implement the products of a ready-made curriculum adopted by the principal and school staff, or by the school staff only. In a broader sense SBCD may be perceived as a decision-making process, encompassing the activities of developmental planning, implementation, and evaluation of a whole school program involving all those staff members—principals, teachers, students, and parents—who want to participate. This broad scope definition encompasses all aspects of educational experiences for which the school assumes responsibility such as school organization, institutional inservice education, resources, community involvement, and so forth.

1. Historical Perspectives

In the late 1950s and in the 1960s a great many curriculum centers were established across the world. Despite their variety, there were several features that all had in common. Basically, they employed project teams for producing instructional materials, often concentrated on traditional subject matters, used highly qualified professional expertise, had a predetermined aim on a macro-social level, and developed curricula via a "scientific" process. The aim of these centers was to produce curricula which have a long-term life span (thus hindering the introduction of fast relevant changes). Teachers received ready-made materials often with detailed (and restricting) instructions, with or without an introductory familiarizing course.

The new curricula developed by this approach failed to prove themselves, in spite of their professional quality. There were very few signs of their impact in the classroom, not even in science curricula where the most serious efforts were made (Goodlad and Klein 1970).

Connelly (1972), who criticized this top-down approach, perceived the process of curriculum development as having two phases: the preparation of curriculum materials by external developers, and the planning of classroom instruction by "developers as users." The latter are the teachers who best know the situational conditions of teaching–learning in their classes. The teachers receive instructional materials prepared by professionally trained experts and then adapt them to the needs of their own classroom. But in the late 1970s and early 1980s, curriculum experts tended to view teachers and schools as contributors to the curriculum development process, rather than as mere receptive partners. Consequently SBCD became legitimized as a complementary system to centralistic curriculum development activities (Skilbeck 1985, Sabar 1987). Those who supported SBCD perceived the school as a full partner in planning, developing, implementing, and evaluating curricula.

The increased recognition of the important role that teachers and schools may and should play in curriculum improvement came as a result of several social and educational developments: the implementation of the new, centrally developed curricula; widespread democratization in various areas of life, where decision-making power gradually became decentralized; and the continual debate on the need to raise the prestige and the occupational status of teachers. Research findings and the work of curriculum theorists also contributed to this change. Curriculum evaluation studies suggested that the curriculum reforms of the 1950s failed to achieve the expected changes in the quality of education, mainly because of the lack of teachers' participation in the process of curriculum development (McLaughlin and Berman 1978). These finds were reinforced by Goodlad's (1980) concept of the school as a creative workshop, and by Schwab's (1983 p. 245) unequivocal statement that ". . . teachers must be involved in deliberation and decisions about what and how to teach."

2. Characteristics of SBCD

Successful school-based curriculum development can take place only within the framework of institutions or organizations which operate as a pedagogically autonomous entity. The pedagogical autonomy enables curriculum-related decisions to be made without the intervention of external authorities. It should be noted, however, that school-based curriculum development ought not to be, and indeed cannot be, reduced to teacher-based curriculum development, important as teachers' roles are at every stage. It should be par-

ticipatory: that is, decisions should be shared with all those involved in the educational experience. It should reflect the parents' perceptions of, and expectations for, their children's education and, as far as possible, it should consider the students' interests, inclinations, wishes, and aspirations.

The school must apprehend its role in curriculum development as a close, yet ever changing partnership with other institutions and agencies in society. It makes little sense to treat the school as the sole and exclusive determinant of the curriculum. School decisions should be congruent with, and should be related to, the wider national goals in education.

> To give to the school a central role in curriculum development is to raise challenging questions about the source and authority of the aims and values it adopts, the manner in which it selects and arranges curriculum content, and its capability as an organization to handle the time-consuming and often difficult tasks of planning, designing, implementing, and evaluating curricula. Changes in school managements, organization, and climate are required if schools are to be effective in their curriculum roles. (Skilbeck 1985 p. 3)

As a consequence, changes in the life of the institution and its need for resources and support must be addressed.

According to Harrison (1981), schools which operate SBCD have a dynamic interaction between the following subsystems of the school: task and structure, resource utilizations, and human relationships.

2.1 Task and Structure

SBCD can operate only in a school with a readiness for it. It can be neither imposed nor dictated. There is need for a democratic organizational structure, in which a horizontal communications system rather than a bureaucratic vertical one is operating. The latter communication pattern is mainly one-way, top-down directed, while the former is characterized by channels that are open in all directions.

The open horizontal structure is enhanced by clear and broad oral and written communications. This structure enables the decentralization of authority, and hinges upon team work and good communication within and between teams (Brown 1980). A well-functioning team requires leadership, which would normally be accepted upon recognition of expertise, and not just authority. Leadership need not necessarily come from the principal, but a supportive principal is certainly a key to the facilitation and implementation of teachers' SBCD decisions (Harrison 1981).

2.2 Human Relationships and Resource Utilization

Training in group decision-making processes, clear goals that are accepted by everyone, and wide representation of teachers, reflecting various approaches to curriculum, lead to a climate of more widely-shared responsibility and higher motivation for success.

Judicious allocation of time, working space, and funds is required to guarantee the smooth operation of SBCD, as well as easy access for experts, continuous dialogue, and a built-in feedback system. While all the above are necessary conditions for operations for all schools, the following are site-specific issues: How are the students and parents incorporated in the decisions? How does a school distribute the implementation of its various decisions among teams? How are the resources organized? What are the modes of cooperation with external agencies for expert advice and feedback?

All these issues are to be decided on and resolved by each school. By definition, there can be no uniform solution to SBCD for all schools. A uniform model is contradictory to the concept of SBCD.

3. Degree of Scope and Variables Involved in SBCD

As mentioned above, in practice SBCD projects differ from each other with regard to the degree and the scope of variables involved: Who of the potential partners actually participates? Where is the seat of responsibility for curriculum development decisions, whether externally based, generic or site-specific? and What conception of the realities of the setting is adopted? (Short 1983). In the matrix of Fig. 1, these realities determine the levels of adaptation. The lowest level is the fidelity adoptions, which means using materials developed by others and carrying out all instructions provided by external developers with a high level of fidelity. At this level, practically no curriculum adaptation takes place. The highest level is complementary developing, which involves revising available materials as well as completely new local development activities by teachers and other partners.

To illustrate the meaning of levels of adaptation, Fig. 1 presents a revised matrix of Short (1983), on which is marked a particular case of SBCD. The development takes place within the school, that is, it appears at the site-specific location. The participants are experts and teachers who decided to carry out complementary developments, that is, to adapt existing materials. They are involved in selecting from the available materials, revising some parts of it, and also developing additional complementary materials. In this case the level of adaptation is quite high.

4. Advantages and Disadvantages of SBCD

As SBCD developed concurrent with the growing sense of professional disappointment in external curriculum projects, it has emphasized the role of the school and the teacher in the process of curriculum development.

A school which has introduced SBCD becomes an attractive place for teachers to work because its climate is supportive and motivating. Communication within the school becomes easier. In such schools the status of the teacher is high, since the conditions enhance professional growth and development. Effective utilization of existing curricular materials is promoted and the improvement of the quality of teaching is facilitated (McLaughlin and Berman 1978). Teachers may more easily combat burnout through working in teams, having higher motivation, interest in work, and professional satisfaction.

Students feel that learning is more relevant to their needs, as their views constitute input to the school's curricular planning. The curriculum is flexible and can easily integrate emerging topics of immediate relevance. Parents are also welcome to contribute to the curriculum, and are encouraged to specify their educational perceptions and preferences.

While the advantages of SBCD are easy to identify, one should be aware of the great investment required for the school to implement such programs successfully.

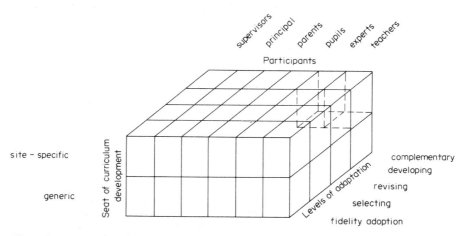

Figure 1
Matrix for identifying curriculum development strategies

The disadvantages and pitfalls are many. The main weakness is the question of quality. Teachers' inadequacy to prepare materials raises a central issue for critics of SBCD, based on quality. The professional competency of most teachers is in the field of performing, rather than in writing the "libretto" for the performance. Teachers who are trained and expected to carry out instructions may not necessarily have the abilities to construct materials. Teachers already have a heavy burden of teaching hours, and consequently imposing the extra task of materials development may reduce the time available for teaching-related activities.

Another concern is that SBCD is very much dependent on school initiative, human and financial resources, and community support. Schools differ from each other with regard to access to resources, and thus SBCD may endanger national goals of equality. Also, due to mobility, many of the staff in any one school in any one year may not have participated in the curriculum decisions that are being implemented in the next year and thus may not share the commitment which is characteristic of (and necessary for) SBCD.

Another disadvantage of SBCD is that external professional criteria are exchanged for internal public and community control. This change endangers the quality of school work; it is liable to introduce mediocracy and compromises, or it may bring politicization and conflict into the schools, even at the elementary school level.

It seems, therefore, that the professional advantages that were listed as the strengths and characteristics of many of the central curriculum bodies cannot be exercised by teachers in a school, if only because of lack of expertise, time resources, and evaluation procedures. Therefore the question arises: should SBCD engagement be a high priority component of the teacher's role? The answer to this is manifold. First, there is little hope that the teaching profession will, in the forthcoming years, attract candidates of the high intellectual capabilities, desire for autonomy, and independent decision-making traits needed for SBCD. On the contrary, it is more likely that in competition with other, more prestigious and better-paid professions, it will tend to lose such candidates. Second, large-scale engagement of teachers in developing instructional materials will necessarily require increased expenditure. There are good reasons to believe that national educational systems will not be willing to bear these expenses. Third, educational technology will increasingly intrude into the field of education and will proliferate commercially-produced instructional materials. Also the accountability of schools to central educational authorities may hinder the diffusion of SBCD, especially if school-leaving examinations continue to be centrally administered.

5. Future Prospects and Relevant Research

As more and more educational institutions adopt the SBCD approach, more attention needs to be given to curriculum development competencies in teacher education.

It is expected that the burden of schools in the field of curriculum development will not decrease; in fact, with society's expectations from the educational system, it will even increase. Consequently a new type of relationship between central curricular bodies and the local school periphery may emerge, each side contributing its own expertise. There is a growing need for descriptions of existing models of SBCD, each one specifying its own problems as well as attempted and successful solutions. Also the role of curriculum specialists in the SBCD context should be defined and institutionalized as they become a crucial factor in determining the quality of the SBCD product.

There are four main areas of problems that still require the accumulation of much research and experience:

(a) clarifying the functions of schoolteachers in the curriculum developmental process and identifying ways to utilize their expertise in various phases of curriculum development and implementation:

(b) including SBCD skills in preservice and inservice teacher education programs:

(c) establishing a variety of modes of collaboration between teachers' curriculum activities and professional curriculum bodies: and

(d) specifying clearly the extent and the conditions of students' and parents' involvement in SBCD.

Bibliography

Bolam R (ed.) 1982 *School-focussed In-service Training*. Heinemann, London

Brown L D 1980 Planned change in underorganized systems. In: Cummings T (ed.) 1980 *Systems Theory for Organization Development*. Wiley, Chichester, pp. 181–203

Connelly F M 1972 The functions of curriculum development. *Interchange* 3: 161–77

Eggleston J (ed.) 1980 *School-based Curriculum Development in Britain: A Collection of Case Studies*. Routledge and Kegan Paul, London

Goodlad J I 1980 What schools should be for. *Learning* 9: 38–43

Goodlad J I, Klein M F 1970 *Behind the Classroom Door*. Charles A. Jones, Worthington, Ohio

Harrison M 1981 School based curriculum decision making: A personal view-point. *Curric. Perspect.* 2(1): 47–52

Klein M F 1986 Alternative curriculum conceptions and designs. *Theory Prac.* 25(1): 31–35

McDonald J B 1971 Responsible curriculum development. In: Eisner E W (ed.) 1971 *Confronting Curriculum Reform*. Little, Brown, Boston, Massachusetts

McLaughlin M W, Berman P P 1978 *Federal Program Supporting Educational Change*, Vol. VIII, *Implementing and Sustaining Innovation*. Rand R-158918-HEW, May 1978, Santa Monica, California

Sabar N 1987 School based curriculum development: The pendulum swings. In: Sabar N, Rudduck J, Reid W A (eds.)

1987 *Partnership and Autonomy in School Based Curriculum Development*. University of Sheffield Division of Education, Sheffield

Sabar N, Silberstein M, Shafriri N 1982 Needed: Curriculum coordinators for teachers developing learning materials: A systematic analysis of coordinators' characteristics for better planned training. *Curric. Inq.* 12(1): 53–67

Schwab J J 1983 The practical 4: Something for curriculum professors to do. *Curric. Inq.* 13(3): 239–65

Short E C 1983 The forms and use of alternative curriculum development strategies: Policy implications. *Curric. Inq.* 13(1): 43–64

Skilbeck M 1985 *School Based Curriculum Development*. Harper and Row, London

Using the Curriculum

Curriculum Diffusion

K. A. Leithwood

Curriculum diffusion refers to the spread of information about innovative instruction or instruction-related practices. In this article, meanings associated with the terms curriculum and diffusion are clarified; approaches to research about processes of diffusion and the status of knowledge resulting from that research are examined; and several critical but unresolved issues facing those who would engage in curriculum diffusion are discussed.

1. Definition of Terms

Meanings associated with the term "curriculum" are multiple and varied, as amply illustrated throughout this volume. For present purposes, the term will refer to decisions about the educational experiences of students; a curriculum is a set of decisions about what outcomes are desired for students as a result of such experiences, and the instructional activities likely to facilitate the achievement of these outcomes.

Outcomes desired for students are value based and typically derived from socially shared images of the educated person. They have been variously classified: for example, cognitive, affective, and psychomotor (Bloom 1956); knowledge, skill, and affect (Robinson 1979); knowing about, knowing that, and being able to.

In conventional school settings, instructional activities consist of categories or dimensions of teacher behaviour which are thought to significantly influence student learning. Both theories of instruction and research on teacher effectiveness (Peterson and Walberg 1979) represent attempts to discover such categories and specific behaviours within categories that aid growth in student achievement. Leithwood's (1981) review of literature provides examples of 10 categories; platform, objectives, students entry behaviours, assessment tools and procedures, instructional material, learner experiences, teaching strategies, content, and time. In addition to a set of decisions about desired student outcomes, then, a curriculum is also a set of decisions about those instructional behaviours hypothesized as sufficient to realize those outcomes.

The term diffusion is less contentious than curriculum although it refers to a complex and not well-understood process. Diffusion and dissemination are used synonymously in reference to the process by which new ideas are communicated to the members of a social system (Zaltman et al. 1973, Rogers and Shoemaker 1971). Such communication may or may not result in changed practices by members of that social system. In order for practices to change, new ideas which are diffused must be "adopted" (a decision made to use the new ideas) and then "implemented" (put into practice). The diffusion process thus represents the early stages of a larger change process. Interests in the long-term status of new ideas that are both adopted and implemented further extends this process into a stage labelled institutionalization (Berman and McLaughlin 1978). At this stage, ideas considered new at the earlier stages become part of the standard operating procedures and way of thinking by those members of the social system. The ideas cease to be new.

Although just one stage in a larger change process, diffusion includes at least three distinct substages. These include (a) the sending out of information about the new idea, for example through a newsletter, memo, professional journal, or publisher's conference; (b) the receiving of the information by a potential user of the new idea (the teacher is given a new text by a publisher or picks up the memo from his or her mailbox); and (c) the potential user attending to the information (e.g., reads the memo, skims through the new textbook). Diffusion is complete only when such attention is captured.

The clarification of terms provided above permits a relatively precise and specialized meaning to be attached to the concept of curriculum diffusion. The "ideas" to be diffused are ideas about desired student outcomes and instructional activities likely to aid in their achievement. These ideas may come in kits, as guidelines, or packaged in textbooks. They may appear as the results and implications of educational research, or they may simply be assertions and claims about effective instructional practices. Whether or not such ideas are new depends on the existing practices and knowledge of the person receiving the information. Curriculum diffusion is the process of bringing ideas about student outcomes and instructional activities to the attention of potential users who are unaware of these ideas.

2. Diffusion Research

Little systematic research has been carried out in order to understand better the process of curriculum diffusion, in particular. In other fields, however, research about the process of social changes has focused heavily on the diffusion stage. This is particularly the case in agriculture (Rogers and Shoemaker 1971) and social anthropology. A dominant model or conceptual framework has emerged to guide this research. The model is one in which an innovation is communicated in a variety of ways over time to members of a social system (Feller 1979) considered as "adopter units". Research questions have addressed the effectiveness of different forms of communication. They have also addressed the characteristics of adopter units (age, wealth, cosmopolitanness, and the like) and how such characteristics influence the outcome of the diffusion process. Effects on adoption of innovations with different characteristics such as divisibility, trialability, complexity, and compatibility have been investigated as well and hypotheses generated about the effects of many such characteristics (Lin and Zaltman 1973, Rogers and Shoemaker 1971).

Extant diffusion research appears to offer very limited understandings of the process of curriculum diffusion at present. This situation is partly a function of the small amount of diffusion research carried out in educational settings focused on curricular innovations. The professional or semiprofessional status of the agents working in these settings and the uncertain nature of instructional technology are both examples of ways in which educational settings differ significantly from settings in which much diffusion research has been conducted. In addition, curricular innovations are characteristically complex in nature, often not divisible, poorly tested, and only loosely specified. As a result they offer little "relative advantage" to potential users; they are a class of innovation that has yet to be the object of much systematic inquiry. Wolf (1981) described empirical attempts by four different researchers to obtain support for selected generalizations in the diffusion literature as applied in educational contexts. He reported lack of stability of these generalizations in such contexts. Hughes and Keith (1980) reported support for generalizations from diffusion research about the importance of user's perceptions of the characteristics of curriculum innovations. The dependent variable in their study, however, was degree of "implementation" rather than diffusion.

A second set of limitations on the value of extant diffusion research emerges from problems inherent in the diffusion model itself and its misapplications. These are outlined by Dill and Friedman (1979) and are not described here.

3. Critical Issues

Most of the questions addressed by diffusion research are highly relevant to those who wish to spread information about an innovation. There is a logically prior set of questions, however, particularly relevant to diffusion practitioners; questions about the value of ideas or knowledge to be diffused. These questions cast doubt on the central premise underlying much of the interest in diffusion; that the problem to be solved is how to provide more existing information to those making decisions so that decisions will be better informed. The alternative premise these logically prior questions raise is that decision makers are already swamped with more information than they can possibly process. The problem is that a high proportion of the information is of little value to them.

Knott and Wildavsky (1980) suggest that, in order to be useful to a decision-maker, knowledge or information to be diffused must meet three conditions:

(a) it must address factors over which decision makers have some control through their programs or policies;

(b) it must be valid under conditions faced by decision makers in their own settings (the authors suggest that data linked together by theory enhances the transferability of information); and

(c) it must be positive—information about what will work not what has failed.

A fourth condition should also be added. Knowledge ought to be at least partially procedural in nature if the intended outcome of diffusion is practical action. Procedural knowledge extends beyond descriptive understanding ("knowledge about") to prescriptions or guidelines for action ("knowing that"). In the field of social policy, Knott and Wildavsky (1980) and Lindblom and Cohen (1979) suggest that the amount of available knowledge likely to meet these conditions is modest indeed. The same case can be asserted in the curriculum field, as well.

Bibliography

Berman P, McLaughlin M W 1978 *Federal Programs Supporting Educational Change*, Vol. 8: *Implementing and Sustaining Innovations*. Rand, Santa Monica, California

Bloom B S (ed.) 1956 *Taxonomy of Educational Objectives: The Classification of Educational Goals, Handbook 1: Cognitive Domain*. McKay, New York

Dill D D, Friedman C P 1979 An analysis of frameworks for research on innovation and change in higher education. *Rev. Educ. Res.* 49: 411–35

Feller I 1979 Three coigns on diffusion research. *Knowledge* 1: 293–312

Hughes A S, Keith J J 1980 Teacher perceptions of an innovation and degree of implementation. *Can. J. Educ* 5 (2): 43–51

Knott J, Wildavsky A 1980 If dissemination is the solution, what is the problem? *Knowledge.* 1980 1: 537–78

Leithwood K A 1981 The dimensions of curriculum innovation. *J. Curric. Stud.* 13: 25–36

Lin N, Zaltman G 1973 Dimensions of innovations. In: Zaltman G (ed.). 1973 *Processes and Phenomena of Social Change*. Wiley, New York

Lindblom C E, Cohen D K 1979 *Usable Knowledge: Social Science and Social Problem Solving.* Yale University Press, New Haven, Connecticut

Peterson P L, Walberg H J (eds.) 1979 *Research on Teaching: Concepts, Findings and Implications.* McCutchan, Berkeley, California

Robinson F G 1979 *A System for Curriculum Development.* Ontario Institute for Studies in Education, Toronto, Ontario

Rogers E M, Shoemaker F F 1971 *Communication of Innovations: A Cross-cultural Approach,* 2nd edn. Free Press, New York

Wolf W C 1981 Selected knowledge diffusion/utilization know-how: Generalizability within educational practice. *Knowledge* 2: 331–40

Zaltman G, Duncan R, Holbek J 1973 *Innovations and Organizations.* Wiley, New York

Demonstration Programs

L-E. Datta

Demonstration programs involve the operation of an educational facility or the delivery of educational services in order to establish the characteristics and requirements of certain innovations in practice and to show their feasibility and value. Three elements distinguish demonstration programs from other forms of educational research: operation, scale, and purpose.

Demonstrations involve operation of an educational service, often throughout an entire school or group of schools, or through a common element such as a reading laboratory in several schools. Such operations may require installation of curricula, use of instructional materials and technologies, or application of administrative arrangements that were not available previously in the facility. Alternatively, demonstrations may be arranged through upgrading existing practices, such as expanding the use of microprocessors for instructional purposes from one classroom to the entire school. And, increasingly, operations involve selection of exemplary educational programs already functioning well to serve demonstration functions without changes in the existing program.

With regard to scale, demonstration programs are usually larger and more coherent than is required for testing curriculum elements or practices that eventually may be integrated into a demonstration. They are smaller, however, than would be required systematically to assess the consequences of an innovative approach. Most of the resources for demonstrations are invested in service delivery rather than in evaluation.

The primary purpose of demonstrations is to show in practice what an educational innovation looks like and to offer potential adopters a site where they can see for themselves how the innovation functions. Demonstrations can thus precede larger scale pilot or experimental programs, providing the opportunity to establish the feasibility and value of an innovation. They can also follow such programs and be used for the training and dissemination of the models of the innovation in operation.

Variants of this purpose have been fairly frequently used: convincing, developing, co-opting, and inspiring. In one form, demonstrations are intended to provide more convincing evidence than the written word for ideas which seem to work. Support for such exemplary programs is based on the notion that educators who come and see are more likely to return and do than those who merely read about the innovation. Demonstrations intended for convincing are often staffed with personnel trained to help visitors consider the advantages of the program for their own uses and are part of dissemination networks.

In a second form, demonstration programs are regarded more as living educational laboratories, whose lineage traces back to the early 1900s and the laboratory schools associated with teacher colleges. Support for these projects is based on the notion that embedding development of new educational ideas in an operational facility staffed to integrate research and practice is a valuable, if not better, way to improve education than is relying only on shorter term, single purpose studies. Collaborative research programs and "contract schools" are contemporary variants on the principles of laboratory school-like demonstrations.

In a third form, demonstration programs are intended to lever changes which otherwise might be resisted. Funds and the technical assistance often associated with demonstration program status are offered in exchange for school adoptions of innovations planned elsewhere. The assumption underlying such support is that providing some measure of local participation in shaping how new goals will be achieved or new practices established will ease adoption of changes.

And, in a fourth variant, some demonstration programs are intended to stimulate readiness for major shifts. They are established to exemplify what currently is far beyond the resources, practice, or philosophy of most educational programs, but what might be desirable in the future. The assumption underlying this variant is that the appetite for quite different and possibly more costly programs could be most sharply whetted by seeing an operational model.

Support for demonstration programs both within countries and through international agencies has been generous since the early 1960s. Demonstrations have included delivery of elementary-level schooling through satellite transmitted radio and television in countries as diverse as Guatemala and India; operation of model technical secondary schools combining long-term economic planning with new instructional techniques merging literacy and vocational skill acquisition; programs aimed at adults as part of still more complex economic development schemes, such as the projects in the Philippines offering literacy training in improved boat construction and fishing techniques and changes in the distribution and marketing system for the catch; and the operation of demonstration bilingual education and compensatory education programs in countries with substantial numbers of children of immigrant workers or from very low-income families.

Research on the effectiveness of demonstration programs has focused on two issues. The first is documenting the immediate effectiveness of the demonstration in reaching its goals; the second, on the longer term value of demonstrations. The first effort has led to a considerable body of publications based on the programs themselves (e.g., on the effectiveness of preschools), in which the results of the demonstrations are stand-ins for more experimental tests of the concepts themselves in optimum form. It has also yielded extensive analyses of the evaluation methodology appropriate for demonstrations. Expansion of qualitative and case study methods has been stimulated as evaluators have dealt with methodological problems of inference and contextualization of findings when true experimental studies are neither possible nor appropriate.

The studies of the validity of the assumptions underlying the uses of demonstrations have been more abundant for the first and third than for the second and fourth purposes. Research suggests that support of demonstrations primarily for the purpose of levering changes that otherwise might be resisted works only when other local purposes happen to coincide with the ostensible purposes of the demonstration. These studies indicate that demonstrations are neither very subtle nor long-lasting instruments of that kind of social change.

In contrast, recent studies of educational change have generally shown that while the dissemination process is considerably more complex than simple availability of lighthouse programs, having operational facilities to visit does contribute significantly to dissemination. Both frequency of adoption and appropriate adaptations seem fostered by demonstration sites, in combination with other elements of a dissemination system, and user satisfaction—including those who decide not to adopt the innovation—seems higher for those with the opportunity to observe the innovation in practice than those without.

Bibliography

Acheson K (ed.) 1977 *The Five Dimensions of Demonstration*. Teacher Corps Research Adaptation Cluster, Norman, Oklahoma. ERIC Document No. ED 183 558

May M J 1981 Demonstration project for handicapped young children: A review. *Young Child.* 36: 26–32

Vanecko J L 1978 *ESEA Title I Allocation Policy: Demonstration Study*. Abt, Cambridge, Massachusetts. ERIC Document No. ED 187–794

Curriculum Adoption

S. F. Loucks

Curriculum adoption refers to actual utilization of a particular educational program in a school system following a formal decision made by the appropriate authorities.

Curriculum adoption has taken on many meanings in the course of 30 years of attempts to understand its role in the process of educational change. In the 1950s and 1960s adoption was generally viewed as the endpoint of diffusion: when ideas or innovations were "adopted" they were considered to have been effectively diffused. To understand the adoption of new curricula such as "new mathematics" they were studied as they spread from school to school. Factors of interest were characteristics of the curricula (e.g., complexity, compatibility, relative advantage), channels of communication (e.g., person-to-person contact, print materials), innovativeness of the adopters (i.e., did they adopt early or late?), and nature of the school or district (e.g., size, existing communication structures) (Rogers and Shoemaker 1971). Adoption was the endpoint of individual-to-individual or organization-to-organization diffusion,

the point in time when a decision was made to use the new curriculum.

In the 1960s, a profusion of curricula were developed to attack problems of illiteracy, lack of scientific knowledge, and education for underserved populations (including the handicapped, poverty level, and non-college bound). By the 1970s, evaluation studies indicated that many of these curricula were unused or underused. Seeking to understand this phenomenon, researchers began to focus more carefully on the change process as it occurred within organizations such as schools and school districts. Thus evolved a new definition of curriculum adoption. Rather than the endpoint of interorganizational diffusion, it was seen as the first phase in the process of intraorganizational change (Havelock 1970). This new definition is used in the balance of this article.

Curriculum adoption is the process which leads up to and includes the decision to proceed with or use a curriculum. It is the first phase of the change process, also labeled the "initiation" or "mobilization" phase.

Subsequent phases are implementation or initial use (phase 2), and routinization or institutionalization (phase 3) (Fullan 1982).

Although many isolated and small-scale studies have been done of factors influencing adoption of a particular curriculum, the processes of initiating, mobilizing, and planning to prepare for a change are not yet understood. This is partially due to the lack of valid measures of adoption. Most often, studies of adoption employ survey questionnaires mailed to decision makers—a methodology of questionable value, since it often relies on hear-say, rarely defines terms precisely, and cannot explain instances of no response.

Curriculum adoption is accomplished in many ways. Sometimes it is effective; other times, as research indicates, an adoption decision merely creates the illusion that change has occurred. Attempts to understand successful adoption have identified many influencing factors. Six factors are described here.

The availability and quality of curricula influence their adoption. Studies have found curricula to exist in profusion in some areas, such as elementary school reading and mathematics, and to be of limited variety in others, such as teacher inservice training and career education (Louis and Rosenblum 1981). Time and resources are limited for development of curricula by those who ultimately use them. And quality of available curricula varies widely. One approach to quality control taken in the United States is a federal panel which "validates" programs on their evidence of effectiveness (the Joint Dissemination Review Panel) (Crandall et al. 1982). Research studies have found more effective adoptions where curricula are of proven quality (Louis and Rosenblum 1981).

A second factor influencing adoption is the access to information about available curricula. Most effective are person-to-person contacts through conferences, workshops, and professional networks. Such contacts occur most often in more densely populated areas, thus rural areas have special problems accessing information needed for wise adoption decisions (Fullan 1982).

Adoption never occurs without an advocate, a third important factor. Support of decision makers such as high-level district administrators is necessary, since the position combines ready access to information, authority, and resources. Also critical is advocacy by the actual users of the curriculum, who appear to use their peers for the major source of new ideas. Research has found teachers to be willing to adopt new programs under the right conditions, which include a curriculum that is clearly usable, support from building and district administrators, the opportunity to interact with their peers, and outside resource help when needed (Crandall et al. 1982). Finally, advocacy by members of the community can powerfully influence adoption through pressure and support, although they can also cause rejection of a new curriculum by direct opposition.

Individuals and agencies that link external resources to adopters are a fourth factor in effective adoption.

Research indicates that with the help of such linking agents, especially on a person-to-person basis, teachers and other potential users can locate curricula that meet their needs, and organizations such as school districts can identify materials and resources that meet organizational goals and external mandates (Havelock 1970). Special attention is given to developing the capabilities of linking agents in several countries, including Belgium, Sweden, and the United States.

The availability of external funds is a powerful stimulant for curriculum adoption. However, research has found that these resources are applied in two ways. The first, labeled the "problem-solving" approach, uses extra resources to identify and meet particular needs of the population served by the organization. The "bureaucratic" approach uses extra resources for expenditures other than identified needs, often in a response to a mandate or community pressure, where the political and symbolic value of the adopted curriculum is often of greater significance than its educational merit. Here implementation, or actual behavior change, rarely follows adoption (Berman and McLaughlin 1975).

A final factor influencing curriculum adoption is new legislation or policy, without which changes targeted at underserved populations are rarely considered. Often mandates aimed at changes in curriculum are general and ambiguous; they are easier to adopt than they are to implement. The adoption of nationally or regionally directed policies is of concern in several countries, including Canada, the Netherlands, and the United States (Fullan 1982, Van den Berg and Vandenberghe 1981).

Curriculum adoption is important because it sets in motion the direction or content of a change. During the adoption phase, goals, however ambiguous, are set, and new materials or methods are decided upon. The way is paved for actual changes in behavior, having direct implications for the next phase, implementation.

Bibliography

Association for Supervision and Curriculum Development (ASCD) 1980 *Considered Action for Curriculum Improvement, 1980 Yearbook.* ASCD, Alexandria, Virginia

Berman P, McLaughlin M W 1975 *Federal Programs Supporting Educational Change,* Vol. 4: *The Findings in Review.* Rand, Santa Monica, California

Bolam R 1981 *Strategies for Sustaining Educational Improvement in the 1980s.* Organisation for Economic Cooperation and Development/Centre for Educational Research and Innovation, Paris

Crandall D, Loucks S et al. 1982 *A Study of Dissemination Efforts Supporting School Improvement.* Network, Andover, Massachusetts

Fullan M 1982 *The Meaning of Educational Change.* Ontario Institute for the Study of Education, Toronto, Ontario

Havelock R 1970 *A Guide to Innovation in Education.* Institute for Social Research, Ann Arbor, Michigan

Louis K, Rosenblum S 1981 *Linking R and D with Schools: A Program and its Implications for Dissemination and School*

Improvement Policy. Abt Associates, Cambridge, Massachusetts

Miles M et al. 1978 *Designing and Starting New Schools: A Field Study of Social Architecture in Education*. Center for Policy Research, New York

Rogers E M, Shoemaker F F 1971 *Communication of Inno-vations: A Cross-cultural Approach*, 2nd edn. Free Press, New York

Van den Berg D, Vandenberghe R 1981 *Onderwijsinnovatie in Verschuivend Perspectief* [Educational Innovation in a Changing Perspective.] Catholic Educational Center, Netherlands

Curriculum Implementation

M. Fullan

Curriculum implementation is the process of putting a change into practice. It differs from the adoption of a change (the decision to use something new) in that the focus is on the extent to which actual change in practice occurs and on those factors which influence the extent of change. The idea of implementation and the factors affecting active use seem simple enough, but the concept has proven difficult to define. The following aspects of implementation are examined in order to identify the main issues: (a) implementation in perspective; (b) approaches to defining implementation; (c) components of implementation; (d) factors affecting implementation; (e) measurement and evaluation; and (f) planning for implementation.

1. Implementation in Perspective

There is no need to dwell on the fact that the vast majority of curriculum development efforts in the 1960s and 1970s did not get implemented in practice. Implementation is critically important because it refers to the means of accomplishing desired educational objectives. In perspective, most researchers see three broad, overlapping phases to the educational change process: (a) initiation, development, or adoption; (b) implementation or use; and (c) institutionalization and other outcomes (Berman 1981). It can be seen that the amount and quality of change which occurs or fails to occur at (b) will significantly affect what outcomes are achieved in any given change effort.

It is also important to raise the question of whether implementation per se is always desirable. While change for the sake of change is not by definition good, neither is implementation. It depends on the answers to two questions: Are the objectives and goals which the particular change purports to address highly valued (by whichever criterion groups are used)? What is the technical quality of the change in relation to accomplishing the goals in question?

With the above perspective as context, various aspects of the implementation question can now be examined in more detail. It is necessary to recognize (a) that there are at least two different schools of thought or approaches to defining and researching implementation (see Sect. 2); (b) that actual use must be examined (involving different components—see Sect. 3); (c) that factors influencing use should be identified (see Sect.

4); (d) that measurement and evaluation issues arise at all phases and aspects of the change process (see Sect. 5); and (e) that no matter how adept people become at researching and explaining the implementation process, it is entirely another matter to develop effective planning procedures for bringing about better implementation (see Sect. 6).

Finally, while most of the references used in this article are from Canada and the United States, it is the case that interest in implementation problems is a worldwide phenomenon. [For some sources outside North America see Frey and Haft 1982, Lewy and Nevo 1981, and the international projects on educational implementation coordinated by the Centre for Educational Research and Innovation, the Organisation for Economic Co-operation and Development (CERI/OECD), and International Movements Toward Educational Change (IMTEC) in Oslo, Norway.]

2. Approaches to Defining Implementation

Implementation consists of putting into practice something which is new to the person who is attempting to bring about a change. Changes can be in the form of externally developed innovations or ones which are locally or self-developed. In either case, individual implementers are involved in a process of change. There are two distinct approaches to implementation in the research literature, one of which is labeled the "fidelity or programmed approach," the other the "mutually adaptive or adaptive approach." The two approaches are based on different assumptions and methodologies, and therefore it is necessary to separate clearly their main features.

The fidelity or programmed orientation as the label implies rests on the assumption that the main goal of implementation for selected changes is to bring about and assess the extent to which actual use corresponds "faithfully" to the kind of use intended by the developer or sponsor of the innovation. The assumption is that the change has certain program requirements established by its developer(s), which in turn can be installed and assessed for any group of users attempting to use the new practice. While minor variations might be tolerated, the emphasis is clearly on ensuring that practice conforms to the developer's intentions (Berman 1981,

Fullan and Pomfret 1977, Crandall et al. 1982, Hall and Loucks 1977).

The adaptation approach on the other hand, assumes that the exact nature of implementation cannot and/or should not be prespecified, but rather should evolve as different groups of users decide what is best and most appropriate for their situation. There are different degrees of adaptation which might be envisaged ranging from minor adaptations (which is quite close to fidelity) through mutual adaptation (in which an external idea or innovation influences what users do while users more or less equally transform the idea for their situation), to evolutionary changes (in which the users evolve all sorts of uses according to their own interests, i.e., the adaptation is not mutual). Problems of mutual adaptation are discussed by Berman (1981), Fullan and Pomfret (1977), and Fullan (1981).

While there are different points on the fidelity–adaptive continuum, it is the case that different researchers and planners tend to stress one or the other approach. Those with a fidelity orientation formulate indicators to assess the degree of homogeneous implementation performance, while those with an adaptive orientation expect, encourage, and look for variations in practice. Fidelity emphasizes a priori specificity and structure, while adaptation is based on relatively unstructured, more open-ended premises (Fullan 1981). Berman (1981) suggests the interesting proposition that programmed (fidelity) approaches are appropriate under certain conditions (clear and consensual goals, well-worked out innovations, minor focused changes, etc.) while adaptive approaches are more effective under the opposite conditions (conflict over goals, incomplete development, major changes). Regardless of the situation however, the values of individual decision makers frequently determine whether a more structured (programmed) or more pluralistic (adaptive) approach is favored (see Fullan 1981 for some comparison of the United States and the United Kingdom in this regard).

Clearly, the assumptions and approach taken to implementation, influences to a great extent how research on implementation is conducted. Programmed changes have the advantage of being more clear, more specific, and easier to assess; but they also may be inappropriate for all or some situations and/or lead to rejection by individuals and groups who do not wish to use the particular version being advocated. Adaptive changes have the advantage of allowing for more individual choice, and development suited to a variety of situations; but they frequently create confusion about what should be done, and certainly from a research point of view are exceedingly difficult to assess (as the change is continually evolving, and varies across situations).

3. Components of Implementation

Components of implementation refer to what is meant by change in practice. Several researchers have stressed that change in practice is multidimensional, that is, there are a number of components of existing practice which are altered as a result of implementing something new. Leithwood (1981) spells out eight distinct dimensions of curricular implementation in describing changes in global conceptions, objectives, content, instructional material, teaching strategies, and the like. In a recent large-scale study of innovative practices in the United States, Crandall et al. (1982) have further developed the conceptual and methodological basis for measuring components of implementation in use.

In short, given curriculum changes, whether they are externally or locally developed, involve a number of changes in terms of what teachers (and others) think and do. Altering aspects of one's beliefs, using new curricular materials and technologies, employing new teaching strategies and learning diagnoses are all aspects of components of implementation. Further, the notion of components can be applied to both fidelity and adaptive approaches with the former consisting of identifying and measuring components contained in the developer's version, while the latter involves identifying and assessing what has changed in practice from what a person was previously doing regardless of other people's images of the change (Crandall et al. 1982).

4. Factors Affecting Implementation

Taken as a whole, implementation is a process over time by which people, events, and resources determine whether or not practice is altered when something new is attempted. Although the list of factors in any one situation can be quite large and variable, research since about 1965 has succeeded in identifying a number of factors commonly found to influence change in practice. These factors can be divided into four broad categories: (a) characteristics pertaining to the curriculum change being attempted; (b) local contextual conditions at the school district and school levels; (c) local strategies at the district and school levels used to foster implementation; and (d) external (to local) factors affecting the likelihood of implementation (Berman 1981, Fullan 1982). Research on each of these four sets of variables is reviewed briefly. In interpreting the role of these factors, two points should be borne in mind. First, the influence of any given characteristic is a function of how much impact it has on users. The meaning of change to those using it is a crucial aspect of effective implementation (Fullan 1982). Second, the factors cannot be understood in isolation from each other. It is the combination of characteristics occurring in specific settings which determines implementation outcomes.

4.1 Characteristics of the Change

Changes have different characteristics or attributes when perceived by those attempting to develop and/or those attempting to use them. These attributes can influence how likely real change is to occur in practice. In some pioneering work, Rogers and Shoemaker

(1971) identified a number of attributes of innovation which they found contributed to adoption—relative advantage, compatibility, complexity, trialability, and observerability. Note, however, that their research synthesis was based on adoption outcomes (the decision to use, not actual use), and was by and large conducted on individual decision makers (e.g., farmers adopting a new technology) rather than on individuals in organizational contexts such as school systems.

Since Rogers and Shoemaker's work there has been some concentrated research on the relationship between attributes of curriculum changes and subsequent implementation. Four main factors identified in several major research studies are: need and compatibility, clarity, complexity, quality and practicality of materials (Crandall et al. 1982, Emrick and Peterson 1978, Louis and Rosenblum 1981).

Curriculum changes, as with other social innovations are not always based on an assessment of need, especially as perceived by people responsible for working with the change. This is not to say that only changes which everyone agrees to should be attempted, but the research does suggest that the question of perceived need and compatibility makes a difference in terms of whether something happens.

Clarity (about goals and means) is another perennial problem in the curriculum change process. Even when there is some agreement that certain changes are needed, the adopted change may not be at all clear about what people should do differently. Problems related to clarity have been found in virtually every study of significant change. The role of clarity in the fidelity and adaptive approaches is particularly instructive for understanding the differences in the two approaches. In the fidelity approach, developers attempt to be highly specific, while in the adaptive approach there is much more open-endedness allowing for decisions to be made along the way (Shipman et al. 1974, Elliott 1976–77). In either case, the degree of clarity on the part of people attempting something new is related to the degree of change in practice which occurs. Further, even with highly programmed changes, research has found that clarity is not something which happens all at once. The development of clarity (or confusion) is a process which depends on the combination of factors and events discussed in this section. Nor is greater clarity an end in itself: very simple and insignificant changes can be very clear, while more difficult and worthwhile ones may not be amenable to easy clarification—a matter related to the third attribute, complexity.

Complexity refers to the difficulty and extent of change required of the individual involved in implementation. The actual amount depends on the starting point for any given individual or group. Many changes such as open education, systematic direct instruction, inquiry-oriented studies, involve an array of activities, diagnostic skills, teacher strategies, pedagogical understandings, and the like if effective implementation is to be achieved. While complex changes create more problems, they may result in more significant changes because more is being attempted.

The final factor associated directly with the nature of the change concerns the quality and practicality of the learning materials being used. Although it seems self-evident that quality is important, many curriculum changes fail to get implemented because the learning materials are insufficiently developed. The rather large-scale curriculum development efforts in the 1960s and early 1970s in the United States suffered because of inadequate attention to the quality, usability, and appropriateness of materials (Welch 1979). More recent research shows that many of the curriculum development efforts of the late 1970s are faring better. In an evaluation of the use of innovations in the National Diffusion Network (NDN), Emrick and Peterson (1978) found that "well-articulated adoption materials, which . . . are complete, well organized, comprehensive and detailed" and address "how-to" concerns are more effective at the implementation stage." The National Diffusion Network is a nationwide system in the United States to assist local districts and schools in selecting and using proven innovative programs. Using criteria of quality and effectiveness a panel screens potential programs for the purpose of selecting (validating) quality programs. Once validated they are disseminated through a system of state facilitators who help local decision makers select programs and who arrange for the developer of the programs to provide inservice training assistance to implementers.

More recent research has also found that perceived quality makes a difference in how likely and how well teachers implement a curriculum change (Crandall et al. 1982, Louis and Rosenblum 1981). Once again the difference between fidelity and adaptive approaches can be noted. In the former case, details of quality are attempted to be resolved at the developmental stage, while for the latter it is recognized that further development must be worked out by individuals and groups who are involved in implementing the particular change.

4.2 Local Conditions

It is necessary to distinguish between local conditions and local strategies relative to specific changes. Local conditions concern the climate and individual characteristics—at the county/district level, at the school level, and at the community level—which affect whether curriculum changes will be considered and under what conditions they are likely to be implemented. Some of the main factors found to influence change in practice are district leadership, school board and community support, the role of principals, school climate (e.g., professional collegiality among teachers), individual and collective emphasis on, and sense of efficacy about, instructional matters, and unanticipated critical events.

District leadership encompasses a number of variables which influence implementation. The nature of leadership sets the broad conditions for change in the district. Central office staff who show an active interest in determining which changes are needed, in supporting adopted changes during the initial implementation period, and in assessing their impact have an influence on the quality of implementation (see for example, Berman and McLaughlin 1977, Emrick and Peterson 1978). Through leadership in planning, through communication, and through decisions about resources, and selection and development of other leaders in the district, central administrators have an influence on the climate for change in the district as a whole.

If school districts are governed by local or regional boards of education as most are, such boards may have an indirect impact on implementation through the resource decisions they make, but there is not much evidence that they directly influence implementation, although there is some research which indicates that parent involvement in elementary schools can influence implementation (Fullan 1982). In any case, the large variety of organizational structures and cultural differences and the scarcity of research on the role of school boards in implementation does not put us in a position to draw clear conclusions.

On the other hand, there has been considerable research over the past few years on the role of the school principal. All major research on innovation and school effectiveness shows that the principal strongly influences the likelihood of change, but it also indicates that most principals do not play instructional leadership roles (Leithwood and Montgomery 1982). At the school level the principal frequently sets the climate of communication, support, and decision making which can foster or inhibit change in practice. Indeed, the next factor— school climate—brings together teacher–teacher and teacher–principal relationships. There is a good deal of evidence which says that interaction among users during attempts at change is the key to effective implementation. New meanings, new behavior, new skills depend significantly on whether teachers are working as isolated individuals or are exchanging ideas and support about their work (Rutter et al. 1979). While it is possible for teachers to develop such collegiality among themselves, the actions of the principal in relation to potential changes makes it more or less likely that school climate conducive to implementation will evolve.

It is not simply collegiality and school leadership per se which determine implementation outcomes, but also the question of the substance of concerns over which people interact. It is significant that two different bodies of research—that on school innovation, and that on school effectiveness— have made similar discoveries. Both found that better implementation and learning occurs when the principal and teachers set instructional matters as a high priority, and have a sense of efficacy that they can improve instruction through their efforts (see Edmonds 1979, Rutter et al. 1979).

Finally, there are a number of unanticipated events which occur with enough frequency to be cited as having a signficant impact on the extent of change. These include teacher turnover, changes in leadership at the school or district level (e.g., through promotion), collective bargaining, strikes and other events which affect the quality of teacher–school board relationships (Berman 1981, Louis and Rosenblum 1981, Crandall et al. 1982).

4.3 Local Strategies

Local strategies refer to the planning and policy actions taken in relation to implementing specific curriculum changes. Two core aspects of implementation strategies involve choices about inservice or development activities, and communication–information systems. Since implementation (whether voluntarily sought or externally imposed) involves learning how to do something new, it follows that opportunities for inservice education in relation to specific changes are critical. There is a compelling body of research which demonstrates that little change in practice occurs when staff development activities are absent, or when they consist of one-time orientation sessions without follow-up; by contrast when staff development activities are conducted prior to and during implementation, significant change in practice can occur (McLaughlin and Marsh 1978).

Decisions about how to address communication problems are very complex. They range from questions about how much participation in decisions should occur (at each phase of adoption, implementation, continuation), whether and how to gather and use evaluative and other information on implementation problems as well as learning outcomes, and how to maintain a communication system among the different parties. There are too many variables and too many cultural differences at work to be able to draw firm conclusions. Lack of participation in initial decisions, for example, may not make a difference as long as the selected innovation meets a need, and there is intensive staff development support. Similarly, formal evaluation at the early stages of implementation may not be necessary or even helpful (see Sect. 5 below). However, it should be noted that other factors listed earlier address critical communication needs. Assessment of need, active leadership, principal and teacher–teacher interaction, staff development all serve to increase the communication between administrators and teachers about what should be done, and how to do it. Stated another way, while communication systems vary in their degree of formality, a regular, systematic exchange of information about implementation requirements is necessary for change in practice to occur (Fullan 1982).

4.4 External Factors

Factors external to the local school system can be seen as facilitating or inhibiting curriculum implementation. Three factors which illustrate this dilemma are policy change, financial or material resources, and technical assistance. The passage of a new piece of legislation or other government policy decisions in the curriculum/ program area result in a certain amount of formal pressure for changes to be implemented, but the mere existence of the policy does not result in much implementation unless several of the other factors listed in this section are also conducive to change.

Similarly, the availability of financial or material resources does not guarantee curriculum change as there are a variety of opportunistic reasons why school systems seek additional resources (Berman and McLaughlin 1977). Forms of external assistance, depending on their characteristics, can also be more or less helpful. External assistance (e.g., from government staff, project developers, etc.) given only at the orientation stage does not result in much change in practice, unless the local conditions and strategies reinforce the external assistance. Two recent large-scale studies in the United States found that external training, given by a variety of consultants combined with follow through support which is coordinated with local consultants or staff represents a very effective combination in bringing about change in classroom practice (Crandall et al. 1982, Louis and Rosenblum 1981).

5. Measurement and Evaluation

There are three major components involved in assessing curriculum implementation as indicated in Fig. 1.

In examining specific curriculum changes, it is possible to gather evaluative data on (a) factors affecting implementation (as outlined in Sec. 4), (b) implementation or the state of change in practice at any given time (Sect. 3), and (c) the impact of implementation on student learning, attitudes, organizational capacity, and other outcomes. Questions of measurement and instrumentation are discussed for each of the three components starting with outcomes. It can also be anticipated that the criteria of evaluation are more or less specific depending on whether one takes (and/or whether the innovation is conducive to) a fidelity or adaptive approach.

5.1 Outcomes

This article is not directly concerned with the evaluation of learning outcomes. However, the relationship to implementation should be understood. Implementation (or bringing about changes in practice) is the means to accomplishing desired outcomes. Several difficulties arise when an attempt is made to assess outcomes and relate them to implementation changes. First, learning outcomes will be considered, followed by some comments on other types of outcomes.

One of the first issues concerns the measurement of learning outcomes. Since the early 1970s there have

been considerable developments in instrumentation for testing basic skills and knowledge (Lewy and Nevo 1981). Beyond this there is a great deal of controversy about how and whether to measure some of the higher cognitive development (e.g., problem-solving ability) and social development (e.g., ability to work in groups) objectives in education.

Even if valid information can be obtained on learning outcomes, the next question concerns what it indicates about implementation. Such information by itself tells very little. It indicates what students are learning and not learning, but provides no information on the source of the problem. For the latter information it is necessary to delve into the question of what changes in practice have in fact occurred, and in turn what factors affected these changes.

Two final issues remain: the question of other types of outcomes, and the matter of fidelity versus adaptive orientations to curriculum evaluation. In addition to learning outcomes, curriculum changes result in other individual and organizational changes. Crandall et al. (1982), for example, assessed the impact of specific program changes on teacher attitudes and benefits, organizational changes (e.g., increased or decreased communication, morale), and overall attitude toward engaging in school improvement activities (such as curriculum change). Louis and Rosenblum (1981) assessed a similar range of outcomes. Shipman et al. (1974) using a more open-ended approach uncovered a variety of outcomes in examining a major curriculum project in the United Kingdom. In brief, it is necessary to consider a number of intended and unintended consequences when examining the impact of curriculum change.

The final issue which complicates a researcher's ability to evaluate curriculum change relates to the fidelity/adaptive distinction. Obviously, the more that a curriculum change is amenable to clear, specific, a priori definition the more it is possible to measure instances of change in relation to corresponding outcomes. But, as has been seen, it is not appropriate or even possible to approach all curriculum changes with this orientation.

For all of the above reasons, the vast majority of the research literature does not contain studies in which both implementation and outcomes are assessed and their relationship examined. There are careful studies examining one or the other, but studies which investigate the relationship of implementation to outcomes are still in the early stages of development and face some intrinsically difficult problems.

5.2 Implementation

By contrast, there have been substantial developments in the direct measurement of implementation, that is, the extent of change in practice, especially from the fidelity perspective. In particular, the assessment of components of implementation, coupled with the measurement of levels of use vis-à-vis each component has received considerable attention. Hall and Loucks (1977) and colleagues at the University of Texas were

Figure 1
Components of implementation evaluation

responsible for many of the conceptual and methodological procedures for assessing the levels of use of innovations by individual users. They employ an eight-level distinction ranging from nonuse through mechanical use, to renewal. The procedures have been refined and applied to a large number of different program innovations. The separation of dimensions or components of implementation is a more recent phenomenon. Leithwood (1981) identified eight different dimensions of curriculum change (e.g., materials, teaching strategies, etc.). Hall and Loucks (1977), and Crandall et al. (1982) in building on this work, define components in relation to each innovation thereby allowing the number of components to vary depending on the innovation being assessed (e.g., use of particular materials, use of a particular diagnostic test, using a certain question-asking technique, etc.). In all of these efforts researchers have refined methods involving interviews, questionnaires, and content analysis.

Using more open-ended procedures, researchers interested in adaptive or evolutionary patterns of implementation have also attempted to identify and describe what changes in practice have been happening. Shipman et al. (1974) explored some of these issues from "inside a curriculum project." In a collaborative research mode, Elliott (1976–77) worked with a group of teachers to develop a number of changes in classroom practice. Crandall et al. (1982) in addition to assessing implementation in relation to the developer's model, also described changes in practice regardless of the expectations of developers. Thus, whether interest lies in innovations from a developer's perspective, or more broadly in what changes are occurring, it is possible to assess and describe the nature and extent of change in practice.

5.3 Factors Affecting Implementation

In Section 4, the list of factors found to affect the extent of implementation was divided into four broad categories. In evaluating implementation, it is important to include these types of factors in the evaluation design. It is necessary to understand the role of these local and external conditions and strategies in order to understand implementation outcomes. Researchers have used a combination of documentary or content analysis, observation, interview, questionnaire, and case-study methods to gather information on factors influencing implementation. Fullan and Pomfret (1977), and Fullan (1982) contain summaries of many of these studies. For large-scale projects, documentary, questionnaire, and interview instrumentation have been particularly comprehensively developed by Crandall et al. (1982), and Louis and Rosenblum (1981). One of the more intriguing methodological developments involves the use of the case study, especially multiple case studies to portray implementation processes more wholistically while at the same time struggling with problems of reducing and displaying the amount of information more concisely and explicitly.

6. Planning for Implementation

The topic of planning for more effective implementation is extremely complex. In this conclusion some of the main issues can be introduced. The first matter is that "understanding" the implementation process is not the same as being able to "influence" it for the better. Some factors may be unchangeable or a researcher may not have the authority to alter them. Planning for more effective implementation then, involves a new set of considerations. The second issue is that a good deal is known about the factors which make it more or less likely that change in practice will occur (see Sect. 4). By deriving implications from this knowledge some of the main planning goals and tasks can be identified. It is known that change in practice occurs when certain elements occur in combination: attention to the development of clear and validated materials; active administrative support and leadership at the district and especially the school level; focused, ongoing inservice or staff development activities; the development of collegiality and other interaction-based conditions at the school level; and the selective use of external resources (both people and materials).

This broad list can be used to generate a list of more particular strategies. Materials production and availability can be promoted through systems like the National Diffusion Network in the United States (Crandall et al. 1982). Leadership programs for district and school personnel can be used for long-term development of leadership capacity. Specific inservice activities can be designed and can significantly affect implementation provided that they are ongoing, specific, and combined with other factors.

The third complexity is that specific planning implications only make sense from the perspective of the situation and role of individuals. Therefore, there are many different planning guidelines that would have to be developed depending on whether one is a government official, a teacher, a parent, a principal, a consultant, and so on (Fullan 1982).

In conclusion, knowledge about curriculum implementation has increased substantially since the early 1970s. During this period, intensive research endeavors and accomplishments on a number of fronts have been made.

Bibliography

Berman P 1981 Educational change: An implementation paradigm. In: Lehming R, Kane M (eds.) 1981 *Improving Schools: Using What We Know.* Sage, Beverly Hills, California, pp. 253–86

Berman P, McLaughlin M W 1977 *Federal Programs Supporting Educational Change*, Vol. 7: *Factors Affecting Implementation and Continuation.* Rand, Santa Monica, California

Crandall D et al. 1982 *Master Report Series of the Study of Dissemination Efforts Supporting School Improvement.* The Network, Andover, Massachusetts

Edmonds R 1979 Effective schools for the urban poor. *Educ. Leadership* 37: 15–18

Elliott J 1976–77 Developing hypotheses about classrooms from teachers' practical constructs: An account of the work of the Ford Teaching Project. *Interchange* 7(2): 2–22

Emrick J, Peterson S 1978 *A Synthesis of Findings Across Five Recent Studies in Educational Dissemination and Change.* Far West Laboratory, San Francisco, California

Frey K, Haft H (eds.) 1982 *Compendium Curriculumforschung.* Universität Kiel, Institut für die Padagogik der Naturwissenschaften, Federal Republic of Germany

Fullan M 1981 The relationship between evaluation and implementation. In: Lewy A, Nevo D (eds.) 1981 *Evaluation Roles in Education.* Gordon and Breach, London, pp. 309–40

Fullan M 1982 *The Meaning of Educational Change.* Teachers College Press, New York

Fullan M, Pomfret A 1977 Research on curriculum and instruction implementation. *Rev. Educ. Res.* 47: 335–97

Hall G E, Loucks S F 1977 A developmental model for determining whether the treatment is actually implemented. *Am. Educ. Res. J.* 14: 263–76

Leithwood K A 1981 The dimensions of curriculum innovation. *J. Curric. Stud.* 13: 25–36

Leithwood K A, Montgomery D J 1982 The role of the elementary school principal in program improvement. *Rev. Educ. Res.* 53: 309–39

Lewy A, Nevo D (eds.) 1981 *Evaluation Roles in Education.* Gordon and Breach, London

Louis K, Rosenblum S 1981 *Linking R and D with Schools: A Program and its Implications for Dissemination.* National Institute of Education, Washington, DC

McLaughlin M W, Marsh D D 1978 Staff development and school change. *Teach. Coll. Rec.* 80: 69–94

Rogers E M, Shoemaker F F 1971 *Communication of Innovations: A Cross-cultural Approach*, 2nd edn. Free Press, New York

Rutter M, Maugham B, Mortimer P, Ouston J, Smith A 1979 *Fifteen Thousand Hours: Secondary Schools and their Effects on Children.* Harvard University Press, Cambridge, Massachusetts

Shipman M D, Bolam D, Jenkins D R 1974 *Inside a Curriculum Project: A Case Study in the Process of Curriculum Change.* Methuen, London

Welch W 1979 Twenty years of science curriculum development: A look back. In: Berliner D (ed.) 1979 *Review of Research in Education*, Vol. 7. American Educational Research Association, Washington, DC

Curriculum Adaptation

A. Blum and A. B. Grobman

Curriculum adaptation involves the modification of a course of study for groups of students different from those for whom the course was originally designed.

The term curriculum adaptation is used both at the classroom level and at the level of an entire educational system. It applies to all kinds of curricular changes a teacher decides on, when implementing a written curriculum in his or her own classroom. In this sense Haussler and Pittman (1973) use the term adaptiveness as the "quality of the curriculum which allows the teacher, in consideration of his own style, to function within the curriculum," and to consider each student as a unique human being.

Curriculum adaptation is more often used to describe "the appropriate transfer of a curriculum from one society into another, which is different from the first" (Tütken 1972).

1. Need for Adaptation

Curriculum development is an expensive endeavor. During the 1960s, in the United States alone over US $100 million were spent on curriculum development in science education (Holton 1969). It is also a time-consuming enterprise, especially where budget or personnel constraints allow only for a step-by-step operation, in which courses for different age and ability levels cannot be developed side by side. Moreover, a new curriculum has a validity of limited duration. Grobman (1969) suggested that science curricula should

be revised every five years, but due to the high expenses of producing new curricula most educational programs are used for a much longer period of time.

Time and money are not the only constraints in the development and implementation of educational curricula. Local personnel are another constraint. Over 1,000 scientists were involved in the development and rewriting of the various BSCS (Biological Science Curriculum Study) versions (Hurd 1969). Only in a few countries is there a balance between the need for new curricula and the resources available for this purpose. In most nations, and above all in the developing world, the urge for quick but also profound change outweighs the manifold resources. A possible shortcut to overcome the constraints, at least partially, is to adapt curricula developed elsewhere. (Thus, BSCS was translated into 21 languages and adapted for use in over 40 nations.)

2. Issues in Adaptation

The main issues concerning adaptation are changes which are deemed necessary because of the different ecological and sociocultural environments, different historical and political perspectives, and different classroom situations.

Discussions of plants and animals from the local environment make textual materials more relevant for students. Thus for students in the United Kingdom and much of the United States, references to oak, willow, or pine trees would be familiar, but for students in tropical areas of India or the Philippines, they would not. In an adaptation, those examples might be replaced with palm, banana, and banyan trees. In Japan the silkworm is used for many of the genetic experiments for which the fruit fly is employed in the United States.

While the ecological differences are usually taken care of in curriculum adaptations, this is not always the case for sociocultural differences.

Holmes (1977) maintains that "systems of education have their own nation-specific ethos . . . societal features include internalized national attitudes to politics, religion, economics, social class, and so on."

Nevertheless, most countries that adopted the Scottish Integrated Science (SIS) curriculum share common characteristics which often contrast sharply with those found in Scotland. Yet in some of these countries, SIS was adopted virtually without change.

The adoption or adaptation effort is often speeded up when metropolitan publishers with subsidiaries in the new nations help to promote the publication of the new texts, sometimes involving local educators only on a token basis. Regional curriculum development centers in developing regions tended to start with the adaptation of foreign programs in order to get a quick start, but as soon as possible shifted towards indigenous programs (Maddock 1982).

Curriculum projects which emphasize cultural heritage (e.g., the Harvard Project Physics) or which used specific ecosystems like Biological Sciences Curriculum Study (BSCS) gave permission to adapt their materials only under the condition that the materials would be adapted to the ecological and cultural backgrounds of the adapting country. In this way they reinforced the wish of the adaptors to produce something of their own. A thoughtful recombination of existing elements to a new whole can, indeed, be creative.

Typical examples of changes due to pride in local cultural achievements are the Russian BSCS adaptation, in which the achievements of Russian scientists were emphasized rather than those of scientists from other parts of the world, and the Italian Harvard Physics Project adaptation, in which Galileo is given more space than in the American original.

Another reason for the need to adapt a curriculum may be the differences in time allocation for studying a particular program. Thus, for example, the BSCS standard course was designed for 10th grade students in the United States, who meet in biology class for five periods a week throughout the academic year. In England and Wales, the biology program occupies one or two periods a week over a five-year time span. Thus the adaptation of the course for use in England and Wales had to accommodate the growing intellectual capabilities of the students over the five-year period. Even if a particular course is taught at the same grade level in various systems, the placement of cognate courses may necessitate making provision for the adaptation of the

materials. Thus, for example, if physics and chemistry precede biology, a deeper understanding of molecular biology can be expected in the biology course during the same span of time that would be devoted to it, than in countries where those physical sciences follow biology in the sequential presentation.

Another kind of adaptation is required for students who are academically or physically disadvantaged. For slow learners, the standard BSCS course, for example, was adapted by reducing the amount of reading and the complexity of the vocabulary while concurrently increasing the "things to do" in the laboratory. In other programs, special adaptations were made for physically handicapped students (Goodrich and Kinney 1985). A systematic approach to curriculum adaptation is described by Blum et al. (1981).

3. How Curricula are Chosen for Adaptation

The process of curriculum adaptation can be divided into two separate stages: selection of a suitable curriculum (or curricula) for adaptation, and adaptation itself. The selection is sometimes, but certainly not always, based on a review of several curricula that seem, at least prima facie, to be amenable for adaptation. It is also assumed that the adaptors have a clear idea about the needs of their target population and are determined to choose the best curricula. In reality, however, the picture can be very different.

Blum (1979) describes various procedures used to select curricula for adaptation: (a) only one choice possible; (b) first seen, first chosen; (c) first offer at recommendation accepted; (d) intuitive choice among some feasible projects; (e) intuitive but reasoned choice among feasible projects; (f) choice based upon predetermined criteria; (g) synthesis of a new curriculum based on others.

Some examples of such selection procedures follow.

When the West Indian Science Improvement Project (WISCIP) was set up in the Caribbean region, various curricula from the United Kingdom, the United States, and Australia were considered for adaptation. After a first screening, the American projects were rejected because of the high costs involved in their implementation and because the Caribbean educational system is closer to the British than to the American system. Finally, five project outlines were put before an assembly of teachers and SIS was chosen by a majority vote.

When Swaziland decided to set up an integrated science project based on adaptations, a workshop was held and again five programs were scrutinized as regards to suitability for local adaptation. This time a set of 40 criteria were employed under the headings: (a) aims; (b) content selection; (c) content organization; (d) learning experiences; and (e) resource materials. The WISCIP came out clearly ahead on content selection and resource materials and narrowly on learning experiences and consequently it was selected for adaptation.

A more sophisticated strategy, and in the end probably a more effective one, is to screen a number of projects, but instead of selecting one of them, adaptors synthesize a new curriculum by recombining the most suitable elements from several of them. This approach was taken by the originators of the Tel Aviv Elementary Science Project.

It could be argued that such a synthesis of elements taken from various projects, each of which reflected a different rationale, may destroy the unique character of the original programs. This may be so, but the argument is not relevant for the adaptors–synthesizers, who above all are guided by what they believe to be the best interests of their students. Often the original curriculum projects participate in the adaptation process to ensure that the spirit and flavor of the original course are accurately reflected in the adaptation (Grobman 1976).

In some cases, a curriculum which was adapted for use in a developing country was further adapted for use in another developing country. Thus, the Colombian adaptation of the BSCS course was the basis for an adaptation for use in Puerto Rico instead of the latter being derived directly from the original BSCS materials. (The adaptation of the SIS based WISCIP curriculum into the African SWISP has already been mentioned.)

4. Adaptations of the Second Order

So far most adaptation efforts have gone into the adaptation of written texts and the simplification of equipment. It was also assumed that the culture into which the programs were adapted was one based on the written word. Little has been published about adaptations of the second order—for students in cultures in which communication is through the spoken word, or through visual and manipulative signs (Blum 1979). Some attempts—mostly intuitive—are already being made, for example, in the adaptation of FAST (Foundational Approach Science Teaching, a Hawaiian curriculum project) to the Marshall Islands and SCIS for the Pueblo community. Insights gained in these adaptation projects should be carefully studied, so that generalizations might be crystallized in order to improve further adaptations of the second order.

Bibliography

Blum A 1979 Curriculum adaptation in science education: Why and how? *Sci. Educ.* 63: 693–704
Blum A, Kragelund Z, Pottenger F 1981 Development and evaluation of a curriculum adaptation scheme. *Sci. Educ.* 65: 521–36
Davey T 1972 Problems and developments in the teaching of biology in Malaysian schools. *J. Biol. Educ.* 6: 93–97
Goodrich J A, Kinney P G 1985 *ADAPTIPS—Adapting Curricula for Students who are Deaf–Blind.* College of Education, Kentucky University, Lexington, Kentucky.
Grobman A B 1969 *The Changing Classroom: The Role of the Biological Sciences Curriculum Study.* Doubleday, New York
Grobman A B 1976 Factors influencing international curricular diffusion. *Stud. Educ. Eval.* 2: 227–32
Haussler P, Pittman J 1973 *System zur Analyse naturwissenschaftlicher Curricula.* Beltz, Weinheim
Holmes B 1977 Science education: Cultural borrowing and comparative research. *Stud. Sci. Educ.* 4: 83–110
Holton G 1969 Collaboration between curriculum development projects in developed and developing countries. *Israel—Rehovot Conference on Science and Education in Developing Countries.* Weizmann Institute of Science. Rehovot
Hurd P De H 1969 *New Directions in Teaching Secondary School Science.* Rand McNally, Chicago, Illinois
Karplus R 1974 SCIS Safari. *SCIS Newsletter* 26: 3–4
Lockard D (ed.) 1977 *Reports of the International Clearinghouse on Science and Mathematics Curricular Developments.* University of Maryland, College Park, Maryland
Maddock M N 1982 *Some Trends in the Evolution of Science Curriculum Centers in Asia.* UNESCO Regional Office for Education in Asia and the Pacific, Bangkok
Tütken H 1972 Zur Adaptierung ausländischer Curricula. In: Robinson S B (ed.), 1972 *Curriculumentwicklung in der Diskussion.* Klett, Stuttgart

A. Blum

Curriculum Adaptation within the Class

M. A. Smylie

Curriculum adaptation within classrooms refers to the transformation and modification of curricula by teachers for classroom instruction. Research on teaching and the implementation of curriculum and instructional programs consistently reveals that teachers adapt the goals, objectives, and content of formal curricula to their specific classroom contexts (Berliner 1982, Fullan 1982). Despite mandates from state departments of education and local school districts, teachers routinely modify curricula by additions, deletions, and changes in sequence and emphasis (Clark and Peterson 1986).

1. Differences in Coverage, Time Allocation, and Instructional Emphases

Curriculum adaptation at the classroom level is evident in differences between formal curriculum requirements and the amount of curriculum actually covered during classroom instruction. Several studies reveal dramatic differences in how much of a particular curriculum is taught despite specific mandates about content coverage (Berliner 1982). For example, the extensive Beginning Teachers Evaluation Study identified many teachers who were selective in covering state-required curricula and some teachers who ignored state curriculum requirements altogether and failed to teach certain aspects of different subject areas (Fisher et al. 1978).

Another way that curriculum adaptation within classrooms is evident is in differences in the amount of time that teachers allocate for instruction among subject areas. In an in-depth study of teaching in elementary schools, Carew and Lightfoot (1979) demonstrated that teachers' specific curriculum interests and concerns can dominate instructional time devoted to particular curricular areas. In one first-grade classroom, they found that 75 percent of all academic interactions between the teacher and students were focused on reading, to the virtual exclusion of other subject areas. The Beginning Teacher Evaluation Study reveals substantial variations in the time teachers allocate to different curricula (Fisher et al. 1978). Some teachers in that study allocated as much as two-and-a-half times more instructional time to reading and language arts than other teachers at the same grade level, even though they were all constrained by the same length of school day. Wider variations were found in other subject areas, such as mathematics and science. For example, time allocated to mathematics instruction differed as much as 300 percent among teachers at the same grade level within the same length of school day.

Curriculum adaptation is also evident in variations in instruction provided to groups of students of different academic achievement levels within the same classroom. Research on instructional grouping finds that teachers often teach different curricula, present less curricular content, and cover that content in less comprehensive ways with groups of low-achieving students than with groups of higher achieving students (Good and Marshall 1984). The research also reveals differences in the amount of time allocated to specific curricula and in the levels of comprehension that are required of low-achieving and higher achieving groups of students within the same classroom.

Even where teachers select the same curriculum for low-achieving and higher achieving groups of students within their classroom, research finds substantial differences in instructional emphases between these groups (Good and Marshall 1984). Low-achieving students are more frequently taught about the concrete and practical aspects of the curriculum for skill development. Higher achieving students are introduced to the more abstract and theoretical dimensions of the curriculum for developing deeper meaning and understanding of the subject matter. Instruction is usually paced at a slower rate for low-achieving students than for higher achieving students and low-achieving students are generally assigned easier and less varied work that under-

emphasizes the higher level substantive aspects of the curriculum.

2. Teachers' Decision Making

Differences in curriculum coverage, time allocations, and content and instructional emphases are functions of teachers' decisions related to translating formal curricula into specific instructional tasks and activities. Curricula may be adapted during preactive planning for instruction (Clark and Peterson 1986). Decisions that teachers make during preactive planning to transform curricula are based on their considerations of several different factors (Clark and Peterson 1986, Fullan and Pomfret 1977, Shavelson and Stern 1981). First, teachers may consider various characteristics of the curriculum itself, including its goals and objectives, subject matter content, and emphases. They may examine the recommended tasks and activities and their sequencing as well as the instructional materials that accompany or are recommended for teaching the curriculum. They may consider the explicitness, complexity, and difficulty of the content, tasks and activities, and materials. Then, teachers may compare these various characteristics of the curriculum to their own interests; their knowledge and understanding of the subject area; and their theories, values, and beliefs related to the curriculum and to pedagogy. They may weigh the various characteristics of the curriculum against their students' interests, abilities, and learning needs as well as their expectations for student academic performance.

Teachers may also consider the implications of curriculum implementation with respect to maintaining student attention and involvement in instructional activity and the problem of student control. For example, teachers may view specific tasks and activities included in the formal curriculum to be too difficult, complex, or abstract for students and conclude that these characteristics of the curriculum may lead to boredom, inattention, disengagement, failure, frustration, and perhaps to student misbehavior and interruption of teaching. Finally, teachers may draw upon their previous experiences with the particular curriculum, including their assessments of students' interest and learning and how difficult and enjoyable it was to teach the curriculum, to determine whether and how that curriculum might be modified.

Research on teacher decision making is not clear about which of these factors are considered and when and how they are considered in teachers' preactive planning decisions to determine how specific curricula should be taught (Shavelson and Stern 1981). The importance attributed to any one factor seems to depend in large part on the individual teacher and that teacher's assessment of the specific classroom context. However, particular factors may come to dominate teachers' preactive planning decisions. For example, Schwille et al. (1981) found in their study of mathematics instruction in elementary schools that teachers' perceptions of the effort required to teach a particular curriculum, their perceptions of the difficulty of the curriculum for students, and their personal feelings of enjoyment while teaching that curriculum are primary factors that govern teachers' decisions related to curriculum coverage and emphasis.

Preactive planning decisions shape the broad outlines of what curricula are likely to be taught, how much content is covered, the emphases that are likely to be given, and the teaching strategies that are likely to be used during classroom instruction. Often, however, preactive planning decisions are altered as a result of specific classroom experiences. Teachers make interactive decisions during the course of instruction that may result in additional transformations of formal curricula (Clark and Peterson 1986). While teachers infrequently abandon original plans completely or interrupt the flow of instructional activity to introduce new curricula or instructional routines (Shavelson and Stern 1981), they continuously make judgments and alter the content and course of lessons according to their assessments of students' responses to instruction, and according to unanticipated classroom events (Green 1983).

Teachers observe students' answers to questions, the questions students ask, and the comments they make during lessons. Teachers also examine students' levels of attention, involvement, and interest, and the amount of difficulty they experience in understanding new content and successfully completing specific tasks and activities. Information from students' responses and reactions is gathered throughout the course of instruction and assessed in conjunction with other information, such as the teacher's knowledge and perceptions of students' academic abilities and learning needs, expectations for student performance, and theories and beliefs about the curriculum and pedagogy. On the basis of these assessments, teachers may elaborate, deviate from, or otherwise alter the curriculum on a moment-to-moment basis during the course of classroom instruction. These assessments may also be considered after instructional tasks and activities are completed to evaluate the implementation and instructional success of the curriculum and to determine how the curriculum might be adapted further in subsequent preactive planning decisions.

Bibliography

Berliner D 1982 The executive function of teaching. Paper presented at the annual meeting of the American Educational Research Association, New York, March 1982

Carew J V, Lightfoot S L 1979 *Beyond Bias: Perspectives on Classrooms.* Harvard University Press, Cambridge, Massachusetts

Clark C M, Peterson P L 1986 Teachers' thought processes. In: Wittrock M C (ed.) 1986 *Handbook of Research on Teaching*, 3rd edn. Macmillan, New York, pp. 255–96

Fisher C, Filby N, Marliave R, Cahen L, Dishaw M, Moore J, Berliner D 1978 *Teaching Behaviors, Academic Learning Time and Student Achievement: Final Report of Phase III-B, Beginning Teachers Evaluation Study.* Technical Report V-1. Far West Laboratory for Educational Research and Development, San Francisco, California

Fullan M 1982 *The Meaning of Educational Change.* Teachers College, New York

Fullan M, Pomfret A 1977 Research on curriculum and instruction implementation. *Rev. Educ. Res.* 47(1): 335–97

Good T, Marshall S 1984 Do students learn more in heterogeneous or homogeneous groups? In: Peterson P, Wilkinson L, Hallinan M (eds.) 1984 *The Social Context of Instruction: Group Organization and Group Processes.* Academic Press, Orlando, Florida, pp. 15–38

Green J 1983 Research on teaching as a linguistic process: A state of the art. In: Gordon E (ed.) 1983 *Review of Research in Education*, Vol. 10. American Educational Research Association, Washington, DC, pp. 151–252

Schwille J, Porter A, Belli A, Floden R, Freeman D, Knappen L, Kuhs T, Schmidt W 1981 *Teachers as Policy Brokers in the Content of Elementary School Mathematics.* Institute for Research on Teaching, Michigan State University, East Lansing, Michigan

Shavelson R J, Stern P 1981 Research on teachers' pedagogical thoughts, judgments, decisions, and behavior. *Rev. Educ. Res.* 51(4): 455–98

Course Offering

W. H. Schubert

Course offering refers to the entire range and character of courses provided by a school or other educational institution. The term may also denote those courses (including workshops, independent studies, laboratories, and other formalized teaching/learning situations) provided during a given time period, for example, academic year, semester, quarter, or special session. Furthermore, a less frequent use of course offering signifies course description, that is, the content of any given course as represented in a course syllabus or outline. On a large scale and taken in plural form, however, course offering refers to entire programs of studies.

Colleges, universities, and technical-training institutes have the most formalized descriptions of course offerings. They are usually detailed in academic bulletins or college catalogs. Course offerings of elementary or secondary schools also have formalized descriptions however, these are less thoroughly described. Regardless of the elaboration of written statement, course offerings constitute a form of curricular policy. When written, such policy serves as a clarification, explication and advertisement for that which is offered to those who use or are contemplating use of the services of an educational institution.

The overt offerings of an educational institution are sometimes referred to as the explicit curriculum (Eisner 1979). These overt offerings are usually designated as one of two kinds of offerings: required courses and elective courses. Both are part of the explicit or overt curriculum. Required courses are those that must be taken, and elective courses are those that may be chosen by the student.

In order to provide greater perspective on the idea of course offering, the concept should be seen as a salient dimension of curriculum and program design taken as a whole. It is emphasized that a survey of lists of courses offered by an educative organization provides only superficial comprehension of the depth and subtlety of course offering.

Still today, curriculum scholars argue that those who wish to understand course offerings must study the systemic impact of principles drawn upon to create the particular configuration of required and elective courses that a given curriculum provides. Posner and Rudnitsky (1982) have developed systematic guidelines for teachers to use in the design of course offerings. They describe how to develop a rationale that gives focus to initial ideas about a course to be constructed, and proceed from that point to enable teachers to refine intended learning outcomes, to cluster and organize them into instructional units, select appropriate teaching strategies, and plan for evaluation.

Great complexity is added to this process when networks of courses are the topic of concern, for example, all required and elective offerings. It is almost without variance that authors of texts on curriculum development, design, planning, and decision making (terms that are frequently used interchangeably) emphasize the necessity of acquiring an integrated view of purposes, learning experiences, organization, and evaluation for the whole configuration of course offerings as well as for individual courses.

Finally, it is useful to provide perspective on course offerings by juxtaposing them with that which is not offered. To that end, Eisner (1979) contrasts the explicit curriculum with implicit and null curricula. Sometimes known as the hidden curriculum (Snyder 1970), implicit curriculum refers to the multitude of unintended side effects of the explicit curriculum (see *Hidden Curriculum*). This curriculum teaches a great deal, and there are some (e.g., Apple 1979) who argue that this hidden curriculum reproduces values and social hierarchies of social classes in any culture. Eisner's (1979) use of null curriculum refers to the plethora of possible courses, given today's knowledge explosion, that could be offered but are not. A person who wishes to seriously consider the issue of course offerings, in addition, must not neglect attention to courses offered by nonschool agencies, for in the present era of expanded communication an ecological perspective is needed to enjoin many conceptions of course offerings that extend beyond schooling to the culture at large (Schubert 1982).

In summary, course offering refers to the explicit curriculum, both required and elective courses, as they are described and practiced. To comprehend the complexity of course offerings it is necessary to see them in a broad curricular perspective, and also to juxtapose them with both intended and unintended offerings provided by many educative organizations.

Bibliography

Apple M W 1979 *Ideology and Curriculum*. Routledge and Kegan Paul, London
Eisner E W 1979 *The Educational Imagination: On the Design and Evaluation of the School Program*. McCutchan, Berkeley, California
Posner G J, Rudnitsky A N 1982 *Course Design: A Guide to Curriculum Development for Teachers*, 2nd edn. Longman, New York
Schubert W H 1982 The return of curriculum inquiry from schooling to education. *Curric. Inq.* 12: 221–32
Snyder B R 1970 *The Hidden Curriculum*. Knopf, New York

Curriculum Pacing

U. P. Lundgren and M-A. Colliander

In the *International Dictionary of Education* (1977 p. 257) pacing is defined as guidance by a teacher to increase pupils' reading speed. This meaning of the term pacing can be related to three different fields of pedagogical activities. First, pacing as an integral element of the teacher's acts in monitoring the performances of the students or of a group of students. Second, pacing within programmed learning refers to the rate at which the student proceeds through a series of tasks. Third, pacing indicates the student's learning

rate as a function of his or her interest and ability in contrast to a predetermined rate (Good 1973). In the current literature the term pacing refers to focusing on the individual learner and the time needed by that individual to achieve a given objective (Barr 1975). In contrast, in regular classroom instruction the concept "curriculum pacing" refers to determining the time needed for a group of students (usually a class) to master a given curriculum or a part of a curriculum in the regular classroom setting. It concerns how the time is allocated for a particular curriculum unit, and how much time is actually required by a class or a group to master the objectives of a curriculum unit. In dealing with curriculum pacing, both sides of its Janus face have to be analyzed, that is, how in practice curriculum pacing is carried out and what the determinants of pacing are for a particular group of students within a given curriculum framework.

There is little empirical knowledge about curriculum pacing. As noted above, educational research has dealt only with the problems of pacing the learning of the individual student (Good et al. 1978). It should be noted that even this type of research is relatively new. In 1963 Carroll pointed out in his article on mastery of learning that research on time factors were few (Carroll and Spearritt 1967). In the 1980s the picture is somewhat different. However, the majority of studies are rather normative, that is, telling what the pacing ought to be, rather than studying pacing (Barr 1975, Keeves 1976, Filby 1977, Kemmer 1978, Frederick 1980, Karweit and Slavin 1980, Stallings 1980).

How curriculum pacing is decided upon depends on the decision structure within an educational system. In centralized systems, like those of most European countries, there are parliamentary decisions which frame the time allocated to various parts of the curriculum. In decentralized systems, school decisions are made at the local level. Considering the constraints of a given framework, the teachers decide when to proceed from one particular curriculum unit to the next, basing their decisions on judgments as to whether their students have satisfactorily mastered the objectives of the unit already taught in the class.

It is of interest to examine how decisions about pacing are affected by decisions both outside and inside the classroom. Since rational decision making requires the utilization of a reliable body of knowledge, it may confidently be stated that decisions about pacing are not rational decisions.

The decisions outside the classroom relative to the time allocated for teaching a subject or for teaching various units of the curriculum are affected by the social context within which educational policy is formulated. This means that these decisions are affected both by context factors of an educational system and by the interests of various agents participating in the process of policy formulation. The following contextual factors can be identified:

(a) *Traditions.* How much time has earlier been given to a specific curriculum or to specific units within a curriculum.

(b) *Available teachers.* The time that has previously been allocated results also in a certain number of teachers qualified to teach these curriculum units (school subjects). Changes in time allocated to a part of the curriculum will have consequences for teacher employment. This is especially important in the case of nationwide curricula, where even very small changes in time allocation can have significant consequences for the division of labor within the educational system.

(c) *The power of various interest groups.* Changes in the time allocated to various parts of a curriculum have consequences for the balance of employment between teachers of different specializations. Therefore, teacher unions have vested interests in determining how time should be distributed across subjects taught in schools. Examples of other interest groups are national societies for specific scientific fields and school subjects, parent associations, and so on. By increasing their influence on educational systems these groups have gained increased power in affecting decisions about time allocation to various subjects.

(d) *Political programs.* Political programs influence the objectives specified in a curriculum and the time given to specific units of a curriculum. This may result in expanding the time for a particular subject in the whole system, and in emphasizing its importance as well as allocating more time to various curriculum units for a group of students specializing in a particular field of studies.

(e) *The public sphere.* The public debate and public program evaluations can mobilize power in favor of a specific part of a curriculum.

(f) *The structure of the curriculum.* The structure of the knowledge transmitted within a curriculum can influence the time given to various units. In cumulative knowledge structures, basic units will be given more time. The interrelation between the various school subjects is also of importance here. For example, can more time be allotted to mathematics based on the justification of its basic importance for science?

The relationship among these pressure factors and their relative weight in affecting curriculum decisions depends on the kind of curriculum decision to be taken. At present very little is known on how actual decisions on time distribution in a curriculum are made.

Within the classroom the teacher is constrained by the decisions made outside the classroom. The decisions of the teacher must then be understood as decisions where the possibilities for alternatives are limited (Shavelson 1981). Dahllöf (1971, 1978) showed in a study of ability grouping that classes of different composition with respect to general ability spent different time on elementary units in the curriculum. He identified a steering group constituted by the students between percentile 10–25 (on general ability). This steering group seemed to set the pace for the class on the elementary units. Lundgren (1972, 1977), Gustafsson (1977), and Pedro (1981), followed the curriculum pacing for a sample of high-school classes in Sweden during one year. In this study, in which observations of classroom teaching were also carried out, the steering group hypothesis was confirmed. The Dahllöf–Lundgren theory—the frame factor theory—offers an explanation of what constitutes the framework for decisions on curriculum pacing inside the classroom. For elementary units in the curriculum, that is, units that give the prerequisites for the mastering of other units or have a basic importance for the general goals, the teacher has to find a point of balance between the variation among the students in ability and motivation on the one hand and the mastering of the content transmitted on the other. This means that the teacher consciously or unconsciously identifies which group in the class is crucial for the pacing of the whole class. If the steering group is constituted by the least motivated and the least able students, in a class with a great variation in ability and motivation, the effort to reach mastery for this group creates discipline problems for the other students. Where the steering group is located depends on:

(a) The time factor—the amount of global time allocated to teaching a particular unit in relation to the quantity of objectives and the amount of content to be covered. This is one of the frame factors whose control is outside of the teacher's authority.

(b) The composition of the class—the heterogeneity of the class as to the ability of the learners, their motivation, perseverance, and discipline, is another factor which affects curriculum pacing.

(c) Class size—this factor may be related to the class composition.

(d) Teaching materials—how well the teaching materials are structured and the extent to which individualized instruction can be carried out.

(e) Physical space—how the physical environment provides opportunity for individualized instruction, group work, and so on.

These are frame factors because they are factors over which the teacher has no control and to which the teaching must therefore be adjusted. (To some extent teaching materials and motivation of the learners may be determined by the teacher's behavior and therefore they may be partially outside of the domain of the frame factors.) Thus the decisions outside the classroom constrain, and constitute the outer limits for the curriculum pacing. Within these frames curriculum pacing is determined by the ability of the teacher to develop effective teaching strategies.

Curriculum pacing is a central issue for curriculum construction, implementation of educational policy, and assessment of the outcomes of teaching. It is also a central issue for developing strategies for teaching. Thus, it is one of the key issues in curriculum theory and curriculum development (see *Curriculum Theory*). There are few theories or theoretical models explaining how curriculum pacing is actually done in the classroom

teaching. As the decisions on the amount of time allocated to various parts in the curriculum constrain both teaching strategies and the actual teaching process, the development of knowledge about curriculum pacing must include both the study of classroom practices and the study of the construction of the frames determining the outer limits of classroom teaching.

Bibliography

Barr R 1975 How children are thought to read: Grouping and pacing. *Sch. Rev.* 83: 479–98
Bernstein B 1975 *Class, Codes and Control*, Vol. 3: *Classification and Framing of Educational Knowledge*. Routledge and Kegan Paul, London
Block J H (ed.) 1971 *Mastery Learning: Theory and Practice*. Holt, Rinehart and Winston, New York
Bloom B S 1968 Learning for mastery. *Eval. Comment* 1(2)
Carroll J B 1963 A model of school learning. *Teach. Coll. Rec.* 64: 723–33
Carroll J B, Spearritt D 1967 *A Study of A "Model of School Learning."* Center for Research and Development on Educational Differences, Harvard University, Cambridge, Massachusetts
Dahllöf U 1971 *Ability Grouping, Content Validity and Curriculum Process Analysis*. Teachers College Press, Columbia University, New York
Dahllöf U 1978 *Curriculum Evaluation, Frame Factors and Teaching for Mastery*. Reports on Education 2. Uppsala
Filby N N 1977 Time allocated to reading and mathematics: How it varies and why. *Calif. J. Teach. Educ.* 4: 12–22
Frederick W C 1980 Learning as a function of time. *J. Educ. Res.* 73: 183–204
Good C W (ed.) 1973 *Dictionary of Education*. McGraw-Hill, New York
Good T L, Grows D A, Beckerman T M 1978 Curriculum pacing: Some empirical data in mathematics. *J. Curric. Stud.* 10: 75–81
Gustafsson C 1977 *Classroom Interaction: A Study of Pedagogical Roles in the Teaching Process*. CWK/Gleerup, Lund
Karweit N, Slavin R E 1980 *Time on Task: Issues of Timing, Sampling and Definition*. University of Maryland, College Park, Maryland
Keeves P 1976 Curricular factors influencing school learning. *Stud. Educ. Eval.* 3: 167–83
Kemmer F 1978 The allocation of student time. *Administrator's Notebook* 8: 1–4
Lundgren U P 1972 *Frame Factors and the Teaching Process: A Contribution to Curriculum Theory and Theory on Teaching*. Almqvist and Wiksell, Stockholm
Lundgren U P 1977 *Model Analysis of Pedagogical Processes*. CWK/Gleerup (2nd edn. 1981), Lund
Page G T, Thomas J B (eds.) 1977 *International Dictionary of Education*. Nichols, New York
Pedro E 1981 *Social Stratification and Classroom Discourse. A Sociolinguistic Analysis of Classroom Practice*. CWK/Gleerup, Lund
Shavelson R J 1981 Research on teachers' pedagogical thoughts, judgments, decisions and behavior. *Rev. Educ. Res.* 51: 455–98
Sjogren D D 1967 Achievement as a function of study time. *Am. Educ. Res. J.* 4: 337–44
Stallings J 1980 Allocated academic learning time revisited, or beyond time on task. *Educ. Res.* 9: 11–16

Curriculum Studies in Teachers' Education

M. Silberstein

Curriculum studies in teacher education are aimed at equipping teachers with the knowledge and skills necessary to implement curricula, use available instructional material, and participate in developing new curricular materials.

Many past and present programs in teacher education have contained elements of curriculum studies, though they have not been explicitly defined as such. Student teachers are frequently asked to set objectives, select instructional activities, evaluate students' progress, and otherwise join in a variety of experiences related directly or indirectly to planning and implementing curriculum.

In the 1980s, an increasing number of experts recommended that curriculum studies be introduced as a specific course in teacher education programs, and called for adequate designs to fit this purpose (Ben-Peretz 1984, Goodman 1986).

1. Introducing Curriculum Studies in Teacher Education Programs

Educators of teachers urge that the development of curriculum literacy and critical competency in curriculum planning should become a major component of preservice teacher training programs. Several factors have contributed to this perceived necessity. The first has been the failure experienced in implementing innovative programs. It is well-known that numerous innovative curricula have failed to produce their expected impact in terms of classroom events and student outcomes. Much of the responsibility for these failures was attributed to teachers, who lacked the requisite understanding, commitment, and competency (McLaughlin and Marsh 1978).

Secondly, the conception of the teacher's role has changed and become more demanding. Teachers are now encouraged to participate in planning, developing, and implementing curricula. They are more often expected to act as coursework assessors, and as selectors of learning material. Teachers are asked to devise learning systems, to construct syllabi, and to cope with the conflicting demands in educational systems. They have had to manifest judicious consumer behaviors and to implement "core" curricula with externally imposed goals and achievement requirements on the one hand, and to behave autonomously in producing their own curricula (at least in selected study areas) on the other. To successfully fulfill such complex roles, teachers need to obtain systematic knowledge about various aspects of dealing with school curricula. Shulman (1986) suggested that "curriculum knowledge" should be one of the foundations on which prospective teachers build their "pedagogical content knowledge" which, well-integrated with field experience, will eventually render them expert in teaching a particular subject.

The role conceived for teachers in curriculum making, and the image that educators and curriculum developers have of the prospective teacher functions in the classroom, both have deep implications for determining the parameters of curricular training programs. The once popular view, supported by curriculum innovators (but resisted by teacher educators), that teachers should act as "users" of prepackaged curricula, and should strive to execute the intentions of external developers with a high level of fidelity, is no longer tenable. Instead, the prevailing view now is that teachers should act as autonomous professionals and be competent to make decisions on a great variety of curricular and instructional issues.

This high expectation that teachers should be both knowledgeable and skillful in the field of curriculum making seems to justify the incorporation of curriculum studies in the training of teachers.

2. Conceptual Schemes in Suggested Programs

Two conceptual schemes of curriculum study courses emerged: a generic type, applicable to any subject taught in school, and a content-bound type, applicable only to a specific curricular area.

2.1 A Generic Paradigm

Ben-Peretz (1984) suggested an integrated program of curriculum theory and practice, aimed at training prospective teachers in planning and implementing curricula. She claims that competencies in curricular decision making touch upon five areas of experience: subject matter, learner, milieu, teacher, and curriculum making. The five areas of expertise are represented in Fig. 1. Ben-Peretz identifies key questions in each area of expertise, around which planners might build detailed instructional programs. For instance, questions related to the learner are:

(a) What perceptions of learners and their involvement in the learning process are expressed in the materials?

(b) What opportunities for learner development are included in the curriculum?

(c) What is the form of instruction—individual or group?

(d) What learning styles are anticipated by the materials?

Additionally, Ben-Peretz suggests that teacher education programs should contain the following elements: awareness of theoretical "choice points" in curriculum development; training of abilities in curriculum analysis; experience in curriculum development; reflection on

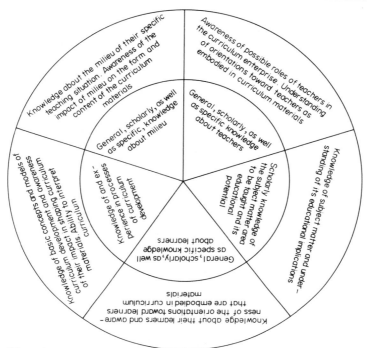

Figure 1
Areas of curricular expertise required of curriculum developers and teachers

curriculum implementation studies; and cooperative and collaborative skills in working with colleagues.

Silberstein and Tamir (1986) proposed a modular program to train student teachers for functioning both as autonomous consumers of available instructional material and as producers of their own curriculum materials. This program is also of a generic type. It is based on identifying and mapping those areas of decision making and action in which teachers should be involved in the course of their routine work. Curriculum making is conceived as a multi-phase process. Accordingly, the following five areas of teacher activity were identified: (a) using course syllabi and producing syllabi; (b) using available curricular materials or, alternatively, producing new ones; (c) instructional planning; (d) managing and controlling curriculum in operation; and (e) handling outcomes and feedback data.

A modular set of program materials was developed which covered the above-mentioned five process topics. Since the input of two different kinds of expertise is assumed, namely curriculum making and teacher training, the program is supposed to be a collaborative enterprise of teacher educators and external curriculum developers.

2.2 A Subject-matter-oriented Paradigm

Based on the progressive pedagogical theories of Dewey and James, and on the critical curriculum theories of

Apple and Eisner, Goodman (1986) designed a course for student teachers in how to develop a critical approach to curriculum design. Within the framework of the course, the students were asked to implement (on the practicum site) an original social study unit based on their own and/or their pupils' intellectual interests. The course reflects the perspective that decision making in curriculum development entails simultaneous consideration of several issues: subject-matter structure, past experience of the teacher and pupils, educational and social goals, available resources and materials, and so on.

The program is built on five sequential phases:

Phase I: Developing curriculum themes. Student teachers learn to choose meaningful topics and to map their contents, creating webs of issues, concepts, and themes.

Phase II: Exploring resources. Student teachers are exposed to relevant types of resources which both adults and pupils may use.

Phase III: Developing learning activities. Student teachers learn to develop and organize learning activities for their units.

Phase IV: Evaluation of pupils. Student teachers learn to develop and use alternative methods of evaluating learning outcomes.

Phase V: Evaluation of the unit. Student teachers learn to evaluate the merits and the implications of the units they prepared.

It should be noted that in all of the programs described above, teachers are perceived as fulfilling the role of an active and judicious consumer of readily available curricular resources. They are expected to choose, modify, and adapt existing curricular resources to their specific instructional situation. To achieve these goals, teachers are supposed to become reflective and critical performers of two main functions; they must *localize* existing curricular materials by taking into account the particular and unique teaching–learning circumstances, and they must *personalize* the learning materials by considering their own educational philosophy, beliefs, and values.

Beyond this common feature, two main differences may be noted. Some programs focus on educating teachers to serve as critical implementors and lesson planners; in other programs the objectives are broader, and they comprise the education of the teacher both as consumer and producer of curricular products. Another difference is a structural one. Ben-Peretz suggests that a program draw synchronously from the five areas of experience in analyzing curricular materials. Goodman, Silberstein and Tamir approach curriculum making as a developing phenomenon and for the sake of analysis and instruction, they recommend an organization of curriculum studies into sequential steps of decision making and action.

3. Research and Development Needs

Curriculum studies in teacher training programs may serve two purposes: the provision of meaningful and challenging experiences in curriculum theory and practice, which reduces the observed gap between the intent of a program and its implementation; and secondly, the preparation of teachers to fulfill an active role in developing school-based curricula.

While the market abounds in textbooks for teaching curriculum theory and practice, very few of them, if any, deal with these problems in a way which best responds to the teacher's learning needs. Most textbooks serve the needs of educational administrators, supervisors, and professional curriculum workers. Curriculum study courses to fit the needs of teachers should be developed. Such work would imply broadening the scope of research on school-based curriculum problems, insofar as contemporary research focuses mainly on outcomes of school-based curriculum development. It seems desirable to extend the research, and to examine the process of relevant decision making and the development of activities in school-based curriculum making.

Bibliography

Ben-Peretz M 1984 Curriculum theory and practice in teacher education programs. In: Katz L G, Raths J D (eds.) 1984 *Advances in Teacher Education*. Vol. 1. Ablex, Norwood, New York, pp. 9–27

Goodman J 1986 Teaching preservice teachers a critical approach to curriculum design: A descriptive account. *Curric, Inq.* 16(2): 179–201

McLaughlin M W, Marsh D D 1978 Staff development and school change. *Teach. Coll. Rec.* 80(1): 69–94

Shulman L S 1986 Those who understand: Knowledge growth in teaching. *Educ. Res.* 15(2): 4–14

Silberstein M, Tamir P 1986 Curriculum development and implementation as a component of teacher education in Israel. *Teach. Teach. Educ.* 2(3): 251–61

Section 4

Curriculum Evaluation

Overview

The articles in Section 4 are grouped into five subsections. Section 4(a), General Framework, has three articles on general features of curriculum evaluation. Worthen reviews alternative approaches to *Program Evaluation*, but observes that some of the frameworks reviewed are sufficiently multifaceted to place them in more than one category. Lewy compares features of *Formative and Summative Evaluation* and discusses the effect of distinguishing between these two evaluation types on educational evaluation in general and on curriculum evaluation in particular. Finally, Sanders delineates the major areas of *Curriculum Evaluation Research*.

Section 4(b) contains articles on the main Approaches to Evaluation. Several attempts have been made in the past to classify curriculum evaluation models, and the articles appearing here are by no means a new attempt to provide a classification scheme. Rather, they represent those models which are most frequently referred to in evaluation reports. Additional evaluation models are briefly described in the main articles. The first article in this subsection presents *Tyler's Evaluation Model*, the first of the evaluation models which marked the emergence of Curriculum Evaluation as a field of study. It is followed by a short article on *Goal-free Evaluation*, which can be considered as an extension of Tyler's model in so far as it expands the scope of the variables which deserve attention in a curriculum-evaluation study. The decision-oriented approach, as conceptualized by Alkin and by Stufflebeam, and further developed by Borich in his article entitled *Decision-oriented Evaluation*, differs from the previous ones in its definition of the evaluation target. While both Tyler's model and the goal-free model derive the evaluation target from the curriculum itself or from its implementation in schools, the decision-oriented model derives its evaluation targets from the interest of those who are in charge of making decisions concerning the curriculum. Concern for the stakeholders' interest also appears in the *Responsive Evaluation* model, but here emphasis is placed on the continuous adaptation of the evaluation goal-setting and data gathering as the people responsible for evaluation become acquainted with the program and the evaluation context. The *Illuminative Evaluation* model shares basic tenets with the *Responsive Evaluation* model, but it adopts a holistic approach and recommends condensing the maximum amount of valid experience and informative commentary about the system studied into a readable report which will stimulate talk and bring together key topics, unresolved questions, and practical thinking. Three additional interrelated articles appear in this subsection. They deal with *Naturalisic Evaluation*, *Qualitative Evaluation*, and *Educational Connoisseurship and Criticism*. Dorr-Bremme, the author of the first article, indicates that the term *naturalistic evaluation* functions as a generic label and entails nothing about the data to be collected. Thus, a naturalistic evaluation study is not necessarily a qualitative one and vice-versa, despite the fact that in practice there is considerable overlap between these two approaches. The third article, by Barone, deals with an approach to evaluation which is described by its originator as an artistic approach making judgement about an entity. In contrast to some variants of qualitative evaluation, which are based on systematic data collection, the connoisseur and the curriculum critic react in a holistic way to the evaluation target without relying on empirical data at all.

The articles in Section 4(c) deal with evaluation activities, which are carried out in a particular phase of the program's life cycle, although some of them can be carried out at several points, in which case they manifest almost all the attributes which characterize an overall approach to curriculum evaluation. *Needs Assessment Studies* precede actual development activities. Then, at the initial stages of developing a new program, individual components of the program can be subjected to formative evaluation using one of the patterns described in the articles *Prototype Evaluation, Feasibility Studies*, and *Error Analysis*. The merit of curriculum materials can be examined by using procedures described in the articles on *Curriculum Tryout, Curriculum Validation*, and *Curriculum Analysis*. The question as to whether a program is adequately used in classes, or whether it is to be used at all, is dealt with in the article on *Implementation Evaluation*. Finally, the outcome of a program can be identified by follow-up studies as described in the article *Long-term Curriculum Evaluation*.

Section 4(d) is concerned with selected techniques and strategies used in curriculum evaluation. Schubert's article on *Experimental Curriculum* describes a technique used more frequently by curriculum management people than by evaluation experts. Thus, for example, in the Soviet Union from 1986, when a decision was made to introduce curriculum reform in the whole educational system as of 1990 or later (which was set as the date for implementing the reform), the local educational authorities were encouraged to develop and use innovative experimental programs. These programs were scrutinized by the leaders of the educational system and were exposed to public criticism before decisions were made about the obligatory content of the curriculum (see Muckle 1988). Eraut's article, *Intrinsic Evaluation*, is concerned with passing judgment on the intrinsic value of curricular products and processes. A technique for generating empirical data about phemonena which are not amenable to observation is described in the article on the *Delphi Technique*. This technique was developed by people dealing with complex problems of defense and has frequently been used and usually misused in curriculum evaluation. The article entitled *Criterion-referenced Measurement* reviews the problems in a measurement technique which was developed and has been extensively used in the context of curriculum evaluation.

Section 4(e) contains articles about *Curriculum-specific Criteria*, namely, criteria encountered in curriculum evaluation studies but not frequently in other areas of evaluation. In his article entitled *Impact Analysis of Curriculum*, Alkin lists a broad array of criteria for assessing the effect of a particular curriculum. The main categories are changes in teaching practice, administrative and management patterns, community and parental relationships, and teacher behavior. The intrinsic value of the curriculum constitutes the focus of the articles by McClure and Ben-Peretz. In his article on *Curriculum Balance*, McClure provides a criterion for examining the overall context of the school program. Ben-Peretz's article, *Curriculum Potential*, addresses the issue of evaluating small units of curricular materials. The article on *Prerequisite Knowledge* focuses on the adequacy of curriculum materials for learners of a particular type. Finally, Levin discusses problems in *Evaluating Computerized Curriculum Materials*.

Bibliography

Muckle J 1988 *A Guide to the Soviet Curriculum*. Croom Helm, London

A. Lewy and M. C. Alkin

Three Decades of Curriculum Evaluation

Introduction

M. C. Alkin and A. Lewy

Curriculum Evaluation became a recognized field of study in the 1960s in the wake of the New Curriculum Movement in the English-speaking countries. This movement adopted the view that curriculum materials needed to be scientifically validated before being put to widespread use in schools. To carry out this task adequately it became necessary for curriculum evaluation to achieve the status of an academic endeavor.

Curriculum Evaluation has its roots in the wider disciplines of curriculum studies and educational evaluation, however, it has acquired all the attributes of professional status. It has its own professional organizations, publishes several newsletters and journals, and runs professional meetings. Since 1960 dozens of books have been published which in one way or another make reference to Curriculum Evaluation in their title, and by 1987 the ERIC information base had accumulated almost 4,000 items related to this field. Universities around the world offer courses and award diplomas in Curriculum Evaluation.

Despite the newness of Curriculum Evaluation as a professional activity, early instances of studies in this field occur. Madaus et al. (1983) encountered interesting instances of such studies undertaken 150 years before the debut of evaluation in the 1960s, and Devereaux (1933) described educational films from the beginning of the twentieth century employing evaluating designs which would be acknowledged as legitimate formative evaluation designs even at the end of the 1980s.

Since the 1960s the focus of interest in Curriculum Evaluation has changed several times, corresponding with the shifts of interest of those who were in charge of developing new curricula. At the outset of the New Curriculum Movement, both development teams and evaluators strove to strengthen the scientific qualities of those evaluation activities which have come to be labelled as formative evaluation. Thus, the 1960s was the decade of generating curriculum evaluation models, most of them specifying the desired characteristics of studies with a formative role in program development. The early 1970s witnessed concern about using developed programs in classes and in response to this concern evaluation experts turned their attention to implementation evaluation, developing theories and creating research instruments for dealing with this.

Disillusionment caused by the fact that evaluation failed to fully answer the needs of development teams by not providing sufficient information that curriculum planners could use, led evaluation experts to seek remedies. Firstly, they enlarged the repertoire of curriculum evaluation strategies; the Naturalistic Evaluation paradigm together with the use of qualitative databases and analysis techniques gradually proved equal if not superior to traditionally used experimental designs and sets of "hard" data. Secondly, a joint committee appointed by twelve professional organizations in the United States published the Standards of Evaluation of Educational Programs and Materials (1981) with the aim of increasing the quality and utility of curriculum evaluation studies. Thirdly, the application of evaluation results was systematically examined with the result that evaluation findings found greater application.

During the 1980s the trend in curriculum evaluation was to examine the relationships between the curriculum and context variables of the social system such as values, development trends, economic factors, and politics.

Curriculum Evaluation during 1960–1990 developed within the framework of the social sciences in two seemingly opposite directions, since both conceptually and organizationally it became differentiated from the main body of Educational Evaluation as an independent field of enquiry. However, it then became intricately linked to a broader discipline known as Program Evaluation, abandoning its independent professional status and becoming part of a cross-disciplinary endeavor which dealt with the evaluation of a wide variety of social intervention programs in areas such as health, community development, city planning, business management, and agricultural production.

The articles contained in this Section reflect concerns and issues of the past thirty years, and not only those which prevailed at the time of publishing this *Encyclopedia*.

Bibliography

Devereaux F L 1933 *The Educational Talking Picture*. University of Chicago Press, Chicago, Illinois
Joint Committee on Standards for Educational Evaluation 1981 *Standards for Evaluation of Educational Programs, Projects, and Materials*. McGraw-Hill, New York
Madaus F, Stufflebeam D L, Scriven M S (eds.) 1983 *Evaluation Models: Viewpoints on Educational and Human Services Evaluation*. Kluwer-Nijhoff, Boston, Massachusetts

General Framework

Program Evaluation

B. R. Worthen

Educational programs (and other publicly funded programs) have continued to increase in size and expense. Not surprisingly, taxpayers and public officials have increasingly urged that these programs be made more accountable to their publics. Indeed, "accountability" for expenditures of public funds has become the hue and cry of an ever-increasing number of economy-minded social reformers. In several countries, policy makers at both national and local levels now routinely authorize funds to be used for the express purpose of evaluating educational programs to determine their effectiveness. Thus, "program evaluation" has come into being as both a formal educational activity and as a frequently mandated instrument of public policy. Many private educational enterprises have similarly turned to program evaluation as a means of answering questions about the benefits received from monies expended on various educational programs.

To define program evaluation, it is necessary to define its component parts. In an educational context, a program can be thought of as any educational enterprise aimed at the solution of a particular educational problem or the improvement of some aspect of an educational system. Such a program would typically be sponsored by public or private funds, possess specified goals, and exhibit some structure for managing the procedures, materials, facilities, and/or personnel involved in the program.

Evaluation can be defined most simply as the determination of the worth of a thing. In its simplest form, therefore, program evaluation consists of those activities undertaken to judge the worth or utility of a program (or alternative programs) in improving some specified aspect of an educational system. Examples of program evaluations might include evaluation of a national bilingual education program, a university's preservice program for training urban administrators, a ministry of education's staff development program, or a local parent education resource center. Evaluations may be conducted for programs of any size or scope, ranging from an arithmetic program in a particular school to an international consortium on metric education.

A curriculum evaluation may qualify as a program evaluation if the curriculum is focused on change or improvement, as implied in the previous definition of "program." Program evaluations, however, often do not involve appraisal of curricula (e.g., evaluation of a computerized student recordkeeping system or evaluation of the extent to which funds from a national program for the hearing impaired are actually used to provide services to children with hearing impairments). For this reason, the closely related but more specialized topic of curriculum evaluation is not discussed further in this section (see *Curriculum Evaluation*).

1. Purposes of Program Evaluation

Most program evaluators agree that program evaluation can play either a formative purpose (helping to improve the program) or a summative purpose (deciding whether a program should be continued). Anderson and Ball (1978) further describe the capabilities of program evaluation in terms of six major purposes (which are not necessarily mutually exclusive). They are:

(a) to contribute to decisions about program installation;

(b) to contribute to decisions about program continuation, expansion, or "certification";

(c) to contribute to decisions about program modifications;

(d) to obtain evidence to rally support for a program;

(e) to obtain evidence to rally opposition to a program;

(f) to contribute to the understanding of basic psychological, social, and other processes (only rarely can this purpose be achieved in a program evaluation without compromising more basic evaluation purposes).

2. The History of Program Evaluation

The informal practice of program evaluation is not new, dating back at least to 2000 BC, when Chinese officials were conducting civil-service examinations, and continuing down through the centuries to the beginnings of school accreditation in the late 1800s. The first clear evidence of formal program evaluation, however, appears to be Joseph Rice's 1897–1898 comparative study of spelling performance of 33,000 students in a large United States school system. Few formal evaluations of educational programs were conducted in the next few decades, with Tyler and Smith's Eight-year Study of the 1930s being the next notable effort to evaluate the outcomes of an educational program. During the late 1950s and early 1960s (the post-Sputnik years), cries for curriculum reform led to major new curriculum development programs and to subsequent calls for their evaluation. The relatively few evaluation studies that resulted revealed the conceptual and methodological impoverishment of the field—or perhaps more accurately, the "nonfield"—of evaluation in that era. In many cases, the designs were inadequate, the data invalid, the analyses inaccurate, and the reports irrelevant to the important evaluation questions which should have been posed. Most of the studies depended on idiosyncratic combinations and applications of concepts and techniques from experimental design, psychometrics, curriculum development and, to a lesser extent, survey research. Theoretical work related to educational evaluation, per se, was almost nonexistent. Few scholars had yet turned their attention to the development of generalizable evaluation plans which could be adopted or adapted specifically to educational evaluation studies. In the absence of a "formal subject matter" or educational evaluation, evaluators of educational programs were left to glean what they could from other fields to help them in their work.

Since a large number of persons serving in evaluation roles during the late 1950s and 1960s were educational and psychological researchers, it is not surprising that the experimental tradition quickly became the most generally accepted evaluation approach. The work of Campbell and Stanley gave enormous impetus to predominance of experimental or quasiexperimental approaches to program evaluation. Although some evaluators cautioned that correct use of the experimental model may not be feasible, the elegance and precision of this model led most program evaluators to view the experimental method as the ideal model for program evaluations.

Not all program evaluators were enamored with the use of traditional quantitative methods for program evaluations, however, and their dissatisfaction led to a search for alternatives. Qualitative and naturalistic methods, largely shunned by program evaluators during the 1960s as unacceptably "soft," gained wider acceptance in the 1970s and thereafter as proposals for their application to program evaluations were made by Parlett and Hamilton, Stake, Eisner, Guba and Lincoln, and others. Sharp disagreements developed between proponents of the newer qualitative approaches and adherents to the more broadly accepted quantitative methods and the 1970s were marked by polemics as the two schools of thought struggled for ascendancy. The

late 1970s and the early 1980s saw the dialogue begin to move beyond this debate as analysts accelerated their discussions of the benefits of integrating both types of methods within a program evaluation (for instance see Cook and Reichardt 1979, Worthen 1981, and the especially useful summary by Madey 1982).

Concurrent with program evaluators' struggle to sort out the relative utility of quantitative and qualitative methods, a separate but closely related development was taking place. Beginning in the late 1960s, several evaluation writers began to develop and circulate their notions about how one should conduct educational evaluations; these efforts resulted in several new evaluation "models" being proposed to help the practicing program evaluator. Although these seminal writings in educational evaluation (discussed in Sect. 3) were doubtlessly influenced by the quantitative–qualitative controversy and some proved more comfortable companions with one or the other methodological persuasion, several were broader in conceptualization, providing guidelines for conducting program evaluations that could use either quantitative or qualitative data. As these frameworks for planning evaluation studies were applied and refined, program evaluators began to turn to them as promising sources of guidance. Collectively, these writings, the so-called evaluation models, represent the formal content of program evaluation and are discussed in the following section.

3. Alternative Approaches to Program Evaluation

Because of space restrictions, only some of the more popular current approaches used in conducting program evaluations can be presented in this section. Many of these (and other) approaches to program evaluation are summarized in Worthen and Sanders (1987) and the work of authors mentioned but not referenced herein (and in other sections of this entry) can be found in that source. For convenience, these conceptual frameworks for evaluation are clustered into five categories, although some of the frameworks are sufficiently multifaceted that they could appear in more than one category. Most of these "models" have focused broadly on program evaluation, although some are focused more specifically on curriculum evaluation. It should be noted that these frameworks deal with methods, not techniques; discussion of the many techniques which might be used in program evaluations is beyond the scope of this article.

3.1 Performance–Objectives Congruence Approaches

This approach to program evaluation was originally formulated by Ralph Tyler, who conceived of evaluation as the process of determining the extent to which the educational objectives of a school program or curriculum are actually being attained. He proposed a process in which broad goals or objectives would be established or identified, defined in behavioral terms, and relevant student behaviors would be measured against this yardstick, using either standardized or evaluator-constructed instruments. These outcome data were then to be compared with the behavioral objectives to determine the extent to which performance was congruent with expectations. Discrepancies between performance and objectives would lead to modifications intended to correct the deficiency, and the evaluation cycle would be repeated.

Tyler's rationale was logical, scientifically acceptable, readily adoptable by program evaluators (most of whose methodological upbringing was very compatible with the pretest–post-test measurement of student behaviors stressed by Tyler), and had great influence on subsequent evaluation theorists. Hammond's EPIC evaluation model followed Tyler's model closely, adding only a useful program-description "cube" which elaborates instructional and institutional variables often overlooked in previous evaluations. Provus' discrepancy model of program evaluation is clearly Tylerian and gains its name from the constant setting and juxtaposition of program standards against program performance to yield "discrepancy information" needed for program improvements. Popham's instructional objectives approach also clearly stems from Tyler's earlier conceptions.

Useful as this approach to evaluation is viewed by its many adherents, critics such as Guba and Lincoln (1981) have noted that it lacks a real evaluative component (facilitating measurement and assessment of objectives rather than resulting in explicit judgments of worth), lacks standards to judge the importance of observed discrepancies between objectives and performance levels, and depends on a highly utilitarian philosophy, promoting a linear, inflexible approach to evaluation.

3.2 Decision–Management Approaches

The most important contributions to a decision-oriented approach to program evaluation are Stufflebeam's Context, Input, Process, and Product (CIPP) evaluation model and Alkin's Center for the Study of Evaluation model, which follows a similar logic to the Context, Input, Process, and Product model but distinguishes between program implementation and program improvement, two subdivisions of what Stufflebeam terms process evaluation. In both models, objectives are eschewed as the organizer for the study and the decision to be made by program managers becomes pivotal. Stufflebeam has provided an analysis of types of decisions program managers are required to make and proposes a different type of evaluation for each type of decision. In both of these decision-oriented models, the evaluator, working closely with the program manager, would identify the decisions the latter must make and collect sufficient information about the relative advantages and disadvantages of each decision alternative to enable the decision maker to make a

judgment about which is best in terms of specified criteria. Thus, evaluation became an explicitly shared function dependent on good teamwork between evaluators and decision makers.

This approach has proved appealing to many evaluators and program managers, particularly those at home with the rational and orderly systems approach, to which it is clearly related. It was viewed by others, however, as failing to determine explicitly the program's worth and being dependent on somewhat unrealistic assumptions about the orderliness and predictability of the decision-making process.

3.3 Judgment-oriented Approaches

This general approach to evaluation, which historically has been the most widely used evaluation approach, is dependent upon experts' application of professional expertise to yield judgments about a program being observed. For example, the worth of a program would be assessed by experts (in the view of the evaluation's sponsor) who would observe the program in action, examine its products or, in some other way, glean sufficient information to render their considered judgment about the program. Site visits initiated by funding agencies to evaluate programs they support and visits by accrediting agencies to secondary schools and universities are examples of judgment-oriented program evaluations. Scriven, in his article *The Methodology of Evaluation* (Worthen and Sanders 1973), stressed judgment as the sine qua non of evaluation and, in his insightful examination of educational evaluation, did much to rescue this approach from the disrepute into which it had fallen in evaluation's headlong rush to gain respectability as a science. He stunned orthodox objectives-oriented evaluators by his suggestion that evaluators might go beyond measuring a program's performance to also evaluate the program's goals and later compounded the shock still further with his suggestion that evaluators should do "goal-free" evaluations, in which they not only ignore the program's goals but actually make every effort to avoid learning what those goals are. Thus, judgments about programs were based on the actual outcomes of the program, intended or not, rather than on the program's objectives or on decisions faced by program managers.

Another important judgement-oriented evaluation model is Robert Stake's Countenance Model, in which he suggests that the two major activities of formal evaluation studies are description and judgment (the "two countenances") of the program being evaluated. Within the description phase, Stake follows Tyler's rationale of comparing intended and actual outcomes of the program. However, he argued that in the judgment phase standards and procedures for making judgmental statements must be explicated to ensure the publicness of evaluative statements, although he failed to provide any suggestions as to how to weight or combine individual standards into overall judgments about the program.

Eisner's "connoisseurship model" casts program evaluators as educational critics whose refined perceptual capabilities (based on knowledge of what to look for and a backlog of relevant experience) enable them to give a public rendering of the quality and significance of that which is evaluated. In this model, the evaluator is the "instrument," and the data collecting, analyzing, and judging that Stake tried to make more public are largely hidden within the evaluator's mind, analogous to the evaluative processes of art criticism or wine tasting.

Collectively, these judgment-oriented approaches to evaluation have emphasized the central role of judgment and human wisdom in the evaluative process and have focused attention on the important issues of whose standards (and what degree of publicness) should be used in rendering judgments about educational programs. Conversely, critics of this approach suggest that it often permits evaluators to render judgments that reflect little more than figments of fertile imaginations. Others have noted that the presumed expertise of the evaluators is a potential weakness and worse, strong arguments can be made that serious disadvantages can accrue if a program is evaluated only by content experts (Worthen and Sanders 1987). Finally, many program evaluators are disinclined to play the single-handed role of educational judge (which they feel smacks of arrogance and elitism) proposed by some of these approaches.

3.4 Adversarial Approaches

Adversarial evaluation is a rubric that encompasses a collection of divergent evaluation practices which might loosely be referred to as adversarial in nature. In its broad sense, the term refers to all evaluations in which there is planned opposition in the points of view of different evaluators or evaluation teams—a planned effort to generate opposing points of view within the overall evaluation. One evaluator (or team) would serve as the program's advocate, presenting the most positive view of the program possible from the data, while another evaluator (or team) would play an adversarial role, highlighting any extant deficiencies in the program. Incorporation of these opposing views within a single evaluation reflects a conscious effort to assume fairness and balance and illuminate both strengths and weaknesses of the program.

Several types of adversarial proceedings have been invoked as models for adversary evaluations in education, including judicial, congressional hearings, and debate models. Of these, most of the sparse literature in this area has focused on adaptations of the legal paradigm, providing insights into how concepts from the legal system (for instance, taking and cross-examination of human testimony) could be used in educational evaluations. Owens, Wolf, and others have adapted the legal model to educational evaluations, while Worthen and Rogers have described use of the debate model in an adversary evaluation and have dis-

cussed pitfalls and potentials of the legal and other forensic paradigms in conducting program evaluations.

Despite the publicity given this approach to evaluation, as yet there is little beyond personal preference to determine whether program evaluations will profit most from being patterned after jury trials, congressional hearings, debates, or other arrangements.

3.5 Pluralist–Intuitionist Approaches

Ernest House has used this descriptor to characterize several evaluation models, contrasting them with more "utilitarian" models. In this approach to evaluation, the evaluator is a portrayer of different values and needs of all the individuals and groups served by the program, weighing and balancing this plurality of judgments and criteria in a largely intuitive fashion. Thus, the "best program" is largely decided by the values and perspectives of whomever is judging (an obvious fact nonetheless ignored in most other evaluation approaches). Examples of pluralist–intuitionist evaluation "models" are those proposed by Stake, Parlett and Hamilton, Rippey, and MacDonald's democratic evaluation. There are unique contributions of each of these proposals. Stake urges program evaluators to respond to the audience's concerns and requirements for information, in terms of their value perspectives, and argues that the evaluation framework and focus should emerge only after considerable interaction with those audiences. Parlett and Hamilton draw on the social anthropology paradigm (and psychiatry and sociology participant observation research) in proposing progressive focusing of an evaluation whose purpose is to describe and interpret (not measure and predict) that which exists within an educational system. Rippey focuses on the effects of programs on the program operators and views evaluation as a strategy for conflict management. MacDonald views evaluation as primarily a political activity whose only justification is the "right to know" of a broad range of audiences. Yet a common thread runs through all these evaluation approaches—value pluralism is recognized, accommodated, and protected, even though the effort to summarize the frequently disparate judgments and preferences of such groups is left as an intuitive process which depends heavily on the sagacity and impartiality of the evaluator.

Critics of this approach to program evaluation discount it as hopelessly "soft headed" and argue that few if any program evaluators are such paragons of virtue and wisdom as to be skillful in wielding the seductively simple, yet slippery and subtle tools this approach requires. Champions of pluralistic, responsive approaches reply that they can be readily used by any sensitive individual and that they are infinitely richer and more powerful than other approaches and, indeed, can subsume them, since they are flexible and do not preclude the use of other approaches within them, should that be desired by the evaluator's sponsor.

4. An Appraisal of Current Program Evaluation Models

Collectively, the writings reviewed briefly in Sect. 3, the so-called evaluation models, represent the formal content on which educational program evaluators draw. It is, therefore, appropriate to ask how useful they are.

The answer is "very useful, indeed," even though they collectively have not moved evaluation very far toward becoming a science or discipline in its own right (a dubious aspiration, nonetheless sought by many evaluators). In a recent analysis, Worthen and Sanders (1987) suggested that (a) the so-called evaluation models fail to meet standard criteria for scientific models, or even less rigorous definitions of models, and (b) that which has come to be referred to as the theoretical underpinnings of evaluation lack important characteristics of most theories, being neither axiomatic nor deductive, having no real predictive power, and being untested and unvalidated in any empirical sense. That same analysis, however, suggested that these conceptions about how evaluations should be conducted—the accompanying sets of categories, lists of things to think about, descriptions of different evaluation strategies, and exhortations to which one might choose to attend—influence the practice of program evaluation in sometimes subtle, sometimes direct, but always significant ways. Some program evaluators design evaluations which adopt or adapt proposed models of evaluation. Many evaluators, however, conduct evaluations without strict adherence (or even intentional attention) to any "model" of evaluation, yet draw unconsciously in their evaluation philosophy, plans, and procedures on that which they have internalized through exposure to the literature of program evaluation. So the value of the "models" lies in their ability to help us to think, to provide sources of new ideas and techniques, to serve as mental checklists of things we ought to consider, or remember, or worry about. Their value as prescriptive guidelines for doing evaluation studies seems much less.

5. Impediments to Improving Program Evaluation

Despite the advances made in program evaluation, there is obviously room for a great deal of improvement. In this section, four areas that need improvement for educational evaluation to reach its full potential are discussed briefly.

5.1 Evaluation Lacks an Adequate Knowledge Base

Since the early 1970s, Stufflebeam, Worthen and Sanders, Smith, and others have issued a call for evaluation to be researched to develop an adequate knowledge base to guide evaluation practice. That call is still largely unanswered, despite some promising research which has been launched on evaluation methods and techniques. A program of research aimed at drawing from other disciplines new methodological metaphors and techniques for use in educational evaluation existed at the Northwest Regional Educational Laboratory for nearly a decade and has introduced program evaluators to promising new metaphors and techniques drawn from areas such as architecture, philosophic analysis, investigative journalism, and literary and film criticism. A second National Institute of Education-sponsored research effort at the University of California at Los Angeles focused largely on descriptive studies of evaluation practices in educational agencies. In addition, a few research studies aimed at generating knowledge about either particular evaluation strategies and procedures or factors affecting evaluation utilization have begun to appear.

These positive developments notwithstanding, there is still little empirical information about the relative efficacy of alternative evaluation plans or techniques or many evaluation components germane to almost any model. For example, virtually no empirical information exists about the most effective way to conduct a needs assessment or weight criteria in reaching a summative judgment. Little is known about the extent to which various data collection techniques interfere with ongoing educational phenomena. Techniques for identifying goals are developed anew with every evaluation, since there is no evidence that any one way of conducting these activities is more effective than any other. Elaborate systems are developed for providing evaluative feedback, but there is little research evidence (as opposed to rhetoric and position statements) about the relative effectiveness of feedback under differing conditions and scheduling. One could go on to create an exhaustive list of phenomena and procedures in evaluation which badly need to be systematically studied, but the above should suffice to make the point. Smith (1981) has summarized the needs for research on evaluation as requiring more knowledge about (a) the contexts within which evaluation is practiced, (b) the nature of evaluation utility, and (c) the effectiveness of specific evaluation methods. Nearly a decade later those needs still remain largely unmet.

5.2 Evaluation Studies are Seldom Evaluated

The necessity of "meta-evaluation" has long been apparent to evaluators and completion of the *Standards for Evaluations of Educational Programs, Projects, and Materials* (Joint Committee on Standards 1981) marked a welcome milestone. Although many evaluation writers had proposed their own sets of meta-evaluation criteria, none carried the profession-wide weight reflected in the comprehensive standards so carefully prepared by the Joint Committee. These standards include criteria within each of the following categories: utility standards; feasibility standards; propriety standards; and accuracy standards.

Despite the wide acceptance and availability of these standards, however, there is no evidence that program evaluations are being subjected to any closer scrutiny than was the case before their publication. Even casual inspection reveals that only a small proportion of evaluation studies are ever evaluated, even in the most perfunctory fashion. Of the few meta-evaluations which do occur, most are internal evaluations done by the evaluator who produced the evaluation in the first place. It is rare indeed to see evaluators call in an outside expert to evaluate their evaluation efforts. Perhaps the reasons are many and complex why this is so, but one seems particularly compelling—evaluators are human and are no more ecstatic about having their work critiqued than are professionals in other areas of endeavor. Indeed, it can be a profoundly unnerving experience to swallow one's own prescriptions. Although the infrequency of good meta-evaluation might thus be understandable, it is not easily forgivable, for it enables shoddy evaluation practices to go undetected and worse, to be repeated again and again, to the detriment of the profession.

5.3 Program Evaluators Fail to Understand the Political Nature of Evaluation

Cronbach and co-workers (1980) have presented the view that evaluation is essentially a political activity. They describe evaluation as a "novel political institution" that is part of governance of social programs. They assert that evaluators and their patrons pursue unrealistic goals of finding "truth" or facilitating "right" decisions, rather than the more pertinent task of simply enlightening all participants so as to facilitate a democratic, pluralist decision-making process. While some may reject this view as overstated, it underscores the fact that program evaluation is inextricably intertwined with public policy formulation and all of the political forces involved in that process. Evaluators who fail to understand this basic fact expend unacceptably large amounts of human and financial resources conducting evaluations that are largely irrelevant, however impeccably they are designed and conducted.

5.4 Program Evaluators are too Narrow in their Choice of Evaluation Approaches and Techniques

It may be that innocence about the political nature of the evaluation enterprise contributes to the naive hope that evaluation will one day grow into a scientific discipline. That day, if attainable, would seem far off. Education itself is not a discipline but rather a social process field which draws its content from several disciplines. It seems unlikely that educational program evaluation, which also borrows its methods and techniques from many disciplines will gain the coherence that would

result in it becoming a discipline in its own right. Perhaps that is just as well, for much of the richness and potential of educational program evaluation lies in the depth and breadth of the strategies and tools it can employ and in the possibility of selectively combining them into stronger approaches than when used singly (Worthen 1981). Yet eclectic use of the evaluator's tools is a lamentably infrequent occurrence in program evaluations. Disciple-prone evaluators tend to cluster around their respective evaluation banners like vassals in a form of provincial bondage. For program evaluation to reach its potential, such intellectual bondage must give way to more mature and sophisticated approaches that draw appropriately on the richness and diversity of the many approaches, models, and techniques that characterize program evaluation today.

Bibliography

Anderson S B, Ball S 1978 *The Profession and Practice of Program Evaluation*. Jossey-Bass, San Francisco, California

Cook T D, Reichardt C T 1979 *Qualitative and Quantitative Methods in Evaluation Research*. Sage, Beverly Hills, California

Cronbach L J, Ambron S, Dornbusch S, Hess R, Hornik R, Phillips D, Walker D, Weiner S 1980 *Toward Reform of Program Evaluation: Aims, Methods and Institutional Arrangements*. Jossey-Bass, San Francisco, California

Guba E G, Lincoln Y S 1981 *Effective Evaluation: Improving the Usefulness of Evaluation Results through Responsive and Naturalistic Approaches*. Jossey-Bass, San Francisco, California

Joint Committee on Standards for Educational Evaluation 1981 *Standards for Evaluations of Educational Programs, Projects, and Materials*. McGraw-Hill, New York

Madey D L 1982 Some benefits of integrating qualitative and quantitative methods in program evaluation, with illustrations. *Educ. Eval. Policy Anal.* 4(2): 223–36

Smith N L 1981 Developing evaluation methods. In: Smith N L (ed.) 1981 *Metaphors for Evaluation: Sources for New Methods*. Sage, Beverly Hills, California

Worthen B R 1981 Journal entries of an eclectic evaluator. In: Brandt R S, Modrak N (eds.) 1981 *Applied Strategies for Curriculum Evaluation*. Association for Supervision and Curriculum Development, Alexandria, Virginia

Worthen B R, Sanders J R 1973 *Educational Evaluation: Theory and Practice*. Jones, Worthington, Ohio

Worthen B R, Sanders J R 1984 Content specialization and educational evaluation: A necessary marriage? Occasional Paper No. 14. Western Michigan University Evaluation Center, Kalamazoo, Michigan

Worthen B R, Sanders J R 1987 *Educational Evaluation: Alternative Approaches and Practical Guidelines*. Longman, New York

Formative and Summative Evaluation

A. Lewy

The terms *formative* and *summative* appeared first in the context of curriculum evaluation. Scriven (1967), who coined these terms, specified the differences

between them, and stated that both formative and summative evaluation may examine the worth of a variety of entities such as products, processes, personnel, or learners. Nevertheless, for several years these terms were uniquely applied to describing various types of curriculum evaluation activities. Only later did they become generalized and employed in the context of learner evaluation (Bloom et al. 1971) and educational actions other than curricula (Cronbach et al. 1980). The distinction between formative and summative evaluation contributed to broadening the range of disciplined inquiries recognized as evaluation studies, by attributing scholarly significance and professional status to evaluation activities conducted in the course of program development. Prior to the emergence of these terms, program evaluation, insofar as it was carried out, typically meant the comparison of the outcomes of competing programs for the sake of advising the decision maker about selecting or continuing educational programs. The evaluators, taking a stance of impartial aloofness and employing some legitimate form of experimental design, made an attempt to compare the relative merits of neatly packaged or fully structured competing programs. The failure of studies of this type to provide conclusive results on the one hand, and the conviction of evaluators that they can, and should, contribute to the improvement of education programs at various stages of their development on the other hand, gave issue to relatively small-scaled studies focusing on particular aspects of programs in the course of their development. Such studies, which in many cases waived the demanding patterns of experimental design and frequently revealed little interest in comparisons, came to be labelled formative evaluation studies. At the same time, comparative studies examining the outcomes of finished programs, with the aim of providing recommendations about program selection and continuation, which up to that time had been considered the sole permissible genre of evaluation, were redefined as a particular type of evaluation study within the framework of a variety of summative evaluation studies.

Attempts at conducting evaluation studies of instructional programs in the course of their development had been made before the emergence of the formative–summative distinction (Markele 1967). But the introduction of these terms constituted a point of departure for systematically exploring and conceptualizing the differences between the two types, and for disseminating the idea that it is both permissible and highly desirable to conduct evaluation studies in the course of program development, with a design deviating from that of the classical comparison studies.

1. The Formative–Summative Dichotomy

Two decades after the emergence of these innovative terms, a full consensus has not been reached as to their precise meaning. Therefore some experts tend to disregard the summative–formative distinction and focus on other, in their view, more clearly defined evaluation study dichotomies, such as prospective versus retrospective, responsive versus preordinate, natu-
ralistic versus experimental, holistic versus analytic, process versus outcome, and so on. Some of these have been erroneously interpreted as parallel to (if not fully identical with) the formative–summative distinction. In response to this confusion Scriven, the originator of these terms, provided definitions of formative and summative evaluations, which emphasize their orthogonality to the dichotomies mentioned above. According to Scriven (1980), formative evaluation is conducted during the development or improvement of a program or product (or person). It is an evaluation conducted for in-house staff and normally remains in house, but it may be done by an internal or external evaluator, or (preferably) a combination. Summative evaluation, on the other hand, is conducted after completion of a program (or a course of study) and for the benefit of some external audience or decision maker (e.g., funding agency or future possible users), though it too may be done either by an internal or an external evaluator or by a combination.

Scriven adheres to the view that there are no basic logical and methodological differences between formative and summative evaluation. Both are intended to examine the worth of a particular entity. Only timing, the audience requesting it, and the way its results are used can indicate whether a study is formative or summative. Moreover, the same study may be viewed by one client as formative and by another one as summative.

2. The Relative Importance of Formative and Summative Studies

While the scholarly status of formative evaluation studies was established only recently, they have swiftly dominated the field of program evaluation. Cronbach et al. (1980) claim that formative evaluation is more impactful and therefore more significant than summative evaluation. In their opinion, evaluation employed to improve a program while it is still fluid contributes more to the improvement of education than evaluation used to appraise a product already placed on the market. To be influential in course improvement, evidence must become available midway through program development and not in the home stretch, when the developer is naturally reluctant to tear apart a supposedly finished body of materials and techniques. Similarly, providing feedback to the teacher and learner about success or failure in mastering specific skills or components of the program constitutes an essential part of the teaching–learning process. It makes it possible to spot weak points of the program and to identify those learners who need corrective teaching. Formative information of this type contributes more to the improvement of learning than do results of end-of-course testing.

The superior usefulness of formative evaluation is so stressed in the writings of numerous evaluation experts that people dealing with specific programs often display no interest in conducting summative evaluation studies.

Scriven deplores this attitude and points out that both types of study have unique and essential roles. Summative evaluation is an inescapable obligation of the project director, an obvious requirement of the sponsoring agency and a desideratum for schools.

3. Characteristics of Formative and Summative Studies

Despite the tremendous growth in the number of formative and summative evaluation studies published in the 1960s and 1970s, theoreticians have not produced rules as to the procedures appropriate for either type of study. An exception is within the field of formative and summative evaluation of students' learning. As to other targets of evaluation, Scriven plays down the differences between formative and summative studies. Nevertheless, several reviews of empirical studies have pointed out systematic differences.

Stake (1977) provides a series of terms which characterize differences in information sought by users of formative and summative evaluation. Formative evaluation focuses on relatively molecular analyses, is cause seeking, is interested in the broader experiences of the program users, and tends to ignore the local effect of a particular program, while summative evaluation focuses on molar analyses, provides descriptive information, is interested in efficiency statements, and tends to emphasize local effects.

Alkin (1974), analysing 42 evaluation reports, and questionnaires completed by the 42 project directors, lists additional characteristics of formative evaluation studies. Their design is characterized as exploratory, flexible, focusing on individual components of the program, and as emphasizing iterative processes. While not comparative, it seeks to identify influential variables. A formative evaluation study uses a great variety of instruments which are either locally developed or standardized; it relies on observation and informal data collection devices, mostly locally chosen. In contrast, summative evaluation studies tend to use well-defined evaluation designs, as unobtrusive and nonreactive as possible; they are comparative and concerned with a broad range of issues, for example, implications, politics, costs, competing options. The instruments used in summative evaluation are publicly accepted, reliable, and valid instruments, reflecting concerns of the sponsor and of the decision-maker.

The rules provided by Bloom et al. (1971) for conducting formative and summative evaluation of students' learning are more specific. For formative evaluation, it is first necessary to analyze the instructional materials, to map the hierarchical structure of the learning tasks, and to administer achievement tests after completing a short learning unit covering study materials for 6 to 10 periods of study. A sample of test items appearing in the formative tests, or equivalent items, should constitute the summative evaluation test to be administered at the end of the course, with the aim of providing a basis for grading or certifying the learner.

4. The Consequences of the Formative and Summative Distinction

The formative–summative distinction has increased the range of evaluation studies and contributed to the improvement of educational planning. But two decades of utilizing these terms produced little consensus concerning their distinct features. The allegation that they differ only from the point of view of decisions they are supposed to support, and that no distinction should be made between them from the point of view of design, methodology, etc., has been endorsed by many evaluators without its veracity having been empirically examined. At the same time, other evaluators have asserted that methodological rigor is required only in summative studies, while in formative ones the evaluator may rely on less rigorously validated data and analysis procedures. This claim has never been confirmed by evaluation experts, but nevertheless it, unfortunately, has lead to the burgeoning of sloppily designed formative evaluation studies.

To avoid such theoretical and empirical pitfalls, there is a need to conduct empirical studies to ascertain the characteristic method and design features of formative and summative evaluation. Such studies might facilitate the use of formative and summative evaluation, and enhance their quality.

5. Recent Trends

During the 1980s the practice of formative evaluation was perceived as an indispensable component of planning programs and monitoring learning. Recent publications related to this topic tend to illustrate its utilization to innovative educational media, such as telecourses, computer software, interactive video cassettes, and video discs. The conceptual issues dealt with in this field elaborate on, and try to refine, existing models. Thus, for example, Chelimsky (1987) specifies the differential roles of formative evaluation at various phases of the process of program development, and addresses issues of the policy of formative evaluation. Medley-Mark and Weston (1988) examine the suitability of various data types (such as retrospective comments to instructional materials versus comments made during the process of working on a task) for fulfilling a particular formative evaluation role. But the methodology of formative and summative evaluation has remained founded on the seminal ideas of the 1960s.

Bibliography

Alkin M C 1974 *Evaluation and Decision Making: The Title VII Experience.* Center for Study of Evaluation, University of California, Los Angeles, California
Bloom B S, Hastings J T, Madaus G F 1971 *Handbook on*

Formative and Summative Evaluation of Students' Learning.
McGraw-Hill, New York

Chelimsky E 1987 The politics of program evaluation. *New Direction in Prog. Eval.* 34: 5–21

Cronbach L J et al. 1980 *Toward a Reform of Program Evaluation.* Jossey-Bass, San Francisco, California

Markele S M 1967 Empirical testing of programs. *Sixty-sixth Yearbook of the National Society for the Study of Education.* University of Chicago Press, Chicago, Illinois

Medley-Mark V, Weston C B 1988 A comparison of student feedback obtained from three methods of formative evaluation of instructional materials. *Instructional Sci.* 3–27

Sanders J R, Cunningham D J 1973 A structure for formative evaluation in product development. *Rev. Educ. Res.* 43: 217–36

Scriven M 1967 The methodology of evaluation. In: Tyler R W (ed.) 1967 *Perspectives of Curriculum Evaluation.* Rand McNally, Chicago, Illinois

Scriven M 1980 *Evaluation Thesaurus*, 2nd edn. Edgepress, Inverness, California

Stake R 1977 Formative and summative evaluation. In: Hamilton D et al. (eds.) 1977 *Beyond the Numbers Game: A Reader in Educational Evaluation.* Macmillan, London, pp. 156–57

Curriculum Evaluation Research

J. R. Sanders

There are several ways to organize the research on curriculum evaluation. One might classify studies of curriculum evaluation into empirical and nonempirical groups. One might use the tasks of curriculum evaluation as a categorization scheme, that is, research on (a) delineating, (b) obtaining, (c) providing, and (d) using evaluation information (Stufflebeam et al. 1971, Straton 1977, Stufflebeam and Welch 1986). One might also group research on curriculum evaluation by the various approaches proposed for conducting curriculum evaluation (Van der Klaauw and Lubbers 1979, Fraser 1982, Madaus et al. 1983, Worthen and Sanders 1987). There are many other possible organizers for research on curriculum evaluation.

The choice of organizers is somewhat arbitrary, but important, because it creates a certain mindset about what is known about curriculum evaluation and what still needs to be studied. The organization to be used here is in accordance with the tasks of curriculum evaluation. This framework was chosen because it has been used elsewhere, and other useful organizers can be subsumed within it.

The term research is used to include both empirical and nonempirical inquiry aimed at expanding knowledge and understanding of curriculum evaluation. Curriculum evaluation refers to the process of studying the merit or worth of some aspect, or the whole, of a curriculum. Curriculum could include the design of, needs for, processes of, materials for, objectives of, environment of, policies for, support of, and outcomes of educational experiences (Schubert 1982).

1. Research Delineating Curriculum Evaluation

Research on delineating the questions that curriculum evaluation should address has been sparse. Stufflebeam and Welch (1986) identified a few studies aimed at identifying the kinds of questions a curriculum evaluation should address. Worthen and Sanders (1987) identified several checklists that have been developed

for evaluating curriculum materials and school curriculum, but few were research based. They also reported research showing that evaluation user involvement in delineating the questions to be answered by evaluation does affect the eventual use of evaluation information. Questions addressed by curriculum evaluation have been found to come from evaluation models, curriculum checklists, research literature, and from clients.

Straton (1977) suggested research that needs to be conducted on the delineation process in curriculum evaluation. Needed research includes studies of alternative methods for identifying evaluation questions and of alternative methods for selecting evaluation questions. It also includes studies of the information that different audiences value in curriculum evaluation.

2. Research on Obtaining Information for Curriculum Evaluation

Research on obtaining information for curriculum evaluation has concentrated on techniques to enhance the quality of information being gathered. Research on methods for enhancing the validity and reliability of testing can be found in most testing textbooks. Likewise, references to research on enhancing the quality of surveys, interviews, observations, site visits, and other data collection methods can be found in many research methods textbooks. Straton (1977) and Worthen and Sanders (1987) have provided extensive references to research on information gathering methods used in curriculum evaluation.

Straton (1977) identified research that is needed on information collection processes in curriculum evaluation. This research includes studies of alternative data collection methods (e.g., approach, format, length, administration, sampling procedures) used for different kinds of evaluation questions and with different populations. Criterion variables would include cost and data quality.

3. Research on Providing Curriculum Evaluation Information to Various Audiences

The research on providing curriculum evaluation information has grown substantially since 1970. This research is often concerned with methods of providing information so that the chances that it will be used are enhanced, thus linking the providing and using processes in curriculum evaluation.

Worthen and Sanders (1987) reported research indicating that written reports are not always the most effective way to provide information in curriculum evaluation. Studies have found that teachers tend to rely on verbal information and look for it at the time it is needed. Other research on providing information has indicated that the technical quality of a study will affect its use by administrators and policy makers, as will its timeliness, use of nontechnical language, use of illustrations and examples, and focus on practical matters that audiences can do something about. Most guides to curriculum evaluation advise tailoring report format and style to those who will be expected to use the results of curriculum evaluation.

Straton (1977) identified needed research in the area of providing curriculum evaluation information. Needed research includes studies of alternative media for communicating different types of message to different types of audience. Audience studies, looking at difficulty level of communications, timing of delivery of information, and interest in different levels of thoroughness in reporting, are also needed.

4. Research on the Use of Curriculum Evaluation

The research on curriculum evaluation use began receiving a considerable amount of attention in 1975. Worthen and Sanders (1987) have provided extensive references to this research.

The findings of research on curriculum evaluation use have indicated that use takes on many forms: some is direct use to make decisions or changes; most is indirect conceptual learning that eventually shapes the thinking of decision makers; and some is proforma use to fulfill some mandated reporting function. Factors found to affect the use of curriculum evaluations have included credibility of the evaluator and the evaluation, the evaluator's commitment to getting the evaluation used, the quality of the evaluation itself, the interest of decision makers in the evaluation, the extent to which the evaluation focused on local needs, the way in which the evaluation findings are presented, and the translation of evaluation results into specific recommendations for action.

Methods for getting curriculum evaluation results used have been found in several field research projects. These methods include staff development through workshops and inservice programs, participation on committees, discussions with parent groups, school board policies governing the use of curriculum evaluations, demonstrations of how using evaluation findings will save money, and the evaluator being available at the right places at the right times.

Studies of the processes of decision making by teachers, principals, and other educational decision makers, the kinds of information they need and use, and methods for making that information available are needed. Studies of methods for integrating curriculum evaluation into curriculum decision making by teachers, administrators, and school board members are also needed.

5. Summary of the Research on Curriculum Evaluation

Although research on the process of curriculum evaluation accelerated during the 1970s, there is much that is remaining to be done. There is little known about how curriculum evaluation is conducted in schools of different size or across international boundaries. Stufflebeam and Welch (1986) concluded that, overall, research on curriculum evaluation is spotty and inconclusive. It is limited in its usefulness for guiding evaluation practice and for developing an agenda for further research. There is a need for a better research base to help in advancing the theory and practice of curriculum evaluation. Straton (1977) began building the research agenda, and many of the questions he listed are still unanswered. Research on curriculum evaluation remains a priority for those who depend on evaluation to guide curriculum change.

Bibliography

Fraser B J 1982 *Annotated Bibliography of Curriculum Evaluation Literature.* Israel Curriculum Center, Ministry of Educational Culture, Jerusalem

Madaus G F, Scriven M, Stufflebeam D L 1983 *Evaluation Models: Viewpoints on Educational and Human Services Evaluation.* Kluwer-Nijhoff, Boston, Massachusetts

Schubert W H 1982 Curriculum research. In: Mitzel H E (ed.) 1982 *Encyclopedia of Educational Research*, 5th edn. The Free Press, New York

Straton R G 1977 *Research of the Evaluation Process: Current Status and Future Directions.* The University of Sydney, Sydney

Stufflebeam D L, Foley W J, Gephart W J, Guba E G, Hammond R L, Merriman H O, Provus M M 1971 *Educational Evaluation and Decision Making.* F E Peacock, Itasca, Illinois

Stufflebeam D L, Welch W L 1986 Review of research on program evaluation in United States school districts. *Educ. Admin. Q.* 22: 150–70

Van der Klaauw C F, Lubbers M 1979 *Evaluation of Education: A Review.* Department of Educational Research, Erasmus University, Rotterdam

Worthen B R, Sanders J R 1987 *Educational Evaluation: Alternative Approaches and Practical Guidelines.* Longman, New York

Approaches to Evaluation

Tyler Evaluation Model

R. M. Wolf

The Tyler evaluation model refers to an approach to the evaluation of educational enterprises drawn from Ralph Tyler's rationale for curriculum development, instruction, and evaluation. The full formal presentation of this rationale appears in *Basic Principles of Curriculum and Instruction* (Tyler 1950) although its origins can be traced to Tyler's earlier work in the 1930s and 1940s (Tyler 1935, 1942, Smith and Tyler 1942).

The Tyler rationale is a rational–empirical approach to the development and evaluation of curricula. It is centered around answering four fundamental questions in the development of any curriculum and plan of instruction. These are:

(a) What educational purposes should the school seek to attain?

(b) What educational experiences can be provided that are likely to attain these purposes?

(c) How can these educational experiences be effectively organized?

(d) How can it be determined whether these purposes are being attained?

Tyler goes on to suggest methods for studying these questions. While he does not furnish answers to the questions since the answers will vary from one level of education to another and from one institution to another, Tyler does provide a framework for dealing with the questions.

Tyler's rationale consists of three major elements: (a) objectives, (b) learning experiences, and (c) evaluation. Each element can only be fully understood in relation to the others. Schematically, the Tyler rationale can be represented as in Fig. 1.

Objectives refer to one's intentions for an educational endeavor. They represent the desired performances or behaviors that students are to acquire as a result of going through the program. Objectives can range from the acquisition of specific skills to the development of new ways of thinking and feeling. The term "learning experiences" refers to those activities and experiences that learners undergo in order to acquire the desired performances and behaviors. Learning experiences is a broad term that includes both individual and group activities that are carried on both in and out of class for the purpose of attaining the objectives of a program. Evaluation refers to activities undertaken to determine the extent to which the objectives of the program are being attained.

The representation in Fig. 1 is a dynamic one as signified by the two-directional arrows linking each element with each of the others. Beginning with the objectives, the arrow pointing to learning experiences indicates that objectives serve as a guide for the selection and/or creation of learning experiences. The point here is that the nature of one's objectives will be the critical determinant of the learning experiences which constitute the operational program. The arrow pointing to evaluation denotes that the objectives serve as specifications for the development of evaluation procedures and instruments.

The two arrows stemming from objectives in the representation are easily explained. The meaning of the other arrows is less apparent but no less important. The arrow pointing from learning experiences to evaluation is indicative of the fact that learning experiences can provide exemplars for the development of evaluation tasks. The activities that students engage in during the learning phase of a program should furnish ideas for evaluation situations. In fact, there must be a basic consistency between learning experiences and evaluation tasks for learners. If there is not, something is amiss in the program.

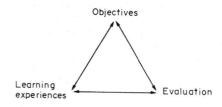

Figure 1
Representation of the Tyler rationale

411

The two arrows pointing from evaluation to objectives and to learning experiences are especially important. In the case of the former, the arrow signifies that evaluation procedures should furnish information about the extent to which the objectives are being attained. This is an important function of evaluation. Evaluation information can also furnish information that may result in the modification of some objectives and possible elimination of others. Particular objectives may have been included as a result of noble intentions on the part of a group of educators but evaluation may yield information that indicates that the objectives were clearly not attained. This may necessitate that educators reconsider the objectives. Should the objectives be modified or perhaps eliminated? Are the objectives realistic for the group of students served by the program? Are the resources necessary for achieving the objectives available? Such questions will, of course, have to be answered within the context of a particular situation. The point in raising these questions is to illustrate how the results of evaluation can provide information that is pertinent to a review of objectives.

The arrow pointing from evaluation to learning experiences is suggestive of two important notions. First, just as evaluation activities can furnish information about the extent to which objectives are being attained, they can also provide information bearing on which learning experiences appear to be working well and which ones are not. In any educational enterprise there will be a variety of learning experiences. It is unrealistic to expect that all will be equally effective. Evaluation procedures can furnish information as to which learning experiences are succeeding, which ones may be in need of modification and which ones should perhaps be eliminated. This involves the notion of formative evaluation developed by Scriven (1967). A second important idea suggested by the arrow pointing from evaluation to learning experiences is that tasks, exercises, and problems developed by evaluation specialists may be suggestive of new learning experiences. The incorporation of novel and imaginative evaluation materials into the evaluation of a program has, on occasion, contributed significantly to the improvement of learning. Of course, the appropriation of such materials for the improvement of the quality of the learning experiences renders the materials useless for further use in evaluation. However, this is usually considered a small price to pay for the improvement of the quality of the learning experiences.

Finally, the arrow pointing from learning experiences to objectives denotes that learning activities can result in encounters between teachers, learners, and learning materials that can suggest new objectives. Alert and sensitive teachers can identify potentially important new objectives. Thus, what started out as incidental learning can be incorporated into an educational program.

The above description of the Tyler rationale, albeit terse, conveys two important notions. First, the objectives of an educational program constitute the essential standard against which success must be judged. Second, evaluation is considered to be an integral part of the educational process and not something apart from it. The first notion, the centrality of educational objectives, has two important implications for evaluation work. First, since objectives are statements of desired student performances and behaviors, evaluation of an educational program must be based on how well students achieve the objectives rather than on other grounds such as the content of a program, quality of materials used, etc. Second, to ensure that evaluation is carried out in accord with the stated objectives, it is necessary to systematically develop evaluation instruments that faithfully and fully reflect a program's objectives. The use of test blueprints, checks on content validity, and the like, are mechanisms for ensuring the rational development of evaluation instruments.

The second notion, that evaluation is an integral part of the education process, is not only central to the Tyler rationale but paved the way for the development of the idea of formative evaluation (Scriven 1967) as well as furnishing a means for integrating evaluation and curriculum development. This integration had long been advocated by specialists in the curriculum field but there was no way of realizing this goal until Tyler formally incorporated it into his rationale.

The use of a variety of evaluation procedures that would reflect the whole range of a program's objectives rather than a mere end-of-program test is also directly attributable to Tyler. The evidence produced through the use of a variety of procedures allows educators to determine how well program objectives are being achieved as well as how effective particular learning experiences are. Thus, the Tyler evaluation model combines both rational approaches (in the development of procedures and instruments) with an empirical study of program functioning. The combination of a rational and empirical approach to the process of curriculum development and evaluation is considered one of the strongest features of the Tyler rationale.

While the Tyler rationale has been widely accepted as a framework for curriculum development and evaluation, it has not gone without criticism. Kliebard (1970) conducted a thoroughgoing analysis of the Tyler rationale. He finds it deficient in several respects despite his being generally approving. Kliebard's criticisms center around the way in which objectives are formulated and the general narrowness of the approach to evaluation. Also, according to Kliebard as well as others, restricting evaluation to achievement of program objectives prevents one from judging whether a program is serving larger interests. For example, a program may have trivial objectives and could be judged successful for achieving them. However, the students enrolled in the program may be being educationally shortchanged insofar as their future development is concerned. Despite these criticisms, however, the Tyler rationale and the specific approach to evaluation he has long advocated have been one of the most widely accepted and used means for approaching the process of curriculum development and evaluation.

Bibliography

Kliebard H M 1970 The Tyler rationale. *Sch. Rev.* 78: 259–72
Scriven M 1967 The methodology of evaluation. AERA Monograph Series on Evaluation No. 1. In: Stake R E (ed.) 1967 *Curriculum Evaluation*. Rand McNally, Chicago, Illinois
Smith E R, Tyler R W 1942 *Appraising and Recording Student Progress*. Harper, New York
Tyler R W 1935 Evaluation: A challenge to progressive education. *Educ. Res. Bull.* 14(1): 9–16
Tyler R W 1942 General statements on evaluation. *J. Educ. Res.* 35: 492–501
Tyler R W 1950 *Basic Principles of Curriculum and Instruction*. University of Chicago Press, Chicago, Illinois

Goal-free Evaluation

B. Stecher

Goal-free evaluation is an approach to evaluation in which merit is determined from an examination of program effects without reference to goals or objectives. This focus on results rather than intentions was proposed by Michael Scriven to counteract the bias that can result when attention to stated program goals narrows the range of potential outcomes that are investigated by an evaluator. In contrast, the goal-free evaluator is charged to examine all program outcomes—staunchly ignorant of project objectives—and make no distinctions between "anticipated outcomes" and "side effects."

The notion of goal-free evaluation evolved out of a concern that evaluation was too easily circumscribed by program goals and thus too strongly influenced by program managers and planners. "The rhetoric of intent was being used as a substitute for evidence of success" (Scriven 1972). Moreover, official goals are often narrow, vague, purposefully overstated, or purposefully understated. Thus, adherence to goals severely limits the scope and meaningfulness of an evaluation. By changing the focus from "what the program was trying to do" to what it was actually doing, Scriven's goal-free evaluator is free to determine merit without such program-based bias.

This is somewhat analogous to the double-blind technique used in scientific experiments. In a double-blind medical study, for example, neither the subject nor the administering physician knows who is receiving the treatment drug and who is receiving the placebo. This eliminates many potential confounding explanations for the observed effects. Scriven referred to goal-free evaluation as triple-blind, for, in addition, the evaluator does not even know the intentions of the intervention.

Goal-free evaluation is not a fully realized evaluation model with formal definitions, specification of structural relationships, frameworks for data collection and reporting, operating procedures, and so on. It is primarily a philosophical principle for guiding the evaluation process. For the most part, the goal-free evaluator must use his or her best professional skill to discover and document program effects. However, Scriven did offer some additional suggestions about how it is possible to determine which observed effects can be attributed to the program under investigation. Likening goal-free evaluation to criminal investigation, he called the process the modus operandi method. The name refers to the manner in which investigators try to establish causal connections. The method consists of a careful examination of all potential causes for observed effects and the establishment of solid connections, link by link, to prior program activities or rival influences.

There have been numerous criticisms of goal-free evaluation; the most frequent is that it simply substitutes the goals of the evaluator for those of the program manager. After all, the evaluator must have some criteria for making favorable or unfavorable judgments. Advocates of goal-free evaluation would argue that this is merely a misunderstanding. It derives, in part, from a failure to recognize that the important criterion in an evaluation is not the degree to which the program meets its goals, but the degree to which it meets demonstrated needs. Merit is derived from the congruence between program effects and the needs of the affected population, not from the correspondence between effects and goals. Consequently, the critical task for the evaluator is to determine the needs of the affected population, and these become the basis for judgments about program effects. In fact, Scriven (1981) referred to goal-free evaluation as "needs-based evaluation."

Another way in which Scriven addressed the concern about the role of goals in program evaluation is to note the similarity between goal-free evaluation and consumer product testing. A product—be it automobile or copying machine—should be evaluated from the perspective of the consumer and the society, not the producer. It would be incorrect to use the goals of Nissan Motors or Xerox as the basis for the evaluation of their products. It would also be improper to substitute the evaluator's goals. Instead, a good product evaluator determines the functional needs of the consuming audience and uses these as the criteria for assessing the merits of the product. The goal-free evaluator takes a similar approach to program evaluation; in fact, Scriven

(1981) also referred to goal-free evaluation as "consumer-based evaluation."

Despite its interesting philosophical basis, goal-free evaluation has not enjoyed wide popularity as a practical evaluation approach. This is due to many factors, including the resistance of program personnel to such uncontrolled examination of their actions, the reluctance of most evaluators to accept such large responsibility, and important disagreements with Scriven about the appropriate role for evaluation. Many evaluators place greater emphasis on the provision of information to decision makers and less on abstract judgment of merit.

Yet, proponents of goal-free evaluation have had some impact on the practice of evaluation. By emphasizing the independence of the evaluator, the importance of examining all program effects, and the need to subject program goals themselves to scrutiny (when conducting a goal-based evaluation), goal-free evaluation has affected the actions of many evaluators. Though not widely employed as a practical evaluation approach, goal-free evaluation has caused evaluators to be more attentive to a wider range of program outcomes, and the ideas embodied in this approach are mentioned frequently in other scholarly writing about evaluation.

Bibliography

Alkin M C 1972 Wider context goals and goal-based evaluators. *Eval. Comment* 3(4)
Popham W J 1975 *Educational Evaluation*. Prentice-Hall, Englewood Cliffs, New Jersey
Scriven M 1972 Pros and cons about goal-free evaluation. *Eval. Comment* 3(4): 1–4 Reprinted in Hamilton D, Jenkins D, King C, MacDonald B, Parlett M (eds.) 1977 *Beyond the Numbers Game: A Reader in Educational Evaluation*. Macmillan, London, pp. 130–1
Scriven M 1981 *Evaluation Thesaurus*, 3rd edn. Edgepress, Point Reyes, California
Stufflebeam D L 1972 Should or can evaluation be goal-free? *Eval. Comment* 3(4)

Decision-oriented Evaluation

G. D. Borich

Decision-oriented evaluation is a process that produces information for selecting among alternative courses of action. An evaluation is decision oriented if it (a) services a decision, (b) implies a choice among alternatives, and (c) is used in committing resources for the next interval of time before another decision is to be made. Properly conceptualized, decision-oriented evaluation is a perspective for organizing and focusing the concepts of evaluation toward the broadly defined requirements of decision making rather than a specific method or technique by which decisions are made.

1. Some Decision-oriented Definitions and Concepts

The Phi Delta Kappa National Study Committee on Evaluation (Stufflebeam et al. 1971) represented one of the first attempts to consider evaluation from a decision-making perspective. They defined educational evaluation as "the process of delineating, obtaining, and providing useful information for judging decision alternatives" and divided evaluation into four distinct activities, each with its own decision-making purpose. Similarly, Hagedorn and co-workers (1976), writing to mental-health professionals, defined evaluation as "a systematic set of data collection and analysis activities undertaken to determine the value of a program to aid management, program planning, staff training, public accountability, and promotion." This definition reflects the same view of evaluation as that which prevailed in education, that of an information feedback process to aid administrators and project management.

The primary impetus for the development of decision-oriented evaluation was a desire to maximize the utilization of evaluation results. For the Phi Delta Kappa National Study Committee on Evaluation utilization was to be fostered by having the evaluator serve "as an extension of the decision maker's mind." The Commission suggested that the evaluator must assume, in addition to a technical role, an interface role in which he/she interacts with the decision maker for the purpose of delineating decision alternatives and providing information for selecting among alternative courses of action. This role requires the evaluator to work with the decision maker in creating an awareness of the decisions to be made, spelling out the decision alternatives, and identifying the evaluative criteria to be utilized in the evaluation.

A similar decision-oriented view of evaluation can be found in the work of Alkin (1969). Alkin's definition of evaluation advanced the notion that evaluation is a process of ascertaining decision areas of concern, selecting appropriate information, and collecting and analyzing information in order to report summary data useful to decision makers. This definition, while affirming that evaluation should be an information-collection process used to make decisions about alternatives, goes further to suggest that "the manner in which the information is collected, as well as the analysis procedures, must be appropriate to the needs of the decision maker or a potential decision involved public." This definition laid the groundwork for a broad distinction between the decision-oriented evaluator whose role it was to delineate decision alternatives and to provide information for selecting among them, and the researcher whose role it was to discover or explain theoretical phenomena. Emphasized was the notion that the most important function that an evaluator can perform is to report summary data to the decision maker in the form of practical and unambiguous statements about what alternative course of action should be taken.

2. Decision-oriented Evaluation Paradigms

Given the diversity of evaluation contexts within any particular field, there is considerable diversity in the specific decision-oriented approaches and procedures utilized. Different decision makers have different values, priorities, and political presses on their activities. Other influences which may vary from setting to setting include administrative levels and leadership styles of decision makers, variety of organizational goals, and disparity in the communication networks that both form and inform decisions. Each context and information need places different constraints on the activity of evaluation. Some evaluation approaches and procedures will be inadequate or inappropriate in some contexts and perfectly matched with the decision-oriented information needs in others. From these practical considerations have emerged different procedural frameworks for conducting decision-oriented evaluations. Although varied in their explicit references to decisions, these frameworks—or models—are decision oriented in that they are devoted almost exclusively to the gathering and reporting of information relevant to the needs of decision makers for the purpose of selecting among alternative courses of action.

2.1 Educational Psychology Models

When applied in the context of a specific program or intervention, decision-oriented evaluation often takes the form of an evaluation of the objectives of that program or intervention. The decision is usually one of adopting or revising the program based on the degree to which the program did or did not meet its objectives. Generally these evaluation models employ the following steps: (a) identifying objectives, (b) stating objectives in measurable behavioral terms, (c) devising and administering measurement instruments, (d) comparing obtained results with the objectives prespecified in step (a), and (e) reporting to decision makers discrepancies between obtained results and objectives for the purpose of program revision or adoption. Common features of educational psychology models include (a) their almost exclusive application to the evaluation of curriculum and instruction, (b) the high priority they place on defining objectives, and (c) their limited focus on comparisions of "what is" with "what should be," with discrepancy information constituting the bulk of evaluation results. One educational psychology model commonly used for the purpose of gathering and reporting information relevant to the needs of decision makers was that developed by Provus (1971). Provus proposed

a five-stage evaluation process: design, installation, process, product, and program comparison.

The design stage has as its objective a description of all intended program inputs, processes, and outcomes. The installation stage is concerned with field operations and the discrepancy between the intended and actual manner in which the program was installed. The process stage has as its objective the measurement of enabling or short-term outcomes. In the product stage the evaluator determines if terminal or long-term outcomes have been attained at the level specified by the objectives. In the final program comparison stage, the evaluator compares the experimental program with some competing program to show that benefit is commensurate with cost.

At each stage of this process there are three activities: (a) agreeing on program standards (usually program goals or objectives), (b) determining if a discrepancy exists between aspects of a program, and (c) using discrepancy information to identify program weaknesses. Discrepancy information at each stage is used to inform decision makers whether or not to proceed to the next stage or to revise program standards or operations.

Although the evaluator's role as an information provider is not as explicit in the educational psychology models as in the following set of models, these models identify the decision areas of concern, select appropriate information, and collect and analyze information in order to report summary data useful to decision makers. As is the case with other decision-oriented approaches, these models limit the evaluator's freedom in an evaluative context to activities that are congruent with the information needs of the decision maker.

2.2 Educational Decision Models

Some writers in the field of evaluation have explicitly put forth the notion that the role of evaluation is to provide decision makers with information. The following premises characterize this notion of evaluation: (a) the decision maker determines what is to be evaluated and may even choose the measures to be used, (b) the evaluator's role is that of an advisor to the decision maker, (c) the work of evaluation consists almost exclusively of information gathering and reporting, (d) the information gathered must be relevant to the decision maker's needs, and (e) the information that is important is dictated by the decision to be made.

The CIPP evaluation model (Stufflebeam et al. 1971) is particularly representative of this approach. This model divides evaluation into four distinct stages—context, input, process, and product evaluation, thus the acronym CIPP. Each of these stages is intended to represent a cluster of decisions to be served by the information provided within them. Context evaluation has as its objective to specify the operational context and to identify problems and underlying needs within the decision maker's domain. Input evaluation is concerned with identifying and assessing alternative means of achieving specified ends. Process evaluation has as its objective to inform decisions pertaining to procedural design or implementation and to make adjustments and refinements that seem to be called for from monitoring the program. The goal of product evaluation is to relate outcome information to objectives and to context, input and process data, eventually leading to a series of decisions (e.g. to terminate, revise, or recycle the program as is). At each stage outcomes are compared to stated objectives and differences between expected and actual results are reported to decision makers.

2.3 Educational Science Models

In this third view of the decision-oriented perspective, evaluative inquiry is conducted in much the same manner as in the previous models, except that the decisions to be made pertain almost exclusively to choices among alternative courses of action representing competing programs. The terms evaluative research and applied research reflect this attempt to use experimental design and the tools of classical research methodology for making practical choices among programs.

This evaluation process proposes a causal model consisting of three components: inputs (usually client or student characteristics or attributes), the programs (those experiences to which clients or students are exposed), and outcomes (certain targeted skills and abilities measured at program completion). The purpose of educational science models is to establish causal connections between these components. Regression or linear model techniques are used to compute predicted outcome scores on the basis of various input data. Then groups of students, subjected to various program alternatives, are tested to determine whether those in each program exceed, match, or fall short of what would be expected from input data alone. Program impact is inferred if outcome variance cannot be explained by input data alone and if the performance of clients or students in the experimental program represents a statistically significant improvement over the performance of those in a comparison program.

Although educational science models have not proliferated, a sorting through of evaluation studies reveals a strong reliance on the scientific method and an even heavier emphasis on the experimental designs and statistical tools of research. In this model statistical decision rules (e.g., $p < .05$) unequivocally determine program effectiveness and, hence, identify which alternative course of action (program) should be selected. Implicit in this paradigm is the translation of decisions about programs into notions of cause and effect.

Other quantitative approaches to decision-oriented evaluation can be found in the decision-theoretic work of Guttentag (1973) and the Bayesian statistics of Thompson, Schnelle, and Willemian (reviewed in Larson and Kaplan 1981). These highly quantitative procedures for informing decisions about programs attempt to bridge the gap between the complex multivariate world in which programs operate and unambiguous "go/no-go" decisions that are envisioned by decision makers who operate within it.

3. Other Perspectives

Some authors have taken exception to the decision-oriented perspective and, in particular, to the applied research model. The primary criticism of the decision-oriented definition of evaluation is that evaluator and decision maker share the function of evaluation unequally. The role of the evaluator is to provide the decision maker with meaningful information; the decision maker defines the information that is needed and makes the actual judgment of value or merit. The criticism of the applied research model is that all of the contextual and moderating factors that can affect a program's performance are covaried or randomized out of the evaluation, reducing the evaluation to a theoretical statement about program impact in a statistically sterilized environment. The role of the evaluator is to provide a "clean" interpretation of program effectiveness for the decision maker, sometimes at the expense of a more complex but more valid interpretation.

One approach to evaluation which is at variance with the decision-oriented notion is value-oriented evaluation (Borich and Jemelka 1981). A value-oriented definition of evaluation stresses the value judgments made in evaluating programs and describes the act of judging merit or worth as central to the role of the evaluator. Scriven (1983) has argued that value judgments are a crucial part of all sciences, particularly methodological value judgments, and there appear to be no reasons to dismiss them in the evaluation of programs. He calls for goal-free evaluation, insisting that all aspects of a program should come under the scrutiny of an evaluator and that nothing should be taken as given, including the decisions to be made and the alternative courses of action to be taken.

A value-oriented definition of evaluation begins with the premise that evaluators or decision makers seldom know all of the decisions and alternative courses of action with which they or others will make a judgment of program merit. A value-oriented conception assumes that programs operate in environments characterized not by value consensus, but by value pluralism, and that different value positions should be objectively examined for the decisions and alternatives they hold. Thus, people gain from this definition the notion that evaluation includes not only the collection of data from which judgments of merit can be rendered, but also the objective determination of criteria upon which these judgements should be based. In essence, a value-oriented definition of evaluation implies that the program being evaluated ultimately must be justified in terms of the values of those it is to serve. These values should, but may not always, coincide with those values that are perceived to be important by the decision maker.

Another competing notion of evaluation is systems-oriented evaluation. The systems-oriented definition of evaluation assumes a view of programs as systems and reflects a theoretical/philosophical stance in the sciences called general systems theory. While traditional scientific inquiry attempts to understand humans within their environment by isolating the effects of single variables, holding everything else constant, the general systems paradigm posits that it is impossible to understand complex events by reducing them to their individual elements. Hence, a basic tenet of general systems theory is the often-heard exhortation of the Gestalt school of psychology that the whole is more than the sum of its parts; to understand the whole it is necessary to study the whole.

General systems theory holds that the complexity of any system, including programs, cannot be understood through analytical reduction and experimental control. Rather, programs are viewed as organismic entities that evolve and decay, depending on their relationship to other programs and the larger context to which they contribute. Furthermore, because all programs are ultimately seen as interrelated, changes in any program will have implications throughout the larger system of which the changed program is a part. This viewpoint differs from the decision-oriented perspective in which the immediate context is the focus of inquiry and the limits of the evaluation are bounded by the decision maker's information requirements and prescribed alternative courses of action.

Still other notions pertaining to the relevance of decision-oriented evaluation have emerged from the work of Cronbach et al. (1980) and from Guba and Lincoln (1981). Departing from an earlier distinction between decision-oriented and conclusion-oriented inquiry, Cronbach and co-workers question the appropriateness of an inquiry that focuses exclusively on decisions. Cronbach and co-workers point out that the theory of evaluation has been developed almost wholly around the image of command. By "image of command" these authors refer to a mistaken belief that there is a clearly identifiable decision maker on the horizon who makes decisions on the basis of informative input, including that provided by the evaluator. These writers point out that the actual context in which evaluation occurs is not consistent with the context of command assumed to exist in virtually all program settings. Their point is that only when a large confluence of data becomes available is a "decision" actually made, and even then, the decision is made interactively over a long period of time by a large number of persons (policy makers, bureaucrats, program monitors, project personnel, vested-interests, and others) who make up what constitutes a "policy-shaping community." These authors advance the notion that the process of decision making does not terminate in a clearly defined decision but is a cumulative, never-ending process characterized by negotiation and accommodation among members of the policy shaping community (PSC) who continually reassess and modify the decisions to be made and the alternative courses of action to be taken. Cronbach and his colleagues describe the evolution of decisions in the policy shaping community this way:

> Most action is determined by a pluralistic community, not by a lone decision maker. Parties having divergent perceptions and aims bear down on lawmakers and administrators. Information can change perceptions but is unlikely to bring all parties to agree on which facts are relevant or even on what the facts are. If the term *decision* is understood to mean formal choice at a particular time between discrete alternatives, decision making is rarely to be observed. When there are multiple participants with multiple views, it is meaningless to speak of one action as the rational or correct action. The active parties jockey toward a politically acceptable accommodation.

Hence, these authors suggest that the proper role of evaluation is not to service decisions but to participate in and contribute to the negotiation and accommodation process by raising new issues, stimulating new debate and illuminating the complexities of the problem at hand. For these reasons evaluations should focus on programs as implementations of policy and not on specific alternative courses of action to be taken in a particular context. Their reasoning is that by the time decisions are about to be made, the alternative courses of action to which they relate will have lost their significance, while the policy which underlies these alternative actions will have remained a relevant social issue.

Guba, one of the original founders of the CIPP decision-oriented model, also has recently voiced some changed views on the relevance of decision-oriented evaluation. Although acknowledging that the decision maker or client is entitled to issue directives to the evaluator, Guba and Lincoln (1981) warn that:

> . . . the evaluator need not be naive. He must recognize that the client may have many covert reasons for putting the charge in a particular way. He may, for example, select for evaluation only those program aspects that appear to be successful, cover up program failure by focusing on partisan testimonials, make evaluation gestures designed to promote a favorable public image, respond to goverment mandates that he does not take seriously but must be complied with overtly and the like. Sheer ignorance may also shape the client's directives.

Looking retrospectively at the CIPP model itself, Guba and Lincoln's views essentially echo those of Cronbach and co-workers ". . . it made what are probably unwarranted assumptions about the rationality of decisions, about the openness of the decision-making process (essentially political) and about the ease with which operational decision makers can be identified (in complex organizations or loosely coupled organizations decisions appear to "bubble up" rather than be made explicitly at some particular time and place)."

The assumption of a context of command or the notion that evaluation is or should be decision-oriented has not been a result of accident or serendipity. Rather, the evolution of decision-oriented evaluation has resulted from the belief that evaluation's central role is to respond to the pragmatic needs of the decision maker and to the information requirements of those in most immediate control of the program. Hence, more complex decision making patterns involving negotiation and accommodation within a larger network of stake holders as well as more holistic and value-based criteria for program effectiveness, generally, are not assumed to be characteristic of the decision-oriented perspective.

Bibliography

Alkin M C 1969 Evaluation theory development. *Eval. Comment* 2(1): 2–7

Borich G D, Jemelka R 1981 *Programs and Systems: An Evaluation Perspective*. Academic Press, Orlando, Florida

Cronbach L, Ambron S, Dornbusch S, Hess R, Hornik R, Phillips D, Walker D, Weiner S 1980 *Toward Reform of Program Evaluation: Aims, Methods and Institutional Arrangements*. Jossey-Bass, San Francisco, California

Guba E G, Lincoln Y S 1981 *Effective Evaluation: Improving the Usefulness of Evaluation Results Through Responsive and Naturalistic Approaches*. Jossey-Bass, San Francisco, California

Guttentag M 1973 Subjectivity and its use in evaluation research. *Eval.* 1(2): 60–65

Hagedorn H J, Beck K J, Neubert S F, Werlin S H 1976 *A Working Manual of Simple Program Evaluation Techniques for Community Mental Health Centers*. National Institute of Mental Health, Rockville, Maryland

Larson R C, Kaplan E H 1981 Decision-oriented approaches to program evaluation. In: Wooldridge R (ed.) 1981 *New Directions for Program Evaluation: Evaluation of Complex Systems*. Jossey-Bass, San Francisco, California

Provus M M 1971 *Discrepancy Evaluation for Educational Program Improvement and Assessment*. McCutchan, Berkeley, California

Scriven M 1983 The evaluation taboo. In: House E (ed.) 1983 *New Directions for Program Evaluation: Philosophy of Evaluation*. Jossey-Bass, San Francisco, California

Stufflebeam D L, Foley W J, Gephart W J, Guba E G, Hammond H D, Merriman H O, Provus M M 1971 *Educational Evaluation and Decision Making*. Peacock, Itasca, Illinois

Responsive Evaluation

R. E. Stake

Responsive evaluation is an approach to the evaluation of educational and other programs. Compared to most other approaches it is oriented more to the activity, the uniqueness, and the social plurality of the program.

The essential feature of the approach is a responsiveness to key issues, especially those held by people at the site. It requires a delay and continuing adaptation of evaluation goal setting and data gathering while the people responsible for the evaluation become acquainted with the program and the evaluation context.

Issues are suggested as conceptual organizers for the evaluation study, rather than hypotheses, objectives, or regression equations. The reason for this is that the term "issues" draws thinking toward the complexity, particularity, and subjective valuing already felt by persons associated with the program. Issue questions such as, "Are the admission criteria appropriate?" "Do these simulation exercises confuse the students about authoritative sources of information" are raised. The evaluator inquires, negotiates, and selects a few issues around which to organize the study.

To become acquainted with a program's issues the evaluator usually observes its activities, interviews those who have some stake in the program, and examines relevant documents. These are not necessarily the data-gathering methods for informing and interpreting the issues, but are needed for the initial planning and progressive focusing of the study. And even later, management of the study as a whole remains flexible whether quantitative or qualitative data are gathered.

1. Observations and Judgments

A responsive evaluation study is, of course, directed toward the discovery of merit and shortcoming in the program. It is attentive to the multiple and sometimes contradictory standards held by different groups. Ultimately the evaluators will either make strong summary statements of the program's worth, or they may provide descriptive data and the judgments of others so that report readers can make up their own minds about program worth.

There is a common misunderstanding that responsive evaluation requires naturalistic inquiry or qualitative research. Not so. The evaluators and program staff and evaluation sponsors discuss alternative methods. They negotiate. Knowing more about what different methods can accomplish, and what methods this evaluation "team" can do well, and being the ones to carry them out, the evaluators ultimately determine what the methods will be.

With preliminary emphasis on becoming acquainted with the history and social interactions of the program, it is often decided that the methods of study should be naturalistic or phenomenological. Other times it will become highly quantitative, possibly goal oriented. It depends on the situation. For it to be good responsive evaluation the methods must fit the "here and now," having potential for serving the evaluation needs of the various parties concerned.

It is in fact rather uncommon for a responsive evaluation study to emphasize the testing of students or other indicators of successful attainment of objectives. This is because such instrumentation has so often been found not to be cost effective. Available tests are often not good approximations of the several outcomes intended. And even when possible, developing new tests is very expensive. Test results have too often been disappointing, with educators probably justifiably believing that more was learned than showed up on the tests. With the responsive approach, tests may be used, but usually are kept in a subordinate role. They are needed when it is clear that they actually can serve to inform about the quality of the program.

People are used more as sociological informants than as subjects here. They are questioned not so much to see how they have changed but to indicate the changes they see.

2. Subjectivity and Pluralism

Those who object to the responsive approach often do so on the grounds that too much attention is given to subjective data, for example, the testimony of participants. To obtain a description of what is happening, the evaluation researchers try through triangulation to show the reliability of observations. Part of the description, of course, especially that about the worth of the program, is revealed in how people subjectively perceive what is going on. Placing value on the program is not seen as separate from perceiving it.

The researchers' own perceptions are also recognized as subjective—in choosing what to observe, in observing, and in reporting the observations. One tries in responsive evaluation to make those value commitments more recognizable. Issues are not avoided because they are inextricably subjective. When reporting, care is taken to illuminate the subjectivity of data and interpretations.

Objection to a responsive approach is also expressed in the belief that the program staff, the funding agency, or the research community should specify the key questions. Their questions are worthy of study, but in program evaluation for public use, should never be used exclusively. There is a general expectation that if a program is evaluated, a wide array of important concerns will be considered. Embezzlement, racial discrimination, inconsistency in philosophy, and thwarting of creativity may be unmentioned in the contract, and barely in the evaluation specialist's range of view, but all such shortcomings belong to the evaluation expectation, and the responsive evaluator at least tries not to be blind to them.

Further it is recognized that evaluation studies are administratively prescribed not only to gain understanding and inform decision making but to legitimatize and protect administrative and program operations from criticism, especially during the evaluation period. And still further that evaluation requirements are sometimes made for the purpose of promulgating hoped-for standards.

By seeking out stakeholder issues, the responsive evaluator tries to see that these efforts at extending control over education are not undermining legitimate interests. Responsive evaluation is not intended as an instrument of reform, though reformists might find it useful. It is intended to serve the diverse people most affected personally and educationally by the program at hand—though it is bound to produce some findings they will not like.

3. Organizing and Reporting

The feedback from responsive evaluation studies is expected to be in forms and language attractive and comprehensible to the various groups. Thus, even at the expense of inequitable disclosure, different reports may be prepared for different groups. Portrayals and verbatim testimony will be appropriate for some, data banks and regression analyses for others. Obviously a budget will not allow everything, so these different communications need to be considered early in the work.

It is not uncommon for responsive evaluation feedback to occur early and throughout the evaluation period, particularly as a part of refining the list of issues to be pursued. The evaluator may ask, "Is this interesting?" and might, based on the answer, change the priorities of inquiry.

As analyzed by Ernest House (1980) responsive evaluation can be considered "intuitive" or indeed subjective, closer sometimes to literary criticism, Elliot Eisner's connoisseurship, or Michael Scriven's modus operandi evaluation than to the more traditional social science designs. But it differs from them in the most essential feature, that of emphasizing the issues, language, contexts, and standards of stakeholders.

When Stake proposed this "responsive evaluation" approach at an evaluation conference at the Pedagogical Institute in Göteborg, Sweden in 1974, he drew particularly upon the writings of Barry MacDonald, Malcolm Parlett, and David Hamilton, all stressing the necessity of organizing the evaluation of programs around what was happening in classrooms and boardrooms, drawing more attention to what educators were doing and less attention to what students were doing.

It is difficult to tell from an evaluation report whether or not the study itself was "responsive." A final report seldom reveals how issues were negotiated and how audiences were served. Three examples of studies which were clearly intentionally responsive were those of Stake et al. (1978), MacDonald (1975), and Murray et al. (1981).

Bibliography

Eisner E W 1976 Educational connoisseurship and criticism: Their form and functions in educational evaluation. *J. Aesthetic Educ.* 10: 135–50

House E R 1980 *Evaluating with Validity.* Sage, Beverly Hills, California

MacDonald B 1975 *The Programme at Two: An UNCAL Companion to Two Years On.* Centre for Applied Research in Education, University of East Anglia, Norwich

Murray C A et al. 1981 *The National Evaluation of the Cities in Schools Program,* Final Report. American Institutes for Research, Washington, DC

Parlett M, Hamilton D 1976 Evaluation as illumination: A new approach to the study of innovatory programmes. In: Tawney D H (ed.) 1976 *Curriculum Evaluation Today: Trends and Implications.* Macmillan, London

Scriven M 1974 Evaluation perspectives and procedures. In: Popham W J (ed.) 1974 *Evaluation in Education: Current Applications.* McCutchan, Berkeley, California, p. 7

Stake R E 1980 Program evaluation, particularly responsive evaluation. In: Dockrell W B, Hamilton D (eds.) 1980 *Rethinking Educational Research.* Hodder and Stoughton, London

Stake R E, Easley J, Anastasiou K et al. 1978 *Case Studies in Science Education.* University of Illinois, Urbana, Illinois

Illuminative Evaluation

M. R. Parlett

The basic emphasis of illuminative evaluation applied to education is on investigating and interpreting a variety of educational practices, participants' experiences, institutional procedures, and management problems, in ways that are recognizable and useful to those for whom the study is made. The research worker contributes to decision making by providing information, comments, and analysis to increase relevant knowledge and understanding. Illuminative evaluation is characterized by a flexible methodology that capitalizes on available resources and opportunities, and draws upon different techniques to fit the total circumstances of each study.

Illuminative evaluation falls within the general definition of a "systems" approach. Thus, it is holistic in outlook; studies tend to be far-ranging, concerned with the entire network of interrelationships rather than focusing on circumscribed programme features and correlations between individual "variables". As in systems thinking generally, illuminative evaluators are concerned with phenomena of organized complexity; they assume that events can usefully be treated as interrelated; they accept the likelihood of multiple causality and see their task as unravelling what is usually a complicated web of causes and effects. The outcome of an illuminative study is some overall model or "map" which attempts to make sense of the system as an organized and coherent totality, in ways which will inform those for whom the study is directed.

The aim is to increase understanding of policy questions related to the educational programme, instructional innovation, school setting, organizational problem, or other "system" studied. The approach is designed to illuminate (or throw light upon) its character and special features as a working system, along with the wider context in which the system operates. The approach is also evaluative in that attention is necessarily paid to qualities, to costs and effects, to desirable and unintended outcomes, and the value (or lack of it) of parts of the system or the whole of it, as perceived by the various constituencies or pertinent subgroups with different investments, perspectives, and allegiances.

1. A Coordinated Approach

Illuminative evaluation represents a coordinated research approach—its purposes, working philosophies, strategic methodology, built-in values, and conceptual orientation combine together in a distinctive and necessary way. Each feature contributes to the whole. It needs to be understood as an integrated and "total" approach to investigation—not as simply an espousal of qualitative methodology, ethnographic field work, face-to-face methods of enquiry, and narrative reporting— although these do feature strongly in most studies.

Another way of depicting the approach is in terms of its being responsive, naturalistic, heuristic, and interpretive.

1.1 Responsive Features

Illuminative researchers aim to be responsive in several ways. It is a tenet of the approach that studies be of use and interest to the educational practitioners and policy makers who represent the target audiences. If this is to be more than a pious wish, it means paying special attention to the audiences of each study—their requirements for information, their interests, questions, and needs. It means designing the study in ways that do not affront their common sense, with reports being written lucidly, with minimal resort to jargon, and with attention paid to presentation and brevity. If an illuminative evaluation report is found by policy makers and practitioners to be irrelevant, long-winded, or superficial, the study has failed within its own terms.

The approach requires investigators to be responsive in other ways too. Thus, while all research and evaluation constitutes intervention of some kind in the lives of organizations and persons, the close-up, on-site investigative techniques favoured by illuminative evaluators increase the requirements for researcher sensitivity, the building of trust, and responsibility in the way the study is reported so as to maintain anonymity.

Another way in which the approach is responsive is that studies are kept as brief as possible. Although the orientation derives much from anthropological techniques here is one sharp disjunction from field work as commonly practised by ethnographers. Studies which take years to carry out and to write up are rarely adequate for evaluation purposes. Illuminative evaluation can be adapted to carrying out short, intensive studies when these are called for by special circumstances.

1.2 Naturalistic Features

In illuminative studies, educational and other relevant phenomena are examined as they occur "naturally" in real-life institutional settings. No attempt is made to bring them under artificial conditions for purposes of investigation. Moreover, every effort is made to look "beyond the display counter" and to do justice to the observable realities "at the back of the shop". Organizational life is studied in all its natural complexity, with attention paid to the unexpected and the atypical as well as to the routine and obvious.

Overall, the concern is to document the programme or set of issues being studied in an informative and revealing manner, drawing together factual and statistical material, opinions, observations, and historical perspectives, to provide a fuller basis for comprehending and appreciating the special nature of the system studied. The data handled are undoubtedly complex. An attempt is made to do justice to the complexity without being submerged by it in the course of study or passing it on to readers in a way that is confusing or inaccessible.

1.3 Heuristic Features

In working practice, the systemic nature of the approach calls for a heuristic design—that is, an evolving strategy of study, continuously updated to accord with the investigators' emerging understandings of the system as a whole, as well as accommodating changes in the system that result from the flux of unfolding events during the course of study. In this regard, the illuminative investigator proceeds like a clinical diagnostician or, perhaps, a historian documenting a particular event: the course of enquiry cannot be charted in advance.

In turn, flexibility of design necessitates having facility with a range of methods—mainly direct observation, interviews, focused group discussions, unobtrusive measures, questionnaires, analysis of background documentary materials and of statistical and other information already collected. Techniques are deployed in various combinations according to the exact nature of the enquiry at different stages, with problems defining methods rather than vice versa. Illuminative evaluations therefore have a custom-built plan of study, rather than one "off the shelf", one which acknowledges the programme's specialized features, the requirements and interests of policy makers, and the constraints, resources, and boundary conditions relating to the particular study.

1.4 Interpretive Features

Despite the importance placed upon accurate and full description and reporting, illuminative evaluators believe there is a need to go further. The aim is to provide a distillation of local thinking, to concentrate the wisdom, as it were, dispersed in many different perspectives, and to draw threads together in such a way as to "sharpen discussion, disentangle complexities, isolate the significant from the trivial, and raise the level of sophistication of debate" (Parlett and Hamilton 1972).

In order to focus discussion, heighten awareness, and promote a fresh appreciation of the system studied and the related issues of policy, the investigator goes beyond simple description. Underlying structures and relationships do not declare themselves in obvious ways—they have to be discovered, even created. In this respect, illuminative evaluators align themselves with the functionalist anthropologist Bronislaw Malinowski (1961): "The principles of social organization, of legal constitution, of economics and religion, have to be constructed by the observer out of a multitude of manifestations of varying significance and relevance. It is these invisible realities, only to be discovered by inductive computation, by selection and construction, that are scientifically important in the study of culture."

2. History, Context, and Applications

Illuminative evaluation (Hamilton et al. 1977) has been in the forefront of the movement away from evaluation based heavily on preordinate designs, specification of objectives, operationalization of variables, the collection of more or less exclusively numerical data, and the primacy of statistical methods of analysis. While illuminative evaluation needs to be seen in the context of a vigorous critique of the traditional research paradigm used in evaluation, the chief priority since 1972 has not been on dismantling the previously dominant model but on practising and perfecting an investigative approach located within a different paradigm, which is a genuine, viable, and radical alternative.

Illuminative evaluation originated in work carried out at the Massachusetts Institute of Technology in 1967–1968 and at the University of Edinburgh in the early 1970s. The basic ideas and methods of working were largely discovered through trial and error, in relative ignorance of similar approaches. Discoveries of roots, connections, and overlaps swiftly followed. These helped to solidify and extend the approach which was first fully elaborated and designated as illuminative evaluation by Parlett and Hamilton (1972).

There are family resemblances to a broad variety of naturalistic enquiries in evaluation and to the participant observation-based fieldwork research into schools developed by Smith.

Illuminative evaluation is most often linked with responsive evaluation and shares with this approach concerns to inform decision makers; to represent the complexity and detail of programmes studied; and to use a variety of investigative techniques in order to achieve a portrayal of the system studied.

Illuminative evaluation has been applied in many different forms and contexts (and not only within education). There have been numerous studies in higher education settings, examining undergraduate life and subcultures, student assessment, laboratory instruction in the sciences and engineering, and experiments with new approaches to teaching. One study carried out retrospectively concerned a major innovation in undergraduate physics instruction that had failed (Friedman et al. 1976). On a larger scale, there has been a national study of mainstreaming or integration of visually impaired children in England and Wales (Jamieson et al. 1977); a study of the cost-effectiveness of an internationally sponsored community development and parent education project in rural Chile (Richards 1984); and a government-funded study of vocational preparation schemes in the United Kingdom. Major studies have also been made of open-plan schooling (Hamilton 1977) and of professional decision making in special education.

While a number of evaluation reports have been published (completely or in extract) most have circulated locally. Few have been confidential or restricted. Most (to the author's knowledge) have been well received. Over 120 persons have been given formal training in the approach by Parlett alone and a growing number of Ph.D. theses in several different countries have been based on the approach.

3. Negotiation and Setting Up the Study

In any exercise labelled "evaluation" there are questions regarding policy. Take the following examples: (a) Is this scheme worth trying to replicate elsewhere? (b) What improvements can be made in the running of the organization and the effectiveness of initiatives? (c) Is refunding desirable and on what basis should the effort be judged? (d) What have been the principal benefits attributable to the programme that was funded?

These are the kinds of questions that lead organizations, funding bodies, sponsors, and managers of programmes to consider having an evaluation carried out. Part of a comprehensive study must be to consider the circumstances of its being required. The illuminative evaluator places a premium on discovering: What is really at stake? Do the policy makers want to examine management problems, find a scapegoat, resolve a conflict, cut down a programme to size? And what

intentions do sponsors and others have for how the report will be used? To satisfy funding agencies, convince consumers (such as parents), reassure committees, boost the bargaining power of the director? These motives are not disparaged; they are part of the "real world" contexts in which evaluators have to operate.

In illuminative evaluation care and time is taken to surface and wherever possible make explicit the foundations of the study. The evaluator seeks to avoid becoming an unwitting tool of a single power base or pressure group. Illuminative evaluations require a high level of mutual trust if the more delicate (and usually more telling) policy questions are to be opened up to detailed scrutiny. Starting off a study on "the right foot", following extensive negotiation, has been found to be essential and not merely desirable, given the nature and priorities of the approach in action.

Illuminative evaluators treat as a major part of the method how to present the study and win confidence while maintaining its integrity; how to establish working contracts; and how to renegotiate, expanding or contracting the scope of work, if necessary, as the study proceeds.

4. Progressive Focusing and Theme Building

In parallel with the initial "negotiation phase" of a study is the "immersion" period: a time of rapid familiarization. Investigators listen and observe, ask numerous questions, read widely, consult a variety of individuals already knowledgeable with the system. Unless a basic familiarity is achieved there is little prospect of subsequent design decisions being adequate or of investigators winning the confidence of programme or organizational members.

Studies then become more selective, with more focused subsidiary investigations being carried out to explore particular themes in depth. Such themes may include problems frequently referred to by teaching assistants; particular sources of pride and felt satisfaction discerned among programme participants; topics avoided or glossed over by administrators; areas of consensus and disagreement among teachers; discrepancies between what is supposed to happen and what in fact happens at the level of day-to-day activities; issues that predominate in off-duty staff talk; and key assumptions about a programme's educational mission that seem to be unquestioned yet central to its operations. These "emerging themes" represent strands of observation and argument which give form and direction to the evolving study. They derive from knowledge gathered in the field as well as from preliminary review of relevant documents, reports of previous studies, and so on, and are "progressively focused" upon in greater detail as the study continues. New themes are added right up to the end of the study. Themes are not cast in permanent fashion but remain "interim" for as long as is compatible with the requirement also to achieve closure and to complete the study. Working themes are likely eventually to become chapter headings and subsections in the report, with the various "points" linked to each theme becoming individual paragraphs.

Perhaps the most distinctive feature of illuminative evaluation is its explicit and conscious concern with progressive focusing and accompanying distillation. In any relatively open-ended study which emphasizes detailed documentation, there is a surfeit of material and numerous possible ways to assemble and summarize it. The illuminative evaluator is like a historian attempting to write an account of a war. So much material is available, so many dimensions of the war-in-context can be covered that a simple commission could easily grow into a life work. The illuminative evaluator has the same obligation as the historian to make judicious selections, devise a manageable structure, and impose intelligent form and meaning to material he or she has gathered.

This form of interpretive work—choosing areas of concentration and key topics and framing the study around these in a series of midway conceptualizations—lies at the centre of illuminative evaluation practice. Progressive focusing on selected themes provides the management criteria for channelling investigative resources and also reduces the likelihood of "data overload" and "not being able to see the wood for the trees". The iterative recycling of emergent themes is also a route to achieving greater clarity, "thickness" of description, and enables the policy relevance of the emerging structure of argument to be selectively tested.

The refinement of themes also provides the procedural vehicle for a critical examination of themes and planning of further enquiries. Asking the questions: "What evidence can be cited?" and "What is the quality of the data being relied upon?" may point to the need for a different form of enquiry or some cross-checking by other methodological means. Such "triangulation" (a term drawn from surveying) refers to key events, processes, practices, outcomes, etc. being examined by different techniques, generating data of various kinds which when considered together give a powerful indication of accuracy and repeatability independently of the mode of enquiry.

5. The Analogy with Map Making

Illuminative evaluators are like map makers: their job is to represent the system studied and to condense information and analysis. There is continual to and fro movement between the reality to be depicted and the emerging representation of that reality. Like makers of maps, illuminative evaluators have to decide what to include and leave out. In the case of maps, the criteria are governed by the use to which the map will be put (e.g., meteorologists want isobars, political analysts want regional voting patterns) as well as by resource considerations—some information is simply too difficult or expensive to justify collection.

Illuminative evaluators have comparable decisions to reach: Who exactly will read the report, what do they need to know, what will constitute a sufficiently detailed analysis? If the report is long, with many diffuse themes, it is likely to be found irrelevant (like a needlessly cluttered map). On the other hand, a superficial report with little in it (an uninformative map) is equally a waste: it will be easily dismissed or, worse, used to justify simplistic policies. Choosing the appropriate level of detail, scope of enquiry, and apt themes, constitutes the creative work to be done.

The necessary activities of selection and organization are represented by critics of the approach as private, almost artistic processes which cannot be taught and learned as research methods. In practice this is not the case. Most people's "natural" way of mentally ordering everyday experience is to make connections, build some kind of "internal map" of what they are finding out, and to focus on matters of interest and importance to them. In other words, they operate somewhat like the observing and interpreting field investigator. Of course, the ordering of material, the weighing of alternative emerging themes, the self-aware review of inclusion and exclusion criteria, the scrupulous assessment of evidence, and much else that comprises the necessary work of illuminative studies, obviously go far beyond natural ways of knowing and may even contradict them (e.g., by earmarking data that do not fit preconceptions). However, the underlying basis for the necessary interpretive work does not appear to need learning from scratch; instead the capability needs to be revalidated (especially among social scientists taught to distrust their powers of discernment and commonsense ways of knowing), and also made more public and practised with reflexive rigour.

The analogy of map making is helpful in another respect. E. H. Carr, the historian, has written: "To praise a historian for his accuracy is like praising an architect for using well-seasoned timber or properly mixed concrete in his building. It is a necessary condition of his work, but not his essential function." The same goes for illuminative evaluators. A concern frequently expressed before (and only rarely after) an illuminative evaluation study is "How will we know what you say is accurate?" The same question directed at map makers might elicit the reply that once a map is made it can be checked against other sources of information, including the users' experience. Likewise with evaluation reports: those acquainted with the system can normally check most of its observations, challenge its conclusions, and certainly assess its usefulness as an attempt to capture a recognizable reality. This form of quality check is about as demanding as any.

Illuminative evaluation is, in summary, a way of carrying out an investigation into a working system, mapping it for the benefit of interested and responsible readerships. Investigators may serve as conduits—portrayers of individual and collective comment and opinion, summarizing suggestions for changes and system improvements. This "phenomenological mapping" overlays and interlocks with other accounts of the system developed—for example of its history and structure, its purposes and theories of practice, its resources and the use made of them, its stated intentions and the variety of actual consequences. A complete study provides a small atlas of different kinds of programme maps.

A fully successful illuminative evaluation is one which condenses a maximum amount of valid experience and informative commentary about the system studied into a readable report which stimulates talk and brings together key topics, unresolved questions, and practical thinking. Ideally the report is a freely circulating document; it commands respect from different constituencies as a faithful account of their working world; it is "eye-opening" to different groups or interests; and it facilitates substantive discussion and policy formation. Exceedingly hard though not impossible to bring about, such a result certainly is not achievable without utilizing the approach to its full, including careful negotiation; a custom-built design which evolves in the course of study; progressive focusing on to organizing themes; triangulation; the use of multiple enquiry techniques; maintaining the feelings and rights of those participating; attending closely to the ethics of investigation and reporting; writing lucidly for specific audiences; and taking into account the multiple contexts in which the report will represent an intervention.

Bibliography

Carr E H 1961 *What is History?* Macmillan, London

Friedman C P, Hirschi S, Parlett M R, Taylor E F 1976 The rise and fall of the personalized system of instruction in physics at Massachusetts Institute of Technology. *Am. J. Phys.* 44(3): 204–11

Hamilton D F 1977 *In Search of Structure: Essays from an Open Plan School.* Hodder and Stoughton, London

Hamilton D, Jenkins D, King C, MacDonald B, Parlett M R (eds.) 1977 *Beyond the Numbers Game: A Reader in Educational Evaluation.* Macmillan, London

Jamieson M, Parlett M R, Pocklington K 1977 *Towards Integration: A Study of Blind and Partially Sighted Children in Ordinary School.* NFER Publishing Co., Slough

Malinowski B 1961 *Argonauts of the Western Pacific.* Dutton, New York

Parlett M 1974 The new evaluation. *Trends Educ.* 34: 13–18

Parlett M 1981 Illuminative evaluation. In: Reason P, Rowan J (eds.) 1981 *Human Inquiry: A Sourcebook of New Paradigm Research.* Wiley, Chichester, pp. 219–26

Parlett M, Hamilton D 1972 Evaluation as illumination: A new approach to the study of innovatory programs. Occasional Paper No. 9, University of Edinburgh, Centre for Research in the Educational Sciences. Reprinted in: Glass G V (ed.) 1976 *Evaluation Studies Review Annual*, Vol. 1. Sage, New York

Richards H 1984 *The Evaluation of Cultural Action.* Macmillan, London

Naturalistic Evaluation

D. W. Dorr-Bremme

Evaluation is a name applied to several different endeavors in the field of education. Here, however, it means but one of these: the act of gathering information and juxtaposing it with some set of criteria to make judgments regarding the strengths and weaknesses, merits or worth of an educational innovation, program, or product. Naturalistic evaluation is any evaluation in this sense in which information is systematically acquired through a naturalistic mode of inquiry. The quintessential example of naturalistic inquiry is anthropological or sociological fieldwork, in which the researcher spends an extended time on site studying a group's culture or social life in naturally occurring circumstances. Thus, naturalistic inquiry can be distinguished from experimental inquiry and other modes of inquiry oriented by psychometric principles. Collectively, the latter are often associated with such terms as quantitative research, scientific research, hard data, variables, hypothesis testing, and statistical. In contrast, naturalistic inquiry—and so naturalistic evaluation—is commonly associated with such phrases as qualitative research, ethnographic research, fieldwork, case study method, soft data, ecological, descriptive, and interpretive (Bogdan and Biklen 1982).

It bears emphasizing that as most often used, the term naturalistic evaluation functions as a generic label. It references only one major aspect of an evaluation: the general approach followed by the evaluator in collecting and analyzing data. The label, then, entails nothing about the particular procedures or criteria employed to assign value or values to the program, innovation, and so on, etc., which is evaluated.

As the distinguishing feature of naturalistic evaluation, the naturalistic mode of inquiry deserves elaboration here. It consists of and is defined by (a) an orientation—a way of thinking about and portraying the activities of human social groups, and (b) an inquiry method—a systematic process for coming to understand human social activities in context.

1. The Naturalistic Orientation

The naturalistic orientation flows logically from theoretical concepts and research findings in several disciplines. Chief among these are anthropology and sociology. Increasingly, ethnomethodology (the study of everyday, practical reasoning), linguistics, and sociolinguistics or pragmatics have come to influence the naturalistic perspective. The philosophy known as symbolic interactionism has also influenced the naturalistic viewpoint.

Work from these fields warrants certain premises about the nature of humankind and human social endeavor. These premises, in turn, underlie the naturalistic orientation. They are as follows:

(a) Social groups—even those that exist side by side in a particular community or school; even those with overlapping memberships—can, and in many instances do, generate and sustain different "systems of standards for perceiving, believing, evaluating, and acting" (Goodenough 1971).

(b) Thus, their memberships routinely perceive and interpret phenomena differently and routinely act on the basis of their interpretations, whatever may be ascertainable as "fact" by standards of "scientific" measurement.

(c) A given social group's standards for sensibly and appropriately interpreting phenomena, ascribing meaning and value, and choosing actions can vary with features of the social context or situation—features which themselves are interpreted by members at successive levels of generality, for instance, this moment in this situation in this event in this phase of the program.

(d) The social life of any societal group, whatever its scope, is systematically ordered. Members' ways of conceptualizing and organizing their activities in many domains of social life are interdependent in dynamic, ecological balance, just as are the various life forms in an ecological niche.

(e) Despite the evident complexity of a group's organized social endeavor, the contexts, the standards for interpreting phenomena and selecting actions, and the relationships among societal elements that its members know and experience are accessible to nonmembers. They are apparent in the patterns that recur in time and across time in members' everyday talk and actions. They are clarified by members' accounts of their activities, especially those that they give as they engage in the activity in question.

These premises orient the naturalistic evaluator's (or researcher's) general goals and specific ways of thinking during inquiry. The naturalistic evaluator assumes that it is in terms of their own particular social realities, in terms of their own standards for appropriately making sense of phenomena and determining appropriate actions, that participants come to interpret, to enact, to judge, and so on, the program to be evaluated. From the naturalistic orientation, then, valid description and explication of the program at issue consists, at least initially, of reporting phenomena and how they function in relationship to one another from the perspectives of program participants. Therein lies the naturalistic evaluator's central goal. To achieve it, he or she takes reality and meaning as problematic as inquiry proceeds. This entails continually reflecting on such questions as: what contexts do participants in this setting know and act in terms of? By what features do they identify them? What meanings, values, and relationships do participants routinely ascribe to specific things, forms of behavior, social roles, and individuals? What standards do participants have for selecting actions that are accepted by other participants as appropriate and sensible in context? What does this person mean by what he or she is doing now? From participants' viewpoints, what relationships of function obtain among aspects of their immediate social environment and aspects of the larger worlds which impinge upon it?

In summary, the hallmarks of the naturalistic orientation are (a) a primary focus, during both inquiry and reporting, upon participants' perspectives; (b) a holistic approach, that is, an effort to understand and portray events in context, as they function in the web of interdependent relationships known to participants; and (c) a commitment to using the evaluator himself or herself as the primary instrument of data collection and analysis: a belief that only a human being operating experientially in the program setting can "peel back" and comprehend the layers of context, meaning, and systemic interdependency among phenomena that constitute participants' social realities.

2. The Naturalistic Method

The naturalistic inquiry method follows directly from the naturalistic orientation. The naturalistic evaluator begins inquiry with a few, very broad questions. In general, he or she wants to know "What is going on here that seems to be occasioned by, enacted in the name of, and functionally relevant to the program at issue?" Other, only slightly more specific questions, are usually framed in the light of the program's nature, the evaluation's intended purposes, and/or the concerns and interests of various evaluation audiences. Having established these initial questions, the naturalistic evaluator begins a cycle of inquiry steps that recurs for the duration of the effort. These steps consist of (a) gathering data on site, (b) analyzing and reflecting on the data, (c) refining and posing new (usually more specific) questions to guide continuing inquiry, and (d) returning to the site(s) for further data collection. In this cycle, hunches and hypotheses are successively generated, examined in view of the increasing data, and validated, reshaped, or disconfirmed.

Nearly anything the naturalistic evaluator notices or experiences on site can become data. He or she observes and listens to what program participants and relevant others do and say in their everyday lives, attending to when and where they do and say it. Planned interviews and impromptu conversations with participants are also important information sources. Audiotapes of interviews and videotapes of key activities can be made. Often, too, formal and informal documents are read and analyzed.

In narrative field notes, the naturalistic evaluator records what participants say as fully and as literally as possible. He or she also records personal impressions and inferences, carefully keeping these separate from the record of participants' words and deeds. At the end of a day on site, these notes are reviewed and filled in as necessary. Then, they are examined to identify emerging themes and patterns: phrases, actions and action sequences, expressed thoughts and feelings, and so on, that seem to recur in the data and to fit together. The evaluator also looks for apparent contradictions and discrepancies in the field-note record, pinpoints topics on which information seems incomplete, and tries to monitor how his or her preconceptions and biases may be influencing the accumulating record and evolving interpretations of "what is going on."

As the naturalistic evaluator reflects on his or her field notes in these ways, hunches and further questions suggest themselves. These serve to direct the ongoing inquiry when the evaluator returns to the program site(s). And as the evaluator repeats these steps and gathers additional and more detailed information, the evaluator's first, tentative hunches evolve into firmer hypotheses and, with still further inquiry, into findings.

Naturalistic evaluators disagree on whether reports should provide more than description and explication of the program which emphasizes participants' perspectives. Some argue for doing only this, allowing various evaluation audiences to reach their own judgments of value. Others are willing to make evaluative judgments, usually with the caveat that criteria from diverse frames of reference be used for doing so.

3. Current Status and Uses

Naturalistic evaluation remains less common than evaluation based on the experimental and psychometric traditions. Nevertheless, it has been conducted in education with increasing frequency since the mid-1970s. Its wider acceptance and use have been stimulated by broadened definitions of evaluation and the emergence of diverse evaluation models (see Guba and Lincoln 1981 pp. 1–22 for a brief history).

Many of the more recent evaluation models have called for more open-ended and flexible inquiry, an emphasis on program activities and processes, orientation to the evaluation audiences' specific information needs, and multiple criteria for assigning value(s) to program components. Naturalistic evaluation is more consonant with these emphases than with those of the more conventional models, in which program outcomes are measured against formally stated program objectives.

More broadly, naturalistic evaluation is a strong approach when the purpose of evaluation is to refine and improve the enactment of a program, to increase the effectiveness of its management, and/or to examine its implementation or adaptation in particular localities. It is also useful when the principal objective is to improve the technical assistance or support services provided by program sponsors to participants in local settings. Frequently, naturalistic evaluation in a few of many program sites is used to prepare for, supplement, or follow up a larger evaluation using survey and test-score measures.

The advantages of naturalistic evaluation for the above purposes are several. The naturalistic evaluator typically provides richly detailed description and holistic explication of program processes and outcomes as they occur amidst the complexity of the "real world." The naturalistic approach is likely to identify program effects and influences on the program that are missed in evaluations oriented by experimental and/or psychometric premises, and by less theoretically informed and systematic "qualitative" methods as well. And since naturalistic evaluation portrays program processes and effects in terms consonant with participants' ways of experiencing reality, it enables program managers and sponsors to act on the evaluation in ways that take into account and respond to the needs, concerns, and viewpoints of participants in local settings.

While the advantages of naturalistic evaluation are many, it has some practical disadvantages. Naturalistic inquiry requires considerable amounts of time and labor. It tends, therefore, to be costly—a practical disadvantage in most circumstances. In particular, costs tend to restrict the number of settings the naturalistic evaluator can study thoroughly. This becomes a drawback when the number of program settings is great, since it is then difficult for the naturalistic evaluator to provide data that meet the usual standards for generalizability. Furthermore, where evaluation information is required in a short time, the naturalistic approach can be impractical. Some useful impressions can be gleaned quickly by holding the naturalistic orientation in mind and abbreviating the number of inquiry cycles. But to comprehend program activities validly (that is, from participants' perspectives and holistically) is nearly impossible in a brief period. In addition, naturalistic inquiry generates great amounts of narrative data: reducing, analyzing, and reporting it can take from two to three times the period spent in data collection. All this helps to explain why naturalistic evaluation is most often undertaken as an adjunct or supplement in evaluations based principally on statistically manipulable measures. Some exclusively naturalistic evaluations have been done, however, of both national and local programs. And in general, naturalistic evaluation has become an increasingly important alternative in the repertoire of evaluation inquiry.

Bibliography

Bogdan R C, Biklen S K 1982 *Qualitative Research for Education: An Introduction to Theory and Methods.* Allyn and Bacon, Boston, Massachusetts

Goodenough W H 1971 *Culture, Language, and Society*, Addison-Wesley Modular Publications No. 7. Addison-Wesley, Reading, Massachusetts

Guba E G 1978 *Toward a Methodology of Naturalistic Inquiry* in *Educational Evaluation*, CSE Monograph Series in Evaluation No. 8. Center for the Study of Evaluation, University of California, Los Angeles, California

Guba E G, Lincoln Y S 1981 *Effective Evaluation: Improving the Usefulness of Evaluation Results through Responsive and Naturalistic Approaches.* Jossey-Bass, San Francisco, California

Spradley J P 1980 *Participant Observation.* Holt, Rinehart and Winston, New York

Qualitative Evaluation

G. Willis

Qualitative curriculum evaluation, also known as "educational criticism," cannot be defined by a fixed set of procedures, nor by a specific kind of data. It is not an effort to develop universal, invariant, or even unambiguous knowledge and valuations about educational situations and thus can be contrasted sharply with the typical positivistic pursuits which have dominated Western educational research during much of the twentieth century. Nor should it be confused with forms of research (such as some kinds of ethnography) which deal with qualitative data but from a scientific or technological perspective, thus deriving limited valuations or no valuations at all.

Consistent with, and partially developed in its modern form, from such sources as phenomenology, hermeneutics, and critical theory, qualitative curriculum evaluation aims at expanding reflective human understanding of specific educational situations and promoting moral action within these situations and their social contexts. To do so, qualitative curriculum evaluators immerse themselves in educational situations, not only to discover their tangible characteristics, but also to discern personally their salient but intangible qualities. Each evaluator derives meanings and valuations (including tendencies to action) which he or she shares with others in order to provide new and multiple perspectives on each situation under investigation. However, since neither meanings nor valuations exist apart from context, qualitative evaluators extend their investigations to the personal and social contexts of specific situations. Hence, qualitative curriculum evaluation can be defined as reflective effort to develop the fullest possible range of knowledge (including personal knowledge) about specific educational situations, and to derive meanings and valuations about situations within the fullest possible range of knowledge about their contexts in order to enlarge understanding and to promote moral action. To fulfill these aims, qualitative curriculum evaluation treats curriculum in the fullest possible way, as the experience of the student. In general, it encourages reflection by using naturalistic methodology, proceeding through a case study format, and incorporating four phases of criticism (observation, description, interpretation, and appraisal).

Since qualitative curriculum evaluation includes empiricism and employs enumeration whenever appropriate, it cannot be differentiated from other forms of curriculum evaluation by reference to quantification or lack thereof. Other forms of evaluation consistent with a scientific or technological perspective ordinarily strive for objective, usually hypothetical–deductive knowledge about educational situations by limiting themselves to controlled research designs and statistically derived generalizations about empirical data only. A major contrast between qualitative and scientific or technological studies is, therefore, that the latter are often neither about the fullness of educational situations nor valuations. Their principal concern is precise measurement of specified characteristics of situations. For instance, they may provide evidence about whether certain goals of a program or curriculum have been realized, but may say nothing, in and of themselves, about many other matters, such as whether the goals were worth attempting to realize in the first place. Though the latter kind of study has been used extensively in Western education during the twentieth century, qualitative curriculum evaluation is actually much older. In fact, in rudimentary, undeveloped form it is the means used by virtually all people to derive meanings and valuations in their own lives. Since the mid-1970s it has been developed and refined especially by advocates in the United States and the United Kingdom and has made substantial inroads into the former dominance of self-limited scientific and technologically oriented evaluation studies.

1. Origins

For centuries people have made decisions about how to live their lives and what to study in schools. In so far as most of these decisions have been made in naturalistic, informal ways, the origins of qualitative curriculum evaluation are lost in antiquity. However, the curriculum itself can be conceived in several different ways, and it can be evaluated formally in different ways more or less consistent with these conceptions. The curriculum has been commonly conceived throughout history as subject matter or the course of studies. As subject matter it can be evaluated in terms of how accurately it reflects the underlying reality of the universe and how logically it is arranged. This kind of metaphysical and epistemological analysis of subject matter was for centuries the principal means of evaluating the curriculum in Western education. The curriculum can also be conceived as the activities which students undertake in schools, and it can be evaluated in terms of the utilitarian results of these activities. This point of view underlies the scientific or technological orientation to curriculum evaluation. It has developed primarily in the twentieth century, abetted by the testing and measurement movement, and recently has been associated with efforts to improve programs and promote accountability.

A third way of conceiving the curriculum has also developed in the twentieth century. Arising originally from the thought of John Dewey and progressive education, it has recently been shaped by other sources. In this point of view the curriculum is the experience of the individual student. This experience is influenced by the entire environment to which the student is exposed, including the course of studies, and it is comprised of both an external side (the overt activities which the student undertakes) and an internal side (the beliefs, ideas, attitudes, feelings, and the like which the student holds or undergoes). In this view the curriculum can be evaluated by assessing the quality of the student's experience, but this assessment must include all phases of the entire interaction, including the student's autonomous participation.

In this view, evaluation depends on the ability of the evaluator to apprehend the overall situation adequately and fully, to portray it accurately and compellingly, and to make valuations about it wisely. Hence, qualitative curriculum evaluation updates the ancient, informal means of making decisions about schools through personal observations by refining the evaluator's essentially artistic skills of perception and portrayal, and essentially philosophic skills of critical analysis (now extended from subject matter only, to the fullness of educational situations, including contexts and the experiences of individual students). Although there are many examples of qualitative, naturalistic studies of schools extending back to the beginnings of the twentieth century and beyond, the first modern statement to argue that curriculum evaluation is, in fact, educational criticism dealing with the experience of students was probably made by Mann (1968–69). In the 1970s books began to appear taking this same position. Hamilton (1976) pointed out how typically technological–utilitarian evaluations borrow methods developed to measure agricultural production, and with several colleagues (Hamilton et al. 1977) collected a series of essays further extending this critique and developing the modern notion of naturalistic evaluation. Willis (1978) described the art of educational criticism as "qualitative evaluation" and provided a series of essays, many of them written by practising critics, which further defined the theoretical

basis for, and offered concrete examples of, educational criticism. However the leading spokesperson for this point of view has been Eisner, who in an influential essay (Eisner 1977) described the skills essential to high quality, formal educational criticism and two years later published the first book (Eisner 1979) to develop a complete rationale for educational criticism. In another influential essay (Eisner 1981) he clearly differentiated artistic and scientific approaches to educational research and evaluation. Such books and articles provide a modern basis for qualitative curriculum evaluation as educational criticism, though many other authors, especially in the 1980s, have added their own statements.

2. Procedures and Aims

The methodology of qualitative curriculum evaluation is naturalistic. Naturalistic methodology has been described at length by Guba and Lincoln (1981), who define it in terms of two dimensions. First, the evaluator attempts to encounter the situation as it is. The point is to change the situation as little as possible through the evaluator's presence or by deliberately altering the situation to make it conform to a preordinate research design, which may, in fact, deal with only part of it. Second, the evaluator brings as few preconceptions as possible to the situation. The point is to let meanings and valuations arise as fully as possible out of the situation itself. Naturalistic methodology leaves open a wide variety of ways of encountering the situation fully. The evaluator may or may not attempt to gain an insider's perspective by becoming an organic part of the situation, but in either case the evaluator observes the situation at sufficient length to gain a thorough understanding of it and gleans additional evidence about it from a variety of sources.

Understandings developed naturalistically are usually reported in a case study format. (For a discussion of the case study, see Stake 1978.) Case studies do not attempt to report generalizations abstracted from specific situations. Rather, they attempt to portray the truth about specific situations concretely, vividly, and in context. This is not to say that an evaluator can never suggest any generalizations through a case study nor that an audience cannot infer any generalizations, but it is to say that meanings and valuations conveyed by vivid portrayals of specific situations must be carefully scrutinized for how well they fit the particulars of any other situations.

The phases of criticism present in any thorough evaluation study have been described by McCutcheon (1979). These phases are always interrelated but tend to be more fully developed and carefully balanced in educational criticism than in scientific or technological evaluation studies. The first of these phases, observation, includes whatever means the evaluator uses to gain information and insight. This phase may therefore include not only the direct observations of the evaluator, but also interviewing, the examination of records, the use of unobtrusive measures, and the evaluator's reflective consideration of all evidence. The second phase, description, is how the evaluator chooses to portray the situation. Here the evaluator must choose from among the many things which could be portrayed and the many ways of creating this portrayal. The aim is communicating to the audience of the evaluation significant truths about the situation itself and its larger context. Descriptions are usually written narratives but may include oral, visual, and other forms of communication as well. The third phase, interpretation, is the ascribing of meaning to the situation. (For a detailed discussion of interpretation, see McCutcheon 1981.) Meanings may arise either internally or externally to the situation. Internal meanings arise when participants ask themselves what it means to them personally to live within the situation. External meanings arise when specifics of the situation are compared with ideas, theories, other events, or other situations which provide new ways of viewing or understanding the situation. Both internal and external meanings are ways of attributing significance in context. The fourth phase, appraisal, is the directly evaluative part of educational criticism. Despite the tendency of scientific and technological studies merely to report purportedly objective facts about a situation, there simply is no evaluation until someone derives valuations about it. This means that the critic must comment on the *merit* and *worth* of the overall situation or its parts. Merit deals with value in terms of how well done something is; worth with the value of doing it in the first place. In general, the best studies make clear the basis for the critic's valuations. All four phases are present in any good critical study, which itself can be evaluated in terms of the adequacy of the fit between evidence and situation, the internal consistency of the study's various parts, the significance of its meanings and valuations, and the compellingness of its portrayals.

Since qualitative curriculum evaluation is thus a way of making public the fullest possible range of knowledge about educational situations and their contexts, its general aims of enlarging understanding and promoting moral action are actually one and the same and can best be realized when different insights are openly portrayed and actively tested. Therefore, educational criticism is not limited to formal evaluators; virtually anyone—especially teachers and students—may engage in it, and all honestly held and openly shared meanings and valuations contribute to the realization of these aims (Willis 1981). In this sense qualitative curriculum evaluation is not merely a way of assessing the curriculum, however conceived, but also a means of increasing the quality of the educative experience of all those who engage in it.

Bibliography

Eisner E W 1977 On the uses of educational connoisseurship and criticism for evaluating classroom life. *Teach. Coll. Rec.* 78: 345–58

Eisner E W 1979 *The Educational Imagination: On the Design and Evaluation of School Programs.* Macmillan, New York

Eisner E W 1981 On the differences between scientific and artistic approaches to qualitative research. *Educ. Res.* 10 (4): 5–9

Guba E G, Lincoln Y S 1981 *Effective Evaluation: Improving the Usefulness of Evaluation Results Through Responsive and Naturalistic Approaches.* Jossey-Bass, San Francisco, California

Hamilton D 1976 *Curriculum Evaluation.* Open Books, London

Hamilton D, MacDonald B, King C, Jenkins D, Parlett M (eds.) 1977 *Beyond the Numbers Game: A Reader in Educational Evaluation.* Macmillan, Basingstoke

McCutcheon G 1979 Educational criticism: Methods and application. *J. Curr. Theor.* 1 (2): 5–25

McCutcheon G 1981 On the interpretation of classroom observations. *Educ. Res.* 10 (5): 5–10

Mann J S 1968–69 Curriculum criticism. *Curr. Theory Network* 2: 2–14

Stake R E 1978 The case study method in social inquiry. *Educ. Res.* 7 (2): 5–8

Willis G (ed.) 1978 *Qualitative Evaluation: Concepts and Cases in Curriculum Criticism.* McCutchan, Berkeley, California

Willis G 1981 Democratization of curriculum evaluation. *Educ. Leadership* 38 (8): 630–32

Educational Connoisseurship and Criticism

T. E. Barone

Educational connoisseurship and *educational criticism* are terms coined by Eisner (1977) to describe two facets of an arts-based approach to educational inquiry. Connoisseurship refers to a capacity to appreciate subtle and important qualities in educational phenomena. Criticism is the means of disclosing these appreciations, usually in the form of a critical essay.

1. Educational Connoisseurship

The connoisseur of fine arts is someone whose perceptive powers have been highly developed through intense experiences with the products of various modes of artistic expression. He or she is able to recognize and appreciate the significant nuances within the art object.

Eisner (1985) argues that connoisseurship also extends to more mundane areas of life such as wine-tasting, sports, and other aspects of nature and society. One can develop a level of connoisseurship in educational matters by becoming a sensitive student of curriculum artifacts and classroom life. This demands, first, attention to curricular and pedagogical phenomena, and secondly, the opportunity to compare the features found in one setting or object with others found elsewhere. This can result in refined powers of discrimination and a set of ideas that allow the critic to place what is seen into an intelligible context.

2. Educational Criticism

The perceptual activities of the educational connoisseur are essentially private in nature; educational criticism is the art of publicizing what the connoisseur has appreciated. Usually this disclosure takes the form of a written text, especially an essay.

A critique will often be a blend of two modes of language. The first mode is used when the critic aims to publicize his or her emotional and intellectual responses to the patterns of qualities experienced. This is the metaphorical mode, with language that is artful, suggestive, connotative, evocative, literary. Only figurative language possesses the power to allow a foreign audience direct imaginary access to these experiences, through the rhythms evoked in the structure and form of the writing, by the imagery within the words and phrasing, and so forth.

At other points the critic's narrative requires an explicit, denotative, linear mode of language, one that often takes the form of propositional statements. Factors that determine the quality and manner of the blending of these language modes include the nature of the intended audiences and the talents and proclivities of the critic.

3. Structural Dimensions of Educational Criticism

Each of these language modes is also associated with certain structural dimensions of the critique. McCutcheon (1976) has identified three such dimensions: description, interpretation, and assessment. These dimensions are useful for analytical purposes although, in fact, each dimension implies the others to some extent. For example, there is always assessment implicit in description.

Within the descriptive dimension the critic attempts vividly to portray, or render salient, qualities within curriculum artifacts or educational events. The critic's task is thus to re-educate the readers' perceptions enabling them to experience vicariously various aspects of these artifacts or events, and to help them to see aspects that would otherwise be missed. Description is best accomplished using the metaphorical mode of language.

In the interpretative dimension the critic attempts to make sense of the qualities described. Critics have cited the notion of "thick description" as crucial to the role of interpretation in criticism. The critic attempts to explicate the "deep structure" of educational phenomena perceived, construing their significance by viewing them as part of a nexus of social meaning.

Interpretation may involve placing features of an intended curriculum or ongoing program within an historical context or even drawing on a variety of theories from the social sciences for illumination. The interpretative dimension often requires a language that is denotative and discursive, comprised of propositional statements, as does the third dimension, evaluation.

Both the descriptive and interpretative dimensions can be found within science-based modes of qualitative educational inquiry (although usually in forms different from those found in criticism). The evaluative dimension most clearly distinguishes it from those other inquiry modes. Proponents of criticism argue that appraisal is also implicit in the work of social scientists (just as appraisal is implicit in the descriptive and interpretative dimensions of educational criticism). But it is also the task of the educational critic to *explicitly* appraise features of the critical object according to personally held educational criteria. These criteria may even be spelled out in order to make the perspective of the critic more obvious to the reader, and itself open to criticism. In reading an educational criticism, one should be aware of the voice of the critic speaking about educational phenomena from within a distinct set of educational values. The reader should, therefore, be in a better position to judge the persuasiveness of the critic's appraisal of those curriculum materials or educational practices.

4. Two Categories of Educational Criticism

Two distinct categories of educational criticism are identifiable, based on the kinds of educational phenomena treated within each. Biological metaphors have been borrowed to label these categories: the in vitro or "test tube" category of criticism, and the in vivo or "in life" type. Within the former the critic analyzes curricular phenomena such as program blueprints, sets of plans and intentions, curriculum materials of all sorts, or the physical surroundings in a school or classroom, all *apart* from their operation or usage in educational events. These materials are treated in some ways as analogous to pieces of plastic art such as paintings and sculpture, or to literary texts, or to architecture.

Examples of in vitro criticism are few in number. Prominent examples are by Vallance (1977), who applied a set of guidelines distilled from critical descriptions of paintings to a curriculum package called "The Great Plains Experience," and Munby (1979) who reviewed the curriculum "Philosophy for Children." Both critically appraised the materials as a completed work, a static artifact. Both also expressed some discomfort about this approach since program plans and materials usually undergo a process of adaptation, implementation, and modulation by a teacher, and students seldom see the curriculum in the form examined by the critic.

In vivo criticism takes into account that materials exist not in a vacuum but as an integral part of a usually complex educational landscape. In vivo critics thus focus on the curriculum-in-use, or the experienced curriculum: the transactions that occur within the lives of people in schools and classrooms. Unlike paintings, sculptures, or pieces of architecture, the "objects" of concern are events that are played out spatio-temporally, like dances or dramas. Even further, the events analyzed by in vivo critics are "actual" rather than staged. Educational criticism may, therefore, contain features found in social criticism as well as art criticism. Genres of literary nonfiction are potential sources of strategies for effectively criticizing the experienced curriculum (Barone 1980).

Usually the focus of in vivo criticism is an ongoing education program. Individual examples of in vivo critiques include Donmoyer (1980) and Barone (1987). Collections of in vivo critiques are included in Eisner (1985), and issues of *Daedalus* (1981, 1983) devoted to high school and outstanding school arts programs. Another collection of essays that closely resemble in vivo criticism can be found in Lightfoot (1983), although the author prefers the term "social science portraiture."

5. The Critical Process

An educational critic seldom enters the critical process with a preconceived set of hypotheses to be tested, or preformulated questions to be answered, or with a precise set of methodological procedures to be employed. Instead, both the emergent pattern of inquiry and the form and substance of the final product are highly dependent on the unique interactions between the educational perspective of the critic and the phenomena confronted in the particular setting. Nevertheless, several phases have been identified in the process (Barone 1982).

When the educational critic first confronts the critical phenomena there is an initial haziness: the qualities are not yet subordinate to an explicit overall structure or pattern and so appear to be random. In the second phase, relationships between various phenomena begin to be perceived and tentative patterns of qualities discerned. Only in phase 3 does the process climax, as a theme emerge as a mediator for structuring the phenomena that besiege the critic. In phase 4 the thematic structure serves to guide the inquiry and writing tasks, while simultaneously growing in clarity and definition itself. The implications of this controlling idea are "teased out" as it serves to select from among, and reveal relationships between, qualitative phenomena. It also becomes a premise for inferring subthemes.

Finally, in phase 5, closure is reached and the critique is judged adequate and complete.

6. Issues of Credibility and Generalizability

Opponents to the legitimation of educational criticism as a research genre have objected to the subjective nature of the inquiry approach. Its findings, they submit, are highly suspect due to a lack of rigorous methodological safeguards to insure elimination of personal biases and distortions. Proponents have responded by noting that there are value judgments, and hence subjectivity, involved in all forms of research, including science-based research. These value judgments are more implicit and less obvious, but nevertheless unavoidable, in several phases of science-based research: in the formation of the research question, in the choice of tools to be employed, in the interpretations of information collected (McCutcheon 1976 p. 65). Educational criticism may, therefore, possess the advantage of avoiding the illusion of objectivity inherent in other inquiry modes.

Proponents of educational criticism view science-based research as undergirded by a false epistemology, one that honors the correspondence theory of truth. In such research the aim is to discover reality apart from the human mind and to represent this unmediated reality in a statement of findings. Proponents hold that the meaning of phenomena is inevitably construed, and thereby influenced, by previous experience and present perspective. The educational critic may, however, strive to promote a type of intersubjectivity through his or her critique, persuading readers of its credibility and usefulness. Eisner (1985) has cited two processes that are important if an individual critique is to receive this "consensual validation." These are (a) structural corroboration and (b) referential adequacy.

Structural corroboration concerns the coherence of the evidence and arguments presented by the critic. Have general statements and opinions been supported by evidence that builds into a persuasive (i.e., unified and coherent) picture? Have pieces of evidence been effectively assembled to create a structured pattern, a comprehensive entity of information?

Referential adequacy means that new insights attained through educational connoisseurship must be based on empirical phenomena observable by others and conveyed in a critique that adequately refers to those phenomena. Referential adequacy is most appropriately applied to criticisms in which the audience has direct access to the object or situation criticized, allowing them to check the relationship between the critic's subject matter and his or her rendering of it.

Donmoyer (1981) suggested that even a lack of direct access need not present an insurmountable problem for criticism in regard to its credibility. The understanding of a critical text is seen as a means to an end rather than an end in itself. The credibility of a piece of criticism lies in its usefulness for promoting in the reader a "psychological generalization" process that is distinct from the kind of nomothetic generalization found in science-based research. The latter kind of research is concerned with the discovery and/or construction of general abstract theories. Psychological generalization, on the other hand, is concerned with creating anticipatory images in the reader of a criticism. Having confronted these images in a criticism, the reader can then assess their appropriateness for other educational situations to which he or she does have direct access.

7. Critics and Audiences

Advocates of educational connoisseurship and criticism see a potential value in its use for a variety of educational constituencies. Beneficiaries might include teachers who desire insightful feedback on their pedagogical methods, administrators and policy makers who make complex decisions on educational matters, parents who would like a fuller picture of the school activities engaged in by their children, and members of the general public who need to be brought closer to the complexities of education than lists of test scores can bring them.

Who, then is the educational connoisseur and critic? Eisner (1985) sees criticism less as a role than as a function. Despite the seemingly elitist connotations of the labels, the connoisseur/critic need not be a member of a "privileged" cadre of evaluators but might be a student, administrator, school board member, or university professor. Peer criticism among teacher colleagues within institutions might lead to more effective pursuance of educational aims. Anyone familiar with schooling is an educational connoisseur to some extent, and can thus aspire to educational criticism. Indeed, Gray (1981) has argued that the term "educational criticism" has clarified and made visible what many practitioners and supervisors have long engaged in under other names. Careful observation, qualitative

interpretation and assessment of practice already occur in many educational institutions, although usually in forms less elaborate and polished than those found in published educational criticisms.

Bibliography

Barone T E 1980 Effectively critiquing the experienced curriculum: Clues from the "new journalism". *Curr. Inq.* 10 (1): 29–53

Barone T E 1982 The Meadowhurst experience: Phases in the process of educational criticism. *J. Curr. Theor.* 4 (1): 156–70

Barone T E 1987 On equality, visibility, and the fine arts program in a black elementary school: An example of educational criticism. *Curr. Inq.* 17 (4): 421–46

Daedalus 1981 Vol. 110 (4) (issue devoted to America's schools: Portraits and perspectives)

Daedalus 1983 Vol. 112 (3) (issue devoted to the arts and humanities in America's schools)

Donmoyer R B 1980 The evaluator as artist. *J. Curr. Theor* 2 (2): 12–26

Donmoyer R B 1981 Alternative conceptions of generalization and verification for educational research: Toward a rationale for qualitative ideographic inquiry. Doctoral dissertation, Stanford University

Eisner E W 1977 On the uses of educational connoisseurship and criticism for evaluating classroom life. *Teach. Coll. Rec.* 78: 345–58

Eisner E W 1985 *The Educational Imagination: On the Design and Evaluation of School Programs*, 2nd edn. Macmillan, New York

Gray J U 1981 Vintage connoisseurship: A practitioner's view of educational criticism. *Curr. Inq.* 11 (4): 343–58

Lightfoot S L 1983 *The Good High School: Portraits in Character and Culture*. Basic Books, New York

McCutcheon G 1976 The disclosure of classroom life. Doctoral dissertation, Stanford University

Munby H 1979 Philosophy for children: An example of curriculum review and criticism. *Curr. Inq.* 9 (3): 229–49

Vallance E 1977 The landscape of "The Great Plains Experience": An application of curriculum criticism. *Curr. Inq.* 7: 87–105

Curriculum Evaluation Strategies

Needs Assessment Studies

T. M. Suarez

Needs assessment is an information-gathering and analysis process which results in the identification of the needs of individuals, groups, institutions, communities, or societies. In education the process of needs assessment has been used, for example, to identify the needs of students for instruction in a given subject area; to determine weaknesses in students' overall academic achievement; to determine the needs of teachers for additional training; and to determine the future needs of local, regional, and national educational systems. It is the intent of needs assessments to identify areas in which deficits exist or desired performance has not been attained. The results of needs assessments are then used for further action such as planning or remediation to improve the situation.

Educational needs have been assessed and analyzed for centuries. However, formalized assessments of educational needs were not conducted on a widespread basis until the middle of the twentieth century (Suarez 1981). At that time, public and professional demands for more systematic and accountable processes of providing education led to the emergence of information-based models for educational planning and evaluation. This was particularly true in the United States where widespread federal aid to education with accompanying accountability requirements was instituted in the mid-1960s. Among the information-based processes which emerged during that time was the systematic determination of needs as a basis for program planning and development. This process was called needs assessment.

Since then development and activity regarding needs assessment have been intense. Many educational needs assessments have been conducted to meet an array of intents using a wide variety of designs and procedures. Because of the wide range of situations in which needs assessments have been found to be appropriate, there does not appear to be a single set of concepts that can be used to describe the process. Instead, needs assessments are described or designed on the basis of their purpose and the types of needs that are identified.

1. The Purposes of Needs Assessments

Providing information for planning is the most common reason given for conducting needs assessments. Needs assessments for planning may result in the identification of goals, the determination of the extent to which desired goals are being achieved, or the specification of areas in which efforts and resources should be placed. Such assessments may be used to develop plans for immediate action or to develop long-range plans for the future.

The diagnosis or identification of problems or weaknesses is another common purpose for needs assessments. Needs assessments for this purpose focus on identifying the areas in which the educational process or system is ineffective so that remedial actions may be taken.

Needs assessments are components of several evaluation models. These assessments are part of the evaluation process and may have as their purpose determining areas of weakness prior to the implementation of a given form of instruction or treatment, determining gaps in implementation, or determining the status of performance at intervals during the development or implementation of a treatment. The results of these assessments become part of the evaluation findings or, in the case of needs assessments prior to treatment, the basis upon which the evaluation criteria for judging the effectiveness of treatments are determined.

Needs assessments are also conducted to hold educational institutions accountable for their efforts. The most common forms of these types of needs assessments are mandated large-scale assessments of student educational outcomes. Results of these assessments are used to determine if the educational efforts of schools or school systems are effective and to identify subject areas or locations in which educational achievements are less than desired.

2. The Concept of Need

To understand a needs assessment it is necessary to understand the concept of need upon which the process is based. This requires an understanding of the definition used in the study for the term "need," a specification of whose needs are of interest and the type of need that is to be identified.

A variety of concepts of the term "need" are used in

both the discussions and practice of needs assessment. Controversy regarding the definition of "need" for needs assessments, together with a proliferation of studies using different definitions, has limited the development of universally accepted conceptual or theoretical models of the process. The majority of needs assessment studies, however, has been based on a variation of one of three definitions of the term "need."

The most widely used definition of "need" for needs assessments is that of a discrepancy. This definition, introduced by Kaufman (1972), suggests that needs are areas in which actual status is less than targeted status. Targeted status has come to encompass ideals, norms, preferences, expectations, and perceptions of what ought to be. Needs assessments based on this definition require procedures for selecting or determining targeted status, gathering information to determine current status relative to the target status, and comparing the two to discover discrepancies and identify needs.

Another commonly used definition of need is that of a want or preference. Identification of needs does not require the determination of a discrepancy. Instead, it requires determining the perceptions of needs of selected individuals or groups. Although there are writers who oppose the use of this definition, many needs assessments are based on this definition, particularly in those situations where public and professional opinion regarding needs are used as a basis for establishing educational goals or policy.

A more stringent and less used concept of need for needs assessment studies is that of a deficit. A need is said to exist if the absence or a deficiency in the area of interest is harmful. Scriven has expanded this definition to describe a need as a state in which a minimum satisfactory level has not been reached or cannot be maintained. Few needs assessment studies have been conducted using this definition due to the difficulty in determining the point at which a deficit or minimum satisfactory level can be said to exist.

In addition to understanding the definition of need that is used, it is also necessary to know whose needs or what needs are to be identified. When conducting needs assessments in education the needs of participants (individuals, subgroups, or groups), the educational institution, or society at large may be of interest. Needs may also be determined in relation to such aspects of the educational process as implementation, availability of resources, or facilities. Related to the target of the needs assessments are the types of needs that will be determined. Needs are usually described as those which are of an outcome nature, for example, performance or basic needs, and those which contribute to outcomes, for example, treatment or incremental needs.

3. Needs Assessment Strategies and Procedures

Because needs assessments are conducted for a variety of reasons in many different settings and to identify many types of needs, the strategies and procedures used

to conduct such assessments also vary a great deal. There are, however, several procedures or stages which are common to many needs assessment studies.

3.1 Preparing to Conduct a Needs Assessment

Like other forms of inquiry, preparing to conduct a needs assessment requires decisions to conduct such a study, determining the purposes the assessment is to serve, and delimiting the areas in which the study is to concentrate. In addition, because educational needs are based to a large extent on the values of the institution or society in which they are to be determined, procedures must be incorporated into the process to ensure that these values are represented. This is most often accomplished by involving a variety of interested or involved individuals or groups in the process. A preparation activity for these assessments is the identification of those who will be involved in or affected by the study and the procurement of their commitment to participate.

3.2 Determining the Standards by which Needs will be Identified

When planning is the purpose of a needs assessment, educational goals are often the standards against which status is compared to determine needs. A common practice for these types of needs assessments is the determination of goals prior to the assessment of needs. When goals have been determined, the needs assessment is then conducted to determine if there are discrepancies between identified goals and current status. The process of goal determination involves identifying the individuals and/or groups who should participate in the determination of goals and involving them in the process. Two major procedures for goal determination are usually used: (a) generating the set of goals, and (b) selecting goals from present lists of goal statements. When goals already exist in the area of interest, this step is omitted and current status is compared to the existing goals.

Norms are another standard often used in the determination of educational needs. The norms most often used are those associated with standardized tests. Needs are determined by comparing performance on the tests with existing norms, that is, the performance of the population upon which the test was standardized. Other norms used for needs assessments are previous behaviors of similar groups, for example, number of graduates entering college in previous years.

Minimum satisfactory level is a standard not often used but widely advocated for needs assessments. Determining minimum satisfactory levels of performance requires determining the level of performance at which goals cannot be met or harm due to educational deficits will be the result. These types of standards are most often applied in biological and medical situations and are based on research evidence or experience. There is little research evidence regarding the minimum level of education that is needed to predict future achievement with certainty. Most minimum educational levels are therefore determined on the basis of experience as represented by public and professional opinion.

Other standards used to determine needs are desires or wants, perceptions of what should be the status of performance, and requirements. The first two are determined by public or professional opinion. Requirements are found in existing laws, policies, and regulating procedures.

3.3 Designing the Needs Assessment

Good designs for needs assessments begin with a clear specification of the focus of the study. This includes a delineation of the specific purposes of the study, the areas in which needs are to be assessed, and the type of needs to be identified.

A clear focus for the assessment will dictate most of the data collection, analysis, and reporting procedures. Needs assessments designed to gather community opinions of educational needs, for example, would require the methods of opinion-survey research. Procedures such as selecting appropriate sampling methods would be of prime importance. Data collection procedures might include the administration of surveys or the use of ranking procedures such as card sorts or budget allocation simulations. To conduct assessments designed to determine student performance needs, one might administer tests, analyze school work, survey teachers, or examine existing records. Still other assessments, designed to determine needs and their cause, would require the use of experimental research techniques.

Complete designs would include procedures for analyzing data and reporting results. For many needs assessments it is necessary to conduct discrepancy analyses to identify needs. These may be conducted by determining differences among two sets of data, combining analyses of several sets and types of data, and developing criticality indices or functions (Witkin 1977).

3.4 Assigning Priorities to Needs

Needs assessment studies may result in the identification of many needs. To be of maximum use, identified needs should be placed in order from most to least crucial. Procedures for setting priorities include ordering needs by the strength of their ratings of importance, by the extent of the discrepancy between targeted and actual status, by the importance ratings and extent of discrepancy, and using previously established decision rules (Witkin 1977).

3.5 Using the Results

A particular characteristic of needs assessment studies is the intended utility of the results. Whether for planning, problem solving, setting criteria for evaluation results, or praising or censuring education efforts, the final stage in the process is intended to be one of active use of the findings.

Bibliography

Kaufman R A 1972 *Educational System Planning*. Prentice-Hall, Englewood Cliffs, New Jersey

Kaufman R A, English F W 1979 *Needs Assessment: Concept and Application*. Educational Technology Publications, Englewood Cliffs, New Jersey

Scriven M, Roth J 1978 Needs assessment: Concept and practice. *Exploring Purposes and Dimensions: New Directions for Program Evaluation* 1: 1–11

Suarez T M 1981 Needs assessment. In: Lewy A, Devo D (eds.) 1981 *Evaluation Roles in Education*. Gordon and Breach, London

Witkin B R 1977 Needs assessment kits, models and tools. *Educ. Technol.* 17(11): 5–18

Prototype Evaluation

M. C. Alkin

A prototype represents an instructional designer's initial solution to a product development problem. Prototype evaluation assesses the product's instructional effectiveness and identifies areas for revision. This product development and evaluation phase precedes operational development, namely, the formative evaluation phase concerned with a product's practicality and usefulness in a real setting (Baker and Alkin 1973).

Evidence indicates that the maximum benefits occur if prototype evaluation begins during the early stages of product development. The process is applied to a "lean version" of the product in mock-up form. Errors in such areas as sequence, content, and wording can be detected and corrected before expensive, polished versions of the prototype are manufactured.

Review of the prototype by subject experts provides the first source of data for product revision. Experts can give information on selection of appropriate goals and objectives, accuracy of content, relevance of the content to objectives, and appropriateness of language style and level.

After screening by subject matter experts, the prototype is ready to be tried out on representative learners. Current consensus indicates that at the prototype stage individual sessions with a small number of subjects are most cost effective (Dick 1980, Markle 1969). This method allows the prototype evaluator to obtain detailed information from subjects in a relatively short period without wasting the time of a large sample of learners on an instructional product which may be of limited effectiveness.

During student tryout, the prototype evaluation provides information on clarity of instructions, sufficiency of the instructional methodology (instructional cues, feedback, practice), usefulness of examples, organization of material, and appropriateness of language. In addition, the developer must determine which sequences cause difficulty and confusion for the learners.

Evidence of instructional effectiveness may come from student performance on such measures as practice exercise responses, performance checklists, and end of sequence tests. However, some of the most important data are obtained through the use of less formal measures such as observation, work samples, subjects' scribbled notes, and clinical debriefing.

Learner attitudes toward the instructional product are also investigated during the prototype evaluation. Attitudes are assessed by informal methods prior to the use of formal questionnaires. Observation of such body language as frowns, sighs, and grimaces, as well as subject debriefing, provide valuable attitude data.

In summary, prototype evaluation is the process of assessing the components of an instructional system during the earliest stages of development to determine instructional quality. The purpose of prototype evaluation is to improve the product prior to its final production. Information on program effects and on areas in need of revision is gathered from subject matter experts and representative learners. The end product of the process should be an instructional package directed towards the appropriate product goals, properly sequenced, and understandable by users. At the conclusion of prototype evaluation, program developers should feel confident of the instructional effectiveness of the product and ready to consider product implementation in real-life contexts.

Bibliography

Baker E L, Alkin M C 1973 ERIC/AVCR annual review paper: Formative evaluation of instructional development. *Audio. Vis. Commun. Rev.* 21: 389–418

Cunningham D J 1973 Evaluation of replicable forms of instruction: A classification of information needs in formative and summative evaluation. *Audio. Vis. Commun. Rev.* 21: 351–67

Dick W 1980 Formative evaluation in instructional development. *J. Instr. Dev.* 3(3): 3–6

Markle S M 1969 *Good Frames and Bad: A Grammar of Frame Writing,* 2nd edn. Wiley, New York

Thiagarajan S 1978 Instructional product verification and revision: 20 questions and 200 speculations. *Educ. Commun. Technol. J.* 26: 133–41

Error Analysis

T. N. Postlethwaite

Error analysis consists of analysing students' work— homework, school work, tests—to identify the major errors they are making, or to identify mislearning which is occurring. Error analysis is usually undertaken at two or three points in the curriculum development cycle. The first point is at the small-scale tryout stage of new curriculum materials. The second point is at the larger-scale tryout stage; however, this stage is only undertaken in a few countries. The third point is at the quality-control stage when a probability sample of children is tested after the curriculum has been fully implemented in all schools.

The error analysis undertaken at the first point is more comprehensive than at the second and third points. The error analysis conducted for all three points consists of two analyses.

The first is to discover where an objective is being achieved by only a "few" students. "Few" must be operationally defined by the curriculum team. It is often defined as fewer than 40 percent of students.

At the small-scale tryout stage where perhaps only six classrooms are being used, the pattern of percentage correct for the first three items (one item measuring one objective) could be as shown in Table 1. It can be seen that the objective measured by Item 1 is well-achieved, by Item 2 is poorly achieved, and by Item 3 is well-achieved in some classes and poorly achieved in other classes.

What is "going wrong" with Item 2? At this point, the evaluator turns to the item analysis. This is also the analysis which is used for the larger-scale tryout and quality-control stages. For all students the analysis may be as presented in Table 2 for a multiple-choice item with five possible responses.

Table 1

Percentage of correct responses in a sample of six schools

	Schools						Average
	A	B	C	D	E	F	
Item 1	90	80	85	87	93	78	85.50
Item 2	20	30	27	19	15	22	22.16
Item 3	90	80	15	20	50	90	57.50

Table 2
Item analysis for Item 2

| | Omit | | Responses | | | |
		A	B	C^a	D	E
Item 2:						
Percentage of students selecting	0.6	8.0	52.2	22.2	7.6	9.4
Discrimination	−0.04	−0.09	0.26	0.12	−0.12	−0.14

a The correct response

Response C is considered to be the right answer or best answer. Responses A, B, D, and E are wrong answers but have been constructed such that they are errors which the students are likely to make. These responses are usually based on teachers' experience. Only 22.2 percent of the students obtained the correct answer. However, Response B was answered by 51.2 percent of all students and the discrimination index, which is typically a point biserial correlation, is positive. This indicates that the better students on the test as a whole are opting for Response B. Assuming that the item is a good item, then an error in learning has been discovered.

The next question is why or how has this error arisen? At the larger-scale tryout and quality-control points all that can be done is to examine the curriculum materials and hope that it is possible to identify what might be the cause. At the small-scale tryout stage the evaluators have usually collected other information of a qualitative nature from the teachers and students about problems they have had with the curriculum text or with the teaching–learning strategy used. By referring to the qualitative data it is usually possible to identify the cause. The two most frequent causes are that the level of language used is too difficult for the students or that the sequencing is inappropriate. The curriculum team is then in a position to revise the materials and/or the accompanying teacher guide.

The examples given above have used tests with multiple-choice format. However, it is also possible to use students' homework or classwork for such an analysis. There are certain types of achievement for which multiple-choice tests are inappropriate (Thorndike and Hagen 1969). The basic technique is to go through the set homework or school work of the group or sample of students in question and make a frequency count of the "errors" occurring. This yields information about the most frequent errors and again it is usually possible to identify "causes" in the small-scale tryout but not in the larger-scale tryout and quality-control stages.

Three other ways in which error analysis is used are worthy of brief mention. The first is the construction of distractors in multiple-choice items such that the wrong answer chosen by the student indicates to the teacher the likely error. Take for example the item

$$(-17) + (-14) = \text{A.} \quad -31$$

$$\text{B.} \quad +31$$

$$\text{C.} \quad -3$$

$$\text{D.} \quad +3$$

If a student answers B, the most likely error is that the student is confusing $(-) + (-)$ with $(-) \times (-)$. The second use links errors to the way in which teachers explain rules and principles. For example, it was found that some children in a particular target population were calculating $3 + (-7)$ as 10 and $(-6) + (-15)$ as 9. A small study then discovered that these errors were being made only in classes where teachers were attempting to teach the concept and operation of negation numbers using a number line—for example a line with unit intervals along it from -30 passing through zero to $+30$.

A third way (Lundgren 1976) in which error analysis is used is in the drawing of profiles of achievement of individual students as compared with what objectives they are meant to learn. Objectives are classified by theme and behaviour (in the taxonomic sense). Hence, there may be one category which involves the calculation of simple multiplication. If 12 items are involved in the testing of the objective, the profile indicates how many of the items are correctly answered. This, in turn, indicates to the teacher where remedial work is needed with an individual student.

Bibliography

Johnstone A H 1981 Diagnostic testing in science. In: Lewy A, Nevo D (eds.) 1981 *Evaluation Roles in Education*. Gordon and Breach, New York
Klahr D (ed.) 1976 *Cognition and Instruction*. Erlbaum, Hillsdale, New Jersey
Lewy A (ed.) 1977 *Handbook of Curriculum Evaluation*. UNESCO, Paris
Lundgren U 1976 *Model Analysis of Pedagogical Processes*. Stockholm Institute of Education, CWK, Gleerup
Postlethwaite T N, Nasoetion N 1979 Planning the content of teacher upgrading programs: An approach in Indonesia. *Stud. Educ. Eval.* 5: 95–99
Thorndike R L, Hagen E 1969 *Measurement and Evaluation in Psychology and Education*. Wiley, New York

Feasibility Studies

L. A. Sosniak

When presented with a proposed curriculum or a plan for developing a curriculum, at least two broad questions need to be addressed. First, to what extent is the curriculum worthwhile for the educational circumstances in question? Second, how likely is it that the curriculum can be implemented successfully? Attempts to answer these questions constitute feasibility studies of curriculum.

Curriculum feasibility studies are likely to be informal. A decision about feasibility will typically be based on the best judgment of the curriculum specialist or instructional leader in a school or school district. Such a decision is made after careful reading of the materials or proposal and after considerable discussion with staff in the school or district who would be responsible for implementing the curriculum. An extended, highly systematic study of a proposed curriculum is both unlikely and not necessarily desirable. It is unlikely because typically a substantial number of curricular suggestions are put forward each year. If each was subject to systematic evaluation, the cost to a school system would be staggering. Any curricular suggestion judged to be worthy after an informal evaluation can always be pilot tested before being fully implemented in a school or district. Even then, because a pilot situation is seldom—if ever—identical to the circumstances under which the curriculum would be implemented on a large-scale, the "hard data" provided by such an evaluation may cost far more than it is worth. Therefore, a costly, highly systematic feasibility study may also be undesirable. Further, a curriculum is a plan for instruction, and as such is never completely standardizable. The curriculum-in-action will always be moderated by the teachers and students working with the guide. Consequently, effectiveness in one setting is no guarantee of effectiveness in another (Eisner 1985 pp. 196–97).

Although feasibility studies are likely to be informal, they involve a wide variety of specific concerns. These include philosophical, pedagogical, political, and economic issues. Each of these will be considered under a separate heading.

1. Philosophical Issues

A curriculum, or an idea for one, may be right for one situation but wrong for others. Determining whether it is right for one's own situation typically begins with an analysis of the fit between the curriculum and the philosophy of one's own school or school system. A test of philosophical fitness can be applied both to the aims or objectives of the curriculum and the means of realizing the curricular intentions. That is, a first consideration might be the extent to which the aims or objectives of the curriculum are consonant with the stated and implicit local educational philosophy. An equally important consideration would be whether the procedures explicit and implicit in the new curriculum are also consistent with the local philosophy for the ways students and teachers should work—individually and together (Peters 1959).

If the philosophy embedded in the curriculum is not consistent with the local educational philosophy, it might be worthwhile to ask whether it is in harmony with the philosophy the school or district is moving toward. If the answer is still no, there may be little reason to look at the curriculum proposal any further. If the philosophy embedded in the curriculum is appropriate, there is one further philosophical question to consider: the question of whether the curriculum proposed constitutes an improvement over the present state of educational affairs. As Schubert (1986 p. 373) reminds us, a curricular change is no guarantee that the change will be for the better.

2. Pedagogical Issues

A new curriculum can be analyzed with a view to a variety of pedagogical considerations. Some of these focus specifically on the fit between the curriculum and the students with whom it will be used; others focus on the integrity of the curriculum itself; still others focus on the relationship between the curriculum and the teachers who will be expected to translate it into classroom instruction.

One would probably want to consider, first, whether the educational claims for the curriculum are realistic. Is it likely that the students will be able to learn what the curriculum promises? Do they have the prerequisite knowledge necessary for working through the curriculum? Is it likely that the students will have mastered the most important knowledge and skills of the curriculum even before they begin working through the new course of study? A related, more specific consideration is the degree to which the content and methods of the curriculum are appropriate for the students who will be working through the course of study. On the whole, are they geared to the proper level of difficulty for the students in your school or district? Are they relevant to students' lives?

One can also look at the extent to which the curriculum is coherent within itself. Is the content well-chosen given the aims of the curriculum? Are the explicit and implicit methods of instruction appropriate for both the curricular aims and content? Is the curriculum consistent in its philosophy and methods from beginning to end?

The importance of considering the appropriateness of the curriculum for the teachers who will be using it cannot be overestimated. Recent examinations of curriculum implementation repeatedly show that new curricula often fail to be adopted or to be used as intended because of the difficulties they pose for classroom teachers (Jackson 1983, Tyler 1979). Three considerations seem especially important. First, are the teachers likely to understand and value the aims of the curriculum? Second, are the teachers likely to be knowledgeable about the content and methods of the curriculum? Third, are the methods of instruction for the new curriculum likely to fit well with the teachers' current methods for organizing instruction?

3. Political Issues

A curriculum that seems philosophically and pedagogically appropriate for one's situation may prove troublesome nonetheless. When studying the feasibility of implementing a new curriculum, it is important to consider the politics—within the school as well as within the community served by the school—that may interfere with successful implementation of the curriculum. Will both moral and organizational support be available to teachers from high-level administrators within the school or district? Teachers need to be given time, incentive, and payoff for changing their practices and course content (see, for example, Lazerson et al. 1984); they need, especially, the room to flounder and be less-than-successful initially when working with unfamiliar and complex content and methods (Little 1984). Recent analyses of curriculum change indicate further that teachers resist imposed change; the wholehearted support of teachers typically requires involving them meaningfully in the construction or selection of the curriculum (Noddings 1979).

Controversy in the community around a particular curriculum also has proved to be especially troublesome. Two issues seem important to consider in this regard. First, does the curriculum fall within the role of the school as the parents of the school children envisage it? Some new curricula may be seen by the community as usurping the role of the parent in a child's education. Second, does the point of view espoused by the curriculum match the values of the community? If even a small but vocal portion of the community believes that the curriculum espouses a point of view that conflicts with their beliefs or values, the curriculum may be impossible to implement successfully.

4. Economic Issues

Although one wouldn't want to make decisions about school curricula solely on the basis of cost, it would be foolhardy and irresponsible to ignore the matter of cost entirely. Changing from one curriculum to another involves a variety of "costs." Some costs are quite obvious while others are "hidden;" some can be measured in dollars and cents while others may not be quantifiable (Wolf 1984 Chap. 7). The price of the new materials required is just a small part of the total investment necessary to implement a new curriculum.

If the new curriculum is to be added to the current school program (rather than replacing a portion of the existing curriculum), one would certainly want to consider student time as a cost. The time students would be required to invest in the new curriculum would have to be subtracted from other portions of the school program. Time is an important variable in any cost estimation even if the new curriculum is intended to replace a portion of the existing school program. It is important to consider the time teachers would have to invest preparing to use a new curriculum (individually and in staff development programs), as well as the time that administrators and other extraclass professional staff would have to devote to implement and maintain the new course of study.

Some curricular proposals may require additional staff. Others may require additional space (for classrooms, offices, or supply rooms) or substantial remodeling of existing space. Still other curriculum proposals may require that a school be kept open longer hours—adding to the cost of heat, light, janitorial services, and so forth.

Finally, all new curriculum proposals are likely to require some new materials. The type of materials—and related costs—can vary considerably. Textbooks which can be used for a period of years will obviously be significantly less expensive than "consumable" materials (e.g., workbooks, science materials) which would have to be replaced each year. Equipment (including movie projectors, microcomputers, and tape recorders) will have to be maintained. Both the nonrecurring and the recurring costs of materials need to be kept in mind.

5. Conclusion

Decisions about the feasibility of a proposed curriculum or a plan for developing a curriculum involve multiple considerations. The educational significance and appropriateness of the curriculum for one's particular circumstances are certainly the most important. However, economic and political considerations ought not to be given short-shrift.

Bibliography

Eisner E W 1985 *The Educational Imagination: On the Design and Evaluation of School Programs*, 2nd edn. Macmillan, New York
Jackson P 1983 The reform of science education: A cautionary tale. *Daedalus* 112: 143–66
Lazerson M, McLaughlin J B, McPherson B 1984 New curriculum, old issues. *Teach. Coll. Rec.* 86 (2): 229–319
Little J W 1984 Seductive images and organizational realities in professional development. *Teach. Coll. Rec.* 86 (1): 84–102
Noddings N 1979 NIE's national curriculum development conference. In: Schaffarzick J, Sykes G (eds.) 1979 *Value Conflicts and Curriculum Issues*. McCutchan, Berkeley, California

Peters R S 1959 *Authority, Responsibility and Education.*
George Allen and Unwin, London
Schubert W H 1986 *Curriculum: Perspective, Paradigm, and Possibility.* Macmillan, New York
Tyler R W 1979 Educational improvements best served by curriculum development. In: Schaffarzick J, Sykes G (eds.) 1979 *Value Conflicts and Curriculum Issues.* McCutchan, Berkeley, California
Wolf R M 1984 *Evaluation in Education*, 2nd edn. Praeger, New York

Curriculum Tryout

A. Lewy

The curriculum reform of the 1960s and 1970s brought forward the demand for empirical tryout of instructional materials and curricula prior to their widespread use. The high cost of producing new curricula was one of the factors that motivated sponsors to demand empirical evidence of the quality of new programs. But apart from such demands, one of the basic tenets of the curriculum movement of the 1960s was that only empirical evidence can demonstrate the quality of an educational program. The leaders of the curriculum movement strove to realize Campbell's (1969) vision of the experimental society, where preliminary tryout of social action is adjunct to planning.

1. Phases of Curriculum Tryout

The tryout of new curricula is carried out in successive phases with increasing numbers and type diversification of students. Nevertheless, it does not fully cover the entire span of planning activities. Formative evaluation of new curricula already starts at the pretryout stage, when the development team defines the program objectives, selects the contents, and makes decisions about the outline of the course of the study. The tryout of the curriculum can start only at a phase when instructional materials to be used by learners are already available; but it is not necessary to wait until all study materials for a whole course of study become available. The tryout may and should start at a phase when only selected components of the program are available to the learner. Evaluation experts use various terms for denoting the successive stages of program tryout, such as: prototype testing, revision cycles, and product tryout; or laboratory phase, hothouse phase, and utilization phase.

While there may be slight differences among these sets of terms, in practice they delineate three phases parallel to what will be labelled here as: laboratory tryout, pilot tryout, and field tryout.

1.1 Laboratory Tryout

Individual components of the program can be tried out on individual students invited to the curriculum laboratory at the very earliest stages of the development activities. The curriculum team itself, together with the evaluator, observes the learner's behavior, takes note of his or her responses to the instructional materials, and, if needed, suggests specific modifications. One of the problems of the laboratory tryout is that certain learning activities must be presented to the learner in a predetermined sequence. In an ordinary school situation lessons are presented to the learner in a day-by-day sequence. During the laboratory tryout phase, a considerable amount of time is often needed to prepare the materials and it may therefore occur that the interval between the tryout of one lesson and that of the subsequent one is much longer than it would be in an actual school setting.

1.2 Pilot Tryout

As soon as a fully completed preliminary version of a course is available for learners, it can be tried out in a regular school setting. At this phase the team members themselves usually serve as classroom teachers. The purpose of such a tryout is to examine whether the program can be implemented within the system and to ascertain the conditions (in terms of space, equipment, teacher training, learners' prerequisite knowledge) necessary for ensuring the success of the program, and what modifications, if any, are needed to improve the quality of the program. Harlen (1973) lists a series of issues to be examined at this phase: Do the children enjoy the program? Can they cope with the assignments they are given? Do they participate in the scheduled activities? Are the teachers aware of the unique features of the program? Do they accept or identify themselves with the basic tenets of the program?

1.3 Field Tryout

On the basis of the findings of the pilot tryout, a revised version of the program is produced, which is then tried out by school teachers in the regular settings of their classes, and without any direct intervention on the part of the development team. The purpose of this phase is to examine the "exportability" of the program, that is, to ascertain whether it can be used in school without the ongoing support of the development team, as well as to demonstrate the merits of the program to its potential users.

2. Procedures and Instrumentation

Curriculum tryout moves from relatively "soft" methodology at the initial phases toward more strictly prescribed design as an advance is made toward the later tryout phases. At the laboratory phase it is necessary to be content with observing a few learners. Nevertheless, studies have shown that even such limited tryouts (with nonrepresentative samples of the target population) may contribute to the improvement of programs (Markele 1967). The major methodological problem at this phase is usually referred to as "distortion filter." The evaluator does more than note what he or she observes; he or she interprets or "filters" what is observed. The ideal tester of instructional materials should be sensitive to subtle manifestations of the pupil's problems. At the pilot phase the utilization of a judgmental sample is recommended. The evaluators, utilizing a variety of instruments, collect information about various aspects of the functioning of the program. They collect information about classroom processes by direct observation supplemented by teachers' remarks at the margins of the textbook pages, by interviews, and by questionnaires. Formal testing plays a relatively minor role at this phase. Evidence of achievement is provided through observing the learners' behavior in the classroom and by "curriculum embedded tests," that is, assignments and homework presented to the learner during the actual teaching–learning process. Only at the field-trial phase does it become feasible to employ random sampling procedures and to compare the outcomes of the program being evaluated with those of alternative programs.

3. Utilizing Findings of Curriculum Tryout

Recent research has focused on the question of what use is made of findings obtained from curriculum tryout, and what factors affect the degree of utilization of such findings. Harlen (1973) reports that data collected through direct observation of classroom processes and through teachers' written comments about flaws detected in the instructional materials are used more frequently as a basis for modifying programs than the results of achievement tests. A survey of evaluation studies conducted in the United States revealed that the credibility of the evaluation results is a crucial factor in determining the degree of their utilization (Boruch and Cordray 1980). This is true mainly with clients who have difficulty in understanding certain technical aspects of the report. In such cases, confidence in the evaluator is very important, and this is one reason why the stability of the evaluator is critical. The interpretability of the information is another critical factor. Printed information is frequently misinterpreted by users and there is a need for oral reporting as well. Absence of regular meetings between evaluators and curriculum developers invites errors in interpretation. Surprisingly enough,

lack of timeliness is not mentioned among the obstacles to utilizing results of tryout. This is true mainly with regard to the phases of laboratory tryout and pilot tryout in which the data are based on direct observation, and certain preliminary summaries are produced almost immediately after collection of the data. When these findings are made available for the development teams in the form of oral reports they are put to use long before the written report is completed. Lewy (1977) found that the tryout process provides a moratorium for the development team to reconsider issues which may have been overlooked during the strenuous work of program writings, when they were required to meet strict deadlines. Such considerations are combined with the reported tryout findings, and used for modifying the program. Cronbach (1980) claims that the tryout process creates among the team members an awareness of the importance of certain criteria used for evaluating the program, and in this way affects the quality of their work. The mere existence of tryout may keep certain flaws from occurring. In addition, it contributes to the accumulation of knowledge which teaches team members to avoid certain flaws in the future. Thus the effects of tryout make themselves felt not only with regard to the target program, but also in forthcoming planning activities.

No studies have been conducted either on the direct contribution of program tryout and modification to the outcomes of program utilization or on the payoff of repeated tryouts. Information about these two issues seems to be crucial for future decisions with regard to the planning of curriculum tryouts.

Bibliography

Boruch R F, Cordray D S (eds.) 1980 *An Appraisal of Educational Program Evaluation: Federal, State and Local Agencies.* Northwestern University, Evanston, Illinois

Campbell D T 1969 Reforms as experiments. *Am. Psychol.* 24: 409–29

Cronbach L 1980 *Toward Reform of Program Evaluation.* Jossey-Bass, San Francisco, California

Harlen W 1973 Science 5-13 Project. In: Schools Council (eds.) 1973 *Evaluation in Curriculum Development: Twelve Case Studies: Papers from the Schools Council's Project Evaluators on Aspects of the Work.* Macmillan, London

Lewy A (ed.) 1977 *Handbook of Curriculum Evaluation.* Longman, New York

Markele S M 1967 Empirical testing of programs. *Sixty-sixth Yearbook of the National Society for the Study of Education, Part II.* University of Chicago Press, Chicago, Illinois

Curriculum Validation

W. H. Schubert

The question of validating the curriculum involves considerations of whether the educational program provides what its stated intent indicates. This relates quite

directly to conceptions of validity (construct, context, content, external, internal) as treated in evaluation and research design literatures. While curriculum validation clearly relates to these areas, it extends to even more complex philosophical issues in the question: How can one know a good curriculum?

This question directly invokes epistemological and axiological problems. Epistemological concerns about the character of defensible ways of knowing are raised when one asks how curricular purposes and content can best be determined. Smith et al. (1957) identify four procedures for curriculum developers to use in making such decisions: judgment, experimentation, analysis, and consensus. The consideration of these procedures as alternative methods of decision making in turn invokes basic questions about defensible ways to come to acquire or create knowledge. Thus, the relative merits of such epistemological bases as intuition, experience, utility, authority, tradition, and the scientific method are central to the problem of curriculum validation.

The question of validation procedure is merely technical unless it is coupled with substantive inquiry about the nature of what should be taught. The term "should" is a question of value and thus is rooted in the axiological realm. To what standard of judgment should those who determine curricular purpose and content turn in striving for validation? Smith et al. (1957) also address this question by using a criterial approach. They ask if justification of purposes stems primarily from provision of basic needs, social adequacy, or democratic ideals. The latter serve as criteria for validating educational objectives. Similarly, these authors suggest the following criteria for the selection of curricular content: (a) significance to an organized body of knowledge; (b) longevity of use or the "test of survival"; (c) utility; (d) interest of learners; and (e) contribution to the growth and development of democratic society (p. 131–50).

Smith et al. (1957) emphasize the importance of consistency among objectives. It is central to curriculum validation to insure that objectives are noncontradictory. It is too frequently discovered, upon careful analysis, that objectives within different subject matter areas or at different grade levels contradict one another. They can even be shown to have counteractive effects upon one another. Recent investigations by Goodlad in the United States have revealed that purposes of state departments of education are often lost or massively distorted by school districts, that are supposed to implement them. Moreover, the character of curriculum changes as it is mediated and interpreted through national and state decision-making hierarchies and through every dimension of local schooling: district administrators, building administrators, supervisors, teachers, and students. As each of the members of the curriculum development and implementation process acts in a capacity that modifies the selection of learning experiences, instructional approaches, patterns of organizing learning environments, and evaluation strategies, the character of the curriculum is altered. Such interdependencies are seldom accentuated as fully as in the selection of instructional materials by schools. Selection of materials that are not consonant with purposes distorts the validity of the entire program. The Educational Products Information Exchange (EPIE) Institute attempts to overcome this problem by providing a consumer service to schools that enables them to explicate the intent, content, instructional strategies, and evaluation procedures implicit in materials; thereby, schools are helped to match characteristics of materials with the needs and interests of teachers, students, the public, and governmental policy. Moreover, EPIE uses a process of learner verification and revision whereby student input is used to test the assertions of publishers about their materials.

While the process of curriculum validation frequently involves the efforts of experts who identify assumptions embedded in the substance and process of determining the curriculum, and while they diligently try to understand the interactive effects among different curricular components, more subtle and complex processes are at work. All individuals who participate in the curriculum process, especially students, act to validate it by judging its merits in relation to their own needs and experiences (Hopkins 1954). A great deal remains to be learned about this activity as it relates to formal conceptions of curriculum validation. While students' perceptions of the curriculum are sometimes used as feedback to curriculum planners, conceptions of active student involvement in curriculum creation are a new frontier for curriculum validation.

Bibliography

Educational Products Information Exchange (EPIE) Institute 1979 *Selecting Instructional Materials*. EPIE, Stoney Brook, New York

Hopkins L T 1954 *The Emerging Self in School and Home*. Harper, New York

Smith B O, Stanley W O, Shores J H 1957 *Fundamentals of Curriculum Development*, rev. edn. Harcourt, Brace and World, New York

Curriculum Analysis

T. Ariav

Curriculum analysis is the systematic examination of curricula with respect to a set of concrete concerns. This set of concerns, or scheme, is a conceptual framework that guides the analysis. A large variety of such schemes has been proposed over the years, but ultimately each particular scheme applied is selected or formed in a way that reflects that user's particular interests and needs. The uniqueness of the analysis process lies with the potential to illuminate the intrinsic educational worth of a curriculum, to reveal its implicit underlying paradigm and value base, to shed light on its possible strengths and weaknesses, and to unearth its social and personal meaning. Although curriculum analysis can be applied to various conceptions of the term *curriculum*, it is mostly used in the context of curriculum materials.

The analysis process is meant to highlight the overt characteristics of a curriculum and disclose its hidden features. It centers on the required or desirable overt features in curricula and examines the extent to which they are absent or present. Examples of such features are: interrelationships between objectives and learning activities, readability, internal coherence between the rationale and the actual teaching–learning materials, biases and stereotypes, type of evaluation procedures, structure and sequence of instruction, content accuracy and importance, and graphic design.

In most cases, however, the process of analysis extends itself to examine the social ideology and epistemological assumptions that are hidden in curricula. Examples of features in that group are: the meaning of experience in the learning process, relationships between information and ideas, levels of thinking, and the social significance for the immediate community as well as the society at large.

An effective way of defining curriculum analysis is to contrast it with curriculum evaluation and curriculum criticism. Related literature has not made a clear distinction among these three concepts. However, evaluation differs from analysis on functional and historical–theoretical grounds (Ariav 1986), while criticism differs in the means applied and their value base. These two contrasts are outlined below, followed by a discussion of the variety of schemes.

1. A Contrast with Evaluation and Criticism

Curriculum analysis had just started to evolve at the time when curriculum evaluation was already a maturing field of disciplined inquiry. The curriculum reform of the 1960s overwhelmed practitioners and curricularists with instances of decision making concerning curriculum selection, adaptation, implementation, and development. The need for practical guidelines and procedures in these decision-making processes was the impetus for the development of over 50 schemes for curriculum analysis (e.g., Eraut et al. 1975, Gow 1977, Gall 1981). Unlike evaluation, analysis is rooted in practice rather than in the research tradition. As a young area of disciplined inquiry, curriculum analysis still lacks a well-established theoretical base and a broad historical perspective.

The purpose of curriculum analysis is to assess how worthwhile a curriculum is regardless of the success of its use in practice. It is, therefore, not concerned with the observed effects of curriculum materials in use because these outcomes are affected by the whole instructional context and not only by the quality of the instructional materials. Curriculum analysis deals mainly with materials before they are used in the classroom. The differences between curriculum evaluation and curriculum analysis are not only in purpose, focus, and methods but also in the audiences for which they are targeted, the kind of educators who perform them, and the roles of these two areas in the curriculum field.

Curriculum analysis is usually intended to be performed by trained school or school-district personnel, with relatively limited specialization in this activity. It is often targeted at field-based educators such as teachers, principals, librarians, curriculum coordinators, and curriculum developers. Evaluation, on the other hand, is often based in academic institutions and research and development centers; conducted by teams of experts, during a relatively long period of time; supported financially by grants; and targeted at state or district administrators, politicians, granting agencies, purchasing personnel, publishers, parents, and community lay people. The literature on curriculum analysis identifies a long and diversified list of roles which seem to be more pragmatic and specific than those of evaluation. These vary from helping teachers to improve instruction, and developing awareness of curricular issues, to identifying trends in curriculum materials and assisting in curriculum mapping.

Curriculum analysis is therefore neither a methodology for evaluation nor is it only one aspect of, or a preliminary state in, evaluation. The two activities can be performed independently of one another, in a sequence where analysis precedes evaluation or vice versa, or in a collaborative mode where the two are interrelated.

Curriculum analysis has also been confused in the literature with curriculum criticism. The latter assumes an *a priori*, grand social or personal theory as a basis for examining curricula. It uses such theories as methodologies for curriculum research and curriculum theorizing. One stream of curriculum criticism is associated with the neo-Marxist tradition, claiming that the curriculum in capitalist societies perpetuates the bourgeois myths of the supremacy of the dominant classes. Another stream is rooted in phenomenology, theology, and existentialism, focusing upon the individual student in a hostile milieu, surrounded by an environment rich with conflicting messages, hidden factors, and multiple expectations.

Curriculum analysis, in contrast, is a practical methodology that seeks to help those directly involved with the instructional situation. Users of curriculum analysis are not bound to monolithic views but are expected to choose from various educational theories and views that are reflected in different available schemes. Moreover, users are encouraged to develop their own idiosyncratic schemes independent of, or based on, existing schemes. Both curriculum criticism and analysis share a similar purpose but diverge on methodological grounds and vantage points.

2. Schemes for Curriculum Analysis

Schemes for curriculum analysis are instruments that ensure a systematic, articulated, and deliberate analysis process. The variety of existing schemes reflects different interests in this process, ranging from purely theoretical inquiry to the support of praxis-based instructional decision making. The centrality of schemes in curriculum analysis is manifested in the fact that most studies in this area focus upon the utility and value of specific schemes. An extensive development of such schemes has been witnessed in recent years.

The underlying assumption behind the development of schemes is that by providing a conceptual framework the process of judgment would be raised from the mainly intuitive, nonsystematic, and often indefensible level to a more explicit and conscious level. Although only a few schemes were practically applied and field tested, evidence shows that they were found to be of special importance and usefulness in decision making regarding curriculum selection and implementation (Tyler et al. 1976, Mahung 1980). Specifically, schemes help teachers to avoid conceptual confusion, justify instructional decisions, extend their thinking into new avenues, set priorities, and exercise criticism regarding the use of materials (Partington 1984).

Schemes are composed of items which either ask whether a specific element exists in the curriculum, or require that a certain characteristic be fulfilled. These questions and criteria are usually grouped into categories. Items have sometimes an attached measure (e.g., rating scales, tabulations, and check-lists) that helps to quantify or portray the results of the analysis process. The type of items and their categorization in a scheme reveals and reflects its specific approach to the process of curriculum analysis. Schemes, therefore, function as specific bases for looking at curricula and thereby provide clients with alternate means to be used for differentiated needs.

The variety of schemes is substantial. Schemes are developed for different subject matters, grade levels, types of materials (e.g., printed materials, computer software, and audiovisual materials), and functions (e.g., to reveal consistency, biases, underlying values and thought processes). Schemes range from a page to a book in length and vary in such respects as structure and philosophy. They have been developed by curriculum experts, teacher educators, psychologists, and subject matter specialists, among others. Schemes are also disseminated in various publications such as pro-fessional journals, books, dissertations, papers presented at conferences, and publications of educational organizations or institutions.

In general, schemes for curriculum analysis can be mapped along the following dimensions. For whom is the scheme designed? What is to be analysed with it? What is the purpose of the analysis? For what subjects and grades is the scheme applicable? What kind of measures are available to assist the decision-making process? What are the major domains of the scheme? How are the various items in each domain presented? What are the assumptions and values that underlie the scheme? Is the scheme coherent, comprehensive, and clear? How easy is it to use and apply? This "meta-analysis" is useful both for selecting a scheme from the pool of those available and for the design of new schemes.

The flooding of the educational market by a large variety of curriculum materials requires a systematic study of this topic especially in educational systems which strive to enhance the teacher's autonomy. This implies that knowledge and skills in this activity should be introduced in preservice and inservice teacher education programs.

Bibliography

Ariav T 1986 Curriculum analysis and curriculum evaluation: A contrast. *Stud. Educ. Eval.* 12: 139–47

Eraut M, Goad L, Smith G 1975 *The Analysis of Curriculum Materials*. Educational Area. Occasional Papers 2, University of Sussex, Brighton

Frymier J 1977 *Annehurst Curriculum Classification System; A Practical Way to Individualize Instruction*. Kappa Delta Pi, West Lafayette, Indiana

Gall M D 1981 *Handbook for Evaluating and Selecting Curriculum Materials*. Allyn and Bacon, Boston, Massachusetts

Gow D T 1977 *Curriculum Analysis: An Aid to Selection, Adaptation, and Implementation of Curricula*. Learning Research and Development Center, Pittsburgh, Pennsylvania

Mahung S 1980 Evaluating curriculum materials using conceptual analysis. In: Munby H, Orpwood G, Russell T (eds.) 1980 *Seeing Curriculum in a New Light: Essays from Science Education*. Ontario Institute for Studies in Education (OISE), Toronto, Ontario, pp. 100–10

Partington G 1984 How can curricula be analyzed? The case of History syllabuses. *Aust. J. Educ.* 28(2): 202–11

Tyler L L, Klein M F, Lane M 1976 *Evaluating and Choosing Curriculum and Instructional Materials*. Educational Resource Associates, Los Angeles, California

Implementation Evaluation

K. A. Leithwood

In the field of education, interest in implementation evaluation can be said to have officially begun with the Charters and Jones (1973) article: "On the risk of appraising non-events in program evaluation." Prior to the early 1970s educational evaluators focused primarily on assessing program outcomes. Subsequently, their perspective broadened to include descriptions of the educational processes responsible for these outcomes. Scriven's (1976) distinction between formative and summative evaluation exemplified this broadened perspective, as did the development of evaluation models incorporating procedures for describing educational processes. This article describes the main purposes to be served by implementation evaluation, one aspect of this broadened perspective, and clarifies concepts central to the process. Generic tasks associated with doing implementation evaluation are identified. How these generic tasks are carried out depends on orientation to the implementation process. Three such orientations are described along with the implications of each for implementation evaluation. Examples of evaluations based on each orientation are also mentioned.

1. Purposes for Implementation Evaluation

Implementation evaluation may assist in making accountability and management decisions as well as serving research and development functions. Accountability decisions are aided when information is provided about whether, or the extent to which, an innovation has been put into practice according to design; whether what was delivered or paid for is being undertaken as planned (Leithwood and Montgomery 1980).

Implementation evaluation may also be designed to help specify the practices implied by the innovation; identify those conditions under which implementation is likely to succeed, including problems likely to be encountered under those conditions and strategies available for their resolution; determine the feasibility of innovation implementation, including the capabilities required of the implementors and whether policy changes are warranted in the light of unintended effects; and decide when the innovation has been sufficiently well-imple-mented to warrant an assessment of its effects on student learning. Implementation evaluation providing information about these issues assists with management decisions.

It is primarily a research and development function that is performed when evaluation attempts to explain the innovation's successes and failures. Such information helps, given disappointing outcomes, for example, to determine whether the innovation was fairly tried and did not work or whether it might work but was not adequately tried. It may also try to explain causal relationships between components of the innovation and effects on student achievement and to understand the relationship of the innovation to situational variables.

Accountability, management, and research are not independent functions. A decision maker might profit from information relevant to several or all of these purposes at a given time.

2. Concepts Central to the Process of Implementation Evaluation

Three concepts are central to the focus of this article: (a) the innovation being implemented; (b) the process of implementation; and (c) what is implied by the term *evaluation*.

2.1 Innovation

At least two quite different meanings can be attached to the term *innovation*. An innovation may be defined as a new idea, method, or device; the term *new* is defined as either having been made but a short time (recent) or novel (unfamiliar, strange, having no precedent). If the meaning recent or having been made but a short time is attached to the term *innovation*, then a recently published textbook perfectly consistent with the existing practices of a teacher is an innovation. If, on the other hand, novelty is the meaning associated with the term *innovation*, the things properly labeled as such are much fewer. That is, an educational idea or curriculum product would not be called an innovation unless the actions it suggested had no precedent in actual practice, or were not to be found in what the implementor was currently doing (Leithwood 1982).

As novelty, the term *innovation* has a subjective referent. For example, what any given group of teachers is currently doing in their classrooms is likely to vary substantially. Whether or not an innovation is novel, then, depends on the implementor. For the implementor whose practices are already consistent with those suggested by the innovation, there is no reason created by the innovation for that implementor to change. The same innovation, however, may imply many changes in practice for other implementors with practices discordant in some fashion with those suggested by the innovation. In this article only those things that have novel features for the individuals who choose to use them are considered to be innovations. Furthermore, few innovations imply wholesale changes in the practices of those who would implement them. Such practices are multidimensional and usually far more complex than the developer of an innovation ever prescribes.

2.2 Implementation

An innovation has been defined as a suggested change in existing practices within one or more of a number of dimensions of these practices (e.g., Fullan 1982). Implementation is the process of reducing the differences between existing practices and practices suggested by the innovation. Whether modifications are being implemented in an existing set of practices or an entirely new set of practices is being implemented, the process occurs over time. Differences between existing and innovative practices are only gradually reduced. The behavior of people must change if most innovations are to be implemented and changes in behavior depend on the acquisition (learning) of new knowledge, skills, attitudes, and values. The process of reorganizing and adding to what one thinks, what one is able to do, and how one feels, is a slow and gradual process. It is sometimes useful to view this slow, gradual process of behavioral change as occurring in stages. In this view, implementing an innovation can be seen as growth, on the part of those who wish to use an innovation, from their existing practices through relatively immature approximations of practices suggested by the innovation, to (eventually) relatively sophisticated use of the innovation.

When implementation is viewed as occurring in stages, the question as to what stimulates or inhibits change from one stage to the next arises. Indeed, successful implementation depends significantly on how well a person answers that question. From what has been said about behavioral change, it is clear that impediments or obstacles to growth include lack of the knowledge and skill required for the next more mature level of implementation activity, and negative feelings about implementation activities. During implementation of many innovations the unavailability of particular resources and the nature of the existing organization will also be a serious obstacle to change.

In sum, implementation is a process of behavioral change, in directions suggested by an innovation, occurring in stages, over time, as obstacles to such change are overcome.

3. Evaluation

This concept refers to the process of describing and making judgments about the worth of a phenomenon of interest: in this case, the nature of the implementation process and the degree to which the innovation has been implemented. Based on how the concepts innovation and implementation have been defined, four tasks may be considered a generic part of any implementation evaluation. These tasks include:

(a) identifying those dimensions of the implementor's practices that need to change in order for the innovation to be implemented;

(b) describing the nature of practices within those dimensions that are considered to be desirable when the innovation is fully implemented;

(c) within the identified dimensions, specifying stages of change in practices from those practices most inconsistent with the intention of the innovation to those practices associated with the meaning of full implementation;

(d) describing the implementors' current practices in relation to such stages.

For management purposes, the additional task of identifying obstacles implementors encounter in moving from one stage to the next in the implementation process might also be considered fundamental. Such data is a prerequisite for the systematic choice of useful implementation strategies.

4. Alternative Orientations to Implementation

Incremental reduction in the gap between current practices and those suggested by an innovation is a widely accepted conception of the implementation process in education. Much more controversial, however, are beliefs about how that process occurs. Table 1 summarizes the assumptions underlying three orientations to implementation that are widely reflected in the literature. Each orientation carries its own implications for how the generic implementation evaluation tasks are best carried out.

Muddling through is the most conservative approach to implementation. It is premised on a pessimistic estimate about the value of planning and about the likelihood of people acting systematically and rationally toward realizing a set of predetermined outcomes. This alternative sees implementation as a political process, stressing the negotiation of change among those with different, vested interests. With this orientation to implementation, it is more accurate to suggest that one is moving away from a problem rather than toward a goal. At any given time, extremely small changes are made and the consequences are assessed before additional, small steps are taken. In the belief that the effort would not be warranted, little attempt is made to predict consequences in advance or to plot longer-term goals; at any point in the process, the change may be coopted by existing practices or abandoned altogether in favor of actions more consistent with local definitions of the problem.

Given a muddling through orientation to implementation, evaluation is most likely to be retrospective. Evaluation may recover what has happened by tracing the stages of change which implementors have experienced. Dimensions of change and full implementation are likely to be defined by those practices which have been discovered to work (or at least tried) by the time the evaluation is carried out. There is likely to be much opinion data available from implementors concerning the obstacles they have experienced during the implementation process. Such evaluation may serve accountability purposes, in a modest way. As practiced, however, its strength is the rich description of actual processes leading to a better appreciation of those processes, often under conditions which have made little use of extant knowledge about the management of change. Scheirer and Rezmovic (1982) discovered that ethnographic observations were the mode of data collection significantly more often when implementation evaluation was conducted with a muddling through orientation to change. Such data collection methods do not depend on prior specification of the dimensions of change or the meaning of full implementation. Examples reflecting such an approach to implementation and its evaluation have served research pur-

Table 1
Assumptions underlying alternative perspectives on the implementation process

	Alternative perspectives on the implementation process		
Assumptions	Muddling through	Adaptation	Fidelity
1. Role of innovation	Stimulates change	Provides a partial solution	Is the solution
2. Implementors	Proactive	Responsive	Passive
3. Content	Does not figure in decisions	One important consideration in decisions about change	Dominates decisions about change
4. Outcomes	Unpredictable	Partly predictable: within range specified by innovation	Predictable; as specified by innovation
5. Nature of change process	Incremental; direction uncertain	Incremental: growth in valued direction	Nonincremental; an "event"
6. Pivotal change strategy	Negotiations among all stakeholders	Participative, intermediate range planning	Strategic planning from the top
7. Actions required for full implementation	Determined by implementors during the process	Loosely specified at outset; modified during the process	Can be fully specified at the outset

poses; for example, Gross et al. (1971) and Hamilton (1975).

The fidelity perspective is least like muddling through. It is highly optimistic about achieving predetermined goals through the use of systematic, rational processes. An innovation worth implementing is viewed as a relatively complete solution to a clearly defined problem in a school or school system. Implementors are encouraged to focus their attention on the innovation and its use and to trust that full implementation will solve the problem. Linear and mechanistic are descriptors frequently applied to this alternative.

From a fidelity perspective, implementation is often assumed to be nonproblematic and to occur as a result of reasonable people quickly grasping the value of an innovation and readily following its prescribed practices. For this reason, instances of implementation evaluation conducted from this perspective are rare. Were they to be carried out, the innovation developer would be the most likely to identify dimensions of practice to change and to specify the meaning of full implementation. The evaluator would then collect data about whether or not the innovation was being implemented: when implementation of an innovation is considered nonproblematic, there is little need to consider either stages of implementation or obstacles to implementation.

On the surface adaptation appears to be the sane, middle ground between two extreme positions. It is not just a compromise based on what is possible; many also regard it as desirable on ethical and moral grounds because it permits some self-direction for implementors while recognizing the legitimate role of policy makers in setting educational goals. Adaptation requires the innovation to be reasonably well-developed at the outset (unlike muddling through) but assumes that it will have to be modified to fit effectively into the local context (unlike the fidelity alternative).

From an adaptation perspective, implementation evaluation includes collaboration among advocates of the innovation and implementors concerning the dimensions of practice to change, the meaning of full implementation and sometimes the stages of implementation as well. There are two well-developed sets of procedures for implementation evaluation from an adaptation perspective. One set of procedures was developed by Hall and associates in the context of the Concerns Based Adaption Model (CBAM) (e.g., Hord 1987). This procedure requires the evaluator to recover different configurations of use with respect to the innovation and then assess the degree of implementation of each configuration using a prespecified description of levels of use. Interviews are used to collect these data. A second set of procedures was developed by Leithwood and associates specifically to help implement curriculum innovations (e.g., Leithwood and Montgomery 1987). This procedure requires teams of practitioners to develop descriptions of stages of growth in the implementation of each curriculum innovation (called innovation profiles). Then, using interview or observation data, implementors' practices are matched with stages in the profile as a means of describing the degree of implementation.

5. Conclusion

Independent of orientation to implementation, for judgments to be made regarding the nature and degree of implementation of an innovation, existing practices must be described. Interviews, questionnaires, and direct observations are the most heavily relied on types of instruments used for collecting the data required for such description. The strengths and weaknesses of such instrument types for implementation evaluation have been examined (e.g., Leinhardt 1980). Perhaps the most noteworthy result of such an examination is recognition of the difficulty in choosing one best type of instrument. Which type of instrument is best depends on purposes for the evaluation and on the dimensions of practice within which change is being assessed. Changes in teachers' instructional strategies, for example, are overtly evident and so lend themselves to direct observation. A teacher's goals, however, are not visible and so require some type of self-report such as an interview or questionnaire.

Bibliography

Charters W W Jr, Jones J E 1973 On the risk of appraising non-events in program evaluation. *Educ. Res.* 2(11): 5–7

Fullan M 1982 *The Meaning of Educational Change.* OISE Press, Toronto, Ontario

Gross N, Giacquinta J B, Bernstein M 1971 *Implementing Organizational Innovations.* Harper and Row, New York

Hamilton D 1975 Handling innovation in the classroom: Two Scottish examples. In: Reid W A, Walker D F (eds.) 1975 *Case Studies in Curriculum Change.* Routledge and Kegan Paul, London, pp. 179–207

Hord S 1987 *Evaluating Educational Innovation.* Croom Helm, London

Leinhardt G 1980 Modeling and measuring educational treatment in evaluation. *Rev. Educ. Res.* 50(3): 393–420

Leithwood K A 1982 Implementing curriculum innovations. In: Leithwood K A (ed.) 1982 *Studies in Curriculum Decision Making.* OISE Press, Toronto, Ontario, pp. 245–67

Leithwood K A, Montgomery D J 1980 Evaluating program implementation. *Eval. Rev.* 4(2): 193–214

Leithwood K A, Montgomery D J (eds.) 1987 *Improving Classroom Practice Using Innovation Profiles.* OISE Press, Toronto, Ontario

Scheirer M A, Rezmovic E L 1982 *Measuring the Implementation of Innovations.* American Research Institute, Annadale, Virginia

Scriven M 1967 The methodology of evaluation. In: Tyler R W (ed.) 1967 *Perspectives of Curriculum Evaluation.* Rand McNally, Skokie, Illinois, pp. 39–83

Long-term Curriculum Evaluation

P. Tamir

Retrospective curriculum evaluation is a process by which the merits of a particular instructional program are determined on the basis of its long-term effects. The rationale and goals of many curricular innovations include long-term effects. For example, Bruner (1960) suggests that "massive general transfer may be achieved by appropriate learning, even to the degree that learning properly under optimum conditions leads one to learn how to learn" (p. 6). Cronbach (1963) is even more explicit and asserts that "outcomes of instruction are multidimensional . . . hence the outcomes observed should include general outcomes ranging far beyond the content of the curriculum itself—attitudes, career choices, general understandings and intellectual powers, and aptitude for further learning in the field" (pp. 675, 683). Thus, one major justification of retrospective curriculum evaluation is its potential for evaluating long-term effects.

The second justification is even more compelling; it suggests that *only* long-term evaluation can adequately assess certain merits of a given program. This suggestion is based on Ausubel's theory of meaningful learning, which asserts that the best and, perhaps, the only way to find out whether learning has been meaningful is by looking at the impact of the learning on subsequent achievement. Although details may be forgotten, the cumulative effects of having learned them remains on the cognitive structure of the learner. On the other hand, Ausubel seriously questions the validity of results obtained in an immediate final examination for assessing the worth of a curriculum, since "motivated students can learn for examination purposes large quantities of overly sophisticated and poorly presented material that they do not really understand" (Ausubel 1968 p. 578).

1. Examples of Retrospective Evaluation

The following examples are illustrative cases of retrospective evaluation.

In 1966 Ausubel evaluated the Biological Science Curriculum Study (BSCS) approach by content analysis of its three versions which were designated as Blue, Yellow, and Green. He wrote:

> The Blue Version presents biological material of college level difficulty and sophistication to students who had not had the necessary background in chemistry, physics, and elementary biology for learning them meaningfully. . . . It is so impossibly sophisticated for its intended audience as to be intrinsically unlearnable on a long-term basis. . . . It is not only unnecessary and inappropriate for the beginning course, but also hinders learning and generates unfavorable attitudes toward the subject.
>
> If biochemical content is included, it is probably better to provide a minimal background in chemistry and to consider biochemical topics at a somewhat lower level of sophistication (Yellow Version), than to provide almost no background in chemistry and to consider biochemical topics at a very high level of sophistication (Blue Version).
>
> Only the Green Version has a unifying theme . . . is reasonably well organized and integrated and makes an original contribution to and introduces a new (i.e., ecological) approach in the teaching of high school biology. (Ausubel 1966 pp. 176, 177, 180–81, 183)

When the results of achievement tests administered immediately at the end of the course were compared it was found that Blue Version students outscored Green and Yellow Version students (The Psychological Corporation 1967). Yet, when the long-term effects of the three versions were compared by evaluating students in their first year biology course at the university several differences were observed. Some of them are the following.

(a) BSCS students, compared with traditional students, were less likely to fail or drop out of introductory biology.

(b) Among the BSCS versions, "Blue" students showed the highest rates of failure and attrition, but "Yellow" students rarely failed or dropped out.

(c) Green Version students, compared with all other students, demonstrated the highest rate of retention with respect to ecology.

(d) Yellow Version students had the most positive, and Blue Version students the least positive attitudes toward biology.

(e) In their performance in tests that required critical thinking and an understanding of science, BSCS graduates tended to rely on higher cognitive abilities more than did non-BSCS graduates.

It may be seen that the results of the retrospective evaluation confirmed many of Ausubel's predictions, especially in relation to the inadequacy of the Blue Version for most 10th-grade students and the meaningful learning offered by the Green Version. On the other hand, in spite of Ausubel's assertions, Yellow Version students have demonstrated significant and consistent superiority in various aspects of achievement and attitudes (Tamir 1970).

Another example of retrospective evaluation is the evaluation of the chemistry program known as CHEM Study. It was found that:

> CHEM Study students have a distinct advantage in selective courses.
> The improved completion record of CHEM Study students in college chemistry courses suggests that they are more persistent, hence more interested in chemistry, due to their background. This record indicates that it is just as advantageous for the marginal students to have had CHEM Study as it is for the best. (CHEM Study 1967)

A study of first-year university students' perceptions of their high-school biology (Tamir et al. 1980) revealed, among other things, firstly, that students valued most highly the help of prior biological knowledge for the understanding and retention of new material presented in lectures, and secondly that students who specialized in high-school biology, as well as those who studied the Israeli BSCS adaptation, had considerable advantage over others in understanding the lectures and in their work in the laboratory.

2. The Nature and Limitations of Retrospective Evaluation

As already explained, the essence of retrospective curriculum evaluation is the long-term transfer paradigm which assumes the existence of relationships between early and subsequent levels of education. These relationships can be identified in two ways: (a) evaluation of actual students' behaviors at an advanced stage in reference to their learning experiences at earlier stages; and (b) examination of students' perceptions of the contribution of an earlier program (e.g., high school) to their subsequent studies (e.g., university).

Retrospective studies have certain limitations. One limitation of retrospective evaluation is the lack of control of events that have occurred in the interval between the two stages (e.g., high school and university). Another is that the samples are, by necessity, selective, since they include only those students who have moved from the lower to the higher level (e.g., from high school to the university).

Two alternative strategies have been traditionally used to study long-term effects: cross-sectional and longitudinal. Both strategies have severe limitations. Thus in longitudinal studies the same students are supposed to be followed for several years and their behaviors are measured at different points of time. However, not only is it difficult and costly to locate the subjects, but it is often impossible to maintain the original sample, hence attrition becomes a major handicap. Cross-sectional studies are free of this handicap, but suffer from the fact that different students represent different stages of growth, and one can never be sure of the magnitude of the effects of individual differences. The strategy suggested here, namely retrospective evaluation, overcomes the limitations mentioned above, since it deals with the same sample and there is practically no attrition.

3. Conclusion

Retrospective curriculum evaluation is built on sound theoretical grounds and its value has been demonstrated by several empirical examples. It may serve three major purposes: (a) the evaluation of long-term effects; (b) the evaluation of the meaningfulness of learning within the framework of a particular curriculum; (c) the long-term views and perceptions of students who are the major clientele of any given curriculum.

Bibliography

Ausubel D P 1966 Evaluation of the BSCS approach to high school biology. *Am. Biol. Teach.* 28: 176–86
Ausubel D P 1968 *Educational Psychology: A Cognitive View.* Holt, Rinehart and Winston, New York
Bruner J S 1960 *The Process of Education.* Vintage, New York

CHEM Study 1967 A study of CHEM study students after reaching college. *CHEM Stud. Newsletter* 7: 1

Cronbach L J 1963 Course improvement through evaluation. *Teach. Coll. Rec.* 64: 673–83

Tamir P 1970 Long-term evaluation of BSCS. *Am. Biol. Teach.* 32: 354–58

Tamir P, Amir R 1981 Retrospective curriculum evaluation: An approach to the evaluation of long-term effects. *Curric. Inq.* 11: 259–78

Tamir P, Amir R, Nussinvoitz R 1980 High school preparation for college biology in Israel. *Higher Educ.* 9: 399–408

The Psychological Corporation 1967 *A Report of Biology Science Curriculum Study Evaluation Program 1964–1965.* The Psychological Corporation, New York

Evaluation at Various Phases of Curriculum Development and Use

Experimental Curriculum

W. H. Schubert

Experimental curriculum, broadly conceived, refers to the attempt to provide a course offering that is different from those currently provided. In addition, the term experimental implies that the offering in question involves formal or informal hypotheses and draws attention to probable consequences. Experimental curricula sometimes use an experimental research design to assess results, but this is not always the case.

The variety of different interpretations of experimental curriculum can be explained in part by the fact that conceptions of curriculum itself vary (Eisner and Vallance 1974, Schubert 1980). For example, if curriculum is defined as a written course of study or document, then experimental curriculum would refer to the extant variation of implementation and outcomes that accrues from a change of policy. If, however, curriculum is defined as all of the experiences which the students have under the auspices of a school, experimental curriculum could pertain to any intervention that had impact upon learning experiences for which the school could be held responsible.

There is great varation as to the breadth or scope of a curricular experiment. It may range from a national policy alteration, to the adoption of a new curriculum by a school district (see *Curriculum Adoption*), or even to the attempt by an individual teacher to try something novel. It may be an attempt to experiment with an entire program, or to do so with a salient feature that runs through a program but does not alter the whole directly, or it may even refer to one relatively minor aspect of a program.

A curriculum experiment may focus upon any one or several of the following topics that perennially appear under the curriculum rubric: purposes, learning experiences or content, scope and sequence, methodology or instruction, learning environments, and evaluation or accountability practices.

The variety of types of experimental curricula can be exemplified by a brief sampling drawn from the history of curriculum in this century. John Dewey designed his Laboratory School at the University of Chicago (1896–1904) as an experiment in the sense that it set out to actualize the theory that a school curriculum could become a community that fostered both social and individual growth (see *Community Participation*). Beginning in 1932, the Progressive Education Association designed an experiment to compare students from traditional and progressive curricula of the Deweyan genre, known as the Eight-year Study. The unique nature of this project points to two very different orientations to experimental curricula. One form of experimentation consisted of the use of instruments developed to quantitatively and qualitatively portray outcomes of experimental and control groups. However, a second form of experimentation consisted of a deliberation among personnel from the 30 experimental schools about what was worthwhile to teach and learn. In this orientation, experimentation took the form of an encounter among teachers, students, administrators, and consultants who seriously reflected together and revised practices on a continuous basis. This kind of curriculum experimentation is reflected in the teacher-as-researcher movement in England and Wales (Stenhouse 1975). It interprets science as problem solving and interprets curriculum itself as an interaction among commonplaces that Schwab has labeled teacher, learner, subject matter, and milieu (Schwab 1978). Herein lies a practical notion of curriculum experimentation in which hypotheses are tested informally in the consequences of action.

Much more formal is the outgrowth of the dominant form of evaluation research which carefully specifies treatment, verifies its implementation, and tests preordained objectives against outcomes by the use of sophisticated statistical tools or ethnographic observations. Massive national curriculum reforms such as the post-Sputnik projects (Atkin and House 1981) in science and mathematics and antipoverty programs such as Head Start in the United States are often criticized on the grounds that the implementation of specified treatment is not verified.

Thus, it is both large- and small-scale efforts of considerable variety that have historically been regarded as experimental curricula. They range from national

451

movements to innovative action taken in a specific classroom situation.

Bibliography

Atkin J M, House E 1981 The federal role in curriculum development, 1950–1980. *Educ. Eval. Policy Anal.* 3(5): 5–36

Eisner E W, Vallance E (eds.) 1974 *Conflicting Conceptions of Curriculum.* McCutchan, Berkeley, California

Schubert W H 1980 *Curriculum Books: The First Eighty Years.* University Press of America, Lanham, Maryland

Schwab J J 1978 *Science, Curriculum, and Liberal Education: Selected Essays.* University of Chicago Press, Chicago, Illinois

Stenhouse L 1975 *Introduction to Curriculum Research and Development.* Heinemann, London

Intrinsic Evaluation

M. R. Eraut

The term "intrinsic evaluation" was first introduced by Scriven (1967) to characterize an approach to the evaluation of curriculum proposals and materials which focused on their intrinsic nature rather than their effects. Though he gave little methodological guidance, Scriven argued that all evaluations should include an evaluation of goals and that pure empiricism was impossible. The intrinsic component of an evaluation study should also include a consistency analysis in which divergencies between (a) espoused, (b) implicit, and (c) tested-for goals are disclosed; and a content analysis to appraise the accuracy, coverage, and significance of the content. While an evaluator might himself or herself be responsible for the former, the latter would necessitate consultation with external experts in the subject matter field.

Three possible roles may be played by intrinsic evaluation in the development and evaluation of curriculum materials. Firstly, in formative evaluations independent analysis by an evaluator and/or external experts can begin as soon as draft materials are available. Aims of this early analysis might be to disclose the developers' assumptions about the feasibility, desirability, and utilization of their materials; to relate these assumptions to the standards and values of various external groups; to anticipate issues that might emerge as significant during subsequent field testing; and to collect suggestions for possible improvements. The audience for this intrinsic evaluation would be the development team and its consultative committee; and its purpose both to assist in the formative evaluation and to prevent the developers from early commitment to assumptions that might ultimately prove disadvantageous.

The second role is in the initial stage of a summative evaluation when the audience is the evaluator. In this role the analysis is essentially hypothesis forming and its purpose is to guide subsequent empirical investigation. In addition to providing the basis for any assessment of student performance, an intrinsic evaluation can be combined with knowledge of common school practices to predict likely patterns of use and to anticipate possible incongruencies between intended and observed practice.

Then thirdly, intrinsic evaluation may contribute to the final stage of a summative evaluation by highlighting the major assumptions embedded in the product, evaluating its goals, reporting the findings of content and consistency analyses, and briefing decision makers on the similarities and differences with alternative products. It is only at this stage that the independence of the evaluator is crucial for external credibility.

Other articles in this Encyclopedia describe evaluation activities which rely heavily on intrinsic evaluation. These are rarely performed by people who receive any training for the task; and, while checklists of questions abound, there are few publications which discuss the methodology in any detail. The development of techniques for intrinsic evaluation is still in its infancy, so this article is limited to a review of those approaches which appear to offer the greatest potential.

Content analysis as a systematic technique has been most fully developed in the context of communication research. In essence it involves creating some system for categorizing content, defining a unit of analysis and a set of categorizing rules, and applying them to obtain a profile which depicts the content balance of a communication in terms of the chosen categories. The unit of analysis may be a chapter, a page, a topic, a period of allocated time, or an assignable unit. Several profiles may be used to present a more complete picture, but each needs to have a coherent theoretical base for its characterization. For example, thematic categories indicate the selection and focus of thematic content; categories based on classifications of objectives can indicate levels of thinking demanded of pupils; and other category systems can be devised to show the balance of pupil activities, the difficulty of the language, or the abstraction of the content. While some may be based on existing theories, others may be specifically developed to suit the particular documents being analysed. The most fully developed are probably those relating to the detection of bias against minority groups.

A rather different approach is needed for analysing the structuring and sequencing of content. While Posner and Strike (1976) provide an excellent theoretical framework, there still remain many methodological problems.

How, for example, is it possible to assess the validity of the claim by an author or an evaluator that their materials are indeed organized in the way they describe? Can an analyst identify underlying structures without underestimating the richness of good content? Do instructional designers' checklists adequately characterize quality in curriculum materials? As yet there is little systematic advice available.

A different style of intrinsic evaluation can be found in writings on curriculum criticism. This notion was introduced by Mann (1969) who argued that the purpose of the critic was to disclose meaning and to relate materials to their social context, making use of their own personal knowledge and stressing their ethical and aesthetic concerns.

Werner (1980) addresses the important issue of validity and suggests three basic validation principles for curriculum criticism: an explicit methodological framework and purpose; public dialogue about the appropriateness of the framework and the validity of the critic's interpretations within it; and evidence that it has contributed to better understanding of the curriculum. All three principles might usefully be applied to intrinsic evaluation in general.

Bibliography

Mann J S 1969 Curriculum criticism. *Teach. Coll. Rec.* 71: 27–40

Posner G J, Strike K A 1976 A categorization scheme for principles of sequencing content. *Rev. Educ. Res.* 46: 665–90

Sanders J R, Cunningham D J 1973 A structure for formative evaluation in product development. *Rev. Educ. Res.* 43: 217–36

Scriven M 1967 The methodology of curriculum evaluation. In: Tyler R W, Gagné R M, Scriven M (eds.) 1967 *Perspectives of Curriculum Evaluation.* American Educational Research Association Curriculum Evaluation Monographs 1. Rand McNally, Chicago, Illinois

Stake R E 1970 Objectives, priorities and other judgement data. *Rev. Educ. Res.* 40: 181–212

Werner W 1980 Editorial criticism in curricular analysis. *Curric. Inq.* 10: 143–54

Delphi Technique

N. P. Uhl

The Delphi technique, named after the oracle at Delphi in ancient Greece, is a communications process which permits a group to achieve consensus in the solution of a complex problem without face-to-face interaction or confrontation by the individual members of the group. By eliminating face-to-face interaction, this process avoids such problems as the influence of dominant individuals on group decisions, the loss of time and energy on irrelevant or biased discussions, the distortion of individual judgment by group pressure, the inclination to reject novel ideas, and the tendency to defend a previous position. At the same time, it assures independent thought, anonymity, and the assessment without pressure of the ideas of others in the gradual formation of a considered opinion.

In general, the procedure is as follows: (a) participants are chosen and are asked to give anonymous opinions, suggestions, recommendations, or predictions (depending on the topic) to a series of questionnaire items; (b) each participant receives feedback, such as the median response of all participants, and a second round of responding begins in order to ascertain the intensity of agreement or disagreement with the group median response; (c) again feedback is given to the participants in terms of the group median and also the reasons why some participants do not agree with the median response; (d) after reviewing the reasons for the minority opinions, the participants again respond; (e) steps (c) and (d) can be repeated although convergence of opinion usually does not increase greatly after one round of these two steps. A detailed chronological description of how these five steps were employed in an actual study can be found in Uhl's (1971) investigation of institutional goals using the Delphi technique. It is interesting to note that while most studies incorporating the Delphi technique have used questionnaires, a few studies have adopted the technique for computer use which permits participants to respond through separate terminals. Linstone and Turoff (1975), in the most recent compendium of Delphi studies, describe such a study.

The Delphi technique was originally developed by the Rand Corporation in the 1950s to deal with complex defense problems and since the mid-1960s its use has expanded at a prolific rate. It is being used by business, government, industry, medicine, regional planning, and education in a wide variety of situations including futures forecasting, goal assessment, curriculum planning, establishment of budget priorities, estimates concerning the quality of life, policy formulation, as well as problem identification and formulation of solutions. While the Delphi technique was considered primarily a forecasting tool in its earlier uses, it is currently being utilized more and more as a process to improve communications and generate consensus in the solution to almost any type of complex problem.

The use of the Delphi may be warranted if any or all of the following conditions exist: (a) the resolution of a problem can be facilitated by the collective judgments of one or more groups; (b) those groups providing judgments are not likely to communicate adequately without an intervening process; (c) the solution is more likely to be accepted if more people are involved in its development than would be possible in a face-to-face meeting; (d) frequent group meetings are not practical because of time, distance, etc.; and (e) one or more groups of participants are more dominant than another.

It is surprising that of all the studies performed using the Delphi technique, very few are of a methodological nature. As a result, Delphi has a poor theoretical base and little is known about the variables that affect the process. This lack of a theoretical framework is its main

weakness. A systematic research program is needed to determine how and why the method functions.

Bibliography

Linstone H, Turoff M (eds.) 1975 *The Delphi Method: Techniques and Applications.* Addison-Wesley, Reading, Massachusetts

Uhl N P 1971 *Identifying Institutional Goals: Encouraging Convergence of Opinion Through the Delphi Technique*, Research Monograph No. 2. National Laboratory for Higher Education, Durham, North Carolina

Criterion-referenced Measurement

R. K. Hambleton

Criterion-referenced tests are constructed to permit the interpretation of examinee test performance in relation to a set of well-defined competencies (Popham 1978). In relation to the competencies, there are three common uses for criterion-referenced test scores: (a) to describe examinee performance, (b) to assign examinees to mastery states (e.g., "masters" and "nonmasters"), and (c) to describe the performance of specified groups of examinees in program evaluation studies. Criterion-referenced tests are presently receiving extensive use in schools, industry, and the military in the United States because they provide information which is valued by test users and different from the information provided by norm-referenced tests. This article will introduce basic criterion-referenced testing concepts, compare these tests to norm-referenced tests, consider some aspects of criterion-referenced test development, and describe several promising applications.

1. Basic Concepts

One of the first articles on the topic of criterion-referenced testing appeared in the *American Psychologist* (Glaser 1963). Over 700 papers on the topic have been published since then, and the scope and direction of educational testing has been changed dramatically. Glaser was interested in assessment methods that would provide necessary information for making a number of individual and programmatic decisions arising in connection with specific objectives or competencies. Norm-referenced tests were seen as limited in terms of providing the desired kinds of information.

At least 57 definitions of criterion-referenced measurement have been offered in the literature. Popham's definition which was introduced earlier in this article is probably the one which is most widely used. Several points about the definition deserve comment. First, terms such as objectives, competencies, and skills are used interchangeably in the field. Second, the competencies measured by a criterion-referenced test must

be well-defined. Well-defined competencies make the process of item writing easier and more valid, and improve the quality of test score interpretations. The quality of score interpretations is improved because of the clarity of the content or behavior domains to which test scores are referenced. There is no limit on the breadth and complexity of a domain of content or behaviors defining a competency. The intended purpose of a test will influence the appropriate breadth and complexity of domains. Diagnostic tests are typically organized around narrowly defined competencies. End-of-year assessments will normally be carried out with more broadly defined competencies. Third, when more than one competency is measured in a test it is common to report examinee performance on each competency. Fourth, Popham's criterion-referenced test definition does not include a reference to a cutoff score or standard. It is common to set a minimum standard of performance for each competency measured in a criterion-referenced test and interpret examinee performance in relation to it. But, the use of test scores for describing examinee performance is common (e.g., the best estimate of student A's performance in relation to the domain of content defined by the competency is 70 per cent) and standards are not needed for this type of score use. That a standard (or standards) may not be needed with a criterion-referenced test will come as a surprise to persons who have assumed (mistakenly) that the word "criterion" in "criterion-referenced test" refers to a "standard" or "cutoff score." In fact, the word "criterion" was used by Glaser (1963) and Popham and Husek (1969) to refer to a domain of content or behavior to which test scores are referenced.

Three additional points about criterion-referenced tests deserve mention: (a) the number of competencies measured by a criterion-referenced test will (in general) vary from one test to the next, (b) the number of test items measuring each competency and the value of the minimum standard will (in general) vary from one competency to the next, and (c) a common method for making mastery–nonmastery decisions involves the comparison of examinee per cent (or proportion-correct) scores on competencies to the corresponding minimum standards. With respect to (c), when an examinee's per cent score is equal to or greater than the standard, the examinee is assumed to be a "master" (M), otherwise the examinee is assumed to be a "nonmaster" (NM). There are however more complex decision-making models (for a review, see van der Linden 1980).

It is common to see terms like criterion-referenced tests, domain-referenced tests, and objectives-referenced tests in the psychometric literature. Popham's definition for a criterion-referenced test is similar to one Millman and others proposed for a domain-referenced test. There are no essential differences between the two if Popham's definition for a criterion-referenced test is adopted. The term "domain-referenced test" is a descriptive one and therefore it is less likely to be misunderstood than the term, "criterion-referenced test." One reason for continuing to use the term, "criterion-referenced test," even though it is less descriptive and its definition has become muddled in the psychometric literature, is that there is considerable public support in the United States for "criterion-referenced tests." It would seem to be a waste of valuable time to mount a campaign for a new term (Popham 1978).

Objectives-referenced tests consist of items that are matched to objectives. The principal difference between criterion-referenced tests and objectives-referenced tests is that in a criterion-referenced test, items are organized into clusters with each cluster serving (usually) as a representative set of items from a clearly defined content domain measuring an objective, while with an objectives-referenced test, no clear domain of content is specified for an objective, and items are not considered to be representative of any content domain. Therefore, interpretations of examinee performance on objectives-referenced tests should be limited to the particular items on the test.

2. Norm-referenced and Criterion-referenced Tests

Proponents of norm-referenced and criterion-referenced tests in the United States waged a battle in the 1970s for supremacy of the achievement testing world. A third group argued that there was only one kind of achievement test from which both criterion-referenced and norm-referenced score interpretations could be made when needed. It is now clear that there was no winner although in the 10-year period the uses of criterion-referenced tests did increase substantially in the United States. Also, there was a reduction in the amount of norm-referenced testing taking place. There was no winner because it is clear that it is meaningful to distinguish between two kinds of achievement tests and both kinds of tests have important roles to play in

providing information for test users. Norm-referenced achievement tests are needed to provide reliable and valid normative scores for comparing examinees. Criterion-referenced achievement tests are needed to facilitate the interpretation of examinee performance in relation to well-defined competencies.

Although the differences between norm-referenced tests and criterion-referenced tests are substantial, the two kinds of tests share many features. In fact, it would be a rare individual who could distinguish between them from looking at the test booklets alone. They use the same item formats; test directions are similar; and both kinds of tests can be standardized.

There are a number of important differences, however, between them. The first difference is test purpose. A norm-referenced test is constructed specifically to facilitate comparisons among examinees in the content area measured by the test. It is common to use age-, percentile-, and standard-score norms to accomplish the test's purpose. Since test items are (or can be) referenced to competencies, criterion-referenced score interpretations (or, more correctly, objectives-referenced score interpretations) are possible but are typically limited in value because of the (usually) small number of test items measuring any competency in the test. Criterion-referenced tests, on the other hand, are constructed to assess examinee performance in relation to a set of competencies. Scores may be used (a) to describe examinee performance, (b) to make mastery–nonmastery decisions, and (c) to evaluate program effectiveness. Scores can be used to compare examinees but comparisons may have relatively low reliability if score distributions are homogeneous.

The second difference is in the area of content specificity. It is common for designers of both test types to prepare test blueprints or tables of specifications. It is even possible that norm-referenced test designers will prepare behavioral objectives. But, criterion-referenced test designers must (typically) prepare considerably more detailed content specifications than provided by behavioral objectives to ensure that criterion-referenced test scores can be interpreted in the intended way. This point will be considered further in the next section. Thus, with respect to content specifications, the difference between the two types is in the degree to which test content must be specified.

The third difference is in the area of test development. With norm-referenced tests, item statistics (difficulty and discrimination indices) serve an important role in item selection. In general, items of moderate difficulty (p-values in the range 0.30 to 0.70) and high discriminating power (point biserial correlations over 0.30) are most likely to be selected for a test because they contribute substantially to test score variance. Test reliability and validity will, generally, be higher when test score variance is increased. In contrast, criterion-referenced test items are only deleted from the pools of test items measuring competencies when it is determined that they violate the content specifications or standard principles of item writing, they are biased, or if the available item statistics reveal serious non-correctable flaws. Item statistics can be used to construct parallel forms of a criterion-referenced test or to produce a test to optimally discriminate between masters and nonmasters in the region of a minimum standard of performance on the test score scale.

The fourth and final major area of difference between criterion-referenced tests and norm-referenced tests is test score generalizability. Seldom is there interest in making generalizations from norm-referenced achievement test scores. The basis for score interpretations is the performance of some reference group. In contrast, score generalizability is usually of interest with criterion-referenced tests. Seldom is there interest in the performance of examinees on specific sets of test items. When clearly specified competency statements are available and assuming test items are representative of the content domains from which they are drawn, examinee test performance can be generalized to performance in the larger domains of content defining the competencies. It is this type of interpretation which is (usually) of interest to criterion-referenced test users.

3. Content Specifications

Behavioral objectives had a highly significant impact on instruction and testing in the 1960s and 1970s. But, while behavioral objectives are relatively easy to write and have contributed substantially to the specification of curricula, they do not usually lead to clearly defined content descriptions defining competencies. Popham (1974) described tests built from behavioral objectives as "cloud-referenced tests." Several suggestions have been made for addressing the deficiency in behavioral objectives and thereby making it possible to construct valid criterion-referenced tests. These suggestions include the use of item transformations, item forms, algorithms, and structural facet theory. Possibly the most versatile and practical of the suggestions was introduced by Popham (1978, 1984) and is called domain specifications, item specifications, or expanded objectives. Domain specifications serve four purposes: (a) provide item writers with content and technical guidelines for preparing test items, (b) provide content and measurement specialists with a clear description of the content and/or behaviors which are to be covered by each competency so that they can assess whether items are valid measures of the intended competencies, (c) aid in interpreting examinee competency performance, and (d) provide users with clear specifications of the breadth and scope of competencies. Some educational measurement specialists have even gone so far as to suggest that the emphasis on content specifications has been the most important contribution of criterion-referenced testing to measurement practice (Berk 1984).

Using the work of Popham (1978) as a basis, Hambleton (1990) suggested that a domain specification might be divided into four parts:

(a) Description—a short, concise statement of the content and/or behaviors covered by the competency.

(b) Sample directions and test item—an example of the test directions and a model test item to measure the competency.

(c) Content limits—a detailed description of both the content and/or behaviors measured by the competency, as well as the structure and content of the item pool. (This section should be so clear that items may be divided by reviewers into those items that meet the specifications and those items that do not.) Sometimes clarity is enhanced by also specifying areas which are not included in the content domain description.

Description
The student will identify the tones or emotions expressed in paragraphs.

Sample directions and test item
Directions: Read the paragraph below. Then answer the question and circle the letter beside your answer.

Jimmy had been playing and swimming at the beach all day. Now it was time to go home. Jimmy sat down in the back seat of his father's car. He could hardly keep his eyes open.

How did Jimmy feel?

A. Afraid   B. Friendly   C. Tired   D. Kind

Content limits
1. Paragraphs will describe situations which are familiar to grade 3 students.

2. Paragraphs should contain between three and six sentences. Readability levels should be at the third grade (using the Dale-Chall formula).

3. Tones or emotions expressed in the passages should be selected from the list below:

sad	mad	angry	kind
tired	scared	friendly	excited
happy	lucky	smart	proud

Response limits
1. Answer choices should be one word in length.

2. Four answer choices should be used with each test item.

3. Incorrect answer choices may be selected from the list above.

4. Incorrect answer choices should be tones or emotions which are familiar to students in grade 3 and which are commonly confused with the correct answer.

Figure 1
A typical domain specification in the reading area

Table 1
Steps for constructing criterion-referenced tests

Steps	Comments

1. Preliminary considerations
 	
  (a) Specify test purposes.
  (b) Specify groups to be measured and (any) special testing requirements (due to examinee age, race, sex, socioeconomic status, handicaps, etc.).
  (c) Determine the time and money available to produce the test.
  (d) Identify qualified staff.
  (e) Specify an initial estimate of test length.
	This step is essential to ensure that a test development project is well-organized and important factors which might have an impact on test quality are identified early.

2. Review of competency statements
 	
  (a) Review the descriptions of the competencies to determine their acceptability.
  (b) Make necessary competency statement revisions to improve their clarity.
	Domain specifications are invaluable to item writers when they are well-done. Considerable time and money can be saved later in revising test items if item writers are clear on what it is that is expected of them.

3. Item writing
 	
  (a) Draft a sufficient number of items for pilot-testing.
  (b) Carry out item editing.
	Some training of item writers in the importance and use of domain specifications, and in the principles of item writing is often desirable.

4. Assessment of content validity
 	
  (a) Identify a sufficient pool of judges and measurement specialists.
  (b) Review the test items to determine their match to the competencies, their representativeness, and their freedom from bias and stereotyping.
  (c) Review the test items to determine their technical adequacy.
	This step is essential. Items are evaluated by reviewers to assess their match to the competencies, their technical quality, and their freedom from bias and stereotyping.

5. Revisions to test items
 	
  (a) Based upon data from 4(b) and 4(c), revise test items (when possible) or delete them.
  (b) Write additional test items (if needed) and repeat step 4.
	Any necessary revisions to test items should be made at this step and when additional test items are needed, they should be written, and step 4 carried out again.

6. Field test administration
 	
  (a) Organize the test items into forms for pilot testing.
  (b) Administer the test forms to appropriately chosen groups of examinees.
  (c) Conduct item analyses, and item validity and item bias studies.
	The test items are organized into booklets and administered to appropriate numbers of examinees. That number should reflect the importance of the test under construction. Appropriate revisions to test items can be made here. Item statistics are used to identify items which may be in need of revision: (a) items which may be substantially easier or harder than other items measuring the same competencies, (b) items with negative or low positive discriminating power, and (c) items with distractors which were selected by small percentages of examinees.

7. Revisions to test items (a) Revise test items when necessary or delete them using the results from 6(c).	Whenever possible, malfunctioning test items should be revised and added to the pools of acceptable test items. When revisions to test items are substantial they should be returned to step 4.

8. Test assembly
 	
  (a) Determine the test length, and the number of forms needed and the number of items per objective.
  (b) Select test items from the available pool of valid test items.
  (c) Prepare test directions, practice questions, test booklet layout, scoring keys, answer sheets, etc.
	Test booklets are compiled at this step. When parallel-forms are required, and especially if the tests are short, item statistics should be used to ensure matched forms are produced.

Table 1 *continued*

Steps	Comments
9. Selection of a standard (a) Initiate a process to determine the standard to separate "masters" and "nonmasters."	A standard-setting procedure must be selected and implemented. Care should be taken to document the selection process.

10. Pilot test administration
   (a) Design the administration to collect score reliability and validity information.
   (b) Administer the test form(s) to appropriately chosen groups of examinees.
   (c) Evaluate the test administration procedures, test items, and score reliability and validity.
   (d) Make final revisions based on data from 10(c).
	At this step, test directions can be evaluated, scoring keys can be checked, and reliability and validity of scores and decisions can be assessed.

11. Preparation of manuals
   (a) Prepare a test administrator's manual.
   (b) Prepare a technical manual.
	For important tests, a test administration manual and a technical manual should be prepared.

12. Additional technical data collection (a) Conduct reliability and validity investigations.	No matter how carefully a test is constructed or evaluated, reliability and validity studies should be carried out on an ongoing basis.

(d) Response limits—a description of the kind of incorrect answer choices which must be prepared. The structure and content of the incorrect answers should be stated in as much detail as possible. On the other hand, when performance tasks are used to assess mastery, this section includes the details concerning scoring.

An example of a domain specification is shown in Fig. 1. Once properly prepared domain specifications are available, the remaining steps in the test development process can be carried out.

4. Criterion-referenced Test Development

It is essential to specify clearly the domain of content or behaviors defining each competency which is to be measured in the test being constructed. The mechanism through which the competencies are identified will vary from one situation to the next. For high-school graduation exams, the process might involve district educational leaders meeting to review school curricula and identifying a relatively small set of important broad competencies (e.g., reading comprehension, mathematics computations). When criterion-referenced tests are needed in an objectives-based instructional program, it is common to define a curriculum in broad areas (and, sometimes into a two-dimensional grid). Then, within the cells of the grid the sets of relevant objectives, often stated in behavioral form, are specified, reviewed, revised, and finalized. With certification exams, it is common first to conduct a "role delineation study" with individuals working in the area to identify

the responsibilities, subresponsibilities, and activities which serve to define a role. Next, the knowledge and skills which are needed to carry out the role are identified.

A set of 12 steps for preparing criterion-referenced tests adapted from Hambleton (1990) is suggested in Table 1.

5. Applications of Criterion-referenced Tests

Criterion-referenced tests (or domain-referenced tests, mastery tests, competency tests, basic skills tests, or certification exams as they are alternately called) are being used in a large number of settings in the United States to address many problem areas. Criterion-referenced tests are finding substantial use in American schools. Classroom teachers use criterion-referenced test score results to locate students correctly in school programs, to monitor student progress, and to identify student deficiencies. Special education teachers are finding criterion-referenced test scores especially helpful in diagnosing student learning deficiencies and monitoring the progress of their students. Criterion-referenced test results are also being used to evaluate various school programs. While it is less common, criterion-referenced tests are finding some use in higher educational programs as well (e.g., those programs based upon the mastery learning concept). Also, criterion-referenced tests are in common use in military and industrial training programs.

In recent years, it has become common for state departments of education and (sometimes) school districts to define sets of skills (or competencies) which students must achieve in order to be promoted from one grade to the next, or in some states, to receive high-school diplomas. The nature of these criterion-referenced testing programs varies dramatically from one place to another. For example, in some places, students are held responsible for mastering a specified set of skills at each grade level, in other states, skills which must be acquired are specified at selected grade levels, and in still other states, only a set of skills which must be mastered for high-school graduation is specified.

One of the most important applications of criterion-referenced tests is to the areas of professional certification and licensure. It is now common in the United States, for example, for professional organizations to establish entry-level examinations which must be passed by candidates before they are allowed to practice in their chosen professions. In fact, many of these professional organizations have also established recertification exams. A typical examination will measure the competencies which define the professional role and candidate test performance is interpreted in relation to minimum standards which are established. There are now over 900 organizations, including most groups in the medical and allied health fields, who have instituted certification and recertification exams (Hambleton and Rogers 1986).

Bibliography

Berk R A (ed.) 1984 *A Guide to Criterion-Referenced Test Construction*. Johns Hopkins University Press, Baltimore, Maryland

Glaser R 1963 Instructional technology and the measurement of learning outcomes. *Am. Psychol.* 18: 519–21

Hambleton R K 1990 Criterion-referenced testing methods and practices. In: Gatkin T, Reynolds C (eds.) 1990 *Handbook of School Psychology* (2nd edn.). Wiley, New York, pp. 388–414

Hambleton R K, Swaminathan H, Algina J, Coulson D B 1978 Criterion-referenced testing and measurement: A review of technical issues and developments. *Rev. Educ. Res.* 48: 1–47

Hambleton R K, Rogers H J 1986 Technical advances in credentialing exams. *Evaluation and the Health Professions* 9: 205–229

Popham W J 1974 An approaching peril: Cloud referenced tests. *Phi Delta Kappan* 55: 614–15

Popham W J 1978 *Criterion-Referenced Measurement*. Prentice-Hall, Englewood Cliffs, New Jersey

Popham W J 1984 Specifying the domain of content or behaviors. In: Berk R (ed.) *A Guide to Criterion-Referenced Test Construction*. Johns Hopkins University Press, Baltimore, Maryland, pp. 29–48

Popham W J, Husek T R 1969 Implications of criterion-referenced measurement. *J. Educ. Meas.* 6: 1–9

van der Linden W J 1980 Decision models for use with criterion-referenced tests. *Appl. Psychol. Meas.* 4: 469–92

Narrative and Story-telling Approach

D. J. Clandinin and F. M. Connelly

One of the dilemmas of educational studies is that it is often the case that the more rigorous and scientific educational research becomes, the less it becomes connected to human experience. The objectivists call those who study experience "soft" and "subjective"; conversely experientalists claim that the scientific study of education depersonalizes, dehumanizes, and objectifies people. Narrative and story telling, two intimately related terms, are increasingly evident in the literature which swirls around these compelling scientific-humanistic modes of inquiry. They are terms representing ideas about the nature of human experience and about how experience may be studied and represented and which tread a middle course between the extremes. Narrativists believe that human experience is basically storied experience: that humans live out stories and are story-telling organisms. They further believe that one of the best ways to study human beings is to come to grips with the storied quality of human experience, to record stories of educational experience, and to write still other interpretive stories of educational experience. The complex stories that are written are called narratives. Properly done these stories are close to experience because they directly represent human experience; and they are close to theory because they give accounts that are educationally meaningful for participants and readers.

There are a number of qualities of narrative approaches to educational studies which make them different from other forms of research. To begin with narrative has a story quality. Secondly, stories are interesting in themselves in the same sense that a fictional story is interesting. They have what some authors call an "invitational" quality and are compelling for both academics and practitioners. Given the limited space available the following discussion is restricted to an account of the theoretical origins of narrative studies, a brief description of narrative studies in education and to several narratively based curriculum lines of inquiry.

1. The Inquiry Contexts of Educational Narrative Studies

Narrative has a long history in literature. Perhaps because it focuses on human experience, perhaps because story is a fundamental structure of human experience, and perhaps because it has a holistic quality, narrative is exploding into other disciplines. Narrative is a way of characterizing the phenomena of human experience and its study which is appropriate to many social science fields.

Literary theory is the principle intellectual resource (e.g. Hardy 1968). The fact that a story is inherently temporal means that history (White 1981) and the philosophy of history (Carr 1986), which are essentially the study of time, have a special role to play in shaping narrative studies in the social sciences. Therapeutic fields are making significant contributions (e.g. Schafer 1981). Psychology has only recently discovered narrative although Polkinghorne (1988) claims that closely related inquiries were part of the field at the turn of the century but disappeared after the Second World War when they were suffocated by physical science paradigms. Sarbin (1986) is a frequently cited psychology source. Among the most fundamental and educationally suggestive works on the nature of narrative knowledge is Johnson's philosophical study of bodily knowledge and language (1989). Because education is ultimately a moral and spiritual pursuit, MacIntyre's narrative ethical theory (1981) and Crites' theological writing on narrative (1986) are especially useful for educational purposes.

2. Related Educational Studies

Most educational studies of narrative have counterparts in the social sciences. Polkinghorne's (1988) history of "individual psychology" from the mid-1800s describes narrative-related studies which have educational counterparts. He discusses case history, biography, life history, life-span development, Freudian psychoanalysis and organizational consultation. The focus in all of this work is an individual's psychology considered over a span of time. Narrative inquiry may also be sociologically concerned with groups and the formation of community (Carr 1986).

Goodson's (1988) historical discussion of "teachers' life histories and studies of curriculum in schooling" gives a sociologically oriented account of life history in sociology, anthropology, and educational studies. Goodson sees autobiography as a version of life history work. However, many writers focus on teacher careers and professionalism (e.g. Sikes et al. 1985) and thus it seems useful to maintain a distinction between biography/autobiography and life history. Goodson assigns to the "Chicago school" the main influence on life history work through sociologists such as Park and Becker. Polkinghorne (1988) emphasizes Mead's (also "Chicago School") philosophical theories of symbolic interaction.

Pinar (1988) and Grumet (1988) have outlined an autobiographical tradition in educational studies. Berk (1980), in a discussion of the history of the uses of autobiography/biography in education, states that autobiography was one of the first methodologies for educational study. Shifting inquiry from the question "What does it mean for a person to be educated?" to "How are people, in general, educated?"

appeared to lead to the demise of autobiography/biography in educational studies. Several writers have explored relations between autobiography/biography and narrative (e.g. Connelly and Clandinin 1987).

Some closely related lines of inquiry focus specifically on story: oral history and folklore, children's story telling, and the uses of story in preschool and schooling language experience. Dorson (1976) distinguishes between oral history and oral literature which yields a wide range of phenomena for narrative inquiry and which suggest educational inquiry possibilities such as material culture, custom, arts, recollections, myths and so on. Myths, Dorson notes, are the storied structures which stand behind folklore and oral history, an observation which links narrative to the theory of myth. Van Maanen (1988) provides an introduction to the ethnography of story telling both as subject matter and as ethnographers' written form. The best known educational use of oral history in North America is the Foxfire project (Wigginton 1989).

Applebee's (1978) work is a resource on children's story telling and children's expectations of story from teachers, texts and others. Sutton-Smith's (1986) review of the literature distinguishes between structuralist approaches, which rely on "schema" and other cognition theory terms and meaning in a hermeneutic tradition. A curricular version of this literature is Egan's (1986) suggestion that school subject matter be organized in story form. He suggests a model that "encourages us to see lessons or units as good stories to be told rather than sets of objectives to be obtained" (p. 2).

Applebee's work is an outgrowth of the uses of story in language instruction: a line of enquiry sometimes referred to as the work of "the Cambridge group". Much of this work has a curriculum development/teaching method focus but there are also theoretical and research traditions (e.g. Applebee 1978. Recently this work has begun to establish a counterpart in studies of adult language and second language learning (Allen 1989). In their work on curriculum, Connelly and Clandinin (1988) see teachers' narratives as a metaphor for teaching–learning relationships. In "understanding ourselves and our students educationally, we need an understanding of people with a narrative of life experience. Life's narratives are the context for making meaning of school situations" (Connelly and Clandinin 1988 p. 27). This narrative view of curriculum is echoed in the work of language researchers (Calkins 1986) and general studies of curriculum (Lightfoot and Martin 1988).

Because of its focus on experience and the qualities of life and education, narrative is situated in a matrix of qualitative research. More specifically, Eisner's (1988) review of the educational study of experience implicitly aligns narrative with qualitatively oriented educational researchers working with experiential philosophy, psychology, critical theory, curriculum studies, and anthropology. Whereas Eisner came at his problem from the point of view of experience, Elbaz (1988) focused on teacher thinking studies. Because her interest is also a narrative one, her review creates a profile of the most closely related narrative family members. One way she constructs the family is to review studies of "the personal" to show these studies have an affinity with narrative. Another entry point for Elbaz is "voice" which, for her, and others (Clandinin 1988), aligns narrative with feminist studies. Elbaz's principal concern is with "story". Using a distinction between story as "primarily a methodological device" versus story as "methodology itself", she aligns narrative with many educational studies which, while the researcher may not be conscious of using story, report data either in narrative form or use participant stories as raw data. On this basis works such as Schulman's (1987) on expert teachers, Reid's (1987) policy analysis and Lincoln and Guba's (1985) naturalistic approach to evaluation qualify as narratively related work.

There is a collection of educational literature which is narrative in quality but which is not found in review documents where it might reasonably appear, (e.g. in Wittrock 1986). We call this literature "teachers' stories and stories of teachers". This name refers to second-hand accounts of individual teachers, students, classrooms and schools written by teachers and others (e.g. Paley 1981). Jackson's (1968) book plays an especially generative role with respect to the literature of "teachers' stories and stories of teachers".

This overview of narrative and story-telling approaches in and out of education is intended to help locate narrative in a historical intellectual context. On the one hand, narrative inquiry may be traced to Aristotle's *Poetics* and Augustine's *Confessions* (See Ricoeur's 1984, use of these two sources to link time and narrative) and may be seen to have various adaptations and applications in a diversity of disciplines including education. Dewey's (e.g. 1934, 1938) work on time, space, experience and sociality is also central. On the other hand, there is a newness to "narratology" as it has developed in the social sciences, including education. The educational importance of this line of work is that it brings theoretical ideas about the nature of human life as lived to bear on educational experience as lived.

Bibliography

Allen J P B 1989 The development of instructional models in second language education. *Ann. Rev. Appl. Ling.* 9: 179–92

Applebee A N 1978 *The Child's Concept of Story: Ages Two to Seventeen.* University of Chicago Press, Chicago, Illinois

Berk L 1980 Education in lives: Biographic narrative in the study of educational outcomes. *J. Curric. Theor.* 2(2): 88–153

Calkins L M 1986 *The Art of Teaching Writing.* Heinemann, Portsmouth, New Hampshire

Carr D 1986 *Time, Narrative, and History.* Indiana University Press, Bloomington, Indiana

Clandinin D 1988 Understanding research on teaching as feminist research. Paper presented at the annual meeting of the Canadian Society for the Study of Education, Windsor, Ontario

Connelly F M, Clandinin D J 1987 On narrative method, biography and narrative unities in the study of teaching. *J. Educ. Thought* 21(3): 130–39

Connelly F M, Clandinin D J 1988 *Teachers as Curriculum Planners: Narratives of Experience.* Teachers College Press, New York

Crites S 1986 Storytime: Recollecting the past and projecting the future. In: Sarbin T R (ed.) 1986 *The Storied Nature of Human Conduct.* Praeger, New York, pp. 152–197

Dewey J 1934 *Art as Experience.* Milton Balch, New York

Dewey J 1938 *Experience and Education.* Macmillan, New York

Dorson R M 1976 *Folklore and Fakelore: Essays Toward a Discipline of Folkstudies.* Harvard University Press, Cambridge, Massachusetts

Egan K 1986 *Teaching as Story Telling: An Alternative Approach to Teaching and Curriculum in the Elementary School.* Althouse Press, Faculty of Education, University of Western Ontario, London, Ontario

Eisner, E W 1988 The primacy of experience and the politics of method. *Educ. Res.* 17(5): 15–20

Elbaz F 1988 Knowledge and discourse: The evolution of research on teacher thinking. Paper presented at the Conference of the International Study Association on Teacher Thinking meeting of the University of Nottingham

Goodson I F 1988 Teachers' life histories and studies of curriculum and schooling. In: Goodson I F (ed.) 1988 *The Making of Curriculum: Collected Essays.* Falmer Press, London

Grumet M R 1988 *Bitter Milk: Women and Teaching.* University of Massachusetts Press, Amherst, Massachusetts

Hardy B 1968 Towards a poetics of fiction: An approach through narrative. *Novel* 2: 5–14.

Husén T 1989 Educational research at the crossroads? *Prospects* 19: 351–60

Jackson P W 1986 *Life In Classrooms.* Holt, Rinehart, and Winston, New York

Johnson M 1989 Embodied knowledge. *Curric. Inq.* 19(4): 361–77

Lightfoot M, Martin N (eds.) 1988 *The Word for Teaching is Learning: Essays for James Britton.* Heinemann Educational Books, London

Lincoln Y S, Guba E G 1985 *Naturalistic Inquiry.* Sage, Beverly Hills, California

MacIntyre A 1981 *After Virtue: A Study in Moral Theory.* University of Notre Dame Press, Notre Dame, Indiana

Paley V G 1981 *Wally's Stories: Conversations in the Kindergarten.* Harvard University Press, Cambridge, Massachusetts

Pinar W F 1988 "Whole, bright, deep with understanding": Issues in qualitative research and autobiographical method. In: Pinar W F (ed.) 1988 *Contemporary Curriculum Discourses.* Gorsuch Scarisbrick, Scottsdale, Arizona, pp. 135–53

Polkinghorne D E 1988 *Narrative Knowing and the Human Sciences.* State University of New York Press, Albany, New York

Reid W A 1987 Institutions and practices: Professional education reports and the language of reform. *Educ. Res.* 16(8): 10–15

Ricoeur P 1984 *Time and Narrative*, vol. I. University of Chicago Press, Chicago, Illinois

Sarbin T R (ed.) 1986 *Narrative Psychology: The Storied Nature of Human Conduct.* Praeger, New York

Schafer R 1981 Narration in the psychoanalytic dialogue. In: Mitchell W J T (ed.) 1981 *On Narrative*. University of Chicago Press, Chicago, Illinois, pp. 25–50

Schulman L S 1987 Knowledge and teaching: Foundations of the new reform. *Harvard Educ. Rev.* 57(1): 1–22

Sikes P J, Measor L, Woods P 1985 *Teacher Careers: Crises and Continuities*. Falmer Press, London

Sutton-Smith B 1986 Children's fiction making. In: Sarbin T R (ed.) 1986 pp. 67–90

Van Maanen J 1988 *Tales of the Field: On Writing Ethnography*. University of Chicago Press, Chicago, Illinois

White H 1981 The value of narrativity in the representation of reality. In: Mitchell W J T (ed.) 1981 *On Narrative*. University of Chicago Press, Chicago, Illinois, pp. 1–23

Wigginton E 1989 Foxfire grows up. *Harvard Educ. Rev.* 59(1): 24–49

Wittrock M C (ed.) 1986 *Handbook of Research on Teaching*, 3rd edn. Macmillan, New York

Transactional Evaluation

R. M. Rippey

Program evaluations and experimental studies of instruction often omit reports of the vicissitudes of change. How did persons involved in new programs contend with discrepant personal needs and aspirations, and institutional demands and sanctions? Transactional evaluation (TE) examines this question.

Classical organizational theory posits a transactional dimension interstitial between the nomothetic (institutional) and the ideographic (personal). New programs and educational experiments strain the academic system and its constituencies. Productive energy is diverted to transactions aimed at reducing the stress. If new roles and demands resemble the old, little energy need be diverted. Unfortunately, personal needs and institutional demands are frequently incongruent. Thus some persons refuse to implement, others are deflected in their purpose, and some experiments unwittingly report on consequences of nonevents.

Although it is useful to know when an innovation fails, it is better to understand why. Programs can fail because they are deficient or because they are badly implemented. Close supervision can force implementation in laboratory settings but rarely in field settings. Thus, effective programs can flounder when disseminated.

Evaluations sometimes overlook the reciprocal character of both the change and the educative process. The changer changes and the teacher learns. One of Ralph Tyler's contributions to curriculum theory was reconceptualizing teaching from a one-way street to a rotary where objectives, instruction, and evaluation interacted. The occasional transformation of this rotary into a cul-de-sac may result from misperceiving the bidirectional character of curriculum reform. Teachers do not apply new educational practices as prescribed any more than students respond uniformly to all stimuli. Resistance of teachers and students against new demands can range from lack of enthusiasm to outright hostility.

1. Development of the Concept

Coffey and Golden, in concluding their chapter in the 1957 National Society for the Study of Education (NSSE) yearbook, suggested that the more profound an educational change, the more vigorous the resistance generated. Therefore, changes should begin modestly and experimentally, involving the most enthusiastic as implementors. They further advised careful evaluation. This commonsense approach unfortunately did not answer the question of what to do with the most energetic detractors.

Rippey (1973) asserted that the loyal opposition could serve on an evaluation team as members of the "adversary" squad. The resulting transactional evaluation model differed from its predecessors in four respects: intents, methods, roles, and composition. Its intent was to expand data collection to include social and interpersonal impediments to change. Its methods were conventional except for a special type of questionnaire whose items were not only supplied by evaluation specialists but also solicited from implementors and their critics. The evaluator role was modified to allow for substantial intervention and intimacy. The evaluation team incorporated previously excluded clients and apostates.

Subsequent applications have generally used this model. However, three modifications are: (a) although initially conceived as a means of facilitating change, it has been used to determine the need for change— Harder (1979) used transactional evaluation on a year-long basis in a high-school history class to ascertain student interests and problems; (b) although conceived as formative evaluation, Seidel (1978) used transactional evaluation for "summative evaluation of a *system*" for introducing computer-assisted instruction into the Washington DC public schools; and (c) Schwartz (1977) utilized transactional evaluation not only in evaluating a university-based teacher-training program, but also in working with the evaluation team in formulating the evaluation design.

2. Theoretical Issues

Since transactional instruments seek to uncover sources of conflict among pluralistic interest groups, they capitalize on rather than minimize subject–item interactions. Since they intend to discover skewed perceptions, the validity of each item will be in the eye of the beholder. Since they intend to capture the essence of specific programs in unique settings, their generalizability is nil. However, the transactional instrument itself is only part of a proper evaluation and overall validity can be confirmed by analysis of agreement among the multiple sources and methods comprising the comprehensive evaluation.

The objectivity of an intimate and influential evaluator raises questions. However, an evaluator who is remote may fail to capture the essence of a project and may lack access to key information. The evaluator who conceals beneficial informed judgment from a project director, or ignores sensitive political issues may be negligent or naive. On the other hand, can such an evaluator produce an honest account and does such an evaluator interfere with valid findings?

External audits of evaluation reports reveal varied quality independent of intimacy or austerity. Talmage illustrates that dangers to honest accounting may occur subsequent to rather than prior to an evaluation (Rippey 1973). The imperative of replication affects the intimate and the aloof alike.

Data support the modified evaluator role. Cicerelli concludes that National Opinion Research Center community studies of Project Head Start contributed to the resolution of specific social conflicts (Rippey 1973). In a four-year study of college student attitudes toward instruction, Schroder showed that student-contributed transactional evaluation items produced more information than faculty constructed items. Student attitudes appeared to improve as a result of the process. Costs were negligible. Livingston showed increased reading comprehension and speed scores for students assigned to randomly selected reading classes in comparison to equivalent control groups. The experimental groups used frequent transactional analysis assessments of student needs which helped teachers plan instruction.

Transactional evaluation is not restricted to education and has been used by Seidel (1978) in industrial, governmental, and training settings. His data suggest that transactional evaluation is helpful in resolving ambiguity and polarization in collaborative team ventures. However, he believes that it will not be effective in troubled organizations where authority and responsibility have been separated.

Transactional evaluation can lead to more illuminating program evaluations. At the same time, it can increase compliance with and acceptance of experimental treatment and evaluation protocols. Thus it constitutes a useful option for the evaluator's armamentarium.

Bibliography

Harder P J 1979 Student comments change curriculum. *Soc. Stud.* 70: 125–28

Rippey R M 1973 *Studies in Transactional Evaluation*. McCutchan, Berkeley, California

Rippey R M 1977 Transactional evaluation and the improvement of instruction. *Educ. Technol.* 17: 7–11

Schwartz H 1977 The use of multiple research methodologies to evaluate an inservice curriculum, Paper presented at the 61st annual meeting of the American Educational Research Association, New York. ERIC Document No. ED 137 335

Seidel R J 1978 Transactional evaluation: Assessing human interactions during program development, Report No. Hum RRO Professional Paper 8–78. ERIC Document No. ED 159 579

Tyler R W 1949 *Basic Principles of Curriculum and Instruction*. University of Chicago Press, Chicago, Illinois

Curriculum-specific Criteria

Curriculum Potential

M. Ben-Peretz

The term curriculum potential refers to the totality of learning experiences which can be derived from a particular set of resources in order to attain a broad range of educational goals. The curriculum potential of two types of resources is of significance for education. The term may be used in reference to scholarly materials such as articles, data sets, scientific reports, and so on, any of which may be used by curriculum developers in constructing curriculum materials (see *Curriculum Development*). Alternatively, it may be used in reference to available curriculum materials, textbooks, worksheets, audiovisual aids, and so on, which are to be used by teachers for planning classroom activities.

1. Curriculum Potential of Scholarly Materials

Most curriculum materials, in the various disciplines which serve as school subjects, are based on studies and publications of scholars and scientists. These publications, however, are designed for fellow scholars and cannot usually be presented to school learners in their original form. Moreover, curriculum developers are interested in using scholarly materials as instruments for attaining specified educational goals. Accordingly, they seek to determine the curriculum potential of scholarly materials of various types (Schwab 1973). Curriculum developers thus select the specific instances of scholarly materials to be introduced into the curriculum and decide on necessary changes such as deletions, additions, simplifications, and combinations.

Schwab (1973) suggests three aspects of curriculum potential of scholarly materials for possible translation into curriculum materials: the content conveyed; the inquiry process of which they are the outcome; and the access disciplines which are required to reveal their full purport. Thus, a section of historical material is an account of events at a certain time and place. This is the content conveyed by the material. Yet, this account is also the outcome of an originating discipline, history, which confers order and meaning on a series of events through the application of principles and methods of historical inquiry. Access to the understanding of historical writings calls for abilities of interpretation which can be developed through analysis of the different ways in which historical events can be approached. Each of

these aspects suggests a rich repertoire of curricular possibilities which, according to Schwab, should be carefully considered by curriculum developers seeking potential contributions for learners.

Fox (1972) describes the deliberative process for revealing curriculum potential in a practical situation. Participants of a curriculum development team, representing collective competence and experience, identify and transform the curriculum potential of scholarly materials into curriculum materials. They formulate and reformulate the nature of a curriculum problem—an example might be learners' lack of motivation—and suggest alternative solutions, which they derive from analyzing different aspects of the scholarly materials.

Various principles may guide the discovery of curriculum potential in the process of curriculum development. Martin (1970) identified two main principles, the "structure of the discipline" principle and the "inquiry" principle. The "structure of the discipline" principle requires identifying the basic concepts of a scholarly discipline which embody issues of major significance in the field. The "inquiry" principle calls for determination of the special ways in which scholars formulate their questions, and the methods of investigation which they use. Curriculum potential according to these principles is perceived as the learning about structures of disciplines through inquiry.

2. Curriculum Potential of Curriculum Materials

Implementors and evaluators tend to view curriculum materials as the embodiment of developers' intentions, yet the materials may be viewed as expressing more than these intentions. Once curriculum materials have left their originators' hands they may be interpreted and used in many ways. Thus, different interpretations would be available to teachers for implementation in their unique and changing classroom situations. New frames of reference, as well as practical experience, may lead to the discovery of novel curricular possibilities embodied in the materials.

Connelly and Clandinin (1988) elaborated the notion of curriculum potential and its use in teacher planning, stating that teachers shape curriculum materials according to their pedagogical purposes. Teachers who read

465

materials from a personal point of view may ask themselves what could be done with them in their own teaching situation.

Ben-Peretz (1990) developed special strategies of curriculum interpretation for the uncovering of curriculum potential, and for assisting teachers in flexible and adaptive planning.

A passage in biology curriculum materials concerning research on water consumption by plants may be originally intended to serve as an introduction to the concept of scientific inquiry. According to developers' specifications, students may be asked to discuss the specific knowledge it imparts and the process used to generate that particular knowledge. The same passage, reinterpreted, may be viewed as illuminating the interaction between society and science and the relevance of applied science to everyday life. It can be viewed as a vehicle promoting positive attitudes towards research and identification with scientists. The planned introduction to an instance of inquiry can thus be transformed into a series of learning activities and experiences that were not planned by the developers. These activities constitute a realization of some of the curriculum potential inherent in the materials. The choice of curriculum potential to be realized in a specific educational situation is usually determined by perceived student needs and teacher preferences.

The competencies of teachers or curriculum analysts, their knowledge of subject matter, feeling for classroom reality, experience in the development of curriculum materials, and openness to new ideas all contribute to the discernment of curriculum potential. Innovative uses of materials arising from particular concrete classroom situations, student questions, and teacher insights are sources for a broad spectrum of curriculum potential.

"Maps" of curriculum potential can be composed to accompany curriculum materials. Curriculum analysts, using different frames of analysis, would reveal and describe possible uses and learning outcomes of materials. Guiding questions for analysis are: in what ways might a given curriculum item be used? How might an item be modified for different pupils and varying education situations?

3. Teacher Education for Curriculum Potential Analysis

Special teacher education programs are required to enhance teachers' competencies in the discovery and use of curriculum potential. The daily experience of teachers is liable to narrow their outlook with regard to the multiple potential uses of curriculum material. Teachers may tend to adhere to obvious interpretations of materials, especially to those with which they are already familiar. Specially devised strategies and experiences are therefore needed to enhance teachers' awareness of divergent aspects of available curriculum materials and to facilitate appropriate use of this divergency.

Haysom and Sutton (1974) have developed sets of strategies and experiences to guide teachers in their attempts to interpret curriculum materials. These strategies and experiences include exercises in curriculum analysis using a variety of analytical schemes. Other activities focus on matching sections of curriculum materials to learning outcomes or learner experiences, which are determined by teachers regardless of developers' intentions. Classification of items of curriculum materials according to categories imposed by teachers is yet another tool for curriculum interpretations. These activities encourage teachers to make their own sense of available materials. The teacher who is thus trained may be better equipped to disclose curriculum potential and to suggest and elaborate on a wide range of learning activities originating in a given set of curriculum materials.

Bibliography

Ben-Peretz M 1975 The concept of curriculum potential. *Curric. Theory Network* 5(2): 151–59
Ben-Peretz M 1990 *The Teacher-Curriculum Encounter: Freeing Teachers from the Tyranny of Texts.* SUNY Press, Albany, New York.
Connelly F M, Clandinin D J 1988 *Teachers as Curriculum Planners: Narratives of Experience.* Teachers' College Press, New York
Fox S 1972 A practical image of "The Practical." *Curric. Theory Network* 10: 45–47
Haysom J T, Sutton C R 1974 *The Science Teacher Education Project.* McGraw-Hill, New York
Martin J R 1970 The disciplines and the curriculum. In: Martin J R (ed.) 1970 *Readings in the Philosophy of Education: A Study of Curriculum.* Allyn and Bacon, Boston, Massachusetts, pp. 65–86
Müller-Wolf H M 1980 Soziales und affektives Lernen als Grundkomponente des Curriculum Internationale Erziehung. In: Kron F W (ed.) 1980 *Persönlichkeitsbildung und Soziales Lernen.* Klinkhardt, Bad Heilbrunn
Schwab J J 1973 The practical: Translation into curriculum. *Sch. Rev.* 81: 501–22

Curriculum Balance

R. McClure

Curriculum balance commonly refers to the relative emphasis given to subjects selected for inclusion in a school program. In the twentieth century, schools generally have attempted to distribute curricular offerings among the liberal arts, including the humanities; the physical and natural sciences; and, in many countries, vocational, career, and technological education.

There is no international criterion that delineates a balanced curriculum. Indeed, in countries that do not have a national curriculum there is seldom agreement among curriculum planners as to what constitutes balance. Curriculum makers judge the existence of balance on data about their clients and their potential needs, and on the requirements and values of the society served by the schools. Thus, in some countries where there is a societal need for skilled workers, the curriculum will emphasize the technological. In countries where there is a strong tradition of societal support for the liberal arts, the curriculum will focus on the arts, humanities, and social sciences. Historians and anthropologists can learn a great deal about a culture by identifying the subjects selected for the curriculum and the relative emphasis the society places on those subjects.

Time is the major characteristic used to determine curriculum balance. Decisions about content areas and the amounts of time devoted to them in the curriculum are major indicators of the values held by those who make the decisions. Time influences the opportunities students have to learn, and it affects their perceptions of what is valued by the school.

Related to the amount of time is the placement of that time. Almost all schools, for example, devote the early years of schooling to acquisition of basic skills (see *Basic Skills*). In the later years, the program concentrates on subjects more closely related to the needs and aspirations of the society and the views held by the school about what students will need in order to function in that society. Consideration of balance, therefore, will vary depending on where a student is in his or her educational program.

The time of the day or week or even the school year when a subject is offered affects balance. For example, most teachers of young children will spend the last afternoon of the week on topics they perceive as requiring less cognitive energy. Art, physical education, and music are often relegated to this time period and students and others therefore perceive those subjects as less important. Conversely, subjects that are viewed as more demanding—grammar, mathematics, science—will be scheduled earlier in the day and in the week. In some schools, the "more difficult" subjects are even scheduled by the season of the year, apparently on the assumption that students learn more during cooler seasons and that "less trying" subjects are best acquired in warmer weather. Clearly, the uses of time shape the views of students and others about the relative values of curricular topics.

For a student to spend time on a curricular subject means, of course, that it has been decided to include that subject in the program. The corollary, whether conscious or not, is that it has also been decided *not* to include a topic in the curriculum. What to include and what to exclude are critical decisions for curriculum developers. They are value-laden and require great skill to be done well. In all societies, decisions of inclusion and exclusion are political as well as substantive and pedagogical. When such decisions are skewed to gross political influence, curricular imbalance is certain.

Another determiner of balance has to do with those student behavioral outcomes anticipated by curriculum planners. Although students possess individual dominant learning styles, they have the capacity to learn and act in a wide variety of ways. For balance to exist, the school must plan for and expect teachers, other school personnel, and students to employ a variety of cognitive, affective, and psychomotor styles. For the school to single out and value a narrow range of teaching and learning styles would deny students the opportunities they need and would create curriculum imbalance.

Decisions to include opportunities for students to acquire a variety of thinking and behavior styles affects the selection of specific program content. Subject matter disciplines employ different ways of knowing, different ways of conceptualizing, and different skills, even when addressing the same topic. Botany, painting, literature, and history can all deal with the same subject and enrich students' reality. For a curriculum to be balanced, attention must be given to a variety of ways of knowing.

With the advent of increasing interest in the role of student evaluation in the learning process, there has been, since the 1960s, increased attention to the assessment of outcomes. The nature of what is to be assessed and how also determines the existence of curriculum balance. In practice, student evaluation is largely concerned with measuring lower level cognitive skills. Even when curricular objectives call for student competencies in a variety of subjects and the evidence of a broad range of behaviors, formal assessment procedures are very limited in what they measure. Such dissonance between goals and the measurement of their achievement causes imbalance in the curriculum.

In summary, criteria for determining balance in the curriculum vary greatly among countries because of differences in values, views of learner needs, and societal expectations. Time devoted to curricular subjects is the variable most often used to establish that balance exists. Content selection or exclusion is also an important consideration in determining curriculum balance, as is the nature and content of student assessment.

Bibliography

Alexander W M 1967 *The Changing Secondary School Curriculum*. Holt, Rinehart and Winston, New York

Eisner E W 1978 The impoverished mind. *Educ. Leadership* 35(8): 615–23

Goodlad J I, Von Stoephasius R, Klein M F 1966 *The Changing School Curriculum*. Fund for the Advancement of Education, The Ford Foundation, New York

Halberson P et al. 1961 *Balance in the Curriculum*. Association for Supervision and Curriculum Development, Washington, DC

Neagley R L, Evans N D 1967 *Handbook for Effective Curriculum Development*. Prentice-Hall, Englewood Cliffs, New Jersey

Peddiwell J A, Benjamin H R W 1939 *The Saber-tooth Curriculum: Including other Lectures in the History of Paleolithic Education*. McGraw-Hill, New York

Prerequisite Knowledge

M. Rabinowitz and W. H. Schubert

The idea of "prerequisite knowledge" is implicit, if not explicit, throughout the processes of curriculum development and curriculum design. It is particularly relevant to the topic of curriculum organization referred to as sequence. Sequence refers to the problem of determining the order of teaching and learning experiences that leads to the acquisition of knowledge, skills, values, appreciations and so on.

Piaget broadly addressed the issue of sequencing in his presentation of the principle of moderate novelty. The two basic assumptions underlying this principle are (a) when a person sees some stimulus event, he or she understands that event by relating it to some preexisting knowledge structure (i.e., they assimilate it); and (b) in order to understand the stimulus event people need to adapt their knowledge structures to better match this event (i.e., the knowledge structures must accommodate). The principle of moderate novelty states that information should not be presented at a level that is very consistent with existing knowledge structures, because there would be assimilation but no accommodation. Nor should information be presented at a level too far afield from existing knowledge structures; the person would not be able to assimilate the information at all. Rather, the information should be presented at a level of moderate novelty where both assimilation and accommodation can occur. While application of this principle clearly has problems (for example, how novel is moderately novel in a given domain?), it serves as an intuitive way in which to discuss the issue of sequencing.

Given this orientation, curriculum theorists are implicitly, or explicitly, making statements regarding the learner's knowledge structures at the time of instruction. The interesting question, then, regarding curricular sequencing decisions is: What knowledge and experiences are required as a condition for subsequent knowledge and experiences? The justification of responses to this question invokes a range of logical, epistemological, and psychological assumptions about the nature of knowledge and learning. The answer to this question often determines the defensibility of curricular sequence. As a way of evaluating curricular decisions, then, readers are encouraged to inquire into the validity of these assumptions. Such an investigation would involve the study of philosophy and psychology, as well as curriculum theory.

The history of curriculum theory and practice yields a number of commonly presented positions on what constitutes prerequisite knowledge in the process of determining curricular sequence (Schubert 1986). However, while these various positions are all based, either explicitly or implicitly, on a range of psychological or philosophical assumptions, they vary considerably in the degree to which they rely on empirical support for validation of assumptions. In addition, the relation between these assumptions and the actual curricular decisions made is often tenuous or nonexistent. In fact, it should be noted that some of the most widely practiced notions of prerequisite knowledge are among the least defensible, if one takes as important legitimation by research and theory in psychology and philosophy.

1. Bases for Curriculum Sequence in Conceptions of Prerequisite Knowledge

Perhaps the most widely accepted practice of sequencing curriculum is to follow the textbook or other published materials such as mastery learning packets, workbooks, programmed learning booklets, and computer-assisted software. To follow the text, however, is not in itself a form of sequence; rather, it is based on whatever configuration of assumptions was held about the nature of prerequisite knowledge by the authors of the instructional materials in question. The issue, then, is to identify the basis of sequencing in assumptions about prerequisite knowledge.

One principle of curricular sequence is based on the premise that instruction should move from the simple to the complex. The premise is based on the work of Robert Gagné (1977) whose hierarchical theory of instruction is based on learning theory that suggests that knowledge is acquired by proceeding from data and concepts to principles and constructs. Thus, the assumption regarding knowledge structures is that data and concepts are bases for principles and constructs. The practice of sequence that flows from simple to complex is usually much less tied to rigorous research standards than in the case of Gagné's work. That which is simple and that which is complex can be difficult to determine. For example, it is commonly assumed that one must learn to add, subtract, and multiply before learning to divide. While this seems quite true with regard to long division problems, the position is usually expanded by elementary school arithmetic teachers to imply that first one must learn to add, then learn to subtract, and proceed to multiplication, followed by division. In the 1960s and 1970s the British Nuffield approach to teaching mathematics to young children asked the simple but insightful question of whether this was an appropriate notion of moving from the simple to the complex. For example, one need not master algorithms of addition, subtraction, and multiplication in order to conceptualize how to divide a cookie. Thus, it becomes highly problematic to determine just what is simple and what is complex, since definitions of these terms have varied so much in curriculum policy and practice.

A similar premise is that instruction should move from the concrete to the abstract. This premise is tied to the research of Jean Piaget who suggested that it isn't until the stage of formal operations that the child is able to think and represent information abstractly. Before that stage the child is tied to the concrete, or the here and now. Recent psychological research, however, is suggesting that the child may be capable of abstract thought earlier than expected (see Gelman and Baillargeon 1983, for a review of this literature). However, given this approach, curriculum sequence is based on the developmental appropriateness of the materials. When interpreted mechanistically as stage-appropriate curriculum, the approach harkens back to developmentalists at the turn of the century such as G. Stanley Hall, who built a theory of prerequisite knowledge derived from J. H. Herbart's cultural epochs theory. This theory asserted that the development of human beings parallels or recapitulates the development of human history. For example, the child begins life as uncivilized and by age nine or so might profit from such survival-oriented literature as *Robinson Crusoe*.

A third premise is the assumption that knowledge structures are organized around specific disciplines. Throughout the nineteenth century, for instance, faculty psychology reigned supreme as the basis for decisions about how to sequence curriculum. Certain subjects (e.g., Greek, Latin, geometry) were deemed prerequisites because they trained the faculties of the mind. Research studies by William James and especially by E. L. Thorndike discounted this notion and led to a reduction of ancient languages in the curriculum; however, psychological and philosophical research, in the 1980s is once again arguing for a modified version of faculty psychology (see Gardner 1983, Fodor 1983). Today, however, we still find remnants of faculty psychology used in justification of the presentation of school subjects.

Related to this third premise, the work of Bruner (1960), surrounded by post-Sputnik curriculum reform efforts, suggested a more direct effort to build curriculum around the structure of disciplines of knowledge. Many argued that each discipline had an inherent structure and if it could be learned, other knowledge within the discipline would be readily understood. For some time debate raged on what exactly the structure of a given discipline was and whether or not all disciplines, in fact, had an inherent logic or structure (see Ford and Pugno 1964, and Elam 1964). While one might, for example, assert that a coherent structure is

evident in mathematics or is symbolized in the periodic chart of the elements in chemistry, one might question the existence of a governing structure in English literature, sociology, ancient history, or women's studies. Still, much work was done to develop curriculum packages based on one or another conception of the structure of disciplines. An interesting distinction can be made between this premise and the preceding three. With the earlier premises, the orientation was aimed directly at what kind of prerequisite knowledge the learner must have to learn new material. With the current premise, however, the orientation is aimed at the structure of the domain, not the structure of knowledge of the learner. Thus, while this premise has been a very influential one in curriculum theory, it is not as tied to the notion of prerequisite knowledge as the others.

While the preceding premises are based fairly explicitly on psychological theories regarding the kinds of knowledge structures learners have at different points in their education, many conceptions of curricular sequencing are implicitly tied to issues of prerequisite knowledge and available knowledge structures. For example, John Dewey's theory of the progressive organization of curriculum (Dewey 1916) simply asserts that teachers and students work together to discover that which is developmentally appropriate for their unique configuration of experiences and that they reflect on the desirability of pursuing such developmentally appropriate experiences in view of the good that would be likely to emerge from them. The teacher as curriculum developer would, therefore, begin by treating the expressed interests and concerns of students as the appropriate prerequisite knowledge, and through discussion, help students probe more deeply into their interests to discover that at a fundamental level they are connected with the interests of other students. Connections are possible due to the assumed existence of common human interests which Robert Ulich characterized as "great mysteries and events of life: birth, death, love, tradition, society and the crowd, success and failure, salvation, and anxiety" (Ulich 1955 p. 255). The progressive teacher then builds upon these deeper human interests as prerequisites to introducing the disciplines of knowledge as they provide relevant insights to illuminate problems associated with common human interests. Dewey (1916) referred to this movement from daily interests, to common human interests, to the disciplines of knowledge as movement from the *psychological* to the *logical*. Thus, each phase of this process constitutes a broadly conceived notion of prerequisite knowledge for the next phase.

In addition, the expanding horizons curriculum that emerged in the 1930s is still accepted as conventional wisdom in much curriculum practice in the 1980s. This principle of prerequisite knowledge, pervasively evident in reading and social studies textbooks at the elementary-school level, asserts that curriculum should proceed from the home and neighborhood, and expand outward to the community, state, nation, and world. Egan (1979,

1983) argues persuasively against this view, asserting that children and youth learn better by starting with the distant, the fantastic, and moving from fantasy back to reality. Moreover, he suggests a developmental sequence, based on literary and anthropological theory, that moves through mythic, romantic, philosophic, and ironic stages, utilizing a story form of sequence that begins with a problem and evolves to a climax and resolution to the problem. While Egan's theory is in some respects reminiscent of Rousseau, and of Whitehead's rhythms of education (Whitehead 1929), the position has had little impact on changing the dominance of the expanding horizons curriculum thus far; however, critiques and new proposals usually take considerable time to become realized in curriculum practice.

The preceding was a brief overview regarding the variety of positions on what constitutes prerequisite knowledge. The reader should be aware, however, that only a limited selection was offered here. For a more elaborate discussion of the variety of positions offered, the reader is referred to Posner and Rudnitsky (1986 Chapter 6). The fact that there is such a wide variety of positions, however, argues for the need to take into account recent psychological and philosophical research in order to test the defensibility of the variety of arguments.

2. The Issue of the Availability versus the Accessibility of Prerequisite Knowledge

The primary argument centers on what knowledge is necessary or must be available to the learner in order for new knowledge to be acquired. Thus, the issue centers on whether the learner has available, or does not have available, some piece of prerequisite knowledge at the time of learning. However, it also seems relevant to question whether available knowledge can be accessed at the time of instruction. A distinction can be made between the *availability* of knowledge and the *accessibility* of knowledge (Rabinowitz and Glaser 1985). Availability refers to whether some piece of knowledge has been previously stored for the learner to access at the time of learning. Accessibility, however, refers to either whether or not, or the manner in which, prior knowledge can be accessed at the time of learning. Just because information has been previously learned and stored does not imply that the learner will be able to access this knowledge when it is needed at the time of learning. Knowledge is stored, or represented, in a variety of ways and the manner of this representation will affect how, and under what conditions, this knowledge will be accessed.

With most tasks, there is more than one way for prerequisite knowledge to be accessed. In many situations we all seem to have the ability to arrive at an answer directly. To take two very simple examples, when asked their name or current address, most people have answers available almost immediately. There is

little sense of doing anything special to obtain the information. However, in other situations, there seems to be a need to run through some procedure in order to derive the answer. Take the question, "How many windows are there in the place where you are currently living?" Most people probably do not have this information encoded in such a way that it can be readily retrieved. A person can derive this information, however, by picturing him- or herself walking through the house counting the number of windows.

This distinction is consistent with the philosophical distinction of "knowing how" and "knowing that"; in the fields of psychology and computer sciences, these two types of knowledge are respectively referred to as procedural and declarative knowledge (Winograd 1975). We know how to ride a bicycle or tie our shoes, usually without being able to specify the actions that we take in so doing—knowing how. This kind of knowing seems quite different from knowing facts, such as the name of the president or the product of three times four—knowing that.

Regarding the issue of prerequisite knowledge, assume that knowledge of simple addition is a prerequisite for some other task. In needing the answer to the problem $7 + 2$ as a component of some other task, one person might be able to access a store of facts and retrieve the answer 9—he/she used declarative knowledge or he/she "knew that." Another person (a young child) might generate the answer by first counting to 7, then counting two more and observing the end result—he/she used procedural knowledge or he/she "knew how." Even though both people were able to access the relevant piece of information for the task, they accessed the information in two very different ways. Do both people have the prerequisite knowledge for the task?

A related aspect to this argument is that most tasks require that people apply their attentional resources to the task for success at learning—resources of which they only have a limited supply. Declarative knowledge is usually associated with automatic processing; there is little sense in doing anything special to obtain the information; it is accessed by a fast and fairly effortless process. In order to access information from procedural knowledge, however, a more reflective process is often required: one which is more dependent upon a person's attentional resources, one which is dependent on a slower, more effortful process. The necessity of relying on a slower more effortful process imposes a limit on the amount of information with which people can work. For example, in a discussion on reading, Perfetti and Lesgold (1978) suggested that capacity during reading comprehension is limited by momentary data-handling requirements. They proposed three components in reading that, when not fully developed, could increase a working-memory bottleneck: (a) access to long-term memory, (b) automation of decoding, and (c) efficiency of reading strategies. Having to work consciously at accessing any of these three types of prerequisite knowledge diverts attentional resources that could be applied to other processing. By automatizing each of these component processes as much as possible, the reader has more resources to apply to the other components or to higher level skills, such as using context, prior knowledge, and inference to aid comprehension.

Thus, it seems important for curriculum theorists to take into account, when discussing the issues of sequencing and prerequisite knowledge, not just what knowledge is important, but also how that knowledge is represented and accessed. Answers to both these issues are required as a condition for success in the acquisition of additional knowledge.

Bibliography

Bruner J S 1960 *The Process of Education*. Vintage, New York

Dewey J 1916 *Democracy and Education: An Introduction to the Philosophy of Education*. Macmillan, New York

Egan K 1979 *Educational Development*. Oxford University Press, New York

Egan K 1983 Children's path to reality from fantasy: Contrary thoughts about curriculum foundations. *J. Curric. Stud.* 15(4): 357–71

Elam S M (ed.) 1964 *Education and the Structure of Knowledge*. Rand McNally, Chicago, Illinois

Fodor J A 1983 *The Modularity of Mind*. Massachusetts Institute of Technology (MIT) Press, Cambridge, Massachusetts

Ford G W, Pugno L (eds.) 1964 *The Structure of Knowledge and the Curriculum*. Rand McNally, Chicago, Illinois

Gagné R M 1977 *The Conditions of Learning*, 3rd edn. Holt, Rinehart, and Winston, New York

Gardner H 1983 *Frames of Mind*. Basic Books, New York

Gelman R, Baillargeon R 1983 A review of some Piagetian concepts. In: Flavell J H, Markman E M (eds.) 1983 *Handbook of Child Psychology*, Vol. 3: *Cognitive Development*, 4th edn. Wiley, New York, pp. 167–230

Kliebard H M 1986 *The Struggle for the American Curriculum, 1893–1958*. Routledge and Kegan Paul, Boston, Massachusetts

Perfetti C A, Lesgold A M 1978 Discourse comprehension and sources of individual differences. In: Just M A, Carpenter P A (eds.) 1978 *Cognitive Processes in Comprehension*. Erlbaum, Hillsdale, New Jersey, pp. 141–83

Posner G J, Rudnitsky A N 1986 *Course Design*. Longman, New York

Rabinowitz M, Glaser R 1985 Cognitive structure and process in highly competent performance. In: Horowitz F D, O'Brien M (eds.) 1985 *The Gifted and Talented: Developmental Perspectives*. American Psychological Association, Washington, DC

Schubert W H 1980 *Curriculum Books: The First Eighty Years*. University Press of America, Lanham, Maryland

Schubert W H 1986 *Curriculum: Perspective, Paradigm, and Possibility*. Macmillan, New York

Ulich R 1955 Comments on Ralph Harper's essay. In: Henry N B (ed.) 1955 *Modern Philosophies and Education*, the 54th Yearbook (Part I) of the National Society for the Study of Education. University of Chicago Press, Chicago, Illinois, pp. 254–57

Whitehead A N 1929 *The Aims of Education and Other Essays*. Macmillan, New York

Winograd T 1975 Frame representations and the declarative–procedural controversy. In: Bobrow D G, Collins A (eds.) 1975 *Representation and Understanding: Studies in Cognitive Science*. Academic Press, New York, pp. 185–210

Impact Analysis of Curriculum

M. C. Alkin

Curriculum impact analysis is the study of changes in the total society influenced by implementing curricula. A new curriculum might itself lead to dramatic changes in the school context. More typically, however, curriculum changes combine with other factors (community values, changes in resource availability, demographics, etc.) to have an impact. Furthermore, it should be noted that the impact of a new curriculum is not always immediate—often, the effects are not felt for some time. In this section, curriculum impact refers to instances when curricula contribute to changes in the school context.

What are the areas of impact? Curricula are designed to have impact on students' subject matter mastery; thus, investigations of curricula typically focus on how closely learners reach prescribed objectives. Looking only at learner behavior changes, however, ignores other important factors. Several researchers have urged that changes in teaching practices, administrative and

management patterns, community and parental relationships with the school, and learner social behavior be studied also. Curricula must be judged in terms of the various impacts (intentional and unintentional, long range and short range) which they have on all elements of the school system.

1. Teaching Practices

Various curricula demand that certain types of relationships be established between teacher and student. The consultative role demanded by heuristic learning, for example, requires the development of new communication patterns from a teacher who is accustomed to lecturing. Similarly, a "back-to-basics" curriculum (see *Back to Basics Movement*) may require that much more structured roles be developed by teachers who have used an open education curriculum. Curricula which mandate a team teaching approach require instructors to form new kinds of relationships with fellow teachers and to be more sensitive in the ways they interact with parents and community members.

Some curricula demand a change in the way a subject matter is presented. Curricular approaches which require such techniques as individualization, discovery learning, or the extensive use of audiovisual materials have a direct effect on teaching practices. Teachers who are accustomed to other instructional modes may have to change their practices to accommodate such curricular changes. Schramm (1977), for example, has noted the changes in teaching practices caused by the introduction of nationally sponsored multimedia curricula in several developing countries.

But teachers do not always completely adopt the instructional mode prescribed for a given curriculum. Teachers may modify a curricular approach or continue to use methods which differ from those specified. Thus, examinations of the impact of curricula must examine the methods that teachers actually use, not just those that they were supposed to have used.

Teachers also make use of practices developed in one curriculum when teaching other courses. As an example, a particular program may use individualized instruction. If a teacher chooses to individualize courses which are not using that program, or if the teacher vigorously rejects individualization in all other contexts, the curriculum has had an impact on teaching practices.

The impact of a curriculum on teacher morale will affect the curriculum's impact on student learning. Gordon et al. (1979), for example, found that teachers using Project Follow Through curricula were led to pursue further professional career development activities. This would indicate a positive impact on attitude. Other curricula may create negative teacher attitudes.

2. Administrative and Management Patterns

Administrative patterns are influenced by curricular decisions in numerous ways. To fully understand schools, analysts must consider curricula's impact on this educational subsystem.

The introduction of new curricula may cause unrest, lack of understanding, and sometimes misunderstanding among teachers, parents, and the community. Administrators must develop effective communication channels to ameliorate communication problems. The changes must be explained to faculty and their support gained. Parent and community groups must be reassured (Mann 1977).

Curricula have impact on administrative resource allocation decisions. The adoption of a laboratory approach in the science curriculum, for example, can have a tremendous impact on the school budget. Finding both the space and the money to implement a new curriculum can require shifting resources formerly allocated to other areas. Administrators might find them-

selves facing entrenched groups not ready to accept resource reductions.

Curricula also impact on school staffing decisions. A school which stresses an academic curriculum needs different kinds of teachers than a school which places importance on a vocationally oriented curriculum. The introduction of a curriculum which calls for individualization may require that the administrator hire additional paraprofessional staff. A new curriculum may be usable by the existing staff, but the staff may need inservice training to successfully implement it.

The impact of curricular change on roles and role relationships has been recognized by several researchers. Fullan and Pomfret (1977), for example, assert that this is the main problem in curriculum implementation. In a curriculum which calls for team teaching, assignment to teams must take into account the relationships among team members. New curricula can also result in administrative role changes. An open education curriculum calls for a consultative role: a traditional academic curriculum, on the other hand, demands a much more formalized role.

Existing curricula have impact on administrative behaviour as well. The organization of curricula affect the way in which administrators receive and maintain their power and leadership roles (Goodlad et al. 1979). Some curricula are organized so that the administrator can establish a leadership position through acknowledgement as the most experienced subject matter expert. In other instances, it is unrealistic to expect that an administrator should have a high degree of knowledge about all of the specialized fields which are included. Thus, the administrator must use different tactics to establish a leadership role.

3. Community and Parental Relationships

A curriculum's impact on parents and the wider community is often overlooked. Curricula which deal with topics that typically provoke a reaction in parents such as sex education, evolution and creation, and political systems could cause disruption in parental and community support for the schools. Schools must assess the impact of such curricula on the community in order to successfully implement them. Unfortunately, it is sometimes impossible to predict community reaction.

Recently, multicultural curricula have been introduced in several countries both to challenge the "melting pot" philosophy and to improve school–community relations. Stahl (1979) found that use of a curriculum which recognizes the contributions and culture of Oriental Jews in addition to those of European Jews has resulted in better relations between parents and teachers in the schools.

Gordon et al. (1979) present one illuminating example of the many kinds of impacts which curricula can have on parents and communities. They discovered that Project Follow Through curriculum projects had a consistent impact on both the home–school partnership and the career development of parents and community aides. Parents used the desirable teaching behaviors which they had learned through the curricula with younger children not yet involved in the projects. The rate of parental volunteerism increased significantly as a result of the programs, and parents became actively involved in the political processes of their communities. A further impact of the curricula was to increase parental motivation to continue their own education.

4. Learner Behavior

Curricula also impact on learner behavior—the way students think, learn, and approach life. Examples of these process outcomes (as opposed to cognitive outcomes) include student attitudes toward school, their expectations, self-images, and preparation for adult life. A number of writers have addressed this issue, but examples of a few recent studies will illustrate the point.

Stallings (1975) provides an informative view of this aspect of learner behavior in her evaluative studies of Project Follow Through. Since a variety of curricula were used, Stallings was able to compare the effects of various curricula on learner process behavior. She discovered that independence, cooperation, and nonverbal problem-solving ability were highest in classrooms where the curriculum called for self-selected activities, individualization, use of audiovisual materials, and a wide variety of activities. Classes using this type of curriculum also had significantly lower rates of absenteeism. She found that curricula which stressed work with textbooks and workbooks produced high learner task persistence. In classes which utilized a behaviorist curriculum, students tended to feel responsible for their own failures but not for their successes; they attributed their success to the teacher or the materials.

Kerkhoff (1977) investigated the effect of English and American curricula on shaping the educational expectations of boys. His hypothesis that the English curriculum would produce more realistic expectations earlier in adolescents was generally supported, but British boys overestimated the importance of ability. He found overall that the older American boys had the most realistic expectations of all.

Ballard et al. (1977) looked at the curriculum impact of a peer tutoring program on educable mentally retarded students. They were interested in discovering if working in a peer tutoring environment would improve the social acceptance of the retarded students and found that the social acceptance of those retarded students who had been in the tutoring curriculum was significantly improved over that of those retarded students who had not been involved. On a related note, Stahl's (1979) findings suggested that the inclusion of a multicultural curriculum results in a more positive self-image of Oriental Jewish students.

Macdonald (1975) theorized that schools develop and transmit social patterns to learners. He suggests that most school curricula require learners to play a passive role. He maintains that the impact of this learned role has serious long-range implications since he believes that this role is not what will be expected of students in their adult lives. He speculates that one short-range impact is the development of boredom and a lack of seriousness in students; a long-range implication is a dysfunctional attitude toward later careers. Finally, Macdonald suggests that the curriculum of modern schools produces students who work for social rewards rather than personal satisfaction.

5. Summary

Curriculum impact analysis views the school as a social system made up of learners, teachers, administrators, parents, and the wider community. While recognizing that curricula are designed to increase student subject matter learning, consideration of impact must focus on issues beyond changes in learner cognitive knowledge. Analysis of the impact of curricula must assess a curriculum's effects on teaching practices, administrative and management patterns, parent and community relationships with the school, and learner behavior in areas other than subject matter knowledge.

Bibliography

Anderson R E 1979 The deterioration of the college-educated labor market: Implications for secondary schools. *Teach. Coll. Rec.* 79(2): 274–78

Ballard M, Corman L, Gottlieb J, Kaufman M J 1977 Improving the social status of mainstreamed retarded children. *J. Educ. Psychol.* 69: 605–11

Fullan M, Pomfret A 1977 Research on curriculum and instruction implementation. *Rev. Educ. Res.* 47: 335–97

Goodlad J L, Sirotnik K S, Overman B C 1979 An overview of "A Study of Schooling." *Phi Delta Kappan* 61: 174–78

Gordon J I, Olmsted P, Rubin R, True J 1979 How has Follow Through promoted parent involvement? *Young Child.* 34: 49–53

Hanson E 1979 *Educational Administration and Organizational Behavior.* Allyn and Bacon, Boston, Massachusetts

Kerkhoff A 1977 The realism of educational ambitions in England and the United States. *Am. Sociol. Rev.* 42: 563–71

Macdonald J B 1975 The quality of everyday life in school. In: Macdonald J B, Zaret E (eds.) 1975 *Schools in Search of Meaning.* Association for Supervision and Curriculum Development, Washington, DC

Mann D 1977 The politics of changing schools. *National Association of Secondary School Principals (NASSP) Bull.* 61: 57–66

Schramm W 1977 *Big Media, Little Media: Tools and Technologies for Instruction.* Sage, Beverly Hills, California

Stahl A 1979 Adapting the curriculum to the needs of a multiethnic society: The case of Israel. *Curric. Inq.* 9: 361–71

Stallings J 1975 Implications and child effects of teaching practices in Follow Through classrooms. *Monographs of the Society for Research in Child Development* 163: 40 (7–8)

Evaluating Computerized Curriculum Materials

T. Levin

While the information and technological revolutions are having major implications on all aspects of society, their effects are particularly evident in education. Microcomputers are rapidly becoming an important focus in the classrooms, and are making a strong impact. Educators are becoming more aware of the potential of microcomputers as powerful and flexible tools for instruction and learning. However, no matter how great their potential may be, the usefulness of computers is determined by the quality of the programs available for them.

The use of computerized curriculum materials is a relatively new practice; it is highly innovative, and therefore still experimental in both nature and design. Problems and uncertainties make it necessary to evaluate these materials before they go into general use; consequently, a relatively new field is opening up for evaluators.

In this article, the term "computerized curriculum materials" is used synonymously with "computer programs," "courseware," and "software." All refer to activities which involve a computer in one way or another to promote learning and instruction.

The evaluation of computer programs is highly influenced by current concepts, procedures, and standards of evaluation in general. At the same time, since it is concerned with a fundamental innovation, there are some differences in the needs of software evaluation as well as in the form the evaluation takes.

It is generally accepted that the four basic roles of curriculum evaluation are applicable to courseware evaluation. These functions are to contribute to: (a) program improvement, (b) program selection, (c) program implementation, and (d) an understanding of the psychological, social, instructional, and other processes involved in using computers in various educational contexts. Still, there are differences in the priorities given to these roles, and in the emphasis and methodologies used in the evaluations.

For example, selection procedures for computer programs are different from those used for printed materials. Publishers of printed materials are relatively casual about instructional quality, since they assume that teachers usually modify curriculum materials to suit their needs. Therefore, textbook committees often base their decisions on such factors as cost, durability, educational philosophy, and range of topics covered—while giving little attention to instructional effectiveness. With courseware, however, the teacher has less of a role as an adaptor or modifier; many programs are oriented toward independent learners. Therefore, selection procedures for software are more crucial than for printed materials, and require a more active role by the evaluators.

1. Evaluation: Unique Issues and Problems

The need for and nature of the evaluation of computerized materials have changed quickly in direct proportion to the rapid changes in hardware, courseware, and users. The expressions of need have become more intense, and indicate a great variety of educational needs. After less than a decade of massive development, there are six different modes of information delivery and interaction for instructional purposes: drill and practice, tutorial, educational games, simulations, problem solving, and educational tools. Each mode has a different purpose, a different use, and a different set of intrinsic characteristics. New applications are springing up frequently, and each must be evaluated on its own terms.

There is a diversified audience that needs sound information about computer programs: policy makers, school officials, producers of educational materials, financial supporters of innovations, teachers, students, parents, and researchers. Professional users of educational software have increased greatly in numbers, and differ in their knowledge of computer applications. They have different concerns, such as improving the productivity of the educational system; improving the learning of a particular subject matter; maintaining or increasing educational equity; and preparing students for the information and technological age. Therefore, there is a need to evaluate educational software in the light of broader curricular priorities, for an increasingly diverse market of consumers.

The multiplicity of courseware, of needs, and of consumers affects the criteria for evaluation and the methodologies used.

2. Evaluation Criteria

Evaluation instruments require a set of general parameters that define good educational courseware. Determining these parameters is the most difficult part of the evaluation process, for two distinct reasons. First, courseware products are markedly different in their approaches. This diversity does not fit well with a standardized evaluation instrument.

For example, a tutorial program presents concepts, principles, and rules; evaluates comprehension; and provides practice through branching after a diagnosis of mistakes and mastery. The usual cognitive objectives are knowledge acquisition and comprehension. A simulation program, on the other hand, uses a real situation or models the characteristics of a real phenomenon, thus requiring students to interact with and become part of the situation. Its major goal is to teach problem solving; it can be used either before or after the student learns the basic principles. Therefore, it is unlikely that a single set of attributes could accurately and meaningfully assess the intrinsic qualities of programs of both types, or their effects on the processes and the products of instruction and learning.

The second reason why it is difficult to establish parameters for evaluation is that instructional and learning theory are not monolithic. What is considered crucial within one school of thought may not be so by another. An obvious example is the divergence between highly structured, didactic instruction and exploratory, discovery-based, inductive learning. Moreover, since the computer is a relatively new medium for education, it is necessary to broaden our understanding of the nature of learning and instruction to include the characteristics of the computer. Communication models and theories suggest how people interact with a medium; their principles should, therefore, be applied to the use of computers.

There are no widely accepted criteria for the features of an effective computer program. The diversity of opinions regarding the characteristics of an ideal courseware product is becoming more pronounced as computer technology extends its potential. The more an instructional methodology uses the capabilities of a computer (such as in several simulations or problem-solving types of programs), the more difficult it is to define relevant evaluation criteria.

A number of organizations and individuals have suggested certain attributes to be considered when evaluating courseware (NEA 1983, Roblyer 1981, Gold 1984). Although the criteria differ in form (scales versus discrete coding; descriptive versus judgmental; qualitative versus quantitative) and in specificity, most are organized around the same three facets of a program: (a) content and goals, (b) instructional quality, and (c) technical quality. A few of the forms reflect a need for distinguishing between attributes that are unique to educational software and those that apply to all media of instruction (Cohen 1983). In addition, the various schemes generally agree that the important issue is not simply whether a criterion is being used, but how it is used to make the program significant. The best source on current criteria is *Evaluation of Educational Software: A Guide to Guides* (Jones 1983), produced by the Southwest Educational Development Laboratory.

Because of the diversity of opinions and approaches, educators use a broad range of resources to create and justify their sets of criteria.

3. Sources for Establishing Criteria

Courseware criteria are mostly commonly based on the goals set for the use of computers in education. Educators are just beginning to discover the kinds of instruction that are appropriate for computers, yet they are already able to cite a number of reasons for using the new technology: (a) to extend the students' creative and intellectual activities, (b) to provide new tools for self-expression and exploratory thinking, (c) to motivate learners, and (d) to teach topics more effectively and efficiently than by conventional means.

With these rather general and varied goals in mind, evaluators search for criteria to answer three basic questions: (a) Is the program suited to the computer for the intended purposes and users? (b) Does the program take advantage of the computer's capabilities? (c) Does the program follow good educational practice? (Kleiman et al. 1984). Additional attributes are drawn from theories of learning, cognition, and motivation; theories and models of instruction and curriculum design; models of human communication with media, and previous research into courseware.

Jay (1983), for example, suggests several generic computer attributes based on five principles of human information processing. He translates memory and attention demands into such attributes as amount of text on screen, timing, the use of scrolling, levels of processing, and duration of an activity. Following principles of student behavior as a function of the type of student, Jay translates the type of message and its intent into attributes such as degree of abstractness and sentence format.

Guidelines for other criteria were gleaned from research into what makes computer materials motivating and instructionally effective. The best-known example is Malone's (1981) three attributes of educational games: competition, fantasy, and curiosity. These general features can be refined through the use of hidden information, speeded responses, choice, randomness, audiovisual effects, and so on.

Another point on which to evaluate an educational program is the relationship between motivational and instructional features. Are the game-like graphics, sound effects, and the like used as extrinsic rewards for successful performance, or is there some integral relationship between the problem posed and the special effects employed (Lepper 1985)?

Some of the critical variables derived from intrinsic motivational concepts are: the goal structure of an activity; difficulty of achieving the goals; relevance of the goals to valued personal activities; responsiveness of the environment; and perceived personal freedom.

Another source, less specifically apparent in many evaluation forms, concerns the social implications of educational materials. As emphasized by Rothe (1983) and Bork (1985), the assumption is that there is little neutrality in the selection of knowledge, content, learning outcomes, language usage, ethics, or cultural perspectives; therefore, value stance and perspectives should be included as criteria.

4. Methodology

Four broad methodologies are typically used in courseware evaluation: checklist, analytical (open-ended) review, observation, and experimentation. They serve different purposes and are used at different stages of the courseware development, so practical evaluation procedures often combine several of them.

4.1 Checklist

A checklist can systemize the evaluation process by having a number of people (teachers, specialists, or students) rate the program according to the same set of evaluative dimensions. The ratings help the evaluator focus on the important features of the program, and provide relatively objective information.

4.2 Analytical (Open-ended) Review

Another method involves detailed, unstructured documentation of the positive and negative features of a program. By giving users and specialists the freedom to describe and judge various aspects of a program, the evaluator may detect strengths and weaknesses which may not be touched by the most detailed checklist of criteria. This method provides subjective information from people who may have different perspectives on the worth of a program.

4.3 Observation

Observation of the interaction between the student and the program is a highly effective way to find out how students and teachers relate to the learning materials (as well as to the medium). Although observation is a routine method for evaluating printed materials, it takes on more importance in computerized programs because our lack of knowledge leads to the sometimes naive assumption that students interact with computerized text in the same way as they do with printed text.

Observation of the users' reaction can sometimes change an evaluator's own assessment of a program. Something that an evaluator thought was challenging and intriguing may prove not to be so to students, and vice versa.

Ideally, interactional observation should be conducted at three levels: (a) observing a number of students on an individual basis, (b) observing students under real classroom conditions during an actual instructional program, and (c) conducting a formal field trial to examine the effectiveness of the instructional and learning process.

4.4 Experimentation

The use of experimental designs is a controversial issue in evaluation study, and especially with media-related educational programs (Clark 1985). Yet, if used properly, it is an acceptable methodology, particularly for exploring the relative effects of specific attributes of courseware and for estimating the growth in learning.

5. Evaluation Efforts

Four levels of evaluation are reported in the literature. The following categorization (Holznagel 1983), al-though somewhat artificial, indicates the various expectations of potential users.

The first level, which requires the least amount of time and effort, is a screening stage that provides data of a subjective and general nature. It involves a cursory examination of a program for completeness, suitability for the intended hardware and population, and technical quality.

The data obtained at the second level are more objective, but are still in a descriptive form. They include identification of the program's source, cost, class level, content, objectives, and components. Some subjective judgments are made when data are not expressly provided.

The third level primarily involves the professional judgment of one or more people experienced in the use of computers in the subject, grade level, or other category at which the program is aimed. The time spent can range from 2 to 20 or more hours, depending on the complexity of the package, its length and the time available.

The fourth level comprises expensive and time-consuming techniques such as in-depth observation of students using the materials, analysis of pre–post results, and analysis of computer records. This category provides subjective or objective information on the important characteristics and effects of the materials.

6. Organizations and Structures

Several major organizations collect evaluation data on educational software. The best-known in the United States are the MicroSIFT project at the Northwest Regional Educational Laboratory (NWREL) and the Educational Products Information Exchange Institute (EPIE). Both use standard evaluation forms including predefined criteria and open-ended comments. Each evaluation report is a composite of the opinions of several professionals, including teachers.

The reports by the MicroSIFT project are sent quarterly to more than 150 clients, including states, regional services, and school districts, and the data are added to the RICE database (Resources in Computer Education). The reports by EPIE are published as Micro-Courseware PRO/FILES (EPIE Institute Teacher College, Columbia University, New York, United States).

Another source of data is a group of professional journals and magazines in computer education, published privately and by professional associations. These include the AEDS (Association for Educational Data Systems) monitors, *Computing Teacher*, and Electronic Learning from Scholastic Magazines. The reports are open-ended comments with checklist summaries. EPIE collates citations and ratings from 30 such reviews in the United States alone (TESS 1985).

Because many countries have decentralized authorities, there are numerous other organizations that are more local in scope. These are often within a formal governmental structure, sometimes located at a university. In Canada, for example, a number of provinces have established software evaluation offices to recommend (or not recommend) programs for use in the schools.

7. Future Perspectives

Given the multiplicity of criteria and the various priorities among uses and users of educational software, there is much to be developed in this challenging activity of courseware evaluation. While it can build on the large body of evaluation experience with traditional curriculum materials, software evaluation must be adapted to the uniqueness of computer programs. It appears that courseware evaluation should be formative in its focus; flexible and eclectic in its research methodologies; and highly sensitive to both the contexts in which the programs are to be used (Prosser 1984), and to the characteristics of its users (Bates 1981)—students and teachers alike.

The dynamics between courseware development and evaluation must stay transactive; this will help new awarenesses and creative advances in courseware development to be reflected in evaluation activities, and vice versa. Since computer materials range in significance from a single game to a set of activities to a complete curriculum or instructional package, more is likely to be learnt from the evaluation of some programs than from others.

Walker (1986) strongly advocates that major evaluation efforts be devoted to novel, fully developed programs with a sound basis in theory, rather than to discrete, fragmentary elements of a program. Apparently, such a molecular approach, rather than an atomistic approach, is likely to yield more valid information and to be more worthwhile both conceptually and economically. This will enable a better understanding not only of the effects of courseware, but also of the origin of these effects—not just whether and how a computer program works, but also why it works in a variety of contexts, as well as with various groups of users.

Bibliography

Bates T 1981 Towards a better research framework for evaluating the effectiveness of educational media. *Br. J. Educ. Technol.* 12: 215–33

Bork A 1985 Ethical issues associated with the use of computers in learning environments. Unpublished paper, Educational Technology Center, Information and Computer Science, Irvine, California

Clark R E 1985 Confounding in educational computing research. *J. Educ. Comput. Res.* 1: 137–48

Cohen V B 1983 Criteria for the evaluation of microcomputer courseware. *Educ. Technol.* 23: 9–14

Gold P C 1984 Educational software—new guidelines for development. *AEDS J.* 18: 41–50

Holznagel D C 1983 Evaluating software. *AEDS J.* 17: 33–40

Jay T B 1983 The cognitive approach to computer courseware design and evaluation. *Educ. Technol.* 23: 22–26

Jones N B (ed.) 1983 *Evaluation of Educational Software: A Guide to Guides.* Southwest Educational Development Laboratory, Austin, Texas, and NEREX, Chelmsford, Massachusetts

Kleiman G, Humphrey M M, Buskirk T van 1984 Evaluating educational software. *J. Comput. Maths. Sci. Teach.* 3: 33–37

Lepper M R 1985 Microcomputers in education: Motivational and social issues. *Am. Psychol.* 40: 1–18

Malone T W 1981 Toward a theory of intrinsically motivating instruction. *Cognit. Sci.* 4: 333–69

NEA Educational Computer Service 1983 *Guide to the Software Assessment Procedure Review Document #1: Courseware.* NEA Educational Computer Service, Bethesda, Maryland

Prosser M T 1984 Towards more effective evaluation studies of educational media. *Br. J. Educ. Technol.* 15: 33–42

Roblyer M D 1981 When is it "good courseware?" Problems in developing standards for microcomputer courseware. *Educ. Technol.* 21: 47–54

Rothe J P 1983 Critical evaluation of educational software from a social perspective: Uncovering some hidden assumptions. *Educ. Technol.* 23: 9–15

TESS 1985 *The Educational Software Selector*, 2nd edn. Educational Products Information Exchange (EPIE) Institute, Water Mill, New York

Walker D F 1986 Evaluation of educational software. In: *Proc. Conf. Courseware Design and Evaluation*. Israel Association for Computers in Education (IACE)

Part 2

Specific Study Areas

Part 2

Specific Study Areas

Introduction

Curriculum Areas

Curriculum development entails the selection and organization of intended learning outcomes. The source of all curricula is that portion of the content of a culture that is transmissible through learning. Some cultural content is derived from systematic inquiry carried out within various scholarly disciplines. Much potentially learnable content, however, evolves spontaneously out of the ongoing life within a society. From these two bodies of available content, choices must be made, consistent with some set of educational goals, as to what will be taught in some anticipated instructional situation.

In some instances, the selection occurs at the microcurricular level. Specific items are selected to be learned, items that are taxonomically classifiable into three "domains," designated cognitive, psychomotor, and affective (Bloom 1956). One cognitive sub-domain consists of cognitions, for example, facts, concepts, generalizations; the other comprises five intellectual operations, namely, comprehension, application, analysis, synthesis, and evaluation. The psychomotor domain embraces those performance capabilities which entail perception and movement (Harrow 1973), while the affective domain encompasses acquired feeling dispositions (Krathwohl et al. 1964).

Once selected, curriculum items are usually synthesized into macrocurricular categories defined on the basis of their substance rather than their taxonomic form. Alternatively, however, the selection process itself can be directed at previously defined macrocurricular categories, rather than at specific items of learnable content. In this instance, the selected categories must then be analyzed to identify the specific microcurricular items subsumed by them.

The term "curriculum area" is used in reference to both (a) the categories of human experience and scholarship from which curriculum items may be selected, and (b) the macrocurricular categories into which selected items are subsequently organized for learning and instruction. Thus, a curriculum area comprises a set of potential or adopted curriculum items that àre viewed as substantively related.

Curriculum areas exist at various hierarchical levels. At the lowest level, a number of specific entities that are intended to be learned are grouped together according to some classificatory principle or organizing theme. The category thus created, a curriculum "area," can then be incorporated with other areas which are, in some respects, similar to it into a still higher macrocurricular category, which in turn can be classified under an even more comprehensive rubric. Together, all such categories define an instructional program or curriculum.

More commonly, curriculum areas are established analytically, rather than synthetically. Broad macrocurricular classifications are analyzed and repeatedly subdivided into lower order categories, until the level of the specific microcurricular items is reached.

While the terminology for curriculum areas is not standardized or even consistent, the term "subject" is widespread and central. Subjects are often classified under "fields" and are usually first subdivided into "courses."

The "course" is a fundamental instructional category because it represents the level at which "credit" for acceptable achievement is commonly awarded, recorded, and reported. It is usually associated with a specified period of time, during which instruction will occur and some acceptable amount of learning is expected to be demonstrated.

Courses are usually subdivided either into substantively logical "topics" and "subtopics" or into somewhat larger and substantively diverse "instructional units" which reflect application contexts or are believed to offer certain pedagogical advantages. Topics usually comprise a number of "lessons," each occupying an instructional period, whereas units may be divided into various learning activities or experiences requiring more or less than one period for completion.

Every course and subcomponent has associated with it certain curricular content, representing whatever is intended to be learned within it. This content may derive from a single "subject" or from more than one subject within a "field" (fusion) or even from more than one field (unified studies). The term "core curriculum" (Wright 1952) has such a variety of meanings that it is virtually useless, but one type of "core course" that has emerged relatively recently is designed to address a variety of problems, either designated or unspecified, drawing its curricular content from any or all "fields," as appropriate for each problem investigated.

Which curriculum areas are included in an instructional program depends on the level and mission of the program and varies from one national tradition to another, as well as among philosophical positions. Historically, the number of areas has increased markedly over the centuries, particularly during the recent century. In the Western world, the areas designated the "trivium" and "quadrivium" in ancient Greece and Rome were abandoned during the "dark ages" and replaced in the medieval period with the professionally oriented areas of medicine, law, and theology. The trivium of logic, grammar, and rhetoric and the less prestigious quadrivium of music, arithmetic, geometry, and astronomy were rediscovered as the "seven liberal arts" during the Renaissance, narrowed to grammar and dialectics in the Scholastic era, and finally absorbed into a much wider range of areas during the nineteenth and twentieth centuries (Brubacher 1947 pp. 249–317). The combined effect of the rise of science and its derived technologies and the extension of educational opportunity beyond a small elite was a substantial proliferation of curriculum areas at all educational levels.

At the higher education level, many curriculum areas tend to correspond with the scholarly disciplines within which systematic inquiry proceeds, and these are classified into large "divisions" or "subject fields" with titles such as arts and humanities, mathematics and natural sciences, and social and behavioral sciences. Other curriculum areas at this level derive from the various professions and their constituent specialities (Carnegie Foundation for the Advancement of Teaching 1977 pp. 100–20).

Comparable areas based on subprofessional occupations (e.g., business, agriculture, electronics) are found at the secondary-school level, together with academic areas that either reflect individual disciplines, such as physics and history, or combinations of disciplines, such as social studies and general science. A third type of curriculum area at this level represents nonvocational aspects of life, such as health and practical arts.

At the elementary-school level, curriculum areas are usually even more general and are oriented less explicitly to disciplines and occupations. Fields such as mathematics and science may remain undifferentiated, and numerous cognate subjects may be combined as "(vernacular) language arts," while others, such as music and visual arts, remain separate. Matters pertaining to children's physical, social, and spiritual development may also be organized as curricular areas. One "thesaurus" for classifying curriculum materials in the elementary school (known as the Annehurst Curriculum Classification System), provides for 10 "topics" under each of 10 "subject divisions" for each of 10 "subject areas" constituting each of 10 "disciplines" (Frymier 1977 pp. 281–91).

Various alternative ways of grouping curriculum areas have been suggested. Thus, the courses included in an undergraduate college program can be classified under the five headings: advanced-level skills, major subject, minor subject, meeting breadth requirements, and fostering "general understanding" (Carnegie Foundation for the Advancement of Teaching 1977 pp. 126–27). Similarly, Broudy et al. (1964) proposed that curriculum areas in the secondary school be grouped into five categories: symbolic skills; sciences; developmental studies of cosmos, society, and culture; value exemplars; and molar problem solving. This taxonomy is consistent with the architectonics of knowledge formulated by Phenix, with its qualitative dimension defined by the relative emphasis upon fact, form, and norm and its quantitative dimension by the focus on the singular, the general, or the comprehensive (Elam 1964 pp. 44–74). From the nine cells of this configuration, Phenix (1964) derived six realms of meaning: synectics, empirics, symbolics, aesthetics, ethics, and synoptics.

Bibliography

Bloom B S (ed.) 1956 *Taxonomy of Educational Objectives: The Classification of Educational Goals, Handbook 1: Cognitive Domain.* McKay, New York

Broudy H S, Smith B O, Burnett J R 1964 *Democracy and Excellence in American Secondary Education: A Study in Curriculum Theory.* Rand McNally, New York

Brubacher J S 1947 *A History of the Problems of Education.* McGraw-Hill, New York

Carnegie Foundation for the Advancement of Teaching 1977 *Missions of the College Curriculum: A Contemporary Review with Suggestions: A Commentary.* Jossey-Bass, San Francisco, California

Elam S M (ed.) 1964 *Education and the Structure of Knowledge.* 5th annual Phi Delta Kappa Symposium on Educational Research. Rand McNally, New York.

Ford G W, Pugno L (eds.) 1964 *The Structure of Knowledge and the Curriculum.* Conference, San José State College, 1963. Rand McNally, Chicago, Illinois

Frymier J R 1977 *Annehurst Curriculum Classification System: A Practical Way to Individualize Instruction.* Phi Delta Kappa, West Lafayette, Indiana

Harrow A J 1973 *A Taxonomy of the Psychomotor Domain: A Guide for Developing Behavioral Objectives.* McKay, New York

Krathwohl D R, Bloom B S, Masia B B 1964 *Taxonomy of Education Objectives: The Classification of Educational Goals, Handbook 2: Affective Domain.* McKay, New York

Phenix P H 1964 *Realms of Meaning: A Philosophy of the Curriculum for General Education.* McGraw-Hill, New York

Wright G 1952 *Core Curriculum Development, Problems, and Practices.* Bulletin No. 5. United States Office of Education, Washington, DC

M. Johnson

Section 5

Language Arts

Overview

The articles in Section 5 are divided into four subsections. The first group of articles in Section 5(a) deals with some of the broader issues of the relationships between School Learning and Language Development.

Fillion's article, *Language Across Curriculum*, shows how, in the wake of the Bullock Report, functional work in the language arts across the curriculum assumed a central role in education in the United Kingdom, particularly at the primary stage which starts at age five. The approach rests on multiple opportunities for purposeful talk, reading, and writing in all areas of the curriculum. The lack of prescribed goals for development of subsidiary skills and the absence of workbooks may evoke an image of unbridled diversity, but this is not the case. Daily monitoring of each child's work is an integral part of the individualistic teaching approach of primary schooling in the United Kingdom. Moreover, educators are in close agreement about what they expect from students at different stages of learning.

School entrants' introduction to reading and writing would not be possible without their attaining a suitable level of language competency. Johnson's article provides background information about factors influencing the rapid rate of children's *Vocabulary Development* during the preschool years and the effectiveness of different approaches to vocabulary enrichment.

Section 5(b) discusses issues in Initial Reading instruction. The articles by Rousch, Chall, and Merritt deal with the controversial topic of approaches to initial reading instruction. Rousch juxtaposes the underlying assumptions and implications of what he terms the *traditional* and *nontraditional* theories of beginning reading instruction. Merritt describes phonic reading instruction and discusses some of the inherent problems accompanying the use of phonic methods in the English language. Chall presents a cogent analysis of developments in reading instruction in light of up-to-date research results.

Feitelson charts the development of the concept of *Reading Readiness* and shows how it relates to the way beginning reading is approached in different countries. She also questions the tendency of reading readiness work to focus mainly on preparation for the technical aspects of reading.

The traditional rationale and practices of sight-word instruction, as well as developments in this area, are insightfully described by Fleet in the last article dealing with issues in Initial Reading instruction.

Hill's review of holistic and targeted competency approaches in secondary reading instruction opens Section 5(c). It is followed by the late Harry Singer's exhaustive examination of reading comprehension development from early childhood through high school and his discussion of comprehension teaching strategies. Instruction in critical reading teaches children to evaluate what they have read and understood. Parker and Unsworth present the skills, research, and teaching practices pertaining to this increasingly popular area.

The article by Samuels and Schermer shows how *Reading Rate* and *Reading Flexibility* are related to each other, and also to text familiarity and difficulty, as well as readers' motivation and skills. Listening and reading share the common goal of comprehending meaning and both are receptive skills. Mead's article examines listening instruction in relation to other factors.

The articles by Crocker, Purves, Peters, and Holbrook mark a transition to the expressive components of mother tongue instruction, namely speech and writing. Their analyses of *Speech Instruction, Composition Instruction, Spelling Instruction, Handwriting Instruction*, and Van Nord's analysis of *Study Skills*, demonstrate that, in different areas, students' time and efforts are often taken up by learning experiences whose effectiveness has not been proven.

Section 5(d) deals with what is increasingly recognized as a major goal of language arts instruction namely, students' independent reading. Greaney reviews research results about *Reading Interest* and practices on the international scene. Chall and Marston conclude this section with findings about the development of lifetime reading habits.

D. Feitelson

Language Arts

Introduction

M. L. King

The language arts are those human endeavors concerned with using language to represent meaning to oneself and others in order to attain personal purposes in a social world. The term, more frequently applied to a curriculum band in elementary schools than in secondary schools, emerged from the social milieu following the First World War when pragmatic conceptions of education began to influence the teaching of language (specifically English) in schools. The term signifies an intention to move away from teaching language for its own sake, as subject matter, to a larger concern for the development of individuals who could use language effectively and confidently for an increasingly wider range of purposes.

1. Purpose and Scope

One of the major uses of language is communication; the other is learning. Language arts teaching should enable individuals to communicate effectively with others and to understand as fully as they can what others communicate to them. But language also plays a role in the way people learn about their social and physical environments, represent and shape these experiences, conceptualize and respond to their personal feelings and attitudes, and make this knowing available to themselves and others (Britton 1970, Donaldson 1978).

The scope of the language arts is broad, encompassing all of the art and skill people use in producing and receiving meaning through oral and visual symbols. These include the main channels of encoding (speaking and writing) and decoding (listening and reading), and written and spoken messages. Within these four modes are a range of language activities, knowledge, and skills that are best considered within a framework of language in use. When the language arts are conceived as content to be mastered, there is a tendency to address the components separately; that is, to teach composition, literature, language (particularly grammar), spelling, handwriting, and drama with little reference to each other and often as separate courses.

2. Language Learning and Competence

Concern for effective use of language on the other hand requires consideration of how children learn language and how language functions in society. The stellar success that children have in learning language in the home surely has implications for language teaching in school. Language research shows quite convincingly that children learn language by using it in the meaningful interactions that occur within the daily life of the family (Macnamara 1972, Donaldson 1978, Bruner 1972). These studies seriously challenged the notion, posited by Chomsky (1965), that human beings have a special competence, a language acquisition device, as opposed to a biological inheritance, for learning language. While Chomsky's view emphasized the creative aspects of language production, recent research shows that language learning is a constructive process in which children learn language as they build a system of meanings (Halliday 1975). Chomsky was primarily interested in people's ability to generate sentences and to transform ideas in the mind into the linear syntactic representation required in speech and writing. Other linguists, however, were concerned with a more complex human capacity—the ability to produce language that was appropriate in a given social situation (Hymes 1971, Halliday 1973). This expanded view of communicative competence represents a person's capacity to use language to share meanings and incorporates a repertoire of social rules as well as linguistic ones. This latter view is more consonant with the way children learn language and the goals of the language arts as set forth above, than with Chomsky's limited concept of competence.

3. Integrative Perspectives

Several scholars have contributed to the understanding of the integration of the language arts, but the work of three is particularly relevant to curriculum decisions in teacher education. Halliday (1973) has described how language functions in the social world; Moffett (1968) has defined the "universe of discourse" within a trinity of communication, and Britton (1971) with the language user in mind, has proposed a scheme which he believes applicable to "language across the curriculum."

Children arrive at school as social beings who intuitively view language as functional, as serving them; they know what language is on the basis of what they can do with it (Halliday 1973). They have had experience in a broad range of language functions which Halliday has labeled "relevant models" and defined as language: (a) to get things done, instrumental; (b) to control behavior, regulatory; (c) to relate to others, interactional; (d) to express self, personal; (e) to find out, heuristic; (f) to pretend, imaginative; and (g) to tell someone something, informative. These basic uses of language continue throughout life, but operate at different levels of abstraction depending on the context of situation.

Halliday (1975) claims that these early functions are consolidated and integrated into an adult system of functions which serves individuals in three ways: to interact with and communicate with others, an interpersonal function; to deal with ideas, to think and to learn, an ideational function; and to create oral and written texts, a textual function. All language interactions are processes for creating text; they occur in an environment and the text generated at any one time is interwoven and shaped by the relevant factors in that situation (Halliday 1975). When producing language (text), the speaker/writer selects from the language options available, that is, words, syntax, and phonology to form text that is coherent within itself and relates to the social context. Each language-evoking context is characterized by a meaning structure which sets it apart from other situations and can be described in three dimensions: the ongoing activity (field), the role relationships among the participants (tenor), and the symbolic rhetorical channel of language used (mode). This model enables teachers and curriculum specialists to see the interdependence of the language produced in the classroom and other important factors in the learning context, such as the ongoing activity and the relationships between speaker/writer to their audience and to the content being considered.

From the perspective of the language user, Britton developed a matrix of language function, also based on the idea of "context", but with context interpreted as "universe of discourse." Thus, he sees language operating in a universe of conventions and presuppositions maintained by the mutual acknowledgement of communicating subjects (Britton 1971). At the center of Britton's spectrum is the expressive function which he proposes becomes more explicit and referential when so demanded by the situation. Expressive language is language close to the speaker/writer in which he or she expresses feelings, tests out ideas, and thinks aloud on paper. It is the language in which "we are likely to test the growing points of our formulations and analysis

of experience" (p. 246). While expressive language is maintained throughout life, Britton proposes that individuals develop toward two major categories of discourse functions: transactional and poetic, as illustrated in Fig. 1.

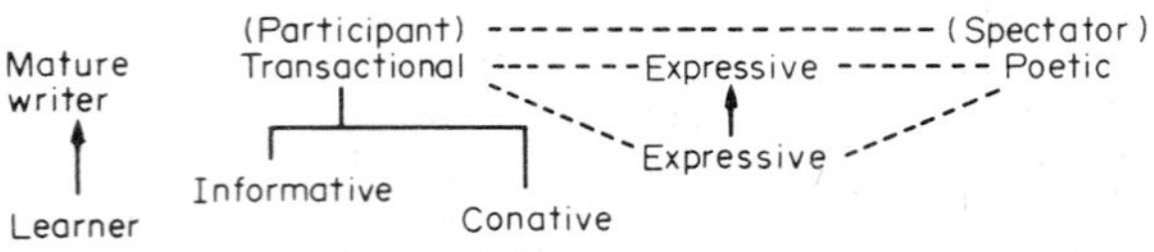

As language develops towards the transactional function, there is a need to get things done, to inform, control, and persuade. This category has two subdivisions of informative and conative uses, with the latter further divided into regulative and persuasive functions. Language also develops in another direction where individuals assume a different role toward experience and audience. The speaker/writer is not seeking to participate directly as in the transactional mode; rather he or she takes a different stance, that of spectator. Here, language serves as a means to recapture experience—to savor, to reformulate events, and to shape them into a verbal construct. Language in this sense is poetic or "presentational," the shape and form are an important part of the construct; language functions to create artistic forms of story, novel, poetry, which call for "global contextualization" (p. 248).

Britton subdivides the informative uses of language on the basis of a scale of abstractions as formulated by Moffett (1968). Although Britton's matrix has more categories than Moffett's, it is based on similar assumptions about the relationships that exist between speaker, listener, and subject in communicative situations. The levels of abstraction result from the distance between the speaker/writer and the temporal distance from the topic. Thus, at one end of the scale the immediate present is recorded or commented on and at the other, the classified event becomes the subject for speculation and theorizing.

Moffett constructs his "universe of discourse" on the basis of a set of relationships that exists between a triad of *I*—the producer, *It*—the subject, and *You*—the receiver. He argues that shifts in relationships in time and space between producer-to-subject and producer-to-receiver affect the degree of abstraction with which a topic is represented in language. Table 1 shows how levels of abstraction and potential forms of discourse are related to the distance between speaker and topic.

Figure 1
Transactional and poetic discourse functions

Table 1
How levels of abstraction and potential forms of discourse are related to the distance between speaker and topic

Topic (It)	Abstraction	Discourse
What is happening	Chronology of perceptual selectivity	Drama, recording, conversation
What happened	Chronology of memory selectivity	Narration, report, letters
What happens	Analogy of classification	Generalizing, exposition, essay
What may happen	Theorizing, logical argumentation	Scientific work

4. Implications for the Curriculum

Together, the models provide a very useful framework for integrating the numerous knowledge/skill components within the language arts and indicating how they function across the schools curriculum. Literature's special role is designated in Britton's spectrum as content as well as process in the poetic realm, while the study of language falls largely in the transactional category. The focus on language use implies that in the study of language, the traditional emphasis on the structure should be extended to encompass language use in society including language variations and changes over time. Understanding the problems and special needs of second language learners is likely to be easier when they are considered in relation to the learners' potential use of the language in particular contexts.

Of special value is the way the theories relate language to the real world, especially the universe of discourse, and show how the relationships between language producer, topic, and receiver effect the kind of thinking required and the type of speech or writing generated. A curriculum based on language function is close to the way language is used in life. It is an integrated system in which language skills are learned as a part of a global meaningful activity. Such natural integration does not preclude separate attention to and practice in skills, such as constructing sentences, reading, listening, handwriting, and spelling; but does imply that skills are most naturally learned through use.

Language also serves a metalinguistic function which is implied in Halliday's textual function and is surely incorporated in Moffett's and Britton's concern for audience and "shaping" of various forms of discourse. However, attention to language itself is more likely to occur in writing than in speaking because of the need to transcribe thoughts into visual form and to make meanings clear and free from contextual factors. The metafunction is apparent also when learning subject matter through language. Often, the learner finds it necessary to disembed the meanings from the language in which they are expressed in order to understand the mathematical or historical ideas.

5. Research Reflects Concern for Process and Function

Language arts research since the late 1950s reflects the new understandings about the process of language learning and the functions of language in the social world. Emphasis has been on how meanings and language develop together in home and in school. Less research attention has recently been given to the study of teaching method and more to discovering how children learn to talk, to read, and to write—and the conditions of the home and school that foster such development. Studies reveal that children are active learners who, with the help of their parents, construct their own system of language and meanings (Bruner

1972, Halliday 1975). In various areas of language competence children appear to first develop a system of operation that is not adult-like, but is discernible and predictable. For example, they construct a protogrammar before entering the adult system (Halliday 1975), invent a unique system of spelling (Read 1971), and utilize a set of identifiable principles in creating written messages (Clay 1975).

Children learn their oral language skills through interaction with adults in which they seek to negotiate meaning. Given the opportunity to do so, children also bring these same processes to reading and writing. When reading they seek meaning from the text; they interact with the author's words, that is, they negotiate meanings embedded in the language. Children reveal this process in the kinds of errors or "miscues" they make when reading aloud. These errors indicate how they are reading, that is, predicting meanings, sentence structures, and pronunciation of words (Goodman and Burke 1972).

Recent research in writing has focused on the writing process; children's development in writing, and the functions of writing in the home, school, and society. It is clear that when children write from their own intentions, their purpose is to convey meaning. And they use whatever knowledge of signs, symbols, and pictures they know to create the message. There is considerable evidence that children know a great deal about written language before coming to school which is often ignored as the established curriculum unfolds. Further, during the first three years in school children demonstrate that they understand that written texts differ from spoken ones in the way they use words, reference, and other text elements to make their writing cohesive and explicit.

Research has brought a much greater understanding of the writing process in respect to both what children do when they write and the cognitive demands they face in the process. A big problem young children confront in writing is that of sustaining the flow of language and thought without the support of conversational input which they have in oral language (Bereiter and Scardamalia 1982). Finally, studies of writing in school and society have provided very useful information to educators about the way written language actually functions to achieve purposes of communication and reflection.

Bibliography

Bereiter C, Scardamalia M 1982 From conversation to composition: The role of instruction in developmental process. In: Glaser R (ed.) 1982 *Advances in Instructional Psychology*, Vol. 2. Erlbaum, Hillsdale, New Jersey

Britton J N 1970 *Language and Learning*. Allen Lane, London

Britton J N 1971 What's the use? *Educ. Rev.* 23(3): 205–19

Britton J N, Burgess T, Martin N, MacLeod A, Rosen H 1975 *The Development of Writing Abilities (11–18)*. Schools Council Project on Written Language of 11–18 year olds. Macmillan, London

Bruner J S 1972 The ontogenesis of speech acts. *J. Child Lang.* 1(2): 1–19

Chomsky N 1965 *Aspects of the Theory of Syntax*. MIT Press, Cambridge, Massachusetts

Donaldson M 1978 *Children's Minds*. Fontana, London

Goodman Y M, Burke C L 1972 *The Goodman–Burke Reading Miscue Inventory*. Macmillan, New York

Graves D 1983 *Writing: Teachers and Children at Work*. Heinemann, Exeter, New Hampshire

Halliday M A K 1973 *Explorations in the Functions of Language*. Arnold, London

Halliday M A K 1975 *Learning How to Mean: Explorations in the Development of Language*. Arnold, London

Harste J, Burke C L, Woodward V 1982 *Children, Their Language and World: Initial Encounters with Print*. Final Report to NIE. Language Education Department, Indiana University, Bloomington, Indiana

Heath S B 1982 Toward an ethnohistory of writing in American education. In: Whiteman M F (ed.) *Variations in Writing: Functional and Linguistic–Cultural Differences*, Vol. 1. Erlbaum, Hillsdale, New Jersey

Hymes D 1971 Competence and performance in linguistic theory. In: Huxley R, Ingram E (eds.) *Language Acquisition: Models and Methods*. Academic Press, New York, pp. 3–28

King M L, Rentel V M 1981 Conveying meaning in written texts. *Language Arts* 58(6): 721–28

Macnamara J 1972 Cognitive basis of language learning in infants. *Psychol. Rev.* 79: 1–13

Mallett M, Newsome B 1977 *Talking, Writing and Learning, 8–13*. Schools Council, London

Moffett J 1968 *Teaching the Universe of Discourse*. Houghton Mifflin, Boston, Massachusetts

Read C 1971 Preschool children's knowledge of English phonology. *Harvard Educ. Rev.* 41: 1–34

School Learning and Language Development

Language Across Curriculum

B. Fillion

Language across the curriculum refers to an emerging body of educational theories and practices concerned with the whole school's influence on pupils' language development, and with pupils' uses of language in the process of learning. Language across the curriculum is primarily concerned with pupils' ability to use reading, writing, and talk for an increasing range of personal, social, and educational purposes, rather than with conventional correctness or with explicit knowledge about language. In place of traditional school emphasis on language as a subject, with particular skills and conventions to be taught, language across the curriculum stresses concern for how pupils learn to use language, how they use language to achieve understanding and appreciation of their experiences (including the curriculum content introduced in schools), and how language use influences cognitive development.

Although language across the curriculum is based on particular points of view about language development and the relationship of language to learning, its advocates have generally been reluctant to translate its principles into particular teaching methods. Relying extensively on descriptive studies of actual school practices and close observations of children using language, language across the curriculum has tended to pose questions and provide the focus for teachers' explorations of language development and learning, rather than advocating the adoption of teaching techniques or educational practices.

Language across the curriculum, sometimes discussed as "writing across the curriculum," "language and learning across the curriculum," and "school language policies," was popularized by the United Kingdom Department of Education and Science's Bullock Report, *A Language for Life* (1975), an extensive study of language development and language education made in response to widespread public concern about pupils' language skills and linguistic performance, particularly in reading. Heavily influenced by the theories and research of James Britton, Nancy Martin, Douglas Barnes, and other United Kingdom educators, especially at the University of London Institute of Education, the Bullock Report supported two key premises of language across the curriculum. First, that language development

results primarily from the purposeful use of language and that through the control of pupils' language use the entire school and curriculum influence children's language development. Second, that language has a powerful heuristic function and is inextricably involved in virtually all school learning and in cognitive development generally.

Two principal recommendations of the Bullock Report, based on these premises, are that every school should develop an organized policy for language across the curriculum, involving every teacher at every grade level in the pupils' language and reading development, and that every teacher's initial training should include substantial course work on language in education, regardless of the teacher's intended subject matter or grade level (Department of Education and Science 1975 pp. 514–15).

1. Language Use and Development

The Bullock Report reviewed recent theories and research concerning children's language acquisition and development in the home and school, and concluded that development is most usefully characterized as a facility in using language for an increasing range of purposes, rather than as the accumulation of discrete skills, such as word recognition, spelling, and punctuation, or as the elimination of errors. While allowing the importance of such small-focus skills and surface correctness, the report emphasizes that the real basics in language development are motivation, intention, and the opportunity to use language for one's own purposes, including the purposes generated by school learning.

This shift in emphasis, from language teaching to language learning, from skill-building techniques to the child's intentional uses of language, and from teacher as corrector to teacher as audience, brings the whole school under scrutiny as a language-learning environment. The search for ways to improve pupils' reading and writing is no longer restricted to one particular teacher or subject area but includes all areas of the curriculum in which language is used. While stressing that children's language development should not be left to chance, and that the provision of environments that promote language use for varied purposes may not be sufficient in itself, the Bullock Report and language across the curriculum advocates share the assumption that virtually all children have tacit powers of language and a natural capacity for language learning that schools often fail to exploit.

Arguing that "language competence grows incrementally, through an interaction of writing, talk, reading, and experience" (Department of Education and Science 1975 p. 7), rather than through the acquisition of skills taught in isolation, the Bullock Report advocates an educational approach to language development patterned after successful language acquisition in early childhood: the creation of situations "in which, to satisfy his own purposes, a child encounters the need to use more elaborate forms and is thus motivated to extend the complexity of language available to him" (p. 67). The provision of such situations, the development of pupils' motivation and intentions, and teachers' careful monitoring of pupils' language need not be restricted to particular "language arts" portions of the curriculum; opportunities for purposeful talk, writing, and reading exist throughout the school day, and in all areas of the curriculum.

Although various descriptions of language uses have been advanced by educators and linguists, language across the curriculum has been most directly influenced by James Britton's characterization of the functions of language, and his account of language development related to them. Britton (1970), argued the importance of two key roles of language in people's lives: the participant role and the spectator role. Language in the participant role is language used as a means to some practical end beyond itself, such as informing, persuading, and direction giving. These are necessary parts of transactions and of participation in the ongoing affairs of the world. Language in the spectator role is used primarily to recount, reflect on, and enjoy experiences—real or imagined—in which the account, the recollection, or the language itself becomes the main concern, rather than a means to some practical end. The practical importance of language in the participant role, language to get things done, is well-recognized and reflected in virtually every school's emphasis on the development of communication skills. Less well-recognized is the importance of language in the spectator role, in ordering and shaping perceptions of the world, and the beliefs, attitudes, and values which influence actions. Britton argues that a central developmental task of human beings as symbol-using animals is the construction of adequate representations of reality, largely through language. Consequently, a fundamental purpose of education is to promote pupils' use of the full potential of language in this enterprise, in both the participant and spectator roles.

According to Britton, language development occurs when individuals, responding to various situations and their own intentions, use language for an increasing range of purposes and audiences. Beginning with infor- ·

mal, everyday expressive language—language used with one's self and intimates—a command is gradually gained over the functions of the spectator and participant roles, and the linguistic resources necessary for them are developed. Personal, expressive language is important both as the starting point for linguistic development, and as the language in which people explore, mull over, and begin to come to terms with new and unfamiliar ideas and experiences. Audiences stimulate and provide feedback on language and ideas and serve as conversational partners in shaping discourse and meanings.

In an extensive study of writing development in adolescents, Britton and his colleagues (1975) investigated the functions and audiences for pupils' school writing, establishing three major functions associated with the roles of language. Transactional writing—basically writing in the participant role to inform, persuade, and direct—was found to dominate the secondary-school writing of pupils in the United Kingdom, with very little poetic (spectator) writing, and even less expressive writing (writing close to informal speech). Pupils wrote primarily to the teacher "as examiner," rather than to themselves, peers, or the teacher as "trusted adult." The dearth of expressive writing was considered important for two reasons: (a) because of the importance of such writing as a means of learning; and (b) because of its importance to the development of writing ability generally. The lack of expressive writing may prove especially debilitating for poorer writers, depriving them of a necessary stage in the development of more formal transactional and poetic writing.

Britton's findings suggest that secondary schools in the United Kingdom are failing to provide a sufficient range of writing functions and audiences to promote pupils' full development as writers. Similar findings of restricted language use in school are also revealed in a United States study of secondary-school writing (Applebee 1981) and in a United Kingdom study of school reading (Lunzer and Gardner 1979). Each of · these surveys of actual practice suggest that pupils' use of language in the schools, at least at the secondary level, is significantly restricted and unlikely to promote the language development that is desired and possible. The Lunzer and Gardner study notes that in secondary schools the pressure to cover material and teachers' general pessimism about pupils' reading ability have combined to reduce the role of in-class reading, and talk about reading, and to increase the role of teacher talk as a means of instruction. Thus, instead of attempting to improve pupils' reading ability, teachers seem to have retreated from the problem by reducing the role of written language in the classroom. Similarly, Applebee notes that secondary teachers in the United States often reduce pupils' writing to fill-in-the-blanks exercises. In each case, teachers appear to be doing much of the linguistic work for their students: bypassing pupils' language use in order to get on with their courses. As Applebee points out, "teachers seem not to realize that the part of the task which they have taken over also involves important skills that are as relevant to the students' subject-area learning as to their writing instruction" (1981 p. 100).

2. *Language and Learning*

No serious examination of the uses of language proceeds very far without consideration of the relationship between language and learning. Both in and out of school, learning often involves and occurs through language and provides a powerful motive for its continued development. Children describing their toys and travels to friends, and secondary pupils exploring concepts in term papers for their teachers, are all involved both in shaping their own understandings and in extending and developing the language resources necessary to accomplish their intended purposes. The practical matter of participating in the world's affairs and the human need to interpret and make sense of experience as spectators involve learning, language development, and the interaction of language and learning.

James Britton's *Language and Learning* (1970), which has had such a marked influence on language across the curriculum, begins with a discussion of language as a primary means whereby human beings construct the mental representations of reality that guide their perceptions and actions: "learning" in the most fundamental and global sense. Similarly, the Bullock Report, following its introductory chapters on the reasons and intentions of the study, introduces its discussion of language development with a chapter on "Language and Learning," reiterating Britton's contention that language is first and foremost an intellectual tool by which experiences are interpreted and organized into generalized representations, formulating and reformulating what is known about the world. Especially in the processes of talking and writing, but also in the internal language that accompanies reading and listening, knowledge is actively brought into being and at the same time the mental operations that constitute cognitive growth are developed.

Most language across the curriculum theorists share these views of knowledge as essentially personal and subjective, of learning as the process by which the learner actively assimilates, understands, and interprets new information and skills, and of language as a major intellectual tool. Except perhaps for simple rote memorization, and purely retained visual imagery and muscular movements, the process of learning always involves the reformulation, interpretation, and contemplation of experiences and given information, and talk and writing are significant parts of that process, even if the talk occurs subvocally as inner speech.

Pupils' language, and especially their informal, personal "expressive" language, is important to the learning process in four critical ways, all of which have implications for teachers and subjects across the curriculum. First, language is involved in developing pupils' interest and their commitment to learning, because it is through talking or writing about a subject that they are likely to locate the links between given topics and information and their own concerns and experiences. Second, language is part of the process by which pupils get from information "out there" to their own understanding and appreciation of it. The process of interpreting and understanding information and concepts, or experiences, is largely a matter of establishing the relationship between new and prior knowledge and experiences, and these links are normally forged through language. The practical implications of both of these points are developed in *Writing and Learning Across the Curriculum, 11–16 Years* (Martin et al. 1976) and in the work of Torbe and Medway in *The Climate for Learning* (1981).

A third important relationship between language and the learning process is that, although the precise relationship of thought and language remains a matter of controversy, there is little doubt that in the process of solving problems and coming to understand complex experiences—processes that often involve various forms of talk and writing—pupils develop mental operations which help them with subsequent thinking and learning. This point is succinctly made in the Bullock Report's case for language across the curriculum: "While many teachers recognise that their aim is to initiate a student in a particular mode of analysis, they rarely recognise . . . that the mental processes they seek to foster are the outcome of a development that originates in speech" (p. 189). Fourth, it is only through expressed language that the learner's mental operations and learning processes become available for inspection and consideration, by the learner or the teacher. In Britton's telling phrase, language is "the exposed edge of thought," providing teachers and the learners themselves with the means to assess and work upon the learner's cognitive processes and development.

Martin and her associates (1976) investigated the pedagogical implications of Britton and his co-workers' writing research in a Schools Council study of the relationship of writing and learning across the curriculum at ages 11 to 16. Working with teachers in various school subjects, the researchers explored the ways that different kinds of writing and talking (expressive, transactional, and poetic) seemed to promote or inhibit students' understanding, appreciation, and use of learning materials and information in different disciplines. They concluded that the restriction of children's talking and writing, and the exclusive use of transactional writing, deprived pupils of important ways of developing a commitment to learning, and of coming to understand the material presented to them. The project further concluded that two major obstacles to language across the curriculum existed in most secondary schools: first, the organization of the schools inhibited cross-disciplinary discussions of language and learning; and second, the teachers generally failed to consider the implications of language as a major intellectual tool and therefore failed to realize the potential of pupils' talking and writing as a means of learning.

Barnes (1976, Barnes et al. 1971) investigated the role of spoken language in learning, analyzing pupils' small-group talk in various school subjects. He concluded that informal, "exploratory" language plays an important role in moving pupils toward understanding and appreciation of the information and ideas presented to them in the curriculum. Barnes observes that schools often require and permit only "final draft" language from pupils, to demonstrate their mastery or memorization of information, and restrict the exploratory language by which pupils might achieve such mastery.

In their study of secondary-school reading in the United Kingdom, Lunzer and Gardner (1979) found that pupils' use of reading to learn could be improved by the development of more "reflective" reading, through a combination of instruction and talk about the reading, and that such improvement could occur in the classroom context of ongoing learning and discussion of subject matter. However, few teachers provided such contexts in their classrooms, and many teachers expressed reservations about pupils' ability to use reading to learn. In the secondary schools studied, the pupils' main opportunity to use reading to learn—to read reflectively—was in their homework assignments, when they had no access to teacher help. Thus, the development of an important heuristic skill is left largely to chance, and when it fails to develop, teachers further reduce pupils' opportunity to learn it by reducing classroom use of reflective reading in favor of presenting material to the class orally.

With learning, as with language development, language across the curriculum investigations have raised serious questions about both ends and means. In language development, schools often appear to have turned enabling objectives such as skills acquisition into ends in themselves. Similarly, in subject matter learning, the development and use of personal knowledge often seem to be sacrificed to the mere acquisition and recall of information. In each case, this confusion of means and ends obscures the role of pupils' natural intentions and thus deprives them of powerful motivation for both language development and learning. It also leads teachers to ignore the crucial role of pupils' language use in language development and in the learning process.

3. Language Across the Curriculum: Problems and Prospects

Despite the currency of the phrase "language (or writing) across the curriculum" in contemporary educational discourse, it is unclear whether it has achieved the status of a widespread educational movement. There are several reasons for its uncertain status and prospects. First, as the Martin et al. study (1976) indicated, school organization, especially at the secondary level, does not easily support cross-disciplinary cooperation in matters of curriculum and instruction, particularly when the issue—language development—is widely perceived as the responsibility and province of one particular subject area. A basic problem in implementing the Bullock Report's recommendations about school language policies has been to involve teachers of subjects other than English (National Association for the Teaching of English 1976). One solution to the problem has been to emphasize learning, rather than language, as the key term in the revised phrase "language and learning across the curriculum" (National Association for the Teaching of English 1976, Torbe and Medway 1981), but this de-emphasis of language may result in a loss of focus and interest as well.

A second problem in the acceptance and implementation of language across the curriculum has been the advocates' reluctance to recommend particular teaching methods, even though the general theory of language across the curriculum has clear implications for teaching and educational practice. For instance, pupils should have encouragement and opportunity to use informal, expressive, exploratory language—both spoken and written—in discourse about new information and subject matter before they are expected to write formally, using the established conventions of the discipline. Such methodological implications of language across the curriculum have been published in various documents, such as the 1969 London Association of Teachers of English discussion paper, "A Language Policy Across the Curriculum" (Barnes et al. 1971). Nevertheless, language across the curriculum advocates have generally resisted the reduction of their ideas into particular methods, partly because of the advocates' lack of experience in subjects other than English, and partly because the ideas, translated into methods divorced from their intent, tend to become trivialized (Martin et al. 1976). That is, despite their seeming simplicity, the methods implied by language across the curriculum also imply profound changes in many teachers' attitudes, beliefs, and relationships with pupils. For example, many secondary teachers give much higher priority to subject matter acquisition than to pupils' heuristic or linguistic development and would prefer to help pupils around their language problems—by reducing the role of written language in the classroom—than to help them solve the problems through increased reading and writing. Following Martin and the National Association for the Teaching of English observation that any effective school changes must involve teachers in the change process, the general approach of language across the curriculum has been to invite teachers to investigate the relationship of language and learning in their own classes and school, and to draw their own conclusions about how pupils' talk, writing, and reading can contribute to more efficient and effective learning of their subjects. However effective this approach may be in creating long-term change, it is much more difficult in schools to sustain basic inquiry than to urge the adoption of particular methods, materials, or approaches.

A third problem of language across the curriculum has been its lack of an experimental research base. The case for language across the curriculum continues to rest primarily on the claims of theory and descriptive research, and especially on United Kingdom accounts and analyses of "best practice," and teacher testimonials. There is as yet no substantial body of experimental research demonstrating conclusively that increasing pupils' talk and writing, or their use of expressive language in schools, or the promotion of more reflective reading will substantially improve pupils' commitment to learning, or their performance in academic subjects, or on established and accepted measures of language development.

Finally, the basic beliefs and assumptions of language across the curriculum about the nature of knowledge, learning, language development, and the ends of education may not be widely shared by teachers or the public at large. Convincing teachers to view language as an intellectual tool, rather than as a body of skills to be corrected and improved, was a major problem for the Martin study, and many teachers would probably have difficulty accepting the view that knowledge is essentially personal and subjective, rather than a body of information to be acquired. There is by no means universal acceptance of the language across the curriculum assumptions that many pupils' commitment to learning can be increased, or that the development of learning skills should have equal priority with the acquisition of subject matter, especially in the secondary schools.

Nevertheless, despite these problems, from the late 1970s there has been considerable interest among theorists, researchers, and practitioners throughout the English-speaking world in the basic concerns and precepts of language across the curriculum, and in their implications for language development and educational practice. Language across the curriculum has been accepted as official policy in some jurisdictions, such as Ontario, Canada (Ontario Ministry of Education 1978), and has provided the impetus for numerous revealing investigations of school practice, such as the Britton, Martin, Applebee, and Lunzer and Gardner studies cited earlier. More recently, the concern for writing has stimulated language across the curriculum research and development in postsecondary education (Fulwiler and Young 1982). Whether language across the curriculum is or becomes a widely accepted educational movement or is dismissed as a fad, the basic issues and questions it has raised about language development, learning, cognitive growth, and the ends of education will continue to be central concerns for researchers, theorists, and practitioners in the foreseeable future.

Bibliography

Applebee A N 1981 *Writing in the Secondary School: English and the Content Areas*. National Council of Teachers of English, Urbana, Illinois

Barnes D 1976 *From Communication to Curriculum*. Penguin, Harmondsworth

Barnes D R, Britton J, Rosen H 1971 *Language, the Learner and the School: A Research Report*. Penguin, Harmondsworth

Britton J N 1970 *Language and Learning*. Penguin, Harmondsworth

Britton J N, Burgess T, Martin N, McLeod A, Rosen H 1975 *The Development of Writing Abilities (11–18)*. Macmillan, London

Fulwiler T, Young A (eds.) 1982 *Language Connections: Writing and Reading Across the Curriculum*. National Council of Teachers of English, Urbana, Illinois

Lunzer E A, Gardner K 1979 *The Effective Use of Reading*. Heinemann, London

Marland M 1977 *Language Across the Curriculum: The Implementation of the Bullock Report in the Secondary School*. Heinemann, London

Martin N, D'Arcy P, Newton B, Parker R 1976 *Writing and Learning Across the Curriculum, 11–16 Years*. Ward Lock Educational, London

National Association for the Teaching of English 1976 *Language Across the Curriculum: Guidelines for Schools*. Ward Lock, London

Ontario Ministry of Education 1978 *Language Across the Curriculum: A Resource Document for Principals and Teachers*. Ontario Ministry of Education, Toronto, Ontario

Torbe M, Medway P 1981 *The Climate for Learning*. Ward Lock, London

United Kingdom, Department of Education and Science 1975 *A Language for Life*, Report of the Committee of Inquiry appointed by the Secretary of State for Education and Science (The Bullock Report). Her Majesty's Stationery Office, London

Vocabulary Development

D. L. Johnson

Through words, concepts enter the arena of social communication and all during life concept and word interact, each building on the other. Thus, the development of vocabulary is intimately tied to the development of thought, and influences on one are influences on the other. For the child, understanding the meaning of words is the most important aspect of vocabulary development.

A frequently cited theory of vocabulary development is Clark's (1973) Semantic Feature Hypothesis which holds that each word is made up of features or components of meaning. Children learn word meaning by adding features. Thus, the word *wide* is incompletely understood if it is only taken to mean *big* because this aspect would also be a feature of *tall* or *long*. When the child adds the feature that *wide* refers to size on the horizontal dimension, its meaning is more nearly complete. The theory does not account for all instances of word acquisition. For alternative views of conceptual and vocabulary development in young children see Carey (1978) and Anglin (1977). A volume edited by Kuczaj and Barret (1986) deals with this issue in detail.

Carey (1978) has demonstrated that new word acquisition may be a lengthy process. Preschool children were shown materials in a new color, olive, and told that this color was chromium. Subsequent exposure to the color or word revealed that most of the children did not have a reliable understanding of the word even after several months of weekly experiences with it. Quite likely other words acquired by the child take an equally long time to become known; exactly how long depending on the initial meaning of the word for the child, existing syntactic structures, presence of other related words, and the frequency of contact with the word. It is obvious that many words must exist in a child's mental dictionary, or lexicon, in very tenuous form. New entries are held in the lexicon and processed further with additional experience. Each encounter with the word offers opportunities to contrast it with other words and thus add semantic features contributing to the word's meaning.

Early vocabulary growth is remarkably rapid. From an average of three words at 1 year, children have acquired 272 words at 2 years, 896 words at 3 years, and 1,540 words at 4 years (Smith 1926). Estimates of the number of words known by the typical 6-year-old range from 2,562 to 14,000. The wide range of estimates depends on the language sampling method used, how words are defined, and how word knowledge is defined. The larger estimates include inflected and derived words. Thus, jump, jumped, and jumping can be counted as three words with inflections or one word without. If the larger estimate is accepted, the rate of acquisition of new words from 18 months to 6 years comes to about 9 words per day, or roughly one per waking hour. The magnitude of this intellectual feat is enhanced when one considers that word learning requires learning the word's place in the syntactic structure, its relationship to other words, and its semantic or meaningful properties. All of this is made more complex by the fact that many words have multiple meanings, for example, *bar* or *trace*, and so the child must learn the particular meaning the word has in various contexts. Furthermore, words of the same realm convey different shades of meaning, for example, *smile* is learned quite early, *grin* later, and the difference between *sneer* and *leer* is a subtle distinction that is acquired much later. Word meanings are also embedded in social role learning. Gibson (1975) has pointed out that young children define *promise* as *tell* or *say* and do not grasp its full

meaning until they understand the role obligation involved. Words belong to conceptual realms and are not equally difficult to acquire. Thus, the acquisition of *first* may require many exposures in a variety of contexts, but related words, *second*, *third* and *fourth* may be learned rapidly once the child has acquired the concept of relational numbers.

Much of the uncertainty about the typical size of vocabulary at various ages stems from the fact that word knowledge is often incomplete. Words are understood to a greater or lesser degree. As Dale (1965) has stated it, there are four levels of word knowledge: "(a) I have seen it before, (b) I've heard of it, but I don't know what it means, (c) I recognize it in context, (d) I know it."

Another factor to consider is that there are several different vocabularies: speaking, listening, writing, and reading. Typically one's vocabulary is greater for reading than for writing, and for listening than for speaking.

The rate of vocabulary development varies greatly from one child to another. The sources of individual differences tend to be the same as the sources of differences in intelligence scores, as vocabulary knowledge and measured intelligence are highly correlated. Vocabulary knowledge is often used to index intelligence, and vocabulary tests are included in such standard intelligence tests as the Stanford–Binet and the Wechsler series. Vocabulary is a highly stable characteristic and is resistant to decline with advanced old age or brain damage.

Individual differences in vocabulary are related to socioeconomic variables such as parental income, occupation, and education (Lassman et al. 1980). However, more important is how parents encourage the child's verbalization through conversation, word games, reading to the child, providing reading materials in the home, and indicating to the child that learning in general and word knowledge in particular are valued (Jordan 1978). The evidence for sex differences in vocabulary is contradictory and it is most likely that they do not exist in any systematic way.

Acquistion of new words in the preschool years takes place in the family or nursery school setting. First words are typically learned through the direct teaching of parents, for example, "This is daddy, see daddy, can you say, 'daddy'?" but most words from age 2 on are acquired informally, without benefit of teaching or use of dictionary. In the early elementary years, formal vocabulary instruction takes place in the context of learning to read. A major issue in beginning reading instruction is whether to adopt a basal approach in which reading vocabulary is selected from high frequency words likely to be in the child's lexicon or to adopt a code emphasis which focuses on spelling–sound correspondences. Early reading programs also vary in number of words taught, rate of introduction of new words, and the number of repetitions of words. Children have a vocabulary of about 3,000 words by the age of 7 and add about 1,000 words per year in school thereafter.

The average high-school senior knows about 14,000–15,000 words and the average college senior knows approximately 18,000–20,000 words (Dale 1965).

While there is much advice in the educational literature on ways to stimulate the vocabulary development of older school children (see Dale et al. 1971, Petty and Jensen 1980, Johnson 1986, McKeown and Curtis 1987), there is little sound evidence that any one approach is superior. Relatively little comparative evaluation research has been done and attempts to evaluate teaching programs have been plagued by difficulties in defining vocabulary knowledge, assessing knowledge in the different vocabularies, dealing with the degree of permanence of knowledge, and matching methods with developmental level of child. Petty et al. (1968) and Bowker (1980) have reviewed published research on vocabulary instruction. What seems to emerge is the following set of generalizations: (a) making dictionaries and encyclopedias available is essential, but the most popular form of instruction, having pupils look up words in a dictionary and write sentences including the words is not effective because it is uninteresting; (b) wide reading expands vocabularies, but is not sufficient in itself; (c) active methods where new words must be used are more effective than passive methods in which new words are only seen or heard; (d) the analysis of words into parts and learning the meaning of suffixes, prefixes, or the analysis of roots, such as Greek or Latin, have some usefulness, but less when this analysis is a matter of drill than when the techniques are made personally interesting to the pupils; (e) discovery methods seem to be most effective. Students are introduced to words in a variety of ways and required to carry out different activities with them; (f) the role of the teacher is important in enhancing motivation and in modeling word usage. All authorities agree that new words are most potent when they have particular significance for the individual or when they can be used in immediate experience to meet some need.

Bibliography

Anglin J M 1977 *Word, Object, and Conceptual Development.* Norton, New York
Bowker R 1980 Vocabulary instruction and the state of knowledge. *Resources in Education* 1980. Oryx, Phoenix, Arizona, pp. 192–258
Carey S 1978 The child as word learner. In: Halle M, Bresnan J, Miller G A (eds.) 1978 *Linguistic Theory and Psychological Reality.* MIT Press, Cambridge, Massachusetts
Clark E V 1973 What's in a word? On the child's acquisition of semantics in his first language. In: Moore T E (ed.) 1973 *Cognitive Development and the Acquisition of Language.* Academic Press, New York
Dale E 1965 Vocabulary measurement: Techniques and major findings. *Elem. Engl.* 42: 895–901
Dale E, O'Rourke J, Bamman H A 1971 *Techniques of Teaching Vocabulary.* Benjamin/Cummings, Menlo Park, California
Gibson E J, Levin H 1975 *The Psychology of Reading.* MIT Press, Cambridge, Massachusetts
Johnson D D (ed.) 1986 Introduction to a themed issue on vocabulary instruction. *J. Read.* 29: 582–668
Jordan T E 1978 Influences on vocabulary attainment: A five year prospective study. *Child Dev.* 49: 1096–106
Kuczaj S A, Barret M D (eds.) 1986 *The Development of Word Meaning: Progress in Cognitive Developmental Research.* Springer Verlag, New York
Lassman F M, Fisch R O, Vetter D K, La Benz E S 1980 *Early Correlates of Speech Language and Hearing: The Collaborative Perinatal Project of the National Institute of Neurological and Communicative Disorders and Stroke.* PSG Publishing, Littleton, Massachusetts
McKeown M G, Curtis M E (eds.) 1987 *The Nature of Vocabulary Acquisition.* Erlbaum, Hillsdale, New Jersey
Petty W T, Jensen J M 1980 *Developing Children's Language.* Allyn and Bacon, Boston, Massachusetts
Petty W T, Herold C P, Stoll E 1968 *The State of Knowledge About the Teaching of Vocabulary.* National Council of Teachers of English, Champaign, Illinois
Smith M E 1926 An investigation of the development of the sentence and the extent of vocabulary in young children. *Univ. Iowa Studies on Child Welfare* 3(5): 1–92

Initial Reading

Decoding

P. D. Rousch

Decoding implies the analysis of spoken or written symbols of language with the purpose of extracting meaning. However, Harris and Hodges (1981 p. 80) claim that decoding in actual reading practice has come to mean word recognition. The implication is that while modern use of the term assumes a meaning emphasis, practice in a pedagogical sense has restricted the term to a small unit of language.

1. Alternative Views

Decoding in reading practice has traditionally required the oral realization of printed features of the language. This view of decoding requires the matching of each of the letters of an alphabet with a range of sounds. The assumption underlying decoding in this sense is that written language is an evolution of the oral form and is, in effect, a means of mapping oral language onto print. The corollary of the theory is that in order to read, it is first necessary to produce a matching of letters with their 1334appropriate sounds. The logical development of the proposition is that "phonics instruction", or the method of teaching reading through the realization of matched symbols and sounds, or clusters of these, has dominated reading instruction over the years. The ultimate aim of this pedagogical practice is to achieve word recognition.

In more recent years there has been a questioning of the decoding assumptions. The alternative view is that decoding does occur in reading, but it is in reality a process that results in understanding, rather than letter/sound matching. In other words, readers decode to meaning, as occurs in the comprehension of morse code. The leading proponent of this view is Kenneth Goodman who suggests that all reading requires decoding to meaning, otherwise it is not reading. The capacity to match sounds and letters is therefore regarded as "recoding", or expressing the printed symbols in an oral form without paying attention to meaning. This view implies that not only is decoding from print to sound an impediment to reading, it is also an inappropriate use of the term "decoding", hence the term "recoding" used in its stead by its critics.

2. Applying the Two Theories—The Traditional

Historically, the pattern of traditional reading pedagogy has moved between phonics instruction to whole word instruction, the aim being to achieve decoding in the word recognition sense. Phonics assumes that the letters of the alphabet (graphemes) have a relationship with sound patterns (phonemes) that permit reasonably close mapping of one onto the other in a way that enables the learner to "sound out" new or unfamiliar words. In this practice it is necessary to teach clusters of sounds, represented by groups of realizable letters such as *ou*, *bl*, *ck*, *ch*, as well as individual sound/symbol relationships.

Whole word instruction entails the teaching of new words as a whole, as a result of which it is expected that children will deduce the sound/symbol relationships within or, if not, they will be taught them subsequent to word recognition. Very often the whole word approach is taught by the use of "flash cards" each of which contains a word. The cards are then "flashed" in turn before the child whose task it is to recognize the words. In some quarters the practice is termed "the look and say approach".

Both phonics and whole word methods are predicated on written language being a direct representation of oral language, which is primary. They also assume precise word knowledge as a prerequisite for reading success in a comprehension sense.

A major objection offered by critics of this traditional view of decoding is that the material written for young children is consequently artificial and uninteresting, particularly if phonics underlies the scheme. The need to write material with easily-sounded words, it is claimed, often results in such sequences as:

A fat man is in a can.

Similarly, whole word approaches are often criticized for their reliance on the memory of the child who, it is claimed, will guess wildly because of lack of insights into sound/symbol relationships.

3. Applying the Two Theories—The Nontraditional

Nontraditional theories of reading assume that decoding implies "decoding direct to meaning". Such theories discount the need to teach sound/symbol relationships or whole words in a formal sense. Proponents of the view claim that such traditional practices are not only unnecessary but they are also inefficient and stand in the way of the child becoming literate. The argument is based on the proposition that oral and written language are alternative elements and one is not derived from the other. The theory is, therefore, predicted on the belief that print is not a written representation of speech.

The application of the nontraditional theory assumes that children can be taught to read by focusing on the prime purpose, namely the meaning of the extract, and by using their intuitive knowledge of how language works, decode to meaning. The meaning focus is achieved by using natural language in experimental situations familiar to the child. The role of sound/symbol relationships, rather than being ignored, is seen as a further strategy available to the reader when predicted meaning is not realized and the reader is forced to refocus in a sharper manner upon the precise visual features.

Perhaps the distinguishing characteristic of the nontraditional theory is its focus on the whole rather than on the parts. In brief, this means emphasizing the total message and not the individual words.

The modern proponents of the theory are the psycholinguists, who argue that reading is not an exact, errorless activity, but rather one in which the reader interacts with print, with meaning uppermost in the mind. It is inevitable, according to theory, that deviations from the text will occur because the proficient reader uses the print only to the extent that meaning needs to be predicted. Naturally, because of this minimal use of graphic information, errors will occur from time to time. This should not be seen to be a problem but rather an indication that true decoding is occurring. Where it does become a problem, however, is when the predicted meaning is not met and the reader fails to regress to focus more carefully on the particular aspect of the print that caused the original confusion. This cycle of predicting, confirming, and regressing is seen as the inevitable behaviour of the proficient reader. Since this is regarded as desirable behaviour the implication is that beginning readers should be taught reading in a similar cyclical sense, and the practice of starting with sounds and letters should be discarded. The application of the nontraditional theory is stated to be "a psycholinguistic method". The psycholinguists claim, however, that this is a misnomer, and what they are really trying to inculcate in teachers and researchers is an understanding of the principles underlying the reading process, rather than mandate a particular pedagogical approach.

4. Summary

Decoding is, in practice, viewed from two conflicting perspectives. The traditional practice requires beginning readers to focus on the elements of language at the word level, while undertaking a range of tasks designed to build competence in subskills.

The alternative view is that decoding implies meaning gathering through a focus on the totality of language. Print is seen as an alternative mode to oral language and independent of it. Therefore it is unnecessary and illogical to process print by first passing through an oral rendition of it.

Bibliography

Bereiter C, Engelmann S 1966 *Teaching Disadvantaged Children in the Preschool*. Prentice Hall, Englewood Cliffs, New Jersey
Gollasch F V (ed.) 1982 *Language and Literacy: The Selected Writings of Kenneth S. Goodman*. Vol. 1: *Process, Theory, Research*. Routledge and Kegan Paul, London
Harris T L, Hodges R E 1981 *A Dictionary of Reading and Related Terms*. International Reading Association, Newark, Delaware
Smith F 1971 *Understanding Reading: A Psycholinguistic Analysis of Reading and Learning to Read*. Holt, Rinehart and Winston, New York

Phonics

J. E. Merritt

Phonic methods of teaching reading are those which emphasize the learning of letters and letter combinations (known as "graphemes") and the sounds they can represent (known as "segmental phonemes") as a means of word recognition. The main opposition to a phonic emphasis in the teaching of reading comes from those who believe that reading for meaning should be the first priority, with the learner's own language experience playing a major part in word recognition.

There are two main approaches to phonics teaching—synthetic phonics and analytic phonics.

In synthetic phonics, the learner starts with the elements from which words are constructed, that is, letters and sounds, and is then taught to "build" words by blending together the sounds represented by successive letters or letter combinations, for example, c–a = ca; ca–t = cat. Longer words which can be handled in a similar way are introduced gradually. Words whose spellings are irregular, for example, *one*, *any*, *do*, or *the* which are needed for making up phrases and sentences, are taught as whole words to be recognized on sight. They are then used in sentences such as "The man is in the tan van." The learner gets a great deal of practice with a restricted set of phoneme–grapheme correspondences of this kind in the early stages and more complex spelling patterns are introduced very gradually.

In analytic phonics, the learner starts by looking at whole words and then learns about the parts. This is done by studying words which have elements in common and noting similarities and differences in spelling and pronunciation. The attention of the learner may be expressly directed to phoneme–grapheme correspondences or the learner may be encouraged to discover them as a result of working through carefully structured teaching materials. Lists of words are often used to demonstrate particular spelling patterns, for example, *weed–seed–reed*, or *knife–knit–kneel*.

In both approaches it is usual at various stages to introduce explicit phonic generalizations, that is, general rules for pronunciation such as, "When a word begins with *kn* the *k* is silent." This practice is somewhat problematic in the case of English where the relationship between sounds and spellings is very complex. The problem is exacerbated by the fact that there are some 45 segmental phonemes but only 26 letters in the alphabet. Although it is possible to identify many "word families" in which spellings do follow a general pattern, i.e., groups of words such as *cake–rake–lake*, or *night–light–sight*, rules for pronunciation based solely on letters and sounds provide an unreliable guide. In the case of the letter "o" for example, the "final e" rule which applies to words such as *bone*, *code*, *dole*, *home*, and *note* is breached by such everyday words as *gone*, *done*, *dove*, and *prove*. Thus phonic methods present more problems in English than they do in languages such as Spanish or Finnish where spelling patterns are fairly straightforward.

Attempts to compensate for spelling complexity have included the use of diacritics—special markings of the kind used in dictionaries as guides to pronunciation. Coloured letters or backgrounds have also been used for this purpose. Neither approach has met with significant success. There have also been many attempts to introduce simplified spellings but they have all foundered. The use of simplified spelling in an alphabet used for initial teaching only met with rather more success but it is not widely used. (Its use has not been entirely restricted however to phonic methods of teaching.)

There is a further complication in English in that spellings have in many cases tended to follow word meanings rather than sounds. This can be seen in the spelling of words such as *hear–hearing–heard* or *bath–bathing–bathed*. Consequently, the logic of analytic phonics has had to be supplemented by structural analysis—an approach to word identification in which words are broken down into pronunciation units that relate to morphemes rather than graphemes. This involves the identification of roots, affixes, compounds, hyphenated forms, and inflected and derived endings.

There are certain other skills that are also involved in word recognition, as can be seen from the following examples:

(a) He stood it on the grombed
(b) He grombed it

In (a), "grombed" is clearly a noun and will usually be pronounced as a two-syllable word by analogy, perhaps, with "tripod". In (b), the self-same word is clearly a past participle and will usually be pronounced as a word of one syllable, by analogy, perhaps, with "combed" or "entombed". Thus the reader often needs to draw on more general language skills in pronouncing unfamiliar words. These additional skills are used even more widely in recognizing a large number of familiar words which have different meanings and sometimes different pronunciations, but which share the same spelling, for example, "the wind blows" vs. "wind it up"; "made of lead" vs. "lead on". For this reason phonic methods as such cannot, strictly speaking, be regarded as wholly independent or alternative methods of teaching reading, but must be seen as ancillary to other approaches.

One of the major arguments used against an emphasis on phonic methods is that they may interfere with normal fluent reading by giving the response to letters and sounds a role that is too dominant. Given, for example, a sentence such as, "Mary went on her holidays in an . . ." it is suggested that the reader identifies the next word as "aeroplane" by making an intelligent prediction and then checks the letters for consistency with the prediction. This normally requires only a minimal check on some of the critical features, for example, the initial and final letters and word length. Working out each word from scratch from the set of possible pronunciations for each letter, or group of letters, would, it is argued, be a much longer process and the result would still need to be checked against context as in the examples cited earlier.

No matter what method of teaching reading is adopted, users of any alphabetic writing system do need to have certain phonic skills. The point at issue in any debate about phonics is not whether they are necessary, or even how effective they may be initially, but about the effect of any particular approach on the subsequent development of fluent reading.

Bibliography

Balmuth M 1982 *The Roots of Phonics: An Historical Introduction*. McGraw-Hill, New York

Chall J S 1967 *Learning to Read: The Great Debate: An Inquiry into the Science, Art, and Ideology of Old and New Methods of Teaching Children to Read*. McGraw-Hill, New York

Cordts A T 1965 *Phonics for the Reading Teacher*. Holt, Rinehart and Winston, New York

Tzeng O J L, Singer H (eds.) 1981 *Perception of Print: Reading Research in Experimental Psychology*. Erlbaum, Hillsdale, New Jersey

Initial Reading

J. S. Chall and S. A. Stahl

How best to teach children to read has frequently been a subject of keen debate (Chall 1967, 1983a). In the United States and the United Kingdom, the research on, and practice of, beginning reading tended to stress either an emphasis on "decoding" (also referred to as phonic methods) or "meaning" (also referred to as global methods). In the United States, the preferred beginning approach from about 1930 to the late 1960s was a "meaning emphasis." In the late 1960s, a greater emphasis in research and practice was placed on decoding (Chall 1983a, Resnick and Weaver 1979).

Mathews (1966) and Balmuth (1981) trace this controversy back to the the time of the ancient Greeks. Downing (1972, 1979) notes similar debates in Europe, Asia, and Latin America. Even in Hong Kong, where the Chinese language would seem to lend itself to a global, meaning emphasis, there have been suggestions that greater attention be paid to the phonetic and orthographic patterns of the Chinese ideograph in beginning reading (Leong 1973). Steinberg and Yamada (1978–79) and Tzeng and Singer (1978-79) note a similar debate in Japanese.

Research in Beginning Reading (Chall 1967) reviewed a half-century's research on beginning reading methodology from the United States, the United Kingdom, and Australia and found, from an analysis of the research from the classroom, laboratory, and clinic, that code-emphasis approaches produced better achievement than meaning-emphasis approaches through the third grade (age 8–9), the highest grade studied. This was so not only for word recognition and decoding, where an advantage might be expected, but also for silent reading comprehension. The research also indicated that earlier and more systematic instruction in phonics produced better reading achievement than later and less systematic instruction. This review inevitably drew its share of critics but, by 1975, Popp found that widely used beginning reading programs published in the United States during the early 1970s had earlier and more systematic phonics programs than those published in the 1950s and 1960s analyzed by Chall (1967).

The United States Office of Education's (USOE) Cooperative First Grade Studies (Bond and Dykstra 1966–67, Dykstra 1968) presented further evidence on beginning reading approaches. Overall, these 27 studies which compared various methods also found that stronger phonics programs tended to produce better achievement than meaning emphasis approaches. However, some argued that these studies indicated no difference in methods, because of the large intersite variations in achievement found for each of the methods. Other large-scale evaluations of different approaches to teaching in the early grades, such as Project Follow Through (Abt Associates 1977, Stallings

1975) have also reported large intersite variations. These variations were also interpreted by some to mean that the effects of the individual programs, especially the teacher, outweighed the effects due to method.

With regard to the USOE studies, many rejected the higher achievement found for the stronger and more systematic phonics programs and focused instead on the influence of the teacher. It should be noted that teacher factors were not in the design of the study. The USOE study which focused directly on the teacher (Chall and Feldmann 1966) found, in addition to the positive influence of general excellence in teaching, other factors more relevant to method, such as an appropriate level of difficulty, a thinking approach to learning, and a code emphasis, resulted in higher reading achievement.

Other recent reviews of research on the decoding/ meaning issue (Calfee and Drum 1978, Resnick and Weaver 1979, Pflaum et al 1980, Williams 1979) also report an advantage for code-emphasis beginning reading instruction.

The above research reviews did not generally address the question of type of code emphasis. With additional research during the late 1960s and 1970s, it was possible to make some comparisons between "direct-synthetic" approaches (which generally teach letter sound correspondences directly and blend these into words) and "indirect-analytic" approaches (which teach whole words first and then analyze them into constituent sounds). In indirect-analytic approaches, blending is usually not practiced.

In a second edition of *Learning to Read: The Great Debate*, (Chall 1983a) an analysis of such studies revealed that direct-synthetic approaches tended to produce better achievement than indirect-analytic approaches in the first three grades. The research reviewed included that from classrooms and laboratories. Most of the laboratory studies used a paradigm in which students were instructed in decoding and word recognition and tested for transfer to reading (decoding) novel words.

Several trends were found in the above studies. First, students given letter-sound training outperformed those given only whole word training. Further, students given blending training in combination with letter-sound or letter-name training outperformed those without training in blending. The Richardson and DiBenedetto (1977) review of many of these studies and the meta-analysis of Pflaum et al. (1980) also confirmed the importance of sound blending training. Indeed, they found it to be the only significant effect in their analysis.

The advantages of a direct-synthetic approach have also been reported by the multiple regression study of Kean et al. (1979). A wide variety of teacher, student, and method characteristics were used to predict reading achievement at the fourth grade (age 9–10). Of the methods studied, only the direct-synthetic approach had a significant, positive effect on reading achievement.

The Initial Teaching Alphabet (i.t.a.), a modified alphabet consisting of 44 characters each corresponding to one of the 44 major English phonemes, received considerable interest as a beginning reading method during the 1960s. It was intended to minimize the difficulties due to the irregularity in English sound–symbol correspondences for beginning readers. After the beginner was fluent in i.t.a., the traditional orthography was to be used. Research on i.t.a. found it to be more effective than traditional orthography *before* the transfer (Bond and Dykstra 1966–67, Calfee and Drum 1978, Warburton and Southgate 1969). Although some authors still advocate its use, by 1975 fewer than 10 percent of the schools in the United Kingdom were reported using it (Downing 1979) and perhaps fewer in the United States. In addition, some linguists have criticized modified alphabets since English orthography, although somewhat irregular in its sound–symbol correspondences, corresponds well to an underlying abstract level of phonemic knowledge. Use of a modified alphabet would obscure the underlying relationships implicit in regular orthography.

The Words in Color method uses regular orthography but codes letters by color to help identify sounds. Identical colors are used for identical sounds. For example, in "science" both the "sc" and "ce" would be coded the same color as the "s" in "us." Once the sounds have been learned the color coding is dropped.

Other approaches to beginning reading have been suggested as a result of the observations of many researchers that children who lack the skill to segment a spoken word into its constituent phonemes are less likely to succeed in beginning reading. Some authors have suggested teaching phonemic segmentation as a prerequisite to reading, using procedures similar to those described by Elkonin (1973) in the Soviet Union. Others have suggested, since segmentation of spoken words into syllables is easier than segmentation into phonemes, that the syllable be the initial unit of reading. These programs remain experimental.

In spite of the research evidence cited above, there remain serious critics of code-emphasis instruction in beginning reading. Goodman and Goodman (1977), Goodman (1967), and Smith (1971, 1973, 1978) have argued that phonics is, at best, unnecessary for learning to read, and at worst, a distraction from purposeful reading. Goodman (1967) has suggested that, based on his analysis of oral reading errors, or "miscues," the overwhelming majority of miscues are semantically and syntactically consistent with the preceding content. Phonics, by concentrating the child's attention on the graphemic–phonetic level of language, he notes, distracts the child from the more important task of reconstructing the meaning of the passage. Smith, based on his studies of word recognition in adults has argued that

proficient readers go directly from the visual print to the deep structure of language, and that print is not normally "decoded" into aural language. To teach young children to do so, he claims, is both unnatural and inefficient, due to the overwhelming number of phonic rules that must be learned.

Other authors have interpreted the oral reading miscue and word recognition literature differently. For example, beginning reading errors have been shown to be consistent with the type of reading instruction the child received—either phonics or whole word. Some authors argue that adults *do* recode words phonemically as a way of accessing their meaning, while others suggest that mature readers use patterns of orthographic regularity to speed recognition of words. These positions would appear to argue for the need for explicit phonics instruction for beginners.

Other authors have suggested that one detriment to efficient reading comprehension is lack of automaticity in word decoding. These authors suggest that only through practice in decoding, can such automaticity, and consequent good comprehension, be achieved. As noted in the classroom studies reviewed earlier, methods which produced better word recognition generally also produced better reading comprehension in the early grades (Chall 1967, 1983a).

As in most longstanding debates, it is helpful to consider why it has persisted so long. As Downing (1979) points out, language can be viewed in terms of both language features and language function, and both of these aspects must be stressed in order to foster growth in reading. Cast in this dichotomy, critics such as the Goodmans and Smith argue that phonics instruction focuses the child's attention too closely to the features of written language, or the alphabetic principle. Instead, they argue that beginning reading instruction should concentrate on the functions of language, or its situational and universal meanings, as children do when learning speech (Goodman and Goodman 1977). But to concentrate on only the functional aspects of language would be to ignore the accumulating evidence that early and systematic phonics instruction produces better readers, not only in word recognition, but also in comprehension. It would seem, therefore, that effective written language instruction should incorporate both featural and functional aspects of written language. Both Beck (1977) and Downing (1979) have put forth proposals of how this can be done effectively.

Another way of viewing the debate is to view reading as a developmental process with characteristic stages. In this view, decoding instruction is seen as a first stage in reading acquisition, followed by a stage in which the child's decoding skills are practiced on reading material whose content is already known, in order to develop fluency in decoding text. Once the child has reached an adequate level of fluency, the child is then able to learn new information through reading. Such a proposal would suggest a decoding emphasis. This decoding training is not to be considered as an end in itself, but as part of a process leading to fluent and flexible reading of complex connected texts (Chall 1983b).

Bibliography

Abt Associates 1977 *Education as Experimentation: A Planned Variation Model.* Vol. 4, Effects of follow through models. Abt Associates, Cambridge, Massachusetts

Balmuth M 1981 *The Roots of Phonics: A Historical Introduction.* McGraw-Hill, New York

Beck I L 1977 Comprehension during the acquisition of decoding skills, In: Guthrie J T (ed.) 1977 *Cognition, Curriculum, and Comprehension.* International Reading Association, Newark, Delaware

Bond G, Dykstra R 1966–67 The cooperative research program in first grade reading instruction. *Read. Res. Q.* 2: 5–142

Calfee R C, Drum P A 1978 Learning to read: Theory research and practice. *Curric. Inq.* 8: 183–249

Chall J S 1967 *Learning to Read: The Great Debate.* McGraw-Hill, New York

Chall J S 1983a *Learning to Read: The Great Debate*, 2nd edn. McGraw-Hill, New York

Chall J S 1983b *Stages of Reading Development.* McGraw-Hill, New York

Chall J S, Feldmann S 1966 First grade reading: An analysis of the interactions of professed methods, teacher implementation, and child background. *Read. Teach.* 19: 569–75

Downing J A (ed.) 1972 *Comparative Reading: Cross-Natural Studies of Behavior and Processes in Reading and Writing.* MacMillan, New York

Downing J A 1979 *Reading and Reasoning.* Springer-Verlag, New York

Dykstra R 1968 The effectiveness of code- and meaning-emphasis beginning reading programs. *Read. Teach.* 22: 17–23

Elkonin D B 1973 In: Downing J A (ed.) 1973

Goodman K S 1967 Reading: A psycholinguistic guessing game. *J. Read. Specialist.* 6: 126–35

Goodman K S, Goodman Y M 1977 Learning about psycholinguistic processes by analyzing oral reading. *Harvard Educ. Rev.* 47: 371–33

Kean M H, Summers A A, Raivetz M J, Farber I J 1979 *What Works in Reading? Summary and Results of a Joint School District/Federal Reserve Bank Empirical Study in Philadelphia.* Philadelphia School District, Pennsylvania, Office of Research and Evaluation. ERIC Document Reproduction Service No. ED 176 216

Leong C 1973 Hong Kong. In: Downing J A (ed.) 1973

Mathews M M 1966 *Teaching to Read, Historically Considered.* University of Chicago Press, Chicago, Illinois

Pflaum S W, Walberg H J, Karegianes M L, Rasher S P 1980 Reading instruction: A quantitative analysis. *Educ. Res.* AERA 9: 12–18

Popp H M 1975 Current practices in the teaching of beginning reading. In: Carroll J B, Chall J S (eds.) 1975 *Toward a Literate Society: A Report from the National Academy of Education.* McGraw-Hill, New York

Resnick L B, Weaver P A (eds.) 1979 *Theory and Practice of Early Reading.* Erlbaum, Hillsdale, New Jersey

Richardson E, DiBenedetto B 1977 Transfer effects of a phonic decoding model: A review. *Read. Improvement* 14: 239–47

Smith F 1971 *Understanding Reading: A Psycholinguistic Analysis of Reading and Learning to Read.* Holt, Rinehart and Winston, New York

Smith F 1973 Decoding: The great fallacy. In: Smith F (ed.) 1973 *Psycholinguistics and Reading.* Holt, Rinehart and Winston, New York

Smith F 1978 *Reading without Nonsense.* Teachers College Press, New York

Stallings J 1975 *Implementation and Child Effects of Teaching Practices in Follow Through Classrooms.* Monographs of the Society for Research in Child Development, Serial No. 163, Vol. 40, Nos. 7–8. University of Chicago Press, Chicago, Illinois

Steinberg D D, Yamada J 1978–79 Are whole word kanji easier to read than syllable kana? *Read. Res. Q.* 14: 88–99

Tzeng O T, Singer H 1978–79 Failure of Steinberg and Yamada to demonstrate superiority of kanji over kana for initial reading instructions in Japan. *Read. Res. Q.* 14: 661–667

Warburton F W, Southgate V 1969 *Initial Teaching Alphabet: An Independent Evaluation.* Murray, London

Williams J 1979 Reading instruction today. *Am. Psychol.* 34: 917–22

Reading Readiness

D. Feitelson

"Reading readiness" is a descriptive term which gained wide popularity in the field of reading research in North America. In the period of greatest popularity of beginning reading instruction by "look and say" approaches, reading readiness referred mainly to assessment procedures which attempted to predict whether candidates for school entry were likely to be successful students by the end of first grade. More recently, the term reading readiness has come to be associated with instructional materials and techniques designed to help preschoolers develop skills considered useful in learning to read. School entry age and approaches to beginning reading instruction vary widely across countries. One conse-

quence of this is that conceptions in regard to prerequisites for reading are far from uniform.

Interest in readiness for reading developed in the 1930s and 1940s. An apt definition of reading readiness, which particularly suits the thinking of those times is "a state of general maturity which, when reached, allows a child to learn to read without excess difficulty" (Harris and Sipay 1975). Accordingly, reading readiness was conceived as a developmental stage, before which there was little point in starting formal instruction.

At a time when educational practices were greatly influenced by innovators and researchers like Dewey and Huey, both of whom believed that reading should be learned informally at around age 8 or later (Dewey 1898, Huey 1908), the best policy in regard to lack of readiness, seemed to be to postpone school entry, or at least onset of formal reading instruction. Initially, reading readiness tests were thus mainly a selection device, aimed at helping educators cope with the issue of individual differences among children who were entering school solely according to the criterion of chronological age.

Great efforts were invested in identifying factors which would prove good predictors of success in learning to read. Among the factors which were frequently mentioned and often included in reading readiness assessment batteries were (a) mental age; (b) different aspects of language proficiency; (c) visual discrimination ability; (d) health indices; (e) acuity of hearing and vision; (f) laterality; and (g) emotional and social maturity (Tinker and McCullough 1962).

The issue of prerequisite mental age occupied researchers most especially. In the wake of several studies, the consensus was that a mental age of between 6 and 6½ years would ensure better results than attempts to initiate reading instruction before the required stage of mental development was reached. However, it was also recognized that precocious children who attained a necessary level of development at younger chronological ages, were apt to do better than their more slowly developing peers (Tinker and McCullough 1962).

Viewing reading readiness as a definite stage of development which can be assessed, assumes that curricula and teaching approaches are fixed entities (MacGinitie 1969). While reading specialists of the day may perhaps not have been consciously aware of the fact, the unanimous endorsement of classic "look and say" over a relatively long period of time did, in fact, entail such a conception.

Developments in the 1960s and 1970s have led to considerable modifications in basic approaches to the issue of reading readiness. Studies of early readers and experiments in which young children were successfully taught to read rendered the belief in a fixed developmental threshold obsolete. Also, American society became much more aware of the role of social differences in school achievements. Moreover, contrary to earlier times, this awareness was now interpreted as a challenge rather than a determinant. Consequently, the term reading readiness came to be used in an affirmative sense, in relation to exercises and/or instructional materials designed to prepare preschoolers for the kind of tasks they would have to face when learning to read. A great increase in high-level theory-based reading research, which coincided with these developments, had led among other things to the identification of numerous skills which were believed to be prerequisites for learning to read. In addition to factors which had already been recognized earlier such as language proficiency, visual discrimination, and directionality, further factors which were now thought important were auditory discrimination, the ability to segment speech into words and words into their components, conceptual enrichment in regard to reading-related terminology, and facility in recognizing and naming letters (Gibson and Levin 1975).

The great involvement with reading readiness in North America, whether in the form of assessment in earlier times, or as pretraining preceding actual instruction later on, has not been mirrored to the same extent in other countries. Ages at which children in different countries start to learn to read vary considerably. Among the 13 countries included in Downing's (1973) comparative survey of reading, reading instruction begins at age 5 in two, around age 6 in seven, and at 7 or even later in the remaining four. There is also evidence, that in general practitioners tend to feel comfortable with local practices as they developed in their respective countries. Thus in the United Kingdom, where reading instruction begins at age 5, there is considerable advocacy for an early start (Bullock 1975), whereas in Denmark, where children do not enter school until age 7, a relaxed, late introduction is lauded (Jansen 1973). However, there is consensus in other areas. Both British as well as Danish experts caution against basing decisions in regard to onset of instruction on test results. Also, in both cases it is clearly brought forth that reading instruction should best proceed by engaging in reading activities per se, and that artificially segmented pretraining by formal pencil-and-paper tasks should be avoided. In many other countries included in Downing's (1973) survey, beginning reading instruction is also approached fairly directly, with no intermediary preparatory stage or systemwide diagnostic pretesting.

Once American prereading programs are reexamined in the light of this overwhelming consensus, the striking fact emerges that the rationale for including specific skills seems often to be based mainly on correlational evidence. Good performance on auditory or visual discrimination tasks, letter knowledge, language measures, and the like in kindergarten or at school entry were predictive of satisfactory reading achievement by the end of first grade. However, when rigorous research criteria were applied, the effectiveness of pretraining on many of these skills was not unambiguously established. For instance, visual discrimination exercises are included in many reading readiness programs. But a growing number of studies indicate that there is at present no clear evidence that this kind of training facilitates learning to read. The case of letter names is another good example. Not only did experimental studies not replicate the positive relation of knowledge of letter names with reading achievement documented in correlational studies (Gibson and Levin 1975), but, there is even evidence from the Soviet Union that teaching letter names interfered with learning to read (Downing 1973). The fact that in other countries educators refrain from preteaching letter names indicates also that their day-to-day experiences confirmed this conclusion. This example may have far-reaching implications, in that it seems to demonstrate that in some cases indiscriminate engagement in reading readiness training may be not only superfluous but even counterproductive.

It is somewhat surprising that for such an extended period of time, attention in the area of reading readiness has been devoted mainly to skills connected with the decoding aspects of learning to read (see *Decoding*). In recent years the consensus of specialists in many countries is that the main difficulty in attaining literacy is related to problems of reading comprehension rather than to decoding per se (Spiro et al. 1980). If this is confirmed, it would seem that efforts aimed at improving young children's potential reading comprehension skills might be a particularly good way to prepare them for the tasks they will have to cope with in school.

Research on reading comprehension processes is presently proceeding at many centers of learning. Within educational research, massive exposure of children to books and to a variety of reading activities including being read to are strategies which are becoming increasingly popular. Essentially such approaches replicate experiences middle-class children typically seem to have in their own homes. Links between early experiences of this sort and later high-level reading proficiency have been documented relatively frequently (e.g., Chomsky 1972). However, until recently, attempts to establish causal relationships were lacking. A recent series of experimental studies have shown that intensive reading to Israeli low socioeconomic status preschoolers resulted in improved performance on reading comprehension measures (Feitelson 1988, Feitelson et al. 1986). The theoretical assumptions on which these experiments were based are that reading to children exposes them to typical "book language" which is very different from everyday face-to-face speech. Also in terms of content and vocabulary, books are more likely to enrich a child's experiences beyond the immediate here and now, thus providing stored knowledge which will in turn be helpful in grasping story scenarios.

There seems reason to believe that future trends in reading readiness will lead away from pretraining in specific subskills which in the past were believed to further decoding processes. Instead, interest appears to be turning to more general ways of developing comprehension and language skills.

Bibliography

Bullock A 1975 *A Language for Life: Report of Committee of Inquiry. Appointed by the Secretary of State for Education and Science under the Chairmanship of Sir Alan Bullock. (Committee of Inquiry into Reading and the Use of English).* Her Majesty's Stationery Office, London

Chomsky C 1972 Stages in language development and reading exposure. *Harvard Educ. Rev.* 42: 1–33

Dewey J 1898 The primary education fetich. *Forum* 25: 315–28

Downing J A 1973 *Comparative Reading: Cross-national Studies of Behavior and Processes in Reading and Writing.* MacMillan, New York

Feitelson D 1988 *Facts and Fads in Beginning Reading: A Cross-language Perspective.* Ablex, Norwood, New Jersey

Feitelson D, Kita B, Goldstein Z 1986 Effects of listening to series-stories on first graders' comprehension and use of language. *Res. Teach. Eng.* 20: 339–56

Gibson E J, Levin H 1975 *The Psychology of Reading.* Massachusetts Institute of Technology, Cambridge, Massachusetts

Harris A J, Sipay E R 1975 *How to Increase Reading Ability: A Guide to Departmental and Remedial Methods*, 6th edn. McKay, New York

Huey E B 1908 *The Psychology and Pedagogy of Reading.* MacMillan, New York (reissued 1968 MIT Press, Cambridge, Massachusetts)

Jansen M 1973 Denmark. In: Downing J (ed.) *Comparative Reading.* Macmillan, New York

MacGinitie W H 1969 Evaluating readiness for learning to read: A critical review and evaluation of research. *Read. Res. Q.* 4: 396–410

Spiro R J, Bruce B C, Brewer W F 1980 *Theoretical Issues in Reading Comprehension: Perspectives from Cognitive Psychology, Linguistics, Artificial Intelligence and Education.* Erlbaum, Hillsdale, New Jersey

Tinker M A, McCullough C M 1962 *Teaching Elementary Reading*, 2nd edn. Appleton–Century–Crofts, New York

Basic Vocabulary Instruction

A. Fleet

Instruction in basic vocabulary has traditionally been a major component of any teacher's reading programme in the early grades of school. The task has been seen in terms of increasing the number of words children can recognize in print at first glance, rather than in terms of broadening an individual's experiential vocabulary in the oral or written forms.

The notion of "basic vocabulary" is aligned with a "building blocks" approach to reading instruction and reflects a primary focus on initiation by the teacher rather than self-direction by the learner. The teacher's approach to the task depends largely on his/her view of the reading process. Teachers may tend to favour either a "bottom-up" approach in which small units of print are taught before large, or a "top-down" approach in which chunks of the message are dealt with before concentrating on the print in detail (Cambourne 1979).

The underlying rationale for instruction in basic vocabulary is to give the beginning reader tools with which to work, to make the task easier by enabling the child to recognize the words most commonly encountered in classroom print and to thereby boost self-confidence and encourage continued effort in learning to read.

In deciding how to teach basic vocabulary, a teacher must first identify the words for instruction. Two approaches are common at this stage: one is to focus on the language contained in the basal reading series in use in the classroom; the other is to focus on a group known as "basic sight words". The concentration on the controlled vocabulary of a reading scheme, arranged in terms of linguistic patterns and phonic regularities within words, is gradually losing support in much of the educational community with increased understanding of how children learn, about the nature of the reading process, and about the limiting nature of some forms of reading instruction.

To accommodate these understandings, and in support of a different philosophical position, several publishers have used an alternative approach by compiling reading schemes which use the topics and phrases common to children's natural language. Examples of this approach can be found in the *Breakthrough to Literacy* scheme, the *Developmental Language Reading Program*, and the *Young Australia Readers* (2nd edn.).

If the teacher chooses to focus on "basic sight words", there will be three main sources for these words which are meant to be identified immediately, with no form of word attack, no "sounding out" or "breaking down" or other form of analysis prior to recognition. These sources are: (a) sight word lists compiled by researchers, (b) individual children's personal interest words, and (c) classmembers' common interest words.

(a) *Basic sight word lists*. Researchers have analysed children's reading materials to identify those words which an early reader will most often encounter. The Dolch (1936) list of 220 words is the most well-known of these lists and is divided into levels of difficulty with a supplementary list of 95 common nouns. This list is somewhat dated and includes some words which are culturally or geographically specific (e.g. squirrel). A more recent list (of 300 words) which claims to rectify some of the errors of selection in earlier lists is that by Fry (1980). These lists generally focus on function words rather than contentives.

(b) *Children's personal interest words*. For the majority of children, their first sight word will be their own name, as in their egocentric stage of development, the word stands for the central character in their lives. They will also be exposed to the word regularly as enthusiastic parents and teachers write it on all the child's belongings and early art works. From that early beginning, children will be most likely to acquire words which have particular relevance to their own lives. A total literacy programme was built on this likelihood by Sylvia Ashton-Warner (1972) working with Maori children on an "organic" approach to basic vocabulary.

(c) *Classmembers' common interest words*. These words are the "basic vocabulary" for any theme or particular unit of study, or are part of the classroom

environmental print. With these words, the teacher's focus would usefully be the expanding of children's experience and oral vocabulary through problem-solving and discussion so that children are expanding their conceptual frameworks, having a need to communicate in a common vocabulary, and gaining a broader foundation for the recognition of printed words.

Assuming that a teacher wishes to teach a basic vocabulary, or to at least encourage the development of a bank of sight words, there is a variety of options available depending on the teacher's philosophical orientation, ranging from a highly directed approach reflecting the work of the behaviourists to a more interactive approach reflecting the cognitivist approach to education, and in particular the thinking of the psycholinguists (see *Literacy, Initial*).

Cognitivist learning theory would note the inadvisability of drilling words out of context with children who see no purpose in the task and have no opportunity to apply any learning which might occur. They would state that if the printed word being drilled does not link to an experiential concept in the child's head the task is irrelevant to constructive use of print. The behaviourists on the other hand would argue that once the words are learned, the child has been given greater power to read in the future.

Strategies which reflect a cognitivist orientation include a range of language in use and game activities which will immerse the children in the vocabulary which the teacher feels will benefit them. Young children have learned their first oral vocabulary from interaction with proficient language users who continually model the applied use of the language, immersing the child in "a language bath", and expecting the child gradually to comprehend, respond, and eventually produce approximations of the oral language—finally moving towards proficiency of use.

In much the same manner, children may be immersed in written language which they will learn through purposeful interaction. Class teachers and families may involve the children in print-related activities in many situations which enable children repeatedly to see common or interesting words in circumstances they can relate to and understand. The focus should be on total messages in natural contexts rather than on single words in isolation. (Although there is no doubt that children can memorize single words in isolation, there is considerable doubt about the usefulness of the exercise.) For example, a range of activities might include:

(a) Chanting—children can dictate class chants such as:

> We like yummy things
> Yummy in the tummy things:
>> Josie likes _____
>> Tony likes _____
>> Sean likes _____
>> Maria likes _____
> We like yummy things,
> Yummy in the tummy things!

The teacher writes up the poem (or sentence frames, or nursery rhyme) which the children chant. They will largely have memorized the rhythm and inherent sense of the chant, but at some point the association of print and oral language mesh and words are identified; a basic vocabulary is learned.

(b) Labelling objects—
This is the door.
Here is the nature table.

The teacher may have such sentences prewritten and then involve the children in actual labelling and discussion of the purpose of labelling. This approach reflects belief in principles of learning through exposure and imitation. Follow-up activities may include matching the sentences (put duplicate sentence strips in a pile on the floor) or matching individual words (put words in a "grab bag"). The word cards can also be used in card games such as "Go fish" (asking partner for matching word, taking one from centre pile if partner does not have it in hand) or "Concentration" (cards all face down, two of each word, children turn up any two at a time, keeping them if they match, replacing them if they do not).

(c) Writing—Children can write every day in the manner advocated by the research of Donald Graves (1981). Communication rather than spelling is the initial goal, and the interrelatedness of writing and reading is self-evident; the child as writer is his/her own reader. Children will "use vocabulary" as they write; they will learn the principles of spelling after they have a solidified concept of self as writer. The ability to write a word "correctly" is different from either the intent to communicate with that word or to recognize it immediately when it is written, but by writing, every child will use a "basic vocabulary".

(d) Reading—Children may be able to recode (pronounce) words they do not know (understand) which is not reading in any functional sense. Rather, regular involvement in sustained silent reading periods or shared book activities will enable children to interact with print and process what they are seeing.

There is little applicable research on why children need sight words or which approaches are most useful to teach the words, because the only accessible format is the teaching and testing of restricted word lists in laboratory situations rather than in the multi-dimensional learning environment of the classroom within the larger world. Children will learn to recognize different words at different times depending on the nature of instruction (Clay 1979), breadth of environmental experience as studied in Goodman's work (see Gollasch 1982), and degree of involvement in personalized print-related tasks (Butler and Clay 1979). The conceptualization of what is basic in vocabulary instruction will depend on the teacher's understanding of the nature of the reading process.

Bibliography

Ashton-Warner S 1972 *Teacher.* Bantam, New York

Butler D, Clay M 1979 *Reading Begins at Home.* Primary Education, Melbourne

Cambourne B 1979 How important is theory to the reading teacher? *Aust. J. Read.* 2(2)

Clay M 1979 *Reading: The Patterning of Complex Behaviour.* Heinemann, Auckland

Dolch E W 1936 A basic sight vocabulary. *Elem. Sch. J.* 36: 456–60, 37: 268–72

Fry E 1980 The new instant word list. *Read. Teach.* 34: 284–89

Gollasch F V (ed.) 1982 *Language and Literacy: The Selected Writings of Kenneth S. Goodman.* Routledge and Kegan Paul, London

Graves D 1981 *A Case Study Observing the Development of Primary Children's Composing, Spelling and Motor Behaviour During the Writing Process.* Final Report, National Institute of Education, Grant No. G-78-0174, University of New Hampshire

Rousch P, Cambourne B 1978 *A Psycholinguistic Model of the Reading Process as it Relates to Proficient, Average, and Low Ability Readers.* Report to the Education Research and Development Committee, Riverina College of Advanced Education, Wagga Wagga

Sloan P, Latham R 1981 *Teaching Reading Is. . .* Nelson, Melbourne

Smith F 1978 *Reading.* Cambridge University Press, Cambridge

Smith F 1981 *Writing and the Writer.* Holt, Rinehart and Winston, New York

Advanced Level Instruction

Reading Methods in Secondary Schools

W. R. Hill

The belated emergence of formal programs in secondary reading education produced a reading methodology which incorporates much instructional practice from the elementary school. To a lesser degree, it reflects approaches which evolved from university psychology laboratories, reading clinics, and college reading-study courses. Understandably, the literature on secondary reading methodology includes numerous strategies and tactics. Program surveys have revealed considerable overlapping of practices, and attempts to type these procedures by developmental, remedial, or content classroom preference have not been useful.

A more efficient review may be effected by treating the most common patterns of secondary reading methods according to the three broader reading–learning constructs they tend to exemplify. The first, holistic reading approaches, emphasize pupil purposeful reading—meaningful processing, affect, and communication related to the message content of the language experiences, reading selections, and print sources which serve as the focus of instructional attention. The second, targeted competency approaches, stress the association and reinforcement of specific reading responses to particular print task stimuli. The ultimate goal is to produce a hierarchy of specific reading knowledges and skills upon which the reader will draw to meet real reading situations.

The third pattern emphasizes the development of metacognitive readers and consists of a group of instructional strategies intended to encourage deeper processing of text meaning and to improve independent learning from text. Reading educators recommend the interactive use of these three general approaches in developmental, remedial, and content area reading at the secondary level.

1. Holistic Approaches

Although varied in form, these approaches tend to implement the following premises: that learning and application of reading vocabulary and processes are most effective when derived from successful, purposeful, and realistic print message situations; that increasing the amount of continuous on-task reading of materials of pupil-appropriate interest and readability will improve instructional productivity and learning efficiency; that reading instruction should facilitate the synergy of language, thinking, and learning processes; and as pupils mature, that reading instructional materials should reflect a broader representation of school- and life-related use of print sources and genre (Bruner 1967).

1.1 Whole Language Instruction

The major premise of whole language pedagogy is that reading, writing, listening, and speaking are interactive processes and should not be separated by curriculum decision or instructional procedure. Whole language theory gained initial favor among primary school language and secondary English teachers, and the philosophy carries implication for secondary reading instruction. The earliest and most structured of these approaches, the Language-Experience Approach, has been used in upper schools in remedial instruction, particularly with illiterates and the language different pupil. It has been used as a supplementary short term strategy by content area teachers.

Typically, Language-Experience Reading instruction implements variations of the following sequence: evoking an event, experience, or problem from the pupil or group; stimulating and sharing associated or analytical thinking; eliciting and organizing pupil statements about the experience; making a printed message record from these oral statements; using this record for oral and silent rereading, vocabulary development, varied tasks of comprehension, and rewriting or creative extension; and filing and reusing the record for later reinforcement of vocabulary and skills practice (Hall 1978).

1.2 The Guided Reading Lesson

The Guided Reading Lesson is a methodological format by which a teacher guides a group of readers through a reading selection to discover the meaning of the content while significant vocabulary and reading–thinking processes are introduced or reinforced as related activities. The Guided Reading Lesson has been adapted in secondary developmental, remedial, and content settings for a whole class, smaller groups, or individuals. The lesson will vary with the nature of the selection, instructional objectives, and pupils. Developmentally, the approach is more productive when employed with selections or stories of appropriate graduated readability which are chosen or developed to fit a planned scope and sequence of reading and language learning.

A typical Guided Reading Lesson sequence involves: teacher identification of objectives to be implemented in reading and rereading the selection; pupil readiness for the selection through motivational and preteaching activity; group determination of first reading purposes; initial silent reading to gain a general understanding of the selection as guided by the set purposes and teacher intervention; feedback from teacher monitoring and discussion of first reading to identify content, processes, and purposes needing further attention; selective silent and oral rereading guided by deeper reading purposes and adjunct teaching aids; and follow-up activities in the form of practice exercises, creative language projects, or supplementary related reading (Hill 1979).

The Guided Reading Lesson has been adapted for use in larger secondary content area classes. The best known is the Instructional Framework, which consists of three stages: prereading activities, guided reading, and independent use activities. Guided reading in this approach involves paper–pencil "reading-study guides" whose object is to combine the learning of content with the use of pertinent reading–thinking processes. These guides may be used for in-class group instruction or for independent assignment. The most common forms are organizational or pattern guides; specific skill practice guides; differentiated guides to adjust for pupil differences, and interlocking guides which treat several levels of comprehension tasks (Vacca R and Vacca J 1989).

1.3 Individualized Reading

Conceived as a distinctive reading instructional approach, Individualized Reading involves: the collection of a substantial library of print materials of varied difficulty, topic, and genre; pupil self-selection of materials to read; pupil self-determination of purposes for reading (sometimes aided through teacher conference); pupil self-pacing in reading materials; and individual teacher–pupil conferences once or twice a week to monitor progress, to resolve meaning or approach difficulties, and to aid in determining future reading directions. Pure form individualized reading theorists eschew the use of reading instructional and practice materials, although most programs incorporate or complement the method with some group teaching of vocabulary and skills.

In the secondary school, individualized reading has been employed in special programs or as a loosely structured complement to more traditional instruction in reading and literature courses. Relatively little rigorous comparative research on individualized reading has been conducted in the upper grades. As a long-term singular approach to developmental reading instruction,

individualized reading poses problems in maintaining a sequenced curriculum, in obtaining and administrating numerous reading materials, and in teacher stress generated by frequency of program conferences and by immature pupils and reluctant readers. In general, its advantages lie in developing better reading affect, broader reading interests and contacts, larger reading vocabulary, and increased habits of personal reading (Sartain 1970, Guthrie 1981).

Several modifications of the individualized reading approach need mentioning. In a high intensity reading laboratory version for remediating disadvantaged readers, individualized reading is implemented through teacher conferences, a well-stocked personal reading center, and is combined with a highly structured but individualized competency mastery program in vocabulary and language. More loosely structured programs combining bibliotherapy with individualized reading for populations of disturbed adolescents have been reported with promising results (Fader 1976). Variations of individualized reading have gained some popularity in the form of all-school or all-class compulsory sustained silent reading sessions of increasing length (Bamberger 1973).

1.4 Reading-study Systems

A reading-study system represents a highly structured example of a holistic approach to the reading–learning–retention tasks of study. More than a score of such systems now appear in the reading and study literature, and are usually identified by acronyms such as SQ3R, and POINT, and PQRST which serve as mnemonic aids in the learning of the sequenced steps. Although some minor variations occur in the nature and sequencing of the parts, most systems provide for the development of purposes or questions to guide the reading and study activity, an overviewing of the material to be mastered, multiple readings geared to different tasks of interpretation and retention, a selective system of note taking, and some provision for overlearning such as self-testing, memorization, or reorganization of essential information (Graham and Robinson 1984).

Individually, the efficacy of such components has been supported by independent research, and there is some evidence to support the reading–learning usefulness of whole systems. However, surveys and methods studies have established neither the popularity nor the superiority of these systems to date. It should be added that teaching and research on study instruction has been criticized justly (Poulsen 1974).

1.5 Cognitive Organizers and Overviews

Cognitive organizers, supplemental information which provides a subsuming structure of concepts presented in the target passage, represent a holistic use of adjunct reading aids. Common organizer forms include brief prose selections, flow charts, diagrams, and tape recordings, usually presented before reading the content selection. Research on the instructional value of organizers suggests they benefit immediate comprehension more than retention. Expository prose forms function more effectively than analytical or iconic forms for pupils with lesser topic background and reading ability. Teaching the organizer as a structured overview may improve its effectiveness (Singer and Dolan 1989).

2. Targeted Competency Approaches

The construct of reading ability as a task-differentiated use of one or more of a bank of specific skills or behaviors which are learned through targeting of intensive skill practice, reached its apex when and where behavioral reinforcement learning theory exerted notable influence upon school practice. Targeted competency methods are closely married to their accompanying instructional software and hardware. Representative of these materials used in secondary reading programs are vocabulary and skills practice workbooks, published exercise duplicate masters, multilevel programs of competency tests and related exercises, programmed workbooks, film series for reading-rate improvement, video display programs, and multi-component skills programs featuring the combined use of tape recorders, visual task projectors, and print materials.

The preferred sequence of specific competency instruction provides for: stating the targeted competency in terms of the desired behavioral product (e.g., "to be able to identify correctly the implied main idea in nine of ten paragraphs"); preassessing pupil capability in using the targeted competency; developing readiness for learning the competency, including explanation of its nature and function and demonstration of its use in representative reading situations; providing closely monitored pupil association of the task stimulus and appropriate response, repeated to point of mastery; reinforcing initial learning of competency with independent practice in materials of graduated difficulty; assessing pupil mastery to determine need for reteaching; and providing systematically delayed practice and transfer application of the competency in realistic reading situations.

Evidence of the efficacy of specific competency instruction is somewhat mixed. Closely controlled short-term laboratory and classroom studies indicate that average or better subjects will probably demonstrate learned mastery in the competency, but maintenance and transferred application of the competency is less probable. A notable weakness of competency-oriented methodology is implicit in Durkin's evidence that classroom skill instruction emphasizes testing rather than explanation and guidance (Durkin 1978).

3. Metacognitive Targeted Strategies

A growing body of field evidence indicates that many secondary pupils fail to employ metacognition when reading serious prose (Baker and Brown 1984). That is, they do not use cognitive processes to direct and control their comprehension and learning from text. When reading independently, they fail to set purposes, monitor meaning gained against those purposes, and interactively and flexibly use schema driven and data driven information processes in order to get beyond the surface level of print information (Anderson 1984). Among the more promising of the instructional methods emerging to compensate for these deficiencies are the refinement of pupil question raising, modeling schema generation techniques, the systematic teaching of information restructuring techniques including summarizing and semantic mapping, and meaning elaboration practices (McNeil 1987).

Bibliography

Anderson R 1984 Role of the reader's schema in comprehension, learning, and memory. In: Anderson T et al. (eds.) 1984 *Learning to Read in American Schools*. Lawrence Erlbaum Associates, London, pp. 243–67

Baker R, Brown A 1984 Metacognitive skills and reading. In: Pearson D (ed.) 1984 *Handbook of Reading Research*. Longman Inc., New York, pp. 353–93

Bamberger R 1973 Leading children to reading: An Austrian venture. In: Karlin R (ed.) 1973 *Reading for All*. Fourth International Reading Association World Congress on Reading, Buenos Aires, 1972. International Reading Association, Newark, Delaware, pp. 192–99

Bruner J 1967 *Toward a Theory of Instruction*. Harvard University Press, Cambridge, Massachusetts, pp. 113–28

Durkin D 1978 What classroom observations reveal about reading comprehension instruction. *Read. Res. Q.* 14: 481–535

Fader D 1976 *The New Hooked on Books*. Berkeley, New York

Goodman K 1986 *What's Whole in Whole Language?* Heinemann, Portsmouth, New Hampshire

Graham K, Robinson H 1984 *Study Skills Handbook: A Guide for All Teachers*. International Reading Association, Newark, Delaware

Guthrie J 1981 Reading in New Zealand: Achievement and volume. *Read. Res. Q.* 17: 6–27

Hall M 1978 *The Language-Experience Approach for Teaching Reading: A Research Perspective*, 2nd edn. International Reading Association, Newark, Delaware

Hill W 1979 *Secondary School Reading: Process, Program, Procedure*. Allyn and Bacon, Boston, Massachusetts

McNeil J 1987 *Reading Comprehension: New Directions in Classroom Practice*, 2nd edn. Scott, Foresman and Co., Chicago, Illinois

Poulsen S 1974 *How-to-Study Methods: Where Did They Go?* Danish Institute for Educational Research, Report No. 8, Copenhagen. ERIC Document No. ED 197 709

Sartain H 1970 *Individualized Reading: An Annotated Bibliography*. International Reading Association, Newark, Delaware

Singer H, Dolan D 1989 *Reading and Learning from Text*. 2nd edn. Lawrence Erlbaum Associates, London

Vacca R, Vacca J 1989 *Content Area Reading*, 3rd edn. Scott, Foresman and Co., Chicago, Illinois

Comprehension Instruction

H. Singer

Comprehension instruction has increased as research has discovered how people comprehend printed materials. This article traces the research through three definitions of reading and draws out their implications for teaching comprehension. Then it explains the current definition's two components, text data and reading resources. It concludes with strategies for developing comprehension at the preschool, elementary-school, and high-school levels of instruction.

1. Definitions of Reading

Prior to 1917, reading was defined as the ability to transform printed words into oral responses. Teachers then emphasized accuracy in word identification and oral reading, but did not teach comprehension as such when students could read aloud accurately, fluently, and with appropriate intonation. Teachers assumed that without any further instruction students could use their reading ability to learn from texts in any content area.

In 1917 research led to a change in the definition of reading. Noting that student responses in trying to comprehend a paragraph were analogous to processes in solving a mathematics problem, Thorndike (1917) defined reading as reasoning. Acting on this definition, teachers began to limit oral reading to diagnosis and audience situations, and started to emphasize silent reading as soon as possible so that students could focus their attention on use of their reasoning processes during reading.

The next major change in comprehension instruction stemmed from a study which showed that readers varied their processes of reading according to changes in their purposes, and in the type and difficulty of their reading materials (Judd and Buswell 1922). This research eventually led teachers to instruct students to establish their purposes prior to reading, search for information to satisfy these purposes during reading, and use their reasoning processes after reading to answer questions on information stored in memory.

Researchers and teachers also realized that students acquire a profile of reading abilities as they progress through school. This profile reflects students' previous reading experiences, aptitudes, interests, and school subjects. Consequently, teachers began to teach students to read and learn from text in each content area. They also continued instruction in reading and learning from text throughout the grades so that students could learn to comprehend increasingly more difficult tasks.

Further research on cognitive processes and abilities led to a more complex definition of comprehension (see *Cognitive Processing in the Classroom*). Holmes (1954, 1965) stated that reading ability consists of two major components: speed of reading—the ability to read relatively easy material rapidly, and power of reading—the ability to read relatively difficult material analytically. Underlying each of these components are a multiplicity of abilities and processes readers mobilize to solve problems in reading. At one moment, they might mobilize their abilities and processes for identifying a printed word; at another, for attaining a contextually defined word meaning; and at still another, for making an inference, interpretation, or evaluation. They not only switch from one problem to another, they may also have to try to solve a problem in more than one way. For example, if they cannot readily retrieve or construct the meaning of a word, they might next try to analyze it into its constituent meanings (prefix, root, and suffix) and integrate them, or try to infer a word's meaning from the context. Thus, readers must learn to mobilize different abilities and processes according to changes in their purposes and the demands of the reading task. Throughout the process of reading, active readers also direct, monitor, and evaluate their cognitive processes (Brown 1981) which interact with their affective reactions to the text and themselves (Athey 1982). Thus, reading comprehension consists of an interaction between text data and reader resources (Rumelhart 1977, Singer 1983). Consequently comprehension instruction now focuses on text characteristics, reader resources, and interactions between them.

2. Text Characteristics

Texts have three major features: (a) cohesion, a means of tying sentences together through various devices, such as pronouns or any grammatical element that represents information in previous sentences; (b) content that can be divided into events (participants and what happens to them) and nonevents (setting, background, collateral information, and evaluation); and (c) staging, ways of featuring information, for example, by its location in a passage or by use of rhetorical devices such as problem–solution and question and answer (Grimes 1975). If students learn to recognize and use these and other organizational features of a text, they will tend to process and recall information better.

Teachers can obtain better comprehension in their students by selecting texts at difficulty levels that are appropriate to their students. Readability formulas have been used to select such texts, but these formulas are not infallible. They are based on sentence length and either word frequency or word length. Sentence length is related to syntactic ability and perhaps memory; word frequency or length tends to correspond to semantic ability. But shorter sentences and words do not always make texts easier to understand. Some longer sentences are comprehended and remembered better because they explicate causal relationships and make their facts significant (Pearson 1976, Stein and Bransford 1979). For example, a text that explains why arteries are larger and more elastic than veins makes these facts more meaningful than if it just communicates the ways in which they differ. In short, a text should have adequate explanations for its facts, not just an arbitrary list of information.

Texts also vary in organizational features, such as use of headings and subheadings, and in placement of information. For example, when objects are grouped with their properties rather than separated into categorized lists, students tend to acquire and retain the information better (Frase 1969). Texts are also more memorable when facts are close to the main ideas or the topics they support.

Most important to comprehension is a text that students can relate to their prior knowledge and use for constructing new knowledge. Such a text uses many familiar examples. When new concepts are introduced, the text may use analogies to bridge the gap between prior and new knowledge (Hayes and Tierney 1982) or supply the necessary information for the student to refine pre-existing knowledge or construct new knowledge categories (Bransford 1981). In short, an appropriate text should start at the level of a student's knowledge framework and build upon it.

Thus, selection of a text is a crucial initial step in teaching comprehension. The text should have examples that activate and make contact with students' prior knowledge and experience, use analogies to explain new concepts, provide information necessary for constructing new knowledge categories, explicate causal relationships, place related information together, and be written at a level of abstraction that can be related to and build upon a student's knowledge framework. Appropriate, adequate, and well-organized texts facilitate comprehension by enabling readers to mobilize their resources for comprehending it.

3. Reader Resources

3.1 Resource List

Readers allocate their attention among their knowledge resources and between text data and reader resources to construct the meaning of a text (Rumelhart 1976, Adams and Collins 1977, Singer 1983b). Their resources consist of word recognition abilities, word knowledge, syntactic processes, semantic and conceptual abilities, and world knowledge. These resources may operate simultaneously in parallel and in interaction with each other and the text. If readers become automatic in word identification ability, they can then devote their attention to use of their other resources (LaBerge and Samuels 1976). If they are not automatic, they can approximate the process through repeated readings of the same text (Samuels 1979). They can use their cognitive processes for inferring which words are appropriate for a given sentence, such as "The run on the

bank tired the men" vs. "The run on the bank depleted its supply of money." They can mobilize their syntactic ability to parse sentences into meaningful phrases. They can draw upon their knowledge structures to give meaning to words (Anderson et al. 1977). For example, if they know a flower has particular properties and then learn that a rhododendron is a flower, they also know its properties. They can use their world knowledge to supply omitted but commonly understood information, such as the causal links in the sentence, "The cigarette caused the forest fire."

3.2 Scripts, Purposes, and Perspectives

Sequences of events in world knowledge are called scripts. Each script consists of schemata or knowledge structures, which contain organized information about objects, events, and situations. These knowledge structures are abstractions that are instantiated by particular objects, events, or situations. A script may be about procedures to follow that individuals use when in a restaurant, in sailing a boat, or when flying a kite; in short, scripts pertain to a sequence of expected events within a situation or story (Schank and Abelson 1977). The reader's purpose or perspective mobilizes or activates a particular script which enables the reader to obtain a coherent interpretation of events in a situation or story. Because schemata and perspectives can vary from reader to reader, teachers can expect readers to attain different but equally plausible interpretations (Pichert and Anderson 1977).

3.3 Instructional Implications

A knowledge of reader resources and their mobilization has these implications for instruction: (a) it develops in students all the necessary resources for comprehending text; (b) it has students acquire automaticity in word identification for all high frequency words by having them read an abundance of relatively easy material in elementary school, and develops students' ability to identify and know the meanings of technical terms so that they can allocate their attention to other aspects of comprehension; (c) it teaches students to organize their knowledge and to actively use and integrate new knowledge with their prior knowledge as they read; (d) it encourages students to expand and enhance their vocabulary, scripts, and general knowledge through wide reading and participation in a broadly based educational curriculum; and (e) it expects readers to have a profile of reading abilities, to need instruction in each content area, and to vary in interpretation of texts because of differences in their abilities, educational experiences, cultural backgrounds, and perspectives (Tierney and LaZansky 1980). Reader resources and their interaction with text begin to develop at the preschool level. While the word recognition and syntactic components can approach maturity at the elementary-school level, the other resources continue to develop throughout school and a person's lifetime.

4. Development of Comprehension

4.1 Preschool Level

Development of reader resources in relation to text begins when parents or teachers start to read to children, sometimes as early as age 3. The children learn that reading is an enjoyable and worthwhile activity and that stories have certain characteristics. Initially they learn that stories have a beginning, middle, and end, and the characters in them try to solve a problem in one or more ways and eventually are successful or else give up. Thus preschoolers begin to acquire the knowledge structures of story grammar and use them to guide their listening and retrieval of information from memory (Singer 1982).

4.2 Elementary-school Level

(a) *Picture-story method.* At the kindergarten level, teachers may bridge the gap between prior and new knowledge by having students draw pictures and tell stories about them. Typically a child's story is only a sentence. The teacher writes the story under the picture and subsequently students read their own picture stories. Gradually students acquire a repertoire of printed words they can recognize at a glance. These sight words may consist of pronouns (I, we), nouns (father, mother, sister, brother, school, bus, home), verbs (saw, went), and perhaps noun determiners (the, a). When these words are printed on cards and the number of cards is augmented by pictures of nouns, the students can use them to construct their own sentences. This instructional activity leads into the next stage in the development of comprehension, the language experience approach.

(b) *Language experience approach.* Children construct short stories based on some common experience. They dictate the sentences about their experiences to the teacher who writes them on the board. The students then read their story. Eventually the students learn to write and read their own and other students' stories. After this language experience approach to beginning reading, the students may go into a more formal instructional program consisting of individualized reading or a basal reader, or preferably both (Singer 1982).

(c) *Individualized reading.* Individualized reading consists of self-selection of books with guidance from the teacher. The teacher checks the student's comprehension of a previously read book by having the student recall the story and answer a few questions about the characters, plot, outcome, and the student's evaluation of the book.

(d) *Basal reader.* A basal reader is a more systematic way of developing comprehension and is the most widely used tool for teaching reading. Its vocabulary is carefully controlled; each new word is taught by the teacher, used immediately in a story, and then cumulatively with other new words in subsequent stories until students have acquired word recognition techniques for independently identifying novel words (Singer 1984).

A teacher's manual which accompanies the basal reader contains prepared lessons for teaching word identification and comprehension. Each comprehension lesson usually consists of five steps. The teacher establishes a purpose for reading the story by arousing students' curiosity, introduces new vocabulary, relates the story to students' prior knowledge and experience, guides the reading of the story through questions, and has students read the rest of the story silently to answer previously posed questions or to prepare for answering questions at the end of the story. Teachers may also have students learn to skim and scan by having them search through the story again to find answers to specific questions.

Thus, the basal reader teaches comprehension primarily through questions that direct students to focus attention on important components in the text. If the questions are based on story grammar concepts and teachers ask these questions at appropriate points in the story, students are more likely to learn to segment stories at the same junctures. In other words, they become able to classify story content into the relevant story grammar structures and can then store the content in memory in an organized way. They can subsequently use their story grammar structures to retrieve the story from memory (Beck et al. 1982).

4.3 High-school Level

A gradual shift occurs from emphasis on narrative texts at the beginning of elementary school to expository texts at high school. But narrative and expository texts are actually on a continuum. Some stories, like expository texts, may contain information consisting of facts, concepts, and generalizations. Likewise, some expository texts may also contain stories, such as a scientist in a particular setting who is trying to solve a problem and reach a goal. Since narrative and expository material overlap, students must draw upon similar abilities and processes to comprehend them.

However, these types of materials also differ in structure and content. At the beginning stage of reading acquisition, stories are familiar and frequently within children's own experiential repertoires. Subsequently they will have to learn to comprehend less familiar stories and even less familiar expository content. As this change occurs, teachers shift from instructional emphasis on teaching students how to read to strategies for teaching students to comprehend or learn from texts.

5. Strategies for Teaching Comprehension

Students are more likely to learn and retain information that they have to expend effort on to attain. Therefore the goal of instructional strategies is to help readers learn how to select and process important information, information that is relevant to their purposes and goals in learning from text. The strategies overlap, but they tend to fit into four major categories: comprehensive teaching strategies, strategies for enhancing text characteristics, reader resources, and interactions between text and reader.

5.1 Comprehensive Teaching Strategies

(a) *Directed reading activity.* This strategy is similar to the five step basal reader strategy applied to expository text (Stauffer 1969). The teacher explains the purpose or goal for reading the text, relates the text to students' prior knowledge, teaches the technical terms, guides the students through the text, explains and demonstrates how to read and interpret it, how to make use of the rhetorical devices in it, and how to evaluate whether the goal has been reached, for example, whether an answer to a question has been found and how to check whether the answer is correct. If students have difficulty in comprehending the text, teachers usually explain the content. But they should next have the students go back to the text to perceive the way the text explains the content. Thus, teachers can teach students how to learn from texts (MacGinitie 1981).

(b) *Mathemagenic behavior.* Activities that initiate or stimulate learning are known as mathemagenic behaviors. The teacher-provided activities for mathemagenic behavior are directions given to the reader, questions embedded in text, establishment of purposes and goals by the reader, information in text that enables readers to achieve their goals, and assessment of goal achievement by an examination that is coherent with the text, reader purposes, and the teacher's adjunct aids (Rothkopf 1982).

5.2 Text Characteristics Strategies

(a) *Text annotations.* If students are to learn anything new, texts must be relatively difficult for them. However, teachers can help students bridge that gap between what they know and what they must learn by defining terms with examples related to the students' experience, inserting needed background knowledge to clarify ideas, using analogies to relate new knowledge to prior knowledge, suggesting where students might

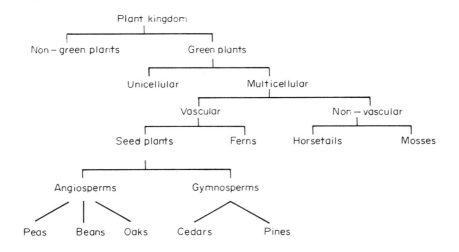

Figure 1
Graphic organizer for the concept angiosperms[a]
[a] *After Thelen 1982a (reprinted with the permission of the International Reading Association)*

draw diagrams or maps to represent relations among ideas in the text, adding questions to focus attention on relevant information, and indicating where students should process the text more carefully. Teachers might also suggest where readers might consider alternative purposes and perspectives and justify their interpretations (see *Critical Reading Instruction*). They might be stimulated to think of applications of text information or their conclusions to new situations (Tierney and Pearson 1982). These teacher annotations can be in the form of materials inserted in the text (Singer and Donlan 1980).

(b) *Graphic organizers*. Texts can be divided into two components: structure and content. The text structure consists of chapters, sections, paragraphs, and sentences. These are tied together by rhetorical devices, such as problem–solution and cause–effect, and by cohesive ties, such as pronouns. The structure is also signalled by conjunctions and prepositions. Students can learn to use these structural devices to organize the content into hierarchically organized semantic relationships. For example, Fig. 1 shows a graphic organizer for the concept of angiosperms. Teachers can elicit from students their prior knowledge of flowering plants (angiosperms), organize it graphically, and show students where new knowledge components fit into this graphic organizer (Thelen 1982).

(c) *Mapping or diagramming text*. Students can learn to diagram the explicit and implicit relationships among agents, causal relationships, actions, objects, and recipients of actions in texts. For example, the biblical story of Solomon as a wise judge can be mapped or diagrammed as shown in Fig. 2.

(d) *Learning from text guides*. Teachers can help readers comprehend expository texts by constructing a written guide. The guide contains information that the teacher has selected from the text and categorized into literal, inferential, interpretive, and generalized levels. The guide, acting in place of the teacher, directs the student to check whether information stated in the guide actually occurs in the text, determines whether an

inference or interpretation made in the text or by the reader is valid, and finally justifies whether the literal information and inferences or interpretations fit into a generalization. Thus, the guide teaches the student to attend to important text information and leads the student from a literal to a generalized level of thinking (Herber 1970). This guide can be extended to the affective domain by asking readers to determine their emotional or critical reactions to the information in the text or to interpretations, generalizations, and conclusions of the author or themselves (Singer and Donlan 1980).

(e) *Discussion or quest guides* (*questions that stimulate thinking*). Similar to a learning from text guide, a discussion guide, conducted by the teacher, first asks the class to select or recall the factual or literal information; then through lifting questions (What do these facts mean or what do they have in common?), the teacher leads the students to form an interpretation or a concept; next the teacher may ask the group to form a generalization (What concepts are related? Is this relationship always true?) Thus, through discussion, the teacher can lead a group from recall of literal information to the formulation of generalizations (Taba 1965, Singer and Donlan 1980).

5.3 Reader Resource Strategies

(a) *Advance organizers*. A brief but abstract overview of a passage prior to reading may enable individuals to activate the concepts necessary for grasping the situational context and for subsuming the text's events. An organization and explication of a text's technical vocabulary may also serve as an advance organizer (Ausubel 1960, Earle and Barron 1973). However, if students do not have the necessary repertoire, then an advance organizer will not be effective. Instead, the text will have to develop them and their interrelationships.

(b) *Schema strategies*. These are a group of strategies for developing knowledge structures for objects, events, and situations. When teaching new terms (nouns), objects should be presented in an organized way. The

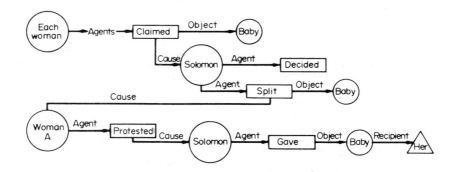

Figure 2
Diagram of the biblical story of Solomon[a]
[a] After Singer 1979a (reprinted with permission of Deakin University Press)

term should be listed with its properties or attributes, its exemplars, class membership or immediate superordinate and related concepts (Pearson and Johnson 1978). For example, a ship has attributes of rudder, bow, and keel; it has exemplars such as USS Orion, Lusitania, and Queen Mary. A ship can be subsumed under a superordinate of vessel, and it is related to other concepts, such as plane. Such organized instruction may facilitate students' acquisition of knowledge structures.

Teachers can explain to students that an abstract structure can subsume a multitude of propositions. Students can also use an abstract structure to generate an infinite number of propositions. For example, one abstract structure is: An agent acts on an object. This structure can subsume or generate such sentences as "Debbie hit the ball," "Matthew ate a sandwich," "David rode the bike," and "Simon climbed a tree."

Students can also learn that conjunctions relate one proposition to another. For example, the abstract structure may be proposition A has a causal effect on proposition B. This structure can subsume or generate these sentences: "Samson lost his strength because his hair was cut" or "Mary went to the store to buy a loaf of bread." Students can learn to use these structures for comprehending and generating sentences and for mapping stories (Singer 1979).

Readers have abstract scenarios or scripts in their heads. As they read, they can generate a script to subsume events and attain a coherent interpretation of a text (Schank and Abelson 1977). For example, individuals can generate a problem-solving schema that can subsume the events in a story. The schema consists of an agent seeking to solve a problem, making one or more attempts to overcome a barrier, and finally succeeding or giving up in frustration, or seeking an alternative goal (Adamsand Collins 1977). Students can learn to relate these problem-solving categories to short stories and thus improve their comprehension of the stories (Singer and Donlan 1982).

(c) *Summarization*. If students summarize text information in their own words, they are more likely to remember it. Summarization rules call for (a) deletion of nonessential information; (b) identification or construction of topic sentences; (c) construction of superordinate terms; and (d) integration of these terms into generalizations. The end result is construction of a text's general and supporting statements (propositions) (van Dijk and Kintsch 1977, Brown1981).

5.4 Interaction Strategies

(a) *SQ3R*. An early strategy for teaching comprehension consists of students *s*urveying a text, formulating *q*uestions, such as turning section headings into questions, then *r*eading to answer their questions, *r*eciting the answers, and *r*eviewing the text to check their answers (Robinson 1961).

(b) *Active reader*. Teachers initially guide students toward comprehension with teacher-posed questions, often at the literal, inferential, interpretive, and evalu-

ative levels. They can also ask children questions which can only be answered by drawing upon background knowledge.

In general, teachers should strive to match their questions to children's interpretations of texts (Bransford 1981). However, if students are to develop independence in learning from text, whether narrative or expository, the teacher has to shift responsibility to the students by having them set their own goals, arouse their own curiosity, formulate their own questions, monitor their progress to the goal, and evaluate their accomplishments. For example, teachers may develop independence by asking students what they would like to learn from a given text, where they might find the information, how the information may be related to what they already know, why the facts in the text are significant, how they can be used, and how they would know they had accomplished their goal. Thus, teachers can develop students into active readers who read to answer their self-generated questions, and in doing so, direct, monitor, and evaluate their own cognitive processes and affective reaction to the text and themselves.

The active reader strategy can begin as early as children start to read and can work with both narrative and expository prose. For example, instead of directing children in kindergarten to respond with answers to the teacher's questions about a picture, the teacher can elicit their questions by asking, "What would you like to know about this picture?" The children can then search for answers to their own questions as they progress through a story (Singer 1979). Story grammar, which children have acquired as early as grade 1, provides a set of structures for generating questions that can vary from story-general to story-specific (Singer and Donlan 1982). However, story grammar does not contain rules for emotional reactions, interpretations, and moral or thematic formulations (Guthrie 1978); these and other story components, such as knowledge of satire and irony, are gradually acquired from texts and instruction as students progress through school. Students also need to gain structures for guiding their learning from expository materials, particularly for unfamiliar and therefore relatively difficult material, such as categorizing text information into a hierarchy of facts, concepts, and generalizations. As students learn and internalize a strategy, the teacher can phase out instruction in its use. Students can then apply their internalized strategy for self-direction and active learning from text.

6. Summary and Conclusion

Instruction in comprehension has progressed as a result of research from no instruction in comprehension to multiple strategies for developing comprehension and for teaching students to be active in learning from text. Researchers have recently developed a multitude of hypotheses for teaching comprehension, but they still need to be validated in classroom settings. Those that are valid will add considerably to the teacher's repertoire of strategies for teaching comprehension (Singer 1981).

Another change in teaching comprehension is that it no longer occurs only in elementary school, but in all grade levels and all content areas. Students may learn how to read in elementary school, but as they progress through school they can continue to learn how to learn from text.

Bibliography

Adams J, Collins A A 1977 *A Schema–Theoretic View of Reading*. Bolt, Beranek and Newman, Boston, Massachusetts

Anderson R C, Spiro R J, Montague W E (eds.) 1977 *Schooling and the Acquisition of Knowledge*. Erlbaum, Hillsdale, New Jersey

Athey I 1982 Reading: The affective domain reconcept realized. In: Hutson B A (ed.) 1982 *Advances in Reading/Language Research*, Vol. 1. JAI Press, Greenwich, Connecticut

Ausubel D 1960 The use of advance organizers in the learning and retention of meaningful verbal material. *J. Educ. Psychol.* 51: 267–72

Beck I L, Ohmanson R C, McKeown M G 1982 An instructional redesign of reading lesson: Effects on comprehension. *Read. Res. Q.* 17(4): 462–81

Bransford J D 1981 Schema activation and schema acquisition. Comments on Richard C. Anderson's remarks. In: Anderson R C, Osborn J, Tierney R J (eds.) 1981 *Proceedings of the Conference: Learning to Read in American Schools: Basal Readers and Content Texts*. Center for the Study of Reading, Champaign, Illinois

Brown A 1981 Metacognition: The development of selective attention strategies for learning from texts. In: Kamil M (ed.) 1981 *Directions in Reading: Research and Instruction*. The 30th Yearbook of the National Reading Conference. National Reading Conference, Washington, DC

Earle R, Barron R F 1973 An approach for teaching vocabulary in content subjects. In: Herber H L, Barron R F (eds.) 1973 *Research in Reading in the Content Areas: Second Year Report*. Reading and Language Arts Center, Syracuse University, New York

Frase L T 1969 Paragraph organization of written materials: The influence of conceptual clustering upon the level and organization of recall. *J. Educ. Psychol.* 60: 394–401

Grimes J E 1975 *The Thread of Discourse*. Mouton, The Hague

Guthrie J 1978 Research views: Fables. *Read. Teach.* 31: 724–26

Hayes D A, Tierney R J 1982 Developing readers' knowledge through analogy. *Read. Res. Q.* 17: 256–80

Herber H L 1970 *Teaching Reading in Content Areas*. Prentice-Hall, Englewood Cliffs, New Jersey

Holmes J A 1954 Factors underlying major reading disabilities at the college level. *Genet. Psychol. Monogr.* 49: 3–95

Holmes J A 1965 Basic assumptions underlying the substrata factor theory of reading. *Read. Res. Q.* 1: 5–28

Judd C H, Buswell G T 1922 *Silent Reading: A Study of the Various Types*. Supplementary Educational Monographs, No. 23. University of Chicago Press, Chicago, Illinois

LaBerge D L, Samuels S J 1976 Toward a theory of automatic information processing in reading. In: Singer H, Ruddell R (eds.) 1976 *Theoretical Models and Processes of Reading*, 2nd edn. International Reading Association, Newark, Delaware

MacGinitie W H 1981 Readability as a solution adds to the problem. In: Anderson R C, Osborn J, Tierney R J (eds.) 1981 *Learning to Read in American Schools: Basal Readers and Content Texts*. Conference Proceedings. Center for the Study of Reading, Champaign, Illinois

Pearson P D 1976 The effects of grammatical complexity on children's comprehension, recall, and conception of certain semantic relations. In: Singer H, Ruddell R (eds.) 1976 *Theoretical Models and Processes of Reading*. International Reading Association, Newark, Delaware

Pearson P D, Johnson D D 1978 *Teaching Reading Comprehension*. Holt, Rinehart and Winston, New York

Pichert J W, Anderson R C 1977 Taking different perspectives on a story. *J. Educ. Psychol.* 69: 309–15

Robinson F P 1961 Study skills for superior students in secondary school. *Read. Teach.* 15: 29–33

Rothkopf E Z 1982 Adjunct aids and the control of mathemagenic activities during purposeful reading. In: Otto W, White S (eds.) 1982 *Reading Expository Material*. Academic Press. New York

Rumelhart D E 1976 *Toward an Interactive Model of Reading*. Technical Report No. 56. Center for Human Information Processing, University of California, San Diego, California

Rumelhart D E 1977 Understanding and summarizing brief stories. In: LaBerge D, Samuels S J (eds.) 1977 *Basic Processes in Reading: Perception and Comprehension*. Erlbaum, Hillsdale, New Jersey

Samuels S J 1979 The method of repeated reading. *Read. Teach.* 32: 403–08

Schank R C, Abelson R P 1977 *Scripts, Plans, Goals, and Understanding: An Inquiry into Human Knowledge Structures*. Erlbaum, Hillsdale, New Jersey

Singer H 1979 *Reading Comprehension: Interacting with Text*. Deakin University Press, Victoria

Singer H 1981 Hypotheses on reading comprehension in search of classroom validation. In: Kamil M (ed.) 1981 *Directions in Reading: Research and Instruction*. 30th Yearbook of the National Reading Conference. National Reading Conference, Washington, DC

Singer H 1982 An integration of instructional approaches for teaching reading and learning from text. In: Reed L, Ward S (eds.) 1982 *2 Basic Skills: Issues and Choices*. Central Midwest Regional Educational Laboratory, St. Louis, Missouri

Singer H 1983 The substrata-factor theory of reading: Its history and conceptual relationship to interaction theory. In: Gentile L, Kamil M, Blanchard J (eds.) 1983 *Reading Research Revisited*. Merrill, Columbus, Ohio

Singer H 1984 Word recognition. In: Rauch S, Sanacore J (eds.) 1984 *Handbook for the Volunteer Tutor*. International Reading Association, Newark, Delaware

Singer H, Donlan D 1980 *Reading and Learning from Text*. Little, Brown, Boston, Massachusetts

Singer H, Donlan D 1982 Active comprehension: Problem-solving schema with question generation for comprehension of complex short stories. *Read. Res. Q.* 17: 166–86

Stauffer R G 1969 *Directing Reading Maturity as a Cognitive Process*. Harper and Row, New York

Stein B S, Bransford J D 1979 Constraints on effective elaboration: Effects of precision and subject generation. *J. Verb. Learn. Verb. Behav.* 18: 769–77

Taba H 1965 The teaching of thinking. *Elem. Engl.* 42: 534–42

Thelen J 1982 Preparing students for content reading assignments. *J. Read.* 25: 544–49

Thorndike E L 1917 Reading as reasoning: A study of mistakes in paragraph reading. *J. Educ. Psychol.* 8: 323–32

Tierney R J, LaZansky J 1980 The rights and responsibilities of readers and writers: A contractual agreement. *Lang. Arts* 57: 606–13

Tierney R J, Pearson P D 1982 Learning to learn from text: A framework for improving classroom practice. In: Reed L,

Ward S (eds.) 1982 *2 Basic Skills: Issues and Choices: Approaches to Basic Skills Instruction.* Central Midwest Regional Educational Laboratory, St. Louis, Missouri

van Dijk T, Kintsch W 1977 Cognitive psychology and discourse: Recalling and summarizing stories. In: Dressler W U (ed.) 1977 *Current Trends in Textlinguistics.* De Gruyter, Berlin, New York

Critical Reading Instruction

R. L. Parker and L. Unsworth

Critical reading is a process of evaluating the validity, relevance, effectiveness, or worth of what is read according to a set of criteria. These criteria are related to logical reasoning and deal with internal properties of the text as well as to external criteria related to the readers' knowledge of the subject matter being read, and to individual readers' biases, cultural and sociopolitical attitudes, and purposes in reading the text. Hence "critical reading may involve internal and/or external critical evaluation" (Harris and Hodges 1981). There is some evidence of specific skills in critical reading (Wolf 1969) and the necessity of teaching such skills is widely asserted in pedagogical texts. Skills dealing with internal critical evaluation include detecting fallacies in logical reasoning and recognizing propaganda techniques. Those based on external criteria include: distinguishing fact from opinion, detecting authors' biases, and evaluating authors' qualifications. Despite variances in terminology and definition with respect to these aspects of critical reading, it is widely held that there is a close relationship between them and components of critical thinking.

Most texts on the teaching of reading include lists of critical reading skills which refer to similar competencies despite a lack of uniformity in nomenclature and classification systems used. Evaluating written material according to logical reasoning is believed to be facilitated through the development of skills such as:

(a) distinguishing between causal and correlational relationships;

(b) detecting analogies which are false due to an inappropriate difference between the items being compared in an area fundamental to the purpose of the analogy;

(c) detecting false dichotomies which result from a failure to take all possibilities into account;

(d) recognizing overgeneralization or conclusions based on insufficient evidence;

(e) judging the accuracy of premises and determining whether a conclusion should follow necessarily;

(f) recognizing contradictory statements;

(g) recognizing digressions to irrelevant issues;

(h) recognizing stereotyping as a process of overemphasizing characteristics thought to be common to a class of objects or people and underemphasizing the uniqueness of individual members of the class.

Critical evaluation is also facilitated through an awareness of propaganda techniques which may be detected by reference to internal characteristics of the text. Educators have focused on the following:

(a) Bad names—terms with unpleasant connotations used to invoke negative feelings toward the subject.

(b) Glad names—terms with pleasant connotations used to invoke positive feelings toward the subject.

(c) Testimonial—a declaration of endorsement for a recommendation relating to an individual, proposal, belief, theory, or product.

(d) Transfer—authoritative individuals or institutions in a particular field endorse some idea, theory, belief, proposal, individual, or product to which their realm of expertise is peripheral or irrelevant.

(e) Plain folks—emphasizes identification with common people.

(f) Card stacking—presents only information favorable to the subject.

(g) Bandwagon—the subject of the information is presented as something everybody aspires to as the acceptable and desirable norm.

A sound knowledge of the field in which the reading is being done is an essential prerequisite to critical reading. However, in our complex world, this is obviously unattainable in many instances. Here, critical evaluation will necessitate recourse to external criteria, or other references and sources. The ability to suspend judgment until a frame of reference can be established from valid external sources is essential to effective development of the following critical reading skills:

(a) distinguishing between fact and opinion;

(b) identifying assumptions made by an author;

(c) judging the author's qualifications;

(d) establishing the reliability of the publication;

(e) determining the currency of the information;

(f) distinguishing between primary and secondary sources;

(g) detecting the author's bias.

Because a reader's response to written material is partly determined by cultural and sociopolitical attitudes, these produce some largely idiosyncratic, external criteria for critical evaluation. The detection of bias related to particular issues such as sexism, racism, ageism, handicapped people, and so on, depends, therefore, on readers' recognition of their own biases in reacting to written material.

1. Research Evidence

As is the case with many other aspects of the study of reading, there is remarkably little research which bears on the issue of critical reading. Nevertheless, those studies that are available, taken with evidence on other aspects of the reading process and strategies for teaching, can lead to some useful insights into the nature of critical reading and implications for the classroom.

There is evidence to suggest that students' levels of competency differ from one age level to another, and from one nation to another. There is general agreement that younger children have not developed the capacity to read critically: there is also evidence which confirms the belief that one of the characteristics of older, less proficient readers, is that they use limited critical reading strategies. The International Association for the Evaluation of Educational Achievement (IEA) Study of Literature (Purves et al. 1973) leads to the conclusion that there are highly significant differences across nations in the way secondary-school pupils interpret literature. While some of the differences reported may be attributed to cultural differences, it seems reasonable to conclude that the nature of the teacher's approach to literature education is a significant factor. This conclusion is well-supported by the results of Project SOAR (Whimbey et al. 1980), a project concerned with "a method of teaching comprehension and analytical skills that emphasises the connection between the two." This study also confirms the relationship between critical reading and analytic reasoning.

It appears that not only are there differences in levels of performance for pupils of different ages, but there are also differing expectations on the part of teachers of the place critical reading should have in the curriculum. While 50 per cent of college students' reading time is concerned with critical reading, middle and secondary teachers do not feel that critical reading activities are important. Current conceptions of the reading process, and the view that critical reading and critical thinking are closely related, lead to the conclusion that young readers can, and should, be taught to read critically.

2. Teaching Practices

Traditional views of teaching critical reading are well-summarized by a number of recognized texts on reading (Harris and Smith 1980, Smith and Robinson 1980, Spache and Spache 1973). More recent evidence suggests the following guidelines for the development of effective critical reading instruction:

(a) the selected materials need to be wide ranging in nature and level of difficulty;

(b) the teaching of critical reasoning can be taught effectively as early as first grade (age 6);

(c) the teaching of critical reading can be commenced from as early as first grade, provided that the materials are suitable to the grade level;

(d) the use of controversy (i.e., analyzing a number of articles dealing with a controversial issue) is a useful strategy;

(e) comprehension (understanding meaning) and critical reading (evaluating that meaning) should be taught as distinct but related processes (Lehr 1982);

(f) the use of discussion following individual reading optimizes the effectiveness of instruction;

(g) writing should be encouraged as a logical extension of critical reading (e.g., students could be asked to write articles for particular purposes, to compose advertisements, etc.);

(h) the development of more effective questioning by teachers is essential to the development of critical thinking and reading.

Bibliography

Ericson B 1987 Increasing critical reading in Junior High classrooms. *J. Read.* 30(5): 430–39

Harris L A, Smith C B 1980 *Reading Instruction: A Handbook*, 3rd edn. Holt, Rinehart and Winston, New York

Harris T, Hodges R E (eds.) 1981 *A Dictionary of Reading and Related Terms*. International Reading Association, Newark, Delaware

Lehr F 1982 Developing critical reading and thinking skills. *J. Read.* 25: 804–07

Purves A C, Foshay A W, Hansson G 1973 *Literature Education in Ten Countries*. Wiley, New York

Reardon S J 1988 The development of critical readers: A look into the classroom. *New Advocate* 1(1): 52–61

Smith N, Robinson H 1980 *Reading Instruction for Today's Children*. Prentice-Hall, London

Spache G D, Spache E B 1973 *Reading in the Elementary School*, 4th edn. Allyn and Bacon, Boston, Massachusetts

Whimbey A, Carmichael J W, Jones L W, Hunter J T, Vincent H A 1980 Teaching critical reading and analytic reasoning in Project SOAR. *J. Read.* 24: 5–10

Wolf W 1969 A factor analytic study of the Ohio State University Critical Reading Tests. *J. Res. Dev. Educ.* 3: 100–09

Reading Rate and Reading Flexibility

S. J. Samuels and N. Schermer

Reading rate and reading flexibility are topics which can be discussed independently, but because the rate and flexibility issues are so closely linked, in this article, the two topics will be discussed together. Reading flexibility refers to the ability of an individual to adjust reading rate according to the difficulty of the material and the purpose for reading. Ability to alter reading rate according to text difficulty and purpose for reading is considered to be an important characteristic of the proficient reader. Consequently, instruction in reading flexibility receives considerable time and attention in courses for the development and improvement of reading skills. This article begins with a model which presents factors which influence reading rate and flexibility. Research studies which fail to find flexibility of reading rate are then reviewed and errors in the research pointed out. Finally, studies which have found flexibility in reading are described.

1. A Model of Reading Flexibility

There are three factors which should influence the rate at which an individual reads a text. These three factors are linked to each other and so the model takes on the form of a triangle. The first factor which influences flexibility is what may be called text difficulty. The second factor is purpose for reading, and the third factor is reading skill.

Common observation would lead one to believe that the difficulty of a text should influence the rate at which the text can be read. In order to understand a text which is difficult, the text has to be read slowly, whereas a text which is simple can be read quickly. Several variables can contribute to text difficulty. One of the variables which can make a text difficult to understand is the topic which may be unknown to the reader. Consequently, the reader has little background and experience to bring to the text in order to make sense of the ideas presented. Another variable which can make a text difficult is ideas which are complex. When ideas are complex, they often require longer and more syntactically difficult sentences to express them. Thus, the combination of complex ideas and sentences make the text harder to comprehend. Another element in a text which can make a text difficult to understand is lack of clarity of the writing and the inability of the writer to organize and express ideas in a manner which is easy to comprehend. To summarize the three variables which can contribute to text difficulty, they are: lack of background knowledge, complexity of concepts and the sentences needed to express them, and clarity of the writing style.

The second factor which should influence the ability of the reader to vary the rate of reading is reading skill. A skilled reader may be able to read a newspaper article on a well-known topic at the rate of 200–300 words a minute. But, if the same reader encounters a topic about which little is known, the reader will have to slow up. What is being suggested is that the skilled reader has an option to read at a variety of rates, to read at a rapid or a slow rate, depending on text familiarity and difficulty. On the other hand, the poor reader may have difficulty recognizing printed words and may have difficulty with the strategies needed to understand a text, and consequently may not have an option to read either rapidly or slowly, as the case may require. The poor reader may have to read all texts, regardless of difficulty, at the same painfully slow rate.

The third factor in the model which should influence rate of reading is one's purpose for reading. If, for example, one's purpose for reading is to prepare for an important examination where mastery of detail is required, then slow reading would probably be necessary, but, if the purpose for reading is to get a superficial overview of a topic in a text, then rapid reading may be appropriate.

2. Flexibility and Rate

Based on a number of studies which have failed to find flexibility of reading speed (Rankin and Hess 1970, Boyd 1966, Hill 1964), one might conclude that students are not flexible readers. However, studies which fail to find flexibility often have a serious error in the tests and the procedures which are used, and this error is the failure to let the student know if the purpose for reading is for detail or for general overview. Test directions which state "Read quickly but carefully" are confusing to the reader. When the student knows before reading the text how specific the test questions will be, one finds substantial and appropriate flexibility in reading rate (Miller 1978, Samuels and Dahl 1975, McConkie et al. 1973).

3. Normal Rate of Reading

How fast one should be able to read is influenced by numerous interacting factors such as reader skill, familiarity with the text topic, and purpose for reading. Thus, it is difficult to answer this question. The major bottleneck on reading speed for skilled readers is thinking time, or the time necessary to understand the text. One may take the rate of 250 words per minute as a rough estimate of the normal rate of reading for skilled readers for materials of average difficulty.

Bibliography

Boyd R 1966 Rate of comprehension in reading among sixth form pupils in New Zealand schools. *Read. Teach.* 20: 237–41

Hill W R 1964 Influence of direction upon reading flexibility of advanced college readers. In: Thurston E, Hafner L (eds.) 1964 *New Concepts in College-adult Reading, Thirteenth Yearbook of the National Reading Conference.* National Reading Conference, Milwaukee, Wisconsin

McConkie G W, Rayner K, Wilson S J 1973 Experimental manipulation of reading strategies. *J. Educ. Psychol.* 65: 1–8

Miller P A 1978 Considering flexibility of reading rate for assessment and development of efficient reading behavior.

In: Samuels S J (ed.) 1978 *What Research Has To Say About Reading Instruction.* International Reading Association, Newark, Delaware, pp. 135–64

Rankin E, Hess A K 1970 The measurement of reading flexibility. In: Schick G, May M (eds.) 1970 *Reading Process and Pedagogy.* Nineteenth Yearbook of the National Reading Conference, Milwaukee, Wisconsin

Samuels S J, Dahl P R 1975 Establishing appropriate purpose for reading and its effect on flexibility of reading rate. *J. Educ. Psychol.* 67: 38–43

Listening Comprehension

N. A. Mead

During the 1950s and early 1960s, there was a flurry of research and instructional development in the area of listening within the classroom. Since that time there has been much less activity. Devine's (1978) summary of listening research primarily restates the conclusions which were reached by earlier reviewers. Most of the research involved:

(a) defining listening, either as a unitary skill or a series of subskills;

(b) exploring the relationship between listening and other factors, primarily motivation, verbal aptitude, and reading skills;

(c) developing and evaluating listening instructional approaches;

(d) developing listening tests.

The results of listening research have not produced a single, empirically based definition of listening. Instead, a series of descriptions have emerged that have been used as a basis for listening instruction and measurement. These definitions are primarily based on a logical analysis of the listening process. Many follow established descriptions of listening comprehension.

1. A Model of Listening

The listening process includes four interrelated components: hearing, attending, comprehending, and remembering. Hearing takes place when sound waves hit the tympanic membrane of the ear. Humans are constantly barraged by all sorts of aural stimuli. Only a few of these become the focus of attention. The listener then assigns meaning to the sounds. This is the comprehending component. Finally, these meanings are stored in memory for later recall.

Lundsteen (1979) proposes a tentative hierarchy of listening skills that expands upon the general model. She uses this hierarchy as a guide for instructional activities for elementary and secondary level students, and identifies two important skills that students must obtain as prerequisites for comprehension. First, stu-

dents must be able to distinguish between hearing and listening—to discriminate incomprehensible sounds from verbal messages. Second, students must demonstrate two-way responsibility as a speaker/listener—a shift from presenting information to attending to information others are presenting. Lundsteen goes on to provide a list of comprehending skills that range from the simplest to the most complex: (a) selecting facts and details, (b) sequential ordering, (c) selecting main idea, (d) summarizing, (e) relating one idea to another, and (f) inference making. She adds a higher level to the hierarchy that she calls critical listening. This level requires more than understanding what is said and includes skills such as analyzing, interpreting, and evaluating information.

A model of listening must also take into account other, noncognitive, aspects of listening. Listening primarily involves comprehending the meaning of words. However, listening also requires interpreting nonverbal signals. Some of these signals are received aurally. For example, tone of voice, pauses, volume, rate, and accent provide additional communicative information. Nonverbal signals are also received in other ways. For example, much information is conveyed through facial expressions, gestures, and posture. Listening involves understanding both cognitive and affective meanings. The listener must comprehend what is said and also recognize the feelings behind what is said.

Wilkinson et al. (1974) propose a model of listening that takes into account cognitive, affective, situational, and cultural factors. They used this model to design a comprehensive listening test for elementary and secondary level students. First, listening involves comprehending the content of what is said. Secondly, it requires understanding additional meaning that is conveyed by the way the speaker stresses or emphasizes words; this aspect of language is referred to as phonology. Thirdly, listening involves understanding the contextual constraints of language—the basic requirements of grammar, word meanings, topic and so forth. Fourthly, listening requires knowing the appropriateness of language for a given situation; this aspect of language is referred to as register. Finally, listening involves recognizing the roles and relationships of the speakers from the language they use.

2. Relationships between Listening and Other Psychological Factors

Several psychological factors influence the listening process: motivation, attitudes, and other verbal abilities. Attending to a message is a prerequisite for comprehending it, and attention is influenced by the motivation and interest level of the listener. In listening, the distinction between competence and performance is very important. A person may be fully capable of understanding a spoken message. However, in many cases the person may not find the message relevant and may ignore the message.

Also, comprehending happens within the listener and is highly dependent upon the attitudes of the listener. A listener sometimes selects only those messages that he or she wishes to hear and/or interprets messages in terms of his or her preconceived notions. Research indicates that good listeners are likely to be less dogmatic and more open to new ideas.

The relationship between listening and other verbal abilities has been well-established. The research has substantiated relatively high positive correlations between listening and intelligence and verbal aptitude. Likewise, the relationship between listening and reading has been well-established. In fact, evidence indicates that tests of listening correlate as well with tests of verbal aptitude and reading skills as they do with one another (Kelly 1965). However, Spearitt (1962), in a factor analysis of 34 tests given to 300 sixth grade pupils (age 11–12) was able to identify a separate "listening comprehension" factor.

3. Listening and Other Language Skills

Even though the research does not clearly identify listening as a separate trait, listening can be identified as a skill that develops separately and contributes to the development of other language skills. Stitch et al. (1974) have developed a model of communication skills development which describes the progressive acquisition of oral and written skills. They first identify basic capacities of hearing, seeing, and motor movements. These develop into the skills of listening, looking, uttering, and marking. Comprehending meaningful speech and producing meaningful utterances—listening and speaking—come next. Lastly, reading and writing skills develop.

The school experience supports an integrated model of language skills development which capitalizes on the similarities of listening, speaking, reading, and writing and the sequential acquisition of these skills. When children enter school they are placed in an environment that is dominated by oral communication. Students receive much of their instruction through listening and are often asked to demonstrate their understanding of that input by speaking. Later, listening and speaking are used to facilitate the development of reading and writing skills.

Listening is perhaps most closely linked to reading. Both are receptive skills and have as a common goal comprehending meaning. Reading is more difficult than listening, because it is a two level process that requires understanding graphic symbols that stand for phonetic symbols. In the instructional setting, listening can be used to build vocabulary and to teach sound–symbol relationships and thus can facilitate learning to read. Later, listening can be used to teach higher level intellectual skills, such as those indicated by Lundsteen as critical listening skills. A natural progression would be to teach these higher level skills in the listening context before they are introduced in the context of reading and writing.

Listening and speaking are both oral communication skills; the former is a receptive activity and the latter a productive activity. Usually listening and speaking take place in face-to-face situations and are interactive activities. The individual acts both as listener and speaker with other speaker/listeners. Thus, in the instructional setting, both listening and speaking skills development can be enhanced by integrating the two activities. Also, since listening is a receptive skill, listening activities can be used in the classroom as stimuli for speaking and writing production.

Perhaps listening is least like writing—the former is oral and receptive and the latter is written and productive—and yet even these two skills are related. Research has shown that deaf children, who do not have the benefit of an oral environment, do not develop the style, variety, and more sophisticated structures in their writing that hearing children do. In elementary classrooms, listening activities are often used as stimuli for writing. Also, at higher levels, teachers have found that asking students to think about listening and speaking experiences can provide students with a source for vivid auditory images for their writing.

4. Evaluation of Listening Instruction

Experience indicates that listening plays an important and logical role in language arts instruction. However, research related to the effectiveness of focused listening instruction is less clear. Weaver (1972), in a review of evaluations of listening instruction programs, found that significant gains were identified in about half of the programs; but no gains were identified in the other half. However, inspection of the contents of the programs indicated that they differed greatly in terms of the skills they cover. Furthermore, it appears that the effectiveness of the programs depended to some extent upon the match of the instructional objectives and the evaluation instruments.

Assessment of listening skills is first and foremost hampered by a difference of opinion about what listening is. Nevertheless, any evaluation of listening skills should take into account the unique aspects of listening that have already been identified and agreed upon. The qualities of spoken language are different from those of written language. Typically, speaking is less organized, less complete, and more redundant than writing. Therefore, it is important that a listening assessment requires students to listen to natural spoken language rather than written language that has been presented orally. It is less obvious how to deal with the nonverbal and interactive nature of listening in an assessment situation. It is possible to use audiotapes or videotapes that include nonverbal information. However, nonverbal signals tend to be subtle and individualistic and thus difficult to include in an assessment. It is possible to assess students in live, face-to-face situations. However, it is difficult to sort out failures in the listener from failures in the speaker.

Other technical concerns should also be considered in the assessment of listening skills. Since motivation and interest play an important part in the listening process, it is important that listening tests provide, to the extent feasible, interesting material that listeners will find to be relevant listening tasks. Also, as in reading assessment, consideration must be given to the background and experience of the students. Tests must be constructed that do not give an advantage or disadvantage to any particular subpopulation.

In summary, most researchers follow a general model of listening that includes hearing, attending, comprehending, and remembering. However, researchers do not agree upon the specific subskills involved in listening. Listening is related to motivation, attitudes, and verbal ability and is also closely tied to the other language skills: reading, speaking, and writing. There are numerous possibilities for integrating listening into the language arts curriculum. However, possibly because of failure in evaluation methodologies, the effectiveness of focused listening instruction has not been conclusively determined.

Bibliography

Barker L L 1971 *Listening Behavior*. Prentice-Hall, Englewood Cliffs, New Jersey
Devine T G 1978 Listening: What do we know after fifty years of research and theorizing? *J. Read.* 21: 296–304
Kelly C M 1965 An investigation of construct validity of two commercially published listening tests. *Speech Monogr.* 32: 139–43
Lundsteen S W 1979 *Listening: Its Impact on Reading and the Other Language Arts*. National Council of Teachers of English, Urbana, Illinois
Spearitt D 1962 *Listening Comprehension—A Factorial Analysis*. Australian Council for Educational Research, Series No. 76, Melbourne
Sticht T G, Beck L, Hauke R H, Kleiman G M, James J H 1974 *Auding and Reading: A Developmental Model*. Human Resource Research Organization, Arlington, Virginia
Weaver C H 1972 *Human Listening: Processes and Behavior*. Bobbs-Merrill, Indianapolis, Indiana
Wilkinson A M, Stratta L, Dudley P 1974 *The Quality of Listening*. Macmillan, Basingstoke

Speech Instruction

W. J. Crocker

Most human beings learn, through experience and some informal instruction, to speak and listen well-enough to meet their normal needs for communication. As Dell Hymes said:

> [The child] acquires competence as to when to speak, when not, and as to what to talk about with whom, when, where, and in what manner. In short, a child becomes able to accomplish a repertoire of speech acts, to take part in speech events, and to evaluate their accomplishment by others. (Hymes 1972 p. 271)

Though most people learn to do these things, there are obvious social, vocational, and recreational advantages to be gained from learning to do them well. The teaching of speech is concerned with systematically helping people to develop their abilities in oral communication.

There have been professional teachers of speech for many centuries. At different periods they have defined effectiveness in communication in different ways and concentrated on different kinds of speech acts.

1. Historical Background

The first speech teacher on record was a Greek named Corax who ran a school of public speaking in Sicily about 466 BC. Corax wrote a treatise on the art of rhetoric in which he pointed out that effectiveness in speaking depended not merely on innate ability but on the application of certain principles that were teachable and learnable. He was not the first to point this out. Advice on how to speak effectively went back at least to the precepts of Kagemni and Ptah-Hotep found on Egyptian papyri roughly dated 2900 BC. But Corax organized his principles into a system which became a subject for disciplined study.

1.1 Teaching Rhetoric

The major concern of rhetoricians is the study of formal speech acts such as political speeches, forensic argument, and sermons. They see effective communication as a process of eliciting desired responses.

From the time of Aristotle, rhetoric was organized into five broad divisions, now called invention (dealing with purposes, issues, and persuasive appeals), disposition (structure or organization), style (choice of language), memory (recall of ideas and organization), and delivery (vocal and visual aspects of presentation). Successive generations of scholars have refined, modified, or extended rhetorical principles, except that memory is rarely included in any modern rhetorical system. In the twentieth century, many rhetorical principles have been subjected to experimental investigation and modified where appropriate.

Speech teachers who follow the rhetorical approach guide their students to discover (through experience in giving speeches, which are critically analysed, and through the analysis of other people's speeches) principles which help them to develop their own skills. The knowledge and skills which the student learns are directly applicable to such activities as teaching, mass communication, and advertising. Moreover, the student acquires a general ability to analyse issues and to present views persuasively in any situation.

1.2 Teaching Techniques

During the eighteenth and nineteenth centuries there was considerable interest in speech as an art form. Throughout all English-speaking countries, famous preachers and platform speakers drew great crowds. Public readings and recitations were very popular. (This fashion was paralleled in the Arab world by Khataba and Zajal.) The skills involved were closely related to those of the actor. Consequently, speech teaching concentrated on the skills of delivery and, to some extent, of style.

The techniques approach to speech teaching is more concerned with skills than with ideas or with general principles. Effectiveness is seen as presenting messages clearly, accurately, and attractively. The usual teaching procedure is:

(a) the technique is explained and studied;

(b) the student practises the technique;

(c) the teacher gives constructive criticism of the performance;

(d) these three steps are repeated until mastery has been achieved.

This approach has sometimes led to absurd practices. Nevertheless, it remains popular because, when competently used, it does meet specific needs. For example, in many language communities there is a high status dialect which has economic and social advantages. People wishing to learn the high status dialect go to a teacher of speech techniques. In some countries, a "standard" dialect is taught in schools and the techniques specialist advises and trains the teachers. This method can help with many vocational skills, such as acting, preaching, radio announcing, chairing meetings, counselling, storytelling, and so on.

Some people have markedly defective speech caused by faulty articulation, poor voice production, stuttering, cerebral dysfunction, and so on. To meet the needs of such people, speech trainers have combined with linguists and physicians to produce speech therapy which since the early 1930s has become a quite separate and rapidly growing branch of speech education.

1.3 Teaching Interpersonal Interaction

Around the early 1960s, several books were published which synthesized a great deal of research on the nature of the communication process. These books had a considerable impact on speech departments in American universities and resulted in a deluge of articles and books questioning established speech teaching practices and describing new courses. All this ferment culminated in the New Orleans Conference on Research and Instructional Development as a result of which the Speech Association of America changed its name to the Speech Communication Association and established the interactional approach as the new orthodoxy for speech education in America.

Teachers following this approach regard communication as a process of reciprocal creation of meaning and effectiveness, maximizing the satisfactions of all interactants in a communication situation. Through simulation, introspection, games, and observation, teachers explore with their students the nature of the communication process. They test their conclusions against the research evidence.

Some speech teachers following this approach believe that their task is solely to lead their students to understanding. Most, however, accept that they should also help their students to acquire some skills. The skills that are emphasized in this approach are quite different from those which are central in the techniques approach. Here the teacher is concerned that students should develop, for example, the ability to reject a person's behavior without rejecting the person, the ability to take account of a total situation (e.g., with regard to degree of formality, time of day, others' perceptions), the ability to recognize role relationships, and the ability to recognize nonverbal cues. Students develop an enhanced sense of responsibility and self-worth.

Developing oral communication competence in this way can have obvious vocational benefits. Most teachers, however, stress general relational values.

2. Current Practice

The approaches to speech teaching which have been described may be found, singly or in combination, in schools and other educational institutions.

2.1 In Schools

Speech education received scant attention in schools in the past. The work of Piaget, Vygotsky, Luria, Bernstein, and others, however, made educationists aware of the relationship between speech competence and learning. Other writers pointed out the social, vocational, and psychological importance of speech skills. Consequently, in the 1960s and 1970s, increasing emphasis was given to speech in language curricula in many places from the laroplaner for Swedish in Sweden to the English syllabi in the Australian states. The United States Congress, in 1978, amended the Elementary and Secondary Education Act and included "effective communication both written and oral" among the basic skills which must be taught in American schools. Some indication of British attitudes can be seen in the "Manifesto for Change" published in the *Times Educational Supplement* (30 January 1981 p. 18) which states that "the school system fails young people by its absorption with the written word. In modern society, oral fluency is of even greater importance because communication is increasingly oral".

There seems to be worldwide agreement now that it is a responsibility of schools to help each child to develop to the utmost his or her ability in oral communication. Furthermore, it is recognized that the most important contribution the school can make towards the achievement of this aim is to provide children with a wide variety of satisfying and successful experiences of communication. These experiences should arise out of the child's interests rather than be imposed by the teacher.

As the Bullock Report pointed out, however: "A stimulating classroom environment will not necessarily of itself develop the children's ability—The teacher has a vital part to play and his role should be one of planned intervention" (Bullock 1975 p. 526). A teacher can intervene by giving students opportunities to experience as many kinds of speech in as many situations as possible and by helping them evaluate their own effectiveness. A teacher can also teach some rhetorical principles, some speech techniques, and some interactional skills (as described above) appropriate to the needs of students. Finally, individual guidance can be given to students with defective speech or with outstanding talent.

Research into the teaching of speech in schools is proceeding in many places. In the United States a National Project on Speech Communication Competencies (Allen and Brown 1976) summarized research, defined communication in functional terms, and suggested instructional goals. The report identified four categories of communication functions (controlling, informing, ritualizing, and imagining) and competencies needed for each. This report has influenced work done by the Speech Communication Association and the National Institute of Education, Washington (Lieb-Brilhart 1980). Speech teaching seems likely to become, very slowly, more purposeful and systematic.

2.2 Other Educational Settings

People with or without formal qualifications can set themselves up as teachers of speech and charge what-

ever fees they care to. People in all parts of the world attract private pupils who may wish to change their dialect, modify their accent, become effective platform speakers, acquire a vocational skill, or practise the speech arts such as *nachgestaltendes Sprechen* (interpretative speaking of verse and prose). There is a growing demand from business and corporations for communication consultants. Independent teachers are also employed by organizations such as the Workers' Educational Association in Britain and *Arbetarnas Bildningsforbund* in Sweden which organize adult study groups.

In the United Kingdom, independent teachers set up examining bodies such as Trinity College London and the London Guilds to award teacher qualifications and maintain standards. These bodies tended to stress correctness and artistic delivery but now they (especially the English Speaking Board) are more functional in their approach. Similar examining bodies have been established in other parts of the world. Some (such as *Suomen Puheopista* in Finland and the Australian Music Examination Board) work in association with universities.

In the United States, most universities and colleges have a department of speech communication. These prepare teachers but also offer courses in such areas as interpersonal and small group communication, business communication, radio and television, public address, oral interpretation, and speech sciences. Elsewhere, university courses in speech have been rare, except for work in phonetics and speech science, but they are slowly becoming more widespread (Casmir and Harms 1970).

Vocational speech skills, as noted above, are taught in colleges of technical or further education in many parts of the world. Speech pathology and audiology (or logopedics) are usually taught partly in universities or colleges and partly in speech clinics.

3. Future Trends

The establishment of speech communication courses in universities in various parts of the world will augment the large amount of research which has been, and is being done in the United States. One area of investigation is into the nature of the communication process with investigators proceeding from a constructivist, neomarxist, semiotic, or other perspective. Other researchers are clarifying factors influencing effectiveness in communication and still others are applying theory to specific contexts such as intercultural communication, communication in organizations, and instructional communication. In education, the trend seems to be to try to define communication competence in terms of particular skills for different ages and to discover the best methods of teaching them. There are a number of specific educational concerns such as assessment, sequential programming, and the treatment of communication apprehension.

The growth of organizations such as the International Communication Association and the Communication Association of the Pacific (especially in Japan and Korea), and the formation of new national groups such as the Australian Communication Association (1979) are indicators of a growing demand for speech teachers throughout the world.

Bibliography

Allen R R, Brown K L (eds.) 1976 *Developing Communication Competence in Children*. National Textbook Company, Skokie, Illinois

Bullock A (chairman) 1975 *A Language for Life*. Report of the Committee of Inquiry appointed by the Secretary of State for Education and Science. Her Majesty's Stationery Office, London

Casmir F, Harms L S (eds.) 1970 *International Studies of National Speech Education Systems*. Burgess, Minneapolis, Minnesota

Friedrich G W (ed.) 1980 *Education in the Eighties: Speech Communication*. National Education Association, Washington, DC

Hymes D H 1972 On communicative competence. In: Pride J B, Holmes J (eds.) 1972 *Sociolinguistics: Selected Readings*. Penguin, Harmondsworth

Lieb-Brilhart B 1980 Oral communication instruction in the USA. In: Crocker W J (ed.) 1980 *Developing Oral Communication Competence*. University of New England, Armidale, New South Wales

Composition Instruction

A. C. Purves

Instruction in composition is one of the oldest aspects of education in most societies. This article will briefly survey the history of the teaching of composition, and examine current methodologies and issues.

Instruction in composition first dealt with oral composition, particularly in Greece, Rome, and medieval Europe, as well as in China and India, where written composition or the training of scribes played an important part in schooling. In the West, composition was dominated by the principles of Aristotle and later rhetoricians such as Quintilian, Longinus, Cicero, and Seneca. With the advent of the printing press, instruction turned to written composition, which became fully established in the curriculum by the eighteenth century. Throughout its history, instruction in composition has been an area of controversy, the main bone of contention being the relative importance of content and form, and the pedagogical consequence of dealing with the student's ideas and reasoning, or with correctness and elegance of expression. Many rhetoricians dealt with what was called invention or the gathering and arranging of ideas; others focused on disposition or the ordering of words, phrases, and sentences; still others with elocution, which covered oral presentation. Elocution has dropped out of the controversy with the dominance of print, but the relative importance of invention and disposition has remained controversial.

In current discussion, the terms have changed somewhat and the pedagogical issue is whether the focus should be on what is called prewriting or on revision and editing. Instruction in writing generally treats prewriting, composition, revising, and editing as the major stages in the process of composition. Prewriting includes all those activities that take place before the student actually sits down to write the first draft of a composition; composing includes all the activities related to the production of a draft; revising, the activities in reordering or modifying a composition between first and final draft; and editing, the activities in the production of a final copy.

1. Prewriting

Currently, prewriting is seen as being almost synonymous with invention, being the act of discovery of what is to be said and the ways by which it might be organized and displayed. Prewriting generally refers to mental acts, although it may refer to such activities as discussion, outlining, and note making. A number of pedagogical approaches have been advanced, the most classical being the discussion of arguments and strategies of argument as well as logical analysis of the topic. Alternative models of topic analysis include problem solving, dramatism, and tagmemics (Young, in Tate 1976). Each approach suggests that, once given the assignment, students together with a teacher or separately should analyze the assignment in terms of the content, purposes, and audience of the composition. The different approaches, however, stress one of the three aspects of an assignment more than another. Some, such as the problem-solving approach, stress originality over conventional or appropriate ways of handling the assignment. Some also emphasize the role of the writer and the personal involvement of the writer in the assignment as opposed to the analysis of the audience and what will interest the reader. Most of these approaches suggest that much work should be done before writing begins. Recently, however, it has been suggested that invention occurs within the act of writing, and that students should not think first but should engage in what is known as free writing, the act of putting pen to paper in order to let the ideas about the topic form during the actual writing. Then what has been drafted should be analyzed and revised in order to produce a finished product (Macrorie 1970, Elbow is supported in part by the work of Britton et al. (1975), in their discussion of the importance of "expressive" writing, particularly for younger children. "Expressive" writing is defined as writing in which the writer seeks to explore his or her own ideas about a topic with little regard to others as an audience. If a teacher stresses expressive writing, he or she will spend less time on analytic strategies and more time on having the student make language flow on paper.

2. Composing

In the 1970s there has emerged a large corpus of study of students of various ages as they are engaged in writing a composition (Emig 1971, Graves 1975, Britton 1975, Flower and Hayes 1979, Lindell 1974). Most of these studies have either interrupted the composer in the act of writing or have transcribed the composer's comments while writing. A few studies have timed the act of composing. The results of these studies indicate that the composing process is complex and that prewriting and revision are not necessarily separated in sequence from the actual writing. They also indicate that the writer is simultaneously concerned with the content (what is said) and the form or style (how it is said) in the composition. There is also little information on the role of intervention by the teacher in the act of writing. One study (Zoellner 1969) indicated that writing improves if there is feedback during the course of writing rather than after it, but the pedagogical means of providing that feedback have not been developed. In most cases, instruction focuses on prewriting and revision.

3. Revising and Editing

It is in these two areas that much of the direct instruction in writing takes place. The instruction usually focuses on one of two aspects of the text: development and organization of ideas; or style, form, and mechanics. In general, the process of instruction is for the teacher or another student to make comments on one of these two aspects of the text and for the student to then make appropriate changes. In addition, however, in many countries there is instruction and practice dealing with one or both of the aspects separate from the writing of a complete composition. Instruction may, for instance, deal with the analysis of classical texts in order to discern their organization and development followed by imitation of the patterns found. Instruction may also involve the practice of paragraph structures or essay structures following a particular format (cause–effect, classification, narration, and the like). In many countries, moreover, a great deal of instructional time is spent on sentence practice, grammar, syntax, punctuation, and spelling or vocabulary development. Some of this study may involve the learning of rules and the correcting of poor or incorrect sentences. In the United States since the early 1970s, much of the practice involves "sentence combining," a strategy derived from transformational grammar, in which students take a series of unconnected single sentences and rewrite them as a complex sentence.

John had a ball.
The ball was red.
The ball was big.
John had a big red ball.

Recent research has shown that practice in sentence combining, with or without grammatical instruction, increases the stylistic maturity of many students and also increases the scores they receive on tests of composition (O'Hare 1973). The extent to which sentence combining is practiced in other languages is unclear, but informal reports indicate that similar kinds of activities are relatively widespread.

The effectiveness of instruction in grammar separated from the actual writing, revision, and editing of student compositions has been questioned in many countries, and the most recent study (Elley et al. 1976) indicates that such instruction has little effect on writing performance; in fact, there appeared to be little change in performance over three years of instruction of various sorts.

4. Approaches to the Teaching of Writing

At the present time, there is little consensus on how the various approaches to the teaching of writing might be described. Broadly speaking, the approaches appear to fall into a heritage model, using classical texts and imitation; a competence model, using analysis and emphasizing correctness; and a process model, using free expression and emphasizing growth (Mandel 1980). More specifically tied to methodology and composition, there appear to be five dominant approaches:

(a) fixed product: an approach that aims at teaching a select number of specific types of writing (e.g., the business letter or the academic essay) and that emphasizes correct forms, structures, and language;

(b) variable product: an approach that aims at teaching a variety of different forms and types of composition dependent on audience and task, and that emphasizes appropriate structures, forms, and language;

(c) phase instruction: an approach that emphasizes the various stages of writing (prewriting, writing, and revision), and that aims at developing security in the process;

(d) content instruction: an approach that aims at writing skill indirectly, and that emphasizes the learning of appropriate discourse about a subject (e.g., literature or history);

(e) knowledge instruction: an approach that emphasizes the teaching of information about language and writing and aims at correct use of structures, forms, and language through the acquisition of such knowledge.

Each of the five approaches has a relatively long history and each has a number of advocates in many countries around the world. In practice, teachers do not use a single approach exclusively (most teachers are eclectic and pragmatic), yet it appears that one or another of these approaches tends to dominate the thinking of a particular teacher. Each approach clearly bears implications for what would go on in class, what sort of assignment for a composition is made, and what sort of feedback would be given. Until recently, research has been relatively silent on which of these approaches is most effective, in part because effectiveness must be seen in terms of the criterion for good writing that would be used and the type of student being taught (e.g., whether they are native or nonnative speakers of the language, their age, and their degree of motivation).

5. Research in Cognitive Approaches to Writing

Beginning in the late 1970s a number of cognitive psychologists began to turn their attention to composition. To a certain extent their work supports much of what has been said earlier, but they have complemented the work by rhetoricians by studying closely the process of composition and seeking to establish a hierarchical framework that might be pedagogically useful. First of all, they have tended to treat writing and development in writing as distinct from speech and general language development. Written language in most language systems has its own conventions and purpose separate from spoken language. Written language posits a different relationship between writer and reader than that between speaker and listener. It may, in fact, be supported by a different kind of thought than that associated with spoken language (Dillon 1981, Applebee and Langer 1987).

One researcher (Bereiter 1980) suggests that the writer must put into operation a number of schemes in order to write: a general executive scheme, a genre scheme that selects the general structure of writing (a letter rather than an essay), a content processing scheme, and a language processing scheme. Each of these schemes has a number of subschemes. As the writer gains experience the repertoire expands. Bereiter suggests in Fig. 1 a general developmental pattern as the individual moves from speech to writing, and on through various stages of writing in each of which stages a new cognitive dimension is added. He suggests that schools focus primarily on performative and communicative writing, with unified and epistemic writing being the desired outcomes. He also suggests that research needs to address itself less to the normal outcomes of schooling and more to the possible gains that schooling could effect.

Cognitive research in writing has examined various aspects of the prewriting stage and the application of various heuristics. It has also focused on the revising and editing phases and the various strategies and demands that are involved. The research has also investigated the effects of teaching what Scardamalia and Bereiter (1981) call "procedural facilitators." These can range from such simple strategies as asking the writer to "say more" to presenting the writer with complex models of syntactic patterns to imitate in the revision. Generally, the results of using these facilitators showed increases in length and quality of the writing. This research suggests that instruction in part focuses on the actual text and in part on various mental representations of the text (from graphical representations to plans for a whole text), so that not only is the immediate task affected, but the student is able to use the representation in the next task.

The studies carried out by Bereiter and his associates have shown that young beginning writers (from age 11 onward) can be helped to plan and evaluate their compositions if they are provided with procedural facilitation. This is a method in which children's potential is utilized by assisting them in rhetorical decisions by means of procedural cues while no hints as to content are given. The Bereiter group has also shown that the

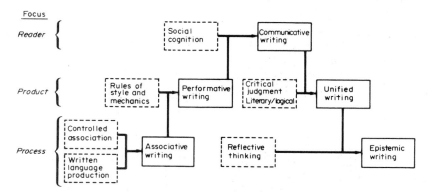

Figure 1
A model of skill systems integration in writing development

slower speed and mechanical constraints associated with writing are largely responsible for the relative shortness of written compositions and this in turn is largely responsible for the low judged quality of compositions. When students are prompted to write more, they often can double or triple the quantity of compositions, which tend to be judged better than dictated texts. It is assumed that in writing, students have to make a greater cognitive effort in constructing or reconstructing mental representations of the text at higher levels than in dictation and this ultimately pays off. It is assumed that this extra cognitive effort helps students, after being prompted, in producing new language strings which are coherent, whereas in simple dictation exercises where the child talks to the teacher scribe, the new strings are often less coherent.

This line of research clearly suggests the efficacy of an approach that combines phase instruction with variable product instruction. The research is beginning to establish that instruction in general procedures rather than strict rules has an effect on student performance. At this point, however, the procedures are only being defined and the instructional technique needs fuller development before it can be tested against other approaches to instruction.

6. The Use of Computers in Instruction

A recent development in the teaching of composition has come with the use of the computer, particularly the word-processing computer. In the 1960s there were some experiments with programmed instruction in writing and with computer-assisted instruction. Most of these early lessons dealt with grammar, usage, and mechanics. Attempts to deal with more complex issues of rhetoric were not successful. The advent of the word processor, however, with its ability to store a text and with its various editing capabilities, is beginning to affect writing instruction in some countries. Work in this sort of instruction is just beginning, but one can see that the computer can be used as a tool for both phase instruction and variable product instruction, and has the potential for strengthening the cognitive approach to writing instruction.

Until recently there had been predictions that writing was going to disappear amidst the new technologies.

The new technology now suggests that writing will stay, but that the teaching of writing may indeed have to be transformed, and transformed along lines set forth by the cognitive researchers.

Bibliography

Applebee A, Langer J 1987 *How Writing Shapes Thinking.* NCTE, Urbana, Illinois
Bereiter C 1980 Development in writing. In: Gregg L W, Steinberg E R (eds.) 1980 *Cognitive Processes in Writing.* Erlbaum, Hillsdale, New Jersey
Britton J, Burgess T, Martin N, McLeod A, Rosen H 1975 *The Development of Writing Abilities* (11–18). Schools Council on written language of 11–18 year olds. Macmillan, London
Dillon G L 1981 *Constructing Texts: Elements of a Theory of Composition and Style.* Indiana University Press, Bloomington, Indiana
Elbow P 1973 *Writing Without Teachers.* Oxford University Press, New York
Elley W B, Barham J H, Lamb H, Wylie M 1976 The role of grammar in a secondary school English curriculum. *Res. Teach. Engl.* 10: 5–21
Emig J 1971 *The Composing Processes of Twelfth Graders.* National Council of Teachers of English (NCTE) Research Report No. 13. NCTE, Urbana, Illinois
Flower L, Hayes J R 1979 *A Process Model of Composition.* Carnegie-Mellon University, Pittsburgh, Pennsylvania
Graves D H 1975 An examination of the writing process of seven-year old children. *Res. Teach. Engl.* 9: 227–41
Lindell E 1974 Vad menas med bra sprok?: Några del resultat från? [What is meant by good education?]. Projekt FRIS. Pedagogisk-psykologiska problem, No. 251. School of Education, Malmö
Macrorie K 1970 *Telling Writing.* Hayden, New York
Mandel B 1980 *Three Language-Arts Curriculum Models: Pre-Kindergarten Through College.* National Council of Teachers of English, Urbana, Illinois
O'Hare F 1973 *Sentence Combining: Improving Student Writing Without Formal Grammar Instruction.* National Council of Teachers of English, Urbana, Illinois
Scardamalia M, Bereiter C 1981 From conversation to composition: the role of instruction in a developmental process. In: Glaser R (ed.) 1980 *Advances in Instructional Psychology,* Vol. 2. Erlbaum, Hillsdale, New Jersey
Tate G (ed.) 1976 *Teaching Composition: 10 Bibliographical Essays.* Texas Christian University Press, Fort Worth, Texas
Zoellner R 1969 A behavioral pedagogy for composition. *College Engl.* 30: 267–320

Spelling Instruction

M. L. Peters

Spelling instruction has long reflected ideological conflicts in education in the continuing incidental/systematic controversy, that is to say in the debate as to whether spelling is caught or taught.

In support of "incidental" teaching the practice of reading has long been assumed to determine good spelling. Those who support "systematic" teaching have mainly concerned themselves with list making and list learning. They have also paid much attention to the rules of spelling.

In the light of the "visual" nature of spelling, and in the context of psycholinguistic studies since the late

1960s, spelling has been seen in terms of the serial probability of letters within words, and the generalizing of the most common letter sequences.

"Creative" and "inventive" spelling exploits children's knowledge of letter-strings, as does carefully programmed computerized spelling. As research into children's writing has become less "text based" and more "writer based", concern with spelling as a support system ensures the place of spelling in the curriculum.

1. The Incidental/Systematic Controversy

As early as 1897, when the teaching of spelling was a universal practice, the possibilities of its being "caught" were beginning to be considered. Rice, in that year, wrote an article called, "*The Futility of the Spelling Grind*", and this was followed by, for example, Cornman (1902) criticizing the systematic teaching of spelling and suggesting, with statistical evidence, that spelling could be approached through other activities such as written work and reading. Though the possibility of spelling being "caught" rather than "taught" was challenged soon after by Wallin (1910) with further statistical evidence in favour of the "taught" rather than "caught" school, the controversy had come to stay, simmering in the United States, but not boiling until the second quarter of the century with Grace Fernald, who in *Remedial Techniques in the Basic School Subjects* (1943 p. 206) emphasized that "the most satisfactory spelling vocabulary is that supplied by the child himself" in the course of his own expression. Kyte (1948) supported this view with reservations, advocating the withdrawal of good spellers from formal spelling lessons. Even these, he said, would need to be regularly tested, to ensure that they maintained their competence.

Meanwhile, in 1941 in England, Nisbet pointed out that children are likely to "catch" only one new word out of every 25 they read. With older people who are unsophisticated readers, this may also be true, but with serious, slower, more focused readers such as students, the gain in spelling ability from mere reading could be expected to be greater, particularly in more technical words that may be new to the student, who might pick up the spelling from the significant etymology of the word. Some years before this, Gilbert (1935) had found that college students' spelling certainly improved as they read, the extent of the improvement depending on the type of reading and the reader's purpose. Words that had been recently brought to their attention were "caught" more effectively than words encountered more remotely, and good spellers learned more words than poor spellers.

It is clear then that the more competent the reader, the greater resources for spelling reference. As Mackay et al. (1978) point out "The fluent reader has an internalized model of the orthography, although he is unlikely to be able to say what this model looks like". But this is not to say that the model provides a sufficient condition for spelling competence. The model may be internalized, without the strategies for utilizing this being exploited. So good reading ability is not enough to ensure good spelling. The role of incidental learning had become respectable.

"Incidental learning is indirect learning", wrote Hildreth (1956 p. 33), "which takes place when the learner's attention is centred not in improving the skill in question, but on some other objective . . . " and she qualified this a moment later with, "Teachers should not think of incidental learning and integrated teaching as excluding systematic well-organized drill. Rather from the child's attempts to write will come evidence of his need for systematic word study." So not only may spelling be "caught", but the need to learn to spell also. Incidental and systematic teaching are thus mutually supportive and interactive.

2. Spelling Strategies

2.1 List Learning

To return to "systematic" teaching of spelling, stressed as important by, for example, Smith (1975), this has concerned itself mainly with the compiling and teaching of lists, lists of words which are often remote from and irrelevant to a child's world and what he or she wants to write about that world. As Fernald (1943 p. 210) wrote, "formal word lists will always fail to supply the particular word a person should learn at a particular time".

If the teaching of spelling depends on fulfilling the felt need of a child to spell a word, there must be a safe resource from which the child can obtain the word he or she wants to write, and an efficient and economical strategy by which he or she can learn that word when it has been provided. So lists of words are valuable only if they are derived from words asked for by the child.

2.2 Rule Learning

Again, those who support the "systematic" approach have paid much attention to teaching spelling through rules. But it is now generally agreed that using spelling rules in school is unproductive since the rules frequently include concepts not yet acquired developmentally and are unreliable since rules ignore exceptions, are often misleading and are not exploited outside the rule-learning situation, that is, in the child's "free writing" (McLeod 1961, Vallins 1965). Sloboda (1980) doubts if the achievement of good spellers does indeed stem from rules.

3. The Visual Factor

The most important factor in the teaching of spelling is now considered to be the visual factor (Simon 1976). It is common practice for adults to practise visual checking, that is, to write down possible spellings for a word when in doubt, to "see if it looks right", and the success of this practice is demonstrated by Tenney (1980). Such visual checking depends on an extensive experience of the serial probability of letters within words. For it is what Beers (1980 p. 43), looking at spelling developmentally within a cognitive framework, speaks of as "being continually exposed to written words and their similar letter combinations with different pronunciations" that brings about awareness of stability in the visual presentation of spellings. It is accepted that a word that has been written is probably correct if it conforms to a close approximation to English, that is, if there are precedents for such spelling in a person's own language, for spelling is language-specific. It is known that the serial probabilities of letters in a first language are better known than the serial probabilities of letters in an unknown or unfamiliar language.

In the teaching of spelling, therefore, it is important to make children aware of high-frequency letter-strings and words already in their own vocabulary in which these letter-strings occur. For spelling, a system of systems, has been defined as "a kind of grammar for letter sequences that generates permissible combinations without regard to sound" (Gibson et al. 1962).

If spelling is dependent upon a "kind of looking" (Hartmann 1931) (which is not at all the same as acuity of vision) it depends on looking with "interest, intent, and intention to reproduce a word" (Peters 1970) and the reproduction is obviously in writing. Schonell (1942 p. 277) emphasized that in learning to spell a word the "visual, auditory, and articulatory elements must be *firmly cemented in writing,*" and this implies well-formed legible handwriting.

4. Imagery

Another teaching strategy employed with various refinements is teaching by imagery. Now Sloboda demonstrates that though visual imagery seems unlikely to be at the root of good spellers' success, it is task-dependent and supports other strategies. Thus Fernald (1943) exploits imagery in the child's finger-tracing of a word with concurrent tactile, visual, articulatory, and auditory inroads. Such a strategy directs the child's attention to letter sequences and word structure, which is obviously crucial to the teaching of spelling.

Furthermore, in order to exploit the visuo–motor nature of the spelling skill it is important to teach children, as Fernald does, to look carefully at words and to write them without copying, for it is this strategy that helps the child to generalize from common letter sequences to new and previously unknown spellings.

5. Generalization

Gibson and Levin (1975) consider that learning to generalize must be something a child learns on his or her own. But learning to generalize can be built into the strategy for learning, as teachers point out to children,

and encourage them to note and explore the occurrence of letter strings in different words.

Such familiarity with letter-strings, as has been seen, does not come from reading, since in reading a person does not look at every word as they read, reading being predictive rather than reactive. Yet it is as Frith (1980a p. 505) says "by looking at written or printed words carefully—that is their letter-by-letter sequences—we gain incidental knowledge of the orthographic peculiarities of the different underlying systems". It is this looking carefully at the structure of a word that makes for successful generalization, and this is what makes a good speller. "Creative" and "inventive" spelling, at the prespelling stage exploits and eventually cultivates children's knowledge of letter-strings (Read 1971, Chomsky 1970). It is from studies of such "invented" spellings (a more positive alternative to the traditional concept of spelling errors) that Henderson (1980) demonstrates the systematic, though gradual development of children's knowledge of word structure, how they move away from the idea that pronunciation is the major control in English spelling. And it is looking carefully at letter-by-letter sequences that can be exploited successfully in computer-assisted learning, if, in learning-to-spell-programmes, the child, having typed a word incorrectly, is instructed to look carefully before retyping without copying.

6. Word Structure Without Regard to Sound

Unlike "phonics for reading", learning to spell depends on looking carefully at words containing the same letter sequences without regard to sound, for example, in phonics for reading, "bone" would be taught with words like "stone", "alone", "throne", and so on, but in spelling this would be extended to include words like "one", "done", "none", and "gone". For it is using word-groupings of this nature that children are given the opportunity of associating an unknown word with one they already know, for example, "shoulder" is a relatively easy word to write if associated with "should" (see *Phonics: Reading Instruction*).

7. Lexical Spelling

What also makes for good spelling is the use of subtle regularities at a deeper linguistic level. Chomsky (1970) has shown that uncertainty about a spelling can be resolved by relating words lexically, thus "medicine" can be related to "medical", "sign" to "signal", "national" to "nation" but this only helps in certain specific lexical relationships and is not infallible (Marsh et al. 1980, Simon and Simon 1973).

It looks then as if the incidental/systematic controversy is outmoded. That is to say children learn the words they feel they need incidentally but in a systematic manner. Increasingly children are taught to learn the word they need by such strategies as "looking with interest, intent, and intention to reproduce", without copying the word, and by learning lists compiled from such "asked for" words.

The growing trend in research on children's writing has been to focus on the process of writing, not on the product, in other words on what is going on when children are writing rather than what they actually write (Stahl 1977). When children are writing there are so many things to be dealt with at the same time that to pay conscious attention to all of these would be, Scardamalia (1980) writes, "to overload the information process and capacity". For her, spelling is only one of a number of supportive aspects of writing which must clearly be automatic if children are to be free to attend to other aspects related to content, in other words if children are to be free to write what they want to write without being overloaded, without circumlocuting, and with contextual precision.

To this end there is considerable consensus that spelling should be taught systematically by efficient and economical strategies but that the words that are taught should be those which a particular child wants to write so that from letter sequences studied within such words, generalization will occur.

Bibliography

Beers J W 1980 Developmental strategies of spelling competence in primary school children. In: Henderson E H, Beers J W 1980

Chomsky C 1970 Reading, writing and phonology. *Harvard Educ. Rev.* 40: 287–309

Cornman O P 1902 *Spelling in the Elementary School*. Ginn, Boston, Massachusetts

Fernald G M 1943 *Remedial Techniques in Basic School Subjects*. McGraw-Hill, New York

Frith U 1980a Unexpected spelling problems. In: Frith U (ed.) 1980b

Frith U (ed.) 1980b *Cognitive Processes in Spelling*. Academic Press, New York

Gibson E J, Levin H 1975 *The Psychology of Reading*. MIT Press, Cambridge, Massachusetts

Gibson E J, Pick A, Osser H, Hammond M 1962 The role of graphemephoneme correspondence in the perception of words. *Am. J. Psychol.* 75: 554–70

Gilbert L C 1935 Study of the effect of reading on spelling. *J. Educ. Res.* 28: 570–76

Gregg L W, Steinberg E R (eds.) 1980 *Cognitive Processes in Writing*. Erlbaum, Hillsdale, New Jersey

Hartmann G W 1931 The relative influence of visual and auditory factors in spelling ability. *J. Educ. Psychol.* 22(9): 691–99

Henderson E H 1980 Developmental concepts of words. In: Henderson E H, Beers J W 1980

Henderson E H, Beers J W 1980 *Developmental and Cognitive Aspects of Learning to Spell: Reflection of Word Knowledge*. International Reading Association, Newark, Delaware

Hildreth G H 1956 *Teaching Spelling*. Henry Holt, New York

Kyte G C 1948 When spelling has been mastered in the elementary school. *Jun. Educ. Res.* xli: 47–53

MacKay D, Thompson B, Schaub P 1978 *Breakthrough to Literacy Teachers' Manual*. Longman, London

McLeod M E 1961 Rules in the teaching of spelling. *Studies in Spelling*. University of London Press, London

Marsh et al. 1980 The development of strategies in spelling. In: Frith U (ed.) 1980b

Nisbet S D 1941 The scientific investigation of spelling instruction in Scottish schools. *Br. J. Educ. Psychol.* 11: 150

Peters M L 1970 *Success in Spelling: A Study of Factors Affecting Improvement in Spelling in the Junior School*. Cambridge Institute of Education, Cambridge

Read C 1971 Preschool childrens' knowledge of English phonology. *Harvard Educ. Rev.* 41: 1–34

Rice J M 1897 The futility of the spelling grind. *Forum* 23

Scardamalia M 1980 How children cope with the cognitive demands of writing. In: Frederiksen C H, Whiteman M S, Dominic J F (eds.) 1980 *Writing: The Nature, Development and Teaching of Written Communication*. Erlbaum, Hillsdale, New Jersey

Schonell F J 1942 *Backwardness in Basic Subjects*. Oliver and Boyd, Edinburgh

Simon D P 1976 Spelling: A task analysis. *Instruct. Sci.* 5: 277–302

Simon D P, Simon H A 1973 Alternative uses of phonemic information in spelling. *Rev. Educ. Res.* 43: 115–37

Sloboda J A 1980 Visual imagery and individual differences in spelling. In: Frith U (ed.) 1980b

Smith H A 1975 *Teaching Spelling*. Henry Holt, New York

Stahl A 1977 The structure of children's composition: Developmental and ethnic differences: Research in the teaching of English. In: Gregg L W, Steinberg E R (eds.) 1980

Tenney Y J 1980 Visual factors in spelling. In: Frith U (ed.) 1980b

Vallins G H 1965 *Spelling*. Deutsch, London

Wallin J E 1910 Has the drill become obsolescent? *Jun. Educ. Psychol.* 1: 200–13

Handwriting Instruction

A. P. Holbrook

Handwriting is a means of encoding and communicating human thought. As a tool of communication it naturally has a key role to play in education, yet very few countries have a national handwriting policy. Moreover, it is hard to obtain a comprehensive picture of teaching practice from the available literature, almost all of which is concerned with the teaching of the roman alphabet, and in particular, the position in the United States and the United Kingdom. Nevertheless it is possible to identify a common aim, the development of an individual style that is, first and foremost, legible as well as fast, fluent, and aesthetically pleasing. Prior to the 1960s there was little empirical research in the field. Since then considerable advances have been made, but the findings are slow to filter into the classroom. Thus, the foundations of current practice are, on the whole, traditional rather than empirical.

If handwriting is to be an effective tool of communication it must be legible. The main components of a legible hand are alignment, spacing, stroke, size, slant, proportion, and letter formation. Of these, letter formation has been found to be the most important factor in determining legibility. The ease and legibility with which specific letters or groups of letters are formed has been the subject of several studies (Askov et al. 1970 pp. 100-01, Peck et al. 1980 p. 284). Scales designed to measure legibility are available but do not appear to be widely used.

Children are generally motivated to write at an early age. Their readiness, however, is contingent upon the acquisition of certain sensory-motor skills. Indicators of readiness are: the ability to make visual discriminations, an understanding of left to right progression, adequate muscular coordination, and hand dominance. In a recent study of preschool and kindergarten children, five sequential stages in handwriting development were identified: (a) controlled scribbling; (b) discrete lines, dots, and symbols; (c) straight lines and circular uppercase letters; (d) uppercase letters; (e) lowercase letters, numerals, and words. It was also found that the most radical change in development, in terms of process, product, quality, and quantity of handwriting, occurred at 4.6 years of age (Tan-Lin 1981).

Relatively few empirical studies have been concerned with handwriting as a dynamic process, that is, the act of letter formation. Research, discussion, and instruction have been dominated by consideration of the finished (static) product. The advent of computers into the field may well result in a shift in perspective, because computers can record and display deviations in letter formation even as they occur (Macleod and Proctor 1979, Lally 1988). Meanwhile, classroom practice continues to focus on the production of model letter forms. The letters are taught in isolation, or, as is becoming more common, in the context of words. At first children are taught to print, then at about the age of 8 the transition is made to cursive. The results of research into the optimum time for this transition have been inconclusive. Furthermore, the time of transition has not been found to affect performance in other language skills (Askov et al. 1970 p. 108), even though a relationship between performance in handwriting and such skills has been demonstrated (Peck et al. 1980 pp. 288–89).

There are a number of handwriting models in use today. In virtually all of them the print form is a simplified, unjoined version of the cursive that will follow. The widely used manuscript model is the main exception. It is characterized by round, upright letterforms that resemble type. The change from manuscript to cursive requires that a completely new handwriting alphabet be learned. As a result many have questioned the desirability of the switch and advocate the retention of manuscript, either on its own, or together with

cursive, throughout primary school (Graham and Miller 1980). *The Simple Modern Hand* is a relatively new and popular handwriting model based on the italic style. In this and many other models, the transition to cursive is facilitated by the addition, to the print letters, of ligatures (entrance and exit strokes). Some modified cursive models, for example, *Marion Richardson*, feature upright and rounded letters, but most have their roots in the sloping, elliptical, copperplate, and italic styles. These foundational styles are the product of specific nib types. Only recently have moves been made to develop handwriting styles to suit the widely used ball-point and felt-tipped pens. There is no conclusive evidence to support the exclusive use of any one writing instrument or surface in the early stages of handwriting instruction (Ayris 1981, Peck et al. 1980, pp. 295–96), but in general a soft pencil is used, and later on a pen (the handwriting model usually specifies the type of pen).

The most effective teaching strategies are seen to be those that establish correct habits of posture, grip, and paper position right from the start. The clear and consistent demonstration by the teacher of the rules of letter formation (i.e., where to start and end letters), is also considered to be desirable. Recent research has shown that rule-based instruction at the kindergarten level results in better performance in copying letters, and an improvement in the ability to discriminate between letters (Peck et al. 1980. pp. 288–89). Copying letters, either from the board, or from a copybook, is a long-established practice, the efficacy of which has been demonstrated in several empirical studies (Peck et al. 1980 pp. 284–85). Other instructional strategies shown by research to lead to an improvement in handwriting performance include training to discriminate between letters, the tracing of letters, the combination of visual instruction in, and verbal demonstration of, letter formation, the use of evaluative overlays, and the use of televised lessons reinforced by teacher follow-up (Shepard 1985). In the remedial area, the individual diagnosis, and task analysis approaches have proved successful, so too the combination of visual and verbal feedback and the use of incentives (Askov et al. 1970 pp. 100–03, 104–08, Peck et al. 1980 pp. 284–88, 290–95).

Instead of pulling the pen across the page, left-handed writers push it, or even hook it, the latter process being extremely awkward and the product less desirable (Enstrom 1962). There does not seem to be any significant difference in the handwriting speed and quality of left- and right-handed writers (Askov et al. 1970 p. 103). However, the former do tend to make more reversal and inversion errors in their letters. It is evident from the above discussion, that teachers need careful training in handwriting skills and the opportunity for the observation of individual students, yet the literature suggests that teacher preparation in the area, and the face-to-face teaching time allocated to handwriting instruction is inadequate (Graham and Miller 1980 pp. 1–2).

Bibliography

Alston J, Taylor J 1987 *Handwriting. Theory, Reseach, and Practice.* Croom Helm, London.

Askov E, Otto W, Askov W 1970 A decade of research in handwriting: Progress and prospect. *J. Educ. Res.* 64: 100–11

Ayris B M 1981 The effect of various writing tools on the handwriting legibility of first grade children (Doctoral dissertation, University of Florida) *Dissertation Abstracts International* 1981 42: 2485A-2486A (University Microfilms No. 8127411)

Enstrom E A 1962 The relative efficiency of the various approaches to writing with the left hand. *J. Educ. Res.* 64: 573-77

Graham S, Miller L 1980 Handwriting research and practice: A unified approach and review. *Focus on Exceptional Children* 13(2): 1–16

Gray N 1979 Towards a new handwriting adapted to the ballpoint pen. *Visible Lang.* 13: 63–69

Lally M 1988 Using micros to teach handwriting. In: Wills S, Lewis R (eds) 1988 *MICROS PLUS: Educational Peripherals.* Elsevier Science Publishers, North Holland

Macleod I, Proctor P 1979 A dynamic approach to teaching handwriting skills. *Visible Lang.* 13: 29–42

Peck M, Askov E, Fairchild S 1980 Another decade of research in handwriting: Progress and prospect in the 1970s. *J. Educ. Res.* 73: 283–98

Shepard E T 1985 A comparison of two methods for teaching transitional cursive handwriting: Students taught by educational television and its guide and students taught as planned by the individual teacher. (Doctoral dissertation, University of Alabama) *Dissertations Abstracts International* 1985 46: 09A (*Dissertation Abstracts ONDISK* DAI vols 45/07–49/06)

Tan-Lin A 1981 An investigation into the developmental course of pre-school/kindergarten aged children's handwriting behavior (Doctoral dissertation, Southern Illinois University) *Dissertation Abstracts International* 1981 42: 4287A (University Microfilms No. DA 8206504)

Study Skills

J. E. Van Nord

Study skills are defined as those techniques, such as summarizing, note taking, outlining, or locating material, which learners employ to assist themselves in the efficient learning of the material at hand.

The task of learning required information, either from the text or classroom lecture, is a complex one which calls upon the student to employ many techniques and skills. Traditionally, educators have assumed that by providing instruction in study skills the learning task will become easier. Current research in the area now shows that this may not be the case and that there are factors other than the application of specific study techniques which influence the learning task.

Those who work with students are now using not only the basic techniques of the past, but are developing new methods and approaches to the learning process which may assist the student in learning more efficiently.

1. Historical Background

The student's approach to learning is highly individualistic with a wide variation of techniques observable. One student may prefer the quiet of the library, another, the student lounge; one may underline a text, another take notes; one may study intensively for several hours, another may take many breaks. The variations are endless. Educators felt that the study process could be more productive if learners were taught specific skills and techniques which would formalize the study process and thereby make it more efficient. This led to the development of study manuals or courses.

Such courses have proliferated although there was little scientific evidence of their value. Laycock and Russell (1941) found that of 38 manuals published between 1926 and 1939 few were based on research findings. Research interest in study skills courses grew. Entwisle (1960) reviewed 22 studies of college-level study skills courses conducted during the 1940s and 1950s. She found that such courses generally resulted in an improvement in grades, but that such gains were not necessarily related to course content or the duration of the course; it was the highly motivated student who was most successful. These courses usually included material on reading skills, study habits, test taking, and individual or group counseling.

Berg and Rentel (1966) also found that motivation was the key factor for students enrolled in study skills courses. Weigel's (1967) study of freshman psychology students found that knowledge of and use of study skills was not a good predictor of academic success. Many students knew various study techniques, but did not apply them.

2. Study Skills Tests

Standardized tests which attempt to test not only study skills, but also such factors as study attitudes and habits, reading comprehension, research skills, and test anxiety have been developed as interest in study skills has increased. The *Eighth Mental Measurements Yearbook* (1978) lists nine tests which attempt to test some aspect of study skill knowledge or performance. Few are recommended usually because of inadequate norms or validation data.

The most commonly used American test is the *Survey of Study Habits and Attitudes* (1953–1967). The latest editions, *Form C* for college (1966) and *Form S* for high school (1967) include 100 items grouped into four scales:

delay avoidance, work methods, teacher approval, and educational acceptance. The survey is often used as a predictor for academic success. McBee and Duke (1960) found that in their modification of the test for junior-high-school students the items are relevant in the subject areas of reading, arithmetic, and science.

The *Survey of Study Habits and Attitudes* (1953–1967) is not entirely appropriate for the British student. To remedy this, Entwistle et al. (1971) have developed the Student Attitudes Inventory. They report that the reliability of the scales is high although some subscales give low correlations and that there is difficulty in predicting achievement especially for college or university students.

3. Traditional Study Techniques

3.1 Text Study

The most commonly taught study skill technique is the SQ3R and its adaptations originally developed by Robinson (1970) in the 1940s to provide soldiers with higher level study skills which would assist in their training for specialized positions. Robinson discusses such items as concentration, motivation, time management, test taking, and the application of the technique to various subject areas. SQ3R is comprised of the following steps:

(a) Survey: look over the headings in a chapter to see what points will be discussed. Read the chapter summary paragraph.

(b) Question: turn each heading into a question.

(c) Read: read the chapter to find the answer to the questions posed.

(d) Recite: after reading the first section recite the answer to the posed question. Recitation may take the form of notes or an outline. For each section of the chapter repeat the question, read, recite procedure.

(e) Review: at the completion of the chapter reread the notes and recite the major points under each topic.

Educators have found the SQ3R study method a useful technique for students from junior-high age through adults.

Several adaptations of the method have also been developed. The Study Management System has been used with college age students. This system asks students to: (a) survey the chapter; (b) question by again scanning the chapter and formulating questions; (c) recite by reading several paragraphs, then writing a closed book summary, open the book and check the summary; and (d) review at the end of the chapter by rechecking the written summaries.

3.2 Note Taking

Note taking is a crucial aspect of the study process. Pauk (1962) recommends two techniques which work well and are especially useful in the review for examination process.

If class lectures and the text are closely related he recommends the student to divide the note book paper into three columns. In one column the learner records brief notes concerning the important topics presented at the lecture. During the "recite" component of SQ3R, notes on related text material are entered on the same sheet in a second column. As the student reviews both lecture and text notes, a recall clues or summaries section is filled in with brief notations which will be the key or index to the notes. An observations and conclusions section beneath the three columns may be used for student questions about the material, or conclusions drawn concerning the material covered.

As the student prepares to review for a test, the notes should be covered except for the clues or conclusions section.

4. Contemporary Trends

Recently there has been a growth of interest in the cognitive process and learning styles which has been reflected in the recent research on study skills. Researchers believe that the particular method of study used by a learner is not the most important factor in the learning process; it is factors within the learner which determine what is learned. They feel that learning style—whether field dependent or independent, holistic or atomistic—is a critical factor in the learning process. Motivation and how the learner processes new information are also crucial. The process by which the brain handles new information is often described in terms similar to those used in describing computer functions. For example, data input is through the sensory organs after which it is processed by the memory system. The data are then structured and categorized in a meaningful manner after which they are stored for retrieval at the appropriate time. These same terms could be used to describe the operation of a computer.

Anderson and Armbruster (1980) are among the most active researchers today. They believe that there are two components which influence the learning process. (a) State variables are defined as the status of the student and the material at study time; student variables include knowledge of the criterion task (expected use of the material), content knowledge, and motivation; and text variables include the organization and content. (b) Processing variables are defined as the method by which the material on the page transfers to the learner's brain. Aspects of this process include focusing of attention, encoding, and retrieval of the information when required. It is their contention that the more knowledge students have about the task they will be required to perform the more effective their studying will be and the more willing they will be to modify their techniques of study to meet the task. They feel that any method which requires the student to deep-process the information will be the most successful.

5. *Contemporary Study Skills Tests*

The present upsurge of interest in learning and study skills has not yet led to the development of many new standardized tests. Biggs (1978) appears to be one of the few attempting to develop such an instrument. His Study Process Questionnaire evaluates the study process by focusing on the values, motives, and study strategies of the student. His contention is, "Performance (in studying) is then presumed to be affected by personality and environmental factors *via* the study process complex" (Biggs 1978 p. 266). The questionnaire examines personality in terms of IQ and home background, and subject content, teaching methods, and type of course evaluation are examined as components of the environment or institutional aspects of the study process. Validation and evaluation of the questionnaire are currently being made in Australia and the Phillipines.

6. *Contemporary Techniques*

Anderson and Armbruster's (1980) synthesis of research on study skills indicates that any study technique can be successful if the learner is deeply involved in the process. Note taking, underlining, self-questioning, and summarizing require focused attention; students must deep-process the information in their own words in a manner which enables them to retrieve the information as it relates to the expected future use of the information.

An efficient learning procedure requires that the learner be able to retrieve the information read or heard at some future date. Traditionally, this has taken the form of some manner of notetaking. Two new methods, mapping and networking, have emerged as techniques which will make learning more efficient. Although neither method has had sufficient validation through scientific testing, both appear promising because they graphically show the interrelationships of the ideas presented in the material. Outlining, which has been one of the more common methods of note taking can show points subsumed under the main topic, but it cannot represent the interrelationship of ideas.

[Mapping] has seven fundamental relationships between two ideas, A and B: when B is an instance of A, B is a property or characteristic of A, A is similar to B, A is greater or less than B, A occurs before B, A causes B, and A is a negation of B. (Anderson 1979 p. 94)

Networking also graphically represents the interrelationship of ideas, but in a somewhat different manner. Linkages to components of the topic are made by arrowed lines and letters. Three types of idea structures are represented through networking (see Fig. 1).

Anderson's (1979) steps in the study process are illustrated in Figs. 2 and 3, through both the networking and mapping procedures.

Although networking and mapping show promise as learning tools, both are extremely time consuming to construct and may require the student to learn more than is necessary for the task at hand.

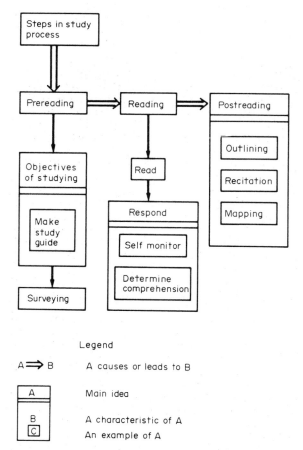

Figure 2
Map of Anderson (1979)

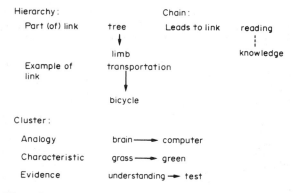

Figure 1
Network components

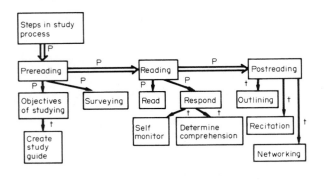

Legend

P   Part of link
†   Type or example link

Figure 3
Network of Anderson (1979)

7. Summary

Knowledge of a specific study skill technique does not guarantee that the student will use the technique or that use of the technique will result in improved learning as verified through improved grades. There are many other factors which influence the learning process. The learner must be able to read, write, or listen at the appropriate level. The vocabulary of the content area must be understood as well as such components of writing as sentence and paragraph structure, stylistic devices, and signals. The learner must also be able to interpret visuals such as graphs and tables. Other factors which may influence the learning process are the learning style of the student or the manner in which the class is taught. It is the responsibility of the instructor to provide the student with learning techniques appropriate to a specific subject, to indicate the tasks expected of the student, and to show how these techniques may be applied to other subjects.

Unless the student can see the value of a specific technique, whether it is SQ3R or mapping, he or she will not use it. Most methods appear to require additional work on the part of the student; it is far easier to maintain the status quo unless there is sufficient motivation to do otherwise.

Bibliography

Anderson T H 1979 Study skills and learning strategies. In: O'Neil H F, Spielberger C D (eds.) 1979 *Cognitive and Affective Learning Strategies*. Academic Press, New York, pp. 77–97

Anderson T H, Armbruster B B 1980 *Studying*. Technical Report No. 55. ERIC Document No. ED 181 427. Bolt, Beranek and Newman, Cambridge, Massachusetts

Berg P C, Rentel V M 1966 Improving study skills. *J. Read.* 9: 343–46

Biggs J B 1978 Individual and group differences in study processes. *Br. J. Educ. Psychol.* 48: 266–79

Eighth Mental Measurements Yearbook 1978 Edited by O K Buros, Vol. II. Gryphon Press, Highland Park, New Jersey

Entwisle D R 1960 Evaluation of study skills courses: A review. *J. Educ. Res.* 53: 243–51

Entwistle N J et al. 1971 The academic performance of students: Prediction from scales of motivation and study methods. *Br. J. Educ. Psychol.* 41: 258–67

Laycock S R, Russell D H 1941 An analysis of thirty-eight how-to-study manuals. *Sch. Rev.* 49: 370–79

McBee G, Duke R L 1960 Relationships between intelligence, scholastic motivation, and academic achievement. *Psychol. Reports* 6: 3–8

Pauk W 1962 *How to Study in College*. Houghton Mifflin, Boston, Massachusetts

Robinson F P 1970 *Effective Study*, 4th edn. Harper and Row, New York

Weigel R 1967 The relationship of knowledge and usage of study skills techniques to academic performance. *J. Educ. Res.* 61: 78–80

Reading Habits

Reading Interest

V. Greaney

Dictionary definitions of interest indicate the term has numerous meanings. Applied specifically to reading, interest refers to the tendency of people to voluntarily seek reading material and to devote time to reading. It also refers to those topics and materials which are selected for reading. Thus the topic reading interest has a number of different aspects. In this article procedures for measuring reading interest are listed; individuals' reasons for reading are explored; the volume of material read and the amount of time devoted to reading are examined; preferences for different types of reading material are reviewed and factors associated with the methods for development of interest in reading are outlined.

1. Measurement

Reading interest has been a subject of investigation in the areas of librarianship, journalism, education, psychology, sociology, commerce, literature, and history. Given this diversity of disciplines it is not surprising that many different approaches have been used to measure reading interest. These include formal questionnaires and interest inventories in which preferences are listed. Historical records, detailed diaries of leisure activities, book reports, records of library books chosen, and book sales have been analyzed. Studies have attempted to determine children's and adults' interests by having individuals select choices from lists of fictitious titles that are annotated, read sample pages, rate pairs of books, or examine pictures of books. Children have indicated their preferences after hearing selections read to them. Estimates of preferences have been obtained from secondary sources such as parents, teachers, and librarians.

The overall standard of research on reading interest leaves much to be desired especially from the points of view of experimental design, statistical analysis, and definition of terms. Many of the studies are based on small samples of data derived from single classes, libraries, or geographical regions. Some reviewers have tended to analyze trends in reading from series of poorly designed studies. There is a conspicuous dearth of longitudinal data. Most of the studies have focused on the relationship between reading interest and one other variable, thereby omitting potentially important variables from consideration. Some studies have failed to recognize that recall has limitations, that stated reading preferences need not necessarily indicate interest, that preferences are related to amount of exposure to material, that number of books bought or borrowed is quite different from number of books read, that the more interesting of two reading alternatives may be uninteresting, that book categories are quite arbitrary (e.g., the same book could be classified as "birds", "adventure", or "science"), that sales are not necessarily good indicators of interest especially in totalitarian societies, and that the term reading may refer to more than leisure reading.

2. Reasons for Reading

Reasons for reading vary according to individual needs and factors such as age, cultural background, level of education, social status, and religious and political values. In addition to self-motivation, motivation to read is often provided by family members, friends, peers, teachers, librarians, and society at large. In the past, an ability to read (especially books such as the Bible or the Koran) conferred a status on the individual. More recently, especially in developed countries, the situation has altered; an ability to read is assumed while an inability to read tends to isolate the individual.

The need for information is a primary motivator of both children and adults. This need can be satisfied not only by newspapers, books, and magazines but also by instructions, captions, signs, maps, forms, and letters. People read material which might help them to learn more about their occupations or about their hobbies. Together with television and radio, reading tends to be the primary source of information on foreign issues, urban problems, and cultural values. Reading can satisfy intellectual and political demands. Students use reading to acquire knowledge which is related to scholastic success; indeed in many societies young people view this as the primary motive for reading.

Reading also provides a source of pleasure. Studies have shown that preschoolers, older pupils, and adults read simply for the joy of reading. This seems to be particularly true of those readers who describe themselves as "book readers". For many, especially children, pleasure is derived from identifying with leading fictional characters.

3. Volume and Amount of Time

In developed countries most adults and children appear to read quite extensively both during work and leisure hours. In the United States, for instance, it has been reported that the average adult person reads for 1¾ hours on a typical day; most of this time is given to reading newspapers, magazines, books, and job-related materials (Sharon 1974). Males aged 16 or older tend to read more than females. British findings indicate that children read approximately three books per month, and that there has been little increase in the amount of book reading between the mid 1950s and the early 1970s (Himmelweit et al. 1958, Whitehead et al. 1975). In Ireland, fifth-grade pupils devoted an average of 5 percent of their leisure time to reading (Greaney 1980). New Zealand boys and girls ranked reading as one of their top three interests (Elley and Tolley 1972), while in Korea, Malaysia, and Singapore, it was reported that reading took up more leisure time than television (Gopinathan 1978). It should be stressed that averages in this context may be quite misleading. Many studies have reported large minorities of nonreaders and a small percentage of very heavy readers; for instance, in one United States study it was found that 39 percent never read a book (Yankelovich et al. 1978), while in another it was estimated that 10 percent of the population read 80 percent of the total books read (Gallup 1972).

Amount of time devoted to out-of-school reading is related to several measures of reading achievement, including gains in reading between grades two and five; the relationship is about the same magnitude as the strongest relationship reported for within-school use of time and achievement (Anderson et al. 1988).

Studies in a number of countries have identified factors which are related to volume of reading. Towards the end of primary school there is a general agreement that children experience the "reading craze". As they get older, however, there is a pronounced decrease in leisure reading. Females tend to devote more leisure time to reading than males except in developing countries where their rate of illiteracy is relatively high. In particular girls read more books than boys.

Leisure reading and in particular book reading requires a minimum level of reading proficiency on the part of the reader. Very many studies have reported significant relationships between amount of leisure reading and level of reading attainment. Leisure reading is not a conspicuous feature of life in less developed countries, especially in rural areas of Africa, Asia, and Latin America. Although the relationship is not very strong, frequent leisure reading is most characteristic of those of higher social backgrounds. Children from working-

class backgrounds tend not to read very much. Readers of fiction along with readers of history, plays, and poetry tend to be the most consistent readers, while the fewest consistent readers exist among those who prefer material on health, hobbies, sea, and sport (McElroy 1978). In addition to interest, the amount of leisure reading is related to the availability of reading material. Reading material may come from a variety of sources, including public and school libraries, personal purchase, friends, and relatives. In many areas reading material in the indigenous languages is relatively scarce. Readership of books and newspapers in a second language tends to be low. In some countries (e.g., Korea) different forms of script pose problems for readers.

4. Content

Material which people select for reading during their leisure hours may be categorized as books, newspapers, comic books, and magazines. Much more is known about book-reading preferences than preferences for other forms of reading material.

4.1 Books

In recent decades changes in the reading interests of children and adolescents tend to reflect technological and social changes in society; some subjects that were formerly taboo (e.g., sex, conscientious objection) are now appearing in books. In general, however, reading interests of children in particular have changed surprisingly little. At the adult level, reading interests are perhaps more susceptible to changes in public taste and economic and social conditions.

At a very early stage, children in developed countries are normally introduced to picture books. Later, stories are read aloud and popular ones, such as A. A. Milne's *Winnie the Pooh*, tend to be reread many times. Fairy tales, animal stories, and stories based on well-known television characters are most popular. Among primary-school children, favourite subjects include adventure, fantasy, mystery, social studies, sports and games, humour, and animals. As they get older, sex differences become more apparent. Boys show a preference for books on general information, sports, science, hobbies and in recent years, books on violent themes. Girls prefer books based on people, fantasy, humour, and romance. Though boys tend to read more nonfiction, girls tend to read more overall. Series books such as *The Hardy Boys*, *Nancy Drew*, *Dr. Doolittle*, and books by Enid Blyton have proved particularly popular in many countries. They have been strongly criticized however for the quality of plot, characterization, theme, and style. At the same time award-winning children's books (by adult standards) have not fared so well in the market place. An analysis of children's favourite books (Abrahamson 1980) revealed that children like books that involve confrontation with a problem, and include series of adventures and characters with opposing viewpoints. Poetry is relatively less popular, especially among boys. Poems which involve either rhyme, humour, animals, or everyday experience tend to be liked; poems that lack a story line or that are difficult to understand are unpopular. Although the reading interests of poor and good readers as measured by achievement tests are quite similar, good readers appear to devote more time to reading books for leisure.

Among adolescents, book-reading interests vary substantially and gradually expand to include those of adults. Adolescent readers seem to be interested in personal experience and in fictional and nonfictional characters who face the problems which accompany establishing personal identities in the adult world. Suspense, humour, violence, sport, and social responsibility are popular themes. The desire for happy endings is not as prevalent as it was in earlier years. Although there is a general overlapping of interest, boys show a preference for sport, hobbies, sex, crime, adventure, and war, while girls tend to prefer books on people, social relationships, and mystery without violence. Adolescent girls tend to read more than boys, though boys again tend to read more nonfiction. Poetry does not have a heavy readership.

Fiction appears to be the most popular category among adults. In the United States, for example, an analysis of the most frequently purchased books between 1965 and 1975 revealed that character-based fiction and erotic fiction accounted for over half the books purchased (Guthrie and LeGrand-Brodsky 1980). Fiction readers tend to read fewer books from other categories than other readers (McElroy 1978). Readers of social science, physical science, and history read with a great deal of variety and tend to be highly educated. Adult reading habits in many countries are nationally centred with preference being shown for national authors. As people get older, there is a tendency to select books on history, biography, travel, and religion. Adult poetry reading is relatively rare and readers tend to be female.

4.2 Newspapers

For most readers, newspaper reading represents the most common type of leisure-reading activity. It is difficult to generalize about the most popular newspaper sections since coverage of such topics as world news varies considerably from country to country and also within countries. Many major newspapers strive to cater for a general readership, while others are published for specific interest groups such as the business community, sports enthusiasts, those interested in human-interest stories, adherents to a particular political party or ideology, and residents of a defined geographical area. In Western countries, older children tend to read the comic sections, adolescents the front page and the comic, sports, and television sections, and adults show a preference for general news, local news, entertainment, and sports. Larger units of text tend to be read less frequently than shorter ones, and headlines and photographs are read much more often than units of text.

4.3 Comic Books

Comic-book reading tends to be very popular among children and in certain countries (e.g., Philippines) among sections of the adult population. In addition to humour, comic books have expanded to cover other areas such as mystery, war, romance, and sport. Comic books appear to be more popular among weaker readers than among better readers who prefer books. Although comics tend to have relatively low readability levels, they generally require certain levels of reading competence. Most surveys indicate that boys devote more time to comics than girls. The popularity of the comic book appears to peak around 12–14 years of age.

4.4 Magazines

Magazines attract a sizeable readership among adolescents and adults. In the United States, for instance, where 12,000 magazines are published annually, 4 out of 10 persons read magazines for an average of 33 minutes each day. Among adolescents, boys and girls are interested in magazines devoted to pop music and general teenage culture, but tend to have quite different preferences in specific areas; boys seem to prefer magazines devoted to sports, science, and war, while girls seem to favour those devoted to fashion, home, and beauty care. Similar differences in preference are found at the adult level. General-interest magazines (e.g., *Reader's Digest*) are most popular. News magazines tend to be read for relatively long periods of time and are very popular among key decision makers. High socioeconomic status is associated with readership of literary and political reviews and low status with romance and detective magazines (Sharon 1974).

5. Developing Interest in Reading

There is considerable evidence that schools give little attention to fostering favourable attitudes to reading. Schools are primarily concerned with reading skills; relatively little is done to encourage independent reading for pleasure. The findings of studies suggest that parents can help their children to develop an interest in reading by reading themselves, by providing books, comics, and magazines, by reading aloud to them when they are young or by having the children read aloud, by encouraging library or book-club membership, and by making the newspaper available in the home.

At the global level, the major problem in developing an interest in reading is posed by the inability of 800 million people to read. In addition, in many countries, especially in Asia, Africa, and Latin America, the needs of potential readers are not being adequately served due to the lack of appropriate inexpensive reading materials, local publishing firms, and adequate distribution systems.

Bibliography

Abrahamson R F 1980 An analysis of children's favorite picture story-books. *Read. Teach.* 34: 167–70
Anderson R C, Wilson P T, Fielding L G 1988 Growth in reading and how children spend their time outside of school. *Read. Res. Q.* 13: 285–303
Elley W B, Tolley C W 1972 *Children's Reading Interests: A Wellington Survey.* New Zealand Council for Educational Research and the Wellington Council of the International Reading Association, Wellington
Gallup G H 1972 *The Gallup Poll: Public Opinion, 1935–1971.* Random House, New York
Gopinathan S 1978 *A Measure of Reading: I.E. Survey of Reading Interests and Habits.* Institute of Education, Singapore
Greaney V 1980 Factors related to amount and type of leisure time reading. *Read. Res. Q.* 15: 337–57
Guthrie J T, LeGrand-Brodsky K 1980 Research: A signal of values. *J. Read.* 23: 354–57
Himmelweit H T, Oppenheim A N, Vince P 1958 *Television and the Child.* Oxford University Press, London
Huus H 1979 A new look at children's interests. In: Shapiro J E (ed.) 1979 *Using Literature and Poetry Affectively.* International Reading Association, Newark, Delaware, pp. 37–45
McElroy E W 1978 Subject variety in adult reading: 11. Characteristics of readers of ten categories of books. *Library Q.* 38: 261–69
Robinson H W, Weintraub S 1973 Research related to children's interests and to developmental values of reading. *Library Trends* 22: 81–108
Sharon A T 1974 What do adults read? *Read. Res. Q.* 9: 148–69
Whitehead F, Capey A C, Maddren W 1975 *Children's Reading Interests.* Evans, London
Yankelovich, Skelly and White Inc. 1978 *The 1978 Consumer Research Study of Reading and Book Purchasing.* Book Industry Study Group, Darien, Connecticut

Independent Reading

J. S. Chall and E. W. Marston

Research on independent reading has continued from the end of the nineteenth century into the present. It has been carried out by scholars in educational psychology, reading, children's literature, and library science; by educational policy makers; and by the communications and publishing industries. It is extensive and diverse. Taken as a whole, the research displays widely substantiated findings relating to the course of development of lifetime reading habits.

Two reservoirs of research will be discussed. The first has to do with reader characteristics in relation to the extent of independent reading. The second concerns the textual factors related to reader interest.

1. Reader Characteristics Related to Extent of Reading

Most of the research on reading habits has included age and sex among the independent variables. Research on adults has commonly included socio-economic status (SES), as measured by level of education and occupation. Research on children and adolescents has sometimes included IQ and/or reading achievement scores, and SES measures.

At all ages, more readers are found among those groups having higher proportions of skilled readers. The most powerful correlates of independent reading are education in adults (Ennis 1965, Sharon 1973, Murphy 1973, Yankelovich et al. 1978) and academic ability in children and adolescents (Terman and Lime 1931, Himmelweit et al. 1958).

Among all age groups, females have consistently been found more likely to be readers, particularly of books

(Terman and Lime 1931, Himmelweit et al. 1958, Ennis 1965, Sharon 1973, Murphy 1973, Purves 1973, Johnson 1973, Landy 1977, Yankelovich et al. 1978). Several explanations have been offered. Some argue that reading is largely perceived as a "feminine" activity (Steinberg 1972, Dwyer 1973). Others argue that differences are related to reading ability. Males tend to have the larger proportion of unskilled or disabled readers (Dwyer 1973). The sexes may also differ in their motivations for reading, in ways that affect quantity. Adult males are more likely to read for information, and females for pleasure, with the pleasure motivation resulting in more extensive reading (Yankelovich et al. 1978).

In children and adolescents, age is an index of cognitive growth and academic progress. The age-related findings have consistently displayed the following: with the acquisition of initial reading skill, there is an increase in amount of reading with increase in age. Near or during adolescence, there is generally a decline (Terman and Lime 1931, Himmelweit et al. 1958). Some resume reading in adult life, while others do not (Ennis 1965). Whereas most adults may read newspapers and magazines, relatively few are readers of books (Ennis 1965, Sharon 1973, Murphy 1973, Yankelovich et al. 1978). In the studies cited, education was the major contributing factor in book reading among adults.

Young adults are likely to be the heavier readers, with a decline in reading after the age of 55 or 60 (Ennis 1965, Sharon 1973, Murphy 1973, Yankelovich et al. 1978). This may relate to differences in education; young adults have the higher proportion of high-school and college graduates. However, decline in reading has been found after the age of 55 even among college graduates (Ennis 1965).

These findings suggest that reading tends to flourish during some portions of the life cycle, and to be at risk during others. Adolescence seems to be a watershed in the formation of independent reading habits.

In children and adolescents, the socioeconomic status of the home has generally shown a moderate relationship with extent of reading. Overall, low SES is associated with less reading, and this gap seems to increase with age (Johnson 1973). A low income would tend to deprive homes of reading resources. Socioeconomic status may also imply level of commitment to reading. There is evidence that process variables, the things parents do, are most important in the formation of attitudes toward reading (Hansen 1973). Further research is needed on the long-term effects of parent behaviors across a variety of ages.

Other process variables seem promising for further study. For example, it is often assumed that people would read more if they had more time. Reading is seen as having to compete with other activities. Recent research suggests that the opposite is true, that readers are busy people engaged in a variety of activities (Himmelweit et al. 1958, Landy 1977, Yankelovich et al. 1978, Marston 1982).

A second reservoir of research to be discussed concerns factors within texts that contribute to their acceptance or rejection by various groups of readers.

2. Textual Factors in Relation to Reader Interest

In research on adults, accessibility, readability, and interest have been found to affect patterns of independent reading, with accessibility being the major determinant (Waples and Tyler 1931, Waples et al. 1940). When prior conditions of accessibility and readability have been met, reading may be affected by the topic, theme, genre, or style.

The research on reading interests identifies ways in which readers tend to be alike. Narrative seems to have universal appeal; works tending toward the philosophical, meditative, or didactic to be generally shunned (Purves and Beach 1972, Marston 1976). Adults seem most interested in topics relating to their own lives (Waples and Tyler 1931). Adolescents value books that contribute to their understanding of the world (Whitman 1964). Males of all ages have consistently been found to avoid books emphasizing sentiment (Lazar 1937, Thorndike 1941, Purves 1973). Among children and adolescents, age-related changes in interests may be characterized as increasing interest in the real world (Terman and Lime 1931, Purves 1973). There is some evidence that this appears earlier in males, and seems to appear at younger ages in recent years (Marston 1976). Some researchers have asked whether readers of different ages perceive different aspects of reality. This issue has been studied in relation to the developmental theories of Freud and Piaget.

While reading achievement does affect extent of reading, it does not seem to have much effect on what children want to read about. Both reading achievement and SES have shown only slight relationships with reading interests (Terman and Lime 1931, Lazar 1937, Thorndike 1941, Thorndike 1973). The differences produced by SES and achievement levels resemble those associated with age; less-able, less-affluent readers resemble younger, less-experienced readers (Marston 1976). In general, students want to read what is read by their peers.

3. Implications for Theory and Practice

The research on reading habits identifies groups within the population whose lack of inclination to read is likely to be of concern. The research on reading interests defines principles applicable in book selection, for those concerned with providing for groups of readers. Both areas of research, viewed developmentally, contribute to the understanding of what goes into the making of readers.

Bibliography

Dwyer C A 1973 Sex differences in reading: An evaluation and a critique of current theories. *Rev. Educ. Res.* 43: 455–67

Ennis P 1965 Adult book reading in the United States: A preliminary report. ERIC Document No. ED 010 754

Hansen H S 1973 The home literary environment: A follow-up report. *Elemen. Engl.* 50: 97–98

Himmelweit H T, Oppenheim A N, Vince P 1958 *Television and the Child: An Empirical Study of the Effect of Television on the Young.* Oxford University Press, London

Johnson S 1973 *A Survey of Reading Habits: Theme 4, Literature.* Education Commission of the States. National Assessment of Educational Progress, United States Government Printing Office, Denver, Colorado

Landy S 1977 An investigation of the relationship between voluntary reading and certain psychological, environmental, and socioeconomic factors in early adolescence. Masters' thesis, University of Regina. ERIC Document No. ED 145 409

Lazar M 1937 *Reading Interests, Activities, and Opportunities of Bright, Average, and Dull Children.* Teachers College, Columbia University, New York

Marston E W 1976 An analysis of selected studies of reading interests and preferences of children, adolescents, and young adults. Unpublished Special Qualifying Paper, Harvard Graduate School of Education, Cambridge, Massachusetts

Marston E W 1982 A study of variables relating to the voluntary reading habits of eighth graders. Unpublished doctoral thesis, Harvard Graduate School of Education, Cambridge, Massachusetts

Murphy R 1973 *Adult Functional Reading Study.* Final Report, Project No. 0-9004, Educational Testing Service, Princeton, New Jersey

Purves A C 1973 *Literature Education in Ten Countries: An Empirical Study.* International Studies in Evaluation, 2. Wiley, New York

Purves A C, Beach R 1972 *Literature and the Reader: Research in Response to Literature, Reading Interests, and the Teaching of Literature*. National Council of Teachers of English, Urbana, Illinois

Sharon A 1973 *Reading Activities of American Adults*. Final Report, Project No. 0-9004, Educational Testing Service, Princeton, New Jersey

Steinberg H 1972 Books and readers as a subject of research in Europe and America. *Int. Soc. Sci. J.* 24(4)

Terman L M, Lime M 1931 *Children's Reading: A Guide for · Parents and Teachers*, 2nd edn. Appleton, New York

Thorndike R L 1941 *A Comparative Study of Children's Reading Interests, Based on a Fictitious Annotated Titles Questionnaire*. Teachers College, Columbia University, New York

Thorndike R L 1973 *Reading Comprehension Education in Fifteen Countries: An Empirical Study*. International Studies in Evaluation 3. Wiley, New York

Waples D, Berelson B, Bradshaw F R 1940 *What Reading Does to People: A Summary of Evidence on the Social Effects of Reading and a Statement of Problems*. University of Chicago Press, Chicago, Illinois

Waples D, Tyler R 1931 *What People Want to Read About: A Study of Group Interests and a Survey of Problems in Adult Reading*. University of Chicago Press, Chicago, Illinois

Whitman R S 1964 Significant reading experiences of superior English students. ERIC Document No. ED 026 394

Yankelovich, Skelly, and White Inc. 1978 *Consumer Research Study on Reading and Book Purchasing: Selected Findings*. Book Industry Study Group, Darien, Connecticutt

Section 6

Foreign Language Studies

Overview

Section 6, Foreign Language Studies, is divided into three subsections. Section 6(a), Foreign Language Curricula, deals with general aspects of foreign language education. Dunlop et al. provide an overview of various areas of research in the field of teaching foreign languages. Their article, *Foreign Language Education*, reviews the history of teaching foreign languages from ancient times, when the Sumerians and Romans taught the living language through oral conversation and text analysis, to the start of the 1990s, when teaching of foreign languages takes advantage of technological devices and research findings in the fields of communication sciences and educational psychology. The article summarizes research related to factors affecting the policy of teaching foreign languages in various educational systems, the differences across countries in setting aims for foreign language teaching, the relative advantages of various teaching methods, and the determinants of success in learning a foreign language.

The articles by Stern and Green review problems related to curricula of foreign language studies in primary and secondary schools. Stern describes vagaries in the field of teaching foreign languages in the primary school and examines the implications of findings derived from cross-national comparative studies on the place of teaching foreign languages in the school, and the optimum age for beginning this. With regard to secondary school curricula, research touching on the following topics is summarized in Green's article: cross-national differences in the language policy, utilization of technical aids such as language laboratories and microcomputers, materials used in the schools, and examinations and testing.

Section 6(b) contains articles that summarize research on special issues, concepts, and problems in the field of foreign language teaching. Two articles deal with the teaching-oriented components of scientific disciplines in the domain of language studies. In his article on *Educational Linguistics* Spolsky defines this area of studies as a subfield of applied linguistics. The scope of this area may be defined by topics it encompasses, such as language education policy, first and second language teaching, reading, literacy, bilingual education, composition, and language testing; or by the fields from which it derives its theoretical foundations, including theoretical linguistics, sociolinguistics, psycholinguistics and anthropological linguistics. Olshtain, in her article on *Pedagogic Grammar*, describes the differences between scientific and pedagogical grammar. The former is based on a formal theory of language and is expected to provide an exhaustive representation of what a native speaker knows, while the latter is concerned with the needs of the learner in the process of acquiring linguistic knowledge.

A second group of articles in Section 6(b) deals with problems and techniques encountered in the process of developing foreign language curricula and using them in the class. Trim deals with *Language Needs Analysis* and introduces the concept of "minimum language needed" for a particular purpose. This concept is linked to that of *Language for Special Purposes* (LSP), which is examined by Sager. The article deals with three dimensions of this concept: the linguistic, the semiotic, and the educational.

549

Several articles in this group deal with problems related to similarity and differences between the native language and the target foreign language of a particular learner. Sajavaara examines the changes which have occurred in using *Contrastive Linguistic Analysis* for the purpose of developing foreign language curricula. Berman deals with *Interference*, or negative transfer from the learner's mother tongue to the target foreign language. She distinguishes between phonemic, lexical, and syntax level instances of interference. A more direct approach to study difficulties in acquiring a foreign language is the technique of *Error Analysis*. Sajavaara distinguishes between the traditional approach to error analysis, which focused on developing typologies of errors, and more recent approaches, which consider systematic errors as the markers of the learner's progress towards higher levels of competence. A related topic, summarized by Schumann, is the notion of *Interlanguage*, which is used to refer to the speech of a second language learner before reaching full proficiency in the target language of his/her study.

Two techniques of teaching foreign languages are dealt with in separate articles. The first, *Immersion Education*, is based on the imitation of the natural setting where the mother tongue was acquired. The second, the *Language Laboratory*, is based on creating an artificial environment to teach the target foreign language. Swain characterizes immersion education as a type of bilingual education. Methodologically it operates on the principle that the second language is best acquired as the child acquires the first language. Intensive work in this area has been done in the bilingual setting of Canada, where children with English speaking backgrounds studied in schools in which the medium of instruction was French. Language laboratories, as indicated in Higgins' article, take advantage of recent developments in audio and video recording techniques. Such techniques enable highly individualized learning environments to be created, in which the learner may receive immediate feedback about his/her performance.

Research on *Foreign Language Testing in the Classroom* is summarized by Cohen. He presents a three-dimensional model for classifying foreign language achievement-test items. The three dimensions are: discrete-point/integrative, nonpragmatic/pragmatic and indirect/direct. In Clark's article on *Testing Speaking Proficiency in Foreign Language* the distinction is made between speaking about specific content elements of a course and communicative competency in real-life situations.

Section 6(c) contains eleven articles in which the authors examine problems related to teaching specific languages which are taught as a foreign language in numerous countries, either as a Language of Wider Communication or as a Language of Cultural Significance.

A. Lewy

Foreign Language Education

Introduction

E. Olshtain

Second or foreign language education has been part of the school curriculum for many centuries. Since ancient times approaches, methods, and ways of teaching languages have changed and developed to fit a shift of emphasis from the learning of language for the sake of intellectual analysis to learning language for practical, communicative needs.

Changes in methodology have been affected by changes in the understanding of the nature of language and the nature of language learning. Such changes have been related to research in the field of language learning as well as to the development of linguistic and learning theories. Sociolinguistic considerations of the wider context in which language learning and teaching is taking place have further expanded the host of factors related to policy making and curriculum development.

An important distinction in the context of learning foreign languages focuses on whether the language is acquired in a natural setting (where the target language is spoken and used intensively in society) or a formal, school setting where the target language, from the learner's point of view, is limited to classroom use. The natural context is thus equated with *second language learning* while the formal context is referred to as *foreign language learning*. When such a distinction needs to be avoided, the term *additional language* is often used, in other words, a language different from the first language and added at a later stage.

Learning an additional language is a process affected by three sets of factors: factors related to the target language; factors related to the learning context; and factors related to the learner. Factors related to the target language comprise: (a) linguistic features; (b) social functions; (c) availability; and (d) interference from the first language. Linguistic features consist of idiosyncratic aspects of the target language which might create difficulty in learning, such as diglossia in Arabic, a different writing system, a complex paradigmatic structure, and so on. Social functions which the target language fulfills in the learner's world might facilitate or impede the learning process. For instance, a target language which serves as a language of wider communication (LWC) usually has prestige and status in society while the language of a dominant group might be limited to the necessary interaction with that language group and present negative motivation beyond such restricted use. Availability of the target language depends on its use in the support system outside school; a language widely used in the environment enables informal exposure, unlike a language that is limited to the classroom. The first language always presents facilitation of learning as the students know a lot about that language before they start to learn the additional language. However, there is often negative interference between conflicting forms or usages in the two languages which might create some difficulty in the learning process.

Factors related to the learning context comprise: (a) the role of the teacher; (b) the role of the learner; (c) the role of materials and media; and (d) the role of feedback in the learning process. Modern language teaching methodology views the teacher as a multifaceted, central figure in the teaching/learning process acting as resource person, evaluator, and facilitator in the classroom. Teachers need to be knowledgeable not only in the target language which they teach but also in a wide variety of didactic methods, in group dynamics, in evaluation, and in curriculum development. Similarly, the role of the learner has changed. The language learner is no longer viewed as a passive receiver of the learning process but as a contributing participant. Thus, learners are often given the opportunity to share in the decision making or at least in the implementation of the process. Teaching materials consisting of textbooks, computer courseware, media, and other elements enable both teachers and learners to fulfill their roles in the teaching/learning process allowing for choices and adaptations. As the learner becomes more responsible for his/her participation in the learning process he/she also becomes more dependent on feedback which guides the continuation of the process. All of these factors together make up the learning context.

Factors related to the learner derive from the centrality of the learner in modern education. Thus, individual aptitude, attitudes, needs, and motivation become key factors in contributing to success or failure in the learning process. Second language acquisition research since the 1970s has greatly contributed to our understanding of how individual learner factors relate to success in language acquisition. Aptitude, often replaced by cognitive and academic proficiency in the mother tongue, has been found to act as a useful predictor for success in the formal classroom setting, while attitudes towards the target language, its culture, and the people who speak it have been found to be quite significant in second language settings. Both can further affect the individual motivation that students develop towards the learning of the second or foreign language, such motivation ultimately consisting of the willingness to invest effort, time, and interest in the learning of the target language. Motivation is further affected by learners' perception of their needs for the target language. If they perceive the language as a valuable instrument for advancement they might be more willing to invest the effort of learning it than if they see it only as another school subject.

The articles presented in this Section deal with all three sets of factors with respect to additional languages in general and to the history of language teaching methodology. This Section also contains specific articles on the teaching of certain languages as a target language.

Foreign Language Curricula

Foreign Language Education

I. Dunlop, R. Titone, S. Takala, H. Schrand, E. Lucas, R. Steele, E. Shohamy, J. P. B. Allen, E. Olshtain, B. Spolsky, S. D. Krashen, E. Bialystok

A foreign language is a language which is not the mother tongue and which is associated with a country or countries whose mother tongue it is. Learning to speak or write a foreign language means a person acquiring the ability to express themselves in different sounds with a different rhythm of speech using different words (and perhaps a different script), different grammar, different idioms, and different phraseology in differing styles which are appropriate to different situations. Learning to understand a foreign language entails learning to decode the sounds, rhythm, and meaning of words and sentences as well as to interpret the cultural associations of these utterances both in speech and writing. Most language learning takes place in schools where foreign languages are, in the majority of cases, taught by nonnative speakers of the languages being taught; and in countries where that foreign language is not used as a language of communication internally. Some authors make a distinction between "second language learning" and "foreign language learning." Others do not. Where this useful distinction is made, "foreign language teaching" means that this language is taught as a school subject or learned as an adult at university or other adult teaching organization, while "second language learning" refers to a situation where that language is the language of instruction in schools (i.e., is used for teaching other subjects) or where that language is used as a lingua franca internally in a country because there is no other common language (Marckwardt 1963). The teaching of immigrants is regarded as second language learning. Obviously there are other circumstances in which people learn a foreign or second language (for example, language schools in the country of origin of that language; by private tutoring; through individual study, etc.) but most people learn a foreign language at school in the first instance, and therefore foreign language learning and foreign language teaching have always been strongly linked, although where there is no unified and generally acceptable theory of learning there can be no generally acceptable or unified theory of teaching (Gage 1972).

The importance that countries attached to foreign language learning grew as the need to communicate in the modern world became more insistent and as the provision of secondary as well as primary education increased. The importance given to different aspects of foreign language learning changed from an emphasis on writing, reading, and translation skills to include oral ability as communications between countries improved. However, the early 1980s saw signs of a possible reversal of this direction with an increasing amount of attention being paid to the receptive skills of reading and listening in the initial stages of learning (Davies 1980). As countries allocated between 8 and 22 percent of their annual school budget to foreign language instruction (Lewis and Massad 1975), educationalists and educational administrators as well as teachers and students of linguistics tried to determine what brought achievement in foreign language learning. The International Association for the Evaluation of Educational Achievement (IEA) carried out surveys of language teaching in schools in 16 countries (Lewis and Massad 1975, Carroll 1975) and found that both for French as a foreign language and English as a foreign language the home background of the student is not significant in foreign language achievement but that the following factors are: the amount of time given to language study over the years; a student's attitude and aspirations as regards the language being studied; teachers' competence (as perceived by themselves) in the foreign language; and use of foreign language in the classroom (although use of the mother tongue is not banned). Nevertheless, the debate about foreign language methodology continued, as it has throughout the century, as different theories of learning, language, linguistics, and teaching were enthusiastically proposed or discarded. The subsections of this article, therefore, attempt to reflect this past and continuing debate. Each author has taken a different aspect of language learning or teaching and their contributions have been arranged in order to move from the history of language teaching and its aims to descriptions of various methods of teaching and learning, given in roughly chronological order. The final section draws together these threads in its exposition of the determinants and process of language learning. This arrangement causes some overlapping, as is inevitable in descriptions of methodology particularly, but it enables each author's contribution to be read separately while still being linked to the other contributions that come before or after it. It also provides an overview of the majority of the main areas of discussion that have occupied teachers, linguists, and administrators concerned with language learning and teaching during the first 80 years of the twentieth century.

1. The History of Foreign Language Teaching

Certain well-defined trends in methodological approaches to foreign language teaching can be discerned throughout history. As a generalization it can be said that the oldest way of teaching language was through the direct method and text interpretation; after the Renaissance the tendency was to center teaching upon grammatical theory and translation; functional methods became a focus of interest towards the end of the nineteenth century; while the search for an integrated approach has characterized the period since the early 1960s.

Foreign language teaching in ancient times (2500 BC–AD 900) was characterized by exclusive emphasis on the learning of the living language through oral conversation or text analysis. Sumerians, Egyptians, Romans, and the early medieval scholars always favored some sort of direct approach.

From the Renaissance to the eighteenth century, Latin, Greek, and Arabic fulfilled the role of lingua franca in different parts of the learned world. They were learned mainly through direct contact with the written texts, or "classics," and grammar was mainly considered in terms of Quintilian's idea of text interpretation. Latin, Greek, and Arabic were the languages of theology, philosophy, literature, and science.

At the beginning of the nineteenth century there was a resurgence of grammar, especially in the works of German teachers such as Seidenstücker and Plötz (Titone 1968), but then came the so-called Reform Movement in Europe and the United States and the direct method or natural method was strongly advocated by a number of practical educators and theoreticians.

Starting from the 1920s or shortly before (O. Jespersen, H. E. Palmer, preceded by H. Sweet) new ideas and principles for language teaching were developed within the theoretical orientations of the oral approach, structural linguistics, and the various forms of the communicative (functional) approach (Titone 1968).

The main tendency today is to combine, either in practice or theoretically, the experience and principles of various methods according to a kind of eclecticism or, more scientifically, an "integrated approach." Flexibility has taken the place of belief in one particular "method." A major impact has been made upon methodology by the contributions of the communication sciences and educational psychology. A large body of research findings—especially those from applied linguistics and psycholinguistics—have helped direct teachers along more effective lines of action.

Instructional experience and research have received great impetus from the new interest in child bilingualism and foreign language teaching at a very early age (Stern 1969).

2. Foreign Language Teaching Policy

Contrary to a commonly held view, several languages are spoken in most countries of the world. There are many times more languages than there are states (Mackey and Verdoodt 1975). The crucial role of language for individuals, social groups, and states has made it important for states to define national language policies. Depending on their internal linguistic situation, the relative political power of different linguistic groups, views on language rights and language equality, and other similar factors, states may choose to promote a policy of a unilingual, bilingual, or multilingual society. This general language policy, whether it has explicit statutory legitimation (e.g., Canada and Finland) or implicit social legitimation by tradition (e.g., the United States), is one of the major determinants of a nation's language teaching policy. Another major determinant is the nation's political and economic orientation towards other nations, which partly explains clear shifts in language teaching policy in some countries, especially after the Second World War. The term "foreign language teaching policy" refers to the plans and practical measures undertaken to fulfill a country's needs for people with knowledge of foreign languages. The need to teach citizens to understand and use either a second language or a foreign language arises from language contacts both within the country and with other countries.

2.1 Emergence of Foreign Language Teaching Policy

Systematic attempts to define a national policy of foreign language teaching are of a relatively recent origin. The growing need for such a policy is due to a number of developments. The fact that the teaching of foreign languages has expanded to encompass larger sections of the population including both younger and adult learners means that language teaching has become increasingly more institutionalized. It has become more organized and systematic, which means that roles and tasks have been specified in greater detail. Language teaching is not the activity of individual teachers only. It is a system of activities at several levels. In order to understand language teaching in all its complexity, it is necessary to be aware of its various levels and subsystems and of their interrelationships. It is also necessary to relate language teaching to its broader educational and societal context.

International organizations have contributed to exploring problems related to defining national language teaching policies. Two seminars sponsored by the UNESCO Institute for Education in the 1960s addressed problems related to an early start of foreign language learning (Stern 1967). Since the early 1960s the Council of Europe has actively worked for the improvement of foreign language teaching in Europe. Through a number of seminars, symposia, and projects (Trim et al. 1980) its work has stimulated foreign language teaching in member countries and beyond. More recently the final act of the Helsinki Accords (1975) commits the signatory states "to encourage the study of foreign languages and civilization as an important means of expanding communication among peoples."

In the United States the growing enthusiasm for teaching foreign languages in the elementary schools (FLES), the National Defense Education Act (1958) in the aftermath of Sputnik, and the Bilingual Education Act (1968) all encouraged the expansion of language teaching. Quite soon enrollments dropped and many colleges and universities stopped requiring a foreign language for admission. A commission on foreign languages and international studies was set up by President Carter in 1978 and its report "Strength Through Wisdom" was published the following year. The commission reviewed the current situation and made a number of recommendations to improve it. In Finland a national commission has recently (1979) outlined a comprehensive plan for foreign language teaching policy for the next few decades.

2.2 Components of Foreign Language Teaching Policy

As linguistic conditions and social systems differ, foreign language teaching policy may range from an explicit, detailed, and binding document to implicit tradition. Thus each country will have to decide what criteria its foreign language teaching policy has to fulfill.

It is obvious that even countries where some "language of wider communication" is spoken will find that there is a need to have some knowledge of other languages. The first stage in defining a foreign language teaching policy usually consists of assessing the country's need for people with a requisite type and extent of knowledge of different languages. Several studies conducted in Sweden in the early 1960s were among the first systematic attempts at needs assessment (see *Needs Assessment Studies*). Since then a number of needs assessments have been carried out in several countries. Typically they have dealt with language needs in business and industry (e.g., Emmans et al. 1974, BOTB 1979). Recently more detailed methods have been developed for identifying the needs of people learning foreign languages (Richterich and Chancerel 1980).

An important decision concerns the degree of choice made available to students. Should all students be required to study a foreign language irrespective of their motivation and linguistic ability? Should they all study the same languages for the same number of years, have the same number of lessons per week, and pursue essentially the same objectives, or should there be different options on these points? Some countries (e.g., Hungary, Norway, the Soviet Union, Sweden) have

decided in favor of making the first language the same for all students whereas some other countries (e.g., Finland) offer students a choice of the first language.

Another major area for planning is related to continuity in language teaching and learning. The Finnish Commission outlined in broad terms the general approach of teaching and the general progression of objectives on different levels of the educational system. Such an outline is designed to improve articulation between different types and levels of educational institutions which provide language learning services.

Foreign language teaching policy also has to tackle the quantitative and qualitative targets of language teaching. Thus it may be found useful to estimate how many people will need to know particular languages and what kind of knowledge they will need to have.

After the scope and general orientation of language teaching has been determined there is a need to set up an efficient administration and organization to take care of the initial and inservice education of language teachers, to promote syllabus design and materials construction, and to make language learning services available from compulsory education to adult education (Strevens 1977).

The system of language teaching is a complex whole. Its successful performance requires continuous research, development, and evaluation as well as a close link between theory and practice. Foreign language teaching policy is designed to coordinate all these activities and to help language teaching become a self-corrective system.

3. Aims in Language Teaching

In most Western European countries the first two to three years of foreign language teaching are devoted to the presentation of the basic grammatical resources of a language; its categories of form and meaning; its fundamental inventories of syntax, lexis, and verbal functions; and their development in the sense of skills in the areas of listening comprehension, reading comprehension, speaking, and writing.

Less recent curricula define grammar and vocabulary loads (the latter ranging from 1,500–4,000 items) for the first few teaching years and confine themselves to the instruction that teaching should be appropriate to the needs of the child and informative about the foreign culture with the aim of arousing interest in the foreign country and enabling students through imitation of speech patterns to produce the target language orally both in the context of monolingual instruction and in role plays representing situations from the everyday target language reality.

As from 1970, statements on skills, topic areas, situations, and learning objectives became more precise and an attempt to include linguistic progressions in curricula in the form of lists of sentence patterns and grammatical categories became increasingly more apparent. The

Council of Europe initiated two studies in the mid-1970s on foreign language teaching in Europe: the Threshold Level (1975) and Waystage (1976). How effective they will be as curricular framework for foreign language teaching in European schools cannot yet be predicted.

There are increasingly varied views in individual Western European countries as to the objectives of foreign language teaching after the first two to three years, although there is general agreement that speech practice should remain an element in the fields of cultural and literary studies which follow the phase of language acquisition.

Adult foreign language teaching is mainly directed towards students who come to courses as a way of gaining further professional qualifications; as a way of spending their leisure time; to a lesser extent for personal reasons (relatives in the target language area); to prepare for school entrance or leaving examinations; or, in general, to make up for missed education.

Adult courses such as those held in the Federal Republic of Germany, the Netherlands, Austria, Switzerland, and France are guided by principles of objective achievement measurement and bound by obligatory examination regulations, assignments, and criteria of assessment. In most European countries and in the United States, the objective of these courses is the development of practical language skills in the areas of listening, speaking, reading, and writing. The following criteria of identification and selection in the relevant curricula help to describe such courses:

(a) Speech intentions—the Council of Europe's Threshold Level lists the speech intentions (e.g., social contact: addressing someone and reacting to being addressed or introducing oneself and other people and reacting to introduction) which the student should have at his or her command after a certificate-orientated English course.

(b) Topics—a definition of the topics/topic areas (e.g., sport, radio, cinema, leisure activities) which provide the framework for the learner's utterances in English.

(c) Situations—this list has the same aim as the topic list. Some examples are: Shopping, At the Post Office.

(d) Texts—this catalog of learning objectives contains the texts which the students should be able to understand and/or produce after completing an English course.

(e) Vocabulary/structures—this list defines the nature and volume of the linguistic material which the student should have at his or her command.

The primary objective of these courses is comprehensibility; linguistic correctness is demanded only when mistakes are liable to render something incomprehensible.

4. Language and Language Teaching

Foreign language teaching since the 1950s has gone through three main cycles each of which has been affected by theories of language, linguistics, and learning.

Structural linguistics, of the kind that ignored meaning in language, combined with some behaviorist theories of learning to produce methods of teaching which were variously called "the audiolingual method," "the direct (or modified direct) method," and "the S-R (or stimulus–response) approach." The main ideas of this approach are:

(a) language is speech not writing;

(b) a language is a set of habits;

(c) [teachers should] teach the language not about the language;

(d) languages are different. (Moulton 1962)

The ideas of contrastive linguistics and contrastive analysis were also influential in persuading many language teachers and writers about teaching that for the learner "those elements that are similar to his native language will be simple for him, and those elements that are different will be difficult" (Lado 1957) and that the way to find out differences is through scientific contrastive analysis of the native language of the speaker and the target language to be learned, especially as regards phonemic differences between the languages being contrasted.

The difficulties inherent in the contrastive approach were also, however, pointed out (Denison 1962) though perhaps these warnings were not sufficiently regarded. The audiolingual approach can best be characterized in Carroll's words:

> The audiolingual habit theory . . . has the following principal ideas: (a) that since speech is primary and writing secondary, the habits to be learned must be learned first of all as auditory discrimination responses and speech responses; (b) that habits must be automatized as much as possible so that they can be called forth without conscious attention; (c) that the automatization of habits occurs chiefly by practice, that is by repetition. (Carroll 1965)

Chomsky, however, reacted sharply both to the linguistic and to the psychological views on which the audiolingual method was based. He did not accept that language was a set of habits and described the "rule-governed creativity involved in the everyday use of language" (Chomsky 1964), while pointing out that if language is "generative" it cannot be learned merely as a set of habits. Although Chomsky's work was difficult for teachers to access, his description of language as "rule-governed behavior" revived the old arguments about grammar–translation methods versus a more direct method approach. Carroll described "the cognitive-code learning theory [which] may be thought of as a modified up-to-date grammar–translation theory. According to this theory, learning a language is a process of acquiring conscious control of the phonological, grammatical, and lexical patterns of a second language largely through study and analysis of these patterns as a body of knowledge" (Carroll 1965).

A combination of an S–R and a "generative" approach was seen as a resolution of these two points of view in teaching (Dunlop 1970) and "a meaningful synthesis" was suggested in Carroll's "cognitive habit-formation theory" (Carroll 1971). Lenneberg's biological theory of language had also stated that primary language acquisition occurs between the ages of 2 and 3 and puberty by "an interaction of maturation and self-programmed learning" (thus implying that human beings have a language learning "mechanism" which was later called LAD or "language acquisition device". "After puberty, the ability for self-organization and adjustment to the physiological demands of verbal behaviour quickly declines" (Lenneberg 1967). The implication of Lenneberg's theory for foreign language learning is that up to the age of puberty, the child's innate language learning ability will enable it to structure the foreign language being learned; whereas after that age (for example, in adult learning) this innate language learning ability would have declined and the adult learner would need a more structured approach to learning a foreign language and more explanation of the rules governing that foreign language. Another implication of Lenneberg's theory is that there is little point in comparing the way a child learns its own language with the way a person learns a foreign language after the age of puberty. A distinction therefore needs to be made between different approaches to language learning and teaching at different ages; a distinction which is not always made clear in the literature.

However, in the 1970s and early 1980s, the third cycle of modern language teaching discussions concerned "communicative competence." Here language competence is seen as including:

(a) formal possibility (i.e., is a sentence possible grammatically?);

(b) feasibility (a sentence may be possible grammatically but hardly feasible);

(c) appropriateness to context;

(d) possibility of occurrence. (Hymes 1970)

The notional–functional syllabus (Wilkins 1976) concentrates on language for the communication needs of the student and these will include social behaviors as well as grammatical competence at this level of performance, and appropriateness of language to the relationship of the speakers, for example in "stranger to stranger" situations (van Ek 1975).

At the time of writing, communicative competence is still an aim rather than a reality in the classroom and "learner centered" learning is very often at the center of discussion together with approaches like community language learning, suggestopedia, and the silent way. The idea of individual learning strategies attracts attention, as does monitor theory and there is an interest,

for the future, in self-access materials and individualized work as an expanding field of activity in language learning. In this connection, computers in language teaching are attracting notice and CALL (Computer-Assisted Language Learning) includes, among other things: games and simulations; interactive audio and video; hypermedia; testing; conventional language teaching exercises; authoring programs and languages; and the application of business software to language learning activities.

5. The Grammar–Translation Method

The grammar–translation method, which developed from Cartesian logic (Kelly 1971) is based on medieval practices in teaching classical languages where emphasis is placed on memorization of grammatical rules and analytic translation of texts sometimes known as construing.

The method spread during the eighteenth and nineteenth centuries. Ignoring the direct and natural approaches of Comenius and Locke, its exponents such as Hamilton in England, Jacotot in France, and Ollendorf and Plötz in Germany developed a system of interlinear translation, and used synthetic passages built around rules, exceptions, and selected vocabulary.

Proponents of the method believe that: language is logical and static and is based on written models (Grittner 1969); modern languages conform to rules of Latin where inflections are important; grammar is prescriptive and is based on rules which must be followed; certain forms of language are good while others are bad; modern vernaculars are deteriorations of an earlier better language; language should be studied through rules which are more important than the example; language knowledge is assessed in terms of knowledge of rules and ability to translate.

Nineteenth century textbook writers were mainly concerned with codifying the foreign language into rules of morphology and syntax to be explained and memorized (Titone 1968). Textbooks contained definitions of rules and exceptions, lists of paradigms and classes of words, passages for translation into and from the target language, and some exercises. There was little simplification of texts and complete disregard for natural language.

In the grammar–translation method the main preoccupation of the teacher is correctness and not fluency (Kelly 1971). The teacher monopolizes the lesson, expounding texts, correcting answers, and testing students. There is little difference in the form of lessons in upper and intermediate classes. Teaching is deductive. Reading is done intensively. The teacher's aim is completion of exercises in the book.

Linguists of the nineteenth and twentieth centuries have criticized the grammar–translation method because it is based on traditional grammar which they regard as unsystematic, arbitrary, and confusing. The method is considered ineffective for teaching students to speak the language (although it has proved effective for teaching gifted students to understand written texts). Students are taught about the language rather than its use. Teachers often lecture in the native language and may not be able to speak the target language.

A survey conducted by the International Bureau of Education in 1964 indicates that most countries had adopted other methods. Of 83 countries surveyed, only 15 were still using the grammar–translation method. Many were using the direct method.

6. Pattern Practice

Structural linguists attempted to isolate the basic syntactic structures of the language. Language teachers thought that if second and foreign language learners could acquire the basic structures or patterns in a systematic manner, they would make faster progress in mastering the language. Structuralism coincided with behaviorism which views language learning as habit formation. It was claimed that the listening, speaking, reading, and writing skills could be acquired through a conditioning process based on the theories of B. F. Skinner whereby correct habits are reinforced by automatic repetition and reward. A language teaching approach developed from this called the audiolingual method which emphasized the oral skills and techniques of memorization and systematic pattern practice or structure drills (*exercises structuraux*). Patterns were drilled to a point of automatic response in the belief that the learner would then merely have to slot in lexical items appropriate to the conversational situation. At the same time educational technology produced the language laboratory which, with the use of two-track tapes, encouraged listening and drilling exercises.

A pattern is usually introduced to the learner in a dialogue to be memorized, or in a reading passage, before it is drilled. The subsequent practice is usually of two general types, substitution and transformation (see Dakin 1973 for other types). In substitution drills the same element of the pattern is replaced in each item in response to a cue. The teacher first gives an example (e.g., He talks) and a cue (e.g., to run). The correct response will then be "He runs," following which the teacher gives another cue, and the student another response, and so on. Sometimes this substitution will cause a morphological change to another element in the pattern (singular/plural; masculine/feminine, etc.).

In transformation drills, the utterance is changed according to a pattern as in the transformation of a statement into a question. For example, given the pattern: "He talks" → "Does he talk?" as an example, the correct response to the cue "He runs" will be "Does he run?"

The same pattern is practiced over a number of items so that the learner is able to give the correct automatic response, thus reinforcing mastery of the structure. The learner is assumed to induce from this repetition a generalization about the structure.

Since the aim is to reinforce accurate manipulation of the structure, the drill is usually presented in a three-phase or a four-phase mode after the initial example. Typically, the first and second phases are the teacher's cue and the learner's response. Following this the student is given immediate confirmation of the correct response (phase three) and time to repeat the response once again (phase four).

Pattern practice did not achieve the anticipated dramatic improvement in the learner's general command of the language. Some learners found the mechanical repetition of drills in the language laboratory boring. Others could repeat the patterns perfectly but were unable to use them in spontaneous conversation. Teachers then realized that mastery of discrete grammatical structures does not enable the learner to integrate them into the overall system of the language. The items in the drills focused on grammatical form and reduced the importance of vocabulary; so each item had limited meaning and the semantic link from one item to the next was quite arbitrary and often absurd.

Chomsky led the attack against the theory of language as a set of habits. The original audiolingual method which relied heavily on pattern practice was adapted to give more importance to meaning and contextualization. Some pattern practice can be useful in the early stages of language learning but patterns remain hollow until the learner uses them to express a personal meaning in conversation where spontaneous interaction and the social setting are important factors.

7. Inductive Versus Deductive Foreign Language Teaching

The inductive and deductive approaches in foreign and second language teaching refer to procedures for introducing material in teaching. Specifically, inductive teaching means that the students are introduced to a number of examples from which they, themselves, develop (induce) a rule or generalization which governs or subsumes the examples. Deductive teaching means that students are introduced to a statement, generalization, or rule and move from it to provide specific examples, applications, and practice. Thus, the specific instances are deduced from the general rule.

The history of second/foreign language teaching methodology has witnessed an ongoing debate concerning the preferability of induction or deduction. Specifically, should foreign language be taught in a way that facilitates the induction of underlying rules, or should these rules be introduced from the beginning? The debate is related to other controversies in the field, such as formal versus informal language learning (in informal learning the learner induces from the data certain rules and meanings, while in formal learning, rules and meanings are generally presented to the student), and the function which language rules play in the learning process.

Historically, different teaching methods have been associated with either the inductive or the deductive approach. In general, formalists who tend to focus on language analysis have relied mostly on deductive teaching, while activists who stress language use, have relied more on inductive teaching. Thus, the grammar–translation method is generally associated with the deductive approach, since grammar is taught explicitly and is viewed as a significant teaching goal. The direct method is usually associated with the inductive approach since its focus is on structural practice and students are left to form their own generalizations about grammatical structures based on what they have been practicing. In the audiolingual era the learner was encouraged to induce grammatical rules, and teaching materials were constructed accordingly. The cognitive-code approach called for a return to explaining grammar rules first. It was claimed that this approach involves students' reasoning processes in language learning. The current approaches are concerned with communication and use of language according to the specific needs of the learner. These approaches emphasize inductive learning since the learner is encouraged to induce information from authentic real-life experiences and to make generalizations from language input.

It should be noted that induction/deduction is not limited to teaching grammar but applies to other areas in language teaching as well. In teaching reading, for example, students can be encouraged to seek comprehension by inferring meaning of unknown words from the context (inductive approach), or by referring to a translation and bilingual dictionary for unknown elements (deductive approach).

Proponents of the inductive approach believe that it facilitates the induction of underlying abstractions of the language and that the learner absorbs and internalizes better when he/she has discovered the underlying abstraction for himself or herself. Furthermore they believe that such learning increases retention. Proponents of the deductive approach believe that introducing the rule at the beginning allows the learner to apply the rule during the practice segment of the lesson rather than to spend time confirming its hypothesis.

However, very little empirical evidence is available to confirm either of the claims or to show that the two approaches are basically different. Seliger (1975) conducted an experiment utilizing both approaches and found no difference in learning the material, although he did find that retention was better under the deductive approach. In this article Seliger refers to a study conducted by Politzer in which differences between the two approaches were examined and it was found that the early introduction of the explanation of the rule is more advisable than its postponement. Carroll (1971) states that research has shown that neither approach alone is adequate; there must be considerable alternation between rules and examples. Chastain (1976) claims that induction/deduction does not represent a dichotomy but rather a continuum. Other scholars have expressed the view that there is no evidence that what is induced is of more value than what is provided deductively, nor that what is discovered in the inductive approach is better retained. In the classroom situation it was observed that the teacher provides the rule in both approaches, and the only difference is in the number of examples used. Furthermore, not all students were capable of inducing and they tended to wait for the teacher's explanation. There is also no evidence that the deductive approach is more cognitive than an inductive discovery procedure since induction requires similar cognitive processes.

The strongest criticism of the two approaches is that they must be viewed in relation to other variables, such as the conditions of learning, the situation, the learning material, the subject matter, and most importantly, the learner. The learner's goal in learning the language, age, learning style, aptitude, and strategies all influence his/her ability to utilize generalizations or rules made available by the deductive approach, or in the case of the inductive approach, to be able to identify certain attributes of the learning concept.

Any attempt to arrive at a conclusion about the advantages or disadvantages of either induction or deduction in teaching requires careful examination and consideration of the above variables, in order to determine if these approaches are justified constructs that really make a difference in language teaching and learning.

8. The Eclectic Method

Eclecticism, a mode of thought which takes ideas from different philosophical systems and attempts to fit them into a logically coherent unity, has existed since ancient times. In second language teaching, the eclectic method tends to be adopted by those who wish to avoid rigid partisan commitments, and who believe that they can see the merits in each of two opposed arguments. D. D. Runes, in his *Dictionary of Philosophy*, distinguishes between "passive" or ad hoc eclecticism, which consists of the arbitrary juxtaposition of doctrines from different systems and which is often found in the work of scholars of no great originality, and "active" or rational eclecticism, associated with those creative thinkers who succeed in assimilating the seemingly contradictory principles of several systems into a more comprehensive viewpoint. All authorities agree that the eclectic approach, whether in its frequently disparaged passive form or in its more highly valued active form, has much to commend it from a practical point of view, and tends to emerge at times when established schools of thought have become inflexible and dogmatic, or are otherwise revealing their defects.

Eclecticism is a position often favored by practical teachers who like to experiment with new ideas, but who have to reconcile these with the need to maintain a set of techniques which can be shown to work in a particular situation. The eclectic approach in language teaching has a long history. For example Henry Sweet, writing at the end of the nineteenth century, sought "a mean between unyielding conservatism on the one hand and reckless radicalism on the other" (Sweet 1899 p. vii). More recently Rivers is consistent with Runes when she distinguishes "true eclecticists" from "drifters who adopt new techniques cumulatively and purposelessly." According to Rivers (1981 p. 55), true eclecticists are willing to experiment but they are wary of bandwagons. They seek to maintain a judicious balance in their teaching, and they gradually evolve a method which suits their own personality and circumstances.

At the present time there appears to be a growing awareness that the bandwagon effect in second language teaching should be recognized and guarded against. Thus, much recent work has emphasized the fact that language learners do not constitute a single homogeneous group, but manifest a great variety of backgrounds, personalities, and individual learning styles. It follows that there can be no single method or theory which is capable of accounting for all aspects of language and language learning. Recent writers have begun to question whether there is any need to invest further time or effort in the search for decisive innovations or for unified, multipurpose formulas such as the grammar–translation method, the direct method, or the audiolingual method. Instead, it is claimed that emphasis should be placed on the responsibility of individual teachers to make informed, intelligent choices from among the large number of competing theories and methodologies which are currently available.

One of the most clearly articulated statements of rational eclecticism in language teaching is to be found in Palmer's *Principles of Language Study* (1922). Palmer recognized that language teaching is an art rather than an exact science, and that therefore there are bound to be disagreements about the best procedure to adopt to achieve a particular end. If the widely varying needs of students are to be taken into account it is essential that dogmatic theorizing should be avoided and that a varied and flexible approach should be maintained to classroom methodology. Faced, for example, with the necessity of deciding on the relative merits of "conscious" and "subconscious" methods of study, teachers often find themselves in a dilemma: either they can adopt one alternative and reject the other, thus encouraging the development of an unbalanced and artificially restricted teaching method, or they can attempt to create a compromise between the two approaches, which carries with it the danger that they might end up with the worst of both worlds—a combination of disrupted drill-work and partial and misleading explanations.

Having rejected these two unsatisfactory alternatives, Palmer suggests instead that a method of teaching should be developed in which inductive and deductive principles are used concurrently in the same program, but not in one and the same operation. The application of this principle, which Palmer calls the "multiple line of approach," results in a cycle of activities—drills fol-

lowed by free work, rational explanation alternating with spontaneous assimilation—in which the various learning principles support and complement one another, rather than being allowed to fall into conflict. Only in this way, according to Palmer, can justice be done to the great richness of language, or provision be made for the many and diverse needs of the learner.

A cyclical, interaction model as advocated by Palmer tends to be preferred by those who recognize the need to reconcile on a practical level approaches which may seem to be in conflict on a theoretical level: for example, cognitive-code learning theory and audiolingual habit theory, or structural, functional, and experiential concepts of curriculum. This reconciliation is typically brought about by adopting a combination of teaching strategies, but with varying degrees of emphasis depending on the teacher's assessment of the students' needs. The question of what determines the most efficient fit between the teaching strategy and the learner can only be decided empirically, either by practical experience in the classroom, or by research designed to compare the results of different types of educational treatment.

9. The Notional–Functional Syllabus

The notional–functional syllabus is an approach to language syllabus design and therefore concerns decisions leading to the organization and selection of language content for teaching/learning purposes. The early proponents of the notional–functional syllabus presented it as an analytic approach to syllabus organization (Wilkins 1976) which does not view language components as building blocks to be accumulated progressively but as types of language behavior which represent the global way in which people use language. The term "notions" in the notional–functional syllabus refers to concepts which people use in verbal communication and hence it represents a wide variety of levels of abstraction; general notions relate to universal themes such as time, space, motion, and so on, while specific notions are topic related, for example, travel, sports, work, and so on. The term "function" refers to the functional meaning of an utterance, that is, the social purpose of that utterance. The notional–functional syllabus is organized in terms of the purposes for which people are learning language and the kinds of language performance that are necessary to meet those purposes (Wilkins 1976 p. 13).

The notional–functional syllabus began as a new trend in the United Kindgom and Europe during the early 1970s, and was first realized in syllabus format with the publication of van Ek's (1975) *Threshold Level* of language proficiency for the Council of Europe. It reached the United States in the late 1970s following Wilkins' (1976) publication of *Notional Syllabuses* and the plenary debate on the notional–functional syllabus held at the 12th Annual TESOL Conference in Mexico City (Campbell, Rutherford, Finocchiaro, and Widdowson in Blatchford and Schachter 1978). This rather rapid spread of notional–functional syllabus thinking had a considerable pragmatic impact on the field of material development since a large number of textbooks appeared, which claimed to be based on this approach.

The initial development of the notional–functional syllabus drew from both theoretical and practical sources. On the one hand, there was a strong shift of linguistic interest from formal and distributional properties to communication properties of language, for example, speech act analysis, conversational implicature, presuppositions, and so on. On the other hand, the focus of language teaching shifted from linguistic objectives to learner's needs. The notional–functional syllabus recognizes the fact that the content of learning must be sensitive to the needs of the learners. Accordingly, such needs must be defined in terms of the different types of communication in which the learner may engage during or beyond the course of study.

The construction of a language syllabus inevitably requires a quantification of language data since it aims at the organization and specification of the content of language teaching. Syllabi may differ in the principles which guide the selection of language elements, in the criteria which are used to arrive at a suitable arrangement of these elements, and in the expected goals or outcomes of the teaching/learning process. The essence of the notional–functional syllabus is the priority it gives the semantic content of language learning (Wilkins 1976) and in the full account of the conventions of social use which it aims to provide (Wilkins 1981). Thus, the difference between the grammatical syllabus and the notional–functional syllabus lies in the definition of their language content—the grammatical syllabus is defined in formal terms such as grammatical patterns and lexical items, while the notional–functional syllabus is defined in semantic and functional terms. Three kinds of categories are distinguished in the notional–functional syllabus: semantico-grammatical or conceptual categories, modal categories, and communicative functional categories. The first type (semantico-grammatical) relates to the ideational or propositional meaning of an utterance which is expressed through the grammatical system of the language. The second type deals with the modality of meaning through which the speaker expresses his/her own attitude towards what is being said, and the third refers to the function of the utterance in the larger context within which it occurs.

The point of departure of the notional–functional syllabus is not, as has sometimes been the claim of ardent followers, a rejection of grammar-based or situation-based approaches, but these are viewed as inadequate bases for the development of language programs, since they lack the incorporation of communicative properties of language, and do not sufficiently emphasize the function that forms are supposed to fulfill. Moreover, such syllabi differ in the definition of the kind of knowledge or behavior that the course should aim at.

Thus, the grammatical syllabus is based on the assumption that it is necessary to know the language system and how to exploit it in order to reach communicative ability while notional–functional-syllabus proponents claim that usable language will become available to the learner sooner than in a structure-based approach and that the learners' motivation will increase due to the demonstrable social value of what they are learning (Wilkins 1981).

Perhaps the most significant claim maintained by the notional–functional approach is related to its attempt to account for communicative competence within the actual design of the syllabus itself. It is on this issue that the notional–functional syllabus has had to face serious criticism and theoretical challenge since most of the criticism was raised by scholars supporting the communicative approach to language teaching. Widdowson (in Blatchford and Schachter 1978) questions the claim that communicative competence can be accounted for in the notional–functional syllabus. He considers it yet another inventory of units or items and not a continuum, which would be the only way to truly represent communication. What has changed, according to Widdowson, is the nature of the units: instead of structural isolates, there are notional isolates.

The major weakness of the notional–functional syllabus, according to Brumfit (1981) and Paulston (1981) concerns the lack of emphasis on systematicity. They maintain that language learning can be brought about successfully only when the presentation is systematic and allows for generalizations. Furthermore, Brumfit is concerned with the fact that to date it is not feasible to define all notions and the relations that hold among them and hence the principles of organization into a syllabus are not sufficiently operational.

In spite of the widespread implementation that has followed the theoretical claims related to the notional–functional syllabus, it seems that the approach, as such, is still suffering from serious limitations. There is not, as yet, a complete understanding of the functional system of any one language, much less of the differences across sociocultural boundaries. This lack of theoretical foundation has resulted in the lack of systematicity in language content organization for teaching/learning purposes. In order to implement Wilkins' (1981) suggestion to use the specification of language events (those needed by the learners) as the general organizing principle for the syllabus, it would be necessary to know much more about speech acts and sociocultural rules. Future sociolinguistic research might provide such knowledge. Still, with all the limitations evident in the notional–functional syllabus, its contribution to the field of language syllabus design and material development has been considerable: it has forced planners to focus on communication as the major goal for language courses and to incorporate learners' needs as a major factor in the definition of this goal. This has, no doubt, resulted in more relevant language courses and teaching materials.

10. Community Language Learning

Community language learning is the name of a method of teaching foreign languages developed by Charles A. Curran (1976) (see also Stevick 1980). The method, which is part of a general approach to education that Curran labeled "counseling–learning" has as its central principle the notion that the relation between the persons involved should not be teacher and student but rather counselor and student. The counselor, who, by the nature of the situation, knows what it is that the other wants (or needs) to learn, is responsible not just for this knowledge, and for managing and directing the learning, but also for understanding the personal psychological needs of the learner. The counselor then must try to provide a situation of security in which learning can take place.

In a community language learning lesson, the students are seated in a circle with the counselor moving freely outside. In the first phase, the students record a brief conversation that consists of their individual repetitions of the counselor's translation into the foreign language of utterances they have selected as something they want to say to each other. After the tape has been made, it is played over twice. The counselor then writes down the text. Word for word translations are provided. After a period of short contemplation, students are permitted to ask questions of each other and of the counselor. There are other techniques used, but central to them all is the counseling response: the attempt of the teacher to assume, as far as humanly possible, the student's frame of reference, to bring to the lessons "a deep understanding of the students' anxieties, insecurities, and feelings of inadequacy," so that they may "grow confident and secure in their ability to trust the knower and to abandon themselves to the knowledge which he represents" (Curran 1976 p. 5).

11. Suggestopedia

Suggestopedia is the name of a method of foreign language teaching proposed and being developed by Georgi Lozanov (Lozanov 1979, Stevick 1980). Suggestopedia holds that unconscious learning is as important as conscious, and that students can learn languages (among other things) much faster if they are released from socially imposed limitations and provided with a relaxed atmosphere for learning. Learning can be enhanced by double "planeness," when there is support on the unconscious level for the learning taking place overtly. Supporters claim that students in suggestopedic courses learn 2,000 words in 60 hours of instruction. A number of techniques used in the method have been described: students adopt new identities (names and backgrounds) during the course; teachers do not correct, blame, or praise; translation in the student's language is provided to relax tension; the classroom is specially designed with appropriate colors and furniture; various ritual patterns (words or actions or objects) are repeated regularly; background music of a special kind is used in closing parts of lessons; and three basic principles are maintained: "the principle of joy and easiness," the close connection of conscious and unconscious, and the principle of "suggestive interaction." Most published descriptions of the method are by followers.

12. The Silent Way

The silent way is a method of teaching foreign languages developed by Caleb Gattegno (Gattegno 1976, Stevick 1980). Gattegno, who has been active in many spheres of education, argues that language learning is a part of becoming a better and freer person, "an exciting adventure involving the whole self" (1976 p. 10). His approach, very much in tune with the various modern schools of humanistic psychology, and in this way similar to suggestopedia and community language learning, puts considerable emphasis on the affective dimension of language learning. The "silence" in its name is that of the teacher who (contrary to one of the major principles of the audiolingual method), does not offer native-like models for imitation, but works rather to elicit, when possible by silent cues, student utterances in the foreign language; moreover, the teacher is expected to react neutrally and nonevaluatively to student responses, avoiding either praise or blame.

Silent way courses start with students pronouncing color-coded syllables from wall charts. If the sound is quite new, the teacher may give a single audible example; otherwise, the students are moved towards minimally acceptable pronunciation by silent cues. Once the sounds are satisfactory, the teacher moves on to the second phase, which involves numbers, and the third, which uses colored wooden or plastic rods of various lengths. Using the charts and the rods, the teacher leads the class to talk about the number and color of the rods and their changing locations. Only one element is worked on at a time. There is no memorization or translation.

Among the principles espoused by Gattegno are the following:

(a) Learning is more important than teaching.

(b) The teacher must listen and observe but not interfere.

(c) Structures are more important than vocabulary.

(d) Language learning should involve physical activity.

(e) The class must be treated as a social unit.

(f) Learners must be allowed to experiment.

Supporters of the system report considerable success with it.

13. Monitor Theory

Monitor theory, developed by S. Krashen, consists of five hypotheses about second language acquisition.

(a) *Acquisition-learning hypothesis.* Second language competence can be developed in two different ways: Acquisition is subconscious, gained through experience using the language in communicative situations. Learning is conscious knowledge, usually gained through formal study.

(b) *Natural order hypothesis.* Structures are acquired (not learned) in a predictable order, common to all second language acquirers. The "natural order" is largely independent of the influence of the first language and is also independent of the classroom syllabus, or teaching order.

(c) *Monitor hypothesis.* Fluency in second languages derives from what has been acquired. Learning functions only as a monitor, or editor. Learning is used only to make formal corrections on the output of the acquired system, either before or after the utterance is actually produced.

Monitor use is very limited. To access conscious rules, learners or performers need to have enough time. Normal conversation does not provide enough time for extensive monitor use for most people. Even when performers have time, they often do not use the conscious rules they know—performers also need to be focused on form, or thinking about correctness, to utilize rules. Also, the performer needs to know the rule. These conditions predict significant use of the conscious grammar only when all three conditions are met, for example, when students take traditional grammar tests.

(d) *Input hypothesis.* Language is acquired in only one way: by understanding input language containing structures not yet acquired. This is done by focusing on what is said, on the message and not the form. Context, or extralinguistic information, is utilized in doing this.

Theoretically, speaking is not necessary for language acquisition. Speech (output) is a result of language acquisition, not its cause. Speaking may help indirectly, however, by inviting comprehensible input via conversation.

When there is sufficient comprehensible input, necessary structures are automatically provided: it is not (and should not be) necessary to deliberately program or sequence structures into the input.

(e) *Affective filter hypothesis.* Affective variables do not influence the actual operation of the "language acquisition device" but act externally. When performers are anxious, or not motivated, a mental block, or "affective filter" prevents the input from reaching the parts of the brain responsible for language acquisition.

"Monitor theory" implies that the language class should provide comprehensible input that is interesting and/or relevant in a situation that encourages a low affective filter. For the beginner, the classroom can be an excellent place to obtain comprehensible input. Input on the "outside" may be hard to obtain or be incomprehensible. The goal of the class is to bring the student to the point where he or she can begin to understand input outside the class and improve on his or her own. Grammar teaching is useful for the monitor function

and as part of general education (linguistics) but is peripheral. The central goal of any language teaching program is to encourage acquisition. (Evidence for monitor theory is found in Krashen 1981, 1982.)

14. The Natural Approach

Developed by T. Terrell at the University of California at Irvine, the natural approach is fully consistent with monitor theory. The natural approach follows five basic guidelines:

(a) The teacher uses only the target language in the classroom.

(b) Student responses are not corrected for speech errors unless communication is seriously disturbed.

(c) Classroom activities center on topics of personal interest to the student. The teacher attempts to present comprehensible and interesting messages, but does not drill particular grammatical forms.

(d) Study of formal grammar is limited to homework and written grammatical exercises, which are corrected.

(e) Speech is allowed to "emerge." The focus of the natural approach classroom is on comprehension. In early sessions, students are not expected to produce in the target language. Subsequent activities invite single word responses and eventually longer student responses are encouraged, but not forced.

Reports of natural approach teaching have been quite positive. Voge (1981) compared university natural approach students to those in a grammar-oriented class, also taught exclusively in the target language (German). Natural approach students were comparable in grammar (despite less grammar study) and were superior in communication and fluency measures. Informally, it has been noted that natural approach students begin to utilize the second language spontaneously within a few sessions, even if they are not required to, and appear to be more willing to use the language outside the class, as compared to traditional students.

The natural approach can be used at the elementary level with a de-emphasis of the grammar–homework component, since children have less capacity and need for conscious learning. The grammar component can be optional in adult education, reflecting individual variation among adults in conscious learning.

15. Foreign Language Acquisition

The influence of psychological factors on language learning comes primarily from two sources: individual variation in a learner's success with the task and the more universal constraints that govern human learning. The first of these is addressed by discussing selected determinants of achievement in foreign language learning and the second by examining some of the cognitive processes implicated in language learning. Most of the discussion assumes a situation of foreign language learning in which the language is not spoken in the community. Some implications for second language learning in which the target language is the language of the community, are also discussed.

15.1 Determinants of Achievement

Most normal children master their native language with apparently little difficulty and astonishingly little variability. Second or foreign language learners, however, be they children or adults, show enormous differences in their success with the task. It is this disparity in the degree of challenge that second or foreign language learning presents to individuals that has led to the pursuit of a set of predictors or determinants of achievement. The assumption is that successful learning is associated with a constellation of factors relating to the individual, the learning situation, and other environmental features. Moreover, it is assumed that the identification of such a set will not only provide instructional models for those who are less successful, but also indicate aspects of the processes and strategies involved in language learning.

Because foreign language classrooms yield such varying degrees of proficiency in students and because such classrooms remain a major setting for language learning, the pursuit of a set of classroom-related determinants of achievement becomes particularly important. Why do two learners who presumably have the same instructional opportunity differ so greatly in attained proficiency? Two types of factors have been examined in response to such disparities: first, individual factors which explore a number of skills or abilities that may be relevant to language achievement; and second, environmental factors which relate aspects of the social and personal context of learning to attained proficiency.

(a) *Individual learner factors*. A variety of the relevant individual learner factors can be described in terms of their relative emphasis on cognitive or affective descriptors. Cognitive includes all such characteristics as intelligence, aptitude, or ability. Affective includes both attitudinal and personality variables that distinguish individuals in ways unrelated to cognitive ability. Numerous tests of each have been developed, and the results of such tests related to language achievement.

One set of cognitive factors, broadly called "cognitive style" refers to the way in which individuals approach the learning task and operate upon information. Examples include constricted versus flexible control (Kogan 1971), broad versus narrow categorizing, and field dependence versus field independence (Witkin et al. 1962). Most of the research, however, has been addressed to the variable of field dependence/independence.

This latter variable indicates differences in the way in which information is analyzed and structured in the perceptual and cognitive domains. The underlying skill is the individual's ability to deliberately focus on relevant information while ignoring misleading or irrelevant cues. The usual assessment is the Hidden Figures Test in which subjects have to identify a simple geometric figure within a complex design. The hypothesis has been that field independent learners may be able to focus on the relevant language stimuli without being distracted by the inappropriate ones whereas the field dependent learners may be unable to disentangle the complex language input.

Evidence for the advantage of field independence in classroom foreign language learning fluctuates as a function of the type of investigation, the task used, the program of study, and the age of the learners. Facilitating effects of field independence, for example, have been reported for older learners as opposed to younger ones (Naiman et al. 1978), oral tasks as opposed to written ones (Naiman et al. 1978), and formal tasks as opposed to communicative ones (Tucker et al. 1976). Even these findings, however, have proven to be highly sensitive to variation and are not always replicated.

Other cognitive factors include more quantifiable differences such as language learning aptitude, measures of IQ (especially on the verbal intelligence component of those tests), and nonlanguage academic achievement as indicated by grade scores and subject matter standardized tests. The factor which has received the most attention in this domain is that of language learning aptitude.

Research on the description and role of language learning aptitude for second language achievement has proceeded largely through standardized tests—the Modern Language Aptitude Test, the Pimsleur Language Aptitude Battery, and the Illinois Test of Psycholinguistic Abilities. For the first two, components of the concept "language learning aptitude" were identified and items constructed to measure those abilities. Early research was, in fact, aimed precisely at discovering the component skills which could be tested and used to predict foreign language achievement. For Pimsleur (1966b), the relevant components were verbal intelligence, motivation to learn the language, and auditory ability. Carroll (1977) included abilities such as: phonetic coding ability which is the "ability to listen to second language sounds or words, to identify them as distinctive, and then to store them in memory so that they can later be recalled accurately on an appropriate occasion"; grammatical sensitivity which is the "ability to understand the grammatical functions of different kinds of language elements (words, particles, suffixes, etc.) and the rules governing their use"; and inductive reasoning ability which is the "ability to infer, from the way in which different words and grammatical constructions are used in the second language, the rules governing the use of the words and constructions."

Research based on such tests has shown these scores to be moderate but consistent predictors of classroom achievement. The interpretation of results, however, is problematic in that the reliability varies with the age of the subject, the language being learned, and the type of achievement criterion used. In addition, the relationship between aptitude and intelligence varies as a function of the aptitude trait being assessed, again complicating the interpretation of this construct. In general, however, there is a fairly strong relationship between variables such as aptitude, intelligence, and language achievement for learners in foreign language classrooms, although the predictive power of such traits decreases as the criteria for proficiency become more communicative than formal and the learning setting becomes more natural than instructional.

Some of the descriptions of the affective domain include the major personality dimensions, such as ego permeability, extroversion/introversion, empathy, tolerance of ambiguity, and sensitivity to rejection. The hypothesis is that particular personality types should be more successful in foreign language learning, presumably because of their willingness to expose themselves to threatening or unusual language situations, to surrender their own language and identity and appear foolish in the attempt to adopt another, to find meaningful interaction with others who speak another language important, and so on. All of these factors are independent of cognitive considerations such as the relative ability of individuals to profit from the experience.

In investigating classroom implications of such variables, students are assessed for their profile along a number of personality dimensions or observed in their classes for the amount and type of participation, and then tested for language achievement. The hypothesis is that certain characteristics, such as extroversion or high self-esteem provide an advantage in foreign language learning. Data from such studies are erratic, but a serious limitation to such inquiries has been the lack of reliable instruments for assessing the personality variables initially. The problem is compounded by the usual tendency to operate within an undifferentiated definition of achievement, a point which will be returned to presently.

Within the domain of affective variables, however, the most energetic pursuit has been in examining the role of motivation to learn the target language and attitude toward the target language and culture. The social implications of such variables are reflected in the degree to which learners assimilate into the target community. Such assimilation patterns, in conjunction with descriptions of power relations that exist between the learner and the community, are very influential in second language learning in a natural environment. But in classrooms, too, attitudinal constructs account for some of the variation in success.

An important distinction which followed from the early studies was that between two motivational orientations: integrative and instrumental (Gardner and Lambert 1972). An integrative motive was defined as one in which the target language was being learned for the purpose of learning about the target cultural community and ultimately being accepted as a member of that community. An instrumental motive was one in which the language was being learned for some utilitarian goal, such as getting a job, completing a course, and the like. The hypothesis was that more successful second language learning occurred within an integrative orientation, rather than an instrumental one. Moreover, it was expected that the integrative orientation would be especially important in foreign language classrooms to compensate for the fact that the target language was not spoken in the community or in the student's home.

Early research with college students which assessed attitude and motivation primarily by means of questionnaires and related these profiles to achievement tended to support these hypotheses. In school settings, positive attitudes and appropriate motivation have been associated with perseverance in the course, participation in extracurricular activities, adoption of effective learning strategies, and participation in and benefit from exchange programs—all of which contribute to successful language learning.

Research directed at the distinction between the two types of motivation, however, has been less decisive. Studies are reported which claim no superiority for an integrative motive and others even report an advantage bestowed by an instrumental motive (e.g., Genesee 1978). In addition, the questionnaire method for assessing motivation has been severely criticized. Finally the interactions between ability, attitude, and achievement found in most of the attitudinal research emphasized the need to consider the contextual or environmental aspects of foreign language learning.

(b) *Environmental factors.* Students learning a second or foreign language inevitably find themselves in a certain political, cultural, and sociolinguistic milieu which exerts a major influence on their attitudes towards the target language group and on their motivation to learn the target language. For foreign language learning, a variety of environmental factors have been reported to affect achievement scores. Burstall et al. (1974) in a survey of French teaching in England and Wales, reported significant effects indicating that girls scored higher than boys, status of parental occupation was directly related to achievement, students in small schools scored better than students in large schools, and students in small classes scored better than students in large classes. A larger survey of French instruction in eight countries by Carroll (1975) reported positive effects on achievement by sex, school type, and teacher sex, and mixed effects by parental interest in which it was at some times positively and at other times negatively related to achievement.

The effect of the social and political environment is particularly critical for second language learning. Studies have shown, for example, that patterns of majority and minority language use influence the acquisition of the grammatical features of the minority language, even when students are schooled in that minority language. For example, Canadian francophones living in communities in which French is the minority language and English is the majority language learn a less elaborated form of French, even though all schooling occurs through French. Thus the development of language proficiency is influenced by social factors which lie outside the school.

The attitudes of minority groups towards the majority group and towards their own identity are also an important factor determining educational outcomes. Specifically, groups which manifest school failure such as Finns in Sweden, North American Indians, Spanish speakers in the United States, and Franco–Ontarians in Canada tend to have ambivalent or negative feelings towards the majority culture and often also towards their own culture. This pattern has been clearly documented for Finnish immigrants in Sweden by Skutnabb-Kangas and Toukomaa (1976). As with all studies that report a relationship between negative attitudes and poor achievement, however, it is impossible to attribute causality to either factor.

Although no decisive profile of the good language learner in the perfect environment has ever been constructed, neither has it ever been shown that good ability, positive attitude, and a supportive environment do not contribute substantially to success. But measurements of individual differences are inherently nonproductive if they merely generate lists of unrelated features that bear no principled relationship to outcomes. In order to be more precise about such possible relationships, however, a more refined concept of "proficiency" which is sensitive to contextual differences and needs in various learning situations is required.

15.2 Process of Language Learning

The criteria for successful language learning depend on who is learning the language, under what circumstances, and for what purposes. Thus descriptions of the process of learning which address the psychological mechanisms responsible for learning cannot be considered in isolation from these factors. In particular, the concept of successful mastery varies enormously, and hence a description of "proficiency" is logically prior to the consideration of process descriptions of language learning.

(a) *Nature of language proficiency.* Evidence for distinction of at least two components of language proficiency for second language learners is pervasive. It is known, for example, about learners who studied a language in classrooms yet seemed particularly ill-equipped to communicate in the streets. Or the immigrant whose control of the new language permitted flawless negotiation in the streets, but whose control of the language under more formal conditions of examination would certainly appear to diminish. Such examples, although commonplace, are problematic to a concept of proficiency which requires a single assessment of mastery that ties that learner to a particular stage in acquisition.

One approach to the description of proficiency has been to devise a scheme in which the global concept of proficiency is analyzed into isolable component skills which can be independently invoked to describe proficiency in specific situations. Such schemes have been developed for a variety of purposes: as a guide to the development of testing instruments, as a model for making decisions about entrance into and exit from bilingual education programs, as a means of understanding the psycholinguistic processes involved in second language learning, and as a guide to the construction of second language teaching materials.

For foreign language education, the most productive division of abilities has distinguished communicative language competence from academic language competence. The former refers to the ability to use language for its interpersonal functions, in informal settings, where the focus is on negotiation of meaning. The latter refers to the ability to use language for its ideational functions, as a tool of thought, in accordance with the conventions of text and other formalized uses of language. The role of the determinants of achievement which appeared to exert a somewhat erratic influence on performance, becomes more systematic when proficiency is defined in these more specialized ways.

One application of this distinction of aspects of proficiency is in understanding the role of age in second language learning. Part of the fascination with the theoretical pursuit of an "optimal age" for second language learning has been because commonsense observations have posed a firm answer: younger is better. While early theory and research based on a neurological model tended to confirm that assumption, more recent studies have challenged the physiological basis of those claims and proposed interactions between age and aspects of proficiency (Krashen et al. 1979).

In global judgments of proficiency, the tendency is to compare the second language learner with a native speaking peer. Thus, children may be assessed in terms of their ability to communicate on the playground, while adults would be required to participate in mature conversations and use the language to manage their lives, including, therefore, competence with the literate forms of the language. When attention is paid to these aspects of proficiency required by the two age groups, comparisons between adults and children show quite different patterns. In many cases, the usual "child advantage" disappears, and for some comparisons, it is in fact the adults, or at least the more mature learners, who display greater competence and greater efficiency of learning (Snow and Hoefnagel-Höhle 1978).

Finally, the need for a distinction between communicative and academic uses of language is supported by study of the success or failure of immigrant children who appear to know the language well when communicating with their peers, yet fail in school where more specialized uses of the language are required. These relationships have been reported in a variety of countries and for a variety of language programs (Skutnabb-Kangas and Toukomaa 1976, Cummins 1981).

In general, then, attention must be paid to the criteria by which proficiency will be established for a learner in a given situation. Using a language is complex, and judgments of the ability to carry out that skill must reflect that complexity.

(b) *Description of process.* The process of learning can be described as the interaction between the determinants of achievement and the concept of proficiency. In cognitive terms, the mechanisms underlying the acquisition of knowledge in all these cases are the same, but the specific outcomes of learning in terms of what material can be learned easily, what skills are developed, and what strategies are deployed, depend upon these factors. Thus the process itself can never be observed directly but only described inferentially in terms of the type of skill which is developed.

The models of process based on psychological principles explain the relationship between determinants of achievement and aspects of proficiency from the perspective of the learner. These models vary in detail, some being based more directly on cognitive developmental models or information processing models than others. None, however, has direct evidence for psychological claims of learning processes.

One of the earliest cognitive models was the "creative construction hypothesis" proposed by Dulay and Burt (1974). They argued that a second language is constructed in much the same way as a child constructs a first language—input is organized in terms of a cognitive apparatus which is designed to respond to meanings. This requirement for construction precludes influences such as language transfer from first language knowledge or comparison between the two languages. The primary constraint on order and ease of acquisition in a second language is cognitive, and the effects of linguistic factors such as similarity between languages and social factors such as environmental constraints are minimized.

One of the problems with the creative construction hypothesis is that it underestimates the influence of instruction and the possibility of a learner profiting by interlingual comparisons. Consequently Krashen (1981) proposed a model in which two processes are identified—acquisition, which corresponds roughly to the creative construction process, and learning, which incorporates intervention, either by the learner or some instructional program. Krashen argues that these two processes are distinct, and the knowledge accrued by each is functionally differentiated. Specifically, he posits that the language which is acquired can be used as a response initiator and in fact is the source of most spontaneous uses of language. The language which is learned, by contrast, can function only as a "monitor" for the purpose of editing speech under restricted conditions.

While Krashen's model succeeds in accounting for a large number of reported phenomena in second language learning, the explanation still has a number of theoretical problems. Difficulties with the underlying cognitive mechanisms for example, have been pointed out by McLaughlin (1978), and with the categorical nature of the learning/acquisition dichotomy by Sharwood Smith (1981). Nonetheless, the model has succeeded in stimulating interesting discussion about the cognitive processes responsible for second or foreign language learning. (For Krashen's response to this criticism, see Krashen 1979.)

Most models of the language learning process allow a role for the learner to deliberately intervene in the task and take some responsibility for progress in language learning. The result is a set of "strategies" for language learning, which may operate at either a conscious or an unconscious level. Learning, productive, communicative, and receptive strategies have been identified and those which characterize successful language learners have been described. These strategies have been examined empirically for their specific effect on language learning (Bialystok 1979). The general finding of all such inquiries is that learners can actively participate in the language learning process and influence the outcomes in a positive way through the adoption of efficient strategies.

Finally, most current models of the language learning process attempt to account for proficiency in at least the two ways identified as communicative or formal. Krashen, for example, constructs a profile of the type of learner and the type of environment that is more likely to promote the development of one or the other aspects of proficiency. Monitor overusers, who are excessively concerned with language structure, would excel in formal, possibly classroom situations, while monitor underusers (whose emphasis is on meaning) would likely thrive in communicative situations. More generally, emphasis on learning results in formal language proficiency while emphasis on acquisition results in communicative language proficiency.

This view of language learning processes which isolates aspects of proficiency provides only a rough framework in which more specific questions may be raised. For example, the problem of age as shown above, can be reformulated as a relationship between a certain type of learner who has particular cognitive and linguistic limitations and the type of proficiency that learner is expected to achieve. Similarly, the questions of stages of learning must be restated in terms of more specific descriptions of proficiency. The role of the environment is obviously crucial to language learning, but the most likely effect of such factors is on the ease and enjoyability of the task rather than the process. It is unlikely that the human mind incorporates a new language in fundamentally different ways from the procedures for learning other information. And while cognitive psychologists have by no means solved all the mysteries of human learning, it is to those models that researchers must look for clues to the questions posed about how people learn foreign languages.

Bibliography

Bialystok E 1979 The role of conscious strategies in second language proficiency. *Can. Mod. Lang. Rev.* 35: 372–94

Blatchford C H, Schachter J (eds.) 1978 *On TESOL '78 EFL Policies, Programs, Practices.* Teachers of English to Speakers of Other Languages, Washington, DC, pp. 15–19

British Overseas Trade Board (BOTB), Study Group on Foreign Languages 1979 *Foreign Languages for Overseas Trade,* A Report. BOTB, London

Brumfit C J 1981 Notional syllabuses revisited. A response. *Appl. Linguist.* 2: 90–92

Burstall C, Jamieson M, Cohen S, Hargreaves M 1974 *Primary French in the Balance.* National Foundation for Educational Research, Slough

Carroll J B 1965 The contribution of psychological theory and educational research to the teaching of foreign languages. *Mod. Lang. J.* 49: 271–81

Carroll J B 1971 Current issues in psycholinguistics and second language teaching. *TESOL Q.* 5: 101–14

Carroll J B 1975 *The Teaching of French as a Foreign Language in Eight Countries.* Wiley, New York

Carroll J B 1977 Characteristics of successful second language learners. In: Burt M L, Dulay H C, Finocchiaro M B (eds.) 1977 *Viewpoints on English as a Second Language.* Regents, New York

Chastain K D 1976 *Developing Second Language Skills: Theory and Practice.* Rand McNally, Chicago, Illinois

Chomsky N 1964 *Current Issues in Linguistic Theory.* Mouton, The Hague

Cummins J 1981 The role of primary language development in promoting educational success for language minority students. *Schooling and Language Minority Students: A Theoretical Framework.* Evaluation, Dissemination and Assessment Center, California State University, Los Angeles, California

Curran C A 1976 *Counseling–Learning in Second Languages.* Apple River Press, Apple River, Illinois

Dakin J 1973 *The Language Laboratory and Language Learning.* Longman, London

Davies N F 1980 Language acquisition, language learning and the school curriculum. *System* 8: 97–102

Denison N 1962 Phonetics and phonemics in foreign language teaching. In: Sovijarvi A, Aalto P (eds.) 1962 *Proceedings of the Fourth International Congress of Phonetic Sciences.* Mouton, The Hague, pp. 571–76

Dulay H C, Burt M K 1974 A new perspective on the creative construction process in child second language acquisition. *Lang. Learn.* 24: 253–78

Dunlop I 1970 *Practical Techniques in the Teaching of Oral English.* Almqvist and Wiksell, Stockholm

Dunlop I 1975 *The Teaching of English in Swedish Schools: Studies in Methods of Instruction and Outcomes.* Almqvist and Wiksell, Stockholm

Dunlop I 1985 How do people learn languages? *Zielsprache Englisch* 4: 1–7

Emmans K A, Hawkins E W, Westoby A 1974 *The Use of Foreign Languages in the Private Sector of Industry and Commerce.* Language Teaching Centre, University of York, York

Fishman J A, Cooper R L, Ma R et al. 1971 *Bilingualism in the Barrio.* Indiana University Press, Bloomington, Indiana

Gage N L 1972 *Teacher Effectiveness and Teacher Education: The Search for a Scientific Basis.* Pacific Books, Palo Alto, California

Gardner R C, Lambert W E 1972 *Attitudes and Motivation in Second Language Learning.* Newbury House, Rowley, Massachusetts

Gattegno C 1976 *The Common Sense of Teaching Foreign Languages.* Educational Solutions, New York

Genesee F 1978 Individual differences in second-language learning. *Can. Mod. Lang. Rev.* 34: 490–504

Grittner F M 1969 *Teaching Foreign Languages.* Harper and Row, New York

Hymes D H 1970 On communicative competence. In: Gumperz J J, Hymes D H (eds.) 1972 *Directions in Sociolinguistics: The Ethnography of Communication.* Holt, Rinehart and Winston, New York

Jespersen O 1904 *How to Teach a Foreign Language.* Allen and Unwin, London

Kelly L G 1969 *Twenty-five Centuries of Language Teaching.* Newbury House, Rowley, Massachusetts

Kelly L G 1971 English as a second language: An historical sketch. *Engl. Lang. Teach.* 25: 120–32

Kogan N 1971 The nature of cognitive styles. In: Lesser G S (ed.) 1971 *Psychology and Educational Practice.* Scott Foresman, Glenview, Illinois

Krashen S 1979 A response to McLaughlin, "The Monitor Model: Some Methodological Considerations". *Lang. Learn.* 29: 151–67

Krashen S D 1981 *Second Language Acquisition and Second Language Learning.* Pergamon, Oxford

Krashen S 1982 *Principles and Practice in Second Language Acquisition,* Pergamon, Oxford

Krashen S D 1985 *The Input Hypothesis: Issues and Implications.* Longman, London

Krashen S D, Long M A, Scarcella R C 1979 Age, rate and eventual attainment in second language acquisition. *TESOL Q.* 13: 573–82

Lado R 1957 *Linguistics across Cultures: Applied Linguistics for Language Teachers.* University of Michigan Press, Ann Arbor, Michigan

Lenneberg E H 1967 *Biological Foundations of Language.* Wiley, New York

Lewis E G, Massad C E 1975 *The Teaching of English as a Foreign Language in Ten Countries.* Wiley, New York

Lozanov G 1979 *Suggestology and Outlines of Suggestopedy.* Gordon and Breach, New York

Mackey W F 1965 *Language Teaching Analysis.* Longman, London

Mackey W F, Verdoodt A 1975 *The Multinational Society: Papers of the Ljubljana Seminar.* Newbury, Rowley, Massachusetts

McLaughlin B 1978 The monitor model: Some methodological considerations. *Lang. Learn.* 28: 309–32

Marckwardt A H 1963 English as a second language and English as a foreign language. *Publ. Mod. Lang. Assoc.* 78(2): 25–28

Moulton W 1962 Linguistics and language teaching in the United States 1940–1960. In: Mohrman C, Sommerfelt A, Whatmough J (eds.) 1962 *Trends in European and American Linguistics.* Spectrum, Utrecht

Naiman N, Frohlich M, Stern H H, Todesco A 1978 *The Good Language Learner: A Report.* Ontario Institute for Studies in Education, Toronto, Ontario

Obler L K, Zatorre R J, Galloway L, Vaid J 1982 Cerebral lateralization in bilinguals: Methodological issues. *Brain Lang.* 15: 40–54

Palmer H E 1917 *The Scientific Study and Teaching of Languages.* World Book, Yonkers-on-Hudson, New York

Palmer H E 1922 *The Principles of Language Study,* 2nd edn (Reprinted 1964). Oxford University Press, London

Paulston C B 1981 Notional syllabuses revisited: Some comments. *Appl. Linguist.* 2: 93–95

Pimsleur P 1966a *Pimsleur Language Aptitude Battery.* Harcourt, Brace and World, New York

Pimsleur P 1966b Testing foreign language learning. In: Valdman A (ed.) 1966 *Trends in Language Teaching.* McGraw-Hill, New York

Richterich R, Chancerel J-L 1980 *Identifying the Needs of Adults Learning a Foreign Language.* Pergamon, Oxford

Rivers W M 1981 *Teaching Foreign-language Skills,* 2nd edn. University of Chicago Press, Chicago, Illinois

Schumann J H 1978 The acculturation model for second-language acquisition. In: Gingras R C (ed.) 1978 *Second-language acquisition and Foreign Language Teaching.* Center for Applied Linguistics, Arlington, Virginia

Seliger H W 1975 Inductive method and deductive method in language teaching: A re-examination. *IRAL* 13: 1–18

Seliger H W 1977 Does practice make perfect? A study of interaction patterns and L2 competence. *Lang. Learn.* 27: 263–78

Sharwood Smith M 1981 Consciousness-raising and the second language learner. *Appl. Linguist.* 2: 159–68

Skutnabb-Kangas T, Toukomaa T 1976 *Teaching Migrant Children's Mother Tongue and Learning the Language of the Host Country in the Context of the Sociocultural Situation of the Migrant Family.* Finnish National Commission for UNESCO, Helsinki

Snow C E, Hoefnagel-Höhle M 1978 The critical period for language acquisition: Evidence from second language learning. *Child Dev.* 49: 1114–28

Stern H H 1967 *Foreign Languages in Primary Education: The Teaching of Foreign or Second Languages to Younger Children.* Oxford University Press, London

Stern H H (ed.) 1969 *Languages and the Young School Child.* Oxford University Press, London

Stevick E W 1980 *Teaching Languages: A Way and Ways.* Newbury House, Rowley, Massachusetts

Strevens P 1977 *New Orientations in the Teaching of English.* Oxford University Press, London

Sweet H 1899 *The Practical Study of Languages: A Guide for Teachers and Learners.* Dent, London (Reprinted 1964, Oxford University Press, London)

Terrell T 1977 A natural approach to second language acquisition and learning. *Mod. Lang. J.* 61: 325–37

Titone R 1968 *Teaching Foreign Language: An Historical Sketch.* Georgetown University Press, Washington, DC

Titone R 1981 Research trends in foreign language teaching. *Rass. Ital. Linguist. Appl.* 13(3): 35–56

Trim J L M, Richterich R, van Ek J A, Wilkins D A 1980 *Systems Development in Adult Language Learning: A European Unit/Credit System for Modern Language Learning by Adults.* Pergamon, Oxford

Tucker G R, Hamayan E, Genesee F 1976 Affective, cognitive, and social factors in second language acquisition. *Can. Mod. Lang. Rev.* 32: 214–26

van Ek J A 1975 *The Threshold Level.* Council of Europe, Strasbourg (Reprinted 1980 *Threshold Level English.* Pergamon, Oxford)

van Ek J A, Alexander L G, Fitzpatrick M A 1980 *Waystage English.* Pergamon, Oxford

Voge W 1981 Testing the validity of Krashen's input hypothesis. Paper presented at the International Congress of Applied Linguistics, Lund

Widdowson H G 1978 *Teaching Language as Communication.* Oxford University Press, Oxford

Widdowson H G 1979 *Exploration in Applied Linguistics.* Oxford University Press, Oxford

Wilkins D A 1976 *Notional Syllabuses: A Taxonomy and its Relevance to Foreign Language Curriculum Development.* Oxford University Press, Oxford

Wilkins D A 1981 Notional syllabuses revisited and notional syllabuses revisited: A further reply. *Appl. Linguist.* 2: 83–89, 96–100

Witkin H A, Dyk R, Faterson H F, Goodenough D R, Karp S A 1962 *Psychological Differentiation: Studies of Development.* Wiley, New York

Zettersten A 1985 *New Technologies in Learning.* Pergamon, Oxford

Foreign Language Curricula: Primary Schools

H. H. Stern

What is meant by foreign languages in the primary school largely depends upon what distinguishes primary from secondary education. Since this varies from country to country, foreign language teaching in the primary school (henceforth primary or early language teaching), for the purposes of this article, is defined as the teaching of a nonnative ("foreign" or "second") language as part of the school curriculum at any stage of schooling between the beginning of mandatory education (from age 4 or 5 upwards) to the end of pre-adolescent schooling (at the age of about 10 or 11). In the United States, the acronym FLES (foreign languages in the elementary school) was introduced during the 1950s and widely used in subsequent decades. The term early language learning (ELL) has recently been proposed to cover "all forms of language learning by preteens: bilingual education, second-language instruction, foreign language learning, exploratory language courses, and interdisciplinary language-learning activities" (Rivers 1981 p. 462). In the United Kingdom and some other countries of Western Europe, yet another acronym, ETML (early teaching of modern languages) has been employed since the 1970s.

The development of primary language teaching in the second half of this century is not only of interest to primary school and foreign language educators. It is also of considerable relevance to students of curriculum as an illustration of the ups and downs of a curriculum innovation.

1. Historical Orientation

Until about 1950, the placing of nonnative languages in the school curriculum was more a matter of tradition and practical convenience than of a rationally developed educational policy. Right through the history of formal education it is possible to find many examples of early language teaching, for example, the teaching of Latin and French in private education or the teaching of French and English as languages of schooling in colonial school systems. In the first half of the twentieth century, however, the unquestioned place of foreign languages in the well-established state school systems of the Western world was predominantly the secondary school while the primary school was considered to be the right place for native language education.

It was largely the reforming zeal, the internationalism, and the desire for a radical improvement in foreign language learning during the postwar era, particularly in the 1950s, that led to the advocacy of primary language teaching. To some extent, purely practical curriculum considerations suggested this innovation: lightening the overcrowded timetable of the secondary school, thus allowing more time for foreign language learning and distributing the time available over a longer period. Finally, it was also a response to psychological thinking in the 1950s about education in relation to child development, that is, to put a subject into the curriculum at the "teachable moment," that is at the time of natural developmental readiness. These psychological considerations received a certain amount of scientific support through the pronouncements of a few prominent psychologists and neurologists who considered the early years of life before puberty as crucial for both first and second language acquisition (Penfield and Roberts 1959).

The main initiative for this reform came from the United States where FLES became a popular and widespread educational movement. But the interest in early language learning as a way out of the foreign language impasse found an echo in many other countries across the world, including the Soviet Union and several European nations. In the late 1950s, UNESCO recognized primary language teaching as a movement of worldwide significance and of considerable potential for international educational development. Accordingly, an international study and expert meeting was organized at the UNESCO Institute for Education in Hamburg in 1962, with the purpose of gathering the experience of some 32 countries, evaluating what had been achieved, and planning future developments (Stern 1967).

The first report which resulted from this study endorsed foreign languages in primary education. It encouraged internationally sponsored research on practical experiments in different countries. The most important reasons it advanced for early language learning were educational and sociopolitical. The severely unilingual and unicultural training of traditional primary education, the report argued, should be "mitigated by contact with another language and culture" (Stern 1967 p. 118), because "the political, economic, and cultural interdependence of the world today demands a crossing of language and national barriers in the early phases of schooling." It recommended that the acquisition of a second language be treated as part of basic literacy. On the frequently advanced neurological and psychological reasons for an early start it expressed itself more cautiously than was commonly done at the time by advocates of primary language teaching, and it firmly rejected the notion of an unqualified optimal age. It thus counteracted excessive expectations and stressed the need for careful planning for the move of languages into the early stages of schooling, a caution that has unfortunately not always been adequately heeded.

In the early 1960s the trends of development, described in the Hamburg study, continued for a while and languages began increasingly to be accepted in several countries across the world as subjects to be learned at different stages of primary education. However, the call for systematic experimentation and coordinated research on an international scale, voiced in the UNESCO report, was followed only to a limited extent. Two major experiments which were initiated at that time stand out. One was the Primary French Pilot Scheme in England and Wales, a nationwide project involving research, development, and evaluation, which was initiated in 1963–1964 and continued for 10 years (Burstall et al. 1974, Hawkins 1981). The other was a more loosely organized Canadian series of projects on early French immersion which began in one school in Montreal in 1965 and then spread across Canada over the subsequent 15 years (see *Immersion Education*).

In order to stimulate further international cooperation and research, the UNESCO Institute for Education, Hamburg, convened a second international meeting on languages in primary education in 1966, sponsored jointly by UNESCO and the Council for Cultural Cooperation of the Council of Europe. The second report resulting from this meeting was even more insistent than the first that an internationally coordinated research approach to the many questions that primary language teaching had given rise to would be advantageous (Stern 1969). Although the UNESCO initiatives no doubt helped those who experimented with primary language teaching to become more aware of the issues involved and to take note of the experience gained in different countries, no international research project specifically directed to this question was actually initiated.

In another respect, too, the second UNESCO study did not achieve what it set out to do: it attempted to make clear that primary language teaching implies a new view of the nature of primary education, and that it is this new view much more than the presumed greater effectiveness of early language learning that justified its inclusion into the primary-school curriculum. According to the older view, the report argued, primary education was regarded as vernacular education. This meant that children were expected first to settle down in one cultural and linguistic milieu, their own, before advancing next to foreign languages and cultures, and this distinction was seen as one of the main characteristic differences between primary and secondary education. The newer conception sketched by the report was that of a primary education which no longer operates purely in terms of the native language. Since at least half the populations of the world have been estimated to be bilingual and since everyone lives in a world in which many different languages are spoken, the report went on, it is not defensible to create through schooling an artificial and rigidly unilingual setting. "If education is to reflect the realities with which we have to live, other languages and other cultures should impinge on children from the earliest stage of formal education" (Stern 1969 p. 26).

The implications for the primary school of this philosophy of language education were never adequately discussed in the 1960s nor have they indeed been fully worked out even today. Instead, those who promoted languages in primary education continued to base themselves mainly on two assumptions both of which are questionable: one was that the early years of schooling are inherently optimal for language learning; and the other was that teaching foreign languages by traditional methods in secondary schools was hopelessly unsatisfactory and that a new approach required new teachers in a new language teaching environment, "uncontaminated" by the traditions of the past. Both assumptions have turned out to be overoptimistic as claims for primary language teaching, and unjustifiably derogatory towards secondary language teaching.

In the subsequent years, up to the early 1980s, the place of languages in the primary-school curriculum remained uncertain (Hawkins 1981). For example, by the early 1970s, the FLES movement in the United States had lost its main impetus, and improvements in language teaching were largely looked for in other directions. Nevertheless, the Commission on Foreign Language and International Studies, set up in 1978 by the United States President Jimmy Carter, a year later in its report, which was highly critical of United States foreign language learning at all stages, recommended that "language study begin in the early grades" (United States of America 1979 p. 29). In the United Kingdom, where primary language teaching had been spreading to a remarkable extent, this movement received a severe blow as a result of the research report on the 10-year Primary French Pilot Scheme which, although very informative and encouraging in certain respects, concluded in 1974 that, overall, "the weight of the evidence has combined with the balance of opinion to tip the scales against a possible expansion of the teaching of French in primary schools" (Burstall et al. 1974 p. 246). This negative view led to a conflict between those in the United Kingdom who viewed primary language teaching in a more favorable light and those who believed that the findings of the Burstall report were realistic. As one respected British language educator summarized it: "one more panacea had failed" (Hawkins 1981 p. 190).

Against this, it should be noted that more encouraging experiences were reported from several other countries in which a more optimistic view of languages in the primary curriculum has prevailed. In the Federal Republic of Germany an experiment on English as a foreign language involving over 1,000 children was carried out between 1970 and 1975 under more favorable conditions than the much larger British French Pilot Scheme and also with more positive results which led the investigators to recommend the general introduction of English as a foreign language into all primary-school curricula of the Federal Republic (Doyé 1979). In some school systems, a foreign language has become accepted as a normal component of the primary curriculum. A survey, undertaken in 16 European countries in the mid-1970s concluded "that the European picture is one of a general trend towards lowering the starting age for modern languages" (Hoy 1976 p.14). English in the Swedish comprehensive school, for example, is introduced at the age of 8 and experimentally as early as the age of 6. In Canadian educational systems, the place of French in anglophone and English in francophone primary education is undisputed. Points at issue are not whether the language should be offered in the primary school, but at what grade level it should be introduced and how much time it should be given daily. Not only have many Canadian school systems successfully introduced "early immersion" in French as a second language from kindergarten or age 6 (see *Immersion Education*), but also second language instruction of a more conventional kind, such as a daily second language lesson of 20, 30, or 40 minutes, beginning at age 6, 9, or 11 is so widespread that in Canadian school systems French or English as a second language has typically become a primary school subject. It may, in fact, in some areas be offered more widely in primary than in secondary schools.

It should also be borne in mind that in many countries, young children whose parents are immigrants or migrant workers often receive instruction in the language of the host countries. Many others who live in bilingual or multilingual countries are introduced to a regional language, the national language, or a language of wider communication during the primary school years. Consequently, examples of bilingual, and even trilingual, primary school curricula are not at all uncommon (McLaughlin 1978).

The net outcome of this rather uneven development since the 1950s has been that today there is far more foreign and second language instruction in primary schools than previously. Above all, there has been a shift from a philosophy of primary education as exclusively vernacular schooling to a primary education which may include a foreign language or a bilingual–bicultural or even a multilingual–multicultural element. An important consequence of this recognition of languages in primary education is that foreign language teaching has been taken out of its relatively exclusive and isolated position as a high school or university curriculum subject and may today be found at any level from the kindergarten to adult education.

Nevertheless, the fact that this shift of languages into the primary school has not been universally accepted must not be overlooked. In the words of an international review of languages for younger children, carried out in 1977, it is a fair summary, even today, to say that: "the provision of languages in the education of younger children has not come to be considered the *sine qua non* of effective language learning over the last 25 years. Its place in the curriculum of primary education continues to be a matter of debate and controversy" (Stern and Weinrib 1977 p. 15).

2. A Critical Analysis of Four Major Issues

Why is it that in over 30 years of primary language teaching, the issue is still controversial? A full and critical review of primary language teaching from its beginnings to the present has not yet been made. The answer to the question must therefore be tentative. But to attempt to find an answer would probably be useful not only for the future of primary language teaching but also for the study of the dynamics of curriculum change and for primary education in general. Here some explanations can only be suggested.

As a generalization from the historical review it appears that primary language teaching as an educational innovation has established itself quite satisfactorily and is likely to continue, but it has encountered a number of difficulties which it must attempt to overcome. Four problem areas stand out: (a) the optimal age controversy; (b) questions of pedagogical development; (c) the role of research; and (d) questions of policy and decision making.

2.1 The Optimal Age Controversy

For most curriculum subjects it would be difficult to offer conclusive evidence that a particular age or stage in life presents a uniquely right teachable moment. It is usually sufficient to show that the teaching of the subject is possible and appears approximately right at a given stage of the educational process. Unfortunately, when foreign language teaching for younger children was proposed in the 1950s it was not always done with such realistic and modest expectations in mind. Instead, some advocates of this reform were convinced that the early years are decisively better for foreign language learning than later years. This claim was nourished by the widespread popular belief that young children possess natural and almost magical language learning powers and that it is therefore just common sense to start foreign language teaching early. This belief in the early years of schooling as the optimal stage for language learning received welcome support in the 1950s through the neurological speculations of a renowned neurologist, Wilder Penfield (Penfield and Roberts 1959), concerning the plasticity of the young brain and its implications for second language learning, and, a few years later, through the nativistic theories of language development of a physiologist, Eric Lenneberg (1967).

Since the 1950s the controversy on the optimal age for second language learning has not ceased nor has it been resolved. While in the course of time the neurological data became increasingly difficult to interpret, different psychological theories on the cognitive and affective characteristics of young language learners were advanced to account for the advantages of early language learning. Against all these claims, other scholars produced arguments and evidence to show that early language learning had been overrated and later learning underestimated. The practical teaching experiments demonstrated that primary language teaching was feasible and had educational and practical merit, but they did not provide overwhelming evidence for the distinct advantages of an early start over later language learning (Hawkins 1981, Rivers 1981).

Thus, the optimal age question has remained a central theoretical issue in the development of primary language teaching. In some ways this is good. It has caught the imagination of researchers and practitioners. Without a certain innocent belief in the optimal age, primary language teaching might never have got off the ground, and researchers might not have felt impelled to question it and thus to begin to theorize about the age issue and to compare child and adult language learners.

On balance, however, the preoccupation with the optimal age controversy has distorted research on language learning as well as the practical teaching experiments. Instead of spending time and effort trying to prove that either the early or the later years are optimal for language learning, it would be more productive and more helpful to the teaching experiments to study by empirical research methods the specific characteristics of second language learning at different stages in a lifetime in order to maximize the educational effort without feeling compelled to demonstrate the superiority of one stage over another. Even today, educational policy makers are often misled by the futile search for the optimal starting age, and they fail to recognize that the decision about primary language teaching is principally one of educational values and judgments about the quality and purposes of language education and much less about the biological development of children as language learners.

2.2 Questions of Language Pedagogy

A curriculum innovation usually requires a new pedagogy, new materials, and often the training or retraining of teachers. The danger is that the task of curriculum development is underrated. In this respect, primary language teaching has had a mixed record. Some disappointments in its development can be accounted for by lack of planning and inconsistency in the provision for teaching.

Implicit in the advocacy of primary language teaching in the 1950s and 1960s was dissatisfaction with language teaching at the secondary stage. But what the deficiencies of language instruction at that stage really were was never clearly identified or systematically studied. It was—perhaps naively—hoped that new methods which came into vogue around 1960 would remedy the weaknesses. It was also rather rashly believed by some proponents of early language teaching that the primary teachers as new language teachers would be more receptive to new ideas and less hampered by the traditions and conventions of language teaching in secondary schools.

These hopes were only partially fulfilled. It should be recognized that many new and valuable teaching approaches were indeed initiated, new curriculum materials for teaching younger children were developed, and a teaching methodology appropriate for primary classrooms was gradually established (Freudenstein 1979). In spite of these advances, primary language teaching—not surprisingly—has met with many problems and difficulties. Most primary school subjects, for example, reading or mathematics, which have been in the field much longer, have also become embroiled in controversies and have had to overcome numerous obstacles. Here are some of the issues that primary language teaching has had to contend with:

(a) Inadequate teacher preparation has been a main concern. The question has been whether it would be better to employ well-trained language specialists who know a great deal about the foreign language in question, but relatively little about the primary school, or whether the general primary school practitioners should include the foreign language in their repertoire at the risk of being less proficient as linguists (Stern 1969).

(b) A matter of much debate has been the time allowance for foreign languages which is usually time taken away from other areas of the curriculum. Initially, very short time allocations were made, such as 20 minutes a day, partly because it was believed that young children's span of attention would not tolerate longer periods of language learning and partly because the primary schools were unwilling to give up more time. Time variations from 20 minutes up have been investigated, and these studies have shown (i) that total amount and distribution of time can have a significant influence on language proficiency levels attained, and (ii) that the time given to the foreign language has little or no negative effect on other school subjects in spite of the slight reduction in their time allocation (Stern and Weinrib 1977).

(c) Primary language teaching was introduced at a time when doctrinaire theories of language and language learning imposed a narrow and rigid teaching methodology with an emphasis on drill, mechanical practice, and mindless imitation which, in many respects, conflicted with the cognitive and social orientation of the primary school. Recent developments in the study of language suggest an approach to language pedagogy which need no longer be out of step with the philosophy of the primary school. But many primary language teachers have still not lived down the language teaching beliefs of the 1960s.

(d) An important related question has been the integration of the foreign language into the general curriculum of the primary school. The foreign language can be expected to contribute to the language and social education offered by the primary curriculum. From this point of view it has been argued that the acquisition of foreign language skills is perhaps less important in the primary school than the creation of a general language awareness and a curiosity about other languages and cultures. Curriculum suggestions for such broader language explorations have recently been made with the intention of integrating native and foreign language studies in the primary school.

(e) One of the main unsolved problems is the lack of coordination or "articulation" between language programs at the primary stage and their follow-up programs at the secondary level. It is recognized that the success of primary language teaching crucially depends on continuity and the planning of the program in its entirety at the primary and secondary stage. While the principle of continuity and articulation is widely acknowledged, it has proved difficult to implement it in practice (Hoy 1976).

(f) Although varied curriculum materials and useful practical "know-how" on teaching languages to younger children are available, a great deal more needs to be done to provide satisfactory long-term programs which offer worthwhile linguistic and cultural content of true educational merit and involve children in interesting language-related activities so that the foreign language curriculum of the primary school is educationally comparable to, say, the best science, mathematics, or native language programs at the same stage of child development.

2.3 The Role of Research

Primary language teaching, like any other major curriculum innovation, should have been and should still be supported by a program of research and evaluation partly to answer some of the basic questions to which it gives rise and partly to monitor its progress. That primary language teaching would benefit from a research component was known from its early beginnings. The two UNESCO-sponsored initiatives in 1962 and 1966 were prompted by the conviction that the collective experience in different countries and research on an international scale would be useful to the development of this innovation. But as was seen in the historical review, the call for research was only taken up to a very limited degree, and after the two UNESCO meetings in Hamburg (with the exception of some work sponsored by the Council of Europe) it was not internationally coordinated. A few projects, already mentioned, in the United Kingdom, Canada, and the Federal Republic of

Germany, and others such as the Swedish EPAL project (Holmstrand 1979) and a few studies in the United States (McLaughlin 1978) provided a much needed database and have helped language educators to realize the strengths and limitations of primary language teaching. In retrospect, it should be noted that the scope and amount of the research effort were often too limited and the total effort was not sustained enough both within educational systems and internationally. Curriculum activities were not supported by any research, and as was seen in an earlier section, critical questions, such as the age issue, have remained unresolved.

2.4 Policy Questions and Educational Decisions

While more research is certainly needed to assist the policy maker and curriculum developer, primary language teaching, finally, illustrates the legitimate limits of research. Some of the difficulties and uncertainties in primary language teaching can be accounted for by the fact that these limits have not always been recognized.

Ultimately the place of languages in the primary curriculum cannot be conclusively answered by research alone. The decision on the stage of education at which to introduce a second language must be based on educational, cultural, and political judgments. Basically the question is whether language education or literacy in the primary school are to be conceived in "unilingual" and "ethnocentric" terms, or whether, and at what stage, the curriculum should reflect the ethnic pluralism and language contact which characterize most communities across the world today. There is no question any more that foreign languages can be taught at any stage in the primary school. Whether they should be taught and at what stage they should be introduced, are matters for the policy maker to decide. As was pointed out some years ago in the previously mentioned survey of primary language teaching (Stern and Weinrib 1977 p. 20), the decision-making process of the policy maker can perhaps be helped by using the following three criteria as a guiding principle in answer to the question of at what stage in the educational process to introduce a foreign language:

(a) the estimated time necessary to reach a desired level of language proficiency by a specified stage in the school career of the majority of learners; (b) the educational value attributed to learning foreign languages at a given stage of the curriculum; and (c) the human and material resources required to develop and maintain an educationally sound and successful foreign-language program.

3. Conclusion

To the question raised earlier, why primary language teaching is still controversial and why it has encountered so many difficulties and disappointments, the answer that has been given can be summarized as follows: (a) it misguidedly insisted on demonstrating that early language learning is better than later learning (rather than being satisfied with proving that early learning is feasible and educationally defensible); (b) it underrated the pedagogical issues and did not treat them consistently enough; (c) it did not pursue a sufficiently sustained, broad, and internationally coordinated program of research and development; and, lastly, (d) decision makers in this area did not recognize the limitations of the research evidence and the need for making informed value judgments about the stage and scope of language teaching in the primary school curriculum. No doubt other educational innovations have not been implemented more satisfactorily. Putting this critical analysis into perspective it should be remembered that primary language teaching has not been a failure but it has not been the spectacular success that some proponents may have hoped it would be. For the student of primary education and language pedagogy, and for the student of curriculum processes, primary language teaching offers an instructive example of the complex interaction between theoretical issues, empirical research, educational practice, and policy questions.

Bibliography

Andersson T 1953 *The Teaching of Foreign Languages in the Elementary School.* Heath, Boston, Massachusetts

Burstall C, Jamieson M, Cohen S, Hargreaves M 1974 *Primary French in the Balance.* National Foundation for Educational Research, Slough

Doyé P 1979 Primary English. A research project on the teaching of English in German primary schools. *Engl. Lang. Teach. J.* 34: 29–34

Freudenstein R (ed.) 1979 *Teaching Foreign Languages to the Very Young: Papers from Seven Countries on Work with 4- to 8-year-olds.* Pergamon, Oxford

Hawkins E W 1981 *Modern Languages in the Curriculum.* Cambridge University Press, Cambridge

Holmstrand L S E 1979 *The Effects on General School Achievement of Early Commencement of English Instruction.* Uppsala Reports on Education, No. 4. Department of Education, University of Uppsala, Uppsala

Hoy P H 1976 *The Early Teaching of Modern Languages: A Summary of Reports from Sixteen Countries.* Symposium on Modern Languages in Primary Education. Council of Europe, DECS/EGT (76) 39, Strasbourg

Krashen S D, Long M A, Scarcella R C 1979 Age, rate and eventual attainment in second language acquisition. *TESOL Q.* 13: 573–82

McLaughlin B 1978 *Second-language Acquisition in Childhood.* Erlbaum, Hillsdale, New Jersey

Lenneberg E H 1967 *Biological Foundations of Language.* Wiley, New York

Penfield W G, Roberts L 1959 *Speech and Brain-mechanisms.* University Press, Windsor

Rivers W M 1981 *Teaching Foreign Language Skills*, 2nd edn. University of Chicago Press, Chicago, Illinois

Stern H H 1967 *Foreign Languages in Primary Education: The Teaching of Foreign or Second Languages to Younger Children.* Oxford University Press, London. [1965 *Les Langues étrangères dans l'enseignement primaire: L'Enseignement d'une seconde langue ou d'une langue étrangère à de jeunes enfants.* UNESCO Institute for Education, Hamburg]

Stern H H (ed.) 1969 *Languages and the Young School Child: An International Collection of Studies*. International Meeting of Representatives of Institutions and Experimental Schools Concerned with Second Language Teaching in Primary Education Research and Development, Hamburg, 1966. Oxford University Press, London

Stern H H, Weinrib A 1977 Foreign languages for younger children. *Lang. Teach. Ling. Abstr.* 10: 5–25

United States of America 1979 *Strength Through Wisdom: A Critique of US Capability*. Report of the President's Commission on Foreign Language and International Studies. Government Printing Office, Washington, DC

Foreign Language Curricula: Secondary Schools

P. S. Green

Despite a trend to reduce the starting age, foreign language teaching still generally begins in the secondary school, which for most countries means not before the age of 10. There are, however, substantial differences both between and within countries, and furthermore the teaching of foreign languages has recently undergone and is still undergoing considerable change.

A reliable and relatively up-to-date picture is given by the research carried out in the 1960s and early 1970s by the International Association for the Evaluation of Educational Achievement (IEA). Seven subject areas, among them English and French as foreign languages, were studied in schools in 22 countries.

The investigation of English involved 10 countries (Belgium, Chile, the Federal Republic of Germany, Finland, Hungary, Israel, Italy, the Netherlands, Sweden, and Thailand) and that of French 8 countries (Chile, England and Wales, the Netherlands, New Zealand, Romania, Scotland, Sweden, and the United States). Thus, large and small, industrial and non-industrial nations, with differing political systems, with one or more national languages, and on different continents, were represented. English was a major foreign language in most of the non-English-speaking countries, French in the English-speaking countries. In Hungary, the first foreign language studied was Russian. Only a few countries (e.g. Hungary, Israel, and Sweden) offered a foreign language to a majority of pupils. The starting age varied from 10 to 15 and the number of years of study from two to nine. In most countries, pupils were taught in groups differentiated according to ability. A general tendency was observed for the starting age to be lowered, for a larger proportion of the ability range to be offered a foreign language, for changes in teaching methods to be taking place, and for technical aids to be introduced (Lewis and Massad 1975, Carroll 1975). These tendencies will be examined in more detail through specific examples.

1. Language Policy

National policy about foreign language teaching in schools ranges from almost total control to almost total freedom. Sweden, for example, with a single system of compulsory comprehensive schooling for the vast majority of pupils and a national school curriculum, lays down that English shall be taught to all from the third to the ninth year of compulsory schooling for a certain number of hours per week, and in groups undifferentiated according to ability. Furthermore, the aims of English teaching are specified as well as the syllabus and methods of teaching and assessment. A key control of the content of English teaching is exercised by the state licensing of textbooks. The United Kingdom, on the other hand, has no single school system and did not introduce a national curriculum until 1987, full implementation of which will not occur before 1991–92. Whilst the curriculum stipulates that all pupils shall learn a foreign language throughout secondary schooling, it allows great freedom in the choice of language, materials, and methods.

A supranational policy was agreed upon by the 22 member states of the Council of Europe in 1969, when the Committee of Ministers adopted a resolution that at least one widely spoken European language should be taught to all pupils from the age of about 10. In 1981, the West European Commission of the *Fédération Internationale des Professeurs de Français* (FIPF) transmitted a resolution to the bodies of the European Community urging, amongst other things, "that the learning of at least two (foreign) languages as early as possible should also be established in countries which have not yet met such requirements".

Very many countries in the world have more than one indigenous language. Where there are few indigenous languages and they are spoken by significant proportions of the population, as in Switzerland, it may be national policy to teach everyone a second indigenous language. Where there are many, a nonindigenous language may be the official language and therefore the language of instruction in schools. This is true of many African countries and former colonies, such as Nigeria (English) and Zaire (French). If one indigenous language has a dominant position, it may officially replace the former colonial language as the official language and language of school instruction, as with Arabic in Algeria or Bahasa Malaysia in Malaysia. In some situations it may be more appropriate to speak of a second language than a foreign language, but it should be noted that the term "second language" is not used in any one universally accepted way (see discussion in Christophersen 1973 pp. 29–33).

Political, economic, geographical, and historical reasons have led to a situation where English, French,

German, Russian, and Spanish are probably the most commonly taught foreign or second languages in secondary schools.

2. Teaching Methods

The history of language teaching methods has been likened to the swing of a pendulum. At one end of the swing is a method in which the pupils are taught explicit rules of grammar and lists of vocabulary and deduce sentences of the foreign language from them, often by translating sentences of their own language. At the other end is a method in which the pupils are "immersed" in the foreign language and learn by practice rather than by rules, which are induced from the examples encountered of the foreign language. Many different names and labels have been attached to various developments of these extremes (Hawkins 1981 pp. 307–8), but they are often loosely characterized by language teachers as the grammar-translation method and the direct method.

One of the most violent swings of the pendulum took place just after the Second World War. What is generally called the audiolingual method (or in Europe, the audiovisual method) seemed for a time to be an unassailably strong combination of linguistic theory (structural and contrastive linguistics), learning theory (behaviourist psychology), technological advances (tape recorder, language laboratory, filmstrip projector), and practical experience gained in the American Army Specialized Training Programme. The influence of the method on language teaching in schools was very great, especially through the teaching materials that it engendered.

The audiolingual method suffered a decline when, on the one hand, its theoretical bases came under increasing criticism from linguists and psychologists and, on the other hand, a number of school-based research projects failed to demonstrate its superiority over other methods. In the United States, for example, the massive Pennsylvania Project found that students following a traditional (cognitive) method were equal or superior in performance to those following an audiolingual method (Smith 1970). In Sweden, the series of GUME projects was unable to establish any significant difference between the results of "implicit" and "explicit" approaches to grammar teaching in schools (Levin 1972).

The inconclusive outcomes of these and other comparative method studies led Allwright to propose a moratorium on such "prescriptive" research and to recommend instead a concentration on "descriptive" research, that is, the study of successful language teaching in an attempt to identify the elements in it that correlate with good learner performance (Allwright 1972). That was the approach of a major study funded by the Nuffield Foundation to investigate successful language teaching in British schools (Sanderson 1983). What foreign language teachers actually do in the classroom was also the subject of an international study conducted by Peck (1988).

The decline of the audiolingual method has not brought about a resurgence of a cognitive approach. The swing this time has been from concentration on the form of the language, which audiolingual pattern practice inevitably entailed, to attention on its content and an emphasis on meaning—from medium to message. The term most associated with current discussion of method is "communicative". There are two reasons for this trend. The first is the realization that linguistic competence, or knowledge of language usage, does not on its own confer communicative competence, or knowledge of language use. The second is the insight that language used with "force", with real intent to mean, is more readily acquired. A distinction is drawn between language learning, with attention to form and the conscious learning of rules, and language acquisition, with attention to meaning and the unconscious acquisition of grammar. A sharper focus on meaning has led to an interest in what learners do when the means at their disposal are inadequate for the message they wish to convey. This study of "communication strategies" (Faersch and Kasper 1983) has as yet remained largely academic and had only a minor impact on teaching methods.

Other trends which can be discerned in current discussions of methods are the attempt to individualize language teaching programmes, to make them more learner centred, and experiments with other forms of timetable organization than the traditional "drip-feed" method of a few lessons a week for several years.

3. Technical Aids

An invention of the war years, the tape recorder, with its ability to bring native speakers' voices into the classroom tirelessly and (unlike the gramophone) flexibly, was hailed as a gift to language teachers with greater potential than any invention since the chalkboard. Yet a survey of pupil attitudes which formed part of the official evaluation of primary school French in the United Kingdom revealed an almost universal hatred of the tape recorder. That may have been the outcome of excessive use of the tape recorder as a model for repetition in the heyday of the audiolingual method.

The language laboratory was a development of the tape recorder that was introduced into schools first in the United States at the end of the 1950s and then in other countries in an explosive expansion during the 1960s. That expansion probably passed its peak as educational spending suffered from worldwide recession and as the unrealistic hopes that many teachers, learners, and administrators had of the new equipment failed to be realized and a decade of comparative research studies failed to provide conclusive evidence of the effectiveness of language laboratories in schools (Green 1975). A more recent picture of the use made of language laboratories in schools is given by a survey of 322 labs and 2,109 teachers in Lower Saxony in the Federal Republic of Germany (Kleinschmidt and Nübold 1981) (see *Language Laboratories*).

Although the tape recorder in both classroom and language laboratory may have suffered from a period of overenthusiastic use of it for behaviouristic drilling, there is no doubt that it has profoundly influenced language teaching, particularly in the attention that it has made it possible to pay to listening comprehension. The advent of the compact cassette has made tape recorders both cheaper and easier to use, and commercially produced course materials very commonly include cassette recordings.

Audiovisual courses extended the visual side of language teaching, which had been limited to book and wall pictures, through the use of slides and filmstrips. Later, language teachers began to realize the great potential of the overhead projector, with its scope for teacher- and pupil-produced visuals, the possibility of introducing simple movement into pictures, and the convenience of daylight projection. In some countries it has become a major language teaching aid. More recently, the boom in domestic video recorders has brought their cost within the reach of schools in some countries, enabling them to use sophisticated television programmes in language teaching.

The latest development in technology to have an impact on language teaching is the microcomputer. As with video recorders, a dramatic increase in sophistication has been accompanied by an equally dramatic reduction in cost. There are already numerous articles on microcomputers and language teaching, and teachers are beginning to form working groups to develop programmes. Commercial programmes are already on the market. It is to be hoped that fascination with the hardware will not blind language teachers, as it did with language laboratories, to the importance of the software, the actual teaching programmes. The first indications are none too encouraging, for many of the programmes seem to be a return to the sort of uncontextualized grammar drill that classroom language teaching has been moving away from.

4. Syllabus

The syllabus for foreign languages in schools has traditionally been defined in terms of an inventory of grammatical structures and a list of vocabulary items. The aim has been for the pupil to learn (part of) the grammatical system and a useful vocabulary, the latter sometimes based on a frequency count, like *le français fondamental*. Such syllabi are often called structural syllabi. The disadvantage is that they can easily lead to teaching materials in which the language is chosen more for its exemplification or practice of particular grammatical structures than for its practical usefulness. Semantically unrelated items are often juxtaposed because they are structurally related (as in so-called structure drills), and at worst the language may not only lack any

real context but be quite unlike any naturally uttered language. The usefulness of the language taught in a structural syllabus is often very low in the initial stages because the order in which grammatical items are introduced is dictated by principles of structural grading (e.g. simple tense before compound tense).

More recently, there has been a movement to define the learning syllabus in terms of what the learner should be able to do with the language. Such syllabi are often called functional or notional-functional syllabi, because they specify language functions such as apologizing or asking for information with reference to general notions such as time or space, or more specific notions such as shopping or health. The work of the Council of Europe in defining communicative objectives for adult language learners, for example the Threshold Level in English, has had a widespread influence in popularizing functional syllabi for school learners as well.

Functional syllabi have been criticized because they are merely taxonomies and not capable of being systematized into rules like a grammatical syllabus giving the learner the power to generate new language. The importance of that argument depends crucially on the view taken of language learning, for neither the grammatical nor the functional syllabus automatically defines a methodology for teaching it.

5. Organization

Typically, language teaching in schools is organized into a number of lessons per week (usually from two to six) for a number of years. For methods that attempt to immerse the learner in the foreign language it is a form of organization that has been likened to "gardening in a gale" (Hawkins 1981): the tender seedlings of the foreign language, planted and nurtured by the teacher for 40 or 50 minutes, are exposed to the gale of the native language that blows across them for several hours as soon as the classroom doors open. It has been suggested that if the number of hours of instruction that a learner gets were concentrated into a shorter period without the distracting interruptions of other subjects, then learning would be more effective. Such intensive courses are difficult to reconcile with the other demands of the school curriculum and are therefore uncommon at the school level of language learning, though there have been experiments with them (Hawkins 1988).

Language learning in schools may be made more intensive not only by increasing the number of hours per week devoted to teaching the foreign language but also by teaching other subjects through the medium of the foreign language. Experiments along these lines have taken place in a number of countries. In the Soviet Union, there are some thousand or more special language schools offering both intensified teaching of a foreign language and instruction in other subjects through the medium of it, to linguistically gifted pupils.

A form of reorganization of language teaching in schools that has attracted international attention is what has become known as the graded test movement in the United Kingdom. Recognizing that, in the United Kingdom, pupils exit from the language learning process at many different points, the movement has sought to define a series of short-term objectives (usually defined in communicative terms) called grades or levels, each of which offers the learner a relevant and worthwhile, if limited, achievement in itself. Each level represents about one year's work for the average learner, is usually tested by a criterion-referenced test and rewarded with the award of a certificate. As learners need varying amounts of time to achieve grades there is a flexible system of teaching and testing not rigidly linked to age or years of instruction (Harding et al. 1980).

A special problem of organization is posed when pupils enter the secondary school having already learnt a foreign language in the primary school. The need for coordination of the two levels in such cases has been generally recognized, but in practice there have often been severe difficulties in the way of achieving it. Secondary schools may be served by several different primary schools, some not teaching a foreign language at all, whilst others adopt different starting ages and time allocations and different materials and methods from each other. Even where such matters are regulated by a national curriculum, effective coordination may be hampered by resistance to change on the part of the secondary teachers.

6. Materials

For many years, the materials available to teachers were principally textbooks, typically written by other teachers and designed to last about one year. They were supported by separate readers, grammars, and vocabularies. Direct method teachers also made extensive use of wall pictures. In the postwar era, this pattern tended to change in a number of ways. Firstly, the development of audiovisual aids, coupled with an increased emphasis on the spoken word, meant that the textbook was sometimes no longer at the centre but simply part of a multimedia package of materials, which could include tapes, filmstrips, flashcards, readers, wallcharts, exercise books, workcards, and teacher's manuals. Such a course could no longer be produced by a single teacher but needed a team of linguists, artists, and native speakers.

Secondly, the objectives of teaching materials are increasingly defined in functional rather than grammatical terms. To take an example: a German textbook of 1965, *English for Today*, stresses the procedure for acquiring the grammatical forms and sentence patterns of the language, building each unit around a particular grammatical structure such as the future, whereas a Far Eastern course of 1980, *Communication Targets*, stresses English in use, taking as the core of each unit a particular communication requirement such as expressing intention.

It is possibly through changes in textbooks as much as any other channel that the majority of language teachers in schools become aware of changes in the aims and methods of language teaching, and it is no doubt in recognition of that fact that in many countries teaching materials are subject to some form of ministry approval before they can be introduced into schools.

7. Examinations and Testing

A further potent influence on language teaching in schools is the way in which the language proficiency of pupils is tested. Whether the tests are produced by the school itself or by some external agency, those that count towards important grades such as school-leaving grades are generally subject to some form of national control. It is important that there is no disparity between the teaching syllabus and methods and the testing syllabus and methods, otherwise the backwash effect of the latter inevitably begins to erode the former. The "heavy hand" of the examinations is sometimes justifiably blamed for holding back developments in classroom methods. That may not only be due to the conservatism and inertia of large institutions like examinations boards but also to the difficulty of devising valid and reliable instruments to test new aims in teaching.

Traditional language testing employs techniques such as dictation, translation, free or guided (picture) composition, reproduction, and oral interview. In the audiolingual era, they were criticized as being too subjective, too integrative (i.e. mixing up different skills), and not susceptible to statistical tests of reliability and validity. Language tests therefore became more objective and discrete (keeping language skills separate), and were often statistically standardized. The use of the multiple-choice format, which permits item analysis and facilitates mass testing, became widespread. Integrative tests are now returning with the demand for tests of real communicative use of language, but it is probably true to say that many exams still favour accuracy at the expense of communicative efficiency, and writing at the expense of speaking.

Until recently, most school foreign language examinations have resulted in a single overall grade of language proficiency, even though the exam may have separate subtests of listening and reading skills, etc. Also, the grades are very often arrived at by norm referencing rather than criterion referencing, that is, candidates are measured against each other rather than against a fixed criterion of performance. Such grades may be of little value to those who need to interpret them such as employers or university selectors. An "A" in French means no more than that the candidate was among the best of those tested, unless there is some definition of what such a candidate is able to do with the language. Nor does it give any indication of the areas in which the candidate's strengths and weaknesses lie. The General Cerificate of Secondary Education (GCSE), a 16 plus examination introduced in the United

Kingdom in 1988, attempts to set communicative tasks for foreign languages, give meaning priority over form in the assessment, and award criterion-referenced grades with some profiling.

8. Success

The IEA studies of English and French as foreign languages examined differences in achievement between pupils, schools, and countries. Of course, the differing levels of achievement have to be considered in relation to a whole series of other variables and, indeed, one of the main purposes of the studies was to identify the factors bearing on pupil progress in achieving foreign language skills. Such factors appeared (with some differences for French and English and between countries) to be home background, type of school, amount of exposure to the foreign language, quality of instruction (including use of the foreign language in the classroom), pupil interest, and general verbal ability. Sex was an important factor in some countries (English speaking and Sweden, for example), with girls being favoured.

How pupil attitudes towards foreign languages may be positively influenced by the organization of the syllabus was strikingly demonstrated in a British Schools Council evaluation of the effect of graded tests and objectives on the attitude of pupils towards learning French. After one year, pupils who had followed a graded objectives syllabus had markedly superior attitudes, whether they had passed the test or not, to a control group who had continued with the normal syllabus (Buckby et al. 1981).

Insights like this may be very important in situations where motivation for learning a foreign language is generally low. This seems to be the case particularly in English-speaking countries, which may have to do with the status of English as a world vehicle language. Certainly, quite apart from IEA, national assessments of foreign languages in schools in the United Kingdom and the United States paint a depressing picture of low achievement and interest. In the United Kingdom, a report by the schools inspectorate in 1977 found "widespread underperformance of pupils of all levels of ability" and 60 percent of pupils dropping out of language learning after only three years. In the United States, the President's Commission on Foreign Language and International Studies in 1979 found "Americans' incompetence in foreign languages is nothing short of scandalous, and it is becoming worse". It also recorded that, at the time of the Commission's survey, only 15 percent of all high-school students (in grades 7–12)

were studying a foreign language (down from 24 percent in 1965) and, furthermore, that only 5 percent took the study of French, German, or Russian beyond the second year.

The situation in non-English-speaking countries seems brighter: IEA found high levels of achievement in, for instance, Sweden and the Netherlands—a finding that would not surprise English-speaking visitors to those countries.

Bibliography

Allwright R L 1972 Prescription and description in the training of language teachers. In: Qvistgaard J, Schwarz H, Spang-Hanssen H (eds.) 1974 3rd Int. Congress Applied Linguistics, Copenhagen, 1972, Vol. 3: *Applied Linguistics: Problems and Solutions.* Groos, Heidelberg, pp. 150–66

Buckby M, Bull P, Fletcher R, Green P S, Page B, Roger D 1981 *Graded Objectives and Tests for Modern Languages: An Evaluation.* Schools Council/Centre for Information on Language Teaching and Research, London

Carroll J B 1975 *The Teaching of French as a Foreign Language in Eight Countries.* Wiley, New York

Christophersen P 1973 *Second-Language Learning: Myth and Reality.* Penguin, Harmondsworth

Faersch C, Kasper G (eds.) 1983 *Strategies in Interlanguage Communication.* Longman, London

Green P S (ed.) 1975 *The Language Laboratory in School, Performance and Prediction: An Account of the York Study.* Oliver and Boyd, Edinburgh

Harding A, Page B, Rowell S 1980 *Graded Objectives in Modern Languages.* Centre for Information on Language Teaching and Research, London

Hawkins E W 1981 *Modern Languages in the Curriculum.* Cambridge University Press, Cambridge

Hawkins E W (ed.) 1988 *Intensive Language Teaching and Learning.* Centre for Information on Language Teaching and Research, London

Kleinschmidt E, Nübold P 1981 *Untersuchung zur Situation des Sprachlabors an niedersächsischen Schulen.* [A Study of the Position of Language Laboratories in Schools of Lower Saxony]. Arbeitsgruppe Sprachlabor [Working Party on Language Laboratories], Technical University of Braunschweig, Braunschweig

Levin L 1972 *Comparative Studies in Foreign Language Teaching.* Almqvist and Wiksell, Stockholm

Lewis E G, Massad C E 1975 *The Teaching of English as a Foreign Language in Ten Countries.* Wiley, New York

Peck A J 1988 *Language Teachers at Work.* Prentice Hall, London

Sanderson D A 1983 *Modern Language Teachers in Action.* University of York/Nuffield Foundation

Smith P D 1970 *A Comparison of the Cognitive and Audiolingual Approaches to Foreign Language Instruction. The Pennsylvania Foreign Language Project.* Harrap, London

Factors Relating to Foreign Language Studies

Educational Linguistics

B. Spolsky

Educational linguistics is a term recently coined to refer to the field or fields concerned with the interaction of language and education.

Educational linguistics might be considered as a subfield of applied linguistics, though this term is itself often used to refer only to language teaching. In some British usage, educational linguistics is restricted to mother tongue education. Educational linguistics as it has developed since the early 1970s is perhaps best considered as a kind of applied educational sociolinguistics, for it draws most heavily on sociolinguistics with its central interest in language use, and is less concerned with the questions of language structure that are the focus of theoretical linguistics.

The scope of educational linguistics may be defined by the areas that it encompasses, such as language education policy, first and second language teaching, reading, literacy, bilingual education, composition (see *Composition Instruction*), language testing; or by the fields from which it derives its theoretical foundations, including theoretical linguistics, sociolinguistics, psycholinguistics and anthropological linguistics; or by its subfields, which include first and second language acquisition studies, mother tongue teaching, second language pedagogy, immigrant and minority language education, and language planning. The unified nature of the field emerges most clearly when the background, rationales, operations, and outcomes of language education are looked at.

The background of language education is twofold: the situation in which it takes place and the communicative competence of the learners who are to be educated. In analysing the situations in which language education occurs, the focus may be on the society (what languages are used for what purposes in the community under consideration?) or the individual (what is the communicative competence of the person whose education is being examined). When focusing on the society, a first major distinction arises between homogeneous speech communities (ones that share a single language variety, albeit one with distinct registers and styles for different roles and purposes) and heterogeneous speech communities (ones where several varieties are in systematically structured alternative use

in the same community). In the case of the heterogeneous communities, there are various kinds of societal bilingualism. The paradigmatic case of societal bilingualism is diglossia, where one variety is used for more or less informal functions (such as home) and another is used for more or less public or formal functions, usually including school. The complexity and nature of the underlying sociolinguistic situation is clearly fundamental to the development of a workable language education policy, and provides some explanation of the communicative competence with which it is concerned.

1. Communicative Competence

Studies of communicative competence, bridging sociolinguistics which looks at language complexity and variation and psycholinguistics which looks at language processing and acquisition, provide the second major background focus of the field. A number of important findings or assumptions have developed in the course of recent studies in these two interrelated areas. The most important are probably the following:

First, language education must be concerned with the whole communicative competence of the child or person being educated. By communicative competence is meant the ability to participate in a society as a speaking and communicating member: it involves not just competence in the underlying linguistic system (what Chomsky called linguistic competence) but also in language use, attitudes and beliefs about language, and knowledge of the complex patterns of discourse used by the society (Chomsky 1965). Approaches that are concerned only with a single variety, or with such a narrow issue as the shibboleths or standard grammar rules of a prestigious written variety, are unlikely to meet the needs of those being educated. To do this, it is necessary to know the patterns of language use in the communities from which children come, the values ascribed to language by different sectors of society, the actual language ability of the children in the various settings in which they are called on to communicate, and the modifications in ability that will best fit the children to function as communicating members of the society they are preparing to join.

Second, language acquisition is a complex process that occurs naturally in all children. In normal circumstances, children acquire the socially expected control of the variety or varieties to which they are exposed before coming to school. As a result, the formal language education of the school must be seen in the context of the informal language education that takes place outside it. This fact helps explain the differences between foreign language teaching where the only context for language use is the classroom, and second language teaching where there is use of the language in other situations outside the school; these external uses provide opportunity for practice and additional learning and have important effects on attitudes of the learners to acquiring the language (Spolsky 1978). Thus educational linguistics stresses the broad range of communicative competence and the full social context in which language operates.

Third, whatever complex relations might exist between language and cognition (and exploration of this issue remains an urgent concern of educational linguists, so far without convincing evidence of the nature of the relations), all living languages offer evidence of comparable complexity and so of comparable potential for cognitive development. While languages have lexicons more developed in one area than another, and while each has its favourite grammatical devices, there is no linguistic evidence of an inherently inferior language, and no linguistic support for the notion that one language is intrinsically better than another (Labov 1969). Thus, notions that one language is more beautiful or logical than another, or that certain dialects are illogical because they lack a grammatical feature found in another (as some psychologists have complained that Black English is illogical because it omits the verb "to be" in the present tense, a characteristic it shares with such languages as Russian and Arabic), or that learning a particular language (e.g., Classical Latin) will automatically lead to improved reasoning ability, find no support in research or theory.

At the same time, and this is the fourth basic assumption, all varieties of language are socially valued, and this social value rather than inherent linguistic value or quality is usually what determines language education policy. A variety's social value derives from the roles with which it is associated: thus, in a strongly religious community, the variety of language associated with the religion or the language of its sacred texts is likely to have the highest prestige; in a modern industrialized society, the standard variety of the dominant social group is usually the prestige variety; in the academic world, the style and variety of writing called academic prose has the highest prestige. This factor of prestige is clearly crucial in the determination of rationales and goals for language education. It also explains the development of tension in bilingual and multilingual societies, where the languages concerned have different and competing claims for prestige. In Belgium, for instance, the struggle over the competing political and ethnic

values associated with standard French and Dutch overshadows the pedagogical gaps between these standard languages and the local varieties of each spoken by most Belgian children (Bustamente et al. 1978). In many nations, the competition between a national language and an international one creates major tension in educational policy. In diglossic situations, the enormous prestige of the standard language, particularly when it is a classical language associated with a religious tradition, makes it difficult even to acknowledge the existence of the local variety.

A fifth basic lesson of recent work in educational linguistics is the recognition of the inadequacy of accounts of language situations, whether social or individual. There have generally only been sketchy descriptions of language situations and inadequate methods of measuring the actual level of language control achieved by children before they start formal education: as a result the development of aims and curricula for language education programmes is often misguided. It is thus an urgent concern of educational linguistics to map more clearly actual communicative competence; with the disappointing shortcomings of psychometric techniques (see Sect. 4), ethnographic approaches are now being applied to the process.

2. Rationales for Language Education

In the study of rationales, the concern is with the attitudes which underly the development of language education policy and which affect various aspects of its implementation (see *Rationale: Curriculum*). In educational linguistics, these rationales might be linguistic (the notion that acquisition of a variety of language is good in itself), psychological (the notion that mastery of a variety of languages has value for personal, emotional or intellectual growth), sociopolitical (the notion that control of a variety of language has value for a social or political unit), cultural (the notion that knowledge of a variety of language provides access to specific bodies of religious or cultural knowledge), or pedagogical.

When rationales are studied, a distinction needs to be made between the various people and institutions able to influence language education policy: the central or the local government, the general or the local community, religious or cultural leaders, the educational establishment, the local teachers, the parents, and the students themselves. The existence of so many competing sources of pressure provides the potential for conflict. In heterogeneous communities, the potential is often realized, and the study of language education becomes a study of political struggle. There are many cases that illustrate this fact. In nineteenth-century Africa, the colonial powers were divided into those who favoured initial education in the vernacular (the British, the Germans, and the Belgians) and those who insisted on education from the beginning in the metropolitan language (the French and the Portuguese); these traditions, plus the complex linguistic patterning artificially created by the European conquest of Africa, left most newly independent African countries with a horrendous heritage of conflicting forces in the struggle over language education policy (Whiteley 1974). In the Soviet Union, the swing between centripetal and centrifugal tendencies in language policy has sometimes favoured the maintenance of selected local languages but has usually worked towards the gradual spread and primacy of Russian (Lewis 1980). Nationalist movements provided the basis of postindependence language revival programmes in Algeria, Indonesia, Ireland, and Israel. In the United States, struggles for ethnic identity and access to economic resources were focused on the development of bilingual education. In Western Europe, the ambivalent attitude to foreign workers has been shown in the linguistic treatment of their children in schools. These are only a few of the cases that show the potential complexity of competing rationales for language education policy.

It is in the area of rationales that a number of unfounded but influential opinions about language education might be suitably considered, many of which educational linguists are attempting to demonstrate to be false, but all of which are likely to influence policy makers, parents, and educators. The first of these is the notion that there is a single correct variety of language which school must teach. In actual fact, sociolinguistic research has shown that all societies have a complex pattern of social values attached to a wide range of registers, varieties, styles, and languages. A person who can handle only one level of language is considered handicapped: excessive formality is frowned on as much as excessive informality. A second misleading notion is the idea that language education should be concerned with reading and writing alone. Speaking and listening skills are just as important in most communities and deserve full attention from the school, whether in mother tongue or foreign language teaching. The analysis of oracy and literacy has shown that they include many similar features: the line between them is somewhat technical and superficial, and many of the structural features associated with literacy are to be found in varieties of spoken language. A third mistaken notion has already been discussed: there is no evidence of inherent inferiority in any particular language. A fourth notion that has not stood up to empirical testing is the dictum of UNESCO experts and others that reading must be taught in the mother tongue (Spolsky 1981). There are many situations in which high levels of literacy are achieved in a second language. Studies in the sociolinguistics of literacy are helping to produce an understanding of the factors that account for these differences. A fifth incorrect notion is the idea that bilingualism is in some way harmful. This notion, derived from the work of psychologists who carried out their studies in societies where bilingualism was stigmatized as a mark of membership of a linguistic minority, has been refuted by studies of cases where bilingualism is a mark of membership of an elite group. Studies that hold language prestige constant show the potential benefits in cognitive ability and creativity of being bilingual.

Reference may be made here to the growing understanding of the effects of attitudes, whether on the part of teachers (the so-called Pygmalion effect) or of learners or of other significant participants.

Studies have shown the importance of both degree and kind of attitude to language learning: learners are much more likely to reach a high level of control of a variety of language when they are learning it in order to become a member of the community speaking the language than when they are learning it for some other purpose (Gardner and Lambert 1972). Thus, immigrants in societies that permit or encourage integrative social mobility are more successful than those who are in a less welcoming environment, and both are likely to attain higher levels of control than learners who are acquiring a language for its symbolic educational value. In this last case, language learning seems most affected by attitude to school learning in general, and success in it will correlate highly with other kinds of school success.

3. Language Education Policy and Implementation

When the actual operations involved in language education are looked at, language education policy may be considered first, followed by a consideration of implementation. Basically, language education policy may choose to extend and improve the variety of language that a child brings from home (mother tongue education, vernacular education, language arts education, teaching of reading and writing), to add another variety for limited use (foreign language or classical language education) or for general use (bilingual education), or to replace the home language with another language immediately (the home–school language switch, submersion, second language education), or later (transitional bilingual education), or temporarily (immersion foreign language teaching). More than one additional or replacive language may be taught. The policy may or may not be congruent with the actual situation: thus, failing to recognize the actual home or community language situation, a school may use a mother tongue approach when the pupils are in fact learning a foreign or second language.

A fundamental policy question is age of beginning and the amount of time devoted to language instruction. Assuming that the mother tongue is to be taught, the most general pattern is to teach it first, but in certain colonialist or postcolonialist situations, instruction in the mother tongue has been delayed until secondary school (e.g., the teaching of Maori in New Zealand during the period while there were still many native speakers) or later (Tahitian is offered in France as a university-level subject but not taught in the schools on the islands of Tahiti themselves). There is considerable controversy over the age of beginning second or foreign language instruction. There was a widely held consensus that young children learned second languages more easily than adults; on this basis, there was considerable argument for an early start. More recent research makes clear that older learners acquire certain aspects of language (especially those involving conscious learning of the more formal aspects) with greater speed than younger children; this is used in some places to argue for delaying a start of the second language and giving greater attention to the mother tongue or the standard language. It does however seem to be supported by current research that an early start, combined with appropriate methods, leads ultimately to higher levels of mastery (Freudenstein 1979, Genesee 1978).

The amount of time devoted to language instruction is similarly varied. While a number of experiences (the United States Armed Services Training Program and the Foreign Services Institute methods that developed from it, the *Ulpanim* in Israel, the immersion bilingual programmes in Canada, to name a few of the better known) have made clear the value of intensive programmes for learners of all ages, so that it is clear that the attainment of mastery of a second language comparable to that of a first requires comparable exposure, political and practical considerations usually mean that only a few hours' instruction a week are available, with obvious increase in the demand for efficiency and decrease in the level of control that can reasonably be expected.

Implementation covers the full range of language education pedagogy: method, approach, materials, and teachers. In this field as in many others, pedagogical history is marked by the regular announcement and temporary acceptance of new panaceas for old ills: a list need only be made of some of the labels (the more significant of which appear elsewhere in these volumes) that have been popular in the various parts of the field: in reading, phonics, look–see or whole word, speed reading; in heterogeneous speech communities: mother tongue, vernacular, transitional or maintenance enrichment, compensatory bilingual, or bilingual–bicultural monoliterate or biliterate, second language; in a foreign or second language teaching: new method, natural method, direct method, audio-lingual method, cognitive method, language for special purposes or for academic purposes, notional, functional, or notional–functional, etc. Curricula and textbooks have multiplied, sometimes but not always reflecting growth in understanding of the complex learning processes involved (see, for example, Mackey 1965).

Also, with the increase of modern technology and as a result of pressures for higher achievement with restricted exposure, language education too has joined the subjects that are considered to benefit from modern equipment: record players, tape recorders, elaborate systems of tape recorders organized into what has been called a language laboratory, film, television, programmed instruction with or without computer control, have all been applied to various aspects of language education, with varying levels of success.

In this multiplicity, several recent notions seem to be basic to language education in general and foreign or second language instruction in particular. First, there seems to be a difference between the kind of automatic unconscious learning most commonly associated with the natural acquisition of a mother tongue or of a second language in the country where it is spoken, and the learning of the more formal and consciously acquired aspects of language; each of these has a part to play, but each seems to develop with some degree of independence (Carroll 1981, Bialystok 1981). Second, there are differences about learner's aptitude and attitude that make it impossible ever to assume that one method or approach will be appropriate to all (Rivers 1980). Third, the organization of new material can be structural or functional, according to the aim of instruction and kind of learners involved, but whatever order is chosen, it will need to take into account the learner's own conscious and unconscious readiness to learn (Breen and Candlin 1980).

The selection and training of teachers is also a matter of considerable variation and dispute. In traditional societies, the status of language teachers ranged from the Greek slave in Rome to the Priestly Scribe in ancient Israel. In modern societies, those who teach the mother tongue or foreign languages usually share the social status of other teachers, although it is generally the case in tertiary education that those who teach use of language have lower status than those who teach about it. The question of who should teach a language, a native speaker of the variety being taught or a native speaker of the learners' variety, is more usually resolved on political or economic grounds than on pedagogical ones. Similarly, the question of the best training for language teachers depends on who has control of the universities or institutions where they are trained, which thus determine whether the major emphasis of training be on the language to be taught, on its literature, on linguistics, or on general educational theories and practices.

4. The Assessment of Outcomes

The measurement and evaluation of outcomes is the fourth central concern of educational linguistics. A distinction must be made between attempts at measurement of effects of various programmes (evaluation or experiment) and the field of language testing which must be considered in its own right. As in other areas of education, attempts to apply the agricultural model (experimental and control groups, treatment with a single factor changed) have turned out to be singularly ineffective in the area of language education. For example, a large number of reported studies of various models of bilingual education concerned with the issue of teaching literacy in the vernacular or in the standard language first have produced contradictory results. Recent studies of immersion programmes in Canada have shown that it is possible to teach English-speaking children to read first in French without harm to their later English reading; at the same time, a recent longitudinal study in the United States has shown that teaching Navajo children to read in Navajo first has in fact led to a marked improvement in their English reading ability (Rosier and Holm 1980). But these studies have highlighted the need for long-term multimeasurement studies, showing the futility of attempts to decide with immediate pre- and post-testing the effects of educational innovation. Similarly, short-term studies of the effect of changes in foreign language teaching methods have usually shown little more than that learners learn what they are taught.

The field of language testing is described in greater detail elsewhere in these volumes. There have been several important developments. The first was the move to apply psychometric techniques and principles to language testing. While many parts of the world continue to make use of unreliable and unvalidated subjective examinations, the notion of an objective and standardized language test has received wide acceptance. There has been considerable exploration of the possibilities and limitations of these objective tests, and, more recently, a good deal of research into the possibility of adding reliability and validity to more integrative testing techniques such as writing or dictation or interviews and into the possibility of developing other tests of integrative abilities such as the cloze test. An important controversy continues over the nature of language proficiency and the number of factors of which it may be composed (Klein-Braley and Stevenson 1981).

Organizationally, the field of educational linguistics remains comparatively unrepresented: educational linguists are found and trained in various parts of the university, most often where there is collaboration between scholars in education, linguistics, anthropology, and language departments.

Bibliography

Bialystok E 1981 Some evidence for the integrity and interaction of two knowledge sources. In: Andersen H W (ed.) 1981 *New Dimensions in Second Language Acquisition Research*. Newbury House, Rowley, Massachusetts

Breen M P, Candlin C 1980 The essentials of a communicative curriculum in language teaching. *Appl. Linguistics* 1: 89–112

Bustamante H, Van Overbeke M, Verdoodt A 1978 Bilingual education in Belgium. In: Spolsky B, Cooper R L (eds.) 1978 *Case Studies in Bilingual Education*. Newbury House, Rowley, Massachusetts

Caroll J B 1981 Conscious and automatic processes in language learning. *Can. Mod. Lang. Rev.* 37: 462–74

Cazden C B, John-Steiner V P, Hymes D 1972 *Functions of Language in the Classroom*. Teachers College Press, New York

Chomsky N 1965 *Aspects of the Theory of Syntax*. MIT Press, Cambridge, Massachusetts

Freudenstein R (ed.) 1979 *Teaching Foreign Languages to the Very Young*. Pergamon, Oxford

Gardner R C, Lambert W E 1972 *Attitudes and Motivation in Second-language Learning*. Newbury House, Rowley, Massachusetts

Gardner R C 1985 *Social Psychology and Second Language Learning: The Role of Attitudes and Motivation*. Edward Arnold, London

Genesee F 1978 Is there an optimal age for starting second language instruction? *McGill J. Educ.* 13: 145–54

Hymes D 1979 Language in education: Forward to fundamentals. In: Garnica O K, King M L (eds.) 1979 *Language, Children, and Society: The Effect of Social Factors on Children Learning to Communicate*. Pergamon, Oxford

Klein-Braley C, Stevenson D K (eds.) 1981 *Practice and Problems in Language Testing I*. Lang, Frankfurt

Labov W 1969 The Logic of non-standard English. In: Alatis J (ed.) 1969 *Monograph Series on Languages and Linguistics*. Georgetown University Press, Washington, DC

Lambert W E, Tucker G R 1972 *Bilingual Education of Children: The St Lambert Experiment*. Newbury House, Rowley, Massachusetts

Lewis E G 1980 *Bilingualism and Bilingual Education: A Comparative Study*. University of New Mexico Press, Albuquerque, New Mexico, Pergamon, Oxford

Mackey W F 1965 *Language Teaching Analysis*. Indiana University Press, Bloomington, Indiana

McLaughlin B 1987 *Theories of Second-Language Learning*. Edward Arnold, London

Paulston C B (ed.) 1988 *International Handbook of Bilingualism and Bilingual Education*. Greenwood Press, New York

Rivers W M 1980 Foreign language acquisition: Where the real issues lie. *Appl. Linguistics* 1: 48–59

Rosier P, Holm W 1980 *The Rock Point Experience: A Longitudinal Study of a Navajo School Program. (Saad Naaki Bee Na'nitin)*. Center for Applied Linguistics, Washington, DC

Spolsky B 1978 *Educational Linguistics: An Introduction*. Newbury House, Rowley, Massachusetts

Spolsky B 1981 Bilingualism and biliteracy. *Canadian Modern Lang. Rev.* 37: 475–85

Spolsky B (ed.) 1986 *Language and Education in Multilingual Settings*. Edited with introduction. Multilingual Matters, Clevedon & College-Hill Press, San Diego

Spolsky B 1989 *Conditions for Second Language Learning: Introduction to a General Theory*. Oxford University Press, Oxford

Spolsky B 1989 Communicative competence, language proficiency, and beyond. *Appl. Linguistics* 10: 138–56

Stern H H 1983 *Fundamental Concepts of Language Teaching*. Oxford University Press, Oxford

Whiteley W H (ed.) 1974 *Language in Kenya*. Oxford University Press, Nairobi

Pedagogic Grammar

E. Olshtain

A pedagogic grammar is a collection of explicit generalizations about a language. The linguistic generalizations contained in a pedagogic grammar are derived from one or more scientific grammars and have been converted into practical teaching material. Notwithstanding the systematic relationship that holds between the scientific and pedagogic grammars, they differ significantly with respect to two important features: (a) their inherent goals, and (b) the manner in which they represent the linguistic rules.

The major aim or underlying motivation of a scientific grammar is to describe and explain linguistic knowledge. Such a grammar seeks therefore, to develop the best theoretical model or framework to provide a vocabulary to discuss the elements of language such as sounds, words, phrases, clauses, sentences, and discourse units, as well as linguistic rules that define and explain how these elements are used. The writer of a scientific grammar aims to give a systematic account of the idealized linguistic knowledge or competence which underlies the actual use of language in concrete communicative situations.

A scientific grammar is based on a formal theory of language and it is expected to provide an exhaustive representation of what a native speaker knows. As such it should specify all the sentences of a language in terms of the widest possible generalizations. Furthermore, a scientific grammar should answer requirements of simplicity and efficiency in the way the rules are organized in order to ensure maximal generality.

The goal of a pedagogic grammar is quite different from that of a scientific grammar since its major objective is to impart knowledge. Such a grammar must concern itself with the needs of the learner and the process of acquisition of linguistic knowledge in order to aid and facilitate this process. A pedagogic grammar is therefore, by definition, prescriptive in nature, since it must guide the learner in using language properly.

A writer of a pedagogic grammar seeks to develop a comparatively informal framework of verbal definitions and explanations of linguistic realizations. In order to make such explanation more accessible to the learner they are often accompanied by graphic devices. Furthermore, rules in a pedagogic grammar must be illustrated with examples and followed by suitable exercises to enable the learner to acquire and internalize these rules.

In the process of converting linguistic rules into pedagogic generalizations, the writer of a pedagogic grammar has to follow didactic considerations. The ordering of the rules is, therefore, guided by usefulness, frequency, conceptual familiarity, and contrast with the mother tongue of the learners. A careful process of sequencing, grading, and recycling of information needs to be applied to the ordering of the rules, thus rendering a grammar which is very different in nature from the scientific grammar or grammars upon which it is based. Some of the rules in the pedagogic grammar give only partial information and therefore violate the true linguistic validity of these rules but such partial definitions may be the result of careful pedagogic considerations and therefore necessary for the acquisition process.

A pedagogic grammar can be intended to teach a second or foreign language to speakers of other languages. In this case the aim would be to lead the learner towards competence that resembles the native speaker's knowledge of the target language. A school grammar, is however, also a pedagogic grammar which aims to help native speakers of a language to use their language more expressively and normatively. Both types of pedagogic grammars follow the same principles as described here although their goals are different.

Bibliography

Allen J P B 1970 Pedagogic grammar. In: Allen J P B, Corder S P (eds.) 1970 *The Edinburgh Course in Applied Linguistics*, Vol. 3. Oxford University Press, London

Berman R A 1979 Rule of grammar or rule of thumb? *Int. Rev. Appl. Ling. Lang. Teach.* 17(4)

Corder S P 1974 Pedagogical grammars or the pedagogy of grammar? In: Corder S P, Roulet E (eds.) 1974 *Linguistic Insights in Applied Linguistics*. Association Internationale pour la Recherche et la Diffusion des Méthodes Audio-Visuelles et Structure-Globales, Brussels

Thomas O, Kintgen E R 1974 *Transformation Grammar and the Teacher of English*. Holt, Rinehart and Winston, New York

Language Needs Analysis

J. L. M. Trim

Analysis of language needs is an essential aspect of any systematic approach to language learning. Few people, if any, can learn a foreign language to perfection. How are the limited human and material resources to be used to the best effect? Not by plodding through grammar and general vocabulary from "elementary" through "intermediate" to "advanced", but by forecasting the communicative demands upon learners, establishing priorities in terms of use, then establishing corresponding operational objectives and gearing methods, materials, and evaluation to them. Attempts to establish

the language needs of industry and commerce (Emmans et al. 1974) encountered difficulties in distinguishing need from demand and motivation. More detailed breakdowns of activities (LCCI 1972, Schröder et al. 1978) have served as the basis for languages for special purposes (LSP), and academic purposes (LAP). Such specialized courses now abound. A detailed specification of the minimum English language required of a foreign visitor for everyday transactions and basic social relations was produced for the Council of Europe by Van Ek and Alexander (1980), covering situations, topics, required behaviours, functions (e.g., apologizing, offering, requesting, explaining), and notions to be expressed and the language necessary to do so. This was later applied to French, German, Spanish, and Italian. Military needs have been analysed by Development and Evaluation Associates. A general model was produced by Munby (1978) and procedures for eliciting information by Richterich and Chancerel (1980). This model was applied to the needs of students in polytechnics in the United Kingdom. Now increasingly stressed are: (a) the need for learners to develop strategies of communication; (b) the integration of needs analysis into a more general assessment of learning/teaching situations (needs, characteristics, motivation, resources, constraints); (c) dynamic monitoring of feedback-sensitive systems rather than a once-and-for-all analysis as a preliminary to planning. "Objective", practical, operational needs are easiest to establish. For children at school, whose communicative needs are long term and less predictable, other needs (personal affective and cognitive development, attitude formation, cultural sensitization) are of great importance but more difficult to define, describe, and quantify.

Bibliography

Emmans K, Hawkins E, Westoby A 1974 *The Use of Foreign Languages in the Private Sector of Industry and Commerce.* Language Teaching Centre, University of York, York

London Chamber of Commerce and Industry (LCCI) 1972 Market survey on non-specialist use of languages in industry and commerce. Papers for a conference organized by the Centre for Information on Language Teaching and Research (CILT), 5–7 July 1972

Munby J L 1978 *Communicative Syllabus Design: A Sociolinguistic Model for Defining the Content of Purpose-specific Language Programmes.* Cambridge University Press, Cambridge

Richterich R, Chancerel J L 1980 *Identifying the Needs of Adults Learning a Foreign Language.* Pergamon, Oxford

Schröder K, Langheld D, Macht K 1978 *Fremdsprachen in Handel und Industrie: Unter Besonderer Berücksichtigung Mittlerer Betriebe in Schwaben und im Raum München. Dokumentation und Auswertung einer Umfrage.* Universität Augsburg, Augsburg

Setzler H H et al. 1979 *Method for Determining Language Training Objectives and Criteria: Final Report of Recommendations, Executive Summary.* Development and Evaluation Associates, New York

Van Ek J A, Alexander L G 1980 *Threshold Level English.* Pergamon, Oxford

Language for Special Purposes

J. C. Sager

The study of language for special purposes (LSP) is that area of applied linguistics concerned with the teaching of subsets of language to groups of users who require specialized communication skills in specific areas of working life. Its theoretical foundations are the analysis and description of special languages, in terms of linguistic, pragmatic, and extralinguistic phenomena; its practical applications are exemplified by the teaching of skills such as report writing to engineers, foreign-language reading comprehension to scientists, and control-tower language to pilots. Language for special purposes is thus interdisciplinary, combining aspects of linguistics, semiotics, and education.

1. Origins and Scope

The origins of LSP can be traced to the Prague School of Linguistics of the 1920s, which stressed the functional aspect of language and its stylistic variation according to the situations in which it is used. Its recent impetus owes much to the development of sociolinguistics and pragmatics. The importance of LSP in education can be attributed to various factors: the need for trained personnel in diverse, rapidly developing fields of science and technology; the increasing interdependence of fields of knowledge, which puts specialists from different disciplines in close contact with one another; and the growing importance of international information exchange, requiring communication across language barriers on specialized topics.

Subject specialization entails a concomitant specialization of means of communication; these specialized communication skills can, and often should, be taught independently of the subjects themselves. Whilst these factors have long been recognized as far as foreign languages are concerned, they are now also applied to the teaching of the native language, in an attempt to overcome the barriers to communication which result from the use of special languages within a given language community.

Special languages are semiautonomous, complex, semiotic systems, based on and derived from general language (Sager et al. 1980). The subdivision of language into special language and general language, and the delimitation of special languages and their situational subsets is fundamental to all research in LSP. The criteria which are used to achieve this do not correspond to those underlying the traditional divisions of knowledge. Nor must the process be confused with the collection of a subject-specific vocabulary. The communication skills required by an individual in the course of his or her work extend beyond the narrow limits of a particular discipline. A doctor, for instance, may communicate with patients, nurses, administrators, and other doctors within the course of his or her work; each communication act requires its own particular

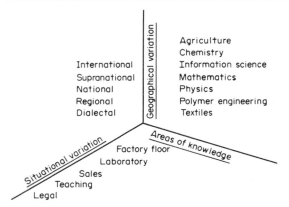

Figure 1
Model of a multidimensional pragmatic space

form. Geographical and situational factors increase the variety of the speech acts performed by an individual. Conversely, a given special language may be employed within a variety of different occupations. For instance, the special language of a scientific discipline such as mechanics or optics may also be an established part of an associated craft or trade. The range and variation of special languages may be characterized by a model of a multidimensional pragmatic space (see Fig. 1).

2. The Linguistic Dimension

To a far greater extent than geographical and social sublanguages, special languages are determined and delimited by the nature of the concepts—and so of the subject field—to which they refer. This is reflected in the specialization, not only of vocabulary, but also of the forms of speech act which are stipulated. Laboratory reports, parts lists of machines, and procedural descriptions are forms of the language of experimental and applied sciences; speculative sciences and philosophy generally use a more discursive line of argument, often presented in essay form. The subject also prescribes the extent to which there is a need for non-linguistic reference and communication, in the form of other symbolic notation, taxonomic systems, and diagrammatic representations. Special subject languages can be classified according to the degree to which they differ from general language and move towards the borderline of artificial languages.

Current research into the linguistic dimension of LSP is principally concerned with text and discourse analysis of written and spoken language. From the lexical, morphological, and syntactic perspectives, statistical studies have revealed that the resources available to a language are used very sparingly within particular types of speech act (Hoffman 1981). Stylistic analysis proceeds from more general concepts, such as "precision", "conciseness", and "objectivity", in order to further characterize special language speech acts according to pragmatic criteria.

3. The Semiotic Dimension

Linguistic phenomena are only part of the complex process of communication to be analysed within the context of LSP. Features such as mode of articulation, facial expression, and the organization of written texts are also important, as all these factors convey meaning and are characteristic of particular areas of communication. The intention of a message is often conveyed extralinguistically through the situation surrounding the speech act. The importance of what is not said, but signified by other means, increases as the size of the linguistic community involved in special communication becomes smaller.

Some special languages may incorporate alternative written codes or whole systems of communication parallel to linguistic means of expression. In their specificity of reference and independent syntax they tend towards artificial languages. The language of chemistry has a number of parallel systems for designating chemical compounds which demonstrate a whole spectrum of semiotic codes. These range from common chemical names, proper names derived according to the morphological rules laid down by international agreement between chemists, through structural diagrams to physical models showing precise structural relationships. As the relationship between signifier and signified becomes less arbitrary and more explicit, so the linguistic content of the code is reduced. Many special languages have adopted other semiotic systems, such as graphs, tables, and diagrams, in direct response to the arbitrary, inexact, and lengthy nature of linguistic designation. In doing so, they have transcended the boundaries of natural language.

4. The Educational Dimension

Special languages are a different type of sublanguage from dialects and sociolects, and thus require a different approach in teaching. Dialects and sociolects are usually acquired unconsciously by a process of conditioned learning; a special language is always learnt as a second language, requiring the knowledge of general language which initially serves as a metalanguage. Therefore, in some senses the learning of a special language is akin to the acquisition of a foreign language. It also requires a knowledge of the special subject for which the language has been developed. The deliberate nature of special language acquisition entails a high degree of commitment on the part of the learner.

Languages for special purposes teaching is founded on the assumption that alternatives to the general "academic" language teaching syllabus of schools and universities are desirable (Gorosch 1970). As special languages are a reflection of the intellectual and socioeconomic development of a speech community, they develop and undergo frequent changes in response to changes in the society. Task-specific, goal-oriented learning in short units is considered more effective in a world of continuous education. The designer of an LSP course must define prime objectives and subgoals based on a consideration of the resources available, the relevance of instructional technique, and most importantly, the communicative requirements of the learner (Turner 1981).

A learner's communicative needs are dictated principally by the interaction of two factors: command of general language, and knowledge of the area in which the use of LSP is planned. For learners already having a good command of the appropriate general language, LSP teaching occurs as a regular part of specialist education, and is provided by subject teachers, as distinct from language teachers, who may supplement this work with special communication courses. Such courses may be the only form of LSP instruction given if the learner is already familiar with the subject area concerned, or, as in the case of translators and interpreters, is not receiving education in the special subject.

A different approach to LSP teaching is required when the students have little or no knowledge of the general language concerned. If the learners are well-versed in the subject matter, this expertise can serve as a structural basis for courses designed to give them limited general language skills, as well as the particular LSP skills that they need. However, if the learners are not subject specialists, the aims of an LSP course are necessarily more limited. Such courses are often tailor-made for small groups, for example shop floor language for a group of immigrant workers, military command language for a multinational United Nations peace-keeping force (Mackay and Mountford 1978).

The diversity of linguistic factors used to characterize LSPs is matched by a wide variety of courses, each emphasizing a different combination of these factors. Curriculum development, which is of overriding importance in LSP, is based on careful needs analysis, which in turn depends on detailed linguistic and pragmatic case studies. With the extension of LSP to all sections of education, from degree courses in translation and interpreting through purpose-specific short courses of very limited objectives to self-instruction courses, theoretical research has intensified, leading to the creation of specialized journals. Since 1977 there have been biannual LSP conferences in Europe, e.g. Bielefeld 1979, Copenhagen 1981, Bordeaux 1983, Louvain 1985, Vaasa 1987, Budapest 1989, under the aegis of the International Association of Applied Linguistics (AILA). The proceedings of these conferences bear testimony to the wide range of topics considered relevant to LSP (Lauren and Nordmann 1989).

Bibliography

Allan J P B, Corder P (eds.) 1973 *The Edinburgh Course in Applied Linguistics*. Longman, London

Drozd L, Seibicke W 1973 *Deutsche Fach- und Wissenschaftssprache*. Brandstetter, Wiesbaden

Fachsprache 1979– Braumüller, Vienna

Gorosch M 1970 Goal-oriented modern language teaching. *CEBAL* 1. Busck, Copenhagen, pp. 67–83

Høedt J, Turner R (eds.) 1981 *New Bearings in LSP*. Copenhagen School of Economics, Copenhagen

Hoffman L 1976 *Kommunikationsmittel: Fachsprache*. Academie, Berlin

Hoffman L 1981 The linguistic analysis and teaching of LSP in the German Democratic Republic. In: Høedt J, Turner R (eds.) 1981

Lauren C, Nordmann M (eds.) 1989 *Special Language: From Humans Thinking to Thinking Machines*. Papers presented at the 6th European Symposium on LSP at the University of Vaasa, August 1987. Multilingual Matters, Clevedon & Philadelphia

Mackay R, Mountford A 1978 *English for Specific Purposes: A Case Study Approach*. Longman, London

Reading in a Foreign Language 1982– University of Aston, Birmingham

Sager J C, Dungworth D, McDonald P 1980 *English Special Languages: Principles and Practice in Science and Technology*. Brandstetter, Wiesbaden

Selinker L, Vroman R 1972 *Working Papers in English for Science and Technology*. University of Washington, Seattle, Washington

Swales J 1971 *Writing Scientific English: A Textbook of English as a Foreign Language for Students of Physical and Engineering Sciences*. Nelson, London

Trim J L M (ed.) 1973 *Systems Development in Adult Language Learning: A European Unit/Credit System for Modern Language Learning by Adults*. Council of Europe, Strasbourg

Trim J L M 1976 Languages for adult learners. *Lang. Teach. Ling. Abstr.* 9: 73–92

Turner R 1981 A note on "special languages" and "specific purposes". In: Høedt J, Turner R (eds.) 1981

UNESCO ALSED LSP Newsletter 1978– Copenhagen School of Economics, Copenhagen

Widdowson H G 1979 *Explorations in Applied Linguistics*. Oxford University Press, Oxford

Contrastive Linguistic Analysis

K. Sajavaara

Contrastive linguistic analysis is a subdiscipline of comparative linguistics concerned with the comparison of two or more languages or subsystems of languages to determine the differences or similarities between them.

Comparative studies have a long history in linguistics. Different stages in the development of a language or several languages have been compared for the purposes of comparative historical linguistics. Typological linguists have looked at the classification of languages in terms of features occurring in them. Bilingual dictionaries and grammars have always included an element of comparison.

After some pioneering contrastive studies with a primarily theoretical bias in the early twentieth century, contrastive linguistic analysis got its major impetus from attempts in the United States in the 1940s and 1950s to work out effective and economical foreign language teaching methods. The most efficient language teaching materials and techniques were thought to require a scientific description of the language to be taught, carefully compared with a parallel description of the learner's native language (Fries 1945). The underlying theoretical assumption was the idea, expressed influentially by Lado (1957), that the degree of difference between the two languages also correlated with the degree of difficulty. Later on, attention was also called to the similarities between the languages, and it was found that both differences and similarities can be equally problematic.

In the United States, a series of extensive contrastive linguistic analyses were undertaken in the 1960s between English and a number of languages, and in Europe several contrastive projects were launched somewhat later (Fisiak 1980). Although the objectives were normally clearly applied, the results applicable for specific purposes have remained minimal, which has given rise to certain doubts about the validity of contrastive studies.

To avoid undue confusion in the expectations concerning the applicability of contrastive analysis, it is necessary to distinguish between two types of analysis, theoretical and applied (Fisiak 1980). As well as giving an extensive account of the differences and similarities between the languages contrasted, theoretical studies provide an adequate model for cross-language comparison and determine how and which elements are comparable. Theoretical contrastive linguistic studies are also useful in adding to the knowledge about the languages contrasted. No claims are made as to the applicability of the results for specific purposes.

Applied contrastive studies aim at gathering contrastive information for specific purposes, such as language teaching, translation, and bilingual education. The major concern is the identification of potential trouble in the use of the target language.

A confusion between the aims of the two types of contrastive analysis has often resulted in the assessment of purely theoretical research against applied objectives, or theoretical analysis has been performed for the purposes of language teaching. This has strengthened the doubts about the applicability of contrastive studies.

Traditional contrastive analysis proceeds through the description of the same features or phenomena (e.g., linguistic categories, rules or rule systems, realizations of semantic concepts, or various functions of language) in the two languages to their juxtaposition on the basis of translation equivalence as assessed by a bilingual informant.

The main concern of early applied contrastive studies was a reliable prediction of the learner's difficulties. This was later to be called the strong hypothesis of contrastive analysis. The strong hypothesis did not prove to be valid because similarities and differences between the languages were not the sole cause of problems for the learner. Error analysis was therefore offered as an alternative for contrastive studies, and the predictive role of contrastive studies was superseded by an explanatory one in this weak version of the contrastive hypothesis.

Despite continued criticism, contrastive analysis remains a useful tool in the search for the sources of potential trouble. It cannot be overlooked either in syllabus design, or in the preparation of textbooks and teaching materials.

Recent contrastive studies have introduced various psychological, sociological, and contextual factors together with the purely linguistic ones, because the mapping of the language codes has proved to be insufficient. Some explanation is also needed for the variability of learner performance. Since language use is based on internalized categories of rules and structures and various processes, speakers observe phenomena that they have learned, or which they choose to observe. A student may hear, and thus also produce, a certain pattern differently from the teacher, because the student's perception is not necessarily governed by patterning adopted for theoretical or pedagogical purposes. Learners' problems can only be understood if it is known how they feel, what they attempt to hear, what they actually hear, what the structures are that they actually perceive, and how these differ from the perceptions of native speakers in similar situations.

The main target of pedagogic contrastive linguistic studies is to determine phenomena characteristic of bilingual speakers using their second language as against the use of their first language, their reactions to native-speaker speech, and a native speaker's reactions to their speech. The theory and methodology of linguistics has to be supplemented with those of sociology, psychology, neurology, and other related disciplines for the analysis of pragmatic patterning, cognitive mechanisms, and information processing systems involved (Sajavaara and Lehtonen 1980).

Bibliography

Fisiak J 1980 Some notes concerning contrastive linguistics. *AILA Bull.* 27: 1–17
Fisiak J 1981 *Contrastive Linguistics and the Language Teacher.* Pergamon, Oxford
Fries C C 1945 *Teaching and Learning English as a Foreign Language.* University of Michigan Press, Ann Arbor, Michigan
Lado R 1957 *Linguistics Across Cultures: Applied Linguistics for Language Teachers.* University of Michigan Press, Ann Arbor, Michigan
Sajavaara K, Lehtonen J (eds.) 1975 *A Select Bibliography of Contrastive Analysis.* Jyväskylä Contrastive Studies 1. University of Jyväskylä, Jyväskylä
Sajavaara K, Lehtonen J 1980 *Papers in Discourse and Contrastive Discourse Analysis.* Jyväskylä Contrastive Studies 5. University of Jyväskylä, Jyväskylä

Interlanguage

J. H. Schumann

Interlanguage is a term used to refer to the speech of a second language learner at any point between the native language and full target language proficiency. The notion developed out of studies of first language acquisition which viewed child language as a series of evolving grammars. This idea was carried to second language acquisition studies by Nemser who referred to the evolving second language as "approximate systems," Corder who called it an "idiosyncratic dialect," and Selinker who named it "interlanguage" (Richards 1974). Selinker's term took hold and now studies of second language learner speech are referred to as interlanguage studies. From within the field of second language learning itself, the historical development of the notion of interlanguage can be seen as an evolution from contrastive analysis which compares the grammatical structures of the native language and the target language in order to predict learner errors, to error analysis which seeks to explain the source of errors once they have been made, to interlanguage analysis which attempts to capture the systematicity of learner speech by examining both its deviations from the target language and its correct forms (Hakuta and Cancino 1977).

Interlanguage studies so far have examined the acquisition of negation, questions, morphemes, lexicon, discourse, relative clauses, and phonology.

Interlanguage development has been related to the process of pidginization (Schumann 1978), creolization, depidginization, and decreolization. Pidginization is the acquisition of a second language to which learners have only restricted input. This results in a reduced and simplified form of speech. Depidginization occurs when learners gain increased access to speakers of the target language and their pidginized speech gradually evolves in the direction of the target. Creolization occurs when the pidgin language is acquired by a generation of children whose parents speak the pidgin. Since the pidgin grammar is inadequate for a native language, the creolizing children elaborate that grammar in order to meet their communicative needs. Decreolization occurs

when the creole community gains access to speakers of the language on which the creole is based and the creole begins to evolve toward that language.

The early stage of interlanguage development (called the basilang) is seen as a form of reduced and simplified speech as in pidgin languages. The later stages (called the mesolang and acrolang) are viewed as reflecting the complications and expansions that are seen in depidginization and decreolization. Creolization, or language acquisition directed by the learner's innate capacities and native language, can occur at any of the stages of interlanguage development.

Most research on interlanguage has implicitly assumed that there is a single continuum of development between the native and target languages. However, recent proposals by Meisel et al. (1981) based on studies of the acquisition of German by guest workers in the Federal Republic of Germany indicate that interlanguage development may occur on a multidimensional continuum. In other words, different learners or even the same learner in different parts of his/her interlanguage grammar may be assimilating to either the standard variety, the local variety, or the immigrant variety of the target language.

Bibliography

Brown H D 1973 *A First Language: The Early Stages*. Harvard University Press, Cambridge, Massachusetts
Hakuta K, Cancino H 1977 Trends in second-language-acquisition research. *Harvard Educ. Rev.* 47: 294–316
Hymes D 1971 *Pidginization and Creolization of Languages*. Cambridge University Press, Cambridge
Meisel J, Clahsen H, Pienemann M 1981 On determining developmental stages in natural second language acquisition. *Stud. Second Lang. Acquisition* 3(1): 109–35
Richards J C 1974 *Error Analysis: Perspectives on Second Language Acquisition*. Longman, London
Schumann J H 1978 *The Pidginization Process: A Model for Second Language Acquisition*. Newbury House, Rowley, Massachusetts

Interference

R. A. Berman

The notion of interference in foreign language teaching and learning is based on the psychological principle of transfer of learning, referring in its most general form to "the hypothesis that the learning of Task A will affect the subsequent learning of Task B" (Jakobovits 1970 p. 188). In foreign language learning, this principle entails the claim that "individuals tend to transfer the forms and meanings . . . of their native language and culture

to the foreign language and culture" (Lado 1957 p. 2). The term interference in this context refers to negative transfer, leading to errors and misusages in the foreign language which can be attributed to the inappropriate transfer of forms and usages from the native language to the new one being learned. Although the existence of such a mechanism has long been recognized in the theory and practice of foreign language teaching (for instance, in Jespersen 1904), use of the term interference is generally attributed to Weinreich's classic study of bilingualism, where it is defined as "the rearrangement of patterns that result from the introduction of foreign elements into the more highly structured domains of language, such as the bulk of the phonemic system, a large part of the morphology and syntax, and some areas of the vocabulary" (Weinreich 1953 p. 1).

Examples of phonemic interference would include the tendency of speakers of Japanese to substitute the sound /l/ in contexts where English requires an /r/ sound; or the different sounds substituted by speakers of different native languages for English *th* as in the words *thing*, *throat*: German speakers tend to use an /s/ sound, Hindi speakers will substitute an aspirated /t/ sound, and speakers of Thai or Hebrew substitute a regular /t/ sound, whereas speakers of varieties of Spanish that have a /th/ sound in their native tongue will pronounce this in a suitable way in using English, too. An example of lexical interference would be cases where an English speaker learning Spanish uses the same word for body parts such as *leg*, *neck*, or *liver* in referring to both human beings and animals, since English does not use distinct body-part terms in such cases, whereas Spanish does. And an example of interference at the level of syntax is provided by a Hebrew speaker who says *pin hair* for *hairpin* or *tape scotch* instead of *scotch tape*, since in Hebrew the head noun precedes its modifier in noun compounds like these, while in English the head noun comes last.

The idea of interference or negative transfer as playing a major role in foreign language learning, and the claim that it should be deliberately considered in programs for teaching foreign languages, was first articulated in the 1940s, under the influence of the structuralist orientation of descriptive linguistics at that time, and the impact this had on language teaching theory and practice. This in turn gave rise to the area of contrastive analysis, devolving upon the claim that the most effective way to teach a new language is to base instruction on a systematic analysis and comparison of the so-called source language (the student's native tongue) and the new language to be learned (the target language). This view held that careful comparison of the first and foreign language at all levels of linguistic structure—phonology, morphology, syntax, and the lexicon—would make it possible to predict potential sources of learner error and, by anticipating such errors, hopefully eradicate them in advance by suitably organized and controlled materials of study. In recent years, scholars have come to query the validity of what has been termed the "strong" version of the contrastive analysis hypothesis, or so-called contrastive analysis a priori (Schachter 1974). The view that negative transfer is the dominant process underlying foreign language learning is interpreted as running counter to more cognitively oriented views of the learning process. On the one hand, language learning can be conceived of as a creative process

of rule—internationlization rather than the acquisition of new habits by means of stimulus–response associations, reinforcement, and so on. On the other hand, more abstract views of the nature of language structure and linguistic knowledge associated with contemporary linguistic theory have also queried the validity of item-by-item kinds of comparisons between languages (Berman 1978).

Two main types of research in recent years have led to a modification of the originally extreme, and pedagogically overly optimistic, claims made for the effectivity of contrastive analysis and the central role of interference as the major stumbling block in foreign language learning. Findings of error analysis in the foreign language usage of students of different ages and language backgrounds revealed that many errors were shared by all those learning, say, English, irrespective of their specific mother tongue. It further transpired that some kinds of errors were common to adolescents or adults learning a foreign language and to young children acquiring their native tongue. Both types of data pointed to the inadequacy of interference, in the sense of inappropriate transfer of native patterns of usage to the language being learned, as the sole, or even the major, source of difficulty and error in learning a new language. Instead, scholars proposed the idea of an interlanguage (Selinker 1972) to characterize the various ways in which learners' forms and usages may deviate from those of the standard, adult target. Today, there is quite general agreement that such deviations have their origin in a multiplicity of factors, of which interference is only one.

As in all swings of the pendula in education and other disciplines, reaction against a given notion may lead to its being abandoned totally, where in principle it could be reintegrated to take into account fresh insights in the field. Thus, the role of interference in foreign language learning, and hence in teaching, can be re-evaluated as follows. It is only one of many factors impinging on the process of learning a new language, but it does play a role therein. Interference may have more of an impact in some areas of language structure than in others: for instance, with respect to pronunciation, the entire notion of a foreign accent depends crucially on interference from the speaker's native tongue; while in the realm of syntax, word order tends to be particularly resistant to reorganizations that differ critically between the source and target languages. And there is some indication that interference may be more critical at some stages (initial rather than more advanced phases) and in some settings (formal classroom rather than naturalistic contexts of use) than in others. The still lively debate as to the precise nature, let alone the role of so-called interference, might be clarified by greater attention to its converse (in the form of positive transfer or facilitation), since it is clear that some types of learning may be aided rather than hindered by the fact that in trying to master a foreign language, the learner already knows what a language is, and what it can be used for.

An excellent review of current evaluations of the import of L1 interference is provided by Ellis (1985). A recent collection of studies devoted entirely to transfer in second language production deals with the issue in a wide range of contexts, including grammatical aspect, object reference, passives, and word order at both the sentence-level and in extended discourse (Dechert & Raupach 1989).

Bibliography

Berman R 1978 Contrastive analysis revisited: Obligatory, systematic, and incidental differences between languages. *Interlanguage Stud. Bull.* 3: 212–33

Ellis R 1985 The role of the first language. In: *Understanding Second Language Acquisition.* Oxford University Press, Oxford

Dechert H W, Raupach M (eds.) 1989 *Transfer in Second Language Production.* Ablex, Norwood, New Jersey

Jakobovits L 1970 *Foreign Language Learning: A Psycholinguistic Analysis of the Issues.* Newbury House, Rowley, Massachusetts

Jespersen O 1904 *How to Teach a Foreign Language.* Allen and Unwin, London

Lado R 1957 *Linguistics Across Cultures: Applied Linguistics for Language Teachers.* University of Michigan Press, Ann Arbor, Michigan

Schachter J 1974 An error in error analysis. *Lang. Learn.* 24: 205–14

Selinker L 1972 Interlanguage. *Int. Rev. Appl. Ling.* 10: 201–31

Weinreich U 1953 *Languages in Contact: Findings and Problems.* Linguistic Circle of New York, New York (1963 Reissued by Mouton, The Hague)

Error Analysis

K. Sajavaara

Correction of errors has always been a common practice in foreign language teaching. A systematic analysis of learners' errors was introduced in the wake of contrastive analysis. It was initially offered as a substitute for, or a complement to, contrastive analysis, when the latter failed in its original task of predicting learners' errors. The study of language learning problems was to begin with the investigation of the phenomenon, that is, negative transfer or interference, which was supposed to account for the problems, while contrastive analysis was assigned an explicatory role only. Variability in learner performance could not however be explained by means of error analysis alone, and the basic problems found in contrastive analysis, such as comparability of specific items and equivalence, still remained.

In error analysis, errors have often been given much too strong an emphasis at the cost of the communicative task of language, and therefore error analysis gradually gave way to the analysis of the learner's language as a whole. Static error analysis was replaced by research in which errors are seen to be essential ingredients in a dynamic process of language learning instead of malignant growths to be weeded out. A learner's deviant language is thus seen to be an unavoidable interim stage towards second language proficiency.

Traditional error analysis consists of five stages. In error recognition, an attempt is made to distinguish systematic competence errors from performance errors, that is, mistakes and lapses, easily corrected by the learner when pointed out (Corder 1981). Error recognition depends crucially on correct interpretation of the speaker's intentions. In the following stages, the errors are described according to a model and classified. In the explanation of the errors, three causes are usually distinguished: interlingual errors caused by interference from the mother tongue, intralingual errors caused by

the target language system, and teaching-induced errors. At the final stage, the errors are compared with target language norms to assess their influence on the success of communication. The decisions about the nature of feedback to be provided to learners are crucially dependent on the systematicity of the errors.

More recent approaches to error analysis consider systematic errors to be markers of the learner's progress, and learner performance has come to be characterized as interlanguage, also described as transitional competence, approximative system, or idiosyncratic dialect. It is characterized as a distinct linguistic system resulting from the learner's attempts to achieve target language norms. Interlanguage is supposed to derive its features from five processes: language transfer, transfer of training, strategies of second language learning, strategies of second language communication, and overgeneralization of foreign language linguistic material (Selinker 1972). With many learners, progress in interlanguage development stops at the point at which some deviant features still remain in learners' performance. The true nature of such fossilization is unknown.

Strategies of second language learning have been exposed to intensive research, which has been mainly concerned with transfer and overgeneralization. A great deal of research which has been devoted to transfer has been unable to reveal its true nature. This would require a clearer picture of the processes involved in speech reception and production. Communication strategies mostly refer to procedures adopted by learners to overcome problems in second language communication; they include avoidance, paraphrasing, borrowing, and call for assistance. The research in the second language acquisition process has only recently begun, but in addition to certain features universal to all language acquisition, some phenomena characteristic of second language acquisition only have also been specified (Wode 1981).

One of the prominent aspects of learner performance is simplification, which seems to be due to several types of reduction processes at work in learner speech (Faerch and Kasper 1980). Similar simplification is also characteristic of foreigner talk, baby talk, caretaker speech, and teacher talk, but here simplification results from attempts to assist the interlocutor in the task of comprehension. The study of simplification has established a link between error analysis and the research in pidgins and creoles, in which phenomena similar to those occurring in second language acquisition can also be found.

Traditional error analysis works with naturalistic data drawn from various types of productions by language learners, above all translations and compositions. Free delivery of speech, various types of narration tasks, retelling of stories, cloze tests, multiple-choice tests, and direct observation of learner behaviour have also been used. Elicitation of errors has often proved necessary to expose learners to situations in which certain types of structures could be expected to occur.

The main problem in error analysis is the same as in contrastive analysis. The theory and methodology of linguistics is insufficient to explain the phenomena involved. A wider framework is needed involving psychological, sociological, neurological, and other related insights into cognitive mechanisms and information processing in the brain and the speech channel as a whole.

Bibliography

Arabski J 1979 *Errors as Indicators of the Development of Interlanguage*. Uniwersytet Slaski, Katowice

Corder S P 1981 *Error Analysis and Interlanguage*. Oxford University Press, London

Faerch C, Kasper G 1980 Processes and strategies in foreign language learning and communication. ISB-*Utrecht* 5: 47–118

Johansson S 1978 *Studies of Error Gravity: Native Reactions to Errors Produced by Swedish Learners of English*. Gothenburg Studies in English 44. University of Gothenburg, Gothenburg

Nickel G 1981 Aspects of error analysis (EA): Errare humanum est. AILA (International Association for Applied Linguistics Spain), *Bull.* 29: 1–28

Palmberg R 1980 *A Select Bibliography of Error Analysis and Interlanguage Studies*. Åbo Akademi, Åbo

Richards J C 1974 *Error Analysis: Perspectives on Second Language Acquisition*. Longman, London

Richards J C 1978 *Understanding Second and Foreign Language Learning*. Newbury House, Rowley, Massachusetts

Selinker L 1972 Interlanguage. *IRAL (International Review of Applied Linguistics in Language Teaching)* 10: 209–31

Wode H 1981 *Learning a Second Language*. Narr, Tübingen

Attitude Toward Learning Foreign Language

L. W. Anderson

The role of emotion in the acquisition of a foreign language has been examined and discussed by several scholars in the field. Bégin states a fairly common belief concerning the role of emotion when he writes that "the efficiency and depth of (a student's) learning is a function of his (or her) subjective evaluation of the target language" (Bégin 1971 p. 30). Several studies of the relationship between emotion and foreign language learning lend partial support to this contention. At the same time, however, several questions can be asked about the hypothesized emotion–learning relationship. First, what is the nature of this emotion? Second, what measures of emotion have been used and how good are they? Third, what is the nature of the relationship between emotion and foreign language learning? Each of these questions forms the basis for one of the major subsections that follows.

1. The Nature of Emotion in Foreign Language Learning

Quite frequently, attitude is used as a generic term referring to all types of emotion. If the literature is examined, however, it must be concluded that attitude is a specific type of emotion. An attitude is a "learned predisposition to respond in a consistently favorable or unfavorable manner with respect to a given object" (Fishbein and Ajzen 1975 p. 6). Based on this definition, then, an emotion must possess several critical attributes if it is to be labeled an attitude.

First, the emotion must be directed toward an object or target. Second, the link between the emotion and target must be learned. Third, attitudes are emotions of moderate intensity (since the person only has to respond to, not seek out, the target). Fourth, the emotion must exist on a continuum from negative to positive (or more specifically from unfavorable to favorable). Fifth, the emotion must be experienced consistently when the target is encountered.

In the foreign language literature, Carroll's concept of "liking for foreign languages" is the most consistent with this definition of attitude (Carroll 1962 pp. 115–16). The target is the foreign language itself. The link between liking and the specific foreign language is clearly learned. Liking is a moderately intense emotion (with loving being of greater intensity). The endpoints of the underlying continuum are liking and disliking. Finally, the consistency of the liking is an empirical question; a question closely aligned with the psychometric concept of reliability.

Other emotions described in the foreign language literature are related to, but quite distinct from, attitude. These emotions differ from attitude primarily in intensity and sometimes in target. In some cases the endpoints of the underlying continuum are not apparent. One such emotion is interest.

Interest involves greater emotional intensity than does attitude. The key word found in definitions or discussions of interest that is missing in definitions or discussions of attitude is "desire"; most frequently, desire to seek out the target. Pimsleur and Struth, for example, define interest as the student's desire to study a foreign language. (Pimsleur and Struth 1969 p. 85). In addition to Pimsleur and Struth, interest in learning a foreign language has been examined by Carroll (1975), Gardner and Lambert (1972), and Gardner et al. (1979).

Spolsky also has studied interest. Rather than the target of this interest being the learning of the language, however, the target is the people who are fluent in the use of the language. Spolsky highlights the importance of this type of interest when he writes that "learning a second language is a key to possible membership of a secondary society; the desire to join that group is a major factor in language learning" (Spolsky 1970 p. 282).

A third emotion—one quite distinct from both attitude and interest—is a person's orientation toward learning a foreign language (Lambert 1963). Put simply, this orientation has to do with a person's reason(s) for learning the language. Two categories or types of orientation have been identified: instrumental and integrative. Reasons are considered instrumental if they are utilitarian in nature (e.g., to fulfill an educational requirement, to get a better job). Reasons are considered integrative if they indicate a desire to learn more about the people and/or culture of the country or countries in which the language is spoken. One of the variables included in the International Association for the Evaluation of Educational Achievement (IEA) eight-country study, perceived utility of French, is similar to orientation. Quite obviously, the target can be expanded to include the perceived utility of studying or learning any foreign language.

The difference between orientation and the previously mentioned emotions becomes evident when the fact that both instrumental and integrative students can respond favorably to the language being studied is considered. Similarly, both instrumental and integrative students can desire to study the language. In fact the results from several studies suggest that orientation and interest are factorially independent (Gardner and Lambert 1972).

A final emotion examined within the context of foreign language learning is the perceived importance of studying or learning a foreign language. Perceived importance of studying or learning the language is different from all of the previously mentioned emotions in that the perceptions are typically sought from members of society at large, not only from those currently engaged in foreign language study. The Survey Research Center of the University of Michigan, for example, interviewed a nationally representative sample of Americans (Eddy 1979). One part of the interview focused on the extent to which studying foreign languages at various levels of schooling was perceived to be important.

In summary, then, several emotions have been identified in the field of foreign language learning. Among the most frequently studied are liking for foreign languages, interest in learning the foreign language, desire to become a member of the group whose native language is the foreign language, reasons for studying or learning the foreign language, and perceived importance of studying or learning the language. The differences among these emotions tend to be in intensity and target. Interests for example, are more intense emotions than are attitudes. The targets of the emotion may be the language itself or the people whose native tongue is the language.

2. Measures of Attitudes and Related Emotions

The measurement of foreign language attitudes and related emotions has relied almost exclusively on self-report, Likert-type inventories, or scales. While many of the instruments are targeted to a specific foreign language (quite often, French), appropriate modifications can be made quite easily to adapt the instrument to other languages.

In general, the technical quality of the instruments is quite good. When presented, estimates of internal consistency range from 0.60 to 0.80. Thus the reliability of the instruments is quite sufficient for making group comparisons. Quite obviously, the instruments have "face validity." Furthermore, the instruments possess a reasonable degree of criterion-related validity, the criterion being proficiency in the foreign language.

(a) *Liking for foreign languages* (Carroll 1962)—in actuality, this "instrument" consists of a single item. The respondent is asked to indicate the extent to which he or she likes to study foreign languages. Since this is a one-item instrument, the psychometric quality is suspect.

(b) *Attitude toward learning French scale* (Gardner et al. 1979)—this inventory consists of five positively-worded and five negatively-worded statements. The five alternative responses are modifications of the standard Likert responses of strongly agree, agree, undecided, disagree, and strongly disagree.

(c) *Interest in foreign languages* (Gardner et al. 1979)—this inventory is similar in structure to the attitude toward learning French scale mentioned earlier. The respondent is presented with 10 statements and is asked to select from modified Likert alternatives.

(d) *International Association for the Evaluation of Educational Achievement* (IEA) *interest in French scale* (Carroll 1975)—this inventory contains 10 items presented in a modified Likert format. It has been translated into six languages.

(e) *Orientation index* (Gardner and Lambert 1972)—this inventory presents the respondent with eight alternative reasons "typically given for studying French." The respondents are asked to indicate the reason(s) that best describe their reason(s) for studying the language. The odd-numbered statements represent instrumentally oriented reasons; the even-numbered statements represent integratively oriented reasons.

(f) *IEA perceived utility of French scale* (Carroll 1975)—this inventory is very similar in format to the IEA interest in French scale. The items also are substantively similar to those included in the orientation index.

(g) *Indirect questionnaire* (Spolsky 1970)— this questionnaire contains four lists of 30 adjectives such as "busy," "stubborn," and "sincere." The respondent is asked to respond differently to each list. In order, from list 1 to list 4, the respondent is asked to indicate how well each adjective describes him or her, how well each adjective describes the way he or she would like to be, how well each adjective describes people whose native language was the same as his or hers, and how well each adjective describes people who speak the target language.

3. The Relationship Between Emotion and Learning

The vast majority of the scholars in the field of second language learning view emotion as the predictor (and, often, the cause) of foreign language learning. Since few, if any, of the studies have been experimental in nature, the predictor–outcome rather than the cause–effect relationship will be described in this subsection.

Several indicators of foreign language learning have been identified in the various studies. Course grades or marks, and proficiency in reading, listening, and speaking have all been used as indicators. Similarly, as has been indicated in the previous two subsections, several types and indicators of emotion have been included in the studies. The strength of the emotion–learning relationship tends to depend on the type of emotion and type of learning indicator investigated.

When all types of emotion are considered, the relationship between emotion and learning tends to be the strongest when course grades or marks are used as the indicator of learning. It should be pointed out, however, that no more than 16 percent of the variation in course grades can be predicted from any emotion. Emotion also tends to be related to reading proficiency, but the relationship is typically less strong than the emotion–course grade relationship. Emotion has seldom been found to be related to proficiency in speaking or listening, however.

Different emotions tend to be differentially related to the various learning indicators. The best, and most consistent, predictor of indicators of foreign language learning is interest. Virtually every study including interest as a predictor variable found that interest was significantly related to measures of second language learning. In contrast with interest, attitudes tend to be unrelated to foreign language learning. These contrasting findings tend to support the distinction between interest and attitude made earlier; interest being of greater intensity than attitude. Stronger relationships would be expected between emotion and learning when emotions of greater intensity are examined.

The results of several studies have suggested that students with an integrative orientation are more proficient than those with an instrumental orientation (Gardner and Lambert 1972). At least one study, however, fails to support this relationship (Spolsky 1970). In addition the results of the IEA study provide conflicting evidence concerning the orientation–learning relationship. The relationship of perceived utility of learning French and indicators of language learning tended to be positive, negative, or virtually zero depending on the country and the age level of the students.

In contrast with the emotion-as-predictor perspective, a few scholars have viewed emotions as outcomes of foreign language learning (Bégin 1971, Lambert et al. 1973). In each case, however, emotion was hypothesized to be an outcome of the method of teaching or learning the foreign language, rather than level of proficiency alone. When emotion has been viewed in this manner, the results have been quite positive. Perhaps Bégin best summarizes these results when he writes "the most striking finding of this research is perhaps the continuous intensification of the desire to speak French in the experimental group, as opposed to the increased frustration commonly experienced by students who try to communicate in a target language" (Bégin 1971 p. 117).

4. Discussion

The relationship between emotion and foreign language learning is quite complex. Part of this complexity stems from the inclusion of different emotions, often under the general rubric of attitude. Despite this complexity, however, several conclusions can be drawn. High intensity emotions (such as interest) have been found consistently to be related to foreign language learning. The extent to which these emotions actually influence foreign language learning, however, is a matter of speculation, rather than evidence. In contrast, however, particular methods of teaching a foreign language (typically involving intensive training and immersion into the culture of the people who speak the target language) can influence the feelings of the students toward the target language.

Bibliography

Bégin Y 1971 *Evaluative and Emotional Factors in Learning a Foreign Language.* Les Editions Bellarmin, Montreal

Carroll J B 1962 The prediction of success in intensive language training. In: Glaser R (ed.) 1962 *Training Research and Education*. University of Pittsburgh, Pittsburgh, pp. 87–136

Carroll J B 1975 *The Teaching of French as a Foreign Language in Eight Countries*. Almqvist and Wiksell, Stockholm

Eddy P A 1979 Attitudes toward foreign language study and requirements in American schools and colleges: Results of a national survey. *ADEL Bull.* 11(2): 4–9

Fishbein M, Ajzen I 1975 *Belief, Attitude, Intention and Behavior: An Introduction to Theory and Research*. Addison-Wesley, Reading, Massachusetts

Gardner R C, Lambert W E 1972 *Attitudes and Motivation in Second Language Learning*. Newbury, Rowley, Massachusetts

Gardner R C, Smythe P C, Clement R 1979 Intensive second language learning in a bicultural milieu: An investigation of attitudes, motivation and language proficiency. *Lang. Learn.* 29: 305–20

Lambert W E 1963 Psychological approaches to the study of language: On second language learning and bilingualism. *Mod. Lang. J.* 47: 114–23

Lambert W E, Tucker G R, d'Anglejan A 1973 Cognitive and attitudinal consequences of bilingual schooling: The St. Lambert experiment through grade five. *J. Educ. Psychol.* 65: 141–59

Pimsleur P A, Struth J F 1969 Knowing your students in advance. *Mod. Lang. J.* 53: 85–87

Pimsleur P A, Mosberg L, Morrison A V 1962 Student factors in foreign language learning: A review of the literature. *Mod. Lang. J.* 46: 160–70

Spolsky B 1970 Attitudinal aspects of second language learning. *Lang. Learn.* 19: 271–83

Immersion Education

M. Swain

Immersion education is a type of bilingual education which can be described in terms of methodological, structural, and background characteristics. Methodologically, immersion education operates on the principle that a second language is best acquired in the same way a child acquires a first language, through extensive exposure to and use of the target language in real communicative situations. Thus, in immersion education the teachers use the target language exclusively to teach the academic curriculum and to communicate with their students.

The structure of the immersion program involves a number of crucial aspects. First, the students are homogeneous with respect to their knowledge of the target language and with respect to the home language they speak. They are members of the dominant, majority culture. Secondly, the teachers are bilingual in the students' home language and target language. Although the teachers only speak the target language in class, they make considerable use of the children's home language in the sense that they understand everything the children say to them. Thirdly, the home language is incorporated into the curriculum. In the primary-level program, first language literacy skills are introduced after several years of immersion schooling in the target language. At later grade levels, the first language is also used as a medium of instruction for specific academic subjects. The two languages continue to serve as languages of instruction throughout schooling. Variations in the immersion concept entail two basic dimensions: the grade level at which the child enters the program (kindergarten to age 15); and the percentage of time the second language is used as the medium of instruction both within an academic year and sequentially across grades in a program. Finally, participation in the immersion program is optional. Parents have always had the alternative of enrolling their children in a unilingual program where their first language is the only language of instruction.

In Canada, the increasing emphasis on bilingualism since the early 1970s and the lack of satisfaction with traditional programs of French as a second language have been largely responsible for the initiation and development of French immersion programs. The pressure to implement this innovative approach to second language teaching has come mainly from parents rather than school board officials or other educational personnel.

In spite of parental enthusiasm for immersion education, both the parents and the school authorities have insisted that the programs be carefully monitored. They were concerned that there might be retardation of the immersion students' development of first language skills; that there might be negative effects on cognitive functioning and general intellectual development; that the immersion students' learning of content material might not be comparable to that of students in unilingual programs; and that the immersion students' French might, after all, not be significantly better than that of students studying French as a second language through a more traditional, structurally oriented method. They also hoped that the immersion students would retain a sense of personal identity while learning to respect the target language group.

These concerns have formed the basis of the numerous evaluations of immersion programs across Canada which have been undertaken over extensive periods of time by a number of different researchers (see Swain and Lapkin 1982, 1986, and Genesee 1987 for a synthesis of this research). A summary of the findings as they relate to these questions follows.

The first language literacy-related skills of children who enter a total French immersion program at the kindergarten level remain significantly behind those of comparable students in unilingual English programs until a year or two after English language arts is introduced into the curriculum. At that point, the immersion students' performance on tests of English achievement is equivalent to that of English-instructed students. In later years, the immersion students have demonstrated superior performance in some aspects of measured English language skills relative to their English-educated peers. Overall, in no immersion program has there been any long-term retardation observed in the development of the immersion students' first language skills.

No negative effects on the cognitive functioning and general intellectual development of immersion students relative to comparable students in the English program have been observed. Indeed, the results indicate a trend towards their enhancement.

Immersion students have been tested in English for achievement in such academic areas as mathematics, science, and social studies which have been taught in French. In general, the immersion students' performance is equivalent to students taught these subjects in English.

The French of the immersion students is far superior to that of students taught French in short daily periods using a more structured grammar-based syllabus. In the long run, the reading and listening comprehension of the immersion students in French approaches that of native speakers of French. However, their speaking and writing remain identifiable as nonnative.

Self-views of the immersion children are healthy and typical for their age. Their views of French Canadians are as positive as those of their English-educated peers, tending at times to be more positive.

These results indicate that, overall, immersion education, an innovative approach to second language teaching in which the target language is used as the major language of instruction, facilitates second language acquisition at no cost to first language development, academic achievement, or to general cognitive or social development. The generalizability of the immersion results to other situations where the background and structural variables are similar seems warranted given the consistency of the results across a large number of immersion programs in Canada. Where any of the characteristics differ, the results may also be expected to differ. The effectiveness of using the target language as a vehicle of communication and instruction to enhance second language acquisition seems, however, to be an important and generalizable finding.

Bibliography

Genesee F 1987 *Learning Through Two Languages: Studies of Immersion and Bilingual Education.* Newbury House, New York

Husén T, Opper S (eds.) 1983 *Multicultural and Multilingual Education in Immigrant Countries.* Pergamon, Oxford.

Swain M, Lapkin S 1982 *Evaluating Bilingual Education: A Canadian Case Study.* Multilingual Matters, Clevedon, Avon

Swain M, Lapkin S 1986 Immersion French in secondary schools: "the goods" and "the bads". *Contact* 5(3): 2–9

Language Laboratories

J. J. Higgins

A language laboratory can be looked at either as a configuration of machines constituting a learning environment and heavily conditioning the types of learning activity that occur in it, or else as a relatively neutral carrier of software reflecting a diversity of approaches to learning. There is some evidence of a shift from the first to the second position since the early 1970s, and this article examines the background to that shift.

1. Hardware Development

The first use of the term "language laboratory" was by Ralph H. Waltz of Ohio State University in articles published in 1930, but the use of audio machinery as a language teaching aid goes back 26 years before that (Hocking 1964). The defining characteristic of the language laboratory is that it provides a bank of listening stations, each fed from a central source of recorded sound, and with each student isolated by headphones from overhearing or being overheard. An installation that provides this and nothing else is known as audio-passive (AP). If a microphone is added to this into which the student can speak so that student output is fed both to his or her own headphones and to a monitoring station manned by a teacher, this is called an audio-active (AA) installation. If each student position is equipped with a twin-track tape recorder, carrying the master program on the top track and the individual's responses on the bottom track, and permitting subsequent playback and comparison, this is called an audio-active-comparative (AAC) installation, and this is what the term language laboratory generally implies today. Most early labs were AA only, and the widespread use of AAC laboratories had to wait for the commercial development of the tape recorder in the early 1950s. Permanent laboratories of the 1950s and 1960s normally had forward-facing rows of built-in booths with underfloor wiring and transparent front panels, emphasizing the lockstep approach to class language teaching. The teacher's console has grown in complexity over the years. Modern consoles normally provide remote switching of the mechanical functions on the student machines (play and record, rewind, etc), monitoring of an individual, two-way conversation with an individual, group call, and some kind of conference facility, giving pairs or small groups of students a voice link.

Even though forward-facing ranks of booths make the most economical use of space, the modern trend is toward a different shape, with booths facing the outer walls and a central area left free for face-to-face activities. The monitor has no eye contact with the student when the booths are in use, so the learner's privacy and self-reliance are reinforced. Another recent development has been the use of "minilabs", usually based on cassettes rather than open-reel recorders, using lightweight components, and capable of being assembled on a trolley for transport from room to room. The term minilab used to be applied mainly to AA equipment, but the modern minilab is a full AAC installation.

The design and capabilities of the individual student's booth have remained remarkably stable since the early 1950s, although various devices have been used experimentally. Most laboratories come equipped with a screen and some projection equipment, but few institutions make much use of them, defeated by the need for room blackout and better resource management. (Exceptions to this can be found in France, where the visual element in audiovisual has always been stressed.) Some wealthy institutions, universities, or military training establishments, have equipped student booths with individual video monitors fed from a central video recorder. In the 1960s, Tandberg developed a repeater laboratory which provided a second tape recorder at each student position which constantly copied the last five seconds of the master programme on to an endless loop of tape. The student could press a button to secure unlimited repetition of a phrase he or she was unsure of, obviously a real boon in activities like phonetic dictation. However this was never put into full commercial development.

2. The Future

In its present form, the language laboratory cannot be anything but quasi-interactive. The programme recorded on tape is not modified by the learner's responses, and the student controls nothing except pace and amount of repetition. An ingenious application of a twin-track recorder has been proposed for a comprehension exercise: one starts with a recording on track one ending with a polar question, and continuing with two different recordings on the parallel tracks, each corresponding to one possible answer to the first question. This satisfied the hunger felt by teachers for some kind of branching. This is now being met in a different way by the combinations of tape recorders and microcomputers. By 1982, at least two companies, Atari and Tandberg, had language teaching products in which a computer input selects a segment of tape, permitting multiple branching. Neither machine was fully AAC in 1982, but the development of that facility is to be expected. However, recorded tape, whether open reel or cassette, is a serial medium, and branching to different parts of the tape is relatively slow. The language laboratory of the future will probably incorporate a tape for recording and comparison, but will rely on a laser-read disc, possibly a videodisc, to provide access to a large body of possible inputs (so-called random access). Innovative work on these lines has already begun, notably at Brigham Young University, Utah, with a videodisc project called *Montevidisco*, for learners of Spanish. The disc contains a simulation of a visit to a Mexican town, and permits real interaction since what the students see and hear is governed by the commands they enter or the answers they give to questions. Students also record utterances on to an audio cassette, for later monitoring (Gale 1983). For the time being the costs of the hardware are high, but they are likely to diminish as the domestic videodisc market expands.

3. Software

In the early days, audio aids were thought of almost exclusively as pronunciation aids, and most language laboratory material consisted of words, phrases, and passages for repetition. However, the 1940s and 1950s were the heyday of structural linguistics, behavioural psychology, and pattern practice methodology, and with all of these the language laboratory configuration was well in tune. Under these influences the staple diet of the laboratory become the "anticipation drill", which requires the student to respond to a cue, forming the response by analogy with an example. The response is given immediately before hearing the correct response (hence the "anticipation" of the name), and a pause then follows in which the correct answer can be repeated. A drill with all these elements (cue, student's response, correct response, and repetition) was called four-phase, and this was the normal pattern up to the mid-1960s. Since then, the three-phase drill (omitting the repetition) has become far commoner, since the repetition phase was seen to reinforce the boring and mechanical aspects of laboratory practice. Drills can be classified according to the relationship between each cue and response, for example, substitution drill (replacing one word with another given in the cue), replacement drill (replacing nouns with pronouns or similar changes), transformation drill (present to past, active to passive, etc), question and answer drill, and so on. No standard nomenclature was ever agreed upon, and it became apparent that such classification was irrelevant since the essential relationship was not that between cue and response but between example and response. Under the influence of two groups of people working on laboratory materials for English as a foreign language, one in Kursverksamheten in Sweden and the other in the British Council English Language Teaching Institute in London, it became established as a principle that the contexts for drills should be as rich and lifelike as possible. Each drill response should be a natural response to the same prompt in real-life conversation; the items in a drill should all refer to the same context or draw on the same body of data. Most published drills nowadays embody these principles. Earlier materials had often paid little attention to meaning, concentrating on form and word order (sometimes referred to as "fluency"). Dakin (1973) articulated a resistance to meaningless drills and illustrated how a semantic or problem-solving element could be built in to practice activities, but it is still the case that many laboratory drills can be executed correctly without the student understanding what he or she is saying.

4. Other Applications

Rehearsed dialogue has long formed a part of laboratory practice (Higgins 1969). Nowadays, one often meets "open dialogue" in which the student, after hearing a model, responds to the cues with data about himself or herself. Naturally such responses cannot be corrected on the tape, so the only feedback will come from sporadic monitoring by the teacher.

There has been a strong tendency recently towards using the laboratory mainly for listening activities, or to treat it as a kind of listening library. One activity that takes special advantage of the laboratory configuration is "jigsaw listening". Several different recordings (e.g. three different accounts of a road accident) are dubbed to separate blocks of booths. Students sit at booths and make notes on what they hear. They must then find students who have heard the other recordings, compare notes with them, and discuss the solution to the task (e.g. assess blame for the accident).

Another important area of application is in oral examining, pioneered by the Association of Recognised English Language Schools in Great Britain. Using the laboratory can ensure common conditions for all candidates and remove much of the subjectivity and unreliability found in the assessment of oral interviews. Exercises in dictation and in both consecutive and simultaneous interpreting are also highly appropriate to the laboratory.

5. Conclusion

When the popularity of laboratories began to spread, they were given a great deal of commercial promotion and were often installed more for prestige than to answer felt needs. In the 1970s, there was an almost Luddite reaction. The profession abounds with tales of useless and abandoned laboratories, and with teachers who take pride in not using them. Coincidentally, much of the linguistic and learning theory underpinning the traditional laboratory drill was discredited. Notional approaches emphasize the variety of ways in which messages can be encoded, and communicative methodology deals with language which is not predictable. But there are signs of a renewal of interest as it is realized first that the machines are perhaps more flexible than was thought, and second, that some mastery of code and "fluency" in its old-fashioned sense are necessary to achieve adequate levels of communication.

Bibliography

Council for Educational Technology 1987 *Language Laboratories* USPEC, Information Sheet No. 4. Council for Educational Technology, London
Dakin J 1973 *The Language Laboratory and Language Learning*. Longman, London
Davies N 1974 The language laboratory: An annotated bibliography. *System* 1(2): 52–67
Gale L E 1983 Montevidisco: An anecdotal history of an interactive videodisc. *Calico J.* 1: 42–46
Hayes A 1980 *Language Laboratory Management*. British Council, London
Higgins J J 1969 *Guide to Language Laboratory Material Writing*. Universitetsforlaget, Oslo
Hocking E 1964 *The Language Laboratory and Language Learning*. National Education Association of the United States, Washington, DC
Stack E M 1971 *The Language Laboratory and Modern Language Teaching,* 3rd edn. Oxford University Press, New York

Foreign Language Testing in the Classroom

A. D. Cohen

Foreign language testing in the classroom concerns the daily use of tests or quizzes by classroom teachers of foreign languages. This article will give a rationale for frequent testing or quizzing, provide means for classifying test items and procedures, consider the process of test taking, and offer some suggested means for heightening the respondents' awareness about more effective test taking.

1. Use of Frequent Tests and Quizzes

Foreign language tests and quizzes intended for daily classroom use can be distinguished from tests intended to assess overall achievement (e.g., an end-of-course exam) or general language proficiency (e.g., a diagnostic placement test). Quizzes are brief, perhaps relating just to the highlights of the day's assignment and class activities. The focus may be quite narrow, in terms of both the extent of coverage of what was taught/learned and the degree of variety of items and procedures. Teachers can benefit from feedback as to how much learning is going on and as to the effects of what is taught on what is learned. As foreign language students are constantly formulating and reformulating hypotheses about the way that the new language works, they need feedback as to the accuracy of these hypotheses.

Frequent informal quizzes may be used as a vehicle for checks on student mastery and as a lead up to a more elaborate test.

Although for some teachers, even informal quizzes are considered too formal, alternate means of assessment, such as teachers' intuitions, a show of hands, a nod of the head, or simply the absence of student questions, may prove too impressionistic or even inaccurate. For one thing, cross-cultural differences among students and between students and teachers may result in teachers being unable to perceive whether students are in fact having trouble learning the language. In certain cultures student signals regarding trouble areas may not be at all overt.

2. Classifying Test Items and Procedures

There are a number of items or procedures that make up a quiz or test. A test item is one entry or question on a quiz or test, and a sizeable item or task (e.g., writing a summary of an article or doing a dictation) is referred to as a test procedure. Any feature or form that a given item elicits is referred to as a testing point. If the intent of an item is to test only one point at a time—that is, only one element (e.g., negative singular past auxiliary "didn't") from one component of language (e.g., syntax) assessed in one skill (reading)—then the item is referred to as discrete-point. If an item tests two or more points at a time, then it is referred to as integrative.

There exists a continuum from the most discrete-point items on the one hand to the most integrative, global items and procedures on the other. There is also a continuum from more indirect to more direct tests. A direct test samples directly from the behavior being evaluated (e.g., testing talking on the phone by having the student engage in an actual phone conversation), while an indirect test is contrived to the extent that the test is different from a normal language-using task (e.g., a written test of speaking ability). Thirdly, there is a continuum from pragmatic to nonpragmatic tests, depending on the extent to which respondents are motiv-

ated by the task to participate in the communication act, receptively or productively (e.g., students engaging actively and eagerly in a simulated dialog without focusing on form would provide the teacher with pragmatic test data).

The three continua can be depicted in a three dimensional model as shown in Fig. 1. To illustrate the model, if a student is tested on his or her ability to give a talk in front of the class, is talking about a topic that engages him or her actively in the content, and is tested on usage of specific verb tenses only, it could be said that the test is largely a "direct" test of particular language behavior (i.e., giving a talk), that it is concentrating on discrete points (i.e., verb tenses), and that it is pragmatic to the extent that the student is truly motivated to give the talk.

Any given test item or procedure also has a format for eliciting data from a student and a format for the student in turn to respond to the elicitation. The item stimulus may make use of an oral, written, or nonverbal medium, or some combination of these. The same is true for the item-response format. Viewing item format as the joining of the medium for the item stimulus with the medium for the item response, it can be shown that there are at least nine possible item-stimulus and item-response formats—even before considering combined formats like an oral and nonverbal (i.e., gestural or pictorial) stimulus and a written response. What emerges from the combination of an item stimulus and an item response can be referred to as an item type. Thus, for example, the item stimulus may be written (e.g., a reading passage) and the item-response format may also be written (for example, the respondent may be required to give both a fixed response—such as selecting one of the alternatives in a series of multiple-choice items—and a free response—giving a written rationale for selecting the alternative considered the correct answer and for rejecting each of the other alternatives).

Breaking test items down into their distinctive elements with respect to stimulus and response formats is intended to demonstrate how with a few elements the teacher may construct a variety of classroom quizzes and tests. For example, a teacher can choose from different written stimulus formats (e.g., individual words, a phrase, a sentence, a passage) and from different oral or written response formats (e.g., distinguishing, ordering, combining, identifying, completion, paraphrase, structured or free response, matching, note taking, rewriting) (Cohen 1980 Chap. 4).

3. The Process of Test Taking

Studies have begun to appear that look ethnographically at how learners actually accomplish testing tasks (Mehan 1974, Mackay 1974). For example, with respect to a teacher's oral questioning of young children, it has been suggested that "the interrogator and respondent work together to jointly compose the 'social fact' we call an 'answer-to-a-question'" (Mehan 1974). On the

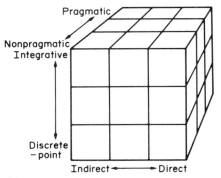

Figure 1
A model for classifying foreign language test items and procedures

basis of his research efforts, Mehan indicated that it may be misguided to conclude "that a wrong answer is due to a lack of understanding, for the answer may come from an alternative, equally valid interpretation." In other words, students may get an item wrong for the right reasons or right for the wrong reasons.

Studies investigating cognitive processes that learners use in taking foreign language tests are beginning to appear. Among the cognitive processes that were identified in a study by Cohen and Aphek (1979) were the following:

(a) Incomplete analysis: not necessarily processing receptively (in reading) the entire item stimulus, but only part of it, and answering that part (usually out of lack of understanding of a word or phrase in the item stimulus); lifting material intact from an item stimulus or from a passage for use in an answer; using prepackaged, unanalyzed material and combining it with analyzed forms.

(b) Field dependence: being distracted by elements that were in the immediate environment but irrelevant to the language processing being called for—for example, using a plural verb with a singular subject because the intervening indirect object was plural.

4. Heightening Awareness about Effective Test Taking

The research literature shows mixed benefits from practice in taking foreign language tests. It would appear that positive effects from practice show up more on discrete-point tests than on integrative ones (Kirn 1972, Bowen 1977, Schulz 1977). It may be, however, that students can benefit from heightened awareness about effective strategies to follow in taking any type of foreign language test.

The following is a sample set of strategies based on the findings from the above-cited study by Cohen and Aphek (Cohen 1980 pp. 52-53):

(a) Read the directions carefully and pay attention to the entire stimulus.

(b) Pay attention to the relationship of elements to one another, and try to avoid being distracted by elements that are irrelevant to the task at hand.

(c) When having to deal with unfamiliar or confusing forms in a test, scrutinize these carefully within the entire context and avoid being misled by features which are conspicuous but which lead to the wrong analogy.

(d) Avoid the temptation to select a form simply because it appears often or is popular.

(e) Do not assume that there is always a trick to answering an item, but if the item is tricky, try to identify all the necessary operations.

(f) Deal with all material both in the item stimulus and in the response, guessing where necessary.

(g) Use translation sparingly; avoid using it as a crutch.

(h) Try thinking in the target language while answering items.

(i) Go along with instinct. Do not be too quick to change answers which may be correct to begin with.

In summary, the purpose of this article was to provide a rationale for frequent quizzes, offer a system for classifying the various elements that go into test items and procedures, consider cognitive processes students use in taking foreign language tests, and then raise the issue of making students aware of more effective means of taking foreign language tests. The classroom teacher is encouraged to participate actively in the creative construction of classroom quizzes and tests. It may also be beneficial for teachers to discover more about how the students are arriving at answers to the various test items and procedures, and even to discuss with all or certain students how to be more successful test takers.

Bibliography

Bowen J D 1977 Practice effect in English proficiency testing. In: Brown H D, Yorio C A, Crymes R H (eds.) 1977 *On TESOL 77*. TESOL, Washington, DC, pp. 295–308
Cohen A D 1980 *Testing Language Ability in the Classroom.* Newbury House, Rowley, Massachusetts
Cohen A D, Aphek E 1979 *Easifying Second Language Learning.* Report financed by the Jacob Hiatt Institute, Jerusalem. ERIC Document No. ED 163 753
Kirn H E 1972 The effect of practice on performance on dictations and cloze tests. (M.A. Thesis, University of California, Los Angeles, California)
MacKay R 1974 Standardized tests: Objective/objectified measures of 'competence.' In: Cicourel A V, Jennings K H, Jennings S H M, Leifer K C W, MacKay R, Mehan H, Roth D R (eds.) 1974 *Language Use and School Performance.* Academic Press, New York, pp. 218–47
Mehan H 1974 Ethnomethodology and education. In: O'Shea D (ed.) 1974 *The Sociology of the School and Schooling.* National Institute of Education, Washington, DC
Schulz R A 1977 Discrete-point versus simulated communication testing in foreign languages. *Mod. Lang. J.* 61: 94–101

Testing Speaking Proficiency in Foreign Language

J. L. D. Clark

"Speaking proficiency testing" is commonly used to refer both to achievement testing over specified elements of course content and to the more generalized assessment of communicative proficiency—the ability to use the spoken language for real-life purposes outside of the classroom setting. Both types of measurement are considered below, beginning with a survey of test formats available for speaking testing in general, and followed by a discussion of the extent to which each of these formats may be considered appropriate for achievement-oriented or communicative proficiency-oriented testing.

Speaking test formats may usefully be classified as "indirect," "semidirect," and "direct." Indirect speaking tests are those which do not require actual speech production on the part of the person being tested; one example is the pronunciation test devised by Lado (1961) in which the examinee is asked to sound out mentally the pronunciation of each of a series of printed words (e.g., wood, food, understood) and to mark the one pronounced differently from the others. Although reasonably high correlations have been obtained between such indirect tests and tests of active speech production, their lack of face validity as reflective of actual speaking performance constitutes a serious drawback to their general acceptance and use as prima facie indicators of speaking skill, both for achievement and communicative proficiency testing purposes.

"Semidirect" and "direct" tests both involve active speech by the examinee, but differ in the way that the test stimuli are presented. Semidirect tests use booklets, audiotapes, or other mechanical means to present the test instructions, speaking cues, and other stimuli, and do not require the presence of a live examiner. Typical semidirect tests include the MLA-Cooperative Speaking Tests in French, German, Italian, Russian, and Spanish, used extensively in the United States in the mid-1960s (Educational Testing Service 1965); and the more recently developed speaking tests administered in the large-scale International Association for the Evaluation of Educational Achievement (IEA) study of the teaching of French in eight countries (Carroll 1975). The tests in both programs use an audiotape-and-booklet format in which are presented such tasks as repeating aloud sentences heard on the tape, answering spoken questions, and "telling a story" about printed pictures. Test administration, including the tape recording of the examinee's responses for later scoring, is usually carried out in a language laboratory, permitting simultaneous administration to a number of examinees.

Direct speaking tests require the examinee to engage in a face-to-face communicative exchange with one or more live interlocutors, typically in a setting intended to approximate natural conversation. The most widely known and extensively documented direct test is the so-called "FSI" or Foreign Service Interview developed in the 1950s by the Foreign Service Institute of the United States Department of State. The FSI interview consists of a structured conversation of gradually increasing complexity and linguistic sophistication, carried out over a period of approximately 15–30 minutes between the examinee and a trained interviewer. On completion of the interview, the examinee's performance is evaluated on a verbally defined scale of 0–5, ranging from "no functional proficiency" in the language to that of

an educated native speaker. Other direct speaking tests based generally on the FSI approach have been developed in England by Carroll (1980) and for the Australian Department of Immigration by Ingram and Wylie (1981).

To probe examinee performance in speaking situations involving types of interlocutors or communicative tasks that cannot be suitably reflected in general examiner–examinee conversation, the direct interview is often supplemented by role-playing exercises or by various interpreting situations in which the examinee is asked to be the communicative go-between for two examiners serving as monolingual speakers of the test language and the examinee's native language, respectively. The linguistic complexity of the interpreting task can be varied, according to the proficiency level of the examinee, from basic "survival" functions (for example, ordering a meal in a restaurant) to highly sophisticated language-use tasks (for example, buying a restaurant chain).

The choice between semidirect and direct testing approaches for a particular testing application depends in large part on the measurement purpose to be served. If the intent is to evaluate functional proficiency in "real-life" communicative settings, the direct format has several significant advantages, including especially its capacity to incorporate and reflect, within the testing procedure itself, the continual give-and-take associated with live communication—a fundamental aspect of natural speech that cannot for all practical purposes be accommodated within the administrative constraints imposed by the semidirect format. A second major advantage of the direct interview approach as a measure of general communicative proficiency is that the associated scoring scales are based, for the most part, on broad, functionally defined levels of performance rather than on more highly discrete elements of linguistic control. Semidirect tests, by contrast, are generally designed to yield total numerical scores reflecting the accumulation of discrete performance "points." The resulting scores are not directly interpretable in functional communication terms, although such interpretations could be made following correlational analyses establishing a satisfactorily high congruence of these scores with the results of more highly face- and content-valid tests which do use functional level descriptions.

If the testing intent is to measure the examinee's control of each of a series of discrete language aspects (such as proper pronunciation of certain phonemic contrasts or the oral production of specified tense forms), the direct interview approach is considerably less efficient and more subject to inter-interviewee variation in stimulus presentation and scoring than would be the case with a semidirect test specifically designed to assess the desired linguistic elements in a straightforward and unambiguous way. For example, in a direct conversational interview, checking the examinee's ability to differentially pronounce French *wi* and *yi* would involve a possibly futile wait for utterances embodying these sounds to appear naturally in the course of the examinee's conversation. By comparison, in a controlled semidirect format, a variety of techniques could be used to probe this distinction explicitly, such as reading printed sentences aloud or repeating spoken words or phrases containing the specified elements.

In a few cases, semidirect techniques have been used for general proficiency testing. For example, the *Recorded Oral Proficiency Examination* (Lowe and Clifford 1980) presents FSI-type questions by means of a tape recording, with the examinee's responses evaluated on a global proficiency scale. This test, which has shown high correlations with the direct interview procedure, is used in situations where it is not administratively feasible to send a trained FSI interviewer to the testing site. In other instances, direct testing procedures have been used to present discrete-point tasks, such as producing specified syntactical patterns or lexical items in response to questions posed by a live examiner. This approach, exemplified in a number of "language dominance" tests for Spanish–English bilingual schoolchildren, utilizes the examiner in a highly mechanical way that does not take maximum advantage of the flexibility and communicative realism available in the direct testing mode.

As a class, direct interview tests are often considered to be less reliable than the more highly structured semidirect tests. However, several recent studies have shown highly satisfactory scoring reliabilities for the direct interview procedure, figures which are quite in keeping with those reported for semidirect tests.

From the standpoint of practicality, semidirect tests provide some administration time and personnel economies over direct tests. However, both types must be individually scored, and in the case of semidirect tests, evaluation of the examinees' tape recorded responses may be laborious and time-consuming if the scoring procedure is not carefully planned. In direct testing, evaluation of examinee performance is usually carried out "live," and requires little or no additional time beyond that needed for test administration per se.

In summary, both direct and semidirect speaking proficiency tests offer specific advantages and drawbacks depending on the intended purpose of the testing. Semidirect procedures may, in general, be recommended for the diagnostic testing of particular linguistic features. Direct speaking tests involving face-to-face conversation with a live examiner provide a much higher degree of face and content validity as measures of general communicative proficiency. The associated verbally defined scoring scales, expressed for the most part in terms of the particular types of language-use situations in which the examinee would be expected to function effectively, add to the usefulness of the direct testing approach for this assessment purpose.

Bibliography

Carroll B J 1980 *Testing Communicative Performance: An Interim Study*. Pergamon, Oxford

Carroll J B 1975 *The Teaching of French as a Foreign Language in Eight Countries*. Almqvist and Wiksell, Stockholm

Ingram D E, Wylie E 1981 *Australian Second Language Proficiency Ratings* (ASLPR). Mount Gravatt College of Advanced Education, Brisbane

Lado R 1961 *Language Testing: The Construction and Use of Foreign Language Tests: A Teacher's Book*. Longman, London

Lowe P, Clifford R T 1980 Developing an indirect measure of oral proficiency. In: Frith J R (ed.) 1980 *Measuring Spoken Language Proficiency*. Georgetown University Press, Washington, DC, pp. 31–39

Teaching Specific Foreign Languages

Arabic

E. M. Badawi

The demand for facilities in teaching Arabic as a foreign language (TAFL) has increased tremendously due to the political–economic situation in the Middle East. Yet today's learners of Arabic, in spite of recent advances made in the area of foreign language teaching, still find Arabic as difficult to learn as their predecessors had always found it. This is due to the virtual absence of clearly defined language objectives, professionally trained personnel (teachers, curriculum designers, material writers, methodology experts, researchers, etc.), properly designed teacher-training programs, evaluated curricula, and coordinated research.

Perhaps the most serious problem facing TAFL is the lack of clearly defined language objectives, which is the result of the lack of a clear understanding of the language itself and its sociolinguistic role in present-day Arab societies.

Traditionally, Arabic has been considered to comprise two complementary varieties: Fusha, mainly written, and ᶜammiyya, spoken. Teaching materials have been devised accordingly. Present research, however, has demonstrated the inadequacy of such a classification. As many as five varieties, each exhibiting its own distinctive linguistic properties and social functions, are said to exist within each Arab community. Arranged on a descending scale reflecting the degree of schooling they each represent these are: classical Arabic, modern standard Arabic, educated colloquial, standard colloquial, and illiterate colloquial.

Extensive research is still needed before applicable descriptions of these varieties emerge. There is, for example, a dire need for scientifically constructed word lists, morphologies, syntax, and sociolinguistic attributes for each of the varieties. At the beginning of the 1980s, subjectivity still played a major role in assembling materials, vocabulary, structures, and readings for TAFL teaching books. Colloquial courses also lean too heavily on grammars of literary Arabic.

The lack of clearly defined language objectives for TAFL has generally resulted in:

(a) educated and illiterate colloquial effectively not being a part of regular teaching. While educated colloquial could be described as the most versatile and dynamic of the five varieties, there is no single course or book that teaches it. Foreign students wishing to identify with educated Arabs have to "merge" the modern standard Arabic and standard colloquial they have learned for an "approximation" of educated colloquial;

(b) some TAFL programs claiming to teach only classical Arabic (mainly for the purpose of worship in Islamic non-Arab countries such as Pakistan and Nigeria) use modern standard Arabic reading materials originally produced for Arab children;

(c) programs professing to teach only modern standard Arabic (mainly in Western countries) burden the student with detailed features of classical Arabic (e.g. the full cumbersome system of vowel endings);

(d) colloquial courses are loosely structured: features of educated colloquial and illiterate colloquial are confused with standard colloquial.

At present there are few trained personnel in TAFL, but teacher-training programs are being energetically created in Arab universities. Worldwide programs in TAFL may be classified, with a certain degree of overlapping, as:

(a) *Preuniversity programs.* Classical Arabic is taught for religious purposes to millions of children in Africa and Asia (e.g. 8,000 schools in Pakistan). The utilitarian function of European and local languages, together with inferior learning facilities in the case of Arabic, put the latter at a great disadvantage. Schools in European countries are increasingly offering modern standard Arabic mainly to children of Arab immigrants. France has over a hundred such schools. In the United States, a number of high schools, mainly in Michigan, offer modern standard Arabic with development funds obtained from the United States Office of Education since the early 1960s. In the Middle East, schools offer modern standard Arabic/standard colloquial to non-Arab children.

(b) *Vocational programs.* Arabic is rapidly becoming the tool of the anxious business person, having for centuries been mainly the domain of the serene theologian/academic. Accordingly, vocational TAFL programs offering modern standard Arabic/standard

605

colloquial have sprung up inside and outside the Arab world, but unfortunately far ahead of a proper structuring of the language. They largely depend on the personal qualities of their usually untrained instructors rather than on evaluated programs. Some long-established centers, however, have excelled in some particular areas of this complex field. Examples of these are: the five-year simultaneous translation modern standard Arabic and standard colloquial programs at Leipzig, the modern standard Arabic text-translation program at Beijing's Foreign Language Institute, the computer-assisted self-instruction program in modern standard Arabic at Houston, Texas, the course on "spoken formal" Arabic at the Foreign Service Institute (FSI) in Tunis and the rapid modern standard Arabic reading-for-comprehension program developed at the American University in Cairo, which represents a breakthrough in the history of TAFL.

(c) *University-type programs.* These offer literary and/or colloquial Arabic as parts of a relevant degree package (Abboud 1966, Mitchell 1969).

The publication of Wehr's *Dictionary of Modern Written Arabic* in the 1960s and Abboud et al.'s *Elementary and Intermediate Modern Standard Arabic* in the 1970s has offered improved opportunities for learning modern standard Arabic.

To achieve meaningful communication within any Arab society, a student must acquire at least modern standard Arabic and a colloquial variety of Arabic. Whether these two are studied simultaneously or consecutively, the dearth of evaluated learning strategies leads to inevitable confusion on the part of the student who has to learn two related but often conflicting language systems. Empirical research must tackle this basic TAFL issue. Research, coordinated and carried out according to an agreed schedule of priorities, is needed before real advances in TAFL can be made. At present, funds are being directed to satisfying the day-to-day needs for more materials, glossaries, tests, better classroom techniques, and so on (see recent issues of *Al-ᶜarabiyya*). While all this is important, it is first of paramount importance to undertake more basic language-survey type of research (as described above).

Bibliography

Abboud P F 1966 *The Teaching of Arabic in the United States: The State of the Art.* ERIC Document No. ED 024 051

Al-ᶜarabiyya, Journal of the American Association of Teachers of Arabic

Mitchell T F 1969 The teaching of Arabic in Great Britain. *The Linguistic Reporter* 20: 1–7

Stoetzer W 1977 On levels of contemporary Egyptian Arabic. *Der Islam* 54(2): 300–04

Zughoul M R 1980 Diglossia in Arabic: Investigating solutions. *Anthropol. Ling.* 22(5): 201–17

Chinese

Huan Wang, Du Rong, Chin Chuan Cheng

The language known as Chinese is spoken by one of the numerous nationalities in the People's Republic of China, the Han, who make up over 90 percent of the total population. It is a tonal language with a writing system of several thousand ideograms or characters. Before the Second World War, modern Chinese was seldom taught as a foreign language. It was first taught on a large scale in the United States in 1943. After the founding of the People's Republic of China, Chinese began to be taught as a discipline to foreign students in China. Beijing Language Institute is a college specially devoted to this purpose, though there are now other universities which also offer courses of elementary Chinese for foreign learners.

1. The Standard Language

The standard spoken Chinese known as *putonghua* (common speech) is mainly the Beijing dialect. It has four tones plus a neutral tone. That is to say, every syllable, usually represented by a character, must be pronounced in one of the five tones. There is no syllable without a tone. The same syllable with two different tones may be represented by two different characters and carry two different meanings. Each character is either a word or a morpheme. Many of the words of the basic vocabulary are monosyllabic but most of the words in current Chinese consist of two characters. Disyllabic words have been increasing rapidly, and there are even words of more than two syllables.

Many of the Chinese characters are rather complicated in structure and thus difficult to write. Since the 1950s more than 2,200 of them have been simplified.

Chinese is a language with a large number of dialects. The differences between the dialects are mainly differences in pronunciation, which may make oral communication impossible among people from different districts. Only the writing system is intelligible throughout the country.

In order to popularize *putonghua*, a new phonetic alphabet has been adopted known as *Hanyu pinyin* (the Han speech transcription) which uses the Roman alphabet plus four tone marks. It is now used by all Chinese dictionaries to indicate the pronunciations. The popularization of *putonghua* has been quickened in recent years through radio broadcast, television programs, movies, and so on, but there is a very long way to go before all the people in the People's Republic of China can talk in *putonghua*.

2. Teaching Modern Chinese in the People's Republic of China

Chinese taught by sinologists prior to the Second World War was classical Chinese, a dead language like ancient Greek or Latin. The first special course for teaching modern Chinese was designed in the United States in 1943. After the founding of the People's Republic of China and the establishment of diplomatic relations between China and various socialist countries in Eastern Europe, a constant exchange of students was begun between the People's Republic of China and the socialist countries. The East European students had to study Chinese intensively for a year or two before they could study other disciplines in Chinese universities. The organization which first gave this course in Tsinghua University and later in Peking University was the predecessor of the present Beijing Language Institute which was founded in 1973. The institute now receives several hundred foreign students every year from all corners of the world.

It is only since the founding of the People's Republic of China that the number of students of Chinese has increased by leaps and bounds. The new regime has brought drastic changes to the Chinese language, especially to its vocabulary. Since 1949, unprecedented changes in people's political and social life have caused such changes in the language that for a person who left China before 1949 it may now be difficult to understand the language spoken there in the 1980s.

The Beijing Language Institute was for a long time the only college where foreign students could study Chinese, but in the 1980s courses of elementary Chinese are also being offered at many other universities such as Peking University, Beijing; Nankai University, Tianjin; and Nanking University, Nanjing. Several textbooks have been compiled by the Beijing Language Institute, the most up-to-date one being the *Elementary Chinese Reader* in four volumes published in 1979–80. It was designed for classroom teaching conducted in the People's Republic of China. Another textbook compiled specially for students abroad called *Practical Chinese Reader* was published in 1981.

At the Beijing Language Institute both the compilation of textbooks and the classroom teaching is guided by the following principles:

(a) Students are interested in learning the language so that they can use it for various practical purposes. They are less interested in learning theories about the language.

(b) Students must acquire the basic skills of listening, speaking, reading, and writing within a year: that means apart from basic Chinese grammar they must learn around 3,000 words and phrases made up of around 1,200 characters.

(c) The mastery of the language can best be attained through intensive practice, and therefore the major role of the teachers is to provide opportunity for the practical use of the language.

(d) The knowledge of grammar is supposed to facilitate the utilization of the language.

Students are roughly divided into two groups, those who will later study natural sciences and those who will study liberal arts. The former group is taught the technical vocabulary of their speciality. Students of liberal arts participate in a second year of advanced language training, which includes learning classical Chinese.

3. Teaching Chinese as a Foreign Language Outside the People's Republic of China

In the United States in the 1950s and 1960s, most of the college students who studied Chinese seriously beyond the second year were interested in using their knowledge of Chinese to do academic work. Indeed, many of them with the support of National Defense Education Act fellowships have become China scholars. Since the early 1970s, however, Chinese classes have been getting more and more students from disciplines other than humanities. Now people expect to find a number of opportunities in international trade, business, and law. Students from hard sciences also find Chinese useful in their international communication. In other words, more students expect to use Chinese as a tool rather than as an object of study. This naturally entails certain adjustments on the part of the teacher in the selection of reading material, emphasis of contents, and so on. The teaching profession is gradually realizing this shift of student interest.

Since the early 1950s, discussions concerning Chinese language teaching have on the whole focused on methodology and lesson contents. Some teaching innovations have been started, however, because of the advent of the computer. At the University of Illinois, for example, computer-assisted instruction has been used in teaching pronunciation, writing of Chinese characters, and other aspects of the language (Ching-Hsiang Chen and Chin-Chuan Cheng 1976).

Another innovation has to do with course design. In August 1973 an interagency conference was held at the Foreign Service Institute to address the need in the United States Government language training community for improving Chinese material to reflect current usage in Taipei and Beijing. The Chinese Core Curriculum Project involving various coordinators and Chinese language teachers was set up in 1974. A set of materials has been produced. The modular approach by the Chinese Core Curriculum Project (1977) is still undergoing field testing at Brown University, the Defense Language Institute, the Foreign Service Institute, the Language Learning Center, the United States Air Force Academy, the University of Illinois, and the University of Virginia. The course includes a number of core, resource, and optional modules. The instructor takes the role of conversational partner rather than the conventional roles of lecturer or drill master. Instructions are already recorded on tapes. This course, therefore, begins each unit with a tape assignment. For example, a unit of a core module starts with self-study of two tapes followed by review and drill in class.

As they study Chinese, American students face these three extra dimensions of learning in comparison with their study of a European language: the addition of tone, the lack of cognates, and a nonalphabetic writing system. They must take many years of study to master the Chinese language. This applies also to all non-Chinese persons learning Chinese as a foreign language.

Bibliography

Beijing Language Institute 1979–80 *Elementary Chinese Reader*, Vols. 1–4. Foreign Language Press, Beijing

Beijing Language Institute 1981 *Practical Chinese Reader*. Foreign Language Press, Beijing

Chin-Chuan Cheng 1977 In defense of teaching simplified characters. *J. Chinese Ling.* 5: 314–41

Ching-Hsiang Chen, Chin-Chuan Cheng 1976 Computer-assisted instruction in Chinese: An interim report. *J. Chinese Ling.* 4: 278–98

Chinese Core Curriculum Project 1977 *Standard Chinese: A Modular Approach*. Defense Language Institute, Monterey, California

DeFrancis J 1963 *Beginning Chinese*. Yale University Press, New Haven, Connecticut

DeFrancis J 1975 Sociolinguistic aspects of Chinese language-teaching materials. *J. Chinese Ling.* 3(2/3): 245–56

Kratochvil P 1968 *The Chinese Language Today: Features of an Emerging Standard*. Hutchinson University Press, London

Lindbeck J M H 1971 *Understanding China: An Assessment of American Scholarly Resources*. Praeger, New York

Tai J 1975 Vocabulary changes in the Chinese language: Some observations on extent and nature. *J. Chinese Ling.* 3(2/3): 233–44

English

C. B. Paulston

English as a foreign language (EFL) is concerned with the teaching of English to speakers of other languages (TESOL). Sometimes the reference is to English as a second language (ESL), and this article attempts first to clarify the various acronyms of the field and their reference. The article continues with a discussion of the various domains of TESOL and closes with a brief look at the major trends in the field.

1. EFL, ESL, and TESOL

The original term for teaching English to those who did not know it and for the area of expertise associated with it, was English as a foreign language, known for short as EFL. On the whole, this continues to be the British usage in referring to overseas teaching of English. In the United States, the term ESL, English as a second language, became increasingly used, and today there are no less than three definitions of the term. American publishers increasingly avoided the term EFL in favor of ESL as they considered the term "foreign" to be pejorative and so to be avoided in the selling of textbooks. This usage is simply synonymous with EFL and begs the question of any difference between the two. The second usage of ESL refers to the learning of English in an English-speaking environment, such as by foreign students in England or in the United States. Finally, the third usage of ESL defines a second language as the nonhome but official language of a nation which must be learned by its citizens for full social, economic, and political participation in the life of that nation. Australian Aborigines, United States Chicanos, and British Gaelic speakers as well as immigrants all learn English as a second language according to this defi-

nition. All three usages are common, but the third is to be preferred because it is the relationship between the super- and sub-ordinate groups within a nation which gives second language learning its significant characteristics and which distinguishes it from learning a foreign language where attitudes are fairly neutral.

Exactly in order to avoid the dichotomy, EFL and ESL became united in TESOL, teaching English to speakers of other languages, which stands both for the field and for the international professional organization, which was founded in 1966. Unless a technical differentiation is intended, TESOL is the better cover term for the field.

2. The Domains of TESOL

The teaching of English to speakers of other languages, as a professional field, is a relative newcomer to language teaching compared to the teaching of Greek and Latin. Similar to those languages, the spread of English has also reflected social conditions such as emigration, colonialism, military power, and trade as well as advanced scientific knowledge, and in the case of English, advanced technology. The result necessarily has been a many-faceted picture of English teaching around the world.

Basically the field can be subdivided into four areas: EFL, ESL, bilingual education, and ESOD (English to speakers of other dialects) (Robinett 1972).

2.1 EFL (English as a Foreign Language)

The study of English began primarily as learning English as a cultural acquisition which would enable the learner to read the classics like Shakespeare and Milton in the original. The purpose, objectives, and methods of this type of English study are very similar to the study of French, German, and Italian as foreign languages.

Today, however, straight EFL overlaps with, and is superseded by, English as an LWC (language of wider communication), as the major lingua franca of the world. Until the First World War, French had been the major language of wider communication within Europe, but after the Second World War this role has been taken over worldwide by English. This fact is reflected in the considerable investment in English teaching—in curriculum, textbooks, and teacher training—held by Third World countries where English is not seen primarily as a cultural acquisition nor as a colonial legacy but practically as an instrumental means of international communication in an electronic world. It is also reflected in the popularity of the adult English classes sponsored by the British Council and the United States Binational Centers around the world. The Regional English Language Centre (RELC) in Singapore is another case in point.

As far as language attitudes are concerned, the study of EFL is the most neutral of the field. There are no external social, religious, or political pressures which enforce the study of English but rather it is a voluntary choice for instrumental or integrative purposes.

2.2 ESL (English as a Second Language)

In many parts of the world the study of English takes place because English is an official (or critically important public) language of that nation. This situation is almost always the result of earlier annexation or colonization. Actually, the situations vary widely from countries which are commonly thought of as monolingually English, such as Australia and the United States, to countries which are notedly multilingual such as Nigeria and India.

The purposes and motivations for maintaining English as the official language vary as the situation's social, economic, religious, and political factors vary. In Nigeria, for example, it has served both to neutralize ethnic group interests as well as to promote Pan-Africanism, and so a former colonial language remains tolerated as the official language among several national languages. In India, English remains preferred by many as the national language to the alternative of Hindi with its strong associations to a specific religious sect. In Singapore, English is a practical means of a multiethnic population for carrying on trade with the West. In the United States, English became unofficially (there exists no federal legislation on the matter) the official language for primarily practical concerns, until monolingualism became the idealized norm, although 16.3 percent of the population report a non-English mother tongue (Waggoner 1981). The United States is one of the few countries outside Britain in which nationalism has been an issue in English teaching.

The situations vary widely, and so do the attitudes toward the study of English that accompany them. All

ESL situations share, by definition, an imposition of English on the learner and often this is perceived as a derogatory comment on the home culture with concomitant social strife. Spanish-speaking Puerto Rico is a good example of such tension. On the other hand, predominantly Spanish-speaking Gibraltar gladly welcomes English. The reasons for the various attitudes towards and the relative efficiency of learning ESL are ultimately to be found in the social settings (Saville-Troike 1976).

2.3 Bilingual Education

The domain of bilingual education within the field of TESOL refers to programs where equal emphasis is placed on learning the native language as well as English. Typically, the literature and discussions of bilingual education do not include elitist schooling which adds a component of EFL to the curriculum of private schools, but rather tend to include the concerns of minority group children in public schooling where English is taught as a second language. An exception are the Canadian immersion programs where Anglophone children study in French and English, but another defining characteristic of bilingual education holds: the children study subject matter, such as history, through the medium of French, the target language (see *Immersion Education*).

Considerable conflict exists over the goals of bilingual education. In the United States, for example, the programs officially are denoted as transitional bilingual education and seen as a more efficient way of teaching the national language where the tacit goals are language shift through bilingualism and assimilation into mainstream culture. (Alaska is an exception.) Many Chicanos, Indians, and Puerto Ricans resent these goals and prefer to maintain their cultural identity of which language is an integral part. Their social goal is cultural pluralism with structural incorporation, that is, access to goods and services and to social institutions like education and justice. The goals of bilingual education, as they see it, are maintenance bilingual education programs, where the programs teach not only the native language but also the native culture. Bilingual programs in which the children speak the national language and which are voluntary tend to avoid such strife.

There is very little systematic knowledge of techniques and procedures for teaching children a second language at the elementary level which is coherently anchored in a theory of language acquisition. The elaboration of such a body of knowledge is an important priority for the future development of bilingual education (Paulston 1980) (see *Bilingual Education*).

2.4 English to Speakers of Other Dialects

The last domain of TESOL refers to ESOD (English to speakers of other dialects) or more commonly known as SESD (standard English as a second dialect). Standard English as a second dialect deals with teaching English to those whose home language is a distinct English dialect which differs markedly from standard English, such as the Maoris in New Zealand, the Native Americans in Alaska and Canada, Afro-Americans in the United States, creole speakers in the Caribbean, and so on. Even though the social settings differ widely, the educational problems remain markedly similar.

Since the early 1970s, Caribbean Creoles and black English have been the focus of intense scholarly interest and work which are reflected in the teaching of Standard English (Alleyne 1980). There were originally attempts to adopt foreign language teaching techniques, but such methods have not turned out very well, and most scholars believe with Allen that "A Second Dialect is not a Foreign Language" (1969). Some major issues have been: (a) applying linguistic descriptions to studies of interference in reading and writing and consequent implications for teaching; (b) teaching the legitimacy of the dialects as a linguistic system in its own right; (c) the identification of culture-specific speech acts and the legitimacy of the culture itself; (d) language attitudes; and (e) Labov's *The Study of Non-standard English* (1968).

Altogether, the domains of TESOL range over a wide variety of situations and needs. The particular situation of the learner needs always to be taken into account because the social, political, cultural, and economic factors tend to be of far more significance in influencing educational results than any language teaching methods per se.

3. Recent Trends

Foreign language teaching turns primarily to psychology for theory, models, and explanatory frameworks. With the recent concentration on student learning rather than on teaching, cognitive psychology has succeeded behavioral psychology as a more viable approach. Neurolinguistics is an area of study which has recently received much attention, but at this point it is premature to make any direct application to language teaching. In psycholinguistics, the amount of so-called second language acquisition research attests to the increasing emphasis and importance of empirical and quantificational research in language teaching.

In general, language teaching remains eclectic in its methods (Paulston and Bruder 1976, Rivers and Temperley 1978, Robinett 1978). The audiolingual method has been discredited but no one method has taken its place. Instead there is a plethora of methods among which may be mentioned community counseling–learning, notional–functional syllabi, rapid acquisition, the silent way, suggestopedia, and total physical response. These methods vary widely, and each has its supporters as well as detractors. Actually, as long as teachers and students have confidence that they are in fact learning, and all are happy in the process, methods probably do not make too much difference. Probably the most widespread method in TESOL in spite of all the scholarly

criticism remains the grammar-translation approach, but the social incentives are so strong that students learn in spite of the methods.

By far the most important development in TESOL has been the emphasis on a communicative approach in language teaching (Coste 1976, Roulet 1972, Widdowson 1978). The one thing that everyone is certain about is the necessity to use language for communicative purposes in the classroom. Consequently, the concern for teaching linguistic competence has widened to include communicative competence, the socially appropriate use of language, and the methods reflect this shift from form to function.

One more development in TESOL deserves mention, namely the publication of *A Grammar of Contemporary English* (Quirk et al. 1972) and its shorter version *A Concise Grammar of Contemporary English* by Quirk and Greenbaum (1973). As reference grammars, they are not intended for EFL/ESL students, but they nevertheless provide a wealth of information for the English textbook writer, teacher, and serious student alike.

Bibliography

Allen V F 1969 A second dialect is not a foreign language. In: Alatis J (ed.) 1969 *Linguistics and the Teaching of Standard English to Speakers of Other Languages or Dialects*. Georgetown University Press, Washington, DC

Alleyne M 1980 *Comparative Afro-American: An Historical-Comparative Study of English-based Afro-American Dialects of the New World*. Karoma, Ann Arbor, Michigan

Coste D 1976 *Un Niveau seuil: Systèmes d'apprentissage des langues vivantes par les adultes*. Council of Europe, Strasbourg

Ellis R 1988 *Classroom Second Language Development*. Prentice Hall, New York

Kachru B 1986 *The Alchemy of English: The Spread, Functions and Models of Non-Native Englishes*.

Labov W 1968 *The Study of the Non-standard English of Negro and Puerto Rican Speakers in New York City*. ERIC, Center for Applied Linguistics, Washington, DC

McLaughlin B 1987 *Theories of Second-Language Learning*. Edward Arnold, London

Paulston C B 1980 *Bilingual Education: Theories and Issues*. Newbury House, Rowley, Massachusetts

Paulston C B, Bruder M N 1976 *Teaching English as a Second Language: Techniques and Procedures*. Winthrop, Cambridge, Massachusetts

Quirk R, Greenbaum S 1973 *A Concise Grammar of Contemporary English*. Harcourt Brace Jovanovich, New York

Quirk R, Greenbaum S, Leech G, Svartvik J 1972 *A Grammar of Contemporary English*. Harcourt Brace Jovanovich, New York

Rivers W M, Temperley M S 1978 *A Practical Guide to the Teaching of English as a Second or Foreign Language*. Oxford University Press, Oxford

Robinett B W 1972 The domains of TESOL. *TESOL Q.* 6: 197–207

Robinett B 1978 *Teaching English to Speakers of Other Languages: Substance and Technique*. McGraw-Hill, New York

Roulet E 1972 *Théories grammaticales, descriptions et enseignement des langues*. Nathan, Paris [1975 *Linguistic Theory*,

Linguistic Description and Language Teaching. Longman, London]

Saville-Troike M 1976 *Foundations for Teaching English as a Second Language: Theory and Method for Multicultural Education.* Prentice-Hall, Englewood Cliffs, New Jersey

Waggoner D 1981 Statistics on language use. In: Ferguson C F, Heath S B (eds.) 1981 *Language in the USA.* Cambridge University Press, Cambridge, Massachusetts

Widdowson H G 1978 *Teaching Language as Communication.* Oxford University Press, Oxford

French

R. Bergentoft

According to estimates made at the beginning of the 1980s, French is the mother tongue of 90 million people. This figure breaks down into 60 million Europeans, 12 million people in the Americas, and 18 million elsewhere in the world. In addition, 196 million people living in non-French-speaking countries are estimated to know French. According to a worldwide survey of teachers of French (*Le Français dans le Monde* 1981), there are about 250,000 teachers of French as a foreign language in the world today. The number of persons studying French as a foreign language is estimated at about 25 million or more. There is an element of uncertainty about all these figures, because statistics are incomplete or nonexistent for certain countries and because numbers will fluctuate over time. In addition, the criteria for "knowing" French tend to vary.

Why is it that almost 200 million people in five continents are able to speak French and about 25 million young persons and adults are studying French as a foreign language? One basic reason is that many countries and individuals consider a knowledge of French important to their own community or to themselves as individuals. It is often necessary or desirable for use in business and trade dealings, in order to keep up with technical research, for cultural enrichment, or for some other reason. Also French is still used in the former French colonies, and the inhabitants account for a proportion of the figure for French speakers.

The status of French, however, is not uncontested. English is gaining ground in many places at the expense of French (and often, too, at the expense of other languages). French long ago ceased to be a compulsory secondary-school language in the United States, and its status as first foreign language in schools in the United Kingdom has begun to be challenged. Except in Canada, French is usually studied as the second or third foreign language, often as an alternative to other languages or other groups of subjects. There are several countries where French is holding its own, and in some cases it is doing more than this. In some instances this is due to extensive efforts by the French government, especially in the recent past, to strengthen the standing of the French language throughout the world. *Le Conseil International de la Langue Française* plays a leading part in this connection, as do the *Centres Culturels, Instituts Française,* or cultural services attached to the French Embassies. In many countries—not least in Latin America—the Alliance Française, formed in 1883, helps to disseminate knowledge of the French language and culture.

1. Goals of French Teaching

Recently there has been a certain shift of emphasis from grammar and written French, in favor of communicative, and especially oral, skills in language learning. This change is generally a slow process, however, and in some quarters it is barely discernible.

Goal descriptions are short and generalized in some countries, while in others they are relatively comprehensive and detailed. The following example illustrates how a curriculum coming into force in the 1982/83 school year describes the goals for the first three years of French as a second foreign language (chosen in preference to German or as an optional subject) for students aged 13–16 in a Swedish comprehensive school.

In the curriculum French and German are included for the following reasons:

(a) international contacts are of great importance to Sweden, and the pupils' opportunities to establish such contacts are increased if they are proficient in a second foreign language;

(b) pupils must be made aware of the fact that language is an expression of diverse living conditions and cultures, and of different concepts existing in different countries;

(c) a knowledge of French/German is useful for the pupils in their higher education and future working life.

The aims of including French and German in the school curriculum are so that pupils gain such skills during their course of studies that they can:

(a) understand spoken French/German

(b) make themselves understood when speaking French/German

(c) read and understand various types of text

(d) use a simple form of the written language.

Further the teaching should encourage the pupils

(a) to want to and to dare to use French/German

(b) to take an interest in everyday life, working life, social conditions, and culture in the French-speaking/German-speaking countries.

The main listening and speaking components are as follows:

(a) The teaching of French/German is primarily intended to provide the pupils with a degree of oral proficiency. Aural/oral exercises must therefore be given a prominent place in the syllabus. The language used in the aural/oral practice should be natural and realistic so that the pupils feel that what they learn is useful outside school.

(b) The pupils should learn, first and foremost, those words, phrases, and grammatical structures which they need to know in order to express themselves in different oral situations. In addition to this active vocabulary they should be familiar with a considerably greater number of words, phrases, and grammatical structures so that they can understand what they read and hear in French/German.

(c) The study of grammar should be directed towards practical ends so that the pupils can express themselves reasonably correctly and be understood. Apart from the grammar which pupils acquire as active language, there are some grammatical structures which they must be aware of, but which they themselves will not need to use. Practice should be aimed at the pupils understanding such forms when they meet them in their reading or when listening to French/German.

(d) Oral/aural exercises, chiefly in dialogue form, provide practice in pronunciation and intonation. In order that the pupils' pronunciation shall be as good as possible, they should listen regularly to recorded native speakers of French/German and practice repeating what they hear. The norm for pronunciation should be educated speech without any strong dialectical variation.

Texts should provide the pupils with information and enjoyment. They should be of various kinds, for example, narrative and descriptive texts, messages, and instructions. Authentic text material should also be used.

The teaching should include:

(a) reading of linguistically simple texts which can form the basis of language exercises of various types

(b) reading of linguistically more difficult texts with increasing emphasis on free choice of reading material

(c) practice, when reading texts, in differentiating between important and nonessential information, and in drawing conclusions, and in forming an opinion about the content

(d) practice in using a dictionary.

Written exercises of various types serve to reinforce the oral exercises and help in the consolidation of words, phrases, and grammatical structures. The pupils should also, as early as possible, be allowed to practise expressing themselves in French/German. More creative writing, for example, short essays, should be a regular feature in the syllabus.

The teaching should include:

(a) information on everyday-life, working-life, social and geographical conditions, culture, and current problems in French-speaking/German-speaking countries. These aspects should be dealt with in various ways and compared with the equivalent conditions in Sweden

(b) the discussion of important current events in the French-speaking/German-speaking countries

(c) the opportunity for pupils to practise giving information in French/German about Swedish conditions

(d) a discussion of the importance of language competence in different occupations.

More specific goals are sometimes established in adult education, in order for example to describe command of language relating to a particular purpose or vocation, for example, French for science or French for catering.

2. Aids to French Teaching

The use of different teaching aids naturally varies a great deal, depending on the resources of the country and school concerned. Whatever the aids, however, the teacher seems to be the most important factor determining learning results. These depend not least, on his or her ability to motivate students. Motivation appears to be more common among students feeling that they can shape their own situation through their schooling, and not least perhaps through their proficiency in the French language. Students who feel unable to shape their own futures are just as liable to be found in a village school in Chile or Laos as in a comprehensive school in a British or Japanese industrial city.

The design of teaching materials has proved to have an important bearing on the quality of instruction. During the 1960s and 1970s, this resulted in considerable emphasis being placed, particularly in certain parts of the United States and Europe, on the production of teaching kits aimed at accommodating the syllabus for a particular subject over a period of one or more years. This was thought to be a particular help to teachers with little or no training and was expected to improve, or at least equalize, teaching standards. These comprehensive packages often made teaching excessively hidebound. As a reaction to this, some teachers went to the opposite extreme and began teaching French and other subjects based on newspaper cuttings and other authentic material, instead of on textbooks. Consistently applied, teaching without a textbook often means a great deal of extra work for the teacher and entails improvisation which is not always good for teaching standards. Most French teachers probably prefer teaching via media, the rule being that departures from the textbook are proportional to the teacher's communicative proficiency. It is worth pointing out in this connection that aids such as dictionaries are often out-of-date and therefore difficult to utilize rationally.

Some countries have extensive interchange of trainee teachers, that is, "assistants" from the target language country. Arrangements of this kind are common, for example, between the United Kingdom, France, and the Federal Republic of Germany. They have a galvanizing effect on teaching while at the same time providing useful inservice training for the participating teachers and their colleagues.

Tape-recorded radio and television broadcasts provide a rich and varied source of contemporary sociocultural information embedded in language activity.

A communicative approach has been the subject of a great deal of research and practical implementation in many countries for several years but has, since 1970, gained particular impetus under the auspices of the Council of Europe. The following passage is taken from the recommendations adopted by the Committee of Ministers of the Council of Europe. The reasons for learning and teaching modern languages are:

> To promote, encourage, and support the efforts of teachers and learners at all levels to apply in their own situation the principles of the construction of language-learning systems (as these are progressively developed within the Council of Europe "Modern languages" programme):
>
> (a) by basing language teaching and learning on the needs, motivations, characteristics, and resources of learners,
>
> (b) by defining worthwhile and realistic objectives as explicitly as possible,
>
> (c) by developing appropriate methods and materials,
>
> (d) by developing suitable forms and instruments for the evaluation of learning programmes.

3. Research on the Teaching of French

The teaching of French as a foreign language at three age levels was studied in eight countries by the International Association for the Evaluation of Educational Achievement (IEA). The focus was on outcomes with regard to reading, speaking, and writing. Among the determinants of outcomes, Carroll (1975) in his report of the study particularly analyzed the role played by time defined by (a) age of introducing the language, (b) number of years of instruction, and (c) number of periods of instruction per week. There was no indication of it being particularly advantageous to introduce French at an early age; rather, there was evidence pointing in the opposite direction. Achievement in reading, listening, and writing correlated between 0.6 and 0.8 with length of time of study over the various countries. Figure 1 shows the scattergram in reading. Students in the last year of secondary education in England are at the top with more than seven years of study, and the United States students are at the bottom with only two years of study.

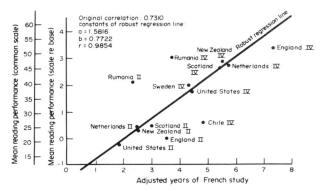

Figure 1
Scattergram of French reading achievement in eight countries with respect to length of time of study[a]

[a] Source: Carroll 1975 p. 182.

Carroll concludes that some six years of instruction in French at the usual pace with 3–5 hours per week would be required in order to bring the students up to a reasonable level of competence in French.

Nyström (1978) compared in detail the teaching of French in England, Scotland, and Sweden. Although the instructional objectives in the three countries were rather similar, the teaching strategies employed varied considerably. Little individualization was used in any of these countries in spite of the need to diversify both objectives and methods according to the level of ability of students. Nyström confirms Carroll's findings of the importance of verbal ability. She also shows the importance of social background, particularly in a country where knowledge of French traditionally has been a stamp of good education. A more "dynamic teacher–learner interaction," that is to say, a moderate use of French as the medium of instruction improves the quality of outcomes.

Bibliography

Birkmaier E M 1973 Research on teaching foreign languages. In: Rivers M W (ed.) 1973 *Second Handbook of Research on Teaching: A Project of the American Educational Research Association*. Rand McNally, Chicago, Illinois, pp. 1280-302

Blancpain M, Reboullet A 1976 *Une Langue, le français aujourd'hui dans le monde*. Hachette, Paris

Bouacha A 1978 *La Pédagogie du français langue étrangère: Orientations, théoriques, pratiques dans la classe*. Hachette, Paris

Burstall C 1970 *French in the Primary Schools: Attitudes and Achievement*. National Foundation for Educational Research, Slough

Carroll J B 1963 Research on teaching foreign languages. In: Gage N L (ed.) 1963 *Handbook of Research on Teaching: A Project of the American Educational Research Association*. Rand McNally, Chicago, Illinois, pp. 1060–100

Carroll J B 1975 *The Teaching of French as a Foreign Language in Eight Countries*. Almqvist and Wiksell, Stockholm

Le Français dans le Monde No. 148, No. 161 1981 *Des Professeurs de Français*. Hachette, Paris

Nyström A 1978 *French as a Foreign Language: A Comparative Study on Factors Affecting Student Achievement*. Almqvist and Wiksell, Stockholm

Politzer R L, Weiss L 1970 *The Successful Foreign-language Teacher*. Center for Curriculum Development, Philadelphia, Pennsylvania

The 1980 Compulsory School Curriculum. 1980 National Board of Education, Liber, Stockholm

German

H. J. Krumm

Learning and teaching a foreign language is not only a field for educational and linguistic efforts, but to a large extent it is also a matter of cultural relationships and thus depends on cultural politics. This is especially true for German as a foreign language, because German plays a different role in various German-speaking countries: Austria, the Federal Republic of Germany (FRG), the German Democratic Republic (GDR), and in Switzerland which is a multilingual country. The Federal Republic of Germany and the German Democratic Republic to some extent undertake similar efforts to support the teaching of German in other countries through the Herder Institute (GDR), and the Goethe Institute and the German Academic Exchange Service (FRG) (Sturm 1987).

The teaching and learning of German is largely determined by its situational context. Since in the past it was mostly taught as a third foreign language or as an elective subject, the efforts related to teacher training, curriculum materials, and research, were more limited in their scope than those related to teaching English or French as foreign languages. Within the German-speaking countries, German as a foreign language was taught only to a rather small group of foreign students and experts. The presence in the Federal Republic of Germany of more than 4 million migrant workers and their families (from Turkey, Greece, Yugoslavia, Italy, Spain, Poland, and Portugal) since 1975 has changed this situation completely: for a large number of people living in the Federal Republic of Germany, German has the status of a second language which they need to speak in order to live in a German-speaking community. This situation has increased interest in the teaching of German and generated activities in the field of research, materials development, and teacher training. It has also affected the teaching of German abroad.

1. The Scientific Study of Teaching German as a Foreign Language

For many years, the scientific basis of the teaching and learning of German as a foreign language was rooted in the field of German philology: people who had studied German linguistics and/or literature were those who were involved in teaching, teacher training, or research in the area of German as a foreign language. Consequently, the German departments in universities in many countries have concentrated on German philology. Structuralistic description of the German language and behavioristic learning theories were considered to be a sufficient basis for developing teaching methods. As learning theories emerged changes occurred in the teaching methods and in the underlying linguistic theories.

The development of applied linguistics led to increased expectations on the part of teachers and textbook authors, especially in the field of contrastive linguistics: it was hoped that a contrastive analysis of the mother tongue and target language would reveal learning problems (interferences) and allow for better teaching. Such studies, specifically those contrasting English and German, have made teachers aware of certain areas where structures, which the learners have already acquired in their mother tongue, can be used for learning a foreign language. In combination with error analysis studies it became possible to systematize mistakes in foreign language learning and to construct teaching materials to reduce the frequency of such mistakes (Kufner 1962, Nickel 1971). In the light of studies in psycholinguistics (Krashen 1981) and pedagogical grammar (Bausch 1979) it became evident that learning a foreign language is a process in which several factors interact and which cannot be fully understood without taking into consideration the conditions of the learning situation and the proclivities of the learner. The necessity of an interdisciplinary approach incorporating elements from the fields of social sciences, communication theory, psychology, psycholinguistics, cultural studies, and other sciences is now widely acknowledged. One particular discipline should not be focused on, neither should an attempt be made to accumulate in an additive manner all the theories and findings of different sciences; instead actual problems should be approached by examining practical teaching and learning situations, as well as the contribution of each particular theory in explaining observed phenomena (Krumm 1978). *Sprachlehr- und Sprachlernforschung* (Koordinierungsgremium 1983), an interdisciplinary research based on classroom observation and learner language analysis, was established at German universities. German as a foreign/second language became a regular subject in the academic curriculum.

With respect to migrant workers and their families, additional problems arose: they learn German as a second language and use it in competition with their mother tongue. Their children, most of them born in

Germany, have to learn German parallel to the language spoken in their home which may cause deficiencies in both languages (Stölting 1980). For dealing with such problems it is necessary to integrate findings from sociolinguistics, psycholinguistics, and contrastive analysis of languages. Awareness of cultural differences such as religion, family life, and social behavior are also of great importance. In the Federal Republic of Germany, a new field of interdisciplinary research called *Ausländerpädagogik* (pedagogy for teaching foreigners) was established to deal with such problems.

2. *Aims, Objectives, and Content*

There are two traditional objectives for the teaching and learning of a foreign language: first the mastery of the language for a particular purpose or several specified purposes, and secondly the acquaintance with another culture (often seen as part of a person's getting to know his or her own culture better as well). For migrant workers and their families other aims become more important: the possibility of participating in and being integrated into the German society. In the structuralistic tradition of language teaching, the objectives were also formulated in structuralistic terms or lists of words and structures. The influence of speech act theory and systematic studies of the learners and their specific needs led to a redefinition of objectives so that they would better reflect the communicative aims and social needs of the learners. This new approach was stimulated by the Modern Languages Project of the Council of Europe: the Council wanted "to make the process of language learning more democratic by providing the conceptual tools for the planning, construction, and conduct of courses closely geared to the needs, motivations, and characteristics of the learner. . ." (Trim 1978). On an intermediate level the *Kontaktschwelle* defines the objectives in terms of social domains, communicative roles and skills, speech acts, and topics. On a more advanced level the Goethe Institute and the German Adult Education Association cooperated in developing a certificate program (Goethe Institute 1977), where the objectives for listening and reading comprehension as well as for oral and written performances are defined in terms of four characteristics: intentions, topics, situations, and texts.

Teaching materials often lag behind such developments. In the 1970s, for instance, the discrepancy between communicative objectives and structuralistic materials was strongly felt. In the Federal Republic of Germany, a group of experts examined most of the available textbooks and evaluated them on the basis of pedagogic, linguistic, and cultural criteria (Engel et al. 1977–79). By the beginning of the 1980s there were strong arguments for a differentiation of aims and materials for teaching German in developing countries and in industrialized countries (Gerighausen and Seel 1982). Yet another different set of aims should be established for migrants living in Germany. These should reflect the particular need of a minority group and the relationship between different cultures (Barkowski et al. 1986).

3. *Teaching and Learning Strategies*

Even at the beginning of the 1980s, methodological decisions about foreign language teaching could hardly be based on empirical research findings. Some researchers pointed out the similarity between the acquisition of the first and a second language, and claimed that foreign language teaching might gain from the knowledge accumulated in the field of "natural" first and second language acquisition (Felix 1982). This identity hypothesis, however, was criticized on several grounds: it does not take into account the specific factors of the teaching situation (e.g., learners' strategies, teacher induced errors), and it generalizes from empirical data about some morphological and syntactical elements of the language to the learning (Bausch and Kasper 1979). Most studies aimed at developing instructional materials focused on the needs of immigrant children. Such studies are primarily based on a linguistic approach (Clashen et al. 1982), or on the combination of contrastive analyses, socio- and psycho-linguistic data, and classroom observation data (Stölting 1980 for Yugoslavian children, Meyer-Ingwersen et al. 1977 for Turkish children, Barkowski et al. 1981 for teaching adult migrants).

The dominant approach in the teaching of German as a foreign language is the communicative methodology (Piepho 1981, Neuner et al. 1981): the learners are provided with opportunities for spontaneously reacting to authentic materials in the target language and to use German within the classroom for communicative purposes. This requires the utilization of flexible materials and media. Communication between members of different cultures does not work if teaching is restricted to linguistic items. Intercultural objectives and the training of intercultural perception have therefore become important elements of the foreign language curriculum (Krumm 1989, Wierlacher 1987). Unfortunately, many teachers are not familiar with these developments in the field of linguistics (functional understanding of language), education (learner-centeredness and intercultural education), and methodology (communicative approaches), and hence the necessity of inservice training has been generally acknowledged. Many institutions for training teachers of German as a foreign language offer training programs which include microteaching, the utilization of video models, and the like in order to motivate teachers to change their attitudes towards language, the learner, and their own roles as teachers (AUPELF 1987).

Bibliography

AUPELF The British Council, Goethe-Institut 1987 *Training Foreign Language Teachers*. Triangle No. 6. Didier, Paris

Baldegger M, Müller M, Schneider G, Naf A 1981 *Kontaktschwelle Deutsch als Fremdsprache: Grundlagenpapier des Europarates*. Council of Europe, Strasbourg

Barkowski H et al. 1981 *Handbuch für den Deutschunterricht mit ausländischen Arbeitern*. Scriptor, Königstein

Barkowski H, Fritsche M, Göbel R, v.d. Handt G, Harnisch U, Krumm H-J, Kumm S, Menk A-K, Nikitopoulos P, Werkneister M 1986 *Deutsch für Ausländische Arbeiter*, 3rd edn. Werkmeister, Mainz

Bausch K-R (ed.) 1979 *Beiträge zur didaktischen Grammatik: Probleme, Konzepte, Beispiele*. Scriptor, Königstein

Bausch K-R, Kasper G 1979 Der Zweitsprachenerwerb: Möglichkeiten und Grenzen der großen Hypothesen. *Linguistische Berichte* 64: 3–35

Clashen H, Meisel J M, Pienemann M et al. 1982 *Deutsch als Zweitsprache*. Narr, Tübingen

Engel U, Krumm H-J, Wierlacher A 1977–1979 *Mannheimer Gutachten zu ausgewählten Lehrewerken Deutsch als Fremdsprache*. Groos, Heidelberg

Felix S 1982 *Psycholinguistische Aspekte des Zweitsprachenerwerbs*. Narr, Tübingen

Gerighausen J, Seel P C 1982 Regionale Lehrwerke. In: Krumm H-J (ed.) 1982 *Lehrwerkforschung-Lehrwerkkritik, Deutsch als Fremdsprache*. Goethe Institute, Munich

Goethe Institute (eds.) 1977 *Zertifikat Deutsch als Fremdsprache (DAS)*, 2nd edn. Goethe Institute, München/Deutscher Volkshochschulverband, Bonn

Koordinierungsgremium 1983 *Sprachlehr- und Sprachlernforschunng—Begründung einer Disziplin*. Narr, Tübingen

Krashen S D 1981 *Second Language Acquisition and Second Language Learning*. Pergamon, Oxford

Krumm H-J 1978 Sprachvermittlung und Sprachlehrforschung, Deutsch als Fremdsprache. *Jahrbuch Deutsch als Fremdsprache* 4: 87–101

Krumm H-J 1989 Kulturspezifische Aspekte der Sprachvermittlung Deutsch als Fremsprache. *J. Deutsch Fremdsprache* 14: 121–26

Kufner H L 1962 *The Grammatical Structure of English and German: A Contrastive Sketch*. University of Chicago Press, Chicago, Illinois

Meyer-Ingwersen J, Neumann R, Kummer M 1977 *Zur Sprachentwicklung türkischer Schüler in der Bundesrepublik*. Scriptor, Kronberg

Neuner G, Krüger M, Grewer U 1981 *Übungstypologie zum kommunikativen Deutschunterricht*. Langenscheidt, Berlin

Nickel G (ed.) 1971 *Papers in Contrastive Linguistics*. 2nd Int. Conf. Applied Linguistics, Cambridge, UK, 1969. Cambridge University Press, Cambridge

Piepho H E 1981 *Deutsch als Fremdsprache in Unterrichtsskizzen*. Quelle and Meyer, Heidelberg

Rall M, Engel U, Rall D 1979 *DVG für DaF: Dependenz-Verb-Grammatik für Deutsch als Fremdsprache*. Groos, Heidelberg

Stölting W 1980 *Die Zweitsprachigkeit jugoslawischer Schüler in der Bundesrepublik Deutschland*. Harrassowitz, Wiesbaden

Sturm D 1987 *Deutsch als Fremdsprache Weltweit*. Hueber, Munich

Trim J L M 1978 *A European Unit/Credit System for Modern Language Learning by Adults*. Council of Europe, Strasbourg

Wierlacher A (ed.) 1987 *Perspektiven und Verfahren Interkultureller Germanistik*. Iudicum, Munich

Hebrew

R. Nir

A basic distinction should be drawn between the teaching of classical Hebrew (i.e., Biblical and post-Biblical) and that of modern Hebrew (i.e., the language currently spoken in Israel). This article will be mainly concerned with the formal teaching of modern Hebrew to speakers of other languages in Israel and the diaspora.

1. History

Around AD 200, after having served the Israelis and the Jews for over 1,400 years, Hebrew ceased to be a spoken language. Henceforth, for 17 centuries, it became "the language of the book," and was used by Jews to read the Holy Scriptures and to recite their prayers. During that period the teaching of Hebrew was linked with the study of the Pentateuch, the Mishnah, and the Book of Prayers. Colleges and universities taught Hebrew with a religious aim: to seek in the Scriptures support for Christian doctrines and interpretations. The Reformation, being a Bible-centered movement, accelerated the spread of Hebraic learning among European Christians. By the end of the seventeenth century

Hebrew became a universally recognized discipline in European higher educational institutions, alongside Greek and Latin. In the nineteenth century some impressive archeological findings aroused interest in the Hebrew language; the "archeological movement" found exponents in Europe as well as in North America, and as a result various universities created departments of Semitic studies in which Hebrew was taught beside other Semitic languages.

Until the end of the nineteenth century Hebrew was taught in Jewish communities not as a separate subject, but merely as a part of Jewish culture through the Holy Scriptures. However, in some Jewish schools in Europe special Hebrew grammar lessons were introduced during the Enlightenment (ca. 1770–1880). By the end of the century the revival of Hebrew as a spoken language had begun. This caused major changes in the teaching of the language, first in Palestine and subsequently in the Jewish diaspora. In Palestine, it gradually became an all-purpose spoken tongue. The chief proponent of the revival was E. Ben-Yehuda (1858–1922) (see Sivan 1980). He declared that in order to survive as a national entity the Jews must employ Hebrew for purposes of ordinary intercourse. He claimed that Hebrew should serve as the exclusive classroom language for all subjects, even though for most of the students and teachers it was not a native language. The generation that grew up in these schools later formed the first genuinely Hebrew-speaking families.

After several waves of immigration the number of Jews in Palestine increased from several thousands, at the beginning of the present century, to about 650,000 in 1948, when the state of Israel was proclaimed. The immigrants learned Hebrew as a second language in evening classes, whereas their children learned the language informally by direct exposure.

Since 1948 the teaching of Hebrew in Israel has been conducted in institutions called *ulpanim* (singular-*ulpan*). The success of the *ulpanim* is partially due to the students' high motivation—to gain as quickly as possible a basic working knowledge of the language, which was indispensable for their integration.

The *ulpan* was created as a unique type of school, geared to the needs of a rapidly developing country with large numbers of immigrants; but its methods became, to a certain extent, a model for the instruction of Hebrew as a foreign language in Europe and in the United States (elementary Hebrew courses are often called "*ulpan* classes"). Since the early 1960s a growing number of universities and colleges in North America have been offering modern Hebrew courses, and classical Hebrew has become limited to seminaries and a few universities.

2. Traditional Methods

In the old *heyder* (a religious nongraded elementary school for Jewish boys) Hebrew was learned as the language of the Holy Scriptures. The texts were translated word by word or phrase by phrase mainly into Yiddish. This traditional translation method of learning the language prevailed until the end of the nineteenth century. By that time the natural method was advocated as the major tool for teaching foreign languages (Sweet, Viëtor, Franke). As regards teaching Hebrew, some prominent Hebraists such as D. Yellin and I. Epstein, suggested the teaching of "Hebrew in Hebrew," demanding the discontinuance of translation as a means of instruction. Their motives were nationalistic rather than pedagogical: they believed that the direct method, when applied to the teaching of Hebrew, would be an effective tool for the revival of the ancient language.

In 1937, N. Levin, then the chief inspector for the Jewish agency of Hebrew courses for adults in Palestine, published a curriculum for Hebrew as a foreign language, in which he recommended an eclectic method encompassing pedagogic principles from both the direct method (which he called the Berlitz Method) and the grammar-translation method. Indeed, until 1948 teachers employed various combinations of the two (Sivan 1980).

3. The Ulpan Method and Recent Developments

The *ulpan* method is basically an adaptation of the direct method. The idea of teaching directly through the target language well-suited the heterogeneous population that came to Israel from many different countries. Other influences can be traced to the American Army method and even back to the Reform movement. The vocabulary taught in the *ulpanim* has been a basic and functional one, and the students were required to utilize it by communicating in Hebrew at a very early stage. The use of conversation, role playing, and simulation games became widespread. Hebrew grammar was taught "functionally," and the subject matter was selected so as to serve the primary needs of the learner.

During the 1950s, the teaching of Hebrew as a foreign language in Israeli *ulpan* and in North America was in its preaudiolingual phase. The *ulpan* applied conversation as its chief technique, and in some instances the responses to the teacher's stimuli were in the form of "speaking chorus" (a technique borrowed from the American Army method).

In the mid-1960s the influence of the audiolingual approach to the teaching of foreign languages became stronger. New textbooks were published, based on structural linguistic principles. Graded pattern drill was introduced in the *ulpan*, while the basic orientation towards the direct method still prevailed. Contrastive analysis, which was an important branch of applied linguistics in the 1960s, has also left its traces on the teaching of Hebrew as a foreign language in Israel. Teachers were trained to interpret their students' errors as stemming from intervention of their native tongue; lists including typical errors of various groups of immigrants were made up to alert the teachers.

Surprisingly, very few field studies of the *ulpan* achievements have been conducted. One of these studies was aimed at describing certain aspects of student learning in the so-called "intensive" *ulpan* (Nir et al. 1978). In a survey of these *ulpanim*, where students get approximately 500 hours of Hebrew instruction in absorption centres in a five months' course, some significant relationships were found between student background characteristics and success in reading comprehension of Hebrew texts (as measured by cloze tests). Some of the variables that proved to be of predictive value were age, religion, and occupation: young people, Orthodox Jews, and teachers did particularly well. The study also revealed that in spite of the remarkable progress of most of the students in speaking Hebrew, they were incapable of coping with a news item in a daily newspaper without a teacher's assistance, after a period of five months of learning Hebrew intensively.

The *ulpan* student is trained to acquire communicative competence as early as possible, so that he or she may communicate in Hebrew in real-life situations, even with a rather restricted command of vocabulary. This explains the fact that the *ulpan* method adopted some of the principles that have been recently propagated by the "communicative approach." The communicative approach suits *ulpan* students, who are generally driven both by an "integrative" motivation, as they tend to identify themselves with the surrounding society and its tradition and cultural values, and by an instrumental need for the language. On the other hand, university courses, whether in Israel or in North America, train their students mainly in reading comprehension. To achieve this end the Hebrew University of Jerusalem published a series of graded textbooks based on audiolingual strategies. In these textbooks the structural aspect is given priority over the semantic. These texts are now widely used in Hebrew as a foreign language courses in Israel and in other countries.

Other teaching materials include a series of primers in simplified Hebrew, a series of film strips and records (*Habet Ushma—Say and listen*), a set of television films with accompanying textbooks (*Ivrit Besiman Tov—Hebrew in Good Time*), a Linguafon course, and so on. Two newspapers in easy Hebrew are published in Israel and are used in courses to train learners in following the daily news. In recent years the teaching of Hebrew as a foreign language has been influenced by developments in linguistics, psycholinguistics, and sociolinguistics. This is reflected in the introduction of special courses in these subjects in universities and in colleges geared to train teachers for teaching Hebrew as a foreign language.

Bibliography

Cais J, Enoch P, Stern J 1966 *Hebrew by the Audio-visual Method*. Chilton, Philadelphia, Pennsylvania

Haramati S 1966 Teaching Hebrew to immigrants in Israel. *Mod. Lang. J.* 50: 526–34

Nahir M (ed.) 1981 *Hebrew Teaching and Applied Linguistics*. University Press of America, Washington, DC

Nir R, Blum-Kulka S, Cohen A D 1978 *The Instruction of Hebrew in the Intensive Ulpan in Israel*. Szold Institute for Research in the Behavioral Sciences, Jerusalem (in Hebrew)

Rieger E 1953 *Modern Hebrew*. Philosophical Library, New York

Sivan R 1980 *The Revival of the Hebrew Language*. Rubinstein, Jerusalem

Rivers W R, Nahir M 1989 *A Practical Guide to Teaching of Hebrew*. University Publishing Projects, Tel Aviv

Italian

R. Titone

The teaching of Italian as a foreign language is undergoing a new historical development. The Italian language has passed from a stage where it represented an international literary bond to a stage where it is more and more often used as a utilitarian or instrumental tool for communication in various pragmatic fields. As a consequence, the teaching of Italian as a foreign language has taken on a new impetus and has been directed along new methodological paths.

1. Teaching Agencies

A number of educational and cultural agencies have been concerned in Italy and abroad with spreading the knowledge of the Italian language. The first in time dates from the 1930s and has been named after the great Italian poet, Dante Alighieri. Other institutions of a university or extramural character that run courses teaching Italian as a foreign language are: the Italian University for Foreigners in Perugia, summer schools attached to various Italian universities, private schools, the Italian Center for Applied Linguistics (CILA) in Rome, the Center for Applied Linguistics and Language Didactics (CLADIL) in Brescia, the Cultural Office of the Italian Ministry of Foreign Affairs, and so on.

2. Methodological Trends

The teaching of Italian has followed basically the same evolutionary trends as contemporary language pedagogy. From an early stage of teaching being literature oriented it passed to a second stage of grammar-centered instruction, and finally to a third stage characterized by a functional approach. The latest developments have been determined by the work of the Italian Center for Applied Linguistics which has a special branch devoted to the pedagogical renewal of Italian teaching abroad.

3. Instructional Projects and Strategies

3.1 In Italy

New materials and newly framed teacher training seminars have been produced and organized by agencies such as the Italian Section of the CILA, the *Italiano Come Lingua Straniera* (ITALS) Project of the CLADIL, sections of the Italian Linguistic Society (SLI), and the educational laboratory of the Italian Treccani Encyclopedia. A special Office of the Italian Ministry of Foreign Affairs has sponsored numerous teacher training seminars around the world attended by about 2,000 teachers of Italian as a foreign language.

3.2 Abroad

Foreign experts in the teaching of Italian as a foreign language have worked intensively especially since the early 1960s. They are located particularly at the Universities of Zagreb, Budapest, Moscow, Delft, Sussex, Cambridge, Delaware, Toronto, and in many Italian Cultural Institutes around the world. A few years ago an International Italian Teachers Association (AIPI) was founded, gathering specialists from different countries and continents.

4. Research in the Teaching of Italian as a Foreign Language

The only center devoted to experimental research in the teaching of Italian as a foreign/second language is the Italian Center for Applied Linguistics (CILA) located in Rome and directed by Renzo Titone. A list of pedagogical experimental projects follows:

(a) Range of vocabulary and grammar use—statistical frequency at various levels.
(b) Use of prepositions in Italian and Spanish in light of applied contrastive linguistics and error analysis.
(c) Chief difficulties in learning Italian on the part of Spanish speakers at the phonetic and morphosyntactic levels.
(d) Use of prepositions in Italian and Portuguese: contrastive and error analysis.
(e) Use of the auxiliaries "*essere*" and "*avere*" in passive constructions for Polish learners.
(f) Phonetic and morphosyntactic errors made by Maltese learners.
(g) Language education of immigrants' children in different host countries.
(h) A typology of phonetic and spelling errors made by German learners.

(i) Difficulties in learning Italian on the part of Slovenian students.
(j) Emphasis in Italian and French sentences.
(k) Construction of teaching units for Spanish students.
(l) Construction of courses of Italian for Brazilian students.
(m) The role of grammar in audiolingual courses of Italian.
(n) Allocation in Italian and Spanish with special regard to forms of honor.
(o) Various teaching materials (handbooks and recordings) for students of different countries and areas (Spain, Brazil, South Tyrol, etc.) and for special purposes (scientific Italian for physics, chemistry, and mathematics).

Finally the same center has organized numerous teacher-training courses and workshops on an experimental basis with a view to finding better models of inservice teacher education.

Bibliography

Freddi G 1976 *Il Progetto ITALS*. Lingue e Civiltà [Italian as a foreign language]. Centro di Linguistica e Didattica delle Lingue (CLADIL), Brescia
Katerinov K 1980 *Lingua e vita d'Italia*. [Language and life in Italy]. Mondadori, Milano
Titone R (ed.) 1975, 1980 *L'Italiano come lingua seconda*. [Italian as a second language]. Rassegna Italiana di linguistica applicata, Bulzoni, Roma

Japanese

K. Nomoto

The Japanese language employs a set of phonemes which are relatively easy to pronounce, and its grammar exhibits few anomalies. Still, it is considered a difficult foreign language to master because its grammar reflects a unique way of thinking that is completely alien to European languages. Japanese is a tone language with only a little over 100 different syllable units; these are basically open and of equal length. Tonemes, syllable length, and openness must be mastered if the foreign speaker is to overcome his or her accent.

1. Grammar and Vocabulary

Japanese grammar is simple in that it does not possess gender or number. The relationship of nouns to other sentence elements is marked by suffixes. Verbs are qualified by auxiliaries that are concatenated in a prescribed order. The basic word order is subject–object–verb, with the modifier preceding the modified. Since the Japanese language allows context- or situation-dependent uses of phrases, the subjects and personal pronouns can be omitted whenever they are clearly indicated by the context. One of the most difficult tasks for foreigners to master is the honorifics. Honorific verbs refer to the omitted subjects and pronouns and function in part as substitutes for them. Speakers of Japanese, therefore, always have to grasp well the situation and the context in order to use the honorifics correctly.

There are stylistic differences, related to the honorifics, between oral and written language and between male and female usage. When Japanese is taught as a foreign language, the student starts with the formal style, which does not have male/female differences. However, the transition from this neutral language to the commonly used stylistic forms often presents great difficulties.

The lexicon presents the following characteristics: most words are longer than in European languages; this is due to the small number of syllable variations. There are three lexical groups: *wago*, words that are originally Japanese: *kango*, loan words from Chinese and words formed in Japanese by the use of Chinese characters; and *gairaigo*, loan words from languages other than

Chinese, mainly from European languages. Finally, there are many words with different origins that express similar contents. For example, there are three words which describe a place for a traveler to stay overnight. They are *ryokan*, which is of Chinese origin, *yadoya*, of Japanese origin, and *hoteru*, which is a non-Chinese loan word taken from *hotel*. Since these words are not fully interchangeable, foreigners learning Japanese must acquire a relatively large vocabulary. Verbs of Japanese origin describe basic behaviors and actions. Loan words from European languages constitute 10 percent of the entire vocabulary; however, in everyday usage they cover only 3 percent of the total vocabulary. More than 80 percent of the non-Chinese loan words are of English origin, but their pronunciation and meaning vary greatly from the original, and they are rather troublesome for foreign students.

2. Japanese Writing

Characters consist of *kanji*, Chinese characters imported from China long ago, and *kana* syllabaries formed on the basis of Chinese characters but applied to Japanese. *Kana* syllabaries are subgrouped into *katakana* and *hiragana*. The Japanese writing system uses all three types of characters and is not as simple as the Chinese writing system. The Chinese characters are equipped with two types of pronunciation, one originating from Chinese sounds and called *on* reading, the other originating from Japanese sounds that reflect the meaning expressed by each Chinese character called *kun* reading. These nonunique ways of the pronunciation attached to Chinese characters contribute to the complexity of the written language. In addition to these characters, Roman letters and Arabic numerals are also used. Japanese can be written using only Roman letters. However, printed and handwritten materials using only Roman letters are scarce. It is, therefore, necessary to learn the complex writing system in use in order to cope with the present situation.

3. Learning Japanese

The number of foreigners studying Japanese in Japan increases from year to year. In 1981, the Agency for Cultural Affairs in the Ministry of Education reported the number to be 22,241. The number of students of Japanese abroad was reported by the Japan Foundation to be 263,300 in 1977. The largest number of learners was found in Asia, where 194,000 students were studying Japanese with 600 instructors in 304 institutions. It is also reported that in the People's Republic of China, more than 1,000 students are studying Japanese as a regular subject at 35 institutions and universities. A further 1,000,000 Chinese are reported to be studying Japanese at their workplace or through radio programs at home.

Bibliography

Kindaichi H 1976 *Japanese Language*. Tutle, Rutland, Vermont
Miller R 1980 *The Japanese Language*. University of Chicago Press, Chicago, Illinois

Russian

A. A. Leontiev

The specific characteristics that set the teaching of Russian as a foreign language apart from the teaching of many other languages are connected with its flective and synthetic features and its phonetic and grammar phenomena (palatal consonants, degrees of vowel reduction, a complex system of aspect relations), as well as with the Russian and Soviet cultural peculiarities that are reflected in the language. However, the existence of these peculiarities does not make Russian particularly "difficult" to learn in comparison with other foreign languages.

The motives for studying Russian as a foreign language vary from country to country. For example, in Bulgaria these motives are related to conformity of spiritual cultures, proximity of languages, and the role Russia has played in the history of the Bulgarian people, as well as the uniformity of the two social systems. In the United States pragmatic motives are typical, as well as an interest in Russian and Soviet literature. In many developing countries, Russia is the language of vocational education and scientific texts.

Russian as a foreign language is studied in more than 100 countries, including (according to official Soviet Union data) 54 countries where it is studied in schools. The average number of students is about 23 million at any one time. In Western and Socialist countries this figure has been consistent at approximately the same level since 1970; in Africa it has increased by threefold in the same period; in South and Southeast Asia there has been a twofold increase; in the Near and Middle East an almost threefold increase; and in Latin America almost twice as many students now study Russian as compared to 1970. In 1981 there were 19 million school children studying Russian all over the world. The countries with the largest percentage of students studying Russian in schools where Russian is taught are Poland, Czechoslovakia, Hungary, Bulgaria, the United States, the United Kingdom, and France; the countries with the largest number of students studying the Russian language and literature are Poland, Czechoslovakia, Hungary, Cuba, Vietnam, the United States, the Federal Republic of Germany, Finland, Japan, and

Mongolia. In more than 30 countries Russian is taught over the radio and television. At present it is spoken (with different degrees of proficiency) by over 500 million people. This number makes it one of the world languages. Russian is a working language in the United Nations, UNESCO, and other international institutions.

The teaching of Russian as a foreign language in schools takes place mainly at the secondary level. In universities and colleges Russian is taught primarily in philological departments (including departments of Russian language and literature), although some instruction takes place in other departments. Russian instruction is also given at adult study circles and courses and in regular and correspondence courses designed to improve the language skills of teachers of Russian as a foreign language and scientists studying the language and literature. In the Soviet Union instruction is given to foreign students on college and university preparatory courses (where Russian is taught as the language of professional instruction).

The dominant method of teaching Russian as a foreign language is through the conscious-practical method based on the principle of active communication. Other methods such as the audiovisual, audiolingual, and suggestive methods are also used, though they are less popular. The principal textbooks are published in the Soviet Union, the most prevalent being the series *Russian for Everyone* written by Z. Yevleva, E. Stepanova, and L. Trushina, and edited by V. Kostomarov. So far five editions have been published and in 1979 it was awarded the Soviet Union State Premium prize. The series consists of the proper textbook, a reader, an exercise book, a grammar book, a speech practice book, a film course, a "language and culture" supplement, and a set of records. There are several variants of the series designed for different native language speakers. Among other standard textbooks and instruction series upon which national variants are based are *The Russian—1, 2, 3* (for elementary-school children), *The Horizon* (for teenaged children), *Start* (for college preparatory courses), and *Tempo* (for adult study circles and courses). In many countries Russian language teaching is based upon the textbooks written by teams of authors composed of people from the native country as well as from the Soviet Union (e.g., USA, UK, Finland).

In 1967 the International Organization of Russian Language Teachers and Literature (MAPRYAL), was founded with V. V. Vinogradov as president. The organization unites 162 collective and individual members from 63 countries and is governed by an executive council. It regularly holds international congresses. These have been held in Moscow (1969), Varna (1972), Warsaw (1976), Berlin (1979), and Prague (1982). The organization's journal *Russian Language Abroad*, has been published at the rate of six issues a year in Moscow since 1967 and offers theoretical articles and instruction materials to be used in the classroom. In 1981 42,000 copies were sold. In Western countries there exist a number of independent national associations.

The Pushkin Institute of Russian Language was established in 1973 as an extension of the Moscow University science-methodical centre for Russian language (founded in 1966) and is now the leading instructional institution. It comprises departments of research and education and provides trade-improvement courses for foreign teachers of Russian and foreign students of philology. In 1982 it had approximately 3,400–4,000 students annually in regular classes as well as 1,500 on correspondence courses. The institute coordinates the activity of about 500 departments of Russian as a foreign language in Soviet institutes and has branches in Brazzaville (Congo), Bratislava (Czechoslovakia), Budapest (Hungary), Warsaw (Poland), Havana (Cuba), Prague (Czechoslovakia), and Ulan Bator (Mongolia). In addition there are national institutes and centres of Russian language in a number of countries working mainly in the field of instruction. There are also national journals on Russian language problems (e.g., *Język zosyiski* in Poland, *Bulgarska rusistica* in Bulgaria, and *Ruštinar* and *Ruský jazyk* in Czechoslovakia). The Russian Language Publishing House in Moscow produces textbooks, manuals, readers, scientific and methodological literature, and dictionaries.

Bibliography

Leontiev A A 1973 Some problems in learning Russian as a foreign language: Essays on psycholinguistics. *Soviet Psychol.* 11(4): 1–117 [1974 *Psycholinguistik und Sprachunterricht.* Kohlhammer, Stuttgart]

Kostomarov V G 1975 *Russkii yazyk sredi drugikh yazykov mira.* [Russian among other languages of the world.] Prosveshchenie, Moscow

Russkii yazyk: Entsiklopediya. 1979 [Russian language encyclopaedia.] Sovetskaya Entsiklopediya, Moscow

Russkii yazyk v sovremennom mire. 1974 [The Russian language in the modern world.] Nauka, Moscow [1977 *Die russische Sprache in der heutigen Welt.* Enzyklopädie, Leipzig]

Spanish

M. E. Ruiz

The teaching of Spanish, or any other language, as a foreign language implies the introduction of people to the language and their familiarization with it. The form of Spanish most commonly taught as a foreign language is Castilian as it is spoken in the central region of Spain—Castille.

In order to teach a language it is helpful to know a little about its history, its structure, and some of the physical problems that may be encountered in mastering its pronunciation.

Castilian has developed principally from the Latin, together with other Romance languages spoken in Spain, of which the two main ones are Catalán and Gallego. The Basque language has considerably more obscure origins, still in dispute. In addition to Latin, the two main influences in the development of modern Castilian have been the Germanic and Arabic languages. These were introduced during the invasion of the Goths from the north and then of the Moors from the south. The Romance languages, which include Italian, French, and Portuguese, have many points in common, making them mutually quite comprehensible. Many words have the same root and the grammatical structure of the sentence is very similar. Thus it is much easier for those whose native languages belong to the Romance group to master Spanish than for those whose mother tongue does not.

Spanish as a foreign language is not often taught as either the second or third language in the United Kingdom or other countries of Europe. In most of the latter countries, English is the second language, followed by French or German.

In the Netherlands, for example, as in all European countries where there is a community of Spanish expatriates, the teaching of Spanish tends to be limited to keeping them in contact with their mother tongue and culture. In Belgium a similar situation prevails. Courses are also available for others interested in learning Spanish. One such course is based on the book *Lengua y Vida Españolas*.

The teaching of Spanish in the United Kingdom is rarely introduced in schools before the sixth form, that is, until the age of 16 or 17. In the first year the O'level syllabus is covered, which concentrates on the linguistic aspect, giving a good grammatical grounding supported by conversation classes, preferably supplied by a native Spanish speaker. In the second year the student is introduced to literature and taken up to A'level.

Adult teaching methods approach the language slightly differently, usually because there need not be an examination at the completion of the course. At the Oxford University Language Teaching Centre and the Oxford College of Further Education the conversational element is stressed. Classes are conducted in Spanish and backed by grammatical instruction when the need arises. A language laboratory is also always available for the student to continue studying independently. The British Broadcasting Corporation has organized beginners' and continuation courses, providing books and tapes. There have been television courses on current affairs, giving the student ample opportunity to improve his or her understanding of the language, while getting used to the accent and at the same time becoming more familiar with Spain, its culture, and its people. *Radio Naçional de España, Servicio de Transcripciones* also provides tapes on current affairs, such as *Panorama de España* and *Crónica de un año*. Longman's have published courses, which are not only used in the United Kingdom but also in other European countries, for example, *Eso Es* in two stages. The Spanish Embassy in many countries as well as the education authorities and institutions have evolved their own courses, often based on existing courses but adapted to their own needs, or even using a combination of parts of many courses. However, all these audiovisual, audiolingual, teach yourself, and other methods of teaching still need some grammatical backing, and there again many works have been published. *An Essential Course in Modern Spanish* by Ramsden is widely acclaimed both from the point of view of its completeness and from that of its ease of comprehension. At the University of Manchester tape drills have been produced to accompany Ramsden's book.

In Europe, English is considered the International language in science, technology, and for business transactions. The volume of trade within the EEC, which is related to the gross national product of its member nations far outweighs any trade with Spain or the other Spanish-speaking nations. This situation explains the lack of importance given to the teaching of Spanish, since the remaining reasons for learning it are: general interest, a desire to establish social contacts (for example on vacation) or a career as a professional linguist.

In contrast to this in the United States, particularly in California, the teaching of Spanish is of much greater importance because of the proximity of the Latin–American countries. The language is introduced to the children at primary-school level although some will already have had contact with Spanish-speaking children at an even earlier age. Their vocabulary is increased by using picture cards, posters, cut outs, dramatization of daily situations and of well-known stories, and dialogues such as role reversal of teacher and pupil which may be much more extensively used than with the older student. The younger pupils also tend to find less difficulty in adapting to differences in pronunciation, to sounds with which they are unfamiliar.

Without going into the phonetics of the Spanish language in any detail, the main difficulty presented by Spanish pronunciation, to the foreigner, is the sound of the jota, phonetic symbol "x" as in the Scottish "lo*ch*". Confusion may arise between the soft c or z whose pronunciation is "θ" (the English "*th*in") in Castilian, but in some Southern regions of Spain and in Latin America it is pronounced as an s, as in "*sea*". Otherwise the Spanish pronunciation is quite straightforward, each vowel having a single sound. There are no diphthongs; even when two vowels follow each other, each retains its own sound. The three extra "letters" in the Spanish alphabet are: "ch" (t∫) as in "*ch*at", "ll" (j) as in "*y*es" (these letter combinations have individual status in the Spanish alphabet) and "ñ" (ɲ) as in "o*ni*on". The letter "h" is always silent. The rules for pronunciation of the letters, once learnt, never vary.

In common with all other languages it is not possible to make general rules concerning the teaching of Spanish to foreigners. It has been mentioned that Spanish as a Romance language has many points in common with French, Italian, and Portuguese. These common features are useful points of reference for the development of a course.

Although not as abundant, there are still significant points of comparison with other European languages that share common Latin roots and common points of grammatical construction. At the other extreme it is clear that the methods will have to be entirely different when there is no common base whatsoever between Spanish and a mother tongue such as Japanese or Chinese.

It must therefore be concluded that there can be no absolute rules concerning the techniques of teaching Spanish or any other language as a foreign language. The teaching must be adapted to the requirements of the student.

Bibliography

British Broadcasting Corporation (BBC) 1978 *Dígame: A Combined Television and Radio Course for Beginners in Spanish.* BBC, London

British Broadcasting Corporation (BBC) 1979 *Por Aquí: Spanish Comprehension.* Radio Continuation Course. Longman, London

British Broadcasting Corporation (BBC) May 1979 *Realidades de España: Television Course (Adv.).* BBC, London

Lorenzo Criado E 1978 *Lengua y Vida Españolas.* Editorial Mangold, Madrid

Masoliver H et al. 1975 *Eso Es: Audio Lingual Course for Beginners.* London

Radio Nacional de España 1982 *Panorama de España* and *Crónica de un Año.* (Tapes with duplicated texts.) Radio Nacional de España, Apartado, Madrid

Ramsden H 1959 *An Essential Course in Modern Spanish.* Harrap, London

Ramsden H n.d. Tape drills to accompany *An Essential Course in Modern Spanish.* Manchester University, Manchester

Swahili

M. Hauner

The teaching of Swahili as a foreign language can be divided into two broad categories: (a) teaching of Swahili in East Africa, and (b) teaching of Swahili outside East Africa, particularly in Europe. These two categories can be paralleled with historical developments.

1. Teaching of Swahili in East Africa

This category can be subdivided historically into (a) the time before European colonization (before the end of nineteenth century) when Swahili was taught informally by trade contacts existing between the Swahili people of the coast of East Africa and the ethnic groups in the interior, for example, the Giryama of Kenya and the Nyamwezi of Tanzania, etc. and (b) the period following European colonization when European and other white missionaries, business people, and farmers arrived, and Germany and the United Kingdom set up formal colonial empires. During the colonial era (1890s to 1960s), Swahili was used in administration in East Africa, and therefore was taught in local schools in order that the local inhabitants, the vast majority of whom spoke other languages, would become proficient in Swahili.

2. Teaching of Swahili Outside East Africa

Category (b) overlaps historically with the early stages of the period when Swahili began to be taught outside East Africa after the German, British, and French missionaries found that it was a *lingua franca* throughout East Africa, and could conveniently be exploited as such in missionary education. Missionaries laid the foundation of a systematic study of Swahili. J. L. Krapf, a German missionary, had the first systematic grammar published in 1850, and a substantial dictionary (433 pages) in 1882. Between the 1880s and 1930s, formal courses in Swahili were offered at universities in Austria (*Institut für Ägyptologie und Afrikanistik an der Universität Wien*), Belgium (*Université Coloniale de Belgique*, Antwerp, and *Université de Louvain*), England (Universities of London, Oxford, and Cambridge, and Germany (*Seminar für Orientalischen Sprachen an der Universität zu Berlin*, and *Hamburgisches Kolonialinstitut*). Courses were offered to members of the colonial service, missions, and business firms, and to university students. Individual missionary orders also organized their own language courses.

After the independence of Kenya (1963), Tanganyika (1961), and Zanzibar (1963), Swahili continued to play a role in those countries' educational systems. By 1982 in Tanzania (formed in 1964 by the unification of Tanganyika and Zanzibar), Swahili was taught and/or was the language of instruction in preschool, primary, and secondary education, and at the University of Dar es Salaam (Department of Swahili). In Kenya it is studied in primary and secondary schools, and at the University of Nairobi (Department of Linguistics), while in Uganda it has no formal place in the curriculum. Since most of the languages spoken in Tanzania belong to the Bantu group, as does Swahili, it is less difficult for most Tanzanians to learn than it is for Kenyans and Ugandans, many of whom speak non-Bantu languages. Swahili is also taught at schools in Zaire, Rwanda, and Burundi.

During the late 1950s, when independence in East Africa was becoming iminent, Swahili was one of the first African languages to find its way into university curricula of countries which had had no colonial empires in Africa. Thus Swahili was offered in the Soviet Union (Leningrad and Moscow) in the late 1950s, followed by Poland, Czechoslovakia, and the Democratic Republic of Germany, and has been taught ever since. The Scandinavian countries followed, too, as did the United States from the early 1960s, and today Swahili is taught on every continent, from informal private coaching to advanced university courses. While most countries concentrate their Swahili teaching at universities, short-term practical courses aimed at expatriate workers are organized independently, too. University-level teaching of Swahili in the 1980s has been reported for the following countries: Australia, Austria, Belgium, Brazil, Burundi, Canada, People's Republic of China, Czechoslovakia, Denmark, Egypt, United Kingdom, France, the Democratic Republic of Germany, the Federal Republic of Germany, Ghana, Hungary, India, Italy, Israel, Japan, Mozambique, Nigeria, Norway, Poland, Rwanda, South Africa, Soviet Union, Sweden, Switzerland, United States, Zaire, and Zambia.

Since the adoption in Tanzania of a socialist system of government in 1967 (Ujamaa), Swahili courses overseas have gained in popularity among university students in general, and among black students in particular. As more foreign aid was coming to Tanzania after 1967, more foreigners went there, as well as to Kenya, as workers connected with aid projects. Many worked in exclusively Swahili-speaking environments, and needed some knowledge of the language. In 1979 in the United States alone there were at least 130 university-level Swahili courses offered.

3. Swahili Published Courses

There are numerous published courses of Swahili available now in many languages, most of them introductory-level ones. Some are accompanied by magnetic tapes or cassettes. A well-constructed tape enhances the study greatly. Intermediate to advanced courses are rare, and students and teachers tend to use secondary materials like Swahili stories, novels, magazines, and newspapers published in East Africa, and recordings of Swahili speakers. There are Swahili dictionaries and vocabularies available in many languages, as well as a Swahili–Swahili one, produced in Tanzania (1981).

4. Teaching/Learning Problems

Swahili is not a tonal language, and its phonology is not complex compared to other African languages. Because its basic grammar is regular, its spelling phonetic, and its pronunciation easy for most students, the beginning stages of learning Swahili are relatively easy. At the intermediate and advanced levels, Swahili syntax and semantics are complex and demanding. The study of Swahili poetry of the "classical" type requires a knowledge of Arabic as the incidence of Arabic loan words is high and it is almost exclusively written in the Arabic script. Except for its use in poetry, the Arabic script was abandoned under colonial influence starting around the turn of this century. It is rarely taught nowadays as part of Swahili courses.

Bibliography

Akida H et al. 1981 *Kamusi ya Kiswahili Sanifu.* (A Standard Swahili–Swahili Dictionary.) Oxford University Press, Dar es Salaam, Nairobi

Ashton E O 1944 *Swahili Grammar, Including Intonation.* Longman, London

Duffy D, Frey M M 1979 *Directory of African and Afro-American Studies in the United States.* Crossroads, Brandeis University, Waltham, Massachusetts

Hinnebusch T J, Mirza S M 1979 *Kiswahili, Msingi wa Kusema, Kusoma na Kuandika* [Swahili, a foundation for speaking, reading and writing]. University Press of America, Washington, DC

Jahadhmy A A 1966 The teaching of Swahili as a foreign language. *Swahili* 36: 100–04

Kiswahili Journal of the Institute of Swahili Research, University of Dar es Salaam, Nairobi

Perrott D V 1951 *Teach Yourself Swahili.* Teach Yourself Books, Hodder and Stoughton, London

Whiteley W H 1969 *Swahili: The Rise of a National Language.* Methuen, London

Section 7

Humanities Curricula

Overview

The articles contained in this section review research related to the teaching of humanity subjects taught in schools. Kridel describes trends in the *General Education Curriculum* indicating that the basic purpose of such curricula is to educate individuals to a common culture, however conceived. This article which deals with humanities education in general terms precedes a series of articles which focus on individual school subjects.

Philosophy in precollege education is taught mostly as an elective subject and programs differ widely from country to country. Lipman reports on an interesting attempt to include elements of philosophy into the primary school curriculum in his article, *Philosophy Programs: Primary Schools*, and Zahn addresses issues related to philosophy programs in secondary schools in the article, *Philosophy Programs*. Thomas provides a cross-cultural overview of *Religious Education* in schools and examines the forms and aims of religious education in an age of mass communication.

The major humanities subject taught in schools across the whole world is literature. In teaching literature, more than in most school subjects, great emphasis is put on shaping attitudes toward the topic of the studies and creating an appetite for reading books of lasting value. Three articles deal with issues related to literature. Purves surveys the history of literature curricula in schools, examines the nature of current curricula and summarizes the current state of curriculum research in his article, *Literature: Educational Programs*. Beach discusses the importance of acquiring a positive attitude towards reading and examines the impact of parents, home environment, and school on developing such an attitude. The article by Lamb and Sanati contains a survey of *Children's Literature* in three different cultural settings: in the Western countries, in the Soviet Union, and in Iran.

The last article in this section, *Classical Languages Curricula* by Vester, deals with the place of classical languages (ancient Greek and Latin) in the contemporary secondary school, the content and the aims of teaching classical languages, and the impact of research related to teaching modern languages on the teaching of classical languages.

A. Lewy

Humanities Education

Introduction

M. R. Grumet

The problems of definition and scope associated with the humanities are essential to their methods and purpose. As inquiries that probe the nature of the human species, the humanities study the history of human action and examine the objects shaped by human experience and imagination. The study of philosophy, the interpretation of literature and history, and the criticism of art, music, and theatre all question the limits, depths, and capacities of the human spirit. The question, "What are the humanities?" may not be answered with an inventory of disciplines, methods, forms, and purposes, for this is the question that the humanities are organized to pursue. Although the project of definition has been sustained by humanities scholars throughout centuries of Western civilization, humanities educators have been intolerant of their disciplines' refusal to provide conclusive answers to the questions they pose. Beyond testifying to a human capacity to organize, interpret, and give value to experience, humanities texts are often required to provide examples of reason, imagination, and compassion. Educators have struggled to achieve a consensus regarding those works, and the values and methods that provide the best models for the young. The design of a contemporary humanities curriculum must address the competing claims of reason and emotion, language and experience, the integrity of the disciplines and the relativism of all knowledge, an elitist tradition, and a plural culture.

The Classic Ideal of Humanities

Many of these issues are as ancient as the humanities themselves. The classical conception of the humanities originated in the Hellenistic tradition of *paideia* which signified the general education required to develop a harmonious and balanced person. The Romans drew the idea of human sympathy through *paideia* into their conception of education as *humanitas* which grounded the Greek ideal in the concerns fostered by family and community. Silverman's history of the humanities identifies the rhetoric of Isocrates as the keystone of Hellenistic education. This art of rhetoric was the rich expression of civic virtue and practical knowledge and

not merely a formal or stylized argument. The Roman *artes liberales* adopted Isocrates' conception of rhetoric as an art of discourse suited to the discussion of government and ethics. Whereas Plato distrusted language and regarded metaphysics to be a higher form of human reason than the art of argument, Isocrates, equating eloquence with understanding, identified language as the essence of humanity and celebrated its capacity to express the relationships that give order and meaning to human experience (Silverman 1973).

In the Middle Ages the *artes liberales* evolved into the arts of words, known as the trivium: grammar, dialectic, and rhetoric; and into the arts of things, known as the quadrivium: arithmetic, geometry, music, and astronomy. Silverman argues that the classical conception of the humanities, or *artes liberales*, emphasized their methodological or structural coherence rather than pure content. The disciplines were related to each other through the principles of philosophy or metaphysics. A general education required an understanding of the principles of each discipline and of their interrelationships rather than the specialist's mastery of detail and methodological proficiency.

It is from the harmony of *paideia* and the meta-disciplinary coherence of the *artes liberales* that the contemporary expectation that humanities education should integrate its disciplines is derived.

Cultural Criticism or Consensus

The mutual estrangement of what C. P. Snow (1962) has called the two cultures, namely the arts and the sciences, and the identification of the humanities with the arts only, followed the seventeenth century's embrace of natural philosophy. As sciences became identified with general laws of prediction and control contained in codes and symbols that precluded language, the humanities became identified with texts associated with particular persons. The poems, philosophies, narratives, and histories that constitute the humanities express the material conditions of human life as well as the imagination that resists and transforms these constraints and determinations. Although the Greco-Roman integration of the arts and sciences and the civic and ethical focus of the rhetorical tradition support the claim that the study of the humanities develops and reinforces a common culture, the humanities provide, as well, visions that are more often subversive than conventional. It is the capacity to challenge a culture at the same time as employing its ancient forms that Trilling celebrated in his famous essay, *On the Teaching of Modern Literature* (Trilling 1965). Within the humanities are expressed those emotions and instincts whose repression has been exacted by the civilization that readmits them as art. The humanities traditions encompass many contradictory themes. They are grounded in reasoned argument yet express emotion and deep commitments. They require the study of specific texts, eschewing generalization and abstraction, yet are understood to provide the basis for a common culture. They are associated with a highly educated, class-bound elite, yet are expected to express universal concerns that all people can grasp. They are expected to build community although they undermine consensus. They represent the integration of human faculties yet rely on specific disciplines of interpretation, often defined in opposition to the natural and social sciences.

As the articles in this Section all argue, every humanities curriculum, whatever its discipline, rests on the politics and processes of interpretation. Drawing on the philosophical studies of Dilthey and Gadamer, humanities educators have turned to hermeneutics to resolve conflicts between individual and collective determinations of meaning. Hermeneutics, the study of interpretation, summons students to examine the social, historical, and cultural roots of the symbol systems that encode the meanings they discover in text. By emphasizing the social sources of meaning and inviting students to draw deliberate and reasoned distinctions between those traditions of thought they have inherited and those they choose to bring forward into their own futures, hermeneutics challenges students to think, read, write, and converse critically.

Humanities Curriculum in the United States

A humanities curriculum assumes many shapes throughout its history, each expressing the conflicts, compromises, or consensus of its constituents.

Colonial education borrowed the classic curricula of European universities to educate clergy and statesmen to civic virtue, initiating them into the linguistic and philosophical traditions that would link a frontier culture to its European past. The common school movement of the nineteenth century was preoccupied with establishing the conventions of the classroom and extending literacy and socialization to the frontier, as well as to the new urban centers. This regimen was relieved by the progressivism of the 1920s and 1930s. Bringing expression and the arts into the schoolroom, John Dewey promoted curricula that integrated schooling with practical experience. Dewey had maintained

that the compartmentalization of the disciplines imposed artificial boundaries and dichotomies on a natural intelligence that drew upon all of its cognitive, volitional, and affective resources in solving the problems of everyday life. The "core" curriculum that Flexner brought to the Lincoln School of Teacher's College organized the disciplines around themes related to life situations employing the "project method" (Cremin 1961).

As the United States and the Soviet Union competed for technological supremacy in the 1950s, the humanities languished until the youth of the 1960s repudiated war, materialsm, and schooling, and educators turned to the humanities again. In the late 1960s and early 1970s humanities courses were used as a lure to draw youth back to the culture they saw as morally and spiritually defunct, and back to curricula they saw as empty and alienating.

Oehler's study of humanities programs in secondary schools in the United States in the early 1970s noted that the seven disciplines that appeared most frequently in these programs were: art, music, literature, drama, philosophy, history, and art history. Instructional materials most frequently employed were films, books, graphics, recordings, and music. Preferred class size was small to permit class discussion, and humanities classes were most frequently taught by teams of between two and four teachers. Most courses were voluntary but chosen by students described as superior or above average and college bound. Oehler reported very little use of prepackaged materials or of state curriculum guides. His research suggests that these interdisciplinary curricula were developed locally by the teachers who taught them. Stated aims of the programs were to help students clarify personal values, to develop creativity, to understand the great ideas of Western civilization, to develop an understanding and commitment to universal values, to develop an appreciation of aesthetic values, and to transmit a cultural heritage (Oehler 1973).

Silverman has identified four major curricular motifs that structured these interdisciplinary humanities courses: aesthetic education, the cultural epoch, great themes, and great books. Critical of the epistemological confusion of these efforts, Silverman charges them with substituting expressiveness for understanding, approximate and superficial study for probing scrutiny of specific texts, and facile relativism for ethical philosophy (Silverman 1973).

Humanities and Class Structure

The Latin root *liber* originally referred to the bark of a tree, then to a book, as in "library" and "libel." The adjective *liberalis*, pertaining to free man, was originally, according to the *Oxford English Dictionary*, "a distinctive epithet of the arts and sciences that were considered worthy of a free man, as opposed to servile or mechanical . . . pertaining to or suitable to persons of superior social station, becoming a gentleman." The humanities tradition was bonded to class and gender and for centuries was designated as the formal education that marked its students as those suited by both birth and training to civic responsibility and power.

When inherited wealth was the qualification of the ruling class, humanities education was employed as a preparation for the responsibilities of civic leadership. Those countries that employ qualifying exams to distribute their adolescents between schools leading to industry and schools leading to university have tended to maintain classical languages, history, and literature in a rigorous humanities curriculum leading to higher education. As comprehensive secondary schooling was organized to encourage social equality, humanities curricula substituted modern languages for their classical forebears. In the United Kingdom as access to higher education has been extended by bringing secondary students together in comprehensive schools, reading and writing in Latin has frequently been replaced by classics in translation. Whereas the knowledge of antiquity had provided a special and esoteric code that distinguished the elite from the masses, the democratization of the humanities curricula coincided with the emergence of science and technology as the social and epistemological codes promising employment and status. In Italy, where the classical lyceum used to enroll three times as many students as the science lyceum, there were, in 1980, twice the number of students in the science lyceum than there were in the classics program (Merritt and Leonardi 1981). Williamson argues that socialist countries such as the Soviet Union and the German Democratic Republic permitted the sciences and the children who study them to form an educated elite, which, while it provided the skills required by modern industry, undermined the claim to a classless society (Williamson 1979).

In Third World countries where humanities education is often associated with colonial rule, it is often seen as an obstacle to economic growth, a social distinction that alienates a small urban and affluent minority from the poor and rural populace of the country. In India, from 1960 to 1961 there were over 1,192,000 professionals in the labor force. Ninety percent of them held degrees in law, arts, and commerce in a country of great graduate unemployment where two-thirds of all those employed work in agriculture. Julius Nyerere's self-reliance plan for Tanzania's education turned away from the humanities curriculum of urban culture and toward a practical education in agriculture (Williamson 1979 p. 21).

In the United States the humanities have been criticized for presenting a portrait of humanity that excludes the culture and experience of the working class, of racial minorities, and of women. Critics have challenged the exclusion of texts that reveal the experience of those engaged in manual labor, the absence of folk arts from the museums and art history courses, and the confinement of history to the accounts and exploits of men.

As departments and programs for black studies, Third World studies, and women's studies developed in the universities, source material and course outlines were developed for public secondary and elementary schools, many supported by Title IX funds. In the 1970s humanities curricula became noticeably diversified, offering more courses in comparative religions, the literature of minorities and women, and the art and cultures of Africa and Asia.

Even though the humanities have been attacked for perpetuating class, racial, ethnic, and sex bias, they are still pictured as disciplines that promote understanding and tolerance. A 1974 report describing civic and social education in the member countries of the Council of Europe celebrates the methods of humanities curricula that contribute to world citizenship and morality rather than their content. Written interpretation and group discussion promote social awareness, independent thinking, and pupil involvement in school and community life (Rust 1974).

The Methods of the Humanities

Even more critical than the content of the humanities courses are the methods they employ. The support for humanities education that emerged in the 1960s expressed the need to humanize the curriculum, to make it relevant and responsive to students' lives. Accordingly, humanities curricula were organized around questions drawn to address students' feelings and experience as well as their sense of ethics. Related to "values education" these courses used texts as springboards for discussion about the nature of society or violence, of love or of loneliness. At their best these courses encouraged the active participation of their students. At their worst they slid into dogma, or rambling discussions which lacked method, specificity, clarity, and focus. Multidisciplinary courses encouraged team-teaching and diminished the professional and intellectual isolation of public secondary school teachers. When bi-disciplinary courses increased the depth of study by accompanying the study of literature with that of the history or art of the period, they provided students with occasions for careful analysis and thoughtful interpretation. When literature was coupled with the social sciences, it was frequently used to illustrate psychological or sociological theory. The complex history and structure of a particular text were relinquished so that a theme such as class struggle or alienation could be emphasized.

Threatened by the instrumentalism and vagueness of affective education on one side, humanities education was even more vulnerable to the commodification of curriculum into kits and packages. By reducing individualized instruction to a format of isolated busy work, elementary and secondary school curricula abandoned the careful study and discussion of texts for exercises in reading comprehension followed by endless pencil and paper puzzles and exercises requiring one word answers or the correct choice from a multiple choice offering. Stripped of the discourse conventions that stimulate critical and creative thinking, the study of literature and history had become technical, and humanities teachers had become timekeepers and distributors of materials (Carlson 1982). Students were not reading, writing, or speaking with enough frequency to foster a rich appreciation for language or an extensive repertoire of expression. The reconceptualist critique of education was a response to the failure of humanities education to provide students and teachers with an opportunity to interpret and reflect on the culture they shared (Pinar 1975).

Dismayed by low reading scores and poor writing skills, educators responded with an emphasis on basic skills and competency exams designed to require minimum competence in the common branches of the curriculum as a prerequisite for promotion and/or graduation. The 1980 Report of the Commission on the Humanities discouraged "narrow utilitarian approaches to literacy" and called for the reintroduction of basic skills into humanities disciplines where writing, reading, speaking, and thinking are cultivated; "through history, the ability to disentangle and interpret complex human events; through literature and the arts the ability to distinguish the deeply felt, the well wrought, the continually engrossing from the shallow, the imitative and the monotonous; through philosophy the sharpening of criteria for moral decision and warrantable belief" (Report of the Commission on the Humanities 1980 p. 12). The Commission commended a project in aesthetic education developed by the Central Midwestern Regional Educational Laboratory (CEMREL) designed to provide a vocabulary for aesthetic criticism as well as regional centers to provide aesthetic education for teachers, and a Philosophy for Children Program developed by Matthew Lipman of the Institute for the Advancement of Philosophy for Children at Montclair State College, New Jersey. Both of these programs provide a rationale for the devel. opent of critical thinking. The Humanities Curriculum Project (1970) in England was similarly focused on the discipline of discussion, engaging its teachers in developing a protocol for critical discourse in the classroom.

Another project closely tied to the contexts where it is realized is the Program for the Development of Humanities Disciplines within the Schools (PDHDS). It brings humanities scholars into public schools where they work with teams of teachers to research, revise, or create new humanities curricula. The program is investing its resources in teachers by sharing the power of humanities scholarship with them and by inviting them to engage in research and curriculum development that are stimulating and intellectually compelling. Related projects inviting public school and university collaboration are the Yale/New Haven Teacher Institute, and Bay Area Writing Project which gathers teachers from 56 sites together in the summer to share ideas and study.

Bibliography

Carlson D 1982 Updating individualism and the work ethic: Corporate logic in the classroom. *Curric. Inq.* 12: 125–60

Commission on the Humanities 1980 *The Humanities in American Life: Report of the Commission on the Humanities.* University of California Press, Berkeley, California

Cremin L 1961 *The Transformation of the School: Progressivism in American Education, 1876–1957.* Vintage Books, New York

Humanities Curriculum Project 1970 *The Humanities Project: An Introduction.* Heinemann Educational Books, London

Merritt R, Leonardi R L 1981 The politics of upper secondary school reform in Italy: Immobilization or accommodation? *Comp. Educ. Rev.* 25: 369–83

Oehler Jr J S 1973 *A Study of Secondary School Humanities Programs in the United States.* University Microfilms, Ann Arbor, Michigan

Pinar W 1975 *Curriculum Theorizing: The Reconceptualists.* McCutchan, Berkeley, California

Rust W B 1974 *European Curriculum Studies No. 9—Social and Civic Education.* Manhattan Publishing, New York. ERIC Document No. ED 102 078

Silverman J 1973 *A Criticial Analysis of the Philosophical Foundations of Secondary School Humanities Programs.* University Microfilms, Ann Arbor, Michigan

Snow C P 1962 *The Two Cultures and the Scientific Revolution.* Cambridge University Press, New York

Stake R 1972 Responsive evaluation. *New Trends in Evaluation, No. 35.* Institute of Education, University of Goteborg, Goteborg

Trilling L 1965 On the teaching of modern literature. In: Trilling L (ed.) 1965 *Beyond Culture: Essays on Literature and Learning.* Viking Press, New York

Williamson B 1979 *Education, Social Structure and Development.* Holmes and Meier Publishers, New York

Willis G 1978 *Qualitative Evaluation.* McCutchan, Berkeley, California

General Education Curriculum

C. Kridel

General education curriculum is a programmatic resolution to the basic dilemma: "What knowledge is of most worth?" Countless definitions of general education have emerged throughout the twentieth century, as different educators attend to this dilemma, so emerge the diverse conceptions. Yet, a basic purpose of general education has developed, namely to educate individuals to a common culture, however conceived. Fundamental to this purpose is the educator's belief in shared learning experiences for all students. The interpretations of common heritage and shared experience then provide the framework for the various definitions and conceptions of general education.

What remains consistent among the varying perspectives is the relationship of general education to other administrative components of the curriculum. Since in the secondary school it continues to be a counterpart to vocational education, general education becomes that component of the curriculum that provides a "basic knowledge of life" (or aspects of common culture and heritage) but does not necessarily carry the burden of providing knowledge for occupational ends.

In a larger administrative sense secondary general education may become a program, or curricular track, in and of itself. The general program becomes an option for students along with an academic program (typically college preparatory) or a vocational program. It should be noted that the common usage of "general program" is markedly different from the specific conceptions of general education that will be described.

When general education is discussed at the post-secondary level it typically is juxtaposed to specialized education. The curricular components at this level include general education, the academic major (specialized knowledge), and the elective.

These administrative perspectives serve merely to display general education as a component within the entire school program. The specific conception and development of those educational experiences that constitute general education vary widely; they are not determined necessarily by an administrative perspective but, instead, by a foundational, normative conception of what constitutes a common body of knowledge for all students.

1. Issues in General Education Curricula

When educators begin determining what knowledge constitutes a general education program, a variety of curricular issues emerge. The process of resolving them is what gives character to programs and provides the different conceptions of general education.

A basic issue of general education results from the most commonly held definition: general education is the encyclopedic mastering of important information. This curriculum emphasizes a vast array of information, comprehensive in scope and carefully structured. Yet knowledge, however common and important, is conceived within the traditional subject disciplines; no effort is made to integrate this general education curriculum. In addition, knowledge is presented as a body of information to be mastered, independent of the experiences of the learners. Little effort is made to portray the relevance of the information for the learner. While curriculum integration and recognition of ex-

perience are not presupposed for general education, their absence may greatly weaken a program.

A long-standing criticism of general education stems from accusations of elitism, regularly associated with liberal education curricula at the post-secondary level. Knowledge represented in general education programs often reflects the values of a Western European aristocracy which, as inherently maintained by educators, will "elevate" students into society and allow them to share a common cultural heritage. Knowledge is justified for its own sake and offers no utilitarian ends, thereby perpetuating the notion of general education for the privileged class. As general education became associated with fostering democratic principles and educating all youth, such accusations created serious problems for the curriculum developer.

Related to the criticism of elitism is the problem of indoctrination and the imposition of values. When one identifies knowledge for all students, one's own values as well as those of school and society become embedded in the selection of content. This content may present "a common heritage" to the learner, yet the culture is constructed from a set of imposed and, perhaps, questionable values and mores. Indoctrination becomes more of a concern for those educators who view the purpose of general education to develop autonomously thinking citizens of a free society. The development of such persons seems negated by a predefined, value-imposed curriculum.

2. Types of General Education Programs

From the basic curricular issues described above (as well as various others), the curriculum developer is left to construct a general education program. Four fundamental types of programs best represent the many different examples of general education curricula.

2.1 General Education within Separate Subjects

The most traditional and commonly held conception of general education is that of common learnings as identified within the separate subjects of the school curriculum. The accumulation of a specified number of courses (or units) constitutes the general education program. The focus of curriculum development becomes the identification of basic, important knowledge that will be learned by all students; emphasis is placed upon determining content and deciding the representation and amount of instructional time devoted to the separate subjects. Little effort is made to integrate the general education knowledge within these separate subjects. Conant's (1959) Carnegie Corporation report best represents this perspective. General education graduate requirements for all students included four units of English, three or four units of social studies, one unit of mathematics, and one unit of science.

This perspective of general education reflects a larger view of school curriculum, one imposed by college entrance requirements. The Carnegie Foundation in 1909 proposed the Carnegie Unit as the standard form of measurement for high-school credit (a unit is determined by the completion of 120 study hours in a subject during the school year). The widespread acceptance of the Carnegie unit, though solely for the quantitative measurement of assessing credit for college admission, served to help separate the school subjects. When the curriculum is conceived in this manner, general education curriculum development becomes a matter of selecting and totaling units.

2.2 General Education as Core Curriculum

While attending to the importance of developing common, basic educational experience for all youth, many curriculum designers have sought to integrate knowledge into a core curriculum (see *Core Curriculum*). According to Alberty (1947), core curriculum is "that aspect of the total curriculum which is basic for all students, and which consists of learning activities that are organized without reference to conventional subjects lines" (p. 154). Many core programs have underscored a conception of "democracy as a way of life" and used the classroom relationship between teacher and students to portray this democratic ideal.

Alberty and Alberty (1962) identified five types of core programs which are distinguished according to the degree of curricular integration. Type 1, separate subject core, while officially identified as core curriculum, is more within the general framework of separate subjects, common learning in general education (as previously described). Type 2, correlated core, allows teachers of two required core courses to show interrelationships between their separate subjects. Students continue to meet within a traditional, separate subject format, but content of the separate disciplines is related. Type 3, fusion core, consists of broad problems, units of work or unifying themes which are chosen because they afford the means of teaching effectively the basic content of certain subjects or fields of knowledge. These subjects or fields retain their identity, but the content is selected and taught with special reference to the unit, theme, or problems. A Type 4, broad problems core, is based upon common problems, needs, and interests of students within a framework of problems areas. This core consists of a number of fields of knowledge which are unified; knowledge is no longer conceived according to traditional subject fields. A Type 5, no preplanned structure core, consists of broad units of work or activities planned by the teacher and students in terms of needs as perceived by the group. A basic curriculum design is established, yet no curricular experiences are predefined.

2.3 General Education as Learning Traits

In some instances general education programs, while facing the difficulty of specifying content, have turned to the identification of traits or abilities which emerge from general education experiences. Thus, the focus of the program becomes the establishment of common traits that all students will develop as opposed to focusing upon content. The Harvard Redbook, *General Education in a Free Society* (1945), is an example of this perspective, though it also identifies guidelines for selecting content for secondary general education (as well as for colleges and in some instances for elementary schools). The Redbook identifies abilities, or "traits of mind," that develop through general education experiences. These are thinking effectively, communicating thought, making relevant judgments, and discriminating among values.

Since this conception of general education focuses not so much on specific content as on the outcomes of knowledge, flexibility is provided in the selection of content. A recent example of this perspective is Harvard's efforts in 1978 to revise their general education program. In this conception general education becomes the student's ability to think and write clearly and effectively; to appreciate ways in which we gain knowledge; to know other cultures and other times; to understand and experience moral and ethical problems; and to achieve depth in some field of knowledge. From these learning traits specific course requirements and criteria were established. General education as learning traits seems more common at the postsecondary level in part because of the teachers' (faculty's) autonomy in selecting content.

2.4 General Education as Realms of Meaning and Modes of Inquiry

A unique aspect of general education curriculum emerged in the 1960s with the publication of Phenix (1964) and Bell (1966). Phenix took general education curriculum to a more abstract level when he defined general education as "the process of engendering essential meanings" (p. 5). These meanings emerged as individuals engaged in educational experiences within six identifiable realms (or patterns): symbolics, empirics, aesthetics, synnoetics ("direct awareness" through personal or relational knowledge), ethics, and synoptics (comprehensive, integrative meanings). Phenix identified specific guidelines for selecting content, yet the unifying, common experience was not solely in content but in experiencing all six realms of meaning. "Without these [six realms] a person cannot realize his essential humanness" (p. 270).

Bell introduced the idea of a "third-tier" program where conceptual inquiry serves as a methodological basis for the unity of general education. Content continued to center upon the disciplines, but the manner in which this material was conceptually organized and presented to the student—the modes of inquiry—became an organizing feature of the curriculum and a topic for study and reflection. Bell assumed this form of general education would occur after secondary' education where emphasis had already been placed upon primary learning skills and factual data.

3. Conclusion

One should not be surprised by the diversity and lack of consensus among general education programs. The complexity of the most basic question of general education—what knowledge is of most worth—somewhat necessitates a variety of programmatic interpretations. Two factors, however, do cause difficulty for those involved in the revision of general education. The first is the dominance of a separate subject curriculum: fostered by college entrance requirements and perpetuated by the case of student evaluation, a separate subject curriculum can easily overlook many of the important issues in general education. The second is that many revisions have "gone astray" because those in charge did not have a general education of the field of general education, that is, curriculum design and development was initiated with little knowledge of past efforts in general education. Yet, as educators continue their efforts to revise and reconceive the curriculum, knowledge of society, the learner, the disciplines, and the field of general education itself will provide many refinements as well as fresh conceptions for general education curricula.

Bibliography

Alberty H 1947 *Reorganizing the High School Curriculum*. Macmillan, New York

Alberty H B, Alberty E J 1962 *Reorganizing the High School Curriculum*, 3rd edn. Macmillan, New York

Bell D 1966 *The Reforming of General Education: The Columbia College Experience in its National Setting*. Columbia University Press, New York

Boyer E L 1983 *High School*. Harper and Row, New York

Boyer E L, Levine A 1981 *A Quest for Common Learning: The Aims of General Education*. The Carnegie Foundation for the Advancement of Teaching, Washington, DC

Conant J B 1959 *The American High School Today: A First Report to Interested Citizens*. McGraw-Hill, New York

Harvard Committee 1945 *General Education in a Free Society*. Report of the Harvard Committee. Harvard University Press, Cambridge, Massachusetts

Harvard Committee 1978 *Report on the Core Curriculum*. Offices of the Dean, Faculty of Arts and Sciences, Harvard University, Cambridge, Massachusetts

Goodlad J I 1984 *A Place Called School*. McGraw-Hill, New York

Leonard J P 1946 *Developing the Secondary School Curriculum*. Rinehart, New York

Phenix P H 1964 *Realms of Meaning: A Philosophy of the Curriculum for General Education*. McGraw-Hill, New York

Philosophy Programs: Primary Schools

M. Lipman

The early 1970s saw the first stirrings of efforts to introduce philosophy as a systematic discipline into elementary-school classrooms. Over the next decade, what had begun tentatively and experimentally had become established as an accepted discipline and had expanded into every American state as well as into many other countries. Parents and administrators seemed to base their approval on the significant bettering of children's academic performance that resulted from the sharpening of their logical skills. And children, responding readily to the opportunity to discuss their concepts, values, and ideals in an open and objective manner, also appeared favorably disposed. Some consideration needs to be given to the historical sources of so intriguing and so unexpected an educational development.

It will be recalled that Greek philosophy underwent a drastic change during Plato's lifetime. Previously it had been literary—aphoristic, poetic, dramatic—and in practice conversational. Indeed, so nontechnical and dialogical was it that Socrates, apparently with little difficulty, could converse philosophically with children. The earlier phase of philosophy, in consequence, was nonacademic and exoteric. But by the time the Academy had been established, it had become customary to present philosophy in lectures and to write it in exposi-

tory prose. Within a generation, it had become esoteric and academic. Ever since, philosophy "proper" has been the academic philosophy of the college and the university, only occasionally seeping down, in somewhat popularized versions, into the upper reaches of the secondary school, the lycée, or the gymnasium.

One senses in Socrates the conviction that philosophy is thinking at its best, and that to educate children is to provoke them to think well, from which it follows that philosophical activity must be central to the educational process. The emphasis here is upon philosophy as an activity—a dialogical, self-monitoring, self-corrective activity—rather than upon the products of such an activity: those distinctions, canons, theories, and systems which proceeded to become the content of philosophy as an academic discipline and an historical tradition. It is within this perspective that philosophy for children can be viewed as the reawakening of something long dormant rather than as a transient and momentary educational mannerism.

Those who prepare the groundwork for the introduction of philosophy into the elementary school appear few and far between in the earlier phases of the modern era. In Renaissance France, Montaigne sees the readiness of the child for philosophy, but the philosophy he has in mind is the philosophy of the adult tradition. A century later, Locke advises parents and teachers that children treated with respect and without condescension will be able to engage with little difficulty in philosophical conversation. Still another century passes before Richard and Maria Edgeworth break fresh ground with their *Practical Education*, in which they recognize in the child's ability to reason philosophically the foundation of the educational process. Yet one more century must go by before John Dewey brings the wheel around full circle by proposing that educators must set as their primary goal the fostering of thinking rather than the acquisition of knowledge, and that the school as an institution be judged by its effectiveness in getting children to think for themselves.

Meanwhile, other twentieth-century developments help set the stage: the emergence of the philosophy of language with special attention being given to ordinary language and to nonformal logic, as in Wittgenstein, Austin, and Ryle; the recognition of the social and cooperative impulses of the child, as in G. H. Mead, Piaget, and Vygotsky; the spotlighting of the educational importance of analytical or "metacognitive" skills, as in Bruner and Flavell; and the growing awareness that if the "acquisition of knowledge" approach to education stressed the learning of terms (of which isolated facts would be one example), then the "thinking" approach to be devised would have to stress relationships: logical, social, geographical, aesthetic, geometrical, ethical, arithmetical, and so on.

Philosophy for children always has dialogue at its core, whether the children are 15 years old or in kindergarten. To provoke the dialogue, there must be a classroom experience which models and expresses the involvement of children and ideas, and which can be reflected upon and analyzed in the ensuing discussion. This initial experience can be provided by the children script-reading an episode from a specially written philosophical novel, or by a puppet performance, or by the reading of a poem—anything that will dramatize the interplay of ideas in the life of the mind. As the conversation brings one or another philosophical notion into focus, the teacher is able to draw upon the resources of instructional manuals which provide discussion plans, reasoning games, and other philosophical activities, so as to lend further structure and direction to the discussion, with the aim of converting the classroom eventually into a community of inquiry. Needless to say, most teachers require extended and intensive education before they can properly hear the philosophical implications of children's conversations, and before they can effectively orchestrate classroom dialogue so as to follow the ideas where they lead.

Another factor which contributes to the success of philosophy in the elementary school is the mobilization of the reasoning skills which are among the philosopher's most characteristic stocks-in-trade. The adroitness with which philosophers demand reasons, draw inferences, seek definitions, and ferret out underlying assumptions is evidence that they are highly practiced in the very analytical skills which interpenetrate every area of learning. Little wonder that contemporary educators find it profitable to study the moves philosophers make in the course of their discussions, for it is when children learn to make such moves that their reading and writing becomes more meaningful. Nor should it be surprising that educational research has shown, on repeated occasions, that the introduction of philosophy into the elementary school, when taught by properly trained teachers, produces significant improvement not only in reasoning, but in the established educational disciplines as well.

Perhaps the most important change brought about by elementary school philosophy is the improvement of student judgment. As classroom discussion proceeds, students repeatedly encounter problems for which there are no clear-cut answers. Subtle differences in context are discovered, with the result that one must make appropriate revisions in the meanings of terms, the assumptions one makes, and the inferences one draws. It is found necessary to appeal to more and more compelling reasons, that is, to criteria, and it is those criteria that students finally learn to employ to guide them in making appropriate judgments about the issues under discussion. It is by means such as these that primary school philosophy students become more reasonable and more judicious.

Such philosophy as is to be found in the secondary school is generally taught in the final year or two before graduation, and far more resembles college philosophy than philosophy for children. It would not be absurd to suppose, however, that children exposed to eight or ten years of philosophy before they arrive at the typical high-school or college introduction to philosophy are likely to place very different demands upon the methods of instruction than those which are at present familiar. If at the moment the impact of a university-level subject upon children is being watched, it may not be out of place to wonder about the eventual impact of philosophically sophisticated young people upon the university.

See also: Philosophy Programs

Bibliography

Glatzel M, Martens E 1982 *Philosophieren im Unterricht 5–10*. Urban and Schwarzenberg, Munich

Lipman M 1988 *Philosophy Goes to School*. Temple University Press, Philadelphia, Pennsylvania

Lipman M, Sharp A M (eds.) 1978 *Growing Up With Philosophy*. Temple University Press, Philadelphia, Pennsylvania

Lipman M, Sharp A M 1980 *Philosophy in the Classroom*, 2nd edn. Temple University Press, Philadelphia, Pennsylvania

Matthews G B 1980 *Philosophy and the Young Child*. Harvard University Press, Cambridge, Massachusetts

Matthews G B 1984 *Dialogues with Children*. Harvard University Press, Cambridge, Massachusetts

Pritchard M S 1985 *Philosophical Adventures with Children*. University Press of America, Langham, Maryland

Philosophy Programs

L. Zahn

In the Western world, the school as an institute of training and of education has its roots in philosophy. The term "school" in Greek means leisure, referring to the fact that Greek philosophers thought of school (the academy of Plato, the lyceum of Aristotle, the Stoa) as a place of communication during their free time. In this leisure time, Greek citizens could forget daily concerns and devote attention to their own existence, trying to understand themselves, their aims, motives, and in general, the meaning of their lives. The inscription on the temple of Apollo at Delphi, "know thyself," has remained throughout the ages what Hegel called the "absolute commandment of philosophy." The human race should not merely acquire an extensive body of knowledge, but should learn to appreciate itself as the bearer of all ways of knowing. The word philosophy (philo-sophia) means friend of wisdom.

1. The Content and the Method of Philosophical Teaching

In classical Greek philosophy, questions concerning the substance of appearances fell into several different areas. *Metaphysica generalis* investigated general modes of being and statement, and contained the fields of ontology and logic. *Metaphysica specialis* dealt with questions of God, world, and humankind and contained the disciplines of theology, psychology, and cosmology. Psychology in turn was subdivided into the theory of knowledge and what Kant called a practical philosophy, embracing the questions of rational behavior, ethics, and politics. Hegel was the last thinker who tried to unite these disciplines into a systematic survey of all knowledge. Despite his efforts, new and independent disciplines emerged in the domain of philosophy such as aesthetics, philosophy of history, linguistics, legal or social philosophy, theory of learning, anthropology, and so on. This expansion of the contents of philosophy made it necessary to select topics for study and therefore teaching no longer follows a single obligatory pattern. The oldest method of transmitting teaching is the Socratic dialogue. In the Middle Ages, the scholastic method developed from a fixed supernatural revelation in Holy Writ. This approach was rejected after the advent of Kant's transcendental method, which focused on investigating the relationships between objectivity and our reasoning. For Fichte, von Schelling, and Hegel the state of consciousness manifests itself in the phenomenal world, and the dialectic method attempts to reconstruct this as a process of experience mediated through contradictions. All these methods are rejected as purely speculative by the theoreticians of positivism. For them, the method of philosophy is reduced to the gen-

eralization of scientific processes into logical rules and models, what Popper calls a "logic of research." Opposed to these explanatory methods, the hermeneutic method, basing itself on history and tradition, seeks to understand manifestations of culture, and interpret them in accordance with the present state of knowledge.

2. Forms of Academic Teaching

In ancient times, two different forms of philosophical teaching prevailed: dialogue and systematic exposition. The first was practiced by Socrates and Plato and the last by Aristotle. Both approaches exist in our time too. Today the dialogue appears in a new guise as the modern "discourse." Philosophy is conceived as an argumentative construction concerned with existential questions, and with questions related to the aims of human action. According to this concept, philosophy has a lifelong task. Its practice assists in acquiring a qualified common sense. The form of teaching which may best lead to the attainment of this aim is the seminar. Von Humboldt referred to it as the "successful conversation." The other tradition of teaching, common in continental countries, viewed philosophy, in contrast to individual scientific disciplines, as a discipline concerned with systematizing and integrating the totality of human knowledge. This view coincides with Hegel's contention that truth can be found only in the unity of the whole, which gives meaning to particular bits of knowledge.

3. The Teaching of Philosophy in Grammar Schools

Until about 1800 most European countries had similar patterns of teaching philosophy, which consisted of first learning Latin, then philosophy, and finally specialized studies. Philosophy was taught with the aim of acquiring a general orientation to human knowledge. Since Kant had stigmatized "school philosophy" as mere dogmatism and had raised the intellectual complexity of the subject, it turned out to be very difficult to teach it in grammar school. At preuniversity level, instead of teaching philosophy, it was recommended that logic and psychology be taught as propaedeutic subjects, but these recommendations were rarely realized. After the First World War, educational programs prescribed the teaching of text-orientated philosophy concerned mainly with the history of ideas and after the Second World War, interest shifted towards teaching ethics within the framework of philosophy studies. In the 1980s, philosophy in high schools is mostly an elective subject (see *Elective*

Subjects). In some educational institutes it is offered as a substitute for religious studies. Ecology and the peace movement have given strong impetus to teaching social, political, and moral philosophy. A survey conducted by UNESCO (1953) in 16 European countries pointed out the great divergence of high-school philosophy courses from the point of view of scope, content, and aims.

Bibliography

Püllen K 1958 *Die Problematik des Philosophieunterrichts an höheren Schulen: Ein Beitrag zum Verhältnis von Philosophie und Bildung.* Schwann, Düsseldorf
Schmucker-Hartmann J 1980 *Grundzüge einer Didaktik der Philosophie.* Bouvier, Bonn
UNESCO 1953 *The Teaching of Philosophy: An International Enquiry of UNESCO.* UNESCO, Paris

Religious Education

R. M. Thomas

Because there exists no universal agreement about the meaning of either religion or education, there is likewise no agreement about what constitutes the field of religious education. Therefore, at the outset of this review of religious-education studies, it is useful to identify which meanings will be assigned to these two terms.

Writers who conceptualize religion in a broadly inclusive way define it variously as "the collective expression of human values," as "the zealous and devout pursuit of an objective," or as "a system of values or preferences—an inferential value system." Such definitions are so broad that they encompass not only the belief systems of Christianity, Islam, and Hinduism but also those of communism, democracy, logical positivism, and even anarchism.

Other writers place far greater limitations on the term religion, proposing that a conceptual scheme qualifying as religion must be an integrated system of specified components, including the nature of a supreme being or of gods (theology), the origin and condition of the universe (cosmology), rules governing human relations (ethics, morals), the proper behavior of people toward superhuman powers (rites, rituals, worship), the nature of knowledge and its proper sources (epistemology), and the goal of life (teleology). Under this second sort of definition, Christianity, Islam, and Hinduism are religions but communism, democracy, logical positivism, and anarchism are not.

The second of these conceptions of religion seems to be the one intended by most people who write or speak about religious education, so it is the one adopted here for identifying matters which rightly belong in the field of religious education.

Just as religion has been defined in various ways by different writers, so has education. In its broadest sense, education can be equated with learning. And learning can be defined as "changes in mental process and overt behavior as a result of experience." However, for the purposes of the following review, education is defined in a narrower sense to mean "the activity carried on by a society's institutions of systematic, planned instruction." Such a definition eliminates from consideration kinds of learning informally acquired during people's daily social interaction, as through their conversations in the family or through models of behavior offered by their companions. It eliminates as well learning acquired through the incidental use of libraries, book shops, newspapers, and recreational radio and television.

When the forgoing preferred definitions are combined, they identify the realm of religious education as being that of "systematic, planned instruction in beliefs about the nature of the cosmos and of a supreme power, about rites and worship, about personal moral values and the ethics of human relations, and about the meaning and goal of life."

It is well at the beginning also to recognize a distinction between religious instruction and instruction about religions, since both of these types can be classified under the rubric religious education. The term religious instruction traditionally has meant teaching the doctrine of a given religion with the intention of convincing the learners that this religion is the true one, and its tenets and practices are to be honored as the correct ones. Such religious instruction, aimed at converting learners both intellectually and emotionally to a set of convictions, continues to be by far the dominant form of religious education in all parts of the world. In contrast, instruction about religions is a relatively recent development, with the teacher describing various religions rather than seeking to convert learners to a particular faith. Studies bearing on both of these varieties of religious education are included in the following pages.

The review of studies is organized around six aspects of religious education. Each aspect is described and trends in its development are traced. The six are (a) forms of religious education, (b) aims or objectives, (c) instructional methods and media, (d) educational personnel, (e) administration and finance, and (f) evaluating religious education. The review of these six is prefaced by a brief overview of the estimated number of followers of the major religions of the world. The article closes with an estimate of the state of recent research on religious education.

1. Major Religions and Their Followers

The best present-day description of the spread of religions was published in 1982 in the *World Christian*

Encyclopedia, the product of a 14-year research effort by D. B. Barrett that included identification of the world's major and minor religions and of the location and numbers of their adherents. By 1980, in an estimated total world population of 4,374 millions, the major religions reported the following numbers of advocates (with the percentages of the world population represented by each religion indicated in parentheses). Christianity had 1,433 millions (32.8 percent), non-religion and atheism 911 millions (20.8 percent), Islam 723 millions (16.5 percent), Hinduism 583 millions (13.3 percent), Buddhism 274 millions (6.3 percent), Chinese folk religion 198 millions (4.5 percent), tribal and shamanist religions 103 millions (2.4 percent), new religions 96 millions (2.2 percent), Judaism 17 millions (0.4 percent), and others 36 millions (0.8 percent) (Ostling 1982 p. 66). Compared to estimates in 1900, Christianity's percent of the world population by 1980 had diminished only slightly (34.4 to 32.8) while the percentages of Moslems, Hindus, and new religions had grown slightly. The greatest increase of any category over the 80-year period was in people professing either no religion or else atheism (from 0.2 to 20.8). Chinese folk religion had dropped dramatically (23.5 to 4.5), Buddhism had decreased by 1 percent and Judaism by 0.4 percent. While these figures illustrate gross trends in religious affiliation, they fail to make clear the changes that have occurred within a given religion. Christianity, in particular, has experienced a marked shift in the proportion of adherents from one denomination to another. For example, Barrett reported that in 1900 two-thirds of all Christians lived in Europe and Russia, but he estimates that by the year 2000 three-fifths of them will live in Africa, Asia, and Latin America. Likewise, the traditional Reformation denominations (Lutherans, Presbyterians, and the like) no longer have the majority of followers, but are outdistanced by evangelical groups (Ostling 1982 p. 67).

The continuing strength of religions and the changes in the percentages of adherents in different groups are partially the result of differing degrees of success of religious education. And the marked growth in nonreligious people is likewise a result of educational efforts that discredit religion. Often these efforts are sponsored by such political movements as communism.

2. Forms of Religious Education

The term forms refers to the various combinations of time and location used for providing religious instruction. The following overview proceeds from forms that involve the largest amounts of time to those that involve the least, a range extending from full-time boarding schools to only occasional religious study. The limited research about the relationship between the amount of time spent on instruction and the thoroughness of religious learning supports the commonsense notion that the more time spent in religious study, the greater the religious knowledge acquired and the deeper the

religious conviction (Hartman 1979, Himmelfarb 1977). Consequently, the forms described early in this overview can be expected to lead to greater achievement of the religious goals than do the ones described later.

2.1 Full-time Boarding Schools

The institutions providing the greatest amount of time for religious instruction are schools in which students live full time, following a curriculum that is entirely or dominantly religious. In such settings, students' class time and out-of-class study hours not only focus on religious issues, but mealtimes and leisure hours are often imbued with religious teachings and rituals as well.

Full-time boarding schools trace their beginnings back to ancient days. In modern times most residential schools of this type are found in Asia and Africa, attended almost exclusively by boys and young men. While such institutions also exist in Europe and in the Americas—principally at the college or seminary level—they are far fewer in number and more often include secular subjects in the curriculum (mathematics, social science, science) than do the traditional Asian and African varieties.

In Islamic regions the residential schools are much alike, focusing chiefly on the Koran and other Islamic scriptures and on the Arabic language, even though the schools are known by different titles in different regions—madrasah in Arabic countries, khalwa in the Sudan, pesantren in Indonesia, and pondok in Malaysia. In Hindu India, where the schools center on the study of the Vedas and other Hindu writings and often on techniques of meditation, they are known as ashrams. In Buddhist Thailand they are wat schools.

In terms of worldwide trends, full-time religious schools have been diminishing both in number and in the proportion of their religious subject matter in comparison to secular subjects. In developing nations, this decrease in religious schools apparently has been caused chiefly by the developing societies' "modernization programs," with modernization meaning the adoption of the socioeconomic values and technology of industrialized Western nations. Graduates of a traditional religious curriculum find themselves poorly equipped for the job requirements of the newly evolving vocational world, so that learning to be a "good person" in a religious sense no longer suffices for succeeding socially and economically in a society stressing new values.

2.2 Full-time Day Schools

Next to boarding schools, the intensity of religious education is greatest in full-time day schools that concentrate exclusively on religious studies. They are much like the religious boarding schools in curricula and organization. Often the two types are identical, with the same school enrolling both resident students and ones who live at home and attend classes only during the day.

More numerous than day schools that teach only religious subjects are those whose curriculum includes a combination of religious and secular studies. An example of this type is the Islamic madrasah in Indonesia, the nation with the largest Moslem population in the world at over 130 million. The Indonesian version of the madrasah was first inaugurated in the second decade of the twentieth century by Islamic reformers to make religious education more relevant to the requirements of modern secular life, yet retain the essential elements of traditional Moslem schooling. In present-day Indonesian madrasahs, which numbered over 30,000 by the mid-1970s, between 50 and 75 percent of class time is devoted to secular studies (Indonesian language, mathematics, science, social studies, local language or English, the arts) and the remainder to Moslem topics (the Koran, the Hadits or sayings of the Prophet Muhammad, principles of Islamic faith, Islamic law, Arabic language, and others) (Postlethwaite and Thomas 1980).

To learn that a day school includes both secular and religious studies fails to inform us clearly of the amount of religious education students receive, since the amount of time dedicated to religious subjects varies so greatly from one school to another. In fact, the practice of combining religious and secular subjects in most school systems consists of dedicating only one class hour a day or only one or two hours a week to religious topics, with the rest of the school hours focusing entirely on secular studies. In school systems that enroll pupils from various religious sects, religious studies are often provided through a released-time arrangement, with pupils released an hour or so a week from their secular studies to follow instruction offered by a religious teacher of their own persuasion. Such teachers are often priests, pastors, or knowledgeable laypersons. Under these arrangements, religious education is systematic but in a relatively small amount.

2.3 Supplementary Day Schools

In many parts of the world, pupils not only attend a secular school, but also daily attend one that concentrates on religious studies. Such a pattern of paralleling secular schooling with religious education appears to have evolved in two principal ways in different societies.

In one case a dominant, traditional religious-school system has been largely displaced in recent decades by a secular public system. The displacement has occurred either because parents have come to judge religious education as inadequate preparation for youths to progress in a modernizing socioeconomic system or because the government requires that all children follow a curriculum that includes an array of secular subjects not taught in the traditional religious schools. Under such conditions, the displaced religious school assumes a supplementary-education role, offering its daily lessons during hours before or after the secular-school sessions. One example of this pattern is provided by the present-day *faifeau* (pastor) or catechist schools in the Samoan Islands of the South-Central Pacific. These schools were introduced in the mid-nineteenth century by Christian missionaries, who established the institutions in villages throughout the islands to give instruction in religious topics and in reading the Bible in the Samoan language. Eventually such secular topics as geography, history, and arithmetic were added to the curriculum. Faifeau schools served as the chief educational institutions in the islands until far into the twentieth century. However, today they have been largely replaced by secular public schools, particularly in American Samoa. At present, faifeau schools, as a way of adjusting to changing times, are conducted for only an hour or two in the early morning or evening and/or when pupils are on vacation from secular schools. In Malaysia a similar pattern of development has occurred, with pupils attending in parallel both a secular school and a traditional Islamic pondok.

The second type of parallel school has developed, not from religious schools gradually being displaced by secular education, but rather from parents' desire to have their children obtain systematic religious education in addition to the secular instruction received in a public school system. An example is the Jewish supplementary school in the United States, a ccommon type of religious education in the nation which by 1980 contained the world's largest Jewish population at 7.1 million. The typical supplementary school meets in the late afternoon twice during the week, such as on Tuesday and Thursday for an hour or two, and on Sunday for perhaps three hours. At the elementary level the subjects of study are Jewish history and culture, the biblical Old Testament, and Hebrew language. At the secondary level such subjects as Jewish law, ethics, and comparative religion are frequently added.

2.4 Occasional Classes

Much religious education, particularly since the spread of secular schooling, has been only an occasional event, such as a child's attending Sunday school or an adult's attending a church, mosque, temple, or synagogue for an hour or so once a week. Or people may engage in religious study at home by means of radio or television broadcasts, self-instructional lessons distributed by a religious organization, or a small group of adherents meeting to analyze holy scripture.

3. Aims and Objectives of Religious Education

The goals of religious education can be viewed from a variety of perspectives, three of which are (a) the overt versus the implied, (b) indoctrination versus comparison, and (c) the cognitive versus the affective.

3.1 Overt Versus Implied Objectives

The objectives of religious education may either be stated directly or only be implied by the methods of instruction and the observed outcomes of religious-training programs. Typical openly stated objectives are illustrated by the following examples drawn from official descriptions of religious groups' educational goals or from proposals by scholars in the field.

An example from Islam is a statement endorsed by 313 Moslem scholars attending the First World Conference on Moslem Education held at Mecca in 1977:

> Education should aim at the balanced growth of the total personality of Man through the training of Man's spirit, intellect, the rational self, feelings, and bodily senses. Education should therefore cater for the growth of man in all its aspects: spiritual, intellectual, imaginative, physical, scientific, linguistic, both individual and collectively and motivate all these aspects towards goodness and the attainment of perfection. The ultimate aim of Muslim education lies in the realization of complete submission to Allah on the level of the individual, the community, and humanity at large. (Husain and Ashraf 1979 p. 44)

A widely adopted Christian statement of goals derives from a National Council of Churches of Christ (USA) study paper:

> The objective of Christian education is to help persons to be aware of God's self-disclosure and seeking love in Jesus Christ, and to respond in faith and love—to the end that they may know who they are and what their human situation means, grow as sons of God rooted in the Christian community, live in the Spirit of God in every relationship, fulfill their common discipleship in the world, and abide in the Christian hope. (Cully 1963)

As a more detailed proposal, M. C. Miller (1977 pp. 54–58) has suggested five goals as appropriate for Christian education. First is the objective of developing an attitude of respect and concern for others. "If we are persuaded to love God and to love others as ourselves, we are dealing with an attitude toward the whole of life." Second is creating amicable relationships, "the I–thou relationship." Third is learning religious content, in the sense of education as an intellectual discipline— "to develop beliefs that are consistent with our view of the world as derived from all sources, especially science." Fourth is establishing personal morality by recognizing religion's "supreme importance for the meaning of living." Fifth is developing social ethics so that the individual is not just personally "good" but also works for the common welfare—"civil rights, racial harmony, open housing, or the liberation of oppressed groups."

In contrast to overt objectives are those which we can only infer are being pursued, for they are not openly described. The inference is drawn from the nature of the methods and materials used, or from the beliefs and behaviors the learners eventually exhibit. There are at least three reasons why goals may be left unstated.

First, the program planners may believe their objectives are self-explanatory, that is, so obvious to anyone that they need not be explained. For example, religious educators may feel it unnecessary to state that the aim of studying the Torah for Jews, the Koran for Moslems, the Vedas for Hindus, or the Bible for Christians is to understand God's will and thereby know how to attain a desired life after death.

A second reason is that religious educators may not recognize that certain unintended outcomes result from the methods and materials they are using. In this case, the goals are being attained unintentionally or out of ignorance. For instance, Adamu (1973 p. 54) quotes Alhaji Aminu Kano as criticizing the Koranic schools of Northern Nigeria for having a curriculum:

> "arbitrary in form, bookish in style, and hopeless for promoting social ideals and usefulness. It has done nothing but make the work in the school lifeless and killing." The Koranic schools, he points out, have utterly failed to appeal to the child, "but succeeded in promoting drudgery, loading the child's mind with fantastic facts which she or he never understands." Consequently, the child becomes mentally disabled, and the products of such schools are a mass of static adolescents "who make a static society."

In leveling these charges at the religious schools, Aminu did not propose that the teachers were intentionally producing dolts and laggards, but rather that they were unwittingly achieving such undesirable ends.

> The present-day Koran teacher, beside being a most disqualified teacher or educator, appears to be a menace to the children's world and in the educational field; for not only is he hopelessly ignorant of modern conceptions, but is not ready to accept them. (Aminu in Adamu 1973 p. 55).

It should be noted, however, that not all unintended outcomes are negative ones. For example, the Buddhist wat schools of Thailand serve as a vehicle of upward social mobility for boys of lower-class families, an outcome not advertised as a purpose of the schools but one which, nevertheless, most parents likely recognize when they enroll their sons.

A third reason certain objectives may be left unstated is that the religious educators or their sponsors are intentionally exploiting their followers. That is, the leaders promote their own welfare rather than that of the learners, a condition that the leaders do not wish their followers to discover. Such educators have been accused of intentionally teaching in ways that cause learners (a) to be afraid to inquire into controversial theological and social issues, (b) to feel guilty about ever doubting the leaders' word, (c) to obey the leaders without question, (d) to accept a subservient or degrading role in life as being the learners' just due, (e) to hate people of other sects or ethnic groups, and (f) to sacrifice one's own needs and desires in order to enhance the leaders' wealth, comfort, and power. The traditional Hindu caste system has been used by critics as an illustration of this phenomenon. Critics have claimed that the system was created in ancient times by the conquering Aryans who devised the caste features of Hinduism as a way of ensuring their own superior power and welfare in relation to the peoples they sought to dominate. Much of traditional Hindu education for the upper castes has consisted of students' mastering the rules and rituals that define the rights and responsibilities for each caste as described in such writings as the *Laws of Manu* (*Manu Smriti*) (Bühler 1886) and the *Rules of Vedic Domestic Ceremonies* (*Grihya-Sutras*) (Oldenberg 1886). Although the caste system—and particularly its relegating certain groups to untouchable status—has been repudiated in modern times by the Indian government, the system and its educational components live on.

Charges of fostering similar unstated exploitative aims have been directed at other religious groups as well. Some of the most caustic charges have been issued by followers of such social commentators as Karl Marx who have viewed religion as "the opiate of the masses."

While it is possible that the originators of a particular sect—like the originators of certain socioeconomic and political systems—may consciously devise methods that foster their own welfare at the expense of their followers, people who subsequently perpetuate the religion's educational techniques may not be moved by such a motive, at least not consciously. They may simply propagate the faith and its methodology because they accept the particular religious tradition as the true way. In that case, such educators qualify for inclusion in the second category described above, that of religious instructors who unwittingly further unstated ends.

Accusations about exploitative unstated goals—or what has sometimes been called a hidden curriculum—have been important in religious education for several reasons. First, they have stimulated reforms in objectives and in instructional methods within those religions at which the accusations have been directed. (Illustrative reforms are described below under Sect. 4.) Second, criticism has motivated religious educators who believe such accusations are undeserved to develop more convincing rationales and explanations of their work. Third, the accusations have sufficiently alienated some followers from a particular religion that they have either rejected organized religion entirely or else adopted markedly different religious-education practices. One different practice is that of replacing the goal of religious indoctrination with one of comparing religions so that each learner can achieve a "free, enlightened choice of faith," as explained in Sect. 3.2.

3.2 Indoctrination Versus Comparison

The dominant, almost exclusive purposes of religious-education programs have been (a) to convince learners that a particular religion is the one true faith and (b) to school the learners in the doctrine and practices of that faith. In short, the goal of such programs is evangelism or indoctrination. However, in recent times a growing number of programs have been designed to teach students about various religions and even about such nonreligious philosophical positions as humanism, which stresses a commitment to human values without necessitating belief in a god, in religious ritual, or in a life hereafter. The goal of this second variety—the comparative-religion approach—is to help students "find a faith to live by." They are to find this faith not as a result of indoctrination in a single religion but by their own enlightened choice, which "can only be made when the pupils have studied with some seriousness the nature of religious and nonreligious systems of belief and the grounds which men of goodwill and sincerity on both sides find convincing" (Holm 1975).

The aim of such religious study, which is both non-denominational and comparative, is illustrated in the syllabus ratified by the Swedish parliament in 1969 to guide the religious instruction required at all levels of Sweden's comprehensive school system. Under this reformation of religious education:

> Instruction shall be broadminded and objective in a way that factual knowledge concerning different religious beliefs and philosophies is presented without seeking to exert pressure on the students to embrace one particular ethic. This instruction should be carried out in such a way that the students understand the seriousness and importance of the questions with which they are dealing. It should enhance their personal development and help bring about an understanding of the value of a personal ethic. The students should also gain understanding and respect for different points of view in questions of ethics and religion. (Fägerlind 1974 p. 38)

The comparative-religion approach is rarely the type conducted within an established sect or denomination, such as in a Sunday school or in a church-sponsored day school. Nearly all church-sponsored schools limit teaching to their own doctrine or else they compare other belief systems unfavorably to their own. In contrast, comparative-religion programs are most often found in secular schools—public or private—of nations like the United Kingdom, Australia, the Federal Republic of Germany, and Sweden that (a) require religious education in all schools and (b) have varied religious and nonreligious groups represented in the society, with enough adherents in the major groups to threaten political disorder if a single religion's doctrine were imposed on students in the schools.

3.3 Cognitive Versus Affective Objectives

The term cognitive refers here to intellectual comprehension, to those parts of religious education that can be communicated to someone else in words, committed to memory for later recall, analyzed, and used for guidance in making decisions in life. Students are most frequently expected to achieve cognitive objectives by memorizing holy scripture and answers to common doctrinal questions (catechisms) and by hearing an expert apply religious doctrine to life situations. Some programs, particularly at the more advanced levels, move beyond the passive–receptive mode of cognitive learning to the more active–productive intellectual activities of debating, analyzing, and synthesizing religious issues.

In contrast to the cognitive aspect, the affective is the emotional component of religious education, the array of feelings that cannot be conveyed adequately in words, like the sensation referred to in a Christian hymn as "the peace that passeth understanding." Such affect includes mysticism, in the sense of realities beyond perception and intellectual comprehension, realities that are directly accessible through intuition, inspiration, or meditation.

While for purposes of analysis, the cognitive and affective have been contrasted, religious education programs generally attempt to achieve both types of goals. As Brink (1977 p. 409) has suggested, "Religion does not and should not aim at intellectual conversion. Religion should strive for total conversion, that is, one which involves feeling, willing, and acting as well as thinking."

Different religious-education programs consist of different proportions of cognitive and affective goals, just as different religious sects may place more emphasis on one type of goal than another. For example, within the typical Unitarian and Christian Science versions of Christianity there has been a greater emphasis on intellectual comprehension and cognitive analysis than was found in the Catholic Church's ritual of the past which was conducted in Latin for non-Latin-speaking congregations who were expected to gain more affectively—or spiritually—than cognitively as a result of their religious experience. In a similar fashion, affective outcomes, as contrasted to cognitive ones, have been particularly important components of the Sufism movement in Islam, the Yoga version of Hinduism, and the Zen variety of Buddhism. The instructional methods in programs emphasizing affective objectives typically depend less on intellectual analysis and more on the generation of altered states of consciousness (meditation), on visual and tactile symbols (a cross, a star, a crescent moon, a statue, beads), and on the repetition of prayers, chants, and mantras (sacred verbal formulas).

Often a religious body emphasizes cognitive goals in one portion of the church program and affective goals in another. For example, Christian churches frequently provide Bible-study classes whose chief purpose is to teach the history and tenets of the religion, while separate prayer meetings or revival sessions are conducted to further the sect's emotional or spiritual outcomes.

4. Instructional Methods and Media

At present, as in the past, the predominant—and often exclusive—methods of instruction are those of having students (a) memorize passages of the holy scriptures, (b) participate in rituals, and (c) read or listen to sermons or interpretations of what the scriptures mean and how they can be applied to one's life. The interpretations are usually presented by someone in a position of authority—a priest, minister, teacher, or religious scholar. At the more advanced stages of study, students may engage in discussions or debates in which they actively analyze theological and ethical issues, supporting their opinions with quotations from the scriptures.

While such traditional instructional methods continue throughout the world to be by far the most popular teaching techniques, their dominance has been challenged recently by a variety of different instructional methods. The new techniques are chiefly adaptations of innovative methodology developed in secular schools and founded on recent advances in educational psychology and instructional technology. As a consequence, increasing numbers of programs, particularly in Western nations, have focused their curricula on children's interests (student-centered approaches) or on problems in society (social-issue approaches) rather than on direct study of the holy scriptures. Religious educators' interest in thus replacing or supplementing traditional teaching methods has been motivated by their dissatisfaction with what they judge are serious shortcomings of conventional methodology.

One of the most common topics of pedagogical debate has been that of the effectiveness of rote memorization. In virtually every religious tradition, memorizing passages of scripture or catechisms and being able to repeat them word-for-word has been considered a keystone of religious instruction. In typical Moslem schools, children spend years memorizing the entire Koran and chanting it in a prescribed manner. Pride in the ability to perform this act continues to be so great that in such a country as Malaysia, where Islam is the official state religion, an annual nationally televised contest is conducted to determine which youths intone passages of scripture most eloquently.

Supporters of rote-memorization methodology contend that a student's committing scriptures to memory not only makes them constantly available as guides to living but that the demanding feat of memorization itself builds character. Advocates of such mastery also often hold that the literal repetition of holy words itself conveys mystical values that extend beyond the analytical meaning of the passages themselves.

> Every Muslim agrees that the Quran itself as the word of God is untranslatable, not only in the ordinary sense in which all great literary works are untranslatable, but because its meaning cannot be divorced from its rhythms and the incomparable harmony which its sounds create. (Husain and Ashraf 1979 p. 116)

However, critics have charged that too often students memorize phrases whose meaning they do not truly comprehend—they simply parrot the words—so the material fails to furnish the guidance and consolation needed in their daily lives. Schmitt (1982 pp. 94–95), commenting on present-day German parents' opinions of the mandated religious-education classes they had attended in secondary school, reports that "adults often express dissatisfaction and unpleasant memories. They recall that much memorizing of biblical texts and hymns was required, absolute but hardly practicable moral principles were laid down, and uncritical acceptance of church teachings demanded."

Linked to the issue of rote memorization is the claim that religious education is too often seen by the learners as irrelevant to their interests and needs. Youths frequently consider religious instruction old fashioned, perhaps pertinent in the past but inappropriate to the present as they experience it. This problem has become particularly acute with the spread of advanced technology that finds secular subjects taking precedence over religious studies in preparing youths for the goals they hope to achieve.

Furthermore, traditional methods of instruction—reading and memorizing scripture, listening to sermons, performing rituals—often seem less appealing than newer instructional approaches found in secular education, such as simulation games, sociodrama, motion pictures, television, and discussions focusing on problems important to modern youth. Not only has the cognitive significance of conventional methodology been cast in doubt, but traditional ways of achieving the desired affective or mystical outcomes of religious experience have also been questioned.

Stimulated by such criticisms, religious educators have sought new methods and media to replace or, more often, to supplement traditional approaches, new methods which better ensure that (a) learners truly understand the meaning of scriptures and not merely memorize the words, (b) the methods and materials capture the learners' interest in competition with other attractions in their environment, (c) the learners know how to apply religious teachings in their daily lives, and (d) religious education reaches as large an audience as possible. The following samples of six types of innovative practices illustrate the range of methods with which religious educators have experimented in recent years.

4.1 Participatory Sermons and Study Groups

Stokes (1977) has described a variety of innovations in certain American Protestant churches in the 1970s intended to elicit more active learning than likely occurs when a congregation listens passively to a sermon. One approach has been the participatory sermon during which the members of the audience respond to questions posed by the minister during the sermon. The response may take the form of a minister/congregation dialogue during the sermon or may follow the sermon as an open discussion, debate, or panel discussion. In some cases the discussion takes place in small groups later in the week.

4.2 Student-centered Projects

One trend, particularly in Western societies, has been that of identifying interests of young people at different age levels, then designing religious-study projects directed at those interests. An example of such student-centered instruction is a Swedish program which began with an investigation of the personal concerns of pupils aged 10 to 12, an investigation that involved pupils completing unfinished stories about children in pictured conflict situations. The survey showed that two of the primary concerns of pupils were about loneliness and about the effects of violence, suffering, and war. The results of the survey were then used to formulate themes for religious-education projects enabling instructors to identify passages of the Bible which bore on these concerns and to devise discussions that engaged children in identifying ways the themes and Bible passages could influence their lives. In effect, the starting point for specifying topics to study was not the Bible or adult interests, but rather was a series of children's interests in matters of life and death, responsibility and guilt, suffering and compassion, fear and security, loneliness and fellowship (Fägerlind 1974).

4.3 Social-action Programs

The 1960s witnessed marked social unrest in many nations, an unrest reflected in religious-education programs often turning from Bible study to social action. The action took the form of political demonstrations and direct social service intended to redress the neglect or oppression being suffered by minorities, or to correct conditions detrimental to the general quality of life in the community.

According to a survey of North-American Protestant churches (Stokes 1977), the social involvement of the 1960s changed in the 1970s to include greater attention to Bible study and serious theological thinking, so that the version of the 1970s deserved the label action/reflection model. In keeping with this conception of religious education, a film produced by the United Presbyterian Church suggested four models of adult learning that might be combined: (a) the conventional Bible class in church, but taught in newer ways (cognitive learning); helping others, as in giving service in a teenage crisis center (personal–social skill training); small, intimate discussion group (affective learning); and participation in issue-oriented movements, such as gaining equal rights for women or for minority groups (action/involvement learning).

4.4 Dramatics

The use of drama in religious education is nothing new, for drama and pageantry have long been used to portray religious events. As evidence, the present-day term for string-operated puppets—marionettes—derives from the description of the supporting characters (little Marys) in medieval Christian plays which featured the Virgin Mary. However, the variety of ways dramatics contribute to religious instruction today is far greater than in the past.

Formal dramas in which actors memorize speeches created by a playwright continue to be popular. Puppetry also continues in use. However, in their modern form, dramatics are not confined to stage productions but can be audio recorded on tape to simulate radio drama or video recorded through a television camera to form a motion picture. Or, as another approach, members of a study group may read aloud segments of a play, then use the segments as the subject of a discussion of theological or moral issues.

Less traditional forms of drama, requiring greater ingenuity on the part of the actors, are creative dramatics, role playing, sociodrama, and psychodrama. In each of these, the actors spontaneously devise their own speeches and actions in response to the behavior of the others in the play. Such dramatic forms can reflect daily life and thereby furnish the actors practice in ways of responding to real-life decision-making demands. Creative dramatics is a general term identifying modes of spontaneously developing characters and their actions. Typically the characters are told whom they represent and the conflict situation in which they find themselves. Then they are to interact with each other as they imagine such characters would in real life. Role playing, as a form of creative dramatics, emphasizes the kind of person a character is and the way that person would feel and behave under various conditions. Sociodrama lays stress on the social interaction of characters, and psychodrama emphasizes the internal struggles that operate within an individual's personality (see *Psychodrama; Sociodrama*).

4.5 Multimedia Approaches

A significant feature of many religious-education programs has been the introduction of a broad variety of communication media found in modernized secular education and in public-information and entertainment fields. These media have included such stimuli for discussion sessions as filmed interviews with famous personalities or with people who have had striking religious experiences, posters illustrating personal and social issues, photographs of people in problem situations, "you-are-there" radio broadcasts of Biblical occasions, comic-book versions of religious history, picture Bibles for children, and filmstrips of places and events associated with a religion. Increasing numbers of motion pictures have been produced by religious organizations, and regular entertainment films have been used in movie forums as subjects of analysis to determine to what degree the films reflect values advocated in religious education. To aid European educators in conducting such forums, the Dutch-based Interfilm organization furnishes information about available films and ways they can serve in religious instruction.

4.6 Radio and Television

Since the early 1970s an unprecedented increase in the use of radio and television for religious education has been witnessed on an international scale. While in many nations occasional religious programs appeared on radio and television in the past, it was not until the latter 1970s that evangelical religious programs achieved the prominence they currently display. By the beginning of the 1980s in the United States there were more than 300 radio stations dedicating their entire time to religious material, and hundreds of commercial stations sold portions of their broadcast time to religious groups.

But more dramatic than radio has been the growth of television broadcasting. By 1981 in the United States there were 36 television stations maintaining full-time religious schedules, with some stations operating 24 hours a day. Hundreds of additional commercial-television stations sold their entire Sunday morning and much of their late evening time to religious groups. As a consequence, evangelical programs now reach into millions of homes on a regular basis. While most broadcasts have originated in the United States, their influence has not been confined to that nation. One religious leader's radio and television programs have been broadcast on 650 stations in 18 countries and translated into seven languages (Hadden and Swann 1981).

As a result of these developments, religious education—particularly of an evangelical variety—reaches a larger audience than ever before, is available to listeners in their homes, and is produced in a format that matches the technical and dramatic quality of modern-day commercial television.

5. Educational Personnel

Religious-education instructors throughout the world are more diverse in their qualifications than are instructors teaching secular subjects. Teachers of religion range in background from those with advanced university degrees in theology and in teaching methodology to others who have had no teacher training and who hold only a slight knowledge of religion. There appear to be several reasons for such diversity.

First, religious instruction is carried on in more varied ways than is secular schooling. As noted earlier, religious education assumes many forms—full-time study in school, part-time study in school, once a week in a church or mosque, in casual study sessions of a small group, during an informal visit to a neighbor's home, and others. The skills a person needs to offer religious instruction in one of these settings can differ markedly from those needed in another.

Second, governments usually maintain more official control over secular than over religious instruction. Part of the reason for this is that freedom of religious belief is a far more common political policy than freedom of secular education. Whereas governments commonly regulate what is taught in schools and stipulate who is qualified to teach (especially in state-supported or public schools), they are far less likely to set regulations about who is qualified to offer religious instruction, particularly in countries with sects that might pose a political threat if their independence was hampered. Thus, even in as formal a setting as the school, marked diversity exists in the kinds of people offering religious instruction. For example, in the Netherlands, laypersons teach in the Sunday school, regular classroom teachers provide religious instruction in primary schools, and clergymen or theologically trained laymen teach religion in secondary schools. Furthermore, in Moslem regions there is a long tradition of permitting anyone who has attended a Koran school to set up such an instructional center of his own without his having any formal teacher training. Governments seeking to change such a tradition could expect stiff resistance from the Islamic community. In short, few if any nations that endorse the practice of religion will prevent anyone from organizing at least informal religious-instruction sessions.

Third, there is greater consensus about what should constitute teacher education for giving instruction in secular subjects than for teaching religion. In other words, educators agree more on the content and skills needed for teaching such subjects as geography, physics, or music than for teaching religious doctrine. Hence, it has been easier to specify qualifications that should be met by instructors for secular subjects than those to be met by religious educators.

For the future, it seems likely that the issue of what preparation is needed by religious-education personnel will continue to be debated. However, because of widespread governmental policies of religious freedom and the lack of agreement about the skills and knowledge needed for offering religious instruction, it seems unlikely that the present diversity in qualifications for teaching religion will diminish.

6. Administration and Finance

A wide variety of systems for administering religious education operate throughout the world. In some cases a large international network of churches of a particular denomination, such as those within Catholicism, is administered through a hierarchy of authorities that provide goals, curriculum materials, teacher training, supervisory personnel, interchurch conferences, newsletters, evaluation procedures, and financial aid to the religious-education programs within the network. In other cases a national or regional body performs these services. In still other instances, individual churches independently devise their own religious instruction, drawing upon whatever materials and methodologies they choose from those available in the general field of religious education.

Over recent decades, organizational trends have moved in two opposite directions. On the one hand, formerly independent groups have linked together to produce larger, overarching administrative units. This has been the ecumenical movement in which different denominations have sought to emphasize their likenesses rather than differences and to cooperate in such activities as the production of syllabi and the conduct of interfaith religious-education conferences. At the same time, segments of existing large administrative units have broken away from the parent body, or at least have loosened their administrative ties, so as to gain more autonomy. This kind of splitting off from an established structure, which over the centuries has produced a multitude of subsects and denominations, has been particularly evident in developing nations, that is, in formerly colonized regions which, after the Second World War, gained political independence. During col-

onial times in these countries, Christian missionaries had conducted much of the available religious and secular schooling, with the administration of both churches and schools controlled by the sponsoring denominations in Europe or North America. But since the early 1950s, as part of the general movement of colonized peoples toward political independence, an increasing number of church groups within formerly colonized countries have chosen to become self-sufficient in church administration. Nevertheless, while assuming more administrative control, such groups still usually maintain at least a liaison relationship with their original church abroad, availing themselves of both funds and religious-education practices from Europe and the Americas.

An administrative issue of continuing importance throughout the world has been the relationship between church and state. Some nations have a state religion (either official or unofficial), with the authority to oversee religious education vested in a central ministry or department of education or subsumed under the authority of a minister of general education. The governments in such countries frequently mandate the teaching of religion as a regular subject of instruction in all schools, public and private. Such is the practice in Finland, Norway, France, the Federal Republic of Germany, the Netherlands, Italy, Spain, much of Latin America, Thailand, Indonesia, countries of the Middle East, and others. Although religious instruction is officially required in these nations, provision is often made—as in the United Kingdom, Finland, the Federal Republic of Germany, and Italy—for children to be exempt from the requirement if their parents are either nonbelievers or if an instructor is not available for the faith to which the parents subscribe. New Zealand is one of the countries that follow a released-time policy by which pupils are released from their secular studies each week for sessions of religious instruction offered by someone of their faith.

In some countries, religious-instruction policy is not uniform throughout the nation but varies from one region to another. In Canada religious instruction in the schools has been obligatory in three provinces, permitted in three others, not permitted in two, and offered as an elective course in the remaining two. In Scotland the responsibility for implementing religious-instructional policy rests with local authorities.

In still other nations, religious instruction—in the form of espousing a particular faith—is prohibited in the schools. Such is the case in the United States of America and in countries ruled by single-party Marxist governments, such as the Soviet Union, a variety of nations in Eastern Europe, the People's Republic of China, the Democratic People's Republic of Korea, and others.

Financing religious education has always depended heavily on private sources, chiefly on contributions that followers of a religion voluntarily make to the church and on fees parents pay to support their children's studies. However, public funding is also often involved, with the role of government in financing religious education varying greatly from one nation to another. In the Netherlands, both secular state schools and ones operated by religious groups (confessional schools) are completely underwritten by the government. In Indonesia, the Ministry of Religion fully finances Islamic madrasahs in certain sections of the country, while the Ministry of Education subsidizes Christian schools that meet government standards. In the United States, schools below the university level that are sponsored by religious bodies receive no government funds, although they enjoy tax-free status by virtue of their religious nature.

It seems apparent that the financial viability of religious-education programs is significantly influenced by the funding policies of the governments under which they operate. The chances that religious education will thrive appears greater in nations that contribute public funds towards its support.

7. Evaluating Religious Education

Many kinds of data and methods of data collection have been used for evaluating the success of religious education. Some assessments are in simple quantitative terms. One crude measure of success is the total number of professed followers of a religion. A second is the number of converts or new church members during a particular period of time. A third is the number of people enrolled in religious-education programs. However, because such figures, even when accurately reported, tell nothing of the quality of religious education, other sorts of assessment have been used to appraise qualitative aspects.

Perhaps the most obvious approach to judging quality has been that of assessing an individual's religious training by how well his or her behavior matches the model of a true adherent of the faith. In the case of a traditional Hindu, this means observing him to learn how well he follows his caste's rules pertaining to occupation, social intermingling, marriage, food taboos, and prayers and rituals for various occasions. In the case of a Moslem, it means observing how well he fulfills the five pillars of faith (declaring that there is no God but Allah and that Muhammad is his messenger, praying five times daily, giving alms to the poor, fasting during the prescribed lunar month each year, and making a pilgrimage to the holy city of Mecca at some time during one's life). In addition, the proper Moslem abides by a variety of other expectations, such as attending services in the mosque at midday on Friday and abstaining from drinking alcoholic beverages.

Assessing the adequacy of religious education by observing individuals' behavior has typically been an informal mode of evaluation, popular since the earliest days of religions. However, more formal evaluations have also been performed, as in the Catholic practice of believers confessing to a priest the ways in which they have fallen short of the goals of their religion. Another

formal mode of long standing is the oral examination in which a religious teacher questions the learner over doctrine and church history. In more recent times, such examinations have been in written form, permitting the simultaneous testing of a group of learners by a single instructor.

Finally, built-in assessment is provided by all instructional methods that require an active response on the part of the learners. Observing the learners' performance during group discussion, role playing, social-action projects, picture or story interpretation, and creative-writing assignments informs the instructor of how well the students have mastered the knowledge and skills being taught.

8. The State of Religious-education Research

Studies of religious education have been of many varieties. A large number qualify as think pieces, philosophical proposals or analyses based on an author's casual observation, personal experience, and logical reasoning. Often the author's purpose is to convince readers to adopt a viewpoint he espouses. Wyckoff offers three reasons why the Federal Republic of Germany may well be the leader in this type of study:

> First, the size and cohesiveness of the corps of professional teachers makes feasible production of books and journals of high scholarly quality. Second, the theologians and educators who train the teachers in theological faculties and in the faculties of graduate educational institutes constitute a large coterie of scholar–teacher–writers. Third, there is in each German state a highly trained supervisory group of scholar–administrator–writers. The result is a volume and quality of writing on religious education that exceeds that of any other country in the world. (Wyckoff 1979 p. 101)

In a variety of nations, historical research is also common, with authors attempting to explain the evolution of such institutions as the Sunday school, the Salvation Army, and catechetical instruction. Other studies are descriptions of educational practice, often based on data gathered by means of a survey of a variety of programs. Surveys are also conducted of people's attitudes on religious issues.

Another type of investigation utilizes content analysis, a process consisting of a researcher examining published materials to discover how much their content fits selected analytical categories. For example, history and science textbooks may be analyzed to determine whether the way they picture the creation of the world fits the view given in holy scripture. Or motion pictures may be inspected to determine if moral values they reflect are in keeping with values advocated in religious doctrine. A further kind of study seeks to show ways learners have changed as a result of religious instruction, with comparisons sometimes made of the effects of instruction at different age levels.

The question of how many studies have been carried out across the world in recent years cannot be answered, because research has been conducted in so many different places and issued in such diverse forms. There appears to be no agency dedicated to the task of cataloguing the myriad studies. However, a growing number of lists of research have been published so that some information is available about types and numbers of investigations for limited sections of the world. For example, a volume edited by Strommen (1971) reviewed studies readily available in Western published sources for a period prior to the 1970s. In 1979 Peatling (1979) updated Strommen's work by listing 134 empirical investigations on religious- and moral-education topics reported in European, North American, and Australian sources over the period 1968–1979. Since 1979 the journal *Religious Education* has issued brief yearly reviews of empirical research, with each review followed by more detailed abstracts of studies in book form under the title *Annual Review of Research: Religious Education*, sponsored by the Religious Education Association.

Periodically *Religious Education* also publishes abstracts of doctoral studies reported in *Dissertation Abstracts International*. However, because *Dissertation Abstracts* draws chiefly on work done in North American universities, its coverage of studies in religious education is quite limited. The present writer's observations of universities in the Far East suggests that most research on educational matters in many countries is carried out in the form of master's degree or doctoral theses which never enter lists of research and therefore have little chance of coming to the attention of either the regional or worldwide academic community.

While the cataloguing of research continues to be incomplete, those listings which have been compiled provide some limited notion of trends in methodology, at least in Western nations. For example, Peatling (1979) concluded from his review of empirical investigations that objective assessments, rather than only subjective appraisals, are being increasingly used in religious-education research, which is a development he commended. Furthermore, researchers have utilized a broad variety of tests and rating devices, many of which are in sufficiently standard use in psychology and education that they provide the basis for reliable comparisons across different studies. However, Peatling also noted two methodological shortcomings. One was a paucity of studies that provide pretesting followed by a carefully designed educational intervention or treatment which, in turn, is followed by posttesting to determine the effect of the intervention. The other was a shortage of:

creative methods peculiarly suited to exploratory research. . . . If this indicates any feeling that the important questions have been explored, then a lot more realism and some serious thinking is an urgent necessity. Large samples, rigorous designs, and sophisticated analyses all build upon careful exploratory research: the two have a true symbiotic relationship. (Peatling 1979 pp. 425–26)

What appears to be needed in the future is a greater quantity of research on religious-education issues, wider application of modern research techniques, and better methods for providing access to studies from around the world. Advances in data-storage and retrieval techniques by electronic computers linked into a network of the world's libraries promise greater availability of studies on religious education in the years ahead.

Bibliography

Adamu H A 1973 *The North and Nigerian Unity*. Daily Times, Lagos
Anderson K J 1986 *Religion in the Public Schools*. American Association of School Administrators, Arlington, Virginia
Barrett D B (ed.) 1982 *World Christian Encyclopedia: A Comparative Survey of Churches and Religions in the Modern World, AD 1900–2000*. Oxford University Press, London
Brink T L 1977 A psychotherapeutic model for religious education. *Religious Educ.* 72: 409–13
Bühler G 1886 *The Laws of Manu: Manu Smriti*. In: Müller F M (ed.) 1886 *The Sacred Books of the East*, Vol. 25. Clarendon Press, Oxford
Cox E 1983 *Problems and Possibilities for Religious Education*. Hodder and Stoughton, London
Cully K B (ed.) 1963 *The Westminster Dictionary of Christian Education*. Westminster Press, Philadelphia, Pennsylvania
Fägerlind I 1974 Research on religious education in the Swedish school system. *Character Potential* 7(1): 38–47
Felderhof M C 1985 *Religious Education in a Pluralistic Society*. Hodder and Stoughton, London
Hadden J K, Swann C E 1981 *Prime Time Preachers: The Rising Powers of Televangelism*. Addison-Wesley, Reading, Massachusetts
Hartman E E 1979 A follow-up study of graduates of selected Hebrew elementary educational institutions. *Religious Educ.* 74: 416
Himmelfarb H S 1977 The non-linear impact of schooling: Comparing different types and amounts of Jewish education. *Sociol. Educ.* 50: 114–32
Holm J L 1975 *Teaching Religion in the School: A Practical Approach*. Oxford University Press, London
Husain S S, Ashraf S A 1979 *Crisis in Muslim Education*. King Abdulaziz University, Jeddah
Miller C M 1977 Theology and the future of religious education. *Religious Educ.* 72: 46–60
Oldenberg H 1886 The Grihya-Sûtras: rules of Vedic domestic ceremonies. In: Müller F M (ed.) 1886 *The Sacred Books of the East*, Vols. 29, 30. Clarendon Press, Oxford
Ostling R N 1982 Counting every soul on earth. *Time* May 3: 42–43
Peatling J H 1979 Annual review of research: Religious education. *Religious Educ.* 74: 422–41
Postlethwaite T N, Thomas R M 1980 *Schooling in the ASEAN Region*. Pergamon, Oxford
Schmitt G 1982 Teaching religion in German secondary schools. *Religious Educ.* 77: 88–100
Stokes K E 1977 Protestantism. *Religious Educ.* 72: 121–31
Strommen M P 1971 *Research on Religious Development: A Comprehensive Handbook*. Hawthorn, New York
Thompson N H 1988 *Religious Pluralism and Religious Education*. Religious Education Press, Birmingham, Alabama
Tulasiewicz, Brock C 1988 *Christianity and Educational Provision in International Perspective*. Routledge, London
Weesen D J 1986 *Educating Religiously in the Multifaith School*. Detselig Enterprises, Calgary, Canada
Wyckoff D C 1979 German religious education: An analysis. *Religious Educ.* 74: 100–5

Literature: Educational Programs

A. C. Purves

A curriculum in literature has been a staple of schooling around the world for centuries. Literature, which may best be defined as the verbal expression of the human imagination regardless of medium or mode of expression, has existed since before the earliest recording of human history; in fact it has formed the vehicle for much of human knowledge and belief, both religious and secular. This article will briefly survey the history of literature in schools, examine the nature of current curricula, and summarize the current state of curriculum research.

1. Historical Background

Literature has formed a part of the curriculum since the dawn of history, for it is through literature—songs, stories, dramas—that people have passed their knowledge from generation to generation. Various literary forms have been the vehicle for metaphysics, science, history, ethics, as well as entertainment. In many societies, the bard or the storyteller ranked as highly as the priest; in fact, in some societies, such as the Semitic and the American Indian, storytellers were priests.

One may see vestiges of this use of literature in schools today. From the Renaissance onward, students have been expected to read certain classical or national works so as to join the ranks of the educated. In Europe, up until the nineteenth century, Greek, Latin, and Hebrew writers were most important. Slowly, native writers were admitted to the canon as instruction turned more and more to the vernacular: in Italy, Dante and Petrarch; in France, Montaigne and Racine; in England, Shakespeare and Milton.

Literature and literary forms were early used as an aid to memory, and many early primers contained verses and stories to help children learn numbers, days of the week, or other daily lore. These forms also contained various ethical lessons as well as some explanations of natural phenomena; the "pourquoi tale" is well-known to folklorists as a means of exploring the origins of natural phenomena or social customs.

In many ways, then, literature played an important part in the school curriculum but except for knowing the masters, there was virtually no literature curriculum as such. Students read literature as a vehicle to learn how to read or they read literature as a means of learning another language, or they read literature in order to acquire "classical" learning. By the end of the nineteenth century, however, literature began to be an object of study. Literary history and philology served as the disciplines behind that study, but in the 1920s and the 1930s they came to be challenged by other approaches, particularly that of analytic criticism influenced by schools of thought developed in the Soviet Union, Czechoslovakia, the United Kingdom, and the United States, and that of psychological criticism derived from Jung and, particularly, Freud.

2. Current Curricular Structures in Literature

A review of data from various countries and of histories of literature teaching in the United States and in Europe have suggested that three radically different deep structures operate in literature education today and describe a culture's influence on its literature curricula. In any one historical era or in any one country these structures may appear in a less than pure state; even so, they remain distinguishable. Like many concepts throughout the history of ideas, these deep structures have social origins (Applebee 1974, Van de Ven 1988).

2.1 The Imitative Structure

Historically, the imitative is the oldest structure, originating in the West when Latin and Greek held sway, and students were educated by memorizing and imitating classical models. In the United Kingdom its strongest proponent was Matthew Arnold, who advocated a cultured elite that would recognize literary excellence by "touchstones." Most of the spokespersons for the imitative were nationalists. On the European continent, people like Sainte-Beuve and Taine re-established the importance of French literary history and biography, setting out nationalistic models of excellence which could presumably become the basis for education within the culture. In the United States, Emerson became the spokesman for the Americanism of American writers.

In the twentieth century, T. S. Eliot advocated a national literature as providing a force for social cohesion and, by extension, he saw the schools as providing the means whereby that national literature could work its cohesive effect. Eliot saw the elite as tied to the larger populace through the bonds of a common language and common schooling.

Whether the end is Arnold's class cohesion or Eliot's cultural cohesion through the weight of tradition, nearly every national curriculum is partly based on the assumption that literature forms a heritage and that reading, absorbing, and imitating that heritage will transmit cultural values to the young. Following the curricular implications of Sainte-Beuve, Emerson, or Eliot, a historical curriculum tends to emerge, either rigidly national or more broadly conceived (e.g., Anglo–American or Scandinavian). Following Arnold, what observers in the United States have come to call a "humanities curriculum" tends to emerge, which emphasizes the sweep of Western (or Asian, or African) literature and stresses great ideas more than great writers. The difference is one of breadth of perspective, an important difference but not a radical one. The Finnish curriculum of the 1960s expresses a narrower view: "The objective of instruction in the lower and middle grades of the secondary school is that students should understand and internalize what is read . . . . Special attention must be paid to the manifestation of the national spirit in literature." In Iran the national report says, "Literary history is highly uncritical . . . . In the early years it is told in hyperbolic generalizations." In Sweden and Chile the emphasis seems to be more on the literature of high culture than on the literature representing a national spirit, though the national emphasis is present, as it is in most countries (Purves 1973).

For the teacher, the imitative curriculum provides a clear sense of standards that upholds the selection of works taught by the authority of the past, although there may well be various forms of revisionism, as can be seen in ethnic and women's studies. Characteristically, the imitative curriculum refers to historically and culturally established "standards of excellence" when seeking answers to such questions as "What will these students need to know and understand in today's world?" and "How can this subject matter best be conveyed to them?"

2.2 The Analytic Structure

The analytic structure, a scientific or semiscientific structure, is based on the work of literary critics and aestheticians. Analytic criticism is a relatively recent phenomenon (although there are roots in the nineteenth century, particularly among the philologists).

The thrust of the structure was that literature cannot be taught; one can only teach criticism: the application of logical discourse to a work of literature and the superimposition of some theoretical structure on the work—whether that structure be linguistic, rhetorical, or interpretive. Able to apply his or her skills to any verbal structure, the trained literary critic often becomes a cultural critic or a critic of political figures, as can be seen in the pages of many intellectual journals.

Literature education based on the analytic structure stresses the development of students' critical faculties, their abilities to comprehend, analyze, and respond to works studied. In the classroom, the analytic curriculum takes many forms, which appear to depend partly on the school of criticism dominant in the culture at the time. In general, however, the principles of structured inquiry are stressed. There is considerable reference in curriculum rationales to "critical skills," processes, and the performance of certain operations. Whether through didactic or heuristic teaching, students are provided with structures to consider, problems to solve, devices to use, and procedures to master. The emphasis is on the development of students' technical proficiency in confronting, analyzing, and responding to literature.

The analytic deep structure is evident to some extent in many countries. In Belgium there is frequent mention of *analyse textuelle*, in the United States, of study of genres. In Finland the emphasis in the 1960s was psy-

chological: "An artistic creation deserves special attention as a psychological document. An author is not approached through the important dates and events in his life, but instead his work must be studied to reveal his personality, temperament, and development as a writer." In Sweden, the analytic structure competes with the imitative, particularly at the upper levels. Literary education based on an analytic deep structure is training in verbalizing about the literary response rather than imitative training of the aesthetic sensibility; and in many countries, the literature section of university entrance examinations involves the analysis and interpretation of unfamiliar texts (Purves 1973).

2.3 The Generative Structure

The generative structure was influenced by the impact of Freud on criticism and John Dewey on literature education. Freudian criticism first analyzed the psyches of writers and characters but then turned to analyses of the critic's response and to the responses of other readers. It asserts the individuality of readers (a point recently supported by cognitive psychologists looking at schema theory and by certain linguistic philosophers).

The influence of John Dewey comes from his philosophical support of the Freudian position, particularly as it is set forth in "Knowing and the Known" (Dewey and Bentley 1973), and later made specific to literature in Louise Rosenblatt's (1968) *Literature as Exploration*. She speaks of the fact that the "poem" is the result of a transaction between reader and text, that the poem read is not the poem written. The point has been reaffirmed by the structuralist and poststructuralist critics in France who refuse to accept the purity of the poem and see it as a set of structures imposed by poet and critic. Rosenblatt sets forth the pedagogical implications of this critical position:

> Teaching becomes a matter of improving the individual's capacity to evoke meaning from the text by leading him to reflect self-critically in this process. The starting point for growth must be each individual's efforts to marshal his resources and organize a response relevant to the stimulus of the printed page. The teacher's task is to foster fruitful interactions—or, more precisely transactions between individual readers and individual works. (pp. 26–27)

The generative curriculum stresses individual and personal growth through reading rather than the development of critical skills. In the classroom, the generative structure often takes the form of unstructured inquiry, focusing on students' experiences with literature but having no predetermined end in sight beyond the inquiry itself, which is presumed to have value in leading to the students' own goals rather than to teacher-determined objectives.

In practice, this deep structure has found expression in relatively few curricula, most commonly in those school systems where comprehensive education has made its greatest inroads. It is referred to in England and Wales ("the student should express what he *felt* and *thought*"), in New Zealand ("for criticism and appreci-

Table 1
Dimensions of content and behavior for the curriculum in literature

Content areas		Specific literary texts	Contextual information	Literary theory	Cultural information
Behaviors					
(a)	Be familiar with	I	I	A	I
(b)	Apply knowledge of specific literary texts to	IG		A	
(c)	Apply literary history to	I			
(d)	Apply literary theory to	A			A
(e)	Apply cultural information to	I			
(f)	Respond to	IAG			IG
(g)	Express a pattern of preference for	I			
(h)	Express a response to	GA			IG
(i)	Express a consistent pattern of responses to	A			
(j)	Have positive attitudes and interests in literature	IAG	I	A	I

I–imitative   G–generative   A–analytic

ation, absolute sincerity should be the basis") and in the *läroplan* in Sweden, as well as in the pronouncements of some curriculum writers in the United States. It now appears most strikingly in curricula for students at the upper-elementary or early-secondary levels, but it has gained little currency at the upper-secondary level, perhaps because these curricula are still dependent on the university, which still holds to either the imitative or the analytic structure (Purves 1973).

2.4 Comparison of the Three Structures

In order to compare the structures or to determine which structure defines a particular curriculum, content, behaviors, and sequence manifest in the curriculum need to be examined. The content and behaviors emphasized may be seen in a comparative grid (Table 1).

2.5 Content Areas

(a) Specific literary texts—this refers to any literary text considered as an entity in itself.

(b) Contextual information—this includes the literary, political, social, intellectual, and cultural history surrounding a text as well as biographical information about an author, and information about the various expressed opinions concerning a particular literary work.

(c) Literary terminology and theory—this includes such terms as "metaphor" or "symbol" and theories of aesthetics or literary study.

(d) Cultural information—this includes the basic themes and sources of literary allusion (e.g., the

Bible; Greek, Norse, or Persian mythology; folk literature; and children's literature).

2.6 Behavioral Categories

(a) Be familiar with: the behavior includes what could be called "knowledge of."

(b) Apply knowledge of specific literary texts to: this behavior refers primarily to the use of knowledge of one text in the comprehension of another, to the making of analogies between texts.

(c) Apply literary history to: the use of a historical context derived from background knowledge and remembered features from other works.

(d) Apply literary theory to: this behavior refers primarily to the application of one's knowledge of terminology and theory to a literary text.

(e) Apply cultural information to: this behavior refers primarily to the application of knowledge to a literary text.

(f) Respond to: response is defined as the ongoing interaction between the individual and the literary work. One of its indices will be the absence or presence of the tendency to continue reading the work. It may be defined variously as interest, appreciation, and taste, or conversely, boredom and rejection. It can never be made explicit, but must instead be revealed indirectly through the observation of the works preferred or rejected by the individual. The educational goal is generally the development of an increasing range and flexibility of response.

(g) Express a pattern of preference for: this behavior refers to an overt act of response by which a person signifies a liking for certain literary works more than others.

(h) Express a response to: this behavior refers to the second overt act of response whereby the individual selects aspects of his or her response which he or she thinks important to communicate. This expressed response exists in a pattern which can be described (one method of description is contained in Purves and Rippere 1968). This pattern will result from educational, social, and cultural forces as well as from the private interaction between the individual and the text.

(i) Express a pattern of response to: in certain educational systems, the development of a particular pattern of response may be a goal (e.g., that the individual will analyze a work according to a series of conventions, or that he or she will consistently use a single set of criteria for judging a poem, or that he or she will seek to view each work in a historical setting). Others may believe that while some stances or processes are valuable, and, at appropriate stages, to be aimed at, nonetheless the students should be discouraged from adhering to a fixed pattern but should explore their singular reactions to a unique work of art.

(j) Have positive attitudes and interest in literature: this behavior encompasses the internalization of positive attitudes towards literature and literary works and the development of strong reading habits. It also refers to the habit of using the way a person responds to literature and literary events as a basis for responding to nonliterary events (e.g., to seeing that the relationship between literature and life is a two-way street—one sees one in terms of the other and the experience of one feeds the capacity to experience the other).

As can be seen, the imitative curriculum emphasizes more cells, because it is more knowledge based, focusing on knowledge of works, authors, and trends. The analytic also stresses knowledge but knowledge of terms and critical constructs. The imitative like the generative commands a variety of affective behaviors as well, but again the attitudes are directed towards the content rather than the students themselves.

With regard to sequence of materials, the imitative curriculum generally follows a chronological approach, although chronology may be tempered by divisions which look at specific genres or themes. The analytic curriculum often uses a generic division, and the generative curriculum a thematic division. Other organizations of the sequence of material may include a rhetorical or formal approach, taking up topics such as point-of-view, structure, or metaphor separately. These topics may be treated discretely in the analytic approach, but more often they occur as aspects of a general historical, generic, or thematic sequence.

3. Curriculum Research and New Developments

Studies in the teaching of literature and the literature curriculum have focused primarily on the psychology of the reader, and in particular on the epistemological question of whether understanding of a text is primarily a reaction to a stimulus or whether it is directed by the reader. The challenge to the primacy of the text has come from philosophic sources, particularly the disciples of Roman Ingarden and European poststructuralists, and also from cognitive psychologists concerned with schema theory.

Research in reading comprehension suggests that when a person reads, they project a schema upon the text. Even a young child begins a sentence or story with the expectation that it will have certain features. Reading, then, appears to follow a pattern of prediction followed by confirmation; it is not a purely inductive process. A group of cognitive psychologists says: "Text understanding proceeds by progressive refinement from an initial model to more and more refined models of the text . . . . The initial model is a partial model, constructed from [schemata] triggered by the beginning elements of the text" (Collins et al. 1977). Schema theory dates back to the 1930s and is related to both gestalt psychology and George Kelly's psychology of personal constructs. Schemata also resemble the semiologists' "code." R. P Abelson (1973) suggests six levels of schemata: elements, atoms, molecules, plans, themes, and scripts, each defined in terms of the lower ones. Whether these levels may also be seen developmentally remains to be determined, but they do appear to have linguistic analogues. The work of these researchers appears to be confirmed by developmental psychologists and others. In an essay on metaphor, Andrew Ortony (1979) shows how schemata enable metaphor to be defined more sharply. In fact, Spiro (1979) has even argued against a reader's overreliance on the text and distrust of the schemata that the reader possesses, a clear support of the role of the reader. It is suggested that readers acquire schemata in a variety of ways—from apprehension of the phenomenal world, from hearing various kinds of discourse, from prior reading, to name the most obvious.

It would appear that these levels of schemata are also modes of perceiving discourse, which is to say, choices as to what to attend to as a person reads. When it comes to critical strategy, or the mode in which a reader discusses a text (whether, for example, to concentrate on structure, language, meaning, or symbol), earlier research suggests that readers possess a strategy much as they possess schemata (Purves 1973). In many readers, a strategy of discourse or of response tends to persist across selections read and to be culturally bound. In the United States, for example, the pattern consists of concern for symbol, theme, and moral and is held by those students who perform well on comprehension tests. Thus schemata, whether they relate to the perception of content, to the procedure for determining meaning, or to the style of talking about a text, are acquired or learned, and they appear to constitute the major form of variation among readers.

The impact of schema theory and research in reader response on the curriculum in literature is beginning to be felt. In some respects, schema theory supports the principle of the heritage curriculum, and particularly the early inclusion of mythology, folk and traditional literature, and "classical" texts that represent pervasive genres and themes within or across cultures. The argument for this inclusion stems from a clear sense that students absorb the genres and themes and are thus better prepared to read other literary texts, most of which build upon these forms and themes.

Schema theory also supports certain aspects of both the analytic and generative curricula models. That kind of schema that underlies the characteristic approach to a literary text—and perhaps any text held by a reader—can be broadened or narrowed through instruction, and it would appear that the development of an ideal reader would include exposing that reader to a variety of approaches. In many ways, these approaches manifest themselves in the questions a reader asks in response to a text. If the only question asked and rewarded is, "What does it mean deep down underneath?", that question will dominate the critical approach of a reader. Other cultures and other periods within a dominant culture have suggested alternatives to that question, and it would seem therefore that students should be exposed to a variety of critical schemata, including those which are personal and affective, those which are analytic, those which are interpretive, and those which are evaluative.

A third area of curricular concern arising from schema theory lies in the teaching and learning of strategies or heuristics for reading a text. Hansson (1990) has shown that "reading" must include articulating an oral or written response to a text. Research in this area is barely under way but it seems promising in its implications for the curriculum (Langer 1989). The thrust of this research is towards isolating those general patterns of thinking that readers employ when they analyze or make meaning of what they read. Included in this research are such questions as what aspects of a text are most salient to examine if one is to answer a particular question such as "What does this passage mean?" or "How are form and content related?"

More generally, research and theory building has laid the groundwork for a developmental approach to the literature curriculum. Most curricular sequences have derived from a conception of the literary material as chronological, analytic, or biographical. The works included were, to some extent, graded on their difficulty or estimated appropriateness to the age group. The focus on the cognitive operations involved in reading texts, especially literary texts, suggests a more deliberate planning of the sequence not only of texts but also of the kinds of mental operations involved in reading and therefore of the kinds of activities that go on in classrooms. Beginning to emerge are curricula based on the increasing complexity of literary structures and on the increasing complexity of mental operations involved in progressing from description to analysis to interpretation and evaluation.

Bibliography

Abelson R P 1973 Structure of belief systems. In: Schank R C, Colby K M (eds.) 1973 *Computer Models of Thought and Language*. Freeman, San Francisco, California, pp. 287–340
Applebee A 1974 *Tradition and Reform in the Teaching of English*. NCTE, Urbana, Illinois
Collins A, Brown J S, Larkin K M 1977 *Inferences in Text Understanding*. Technical Report No. 40. Center for the Study of Reading, Urbana, Illinois
Dewey J, Bentley A F 1973 Knowing and the known. In: Handy R, Harwood E C (eds.) 1973 *Useful Procedures of Inquiry*. Behavioral Research Council, Barrington, Massachusetts
Hansson G 1990 *Reading and Understanding Literature*. Centre for the Learning and Teaching Of Literature. Albany, New York
Langer J 1989 *The Process of Understanding Literature*. CLTL, Albany, New York
Ortony A 1979 Beyond literal similarity. *Psychol. Rev.* 86: 161–80
Purves A C 1973 *Literature Education in Ten Countries*. International Studies in Evaluation, 2. Wiley, New York
Purves A C, Rippere V 1968 *The Elements of Writing About a Literary Work: A Study of Response to Literature*. National Council of Teachers of English, (NCTE) Research Report No. 9, NCTE. Champaign, Illinois
Rosenblatt L M 1968 *Literature as Exploration*. Noble and Noble, New York
Spiro R J 1979 *Etiology of Reading Comprehension Style*. Center for the Study of Reading, Urbana, Illinois
Van de Ven P 1988 Some histories of mother tongue teaching in western Europe. II: A tentative survey. *Mother Tongue Educ.* 3: 35–44

Attitude Towards Literature

R. W. Beach

The development of a positive attitude towards literature—the desire to seek out and read literature that fulfills certain needs—plays an important role in a student's success in school. A favorable attitude towards reading is related to success in school and a positive student self-concept. Svensson (1985) found a significant relationship between secondary students' amount of literature reading and the quality of their literary interpretations. The 1986 NAEP literature assessment found that the amount of reading for pleasure is related to positive achievement on the literature assessment (Ravitch and Finn 1987). Moreover, students become avid readers because they perceive reading as affording active engagement in pleasurable responses (Nell 1989).

The research on attitudes towards literature includes studies on overall attitude towards literature, attitudes towards instruction, response to literature, and reading interests. This research also examines the influence of instruction, social and cultural attitudes, and readers' needs and abilities on attitudes, responses, and interests.

1. Measurement of Attitudes

The quality of research attempting to measure such a subjective phenomenon as readers' attitudes rests on the validity, reliability, and appropriateness of the measurement techniques employed (Chester and Dulin 1977). These measures or techniques include direct observation of student behavior, questionnaires, rating scales, or interviews about amount of reading, propensity to seek out literary titles, willingness to discuss reading, preferences for reading versus other activities, feelings about literature, or preferred instructional methods (Alexander and Filler 1976). The validity of some measures is hampered by the fact that behaviors such as checking out books may not reflect students' actual feelings.

2. Student Variables and Attitudes Towards Literature

It is difficult to generalize about students' attitudes towards literature. Some students have highly positive attitudes towards literature whereas others do not. Some students have no definite attitude because they spend little time reading. As many surveys indicate, many people, particularly poor readers, spend little time reading. In one survey, one-half of the poorer readers spent less than one hour a week reading for pleasure (Purves 1973). A survey of 13,395 British adolescents from ages 11 to 16 indicated that 63 percent of the males and 53 percent of the females devoted none of their leisure time to reading; a steady decline in the amount of reading occurred from ages 11 to 16 (Hincks and Balding 1988).

Research investigating the relationships between a number of student variables and attitudes indicates that there is no strong relationship between intelligence, reading ability, socioeconomic status, or sex and attitudes toward literature, although in some studies, females with high reading ability show more positive attitudes (Purves and Beach 1972) and adolescent females with strong self-concepts have more positive attitudes than females with low self-concepts (Stevenson and Newman 1986).

The factors that seem to have a stronger relationship with attitudes are high positive school achievement, self-concept, and age. The research correlating achievement and attitudes generally indicates that as students begin to perceive that the development of a positive attitude towards reading literature leads to success in their literature classes, they develop a stronger sense of the worth of reading. As their achievement improves, they develop a stronger "reader" or "student" self-concept, particularly when they receive positive reinforcement from parents, peers, and/or teachers (Purves 1973). If they conceive of themselves as unsuccessful readers, they may avoid reading, which diminishes their success in school (Alexander and Filler 1976). In some studies, sex interacts with achievement (Purves and Beach 1972). Often low-achievement males tend to have more negative attitudes towards literature; in some cases, this reflects cultural attitudes.

Age or grade level can impinge on this relationship between attitudes and achievement. Students at different age or grade levels bring different developmental needs to their reading—the need for escape, enjoyment, vicarious experience, and so on (Spiegel 1981). Fulfilling these needs enhances attitudes, as is evident by further self-selection (or "binges") of particular authors, genres, or titles that meet those needs. For example, early adolescents have a strong need for anticipatory vicarious experience of social behaviors/roles. Thus the amount of voluntary reading of literature reaches a high point during early adolescence (Purves and Beach 1972), particularly for females reading traditional (and often stereotyped) romances in anticipation of later social experiences.

3. The Influence of Parents, Home Environment, and School on Attitudes

The International Association for the Evaluation of Educational Achievement (IGA) literature study (Purves 1973), the largest study ever conducted on attitudes towards and response to literature, indicated that across 10 different countries the one factor that was most likely to contribute to a positive attitude towards literature was the degree to which students had an opportunity to read and learn literature both in the home and at school. The influence of home begins at an early age. Use of the *Preschool Reading Attitudes Scale* indicated a wide variation in 3-, 4-, and 5-year old children's attitudes towards reading (Saracho 1984/1985). Students who are read to by parent(s) or adult(s) during preschool years (when compared to students who are not read to at an early age) develop what researchers define as a "literacy set," which results in later superior reading and writing skills (Bettelheim and Zelan 1982).

The first years of school, when children are learning to read, is another crucial stage in the development of attitudes towards literature. As children acquire the ability to comprehend and enjoy stories on their own, they begin to recognize the intrinsic value of learning to select and read stories that fulfill their needs and interests. However, analyses of many of the beginning reading textbooks series indicate that these series contain stories or selections with little literary quality (Bettelheim and Zelan 1982). One reason for the non-literary, pedestrian nature of much of this material is that it is specifically written to teach decoding skills. These unappealing, unimaginative selections undermine the development of a positive attitude towards reading. Comparisons of reading series used in different countries found considerable variations in the literary quality of the series. During the elementary grades, the extent to which parents encourage reading in the home also influences attitudes.

Contrary to popular opinion, the amount of television viewing does not substantially interfere with amount of reading (Whitehead et al. 1977, Witty 1967). However, in one study, heavy viewing children who were light readers chose books of lower quality (Neuman 1982).

The availability of books and magazines in the home and school has a strong effect on attitudes. In one study conducted in two New Zealand primary schools with nonreader students, after large numbers of books were made available to the students, their attitudes towards reading and amount of reading increased significantly (Alexander and Filler 1976).

Students' awareness of the fact that optional titles and more satisfying books are available influences attitudes. If students know they have a wide range of options to choose from, they can reject books until they discover books that meet their needs. Students are also influenced by their familiarity with the story content or characters, familiarity conveyed through book jacket blurbs or booktalks (Whitehead et al. 1977).

4. The Influence of Instructional Methods on Attitudes

Instruction can also influence attitudes towards literature. Literature instruction typically involves eliciting students' responses to texts in the hope that, through responding, students will develop fuller understanding of their reading. The extent to which students are able to express their responses affects their attitudes towards literature. If students are able to openly express their own responses, they can anticipate responding in the classroom according to their own unique experiences with the text. If, on the other hand, they anticipate responding in terms of a limited format (answering reading check questions or reciting memorized passages) then they develop less positive attitudes towards literature (Purves and Beach 1972).

Most of the research on the effects of certain instructional methods on students' attitudes suffers from simplistic designs, vague description of the methods employed, and the use of invalid outcome measures. A number of studies have compared "extensive reading" with "intensive reading" programs; in extensive reading programs, students read a large number of books with general discussion of the books; intensive reading programs involve detailed discussion of a few books. Most studies indicate that extensive reading programs have a more positive effect on literature attitudes than intensive ones (Alexander and Filler 1976). Unfortunately, voluntary reading in the classroom is often a low priority for teachers relative to time devoted to reading skills instructions (Morrow 1980). Voluntary reading of literature increases dramatically when teachers incorporate enjoyable literature activities in the classroom (Morrow and Weinstein 1986).

One problem with many secondary literature curriculums is that teachers rely on the same established texts by white, male authors; texts that may have limited appeal to students of different gender or ethnic backgrounds. Of the twenty most frequently taught texts in high school literature classes, only one was written by a woman and one by a minority writer (Applebee 1989). By allowing students to choose their own titles in a voluntary, "free-reading" program, students may select from a wider variety of texts beyond the established literary canon.

In addition, students seem to have a more positive attitude towards the "phase-elective" English curriculum in which they choose from among a range of short courses focusing on specific genre, themes, or topics ("the mystery novel," "the ballad," "the haiku," etc.) than towards a more traditional literature curriculum. Because much of their instruction is devoted to "basic skills", students in lower "tracks" are often read less literature than students in the upper "tracks" (Barnes and Barnes 1985; Ravitch and Finn 1987), which limits their potential for developing a positive attitude towards reading.

5. The Influence of Social and Cultural Attitudes on Attitudes Towards Literature

Literature often portrays human realities in a manner that either reinforces or challenges readers' social and cultural attitudes. These social and cultural attitudes in turn influence readers' attitudes towards literature. A number of studies examining the relationships between attitudes and responses indicate that younger readers prefer stories with happy endings, a phenomenon that reflects their more optimistic attitude towards life (Purves and Beach 1972). Readers who are "reality bound" and have difficulty suspending their disbelief have difficulty transporting themselves into fictional worlds, reacting negatively to texts that do not conform to their sense of reality (Culp 1977). They then select those texts that conform to their attitudes or beliefs.

The research on the relationships between attitudes and responses has focused on two levels. The first level involves the influence of specific cultural or social attitudes towards topics portrayed in texts (government, war, love, religion, etc.). For example, students with more liberal attitudes towards teaching responded in a more negative, disapproving manner to a "traditional" teacher in a short story (Beach 1983).

The second level examines the influence of general cognitive or intellectual dispositions (tolerance for ambiguity, cognitive flexibility, level of moral reasoning, etc.). Readers who conceive of the world in a highly rigid, inflexible manner or who are intolerant of ambiguity react negatively to complex, ambiguous events or characters or to works that challenge their attitudes. Further, readers who reason at a relatively low level of moral reasoning will usually respond negatively to characters who reason at a high level of moral reasoning (Gilligan 1981).

While readers' social and cultural attitudes influence their attitudes towards literature, reading also influences attitudes, affecting some readers more than others (Culp 1977). One of the traditional justifications of literature instruction is that literature "humanizes" or improves readers' values. However, the somewhat limited research on the effects of reading on attitudes coupled with the larger body of research on attitude formation indicates that attitudes as shaped by family, school, or peers are relatively stable and are therefore unlikely to be influenced by reading literature over a short time period (Beach 1979). For example, reading novels portraying minority characters may not alter students' social attitudes towards that minority.

The extent to which students are influenced by texts is related to their understanding or willingness to assimilate segments of a text. Readers who are willing to empathize or accept a text are more open to influence than those readers who distance themselves from the text.

There is little research charting the long-range socializing influence of reading literature on attitudes. One study of the influence of reading on Israeli youth's political beliefs indicated that fiction had a stronger influence than nonfiction on their beliefs and that their cognitive beliefs were influenced more than affective orientations (Adoni and Shadmi 1980).

Research on the effects of reading on attitudes is directly related to issues surrounding censorship. Advocates of censorship argue that reading certain works will adversely affect students' attitudes and behaviors, particularly if those attitudes and behaviors run counter to the community's or country's accepted norms. However, given the findings of the research that the relatively stable attitudes readers bring to their reading are unlikely to be altered by reading one or two books calls into question arguments for censorship (Beach 1979).

6. Reading Interests Research

Research on reading interests attempts to determine those types or genres most preferred by readers at different grade levels as well as factors influencing those interests. Some research indicates that of the various paper and pencil measures used to determine interests— check lists, questionnaires, fictitious annotation booklists, text sample ratings, and paired comparisons— fictitious annotations booklist measures are particularly valid largely because students' responses are not then biased by exposure only to available texts (Lehtovaara and Saarinen 1964). Students may have a latent interest in science fiction even though they have been exposed to little science fiction. Teachers can also examine interests in certain topics according to differences in students' grade level, sex, ethnicity, ability, and achievement (Bank 1986).

Although it is difficult to reach a consensus on what constitutes literary quality, there is no relationship between interests and quality; it is not until late adolescence that quality begins to influence preferences. Children prefer relatively clearly developed story lines with imaginative, unusual characters; they are less enthusiastic about didactic, highly realistic stories (Purves and Beach 1972). Secondary students prefer novels and short stories to essays, drama, and poetry (Ravitch and Finn 1987).

Reading interests during adolescence shift markedly according to changing developmental needs and social experiences. Early adolescents prefer adventure, animal stories, sports, detective or mystery series, romance and obvious humor, reading that provides escape, and entertainment. Middle adolescent readers prefer reading that helps them vicariously understand and test out social experiences and problems: biography, historical novels, romance, mystery, and particularly "adolescent novels" portraying characteristic adolescent experiences with dating, parents, peer groups, sex, self-concepts, and so on. In their search for personal values, late adolescents prefer adult fiction portraying characters' transition into adult life and involving social and philosophical conflicts. Sex differences continue to be quite distinct up through midadolescence. For example, fifth grade males rated stories as much less interesting when the protagonist was a female, while female students' preferences were not as pronounced (Bleakley et al. 1988). Television and movies influence preferences by popularizing certain titles (Whitehead et al. 1977).

Teachers and librarians need to be able to determine students' reading interests in order to recommend books students will enjoy. Providing students with books of high interest contributes to the success of recreational reading programs based on students' voluntary self-selection of books. In these programs, students learn to select books that are consistent with their needs and interests, an experience that enhances their positive attitudes towards literature.

Bibliography

Adoni H, Shadmi E 1980 The portrait of the citizen as a young reader: The functions of books in the political socialization of youth in Israel. *Res. Q.* 16: 121–37

Alexander J E, Filler R C 1976 *Attitudes and Reading*. International Reading Association, Newark, Delaware

Applebee A 1989 *A Study of Book-length Works Taught in High School English Courses.* Center for the Learning and Teaching of Literature, SUNY at Albany, Albany, New York

Bank S 1986 Assessing reading interests of adolescent students. *Ed. Res. Q.* 10: 8–13

Barnes D, Barnes D 1985 *Versions of English.* Heinemann, London

Beach R W 1979 Research on effects of and response to reading. In: Davis J (ed.) 1979 *Dealing with Censorship.* National Council of Teachers of English, Urbana, Illinois

Beach R W 1983 Attitudes, social conventions and response to literature. *Jr. Res. Dev. Ed.* 16: 47–54

Bettelheim B, Zelan K 1982 *On Learning to Read: The Child's Fascination with Meaning.* Knopf, New York

Bleakley M, Westerberg V, Hopkins K 1988 The effect of character sex on story interest and comprehension in children. *Amer. Ed. Res. J.* 25: 145–55

Chester R, Dulin K L 1977 Three approaches to the measurement of secondary school student's attitudes towards books and reading. *Res. Teach. Engl.* 11: 193–200

Culp M B 1977 Case studies of the influence of literature on the attitudes, values and behavior of adolescents. *Res. Teach. Engl.* 11: 245–53

Gilligan C 1981 Moral development. In: Chickering A W et al. (eds.) 1981 *The Modern American College.* Jossey-Bass, San Francisco, California

Hincks T, Balding J 1988 On the relationship between television viewing time and book reading for pleasure: the self-reported behaviour of 11–16 year olds. *Reading* 22: 40–50

Lehtovaara A, Saarinen P 1964 *School-age Reading Interests: A Methodological Approach.* Suomalaisen Tiedeakatemia, Helsinki

Morrow L 1980 Attitudes of teachers, principals, and parents toward promoting voluntary reading in the elementary schools. *Reading Res. Inst.* 25: 116–130

Morrow L, Weinstein C 1986 Encouraging voluntary reading: The impact of a literature program on children's use of library centers. *Reading Res. Q.* 21: 330–346

Nell V 1989 *Lost in a Book: The Psychology of Reading for Pleasure.* Yale University Press, New Haven.

Neuman S B 1982 Television viewing and leisure reading: A qualitative analysis. Paper presented at Annual Meeting of American Education Research Association, New York, March 19–23, 1982. ERIC Document No. ED 214 106

Purves A C 1973 *Literature Education in Ten Countries: An Empirical Study.* Wiley, New York

Purves A C, Beach R W 1972 *Literature and the Reader: Research in Response to Literature, Reading Interests, and the Teaching of Literature.* National Council of Teachers of English, Urbana, Illinois

Ravitch D, Finn C 1987 *What Do Our 17-year-olds Know?* Harper & Row, New York

Saracho O 1984/1985 Young children's attitudes towards reading. *Ed. Res. Q.* 9: 19–27

Spiegel D L 1981 *Reading for Pleasure: Guidelines.* International Reading Association, Newark, Delaware

Stevenson H, Newman R 1986 Long-term prediction of achievement and attitudes in mathematics and reading. *Ch. Dev.* 57: 646–657

Svensson C 1985 *The Construction of Poetic Meaning.* Liber, Linkoping, Sweden

Whitehead F, Capey A, Maddner W, Wellings A 1977 *Children and Their Books.* Macmillan, London

Witty P 1967 Children of the television era. *Elem. Engl.* 44: 528–35

Children's Literature

P. Lamb and M. Sanati

The term "children's literature" refers to works of fiction and selected nonfiction written for children. While no categorization is universally accepted, there is general agreement that the following are included: folklore, fantasy, picture books, historical fiction, information books, and poetry.

There is some disagreement about the features which distinguish literature written for children from that written for adolescents and/or adults. C. S. Lewis suggests that he wrote for children when a children's story was the best art form for his message (Lewis 1963). A skillful author certainly does not write less skillfully when the intended audience is juvenile. The following aspects of a literary work are among those carefully considered by most authors, whether the intended audience is children, adolescents, or adults: (a) plot—what happens, the plan of action; (b) theme—the message or messages conveyed by the author; (c) characterization—the people, animals, and/or inanimate objects the author writes about; (d) setting—when and where the story takes place.

However, because children are not miniature adults, and possess the specific characteristics related to a particular stage of development, authors who write for children probably write somewhat differently than they would if their intended audience consisted of adolescents or adults. For example, Smith (1967) notes the following: As children have limited experience, the plot of a children's book must have a narrow circle of reference. Children have more limited attention spans than most adults, and are able to deal with fewer elements at once. Finally, and perhaps most importantly, children have more limited linguistic experience than adults. Thus, it is probably correct to speak of a literature specifically designed for children.

Educators are interested in children's literature as an instrument to be used in the context of value clarification studies, for the purpose of enhancing self-understanding and self-confidence, and as reading materials in language arts programs. Accordingly, they are inclined to use nonliterary and nonaesthetic criteria for determining the worth of children's books, preferring criteria of ethical, psychological and pedagogical utility. "Their questions or criteria will be: What does it teach? Does it disturb or reassure children? Does it cultivate racial tolerance?" (Smith 1967). Educational studies dealing with children's books tend to focus on questions of utility rather than on questions of literary merit.

This focus is especially apparent in analyzing two educational trends which are currently very strong in the United States, both of which emphasize the *uses* of children's literature rather than literary analysis or reader response. Widespread criticism of "reading schemes", basal readers (unnatural language, stereotypic content, poor literary quality of selections, etc.) has helped foster what has come to be known as "literature based reading programs" (Smith 1988), in which a literary selection, used in its entirety and in its original form (no vocabulary or syntactic controls applied), serves as the medium for reading instruction. Skills, related to word recognition and reading comprehension as well, as taught based on the material being read (e.g. *Charlotte's Web*). Although such programs almost certainly enhance motivation and promote lifetime interest in reading, concern has been expressed because attention to significant literary elements (e.g. motifs, recurring themes, important elements such as characterization) may be limited or even omitted in favor of teaching skills. Furthermore, if literary selections become vehicles for teaching skills, aesthetic response to that selection may be totally ignored. A related trend is known as "whole language" (Newman 1985), stressing the integration of reading, writing, speaking, and listening. Obviously all these facets are closely related. Nevertheless, using a literary selection primarily as a vehicle for creative drama or as a stimulus for composition may well be viewed as trivializing that selection.

As is true of most trends, the success or failure of these two will depend largely on the effectiveness of the classroom teacher and the resources available to him or her. Hopefully effective teachers will recognize the importance of developing knowledgeable readers who respond with some sophistication to authors' style, creative uses of language, and imaginative manipulation of literary elements. Children's literature is far too important to serve merely as a vehicle for teaching reading skills or integrating several facets of the language arts.

1. Children's Books in Various Cultures

The earliest literature, for adults as well as children, was transmitted by mouth and received by ear. Chants, songs, stories, and explanations of natural phenomena were handed down from one generation to the next in this manner. Favorites were told or sung again and again, spread from tribe to tribe and group to group. Sometimes minstrels or professional storytellers passed on the tales, legends, and ballads, usually after polishing and embellishing them. Much, if not most, of our folk literature originated long before the invention of the printing press.

The topics, the themes, and the styles of children's books inevitably reflect the culture in which authors write and the purposes for which they write, and

society's view about the nature of childhood strongly influences those who write for children.

This section contains a review of the development and current status of children's literature in three different cultural settings: in the Western countries, in the Soviet Union, and in Iran.

The trend observed in Western countries is the diminishing emphasis on didacticism and an increasing variety of topics, genre, and style. In the Soviet Union, where the government has until recently created, supported, and controlled all publication, for many postrevolutionary years fantasy was forbidden and deemed unfit for young minds. At present, changes in children's literature here reflect a movement away from didactic works designed to create "ideal" Soviet citizens and toward a freer, more child-oriented imaginative literature.

Iran's modern history until 1980 manifested an interest in preserving its ancient tradition and political system, and at present children's literature reflects a movement away from books designed to promote the status quo by idealizing courtliness and toward a more realistic and even subversive children's literature that conveys, through allegory and fantasy, the possibility of opposition to aristocratic ideals.

Three basic approaches to teaching literature have been identified: the imitative, the analytical, and the generative. The children's books in these three cultural settings can be said to represent these different approaches. The imitative approach is characteristic for Iran, where the educational system is a conservative force trying to transmit cultural values through the memorization of texts and recapitulation. The analytical approach aims to develop the ability to comprehend texts critically. The teaching of literature as well as children's books in the Soviet Union both try to strengthen critical analysis of situations. Rotkovich (1980) notes that teaching literature in the Soviet Union moved away from "holistic analysis" (i.e. the study of the content and form of the whole work) towards "composition analysis," which studies the internal structure and the patterns of imagery within a work in order to understand the whole. The Western pattern tends to encourage the generative approach, the goal being to facilitate the intellectual growth of the young reader.

1.1 Children's Books in Western Countries

Very few children in Western countries in the seventeenth and eighteenth centuries were literate, and those who were read either books written for adults or those written to teach children important lessons. Adult books differed sharply from children's books, the latter being designed to instruct, to correct, and to demonstrate the horrible consequences of normal childhood exuberance and egocentrism. Termed didacticism, that tradition was to dominate children's books for hundreds of years and persist as an influence into contemporary times (Sutherland and Arbuthnot 1986). Books of this sort were frequently written in rhyme or in question–answer format, and dealt with such topics as manners, customs, and morals.

In 1976, Charles Perrault published, in Paris, *Contes de ma mère l'Oie* [Tales of Mother Goose], which is considered the first book of any consequence to be written specifically for children (Hazard 1944). Although *Pilgrim's Progress*, which John Bunyan had published in England (part 1 appearing in 1678, part 2 in 1684) was written for adults, children who could read apparently enjoyed it as well.

Defoe's *Robinson Crusoe*, which appeared in 1719, ran counter to the puritan tradition exemplified by *Pilgrim's Progress* and although likewise written for adults, was popular with children.

Gulliver's Travels, published anonymously in 1726, was well-received by youngsters, much to the surprise of its author, Jonathan Swift, who wrote the book for adults, as a satirical social commentary.

Jean-Jacques Rousseau in France and John Locke in England shared the belief that children were not inherently bad, and that experience, particularly direct experience, was a valuable teacher. At the same time, people came to believe that education was every child's right, and a few public libraries were established. While all these factors influenced children's literature, didacticism was by no means eliminated.

In 1812, Jacob and Wilhelm Grimm published *Kinder und Hausmärchen* [Children and Home Tales], translated into English in 1823 and entitled *Grimms' Fairy Tales*. The Grimms were serious scholars who tried to preserve the form as well as the content of the old tales they collected.

Hans Christian Andersen's *Fairy Tales* appeared in England in 1846. Andersen too was a careful collector of folk tales, but unlike the Grimms he changed, elaborated, and perhaps enriched them. Andersen's tales may have been the precursors of the genre currently known as "realistic fiction."

Several series of children's books, some still popular today, were introduced in the middle of the nineteenth century. The first of a series of *Elsie Dinsmore* books, written by Martha Finley, appeared in 1868. The best known of Louisa May Alcott's books about the March family, *Little Women* and *Little Men*, were published in 1868 and 1872 respectively. Robert Louis Stevenson's *Treasure Island*, published in 1883, became a classic, read by children everywhere. With Mark Twain's *Adventures of Tom Sawyer* (1876) and especially *Adventures of Huckleberry Finn* (1884), which were instantly popular, didacticism was moribund at last. By the end of the nineteenth century, it was no longer considered essential to teach a lesson through every book written for children. Authors were writing to provide pleasure, adventure, and delight for children.

The increasing popularity of the picture book in the twentieth century, some without words at all [e.g. *Changes, Changes*, by P. J. Hutchins (1971)] has generated a controversy over the literary value of such books. Can a book without words be considered literature? Can it be assumed that since the story unfolds in the mind of the viewer (reader?) as guided and stimulated by the illustrations, these books are indeed literature? The value of such books is not questioned: "These books encourage children to interpret and embellish a story; they are a good catalyst for a discussion of the author's (perhaps one should say illustrator's) intent and for the child's creativity" (Sutherland and Arbuthnot 1986). It might be added that the increasing importance of the picture book is strong evidence that early childhood is accepted as an important developmental period. During the twentieth century there has been a tremendous increase in the number and quality of nonfictional books for children. These are informative books—yet not textbooks—from which children can gain knowledge in various fields on their own. Today, the choices available to young readers seeking information are greater than ever.

Current informational books deal with a variety of things ranging from railroads and tugboats, to matrices and making mobiles, to ecology and pollution. Children and adolescents eager to pursue independent research, or explore a topic of interest, have no difficulty locating information in most school and/or public libraries, provided they are given the necessary guidance and training in the requisite locational and reference skills.

Contemporary authors have also dealt with death, divorce, homosexuality, drug and alcohol abuse, how it feels to have a retarded sibling, and how it feels to be black, all in the form of "realistic fiction."

1.2 The Soviet Union

In Czarist Russia, little effort was made at producing anything other than translations of folk tales and fairy tales, and collections of Russian fables, epics, and folk tales. Yet even in prerevolutionary times, the study and reading of literature was woven into the lives of Russians, from the peasant child who heard tales around a fireside to the aristocrats who reared their children either on translations of Western literature, or on the hundreds of stories written for children by such luminaries as Leo Tolstoy (1820–1910). Tolstoy was responsible not only for an effort to compile a textbook that would guide a child's moral growth, but also for some 629 fables and stories aimed at the same end. Another famous prerevolutionary classic in the same genre was Pyotr Ershov's *The Little Humpback Horse* (1834), a satiric fairy tale in rhyme that included folklore elements. Although this book was suppressed by the Czar for 30 years, it was finally published (and translated into English) and is still a popular part of children's reading in the Soviet Union.

The cultural revolution that accompanied the political revolution stressed the importance of literature as a source of truth and idealism, and as an instrument capable of effecting social awareness and change. Consequently, such writers as Pushkin, Gogol, Turgenev, Dostoevsky, Tolstoy, and Chekhov were among the prominent writers of short tales included in the reading curriculum of the young. By 1919, in addition to compulsory general, political, and cultural education, an Institute for Children's Reading was established, and such writers as Gorky and A. S. Serafimovich were instrumental in the development of a public school literature curriculum. In the 1920s, K. Chuckovsky, S. Marshak, A. Barto, and S. Michalkov, translated English nursery rhymes into Russian, and their effort opened the door for literary material for preschoolers.

After 1923, children's literature became a field for playing out various opposing attitudes towards educating the Soviet child into knowing the goodness of the common person and the importance of production and technology in the creation of the state; for example, real adventures in the life of scientists and explorers and numerous biographies of Lenin were produced. V. Katayev's *The Cottage in the Steppe* is a novel about prerevolutionary days and the involvement of two young boys in the Revolution and Civil War. The 1930s and 1940s saw a period that attempted to discredit fantasy and to purge literature of whatever was not realistic. War stories were numerous and reinforced the patriotism and idealism emphasized in the training of youth. A. Nadekhdina's *The Eaglet*, a story about 16 children who lost their lives during the siege of Leningrad, was one of the best-known stories of this genre. The post-Stalin period from 1956 onward saw an end to the battle against fantasy. The most famous work of fantasy that emerged out of this era is N. Nosov's *The Adventure of Dunno and His Friends* (1954). The 1960s and 1970s saw the publication of a great deal of adolescent and juvenile fiction, many fine nature stories, and an abundance of books of poetry.

1.3 Iran

The history of children's literature of Iran, though short, is the history of a nation's changing values. The great poets whom the Iranians revered became those they expected their children to revere, the most popular and accessible of these being Firdausi. Though he was a court poet, his stories became part of popular storytelling for centuries after his death. One of the greatest epics ever produced is Firdausi's *Shahnama* (1000-10)— a magnificent collection of tales in the form of 60,000 couplets based on oral tales, folk history, and mythology. Its material goes back to the beginnings of time, and its central theme is the struggle and rise of the Persians dramatized as the fight between good and evil; the story reaches its climax in the adventures of one of its greatest heroes, Rustam, whose superhuman moral, physical, and national strength protected the land for hundreds of years and was the ideal of children generations later. In a country that has had an illiteracy rate of 75–80 percent, the success and popularity of this epic is probably due to its subject and particularly to its rhymes that lend themselves to memorization as well as its frequent repetitions that link its many episodes and scenes together.

The 1940s through the 1960s saw the translation of German and French folk and fairy tales, and the adaptation of major Persian classics in children's editions. Through the efforts of the Library Association, the Children's Book Council, and the Institute for the Intellectual Development of Children and Young Adults, an increased effort was made to produce children's books of better quality. Book illustrators improved and won several international awards, and writers became more daring and imaginative in producing original works intended to stimulate the minds of the young. The most famous of these was a teacher whose satiric treatment of social injustice was almost banned by court censorship. Samad Behrangi's *The Fish That Was Black and Small* (1967) camouflages social criticism as an animal tale— in the story of a little black fish who loses its life in the struggle to find a better life. Since the revolution, the number of books written expressly for children and evaluated by the Children's Book Council has increased, but the majority are didactic in intent and aimed towards inculcating an understanding of revolution and Islam.

2. Content Analysis of Children's Books

The major themes dealt with in children's books changed in the course of the centuries. The 1940s have been frequently described as the beginning of a new period in juvenile literature characterized by increased realism. Current children's books contain reports on economic trends and social problems such as immigration and school integration, and include true-to-life, accurate stories about physically handicapped children, those belonging to single parent families, and so on. Several researchers have tried to apply the technique of content analysis to describe the changing trends in the themes of children's books. For example, Bekkedal (1973) discerned in these trends three subject areas: human relations, values and cultural context, and racial and ethnic group differences.

Children's books generally present positive images of obedient, lovable, intelligent children who live in harmony with their parents. There is a trend away from writing about rural locations toward writing about urban locations and smaller families. While a variety of family settings are depicted, an underrepresentation is observable of family types differing in some way from the majority such as children of divorced parents, of families that move frequently or are lower class, and so on. Books about the physically handicapped are increasingly diverse and contain honest appraisals by other children of the handicapped child's behavior. Books dealing with death within the family attempt to help children overcome anxieties and adjust to the inevitable facts of life. Values commonly dealt with in children's books are sexual morality, good manners, justice, work, obedience, natural conservation, interdependence, and personal responsibility.

The first intensive study of values represented in children's literature examined the appearance of symbols of nationalism in books and their relationship to the popularity of books. As might have been expected, it was found that a hostile attitude made a book unpopular in the nation criticized.

There is a tendency toward increasingly realistic treatment of racial and ethnic minorities, and a decrease in racial and ethnic stereotyping in juvenile literature, so that members of minority groups appear as major characters in books published in the 1960s and 1970s. The differing roles of boys and girls, mothers and fathers as portrayed in books, and the proportion of male and female characters have been examined in several studies. Studies about handling the subject of war in children's books present some interesting contrasts. While earlier books are filled with racist remarks about the enemy and emphasize the glory of battle, more recent ones tend to describe the misery of war and its devastating effect upon individual families.

3. Illustrations in Children's Books

Illustrations in children's books may fill a variety of functions. In picture books, counting books, concept books, and so on the illustrations carry the entire message for young children. In picture story books, the illustrations support the verbal message read to or by the child. In most children's books the illustrations extend the meaning of the text, evoke an appropriate mode, establish the setting for the events, portray the fictional characters, or, in books designed for older children, simply provide decoration.

Probably the first picture book prepared for children was the *Orbis Pictus* written by Comenius in Latin in the seventeenth century and shortly after its Latin publication, translated into most European languages. It contains drawings illustrating the words appearing in the book. Seventeenth-century children's books contain woodcut illustrations which are not generally of a high aesthetic level. The technical achievements of the eighteenth and nineteenth century, the advent of metal engraving and the invention of lithography increased the aesthetic qualities of the illustrations in children's books. These technical advances coincide with the first well-known artist who became famous for his work in illustrating children's books, Thomas Bewick (1753–1828). Nineteenth-century book illustrations are characterized by an attempt to provide recognizable representations of things and events combined with elegant elaboration. Contemporary children's books reflect the impact of most major movements in art. Smith (1967) lists several gains which can be derived from illustrations and cautions against dangers inherent in them: good illustration makes possible a two-way attack upon the reader's attention: visual and verbal. The visual patterns provide a stimulus for the child's own verbal storytelling and constitute a source of information. Finally, they provide a visual aesthetic experience. The potential dangers in illustrations need to be recognized. Superior visual storytelling can obscure inferior verbal storytelling or hide the literary merits of the text. The child may be overpowered by the pictures to the extent of losing interest in the text. Reliance on pictures may confine the child's imagination to the visual world of the artist's conceptions.

4. Censorship

In pluralistic societies, various points of view can be and are expressed freely subject to the restrictions of accuracy of data and good taste. Nevertheless, in every society there are groups and individuals who believe that all materials written for children should be reviewed, and access denied to any materials (fiction, nonfiction, and nonprint media) which could be considered controversial or potentially damaging to children and youth.

The issues are very complex; there is almost never enough money to purchase all the materials produced related to a given topic, whether or not the topic is controversial. In determining which books on sex, minority groups, revolutions, or civil wars to buy or not to buy, criteria are applied by individuals or groups. The first criterion is that any material purchased or selected must first of all be of "good" quality. Who determines whether or not a book is "good"? What are the standards to be applied in determining whether or not a book or film is in "good taste"? Too often, good taste is what the selector likes and poor taste is what the selector does not like. In deciding how limited financial resources are to be allocated, a process remarkably like censorship can occur. We are all censors in this sense, and teachers and parents play a significant and sensitive role in selecting the books to which children will be exposed. There should be distinct and significant differences between censorship and selection. "Selection" implies careful, objective decision making about materials, and the decisions are usually made by a group, not a single individual. Kamhi (1981) reports the results of a recent nationwide (US) survey indicating that contemporary fiction was the most commonly censored material. Seiferth (1981) surveyed approximately 1,000 high-school principals. Results indicated that pornography was frequently subject to censorship, obscenity occasionally, and racist/sexist language never.

Purchasing and selection decisions should be based upon thoughtfully developed criteria which will guide the process and will, hopefully, ensure the selection of a broad range of the best materials available. All the factors, including those which combine to limit and restrict children's and adolescents' exposure to the widest possible range of beliefs, ideas, theories, and concepts must be considered. A well-educated human being does not emerge from an environment characterized by fear, short-sighted decision making, or one in which those responsible for a child's education operate from a base of expedience. Censorship involves far more than burning copies of books or cutting out pages which might be considered offensive.

Restricting children's free access to materials inevitably restricts their growth and development. Children cannot be protected from life's realities by burning books or expurgating them. A literary work which is totally inoffensive is probably also of little value; its theme is likely to be trivial and the book is then hardly worth the time spent reading it. When parents, librarians, and teachers through ignorance and/or fear retreat and permit themselves to be manipulated by whichever political, ethnic, or racial group is ascendant at the moment, they are hurting the children and youth for whom they are responsible and the society those people will someday lead as well.

5. Measuring Responses to Literature

Purves (1973) conducted a cross-national comparative study of achievement in literature education in 10 countries. Students were asked to read three short literary passages, and select a few questions from a list of 20 questions representing various approaches to dealing with literature. The children's responses were classified according to four major categories: personal involvement, moral interpretation, aesthetic comments, and contextual classification. The results suggested that older students are more consistent than younger ones in their response to a given story. The response of the students also varied according to the content of the story. Some stories elicited more questions of personal involvement or moral interpretation than other ones. National differences in response patterns did exist but there were also many similarities. It appeared that in some countries (Belgium, Chile, Iran, Italy) the personal involvement response was enhanced to the detriment of the aesthetic response patterns, whereas in others (Finland, New Zealand, and Sweden) the opposite was true.

Applebee (1978) reports comprehensive analyses of the responses to literature of children of various ages. The 6-year-olds responded orally to the question "What is your favorite story? Tell me about it." The five titles most frequently cited by 6-year-olds included "Jack and Jill," "Cinderella," and "Goldilocks." "The Lion, The Witch and The Wardrobe," "Sleeping Beauty," and "Snow White" were among the favorite stories cited by the 9-year-olds. Applebee related the responses of the 9-year-olds, both oral and written, to Piagetian stages, and accounts for the more sophisticated responses of the 9-year-olds in terms of their being at the concrete operational stage rather than at the preoperational stage. Six-year-olds (50 percent) typically retold the story, including title, opening and closing lines, and dialogue. The 9-year-olds (40 percent) tended to summarize the events, and state the theme of the story. Following this reasoning, Applebee characterizes the responses of the adolescents as being typical of those who have reached the stage of "formal operations." The Purves–Rippere (1968) categories (enlargement, perception, interpretation, evaluation, and miscellaneous) were used in analyzing the responses of subgroups of 6- and 9-year-olds in discussions of favorite stories and of a single favorite story; 92.9 percent of the responses of the 6-year-olds and 78.0 percent of those of the 9-year-olds were categorized as "perceptive"; 6.3 percent of the 6-year-old responses and 16.0 percent of the 9-year-olds' responses were considered "evaluative."

Schlager (1978) also takes a Piagetian/developmental approach to literary response: "Books that reflect the child's perception of the world are the books children clamor for. The toddler delights in aspects that will be of little interest to the 7- to 12-year-old. The interests of middle childhood are likewise not of interest to the young adolescent."

Ann Terry (1974) conducted a survey of children's poetry preferences. Her subjects were 1,276 pupils enrolled in grades four, five, and six (ages 9 to 12) in the United States (Florida, Ohio, Pennsylvania, and Texas). The major purpose of the study was to determine the poems which children liked best and those which they liked least. Terry also analyzed the relationship between pupils' choices and their sex, grade level, and type of school setting. The most popular poems were analyzed in terms of form, content, poetic elements, and age of the poem. She concluded that interest in poetry reaches a peak at grade four and then declines. Although few sex differences were noted, in general girls appeared to like poetry better than boys. Inner-city children showed the greatest enthusiasm for poetry, and suburban children showed the least. There was a general preference for contemporary poems, humorous poems, and poems about familiar experiences and animals. The poetic elements of rhyme, rhythm, and sound appeared to have the strongest influence on children's choices.

Cooper (1972) reviewed a number of attempts to measure appreciation of literature grouped into two categories: discriminations among selections, and content analysis. Robinson and Weintraub (1973) summarized research related to the developmental value of reading, which examined whether children acquire culturally adaptive values through reading. The authors indicated that there are no dependable research techniques for determining the effects of reading on children, perhaps because of the multiplicity of factors that may impinge on behavior or attitude change. There is some evidence that although a single book has relatively little impact on the child, there is a discernible effect derived from reading a broad selection of books. Several studies examined the impact of reading on understanding one's self and on developing a positive self-awareness. The premise that reading is a factor in promoting mental/emotional health constitutes a basis for bibliotherapy. Fisher (1968) arranged discussion groups dealing with the content of reading and found that such groups changed their attitudes more than the groups that only read the literary selections. An extensive study conducted by Lorang (1968) indicates that 86 percent of children said that books had aroused their emotions, 53 percent tried to emulate a character of a book, and 42 percent did something because they read about it in a book.

The data and opinions summarized here indicate that children's choices, and their response to literary selections, are strongly influenced by age and the child's stage of emotional and psychological development. Sociological and cultural factors also play a significant role. While it is important to discover what children like and dislike, this should not limit what is supplied to them. If the selection is inappropriate to the child's developmental level, it will probably be rejected. It is possible, however, that children's reactions will not change unless and until the adults in their world make an effort to broaden and expand the focus to which children might respond in a positive manner.

Bibliography

Applebee A N 1978 *The Child's Concept of Story: Ages Two to Seventeen.* University of Chicago Press, Chicago, Illinois

Ayman L 1969 The progress of children's literature in Iran during the past decade. *Int. Libr. Rev.* 1: 197–99

Bekkedal T K 1973 Content analysis of children's books. *Library Trends* 22: 109–26

Clay M 1979 *Reading: The Patterning of Complex Behaviour.* Heinemann, Portsmouth, New Hampshire

Cooper C 1972 *Measuring Growth in the Appreciation of Literature.* International Reading Association, Newark, Delaware

Doderer K (ed.) 1975 *Lexikon der Kinder- und Jugendliteratur: Personnen-, Länder- und Sachartikel zu Geschichte und Gegenwart der Kinder und Jugendliteratur.* Beltz, Weinheim

Fisher F L 1968 Influences of reading and discussion on the attitudes of fifth graders toward American Indians. *J. Educ. Res.* 62: 130–34

Hazard P 1944 *Books, Children and Men.* The Horn Book, Boston, Massachusetts

Kamhi M 1981 *Books and Materials Selection for School Libraries and Classrooms: Procedures, Challenges and Responses.* Education Resources Information Center, ERIC Document No. ED 210-772. American Library Association, Chicago, Illinois

Lewis C S 1963 On three ways of writing for children. *The Horn Book Magazine* 39(5): 459–69

Lorang M C 1968 *Burning Ice: The Moral and Emotional Effects of Reading.* Scribner, New York

Newman J M 1985 *Whole Language: Theory in Use.* Heinemann, Portsmouth, New Hampshire

Purves A C 1973 *Literature Education in Ten Countries: An Empirical Study.* Wiley, New York

Purves A, Rippere V 1968 *Elements of Writing about a Literary Work.* National Council of Teachers of English, Urbana, Illinois

Robinson H M, Weintraub S 1973 Research related to children's interests and to developmental values of reading. *Library Trends* 22: 81–108

Rotkovich I A 1980 The history of literature teaching in the Soviet schools. *Soviet Educ.* 22(7): 3–160

Schlager N 1978 Predicting children's choices in literature: A developmental approach. *Children's Literature in Educ.* 9: 136–42

Seiferth B 1981 *Censorship: Cause for Concern?* Education Resources Information Center. ERIC Document No. ED 208 589

Smith F 1988 *Understanding Reading: A Psycholinguistic Analysis of Reading and Learning to Read,* 4th edn. Lawrence Erlbaun Associates, Hillsdale, New Jersey

Smith J S 1967 *A Critical Approach to Children's Literature.* McGraw-Hill, New York

Sutherland Z, Arbuthnot M H 1986 *Children and Books,* 7th edn. Scott Foresman Little Brown, Glenview, Illinois

Terry A 1974 *Children's Poetry Preferences: A National Survey of Upper Elementary Grades.* National Council of Teachers of English, Urbana, Illinois

Writing in the Humanities

J. M. Willinsky

Writing has always had a presence in interdisciplinary programs that wear the humanities' label and in the disciplines of literature, philosophy, history, and the arts that traditionally make up the humanities. Yet, after suffering a certain lapse in their fortunes, the study and practice of writing have experienced a renewal of interest from the humanities. In classical and medieval times, composition was at the core of the liberal arts, a heritage which carried well into the nineteenth century with the prominent place given to the study of rhetoric and grammar. While teachers have continued to seek high levels of expository writing from their students, composition has given way during the course of this century to the study of literature as the pre-eminent language art in the humanities.

However, writing has been the subject of a number of innovations in the curriculum which enhance its potential as a tool for learning and empowerment in the humanities. One effect of these innovations has been to reveal a rift between those educators who envisage the humanities as developing an appreciation of the cultural heritage which gives continuity to a society (Shattuck 1987), and those who see it as drawing from the study of culture the means of remaking that society (Greene 1983). The revival of writing in the humanities curriculum, led by this latter group, has taken two forms: (a) a pedagogical interest in teaching writing as a process that can lead to articulate participation in the culture, and (b) a poststructuralist concern with the way writing organizes the discourses that shape a culture.

These two developments represent refinements of a Hellenistic concern, if with a postmodern twist, for marshalling the rhetorical powers of language. Programs such as the National Writing Project in the United

States would develop the student's voice with an almost classical regard for composition as training for taking part in the *polis*. These ancient and contemporary curricula would also weave together oral and written cultures, as they did once in the study of Homer and Plato, and would today in bringing the experiences of the community into the discourse of the school. A third aspect of this classical heritage is a reluctance to treat creative writing as a separate entity in the curriculum. In an approach pioneered in Britain, writing is employed in a variety of creative forms to facilitate learning across the curriculum (Martin et al. 1976). However, this new approach to writing can also be seen to break radically with the past; the classical emphasis on mastering the rules of rhetoric, grammar and logic, which constituted the medieval trivium in the liberal arts, has been supplanted by the contemporary treatment of writing as a working process for teacher and student which entails drafting, revising, editing, and publishing their work.

The key to bringing writing back to the core of the humanities has been its integration with the disciplines. Literature has proven an excellent starting point for that integration, and instances of students working creatively and critically in the company of accomplished authors include Hansen's (1987) use of writers' journals with young readers and Bleich's (1978) reader-response pedagogy in which college students build a personal commentary on literary works into a critical engagement with the text. A more traditional example is Koch's (1973) method of teaching great poetry to children which follows a classical pattern of using poems by Shakespeare, Blake, Stevens and others as models for the students' writing; Koch improves on the old approach by bringing forward only one or two of the larger structural and thematic elements on which students build their own poetry.

Another successful method of integrating writing instruction with the liberal arts has been inquiry-centered writing. Students begin with a self-defined problem or question to pursue within a given subject area; and, with guidance from the teacher, plan their research, take notes, and prepare their reports for the rest of the class or a wider audience. The research on composition has found this one of the most effective means of improving students' writing (Hillocks 1986). Freire (1970) has developed a related pedagogy for adult literacy programs in Third World countries in which the students' inquiry into their immediate culture produces a powerful language for turning literacy into a humanistic and political enterprise.

Complementing this incorporation of the writing process into the humanities is the critical inquiry of deconstruction and feminism, both of which challenge the structure of discourse. By examining how meaning, genre, and authority are constructed through writing and how unacknowledged ideologies of gender, race, and class are inscribed, this method of analysis examines the written organization of discourses across the humanities (Atkins and Johnson 1985). The unsettling of the text can also lead back to the students' writing as these challenges to traditional forms suggest the possibility of new writing strategies (Yaeger 1988).

The critical and productive restoration of writing to the core of the humanities is an attempt to balance the give and take in students' education. The manner in which students write in the humanities has important consequences for the nature of their engagement with the culture. Depending on the educator's approach to writing in the humanities, students may have the opportunity to record their appreciation of various aspects of the culture, learn by working creatively with the culture, assess cultural aspects of discourse, and achieve a new degree of expression for themselves within the culture.

Bibliography

Atkins G D, Johnson M L (eds.) 1985 *Writing and Reading Differently: Deconstruction and the Teaching of Composition and Literature.* University Press of Kansas, Lawrence, Kansas

Bleich D 1978 *Subjective Criticism.* Johns Hopkins University Press, Baltimore, Maryland

Freire P 1970 *The Pedagogy of the Oppressed.* Herder and Herder, New York

Greene M 1983 The humanities in question. In: Finkelstein D (ed.) 1983 *The Humanities in Education: Rebirth or Burial in the 1980s.* Prakken, Ann Arbor, Michigan, pp. 14–19

Hansen J 1987 *When Writers Read.* Heinemann, Portsmouth, New Hampshire

Hillocks G Jr 1986 *Research on Written Composition: New Directions for Teaching.* ERIC, Urbana, Illinois

Koch K 1973 *Rose, Where Did You Get that Red? Teaching Great Poetry to Children.* Random House, New York

Martin N, D'Arcy P, Newton B, Parker R 1976 *Writing and Learning Across the Curriculum: 11–16 Years.* Ward Lock, London

Shattuck R 1987 *Perplexing Dreams: Is There a Core Tradition in the Humanities?* American Council of Learned Societies, Washington, DC

Yaeger P S 1988 *Honey-Mad Women: Emancipatory Strategies in Women's Writing.* Columbia University Press, New York

Classical Languages Curricula

H. Vester

The term classical languages generally means Greek, the language of the ancient Greeks, and Latin, the language of the Romans, as distinct from other languages of antiquity (e.g., Hebrew). In the course of history, both of these languages and their literatures have played an important role in general education.

Today, in a science-oriented era, they have lost their former central position but have retained a place in the curriculum of secondary schools. The purpose of this article is to clarify their present situation and to describe the aims and methods of classroom instruction.

1. Contents and Aims

The subjects of instruction in the classical language are their linguistic systems and their literature and culture. Course duration and the number of weekly periods, which determine the emphasis of linguistic and literary studies, vary greatly from school system to school system. Whereas in a number of schools in the Federal Republic of Germany it is still possible for Latin courses of nine years' duration and Greek courses of five years' duration to be implemented, in most school systems, long courses seem to be rather an exception. It is also fair to say that, as in previous centuries, the position of Greek is weaker than that of Latin, to the extent that in most school systems it is only a minute percentage of pupils and students who study the language of the ancient Greeks.

The systematic teaching of the language and an introduction to its literature have always been and still are the basis of classroom instruction. However, owing to the shortage of available time, different courses have evolved, especially in Latin, which do not aim at covering the totality of the language. The remedial Latin programs and Latin-based language-readiness courses in the United States, and the classical studies courses in the United States and in the United Kingdom, concentrate on the most relevant aspects of Greco–Roman civilization and culture, and incorporate the ancient authors only in translations. Wherever the works are studied in the original there is a great consensus to be found as to the choice of authors: Homer, Sophocles, Euripides, Plato, and Thucydides in Greek; Virgil, Horace, Caesar, Cicero, and Tacitus in Latin. These names are found in virtually all reading lists in European and American schools and colleges. More recently, some alternatives have been suggested: authors in whose works everyday life is reflected, such as Plautus, Terence, Petronius, or medieval and humanist writers such as Archipoeta, Thomas Morus, and Erasmus. Beside the study of entire books or substantial portions of them, a topical approach to classroom studies has been developed. The focus is on anthropological problems and political and philosophical ideas, with shorter passages from various authors and epochs being combined to contribute to a single theme.

Aims and arguments for the study of classical languages have been characterized by a comparatively high stability over time and place. On the other hand, owing to changes in the instructional situation, these, too, were bound to change and to exhibit great differences, denoting that not all potential objectives can be valid for all types of courses. Since the early 1920s, important statements on the aims of classical instruction have been corroborated by empirical studies. The type of research applied to the classics will be illustrated by representative examples from Latin.

1.1 The Classical Investigation

At the beginning of the 1920s, the American Classical League made an extensive and comprehensive investigation into the aims of classical instruction as conceived by teachers and high-school and college students. The Classical Investigation defined the primary and indispensable objective of the study of Latin as a progressive development in the ability to read and understand Latin. Out of a list of 21 objectives under three general headings (instrumental and application, disciplinary, and cultural) extending beyond the Latin classroom, 10 statements could be regarded as valid indications of motivation for the study of Latin (American Classical League 1924 pp. 29–82). Recently, these ultimate objectives have been "consolidated and rephrased in keeping with contemporary challenges and opportunities as follows:

(a) To enhance skills in use of the English language.

(b) To build a firm foundation for the study of modern foreign languages, especially the Romance languages.

(c) To impart an understanding of Greco–Roman civilization and culture as a key to understanding ourselves.

(d) To develop a systematic acquaintance with the workings of the Latin language and an ability to handle the language, with Latin being used as an example of how language works" (Lawall 1981 p. 14).

These aims and objectives may not always have represented reality, but they certainly do represent the ideals toward which good teachers strove and should still strive.

1.2 Validation of Aims and Objectives by the German Classical League

Fifty years after the Classical Investigation, in the context of worldwide curricular reforms, the classics were in greater turmoil than ever before. They were being pressured by curricular theory to put forward the relevance of their objectives in a modern curriculum and to validate them by empirical research. A committee of the German Classical League not only analyzed the effects of classical instruction with the aid of taxonomical categories but also attempted to validate significant statements about Latin instruction by means of a study of teachers and a nationwide achievement test (Bayer 1973). After some experimentation with B. S. Bloom's taxonomy of educational goals in the cognitive domain, the committee decided to follow a slightly different concept. They developed a matrix combining four content areas (language, literature, society/state/

history, basic anthropological problems) with four stages of behavioral objectives (knowledge, reorganization of knowledge, transfer, problem solving), and formulated a full list of 76 objectives and 32 test questions pertaining to them.

The results of the investigation may be summarized as follows. The teachers who answered the questionnaire expected that in the content areas of language and history nearly all objectives of the matrix would be implemented. In the other two areas, however, they expected only two-thirds to be realized. The test designed to control the results of teacher validation led to similar conclusions in general. It could also be shown that the outcomes validated were related to course duration. The longer the Latin instruction, the greater the chance to achieve the proposed goals. The most significant point of this study seems to be that the concrete learning outcomes that were hypothesized could be proved real to a considerable degree. It is worth noting that, since the early 1970s, instruction in the long-term courses has been far more directed toward literature and anthropological issues.

1.3 The Washington and Philadelphia Studies

At about the same time, two very important studies on the transfer effect of early Latin instruction (for ages 10 to 12) on the mastery of English were carried out in the United States: the Washington (District of Columbia 1971) and Philadelphia studies (Offenberg et al. 1971). The projects they described were conducted as part of the Foreign Languages in the Elementary School (FLES) program aimed at compensating for the language deficiencies of deprived children. Several thousands of elementary-school children were given 20 minutes of Latin instruction daily, the instruction not being geared to a systematic approach to the language. The underlying hypothesis of the project was that the study of specific linguistic and semantic aspects (words, roots, suffixes, prefixes) of Latin might help to break down language barriers. The results of the two studies were similar and conclusive. The achievement of Latin pupils in mastering the English language (vocabulary, reading comprehension) was in general significantly higher than that of the control groups (pupils without Latin instruction, or with Spanish or French instruction). The compensatory program in Philadelphia was widely extended to take in a great number of other school districts. The Philadelphia study was replicated in Indianapolis (and elsewhere) with comparable results. It was even possible to demonstrate a significant increase in mathematical skills in the experimental group (Sheridan 1976).

This section may be summarized by saying that the FLES Latin idea has caught on, and that, toward the end of the 1980s, such programs have been implemented in the public school systems of more than a dozen cities, and hundreds of smaller districts and individual schools have either started or are considering FLES Latin programs.

2. Methods and Media

The choice of teaching materials and media is, in the first place, determined by the relevant aims and objectives. Nevertheless, numerous other factors make themselves felt, shaping instructional procedures. Since the early 1960s, the patterns of classics teaching have been fundamentally changed by the quest for relevance, the developments in linguistics in general and in the methodology of modern language teaching, and by the invention of technical teaching devices.

2.1 The Quest for Relevance

It was a combination of motivational considerations and linguistic concepts that paved the way for completely new types of textbooks. No longer is it the disconnected sentence, illustrating some point of grammar, that is the core of present-day books but a "real text" which, by virtue of its form and content, is likely to motivate pupils. Quite frequently the reading passages of several units, or even the whole book, are grouped under one topic or are rendered coherent by the characters involved. Far more than in textbooks of bygone days, it is the everyday life of the ancient world that is depicted, while the "virtues of the Romans and Greek" recede to the background. Real human beings appeal to the mind of the young reader.

Accordingly, the most significant innovation in some textbooks is the regular presentation of formal grammar after the reading section, reversing the traditional practice. In order to enhance the pupils' interest in the story, several books present as little formal grammar as seems justified. Translation into the target language is now widely abandoned or regarded as one type of linguistic exercise among many others.

2.2 The Influence of Linguistics and Modern Language Teaching

Grammatical explanations and linguistic drills in present-day books quite frequently follow patterns that were developed by contemporary linguistic and methodological innovations in modern language teaching. In 1957, W. E. Sweet tried to apply the findings of structural linguistics to Latin. This approach implies that talk about the language should be kept to a minimum and Latin should be learnt by hearing it, reading it, and writing it (Sweet et al. 1966 p. 5). Some other textbooks have followed a similar strategy—incorporating the oral use of Latin, not towards developing oral proficiency in a language that is no longer spoken, but towards promoting the primary goal of Latin instruction: reading. Although the new proposals were never widely adopted by teachers, they were accepted by enough to inject a strong influence into almost all Latin classes today.

There are, however, other contemporary approaches to teaching grammar, which again demand more talk about the language. They are oriented towards the French linguist Tesnière's (1959) conceptions of sentence structure. The basis of this procedure is the analysis of any syntactical dependencies in relation to the verb. Some scholars are also trying to utilize the analytical methods of textual grammar to improve reading, translation, and interpretation work. The findings of a series of word-frequency studies, which enable textbook writers to distinguish between basic and author-specific words, are being applied to vocabulary building (Mathy 1952, Krope 1969).

2.3 The Impact of Educational Technology

The 1960s may be looked upon as a phase of technical innovations in classroom instruction. In the guise of programmed instruction, language laboratory work (see *Language Laboratories*), and computer-assisted instruction (CAI), technology entered Latin and Greek classes. Not only were specific sections of structural points programmed but also complete courses. For whatever reasons, however, actual classroom teaching has never been widely influenced by such materials, though more so in the United States than in Europe. There is still room for experimentation and research in this field.

As to work in the language laboratory, some teachers did experiment with this type of activity, but few materials were ever published. Soon after the general crisis of language laboratory work, these innovations were again given up in many places. Computer-assisted instruction is supplemental to regular classroom work; and it must be borne in mind that all technical devices were hardly ever considered as exclusive alternatives to direct teaching but as being subsidiary in nature.

Little research seems to be available as to the effects of all these innovations in methodology and technology on classroom instruction. Their personal and subjective experiences have led many teachers to believe that certain modern features, such as the new look of the textbooks, definitely can enhance the pupils' motivations. In general, however, these recent developments have yielded a paradoxical result "that the increased emphasis on learning to read Latin and Greek as Latin and Greek is not accomplishing that purpose as effectively as might be expected or certainly desired" (Latimer 1973 p. 18). Latimer suggested that a more precise definition of reading ability as it relates to Latin and Greek was needed. Though this problem has not yet been solved, it seems obvious that, in contrast with comprehension of modern languages, the reading of an ancient text in the original is a mental process *sui generis* which is made complex not only by the structure of the language but also by the distance of the subject matter.

Such an understanding affords a unique training of intellectual abilities, which still justifies the presence of the classics in modern curriculum.

Bibliography

American Classical League, Advisory Committee 1924 *The Classical Investigation,* Part 1: *General Report.* Princeton University Press, Princeton, New Jersey

Bayer K (ed.) 1973 *Lernziele und Fachleistungen: Ein empirischer Ansatz zum Latein-Curriculum* [Objectives and achievements: An empirical approach to the Latin curriculum]. Der Altsprachliche Unterricht, Beiheft VI. Klett, Stuttgart

District of Columbia, Public Schools 1971 *A Study of the Effect of Latin Instruction on English Reading Skills of Sixth Grade Students in the Public Schools of the District of Columbia, School Year 1970–71.* District of Columbia Public Schools, Washington, DC. ERIC Document No. ED 060 695

Happ H 1976 *Grundfragen einer Dependenz-Grammatik des Lateinischen* [Basic problems of a dependence-grammar of Latin]. Vandenhoeck and Ruprecht, Göttingen

Krope P 1969 Die 1,000 häufigsten Wörter der Schullektüre aus Caesar, Livius, Cicero. [The most frequent 1,000 words in school readers of the works of Caesar, Livius and Cicero]. *Der altsprachliche Unterricht,* Beilage 2u 12(5): 1–12

LaFleur R A (ed.) 1987 *The Teaching of Latin in American Schools. A Profession in Crisis.* The Scholars Press, Atlanta, Georgia

Latimer J F 1973 *The New Case for Latin and the Classics.* Occasional Papers 19. Council for Basic Education, Washington, DC

Lawall G 1981 Latin: Directions for the 1980s. *The Maine Classicist* I(2): 3–35

Mathy M 1952 *Vocabulaire de Base du Latin.* Préface de J Marouzeau. Desclée, De Brouwer, Paris

Mavrogenes N A 1987 Latin and language arts: An update. *Foreign Language Annals* 20: 31–36

Offenberg R M et al. 1971 Evaluation of the elementary school (FLES) Latin program 1970–71. School District of Philadelphia, Pennsylvania. ERIC Document No. ED 056 612

Phinney E 1987 The current classical scene in America. *Joint Assocation of Classical Teachers Review* 2nd Series 2: 2–7

Sheridan R S 1976 *Evaluation Report of Title III Project.* Indianapolis Public Schools, Indianapolis, Indiana

Sweet W E, Craig R S, Seligson G M 1966 (1957) *Latin: A Structural Approach.* University of Michigan Press, Ann Arbor, Michigan

Tesnière L 1959 *Eléments de syntaxe structurale,* 2nd edn. Préface de Jean Fourquet. Klincksieck, Paris

Wulfing P (ed.) 1986 *Gesprächskreis Europa.* Romiosini, Köln

Wulfing P (ed.) 1989 Bericht über die Situation des Alten Sprachen in einigen europäischen Ländern. *Der altsprachliche Unterricht* 89(2): 69–80, 89(3): 84–93

Section 8

Arts Curricula

Overview

The Section on arts curricula is divided into two parts. The first part surveys art subjects traditionally taught in schools, and the second part deals with innovative subjects which have appeared in school programs only in the second half of the twentieth century.

The first entry in this Section, by Otto, defines the term "aesthetic education," reviews trends in this field since the 1930s, and proposes a three-dimensional model for examining interdisciplinary aspects of separate art subjects (such as art, music, and so on). Efland presents a broad historical overview of ideas and practices which have influenced art education programs in the twentieth century, and reviews cross-national differences in later twentieth century school programs in the United States, England and Wales, the Federal Republic of Germany, the Soviet Union, France, Japan, and the developing countries. Morris examines the concept of *Attitude Towards Art* and its interrelationship with art education in the context of school and life-long education.

The task of the schools in art education is complemented by the educational activities of museums. Originally, museums served in the capacity of custodians of the artistic, historical, and scientific heritage of humankind. In the twentieth century the museum is no longer considered as a passive keeper of art treasures, but has gradually assumed the role of an educational institution. The educational activities of museums, both for adults and children, are the topic of Lee's article.

One of the oldest arts subjects in the school is music. It was a major component of the school program in ancient Greece as well as in the church schools over the centuries. Learning to sing had an instrumental value for participating in church services and also for boosting patriotic feelings. It was this instrumental value of singing which has kept music teaching alive in schools, and not merely the enjoyment of music. Garretson describes *Music Curricula* in modern schools and examines the significance and the value of music in modern life.

The last article in this subsection is on *Handicrafts*, which is at the edge of arts studies. Schleicher's article on this topic describes goal definitions of this subject in various school systems, which contain also principles of industrial arts, but also manipulative skills, career education, polytechnic education, and so on.

The second part of this Section reviews innovative topics or subjects taught in schools. The first entry deals with creativity programs. Tannenbaum views creativity as a generic term that refers to activities in various areas of human life, and not only to art. He notes that the concern of schools for encouraging creativity has a relatively long history; nevertheless only in the second half of the twentieth century have creativity programs been put into use in schools. Tannenbaum reviews such programs and summarizes various studies on their effectiveness.

Dance as an independent school subject appeared in the curriculum of numerous schools after the 1960s. Dimondstein argues that dance studies have to touch upon the historical, aesthetic, and performance aspects of dance, as well as on its connection to other areas of life. Dance instruction took place in schools during ancient and medieval times, but it was linked to religious rituals or to social functions, while today the expressive-artistic and folkloristic aspects of dance constitute the focus of interests.

Educational programs, and research related to these programs in the field of *Film Studies* and *Theater Studies*, are described by Shuchat-Shaw and by Child. Two other innovative subjects which appear in contemporary school programs—*Visual Education* and *Media Literacy*—are linked to each other. The first of them, by Cochran, deals with learning to comprehend and appreciate the many forms of visual information presented singly or in sequences. The latter, by Morrow, deals with the ability to understand the message conveyed through various media, including those which are based on using voice cues only. The author emphasizes that, in contrast to the popular view, motion pictures and television commercials are not fully self-explanatory and their comprehension and adequate interpretation is facilitated through systematic study.

A. Lewy

Arts Education

Introduction

P. G. Gluck

It is through the arts that the heritage of a people is so significantly transmitted and their most profound emotions and needs are expressed. Through the languages of art, meanings are transformed, retained, shared, communicated, exchanged, preserved and remembered. It is through experiences in and with the arts that we can see, hear, move and feel with greater sensitivity and purpose. Nevertheless, for a number of reasons the arts have not been perceived as basic to education. Not the least of these reasons is that they do not seem to serve tangible useful ends; and also, because they appear to make few rigorous intellectual demands on our students. Although parents and educators generally acknowledge the value of the arts, there remains a wide gap between their rhetoric and the actual resources and time allocated to quality arts programs.

Even though many of the reform proposals for education recommend that the arts be included, few offer specific and detailed explanations of how this should be done. They do, however, set forth detailed recommendations and standards for the other basic subject areas. Much needs to be accomplished if we are to put in place, at all grade levels, the most fruitful types of sequential arts education programs required for all our students, taught by teachers who are both trained and educated in the arts and in pedagogy. The arts are changing rapidly and it is necessary to know how new forms, new materials, and new technologies might transform the curriculum. These would also require new critical skills. As in other fields, there is often a lag between what is happening in "the art world" and what is explored in the "school world."

In order to be able to create and perform, to analyze, formulate, and express critical judgments, and to share feelings and ideas, students must learn the languages of art. Through aesthetics, art criticism, and art history, meaningful communication is strengthened. Today, "Discipline-Based Art Education" is one of the programs advocating this approach in the visual arts. There are many other areas in arts education in which empirical research, both quantitative and qualitative, is extensive and ongoing. Arts educators need to be more aware of the findings, and to incorporate them into the curriculum. It is also important that arts educators have clearer assessment and evaluation criteria for their disciplines.

It is also important to attend to the expanding vocational opportunities in the arts, and to the education of children and youth from diverse backgrounds and with varying abilities. Finally, we need to emphasize the role of the arts in life-long education and in the fulfillment of leisure. The arts are a rightful legacy for all, and they must be an integral part of school programs at all grade levels.

The articles in this Section provide an international perspective that is of substantial value in helping to shape arts curricula. They fall into two broad categories: those that review particular disciplines within the arts (visual arts education, film, theater, dance, music), and those that address more general and generic subjects (creativity, aesthetic education, attitudes toward art, visual education, museum education, media literacy). The viewpoints reflect the philosophies of the authors and the social, political, and cultural settings in which they work. In some articles, an officially sanctioned view is espoused; in others it is implicit; and in others, repudiated.

Many of the writers deplore the failure of the education community to recognize the value of the arts in education. Too often the arts are treated as marginal and frivolous subjects, and funding for them is cut even further when budgets are tightened. Often the arts are relegated to extracurricular status.

There are also distinctions made between countries with government-mandated policies, and nations in which there is more autonomy. Likewise at issue is whether the official spokespersons truly represent the consensus of the professionals in a particular country.

Rationales for the focus and shape of arts curricula are presented and justified. Some of the authors address the problem of deciding which curriculum to choose out of an array of possibilities, and what to emphasize within it. For instance: what is the relative importance attached to performance or studio work as compared to theoretical, historical, and arts appreciation studies? Some authors explore the important abilities and skills which students should acquire in the arts, for appreciation, creating, and performing. In addition, there is discussion about how influences and attitudes toward the arts affect learning in the arts, and how positive attitudes toward the arts may be developed. At least one of the authors discusses the perennial issues of breadth versus depth, and process versus product in arts curriculum decisions.

Curriculum sources in the arts are being broadened, and more often include non-European cultures in addition to the traditional Western heritages. Although the arts in recent times have themselves drawn upon non-Western cultures for their formal and expressive power, the schools have been much slower to do the same for the arts education curriculum. There are, of course, resources other than the schools that educate students in the arts. They need to experience concert halls, theatres, museums, architecture, and monuments. Contributors discuss the need for the flexible scheduling that permits participation in cultural activities.

Some programs emphasize the role of the arts and the mass media as shapers of modern life, and are seen as forces for social change. The arts are seen as a complex system of symbols, encoding and decoding meanings and values. There is also discussion about the inclusion of popular art and folk art, and there is a recognition that the boundaries that have traditionally separated "high" art from the art of everyday life are no longer intact.

Today, school arts programs are also influenced and shaped by many groups and agencies which have assumed leadership roles. Universities, government, cultural institutions, foundations, the business community and professional organizations, all influence the direction and amount of arts education being offered.

Education in and through the arts develops human potential because it offers skills, values and insights that presumably cannot be acquired from other basic school subjects. Nevertheless, a few of the authors question some of these assumptions and point to the need for further research in this area.

There are issues raised about the nature and types of research in the fields of human development, theories of learning, critical thinking, creativity and perception, as they relate to arts education. There are also concerns about the training of teachers in the arts, about art specialists coming into the schools for special presentations, and the quality of the programs and the uninterrupted spans of class time necessary for them. At issue also are programs for the gifted and the talented, and the ways in which these students are selected. Many countries have specialized schools for the arts, and magnet schools within the community.

Several articles also survey the historical development of, and the rationale for, the arts in education; and how methods of instruction have changed over the years. Conflict sometimes arises as to the location and categorization of certain arts in the school programs, and the effects of those decisions. For example, should dance be part of a physical education program or be a separate entity? Should film studies be part of an art department, part of communications, or a separate program? Those arts with a long history of being part of the curriculum (e.g. music, fine arts) fare better than the relatively new domains such as film, in gaining acceptance as genuine educational disciplines. Even drama, which is an "older" part of the curriculum, is not without its troubles in finding a comfortable home. (The fluctuating fortunes of music and drama, from antiquity to modern times, is itself a fascinating study of moral and other social values.)

Some schools have achieved curricular integration on both levels: by joining the arts with other disciplines (e.g. social studies) and by creating programs that integrate the arts with each other (e.g. dance and theater). However, it is essential that the distinctive attributes of the various arts, and of other disciplines, are not blurred. Furthermore, the search for quality must not be blunted by ideological diversions. The reference here is not to the quality of a particular work of art, about which there may be argument, nor to the particular standards by which a work is judged, for there may often be disagreement about these as well. Rather, it is the generic idea of quality itself—thinking in qualitative terms about the arts. A frequently attempted attack on the generic idea of quality takes the form of accusing those who appeal to it of being undemocratic and elitist.

In a 1974 essay, "Art as Hope for Humanity" the great violinist Yehudi Menuhin wrote:

> I look upon great works of art not only as isolated gifts and benefactions from heaven but also as high points emerging from a continuing living process. It is upon this view that I base my belief in art as hope for humanity. . . . Rhythm in music, proportion and movement in other arts—these are the assurances of continuity, of direction, and of design or logic in everyday life. Without these assurances life must often seem to the bewildered individual and innocent sufferer a "buzzing, booming confusion," without rhyme or reason. Thus not only the creative artist and poet, the musician and painter, but also the humblest craftsman *serves* his society.

Traditional Subjects

Aesthetic Education

G. Otto

Although aesthetic education takes place in every school subject because perception is a condition of all learning, this article will concentrate on aesthetic education in art, music, literature, and physical education. First some reflections on aesthetic education at the beginning of the 1980s will be made, then some comments on trends since the 1930s will be made, and lastly a three-dimensional approach will be suggested which should help to deal with aesthetic education in mass education.

1. Education Programmes at the Beginning of the 1980s

For over a century, music, sport, and art have been traditional school subjects. Literature has typically been a part of mother tongue instruction. The proportion of the timetable allotted to music and art is usually so abysmally small that it would appear to contradict the attainment of such general goals as the production of a "well-rounded person" and the study of society. Typically, too, the proportion of allocated time diminishes as one goes from first to 12th grade. Teacher education varies from country to country sometimes being undertaken in teacher-training colleges, sometimes in art or music colleges, and sometimes in universities.

General educational objectives within subject areas could be categorized along four dimensions:

(a) skill training versus the arousal of creative forces;

(b) product versus process emphases;

(c) emphasis on production versus emphasis on reflection;

(d) emphasis on high achievement within an art versus emphasis on general achievement across several arts.

It is interesting to note that since about 1960 the educational theories within the various "artistic" subjects have developed in a similar way. As a result of various developmental psychology impulses in the period 1920 to 1950 much greater emphasis has been laid on the social relevance of what is taught in school and on the social conditions for a child's development. Socialization theories were stressed. Interest in perception theory grew especially in the United States. Differences can be seen between nations in the way in which the educational functions of art are perceived and the value of their structures for the observation of nonartistic phenomena.

It is to be expected that the determination of criteria for establishing aims and methods in each of the subject areas—music, art, sport, and literature—will become easier and more common to all subjects once certain overriding themes or categories are used (see Sect. 3 below).

2. Trends since the 1930s

From the 1930s to the 1980s there has been a shift from the teaching of detailed content matter in subjects such as music and art to a relatively small elite proportion of the school population to a more eclectic, overarching content coverage in many "artistic" subjects for the mass of children enrolled in school. For example, one major trend has been towards *all* pupils attempting to identify and interpret the general orientations and directions of modern music, literature, and art. Particularly in the Netherlands, the Federal Republic of Germany, and the United States the question has arisen to what extent art is an elite pursuit or to what extent it constitutes a legitimate content for all pupils. What has traditionally been accepted by "society" as art is regarded as obsolete for normal teaching purposes since it cannot compete with the sheer quantity of often trivial visual, verbal, and acoustic materials with which children are now bombarded. It is argued that aesthetic education also needs to include dealing with "pop" literature and music as well as with comics and advertising posters. Such trends are heatedly debated since the traditional way of teaching based on techniques of creative art would appear to be no longer tenable. It is argued that a new theoretical framework is required involving cognition and perception but also giving increased attention to sociological explanations to new directions in aesthetic phenomena.

3. A Three-dimensional Approach

In the 1981 West German Congress of Aesthetic Education a catch phrase evolved: "Aesthetic education is the activation of the senses to achieve new understanding and insight." The implication was that this was for all pupils. This interdisciplinary determination of aims is only possible if those responsible for separate subject areas (art, music, and so on) are able to stand back from their individual field and reflect on the totality of subjects. In this way, an overview can be achieved. Equally, by attempting an analysis of the teaching–learning processes in literature, music, art, and sport it should be possible to extract the common structural elements.

To help in this process it is proposed that three dimensions be used: conceptual, perceptual, and allocational.

3.1 Conceptual

An individual always seeks to develop concepts when confronted with aesthetic objects, processes, and situations. Examples would include: strategies in a ball game or double passing in soccer; principles of construction in a three-nave basilica; categorizing art such as triptych or concetti in cubism; concepts of theatre such as those found in Brecht's educational plays; the structure of a Bach fugue; or the integration of song, literature, dance, and play in musicals. The goal of the teaching–learning process is for students to recognize and identify concepts as well as to use and interpret them.

3.2 Perceptual

Aesthetic perceptual learning is linked not only to a single channel of perception but to the enhancement of the sensitivity of the senses as a whole. The process of perception is linked to preceding sensual experience. Hearing a Bach fugue for the second time is a different experience from that of hearing it for the first time. The second time depends on all accumulated experiences of the first hearing. Accumulated experience typically also includes experience with percepts–maxims laid down within the particular discipline. For example, John Berger (1980) described his two visits to Colmar to view Matthias Grunewald's "Altar of Isenheim" and how his percepts were different on each occasion. Neither percept was arbitrary. His first percept was almost totally concerned with the cognitive structure of the painting in its historical context. The second percept was conditioned by his search for differences between Grunewald's work and other paintings with the same theme. The context had changed for Berger and hence the percepts differed.

Percepts can also overlap and sensual experiences can interact. For example, the movie "Rocky Horror Picture Show" portrayed, visually and musically, an oversensuous Transsylvanian in an artificial world of transvestites. In parts of the film the audience can participate, for instance, by throwing rice when a wedding takes place—a form of interaction with parts of the film. A second step in the perceptual process is the identification with characters in the movie and the adoption, during the film or later, of the characteristics and life-style of such characters.

3.3 Allocational

Individuals classify phenomena as a function of their concepts, percepts, and value systems which, in large part, are conditioned by their view of how society conceives and perceives such phenomena. This, in turn, involves knowledge of the social, economic, political, and "state-of-the-art" context in which a particular artistic work was produced. Thus, the categorization of phenomena is a function of the individual's accumulated store of social knowledge about the phenomena and the contexts in which they were created and how they were perceived by different groups of people.

The perception of roles, traditions, and conventions is a critical factor. For example, soccer, boxing, and wrestling events are perceived primarily in terms of their roles in a society rather than on the content of the sport.

It is proposed that optimal learning will be achieved if all three dimensions—conceptual, perceptual, and allocational—are systematically incorporated into the teaching–learning process. The foundation of aesthetic teaching is the continuous, inevitable learning on the part of students—they see, hear, smell, taste, and feel, regardless of the instruction provided by the school and the school's daily atmosphere. They move about, look at paintings and pictures, listen to music, and read stories with or without schooling. The notions of a desirable curriculum, of sociocultural relevance, and of specific learning objectives being derived from general goals are all encompassed in what has been said above. But the content must be such as to enhance learning qualitatively and quantitatively. Quantity can be achieved by using a very wide variety of objects from across subjects such as art, music, literature, and sport. Quality can be achieved by using all three dimensions simultaneously. This is a tentative theory and it remains to be seen how well it works in practice when applied in a variety of situations.

Only one example will be given here. The example is taken from one ninth-grade class studying the Otto von Bismarck monument in Hamburg and is presented by quoting portions of a report by Otto (1980).

> The architecturally designed monumental statue consists of a round step-like constructed and arranged base, on which the figure of Bismark is mounted. It is about 15 metres high. The Bismark monument has been repeatedly compared with medieval Roland statues. Eight male figures of about double life-size are arranged around the base below the figure. They symbolize the Germanic tribes. The complete structure is 34.30 metres high and is made of Black Forest granite. The sword alone, that Bismark is holding, is 10 metres long. The visitor reaches the monument by walking on the only

possible path through a grove. The visitor is forced to face the Bismark statue from the front and to look up to it. To the right and left are steps which lead to an elevated plateau behind the monument, which contains benches.

The iconographic tradition of the Roland figures is reflected in the Bismark monument. The massive stone structure expresses rigidity and domination. Its knight-like drapery, the anachronistic sword, and the unusual size: these factors evoke an aloofness and distance between the (overdimensional) monument and the (therefore inferior feeling) visitor.

Considering the stated goals of the lesson, the focus on the perceptual, conceptual, and allocational dimensions becomes obvious. The students should learn:

(a) to reflect, to analyse, and to reason visually from their own subjective viewing, and learn to express this;

(b) to realize and grasp that their observation is being directed by the size of the monument and the fact that the visitor is forced to approach it on the dictated path;

(c) to apply various techniques to change and modify the appearance, the impression, and effect of the monument (with photocopies or dittos of photographs and outline drawings);

(d) to explain and visualize several different evaluations of historic persons (critics);

(e) to create visual effects by selection and combination of specific picture materials. (Otto 1980 p. 75)

The following excerpt will show how concepts are recognized, percepts formed, and perceptions connected to actual doing:

All participating students indicated that they had seen the monument. Nevertheless, I suggested meeting in the afternoon to photograph it. Eight boys appeared for the appointment. They began to take shots of the monument from an arbitrary distance, and then chose their distance systematically from various positions around the monument, and from different levels—all different from the conventional way of viewing (180 photographs). During subsequent instruction, the students, under the influence of the photographers, posed the following questions: (a) How did you take the photographs? (b) How should one take the photographs of the monument? (c) What will happen if one takes photographs of the monument from different angles? The described effect of the monument only takes place if it is photographed from a great distance and not from close-up—while climbing around the monument.

"One is supposed to keep one's distance from the monument", a girl says. The photographers explained how the course of the path promotes this effect. (Otto 1980)

The students' questions, such as "Why was the monument erected?" or "Why was a monument like this one erected?" indicated the degree of differentiation in connection with allocation. The lesson continued employing authentic historical texts, caricatures of Bismarck, and newspaper reports from 1906 which was the year of the unveiling of the monument.

This example should have illustrated the connection and reference to the three dimensions important for aesthetic learning, and that the teaching and instruction guaranteed multidimensionality. In this case, aesthetic objects were not only regarded for their formal structures, as many didactic theories suggest, but also from the perspective of the perceiving subject and the social conditions which must be critically questioned.

Bibliography

Ball C et al. 1971 *Towards an Aesthetic Education*. Music Educator's National Conference, Washington, DC

Barkan M 1970 Guidelines curriculum development for aesthetic education. Cemrel (not published)

Berger J 1980 *About Looking*. Writers and Readers, London

Eisner E W 1979 The contribution of painting to children's cognitive development. *J. Curric. Stud.* 11: 109–16

Eisner E W 1981 On the differences between scientific and artistic approaches to qualitative research. *Educ. Res.* 10: 5–9

Eisner E W, Ecker D W 1966 *Readings in Art Education*. Blaisdell, Waltham, Massachusetts

Feyerabend P K 1976 *Wider den Methodenzwang: Entwurf einer Anarchistichen Erkenntnistheorie*. Suhrkamp, Frankfurt

Field D 1970 *Change in Art Education*. Routledge and Kegan Paul, New York

Graumann C F 1966 Die nichtsinnlichen Bedingungen der Wahrnehmung. In: Gottschaldt K, Sander F, Lersch P, Thomae H (eds.) 1966 *Handbuch der Psychologie*, Vol. 1. Hogrefe, Göttingen, pp. 1031–96

Hauser A 1973 *Kunst und Gesellschaft*. Beck, Munich

Hausman J F 1963 Research on teaching the visual arts. In: Gage N L (ed.) 1963 *Handbook of Research on Teaching: A Project of the American Educational Research Association*. Rand McNally, Chicago, Illinois, p. 1101

International Society of Education through Art (INSEA) 1965, 1966, 1969 *Reports of Congresses in Tokyo, Prague and New York*. INSEA, New York

Krichbaum J, Zondergeld R A 1979 *Künstlerinnen: Von der Antike bis zur Gegenwart*. DuMont-Schauberg, Cologne

Otto G 1971 Forschung im Bereich des Kunstunterrichts. In: Ingenkamp K (ed.) 1971 *Handbuch der Unterrichtsforschung*, Vol. 3. Beltz, Weinheim, pp. 3277–340

Otto G 1976 *Didaktik der Ästhetischen Erziehung: Ansätze: Materialen; Verfahren*. Westermann, Brunswick

Otto G 1980 Das Bismarkdenkmal in Hamburg. In: Eucker J, Kämpf-Jansen H (eds.) 1980 *Ästhetische Erziehung 5–10*. Urban and Schwarzenberg, Munich

Otto G 1987 Über der Zusannenhang von Kunst und Unterricht. *Westermanns Pädagogische Beiträge* 38(6): 38–43

Otto, G, Otto M 1987 *Auslegen Ästhetische Erziehung als Praxis des Auslegens in Bildern und des Auslegens von Bildern*, Vols. 1–11. Friedrich, Seelze

Ross M 1984 *The Aesthetic Impulse*. Pergamon, Oxford

Selle G 1981 *Kultur der Sinne und ästhetische Erziehung: Alltag, Sozialisation, Kunstunterricht in Deutschland von Kaiserreich zur Bundesrepublik*. DuMont-Schauberg, Cologne

Warburg A 1932 *Gesammelte Schriften*, Vols. 1 and 2. Teubner, Leipzig

Art: Educational Programs

A. Efland

Though art teaching is as old as art itself, art education identifies its beginnings with the introduction of drawing in the common schools of Europe and America less than 200 years ago. The term "art education" refers both to art teaching as a practice and to that field of inquiry which studies teaching and learning in art. The purpose of art education has been to enable individuals to acquire skills of artistic expression, designing, critical apprehension, and knowledge of art and its history. These teachings have been justified variously as vocational, moral, and citizenship training, and as aiding personal development. Research in this field employs methods common to social and psychological science with typical studies investigating children's artistic development, creativity, relations between socialization and drawing, aesthetic preferences, and the impact of these upon learning. These endeavors, at best, have had an indirect influence upon practices. Having greater impact are the events affecting society, education, and art itself. Thus art education began in response to the social event known as the Industrial Revolution; altered its rationale and character when the progressive education movement was active; and was deeply affected by the art styles of expressionism and abstraction in the first half of the twentieth century.

Its foundations include:

(a) aesthetics with its varied conceptions of art, and its value in human experience;

(b) art history, studio, and criticism as content sources;

(c) curriculum study to conceptualize goals, content, methods, and their interrelation;

(d) history of art education which studies developments in relation to social change, and cultural policy;

(e) empirical research which describes and explains individual and group behaviors associated with art learning and aesthetic response.

1. Nineteenth-century Developments

1.1 Dissatisfaction with Academies of Art

In the early 1800s, drawing instruction was available only in academies of art (Pevsner 1973), and then only to a talented elite pursuing careers as artists. Previously, guilds handled training for artisan designers but ceased with the onset of the Industrial Revolution. The academy's curriculum was anchored in life drawing, where neophytes copied drawings of masters, cast drawing, and eventually drew from the live model. Students trained in this tradition acquired a whole vocabulary of poses, gestures, and ornamental forms, but frequently assumed an air of "exclusiveness" and hence, were disinclined to devote their talents to industry. In many countries, academy training did not lend itself to the needs of burgeoning industries. Eventually, common schools, created for a working-class public, began to assume responsibility for the teaching of drawing.

Pestalozzi was among the first to demonstrate that drawing could be taught to almost all children without special talent, by teachers who were neither artists themselves, nor trained in art. His system approached drawing using geometric elements (straight and curved lines) which were introduced like an alphabet of elementary forms by methods analogous to those used for teaching handwriting and geometry. The method also avoided the complexities of the human figure and the elitist bias of the academy, hence was better disposed to the humbler needs of working-class artisans.

By the 1820s, geometric methods were used in numerous schools in Prussia which provided a technical foundation for students entering trade schools (*Gewerbeschulen*). In 1837, England established her first school of design but by 1849 its program was criticized by artists and industrialists alike. In the reforms that followed the *Gewerbeschule* model was borrowed, but without notable success. Not having a system of drawing in their schools, English students were not able to perform like their German competitors. After the poor showing of manufactured goods at the Exposition of 1851, the English established a national drawing course in their primary schools with the South Kensington School of Design serving as a center for the training of drawing masters (MacDonald 1970). The first statewide system of industrial drawing in the United States was established in Massachusetts in 1870. Walter Smith, trained at South Kensington, emigrated to the United States to implement the plan. Like the English system upon which it was based, instruction began in the primary grades and culminated with normal school training for drawing teachers. France, in contrast to England, established a system of training in the decorative arts based upon academic principles in the period between Louis XIV and Napoleon, and did not experience the critical shortage of artisan designers that aggravated the rest of Europe.

1.2 Froebel and the Kindergarten Movement

By the second quarter of the nineteenth century, believing that children learn through self-activity, Frederich Froebel established a series of "occupations" which would encourage improvization and discovery. His ideas were akin to the romantic views of genius and self-expression then affecting the fine arts and the education of artists. Among the activities he introduced to children were tablet laying using small planes of wood to create designs; paper folding; cutting; plaiting; weaving and twisting; work with peas, cork, wood, and metal rings; thread laying; drawing on checkered paper; designs made by pricking holes in paper with needles; sewing; and work in painting, drawing, and modeling. Froebel's influence was keenly felt in England and the United States but met with censure in his native Germany.

2. Turn of the Century Developments

2.1 Art as Cultural Refinement

As the nineteenth century waned, the demand for drawing in the schools declined since trade and professional art schools supplied the need. Rising cultural aspirations of the middle class turned the school away from narrow vocationalist concerns towards art as an object of refinement and beauty. "Art" had by then replaced the term drawing. "Picture study" was introduced and teachers were urged to adorn the school with reproductions of famous works of art. When speaking of the purposes of such activities, repeated use of such moral sounding words as "ennobling," "elevating," "lofty," "pure," and "virtuous" was made. The aesthetic was justified by the moral.

2.2 Child Study

Child study in Europe and the United States hastened the recognition of child art as an orderly, rational pattern of development that obeyed its own universal laws. In the United States, Hall studied the development of children's interests, responding to the doctrines of Herbart then in fashion. In Munich, Kerschensteiner (1905) compiled a collection of a half-million untutored drawings to document what he termed the growth of the child in the direction of realism. A number of European studies of child growth tended to equate the states of child development with stages of cultural development, where, in effect, the individual recapitulates the history of his or her race.

2.3 The Introduction of New Instructional Materials

In the 1880s and 1890s, a number of publishers began to provide textbooks and manuals which guided children's instruction by appealing to their interests and curiosities. In the United States, a series initiated by Louis Prang utilized colored illustrations which greatly enhanced the teaching of color principles and art appreciation. Prang also developed a line of art supplies including watercolors, colored papers, and crayons (Hicks 1899).

2.4 Free Expression

The ideas of Froebel on self-activity, the revelation of a mental unfolding process, and the rise of new art styles like "Impressionism" and "Expressionism," led many to view the art of the child as a resource worthy of cultivation. Franz Cizek began his juvenile art class at the Vienna Kunst *Gewerbeschule* in 1897. He was opposed to the use of methods based upon copying and imitation, advocating freedom for the child to look at the world and to experiment in congenial ways of self-expression in some artistic medium.

3. Early Twentieth-century Developments

3.1 Growth of Secondary Art Education

As primary education became universal in industrial countries, the secondary school increasingly became the agency which diversified educational offerings to accommodate students with differing vocational or educational aspirations. *Gymnasia*, *lycées*, and high schools were preparatory schools for students entering universities and hence their curricula were influenced by the program of studies of universities. They were also influenced by an examination system used to select students for university. Consequently, art history was more likely than studio study to be found in *Gymnasia* and *lycées*, while in high schools in the United States art studies were patterned after professional art schools. Drawing, painting, sculpture, and applied areas of design were typical high-school studies. By the 1930s, the high school, unlike its European counterparts, evolved into a comprehensive school serving a general clientele rather than the college preparatory student alone. Practical studies in interior design, costume, and commercial art then began to appear. In European secondary schools, art was a general cultural subject, while in the United States it was an elective course (Connell 1980).

3.2 Progressive Education

From the turn of the century until the Second World War, this international movement attempted to organize instruction around the natural curiosities of children. The arts were accorded a greatly enhanced role if taught as self-expression. Troubled by economic depression and rising totalitarianism, the movement modified its preoccupation with self-expression in favor of social reconstruction (Connell 1980). In the United States, art became an instrument for improving home and community. Emphasis was not upon the fine arts in all their remoteness and grandeur, but upon the use of commonplace objects in daily living. Art then became integrated with the teaching of the social studies.

3.3 The Bauhaus

Lasting but 12 years, the Bauhaus (Dorner 1959), founded in 1919 in Weimar, Germany, had a dramatic impact upon art and education. In the aftermath of the First World War, a group headed by Gropius organized a radically new art school which sought to change the position of the visual arts in society by bridging the gap between fine and applied arts and by gearing the training of industrial designers to the possibilities of industrial technology then emerging. Its foundation program was devised by Itten who based it, in part, on the new traditions of art pedagogy originating with Cizek and Kerschensteiner (Franciscono 1971). Materials were investigated in a playful, yet systematic way to enable students to discover structural attributes and apply these to original designs. Traditional life drawing and imitation of classical ornament were abandoned in favor of problem-solving approaches. Attacked by Rightist and Leftist elements in German society, it was closed by the Nazi Party in 1932. Its legacy lives on in the foundation programs of art schools, and in such typical art activities as paper construction, textural studies, and the study of design principles.

3.4 Art Education and Ideology in the Soviet Union

New ideologies appeared in the Soviet Union where art education came to reflect the political doctrines espoused by the state. Soviet art education followed Lenin's view that art was a specific form of social consciousness, a reflection in images of ideology. Art's value lies in its truth-telling attributes necessary for its "progressive" influence upon the masses. An art that reflects the people's ideology is thus a weapon in the class struggle (Skatershchikov 1970). Art in capitalist countries was criticized for its tendency to promote elitist styles for the few, and for its debased popular arts which exploit both artist and public for profit. According to N. P. Krupskaya, an educational leader in the development of primary education, the new generation of Soviet youth must be imbued with a collective spirit and art was one of the means by which this was to be attained. In her view, art works were to inspire feelings of comradeship and joy in the children's collectives. Though child art is creative, she maintained it was necessary to guide its development by observation of surrounding reality.

3.5 Art Education after the Second World War

Albers, Moholy-Nagy, Gropius, and other refugees from the German-speaking world carried Bauhaus ideas into design education in the English-speaking world. The tradition of art-historical scholarship which also originated in Germany came to England and the United States. Lowenfeld from Austria redefined the importance of self-expression drawing upon psychological insights from his work with visually impaired individuals (Lowenfeld 1947), while Schaeffer-Simmern and Arnheim brought the teachings of gestalt psychology into discussions within American art education.

Another effect of the war was the impetus it provided for using children's art to promote world peace and international understanding. Read (1943), in particular, saw in the underlying similarity of children's art from all parts of the globe, a compelling bond of universal kinship uniting people of all nations. This prevailing belief led to the founding of the International Society for Education through Art, INSEA, which was a direct result of an international seminar convened by UNESCO on the teaching of art in general education held in Bristol (UK) in the summer of 1951.

4. Later Twentieth-century Developments

4.1 Art Education in the United States

Postwar American education underwent a period of expansion owing to a rise in the school-age population and expansion of the suburbs around every major city. The number of elementary art teachers rose sharply, most taking positions in the newer suburbs. Urban schools, by contrast, lacked the services of such specialists. By the mid-1960s, the qualitative disparity between inner-city and suburban schools was recognized as an art education problem.

Postwar teaching methods were inspired by Lowenfeld (1947) who suggested ways that children at different stages of artistic development should be stimulated using appropriate media and thematic suggestions. Curriculum was guided mainly by developmental as opposed to subject matter considerations. By the late 1950s, Cold War tensions caused educators to upgrade science and mathematics at the expense of the arts and humanities. The position of the arts within general education was defended by arguments claiming that they stimulated creativeness in all areas of learning, but the more widespread response was to argue for a restructuring of art education using the models that worked to improve teaching materials for science education. Thus, Barkan (1966) suggested that the teaching of art should reflect the structure of art itself, that this would follow the characteristic modes of inquiry employed by artists, art historians, critics, and aestheticians. Previous curricula, he argued, were patterned too exclusively after the artist, neglecting alternative forms of inquiry. By the 1970s, general education was experiencing a "back-to-basics" movement with much of the justificatory rhetoric defending art based on the cognitive character of art learning which provides alternative symbols for representing meaning.

Present American educators are divided into five groups where art and education are concerned. The first group are those who proclaim the importance of self-expression in personal development and see studio studies as the central core of studies. A second group structures curricula around some rationally grounded conception of art as a discipline. These theories tend to suggest the need for content in criticism and art history. A third group focuses upon economic, political, and societal issues affecting the arts—including the arts of popular culture as significant sources of content—and the lives of students. A fourth group explores the study of art from a phenomenological orientation, while an eclectic group rationalizes that no true definition of art is possible, hence the study of art should attempt to enable students to have encounters with varied views of art rather than one (Chapman 1978).

In 1984 the J. Paul Getty Trust established the *Center for Education in the Arts* which has been a vigorous supporter of an approach known as "discipline-based art education" (Greer 1984). Initially limited to the Los Angeles area, it has since established a series of summer institutes in Florida, Ohio, Tennessee, and Minnesota.

4.2 Art Education in England and Wales

Shortly after the Second World War, a series of institutional changes affected the teaching of art at all levels. The colleges of art were absorbed into a system of polytechnics. In the 1970s, colleges of education were drastically reduced in numbers from 150 to 70. The postwar period also saw an expansion of secondary schooling with the "grammar" and "modern" schools being replaced by comprehensive schools in an attempt to lessen social-class inequities. The latter brought a somewhat more adequate provision for instruction in art and craft studies than had existed previously.

English educators hold differing opinions as to what shall be taught and how. One group continues to draw strength from Read's doctrines where art is viewed as self-expression, and where teaching is a kind of benign nurturance. This group approaches art instruction as a studio study. Most English art teachers generally regard art as a "practical" rather than "academic" study; without much emphasis on art history or appreciation. When these latter are taught it is "virtually a different subject to 'art'" (Allison 1984; 1986). Under the Thatcher government emphasis in art study shifted from personal expression to design study oriented to the needs of a technically oriented society. By the mid 1980s, interest in multicultural issues and critical studies became a major focal point in English art education (Mason 1988, Thistlewood 1989).

4.3 Art Education in the Federal Republic of Germany

In an attempt to overcome the chaos and confusion befalling Germany at the end of the Second World War, Weismantel in 1949 organized a *Kunstpaedagogische Kongress* at Fulda to seek a somewhat more unified approach among the tendencies developing in postwar thought. Divisions of opinion were wide and, in part, represented a resumption of views from the Weimar era. One group described as the "from-out-of-the-child" view based curriculum decisions on developmental or "child-centered" considerations. Practices were influenced by the ideas of Gustav Britsch (1926). On the gymnasium level teaching was influenced by Bauhaus ideas emphasizing design elements. A third trend was *Musische Erziehung*, a concept of aesthetic education which embraced all the arts. It possessed an anti-establishment, anti-machine age rationale with human feeling accorded greater educational importance than rational thinking. In 1959 a structured approach was pioneered by Pfennig (1959) who believed that the contemporary arts and arts of the past should be the basis for teaching

in the schools. Building on this tradition Otto's *Kunst als Prozess im Unterrict* (1964) placed art teaching upon a scientific, empirical basis. In the 1965 to 1975 period a new concept of "Kunst visuelle kommunikation" emerged based upon ideas by writers in the Frankfurt School of critical theory. They were characterized by a concern for the socio-political bases of art education and were intent upon restructuring art education as a species of political education. Its advocates criticized their rivals as lacking consciousness of socially oppressive forces in society. Their critique was guided by a Neo-Marxist perspective. Those critical of this view argue that in reducing all aesthetic questions to political or economic issues, one also loses art as a distinctive experience. In recent years, a model of art education was implemented in which students attempt to integrate practical studio studies with critical and analytical studies (Klager 1984).

4.4 Soviet Art Education

Between the end of the Second World War and 1964, two systems of art education coexisted. The first was that which functioned in the public schools which had an organized curriculum with weekly lessons taught in a strict manner. A second functioned in the Pioneer Youth houses where students were taught on an elective, free basis by invited professional artists. No structured curriculum was followed. In 1964 there was an official change in policy which "turned its face to aesthetic values in art education" (Yusov 1978). In effect, it attempted to unite the freer artistic approach of the extracurricular studio circles with the more formal art lesson given in the public school. Throughout the 1970s there was a "wave of liberation" for the arts in which several experimental programs were initiated whereby professional artists were given leadership roles in forming the curriculum. Soviet education as a whole has a deep commitment to the concept of aesthetic education not only limited to the study of the arts but also involved in the teaching of all subjects (Yusov 1978).

4.5 French Art Education

Art teaching is well-established in the French *écoles* and *lycées* though it has retained a traditional emphasis upon representation and figure drawing common in the past. Students in French schools are more apt to be exposed to art appreciation and history than in other industrial countries. French art teacher education has continued to follow a traditional program of study described as rigorous and demanding but which does not reflect the slightest influences from such men as Monet, Cezanne, Van Gogh, or Gauguin. Pedagogical developments of a more experimental nature are found in private schools, and there are signs of a freer approach in programs of teacher training. The student revolts of 1968 were instrumental in modifying French art education. Humanistic tendencies including non-directive teaching, individual autonomy, creativity, and free expression were advocated. The Colloquim of Amiens emphasized the right to develop "des savior-être" (how to be) as well as "des savoir-faire" (how to do). The Official instructions of 1977 place emphasis upon visual communication linking individuals to the community through the play of individual creativity. The design of the visual environment is also emphasized. Another goal defines the role accorded to contact with great works of art which enable students to appreciate the talent of those who are complete masters. In 1987 the French government adopted a law requiring that all students should receive art as a regular part of their schooling (Chavanne 1988).

4.6 Japanese Art Education

Japan has had a well-established program of art education at all levels for over 130 years. Western type drawing exercises were first introduced during its initial modernization epoch (1872–1885). In the early 1900s a large number of American textbooks were translated, a trend which has continued to the present time, excepting the unhappy years of World War II (Okazaki 1984; 1987). Elementary and secondary art curricula are divided between the goals of expression and appreciation (Ministry of Education, Science and Culture 1983). Art in the secondary schools is a required subject. Though stated course objectives are similar to those in North America and Europe, there is a strong emphasis upon acquisition of specific techniques as exemplified by the Kimoko method which is popular among teachers lacking an artistic background (Fujie 1989).

4.7 Art Education in the Developing World

By 1960, many former colonies of Western industrial countries had gained independence and began to redesign their schooling purposes around agendas for national development. Other countries that had not experienced colonial rule also embarked upon programs of modernization. In both, the dual tasks of economic development and nation building sometimes created conflict situations for art education. When educational and cultural policies would favor revitalizing old and venerable artistic traditions to kindle national pride, this would at times work against the goal of preparing individuals to function in the modern world—as artists expressing contemporary values or as designers of products in the international marketplace. Conflicts between traditional and modern aesthetic values would sometimes be expressed as between a local and an alien tradition imposed by outside influences. But the violence done to local traditions is not always from an outside source. For example, programs of modernization frequently require high levels of political centralization and a concomitant weakening of traditional ties of a local (religious or tribal) nature. If traditional arts keep alive latent local loyalties they face being jettisoned in the push for modernization. Art

educational policy has a difficult time in trying to balance between the two tendencies.

Other problems affecting the developing world are poverty and language barriers. Education is a function largely conducted in the languages of Europe hence perpetuating inherited elitism.

5. Research in Art Education

Late in the nineteenth century, child art was studied as a phenomenon in its own right. Early studies by Sully, Kerschensteiner, and Louquet lent credence to the view that artistic development in children is an orderly process, the outward result of an inner mental unfolding process that proceeded by its own rules and logic (MacDonald 1970). Typically these studies attempted to classify the graphic imagery of children either by age or by formal attributes of their drawings. Kellogg (1957), for example, classified close to a million drawings of pre-school-age children from all parts of the world and identified 20 basic scribble forms and a vocabulary of simple graphic forms that are later combined to generate pictorial symbols. Kellogg believed that child art is the same in all parts of the world.

Current studies of artistic development are less dependent upon age-based or formal characteristics and attend to artistic production and response as a social behavior taught and learned in various contexts. Korzenik (1979) noted that children do not draw to depict visual likenesses, but to exchange information through consensually agreed-upon visual symbols. Artistic behavior as an integral part of cognitive development was studied by Lewis and Livson (1979) where, in replicated studies, children's responses on the Goodenough–Harris Test of Intellectual Maturity were compared with the Stanford–Binet and the Wechsler. The first test is based upon the drawing of a human figure while the latter two are based upon verbal measures of intelligence. Though all tests correlated highly, they reported differences in personality and cognitive style between those subjects scoring higher on the Goodenough–Harris Test and the verbal tests. The latter group were described as vigorous, energetic, and task oriented while those doing better on the graphic test were described as shy, dependent, and irritable.

In studies of the drawings of American and Egyptian children, Wilson and Wilson (1979) challenged the longstanding assumption that artistry develops innately, and they have documented the fact that cultural factors also play a major role in facilitating or inhibiting drawing ability. In a subsequent study, Wilson and Wilson (1982) discussed the role of innate versus learned factors in children's drawings. One instance of an innately acquired attribute is what they termed "the perpendicular principle," the persistent tendency to organize pictorial space by placing objects and figures perpendicular to a ground line. While this is a common device used by most children, it does not produce visually convincing results when a child might want to depict figures or other objects on an incline. Thus progress in drawing to a large extent requires the overcoming of innate qualities in favor of the learning of pictorial conventions provided by one's culture.

Since 1967 "Project Zero" at Harvard University has studied the arts from a developmental perspective. In 1982 nearly 150 reports and published studies had appeared including many devoted to the visual arts (Lovano-Kerr and Rush 1982). Gardner (1973), director of the project, focused upon artistic development primarily because it afforded an opportunity to study the psychological processes by which cognition and affect become integrated through the construction of artistic symbols. Emerging from these studies is a much broader view of human cognition in general, one which shows the arts to play a significant role in cognitive development. Though the period between the early 1970s and the early 1980s was fruitful in revealing new knowledge of artistic development, applications to instructional practice had yet to be made.

During the 1980s research moved towards qualitative inquiry, multicultural and cross-cultural studies, and history of art education. Three international conferences on history took place at the University of São Paulo, Brazil since 1984. Conferences on history took place at The Pennsylvania State University (1985, 1989), Halifax, Nova Scotia (1987), and Bournemouth, England (1988).

6. Summary and Conclusions

Modern art education began less than 200 years ago with the rise of schooling in industrial nations. It spread to other nations who borrowed the schooling concept from Europe. European institutional patterns were adopted in many parts of the world, in some cases supplanting traditional systems of education. But schooling patterns in Europe developed with a strong tradition of class consciousness which affected the content of instruction received by various groups. Arts in these nations tend to be characterized by a high degree of pluralism which ranges from contemporary elitist forms of expression to industrial design and popular culture. Paralleling this diversity in the West is a broad range of opinion concerning purposes, methods, and content of art education. Cultural and educational policies in the socialist world differ from those in the West. Thus Soviet education aims at a universal view of art in culture where regional differences are acknowledged, but only as something to be transformed by "progress." The countries of the Third World are faced with the problems of finding appropriate forms of art instruction for the dual tasks of preserving cultural values while preparing for an enlarged economic role in the modern world.

Throughout its nearly 200-year history, art education has attempted to find its place within general education. In countries where aesthetic values have occupied a strong position in the culture the position of the arts is more or less secure. In other nations its position is secured by service to ideology; in still others, the fortunes of art education are a source of perennial debate.

Bibliography

Allison B 1984 England: Old stability, new ferment. In: Ott R and Hurwitz A (eds.) *Art in Education: An International Perspective*. Pennsylvania State University Press, University Park, Pennsylvania

Allison B 1986 *Index of British Studies in Art and Design Education*. Gower Publishing Co., Brookfield, Vermont

Barkan M 1966 Curriculum problems in art education. In: Mattil E L (ed.) 1966 *A Seminar in Art Education for Research and Curriculum Development*. Pennsylvania State University, University Park, Pennsylvania

Chapman L H 1978 *Approaches to Art in Education*. Harcourt Brace Jovanovich, New York

Chavanne M F 1988 *International Inquiry on Art Education*. UNESCO

Connell W F 1980 *A History of Education in the Twentieth Century World*. Teachers College Press, New York, Chap. 10

Dorner A H 1959 The background of the Bauhaus. In: New York Museum of Modern Art 1959 *Bauhaus, 1919–1928*. Charles and Branford, Boston, Massachusetts

Franciscono M 1971 *Walter Gropius and the Creation of the Bauhaus in Weimar: The Ideals and Artistic Theories of its Founding Years*. University of Illinois Press, Urbana, Illinois

Freedman K 1987 Art education as social production: Culture, society and politics in the formation of curriculum. In: Pophewitz T S (ed.) 1987 *The Formation of the School Subjects*. Falmer Press, London

Fujie M 1989 The Kimoko method of painting. (Unpublished) Conference presentation: *Convocation on Japanese Art Education*. The Ohio State University, Columbus, Ohio

Gardner H 1973 *The Arts and Human Development: A Psychological Study*. Wiley, New York

Greer W D 1984 A discipline-based view of art education. *Stud. in Art Educ.* 25(4): 205–18

Hicks M D 1899 *The Prang Elementary Course: Art Instruction in the Primary Schools: A Manual for Teachers*. Prang, Boston, Massachusetts

Kellogg R 1957 *What Children Scribble and Why*. N-P, Palo Alto, California

Kerschensteiner L 1905 *Development of the Graphic Gift* [*Die Entwicklung der Ziechnerischen Begabung*]. Munich

Klager M 1984 Germany: Decentralization in the Federal Republic. In: Ott R and Hurwitz A (eds.) *Art in Education: An International Perspective*. Pennsylvania State University Press, University Park, Pennsylvania

Korzenik D 1979 Socialization and drawing. *Art Educ.* 32(1): 26–29

Lewis H, Livson N 1980 Cognitive development, personality and drawing: Their interrelationships in a replicated longitudinal study. *Stud. Art Educ.* 22: 8–11

Lovano-Kerr J, Rush J 1982 The evolution of visual arts research during the seventies. *Rev. Res. Vis. Arts Educ.* 15: 61–81

Lowenfeld V 1947 *Creative and Mental Growth: A Textbook on Art Education*. Macmillan, New York

MacDonald S 1970 *The History and Philosophy of Art Education*. Elsevier, New York

Ministry of Education, Science and Culture 1983 *Course of Study for Elementary Schools in Japan*. Government of Japan, No. 156

Mason R 1988 *Art Education and Multiculturalism*. Routledge and Kegan Paul, London

Okasaki A 1984 Chinese and Japanese influence on Arthur Wesley Dow's idea of the teaching of art. *Bulletin of the Faculty of Education*. Utsunomlya University 35(1): 163–78

Okasaki A 1987 Cross-cultural problems in the history of art education: The case of Akira Shirahama. *Bulletin of the Faculty of Education*. Utsunomlya University 37(1): 197–202

Ott R and Hurwitz A 1984 *Art in Education: An International Perspective*. Pennsylvania University Press, University Park, Pennsylvania

Otto G 1969 *Art: An Instructional Process [Kunst als Prozess im Unterricht]*. Georg Westermann, Braunschweig

Pevsner N 1973 *Academies of Art, Past and Present*. Da Capo, New York

Read H E 1943 *Education Through Art*. Pantheon, New York

Skatershchikov V K 1970 Leninist principles of esthetic education and the contemporary era. *Soviet Educ.* 12: 101–29

Thistlewood D 1989 *Critical Studies in Art and Design Education*. Longmans, London

Wilson B, Wilson M 1979 Figure structure, figure action and framing in drawings of American and Egyptian children. *Stud. Art Educ.* 2: 36–43

Wilson B, Wilson M 1982 The persistence of the perpendicular principle: Why, when, and where innate factors determine the nature of drawings. *Rev. Res. Vis. Arts Educ.* 15: 1–18

Yusov B 1978 Art education in the Union of Soviet Socialist Republics. *Art Educ.* 31(2): 8–11

Attitude Towards Art

J. W. Morris

The term "art attitude" appears with increasing frequency in art education literature. This is true, in part, because as a specialized concept it has permitted art educators to describe more accurately particular aspects of student responses to art. Unfortunately, art educators have often used the concept casually, without specification, and in contradictory ways. The term art has been used interchangeably with arts, design, aesthetics, and so on while the term attitude has been held synonymous with value, judgment, preference, and so on. This apparent lack of broad understanding across the field has resulted in a proliferation of misuses and problems in practical application of the concept to teaching and research.

Some recent attempts have been made to correct these confounding problems by investigating the theoretical bases to art attitudes. While reflecting upon the literature related to attitudes in general, this work has yielded the following definition for an art attitude: it is a learned and relatively enduring evaluative system of affective predispositions held toward art referents. Implicit within this definition are six major characteristics. That is, art attitudes (a) are affective evaluative concepts which underlay motivations for behavior; (b) are learned; (c) have specific referents; (d) are relatively stable and enduring; (e) vary in quality and intensity; and (f) are interrelated.

Despite these recent attempts to clarify the meaning of art attitudes, broad definitions for attitude referents continue to dominate (e.g., attitude toward art, attitude toward aesthetics, attitude toward art education) in art education methodology, curricular writing, and research. It has been assumed that a general experience with art is sufficient for attitude change and as an influential treatment. With very few exceptions, the rigor which accompanies the methodology of attitude change and research in social psychology is missing in efforts at working with attitudes in art education.

Despite these inadequacies, art education literature indicates that favorable broad experience with art has a favorable influence on attitudes held by students at various levels. Also, general training in art education has a favorable impact on the art attitudes of teachers. In the few instances where more sophisticated and specific approaches have been attempted in classroom settings, Festinger's theory of cognitive dissonance and theories using persuasive communication have been shown to be effective in dealing with a range of art-related attitudes. Although recent results are encouraging for those who advocate the critical role played by attitudes in art education, there remains a need for more specifically defined attitudes, attitude referents, and strategies for attitude change.

Current literature on attitudes toward art reveals one very alarming theme: art attitudes have not always been favorable; correspondingly, support for art in education has not always been elaborate. Different conditions found to be prevalent in different countries cause the nature of art attitudes to be manifest in different ways; however, the results appear similar, as art programs are limited and opportunities for art involvement are few. Funds for art programs are inadequate; there is a lack of understanding by others in education and society as to the value and purpose of art, and there is a feeling expressed by art educators of being alienated from the rest of the educational community. Art educators in the Soviet Union, Australia, the United Kingdom, and the United States, to note a few, report difficulty in counteracting the attitude that involvement with art is not a serious endeavor but is only something to be pursued after work is done and more economical, practical, or socially relevant responsibilities are complete.

One effort to rectify these difficulties has been to consolidate the arts in education and emphasize their interrelated nature. Australia, the United Kingdom, the United States, and Nigeria report such attempts. However, at the same time some question has been raised by art educators in different parts of the world, and especially in the Soviet Union, as to the real benefits of interrelating the arts. The concern expressed by this latter group is that certain dimensions of uniqueness found within each given art form are lost when commonalities are stressed and that underlying, favorable art attitudes held by students are actually less influenced by the integrated approach than by a separate approach.

Other attempts to improve attitudes toward art and the condition of art education around the world have been undertaken by UNESCO. With the support of this international agency, studies have been conducted in Brazil, Hungary, Iran, Kenya, the Republic of Korea, the United Kingdom, and the United States which show the important role that arts play in the lifelong education of people of all ages in varying socioeconomic settings. Also, in 1979, the United Nation's "Year of the Child," UNESCO made a concerted effort to incorporate aspects of art and art education into the year's program as a way of raising the world's attitude toward the arts in general and showing the important role the arts play (or can play) in the lives of children.

Indeed, as the 21st Century approaches, increased value has been placed upon the function the arts play in the lives of people. In numerous countries such as Russia and Japan, approaches to teaching by art educators continue to emphasize cultural taste through artistic production. In other instances curricular revisions have been undertaken to align outcomes of art learning with changing social demands. English revision has been directed toward the preparation of students for the work force, while curricular shifts in the USA reflect increased demands for appreciative components of art study (i.e., aesthetics, art history, art criticism).

The literature of art education also contains the study and research of student-held art attitudes. One of the more substantial of these efforts is the First National Assessment of Art, conducted by the Education Commission of the United States. Results from this study indicate that American students: (a) value art and pursue it in some form; (b) do appreciate art, but do not influence a broad or sophisticated understanding of its nature or function in their culture; (c) have little experience with art museums and galleries; (d) display varying attitudes toward art depending upon socioeconomic background; and (e) feel that school should place more emphasis on art education.

The assessment of art attitudes has been approached both objectively and subjectively, in field as well as laboratory settings, using individuals and specific social groups as targets of study. Scales for objectively measuring art attitudes have been constructed which are based upon various techniques developed by Guttman, Osgood, and Thurstone, for example, but Likert's method of summated ratings appears to be the most widely used approach. Some of the instruments which have been utilized in assessing art and art-related attitudes are: The Beittel Art Acceptance Scale, the Wilson Art Inventory, the Burkhart Uniqueness of Self-concept Scale, and the Stuckhardt Art Attitude Scale.

Some work has been done on the development of alternative methods of attitude assessment in art. These more subjective techniques focus upon the assessment of individually held art attitude systems and the unique context in which these systems are formed. These methods have produced results which appear qualitative in nature, as opposed to the quantitative results yielded from attitude scales.

However, in comparison to other areas of education such as reading, science, mathematics, and music, art education literature contains relatively few studies which deal with attitude assessment. To date, relatively few instruments for art attitude measurement have been constructed; relatively few alternative methods exist, and relatively few attempts have been made to apply proper and feasible attitude assessment procedures to research, study, and curriculum development.

Bibliography

Field D 1977 Recent developments and emerging problems in English art education. *Art Educ.* 30(8): 5–8
Hayman D 1978 The UNESCO arts education programme. *Art Educ.* 31(2): 22–23
Hurwitz A 1976 The US and USSR! Two attitudes towards the gifted in art. *Gifted Child Q.* 20: 458–65
Krosnick J A 1988 Attitude importance and attitude change. *J. Exp. Psycol.* 24: 240–255
Lepman J 1975 *How Children See Our World.* Avon, New York
McGuire W J 1985 Attitudes and attitude change. In: Lindzey G, Aronson E (eds.) *Handbook of Social Psychology* (Vol. 2). Random House, New York
Morris J, Stuckhardt M 1977 Art attitude: Conceptualism and implication. *Stud. Art Educ.* 19: 21–28
National Center for Education Statistics (DHEW) 1978 *Attitudes Toward Art: Selected Results from the First National Assessment of Art.* Washington, DC. (ERIC Document No. ED 166-122)
Richardson D 1978 Issues in Australian arts education. *Aesthetic Educ.* 12: 55–63
UNESCO 1972 *Art Education: An International Survey.* UNESCO, Paris
Wilson B 1988 *Art Education, Civilization and the 21st Century: A Researcher's Reflections on the National Endowment for the Arts. Report to Congress.* The National Art Education Association, Reston, Virginia
Yuson B 1978 Art education in the Union of Soviet Socialist Republics. *Art Educ.* 31(2): 8–11

Museum Education

S. E. Lee and K. Solender

Museums as institutions are custodians of the artistic, historical, and scientific heritage of humankind. They are charged with selecting, preserving, exhibiting, and elucidating objects as worthy examples of the natural and cultural environment, past, and present. The educational function of a museum is both to present and interpret this heritage. What follows is largely related to education in art museums, mainly in America, but applicable tangentially to museums of history, natural history, and science.

In the art world, the museum is *the* primary source for education. By preserving and exhibiting works of art it is educational in the broadest sense. Unlike the library or classroom, an art museum provides information and stimulation through objects rather than the spoken or written word. If in the past the museum was considered a passive keeper of works of art for a privileged and knowledgeable few, the trend in the twentieth century has been for it to become increasingly accessible for use and enjoyment by a broad public. Rather than wait to be discovered, the art museum now invites and encourages visits. This shift in emphasis has been more strongly and systematically developed in the United States than in any other country.

The founders of the earliest major art museums in Boston and New York (1870) were firm believers in the educational values embodied in the charters of their institutions. In 1872 the Metropolitan Museum of Art in New York offered a lecture series for adults and the Boston Museum of Fine Arts began adult classes in 1876. From the outset, American museums were greatly influenced by London's Victoria and Albert Museum, founded in 1852 and dedicated to meeting the challenges of the industrial age by introducing visitors to the decorative arts and crafts of the past. In the 1870s, the educational programs of the Metropolitan Museum and the Cooper Union Museum in New York (now the Cooper–Hewitt Museum of the Smithsonian Institution) and the art museums in Philadelphia and Boston emphasized connections between art and industry. Museum art schools appeared early in American museum development, and a few still operate, though the number has declined.

During the first 30 years of museum growth in America, from 1870 to 1900, more emphasis was placed on building collections and financial support than on educational practices. Between 1900 and 1930, when docents and lecturers were added to museum staffs, the emphasis shifted from the few to the general public. The shift was not achieved, however, without some conflicts in basic philosophy. Benjamin Ives Gilman, secretary of the Museum of Fine Arts in Boston, maintained that art museums were "not didactic but aesthetic in primary purpose." John Cotton Dana, founder of the

Newark (New Jersey) Museum in 1909, argued that museums, as public institutions, have an obligation to actively promote learning for the benefit of the entire community. Most museums found neither approach entirely satisfactory, following instead a middle course based on a balance of the two philosophies.

The economic depression of the 1930s decisively affected American museum efforts to define their educational aims. Realizing that they might be increasingly dependent on public sources for support, some museums began to emphasize their educational programs as justification for their existence. This has resulted in the acceptance of education as a major function of both art museums and general museums. Almost every American museum today offers a comprehensive educational program, and a detailed survey in 1971–72 found that art museum directors rated "educational experiences for the public" even slightly ahead of "aesthetic experiences for the public" (NEA 1974).

The audiences reached by museums can be divided into four main groups: (a) adults; (b) young people, teachers, and schools; (c) college and university students, scholars, and professionals; and (d) artists. Recognizing that visual learning is the form of education least likely to be taught in schools and even in many colleges, museum educators have taken on the task of helping visitors learn to use their eyes, to *see*, in addition to the accustomed task of conveying art historical information.

The museum's heterogeneous adult audience requires a bridge between scholarship and popular education. The principal device used is the educational exhibition, usually accompanied by explanatory labels and a variety of educational aids—brochures, recorded tours, films, lectures, gallery demonstrations, maps, and diagrams. Some are critical of the disruption and distraction such supplementary materials can cause, while others applaud them, believing works of art have been exhibited for too long without context. In planning exhibitions, most museums try to treat visitors as intelligent individuals, encouraging them to make visual connections, see parallels and contrasts, and generally teach themselves through what they see.

Beyond exhibitions, museums provide other educational opportunities for adults in the form of lecture courses, symposia, discussion groups, and films. There has been a tendency for some museums to appear as leisure-time entertainment centers.

Recognizing that traditional museums are often limited in what they can provide for specific community or ethnic groups, the neighborhood museum, set up through alliances with community arts organizations, became increasingly popular in the 1960s and 1970s. Its aim is not only to bring the museum to people who rarely leave their immediate environment, but also to involve them closely in its activities. The exhibitions are often related to the local scene.

Among art museums in the United States, nine out of ten offer some kind of program for school classes, most of them (70 percent) on a regular basis (NEA 1974). Museum goals for youth education programs fall into three categories: helping young people to feel at home in an art museum and understand its value; introducing them to new and enlightening visual experiences; giving children richer opportunities to make art important in itself and for understanding and enjoying the art of others.

Although most art museums try to organize programs for children who come on their own or with their parents—classes for museum members' children being the most typical—the child in a group with his or her schoolmates and teacher is by far the most common arrangement in American museums, usually in a docent-led group tour. The direct experience of original works of art is best achieved by advance preparation in the school classroom. Still, there is the possibility of an exploratory, intuitive experience without previous preparation, if the museum teacher is both flexible and inventive.

Previous approaches to teaching schoolchildren in the museum, the condensed art history lecture and the introductory slide-lecture in an auditorium, have now been replaced by thematic tours. Particularly useful in science and history museums, such tours give students a focus in a vast and potentially overwhelming environment. In art museums, the tour may relate directly to the school curriculum, but elements of art and visual awareness, such as line, texture, and color are often the themes, aided by the traditional museum practice of introducing studio activity—learning to see by doing and making. Many museums use dramatization, dance and movement, creative writing, and other related arts. Most of these programs are aimed at the traditional upper-elementary grades (ages 9–11), although many are for ages 12 to 14, and some include the youngest children.

Many museum educators have become dissatisfied with the one-time group tours and have begun to work closely with schools to conduct programs involving a sequence of visits, providing repeated experiences inside the museum thus making the students comfortable with museum objects, resources, and people. One such program, begun in 1971, was The Cleveland Museum of Art's East Cleveland Project. Built around an extended and concentrated school year, children from inner-city schools came into the museum for two-week "residencies" in the museum's galleries and studios. The overall program was planned and funded by the school system with the museum contribution planned and conducted by museum staff (Newsom and Silver 1978).

A similar program was conducted in several German cities, including Mainz, Trier, Worhus, Cologne, and Munich. In cooperation with the schools, learning units were produced which utilized the personnel and exhibitions of local museums as a complement to the regular school curriculum.

Another development in museum education is the establishment of specialized areas for young people within the larger museum. In the Metropolitan Museum's Junior Museum, facilities include an exhibition gallery, auditorium, art reference library, studio, snack bar, and sales desk.

In recognition of decentralization and in order to reach a broader audience, many museums in both Europe and America have established extension services and outreach programs, sending docents or staff into school classrooms to make presentations, devise circulating exhibitions for school hallways and libraries, or sponsor workshops and mobile units for parks, playgrounds, and city streets. The goal is to interest young audiences in visiting the museum itself, and to supplement inadequate art instruction in the schools.

With high-school students, the American museum encounters special problems. Few museums have high-school programs because rigid daily class schedules prevent students from visiting the museum. Recognizing the importance of the high-school audience, some museums have devised successful offerings. The Cleveland Museum of Art's Advanced Placement course in art history, begun in 1974 for academically talented students, makes broad use of the collection and offers to students a professional academic resource unavailable elsewhere. In 1968, the Metropolitan Museum of Art established a separate department for high-school programs and experimented with ways to interest teenagers in art and the museum (Newsom and Silver 1978).

In some museums, focus on the schoolteacher takes precedence over other audiences. For the Victoria and Albert Museum in London, training teachers to use the museum is a matter of policy. In America, museum educators are increasingly convinced of the need to ally themselves with the classroom teacher. Many have found that their small staffs and limited budgets cannot be stretched to cover all the school groups that demand access to them. Because the same teacher, who knows his or her students and what they should learn in the museum, would be teaching in both places, museums hope that better integration can be achieved. The goal of teacher programs is twofold: to give teachers exposure and practice to make them confident and comfortable not only in the museum but with art, and through teachers to integrate works of art into the education of the young. Over the years, museum staffs have devised a variety of means to these ends. At the St. Louis Art Museum, a teacher resource center offers slides, information sheets, workshops, and a special staff to help teachers use works of art in their curriculum and to train them for their own museum visits (Newsom and Silver 1978).

The educational activities of museums are usually most visible in programs for children, and lectures and tours for adults. But there is another audience: scholars, researchers, artists, college and university students, collectors, dealers, and conservators. The time spent answering inquiries from scholars, meeting with and often advising collectors, and consulting with graduate students, is an important but unmeasurable and often unrecognized educational contribution by the museum to the public. Several museums sponsor scholarly symposia and most art museums maintain extensive book, photograph, and slide libraries to which they allow scholars and students free access. As centers of scholarship, art museums have much in common with universities.

Some museums have joint programs with neighboring colleges and universities, closing the gap between theory and practice, slide and original. Such programs are not limited to classes and seminars but include internships in curatorial and educational departments and apprenticeships in conservation.

Bibliography

Alexander E P 1979 *Museums in Motion: An Introduction to the History and Functions of Museums.* American Association for State and Local History, Nashville, Tennessee

American Assembly, Columbia University 1975 *On Understanding Art Museums.* Prentice-Hall, Englewood-Cliffs, New Jersey

American Association of Museums (AAM) 1969 *America's Museums: The Belmont Report: A Report to the Federal Council on the Arts and the Humanities.* AAM, Washington, DC

Bazin G 1967 *Le Temps des musées.* Desoer, Liège [1967 *The Museum Age.* Universe Books, New York]

Dana J C 1917 *The New Museum.* Elm Tree Press, Woodstock, Vermont

Gilman B I 1918 *Museum Ideals of Purpose and Method.* Riverside, Cambridge, Massachusetts

International Council of Museums (ICOM) 1970 *Museums and Research: Paper from the Eighth General Conference. 29 July–9 Aug 1968, Cologne-Munich.* Deutches Museum, Munich

International Council of Museums (ICOM) 1972 *The Museum in the Service of Man: Today and Tomorrow: The Museum's Educational and Cultural Role: Papers from the Ninth General Conference.* ICOM, Paris

Low T L 1948 *The Educational Philosophy and Practice of Art Museums in the United States.* Teachers College, Columbia University, New York

National Endowment for the Arts (NEA) 1974 *Museums USA: Art, History, Science and Other Museums.* NEA, Washington, DC

Newsom B Y, Silver A Z 1978 *The Art Museum as Educator: A Collection of Studies as Guides to Practice and Policy.* University of California Press, Berkeley, California

Rohmeder J 1977 *Methoden und Medien der Museumsarbeit: Pädagogische Betreuung der Einzelbesucher im Museum.* DuMont Buchverlag, Köln

UNESCO 1973 *Museums, Imagination and Education,* UNESCO, Paris

Wittlin A 1970 *Museums: In Search of a Usable Future.* MIT Press, Cambridge, Massachusetts

Music Curricula

R. L. Garretson

The place of music in general education is a topic of concern to music educators throughout the world. Most would agree that a basic musical education should be provided for students so that music, which is a part of their cultural heritage, can be enjoyed throughout their lives. This point of view becomes apparent when perusing articles or papers in *International Music Education*, the yearbook of the International Society for Music Education (ISME). Music study has various values which should be understood as they serve as the philosophical basis for implementing any system of music education.

Any music curriculum designed to meet the needs of students from elementary through secondary schools has various components including music for everyone in the general school, specialized music schools, special courses for the young adolescent, music theory courses in secondary schools, instrumental music instruction, and performing groups of varying kinds.

Folk music is an integral part of all cultures and may be correlated with the study of social studies to clarify various customs and attitudes of a country. All the arts reflect the culture from which they emanate. Recognition of their interrelationship has resulted in the development of humanities courses and courses limited to music and the related arts. Additionally, some music teachers use the related arts to clarify musical concepts they may be teaching to students in a performing group or ensemble.

1. The Place of Music in the Curriculum

Over the years, music has gained gradual acceptance into the school curriculum in most countries, until today it is considered by educators to be an integral part of the educational system. Music has many values which must be understood if music education curricula are to be properly implemented in the schools.

1.1 Aesthetic and Expressive Values

The aesthetic values of music are one of the primary justifications for including it in the curriculum. Aesthetics may be defined as the study of beauty in art and nature. People have a need for beauty in their lives, as it serves to refine and humanize their entire being. Aesthetic education, or the process of increasing an individual's sensitivity to beauty, is the basic task of the music educator. Teachers should endeavor to broaden students' musical horizons by providing experience with a wide variety of types and styles of music, the objective of which is to make them more discriminating participants and/or consumers of music.

People need to express themselves in as many diverse ways as possible. While many ideas can be expressed through language, it has its limitations. Certain aspects of human experience are best expressed through other media, such as dance, the visual arts, or music. The more opportunities students have for self-expression, the greater will be their potential for self-development. All the arts offer many varied possibilities for the expression of individual feelings in a creative manner.

1.2 Cultural and Personal/Social Values

Music is an integral part of all cultures and it is, therefore, societies' responsibility to pass on to future generations this aspect of their heritage. World peace depends to a great extent upon an understanding of cultures other than one's own. The hopes, fears, and aspirations of all peoples are often expressed in their folk music. A complete understanding of other cultures cannot be achieved unless all aspects, including music, are included in the school curriculum.

All students need to develop self-assurance through having successful experiences in varied activities. Some may find these successes in areas other than music, but a well-rounded curriculum should provide students with a variety of activities and experiences. While individual skills are often developed in music, considerable activity occurs in groups, where achievement is dependent upon a collective group effort. Cooperative attitudes and respect for other individuals may often be fostered through participation in music organizations.

1.3 Therapeutic Values

Music therapy is the scientific application of the art of music to accomplish therapeutic aims, and is used in various institutions including psychiatric hospitals, mental retardation centers, physical disability hospitals, community mental health centers, day care centers, nursing homes, special education schools, correctional facilities, and special service agencies. There is also a trend toward using music as a therapeutic agent in the schools when working with exceptional children. (This practice has become especially prevalent in the United States since the passage of Public Law 94–142.)

Music therapy may help children learn appropriate social interaction, motivate the emotionally disturbed, remediate perceptual motor problems through movement to music, assist the orthopedically handicapped as a form of physical therapy, and help hostile, noncooperative children learn more appropriate behaviors.

1.4 Avocational and Vocational Values

All persons need activities outside their chosen vocation that serve to enrich their lives and renew their spirits. Avocational choices will vary widely, but music is a particularly desirable avocation to pursue, either as an active participant or as a listener, because persons of all ages may become involved. If our musical heritage is to be perpetuated, then dedicated teachers must be trained, and the development of the requisite skills must be begun at an early age (Garretson 1976 pp. 1–5).

2. Components of the Music Curriculum

The types of musical activities offered to students will vary from country to country, but may include general music, that is, singing, rhythmic activities and bodily movement, listening, playing instruments, and creative activities for elementary-school children; special instruction considering the needs of young adolescents, individual and/or group instruction in voice or various band and orchestral instruments, music theory, and a wide range of performing groups, including both vocal and instrumental ensembles.

2.1 Music in the Elementary School

While the nature and extent of children's musical experiences still vary widely, it is generally understood that whether or not music finds its real place in society is dependent upon the success of music education in the schools. Today, lifelong education, or continuing education, is a goal of educators in most countries. For music to be a meaningful part of a person's total life experience necessitates a thoughtfully conceived school curriculum.

Children need to be instilled with the excitement and joy that music holds and appreciate that making music is a worthwhile activity. The ability to discriminate and make musical choices is essential if children are to become intelligent consumers of music throughout life.

In Europe, the elementary school will emcompass various grade levels—kindergarten through fifth grade, grades one through six, and one through eight. Children generally enter the first grade at age 7. In the general school, music instruction is usually taught by the classroom teacher, although music specialists are utilized in some countries beginning in the middle or intermediate grades. Instruction may range from one hour per week to music on a daily basis. Musical activities usually include group singing, listening, bodily movement, playing instruments, and the study of notation. Many European countries, including Finland, Norway, Sweden, Poland, Hungary, Yugoslavia, Austria, and England and Wales (to some extent) have special music schools which children can attend outside the general school. After acceptance tests, students, generally between the ages of 7 and 10, may attend. In Austria, the community music school is open to children between the ages of 8 and 12, and is partially supported by the town or province, but a tuition fee is charged. Because of the lack of economic resources and the availability of trained teachers, not all children can attend these special schools (Sample and Sample 1979).

Some countries have their own unique systems of music instruction. For example, the Kodály method, developed by the Hungarian composer Zoltán Kodály (1882–1967) has been adopted as the state system of music instruction in Hungary. The Orff Schulwerk, developed by the German composer Carl Orff (1895–1982) is widely used in German and Austrian schools. These approaches to music education have had a wide and significant influence and have been adapted for use in many countries. The ideas inherent in the Kodály system are utilized in the Soviet Union, Czechoslovakia, Denmark, Finland, France, Belgium, the Federal Republic of Germany, Switzerland, Argentina, Chile, Peru, Japan, Australia, Canada, and the United States. Orff concepts are utilized in Sweden, Denmark, Belgium, France, England and Wales, Greece, the Netherlands, Israel, Latin America, Portugal, Spain, Turkey, Yugoslavia, Canada, and the United States. New editions of the *Orff Schulwerk* have been printed in the language of most of these countries (Landis and Carder 1972).

There is a trend in some Western countries toward including in the school curriculum some study of the music of Eastern cultures (oriental) and Africa. It is felt that children should learn to recognize the unique musical instruments and idiomatic tonal characteristics of the music, so that increased understanding of these cultures may occur. A particularly valuable resource for information on Eastern or Oriental music, and listed under each country is, *The New Grove Dictionary of Music and Musicians,* edited by Sadie (20 volumes) and published by Macmillan, London 1980.

In the nineteenth century, certain Asian countries, such as Japan, Korea, Vietnam, and the Philippines were influenced by and adopted the Western styles of music which are still taught in many of their schools. Today, however, there is a feeling among music educators that the traditional ethnic music of these countries should also be taught in their schools.

While Arabian countries will accept the scientific knowledge of Western societies, this is not necessarily the case with music. The Arabian musical heritage includes their special tonal system, rhythmic organization, musical forms, and instruments. The techniques of music making or performance are usually passed on from the master teacher to the student and the number of persons able to acquire a musical education is thus limited.

The elementary school in the United States refers to kindergarten through the sixth grade, and generally for children ages 5 to 11. In 1923 Karl Gehrkens made the statement, "Music for every child—every child for music." This phrase became a slogan for the Music Educators National Conference (MENC) and has had a wide-reaching effect upon music education in the United States and subsequently throughout the world.

The long-range goal of music instruction in the United States is the development of children's musicality, that is, increased sensitivity and responsiveness to music, and consists of a variety of activities including singing, listening to music, rhythmic activities and expressive bodily movement, the playing of various instruments, and creative activities comprising both improvisation and creating compositions.

In the early 1960s music educators, particularly in the United States, began to stress the importance of music as an academic discipline and the fact that it had its own structure and content which was just as important as other basic school subjects. The various elements of music include tempo, dynamics, timbre or tone quality, rhythm (duration), melody (pitch), harmony, texture, and form. Related to this development was the emphasis upon conceptual learning and acceptance of the fact that a child could learn any concept or idea provided it was presented in its simplest and most appropriate form. Spiral learning meant introducing to a young child a concept and then gradually expanding upon and clarifying the concept through appropriate musical activities in each subsequent grade level. For example, a sequence of related concepts on pitch and melody are as follows: "sounds (melody) can be high and sounds can be low," "melodies can go up and melodies can go down," "melody has long and short sounds," "notes are placed on a staff to tell us how high or low or long or short each pitch is to be sung," "tones can stay on one pitch or move up and down," "tones can move in steps (scalewise) or by skips or leaps," "a scale is a ladder or arrangement of ascending and descending pitches," and so on. These basic concepts, provided as examples, can continue to be built upon and may eventually lead to an understanding of various scales and modes, including those utilized in the ethnic music of various cultures.

Related to the idea of conceptual learning is the emphasis upon behavioral objectives. Good teaching necessitates careful planning, and objectives stated in behavioral terms, that is, in a way which will help the teacher to determine whether or not, or to what extent, an objective has been achieved. A behavioral objective will include an indication as to what children can be expected to accomplish through a given activity. Both during and after a class period, the teacher may more readily assess the children's accomplishments and better plan for subsequent lessons.

The present approach to music education in the United States might be described as eclectic in nature. Not only are the Orff and Kodály methods used, but they are often used in conjunction with the creative approach of the Manhattanville Music Curriculum Program (MMCP), individualized instruction, and the learning activity package, handbell choirs, and group instruction in recorder, guitar, and piano. As there is a limit to what a teacher can reasonably cover in a given time period, some may place a greater emphasis or stress on one method to the partial exclusion of another. Other teachers may well integrate aspects of these various approaches with one of the graded, basic music series which already contain some of the ideas inherent in the method. In addition to the efforts directed toward the music education of all students, most elementary schools have a children's choir, comprised of selected fifth- and sixth-grade students who are especially motivated toward group participation and effective performance. Ample opportunities exist for performances within the school/community.

One of the unique aspects of American music education is that a considerable amount of the teaching of music is done by music specialists. However, in some school systems, this is only from the fourth grade on. Where the services of special music teachers for all grades are limited, then music specialists are used in an advisory capacity as music consultants to assist the general classroom teachers. Nearly all schools, however, from the seventh through the twelfth grade (junior and senior high schools) employ music specialists in both vocal and instrumental music.

2.2 The General Music Course for Young Adolescents in the United States

The general music course for young adolescents (age levels about 12 to 14) endeavors to build upon those experiences that children have had in elementary school, but takes into consideration the characteristics of puberty—the changing voice and the search for self-identity. The basic objectives are: (a) an increased familiarity with various types and styles of music, basic notation, forms, and vocabulary; (b) the ability to listen intelligently to music; and (c) an appreciation for music, that is, the development of a liking and feeling for music as an art form.

There are two general approaches used in the teaching of general music courses. One is the activities approach which may involve singing, listening, playing instruments (recorders, Orff instruments, handbells, guitars, etc.), reading about music and composers, and the use of learning activity packages by individuals. Students may also maintain personal notebooks that include reports on special musical experiences. Part of the class period may include group activity, while a portion of the time may be devoted to the pursuing of individual interests. This may be accomplished by designating various corners of the room as stations for particular purposes. For example, one corner or station may contain special musical instruments for student exploration and study. Another station may be designated as the listening center with several individual earphones where students may listen to recorded music; still another station may include a number of learning activity packages where students may pursue the study of topics of special interest and proceed at a rate commensurate with their own level of development.

Another approach is through group music performance where students learn about music through actual experience in a nonselective choral group. The focus is usually on one activity, such as singing in parts, with the objective of developing in each student an improved sensitivity to and understanding of rhythm, pitch and intervals, music markings, and interpretation.

The success of such an approach necessitates careful teacher preparation. Besides singing, the teacher will ask many questions—all with the purpose of keeping the class alert and helping them to discover and learn some significant aspect about the music they are performing. The successful teacher may be described as having the following characteristics: a sense of humor, an understanding of the characteristics of young adolescents, and the ability to anticipate problems they will encounter and be prepared to deal with them. Additionally, the teacher will maintain an air of excitement and a sense of accomplishment in the room, will work at a fast pace, and will compliment individual students upon the achievement of specific skills and understandings. The use of positive reinforcement is essential.

2.3 Music Theory Courses

The music theory class is offered in many secondary schools in the United States. It is not for the general student, but for the highly motivated one who has a strong interest in the subject and a reasonable musical background acquired through participation in a performing organization and experience and proficiency on some instrument. The objective of the music theory course is to develop musicianship and broaden the student's understanding of the functional aspects of music.

The content of the music theory course may be outlined as follows:

(a) Music fundamentals—including note names in both treble and bass clefs, rhythmic values (notes and rests), meter signatures, intervals, major and minor scales, chord types, that is, major, minor, augmented, diminished, seventh, and so on. The preceding may be covered by the student in any one of a number of programmed texts available, and subsequently reviewed by the teacher. An alternative approach is for the information to be introduced by the teacher and then reviewed and reinforced through appropriate drills and exercises.

(b) Aural skills to be developed include recognition of intervals, scales, harmonic chords (major, minor, augmented, diminished), meter, and simple forms (binary, ternary, rondo, theme and variations). Ear training is an important part of theory instruction and may be developed through sight-singing (with either syllables or numbers), and melodic dictation.

(c) Harmonization of melodies of four to eight measures in length. Students are provided with a given melody for which they prepare an appropriate harmonization, usually in four-part choral style. The students should write the harmonization, the class should sing it (all parts), and the student and/or the teacher should play it, followed by constructive and helpful comments.

(d) Creative work in which students write compositions of 16 to 32 measures in length is also an important aspect of the theory class, and may be for any medium, or combination of voices and instruments. Initially, setting a poem to music is a good beginning assignment as it provides some structure, and the text provides subtle cues for rhythm, meter, tonality, and chord choice.

(e) Experimentation with electronic music through the use of a tape recorder and/or a synthesizer may also contribute to the objectives of the course.

2.4 Instrumental Music Instruction

Beginning instruction on band and orchestral instruments—brass, woodwind, strings, and percussion—is different in various countries. In some it is available only through private instruction, that is, on a one-to-one basis. In other countries, group instruction is available, either as a part of the regular school curriculum or through special music schools.

In the United States, for example, instruction on brass, woodwind, and percussion instruments begins in the fourth or fifth grade in most school systems, while in others it begins in the seventh grade. Most educators feel that the earlier the instruction begins, the more proficient the students will eventually become. Some, however, advocate postponing instruction for two or three years until the students are physically more mature.

Homogeneous classes, or the teaching of instruments in groups of like characteristics, such as the clarinet and saxophone (single reed instruments), is an approach used by many teachers because of the greater amount of attention that may be given each student. However, especially in smaller schools, more such classes are being taught through a heterogeneous approach, that is, with a combination of all the brass, woodwind, and percussion instruments together. Some schools are able to employ a combination of these approaches by initially scheduling lessons for like instruments separately and after a six-week period changing to a heterogeneous grouping.

In most school systems, students must provide their own instruments which are available on a monthly rental basis from local music stores. Usually a portion of the rental fee may be applied to the purchase price so there is an incentive for parents to eventually buy the instruments.

Most of the instruments rented on this trial-purchase plan include flutes, clarinets, saxophones, trumpets, trombones, and percussion kits (snare drum, sticks, and drum pad). Because of their comparatively higher cost, many schools provide the low brass instruments (French horn, baritone, and tuba), the double reed instruments (oboe and bassoon), and the low single reed instruments (alto and bass clarinets, and baritone saxophone), and an array of percussion instruments.

Instruction on stringed instruments also usually begins in the fourth or fifth grade. Most students in this age group begin on violin, viola, and cello in $\frac{3}{4}$ sizes and string bass in $\frac{1}{2}$ or $\frac{3}{4}$ size. When they reach the seventh grade, students are usually able to play the violin, viola, and cello in full sizes and the string bass in $\frac{3}{4}$ or full size. Violins, violas, and cellos are also available on a rental basis or trial-purchase plan, but a number of schools have some cellos and string basses available for student use.

The Suzuki method of teaching stringed instruments has had a wide influence upon music educators throughout the world. Through this method, children are started on an instrument at a preschool age, and begin by learning familiar folk music by rote and then progressing on to classical music. The emphasis is upon establishing playing technique prior to note reading. This approach is used in many countries primarily by private teachers of music who maintain their own studios, but its influence is beginning to be felt in the public schools and is employed in a number of school systems with children beginning in kindergarten, or even younger when they can be accommodated. Children play violins in $\frac{1}{8}$ or $\frac{1}{4}$ sizes, and the cello in $\frac{1}{8}$ size. (Preschool children may acquire violins in $\frac{1}{32}$, $\frac{1}{16}$, and $\frac{1}{10}$ sizes.) The viola is usually introduced in a later grade.

2.5 Performing Groups or Ensembles

Music educators in all countries take exceptional pride in their performing groups, whether they be children's choirs, men's or women's choruses, mixed choruses, instrumental ensembles, bands, or orchestras. They perform before the public, reflect community and national pride, are enjoyed by many persons, and provide opportunities for genuine musical growth to the participants.

Musical organizations in United States secondary schools vary widely in size, objectives, and music literature studied and performed. Instrumental groups range from string quartets, brass and woodwind quintets, to the wind ensemble and chamber orchestra (about 40 players), to the symphonic band and symphonic orchestra (75 to 80 performers). Choral groups of mixed voices range in size from madrigal groups (12 to 16 voices), jazz and show choirs (16 to 24 singers), to the concert choirs and choruses (60 to 80 singers).

The objective of most of these groups is the achievement of the highest possible performance standards, as well as opportunities to perform periodically throughout the community. Additionally, most teachers endeavor to expose their students to a wide variety of types and styles of music. In the United States there exists a contrasting viewpoint as to the number of public performances musical organizations, particularly vocal groups, should give during the course of a school year. Some feel that maximum exposure is essential, not only as a means of motivating students toward higher performance standards, but also as a means of maintaining a positive relationship with the community. Other teachers strongly resist the temptation to accept all the numerous performance requests and place a limit on outside engagements. Their purpose in limiting the number of performances is so that adequate time will be available to teach students more about music, that is, stylistic characteristics, and the development of music reading skills. To develop music reading skills, some time during each rehearsal period must be devoted to the study of melodic and rhythmic patterns. Singers will improve this skill only through consistent daily practice.

3. Music and Social Studies

Whereas the music specialist is concerned primarily with the development of musical understandings and skills, the classroom teacher quite naturally has a strong interest in using music to enlighten and clarify some concept of a unit topic that the children may be studying in an elementary-school social studies class. Following are some ways in which music may be used to meet this objective (Garretson 1976 pp. 279–80).

(a) Various customs, ideals, and attitudes of the people of a particular culture are often revealed in its music. Examples: "The Shanty Man's Life" (American folksong), which depicts a lumberman's attitude toward work; "When Love is Kind" (Old English Melody), which describes attitudes toward love in old England.

(b) Music often describes various important historical events of a country and some music was written for commemorative purposes. Examples: "Charlie is My Darling" (Scottish folksong), which describes Prince Charles' triumphal entry into Scotland; "The Maple Leaf Forever" by Alexander Muir, which tells about the Battle of Quebec in 1759 between the French and the English.

(c) During times of national crisis, such as war, the people of a country unite and this esprit de corps is reflected in their music. Example: "Yankee Doodle Boy" by George M. Cohan, tells about the American soldier of the First World War.

(d) In the expansion of the United States, and the westward movement in particular, songs describing various types of transportation were popular. Example: "The Railroad Cars are Coming" (American folksong).

4. Music and the Related Arts

All the arts reflect the culture from which they emanate. It is from this understanding that certain courses are taught in which an attempt is made to integrate concepts from various disciplines and to draw parallels or relationships enabling students to comprehend these subjects in their broadest perspective, as well as understanding the interrelationships and effects various events and beliefs have had upon the arts. Several approaches may be described as follows.

4.1 Humanities Courses

The impetus for the organization of humanities courses began in the early 1960s, and courses were organized to be taught in both secondary schools and on the college level. Ideas or concepts were drawn from music, history, philosophy, literature, and the visual arts. Seldom does one person have any degree of expertise in all of these disciplines or areas, so the only logical approach was for such courses to be "team taught" with a specialist from each discipline. When this has occurred and when the entire team is committed to their task, then such courses can be both highly interesting and valuable to students. Adequate time, of course, must be allotted for the team to meet together and to plan their presentations. Without personal commitment, coupled with adequate planning time, such courses can only be less than effective.

4.2 Related Arts Courses

Courses that integrate ideas primarily from music, the visual arts, and literature (also sometimes called humanities courses) are more likely to be successful because with fewer areas to integrate there is less possibility that a particular area will be slighted because of lack of time, or expertise on the part of the teacher(s). While a team approach is still highly desirable, there are persons capable of teaching all these disciplines. Additionally, there are a number of textbooks designed for teaching such related arts courses. One of the dangers or weaknesses of any humanities or related arts course is the temptation for teachers to indicate relationships where none truly exist.

4.3 Concept Clarification

In the rehearsal of any music performing organization, concepts from other arts areas may be utilized for the purpose of clarifying and/or reinforcing musical concepts that will lead toward improved musicality and performance. For example, in rehearsing a motet from the Renaissance period, the conductor may relate that the tempo is to be moderate and steady and the dynamics are to be restrained. If a photograph or color slide of an early Renaissance painting can be shown to the chorus, it can be pointed out, for example, that the colors are likewise restrained with a use of pastels, and as to line and shape, it is delicate and orderly, usually restful in nature, with minimal tension. A minimal amount of rehearsal time may be used for singers to grasp these relationships. Likewise, similar parallels may be drawn between music and art of the Baroque, Classic and Romantic Periods, and Impressionism and Expressionism.

Bibliography

Anderson W, Campbell P S (eds.) 1989 *Multicultural Perspectives in Music Education.* Music Educators National Conference, Reston, Virginia

Bollinger D E 1979 *Band Director's Complete Handbook.* Parker Publishing Company, West Nyack, New York

Choksy L, Abramson R M, Gillespie A E, Woods D 1986 *Teaching Music in the Twentieth Century.* Prentice-Hall, Englewood Cliffs, New Jersey

Garretson R L 1976 *Music in Childhood Education*, 2nd edn.

Prentice-Hall, Englewood Cliffs, New Jersey [1980 *La Musica En La Educación Infantil*. Editorial Diana, Mexico City]

Garretson R L 1988 *Conducting Choral Music,* 6th edn. Prentice-Hall, Englewood Cliffs, New Jersey

Gates J T (ed.) 1988 *Music Education in the United States: Contemporary Issues.* The University of Alabama Press, Tuscaloosa, Alabama

Graham R M, Beer A S 1980 *Teaching Music to the Exceptional Child: A Handbook for Mainstreaming.* Prentice-Hall, Englewood Cliffs, New Jersey

Hoffer C R 1983 *Introduction to Music Education.* Wadsworth Publishing Company, Belmont, California

Hoffer C R 1983 *Teaching Music in the Secondary Schools,* 3rd edn. Wadsworth Publishing Company, Belmont, California

International Society for Music Education 1980 *New Trends in School Music Education and in Teacher Training.* International Society for Music Education, 7th Yearbook. Papers of the International Society for Music Education Seminar in Innsbruck, Austria, 1980

International Society for Music Education 1981 *National Culture: An Inspiration for Music Education.* International Society for Music Education, 8th Yearbook. Papers of the

14th International Conference of the International Society for Music Education in Warsaw, Poland, 1980

Kabalevski C 1965 Music education in the USSR. *Int. Music Educator* 11(2): 353–57

Landis B, Carder P 1972 *The Eclectic Curriculum in American Music Education: Contributions of Dalcroze, Kodály, and Orff.* Music Educators National Conference, Washington, DC

Mark C R 1986 *Contemporary Music Education,* 2nd edn. Schirmer Books, New York

Music Educators National Conference, Committee on Standards 1986. *School Music Programs: Descriptions & Standards,* 2nd edn. Music Educators National Conference, Reston, Virginia

Nye R E, Nye V T 1985 *Music in the Elementary School,* 5th edn. Prentice-Hall, Englewood Cliffs, New Jersey

Reimer B 1989 *A Philosophy of Music Education,* 2nd ed. Prentice-Hall, Englewood Cliffs, New Jersey

Sample D, Sample I 1979 *International Dimensions of Music Education.* ERIC Clearing House on Teacher Education, Washington, DC

Trân V K 1981 *Music Education in Asia.* International Society for Music Education, 8th Yearbook, pp. 44–50

Handicrafts

K. Schleicher

In industrialized and developing societies there is an increasing need for practical, life-related education. Training in crafts is considered to be necessary for several reasons. First, a separation has occurred between the domestic and occupational realms of life, and therefore home does not supply primary experience and training in the field of practical work. Secondly, the technological environment has become more complex and schools are expected to assume a role in helping children to cope with this complexity. Thirdly, teaching in school has become increasingly abstract and divorced from life and thus programmes in practical work shall contribute to a more appropriate balance among the varieties of school and life experiences of children. Nevertheless, numerous educational systems have neither precisely defined nor explicitly stated the aims, objectives, and contents of teaching "handicrafts" in schools. Depending on social needs and economic requirements as well as on the degree of the development of the school systems and on ideological and pedagogical considerations, the following areas of study may be subsumed under the heading "handicrafts": aspects of rural and health education, drawing, arts and crafts, domestic science and home economics, industrial arts, and polytechnic education.

1. Handicrafts Within the Curriculum

Handicrafts are offered more frequently in the primary and in junior-secondary school than in the senior-secondary school and they are primarily directed towards children of below average ability.

Despite the variations across systems, one may observe a certain degree of congruence in offering and teaching these subjects in schools. There is an attempt to provide opportunities for mental and manual experiences with materials (such as wood, metal, textile), with tools (mainly manual ones), and with agricultural and industrial tasks (such as producing and marketing).

The studies aim at integrating practical and theoretical experiences for a better understanding of one's self, of the society, and of the physical environment. They also strive to provide opportunities for understanding how technical, economic, social, and aesthetic factors interrelate in shaping the products we use in our daily life. Handicrafts differ from occupational training insofar as they are not oriented toward preparing the learner for the world of work. They also differ from physical education by not focusing onesidely on physical movements. Handicrafts seek simultaneously to promote nonmanipulative abilities (such as planning and decision making), and manipulative skills (such as sewing, gardening, or trades). They are introduced into the syllabus partly as separate curricular subjects, such as metalwork and home economics, or, alternatively, as a learning activity in other subjects, such as practical exercises, and partly as a strategy to increase motivation for studies. There is a tendency to teach handicrafts in primary grades attached to other subjects (such as social studies and science), in the middle grades as a pre-vocational training in particular manual skills (such as technical drawing and metal work), and in the upper grades as a practical preparation for entrance into the world of work (such as career education). In general, the situation of handicrafts is quite different from other curriculum subjects. Schools enjoy a relatively great freedom in articulating the study of such crafts, since they are seldom offered continuously across all grade levels, and are usually taught separately to boys and girls.

Instruction in handicrafts has been heavily influenced by social and technical changes such as the industrial and the technological revolutions. The status of handicrafts in schools is highly affected by the fact that the subject has never become a university-taught discipline unlike related disciplines such as art, labour studies, and domestic sciences.

2. Historical Development

Handicrafts were introduced into individual educational systems with differing levels of emphasis at different times, depending upon variations in social structure, economic development, and educational policy. In the course of this development, various content and didactic approaches took turns in becoming prominent, which greatly affected and still affect the status of the subject in schools.

After calling attention to the significance of concrete–sensory experiences for thought and learning (Bacon, in 1605, first spoke of "manual arts"), schools stressed the importance of teaching manual skills. Comenius promulgated the didactic meaning of "handicrafts" in education, and Locke proposed the teaching of gardening and working with iron in the schools. In Mecklenburg in Germany it was even officially stated that needlework should be an obligatory subject in village schools (1650). Then, in the eighteenth century, the influence of rapid industrialization and the philanthropic approach imposed two contrasting demands on the teaching of handicrafts. On the one hand, in the "schools for the poor", children were supposed to do gardening or other manual work to be able to support the school financially. On the other hand (as argued by Rousseau and Pestalozzi), visual and practical instruction were considered as tools for broadening the child's range of knowledge, ability to learn by discovery, and fitness for practical life. Consequently, some school programmes for handicrafts developed which were somehow based on psychological principles and for which didactic teaching sequences were organized. Generally however, handicrafts dealt with simple skills and also served to reinforce sex and status differences.

In the nineteenth century, the interest in handicrafts waned for a while under the influence of the new humanism and of the political restoration in Europe. At the same time the Manual Labor Movement in the United States created new links between manual work and

study in the 1830s. However, decisive changes did not come about until the second half of the century, when parallel with the growth of industrialization the system of apprenticeship disintegrated, child labour was gradually restricted, and compulsory school attendance was enforced. In Finland "sloyd" work became obligatory in connection with the introduction of compulsory schooling in 1882, and a few years later in Sweden didactic principles were applied in the teaching of "sloyd" work (e.g. from easy to difficult work, from the known to the unknown). Following the Scandinavian examples, several countries introduced instruction in trades and manual skills as compulsory subjects as, for example in the United Kingdom in 1890, in France in 1892, and in Bulgaria in 1893. Thus the manual training element gained prominence although there was manifold emphasis on the general educational function of handicrafts.

A new appreciation and accentuation of handicrafts ensued in the twentieth century. This was supported in the United States by the growing impact of Dewey's philosophy, in Europe under the influence of the reform pedagogy, and in the Soviet Union through the development of the polytechnic concept.

In the American comprehensive high school, manual training was combined with general education. Educators emphasized the genuine limitation of purely intellectual or purely practical work and accentuated the links between the industrial and social world. Handicrafts were thus seen as useful teaching–learning tools rather than independent school subjects. In contrast, the European approach advocated a theoretically based but work-oriented craft instruction which aimed at the development of work attitudes and social comprehension. With reference to American and German experiences, a polytechnic concept of an industrial training was developed in the Soviet Union (by Blonskii), in order to promote an understanding of industrial culture in Marxist societies. The polytechnic school should offer practical exercises ranging from those in the domestic realm to that of industrial work in a form suited to children.

In summary, it can be said that the chief impulse for the development of handicrafts as a school subject emanated from the central European countries, first in Bohemia and Germany in the seventeenth century motivated by philanthropic sentiments, and later in the eighteenth century in Germany and the United Kingdom within the framework of the industrial schools for the poor. In the nineteenth century, first the Scandinavian "sloyd" work, which was introduced to encourage home manufacturing, added a new dimension to the teaching of manual skills. Then the interest shifted because of pragmatic reasons to the area of rural education and manual arts in the United States, and to a comprehensive "polytechnic education" in Russia. Finally, at the beginning of the twentieth century "work education" in Germany, "industrial arts" in the United States, and "polytechnic education" in socialist pedagogy, all strove towards an integration of the general, social, and preoccupational education.

3. Principles of Instruction for Handicrafts

The objectives, the content, and the teaching practices of handicrafts are more dependent upon traditions and interests of individual states than upon academic criteria. Furthermore, they are moulded by national and regional conditions of school systems rather than by international forums. Consequently, it is only possible to present a few examples of varying emphases in the teaching of handicrafts. Handicrafts are most strongly integrated into one general pedagogic concept within the framework of polytechnic instruction in socialist countries; they find their most diverse expression in countries with decentralized educational systems, such as in the Anglo–Saxon countries, while in developing countries they are strongly affected by the quest for economic and environmentally pertinent considerations.

3.1 Handicrafts as an Element of Polytechnic Education in the Soviet Union

Lenin developed a polytechnic concept in 1920 for the formation of the socialist personality and the increase of industrial production. This concept was modified in the course of the rapid industrialization and social change which took place between 1928 and 1935. Since 1965, the chief tasks of polytechnic training may be identified as follows: to intensify the relationship between schooling and real life, to encourage interest in and an understanding of the scientific and technical revolution, and to support the philosophy of materialism. Within this framework, handicrafts are an element of instruction for work. In the elementary grades (ages 6 to 9), work with paper and plasticine, and gardening are customary; toys and simple teaching aids are made, and technical modelling is encouraged. In the middle grades (ages 10 to 13) practical tasks such as work with wood, metal, and electronics are undertaken in school workshops, and exercises in domestic science and agriculture are usually required. Finally, in the upper grades (ages 14 to 16), knowledge of the natural and social sciences is applied in practical assignments and courses, ranging from the cultivation of seeds to tractor construction. In general, all of these tasks constitute an integral part of a polytechnic education.

3.2 English and Welsh Handicrafts Differentiated by Subject and as a Tool of Instruction

Although the English and Welsh educational system is highly decentralized so that the organization of the curriculum is mainly left to the schools, and the choice of subjects to the pupils, a few trends may be discerned. The demands (for example, of the Hadow Report in 1926) for a realistic and practical "secondary education for all" led to the legal introduction in 1944 of the "secondary modern" and the "secondary technical school", in which handicrafts rapidly achieved great popularity. In the mid-1960s, approximately one-fifth of all secondary-school pupils took part in metalwork, woodwork, or technical drawing lessons, one-third in needlecraft or cookery, and one-tenth in agriculture and rural studies. But participation in domestic science was limited almost exclusively to girls, and in typical crafts courses to boys. Some 10 percent of the total timetable was given to all handicrafts subjects and their share of school examinations (CSE and GCE 'O' level) was approximately half as high as that of natural science subjects. The teaching methods still differed from school to school. Whilst in grammar schools the analytical tradition generally dominated, elsewhere, project work was and is fashionable and seeks to promote links between motivation, practical abilities, logical strategies, and technological understanding. Nevertheless, the notion is increasing that materials are a principal medium of education and that all pupils (and not only the less gifted) should take part in practical instruction, since design problems, a rational consumer behaviour, an understanding of technical and practical matters, insight into the impact and consequences of technology, domestic abilities, and precareer orientations are important for all pupils. Thus, as a general principle, handicrafts do receive serious consideration as a tool of instruction.

3.3 Handicrafts in the Context of North American Industrial Arts

Since public education is principally the concern of individual municipal and state authorities, and since no binding, national "programme standards" have been developed, curricula and teaching not only vary regionally and locally, but also mirror the social and ethnic background of the pupils. In general, however, three chief components are interlocked to form the dominant concept of the "industrial arts": the general–cultural aspect, which proceeds from the significance of manual facility for general human development; the occupation–trade aspect, which seeks to lay the foundations for a later career; and the technological–industrial aspect, which thematizes production methods as well as technological phenomena. In the 1970s, an additional dimension, the psychology of learning and development, was added, which accorded the realm of precareer training a place in the lifelong spectrum of occupational development. Hitherto, however, the "industrial arts" had been offered only as an optional subject, and principally for boys; instruction had been heavily concentrated since the 1920s on basic tool and design skills, that is, on general woodwork, metalwork, architectural drafting, mechanical drawing, and craftsmanship, whilst the pursuit of technological understanding had attracted less attention than career orientation. In the face of diverse interests and the demands of the 1970s, reform educationalists have concentrated efforts on devising interdisciplinary programmes for middle grade learners studying home economics, art, and the industrial arts, thus establishing links between exploratory laboratory workshop and classroom experience.

3.4 Problems of Handicrafts in Developing Countries

Although an attempt has been made to indicate the teaching and structural problems of handicrafts in general and not in terms of national differences, some African countries serve as examples of those developing countries which exhibit comparable developmental structures, or which, alternatively, were under colonial control for a long period. Although preoccupational practical and work training is considered a decidedly important priority, handicrafts meet, in general, with relatively poor recognition from parents and from the public in general; moreover, there is a lack of competent teachers, of necessary teaching materials, and of appropriate syllabi. Nevertheless, there has been a discernible change of attitude since early postcolonial times when school education focused for the most part on "formal literacy". This change has taken the form of an increasing adjustment of instruction to social and local requirements and of an attempt to place greater emphasis on handicrafts within the syllabus.

In Nigeria, although the British organization of the education system was criticized as early as 1922 to 1925 by the Phelps–Stokes Commissions, and demands were made for a more locally and practically relevant education (e.g. in homecrafts, agriculture, woodwork, and village industries), no major change was introduced prior to the country's independence in 1960. Handicrafts were not a component part of school-leaving examinations, and made no contribution to educational and social progress. It was only under the influence of the Nigerian Educational Research Council (established in 1972) that the Government decided in 1977 to introduce into primary schools lessons in domestic science, agriculture, and health education. This innovation led to higher valuation of practical work and to an encouragement of teaching manipulative skills, with the ultimate aim of achieving an education more relevant to life and to local demands. In this attempt, the introduction of handicrafts encounters certain obstacles: appropriately equipped classrooms hardly exist, qualified teachers are scarce, and specialized books are, in general, available only in English (see *Nigeria: System of Education*).

With the granting of independence in Cameroon in 1961, the French- and British-colonized parts of the country were united. Although the previously established administrative and school structures continued, and instruction was furthermore conducted in the respective colonial languages, the way was nonetheless paved for practice- and community-oriented reforms in primary school curricula in both parts of the country. Greater emphasis was put on ruralization and on practical and environmental orientation. Basic manual trade skills were to be imparted, instruction in land economy

given, and work and learning became combined through project methods of teaching. In order simultaneously to compensate for the inadequacy of the schools' equipment for handicrafts, and to intensify the relevance of teaching to the community, locally practising tradesmen were, on the one hand, to be involved in teaching, whilst on the other hand, pupils were to participate in community self-help schemes, such as road-building and irrigation (see *Cameroon: System of Education*; *Rural Education Programmes*).

In general, however, handicrafts may only hesitantly become widely accepted as a subject—or community-oriented project teaching method—and the demand made on primary schools by the African Conference of Education Ministers to strengthen the mutual relationships between school, the working world, and the community has still to be fulfilled.

3.5 International Comparison of Trends

All in all, a comparative consideration shows, on the one hand, that certain points of emphasis embraced by handicrafts relate equally to manual and instrumental work with materials (notably with wood and metal), to basic trade skills (specialization and competence), and to the area of home activity (domestic science). On the other hand however, their location in the syllabus as a whole varies, depending upon tradition, development, and social–political handicaps, with respect to the education system. Thus handicrafts have, in a polytechnic education, a functionally integrated complementary role; in England and Wales, in contrast, they are differentiated by subject or are offered as a principle of instruction, according to pupils' as well as teachers' interests and the specific facilities available in schools; the American "industrial arts", in the third place, aim not only for preoccupational orientation but also for a pragmatic general education; and lastly in Africa, they are oriented towards skilled work which should lead to an education more relevant to life, and to a higher appreciation of practical work.

4. Handicrafts in Need of Pedagogical Legitimation

On the one hand, the historical development of handicrafts shows very clearly to what extent their goals are moulded by economic and social demands, and how little by fundamentally pedagogic considerations. On the other hand, a comparison of the development of curricula in various countries demonstrates that teaching handicrafts is strongly affected by national preconceptions about its importance, and internationally, variables like sex, social strategies, and general achievement levels are highly related to the extent that handicrafts are studied by different groups of children.

A reorientation of curriculum development in the handicrafts seems to be necessary in industrial countries as well as in developing countries. This should start by answering such fundamental questions as the following:

(a) Why do school pupils in the upper grades attribute the greatest usefulness, after mathematics and instruction in their mother tongue, to handicrafts?

(b) How can handicrafts more adequately take into consideration the psychological findings which indicate that cognitive, affective, and motivational developments interact with each other and constitute elements of a general development?

(c) What are the consequences for handicrafts of the fact that demand for manual dexterity is diminishing with the transition from the industrial age to that of technological age?

(d) And to what extent is instruction in handicrafts still justifiable, if absolutely no evaluation is made of which curricula lead to which abilities, modes of behaviour, and attitudes?

Bibliography

Bennett C A 1937 *History of Manual and Industrial Education up to 1870; 1870 to 1917.* Manual Arts Press, Peoria, Illinois

Benson K R, Frankson C E, Buttery T 1975 *Arts and Crafts for Home, School and Community.* Mosby, London

Council of Europe 1972 *The Teaching of Technology.* Council of Europe, Strasbourg

Hanf T, Ammann K A et al. 1975 Education: An obstacle to development? *Comp. Educ. Rev.* 19: 68–87

Hawes H W R 1979 *Curriculum and Reality in African Primary Schools.* Longman, London

Ivanovič K A (ed.) 1975 *Polytechnischer Arbeitsunterricht in der UdSSR: Theoretische Grundlagen und Praktische Durchführung.* Maier, Ravensburg

Lauwerys J A, Scanlon D G (eds.) 1968 *Education within Industry.* Evans, London

Leifer A D, Lesser G S 1976 *The Development of Career Awareness in Young Children.* United States Department of Health, Education, and Welfare, National Institute of Education, Washington, DC

Linderman E W, Linderman M M 1977 *Crafts for the Classroom.* MacMillan, New York

Roberts R W 1971 *Vocational and Practical Arts Education: History, Development, and Principles.* Harper, New York

Russell J E, Bonser F G 1924 *Industrial Education.* Teachers College, Columbia University, New York

Schmitt M L, Pelley A L 1966 *Industrial Arts Education: A Survey of Programs, Teachers, Students, and Curriculum.* United States Department of Health, Education, and Welfare, Washington, DC

Schools Council 1969 *Education Through the Use of Materials: The Possible Role of School Workshops in the Education of Secondary School Pupils* (Working Paper No. 26). Evans/Methuen Educational, London

Schools Council 1980 *Craft, Design and Technology Committee: National Criteria for a Single System of Examining at 16+.* London

Wilkening F 1970 *Technische Bildung im Werkunterricht. Geschichtliche Entwicklung und genenwärtige Problematik.* Beltz, Weinheim

Innovative Study Areas

Creativity: Educational Programs

A. J. Tannenbaum

Creativity has many meanings, probably because it arouses interest among a wide variety of scholars—including philosophers, historians, educators, psychiatrists, and psychologists—who view it from their separate perspectives. Some think of creativity as personal idiosyncrasy while others associate it with special competency. Those responsible for discerning and cultivating it in children take the latter approach, equating it with divergent thought processes, or the ability to produce multiple, unique, and elaborate solutions to problems that can be solved in more than one way. But despite the popularity of this assertion, empirical evidence is by no means clear that superior divergent thinking skills characterize people who are regarded as highly creative by their colleagues or critics.

Discussion of the concept raises a basic problem of communication. On the one hand, using the terms "creativity" and "divergent thinking" as synonyms amounts to assuming a relationship between them that is not substantiated by objective data. On the other hand, it is awkward to deny such a relationship and yet report on research and practice in the field when so many researchers and practitioners who discuss the topic assume that the terms are interchangeable. There is no compromise in such a dilemma. The only way to deal with it is to present rather than ignore the popular belief, but as an hypothesis that needs confirmation, not as an already proven truism. This tacit understanding underlies the following review.

1. Creative Processes

Unlike many psychometrists and educators, those who theorize about the thoughts and emotions involved in creativity are generally not bound by the creativity-equals-divergent-thinking assumption. Instead, they look at broader aspects of human functioning. Among the best-known theories is the one advanced by Wallas (1926) who suggested a four-stage process. The first is preparation, in which a problem is investigated in every possible way. The second is incubation, during which no conscious thought is given to the problem, but the ideas and materials collected in the period of prep-

aration are somehow stored below the conscious level of the psyche. The third stage is illumination, when the "Aha!" feeling is suddenly experienced, often unexpectedly. The final stage is verification, when the new idea is evaluated on the basis of its creator's own standards which may be sharply different from the public's or critic's tastes.

According to Taylor (1975) the Wallas steps toward creative accomplishment are valid, but it is also necessary to recognize hierarchical levels of creativity. From lowest to highest, they are as follows: (a) expressive creativity, or the development of a unique idea with no concern about its quality; (b) technical creativity, or proficiency in creating products with consummate skill, as in shaping a Stradivarius violin, without much evidence of expressive spontaneity; (c) inventive creativity, or the ingenious use of materials to develop new uses for old parts or new ways of seeing old things, as in the case of inventions such as the telephone or incandescent lamp which do not represent contributions of new basic ideas; (d) innovative creativity, or the ability to formulate departures from established schools of thought as alternatives to these traditions; and (e) emergentive creativity, a rarely attained quality of excellence since it incorporates the most abstract, ideational principles in a field of productivity.

Thus, in theory it is possible to conceptualize creative processes as following a sequential pattern, while the forms of creativity can range from fairly mundane to highly sophisticated levels of innovation. Needless to say, it is difficult to measure creative potential in ways that take into account both the sequential patterns and hierarchical forms involved in the process.

2. Measurement of Creativity

Although biographical inventories are used widely to locate creative thinkers among adult groups, for children the emphasis is on performance measures, based primarily on those developed by Guilford (1975). According to Guilford there are four creative thinking abilities: fluency, flexibility, originality, and elaboration. The intellectual operation for these abilities is divergent, and it can apply to all content areas.

2.1 Fluency

Divergent production tests are concerned with measuring the ability to solve problems in as many ways as possible. Ideational fluency denotes skills in generating quantities of ideas in a language context. Examples of this competency include writing large numbers of acceptable plot titles for untitled literary works and imagining many consequences of a change in the environment or in the conditions of life (e.g., suppose the world's supply of oil would dry up; list as many consequences as you can imagine). Associational fluency is the ability to produce many relationships or meaningful associations with a given idea. It is evidenced by the quantity of synonyms a person can attach to any familiar word that has many meanings. Expressional fluency refers to skills in juxtaposing words to meet sentence structure requirements. A person who excels in such tasks is able, for example, to write many sentences while being limited to a uniform number of words and a single set of initial letters for the words in each sentence.

2.2 Flexibility

The skill of being able to discontinue an existing pattern of thought and shift to new patterns is called "flexibility." Two subskills can be recognized, each having a different content and product. Spontaneous flexibility deals with changes in direction of thinking when a person is not instructed to do so. For example, in listing the various uses of a brick, the flexible individual tends to produce ideas relating not only to the weight of the object but also to its size, color, shape, texture, and so on. Adaptive flexibility also deals with changes in direction of thinking to solve problems. However, in this case the content is figural, such as geometric forms which the person uses to make as many objects as possible, or matchsticks arranged in a design that has to be altered in a specific way by removing a given number (occasionally *any* number) of matches. Another example of adaptive flexibility is planning air maneuvers that take the most efficient path in "skywriting" letter combinations.

2.3 Originality

The process of originality resembles that of ideational fluency, except that the focus is on products that are offbeat, unexpected, and sometimes amusing. For example, the "consequences" problem mentioned earlier in relation to ideational fluency is intended to elicit responses that are either indirectly or remotely associated with a given problem situation. For the plot titles, what counts is the number of responses judged to be clever, witty, and pithy.

2.4 Elaboration

The process of elaboration is relevant to skills in planning and organization. For example, a person demonstrates the ability to fill in all of the various details necessary to make a briefly outlined project, such as preparing to mount a stage play, work effectively.

Guilford's pioneering efforts on the theory of creativity as a psychological construct and on the development of creativity tests for identifying such abilities led to the massive work of Torrance, whose test battery (1966) is probably the most widely used in education. Another popular test of creativity is the Wallach and Kogan instrument (1965) which also concentrates on some of the divergent thinking skills described by Guilford. In fact, most of the research in educational settings and most attempts at identifying creative potential involve measures of divergent thinking that resemble those designed by Guilford for his work on the structure of intellect.

3. Tested Creativity and Tested Intelligence

In their use of Guilford-type creativity tests to locate gifted children who would otherwise be overlooked on the basis of IQ, Getzels and Jackson (1962) influenced many educators to include creativity batteries among their instruments for assessing human potential. The researchers compared two groups of students in a university campus high school, one group scoring among the highest 20 percent of that high-school population in IQ but not among the highest 20 percent in creativity, and the other group scoring among the highest 20 percent in creativity but not among the highest 20 percent in IQ. They found that despite a 23-point difference in IQ, the two groups were comparable in scholastic achievement and differed sharply in various personality traits. Getzels and Jackson concluded that the pool of children identified as potentially gifted can be enlarged if creativity tests are used in the identification process. Torrance and Wu (1980) conducted a 22-year follow-up of 5-year-old children identified separately as high-creatives, high-IQ, and high on both. The study shows the high creatives as possessing somewhat better quality images of future careers than did the high-IQ sample. This further confirms the Getzels–Jackson thesis concerning the importance of creativity measures in talent searches.

However, other replications of the Getzels and Jackson study have failed to confirm their hypotheses. Some (Wallach 1970) note serious flaws in the research design. The alternative approach to examining relationships between IQ and creativity has been through correlational and factor analysis. Results of various such studies (Thorndike 1963) suggest that tested IQ and tested creativity partly overlap and are partly independent of each other. This means that divergent thinking is not tapped entirely by conventional measures of intelligence.

4. Stimulating Creativity in the Classroom

Most educational programs designed to cultivate creativity emphasize brainstorming techniques. The aim is to stir up many original solutions and to evaluate them only after every possible alternative has been expressed. Among the pioneers in the field was Alex F. Osborn (1963) whose work has influenced many subsequent efforts of this kind. He developed a five-step process of creative problem solving: (a) problem finding, or the search for the nature of the real challenge from different perspectives; (b) fact finding, in order to understand the situation better and to imagine what the solution might be; (c) idea finding, aimed at calling up ideas from the pre- and sub-conscious and to defer judgment of their quality until they have all been flushed out; (d) solution finding, at which point the ideas are evaluated for their relevance and applicability, and the best one is chosen for implementation; and (e) acceptance finding, or gaining an audience that is willing to support the idea and put it to practical use.

Parnes and his colleagues (1977) built on Osborn's earlier work and suggested the following strategies for creative problem solving:

(a) *Remove the internal blocks to creativity*. In order to prepare children for creative productivity, they must be helped to feel secure in their relationships with others without worrying about the acceptability of their ideas, even if they are extremely offbeat. However, freedom to think carries with it the responsibility for their mistakes.

(b) *Create an awareness of the role of the subconscious*. Even when a problem is removed from direct attention, the subconscious somehow keeps on working at it. Since ideas and fantasies about possible solutions surface only fleetingly, it is important to jot down these thoughts so that they may eventually be clarified and organized.

(c) *Defer judgment*. By so doing, the children can spend more time on a variety of perceptions about a problem and thereby increase the flow of ideas that lead to alternative solutions.

(d) *Create an awareness of the power of metaphor and analogy in triggering new connections and associations*. With the help of checklists and other devices, dealing with analogy and metaphor can be made easy if enough time is spent in practice.

(e) *Provide experiences with mind-stretching exercises*. Forcing the mind to produce many alternative solutions to problems is uncomfortable at the beginning, but ideas flow more and more easily as children grow more comfortable with the task.

(f) *Keep fantasy alive*. Fantasy is not only essential in helping children's mental growth and adjustment; it is also a vital ingredient in creativity. Every effort, therefore, has to be made to discourage the school and the home from communicating the belief to children that such flights of the imagination are signs of immature thinking.

(g) *Remove mental brakes: encourage freewheeling*. Children have to feel assured that their ideas will not be ridiculed and that any far-out thought is worth expressing and sharing with others.

(h) *Discipline the imagination*. Although children should be encouraged to freewheel and fantasize, they

need to realize that after the incubation period ideas will be reviewed critically. Some will be rejected, and those that are retained need to be implemented for humane and useful purposes.

(i) *Increase sensitivity*. Formal awareness training, art exercises, and in-depth discussions of literature can help increase children's sensitivity to others and to their physical environment. It will also enable them to recognize incongruities as well as new relationships and connections that can prove to be meaningful.

(j) *Increase knowledge*. Creativity depends on knowledge previously absorbed. Increasing mastery of information and ideas can help children see relationships that form the basis of new ideas. The point to remember, however, is that while subject content is important, it does not constitute the entire learning experience. Learning to think, to solve problems, and to use knowledge should become an essential part of the school experience.

(k) *Help children to understand why they engage in various exercises related to creative thinking*. Children, parents, and educators have to understand the importance of creative thinking and the exercises that facilitate it in order to maximize the effects of enrichment. Otherwise, such techniques may mistakenly be seen as "fun and games" that only embellish the curriculum rather than breathe life into it.

Most so-called creativity programs in education resemble the Osborn–Parnes design in their emphasis on divergent thinking exercises. They provide children with educational experiences that call for speculation and innovation to a much greater extent than conventional instruction does. As such, they enrich the curriculum significantly even if the thought processes they stimulate may bear only slight resemblance to creative activity.

5. Effects of Stimulating Creativity

It stands to reason that curricula designed to concentrate on divergent thinking will improve children's proficiency in such exercises, and indeed there is ample evidence to show that this is so. However, such studies have to be examined closely for their limitations. For example, there is a review by Torrance (1972) of 142 evaluations of creativity programs which shows that as many as 72 percent of them have proven successful. Yet a sampling of studies for each of the nine types of intervention reveals how difficult it is to interpret the results. In most instances, the treatment consisted of exercises in divergent thinking, and the tests used to assess gain over the experimental period focused on the same thought processes, thus suggesting that experimenters were evaluating the effects of "teaching to the test." Mansfield et al. (1978) point out this weakness, along with several others, in their review of 72 evaluation studies.

It would seem, therefore, that creativity training is a matter of quid pro quo. That is, children who receive practice in divergent thinking generally perform better than those who do not receive such instruction, provided the groups are compared on a test battery that closely reflects the contents of the training program. Since the skills do not seem to transfer easily, the teacher has to apply divergent thinking in every possible curriculum context. Considering the value of these exercises in the overall school program, it is indeed worthwhile for educators to make the application wherever possible.

Bibliography

Getzels J W, Jackson P W 1962 *Creativity and Intelligence: Explorations with Gifted Students*. Wiley, New York

Guilford J P 1975 Varieties of creative giftedness, their measurement and development. *Gifted Child Q.* 19: 107–21

Mansfield R S, Busse T V, Krepelka E J 1978 The effectiveness of creativity training. *Rev. Educ. Res.* 48: 517–36

Osborn A F 1963 *Applied Imagination: Principles and Procedures of Creative Problem Solving*, 3rd edn. Scribner, New York

Parnes S J, Noller R B, Biondi A M 1977 *Guide to Creative Action*, rev. edn. Scribner, New York

Tannenbaum A J 1983 *Gifted Children: Psychological and Educational Perspectives*. Macmillan, New York

Taylor I A 1975 An emerging view of creative actions. In: Taylor I A, Getzels J W (eds.) 1975 *Perspectives in Creativity*. Aldine, Chicago, Illinois, pp. 297–325

Thorndike R L 1963 Some methodological issues in the study of creativity. *Proceedings of the 1962 Invitational Conference on Testing Problems*. Educational Testing Service, Princeton, New Jersey, pp. 40–54

Torrance E P 1966 *Torrance Tests of Creative Thinking*. Personnel Press, Princeton, New Jersey

Torrance E P 1972 Can we teach children to think creatively? *J. Creative Behav.* 6: 114–43

Torrance E P, Wu T 1980 A comparative longitudinal study of the adult creative achievement of elementary school children identified as highly intelligent and highly creative. *Creative Child and Adult Q.* 6: 71–84

Wallach M A 1970 Creativity. In: Mussen P H (ed.)1970 *Carmichael's Manual of Child Psychology*, 3rd edn. Vol. 1. Wiley, New York, pp. 1211–72

Wallach M A, Kogan N 1965 *Modes of Thinking in Young Children: A Study of the Creativity–Intelligence Thinking*. Holt, Rinehart and Winston, New York

Wallas G 1926 *The Art of Thought*. Cape, London

Dance: Educational Programs

G. Dimondstein

Within the American public school system, dance has been traditionally associated with physical education. This is reflected in the place of dance in the curriculum, the training and certification of dance teachers, and the content of learning experiences at the elementary and secondary levels. Currently, the field is marked by conflicting perceptions as to the meaning and function of dance as a separate discipline, from the conventional wisdom of society without, and from the educational community within. Available research while sparse and unstandardized, presents initial data on the status of dance in the schools and its attendant problems.

Dance in education has its origins in the expressive, improvisational forms developed by Isadora Duncan in the early part of the twentieth century. Her approach to movement and the use of the body, as a dramatic departure from ballet, was embraced by some educators as a unique contribution to the development of students. Its pertinence was viewed as evoking in students a consciousness of themselves as individual entities at a time of increasing mass education, allowing for their participation in an educational process based on their own personalities. This approach became a new current in dance education along with the prevailing folk dance and, on a more professional level, ballet. As most practitioners were involved in private schools, and dance (as folk dance) had become institutionalized into public schools, "modern" dance, as it was called, played a greater or lesser role in the ensuing years. Its entry into the public schools has been essentially through the efforts of individual teachers wishing to effect their own

classes, or those few within the educational structure who recognized the arts as fundamental to education.

1. Definition

As an art form, dance may be defined as the expression of ideas, feelings, and sensory impressions in movement forms achieved through the unique use of the body. It is the language of movement which speaks through the vocabulary of space, time, and force; that is, a movement is shaped in relation to the space it occupies, the time it uses, and the energy which gives it power. These elements constitute the materials of dance and are essential in forming its kinesthetic–visual image (Dimondstein 1971).

Movement comes into being only through the combined use of these elements, but there is no objectively defined sequence. Yet, each achieves definition through an investigation of its formal properties: space, through direction, level, and range; time, expressed through the internal rhythms of the body (pulse, heartbeat, breath) and the external metrical rhythms (beat, accent, measure); force, through contrasts of sustained, swinging, percussive, vibratory movements.

2. Distinguishing Characteristics

Within the context of general education, the practice of making dance an adjunct to physical education has tended to equate it with recreation or physical skill, neglecting its characteristics as an art form. Although body control is the basis of all motor activity, control in dance differs from skills or techniques associated with sports or gymnastics. Dance is geared neither toward the refinement of skills in themselves nor toward competitive ends. Whether it is performed as an individual or group activity, its means are not rule bound as in a game, nor are its aims toward predetermined goals.

Dance involves kinesthetic perception, that is, an understanding and appreciation of movement developed through a "muscle sense." Evidence of such perception comes through a conscious awareness of the body: moving through space alone, in relation to others, and to the physical environment; responding to the dimensions of time, both metrical and created; resisting or acquiescing to gravity by restraining or expending energy. All of these function toward the controlled use of the body in expressing ideas and feelings. Thus, while work in dance techniques aids students in developing motor skills, technique alone is not sufficient in the process of discovering the qualities of expression that accompany each movement pattern.

The progression is one of transforming natural or basic movements (walking, running, leaping, swinging, turning) into improvisations (using basic movements to respond spontaneously to specific ideas intitiated by the student or teacher), into dance studies (arranging movements into more organized sequences), into choreography (structuring more complex dances using conventional or invented forms). In addition to the performing aspects, a well-balanced program helps students at all levels to develop critical judgments of their own work and that of others, and to communicate their ideas in appropriate verbal terms. The process may not be sequential and is not determined by age. It is one of presenting creative dance problems which move from simple to increasingly sophisticated solutions, to which students respond according to their sensibility and capacity at any given time.

3. Research

There was little research until the 1960s, a period of general curriculum assessment. Educators, aided by federal money, reconsidered the role of the arts in affecting general education. The perceived dichotomy between dance as a performing art and as an educational discipline led to innovative projects such as "Arts in General Education" (dance related to other subject matter) (Madeja 1973), "Aesthetic Education" (dance as a separate area), and "Artists in Schools" (professional dance residencies) (National Endowment for the Arts 1976). Most existed on a regional basis or were designed for particular school districts; some were initiated by dance educators within school systems through extracurricular local agreements. Evaluations, while programmatic, revealed a range of student achievements from dance used as a unique mode of knowing and feeling, to incremental learnings in other subjects, to a heightened interest in schooling. Such

implications, however, did not penetrate the mainstream of general education.

Limited research within the field reflects internal contradictions both theoretical and practical. A 1967 study conducted to determine the status of children's dance in elementary schools revealed fundamental misconceptions among practitioners as to the nature and function of dance (American Alliance for Health, Physical Education, and Recreation 1971). Although termed "dance," activities fell mostly into categories of rhythmic games, calesthenics, folk and square dance (with major emphasis on the latter). Curriculum leaders were found lacking a rationale as to the contribution of dance to the total development of young children, resulting in no clarity of purpose or coherent design. Problems were identified as inadequate college preparation, lack of inservice programs, and insufficient interest from sports-oriented personnel. Most pervasive is the conclusion that dance is relegated to the fringes of physical education programs and that even when taught in relation to other subjects, it retains a secondary character.

A survey on the status of dance in the secondary schools concerned the training and certification of teachers, and opportunities for students (American Alliance for Health, Physical Education, and Recreation 1971). The findings confirmed the previous study that college programs consisted primarily of physical education courses; some offered dance courses within physical education, a few included dance majors or minors, and almost none provided graduate degrees in dance education. In terms of opportunities for students, dance classes were offered in junior high (ages 12 to 14) with the number and frequency increasing in senior high (ages 15 to 18), with a maximum at age 15. Lacking specialization, most teachers had physical education backgrounds and were found inadequately trained in dance. Significantly, dance classes at this level are available only as "electives" for talented or interested students and do not qualify with other subjects for college entrance (see *Elective Subjects*).

Thus, available research suggests that dance is not regarded as a substantive area within general education, and is not given academic parity in terms of professional preparation, instruction, time, and facilities. Despite the successes of many experimental projects, most states still do not require dance as part of the curriculum and offerings are largely determined by the size of the school population and availability of competent staff. Contributing factors are school administrators unresponsive to granting dance a higher status, curriculum developers with insufficient training and experience to conceptualize programs, and lack of state certification to standardize requirements.

4. Issues and Concerns

Apart from empirical research, controversies continue to generate literature around two central issues: the lack of consensus between physical education and dance education regarding the place of dance in the curriculum, and its function in the larger educational spectrum.

Among physical educators there are several currents, the dominant of which accepts no separation of dance from physical education, but projects a comprehensive program in which both would be complementary rather than competitive. The position taken by dance educators (and some generalists) is that dance is a form of educational development not available in other academic subjects. As such, it is a body of knowledge which requires study of its historical, aesthetic, and performing aspects, as well as its connections to other areas. Therefore, the important issues to be examined are the aims and content of dance as the theoretical framework for curriculum planning and research. These issues project a curriculum geared toward the development of aesthetic perception of dance as an art, that is, an ability to understand the formal, kinesthetic, and expressive elements found in various forms, and to interpret these meanings in relation to other knowledge. Such learnings would be acquired through direct participation, observation of performances, and reading and writing about dance.

To establish dance as a basic part of the school program would be to focus on its distinctive content and its relation to the broad aims of education. The concern is that dance should be separated from physical education and that its relation to other areas of subject matter be one of coexistence. Further attempts to address these issues may be seen in an historical overview of the last two decades. During the early 1970s, there was increased interest in experimental dance groups and a re-emergence of established groups; and, adult dance classes appeared first in aerobics and then in jazz and modern. Much of this began through the initiation of two governmental bodies: the National Council for the Arts and the National Endowment for the Arts. This new audience stimulated interest for dance in schools, who invited dancers and professional companies for residencies, including off-site performances. In the late 1970s, a major economic crisis resulted in severe program cuts, coupled with a "Back to Basics" movement which sought the elimination of all but "basic" courses such as math, reading and writing. Art and music barely survived; dance could not compete. The 1980s has seen a general movement of educational reform. As part of "arts education," dance is, in most cases, included with the visual arts, music, drama, and creative writing. Growing concern for the lack of cultural literacy among America's students has produced critical governmental reports and advocacy statements by renowned educators. Collaborative efforts between governmental agencies, state departments of education, philanthropic organizations and artists alliances have studied and examined how the arts are taught in schools, and problems of graduation requirements, teacher-training and certification, and assessment of arts programs.

An NEA report to the US Congress assessing the current status of arts education revealed that, as of 1985, no state required dance courses of elementary school teachers and only 16 states certify dance specialists at the elementary or secondary level (NEA 1988). A National Dance Association survey (Gingrasso 1987) attributes this to the fact that major support for certification and program development emanated from dance educators who view dance as a creative art that should be codified for all students K–12th grade, rather than from state policy makers who qualify it as a "gym class" to be taught by physical education staff. In regard to curriculum, the NEA reports that middle and senior high schools may have 2, 4 or 6 week units of dance as part of physical education. In a 4-year high school physical education program, one or two terms may offer modern or jazz, generally as an elective chosen by girls; boy's participation is not encouraged. Few physical education instructors are prepared to teach dance, and sports, exercise and dance "do not always coexist congenially" (NEA 1988 p. 62). Dance programs at the secondary level are "typically understaffed, underfinanced, and unrecognized" (NEA 1988 p. 62). Although performing arts high schools offer more technical classes, often courses do not provide a balanced curriculum. Students entering a college dance program therefore receive early training primarily in private studios and community centers. The Report concludes: "Dance in American schools is virtually non-existent, just pockets here and there".

Bibliography

Alter J B in press *Dance-Based Theory: From Borrowed Models to Dance Based Experience.* Peter Lang Publishers, New York and Bern

American Alliance for Health, Physical Education, and Recreation (AAHPER) 1971 Task force, children's dance, dance division. JOHPER (Journal of Health, Physical Education, Recreation) June 1971, Reston, Virginia

American Alliance for Health, Physical Education, and Recreation (AAHPER) 1971 The status of dance in the secondary schools. JOHPER October 1971, Reston, Virginia

American Alliance for Health, Physical Education, Recreation and Dance (AAHPERD) 1981 *Children's Dance.* Reston, Virginia

Bert D 1978 *Philosophy and Human Movement.* Allen and Unwin, London

Chapman S A 1987 Looking ahead to the 1990's *JOPERD* (Journal of Health, Physical Education, Recreation, Dance) Nov/Dec 1987

Dimondstein G 1970 Space-time-force: An aesthetic construct. In: Haberman M, Meisel T (eds.) 1970 *Dance: An Art in Academe.* Teachers College Press, New York

Dimondstein G 1971 *Children Dance in the Classroom.* Macmillan, New York

Dimondstein G 1985 The place of dance in general education. *Journal of Aesthetic Education.* Winter

Gingrasso S 1987 Dance education certification: Current status and significance. JOPERD (Journal of Physical Education, Recreation, Dance) Sep/Oct 1987

Madeja S S 1973 *All the Arts for Every Child*. Final Report on the Arts in General Education Project in the School District of University City, Missouri. The JDR III Fund, New York

Meakin D, Sanderson P 1983 Dance in English secondary schools today. *Journal of Aesthetic Education*. Spring

National Endowment for the Arts 1976 *Artists in Schools*.

National Endowment for the Arts, Washington, DC

National Endowment for the Arts 1988 *Toward Civilization: A Report on Art Education*. US Government Printing Office, Washington, DC

Redfern B 1982 *Concepts in Modern Educational Dance*. Dance Books Ltd

Film Studies

F. B. Shuchat-Shaw

Film studies takes the motion picture as a subject worthy of study in its own right, and as such may be distinguished from the use of film to support teaching and learning in other subject areas. Alternately referred to as motion picture appreciation, or film or screen education, film studies may stand as a separate area in primary and secondary curricula or as a circumscribed unit in language arts, art, mass media, visual communication, or industrial arts education. Frequently it originates as an extracurricular activity before gaining its typical status as an elective.

During its 60-year history in the schools, film studies has construed the motion picture variously as entertainment, art, propaganda, and social realism. The aims of film studies have centered on cultivating in students analytic perspectives on the motion pictures that would enhance aesthetic and technical appreciation, moral discrimination, understanding of its history and sociopolitical role, and production skills. Social concerns and educational ideals prevailing in different periods and nations have contributed to these views and aims and to the rationales for giving (or withdrawing) curricular status to film studies. Also influential are the quality of and national regard for theatrical and nontheatrical films available; prevailing educational perspectives on the arts, media, and technology; and the ongoing experiences of schools using film for instructional support.

Symbol systems and technologies have historically found homes in schools. There they have served as communication tools, skills for youth to cultivate, carriers of ideas and information, and subjects of study. Following Gutenberg's invention of the printing press in 1450, sixteenth-century schools came to depend on books to teach religion and etiquette and to develop reading and writing skills. Seventeenth-century technology enabled Comenius to illustrate childrens' texts with pictures. With the advancing Industrial Revolution, schools in the late nineteenth century used wide-ranging visual displays and realia, Daguerre's photographic technology, and in the twentieth century Edison's motion picture technology. In 1896, Charles Urban began instructional film experiments in England, and by 1927 educators worldwide called for the study of motion pictures in schools.

Despite this continuing pattern, schools have reacted cautiously to technologies, taking experimental steps only after perceiving evidence of their power or value in other social sectors. Moreover, technologies have been feared as often as embraced for the changes they might bring about in social life, cultural values, and educational practices. The notion that technology could effect an educational revolution characterized by control, efficiency, and the democratizing of knowledge has thrilled the instructional science movement throughout this century, while creating anxiety among a majority of educators. Early fears of the educational and moral consequences of children's exposure to film content and form interestingly resembled Socrates' fear of the written word, for its potential to replace the dialectic process with the passive following of arguments and to make recorded ideas accessible to unintended and intended readers alike. Such fears gave significant impetus and shape to the first era of film studies.

1. The Motion Picture Appreciation Movement, 1927–1945

Patterns in social life, educational thought, and the film industry converged during the first quarter of the century to usher in the motion picture appreciation movement, with its moralistic–artistic rationale and approach. With industrial and urban expansion, and in North America the second wave of European immigrants, the schools persisted in their concern for the socialization and moral education of youth. The school's moralistic culture was evident in its criticism of the film industry, which by 1920 was attracting over 100 million children and adults daily, worldwide, to US films made to appeal to patrons of vaudeville and variety shows. Filled with romance, crime, sex, comedy, and mystery, theatricals (feature entertainment films distributed to movie theaters) were feared for their harmful influence on the moral values and conduct of youth. They were far more interesting than dry and overly-long "educationals," the effective use of which was further complicated by content that did not articulate with curricula, and by cumbersome equipment, fire hazards and safety standards, and chaotic distribution. While many educators assumed a negative posture toward film, the instructional science and efficiency movements remained enthusiastic about the nontheatrical industry and the development of portable equipment and film libraries.

The rise of progressive ideals in the 1920s gave energy and clarity to the motion picture moralists, in the United States, England, and France, coincident with their peaking criticism of theatrical themes and the industry's reluctance to release shorts and excerpts to schools where discriminating tastes could be cultivated. While religious and educational leaders pressurized the Motion Picture Producers and Distributors of America (MPPDA) to formulate a code of morals in 1927, a smoke screen that the Legion of Decency would attack several years later, Western Europe was failing in its attempts to produce serious films and waking up to its screen domination by a scintillating Hollywood. As the progressives turned their attention to the role of the social environment in individual growth and social problem solving through community involvement, so did the motion picture moralists mobilize their leaders and committees toward research and action that would equip students with moral discrimination standards and critical viewing skills.

According to Aaron Horn, in 1927 Charles H. Judd, head of the National Education Association's Committee on Cooperation with the MPPDA, blamed the quality of films on the lack of training in intelligent appreciation. Horn himself urged the schools to "face that issue squarely . . . by admitting the photoplay to full standing in the curriculum" (Horn 1927 p. 359). Allen Abbott (1928) of Teachers College, Columbia University, in New York City, led the demand that teachers provide systematic study of film, and the New Jersey teacher education curriculum was the first to include this orientation. The 12 Payne Studies on the relation of motion pictures to youth were undertaken by the Motion Picture Research Council from 1928 to 1932, supported by the Payne Fund, an American philanthropy that had established the National Committee for the Study of Social Values in Motion Pictures (NCSSVMP) in 1927. W. W. Charters, supervisor of the Payne Studies, would throughout the 1930s head efforts of The Ohio State University's Bureau of Educational Research to develop and distribute film teaching materials. As further support, 16 mm portable equipment and safety film became available to schools in 1928, as did series of theatrical shorts and excerpts dramatizing moral issues between 1929 and 1936, largely through Rockefeller Foundation support to the MPPDA, the NCSSVMP, and the Progressive Education Association.

Edgar Dale, already in the forefront of audiovisual instruction, and William Lewin, an English teacher in Newark, New Jersey, emerged as leaders of the movement during the 1930s. Dale's (1933) Payne Studies text promoted analyses of film history, aesthetics, and technique, to develop artistic appreciation and discriminating tastes. Lewin (1934) coalesced the growing interest of the National Council of Teachers of English, emphasizing artistic–literary appreciation and moral discrimination through the use of study guides. Their materials were widely distributed, and by 1938 the MPPDA estimated that 5 million students were studying film. Language arts courses took the lead through the decade, with students engaging in analyses, producing short literary adaptations, writing scenarios and criticism. Between 1939 and 1948, 25 English textbooks from US publishers included units on film (Dale and Morrison 1951).

The 1934 International Congress on Education and Industrial Cinematography, held in Rome, revealed that over 20 nations were teaching through and about film. Europe's increasing exposure to glittering Hollywood talkies and more serious artistic and propagandistic material, produced in France, Italy, Spain, Germany, and England, maintained the dual moralistic–artistic approach to film studies. The English schools took the lead, influenced by Leavis's moral approach to literary study; by studies of the Commission on Educational and Cultural Films from 1929 to 1932, among whose aims was raising standards of critical appreciation through teaching about film as art; and by the establishment in 1933 of the British Film Institute, with its pledge to promote study of film as art and as a record of contemporary life. By 1938, the English Board of Education called for national adoption of motion picture appreciation in schools.

The Second World War disrupted the movement on the Continent, while film studies in the United States and England declined and became transformed during the 1940s and 1950s. More pressing wartime and postwar concerns preoccupied the curriculum. Schools, enthused with the Government's use of military training films, were more interested in teaching with film than about it. Further, contemporary films divided the moralists, as theaters offered escape, patriotism, reconstruction, and newsreels that were welcomed by some and called propaganda by others. The moral and literary approaches to film studies continued in practice but faced challenges and shifts in three directions; toward film literacy, emphasizing motion picture language and technique; towards a sociological approach, emphasizing criticism of social issues depicted and propaganda; and towards film aesthetics, emphasizing artistic form and structure.

With the 1957 launching of Sputnik and the Cold War, film studies was all but eclipsed in the United States. Driven by national interests, principles of academic achievement dominated this period and gave priority to a traditional curriculum. The audiovisual instruction movement defined the role of film in the schools as a resource for increasing efficiency in the teaching of the sciences, mathematics, and foreign languages. In Europe, the literacy, sociological, and aesthetics approaches gained strength and would soon, with the next wave of reforms, influence a renewal of film studies in the United States.

2. Film Studies, 1965–1975

Charged by the Civil Rights Movement and the Vietnam War, a decade of social cause and protest unfolded in communities and schools, on movie screens and television. Schools were pressurized to attend to the values of an establishment responsible for inequalities and discrimination, the war, urban poverty, the spoiling of the environment, and to the voices silenced by such problems. Socially conscious theatricals and documentaries created a new respect and role for film as social realism, social criticism, and art, while television exposed the political power of imagery. Curricula with relevance required reconceptualizations of content and methods for an awakened and visual generation, giving new meaning to film studies in North America and Europe. College and university language arts and humanities education programs developed film studies electives, with significant assistance in England from the British Film Institute. The American Film Institute, established in 1967, and such groups as the National Association of Media Educators, organized in 1970, provided teachers with film education workshops. Evolving community groups, such as The Center for Understanding Media, and a barrage of books and magazines focused on film studies, further supported the movement.

Various approaches to film were prominently represented at all levels in an era of expanding electives and minicourses, interdisciplinary humanities and arts programs. The study of film as language and art followed from the assumption that film was the primary expressive language and communication vehicle for a visual generation whose ideas had been stifled by academic preoccupations, bound by linguistic forms, or simply neglected. The film language approach emphasized grammar, syntax, and structure. The film as art approach, most prominent on the Continent and particularly in France, highlighted form and structure, style and genre; story, theme, and character; film history; contributions of directors, cinematographers, actors, and editors; and aesthetic criticism. The film-making approach coupled film language study with student production, script to screen. While most prominent in English practical education, this approach was popular in the United States, supported in art education by federally and state-funded artists-in-the-schools programs. During this period, the film-making approach was introduced in Finland, where art education assumed a "mass media" focus, and in West German and Dutch art education programs with their "visual communication" focus.

Critical–sociological studies of film as propaganda and social realism constituted parallel developments, particularly in Europe, and in North America after 1970 when mass media criticism gained curricular attention. The propaganda approach followed from the argument that film is a corrupting wasteland that, in the hands of capitalist, profit-seeking elites or free-wheeling,

pleasure-seeking subversives, manipulates viewers to share their values. In this view, schools are responsible for providing vulnerable students with tools to analyze ideologies implicit in film content and form, and with production experiences to demonstrate the subjectivity of the medium. The social realism approach construed film as an expression or critique of the currents, contradictions, and consequences of modern life. From this perspective, students studied and produced film as a means of exploring and understanding, expressing, and acting on vital contemporary issues and problems.

3. Film Studies, 1975–1987 and the Future

Since the mid-1970s, film studies has declined once again in North America. It remains scattered in the elective structure and language arts curriculum of some college-oriented secondary schools, and in fewer elementary and middle schools, where the language, art, and film-making approaches are used. Occasional critical–sociological approaches have tended to address mass media and technology, contexts in which film often takes a secondary role in relation to print, television, and computers which are believed to play larger social roles. Basic skills and traditional subjects have dominated most curricular timetables, to address literacy and employment problems, leaving film to compete with video as an instructional support. With rising concern for achievement, interest has dwindled in what is often perceived as the subjective and freewheeling "turn kids on to media" approach of the previous decade. Artistic respect for feature films in theatrical distribution has declined, with their increasing sensationalism and use of the entertainment formulas associated with television. Disinterest in controversy has kept serious social and political documentaries to a minimum in schools. Technology investments have been made in computers, and to some extent in television for industrial arts, both believed more useful than film in view of prevailing aims.

While film studies has declined in Europe as well, the language, artistic, and critical–sociological approaches continue to be represented. In English, West German, Italian, Finnish, and Dutch secondary schools, the influence of the Frankfurt School's New Criticism has extended to elective media studies the wider project of establishing emancipatory aims across the curriculum (Bennett 1976). Here, film art and entertainment are construed as ideological apparatuses of oppressive capitalist states. The aims of study are to unearth the sources, the ideological content, and the manipulative form of motion pictures, to emancipate students from socially constructed constraints and dependencies, and to move them to social action. In the context of English art education, however, film studies remains practical, despite proposals in 1976 to add analytic–critical and historical–cultural dimensions to the expressive. Finnish art education has led the field in such multidimensionality, on the belief that film and other contemporary media add purposeful content to traditional arts study.

This historical overview reveals that broad social and industrial developments interact with educational ideals to influence the status and character of film studies. The education community's view of film must lead to a curricular rationale that is congruent with wider aims of schools, if film studies is to assume an enduring and meaningful role there.

We have seen that as schools turn to the moral education, artistic development, and expressive experiences of students, film studies emerges; as schools shift toward academic aims, film studies recedes; and as schools address the sociocultural and vocational aspects of wider developments in mass media and technology, film shares curricular attention with other forms. In view of such trends, film may not command separate curricular treatment in the next decades. Instead, its future as a subject of study may depend on the extent to which schools assign academic value and legitimacy to related but broader fields, several of which appear on the horizon in the late 1980s: the critical study of the effects of mass media and technology on cognition and perception, social relations, political biases, and personal values (Postman 1981 p. 382); the study of human communication, symbolization, and semiotics, including linguistic and nonlinguistic symbol systems and all media forms, their historical origins and cultural roles; and the scientific and technical study of communication technologies, including the physics, engineering, mechanics, and programming of those forms likely to have strong vocational value.

Bibliography

Abbott A 1928 Introduction. In: Abbott M A (ed.) 1928 *Motion Pictures for Different School Grades*. Bureau of Publications, Teachers College, Columbia University, New York, p. v

Bennett S 1976 Mass media education—Defining the subjects. *Screen Education*. 18: 15–21

Commission on Educational and Cultural Films 1932 *The Film in National Life*. George Allen and Unwin, London

Dale E 1933 *How to Appreciate Motion Pictures: A Manual of Motion-picture Criticism Prepared for High School Students*. Macmillan, New York

Dale E 1935 *The Content of Motion Pictures*. Macmillan, New York

Dale E, Morrison J 1951 *Motion Picture Discrimination: An Annotated Bibliography*. Bureau of Educational Research, The Ohio State University, Columbus, Ohio

Dennett T, Spence J 1976–77 Photography, ideology and education. *Screen Education*. 21: 42–69

Horn A 1927 Teaching appreciation of the photoplay. *The Educational Screen* VI(8): 359–60

Judd C H 1927 Education and the movies. *The Educational Screen* VII

Lewin W 1934 *Photoplay Appreciation in American High Schools*. Appleton–Century, New York

Lovell A 1968 The Aims of Film Education. Unpublished manuscript, Education Department, British Film Institute, London

Mast G 1971 *A Short History of the Movies*. Pegasus, New York

Olson D R (ed.) 1974 *Media and Symbols: The Forms of Expression, Communication, and Education. The 73rd yearbook of the National Society for the Study of Education*, Pt. 1. University of Chicago, Chicago, Illinois

Ott R W, Hurwitz A (eds.) 1984 *Art in Education: An International Perspective*. Pennsylvania State University, University Park, Pennsylvania

Postman N 1981 The day our children disappear: Predictions of a media ecologist. *Kappan* 62(5): 382–86

Rotha P 1960 *The Film Till Now: A Survey of World Cinema*, 3rd edn. Vision, London

Saettler P 1968 *A History of Instructional Technology*. McGraw-Hill, New York

Selby S A 1978 *The Study of Film as an Art Form in American Secondary Schools*. Arno, New York

Silberman C E 1970 *Crisis in the Classroom: The Remaking of American Education*. Vintage Books, New York

Theater Studies

D. Child

Theater has played many paradoxical roles and has worn many guises in its relationship to education and curriculum. It has been praised and censured, to say nothing of censored, as an educational medium; it has been invited into the curriculum as a subject matter area and as a pedagogic tool and it has been explicitly removed from the curriculum as a frill. In these many treatments it has had much in common with other art forms such as art, music, and dance.

Like its relatives in the arts, theater must answer many of the same questions: Is it educational? If so, does it belong in the inschool curriculum or should it be confined to extracurricular student life in the "out-of-school curriculum" (Schubert 1981)? If it belongs to the inschool curriculum, should it be taught to everyone or only to a select few? Should it be taught at all ages or only a limited range? Should the focus be on process or product? Can it be taught in schools as a subject to be engaged in and enjoyed rather than as yet one more subject to be endured prior to graduation? Who should do the teaching—classroom teachers, subject-matter specialist teachers, or professional theater practitioners? Where should the teaching take place— in the regular classroom, in a special area designed for it, or at an off-campus building? As with many curriculum areas, questions related to theater prior to college have no easy, universal answers.

1. The Concept of Theater

It might be helpful to look at what "theater" means before examining its place in the curriculum. Historically, theater and theatrical activities have gone by many names: theater, children's theater, youth theater, drama, creative drama, creative dramatics, guided drama, developmental drama, and educational drama, are some of them. Shakespeare's Juliet asked, "What's in a name?" Professionals involved in staking out curriculum areas could have answered her: "Everything." Whether theater and drama are part of an underlying continuum or whether theater does or should include or exclude drama, or vice versa, has been the subject of lengthy debates in national and international organizations. The discussions have revolved around the presence/absence of a script and/or an audience and whether the performers were professionals or amateurs.

The Children's Theater Association of America (now the American Alliance for Theater and Education) adopted a continuum view of drama and theater: "Drama in its natural state," that is, ordinary, spontaneous play; "guided drama" (creative drama or child drama); "participation theater drama" (audience members alternately watchers and participants); and "theater" (strictly prearranged art form; clear distinction between actors and audience) (Davis and Behm 1978). The differences between these points have been highlighted by US theorists and practitioners. Among the British, Canadians, and Australians, however, the differences have been noticeably deemphasized, and drama, particularly at the school level, subsumes theater as it is defined in the United States. The International Association of Theatre for Children and Young People, ASSITEJ (Association Internationale du Théatre pour l'Énfance et la Jeunesse), has excluded what Americans call creative drama from its purview. ASSITEJ is concerned with theater performances for child and youth audiences, primarily by companies employing professional actors. There have also been international considerations of whether school is an appropriate place to perform for children (Sweet 1982). Practitioners interested in creative drama and theater performed by children (including high-school students) have joined the International Amateur Theatre Association (IATA/AITA), which sponsors international theater festivals that include high-school actors and symposia on creative drama.

2. Theater as Education

Turning to the issue of whether theater is educational, Watson (1915) traces drama and education from the Greeks through the first decade of the twentieth century. Pericles distributed public funds, as necessary, so all Athenians could attend the plays at the festival of Dionysus and "theater thus became a national educational institution, and an exceedingly powerful one" (p. 361). But Plato was concerned about the educational implications inherently present in the process of impersonating others. He maintained such experiences should be limited in subject matter and character types portrayed lest they harm the developing child's personality. Aristotle's *Poetics* recognizes the cathartic effect that a performance can have for an audience. More recently, Schechner (1985) and Courtney (1986), working crossculturally, have noted how both actor and audience are affected by performances. Likewise, Etherton (1982) described the educational nature of performance and how it may be compromised as it moves from the traditional setting to the sophisticated one in English-speaking Africa. In the Soviet Union the educational possibilities of theater for children were recognized shortly after the 1917 Revolution. "The People's Commissariat for Education organized a permanent office with a Council for Children's Theaters and Children's Festivals" (Hoffman 1978 p. 217).

"The liaison between the arts world and the field of education seems to run the gamut from disdain by the educators to disinterest by the artists. Somewhere in between is a narrow band of cooperation and mutual respect" (Goldberg 1974 p. 85). Many Eastern European children's theaters employ a specially trained administrator, a pedagogue, as a liaison between theater and school. The pedagogue may have been trained as a teacher and "has three functions: to advise the artistic staff, to conduct research, and to coordinate activities with the community's young people" (Goldberg 1974 p. 86).

Sweden and Holland, in the West, train and employ drama pedagogues, but not solely for service as liaisons between schools and theaters. In Sweden, for example, pedagogues work with preschool age groups to retirement-aged citizens, and in hospitals, drug and alcohol treatment centers, recreational centers, as well as schools. In Holland they have worked with prisoners in jails and with the handicapped, using drama as a form of therapy. There are theater companies that perform in schools, but they are not the primary employers of pedagogues (Cranston 1983).

Coventry, England, was the first place to employ a theater company, trained and experienced in both teaching and acting, to work in the local schools. The Theatre in Education (TIE) teams began at the Belgrade Theatre in 1965 (Vallins 1980) and are funded by the local government or the local educational authority. The form has spread throughout Great Britain and Australia but has made little inroad elsewhere. TIE teams work with the teachers and children to produce theater in education, theatrical performances in which actors and audience immerse themselves in curriculum-related experiences related directly to the school and community. TIE team members are not artists-in-residence nor are they actors bringing theater to education.

The key feature of TIE teams is that company members have both educational and theatrical backgrounds to guide their work.

Schools in many countries schedule field trips to theaters for their students or invite traveling troupes to perform in the school. The Soviet Union places a high value on theater for children and provides the beginning first-grader with two things: "the child receives his pass to the school *and* his first ticket to the theatre" (Sats 1979 p. vi). Despite an emphasis on theater attendance during school hours and the use of pedagogues, this does not illustrate theater as part of the inschool curriculum. In most locations school boards restrict theater's availability to the extracurricular activities provided by clubs during school hours or relegate it entirely to the out-of-school curriculum. In Bahrain, students at the secondary level do not study theater or drama, but they may participate in a drama club during the regularly scheduled extracurricular period. An examination of Japanese schools (US Department of Education 1987) indicated that although the children study fine arts and music, theater is explicitly omitted from the Japanese public school curriculum.

Yet two leading theorists (Bolton 1984, Courtney 1980) maintain that drama—which they define as containing both theater and educational drama—should be the heart, not just a part, of the inschool curriculum. During the 1960s and 1970s, however, many school boards and other government bodies were faced with a shortage of funds and vociferous tax payers and scholars calling, "Back to the basics!" When the school boards scrutinized their curricula for areas to cut, they found theater, art, music, and dance, to be only frills, not the basics underlying all cultures. Had the critics consulted Adler, a scholar from outside the field of theater, he might have advised them that "active participation . . . and involvement in artistic activities, e.g., music, drama, visual arts" is integral to enlarging the "understanding of ideas and values" (Adler 1982 p. 23).

A number of state legislatures in the United States, while not going as far as suggested by Bolton and Courtney, have mandated the teaching of theater and the other arts to all public school children within their states from kindergarten to the end of secondary school. Also, two major university systems—Ohio State University and California State University—now require some performing arts credits for admission. As school boards respond to legislative and university pressures to modify their curricula, more children in the United States will have direct experience and familiarity with theater.

3. Theater Study Programs

A comprehensive program might have the following six elements: (a) classroom teachers providing general instruction for their children; (b) itinerant subject-matter specialists providing additional experiences in the classrooms, but at a deeper level; (c) resource teachers working with physically and/or mentally handicapped children whose needs could not be met in the regular classroom; (d) specialist teachers assisting gifted and talented children to develop themselves to their fullest artistic and intellectual potentials; (e) theater artists performing in the schools for large groups and working in individual classrooms; and (f) groups of children visiting the artists as they work in their own theaters and rehearsal studios. It is likely that the theater artists and theater companies not only would be made up of professional actors, but might also be comprised of college and high-school companies. Furthermore, the visiting (and visited) theater artists should be representative of all the workers employed in theater, such as producers, directors, designers, publicists, and stage managers.

Even under this program, however, a curriculum could be set up with objectives that would include elements (a) through (f) above and yet provide little or no opportunity for students to engage in any performance activities. For example, an approach taking theater-as-subject for its model, theater as history, not theater as performance and experience that teaches about society and human nature through doing, would have students analyze playscripts as literature, memorize names and dates of famous playwrights and actors, and identify speeches from noteworthy plays.

An even more serious problem could be ahead, regardless of the model chosen: an insufficient supply of teachers and administrators whose own education incorporated training in theater and aesthetic values. Teacher education programs in the United States, for example, will have to increase their offerings in drama and theater if their graduates are to be able to meet the requirements of the state mandates. Until then, most schools will continue to put on plays, using directors who do not have training or coursework in theater (Peluso 1970).

More positively, there is one type of program using trained professionals to provide students with an arts-oriented inschool curriculum: the elementary and secondary arts "magnet" schools and the high schools for the performing arts. In the United States school boards have established "magnet" schools with specialized curricula as part of their racial desegregation programs. Their goal has been to make programs so attractive that white parents will keep their children within the public school system. These offerings have included theater, dance, and music specializations in addition to courses in the usual school subjects. At the secondary level in the United States, there are currently 63 high schools of the performing arts. These are both public and private high schools and provide intense preprofessional training in the arts. Some other countries annually seek to identify their most talented young people and remove them from the ordinary school system, sending the children to conservatories for training in theater arts. The young people who graduate from the conservatories are then guaranteed work with a state theater company.

"The world of theater is one world. The purpose of theater is one purpose: to make experiential through an emotional and/or intellectual transaction the nature of being human. It has always been so" (Roberts 1982 p. ii). International festivals sponsored by ASSITEJ and IATA/AITA have brought widely dispersed companies from all parts of the world together to verify the truth of Roberts' message, but the message can reach only a minimal audience so long as theater studies are excluded from the inschool curriculum.

Bibliography

Adler M J 1982 *The Paideia Proposal: An Educational Manifesto*. Macmillan, New York

Bolton G M 1984 *Drama as Education: An Argument for Placing Drama at the Centre of the Curriculum*. Longman, Harlow

Courtney R 1980 *The Dramatic Curriculum*. University of Western Ontario, London, Ontario

Courtney R 1986 Islands of remorse: Amerindian education in the contemporary world. *Curric. Inq.* 16(1): 43–64

Cranston J 1983 Impressions of educational drama in Sweden and Holland. *ASSITEJ/USA* 7 (2): 9–12

Davis J H, Behm T 1978 Terminology of drama/theatre with and for children: A redefinition. In: Davis J H, Evans M J (eds.) 1982 *Theatre, Children and Youth*. Anchorage, New Orleans, Louisiana

Etherton M 1982 *The Development of African Drama*. Hutchinson, London

Goldberg M 1974 *Children's Theatre: A Philosophy and a Method*. Prentice-Hall, Englewood Cliffs, New Jersey

Hoffman C (ed.) *Kinder- und Jugendtheater der Welt*. Henschelverlag Kunst und Gesellschaft, Berlin

Leestma R, Bennett W J 1987 *Japanese Education Today*. United States Department of Education, Washington, DC

Peluso J L 1970 *A Survey of the Status of Theatre in United States High Schools* Final Report US Department of Health, Education, and Welfare, Washington, DC (ERIC Document ED 053 117)

Roberts V M 1982 Foreword. In: Davis J H, Evans M J (eds.) 1982 *Theatre, Children and Youth*. Anchorage, New Orleans, Louisiana

Sats N 1979 Foreword. In: Morton M (ed. and trans.) 1979 *Through the Magic Curtain: Theatre for Children, Adolescents and Youth in the USSR: 27 Authoritative Essays*. Anchorage, New Orleans, Louisiana

Schechner R 1985 *Between Theater and Anthropology*. University of Pennsylvania, Philadelphia, Pennsylvania

Schubert W M 1981 Knowledge about out-of-school curricula. *Educ. Forum* 45(2): 184–98

Sweet E C 1982 School: A place for performance? *ASSITEJ/USA* 6: 9–10

Vallins G 1980 The beginnings of TIE. In: Jackson T (ed.) 1980 *Learning through Theatre: Essays and Casebooks on Theatre in Education*. Manchester University, Manchester, pp. 2–15

Watson F 1911 Drama and Education. In: Monroe P (ed.) 1915 *A Cyclopedia of Education*, Vol. 2. Macmillan, New York, pp. 361–66

Visual Education

L. M. Cochran

Visual education refers to learning to comprehend and appreciate the many forms of visualized information (from realistic pictures to charts, graphs, and diagrams) presented singly or in sequences, then using this ability (visual literacy) to gain more knowledge. Visual education also includes instruction in the various ways of creating visuals, from the graphic arts to the use of technological devices such as cameras, video recorders, and graphic computers. Exercises in mental imagery and visual thinking, also, are part of visual education which aims to integrate visual and verbal communication in a holistic approach to learning. In a world where so much information is presented visually, the ability to communicate visually is a "basic skill" (Sinatra 1986 pp. 3–11). Essentially visual education develops these abilities to the point of competence or visual literacy, which is employed by learners in the same manner as verbal literacy in their quest for knowledge in all disciplines.

One term important to understanding visual literacy is "visual languaging," defined by John L. Debes as "the intentional use of culturally acquired signs in culturally established patterns for the purpose of communicating. It includes both creative encoding and perceptual decoding" (Debes and Williams 1978 p. 2). Some educators use the term literacy to refer to competence in verbal languaging (the ability to read and write). Other educators insist that when learners are exposed to visuals, they behave as though they are reading a language (Debes and Williams 1978). When they create a slide show, film, or videotape, they act as though they are writing a language. Therefore the term visual literacy refers to the human languaging ability to interpret and create visual messages.

Using the term visual languaging characterizes interpersonal and intrapersonal communication as a dynamic process. This emphasis on process is important. There is a tendency to evaluate a visual education program only in terms of the visual products produced by learners. Vital as these products are, the important learning occurs during the process of production. A valued justification for visual education lies in the focus on process, process which defies quantification (Cochran et al. 1980).

1. Background

Humans first communicated with each other through gestures which became visual conventions. Many of these gestures have been passed down to us in the form of sign language, and expressive body language. The first written messages known were in pictorial form. In 1659, Johannes Amos Comenius, a clergyman of the Moravian Church, became the first educator to incorporate the teaching of visual education in his textbook: *Orbis Sensualium Pictus* (The Visible World Pictured). This remarkable book espoused his educational theories, revolutionary at the time, which included such modern ideas as "learning should be fun, not drudgery" and "the educational system should serve the learner."

When twentieth-century technology catapulted the pictorial form into a major medium of communication, some educators began urging the use of films and slides for instruction. A group of educators formed the Department of Visual Instruction (DVI) affiliated with the National Education Association (NEA) in the United States. With the advent of recorded sound, DVI became the Department of Audiovisual Instruction (DAVI). The department's focus was on the use of audiovisual materials by teachers to present lessons to learners. In 1970, DAVI dropped its affiliation with NEA and became the Association for Educational Communications and Technology (AECT).

By the 1960s many people had begun to realize that visual communication was more complex than merely showing the right kind of visual material to an audience. A Kodak publication, *Visuals are a Language*, helped focus attention on the linguistic features of visuals. In 1966, John L. Debes began to use the term "visual literacy" (Williams and Debes 1970). This term hit a responsive chord in the minds of teachers who were exploring the uses of photographic production by their students. The First National Conference on Visual Literacy, held in Rochester, New York, in 1969, gave impetus to the formation of a professional organization, the International Visual Literacy Association (IVLA). This provided an interdisciplinary forum for the study and promotion of visual literacy. The International Visual Literacy Association is an affiliate of the Association for Educational Communications and Technology (AECT).

2. Theoretical Approaches

Research in many disciplines contributes to the understanding of visual literacy and the instructional strategies employed in visual education. Visual perception is studied in psychology (Hagen 1980); stimulus characteristics of visuals are examined in art and educational technology (Curtiss 1987, Fleming and Levie 1981); hemispheric assymmetry of the brain researched in neurophysiology suggests that process-oriented paradigms are useful in the study of the ways human learners construct meaning from their environment (Chall and Mirsky 1978); the research methods used by anthropologists and sociologists, as well as documentation of their findings, influence research in visual literacy (Worth 1981). Visual communication as languaging behavior draws upon the field of linguistics with its knowledge of the structure of language and the innate human propensity for developing language (Westcott 1974). The broad field of communication provides many studies in nonverbal communication, in mass communication, and in the interaction of individuals with visual presentations (Petersson 1989). Learning theory in the field of human development also contributes to visual education (Myers 1981). Systems theory provides an approach to studying humans in their environment which helps tie all the disciplines together (LaViolette 1979).

The emerging field of visual education exhibits great diversity in attempting to synthesize the contributions from these many fields of knowledge. Certain generalizations, however, are possible based upon an examination of current visual education practices. These practices treat learners as active seekers after information, who learn about their environment and about themselves as they explore. Such practices reflect a belief in an ecological approach to cognitive psychology. Emphasis on the perceiver's own activity is one of the characteristics of the ecological approach which studies cognition as it occurs naturally (Neisser 1976).

New theories on the cutting edge of knowledge about the human brain are lending more theoretical support to the intuitive convictions of visual educators that feelings are important. Finely tuned emotions may form the basis of all we know (Gray 1979).

3. Practical Approaches

Perceptual abilities are crucial to learning. Visual perception is an interaction between something that occurs outside the person and something that happens inside. Early childhood and primary curricula include materials and activities to foster development of children's visual discrimination. They progress from gross discrimination of objects in the three-dimensional world, to identification of pictures of familiar objects, to interpretation of complex abstract designs of letters and word forms. Figure–ground perception, perceptual constancy, and spatial relationships are other visual perceptual abilities which children must develop in their early years (Buktenica 1968).

Because pictures of places and people resemble actual objects, teachers often assume there is no need to learn to read them. This easy recognition lulls viewers into passive acceptance. Without critically thinking about the events and objects depicted, they miss important information which could be gleaned from the pictures.

From the moment of birth, infants begin the life-long journey of trying to make sense of their world. They use all of their senses in this exploration, constructing conceptual meaning (or schema for followers of Piaget) for the sights and sounds around them. These meanings are constantly modified as the individual explores new experiences, measuring the new against what is already known. Gradually the child learns words for these understandings gained through sensory, primarily visual, experiences. Visual literacy precedes, and is the foundation for, verbal literacy.

Technology is changing the kind of visual experience which teachers can provide for learners. Presentation of information in visual form is important. The variety and quality of informative television programs, video tapes, and computer lessons are constantly improving. Even more important, technology is simplifying and improving the cameras and computer programs whereby learners create their own visual messages. Turtle graphics and the Logo computer language provide very young children with the tools to explore spatial relationships and to construct the mental foundations essential for complex mathematical computations and logical thinking.

Learning to recognize visual eloquence requires opportunities to see and discuss great films and pictures. Learning to create pictures, films, and videotapes leads to increased understanding of visual forms. In so doing, students learn to use the modern devices of communication—a skill required for functional literacy in the twenty-first century (Dunn 1982).

See also: Media Literacy

Bibliography

Buktenica N A 1968 *Visual Learning*. Dimensions, San Rafael, California

Chall J S, Mirsky A F (eds.) 1978 *Education and the Brain*. 77th Yearbook, National Society for the Study of Education, Pt. 2. University of Chicago Press, Chicago, Illinois

Cochran L M, Younghouse P C, Sorflaten J W, Molek R A 1980 Exploring approaches to researching visual literacy. *Educ. Commun. Technol. J.* 28: 243–63

Curtiss D 1987 *Introduction to Visual Literacy: A Guide to the Visual Arts and Communication*. Prentice-Hall, Englewood Cliffs, New Jersey

Debes J L, Williams C M 1978 *Visual Literacy, Languaging, and Learning*. Provocative Paper Series No. 1. Visual Literacy Center, Indiana University, Bloomington, Indiana

Dunn J 1982 *Twilight Zones: Media and Learning*. Video tape by Communications Experience, Frankfort, Kentucky. Available from Ohio State University, Athens, Ohio

Fleming M, Levie W H 1981 *Instructional Message Design: Principles from the Behavioral Sciences*. Educational Technology Publications, Englewood Cliffs, New Jersey

Ginsburg H, Opper S 1969 *Piaget's Theory of Intellectual Development: An Introduction*. Prentice-Hall, Inc., Englewood Cliffs, New Jersey

Gray W 1979 Understanding creative thought processes: An early formulation of the emotional–cognitive structure theory. *Man–Environment Systems* 9: 3–14

Hagen M A 1980 *The Perception of Pictures*, Vol. 1. Academic Press, New York

LaViolette P A 1979 Thoughts about thought about thoughts: The emotional–perceptual cycle theory. *Man–Environment Systems* 9(1): 15–47

Myers P R 1981 Children's memory for sequentially presented words and pictures. *J. Visual Verbal Languaging* 1(1): 7–30

Neisser U 1976 *Cognition and Reality: Principles and Implications of Cognitive Psychology*. Freeman, San Francisco, California

Petersson R 1989 *Visuals for Information: Research and Practice*. Educational Technology Publications, Englewood Cliffs, New Jersey

Sinatra R 1986 *Visual Literacy Connections to Thinking Reading and Writing*. Charles C Thomas, Springfield, Illinois

Westcott R W (ed.) 1974 *Language Origins*. Linstok Press, Silver Spring, Maryland

Williams C M, Debes J L (eds.) 1970 *Proceedings of the First National Conference on Visual Literacy*. Pittman, New York

Worth S 1981 *Studying Visual Communication*. University of Pennsylvania Press, Philadelphia, Pennsylvania

Media Literacy

J. K. Morrow

Media literacy, a coinage popular among progressive educators since before the 1970s, does not enjoy a precise definition. The term can be traced to the common observation that children in industrialized societies now enter school possessing knowledge, mental habits, social attitudes, and nonacademic enthusiasms acquired through exposure to mass media. These influences continue on a frequent and voluntary basis during a student's entire formal education. In the late 1960s John Culkin, an American advocate of "film study" in secondary schools, began urging teachers to move students "toward mediacy," and this was perhaps the first time an educator had overtly connected the concept of media with the concept of literacy (Culkin 1968).

The connection is problematic. Because motion pictures, newspaper photographs, popular songs, and other such forms are essentially self-explanatory and explicit, they do not in fact assume a "literate" audience. Comprehending a television commercial is hardly analogous to decoding a complex notational system such as music, written German, or computer BASIC. "Literate," however, also has a more general meaning—the word suggests a person of discerning, educated tastes—and it is this connotation to which the writers of media literacy curricula appeal. Thus, a "media literate" student would be one who can identify the persuasion devices used by advertisers; who can evaluate photographs, television programs, and so forth along a variety of technical and aesthetic scales; who can explain how such productions are made; and who can create his or her own productions if given the appropriate tools.

1. The McLuhan Thesis

Assessments of mass culture's impact on young people have historically been pessimistic. Though lacking hard data, social scientists in the first half of the century were quick to attribute a broad range of childhood neuroses to Hollywood films, commercial radio drama, mass-market comic books, and television programs (Forman 1933, Wertham 1954).

The Canadian academic Marshall McLuhan (1911–81) attacked this conventional wisdom. In his radical epistemology, the key to "understanding" television was not its ostensible messages but its status in industrialized societies as a sensory stimulus of high intensity and metaphysically benign effects. For McLuhan, the television image's "mosaic" configuration was restoring to Western civilization the plenary awareness and tribal cohesion usurped by centuries of dependence on the visual, fragmented, Renaissance medium of print (McLuhan 1964). Although this thesis arrived with a kind of built-in defense—to counter it was to betray a nostalgia for obsolete, sequential, bookish reasoning—it did not prosper among communications experts. As the decade turned, the British actor–physician Jonathan Miller accomplished a rigorous and scholarly dismantling of the entire McLuhan system (Miller 1971).

McLuhan's emphasis on the sensory contours of media spawned at least one significant curricular innovation—the "visual literacy" movement (Dondis 1973). There is some evidence that typical visual literacy exercises—analyzing the formal elements of a photograph, arranging representational images in narrative sequence, using inexpensive still cameras to fulfill simple picture-taking assignments—promote cognitive growth and enhance self-esteem. McLuhan can also be credited with a revitalization of the high school "screen education" movement (Schillaci and Culkin 1970). His famous maxim, "the medium is the message," kept teachers mindful that sophisticated film criticism does not restrict itself to such "literary" matters as story and dialogue. Collateral meanings are conveyed through camera movement, cutting, lighting, sound, and other technical resources.

2. The McLuhan Antithesis

While McLuhan's particular conclusions about television were largely discredited, his underlying assumption of psychic effects independent of program content did not lose its allure. A quite different appraisal of the inherent powers of the medium emerged in the late 1970s. Far from integrating children's central nervous systems and heralding a Saturnian age of instantaneous gestalt perceptions, television was now seen as ipso facto desensitizing, narcotic, and anti-intellectual (Winn 1977). The anxiety generated by this interpretation eventually prompted the United States Government to fund the development of "critical television viewing skills" curricula at all grade levels.

3. A Multimedia Synthesis

The three movements cited—visual literacy, screen education, critical television viewing—are generally regarded as self-contained programs of study, discontinuous with a student's "major" courses. Many educators, however, would like to make media literacy integral to the mainsteam curriculum.

Murray Suid, an American learning materials specialist, has proposed a curriculum development model called the "media wheel." Around a hub of "content"—the topic or concept under study—are arranged seven basic media groups. These are stage (puppet shows and other varieties of live drama); design (including illustrations, posters, and comic strips); print; photography; sound; films; and television. A wheel-oriented curriculum alternates between two learning modes: the "active" and the "reactive" (Suid and Morrow 1977).

In one demonstration of the model, Suid has asked educators to imagine that a high school social studies class is exploring the concept of "law." Suid suggests that, in the "active" mode, students might produce a slide-tape documenting their visit to a court house (a "visual literacy" activity using the photography medium). They might create a radio play about a lawless society (sound medium). And they might prepare research papers on the history of a particular statute (print medium).

In the "reactive" mode, the teacher might encourage students to analyze attitudes toward authority in television crime shows (a "critical viewing skills" activity). The teacher might have the class watch and discuss a feature film about prison life (a "screen education" activity). And the teacher might invite a police officer to lecture the class on crime prevention (stage medium).

This "model for multimedia learning" suggests that media literacy is not ultimately an academic discipline. Like conventional literacy, it is a set of competencies to be employed throughout a person's schooling.

Bibliography

Culkin J M 1968 Toward mediacy: An extension of film and television study. *Audiov. Instr.* 13: 10–13
Dondis D A 1973 *A Primer of Visual Literacy.* MIT Press, Cambridge, Massachusetts
Forman H J 1933 *Our Movie-made Children.* Macmillan, New York
McLuhan H M 1964 *Understanding Media: Extensions of Man.* McGraw-Hill, New York
Miller J 1971 *Marshall McLuhan.* Viking, New York
Schillaci A, Culkin J M 1970 *Films Deliver: Teaching Creatively with Film.* Citation, New York
Suid M, Morrow J 1977 *Media and Kids.* Boynton Cook, Montclair, New Jersey
Wertham F 1954 *Seduction of the Innocent.* Holt, Rinehart and Winston, New York
Winn M 1977 *The Plug-in Drug.* Viking, New York

Section 9

Social Studies

Overview

This Section is divided into two major subsections. The first subsection contains articles on subjects traditionally taught in schools. These articles review the historical development of these subjects, describe contemporary trends in school curricula, and summarize research evidence about the merits and demerits of innovative educational programs in these fields. The introductory article of this Section, by Morrissett, describes two approaches to organizing relevant knowledge for the school curricula, and provides an analytical comparison of social sciences and the social studies approaches. The first one is based on separate curricula for a series of academically recognized disciplines such as history, geography, economics, and so on. The second one, the social studies approach, focuses on social issues and problems, drawing on the social sciences for essential substantive concepts, without handling the academically recognized disciplines as separate school subjects. The content of the social studies curricula constitutes a federation of disciplinary subjects. The federation is a loose one, involving no denial of the separate identity of, for instance, history, or geography, or civics. The first approach became more common in the school systems of Europe, and the last one became highly dominant in the United States and, to some extent, in other English-speaking countries.

One article of this subsection, by Tabachnick, deals with social studies educational programs in primary schools and another one, by Gillespie, with programs in secondary schools. Both articles survey the emergence of social studies as a school subject, review a variety of definitions of this area of study, and examine the impact of the curriculum movement of the 1950s and 1960s on the content and structure of social studies curricula, and the type of learning strategies employed in them.

These articles are followed by a series of articles, each one dealing with a single social science discipline, or with an area of enquiry, which traditionally constitutes a school subject. The most widespread among these subjects are: history, geography, civics, and home economics, but economics, psychology, and sociology have also been included in this series of subjects. In numerous educational systems these subjects constitute the core of studies about human society.

The second subsection contains articles on a series of innovative school programs, each of them devoted to a specific well-defined problem area. Detailed information is given on the state of art of 23 study areas, which appear in school programs quite frequently. The list of study areas was compiled on the basis of the ERIC thesaurus; thus they represent areas which have generated educational studies of scholarly merit. By no means do they represent a full list of subjects in social studies which are taught in schools. Indeed the list of such subjects is not stable, with new subjects constantly emerging, as well as current ones disappearing. Some of the subjects appearing in the list are well-structured and academically recognized disciplines in the domain of social sciences. They have a considerably long history of systematic research, and have been taught for a long time at the level of higher education. They are new only as subjects taught at the precollege level. An example of this group of subjects is anthropology.

Another group of study areas survives from the time when the "life-adjustment" idea was the dominant trend in selecting topics to teach in schools. The supporters of this approach preferred to deal with problems characterizing areas of life rather than with structured disciplines. The subjects daily living skills and consumer education may serve as examples. Nevertheless one should note that extant programs in these areas have adopted a much broader view than the functional approach, which characterized the life-adjustment curriculum movement in the 1940s. New programs in these areas strive to present a conceptual framework for dealing with practical issues, and also teach the student how to generate new knowledge, which can be used in situations of decision making.

A third group of subjects resulted from adopting an interdisciplinary or a cross-disciplinary approach to organizing social science knowledge for the sake of teaching in schools. As a suitable alternative for the disciplinary structure of knowledge, educators suggested the use of crucial issues of contemporary society, such as conservation or human rights, world peace, and so on. These pervasive problems are examined in the light of theories, principles and generalizations developed in various disciplines of the social sciences.

The study areas dealt with in this subsection differ from each other with regard to a variety of curricular characteristics. While most programs are characterized by a strong bias towards the attainment of affective educational objectives, in addition to the cognitive ones, the balance between the two types of objectives varies not only from one subject to another, but they also manifest great variation across different courses dealing with the same topic.

There are also differences between the subjects in their continuity across the school program. Some of the subjects contain a sequence of materials to be taught during subsequent years for those who wish to specialize in that particular field, while others consist of a series of exercises taught in a short duration course.

The subjects further differ from each other with regard to their links to major disciplinary areas. Thus, for example, environmental studies are strongly linked to natural sciences, consumer education is strongly linked to economics, while human rights education is linked to history and civics. This goes together with the self-sufficiency of various courses. Some study areas are elaborated into a self-sufficient course and are incorporated into the school program as fully fledged subjects. This is the case, for example, with consumer education. If it is included in the school program, it is usually taught as an independent course of study. On the other hand, the topic of human rights is quite frequently taught as an idea emphasized across various school subjects, such as history, literature, economics, civics, and so on, and not as a separate subject. Accordingly, if human rights studies are taught as a topic across the curriculum and not as a separate subject, its syllabus should instruct the teacher how to utilize various subjects for dealing with the idea of human rights, rather than merely listing objectives and specifying topics to be taught in the class.

Finally, subjects differ from each other from the point of view of the role attributed to the school in attaining the specified goals. In numerous study areas the school is considered to be one of several factors which are expected to contribute to the attainment of the program objectives. In such cases the school program should be well articulated with the educational initiatives of the community and other organizations, and with life experiences of the students outside the school, in order to attain the desired goals specified in these programs.

In this Section the innovative study programs in the domain of social behavior are grouped into three clusters on the basis of content.

Study topics dealt with in the cluster headed Society and the Environment comprise issues related to the preservation of the physical environment, to political aspects of modern societies (such as human rights and international education), and to the status of special groups in society (such as women's studies and black studies).

The topics reviewed in the cluster headed Survival deal mainly with functional skills needed to comply with the demands of daily life. Within the framework of this broader area several specific topics, such as consumer habits, drug prevention, family life, and so on are examined in separate entries.

In the cluster headed Communication and Leisure, the entries reflect the trend for schools to include courses into the school program which deal with special problems related to interpersonal communication, various media of mass communication, and leisure activities of the student and adult population.

A. Lewy

Social Studies

Introduction

C. Cornbleth

Although social studies as a school subject has a 75-year history, it continues to lack an agreed-upon definition. If one defines social studies on the basis of school practices, it is clear that while elementary school social studies tends to be multidisciplinary or nondisciplinary, secondary school social studies typically is an umbrella term—like science—which encompasses separate subjects, particularly history but also geography, political science, and economics.

Generally, elementary social studies is intended to promote citizenship, socialization, and patriotism. The purposes of secondary social studies are more variable. A major if implicit purpose is citizenship education. Conceptions of the good citizen range from the passive, compliant member of the local community and nation to the active, informed citizen who is committed to improvement of existing conditions. Social studies programs intended to promote citizenship education include both multidisciplinary and single subject courses. A second major purpose of secondary social studies is more traditionally academic and emphasizes learning within the established academic disciplines for their own sake or for college preparation.

The 30 years of social studies education from 1960–90 have witnessed the so-called New Social Studies curriculum reform movement of the 1960s, the proliferation of elective and multidisciplinary courses in the late 1960s and 1970s, and the return to more conventional or basic social studies courses in the late 1970s and 1980s. In the United States at least, there is continuing debate about the proper purpose, scope, and sequence for social studies education.

Pendulum swings such as those between basic or innovative social studies courses, between an emphasis on information acquisition or inquiry (or reflective or critical thinking), and between attention to or avoidance of affective concerns and values education are likely to persist into the foreseeable future. However, significant trends also are evident in social studies education, even within history, political science, geography, and economics courses. Three interrelated trends are briefly noted here and explored further in several of the entries in this section. The trends are: toward emphasis on social history; toward more attention to the multi-cultural composition of, and contribution to, late twentieth century societies; and toward an increasingly global perspective.

Social history gives attention to the experiences and perspectives of ordinary people. Until the mid-1960s, school history courses tended to emphasize political, diplomatic, and military history and the actions of leaders and recognized heroes. Since then, history textbooks and courses of study have allocated more space and time to ordinary people and everyday life. For example, recent United States textbook accounts of the First and Second World Wars are more likely than earlier ones to provide extended descriptions of life on the "home front" and the effects of the war on various groups and postwar society. This emphasis on social history has made school history courses more multidisciplinary and facilitated the inclusion of accounts of previously ignored groups such as women and minorities.

More attention to the multicultural (ethnic, racial, religious) composition of and contribution to late twentieth century societies, and the experiences and perspectives of women as well as men, can be seen as a reflection of international events and social changes since the First World War and especially since the 1960s. Textbook content analyses and other studies show improvement over this period with respect to the inclusion and treatment of women and minorities in social studies education. However, further improvement is needed to reflect fairly the multicultural nature of present-day societies. For example, an effort has been made to avoid sexist language in United States history textbooks. Yet, the use of terms such as "the people" or "Americans" in descriptions of support for policies or election of a president is misleading when only men could vote until the passage of the 19th amendment in 1920.

An increasingly global perspective takes several forms. One is the modification of more narrowly focused national or regional history courses to encompass a larger part of the world. In the United States, for example, one can trace movement from English history to European history to world history to world civilizations or world cultures, and in some places to global

721

studies. A second form of global perspective, which emphasizes the interdependence of the individual, group, and nation with other people, groups, nations and parts of the world, is evident in history, geography, political science, and economics courses. Even in "new" nations, which tend to emphasize national history in the interests of nation-building, attention is being given to political, economic, and cultural interdependence. A third form of global perspectives addresses global issues such as peace and pollution on a worldwide scale, either in separate courses or units within traditional courses.

Traditional School Subjects

Social Science Versus Social Studies

I. Morrissett

The term "social studies" is seldom used outside the context of precollege education in the United States. In recent years the term has had some usage in the United Kingdom, where it is sometimes equated with sociology. In a search for common ground related to the American concept of social studies, educators from the United States, the United Kingdom, and the Federal Republic of Germany planning a 1980 cooperative conference settled on the term "social/political education" (Morrissett and Williams 1981).

The term "social science" is commonly used in the United States to include the disciplines of anthropology, economics, geography, political science, psychology, and sociology. American historians are sharply divided over whether their discipline is a social science. In other countries, the term "social science" is used less commonly than in the United States, referring more or less to the same disciplines, but with less definitive boundaries.

This article deals with the usages of the terms "social studies" and "social science" in the United States, primarily in precollege education, and with the conflicts that have arisen in connection with those usages.

1. Background of Social Studies

Two parallel developments that took place around the turn of the century set the stage for the interplay between social science and social studies throughout the twentieth century. Several academic groups achieved identity as individual social sciences at this time, as evidenced by the formation of professional associations of economists, sociologists, psychologists, anthropologists, and political scientists. Historians and geographers had already formed their organizations (Hertzberg 1981).

At the same time, attendance in publicly supported schools grew rapidly, and increasing attention was given to shaping the content of education, including that part that later came to be called social studies. Various public and private commissions formulated or reformulated patterns and programs for precollege education. School personnel and university historians played major roles in these efforts, with some participation by political scientists and geographers. Other social scientists, occupied with establishing their professional identities, paid little attention to these activities. The outcome was a pattern of subjects or courses, increasingly referred to as social studies, which, beginning in the 1920s, became the dominant pattern in schools throughout the United States. With some exceptions and modifications noted in Table 1, this pattern is still the dominant one in elementary and secondary schools (Superka et al. 1980, Lengle and Superka 1982).

Throughout this pattern, particularly in the elementary grades, education for good citizenship has been emphasized. Not unlike the stress on nationalistic socialization in the educational systems of all countries, this emphasis was strengthened in the United States by the need to socialize the flood of immigrants that came to America before and after the turn of the century, by an emphasis on "civic education" in the early prescriptions for social studies, and by the heightened emphasis on patriotism that accompanied and followed the First World War. For many social educators throughout the twentieth century, citizenship—meaning good citizenship—has been accepted as the primary goal of social studies.

Table 1
Pattern of social studies subjects dominant in schools in the United States

Grade	Subject
1	Families
2	Neighborhoods
3	Communities
4	State histories and geographic regions
5	American history
6	World cultures, Western hemisphere
7	World geography or history
8	American history
9	Civics or world cultures
10	World history
11	American history
12	American government

2. Social Sciences vis-à-vis Social Studies

Several circumstances have tended to set the social sciences apart from social studies. One is the difference in emphasis on values. Most social scientists have felt an urge to make their disciplines more scientific, an emphasis often interpreted as requiring strict neutrality regarding moral values. Nurtured in universities and often feeling the need to compete with the rapidly growing knowledge and prestige of the physical sciences, social scientists took pride in being objective and "value-free."

Another circumstance setting the social sciences apart from the social studies is lack of communication. With the exception of persons in schools and colleges of education, university professors have paid little attention to precollege education. They may criticize the inadequate preparation of students admitted to the university and may occasionally consult with school curriculum committees, but for the most part they give little thought to what goes on in elementary and secondary education. On those occasions when a committee or commission has been appointed to examine the social science content of the precollege curriculum, the report not surprisingly states that coverage of the particular social science under study is inaccurate and inadequate (Wiley 1977 pp. 87–119).

3. Social Studies vis-à-vis Social Sciences

While social scientists in universities are untroubled by the relationship between social science and social studies—since they give it little or no thought—precollege educators have given the matter a great deal of thought. In 1937 Edgar Wesley, a respected leader, popularized the definition of social studies as "the social sciences simplified for pedagogical purposes" (Wesley 1937). While this definition has been often quoted and widely accepted, it has also been questioned and disputed. Shaver has been its strongest critic, declaring that "This definition has perhaps done more to stifle creative curriculum work in the social studies than any other factor" (Shaver 1967 p. 588). Shaver's comment was made in 1967, at the height of influence of the "new social studies" and in reaction to the emphasis being placed on social science content in social studies at that time.

Shaver was and is one of the strongest advocates of the view that social studies, while drawing on the social sciences for "essential substantive concepts," should have its own agenda and focus independent of the social sciences. The focus of social studies should be on "the preparation of students for . . . reflective and effective political participation in their society—a society whose central commitment [is] to human dignity." In short, the social studies should be "education for rational citizenship." This goal cannot be achieved through "subservience" to the "dictates of the social scientist," allowing "social studies [to be] the handmaiden of the social sciences" in an atmosphere of "overawe of and overdependence on academicians," since social scientists have a "commitment to *adequate description*, not to application in practical circumstances" and give "inadequate attention to the feeling, humanistic elements of citizenship, and to the needs of ethical decision-making that go beyond scientific empiricism" (Shaver 1967, Engle 1960).

Morrissett (1979) has taken sharp issue with some of Shaver's points concerning social science and social scientists. He notes that many social scientists have a commitment to moral values related to their disciplines and to practical applications of their disciplines for social purposes. The majority of social scientists, like their precollege colleagues, are not primarily or exclusively researchers, but teachers who have concern for the welfare of their students. The social sciences should have a place in precollege education, and social educators at all levels should seek a cooperative relationship, not one of competition and confrontation.

Morrissett (1979, 1981) has also taken issue with the role Shaver and others have given to citizenship in the social studies curriculum. He is not opposed to good citizenship, but raises several questions concerning the heavy emphasis placed on it. Putting the dominant emphasis in social studies on citizenship leaves little or no room in the crowded precollege curriculum for social sciences. The heavy emphasis placed on *good* citizenship typically results in deliberate misrepresentation of the realities of civic and political matters; it also places on students an unrealistic moral burden.

4. Recent Changes

Partly as a result of the "new social studies" of the 1960s and 1970s, the social studies curriculum described above has been increasingly modified in recent years (Gross 1977). Courses in economics, sociology, psychology and, to a lesser extent, geography and anthropology have been offered as electives in many secondary schools. In addition, the social studies curriculum has been modified to include courses, units, or emphases that reflect a great variety of social concerns—particularly racial and sexual equity. The increased inclusion of social science courses in secondary schools has tended to make the precollege curriculum a little more like the university curriculum, whereas the increased inclusion of specific materials related to social concerns makes the precollege curriculum somewhat less like the university curriculum, which has been less affected by that trend.

Bibliography

Engle S H 1960 Decision making: The heart of social studies instruction. *Soc. Educ.* 24: 301–04, 306
Gross R 1977 The status of the social studies in the public schools of the United States: Facts and impressions from a national survey. *Soc. Educ.* 41: 194–200, 205
Hertzberg H 1981 *Social Studies Reform: 1880–1980.* Social Science Education Consortium, Boulder, Colorado
Lengle J, Superka D 1982 Curriculum organization in social

studies. *The Current State of Social Studies: A Report of Project SPAN*. Social Science Education Consortium, Boulder, Colorado

Morrissett I 1979 Citizenship, social studies, and the academician. *Soc. Educ.* 43: 12–17

Morrissett I 1981 Romance and realism in citizenship education. *Soc. Stud.* 72: 4–7

Morrissett I, Williams A M (eds.) 1981 *Social/Political Education in Three Countries: Britain, West Germany, and the United States*. Social Science Education Consortium, Boulder, Colorado

Shaver J 1967 Social studies: The need for redefinition. *Soc. Educ.* 31: 588–92, 596

Shaver J 1977 A critical view of the social studies profession. *Soc. Educ.* 41: 300–07

Superka D, Hawke S, Morrissett I 1980 The current and future status of social studies. *Soc. Educ.* 44: 362–69

Wesley E 1937 *Teaching the Social Studies: Theory and Practice*. Heath, New York

Wiley K 1977 *The Status of Pre-college Science, Mathematics, and Social Science Education: 1955–1975*, Vol. 3. National Science Foundation, Washington, DC

Social Studies: Elementary-school Programs

B. R. Tabachnick

That part of the school curriculum which deals with human relationships, and aims to contribute to the development of good citizenship is usually referred to as social studies. In numerous school systems it means a series of separately taught subjects such as geography, economics, civics, and so on; in other educational systems social studies consist of the direct examination of issues and problems encountered in the learner's environment. In elementary schools this latter approach is more common than the separate subjects approach. This article deals with social studies in the elementary school and strives to illustrate approaches to this subject by presenting detailed information about teaching social studies in elementary schools in two countries: the United States and Japan.

1. Early Uses of Social Studies

One of the earliest uses of the term "social studies" to refer to school subjects or disciplines, if not the earliest use, appeared in the United States in 1905 in an article in the *Southern Workman* written by Thomas Jesse Jones. In 1908, Jones expanded this article and published *Social Studies in the Hampton Curriculum* (Jones 1908). In these papers, Jones expressed his concern that young American blacks and Indians would never be able to become integral members of the broader society unless they learned to understand that society, the social forces that operated within it, and ways to recognize and respond productively to social power. Whether Jones' interest was to prepare American blacks and Indians for the full participation and rights of citizens in the society or whether he spoke for powerful groups whose interest was to keep blacks, Indians, and newly arriving immigrants in a willing subservience to the commands of the socially powerful (Lybarger 1980) is a matter of current debate. However, Jones went on to chair the Committee on Social Studies of the Commission on Reorganization of Secondary Education of the National Education Association. That committee's report in 1916 was widely recognized, debated, and finally accepted as identifying a curriculum area for

secondary schools whose purpose was to prepare young people to become productive citizens. The term "social studies" acquired additional legitimation and prestige with the formation in 1921 of the National Council for the Social Studies.

Elementary schools, then as now, were mainly concerned with teaching children to read, to write, and to do arithmetic. In addition to exercises intended to extend their skills in these areas, children studied a bewildering diversity of topics in the general area which would now be referred to as social studies. Teachers and administrators could consider the advice of the National Society for the Study of Education whose yearbooks in 1902 and several subsequent years recommended programs of study in history, geography, civics, and a course in economics stressing occupations, beginning with food, clothing, and shelter for children aged 6, and continuing through "more complex" occupations until children studied printing at age 12 and metal work at age 13 (Wesley and Adams 1946). The teaching of social studies in elementary schools represented even more variety than that reported to be the case for secondary schools, a situation which Edgar Dawson, Secretary of the National Council for the Social Studies, called "a confusion of tongues" (Dawson 1924).

This brief and sketchy review of the earliest days of social studies in elementary schools suggests several problems in understanding what social studies means. There are different categories of discussion about social studies in the elementary school. One type of discussion takes place among scholars who study education and schooling. Some of these scholars specialize in the study of social studies in schools and many of them have responsibilities for preparing teachers to teach social studies in elementary schools. Joining these scholars are professional educators whose responsibility is to develop coherent patterns of curriculum in social studies. Conversations among these educators (some are members of both groups) take place through meetings of national and state associations such as the National Council for the Social Studies, through national, regional, and state meetings of social studies educators including teachers in schools, and through the medium of educational journals and professional books about the teaching of social studies. Periodically, commissions form and professional groups assemble especially for the purpose of reviewing proposals for the social studies curriculum and for making recommendations about needed changes.

A second type of discussion is illustrated by the actions of elementary teachers in their schools and classrooms. Through their actions these teachers define social studies and those definitions are often at variance with the proposals and recommendations for the curricula which have been produced at national, state, and even local school district levels.

This article will examine both levels of discourse, as well as the opinions and influence of a third group, the publishers of school materials, particularly of social studies textbooks used with elementary-school children.

2. What Are Social Studies?

When an attempt is made to define social studies, it is found that the variety and disagreements of the early years of the twentieth century continue into the present day. It should be no surprise that there is debate and conflict. The twentieth century has seen an astonishing degree of social change and social conflict. Technological changes revolutionized the work place, depersonalizing and routinizing production to the extent that workers were forced to recognize their social dependence upon one another in the face of the increasing control over production by management. Advances in technology revolutionized communication, creating access to ideas and places that before were isolated and alien. Conflicting social and political ideas and conflicting economic interests produced two world wars, a series of viciously destructive "lesser" wars, the division of the industrialized nations into two camps, socialist and capitalist. Colonial empires dissolved as traditional political entities. Peoples achieved nationhood and identified themselves as a Third World, signaling that freedom from traditional ties to colonial empires had not produced the independence of self-reliance and self-determination.

Of all school studies, social studies ought to be the most sensitive and responsive to social conditions and social events. Social transitions, confusions, and conflicts of interests in a community are reflected in the varied meanings for social studies proposed by scholars and in the discrepancy between curriculum proposals made for the schools and the actions of teachers within the schools.

There are many ways to answer the question "What are the social studies?" One answer is to examine general definitions for social studies offered by educators whose special interest is in social studies education. A second answer may come from guidelines and statements of purpose for social studies.

Since the report of the Committee on Social Studies in 1916, the purpose of social studies in the schools has been to contribute to the development of productive citizens. That is a very general purpose and easily open to varied interpretations. It is general enough also to invite the observation that productive citizens must know and act on their knowledge in the natural sciences and have mathematical and linguistic skills equal to carrying on the affairs of day to day life. Still, from the earliest times when the term "social studies" was used to refer to school subjects until the present (Butts 1979), educators continue to remind people that the special purpose of social studies education is to contribute to the active and effective citizenship of its students. Identifying the particular point of emphasis of social studies, Wesley and Adams (1946) wrote:

> The term social studies is used to designate the school subjects which deal with human relationships. (Wesley and Adams 1946 p. 17)

They go on to identify the social studies as "a *field* of study, a *federation* of subjects, an *area* of the curriculum. . . . The federation is a loose one, involving no denial of the separate identities of geography or history or civics" (Wesley and Adams 1946 p. 19). Gross and Badger extend this definition by indicating that "the social studies comprise a portion of the school curriculum wherein the content, findings, and methods of the social sciences are simplified and reorganized for instructional purposes" (Gross and Badger 1960). In their definition Gross and Badger are explicit in identifying the methods of social sciences as being important to simplify so that these may be presented to elementary pupils together with content from the social sciences which has also been suitably simplified for presentation. Both definitions leave open the manner of instruction. Teaching could be more didactic or more encouraging of discovery or some combination of both and still meet the sense of these definitions of social studies. Clements et al. stress the active participation of learners and extend the definition of social studies to being concerned with process as well as substance by defining social study as:

(a) The process of learning about variety and change in the actions of people as they arrange to live together in groups. This learning goes on through the gathering and interpretating of social data, as well as through critical examination of the conclusions and generalizations of social scientists.

(b) The development of intellectual skill appropriate to this study.

  (i) Acquiring a language whose content and structure are capable of patterning, ordering, and communicating social realities.

  (ii) Acquiring the "subtlety of mind" that permits the examination of alien individual and cultural forms. (Clements et al. 1966 p. 13)

This definition points to the kind of activity which studies demands, suggests that study is active (a process), and proposes that the way in which ideas are formed is an integral part of the concepts themselves, that is, that there is no separation between method and the content of knowledge produced by that method of inquiry. This definition for social studies is consistent with one form of the emphasis upon the structure of disciplines which received a great deal of attention in the decade 1960–1970. An attempt was made to re-establish the roots of social studies education in the social sciences. Some of the programs produced at that time stressed the transmission of knowledge developed by social scientists while others (more agreeable to the definition by Clements et al. 1966) invented opportunities for elementary children to participate in activities analogous to those through which social scientists create or discover knowledge about social life. These opportunities were an important element in a social studies program whose other elements stressed familiarity with "authentic" social science. Values are not explicitly mentioned in this definition of social studies although some are implied, especially the belief that knowledge is changing, in process, responsive to social context, rather than a fixed and certain entity.

Recent attempts to define social studies suggest that several competing definitions coexist. Barr et al. define social studies as "an integration of experience and knowledge concerning human relations for the purpose of citizenship education" (Barr et al. 1977). They identify three "social studies traditions" which they refer to as citizenship transmission, social science, and reflective inquiry. "Social studies taught as citizenship transmission" promotes citizenship by using a highly structured and closely controlled didactic method to transmit content selected by authorities to illustrate approved values, beliefs, and knowledge. "Social studies taught as social science" aims to promote citizenship through a "mastery of social science concepts, processes, and problems" using a discovery method with students (see *Social Science Versus Social Studies*). "Social studies taught as reflective inquiry" aims to promote citizenship by having students develop problems and search out solutions so that "decision making is structured and disciplined" through a process of reflective inquiry. Critics of the use of these three categories to analyze social studies argue that in creating "pure" and nonoverlapping categories the authors distort the reality of each tradition and of social studies education. The social science and reflective inquiry positions are seen to have weaknesses which can easily be resolved by integrating the two approaches (Helburn 1977). Another criticism rejects the categories as "too forced and arbitrary . . . in the case of citizenship transmission, too negatively laden to encourage discourse" (Shaver 1977). A strength of the approach to defining social studies taken by Barr et al. is that it underscores the continuing alternative meanings which theorists and practitioners give to the same term, social studies, and even to general definitions for that term.

In order to focus understanding of the meaning of social studies, statements have appeared from time to time which list goals or guidelines for the development of the social studies curriculum and the teaching of social studies in elementary classrooms. An example of one of these, published by the National Council for the Social Studies in 1965 was entitled "Themes Representing the Important Social Goals of American Democracy" (Fraser and McCutchen 1965). This list of goals or guidelines aims to achieve a balance between emphasizing needs of individuals and the claims of the society or of social groups. It aims as well to provide a balance between emphasizing the study of social life through the use of such disciplines as economics, anthropology, sociology, political science (there seems to be little emphasis on historical understanding), and balance in emphasizing social action, the development of individual moral and spiritual values, and social understanding and knowledge. Some years after this list of goals appeared, the National Council for the Social Studies established a task force on curriculum guidelines for social studies. The original 1971 position statement of the task force was revised and published in 1979. This statement begins its rationale with "the basic goal of social studies education is to prepare young people to be humane, rational, participating citizens in a world that is becoming increasingly interdependent" (NCSS 1979). The statement strives for a balance between concern for content or substance in the social studies and concern for process; it stresses concern for understanding and concern for social action; statements about the value of detached and objective social science are balanced by statements urging recognition of social injustice and of possibilities for improving social conditions throughout the world.

> As knowledge without action is impotent, so action without knowledge is reprehensible. Those who seek to resolve social issues without concomitant understanding often tend not only to behave irresponsibly and erratically but in ways that damage their own future and the human condition. Therefore knowledge, reason, commitment to human dignity, and action are to be regarded as complementary and inseparable. (NCSS 1979)

The statement develops guidelines within four basic categories: knowledge, abilities, valuing, and social participation. Through the use of such phrases as "knowledge about the real world," it is clear that students are intended to discover the flaws and defects in social life as well as the triumphs and accomplishments which have resulted from human efforts. Intellectual skills and analytic abilities are to be taught and developed as are skills and strategies of social participation. The section on valuing appears internally contradictory, perhaps symbolizing the ambivalent and contradictory responses which practitioners and theorists have toward the responsibilty of schools for helping students clarify and understand social values. At one point the statement says that "neither young people nor society will deal constructively with present social realities through blind acceptance of specified ways of behaving, or of particular positions on public issues, or even of basic cultural values. . . . Cultural pluralism in America and throughout the world rightly hinders the school from seeking or producing uniform values among its students." Two paragraphs later the following appears:

> The school can make clear its own valuing of human dignity by practicing it in the school as a whole and in social studies classrooms. Young children especially must learn the core values in the course of daily living; the school can hardly afford to escape its responsibilities to them. Fair play, justice, free speech, self-respect, decision-making opportunities, the right of privacy, and denial of racism ought to be expected for all students and teachers in every classroom . . . . Candid recognition that the school and its social studies program cannot be value-free may foster the serious consideration of the proper role of the school. (NCSS 1979)

A more recent statement by the National Council for the Social Studies reaffirms the statement of guidelines and moves to resolve some of the contradictions by acknowledging that certain democratic beliefs are to be recognized and taught but that this teaching is to avoid indoctrination, to result from critical examination by students as well as from democratic practices in the daily life of classrooms (NCSS 1981).

3. What Happens in Schools and Classrooms?

In the United States the authority to determine school curricula rests with each of the separate states. In practice, states commonly delegate much of the control over curricula to local school districts. Within school districts, control over curricula is sometimes given to individual schools. State departments of public instruction and school district offices commonly publish curriculum guides which teachers are constrained to follow in a few places and which act merely as suggestions to teachers in most communities and states in the United States. Localities are jealous of their independence from most external controls over what is taught in schools. When proposals were put forward for a national curriculum in social studies, these proposals were fiercely resisted and ultimately rejected (Hanna 1958, *Nations Schools* 1958). Against this backdrop of almost universal rejection and resistance, a surprising degree of similarity in content and in practice has quietly established itself in American schools.

A Virginia study in 1934 and a study completed in Santa Barbara, California in 1940 proposed a curriculum of "expanding environments of man." Dr. Paul Hanna was closely associated with both projects and later elaborated upon them, producing several statements which described a set of curriculum topics beginning with the social context nearest to children in their early school years and gradually moving away to widening and more distant environments. Kindergarten and first-grade children would learn about family, home, and school as social contexts. Second graders would examine ideas about the neighborhood in which the school was situated; third graders would learn about their communities, towns, or cities. In subsequent grades students

were taught about the state in which they lived, the region of states of which their state was a part, the United States as a nation, regions of the world, and the world itself as a vast community, interdependent and in conflict. Hanna identified a set of eight (later nine, then ten) basic human acitivies which could be recognized to exist in each of the communities. Such activities as "organizing and governing" or "protecting and conserving life, health, resources, and property" could be manifested: for the former, in the rules created within a family or the laws passed by a city council or the national legislature; pupils could learn about the change from summer to winter clothing within a family, about police established by local communities, or about parks, or about laws to regulate air pollution established at the national level. Expanding communities provided the sequence of studies while basic human activities provided the scope of studies at each grade level within the system.

An alternative to this approach emphasized social processes or social functions and a spiraling form which saw each major social function (e.g., "using technological resources," "earning a living") examined in increasing depth at designated periods during the six or seven years of elementary schooling (see *Spiral Curriculum*). An early curriculum of this type was proposed by Stratemeyer and her colleagues, who identified persistent life situations as a loose guide within which teachers and their pupils would together create successive social studies (Stratemeyer et al. 1957). A recent proposal for a curriculum of this type is made by Morrissett et al. Their recommendations would have the social studies curriculum developed around seven social roles—citizen, worker, consumer, family member, friend, member of social groups, and self. "While some roles would receive more emphasis than others at certain grade levels, all roles should be taught at each grade level, K–6" (Morrissett et al. 1980).

The pattern of expanding communities has had its critics from the time of its initial presentation. It was denounced as arbitrary, unnecessarily inflexible, logically complete but of little interest to children even though these same children were vitally interested in social interaction and in taking their places as successfully functioning social beings. The expanding communities approach, however, seemed to have a direct appeal to teachers and administrators. By 1945 it was almost universally the program in place for the first three years of the elementary school. By 1955 the general idea of expanding communities had captured the elementary-school social studies curriculum throughout the United States.

The approach to teaching preferred by most writers on social studies is a unit approach to teaching. This organizes teaching around questions, problems, or topics that transcend single social science disciplines. For example, studying the topic "living in families" might use concepts from sociology (roles), economics (producers and consumers), political science (making and changing rules), history (some families long ago), anthropology (nuclear and extended families). Teachers were usually asked (by social studies writers) to plan units by identifying objectives for teaching, varied activities and materials that might have pupils achieve those objectives, and by encouraging pupils to produce a variety of responses (essays, discussions, art work and construction, solutions to formal test items) which might be used to evaluate pupil learning. Teachers were encouraged to invite pupils to plan with them throughout the unit.

As with the expanding communities curriculum, a variation of the unit approach seems to have been very widely adopted. Social studies teaching is most commonly organized around topics and questions which require the use of concepts from many social science disciplines. These are planned by "experts" and transmitted to pupils mainly through textbooks and teacher lectures. Pupil comments during discussions, and written responses to test items examining pupil retention and recall of information are used to evaluate learning. These are among the results discovered through a national survey of science, mathematics, and social studies education (in the United States) commissioned by the National Science Foundation (Weiss 1978). The picture of social studies teaching which emerges from the survey is related to the proposals of social studies theorists in the same way that mutations are related to an original parent species. Knowledge about social events and social interaction is, typically, transmitted as information to be received, stored, and recalled upon demand. Techniques of lecture, class discussions closely controlled by the teacher, short answers or multiple-choice items on worksheets testing recall seem to be most widespread. Textbooks are the mainstay of instruction. Few teachers in grades from kindergarten through grade 6 had ever seen any of the "new social studies" materials developed during the 1960s and 1970s, fewer still had used any of these. Maps, charts, photographs, and posters were widely available and in use among teachers of kindergarten to grade 6; reference books were used by 90 percent of teachers in grades 4–6 and by 77 percent of kindergarten–3 teachers. Other materials that are regularly suggested as enlivening social studies and making the results more authentic and intellectually powerful are seldom used. Artifacts, models, copies of original documents are rarely or never used in most classrooms. Time allocated for social studies is shrinking, with an average of 21 minutes per day spent in grades kindergarten–3 and 34 minutes per day spent in grades 4–6.

In commenting on the results of the survey, Shaver et al. (1979) suggest that most teachers give the highest priority to pupil control and socialization. It can be inferred from these results that livelier, intellectually challenging activities are rejected by teachers because they make it more difficult to control pupils and pupil learning. Small groups working at the same time but at different tasks are noisier and harder to monitor. Fostering a constructive skepticism might encourage pupils to question regulations and decisions taken for bureaucratic convenience. Challenging traditional values might lead to reactions of discomfort and hostility from adults.

On the bright side of the survey results, 15 percent to 25 percent of teachers were using varied materials and some of the newer social studies approaches. Within the continuing expanding communities sequence there has been a significant shift to include more emphasis on other cultures and to include more social science content. The treatment of other cultures and of women and minorities in textbooks has improved considerably. Although it is often only small steps that have been taken, they are important nonetheless. Third World peoples appear regularly as do members of United States minority groups and women. When they appear they are seen in varied and nonstereotyped situations— Nigerian farmers use tractors not merely hand tools; Third World people live in modern apartment buildings as well as in huts. Women and minorities are shown in executive and leadership positions; their contributions to the development of the United States are discussed.

It may be seen that teaching practices in social studies follow institutional and bureaucratic imperatives rather than academic ideals. Clearly, the legitimate claims and constraints of schools and schooling have been little considered by social studies theorists and that lack of consideration has hampered the implementation of warranted change. It is not altogether surprising that this should be the case when teaching is examined about those elements of human life that are the most open to controversy and rival interpretation by competing interests, namely the social life and social history of communities and nations.

4. Social Studies in Japanese Elementary Schools[1]

Social studies education exists as a curriculum area in the six-year elementary schools of Japan. In many respects it is very similar in topics and in teaching method to the patterns for organizing instruction which were described above. Japanese schools have arrived at these patterns by a very different road than have United States schools. Also, the elementary schools exist in a different cultural and bureaucratic context.

All schooling is coordinated by and is the legal responsibility of the national Ministry of Education. A national curriculum is made available to all schools as is money for textbooks. Textbook publishers offer different versions of books that incorporate this national curriculum but all must be approved by the Ministry before they can be made available to local schools.

After the Meiji Restoration in 1867, the Japanese government founded a centralized school system in which the school curriculum was Westernized. Not only

1 The author is indebted to Shigeru Asanuma who assisted in preparing this section.

scientific knowledge but Western philosophy and social sciences were imported. Social knowledge was divided up into three main subjects in schools, geography, history, and moral education. At higher grades of elementary schools moral education (*Shusin*), geography, and history were taught as separate subjects. Moral virtues were reiterated in all grades of elementary schools and were reinforced in national language, history, music, and physical education; moral education was considered to be the core of all subjects except mathematics and natural sciences.

Herbartian pedagogy was imported at the turn of the century and authorized by educational policy makers. The Herbartian instructional formula was compatible with nationalism and with the Confucian tradition in Japanese education. School teachers were forced to use this method; educational administrators periodically checked teachers' plans to confirm that they were teaching properly.

In spite of the standardization of the educational system, there were some exceptional cases. New educational movements in Western countries gave impetus to reform of elementary methods in Japan, for example, Kilpatrick's "project method" (see *Project Method*) and the integration of subjects in Germany as *Heimatkunde* were influential. Japanese progressive educators advocated comprehensive educational programs based on students' life experiences rather than academically organized knowledge.

A unique educational idea was born in the new education movements in the mid-1920s. It is called "*Seikatsu Tsuzurikata*" (life spelling). The term "*tsuzurikata*" is a methodological symbol for educators who believed that children could attain awareness of the social structures and culture of the world surrounding them if they were encouraged to write freely about their own life experiences. Despite political oppression by the government, some radicals attempted to spread this idea nationwide, aiming to create an alternative educational culture, based on children's own social reality, a culture ignored by the traditional educational method. In urban areas, *tsuzurikata* teachers attempted to develop children's own life culture by stimulating their artistic senses using poetry, literature, music, and drawing. In rural areas, a different type of *tsuzurikata* developed because farm families confronted different problems, particularly problems of intense economic hardship. A few teachers, committed to Marxist theory, used *tsuzurikata* as a method for raising the social consciousness of rural children. When the military took control of the government in the mid-1930s, this type of teaching was suppressed. It returned after the war and variations on the form of *tsuzurikata* are still in use today. In 1951 a collection of students' essays *Yamabiko Gakkō* (Echo School) edited by Seikyo Muchaku was a best-selling book.

During the United States occupation of Japan, the teaching of moral education (*Shusin*), national history, and geography was interrupted because the content in these courses was considered (by the United States occupying authority) to be too nationalistic and militaristic. New materials and a new curriculum were quickly developed and a new national course of study was introduced in 1947 (Ohno 1979). This was influenced by Americans but was written by Japanese educators. The curriculum used a problem-solving method to integrate geography, history, and civics through the examination of history and the life experiences of pupils. The sequence followed the expanding communities pattern of the Virginia and Santa Barbara plans.

Many teachers found the new approaches and topics refreshingly different and exciting. Many more were puzzled and resentful. Criticism came from various quarters, pointing to the diffuse nature of the curriculum, a lack of significant social topics and issues and emphasis upon trivial events, and its dependence upon American culture and an American style of teaching. By 1958 the curriculum had become more structured, academic, and textbook centered and it remains so today. The national curriculum follows this pattern:

grade 1 (2 hours per week): school and home
grade 2 (3 hours per week): consumption, production, and communication
grade 3 (3 hours per week): exploring the school district, mapping the community
grade 4 (3 hours per week): our city, geography, industries, transportation
grade 5 (3 hours per week): geography of Japan
grade 6 (3 hours per week): Japanese history

Considerable debate takes place in Japan about social studies education among those who advocate a discipline-centered curriculum, those who wish to preserve "the original (problem-solving/core curriculum) idea of social studies," and those who wish to see topics critical of existing social arrangements. While it has traveled its own road to get there, Japanese social studies appears to have arrived at a destination near to that of social studies in the United States.

Bibliography

Barr R D, Barth J L, Shermis S S 1977 *Defining the Social Studies*. National Council for the Social Studies, Washington, DC

Butts R F 1979 The revival of civic learning: A rationale for the education of citizens. *Soc. Educ.* 43: 359–64

Clements H M, Fielder W R, Tabachnick B R 1966 *Social Study: Inquiry in Elementary Classrooms*. Bobbs-Merrill, Indianapolis, Indiana

Dawson E 1924 The history inquiry. *Ho* 15 June 1924. Cited in: Hertzberg H W (ed.) 1981 *Reform in Social Studies 1880–1980*. Social Science Education Consortium, Boulder, Colorado

Douglass M P 1967 *Social Studies: From Theory to Practice in Elementary Education*. Lippincott, Philadelphia, Pennsylvania

Fraser D M, McCutchen S P (eds.) 1965 *Social Studies in Transition: Guidelines for Change*. National Council for the Social Studies, Washington, DC

Gross R E, Badger W V 1960 Social studies. In: Harris C W (ed.) 1960 *Encyclopedia of Educational Research*, 3rd edn. Macmillan, New York

Hamada Y 1979 *Kaoru Shakaika kyōiku no riron to kōzō* [Theory and organization of social studies]. Gakushū Kenkyūsha, Tokyo

Hanna P R 1958 Design for a national curriculum. *Nations Sch.* September 1958: 43–45

Helburn S W 1977 *Defining the Social Studies*. National Council for the Social Studies, Washington, DC

Hertzberg H W 1981 *Reform in Social Studies, 1880–1980*. Social Science Education Consortium, Boulder, Colorado

Jones T J 1908 *Social Studies in the Hampton Curriculum*. Hampton Institute Press, Hampton, Virginia

Kaigo T (ed.) 1969 *Kyōiko Katei: Sengonihon no kyōiko, Kaikako* [The curriculum: Educational reform after World War II]. University of Tokyo Press, Tokyo

Kaigo T (ed.) 1971 *Nihon Kindai Kyōikushi Jiten* [The encyclopedia of modern Japanese educational history]. Heibonsha, Tokyo

Kokubu I 1955 *Seikatsu Tzurikata Note*. [The note of spelling life]. Shinhyoron, Tokyo

Lybarger M 1980 The political context of the social studies: Creating a constituency for municipal reform. *Theory Res. Soc. Educ.* Fall 1980: 1–27

Morrissett I, Superka D P, Hawke S 1980 Recommendations for improving social studies in the 1980s. *Soc. Educ.* 44: 570–76

Muchaku S (ed.) 1969 *Yamabiko Gakkō* [Echo school]. Kadokawa Bunko, Tokyo

National Council for the Social Studies (NCSS) 1979 Revision of the NCSS social studies curriculum guidelines. *Soc. Educ.* April 1979: 261–73

National Council for the Social Studies (NCSS) 1981 Essentials of the social studies. *Social Studies Professional* Feb. 1981

Nations Schools 1958 What leaders think about a design for a national curriculum. *Nations Sch.* Nov. 1958

Ohno R 1979 The impact of American social studies ideas on Japanese school education. National Institute for Educational Research, Tokyo (unpublished)

Shaver J L 1977 In: Barr R D, Barth J L, Shermis S S 1977 *Defining the Social Studies*. National Council for Social Studies, Washington, DC

Shaver J P, Davis O L, Helburn S W 1979 The status of social studies education: Impressions from three NSF studies. *Soc. Educ.* 43: 150–53

Stratemeyer F B, Forkner H Z, McKim M G, Passow H A 1957 *Developing a Curriculum for Modern Living*. Bureau of Publications, Teachers College, Columbia University, New York

Weiss I R 1978 *Report of the 1977 National Survey of Science, Mathematics, and Social Studies Education*. Center for Educational Research and Evaluation, Research Triangle Park, North Carolina

Wesley E B, Adams M A 1946 *Teaching Social Studies in the Elementary Schools*. Heath, Boston, Massachusetts

Social Studies: Secondary-school Programs

J. A. Gillespie

Secondary-school social studies education has often been equated with the fourth "R" in schooling. Responsible citizenship has been its core goal. The words responsible citizenship have a vast array of meanings across nations. They can stand for the development of skills in political and social situations, the development of national pride, or the increase of international understanding. In effect, the words can imply a whole array of content, skills, and attitudinal objectives. Social studies secondary-school programs can be broadly defined as a complex of content, skills, and attitudes. Four major arenas in secondary social studies will be looked at. First, a review will be conducted of the organization of the curriculum. Then, the relationship between the school and the curriculum will be analyzed. Third, some objectives found in new school programs will be analyzed. Finally, innovations and future directions will be discussed. In each of these arenas, the constraints as well as the opportunities provided in the curriculum will be explored.

1. The Organization of the Curriculum

The basic organization of the curriculum worldwide is by courses. The core course for social studies education is, and has always been, history. National history, world history, and some state or local history have formed a core course or set of courses in the secondary social studies curriculum. Regardless of the more informal goals of this curriculum, the major goal has been to impart knowledge regarding historical events and figures important to understanding national development and world development leading toward the modern nation state and sequence of world affairs.

Most secondary social studies curricula also contain courses on government which focus generally on current national government systems. One trend since the late 1950s in social studies education has been the inclusion of increasingly more economics in either the study of government or as a separate course offering, either required or as a major elective (see *Elective Subjects*). This combination of the study of government and economics forms a second tier of most often taught courses within the curriculum. Therefore, a combination of history and current knowledge about government and economics forms the basic content curriculum for social studies.

Many other courses also form more or less key roles in the social studies curriculum. Geography is often taught at the presecondary level. It is also commonly taught at the secondary level. Sociology, psychology, and contemporary problems are also courses, normally electives, which fall into the curriculum. Throughout the ebb and flow of history, the core courses have remained practically the same with an influx or constraint on elective courses, depending upon movements "back to basics" or toward more "innovation" in the social studies (see *Back to Basics Movement*). Courses in law, moral behavior, and family planning are examples of courses that appear in the curriculum as it stretches to meet contemporary societal demands and then fade from the curriculum as it is constrained by movements to understand basic historical and governmental or economic events.

Generic content is relatively uniform across social studies offerings across the globe. What varies tremendously are the requirements for fulfilling these courses. The locus of control for requirements varies from national to state to local levels. Sometimes these requirements can be added to or subtracted from at every level in the system. The length of requirement also varies considerably. Some students are required to take up to two full years of history; others only a semester or term of subject matter. Therefore, looking at the organization of the curriculum, one can see some important generic similarities and some vast differences moving from nation to nation.

Some serious constraints to the effectiveness of secondary-school social studies programs are built into the system because of this way of organizing the curriculum. Four such constraints will be discussed here. First, in most cases the curriculum acts to reinforce status quo societal values rather than to open doors for change. The social studies curriculum serves as an important socializing force into the system for basic content and with that content, basic values about the society-at-large and the political system. The curriculum thus moves toward the average or median in its content and methodology in almost every system, whether it is utilized to reinforce a historic set of values and attitudes or the aftermath of revolutionary change. The curriculum itself is not a force for change, but rather a force for institutionalizing old or new values that are seen as basic to the development of a society (Anderson 1978).

A second constraint occurs because the curriculum is organized in its basic patterns around content rather than objectives. By organizing the curriculum according to subject matter, such as history, government, or economics, a constraint is put on the ways in which skills are developed and content is organized. The social studies curriculum is not like the mathematics curriculum where addition, subtraction, multiplication, and division skills are the focus for teaching; rather, knowing about a period in history or a set of government institutions serves to organize social studies courses.

This constraint produces a problem which is compounded by the differences in requirements. It is difficult to set standards for attainment of knowledge and skills in social studies education because vastly different subject matters can be taught under the topic of "history." Some teachers focus more on certain periods of history than others; some more on vocabulary and facts; others on analysis of historical problems. There-

fore, by organizing the curriculum by content rather than by objectives, the field lacks generic coherence across schools within a given local area as well as state-by-state or nation-by-nation comparisons.

It is often very difficult to get new ideas and information into the curriculum. This constraint is caused by the lack of communication channels, either formal or informal, to teachers of social studies. Therefore, there is generally a lag of between 10 and 20 years between the curriculum that is taught in the secondary schools and new ideas and information gathered at the university level. For these reasons, the secondary social studies curriculum remains historical even though more contemporary work might infrequently surface in the teaching of a particular teacher. Without important kinds of communication channels to teachers and mandated retraining of teachers, this gap cannot be overcome.

One of the most fundamental constraints in the curriculum is that it is organized as part of an entire school setting. The relationship between formal learning in the classroom and informal learning outside of that classroom is often tangential at best. Because the social studies curriculum focuses on classroom teaching, it often makes difficult the connection between what is learned in the classroom and what can be utilized in school, community, and work settings outside of the classroom. While basic learning in the subject matter is an important goal, the utility of that learning has come into question in countries around the world. As a result of the lack of basic relationship between classroom learning and community life, many individuals have tended to feel that social studies was less important as subject matter than others and ultimately less useful in the everyday lives of citizens.

All of these constraints put together make a powerful lever for the status quo in the social studies curriculum. The opportunity that is presented, however, is equally powerful. If, indeed, the curriculum is a constraint on change for the future, then it can be an equally powerful lever if utilized for future development. Revolutionary governments that have utilized the secondary curriculum as a major mechanism for changing values and opportunities in society have been effective. One need only look at the revolutions in the People's Republic of China and in Iran to see how the utilization of the school curriculum can, indeed, be used to reinforce major societal changes. Again, the use is for reinforcement rather than for the change itself, yet the opportunity in the curriculum is that it can be an equally powerful lever for future change as it has in the past been for reinforcing political realities.

If the curriculum is to be utilized as an opportunity for future change, certain conditions must be upheld. First, the basic organization of the curriculum by subject matter must be removed and an orientation toward objectives, specifically skill objectives, must be maintained. Secondly, teachers must be periodically retrained in new ideas and skills. And finally, communication links must be established between the school and the community in order for reinforcement of new ideas and methods to take hold.

2. *The School and the Curriculum*

The formal curriculum is only one part of the total organization of the school which affects social studies education at the secondary level. Students also learn a great deal from the informal curriculum which is directly influenced by the political and social organization of the school. They learn the "rules of the game" yet they also learn some other basic social studies concepts and ideas. In effect, they learn from what they see in school as much as from what they read (Barker and Gump 1964).

If the informal curriculum is looked at in most schools, the rules which organize the school system can be observed. Most schools are built on an elite or authoritarian set of rules (March 1965). Most of the decision making in the schools goes on at the top. This translates to mean that in most schools the headteacher or principal makes most of the decisions which govern the political and social life of the school system. This kind of atmosphere teaches students lines of authority and control in a society such as the school represents. As long as the schools are seen as a microcosm of the total society, then basically, students are learning lines of authority and control that are fundamentally authoritarian. This is not a constraint in systems where elite authority patterns need to be reinforced, but in western democracies it can promote a dichotomy between classroom teaching and the informal curriculum.

Not all students learn a basic elite model in secondary schools. Larger schools are often bureaucratized to the point where there is a chain of command, and decisions are made at several levels of the system. The basic model of a bureaucracy also characterizes most modern systems. Therefore, it can be argued that the informal curriculum is teaching students basic ways of moving through channels which will be important in communities and work after they graduate.

There are other models which are less frequent, informing students about the basic political and social structure of society. In some schools, there are coalitions of individuals in conflict over school issues. Basic societal issues such as racial desegregation, party ideological differences, war and peace, are brought into the classroom through basic conflicts across students, teachers, and administrators. In these cases, the schools can teach students a great deal about conflict as it applies to their own situation and everyday lives. In some world situations, students have not known peace, but perpetual conflict which has gone on both inside and outside the classroom.

In a very few schools, the informal school curriculum teaches basic participatory values. These schools, which are often special schools or alternative schools, have students participate directly in their governance (McPartland et al. 1971). Research has shown that students in this environment do develop democratic participatory skills which are important to their activities as citizens. They tend to have more political efficacy and to feel a part of the larger political system.

Students, then, do learn a lot from the informal curriculum outside of the classroom. They can learn basic structural norms as well as important political concepts. Recently there has been an increasing amount of research which has shown the relationship of the classroom to other functions within the school in terms of students' attitudes and behaviors (Barker et al. 1978). This research has demonstrated that many other settings such as hallways, gymnasiums, cafeterias, libraries, and administrative offices have equal or more effect on students' basic attitudes and behaviors than the classroom.

A recent study under the auspices of the School Environmental Impact Program has demonstrated a distinct and important role of the cafeteria in secondary-school settings (Gillespie and Kessler 1980). In cases where students have meals within a secondary-school setting, they tend to see the cafeteria setting as a place to interact rather than eat. Therefore, social and political norms are often reinforced and established within this setting as much as, or more than, within the classroom. In fact, in all of the schools studied, the cafeteria had a demonstrably negative effect on student attitudes and behaviors which often overrode the classroom effects.

What is shown in studies such as these is that formal learning in the classroom and the curriculum can be challenged or reinforced by other settings within the school. Basically, students can learn as much or more from the informal curriculum outside of the classroom setting itself as they do from within it. All of this illustrates that the informal curriculum within the school is as important a part of the discussion of the secondary social studies curriculum as course offerings and content.

There are several constraints that the informal curriculum poses for the social studies curriculum. The curriculum itself is built around teaching students about human behavior and the rules of the system. Yet, research studies have demonstrated that one of the chief problems in most school systems involves the inconsistency in the ways that rules are applied. While students have often found that they know what the rules are and those rules are relatively fair, they have complained about rule inconsistency. Its influence on their attitudes and behaviors is generally negative.

When rules are inconsistently enforced by teachers and/or administrators across students or settings within the schools, students tend to develop negative attitudes about the school setting and the political system and society in general. They tend to think that rules either do not apply to them or apply to them uniquely rather than being uniformly enforced across a group of individuals. They also develop a lack of sense of order stemming from the development of rules and a lack of respect in their behavior for the rules of the system.

These are major problems resulting from rule inconsistency which may, indeed, impede learning as much as any constraint on the actual curriculum itself (Gillespie et al. 1980).

One of the most forceful constraints in the school environment has to do with attitudinal characteristics. Research studies have shown that school environments generally do not help to promote self-esteem. This means that students as well as teachers have tended to feel that their own image of themselves and their actions within the school setting were negative. Rule inconsistency and the physical environment can promote lack of self-esteem. Yet, the singularly most important negative correlate has been seen to have been the lack of participation in the decision-making process.

All of these constraints frame the informal school curriculum and have a direct and indirect impact on the formal school curriculum. Yet, these same constraints form opportunities for increasing students' learning. If, in effect, the informal curriculum does have a powerful impact on students' learning of basic social studies ideas and their ability to learn within the school setting, then school environmental change can in and of itself form a model for student behavior. This model is powerful enough to overwhelm classroom effects. Therefore, positive changes in the environment can create opportunities for student learning and self-image which can, indeed, be a powerful tool for learning.

Basically, the informal and formal curricula in the school create an opportunity for experiential learning and the application of ideas learned in the classroom (Gillespie and Patrick 1974). If the formal and informal curricula can be integrated together so that students can see the relationship between classroom learning and extraclassroom learning, then the school itself is set up as a laboratory for learning within which students can learn basic rules, norms, values, and ideals which are important reinforcements for classroom instruction.

3. School Programs

School programs have always largely focused on content objectives, yet there is a wide range of objectives needed in order to promote responsible citizenship. Knowledge is certainly an important core objective. Here basic objectives will be discussed which fall into the categories of knowledge, analytical skills, participation competencies, and valuing. Basically, the core knowledge objectives have remained in the curriculum, while other objectives have gained some prominence since the early 1960s within the secondary school social studies curriculum.

Knowledge objectives themselves have changed over time in social studies education. Basic knowledge objectives were based for a long time on historical facts and situations. Recall of important factual knowledge was the basis for the social studies curriculum, particularly in history and government offerings. With the advent of behavioral sciences and the emphasis in the social

sciences on concepts, there has been a shift in the social studies curriculum from an emphasis on facts to an emphasis on key ideas or concepts as the basis for instruction. Basic concepts such as the Industrial Revolution, war, conflict, and others focus on the history curriculum; basic concepts such as power and authority, war and peace, structure and function are a part of the government curriculum; basic concepts such as supply and demand, prices, and markets are the focus of the economics curriculum. Therefore, there has been a substantial move from situation-specific facts to ideas and trends in almost all social studies offerings.

There has also been a more subtle but equally important move in knowledge objectives from basic description situations to explanations. More and more often the question "why?" is one important focus of the knowledge curriculum. Why is there war and peace? Why is there inflation or depression? As the curriculum has moved from a description of factual circumstances to alternative explanations using key concepts, it has tended to deal with primary issues much more prominently than in the past. All of these moves have made social studies more promising as a discipline in terms of educating responsible citizens.

While the curriculum has tended to deal with important social and political issues due to new knowledge focus, the ways in which these issues are dealt with vary widely. In some cases, critical inquiry skills are the focus of the exploration of issues. In many other cases, they are dealt with factually or descriptively in terms of structural explanations of issues. Normally, issues are dealt with conservatively. In some cases, they are dealt with without considering multiple points of view. Therefore, the introduction of issues into the curriculum which has come about with new knowledge foci does not necessarily promote the full exploration of different sides of issues and multiple causation. It does, however, more adequately than previously, deal with some of the major conflicts in social and political situations.

As the knowledge objectives have expanded, so have analytical skills become increasingly more necessary and more prevalent in the social studies curriculum. There are multiple reasons why analytical skills have become a focus of the curriculum and it is impossible to enter the technological age without thinking in some way about basic analytical skills such as asking questions, being able to gather evidence, being able to analyze key issues, and being able to evaluate the pros and cons of different courses of action. The movement toward analytical skills was given emphasis by new technology. However, it is important that the emphasis on the utility of education also brings about the teaching of analytical skills. Without some means of analysis, there is no way that knowledge itself can be translated into useful community or work situations.

Many new social studies programs have attempted to wed together knowledge and the teaching of analytical skills (Gillespie and Lazarus 1979). Where questions would appear at the end of chapters at one time, now a more analytical method is often used in basic text writing and in some innovative programs, skills are one focus of the objectives of programs.

The teaching of participation competencies formally within the classroom setting is not widespread. It was previously mentioned that the informal school curriculum teaches many of these skills. Yet increasingly, social studies programs across the board are including more attempts at involving students in their school and their local community as a part of learning basic ideas and skills. One of the most common ways in which participation enters into the curriculum is through the learning of citizen roles. Whether these are leadership or "followership" roles, they are often taught in terms of basic role play in the classroom and carried over to situations in the home, the community, or the work place. Increasing community involvement in itself has also contributed pressure for the increased teaching of participation competencies in terms of the basic roles that people play within any group setting.

Another side of participation competencies involves the teaching of decision-making skills and conflict-resolution skills within the classroom. These skills are as generic as the roles, yet less often taught within the social studies curriculum. However, some new innovative programs do give students unique opportunities to learn about decision making in groups within and outside the classroom and to gain practice in conflict resolution. For many years it was assumed that students would learn these skills outside of the school in their everyday lives. This was not the case. Therefore, there has been a major focus, since the early 1960s, to include such skills in the curriculum, especially in Western democracies where participation is valued highly.

One effect of the increase in analytical skills in the curriculum and some teaching of participation skills has been an emphasis on valuing. There has been and there continues to be controversy over the teaching of basic values and valuing skills within the school setting (Lickona 1976). While the controversy continues, schools have taken a larger role in institutionalizing particular values and in teaching valuing skills. The upshot of this objective in the curriculum has been for students to recognize that the basic values are involved in almost any decision which they make and, therefore, whether they are dealing analytically or participating in a community event, they cannot do so without basic values coming to play. The introduction of values into the curriculum, and especially valuing skills, will continue in the future to be controversial. Yet, it is essential if responsible citizenship continues to be the goal of social studies school programs.

With the introduction of all of these new ideas and the expansion of the knowledge objectives in the curriculum, one severe constraint to innovation has rested with the teacher. The curriculum is only effectively implemented by teachers. This involves teachers who are trained in new ideas and skills themselves. Normally, the school programs have outdistanced the teacher

training programs in new ideas and skills and, therefore, the number of classrooms actually utilizing the school programs to their fullest extent is minimal. It is important to note that this teacher variable does not disappear at any level of the system. It is especially strong in the content focus of the secondary-school curriculum. Without some attempt to train experienced teachers in new knowledge, skills, and participation competencies, it is doubtful that these multiple objectives will be successfully implemented in the future.

In addition to the teacher variable, an important constraint is put on new objectives by student priorities. As long as students develop a set mind about school that is basically factually oriented and descriptive, these new objectives, regardless of how they are taught, will have a hard time finding their way into students' habits of thinking and behaving. The ultimate variable, the student, is conditioned by years in a school setting which have often not been conducive to teaching objectives other than knowledge as facts. Until this norm changes and students themselves view education in terms of skills as well as knowledge, it will be difficult to achieve responsible citizenship goals.

The opportunity to teach students multiple objectives, including knowledge and skills and participatory competencies as well as valuing skills is there. Innovations in school programs have created a wealth of materials that supply knowledge in these areas. Unfortunately, the testing of knowledge in these areas and the measurement standards utilized in order to determine the mastery of a social studies field have not kept up with the innovations themselves. Therefore, entrance examinations and other standardized tests often do not test well the innovative materials which are being utilized in the secondary schools. Measurement standards need to change toward an increasing recognition that these objectives need to be tested using standardized procedures or the innovations themselves will not be long utilized by teachers or found useful by students desiring to move forward in the educational system.

All in all, the innovations in school programs have brought about a wide variety of types of programs suited to almost every type of educational objective. The comprehensiveness of the objectives creates one positive effect. It is possible to train students in using multiple objectives toward responsible citizenship in ways that can be effective inside and outside the classroom. Until school programs came to include these multiple objectives, responsible citizenship was a dream rather than a reality.

4. Innovations and Future Directions

In sketching future directions in social studies programs, there are certain factors which must be dealt with. Future speculation is just that; guesswork about what the shape of the future will be. However, there are already signs of forces at work in the society and in the schools which will demonstrably reshape the social studies curriculum and the entire curriculum in general. Some of these things can be controlled and others cannot. A few future directions will be sketched here.

There is one future direction which is a certainty. The social studies curriculum will become increasingly technical. Computers are already dominating much of the social sciences and calling for additional technical skills in order to determine facts and information as well as to gather generalizations about human behavior. Computers have entered high schools in administration for a long time and have become an integral part of the curriculum in sciences. They are quickly becoming an integral part of the curriculum in the social sciences and this trend will continue. Dealing with massive amounts of information and the need for up-to-date data gathering in social studies will increasingly enhance the role of the computer in the curriculum.

The curriculum will also become increasingly technological. A revolution in information processing with many cassettes and much televised communication is occurring at this time. What this technological revolution allows for is the processing of information in compact and useful ways and the updating of information in important ways. Entire textbooks are already taking cassette form and audiovisual dominance of the curriculum has occurred informally through the mass media and will come into the classroom medium as well.

Within not too many years, telecommunications via satellite will be a major classroom influence allowing live programs to be broadcast nationally and internationally on the spot and for two-way communication to occur between students and those involved in current situations. These features will not replace teachers or classroom learning experiences, but they will have a dramatic impact on the types of information which are stressed in the classroom and the access which teachers and students will have to new knowledge.

More speculatively the social studies curriculum will undoubtedly be more controlled by outside forces in the future. Societal forces for war and peace and the ability to decimate entire nations cannot be controlled by educational institutions. Increasingly, war and peace and economic conditions will dictate the conditions under which students learn, increasingly as governments and other forces see the school as a means of manipulating social conditions. Therefore, as society becomes more complex and the forces not controlled by the school become more powerful, the school will be even less in control of its own destiny and what is taught and what is part of the school curriculum. In effect, its role will become narrower and narrower in society as other institutions both improve the information flow and take over functions which have routinely been left to the schools.

Although the school might have less control over its destiny and play a narrower role within society itself due to more powerful political and economic forces, it will also become increasingly necessary as an institution in society. As it becomes more necessary, the role of the curriculum in training students in responsible citizenship will become even more important. Therefore, it can be summarized that the school curriculum will continue in the future, demonstrably changed in shape, form, and scope, and as important, and will be even more vital to the training of society's youth.

Bibliography

Anderson L 1978 *Schooling and Citizenship in a Global Age.* Mid-America Program for Global Perspectives in Education. Bloomington, Indiana

Barker R G, Gump P V 1964 *Big School, Small School: High School Size and Student Behavior.* Stanford University Press, Stanford, California

Barker R G et al. 1978 *Habitats, Environments, and Human Behavior.* Jossey-Bass, Washington, DC

Gillespie J A, Kessler D 1980 *School Environment Impact Program Research Report.* Department of Public Instruction, Indianapolis

Gillespie J A, Lazarus S 1979 *American Government: Comparing Political Experiences.* Prentice-Hall, Englewood Cliffs, New Jersey

Gillespie J A, Patrick J J 1974 *Comparing Political Experiences: A Rationale.* American Political Science Association, Washington, DC

Gillespie J A, deHaas P, Soley M 1980 *School Environment Handbook.* Workshop in Political Theory and Policy Analysis. Indiana University, Bloomington, Indiana

Lickona T (ed.) 1976 *Moral Development and Behavior: Theory, Research and Social Issues.* Holt, Rinehart and Winston, New York

McPartland J et al. 1971 *Student Participation in High School Decisions: A Study of Students and Teachers in Fourteen Urban High Schools.* Johns Hopkins University, Baltimore, Maryland

March J G (ed.) 1965 *Handbook of Organizations.* Rand McNally, Chicago, Illinois

Moral and Values Education

K. Ryan

The individual and the social group have always passed on to the young their values and views about what is right and what is wrong. Without this kind of value transmission, families and larger human groups would cease to function as effective units. The unseen but vital connection among people would be severed. All the basics for cooperation and exchange would be undermined. For this reason, the moral and values education of the young has never been far from the minds of the adult community.

The child psychologist, Jerome Kagan, has recently written that the child's sense of values and morality begins to take shape in the "months just before second birthday" (1981). The child sees some violation of the expected order of things, such as a tear in a curtain and utters "Broke" and indicates disapproval. The child is indicating that he or she has launched a lifelong quest for the meaning of right and wrong, good and bad. Kagan asserts that humans ask the question "How good am I?" long before they ask the question of personal identity "Who am I?"

The child does not travel along the road to moral maturity alone. In primitive societies, the moral and values training of the young is conducted by a small group, the family and the tribe. However, in industrialized society, many groups and institutions contribute to the moral and values education of the young. Even in a modern industrial state, the family is the primary force in this development. Both in terms of its early impact and the amount of time on the task, the family is predominant.

In the contemporary setting, however, there are a number of secondary influences which have substantial impact on the morality and values of the young. Among these are the school, the church, youth-serving organizations (such as the Scouts and the Young Pioneers), the peer group, and mass media, especially television. This article, however, will focus on the relationship between the school and the development of morals and values. The term "moral" refers to what is perceived to be right and wrong. Another way of saying, "What is the moral thing to do?" is to ask "What ought we do?" Values, on the other hand, refer to human preferences, likes, and desires. To have values is to have attitudes or dispositions toward something. Our values or preferences range widely, from things as particular as a liking for a certain kind of food to as general as a love for justice. Those values that refer to people's relationships with others are moral values, and it is these that will be dealt with here. Moral education, then, refers to what the schools do, consciously and unconsciously, to help the young think about issues of right and wrong, to desire the social good, and to help them behave in an ethical manner. What school does "consciously" refers to the intended, planned learnings of the school. It refers to the formal curriculum of subject matter and content and certain skills and attitudes that are intentionally fostered. By "unconsciously" is meant what happens in an unintended manner. This refers to the unplanned learnings of the school, which are sometimes referred to as the "hidden" curriculum. The child struggling to understand what is right and what is wrong and to acquire a set of values is influenced by both these planned and unplanned, overt and covert aspects of school (see *Hidden Curriculum*).

What society does to introduce the young to its values and to teach them its morality has been a concern of philosophers from the time of Plato, Socrates, and Aristotle to the twentieth-century philosophers, such as John Dewey in the United States and John Wilson in the United Kingdom. Most philosophers agree with Plato's view that the goal of education is to make humans both intelligent and good. And, too, most modern nation–states clearly recognize the importance of a moral populace. However, modern nations pick widely differing stances toward moral education. For example, moral education in the People's Republic of China is a high priority. The central government is clearly committed to certain problematic means and goals. On the other hand, in the United States there is much more ambivalence toward moral education. Recent public-opinion surveys show that 79 percent of the American people are in favor of the public schools "teaching morals and moral behavior" (Gallup 1980). However, there is no clear consensus about what moral content should be taught and how it should be taught. Nations, like the United States, committed to cultural pluralism are struggling to find an appropriate and widely accepted content for moral education. Therefore, the "what" of moral education is in many countries a source of concern and controversy. There can, however, be little controversy over the fact that moral education goes on. Whether a society consciously decides on a particular program of moral education or it chooses to ignore or outlaw the subject in its schools, moral education goes on. Children develop particular standards of right and wrong and learn to make specific value choices. Unlike the choice of whether or not to teach the metric system, moral education is an unavoidable process.

1. Theories of Moral Growth and Development

Three psychological theories deal extensively with the phenomenon of human morality, and each explains it in distinctly different ways. Each approach tends to be holistic and isolated, in that it looks at the problem of developing moral maturity and offers answers in complete independence from the other points of view. They are cognitive developmental theory, social learning theory, and psychoanalytic theory.

1.1 Cognitive Developmental Theory

The cognitive developmental approach was pioneered by Jean Piaget and further developed by such psychologists as Lawrence Kohlberg, William Damon, Ralph Mosher, and William Perry. Piaget contributed to the cognitive developmental approach in two ways. First, he posited that the human learner is a stimulus-seeking entity, rather than a creature who learns entirely through conditioning. This structural–developmental view suggests that human beings have certain innate capacities which (a) influence the kind of interactive experiences people have and which (b) determine the reciprocal effects of the experience upon people and their future development. Each person is, in effect, a "self-organizing being." Each "structures" his or her own development, while at the same time being shaped by previously acquired structures. By structural development, then, is meant an active interplay with the environment.

Piaget's second contribution is directly in the area of moral development. What Piaget had observed in intellectual development, he observed also in moral development. That is, the existence of clearly discernible stages or structures of thought. Young people can be identified by distinctly different types of moral reasoning, and these characterize different states of moral development. This basic insight of stages of moral development is a cornerstone of the structural–developmental approach to moral education. In this view people go through similar stages of moral development. The similarity resides in the structures of thought, the way people at a particular stage process moral matter.

The general thesis is that human beings' moral development proceeds developmentally in a stepwise sequence through the various stages of moral reasoning. The capacity for higher reasoning resides in an individual in a potential form, and through the individual's repeated encounters with his or her environment it is called forth. Essential, therefore, to this view is an environment that is morally stimulating and morally challenging. Without the stimulation of an appropriate moral challenge, the individual stays at his or her current stage and does not develop.

While their claim has been disputed, most structuralists assert that there is a high degree of universality about the stages. That is, the ways of thinking, the structures of thought, are the same from culture to culture, even though moral norms may be very different. The behavior may vary widely from community to community, but the basic structures of thought are similar.

Another characteristic of the structural approach is that these stages are irreversible. Once a particular stage of moral thinking is reached, it is not possible to go back to a lower stage. The only exception, here, is the individual encountering extreme trauma. Further, the stages of moral reasoning are invariant. People do not skip from, say, stage two to stage four. Also, the progress into one stage, out of it, and into another stage appears to be quite long and involved.

Perhaps the best-known theory of cognitive moral development is that developed by Lawrence Kohlberg. His theory has been undergoing changes over the years, but in its most well-known form, he describes six stages of moral thinking. The first stage, which children enter about age 3, is the stage of punishment and reward orientation. The child reasons morally on the basis of being rewarded for being good or being punished for being bad. Stage two is called the instrumental–relativist orientation period. The person at this stage thinks about moral issues from a rather selfish perspective and is therefore dominated by the pleasure principle, e.g., what is right or fair is what satisfies maybe someone close to him or her. Stage three is called the "good boy–

nice girl" orientation. What the majority opinion is or what is the stereotypic view is the correct way. Here people try to live by and live up to the expectations of those around them. Stage four is sometimes called the "law and order" orientation. Authority and respect for the social order become dominant here. So is an appreciation of the law as a mainstay of the social good. Stage five is the social contract and individual rights stage. Moral responsibility is seen from the perspective of a social contract, such as the Bill of Rights. At this stage the person is concerned with the rights of the individual and concerned that the procedures of due process are followed. Finally, stage six is that of a universal, ethical orientation. Here an individual habitually reasons according to his or her own conscience according to self-chosen principles, such as justice and respect for the dignity of all human beings. Kohlberg's research has indicated that a few people attain this high level of moral development.

Increasingly, structural developmentalists are suggesting ways that this theory can be applied to the moral development of elementary, secondary, and college students, as discussed later under Sect. 3.

1.2 Social Learning Theory

This second view of moral development derived from the empiricism of John Locke and the behaviorism of John Watson and B. F. Skinner. The view tends to look at human nature as a relatively blank slate on which society writes the experience of the individual. Society here should be viewed as multidimensional, composed of the individual's immediate family, his or her ethnic group and social class, the institutions that are part of his or her life and, also, the total culture into which he or she has been born. These social forces contribute in varying degrees to the individual's learnings. Some of these learnings are moral learnings, learnings about what a person ought to do. Sometimes these moral lessons which are written on the slate or tablet of the individual are good lessons that are learned well. Sometimes they are morally poor lessons that are poorly learned.

The individual learns moral and other social learnings by two methods. The first is direct teaching. The child takes money from the parent's wallet and is spanked. The hope is that he or she learns that stealing is an unpleasant event and not to do it again. The second method is learning through modeling or imitation. The child observes behavior and imitates it. The child sees the parent helping a neighbor in trouble and imitates the helping behavior. The child sees the parent getting what he or she desires by using anger and intimidation, and imitates. Standing behind these two ways of learning is the principle of reinforcement. Those behaviors which are followed by reward are reinforcement and are to be repeated. Behaviors, moral or otherwise, become part of the individual's behavioral repertoire.

How "the moral" enters into this neutral, somewhat dispassionate view of human behavior is important. The psychologist Eleanor Maccoby (1980) writes that "moral behavior is behavior a group defines as good or right and for which the social group administers social sanctions." The "good" or the "correct" come not from within the individual, but from without. Since social learning theorists are uncomfortable with words such as "moral" and "ethical," they substitute their own term: "prosocial." They speak of the need to develop prosocial (as opposed to antisocial) behavior in the young. For the social learning theorist, the parents have a crucial role. They are responsible for providing the early direct learnings and the appropriate prosocial behavior to be imitated or modeled. Parents are the culture's agents for the transmission of the key prosocial behaviors. Their role is the initial socialization of the young.

And while parents have a primary responsibility to teach prosocial behavior, the school, too, has a role. As Emile Durkheim (1973) stated much earlier in this century, the family is too small and too personal a unit to reflect the whole of the social system. The school, then, becomes the microcosm of the society. No longer exclusively in the protective womb of the family, in school the child truly learns how to function in society. And since society is the source of all moral authority, it is important that the school teach the child the society's rules. Social learning theory is the predominant view in psychology and probably the most widely understood by the populace. Moral development, like the rest of learning, is a matter of shaping someone's behavior until it conforms to the shaper's, presumably society's, desires.

While there are many differences between the developmental point of view and the social learning position, none is more important or obvious than their views of thought and action. Whereas the developmentalist focuses on thought, the social learning theorist focuses on action or behavior. The developmentalist focuses on the structure of moral thinking and the social learning theorist focuses on prosocial behavior.

1.3 Psychoanalytic Theory

A third approach to moral development is the psychoanalytic approach. Its founder was Sigmund Freud, the Viennese medical doctor, whose work at charting the unconscious mind began before the turn of the nineteenth century and extended well into this century. The most prominent current spokesman for this position is Bruno Bettelheim.

The psychoanalytic view is based on a view of human nature as driven by irrational impulses which must be controlled. Society's agents, typically parents, must invervene early to introduce restraint and conforming behavior, for both the good of the individual and the society as a whole. As a theory of moral development, a great strength of the psychoanalytic view is that it is rooted in a total view of personality. The moral development of youth—learning self-restraint and discipline—is a major part of the Freudian psychological development.

Freud's psychological model involved three major parts: the id, which is the repository of raw, animalistic urges and desires; the ego, which is the reality principle and works to govern our actions; and, the superego, the last element to develop, which functions as an agent of restraint, and which keeps the person from committing wrong or immoral acts, and that teaches the individual what is right and what is wrong.

However, before this superego develops, each person must go through what is a major struggle in their lives, the resolution of the Oedipal complex. For instance, a son, erotically in love with his mother, comes to see his father as a rival and threat to his relationship with the mother. The Oedipal struggle, then, is to transform this relationship from a sexual one to a harmless, affectionate relationship. The important element in this process for the male child is the fear of castration by the father which is a strong incentive for the boy to give up his erotic desire for his mother. The superego is born out of this trauma. It functions like what is called in plain language, the conscience. It is, in fact, the embodiment of the parents' views in the mind of the child.

The importance of parental influence in the psychoanalytic view cannot be overemphasized. If the parents fail and the superego of the child is stunted or deformed, his or her capacity for mature moral functioning is greatly hampered. The early imprinting of parental influence remains for a lifetime, even though the individual may make later modifications in his or her standards and values. It would seem in this view that teachers and other adults have a role in moral development, but only a secondary role and only as individuals associated with parents. Further, the psychoanalytic view, while having much to say about life, seems to have little to say about schools. Schools and teachers cannot train a child to love. However, they can foster love. Teachers can serve as models for the best in the child's parents and augment an already internalized parental view.

These three positions, then, represent a theoretical background against which the discussions of moral education and moral-education programs are played.

2. Modes of Learning

The child does not come into the world with a set of values or a moral position. These are learned. The ways the child learns can be categorized into four headings, or the four "E's" of moral education: exhortation, example, expectation, and experience.

The first of these, exhortation, refers to people telling children what is right and wrong, urging them to behave in this way and not in that way and, in general, instructing them to live by a certain set of standards. While the exhortation of children is often criticized as being ineffective or too directive, it nonetheless has had a long history in child raising and in education. Also, exhortation can vary from highly emotional demands all the way to more subtle urgings backed up by careful reasoning.

The second "E" refers to the moral model provided by the people in the child's environment. In a school, example is given both by the teacher and by the other students. The student sees a certain type of behavior, either words or actions or both, and imitates. An important aspect of this learning by example has to do with the learner's feeling toward the example. There is a higher probability of the student acquiring a tendency to act in a certain way if he or she has positive feelings toward the teacher than if they have negative feelings. The same is true of the behavior of popular and unpopular fellow students.

The third "E" is expectations. Certain situations and people "call forth" particular responses from others. In these situations the individuals feel the press to behave in designated ways. For instance, a classroom where there is a great deal of pressure to compete, one student with the other, tends to draw out or teach certain ways of acting or behaving. A classroom in which the teacher expects the students to cooperate and help one another aids the students to think and behave altruistically. In the process of conforming to the expectations of a particular classroom environment, certain values are acquired and certain moral learnings take place.

The fourth "E," experience, refers to the act of involvement of students in certain experiences. The student learns by doing. Some learning through experience is brutal. For instance, the student is involved in a debate about the morality of capital punishment and from that experience he or she learns certain moral principles and attitudes. A different type of experience, the more direct experience of doing something, can also instruct morally. For instance, the child who has an opportunity to perform regular service for younger schoolmates, thus begins to define himself or herself as someone who can and ought to help his or her fellow humans.

These four modes of learning all have the potential of contributing to the moral development of the young. All are potential tools for the teacher to use in providing instruction in morals and values.

3. Moral Education Movements

Various cultures at various times have conducted moral education in particular ways. They have, often unknowingly, drawn on various theories of moral growth and modes of learning. Obviously, too, cultures have borrowed from one another a particular way of educating the youth to certain values or a particular system of morality. Currently, there are four movements in education that are attempting to educate children morally. While certainly not inclusive of all that is happening in schools, these four approaches to moral education are reasonably visible and well-articulated. The four are values clarification, cognitive developmental moral education, value analysis, and the set-of-values approach.

3.1 Values Clarification

Values clarification as a movement originated in the mid-1960s and since that time has become widespread. The approach is well-summarized in its title. The role of the school and the teacher is to help the child clarify his or her own values. The school plays a neutral role in that it does not advocate any particular morality. Rather, it sets a process of self-discovery in motion, a process whereby the child identifies his or her own values. The actual means by which values clarification is conducted are quite varied. In effect, values clarification is done through a series of classroom games and exercises that differ in time requirements, complexity, and subject matter, so that teachers of children at all age levels and in all subject matters can engage in values clarification. The purpose of values clarification is to give students an opportunity to grapple with issues of personal preference, to discover or clarify what he or she believes or values. Through the activities, students bring their values to the surface to be seen both by themselves and their fellow students. The role of the teacher in values clarification is to introduce the exercise and facilitate the student's clarification process. The teacher neither participates nor does he or she comment on the students' responses and value statements.

Values clarification does not have a great deal of theoretical underpinning. However, it is based on a particular concept of a value. For something to qualify as a value it must be able to survive a six-step test. For something truly to qualify as a value it must be (a) chosen, (b) chosen freely, (c) chosen from alternatives, (d) privately cherished, (e) publicly acknowledged, and (f) be not only something done occasionally but, rather, done on a regular basis. Given this definition of value, the teacher using values clarification attempts to have students subject their values to the six criteria and discover if their values are, indeed, true values.

In recent years values clarification has been criticized for forcing children to discover their values for themselves, thus playing down the rights and responsibilities of parents and others in society to more directly pass on their values to the young. Further, it has been criticized in that it promotes value relativity, since there is little attempt to challenge or question the values that are presented by students. More recently, however, values clarification has been seen as a possible helpful contributor to moral education, rather than a method that can stand well on its own.

3.2 Cognitive Developmental Moral Education

Since the late 1960s Lawrence Kohlberg and a group of his colleagues have been attempting to apply the cognitive developmental theory to educational programs by developing ways for teachers to assist young people toward higher stages of moral thinking.

Fundamental to their work is the view that higher stage development is promoted by grappling with moral issues. The key to the cognitive developmental approach is to confront children with ethical dilemmas to both stimulate and challenge their thinking. The challenge to a person's normal way of moral thinking brings about intellectual disequilibrium that causes the student to become dissatisfied with his or her current way of thinking and to search for a more complete—and what turns out to be a higher—form of moral thinking.

To stimulate this stage development, Kohlberg would have the teacher present a dilemma and some brief discussion. Then, the teacher divides the class into groups based on their solution to the dilemma and asks each group to come up with its best, that is, most morally powerful, reason. Once the groups have done that, an informal but structured debate takes place, focusing on the question: "What is the right thing to do and why?" Usually the dilemmas are tailored to fit the experiential level of the students. Kohlberg's research shows that a student's stage of moral thinking is unaffected by hearing arguments at lower stages, but it is affected positively by hearing reasoning at one level higher. In effect, the student is drawn toward the more sophisticated structures of moral thought. Therefore, by continuing exposure to the intellectual tension in higher stage thinking, children acquire higher and more comprehensive stages of moral reasoning.

Kohlberg and others are also trying to stimulate moral development through another approach which is called the "just community school." Typically, a just community school is an experimental high school or school-within-a-school. Students volunteer to be part of a community which makes a major effort to involve students in the democratic processes of running their own affairs. A major focus of concern in the just community school is learning to be fair and to take responsibility for the democratic process. At the present time there are several just community schools. However, the effects of these have not been fully evaluated.

3.3 Value Analysis

A third movement within moral education is called value analysis. Essentially, proponents of this view urge that the schools teach a process of moral reasoning, a way to analyze value positions and come to some defensible conclusion. To do this, students are taught the skills of ethical thinking in the same general way they are taught certain scientific methodology or the skills of mathematical problem solving. The essence of this movement is well-captured by Pascal's remark that the most moral thing a person can do is to think clearly.

Advocates of the value analysis approach believe that students should be able, for instance, to provide reasons why stealing should not be permitted. They should be able to deal rationally with questions such as "Is capital punishment ever justified?" There are a number of value analysis approaches available, and all represent a systematic and structured way to attack an ethical problem. The system proposed by Jack Fraenkel is similar to many of these. Fraenkel's analytic approach involves seven steps: (a) to identify the dilemma; (b) to identify the alternatives; (c) to predict the consequences

of each alternative; (d) to predict the short- and long-term consequences; (e) to collect the consequential evidence of each alternative; (f) to assess the correctness of each consequence according to a number of criteria based on the enhancement or diminution of human dignity; and (g) to decide on a course of action. Students practice each of these steps using games and learning aids until they are totally proficient with the whole strategy and are able to apply it with ease to a wide range of ethical situations.

Value analysis, while growing in influence, is not widely practiced. It is also not particularly new, like the first two movements described. The value analysis approach has its origins in two areas. First, it can be traced to philosophical ethics, the study of moral reasoning. The value analysis movement is really taking the subject matter that is part of university-level education and revising it so that it is suitable to be taught to high-school and elementary students.

A second source for value analysis has been the new curricular movements of the last few decades in the social studies. Several of these have stressed the application of rational problem-solving methods to current social problems. Curriculum developers have argued that good citizenship requires the capacity to deal with complex problems, problems often shrouded by conflicting evidence. Therefore, it is essential for the citizen to be trained to deal rationally with the ethical problems surrounding these social issues.

3.4 Set-of-values Approach

This fourth approach is different from the previous three. It is not confined to a particular methodology or set of procedures. On the other hand, it is more comprehensive. In effect, the set-of-values approach aims at imbuing the school experience of the student with particular values that have been consciously chosen by the adult community. These values are seen as necessary for both individual happiness and the social good. Among them might be love of learning, respect for hard work and achievement, respect for property and settling differences in a nonviolent manner, and certain personable habits, such as courage, kindness, and self-respect. The role of the school is to advocate the values and make them part of the life of the student. For instance, a value such as courage and settling disputes in a nonviolent way would be exhibited in the literature and history encountered by the students, and teachers would help students to see their importance. Also, the values would be part of the "hidden curriculum," built into the regulations and school codes. A school using the set-of-values approach might draw freely on the four "E's" mentioned earlier. Students are exhorted to try certain values. Teachers and students are expected to model these values. The values are part of the expectations of the school and are, thus, embedded in the school culture. Finally, the school attempts to give students experiences so that they have practice making the values their own.

The set-of-values approach is a conscious attempt by the adult community to transmit its values to the young. In traditional societies this is not a serious problem. However, modern, pluralistic societies, such as those of the United States, the Soviet Union, or the People's Republic of China have difficulty in transmitting a core of common values and a particular moral view. There is in certain countries, such as the United States and Canada, the fear that the values of the dominant culture may impinge on the values of subcultures. Therefore, certain value expectations are low in priority or ignored. Occasionally, there are some who say that teaching values has no place in public schools for fear that the schools will be found guilty of indoctrinating or inculcating values that are offensive to certain minorities or individuals. However, there are those who consider this objection questionable on several grounds. For one thing, schools, of necessity, teach and affect a child's sense of values and morality. Second, any government is clearly dependent on a set of values for its survival. People who have not been socialized, for instance, to respect property and the rights of others cannot contribute to the maintenance of a stable state. It is to be expected, then, that societies not only have a set of values that need to be transmitted to the young, but that they look to the schools to help them in this process.

4. Moral Education and the State

It is a natural impulse for the state to work to perpetuate itself. To prosper, the state, as the representative of its people, needs to foster, particularly in the young, the attitudes and behaviors that support the state. A major aspect of this political socialization is moral education. In traditional societies, with strong religious orientations, the moral education of the young is, if not easier, at least clearer. The church and the state together attempt to educate the citizen to morality. For instance, in a theocratic state, like present-day Iran, the will of Allah is made known to the citizenry by the head of the government. In serving the state, the citizen is serving God.

The modern nonsectarian and secular state can make no such appeal since it lacks the necessary connection between the will of the Ultimate and the needs of the state. Still, however, the state needs citizens, young and old, who are patriotic, honest, industrious, and responsible.

Throughout most of history, moral education was not as conscious an activity as it is today. While there has always been a wide range of moral behavior, the person considered to be good and what constituted good behavior has been a matter of social consensus. The religious ideal of the society was a prime force in moral education. However, in modern societies which either reject ecclesiastical authority or refrain from supporting one in order not to offend others, there is a new social priority. That priority is to identify what constitutes the good, morally mature person and then support efforts

to help young people attain this goal. While many countries are faced with this problem, the Soviet Union, the People's Republic of China, and the United States can serve as illustrative cases.

The Soviet Union and the People's Republic of China are examples of two major world powers which are deeply committed to the moral education of the young. Lenin, as the primary political architect for the modern communist state, said, "The overall aim of bringing up young people today should be the teaching of Communist morality." Mao Zedong saw the primary aim of education as the moral, intellectual, and physical development of the new communist man. It is of no small significance that moral development is mentioned first.

In the communist state the school is clearly empowered to change youth so as to be closely identified with proletarian thinking, to work for and to experience the collective unity of the new society, and to further the "Revolution." The teacher uses many methods to bring about these aims, but chief among them is to employ the classroom as a microcosm of the collective society. Through the modes of learning referred to earlier (experience, exhortation, example, and expectation) the ideals of the collective life are taught. For instance, the courage of the defenders of Stalingrad is held up for emulation; the industriousness of the citizens of Tachai, the model agricultural commune of the People's Republic of China, is applauded. But, further, students are given opportunities to make social contributions themselves, particularly in the People's Republic of China, where the motto "Serve the People" is ever-present. Youth is expected to make a regular contribution of service for the social good.

Although the Soviet and Chinese efforts toward moral education are quite similar, there are subtle differences. Moral education is a formal subject in the Chinese schools and is taught to students of all ages. In the Soviet Union, moral education is not a matter of formal study until the final year of school. On the other hand, the Soviet Union has an extensive and well-developed system of youth organizations, such as the Young Octobrists and Young Pioneers, where much of the moral education for Soviet citizenship takes place. These youth groups are well-organized and make extensive demands on the time and energies of young people. While the Chinese do not have such an extensive network of youth organizations, youth groups have played a major role in national affairs. This was most notably seen in the Cultural Revolution activities of the late 1960s.

In the United States there is much more ambivalence surrounding moral education than in either the Soviet Union or the People's Republic of China. While the nation has deep religious traditions and the overwhelming majority of citizens define themselves as religious, the state and its schools are officially secular. Also, while there is widespread understanding that certain moral attitudes and behavior are important to enable Americans to live together in peace and harmony, there is uncertainty about the proper role of public schools in an ethnically and religiously pluralistic society. The schools do, however, present the young with the heroic traditions of the country, celebrate the national triumphs, and urge the adoption of the ideals supporting democratic processes. Similar to the Soviet Union and the People's Republic of China, the United States attempts to instill in the young honesty, integrity, industriousness, and responsibility. However, it differs from these countries in the prominence it gives to two other characteristics: objectivity and individuality. Students are more often trained to approach problems, including political and social problems, in an open, objective manner. They are urged to discover for themselves the facts of the situation. They are encouraged to explore controversial social issues to the point that many high schools have a special course devoted to this topic. As opposed to the collective emphasis of communist countries, the schools in the United States stress individuality. The major form of competition that is encouraged is individual competition. This value on individuality in the schools mirrors American dedication to individualism in the economic and cultural spheres. It reflects the spirit underlying democratic socialism that the commonwealth is best served when the individual is encouraged to operate freely and independently. Cooperation and teamwork is learned outside the classroom and less formally in sports and other activities involving teamwork. In general, however, the schools in the United States tend to be less conscious of their roles as moral educators and less direct in the manner in which they go about it.

However, while the schools around the world have varying emphases and approaches, they share a common aim: the creation of the ideal person, an individual whose character reflects the major values and methods of responding to ethic issues of their particular social system.

Bibliography

Bennet W J 1980 The teacher, the curriculum, and values education. *New Directions for Higher Education* 8: 27–34

Damon W 1977 *The Social World of the Child*. Jossey-Bass, San Francisco, California

Durkheim E 1973 *Moral Education: A Study in the Theory and Application of the Sociology of Education*. Free Press, New York

Fraenkel J R 1977 *How to Teach about Values: An Analytic Approach*. Prentice-Hall, Englewood Cliffs, New Jersey

Kagan J 1981 The moral function of the school. *Daedalus* Summer 1981: 151–65

Kohlberg L 1984 *Essays on Moral Development, Vol. 2: The Psychology Of Moral Development*. Harper and Row, New York.

Maccoby E E 1980 *Social Development: Psychological Growth and the Parent–Child Relationship*. Harcourt Brace Jovanovich, New York

Perry W 1970 *Towards a Theory of Intellectual and Ethical Development of College Students: A Scheme*. Holt, Rinehart and Winston, New York

Phi Delta Kappa Foundation 1980 Annual poll of public attitudes toward public education. *Phi Delta Kappan* 62: 33

Ryan K 1986 *Phi Delta Kappan*

Sprinthall N, Mosher R 1973 *Value Development . . . As the Aim of Education*. Character Research Press, Schenectady

Wynne E A 1986 The great tradition in education: Transmitting moral values. *Education Leadership* 43: 4–9

History: Educational Programs

K. Pellens

Although one of the most influential factors in training history teachers is the academic community of historians and researchers in history, they alone can neither plan nor implement teacher training programs, mainly because the selection of topics for research in history is not affected by educational considerations or needs. At numerous universities, the broad field of stimulating historical awareness, usually called the didactics of history, is considered as a field of scholarly activity and includes selecting objectives and content for history programs, transforming historical documents and sources into learning materials, and developing strategies for organizing classroom interactions. Its study is organized in independent academic frameworks, which are supposed to be in permanent critical dialogue with the discipline of general didactics. Nevertheless, their traditional place is among the history disciplines.

At present, the vast majority of research in history is encouraged or controlled by the state or other social institutions. They can influence history teaching through formulating general educational policies, controlling teachers' examination, approving textbooks, and through the monitoring of preservice and inservice teacher educational programs. Only the specialized subject matter competencies constitute the privilege of the academic faculty; the political framework for determining important parameters of teaching practices are set by the educational bureaucracies.

This does not necessarily mean that conflicting powers set up school programs. Quite often, school administrators dealing with teaching a particular subject are experts in that particular field, and vice versa, researchers may have some official bureaucratic position in the school system. Therefore, in dealing with history educational programs, first the relationship of history teaching to historical research on the one hand, and to the state on the other hand, will be examined. The state's role in planning and implementing history teaching will be described. This will throw light on the basic issues in history teaching: the place of time and space in history studies. The role of textbooks and other learning materials in history studies will also be examined. Finally, the relationship of history studies to other disciplines is important.

1. State and Society as Carriers of Historical Research and of Teaching History

State exercise of power is concerned with history; society as a body assuming responsibility for activities not controlled by the state is also bound up with its own history as well as that of neighboring countries. Since, in the modern state, citizens have an increasing influence in shaping decisions, and since accounts of past events mold the citizens' attitude towards the objects of decision, no state can remain indifferent to historical research and instruction. Historical awareness among citizens has political implications for the future. Research and teaching are elements of liberty and emancipation. Many states or societies strive to obtain full control over historical research, others content themselves with partial control through fund allocation. Control of resources has consequences for teaching history. It means that history, research as well as teaching, should be closely linked to problems faced by the state and the society at any particular period of time (Bergmann and Schneider 1982).

2. Types of History-teaching Programs

It is possible to distinguish between monolithic states which control all parameters of teaching history, and states which bear the cost of research and teaching and assume responsibility for organizing relevant activities, but delegate the right of selecting specific topics to the teaching staff. The first type will be referred to as state–didactic type programs and the second as liberal type programs. There are also mixed type programs where the state sets some boundaries for history programs, but leaves the final decision in the hands of the teachers, and thus enables simultaneous use of a number of different programs. Such arrangements result in pluralistic type programs.

2.1 The State–Didactic Type

Several states specify parameters of the history program and no options are given to pupils and teachers to modify its elements. In such cases the aims of teaching history are unilaterally decided by the state and any critical influence on behalf of the society is ironed out. In such states, the program has a monolithic state–didactic character.

The political doctrine which justifies this approach can take on varied forms such as Marxist ideology, the vaguely defined "socialism" of Third World countries, or political doctrines of dictatorships including fascist regimes. At classroom level, however, state policy is implemented with varying degrees of intensity depending on the relationships between state and society,

efficiency and the quality of the educational bureaucracy, local traditions, and individual differences between teachers. Many totalitarian claims meet widely differing inner resistance, and teachers' freedom of action is not fully eliminated.

2.2 The Liberal Type

In many countries and societies, the state refrains from monitoring the teaching of history. It provides guidelines concerning the material to be covered, while the area of content, evaluation, and approach remain the business of the society and of teachers within the society.

The United Kingdom was often presented as representative of this liberal type. Until the late 1980s no national syllabus for history was provided by the central educational authorities and programs were developed locally by teachers. But the liberal British program type was not without problems. Since society and its historical awareness strongly identifies with British history, schools could not resist the relics of such outworn conceptions. The freedom given in such programs can liberate many social energies for the development of historical awareness. But where the society itself is torn in two, this liberal foundation provides no panacea. In spite of efforts on the part of liberal and tolerant teachers in the United Kingdom teaching of the history of Ireland did not create an understanding of the other side.

2.3 The Pluralist Type

Some states may reckon on a broad consensus about the constitution and the basic human rights legislations, but they have to come to terms with minorities, who may not be fully satisfied with these rights. In such cases, the constitution is presented as a normative value emphasizing the protection of the individual and democracy, but at the same time, providing freedom for the citizens to pursue their own goals. In such settings, history programs do not allow a completely free evaluation of all social ideas. Thus, for example, the violation of the state's monopoly of power by minority groups is considered to be a violation of basic human rights. But within well-defined boundaries it provides allowance for particularistic minority ideas or interests and regional perspectives. The plurality of parties with differing priorities and goals appears as a value which makes available to the citizen the effective choice between alternatives. This seems to be the situation in some countries of Central and West Europe (Süssmuth 1980).

3. Unique Questions in the Didactics of History

3.1 Time and Continuity

Many teachers treat the past as one vast continuum. By doing so, they overlook the fact that within a few teaching hours it is not possible to present a millenium or even a century as a continuity. In this respect, utopian ideas about time, and demands mastering the time concept created the problem of covering dense sequences of events. The solution suggested in the 1960s and 1970s to apply the principles of the "exemplar approach" and to teach only selected examples of important ideas and themes were quite reasonable. But one important consequence of this solution was ignored, namely, that the concept of time as an unbroken continuum had to be abandoned. At the same time a qualitative problem arose: continuity has a guiding function only within the framework of the narrowly restricted history of one country. If the teacher tries to subordinate the sequence of events across several countries to the continuum of a single country, facts may be altered resulting in a distorted view of the history.

With these two stipulations borne in mind the idea of dealing with the historical concept of time need not be dismissed. There are many aspects to this concept which can be illustrated through different historical accounts. Time understood as continuity does not take into consideration cases of sudden changes such as downfall, revolution, conquest, and so on, which interrupt the continuous flow of events. In fact history cannot be described by the principle of continuity or discontinuity, but rather by the polarity between these two possibilities. To illustrate such polarity it is necessary to deal with the sequence of events during a relatively short period of time and to weigh against each other differing experiences.

Time understood as a long duration puts individual experiences to the back of the stage and concentrates on social and economic processes. In this sense time is not measured in terms of days or years but rather in terms of decades or centuries lived not as events but as structural transformations. The experience of time, in this context, focuses on the process of change. This too is a legitimate way to attribute meaning to the concept of time.

3.2 Space and Country in History Programs

An examination of the history textbook reveals that categories of space are frequently not properly treated in them. Dealing with ancient times, most history books shift from one region to another (Mesopotamia, Egypt, Greece, Rome) without presenting a synoptic view of events in various parts of the world. Only in teaching the century of great discoveries does the attention focus on a broader space, but even then everything is dealt with from the European point of view. It should be noted that the present-day conception of geographical–physical space cannot serve as a basis for teaching history of the past centuries. Though the physical characteristics of space have hardly changed during the centuries, its psychological characteristics have changed substantially. Today any journey by land or sea, which 100 years ago took a month or two, can now be carried out in a day or less. Any appraisal of political activity, which occurs at a particular point in space, must pay attention to this change (Pellens 1978). The concept of

space in teaching history should be presented properly. Since the concept changes throughout the ages, it must always be treated in a way appropriate to the period being taught (Fürnrohr 1982).

In teaching history it is important to consider the limitation of some space-related concepts, particularly that of political boundaries. Since the nineteenth century, it has been common to mark state boundaries on historical maps as simple lines. Such representation of the boundaries leads to several questions concerning their meaning. What did these boundaries separate and what did they unite? Did they have the same meaning for those who used to live on either side? What mobility across them took place? What changes did they undergo? What effect did the new boundaries have in terms of political behavior and historical consciousness? In many cases the linear marking of the boundaries contradicts the reality: medieval boundaries for the most part were fringe areas; political centers were separated by no-man's-land or exchequer land. Common historical consciousness is not necessarily affected by existing state boundaries.

4. Means and Methods

Many educational programs do not specify the means and methods to be used in the class, leaving the decision about these matters to the teachers. It should be borne in mind that a teacher who was trained to teach in a particular manner may not be aware of the variety of means and methods which can be used. Ideally, if the teacher's freedom of action is increased, it is necessary to ensure that the teacher is familiar with a broad repertoire of possible forms of action. The most influential medium of history teaching is still the textbook. Frequently, books are overloaded with facts and teachers are inclined to lecture about contents presented in the textbooks. Use of supplementary teaching materials, such as historical maps and other audiovisual aids may be functional in increasing interaction between teacher and learner, and reduce time devoted to expository teaching. The shift from teacher-centered teaching toward activity type learning is becoming increasingly widespread. There are programs based on self-learning activities containing sets of learning resources, such as photocopies of historical documents of primary and secondary sources, etc. The student may select assignments which best fit his or her interest and ability (Pellens 1978). Computerized databases were developed for use within the framework of history courses, both by teachers and by students (Slatta 1987). Courses in contemporary history frequently use television, video-records and newspapers as sources for studies (Dolce 1987).

5. Coordination Between Subjects

Since Herodotus and Thucydides there has been a history component in European culture. At times it was highly esteemed; at other times, less so, but it has appeared constantly in the school program, though its relationship to other programs has greatly varied.

For a long period of time, history was subordinated to theology due to sacred elements in perception of kingdom and empire, and salvation-oriented concepts of various periods. Later it was placed in the department of philosophy, and only in the twentieth century did history become a fully independent field of study with its own university department. Its links with other subjects must be considered from a pragmatic rather than from a dogmatic point of view.

In the United States, orientation toward social sciences has been the most common frame. History frequently became part of political instruction. Such coordination is rooted in the fact that both political sciences and history as subjects deal with problems of power, capacity, and social commitment. In France on the other hand, the coordination with geography is the rule as both subjects deal with space and people acting in it. Such coordination does not accentuate the differences in the methodology of the two subjects. It should be noted however, that coordination of subjects does not imply subordination or elimination. Contacts can be worked out between history and several other school subjects. One may move far beyond the traditional triangle of geography, politics, and history and enrich the history studies by linking them to other subjects. Good religious instruction should have a historical component, so should educational programs in literature, art, music, and so on. Skillful coordination may enrich the meaning not only of history studies but that of all other subjects coordinated with it.

6. Desiderata

To increase international understanding and to minimize idiosyncrasies of national programs in teaching history, comparative studies of course outlines should be conducted. In each education system, decisions about course outlines should be made by cross-national committees with the participation of advisors from the neighboring countries.

It is desirable to increase the repertoire of teaching devices and study materials, for the sake of critically examining the society's image about its history. But innovations should be carefully scrutinized as to the system's capability and readiness to adopt them.

Finally, history programs should not confine the freedom of the teacher and of the instruction, but rather they should safeguard them. In order to avoid pressures and distortions of historical perspectives it is desirable that decisions about school programs in history should be made within the framework of open political discussions. A critical grasp of historical sources can loosen rigidity and broaden one-dimensional narrow formulas. The history curricula ought to promote this crucial function of history education.

Bibliography

Ballard M (ed.) 1970 *New Movements in the Study and Teaching of History*. Maurice Temple Smith, London

Bergmann K, Schneider G (eds.) 1982 *Gesellschaft–Staat–Geschichtsdidaktik*. Schwann, Düsseldorf

Burston W H, Green C W (eds.) 1972 *Handbook for History Teachers*, 2nd edn. Methuen, London

Dolce P C 1987 Television, text and teaching immigration history. *Social Studies* 78(5): 213–16

Fenton E 1966 *Teaching the New Social Studies in Secondary Schools: An Inductive Approach*. Holt, Rinehart and Winston, New York

Fürnrohr W (ed.) 1982 *Afrika im Geschichtsunterricht europäischer Länder*. Minerva, Munich

Pellens K (ed.) 1978 *Didaktik der Geschichte*. Wissenschaftliche Buchgesellschaft, Darmstadt

Pellens K 1982 Geschichtsdidaktische Zeitschriften in Europa und Übersee. *Informations* [of the International Society for Didactics of History] 3: 100–17

Pellens K, Quandt S, Süssmuth H (eds.) 1984 *Geschichtskultur—Geschichtsdidaktik*. Internationale Bibliographie Schöningh, Paderborn

Portal C 1987 *The History Curriculum for Teachers*. Falmer Press, London

Slatta R 1987 Students discuss microcomputers and history. *History Microcomputer Review* 3(2):7–14

Süssmuth H 1980 *Geschichtsdidaktik: Eine Einführung in Aufgaben und Arbeitsfelder*. Vandenhoeck und Ruprecht, Göttingen

Geography: Educational Programs

H. L. Schrettenbrunner

Geography curricula prescribe objectives and contents of the subject to be taught at each particular grade level. The specificity of the various types of geography curricula varies considerably. Some contain only vague guidelines or a list of general aims, leaving the teacher free to determine the specific content of the course. Other geography curricula contain more detailed specification of objectives and content to be taught in the school. Several curricula are even more structured,

prescribing also the type of activities to be carried out and the form of classroom organization. Recent geography curricula pertain mainly to the intermediate type of school programs described above.

Another variation which characterizes geography programs across countries is the definition of the boundaries of subject matter. This may range from mere regional descriptions, through physical geography, to human geography, including applied geography and ecology. Some geography programs appear as component elements of broader social studies courses, such as *sciences humaines* or *sciences sociales* in France, *Gemeinschaftskunde* in Germany, and *Geographie mit Wirtschaftskunde* in Austria. In general, during the 1970s there was a tendency to lessen the importance of regional geography and to strengthen human components of the geography studies.

Research on geography curricula on a comparative cross-national level is almost nonexistent, partly due to the divergence of the curricula across countries. Empirical research related to geography curricula mostly focuses on the evaluation of innovative learning packages. International research on the teaching of geography is coordinated by the International Geography Union (IGU) and a respective working group which presents its papers on the occasions of international geography congresses (1988 in Brisbane, see Gerber and Lidstone 1988).

1. Traditional Concepts

Traditional geography courses after the Second World War consisted mainly of content units in regional geography. In these programs, the sequence of units moves from the immediate environment of the learner to more distant geographic areas. The method of presentation is based on a rigid pattern following the sequence of dealing first with geomorphology and geology and other physical properties of a region and then with some human factors, such as settlements, lines of traffic, international commerce, and politics.

The difficulties of covering the descriptive features of a large number of countries have been laid aside by selecting a few countries to study in depth, and by generalizing some concepts derived from the in-depth study to other countries of the same type (thus for example, Tunisia may constitute an example of the oriental type of country). Where geography has been linked to other school subjects, it has usually lost the rigid connection with the discipline of geography and became reduced to a minor component of the broader social studies subject area.

1.1 Social Studies

While the geography courses in the United States vary widely not only from state to state but also from school to school, it can be said that until the 1960s they constituted a weak component of the social studies programs. Nevertheless, this geography component had not been integrated into the course of social science studies. It rather constituted an "insert" into the course and dealt only with the traditional concepts of descriptive regional geography. Teachers had very little systematic training in geography from university geography departments. In France, which has a uniform curriculum across the whole country, geography has been taught in combination with history and social studies by a single teacher within a school. No fun-

damental changes have been implemented in geography curricula during the last century. Program topics are as follows: class 6: home district, different geographical regions; class 7: human and economic geography around the world with one case study from Asia, America, Africa; class 8: Europe; class 9: France, European Common Market, United States, Soviet Union; class 10: general geography, mostly physical; class 11: France and her colonies; class 12: leading countries of the world.

1.2 Regional Geography

As exemplified by the case of France, there may be a link between social studies courses and the traditional regional geography courses. The study of a particular topic in geography is still, however, shaped according to the traditional structure of the subject, that is, moving from the study of the geomorphological and geological aspects to the human and economic aspects of a particular region. The content of such programs may vary according to the freedom given to teachers and to organizational units of the school system in making decisions about the school program.

1.3 Traditional Concepts in the Federal Republic of Germany

Each of the federal states enjoys a high level of cultural autonomy and determines the curricula which are obligatory at a given grade level and in particular school types.

In the 1960s, the main theme was regional geography and courses were concentric; only the position of continents in the sequences varied from state to state. In classes 1 to 4, the neighborhood and district were taught. The sequence of contents could run as follows: class 5: home state; class 6: rest of Federal Republic of Germany; class 7: Europe; class 8: Africa, Asia, Australia; class 9: America; class 11: geology, Germany; class 12, 13: geographical aspects of the leading countries of the world.

1.4 Academically-oriented Schools in the United Kingdom

Traditionally, academically-oriented grammar schools in the United Kingdom preferred traditional regional geography programs which followed the continents around the world (from home country to Africa, South America, Australia to Asia, and the United States to Europe to the United Kingdom and worldwide repetition).

Secondary-modern schools either taught concentric geography (1st year: bread, meat, fruit, world trade routes, mountains; 2nd year: cotton, rubber, dairy products, wood, fish, valleys; 3rd year: coal, sugar, wool, lakes, winds, harbors; 4th year: iron, steel, oil, deserts, population; 5th year: repetition), or they taught systematic geography (e.g. 1st year: food, clothing, dwellings; 2nd: traffic, trade; 3rd: energy, industry; 4th:

world problems; 5th: repetition). Schools could choose between these three main lines, but in the end the syllabi of the university examination boards determined the curriculum in the last few years before the finals. The lower General Certificate of Education (GCE) Ordinary "O" level (taken at age 16) was conservative and required hard facts and good regional knowledge. The higher General Certificate of Education Advanced "A" level (taken at age 18) was more open to thematic and modern geography and led to university courses. The Certificate of Secondary Education (CSE), for less academically-oriented pupils, was based on the concentric and systematic approach.

The following cases of socialist countries show alterations of the regional course because they divide countries in a different manner (capitalist/socialist) and put emphasis also on economic connections between nations.

1.5 Stability of Curricula: The Case of the German Democratic Republic (GDR)

Since the Second World War, there have been a number of geography plans issued (the term "curriculum" is not used) which document the general political line of the German Democratic Republic. The strong division in natural and economic geography is typical of the socialist countries (Sperling 1977).

In 1965, work began on a general reform plan which was subsequently published in 1972. The major themes for geography are: class 5: tasks of geography and map reading, German Democratic Republic ("our socialist home country"); class 6: German Democratic Republic, Federal Republic of Germany, capitalist/socialist countries in Europe; class 7: the Soviet Union, Asia; class 8: Africa, America; class 9: physical geography, natural landscape of the German Democratic Republic; class 10: complex analyses of territories (GDR), home district, integration in socialist countries, economic geography; class 11: geology, cooperation between socialist countries, territorial planning. The plans of the late 1960s seem to be those of the 1980s. Small alterations were made between 1977 and 1979 which lay emphasis on more complex geography (systematic relations between landscape and economy in class 5; complex analyses of territories in classes 9 and 10).

1.6 Traditional Curriculum: The Soviet Union

In the 1960s, the curriculum was revised to keep it up-to-date with new developments in the field. It aimed at a broad general knowledge of the subject and at an insight into technical procedures and practical skills. It was supposed to contribute to the dominant objective of the school system, that is, the optimal preparation of the learners for integration into the working process. All schools throughout the Soviet Union have the same curriculum with an identical time schedule. Geography is an autonomous subject, the coordination with history, social sciences, biology, chemistry, and physics is, however, strong. The division between physical and econ-

omic geography has a long tradition. The articulation of the program is as follows: class 5: fundamentals of physical geography; class 6: geography of continents; class 7: physical geography of the Soviet Union; class 8: economic geography of the Soviet Union; class 9: economic geography of other countries (socialist, capitalist, and developing countries). From 1988 on reforms of schools, educational aims and geographical contents can be noted which can be summarized as a diminution of topographical facts and an emphasis on more complex structures, models, and general geography. The new program runs as follows: class 6: fundamentals of physical geography, class 7: geography of continents and oceans, classes 8 and 9: geography of the Soviet Union, and totally new class 10: economic and social geography of the world (no longer a regional, but a general geographic approach).

2. Drawbacks of Traditional Approaches

Since the 1960s, criticism of the traditional curricula of geography became sharper and gained more influence. Generally speaking the following drawbacks were pointed out:

(a) overemphasis on facts and too little structure in geography;
(b) too much rote learning;
(c) no transferable insights;
(d) neglect of teaching analytical skills;
(e) little pupil involvement;
(f) obsolete content;
(g) no clearly defined educational objectives.

Although it may be assumed that there is a worldwide awareness of these drawbacks, nevertheless, traditional curricula are still in use in many countries partly due to the inertia of authorities, or due to strong legal structures (for example, in Switzerland, partly in the United Kingdom and France) or due to deliberate adherence to the traditional conceptions of the subject (for example, GDR, USSR, Poland, Italy).

3. New Geography Curricula

Because of the effects of the above listed criticisms, the new geography programs contained several innovative features. Still, it should be noted that the features listed below are not manifested in any single innovative geography course; they are rather the totality of all desired characteristics which may have appeared in various programs of the 1970s:

(a) Attention to student comprehension of the structure of the subject rather than knowledge of isolated facts.
(b) A focus on broad, generalizable geography rather than on specific information about individual countries.

(c) Problem-solving activities including generating a hypothesis and testing its validity.

(d) Involvement of the learner in activities (dealing with problems relevant to the child's world, community issues, political problems of concern).

(e) Dealing with recent findings of research within the domain of the discipline and of related fields such as ecology, urban planning, human geography.

(f) Systematic approach to curriculum development (specification of objectives, provision of feedback instruments, trying out the program).

(g) Utilization of a variety of teaching strategies (group work, games, simulations).

(h) Sequencing the curriculum unit on the basis of the objectives to be attained rather than according to the principles of geographic distance.

During the 1970s several countries made minor alterations in their geography curricula in order to comply with some of the demands put forward by the proponents of the new curricula. Thus, for example, since 1978 there has been an observable trend to revise the geography curriculum in the Soviet Union. Reports indicate that there is a trend to utilize knowledge produced by contemporary researchers in the field, to allow a higher level of flexibility in selecting content, to create links between physical and economical geography, and to include in the program topics from ecology and soil conservation. In 1973, the Swiss Geography Teachers' Association started to compile a catalog of educational objectives, so that the teacher could identify intermediate objectives in striving to attain a certain broader educational goal (Aerni 1981). A geography program developed in the United Kingdom utilized microcomputers for incorporating simulation games and databases into the program. Map construction was facilitated by using the computer. The authors of this program emphasize the value of a device called "floor turtle" in pointing out the three dimensionality of the earth surface (Watson 1984). Parallel to such minor program alterations, large-scale curriculum reforms may be observed in geography in several countries. Some of these programs are described below.

3.1 Innovative Programs in the United States: The American Curriculum Movement

In the late 1950s when the low standard of American education seemed evident, the American Association of Geographers (AAG) and the National Council for Geographic Education (NCGE) initiated the High School Geography Project (HSGP). The content of this program reflects a new approach to teaching geography. The units of the course deal with topics like network analysis, analysis of regional systems, diffusion models, and town planning. The learning activities are based on the utilization of new media such as games, simulation exercises, and so on. Macmillan published in 1970 the following packages aimed for a single school year of the high school (15 year olds): geography of cities, manufacturing and agriculture, cultural geography, political geography, habitat and resources, Japan. The diffusion of HSGP may have been hindered by the high price of such packages. On the other hand, its international impact is without comparison in history. The High School Geography Project may well be called the most influential worldwide innovation of geography curriculum (Gunn 1972). Its ideas and methods are known in practically the whole English-speaking world and in most Western countries.

Other American projects of an innovative nature are:

(a) Earth Science Curriculum Project (ESCP), which includes astronomy, meteorology, geology, oceanography, and geography, and was initiated in 1963 by the American Geological Institute. It is also known beyond the United States and has been translated into different languages.

(b) Geography Curriculum Project (GCP), which is discipline oriented and gives basic geographic concepts based on the inquiry learning approach (Elbers 1973). Despite some internationally well appreciated innovative projects, the general state of geography in the USA is deplorably low as several knowledge tests of public opinion research institutes could prove. "Geography Awareness Weeks", the "Alliance Movement" between schools, publishers, universities and planning authorities and "the Guidelines for Geographic Education" have been trying since 1987 to better the situation. New contents and new curricula have been formulated and combined efforts for a more effective in-service training of teachers have been made by school authorities, univerities and the "National Geographic Magazine".

3.2 The United Kingdom: Several Innovative Programs

Due to the parochial structure of the educational system in the United Kingdom, and affected by the innovations implemented in the United States, experimentation with new geography curricula in the United Kingdom started at the end of the 1960s, mostly in classes where final examinations were not imminent; they were mainly promoted by the Schools Council. Such new curriculum packages are:

(a) Geography for the Young School Leaver (for less able learners and for "O" level);

(b) Geography 14–18 (for more able students);

(c) Geography in an Urban Age;

(d) Geography 16–19;

(e) Science 5–13 (more natural science combined with relevant aspects of geography);

(f) Environmental Studies (more skills and concepts);

(g) Social Studies 8–13 (for middle schools, from the Schools Council).

Most of these projects aim at broader objectives linked to the methodology of studying the subject (i.e., map reading, path finding, orientation in landscape, sketching, drawing, fieldwork techniques), and strive to increase the pupil's involvement. They contain modern topics of geography (i.e., urban geography, urban planning, ecology). At the end of the 1980s a long tradition of school-based curricula came to an end, and Great Britain introduced new national curricula. Geographers envisage a certain danger of centralization and the loss of specialities such as local fieldwork, but still more endangered will be the future position of Geography in the timetable (within or without the compulsory subjects).

3.3 Federal Republic of Germany: Curriculum Reform in the Face of the Federal Structure

General discontent with existing curricula was so strong that federal states and the Central Association of German Geographers agreed to launch a comprehensive revision of the school program in geography. Being an experimental project, it could not substitute for the official curriculum, which had a legal status. Nevertheless, after two to four years, most plan commissions had taken over the new ideas represented in the new project.

After 1968, criticism of the regional type of curriculum became so strong that commissions were set up to develop new ideas for geography curricula. The targets of these programs were: more vivid geography courses with more direct relevance to the pupil; less regional geography and no concentric grouping of countries; more modern teaching media; more active pupil involvement.

Between 1968 and 1975, nearly all curricula of all states, classes, and school types were revised. Differences between states still exist, but the major topics of the program across states are as follows: classes 1 to 4: home, neighborhood, district; classes 5 to 6: social geography, Germany, and case studies over the world; class 7: natural geography and the reaction of human beings to challenges; class 8: developing countries (Africa, Asia, South America); class 10 or 11: complex analysis of neighborhood, Germany; classes 12 and 13: geographical aspects of the leading countries of the world, urban geography, planning, ecology. During the 1980s most of the federal states changed the curricula, so that more variance between orders and contents occur. A definite swing-back from a general geography to a more regional approach can be noted.

One of the major innovative programs developed in the Federal Republic of Germany is the *German Geography Curriculum Project* (RCFP) (Marsden 1980). From 1973 to 1978, the RCFP (*Raumwissenschaftliches Curriculum Forschungsprojekt*) was financed from state funds and on the basic ideas of HSGP developed new packages for different classes with similar aims to HSGP, trying to avoid a certain political naivety inherent in the HSGP (Geipel 1972). The following units have been published: Location of an Airport, Development Chances in Nigeria (The case of young Tabi Egbe), Planning for a North Sea Bay Region (The case of the bay of Gelting), Ecological Problems of the Rhine, Soil Erosion and Conservation, Industry at the Coast, and Regional Planning.

These packages were developed as innovations outside the existing state curricula and therefore they do not easily fit the plans of all states (German Geography Curriculum Project 1978). The impact of RCFP can be noted in Austria, the Netherlands, and Italy.

4. Research

Research on geography curricula is scarce if hermeneutic speculations are not included. But it should be borne in mind that most of the changes in curricula are justified by speculative arguments or postulations without reference to empirical evidence. Almost nowhere can quantitative proof be found that traditional geography impedes the intellectual development of children (for an exception see Slater 1976) or that it has negative consequences for the pupil.

Most topics which were dealt with in a quantitative way circled around achievement measures presented in the form of percentages of correct responses. Representativity of the samples is never demonstrated, even when very large numbers of pupils tested may persuade the reader to think so. Only rarely are experimental designs used (Jones 1976, Schrettenbrunner 1980, Gerber and Lidstone 1988).

More complex analyses are scarce, and if there are any, they only test hypothesized relationships among a cluster of five to ten variables. Hypotheses deal with the influence of sex, age, and intelligence on test achievement. Sometimes the profession of the father, experience with nonschool geography, travel experience, qualification of the teacher, or type of school book or curriculum are also found among the independent variables. It is no surprise that explained variances seldom reach 50 percent of the total variance.

It is generally acknowledged that the following flaws should be eliminated:

(a) the paucity of theoretical basis;

(b) the disregard of important variables which may explain variance in pupils' achievement;

(c) insufficient empirical database (deficient planning of experiments owing to lack of cooperation of schools);

(d) inadequate data summary.

The new curricula raised new problems which have not been studied in a satisfactory way:

(a) Does the loss of the regional geography courses lead to topographical disorientation in the pupils?

(b) Does the new content really interest pupils more than the old one?

(c) Do the new curricula really help in the intellectual development of pupils?

(d) Why do teachers partly obstruct the introduction of new curricula?

Curriculum research in the field of geography takes various levels of sophistication and complexity. Below is an attempt to provide a taxonomic classification of such studies, where higher-level studies include the features of all lower-level ones.

4.1 Simple Testing of Achievement (GDR)

During the preparation of the new programs in the German Democratic Republic, the Academy of Pedagogical Sciences assumed responsibility for the scientific supervision; several doctoral dissertations examined which objectives had been attained by the students.

4.2 Development of New Curricula (France)

Until 1980, no summary of relevant research in France had been published; articles published in Institut Nationale du Recherche Pedagogique (INRP) *Recherches Pedagogiques* (Vols. 83 and 85) deal with pupils' opinions about the modern world and about evaluation results, respectively. The main interest seems to lie in examining cognitive and affective student behaviors related to the study of geography.

4.3 Revisions of Curriculum Packages (United Kingdom)

Several local groups in the United Kingdom evaluated new curriculum projects. Slater (1976) analyzed the development of geographical thinking of pupils from classes 3 to 12.

4.4 Evaluations of Innovative Curricula (USA, FRG)

Within the United States, the HSGP is one of the most evaluated geography projects (Binder-Johnson 1972 p. 236). Evaluation activities were carried out jointly by HSGP and the Educational Testing Service in Princeton, New Jersey. Reports have not been published. Apart from pre- and post-test comparisons of test items and pupil and teacher interests in the units, no further examinations have been undertaken. The pupils' interest was regarded as the most important variable for the acceptance of a curriculum unit.

Evaluations of the German RCFP included a sample of over 7,000 pupils; results of interest scales, cognitive test items, and correlations between variables were published (German Geography Curriculum Project 1975–1981, Vols. 13 to 19). Methods of RCFP evaluation were presented at an OECD/CERI conference (Schrettenbrunner 1981). After completion of the RCFP program (1973 to 1978), a special evaluation project was financed by the Science Foundation (DFG) where experimental designs, variance, and factor analyses were applied to determine pupils' reactions to different types of games (Schrettenbrunner 1980). A collection of international empirical studies examining the impact the program units have on attitudes towards geography was published by Schrettenbrunner (1976, 1978).

Bibliography

Aerni K 1981 Zur schweizerischen Schulgeographie. In: Schrettenbrunner H L (ed.) 1981 *Der Erdkundeunterricht*, Vol. 37. Klett, Stuttgart, pp. 5–17

Binder-Johnson H 1972 *Das High School Geography Project*. Tagungsbericht und wissenschaftliche Abhandlungen des Deutschen Geographentages, edited by Association of German Geographers. Steiner, Wiesbaden, pp. 232–38

Elbers D 1973 *Curriculumreformen in den USA: Ein Bericht über theoretische Ansätze und praktische Reformverfahren mit einer Dokumentation über Entwicklungsprojekte, Studien und Berichte*, Vol 28. Max-Planck-Institut, Berlin

Geipel R 1972 Perspective from Germany. In: Gunn A M (ed.) 1972

Gerber R, Lidstone J (eds.) 1988 *Developing Skills in Geographical Education*. The Jacaranola Press, Brisbane

German Geography Curriculum Project 1978 *Das Raumwissenschaftliche Curriculum Forschungsprojekt*. Westermann, Braunschweig

Graves N J 1979 *Curriculum Planning in Geography*. Heinemann, London

Gunn A M (ed.) 1972 *High School Geography Project: Legacy for the Seventies: An Analysis of the High School Geography Project in Relation to New Developments in Geographic Education Worldwide*. Centre Educatif et Culturel, Montreal

Haubrich H 1989 Bericht über internationale Entwicklungen in der Geographiedidaktik. *Geographie und ihre Didaktik* 3(89): 122–35

Irwin H, Baumgart N 1978 Quantitative Analyse der Auswirkungen eines Lernspiels. In: Schrettenbrunner H L (ed.) 1978 *Der Erdkundeunterricht*, Vol 28. Klett, Stuttgart, pp. 29–38

Jones G F 1976 Der Einfluß von unterrichtsmethode und Fähigkeit des Schülers auf den Lernerfolg, das Behalten und die Arbeitszeit. In: Schrettenbrunner H L (ed.) 1976 *Der Erdkundeunterricht*, Vol. 24. Klett, Stuttgart, pp. 110–17

Marsden W E 1980 The West German geography curriculum project: A comparative view. *J. Curric. Stud.* 12: 13–27

Parsons C 1987 *The Curriculum Change Game*. Falmer Press, London

Schrettenbrunner H L (ed.) 1976 Quantitative Didaktik der Geographie, Part 1. *Der Erdkundeunterricht*, Vol. 24. Klett, Stuttgart

Schrettenbrunner H L (ed.) 1978 Quantitative Didaktik der Geographie, Part 2. *Der Erdkundeunterricht*, Vol. 28. Klett, Stuttgart

Schrettenbrunner H L (ed.) 1980 Evaluationsberichte. *Materialien zu einer neuen Didaktik der Geographie*, Vol. 20. Uni-Druck, Munich

Schrettenbrunner H L 1981 Die Evaluation des RCFP. *Schulentwicklung*, Vol. 4. Bundesveirag, Vienna, pp. 208–25

Slater F 1976 Die Entwicklung von geographischen Fragestellungen bei Jugendlichen. In: Schrettenbrunner H L (ed.) 1976 *Der Erdkundeunterricht*, Vol. 24. Klett, Stuttgart, pp. 99–109

Sperling W 1977 *Geographie und Geographieunterricht in der DDR*. List, Munich

Watson D 1984 *Exploring Geography with Microcomputers*. Council for Educational Technology, London

Civic Education

J. Torney-Purta

Civic education (or citizenship education) is that portion of the explicitly stated and implicitly expressed curriculum of educational institutions which socializes individuals to membership in their political community (at both the national and local levels). Its explicit aims usually include loyalty to the nation, knowledge of the history and structure of political institutions, positive attitudes toward political authority, obedience to laws and social norms, belief in fundamental values of the society such as equality, interest in political participation, sense of political efficacy, and skill in analyzing political communications. Sometimes the presentation of material about other nations is included to help the student acquire citizenship in a global context.

In some countries, schools offer or require courses titled Civics, Civic and Moral Education, or Government. In other countries, courses in history or social studies are given the major responsibility for fulfilling these aims. Nonformal civic education programs for adults are becoming increasingly common.

1. Civic Education Policy and the Explicit Curriculum

The stated general aims of civic education show considerable similarity in many countries of the world. Lists of values important for all citizens to acquire have been developed in an independent but parallel fashion in several nations. Butts (an American educational historian) has suggested that this list should include values relating to both unity in society (e.g., justice, equality, authority, participation, and personal obligation for the public good) and pluralism (e.g., freedom, diversity, privacy, due process, and international human rights) (Butts 1980). In the United Kingdom, a similar list of procedural values which should be universally supported has been proposed—freedom, toleration, fairness, respect for truth, and respect for reasoning (Porter 1981). Hilligen (in developing civic education curriculum in the Federal Republic of Germany) arrived at the following list of fundamental values on which members of society should agree: the guarantee of human rights, the establishment of social conditions which enable individuals to develop freely, and the creation of institutions which allow for the free play of social forces (Hilligen cited in Kuhn 1977). Lists of curriculum goals from countries in other world regions share many of these common values (Gross and Dufty 1980, Mehlinger and Tucker 1979, Cummings et al. 1988).

In response to variety in the political and historical context, however, the specific content of civic education curricula also varies across nations. In countries with centralized educational systems, policy relating to the explicit aims of civic education may be found in curriculum statements issued by ministries of education (e.g., Sweden, Nigeria). In some nations, a particular textbook will be prescribed and very similar methods followed over the entire country. In other centralized nations, schools or teachers may choose from lists of approved textbooks in implementing civic education goals.

In some federal systems, there is considerable homogeneity within states or provinces (e.g., Canada). In still other federal systems, decisions about civic education policy are highly decentralized. In the United States, for example, more than 17,000 school boards shape curricula and choose textbooks for local districts. Some homogeneity of objectives exists nevertheless. Mandates in all 50 states require education either about the American Constitution or about United States history. For nearly 70 years, courses in civics have been taught in most districts at ages 14 and 17; courses in American history have been taught at ages 10, 13, and 16. This sequence of courses was established in response to a report by the National Education Association and has been reinforced by the publication of textbooks suitable for these levels by private companies. A number of citizenship education and law-related education projects have recently produced new materials for use in these courses. In the United Kingdom system, which is also highly decentralized, it was assumed for many generations that citizenship skills would be implicitly transmitted to the majority of students, while a small proportion prepared themselves for an examination in British Constitution (and received more explicit instruction). Recently a need for broader approaches reaching larger groups has been recognized. Materials to promote political literacy have been produced and are in use in a number of schools (Porter 1981, Harber 1987). Since 1985 there has been a swing toward more inculcation of traditional values.

Civic education policy may be accounted for by a complex blend of factors. Massive immigration and the need to build national loyalty and patriotism has long characterized American schooling. Recent waves of immigration in Israel and the need to build national unity in newly independent countries of Africa have resulted in similar emphases (Ichilov 1981, Merryfield in press). Rapid economic growth has stimulated programs to replace traditional values with those more suitable to industrial democracy in countries of Asia, Latin America, and the Middle East. At the end of the Second World War, civic education in the Federal Republic of Germany, the German Democratic Republic, and Japan was completely revised (primarily by importing programs) (Torney-Purta and Schwille 1986, Davey 1987, Hanhardt 1978).

It is widely recognized that the family makes a unique contribution to the acquisition of civic values. Countries differ in the extent to which family policy is tied to civic education policy. In some countries civic education has been the subject of partisan political debate; parents have had the opportunity to choose between candidates representing conservative, liberal, and radical views about education for citizenship (Kuhn 1977). In the United States, parents influence the local elections of school boards and often attempt in more indirect ways to shape the civics curriculum. Although parent advisory groups exist in Japan, a strong national teachers' union is more influential in civic education policy.

A wide variety of methods have been suggested for teaching citizenship. A rote approach, which relies on memorization of factual material from lectures and textbooks, is probably the most common. However, research in the United States, the United Kingdom, and several other nations has indicated that taking civics courses has an impact upon knowledge of politics for only a small group of students (and has even less impact on attitudes) (Ehman 1980). In response to the low level of student interest generated by rote methods, a number of countries in several regions have tried to implement approaches which encourage students to inquire into the causes and solutions for social problems. These innovations have had only modest success, even in countries which have invested considerable resources in special curriculum development. Some point to the traditional culture of the school interfering with successful innovation. A recent survey in the United States indicated that the large majority of social studies teachers rely on the textbook and structured methods of learning. It is therefore important to note that studies to improve the presentation of other nations in textbooks have been undertaken multilaterally (under the auspices of UNESCO and specialized textbook institutes, e.g., the International Textbook Institute at Brunswick, FRG) and bilaterally, for example, between the United States and the Soviet Union; between the United States and Japan; and between the Federal Republic of Germany and Poland (Berghahn and Schissler 1987). Education to make students more sophisticated consumers of the mass media has also been undertaken in several nations.

2. The Implicit Curriculum in Civic Education

In addition to the explicit or manifest curriculum, it is widely recognized that an implicit curriculum influences the civic attitudes which students acquire. What is sometimes called "the hidden curriculum" includes the authority relationships and climate for expression of opinion within the school, as well as opportunities for students to participate in decisions about school policy (see *Hidden Curriculum*). Research has demonstrated the powerful way in which fairness in the administration of school rules and students' expectations about their power in school decision making influence attitudes and behavior (Ehman 1980).

Some criticize civic education programs for training students to support the political and economic status quo. They argue that the hidden curriculum of power relationships contradicts the explicit curricular aims and perpetuates injustice (Tapper and Selzer 1978). Sweden provides interesting examples of the role of factors in the hidden curriculum which may hinder change (Englund 1986).

In most Western European countries, the peer group culture is thought of as part of the implicit curriculum. In some nations of Eastern Europe and Israel age-graded youth collectives play an important role in both explicit and implicit civic education (Kedem and Ber-Lev 1989).

3. Cross-national Research in Civic Education

In 1971 a large-scale comparative survey of civic education was conducted by the International Association for the Evaluation of Educational Achievement (IEA) (Torney et al. 1975). Its results address a number of questions about the influence of different aspects of civic education programs. The investigators began by collecting materials describing the objectives of civic education in the participant nations and constructed both cognitive and attitudinal questionnaires to measure the most important outcomes.

Questionnaire data were analyzed for 10-year-olds, 14-year-olds, and students in the last year of pre-university education in the Federal Republic of Germany, Finland, Ireland, Israel, Italy, the Netherlands, New Zealand, Sweden, and the United States. Some countries tested only one or two age groups, however. The stratified samples include more than 30,000 students, 5,000 teachers, and 1,300 principals and headteachers.

The highest scores on the cognitive test among the 14-year-olds were achieved by students in the Netherlands, the Federal Republic of Germany, and Israel. The highest scores on the cognitive test among the preuniversity students were achieved in New Zealand, the Federal Republic of Germany, and Sweden.

When the attitudinal scales were factor analyzed, several independent clusters appeared. The first factor was labeled "support for democratic values" and included scales measuring antiauthoritarianism, support for women's rights, tolerance and support for civil liberties, and support for equality. The second factor was labeled "support for the national government" and included scales measuring positive evaluation of the national government, responsiveness of the national government to citizen demands, and sense of political efficacy. The third factor was labeled "civic interest/participation" and included civic activities, participation in political discussion, and interest in current events television.

Further analysis indicated that there was no single prototype good citizen in these countries (which share many democratic traditions). For example, a student who was high in support for democratic values was not necessarily high in expressed interest in civic participation. Knowledge of civics showed some positive relations to support for democratic values but not to the other clusters of attitudes.

Scores based on the three major attitude clusters were formed, and the countries were compared (14-year-olds and preuniversity students only). In none of these countries did students score above the mean on all three attitudinal factors. All nations where the 14-year-olds had an average score which was above the mean on support for the national government and on civic interest/participation had an average score which was below the mean on support for democratic values (and vice versa). For example, students in the Netherlands and the Federal Republic of Germany showed high levels of support for democratic values but relatively low levels of interest in political activities (and only a modest level of support for the national government and sense of political efficacy). In contrast, students in the United States were positive about their government and interested in participation. However, they had relatively low scores on support for democratic values (and were the lowest of all countries in their support for women's rights).

A regression analysis of the IEA data indicated that an open classroom climate was a positive factor in civic education across countries. Specifically, the extent to which teachers encouraged expression of opinion by students in the classroom was positively related to high cognitive scores, to less authoritarian attitudes, and to more participation in political discussion among students in all countries tested. A measure of the extent to which patriotic rituals were practiced in the classroom (e.g., flag ceremonials or singing patriotic songs) was negatively correlated with cognitive civics achievements. The students in classes where patriotism was stressed were more authoritarian, but they expressed more interest in political discussion. Students who reported extensive use of printed drill materials were less knowledgeable and more authoritarian in several countries. These variables were significant predictors of civic education outcomes even after the effects of home background and type of school had been partialled out. Although civic education programs vary considerably, those which stress the expression of opinion rather than rote and ritual appear to be more successful in achieving both cognitive and attitudinal goals, at least in Western European countries (Torney-Purta and Schwille 1986).

The structure of society as a whole (as well as the implicit and explicit curriculum) appeared to influence the extent to which students supported women's rights and the extent to which they were interested in international politics (in contrast to national politics) (Torney 1977).

The findings indicate the complexity of improving civic education. There was no single modal democratic personality type, but two or three basic patterns with numerous variations among the countries. There appears to be an incompatibility between achieving support for democratic values and achieving support for the government, a sense of political efficacy, and interest in participation. Teachers in these nations agreed that a wide variety of characteristics should be fostered in civic education, but the pedagogy for achieving them was not clear. The traditional approach, stressing knowledge acquisition especially through rote memorization, appears to be counterproductive; it is, however, the approach which is most common in civic education and has been resistant to change. An open classroom climate is the only factor which is clearly positive in its impact in all countries. However, it is difficult to train or retrain teachers to foster such an atmosphere.

Although Japan was not a participant in the IEA project, several studies of textbooks and civic attitudes have been conducted there. Immediately after the Second World War, American curriculum materials were imported. After about a decade, the need to adapt that material to the Japanese situation became obvious. Not only had the "new education" eliminated the nationalistic stress of the 1930s to 1940s, but it had also excised basic Japanese cultural values. The current generation of Japanese students seems to blend the notion of democracy as majority rule with the cultural tradition of group consensus in decision making (Massey 1976). Although democracy as a symbol is important, the symbolic value of peace is greater. Japanese see their country as having a particular role in promoting peace, and democracy is valued as a means to that end. Attitudes of students toward the prime minister were not nearly as favorable as those which American students express about the president. This was attributed to the tendency for Japanese civics textbooks to present a neutral view of political figures (in order not to be accused of partisanship). By the time Japanese students arrive at university they are quite knowledgeable about international issues, but their knowledge of politics does not grow very much during university training (Cogan et al. 1988).

A recent study of political socialization among secondary-school students in Kenya compared students in harambee schools (community controlled and with a strong self-help orientation) with those in schools aided and controlled by the national government (Keller 1978). Although there is little manifest civic education, the large majority of students were supportive of national political authorities. The harambee students were less informed about politics, less interested in a broad range of political issues, and less egalitarian. They were more likely to have discussed development issues and to have been involved in local improvement projects (which they perceived as furthering national development).

4. The Future of Civic Education

There is growing interest in examining programs of civic education as they form part of the social studies curriculum in a variety of nations. Research on social studies, for example the role of discussion of controversial issues or the influence of teacher training, is expanding rapidly (Shaver in press). New interest exists in research on political socialization which includes the influence of family, media, and political organizations as well as schools (Ichilov 1990), in the application of methods of cognitive psychology to the study of political cognition in young people (Torney-Purta 1989, 1990), and in research using qualitative methods to study the implicit transmission of values. All of these areas have implications for civic education policy and practice.

Bibliography

Berghahn V, Schissler H (eds.) 1987 *Perceptions of History: International Textbook Research in Britain, Germany and the United States*. Berg, Oxford

Butts R F 1980 *The Revival of Civic Learning: A Rationale for Citizenship Education in American Schools*. Phi Delta Kappa Educational Foundation, Bloomington, Indiana

Cogan J, Torney-Purta J, Anderson D 1988 Knowledge and attitudes toward global issues: Students in Japan and the United States. *Comp. Educ. Rev.* 32: 282–97

Cummings W, Gopinathan S, Tomoda Y (eds.) 1988 *Values Education: An International Comparison of Origins and Policies*. Pergamon Press, Oxford

Davey T 1987 *Generation Divided*. Duke University Press, Durham, North Carolina

Ehman L H 1980 The American school in the political socialization process. *Rev. Educ. Res.* 50: 99–119

Englund T 1986 *Curriculum as a Political Problem: Changing Educational Conceptions with Special Reference to Citizenship Education*. Almqvist and Wiksell, Stockholm

Gross R E, Dufty D 1980 *Learning to Live in Society: Toward a World View of the Social Studies*. Social Science Education Consortium, Boulder, Colorado

Hanhardt A M Jr 1975 East Germany: From goals to realities. In: Volgyes I (ed.) 1975 *Political Socialization in Eastern Europe: A Comparative Framework*. Praeger, New York

Harber C 1987 *Political Education in Britain*. Falmer Press, Lewes

Ichilov O 1981 Citizenship orientations of city and kibbutz youth in Israel. *Int. J. Polit. Educ.* 4: 305–17

Ichilov O (ed.) 1990 *Political Socialization and Citizenship Education in Democracy*. Teachers College Press, New York

Kedem P, Bar-Lev M 1989 Does political socialization in adolescence have a lasting influence? *Polit. Psych.* 10: 391–416

Keller E J 1978 The political socialization of adolescents in contemporary Africa. *Comp. Politics* 10: 227–50

Kuhn A 1977 Leading positions in political education in the Federal Republic of Germany today. *Int. J. Polit. Educ.* 1: 33–44

Massey J A 1976 *Youth and Politics in Japan*. Lexington Books, Lexington, Massachusetts

Mehlinger J, Tucker J (eds.) 1979 *Social Studies in Other Nations*. National Council for the Social Studies, Washington, DC

Merryfield M in press Research on social studies in Africa. In: Shaver J (ed.) in press. *Handbook of Research on Social Studies Teaching and Learning*. Macmillan, New York

Porter A 1981 Political literacy. In: Heater D, Gillespie J A (eds.) 1981 *Political Education in Flux*. Sage, London

Shaver J (ed.) in press *Handbook of Research on Social Studies Teaching and Learning*. Macmillan, New York

Tapper T, Selzer B 1978 *Evaluation and the Political Order*. Macmillan, London

Torney J 1977 The international attitudes and knowledge of adolescents in nine countries. *Int. J. Polit. Educ.* 1: 3–20

Torney J, Oppenheim A N, Farnen R F 1975 *Civic Education in Ten Countries: An Empirical Study*. Almqvist and Wiksell, Stockholm

Torney-Purta J 1989 Political cognition and its restructuring in adolescents. *Human Devl.* 32: 14–23

Torney-Purta J 1990 From attitudes to schemata: Expanding the outcomes of political socialization research. In: Ichilov O (ed.) 1990 *Political Socialization and Citizenship Education in Democracy*. Teachers College Press, New York

Torney-Purta J, Schwille J 1986 Civic values learned in school: Policy and practice in industrialized countries. *Comp. Educ. Rev.* 30: 30–49

Economics: Educational Programs

M. Kourilsky

Every research discipline has three categories of expertise: (a) that which adds to the theory of the discipline; (b) that which applies the tools of the discipline; and (c) that which studies systematic ways of communicating the theory and application. There are economic theorists, economic application experts, and economic educators. It is this third category of expertise which is the focus of this article. Economic education for children aged 5–18 will be discussed from an historical perspective to the current state of the art with an emphasis on prototype programs and new research directions in the field. Economic education programs exist in the United Kingdom and Canada, and there is some isolated activity in other parts of the world including Scandinavia and Australia. However, the major research activity in this area is currently centered in the United States.

Chief among the goals of economic education is economic literacy. This is the ability of citizens to operate effectively in the economic areas of their lives as workers, voters, and consumers. It is not merely common sense nor intuition. Economic literacy is rational economic decision making utilizing a process of economic analysis and the skills of economic reasoning. Economic literacy, gained through economic education, both elementary and secondary, remains relevant throughout adulthood as people apply logical economic principles, not myths, to the economic realities of their lives. If students are not given economic training before college, it is much more difficult to develop both the conceptual understanding and the analytical skills needed for economic literacy. The attainment of economic literacy hinges upon combining the elements of economic reasoning in a variety of real-world decision-making situations as students and adults.

The field of economic education for kindergarten through 12th grades (K–12), appears to progress in predictable stages within a given country: (a) the recognition and adoption of economic education as an educational priority; (b) the relatively unstructured development and implementation of economic curricula; (c) the recognition of the relationship of child development and learning theory to curricular decision making (in economic education); and (d) the systematic research endeavors necessary to integrate curricular development and decision making (in economic education) with the principles of child development and learning theory.

Until the middle of the 1960s, most of the literature on economic education dealt with the question of whether there was a need for economic education in the curriculum prior to college. That question was answered in the affirmative in the United States as revealed by the United States Task Force Report of 1961. Subsequently similar affirmative answers were obtained in other parts of the world including the Scandinavian countries, the United Kingdom, Australia, and Canada. By the end of the 1960s a strong realization of the desirability of economic education and a commitment to implementing programs was manifested in many countries, but most visibly within the United States. The challenge to economic education in the 1970s expanded to include precisely how to bring about an effective (K–12) curriculum in economics and how to train implementors and disseminators.

The research in the 1970s addressed two major issues with respect to economic education in kindergarten through high school: (a) what facets of economics *can* actually be taught prior to college; and (b) which of those concepts are important to teach. However, the end results of this research were primarily ad hoc curricula. Economic concepts were sometimes ranked on a continuum of easiest to most difficult and introduced accordingly; more often they were assigned arbitrarily to grade levels on the rationale that with proper instructional intervention any concept could be taught at any grade level. There was a deluge of curricula in which scarcity was taught in kindergarten, opportunity cost in the first grade, and so on. Although these curricula reflected some sequencing of ideas, they tended to disregard the developmental stages of learners as well as the depth of inquiry and critical thinking skills necessary to master the concepts. Similar approaches were tried and discarded in the teaching of history. For example, in the United States the Revolutionary War was taught in the third grade, the Civil War in the fourth, and the First World War in the fifth. Economic educators also began to realize that sequencing of concepts alone would not result in learning at desirable levels of cognition (Hansen et al. 1977, Highsmith and Little 1981, Kourilsky 1981).

In the late 1970s and early 1980s economic education experienced significant advancement in its state of the art. Attempts were initiated to broaden the scope of curricula to reflect the developmental/heuristic hierarchy of the learners. Questions addressed in the research literature expanded to include what *should* be taught from a developmental point of view, at what grade level, and to what degree. It was discovered that children as young as kindergarten age could understand a concept like opportunity cost when applying it in choosing a recess game. At the high-school level some learners were developmentally ready to apply the same concept at a much more complex level such as assessing the time value of money (Larkins and Shaver 1969, Kourilsky 1977). Thus it became apparent that concepts could and should be repeated in the curriculum at different grade levels to obtain ascending levels of cognition. This realization is reflected to varying degrees in programs which represent the major models in use today for teaching economics.

1. Current Models for Teaching Economics

The principal current models for teaching economics can be characterized as: (a) media based; (b) experience based; and (c) textbook/materials based. Some contemporary programs that are prototypes of these models and whose effectiveness have been empirically verified and reported in the research literature are described below.

Media-based education places major emphasis on the use of films. In most cases the films are not utilized as a total instructional system but rather are employed as instructional aids. The rationale for using media in teaching economics is to increase cognition through multisensory stimulus and to enhance motivation by depicting concepts in the context of interesting and/or familiar environments.

Trade-offs (Joint Council on Economic Education 1978) and *The People on Market Street* (Disney Corp. 1978) are two widely used media programs. *Trade-offs* is a television/film series consisting of 15 programs designed to improve and expand economics instruction in grades 5–8. Each program is 15–20 minutes long and focuses on a specific economic principle, for example, "demand." The programs are used as motivators for economic lessons, class discussions, and follow-up activities. *The People on Market Street* is a seven-part film series geared to the cognitive sophistication of secondary students. As with *Trade-offs*, each film focuses on one economic concept, but at a higher level of analysis. Series of this type usually include question sets, explanations of economic principles and their current applications, and student activities.

Studies on each of these programs have indicated significant improvement in student knowledge of and attitude toward economics. It is also interesting to note that students of teachers specifically trained in the use of these series significantly outscored those viewing the same with untrained teachers (Walstad 1980).

Experience-based models are based on the premises of active versus passive learner roles, personal as opposed to vicarious involvement, and the importance of decision making in which learners actually bear the consequences of their decisions (see *Experienced-based Studies*).

The most extensively implemented experience-based program is Mini-Society (grades 3–6), with Kinder-Economy (grades K–2), and Maxi-Economy I and II (middle- and senior-high school) being offshoots of the original program (Kourilsky 1977, 1983). Although all three programs concentrate on economics and the experience-based approach, each of the three program designs was carefully tailored for the specific intellectual development stage of the program's intended student users.

Mini-Society is designed as a 10–20 week unit in which the students actually experience and then resolve various economic problems through the creation and development of their own classroom society. The program utilizes two complementary components: the economic experiences themselves and a formal post-experience debriefing procedure for the concepts and ideas derived from these experiences. The formal debriefing paradigm is the key to integrating into the students' formal knowledge base the concepts which emerge from the experience-based activities. The Mini-Society participants are the decision makers as they design and print their own currency, buy and sell student-conceived and student-produced goods and services, and resolve the economic dilemmas they are certain to encounter. Teachers are specifically trained in the 25 predictable economic dilemmas which arise in most economic systems, and in the facilitation of the Mini-Society.

Studies on the effectiveness of the Mini-Society programs have revealed significant gains in economic understanding as well as increases in learner self-concept, autonomy, personal responsibility, and favorable attitudes toward school and learning (Kourilsky and Hirshleifer 1976, Kourilsky 1979b, Cassuto 1980).

The materials-based model usually combines textbook reading with teacher exposition and class discussion. One of the principal rationales for a materials-based model to teach economics is that a written text allows both the student and the teacher to access repeatedly specific text materials without regard to order of appearance in the text. It is assumed that because of the perceived difficulty of digesting economic concepts, learners will benefit from the capability of individualized, repeated, and random access to presented material. A typical learning sequence involves assignment of a chapter to read, teacher presentation of the content of the chapter, and classroom discussion/ activities that are often suggested in the teacher's guide.

Our Working World (Senesh 1973), *Our Economy: How It Works* (Clawson 1979), and *Managing Your Money* (Wolf 1977) are examples of texts widely used in the United States at the grade-school, middle-school, and high-school levels respectively. Although these texts are geared to different grade levels, they can be characterized by a tendency to introduce economic concepts in the context of everyday life applications. All three books have been shown to enhance economic knowledge (Yankelovich et al. 1981).

2. Research in Economic Education

The key research in economic education appears to be moving in new directions with its focus guided by the following premises:

(a) *Children are not miniature adults.* Attempts are being made to systematically integrate economic concepts into curricula according to psychological criteria. Investigations are concerned with whether learners are developmentally ready to learn a particular concept and at what level of abstraction. Economic educators are taking into account in their research that the learners they are addressing, regardless of their intelligence, progress through different stages of cognitive development ranging from preoperational to formal operations (Fox 1978, Kourilsky 1981) (see *Cognitive Development*).

(b) *Research in economic education is more than "show and tell" activities.* The preponderance of papers and articles on "What I did in my class" and "Method A versus method B," is slowly giving way to studies on the underlying principles of learning which are common to large classes of successful programs in economics as well as investigations of models of teaching excellence (Saunders et al. 1978, Kourilsky 1981, Lima 1981).

(c) *The students of the K-12 classroom teachers must be viewed as the ultimate consumers of economic education.* In the past, inservice training, staff development, and economic education workshops were geared toward enriching the teacher's knowledge of economics with little or no systematic assessment of whether such knowledge was transferred to their students. The newest trend is to view the teachers as intermediaries and to conduct research on the acquisition of concepts, skills, and attitudes of their learners—the ultimate consumers of economic education (Kourilsky 1980, Walstad 1980).

Bibliography

Cassuto A 1980 The effectiveness of the elementary school Mini-Society Program. *J. Econ. Educ.* 11: 59–61

Clawson M 1979 *Our Economy: How It Works*. Addison-Wesley, Menlo Park, California

Fox K F A 1978 What children bring to school: The beginnings of economic education. *Soc. Educ.* 42: 478–81

Hansen L et al. 1977 *Master Curriculum Guide in Economics for the Nation's Schools. Part I, A Framework for Teaching Economics: Basic Concepts*. Joint Council on Economic Education, New York

Highsmith R, Little L 1981 *A Scope and Sequence Outline for Teaching Economics K–12*. Economic Literacy Council of California, Long Beach, California

Joyce L 1979 Understanding productivity. *Understanding Economics*, Series No. 2. Canadian Foundation for Economic Education, Toronto, Ontario, ERIC Document No. ED 173 188

Kourilsky M 1977 The Kinder-Economy: A case study of kindergarten pupils' acquisition of economic concepts. *Elem. Sch. J.* 77: 182-91

Kourilsky M 1979a Rx for economic illiteracy. *TELemetry* 7(2): 1–9

Kourilsky M 1979b Optimal intervention: An empirical investigation of the role of teacher in experience-based instruction. *J. Exp. Educ.* 47: 339–45

Kourilsky M 1980 Predictors of entrepreneurship in a simulated economy. *J. Creat. Behav.* 14: 175–98

Kourilsky M 1981 Economic socialization of children: Attitude toward the distribution of rewards. *J. Soc. Psychol.* 115: 45–57

Kourilsky M 1983 *Mini-Society: Experiencing Real-world Economics in the Elementary School Classroom*. Addison-Wesley, Menlo Park, California

Kourilsky M, Hirshleifer J 1976 Mini-Society vs. token economy: An experimental comparison of the effects on learning and autonomy of socially emergent and imposed behavior modification. *J. Educ. Res.* 69: 376–81

Larkins A G, Shaver J P 1969 Economics learning in grade one: The USU assessment studies. *Soc. Educ.* 33: 958–63

Lima A 1981 An economic model of teaching effectiveness. *Am. Econ. Rev.* 71: 1056–59

National Task Force on Economic Education 1961 *Economic Education in the Schools: Summary of the Report*. Committee for Economic Development, New York

Ryba R, Robinson B (eds.) 1980 Aspects of upper secondary economics education in EEC countries. Economics Association of London, ERIC Document No. ED 187 636

Saunders P, Welsh A, Hansen L (eds.) 1978 *Resource for Teacher Training Programs in Economics*, No. 271. Joint Council on Economic Education, New York

Senesh L 1973 *Our Working World*. Science Research Associates, Chicago Illinois

Walstad W B 1979 Effectiveness of a USMES in-service economic education program for elementary school teachers. *J. Econ. Educ.* 11(1): 1-12

Walstad W B 1980 The impact of trade-offs and teacher training on economic understanding and attitudes. *J. Econ. Educ.* 12(1): 41–48

Wolf H A 1977 *Managing Your Money*. Allyn and Bacon, Boston, Massachusetts

Yankelovich S Kelley, White, Inc. 1981 *National Survey of Economic Education 1981—Grades 6–12*. Playback Associates, New York

The People on Market Street. A filmstrip produced by the Disney Corporation, Burbank, California (released 1978)

Trade-offs. A movie series produced by the Joint Council on Economic Education, New York (released 1978)

Sociology: Educational Programs

Y. Kashti and M. Arieli

Sociology as a structured scientific discipline emerged in the nineteenth century and became incorporated into the school program in several European communities at the beginning of the twentieth century and in the United States after the Second World War. It is taught in the higher grades of secondary schools mostly as an elective subject. Nevertheless, topics related to the domain of sociology appear in the school program within the broader framework of social studies at the lower levels of the primary school.

1. The Objectives

The objectives of teaching sociology vary from one course to another, reflecting different approaches to the discipline. Some programs are designed to acquaint the students with the principles of a scientific discipline as part of their general education and as an introductory experience to possible specialization in the subject at university. In this respect, the purpose of teaching sociology is not different from the purpose of teaching other subjects such as history or biology (Fenton 1966). Another objective frequently stressed in sociology programs is guiding students to understand society. The assumption underlying this objective is that learning sociology will assist the students in understanding social phenomena in which they participate or which they closely observe, on the one hand, and in becoming aware of the ways societies and social phenomena are structured and arranged and of the mechanisms which account for social stability and change, on the other hand. It is further assumed that these understandings will contribute to the students' socialization and acculturation as well as to the nature of their social and moral judgments and resolutions. A third objective relates to the belief that the knowledge of sociology may improve the students' social skills, such as objective perception of social situations and the ability to form rational courses of action throughout their social interactions (McLendon 1965, Moreland 1965). These three objectives are not equally acceptable to all curriculum developers and teachers of sociology. Those who raise doubts concerning the nature of sociology as a science are reluctant to teach sociology as a structured discipline and prefer to confront the students with a variety of problems and documents representing social paradigms such as the structural, the conflict, or the interpretive–reflexive approach. Others doubt the possible contribution of sociology to the improving of the objectivity, or the rationality of students' social understanding. The latter tend to stress what they believe to be the ideological nature of any sociological paradigm.

2. The Content of the Courses

Sociology courses manifest a greater variation of content than is found in school programs for other structured disciplines such as physics, chemistry, and so on. Subsequently, the autonomy of the social studies departments at schools and that of individual sociology teachers in setting the curriculum is relatively wide. This state of affairs characterizes, for example, the situation in the United States (Fenton 1967). Even in centralized educational systems, where very specific guidelines prescribe the content of the school program in most subjects, great variation in sociology programs will be found. Some programs include primarily the study of macrosocial structures and arrangements such as institutionalization and stratification, while others concentrate on the study of microsocial processes such as patterns of interaction among actors in various social scenes. Some programs are devoted to general social theory which is regarded as universal, while others are devoted to theories relating to specific institutions, the political, the legal, the economic, and so on, and to specific social contexts, such as the state or the community in which the school functions. Several programs stress formal aspects such as socialization, mobility, or stigma, while others stress substantive areas such as ethnic relations, social integration at school, or the social nature of various professions and occupations. The choice of subject matter and paradigms for the sociology curriculum, like the choice of subject matter for the curriculum of other subjects in the humanities and the arts, is a social act in itself. Since curriculum developers and sociology teachers are often the mediators of prevailing social orders, their choice tends toward sociological approaches and contents which explain the social order that prevails in their communities. This state of affairs may indirectly cause a situation whereby the teaching of sociology functions as a means of ideological legitimation of the prevailing social order (Young 1971). Teachers and curriculum planners regard the arousal of interest and motivation of the pupils in sociology at an earlier stage as difficult. While most educational systems offer sociology as an academic choice, several systems include sociology in the curricula of all secondary schools: academic and nonacademic. It is assumed that students of nonacademic schools who do not identify subjects in the humanities and arts as relevant for them may consider sociological issues which relate to known social problems as relevant and important. This state of affairs may increase the students' motivation to study sociology and view school as an institution where important issues are dealt with. Several programs, such as the Harvard Program (Oliver and Shaver 1966, Shaver 1966), structure their curriculum by selecting important social issues, such as poverty, and presenting them in an interdisciplinary manner. Other programs, such as the program developed by Fenton (1966), stress the study of the independent sociological discipline rather than the study of the interdisciplinary social issue. In some countries the interdisciplinary social approach prevails in the lower grades (Carlton 1972), while the disciplinary approach prevails in the higher grades.

3. Teaching and Learning Methods

The ways sociology is taught relate to the decisions taken by the curriculum planners and the teachers concerning the objectives of the teaching of sociology, the nature of the selected subject matter, and the students' academic and social characteristics. The following are common ways of teaching sociology: (a) analysis of official or research documents which relate to issues of the community to which the students belong; (b) individual or group examination of research questions or hypotheses through questionnaires, interviews, or observations; the processing and the discussing of the data; (c) simulation games, where the students enter the process of role taking and decision making in various social situations; (d) classroom reading and discussing of short essays written by social scientists; (e) classroom discussion of material prepared by the students before the lesson. It seems that the two latter methods are the most common, although the practice of the first three methods is spreading in various countries.

Bibliography

Carlton R 1972 Sociology in the high school curriculum: A problem of cultural delay. *Interchange* 3: 178–87

Fenton E 1966 *Teaching the New Social Studies in Secondary Schools: An Inductive Approach.* Holt, Rinehart and Winston, New York, pp. 290–382

Fenton E 1967 *The New Social Studies.* Holt, Rinehart and Winston, New York

McLendon J C 1965 *Social Studies in Secondary Education.* Macmillan, New York

Moreland W D (ed.) 1965 *Social Studies in the Senior High School: Programs for Grades Ten, Eleven, and Twelve.* National Council for Social Studies, Washington, DC

Oliver D W, Shaver J P 1966 *Teaching Public Issues in the High School.* Houghton Mifflin, Boston, Massachusetts, pp. 98–120

Shaver J P 1966 *Values and the Social Studies.* Boston, Massachusetts, pp. 45–70

Young M F D (ed.) 1971 *Knowledge and Control: New Directions for the Sociology of Education.* Collier-Macmillan, London

Psychology: Educational Programs

K. M. White and H. Marcucella

Psychology is generally defined as the scientific study of human behavior. As pointed out by the American Psychological Association (1980), "The study of psychology is often important for better understanding, as well as for responsible decision making in numerous areas of public concern." Indeed it has been argued that psychology as a course of study probably has achieved much of its popularity through its implicit promise of a pathway to human understanding. Young people, at least in recent decades, have frequently expressed an interest in understanding themselves and others. This goal may take new forms in the 1980s and 1990s—for example, there might be an increasing concern over achieving control (of self, of others, of the environment)—but it seems unlikely that late adolescents and young adults will lose their interest in understanding and predicting human behavior, or that psychology courses will be seen as irrelevant to this goal.

1. College-level Teaching: The Introductory Course

On the basis of 43 site visits and 193 questionnaires, Irion (1976) provides useful information on the college-level introductory psychology course. Irion notes that whether the teaching is done in large classes or small, by junior or by senior staff, the introductory college course represents very big academic business. Extrapolating from his own sample, he estimates that between 70 and 80 percent of all undergraduate students take that one course, and that about 10 percent of this group go on to declare a psychology major. Indeed, the very popularity of the psychology course and the consequent need to handle students in large numbers presents a problem to many institutions where faculty believe that teaching large numbers of students in a survey course will not contribute to promotion and tenure.

Irion (1976) reports that the format of introductory psychology courses is quite variable, with lecture-only format more common in public colleges and both public and private universities than in community and liberal arts colleges. Course content is also variable. Of the schools surveyed, 130 reported using a total of 45 different textbooks—although, as Irion points out, many of these books can be considered more or less interchangeable. A question about the relative importance of various subtopic areas revealed no consistent pattern of emphasis beyond an acknowledgment of the importance of methodology and "experimental psychology" (except in community colleges where personality theory and personal adjustment were ranked highly).

2. High-school Psychology

Psychology has been a part of the secondary-school curriculum for a long time; the United States Office of Education has records dating back to 1900. Engle (1967a) reports that in the United States, psychology was commonly taught in secondary schools in the nineteenth century, and at least five books were published prior to 1890 for use in high schools, of which an estimated half million copies were sold. Interest in high-school psychology (as indicated by introduction into secondary schools) grew steadily in the 1930s, 1940s, and early 1950s and of those courses introduced, only 9 percent were later dropped, sometimes because there were no trained teachers for them (Coffield and Engle 1960). The rate of growth slumped in the late 1950s, and early 1960s; but in the late 1960s and 1970s, high-school psychology has experienced a substantial growth. Indices of this growth include the number of schools offering psychology, the number of students taking courses, the number of teachers teaching psychology, and the number of states with certification requirements.

In the United States, the number of high schools offering psychology increased from 1,080 in 1950 to 5,779 in 1970. The percentage of high schools offering psychology was estimated in the early 1980s at 25–30 percent, compared with 10 percent in 1950. The number of students taking psychology courses has increased as the number of schools offering psychology has increased. Approximately 145,000 students were enrolled in psychology in 1960 to 1961, a total which jumped to 509,000 in 1970 to 1971.

Engle reports a tendency for high-school teachers to consider the application of psychological principles to personal problems of students as their number one objective, whereas psychologists tend to believe that the number one objective for the high-school course should be to develop an appreciation for psychology as a field of scientific knowledge. Teachers placed "personal problems" first and "scientific knowledge" second; psychologists ranked "scientific knowledge" first, and "personal problems" fourth. Noland (1967) reports in a survey of high-school psychologists and counselors in Ohio a similar split between favoring personal adjustment and scientific knowledge. Only 5 percent felt science should be the primary focus. However, when the question was phrased differently, 29 percent felt psychology should be taught "like chemistry or biology." And by far the majority favored a combination of the two approaches.

The content of the courses also reflects this disagreement. Engle (1967b) asked teachers and psychologists to rank order topics appropriate to psychology. Mental health and individuality stay high between 1967 and 1973; development and social behavior rose in importance; learning and motivation, rated highly by psychologists in 1967, dropped in the estimation of teachers in 1973. These topics may be restricted by biases in the available textbooks; Engle derived his list partially from the tables of contents of texts in use, and he found some correlation of the subject rank and emphasis by number of pages devoted to the topic in available texts. Goldman (1983) reported a continued increase in both the number of secondary schools offering psychology and in the number of students enrolling in psychology courses. However, secondary school psychology continued to be plagued by goal and curricular conflicts as well as by inadequate teacher training.

3. Psychology in the Elementary Schools

Psychology and behavioral science topics are taught as part of the science and social studies curricula in the primary grades as well as at the more advanced precollege levels. In a survey of teachers interested in inservice psychology training, it was found that elementary-school teachers included the following psychology and behavioral science topics in their curricula: sex-role development, attitude change and attitude measurement, behavioral surveys, perceptual illusions, power simulations, learning theory, and values and morality. Kasschau (1974) claims that psychological subject matter can be introduced appropriately as early as the fourth grade, especially if the selected topics relate directly to the problems of development and behavior the students are experiencing. Kasschau (1974) also describes briefly some sample curriculum projects suitable for the precollege years—two units on "dealing with the causes of behavior," one for grades 1–3 and one for grades 4–5; "dealing with aggressive behavior" for middle-school and junior-high students; and "the new model me" for high-school students. Prochaska and Prochaska (1983) reported the successful introduction of psychology to gifted fourth-graders. The students were capable of developing research questions and gathering and reporting data.

4. Concluding Comments

It seems clear that the subject matter of psychology—human behavior—pervades school classrooms from the elementary school through to university. The preparation of teachers to teach psychological concepts is variable, and probably declines in adequacy from the top-level university classrooms down through the secondary and elementary schools. The availability of a range of textbooks and curriculum materials seems to have increased at a more rapid rate than trained teachers. Despite some fluctuations in numbers of teachers, students, and classrooms, psychology as a field of study seems here to stay, recognized by many as holding promise for greater understanding of human problems and potentials.

Bibliography

American Psychological Association (APA) 1980 *Inservice Training Guidelines for Secondary School Teachers of Psychology*. APA, Washington, DC

Coffield K E, Engle T L 1960 High school psychology: A history and some observations. *Am. Psychol.* 15: 350–52

Engle T L 1967a Teaching psychology at the secondary level: Past, present, possible future. *J. Sch. Psychol.* 5: 168–76

Engle T L 1967b Objectives for and subject matter stressed in high school courses in psychology. *Am. Psychol.* 22: 162–66

Goldman J J 1983 Recent trends in secondary school psychology: The decade from Oberlin to HBCP. *Teaching of Psychology* 10(4): 228–229

Irion A L 1976 A survey of the introductory course in psychology. *Teach. Psychol.* 3: 3–8

Kasschau R A 1974 Teaching psychology before college: Why, when, and how. *New York Univ. Educ. Q.* 5: 19–25

Noland R L 1967 School psychologists and counselors view the role of the high school psychology course. *J. Sch. Psychol.* 5: 177–84

Prochaska J D, Prochaska J M 1983 Teaching psychology to elementary school gifted students. *Teaching of Psychology* 10(2): 82–884

Home Economics: Educational Programs

H. Taylor Spitze

The focus of home economics is the family in all its forms. Home economists serve families by helping them solve the practical problems of child rearing, of nutrition and health, of interpersonal relationships, of shelter, of clothing, and of the management of family resources to meet family goals.

Home economics is a profession and as such it serves society. It is also a field of study that draws knowledge from root disciplines in physical, behavioral, and social sciences, and in the arts.

According to a recent definition the aim of home economics is "to enable families, both as individual units and generally as a social institution, to build and maintain systems of action which lead (a) to maturing in individual self-formation and (b) to enlightened, cooperative participation in the critique and formation of social goals and means for accomplishing them" (Brown and Paulocci 1979 p. 23).

This aim does not seem to be in contradiction to the creed stated seven decades earlier by Ellen Richards, founder of home economics in the United States, who said that "Home Economics stands for,

(a) the ideal home life today unhampered by the traditions of the past,

(b) the utilization of all the resources of modern science to improve the home life,

(c) the freedom of the home from the dominance of things and their due subordination to ideals, and

(d) the simplicity in material surroundings which will most free the spirit for the more important and permanent interests of the home and society" (Lake Placid Conference 1904 p. 31).

The International Federation for Home Economics, with headquarters in Paris, is the professional organization which enables all home economists to join together. The December 1980 issue of its quarterly journal, formerly the *Bulletin*, now called *Economie Familiale* summarized the most recent quadrennial Congress, held in Manila with the theme "Home Economics, a Responsible Partner in Development."

The speaker whose task was to draw conclusions from the meetings, said, "One conclusion is inescapable. We must begin at the beginning . . . and concentrate on basic survival needs to which home economists may make some contribution. . . . Individuals must have air, water, food, rest, and then physical and emotional safety and freedom from danger before higher levels of belongingness and self-esteem may be addressed" (Green 1980).

Dr. Green identified 11 "pervasive sociological and economic worldwide issues of the next two decades" which had been addressed: (a) population growth; (b) housing and health care and the protection of community networks; (c) effect of technology on quality of life: (d) care of dependent persons; (e) intergenerational relationships; (f) family and work roles and power positions of men and women; (g) special care for high risk groups; (h) balance of technological development and environmental stewardship; (i) support of education for all ages; (j) appropriate government involvement along with private and corporate initiative; and (k) using resources without destroying future supplies. "There is a home economics component in all of these issues," she said.

Dr. Green emphasizes that "home economics works predominately in a preventive, educational, developmental mode rather than through remediation, therapy, or crisis intervention."

These statements help identify the content of home economics for school curricula. Nutrition is taught. In baby clinics in Zaire, the home economist tries to teach mothers that babies cannot live on manioc alone when they are weaned, and in the United States, the concern may be with overeating and heart attacks.

Child rearing is also taught. Boiling water to save children from diarrhea, or immunizations to prevent communicable disease may be foremost in some situa-

tions. In others, the focus may be on time for both parents to love and cuddle their children, or ways to help children grow up secure enough to avoid the need for abusing drugs, or ways to help parents feel secure enough not to abuse their children.

Family relations are taught. In one country home economists may serve as advocates in getting legislation passed to prevent a man from having more than one wife. In another the focus may be on decision making within the family, power among family members, development of respect and trust, or the care of the aging.

Likewise with shelter and clothing, the specifics vary as home economists relate to the use of resources, protection, status, and self-esteem.

Home economics, by whatever name, is taught in primary and secondary schools, vocational and technical schools, colleges and institutes, and in some countries, for example the United States, in universities. It is equally important subject matter for adults as well as for children and youth. Its content is basic to human development and interaction, and it helps all nations to make better use of their human capital. Speaking about the situation in Africa, Florence Sai of Ghana said, "In the beginning women worked, served their menfolk, procreated and slaved for the children, died in the process, many of those who lived led a life of poverty and illiteracy and were onlookers to the affairs of the community and the nation. Africa still has many patches of these dark ages. If there is one subject that is making inroads into changing the situation, it is Home Economics."

The origin of home economics varies from country to country. Home economics began in Nigeria in 1873 when French missionaries included it in the St. Mary Convent School curriculum (Okaru 1977); in Queensland, Australia, it began in the primary schools 100 years ago; and in the United States it began in tertiary education around the turn of the century and has been strong in secondary schools since the passage of federal legislation in 1917. Where home economics has not been taught to both sexes from the beginning, the enrollment in programs at both secondary and tertiary levels is changing now to include males as well as females. The influence of home economics at all levels is growing around the world.

Research in home economics education in the United States has been recently reviewed by Nelson (1981). It has focused on the results, for the learners, of participation in home economics programs, and on the extent to which programs meet the requirements of federal legislation. It includes studies of secondary students, adults, and special populations such as the handicapped or inmates of prisons. Some studies identified life skills that are essential for everyday life in today's society (see *Daily Living Skills*). Others tested special curricula or equipment for teaching mentally retarded or physically handicapped students. Some have been concerned with sex stereotyping, for example, the extent to which textbooks show, in words or illustrations, evidence of this occurring. Other studies identified teacher competencies needed for working with special populations or means for examining teachers' effectiveness. Statewide program evaluations have been made in Illinois and New York, and other studies have focused on developing instruments to use in program evaluation. Some have developed large-scale curriculum projects for special purposes. Nelson also suggested some needs for future research.

Hughes (1981) conducted a nationwide study of secondary vocational consumer and homemaking programs to identify what is taught and who is served and concluded that the findings were encouraging in terms of topics taught, the numbers of students, and the population of males following the programs. Recommendations included offering more comprehensive courses, and more emphasis on nutrition, management, consumer education, parenting, and housing.

Gritzmacher et al. (1981) studied the effectiveness of parenting and child development programs in home economics. Ley and Mears (1981) used a case study approach to study the dimensions of outstanding consumer and homemaking programs. The first of their 10 characteristics of highly successful programs was that the teacher is the key factor. Student involvement was rated second.

Bibliography

Brown M, Paulocci B 1979 Home economics: A definition. In: American Home Economics Association 1979 *Home Economics: A Definition.* American Home Economics Association, Washington, DC, p. 23

East M 1980 *Home Economics: Past, Present and Future.* Allyn and Bacon, Boston, Massachusetts

Green K 1980 Conclusions. *Economie Familiale* 52(4): 66–68

Gritzmacher J E, Shannon T, Watts J 1981 Effectiveness of parenting/child development vocational home economics program. *Illinois Teach. Home Econ.* 24(5): 227–29

Hughes R P 1981 The national "census study" of secondary vocational consumer and homemaking programs. *Illinois Teach. Home Econ.* 24(5): 224–26

Lake Placid Conference 1904 Proceedings of the Sixth Annual Conference September 19–24, 1904, Lake Placid, New York

Ley C J, Mears R 1981 Dimensions of outstanding consumer and homemaking programs: The case study approach. *Illinois Teach. Home Econ.* 24(5): 230–32

Nelson H Y 1981 Review of research in home economics education. *Illinois Teach. Home Econ.* 24(5): 220–23

Okaru V 1977 The teaching of home economics in the secondary schools in Nigeria. *Illinois Teach. Home Econ.* 21(1): 58–60

Sai F 1979 Home economics: A professional subject and a vital aid in the development process. *Int. Fed. Home Econ. Bull.* 51: 11–12

Innovative Study Areas

Anthropology Programs

M. J. Rice

Anthropology emerged in the nineteenth century with two major subdivisions—physical anthropology, with close links to medicine, biology, primatology, and paleontology; and cultural anthropology (known as ethnology in Europe), embracing archeology, linguistics, ethnography, ethnohistory, and applied anthropology. During the twentieth century, anthropology became a recognized academic discipline, but little attention was paid to either the role of anthropology in the training of teachers or teaching of anthropology before college.

Long before the emergence of anthropology as a separate subject, however, content now recognized as anthropological was taught as part of the school curriculum, first as part of geography and later as part of integrated social studies. Geographers such as Humboldt, Ratzel, and Vidal de la Blache had emphasized content dealing with the races of humankind and their diverse cultures. Ratzel's *anthropogeographie* and Vidal de la Blache's *geographie humaine* as well as the French concept of *genre de vie* showed the overlapping concern of geography with anthropology (James 1972).

The dominant method for the teaching of anthropological content is the integrated social studies course used in both the United States and many other countries. Anthropological content is prominent in the Schools Council Project "Time, Place, and Society" in England and Wales (Blyth et al. 1976), as well as in integrated studies in New Zealand. In Mexico, anthropological content is featured as a part of the history course, and in India, it shows up in the form of simple ethnographies in geography texts published by the National Council of Educational Research and Training at New Delhi.

1. Anthropology as a Separate School Subject

Anthropology first gained prominence as a separate school subject and as a conceptual strand in integrated social studies, in the United States in the curriculum reform decade of the 1960s. Contributing factors were an increase in the number of colleges and universities offering anthropology; an increase in the number of teachers taking anthropology as an elective; a demand for more international awareness in education; the disci-

pline movement which organized subject matter for school instruction into separate disciplines and invited the participation of university scholars; and the identification of the method of science with the process of inquiry and induction as practiced by scientists (Bruner 1960).

The two explicitly anthropological curriculum projects were the Anthropology Curriculum Study Project (ACSP) of the American Anthropological Association (for high-school level), and the Anthropology Curriculum Project (ACP) (kindergarten to grade 7) of the University of Georgia.

One other major project with anthropological content was *Man: A Course of Study* (MACOS), a fifth grade (age 10 to 11) behavioral science course of the Educational Development Center (Curriculum Development Associates, Washington).

The interest of curriculum developers and social studies educators was not reflected in adoption for school use. No accurate measures of the diffusion and adoption of anthropological materials are available, but actual adoption for school use slowed down (Weiss 1978) (see *Curriculum Diffusion*).

Several legacies of the anthropological thrust are more important than the identity of anthropology as a school subject. The concept of culture is used more effectively as an explanatory principle of similarities and differences in ways of living; more careful attention is given to accurate and representative case studies; there is less Western ethnocentrism and disparaging comparisons between savage and civilized societies and superior and inferior races have been eliminated; and there is a greater appreciation of how customs and tradition of diverse peoples fit into integrated value–belief–technological–ecological systems. But school anthropology still follows the college example in emphasizing the ethnography of preliterate cultures.

2. Organization, Methods, and Materials

Anthropological content is taught at all school levels. In the elementary and middle grades, such content appears as cross-cultural, with a study of other lands, or ethnic studies components integrated within social studies. As a separate subject, anthropology is most commonly taught as a high-school elective (see *Elective Subjects*).

High-school elective course content reflects teacher preferences without a uniform pattern. The most common offering is a semester overview of physical and cultural anthropology with some attention to archeology. Separate archeology courses, with an emphasis on both actual and simulated digs, vie in popularity with cultural anthropology. A less frequent course variant is two semesters of anthropology, one physical and the other cultural.

Methodologically, great emphasis has been placed on "inquiry" teaching. Except for archeology, however, anthropological inquiry in the schools tends to be literary, depending on reading skills for processing ethnographies. Since the subjects of anthropological study are other human beings rather than the culture in which students live, it is difficult for teachers of cultural anthropology to involve students in empirical data collection and interpretation. Most existing anthropology courses result from teacher initiative; it is thus not surprising to find a preference for open as compared to closed methods of teaching.

3. Values in Teaching Anthropology

Teaching precollege anthropology reflects both ethical and scientific values. The dominant rationale for teaching is ethical: a reduction of ethnocentrism and prejudice, the attainment of cultural empathy and understanding, an appreciation of the universality of humanity and its common problems, and an acquisition of better self-awareness. Teachers who place a heavy emphasis on physical anthropology focus on the humanness of people—on the interactions of evolutionary and cultural forces that make us human.

The value of anthropology as a science is more clearly expressed by teachers of archeology. It is they who are most likely to emphasize scientific methodology in the collection and analysis of data and the careful use of evidence in the reconstruction of the past from limited sources.

An implicit value, expressed in the content, is that anthropological interpretation is especially useful for the understanding of preliterate, peasant, or tribal societies. While some reference is made to cultural or social change, there is little emphasis on the application of anthropology to the study of urban societies, comparative civilizations, or to problems of development. The cultural preferences of precollege courses reflect the dominant emphasis in introductory college texts.

4. Research in Teaching Precollege Anthropology

Research has been limited; most articles relating to precollege anthropology are advocacy articles, rationales without empirical evidence, or descriptions of courses of study (Dwyer-Schick 1976).

Project-related research was primarily testimonial in-house evaluation (Rice and Bailey 1971, Hanley et al. 1970). These evaluations indicate that the material achieved the main instruction objectives although all related goals, such as an increase in cognitive and information-processing skills, were not always attained. Most material developed was not suited for the low ability student.

Teacher feedback was positive in all the projects, and all projects emphasized the importance of trained teachers. Rice (1970) found no difference in the achievement of children taught anthropology by trained as compared with control teachers, a finding different from that of Gonzalez (1973). Rice and Bailey (1971) found that anthropological content was effective in the reduction of ethnocentrism at both elementary and high-school levels. *Man: A Course of Study* also generated a number of studies, summaries of which are given in Dynneson (1975).

5. The Future of Anthropology as a School Subject

As a separate subject, anthropology is one of several social sciences that compete for a place in the school curriculum. While other social sciences are increasingly perceived as relevant to the problems of modern life, anthropology may be increasingly perceived as the study of anachronisms, unless there is a change in emphasis and focus to make it more relevant to the modern world. Anthropology is also more likely to become embroiled in local controversy over curriculum content. This does not mean that anthropological concepts and generalizations will not continue to have an influence on a more empathetic interpretation of non-Western cultures and peoples, as it has had in the past. And certainly the contribution of anthropology might be greater if more systematically included as part of the training in all teacher programs. The teaching of anthropology as a separate school subject, however, will continue to be limited, taught by a few teachers who initiate their own courses because they value the content and methodology of anthropology.

Bibliography

Blyth W A L et al. 1976. *Curriculum Planning in History, Geography and Social Science*. Collins, London

Bruner J S 1960 *The Process of Education*. Harvard University Press, Cambridge, Massachusetts

Dwyer-Schick S 1976 *The Study and Teaching of Anthropology: An Annotated Bibliography*. University of Georgia, Anthropology Curriculum Project, Athens, Georgia

Dynneson T L 1975 *Pre-college Anthropology: Trends and Materials*. University of Georgia Anthropology Curriculum Project, Athens, Georgia

Gonzalez N L et al. 1973 Applied anthropology and the grade school. *Hum. Organization* 32 (3): 295–304

Hanley J P et al. 1970 *Curiosity, Competence, Community: An Evaluation of Man: A Course of Study*. Educational

Development Center, Newton, Massachusetts. ERIC Document No. ED 045 461
James P E 1972 *All Possible Worlds: A History of Geographical Ideas.* Odyssey, Indianapolis, Indiana
Rice M J 1970 *The Effectiveness of Teacher Training as Measured by Pupil Performance.* University of Georgia Anthropology Curriculum Project, Athens, Georgia. ERIC Document No. ED 049 095

Rice M J, Bailey W C 1971 *Final Report: The Development of a Sequential Curriculum in Anthropology, Grades 1–7.* University of Georgia, Anthropology Curriculum Project, Athens, Georgia. ERIC Document No. ED 054 037
Weiss I R 1978 *Report of the 1977 National Survey of Science, Mathematics, and Social Studies/Education.* Center for Education Research and Evaluation. United States Government Printing Office, Washington, DC

Community Education

F. M. Newmann

Throughout the world, "community education" represents diverse concerns which have not been organized into a discrete literature. The phrase refers not only to numerous ways of teaching youth about community life, but also to efforts in community development such as political empowerment of local communities, coordination of social services, economic development, citizen participation, continuing adult education, and extended use of school facilities for these purposes. Interpreted primarily as youth education, community education would include classroom instruction in history, government, social relations, and citizenship; sending students out of school to learn occupational skills, to perform service, to conduct research, or to take political action. Community education might also focus on building solidarity and cooperation within the school itself. Interpreted as community development, community education programs might include a course in fitness for the elderly, dissemination of agricultural technology to farmers, forming a citizen group on land use policy, or using school space for a community health clinic. Societies differ in their approaches to these topics, as evident, for example, in contrasts between social education of youth in the People's Republic of China, the United States, or Nigeria.

Because of multiple meanings of community education, substantial cultural variation in programs, and the difficulty of selecting specific programs to represent the state of the field, this article will not attempt to characterize the content or nature of community education. Instead, it will identify trends that heighten concern for community education across the globe and will describe issues that must be faced in building defensible rationales for programs.

The expansion of formal schooling under the auspices of the state, rather than private associations, highlights the social purposes of education. As public bodies become responsible for extending education to the masses, discussion is likely to center on functional concerns such as training for nation building and community development, reforms for social justice, or the enhancement of ethnic identity. In penetrating beyond the formally stated social purposes of schooling, literature on the hidden curriculum has identified implicit, and often less appealing social purposes such as domination and social control. Whether explicit or implicit purposes of schooling are looked for, the historical movement toward state-sponsored, universal education is likely to emphasize the importance of community needs. Primary needs in one society could be defined as dissemination of agricultural technology, in another as teaching for multicultural tolerance, in another as building an individualistic work ethic.

The expansion of education has been accompanied by its professionalization; that is, the demarcation of educational services as distinct from other areas of community life (such as child rearing, economic production, or worship), including the segregation of children from the general adult population in order to be educated by a special class of adults specifically trained as educators. The organization of education into a professional enterprise has contributed to such problems as youth cultures which seem to require substantial efforts to reintegrate them into community life (because schooling tends to isolate them from skills and values that might otherwise be learned through contact with adults in the family, workplace, church, political group, or voluntary association), and extensive boredom with schooling (tasks of schooling often fail to interest children, in part because of their apparent irrelevance to problems that people encounter in the community beyond school). Societies vary in the extent to which professionalization of education has isolated children from community life, but the trend can be mitigated by requirements (and incentives) for youth work and service in the adult community, by integrating adults of diverse experiences (as both teachers and students) into schools, and by restricting the time that youth spend in school.

A third trend, most evident in technologically advanced societies, that stimulates interest in community education is the emergence of vast corporate institutions, dense urban population masses, geographic mobility, highly specialized division of labor, and other aspects of modernization that destroy traditional communities, leaving many persons without secure attachments or a sense of belonging to stable communities that can offer support throughout the life cycle. Community education becomes attractive as a way to reduce general alienation by helping students strengthen relationships with local community, ethnic–religious heritage, or national efforts to achieve the public good.

Programs of community education, whether as history courses intended to develop student bonding to a national tradition, as work experience in the production of goods to assist a community's economic development, or as a classroom instruction on the nature of global interdependence, raise at least three significant issues that should be addressed if community education is to be grounded in defensible social philosophy (rather than only in symbolic slogans).

In what ways do community education programs communicate a view of knowledge as problematic and tentative or as confirmed truth unlikely to be questioned? Continuous critical and open inquiry into all aspects of life is advocated by some as the essence of education and also as the most effective basis for commitment to humane community life. Others contend that inquiry must be grounded in some unquestioned assumptions and that productive community life rests in part on the inculcation of certain values and bonds that cannot be formed exclusively through autonomous inquiry. These positions may not be reconciled in a conclusive general way, but community education should attempt to articulate situations in which it seems appropriate to favor one side of the dilemma or the other.

Community education concerns the life of groups and aggregates, but it may not necessarily clarify the relationship between individual and collective welfare. To what extent must the individual make sacrifices for a group, and to what extent must the group orient itself toward needs of individuals? A dominant position in Western capitalist nations holds that human dignity depends upon inalienable rights inherent in each individual, suggesting that communities exist primarily to serve individual interests. An alternative view holds that dignity derives from relationships among people forged through collective associations, working together, for example, to achieve transcendent goals such as justice, ecological harmony, spiritual peace, or more simply, caring for one another. According to the first view, communities are organized to promote individual freedom and rights. According to the second, communities are valued because they provide interdependent relationships among people and worthy purposes beyond individual interests. Community education programs may reflect either philosophy, but often without explicit acknowledgement or defense.

Modernization has dramatized the fact of human membership in multiple communities, as persons try to relate to a variety of political–legal constituencies (from neighborhood to nation to an international legal system) and secondary organizations (schools, corporations, unions, religious associations), in addition to primary units such as immediate family and peer groups. Often education programs do not confront social psychological issues involved in maintaining productive relationships in several levels of "community" at once, especially the challenge of making transitions between membership in impersonal, corporate settings and primary, communal settings. The problem is highly visible in areas where planned economic development clashes with communal traditions, less obvious in urban cultures with high technology where many communal traditions have disappeared. A major challenge for community education in either modern or traditional settings is to respond to the considerable evidence that communal forms of life contribute significantly to human dignity, and to facilitate some reasonable balance between participation in close-knit, neighborly communities and in societal aggregates, or "corporate" communities.

Research in community education usually addresses issues specific to particular programs, rather than findings about community education as a whole. Studies have investigated the ways in which school facilities may be shared by a variety of groups in a community, the effect of student volunteer programs on students' social development, the development of moral reasoning in students participating in school governance, the effect of social education on political efficacy, the effect of work experience programs on student's skills and attitudes, the costs and benefits of citizen involvement in schools, and numerous other topics. Most of the published material on these topics consists of program descriptions and proposals rather than empirical research about the effects of various approaches. Relevant literature will also be found under such topics as action learning, citizenship, community schools, community service, experiential education, political education, school climate, socialization, and social studies.

Bibliography

Ardnt C O 1959 *Community Education: Principles and Practices from World-wide Experience*. National Society for the Study of Education, Chicago, Illinois

Bremer J, Bennett I, Kiers D, Laird J (eds.) 1979 *1980 Plus: Community, Participation and Learning*. Australian Association for Community Education, Melbourne

Conrad D, Hedin D 1981 *Executive Summary, Experiential Education Evaluation Project*. Center for Youth Development and Research, University of Minnesota, St. Paul, Minnesota

Hamilton S 1980 Experiential learning programs for youth. *Am. J. Educ.* 88: 179–215

Lynch J 1979 *Education for Community: A Cross-cultural Study in Education*. Macmillan, London

Midwinter E C 1975 *Education and the Community*. Allen and Unwin, London

Minzey J D, LeTarte C E 1979 *Community Education, From Program to Process to Practice. The Schools Role in a New Educational Society*. Pendell, Flint, Michigan

Mosher E (ed.) 1980 *Moral Education: A First Generation of Research and Development*. Praeger, New York

Newmann F M 1975 *Education for Citizen Action: Challenge for the Secondary Curriculum*. McCutchan, Berkeley, California

Oliver D W 1976 *Education and Community: A Radical Critique of Innovative Schooling*. McCutchan, Berkeley, California

White C (ed.) 1981 *Building Bridges to the Law: How to make Lawyers, Judges, Police, and other Members of the Community a Part of your Law-related Education Program*. American Bar Association, Chicago, Illinois

Area Studies

D. Heater

The term "area studies" has a modern ring to it—"an ugly neologism" in the view of one American scholar. Yet the interdisciplinary study of the ancient Graeco–Roman civilization of the Mediterranean basin is as old as the Renaissance and in the systematic form of Classics was the staple humanities diet of European and American universities until the turn of the nineteenth century. Oriental studies, too, flourished alongside Classics, though with fewer students. However, the comparative narrowness of focus on the histories, languages, and literature of these societies must perhaps deny them the title of area studies in the fully fledged modern sense.

The truly comprehensive study of a particular geographical area came to be developed in the United States during and immediately after the Second World War, the supply of substantial funds for this purpose by the National Defense Education Act in 1958 being a significant landmark. Simultaneously in the United Kingdom the Hayter Committee was established in 1959 "to review developments in the Universities in the fields of Oriental, Slavonic, East European, and African Studies . . . and to consider, and advise on, proposals for future development" (University Grants Committee 1961).

Area studies in this new sense may be defined as the study of a culturally coherent geographical area by the use of a comprehensive range of disciplinary tools. How is the burgeoning of this style of academic study to be explained? Four major factors may be discerned. In the first place, government concern—political, strategic, and commerical—must be noticed. East and Southeast Asian studies in the United States reflected traditional, then newer, international interests. In the United Kingdom, European studies developed in parallel with her halting movement into the European Community. In Canada, Canadian studies have evolved to strengthen a sense of national identity and cohesion. Secondly, the development of area studies has been part of the conscious academic attempt to slough off nationalistic, insular, and introspective habits. Some exponents even suggest that area studies are but staging posts to holistic global studies. Most such courses, for example in universities in the United States and the United Kingdom, have indeed been studies of cultures very dissimilar from those of the North Atlantic region. The third factor has been the pedagogical and academic vogue for interdisciplinarity that has flowered in one of its most distinguished forms in the French "Annales" school of historians (e.g. Burke 1972). If individual disciplines are not to be studied for their own sakes, then the subject matter for study must be defined in some other way: a geographical area provides a convenient framework. Fourthly, the rapid and extensive development of the social sciences has transformed the earlier embry-

onic area studies into more thorough, multifaceted analyses of the societies under review.

But is an area study the study of any geographical region irrespective of its size or nature? The usual interpretation involves a region of continental or subcontinental scale with sufficient cultural coherence to render its study intellectually meaningful and manageable within the compass of a course of limited time span. Latin American, European, and Middle Eastern studies fit comfortably into this definition. Nevertheless, cases have been made for classifying as area studies courses on individual countries and even of the globe itself on the grounds that each provides subject matter for the interdisciplinary study of a culturally coherent society (the case for global studies resting on the arguments of international political and economic interdependence and cultural homogenization that characterize the contemporary world). However, if the classification is kept strictly to those courses dealing with continental or subcontinental areas, the parameters of the study are still not easy to define. For example, although many courses on European studies in schools and universities in the United Kingdom confine their attention to West European countries (some even just to the members of the Common Market), the title of "European studies" is surely misleading if the Graeco-Byzantine, Slav, and Soviet experiences of the eastern half of the continent are totally excluded from study.

The evolution of area studies has highlighted a number of organizational and learning difficulties, deriving in large measure from the interdisciplinary nature of the courses. Departmental structures have inhibited some experimentation. If, for instance, Middle Eastern studies are to be taught, what happens to the autonomy of the departments of politics, sociology, geography, history, oriental languages, and comparative religion? Moreover, the question is not merely one of institutional politics. Very pertinent doubts have been raised concerning the ability of students simultaneously to study so many different disciplines and to integrate them for the intellectual illumination of the area under review (e.g. Lucan 1981). Two solutions have been canvassed for this problem. One is to study the area initially from the perspective of a "base" discipline, to which other disciplines are gradually added. The other is to postpone area studies to the undergraduate, even postgraduate, level when a certain elementary command at least of a number of the necessary constituent disciplines can be assumed. The postgraduate Institutes of Latin American Studies established in the 1960s in the United Kingdom following the Parry Report are examples of this approach. For if students do not have command of the methodologies of the various necessary disciplines, the resultant study will never rise above the academically banal. In the United Kingdom, membership of the European Community led to the creation of courses on European studies at the secondary-school level. A number of these operated at the level of "costumes and cuisine". One reason for this academic mediocrity was that no single teacher had sufficient command of the range of subject matter required for effective teaching, and team teaching was difficult to organize. A second reason was that the pupils were unable to operate at any more sophisticated level. Where European studies was a substitute for French for those pupils academically unable to learn a foreign language, such a result was perhaps to be expected. This example raises the final question about whether area studies should in any case always incorporate foreign language study where it is relevant. The very common trend, in fact, is away from languages to the social sciences as the core disciplines: thus are modern area studies to be distinguished from traditional oriental studies and the classics (Williams 1977 pp. 17–20).

Bibliography

Becker J M, Mehlinger H D (eds.) 1968 *International Dimensions in the Social Studies*. National Council for the Social Studies, Washington, DC

Burke P (ed.) 1972 *Economy and Society in Early Modern Europe: Essays from Annales*. Routledge and Kegan Paul, London

Gibb H A R 1964 *Area Studies Reconsidered*. School of Oriental and African Studies, London

Hodgetts A B, Gallagher P 1978 *Teaching Canada for the '80s*. Ontario Institute for Studies in Education, Toronto

Journal of Area Studies 1980 Portsmouth Polytechnic, Portsmouth

Lucan T A 1981 Social studies as an integrated subject. In: Mehlinger H D (ed.) 1981 *UNESCO Handbook for Teaching Social Studies*. Croom Helm, London

University Grants Committee 1961 *Report of the Sub-committee on Oriental, Slavonic, East European and African Studies* (Hayter Report). Her Majesty's Stationery Office, London

Williams M 1977 *Teaching European Studies*. Heinemann, London

Environmental Education

A. M. Lucas

Environmental education is characterized by its goal of providing education *for* the enhancement or preservation of the human environment. It is not sufficient to teach *about* the environment, or even to teach out of school *in* the environment. When the term became common in the early 1970s there was no consensus on its meaning, and many programmes described as "environmental education" did not attempt to produce appropriate behaviour and attitudes, a focus which is implicit in education *for* the environment. However, since the "Belgrade Charter" was adopted at an International Workshop in Environmental Education in 1975, there has been an increasing international consensus that a focus on affective aims is necessary for environmental education. The text of the charter is available in *Connect*, a free UNESCO newsletter (1976 Vol. 1 No. 1).

Many approaches to environmental education within schools can meet the criteria in the Belgrade Charter. Some schools provide a special subject which may have a strong science bias, for example the environmental science syllabus of the Joint Matriculation Board in England and Wales, but others in the same country may require a broad interdisciplinary approach. The course in environmental studies of the University of London Schools Examination Department includes work drawn from geology and economics as well as biology, geography, and other disciplines. Other courses are described in Schoenfeld and Disinger (1977).

Some schools approach environmental education by individual teachers providing an environmental emphasis to their own subject—by the choice of example, homework exercise, and field trip. However, with independent activities in different subjects, students may react adversely to having "pollution pushed at us all the time". To avoid alienation by continual preaching in all subjects, some schools have produced carefully coordinated interdisciplinary curricula designed to build and reinforce appropriate value positions for their pupils (Carson 1978, Chap. 12).

The content of environmental education programmes must vary from continent to continent and from country to country. Human well-being is promoted by a large number of factors, ranging from the social aspects of cultural heritage that are embodied in the remains of the built environment of the ancient civilizations, to the supply of energy, and material for the next meal. Curriculum materials produced in one country necessarily respond to locally important questions and are thus even less transferable than curricular in the biological sciences. But despite the lack of common content there is an international sharing of experience, particularly through the information exchange programmes of UNESCO and the United Nations Environment Program (UNEP). The shared programme descriptions stimulate ideas about approaches that will help in the notoriously difficult area of producing long-term behaviour changes through school programmes.

Unfortunately, much curriculum development consistent with education for the environment has been based on a naive belief that providing knowledge about an environmental issue will produce a "correct" behavioural response. Other teaching schemes have not assumed a direct link between knowledge and attitudes and have concentrated on attitude formation, while sharing the assumption that appropriate action will follow attitude inculcation. Few of the authors of the environmental attitudes reports Lucas (1980) reviewed seemed aware that studies in social psychology have shown repeatedly that there is no strong link between measured attitudes to diffuse concepts, such as "quality of life", "ecological conservation", and subsequent behaviour. Indeed, studies of members of environmental organizations show that attitudes of concern sufficient to prompt joining the organization do not necessarily produce the personal behaviour the organization exists to promote. Studies of attitude formation and the curriculum of environmental education programmes are reviewed in Lucas (1980).

Although successful inculcation of general environmental attitudes is unlikely to produce the behaviours that will enhance or preserve the environment when issues arise, there is some prospect of success if personal attitudes are produced to narrow environmental issues. But unfortunately school-level environmental educators have insufficient time to produce specific attitudes to all the issues that will arise during their pupils' lives. More success might be obtained if the curriculum produced personal moral attitudes such as "I ought to consider the indirect consequences of my actions", taught effective information retrieval skills, and gave practice in applying this attitude in environmental contexts.

The difficulty of choosing specific targets for environmental education at school is reduced if there is a well-developed informal environmental education system accessible to adults, especially if it impinges upon most of the population. Mass media can be utilized in two ways. Firstly, by presenting planned instructional materials with specific learning goals, and secondly, by the production of entertainment material which also helps people think about relationships between humans and the environment in which they live. The Japan Broadcasting Corporation (NHK), for example, has been active in both modes, producing programs for schools which are repeated to encourage parents to watch with their children in an attempt to promote discussion within the family; and transmitting a regular entertainment program "Nature Album" which emphasizes the beauty, grandeur, and wonder of the Japanese environment (Ohno 1981).

Education for the environment cannot succeed if it is directed to school children alone, because they are not in a position to make many of the decisions needed to preserve the present environmental resources, but it might succeed if it deliberately attends to public education on a broader scale.

Bibliography

Carson S McB (ed.) 1978 *Environmental Education: Principles and Practice.* Arnold, London
Linke R D 1980 *Environmental Education in Australia.* Allen and Unwin, Sydney
Lucas A M 1980 Science and environmental education: Pious hopes, self praise and disciplinary chauvinism. *Stud. Sci. Educ.* 7: 1–26
Ohno R 1981 Use of the mass media in environmental education: Japan's experiences. *Environmental Education in Asia and the Pacific.* Bulletin of the UNESCO Regional Office for Education in Asia and the Pacific. 22: 294–99
Schoenfeld C, Disinger J (eds.) 1977 *Environmental Education in Action 1: Case Studies of Selected Public School and Public Action Programs.* ERIC Information Analysis Center for Science, Mathematics and Environmental Education, Ohio State University, Columbus, Ohio

Political Education

W. Langeveld

Political education is the intentional transfer of knowledge, values, attitudes, and skills needed for participation in the political process. Political socialization refers to a broader variety of phenomena encompassing political learning of various types both formal and informal, deliberate and unplanned, at every stage of the life-cycle including nonpolitical learning that affects political behavior.

On the tree of education, the political branch is rather new, although not as new as it might seem. According to an historical–dialectic viewpoint, all education has a political function. Nevertheless, the concept of political education refers to manifest programs and activities within the framework of a special subject, while latent or nondirect facets of activities aimed at importing political skills and attitudes are called "political socialization."

Some philosophies of education perceive "political education" as a contradiction in terms, since education is considered to be an agency for fostering independent thinking, free from any political bias. Accordingly, education should help the learner to understand the functions of the democratic state, without touching upon issues which are considered to be political. The special subject which has some political content is usually called "civics," "social studies," "law education," "moral or value education," and so on, all names which intentionally avoid the adjective "political."

1. Historical Perspectives

Whatever the name of the subject, it cannot be denied that there has in fact always been a kind of political education for the various types of elite, be they military, religious, or commercial. The majority of people, however, were excluded from this kind of education. Ordinary people were politically socialized to be obedient, industrious, pious, and law abiding. Church, labor systems, and the family were the major agents of political socialization. Schools only reinforced this process.

There are many definitions of political education and socialization. The definition of "politics" could be restricted to cover the state and its organs in the widest sense, as David Easton (1965) did, or it is possible to go to the other extreme as the neomarxists do, and see class struggle as the main political conflict, and widen the field of politics to cover almost all aspects of human life. The definition which is chosen determines the aims, content, and methods of political education. It likewise affects the view a person has of the history of (political) education. To those who accept the neomarxist definition, the introduction of a special school subject is just another step in a long process of inculcation of ruling class norms and values in the lower classes. By the former definition, politics appear in the classroom only when a subject like "civics," the "constitution," or "social studies" is part of the curriculum. In this sense, the country with the longest tradition of political education is the United States, followed by the Federal Republic of Germany, and at a distance by France, the United Kingdom, and other countries.

The functions of the subject differed according to the country and the political culture. In the United States, some kind of training was thought necessary for the new immigrants who needed to learn the American way of life and its democratic principles. In the Federal Republic of Germany, the traditional trend has been nationalistic, the main goal being to turn Germans into patriots willing to die for their country. After 1945, the American and British occupation governments decided that a school subject was necessary to reeducate the Germans. The name was *Sozialkunde*, or *Gemeinschaftskunde*, which were replaced by *politische Bildung* when the character of the subject changed. In the United Kingdom after 1945, when the British began to take this matter more seriously, subjects like "civics" were seen to be useful to youngsters from the lower classes. In the 1970s, a program for "political literacy" was developed which is gradually becoming accepted by various kinds of secondary schools.

2. Contents and Aims

The content of the subject varies as much as its history and aims. Traditionally, state law, the constitution, and the institutions of the state, combined with some ethical ideas, formed its substance. With the burgeoning of the social and political sciences, changes slowly took place. As soon as the subject is no longer defined as state law, problems arise about its real identity.

In some states in the United States, the subject is still law related, whereas in other states it is a combination of history, social geography, and sociology (called "social studies"), or it may be some kind of ethics called "moral education" or "values education." In Europe the situation is still more complicated. In the United Kingdom it is usually part of general studies, which cover all kinds of topics from local traffic to ecological problems and "political literacy" programs. In Sweden the programs are a mixture of state law, social questions, and local politics, mixed with international questions. In the Federal Republic of Germany the content differs in the various Länder (provinces) from a conservative kind of partnership education (*Baden-Württemberg*) with the accent on history, to a kind of political education dealing with actual problems relevant to youngsters. In the Netherlands the subject is called "knowledge about society" and the content is very differentiated with emphasis on current topics, world problems (Third World, peace education, disarmament education), and problems that are of special interest to youngsters. In spite of a flood of books and articles about the aims and content of the subject, especially in the Federal Republic of Germany, there is so far no consensus about the content in most countries. As most of these publications have been too theoretical and complicated, their influence on teachers has not been very great.

Educational authorities have hesitated to call the subject "political education," as the term "politics" invites controversies; this predicament has not made it easier to define the subject's identity. To satisfy social demands on schools to deal with contemporary problems, some school systems offer a wide range of new subjects like consumer education, environmental education, disarmament education, mass media education, recreational education, and so on. In traditional school systems, the school program is heavily loaded with conventional school subjects, and there is very little chance to respond to the social demands; this gives educational authorities an excuse for avoiding political education, as such (which would cover most of these claims), while still giving the impression of fulfilling some "equivalent" needs. Authorities do not want to be involved in political disputes, and parents have a fear of indoctrination, by which they generally understand the inculcation in their children of ideas other than their own. A much better definition of indoctrination may be "the transfer of conclusions without giving the necessary arguments and evidence." Parents, however, are often protesting against what they call "indoctrination," even when teachers provide good arguments. It should be noted that the risk of manipulation by the teacher is always there, as youngsters are not able to deal critically with arguments. Therefore, the most satisfactory way of avoiding indoctrination is to present different and conflicting views about social problems and to allow students to make up their own minds. It is this pluralistic approach that is acceptable to educational authorities in most democratic countries where political education is practiced.

3. Themes and Topics Appropriate for Various Age Groups

In most school systems political education starts at the age of 16; it is thus reserved for the last two years of high-school studies. However, there is an increasing awareness that in order to be effective, political education should start at a much earlier age. The need to start political education early is well-understood by totalitarian regimes of various types. Democracies, on the other hand, have trouble accepting this idea, being as they are afraid that schools may become the arena of party politics. Nevertheless, the lowering of the voting age to 18 years in many countries, the role played by youth in today's society and culture, and the higher level of education that is reached by many youngsters as compared to earlier generations, have compelled education authorities to reconsider their views. Political socialization research has shown that children tend to hold political notions even before they enter primary school and that they are able to grasp all kinds of problems which have to do with sociopolitical life. Nevertheless, they cannot deal with more complicated political questions until somewhere between 10 to 13 years of age, and it takes several more years before they are able to treat these problems adequately in all their abstract and ideological dimensions.

To help students understand political issues, school programs should consider guidelines based on the findings from psychology of learning, developmental psychology, socialization theory, and based on experiences accumulated in school practice. After some preparatory work in primary education, systematic studies should start at the age of about 13 years. It is very important to choose the appropriate introductory topics. The themes themselves should have a sound theoretical basis, and the criteria for selection should be scientifically sound. This is where most curricula for political education up to now have failed. At present, selection is usually based on intuition or on vague ideas about what students "ought to know." Real learning experiences are gained only where the students are emotionally involved and where it is clear to them that they will be able to apply what they have learned to real-life situations. This implies that the themes should be directly related to student experiences. Political learning should be directed toward helping them to better solve problems related to their experiences.

When they start formal political education (at about 13 years old), adolescents are highly ego-involved, yet curious to learn about the world around them. They want to know about the behavior of adults and try to find a meaning in social life, norms, values, and so on. They are eager to learn about themselves and their environment. Political education should take its point of origin from what is happening and has happened in the lives of the students, in other words, from their socialization experiences.

The major agents of (political) socialization are the family, the school, peers, and mass media (television, etc.). They offer themes for reflection on the socialization process. Through these themes, political and social concepts are introduced, which may help the students systematize their own past and present experiences, and help them understand that they are part of society and that the society may stimulate or impede their own personal development. They discover that they share some apparently individual problems with many peers and that to solve such problems they have to work together to change social conditions. This approach has little in common with social psychology as it is concentrating on the socio-political forces that affect students' lives. For example, most adolescents are highly interested in pop music, and think they are following their own taste in this matter. Education should show them in what ways they are being manipulated by the mass media and its advertisements and how the "industry of consciousness" is functioning. Concepts from economics and mass psychology are of service here.

Many youngsters think that they make their own school career, and in a way this is true. But they do not see how social forces and mechanisms help or impede the attainment of their goals. The whole social and economic background, the norms and values prevalent in different social classes affect their lives. Consequently, these phenomena should be dealt with within the framework of political education.

This may prevent a feeling of alienation and may create interest in what happens in society. Only when students have intrinsic interest in politics does it become useful to deal with political themes in school programs. Such motivation has to be created, not by talking politics, but by treating topics that are of real interest to students and by showing them their political aspects. Teachers, therefore, have to put themselves in the students' place, and be aware of the students' interests, which may be very different from their own.

Gradually, more complicated problems can be touched upon, until the time when political issues as such can be dealt with. A curriculum like this should be constructed along longitudinal lines and should cover at least three school years (from age 13 to 16).

4. Participation in Political Life

The main aim of political education anywhere is participation in political life in one way or another. Some progressive teachers go so far as to champion participation of the students in demonstrations, actions, and strikes. These teachers tend to find themselves in trouble after a while. They may encounter conflicts with both parents, students, and educational authorities. The school cannot be the basis for social actions. It cannot decide which actions students should participate in and which they should stay out of.

Most teachers are therefore more modest in their aims. Like political scientists, they see reading political articles in newspapers and watching political television programs as a form of participation in the sociopolitical process. If students can be brought to do this, political education has scored quite a success, for it means that the students have become politically involved.

This is a realistic aim, for educational systems function best at the cognitive level and at the level of skill training. They do less well in the affective domain due to their authoritarian atmosphere and hierarchical organization which are incompatible with affective education. Without doubt political education could be much more effective in schools that are organized on a democratic basis, where students have an opportunity to participate fully in all levels of decision making through free and open discussions. Such schools are relatively rare and it is not likely that their number will increase rapidly in the near future. Schools reflect the forces operating in society, and can therefore change only insofar as society itself changes. This does not mean that schools are only reinforcing the status quo. They can have quite an impact on students even if they operate mainly at the cognitive level. By treating the right themes and bringing in the right concepts, schools can make students aware of their political situation,

and this awareness may eventually lead to changes in attitude.

Bibliography

Borelli M 1979 *Politische Bildung in Italien; Revolution und Konterrevolution.* Metzler, Stuttgart

Christian W 1978 *Die dialektische Methode im politischen Unterricht.* Pahl-Rugenstein, Cologne

Easton D 1965 *A Systems Analysis of Political Life.* University of Chicago Press, Chicago, Illinois

Fischer K G 1979 *L'Educazione politica nella Germania Federale; Un'introduzione alla didattica politica.* Felice le Monnier, Florence

Fischer K G (ed.) 1980 *Zum aktuellen Stand der Theorie und Didaktik der Politischen Bildung.* Metzler, Stuttgart

Gillespie J, Heater D (eds.) 1981 *Political Education in Flux.* Sage, London

Langeveld W 1979 *Political Education for Teenagers: Aims, Content, and Methods.* Council of Europe, Strasbourg

Mehlinger H D, Davis O L (eds.) 1981 *The Social Studies.* 80th Yearbook of the National Society for the Study of Education. University of Chicago Press, Chicago, Illinois

Mehlinger H D, Tucker J L (eds.) 1979 *Teaching Social Studies in Other Nations.* Bulletin 60 National Council for the Social Studies, Washington, DC

Stacey B 1978 *Political Socialization in Western Society: An Analysis from a Life-span Perspective.* Arnold, London

Peace Education

C. Wulf

The aim of peace education is to incorporate into the educational process a knowledge of the dangers posed to human life and human social life by war, violence, poverty, and oppression. At the same time, workers in the field of peace education are aware that many of these problems are of a macrostructural nature, relating to social systems at large. They recognize that the resolution of these problems can only be a gradual process, which does not fall entirely within the educator's sphere of influence. Rather it is a question of a lifelong learning process, in which the individual's confrontation of the major issues facing humankind should begin in childhood or puberty, and continue into adulthood (Wulf 1973, 1974).

Peace education efforts are being made in the United States, in Western Europe, in the Soviet Union and Eastern Europe, in Japan, as well as in many of the Third World countries. Of course, approaches differ from one region of the world to another. Third World countries attempt to further peace education by stimulating economic, social, and national development, in some cases even by stimulation of regional development. The socialist countries contend that their whole educational process necessarily contributes to peace, since, according to their ideology, peace is the goal of social development in their societies. In the United

States and Western Europe, peace education has developed a critical approach to its own society and its role in international affairs. By the same token, the beginning of the 1980s has seen a joining of forces on the part of ecologists and peace educators, especially in Western Europe.

Education for peace has a lot in common with other educational fields whose goals are also to help shape the development of young people, albeit with a somewhat different emphasis. These fields include: international education (see *International Education*), survival education, global education, education for world citizenship, and developmental education. In the framework of education for peace, and according to the distinction made by Galtung (1969), peace must not only be conceived of as the absence of war and direct violence (concept of negative peace), but rather, working towards peace as the means to the realization of conditions leading to a maximal reduction in "structural violence" (concept of positive peace). Given this understanding of peace education, not only do war and direct violence between nations or within the international system become topics of discussion, but also conditions within society which foster violence—even including elements of violence in the family and the school system (Haavelsrud 1976, Wulf 1974)—are discussed.

Some of the more important topics treated by peace education are the following:

(a) the East–West conflict, and its nuclear threat to human life;

(b) the North–South conflict and its international vertical division of labor resulting in extensive poverty in the southern hemisphere;

(c) pollution and the destruction of the environment;

(d) the scarcity of food and resources;

(e) the population explosion;

(f) the problem of broadening understanding for human rights and social justice.

Education's inability or unwillingness to handle these problems means failure in its responsibility of preparing young people for the world of the future. Peace education must not limit itself solely to conveying information about the above-mentioned problems. A long hard examination of the issues is needed which ideally leads to a decrease in prejudice and in thinking of the enemy in terms of stereotypes, that is, to a change in attitudes. This process is a complex one. It implies a change in self-awareness leading to a deepened understanding of society and the world.

The prerequisite for this kind of learning process is overcoming widespread apathy and a deep sense of helplessness—obstacles to the development of empathy for, and commitment to, a peace-related learning process. One way of acquiring this kind of practical knowledge is for the young people to see their personal problems as being related to world issues. Through the realization that these issues have ramifications for their own lives they will become motivated to commit themselves to the peace movement. Only when education succeeds in going beyond its function of merely conveying relevant knowledge, can it hope to bring about the necessary change in attitudes and political convictions ultimately leading to political action (Curle 1973, Henderson 1973, Wulf 1973).

Peace education can only be promoted in an atmosphere of nonviolence. Thus, the emphasis must be placed on the development of forms of learning in which participatory and self-initiated learning are possible. The young person must be encouraged to take a great deal of the initiative and responsibility, and to use his or her imagination to develop new ways of solving the problems at hand. In addition, development of the awareness of the historical forces responsible for the world's conflicts and of the basic ability to change these situations plays a decisive role, since it contributes to the development of scenarios for creating a better world. At the same time, it guarantees a future-oriented approach to these problems and to education.

Peace education can be put into effect in many of society's institutions. It can begin within the family setting, where parents serve as models of peace-oriented behavior for their children, and where problems concerning peace are integrated into daily life. These problems can also be made a topic of discussion in schools and institutions of higher learning. There are two principal ways in which this can occur. The first possibility is that the concept of the preservation and advancement of peace be integrated into the discussion of a wide variety of topics. In this sense peace education is seen as a general principle of teaching. The second possibility is that curricula units which deal with peace-related problems be developed, tested, and put into practice. These kinds of units would be appropriate for classes in social studies, literature, or religion. Peace education can also be furthered by the use of mass media. Of course approaches have to be tailored to the specific natures of the mass media. Finally, education for peace can also be carried out in churches, political parties, unions, and at citizens' initiatives. Adults who are active in these organizations are usually those who have recognized that improving conditions for peace is part of their responsibility to following generations. In general, the decisive factor in peace education efforts will be the amount of cooperation between the fields of education, peace-related research, and practical politics.

Bibliography

Curle A 1973 *Education for Liberation.* Tavistock, London

Galtung J 1969 Violence, peace and peace research. *J. Peace Res.* 6: 167–91

Haavelsrud M (ed.) 1976 *Education for Peace: Reflection and Action.* Proc. of the 1st World Conf. of the World Council for Curriculum and Instruction, University of Keele, Sept. 1974. IPC Science and Technology Press, Guildford

Henderson G (ed.) 1973 *Education for Peace: Focus on Mankind.* Association for Supervision and Curriculum Development, Washington, DC

Wulf Ch (ed.) 1973 *Kritische Friedenserziehung* [Critical Peace Education]. Suhrkamp, Frankfurt/Main

Wulf Ch (ed.) 1974 *Handbook on Peace Education.* International Peace Association, Frankfurt/Oslo

International Education

D. Heater

"International education" or "studies" is a convenient generalized term to embrace a number of titles that denote an approach to the subject matter from a particular perspective. Other terms that have been in use at different times or in different countries include: education for world citizenship; education for international understanding; global studies; world studies; and peace studies.

The need to create a more internationally and peace-minded citizenry was stimulated by the horrors of the First World War, though the response was noticeable mainly only in the United States and the United Kingdom. More recent stimuli have been the horrifying experience of the Second World War, the terrifying threat of nuclear war, the consciousness of the frailty of the planet's biosphere, the perception of the interdependence of economies, and the need for justice for conscience's sake as well as for peace.

At the end of the Second World War UNESCO was created as the specialized agency for educational matters and in recognition of the belief that education had a vital role to play in banishing the curse of war. This work is undertaken on behalf of UNESCO by the National Commissions of the member states. The most significant scheme has been the Associated Schools Project (ASPRO) whereby schools and colleges are encouraged and helped to engage in experimental work on four selected themes. These are: world problems and the role of the United Nations system in solving them; human rights; other countries and cultures; and humans and their environment. By 1980 over 1,300 schools and colleges were participating from over 70 countries (Churchill and Omari 1981).

Since the 1920s and more particularly since the early 1960s, both the theory and practice of international education have become increasingly complex. Traditionally, courses have been confined to the secondary level and narrowly conceived as cognitive learning about other countries and the institutions of international cooperation, with the rare possibility in some European schools of a visit to a foreign country. More recently teaching about development and environmental issues has been added to this basic syllabus.

Increasingly, however, it is felt that learning about such matters by pupils sitting at their desks and books is an insufficient way of tackling the task. Indeed, for the more radical opponents of the traditional methods, it is not merely insufficient but positively inappropriate. The argument may be summarized briefly as follows. International education must essentially relate to attitudes rather than knowledge. The acquisition of knowledge alone does not necessarily lead to the adaptation of attitudes. *Tout comprendre, c'est tout pardonner* is liberal mentality at its most naïve. International education should concern itself with the cultivation of such values as empathy and tolerance. These qualities are best inculcated by participative learning processes. Furthermore, recent psychological research has shown how resistant adolescent minds are to attempts at changing an attitudinal mould already cast in earlier years (see e.g., Wolsk 1977).

Some advocates of international studies, however, argue that even this position is little more than a halfway house in pursuit of the really important objectives. These radicals reject the UNESCO proposition "that since wars begin in the minds of men, it is in the minds of men that the defences of peace must be constructed", believing instead that wars are caused by oppression and exploitation. Secondly, the shaping of "correct" attitudes is consequently little short of pointless unless it motivates to action—that is, action for greater justice in the world.

Just as there are different schools of thought relating to the objectives of international education, so there are different views about the way this teaching should be conducted in schools. The most common practice is to provide conventional subjects with a global perspective, or at least to avoid national and nationalistic bias in such training. Syllabi in history, religious studies, and social studies in particular have been revised in this way; the potential of geography for this educational purpose has always perhaps been more clearly recognized. Thus syllabi and the necessary textbooks have been written, for example, in world history and comparative religion. The danger of distorted textbooks, especially in history, as a source of national prejudice has long been recognized. Both the League of Nations Committee on Intellectual Cooperation and UNESCO issued documents on textbook revision. The work of the Georg Eckert Institute for International Textbook Research in Brunswick (FRG) is particularly important. As a result, the most blatant bias has been identified and much expunged from more recently published school books (Boden 1977).

The advocates of using the existing disciplines as vehicles for developing a global consciousness argue that only by thus internationalizing the curriculum can the reality of global interdependence be taught. They reject as artificial an alternative strategy of creating a new, separate subject of world studies. Other educationalists, nevertheless, believe that since by no means all teachers are willing or able to provide their subjects with global frames of reference, the teaching of world studies courses by the few really committed teachers is the more realistic way of progressing (e.g., Hanvey 1975).

The argument for pervasiveness together with the argument about the crucial importance of attitude formation lead many educationalists to emphasize the importance of whole school and extracurricular involvement in this field. Many different schemes have been tried. Some schools celebrate particular days such as United Nations Day. Others, particularly primary schools with more flexible timetables, involve all the pupils in the study of a particular topic, sometimes even involving parents. Yet others collect money to buy educational equipment for schools in underdeveloped countries. In communities with a multiethnic population some aspects of international studies are pursued in microcosm by learning both formally and informally about each others' cultural traditions (Pike and Selby 1988).

The everyday mixing of pupils from different countries and cultures is perhaps the most natural and effective way of pursuing international education. This is achieved for a limited number of pupils in international schools. For the 16–19 age range there are the four United World Colleges based in South Wales, Trieste, Vancouver, and Singapore. Moreover an examination for the 18–19 year old age level has been devised with an international currency. This is the International Baccalaureate, administered from its office (IBO) in Geneva (Leach 1969).

The advocates of international studies often complain that they receive too little support and recognition of the importance of their work. Opponents, or at least sceptics, argue that the study of the whole world is too immense a task for schools. In practice, many courses of study have a particular focus. Consciousness of, or a conscience about, particular international crises lead to courses with particular emphases: peace/conflict studies; Third World/development studies; black/multicultural studies; environmental/ecological studies; human rights education. Awareness of threats to the eco-system has led to particular emphasis on this fact.

Bibliography

Anderson L F 1979 *Schooling and Citizenship in a Global Age.* Social Studies Development Center, Bloomington, Indiana

Boden P K 1977 *Promoting International Understanding through School Textbooks: A Case Study.* Georg Eckert Institute For International Textbook Research, Brunswick

Buergenthal T, Torney J V 1976 *International Human Rights and International Education.* United States National Commission for UNESCO, Washington, DC

Churchill S, Omari I 1981 *Evaluation of the UNESCO Associated Schools Project in Education for International Cooperation and Peace.* UNESCO, Paris

Haavelsrud M (ed.) 1976 *Education for Peace: Reflection and Action.* IPC Science and Technology Press, Guildford

Hanvey R G 1975 *An Attainable Global Perspective.* Center for Global Perspectives, New York

Heater D 1990 *Citizenship: The Civic Ideal in World History, Politics and Education.* Longman, London

Leach R J 1969 *International Schools and their Role in the Field of International Education.* Pergamon, Oxford

Pike G, Selby D 1988 *Global Teacher, Global Learner.* Hodder and Stoughton, London

Remy R C et al. 1975 *International Learning and International Education in a Global Age.* National Council for the Social Studies, Washington, DC

Wolsk D 1977 *An Experience-centered Curriculum: Exercises in Perception, Communication, and Action.* UNESCO, Paris

Women's Studies

M. Johnson

Women's studies is the name given to a multidisciplinary group of topics focusing on content concerning females. Teachers of women's studies courses include scholars from such areas as anthropology, art, biology, economics, education, health, history, law, religion, sociology, and urban studies. An art historian might, for example, organize a course on women as subjects in art from the middle ages to the eighteenth century. Other humanities courses might focus on literary or historical portrayals of women at different points in time. Social scientists study women's place in society, and physical scientists, including some psychologists, investigate women's physical capacities. Scholars in the social sciences and the humanities have been most active in women's studies programs, probably because their subject matter provides so much material for study.

The title of women's studies may refer to courses in secondary schools, colleges, or universities as well as to academic programs within institutions of higher education. Women's studies programs in universities in the United States came into being during the late 1960s and early 1970s as a result of the growth of the feminist movement. Like the black studies programs which preceded them, they evolved from a social–political movement and they drew from a number of academic disciplines. Administratively, the courses are organized into programs rather than departments which are organized around scholarly disciplines. Therefore, women's studies faculty members hold a faculty appointment in the department of their basic discipline and hold another in the women's studies program.

1. Modal Curriculum

A modal curriculum is outlined below which illustrates the multidisciplinary nature of women's studies.

(a) Women painters of the twentieth century (art history).

(b) Women in fiction: from Colette to Joyce Carol Oates (literature).

(c) Psychology of women: a survey course (psychology).

(d) Women in primitive societies (anthropology).

(e) A historical view of women as healers (history).

(f) Women in education (education).

(g) Women's roles in political movements (political science).

(h) Sex-role socialization (sociology).

2. Current Status

About 330 institutions of higher education in the United States offer women's studies programs. Of these, 80 award a B.A., 20 award an M.A., and five award a doctorate (Ph.D. or Ed.D.) in women's studies. In addition, Stanford University in California (USA) has organized a degree in feminist studies. Other programs offer minors or certificates. The majority of university students take only one or two elective courses and most of these students are women. In the United States, the National Women's Studies Association, founded in 1977, has over 2,000 members who are involved in supporting women's studies as an increasingly important academic area. The association holds yearly conferences and supports regional associations as well. The association's internal caucuses indicate the broad scope of scholars in women's studies; among others, they consist of separate groups focusing on community college populations, on prekindergarten through high school populations, and on Third World concerns.

The international scope of the growth of women's studies was demonstrated in May 1980 when UNESCO invited a committee of experts to Paris to discuss research and teaching related to women. These experts, representing Europe, Africa, the Caribbean, North and South America, the Middle East, and Asia, emphasized the contributions to education that scholarships could make in women's studies: for example, work on achievement motivation in males and females, on sex differences in cognitive abilities, on the status of women as teachers, and so on.

The committee of experts also recommended that UNESCO provide assistance toward the design of curriculum research geared to the needs of particular regions, toward the preparation of curricular materials for teaching women's studies in particular regions, and toward the development of research tools for collection of baseline data to be used in women's studies programs. UNESCO's support of such projects and of the scholarships and visiting professorships called for by the committee would greatly expand the exposure of all students to the constantly growing bodies of knowledge encompassed within women's studies.

3. Teaching and Research

The growth of teaching and research materials in women's studies during the decade of the 1980s was formidable. In 1970, textbooks did not exist and research scholarship had only just begun. By 1980, it was necessary to choose from a wealth of rich sources. Many dissertations and theses have been conducted on women's studies as a result of the growing expertise of interested faculty members. University humanities and social and behavioral science departments have found it necessary to seek scholars in women's studies who can direct theses and dissertations in these areas.

The effects of the courses themselves on students' attitudes toward women have become the subject of a number of research studies. Because the curricular material so often touches critical aspects of students' lives and thus creates greater awareness of sex differences, the students frequently demonstrate an increased concern about the effects of socialization on women and

men. Behavioral scientists have pointed to women's studies courses as leading to attitude change (Johnson 1982).

Instructors of psychology of women courses have assessed students' pre- and post-course status on attitudes toward women and on androgyny as a means of measuring the impact of their courses. They frequently make identical assessments of students in other psychology courses for comparative purposes. In addition, male psychiatric residents studying psychology of women have been evaluated in terms of change in values and beliefs about women and mental health. Investigators have also examined the effect of change in self-concept as a function of participation in a women's studies course. Most women's studies specialists have determined that it is still extremely difficult to separate the intellectual aspects of the courses from their emotional impact (Brush and White 1978, Carmen and Driver 1982, Unger 1982, Vedovato and Vaughter 1980).

Research and theory emerging from women's studies appears in traditional scientific journals and books. In addition, several specialized journals have appeared in recent years: *Frontiers: A Journal of Women's Studies* (University of Maryland, College Park, Maryland, USA), *Women's Studies International Forum* (Pergamon Press, Oxford, UK), *International Journal of Women's Studies* (Eden Press, St. Albans, Vermont, USA), *Signs: Journal of Women and Culture in Society* (University of Chicago, Chicago, Illinois, USA), and *Psychology of Women Quarterly* (Human Sciences Press, New York, USA).

4. Future of Women's Studies

The increasing number of women attending colleges and universities, the relevance of the material to students' lives, the scholarly value of uncovering and/or discovering materials and data formerly lost or disregarded—all of these serve to sustain and promote the growth of women's studies programs. The First International Interdisciplinary Congress on Women, held in Israel in December 1981, marked the beginning of a new stage of cooperation and collaboration among scholars of women's studies. In addition to the new content addressed by women's studies, scholars have proposed taking a critical look at current research methodologies. They suggest an evaluation of the questions and methods of current studies and they recommend the use of qualitative research methods. Whatever the method, the results of ongoing research and the continuation of curriculum building in women's studies offer promise of rich opportunities for the interaction of scholars from many disciplines.

Women's studies during the 1980s can be characterized by two factors. First, it has become an international phenomenon. This is best demonstrated by study of the *Women's Studies International Forum*, a bimonthly journal which contains articles written by and about women from Europe, Africa, Australia, Asia, Latin America, and North America. The journal presents research papers; book reviews; discussions of theoretical, methodological, and historical issues; and a forum section which discusses meetings taking place in all parts of the world, and which promotes the formation of networks of women's studies academics in different countries. The second factor emerging during the 1980s has been the increasing effort to integrate or "mainstream" women's studies content into the higher education curriculum (Bowles and Klein 1983, Aiken et al. 1988). Such integration makes possible the dissemination of important knowledge to the majority of students of higher education, many of whom might not elect to take a women's studies course. The international impact and the successful integration of women's studies have joined to give women's studies greater educational legitimacy.

Bibliography

Aiken S, Anderson K, Dinnerstein M, Lensink J, MacCorquodale S A 1988 *Changing Our Minds: Feminist Transformations of Knowledge*. State University of New York Press, Albany, New York

Bowles G, Klein R (eds.) 1983 *Theories of Women's Studies*. Routledge and Kegan Paul, London

Brush L, White M 1978 The paradox of intention and effect: A women's studies course. *Signs: J. Women Culture Soc.* 3: 870–83

Carmen E, Driver P 1982 Teaching women's studies: Values in conflict. *Psychol. Women Q.* 7(1): 81–95

Johnson M 1982 Research on teaching the psychology of women. *Psychol. Women Q.* 7(1): 96–104

Unger R 1982 Advocacy versus scholarship revisited: Issues in the psychology of women. *Psychol. Women Q.* 7(1): 5–17

Vedovato S, Vaughter R 1980 Psychology of women courses changing sexist and sex-typed attitudes. *Psychol. Women Q.* 4: 587–90

Black Studies

W. H. Watkins

The term Black Studies refers to courses and educational programs which deal with topics related to the culture and life of Black people. Born on the White university campuses of the northern United States in the turbulent 1960s, Black Studies has left an imprint on the curriculum, throughout institutions of learning, and as a part of the social struggle for Black equality. Though Black Studies has never enjoyed the status and attention of the established social sciences, it has nevertheless contributed considerably to the Black intellectual tradition in the United States.

1. Background

Following the Second World War, interest and enrollment in US higher education experienced extraordinary growth. Between 1955 and 1965, the number of students (undergraduate and graduate) enrolled in colleges and universities in the United States more than doubled. The three million students enrolled during that decade more than equalled the total number of students during the previous three centuries of American higher education.

By the late 1960s several factors converged to bring large numbers of Blacks to attend White colleges outside the South. First, the Black migration northward dispersed approximately one-half its population to the urban centers of the East, Midwest, and far West. Second, the liberalism of the 1960s fostered the ideas that everyone could benefit from, and should have access to, higher education. Third, higher education became a persistent civil rights demand thought to promote a more just society. Between 1967 and 1971, Black college enrollment rose from under 6.4 to 8.4 percent of total college enrollment.

Inspired by the movement for civil rights and social change, Black and sympathetic White students challenged universities to break with the traditions of academic detachment and the "ivory tower". Black students wanted courses and programs to become "relevant" to the lives of Black people in the ghettos and the rural South. They insisted that the universities become active in attacking racism.

The often angry demand for change most frequently targeted the humanities curriculum, which was denounced as Western and exclusive. The curriculum was said to reflect "arrogant white men in self-congratulatory identification with grand European culture" (Huggins 1985). Black students thus began to challenge the objectivity of mainstream social science.

As the larger civil rights movement provided context, the call for university and curriculum reform pressed forward. Responding to student pressures, prominent college administrators and liberal-minded academics joined the denunciation of American higher education's complicity in stifling the advancement of Black people.

During the latter half of the 1960s, the student demands for a Black Studies curriculum grew more strident. Student disorder became increasingly common. Disruptions at schools such as San Francisco State, Wesleyan, Harvard, Cornell, and many others dramatized the sentiment for curriculum reform. By 1971 there were over 500 Black Studies programs in existence in predominantly White educational institutions. Often hastily established, they ranged from a few courses taught by Black graduate students and adjunct professors to complete autonomous programs with new Black faculty members recruited exclusively for that purpose.

2. The Black Intellectual Tradition

Prior to the 1960s, writings by Black scholars were almost nonexistent in White institutions. While this new hybrid, Black Studies, had little precedent in its own right, it was inextricably linked to the long but obscured traditions of the Black intelligentsia.

As far back as the late nineteenth century, Black historians and social scientists actively engaged in inquiry and explanation. However, works such as the *History of the Negro Race in America from 1619 to 1880* written in 1883 by George Washington Williams (Williams 1968), *Black and White: Land, Labor, and Politics in the South* written by Timothy Thomas Fortune the following year (Fortune 1968), and many others attracted little attention.

A second generation of prominent Black social theorists further established a tradition of scholarly inquiry. W E B Du Bois researched the social, economic, and political conditions of his people. Among his many outstanding works are *The Souls of Black Folk* (Du Bois 1969) and *Philadelphia Negro* (Du Bois 1967) both written at the turn of the century, and *The World and Africa* (Du Bois 1965) written in 1947. Carter G Woodson founded the Association for the Study of Negro Life and History in 1916. Charles H Thompson established the *Journal of Negro Education* at Howard University in 1932. Lorenzo Turner established one of the first African Studies programs at Fisk University in the early 1940s. Through the decades of the 1920s to the 1950s, creative Black novelists and poets helped define a culture forged in the crucible of the American Black experience. A Black intellectual tradition had firmly taken shape.

The contemporary Black Studies of the late 1960s, 1970s, and 1980s is both explicitly and implicitly a product of such tradition. Because Black studies programs were born of social protest, it was unavoidable that they became entangled in the ideological discourse of the times. Many individuals and programs were drawn into the debate on whether the Black Nationalist or social class orientation offered the better explanations. Marxism, while a significant factor in the Black intellectual tradition, has never been the dominant current (Marable 1986).

3. An Interdisciplinary Curriculum

Black studies course offerings have been as diverse as the schools in which they appeared. Hasty organization, lack of clear policy guidelines, and ill-conceived commitments of personnel, space, equipment, money, and time are among the most frequently cited reasons given for initial program confusion. Course titles have ranged from the mundane to the exotic. The University of California's catalog listed among its Black Studies courses: Black Politics in the United States; Black Economic History; Black People and Psychology; Survey of Afro–American Literature; The Black Aesthetic; The Black Experience in Theatre; Black Art in the New World; Afro–American Poetry; The Black Essay; and Survey of Afro–American Literature. Such offerings seem representative of Black Studies programs in general.

The debate on whether or not the Black Studies curriculum is legitimate continues. Some proponents have suggested a core curriculum while others have worked to advance and refine rationale. The National Council for Black Studies in a 1981 report defined the purpose and rationale of the program: (a) to provide skills; (b) to provide a standard and purposefully direct student choice; (c) to achieve liberation of the Black community; and (d) to enhance self-awareness and esteem. Black Studies, the report says, "inaugurates an unflinching attack on institutional oppression/racism."

While conceptualizations of Black Studies have differed, one organizing feature has emerged, namely that Black Studies should transcend the boundaries of traditional disciplines. Most course offerings have fallen within the areas of history and culture. Literature, music, and the arts have also provided subject areas for the field. Of the social sciences, sociology has been most open to the examination of Black issues. Economists and political scientists have been the least willing to outline a specialization on Black American issues (Huggins 1985). Nascent areas such as Women's Studies have provided fertile ground for Black Studies to expand. A review of Black Studies programs in Western Land Grant colleges (Sims 1978) identified courses such as Black Women in History and Black Women in Colonial America. The fields of business and law have been moderately amenable to the inclusion of Black Studies courses.

Black Studies curricula have been tailored to available talent and institutional resources. Few students have chosen to major in Black Studies but rather select courses on an elective basis.

4. Black Studies in the Public Schools

Just as with higher education, Black Studies in the US public schools was hastily constructed in response to pressure and the racial/political climate of the late 1960s and early 1970s. Confrontations over the issue became common between minorities and school policy makers. Even districts with few or no minority groups became concerned with this matter.

Seven states of the United States established the foundation for Black Studies curricula to appear in public schools: California, Connecticut, Illinois, Michigan, Nebraska, New Jersey, and Oklahoma. The motives of these states were mixed. Some were pressured by students and/or community residents; others, foreseeing the trend, acted in a pre-emptive fashion; and yet others acted out of a genuine concern that curriculum reform was now in order.

The first law remotely to address Black Studies specifically involved minority history in California in

1961. The law forbids the State Department of Education to approve any textbook that "does not correctly portray the role and contribution of the American Negro and members of other ethnic groups in the total development of the United States and of the state of California." Furthermore, if such a book is found in any public high school in the state after an investigation by "impartial experts" and a public hearing, the law requires the publisher to pay for the investigation.

California subsequently passed two more laws in the area. A 1965 statute required the State Board of Education to adopt textbooks for civics and history courses at all levels of public school that "correctly portray the role and contribution of the American Negro and members of other ethnic groups in the total development of the United States and of the state of California." A 1968 statute broadened the language to include other minorities. It mandated that grades 1–12 "shall include the early history of California and a study of the role and contributions of American Negroes, American Indians, Mexicans, and other ethnic groups to the economic, political, and social development of California and the United States of America."

The Oklahoma statute of 1965 directs the State Board of Education to require accredited elementary and secondary schools to include the history and culture of Blacks and other minorities in their curricula. It also asked that a bibliography be made available in the areas of minority history and culture.

The Illinois statute of 1967 reads: "The teaching of history shall include a study of the role and contributions of American Negroes and other ethnic groups including, but not restricted to, Polish, Lithuanian, German, Hungarian, Irish, Bohemian, Russian, Albanian, Italian, Czechoslovakian, French, Scottish, etc. in the history of the country and this state." In addition, this law mandated inspection or supervisory visits from the State Board combined with annual reports submitted by the schools demonstrating compliance.

New Jersey in 1967 produced a joint resolution of the state legislature recommending "that the high school curriculum fairly and accurately depicts the role of the Negro in the history of the United States," and that "appropriate materials to achieve this purpose" are included in the curriculum immediately.

The 1969 Nebraska law was the most specific regarding subject areas. It stated that beginning in 1971 all American history courses "shall include and adequately stress contributions of all ethnic groups to the development and growth of America as a great nation" and, specifically, their "contribution to art, music, education, medicine, literature, science, politics, and government, and the war services in all wars of this nation."

Both Connecticut and Michigan approached Black Studies through restrictions on textbooks. A 1969 Connecticut law says, "each town or regional board of education shall, in selecting textbooks for social studies, use textbooks which present the achievements and accomplishments of individuals and groups from all ethnic and racial backgrounds." The Michigan Social Studies Textbook Act of 1966 requires officials to select books which fairly depict the achievements of ethnic and racial groups.

5. Black Studies: Models of Organization

Black Studies operations differ from campus to campus. Determinants include school commitment, budget allocations, faculty, and conceptualizations of organization. Among those models which evolved were the program, the college, the department, the graduate program, the undergraduate center, and the research institute.

(a) *The program.* This commonly used model is based on an interdisciplinary approach, and draws faculty from established departments. Such faculty members remain within their home discipline while contributing courses to Black Studies part-time. Faculty receive joint appointments to the Black Studies department and program. This approach allows Black Studies to draw easily from the curricula of other departments. In most cases, this model is not degree-granting. Students frequently opt for a minor, a certificate, or course hour credits toward other social science majors.

(b) *The college.* This approach establishes a college within the university. While rare, some universities have considered this model before settling on a program model. The college model offers degrees, a self-contained faculty, and the administrative status of other colleges within the university.

(c) *The department.* This model establishes an autonomous department of Black or Afro–American Studies. Such a department is characterized by its own budget, the ability to design its own curriculum, and the power to appoint and dismiss faculty. The department concept eschews the notion that the curriculum of Black Studies is interdisciplinary, but rather claims it as an independent discipline. Major universities such as Harvard, University of Indiana, and the University of California at Berkeley have adopted the department model. It should be noted that since their inception in the early 1970s these department-style operations have evolved to come more into line with the demands and appointment policies of their universities.

(d) *Graduate programs.* In this infrequently used model, the university offers a graduate degree in Afro–American studies. Yale University is among the few that offer an M.A. in the field.

(e) *The undergraduate center.* A center of this type may exist where there is no academic program for Black Studies. Often they provide services such as counseling and career guidance. Additionally, they may host cultural affairs, lectures, and social activities. Such centers, where they exist, reach beyond the university into the larger community.

(f) *The research center or institute.* Research institutes are sometimes unattached to universities. Usually considered prestigious, these institutes attract research scholars of the highest caliber. Typically funded by corporate foundations, the researcher can carry on work removed from the teaching and administrative responsibilities of the academy. Among the best-known research institutes generally associated with Black Studies are The Institute of the Black World (IBW) in Atlanta, the W E B Du Bois Institute for Afro–American Studies at Harvard, the Carter G Woodson Institute for Afro–American and African Studies started by the University of Virginia, and the Urban Center in New York City affiliated with Columbia University.

6. Black Studies: Retrospect and Prospect

The passionate demand for and popularity of Black Studies was short-lived. By 1975 a sharp decline was noted in the enrollment of such programs. Trapped as an interdisciplinary program with little relevance to the job market, many Black Studies operations have lost momentum. In addition, other factors have weakened Black Studies efforts. The once-burgeoning enrollment of Blacks in universities has leveled off. Blacks pursuing academic careers was an "anomaly" of the past decade (Huggins 1985). With regard to Black faculty, all projections point to a decline in the number of Blacks enrolled in doctoral programs.

While there has been attrition, Black Studies endeavors continue. Further contraction seems likely, though student interest in selective courses remains firm. Black and Afro–American Studies programs continue to add another dimension to both scholarly inquiry and to the aim of preparation for all people to live harmoniously in a multiracial society.

Bibliography

Blassingame J W (ed.) 1971 *New Perspectives on Black Studies.* University of Illinois, Urbana, Illinois

Du Bois W E B 1965 *The World and Africa.* International Publishers, New York

Du Bois W E B 1967 *The Philadelphia Negro: A Social Study.* B Blom, New York

Du Bois W E B 1969 *The Souls of Black Folk.* New American Library, New York

Ford N A 1973 *Black Studies: Threat or Challenge.* Kennikat Press, Port Washington, New York

Fortune T T 1968 *Black and White: Land, Labor, and Politics in the South.* Arno Press, New York

Frye C A 1976 *The Impact of Black Studies on the Curricula of Three Universities.* University Press of America, Washington, DC

Frye C A 1978 *Towards a Philosophy of Black Studies.* R & E Research Associates, San Francisco, California

Giles R H 1974 *Black Studies Programs in Public Schools.* Praeger, New York

Huggins N 1985 *Afro–American Studies: A Report to the Ford Foundation.* Ford Foundation, New York

Marable M 1986 Black studies: Marxism and the Black intellectual tradition. In: Ollman B, Vernoff E (eds.) 1968 *The Left Academy: Marxist Scholarship on American Campuses,* Vol. 3. Praeger, New York

Reid I S 1970 An analysis of Black Studies programs. *Afro–Am. Stud.* 1(1): 11–21

Richards H J (ed.) 1971 *Topics in Afro–American Studies.* Black Academy Press, Buffalo, New York

Sims W E 1978 *Black Studies: Pitfalls and Potential.* University Press of America, Washington, DC

Williams G W 1968 *History of the Negro Race in America 1619–1880.* Arno Press, New York

Daily Living Skills

R. J. Riehs

Daily living skills—sometimes called "survival skills" or "life skills"—include those competencies which are commonly used in day-to-day life. They are the capabilities which are necessary for functioning both at home and in society.

There are two worldwide educational trends which emphasize daily living skills. In countries where large portions of the population have had little or no formal education, educational programs are being expanded to provide more students with more instruction in the skills necessary for daily living. In countries where nearly everyone receives several years of schooling, educational programs are being changed by eliminating extraneous or very theoretical items from the compulsory curricula, to make room for a core of more practical or "relevant" competencies in a large number of subject areas.

There has been a tendency among curriculum planners in many countries (particularly since the emergence of competency-based education) to differentiate among three categories of core competencies: basic skills (providing a foundation for further education), life skills,

and job-preparation skills. There is, of course, a tremendous overlap between these categories, and most experts agree that numeracy and literacy are at the cognitive core of each.

1. Literacy

Literacy generally includes not only reading and writing, but also facility with the related language skills of speaking and listening. Even experts within individual countries disagree significantly about how developed these skills must be in order to achieve "minimal" competence. Nevertheless, they do recognize that literacy, at some level, is a prerequisite for normal, daily living in virtually every society. Furthermore, reading, writing, speaking, and listening skills are fundamental learning tools and are therefore essential for further education and continued intellectual growth beyond "minimal" or "survival" levels.

It is worth mentioning here that literacy has not always been recognized as a necessary skill for daily living. At the end of the eighteenth century, "literacy" was frequently judged by the capacity of a person to form the letters of their name. Furthermore, even that minimal level of competence was mastered by less than half of the population in the developed nations of Europe (Resnick and Resnick 1977). It is quite apparent that, over the last 200 years, there has been a substantial increase in societal expectations concerning literacy and a substantial increase in actual skill levels (by whatever definition of literacy used).

There seems to be general agreement that complex technological and/or bureaucratic societies demand higher levels of literacy. However, even in the rural areas of Asia, Africa, and Latin America, there is evidence of a growing determination to increase the level of literacy. The five-year readership promotion campaign in Malaysia (launched in 1980) and the earlier Brazilian literacy movement (MOBRAL) are just two examples of a worldwide trend.

2. Computer Literacy

An emerging "convenience" in a few highly technological societies, computer literacy may well become a necessity of survival in the not-so-distant future. Already, in the Federal Republic of Germany, for example, the Federal States, the *Gesellschaft fuer Informatik*, and various committees of the Ministry of Science have demanded that the basics of computers and informatics be taught in the schools. Similar suggestions can be heard from Scotland's Munn Committee (1977) and in the new curriculum (Lgr 80) implemented in Sweden in 1982.

In several countries computer literacy is regarded as a "daily living skill" for tomorrow's adults. It is therefore appropriately being identified as an area for emphasis in today's schools.

3. Mathematics

Curricular change in mathematics has been markedly tumultuous during the 1970s and early 1980s. There has been an almost worldwide shift in emphasis from the highly theoretical to the more practical—away from "new math", and "back to basics". In other words, there has been an increasing educational focus on daily living skills, job-preparation skills, and basic skills needed for further education.

In the Federal Republic of Germany, a single term—*mathematische Allgemeinbildung*—is used to include all three of the above skill categories, and it is being given increased emphasis in the curriculum. In Sweden, Kenya, and South Australia, new mathematics curricula (implemented in the early 1980s) quite explicitly lay special stress on daily living skills. Each of these programs includes extensive testing to monitor the mastery of individual skills.

Numerous studies are being made to identify precise lists of necessary mathematical competencies. One of the most convenient sources of input is potential

employers. In England, for example, the Shell Centre for Mathematical Education has been doing extensive research on the mathematical needs of school leavers entering employment. The Education for the Industrial Society Project has been performing similar investigations in Scotland, as has the University of Klagenfurt in Austria.

In some school systems, a focus on survival or daily living skills has been seen as a rationale for trimming down the curriculum and, concurrently, trimming down the budget. However, while serious inquiries are identifying some mathematical skills which do not have to be taught, they are identifying many more topics which are not being emphasized and should be. A 1979 survey by the Science Education Center of the University of the Philippines, and a slightly earlier study in the Federal Republic of Germany, are just two examples which support the growing realization that "trimming back" curricula to include basic, necessary, or relevant skills will result, in most societies, in an increase in the amount of mathematics instruction.

4. Multiple Subject Areas

While numeracy and literacy are widely thought of as the academic core of daily living skills, they are not generally considered the only skills necessary for survival in day-to-day life. Unfortunately, it would be quite impossible to construct a universally acceptable list of such skills. The individual items would vary significantly from country to country (depending on the level of technological development, the political system, cultural traditions, and even the climate). Nevertheless, in specific geographical areas, efforts have been made to identify (and implement in the school curriculum) a broad range of competencies used in daily living.

In British Columbia (Canada), for example, the Ministry of Education has introduced a core curriculum identifying the competencies which are generally accepted there as essential—competencies which should be mastered by all students throughout the province. This core curriculum focuses on basic skills in the areas of language, measurement and computation, scientific approach, cultural and physical heritage, analysis research, study and problem solving, and healthful living (Ministry of Education 1977).

The Maryland (USA) State Board of Education has outlined five areas in which students should develop at least miminum competencies (necessary for graduation after 1982): basic skills (numeracy and literacy), survival skills (consumer, parenting, interpersonal, mechanical, and financial), work skills, leisure skills, and citizenship skills.

The important characteristic of the new curricula in both British Columbia and Maryland is the emphasis placed on learning skills which are needed for living, for working, and for learning. Similar movements toward educational relevance in multiple subject areas can be found at various stages of consideration or implementation throughout the world. In Scotland, the Munn Report (1977) provides one instance of curriculum change at the consideration stage. In Australia, the Northern Territory Department of Education reached the implementation stage in seven subject areas in 1981.

The relevance of education to daily living experiences has become a fundamental concern throughout the world. There is a clear understanding that, while in school, individuals must be given more knowledge and must develop more skills than they would have needed to survive a generation ago. Educational planning, then, has focused on providing the opportunities for more learning to more students, and on assuring that programs include the minimal competencies for daily living.

Bibliography

Avakov R M 1980 *The Future of Education and the Education of the Future*. UNESCO, Paris [also published in French]

Behrstock J 1981 Reaching the rural reader. *J. Read.* 24: 712–18

British Columbia Ministry of Education 1977 *Guide to the Core Curriculum*. Ministry of Education, Richmond, British Columbia

Resnick D P, Resnick L B 1977 The nature of literacy: An historical exploration. *Harvard Educ. Rev.* 47: 370–85

Riehs R J 1981 *An International Review of Minimal Competency Programs in Mathematics*. SMEAC Information Reference Center, Ohio State University, Columbus, Ohio

Scottish Education Department 1977 *The Structure of the Curriculum in the Third and Fourth Year of the Scottish Secondary School*. (Munn Report). Her Majesty's Stationery Office, Edinburgh

Consumer Education

P. Idman

Consumer education aims to educate the pupils to become critical, knowledgeable, and rational consumers, conscious of their needs and capable of choosing products in a relatively free and uninfluenced manner. This in its turn is expected to lead to effective economic competition and healthy and correct production corresponding to the consumer's needs and wishes.

The demand that society should ensure through its schools that all its members acquire a basic consumer education goes back a long way. Increasingly, people purchase goods instead of producing articles for their own needs. This development makes it essential for schools to provide individuals with the knowledge and skills that will enable them to function satisfactorily as consumers, both privately and from the point of view of the national economy. The flood of goods offered, the influence exerted by advertising on sales, and the more and more complicated technical nature of these goods, combined with the reduced amount of personal advice given to the shopper, place the individual, as a consumer, in a difficult situation for which he or she lacks preparation and knowledge.

These topics and issues constitute the focus of consumer education as widely interpreted hitherto. Nevertheless, certain problems and trends in the so-called "consumer society", which means the prosperous community that endeavours to increase its material consumption still further, have focused interest on new types of consumer problems. There are two different main problems which have come to influence people's ideas on present-day consumer education and its objectives. One is concerned with disturbance of the environment and with the management of natural resources, the other with the influence exerted on plans made and decisions taken by commerce and industry and by the state and local authorities, and setting limits to freedom to choose a life-style or consumption pattern.

The problem of the effects of production and consumption conditions on the environment and natural resources has had an influence on present conceptions of consumer education. People have also questioned whether the use of consumer education for society is to be assessed simply from an economic standpoint. Insight into the effects of increased production on the relationship between the rich and the poor parts of the world and also on the durability of the resources of the environment and of nature has opened up a new perspective on consumer education. The main aspect of its social usefulness which is now emphasized is the importance of adapting consumption to the environment and natural resources.

The problem of the influence exerted on the plans made and decisions taken by commerce and industry and by state and local authorities arises from the fact that more and more tasks in the community are no longer carried out by a private individual assuming the responsibility or by cooperation between individuals in the household, family, and neighbourhood, but are now performed either by organizations controlled by the community or by commerce and industry. This development has led to increasing interest in the question of how individuals can continue to participate in decision making when the questions to be decided are of importance for their whole life-style and consumption pattern.

A needs assessment study in Sweden identified five specific areas of consumer education (Idman 1977):

(a) Consumption behaviour
(b) Influence on consumption
(c) Private consumption
(d) Consumption policy
(e) Consumer influence

(a) *Consumption behaviour.* Instruction on important factors which can mould both behaviour in general and consumption behaviour is intended to create in the pupils: insight into the factors which form people's consumption behaviour and an understanding of other people's and other groups' consumption habits; reflection on the significance of the conception of welfare, and reasons for defining one's attitude to the aim of one's own welfare; and a critically analytical attitude to different communities' assessments of welfare and to the means for achieving this welfare for all people.

(b) *Influence on consumption.* Education on channels for transmission of assessments and attitudes in consumption and welfare matters and on marketing methods is aimed at creating in the pupils: an insight into the fact that assessments and standards concerning consumption and welfare are influenced and transmitted through a variety of channels; an ability to identify assessments and norms concerning consumption and welfare in the supply of information; awareness of deficiencies in information on consumption and ability to test the material objective basis of an argument; and an insight into the most usual ways of exerting an influence in modern marketing.

(c) *Private consumption.* The purpose of the instruction on matters of private economy is to create in the pupils: the ability to plan their economy and consumption in proper relation both to their needs and wishes and to the available resources and possibilities; an insight into the advantages and drawbacks of different forms of purchase, payment, and saving; and an ability to collect, digest, and assess information relevant to consumption planning, together with an awareness of the consumer's rights to objective all-round information.

(d) *Consumption policy.* Instruction in socioeconomic and consumption policy matters is aimed at creating in the pupils: an insight into the socioeconomic connection and the decision making and responsibility structures which determine production, consumption, and living conditions; an insight into the technical, economic, and political conditions which act on the distribution of the world's joint resources; and a consciousness of the connection which prevails between consumption and production conditions on the one hand and pollution of the environment and exhaustion of resources on the other.

(e) *Consumer influence.* Instruction on the consumers' rights, obligations, and influence is aimed at creating in the pupils: an awareness of consumers' rights and obligations and an ability to protect their interest in regard to consumption; and conditions for participation and willingness to participate in decision making, and use of the channels through which production and consumption conditions can be influenced.

Research pertaining to consumer education of school children relates to the following problems.

Firstly, recent research on the relevance of consumer education to school children emphasizes the importance of consumer education throughout the life of a person (Rader 1972). Young children are vulnerable to manipulation by irresponsible advertisers, and therefore consumer education is relevant to their needs. McKenzie (1970) lists concepts of interest and relevance to children such as consumer consumption, choices, decisions, alternatives, production, consumption, and savings.

Secondly an increasing body of research addresses the problem of children's consumer behaviour. The Consumers' Union survey (1972) points out that even 6-year-old children function as consumers with discretionary spending power. Children of ages 9 to 13 in the United States spend a considerable amount of money on toys and sugar-related snacks. Ninety-eight percent of the children at this age usually or sometimes go with their parents to the grocery store or to the supermarket. It is estimated that in the United States, teenagers spend US $20 billion per year on merchandise, service, and entertainment, beyond the expenses for food, clothing, and shelter provided by their families.

Thirdly, problems related to consumer education are incorporated in several school-subject areas—social studies, language arts, art, mathematics, science, health, and home economics. Numerous studies provide descriptions of successful consumer education programmes. Evans (1972) reports on the successful utilization of visits to the supermarket for teaching consumer problems. He gives examples of learning activities which can take place in different areas of the supermarket. Shurr (1974) uses toys for conveying basic economic concepts, such as what makes a good buy? What is the quality of a product?

Relatively few studies deal with the impact of consumer education programmes. Those reported tend to provide evidence about the success of these programmes in improving consumer habits and in developing a critical attitude toward commercials (Radis 1973).

Bibliography

Consumers' Union of the United States of America 1972 *Elementary Level Consumer Education.* Consumers' Union of the United States of America, Mount Vernon, New York
Evans D W 1972 The supermarket: A consumer's classroom. *Instructor* 82: 60–62
Idman P 1977 *Consumer Education in School: An Experiment in the Production of Educational Material* (Educational and Psychological Interactions, no. 63). School of Education, Malmö
McKenzie R B 1970 The economic literacy of elementary school pupils. *Elem. Sch. J.* 71: 26–35
Rader W D 1972 Working with young consumers in the classroom. *Instructor* 82: 55–59
Radis M W 1973 Consumerism belongs in the classroom too. *Teacher* 90: 54–56
Shurr S 1974 Consumerism. *Teacher* 91: 48–51
Western Provincial Task Force 1976 *Consumer Oriented Studies for Elementary School Children.* Edmonton, Alberta

Drug Education Programs

D. J. Hanson

Drug education takes many forms involving varying permutations of objectives, targets, teaching personnel, and contents and methods. Objectives typically call for either the prevention/elimination of all unacceptable drug use or for the maintenance/reduction of use to levels that minimize negative consequences. The targets are potential users, experimental users, regular users, or the friends, relatives, or associates of any of these groups. The teaching personnel include classroom teachers and personnel drawn from the ranks of the professional and lay communities, from drug users and exusers, and from among the target group themselves. The content of programs ranges from unbiased presentations of drug facts to discussion of the legal, personal, and social ramifications of drug use, to the use of materials with a strong antidrug orientation. Methods include the use of scare tactics, logical arguments (one-sided or two-sided), authorities or experts, self-examination and values clarification, peer approaches, alternative approaches, and others.

1. Background

There exists extensive evidence that the use of alcohol and other drugs has occurred in most societies throughout the world and has probably been known since the Paleolithic Age and certainly since the Neolithic Age. Accounts of alcohol or drug use are found on ancient Egyptian carvings, Hebrew script, and Babylonian tablets. The Code of Hammurabi (c. 2225 BC) devoted several sections to problems created by the abuse of alcohol and in China, laws that forbade making wine were enacted and repealed 41 times between 1100 BC and AD 1400. These and other sources of evidence indicate that concern over alcohol and drug use and abuse are not unique to present societies.

Although drug education can be traced back for many decades, minimal attention was directed to it before the mid-1960s. At that time, recognition of drug abuse as a major problem emerged throughout much of the world. The common reaction was to call for the rapid establishment or expansion of drug prevention education programs. In response to the perceived crisis, numerous educational programs were quickly developed during the late 1960s and early 1970s. Faith in education as the primary preventative agent of undesirable conditions receives widespread support, yet it is important to evaluate the effectiveness of educational programs. By analyzing the effects of various components of drug education, educators may have a more secure foundation on which to design or choose their programs.

2. Curriculum

Basic issues faced in developing a drug education program include objectives, target group, teaching personnel, and content and method.

2.1 Objectives

Objectives of drug prevention education are typically categorized as cognitive, affective, and behavioral. They can also be long or short range and simple or complex. However, in all cases they should be explicit, consistent with other objectives of the larger educational framework, and understood by those charged with achieving them.

A major problem in drug education lies in determining objectives. Among the objectives of such education, the following are often identified: (a) to increase accurate knowledge about drugs; (b) to change attitudes about drugs; (c) to bring about values clarification so as to assist students in making their own decisions regarding drugs; (d) to assist students' emotional maturity and stability so as to reduce motivation for drug use; (e) to deter experimentation with illicit drugs; (f) to prevent chronic use of illicit drugs; and (g) to teach responsible use of legal drugs.

Implicitly, these objectives are all directed toward the larger goal of drug abuse reduction. However, it should be recognized that increasing accurate knowledge about drugs does not necessarily lead to that larger goal. The same has been demonstrated to be true for values clarification and increased emotional security.

Clearly, specifying the objectives of drug education is especially important when evaluations of its effectiveness are to be conducted.

2.2 Target Group

The potential target groups of a drug education program are typically categorized as either the general public or as subgroups of the general public. The latter are sometimes identified on the basis of social role, such as parents, physicians, police, students, politicians, the clergy, and so on. Subgroups can also be identified according to stage of intervention. Such stages are usually categorized as primary, secondary, and tertiary. Primary prevention occurs when the target group is not involved with inappropriate or illicit drug use. Secondary prevention occurs when the group is experimenting with drug use, while tertiary prevention occurs when the group is regularly involved in drug use.

There is increasing evidence that preventative drug education should be introduced in early childhood while beliefs, attitudes, and behavior patterns are in their formative period. Most drug education programs exist in schools, and while school students can be viewed as a single target population, they clearly are not a homogeneous group. The educational needs of nonusers, experimenters, and users/abusers may differ greatly.

Evidence also suggests that the school program should be part of a total community effort since students are affected by the environment outside the school as well as in it. What is learned in school can then be reinforced outside it.

The fact that most drug education programs occur in schools is understandable. Students in school constitute "captive audiences" of relatively young and impressionable individuals. On the other hand, attendance by most nonschool groups is voluntary. Programs for such groups also typically require physical facilities, trained staff, promotional activities, and money. The cost of programs for mass media use tends to be very high. As a consequence of these problems there are relatively few drug education programs for nonschool populations.

2.3 Teaching Personnel

While classroom teachers usually present drug education programs, health professionals, law enforcement officers, exusers (typically young), and student volunteers are frequently used.

There is some disagreement over whether or not exusers should be utilized in prevention programs. Credibility is important in attitude change and research has demonstrated that people tend to like and believe communicators who are similar to themselves. They also tend to be more likely to believe those who speak with the voice of experience. Recognizing that traditionally trained teachers usually do not possess either the ability or the inclination to relate well with drug-using students, many programs have utilized exusers who "know the scene." While students generally report favorable reaction to the use of such individuals, some authorities have suggested that students might idealize their life-style and seek to emulate them.

It is frequently asserted that whoever presents a drug program should ideally be someone students like and trust, someone who knows and will present relevant facts and materials accurately, and someone who is relaxed and comfortable teaching the subject.

2.4 Content and Method

There is general agreement that drug education should be comprehensive and should focus not only on the physiological and pharmacological aspects of drug use and abuse, but also upon the psychological and emotional, the legal, the social, the economic, the political, and the moral implications of drug use and abuse. While drug education has traditionally been located in health and physical education courses, some authorities argue that it should also be infused into other parts of the curriculum.

An area of major concern to drug educators involves the methods to be used in achieving their objectives.

Possible methods include the following:

(a) Negative reinforcement—the negative reinforcement or "scare tactic" approach asserts that the use or misuse of various drugs can result in undesirable consequences (illness, emotional disturbance, death, etc.). The basic assumption is that fear of consequences will prevent use or misuse of drugs.

(b) Logic—the logical argument approach utilizes the presentation of facts which students can use in making personal decisions regarding drug use. The presentation can be either one-sided or two-sided. If one-sided, it may resemble the scare approach. The logical argument approach tends to assume that individuals are logical and rational decision makers regarding their own behavior.

(c) Authority—the authoritative source approach uses traditional experts (medical personnel, law enforcement officers, scholars, etc.) and experiential experts (drug users, exusers, etc.) to present facts and/or opinions on drug abuse. It is assumed that such authorities enjoy a higher level of credibility than the classroom teacher. This approach may or may not utilize scare tactics.

(d) Self-examination and values clarification—self-examination and values clarification attempts to involve students in examining their values, beliefs, and feelings regarding themselves, their lives, and the role of drugs. This approach assumes that students must come to know themselves and their values in order to make informed decisions regarding drugs.

(e) Peers—the peer approach utilizes students to lead (or aid in) discussions or other instructional activities with other students. With training, student leaders can assume the role of teacher. Alternatively, the group may act as a team in exploring the subject. It is assumed that students are strongly influenced by peer pressure and expectation; that students feel more comfortable in discussing and learning about this sensitive topic within their own group; and that, by increasing students' responsibility for their own learning, the approach may increase their motivation to learn.

(f) Alternatives—the alternatives approach seeks to introduce students to alternative activities in order to reduce or eliminate their desire either to become involved, or to maintain their involvement with drugs. It is assumed that individuals crave "highs" and that "natural highs" found in sports or other activities will be perceived as acceptable substitutes for drug highs.

(g) Coping skills—the psychological and social coping skills development approach attempts to achieve its objective through role-playing exercises or any of a diversity of other techniques. It assumes that people who have a broad repertoire of acceptable ways for coping with stressful personal feelings and social situations are less likely to turn to drugs in times of stress.

(h) Self-concept—the self-concept development approach seeks to enhance students' self-concept. It is assumed that students with poor self-concepts, low self-esteem and feelings of inadequacy are both more likely to feel the need to use drugs and simultaneously to be less able to resist peer pressure to engage in drug use.

3. Evaluation

Unfortunately, the vast majority of drug education programs reported in the literature lack any evaluation. Those that do are typically flawed by inadequacies of either research design and/or analysis. Thus, the literature provides little data for guidance in the development or modification of programs. Because some program components can be expected to be more effective with certain types of student or in certain settings, careful evaluation should make it possible to specify the optimal conditions for maximum effectiveness.

Just as early abolitionists assumed that teaching the "evils of alcohol" in schools would lead to abstinence, so too it was believed that if youth were taught the facts about drugs they would tend to abstain. However, it has frequently been argued that drug education has failed to prevent or even reduce the consumption or abuse of drugs and might actually stimulate interest in such substances. The National (US) Commission on Marihuana and Drug Abuse recognized the lack of knowledge regarding the impact of drug education and recommended a moratorium on all drug education programs in the schools, at least until existing programs could be evaluated. It asserted that no drug education program anywhere in the world had proven sufficiently successful to warrant recommendation and speculated that the avalanche of drug education may have been counterproductive.

A review of existing research demonstrates that while most programs evaluated are successful in increasing drug knowledge, far fewer are successful in changing attitudes. A number of studies have reported greater changes in knowledge than in attitude, or have reported changes in knowledge unaccompanied by change in attitude. Clearly the most rigorous test of educational effectiveness involves study of subsequent drug usage. By far the largest number of studies have found no effects of drug education upon use. A few have found drug use to be reduced while others have found it to be increased following drug education.

While there is much correlational evidence that drug users possess greater drug knowledge than do nonusers, there is no evidence that increases in such knowledge actually stimulate use. It is possible that drug education might stimulate use by (a) providing students with facts that overcome beliefs which inhibit use; (b) providing students with facts that overcome the prejudices that had been inhibiting use; (c) desensitizing students about drugs through repeated discussion of drug concepts in environments such as schools, which have traditionally been disassociated from drug use; (d) leading students to think of themselves as potential drug users merely by virtue of their having been included in drug education programs; (e) changing attitudes that were the bastion of defense against drug use; or (f) occasionally including inaccurate or biased information, which undermines the credibility of the basic educational message. On the other hand, it is also plausible that greater knowledge results from use rather than vice versa.

A massive expenditure of funds and energy is being used in numerous countries to deploy a diversity of theories, personnel, techniques, and materials in attempts to influence drug beliefs, attitudes, and behaviors. The generally nonsupportive results of summative evaluation (i.e., evaluation which occurs at the end of a course) in drug education suggest the desirability of conducting formative evaluation. The latter, by occurring during the progress of a program, permits educators to modify the program so as to improve its effectiveness.

The research to date suggests that drug prevention education is most effective when (a) it is planned according to clearly defined objectives, (b) it utilizes personnel, content, and methods appropriate to the target group and for the achievement of its objectives, and (c) it incorporates carefully designed evaluation based upon sound research principles.

Bibliography

Bruvold W H 1988 Issues in alcohol education evaluation and research. *Contemporary Drug Problems* 15: 21–29

Engs R C 1987 *Alcohol and Other Drugs: Self-Responsibility.* Tichenor, Bloomington, Indiana

Girdano D A, Dusek D 1987 *Drug Education,* 4th edn. McGraw-Hill, New York

Gonzalez G M 1988 Should alcohol and drug education be part of comprehensive prevention policy? The evidence from the college campus. *J. Drug Issues* 18: 355–365

Hanson D J 1980 Drug education: Does it work? In: Scarpehi F R, Datesman S K (eds.) 1980 *Drugs and the Youth Culture.* Sage, Beverley Hills, California

Hawley, R A, Petersen R C, Mason M C 1987 *Building Drug-Free Schools: An Educator's Guide to Policy, Curriculum, and Community.* American Council on Drug Education, Rockville, Maryland

Hooper S 1988 *Alcohol and Drugs in the Public Schools: Implications for School Leaders.* National School Boards Association, Alexandria, Virginia

Jones C L, Battjes R 1985 *Etiology of Drug Abuse: Implications for Prevention.* National Institute on Drug Abuse, Rockville, Maryland

Mauss A L, Hopkins R H, Weisheit R A 1988 The problematic prospects for prevention in the classroom *J. Studies Alcohol* 49: 51–61

Singer M, Isralowitz R E (eds.) 1983 *Adolescent Substance Abuse: A Guide to Prevention and Treatment.* Haworth, New York

Family-life Education

L. C. Harriman

Family-life education has its roots in many disciplines including sociology, psychology, anthropology, biology, and education. The goals of programs are often broad based. Family planning, a major goal of programs in developing nations is considered to be a basic human right, as well as an important element in achieving social and economic goals. Family-planning education is viewed as the means by which adults can acquire knowledge of birth control to plan their family size and the spacing of their children. Overall, its objectives are to promote the freedom to choose parenthood and the enrichment of human life.

The concepts of prevention, adaptation, and/or skill development are important bases of family-life education programs in the developed nations. Life-skill programs focus on acquiring specific life skills. Life-theme programs are concerned with promoting understanding of critical life themes, while the key objective of life-transition programs is to facilitate the passage through specific life transitions. The goals of all family-life education programs in developed and developing nations are promoted through both formal and non-formal education activities.

1. Goals and Content

In a world faced with increasing shortages of food, energy, and other resources, developing nations with increasing rates of population growth have come to view population management as a critical need.

Okobiah (1981) reported that in 1950 less developed nations comprised 65.7 percent of the world population. This figure grew to 71.5 percent of the world population by 1975. Hence, it is not surprising that values and goals related to children and decisions about family size and family planning have become one of the most fundamental bases for family-life education in many developing nations. Nor is it surprising, given the current population growth rate, that most family-planning education is directed at youth in premarital age groups and young married couples. The central aim of family-planning education programs in many developing nations is to bring about a change in attitude toward the role children play in family welfare, such that a small family size will come to be desired and accepted as the normal way to achieve other social and economic development objectives. Such objectives include an increased per capita gross national product, improved maternal and child health, reduced infant mortality rates, literacy, an improved status of women, reduced illegitimacy, and reduced illegally induced abortion. Coincidentally, improved individual and family well-being is the expected outcome of meeting both the specific family-planning program goals and the broader social and economic development objectives.

Examples of the ways some of the developing nations have used family-life education as a tool to meet specific family-planning objectives and/or broader social and economic goals can be found in the United Nations Report *Social Welfare and Family Planning* (1976).

In what are now the more developed nations, family-life education grew out of efforts of private organizations to reduce venereal disease and out-of-wedlock pregnancy, and out of concern for other factors affecting family life such as women's employment, changing roles and status, and changes in family structure (Everts and Gershner 1980).

It has evolved so as to include meaningful content for meeting personal and family-life needs of people at all life stages. Fisher and Kerckhoff (1981) offered the following classification scheme as a way of clarifying the focus and objectives of categories of family-life education programs. The life-skills category focuses on skill acquisition and development of inadequate skills such as parenting skills, interpersonal relationship skills, conflict resolution, and child guidance skills, as well as skills in family-resource management, family and marriage enrichment. The development of personal understanding of critical life themes is the focus of life-theme programs. These programs facilitate the examination of specific roles such as parenthood (single parenting, teen parenting, stepparenting, and grandparenthood), being a spouse, career roles, and planning. They also promote cognitive understanding of life stages including childhood, adolescence, adulthood, and aging. Life-transition programs attempt to facilitate adaptation during important life transitions. These include such transitions as marital adjustment, the impact of parenthood, divorce, remarriage, becoming a step-family, retirement, and death.

A philosophy of human rights, rapid social change, and the knowledge explosion have been important influences on the development of family-life education goals and programs.

2. Educational Frameworks

2.1. Nonformal Approaches

In general, family education has increased in nations which have adopted a national family-planning program and/or a family policy. National family-planning programs with broad interdisciplinary approaches have often integrated and coordinated separate related services and family-planning education into the national program. As a result, in some nations a network of education and information dissemination has been established to facilitate one-to-one and group education through home visits, youth organizations, family and women's programs, and other supportive action programs with high potential to impact on public opinion.

Mass media has come to be an important family education tool in many developing nations. Radio, local newspapers, periodicals, billboards, pamphlets, and public educational displays are among the media used in educational information programs. In some areas television also carries family education messages. One such message designed to reach youth in Singapore was "Take your time to say 'yes' . . . to marriage, to having your first child, and your second. A happy family is worth waiting for" (Loh 1978). Posters and leaflets geared to ethnic group concerns and to overcoming language and dialect barriers have also been used in some countries. A unique mass-media family-education effort by the Hong Kong Social Welfare Department was the creation of two characters called "Mr Family Planning" and "Mr Vasectomy." The characters were personified by actors who presented comedy sketches throughout Hong Kong. "Mr Family Planning" was also used in a weekly cartoon series (Lam and Berry 1978). A telephone hotline and youth advisory service has also been established in Hong Kong to provide youth with information on puberty, contraception, and fertility-related problems (Lam and Smith 1980).

Traditional culture forms have served as media for family-planning education messages in India and Indonesia. Songs, drama, puppet shows, plays, traditional ceremonies, and folk dances have all been used (United Nations 1976).

The methods used by family-life educators in nonformal settings in developed nations are numerous and varied. Women's publications and women's organizations have traditionally played an important role in carrying family-life messages. For instance publications have recently played an important role in Yugoslavia for carrying family-planning information. Newspaper articles, pamphlets, newsletters, and learn-at-home packets have also been used to teach the public particularly fathers and employed mothers.

Radio and television are increasingly being used. In Yugoslavia, entire programs have been developed to prepare young people for marriage and for responsible parenthood and to promote family-planning (United Nations 1976). Short one-concept family-education sketches often sponsored by religious organizations have become common in the United States. The Cultural Information Service of New York in cooperation with commercial television has also produced viewers' guides to television programs with family-life messages.

Special study groups, lectures, short courses, conferences, films, small-group discussions, and telephone hotlines are also commonly used techniques among many youth and adult organizations, religious organizations, and private and public agencies involved in nonformal family education.

Family centers, too, have become a more important family counseling and education resource. The United States armed services, for example, have established the "Military Family Resource Center to support and link family programs and to facilitate improved liaison with the civilian community. . . . Most of the military family programs include information services, referral, and coordination of family service providers and resources, relocation aid, spouse employment consultation and job information, family financial management education, and aid to families in crisis" (Wakefield and Yates 1981).

In the Federal Republic of Germany, *Haus der Familie* is a network of conference centers involved in family-life education. The centers are staffed by professional personnel from a variety of disciplines and may include medical personnel, psychologists, social workers, early childhood educators, and physical education teachers. Health, family planning, and parenting are some of the programs in some centers (Moore 1981).

In some programs designed to reach low-income and special ethnic groups, paraprofessionals drawn from the community have been trained to conduct home visits and carry family-life education messages to their neighbors. This approach has been widely used to conduct the United States Federal Extension Service Expanded Food and Nutrition Program, United States Department of Agriculture, Washington, DC.

Short-term skill training programs are also popular in some developed nations. These enrichment programs are usually a series of sessions held over several weeks or compacted into a weekend. They are generally sponsored by private and religious organizations. The programs are led by professionals and involve experiential learning activities designed to improve participants' skills in such interpersonal relationships as marital relationships and parent–child relationships (Sawin 1979).

The formation of special interest self-help support groups has also served as a forum for family-life education. These groups seek family professionals to serve as counselors and/or resource persons during regular meetings.

The conclusions of Scales and Kirby (1981) who conducted a study of nonformal education programs for teenagers in the United States may be applicable to such nonformal program efforts in other developed nations as well. They concluded that nonschool education programs were more likely than school programs to: (a) cover topics such as values, decision making, birth control, communication, abortion, masturbation, and homosexuality; (b) run smoothly, without organized opposition; (c) use mass media, small-group discussions, and experiential learning activities than formal programs; and (d) to involve teenagers in program planning and implementation.

2.2 Formal Approaches

In general, the incorporation of family-life education into formal school programs has been slow, particularly in lower grade level curricula. It is more common in secondary-school and college curricula.

In the Federal Republic of Germany, formal family-life education is carried on through the now compulsory household education program. Richarz (1979) described the objectives of household education as being to enable children and youth to deal with problems of coexistence in home and family life, and to develop behavior and interaction patterns conducive to interdependent living in families and society. In some other nations emphasis is put primarily on one specific area such as parenthood education.

Family-life education is not mandated by federal law in the United States. However, government support has been provided for including family-living and parenthood education as a part of consumer and homemaking education in the public schools.

Since youth is a major target group in the developing nations, family-planning education has been incorporated into the curriculum of primary, middle, and secondary schools in some countries. In some instances it is a unit of instruction and in others it is taught as a separate course. In still other areas it is part of a broader ongoing or experimental life-education program. In the Republic of China (Taiwan), female high-school students receive family-planning instruction as part of a nursing course. Male students receive a brief two-hour orientation on family planning as part of their army military training orientation (Wong and Sun 1980). Lam and Smith (1980) reported that a three-year experimental family-life education program and a parenthood-education program were underway in Hong Kong.

3. Evaluation of Family-life Education

Evaluation studies of family-life education programs generally have been sparse. A brief review of the types of studies conducted and their findings follows.

Perhaps the simplest research design has been to assess the subjective value a program has for participants after the program is completed. Published reports indicate that family-life education is viewed favorably and as helpful by participants (Bee 1952, Behlmer 1961, Harriman 1980, Hennon and Peterson 1981).

Some early studies attempted to measure understanding and knowledge gains. Most of these studies involved experimental and control groups who took pre- and post-tests. Several studies have reported significant gains in knowledge or attitude change of family-life education participants (Bardis 1963, Hereford 1963, Endres and Evans 1969).

Some studies have been designed to collect evidence on the relationship of family-life education to improved personal and interpersonal competence. Some evidence suggests that participation in family-life education may contribute to less stress with the birth of the first child and to being less overprotective with one's children (Dyer 1963, Schvaneveldt 1964). Gains in open-style

communication have also been cited (Wampler and Sprenkle 1980).

Finally, experimental studies have attempted to measure behavior changes occurring as a result of family-life education. These studies are perhaps the most sophisticated and the most sparse. However, when data are available results are generally positive, particularly in the areas of children's behavior change as a result of parent training and in acceptance of contraception as a result of family-planning education (Patterson et al. 1970, Berkowitz and Graziano 1972, Fisek and Sümbüloğlu 1978, Sung 1978).

Producing adequate, comprehensive evaluation studies which show intended and unintended short- and long-term program outcomes is a major concern which needs addressing by family-life educators. A number of factors have been identified which have apparently blocked systematic evaluation of family-life education programs. These include: "(a) Insufficient pressure for program accountability. (b) Inadequate understanding of broad-aimed, continuing education program evaluation and of ways to validly and feasibly conduct it. (c) Reluctance to use money, time, and/or other valuable resources on program evaluation. (d) Unwillingness to require or even ask that clients take the necessary time to provide evaluative feedback. (e) Reluctance to learn evaluative results. (f) Feeling that determining the worth of a program can be done adequately on a subjective and impressionistic basis" (Farmer 1975 p. 25).

4. Summary and Conclusions

Generally, it appears that both in the developed and developing nations the evolution of family-life education has begun with a restricted study and concern with aspects of human sexuality and grown in the direction of more wholistic studies of individual and family development and relationships throughout the human life cycle.

The United Nations World Survey of Home and Family Education (International Federation of Home Economics 1971) indicated home economics to be the principle source of family-life education in 85 countries. A variety of private and public institutions and organizations provide formal and/or nonformal family-life education in the developing and developed nations.

In conclusion, sound family-life education program development is dependent on strong administrative leadership and support; curricula that are realistic and based on a knowledge of needs as the target audience perceives them; community involvement in program development particularly among community leaders and parent groups; awareness of cultural norms and traditions, religious beliefs, and social changes affecting men's, women's, and family groups; competent professionals to implement programs; and preservice and inservice education on a continuing basis for family-life educators (Burke 1970).

Bibliography

Bardis P D 1963 Influences of family life education on sex knowledge. *Marriage and Family Living* 25: 97–103

Bee L S 1952 Evaluating education for marriage and family living. *Marriage and Family Living* 14: 97–103

Behlmer R H 1961 Family life education survey. *Marriage and Family Living* 23: 299–301

Berkowitz B P, Graziano A M 1972 Training parents as behavior therapists: A review. *Behav. Res. Ther.* 10: 297–317

Burke S 1970 *Responsible Parenthood and Sex Education.* Proceedings of a working group of the International Planned Parenthood Federation, London

Cultural Information Service of New York, PO Box 92, New York, New York 10156, USA

Dyer E D 1963 Parenthood as crisis: A re-study. *Marriage and Family Living* 25: 196–201

Endres M P, Evans M J 1969 Some effects of parent education on parents and their children. *Adult Educ. J.* 19: 63–71

Everts J, Gershner V 1980 Preparing family life teachers. In: Stinnett N, Chesser B, DeFrain J, Knaub P (eds.) 1980 *Family Strengths Positive Models for Family Life.* University of Nebraska Press, Lincoln, Nebraska, pp. 473–83

Farmer J 1975 Evaluating family life education programs. *J. Extension* 13: 23–30

Fisek N H, Sümbüloğlu K 1978 The effects of husband and wife education on family planning in rural Turkey. *Stud. Fam. Plann.* 9: 280–85

Fisher B L, Kerckhoff R K 1981 Family life education: Generating cohesion out of chaos. *Family Relations* 30: 505–09

Harriman L C 1980 A newsletter for parents. *J. Extension* 18: 19–22

Hennon C B, Peterson B H 1981 An evaluation of a family life education delivery system for young families. *Family Relations* 30: 387–94

Hereford C F 1963 *Changing Parental Attitudes Through Group Discussion.* University of Texas Press, Austin, Texas

International Federation of Home Economics 1971 *World Survey of Home and Family Education within Formal Education.* UNESCO, Paris

Lam P, Berry K 1978 East Asia review, 1976–77: Hong Kong. *Stud. Fam. Plann.* 9: 234–35

Lam P, Smith D 1980 East Asia review: Hong Kong. *Stud. Fam. Plann.* 11: 316–20

Loh M 1978 East Asia Review, 1976–77: Singapore. *Stud. Fam. Plann.* 9: 246–47

Moore N B 1981 Cross-cultural perspective: Family life education as a force for strengthening families. Unpublished paper. Southwest Texas University, Department of Home Economics, San Marcos, Texas

Okobiah O S 1981 Effects of population change on family life and the child: Implications for home economics programs in Nigeria. *Family Relations* 30: 49–54

Patterson G R, Cobb J A, Ray R S 1970 A social engineering technology for retraining aggressive boys. In: Adams H, Unikel L (eds.) 1970 *Georgia Symposium in Experimental Clinical Psychology.* Pergamon, Oxford

Richarz I 1979 A new concept of household education as a school subject. In: Hutchinson V G (ed.) 1979 *New Trends in Home Economics Education.* UNESCO, Paris

Sawin M M 1979 *Family Enrichment with Family Clusters.* Judson Press, Valley Forge, Pennsylvania

Scales P, Kirby D 1981 A review of exemplary sex education programs for teenagers offered by nonschool organizations. *Family Relations* 30: 238–45

Schvaneveldt J D 1964 The development of a film test for the measurement of perceptions toward maternal overprotection (Unpublished Ph.D. dissertation, Florida State University), *Dissertation Abstracts International* 25: 5250–5251 (University Microfilms No. 65–321)

Stern E A 1969 Family life education: Some rationales and contents. *The Family Coordinator* 18: 40

Sung D 1978 Family planning education as an integral part of day care service in Korea. *Stud. Fam. Plann.* 9: 71–74

United Nations 1976 *Social Welfare ˉand Family Planning.* United Nations, New York

Wakefield R A, Yates A M 1981 *Cofo Memo.* The Coalition of Family Organizations 3(30)

Wampler K S, Sprenkle D H 1980 The Minnesota couple communication program: A follow-up study. *J. Marriage and the Family* 42: 577–84

Wong M, Sun T H 1980 Fairvan, Republic of China. *Stud. Fam. Plann.* 11: (11)

Sex Education

N. Kluge

In most educational systems today, a more or less comprehensive offering of sex education programs is included in the school curriculum. The content of these courses varies from one system to another or even within a single system from one school to another. The narrowly defined programs focus on the topics of human reproduction and sexual function; broader programs include topics related to the emotional and social significance of sexual behavior and touch also upon the topic of family planning.

The special position enjoyed by sex instruction vis-à-vis other subjects results from an appreciation of sexuality and its centuries-old taboos among particular societies and of the associated difficulties for teaching this topic in schools.

1. History of Sex Education

The introduction of sex education in the schools of various countries had widely differing motives. In Sweden, the nation with probably the longest tradition in the area of sex instruction, it was mainly problems of sex hygiene that caused some female doctors at the beginning of the present century to pioneer the concept of an early sex education, particularly for young women. In Norway, it was teachers engaged in social welfare who in the 1920s wished to orient school courses toward real-life situations by introducing instruction on the reproductive processes. In the United States, it was predominantly sociopolitical motives which in the 1960s led to moves to inform school-age children as early as possible about family planning methods. Toward the end of the 1960s in the Federal Republic of Germany, the students and school groups, who were rising in protest, made use of sex education as an instrument to push forward quickly and effectively their demands for emancipation of the individual.

A survey of the school systems in Europe showed that universal and compulsory sex education has been introduced in only five countries: Sweden, Norway, Denmark, the German Democratic Republic, and the Federal Republic of Germany. In the other seven European countries of the survey, only limited portions of the subject have been legalized for instruction and these, too, are left to the initiative of the school authorities or the teacher. The first experiments with schoolroom sex education in the Soviet Union were begun in 1981. After termination of the experimental phase it is intended to implement sex education in all schools (International Planned Parenthood Federation 1975, Kluge 1984).

2. Definition of Human Sexuality and Sex Education

Human sexuality used to be understood in a narrower sense. The concept was limited to the sex characteristics [genitalia, orgasm, and sexual intercourse (coitus)]. The modern interpretation views it as the biological–physiological disposition and behavioral predisposition of the individual, and as being especially dependent on emotional, social, and cognitive learning processes. The sexuality of humans can be linked to three motives: physical desire, social intimacy, and reproductive function.

Sex education means the continuous influence exerted through a guided learning process on the development of human sexuality, whereby sexual attitudes and manners stand at the center of educational interests. The schools and other educational institutions make their specific contribution here on the basis of their institutional environment and their systematic treatment of the topic (Kluge 1978).

3. The Development of Knowledge

Corresponding to this broader concept of human sexuality and sex education, the field of sex education cannot be associated exclusively with one traditional discipline such as biology or medicine. It is to be understood, moreover, as a subdiscipline of the educational sciences, in which the subject under investigation is perceived primarily as human sexuality. Furthermore, it is the role of sex education as an integrating discipline to integrate both the outcomes of sex instruction, and the relevant outcomes in other related subjects, and to initiate inter-

disciplinary projects. The practice of sex education is still characterized by numerous obstacles which have their origins in personal prejudices and social ignorance about human sexuality.

4. School Programs

Sex education programs reflect the varied interpretation of sexuality and of the role of sex education. There are five main categories into which a sex education program can be placed: (a) a one year or a shorter course limited to biological–physiological aspects of sexual behavior; (b) a program where the stated goal is to furnish exclusively sexual–biological knowledge, but the program itself spans all the school years a pupil spends in a particular school system; (c) a popular–scientific sex information program that attempts to orient the parents in providing sexual education to their children; (d) a learning program that expands the learning content to include social, communicative, emotional, and performance-related dimensions. The emphasis on the formative and the psychology-of-learning aspects has led further to (e) a learning program whose content is structured on the didactic principle of the spiral curriculum, which means that a particular topic is repeatedly taught in school with increasing level of depth and comprehensiveness (Kluge 1978) (see *Spiral Curriculum*).

There are only a few sex information programs which have been tried out in actual school situations and for which data have been produced about their merits. Most sex information curricula deal with narrowly defined behavioral objectives. Nevertheless, some examples of program types (c) to (e) are given in the American works of Schulz and Williams (1968) and Schiller (1973). The first book is oriented toward the curiosity of the child and the content is organized according to the principles of spiral learning. The book by Schiller combines sex education in the school with sexual counseling. This is based on the broader concept of sexuality. It includes a multifaceted "model training program" for schools and universities. Most important and not to be overlooked is the inception of an evaluation of the program, which is based on questions directed to the participants of the training program. Examples of areas in which students are questioned are: factual information related to sexual behavior, training needed for teachers, ideas, and suggestions for learning experiences.

5. Results

The learning goals realized by teachers in sex education programs are those primarily associated with sexual biology, physiology, and hygiene. At least two causes mislead teachers into providing one-sided sex information. One is the predominance of such goals in the curricula; the other is a conscious avoidance of confrontations and the fear of lawsuits arising from eventual conflicts with superiors and parents. Student interviews, on the other hand, have shown that young people actually expect to be provided with supplementary information about the emotional function (emotions, onanism, orgasm) and the social function (courtship, customs, principles, social relationships, relations between partners) of human sexuality (Brown 1981).

Whether education leads to sexually permissive behavior in the social contacts of the young—that is, to their being motivated too early—is a question that cannot so far be answered accurately. This probably depends on the quality of sex education, for which parents, educators, and teachers are responsible in equal measure. That human sexual development requires the collective support and promotion of education is no longer in dispute in the field of sexual pedagogy.

6. Problems

For the implementation of sex instruction programs the following objectives remain in the foreground today:

(a) Consideration of the physical, emotional, and social functions of human sexuality requires that the existing learning objectives should be re-examined, and older sex education programs should be revised.

(b) More attention than ever before must be given to the preparation of teachers as sex educators.

(c) To carry out the sex instruction programs, teachers must be especially supported by the school administrations by provision of additional counseling and media.

(d) School administrations must ensure that research aiming to improve sex education practice should no longer be hindered or prevented.

7. Recent Knowledge

In the last few years sex education research has had remarkable success in sex education in schools. It was ascertained that sex instruction programs are contributing to reducing the number of unwanted adolescent pregnancies and the number of unwanted pregnancies in general. The number of abortions and of patients with venereal diseases was also notably reduced. In connection with other actions and under favorable circumstances (free access to the pill, frankness of the society in concerns of sexuality) it was possible to reduce adolescent pregnancies in Sweden, in the United States, and particularly in the Netherlands (more than 60%) with special programs in scholastic sex education (Jones et al. 1986, National Research Council (U.S.) 1987, Kluge 1990). Also the newer tasks of sex education seem to be successful in as far as they are seen as a complement to the family, for example, in information about, and prevention of, sexual assault in the family and AIDs.

If such courses in sexual education are not only confined to biological contents but include other, just as important, targets (emotional, social, or communicative) in the lessons, it is possible to support supplementary behavior, attitudes, and willingness in areas other than the sexual, for example, strengthening of the ego, willingness to make decisions, better contacts between parents and children (Hirschfeld-Balk 1984, National Research Council 1987). These results support the planning of sex education programs with a holistic idea of human sexuality in mind, even if there are immense problems with the realization of this kind of education in practice. It would be helpful for the motivation of an intersubject organization of education to create sex education programs in future which give single subject teachers not only contents and methodological advice, but show them how the different educational programs including media usage worked out. The question of the evaluation of sex education models seems to be most important. The theory that adolescents are seduced to premature or/and more frequent sexual intercourse has not been confirmed by research. Nevertheless this statement is often used by the opponents of sex education in many countries to defame or even abolish sex education in state schools. In the meantime there is a considerable number of sex education programs for parents which are as professional as those for schools (National Research Council 1987, Kluge 1989).

See also: Family Life Education

Bibliography

Bergström-Walan M-B, Eliasson D-M, Fredriksson I, Gustavsson N, Hertopt P, Israel J, Lindberg G, Nelson A 1970 *Modellfall Skandinavien?: Sexualität und Sexualpolitik in Dänemark und Schweden.* Reinbek, Hamburg

Brown L (ed.) 1981 *Sex Education in the Eighties: The Challenge of Healthy Sexual Education.* Plenum, New York

Cook A, Kirby D, Wilson, Alter 1984 *Sexuality Education: A Guide to Developing and Implementing Programs.* Network Publications. Santa Cruz, California

Hirschfeld-Balk U 1984 Sexualerziehung in den USA. In: Kluge N (ed.) 1984 *Handbuch der Sexualpädagogik*, Vol. 1. Schwann, Düsseldorf, pp. 355–67

International Planned Parenthood Federation 1975 *A Survey on the Status of Sex Education in European Member Countries.* The Federation, London

Jones E F, Forrest J D, Goldmann N, Henshaw S, Lincoln R, Rosoff J I, Westoff C F, Wulf D 1986 *Teenage Pregnancy in Industrialized Countries.* Yale University Press, New Haven

Kirby D 1984 *Sexuality Education: Evaluation of Programs and their Effects.* Network Publications, Santa Cruz, California

Kirby D 1984 *Sexuality Education: A Handbook for Evaluating Programs.* Network Publications, Santa Cruz, California

Kluge N 1978 *Einführung in die Sexualpädagogik* [Introduction to Sex Education]. Wissenschaftliche Buchgesellschaft, Darmstadt

Kluge N (ed.) 1981 *Sexualpädagogische Forschung* [Research in Sex Education]. Schöningh, Paderborn

Kluge N (ed.) 1984 *Handbuch der Sexualpädagogik* [Handbook of Sex Education]. Schwann, Düsseldorf

Kluge N (ed.) 1989 *Der Liebe auf der Spur. Das Buch zur TV-/Video-Spielfilmserie über Liebe und Sexualität.* Albanus, Düsseldorf

Kluge N (ed.) 1990 *Jugendesexualität im Spannungsfeld Individueller, Interaktionaler und Gesellschaftlicher Bedingungen.* Dipa, Frankfurt/M.

National Research Council (U.S.) 1987 *Risking the Future. Adolescent Sexuality, Pregnancy, and Childbearing,* Vol. 1. National Academy Press, Washington, DC

Schiller P 1973 *Creative Approach to Sex Education and Counseling.* Association Press, New York

Schulz E D, Williams S R 1968 *Family Life and Sex Education: Curriculum and Instruction.* Harcourt, Brace and World, New York

Safety Education

R. Mortimer

Safety education is the study of those human, machine, and environmental variables which interact to affect the probability of injury or illness to people or damage to property; it embraces a host of situations involving people, such as work, recreation, sport, transportation, home, and natural and human-created disasters; it encompasses not only the safe production of goods or delivery of services but the integrity of the products themselves in the consumers' environment.

The modern study of safety has taken much from the discipline of public health and the epidemiological techniques associated with it. This approach recognizes that accidents are one of the most serious of public health problems, that their causes are usually complex, that they are foreseeable, and that they are not caused solely by the acts of people because machines and environmental factors, in their broadest sense, are also usually involved.

One need for the formal study of accidents developed as an outgrowth of laws relating to working conditions and workers' compensation insurance programs in Europe and the United States. This movement of the late nineteenth and early twentieth century created an awareness of the human toll and costs of occupational injuries and provided the motivation to reduce accidents. The National Safety Council was formed in the United States in 1912 and provided educational services covering the extent and variety of safety problem areas. Educational programs were started in some schools in the United States in the 1920s, and the Center for Safety Education at New York University was founded in 1938, with Herbert J. Stack as its director, to conduct research and provide training of safety professionals. Amos E. Neyhart of Pennsylvania State University pioneered driver education for high-school students in the United States.

In 1970 the United States legislature passed the Occupational Safety and Health Act (OSHA) which resulted in the promulgation of many safety and health standards in the United States industries, upheld by inspection of work places by OSHA personnel. In addition to inspections initiated by request, usually by workers, OSHA personnel periodically inspect at random those industries (and now also government facilities) having the potential for health hazards or relatively high accidental injury reports. A key aim of the OSHA program is to educate workers and management in various aspects of health and safety in industry, mining, and construction. Comparable legislation exists in England (Health and Safety at Work Act 1974), France, the Federal Republic of Germany, and Sweden (Working Environment Act 1977). Each of these acts also requires education and training of workers in safe procedures.

The insurance companies that offer workers' compensation coverage have pioneered safety and health training for workers and management. They also provide consultation to reduce work accidents for the mutual benefit of insurer and policy holder.

Various professional organizations, such as the American Society of Safety Engineers, the American Industrial Hygiene Association, the Safety Systems Society, and England's Royal Society for the Prevention of Accidents, among others, serve a strong educational function by publishing technical journals, holding meetings, and offering short courses.

In the elementary-school curriculum, safety education is often woven into other subjects by examples of safe human behavior in such activities as crossing streets, riding bicycles, or using seatbelts in vehicles, and by fire drills. Safety education in United States high schools culminates in driver education, usually consisting of 30 hours in the classroom and 6 hours of driving. The latter is sometimes augmented by some hours in simulators and on ranges away from other traffic to learn how to control the car. In most countries, except the United States, driver education is done informally or by commercial schools (OECD 1976).

A number of research studies on the effects of driver education on accidents have been done in the United States (Stock et al. 1983) and in England (Raymond et al. 1973). Those studies that have used appropriate control groups have not found consistent benefits of driver education on measures related to accidents or violations. There are also extensive programs now in motorcycle rider education and training for novice riders, using curricula based on a task-analysis approach (McKnight and Heywood 1974) in the United States; other courses are available on a more limited scale for experienced riders. Similar programs exist in the United Kingdom.

795

Some universities offer degree programs in safety. In the United States, the Board of Certified Safety Professionals (BCSP 1982) has recommended a curriculum for the baccalaureate degree in safety, which puts a heavy emphasis on the physical sciences, mathematics, communications skills, human factors/ergonomics, and basic concepts of industrial safety and hygiene. This suggested curriculum reflects the growing technical complexity of the problems confronting safety professionals. The methods used to control hazards (e.g., nuclear power) are often technically complex and require sophisticated methods of analysis to forecast the risks.

A major aspect of safety education is to teach the methods of collecting data that provide indices of the level of safety and measures of the exposure of people, so that the risk associated with various situations can be quantified. Quantification of the level of safety is necessary to determine if a need exists for corrective action, to indicate the kinds of corrections that should be applied, and to evaluate their effectiveness. Thus, for example, the American National Standards Institute Z16.1 defines some aspects of industrial accidents in quantitative terms such as by frequency and severity of injury rates. These measures are augmented by analyses of costs and benefits to realize the most benefit for the financial investment and by cost–effectiveness analysis to choose the most effective corrective action for the cost invested. Systems analytic techniques, such as failure mode effect analysis, failure mode effect and criticality analysis, fault hazard analysis, and fault-tree analysis, are now a part of the education of safety

professionals (Vesely et al. 1981). Journals dealing with such topics are *Hazard Prevention*, the journal of the System Safety Society; and *Professional Safety*, the journal of the American Society for Safety Engineers.

While much emphasis is still being placed upon the education of safety personnel in basic concepts related to the elimination of hazards—such as machine guarding, materials handling, and fire safety—the development of new technologies imposes increasing demands upon the education of the safety staff in sophisticated techniques for the control and reduction of injuries and illnesses caused by hazards in the human environment.

Bibliography

Board of Certified Safety Professionals (BCSP) 1982 *Curricula Guidelines for Baccalaureate Degree Programs in Safety.* BCSP, Champaign, Illinois

McKnight A J, Heywood H B 1974 *Motorcycle Task Analysis.* National Public Services Research Institute, Alexandria, Virginia

Organisation for Economic Co-operation and Development (OECD) 1976 *Driver Instruction.* OECD, Paris

Raymond S, Jolly K W, Risk A W, Shaoul J E 1973 *An Evaluation of the Effectiveness of Driver Education in Reducing Accidents to Young People.* University of Salford, Salford

Stock J R, Weaver J K, Ray H W, Brink J R, Sadof M G 1983 *Evaluation of Safe Performance Secondary School Driver Education Curriculum Demonstration Project.* Report DOT-HS 806-568. Battelle Columbus Laboratories, Ohio

Vesely W E, Goldberg F F, Roberts N H, Haasl D F 1981 *Fault Tree Handbook.* US Nuclear Regulatory Commission Report NUREG-0492, Washington, DC

Education for a Life of Work

Y. Dror

A curriculum preparing for the life of work refers to courses included in general nonvocational school programs, focusing on knowledge, skills, and predispositions which are considered to help graduates succeed in their occupational careers and gain satisfaction and self-fulfilment in work taken on in their adult lives. This definition excludes courses in vocational education, and individual guidance and vocational orientation provided by psychologists and counselors. The content of courses varies across both educational systems and schools within a system. Most frequently, the curriculum contains a selection from a list of topics comprising items like prevocational skills (which can be generalized to a wide variety of occupations), familiarity with the labor market, abilities needed for pursuing occupations of various types, employee–employer relations, legal rights and duties, labor unions, and so on. Since this is a relatively new subject in the school program, the historical circumstances which led to its emergence will first be described; then a review of

approaches determining the content of the program, examples of specific syllabuses in various countries, and a summary of research findings will follow.

1. Historical Background

Until the 1970s there was a full overlap between what was formally defined as preparing for the life of work and vocational education. Those participating in various frameworks of vocational education were considered to receive preparation for the life of work. Changes in the world of work and employment have led toward changes in the content of vocational education mainly because the ability to adjust to new production conditions came to be viewed as a greater asset than the skillful performance of specific tasks. These changes have been precipitated for the following reasons:

(a) The growing state of unemployment among adults and youth has increased the need for providing adequate educational arrangements to help those in search of new employment possibilities.

(b) Numerous developing countries view work as a nation-building activity and therefore training for high technology work has become part of both the political ideology and educational practice.

(c) Economic needs have increased the demand to educate women and minority groups to participate in the high technology labor force of the nation's production system.

(d) The quest for self-fulfilment through work has been intensified and consequently schools are required to deal with the self-awareness of their pupils.

The above circumstances created the need to strengthen the links between learning in school and the practice of work, with the aim of facilitating the transition from school to employment.

During the 1970s several international and national committees and study groups concluded that there was a need to broaden the concept of "education for work" beyond the narrow limits of preparation for a particular type of skilled work or profession (Carelli 1980, Pain 1982, Hoyt 1975, Varlaam 1984, Cumming 1988a).

The progressive, work-oriented educational philosophy of the 1920s and 1930s, and the rise of the open education movement in the 1960s also contributed to broadening the concept of "education for work" by adopting the "learning through discovery" approach, and encouraging pupils to explore various phenomena outside the walls of the school. This movement provided for the inclusion of work activities in the school program, in order to create a balance between verbal and experiential learning. Work—including independent learning, participation in group activities, and in mixed-age study groups—has been considered as a learning experience which contributes to the development of the whole person and not only to his or her intellectual capabilities. Such learning experiences are expected to strengthen the autonomy of children and their desire to contribute to the well-being of the community of children and adults.

2. Basic Principles and Approaches

In dealing with principles of, and approaches to, school programs preparing for the life of work, one may note differences along two dimensions: (a) age groups, and emphasis on primary or secondary school programs, and (b) the industrialization level of a country's production system.

There is a broad consensus that education for work has to begin quite early, in the primary school, or even in kindergarten, and then continue through life. Developmental psychologists claim that primary school children possess the required readiness to learn about work and to carry out activities which contain the rudiments of practical work. Young children have the intellectual

capability to grasp the meaning of work and they manifest positive attitudes toward a variety of productive work activities (Goldstein and Oldham 1979, Cumming 1988a). At this age, the school program emphasizes practical and creative activities such as creating objects by shaping and molding various materials, gardening, and so on.

There are differences between industrialized and developing nations with regard to goals emphasized in education for work. In the first group the emphasis is put on the development of psychomotor skills and the acquisition of basic knowledge-related work of different types. In these school systems issues related to work are taught in the context of acquiring general knowledge. In contrast, in developing nations attention is paid to students' identification with their community and to the education of the individual as a resource for developing his or her country.

In the United States and in England and Wales, work experience is included in several school programs, focusing for instance on: (a) practice in problem solving, (b) information about job opportunities in a particular community, and (c) the rights and the duties of workers. Courses of these types are accompanied by work experience (Watson 1983, Pain 1982, Carelli 1980).

In Poland, education for work begins in the kindergarten. Children assume responsibilities for cleaning the classroom and working in the garden and they are expected to help others in their group. In primary schools the children work and gain experience in productive employment for the benefit of the society. They learn to work with simple tools, take part in planning work activities, and cultivate agricultural lots.

In the Soviet Union (both in the industrialized and the developing republics) practical work constitutes a regular subject in the weekly schedule of the school. Additionally, as in Poland, the pupils are requested to carry out work in the community, and also to spend 10–12 days annually in some kind of project initiated by other community organizations.

At the secondary school level in most countries there are separate academic and vocational education systems. Nevertheless one may observe an increasing trend of including education for work within the framework of the nonvocational streams of the secondary school. This is done in two ways: (a) subjects dealing with general aspects of the life of work such as the recently emerging courses in "science, technology, and society," or courses which focus on specific vocational areas; (b) creating workshops in the school, in which students carry out economically useful, productive work, or creating links with institutions or organizations outside the school which provide work opportunities to the students.

In the Western world, comprehensive schools represent a trend toward integration between general and vocational education, striving to equalize their status and to provide a broad educational basis useful for a wide range of occupational choices. The Western ideal of the comprehensive school emphasizes the flexibility needed to prepare students for rapidly changing occupational opportunities. In the United States, Sweden, and the Federal Republic of Germany schools offer a variety of work-related courses, reducing the sharp differentiation among streams and allowing the students to change courses and streams during the years of their studies. This allows free entrance and exit to the study of a subject, in a way similar to the employment system of the future, and to some extent already of the present.

Work experience curricula in the Western world concentrate on business and commerce, and less on manual work. In the United States academic credit is given for real-life experience both inside and outside of school. The inside-school experiences are frequently connected to the school's student organizations or to school-based enterprise, that is, small businesses employing young people (e.g. the automobile, building and electronics trades, etc.) or which utilize school services (e.g. office, library, students' cafeteria). Examples of outside-school experiences are community activities like working on the local newspaper, annual journal, sports competitions, or community and civic activities for the needy (Hoyt et al. 1977, Stern 1984). Several elements of the "Hereford and Worcester Education and Industry Centre" program in England fit into this pattern, like providing work experience for whole classes, the establishment of minicompanies by the students to gain real economic experience, or students working in agriculture (Watson 1983).

In socialist countries like the Soviet Union, Poland, or Cuba, education for the life of work is provided in two different frameworks: polytechnical schools, and a network of vocational schools with emphasis on work experience. The polytechnics combine a general work-oriented education with a work experience program including, for example, independent acquisition of knowledge needed in a particular job; theoretical work related to applied models (such as learning chemistry through practice in agriculture); workshops; learning from workers who are not teachers; summer work programs. The ongoing contact with the world of work is supposed to assist students in their vocational choice and foster positive attitudes toward work, such as responsibility, flexibility, and mutual aid. The emphasis on work experience curricula in both polytechnical and vocational systems is borne out by the fact that 2,300 schools in the Soviet Union financed by the state and by local manufacturers operate as work-training centers. In such centers students work one day a week producing parts which serve the need of the factories (Carelli 1980).

Several program elements common to all age levels and for all countries deserve special mention:

1. Education for coping with conditions of unemployment is strongly emphasized in Western Europe, but it occurs also in developing countries. It is described as education for change: development of

character, skills, emotions and values; preparation of young people for coping with permanent instability and provision for leisure time activities (Watson 1983).

2. In various countries work experience is included in the curriculum with the aim of preparing students to choose their vocation. Thus, in the United States some courses are linked to a variety of vocational experiences outside of school (Hoyt et al. 1977). In Scandinavia there are structured guidance programs for 13–16 and 16–19 year-olds in schools and also in various types of supplementary education frameworks. In Australia there are programs which deal with understanding of the economic, political, and social forces shaping the world of work (Cumming 1988a). The "preparation for life courses" in England and Wales are introduced in the last two years of secondary schools, and they contain three or four intensive weekly sessions throughout the year (Varlaam 1984).

3. Recommendations issued in the United States, Soviet Union, Europe, and Australia stress the importance of dealing with vocational choice-related decision making and problem solving at the elementary school level. The basic assumption is that choosing a vocation is not an action, and therefore there is a need to prepare students to face recurring changes in their careers in the future. Such programs focus on understanding the significance of work. They deal with the individual's struggle to create links between work and self-fulfilment, and to become a member of a working team and, through it, of society (Hoyt et al. 1977, Pain 1982, Watson 1983, Cumming 1988a). Infusion of career education into the regular classroom has resulted in a growth of career-related decision-making skills (Doty and Stanley 1985).

4. Recommendations about education for work frequently contain statements concerning the disabled, minority groups, and women. Most countries deal with the problem of physically or mentally incapacitated groups by trying to help them to join the productive labor force. Quite frequently, sponsored employment possibilities are created for these groups. In some countries there are "Transition from School to Work" programs concentrating, among other things, upon the career needs of the disabled, minorities, and young women (Watson 1983).

3. Two Examples of Curricula Preparing for Life of Work

In Cuba, preparation for life of work constitutes an important part of the school curricula for all ages. The elementary school operates the so-called "Padrino System," according to which factories and other types of working places adopt a nearby school or a day-center and make their employees available for providing a variety of services within the school. In this way the pupils obtain real working experience. Urban high school pupils are given opportunities to work in agriculture; boarding schools in rural areas take part in regional development programs; and students at polytechnics work in nearby factories. Organized visits to places of work occur in all high schools. Most high schools also have an extra-curricular voluntary program called an "interest circle," in which a group of students with a common interest in a particular area of science or technology links up with production facilities in the community. A technical adviser from a local working place helps them, thus also providing some kind of vocational guidance. Also, preuniversity courses constitute a part of the personal vocational guidance system (Watson 1983).

In Australia, the "World of Work Program" of the Curriculum Development Centre (CDC) has established many projects for students at different age levels. A number of features are common to these programs, as well as to others in Australia: increasing emphasis upon lifelong learning; integrating of theory and practice; participation by young people in their own education, training, and work (Cumming 1988a). Cumming distinguishes among the following main categories of programs preparing for the life of work:

(a) *Classroom-based curricula* including individual, small group and whole class studies in technical subjects for the advancement of personal and vocational skills; cross-disciplinary courses dealing with work-related topics like the course "The Meaning of Work"; video tapes and kits dealing with information about, and attitudes toward, work.

(b) *School-based enterprises* serving the needs of more than one class, such as: mini-enterprises, guided tutoring and counseling, visiting speakers, information bases on working opportunities, contacts with workers and commercial organizations.

(c) *Industry-based experiences* of three types: (a) experience as part of the school's scheduled program; (b) part-time work, afternoon, evening, weekend jobs; (c) tours and excursions to local industrial and commercial projects.

(d) *Community-based curricula* including community projects, mainly involving unpaid work or voluntary community service.

4. Research Findings

Relevant research focuses on attitudes of students, educators, and parents toward the life of work; factors affecting these attitudes; and the outcomes of school programs dealing with the world of work.

4.1 Attitudes

The main factors which influence young people's attitudes towards work are: the local environment, the leisure patterns in the community, the division of labor

within the family, and the availability of different school types (Carelli 1980). The attitudes of the parents toward work and toward education act as powerful influences on the career development of their children. Occupational stereotyping hinders full freedom of occupational choice, and this holds especially for women and for minority group persons. The peer group and the mass media exercise additional influence on the work perceptions of high school students (Watson 1983). Both parents and students attribute a greater importance to the development of occupational competency in the high school curriculum than do the educators. Schools give lower priority to occupational competency than to "academic" pursuits. The school's approach toward career education has a profound influence on the pupils' attitudes toward work in the future. If students see the relationships between what they are being asked to learn in school and what is needed in the world of work, they are better motivated to learn in school.

4.2 Sex Differences, Socioeconomic Status, and Age

Boys' and girls' work-related socializing experiences differ according to the division of labor prevalent in a particular society. Sex-role differentiation related to childwork, sex-typed imagery, aspirational levels, and traditional sex-role preferences and projections affects the process of occupational socialization (Goldstein and Oldham 1979).

There is evidence about the relationship between social status and work orientation. The parents' socioeconomic status imposes constraints on the occupational choices considered by children. These constraints can be slightly eased by intervention strategies begun in the early years (Hoyt et al. 1977). Socioeconomic status has a greater influence upon work orientations in adolescence than it has at earlier ages (Goldstein and Oldham 1979).

Age is the dominant variable in terms of influence upon children's work orientations. The sex and the socioeconomic status of the child is associated with certain vocational choices, only if the age is controlled. The occupational socialization process during childhood is apparently governed by a developmental pattern (Goldstein and Oldham 1979).

4.3 Outcomes of the Educational Process

Empirical studies have examined both the immediate and the long-range outcomes of work-related school programs. In this area, as in others dealing with meaningful issues and where achievement is rewarded on an individual basis, when the student's previous performance serves as a criterion for measuring progress, better outcomes ensue (Hoyt 1975). Moreover, students exposed to career education infusion had better achievement records than students with no infusion programs (Doty and Stanley 1985). As for the long-range outcomes, it was found that education leads to a better job, but how much better is determined by one's gender and race. Training in proper work habits, attitudes, and interpersonal skills was found to be as important to job success as training in the basic skills. To increase the effectiveness of work-related programs, public education systems must do more to guide teachers in transfering skills, so that students will come to view what is taught in school as a future tool for their own career success (Harrison 1986).

5. Conclusions

The following trends can be identified:

1. Education for work contains two main emphases: (a) the individual's preparation for a successful life of work; (b) adequate arrangements for absorbing the student into the world of work for the benefit of society.

2. Education for work contains all the elements of actual work: training in personal skills and the development of work attitudes; learning about the world of work and gaining varied forms of work experience; vocational guidance, and a contribution of the individual to the well-being of the society. All these elements apply to all population groups including the disadvantaged and the disabled.

3. Education for work begins at kindergarten and continues beyond school-age, throughout life.

4. Education for work is supported by a broad range of activities in various subject areas, in the polytechnical schools as well as in schools of other types.

Bibliography

Carelli M D (ed.) 1980 *A New Look at the Relationship between School Education and Work, Madrid Conference, 11–13 September 1979.* Swets and Zeitlinger, Hamburg

Cumming J (ed.) 1988a Curriculum and the world of work: A cross-section of views. *Curric. Perspectives* 1: 54–67

Cumming J 1988b Understanding the world of work through co-operative projects. *Unicorn* 2: 90–98

Doty C, Stanley V E 1985 *Review and Synthesis of Research and Development on Career Education Infusion in the Secondary Classroom 1976–1981.* New Jersey

Fiddy R 1986 Education for employment and unemployment: Is this the age of the trained? In: Wellington J J (ed.) 1986 *Controversial Issues in the Curriculum.* Basil Blackwell, Oxford

Goldstein B, Oldham J 1979 *Children and Work—A Study of Socialization.* Transaction Books, Brunswick, New Jersey

Harrison C 1986 *Education and Employment—Overview.* (ERIC Digest No. 50). Office of Educational Research and Improvement, Washington, DC

Hoyt K B 1975 *An Introduction to Career Education—A Policy Paper of the US Office of Education.* US Department of Health, Education and Welfare and US Government Printing Office, Washington, DC

Hoyt K B, Evans R, Mangum G, Bowen E, Gale D 1977 *Career Education in the High School.* Olympus, Salt Lake City, Utah

Miller J V 1987 *Some Current Issues in Adult, Career and Vocational Education.* Office of Educational Research and Improvement, Washington, DC

Pain A (ed.) 1982 The interaction between education and productive work, educational documentation and information. *Bull. Bur. Int. Educ.* 225(4):

Stern D 1984 School-based enterprise and the quality of work experience—A study of high school students. *Youth Soc.* 4: 401–27

Unger J 1984 Severing the links between school performance and careers: The experience of China's urban schools, 1968–1976. *Comp. Educ.* 1: 93–102

Varlaam C (ed.) 1984 *Rethinking Transition: Educational Innovation and the Transition to Adult Life.* Falmer Press, London and Philadelphia

Watson K (ed.) 1983 *Youth, Education and Employment—International Perspectives.* Croom Helm, London and Canberra

Social Skills Educational Programs

A. R. Brandhorst

Social skill has been defined as the ability to emit behaviors that are positively or negatively reinforced and not to emit behaviors that are punished or extinguished by others (Libet and Lewinsohn 1973). In a somewhat more limited context social skills are defined as those social behaviors, interpersonal and task related, that produce positive consequences in the school classroom setting (Cartledge and Milburn 1980).

Although the acquisition of some social skills has always been an essential element of the socialization process of the young in all cultures, and programs for interpersonal influence training (Carnegie 1981) have long been an element of popular culture in the United States, the development of systematic programs for teaching social skills is a relatively recent innovation. Current interest in social skills curricula can be traced to the development of social learning theory (Bandura 1969). Prior to the development of social learning theory, social abilities were viewed as traits and hence resistant to change. Thus the vast bulk of research on the acquisition and development of social skills has been conducted since 1970. An extensive body of research on social skill acquisition has been collected and organized in major publications (Cartledge and Milburn 1980, Rathjen and Foreyt 1980, Selman 1980). More recently, an additional body of research, associated with social skills in relation to cooperative learning, has been organized (Johnson 1986, Johnson and Johnson 1987, Johnson and Johnson 1989).

1. Inventories of Social Skills

Social skill inventories frequently include skills of identifying group characteristics, skills of interacting with groups, listening skills, empathizing skills, nonverbal communication skills, skills in recognizing one's own feelings, and skills of self-control. The various inventories of social skills generally overlap, emphasizing different ranges of social skills but frequently incorporating common elements.

Compilations of social skill inventories are of limited utility for purposes of building social skill curricula. While an inventory can specify a range of behaviors which a socially skilled individual could exhibit, social skill implies the selection and exhibition of behaviors at appropriate times and in specific situations. Thus social skill training cannot be separated from the contexts in which specific behaviors are to occur. This criterion of contextual embeddedness is a learning principle which social skill training shares with skill mastery in mathematics, vocabulary learning, and tailoring (see Brown et al. 1989). Accordingly much of the future research on learning in context will likely inform research and practice in social skill training.

This reality of social skill training places a major emphasis in skill training on the ability of learners to read social contexts. This range of social skills includes the ability to perceive cues indicative of the mood of a group and classify the group appropriately; it also includes the ability to perceive and classify nonverbal cues indicative of the affective states of individuals. These abilities provide access to the background information essential to the selection of the appropriate behavior.

Research on the perception and classification of nonverbal cues is in its infancy. Rosenthal et al. (1979) present a summary of a decade of research into perception of nonverbal communication. Their development of an assessment instrument, the Profile of Nonverbal Sensitivity, or PONS, marks a major milestone in the operational definition of perception of nonverbal communication.

2. Factors Comprising Social Skill

The forgoing mandates that comprehensive models of social skill training must accommodate both cognitive and behavioral factors. Cognitive factors include interpersonal problem-solving skills and social inferential ability. The interpersonal problem-solving process has been conceptualized to include (a) a problem set; (b) problem identification; (c) generation of alternative solutions; (d) selection of an alternative; and (e) evaluation of the outcome (D'Zurilla and Goldfried 1971). Research on the effectiveness of interpersonal problem-

solving skill training supports the relationship of such training to healthy social adjustment.

Social inferential ability has been studied as a developmental phenomenon (Selman 1980). Selman identified four broad domains of interpersonal understanding and has delineated five stages of development in each domain. His four domains include conceptions of individuals, friendship, peer groups, and parent–child relations. Selman's model proposes a progressive sequence including perception of others as objects, awareness of intentionality in others, awareness of other's knowledge of self's intentions, awareness of stable, predictable traits in personality, and awareness of unconscious motives. The Selman stage model provides a useful framework for the conceptualization of social skills curricula.

Research on social inferential ability has linked the skill to prosocial behavior in children and peer popularity. Intervention programs, however, have produced mainly short-term improvements in cognitive problem solving, with inconsistency of changes across individuals.

Research on the behavioral component of social skills has linked assertive behavior to adjustment. Although effective interpersonal relations require flexibility and accommodation, a capacity for assertive behavior (ability to resist the impositions of others) appears to be a critically important element in the repertoire of the socially skilled individual. Because assertive behavior must be learned, one of the goals of most social skills training programs is the development of this capacity.

3. Social Skills Training Programs

Most effective social skills training programs integrate cognitive, behavioral, and emotional control factors. The primary method used in social skills training programs is role play. The popularity and effectiveness of this method may be traced to the play frame. Extensive research findings have linked anxiety to the inhibition of assertive responses. The play frame, because it is play and not to be taken seriously, reduces anxiety and allows for the completion of successful assertive behavior episodes. The role-play requirement of behavioral participation insures that learners experience control over their own behavior. The simulation qualities of role play provide the learner with contexts with which to associate selective assertive behaviors.

A number of social skills training programs have been described in the literature (Rathjen and Foreyt 1980, Cartledge and Milburn 1980, Goldstein et al. 1980, Gazda et al. 1977). Programs have been developed for a range of distinct populations, including elementary, secondary, and college students, the emotionally handicapped, and adults.

Although the field of social skills training is in its infancy, the extensive attention it has received from researchers suggests that this is a promising new dimension of formal education. Increasing numbers of students with emotional, behavioral, and social adjustment problems seem to be an accompaniment to rapid urbanization and technological change. As these trends accelerate worldwide it is reasonable to expect an increasing need for educational programs directed at the development of social skills. The rising interest in cooperative learning is a bellwether of this trend. As the success of most programs of cooperative learning depend heavily upon the social skills of the learners, social skills training programs should become an increasingly common element in public school curricula.

Bibliography

Bandura A 1969 *Principles of Behavior Modification.* Holt, Rinehart and Winston, New York

Brown J S, Collins A, Duguid P 1989 Situated cognition and the culture of learning. *Educ. Res.* 18(1): 32–42

Carnegie D 1981 *How to Win Friends and Influence People.* Simon and Schuster, New York

Cartledge G, Milburn J F 1980 *Teaching Social Skills to Children: Innovative Approaches.* Pergamon, New York

D'Zurilla T J, Goldfried M R 1971 Problem-solving and behavior modification. *J. Abnorm. Psychol.* 78: 107–26

Gazda G M, Asbury F R, Balzer F J, Childers W C, Walters R P 1977 *Human Relations Development: A Manual for Educators.* Allyn and Bacon, Boston, Massachusetts

Goldstein A P, Sprafkin R P, Gershaw N J, Klein P 1980 *Skillstreaming the Adolescent: A Structured Learning Approach to Teaching Prosocial Skills.* Research Press, Champaign, Illinois

Johnson D W 1986 *Reaching Out. Interpersonal Effectiveness and Self-actualization.* Prentice Hall, Englewood Cliffs, New Jersey

Johnson D W, Johnson F 1987 *Joining Together. Group Theory and Group Skills.* Prentice Hall, Englewood Cliffs, New Jersey

Johnson D W, Johnson R 1989 *Cooperation and Competition. Theory and Research.* Interaction Book Company, Edina, Minnesota

Libet J M, Lewinsohn P M 1973 Concept of social skill with special reference to the behavior of depressed persons. *J. Consult. Clin. Psychol.* 40: 304–12

Rathjen D P, Foreyt J P 1980 *Social Competence: Interventions for Children and Adults.* Pergamon, New York

Rosenthal R, Hall J, DiMatteo M R, Rogers P L, Archer D 1979 *Sensitivity to Nonverbal Communication; the PONS Test.* Johns Hopkins University Press, Baltimore, Maryland

Selman R 1980 *The Growth of Interpersonal Understanding. Developmental and Clinical Analysis.* Academic Press, New York

Communication Skills

J. M. Wiemann

Communication skills, a subset of general social skills, are concerned with the manipulation of symbols for the accomplishment of some purpose. They are distinguished from other sorts of behavior in that they are acquired through training, can be improved with practice, and require conscious knowledge and strategic judgment (Wiemann and Backlund 1980). While communication has many manifestations, oral language and its concomitant nonverbal behavior are the primary materials of communication skills. The concept underlying both teaching and research in this area is that people vary in their ability to communicate (and relate) with others, and that by improving their skills, they will have more effective, satisfying communication experiences.

1. The Idea of "Skill"

The idea of social skill, and hence communication skill, grew out of research into motor skills. The importance of the motor skill analogy is evidenced by the fact that much of the work currently being done with communication skills is still implicitly based on a motor skill model. Argyle (1969) has demonstrated that social behavior can be studied in much the same way as motor skills. He defines skill as an "organized, coordinated activity in relation to an object or a situation, which involves a whole chain of sensory, central, and motor mechanisms. One of its main characteristics is that the performance, or stream of action, is continuously under the control of the sensory input" (p. 180). Argyle's social skill model has the same components as a motor skill model: a motivation or goal which influences and is influenced by the person's perception of the world and the particular situation, especially its communicational requirements, which is translated into responses, both motor and symbolic, resulting in changes in the outside world. These changes (or lack of them) become the stimuli for the next set of perceptions; that is, there is a feedback loop.

From this perspective, human social performance can be conceived of as the intersection of three factors: the performers' capacities to act; the situational demands as perceived by both the performers and others in the situation (these are not always the same); and the strategies used by performers to relate capacities to demands (Welford 1980). Capacities include cognitive ability, attitudes, experience in a variety of situations, and, most importantly, individuals' communication repertoires— that is, the gross number of specific communication tasks they can perform. Communication demands include both prescribed and proscribed behaviors and are context specific. In this sense "context" includes relational parameters as well as spatial and temporal ones. The people must be able to make sense of the combined characteristics of the situation ("Why are we gathered here?"), the location ("Where are we?"), the time and timing ("May I speak now?"), and the role and personal relationships of themselves to the audience ("To whom am I speaking?"). To be effective—that is, to demonstrate the requisite amount of communication skill—people must meet these demands in a way that will facilitate the accomplishment of the communication goals of all parties to the encounter (Wiemann 1978).

It is in the realm of strategy that communication skills are most clearly differentiated from general social skills, and where the motor skill analogy breaks down. General social skills, as motor skills, are typically equated with the use of efficient strategies (Welford 1980). Efficiency usually is not the most important or the most desirable criterion for assessing communication effectiveness. Appropriateness of strategic choices—do they conform to the rules which typically guide behavior in this situation?—is a better standard, and indeed, is the most widely used in communication research. More importantly, it appears to be the commonsense standard against which people judge their own and others' communication.

A second important distinction between communication and social skills is the way in which "strategy" is considered. From the communication perspective, strategy and skill are not equated; rather they are seen as hierarchically related. "Skill" refers to the performance of specific behaviors. "Strategy" is the implementation of various skills and is more general than any skill used to meet a specific goal. In this sense, skills—and the behaviors of which they are composed—are seen as neutral; they are neither effective nor ineffective in and of themselves. Effectiveness is the product of appropriate strategic combinations of skills individuals have in their repertoires.

2. Characteristics of Communication Skills

The identification of communication skills is central to both research and education, and it is because of this that distinguishing communication from general social skill is necessary. There are several important characteristics common to communication skills: (a) the relationship between performance and cognition; (b) functionality; (c) emphasis on effectiveness; and (d) the importance of contexts.

It is generally accepted that both cognition and performance are important in any consideration of communication skills—this in spite of the distinction made by early workers studying "communicative competence" between cognitive competencies ("knowing that") and performance competencies ("knowing how"). Possession of a skill requires both knowledge and performance capabilities. But merely "knowing that" (a skill is such and such) is not to truly have the skill itself. For example, to know the physics of kicking a football through a goal is not the same as being able to execute the kick. The cognitive aspects of a skill are derived solely from observing behavior—either our own or others'. It is skills which connect behavior and knowledge (Wiemann and Backlund 1980).

The general concept which designates the application of skill and knowledge to specific situations is communicative competence (sometimes called interpersonal competence, functional communication, or social competence). Wiemann and Kelly (1981, p. 290), following a review of the philosophical and empirical roots of the concept, defined interpersonal competence as "the appropriate actualization of knowledge and social skill in a relationship." They argued that knowledge without skill is socially useless, and skill cannot be obtained without the cognitive ability to diagnose situational demands and constraints.

One of the implications of their review is that communication skills are functional. That is, they serve to enhance and facilitate desired outcomes and inhibit or prevent undesired ones. The general purpose of a skill is to be effective. When evaluating the social performances of others, it is typical to speak in terms of relative effectiveness (e.g., "She did fairly well in the interview," "I enjoy talking to him on most occasions"). Hence, communication skills are appropriately assessed in terms of how well a performance is carried off— norm-referenced assessment—as opposed to determining presence or absence of skills—objective-referenced assessment (Larson et al. 1978).

The relative usefulness or value of any given skill is underscored by the fact that the context of its enactment, as much as any other variable, determines its effectiveness. Situational demands and constraints, that is, time, place, relationship among the interactants, and so on, are defined by social conventions or rules. Behavior is rule-guided and therefore predictable to the extent that the norms of the social system and their salience to the interactants are known. To be effective, individuals must know cultural rules for various contexts (but not necessarily blindly or unimaginatively obey them) and use those rules as resources to bring off the encounter in a manner satisfying to all participants.

3. Specific and General Skills

One of the goals of people working in this area is to specify necessary skills for effective communication. This specification has been attempted at several levels of abstraction or specificity. At the lowest level, behavioral techniques have been identified that are necessary in narrowly specified situations. For example, "school children should greet their teacher by saying 'good morning' at the beginning of the school day." Note that such a prescription is audience and context specific, and also implies proscribed behavior—for example, "do not hug the teacher." Specification at this level is not very useful from a theoretical point of view because it requires a curriculum to specify a complete set of skills for each age group—clearly an impossible task. More useful are larger categories of behavior which are pertinent in a variety of situations (but may be enacted by different behavioral routines) and which incorporate the desired outcome. To pursue the earlier example, "children should greet their elders in a respectful manner upon seeing them for the first time in a day." Or more generally, "people are expected to greet each other when meeting."

A national research project on communication competencies in the United States identified five "dimensions of communication competence" (Allen and Brown 1976). These are (a) controlling—designing messages to control the behavior of others; (b) feeling—expressing affect and attitude; (c) informing—giving and seeking information; (d) ritualizing—designing messages that primarily maintain social relationships and facilitate social interaction; and (e) imagining—designing messages that are creative or deal with imaginary topics. (See Wood 1977 for an application and operationalization of these skills for elementary and secondary curricula.)

Rubin (1982) has specified four relatively general areas of communicative competence and identified specific skills relevant to each area for high-school graduates and college-aged people. Included are (a) communication codes, for example, effective listening, appropriate nonverbal behavior; (b) oral message evaluation, for example, ability to identify the main idea of a message, to distinguish fact from opinion; (c) basic speech communication skills, for example, ability to express ideas clearly, to defend one's point of view with evidence; and (d) human relations, for example, ability to express feeling to others, to perform social rituals.

Much interest in communication skills has been focused on its application in the provision of human services. Hargie et al.'s (1981) discussion of communication skills in human service professions is illustrative of this interest. They identify nine skills which are relevant to getting and giving information to clients: (a) nonverbal communication; (b) reinforcement; (c) questioning; (d) reflecting; (e) set induction; (f) closure; (g) explaining; (h) listening; and (i) self-disclosure.

On a still more global level, researchers studying communicative competence have tried to identify general competencies of which specific skills are subsets. There seems to be consensus that control and empathy/affiliation are general dimensions of competence which must be attended to in each relationship. That is, each relationship (and interaction) is defined in part by the distribution of control among the participants and the affiliation and empathy they show each other (Wiemann and Backlund 1980, Wiemann and Kelly 1981). Other general, but secondary, dimensions of communicative competence include task orientation, interaction management (actually a subset of control), behavioral flexibility, and social relaxation (the absence of communication apprehension).

4. Conclusion

Knowledge of communication skills has increased dramatically since social scientists first turned their attention to skills in the mid-1960s. But overall understanding of communication skills has not reached a level where prescriptive generalizations are warranted. It can, however, be concluded that instruction in communication skills can be profitably included in school curricula and training programs for professionals, parents, and so on—in short, anyone whose well-being is dependent on good interpersonal relationships.

While increasing individuals' skills will improve their opportunities to have effective and satisfying interactions, there is not a one-to-one relationship between quantity (or even quality) of communication ability and effectiveness. No one individual is totally responsible for a given encounter. All parties to the encounter share responsibility. Each brings to the encounter a set of skills and competencies which must be "matched" with the skills and competencies of the others. That is to say, communication encounters are "interactional" and communication skills training and assessment must be conducted accordingly. In this light, skills can be seen as the means to avoid problems and pitfalls in interaction, rather than as mechanisms for getting everything "just right" communicationally.

Bibliography

Allen R R, Brown K L (eds.) 1976 *Developing Communication Competence in Children*. National Textbook, Skokie, Illinois

Argyle M 1969 *Social Interaction*. Aldine, Chicago, Illinois

Canary D J, Spitzberg B H 1989 A model of the perceived competence of conflict strategies. *Human Communication Research* 15: 630–49

Eisler R M, Frederiksen L W 1980 *Perfecting Social Skills: A Guide to Interpersonal Behavior Development*. Plenum, New York

Hargie O, Saunders C, Dickson D 1981 *Social Skills in Interpersonal Communication*. Croom Helm, London

Lamb M E, Suomi S J, Stephenson G R (eds.) 1979 *Social Interaction Analysis: Methodological Issues*. University of Wisconsin Press, Madison, Wisconsin

Larson C, Backlund P, Redmond M, Barbour A 1978 *Assessing Functional Communication*. ERIC and the Speech Communication Association, Urbana, Illinois

Rubin R B 1982 Assessing speaking and listening competence at the college level: The communication competency assessment instrument. *Commun. Educ.* 31: 19–32

Rubin R B, Graham E E, Mignerey J T 1990 A longitudinal study of college students' communicative competence. *Communication Education* 39: 1–14

Sillars A L, Weisberg J 1987 Conflict as a social skill. In: Roloff M G, Miller G R (eds.) *Interpersonal Processes: New Directions in Communication Research*. Sage, Newbury Park, California

Spitzberg B H, Cupach W R 1988 *Handbook of Interpersonal Competence Research*. Springer-Verlag, New York

Welford A T 1980 The concept of skill and its application to social performance. In: Singleton W T, Spurgeon P, Stammers R (eds.) 1980 *The Analysis of Social Skill*. Plenum, New York, pp. 11–22

Wiemann J M 1978 Needed research and training in speaking and listening literacy. *Commun. Educ.* 27: 310–15

Wiemann J M, Backlund P 1980 Current theory and research in communicative competence. *Rev. Educ. Res.* 50: 185–99

Wiemann J M, Kelly C W 1981 Pragmatics of interpersonal

competence. In: Wilder-Mott C, Weakland J (eds.) 1981 *Rigor and Imagination: Essays From the Legacy of Gregory Bateson*. Praeger, New York, pp. 283–94

Wiemann J M, Brodac J J 1989 Metatheoretical issues in the study of communicative competence: Structural and functional approaches. *Progress in Communication Sciences* 9: 261–84

Wood B 1977 *Development of Functional Communication Competencies: Pre-k–Grade 6 and Grades 7–12*. ERIC and the Speech Communication Association, Urbana, Illinois

Television Studies

A. Dorr

Television studies curricula are designed to teach about television. They may include such topics as why programming is broadcast, how programming is produced, how to produce programming oneself, how to select what to view, how much to view, how to learn from television content, how to evaluate the credibility and accuracy of television content, and cultural imperialism in programming. Other common terms for television studies curricula include visual literacy, critical viewing skills, television literacy, and television viewing curricula. Television studies may also be a unit within broader curricula addressing audiovisual education, media literacy, mass media studies, media education, or media studies.

There is great variation among television studies curricula in their goals, teaching methods, explicitness of curriculum content, comprehensiveness of coverage, intended students, instructional delivery systems, places of instruction, integration into the formal instructional system, and amount of evaluation. Most curricula are fairly new, having been developed in the late 1970s or thereafter. Most are not part of the formal educational system or are just a small unit within the media studies curriculum. Television studies curricula are much more common in highly industrialized countries, countries with many broadcasting outlets, and countries with a high proportion of programming funded by commercial advertising and produced by independent, rather than public or governmental, organizations.

1. Rationale and Goals

Television studies curricula have appeared because the television medium has become an important source of news, information, education, propaganda, persuasion, selling, and entertainment. It shapes, as well as reflects, culture, and in many countries children spend more time in front of the television set than in the classroom. Those who develop and adopt television studies curricula believe that people need to be taught to use this medium well. Television literacy, in their view, is as important to today's citizen as print literacy was to yesterday's citizen. In countries such as the United States and Japan, where the commercial broadcasting systems are strong, the development of television studies curricula is motivated primarily by citizens' many hours of viewing low-brow entertainment programming, their tendency to accept it as realistic, and their exposure to many sophisticated advertisements for products and services that are usually not essential to life. In other countries, television's informational, educational, political, and cultural uses are more likely to prompt curriculum development.

Goals vary among different curricula. Almost all curricula are designed to teach specific facts: how commercial advertising supports program development, how politicians gain broadcast time, persuasive techniques, image creation, stereotyping in character development, the structure of dramatic fare, production techniques, and so on. Some curricula are designed to influence attitudes or behaviors: less at-home viewing, more viewing of high-brow programming, increased understanding of or learning from television programming, more intelligent choosing of the content that will be accepted as accurate, believable, or worth remembering, and greater concern about who controls the production and distribution of content. A few curricula are designed to teach television production.

2. Teaching Methods and Circumstances

Most television studies curricula involve direct instruction through printed materials, lecture, and discussion. Some include viewing common television programs or commercials and analyzing them. A few include viewing television programming produced especially to teach television literacy. Curricula designed for children aged 3 to 10 often include story books, games, role playing, and drawing. Except for those teaching production skills, most curricula provide little or no direct experience with television production. Apparently, few believe that television will be a common means of communication or that understanding of the medium will be increased by knowing how its content is produced. Little research addresses the validity of these assumptions, but the contrast with assumptions about print literacy and writing is striking.

Curricula about commercially supported programming are likely to be directed toward youth aged 4 to 20 years. Curricula about the informational and political functions of broadcasting are ordinarily aimed only at those older than about 12 years. Practical production courses are often directed at older adolescents and young adults. Some curricula are addressed to parents or teachers. It is assumed that when they have correct information and proper values about television they will transmit them to their children or students.

The circumstances under which television studies programs have been developed and taught vary considerably between countries. Illustrative are the following examples supplied by practitioners and researchers in various countries. In Sweden, there is no formal television literacy curriculum in the schools or outside them. General media education goals are integrated, at the teacher's discretion, into instruction in other content areas in the compulsory education system. In Australia and Scotland, the school curricula include media literacy studies. In Australia, they feature television and are enriched by Australian Broadcasting Commission programming. In Canada, the province of Ontario has recently required the teaching of mass media, also featuring television, as part of the regular English curriculum for both intermediate and senior schools. In the United States, in contrast, curriculum development in the 1980s focused exclusively on television rather than media more generally. Some schools developed their own curricula, but most came from people outside the formal educational system. More curricula have been aimed at children than at adolescents. A similar situation exists in Japan. In the United Kingdom, interest in television studies has increased, but most formal courses are still oriented to production, directed at adolescents, and not specifically about television. Similar situations exist in Norway and the Federal Republic of Germany.

3. Evaluation

Most television studies curricula have had little or no evaluation. At most, course enjoyment, learning factual content, and development of production skills have been assessed. At these levels, curricula generally succeed. It is unusual to find assessment of a curriculum's impact on viewing behavior, understanding of television's semiology, selectivity in accepting television messages, or concern about the organizational structure or societal effects of television. Where there has been such an assessment, curricula have been shown to have some salutary effects but probably not enough to allay the concerns that motivated curriculum development in the first place.

Bibliography

Anderson J A 1983 Television literacy and the critical viewer. In: Anderson D R, Bryant J (eds.) 1983 *Children's Understanding of Television: Research on Attention and Comprehension*. Academic Press, New York, pp. 297–327

Centre d'Initiation aux Mass Media 1984 *Initiation aux Mass-media*. Centre d'Initiation aux Mass Media, Fribourg

Dahl A G 1981 *Media Education in Norway*. Ministry of Church and Education, Oslo

Masterman L 1980 *Teaching about Television*. Macmillan, London

Masterman L 1986 *Teaching the Media*. Macmillan, London

Minkkinens S 1979 *A General Curricular Model for Mass Media Education*. ESCO/UNESCO, Paris

Murray J F (ed.) 1980 *Television Studies in Scottish Schools*. Scottish Council for Educational Technology, Glasgow

Piette J, Van Every E 1987–88 Education critique aux medias; Nouvelles avenues de recherche. *Le Telespectateur* 8: 3–4

Ploghoft M E, Anderson J A (eds.) 1981 *Education for the Television Age*. Proc. of a Nat. Conf. on the subject of children and television. Cooperative Center for Social Science Education, Ohio University, Athens, Ohio

Sakamoto T 1981 *The Use of General TV Programmes in School and Community*. UNESCO, Paris

Searching for alternatives: Critical TV viewing: A symposium (a collection of articles) 1980 *J. Commun.* 30(3): 64–125

Watkins L T 1988 Effects of critical viewing skills curriculum on elementary school children's knowledge and attitude about television. *J. Educ. Res.* 81: 165–70

Newspapers in Education

E. F. DeRoche

Newspapers in education is a cooperative program between newspaper businesses and elementary, secondary, and adult education schools and agencies that promote the use of daily and/or weekly newspapers in the teaching and learning of school subjects.

Newspaper businesses are interested in such programs because they want young people and adults to learn to read a newspaper, to learn to use a newspaper as a source of information and entertainment, and to value it as an essential resource in the life of an active, concerned citizen.

1. Educational Use of Newspapers

The educational goals of newspapers in education are to teach children and young people how to use a newspaper effectively as a source of continuing self-education throughout life; to develop an understanding of the role of a free press; and to motivate and assist students to improve their academic skills.

To this end, newspapers in education programs are spreading throughout the world. Programs have been developed in Australia, Canada, England, France, the Netherlands, India, Norway, South Africa, Sweden, and the United States. For example, in Sweden, the newspapers in education program has been part of the school program in basic- and upper-level classes since before the 1960s. It is estimated that in the United States, about a third of the over 1,500 daily newspapers have such programs or services and are distributing an estimated 44.6 million newspapers to one out of 5 schools, one out of 20 teachers, and one out of 10 students.

Many newspaper businesses employ full- or part-time directors or coordinators who work with local school districts and educational agencies in arranging and conducting teacher-training programs and parent presentations. They also assist teachers, curriculum specialists, and administrators in developing curriculum materials and assessing the value of newspaper use in the classroom (Newspaper Readership Project 1980b).

In the early 1970s, only a handful of colleges and universities offered teacher-training courses or workshops on the use of newspapers for teaching and learning programs. In 1982 over 90 undergraduate or graduate credit courses were offered to educators. More and more college professors who teach elementary and secondary methods and curriculum courses are offering students lessons on how to use a newspaper when teaching subject matter.

The French statesman and poet, Lamartine, once wrote: "Mankind will write their book day by day, hour by hour, page by page. . . . The only book possible from day to day is the newspaper." This "living textbook" has been popular among school teachers and administrators for several reasons. Educators are interested in this cooperative program because it responds to their need for providing learners with a medium which brings relevancy and immediacy to school subjects they are studying. Newspapers have been used at all grade levels and in subjects such as mathematics, reading, language arts, social studies, consumer economics, and the like. Educators view this resource as an excellent supplement to textbooks and as a medium worthy of study in itself. In many schools, not only do the students use newspapers as a subject supplement, but they also study the role, purpose, and business of newspapers in society. Such study usually includes an analysis of the history of printing and journalism, the function of the press in a free society, and the financial aspects and occupational opportunities in the newspaper business.

Teachers use the newspaper in their classrooms because they have found it to be an excellent motivational tool. Newspaper content catches the interest of learners, motivates them to want to read, and thus provides the teacher with an opportunity to capitalize on this interest and motivation in teaching school subjects. Teachers have found newspaper content to be an excellent source for learning activities which serve to reinforce skill and concept development.

2. Newspapers as Learning Resources

There are three common ways that teachers use newspapers in their classrooms. Some teachers have students bring articles from the newspaper they may receive at home and discuss the contents of the article with the class. Other teachers set aside two to six weeks and have students study and use the newspaper. This unit of study pattern is probably the most frequently used

method. A third way, one which is promoted by most newspaper curriculum authorities, is to integrate newspaper content into the curriculum or course of study. This method insures that newspapers become an ongoing supplement and resource to both the teacher and learner.

The resources that newspaper businesses provide educators with are many. In addition to the newspaper itself, which is usually offered to schools at a discount price, some newspapers provide supplementary instructional and curriculum materials on a variety of topics. In-paper supplements or inserts whereby the newspaper publishes a page or two just for children and teenagers is one method. Other newspapers create and publish supplements on problems, issues, or concerns of society. The titles of a few examples will illustrate the variety of content: "Dealing With Drugs;" "Energy Conservation;" "Newspapers and Law-related Education." Many newspapers publish teacher how-to-do-it manuals, kits, and activity cards, and filmstrips and slides which include such titles as "Know Your Newspaper," "How to Use the Newspaper to Teach Science," "Newspaper Primary Reading Program," and "Our Living Community."

The Canadian Daily Newspaper Publishers Association and the American Newspaper Publishers Association Foundation sponsor an annual conference that brings newspaper personnel and educators together to discuss newspapers in education trends, techniques, problems, costs, and to review new and existing curriculum materials. Regional conferences are becoming more popular in countries with newspapers in education programs.

3. Research on the Educational Use of Newspapers

Research interests are just beginning, and to date research on the topic is sparse. There have been less than 100 studies, most of which must be carefully interpreted because of sample size, experimental design, and researcher bias. The research that has been done can be categorized into five topics: teacher attitudes, newspaper reading skills, reading achievement, achievement in other school subjects, and reading habits and attitudes.

Studies of teacher attitudes resulting from teacher-training workshops and seminars and from teachers who use newspapers in their classrooms reveal that these teachers generally have more favorable opinions about newspapers, accept the product for educational purposes, have a better understanding of editorial views of newspapers, and favor the use of newspapers as an instructional resource (Canadian Daily Newspaper Publishers Association 1976).

Most studies designed to improve students' skills in reading a newspaper have assessed these skills by using the American Newspaper Publishers Association Foundation's Newspaper Reading Test. This test is specifically designed to assess several reading skills, knowledge of factors related to newspaper sources and services, judgment in evaluating content, and understanding the roles of newspapers in a free society. Results from these studies clearly demonstrate that newspaper use does, in fact, improve student competencies in newspaper reading (De Roche 1979).

Studies of reading achievement using standardized reading tests and comparing newspaper-use classroom groups with nonnewspaper-use groups generally favor the newspaper-use group. That is, students in classrooms that use newspapers as a supplement to textbooks outscored their counterparts who use textbooks on vocabulary, comprehension, distinguishing between fact and opinion, and other reading skills.

A few studies have examined the influence of newspaper use on achievement in subjects such as science, mathematics, social studies, and current events. There is some evidence that newspaper use may influence mathematics and social studies achievement but too few studies have been done to date to substantiate this generalization. Students who use newspapers in their classes do have greater knowledge of current events and the newspaper business than do students not exposed to this medium.

Reading habits and attitudes studies reveal that newspaper use in primary- and secondary-school classrooms positively influences students' newspaper reading habits, increases the amount of time students spend reading a newspaper, and may have a positive influence on reading a newspaper when they are adults (Newspaper Readership Project 1980a, 1980b).

In summary, there is no single newspaper-in-education program. Each program has its unique characteristics that vary according to the size and resources of the local newspaper and attitudes and interests of local teachers and administrators. The most comprehensive programs include a newspapers-in-education coordinator, a teacher–administrator advisory committee, teacher-training opportunities, free or half-priced newspaper subscriptions for the schools, and teachers' manuals, kits, activity cards, newspaper supplements on a variety of topics that become part of the instructional-curriculum package offered to educators. Few programs are evaluated and research on the topic is sparse. Educators involved in the program value these resources and the newspaper itself as an excellent curriculum resource that bridges the gap between classroom subjects and the real world; as an instructional aid that influences student reading achievement, interests, and attitudes; and as an essential medium for supplementing classroom textbooks.

Bibliography

American Newspaper Publishers Association Foundation (ANPA) 1980 *Bibliography: NIE Publications*. ANPA, Reston, Virginia

Canadian Daily Newspaper Publishers Association 1976 *Report of a Survey of Teachers' Attitudes Toward Use of Mass Media in Education*. Toronto, Ontario

DeRoche E F 1979 *Summary of Newspaper in Education Research*. American Newspaper Publishers Association Foundation, Reston, Virginia

DeRoche E F 1980 Newspapers in education: What we know. *Newspaper Res. J.* 2(3): 59–63

DeRoche E F 1981 *Annotated Bibliography of Articles in Educational Periodicals*. American Newspaper Publishers Association Foundation, Reston, Virginia

Newspaper Readership Project 1980a *Children and Newspapers*. Newspaper Advertising Bureau, New York

Newspaper Readership Project 1980b *Daily Newspapers in American Classrooms*. Newspaper Advertising Bureau, New York

Education for Leisure-time

H. Ruskin

Leisure education aims to bring about in the learner certain changes in the way leisure time is used. These changes may be stated in terms of beliefs, feelings, attitudes, knowledge, skills, and behavior, and may take place in formal and informal educational or recreational settings for children, youth, and adults.

1. Definitions

Leisure has been defined both quantitatively in terms of its time, dimensions, and relationships to work or other commitments, and qualitatively as a state of mind, which arises from freedom of choice and a sense of personal satisfaction.

According to the quantitative definition, leisure is that portion of a person's time which is free, non-obligatory, or discretionary, which remains after all other demands for the provision of basic necessities such as work and sleep, and social commitments and constraints have been met.

The qualitative definition emphasizes the essentially personal character of leisure, the extent to which it is a mental and spiritual attitude, a state of mind. Philosophers and scholars, from Aristotle to deGrazia (1964), Pieper (1963), Neulinger (1974), Dumazedier (1967), and Czikszentmihaly (1975) have shown the importance of adopting a qualitative approach in order to understand leisure behavior. Human activity undertaken under the guise of leisure may be either culturally or recreationally oriented. Culturally oriented activities represent a general content and personal context for the more purposive use of leisure time. Recreationally oriented activities generally represent the expression of free choice outside a formal context and/or content.

2. The Objectives of Leisure Education

The achievement of the above-mentioned goals can be made possible by formal and informal educational and community frameworks for children, youth, and adults through the implementation of the following objectives: (a) the development of an ability to judge values regarding leisure-time behavior; (b) the development of an ability to choose and evaluate leisure activities; (c) the development of an ability to determine individual goals and standards for leisure behavior; (d) the development of an awareness and understanding of the importance of a desirable use of leisure time.

3. Curriculum

Leisure education curricula are designed to reach their objectives through the following practices: (a) intellectual, aesthetic, mental, social, and physical experiences; (b) creative expressions in thought, line, form, color, sound, and movement; (c) experiences both in active participation and performance or passive emotional participation (spectating, observing, listening, etc.); (d) social involvement and expressions of companionship, belonging, and cooperation; (e) experiences for and in the outdoors, mainly for urban populations; (f) physical recreation expressions which may contribute to healthy living through the skillful use of the body; (g) experiences and processes which may cultivate a balanced approach to rest, repose, and relaxation.

Specific curricular experiences which may be included in leisure education are reading, music, singing, playing, dancing, participating in games and sports, social and club activities, outdoor recreation, and hobbies in creative fields such as gardening, mechanics, applied arts, fine arts. Specific agencies and human endeavors such as theaters, concerts, libraries, the various means of the mass media, museums, parks, and playgrounds serve the leisure education curricula as means for the enrichment of patterns of leisure behavior.

4. Channels for Leisure Education

4.1 The Total Curriculum

A disciplined, sequential, and scholarly liberal education, covering the broad spectrum of social and natural sciences, humanities, art, music, physical and health education as well as mental and social living may produce educated individuals capable of using a varied and balanced leisure time wisely.

4.2 Specific Educational Subjects

Some subjects are conducive to recreational participation, such as music, physical education, outdoor education, fine and industrial arts, and language, as it relates to recreational reading and creative writing.

4.3 Curricular Units

Topics and subject units of various curricular areas may be used for the purpose of developing favorable attitudes, knowledge, and skills related to leisure activities.

4.4 Cocurricular Activities and Informal Education

Cocurricular activities include two basic categories: (a) an activity which is closely related to a subject area, such as a student newspaper (study of English) and (b) a social activity, club, or event, which is not linked to a particular curricular subject as such, but serves the same social or intellectual objectives of the school and may contribute to leisure-time behavior patterns. Such experiences beyond the classroom should be regarded as an integral part of the educational processes of the school. Emphasis should be placed on spontaneous and enjoyable forms of play and recreation, which provide opportunities for self-expression and which may become lifetime hobbies.

4.5 Counseling and Guidance Activities

Counseling and guidance activities which lead the pupils toward self-direction and self-realization can be included in the program of leisure education. This educational process can persuade students to learn leisure activities which are suitable for them and to help develop specific interests.

4.6 Involvement in School-community Recreation Programs

The school may be directly concerned with broad aspects of living in the community, including leisure and recreational programs of pupils and adults.

5. Research

The literature in areas related to leisure education is voluminous. No attempt is made here to undertake a comprehensive review of the literature. The reader may find this elsewhere (Hoffman and Hoffman 1964, Neulinger 1974, Burton 1971). However, it should be noted that research studies upon which objectives, curricula, and educational channels are being determined in leisure education fall into the following categories:

(a) Psychological studies in areas such as social psychology, child development, socialization processes, attitude theory (formation of and change of attitudes), play theories, motivation, creativity, and sociability.

(b) Sociological studies on patterns of leisure behavior, cultural differences, measurement of leisure, and the meaning of leisure.

(c) Specific studies in leisure and leisure education disciplines, such as art education, physical education, music education, and outdoor education.

Bibliography

Brightbill C K 1966 *Educating for Leisure-centered Living.* Stackpole, Harrisburg, Pennsylvania

Burton T L 1971 *Experiments in Recreation Research.* Rowman and Littlefield, Totowa, New Jersey

Csikszentmihaly M 1975 *Beyond Boredom and Anxiety.* Jossey-Bass, San Francisco, California

deGrazia S 1964 *Of Time, Work and Leisure.* Anchor, New York

Dumazedier J 1967 *Toward a Society of Leisure.* Free Press, New York

Hoffman M L, Hoffman L W (eds.) 1964 *Review of Child Development Research*, Vol. 1. Russell Sage Foundation, New York

Nahrstedt W 1977 *Leisure Education and Animation in Europe.* Edition Freizeit, Dusseldorf/Zurich

Neulinger J 1974 *The Psychology of Leisure: Research Approaches to the Study of Leisure.* Thomas, Springfield, Illinois

Pieper J 1963 *Leisure: The Basis of Culture.* New American Library, New York

Ruskin H 1980 Formal and informal education for leisure centered living: Implications for youth educational frameworks. *Proceedings and Papers of the Second World Conference of Experts on Leadership for Leisure.* World Leisure and Recreation Association, New York.

Outdoor Education

G. L. Mehaffy

Outdoor education is a term still in search of a definition. For some, it refers to school camping; for others, outdoor education implies a focus on the natural environment, whether in a traditional classroom setting or in the out-of-doors. The definitional confusion is highlighted by a recent shift in terminology (and perhaps perspective) away from outdoor education and toward environmental education, which some describe as a much broader field. Evidence of that shift is reflected in the *Encyclopedia of Educational Research*, which in the 1969 edition used the descriptor, "outdoor education." In 1982, the Encyclopedia eliminated that term in favor of "environmental education." The broader term, environmental education, has only added to the confusion. One author noted 25 commonly accepted elements of environmental education and called for a more adequate theoretical and conceptual base upon which to conduct research (Hart 1981). The confusion notwithstanding, a commonly accepted definition of outdoor education has at least four elements: it implies experiences in the outdoors, it is cross-disciplinary, it provides direct experiences for children, and it focuses on real-life situations (Smith et al. 1963 p. 19). The range of activities which are described as outdoor education, however, is so broad as to lack coherence and definition. That lack of adequate definition provides difficulties for the movement—and for anyone attempting to summarize conclusions of research in the field.

1. History

Some countries have made large-scale commitments to outdoor education. For example, Australia has developed more than 30 outdoor education centers since the early 1960s, though still fewer than 10 percent of the school population is afforded the opportunity to participate (Webb 1980). The United Kingdom has had a significant outdoor education program, which was bolstered in 1939 by an Act of Parliament which created the National Camps Corporation. Later, a Field Studies Council was formed, to establish and run field studies centers throughout the country (Kirk 1980). The Federal Republic of Germany, another heavily involved participant in outdoor education, celebrated the 50th anniversary of one of the largest outdoor education centers in the world, *Wegscheide*, a part of the Frankfurt school system (Goering 1971). Indeed, most northern European countries have had programs in outdoor education for many years now.

Within the United States, outdoor education has moved through four distinct phases. Prior to the 1950s, many educators conceived of the summer camp as a novel educational tool. Charles Eliot, president emeritus of Harvard University, described the "organized summer camp" in 1922 as the "greatest contribution America has made to education." His comment was typical of the period. Some claim 1930 as the birth of outdoor education, for in that year two prominent American educators, L. B. Sharp and Bernard S. Mason, completed dissertations on outdoor education at leading American universities. The 1930s and 1940s witnessed a proliferation of outdoor education camps: New York City (Life Camps, Inc.); San Diego; Clear Lake, Michigan (W. K. Kellogg Foundation); and in various other parts of the country (Hammerman 1980).

In the 1950s, the initial development of camps as outdoor education centers turned to camps as extensions of public schools. The literature reflects a concern in this period with learning at school camps: seven studies continued the earlier focus on camping as education.

Yet more than 30 studies examined the educational outcomes of school camps.

By 1960 the term had become outdoor education. An enormous number of programs proliferated in the United States, no doubt in part as a result of the impetus of federal funding. The Elementary and Secondary Education Act of 1965 authorized expenditures for exemplary programs in outdoor education. By 1972 over three million American students were involved in some form of outdoor education, supported by Title III of the United States Office of Education (Hill 1972). By the 1970s, however, the focus had again changed, this time to environmental education. A much wider range of activities and concerns came to be called environmental education, especially some inside classrooms which dealt specifically with environmental issues. The shifting nature of the focus caused more than definitional difficulties; any summarization of research conclusions must be approached cautiously, recognizing the lack of theoretical and conceptual clarity. For example, two surveys of research in environmental education included outdoor education studies as part of their review (Roth 1976). Yet the most recent *Encyclopedia of Educational Research* (1982) limited its review to research studies specifically about environmental education.

The environmental education movement (of which outdoor education is a part) made giant international strides with the participation of the United Nations in the 1970s. In Stockholm, the United Nations Conference on the Human Environment urged environmental education through UNESCO. In 1974 the Environmental Education Program was initiated; by 1975 the first worldwide conference on environmental education was held in Belgrade. Recommendations from that conference are now being disseminated regionally and nationally, along with efforts at implementation (Stapp 1979). Despite the impetus for environmental education, certain regions of the world are handicapped by lack of resources and facilities (such as Africa) (Dyasi 1980). In some areas, teachers are inadequately or inappropriately trained and curricula are already crowded. National examinations provide an inflexibility which restricts curricular innovation (Knamiller 1979).

2. Programs

The number of actual programs in outdoor education is bewildering: summer camp programs, resident school camps, short-term outdoor programs—the list is endless, described by one author as a "smorgasbord" of programs and activities (Hammerman 1980). A survey in 1979 located almost 1,200 ongoing educational programs in the United States alone (Conrad 1980). Recently, particular attention has been given to successful programs in corrections, mental health, and special education. Several volumes have described exemplary practices in these programs (Loughmiller 1979).

3. Research

Obviously, a field with such diversity does not lend itself either to research or to summary statements about research conclusions. A few summaries exist (Staley 1979, Crompton and Sellar 1980), but the field is still inchoate.

L. B. Sharp once remarked that "that which can be best learned in the out of doors through direct experience . . . should there be learned." While that remark has been often quoted, research is only beginning to discover what things can be best learned in the outdoors, and under what conditions. Much of the literature of outdoor education is descriptive in nature, exemplified by a recent description of an exemplary program for the gifted (Grant 1979). Within the small body of research literature, a number of studies have looked at changes in the attitudes of children following an outdoor education experience. The results in general have been inconclusive. Some argue that the lack of conclusiveness is a fault of experimental design while others suggest that long-term attitudinal change cannot be expected to result from short-term experiences. Even stronger negative conclusions are derived from research about changing attitudes toward school. Little evidence exists to support the conclusion that outdoor educational experiences positively affect attitudes towards school; indeed most research suggests little impact on attitudes. The most positive conclusion came from a report of a travelling school camp (Shaw 1960).

In the area of development of more positive self-image, the research results are generally more positive. One researcher found that outdoor education experiences improved the sense of competence, and that feeling intensified as late as 10 weeks after the experiment took place (Beker 1960). Research attention has also been directed toward the development of socialization competencies. In relationship with peers, socialization skills seem to be enhanced by an outdoor education program, though the extent of development of these skills varies with the nature of the experience. Changes in attitudes towards integration have also been examined, beginning with a study of the Life Camps project of the New York City Board of Education (1949). The results in this area, while tentative, generally imply that racial attitudes can be improved by contact in an outdoor setting. Finally, several studies examined student–teacher relationships before and after an outdoor education experience; almost all concluded that there was at least some improvement in that relationship as a result of the outdoor education opportunity (Crompton and Sellar 1980).

The research that has occurred in outdoor education is found primarily in theses and dissertations. Fewer studies have appeared in scholarly journals and the periodic literature. Little impetus for research has been found among professional groups, although in 1964 the Council on Outdoor Education and Camping, at its inception, founded a research committee. That committee, however, has failed to assume a strong leadership role (Donaldson 1972). Part of the problem associated with research in the field may lie with the personality of outdoor educators. As a group, they are perhaps best characterized as action oriented, not inclined to devote their efforts to research. The concerns about the inadequacy of research surface in writings around the world (Linke 1980).

4. Future of the Subject

The future for outdoor education appears mixed. Strong forces are at work to continue an emphasis on environmental and outdoor education. General concern about environmental quality, coupled with international support, will continue to encourage programmatic development. Dissatisfaction with traditional classroom practices will continue to spur efforts to seek viable alternatives. At the same time, financial constraints, increasing litigation, public attacks on the schools, and the back to basics movement will encourage some educators to return to the classroom and traditional curriculum.

The research to date is often historical or descriptive. The experimental research has been limited by flaws: simple designs with inadequate controls have been utilized, the data have been derived from nonrepresentative samples, and unreliable and invalid measuring instruments have been employed. Additionally, many of the researchers are viewed as advocates of outdoor education, not impartial evaluators; their conclusions perhaps colored by their beliefs (Crompton and Sellar 1981). Perhaps the most limiting factor to further research remains an adequate definition of outdoor education. The term still implies an array of educational practices which are loosely joined together by philosophical and educational commitments. Without theoretical and conceptual clarity, research efforts will continue to be fragmented in approach and limited in applicability.

Bibliography

Beker J 1960 The influence of school camping on the self-concepts and social relationships of sixth grade school children. *J. Educ. Psychol.* 51: 352–56

Conrad J (ed.) 1980 *Directory of Selected State Outdoor Education Programs: State Responses to a 1979 Query Conducted by the Council on Outdoor Education/AAHPERD.* ERIC Clearinghouse on Rural Education and Small Schools, New Mexico State University, Las Cruces, New Mexico. ERIC Document No. ED 187 512

Crompton J L, Sellar C 1981 Do outdoor education experiences contribute to positive development in the affective domain? *J. Environ. Educ.* 12: 21–29

Donaldson G W 1972 Research in outdoor education. *J. Environ. Educ.* 3: 9–10

Dyasi H M 1980 Some environmental education activities in Africa. *J. Environ. Educ.* 12: 24–28

Goering O H 1971 Fifty years of outdoor education in the Frankfurt, Germany schools. *J. Outdoor Educ.* 5: 6–9

Grant G 1979 A gifted approach. *G/C/T* 8: 29–37

Hammerman W M (ed.) 1980 *Fifty Years of Resident Outdoor Education, 1930–1980: Its Impact on American Education.* American Camping Association, Martinsville, Indiana. ERIC Document No. ED 193 004

Hart E P 1981 Identification of key characteristics of environmental education. *J. Environ. Educ.* 13: 12–16

Hill W 1972 Model environmental education programs. *J. Environ. Educ.* 3: 28–31

Kirk J J 1980 Environmental education: A reality in the United Kingdom. *J. Environ. Educ.* 12: 29–32

Knamiller G W 1979 Environmental education and the Third World. *J. Environ. Educ.* 10: 7–11

Linke R D 1980 Achievements and aspirations in Australian environmental education. *J. Environ. Educ.* 12: 20–23

Loughmiller C 1979 *Kids in Trouble.* Wildwood, Tyler, Texas

New York City Board of Education 1949 *Extending Education Through Camping.* Outdoor Education Association, New York

Roth R E 1976 *A Review of Research Related to Environmental Education, 1973–1976.* ERIC Information Analysis Center for Science, Mathematics, and Environmental Education. Columbus, Ohio. ERIC Document No. ED 135 647

Shaw M J 1960 The educational effectiveness of the travelling school camp. Unpublished doctoral dissertation, University of California at Berkely (Available from Library Photo Service, General Library, University of California at Berkeley, Berkeley, California 94702)

Smith J W, Carlson R E, Donaldson G W, Masters H B 1963 *Outdoor Education.* Englewood Cliffs, Prentice-Hall, New Jersey

Staley F A 1979 The research, evaluation and measurement dragons in outdoor education. Paper presented at the National Outdoor Education Association meeting, Lake Placid, New York. ERIC Document No. ED 176 937

Stapp W B 1979 International environmental education. *J. Environ. Educ.* 11: 33–37

Webb J B 1980 *A Survey of Field Studies Centres in Australia.* Special Publication No. 4. Australian National Parks and Wildlife Service, Canberra. ERIC Document No. ED 205 375

Library User Education

J. E. Herring

User education in schools represents an attempt by librarians and teachers to teach pupils how to locate and use information effectively. It follows from a recognition that pupils need to acquire skills in identifying the purpose of information, the location of information, and the use of information. Thus user education takes the form not only of instructing pupils in the use of the library, but also of teaching pupils how to learn through effective use of information—in the form of books, journals, newspapers, audiovisual software, and people.

Conventional approaches to library user education mainly took the form of instructing pupils in the location of information in the school library. With the growth of resource-based learning in schools and the wider availability of a range of books and nonbook materials on different subjects, the need for pupils to acquire the skills of using information—in the library, in the classroom, in society—became more apparent.

1. Skills

Traditional user education programmes concentrated on locational skills (Herring 1978) which enabled pupils to find materials, mainly in the school library. Locational skills enable pupils to use the library catalogue, searching by author, by title, or (more importantly) by subject and to use the indexes in books and nonbook materials, to find information relevant to their purpose. Within locational skills, alphabetical skills, which are often underestimated by librarians and teachers but which are vital to any information search, also need to be acquired by pupils.

Locational skills, while useful, are of limited use if they are not allied to other information skills. Until recently, the concentration on teaching only locational skills in schools (Irving 1979) meant that the skills in information use were limited to the use of the library and not directly linked to the curriculum (Fjallbrant 1978, Nordling 1978).

The skills which pupils in both primary and secondary schools need to acquire involve not only the ability to locate materials, but also skills in thinking about the purpose of the information required (Irving 1980, Brake 1980). Pupils should be able to think out their need for information, for example for a project, identifying the topic, the subtopics, and the main keywords within the topic, before embarking on their search for information. In short, pupils need to learn how to learn and how to apply information skills to their curricular work.

Further aspects in the process of information seeking and information use can be seen by examining study skills (Herring 1978). Study skills are mainly relevant to the use of information and include the pupils' ability to extract relevant information from what they read, look at, or listen to; the skill of identifying relevant information; the ability to use skimming and scanning skills; and the skill of relating new knowledge acquired to knowledge already possessed. Additional skills in note taking and the presentation of a project are also relevant.

Thus information skills (Marland 1981) which incorporate the skills of identifying the purpose, the location, and the use of information, will now form the basis of library user education programmes in schools. Such skills are useful not only in the school, in the classroom, and in the library, but can be seen as life skills needed by pupils and adults in a society which is increasingly information conscious and in which information technology is rapidly developing.

2. Stages

User education should begin as early in the child's education as possible. Familiarization with books and libraries can be encouraged at preschool level. In primary schools, pupils can be introduced to basic library skills, especially in the location of materials, but also as an aid to their future understanding of concepts such as classification and information (Herring 1978, Irving 1980). Teaching information skills in relation to project work done in upper-primary school can ensure that pupils have a firm base on which to build their future information use. Thus being aware of what information is (and what kinds of information exist) and how information is classified—in libraries, in books or journals, in society—is a prerequisite for more advanced information use and more advanced learning.

In secondary schools, pupils will continue the process of learning to learn. As pupils' reading ability is enhanced, their ability to access more advanced sources of information, such as periodicals, reference works, and nonbook materials, is increased. While basic skills of finding information and of using libraries need to be repeated in secondary schools, the skills of using information—of evaluating, interpreting, synthesizing, and communicating information—need to be taught, especially to pupils doing advanced level work (Brake 1980).

Bibliography

Brake T 1980 Educating for access into the information culture. *Educ. Libr. Bull.* 23(2): 1–14

Fjallbrant N 1978 Progress and recent developments in Scandinavian libraries. In: Lubans J (ed.) 1978 *Progress in Educating the Library User*. Bowker, New York

Herring J E 1978 *Teaching Library Skills in Schools*. National Foundation for Educational Research, Slough

Herring J E 1987 *The Microcomputer, The School Librarian and the Teacher*. Bingley, London

Herring J E 1988 *School Librarianship*. 2nd edn. Bingley, London

Hyland A M 1978 Recent directions in educating the library user: Elementary schools. In: Lubans J (ed.) 1978 *Progress in Educating the Library User*. Bowker, New York

Irving A 1979 *Educating Library Users in Secondary Schools*. British Library, London

Irving A 1980 Innocents abroad: Information concepts and skills for the international child. *Educ. Libr. Bull.* 23(2): 15–21

Marland M 1981 *Information Skills in the Secondary Curriculum*. Methuen Educational, London

Nordling J A 1978 The high school library and the classroom. In: Lubans J (ed.) 1978 *Progress in Educating the Library User*. Bowker, New York

Taylor T K 1976 School libraries and the academic progress of students. *Aust. Acad. Res. Libr.* 7: 117–22

Section 10

Mathematics Education

Overview

The mathematics curriculum Section is divided into three subsections: traditional subject areas in mathematics studies, innovative topics, and issues in mathematics education.

The first subsection starts with Davis' article on elementary school mathematics programs. The author examines cross-national differences in the organization of mathematics studies and asks: How is curriculum planned? Are there several alternative tracks? Does the regional economy depend on sophisticated mathematics? Travers' article on secondary school mathematics focuses on differences in the content of mathematics courses across various countries and on differences in time allocated to specific topics.

Each of four traditional mathematics curriculum topics are treated in separate articles. Levin describes arithmetic as the child's first encounter with the systematic study of a branch in mathematics, and concludes that the way it is taught in school greatly influences the child's conception of mathematics. Kieran reviews the dramatic changes which have occurred in the algebra curriculum. Past algebra courses focused on teaching manipulative skills, but with the advent of the computer new algebra courses put greater emphasis on conceptual understanding. Mevarech examines the place of analysis in mathematics curricula and summarizes research dealing with the impact of various teaching strategies on achievements in this field. In the last article of this subsection, Fey points out the importance of geometry in construction, modeling, art, and in serving as a basis for the hypothetical-deductive reasoning model.

The second subsection contains 13 articles about innovative mathematics topics, which gained special attention in the new mathematics curricula. Most articles in this section describe the innovative nature of the topic, its place in the mathematics curriculum and trends in research related to teaching that particular topic. Vinner reviews briefly the general features of the *New Mathematics* curricula, and refers to the debate about the worth of these innovative programs. Mathematics applications are treated in two articles. Lesh defines mathematics application as using mathematical concepts in everyday life and claims that average people need to acquire a stock of basic conceptual models, such as probability, measurement, and coordinate systems, in order to pursue career opportunities in a technological society. Usiskin examines the application of mathematics in studying other subjects in the secondary school. Kilpatrick reviews dilemmas related to teaching mathematical problem solving, and compares the advantages and the disadvantages of teaching algorithms versus using heuristic devices.

The teaching of basic *Number and Measurement Concepts* to preschool children is discussed by Voigt; the place of number systems and number theory in the mathematics curriculum is examined by Kieren. Bishop summarizes research related to teaching measurement in schools and points out that intuitive understanding of the quality being measured is more important than the ability to carry out routine measurement tasks. In his article on transformation geometry, Bishop explains how the child's daily experiences facilitates understanding of concepts like motion, transformation, or rotation. Wilson

817

examines whether systematic studies improve the ability of computational and measurement estimation.

Tirosh discusses the role of set theory in studying the logical and philosophical foundations of mathematics, and examines evidence about the desirability of including elementary concepts of set theory in the mathematics curriculum. The teaching of rational numbers is one of the most troublesome topics in elementary mathematics and Lesh summarizes research suggesting how to handle this topic. Fischbein lists arguments in support of teaching *Probability and Statistics*: it serves practical purposes in daily life, it helps in the study of various science disciplines, it develops and refines mathematical thinking. Finally, the desired content of computer literacy studies for children of various ages is examined by Russell.

The third subsection contains articles on major issues related to the mathematics curriculum. Stowasser surveys the history of teaching mathematics since the proto-Sumerian times (before 3000 BC) till our days. Nesher, in her article on *The Language of Mathematics*, reviews research related to two meanings of this term: first, the pedagogical implications of defining mathematical entities, and secondly, the function of the natural language in the process of solving mathematical problems. Pellerey in his article on *Mathematics Instruction* summarizes research about the historical, epistemological, and psychological aspects of mathematics instruction and distinguishes between three components of mathematics instruction, namely the content of the studies, the didactics, and the instructional materials. Aiken summarizes research carried out since the 1950s on *Attitudes Towards Mathematics*. This body of research has dealt with measuring attitude, the development and the correlates of attitude towards mathematics, and the effective ways of modifying such attitudes and overcoming maths phobia.

The impact of recent developments in computing technology is examined in two articles. Hutton examines arguments for and against using hand-held calculators in mathematics education, and concludes that the outcomes of using a calculator are dependent on how it is integrated in the process of the student's work. Olive's article on *Computers in Mathematics Education* describes the dramatic growth in the availability of microcomputers and its impact on the mathematics curriculum, and lists the major foci of research related to this issue.

In the 1980s great attention has been devoted to the impact of learners' awareness of their own thoughts on learning. An area of studies emerged which became known as metacognition, and since 1980 it has been included in the descriptors list of the Educational Resources Information Center (ERIC). Schoenfeld reviews research related to *Metacognition and Mathematics* education. He delineates three areas of research related to this topic: peoples' judgment of their own mental capacities to study mathematics; peoples' ability to monitor their own behavior in the midst of solving mathematical problems; and beliefs that individuals have regarding the nature of mathematical thinking.

Finally White describes *Mathematics as a Humanistic Discipline*, in which free invention and imagination play an important role sharing an aesthetic sense with art, poetry, and music.

A. Lewy

Mathematics Education

Introduction

J. Kilpatrick

The school mathematics curriculum has resulted from the confluence of two traditions. The first, rooted in Babylonian astronomy, Egyptian earth measurement, and ancient commerce, is mathematics as *reckoning*, as a tool required for the affairs of everyday life. Every society attempts to pass on to its children the language and skills it has devised or otherwise acquired for dealing with numerical and spatial problems. When schools are organized to give children a grounding in their common culture, this practical sort of mathematics is what appears in the curriculum. Children are taught to "do sums" and to apply these sums in exercises modeled on adult activities in various fields. The second tradition, rooted in Greek geometry and medieval algebra, is mathematics as *reasoning*, as one of the liberal arts whose mastery marks an educated person. In this tradition, mathematics offers aesthetic satisfaction as well as a means of developing the mind's capacity for abstract thought. Students preparing for university entrance are expected to acquire some facility in using mathematical principles to derive proofs of theorems and solutions to complex problems. The rigorous deductive methods serve as ideals for scientific inquiry; the harmonious patterns, as the essence of artistic symmetry, beauty, and elegance.

The two traditions have, from time to time, led to conflict and confusion. The tradition of mathematics as reckoning usually predominates in the primary school. It largely defines what the public expects schools to provide every child in the way of mathematics education. It is associated with the view that the learning of mathematics requires discipline, repetitive work, and skill at memorization. The tradition of mathematics as reasoning, in contrast, has often been rather elitist. It arose in the secondary school and has become associated with the view that the learning of mathematics entails inquiry, creativity, and the search for meaning. Most mathematicians and many mathematics teachers came to the study of the subject through this tradition. They often fail to appreciate the public's (and some teachers') opinion that mathematics needs to be taught in an instrumental fashion.

As mass education extended into the secondary school, and as primary school mathematics expanded beyond arithmetic, the two traditions became intertwined and transformed. All students need both to reckon and to reason; the problem now is to strike an agreeable balance between these goals and then achieve the goals within the confines of an educational system. The twentieth century's efforts to provide a "higher literacy" (Resnick 1987) to all students have forced a reconsideration of the school mathematics curriculum, especially in the lower secondary years, where the pressures for change have been the greatest and the curriculum is typically regarded as unsatisfactory.

The quickening pace of technological innovation has made it impossible to predict with any accuracy what mathematics a student will need as an adult. The solution many countries attempted during the modern mathematics reforms of the 1950s and 1960s was to provide students with an understanding of the structure of the discipline so that they could later learn what they needed. Since that time, mathematics has changed greatly, primarily under the impact of the computer (Steen 1988). More attention is being given in the school curriculum to teaching applications of mathematics and to making students literate with computers. Mathematics educators continue to promote, especially in the primary school years, approaches to mathematics that stress thinking, exploration, and investigation. Whether such approaches are well understood or accepted by the public and the politicians is another matter.

Broadly defined, the school mathematics curriculum encompasses goals, content, methods, and assessment procedures (Howson et al. 1981 p. 2). Even when people have been able to agree upon the goals, content, and methods, the procedures used to assess students' knowledge and understanding have ordinarily been inadequate. Every country needs some mechanism for deciding who shall receive a university education, and mathematics has historically played a prominent role in whatever mechanism has been set up, which is usually a system of examinations. In recent years, school mathematics has been identified as a gatekeeper that has prevented many students—especially girls and members of minority groups in the society—from pursuing further education. Large-scale assessments of students' mathematical performance across and within countries have documented inequities in access to mathematical knowledge. They have also shown that the general levels of performance in many countries are low. The consensus is that efforts to bring all students into the traditions of mathematics as reckoning and as reasoning have been only partially successful.

These efforts have often taken the form of curriculum development. Around the end of the last century, the school mathematics curriculum came to be seen as something that could be studied and developed. Official commissions examined curricula in various locales and concluded that they could influence mathematics teaching by making recommendations and identifying exemplary practices. By midcentury, mathematics educators had decided that special projects were needed to undertake curriculum change. As they gained more experience in curriculum development, people began to see clear discrepancies between the curriculum desired (as it exists in a ministry of education syllabus or on a project director's desk), the curriculum in action (as it is implemented by teachers), and the curriculum achieved (as it is manifested in the minds of young children). The links between the last two of these has been the focus of much recent attention. No matter what a commission or a project ordains, curriculum development is increasingly seen as an activity of teachers.

Although the community of people concerned with the school mathematics curriculum has witnessed much controversy over such matters as the instructional use of pocket calculators, it is a more cohesive community than exists for most other parts of the school curriculum. Mathematicians, psychologists, and teachers have collaborated in many projects and organizations. A variety of journals—among them, *Mathematics Teaching*, *Educational Studies in Mathematics*, *The Mathematics Teacher*, *For the Learning of Mathematics*, *Zentralblatt für Didaktik der Mathematik*—report to the community on curriculum issues. Institutes such as the Shell Centre for Mathematical Education in Nottingham and the Research Group on Mathematics Education and Educational Computer Centre in Utrecht bring together researchers and curriculum workers to develop materials for teachers and students. Every four years the International Commission on Mathematical Instruction organizes an international congress at which topics and issues concerning the school mathematics curriculum are aired.

During the 1980s the community of mathematics educators became especially concerned about the social and cultural contexts in which mathematics is taught (Bishop 1988). Attention has turned to the mathematics of everyday life and whether and how this mathematics might be used more productively in instruction, so that students might see connections between school mathematics and the world they know. Mathematics is a cultural product; too often it has been taught as though it were fixed, final, and outside of human society. Students have too often been treated as though they brought no mathematical ideas with them to class and could not participate in the mutual endeavor of constructing mathematical knowledge. Mathematics teachers are beginning to accept the challenge of bringing their subject alive and helping to bridge the gap between what the child knows and what society needs in the way of mathematical knowledge and understanding.

Bibliography

Bishop A J 1988 *Mathematical Enculturation: A Cultural Perspective on Mathematics Education*. Kluwer Academic Publishers, Dordrecht

Howson A G, Keitel C, Kilpatrick J 1981 *Curriculum Development in Mathematics*. Cambridge University Press, Cambridge

Howson G, Wilson B 1986 *School Mathematics in the 1990s*. Cambridge University Press, Cambridge

Resnick L 1987 *Education and Learning to Think*. National Academy Press, Washington, DC

Steen L A 1988 The science of patterns. *Science* 240: 611–16

Wirszup I, Streit R (eds.) 1987 *Developments in School Mathematics Education Around the World*. National Council of Teachers of Mathematics, Reston, Virginia

Traditional Subject Areas

Mathematics: Elementary-school Programs

R. B. Davis and F. Goffree

What should actually be taught in schools is surely one of the most fundamental questions in education. It is surprisingly difficult to answer, for at least three reasons: (a) there is great variation from one classroom, school, or nation to another; (b) "official" descriptions of what is supposed to happen are frequently at variance with what actually does happen; and, (c) the way in which a matter is taught and learned is often more important than the choice of the abstract "topic" itself.

For the specific case of elementary-school mathematics—that is, mathematics taught to children between the ages of approximately 5 and 12 years old—it can be said that, over most of the world, this consists mainly of arithmetic, with the possible inclusion of some algebra, some geometry, and, in a few cases, of some experience using computers. In fact the variation is far greater than that answer might suggest.

1. Dimensions of Difference

Differences in elementary-school mathematics programs in various nations tend to reflect differences in the nations themselves. At the most fundamental level, these differences include:

(a) Is education universal, or not? If it is (approximately) universal, how recently was this achieved? (This is important because parents and teachers might be the products of the educational system at an earlier date.)

(b) Does the regional or national economy depend upon sophisticated mathematics, upon quite elementary mathematics, or upon almost no mathematics?

(c) Do all students follow the same course of study, or are there several alternative "tracks"?

(d) How is the curriculum planned and controlled? By central control? Or by local control? Or are decisions left up to the individual schools and individual teachers?

(e) Is primary mathematics taught by a specialist teacher who teaches only mathematics?

For elementary-school mathematics there are some other differences that are embedded deeply in the culture.

For example:

(a) Is arithmetic taught by the use of concrete material aids (such as the abacus used in Japan), or purely by symbols (as, typically, in the United States)?

(b) Are standard Hindu–Arabic numerals used, or are some local number names employed (such as naming numbers by using words for parts of the human body, as in Papua New Guinea)? If a special system is used for naming numbers, is this a place–value system? If so, is it to base 10?

(c) Does the local language lend itself easily to mathematical discussions? More fundamentally, does the local view of the world easily accommodate mathematical modes of thought? [For example, are the students familiar with "If . . . , then . . ." types of statements. With a two-valued logic? With the idea (and practice) of making simple measurements (as of length, weight, etc.)?]

Important as the preceding matters are, two other considerations are even more decisive in determining what is actually taught in elementary-school mathematics:

(a) In what sense are the topics to be "learned"? In what sense are they intended to be known? (How might this knowledge be demonstrated?)

(b) By what process is learning presumed to take place?

2. The General Pattern of "Elementary" or "Primary" Mathematics

The words "elementary" and "primary" have different meanings in different nations. Here, however, the words are used as synonymous, to refer to schooling students whose chronological age is between, roughly, 5 or 6 years old to about 12 years old. Although there are important exceptions, in most of the world education at this level is universal, compulsory, and with a single curriculum for all students.

The age limits can be defined more precisely: one of the earliest starting ages is reported for Ireland, where children begin primary (or elementary) education at about 4 years and 6 months of age. Among the latest starting ages reported are those for Sweden and for Chile; in both countries children begin elementary school when they are about 7 years old.

"Beginning" ages, however, are compounded by the existence in some countries of preschools, for example, in the United States and in the Soviet Union. In the Soviet Union, over 10 percent of all children younger than two years of age are enrolled in preschools, with much larger proportions of older children enrolled. Thus it could be said that Soviet children typically start school earlier than those of almost any other nation. Usually, not much mathematics is taught at the preschool level, but here, too, there are important exceptions, perhaps especially in the United States.

"Elementary" or "primary" school lasts for four years for children in Mozambique, and for 10 years for Japanese children. These represent extremes; for most other children, elementary school lasts for six or eight years, but patterns vary from nation to nation. At the end of elementary school, children may pass on into secondary school, or may enter the world of work, perhaps temporarily, resuming their education at a later date.

3. Some Specific National Patterns

3.1 Mozambique

As indicated above, elementary education in Mozambique means, today, a four-year program, at the end of which students enter the work force. Alternating periods of study with periods of work is national policy and therefore some will resume their education at a later date.

Today's schools in Mozambique were created mainly around 1976, since the nation achieved independence. At the time independence was won, the population was 93 percent illiterate. In 1962, if a student was lucky enough to be in school at all (which was rare), the student was probably taught by an older student. Fourth grade students taught second grade. In 1973, the total number of students in primary schools was 589,000; a year later found 33,000 students in secondary schools. By 1978, these totals had jumped, suddenly, to 1,419,000 and to 82,000, respectively. The teacher shortage is easily imagined; by 1979 more than 90 percent of secondary mathematics teachers had no professional training. The primary situation was presumably far worse. Only 27 percent of the children who began their formal education in 1976 reached the end of primary school after the scheduled four years. Failing in mathematics was one of the main causes for students to fall behind, or to drop out. Today "only some hundreds of students graduate from the ninth grade each year" (Gerdes 1981). Mozambique is making heroic efforts to educate all children, but the level of mathematical achievement cannot as yet be very high.

3.2 Jordan

Jordan is an agricultural country, 80 percent uninhabitable desert. Children enter elementary school at age 6, and complete elementary school 6 years later, by which time they are expected to be proficient in all of the usual arithmetic calculations, using whole numbers, fractions, or decimals. They should know percent, as well as Π and the formula for the area of a circle; they should be good at estimation, and at computing simple and compound interest, and so on. This program is somewhat more comprehensive than the curriculum typically achieved in schools in the United States. Graphs are included, but negative numbers are not. With a population of about 2.25 million, living mainly in a few large cities, Jordan has a centrally controlled nationwide curriculum.

3.3 United States

Diversity is the word for the United States curricula, which officially may be set at the state level, or by individual communities, or by individual schools, or (in some cases) even by individual teachers. Despite this, there is considerable uniformity; the program in general achieves, by the age of 11, an ability to add, subtract, and multiply integers; division may be more equivocal. Computations with fractions are typically unreliable for many students. Virtually no algebra is included, and little geometry. Real-world applications of mathematics are rare.

Individual teachers and individual schools in some cases accomplish much more, including considerable geometry, a beginning to the study of algebra, and sometimes experience in using mathematics in dealing with real-world situations. Some curriculum projects—especially USMES (Unified Science and Mathematics for Elementary Schools)—have introduced an extensive use of real-world situations, such as finding which street intersections most urgently need pedestrian-operated traffic control signals, or designing work clothes for students—but these more ambitious curricula can be found in only a small percentage of United States schools.

An increasing number of schools are teaching the use of hand-held calculators, which are rapidly becoming ubiquitous in the United States. A much smaller number of elementary schools are beginning to teach students to work with—perhaps even to program—digital computers. Computers are also sometimes used in computer aided instruction (CAI) mode, for simulations, or even to teach computational geometry in a form designed especially for young children (Papert 1980).

In some American communities, grades 7 and 8 (ages 12 to 14) are also considered elementary, and may be devoted to reviewing and reteaching introductory arithmetic.

3.4 England and Wales

Until the late 1980s, mathematics instruction in England was distinguished by local, not national, control—by the headteacher and teachers who shaped the program in their school. English instruction is also distinguished by very great use of manipulatable materials, such as geoboards, Cuisenaire rods, "maths labs," "outdoor mathematics," and so on. In recent years efforts have been made to import this English use of concrete materials into the United States, but few schools show any effect of these efforts.

3.5 Japan

Achievement test results and industrial productivity both suggest that Japan is, educationally, one of the most effective nations in the world, if not the most effective of all. The Japanese curriculum begins the study of algebra at the age of 8, and direct measurement of the dimensions of various physical objects in grade 1 (chronological age: 6-year-olds). There is great emphasis on the meaning of mathematical words and symbols; Japanese instruction is not intended to be rote instruction.

By the age of 8, Japanese children are expected to be proficient in multiplication and division, to be familiar with decimal fractions, to have some acquaintance with the idea of functions, and to be able to set up problems on the soroban (or Japanese abacus).

By the age of 9, Japanese children have considerable acquaintance with geometric concepts such as angle measurements, perpendicularity, area, volume, and so on, and are familiar with many geometric shapes in two and three dimensions. Their arithmetic skills include work with decimals and fractions; following the algebraic strand, they can represent functions by using algebraic expressions, by graphs, and by tables.

By the completion of elementary school, a Japanese student has a considerable knowledge of arithmetic computation, of geometric ideas, of the beginning of algebra, and of the measurements of time, distance, money, area, volume, angles, and so on. Children are intended to have experience in devising their own algorithms, to be skillful in the use of the Japanese abacus, and to understand the meaning of what they are doing. They also know some ideas from descriptive statistics, are familiar with direct and inverse proportion, and have some skill in descriptive geometry (or elementary "engineering drawing"). They have begun to deal both with discrete quantities and with continuous quantities, and are familiar with axes of symmetry, ratio and proportion, prisms, cylinders, cones, pyramids, and so on. They are also expected to display some level of originality and resourcefulness.

3.6 The Soviet Union

The Soviet arrangement of schools divides "primary" from "secondary" in a way that is different from most of the nations discussed above. At age 7 a student enters the "8-year school" or the "10-year school." Grades 1, 2, and 3 are designated "primary," and may, or may not, be housed in a separate building. Following the 8- or 10-year school there are recognizable "secondary" schools of various sorts. Thus, to call only grades 1–3 "primary" would probably be to cut that phase too short for comparability with most other nations; but calling grades 1–8 "primary" extends this stage perhaps somewhat too long for good comparability, especially in light of the well-developed preschools that operate in the Soviet Union.

Grades 1–3 deal mainly with arithmetic (but do include a significant beginning in algebra) plus experience in measurement and some study of geometry, including the basic abstract ideas of "point" and "line."

In grades 4 and 5 all three themes—arithmetic, algebra, and geometry—are carried considerably further. In grade 6 the concept of function is studied rather extensively.

By the end of grade 8, the student is expected to be familiar with exponential and logarithmic functions, their graphs, and relationships such as:

$$(\log_a b)\,(\log_b c) = \log_a c$$

Soviet curricula are planned at the national level, and an attempt is made to achieve nationwide uniformity. When one considers the many languages and cultures embraced within the Soviet Union, however, it hardly seems likely that the same program can be offered in remote Eskimo regions, or in Islamic mountain villages, that can be offered in Moscow and Leningrad. The overall strength of the Soviet curriculum is generally recognized, nonetheless, culminating in two years of calculus in the secondary-school program, intended to be offered to all students in the Soviet Union.

4. Quality

The success of the different curricula can be judged against any of several possible standards. When the low literacy and "numeracy" levels in the recent past history of many nations are considered, sometimes only a generation removed from today's students, it is clear that a great effort is being made nearly everywhere in the world. Using, however, the more demanding criterion of the general level of numeracy among a nation's populace, it is clear that, in many advanced societies, skill in elementary mathematics is far from universal. But there is still a yet higher criterion that might be invoked: the best of the modern "experimental" programs have repeatedly demonstrated that 8- to 10-year-old children can have, and profit from, significant experience with real mathematics, with mathematical thinking, mathematical analysis, mathematical conjecturing, with gathering evidence, devising lines of reasoning, seeking and finding regularities and key patterns. This level of education is achieved at present by a small number of teachers and offered only to a small number of students in Hungary, Japan, the United

States, and in other countries. The failure to achieve this level of education more often in elementary mathematics is analogous to teaching reading, but failing to develop an interest in, or a knowledge of, literature and creative expression.

From such considerations—and from the nearly universal tendency to deal with elementary mathematics primarily as meaningless rote—it is necessary to regard elementary-school mathematics curricula as, generally, less than truly successful. Why is this so? Four reasons are often suggested. (a) Because primary education is compulsory, it is a very large undertaking, involving millions of teachers, and such size alone seems nearly to preclude quality. (b) As it is compulsory, primary education embraces a great diversity of students— indeed, just about every kind of child that can exist— and providing adequately for such a range is severely taxing. (c) Teacher turnover at the elementary level is very high; in some nations, more than half of the teachers will leave teaching, and be replaced by newcomers within a period of five years; thus far more teacher education is needed, and there is even greater pressure to keep it simple. (d) Finally, many societies are attempting to pass on to children knowledge and expertise that are unknown to most adults within that society. Given the rate of change of modern societies, this problem is becoming increasingly severe. What was thought to be a problem of developing nations like Mozambique is rapidly coming to be a problem also in the United States where children are learning things about computers that parents and teachers do not generally know.

5. *Levels of Cognitive Development in Children*

It is sometimes argued that elementary-school mathematics must limit itself to modest cognitive goals, if only for the reason that developmental immaturity of the children imposes strict cognitive limits on what they can learn. This argument is not supported by the evidence. Every experimental curriculum that has addressed this question has tended to disprove the absolute nature of these alleged cognitive limits. From Korean Chisanbop to California's Project SEED and Papert's LOGO environments, whenever young children have been given an appropriate opportunity to learn a considerable portion of genuine mathematics, most students have responded well. The limits of elementary mathematics may reflect the limited mathematical goals that a society sets for its citizens, and the limited capacity of many educational delivery systems, but they certainly do not reflect the level of possible student cognitive functioning. Cognitive limits exist, but primarily as limitations on the kind of experience that a child can profit from, and the kind of knowledge he or she can acquire at a given moment in his or her life. If these limitations are taken into account in a proper way, most children can learn a large amount of mathematics and can develop quite sophisticated mathematical capabilities while

in elementary school. At present this happens in very few schools around the world. Very few human beings anywhere ever have an opportunity to learn what mathematical thinking really is.

6. *Senses of "Knowing" and Processes of Learning*

By far the most common assumption in virtually all parts of the world is that primary-school mathematics consists of facts and algorithms, both of which are to be memorized, mainly by rote. These facts and algorithms are learned by a process wherein they are told or demonstrated to the students, after which the students practice reciting the fact, or carrying out the algorithm, until they are able to do so correctly and consistently (Davis and McKnight 1980). This interpretation of what it means to "know" mathematics, though widespread almost to the point of universality, is in fact controversial. Such "meaningless" knowledge—or meaningless performance capability—has been rejected by Bruner, Erlwanger (1973), Alderman et al. (1979), and many others, dating back at least to Dewey. Within recent decades at least three important schools of thought can be identified concerning the nature of the process of learning mathematics (although many variations and lesser alternatives can be found). Firstly the assumption of rote learning, as described above. Secondly the "abstract mathematical structure" school of thought, which argues that the true simplicity of mathematics is not revealed by attempting to retrace the historical path of development, with its detours and wrong turnings and fuzzy concepts, but rather by beginning with the simple, precise abstractions of modern analysis, such as "set," "group," "vector space" and so on. This viewpoint was most prominent in the 1960s and early 1970s. Today it has tended to lose ground to a third position, the "constructivist" point of view.

The "constructivist" position, based partly on the work of Piaget, and expounded more recently by Papert (1980) and others, assumes that knowledge is represented in certain special ways in a person's mind, and that new knowledge can be acquired if, and only if, it can be related to representations previously acquired. Tracing this process backwards, mathematical ideas are seen as ultimately based upon experiences in early childhood, including experience with "horizontal" versus "vertical," the behavior of fluids under the influence of gravity, the behavior of collections of physical objects when the objects are moved about, and so on. This position implies that certain ideas can be learned easily, but others cannot, but the criterion of simplicity is a developmental one, quite different from the "abstract" criteria that see simplicity in such abstract concepts as "transformation group" or "set." Simplicity, for the constructivists, is based upon whatever it is that the individual knows already, which will most often be concrete, or at least experiential. From a constructivist point of view, it is important for a child to have appropriate experiences as a foundation for learning. These experiences may involve such concrete materials or devices as an abacus, or Dienes MAB blocks, or Cuisenaire rods, or geoboards, and so on. In the Soviet Union, where Piaget has not been popular, a version of the constructivist position has been articulated and developed by S. L. Rubinshtein at Moscow University (Davis et al. 1979, Rubinshtein 1935).

The competition between these three views will inevitably shape mathematics in primary schools in the next decade or so. The three views lead to three very different kinds of school mathematics programs.

7. The Challenges Posed by Adult Society

Thus far little heed has been paid to impending changes in the way adult society deals with mathematics, and to implications for school curricula. Hand-held calculators, and even hand-held computers, now exist, and are rapidly becoming both cheap and ubiquitous (see *Calculators in Mathematics Education*). Although it has not yet done so, this must come to have an impact on school curricula. So, too, must the increasing democratization of the world's populations; if we are no longer to educate different classes or different castes, if the distinction between "gentleman" and "peasant" is to be eliminated (including also sex-typing as an important special case), what, then, is to be taught to every person? And what use shall be made of differences in individual ability?

The answers to such questions remain to be worked out in the years ahead.

Bibliography

Alderman D L, Swinton S S, Braswell J S 1979 Assessing basic arithmetic skills and understanding across curricula: Computer-assisted instruction and compensatory education. *J. Children's Math. Behav.* 2(2): 3–28
Davis R B, McKnight C 1980 The influence of semantic content on algorithmic behavior. *J. Math. Behav.* 3: 39–87
Davis R B, Romberg T A, Rachlin S, Kantowski M G 1979 *An Analysis of Mathematics Education in the Union of Soviet Socialist Republics.* ERIC Clearinghouse, Ohio State University, Columbus, Ohio
Erlwanger S H 1973 Benny's conception of rules and answers in IPI mathematics. *J. Children's Math. Behav.* 1(2): 7–26
Gerdes P 1981 Changing mathematics education in Mozambique. *Educ. Stud. Math.* 12: 455–77
Hashimoto Y, Sawada T 1979 *Mathematics Program in Japan.* National Institute for Educational Research, Tokyo
Howson G, Keitel C, Kilpatrick J 1981 *Curriculum Development in Mathematics.* Cambridge University Press, Cambridge
Papert S 1980 *Mindstorms: Children, Computers, and Powerful Ideas.* Basic Books, New York
Rubinshtein S L 1935 *The Bases of Psychology.* Uchpedgiz, Moscow
Servais W, Varga T (eds.) 1971 *Teaching School Mathematics.* Penguin, Harmondsworth
Swetz F J (ed.) 1978 *Socialist Mathematics Education.* Burgundy Press, Southampton, Pennsylvania

Mathematics: Secondary-school Programs

K. J. Travers

The study of mathematics occupies a central place in the school programs of all countries. It has been estimated that in most school systems between 15 and 20 percent of instructional time is devoted to this topic. Only mother tongue, reading, and literature are allocated as much time as mathematics.

The importance afforded mathematics reflects the vital role played by the subject in contemporary society. At the most basic level, a knowledge of mathematics is essential in everyday living. More advanced mathematical concepts and techniques are indispensable tools in commerce, engineering, and the natural and social sciences. Thus, the learning of mathematics can represent firstly, a basic preparation for adult life, and secondly, an entrée to a wide array of career choices. From a societal perspective, mathematical competence is both an essential component in the preparation of an informed citizenry and a requisite for the production of the qualified personnel required by industry, technology, and science.

The secondary years of schooling roughly take place between the ages of 11 to 18 years. In the Western industrialized and the socialist countries, secondary education, at least to the age of 15 or 16 years, is required of all students. Developing countries, on the other hand, while undergoing remarkable growth in their educational systems at the primary (presecondary) levels, are still grappling with the implications of expanded educational provisions for the secondary years of schooling.

1. Types of Mathematics Programs Available

In most countries, the transition from primary to secondary education is marked by a move away from a unitary mathematics program for all students towards a school structure which offers a variety of programs according to the students' abilities, interests, or goals. In some countries, the number of different programs available by the end of secondary school is rather large —a dozen or more. In Japan, for example, 15-year-old students have available to them the "upper-secondary" program (which leads to university study), technical programs, part-time and correspondence programs, training schools for business and other fields, as well as special schools for handicapped students. The majority of the students are enrolled in the upper-secondary program.

Since 1971, Sweden has moved to a more unified system of schooling than it previously had. Prior to that date, Swedish youth (about 90 percent of the 16-year-olds are in school) could choose between three forms of upper-secondary school: *gymnasium*, continuation school, and vocational school. Now, all students enroll in the same school, the *gymnasium*, thereby having access to a broader variety of academic and technical programs. The Swedish *gymnasium* offers 22 streams, five of which lead to further academic study. In some countries, differentiation between courses begins rather early. In the United Kingdom, for example, diversification begins around the age of 12 years.

In the Soviet Union, a single compulsory program is provided for all students through the general eight year school (until age 15). Thereafter, four alternative programs are provided. However, since the mathematics curriculum is virtually identical in these alternatives, a Soviet child is provided with a nearly unitary mathematical program through at least 10 years of schooling.

Quadling (1979, pp. 47–48) has identified four types of mathematics programs at the secondary level.

(a) Academic courses—usually designed for students who will proceed to university studies. These courses tend to present mathematics as an isolated discipline and emphasize theoretical principles and the logical coherence of the subject.

(b) General courses—followed by students of not more than average ability who have no particular career objectives. As more students remain in school beyond the age of compulsory attendance, these courses take on greater importance. For example, they aim to emphasize the relevance of mathematics to the citizen in the modern world.

(c) Technical courses—intended to provide the mathematical knowledge needed in particular fields of employment. Some of these courses (for example, designed for engineers, business, or the electronics industry) may have substantial mathematical content. However, the emphasis is on applications of mathematics to the world of work. Students successful in these courses may go on to advanced study in a technological college or university.

(d) Skill courses—often taken on a part-time basis by employees in particular crafts or trades. Training in the basic mathematical skills (calculation, measurement, application of formulas) is offered. The content of the course is not usually more advanced than that a student has already met in school, but focuses upon special areas of application.

The extent to which a country offers these kinds of programs is a function of the role of secondary schooling in that society. Industrialized countries which tend to have educational systems encompassing all or most of the age cohort through the end of secondary school seek to offer a wide range of programs for the full spectrum of ability and interest groups.

In England and Wales, for example, the "Mathematics for the Majority Project" was undertaken in the 1970s to address the problem of providing for lower achieving children. The project, which was an outgrowth of efforts to take into account the needs of the majority as secondary mathematics programs are developed, approached mathematics through applications, allowing skills to emerge from explorations of practical situations.

In many developing countries, on the other hand, only a small fraction of the age cohort is enrolled in secondary school. A concern for expanding the scope of mathematics programs to address the needs of a broader cross-section of youth was expressed in a recommendation of the Khartoum conference on developing mathematics in Third World countries, which stated, "Mathematics curricula at secondary school level should be designed to be relevant to the needs of that majority of the students for whom this stage will be terminal. As much care should be given to the development of appropriate mathematics curricula for the technical and vocational sectors as for the academic sector" (El Tom 1979 p. 185).

In many countries, the objectives of mathematics instruction are stated explicitly in official publications such as curriculum guides of ministries of education. Halls and Humphreys (1968) examined the official syllabi and directives of the member states of the Council of Europe and classified the aims of mathematics teaching for the academic secondary program in those countries as follows.

(a) *Those dealing with mathematics itself.* The majority of the countries in the Council of Europe subscribe to the view that pupils should be made aware of the significance of mathematics and of the characteristics of the subject.

(b) *Those dealing with the utility of mathematics.* By this is meant not only the use of mathematics in the day-to-day business of life, but also the use of the subject in other academic fields of knowledge, particularly science, technology, sociology, and economics.

(c) *Those dealing with mathematics as an intellectual discipline.* Most countries seem to believe that mathematics imparts a mental training to those who study it. Of the 16 countries reviewed, Halls found reference to those qualities or faculties which are alleged to be honed by mathematics: logic (mentioned by no less than five countries), imagination and creativity (mentioned by three countries), and qualities of precision, clarity, resourcefulness, and judgment.

(d) *Those dealing with moral perceptions or attributes.* The study of mathematics plays an important part of character development. Halls notes that the French perhaps expressed this aspect best when they used in their statements of aims such expressions as, "to teach one to distinguish the true from the false, amid the contradictions of mankind." To this moral dimension, the Germans (Nordrhein–Westfalen) added an aesthetic component, saying that the task of the mathematics teacher is, "to give insight into the many beautiful relationships in numbers and figures that exist and to recognize relationships of size and form . . . in the outside world."

(e) *Those dealing with developing powers of expression.* As a person develops mathematical competence he or she acquires a powerful means of expressing concepts and relationships. The Belgian Catholic directives for the teaching of mathematics, for example, asserted that, "mathematics teachers have a built-in advantage: the subject that they teach requires in a special way a precise language. They must therefore show themselves meticulous not only for the exactness of the subject matter, but for the correctness, and even the elegance, of the form" (pp. 12–13).

2. The Content of Academic Secondary Mathematics Programs

The academic program leading to university and college study receives most attention internationally. Information concerning the content of "nonacademic" programs, such as vocational and apprenticeship courses, is not readily available and, consequently, receives scant attention here.

An analysis of the content of mathematics programs in the academic or scientific stream was conducted by the Second IEA Mathematics Study (SIMS) and reported by Hirstein (1980). The analysis was carried out as a follow-up of a 1959 survey by the Organisation for European Economic Co-operation (OEEC) and presented at a seminar in Royaumont, France. This seminar was important in consolidating recommendations concerning the directions of school mathematics for the 1960s, particularly in Europe (OECD 1961).

A major purpose of the Royaumont and SIMS curriculum surveys was to determine when selected mathematical topics are first taught in school. The results of the investigation for the 22 SIMS countries (which are, primarily, Western industrialized nations) are given in

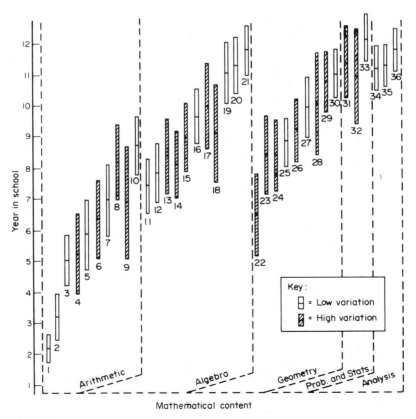

Figure 1
Time of introduction of mathematical topics in secondary schools in 22 countries

Fig. 1. The vertical scale is the year in school when the topic is first introduced. The horizontal scale gives the content classification of the topic. Each vertical bar represents one topic. (A key to these topics is given in Table 1.) The midpoint of the bar (marked by a horizontal line segment) depicts the mean year in school, for the 22 countries surveyed, at which a particular topic is introduced. For example, vertical bar 1 (extreme lower left of the figure), representing addition of two digit numbers, shows that this topic is introduced on average at about year 2.1 and the standard deviation for this topic is about half a year. It could therefore be stated using liberal assumptions about the distribution of years, that about two-thirds of the countries introduce this topic between year 1.6 and 2.6.

Some general observations can be made about the content of the mathematics curriculum as suggested by Fig. 1. By and large, the figure speaks of relative homogeneity of content across the countries. But, on average, the standard deviation when a topic is introduced is about one year.

If variation less than a standard deviation of one year is regarded as "low" and greater than a standard deviation of one year as "high," then the following rough classification of topics across programs of 22 SIMS countries may be made. Topics and illustrative exercises for some topics are given in parentheses in Table 1.

An important observation can be made about the "saw tooth" pattern exhibited by the vertical bars in Fig. 1. Each of the major content areas (arithmetic, algebra, and so on) defines a "tooth." Within each content area, the topics tend to be distributed along the range of years in school. Hence, these classifications impose an artificial structure on the content of the curriculum. Were the pattern to be smoothed to a parabola-like curve then the content classifications would disappear. Instead, topics from across the field of mathematics would be intertwined and developed in a more integrated or unified fashion. It can be concluded, therefore, that internationally, items of subject matter tend to appear in the mathematics curriculum in a unified fashion rather than clustered as arithmetic, algebra, and so on.

3. Selected National Patterns

In order to illustrate the diversity of secondary programs in mathematics which is offered, the following countries have been selected: Hungary, Japan, Tanzania, the Soviet Union, the United States, and England and Wales.

3.1 Hungary

Large-scale curriculum reform activity in mathematics has been taking place in Hungary since the early 1960s. This activity initially began with the Budapest Conference in 1962 when, at a UNESCO symposium, some 20 countries unanimously adopted a set of conclusions and recommendations concerning mathematics

education. On the basis of these recommendations, and following several years of experimental work, the Hungarian Ministry of Education approved in 1974 a definitive curriculum for grades 1 to 8 for the entire country.

Concurrently, the extension of the mathematics curriculum to the higher grades of secondary school was undergoing experimentation. One important consideration in this revision was that of the preparation offered by the secondary-grammar school. Since about 60 percent of those students matriculating cannot enter a university, and since no vocational training is offered by secondary grammar schools, changes in the structure of these schools are now being introduced to take into account the requirements of practical life.

A special mathematics program, the Mathematics II Option, is offered in seven schools in Hungary. Acceptance in this program requires passing both written and oral examinations. This program entails 10, 10, 9, and 9 hours of mathematics study per week for the four years of upper-secondary school, respectively. The program is divided into two parts and is usually taught by instructors chosen for their high level of mathematical knowledge and teaching abilities. The enrichment work includes the topics of Mathematics I, plus methods of numerical approximation in applied fields; inequalities; polynomials, and their roots; statistics; mathematical structures; and graphs and their applications. The official course of study only outlines the requirements of the programs. Teachers are allowed some freedom in determining topics for study and methodological approach to use. Consequently, the Mathematics II classes around the country assume something of their own character and identity.

Recently, the Mathematics II option has been superseded by another optional or "facultative" program. Here, during the last two years of secondary school, students may have up to 7 or 8 hours per week of mathematics instruction, instead of the 3 hours taken by those not in the optional program. The writers of the textbooks and related materials for this program were competitively chosen. Methods of individualized instruction are encouraged through the use of problem sheets and workbooks. Emphasis is placed more on problems of an applied nature than in the regular program.

3.2 Japan

Japan has made great advances in mathematics education since the early 1960s and in the process has attained virtually universal secondary education. Japan requires nine years of schooling from the age of 6. Of those who complete the lower secondary program, most go on to upper-secondary schooling. In 1977, the attendance rate in the upper-secondary school was 93.1 percent. The standard number of school hours (a school hour is 50 minutes) devoted to mathematics in the lower secondary school (years 7, 8, and 9) is four per week. The school year consists of 35 weeks or more.

Table 1
Key to topics in Figure 1

	Low variation		High variation	
Topic no.	Content	Topic no.	Content	
(a) Arithmetic				
1	addition of two digit numbers	4	multiplication of 3 digit numbers	
2	multiplication tables to 10×10 and beyond	6	division of decimal fractions	
3	addition of decimal fractions	8	division of powers (12^2 divided by 6^3)	
5	addition of mixed numbers ($2\frac{3}{5} + 5\frac{7}{12}$)	9	nondecimal numeration	
7	percentage (e.g., 15 percent of what number equals 6)			
10	estimating square roots			
(b) Algebra				
11	subtraction of signed numbers [e.g., $(+10) - (-25)$]	13	plot graph for $y = 3x + 2$	
12	solve $3x - 7 = 2x + 4$	14	solve the inequation $3x + 2 > 8$	
16	solve $3x^2 - 15x + 8 = 0$	15	solve $3x - y = 5$ $x + 2y = 11$	
19	determine roots of $3x^5 - 7x^2 = 0$	17	use field properties of real numbers to prove $(-x)(-y) = xy$	
20	expand $(3x - 2y)^8$	18	solve word problems involving distance, rate, and time	
21	prove $1 + 4 + 9 + \ldots + n^2 = \frac{1}{6}(2n + 1)(n + 1)(n)$ using mathematical induction			
(c) Geometry				
25	solve right angle given a leg and the hypotenuse	22	area of triangle given base and altitude	
27	given two points on a line, find its equation	23	volume of pyramid given base and altitude	
30	derive law of cosines for any triangle	24	similarity of triangles	
		26	state and prove Pythagorean theorem	
		28	isometries of the plane	
		29	vector sums and products	
(d) Probability and Statistics				
33	normal distributions	31	permutations and combinations	
		32	binomial probabilities	
(e) Analysis				
34	find the derivative of $y = 3x^2 - 5x$			
35	find the maximum and minimum values of $y = x^3 - 12x + 5$			
36	find $\int_1^2 (x^3 - 4x + 3)\,dx$			

It should be noted that a topic which is never taught in the lower or middle school (e.g., complex numbers) is destined to have low variation

The content covered during lower-secondary school includes number and algebraic expressions; functions; geometric figures; and probability and statistics. The content is the same for all pupils throughout their three years of study, with individual differences catered for by differentiating the depth of treatment of the topic.

In the upper-secondary school, mathematics is organized according to a sequence of "short courses." A basic course is taken by all students in the 10th year. The standard pattern for the academic program leads to basic analysis and probability and statistics, then to differential and integral calculus. The Ministry of Education teaching guide states that, wherever possible, pupils should be encouraged to use computers or other mechanical aids to computation.

A science–mathematics program leading to specialization in the natural sciences and mathematics is also available. One ingredient is "integrated mathematics," which is studied for 13 to 18 hours per week in the 11th and 12th years of school. The science–mathematics sequence is to include actual experience in preparing programs for the computer, running them, and analyzing the results.

An applied mathematics sequence is available, mainly for students in vocational and practical courses. Here they learn advanced topics needed to support specialized topics in their fields of preparation.

Entrance examinations, particularly from upper-secondary school to universities, are of a highly competitive nature. Since mathematics is usually a key subject in these examinations, the mathematics taught in the schools tends to be influenced by these examinations. Tutorial classes in mathematics which meet outside of regular school hours are available to provide special preparation for the entrance examinations. In Japan, curriculum revisions are undertaken on a regular basis. The most recent version (Nagasaki et al.), to begin implementation in 1990, continues to promote the classroom use of calculators and computers, as deemed appropriate by the teacher. The curriculum guide also recommends that the teacher incorporate the subject matter of mathematics into daily-life phenomena "so as to stimulate students' active learning and foster the ways of mathematically thinking" (p. 31).

3.3 Tanzania

The mathematics program in the United Republic of Tanzania reflects political and social developments which have taken place in that country since the 1950s. Arabic influences, as seen in terms of the Kiswahili language for measures of length, capacity, and time, resulted from the slave trader, ruler, or religious missionary whose caravans passed through both coast and hinterland. The "business mathematics" of the Asian merchant who set up small shops in trading centers has left a visible imprint on the country's culture. Mmari (1980) has noted that it could be argued that through the influence of the Asian in East Africa, com-mercial subjects were introduced in African secondary schools. German colonizers who followed the missionaries established schools to prepare a cadre of African children for colonial service, for working on the plantations, and for serving in houses of business. When after the First World War, the League of Nations placed Tanzania under the British as a mandated territory, the language of instruction changed overnight from German to English and the metric system of measures, introduced by the Germans, was abandoned and replaced by the Imperial system. With a British system of education came preparation for English examinations, including "many hours (spent) grappling with problems on journeys in the underground from tube station X to tube station Y, problems on the life expectancy of the coal miner in Newcastle, and the results of a cricket match in a county in southern England" (Mmari 1980 p. 108).

Since the mid-1960s there have been concerted curriculum development efforts at both primary and secondary school levels in Tanzania and other parts of Africa. A symposium was held in Entebbe, Uganda in 1962 which set in motion a host of activities aimed at "modernizing" both the content and the teaching of mathematics. As a result, the School Mathematics Project for East Africa, which later became School Mathematics of East Africa (SMEA), was launched.

The overall goal of the new Tanzanian program is to produce competent mathematics students who are able to function in their respective vocations. This program emphasizes understanding of a core of mathematics, active participation by the learner, and the practical use of mathematics. The content of the program reveals much of its sources in the School Mathematics Study Group of the United States, the SMEA, and the British School Mathematics Project. Final selection of topics for inclusion in the program was done in consultation with Tanzanian teachers who were invited to suggest what was good for the nation and for the pupils. Because of an emphasis upon the practicability of mathematics, these topics were introduced: simple bookkeeping, plan and elevation, kinematics, rate, ratio, and proportion. Traditional topics were retained in the curriculum, including sequences and series, approximation and accuracy, geometry, and trigonometry.

3.4 Soviet Union

Soviet schools have witnessed a changeover to a new mathematics syllabus since the late 1970s. Steps have been taken towards raising the standard of mathematics instruction by "making better use of the subject for the pupils' development and general education, by getting away from formalistic learning and by arousing the pupils' interest in mathematics. . ." (Kolyagin et al. 1980 p. 71).

The systematic study of algebra takes place in grades 6 to 8 (ages 12 to 15 years). Topics dealt with include functions, equalities and inequalities, exponents (integral and rational), polynomials, rational expressions, absolute and relative errors, linear and quadratic equations. The grade 8 program concludes with the introduction of exponential and logarithmic functions and their graphs. Work with the digital computer is also introduced.

At the final stage of the mathematics program (grades 9 to 10) the study of algebra and analysis includes derivatives, integrals, and probability theory. Geometry is studied concurrently with algebra throughout the grades: the systematic study of plane geometry in grades 7 to 8 and a vector-based approach to solid geometry, together with the development of an axiomatic approach to geometry in the upper-secondary grades.

The identification and nurturing of mathematical talent is an important feature of mathematics education in the Soviet Union. Extracurricular activities, such as clubs and circles and the Olympiads provide such nurturance. Specialized schools for gifted students in mathematics and the natural sciences have also been developed. For example, a mathematics boarding school (one of five reported in the Soviet Union) in Moscow is under the sponsorship of the Moscow State University. Closely associated with this boarding school is the noted mathematician A. N. Kolmogorov, who has played a leading role in forming its mathematics program and devotes part of his time to teaching at the school.

3.5 Curricular Patterns in Decentralized Systems (United States and England and Wales)

The educational systems of the countries whose "national curricular patterns" are described in the preceding sections have one important characteristic in common—they are highly centralized. That is, there is one governmental agency which prescribes the mathematical content which is to be taught, and to some extent, how it is to be taught.

The United States and England and Wales, on the other hand, have decentralized school systems. In the United States, some of the 50 states issue curriculum guides which outline expectations for content coverage for their schools. Often, such decisions are left to the school district and even to the school. In England and Wales, each school has considerable freedom as to what is taught.

Decentralization makes it difficult to characterize a "national pattern" for the curriculum. One source of information about what mathematics are being taught (and learned) in the United States is provided by a periodic survey, the National Assessment of Educational Progress. Standardized tests, such as the Scholastic Aptitude Test and those of the American College Testing Program are used by many universities for admissions purposes and are often cited as sources of information concerning the kind and quantity of mathematics being learned in schools in the United States. Perhaps the best information about what is taught in the schools would be gleaned from an analysis of the content of the half dozen or so most widely used commercially published textbooks series.

In England and Wales, a system of examinations and school certificates has been developed which provides both an index of the subject matter learned in school and entrance qualifications for university and work. Specimen examination papers for British schools provided by Griffiths and Howson (1974) offer considerable information about expectations for mathematical competence at various levels of schooling.

3.6 Early Curriculum Development Projects

Many of the important initiatives for the changes in curriculum which have taken place around the world in the period 1960 to 1980 appear to have been derived from the United States and England and Wales. Indeed, it is tempting to hypothesize a direct causal relationship between decentralization and creativity in curriculum development.

The earliest recorded initiative for curriculum development in school mathematics seems to be at the University of Illinois, in the United States. The University's Department of Electrical Engineering, concerned about the poor preparation of its entering first-year students, sought the assistance of the late Max Beberman, then head of the Mathematics Department at the University's laboratory school. As a result, in 1952 Beberman formed the University of Illinois Committee on School Mathematics which produced curriculum materials, tested them in pilot schools around the country, and conducted institutes to prepare teachers in their use. A more widespread and comprehensive project, the School Mathematics Study Group, emerged in the late 1950s under the leadership of the late Edward G. Begle. The latter project, particularly, was influential abroad, such as in the Entebbe project in Africa mentioned earlier in this article.

In England, J. M. Hammersley, a statistician, held a conference at Oxford in 1957 to consider the improvement of mathematics in schools. This conference, whose membership was drawn from schools, universities, and industry, paid attention to modern industrial applications of mathematics. Successive conferences led to the establishment of the School Mathematics Project at Southampton University. This project, the leading curriculum development activity in England and Wales, was characterized by the dominant role played by teachers and by the importance ascribed to the utility of mathematics.

3.7 Management of Curriculum Development

The early efforts in curriculum development led to the establishment of various structures for managing the process. Most projects were conducted at centers which were usually at a college or university. For example, the Caribbean Mathematics Project was located at the School of Education of the University of the West Indies (Wilson 1978). In the Netherlands, an important national center devoted to school mathematics was the IOWO, the Institute for Development of Mathematics

Education, directed by Hans Freudenthal (1978). An alternative model for managing curriculum development is that of the network of institutes, each assuming responsibility for a particular facet of the development task. In France, there is a network of about thirty IREMs (*Instituts de Recherche sur l'Enseignement des Mathématiques*)—one at almost every university in the country. The IREMs were begun in 1969 in an attempt to assist teachers in implementing the new national mathematics program for secondary schools. They now offer courses for teachers and undertake research and development activities (see, for example, Revuz 1978).

4. Summary Remarks

4.1 Content of Secondary Mathematics Programs

In general, there appears to be a remarkably large common core of mathematical content in the academic programs across countries. One exception is that of geometry. In some European countries (e.g., England and Wales) it has been taught less formally than previously and a variety of approaches—via transformations, vectors, coordinates—has been employed. Elsewhere (e.g., France and Belgium) the move has been towards a modern axiomatic system, more in the spirit of Bourbaki than Euclid (see, for example, Griffiths and Howson 1974). The major differences between countries appear to reside in the time (year of schooling) at which content is introduced. There are clusters of countries which introduce content one or two years earlier than the majority of countries. Furthermore, some countries make heavy use of "spiralling" of content—introducing topics at early years of school then coming back to them repeatedly as the child matures.

4.2 How Many are Taken How Far?

In many countries there have been intensive efforts to reform the school structure and curriculum so that as many students as possible are prepared for higher studies beyond secondary school (e.g., recent changes in Sweden to a single upper-secondary school). Such thrusts, having no less a goal than expanding and upgrading the base of scientific and technological competence of a nation's citizens, are imposing enormous demands upon the educational systems of developing countries.

4.3 The Technology of Computation

Topics in computer science are found in the secondary programs of most countries, often in the upper-secondary grades, but at lower secondary and even earlier in some countries. Typically, however, these topics appear to be only an "add-on" rather than having a pervasive impact on the kind of mathematics taught or the way in which mathematics is taught. Engel (1979) has developed a high school "applications-oriented" mathematics course for which the impact of the computer was revolutionary. The course involves dynamic models which describe a changing world, and includes such tools and concepts as graphs, the language of states and transitions, continuous and discrete processes, recursion and iteration, and probabilistic and deterministic processes.

Papert (1980) has developed curricular materials, based on the computer language LOGO, which signal an important direction for school studies. He has expressed the concern that in many current "computer-based" curricula, the computer is being used to program the child. In Papert's view, however, "the child programs the computer and, in so doing, both acquires a sense of mastery over a piece of the most modern and powerful technology and establishes an intimate contact with some of the deepest ideas from science, mathematics, and the art of intellectual model building".

4.4 The Emerging Secondary Program

The 1960s and 1970s have been times of considerable activity in school curriculum development (see *Curriculum Development*). What will follow? How will mathematics educators, policy makers, and others respond to the new challenges? In the United States the National Council of Teachers of Mathematics (1980) produced an "Agenda for Action" for the 1980s in which eight priorities for mathematics education were listed. Two of these recommendations were that problem solving become the major focus of school mathematics and that full advantage be taken of the power of calculators and computers at all grade levels.

In Hungary, where the extensive experimental work in mathematics programs has already been noted, the Janos Bolyai Mathematical Society and the Hungarian Academy of Sciences is sponsoring research into the needs of mathematics education after the year 2000. Already, some of the findings of these experiments have been incorporated into current curriculum efforts in that country.

In the 1980s the mathematics curriculum continued to be critically examined in the light of the needs of an educated citizenry of the 1990s and beyond. The Second International Mathematics Study of the International Association for the Evaluation of Educational Achievement (Robitaille and Garden 1988, Travers and Westbury 1989) provided cross-national data that helped to focus curricular investigations in several countries. In the United Kingdom, a Committee of Inquiry (Cockcroft 1982) undertook an extensive study of the teaching of mathematics in schools and made recommendations for its improvement. In the United States, the newly-established Mathematical Sciences Education Board of the National Research Council produced a report (1989) that served to identify critical issues in mathematics education, including that of the unacceptably low proportion of students remaining in the study of mathematics throughout high school and college (pp. 6 ff). Concurrently, the National Council of Teachers of Mathematics devised curriculum standards to guide mathematics curriculum reform efforts (1989). A more long range view of what should be the nature of science education (including mathematics) as we move into the next century was presented by *Project 2061* (1989) of the American Association for the Advancement of Science. (The project is named in recognition of the year of the return of Halley's Comet.) This report characterizes mathematics as "a modeling process in which abstractions are made and manipulated and the implications are checked out against the original situation" (p. 101). The report then discusses and provides examples of kinds of mathematical patterns that are available for such modeling, including the nature and use of numbers, symbolic relationships, shapes and uncertainty. The centrality of school mathematics in the curriculum, and continued research and development efforts to improve the curriculum, would seem to be assured by these highly visible national reports.

Bibliography

Amerian Association for the Advancement of Science 1989 *Science for All Americans*. American Association for the Advancement of Science, Washington DC

Cockcroft W H 1982 *Mathematics Counts: Report of the Committee on Inquiry into the Teaching of Mathematics*. Her Majesty's Stationery Office, London

El Tom M E A (ed.) 1979 *Developing Mathematics in Third World Countries*. North Holland, Amsterdam

Engel A 1979 The role of algorithms and computers in the teaching of mathematics at school. *New Trends in Mathematics Teaching*, Vol. 4. UNESCO, Paris, pp. 249–77

Griffiths H B, Howson A G 1974 *Mathematics: Society and Curricula*. Cambridge University Press, London

Halls W D, Humphreys D 1968 *European Curriculum Studies (in the Academic Secondary School)*, Vol. 1: *Mathematics*. Council for Cultural Cooperation, Strasbourg

Hashimoto Y, Sawada T 1979 *Mathematics Program in Japan*. National Institute for Educational Research, Tokyo

Hirstein J J 1980 From Royaumont to Bielefeld: A twenty year cross-national survey of the content of school mathematics. In: Steiner H G (ed.) 1980 *Comparative Studies of Mathematics Curricula-change and Stability 1960–1980*. Institute for Mathematical Didactics, University of Bielefeld, Bielefeld, pp. 55–89

Kolyagin Y M, Lukankin G L, Oganesyan V A 1980 Ways of improving mathematics teaching in Soviet general secondary schools. In: Morris R (ed.) 1980 *Studies in Mathematics Education*, Vol. 1. UNESCO, Paris, pp. 70–86

McKnight C C 1987 *The Underachieving Curriculum: Assessing U.S. School Mathematics from an International Perspective*. Stipes, Champaign, Illinois

Mmari G 1980 Secondary school mathematics in the United Republic of Tanzania. In: Morris R (ed.) 1980 *Studies in Mathematics Education*, Vol. 1. UNESCO, Paris, pp. 106–26

Nagasaki E, Sawada T, Senuma H 1989 *Mathematics Program in Japan*. National Institute for Educational Research, Tokyo

National Council of Teachers of Mathematics 1989 *Curriculum and Evaluation Standards for School Mathematics*. National Council of Teachers of Mathematics, Reston, Virginia

National Research Council 1989 *Everybody Counts*. National Academy Press, Washington, DC

Organisation for European Economic Co-operation (OEEC) 1961 *New Thinking in School Mathematics*. OEEC, Paris

Papert S 1980 *Mindstorms: Children, Computers and Powerful Ideas*. Basic Books, New York

Quadling D A 1979 Mathematics education at upper secondary school, college and university transition. *New Trends in Mathematics Teaching*, Vol. 4. UNESCO, Paris, pp. 47–65

Revuz A 1978 Change in mathematics education since the late 1950s: Ideas and realization: France. *Educ. Stud. in Math.* 9: 171–81

Robitaille D F, Garden R A 1988 *The IEA Study of Mathematics II: Contexts and Outcomes of School Mathematics*. Pergamon Press, London

Suranyi J, Halmos M 1978 The evolution of modern mathematics education in Hungary. In: Swetz F J (ed.) 1978 *Socialist Mathematics Education*. Burgundy Press, Southampton, Pennsylvania, pp. 253–300

Travers K J, Westbury I 1989 *The IEA Study of Mathematics I: Analysis of Mathematics Curricula*. Pergamon Press, London

Wilson B J 1978 Change in mathematics education since the late 1950s: Ideas and realization: West Indies. *Educ. Stud. in Math.* 9: 355–79

Arithmetic: Educational Programs

T. Levin

Arithmetic is the branch of mathematics that deals with numbers, the meaning of numbers, number relations, and computational rules. Contemporary arithmetical studies strive to develop a sensitivity to patterns and laws characterizing number relations and the ability to deal with computational situations through proper comprehension of their mathematical as well as practical significance. As arithmetic is the child's first encounter with the systematic study of a branch of mathematics, the way it is taught in schools influences the child's conception of mathematics and greatly affects attitudes toward its study.

1. Historical View

For a long time arithmetic was conceived as synonymous with skill in performing calculations and as such was not considered a very important school subject. This view of arithmetic is evidently rooted in ancient times when arithmetic was deemed an underdeveloped branch of mathematics, based essentially on calculating devices. Arithmetic was developed by the Romans who made practical use of measuring and counting, and evolved several forms of abaci and finger counting.

Gauss, who was a pioneer in the theory of numbers, called arithmetic the "queen of mathematics," and assigned it its rightful role as a challenging and independent mathematical discipline, clarifying the relationship between arithmetic and algebra.

Arithmetic as a school subject is caught between a regrettable past and a more promising future. Teachers and curriculum planners have realized, albeit relatively slowly, what students and professional mathematicians have known all along, that arithmetic is hard. A real understanding of arithmetic requires considerable mathematical maturity and imagination.

Even before the early 1950s, a reaction against an emphasis on formalized drill in arithmetic curricula began to manifest itself, and in its extreme form insisted that understanding rather than computational proficiency should be the sole aim in teaching arithmetic.

Earlier school arithmetic programs were criticized for being unable to achieve the new goals for two main reasons: (a) the programs neglected the meaning and rational principles which make arithmetic a significant phase of mathematics; (b) the programs gave students little chance to use previously learned ideas and skills in solving their own personal problems. Earlier programs comprised mainly separate and narrowly restricted facts, rules, and algorithms, learned mostly by rote. It had become evident that such a decomposition of arithmetic into a multitude of relatively unrelated components destroyed it mathematically. Thus, calls for changes in arithmetic curricula were heard from nearly all educational leaders, demanding a major emphasis on the notion of meaningful arithmetic or mental arithmetic.

2. Meaningful and Significant Arithmetic

The idea of meaningful arithmetic is not new. It has been present, at least theoretically, since about 1935 (Brownell 1935). The psychological resources and the educational means required to actually implement it in the schools have, however, developed slowly. According to the meaning theory, which conceives of arithmetic as a knit system of understandable ideas, principles, and processes, a true test of learning is an intelligent grasp of number relations and the ability to deal with arithmetic situations with proper comprehension of their mathematical and practical significance. The meaning theory represents an orientation in which there is a sensitivity to pattern, to laws, and an appreciation of relationships between concepts, methods, and techniques. It contends that the teaching of arithmetic needs to foster the actuality of thinking, and the grasping of the inner relation between operations and their reasonable results (Wertheimer 1959).

Influenced by the meaning theory, contemporary arithmetic programs stress two major aspects, the mathematical and the social. Mathematically, such programs strive to help students understand the structure of mathematics, its laws and principles, its sequence and order,

and the way in which mathematics as a system expands to meet new needs. The social aspect of recent programs is characterized mainly by a broad view of the social value of arithmetic. The programs include arithmetical concepts needed for intelligent reading and for the ordinary processes of quantitative thinking, and their scope is large and varied to include present and future everyday situations, other academic disciplines, and situations within the field of mathematics itself.

3. Curriculum Development

Changes in the content of arithmetic curricula have been accompanied by the development of new instructional methods in many parts of the world. Mathematics teachers and educational researchers have evolved new approaches to the teaching of arithmetic, and produced many innovations. These range from concrete apparatus which provide manipulative and sensory experiences to symbol games of various kinds (Dienes and Jeeves 1963, Gattegno 1967).

In the new teaching methods, generally known as the structural or holistic methods, logical mathematical structures are illustrated by reference to concrete or symbolic models or analogies. In general, structural methods advocate a constant and spirited interplay between the general and the particular and between the abstract and the concrete. New and varied criteria for evaluating arithmetic ability are being proffered. The value of speed (rapid computation or rate of computation) and accuracy has been minimized, while the need for attaching more importance to the learning process is stressed.

4. Research

Research has contributed a great deal to the improvement of arithmetic teaching, and influenced the development of different approaches. Studies have dealt with basic research, which focuses mainly on the development of concepts related to quantitative thinking, and applied research concerning the nature of learning and thinking, and the relationship between understanding and computational skills.

Empirical studies support the contention that proficiency in computation cannot automatically develop as an incidental by-product of meaning or understanding, just as it cannot emerge as an incidental by-product of drill. The "meaning versus drill" type of phrase implies an emphasis on one or the other but not both, and represents an unrealistic and unjustified dichotomy. Teaching and learning arithmetic imply the necessity of establishing a proper balance between skill and understanding.

With the current demand by the public for the schools to teach basic skills, however, a new or revived dichotomy has evolved. Although there is general agreement among educators that basic skills should be a component of the school curriculum, there is no common understanding and acceptance of what these basic skills should include. Some groups narrowly limit basic skills in arithmetic to routine computation. Others insist that these skills include also estimating and approximating skills, computer literacy, and so on. Moreover, the availability of computing aids such as computers and calculators, make it imperative to reassess the present utility of various computational skills and emphasize or de-emphasize them accordingly.

Bibliography

Association of Teachers of Mathematics 1977 *Notes on Mathematics for Children*. Cambridge University Press, Cambridge

Brownell W A 1935 *Psychological Considerations in the Learning and Teaching of Arithmetic*. Tenth Yearbook, National Council of Teachers of Mathematics, Teachers College, Columbia University, New York

Buckingham B R 1951 The social point of view in arithmetic. In: Henry N B (ed.) 1951 *The Teaching of Arithmetic*. 50th Yearbook, Part 2, National Society for the Study of Education, University of Chicago Press, Chicago, Illinois

Dienes Z P, Jeeves M A 1963 *Thinking in Structures*. Hutchinson, London

Gattegno C V 1967 *Teacher's Introduction to the Cuisenaire–Gattegno Method of Teaching Arithmetic*. Cuisenaire, Reading

Wertheimer M 1959 *Productive Thinking*. Harper and Row, New York

Algebra: Educational Programs

C. Kieran

Algebra is the branch of mathematics that deals with the symbolizing of general numerical relationships and mathematical structure, as well as the forming and solving of equations. The historical development of algebra as a symbol system passed through three distinct stages. The first, the rhetorical stage, which belongs to the period before Diophantus (ca AD 250), was characterized by the use of ordinary language descriptions for solving particular types of problems and lacked the use of symbols or special signs to represent "unknowns". The second stage, syncopated algebra, extended from Diophantus, who introduced the use of abbreviations for *unknown* quantities, to the end of the sixteenth century. The concern of algebraists during these centuries was exclusively that of discovering the identity of the letter or letters, as opposed to an attempt to express the general. The third stage, symbolic algebra, was initiated by Vieta's use of letters to stand for *given* quantities. At this point it became possible to express general solutions and to use algebra as a tool for proving rules governing numerical relations.

1. Algebra in School

Despite the advances made possible by Vieta's use of letters, school algebra curricula rarely emphasize this aspect of algebra. A considerable portion of the curriculum is devoted to the manipulation of algebraic expressions and the solving of equations. Traditional algebra curricula in most countries also include: (a) the properties of real and complex numbers; (b) linear, quadratic, polynomial, and rational equations; (c) linear, quadratic, exponential, logarithmic, and trigonometric functions, and their graphs; and (d) sequences and series. Not all students study all these topics; the more advanced themes are usually taken only by those students going on to university.

The study of algebra usually begins in high school at the ages of 12–13, although certain countries do begin introducing the more elementary topics to children as young as 6. Most students preparing for college end up with the equivalent of two years of algebra, taken either separately or as fully integrated courses.

The content of high school algebra has changed very little over the years. Even before school attendance became compulsory, the topics covered in beginning algebra courses usually included operations with literal expressions, the solving of both linear and quadratic equations, the use of these techniques to find answers to problems, and practice with ratios, proportions, powers, and roots. In the decades that followed, there was an attempt to include some practical aspects and the use of graphical methods.

In the early 1960s some concern was expressed regarding the large and widening gap between the mathematics being taught in school and the subject as required for postcollege jobs in such fields as nuclear physics, space exploration, communications, and computers. This concern led to the development of the New Mathematics movement in several countries. Algebra in the revised curriculum was to incorporate new topics like inequalities, emphasize unifying concepts like set and function, and be taught so that its structure and deductive character were apparent. However, the changes that have persisted into the 1990s algebra curricula have been more cosmetic than substantial.

Meanwhile, mathematics and its applications have changed dramatically. The advent of calculators and computers as tools in mathematics have changed the way that mathematicians do mathematics and the way that scientists, engineers, and social scientists use mathematics. It is being proposed that it is time to reevaluate the content of the algebra curriculum in order that it begin to reflect these changes.

Past algebra curricula have put a great deal of emphasis on manipulative skill because of its usefulness in calculus, or at least in traditional conceptions of calculus. However, computerized mathematical systems exist that perform the routine manipulations that students spend hours learning to carry out. If computers can do algebraic manipulations like factoring, solving equations, and so on, the importance of developing student skill in these areas is questionable. Thus, an issue that is raised by the advent of technology is one that parallels the issue of calculators and the learning of arithmetic skills; that is, how much proficiency is needed with paper-and-pencil symbol manipulation in order to use a microcomputer intelligently to perform the same calculations? A related question concerns the interplay of practice with the development of conceptual understanding. These questions and others require a great deal of input from the field of educational research before large-scale change can and should occur in school algebra curricula.

2. Research on Algebra Learning

The bulk of past research in algebra learning has not, of course, been carried out in technology-supported environments. It has focused primarily on the difficulties that beginning algebra students experience in making the transition from arithmetic to algebra. Nevertheless, the findings of this body of research provide the foundation for studying the potential contribution of computer technology to algebra curricula. Although research in the learning of computer-intensive algebra is in its infancy, this growing field of investigation has already produced some interesting results.

A project involving the use of computer tools (e.g. curve-fitting programs, generators of tables of values, symbolic manipulators, and function graphers) to develop students' understanding of algebra concepts and their ability to solve problems requiring algebra, before they master symbol manipulation techniques, has been researched by Fey and Heid et al. with entire classes of first-year algebra students. An important feature of this project is the use of the concept of function as a central organizing theme for theory, problem solving, and technique in algebra. Not only has this technology-intensive, resequenced approach to the learning of algebra proved to be quite successful with respect to improving students' abilities to construct and interpret mathematical models and to solve problems, but it has also shown that they can do just as well in tests of symbol manipulation skill as students taught in traditional programs.

In contrast with the above studies where the entire algebra curriculum was reorganized, other studies have investigated how technology might assist in the learning of certain aspects of algebra that have traditionally been areas of difficulty for students. For example, the dynamic capabilities of graphing software have been used to help students make links among the tabular, graphic, and algebraic representations used in coordinate geometry. Still other studies have emphasized the role of programing in Logo as a means of developing students' concepts of variable and their ability to con-

struct formalized rules. Other studies have shown that students can cope more easily with translating a word problem into an equation when that equation is in the form of a short computer program specifying how to compute the value of one variable based on another.

3. Prospects

Algebra education is at a crossroads. With the advent of technology, it is questionable whether it is right to continue with the old style of algebra curricula with its emphasis on the learning of symbol manipulation techniques. Curricula at the beginning of the 1990s integrate neither the power of algebra as the thinking tool developed by Vieta, nor the potential of technology to work hand-in-hand with algebra instruction. Yet, many features of a technology-supported algebra curriculum make it possible to come closer to using algebra as a thinking tool than it was with past curricula. Unfortunately, it is still too soon for research to provide answers to most of the important questions that are now being raised. It is time for leaders in algebra education to work in concert with researchers toward arriving at some consensus as to the goals of algebra teaching in the 1990s and how best to meet those goals.

Bibliography

Coxford A F (ed.) 1988 *The Ideas of Algebra, K-12* (1988 Yearbook of the National Council of Teachers of Mathematics). NCTM, Reston, Virginia

Fey J T 1989 School algebra for the year 2000. In: Wagner S, Kieran C (eds.) 1989 *Research Agenda for Mathematics Education: Vol. 4. Research Issues in the Learning and Teaching of Algebra*. Lawrence Erlbaum Associates, Hillsdale, New Jersey, pp. 199–213

Freudenthal H 1974 Soviet research on teaching algebra at the lower grades of the elementary school. *Educ. Stud. Math.* 5: 391–412

Heid M K, Sheets C, Matras M A, Menasian J 1988 Classroom and computer lab interaction in a computer-intensive algebra curriculum. Paper presented at the annual meeting of the American Educational Research Association, New Orleans, Louisiana April 1988

Hirsch C R (ed.) 1985 *The Secondary School Mathematics Curriculum* (1985 Yearbook of the National Council of Teachers of Mathematics). NCTM, Reston, Virginia

Kaput J J 1989 Linking representations in the symbol systems of algebra. In: Wagner S, Kieran C (eds.) 1989 *Research Agenda for Mathematics Education: Vol. 4. Research Issues in the Learning and Teaching of Algebra*. Lawrence Erlbaum Associates, Hillsdale, New Jersey, pp. 167–94

Kieran C 1990 Cognitive processes involved in learning school algebra. In Nesher P, Kilpatrick J (eds.) 1990, *Mathematics and Cognition: A Research Synthesis by the International Group for the Psychology of Mathematics Education*. Cambridge University Press, Cambridge, pp. 96–112

Wirszup I, Streit R (eds.) 1987 *Developments in School Mathematics Education Around the World* (Proceedings of the UCSMP International Conference of Mathematics Education). National Council of Teachers of Mathematics, Reston, Virginia

Analysis in Mathematics: Educational Programs

Z. R. Mevarech

Analysis is a branch of mathematics dealing with the properties of functions and relations. It especially emphasizes limits and infinite processes, and introduces mathematical concepts, which are fundamentally different to those encountered by the learner in the earlier stages of mathematics study. Among its topics, it includes calculus, function theory, series theory, and often analytical geometry.

1. Placement of First Analysis Course

The question of where in the mathematical curriculum a first course in analysis should be embedded has been addressed since the beginning of the twentieth century. Traditionally, it was a predominantly college or university level course. However, pressures from universities to start its study earlier, and trends prevailing in new mathematics programs to introduce topics as early as possible led numerous school systems to teach "analysis" in high schools.

Early recommendations for the inclusion of analysis (mainly calculus) as an elective course in the 12th grade were adopted by the National Committee on Mathematics Requirements (1923). This committee envisioned analysis as an elite course, appropriate only for a "selected group of students" in "relatively strong schools." The same positions were taken several decades later by the Joint Commission of the Mathematical Association of America (1940), College Entrance Examination Board (1959), and Secondary School Curriculum Committee (1959). In contrast, at almost the same time, the Soviet Union instituted a course in analysis in the ninth- and tenth-grade curriculum (1957).

Shortly after Sputnik's historical orbiting of the Earth, a more ambitious approach was proposed by the Cambridge Conference of School Mathematics founded in 1958. This committee assumed that concepts such as "rate of change" should reach a larger number of people than those who complete all 12 years of mathematics. Accordingly, they proposed to preface a "heuristic brief introduction to analysis in the ninth grade" with a "logically complete course" for grades 11–12. Nowadays, the spiral approach (see *Spiral Curriculum*) to concept development is widely accepted and analysis has become an integral part of high-school mathematics curricula in almost all countries (Spresser 1979, Bell 1978).

These proposals, however, were received with considerable controversy. Some university instructors worried about a possible decrease in algebraic and arithmetic skills that might occur due to the rush to get into calculus. Others argued that the possible benefits of having analysis in high school "may be subject to eventual washout effects" at the college level (Spresser 1979 p. 597).

2. Learning "Analysis"

The new programs in analysis continue to place emphasis on the fundamental structure of mathematical systems, the clarification of formal definitions, the understanding of symbols, and the comprehension of concepts used in this study. In general, the content of a first course in analysis includes topics such as limits of functions, continuity, derivatives, maxima and minima, rate problems, slope of tangent line, and integrals. To meet the demands of most programs, the learning process must be based upon understanding rather than rote learning. The student who gains clear understanding of those ideas will improve his or her ability to apply those methods and will derive a far more adequate basis for further work in this area (Butler et al. 1970).

In attaining mastery on these complex operations, a number of difficulties might arise. First, the large number of prerequisites covering topics from algebra, geometry, and trigonometry often makes the study of analysis more difficult than the study of any other new course in mathematics. Second, the enormous amount of formal work associated with the study of analysis might beget a tendency to emphasize memorization and mechanical performance rather than understanding. Finally, from a psychological point of view, the fact that analysis presents a radically new and different approach to the study of quantitative relations may generate problems in the accommodation of existing schemata to new ones. As a matter of fact, the history of mathematics contains some interesting examples showing the difficulty of accommodation to the idea of the infinite. Problems studied in analysis were known since the fifth century BC (e.g., the four paradoxes of Zeno: the Dichotomy, the Achilles and the Turtle, the Arrow, and the Stadium), but could not be solved until the seventeenth century when modern analysis was introduced by Newton (1643–1727) and Leibniz (1646–1716). Present analysts are still concerned with problems of limits, continuity, differentiations, and integrations of functions in general n-dimensional spaces (Bell 1978).

3. Teaching Methods

Only very recently, mathematics educators have developed instructional methods explicitly aimed at understanding the concepts presented in analysis courses. Two of these methods are the discovery learning strategy (see *Discovery and Inquiry Methods*) and the personalized system of instruction (PSI).

The discovery learning strategy is based on the assumption that students can be guided to discover mathematical rules. Cummins (1977) applied this idea to the teaching of calculus. His method involved four steps: (a) students attack the problem with means they have available, often by arithmetic methods; (b) results are discussed and students are encouraged to make hypotheses; (c) the teacher guides the students to the consideration of more profound questions; and (d) statements accepted as hypotheses remain as such until deduced as theorems.

The personalized system of instruction (PSI) adapted the Keller method (1968) to the teaching of analysis (Thompson 1980). This method consists of (a) unit mastery requirements; (b) individual pacing; (c) reliance on written instructional materials; and (d) student proctors.

Students in the discovery learning group demonstrated a higher level of understanding and developed an equal level of computational skills as compared with control groups who studied under conventional lecture–discussion methods (Cummins 1977). In addition, the PSI group scored higher on a mathematics reading comprehension test than did the traditional group (Thompson 1980).

Undoubtedly, it is possible to help students to attain mastery on higher cognitive processes by designing teaching/learning strategies which enhance understanding. Studies (Butler et al. 1970) have shown that illustrations of various situations drawn from algebra and geometry, explanations of the symbols, usage of calculators for demonstrating the concepts of a difference diminishing progressively toward zero, and giving continuous feedback correctives to the students all facilitate the learning of analysis.

4. The Use of Innovative Technologies in Teaching Analysis

During the 1980s innovative technologies such as computers and interactive video-discs have been utilized for improving the teaching of analysis. Computers have been used in analysis classes to serve at least three functions: (a) to decrease the amount of allocated time usually directed toward mastery of computational skills; (b) to provide concrete data for the discussion of ideas presented in the course; and (c) to provide opportunities for exploring several methods of solutions for a single problem (Heid 1988a). Several commercial programs have been especially designed for the teaching of analysis. One of them is MuMath (Frees 1986, Mathews 1988). MuMath solves equations, performs symbolic manipulations, evaluates functions, and computes limits, derivatives (including partials), and integrals (Mathews 1988). In addition to the specific computer programs, general application-based computer software have also been utilized in analysis courses. These include electronic-sheet, graph functions, and advanced calculators (Bloom 1987, Heid 1988b, Hsiao 1984–85, Marty 1988, Tony 1988). Also teaching analysis as an advanced placement course via conference telephone and computers has been suggested for distance education (Leach 1986).

While computers can perform the computational procedures more easily and quickly than any other technologies known at present, interactive video-disc programs can serve three other instructional functions: (a) to provide explanations and demonstrations of concepts in analysis; (b) to present vividly real life problems that can be solved by applying algorithms learned in analysis; and (c) to model problem-solving and metacognitive processes when new concepts and operations are presented. Henderson and Landesman (1988–89) designed eight interactive video modules for teaching a precalculus course. These include: the number line and inequalities, absolute value and distance, functions and graphs, linear equations and inequalities, quadratic equations and inequalities, the exponential and logarithmic functions and the trigonometric functions. The program allows self-pacing and self-sequencing of the learning processes.

The availability of these powerful technologies has led researchers to look for more effective ways to incorporate them in ongoing instruction in the classroom. Heid (1988a) suggested that the teaching of concepts should precede the teaching of computational skills in both sequence and priority. Using graphical and symbolic manipulation computer programs to perform routine manipulations, she designed an applied analysis course in which students studied the concepts during the first 12 weeks of the course and mastered skills during the last three weeks. Heid (1988a) indicated that the experimental group showed a higher level of understanding and performed almost as well on routine skills as the control group who learned in the traditional way.

5. Future Prospects

Performing higher order thinking operations in our highly technological society is becoming more and more dependent upon one's exposure to analysis courses in mathematics. Yet, mathematical anxiety and low motivation inhibit many students from taking such advanced courses. Computers, interactive video-discs, multimedia, and advanced calculators can assist not only in developing mathematical understanding and overcoming misconceptions related to analysis (Davis and Vinner 1987), but also in reducing mathematical anxiety (Mevarech and Ben-Artzi 1987) and strengthening mathematical self-concept (Mevarech 1985, Mevarech and Rich 1985). Yet, the use of these tools is no guarantee that change will (or could) occur. Special methods combining effective strategies (e.g., mastery learning or cooperative learning), metacognitive skills, and innovative technologies need to be developed for facilitating both understanding and computational skills. Future research should focus on this task.

Bibliography

Allendoerfer C B 1963 The case against calculus. *Maths Teacher* 56: 482–85

Bell F H 1978 *Teaching and Learning Mathematics in Secondary Schools*. Brown, Dubuque, Iowa

Bloom L M 1987 Micro-computer graphics and calculus teaching. *Aust. Maths Teacher* 43: 5–8

Butler C H, Wren L F, Banks J H 1970 *The Teaching of Secondary Mathematics*, 5th edn. McGraw-Hill, New York

Cummins K A 1977 A student experience–discovery approach to the teaching of calculus. In: Grinstein L S, Michaels B (eds.) 1977 *Readings from the Mathematics Teacher*, pp. 31–40

Davis R B, Vinner S 1987 The notion of limit: Some seemingly unavoidable misconception stages. *J. Maths Behav.* 5: 281–303

Frees R 1986 The use of MuMath in the calculus classroom. *J. Comp. Maths Sci. Educ.* 6: 52–55

Greenwell R 1987 Software review. *College Maths J.* 18: 422–24

Heid K M 1988a Calculators on tests—One giant step for math education. *Maths Teacher* 81: 710–13

Heid M K 1988b Resequencing skills and concepts in applied calculus using the computer as a tool. *J. Res. Maths Educ.* 19: 3–25

Henderson R W, Landesman E M 1988–89 Interactive videodisc instruction in pre-calculus. *J. Educ. Technol. Systems* 17: 91–101

Hsiao F S 1984–85 A new approach to teaching calculus. *J. Comp. Maths Sci. Teach.* 4: 29–36

Keller F S 1968 Good-bye, teacher . . . . *J. Appl. Behav. Anal.* 1: 79–89

Leach J 1986 Teaching applied calculus by telephone and computer. *College Board Rev.* 29: 14–15

Marty R H 1988 Using calculators to explore and develop mathematical concepts. *Maths Comp. Educ.* 22: 198–202

Mathews J H 1988 The MuMath calculus tutor. *J. Comp. Maths Sci. Teach.* 8: 53–57

Mevarech Z R 1985 Computer assisted different instructional methods: A factorial experiment within mathematics disadvantaged classrooms. *J. Exper. Educ.* 54: 22–27

Mevarech Z R 1988 Intrinsic orientation profiles and learning mathematics in CAI settings. *J. Educ. Res.* 81: 228–33

Mevarech Z R, Rich Y 1985 Effects of computer-assisted instruction on disadvantaged pupils' cognitive and affective outcomes. *J. Educ. Res.* 79: 5–11

Mevarech Z R, Ben-Arzi S 1987 Effects of CAI with fixed and adaptive feedback on children's mathematics anxiety and achievement. *J. Exper. Educ.* 56: 42–46

National Committee on Mathematics Requirements 1923 *The Reorganization of Mathematics in Secondary Education*. Houghton Mifflin, Boston, Massachusetts

Spresser D M 1979 Placement of the first calculus course. *Int. J. Maths Educ. Sci. Technol.* 10: 593–600

Tony C 1988 Hunting that limit . . . *Maths Sch.* 17: 16–17

Thompson S B 1980 Do individualized mastery and traditional instructional systems yield different course effects in college calculus? *Am. Educ. Res. J.* 17: 361–76

Geometry: Educational Programs

J. T. Fey

Geometry is the branch of mathematics that arises from questions of shape, size, and position in physical space. It has been a core subject in mathematical education at least since the entry to Plato's Academy bore the inscription "Let No One Ignorant of Geometry Enter Here."

The appeal and importance of geometry rest on its major role in four areas of human activity. In practical problems, such as surveying or construction, geometric figures and measurement techniques are essential for planning work and describing results. In science, geometry provides the ideas for modeling astronomical phenomena, the action of physical forces, and the forms of living objects. In the arts, geometric notions of symmetry and projection have been fundamental in creations like the mosaics in Moorish palaces or the introduction of perspective in Renaissance painting. Finally, the Euclidean formulation of geometry as an axiomatic system has served as a model of hypothetical–deductive reasoning for 20 centuries of scholars and students.

1. Geometry in School

Traditional school mathematics curricula have treated geometry in three phases. First experiences in geometry, at elementary and early secondary levels, concentrate on informal study of basic shapes and their properties. Measurement of length, area, and volume is applied to a variety of practical problems. At some stage of upper-secondary education a large portion of the students study the organization of geometric ideas and facts in a formal axiomatic system. Then in later study leading to calculus, a smaller number of students encounter vector and analytic geometry—the blending of geometric and algebraic ideas and methods. Throughout this development of geometric facts, concepts, and techniques for problem solving, the basic theme is geometry as a model of the physical world. The formal axiomatic treatment has, with certain refinements, retained the content and spirit set long ago by Euclid.

Despite the obvious application of geometry to a wide range of important real-world problems and the strong traditional belief that geometry is the ideal vehicle for teaching logical reasoning, the place of geometry in contemporary school curricula is neither satisfactory nor settled. Nearly every curriculum advisory body gives strong support to the inclusion of informal geometry in early instruction. Yet results of most achievement tests show very poor student attainment in geometry, particularly on crucial measurement ideas and skills and geometric problem solving. Not surprisingly, teachers at the elementary level view arithmetic as far more important and they give little time to geometry.

The deepest questions on school geometry today center on the formal treatment of secondary-school years, traditionally based on a version of Euclid's *Elements*. At this stage, the questions are of three types: first, as schools have sought to broaden student participation in secondary and higher education, the range of students studying axiomatic geometry has extended to include many for whom formal reasoning and abstraction are very difficult. Research in cognitive development has suggested that many of these students are incapable of the thinking required in traditional views of the course. At the same time, research in the foundations of mathematics has revealed logical gaps in the Euclidean presentation of geometry and the repairs required make geometry appear a far too complex and subtle subject for the introduction of axiomatic thinking.

Second, the content and methods of reasoning in traditional geometry courses for school level seldom present any geometric idea or fact not known for over 2,000 years. Geometry has developed in many fruitful directions since Euclid's first synthesis. Projective and affine geometries, non-Euclidean geometries, finite geometries, topology, graph theory, differential geometry, algebraic geometry, and the theory of vector spaces (each with multiple subtopics) have been developed and found to provide powerful tools for solving mathematical problems in many disciplines. With few exceptions, these topics, many readily learned by secondary students, have not found a place in the mainstream curriculum of school mathematics.

Third, one of the striking characteristics of recent mathematics is the realization that the major branches of the subject have many structural similarities and that a few general ideas can be used to draw out and capitalize on those similarities. As Descartes showed in the seventeenth century, objects and operations in geometry correspond directly to objects and operations in algebra; in the nineteenth century Felix Klein showed that all geometry (of that day) could be viewed as the study of invariants under transformation of a space; and the various contributors to vector methods showed how that basic notion provides a powerful link between geometry, algebra, and the physical world. Each of these organizing motifs for mathematical ideas now makes a claim as an improvement on the traditional Euclidean approach to geometry.

Finally, the emergence of powerful microcomputer graphics utilities as standard tools for visual reasoning has raised fundamental questions about the proper scope and instructional style of school geometry. A variety of geometric construction programs facilitate student study of shapes and their properties, making it possible for geometry teaching to emphasize exploration and discovery in new ways. Computer graphics have also been essential tools in development of the exciting new world of fractal geometry that models chaos in important dynamical systems. These new methods and visual changes are immensely attractive to students and teachers.

Each of these developments in geometry raises a fundamental question for the school curriculum: what role for axiomatic reasoning? What collection of concepts and methods is appropriate? Which organizing approach is most effective? Since the late 1960s, there has been extensive curriculum development and experimentation on the various approaches. In several countries the formal axiomatic course in geometry has been replaced by a far less rigorous intuitive development of facts and principles, with shorter sequences of proof that might be called "local axiomatics." In these situations, geometric topics have been woven in among topics in algebra, statistics, or arithmetic. In several other countries, geometry programs have been organized around transformation methods in which congruence is the study of rigid motions. In a few countries, school geometry has been recast completely in the language of vector spaces and their transformations. Where new topics like topology, graph theory, or non-Euclidean geometry have been introduced, the approach has been informal and exploratory. There seems no consensus on the proper final resolution of the controversies, only vigorous competing views.

2. Research on Geometry Learning

As problems and new proposals have arisen in school geometry, they have stimulated research and development activity. Various projects have demonstrated the feasibility of teaching geometry from a vector, coordinate, or transformation point of view. Another line of research has sought a theory of cognitive process levels in geometry learning similar to the stage theory of general development proposed by Piaget. There has also been interest, shared by mathematics educators and psychologists, in the development of spatial visualization abilities. This issue has been of special concern because of indications that different spatial abilities might be sex related and basic to understanding observed differences in mathematical performance of girls and boys.

3. Prospects

Since the early 1960s, the debate over school geometry has praised and condemned the "death of geometry." That theme was the focus of a symposium at the 1980 International Congress on Mathematics Education, but such prognoses seem excessively pessimistic. Geometric ideas continue to pervade our everyday experience and the work of people in science and technology. Geometry in school is not dying, it is breaking out of very old and restricting traditions to embrace new content, methods, and applications. It seems clear that spatial intuition, sharpened by informal geometry experience, will continue to be a natural and valuable facet of human thought. The use of vector, coordinate, and transformation methods to describe shape, size, and position of objects in space is of demonstrated utility and of increasing importance for school programs. Further, the abstraction of geometric notions has proven valuable in thinking about a variety of complex problems in other branches of mathematics. The current development of dynamic computer graphics provides yet another promising role for geometric thinking and a responsibility for preparation in school programs.

Bibliography

Lesh R, Mierkiewicz D (eds.) 1978 *Recent Research Concerning the Development of Spatial and Geometric Concepts.* Educational Resources Information Center Clearinghouse for Science, Mathematics, and Environmental Education, Columbus, Ohio

Lindquist M M, Shulte A P (eds.) 1987 *Learning and Teaching Geometry, K–12.* National Council of Teachers of Mathematics, Reston, Virginia

Peitgen H O, Jurgens H, Saupe D 1990 *Fractals for the Classroom.* Springer-Verlag, New York

Schwartz J 1987 The geometric supposer: Using microcomputers to restore invention to the learning of mathematics. In: Wirszup I, Streit R (eds.) 1987 *Developments in School Mathematics Education Around the World.* National Council of Teachers of Mathematics, Reston, Virginia, pp. 623–36

Steiner H-G (ed.) 1980 *Comparative Studies of Mathematics Curricula: Change and Stability 1960–1980.* Institut fur Didaktik der Mathematik, Bielefeld

Innovative Topics

New Mathematics

S. Vinner

The term "new mathematics" is used to denote a movement in mathematics education which took place mainly in the United States, starting approximately in the middle of the 1950s.

The philosophy of the new mathematics was based on two main assumptions: (a) to know a subject means to know its structure, and (b) any subject can be taught in some intellectually honest form to any child at any stage of development (Bruner 1960). Thus, for instance, at the elementary level, to know the structure of mathematics means to know that addition and multiplication of numbers are commutative.

Several years later it was severely criticized by mathematics educators and it ceased to be considered a remedy for all the diseases of mathematics education. Moreover, it was blamed as being the cause of some of them, and new movements (like Back to Basics, Mathematics with Applications, and Problem Solving) took its place. Educators complained that children quite likely know that $3 + 5$ equals $5 + 3$ but they do not known how much $3 + 5$ is. At the secondary levels the deductive nature of mathematics was emphasized. Children were asked to distinguish between numbers and number names; they were taught set theory because it demonstrated the fact that mathematics deals with abstract systems, not only with numbers. Another reason for teaching set theory was the fact that the concept of number in mathematics is established on the concept of set, and therefore the child's way of constructing the concept of number should be the same. In algebra, old terms like "unknown," "equation," "solution," and others were replaced by "variable," "open sentence," "solution set," and others. The new terms were taken from new branches of mathematics developed in the 1920s and 1930s.

The success of the new mathematics movement in the 1950s was for several reasons. Firstly, there was an educational tendency to negate rote learning and to emphasize learning for understanding. Secondly, there was the tendency of university people to become involved in school education. Another factor, perhaps

the most important one, was the "Sputnik trauma." This occurred in American society following the launch of the first Russian satellite, the Sputnik (1957). According to the common opinion then, the Sputnik uncovered the American inferiority in science and technology. The response, people believed, should have been a revolution in mathematics and science education.

In the decade of the new mathematics movement, many projects took place and many textbooks were published. The best known ones are: UICSM (University of Illinois Committee on School Mathematics), SMSG (School Mathematics Study Groups), and CMSP (Comprehensive Mathematics School Program), the Columbia University Secondary School Mathematics, SMP (Secondary School Mathematics Project) in England, and Papy's textbooks in Belgium. Among the most famous names associated with new mathematics are: Max Beberman, Edward Begle, Howard Fehr, Carl Allendorfer, and Robert Davis.

Criticism of the new mathematics programs reached its height in the middle of the 1960s. It was claimed that teachers and parents did not have the mathematical and the pedagogical background to deal with it and, in addition, it was not clear at all whether children, at various ages, were intellectually capable (from the developmental point of view) of learning it.

Although the new mathematics movement ceased to exist, its impact on present mathematics education can still be noticed. Mathematics programs today tend to emphasize comprehension and to encourage creative thinking more than was common before the new mathematics era.

Bibliography

Bruner J 1960 *The Process of Education*. Harvard University Press, Cambridge, Massachusetts
Macarow L 1970 New math. *Sch. Sci. Math.* 70: 395–97
Mueller F J 1966 The public image of "new mathematics". *Maths. Teach.* 59: 618–23
Sharp E 1966 *A Parents' Guide to New Mathematics*. English University Press, London

Mathematical Applications: Primary School

R. Lesh

Mathematical applications means describing real-life situations, or solving problems, using mathematical concepts or principles.

Recent position papers by a number of professional organizations, including the United States National Council of Teachers of Mathematics (NCTM) and the National Council of Supervisors of Mathematics (NCSM), have strongly supported making "applications" a major focus of the school mathematics curriculum (NCTM 1980, NCSM 1977). Commitment to this priority had been demonstrated by the NCTM's 1979 *Yearbook on Applications* and by a 1980 *Resource Book on Mathematical Applications*. Furthermore, since the early 1970s, the National Science Foundation of the United States, as well as comparable agencies in other countries, have funded a variety of research and development projects dealing with applications of elementary mathematics (National Science Foundation 1981). These projects raise the following kinds of curriculum questions: is emphasizing applications the same as emphasizing problem solving—or, in particular, word problems? Do applications have to be added to an already crowded curriculum, or can they be integrated with mathematics concept learning?

1. Teaching Concepts and Applications Jointly

The ability to use elementary mathematics concepts in everyday situations is one of the most important basic skills required for mathematical literacy among average citizens; yet the processes, skills, and understandings that are needed in everyday applications are not necessarily the same as those emphasized by spokespersons for either "basic skills" or "problem solving" (Lesh 1981).

To pursue career opportunities in an increasingly technological society, as well as to understand the events in their daily lives, average people must acquire a stock of basic conceptual models. For example, elementary concepts involving probability, statistics, measurement, coordinate systems, graphing, scientific notation, exponential growth rates, the sensible use of averages, estimates, and approximations, and so on, are often assumed to be "easy," but as research demonstrates, they are exceedingly unobvious to people who have not had specific instruction concerning their use. Most of these ideas do not develop naturally, even for students who have received instruction; practice in the form of typical textbook word problems is of little benefit.

The above observations suggest that a serious emphasis on teaching the practical applications of mathematics may require some new topics to be inserted into the curriculum, and other topics to be deleted (Usiskin 1980). However, it is important to emphasize that applications should not necessarily come *after* formal concepts have been learned, nor should they await the introduction of new topics. Students do not first learn a concept or an idea, then learn to solve contrived problems using the idea, and subsequently (if ever) learn to solve applied problems in which some "real world" knowledge is needed in addition to knowledge about mathematical ideas and principles. Rather, there is a dynamic interaction between basic mathematical concepts and many of the most important applied problem-solving processes. Furthermore, many of the most important applied problem-solving processes contribute both to the meaningfulness and to the utility value of basic mathematical concepts.

Elementary arithmetic, number, and measurement concepts gained their positions in the curriculum precisely because they are useful to the "average person" in a wide variety of situations (Bell 1980). These concepts may become useful only if their teaching is carried out jointly with teaching problems of applications. This is important to stress because, if applications are considered to be important only after learning of basic concepts has occurred, then they probably will, and perhaps should, be omitted from an already overcrowded curriculum.

2. Applications and Word Problems

Emphasizing realistic applications is not the same as focusing increased attention on word problems (Lesh and Akerstrom 1981, Nesher 1980). Seemingly "realistic" word problems appearing in most mathematics textbooks often differ significantly from their real world counterparts with respect to degree of difficulty, processes needed in solutions, and error types most frequently committed (Lesh et al. 1982). Furthermore, if "important" problem-solving experiences are identified based on observations of everyday situations in which mathematics is used, then it becomes obvious that many of the most important problem types are not represented at all in most textbooks (Pollack 1971) and have been neglected in most instructional development projects in mathematics education (Lesh 1981).

Textbook word problems usually describe a series of quasirealistic situations in which a single idea or topic can be "applied." Real problems more often occur in situations where the relevant mathematics must be identified and ideas from several topic areas may be required. For many real-world uses of mathematics, the goal is not to produce an "answer"; rather, the goals might include discovering a procedure that will produce answers to a specific class of nonmathematical decisions, comparisons, or evaluations using mathematics as a tool. Textbook "word cues" are seldom available in the statement of such problems to suggest appropriate solution procedures (Lesh et al. 1982).

3. Applications and General Problem-solving Strategies

The processes that must be utilized in solving applied problems are not necessarily the general problem-solving strategies that have been the subject of so much past research. Problem-solving research and curriculum development have tended to use puzzle-type problems that lack any underlying mathematical content. For such problems, general (but weak) content-independent processes, such as "working backwards," "hill climbing," "beginning the solution process by explicitly identifying the known and unknown quantities," and so on, have seemed important. But researchers focusing on problems based on substantive mathematical content have been finding that in real-life situations, these general processes are used primarily either by poor problem solvers, or by those who lack specific required knowledge in a given domain. Better problem solvers use powerful, content-related processes. They tend to work forward, beginning with a qualitative understanding of the whole situation and gradually work toward a more quantitative, step-by-step approach in which specific data are "plugged into" formulas or answer-giving rules (Simon and Simon 1978).

4. Applications in Mathematics Curriculum

New, inexpensive, and readily available technological tools, such as calculators and computers, are creating the need for new skills and understandings, reducing the importance of mechanistic "answer-giving" skills, creating opportunities to deal with realistic problems with "messy" data, and increasing the importance of "nonanswer-giving" processes, skills, and understandings: for example, finding ways to weight and combine qualitative and quantitative information, planning multiple-step solution procedures, assessing the sensibility or usefulness of trial solutions, and so on. Often, real problems do not occur in the form of well-defined questions with clearly specified goals in which the "problem" is to find legal moves to get from the "givens" to the "answer." Sometimes there is an overwhelming amount of information, all of which is relevant; or some important information may be missing, but an answer must be found anyway. In these cases a mathematical model is used to filter, organize, and interpret information that is "most useful," to find an answer that is "good enough" (Lesh 1981, Nesher 1980).

Interpreting real situations using mathematical ideas is a large part of what is meant by "mathematical understanding," and creating, modifying, and adapting these models is an important part of mathematical problem solving and concept formation. Cultivating these skills should be a priority focus for the mathematics curriculum in the future.

Bibliography

Bell M S 1980 Applied problem solving as a school emphasis: An assessment and some recommendations. In: Lesh R, Mierkiewicz D, Kantowski M G (eds.) 1980 *Monograph for Applied Mathematical Problem Solving*. ERIC/SMEAC, Columbus, Ohio

Bell M S, Bushaw D, Pollak, H, Thompson M, Usiskin Z 1980 *A Sourcebook of Applications for School Mathematics*. National Council of Teachers of Mathematics, Reston, Virginia

Lesh R 1981 Applied mathematical problem solving. *Educ. Stud. Math.* 12: 235–64

Lesh R, Akerstrom M 1981 Applied problem solving: A priority focus for mathematics education research. In: Lester F (ed.) 1981 *Mathematical Problem Solving*. Franklin Institute Press, Philadelphia

Lesh R, Landau M, Hamilton E 1982 Using elementary mathematics in everyday situations. In: Lesh R, Landau M (eds.) 1982 *Acquisition of Mathematics Concepts and Processes*. Academic Press, New York

National Council of Supervisors of Mathematics (NCSM) 1977 Position paper on basic mathematical skills. *Arith. Teach.* 25: 19–22

National Council of Teachers of Mathematics (NCTM) 1980 *An Agenda for Action: Recommendations for School Mathematics of the 1980s*. National Council of Teachers of Mathematics, Reston, Virginia

National Science Foundation 1981 *Source Book of Projects: Science Education Development and Research*. National Science Foundation, Washington, DC

Nesher P 1980 The stereotyped nature of school word problems. *For The Learning of Mathematics* 1(1): 41–8

Pollack H O 1971 Applications of mathematics. In: Beyle E G (ed.) 1971 *Mathematics Education*. Sixty-Ninth Year Book of the National Society for the Study of Education, Part I. University of Chicago Press, Chicago, Illinois

Sharron S (ed.) 1979 *Applications in School Mathematics*, 1979 Yearbook. National Council of Teachers of Mathematics, Reston, Virginia

Simon D P, Simon H A 1978 Individual differences in solving physics problems. In: Siegler R S (ed.) 1978 *Children's Thinking: What Develops?* Erlbaum, Hillsdale, New Jersey

Usiskin Z 1980 What should not be in the algebra and geometry curricula of average college-bound students? *Math. Teach.* 73: 413–24

Mathematical Applications: Secondary School

Z. Usiskin

A mathematical application at the secondary school level is a real-world situation or problem whose understanding or resolution involves mathematics taught at this level, that is, algebra up to and sometimes including calculus. Activities range from manipulation of a known formula to modeling, the process of translating a real situation into its mathematical language.

Traditional applications taught within mathematics

classes include the mensuration formulas for perimeter, area, and volume; trigonometry for finding unknown distances; and exponential functions for describing compound interest and other instances of growth. Outside mathematics classes, applications of secondary-school mathematics have long existed in physics and chemistry classes, but are so often ignored elsewhere in the secondary school that the naive student believes that there are few other applications of mathematics at this level. The recent rapid increase of mathematical sophistication in the biological and social sciences, as well as in business and finance, and the revolution in availability of computing equipment, has created pressure to include more applications in mathematics courses themselves and in the courses involving topics to which mathematics can be applied (Pollak 1979, Bushaw et al. 1980, Blum et al. 1989).

1. Content

Aside from the use of formulas, some rate and mixture problems employing elementary algebra, and the traditional topics mentioned above, few application types appear in all secondary-school mathematics curricula. However, a diversity of applications and contexts receives less widespread use, reflecting the options in selecting content from a field as broad as that of mathematics itself: probability theory for genetics; sampling and simple statistics for the social sciences; linear programming for business; matrices for coding theory; curve fitting for the physical and biological sciences; annuities for consumer finance; and geometric shapes for studies of the structures of animate and inanimate objects. Owing to the lack of uniformity of curricula, applications of secondary-school mathematics appear infrequently in national and international tests and assessments of mathematics achievement.

Presentations of applications range in scope from individual exercises applying the Pythagorean theorem or other propositions, to full courses in statistics or other fields of applied mathematics. Curricula may emphasize the application context, as is common when the educational setting is outside the mathematics classroom; in general application processes such as modeling, simulation, or the translation in and out of prose language and mathematical symbols; or in the mathematical principles themselves involved in the application. Puzzles or contrived verbal problems are usually considered not to be applications, though their teaching is often for the purpose of building translation skills.

The breadth of applications that can be considered and the manner in which a person goes about this consideration can be markedly affected by the equipment at hand. Computers widen the scope and, depending upon the available software, enable iterative, trial-and-error, hypothesis testing, randomness, and graphical procedures that would otherwise be infeasible. Calculators make obsolete the practice of simplifying actual data for school problems so as to avoid computational difficulties (Pollak 1986).

2. Sequence

Mirroring other areas in which it may be asked whether the curriculum should be organized around problems or around disciplinary concepts, a fundamental issue concerns whether mathematical principles should be taught first and then applied to appropriately selected situations, or whether it would be better to begin with real-world contexts and employ these to motivate and develop the mathematics helpful in dealing with them.

Usually the mathematical principles are taught first, reflecting the history of those mathematical topics (e.g., number theory and non-Euclidean geometry) which developed independently of application but were later found to have important use (in coding theory and physics), and exemplifying the general view that the potential utility of any mathematical concept cannot be foreseen (Browder and MacLane 1978). With this sequence, applications are often avoided unless they are presented immediately after the corresponding mathematics, and the student seldom has to decide which mathematics to utilize in a given real problem. While this lack of decision-making experience is often considered as a disadvantage of the sequence, it is close to the reality of people who are given rather specific directions to follow in employing mathematics.

Some areas of mathematics (e.g., probability theory and calculus) developed as a direct consequence of desires to solve real-world problems or understand real-world phenomena. Curricula that follow the order of these histories begin with applications and develop the mathematics as they are needed. This sequence allows easy access to general application processes and is closer to the reality of the person who must search for or invent mathematics to deal with a problem. While this sequence has long been used with individual topics, complete courses or entire mathematics curricula at the secondary level in which the mathematics arises from the applications are a relatively recent phenomenon (Schools Council 1978, Blum et al. 1989).

3. Applied Mathematics, Pure Mathematics, and Problem Solving

Applied mathematics is often contrasted with pure mathematics, that is, mathematics studied without regard for application. Yet, from what is known, school learning and teaching of applied mathematics and pure mathematics are quite similar (Freudenthal et al. 1968). Like their pure mathematical counterparts, applications range from the broadly applicable to the quite specific, from the simple to the difficult, from the elegant to the messy, and from the self-motivating to the obscure. The fundamental difference between pure and applied mathematics with respect to school learning is that there exists in most school systems a rather well-defined curriculum for pure mathematics but there are only a very few applications that all students can be considered to have been taught.

For this reason there are few research studies concentrating on the learning of applications at the secondary-school level. The closest related area of research is that of mathematical problem solving (Silver 1985). The difficulty in applying problem-solving research to the teaching and learning of applications is that real-world situations often have characteristics of complexity and motivational appeal quite different from the corresponding problems as presented in the classroom or laboratory.

In summary, the teaching and learning of applications of secondary-school mathematics on a large scale is a rather recent phenomenon, and both the curricular design and learning aspects of this phenomenon are in their nascent stages.

Bibliography

Blum W, Berry J S, Biehler R, Huntley I D, Kaiser-Messmer G, Profke L (eds.) 1989 *Applications and Modelling in Learning and Teaching Mathematics*. Ellis Horwood, Chichester

Browder F, MacLane S 1978 The relevance of mathematics. In: Steen L A (ed.) 1978 *Mathematics Today: Twelve Informal Essays*. Springer, New York

Bushaw D et al. 1980 *A Sourcebook of Applications of School Mathematics*. National Council of Teachers of Mathematics, Reston, Virginia

Freudenthal H et al. 1968 Proceedings of the colloquium how to teach mathematics so as to be useful. *Educ. Stud. Math.* 1

Pollak H O 1979 The interaction between mathematics and other school subjects. *New Trends in Mathematics Teaching*, Vol. 4. UNESCO, Paris, pp. 232–48

Pollak H 1986 The effects of technology on the mathematics curriculum. In: Carss M (ed.) 1986 *Proceedings of the Fifth International Congress in Mathematics Education*. Birkhäuser, Boston

Schools Council Sixth Form Mathematics Project 1978 *Mathematics Applicable*. Heinemann, London

Silver E (ed.) 1985 *Teaching and Learning Mathematical Problem Solving: Multiple Research Perspectives*. Lawrence Erlbaum, Hillsdale, New Jersey

Problem-solving in Mathematics

J. Kilpatrick

Mathematical problem solving is an individual or group activity in which a question is posed, no route to the answer is indicated, the challenge of answering the question is accepted, and mathematical concepts and principles are used in seeking an answer. As a human endeavor, mathematics has arisen out of the process of solving practical and intellectual problems. Mathematics gives aesthetic pleasure to some people, but for most its principal value derives from its usefulness in providing tools for the solution of problems. Despite the centrality of problem solving in mathematics itself, however, its role in the school mathematics curriculum is not clearly established. Mathematics educators agree that all children should be able to apply the mathematics they have learned in school to the solution of problems they will face, but there is little agreement as to whether the mathematics teacher can, or should attempt to, substantially improve children's ability to solve problems. Some teachers see their task as providing children with the knowledge and skills needed for subsequent problem solving and regard this task alone as sufficient to define the curriculum. Others believe that the curriculum should be organized around the solution of problems and that instruction should be aimed directly at improving problem-solving ability.

The problems most commonly used in mathematics instruction are the so-called "word problems" (sometimes termed "verbal problems" or "story problems"). Word problems are introduced into instruction when pupils have learned a mathematical procedure and the teacher wants to give them practice in applying it. The word problem describes a situation; some information is given, and other information is to be found by applying one or more mathematical procedures. Many word problems involve "one rule under your nose" (Polya 1981 p. 139)—they are solved by the mechanical application of a rule that has just been presented—but some require the pupil to choose among or combine rules. An objection to word problems is that they provide no opportunity to learn skills of problem formulation. Some recent curriculum programs have attempted to develop ways of leaving to the pupil all or part of the process of identifying a problematic situation, formulating a problem out of the situation, and then solving the problem. Increased attention in mathematics instruction is being given to the use of "real problems": problems that are meaningful to the pupil and that require knowledge of the problem setting as well as knowledge of mathematics.

Much mathematics instruction is influenced by the view that the pupil learns to solve problems chiefly through practice and that the teacher's role is simply to provide an ample number of problems and opportunities to solve them. Another, and increasingly popular, view is that the teacher should provide instruction in problem-solving techniques and strategies, but opinions differ as to the nature and extent of this instruction. Programs in which pupils are taught an algorithm to follow in solving problems of a restricted type have met with some success—as long as the algorithm has been well-practiced and the problems restricted. Such programs are much less successful, however, in teaching pupils how to decide whether the algorithm is appropriate for a given problem or how to modify the algorithm to solve problems of a different type. Instead of teaching pupils to follow a fixed sequence of steps, some teachers have attempted to provide them with heuristic advice (Polya 1981) that may help them analyze the problem and transform it into something they can solve. Pupils are not likely to learn to apply such advice unless they are given many opportunities to see it applied, practice its application, and identify cues to help decide when it might be appropriate. Effective instruction in heuristic techniques and strategies is difficult and time consuming to accomplish in the mathematics classroom. Some research indicates that children possess an impressive array of thinking strategies but that in many classrooms they are inhibited from applying them. A considerable improvement in problem-solving performance can occur when pupils' responses are encouraged and accepted and the classroom atmosphere is made less threatening.

Recent analyses of cognition as information processing throw new light on mathematical problem solving as a cognitive activity. These analyses attempt to account for the human mind's ability, with a limited capacity for processing information, to solve complex problems that require planning and strategy. Studies of expert problem solvers and computer simulations of problem-solving processes show that the solution of a complex problem requires: (a) a rich store of organized knowledge about the content domain, (b) a set of procedures for representing and transforming the problem, and (c) a control system to guide the selection of knowledge and procedures. It is easy to underestimate the deep knowledge of mathematics and extensive experience in solving problems that underlie proficiency in mathematical problem solving. On the other hand, it is equally easy to underestimate the sophistication of the control processes used by experts to monitor and direct their problem-solving activity.

Successful problem solving requires an active stance: the pupil should attempt to transform an intractable problem, simplifying it or representing it some other way, rather than waiting passively for an inspiration. When pupils write different versions of problems, modify problems to yield different solutions, and construct original problems, they learn to distinguish between a problem and the various ways it can be posed. The information-processing approach stresses that problem characteristics are major determinants of problem-solving behavior (Goldin and McClintock 1979). Problems can be put into categories according to the information

processing they require so that instruction can be concentrated on the processes needed to solve them. The topic of "problem type," however, needs careful handling by teachers. Experience in several countries shows that a strong emphasis in mathematics instruction on the identification of problem types leads to a narrow approach to problem solving. Pupils are more likely to be flexible in dealing with problems of an unfamiliar type if they have encountered problems (such as those given by Krutetskii 1968) that superficially appear to be of the same type but are not.

To find room for problem-solving activities in a crowded mathematics curriculum, the teacher needs a serious commitment to the importance of problem solving. Teachers find collections of problem material invaluable, but they are unlikely to devote much attention to instruction in problem-solving techniques and strategies if they themselves have not had the opportunity, as students, to solve challenging mathematical problems (Polya 1981) and to reflect on the role of problem solving in mathematics.

Bibliography

Biermann N, Bussmann H, Niedworok H W 1977 *Schöpferisches Problemlösen im Mathematikunterricht*. Urban und Schwarzenberg, Munich

Charles R I, Silver E A (eds.) 1988 *The Teaching and Assessing of Mathematical Problem Solving* (Research Agenda for Mathematics Education, Vol. 3). National Council of Teachers of Mathematics, Reston, Virginia and Lawrence Erlbaum Associates, Hillsdale, New Jersey

Glaeser G 1976 *Le Livre du problème*. Cedic, Paris

Goldin G A, McClintock C E 1979 *Task Variables in Mathematical Problem Solving*. ERIC Clearinghouse for Science, Mathematics and Environmental Education, Columbus, Ohio

Hill C C 1979 *Problem Solving: Learning and Teaching. An Annotated Bibliography*. Pinter, London

Krutetskii V A 1968 *Psikhologiia Matematicheskikh Sposobnostei Shkol'nikov*. Prosveschenie, Moscow [1976 *The Psychology of Mathematical Abilities in Schoolchildren*. University of Chicago Press, Chicago, Illinois]

Mason J, Burton L, Stacey K 1982 *Thinking Mathematically*. Addison-Wesley, London

Polya G 1981 *Mathematical Discovery: On Understanding, Learning, and Teaching Problem Solving*. Wiley, New York

Silver E A (ed.) 1985 *Teaching and Learning Mathematical Problem Solving: Multiple Research Perspectives*. Lawrence Erlbaum Associates, Hillsdale, New Jersey

Number and Measurement Concepts

F. Voigt

The study of the psychological basis of mathematics instruction has a long history in psychology. It was the eminent E. L. Thorndike who searched to translate the results of learning studies into suggestions for classroom instruction. The drilled instruction in specific arithmetic problems was the focus of this associationistic

analysis. A decade later, in the 1930s, Brownell opposed this method of drill, and stressed instead the meaningfulness of mathematical instruction, that is, the rules and regularities underlying mathematical problems. Even though elementary-school mathematics was cast into the waves of reform in the 1960s, computational problems and the practice of elementary operations still fill a large proportion of the time of the child's school experiences. The reform movement has at the same time redirected the attention of psychology to the more basic concepts implicit in mathematics instruction, most notably the natural number concept itself, set theory, and elementary geometry (Resnick and Ford 1981). The precursors of these basic concepts and their developmental integration in the preschool years have been one of the main lines of developmental research into mathematics development since the early 1970s.

1. Logical Definition of Number and Psychological Representation

In mathematical philosophy, two distinct approaches to the definition of the natural number concept have emerged. Ordinal theories of the number concept search the foundation of the natural number in the ordering relations inherent in the series of numbers, for which formalizations have been suggested (as represented for example in the Peano axioms). In contrast, cardinal definitions identify the natural numbers with their cardinal aspect. Following Russell, who is the chief proponent of this logical definition, besides Frege, a number is considered a class of similar classes where the equivalence between these classes is determined via one-to-one correspondence (Brainerd 1979).

Following such logical formalizations, psychological translations of these logical principles have been proposed. Ordinal theories of number development suggest that the child's understanding of transitive and asymmetrical relations (e.g., reflected in a series of sticks of various length) is a prerequisite to the natural number concept. This would not only imply a developmental priority of ordination concepts over the natural number concept, but also a functional relation: specific instruction in ordinal relations and ordinal concepts should foster the child's understanding of natural number. Cardinal number theories in turn consider the child's understanding of concrete representations of the quality of collections and his or her ability to compare various aggregates of objects (via counting or one-to-one correspondence) as the fundamental prerequisite for the number concept. Thus the child's experience with comparison operations in the preschool period should be functionally relevant to the natural number idea and its applications.

The epistemological foundation of the number concept has been the central focus of Piaget's theory of number development. His original question has been: how does the child construct an arithmetical unit in the course of the preschool years? Analyzing various logical structures and their development, Piaget found similar qualitative changes between the preschool years and the elementary-school years (reflected in the transition of the child's thinking from the preoperational to the concrete operational stage). The number concept, and most notably the arithmetic unit, emerges for Piaget from a synthesis of two logical structures: the child's systematic understanding and coordination of classification and seriation (asymmetrical–transitive relations) allow the construction of such a unit. Piaget identified the number concept with the number invariance task, in which the child observes a spatial transformation of one row which has been put initially in one-to-one correspondence with another row. The child's understanding of number is reflected in his or her ability to understand that the numerical relation between the two rows in question is not affected by various spatial displacements.

Empirical studies seem to support the ordinal number theory as far as the developmental priority relations are concerned, that is, the developmental sequence is ordination concepts, then number concept, then cardination concepts (Brainerd 1979). The operationalization of the concepts in question has not been completely solved, though, and thus the present evaluation of the empirical relevance of these theories is unclear. The definition of the number concept itself has some inherent difficulties. While some authors identify the natural number concept with the understanding of basic operations (addition, subtraction, . . .), others refer to the number invariance task of Piaget as representation of the number concept. The empirical status of these theoretical approaches is of some importance in finding a psychological basis for arithmetics instruction. This implies the question in which temporal sequence conceptual skills should be studied in elementary school, a question for which the present approaches have only tentative empirical connections. And it should be of some importance to be able to evaluate the relevance of certain conceptual skills (including ordination and cardination) for the child's further understanding of mathematics.

To circumvent the problems in the operational definition of single concepts, recent research has tried to identify developmental precursors and developmental lines in the preschool years preceding and underlying the conceptual areas in question (number, cardination, ordination). Not surprisingly, this research is directed towards the child's concrete representations and problem-solving strategies in numerical comparisons, counting, and application of simple operations.

2. Ordinal and Cardinal Aspects in Preschool Development

Ordinal and cardinal aspects of number seem to be present over the whole course of the preschool years. The child's beginning understanding of number, as reflected in the increased understanding and coordinate application of principles of counting beginning at 3 years old (Gelman and Gallistel 1978), gives the child access to the inherent order of the series of natural numbers (e.g., preceding and succeeding numbers). Even though the number series could be thought of at the beginning as a chain of associated stimuli, the child discovers early the order underlying this representation and is able to apply it in comparisons (e.g., knowing that a set of six is greater than a set of five). With the further automatization of counting, the child begins to grasp that the process of counting is itself countable: if the child "counts-on" from a set of five, he or she is able to engage in a process of double counting (counting the unity "counted-on"). Double counting serves as a problem-solving strategy in beginning addition and subtraction tasks (Carpenter et al. 1982). Interestingly, this systematic behavior has not been given much attention in elementary grades. The instructional illustrations of the elementary operations (as the use of the number line) introduce new representational tools for the child, but they should be built upon the problem-solving skills the child has already available.

Children at around the age of 4 begin to apply cardinal solution strategies: they solve comparisons of concrete collections of objects via counting or one-to-one correspondence. Still the child is misled by perceptual cues in such comparisons, for example, the length of a row, and it is only after the child coordinates his or her comparison strategies with an emerging knowledge of the meaning of spatial displacements and transformations that cardinal strategies become independent of specific perceptual features. This knowledge is represented most obviously in Piaget's number invariance task. But even before this knowledge has been constructed (by many children at 6 and 7 years), the child abstracts cardinal aspects. Most 5-year-olds know, for example, that the number of objects in a set counted is independent of the order in which the counting process is performed, that is, the cardinal property in counting remains invariant (the last number counted represents the number of objects). One-to-one correspondence is a strategy systematically applied to 6-year-olds, even though some children might be misled by the perceptual properties of the physical arrangement chosen. The child begins elementary school with a systematic knowledge of cardinal strategies, that is, quantitative comparison rules reflected in counting and one-to-one correspondence.

A theoretical perspective that is largely unexplored would derive the child's construction of an arithmetic unit, which is basic to any elementary operation, from its various concrete experiences with ordinal and cardinal aspects of number tasks, abstracting regularities inherent both in the process of counting and in systematic comparison rules.

3. Number and Measurement

The comparison of lengths with a standard unit of measurement appears to be more difficult than quantitative comparisons of discontinuous sets of objects (via application of arithmetical units). Also Piaget's length conservation task (the invariance of length despite various transformations) follows in development after the number invariance task. This suggests that measuring with units (for any system of measurement) builds upon the child's construction of an arithmetical unit. A second logical structure involved in construction of measurement is the child's construction of asymmetrical and transitive relations (e.g., in comparing three sticks of different lengths) managed by 6- to 7-year-olds (indicating the stage of concrete operations). This developmental sequence suggests a clear priority list for the instruction in measurement (Steffe 1971).

It might be noted in conclusion that in Russian psychological studies the measurement aspect of number has been the starting point of arithmetic instruction, most importantly in the work of Galperin and of Davydov. Despite its great originality, the empirical status of this work, either in its possible implications for the understanding of the number concept or in its relevance for elementary instruction in mathematics, is largely unexplored.

Bibliography

Brainerd C J 1979 *The Origins of the Concept of Number.* Praeger, New York
Carpenter T, Moser J M, Romberg T A (eds.) 1982 *Addition and Subtraction: A Developmental Perspective.* Erlbaum, Hillsdale, New Jersey
Fuson K C 1988 *Children's Counting and Concepts of Number.* Springer-Verlag, New York
Gelman R, Gallistel C R 1978 *The Child's Understanding of Number.* Harvard University Press, Cambridge, Massachusetts
Hooten J R (ed.) 1975 Teaching arithmetic in the elementary school. In: Hooten J R (ed.) 1975 *Soviet Studies in the Psychology of Learning and Teaching Mathematics*, Vol. 14. University of Chicago Press, Chicago, Illinois
Piaget J, Szeminska A 1941 *La Genèse du nombre chez l'enfant.* Delachaux et Niestlé, Neuchâtel
Resnick L B, Ford W W 1981 *The Psychology of Mathematics for Instruction.* Erlbaum, Hillsdale, New Jersey
Saxe G B, Guberman S R, Gearhart M 1987 Social processes in early number development. Monographs of the Society for Research in Child Development 52:2 Serial No 216
Steffe L P 1971 Thinking about measurement. *Arithmetic Teacher* 18: 332–38

Number Theory and Systems in Mathematics Programs

T. E. Kieren

Number theory is a well-defined area of mathematics normally subsuming such topics as divisibility, continued fractions, remainders, and equations with whole number solutions. These topics deal primarily with patterns of whole numbers and operations thereon. From the point of view of school mathematics curriculum development and research, it is the more general notion of patterns of whole numbers and operations which is important. Some aspects of number theory are in school curriculum in their own right. However, number pattern study and generation as a thinking tool for students is useful in developing many other mathematical topics. Further, number theoretic considerations are useful in mathematics education research particularly in the area of problem solving.

Although the choice of the counting unit (e.g., by twos, fives, sevens, tens) and its consequences represents an early entrance of number theory into the curriculum, divisibility is normally considered the primary number theory topic in early school mathematics. The notions of even and odd can be seen in the preschool play of children forming two sets of objects from a given set. Divisibility and its related topics, factor and prime, form one part of a basis of the transition from the arithmetic of whole numbers to that of fractions and polynomials. The study of equations in more than one variable with whole number solutions forms a minor part of secondary-school mathematics. Still, whole number solutions to equations of the form $x^2 + y^2 = r^2$ are important in geometry (Pythagoras theorem) and in elementary analysis and linear algebra.

The study of number patterns and their representations is a part of the development of many topics in mathematics. For example, in considering the number of diagonals of a polygon, the number pattern representation models the geometry. Clearly, this use of number patterns as a tool is central to the study of combinatorics, where problems give rise to whole number patterns and the study of such patterns gives rise to a formal representation. Even in the area of analysis, aspects of number theory in the generic sense are used. This can be seen particularly in the study of Cauchy sequences, infinite series, and series as functions. Thus the number pattern representation tools of number theory have a wide value in school mathematics.

Number theory also plays a central role in mathematical problem solving. One important aspect of this role is the fact that many interesting problems in mathematics are number theoretic or at the very least involve representing number patterns. In number theory problem solving, the calculator and computer play increasing roles both for mathematicians and young students of mathematics.

Finally, the clinical observation of children and adults working on number theoretic problems has provided insights into human problem solving and mathematical thinking. Tracing of behavioral patterns and relating them to the number theoretic patterns in the problem is an important aspect of mathematical problem-solving research. For the curriculum maker, number theory in a discipline sense has a minor role in school mathematics. However, number theoretic patterns and representations are part of many aspects of school mathematics.

Number theory problems provide the researcher with a fertile ground for the study of mathematical thinking and problem-solving behavior (Krutetskiĭ 1976).

Number systems are a particular form of mathematical system. Such systems consist of elements, operations on such elements, the axioms which govern interrelationships in that system, and basic definitions and consequences of the definitions and axioms. Considered structurally, number systems are particular examples of algebraic systems. For example, the integers are an example of an integral domain while the rational numbers form a quotient field. Considered analytically, the concept of number and the interrelationships among systems is part of the foundation of analysis. Here such properties as the topology of the real number line, infinite sequences of rational numbers, and the relationship between number system and function are central.

The number systems of school mathematics—whole numbers, integers, rational numbers, real numbers, complex numbers—form a hierarchy of successively more complex structure. The elements of such systems are useful in modeling such questions as "how many" and "how much" in a myriad of ways. Thus number systems have a central role in mathematics curricula both in the pure and applied sense.

In studying how people come to know number systems, three observations can be made. Although, from a mathematical point of view, structural properties are at the foundation of number systems, from a knowledge-building point of view such formal structural number system knowledge must be about or represent patterns in previous experience. Such patterns can arise from physical experiences or from sets of mathematical sentences. Thus knowledge building with respect to number systems proceeds from less to more formal experience.

Number systems admit varying interpretations. These interpretations can be used as a basis for curriculum development, particularly for developing appropriate collections of informal mathematical experiences out of which the concepts and later the definitions and formal structural knowledge can be built (Griesel 1974). For example, rational numbers can be interpreted as measures. Such an interpretation emphasizes the additive nature of rational numbers. Rational numbers can be interpreted also as operators featuring the multiplicative nature of this system. Such attention in curriculum development allows number system concepts to develop which can be tied to transcendent ideas such as transformations.

The axioms of number systems provide them with a logical base. In studying how persons, and particularly children, build up knowledge of number systems, the axioms themselves point to important problems in knowledge building. For example, in the Peano axioms for the natural numbers "every element has a successor." In the behavior of a child counting a disorderly array, one frequently observes that a child will continue counting indicating objects more than once, exhibiting intuitively, if erroneously in the adult sense, this continuity of "successor." To know whole numbers as a personal knowledge system involves the coordination of behavior systems which parallel the axioms. This area of research on the intuitive bases for number systems is of high interest.

Number systems are a central element in the mathematics curriculum. Formal structural knowledge of such systems flows from less formal experience. Such curriculum experience development and the study of actions of persons as they build up number-system knowledge are informed by detailed consideration of the number systems, their axioms, and their interpretations.

Bibliography

Begle E G 1979 *Critical Variables in Mathematics Education: Findings from a Survey of the Empirical Literature.* National Council of Teachers of Mathematics, Washington, DC

Freudenthal H 1973 *Mathematics as an Educational Task.* Reidel, Dordrecht

Goldin G A, McClintock C E (eds.) 1979 *Task Variables in Mathematical Problem Solving.* ERIC/SMEAC, Columbus, Ohio

Griesel H 1974 *Die Neue Mathematik für Lehrer und Studenten.* Schroedel, Hannover

Krutetskii V A 1976 *The Psychology of Mathematical Abilities in Schoolchildren.* University of Chicago Press, Chicago, Illinois

Lesh R A (ed.) 1976 *Number and Measurement.* ERIC Clearinghouse for Science, Mathematics and Environmental Education, Columbus, Ohio

Measuring in Mathematics

A. J. Bishop

Measuring is concerned with quantifying qualities, and in school mathematics those qualities are spatial—length, area, and volume. In school science other qualities would be met, some commonplace, like time and weight, and some less familiar, like current and energy. The same principles of teaching apply to measuring any quality—developing a good intuitive understanding of the quality, encouraging the search for a repeatable unit, and practising the use of conventional units.

The measurement of space has always been of interest to mathematicians as it is to every person. Intuitive ideas of size are critical to the normal functioning of a human being and it is no surprise to find that the school mathematics curriculum contains much reference to measurement. Strictly, only comparatively recently has "measurement" been the concern—prior to that, teaching would be confined to "working with common units". In practice, this meant carrying out extended computations with complicated units (many nonmetric) using strict algorithms or memorized formulas. Nowadays, through knowledge of research, such as that by Piaget et al. (1960), it is recognized that work on measuring in schools needs to consider three very separate aspects.

1. Understanding Intuitively the Quality to be Measured

What this stage emphasizes is the necessity for a good understanding of the quality prior to working with the conventional units. It is of course possible to teach routine algorithms for routine problems, but these will be totally meaningless exercises if the child has not understood how the quality itself varies and under what transformations it remains the same.

Many experiences outside school will familiarize the child with some of the qualities and their variation—cutting string and tying knots, measuring wood, comparing heights, placing one plate on top of another with the "larger" one under the "smaller" one, pouring water from one container into another, stacking things so they don't fall over, and filling boxes. Measurement experiences have been shown to vary from culture to culture (see, for example, Lancy 1978, Harris 1980) suggesting that schools need to provide the child with more structured experiences.

Firstly there is the need to increase the breadth of experience with the quality—to learn for example, that length does not have to be measured in a straight line, and that surfaces have area whether they are rectangular in shape or curved. Secondly there is the need to "sharpen" the vocabulary and the concept. What does the child mean when it says that one object is "bigger" than another? Thirdly the teacher needs to ensure that the child recognizes how and when two shapes have the same measure of a quality and when they don't. Conservation of length, area, and volume have all been explored in research and have all been shown to pose nontrivial problems for children well into secondary school (Hart et al. 1981).

2. Finding and Using a Repeatable Unit

Moving from the intuitive grasp of the quality to the actual quantification of that quality entails locating a convenient and repeatable unit. For example, children who are comparing the heights of two objects and who have progressed beyond mere visual comparison, try to use their own bodies for this—the span of the hands, or the arms, or holding the hands as if one is at the top of the object and the other is at the bottom—and to move from one to the other to make the comparison. The arbitrariness of the choice of the repeatable unit is interesting to explore at this stage as it gives rise to the fundamental problem of measurement—establishing agreed, fixed units. Once again, the cultural background can provide its own unique choices of units (see, for example, Gay and Cole 1967).

3. Learning to Use Conventional Units

This is not just a matter of performing the actual computations but also of dealing with aspects of accuracy and errors. The teaching of measurement in schools is fundamental for mathematical applications and the National Council of Teachers of Mathematics publication (1976) contains many ideas for the teacher. For example, estimating before measuring seems to be an important strategy (Ibe 1973).

Moreover, in mathematics it is necessary to distinguish between counting and measuring—in the first, discrete objects are being dealt with and whole numbers are therefore being used, whereas in the second, qualities of those objects are being attended to, which are continuous. The accuracy of a measurement is related to the acceptable amount of error involved, and the acceptability is judged in terms of the original problem. Distances between towns are conventionally measured in kilometres or miles, but centimetres and millimetres would probably be necessary for determining the tallest child in the school. Extending this example a little further shows how fundamentally linked errors and measurement are. If two children measured say 1.575 m

in height it would be said that they measured the same, within the limitations of the measuring instruments. There would always be the feeling that they could be separated if only available measuring instruments were more accurate. This is a very common feature of scientific research and shows that absolute equality is a remarkably rare phenomenon (see Dantzig 1954).

Bibliography

Dantzig T 1954 *Number, The Language of Science: A Critical Survey Written for the Non-mathematician*, 4th edn. Allen and Unwin, London
Gay J, Cole M 1967 *The New Mathematics and an Old Culture: A Study of Learning Among the Kpelle of Liberia*. Holt, Rinehart and Winston, New York
Harris P J 1980 Measurement in tribal aboriginal communities. *Developing Educ.* 7(4): 23–28
Hart K M, Brown M L, Küchemann D E 1981 *Children's Understanding of Mathematics: 11–16*. Murray, London
Ibe M D 1973 The effects of using estimation in learning a unit of sixth grade mathematics (Doctoral dissertation, University of Toronto) *Dissertation Abstracts International* 1973 33: 5036
Lancy D (ed.) 1978 The Indigenous Mathematics Project. *Papua New Guinea J. Educ.*, Vol. 14 (special issue)
National Council of Teachers of Mathematics (NCTM) 1976 *Measurement in School Mathematics*. NCTM, Reston, Virginia
Piaget J, Inhelder B, Szeminska A 1960 *The Child's Conception of Geometry*. Routledge and Kegan Paul, London

Estimation in Mathematics Education

P. S. Wilson and E. G. Gibb

Mathematical estimation is the association of a quantity, amount, or size with the number of objects in a collection, the result of a numerical computation, the measure of an attribute of an object, the duration of an event, or the solution of a problem. In some cases, an estimate is the only possible quantity (e.g. world population, disease statistics) and in other cases it is more appropriate and efficient than an exact count (e.g. attendance at a sporting event). Widespread use of computing technology presents a need for estimation skills to verify the reasonableness of computations and solution strategies (Levin 1981). In problem solving, an estimate is often sufficient for examining a conjecture, checking the reasonableness of an answer, or making decisions.

The ability to estimate has been identified as one of the basic competencies recommended for all students (Cockcroft 1982, National Council of Supervisors of Mathematics 1989). Estimation skills are necessary for employment (Dawes and Jesson 1979), and motivate problem solving (Polya 1965). Although there is an increasing need for estimation skills, students find estimating difficult (Benton 1986, Morgan 1989), and receive inappropriate help from teachers and textbooks

(Benton 1986, Reys et al. 1982). When asked to estimate, some students mentally calculate the answer and then round to obtain an estimate (Schoen et al. 1981). This approach is probably a result of narrow classroom treatment of estimation which focuses on rounding and is often taught without a context. Providing a context gives meaning to the estimation and allows students to use successful, informal methods (Morgan 1989). Recent research offers possible directions.

1. Computational Estimation

Researchers agree that estimation skills can be taught in a relatively short period of time (Benton 1986, Reys et al. 1982, Schoen et al. 1981). Findings indicate that teaching estimation skills does not interfere with learning to calculate and several studies report improvement in computational achievement. There is conflicting evidence that estimation improves skill in solving verbal problems (Schoen et al. 1981).

The ability to estimate calculations is correlated with general intelligence, mathematical ability, and the number of strategies used (Benton 1986, Reys et al. 1982). Good estimators possess: (a) a quick and accurate recall of basic facts; (b) an understanding of place value; (c) facility with mental computation and rounding procedures; (d) ability to use multiples of 10; and (e) a tolerance for error (Reys et al. 1982). They are quick and flexible in their choices of strategies, often choosing a comfortable strategy over an efficient strategy. Interviews with good estimators revealed three key processes used for computational estimation. The goal of each process is to create a more mentally manageable form. The first process, reformulation, alters numerical data leaving the problem intact. Rounding numbers is an example of reformulation. Translation, the second process, changes the mathematical structure of the problem. Changing the implied operations and creating an equivalent problem is a form of translation. The third process is compensation, which involves making adjustments to compensate for variation caused by reformulation or translation. Some students use intermediate compensation in the middle of the estimating process and some use final compensation at the end.

2. Measurement Estimation

Measurement estimation can be taught but maturation may be an important factor. Sixth graders were found to be much better estimators than fifth graders in the areas of weight, length, circumference, temperature, and capacity. Ability to estimate linear distances correlates with age, and general measurement estimation ability correlates with perceptual ability (Benton 1986). Benton's review of measurement estimation literature identifies several successful student strategies for estimating length. Prior knowledge is the basis of their strategies. Students iterate a known unit or subdivide the unknown length into known subdivisions. Students compare target objects with known objects. They squeeze the unknown length between two known lengths claiming the measurement estimate is larger than length A but smaller than length B. Strategies for estimating area center around partitioning the object into known regions using rearrangement, repeated addition, or a length times width algorithm. Inappropriate strategies include focusing on only one dimension of the area, usually length.

3. Assessment of Estimation

More research is needed in estimation and particularly in how to teach estimation (Benton 1986). Both researchers and teachers must overcome a major difficulty—assessment (Reys et al. 1982). Estimation is a difficult skill to measure, especially when assessing final results rather than processes. Criteria for good estimates are ambiguous because an estimate is tied to the context of the problem. Standardized testing has forced students to look for the right or wrong answer and has dismissed the value of estimated answers. Reys et al. (1982) offer

the following guidelines for assessment. Timing is critical as too much time allows students to calculate answers and too little time encourages wild guessing. In order to adjust for timing, assessment may need to be individual. Good assessment approaches include: open-ended questions, an interval scale for reporting an estimate, responses judged on order of magnitude, and multiple choice questions that test the reasonableness of an answer. It is even possible to discourage computation by designing a problem (e.g. $7/8 + 1$, $17/18 + 8/9$) that is difficult to compute but quite easy to estimate.

4. Summary

There is general agreement that developing skills in estimation should be a major objective of school mathematics because estimation is essential for literate citizenship and more important than precise calculations or measurements for many common situations. Yet estimation is one of the most neglected skills in mathematics curricula. While teachers feel unprepared to teach estimation, students have an increasing need to engage in estimation activities addressing both computation and measurement problems in specific contexts. Recent studies of estimation, including the variety of estimation contexts, useful strategies, characteristics of good estimators, and existing teaching and assessment practices, should provide a strong foundation for the research needed in better ways to teach and assess estimation skills.

Bibliography

Benton S E 1986 A summary of research on teaching and learning estimation. In: Schoen H, Zweng M (eds.) 1986 *Estimation and Mental Computation*. National Council of Teachers of Mathematics, Reston, Virginia, pp. 239–48

Cockcroft W H 1982 *Mathematics Counts*. HMSO, London

Dawes W G, Jesson D J 1979 Is there a basis for specifying the mathematics requirements of the 16-year old entering employment? *Int. J. Maths Educ. Sci. Technol.* 10(3): 391–400

Levin J A 1981 Estimation techniques for arithmetic: Everyday math and mathematics instruction. *Educ. Stud. Math.* 12: 421–34

Morgan C 1989 A context for estimation. *Maths. in Sch.* 18(3): 16–17

National Council of Supervisors of Mathematics 1989 Essential mathematics for the twenty-first century. *Math. Teach.* 82(6): 470–74

Polya G 1965 *Mathematical Discovery: On Understanding, Learning and Teaching Problem Solving*, Vol. 2. Wiley, New York

Reys R E 1986 Evaluating computational estimation. In: Schoen H, Zweng M (eds.) 1986 *Estimation and Mental Computation*. National Council of Teachers of Mathematics, Reston, Virginia, pp. 225–38

Reys R E, Rybolt J F, Bestgen B J, Wyatt J W 1982 Processes used by good computational estimators. *J. Res. Maths Educ.* 13(3): 183–201

Schoen H L, Friesen C D, Jarrett J A, Urbatsch T D 1981 Instruction in estimating solutions of whole number computations. *J. Res. Maths Educ.* 12: 165–78

Set Theory: Educational Programs

D. Tirosh

Set theory, originated by George Cantor at the end of the nineteenth century, is a branch of mathematics that deals with collections of objects. Any collection of objects is a set if (a) the objects are distinct, and (b), there is a rule for deciding unambiguously whether an object is or is not a member (element) of the set. For instance, {1,2,3} is a set which consists of the three elements 1, 2, and 3. The order of succession of the elements in a set does not matter: the set {1,2} is the same set as {2,1}.

The concept of a set is one of the most fundamental and the most frequently used in mathematics. In fact, almost all the mathematical theories deal with sets. For example, arithmetic refers to sets whose elements are numbers. However, set theory investigates general properties of sets regardless of the kind of elements which comprise these sets.

Among the branches of mathematics, set theory plays a special role. Many mathematical concepts such as number, function, and infinity may be formally defined in terms of set theory. Consequently, certain long-standing mathematical problems, such as the problem of comparing infinite quantities, have been rephrased and solved within set theory. Set theory also serves as a vital tool in the study of the logical and the philosophical foundations of mathematics as well as in the study of the structure of mathematics. This theory has thrown light on the common properties of various mathematical theories such as arithmetic, algebra, and geometry, and serves as a connecting link between these fields. Moreover, set theory has had a great influence on many mathematical fields such as analysis, probability, topology, and geometry.

1. Elementary Set Theory and Cantor's Theory of Transfinite Cardinals

Knott (1977) noted that set theory encompasses two distinct groups of definitions and results. One of them is *Cantor's theory of transfinite numbers* and the other is known as *elementary set theory*.

In his theory of transfinite numbers, Cantor defined infinity in mathematical terms and introduced definite and distinct infinite numbers into mathematics. This part of set theory starts with the concept of set and builds up an analysis of the concept of infinity. It has been described as "the first theory of infinity that has all the incisiveness of modern mathematics" (Hann 1956 p. 1593).

Elementary set theory deals with classification of sets and with properties of operations involving sets. One of the set operations is union. The union of two sets A and B is the union set A ∪ B (A union B) that consists of the elements that are in either A or B or both. This

operation has the commutative property, which means that A ∪ B = B ∪ A. The commutative property of the operation of union does not depend on the kind of elements from which these sets are comprised.

Elementary set theory, developed at the beginning of the nineteenth century, illuminates many branches of mathematics such as measure theory, the theory of probability, and mathematical logic. It is this part of set theory that has been considered as the core of the "new mathematics" reform in mathematics education.

2. Elementary Set Theory in Mathematics Curriculum

Elementary set theory was first presented in the elementary and high-school curricula in the middle of the 1950s as the base of many of the new mathematics programs.

The new mathematics reform in mathematics education was a by-product of a revolution in mathematics itself (Begle 1979) and was especially influenced by the work of the Bourbaki group (Howson et al. 1981). The Bourbaki group emphasized the structural nature of mathematics, the use of uniform language and the important role that set theory played in mathematics. This group argued that the various mathematical theories are logically attached to set theory, and used set theory to present mathematics as a unified structure. Mathematicians and mathematics educators attempted to bring the spirit of the work of Bourbaki into the school curriculum. They argued that set theory demonstrates the structure of mathematics and can give unity to the study of various mathematical concepts such as numbers, graphs, functions, relations, geometry, and logic. The work of Bourbaki was one of the major reasons for the judicious use of the notions and the language of set theory in many of the new mathematics projects.

Another source of support for including elementary set theory in the new mathematics programs came from the psychological research of Piaget and from Bruner's cognitive theory of conceptual development. Piaget's studies on children's conception of number (Piaget 1961) showed that the intuitive development of the concept of number is established on the concept of set, and that the intuitive idea of set is developed at a very early stage in the child's thinking. These findings stimulated the inclusion of basic notions of set theory in elementary school programs. Consequently, many of the new mathematics programs instructed the teaching of the basic idea of set at the kindergarten stage.

Bruner, who was concerned with teaching the "structures of the disciplines," argued that "the curriculum of a subject should be determined by the most fundamental understanding that can be achieved of the underlying principles that give structure to that subject" (Bruner 1960 p. 31). The pedagogical idea of teaching children unified themes of the subject, so that they could relate individual ideas to the general structure, was a fundamental reason for the inclusion of elementary set theory in elementary school programs.

Dienes, a mathematics educator who was deeply influenced by both Piaget's and Bruner's work, emphasized that instruction should take into account the structures of mathematics and the cognitive capabilities of the learners. In his book *The Six Stages in the Process of Learning Mathematics* (1973), as well as in other of his books, he argued that in order to teach children abstract mathematical concepts it is necessary to invent an artificial environment which has been specially constructed so that certain mathematical structures may be drawn from it. He developed structural games which were explicitly designed to embody mathematical concepts. Through these games, Dienes hoped to make the children familiar with various mathematical concepts, including properties of sets. Dienes' structural games have gained wide use in mathematics education and many of the new mathematics projects incorporated his special materials in their teaching programs.

At the beginning of the 1960s, when the new mathematics reform reached its height, most of the mathematics courses and textbooks in countries such as France, Belgium, Great Britain, and the United States initiated a discussion on the notion of set. Various mathematical concepts such as number, operation, relation and function were developed through set theory. Articles in favor of the use of set notions in elementary and secondary schools were written by mathematics educators. The terminology that was used in most of the new mathematics programs was mainly taken from the language of set theory. The content of the elementary school curriculum had not greatly changed but stress was placed on the use of the concept of set, set language, set notations, and operations with sets. Elementary school teachers were encouraged to teach set concepts as a means of helping children in (a) clarifying their understanding of cardinal numbers and arithmetic operations, (b) organizing their thinking processes, and (c) providing a good background for the secondary school curriculum.

The traditional secondary school curriculum was radically altered and new topics, such as linear algebra and transformation geometry, were introduced in most of the new mathematics projects. Many projects, especially in Belgium and France, presented mathematics as a unified subject where set theory served as a link between the different topics that were included in these programs.

3. Criticism of the Inclusion of Elementary Set Theory in the Mathematics Curriculum

In the middle of the 1960s, the new mathematics reform was heavily criticized. The inclusion of set theory in the new programs was one of the topics that raised most of the objections. Mathematicians such as Kline, Courant, and Polya argued that set theory is unsuitable for elementary and secondary schools. They claimed that the mathematical background of the students is insufficient for introducing unifying concepts and that a premature introduction of such concepts is worse than useless. Freudenthal (1973 p. 332) criticized the idea of introducing numbers as an outgrowth of sets and argued that "both as regards content and as regards teaching, mathematics starts with numbers." Kapadia (1976 p. 412) criticized the claim that set theory is the foundation of modern mathematics. He also argued that the child's intellectual progress does not follow modern mathematics and noted that "there is no need to fill other mathematical subjects with set theoretic terms. . . . On the contrary, this should be avoided as much as possible." These mathematicians objected to the inclusion of axiomatic set theory in schools. However, most of the new mathematics projects presented only elementary set theory (Servais 1968, Geddes and Lipsey 1968).

Many teachers were not convinced of the value of the changes in the new curriculum and claimed that set theory is too abstract and its language too technical. Teachers encountered difficulties in changing their approach to mathematics and many of them feel that their training was insufficient to teach set theory. Teachers and parents were worried that the new curriculum would cause learners to suffer from a lack of basic computational skills.

The perception of the new mathematics as a failure was one of the causes of the emergence of the "back to basics" movement in the middle of the 1970s. This movement aimed to improve the basic computational skills of learners and was less concerned with the child's acquisition of the structure of mathematics. Since the emergence of the back to basics movement, the status of set theory in many of the elementary school curricula has changed and it is no longer the heart of the curriculum. Teachers are still advised to use the concept of set in introducing the concept of number but set notations and operations involving sets are no longer so prominent in the elementary school curricula of the 1980s. However, many of the secondary-school level programs still introduce mathematics as an integrated subject with unifying concepts such as sets and functions. Set theory notations are widely used and concepts such as set and 1–1 correspondence are incorporated in the instruction of various mathematics topics such as analysis, probability, and computer science. Models of sets are used in many branches of mathematics such as mathematical logic and probability.

4. Cantor's Theory of Transfinite Numbers in Mathematics Curriculum

Cantor's theory of transfinite numbers is considered to be "the finest product of mathematics genius, and one of the supreme achievements of purely intellectual human activity" (Hilbert 1964 p. 139). This theory can provide learners with a wider understanding of the concept of infinity and the concept of number (Hann 1956). It can also serve as a vehicle for understanding the certitude of mathematics methods and the structure of mathematical theories (Russell 1956).

In most countries the theory of transfinite numbers is a university level course for students in scientific faculties. During the new mathematics reform some projects such as the Contemporary School Mathematics (CSM) program in Great Britain and George and Frederique Papy's program in Belgium included this theory in their curriculum for the upper-high-school classes. Most of these projects did not go beyond a discussion about denumerable sets. An evaluation of the extent to which high-school students may acquire the concepts and the procedures related to the theory of transfinite cardinals has hardly been found in the mathematics education research literature.

In 1985, an attempt was made to check the possibility of teaching 10th grade students from academically selective high schools, the basic concepts and proofs of the Cantorian theory of transfinite cardinals (Tirosh 1985). It was found that about 75 percent of the students were able to understand and to use correctly most of the concepts that were taught. Moreover, as a result of the instruction, the students gained a deeper understanding of the important role that definitions and proofs have in mathematics. However, the possibility of teaching the Cantorian theory of transfinite cardinals efficiently in regular high school has not yet been examined.

Nowadays, mathematicians and mathematics educators have raised doubts about the role that set theory should have in mathematics instruction. The research that has been done with regard to set theory concentrates mainly on showing that it is possible to use the concepts, operations, and technical vocabulary of set theory at a very early age (Suppes and McKnight 1961). Nevertheless, not enough research has been done

on the influence of learning set theory on children's acquisition of the structure of mathematics. There is a need for further research that will analyze the influence of teaching set theory on children's acquisition and understanding of mathematics. Such research is essential for determining the proper place of set theory in mathematics instruction.

Bibliography

Begle E G 1979 *Critical Variables in Mathematics Education: Findings from a Survey of the Empirical Literature.* National Council of Teachers of Mathematics, Washington, DC

Bruner J S 1960 *The Process of Education.* Harvard University Press, Cambridge, Massachusetts

Dienes Z P 1973 *The Six Stages in the Process of Learning Mathematics* [trans.]. National Foundation for Educational Research, Windsor

Freudenthal H 1973 *Mathematics as an Educational Task.* Reidel, Dordrecht

Geddes D, Lipsey S I 1968 Sets—Natural, necessary, (k)nowable? *Arith. Teach.* 15: 337–40

Hann H 1956 The crisis of intuition. In: Newman J R (ed.) 1956 *The World of Mathematics.* Simon and Schuster, New York, pp. 1593–611

Howson G, Kietel C, Kilpatrick J 1981 *Curriculum Development in Mathematics.* Cambridge University Press, Cambridge

Kapadia R 1976 Set theory and logic in school. *Educ. Stud. Math.* 6(2): 409–13

Knott R P 1977 A history of set theory notation. *Math. Sch.* 6(2): 17–20

Piaget J 1961 *The Child's Conception of Number.* Routledge and Kegan Paul, London

Russell B R 1956 Mathematics and the metaphysicians. In: Newman J R (ed.) 1956 *The World of Mathematics.* Simon and Schuster, New York, pp. 1576–92

Servais W 1968 Present-day problems of mathematical instruction. *Math. Teach.* 61: 791–800

Suppes P, McKnight B A 1961 Sets and numbers in grade one, 1959–1960. *Arith. Teach.* 8: 287–90

Tirosh D 1985 The Intuition of Infinity and its Relevance for Mathematics Education. Unpublished doctorial dissertation, Tel Aviv University, Israel.

Rational Numbers in Mathematics Education

R. Lesh

Rational numbers are of the form a/b where a and b are whole numbers (positive or negative) and b is not zero.

Test results (Carpenter et al. 1980) consistently show that rational number concepts are among the most troublesome topics in elementary mathematics. They are also among the most important. Ideas like ratio, rate, and proportions are useful in a wide range of everyday applications (Bell 1974) and they provide a basis for the introduction of a variety of algebraic concepts in high school.

Why are rational number concepts so difficult? Some concepts, like proportional reasoning (Noelting 1980),

require formal operational processes. Others, like percents, may require only concrete operational reasoning, but are not intuitive or obvious to students who have not been taught certain specific notation systems (e.g., decimals) or "models" (e.g., Cartesian coordinates) for interpreting and coding their experiences. Some rational number ideas were invented relatively late in the history of science. These hard-won historical achievements are reflected in the names that are associated with the various number systems: for example, natural numbers (versus "unnatural"), positive numbers (versus "negative"), rational numbers (versus "irrational"), real numbers (versus "unreal"), and so on.

Rational number ideas are also difficult because they require students to abandon, modify, or significantly reorganize ideas that were true in more restricted situations, but are no longer true in rational number situations; for example, multiplication always makes things bigger, multiplication is the same as repeated addition, and so on.

Rational number is really a "megaconcept" whose meaning requires students to understand progressively each of the following distinct subconcepts, as well as to understand how the various subconcepts are related to one another (Kieren 1976).

(a) *Fractions*. 3/4 of a pie is read "three-fourths" as though "fourths" are the objects being counted and "three" tells "how many." Fractions do not always describe part–whole relationships. Sometimes (e.g., 4/3 cups of milk), the "part" is bigger than the unit or (e.g., when fractions are used to describe sets of discrete objects rather than continuous quantities) the unit may not be a single, "whole" object.

(b) *Ratios*. The ratio 3/4 is read "3 to 4." "/" indicates a relationship between two distinct (and perhaps qualitatively different) kinds of quantities (e.g., cookies to children).

(c) *Rates*. These describe a single quantity (e.g., speed) in terms of two other quantities (e.g., distance and time). 3/4 miles per hour is read as a single number "three-fourths" as the coefficient for a ratio of two quantities. Only at a sophisticated level is "3/4 miles per hour" considered equivalent to the ratio "3 miles/4 hours."

(d) *Indicated quotients*. 3/4 is read "3 divided by 4." "/" is interpreted as division. This usually happens only when "/" is part of a more complex algebraic statement like $(m + n)/p = x$ or, for example, when it is necessary to change 3/4 to a decimal.

(e) *Linear coordinates*. 3/4 is interpreted as a point on the number line. Salient relationships are those associated with the metric topology of the real number line, that is, betweenness, density, distance, order, and (non)completeness rather than algebraic properties associated with fractions, ratios, or rates. In this interpretation, rational numbers are regarded as a subset of the real number system, rather than as an extension of the integers or natural numbers as in other interpretations. In the Cartesian coordinate system, 3/4 may be interpreted as the line containing all ordered pairs (x, y) where $x/y = 3/4$.

(f) *Decimals*. Rational numbers are represented in base 10 as terminating or repeating decimals.

(g) *Operators*. Rational numbers are interpreted as transformations for geometric shapes (e.g., stretches), quantitative measures (e.g., exchange rates), numbers, or sets.

Important instructional issues include: determining an appropriate sequence to introduce the above topics (Payne 1976), identifying pictures and materials to illustrate qualitatively distinct concepts (Post et al. 1982), and finding ways to relate rational number ideas to other topics (e.g., measurement, calculator use) and to other subject matter areas (e.g., science). All of the above understandings go well beyond the routine computational skills typically emphasized in schools.

Bibliography

Bell M S 1974 What does "everyman" really need from school mathematics? *Maths. Teach.* 67: 196–204

Carpenter T P, Corbitt M K, Kepner H S, Lindquist M M, Reys R 1980 Results of the second NAEP mathematics assessment: Secondary school. *Maths. Teach.* 73: 329–38

Kieren T E 1976 On the mathematical, cognitive, and instructional foundations of rational numbers. In: Lesh R A (ed.) 1976 *Number and Measurement: Papers from a Research Workshop.* ERIC/SMEAC, Columbus, Ohio

Noelting G 1980 The development of proportional reasoning and the ratio concept, Part 1: Differentiation of stages. *Educ. Stud. Math.* 11: 217–53

Payne J N 1976 Review of research on fractions. In: Lesh R, Bradhard D (eds.) 1976 *Number and Measurement: Papers from a Research Workshop.* ERIC/SMEAC, Columbus, Ohio

Post T, Behr M, Lesh R 1982 Rational number concepts. In: Lesh R, Landau M (eds.) 1982 *Acquisition of Mathematical Concepts and Processes.* Academic Press, New York

Probability and Statistics

E. Fischbein

The disciplines of probability and statistics both deal with chance events. The theory of probability sets up formal, mathematical models for measuring chances of possible outcomes in uncertain situations. Inferential statistics use concepts and theorems of the theory of probability in order to make inferences concerning an entire population on the basis of sample data.

1. Importance

The teaching of these disciplines is important for the following reasons:

(a) They play an important role in various branches of physical, biological, and behavioral sciences, and in industry, economics, medicine, meteorology, politics, and so on.

(b) The world is full of uncertainty and therefore school must develop in pupils not only deterministic but also probabilistic ways of analyzing, interpreting, and predicting.

(c) These disciplines constitute an excellent example of the dual nature of mathematical thinking: mathematics is a system of purely ideal concepts and operations and, at the same time, it is a powerful tool for describing, analyzing, and predicting practical situations. As Freudenthal described it: "I like probability . . . because it is the best opportunity to show students how to mathematize, how to apply mathematics . . ." (Freudenthal 1970 p. 154).

(d) The child gets the opportunity to become involved in situations that are similar to a real scientific approach: to formulate predictions on theoretical grounds (a priori calculated probabilities), to perform corresponding experimentations (resulting in relative frequencies OECD), and to compare the two categories of results.

2. Psychological Background

According to Piaget and Inhelder, only at the formal operational stage (ages 12–15) is the child able to gain a full understanding of the concept of probability as a synthesis between the ideas of fortuity and necessity (Piaget and Inhelder 1951). Other researchers argue that even preschool children are able to perform probabilistic estimations, provided the arithmetical computation requested is simple enough (Yost et al. 1963, Davies 1965, Goldberg 1966, Fischbein 1975). The reason for this apparent discrepancy is that Piaget and Inhelder are referring to the formal notion of probability, while other authors consider mostly intuitive estimations.

A major psychological obstacle to learning probability and statistics is represented by the difficulty of using deductive reasoning to interpret chance events. The learner has to understand that the same event may appear to be completely unpredictable when considered as an isolated one, and subject to deductive, predictive considerations if it is envisaged as an element of mass phenomena. Nowadays, mathematics and science education tend, generally, to emphasize univocal, deterministic thinking, while almost completely neglecting the probabilistic approach. Because of this lack of symmetry, the synthesis between the possible and the necessary, on which the concept of probability is based, does not, in fact, occur (Fischbein 1975). The teaching of probability and statistics must, then, start as early as possible, certainly before the full crystallization of the basic intellectual schemes (that is, not later than the age of 12–13).

3. The Teaching

Since the early 1960s, various national and international meetings devoted to mathematical education have strongly recommended the inclusion of probability and statistics in school mathematics curricula: the Commission on Mathematics in 1959; the Royaumont Seminar in 1959; the OECD Conference in Athens, Greece in 1963; the Cambridge Conference in 1963. Every international congress on mathematical education held so far (Lyon, France 1969; Exeter, UK 1972; Karlsruhe, FRG 1976; Berkeley, USA 1980) included a section devoted to the teaching of probability and statistics, and in 1969 a conference held at Carbondale, Illinois, in the United States was devoted to this topic (see Råde 1970).

Once probability and statistics were taught only in universities and colleges: in mathematics departments as an axiomatic body of knowledge and in departments with a practical character (such as biology, social sciences, etc.) mainly as collections of practical procedures with little theoretical background.

Since the 1960s, probability and statistics have become a part of the mathematical curricula of high-school classes. Among the topics generally studied are the relation between probability and relative frequencies; simple and compound events; the concept of sample space; probability of unions and intersections of events; conditional probability; the law of large numbers; binomial, normal and Poisson distributions; confidence intervals; and so on.

Comparatively recently, authors of mathematical curricula began to consider the teaching of introductory notions of probability and statistics in elementary classes as possible and desirable. Various experimental programs were set up, among them those of the School Mathematics Study Group (SMSG) of the Comprehensive School Mathematics Program (CSMP). More recently, the Schools Council Project on Statistical Education (Sheffield, UK) (see Holmes 1981), the Probability Project of Matal (Tel Aviv University, Israel), the Chance and Probability Concepts Project (Loughborough University, UK), and so on, were organized (Barnett 1982, Grey et al. 1982).

At the elementary level, the teaching of probability and statistics is based on empirical grounds. The students are asked to perform defined experiments leading to chance events (such as tossing coins or throwing dice), to record the obtained results, to set up exhaustive inventories of possible outcomes by using tree diagrams and, finally, to compare a priori calculated probabilities with relative frequencies. The main aim of these activities is to improve the child's intuitive background for learning probabilities and statistics.

Bibliography

Barnett V (ed.) 1982 *Teaching Statistics in Schools Throughout the World*. International Statistical Institute, Voorburg

Davies C 1965 Development of the probability concept in children. *Child Dev.* 36: 779–89

Fischbein E 1975 *The Intuitive Sources of Probabilistic Thinking in Children*. Reidel, Dordrecht

Freudenthal H 1970 The aims of teaching probability. In: Råde L (ed.) 1970 pp. 151–67

Garfield J, Ahlgren A 1988 Difficulties in learning basic concepts in probability and statistics: implications for research. *Journal of Research in Mathematics Education* 19(1): 44–63

Goldberg S 1966 Probability judgments by preschool children: Task conditions and performance. *Child Dev.* 37: 157–67

Grey D R, Holmes P, Barnett V, Constable G M (ed.) 1982

Proceedings of the First International Conference on Teaching Statistics. Teaching Statistics Trust, Sheffield

Holmes P 1981 Why teach statistics and what statistics should be taught to pupils aged 11–16. In: Råde L (ed.) 1981 *Proceedings, Göteborg Symposium on Teaching Statistics*. Chalmers University, Göteborg, pp. 10–15

Piaget J, Inhelder B 1951 *La Genèse de l'idée de hasard chez l'enfant*. Presses Universitaires de France, Paris

Råde L (ed.) 1970 *The Teaching of Probability and Statistics*. Almqvist and Wiksell, Uppsala

Yost P, Siegel A, Andrews J 1963 Noverbal probability judgments by young children. *Child Dev.* 33: 769–80

Transformation Geometry Programmes

A. J. Bishop

For many hundreds of years, Euclid's geometry was the only contact school children had with the mathematics of space. Mathematicians had however been developing other formulations, one of which led to a focus on the dynamics of transforming shapes rather than on the details of the shapes themselves. Transformation geometry is not strictly a different geometry, but is rather a different approach to the development of geometric ideas. The transformations studied at school consist of translations, rotations, reflections, enlargements, and shearings.

In his talk at the epoch-making Royaumont seminar in 1959 (OEEC 1961), Professor Dieudonné gave the rallying cry "Euclid must go!" and proposed a complete revision of the geometry taught in schools. The problem as he saw it was firstly with the methods of teaching geometry then used in school and secondly with what might be called the "objects" of geometric study. The fact that in many school systems of the world, transformation geometry has virtually replaced the traditional study of Euclid is testament both to the zeal of the reformers and to the general acceptability of their ideas.

Concerning firstly the methods of teaching geometry which the transformation approach allows, it can be seen that ideas of rotation and reflection are all intuitively familiar to young children. Many actions of the body operate on objects in our environment by means of rotations, for example, throwing and twisting, and mirrors, windows, and water give us reflections (Dienes and Golding 1967–68). It is very easy to provide experiences in schools which extend and clarify these familiar transformations. This appeal to the intuition lays the foundations for geometry as an empirical study in schools. Actual objects can be transformed as can drawn shapes at a later stage. Many paper-folding activities can be developed and connections made with aesthetic ideas of pattern, symmetry, and balance. Even later,

the transformations can be symbolized algebraically and systematically analysed. Combinations of transformations can be explored, and a suitable axiomatic treatment proposed, linking geometry with other branches of mathematics (Wynne Wilson 1977).

The "objects" of this geometric study are not the details of particular shapes but are highly general operations and relationships. However this is not to say that objects such as triangles, circles, quadrilaterals, and polygons generally are ignored. In fact, parallels relate to translations, circles relate to rotations, and perpendiculars relate to reflections, and many Euclidean theorems can be interpreted transformationally. The transformations predominantly studied in schools now are the "rigid" motions of the plan (where distances between points are preserved), that is, translations, rotations, reflections; enlargements and similarities; and affine transformations (where parallelism is preserved), that is, shears, stretches. (More generally one could also include topological transformations here.) The transformational approach to geometry enables it to connect with other parts of mathematics like vectors, matrices, abstract algebra, and group theory.

Bibliography

Bauersfeld H, Otte M, Steiner H G 1974 Proc. of the ICMI—IDM Regional Conf. on the Teaching of Geometry. Schriftenreihe des IDM, Bielefeld

Coxford A F 1973 A transformation approach to geometry. In: Henderson K B (ed.) 1973 *Geometry in the Mathematics Curriculum*. National Council of Teachers of Mathematics, Reston, Virginia

Dienes Z P, Golding E W 1967–68 *Geometry Through Transformation*. Herder and Herder, New York

Organisation for European Economic Co-operation (OEEC) 1961 *New Thinking in School Mathematics*. Organisation for Economic Co-operation and Development (OECD), Paris

Wynne Wilson W 1977 *The Mathematics Curriculum: Geometry*. Blackie, Glasgow

Computer Literacy Programs

H. H. Russell

The concept of "computer literacy" is widely known, although the majority of both children and adults in industrialized countries do not know exactly what a computer is nor how to use one. The concept is known

because the majority of people have seen computers and are aware of the fact that in the very near future they will need to overcome their own "illiteracy." Adults and children will need instruction to accomplish this, therefore teachers are going to have to be trained who can pass on this instruction.

There have been a number of distinct eras in the history of the computer literacy concept. The first era spanned the decade of the 1950s, and during that period the target group for computer literacy courses consisted of graduate students and professors. The courses offered were of a highly sophisticated nature, as were those offered during the second era, roughly spanning the 1960s, a period when the undergraduate students and the business community were the focus of computer literacy programs. By the time the third era arrived, the level of sophistication of literacy courses was reduced appropriately for the new target audience—high-school students. The final stage to date in this downward-simplification sequence began in the 1980s, when the courses focused on the elementary-school student, and others who missed out in the earlier eras. There are very few features in common across all eras, but one is of special significance in the present context. The subject mathematics has remained dominant throughout, and mathematics teachers have remained at the center of most such enterprises.

One definition of computer literacy should be recorded at this point. Anderson and Klassen (1981) propose "whatever understanding, skills, and attitudes one needs to function effectively within a given social role that directly or indirectly involves computers." This satisfies the need to cover the various eras through which the concept has passed, as well as taking into account the wide variation in present-day individual needs. The fact that it focuses attention on the individual and his/her needs rather than on the machine and its capabilities is consistent with growing optimism about the possibility that the machine will serve people rather than the reverse.

A common strategy for presentation of literacy courses during the fourth era is to prepare instructions for the student which can be printed on the video screen. Typically the student sits at a keyboard and the instructions are sufficiently clear on the video screen that he/she can proceed to program the machine to do something. In fact, one such program for literacy type instruction listed among 25 computer literacy modules on the Minnesota Educational Computing Consortium project is labeled "How to get the Computer to do Something." Thus the individual's introduction to the machine can be relatively painless, and it can be done in private. A simple language such as BASIC, usually introduced early in such courses, gives the learner the extended power that even the inexpensive microcomputers possess.

Another approach to literacy holds great promise because it is suitable for young children who are still at the prereading stage in their development and it achieves a fundamental type of literacy through its use of constructs from mathematics and logic. The language involved is LOGO, a special purpose language used by Seymour Papert to lead young students safely through the stages of reasoning identified by Jean Piaget. LOGO is currently available on the type of microcomputers found in elementary schools, and hence this powerful approach is not restricted to the laboratories and to the selected schools which house very expensive machines.

Persons who have learned to use a computer and who have opportunities to continue "hands on" contact have little difficulty in overcoming the computer mystique. They know the machine is limited in its function to what it is programmed to do, and hence they are not susceptible to panic about the possibility of machines turning on their users. In spite of the advantages which contact brings to the computer user, there remains the problem of proliferation of inappropriate use. The fact that the so-called "law of the hammer" is popular among computer instructors supports the need for attention. Ragsdale (1982) describes the law of the hammer which is not really a law but rather a suggestion which illustrates a point. The suggestion is to imagine a 2-year-old being presented with his/her first hammer and then watching to see what needs hammering. The answer is "more than nails." In the case of the first-time computer user, the potential for misuse and overuse is very high indeed, but time will cure this problem. Such a hope is based on the assumption that the most appropriate computer uses eventually will attract the most users.

The time period over which the literacy problems are overcome is not easy to predict. What is clear, however, is that the slow progress of the computer in education which characterized the 1960s and the 1970s is likely to be remedied by the low cost of microcomputers. Research surveys into the availability of machines projected a computer in every school in industrialized countries by the mid-1980s and banks of computers available for all class groups of youngsters soon after.

Although the availability of machines seems to be assured, and the type of programming needed to overcome the literacy problem is already available, it is nevertheless quite unclear what will be the most appropriate type of configuration to deliver the service. During the beginning years of the fourth era it may be necessary, and in fact possible, to make considerable progress with one machine, or less, per class. As machine availability increases and the various uses of the machines are properly assessed, it may be determined that a bank of 10 to 15 machines for a class for part of the day may satisfy most of the commonly agreed needs.

Bibliography

Anderson R E, Klassen D L 1981 A conceptual framework for developing computer literacy instruction. *AEDS J.* 16: 128–50

Papert S 1980 *Mindstorms: Children, Computers and Powerful Ideas.* Basic Books, New York

Ragsdale R G 1982 *Computers in the Schools: A Guide to Planning.* Ontario Institute for Studies in Education (OISE), Toronto, Ontario

Issues in Mathematics Education

History of Mathematics Education

C. Keitel, G. Schubring and R. Stowasser

While the development of mathematics, at least in Western civilizations, is well-documented in the professional literature (Boyer 1968, Struik 1949), much less is known about the history of mathematics education. Mathematics education begins with its institutionalization in very specialized places of learning. It presupposes mathematical knowledge systematically ordered in any way, originating from solving problems, generalizing methods, classifying results, and so on, combined with teaching methods reflecting to some extent the educational goals of very different societies in history.

1. Ancient Times

There is ample evidence from proto-Sumerian times (before 3000 BC) that organized teaching was carried out, presumably in the temple, and that the knowledge taught there was organized systematically. Mathematics was a substantial part of the instruction which included metrological systems based on arithmetical principles and area measures. Around 2500 BC a profession of scribes emerged who were trained at the school. The scribes—who were not identical with the priesthood or with the body of higher officials—performed very important functions which were essential for the legitimating ideology of the state. Although the integration of the Sumerian school and the scribes into the state administration caused a restricted determination of mathematics teaching to practical affairs, the institution of the scribal school—edubba—produced not only the dissemination of mathematical knowledge, but also the systematization and further development of mathematics.

The edubba in the old Babylonian society had its climax about 1800 BC. The scribal profession became more independent as a social body, and the school gained more autonomy. Typically the scribe became proud of doing "pure" mathematics. Problem solving, the main issue of mathematics teaching since its origin, was now more concerned with whimsical problems than with realistic applications.

There is no reliable information about mathematical instruction in the valleys of the Indus and Yangtze rivers in the last millenia BC, but a little is known about ancient Egypt. The chief sources, the Rhind and the Moscow papyri, were intended as manuals for students. The instruction was mostly of a practical nature, and calculation was the main method for handling the exercises; problems were concerned with beer, pyramids, or the inheritance of land. Even Egyptian geometry was mainly a branch of applied arithmetic. The rules of calculation were used only in specific concrete cases without any heuristic reflections.

In Greece, mathematics as a science and as a teaching subject played a drastically different role. The deductive organization of geometry and the philosophical discussion of principles are traditionally attributed to Thales of Miletus (about 624–548 BC). Somewhat later Pythagoras of Samos (about 580–500 BC) associated mathematics teaching more closely with a love of wisdom than with practical affairs. The design of the four branches in the quadrivium: arithmetic (numbers at rest), geometry (magnitudes at rest), music (numbers in motion), and astronomy (magnitudes in motion) has been ascribed to Archytas (circa 400 BC) who was a member of the Pythagorean school. Mathematics education was shaped at the time when a bold attack was made on so many fundamental mathematical problems: the ratio of incommensurable magnitudes, the trisection of the angle, the duplication of the cube, the squaring of the circle, the paradoxes of motion, the validity of the infinitesimal methods, and so on. Since then, some knowledge of mathematics has been considered as a requirement for an educated person, for the study of mathematics illuminates the study of philosophy and sharpens and quickens the mind.

A century later, Euclid of Megara, who was noted for his teaching ability, wrote a most successful mathematics textbook called the *Elements* (circa 300 BC). Perhaps no book other than the Bible can boast as many editions (more than 1,000) as the *Elements*, and no mathematical book has had a comparable influence. It has dominated the teaching of geometry for more than 2,000 years.

The Romans continued the Greek system of general education for the propertied classes of society. (For the socially and economically disadvantaged, mathematics education is a very modern phenomenon.) Elements of arithmetic and geometry were taught in the schools from the time children were 10–12 years old. After this preparatory school, future politicians were trained in "rhetoric schools" in which the disciplines of the quadrivium were taught as supplementary subjects.

After the decline of the Roman Empire, the Islamic civilization kept alive the traditions of the Hellenistic culture. The main contribution was the preservation, reorganization, and improvement of a large body of mathematical literature.

2. The Middle Ages

In the Middle Ages there were only scattered institutions of higher learning where mathematics was taught: private schools or institutions and scholars who were dependent on dynasties, courts, or patronages (mainly in the Islamic countries, Japan, and China). The teaching of elementary mathematics was limited to satisfying the needs of certain professions, especially the clergy. In India the training of the Brahman included the ritual geometry based on special textbooks. In the *madrasa*, the Islamic religious schools, arithmetic and algebra were taught by means of arithmetical textbooks.

In spite of Charlemagne's efforts, education in Western Europe remained confined to the monastery schools, which were fundamentally training schools for the clergy. Mathematics and astronomy were taught there to enable the priests to calculate the exact dates of the religious holidays. The municipal schools that emerged after the thirteenth century in Western Europe included almost no mathematics instruction. People who needed arithmetical skills for their profession could be trained only by private tutors or by the guild of so-called arithmetical masters (*Rechenmeister*). However, institutions were established to teach geometrical skills related to the construction of gothic cathedrals; but this instruction was secret and only for the members of the architect's guild (*Bauhütte*).

3. The Impact of Economic and Political Changes

The economic and political changes in the fifteenth and sixteenth centuries influenced mathematics education in two respects. The revival of the work of Greek scientists enriched and improved mathematics education at the universities, and it helped further the development of mathematics. Beginning in Italy, mathematicians increasingly became specialists rather than encyclopedists. Besides, a public school system was set up with preparatory or Latin schools at the elementary level and the grammar or scholar schools at the secondary level. The schools were first established in Protestant countries after the Reformation, and were later disseminated by the Jesuits in the Catholic countries. Until the end of the eighteenth century mathematics played only a marginal role in general education. The Latin schools included nearly no arithmetic, and in the grammar school curriculum, mathematics had an inferior position.

However, mathematics instruction had to be improved to meet the social needs of the developing mercantile and trading classes. Students were trained in practical skills and computational techniques for vocational purposes in private or public schools in the cities. Hence the need arose for more reliable methods of learning and autonomously treating mathematics. The scholastic "imitatio" was complemented by problem solving; the collection and construction of "problems" became a special task for mathematics teachers; problems and their rules were published in printed textbooks. Textbooks were no longer written in Latin, but in the vernacular.

A more advanced education was given in professional institutions for the nobility or in private instruction for interested amateurs like Euler's *Letters to a Princess*. At the end of the eighteenth century the philosophy of enlightenment exerted enormous influence on the conceptions of education. This justified the establishment of a public school system for general education and the introduction of arithmetic and elementary geometry into the curriculum of primary schools and of mathematics into the curriculum of secondary schools. At the same time Pestalozzi created a decisive progress in the method of mathematics teaching. As a result of psychological considerations of "child-centered" or "natural" learning, the pedagogical conception of instruction was based on the visual–objective and sensual activity of the pupil.

The French Revolution sought to abolish the clergy's domination over education and to establish a school system for the new bourgeois society. Rapidly growing demands for mathematics for engineering and military science combined with attempts to disseminate rationalism through the introduction of modern sciences and mathematics into the curriculum of reformed schools, universities and new institutions. The rise of the French nation in the Napoleonic era was partly attributed to the efficiency of her army which was commanded by officers who were excellently trained at the *Ecole Polytechnique* which had such illustrious mathematics teachers as Lagrange, Laplace, and Monge.

French ideas of mathematically and scientifically oriented education were adopted by Prussian universities and the state school system. A comprehensive educational theory emerged based on the idealistic view of the individual. The Humboldt reforms developed the concept of "*Bildung*" as the paramount goal of all human intellectual and mental development: as a totality of knowledge and judgment, and as the process of education. Science and mathematics had a dual role: to provide essential subjects of *Bildung*, and to represent the learning process at the most advanced level. This established unity of science and education, research and instruction mediated between social and individual demands, at least as a program. During the nineteenth century the concept of *Bildung* shrank to a mere theory of the syllabus in a tripartite school system with three different main goals: in the *Gymnasium* (grammar school) was taught formative Platonic pure mathematics; in technical schools (*Realschule*) was taught applied mathematics related to trade, commerce, and banking; and in "nonacademic" schools was taught computation and applied "social" arithmetic.

Most of the developed countries followed the Prussian model of a tripartite school system. Only in the United States was a comprehensive school system set up. The establishment of a state school system in Prussia was supplemented by the institutionalization of a state teacher training system. School mathematics became an independent body of knowledge, created by new textbooks and collections of exercises, and turned away from Euclid's *Elements*. The formation and separation of a special body of knowledge in school mathematics is important for the formation of a professional class of teachers of mathematics. In other European countries such as England, the formation of teacher associations and professional organizations caused enormous changes in mathematics education by developing new textbooks and instructional materials and setting up common professional meetings and communication centers.

4. The Twentieth Century

At the beginning of the twentieth century, worldwide reforms in mathematics education were brought about by different social problems. In European countries reform efforts started because new technological developments called for unifying mathematics education and teaching it as an applied science in the engineering and natural sciences. A modernized syllabus was introduced in France in 1904 which favored mathematical applications in technology. It was quite similar to efforts in Germany: the Meraner syllabus or Klein program proposed a structuring of the entire mathematics education program based on the concepts of function, heuristic principles, and the didactics of visualizing. The syllabus included geometrical propaedeutic for the seventh and eighth grades (secondary I) and calculus for the secondary II of the *lycée* or *Gymnasium*. The introduction of calculus was the result of a violent reform controversy in Germany. In England, where Euclid had remained the only criterion for university entrance examinations up to 1903, the curriculum was likewise broadened.

In the United States, increasing numbers of immigrants and the availability of comprehensive school education for a greater section of the population necessitated changes in aims, content, and organization of mathematics education. Freer access to schools resulted in the development and extension of examination systems and testing, which became the important criteria for curriculum construction and its evaluation and realization: mathematics education had to match social needs and fulfill economical criteria of efficiency. The

development of general curriculum construction principles tried to embed mathematics education in a concept of social integration.

The International Commission of Mathematics Education (ICME), founded in 1908, was concerned with the implementation and dissemination of ideas to reform mathematics education throughout the world, especially in countries which already had an established secondary-school system. Along with the reform, teacher-training institutions were founded or improved; at teacher colleges and at some universities the first chairs for mathematics "didactics" or mathematics education were founded.

5. After the Second World War

After two World Wars many countries once more made extraordinary efforts to adapt their mathematics and science education to the requirements of a civilization increasingly dominated by science and technology. In the 1950s in the United States attempts to modernize college and introductory courses and enrich them with more demanding mathematical content were frustrated by the low level of understanding and knowledge of mathematics displayed by the students emerging from high school: the mathematics curriculum of the secondary and later the elementary school became a matter of concern for university mathematicians. Science and mathematics now received the social appreciation they had never had before. The result was a wave of reform in school mathematics which proved to be more far-reaching and fundamental than had ever been contemplated in the first instance. Many social groups and forces joined the reform movement which produced a great variety of goals, approaches, and contributions from different scientific positions. Federal agencies and state administrations funded and directed the reform activities. Reform became a school revolution by widening attempts to modernize school mathematics to ambitious comprehensive and advanced mathematics education in all subjects.

In European countries, which followed the reform wave a little later, the context in which mathematics curriculum reforms took place differed considerably from that in the United States. Two characteristics peculiar to the United Kingdom scene strongly influenced the way reforms proceeded: first, they were closely connected with and influenced by the reorganization of the whole educational system towards a comprehensive education for all; and second, the teachers had a strong say in educational decision making, and their professional associations became prominent guides of reform and curriculum development.

In the Soviet Union, which may be noticed here as an extreme example for centralized, long-term bureaucratic reform activities, similar to those in the Federal Republic of Germany or France, work on a new mathematics curriculum, stressing science orientation of the syllabus and textbooks, started in 1966. In following the structures and systematic hierarchy of the discipline to a very great extent, including new topics and transferring others to earlier grades, with a high decree of formalization and theoretical precision, this curriculum bore resemblance to the first big curriculum development projects of the new mathematics era in the United States. Unlike the American mathematics projects, the Soviet curriculum has been able to rely on cooperation of the sociological, psychological, and mathematical disciplines from the beginning in a well-defined organizational frame and has not had to strive for acceptance on the market: it is obligatory for all of the 10-year-olds of compulsory schooling, and at an advanced level it is consistent and universal to a degree unequalled in any comparable big nation.

The dissemination of mathematics curriculum reforms by international organizations like UNESCO and the Organisation for Economic Co-operation and Development (OECD) provided the developing countries with curriculum conceptions for the task which they were facing just after decolonization: the establishment of their own public and compulsory education system.

In most countries the influence of the curriculum reform movement on the reality of mathematics education was less significant than intended. However, this movement created and stimulated the recognition that curriculum development is a continuing necessity and that effective progress is often interrupted by social influences such as differences of opinion about mathematics, teaching, learning, educational management, and evaluation.

Bibliography

Boyer C B 1968 *A History of Mathematics*. Wiley, New York
Grundel F 1928–29 *Die Mathematik an den Deutschen Höheren Schulen*. Teubner, Leipzig
Howson A G, Keitel C, Kilpatrick J 1981 *Curriculum Development in Mathematics*. Cambridge University Press, Cambridge
Høyrup J 1980 Influences of institutional mathematics teaching on the development and organization of mathematical thought in the pre-modern period. *Studien zum Zusammenhang von Wissenschaft und Bildung, Materialien und Studien des Instituts für Didaktik der Mathematik*, No. 20. Instituts für Didaktik der Mathematik, Bielefeld
Jones P (ed.) 1970 *A History of Mathematics Education in the United States and Canada*, 32nd Yearbook of the National Council of Teachers of Mathematics. National Council of Teachers of Mathematics, Washington, DC
Schmidt K A (ed.) 1865 *Enzycolopädie des gesamten Erziehungs-und Unterrichtswesens. Vierter Band: Mathematik*. Schettler, Gotha
Struik D J 1949 *A Concise History of Mathematics*. Dover, New York
Weimer H, Schöler W 1976 *Geschichte der Pädagogik*. Gruyter, Berlin

The Language of Mathematics

P. Nesher

The concept "language of mathematics" refers to two distinct issues. First it deals with linguistic attributes of mathematics, including philosophical approaches to defining mathematical entities and their pedagogical implications. Secondly, it deals with the function of the natural language in the process of solving mathematical problems. Separate sections of the article, therefore, will deal with these two issues.

1. Linguistic Attributes of Mathematics and their Pedagogical Implications

Different pedagogical approaches are derived from the different schools of philosophy, often coupled with different schools of psychology. Schools of philosophy of mathematics differ with respect to the status of the symbolic system (the language) and the mode of existence (ontology) of mathematical entities. The formalist school regards mathematics as a system that has merely syntax and "rules of the game" entailing a pedagogical approach different from one which regards mathematics as a system that has interpretation with given models. Schools differ from each other with regard to setting priorities in selecting contents as well as in recommending methods of teaching. A formalist view might lead to emphasis on the axiomatic foundations of mathematics and its syntax (Thom 1970). An emphasis on model theory of mathematics, however, will lead to the searching for and creating of models for exemplifying some abstract mathematical entities. For example, Gattegno's use of Cuisenaire Rods for teaching natural numbers as an exemplification for Peano's axioms; the multibase models developed by J. Dines to exemplify the place value representation of numbers; or the simulation in LOGO of Turtle Geometry (Abelson and diSessa 1981).

In such educational exemplifications, the physical domain is used as a structural domain of reference, representing the abstract structural domain of the mathematical language. The student first learns the semantics of the formal symbolic system through the semantics of the physical domain. The coherence of the symbolic system is implicitly built into the exemplification model. Using such models carries with it the implication that mathematics has the characteristics of any linguistic system, that is, having both syntax and semantics.

Piaget in his emphasis on constructive processes seems to be closest to the intuitionist school of philosophy of mathematics. Yet Piaget himself made clear distinction between the realm of logic, that is of foundations or validity, and the realm of psychology, that is of causal and genetic explanation (Beth and Piaget 1966). Like the intuitionist school, Piaget's genetic epistemology too, is constructive in its nature, but it focuses on logicomathematical structures as products of human development. Though Piaget himself did not deal directly with schooling, many of his ideas concerning the child's construction of mathematical operations via self-activity and experience are widely accepted in elementary schools.

2. The Natural Language and its Function in Mathematical Problem Solving

Here two separate issues can be identified: (a) the process of learning mathematics with the aid of natural language, and (b) the application of mathematics in other domains represented by natural language.

2.1 Learning

The child learns mathematical language later than natural language and usually in the process of schooling. In learning mathematics, natural language serves as a metalanguage and as a first approximation to acquaintance with concepts later to be articulated by the formalism of mathematical language. Evidence for the child's relying on natural language key words has been found in several studies (Jerman and Rees 1972). These studies show that problem solving is greatly facilitated if the verbal formulation of the problem text includes words such as "more," "altogether," "add," "buy," when the required mathematical operation is "+"; or words like "take away," "lost," "less," and so on when the mathematical operation is "−." Otherwise, the problem becomes more difficult.

It should, however, be noted that identifying the symbols "+" and "−" with such expressions of natural language is only partially correct and it might interfere in the more advanced studies of mathematics such as with operations with signed numbers, where the above-mentioned interpretations of the signs "+" and "−" are meaningless. It was also found that if such key words are mentioned in the text of a "word problem" without a direct correspondence to the required mathematical operation, it may become a source of distraction because relying on the natural language cues, in such cases, leads toward an erroneous solution. Errors of these types are fostered by linking the mathematical operations (such as + and −) to expressions of natural language in the process of learning.

In teaching mathematics via exemplification models, the above difficulty of relying on isolated verbal cues is reduced. By relating to a coherent, structured context, each exemplification model serves both as an interpretation for verbal expressions of natural language, and as an interpretation of mathematical formalism.

2.2 Applications

The question of application is known to be the most problematic in teaching mathematics. The task of solving word problems consists of understanding a situation described in natural language and then of finding out with the aid of mathematical expressions and operations, some additional quantitative information.

Research on problem solving since the early 1970s has progressed from global heuristic methods to addressing the more specific issues. Progress has recently been gained by analyzing the relationship between the syntactic, semantic, and pragmatic components that make up each word problem. For example, it was found that the logical structure of addition word problems—which involve two disjoint sets of objects or events and their union—can be expressed by a variety of linguistic devices such as subordinate–superordinate relations, spatial or temporal connections, and even by verbs. Thus in the following problem: "Two boys walked to the classroom, and three boys ran to the classroom. How many boys arrived at the classroom?" "Walked" and "ran" serve to denote the disjoint sets of boys and "arrive" denotes the union set. (Nevertheless, such interpretation of "walk," "ran," and "arrive" are specific to the pragmatic context of solving mathematical word problems.) Work on additive and multiplicative structures progressed simultaneously in various theoretical frameworks such as the information processing framework (Greeno, in the United States, 1980); the semantic analysis of texts (Nesher and Katriel, in Israel, 1977); and the genetic epistemology approach (Vergnaud, in France, 1982). These researchers have reached agreement concerning the variables affecting children's performance and thereby they could categorize additive word problems and predict their level of difficulty. More specifically, they distinguished three different categories of addition and subtraction word problems, namely, "combine," "change," and "compare," each of which presents different and distinct set of difficulties.

These findings have significant curricular implications, since they predict quite accurately children's behavior in solving word problems. Reducing the global question of teaching mathematical applications to more local analyzable situations seems to be a promising direction for research to follow.

Bibliography

Abelson H, diSessa A A 1981 *Turtle Geometry: The Computer as a Medium for Exploring Mathematics.* MIT Press, Cambridge, Massachusetts
Beth E W, Piaget J 1966 *Mathematical Epistemology and Psychology.* Reidel, Dordrecht
Greeno J G 1980 Some examples of cognitive task analysis with instructional implications. In: Snow R E, Federico P, Montague W E (eds.) 1980 *Aptitude, Learning, and Instruction: Cognitive Process Analyses*, Vol. 1. Erlbaum, Hillsdale, New Jersey

Jerman M, Rees R 1972 Predicting the relative difficulty of verbal arithmetic problems. *Educ. Stud. Math.* 4: 306–23

Nesher P, Katriel T 1977 Semantic analysis of word problems. *Educ. Stud. Math.* 8: 251–69

Pimm D 1987 *Speaking, Mathematically: Communication in Mathematics Classrooms.* Routledge, London

Thom R 1970 Les mathématiques "modernes": Une erreur pédagogique et philosophique? *L'Age de la science* 3: 225–36; *Am. Sci.* 59: 695–99

Vergnaud G 1982 A classification of cognitive tasks and operations of thought involved in addition and subtraction problems. In: Moser J et al. (eds.) 1982 *Addition and Subtraction: Developmental Perspective.* Erlbaum, Hillsdale, New Jersey

Attitude Towards Mathematics

L. R. Aiken

Attitudes are learned predispositions to respond positively or negatively to certain objects, situations, institutions, or persons. As such, attitudes consist of cognitive (beliefs or knowledge), affective (emotional, motivational), and performance (behavior or action tendencies) components. With respect to the subject of mathematics, the affective component—feelings of like or dislike for the subject—has been stressed most often, but cognitive beliefs about the value and utility of mathematics, and, to a lesser extent, the performance component of attitude toward mathematics, have also been assessed and investigated.

1. Measurement

Information on a person's attitude toward mathematics may be obtained in a variety of ways, for example, by direct observations of behavior related to mathematics, by interviews or questionnaires concerning attitude toward mathematics, and by attitude scales. Because of its greater efficiency and apparent objectivity, the last of these has proven to be the most popular.

A scale of attitudes toward mathematics consists of a series of statements expressing positive and negative feelings and/or beliefs about the subject. Although the exact scoring procedure employed depends on the type of attitude scale, a person's score is basically a sum or average of numerical weights assigned to the statements or responses with which the person agrees or disagrees.

The two most popular procedures for constructing attitude scales are Thurstone's method of equal appearing intervals and Likert's method of summated ratings. Illustrative of instruments devised by the former procedure is Dutton's (1951) scale; the scale of Aiken and Dreger (1961) is a product of the latter procedure. Other methods for scaling attitudes toward mathematics are the semantic differential and pair comparisons. Scales of attitudes toward mathematics (or arithmetic) employing these methods and variations on them have been designed for the entire range of school grades and adults.

Scores on the majority of instruments designed to measure attitude toward mathematics represent a composite of several factors or dimensions. During recent years, however, researchers have recognized that attitude is a multidimensional construct requiring more complex assessment procedures. The trend away from single-score instruments and toward multiscore measures of attitude is witnessed by the multivariable scales of Fennema and Sherman (1977), Aiken (1979), and Sandman (1980). Such instruments are designed to assess a combination of affective and cognitive dimensions of attitude, for example, both "feeling for mathematics" and the "recognition of its importance."

Test–retest and internal consistency reliability coefficients of Thurstone- and Likert-type scales of attitude toward mathematics vary with the homogeneity of the scale, the respondent group, and the number of items comprising the scale. The reliabilities of well-constructed scales of attitude toward mathematics are usually in the 0.80s or 0.90s. However, validity coefficients for predicting mathematics course grades and achievement test scores are usually statistically significant but low. When combined with scores on tests of ability, attitude scale scores can contribute to the prediction of mathematics achievement, enrollment in, or selection of, mathematics courses, and withdrawal from such courses. It is likely that scales composed of attitude items focusing less on abstract mental states ("Do you enjoy mathematics?") and more on specific behaviors ("Do you intend to take nonrequired college algebra?") would have even greater validity than traditional attitude scales as predictors of performance on mathematical tasks (Fishbein and Ajzen 1975). In addition, investigations designed to assess the construct validity of various attitude scales would be helpful in determining what is being measured by these instruments.

2. Development

The relationship between attitude toward mathematics and ability in the subject is dynamic and interactive, in that individuals with low ability in mathematics are likely to have more negative attitudes toward the subject and those with negative attitudes are less inclined to make the effort to improve their mathematical abilities.

Attitudes toward mathematics begin developing as soon as children are exposed to the subject, but the junior-high years (age 11–13) appear to be particularly important. This is the time when negative attitudes toward mathematics become especially noticeable.

Whether the increase in negative attitudes at this stage of development is due to the greater abstractness of the mathematical material to be learned, to social/sex preoccupations, or to some other factor is not clear. It is noteworthy, however, that negative attitudes toward mathematics are more common among girls than among boys at the junior-high level and beyond.

Fennema and Sherman (1977) have argued that the less positive attitudes and lower mathematics test scores found in teenage girls, compared with teenage boys, are due to social role expectations and more limited experiences with mathematical tasks rather than to differences in innate ability for the subject. Whatever the correct explanation may be, boy–girl differences in mathematics attitude and ability have been observed in many countries, although the magnitude of the differences varies with type of schooling and other aspects of culture (Nevin 1973, Aiken 1979).

Among those who are in a position to affect children's attitudes toward mathematics are parents and other relatives, teachers, and peers. From the results of a large study of high-school students' achievements and participation in mathematics, Armstrong (1980 p. 30) concluded:

> It is the *active* encouragement of parents, teachers, and counselors which seems to affect participation. The measure of parents' influence as role models, a passive influence, did not correlate with participation. Evidently parents don't need to set good examples regarding mathematics for their children to take mathematics in school. But, they can stress the importance of mathematics and encourage their children to take it by discussing high school course selections and future career options.

A consistent finding of many investigations is that teachers who like mathematics and do their best to make it interesting can definitely create favorable attitudes and positive student motivation in the subject.

3. Correlates

As witnessed by moderate correlations between measures of attitude toward mathematics and measures of interest, anxiety, and motivation in mathematics, attitude is not a distinctly different variable from interest, anxiety, motivation, or other constructs used to label affect toward the quantitative domain. For example, interest is related to attitude, and, like attitude, affects achievement. In an international study, Husén (1967) found that mathematics achievement was correlated at all levels, both within and between countries, with interest in mathematics.

Small but statistically significant correlations have been found between measures of attitude toward mathematics and general intelligence, specific mathematical abilities, socioeconomic status, sex, ethnic group, and a number of personality variables. Positive attitudes toward mathematics are frequently associated with various personality indices of "good adjustment," for example, social maturity, self-control, personality inte-

gration, intellectual efficiency, and the needs for achievement, endurance, order, and dominance.

Since causation cannot be extracted from correlation, the meanings of the relationship of mathematics attitude to other variables are far from clear. For example, what interpretation should be placed on the findings that, on mathematics attitude scales, middle-class students score higher than lower-class students, whites score higher than blacks and Latinos, and well-adjusted students score higher than poorly adjusted students? In the majority of these research studies, demographic, ability, and personality variables are all interrelated in a kaleidoscopic way that defies facile interpretation. After several decades of dissertations and articles reporting significant correlations with mathematics attitude, it should be clear that no statistical procedure, regardless of its complexity, suffices to find the causes and effects of attitude toward mathematics. Unfortunately, very little of a substantive nature can be derived from correlational research alone. Variables must be manipulated and controlled by researchers rather than by statistical equations and computer programs.

4. Modification

Although correlational investigations have abounded, only during the past few years have efforts to change attitudes and anxiety toward mathematics been made in any systematic way. Abetted to some degree by the political and social concerns over women's rights, dozens of articles on the treatment of maths anxiety have been published during recent years. The majority of these efforts have dealt with college-age and adult learners, but some work has also been done with children. Illustrative of these projects are the programs of Peter Blum, Lenore Blum, and Sheila Tobias.

Peter Blum, who has operated a service called the Math Counseling Institute from his Seattle home, has reportedly been successful in applying transactional analysis techniques to assist students in overcoming math anxiety and improving their skills in the subject. A number of colleges and universities have also developed programs to help mathematically anxious students, the best known of which are those begun at Wesleyan University by Sheila Tobias and at Mills College by Lenore Blum. Most of these programs use a combination of remedial instruction to improve students' mathematical skills and psychological counseling to reduce their fears of the subject.

Under the auspices of her Washington DC-based firm, Overcoming Math Anxiety, Tobias has conducted mathematics anxiety reduction seminars with educational and business people and given lectures and workshops throughout the United States. Tobias's underlying philosophy is similar to the credo of Alcoholics Anonymous, in that she believes success in dealing with mathematics anxiety starts with the mathophobe's public acknowledgement that math avoidance is inappropriate in a college-educated adult and must be confronted in order to be cured (Tobias and Donady 1977). Among the therapeutic techniques employed in this approach are desensitization, immersion, and psychological support.

Other intervention strategies designed to reduce mathematics anxiety and improve achievement in the subject include cognitive-therapeutic techniques such as relaxation and visualization, indirect suggestion and hypnosis, modeling, and the use of personal journals and films (Barrow 1984, Basham 1985, Carr 1986, Piggott 1985, Trent 1985). When combined with mathematical skills training and self-efficacy improvement sessions, such techniques may produce noticeable effects in attitudes and achievement in mathematics. Group-therapeutic methods ("mathematics support groups") have also been helpful in working with students suffering from mathematics anxiety.

Although the programs of Tobias, the Blums, and others are laudable, they are probably too little and too late for most mathophobes. Because mathematics avoidance usually begins in early adolescence, efforts to improve attitudes and alleviate anxieties toward the subject need to be directed more toward school children. Every year secondary-school students enroll in courses and make career decisions, which, if devoid of mathematics, will greatly limit their future academic and vocational choices.

Parents and school counselors can certainly help, but the battle against mathophobia falls most squarely on the shoulders of the classroom teacher. And what can he or she do to make students feel more comfortable with the subject and challenged rather than defeated by it? First the teacher must accept the principle that the goal of teaching is to understand the student's cognitive and emotional difficulties with a subject and find ways to reduce them. Then the teacher must discover methods of teaching the material that enable the learner to understand it, not merely to complete the lesson on time.

Every teacher is an individual who will create different methods of accomplishing the goals of instruction with different learners. However, a few general principles can be recommended. In addition to being patient, understanding, and competent in mathematics, perhaps the soundest principle that the teacher can apply in attempting to improve attitudes and alleviate anxieties toward mathematics is to associate the subject with things that are pleasant, interesting, and important to the learner. Furthermore, since the choices that people make are based not only on what they enjoy but also on what they perceive as worth while, the usefulness

of mathematics, both in careers and everyday life, should be demonstrated frequently. Finally, teachers of mathematics should be encouraging and challenging, but at the same time realistic in the goals they set for students.

Bibliography

Aiken L 1979 Attitudes toward mathematics and science in Iranian middle schools. *Sch. Sci. Math.* 79: 229–34

Aiken L R, Dreger R M 1961 The effect of attitudes on performance in mathematics. *J. Educ. Psychol.* 52: 19–24

Armstrong J M 1980 *Achievement and Participation of Women in Mathematics. Report of a Two-year Study Funded by the National Institute of Education* (Rep. 10-MA-00). Education Commission of the States, Denver, Colorado

Barrow R 1984 Use of personal journals to reduce mathematics anxiety. *J. Coll. Stud. Pers.* 25(2): 170–71

Basham R B 1985 Indirect suggestion versus cognitive therapy in the treatment of mathematics test anxiety: a comparative treatment outcome study. *Dissertation Abstracts International* 45(11-B): 3611–12

Carr M J 1986 A film intervention program for changing mathematics attitudes of prospective elementary teachers. *Dissertation Abstracts International* 46(11-A): 3276

Dutton W H 1951 Attitudes of prospective teachers toward mathematics. *Elem. Sch. J.* 52: 84–90

Fennema E, Sherman J 1977 Sex-related differences in mathematics achievement, spatial visualization and affective factors. *Am. Educ. Res. J.* 14: 51–71

Fishbein M, Ajzen I 1975 *Belief, Attitude, Intention and Behavior: An Introduction to Theory and Research.* Addison-Wesley, Reading, Massachusetts

Husén T 1967 *International Study of Achievement in Mathematics: A Comparison of Twelve Countries.* Wiley, New York

Kulkarni S S, Naidu C A 1970 Mathematics achievement related to students' socioeconomic and attitude variables: A pilot study. *Ind. J. Psychol.* 45: 53–66

Mukherjee A, Umar F 1978 Attitudes, attitude change, and mathematics attainments: A study in Nigeria. *Int. Rev. Educ.* 24: 518–21

Nevin M 1973 Sex differences in participation rates in mathematics at Irish schools and universities. *Int. Rev. Educ.* 19: 88–91

Piggott D C 1985 A relaxation and visualization program for mathematics anxiety. *Dissertation Abstracts* 45(7-A): 2021

Sandman R S 1980 Mathematics attitude inventory: Instrument and user's manual. *J. Res. Math. Educ.* 11: 148–49

Tobias S, Donady B 1977 Counseling the math anxious. *J. Nat. Assn. Wom. Deans. Adms. and Couns.* 41: 13–16

Trent R M 1985 The effects of hypnotherapeutic restructuring, systematic desensitization and expectancy control on mathematics anxiety, attitude and performance in females and males. *Dissertation Abstracts* 46(5-B): 1724–25

Mathematics Instruction

M. Pellerey

Mathematics instruction has been a main item of any educational curriculum since the most ancient times. Mathematical discoveries have affected mathematics

instruction for centuries, but only in recent years has a large transformation been proposed. To carry out any transformation one has to take into account not only mathematical claims, but also those coming from epistemological, sociological, psychological, and pedagogical studies. Based on this ground one can then develop a more coherent and useful curriculum and plan carefully designed research programmes.

1. The Historical Perspective

Mathematical thinking began in very ancient times. Certainly it made considerable progress among the Sumerians and Babylonians. The teaching of mathematics developed with its study, and proof of this is found in ancient Egypt. The passage of the Egyptian mathematical culture to Greece, due to the efforts of Talete of Mileto, resulted in a dichotomy, which had already begun in Egypt, between practical or "sensible" mathematics, and rational or "general" mathematics. Only the latter was thought to be true mathematics and to have the highest educative value for the human intelligence. Practical mathematics included: natural numbers, duodecimal fractions used in Greek metrology, measurement of lengths, areas, and volumes.

In elementary teaching, besides these notions, Plato introduced practical computation problems and others related to everyday life and the professions. Rational mathematics, the real discovery of the Greek genius, was based on geometry and deduction. The best example is *The Elements* of Euclid. The teaching of rational mathematics should disengage the spirit from its common sense, and let it dedicate itself only to the intelligible, which Plato considered the only real and absolute truth. Hence this latter form of teaching was reserved for the few spirits qualified and disposed to develop philosophical culture. To the double character of mathematics corresponds its double educative role: one more general, for the totality of free citizens, the other more particular for one who wants to proceed to higher studies (Marrou 1948).

During the centuries that followed and, above all, with the Romans, the centrality of mathematical education considered as a fundamental means for educational development of reason, was progressively weakened, in order to give space to literary studies. Nevertheless, it is possible to perceive in the former statements some characteristics of the position of the teaching of mathematics still present in many countries in the first half of this century. In the elementary school, mathematics was taught through applications and problems of a practical character. In the secondary school, reserved only for a small number, the teaching of mathematics was based on rational geometry, frequently using *The Elements* of Euclid or one of its elaborations.

It is not possible to neglect the transformation of mathematics and its teaching, followed the introduction of Arabic culture into Europe at the end of the Middle Ages, and the developments that followed during the centuries thereafter. A fundamental example is the publication of some of the mathematical works of Leonardo Pisano in the first half of the thirteenth century, of which the most famous is the *Liber Abaci*. From this book, the decimal system for numeration was introduced in Europe as well as the algorithms, or calculation procedures, of actual mathematics. At the beginning, this method was considered difficult and mysterious. In particular, the zero formed a considerable obstacle. Leonardo Pisano named it "zephirus" from which derived the words zero and decipher. The introduction of this new method into teaching did not proceed smoothly. First, some Italian Universities (Bologna and Padua) taught the four elements, then the "Schools of Abaco" brought it slowly to the world of commerce and finance. Finally, by the time of the French Revolution, the decimal metric system was introduced in the elementary and secondary schools, and through the Napoleonic dominations, Arabic arithmetics and the metric system were diffused throughout the whole of Continental Europe. Only England and the United States of America and countries which are linked culturally with them were excluded. Today even in these countries, conversion to the decimal metric system is sought, with great educational and social problems for students of different schools and for adults.

Algebra, which was developed in some of its elements in Babylonia, was further developed by the Arabs and then diffused through Europe, where it was improved. Algebra was first introduced into the universities. Then it was slowly introduced into the secondary schools between the end of the eighteenth century and the beginning of the nineteenth century. As regards calculus, it was the polytechnic schools that introduced it first into France and then in the same period into the rest of Europe. Later on, the teaching of calculus was brought to a higher level.

By the end of the nineteenth century the teaching of mathematics had stabilized along the following lines.

At the elementary level, students were introduced to numbers using the decimal system, and performed exercises in the mechanics of computing using the addition, subtraction, multiplication, and division of natural and decimal numbers up to two decimals. They were brought to recognize the principal geometric figures and to calculate their measurements, to solve problems of a practical nature in measuring, marketing, and so on. The term "brought" is used because, in spite of the insistence of such scholars as Comenius, Froebel, Pestalozzi, and so on, the methods adopted were very repetitive and learning was by rote. There was a strictness which even gave rise to physical punishment. Examples of this same method of teaching at this level could be found in ancient Greece.

In the secondary school, rational geometry was taught according to *The Elements* of Euclid and similar treatises, besides classical algebra and trigonometry. In some countries, and in some schools whose pupils were aiming for entrance into polytechnics, basic knowledge of calculus was taught. Teaching was characterized by a training based on the rhythm of explanation, study, exercise, interrogation, and class work. The standard of mathematics reached in the secondary school was one of the bases used in selection for higher education. This characteristic was also present in ancient Greece.

This situation remained substantially stable for the first half of the twentieth century, except for sporadic initiatives, and the development of professional or technical schools, which emphasized the instrumental character of mathematics, free from the study of rational systems and the comprehension of concepts and procedures.

This situation underwent a profound change in the 1960s and 1970s—the so-called period of the New Mathematics movement.

In 1950 "The International Commission for the Study and Improvement of Teaching Mathematics was established by Gustave Choquet (a French mathematician), Jean Piaget, and Caleb Gattegno (an English educationalist). On that occasion, the progress that had been achieved in mathematics during the first half of the century was verified, a progress due above all to the works of the Bourbaki's school, and the studies of genetic psychology which had promoted, during the previous 30 years, remarkable points of agreement. In both sectors of scientific research, there emerged as an essential, the concept of structure. It was not so much the single objects, the single elements of information, which constituted the basis of mathematical knowledge and its teaching. Rather it was the mutual relationships and the systems of relationships owed by specific properties. In 1952, the commission met at La Rochelle sur Melun in France, with, among the famous mathematicians who were present, Piaget himself. On that occasion, the idea of a radical reform in the teaching of mathematics was put forth. The expected strategy was to be: firstly, a transformation in university education, followed by a transformation in secondary and elementary education. The mathematical model selected was the Bourbaki's system: the base being the concept of group; and the developments—the topological and algebraic structures. Piaget himself pointed out an analogous order in the development of mathematical concepts in children.

In 1951 the University of Illinois Committee on School Mathematics (UICSM) began to work under the guidance of Beberman. The dissatisfaction of university professors with the mathematical preparation of students who came from secondary schools was general. The subjects should have been changed. A principal role had been established for set theory, for relations and functional notions, introduced in these bases, for algebraic laws and the principles related to hypothetical and deductive procedures. Nevertheless Beberman, along with his European colleagues, insisted on the didactic method, stating the need to apply the so-called method of discovery, which begins with the students' activity, providing them with examples so as to arrive

during a second phase at a definition and strict systematization.

An impetuous movement, called the New Mathematics movement, followed this start. In the elementary schools set theory and the operations on sets were considered, before the natural number itself. The mathematical operations were built on corresponding operations between sets. Geometry appeared from the beginning based first on the concept of topological transformation, and later as a projective and metric transformation. The algebraic structures became the framework for both arithmetic and geometry. In the secondary school, the same subjects were developed with greater rigour. In particular, by introducing the vectorial plan, the whole geometric structure was rebuilt, even using algebraic terminology. In a parallel way, there were early introductions to probability and to statistics, subjects completely new to preuniversity education, and even to the university curriculum for future teachers of mathematics.

The push to this modernization did not come solely from within mathematics organizations (Royaumont meetings in France in 1959 and in Cambridge, Massachusetts in 1961), but from outside also. The initial shock led to large funds being made available for a renewal of the teaching of mathematics and science. By the end of the 1960s, the transformation was complete in many countries. The beginning of the 1970s saw the first, sometimes even violent, reactions. The same commission mentioned above encountered divergent positions which led to its division. The first general cause for discord was the didactical method. In fact, the initial intentions vanished, and instead of the discovery method, there prevailed the explanatory and repetitive method. At the same time, research into the results of the teaching of mathematics put in evidence the low assimilation of concepts, and the prevalence of mechanical repetitions, accompanied by a very poor ability to use mathematics in studying real situations and in resolving problems. The content of mathematics also came under attack. In particular, the concept of number based only on set theory was contested (Freudenthal 1973), as were the almost exclusive use of the hypothetical deductive method, the introduction of only axiomatic mathematical entities, the excess algebraization in geometry (for which educative importance was claimed). The support given to the renewal of the teaching of mathematics and science, sometimes in an incoherent way, by the psychology of Piaget, lost force, due to new studies and research in the psychology of mathematics.

This rush of reflections gave rise to two developments; the first, of a reactionary nature, led to the so called "Back to Basics" movement: returning to the essential things—in other words, the return to the situation that characterized the first half of this century; the second led to a better understanding of the problem of mathematics teaching. In fact, its epistemological, sociological, psychological, and pedagogical components were put in evidence. The solution of the didactical problems requires a careful mediation between all contributions, whether scientific or methodological.

2. *The Epistemological Perspective*

In this case it must be remembered that there are four concepts of mathematics present, both on a philosophical level and on a level more directly didactical.

(a) *Descriptive concept.* Mathematics is considered as something already existing in an ideal world. It has a unitary and coherent architecture of its own. The task is to make it known patiently and become masters of it. The principal aims in teaching it are those of considering and understanding definitions, theorems, and demonstrations which are already well-ordered in their logical structure. Thus, there is a "natural" order to be followed in the teaching of arithmetic and geometry without which it is impossible to understand the whole structure in its complexity. This way of thinking on a practical level means considering the textbook as a store of mathematical truths which both teacher and students can draw from.

(b) *Constructive concept.* Mathematics is something referring more to a building up process where concepts, definitions, theorems, and their demonstrations are being fittingly heaped up, rather than to a logical structure pre-existing an understanding of it. There are no mathematical objects independent of the process producing them. Therefore the goals in teaching are based more on promoting the ability to build up concepts, models, theories, and applications in mathematics rather than on reproducing already existing organizations. Mathematics is therefore something more internal, intimately linked to ways of thinking, rather than something external.

(c) *Formal concept.* In this case, attention is concentrated on the form by which the various mathematical propositions can be expressed as well as on the rules allowing their combination. Thus mathematics is spoken of as a language understood above all in its grammatical and syntactic aspects—a language however that is quite formalized, that is to say reduced to very abstract and synthetic symbols. The teaching of mathematics therefore concentrates on the ability to manipulate correctly formulas and propositions written in a symbolic manner. A closer idea can be obtained by thinking of how algebra is studied at present, and also by looking at computation with decimal numbers and fractions.

(d) *Substantial concept.* Instead, here the real substance of things should be borne in mind rather than the form. Interest is focused more on the meanings, the concepts, and the reality lying beneath the formulas or definitions. In teaching, one aims more at the substance of the discourse, at the meaning of various propositions and the content hidden beneath the symbols; and this refers not only to mathematics, but also to its various fields of application. For instance, when speaking of

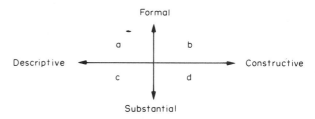

Figure 1
Scheme to show the interaction between mathematical concepts

fractions, decimal numbers and percentages, one tries to build the concept of ratio and therefore have it expressed knowingly in one of its representations.

The influence of the mathematical concept that a teacher or a pupil has accepted, even implicitly, has considerable influence on concrete action. Nevertheless none of these concepts is to be found in a pure state. They interact, and thus it is possible to represent them by means of a diagram (see Fig. 1). Four regions or quadrants can be singled out in it. Region (a) seems to refer more frequently to didactic work done at present in classrooms, and is formal and descriptive—in other words, reproductive and more attentive to correct definitions and manipulations than to the substance of concepts and to skill in interpreting and applying mathematical formulas above all on an elementary level.

Alternatively, there is the concept illustrated by (d). That is, a definition favouring the construction of concepts, processes, models, and applications in mathematics; a definition insisting above all on the meanings of things, and taking into account the skill and knowledge which a child has already acquired during schooldays and later on. Every new concept, every new skill must thus be developed starting from what the child has already mastered, from experience already codified and assimilated, and attained by means of constructive processes within which the child has played an active role.

3. *The Political and Sociological Perspective*

Certainly the most important transformation that has occurred since the early 1950s has been the extending of high-school education to a larger number of citizens. In some countries, compulsory education is now compulsory to the age of 16, in others the age of 14 remains.

The tendency has been to extend compulsory education well-beyond the primary school to grant secondary schooling to nearly all school-goers. From this point of view there would appear to be two impelling problems. The first concerns formulating the concept of mathematics for all, while the second concerns the status and the aims of this teaching as regards the individual and society itself. The lack of such a concept is reflected in the varying opinions concerning the position of the teaching of mathematics in general and in professional training on a postelementary level. Today this is even more urgent because public opinion does not now accord to mathematical, scientific, and technical disciplines the same privileged position they held after the turmoil provoked by the launching of the first Sputnik (Krigowska 1979a, 1979b). It is necessary to reassert the importance of mathematical instruction for society and individuals and provide serious answers to a couple of basic questions: "Why mathematics for all?" and "Which mathematics for all?" If the mathematics taught in the lower stage of secondary school is conceived as the lowest floor of a rigorous global edifice of elementary mathematics, where certain intuitively simple and useful pieces of knowledge can appear for theoretical reasons only on the upper floors, the mathematical education of the majority of pupils (who are not going to climb to these floors) is curtailed. In this situation, this majority only derive from their mathematical education a little knowledge and a few skills which will be useful for their professional training or their future work (Krigowska 1979a, 1979b).

To avoid such a predicament, a clear idea of common mathematical culture should be secured. There is also a need for larger numbers of qualified teachers. This stage of schooling, leading from the child's first experiences in the primary school to lucidity in an adolescent's way of thinking, requires a well-grounded preparation from mathematical and pedagogic viewpoints. All the more because this mass schooling also causes changes in the social structure itself. Similar problems can be found in developing countries, even if they are at times more on a transitional level between primary and secondary schooling.

The problem mentioned above would appear to be particularly marked in some industrialized countries, because there is a tendency to favour an élite able to reach very high levels in computer science and mathematics, while still quite young. This is also due to discontent aroused by the level of skills and knowledge attained by students in mass schooling. Thus a traditional function of mathematics reappears: that of being a good subject to use as a criterion for selection to certain schools and professions. The tendency to give ample space to mathematics in entrance examinations for the various school levels has been consolidating since the birth of the polytechnical schools. It was said that mathematics is replacing Latin in the social discrimination function that classical language once held, and that the former curricular subject could in future be a social-class indicator just as Latin was in the past. This trend would seem to have evidently emerged in secondary schools in a number of countries during these last few years (Revuz 1980).

On the other hand, the necessity of having some concepts and processes typical of mathematics in order to understand and evaluate social and economic phenomena leads to the need for a valid and widespread mathematical culture, even if quite likely different from that taught in the past.

4. The Psychological Perspective

Research in the field of school education has already underlined how a biased or at least an indifferent attitude towards mathematics is rooted in the first experiences of schooling. The most harmful moments would appear to be those connected with the introduction of decimal numbers and their operations in the primary school and with that of algebra in the intermediate school. It would seem that a real sense of uneasiness and extraneousness is slowly increasing among most pupils (Aiken 1970).

It was as early as the 1930s that researchers began to speak of a meaningful learning of mathematics, in the sense that it had to be humanly valid; that is to say not intended only to have students acquiring something new, but also to promoting good insertion of the new into the old. This means that it is not sufficient to introduce new notions, new exercises, and new activities; it is also necessary to consider carefully how these things are related to what each student has already codified and assimilated. Should they prove to be totally without connection, it becomes obvious that the only manner of acquiring them is by mechanical repetition, fixing them in one's mind by means of rote memorizing. This is what has happened to many a young student at school when studying mathematical definitions and formulas.

Bearing this in mind, a scheme could be put forward (see Fig. 2), in which two fundamental dimensions of school learning stand out (Ausubel 1968). The first concerns the manner according to which new knowledge or new skills are incorporated in facts, concepts, and generalizations already assimilated by the student on the whole. Meaningful and rote learning stand at the two extremes of this dimension. The second one concerns the path through which new knowledge and skills are acquired. Discovery learning and reception learning are at the two extremes of this dimension.

(a) Rote learning is characterized by the fact that a new element of knowledge is acquired in an isolated way, without links or connections with what is already known. Because of this lack of relationships between the new contribution and the already developed structure of knowledge, the only practical way of retaining it in the memory is that of

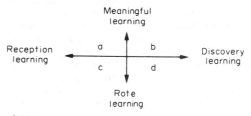

Figure 2
Scheme to show the two fundamental dimensions of school learning

mechanical and stereotyped repetition. There is no transformation either in an external contribution of knowledge or in an internal structure of knowledge. One could add that, as new knowledge remains isolated in the whole of the concepts possessed, it would be difficult to draw on it and use it.

(b) Meaningful learning is instead characterized by the fact that new material being learnt can be connected, and in fact is connected, with other concepts and other skills already acquired and therefore is not embodied in an isolated way, but in a form well-connected with the previous structure of knowledge. The network of relations thus formed makes it easy to remember and use the new knowledge.

(c) Discovery learning instead places accent on the itinerary of learning and, to be exact, on discovery as an independent process and on the fact that the appreciation of the truth of a proposition comes about independently. In normal cases it does not mean discovering something first, that is, in an absolute sense, but rather in a relative one, as if one were the first to do it. This means that the solution of a problem or the demonstration of the truth of an affirmation has not been notified to one by anybody. However, it should be pointed out that an authentic discovery even in a relative sense requires not only the announcing of a valid hypothesis but also the actual verification of the truth of the same.

(d) Reception learning is consequently identified because of the lack of independence in acquiring a concept or in arriving at the truth or falsity of a proposition. In fact all this derives from cultural transmission or direct communication.

Even in this case it would seem that learning placed in quadrant (c) of Fig. 2 prevails in school practice and is learning based on mechanical repetition of what has been explained by the teacher or contained in a textbook. And this would seem more evident in the case of mathematics. Instead, the learning above the horizontal line should be promoted above all on a compulsory school level and this should be based on active exploration by the child under the careful guidance of the teacher and in connection with school training activities on the whole.

Not everything in mathematics, however, can be the object of personal discovery. Quite often, reference is made to the child's discoveries, in the sense that he or she has grasped the meaning of a proposition or singled out the way to solve a problem with the help of the teacher. At this point, a feeling of discovery emerges: it bases itself on the subjective experience of really understanding and of being therefore able to use this discovery in a productive manner. Here one is between a significative communication made by the teacher and a discovery made by the child under the former's guidance. Hence it can be said that good learning must be placed between quadrant (a) and quadrant (b) in Fig. 2. This leads to greater utilization of a meaningful reception in secondary school and is efficient in terms of time. Nevertheless, when introducing new subjects it is necessary to give wide space for constructive activities.

Current cognitive psychological theories emphasize three interrelated aspects of mathematics learning (Resnick 1989). First, mathematics learning is a process of knowledge construction. Effective learning depends on the intentions, interpretations, selfmonitoring, elaborations, and representational constructions of the individual learner. Second, people use available knowledge to construct new knowledge. Effective learning depends on elaboration and extension of prior knowledge. Third, learning is highly tuned to the situation in which it takes place. Memory for isolated facts is very limited. Knowledge is retained in a meaningful and stable way if embedded in some internal and/or external organization. Finally, skills and knowledge are not independent of the context in which they are used and practiced.

On the other hand the analysis of mathematical problem solving showed evident elements of activation of metacognitive processes, that is of the consciousness of the related cognitive and affective processes and the ability to regulate them (Silver 1987). In the same way the importance of the development of strategic thinking has been identified.

5. An Educational Integration

Mathematical education is a process by which a child enters into two basic regions of the mathematical world: into concepts and theories on one side, and mathematical activity on the other. Such initiation, fostered and made easier by teachers, takes place within a well-knit system where as many as four main poles exert their interactive influence:

(a) The culture to which the child belongs; culture is here to be taken in an anthropological sense; such culture expresses itself and is communicated through the mother tongue.

(b) The acts and concepts of mathematical type together with the theories that bind them into a body that is logically coherent and applicatively valid. Such a mathematical body is expressed in linguistic forms, that is, one or more systems made up of language signs according to certain usage rules that are socially determined.

(c) The cognitive structure (or cognitive matrix) of the child; this is to be understood as a more or less organized set of concepts, principles, skills, and attitudes together with their interactions. Within such a cognitive structure, language competence plays a central role; that is to say, the ability to pass from a system of language symbols socially accepted and organized to inner contents or meanings, and vice versa.

(d) The physical world that a child encounters through his or her sensory perception.

The culture to which the child belongs and that is instilled by the mother tongue, is a comprehensive system, from which may be separated a number of cultural subsystems: representational systems, normative systems, expression systems, and action systems. These subsystems interact significantly. This is also true of the elements that make up each of the subsystems: concepts, symbols, knowledge, and ascertaining methods, values, behavioural norms, ways to express and single out deeper feelings, interpretation devices, technological and social mediations.

Mathematical concepts and procedures are more or less deeply embedded in this culture, either in a simple, natural form or in a rather elaborated structure. Such mathematical elements usually belong to conceptual categories whereby situations, facts, and problems fit within an abstract frame for interpretation, explanation, and prediction. Such categories as these may be labelled "mathematical" depending on the relationship they have with established portions of mathematics which are accepted by the scientific community of a given time. However, in school situations contrasts between ideas and words of the native culture, and ideas and words employed in mathematical thinking and communication are often observed.

Mathematical concepts and procedures may be regarded as a "corpus" or common background on which scholars have operated and are still operating with the aim of causing it to grow, of better organizing it to provide a finer inner cohesion, and of employing it when they wish to explain or anticipate situations and facts both of the physical and the social world. This "corpus" is being concretized in quite a number of ways, that include graphic forms, written language forms, more abstract symbolic forms, and so on.

The culture to which a child belongs exerts some influence on these forms of mathematical expression. It is enough to open a textbook written in French and another written in English to see the point: the latter would be more empirical, paying attention to the core of concepts, of procedures, and applications; the former more abstract and formal.

It should be stated that a unique system of signs, or a mathematical language, does not exist; there exists, instead, a set of linguistic forms that evolve according to time, geographical location, and inner regions of the discipline itself. History and geography of mathematical language are very closely related to the history and geography of scientific communities.

The process of mathematical learning that takes place within a school must inevitably start with the code system that the child is already acquainted with through the influence of its family and social environment and with the world of ideas and know-how that make up the

culture to which it belongs. The task, then, consists not only in leading the child to master more elaborated and more formalized codes, but also in leading it to grasp the different functions of such systems with regard to the development of thought and arranging suitable activity.

Instead, too often, a remarkable breakdown is to be perceived between the child's cultural world and language, and the school cultural world and language, so much so that they appear alien to one another. In the case of mathematics, this fact may become a dramatic one, because its categories and procedures are often scarcely represented in a given cultural environment and, besides, both linguistic forms and their functions are wholly ignored by the child. It is bound to develop both with the help of immediate experience and of communication. But, it is chiefly through cultural communication reinforcing direct experience that things and happenings get their meaning. A certain development of the child's language competence is thus asked for.

When dealing with mathematical learning, it is necessary to distinguish between concepts and activities at a very low level and mathematical concepts and activities of a higher level. In the first case, the original or introductory level, a move is made initially from the world of direct experience to the world of its rational representation; in the second case, the representations and schemes worked with are already more or less abstract.

Mathematical concepts at a low level are, then, simplified reproductions of a child's direct experience. The perception process has in this case an all-important role: it consists of selecting and structuring sensory data either according to a conceptual category somehow already present, or according to the attention being focused by outward solicitations, usually by the teacher, with the aim of isolating certain relationships or specific operations. In the second case, one or more relationships pertaining to one or more operations, physical or mental, may emerge: this allows for a wholly singular force to be attached to them, and adequate words to identify them being sorted out.

Two mathematical processes thus open up to the child's mind. The first one applies schemes, albeit very simple ones, of a mathematical nature, to interpret and explain a portion of physical reality. The other one, under the expert guidance of the teacher or of someone else, builds up a conceptual scheme and names it. Nevertheless, in order to speak of building up mathematical concepts or of using them when interpreting schematical facts, phenomena, or physical situations, it is necessary that these schemes, even when they are still incomplete and unfit to settle immediately into a theory or a portion of a theory in mathematics, be open to such future settling without needing deep changes or even reversal from their present state of rationality. This means that from a low level, it must be possible to pass to a superior level, a more abstract and more reflexive level, without meeting with obstacles or contradictions that may be insuperable. The same thing is true for the words and symbols as they are gradually being introduced.

A few simple practical orientations may now be drawn:

(a) Low-level mathematization processes must bank on what a child has already acquired both conceptually and linguistically through the influence of its environmental culture. For instance, in the case of natural number, the child is bound to bestow serious attention on the awareness of phenomena that are of a recursive nature and on their main verbal representation: counting.

(b) If a discrepancy should arise between the schemes and words developed in family and social circles, and schemes and words that are specifically mathematical, one is bound to point out clear differences and alternative roles that are relevant to them: the former more practical, the latter more logical.

(c) Ideal schematization must be achieved using more than a single representation form; those which are closer to a child's interest and practice must be given precedence.

(d) In order to foster significant learning, that is to say with the view of incorporating into a child's cognitive structure the very substance of concepts and procedures, its language competence must improve in both senses: from symbols to inner meaning and vice versa; moreover, the larger possible range of codes should be used.

6. The Curriculum of Mathematics Instruction

The changes that took place since about the early 1960s may be grouped into a threefold trend.

First of all there are people who most carefully point their attention to the changes in mathematical contents, and stress set theory and fundamental structures (algebraical, topological, probabilistic, etc.). Others like to stress the problem of didactic method, that is the means and paths suitable to introduce children to concepts and skills as well as to underline the importance of an active exploration, or a real comprehension, and of a progressive construction.

The third tendency overturns matters. One ought not to start taking into account the internal requirements of mathematics, but the child's needs should be attended to, bearing in mind his or her psychological development and cultural background. From this point of view, mathematics in its content and its methods is subjected to careful pedagogical analysis to set forth those aspects and general claims which are most valid and most productive.

This mathematical education, in its broadest sense, becomes intimately connected with the whole education both in terms of its own appropriate appeal to common educational objectives and in terms of mutual dynamic and productive interaction with the other dimensions of school education, in particular with psychomotor and linguistic education.

In this context one may hint at some general trends with respect to aims, methods, and didactic materials (UNESCO 1973).

6.1 General Aims

(a) A fundamental aim of education in today's society is to provide citizens with a quality education and one that is accessible to everybody.

(b) Another aim focused upon since the early 1970s is the encouragement of students to participate in further continuous education.

6.2 More Specific Aims

(a) To teach up-to-date mathematics, including probability and statistics, besides "numerical mathematics."

(b) To teach mathematics as a unified body by means of broad key-concepts and fundamental structures.

(c) To promote conceptual meaningful mathematics as well as efficient computation skills.

(d) To approach mathematics both as an abstract, autonomous body of knowledge and as a useful, operational tool.

(e) To present mathematics as an ever expanding, open subject.

(f) To show a clearer picture of methodology in mathematical activity.

(g) To pay more attention to developing motivation and positive attitudes concerning mathematics.

(h) To define mathematical literacy for the average citizen in our society.

6.3 Methods

(a) There is a progressive change from passive acceptance of expository teaching to active involvement in inquiry-oriented learning.

(b) New techniques of classroom management are being tried and combined.

(c) New roles for the teachers are emphasized.

(d) Efforts are made to initiate learning from various sorts of problematic situations.

(e) A variety of graphical means are used in the teaching of mathematics.

(f) More emphasis is bestowed on nonlinear presentations and on spiral expansion of concepts.

(g) Coordinated teaching of mathematics with other subjects.

6.4 Materials

(a) Handbooks, work cards, and programmed books must be used extensively with different methods of approaching mathematical contents: they may contain examples and intuitive introductions to formalization or they may compel the student to decodify the formal book, to build instances, diagrams, models, intuitive interpretations, and the like.

(b) Transition from the school book, sparkling with colours, drawings, and ingenious diagrams, to the grey concise severe textbook of adult mathematics is likely to arouse hardships and problems. School must take care of this predicament that needs to be tackled well in advance with a general sound policy about handbooks.

(c) The use of the school book must not only help the student to learn mathematics, but should also give a start in the realm of individual work based on the mathematics book.

7. The Objectives

As for the objectives, even in the field of mathematics, use was made of the matrix suggested by Tyler, which combined two dimensions, that of content and that of activities or cognitive processes changing over to action. The classic taxonomy for the cognitive domain of Bloom et al., and others developed after, caused many problems in the field of mathematics. For this reason, different types were elaborated that kept closer to this realm of learning.

7.1 The Classification of the International Association for the Evaluation of Educational Achievement (IEA)

The *International Study of Achievement in Mathematics* (Husén 1967) arrived at a classification of the objectives of mathematical teaching through a detailed analysis both of possible objectives and of those actually followed in the curriculum of the 12 participating nations. It gave rise to a general view which considers 10 fundamental abilities. They are:

(a) Ability to recall and to reproduce definitions, notations, operations, and concepts.

(b) Ability in rapid and accurate computation and symbols manipulation.

(c) Ability in translating data into symbols.

(d) Ability in interpreting data appearing in symbolic form.

(e) Ability in following a line of reasoning or a proof.

(f) Ability in constructing a proof.

(g) Ability in applying concepts to mathematical problems.

(h) Ability in applying concepts to nonmathematical problems.

(i) Ability in analysing problems and determining the operations which may be applied.

(j) Ability in finding mathematical generalizations.

This succession is included in a matrix of three dimensions. The first dimension specifies the behaviour that the student is acquiring. In fact, the behaviour singled out is threefold: cognitive, affective, and motor. Here only the cognitive type is taken into account. As for the motor type, it includes, for example, ability in using instruments, be they rulers or compasses. The second dimension concerns mathematical topics. Some instances are enumerated here:

(a) Arithmetic

(b) Algebra

(c) Plane geometry, solid geometry, analytical geometry

(d) Trigonometry

(e) Probability, calculus

(f) General aspects

The third dimension concerns the use of the knowledge or of the skills acquired. The reason for separating mathematics considered in itself ("pure mathematics") and mathematics considered as an instrument ("applied mathematics") is probably due to the different emphases placed on mathematical education in different parts of the world.

7.2 The Classification of the National Longitudinal Study of Mathematics Achievement (NLSMA)

Work completed by a group of American researchers belonging to the School Mathematics Study Group (SMSG) and called the "National Longitudinal Study of Mathematical Abilities" (Wilson 1971) is a model with two dimensions. Only the behavioural dimension is considered here.

(a) Computation: this level refers to recalling the fundamental mathematical facts, the terminology, and the skill required in order to carry out algorithms. The accent is placed on the simple evocation of knowledge and on the fulfilment of operations in an appropriate way.

(b) Comprehension: this category covers remembering concepts and mathematical generalization: the student must show comprehension of concepts and of relations among them; translation of data from one mode to another.

(c) Application: this involves the solution of familiar problems, similar to those the student had to face during the process of learning; pupils have to choose an algorithm as a solution and apply it successfully (see *Problem Solving in Mathematics*).

(d) Analysis: the student must go beyond what was done during previous instruction, meeting new mathematics experiences, solving uncommon problems.

7.3 A Synthesis (*Pellerey 1974*)

7.3.1 Reproduction Process

(a) Knowledge of isolated elements, not organized as a whole, in a prevalent repetitive form. Knowledge of organizations, but as purely mnemonic data. This can happen either at a verbal, or at a nonverbal level as in the case of graphics, calculus of algorithms, constructions with a ruler and compasses. All this implies memory or acknowledgement.

Terminology, symbols.
Principles, rules.
Facts, mathematical statements (for example: theorems, definitions).
Development of algorithms.
Solutions of routine problems.
Motor skills (e.g. use of a ruler and compasses).

(b) Knowledge with comprehension of concepts, of organizations that are received as a whole formerly constructed. This present point differs from the former one, because it involves greater activity on the part of the learner (analysis above all), yet without demanding real constructive engagement. Here too one can refer either to verbal or nonverbal levels.

To see relations, regularities to be distinguished (for example: between hypothesis and consequences).

To understand organizations (even logical ones) and organizing principles that pertain to them.

Recoding and translating (through words, graphics and symbols).
Ability to follow a line of reasoning.
Ability to understand problems.
Ability to pursue ways of solving (proposals) for problems.

7.3.2 Production Process

(a) Construction of concepts, organizations, on the bases of experiences or knowledge or information: as these arrive, they are associated or separated.

Construction of concepts, of unified ideas, of symbols.
Construction of schemes, flowcharts, graphs, algorithms.
Formulation of a definition.
Construction of a logical organization (axiomatic).
Representation of data or information.
Constructing games, finding problems.

(b) Solution of problems. It deals with just real problems, in the sense that their solutions are not given by simple processes, such as recalling or recognizing.

To guess, to suppose, to produce hypotheses.
To find some objects (real or mathematical) that satisfy given conditions.
To find all the objects that satisfy given conditions.
To generalize, to extend by analogy.
To find a suitable mathematical model (among known models).
To construct a mathematical model suitable to solve the problem.
To construct an algorithm of solution that standardizes the problem.

(c) To judge. This is a question of defending by argumentation or of rejecting a judgment, a solution, etc., on the basis of principles or criteria coming both from inside and outside the subject.

A statement is meaningful.
A statement is true.
The problem is clearly defined, data are sufficient or data (conditions) are too many or contradictory.
A symbol, a definition, a suggested solution is fine, suitable.
Reasoning is correct.
Solution satisfies the conditions.
Solution is reasonable and/or practical.
Solution is elegant and/or stimulating.

8. Evaluation

Consciousness that the problem of evaluating, especially in mathematics, cannot be faced considering only its technical and methodological aspects without also taking into account its psychological, social, and political factors is widespread. Evaluation takes place, so that important decisions can be made, as these may mean so much for the future of pupils. Often it deals with decisions that have a dichotomous character: pass, fail, for example. However, the reality of personal competencies is better represented by a vector of scores than by only one scale. Consequently, tensions and difficulties spring up. The development of knowledge and personal abilities is a dynamic process, which sometimes does not conciliate with a stratified and a horizontal examination of results already achieved. All these move teachers, administrators, or researchers to think about educational evaluation more like an interactive process which includes knowledge, beliefs, and values of those who are involved: pupils, teachers, administrators, parents, and so on (Kilpatrick 1979).

The use of matrices of the type mentioned in the previous section is becoming more widespread to overcome some of these problems. At the same time, two dimensions are considered: that of content and that related to the cognitive process. From their combination, the object of the observation and the possibility to write the items that allow its realization come out. This activity has been shown to be useful for the single teacher and for the school in general and allowed the construction of item banks, classified according to different schemes. Certainly there is the risk of excessive simplification and of privileging trivial tests instead of using problems that involve a variety of knowledge and abilities.

For reasons like these, one may see introduced more and more different techniques such as systematic observation, analysis of materials, job analysis, questionnaires directed to parents, case study, and so on. A few trends seem to come out from all this. The use of oral examination to evaluate the results of mathematical learning seems to be in decline; external examinations seem to be replaced by a mixed form of internal and external tests with more attention paid to the diagnostic and formative evaluation rather than to pure, simple classification. Psychometric models for examinations are giving way to criterion-based models. Nevertheless, in literature on the teaching of mathematics, general complaints about the absence of instruments to estimate ability in solving problems and creativity are being raised.

9. Research

The IEA research has already been mentioned. It was a cross-sectional study conducted in 12 different nations and at different age levels, in the 1960s. Results were published in 1967 (Husén 1967). Criticism and approval of this initiative as well as changes that occurred in the following years developed into a new study that is still in progress. It considers in a more careful way the curriculum variables of the different countries.

Bauersfeld summed up the inquiring activity in the last 50 years in the following words (Bauersfeld 1979):

> Since the 1920s researches have tried to identify stages of the pupil's learning and investigate the conditions of this success (experimental psychology), and to describe the developmental stages of his thinking (developmental psychology), aiming towards a general learning theory. School-related developmental work of the 1950s and 1960s, on the other hand, was engaged in the curriculum in a wide sense. Mainly by means of projects, pupil's books, learning aids and other media were developed, as well as an analysis of the structure of the subject matter and teaching methods related to it.
>
> Both movements were characterized by a neglect of the teacher's role and of the general context of learning. Consequently, both ran into increasing difficulties. Neither have the big curriculum projects improved mathematics instruction and mathematics learning on a broad scale, nor has research developed a valid general learning theory.
>
> Only competing explanations for partial views of learning have been developed, such as Piaget's genetic theory of epistemology, Gagné's hierarchical model, or Gestalt theories.

On the other hand, Begle (1979) at the end of his intense research activity found in a survey five groups of variables that were the object of research for the effects they have on mathematical education. They are: teachers, curriculum variables; student variables; milieu; and instructional variables. These groups can be further divided into a considerable number of variables, that in the course of time have been more or less widely and systematically subjected to research. Yet in spite of the availability of a large amount of factual information, Begle concluded his research with the following words:

> My final general comment is that this survey of the empirical literature left me feeling quite depressed. There are two reasons for this feeling. On the one hand, I do not see that we have any substantial body of knowledge about mathematics education that we can build on. On the other hand, this lack of a solid knowledge base is in part explained by and at the same time helps to explain the fact that our research efforts have not been based on any broad theoretical foundations. It is true that each author of a research report tries to present some theoretical rationale for his research, but these rationales rarely go beyond references to previous studies or to narrow hypotheses which someone has proposed. But, while I am depressed, I am not despondent. I do believe that there exists, in the literature, a solid body of information about mathematics education. And I do believe that once this information is dug out and organized, then it will begin to suggest testable theories and at the same time will provide a template against which tentative theories can be tested.

The body of knowledge suggested by Begle begins to come to light. Powerful organizing ideas are more and more identified. G. Brousseau (1983), using Bachelard's notion of "epistemological obstacle", was able to explain several conceptual difficulties in developing mathematical culture and to suggest some way of overcoming them. Research on mathematics teaching has analyzed the thoughts and feelings that precede, accompany and follow the act of teaching, identifying their interrelations with the act of learning. These results often seem dependent on the shifting from quantitative methods of research to more qualitative, observational, and interpretative ones (Romberg and Carpenter 1986). One can observe a tendency to develop studies related to real classroom situations. Systematic observations of mathematical instruction, particularly long-term studies of learning processes in natural environments, have given excellent results. Furthermore, they brought about a closer joint activity of teachers in research, and the extension of combined research methods. One can also observe considerable developments to plan more solid theoretical frameworks. Other concerns of study are: the relationship between specific mathematical structures, cognitive structures, and learning sets; the influence they exert on teaching and their results; teachers' outlooks, whether on mathematics or on mathematical education.

Bibliography

Aiken L R 1970 Attitude toward mathematics. *Rev. Educ. Res.* 40: 551–96
Ausubel D P 1968 *Educational Psychology: A Cognitive View.* Holt, Rinehart and Winston, New York
Bauersfeld H 1979 Research related to the mathematical learning process. In: UNESCO 1979 *New Trends in Mathematics Teaching.* Prepared by the International Commission of

Mathematical Instruction, United Nations Educational, Scientific and Cultural Organization, Paris

Begle E G 1979 *Critical Variables in Mathematics Education: Findings from a Survey of the Empirical Literature*. Mathematical Association of America and the National Council of Teachers of Mathematics, Washington, DC

Brousseau G 1983 Les obstacles epistémologiques et les problèmes en mathématiques. *Recherche en Didactique des Mathématiques* 2: 164–98.

Freudenthal H 1973 *Mathematics as an Educational Task*. Reidel, Dordrecht

Freudenthal H 1978 *Weeding and Sowing: Preface to a Science of Mathematical Education*. Reidel, Dordrecht

Griffiths H B, Howson A G 1974 *Mathematics, Society and Curricula*. Cambridge University Press, London

Husén T (ed.) 1967 *International Study of Achievement in Mathematics: A Comparison of Twelve Countries*, Vols. 1 and 2. Wiley, New York

Kilpatrick J 1979 Methods and results of evaluation with respect to mathematics education. In: UNESCO 1979 *New Trends in Mathematics Teaching*, Vol. 4. Prepared by the International Commission of Mathematical Instruction, UNESCO, Paris

Kline M 1980 *Mathematics: The Loss of Certainty*. Oxford University Press, New York

Krigowska Z 1979a *Cenni di didattica della matematica*, Vol. 1. Pitagora Editrice, Bologna

Krigowska Z 1979b Mathematics education at the first level in post elementary and secondary school. In: UNESCO 1979 *New Trends in Mathematics Teaching*, Vol. 4. Prepared by the International Commission of Mathematical Instruction, UNESCO, Paris

Krutetskii V A 1976 *The Psychology of Mathematical Abilities in Schoolchildren*. University of Chicago Press, Chicago, Illinois

Marrou H I 1948 *Histoire de l'education dans l'antiquité*. Seuil, Paris

Morris R (ed.) 1980 *Studies sur l'enseignement des mathématiques*, Vol. 1. UNESCO, Paris

Morris R (ed.) 1981 *Etudes sur l'enseignement des mathématiques*, Vol. 2. UNESCO, Paris

Pellerey M 1974 Obiettivi dell'insegnamento della matematica nella scuola secondaria superiore. *Oreintamenti Pedagogici* 21: 218–38

Pellerey M 1983 *Per un insegnamento della matematica dal volto umano*. SEI, Torino.

Resnick L B 1989 Introduction. In: Resnick L B (ed.) 1989 *Knowing, Learning, and Instruction*. Erlbaum, Hillsdale, New Jersey.

Resnick L B, Ford W W 1981 *The Psychology of Mathematics for Instruction*. Erlbaum, Hillsdale, New Jersey

Revuz A 1980 *Est-il possible d'enseigner les mathématiques?* Presses Universitaires de France, Paris

Romberg T A, Carpenter T B 1986 Research on teaching and learning mathematics: Two disciplines of scientific inquiry. In: Wittrock M C *Handbook of Research on Teaching*, 3rd edn. Macmillan, New York.

Silver E A 1987 Foundation of cognitive theory and research for mathematics problem-solving instruction. In: Schoenfeld A H 1987 *Cognitive Science and Mathematics Education*. Erlbaum, Hillsdale, New Jersey.

Servais W, Varga T (ed.) 1971 *Teaching School Mathematics*. Penguin, Harmondsworth

Steiner H G 1978 *Didaktik der Mathematik*. Wissenschaftliche Buchgesellschaft, Darmstadt

UNESCO 1967 *New Trends in Mathematics Teaching*, Vol. 1. Prepared by the International Commission of Mathematical Instruction, UNESCO, Paris

UNESCO 1970 *New Trends in Mathematics Teaching*, Vol. 2. Prepared by the International Commission of Mathematical Instruction, UNESCO, Paris

UNESCO 1973 *New Trends in Mathematics Teaching*, Vol. 3. Prepared by the International Commission of Mathematical Instruction, UNESCO, Paris

UNESCO 1979 *New Trends in Mathematics Teaching*, Vol. 4. Prepared by the International Commission of Mathematical Instruction, UNESCO, Paris

Wilson J W 1971 Secondary school mathematics. In: Bloom B S, Hastings J T, Madaus G F (eds.) 1971 *Handbook on Formative and Summative Evaluation of Student Learning*. McGraw-Hill, New York

Calculators in Mathematics Education

L. A. Hutton

In the early 1970s, hand-held calculators were placed on the market the world over. These devices were among the first articles manufactured for the general consumer which used the microprocessor, a tiny solid-state silicon chip no larger than this letter "M."

Today, different models with a wide range of functions are available. These range from inexpensive models that only add, subtract, multiply, and divide to programmable models that function as small computers.

Although many students and teachers now own personal calculators, they still have not received wide acceptance into the mathematics curriculum. However, the calculator has been accepted as a computational tool in many upper-level (preuniversity) nonmathematics disciplines, that is, physics, chemistry, business, and so on. At the university level, calculators are used freely by many teachers and often considered part of the expected equipment for students of science, engineering, and economics. For engineering students in the United States the calculator has completely replaced the slide rule. However, at lower grade levels there is less acceptance of the calculator in the mathematics classes. Educators in many countries do not believe that the calculator is appropriate for 13-year-olds and under. For example, in the Federal Republic of Germany, the ministries of education have prohibited the use of the calculator for computation in grades one through six.

In the United States, the National Council of Teachers of Mathematics conducted an extensive survey of the opinions of a broad-based sample of both professional educators and lay persons entitled *Priorities in School Mathematics* (PRISM) (National Council of

Teachers of Mathematics 1981). One of the items considered in this survey was the calculator in the pre-university mathematics classroom. The survey report suggests that there may be greater differences of opinion on the proper use of the calculator in the mathematics curriculum than on any of the other 15 items surveyed.

Textbook publishers' cautious approach to incorporation of the calculator probably reflects this absence of a consensus of opinion. Most textbooks for the 14-year-olds and older have some special problems which are marked for calculator use. However, the traditional curriculum has not been revised to accommodate the calculator. In the United States, Canada, and United Kingdom, as in other countries, there are supplemental publications available to help the teachers who want to use the calculator; however, it is still difficult and requires much individual effort on the part of the teacher to incorporate the calculator into the classroom. The calculator has had wide acceptance only for such tasks as checking answers and replacing trigonometric and logarithmic tables.

Advocates of the calculator see the following advantages: (a) word problems can use realistic data for all age groups; (b) the calculator has a positive motivation effect; (c) its use relieves the student from tedious computation; (d) development of calculator algorithms offer an opportunity to study algorithmic processes; (e) working iterated procedures can lead to a better understanding of concepts such as limits; (f) calculator tests will have to emphasize mathematical concepts and reasoning ability; (g) the ability to operate calculators is an asset on the job market; (h) the use of calculators will improve students' attitudes towards mathematics lessons; (i) with the calculator, many topics such as probability and statistics can be introduced earlier in a more meaningful manner (Suydam 1980).

Some people see the following as dangers of introducing the calculator into the mathematics curriculum: (a) regular use will result in a weakening of basic facts and paper-and-pencil algorithms for computation; (b) use at early ages may hinder development of number concepts; (c) students will become calculator dependent; (d) students will be more likely to accept incorrect answers from the calculator; (e) if students use the calculator, they will not learn to think; (f) students will need to pass various tests without calculators.

Placing the calculator in the classroom will not automatically have all the positive and negative results listed. The outcome of the calculator in the mathematics classroom is dependent on how it is incorporated into the curriculum. A re-evaluation of the global goals of mathematics education is at the core of the calculator decision. No-one can deny that the calculator is rapidly becoming an accepted and often preferred mode of computation in everyday life and business at all levels. It is not so much a question of whether calculator use will hinder performance ability of paper-and-pencil computation as it is a question of the current and future need for paper-and-pencil computation. Is it more

important to know *how* to perform the long division algorithm or to know *when* to divide and how to use a calculator to obtain the answer? Such questions demand a total evaluation of the educational goals of mathematics and a massive restructuring of the curriculum which will not occur quickly. And perhaps a slow meaningful change is most desirable.

In the meantime, consultants and teachers can help to facilitate meaningful integration of the calculator into the traditional curriculum in several ways. Examples of three possible methods are: (a) textbook supplements; (b) games and activities and (c) special problem-solving lessons.

The textbook supplement consists of a page-by-page set of instructions for the teacher. These should include supplemental problems with realistic values. The calculator is not appropriate for all mathematics lessons and, therefore, the supplement should indicate the lessons where its use is not desirable or helpful.

There are many sources of games and activities for the calculator. Also, the value of many traditional classroom games can be enhanced by the calculator. Many games help to teach basic facts and concepts. For example, the following game to aid the learning of the multiplication facts was quite successful in an Indiana (USA) public-school project with 10- to 12-year-old students (Hutton 1980). Students work in pairs, each on a different team, with one calculator per pair. First students enter a multiplication fact of their choice, say, "7 × 9." The second student states the answer verbally, "63" and then presses "=." If the calculator verifies this verbal answer, the second student's team scores a point. If not, the first student's team scores a point. They alternate positions. The team with the most points wins. Students can use problems to which they do not know the answer.

The same project that used the above game also had some success with a special problem-solving lesson. Each week the teachers were given an overhead transparency with the problem format and a teacher's instruction sheet. Students used their calculators to solve the problem. The topics of these special problems were relevant to the students' current interests. For example, the 500 Mile Auto Race is run in May in Indianapolis, Indiana. At this time, one of the lessons concerned the speeds in the race. The lesson involved ratio, proportions, and units. The students were both interested and motivated to find the solutions. With the aid of the calculator they were quickly able to solve a meaningful application of ratios and proportions and thereby reenforce their understanding of these concepts.

The calculator can be an asset to the mathematics curriculum if it is used properly. It will require work by both curriculum specialists and classroom teachers to effect changes in educational attitudes by demonstrating its positive aspects. Undoubtedly, overwhelming general use of calculators will slowly force the schools to recognize their importance. When calculators are incorporated into the mathematics curriculum, hopefully it will be in a manner befitting the technology that developed them.

Bibliography

Hutton L 1980 Calculators: Teachers' attitudes and children's ability. *Math. Teaching* 90: 20–21

National Council of Teachers of Mathematics 1981 *Priorities in School Mathematics: Executive Summary of* PRISM *Project.* National Council of Teachers of Mathematics, Reston, Virginia

Suydam M N 1980 *International Calculator Review: Working Paper on Hand-held Calculators in Schools.* SMEAC Information Reference Center, Ohio State University, Columbus, Ohio

Computers in Mathematics Education

J. Olive and L. L. Hatfield

In this article, the term *computers* refers primarily to personal computers or microcomputers (including powerful hand-held calculators) which are available for student use in school situations, as opposed to the large mainframe computers used by industry and research institutions. The term *mathematics education* refers to the teaching and learning of mathematics in schools.

During the 1980s there has been a dramatic evolution in available microcomputer hardware which can be summed up as more for less. As prices for micros have continued to fall, their capacities have increased dramatically, from machines with only 32K of random access memory to machines with over 1000K. In fact the same computing power of the first micros is available from hand-held calculators, along with much more mathematically sophisticated input–output interfaces. These programable, graphics calculators (referred to by some as supercalculators) should be properly regarded as hand-held computers, and as such offer the possibility of placing a computer in every mathematics student's hand. Such universal access to computing technology must bring into question what and how mathematics is taught and learned in schools, and how it is used in the workplace. The actual impacts of computers on mathematics curricula during the 1980s, however, have been rather modest despite a growing recognition, indeed demand, that the potential impacts and consequences should be significant. "In spite of the intimate intellectual link between mathematics and computing, school mathematics has responded hardly at all to curricular changes implied by the computer revolution" (National Research Council 1989 p. 62).

This article focuses on the most important changes implied by this revolution: changes in the nature of mathematics (which should impact curriculum content), changes in available modes of learning (which impact the teaching/learning process), and changes in the technology (which impact the nature of available learning tools and how teachers and students do mathematics). A brief description of each of these changes is presented. After an overview of the historical development of the use of computers, the actual and potential uses of computers in mathematics education in several different countries is discussed. Research trends from several countries are then presented and the article concludes with suggestions for future trends in both the use of and research concerning computers in mathematics education.

1. Changes in the Nature of Mathematics

Mathematics continues to flourish through the growing power of its applications, and much of its utility is enhanced through the computer. In return, computers influence mathematics through the stimulation of mathematical research, and by the practice of science and engineering. The nature of applications, the models formulated about them, and the results obtained from computer simulations of them all interact to stimulate new ideas and methods. Such changes in the nature of mathematical content must be allowed to impact into mathematical education if students are to be adequately prepared for a complex technological and scientific world. For example, concepts of iteration and recursion can be more readily addressed with simple but powerful computer procedures, thereby providing students with conceptual tools for investigating traditional topics in new ways (e.g., approximation methods for solving equations), as well as new topics (e.g., chaos and fractal geometry).

2. Changes in Available Modes of Learning

Computing technologies have dramatically lessened the human requirements for computation, symbolic manipulation, and memory. At the same time, such tools increase the demand for their users to possess deeper understandings of the meanings and relationships among ideas. The goals of the mathematics curriculum have generally emphasized understanding, but it appears that classroom practices have often emphasized skillful performance at the expense of deep meaning. In a mathematics curriculum infused with applications of computing technologies, it will be critical that students construct rich understandings of fundamental concepts to be able to use the power offered through the technology intelligently. Fortunately, significant interactions with the same technology may promote the development of such understandings.

3. Changes in the Technology

Computing technologies (hardware and software) continue to become more powerful tools for doing mathematics. The memory, speed, precision, cost, ease of use, flexibility, representational capabilities, and responsiveness of microcomputer hardware and software have improved significantly in the 1980s. The new generation of microcomputers offer visual, iconic user interfaces, calculating power, and extensive data storage and retrieval capabilities. The visual interfaces have made computers accessible and usable by even the youngest school-age child. Their calculating power has earned them the title of "the machines of mathematics," while their capacity to handle large amounts of data has turned them into powerful information and management systems. Kaput (1988) offers the following comparisons to illustrate the increase in computing power in the United States from the mid-1960s. In 1965 there were about three electronic computing circuits (the building blocks of all computers) per person, in 1980 about 10,000, and he estimated that in 1990 there would be about two million circuits per person. Another revealing comparison concerns the computing power which controls the Voyager II space probe, launched in 1977, which has transmitted amazing information and video details of the planet Neptune: its on-board computer has less computing capacity than most of the microcomputers used in elementary classrooms.

Software development for educational purposes, however, has not kept pace with the evolution of the hardware or with software development in industry, business, or the sciences. There are very few quality products available for use in schools, although several noteworthy development efforts are now under way. In 1988 Kaput described public schools in the United States as technological ghettos. Specific languages and software tools of increasing power, however, have been developed for educational use. The Logo programing language was specifically developed during the 1970s as a constructive mathematical environment for school-age children and can be found in classrooms throughout the world.

Developments in mathematical computer environments incorporate a vast array of built-in capabilities to permit students and researchers to investigate and construct mathematical theory. With such systems (e.g., *Mathematica*) the gap between the mathematical environment for novice and expert could disappear, thereby allowing students to progress over possibly many years of education within the same fertile context.

Such systems, however, are only available on the most powerful micros which are not yet generally available in schools. The growing availability of Hypertext systems such as HyperCard, however, may help nonspecialist educators create interactive learning environments specifically tailored to their curriculum and student needs. (Hypertext refers to a dynamically linked set of data consisting of text and graphics which can be accessed by clicking specified regions of the computer screen with a pointing device. The system allows for nonlinear movement through sets of data and linking of the data to other computer programs.) Through the use of such systems, computers permit dynamic rather than static representations of mathematical ideas. Unlike the dynamics of film or video, students and teacher can interact with the production system to influence the specific direction and form of the representations. Thus, computers can support an investigative, experimental approach to doing mathematics. Inductive, example-oriented approaches to construction of mathematical generalizations can be used. With the more sophisticated software tools under development, such as symbolic and iconic algebraic systems, more deductive analyses can be coupled with inductive strategies. Statistical toolware permits the interactive exploration of data analyses which can support conceptual development of the underlying mathematical ideas.

Computers can model conceptual connections among multiple representations by displaying several visual and numerical forms of a situation, such as pictorial arrays, equations, data tables or charts, and graphs. If any one of these is changed by the student or teacher, the concomitant effects of the change upon the other forms can be immediately demonstrated. Thus, it is possible to explore the behavior of a mathematical phenomenon more deeply by manipulating and witnessing the covariations among linked representations.

The technology exists to make significant impacts on the way mathematics is learned in schools; but how much of this potential is being put to use in mathematics classrooms? What research efforts have been mounted to assist implementation and assess its impacts?

4. Use of Computers in Mathematics Instruction

In the United States, the first use of computers in schools was confined to time sharing on mainframe or minicomputer systems, which offered poor or nonexistent graphics. During the 1960s and 1970s these systems supported some early forms of Computer Assisted Instruction (CAI), which were fairly inflexible (e.g., Plato), but their main use was to provide programing opportunities for students in scientific languages (e.g., GOTRAN, FORTRAN, BASIC). Computing was regarded as a specialist topic, isolated from the mainstream curriculum.

At the end of the 1970s the microcomputer made its first appearance in schools. At first it was used in much the same way as the mainframe systems, with its built-in form of the BASIC programing language, but quickly came to be used for drill and practice of basic facts—mainly arithmetical knowledge—as CAI software began to dominate the meager market of educational software. The new CAI was different from the earlier CAI only in its use of graphics to supplement text.

Reports from the 1985 National Survey of Instructional Uses of School Computers (Becker 1986) indicated that, even though the number of computers available for instruction in schools in the United States increased dramatically in the two-year period from 1983 to 1985, less than a third of elementary teachers and less than 12 percent of middle- and high-school teachers used computers in their instruction. When computers were used, they were more often used for mathematics instruction at the elementary and middle schools than other subjects, but were more often used for computing subjects in high schools. The major type of use in the elementary schools was drill and practice of mathematical skills, and the major use in the high schools was programing. Overall, less than 15 percent of computer use was for exploration, inductive inquiry, or problem solving.

A nationwide survey of teachers' reactions to computer use in schools in the United States (Wirthlin Group 1989) indicated a favorable attitude towards computers: 85 percent of all teachers surveyed thought that computers have had a positive effect on United States education. The survey also indicated that 70 percent of all teachers did not like software that focused on drill and practice, which indicated a desire to move away from this dominant use of computers in mathematics instruction. In other nations where computers have been used in mathematics education for several years, similar trends have been reported.

All secondary schools in Taiwan offer an optional two-hour computer science class in ninth grade for one semester. This course is usually a course in BASIC programing. There is some use of Logo in mathematics classes in grades five and six. All secondary schools are provided with at least 25 microcomputers. Elementary schools are provided with only one or two computers, but many have purchased more for themselves.

Since 1983, Australia has undertaken a nationwide computers in education program which has been thoroughly evaluated (Bigum et al. 1987). Through 38 case studies of schools in three of the six states, they were able to give an indication of the variety of practices of school computing in Australia. They found that the prime movers for computing in schools was often the cohort of mathematics teachers, giving them an evolutionary advantage amplified by the scarcity of expertise in schools. It appears that many mathematics teachers have begun to make use of computers in their teaching, but their views of curriculum, teaching, and learning often seem unchanged wherein applications of computing are typically accommodated into a traditional scheme. While most teachers seem to have at least a passing familiarity with the terms and jargon of computing, few are able to integrate uses of computers routinely in their lessons. Further, most seem to understand computing in terms of improving the efficiency of current teaching practices; "there is no sense of first questioning current practice before enhancing its legitimacy by carrying out the practice on computer. The practice is not changed, only its means" (Bigum et al. 1987 p. 23). Finally, computing practices of Australian teachers are

seen to be fragile, often subject to disruptive or destructive influences.

Changes in the way computers are used in mathematics education are under way in Japan. The new Japanese mathematics curriculum, as outlined in the new national syllabus and ministerial ordinance announced by the Ministry of Education, Science, and Culture (Government of Japan 1989), places emphasis on the use of computers at lower-secondary (middle) and upper-secondary grade levels of mathematics instruction. The curriculum was recognized as "obviously deficient in introducing computers into mathematics education" (Fujita 1987 p. 201).

The curriculum, scheduled for implementation in the 1990s, attempts to overcome this deficiency. The teaching of flow-charts and the binary system are introduced in lower secondary (middle grades) and the effective use of computers in each content area is recommended, but especially in teaching quantitative relations through experiments and observations.

At the upper-secondary level, the new mathematics curriculum will consist of three courses covering the core subjects, and three courses covering optional subjects. All three of the options courses require the use of computers throughout the course as well as providing specific topics dealing with computer science. In the old curriculum, college-bound students would not have had the opportunity to either use or study computers; in the new curriculum, all college-bound students will have that opportunity. Indeed, for students intending to study mathematical sciences, it will be required.

The new syllabus also specifies new requirements for teacher training and certification. All prospective teachers will be required to take computer-related courses. Prospective mathematics teachers will be required to study the use of computers in mathematics teaching.

The training and preparation of teachers for the infusion of computing technologies in their mathematics instruction is a major issue facing the mathematics education community in every nation. Several projects are being planned in the United States. One such project (Project LITMUS at the University of Georgia) will attempt a system-wide approach to infusion through a leadership model of teacher enhancement which will eventually provide training and support for every mathematics teacher (K–12) in two rural school systems.

In 1985, the Soviet Union launched a national program of computerization. A 70-hour course on Fundamentals of Informatics and Computers was introduced for grades 9 and 10 in all schools. This course has many ties with mathematics instruction in the schools. The course is mainly taught by mathematics teachers. The course is taught without the availability of computers in the majority of schools; however, the Soviet Union expects to equip about 3,000 classes with 12 to 15 computers each. The goal is to deliver approximately 400,000 computers to schools by the 1990 to 1991 academic year, although more realistic estimates suggest that it will be 1995 before every secondary school has a computer class. Educators in the Soviet Union are working towards an integrated use of computers in mathematics classrooms through an amalgamated course in mathematics and informatics (Ershov 1988).

Although most Third World nations can be described as computer-poor, some use of computers is taking place in mathematics classrooms in even the poorest nations. Despite the profound economic problems of Latin American countries, many of their governments are planning a widespread introduction of computers in schools. The mathematics education community in Latin America seems very receptive to the use of computers in mathematics instruction. For example, at the Third Central American and Caribbean Meeting in Teacher Education and Research on Mathematics Education, 10 out of 85 presentations were about the use of computers, especially Logo, in mathematics instruction. As in the United States, most instruction with computers in Latin American schools takes place in computer labs, with drill and practice being the most popular application.

The computer-rich nations have a responsibility to provide research data to developing nations on the most effective uses of computing technologies in education in order for the developing nations to maximize the use of very limited resources. This view was reflected by representatives from the developing countries at the Sixth International Congress on Mathematics Education in Budapest, 1988.

5. Research Issues

Laborde (1989), a member of the Research Group on Mathematics and Computing Education, identified four major foci of mathematics education research in France which addressed the impacts of computers:

(a) Research on the new significance of mathematical concepts which can be modelled or explored on the computer.

(b) Research on the new interactions among knowledge and pupils made possible by the use of the computer.

(c) Research on the change brought about in the didactic contract (teaching/learning situation) by the use of the computer, as the respective roles of pupil and teacher are modified.

(d) Research and development of interactive mathematical learning environments (e.g., Cabri-Géomètre)

These foci match the important changes identified at the beginning of this article and are shared by many mathematics education researchers in most of the industrialized nations.

The British government made an early commitment to the use of computers in schools and in the late 1970s underwrote the development of the BBC microcomputer which has more powerful computing capabilities than most of the microcomputers available in schools in the United States. Several research centers have been actively involved in developing computer learning environments and researching students' learning of mathematics within these environments (e.g., the Centre for Science and Mathematics Education, Chelsea College, London, and the Shell Centre for Mathematical Education at the University of Nottingham). These development efforts are guided by a set of program design and use principles which have emerged from their classroom research (Fraser and Burkhardt 1984).

The Logo Maths Project at the University of London has investigated students' mathematical learning through the use of Logo. Their studies include work with 10 to 14-year-old children. They have investigated learning of both geometric and algebraic concepts (Hoyles and Sutherland 1989). Their results indicate that Logo can be used effectively within the regular mathematics instruction to enhance students' understanding of angle and measurement concepts, and also help students construct a meaningful concept of variable.

Logo research is being conducted on every continent, in countries as diverse as China and Israel. In 1984 several articles on Logo were published in the Chinese journal *The World of Computers*, and in 1985 a group of educators from the United States was invited to conduct workshops for elementary and middle-school teachers in Logo programing and its uses in mathematics education. The Beijing University Press published a Logo Language text book for universities, normal and technical schools in 1985. International conferences on Logo and Mathematics Education have been held in England, Canada, and Israel (Leron 1989).

While results of initial Logo research in North America were varied and inconclusive, more research efforts from many different countries appear to support the conclusions of the project in the United Kingdom. The report of the Logo working group at the Sixth International Congress on Mathematics Education stated that:

> clear progress has been made in a number of key areas:— in understanding the potential of Logo tools for the construction of mathematical representations; in clarifying the role of turtle geometry as offering not only a context for geometrical activities, but also a medium for expressing and exploring a range of algebraic and more general mathematical ideas; finally, in identifying the significant features of the pedagogical context in which children's Logo work is situated. (Fraser 1988 p. 234)

Several other institutions and individuals in the United Kingdom are very active in the field of research and development of computer use in mathematics education. Tall (1986) at the University of Warwick has been developing calculus software and investigating its use with high-school students. A group at the Open University is developing an Intelligent Computer

Assisted Instructional (ICAI) environment for learning early number concepts (Hennessy et al. 1989).

Many of the industrialized nations are supporting research and development efforts in ICAI. The Cabri-Géomètre software, developed in France, has some aspects of ICAI. The United States has several, large scale projects ranging from environments for exploring early number concepts to algebra, geometry, and calculus tutors. The tutor metaphor has dominated the application of artificial intelligence (AI) to educational goals. A geometry tutor is being developed in the Federal Republic of Germany. An intelligent tutor for learning about characteristics of algebraic functions is under development in Israel. The Taiwan government is supporting the development of multimedia techniques for AI tutorial use.

The notion of computerized intelligent tutors, however, has its critics. Kaput (1988) points out that this notion necessitates the ability to represent the domain to be learned within a computer program and, therefore, limits its application to those domains that are themselves (or consist of) formal systems (e.g., algebra, Euclidean geometry). Moreover, the intelligent tutors can only teach the syntax of the formal representations; they do not (because they cannot) deal with what the formalisms are used to represent. According to Kaput these tutoring systems are both pedagogically inappropriate (as they are experienced as meaningless and alienating by students) and superfluous (as more and more powerful formal system manipulation tools become available). Research results from initial pilot implementation studies by developers of such systems appear to support Kaput's first point (Stasz 1988).

Research on other uses of computers in mathematics instruction is also being conducted in many nations. The Taiwan government is supporting three major research and development programs focusing on the use of computers in mathematics education:

(a) CAI for supplemental learning with special (slow or advanced) students. More than 400 lesson units have been developed and are available free to all schools. This program is spread over all schools in Taiwan with instruction for implementation available to all mathematics and science teachers.

(b) The computer as an experimental tool in regular mathematics and science classes. There are 20 research projects in this program, most of which are focused on secondary and tertiary education levels. There are two or three projects at the elementary level.

(c) The implementation of multimedia techniques for tutorial use. There are only one or two development projects in this program which focuses on the use of interactive video-disk technology and artificial intelligence (AI) models for analyzing students' responses.

6. Future Trends

What can be anticipated in the near future with respect to the use of computers in mathematics education? In most of the industrialized countries a strong push for widescale infusion of computing technologies in mathematics instruction at all levels has already begun. National programs are being developed to train teachers to use the available technology in their classrooms effectively. The emphasis in most countries appears to be on the use of the computer (by students) as a tool for exploring mathematical phenomena, for solving real-world problems, for modelling dynamic events, and for theory building. As the technology continues to develop toward more natural human–computer interfacing, the difficulties and reluctance felt by many teachers and students with regard to computer use can be expected to diminish.

While the interest in developing artificial intelligent (AI) tutors is still widespread, there is a growing awareness in the mathematics education research community of the limitations of this endeavor, and of the need for more knowledge of how children construct their own mathematical knowledge within a computerized learning environment. In the United States and Canada, research is being conducted on childrens' constructions of mathematical knowledge in various computer-based learning situations.

Much more widespread use of computer networks for sharing knowledge, creating global data bases, and for collaborative problem solving can be expected. In the United States there are several research and development projects which involve computer networking on a national and international scale. Students are able to create, share, and analyze data from thousands of different locations. They can also share their mathematical and scientific investigations with other students around the world.

Global computer networking can also facilitate collaboration among researchers from different nations. The new era of *glasnost* in the Soviet Union has brought about the possibility of exchanges among Soviet educators and educators in the Western hemisphere. One such collaboration in the area of computer use in mathematics education concerns the School Project of the Soviet Academy of Sciences (Semenov 1989). The emphasis of the project is on how to use technology in mathematics and science education. A collaborative project has been established involving the Massachusetts Institute of Technology (MIT) and Technical Education Research Centers (TERC), both in Cambridge, Massachusetts. A team of Soviet researchers visited Cambridge. They are establishing a Lego-Logo project in schools in the Soviet Union with help from the Logo group at MIT. (Lego-Logo is a learning environment which uses the Logo computer language to control mechanical devices created by children out of Lego construction materials.) This project will share Soviet students' work with Lego-Logo with students and teachers in the United States through TERC's Star Schools computer network.

Such collaborations are necessary to address adequately the far-reaching implications of computer technology on mathematics learning. The speedy communication of ideas among students and teachers from different nations, made possible through computer networks, could also herald the beginning of a global classroom, the implications of which go far beyond mathematics education.

Bibliography

Alvarez M 1989 Construyendo conceptos matematicos con la computadora. In: Oviedo-Valeiro J, Tsijli T, Sanbria R L, Quesada A L (eds.) 1989 *Proceedings of the Third Central American and Caribbean Meeting in Teacher Education and Research in Mathematics Education.* UNED, San Jose, California, pp. 21–24

Becker H J 1986 Instructional uses of school computers newsletter: Reports from the 1985 national survey. Johns Hopkins University Center for Social Organization of Schools, 1: 1–6

Bigum C, Bonser S, Evans P, Groundwater-Smith S, Grundy S, Kemmis S, McKenzie D, McKinnon D, O'Connor M, Straton R, Willis S 1987 *Coming to Terms with Computers in Schools: Report of the Schools Studies of the National Evaluation Study of the Commonwealth Schools Commission's National Computer Education Program.* Deakin Institute for Studies in Education, Victoria

Ershov A 1988 Special IPC-invited lecture: Computerization of schools and mathematical education. In: Hirst A, Hirst K (eds.) 1988 *Proceedings of the Sixth International Congress on Mathematical Education (ICME 6).* Janos Bolyal Mathematical Society, Budapest, pp. 49–65

Fraser R 1988 Theme group 2: Computers and the teaching of mathematics. In: Hirst A, Hirst K (eds.) 1988 *Proceedings of the Sixth International Congress on Mathematical Education (ICME 6).* Janos Bolyai Mathematical Society, Budapest, p. 234

Fraser R, Burkhardt H 1984 *Technology, Triangles and Teaching.* Shell Centre for Mathematical Education, University of Nottingham, Nottingham

Fujita H 1987 The present state and current problems of mathematics education at the senior secondary level in Japan. In: Wirzup I, Streit R (eds.) 1987 *Development in School Mathematics Education Around the World.* National Council of Teachers of Mathematics, Reston, Virginia, pp. 191–224

Government of Japan Ministry of Education, Science, and Culture 1989 *The Course of Study: Arithmetic and Mathematics for Elementary, and Lower and Upper Secondary Schools,* (rev. edn.) [In Japanese]. Japan Society of Mathematical Education, Tokyo

Hennessy S, O'Shea T, Evertsz R, Floyd A 1989 An intelligent tutoring system approach to teaching primary mathematics. *Educ. Stud. Math.* 20(3): 273–92

Hoyles C, Sutherland R 1989 *LOGO Mathematics in the Classroom.* Routledge, London

Kaput J 1988 *Looking Back from the Future: A History of Computers in Mathematics Education, 1978–1998.* Educational Technology Centre, Cambridge, Massachusetts.

Konig G 1989 Computer und mathematikunterricht—Eine bestandsaufnahme zu einzelnen aspekten. *ZDM* 21: 67–72

Laborde C 1989 The audacity and reason of French research in mathematics education (English translation). In: Vergnaud G, Rogalski J, Artique M (eds.) 1989 *Actes de la 13e Conférence Internationale. Psychology of Mathematics Education,* vol. 1. Didactique, Paris, pp. 46–61

Leron U (ed.) 1989 *Proceedings of the Fourth International Conference for Logo and Mathematics Education.* Department of Science Education, Technicon—Israel Institute of Technology, Haifa, Israel

Macao Computers, Science and Technology Agency 1984 *The World of Computers, 8.* Beijing, China

National Research Council 1989 *Everybody Counts: A Report to the Nation of the Future of Mathematics Education.* National Academy Press, Washington, DC

Semenov A 1989 *The School Project of the Soviet Academy of Sciences.* Soviet Academy of Sciences, Moscow

Stasz C 1988 *An Intelligent Tutor for Basic Algebra: Preliminary Data on Student Outcomes.* The RAND Corporation, Santa Monica, California

Tall D 1986 *Graphic Calculus.* Glentop Press, London

Wirthlin Group 1989 *The Computer Report Card: How Teachers Grade Computers in the Classroom.* Wirthlin Group, New York

Yu S 1985 *Logo Language: Teaching Procedures,* Beijing University Press, Beijing, China

Metacognition and Mathematics

A. H. Schoenfeld

Metacognition is a broadly used term referring to individuals' knowledge, understanding, and regulation of their own thought processes. The topic became a focal point of research in education, psychology, and artificial intelligence in the 1970s and was rapidly recognized as representing a fundamental aspect of human thinking and problem solving. Three major aspects of metacognition are discussed in the literature.

The first aspect, metacognitive knowledge, concerns individuals' judgments of their own mental capacities and behavior. Examples of metacognitive knowledge include people's assessments of (a) the amount of information they can memorize without error, (b) the kinds of mental arithmetic they can perform, (c) how well they understand the mathematical subject matter they have been taught, and (d) their abilities to understand and apply mathematical text materials. These kinds of assessments are a critical component of the "feedback loop" providing information to learners as they grapple with new skills. In general, young children's metacognitive knowledge is quite inaccurate; such knowledge becomes more accurate as children mature (Flavell 1979).

The second aspect, control or self-regulation, concerns individuals' ability to monitor, assess, and (if warranted) modify their own behavior in the midst of performing complex tasks such as mathematical problem solving. Research indicates that expert problem solvers are far better at self-regulation than novices. In addition to being more resourceful problem solvers, they are more efficient at using the information they have at their disposal. They spend more time planning their solution attempts, and more time evaluating their solution attempts as they evolve. As a result they are better both at curtailing inappropriate explorations or wild goose chases, and at pursuing potentially promising "leads" in problem solving. This, in turn, leads to more problem-solving success (Schoenfeld 1985, Kilpatrick 1986).

The third aspect, belief systems, concerns the set of (possibly implicit) understandings that individuals have regarding themselves, mathematics, and the nature of mathematical thinking. People's conceptions of what mathematics is, and how mathematics is done, shape the ways that those people behave in mathematical situations. Many students, for example, believe that mathematical ideas and procedures are passed on "from above" by experts to be memorized by themselves. In consequence, they expect to have ready formulas for situations they have studied, and they may simply give up if they have forgotten the formulas, or may fail to analyze situations they would have been capable of understanding had they tried to analyze them. Similarly, many students whose sole experience with problem solving is in working drill-and-practice exercises come to expect that if they can solve a problem at all, they can do so in just a few minutes. Such students may simply stop working on longer problems that would have been solvable had they spent more time working at them (National Assessment of Educational Progress 1983).

1. Evolution of the Concept

Metacognitive abilities are related to "higher order thinking skills," which have a distinguished heritage in the mathematical and psychological literatures. In mathematics specifically they can be traced to the 17th century, to Descartes' reflections on his own thinking (Descartes 1967) and subsequent elaborations on the same theme by Pólya (1945); also to the work of gestaltists such as Wertheimer (1945). Indeed, the best of metacognitive activity bears a marked resemblance to the highest state of intellectual activity described by Piaget (1970): reflective abstraction. In this state individuals are capable of observing their actions "at a distance," reflecting on them, and if necessary, modifying their behavior accordingly.

Despite its lineage, the term metacognition itself is new. (It does not appear, for example, in the 1971 compact edition of the *Oxford English Dictionary* or in the 1979 edition of *Webster's New Universal Unabridged Dictionary*.) More importantly, the way in which the term is used—with metacognitive behavior serving as a component of cognitive process models—is new, and reflects recent advances in understanding and modeling complex thought processes. Recognition that the concept was needed, and progress towards its definition, took place almost simultaneously in three disparate disciplines in the 1970s.

Psychological researchers observed that young children were quite poor at assessing their memorization abilities (Flavell 1979). Students would claim to have memorized a short list of words perfectly, and then make numerous recall errors; they would claim to be able to memorize 100 words while in fact being able to memorize only five or six; and so on. Of course, people who believe that memorizing is easy and that they are good at it will hardly engage in the kind of behavior (e.g., rehearsal) that might help them develop the memory skills they need. Hence students with grossly inaccurate views of their memory skills would have a hard time developing good study habits. It was in such early work on *metamemory* that the interplay between the use and development of one's cognitive skills and one's awareness and assessment of them began to become apparent. Over the following decade, psychological research exploring that interplay was extended from issues of memory to the broader issues of thinking and learning (Brown et al. 1983).

Researchers in artificial intelligence, the branch of computer science that constructs "intelligent" computer programs, made parallel observations. As problem-solving programs became more complex, it became clear that "resource management" was a fundamental issue. Computer programs can store vast amounts of information and do extremely rapid calculations. Their effectiveness, however, depends on which information is accessed and which computations are chosen. Simple flow-chart designs, or other one-dimensional approaches proved inadequate, and a new generation of two-tiered architectures (one for "doing," a second for making decisions) was developed. The upper "executive" tier was assigned monitoring, assessment, and decision-making functions that parallel metacognitive functions in humans (Sleeman and Brown 1982).

Educational researchers reached similar conclusions. In observations of novice problem solvers, Schoenfeld (1985) documented that such students often have adequate factual and strategic knowledge to solve assigned problems; they fail to solve them because they make poor executive decisions, pursuing inappropriate directions and failing to capitalize on potentially useful ones. In contrast, good problem solvers—who often begin working problems knowing fewer domain-specific facts and procedures than the novices—often manage to solve the problems by generating more possibilities, carefully evaluating their options, and opportunistically pursuing the ones that look promising. The research also indicates that people's naive epistemologies (their own naive views of what subject domains such as mathematics or physics are really about) shape what they see in those domains and how they act in them. In the case of naive physics (diSessa 1983), students who have done well in college physics courses often ignore their formal knowledge to provide Aristotelian explanations of everyday phenomena; their own empirical evidence (e.g., "you have to keep pushing a lawnmower to make it move") supersedes their formal instruction in Newton's laws. Analogously, students' empirical experience with mathematics in classrooms (e.g., extensive drill-and-practice on routine exercises, and passive memorization of procedures demonstrated for them; see Cockcroft [1982]) appears to yield the inappropriate student beliefs and behaviors cited above.

2. Instructional Implications

The dominant curricular trend in mathematics education over the past decade has been "problem solving." Virtually nonexistent during the 1970s, a decade that focused on drill-and-practice, and only barely emergent in 1980 (there were three sessions devoted to it at the Fourth International Congress on Mathematical Education in Berkeley, California), problem solving grew exponentially to become the subject with the most heavily attended sessions at the Fifth International Congress on Mathematical Education in Adelaide, Australia, in 1984. As is often the case with curricular movements, problem solving means different things to different people. However, two main themes have emerged in instruction. (There is also a small, though growing, movement toward the use of small group cooperative problem solving in open-ended explorations. This healthy trend needs to be encouraged.) The first theme is an increased use of "word problems" rather than isolated computation exercises. The trend away from pure computation is good, but the definition of problem-solving skill as the ability to solve word problems is far too narrow. The second theme is the inclusion of separate units on problem solving in otherwise standard mathematics textbooks. Such units tend to focus on Pólya-type heuristics, which are often taught as clever tricks for solving particular classes of problems (e.g., "when you see an n, try plugging in values of $n = 1, 2, 3, 4$, and look for a pattern"). Instruction of that type is often mathematically superficial.

The literature on metacognition makes it quite clear that such attempts are not only mathematically superficial, but that they are most likely to be cognitively superficial as well (Collins et al. in press). Collins et al., after reviewing three pedagogical "success models," discuss a framework for the evaluation of learning environments. Along the content dimension—what students should learn about a discipline—they assert than an idealized learning environment should include attention to (a) domain knowledge, (b) problem-solving

strategies and heuristics, (c) "executive" or control strategies, and (d) learning strategies. They also suggest that the success models, by focusing on important aspects of thinking and understanding in the domain, help to nurture (e) belief systems appropriate for learning.

Most mathematics instruction focuses almost exclusively on (a), although the recent emphasis on problem solving has resulted in increased attention to (b). Even so, such instruction leaves metacognitive issues unaddressed, raising the likelihood of students developing maladaptive strategies or understandings in categories (c) through (e). Collins et al. discuss coaching and modeling strategies for attention to control and learning strategies. In coaching, the teacher plays an intellectual role analogous to the physical role of a sports coach. Working with students as they solve problems (possibly in small groups) the teacher may prompt attention to metacognitive actions by asking the students to explain what they are doing, why they are doing it, and how success in what they are doing will help them to solve the problem that they are trying to solve. In modeling, the teacher may give detailed descriptions of problem solutions as he or she works problems. These "out loud" sessions include planning and revision cycles, where the teacher makes explicit those metacognitive decisions that are usually covert and unseen (Schoenfeld 1985, Mason et al. 1982). Students' beliefs about mathematics can be addressed directly in discussions, or more profitably by creating classroom environments conducive to the development of mathematically productive belief systems (Schoenfeld 1987).

In summary, instruction focusing solely on domain knowledge and problem-solving strategies deals with only a fraction of mathematical thinking. Until mathematics instruction comes to grips with a broader spectrum of cognitive and metacognitive issues than are the current focus of concern, success is likely to be elusive. The findings in the (1982) Cockcroft Report and the (1983) National Assessment of Educational Progress Report, though occurring in different countries, indicate respectively the patterns and consequences of instruction that focuses primarily on skill acquisition rather than on substantive understanding.

3. Status and Directions

The simultaneous emergence of metacognition as an important concept in education, psychology, and cognitive science (artificial intelligence included) came about partly because of increased communication among researchers in those fields. The fundamental reason for its emergence, however, is that the paradigms and underlying philosophical perspectives in all those fields began to change radically in the 1970s. Earlier research has been characterized as "product" research, focusing largely on the identification of skills and abilities (e.g., "spatial ability," identified by factor analysis), on ways to measure them, and on ways to find relationships (usually correlational) between those abilities and measures of performance. *How* the abilities contributed to performance was in general unaddressed in formal research, although it was of course the object of speculation; rigorous methodological tools were not available for examining such issues. In the 1970s research began shifting to "process models." In such research the burden of proof is much higher: one must not only identify a construct, but one must explain how it works. Process models, sometimes implemented as computer programs, specify both the precise nature and the function of mental constructs. Such models made it clear that the "purely cognitive" models of the prior decades were inadequate, and that models of thinking processes needed to include metacognitive components.

The concept of metacognition, though of fundamental importance, is still poorly differentiated and poorly understood. Detailed cognitive research, including clinical examinations of students solving problems (Schoenfeld 1985) and computer programs with "meta-level" components (Sleeman and Brown 1982), has pointed to its importance and characterized, in part, how metacognition interacts with cognition. Over the coming decade one can expect to see more precise definitions, most likely resulting in a separation of the cluster called "metacognitive abilities" into its constituent parts: conscious and unconscious control behavior, belief systems, and so forth. With such differentiation should come increased depth (e.g., detailed models that make explicit the functional relationships among domain knowledge, strategies, and control) and breadth (e.g., anthropological studies of classrooms and "real world" experiences of mathematics that help explain how people develop their mathematical epistemologies). The integration of psychological and anthropological research with educational practice and experimentation (e.g., moves toward "open investigations" and small group interactions in mathematics classrooms) should provide a better understanding of the nature of mathematical thinking, and how to teach it.

Bibliography

Brown A L, Bransford J D, Ferrara R A, Campione J C 1983 Learning, remembering, and understanding. In: Flavell J H, Markman E M (eds.) 1983 *Handbook of Child Psychology*, Vol. 3, *Cognitive Development*. Wiley, New York, pp. 77–166

Cockcroft W H (ed.) 1982 *Mathematics Counts—Report of the Committee of Inquiry into the Teaching of Mathematics in Schools*. Her Majesty's Stationery Office, London

Collins A, Brown J S, Newman S 1988 Cognitive apprenticeship: Teaching the craft of reading, writing, and mathematics. In: Resnick L (ed.) 1988 *Cognition and Instruction: Issues and Agendas*. Lawrence Erlbaum, Hillsdale, New Jersey

Descartes R 1967 *Rules for the Direction of the Mind* (E S Haldane and G Ross, trans). Cambridge University Press, Cambridge

diSessa A A 1983 Phenomenology and the evolution of intuition. In: Gentner D, Stevens A L (eds.) 1983 *Mental Models*. Lawrence Erlbaum, Hillsdale, New Jersey, pp. 15–33

Flavell J H 1979 Metacognition and cognitive monitoring: A new area of cognitive-developmental inquiry. *Am. Psychol.* 34(10): 906–11

Kilpatrick J 1986 Reflection and recursion. In: Carss M (ed.) 1986 *Proc. Fifth Int. Congr. Mathematical Education*. Birkhauser, Boston, Massachusetts, pp. 7–29

Mason J, Burton L, Stacey K 1982 *Thinking Mathematically*. Addison-Wesley, London

National Assessment of Educational Progress 1983 *The Third National Assessment: Results, Trends, and Issues*. Education Commission of the States, Denver, Colorado

Piaget J 1970 *Genetic Epistemology*. Columbia University Press, New York

Pólya G 1985 *How to Solve it: A New Aspect of Mathematical Method*. Princeton University Press, Princeton, New Jersey

Schoenfeld A H 1985 *Mathematical Problem Solving*. Academic Press, Orlando, Florida

Schoenfeld A H 1987 What's all the fuss about metacognition? In: Schoenfeld A H (ed.) 1987 *Cognitive Science and Mathematics Education*. Lawrence Erlbaum, Hillsdale, New Jersey, pp. 189–215

Sleeman D, Brown J S (eds.) 1982 *Intelligent Tutoring Systems*. Academic Press, London

Wertheimer M 1945 *Productive Thinking*. Harper and Row, New York

Mathematics as a Humanistic Discipline

A. M. White

The mathematics that is known to most working mathematicians is very different from the subject that school children know. Even college graduates who have studied traditional mathematics in traditional ways may have no idea of the subject that excites and inspires most working mathematicians. The mathematics known to school children is often a dead subject that may or may not have any utility. For a few there is interest and challenge as with solving puzzles. For others there is value in the irrefutable certainty of its theorems; they believe that the only thing "essential for a mathematician is a keen, unerring intellect" (Krull 1987). For many there is fear and anxiety. The mathematics that excites working mathematicians is the free invention of the imagination and shares an aesthetic sense with art, poetry, and music. There is the artistic intuition that sees suitable axiomatic description and generalization of a mathematical situation (Weyl 1985). There is the anticipation of fruitfulness of certain lines of thought and belief. There is a sense of playfulness with which working mathematicians approach their subject (White 1985). The mathematics that is traditionally taught is not the mathematics that tends to be done by working mathematicians, and the students and the teachers are both victimized.

1. Invisible and Obvious

"Mathematics as a humanistic discipline" is a concept that is invisible but also obvious. When a conference with that title was proposed in 1985 to the Exxon Education Foundation, the program officer (a non-mathematician) was surprised—then skeptically hopeful. On the other side, when mathematicians were invited to participate in that conference they immediately understood a meaning and were ready to discuss various aspects from the point of view of their personal understanding.

The initial conference in Claremont, California, 21–23 March 1986, was a spectacular success that stimulated and motivated the 36 participants. A common response was, "I was startled to see so many mathematicians who shared my feelings." A unifying theme that emerged was to move the focus of energy and attention to the student. There was much discussion on how the change of focus could be accomplished. Another theme was the relationship of one's philosophy of mathematics to the method of teaching.

2. Conference Themes

The call to the Mathematics as a Humanistic Discipline Conference stressed the need to develop:

(a) an appreciation for the role of intuition not only in understanding, but in creating concepts that appear in their finished versions to be "merely technical;"

(b) an appreciation for the human dimensions that motivate discovery, competition, cooperation, the urge for holistic pictures in contrast to pieces;

(c) an understanding of the shaky epistemology of even the "hard sciences"—both mathematics and science have philosophical foundations that are more uncertain than is usually conveyed in texts and classroom settings at all levels;

(d) an understanding of the value judgments implied in the growth of any discipline—logic alone never completely accounts for what is investigated, how it is investigated, and why it is investigated; and

(e) an appreciation of the fundamental interrelationships of all knowing, and the political and social forces that create the illusion of separation.

It further pointed to an inclination to study oneself, one's mind, feelings, and world-view as one confronts already established knowledge, and posited the need for new teaching–learning formats that would help wean students from this view of knowledge as certain and to-be-received, and would try to locate the place of the student as a person attempting to understand him- or herself and the problematic nature of knowledge.

The feeling of the conference was that a number of developments in the teaching of mathematics would be desirable in order to bring in the humanistic dimension. Among the suggestions that emerged from the conference were:

(a) giving students opportunity to think like mathematicians, including a chance to work on tasks of low definition, to generate new problems, and to participate in controversy over mathematical issues;

(b) providing greater opportunity for students to be respected as persons (regardless of connection with doing mathematics);

(c) increasing the range of pedagogic options, especially those that suggest interaction among students and provide faculty with a better opportunity to understand them;

(d) designing curriculum to relate mathematics to other areas, such as science, technology, humanities, and ethical issues including personal ethics;

(e) providing opportunities for faculty to do research on issues relating to teaching, and to be respected for that area of research;

(f) inviting students to reflect on their assumptions of mind and personhood for the purpose of what they do in mathematics; and

(g) using mathematics to precipitate thought and discussion on personal idiosyncratic issues that may not lead back to mathematical thinking.

Two related themes of the conference were (a) teaching mathematics humanistically, and (b) teaching humanistic mathematics. The first theme sought to place the student more centrally in the position of inquirer than is generally the case in mathematics classrooms, while at the same time acknowledging the emotional climate of the activity of learning mathematics. What students could learn from each other, and how they might better come to understand mathematics as a meaningful rather than an arbitrary discipline were among the ideas of this first theme.

The second theme, teaching humanistic mathematics, focused less upon the nature of the teaching and learning environment and more upon the need to reconstruct the curriculum and the discipline of mathematics itself. It was suggested, for instance, that the curriculum in the past has neglected to relate mathematical discoveries to personal courage and to other human emotions. In addition, the curriculum has either been silent or has conveyed a lopsided picture of the relation of discovery to verification, mathematics to science, truth to utility, and in general, the relation of mathematics to the culture in which it is embedded.

The concept of "mathematics as a humanistic discipline" is not as well-defined as a geometric series or a triangle, but it is more evocative. Many mathematicians who have heard the phrase are not troubled by the lack of a succinct definition, but are excited by the richness of the fruitfulness that they anticipate.

Others may respond with hostility. The concept, even if ill-defined, challenges traditional ways of teaching and learning mathematics at all levels.

3. *Curriculum*

Mathematics is more than techniques to be mastered and formulas to be memorized. Most teaching and learning, however, is focused on techniques and formulas. Mathematics is open ended. Its concepts, methods, and contacts with other disciplines are expanding. Unsolved problems and unanswered questions abound. Philosophic controversy swirls around it. But most students perceive mathematics as a closed, dead, unchanging subject.

The students' perception comes naturally from texts and lectures that present only the well-established, known results in well-polished form, suitable for instant memorization.

Many agree with the gist of the last paragraph, but lack the resources to teach accordingly. The teachers as well as the students are victimized by such a lack. Not only texts and materials, but support from colleagues and students is necessary to overcome traditional approaches. Most of the participants in the 1986 conference felt a sense of isolation in their individual attempts at reform. Perhaps the most important result of the conference was not the definition of a new concept, but the creation of a new network of mathematicians and teachers who will be mutually supportive of individual and collective efforts to present and study mathematics as a humanistic discipline.

The spirit of this movement is not concerned with a particular curriculum that can be described by listing topics. The spirit of the movement, rather, is concerned with how students experience the curriculum. For example, instead of students being presented with problems to solve, they should be presented with situations that they can explore, and from which they can extract a problem which they then explain and solve or discuss (Stein 1986). Opportunities to experiment, to sharpen one's intuition, one's sense of number, structure, or mathematical culture should be presented. Another example that enriches students' experience is asking students to distort a homework problem until it can no longer be solved by the methods of the text, and then examining the solvable and the unsolvable problems, especially near the boundary between them (White 1985).

Individual students or teams can be invited to invent two homework-type problems, one of which is impossible to solve, and then challenge their classmates to solve both or explain why one is impossible.

Students at every level could come to appreciate that there are unanswered questions as well as unanswerable questions in mathematics by exploring and trying to invent questions. Mathematics is more than solving problems or proving things. Finding a new idea or a metaphor to describe an old idea, evaluating the significance of concepts, and seeing new connections are also reasonable activities in mathematics (Brown and Walter 1983).

These suggestions take time away from teaching the facts. There is so much to cover! When mathematicians (and others) discuss teaching, the pressure to cover the material is often among the main problems discussed.

4. *Counter Voices*

There are, however, other voices. Recently, a former chairman of a Department of Medicine returned to medical school as a full-time student because he was troubled by the problems that he perceived in medical education. He hoped to better understand the student's difficulties. He wrote about his experience in the *New England Journal of Medicine.*

> Learning is a thinking, problem solving process that requires time. Medical school education today involves too little thinking and problem solving. It consists largely of too much fact in too little time. . . .
> Let me be clear and not misunderstood. Facts are essential. Problems cannot be solved without the sequential arrangement of facts. But in medicine, the answer may not be there even after the facts are arranged. Students must learn to handle uncertainty: that too is medicine. Emphasis on facts does not teach this aspect of medicine any more than it teaches problem solving. . . . It is vital to replace the concept of learning as fact gathering to pass examinations with the concept of education as inquisitiveness, sequential thought, problem solving, and the satisfactions that result. (Eichna 1980).

The Association of Medical Colleges in Washington, DC issued a report in 1984 (*Physicians for the Twenty-First Century*) which asserts similar conclusions. Recommendation 1 states:

> In the general professional education of the physician, medical faculties should emphasize the acquisition and development of skills, values and attitudes by students at least to the same extent that they do their acquisition of knowledge. To do this, medical faculties must limit the amount of factual information that students are expected to memorize.

Medical education has been notorious for its demands on coverage of facts. But there are respectable counter voices which recommend a change. Learning and doing mathematics share many attributes with learning and doing medicine, and art.

5. *Less Coverage, More Learning*

Benezet, Superintendent of Schools in Manchester, New Hampshire, wrote more than 50 years ago,

> For some years I had noticed that the effect of the early introduction of arithmetic had been to dull and almost chloroform the child's reasoning faculties. There was a cer-

tain problem which I tried out, not once but a hundred times in grades six, seven, and eight. Here is the problem: 'If I can walk a hundred yards in a minute . . . how many miles can I walk in an hour, keeping up the same rate of speed?'

In nineteen cases out of twenty the answer given me would be six thousand . . . . (Benezet 1935)

In his article Benezet tells of experimental classes which were not formally taught arithmetic until the seventh grade. Those experimental classes learned to estimate, to think, to compare, write more expressively; and when they formally studied arithmetic in the seventh grade, they caught up and surpassed conventionally taught children within a year.

Although the experiment was obviously successful, and the experimental classes outshone the traditional classes in many categories, the school board was nervous and reluctant to allow the experiment to continue and expand. Even with success, one needs courage and support to break with the traditional methods.

6. Conclusion

The pressure from lower-school grades through to college to cover prescribed syllabi at the expense of developing students beyond a superficial comprehension of the subject matter resulted in many school-leavers feeling resentful and hostile towards mathematics at a time when the use of mathematical ideas is increasing in commerce, newspapers, and as the basis of public policy decisions. It is hoped that the network of mathematicians who appreciate mathematics as a humanistic discipline will grow into a movement that is capable of finding ways of bringing meaning and understanding to the mathematics classroom.

Bibliography

Benezet L P 1935–36 The story of an experiment. *J. Nat. Educ. Assoc.* 24 (8/9): 25(1)

Brown S I, Walter M 1983 *The Art of Problem Posing*. The Franklin Institute Press, Philadelphia, Pennsylvania

Eichna L W 1980 Medical school education 1975–79: A students' perspective. *N. Engl. J. Med.* 303: 729–34

Krull W 1987 The aesthetic viewpoint in mathematics. *The Mathematical Intelligencer*, Vol. 9. Springer, New York

Stein S K 1986 The Triex: Explore, Extract, Explain. Paper read at Conference, March 1986, Claremont

Tymoczko T 1986 *New Directions in the Philosophy of Mathematics*. Birkhauser, Boston, Massachusetts

Weyl H 1985 Axiomatic versus constructive procedures in mathematics. *Mathematical Intelligencer*, Vol. 7. Springer, New York

White A 1985 Teaching mathematics as though students mattered. In: Katz J (ed.) 1985 *Teaching as Though Students Mattered*. Jossey-Bass, San Francisco, California

White L A 1956 The locus of mathematical reality: An anthropological footnote. In: Newman J (ed.) 1956 *The World of Mathematics*, Vol. 4, pp. 2348–64

Section 11

Science Education Programs

Overview

The purpose of this Section is to provide a review of the major developments in curriculum and related issues in science education.

The Section is divided into three subsections. The first deals with general curriculum perspectives and discusses the main features which characterize science education over the years. The second describes the unique attributes of programs in the biological and physical science disciplines. The third highlights selected issues which are closely associated with the goals and nature of science education.

In the first subsection, Jenkins attempts to identify the factors which have influenced the nature and extent of science education in the Western world from the beginning of organized schooling in the middle of the nineteenth century to the end of the twentieth. Special attention is given to the revolutionary reforms of the 1960s and their impact on the industrialized, as well as the developing, countries.

Harlen provides a detailed account of science education programs in the primary schools. She identifies the following rationale for primary science: science should be taught as a unified subject, involving children in direct experiences with living and nonliving objects and materials taken from the child's environment and aiming at the development of concepts, skills, and attitudes. She discusses major issues related to the design of curriculum materials such as process versus content, the specification of objectives, and the extent to which programs are prescribed. Her review ends with the observation that the teacher remains the key for successful implementation of any curricular innovation and hence inservice education and continuous teachers' support are the key to effective science education.

Gunstone, in dealing with secondary school science, distinguishes between first and second generation programs. The first were senior secondary single discipline programs with specific concern for high ability students and strong emphasis on the nature of science as well as on laboratory work. They were also characterized by major involvement of scientists. In the second generation programs the role of the scientists declined, the programs aimed at all ages of secondary school as well as at a much wider range of ability levels. Many of these programs integrate several science disciplines and used the processes of science as an organizing framework.

Jenkins identifies general science as a broad course which has its roots in the common experience of children and draws as appropriate upon any of the recognized scientific disciplines. It advocates a broad scope and close relationship to everyday life, thereby providing a "bird's eye view" of the field of science before settling down to more specialized studies.

It is customary to distinguish between the physical sciences which deal with inanimate nature and the life sciences which focus on life and the living world, and the subsection dealing with specific subjects makes this distinction.

In the general review of the life sciences, Tamir begins with a brief historical account which shows how the teaching of biology has changed from a descriptive approach in the

897

first half of the twentieth century into an inquiry-oriented approach in the beginning of the second half, as well as to a more issue and applied orientation in the 1980s. The article continues by stating the role of life sciences in general education, followed by a definition of the major aims of biological education. Several features specifically related to biological education are briefly discussed and the popularity of biology as a school subject is highlighted and explained. Botany and zoology are two specialized fields which in most curricula are taught together under the general title of biology or life science. Nevertheless, as shown in the two brief articles, each of these fields of study has important attributes and presents unique pedagogical challenges.

Other articles on the natural sciences deal with study areas, in which the application of the principles of the biological sciences plays a major role, namely environmental studies, agriculture and nutrition.

Five articles deal with physical science programs. Lunetta defines the aims of physics education and provides a comprehensive curriculum overview followed by major issues such as the organization of physics teaching, materials and media, and the teachers. The article ends with a few comments on the contribution of research and curriculum evaluation to the improvement of physics education.

Ben-Zvi discusses in some detail the development of chemical education at the high school level in the United States to illustrate the relative role of science, society, and the student in shaping up the curriculum. This is followed by a description of chemistry programs in England and by a critical discussion of the role of the laboratory. The article ends with a brief account of some learning difficulties which are specific to chemistry.

Pezaro describes some unique features of *Earth Sciences Programs* which are commonly taught at the middle or junior high school level. This field appears to be less developed than other science education fields. Even less developed is the field of astronomy which is, perhaps, the oldest field of science. Cohen describes only one program designed for elementary school. At the same time, however, he points at some interesting research related to children's interpretation of astronomical concepts.

Lewis describes interesting developments in teaching about energy and illustrates how a central concept in physics has been developed into a separate integrated school subject.

While the final subsection does not deal with specific programs it raises issues which are associated with any science program.

Sutton explains why too early insistence on scientific terminology and on adoption of impersonal styles of reporting may risk meaningful learning by isolating the knowledge of terminology from the totality of understanding of phenomena and concepts.

Klopfer argues that developing students' *Scientific Literacy* has become a central aim of science instruction at every school level. Science literacy is defined as the acquisition of the necessary skills, knowledge, understanding, and attitudes which enable students to behave as successfully functioning adults and responsible members of society.

Harlen deals with teaching *Science Concepts and Skills*, and Solomon describes issues related to the emergence of an innovative study area called Science, Technology, and Society (STS).

Welch claims that developing positive attitudes toward science has been an espoused goal of most of the curriculum development efforts since the late 1950s. He points at the discouraging finding that, by and large, positive attitudes toward science are known to decrease as students progress through their schooling years, but ends with an optimistic note that some potential for enhancing attitude toward science by teacher behavior has been found.

P. Tamir

Reforms in Science Education

Introduction

P. Tamir

Curriculum reform in science education has often been associated with the orbiting of Sputnik in 1957. However, "while Sputnik certainly underlined the climate of concern about scientific and technological manpower in the West, it did not engender it, nor did it prompt the curriculum development movement" (Waring 1979 p. 4). Similarly, Bruner's *The Process of Education* (Bruner 1960) was neither the beginning of this reform nor its crest, although it provided an unmistakable sign to the world that radical changes in the teaching of science were imminent. Bruner's book emphasizes four conceptions which can serve to characterize much of the ferment of the curriculum reform movement of the 1950s and 1960s. The first such conception dealt with the subject matter of science, and reflected the desire to redefine the content and objectives of science education in terms of the structure of the disciplines and the processes of science. The second reconception dealt with the learner's readiness and role as an active participant and discoverer of knowledge, often through direct manipulation of his or her environment. A third and related theme dealt with teaching, emphasizing the notions of discovery and inquiry; and the fourth theme highlighted the role of educational technology in facilitating learning.

Many of the issues which characterize reform in science education are not exclusive to science education, and many of the leading figures such as Bruner, Piaget, Schwab, Gagné, and Ausubel have played central roles in pedagogical and psychological theory "writ large." It has certainly been to the benefit of science education that they chose to devote much of their efforts specifically to this field.

The curriculum reform of the 1950–60s started in the United States and was quickly followed by the United Kingdom and then by other countries. Strangely enough, even in the late 1980s these programs were often still referred to as the "new" curricula. This is so even though a really new reform in science education gradually emerged in the 1980s. The reason for this conservation of the "new" image is that in most countries the new approaches of the 1950s never caught up in many classrooms, thereby sustaining Hurd's (1961) statement that "it is harder to change the curriculum than it is to move a cemetery."

In addition to changes in the science curricula, the reform of the 1950–60s has contributed significantly to the general field of curriculum development and implementation. Several books which tell the stories of particular curriculum development projects have been published in the United States (e.g., Grobman 1969) and in the United Kingdom (e.g., Waring 1970). In the following sections the major characteristics of the new science curricula of the 1950–60s are briefly described, and the major characteristics of the ongoing reform in science education in the 1980s are briefly described.

1. The Nature of the Science Curriculum Reform of the 1950–60s

1.1 The Subject Matter

Klopfer (1971) characterized the contrast between the "traditional" and "new" programs as follows:

> the traditional science courses concentrate on the knowledge of scientific facts, laws, theories and technological applications, while the newer courses put emphasis on the nature, structure and unity of science, and on the process of scientific inquiry. The traditional programs attempt to cover a great number of topics while modern programs prefer depth to breadth. The traditional courses are taught largely by the lecture and recitation method and see confirmation in laboratory exercises which are not essential to the course, whereas the modern programs employ discovery investigations as the basis of course development. (p. 565)

Shulman and Tamir (1973) observed that:

> the new programs have generally attempted to be more accurate and up-to-date scientifically than their predecessors. . . . They strove for greater sophistication from a philosophy and history of science perspective, avoiding the naivete of older texts and their presentation of the "scientific method." The new programs tried to portray the fluidity and dynamum [sic.] of science in contrast to its image as a collection of truths. (p. 1101)

Although Bruner brought the attention of the educational community to the notion of structure, it is Schwab who has explicated and extended the concept for science education. Schwab distinguishes between two closely related and interdependent aspects of structure: the *substantive* and the *syntactic*. The *substantive* consists of "a body of concepts—commitments about the nature of a subject matter functioning as a guide to inquiry," while the *syntactic* involves "the patterns of its procedures, its method, how it goes about using its conceptions to attain its goals" (Schwab 1962 p. 203). Thus, if the structure of science is to be honestly taught, both aspects are to be included. An important aspect of Schwab's notion is that structure is not an inherent characteristic of the discipline, but rather it is an imposed construction. It is no coincidence that the Biological Science Curriculum Study (BSCS)—one of the major curriculum development projects in the United States—in which Schwab played a leading role, came out with three versions, each reflecting a different way of conceiving the subject matter. Yet, even though the three versions differed substantially from each other, they still had nine major themes in common (e.g., "evolution" or "the complementarity of structure and function") and made adequate reference to the seven levels of biological organization, namely: the molecule, the cell, tissue, the organ, the individual, the community, and the world biome (Schwab 1963).

While Schwab's concern has been the transmitting of a valid view of science, other theorists were using structure as a means for facilitating meaningful learning. Thus Gagné's (1970) theory of learning hierarchies revolves around the design of "learning structures." Ausubel's (1968) subsumption theory of learning has been concerned with the ways in which the learning materials can be taught in a way that facilitates their integration into the learner's cognitive structure. Similarly, Piaget's formulations regarding schema of cognitive organization reflect his interest in developing relations among the elements of knowledge. The crucial issue for science educators has been how to structure teaching in such a way that the structure of knowledge will become part of the cognitive structure of the learner.

1.2 The Learner

The "new" curricula have created a different image of the student both as a learner and as a product of learning. As to the learning process, the intent has been:

> to make our pupils feel so far as they may what it is to be, so to speak, inside the skin of the man of science, looking out through his eyes, as well as using his tools, experiencing not only something of his labors, but also something of joyous intellectual adventure. (Nunn, as cited by Waring 1979 p. 38)

Thus the laboratory acquires a major role in the learning process. The learner is conceived as active, as one who constructs concepts by a process of discovery, at least in part of his or her science studies. According to Bruner (1960), an act of discovery may be seen as necessary not only to ensure that the learner integrates the material into his or her cognitive structure, but also to develop the capacity to transfer what has been learned to novel problem situations and to acquire a positive

self-concept as an autonomous problem solver. As to the product of learning, the learner is expected to understand and internalize major modern concepts, principles, and theories, but at the same time to acquire intellectual and manipulative inquiry skills which enable him or her to study natural phenomena and also to distinguish evidence from propaganda, data from fantasy, fact from fiction, reality from illusion, theory from dogma, observation from inference, and the credible from the incredible.

Last but not least, the learner is expected to develop positive attitudes toward science, science learning and science careers.

1.3 The Teacher

The teachers' role in the new programs was supposed to be substantially different from their traditional role. Instead of serving as the source of all knowledge, they were expected to teach science as inquiry by inquiry. They had to learn new subject matter and to adopt new instructional strategies such as: invitations to inquiry; analysis of research; monitoring open-ended investigations in the laboratory and so forth. In spite of detailed teacher guides that have been developed, and large-scale inservice courses, many teachers were unable, or even unwilling, to change their safe existing instructional habits. In states which managed to provide continuous guidance and support to teachers, the implementation of the new curricula has been much more successful than in countries which have not done so. One of the main conclusions of an evaluation of the new curricula is that the teacher is the key to the success of any curricular innovation.

2. A New Curriculum Reform in Science Education

Unlike the revolutionary wave of the 1950s, the new reform of the 1980s has been evolving gradually, and its presence in schools at the end of that decade is still on a very small scale. The need for this reform is based on three premises. First is the recognition that the "new" programs of the 1960s have not been attractive to a large proportion of students and, as a result, many "young people grow up as foreigners in their own culture and leave high school as scientific and technological illiterates" (Hurd 1985 p. 83).

Secondly, while the "new" courses of the 1960s did a good job in presenting the structure of scientific disciplines and in teaching students how to inquire and discover new knowledge, they have not paid attention to the utilization and application of scientific knowledge in everyday life, neither did they provide opportunities for making socially relevant decisions, nor for forming ethical judgments.

Finally, a new line of research, focusing on students' alternative frameworks and naive conceptions of natural phenomena, has emerged and flourished since the early 1970s. This growing body of research is calling for a new approach to curriculum development, which will take into consideration the prevailing pre- and misconceptions, and will structure the learning tasks in ways which facilitate meaningful learning and conceptual change.

Following Hurd (1985), some of the characteristics of a desirable science curriculum in the 1990s and beyond, are:

(a) School science courses should be in accord with the image and ethos of modern science and technology.

(b) Subject matter content should be selected to have personal and social relevance as well as scientific/technological validity.

(c) Scientific literacy is the major goal. Literacy is conceived to be the intellectual skills and knowledge essential to make responsible decisions on issues such as: the use of nuclear power, management of natural environment, control of human population growth, transplants of human organs, and genetic engineering.

(d) Science teaching should provide opportunities to develop students' awareness that value and ethical judgments should be well-grounded in scientific/technological knowledge and that in decision making, due weight must be given to evidence and data.

(e) School science courses should provide the conceptual basis and learning skills essential for lifelong continuing self-directed learning.

(f) A portion of the science curriculum should be organized in terms of ongoing science/technology/social issues, such as food and energy resources, the chemical basis of human behavior, space exploration, and so forth.

(g) The courses, as described above, are to become part of the general education of every student. In addition specialized courses should be offered, at the secondary school, for those students who wish to test their interest and ability to pursue careers in science and technical fields.

As already mentioned, the science curriculum reform of the 1960s has been only partially successful, and many students all over the world have not had a chance to benefit from its offerings. The reform of the 1980s will certainly benefit from the experience of the earlier one. In many ways this newest reform is not an antithesis, but rather a continuation of the curriculum reform which started 40 years before.

Bibliography

Ausubel D P 1968 *Educational Psychology: A Cognitive View.* Holt, Reinhart and Winston, New York

Bruner J S 1960 *The Process of Education.* Harvard University Press, Cambridge, Massachusetts

Gagné R M 1970 *The Conditions of Learning.* Holt, Reinhart and Winston, New York

Grobman A 1969 *The Changing Classroom.* Doubleday, New York

Hurd P D 1961 *Biological Education in American Secondary Schools, 1860–1960,* Biological Science Curriculum Study (BSCS) Bulletin No. 1. American Institute of Biological Sciences, Washington, DC

Hurd D P 1985 Science education for a new age: The reform movement. *Nat. Assoc. Sec. Sch. Princ.* 69: 83–92

Klopfer L E 1971 Evaluation of learning in science. In: Bloom B S, Hastings J T, Madaus G F (eds.) 1971 *Handbook on Formative and Summative Evaluation of Student Learning.* McGraw Hill, New York, pp. 559–642

Schwab J J 1962 The concept of the structure of a discipline. *Educ. Res.* 43: 197–205

Schwab J J 1963 *Biology Teachers' Handbook.* Wiley, New York

Shulman L S, Tamir P 1973 Research on teaching in the natural sciences. In: Travers R M W (ed.) *Second Handbook of Research on Teaching.* Rand McNally, Chicago, pp. 1098–148

Tyler R W 1949 *Basic Principles of Curriculum and Instruction.* The University of Chicago Press, Chicago, Illinois

Waring M 1979 *Social Pressure and Curriculum Innovation.* Methuen, London

Comprehensive Programs

History of Science Education

E. W. Jenkins

The history of science education is concerned with science teaching in the historical context. As such, attention has been focused on the identification and examination of factors which have influenced the nature and extent of science education and determined the educational, political, economic, or other functions and effects ascribed, or attributable, to it. Researchers have drawn, as appropriate, upon a number of the techniques and approaches available to historians and social scientists and have directed their inquiries at different aspects of the educational enterprise, such as finance, administration, resources, teacher supply and training, personnel planning, and curriculum issues. Not surprisingly, therefore, the literature is scattered and diverse. There are a few important texts (Argles 1964, Hurd 1961, Jenkins 1979, Layton 1973, Schöler 1970, Underhill 1941, Waring 1979, Woolnough 1988) and some useful bibliographies (Brock 1975, Heward 1980, Jenkins 1980, Voelker and Wall 1973a, 1973b, Wall 1973) but much remains to be done before the history of science education can take its place as an integral part of history.

As far as schools are concerned, the emergence of science in a recognizably modern form in the industrializing societies of the nineteenth century, together with the development of systems of mass education, raised fundamental issues relating to its educational function. In European countries, scientific disciplines were schooled to challenge the traditional dominance of the classical–literary curriculum at the secondary level and an accommodation was not achieved until the end of the century and then only after fierce controversy over the status and accreditation of the new subjects. The nature of the accommodation varied from one country to another. In Germany, separate schools (*Realschulen, Realgymnasien*) were established as early as 1860. In France, in contrast, no new categories of secondary school to teach scientific subjects were introduced, the appropriate courses being incorporated within existing *collèges* and *lycées* from 1852 onwards. In England and Wales, which failed to develop a national system of secondary education until the twentieth century, most grammar and public schools were slow to incorporate science within their curricula, although much valuable work was done in the so-called higher grade schools, developed under local control from about 1880 onwards in the larger towns and cities and funded on a payment-by-results basis by a central authority, the Department of Science and Art. The assimilation of these latter schools to the secondary system which developed after 1902 meant the loss of much of the practical, vocational, scientific, and technical studies associated with them and led to a diversion of resources from scientific and technical education to the predominantly academic, preprofessional curriculum of the grammar schools (Layton 1978). Ironically, Japan—which, in response to imperialist sentiments and the need for rapid industrialization, systematically imported English educational ideas between 1872 and 1876—had created, by 1903, some 200 secondary-technical schools to coexist with 340 academic secondary schools and provide a distinct, alternative route through the educational system (Terakawa and Brock 1978).

In the United States, despite a small number of important, pioneering academies and colleges (Fay 1931), science education was not institutionalized until the first Morrill Act of 1862, creating land grant colleges to teach agriculture, mechanical arts, and military science, and the establishment, during the following decades, of large numbers of high schools, financed from public funds. The science taught in these schools was strongly influenced initially by the role of the colleges and universities in certification, examination, and accreditation, although this was challenged as more students entered the public school system and stayed there longer. Despite the recognition by the so-called Committee of Ten of the National Education Association (1893) that the high school was not simply a preparatory institution for higher education, it was not until the Depression years that enlarged conceptions of the aims of secondary education began to prevail and significant efforts were devoted to the construction of science courses for students who completed their formal education at the high-school stage (Caldwell 1920, Isenbarger et al. 1950).

In general, the American high school, spared the conflict between classical and scientific studies manifest in social and cultural terms in Europe and lacking the traditional, conservative influences operating upon selective systems of secondary education, has been more flexible than its European counterparts in accommodating a generous variety of science-based courses (academic, vocational, technical) generated in response to perceived local or national needs. However, the sensitivity of school science education to such influences is evident in all countries, particularly in the differentiation of the curricula between the sexes or between schools serving different social functions, in the development of programmes of integrated or general science (Haggis and Adey 1979) and in the construction of courses, derived from the biological sciences, concerned with such issues as health, hygiene, temperance, eugenics, sex education, and citizenship. It is unfortunate, therefore, that the formulation and articulation of science curriculum determinants have not received the attention they deserve (Bybee 1982).

During the nineteenth century and, indeed, for much of the first half of the twentieth century, elementary and secondary education in Europe represented, not successive stages, but alternative kinds of education for different social classes. When science was taught at all in European elementary schools, it was often confined, at least initially, to object lessons, *Naturkünde*, schemes of work in nature study, hygiene, physiology or, in the case of more senior pupils, to courses which stressed the utility and practical applications of scientific knowledge rather than the mental training traditionally associated with the systematic study of science in secondary schools. In the United States, early elementary-school science, also largely identified with nature study, owed much to the pioneering work of Jackman, Comstock, and Palmer [Champagne and Klopfer 1979(a), (b), (c)]. However, as in other countries, such an approach was gradually replaced by more comprehensive elementary science programmes, the work of Craig, Billig, and Parker being particularly significant during the interwar years [Champagne and Klopfer, 1980(a), (b), (c), Craig 1932].

With a few distinguished exceptions, early methods of secondary-school science teaching were based on the textbook and lecture, rather than on the laboratory, but this changed markedly during the closing decades of the nineteenth century. In the United States, the Harvard list of 40 (physics) experiments (Harvard College 1886) and the corresponding pamphlet of chemistry experiments by Josiah Cooke (Rosen 1956) were seminal influences on laboratory-based teaching of high-school physical science. In England and Wales, the development of pupil-based practical work owed much to the chemist, H. E. Armstrong (Brock 1973) whose heuristic approach had some influence in France and Germany and was even exported, although with limited success, to Japan.

By the First World War, there was considerable scepticism of, even hostility towards, some of the more extravagant claims made for laboratory teaching and a variety of other strategies (unit and contract plans, projects, and cooperative studies), increasingly supported by innovations in educational technology, which were developed as educational systems expanded.

The Second World War transformed the role of science and, therefore, of science education in industrialized societies. Science and technology were harnessed, as never before, to the economic, defence, and other interests of the state and the importance of a scientifically literate population was widely recognized (Henry 1947, Nelson 1960, Perkins 1958). These concerns and, in particular, anxiety over an enduring shortage of qualified scientific personnel, prompted a wave of science curriculum development (Lockard 1977) which amounted to something of a revolution. Institutions, organizations, and departments concerned with research and/or development in science education were reinvigorated or established and private and government funds were provided on an unprecedented scale to develop modern science courses which were discipline centred, laboratory based, and founded upon an inductive, problem-solving philosophy designed to encourage students to behave "like practising scientists" (Dede and Hardin 1973). However, these courses differed in their epistemological foundations, in the extent to which they adopted a critical stance towards the scientific enterprise (Millar 1981), in the relative contributions of university and school teachers, learned societies, and science teaching organizations (Layton 1973), and in their dependence upon research findings, especially the learning theories associated with Bruner, Gagné, Ausubel, and Piaget (Mallinson 1975).

During the 1960s and 1970s, science education became an important form of aid to newly independent and developing countries, many of which established their own agencies for curriculum renewal. However, such aid was sometimes given without sufficient awareness of the economic or other constraints operating in the countries concerned or, more significantly, of the cultural context within which science was taught (Maybury 1975, Wilson 1981). In addition, the importance attached by many developing nations to industrialization and, therefore, to training students in physics, chemistry, engineering, and mathematics, has created particular tensions within the science curricula to be provided for pupils, most of whom are destined to spend their lives contributing to a rural and, occasionally, a subsistence, economy. After a period of reduced donor funding in developing countries, the 1980s have brought renewed support for science education as a component of *developmental knowledge*, a term that emphasises the inclusion of health information, agricultural knowledge, home economics, and basic technologies for nutrition and environmental protection as part of the 'text' of science (King 1989).

Paradoxically, the technical assistance and innovation in science education offered by the wealthier nations coincided with a mounting dissatisfaction and, in some countries, disillusionment with what had been achieved by such major investments as the Physical Sciences

Study Committee, the Biological Sciences Curriculum Study, and the Chemical Bond Approach projects in the United States or the Nuffield 'O' and 'A' Level programmes in the United Kingdom (for details on these projects see Lockard 1977.) As the optimism of the 1960s waned, funds for research and development in science education were severely curtailed. However, by the later 1980s, concerns over the quality of science education, prompted by considerations of industrial and economic competitiveness, together with broader issues such as scientific literacy, led to a renewed interest in large scale science curriculum change (Science Council of Canada 1984, Secondary Science Curriculum Review 1987, American Association for the Advancement of Science 1989). In some countries, this change has formed part of a wider initiative, designed to produce a "balanced" science curriculum for all (DES 1985). Also noteworthy during the 1980s has been the attention given to out-of-school and informal science education (UNESCO 1986) and to the public understanding of science (Layton et al. 1986).

Compared with the reforms of a generation earlier, many of the recent initiatives in school science education reflect a more complex 'constructivist' perspective on learning and, in consequence, place greater emphasis on the role of the teacher in developing students' understanding. Some of the reforms have also addressed the relationships between science, technology and society (Solomon 1988) and sought to provide students with an insight into the nature of the scientific enterprise, sometimes by incorporating within curricula elements concerned explicitly with the history and philosophy of science (Bybee et al. 1989, DES 1989).

Bibliography

American Association for the Advancement of Science 1989 *Science for All Americans*. AAAS, Washington, DC

Argles M 1964 *South Kensington to Robbins: An Account of English Technical and Scientific Education since 1851*. Longmans, London

Brock W H (ed.) 1973 *H. E. Armstrong and the Teaching of Science 1880–1930*. Cambridge University Press, London

Brock W H 1975 From Liebig to Nuffield. A bibliography of the history of science education 1839–1974. *Stud. Sci. Educ.* 2: 67–99

Bybee R W 1982 Historical research in science education. *J. Res. Sci. Teach.* 19: 1–13

Bybee R W, Powell J C, Ellis J D, Giese J R, Parisi L 1989 Teaching history and nature of science in science courses: A rationale. Paper presented to Biological Sciences Curriculum Study/Social Science Education Consortium. Colorado Springs and Boulder, Colorado

Caldwell O T 1920 *Reorganization of Science in Secondary Schools*. Bulletin No. 26. United States Bureau of Education, Washington, DC

Champagne A B, Klopfer L E 1979(a), (b), (c) Pioneers of elementary school science. *Sci. Educ.* 63: 145–65, 299–322, 557–90

Champagne A B, Klopfer L E 1980(a), (b), (c) Pioneers of elementary school science. *Sci. Educ.* 64: 7–24, 149–67, 615–36

Craig G S 1932 *Suggested Content for the Grades of the Elemen-

tary School*. 31st Yearbook of the National Society for the Study of Education. Public School, Bloomington, Illinois

Dede C J, Hardin J 1973 Reforms, revisions, re-examinations: Secondary science education since World War II. *Sci. Educ.* 57: 485–91

Department of Education and Science 1985 *Science 5–16: A Statement of Policy*. HMSO, London

Department of Education and Science 1989 *Science in the National Curriculum*. HMSO, London

Fay P J 1931 The history of chemistry teaching in American high schools. *J. Chem. Educ.* 8(8): 1533–62

Haggis S, Adey P 1979 A review of integrated science education worldwide. *Stud. Sci. Educ.* 6: 69–89

Harvard College 1886 *Provisional List of Experiments in Elementary Physics for Admission to College in 1887*. Harvard College, Cambridge, Massachusetts

Henry N B (ed.) 1947 *Science Education in American Schools*. 46th Yearbook of the National Society for the Study of Education, Pt. 1. University of Chicago Press, Chicago, Illinois

Heward C M 1980 Industry, cleanliness and godliness: Sources for and problems in the history of scientific and technical education and the working classes, 1850–1910. *Stud. Sci. Educ.* 7: 87–128

Hurd P D 1961 *Biological Education in American Secondary Schools 1890–1960*. American Institute of Biological Sciences, Washington, DC

Isenbarger K U et al. 1950 *A Half Century of Science and Mathematics Teaching*. A summary of significant developments in the teaching of science and mathematics during the first half of the twentieth century, and an account of the developments of the Central Association of Science and Mathematics Teachers and the part it has played in these developments. Central Association of Science and Mathematics Teachers, Banta, Wisconsin

Jenkins E W 1979 *From Armstrong to Nuffield: Studies in Twentieth-century Science Education in England and Wales*. Murray, London

Jenkins E W 1980 Some sources for the history of science education in the twentieth century, with particular reference to secondary schools. *Stud. Sci. Educ.* 7: 27–86

King K 1989 Donor aid to science and technology education: a state of the art review. *Stud. Sci. Educ.* 17

Layton D 1973 *Science for the People: The Origins of the School Science Curriculum in England*. Allen and Unwin, London

Layton D 1978 Education in industrialised societies. In: Williams T I (ed.) 1978 *A History of Technology*. Oxford University Press, Oxford

Layton D, Davey A, Jenkins E 1986 Science for specific social purposes (SSSP)—perspectives on adult scientific literacy. *Stud. Sci. Educ.* 13: 27–52

Lockard J D 1977 *Twenty Years of Science and Mathematics Curriculum Development*. International Clearinghouse, Science and Mathematics Curriculum Development. University of Maryland, College Park, Maryland

Mallinson G G 1975 *A Summary of Research in Science Education*. Wiley, New York

Maybury R H 1975 *Technical Assistance and Innovation in Science Education*. Wiley, New York

Millar R H 1981 Science curriculum and social control: A comparison of some recent science curriculum proposals in the United Kingdom and the Federal Republic of Germany. *Comp. Educ.* 17: 23–46

National Education Association 1893 *Report of the Committee of Ten on Secondary School Studies*. American Book Company, New York

Nelson H B (ed.) 1960 *Rethinking Science Education*. 59th Yearbook of the National Society for the Study of Education, Pt. 1. University of Chicago Press, Chicago, Illinois

Perkins W H (ed.) 1958 *Science in Schools*. Proc. Conf. of the British Association for the Advancement of Science, April 17–18, 1958, London. Butterworth, London

Rosen S 1956 The rise of high-school chemistry in America (to 1920). *J. Chem. Educ.* 33(12): 627–33

Schöler W 1970 *Geschichte des naturwissenschaftlichen Unterrichts im 17. bis 19. Jahrhundert: Erziehungstheoretische Grundlegung und schulgeschichtliche Entwicklung*. De Gruyter, Berlin

Science Council of Canada 1984 *Science for Every Student, Educating Canadians for Tomorrow's World*. Canadian Government Publishing Centre, Quebec

Secondary Science Curriculum Review 1987 *Better Science: Key Proposals*. Heinemann, London

Solomon J 1988 The dilemma of Science, Technology and Society education. In: Fensham P (ed.) 1988 *Development and Dilemmas in Science Education*. Falmer, London

Terakawa T, Brock W H 1978 The introduction of heurism into Japan. *Hist. Educ.* 7: 35–44

Underhill O E 1941 *The Origins and Development of Elementary School Science*. Scott, Foresman, Chicago, Illinois

UNESCO 1986 *UNESCO Sourcebook for Out-of-School Science and Technology*. UNESCO, Paris

Voelker A M, Wall C A 1973a Historical documents in science education. *Sci. Educ.* 57: 77–87

Voelker A M, Wall C A 1973b Historical documents of significance to science education: A bibliographic listing. *Sci. Educ.* 57: 111–19

Wall C A 1973 An annotated bibliography of historical documents in science education. *Sci. Educ.* 57: 297–317

Waring M 1979 *Social Pressures and Curriculum Innovation: A Study of the Nuffield Foundation Science Teaching Project*. Methuen, London

Wilson B (ed.) 1981 *Cultural Contexts of Science and Mathematics Education: A Bibliographic Guide*. Centre for Studies in Science Education, University of Leeds, Leeds

Woolnough B E 1988 *Physics Teaching in Schools 1960–85*. Falmer, London

Science Education: Primary School

W. Harlen

The origin of modern curriculum development in primary-school science lies in the general discontent felt with science education in the later 1950s. In the West, the kind of science being taught at the secondary level came under review and there was a growing awareness of the need to include, in the presecondary curriculum, something more resembling science education than the traditional nature study. In the rest of the world at that time there was either no science of any kind in the primary school or lessons called science which consisted almost entirely of reading from textbooks.

In the period up to the early 1980s it is possible to distinguish three main phases in primary-school science curriculum development which have somewhat distinct characteristics, though they overlap in time. The first phase consists of the projects begun in the West in the early 1960s. The most prominent ones were, in the United States: the Elementary Science Study (ESS), the Science Curriculum Improvement Study (SCIS), and Science—A Process Approach (SAPA); and in the United Kingdom: The Oxford Primary Science Project, the Nuffield Primary Science Project, and Science 5/13. Each of these developed its own philosophy and view of primary science and produced materials to show what, ideally, these meant when put into practice. They were the visions of educators who expected to bring about rapid changes by publishing new teaching materials. The success of enthusiasts was impressive but unfortunately these were in the minority amongst primary teachers. (A description of science curricula mentioned in this article appears in the yearbooks edited by Lockard, e.g., Lockard 1975.)

The proponents of the first phase projects were spreading their messages to other countries before there

had been time to realize that, beyond the most enthusiastic and able teachers, the response in their home countries was disappointingly small. This gave rise to the second phase of curriculum projects, whose characteristics were that they often began in attempts to adopt ideas, and sometimes sets of materials, taken from first phase projects, but generally ended in designing materials more suited to local conditions and needs. Some of the first of these took place in Africa, where the African Primary Science Project (APSP) began in 1965, but most were in operation in the early 1970s (two projects in Nigeria, two in India, one each in Israel, Sri Lanka, Taiwan, and Japan, for example). Projects which began in the late 1970s (e.g., in New Zealand, Singapore, Indonesia) more often began by examining the kinds of changes required in their primary schools and designing suitable materials, using ideas from other projects selectively, rather than adopting programmes produced elsewhere.

The first two phases had as their main focus the production of classroom materials, for teachers, pupils, or both. The third phase, however, was characterized by concern not only (and in some cases not at all) with producing curriculum materials but with the teaching methods, teacher preparation, and support which are required for science teaching. The first of the developments in this phase was the setting up of the Science Education Project for Africa, which absorbed the earlier APSP and founded a programme of professional training for the trainers of primary teachers. The Southeast Asia Science and Mathematics Experiment at RECSAM, which began in 1973, is a similar enterprise. More modest projects began in the United Kingdom (Progress in Learning Science), the United States (Federation for Unified Science Education), and later in the Arab States

(Defining the Skills of Primary School Science Teaching).

During the 1980s primary science programme development moved into a fourth phase which was informed to a greater extent than previously by research and spurred by concern for creating general scientific literacy as much as improving the education of future scientists. Research into learning and into the scientific ideas which children create in making sense of the world around them has been used to support the importance of using children's existing ideas as starting points for teaching. At the same time developments in assessment methods made it feasible to find out children's ideas and to monitor the development of both conceptual and process skill learning (DES 1988a, Harlen 1990).

1. Definitions and Rationale

The definition of "primary" as a stage of education varies somewhat from country to country. Most commonly, primary is taken to mean the first eight years of schooling (kindergarten to grade 6 inclusive, or ages 5 to 12 or 6 to 13 inclusive). This is the definition adopted by UNESCO in its projects and publications and is the one used here. During these years, "science education" has some widely agreed characteristics, though there is less consensus at the level of specific aims. The four main characteristics which emerge from statements about the curriculum rather than curriculum practice are:

(a) In the primary years science is usually taught as a unified subject, not as separate sciences.

(b) It involves children in direct experiences of living and nonliving objects and materials.

(c) Its goals include development of mental and physical skills, attitudes, and concepts rather than focusing only on the learning of facts and principles.

(d) The subject matter is taken from the child's immediate surroundings.

Arguments put forward in favour of including science in the primary curriculum usually make reference to benefits to the child in terms of general cognitive development, increased satisfaction in everyday life through better understanding of the scientific and technological applications which surround them and improved attitudes and understanding in relation to postprimary science education. Reference is often made to the benefits to society of children being educated to think logically and critically about everyday events and to function effectively and knowledgeably in an increasingly technological world.

Studies which have been carried out on the validity of these claims have produced very little clear evidence of benefits to the child, while benefits to society have been little researched. Comparative studies have been carried out to investigate the effect of new curriculum materials, with an emphasis upon process skill and attitude development, compared with the more traditional textbook approach (Renner et al. 1973, Davis et al. 1976, Vanek and Montean 1977). Overall the results have usually shown no significant difference between the groups, though for some groups and some skills the new materials have been found to have an appreciable effect. Studies in the West of pupils' attitudes to science have commonly shown that attitudes toward science become increasingly negative as pupils pass through the primary school and that this trend is not halted by experience of new science materials (Ayres and Price 1975, Harlen 1975, Krockover and Malcolm 1978, Sullivan 1979, Craig and Ayres 1988).

The difficulties of conducting and interpreting studies of the impact of primary science on pupils are such that it would be unwise to conclude that there is no effect. Instruments capable of detecting change in process skills and in conceptual understanding, as opposed to factual recall, were only developed in the 1980s (DES 1981, APU 1983, APU 1984, APU 1985). Furthermore there are problems of ensuring that the pupils investigated have indeed been exposed to the intended experiences over a sufficiently long period of time. These problems are related to those of implementation to be discussed later. It is, therefore, quite easy to cast doubt on any interpretation drawn from pupil assessment data. At the same time there is evidence from classroom observation studies (Johnson 1970), from teachers (Harlen 1975), and inspectors (DES 1978) that children do benefit from science activities. There is also evidence that language and mathematical performance benefit from breadth of experience rather than a narrow concentration on literacy and numeracy.

2. Issues Relating to the Design and Structure of Curriculum Materials

While sharing the general characteristics mentioned above, there are considerable differences among curriculum development programmes in all phases, reflecting a range of views about the nature and objectives of science experiences for primary-age children. The main issues concern the relative importance given to the development of concepts as compared with process skills and attitudes, the extent to which objectives should be made explicit, and the degree of prescription in the programme. Overlaying decisions on these issues are constraints varying according to whether the development takes place within a centralized or decentralized education system.

2.1 Process Versus Content

This issue concerns the nature of science at the primary-school level. The "process" view is one that holds the development of mental skills and attitudes to be pre-eminent. The skills concerned usually include observing, problem solving, inferring, predicting, hypothesizing, classifying, communicating, interpreting data, controlling variables, and the combinations of skills required for planning and carrying out investigations and experiments. The attitudes in question are not attitudes to science, but attitudes of science, such as curiosity, openness to new ideas, respect for evidence, independence in thinking, satisfaction in understanding the world around. Learning activities which aim to develop these processes naturally have to use some content but this is chosen to serve the practice of the skills rather than to build up a coherent body of knowledge. Indeed content is sometimes deliberately chosen to be trivial (for example, making inferences about the content of "black boxes" or mixing unknown liquids together to develop powers of observation) or is left to the teacher to decide. The purpose is seen as helping children to "learn how to learn" and the information they pick up in the process is regarded as incidental.

In contrast are programmes which are structured in terms of content chosen to build up concepts considered to be fundamental to understanding of the environment and of later science studies. Examples of concepts often included are ones related to properties of matter, energy sources and transfer, living things (life cycle, diversity, interaction and interdependence, adaptation), structure, motion and electric and magnetic interactions. The concepts are to be built up through the children's activity and this will involve them in using some process skills but the emphasis is upon understanding rather than the way of coming to the understanding. Because events in nature are often complex and not easy to understand, these programmes often attempt to simplify the phenomena studied by presenting the children with laboratory exercises in which complicating factors can be excluded.

It is increasingly recognized that both these views are incomplete and philosophically as well as educationally unsupportable (Harlen 1985). The more important developments are directed to achieving process and content goals in combination rather than separately (Young 1983). Such approaches acknowledge that through observing and attempting to interpret observations, children form ideas about the way certain things behave; these ideas are brought to bear in an attempt to understand similar phenomena, when further observation and interpretation may result in the ideas being confirmed, modified, or extended. Thus processes can be seen to play an important part in the building of concepts which gradually become more powerful and widely applicable and concepts enable processes to be refined so that phenomena of increasing complexity can be understood. The content of activities, according to this argument, should be chosen to serve the needs of process development *and* the child's understanding of his or her environment. The dual purpose is particularly relevant for primary science programmes in countries where primary education is the only education for the vast majority of pupils. The main difficulty in combining process and content goals is that the development of enquiry skills and attitudes depends on the methods and organization of teaching rather than on the choice of content. Whilst content can be conveyed effectively through written materials, this is less true for teaching methods. Hence curriculum development must be con-

cerned with teacher education if these multiple goals are to be achieved.

2.2 The Specification of Objectives

Although the role of objectives is not an issue restricted to primary science curriculum development it has been a matter of considerable debate in this area, particularly among those concerned with the first phase programmes. A strong minority school of thought held that the outcomes of children's enquiry could not be predicted and that there should be no attempt to direct that enquiry with specified outcomes in mind. Furthermore it was claimed that some of the more important learning could be prevented by aiming an activity at the achievement of certain ideas or skills. Those who held this view supported it by claims that the experience of an activity is of paramount importance and this will be individual to each child, bringing to it a unique set of existing ideas and experiences. Not surprisingly the supporters of this view were also those who emphasized processes rather than content in the activities.

This issue should perhaps be considered in historical perspective. When the first programmes were being developed in the early 1960s there was no tradition of teaching primary science; the opinion of educators as to what might be the important objectives in this area of the curriculum was, by and large, uninformed by theory or research. That being the case it could be regarded as prudent to hold back from specifying what should be learned until there was more evidence as to the possible and useful outcomes. Evaluation studies of these earlier developments have indeed shed considerable light on this matter and the issue has evolved into one concerning the degree to which objectives should be specified rather than whether they should be specified at all (Harlen 1978).

The subject remains an issue because of the very different relationship to activities of process, concept, and attitude objectives. In programmes which embrace the pursuit of skill *and* concept goals, as opposed to one or the other alone, each activity can generally be regarded as contributing to the achievement of several objectives, some relating to concepts, some to skills, some to attitudes. The concept objectives are related to the subject matter of the activity and can often be expressed as knowledge which can be achieved in one or a few similar activities. For example, the notion that a complete circuit is required for current to flow is an objective of activities with wires, bulbs, and batteries. However the process skills do not have this close relationship with the content of activities. Observation, inference, hypothesizing, and so on, have to be pursued in a very wide range of activities and are not to be achieved by a few activities only. There is no one activity or group of activities which can develop the ability to make predictions, or the attitude of respect for evidence, in the same way that the ideas about a circuit are developed in a few activities. Thus the specification of objectives for each activity risks giving undue attention to content-related learning rather than broader concepts, skills, and attitudes.

A fresh wave of programmes with objectives specified in broader terms is heralded by the form of the National Curriculum in Science (DES 1989a) which has been introduced into England and Wales (shortly to be followed by Northern Ireland). Here objectives take the form of Attainment Targets (17 in number for the whole science curriculum, covering skills, science concepts, and the nature of science), defined at different levels for pupils in the age range 5 to 16 in terms of statements of attainment at each of ten levels. There is also a programme of study, which describes in very general terms the intended learning experiences, but it is significant that it is the statements of attainment, rather than the programmes of study, which are influencing the revision of existing materials and the preparation of new classroom materials.

2.3 The Extent to which Programmes are Prescribed

A closely prescribed programme is one that consists of a series of activities laid out year by year. There is usually a science textbook for the pupils, at least from grade 3 onwards, a teacher's guide, and sometimes a workbook for the pupils. In such schemes, teachers proceed through the programme taking the activities in the order they appear in the programme. In a loosely prescribed programme, activities are suggested but not in a teaching sequence and there are often alternatives from which teachers can choose and create their own teaching programme. The issue of close or loose prescription rests upon the extent to which teachers are thought to be able to take the decisions required to use a flexible programme and the extent to which it is felt that activities can be defined that are suitable, and indeed essential, for all pupils. Widely differing positions were taken by projects in the first phase and by project teams in the same country. The SCIS and SAPA chose to develop closely prescribed programmes in which teachers were provided with detailed directions and all materials were supplied; this ensured that pupils encountered a sequence of activities independent of the teacher's abilities to develop or even understand the sequence. The attempt to by-pass the teacher can, however, mean that activities have to be closely specified so that children follow a recipe—they *do* but do not create enquiries or ideas for themselves. The ESS, on the other hand, like the early projects in England and Wales, chose to provide flexible material in the expectation that teachers would select and adapt it to the needs of their pupils. It is only through allowing this flexibility that a programme can accommodate a philosophy of starting from the interests of children, a strong theme in ESS, the Nuffield Junior Science Project, and Science 5/13. Studies of these projects (Crossland 1967, Harlen 1975), however, suggested that the flexibility presented a problem for most teachers who found themselves unable either to stimulate children's interests or to exploit them in pursuing practical investigations. This result was seen by some as a confirmation that materials should be more structured, so that teachers would not be required to make decisions about activities, but by others as an indication that teachers needed more help than was provided by written materials. These two conclusions were reflected in later developments (for example, of two projects in England and Wales which were sequels to Science 5/13, one developed inservice material to upgrade teachers' skills and the other developed pupil material to supplement the teachers' guides).

3. Implementation of Primary Science Programmes

3.1 Problems

Since the early 1960s, a considerable effort has gone into attempts to introduce active, enquiry-based science into the primary school, but the results have been judged as disappointing (Reay 1979, Martin 1983). A survey in England (DES 1978) showed that only about a half of primary classes had any science at all in the curriculum and the proportion in which the work was developed seriously was about one in 10. Similarly in the United States a study in the same year (Weiss 1978) reported that about 70 percent of school districts did not use any of the materials of the major projects (ESS, SCIS, and SAPA). In countries where science has been included in the national syllabus and has to be taught, by law, there is much evidence that lessons involve hardly anything which can be described as scientific activity; "science" is learned from a textbook or by listening to the teacher.

Reasons for this failure to implement new curricula to any extent are not difficult to find. Firstly, and probably most important, is that the new materials invariably require teachers not only to introduce new content but also to adopt an unfamiliar role in teaching. In this role, teachers have to encourage pupils to raise questions to which answers are to be sought by enquiry, not given by the teacher, to show initiative, to challenge rather than accept ideas given to them and to express their own ideas without fear of giving the "wrong" answer. For a majority of teachers in all countries this requires a major change from the established role of teachers as providers of information. Such a change cannot be made quickly and there is little doubt that the early projects were guilty of expecting teachers to take too great a step in too short a time.

Secondly, the background knowledge of primary teachers is generally weak in science, as much so in developed countries as in developing ones. Although many of the early projects argued that the everyday knowledge of teachers is sufficient to enable them to "learn with the children", this view ignores the importance of teachers' knowledge as a source of confidence. Confidence has been identified as the most important factor in teachers' ability to handle science of any kind. Lack of confidence frequently has been traced to anxiety about inadequate personal knowledge of science, to experience of failure with the subject in the past, and to concern about ability to handle practical activity and supply necessary resources (Parker 1983).

A third factor can best be described as lack of commitment to science as an important part of children's education. Primary education's concern with the "basics" militates against the inclusion of science as long as the subject is not regarded as a basic element in education. The problem here is not simply one of convincing teachers of the value of science in the curriculum but of re-educating ministry or local authority officials, parents, and others who take part, or exert pressure, in decision making about education. The designation of science as part of the "core" of the national curriculum of England and Wales is of considerable significance in this respect (DES 1988b). The message of this designation is to place science on an equal footing with mathematics and language in the primary curriculum.

A fourth point concerns the relationship between assessment and the curriculum. This history of attempts to introduce science into elementary education in England in the late nineteenth and early twentieth century, and the current experience of introducing it into developing countries, illustrate the strong influence of assessment on the curriculum. Where science has not been included in end-of-primary examinations or other mandatory assessment or national surveys, it has withered to a token. Science has the status of a core subject only where it is included in assessment schemes equally with language and mathematics. The strong influence of what is assessed on the curriculum means, however, that it is important to pay attention to the view of science represented in what is assessed and how it is assessed. Greater consistency of assessment with aims relating to process skills and broad understanding has become possible only through developments in the 1980s; until then there was a total lack of experience of effective and valid methods of assessing learning in science at the primary level (Harlen 1983).

3.2 Strategies

Studies of implementation strategies have shown that those consisting principally of the production and distribution of teaching materials have little effect on classroom practice. Since primary teachers generally lack the skills and confidence to make use of new science programmes, some training is required to develop skills and positive attitudes before ideas can be implemented. Single, short courses have limited impact, however. Support for teachers has to be sustained over a period of time and is best given in the form of help within the school rather than at a distant course centre. Science teachers' associations, science fairs, and clubs also seem to be worthwhile in providing opportunities for teachers to meet, help each other, and learn from each other.

Among the more effective strategies for improving primary science practice through inservice work is the use of peripatetic science advisory teachers. Schemes to spread the expertise of selected teachers by releasing them from their own schools to visit others have been tried in many countries (Harlen 1979). A five year evaluation of the scheme operating in England and Wales has provided information about the factors which lead to success of such a scheme. These include training for the advisory teachers, negotiations with the head and staff of a school so that roles and responsibilities are clear and accepted, provision of follow-up support at intervals after the first intensive contact, work with staff on policies, planning and assessing and a programme for monitoring the scheme to provide formative feedback (DES 1989b).

3.3 Teacher Training

The organization and content of courses have received most attention in the third phase of curriculum development. The experience of earlier phase projects showed that teachers able to participate in the production of teaching material, either as authors or trial class teachers, gained a great deal more than others who were given instruction in how to use the final versions of materials. This experience has led to courses which enable teachers to develop—rather than simply accept—arguments for the importance of science, which provide evidence from which children's scientific development can be deduced and which give opportunities to work out ways of promoting this development.

Some projects of the late 1970s have attempted to place teacher training for primary science on a sound research footing. This work involves the identification of the skills required by primary science teachers as a preliminary step to devising instructional strategies for both inservice and preservice teacher education. The main groups of skills are related to:

(a) communication and interaction with children, of which questioning skill is of prime importance;
(b) classroom management and ability to use a range of teaching techniques;
(c) improvising equipment, collecting and organizing resources;
(d) applying knowledge of how children learn so that procedures can be adapted to the needs of individuals;
(e) the science process skills, which the teachers must have themselves before they can encourage, recognize, and assess their development in pupils.

Until the late 1980s few initial training programmes for primary teachers attempted to build up these skills in a systematic way, often because teacher trainers did not themselves possess such skills or know how to transmit them to others. Currently work is in progress in several countries to develop training programmes and to train trainers in their use (Commonwealth Secretariat/UNESCO 1987, Harlen et al. 1990). The focus on teachers' understanding is being informed by research into the science misconceptions of teachers (Summers and Kruger 1989) and this will no doubt lead into the next phase of primary science curriculum development.

Bibliography

Assessment of Performance Unit 1983 *Science in Schools. Age 11:* Report No. 2. Department of Education and Science, London

Assessment of Performance Unit 1984 *Science in Schools. Age 11:* Report No. 3. Department of Education and Science, London

Assessment of Performance Unit 1985 *Science in Schools. Age 11:* Report No. 4. Department of Education and Science, London

Ayres J B, Price C O 1975 Children's attitudes toward science. *Sch. Sci. Math.* 75: 311–18

Commonwealth Secretariat, UNESCO 1987 *Primary Science Teacher Training for Process Based Learning.* Commonwealth Secretariat, London

Craig J, Ayres D 1988 Does primary science affect girls' and boys' interests in secondary science? *Sch. Sci. Rev.* 248: 417–426

Crossland R W 1967 *Report of an Individual Study of the Nuffield Foundation Primary Science Project.* University of Manchester, Manchester

Davis T, Raymond A, MacRawls C, Jordan J 1976 A comparison of achievement and creativity of elementary school students using project vs. textbook programs. *J. Res. Sci. Teach.* 13: 205–12

Department of Education and Science 1978 *Primary Education in England: A Survey.* Her Majesty's Stationery Office, London

Department of Education and Science 1981 *Science in Schools. Age 11:* Report No. 1. Her Majesty's Stationery Office, London

Department of Education and Science 1988a *Science at Age 11: A Review of APU Survey Findings 1980–84.* Her Majesty's Stationery Office, London

Department of Education and Science 1988b *The Education Reform Act.* Her Majesty's Stationery Office, London

Department of Education and Science 1989a *Science in the National Curriculum.* Her Majesty's Stationery Office, London

Department of Education and Science 1989b *Aspects of Primary Education: Teaching and Learning Science.* Her Majesty's Stationery Office, London

Elementary Science Study (ESS) 1966 *Introduction to the Elementary Science Study.* McGraw-Hill, New York

Harlen W 1975 *Science 5/13: A Formative Evaluation.* Macmillan, London

Harlen W 1977 *Progress in Learning Science Project.* International Institute for Education Planning, Paris

Harlen W 1978 Does content matter in primary science? *Sch. Sci. Rev.* 209: 614–25

Harlen W 1979 Towards the implementation of science at the primary level. *New Trends in Integrated Science Teaching.* UNESCO, Paris

Harlen W 1983 *Guides to Assessment: Science.* Macmillan, London

Harlen W (ed.) 1983 *New Trends in Primary School Science Teaching,* Vol. 1. UNESCO, Paris

Harlen W 1985 *Teaching and Learning Primary Science.* Paul Chapman Publishing, London

Harlen W 1990 Pupil assessment in science at the primary level. *Studies in Educational Evaluation*

Harlen W, Macro C, Malvern D, Reed K, Schilling M 1990 *Progress in Primary Science: Workshop Materials for Teacher Education.* Routledge, London

Johnson V L 1970 *An Investigation into the Effect upon Classroom Interaction of the Introduction to Sierra Leone of the African Primary Science Programme.* Education Development Center, Newton, Massachusetts

Krockover G H, Malcolm M D 1978 The effects of the Science Curriculum Improvement Study upon a child's attitude towards science. *Sch. Sci. Math.* 78: 575–84

Lockard D (ed.) 1975 *Science and Mathematics Curricular Developments Internationally 1956–1974.* University of Maryland, Center for Science Teaching, College Park, Maryland

Martin M-D 1983 Recent trends in the nature of curriculum programmes and materials. In: Harlen W (ed.) 1983 *New Trends in Primary School Science Teaching,* Vol. 1. UNESCO, Paris

Nuffield Junior Science Project 1967 *Teachers' Guide.* Collins, London

Parker S J 1983 The preparation of teachers for primary school science. In: Harlen W (ed.) 1983 *New Trends in Primary School Science Teaching,* Vol. 1. UNESCO, Paris

Reay J (ed.) 1979 *New Trends in Integrated Science Teaching,* Vol. 5. UNESCO Paris

Renner J W et al. 1973 An evaluation of the Science Curriculum Improvement Study. *Sch. Sci. Math.* 73: 291–318

Science—A Process Approach (SAPA) 1974 *Overview.* Ginn, New York

Science Curriculum Improvement Study (SCIS) 1974 *Teachers' Handbook.* Lawrence Hall of Science, University of California, California

Science Education Programme for Africa (SEPA) 1977 *Handbook for Teachers of Science* SEPA. Accra, Ghana

Science 5/13 1972 *With Objectives in Mind: Guide to Science 5/13.* Macdonald, London

Sullivan R J 1979 Students' interests in specific science topics. *Sci. Educ.* 63: 591–98

Summers M, Kruger C J 1989 An investigation of some primary teachers' understanding of changes in materials. *Sch. Sci. Rev.* 255: 17–30

Vanek E P, Montean J J 1977 The effect of two science programs (ESS and Laidlaw) on student classification skills, science achievement and attitudes. *J. Res. Sci. Teach.* 14: 57–62

Weiss I R 1978 *National Survey of Science, Mathematics and Social Studies Education: Highlights Report.* ERIC Document No. ED 152 566. Institute of Education, Educational Resources Information Center, Washington, DC

Young B L 1983 The selection of processes, contexts and concepts and their relation to methods of teaching. In: Harlen W (ed.) 1983 *New Trends in Primary School Science Teaching,* Vol. 1. UNESCO, Paris

Science Education: Secondary School

R. F. Gunstone

Secondary-school science education programmes include both integrated or general science and specific single subjects such as physics, chemistry, and biology.

Integrated or general science programmes provide a coverage of some variety of the separate science disciplines, with integrated programmes usually attempting to do this in ways which emphasize some unifying principles of science. Both integrated and single discipline programmes are found at all levels of secondary schooling. However, single discipline science subjects are more common at the senior levels of secondary education.

In the 1970s, specific investigations and general discussions of the purposes of secondary science education were closely intertwined with debate about the relative merits of integrated and single discipline programmes. Many other contemporary issues of concern also embraced this debate. These issues include the nature and sequencing of appropriate content, the purposes of laboratory work and other teaching methodologies, the appropriateness of topic and modular approaches to programmes, the nature of the concepts "relevance" and "scientific literacy", and the extent to which these concepts should influence science programmes.

Science curriculum development efforts since the late 1950s have undergone both an enormous worldwide growth and, in many countries, a subsequent relative decline. These efforts have frequently been directed towards large-scale curriculum projects which have produced both student and teacher materials for science programmes. Such projects have both evolved from relevant research and stimulated new research directions. The first wave of these large projects, usually referred to as first generation projects, was of great significance. Not only did this work mark the beginning of a period of substantial funding for curriculum research and development, it also stimulated effective communication between different educational settings of ideas and data about science programmes.

1. First Generation Projects

In the middle 1950s, there was a growing belief in the United States that secondary-school science in that country was in urgent need of change. This led to the funding of the first of the influential science curriculum projects. The launching of Sputnik 1 resulted in a dramatic increase in funding for science programme development in the United States. Consequently, the growth of these projects accelerated sharply.

Science programmes in use before the first generation projects were seen by some critics as contributing to a scientific and engineering personnel shortage in the country. In responding to this situation, the funded projects worked on senior secondary, single discipline programmes with some specific concern for high-ability students. This single discipline approach was consistent with the existing school curriculum structure. In the physics and chemistry programmes, the number of topics covered was lower than had previously been the practice so as to allow for the development of a smaller number of broad conceptual schemes seen as fundamental to modern thinking in the subjects. This conceptual emphasis was intended to reflect the nature of science. An appreciation of the framework of concepts

and broad ideas on which the structure of the discipline rested was seen as more significant for students than large numbers of facts. Appropriate analyses of the structure of knowledge were influential in the projects. Laboratory work moved away from a process of a sequence of instructions and towards an inquiry approach. The laboratory was now seen as a means of allowing student discovery, and hence engendering some of the excitement seen as characteristic of science. Considerable ancillary materials, such as films and supplementary reading, were developed to accompany students' texts and teachers' guides.

The corresponding biology programme, the Biological Sciences Curriculum Study (BSCS), adopted a similar strategy. It rejected the view of biology as a descriptive science and moved to an experimental perspective. This project also sought to provide for a wider range of student abilities and interests by producing three versions of BSCS Biology, each with a different approach. Unlike other first generation projects, BSCS has continued, producing revisions of the initial programme and developing related programmes.

These first generation projects were also characterized by the major involvement of scientists. Others, such as science educators and curriculum specialists, were also involved. However it was scientists who were the dominant influence. Content and textbooks tended to be the prime concerns of the projects, although curriculum models did shape some development. The relationships between objectives and content were often more logical than in previous courses.

A corresponding upsurge in science programmes occurred in England and Wales under funding from the Nuffield Foundation. Because of their different characteristics, these programmes are not generally termed first generation projects. The first thrust of these projects was again towards specific science subjects for academically able students. Just as the existing curriculum structure in the United States led to one-year senior courses being developed, so the existing English and Welsh curriculum structure led to five-year separate science programmes for children aged 11 to 16. Other differences between the projects from the two countries also have roots in the differences between the two educational systems. There was less concern in England and Wales with the impact on science teaching of poorly qualified teachers. Hence the Nuffield projects did not produce heavily structured programmes and textbooks. These projects involved experienced science teachers rather than scientists, and concentrated on developing materials which would enable the classroom teacher to present science in a more lively and motivating fashion. Laboratory work was a strong component of the materials, with the same shift towards student discovery being evident. Curriculum models were not influential in the development process. Indeed the projects reflected a pooling of substantial teaching experience rather than initial, shaping theoretical positions.

2. The Spread of Science Programme Reform Movements

By the mid-1960s, movements to reform science programmes had taken hold in a large number of countries, both industrialized and developing (Gillon and Gillon 1971). The projects described above were very influential in this movement. Knowledge and experience of the process involved in the early projects assisted the development of strategies in subsequent programmes. Content and teaching ideas from those projects were adapted to meet circumstances in other countries, both through adaptations of whole programmes and through the use of specific ideas in new projects. In some cases, existing programmes were used in new contexts with little or no change.

Since the early 1960s these trends of interaction and influence have become more and more widespread. New programmes have generated new perspectives adopted by others, and research associated with particular programmes has resulted in knowledge and ideas used elsewhere (see *Curriculum Potential; Curriculum Research*). Issues of importance to science programmes over this period are considered in subsequent sections. Descriptions of almost all specific programmes, from first generation projects onwards, are given in Lockard (1963–1977).

Because of the extent to which developed programmes have been adapted to other contexts, this process has been studied at some length. It involves two stages, the selection of a suitable programme for adaptation followed by the actual adaptation itself (Blum 1979) (see *Curriculum Adaptation*). There are many factors involved in making these decisions. At one extreme it may be that only a single programme is available. For example, the first generation physics project produced by the Physical Sciences Study Committee (PSSC) was translated into 14 languages for use in other countries. In addition, the American text was directly adopted in some countries in which English was the language of instruction. This widespread use of a complete programme reflected the fact that PSSC was for some time the only physics project which had produced a textbook and which reflected trends such as student inquiry and conceptual emphases. At the other extreme, some adaptations have considered all relevant projects and synthesized from them a programme to more adequately reflect particular local needs.

Broad social and cultural factors have been important influences on the nature of adaptations. Those developing countries which had previously been colonies have tended to use programmes which originated in the colonizing country. This occurred largely because these were the programmes which were suited to the existing general school structure in the developing countries. Other factors have had effect on the way particular adaptations have been undertaken and on the final programme resulting from the adaptation. These factors include cultural and economic influences on teaching methods, the extent to which vocabulary exists in the language of a people to adequately differentiate particular science concepts, and perceived relationships between religion and science (Wilson 1981).

In a number of countries, some form of central agency has been established to focus, coordinate, or initiate adaptations and new programme development. Some of these agencies, for example, the Institute for the Promotion of Teaching Science and Technology in Thailand, reflect various forms of government-determined priorities for the nation's science programmes. Direct financial and educational assistance to developing countries for new science projects has often been via these agencies. UNESCO has done much to assist the establishment of new projects and to aid appropriate adaptation of existing programmes in developing countries.

3. Second Generation Projects

First generation projects did not always include evaluation as part of their function. However subsequent evaluation and criticism suggested a number of inadequacies in the programmes. These included the failure to attract larger science enrolments in high-school courses, which was one of the prime aims of the projects. There was a lack of concern with the needs of average students, and a failure to define goals and philosophies clearly. Because of the primary concern with content in the projects, inservice training concentrated on the subject matter backgrounds of teachers rather than on methods of teaching. Considerations of how students learn did not influence the projects.

Later projects, usually referred to as second generation projects, reflected these concerns and evolved further issues. The role of scientists in programme development declined, and science educators, educational psychologists, and scholars from related fields such as educational technology and curriculum theory became more heavily involved. Second generation projects marked the beginning of a considerable growth in diversity of approaches. Consequently the form of brief encapsulation of essential features given for first generation projects is not possible. However, there are a number of issues which have been of concern to many second generation programmes. Some of these remain particularly influential in current work on science programmes and are considered in Sect. 4 below.

Most second generation programmes have sought to broaden science education, both in terms of the student population for whom the programme aims to provide, and in terms of the content of the programme. Programmes aimed at all ages of secondary schooling and all abilities have emerged, as have primary (elementary) and tertiary science projects. Numbers of different themes have been used to guide basic programme aims and content selection/sequencing. All of these schemes have been influenced to varying extents by views of the concept of relevance. The definition of relevance has been undertaken in a variety of ways. Theories and data about student attitudes to science, student motivations, and the nature of the learning process were sometimes used. Analytic studies of the disciplines of science were undertaken in order to determine distinguishing characteristics of this broad field of knowledge or to place science in the wider context of human endeavour. Determinations of the scientific knowledge and skills necessary for everyday living in the society in which the programme was to be offered have also been attempted. On occasions it has been just the intuitions of the programme developers which were most influential. In the following overview of themes which emerged from this variety of approaches, prominence is given to those which have continued to be significant.

The broadening of content seen as appropriate for science education resulted in some programmes placing science in the historical/cultural context in which it has emerged. An understanding of forces influencing the growth of scientific knowledge and of the impact of science on the development of other fields of human activity are specific aims of such courses. Some of these approaches have been in single subject programmes. Others have used case studies to consider the history of science. In both of these modes, primary objectives have been that students appreciate the importance of science in the present world, understand the methods of science as a means of extending human knowledge, and are aware of the creative and inquiry attitudes of the scientist. One broad focus is science as a human activity.

This movement extended further to incorporate current social consequences of science, with both scientific and other perspectives being brought to bear on important issues and problems. It was this perspective which contributed to the early development of the environmental education movement in many countries. Attempts to develop an understanding of social issues involving science also provided a rationalization for integrated science, for concern with the processes of science rather than content, for a still wider range of topics seen to be appropriate for science programmes, and for teaching about the social responsibilities of science. All four of these issues also emerged from other perspectives.

Integrated approaches to science programmes have been proposed by some to be the most effective way of catering for a wide range of student abilities and motivations, and for a range of uses for science knowledge and skills in adult life. In addition, integration has been claimed to be the most effective method for presenting the structure of science and for developing scientific literacy. However, all of these claims have been disputed, and the idea of integrated science itself has been criticized as being inadequately defined. Nevertheless, many integrated programmes have emerged. UNESCO sponsorship of the approach has

been a major factor in its widespread acceptance (Reay 1979).

One organizing scheme for the selection and sequencing of content in integrated courses has been the use of themes or topics which embrace more than one of the traditional science disciplines. One example of the use of this scheme is the Nuffield Secondary Science Project. Under this structure the specific disciplines are not identified to students. An extension of that view has led to widespread development of modular programmes. Here the student materials are organized into short segments, often self-contained and again often based on topics. Greater flexibility in programmes is then possible, and choice may be exercised by the teacher or even the student. It has been argued that such an approach can result in a lack of overall structure in the programme, as it is rare to find the possible conceptual and skill links between modules clearly detailed in the materials. One further extension of this view has led to modules which are individualized, such as the Individualized Science Instructional System. This approach aims to allow for quite idiosyncratic rates of progress. Hence, it is argued, the programme can better cope with a wide variety of abilities and interests. In some cases, individualized programmes have also moved farther towards organization via topics, with topics being drawn from personal experience areas such as health, road safety, and hobbies. Student choice of modules is a feature of some such programmes, thus allowing student determination of the scope and sequence of their science course.

An emphasis on the processes of science has been used to give an organizing scheme for integrated courses (for example, see the Schools Council Integrated Science Project). Here processes such as observing, predicting, experimenting, interpreting are given prime importance. Content is selected according to the extent to which it can promote the development of process skills.

The process approach has given laboratory work an expanded role by comparison with first generation projects. This added laboratory emphasis is a feature shared by many second generation projects. In most cases, programmes aim to use the laboratory to develop process and problem-solving skills as well as concepts. Indeed, some programmes intend that the bulk of student learning take place through laboratory activities. Discovery learning has become a widely adopted methodology. Wide use of the laboratory has also been argued on the grounds of increasing student motivation for science. Serious consideration of how learning takes place has also been used to justify laboratory activities, and to direct ways in which such activities are structured. Not only is concern with learning another common feature of these programmes, it has been a prime organizing theme for some projects. The views of learning advanced by Piaget have had particular influence (see, for example, the Australian Science Education Project).

The evolving trends described above have all been heavily influenced by the results of programme evaluations and implementation studies (see *Curriculum Implementation*). Second generation projects have commonly given more attention to the evaluation, both formative and summative, of their products. Other programme evaluations not sponsored by projects have been very influential, as has work which explored ways that project materials have been translated into classroom practice. Trends in science education evaluation/ implementation studies have been intertwined with trends in science programmes. While large-scale, psychometric studies undertaken with earlier projects assisted with further elaboration of possible purposes of and structures for science education, these also gave rise to new questions for curriculum planners as well as evaluators. The gradual growth in case study approaches to evaluation has reflected both evaluation and programme development concerns. For example, case study evaluations of particular projects have given rise to serious questions about the extent to which the trends in laboratory use can be supported. Consequently, there is need for further analyses of the strengths and weaknesses of this approach. Results of early evaluation/ implementation studies gave considerable impetus to the consideration by projects of their role in teacher training. From this, perspectives on both preservice and inservice training for using new programmes change. There was an increasing focus on the rationales of programmes, on methods for implementing ideas in classrooms, and on ways of assessing student learning.

Perhaps the most significant trend whose development has been assisted by evaluation/implementation studies has been the decline in projects which aim to produce a prescriptive learning package (the so-called teacher-proof curricula). As it became clear that individual teachers play an extremely important role in determining the actual programme in practice, so projects moved to the development of a variety of resources from which teachers could select.

In many countries, school-based curriculum development has grown in importance. This movement has been fostered further in some systems by the continued failure of new programmes to increase science enrolments. In these circumstances it has been argued that student attitudes to science, the classroom climate in which students work, the perception of students of the relevance of the science they study remain significant variables. Giving greater responsibility to teachers for the determination of science programmes is seen as one important approach to the problems. A more negative approach has been a decline in science programme development activity.

4. Current Significant Issues

Many of the issues raised in the previous section remain significant in current work. In this section, issues which have been particularly important in shaping recent studies are considered.

The debate between the relative merits of integrated science and separate disciplines remains unresolved, despite considerable effort being devoted to the question. Much work has involved the exploration and specification of relevant dimensions and characteristics of integrated programmes so as to allow more precise description of features of importance in particular programmes. Such data enable more informed and reliable judgments about the relationships between programme aims, materials, and outcomes. Despite this work there still remains a remarkable diversity of views as to what integrated science is, why programmes might be integrated, and how content should be selected for them (Brown 1977). Strident analytic critics of integrated approaches have pointed to a number of other unresolved issues (Chapman 1976). In particular, it is clear that many claims made by proponents about the effects on student outcomes of integrated programmes are often not supported by data. Nevertheless the integrated science movement remains widespread and most influential.

The environmental education movement continues to raise significant questions about science programmes. At the secondary level, this movement began in the 1960s as a means of bringing relevance to biology courses. Today roles are reversed. Rather than considering what environmental education perspectives can contribute to science programmes, the issue under consideration is often what can science education contribute to environmental programmes. This logical extension of the inclusion of social issues in science programmes has led to new perspectives for consideration of science programmes. For example, concern with the personal and immediate environment of the student gives a different view of the influence technology education could have on science education. It is argued that after beginning with some aspect of technology of immediate impact on the student (such as which wood screw is most suited to a particular job), the science needed to understand and answer the question can be introduced. Such combinations of science and personal technology lead some writers to forecast a shift from laboratory to workshop for science education.

This view of a role for technology in science education has significance for the notion of scientific literacy. A concern with establishing the contributions science programmes should make towards general literacy remains prominent. At the secondary level, this tends to be a greater problem in industrialized countries. In countries without the luxury of universal secondary education, national priorities for science and technology can make the content requirements of programmes somewhat more obvious. It is at the primary level in these countries that general scientific literacy is more likely to be considered.

Finally, one area of science learning research which has grown rapidly since the late 1970s is beginning to influence science programme development. This research has grown somewhat parallel to concerns shown for understanding in cognitive psychology. Researchers have used techniques from that area, together with their own, to show a surprising lack of understanding of basic science concepts at all secondary levels. Students have evolved their own explanatory systems for scientific phenomena before entering science programmes. These systems are often logically antagonistic to the tenets of science, and difficult to change. It is common for students to complete science programmes with their initial views unchanged. Data of this kind are giving important new insights into both student learning and the nature of science programmes which aim to develop understanding. Concrete examples of curriculum materials which reflect the personally constructed nature of students' understanding are now appearing, and the major importance of students' understandings in areas other than science cognitions is now well established. Such areas include the affective as well as the cognitive, and ideas/beliefs about teaching and learning and appropriate student roles in these processes. These developments are elaborated in Fensham (1988) and White (1988).

Bibliography

Baez A 1976 *Innovation in Science Education, World-wide.* UNESCO, Paris

Blum A 1979 Curriculum adaptation in science education: Why and how. *Sci. Educ.* 63: 693–704

Brown S 1977 A review of the meanings of, and arguments for, integrated science. *Stud. Sci. Educ.* 4: 31–62

Chapman B R 1976 The integration of science or the disintegration of science education? *Sch. Sci. Rev.* 58(202): 134–46

Fensham P J (ed.) 1988 *Development and Dilemmas in Science Education.* Falmer, London

Gillon P, Gillon H (eds.) 1971 *Science and Education in Developing States.* Rehovot Conf., 1969. Praeger, New York

Jenkins E, Whitfield R (eds.) 1974 *Readings in Science Education: A Source Book.* McGraw-Hill, London

Lockard D (ed.) 1963–1977 *Reports of the International Clearinghouse on Science and Mathematics Curricular Developments.* University of Maryland, Maryland

Reay J (ed.) 1979 *New Trends in Integrated Science Teaching,* Vol. 5. UNESCO, Paris

Welch W 1979 Twenty years of science curriculum development: A look back. *Rev. Res. Educ.* 7: 282–306

White R T 1988 *Learning Science.* Blackwell, Oxford

Wilson B (ed.) 1981 *Cultural Contexts of Science and Mathematics Education: A Bibliographic Guide.* University of Leeds, Leeds

General Science Programs

E. W. Jenkins

General science may be defined as a broad course of scientific study and investigation which has its roots in the common experience of children and draws, as appropriate, upon any of the recognized scientific disciplines. Such courses, therefore, inevitably and properly, differ in their content, although all are of an unspecialized nature and seek to encourage students to develop an intelligent, scientific understanding of their everyday world while providing an adequate foundation for a subsequent and more advanced study of individual scientific disciplines.

In the United States, innovative work in a few schools in the early years of the twentieth century, the encouragement of the Central Association of Science and Mathematics Teachers, and the advocacy by the National Education Association of "introductory science" led to a steady growth in the number of courses of general science provided in high schools in the years leading up to the First World War. However, the new subject was accommodated within the curriculum only with difficulty and amid controversy, partly because of a vigorous dispute over its educational merits and partly because general science was competing for a place in high-school programmes with a number of already well-established, science-based courses, many of which were competently taught and adequately supported by texts and other resources. The report of the National Edu-

cation Association's Committee on the *Reorganization of Science in Secondary Schools* (Caldwell 1920) was of seminal importance for the future of general science since it recommended a clear sequence of presentation of scientific subjects to high-school students, within which general science was assigned a well-defined place. By 1933/34, when general science, biology, chemistry, and physics were commonly offered as a four-year sequence in senior high schools, 54 percent of all students enrolled in the first year (age 14) were following courses in general science, while semester courses in such subjects as astronomy, geology, physical geography, botany, zoology, and physiology had practically disappeared. The best of these general science courses attempted to provide a basic scientific education appropriate to the needs of future citizens and, as such, involved far more than a selection of topics drawn from the individual sciences. In addition, many of the first-year courses were gradually adapted for work with younger students and, by the end of the Second World War, general science was an almost universally accepted component of the curricula of junior high schools. However, such adaptation, coupled with the development of programmes of elementary science, eventually ensured that the conventional first-year course in general science became seriously inadequate (Henry 1947, 1960) and, since the early 1960s, attention has moved away from such courses to schemes of integrated/unified science in which the boundaries between the traditional sciences are, as far as possible, eliminated.

In the United Kingdom, general science was also essentially a development of the interwar years, although its immediate origins lay in two pamphlets published in 1916 by the Association of Public School Science Masters, entitled *The Aims of Science Teaching in General Education* and *Science for All*. It was this association, as its successor the Science Masters' Association, which led the campaign for the introduction of general science into the selective grammar and independent schools from which its members were drawn. By the mid-1930s, syllabi in general science were offered by all the boards conducting the important school certificate examinations and the number of examination entries in general science grew rapidly after 1935 and especially during the period 1939 to 1942. In addition, many secondary schools taught general science to their younger students as an introduction to more advanced examination work in chemistry, physics, or biology. Although revised and detailed proposals for general science were published by the Science Masters' Association in 1938 and reissued in 1950, the position established by general science relative to the specialist sciences during the war years was not maintained. The proportional decline in examination entries in general science during the 1950s gave way to a fall in actual numbers during the 1960s and, by the middle of the following decade, the majority of examination boards had withdrawn their syllabi in this subject in favour of more integrated and/or less comprehensive schemes such as physical science (Jenkins 1979).

The position of general science in schools within educational systems based upon the American or British pattern has, in large measure, followed that described above. Many countries, however, have followed the French system in which separate introductory courses in physics, chemistry, or biology have been offered from the beginning of secondary education.

The literature of general science makes clear that its advocates sought both to widen the scope of school science teaching and to bring this teaching into a closer relationship with the everyday life of students. As such, general science represented a reaction against the formal and academic nature of much secondary-school science teaching and a rejection of the assumption that an introduction into the professional world of precise and abstract scientific ideas could provide an adequate basis of a liberal secondary education for all. Starting with the experiences and interests of the students rather than with the needs or attributes of the scientific disciplines, general science reasserted the usefulness of scientific knowledge by relating such knowledge to those applications likely to be familiar to students. In this way, students were to be helped to understand the scientific conception of the world in which they lived and to appreciate some of the ways in which science and technology interacted with society, influencing and

transforming the intellectual and material condition of humankind. Such a radical conception of school science education inevitably brought the advocates of general science into conflict with some of those individuals and organizations professionally concerned with the future welfare of the scientific disciplines, a concern increasingly buttressed in the 1950s and 1960s by reference to the economic importance of an adequate supply of qualified scientific personnel. This conflict was particularly acute and exposed in countries with selective systems of secondary education in which the academically orientated secondary schools were charged with providing an education preparatory to the universities and the professions. Significantly, it was the nonacademic secondary schools within such systems which provided a more hospitable environment for the growth of alternative courses such as general science.

In practice, many general science courses failed to live up to the high expectations of the early enthusiasts. Some courses were narrowly conceived, their contents confined to topics selected from conventional physics and chemistry programmes. Others, while more broad ranging, were fragmentary and offered no substitute for the intellectual rigour and coherence associated with the traditional scientific disciplines, despite the claim that general science rested on the presumed fundamental unity of methods and principles characteristic of the scientific approach. In addition, the subject has often been taught by teachers who were ill-prepared for the task and who found it difficult to abandon the academic tradition in which they had been nurtured. Not surprisingly, therefore, general science has rarely achieved more than a subordinate and introductory status within school science curricula and this status has been reflected, occasionally, in a lack of adequate laboratory accommodation and equipment and, more often, in selective schools, in a restriction of general science courses to less academically able students or even to girls, most of whom were regarded as unlikely to pursue careers as professional scientists.

However, the value of general science courses should not be underestimated. Such courses have led to a broadening of school science curricula, thereby offering students a "bird's eye view" of the field before they settled down to more specialized study, and have allowed important topics to be taught which would not have been otherwise incorporated within school science programmes. In addition, much of the resource material produced to support general science and the experience gained by teaching it, have been of considerable value in developing the unified/integrated, balanced and modular courses now widely taught in schools as a contemporary response to the enduring challenge to provide a liberal, scientific education. Finally, it must be acknowledged that in many countries in which mass systems of secondary education have yet to be fully developed, general science or courses derived from it, with various degrees of integration and/or local relevance, remain the only scientific education offered to students who complete their education at the elementary stage. Despite these advantages, a general science curriculum that integrates a large portion of the school science disciplines of physics, chemistry, and biology remains to be constructed (Frey 1989).

Bibliography

Caldwell O W 1920 *Reorganization of Science in Secondary Schools*. Bulletin No. 26. United States Bureau of Education, Washington, DC

Eikenberry W L 1922 *The Teaching of General Science*. University of Chicago Press, Chicago, Illinois

Frey K 1989 Integrated science education: 20 years on. *Int. J. Sci. Ed.* 11(1): 3–17

Henry N B (ed.) 1947 *Science Education in American Schools*. 46th Yearbook of the National Society for the Study of Education. University of Chicago Press, Chicago, Illinois

Henry N B (ed.) 1960 *Rethinking Science Education*. 59th Yearbook of the National Society for the Study of Education. University of Chicago Press, Chicago, Illinois

Isenbarger K U et al. 1950 *A Half Century of Science and Mathematics Teaching: A Summary of Significant Developments in the Teaching of Science and Mathematics During the First Half of the Twentieth Century*. Central Association of Science and Mathematics Teachers, Banta, Wisconsin

Jenkins E W 1979 The general science movement. In: Jenkins E W 1979 *From Armstrong to Nuffield: Studies in Twentieth Century Science Education in England and Wales*. Murray, London

Science Masters' Association 1936 *The Teaching of General Science*, Part 1. Murray, London

Science Masters' Association 1938 *The Teaching of General Science*, Part 2. Murray, London

Shelton H S 1939 *The Theory and Practice of General Science*. Murray, London

Specific Subjects

Life Sciences: Educational Programs

P. Tamir

Life sciences, also known as biological sciences, are those branches of science which deal with the study of living organisms and life processes as well as with their interactions with physical–inanimate objects and phenomena both in the present and over time. The distinction between life sciences on the one hand and the physical sciences on the other, is psychological. "Nothing else, after all, has such immediate personal relevance as the phenomenon of life; and biological science, as the study of life, sheds light on what every individual experiences himself and observes around him" (Keeton 1967 p. 11). Life sciences are highly diverse and include a variety of branches, each being characterized by a different substantive structure (i.e. content) as well as by a unique syntactic structure (i.e. processes and methods of inquiry and research). These branches are, to mention a few, morphology, taxonomy, physiology, genetics, microbiology, ecology, zoology, botany, and others. The uniqueness of life sciences as well as their complexity and diversity pose special challenges to educators but at the same time offer unique opportunities for curriculum and instruction.

1. Historical Perspective

In recent studies, it has been shown that, by and large, the teaching of biology is concentrated around textbooks and that learning experiences, including class discussions and laboratory activities, are based mainly on particular textbooks. This is certainly true in countries with centralistic educational systems, but is also true for countries in which education is not centralized. For example, in the United States "three biology textbooks, Modern Biology and the BSCS Green and Yellow versions represent the subject matter taught in two thirds of biology classes with an enrollment of approximately 3,000,000 students . . ." (Hurd 1981 p. 20). Since the textbooks actually represent the teaching goals and the subject matter, and strongly influence instruction, review of their history may serve as a fair description of the development of biology education over the years. According to Schwab (1963), three developmental phases mark this history. In the first phase from about 1890 to about 1929, textbooks

emphasized elementary facts and generalizations of the sciences, but at the same time, since they were written by practicing scientists, they had the advantage of being in close contact with the sources of information and presented, as a result, an accurate account of the knowledge of their time. New knowledge in the field and modifications of previous knowledge found their way relatively quickly into high-school textbooks. By contrast, the books of the second phase (1929–1957), became more and more distantly related to their originating sources. Their authors, mainly teachers and inspectors, were more influenced by, and sensitive to, problems of teaching and learning; however, their line of communication to scientific inquiry grew thinner and thinner, and the gulf between scientific knowledge and the content of textbooks grew wider and wider. In both of these phases, the texts and consequently the curriculum and instruction were almost entirely descriptive. They consisted almost wholly of a mass of poorly connected facts and elementary generalizations. The appearance of the first Russian satellite marks the beginning of the third phase, since biology courses such as those developed by the Biological Science Curriculum Study (BSCS) in the United States and those designed under the auspices of the Nuffield Foundation in the United Kingdom depict biology more as an experimental science with students acquiring some of the skills of scientific investigation and, in part at least, obtaining biological knowledge through such investigations. Even more importantly, the new biology was to be presented as enquiry dealing with doubts and problems, as well as with interaction between ideas and experiments, rather than as rhetoric of conclusions. This third phase can be termed the phase of inquiry since it advocated the teaching of biology as enquiry by inquiry (Schwab 1963).

There is no doubt that biology education has been revolutionized in many countries since the early 1960s. Many college professors would agree with the observation that "each year entering students are better prepared" (Keeton 1967 p. 11, Tamir and Amir 1981). Although reality in many classrooms lags far behind the expectations of the curriculum study groups in which distinguished scientists, science educators, and teachers collaborated to improve science programs, the fact is that in many schools in various countries, students do learn biology as enquiry and are actually engaged in practical laboratory investigations, in problem solving, and in activities which lead to an understanding of the major ideas and inquiry processes which characterize biology. Yet, biology education in the early 1980s seems to be under pressure for another change, this time pertaining not so much to the acquisition of knowledge but rather to its utilization and applications. As one science educator has observed "modern science curricula at all levels pose a curious paradox. For while it is universally acknowledged that human society is largely dependent upon science in the form of modern technology, nonetheless the study of technology as such hardly features in courses at any level. By technology is implied not just the applications of science for human needs but also a consideration of the economic, social, ethical and aesthetic contexts in which these applications are made" (Dowdeswell 1980 p. 21).

Three dimensions characterize the fourth phase in the history of biology education. First, there is an attempt to integrate the social sciences (sociology, psychology) with life sciences to deal with biosocial problems, for example, those which bear on the links and interrelationships between biological and cultural natures. Second, there is an increased emphasis on the study of human biology, a topic rarely studied as such in the 1960s. And thirdly, there is a tendency to move toward issue studies which emphasize solving of real-life problems, decision making, value judgment, and topics which have strong relevance to the life of the individual and the community where he or she lives (Kelly 1980, Hurd 1981).

2. The Role of Life Sciences in Education

The uniqueness of the life sciences has already been attended to because of their immediate personal relevance to the students. Certainly biology as a major field of human knowledge is worth studying on its own merits. Some knowledge of major biological ideas and processes, some familiarity with microorganisms, with plants, and with animals which surround us, and some insight into the structure and function of our own bodies are certainly, much like language, literature, and mathematics, part and parcel of human culture and of basic literacy. In addition, biology has the potential to make some unique contributions to education. Some of these potential contributions will be discussed briefly below.

While the physical sciences are by their nature less complex, the way they are being taught, their heavy reliance on abstractions, as well as their tendency to incorporate mathematics, make them unattractive to many students. It is well-known that when they have a choice, many more students will elect to study biology in favor of either chemistry or physics. For example, in the United States about 90 percent of the high-school students study biology, about 50 percent study chemis-

try, and only about 20 percent study physics. This being the case, the study of biology carries the task of not only presenting the content and processes of the life sciences, but rather of representing the only science that many students would ever experience in their high-school studies. The image of science that many citizens carry into life would be the one acquired through their study of biology.

The diversity of legitimate approaches to the teaching of biology (see below) makes it possible to adjust and adapt curricula and instruction to the needs and capabilities of any student at any age. The richness of the living world enables teachers to build upon the natural curiosity and intrinsic motivation that most pupils hold toward certain biological phenomena.

The biological sciences have special links to central human enterprises such as medicine and agriculture which may be considered in many ways as applied technologies of the life sciences.

Many cultural, economical, and moral issues of paramount importance to our everyday lives are deeply rooted and closely associated with biological processes. Taking advantage of these unique relationships may upgrade the lives of individuals and communities. Issues such as genetic engineering, nutrition, hygiene, birth control (to mention a few) would often be best approached within the context of the biological studies.

3. Aims and Objectives

Various authors and projects have compiled lists of aims and objectives which may guide biology instruction in schools (e.g. Nuffield Foundation 1965, Klinckmann 1970, Klopfer 1971). Silberstein and Tamir (1979) collected 100 objectives from sources such as those cited above and grouped them under three main categories and 13 subcategories. Questionnaires listing all 100 objectives were distributed to a sample consisting of elementary teachers, secondary teachers, inspectors, teacher educators, and scientists.

The results pertain to the relative importance assigned to the subcategories by the respondents. It may be observed, for example, that in the lower elementary level, top priority is given to objectives related to the needs of the individual student and to the affective domain, while the acquisition of most inquiry skills such as formulating hypotheses, designing experiments, and interpreting experimental results is considered inadequate for this level (making observations being a notable exception). While curiosity, open mindedness, ability to cooperate, responsibility, and positive attitudes toward living organisms are already considered important for the early elementary grades, other objectives such as perseverance, accuracy, and self-reliance are conceived to be worth aiming at not before the pupils have reached upper elementary grades. Only at the high-school level do the more abstract inquiry concepts such as hypothesis, assumption, control, and replication and the more complex inquiry skills such as identifying a problem, working with a microscope, designing experiments, reporting results in graphs and in tables become an important component of curriculum and instruction. A similar analysis was carried out in relation to specific biological topics. It was found for example that while it is considered to be important for students aged 11 to 14 to become familiar with the general structure of the cell and to be able to differentiate between animal and plant cells, topics such as cell organelles, active absorption, enzymatic processes, and cell respiration had better be left for students aged 15 to 18.

A useful approach to the delineation of the field of biology for purposes of curriculum construction is presented by Grobman (1969). Following the BSCS approach, he presents a three-dimensional grid. The first dimension consists of the major three groups, namely: microorganisms, plants, and animals. The second dimension consists of nine major themes or conceptual schemes which cut across the different groups of organisms. These are:

(a) nature of scientific inquiry;

(b) the intellectual history of biological concepts;

(c) genetic continuity;

(d) regulation and homeostasis;

(e) complementarity of structure and function;

(f) behavior;

(g) relationship between organism and environment;

(h) diversity and unity;

(i) change through time—evolution.

The third dimension, which cuts across the two already described, refers to seven hierarchical levels of organization which are listed below from less inclusive to the more inclusive: molecular, cellular, tissue and organ, individual organism, population, community, world biome. It is possible to specify objectives in terms of these three dimensions. It is also useful to analyze a given curriculum or text book along these dimensions. For example, while conventional biology emphasizes organs, tissues, and the individual organism, the BSCS Green version, the Australian Web of Life, and the Nuffield 'O' Level texts put great emphasis on populations and communities. At the same time, the BSCS Yellow version and the Nuffield 'A' Level put great emphasis on the cellular level and medium emphasis on the molecular level.

4. Special Features of Life Science in School

Every field of knowledge is distinguished by specific features which relate to the structure of the discipline and to its methods of inquiry. When that field of knowledge becomes a school subject, these features gain special flavor as they interact with the contexts provided by the school environment. A number of these features which characterize the life sciences will be briefly discussed below.

4.1 Children's Conception of Life

Life is the focus of biology education. Many teachers take it for granted that their pupils understand what life is. Yet it was found that while practically all children aged 9 to 15 classify animals as living, only 80 percent correctly classify plants as living and inanimate objects as nonliving, and still fewer (56 percent) classify embryos (seeds and eggs) as living. Movement and growth appear to be the most commonly used indicators of life. Only at the junior-high level do students begin to employ as indicators of life more unique biological attributes such as nutrition, reproduction, and respiration. For many children, the life of man and animals is different from that of plants and embryos. Moreover, life as related to a dormant seed is conceived to be substantially different from that of the same seed as it germinates. The knowledge that living organisms develop from living organisms does not prevent many students from believing that seeds and eggs are not alive. There is no doubt that teachers should be aware of the ambiguities that children associate with the concept of life so that they will be able to choose more effective instructional strategies which will help students form a mature concept of life which is essential for people's understanding of the phenomena around them (see Tamir et al. 1981).

4.2 Use of Living Organisms in the Classroom

An increased emphasis on the use of living organisms has been one of the characteristics of the transition from descriptive to more inquiry- and discipline-based instruction in biology. The use of living organisms poses special problems.

4.3 Human Biology

Human biology as such has not been a common component of the biology programs of the 1960s. Rather it was assumed that human biology would best be studied as part of the general survey of the functional systems of living organisms. One reason for this is that it is often impossible to perform experiments with humans and since biology was to be studied to a large extent by laboratory investigation, it was considered reasonable to integrate human biology with that of other animals which lent themselves more easily to direct observations and experiments. As well, it was believed that a comparative study of human physiology, morphology, and anatomy would provide a useful evolutionary perspective and perhaps help develop a sense of realism and humility in students who are often indoctrinated in other school subjects to adopt a highly homocentric view of the world. More recently, however, this approach has been widely criticized. Silberstein and Tamir (1979) found that 43 percent of their sample of science educators, scientists, and teachers believed that human biology should be studied as a topic in its own right while only 28 percent advocated integration with other biological topics. The desirability of a human biology course dealing with life processes as well as social, anthropological, economical, and cultural aspects of human life is voiced by many science educators (e.g. Kelly 1980, Silberstein and Tamir 1979, Hurd 1981).

4.4 Outdoors—Laboratory—Classroom

Although other school subjects may also use a variety of learning environments, it is in the life sciences where the division of labor between classroom–laboratory and outdoors has become accepted and desirable in many schools. Each of these environments offers unique learning opportunities and only through a synthesis of these diversified faces of biology can the student acquire a faithful holistic image of biology. The BSCS courses mentioned above perhaps with the exception of the Green version do not do justice to outdoors biology. Countries like Australia and Israel in their BSCS adapted programs made special efforts to supplement the BSCS materials by designing their own outdoors learning experiences, so that their students would not be deprived of the rich and unique messages which are delivered by direct contacts with nature.

4.5 The World of "Micro"

All physical and chemical processes have mechanisms which operate at the level of the "micro," namely with tiny particles such as electrons, atoms, and molecules. Students cannot observe the interactions among these particles and therefore have to rely on inferences and abstractions. With the invention of microscopes, humans have gained the means to explore the level of the "micro." For most students this opportunity is provided within the framework of the life sciences which offer ample opportunities to study the structures and functions of unicellular organisms as well as of cells and tissues in higher organisms. These studies with the aid of the microscope are not only important for the study of biology but serve also to extend the world view of students into the dimensions of the micro, very much like the extension of the world view of students beyond our own Earth which is acquired through the study of astronomy. These two extensions are essential components of basic literacy needed by citizens in order to be able to function adequately in our world today.

4.6 Causation, Teleology, and Anthropomorphism

Whereas the physical sciences deal only with explanations indicating cause–effect relationships, the biological sciences evoke in addition two peculiar kinds of explanations known as teleology and anthropomorphism. Teleology deals with means–ends relationships. The origins of these relationships may be related to interactions among three of the major themes of biology, namely: evolution, the complementarity of structure and function, and the mutual relationships between organisms in their environment. Biologists

often refer to ends such as survival or adaptation as if these ends explain why certain structures or functions operate in particular manners. When plants kept indoors bend toward the window this tendency certainly represents an adaptive process by which plants are able to be exposed to more light thereby increasing the rate of photosynthesis. The fact that plants benefit from this adaptation is an illustration of a teleological explanation. However, in fact this kind of explanation tells nothing about the mechanism which causes the plant to bend toward light. The cause of bending is actually a hormonal mechanism which, presumably, has developed through thousands of years, because of its evolutionary survival value. Teleological explanations have a heuristic and historical–philosophical value, but in no way should these values be confused with causal explanations, as many students tend to do. Another kind of confusion is often created through relating to various organisms criteria and processes characterizing human intentional and purposeful behavior. In the case of the plant described above, a student may suggest that it tends toward the window because it seeks light. This kind of explanation implies that the plant has a consciousness much like humans and, hence, it is designated as anthropomorphic. Biology educators have the unique task of teaching students to differentiate between causal, teleological, and anthropomorphic explanations (see Bartov 1978 for practical suggestions).

4.7 Interrelations Between Life Sciences and other Subjects

Since biology teaching shifted from its descriptive phase to an inquiry orientation in the early 1960s, it has established close links with the physical sciences, especially chemistry, and with certain fields of mathematics, notably statistics and probability. The need to deal with these allied fields in the context of biology has raised criticisms and discontent among biology teachers on the one hand, and in chemists and statisticians on the other. The first felt that they unjustly had to deal with topics outside their expertise and spend precious time on marginal issues rather than devoting their time to the real biological matters. The last have complained that biology teachers transmit a distorted version of their disciplines and chemistry teachers, for example, often have a hard time trying to modify and correct these distorted views. In spite of these controversies, chemistry, some physics, and statistics have become integral components of many high-school biology courses, especially in topics such as osmosis, enzymology, microbiology, nutrition and digestion, metabolism, energy transformations, genetics, and ecology. More recently, with the growing interest in the social implications of biology, new bridges are being formed, this time toward sociology, psychology, and anthropology. As already mentioned, life sciences have always had close associations with agriculture and the health sciences. All in all it appears that the life sciences acquire a unique position in the school curriculum by becoming a means for integration among various diverse fields of study. This integrating role gains even more prominence as a move is made to outdoors and environmental education where ample opportunities are provided for interacting with other fields such as geology and archeology.

4.8 Controversial Issues

The new biology which begins to gain prominence in schools also involves questions of ethics, values, morals, and aesthetics. While in previous years, teachers felt responsible for disseminating biological knowledge in a way which created an image of science as an objective field of study, detached from the problems of every day life, the new orientation opens the classroom for discussion and study of controversial issues such as evolution versus creationism, birth control, genetic engineering, chemical pest control, and the like. No discipline other than biology can provide the knowledge base needed for intelligent debates on these controversial issues.

5. Curriculum, Instruction, and Assessment

Biology as a separate subject is not taught in most countries before the age of 11, and in many not before the age of 15. A great number of biology programs are available today all over the world. There is no doubt that many of these programs have followed in many ways the model established by the BSCS in the United States. Space does not allow for a detailed description of the wide range of materials produced by the BSCS (for details, see Klinckmann 1970). Here just one of them, namely the "invitations to inquiry," will be discussed.

Invitations to inquiry are probably the most significant innovation in science teaching since the early 1950s. These are teaching units that bring before students small samples of the operations of biological enquiry, which are graded to the competence and knowledge of the students, but at the same time provide open-ended situations which require the students to be actively engaged in reasoning and problem solving, making use and at the same time developing systematically their inquiry skills. A detailed rationale and guidelines for their use, together with 44 planned instructional units, are presented in the *Biology Teacher Handbook* (Schwab 1963). More recently, the BSCS produced 40 single topic films and 20 inquiry slide sequences, each accompanied by a useful teacher guide. These audiovisuals are also constructed as invitations to enquiry. These unique instructional materials represent a real breakthrough in the attempt to lead science teachers to teach science as enquiry rather than as a dogma. These exemplary instructional materials may be one of the key reasons for the relatively higher success of the curriculum reform in biology compared with that of the physical and social sciences in those schools that made use of them.

The BSCS has recognized the crucial influence of the nature of evaluation on the nature of instruction and learning. A very useful chapter on evaluation is included in the *Biology Teacher Handbook* accompanied by informative examples. Periodical tests as well as final examinations related to both content and processes were designed and made available for each of the BSCS courses. In one area, namely the assessment in the practical mode, the BSCS has left much to be desired. Some useful information based on the experiences of the Israel High School Biology project may be found elsewhere in this volume.

6. Curriculum Dissemination

General considerations and review of curriculum implementation can be found elsewhere in this Encyclopedia. Here it may be appropriate to comment briefly on special problems as well as on the extent to which current biology programs have been disseminated. Compared with programs in the physical and the social sciences, the biology programs which originated in the 1960s have gained on the average, a very high popularity all over the world. In some countries, such as Australia and Israel, virtually all high-school students are studying these inquiry-oriented programs. Because of the dependence of the life sciences on local environments and on local organisms, each country, even when it decided to adopt a BSCS or a Nuffield text, had to make substantive and often quite extensive modifications and adaptations. As new editions are produced, more and more locally developed materials are incorporated, especially in ecology and for outdoor studies. It may be safe to conclude that in the early 1980s, students in different countries, sometimes even in different regions within one country, are studying biology programs which are considerably more inquiry oriented and at the same time much more adapted to local conditions, than those which dominated schools in the late 1950s. In as much as unity and diversity are characteristic of the life sciences as a discipline, biology education worldwide reflects unity in terms of conceptual schemes and inquiry orientation, on the one hand, and diversity in terms of instructional approaches as well as environments and organisms as study targets, on the other.

Bibliography

Bartov H 1978 Can students be taught to distinguish between teleological and causal explanations? *J. Res. Sci. Teach.* 15: 567–72

Dowdeswell W H 1980 The place of biology in technology curricula. In: Kelly P J, Schaefer G (eds.) 1980 *Biological Education For Community Development.* Taylor and Francis, London, pp. 21–22

Grobman A B 1969 *The Changing Classroom: The Role of the Biological Sciences Curriculum Study.* Doubleday, New York

Hurd P D 1981 Biology education. In: Harms N C, Yager R E (eds.) 1981 *What Research Says to the Science Teacher.*

National Science Teachers Association, Washington, DC, Vol. 3, pp. 12–32

Keeton W T 1967 *Biological Science*. Norton, New York

Kelly P J 1980 The structure of biological education. In: Kelly P J, Schaefer G (eds.) 1980 *Biological Education For Community Development*. Taylor and Francis, London, pp. 22–31

Klinckmann E 1970 *Biology Teachers' Handbook*, 2nd edn. Wiley, New York

Klopfer L 1971 Evaluation of learning in science. In: Bloom B S, Hastings J T, Madaus G F (eds.) 1971 *Handbook of Formative and Summative Evaluation of Student Learning*. McGraw Hill, New York, pp. 559–642

Nuffield A' Level Biology 1965 *Project Aims and Outline Scheme*. The Nuffield Foundation, London

Schwab J J 1963 *Biology Teachers' Handbook*, 1st edn. Wiley, New York

Silberstein M, Tamir P 1979 Questionnaire data as a source for curriculum planning. *Stud. Educ. Eval.* 5: 209–14

Tamir P, Amir R 1981 Retrospective curriculum evaluation: An approach to the evaluation of long-term effects. *Curric. Inq.* 11: 259–78

Tamir P, Gal-Choppin R, Nussinovitz R 1981 How do intermediate and junior high students conceptualize living and nonliving? *J. Res. Sci. Teach.* 18: 241–48

Botany: Educational Programs

P. Tamir

Botany is a field of the life sciences that deals with the study of plants. Hence, the discussion of the general issues which relate to aims, curriculum, instruction, and evaluation under life sciences in this Encyclopedia, is valid and relevant also to botany. Here some problems and issues which relate to peculiar attributes of botany in schools will be dealt with.

1. Plants as Producers

To a large extent, plants carry the key to life in their unique capability for photosynthesis, that is, their ability to capture the energy of the sun which they use for their own life and which can be transferred to consumers such as humans and animals. Hence, the study of photosynthesis is an important part of any basic biology course. Often, students are not clear as to the meaning of the concepts and processes related to photosynthesis such as the effects of different wave lengths of light or the ratio between photosynthesis and respiration (e.g., many children believe that respiration in plants takes place only at night). The study of photosynthesis and the factors which affect it have special importance for agriculture which may be conceived as a technology designed to take advantage of photosynthesis for the benefit of humans.

2. Motivating Students to Study Plants

Why should students who do not intend to specialize in biology study plants? Certainly a good answer would be to satisfy their curiosity. As it happens, however, not many students are especially interested in the study of plants (e.g., Tamir and Jungwirth 1974). One way to overcome this lack of motivation is to choose plants of special potential interest for every day life such as ornamentals and cut flowers, poisonous plants, plants from which medicines can be produced, wild plants that can be used as food (e.g., mushrooms), and the like. Another way to motivate students is to create opportunities for outdoor field studies: it was found that under outdoor conditions the interest and curiosity in studying plants are greatly enhanced. Still another way is to identify interesting relations or phenomena associated with plants such as symbiosis (shared life of two organisms).

3. Plants as Study Objects

Many teachers and many courses prefer the use of plants as objects for study in school, not only when the aim is to study processes unique to plants, but also as a means for studying general phenomena and fundamental processes in biology. The main reason for this is that plants are much easier to handle and to work with and their behavior is much more predictable than that of animals. In addition, the use of plants raises neither ethical problems nor negative affective reactions. In order to avoid the decline of interest that is likely to occur if plants dominate biology classes, the integration of the study of plants with that of animals is suggested. A good example of such an integrated text is Keeton (1967). Another way to maintain the interest of students is to integrate morphology, anatomy, and physiology. This is desirable because students are often much more interested in studying life processes than in learning names and structures. Training students to identify names of plants with the aid of a dichotomic key has been found to be a useful way not only to increase the familiarity of students with local flora but also as a means of teaching observation and analytical skills. Plants readily lend themselves to long-term projects and outdoor experiments, as well as to "take home" experiments which students can, and in some schools do, perform at home. The relatively more extensive use of plants compared to animals in school may be an explanation for the relatively high achievement of students in botany (Tamir 1974) compared to zoology.

4. Girls, Boys, and Plants

It has repeatedly been found that while, on average, both boys and girls prefer to study animals, girls are more interested than boys in the study of plants (Tamir and Jungwirth 1974). The reason for this difference is not clear. It may be related, in part, to the greater reluctance of girls to handle animals in the classroom, or perhaps to the greater interest of girls in ornamental plants.

Bibliography

Keeton W T 1967 *Biological Science*. Norton, New York
Tamir P 1974 A comparative study of students' achievement in botany and zoology. *J. Biol. Educ.* 8: 333–42
Tamir P, Jungwirth E 1974 Botany and zoology: A curriculum problem. *J. Res. Sci. Teach.* 11: 5–16

Zoology: Educational Programs

P. Tamir

Zoology is the field of the life sciences that deals with the study of animals. Hence, the discussion of the general issues which relate to aims, curriculum, instruction, and evaluation under life sciences in this Encyclopedia is relevant also to zoology. Here some problems and issues which relate to peculiar attributes of zoology in schools will be dealt with.

1. The Use of Live Animals

The use of live animals poses a serious dilemma to biology teachers. Research has shown that most students are interested in studying live animals by direct observations and are highly motivated to experiment with animals, much more than with either plants or microorganisms (Tamir and Jungwirth 1974). Most students also believe that direct experiences involving the study of animals are superior to learning from secondary sources. At the same time, however, most students exhibit deep concern for and affection toward living organisms in general (Tamir and Hamo 1980). It follows that the use of live animals may have both positive and negative outcomes in terms of students' attitudes to life, to living animals, and to the study of biology (Kelly and Wray 1975). Knowledge of the factors which affect students' attitudes toward the use of animals could help teachers in making more adequate decisions. Silberstein and Tamir (1981) found, for example that if the lead given by high-school students is followed, animals should be used whenever their use appears helpful to learning, provided that undue suffering and cruelty are avoided, and that precautions are taken to reduce the damage to animals as much as possible. The degree of usefulness or harmfulness to humans associated with an animal is the most important factor affecting students' attitude to the use of that animal in observations and experiments. Although a mouse for example is a mammal, more students are willing to use mice than honeybees. Perhaps countries that forbid the use of mammals in schools should reconsider their position and employ different criteria.

2. Advantages of Zoology in Schools

While it is clear that the use of plants offers substantial technical and didactic advantages over the use of animals, nevertheless, animals are the typical representative of life for most children who can easily identify similarities of their own lives and behaviors to those of animals. Teachers can build on the deep intrinsic motivation of students in planning their instruction of zoological topics. Keeping an "animals corner" in class is highly recommended especially at the primary level. Topics such as reproduction, development, hormonal regulation, human genetics, immunization, blood circulation, respiration, and nutrition are often considered by students essential to their understanding of their own lives. Since each of these topics can be taught at different levels of sophistication, a spiral curriculum which allows students to come back to the basic life processes at the level which matches their interests and capabilities is quite common (see *Spiral Curriculum*).

3. Vicarious Experiences

The use of vicarious experiences is of special value in the study of animals. Animals have diverse life styles and, hence, it is often difficult to observe them directly. Although it is exciting to spend, for example, a night outdoors to study the activity of animals, not many students and teachers have opportunities to do so. Another reason for using vicarious experiences is to avoid causing unnecessary damage to animals. Excellent 16 mm films, super 8 loops, and slides are available which can bring the rich and colorful animals' world into the classroom.

Bibliography

Kelly P J, Wray J D (eds.) 1975 *The Educational Use of Living Organisms—A Source Book*. English Universities Press, London
Silberstein M, Tamir P 1981 Factors which affect students' attitudes towards the use of living animals in learning biology. *Sci. Educ.* 65: 119–30
Tamir P, Hamo A 1980 Attitudes of Israeli students to the use of animals in the biology classroom. *Int. J. Stud. of Animal Behavior* 1: 299–311
Tamir P, Jungwirth E 1974 Botany and zoology: A curriculum problem. *J. Res. Sci. Teach.* 11: 5–16

Agriculture: Educational Programs

A. Blum

Agricultural education has vocational, technical, and academic training aspects, and in addition, agricultural elements are used prominently in environmental and development education; in applied science teaching; in fostering aesthetic and emotional values; in developing hobbies and leisure-time skills; in developing students' self-concept and schools' self-reliance; and in compensatory education.

1. The Evolution of Different Types of Programs

Educational programs in agriculture, and more specifically garden work with educational objectives, had a precursor in the cloister schools in which pupils tended the gardens. They did so mainly to chastize the body and to supply the kitchen, but also for educational purposes (Blum 1972). Among the early protagonists of the introduction of agriculture into regular school programs were the outstanding Moravian educator J. A. Comenius (1592–1670) who emphasized the importance of pupils' contact with their direct environment, and J. H. Pestalozzi (1746–1827) in Switzerland who stressed the education towards creative work and vocational training. Also J-J. Rousseau's (1712–1778) ideas of the return to nature had a strong influence on the inclusion of agricultural activities in educational programs. In the United States, Benjamin Franklin proposed in 1749 to teach agricultural practices and to take youth to study the best plantations. The first school garden was probably that of August Herman Francke in Halle, Germany, which was established in 1685. Later, school gardens and farms developed in two directions, although not always strictly separated. By the end of the nineteenth century, nonvocational school gardens and other educational programs involving agriculture—often under the name of rural or nature studies, or rural science—became established in various parts of Europe (Carson and Colton 1962), and also on the initiative of Cornell University's L. H. Bailey in the United States (Snowdon 1973).

Steinecke (1951) distinguished between three categories of school gardens according to their main educational purpose: (a) supply garden (including supply of plants for use in the classroom), (b) work garden, and (c) teaching garden. Most school gardens serve more than one of these aims. During the First and Second World Wars, the growing of vegetables became a prominent feature of agriculture in European schools. The preoccupation with the yield, rather than the study of plants, led in many cases to a low status of rural studies in schools. Agricultural programs were also introduced by the colonial powers into their colonies. Similar to the situation in more developed countries, these programs were usually not very popular.

Nonvocational agricultural programs received a new impetus when environmental education received much attention in the 1970s. In the United Kingdom, Israel, and Australia, for instance, environmental education projects grew out of former gardening and agricultural programs and developed into national curriculum projects. In Israel, city school farms are run jointly by the Ministry of Education and local authorities. In the United Kingdom the City Farms Movement is based on mutual help projects, involving all age groups, including adults, who often use derelict land to improve the neighborhood community. Often they have not succeeded because they copied foreign practices, which were unsuitable to the local conditions (Bergman 1978).

In the United States, 4-H (head, heart, hands, and health) Clubs are organized by agents of the Agricultural Extension Service for children and young people. Lately, this service has expanded from rural areas to inner cities, and the idea was taken up in many developing countries. Also formal school districts in urban centers (e.g., Los Angeles and Cleveland) reacted to the growing estrangement of children from plants and animals by setting up school farms and even operating trailers which periodically bring farm animals to the school compound for observation.

2. Trends in Agricultural Programs

Besides the purpose of vocational training, agricultural programs, in formal and nonformal settings, serve various educational objectives.

2.1 Appreciation of Nature and Environmental Education

Agricultural practices are closely connected with observing nature and learning from it. Careless interference in natural processes can offset the balance of nature. Therefore some agricultural education programs treat agricultural–ecological issues, such as pest control or the use of artificial fertilizers and hormones, for the purpose of educating students to take an informed view when judging major controversies. Examples of such curricula are Agriculture as Environmental Science in Israel, Project Environment in the United Kingdom, and Foundational Approach to Science Teaching in Hawaii. (For these and other science curricula, see Lockard 1975.)

2.2 Agriculture as Applied Science

In the above-mentioned science curricula and in others, simple experiments in the school garden are used as inexpensive, but most meaningful, vehicles to teach science and its application to solve real problems. It is often argued that students should be able to apply scientific principles to their everyday life. In agrarian countries, or in rural areas of more industrialized countries, this can be done well in agricultural science programs. Especially in developing countries, school farms can serve as demonstration models for selected innovations in which scientific principles are applied (e.g., plant propagation, irrigation, and fertilizing).

2.3 Developing a Hobby and Leisure-time Skills

This trend developed mainly in industrialized countries and received renewed interest in the United Kingdom in connection with the "Countryside 1970" movement. According to a Schools Council (1969) statement, rural studies may lead to the development of a lifelong hobby—growing plants or rearing animals to effect an emotional balance for life in an industrialized society. This objective is closely connected with that of leisure crafts in which skills of hand and eye are trained and used (see *Education for Leisure Time*).

2.4 Aesthetic and Other Values

Affective objectives are more often implied than expressed explicitly, but some curricula, for instance in Hawaii (Yoshinaga 1960), emphasize objectives like "fostering international friendship, aesthetic appreciation," and use floriculture as a means to achieve this aim. In Israel, the legislature felt that education towards productivity, dignity of work, and return to the land could be advanced through agricultural programs in elementary schools.

2.5 Agriculture in Compensatory Education

Agricultural programs are sometimes chosen for their compensatory value to mentally and emotionally disadvantaged children and adults. While these programs have benefitted many individuals, they have also contributed to the dubious notion that agricultural education should be offered mainly to underachievers and the nonmotivated (Schools Council 1969).

2.6 Career Education

Today, children no longer follow their fathers' trade. They have to choose among many career opportunities, most of which they are not familiar with. Therefore some school systems (for example, in Sweden and California) include in their junior-high-school programs induction into a variety of occupations, including experience in agriculture.

2.7 Education Towards Self-reliance

Agricultural education programs in agrarian, developing countries serve sometimes to contribute to the financing of the school. This is done for ideological and educational reasons, or simply to pay for the cost of running schools (Müller 1980). Agriculture can provide experiences for developing a significant portion of an individual's self-concept. Little has been done to explore this aspect of agricultural programs.

2.8 Agriculture and Development Education

Many educators are concerned about the unequal distribution of food between poor, overpopulated, and rich, industrialized countries, and the growing danger of a world hunger calamity with its international repercussions. This led to the development of educational programs in which the potential of agriculture is studied in the context of development education.

Bibliography

Bergman H 1978 Agricultural instruction in primary schools: A contribution to rural development. *Dev. Cooperation* 2: 9–11

Blum A 1972 Trends in nonvocational agriculture: An international review. *Agric. Educ. Mag.* 45: 86–87, 91

Carson S McB, Colton R W 1962 *The Teaching of Rural Studies.* Arnold, London

Lockard D (ed.) 1975 *Science and Mathematics Curricular Developments Internationally 1956–1974.* University of Maryland Center for Science Teaching, College Park, Maryland

Müller M 1980 Teaching Self-reliance. *Dev. Cooperation* 4: 26–27

Schools Council 1969 *Rural Studies in Secondary Schools.* Evans, London

Snowdon O 1973 Elementary programs for career education in agriculture. *Agric. Educ. Mag.* 45: 149–50

Steinecke F 1951 *Der Schulgarten: Eine Anleitung zu Seiner Einrichtung und Unterrichlichen Verwendung.* Quelle und Meyer, Heidelberg

United States Department of Agriculture, Science and Education Administration 1978 *4-H Extension's Investment in the Future.* United States Government Printing Office, Document No. 0-265-607, Washington, DC

Yoshinaga E K 1960 *A Guide to Elementary School Gardening in Hawaii.* Agricultural Education Bulletin, No. 13. Department of Public Instruction, Honolulu, Hawaii

Environmental Education Programs

A. M. Lucas

Environmental education is characterized by its goal of providing education *for* the enhancement or preservation of the human environment. It is not sufficient to teach *about* the environment, or even to teach out of school *in* the environment. When the term became common in the early 1970s there was no consensus on its meaning, and many programmes described as "environmental education" did not attempt to produce appropriate behaviour and attitudes, a focus which is implicit in education *for* the environment. However, since the "Belgrade Charter" was adopted at an International Workshop in Environmental Education in 1975, there has been an increasing international consensus that a focus on affective aims is necessary for environmental education. The text of the charter is available in *Connect*, a free UNESCO newsletter (1976 Vol. 1 No. 1).

Many approaches to environmental education within schools can meet the criteria in the Belgrade Charter. Some schools provide a special subject which may have a strong science bias, for example the environmental science syllabus of the Joint Matriculation Board in England and Wales, but others in the same country may require a broad interdisciplinary approach. The course in environmental studies of the University of London Schools Examination Department includes work drawn from geology and economics as well as biology, geography, and other disciplines. Other courses are described in Schoenfeld and Disinger (1977).

Some schools approach environmental education by individual teachers providing an environmental emphasis to their own subject—by the choice of example, homework exercise, and field trip. However, with independent activities in different subjects, students may react adversely to having "pollution pushed at us all the time". To avoid alienation by continual preaching in all subjects, some schools have produced carefully coordinated interdisciplinary curricular designed to build and reinforce appropriate value positions for their pupils (Carson 1978, Chap. 12).

The content of environmental education programmes must vary from continent to continent and from country to country. Human well-being is promoted by a large number of factors, ranging from the social aspects of cultural heritage that are embodied in the remains of the built environment of the ancient civilizations, to the supply of energy, and material for the next meal. Curriculum materials produced in one country necessarily respond to locally important questions and are thus even less transferable than curricular in the biological sciences. But despite the lack of common content there is an international sharing of experience, particularly through the information exchange programmes of UNESCO and the United Nations Environment Program (UNEP). The shared programme descriptions stimulate ideas about approaches that will help in the notoriously difficult area of producing long-term behaviour changes through school programmes.

Unfortunately, much curriculum development consistent with education for the environment has been based on a naive belief that providing knowledge about an environmental issue will produce a "correct" behavioural response. Other teaching schemes have not assumed a direct link between knowledge and attitudes and have concentrated on attitude formation, while sharing the assumption that appropriate action will follow attitude inculcation. Few of the authors of the environmental attitudes reports Lucas (1980) reviewed seemed aware that studies in social psychology have shown repeatedly that there is no strong link between measured attitudes to diffuse concepts, such as "quality of life", "ecological conservation", and subsequent behaviour. Indeed, studies of members of environmental organizations show that attitudes of concern sufficient to prompt joining the organization do not necessarily produce the personal behaviour the organization exists to promote. Studies of attitude formation and the curriculum of environmental education programmes are reviewed in Lucas (1980).

Although successful inculcation of general environmental attitudes is unlikely to produce the behaviours that will enhance or preserve the environment when issues arise, there is some prospect of success if personal attitudes are produced to narrow environmental issues. But unfortunately school-level environmental educators have insufficient time to produce specific attitudes to all the issues that will arise during their pupils' lives. More success might be obtained if the curriculum produced personal moral attitudes such as "I ought to consider the indirect consequences of my actions", taught effective information retrieval skills, and gave practice in applying this attitude in environmental contexts.

The difficulty of choosing specific targets for environmental education at school is reduced if there is a well-developed informal environmental education system accessible to adults, especially if it impinges upon most of the population. Mass media can be utilized in two ways. Firstly, by presenting planned instructional materials with specific learning goals, and secondly, by the production of entertainment material which also helps people think about relationships between humans and the environment in which they live. The Japan Broadcasting Corporation (NHK), for example, has been active in both modes, producing programs for schools which are repeated to encourage parents to watch with their children in an attempt to promote discussion within the family; and transmitting a regular entertainment program "Nature Album" which emphasizes the beauty, grandeur, and wonder of the Japanese environment (Ohno 1981).

Education for the environment cannot succeed if it is directed to school children alone, because they are not in a position to make many of the decisions needed to preserve the present environmental resources, but it might succeed if it deliberately attends to public education on a broader scale.

Bibliography

Carson S McB (ed.) 1978 *Environmental Education: Principles and Practice*. Arnold, London

Linke R D 1980 *Environmental Education in Australia*. Allen and Unwin, Sydney

Lucas A M 1980 Science and environmental education: Pious hopes, self praise and disciplinary chauvinism. *Stud. Sci. Educ.* 7: 1–26

Ohno R 1981 Use of the mass media in environmental education: Japan's experiences. *Environmental Education in Asia and the Pacific*. Bulletin of the UNESCO Regional Office for Education in Asia and the Pacific. 22: 294–99

Schoenfeld C, Disinger J (eds.) 1977 *Environmental Education in Action 1: Case Studies of Selected Public School and Public Action Programs*. ERIC Information Analysis Center for Science, Mathematics and Environmental Education, Ohio State University, Columbus, Ohio

Nutrition: Educational Programs

G. M. Briggs

The term "nutrition education" in its broad sense means the imparting of information about the nutritional aspects of food. More specifically the term refers to the teaching by properly trained and informed persons of researched information about food and nutrition to the extent that there is sufficient understanding, motivation, and an increase in reasoning skills to allow an individual to make intelligent discussions on how one purchases, prepares, and consumes food, not only to prevent malnutrition but for the enjoyment of a long, healthy life. Nutrition is a keystone in health education (see *Health Education*). Thus, nutrition education may be imparted in a variety of settings in addition to schools: in the home, in adult classes, community situations, hospitals, mothercraft centers, extension programs, preschools, informal and informed word-of-mouth communication, example of one's peers, and to a great extent by the mass communication media including radio, television, signboards, newspapers, magazines, the labels on food, and posters in the retail store.

The phrase nutrition training is more limited in scope, generally referring to the training in colleges, universities, and other more formal settings of nutritionists, dietitians, nutrition educators, teachers, and the allied health professions. The phrase food education is closely related to nutrition education but refers primarily to teaching about the use of food in a variety of contexts, not always in terms of the physiological and biological aspects of nutrition. Advertising in the mass media by the food industry is a form of food education but not necessarily nutrition education.

1. Historical Background

Many examples are recorded in the Old Testament and elsewhere of the admonitions of wise persons in ancient civilizations to eat better food for better health. Such records have been found in China, Egypt, Israel, Turkey, Greece, and in other areas of the Middle East. Modern nutrition education and training in schools started in the late 1800s and early 1900s after the development of the chemical and physiological sciences. This allowed an understanding, first, of the early recognized nutrients, fats, proteins, carbohydrates, and a few minerals in protective foods (vitamins were unknown)— along with the processes of their digestion and metabolism for energy formation and for growth and repair.

Most, if not all, of the early teaching of nutrition in elementary and secondary schools in many countries of the world, took place in classes for women in household science and home economics courses. The growth of school canteens and school-lunch programs contributed to the growth of nutrition education in schools and still performs an important function.

Much of the early research in the 1800s and early 1900s leading to advances in human nutrition was performed with experimental and domestic animals. This had great economic importance and was the forerunner of today's development of a large body of nutritional sciences information throughout the world.

2. Need for Nutrition Education in Schools Today

The dramatic growth of modern nutrition education programs since the Second World War has been made possible, first, by modern discoveries of and about vitamins, minerals, amino acids, and fiber and by recent advances in biochemistry, physiology, food science, social sciences, and medicine. These scientific advancements have a ready market in a world now in a vicious cycle of severe hunger and malnutrition related to current widespread social and economic disorders. Unrestricted population growth in countries of limited natural resources has left literally hundreds of millions of individuals with inadequate food supplies and unable to cope.

Since the 1940s, there have been tremendous industrial and cultural changes causing severe malnutrition problems in uneducated persons (and less often in the educated). The modern revolution in the food industry exerts massive influences on what people eat. Traditional food patterns have changed. New types of foods have become widely available in most countries, often highly advertised and attractively packaged, relatively expensive, and of lesser nutritional quality.

In developing countries, the greater incidence and severity of infectious diseases (hookworm and other parasites, tuberculosis, malaria, viral infections, etc.) is closely related to the reduced immunological and other defenses which accompany malnutrition.

Other factors are at work in one form or another in almost all countries that lead to the necessity of programs of nutrition education, especially in schools: lack of knowledge and motivation to buy, store, and prepare tasty, nutritious foods; lack of availability of suitable inexpensive foods; differences in personal preferences along with religious, cultural, or ethical restraints; lack of recognition of increased nutritional needs of groups such as growing children, pregnant women, women during childbearing ages, persons on weight control diets, and the aged; popular reducing diets (usually inadequate); the lack of official and well-researched dietary goals, national nutrition policies, and food guidelines in many individual countries; the lack of adequate nutrition training of physicians and other health professionals; and widespread economic losses from food wastage especially in developing countries from inadequate storage conditions, microbial damage, rodents and other pests, overprocessing of foods, excessive milling of grains, and from inadequate transportation facilities and distribution methods.

These are some of the food and nutrition topics, most of which are vital to the health and well-being of any society, which are taught in schools today. Research in countries around the world including India, the Philippines, Israel, Brazil, Mexico, the United States, the United Kingdom, Canada, the Federal Republic of Germany, Poland, France, Australia, and many others has clearly demonstrated the effectiveness of nutrition education programs in elementary and secondary schools. Only by such teaching in our schools can the vicious cycle of malnutrition from generation to generation be broken (since this information generally is no longer passed on to future generations in the home as it was in the past).

3. Integrating Nutrition in the Curriculum

Nutrition educators are not asking necessarily for more time and new curricula in the schools. As Guthrie (1982) has stated, "Our need is not for more curricula but rather for more intensive and more effective use of those available. . . . Backup resources in the form of books, visuals, games, and workbooks are not only available but tested to document their effectiveness."

Nutrition subjects can be taught as a separate discipline or integrated in biology and science courses, in health and social science courses, and in physical education and home economics courses. At the lower levels, nutrition topics can be integrated in language, mathematics, and social studies curricula. This is already being done in many parts of the world. The list of journals and resources given at the end of this article are examples of where such curriculum material can be obtained.

It is a vital key to the success of any nutrition education program in schools today that the teachers themselves, including all elementary teachers and school food service personnel, have a reliable nutrition course as part of their educational training. This is now possible because major colleges and universities throughout the world have been developing new independent departments of nutritional sciences. Without such training of teachers by nutrition scholars, nutrition education programs have little chance of success.

Bibliography

Cahiers de Nutrition et de Diététique (France)
Ernährungs-umschau (Federal Republic of Germany)
Guthrie H 1982 Nutrition education: Challenges and partnerships. *Food and Nutrition News* 54
Journal of Nutrition Education (USA)
Nutrition and Food Science (UK)
Philippine Journal of Nutrition
Schürch B, Wilquin L 1982 *Nutrition Education in Communities of the Third World: An Annotated Bibliography*. Nestlé Foundation, Lausanne
Voeding (Netherlands)

Physics Programs

V. N. Lunetta

Physics education refers to efforts to teach elements of physics and applied physics to students at all levels of learning. The rationale for teaching physics can be reduced to two global goals: (a) providing experiences that will enable some students to reach the frontiers of physics and the other natural sciences to make scientific and technological contributions in their own right, and (b) providing a foundation of general understanding and reasoning for students who will not specialize in the sciences that will be sufficient for enlightened citizenship in a technological age. These two goals for physics education address both professional and broader cultural needs and are implicit assumptions underlying the development of physics curricula. Yet, curricula based upon these goals have taken a variety of forms, which will be reviewed in this article. The article highlights issues and practices that are particularly relevant to introductory physics education with examples selected primarily from curricula at the secondary school level.

Over the past century and especially in recent decades there has been an unprecedented and exponential explosion of information and productivity in the world of physics and related sciences and technologies. Teaching "the natural philosophy," not too long ago a peripheral part of academe, has become far more central and even "basic" in contemporary schooling. In this scientific age, physics no longer has to fight for academic respectability though it has not fared well in the competition for students, and the nature and orientation of the physics curriculum are still subject to some debate.

Physics curricula over the years have evolved in response to a growth of information, to changing perceptions of the nature of the physics discipline, and to a variety of other factors in the surrounding community and society. These factors have included changing notions about how people learn, changing populations and realities in schools, and changing societal needs and values.

1. Curriculum Overview

The most visible revolution in physics curricula began in the late 1950s at the secondary school level with corollary waves of change at primary and tertiary levels as well. These changes received extensive financial support from government and private sources in both the United Kingdom and the United States, stimulating similar curriculum revision and development in many countries throughout the world. The first of the major curriculum projects of this period and the one having the most profound influence on other projects was prepared by the Physical Science Study Committee (PSSC). The PSSC curriculum development efforts brought together several hundred high school and college teachers with millions of dollars of support to develop the *PSSC Physics* (Haber-Schaim et al. 1976) course designed to:

(a) present physics as a unified yet living and ever-changing subject;

(b) demonstrate the interplay between experiment and theory in the development of physics;

(c) have the students learn the basic principles and laws of physics by interrogating nature itself;

(d) extend the student's ability to read critically, to reason, and to distinguish between the essential and the peripheral;

(e) provide a sound foundation for those students who plan to study science or engineering at the college (tertiary) level.

The Physical Science Study Committee designed an intensive course around a few fundamental areas of physics eliminating applications of physics almost entirely. It also developed a variety of other curriculum materials including an advanced topics course, two physical science courses for junior high school students, and a collegiate edition of the physics text.

In Britain, the Nuffield Foundation initiated a number of science curriculum development projects to renew science teaching in British grammar schools. In 1962 Nuffield (1967) initiated a curriculum leading to the "O-Level" examination for 16- or 17-year-old students. (Secondary school physics experiences in Great Britain are spread throughout five years, and students take different science subjects concurrently in each of those five years, in contrast with separate one-year courses common in the United States.) The Nuffield Physics

Project was intended for the upper 25 percent of students based on academic ability, "and the program was to make science intellectually exciting for [students], and to bring them through their own investigations and arguments, to an understanding of what science is, and as far as possible, of what it is like to be a practising scientist." Thus, the emphasis as in the PSSC course, was on pure science, not on applications of science, and on important scientific processes and conceptual schemes. One of several related efforts was its Advanced Physics Project, a two-year course for students in the sixth form (ages 16–18). The advanced course emphasized use of numerical methods and selective development of mathematical skills.

A third secondary-level physics project having substantial international impact was *Project Physics* (Rutherford et al. 1981), formerly *Harvard Project Physics*, initiated in the United States in 1964. *Project Physics* was intended to increase the appeal of physics to a broader range of high school students by emphasizing the humanistic roots and consequences of physics. The project hoped for an integration of history, culture, technology, and people in the development of physical ideas. It hoped to present physics as an intellectual pursuit rather than as applied technology, to reduce dependence on complex mathematical skills, and to reduce perceptions of difficulty commonly associated with the study of physics. Supplemental "Readers" took students out beyond the normal confines of a physics course and enabled them to pursue special personalized interests. *Project Physics* also advocated some relatively innovative systems for personalizing instruction, managing the classroom, and evaluating students' progress.

At the tertiary level, physics curriculum development during and after the 1960s was less systematic than at the secondary level, with textbooks for physics concentrators becoming generally more massive, mathematical, analytical, and abstract. Though they began to include more "modern" physics, the textbooks tended to provide little contact with philosophical inquiry and with more descriptive, phenomenological study. International attention was garnered, however, by a few creative individual authors, like Eric M. Rogers and Richard P. Feynman, and certain projects, *The Berkeley Physics Course* (1973) being one of the most noteworthy. (The Berkeley project included the production of a series of electronic analogue laboratory activities.)

Many other courses having physics connections were initiated during the science curriculum development wave of the 1960s. One of these, *Man Made World* (Engineering Concepts Curriculum Project 1971) was designed with an applied physics orientation intended to contribute to the technological literacy of high school students of average to above average ability. The course presented some of the ideas covered in conventional physics courses but went beyond them to examine systems and to present concepts and processes such as stability, change, feedback, optimization, simulation,

931

modeling, and programming. Its attention to societal relevance was a precursor to a major movement in that direction among many introductory physics courses, especially those for tertiary-level nonmajors, that flourished a decade or more later. At the primary school level, some excellent activity-centered science programs were developed that included the exploration of many physical phenomena. These materials including the *Elementary Science Study* (1973) in the United States and *The Science 5–13 Project* (1974) in the United Kingdom, to cite only two examples, incorporated some of what is known about human learning and development and provided outstanding source materials for physics curricula at all levels.

Due to changing societal priorities and to increased competition for limited funds, science curriculum development efforts declined sharply in the 1970s and a number of the projects spawned in the 1960s died an early death. The projects sampled in this review, however, have generally been revised and have had worldwide impact with translations in many languages. Though use of the actual project materials in the country of origin has generally declined, commercially prepared textbooks and laboratory handbooks in use two decades later provide evidence of the strong impact of these curriculum projects. Nevertheless, declining enrollments in physics and physical science courses and reduced support for science education in the United States and many places in the British Commonwealth in the 1970s and the 1980s provided reason to wonder about the ability of those societies to cope with the multitude of complex problems at the interface of science and society that were ahead.

2. Resources and Organization for Teaching

2.1 Applied Science/Relevance

The visibility of applications in physics curricula has waxed and waned over the years partially in response to societal values. In the preface to the 1929 edition of *New Practical Physics*, Black and Davis (1929) wrote: ". . . the study of elementary physics should begin with . . . the fundamental principles that underlie the construction and operation of many familiar machines and devices that surround us . . ." In the mid-1950s, however, physics courses were criticized for including a proliferation of technology, and the early waves of new curricula in the 1960s eliminated applications of physics almost entirely. Subsequently, the lack of relevant applications has been cited as one of the causes of the decline in student interest and enrollment.

During the 1970s, a number of groups began to advocate emphasis upon career awareness in introductory science curricula. Concurrently, environmental problems at the interface of science and society were becoming more visible, causing further demands for relevance in science teaching from groups both within and outside the physics teaching profession. Subsequently, groups all over the world have advocated the use of societal problems as foci for study in science. Many of the papers in the *International Group for the Advancement of Physics Teaching* (GIREP) Conference of 1979 document this concern (Ganiel 1980), and a number of texts and supplemental materials emphasizing the societal context (e.g. Lewis 1981) have been prepared. At the collegiate level during the 1970s there was a proliferation of physics offerings for nonmajors with titles like: "The Physics of Sound and Music," "Environmental Physics," and "Physics for Artists," due in part to a growing perception of the need to communicate with the nonscientific community and in part to declining enrollments in physics. In the 1980s, attention to issues at the interface of science, technology, and society (STS) became more organized; professional associations with interests in such issues developed both within and across scientific societies. An increasing array of STS journals and publications became available, and the STS concerns and publications served as stimuli and as resources for the curriculum. Yet at the close of the 1980s, a new wave of concern for the development of depth in concepts of the science disciplines as a most important product of schooling was also powerful and growing.

2.2 The Nature of Science and the Laboratory

There is evidence that students often acquire a simplistic view of science through school science curricula, a view that is isolated from their reality and from the reality of scientific process. Yet, over the years many have written that the physics curriculum should reflect the nature of physics, and developing an understanding of the nature and process of science has been among the more important goals of physics teaching. A primary concern of the major physics curriculum projects was to communicate that physics is more than a collection of facts and static concepts and laws; it is a growing, dynamic network of evolving models and conceptual schemes. In an attempt to communicate this view, the major secondary-level projects of the 1960s planned to highlight some of the history of science and to emphasize the central role of the laboratory. Students were to explore phenomena in the laboratory and to make generalizations about relationships; they were then to further develop these generalizations and models and test them in the laboratory. The process included a mix of both inductive and deductive thinking with much more emphasis on inductive thinking than had been present in the earlier physics courses that preceded them.

Through open inquiry, it was anticipated that students would develop a variety of scientific skills in planning and designing, in observing and interpreting data, and in explaining relationships and developing models. The task of helping students reach the dual objectives of conceptual and methodological understanding is not a simple one, and it has been difficult for publishers to package and for teachers to manage activities that include open inquiry. Emphasis on the role of the laboratory has also oscillated over the years, but in spite of very limited support from research on learning, relatively few physics educators have questioned the importance of laboratory activities.

2.3 Student Grouping/Pacing

The most common pattern of grouping students in physics classes has been by ability and career orientation. The Commission on College Physics in the United States in 1960 recommended two different curricula at the collegiate level, one for students planning graduate study in physics and another for students who were specializing in other fields or planning to teach physics at the secondary level. This pattern enabled physics-oriented students to use calculus early in the study of basic physics while others could be involved in physics with less developed mathematical skills, thus meeting the needs of an increasingly diverse student population. Especially in secondary schools in the United States, however, this homogeneous grouping pattern came under attack in the mid-1960s as an elitist and undemocratic system that discriminated against students with less academic educational and cultural backgrounds. As a result, there was movement toward more heterogeneous groupings of secondary school students, and new systems of management were developed to respond to the increased diversity of students within the same class. In that period, some teachers explored "Keller plan" or "personalized" forms of physics instruction (Sherman and Ruskin 1978). In such courses, students move through core and optional modules at different speeds presumably compatible with their own needs and interests. While some but not all students and teachers preferred such approaches and while learning was not inhibited for many students in those courses, they provided no panacea and were sometimes criticized for promoting "regression toward the mean" rather than excellence in achievement. In the 1980s *Cooperative Learning* (Johnson et al. 1986) emerged as another systematic response to the needs of pluralistic student bodies.

2.4 Materials and Media

Over the past 100 years, there has been an exponential growth in knowledge about the physical world. Concurrently, there has been great growth in the apparatus, material resources, and media available for physics teaching as well. With relatively simple though not necessarily inexpensive apparatus, students today can easily observe some of the fundamental phenomena of physics such as motion in almost frictionless conditions and interference effects in light. They can experimentally determine not only the wave length but also the velocity of light, and they can observe the diffraction of electrons. Many high quality films showing physical phenomena have been prepared, though use of such films in secondary education has been limited by the high costs. On the other hand, some introductory physics classrooms will have relatively easy access to computer and video-disk simulations which can provide new

flexibility and alternative experiences. Simulations can serve as secondary data sources in which phenomena that are too complex, dangerous, expensive, fast, slow, large, small, or too time or material consuming are modelled (Lunetta and Hofstein 1990).

One of the realities of education, especially in secondary schools, is the meagre amount of money available per student to support the purchase of media and laboratory equipment. Thus, many schools are not well-stocked with equipment to support student activity, though many do have a moderate collection of equipment for class demonstration. Thus, there has been a call for using simpler apparatus and for studying the physics of everyday phenomena in the environment. Several groups like the PSSC and UNESCO have designed appropriate apparatus for student activity at low cost, but for a variety of complex reasons, teachers have not rushed to construct, use, and maintain such equipment over an extended period.

The advent of inexpensive electronic calculators revolutionized methods of computing for physics students in the 1990s, and the subsequent advent of microcomputers provides an array of new possibilities for strategies of physics teaching. Computers have the potential to help students develop higher levels of skill and conceptual understanding through computer interfacing with measuring instruments in the lab and through experiences with rapid interactive graphics, dynamic visuals, and interactive simulation. Computers became major research tools in physics and in the other sciences in the years following World War II. Yet, the development of excellent instructional software lagged behind the development of hardware, and the power of computers in instruction is only beginning to be felt.

2.5 The Teacher

From time to time, in response to great variations in the quality of teaching and of teacher preparation, physics curriculum writers have set about the task of creating "teacher-proof" curricula that would be so complete and effective that even the poorest teachers could do little harm. That, however, has proven to be a most elusive goal. Today's teachers generally have access to an array of curriculum resources, but the teacher remains a critical ingredient in the quality of the educational experience for the majority of students.

While there is much that is yet to be understood about how students best learn physics, some large discrepancies are visible between commonly stated goals for physics teaching and what students do in classrooms. These discrepancies may well be among the factors contributing to the disenchantment with science generally and with physics in particular and to the relatively low levels of physical understanding revealed in large data samples gathered by groups like the National Assessment of Educational Progress in the United States. To cite only one example of this kind of inconsistency, testing and evaluation in the classroom often assess only a narrow subset of skills that physics teachers hope to help students develop. Reviews of tests and evaluation systems in introductory courses indicate that they often emphasize the rote cranking of numbers through inadequately understood algorithms and other relatively low-level cognitive activities. In fact, effective evaluation should assess development of conceptual understanding. Similar comments can be made about other dimensions of physics teaching.

There is reason for concern about the quality of preparation of physics teachers, especially at the secondary levels in many Western countries, for people who are well-qualified to teach in the physical sciences are drawn off to more financially lucrative occupations, and their places are often filled by less qualified teachers. On the other hand, national and international professional associations, publications, and communications networks exist today enabling mutual interaction and growth for the community of physics teachers that provide alternative avenues for growth and development (Barojas 1987).

3. Research on Learning and Curriculum Evaluation

One of several byproducts of the growing international collaboration has been the international assessment and comparison of student achievement in science. While early efforts suffered from constraints, they revealed some significant discrepancies from one nation to another that should stimulate international research, understanding, and curriculum development.

Optimally, physics curricula and teaching are firmly rooted in learning theory as well as in the science of physics. While there is much that is still to be known about how people learn, some generalizations can be made that are based upon the research literature. Gagné, Bruner, Ausubel, and Schwab have examined the effects of various aspects of the structure of disciplines on learning. Others, for example Osborne and Freyburg (1985), have examined the development of students' scientific concepts. Throughout the world in the 1980s there was a dramatic increase in the number of studies of students' concepts in physics and other sciences (Novak 1987). These studies reveal some very common patterns of thinking that are frequently inconsistent with views of organized science and indicate the great importance of understanding and responding to the student's prior knowledge and conceptual schemes in teaching new concepts.

Recent research in cognition reveals the importance of conceptual knowledge in influencing the cognitive processes and problem solving of experts in a discipline. Studies of the discipline-specific development of reasoning are highly relevant to the teaching of physics (Watts 1988). There is evidence that in the presentation of certain topics, some introductory texts assume problem solving skills and scientific concepts that have not been developed by large portions of the student population for whom they are intended. Studies of the development of cognitive skills and concepts are currently an area of important research potential for physics teaching.

When the data are reviewed on people's scientific understanding and on enrollments in school science, there is ready evidence of some serious problems. Yet the situation is a complex one, as are most of the problems at the interface of science and society. Curriculum development projects have seldom incorporated thorough research programs, though *Project Physics* did include a careful and extensive program of research and curriculum evaluation. "The results of the final year evaluation suggest that Project Physics was partially successful in achieving the objectives outlined by the course developers." While students taking *Project Physics* did not perform significantly better or worse on cognitive measures than did students in more conventional courses, they did develop more favorable attitudes toward physics. In fact, "seventeen significant course differences" were found in the analysis "all reflecting positively on the [Project Physics] course . . . Perhaps the most important implication is that the attitudinal goals of the course were achieved without a resulting loss in physics achievement" (Welch 1973 p. 374).

While education in physics has not been responsive to all the dimensions affecting the quality of teaching and learning in physics, some excellent curriculum resources now exist as a result of the era of massive curriculum development that began in the late 1950s. In addition, new information and data exist as a result of those experiences that can provide for new steps in curriculum development in the future. The search for an optimal curriculum is a continuing one, for that curriculum will be responsive to changes in the needs of students and society as well as to changes in understanding of physics, learning, schools, teachers, and the evolving cultural context.

Bibliography

Barojas J (ed.) 1987 *Cooperative Networks in Physics Education*. Proceedings of the Inter-American Conference on Physics Education. American Institute of Physics, New York

The Berkeley Physics Course, 2nd edn. 1973 McGraw Hill, New York

Black N H, Davis H N 1929 *New Practical Physics: Fundamental Principles and Applications to Daily Life*. Macmillan, New York

Education Development Center 1973 *Elementary Science Study* (ESS) (Many titles). McGraw-Hill, New York

Engineering Concepts Curriculum Project 1971 *The Man Made World*. McGraw-Hill, New York

Ganiel U (ed.) 1980 *Physics Teaching*. Balaban International Science Services, Jerusalem

Haber-Schaim U et al. 1976 *PSSC Physics*, 4th edn. Heath, Lexington, Massachusetts

Hofstein A, Lunetta V 1982 The role of the laboratory in science teaching: Neglected aspects of research. *Rev. Educ. Res.* 52: 201–17

Johnson R T, Johnson D W, Stanne M B 1986 Comparison of computer-assisted cooperative, competitive, and individualistic learning. *Am. Educ. Res. J.* 23(3): 382–92

Lewis J L 1972 *Teaching School Physics.* Penguin, London-UNESCO

Lewis J L 1981 *Science in Society.* Heinemann, London

Lunetta V, Novick S 1982 *Inquiring and Problem-solving in the Physical Sciences: A Sourcebook.* Kendall/Hunt, Dubuque, Iowa

Lunetta V, Hofstein A 1990 Simulation and laboratory practical activity. In: Woolnough B (ed.) *Practical Science.* Oxford University Press, in press

Novak J D (ed.) 1987 *Misconceptions and Educational Strategies in Science and Mathematics.* Proceedings of the Second International Seminar. Cornell University, Ithaca, New York

Nuffield Foundation, Science Teaching Project 1967 *Physics.* Longman, Harlow and Penguin, London

Osborne R J, Freyburg P 1985 *Learning in Science: The Implications of Children's Science.* Heinemann, London

Rutherford F J et al. 1981 *Project Physics Course*, 2nd edn. Holt, Rinehart and Winston, New York

The Science 5–13 Project 1974 (Many titles). Macdonald Educational, London

Sherman J G, Ruskin R S 1978 *The Personalized System of Instruction.* Educational Technology Publications, Englewood Cliffs, New Jersey

Watts M 1988 From concept maps to curriculum signposts. *Phys Educ.* 23(2): 74–79

Welch W W 1973 Review of the research and evaluation program of Harvard Project Physics. *J. Res. Sci. Teach.* 10: 365–78

Chemistry Programmes

R. Ben-Zvi

Educational programmes in chemistry, as well as in other scientific fields, at the high-school level are, at any given time, affected by three main factors: science, society, and the student.

The first factor—science—refers to the totality of influences from external academic sources which affect the educational programme. Thus, science includes the influence of the subject itself as it develops, the pressure exercised by university entrance examinations, and those university academics who participate in the development of educational programmes. The second factor—society—refers to the societal influences such as the ecological movement, and the quest for scientific literacy. The third factor—student—relates to things such as cognitive level of student understanding, ability to understand concepts, and teaching strategies (individualized learning, open-ended problem solving, etc.).

An overview of the development of chemical education at the high-school level in the United States will be discussed as a model for the relative role of the above three factors mentioned. This will be followed by a description of chemistry programmes in England and Wales, where both the educational system and those involved in programme development are different to those found in the United States. In conclusion, two special topics will be discussed; the place of the laboratory, which is central to both chemical education and science education in general, and learning difficulties which are specific to chemistry.

1. Chemical Education in the United States

In 1872, chemistry was accepted for the first time in the United States as a subject for college entrance. This marks a period in which science was particularly influential. College professors were not only involved in the development of school textbooks but also expressed their demands on school science by the specification of college entrance requirements. The high-school textbooks were mainly watered down versions of college textbooks and the resulting teaching strategy was, on the whole, declamatory and authoritarian, and took into account neither varying student ability nor interest.

In the beginning of the twentieth century, the development of modern high schools eased the domination of higher education and brought about a change in the presentation of science to students. Concurrently, the First World War focused the national interest on industrial chemistry, which resulted in a gradual shift of emphasis from basic scientific principles to an emphasis on practical, applied, and industrial chemistry (Woodburn and Obourn 1965). Judging by the textbooks available in the early 1930s, there were at least 14 different chemistry courses in high schools. In many cases, general chemistry was replaced by applied chemistry; for example, agricultural chemistry, technical chemistry, textile chemistry, or dairy chemistry (Frank 1932). Science had thus been modified by society, and instead of learning what chemistry is, students were taught what chemistry does for the citizen and for society.

The usual chemistry textbooks used in this period became more and more like encyclopedias, crammed with facts which were continually being added to, with little or nothing being discarded. As a result, many chemistry courses consisted of massive doses of facts devoid of conceptual order, unity, or suggestion as to how these facts may have been developed.

The need for a rethinking of science programmes in high schools was certainly apparent in the 1940s, but it was not until the middle 1950s that the National Science Foundation provided funds for the development of new programmes in the various sciences. There are certain common features to the programmes started at that time:

(a) They were developed by academic scientists, that is those who were in the best position to know what science the students needed to study.

(b) The emphasis was on scientific principles and not on engineering and technological applications. The student was asked to "explore, discover, and understand".

(c) The materials were comprehensive and included textbooks, teacher guides, laboratory manuals, visual aids, and examinations.

Specifically in chemistry, two parallel programmes were developed—the *Chemical Bond Approach* (CBA) (1964) and the *Chemical Education Material Study* (CHEMStudy). Although they differed in content and format, both stress the basic principles and concepts of chemistry.

The central themes of the CHEMStudy programme were according to Hurd (1970):

(a) Energy and its role in chemical reactions.

(b) Conservation of mass—energy in terms of the conservation of atoms and electrical charge.

(c) Kinetics and mechanics of reactions.

(d) Dynamic equilibrium.

(e) Competitive factors acting in chemical systems in general.

(f) Electron structure and the geometrical arrangement of atoms.

The central theme of the CBA programme was the study of chemical bonds, reflecting the view that chemistry is the breaking and formation of bonds, and that is what distinguishes chemistry from other related sciences. Students were confronted with the implications of logical arguments, based on theories presented to them through the discussion of mental models and their relationship to facts and observations.

These two chemistry programmes, as well as other science programmes of the late 1950s, signify a period in which the needs of the society merged with the wish of scientists to teach more science. In the post-Sputnik age, priority was given to quickly and efficiently producing young scientists. The developers of educational programmes were well-aware of the needs of the target population—that is, students—but the feeling seems to have been that what is good for the adult scientist is good for the young future scientist—the high-school student. "The school boy learning physics *is* a physicist and it is easier for him to learn physics behaving like a physicist than doing something else" (Bruner 1975).

The idealization of science and the scientists did not last long. When the pressing societal problems did not disappear by the magic touch of science, a new orientation to studying chemistry started to appear in the textbooks. The society factor again became dominant, but this time ecological problems were the main concern of society, and chemistry was presented in many textbooks in the context of pollution, drugs, and warfare.

Since the early 1970s, chemistry teaching in the United States has been constituted by a turn toward a growing awareness of student ability and interest. Thus, for example, introduction of the Interdisciplinary Approach to Chemistry (IAC), was followed by an intensive evaluation study with the aim of examining whether students are markedly able to cope with the complexity level of the new programme.

If an attempt is made to summarize 100 years of chemistry education in the United States, the picture that emerges, on the whole, is that of abrupt changes brought about by forces which were not intrinsic to the teaching of chemistry. No real effort was put into the implementation of the programmes of the late 1950s or into their evaluation. The abandonment of "scientific", post-Sputnik programmes was due more to a shift of emphasis of the external science and society factors, rather than to any objectively evaluated student effect.

2. Chemistry Programmes in England and Wales

The relative balance between the science, society, and student factors and their impact on chemistry education in England and Wales is quite other than that in the United States. In England and Wales, the three sciences—physics, chemistry, and biology—are taught in parallel from the age of 11, while in the United States, students can choose to study one, or more, of the sciences at age 16 to 18. As a consequence of the comparatively early age at which science is studied, the student factor is more in evidence in England and Wales. Science exerts its influence on the high-school system through the university entrance examination boards which interact with the system twice, at the 'O' level or ordinary level taken at age 16, and the 'A' level or advanced level taken at age 18. The pressure is moderated by two other factors. Firstly, initiators of innovations in education are mainly teachers and educators, whose main concern is the student, and the fact that a relatively small group and even a single school can promote examinations. This may explain why changes in the English and Welsh educational programmes tend to be more gradual. The second reason may be that the society is less immediately involved in the English and Welsh educational system.

Two main projects for chemistry education were established in the early 1960s and funded by the Nuffield foundation—one at 'O' level and the other at 'A' level. The 'O' level course was aimed at students most of whom would not continue to study science thereafter. Therefore one of the "self-imposed" criteria was that the programme should present, as far as possible, a complete and comprehensive picture of chemistry, but at the same time, should serve as basis for the studies at 'A' level, for those who continued their studies in this subject.

Because of the relatively early age at which chemistry is studied, the programme develops in three phases: first, it is designed to give the feel for scientific experience, meeting new materials, the basic rules of performing experiments, and the enjoyment and thrill of discovery. In the second phase—*Using Ideas about Atoms and Molecules*—phenomena are explained in terms of the scientific model. The third phase, the last half year, is devoted to a number of optional topics: metal and alloys, giant molecules, chemical industry, historical topics, and so on.

The main objectives of the 'O' level programme are that, as a result of the investigation and the solution of problems, students should have acquired skills in, and understanding of, the following:

(a) Getting new materials from those available.

(b) Looking for a pattern in the behaviour of substances.

(c) Using explanatory concepts and knowing how to check theory by observation.

(d) Associating energy changes and material changes.

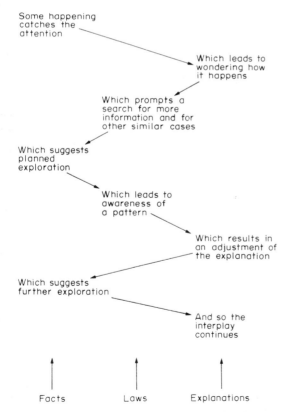

Figure 1
Spiral interplay of facts, laws, and explanations

The course develops as a spiral interplay of facts, laws, and explanations as shown in Fig. 1 from one of the Nuffield guides (1966).

Students are encouraged to think imaginatively about problems with which they are confronted and to suggest further experiments and explanations. The philosophy of the developers was that students should have graded opportunities to be right or wrong and they should be guided and encouraged to become better at deciding whether or not they are right. In other words, no answers or rules should be supplied by an outer source and therefore no student textbook was prepared. Teachers were given two alternative sample schemes as a guide, and thus were encouraged to develop their own ideas and teaching strategies.

The Nuffield 'A' level programme constitutes a continuation of the studies carried out at 'O' level and takes into account students' maturity, containing problems at a more complex level. It is based firmly on the three concepts fundamental to the understanding of chemical systems:

(a) The use of the Periodic Table as a means of providing a unifying pattern for the diverse properties of elements and compounds.

(b) The relationship between structure and the properties of substances.

(c) The ways in which energy transfers can determine the feasibility and outcomes of reactions.

Chemistry was presented as an integrated subject as manifested in the following areas: the previously dominant division into inorganic, organic, and physical chemistry disappeared; facts and concepts, as well as theory and practical work were integrated as fully as possible and the boundaries between pure and applied chemistry were broken.

In summary, it can be concluded that the English and Welsh system shows a clear dominance of the student factor in that the demands of the science factor are carefully balanced by the learning needs of the students.

3. The Place of the Laboratory in High-school Chemistry

Laboratory work in high school has been influenced by two opposing philosophies: (a) the use of experiments as a means for verification of previously studied facts, and (b) the laboratory as the focus of the learning process, as in the programmes of the late 1950s in the United States and the Nuffield programme in England and Wales.

In the latter, experiments are presented as problems to which answers are to be sought. Manipulative skills and techniques are developed, not so much as an end in themselves, but as an aid to the solution of problems. In this respect, the Nuffield programme went furthest: in the 'O' level programme, the teaching is entirely centred around the laboratory. Experiments consist of three parts in each of which the student is actively involved: planning, execution, and deduction.

The major problem of centring a science programme around the laboratory is that it is both expensive in resources and in student time. As a consequence, after the initial enthusiasm, there seems to be a growing concern that although the laboratory cannot be disposed of entirely, its role in science education should be reassessed. The kind of experiments done, their characteristics, and also their number have to be re-evaluated because in many cases the same goals (except possibly for manipulative skills) can be achieved by the use of audiovisual methods, written descriptions of experiments, and by well-planned teacher demonstrations (see, for example, Ben-Zvi and Silberstein 1980).

4. Learning Difficulties in Chemistry

As was mentioned above, the post-Sputnik programmes were characterized by, among other things, the idea of presenting the body of knowledge organized under certain unifying principles. The student is no longer asked to learn by rote a collection of facts but is expected to "understand". However, a thorough understanding of chemistry demands a mastery of reasoning capabilities and requires the student to be at the formal operational stage. Many students, even up to the college level have not reached this stage (Herron 1975).

Students who function at the concrete level are not equipped to deal with ideas such as molecules, atoms, ions, electrons, and so on. The quantitative aspects of chemistry—stoichiometry and calculations based on the mole concept demand proportional reasoning which, again, is a formal manipulative skill. No wonder many students find these ideas impossible to grasp (Novick and Menis 1976).

Understanding of the new, abstract concepts mentioned depends to a large extent on the conceptual framework that students have in various topics related to the study of chemistry. For example, if students have no correct notion of the particular model of matter from their earlier studies (Novick and Nusbaum 1981), they will have difficulties assimilating the more refined models presented in chemistry.

There is another source of difficulties which is intrinsic to the nature of the discipline. Chemists tend to simultaneously use three levels of thought: the level of phenomenology, the level of atomic models involving single entities like one hydrogen atom or one water molecule, and the level of atomic models involving multitudes of entities such as a mole of water molecules. Expert chemists and teachers, know what each of the levels represents and understand that the atomic model was devised to account for facts and observations (at the level of phenomenology) but that in order to do so, it is necessary to function at the multiatomic level. Furthermore, when they use symbols and notations they

know exactly which of the three levels is signified. Students, however, are very confused by this.

The difficulties of coordinating the three levels of thought and the preconceived ideas brought into the chemistry class cause a distorted picture of chemistry. For example, even after studying about the atomic model for some time, many students think that the atom is a small piece of matter, carrying the macroscopic properties of the substance. Some students have also distorted additive (and not interactive) notions about molecular structure and chemical reactions. For example, they conceive the molecule H_2O_2 as composed of a molecule of H_2 and a molecule of O_2, and think that H_2O is formed by the "addition" reaction $H_2 + O \rightarrow H_2O$.

When students have to perform at the multiatomic level of thought, that is, when they have to think about a chemical reaction where many molecules participate, each of which has an internal structure, their performance drops indicating that such situations are overloading their working memory.

All these difficulties have to be taken into account if meaningful learning is expected. A careful content analysis of the subject matter can reveal instances where the use of concrete models and methods of presentations may help students who have not yet reached the formal operational stage. Another way is to define carefully each of the levels of thought and the need to transfer from one level to another. Still another way is to try and lessen the load on the working memory by various strategies, for example organization of the subject matter into "chunks" which can be mastered by the students (Johnstone and Kellett 1980).

Bibliography

Ben-Zvi R, Silberstein J 1980 The use of motivational experiments in the teaching of quantitative concepts in chemistry. *J. Chem. Educ.* 57: 792–94

Bruner J S 1975 *The Process of Education*, 13th edn. Harvard University Press, Cambridge, Massachusetts, p. 14

Chemical Bond Approach Project (CBA) 1964 McGraw-Hill, St Louis, Missouri, p. 383

Chemistry: An Experimental Science 1963 Freeman, San Francisco, California

Frank J O 1932 *The Teaching of High School Chemistry*. Frank, Oshkosh, Wisconsin

Herron J D 1975 Piaget for chemists: Explaining what good students cannot understand. *J. Chem. Educ.* 52: 146–50

Hurd P De H 1970 *New Directions in Teaching Secondary School Science*, 2nd edn. Rand McNally, Chicago, Illinois

Johnstone A H, Kellett N C 1980 Learning difficulties in school science: Towards a working hypothesis. *Eur. J. Sci. Educ.* 2: 175–81

Novick S, Menis J 1976 A study of student perception of the mole concept. *J. Chem. Educ.* 53: 720–21

Novick S, Nusbaum J 1981 Pupils' understanding of the particulate nature of matter: A cross-age study. *Sci. Educ.* 65: 187–96

Woodburn J H, Obourn E S 1965 *Teaching the Pursuit of Science*. Macmillan, New York, pp. 190–98

Earth Sciences Programs

P. E. Pezaro

Earth science offers a convenient vehicle for the integration of the sciences. For this reason it has recently become a popular curriculum subject in many countries, at the middle- and junior-high-school level. The conceptual revolution of the 1960s (plate tectonics) also gives it a unique advantage with respect to new developments and a growing body of knowledge. Different countries have used different approaches to the question of how to bring these developments into the classroom.

Earth science is an umbrella term for the study of different aspects of the earth. The major part of earth science is drawn from the more defined discipline of geology: the study of the earth. This core is complimented by the hybrid fields which bridge between geology and other sciences: geophysics, geochemistry, meteorology, oceanography, pedology, and so on.

The earth sciences currently occupy a unique position in the natural sciences, having recently undergone a major conceptual revolution. Until the early 1960s, the earth sciences were a conglomeration of piecemeal theories, each attempting to explain a small part of the physical world. The introduction and establishment of the theory of plate tectonics (the movement and interaction of vast crustal plates across the face of the earth) revolutionized all previous concepts about the earth and provided a unified framework upon which to hang all previous knowledge and partial theories.

1. Curricula Around the World

This rebirth and conceptual revolution which only began in the early 1960s, and the continued thrust in earth science research, has kept it in the world headlines. Earth science attempts to explain natural phenomenon on a macroscopic level which can be readily understood by a layperson, an advantage which it has over the physical sciences (the microscopic level) and the space sciences (the super-macro-level). By virtue of the non-esoteric nature of this revolution, many countries have adopted earth science as a convenient vehicle for fulfilling the main objectives of teaching science. In these countries, earth science plays various roles according to the philosophical approach of the curriculum planners. In the United States, earth science has traditionally been seen in the main as a preparatory science course for the junior-high-school level. A number of courses have been developed, mainly for the eighth and ninth grades, to provide an overview of the place of science in the natural world. It is thus perceived as providing a good general knowledge for nonscience majors as well as a strong conceptual base upon which to relate the pure science disciplines to be studied in subsequent years by science majors.

In England and Wales and in Australia, earth science topics have tended to be incorporated into integrated science curriculum materials. The Australian Science Education Project (ASEP) developed modular units from many areas of science which were moulded into an overall curriculum design (see *Module Approach*). Some of the units had clear earth science associations. In England and Wales, several of the celebrated Nuffield programs (Nuffield Secondary Science, Nuffield Combined Science) incorporated units on earth science, although many schools in England and Wales teach geology as an independent curriculum subject. This may be due to the United Kingdom's significant contributions to the development of the science of geology, from the eighteenth century until the present day. In Israel, two projects have been developed to introduce geological topics into the existing school curriculum. A "floating" module based on the identification of the common local rocks was developed (Mazor 1976) and an optional course for 10th grade chemistry students based on the chemistry of minerals and rocks was recently completed (Pezaro and Mazor 1979). In the above examples, earth science is considered as an ancillary subject, supporting, illustrating, and extending existing disciplines. This results from the dilemma which has faced the most enthusiastic attempts to introduce earth science as a fully fledged curriculum topic in many countries. Earth science is usually squeezed out in the struggle for curriculum hours, where it must compete with the traditional "giants" of science curricula (biology, physics, chemistry).

2. Some Major Curriculum Projects

2.1 Earth Science Curriculum Projects

The most comprehensive attempts to build a complete curriculum in earth science in the Western world was the Earth Science Curriculum Project (ESCP) in the United States. ESCP was one of the later of the federally funded projects of the 1960s, being developed jointly by the American Geological Institute (AGI) and the National Science Foundation. It culminated with the publication of *Investigating the Earth* (AGI 1967), the most integrative of all the junior-high-school science curricula in the United States. The dissemination stage of the project was very successful and quickly produced a shortage of teachers. Teacher preparation became a major problem as soon as the enrollments in earth science began to rise dramatically [850,000 students (26.2 percent of total enrollments) in 1969: over 3,000,000 students in 1977]. Consequently, two additional projects were initiated, "Environmental Studies" and the "Earth Science Teacher Preparation Project." The teacher shortage was particularly acute because the integrated nature of the subject matter intimidated teachers who had majored in just one of the major science disciplines.

2.2 Crustal Evolution Education Project

Following the era of the 1960s, the 1970s saw new curriculum concepts replace earlier ideas. In the earth sciences, one of the most significant developments in the United States was the Crustal Evolution Education Project (CEEP). This project was established under the auspices of the American Geological Institute and was a direct result of the desire to involve the school student population in the nascent revolution of the earth sciences which had begun with the publication of the notions of sea-floor spreading and plate tectonics. The desire to circumvent the lengthy process of textbook production spawned a new concept in curriculum development: "the articulation of a system of development which brings the latest scientific developments into the classroom whilst research into these developments is still ongoing and far from complete" (Thompson 1980). The involvement of a professional subject association in providing the whole of the project staff for the initiation, planning, and execution of the project constituted another innovation in science curriculum development.

Modules were developed in six centers spread throughout the United States. Individual module themes were chosen according to the areas of interest, expertise, and inspiration of the particular development team. In all, 64 modules were involved. After conventional stages of writing, formative evaluation, revising, and peer review, 32 modules were ultimately published. A wealth of curriculum materials were therefore available to teachers within two to three years, a period considerably less than for "conventional" curriculum materials.

The CEEP project underwent extensive curriculum evaluation, mainly at the formative stage of preparation of the materials. Three types of data were gathered; student background characteristics, student performance variables, and process or climate variables. Initially the modules were tested on a restricted basis, using one of the teachers who had been involved in the module's development. The second stage involved a more systematic collection of data. Between one and four teachers (who had not been involved with the module's development) with at least 100 students each, were monitored with an evaluation package provided by the project evaluation center at Ohio State University. All data were analyzed and used to revise the modules before publication. A final stage of evaluation was on a much larger scale, involving some 12,000 students constituting broadly representative student and teacher populations.

3. Research

Compared to other branches of science education, little systematic educational research has been carried out in earth science. Review of the science education literature in general indicates a paucity of articles in earth science research. Even in the earth science education literature [*Journal of Geological Education* (USA), *Geology Teaching* (UK)] the majority of contributions relate to descriptions of innovative courses or approaches to conventional subject matter, reports on recent geological events of developments in the discipline, or didactic hints and comments.

Considerable educational research has been continued at Ohio State University using the CEEP materials. The materials have been used to explore the feasibility of adapting a novel evaluation technique to science education. Interrupted time series analysis had been virtually unused in educational research until it was applied to the teaching of an instructional unit based on the CEEP modules, in Ohio. This method allowed the sophisticated modeling of the instructional and learning process, and was used to monitor the development of concrete and formal geological concepts in adolescent students over time. It was based on the daily collection of evaluation data, a task which was possible in the research framework but not practical for the average classroom teacher. The tremendous growth in the availability of computers in schools could soon bring this evaluation tool within the easy reach of all teachers. This approach enabled the construction of learning curves for plate tectonics concepts, which indicated clear differences for students at different cognitive levels of development. This result has ramifications for teachers who want to adapt their teaching practices to their students' cognitive levels (Mayer and Kozlow 1980).

4. Summary

Earth science education seems to be still on the upswing around the world. Most curricula tend to be locally orientated, using local examples as much as possible. This makes direct adoption difficult, but lends itself to easy adaptation. The possibility of presenting many earth science concepts in concrete terms makes earth science an attractive first science course and, in fact, it is commonly introduced as such at the middle- or junior-high-school level.

Bibliography

American Geological Institute 1978 *Investigating the Earth*, 3rd edn. Houghton Mifflin, Boston, Massachusetts

Mayer V J, Kozlow M J 1980 An evaluation of a time-series single-subject design used in an intensive study of concept understanding. *J. Res. Sci. Teach* 17: 455–61

Mazor E 1976 *The World of Rocks*. Weizmann Institute of Science, Rehovot

Pezaro P E, Mazor E 1979 *Chemistry of Minerals and Rocks in Israel*. Weizmann Institute of Science, Rehovot

Thompson D B 1980 Plate tectonics for the people: The Crustal Evolution Education Project (1976–79). *Geol. Teach.* 5: 21–25

Energy Education

J. Lewis

Energy education denotes the treatment of the topic of energy within the framework of the school programme. Throughout the twentieth century energy has been a topic within the school curriculum in most countries. However, it is a concept of some difficulty for young people to grasp because it is not tangible and only reveals itself through transformation from one form to another. The difficulties in teaching about energy have only been given the attention they deserve in relatively recent years and it is only in those years that much thought has been given to the wider aspects of energy education now that shortages of energy sources have become apparent. This article considers some of the trends.

1. Energy Education in the Past

At one time energy education was the preserve of the physicists. They gave formal definitions of energy either in terms of capacity to do work or by relating it directly to work as force times distance. This in turn led to a mathematical treatment and a whole series of formulae, such as mgh or $\frac{1}{2}mv^2$, always learnt by heart by students. There was often confusion in the student's mind about "work done by" and "work done on", and the confusion was made even worse when what was learnt in mechanics was somehow different from that learnt in heat: was not energy in one case measured in calories, whilst in the other in quite different units, ergs or joules? These concepts were further complicated in the student's mind because the energy encountered in chemistry seemed to differ somehow from that met in physics.

2. The Beginning of the Change

Since the late 1950s there have been fundamental changes in science education, started by the great curriculum reforms at this time in the United States. There is now a much greater emphasis in teaching on school children gaining experience for themselves, on doing experiments, on "being a scientist for the day": an emphasis on the process of science. This has had its effect on energy education. First came a realization that it is through energy transformation—as energy is transferred from one form to another—that the difficult concept of energy reveals itself. Then apparatus for the precise measurement of the mechanical equivalent of heat gave way to "energy conversion kits" by means of which school children themselves could turn energy from one form to another: for example, energy from a battery could drive a motor, which in turn could drive a flywheel, whereupon at the throw of a switch the energy stored in the flywheel could drive a motor in reverse as a generator, which in turn lit lamps. Yet a further change, relatively trivial in the academic world, but profound in the educational world, was the almost universal move to SI (*Système Internationale*) units: this certainly made energy teaching easier.

3. Science for All

Another profound change has been that science education in recent years has ceased to be the preserve of the academic few, but has become part of the education of all young people and, throughout the world, energy has become a topic within primary education. Again the approach is experimental as youngsters turn energy from one form to another, and UNESCO literature abounds with suggestions for simple experiments using simple apparatus at this level.

4. Useful Energy

The study of energy transformations at the secondary level leads to the idea of conservation of energy. If energy is always conserved, if it is always turned from one form to another and never lost, what is all this fuss about shortage of energy? Inevitably therefore, academic students at the secondary and tertiary levels must be introduced to basic ideas of thermodynamics and in particular to some appreciation of the Second Law of Thermodynamics, and all students need to have a feel for the fact that some forms of energy are more useful than others; some are "high grade" energy forms, some "low grade".

5. Science and Society

There is a further trend which is beginning to affect energy education. At one time science education was primarily concerned with "science for the enquiring mind" or perhaps "pure science" would be the better description. It was felt that this was fundamental, and applied science and technology could safely be left until a later step up the educational ladder. There is now much greater awareness throughout the world that "science for action" should also be a component of science education—and this inevitably has its influence on energy education. At one time students learned a formal definition of thermal conductivity and then how to measure it for good and bad conductors; now they learn something about heat insulation in the home as well, and that is science for action.

However, there is now a realization that there should be another component to science education which might be called "science for citizens". School courses since the early 1950s have included reference to radioactivity, to the properties of alpha, beta, and gamma radiation, to the concept of half-life, but they have tended not to include nuclear power. But with decisions to be made in most countries about nuclear policy, it would seem essential to build up an educated population with some understanding of nuclear energy. This would go into the category of science for citizens.

Criteria established at UNESCO and other conferences concerned with science and technology education for development have all stressed the need to make education relevant to the needs of society. This must have profound effects on energy education. There is an increasing interest in science and society courses at all levels, and an awareness of the importance of energy in agriculture, in the production of minerals, and in industry is likely to pervade education. The quality of life and the quality of the environment will both depend in

the future on energy; whether wise decisions are made about energy and whether limited resources are used in a sensible way will depend greatly on the way young people are educated for that future—and hence the importance of energy education.

Bibliography

Energy programs in the school: Awareness and involvement 1980 *Intercom* 98: 14–15
Kohl J 1981 Utilization of existing energy teaching materials. *J. Environ. Educ.* 12(3): 29–35
Krugger K C 1977 Some guidelines for energy programs. *Today's Educ.* 66(3): 60–62
Schlichting H J 1979 Energy and energy waste: A topic for science education, *Eur. J. Sci. Educ.* 1(2): 157–68
Social Studies Review 1980 19(2)

Astronomy: Educational Programs

M. R. Cohen

Astronomy is the scientific study of all objects and phenomena outside the earth and its atmosphere. It is one of the oldest sciences. Every continent has prehistoric evidence that humans were able to measure time, seasons, and geographic directions from the sun, moon, and stars. The earliest written records reinforce this evidence with additional examples of civilizations measuring time and directions from astronomical observations. Since astronomy was one of the first sciences, it is reasonable to assume that astronomy was also one of the first subjects included in an educational curriculum. Early astronomers and teachers were priests, magicians, philosophers, monks, nobles, and clerics. They combined the practical applications of astronomy with the curiosity of all people to make sense out of the universe. Present-day astronomers and teachers continue to emphasize the practical applications and theoretical aspects of astronomy.

Astronomers cannot deny the ancient traditions of astronomy. At one time astronomy was astrology. While this has changed, constellations that carry the names of astrological signs are still used in astronomy to indicate sections of the sky. This often gives the incorrect impression that astronomy supports astrology. Changing previously held beliefs has always been a problem in astronomy. From an educational point of view the confusion between astronomy and astrology is only one problem. Other ancient religious aspects of astronomy create more serious problems. In some current definitions astronomy is said to be the study of heavenly objects. The inclusion of this religious connotation does more than continue the religious connection of astronomy. It can lead to significant conceptual errors. Heaven is "up" and so the earth is "down." This not only supports the idea of a flat earth, it suggests that space has a bottom. This can confuse a person's under-

standing that the earth is presently in space and that this space extends in all directions from the earth.

Astronomy was critical to the development of science during and after the Renaissance. As with the ancients, the measurements of time and direction were stressed. The older religious connections could not be ignored. They continued to be reflected in many astronomical theories and in the treatment of scientists. It was during this time that formal instruction in astronomy began. At many centers astronomy became part of mathematics. Galileo was the first professor of mathematics and astronomy at Pisa from 1581–1592. The first professor of astronomy, a position often shared with the Royal Astronomer, was appointed at Oxford in 1619. The first professor of astronomy at Harvard was appointed in 1690.

It was not until the present century that wide-ranging undergraduate and graduate programs in astronomy were developed at the university level. The early courses were based on the popular *Manual of Astronomy* (Young 1902). This work was developed into two volumes, one for the solar system and the other devoted to astrophysics and stellar astronomy (Russell et al. 1926, 1927). Present year-long courses in astronomy have maintained this tradition of a two-semester program beginning with the solar system in the first semester and concentrating on astrophysics and stellar astronomy in the second. Astronomers continue to begin their training in other disciplines, notably mathematics and physics. However, engineering, chemistry, geology, and biology have become critical to many astronomical research projects with the introduction of radio and X-ray telescopes, and space exploration.

Astronomy is presently part of many elementary- and secondary-education science programs. Within the secondary-school curriculum, astronomy is usually a small part of the earth science or physics courses. On occasion a course in astronomy is offered, especially if the school has a planetarium. At the elementary-school level astronomy can be found in most science programs beginning in the kindergarten. These include observations of the sun, moon, stars, and planets, discussions of seasons, space travel, and astrophysics, and speculation into topics at the leading edge of astronomy. At all levels of education students are taken to museums, planetariums, observatories, and space research centers. The London School Planetarium opened in 1966 with services for students at all levels.

The most extensive astronomy program for elementary-school children was developed by the Elementary-school Science Project at the University of Illinois (Atkin and Wyatt 1966). A brief outline of the six books in this series will provide an overview of the types of topics included in most elementary, secondary, and introductory college courses in astronomy. The Elementary-school Science Program begins with *Charting the Universe*, a series of activities devoted to measuring astronomical sizes and distances within the universe. They then study *The Universe in Motion*, looking at daily and long-term motions of the sun, moon, stars, planets, and galaxies. They also develop Kelper's laws and moving models of the solar system. The third book is *Gravitation* concentrating on acceleration, force and mass, gravity at the earth's surface, and Newton's universal laws of gravitation. *The Message of Starlight* is the fourth book. It concentrates on various models of light and the characteristics that can be obtained from star light. From a study of light the program moves to *The Life Story of a Star*. Here the properties and various models of stellar evolution are presented. The final book is devoted to *Galaxies and the Universe*. The children begin with our own Milky Way galaxy and move out to other galaxies and the expanding universe.

The Elementary-school Science Project clearly shows that ancient processes and approaches are still applicable to the teaching of astronomy. This project is built on very active participation by the children in the development of each concept or theory. Astronomy

remains a subject with an enormous amount of observational evidence. The practical applications abound and theoretical speculations are impossible to avoid. From an educational perspective, however, it is clear that observations alone are not sufficient for the development of sophisticated science concepts. The work by Nussbaum elucidates the problems children have in interpreting astronomical concepts (Nussbaum 1979). Studying children in the United States and Israel, Nussbaum found five different and distinct stages of children's concepts of the earth in space. At the lowest conceptual level, children, up to the age of 12, visualized the earth as flat with a sky which is parallel to the ground. Down is perpendicular to this flat earth and all down forces are parallel. At the highest level children viewed down toward the center of a spherical earth. Nussbaum's research was replicated in Nepal with similar findings (Mali and Howe 1979).

Archeoastronomy shows the extent to which ancient peoples were able to use their observations to make sense out of the world (Aveni 1981). The best astronomy programs provide students with opportunities to make similar observations. But the research of Nussbaum and Mali and Howe show the need for instruction that fits the observations into theories which are more advanced than those held by the ancients.

Bibliography

Atkin J M, Wyatt S P 1966 *Charting the Universe*. University of Illinois Elementary-school Science Project, Urbana, Illinois

Aveni A F 1981 Tropical archeoastronomy. *Science* 213: 161–71

Mali G B, Howe A 1979 Development of Earth and gravity concepts among Nepali children. *Sci. Educ.* 63: 685–91

Nussbaum J 1979 Children's conceptions of the Earth as a cosmic body: A cross age study. *Sci. Educ.* 63: 83–93

Russell H N, Dugan R S, Stewart J Q 1926 *Astronomy: A Revision of Young's Manual of Astronomy*, Vol. 1: *The Solar System*. Ginn, Boston, Massachusetts

Russell H N, Dugan R S, Stewart J Q 1927 *Astronomy: A Revision of Young's Manual of Astronomy*, Vol. 2: *Astrophysics and Stellar Astronomy*. Ginn, Boston, Massachusetts

Young C A 1902 *Manual of Astronomy: A Textbook*. Ginn, Boston, Massachusetts

Issues in Science Education

Language of Science

C. Sutton

Scientific language has features which deserve particular attention in education, because if they are demanded too soon, they can actually interfere with the growth of understanding. They include:

(a) insistence on clearly defined terms;

(b) suppression of the peripheral aspects of word meanings;

(c) the adoption of an impersonal style of reporting.

All are designed to reduce ambiguity of meaning, and the clash with educational purposes arises only because exploring ambiguities is a necessary part of their resolution in the mind of a learner.

1. Insistence on Definition

Thomas Sprat (1667) writes this about the first Fellows of the Royal Society:

> They have . . . a constant Resolution, to reject all amplifications, digressions, and swellings of style: to return back to the primitive purity when men delivered so many *things* almost in an equal number of *words*. They have exacted from all their members, a close, naked, natural way of speaking . . . bringing all things as near the Mathematical plainness as they can . . .

He expresses the impatience of the group over what they regarded as a "superfluity of talking" and excessive use of the "ornaments of speaking" (not, however, without a certain flourish of his own). Their preference was to try to avoid figurative uses of language altogether, and to let their words refer to something drawn from nature. Boyle (1662) for example, could afford to be scathing about his alchemical predecessors with their vague talk of humours, principles, spirits, and the "elements" of earth, air, fire, and water. He writes:

> . . . to prevent mistakes, I must advertize you, that I now mean by elements . . . certain primitive and simple, or perfectly unmingled bodies; which not being made of any other bodies, or of one another, are the ingredients of which all those perfectly mixt bodies are compounded . . .

This tradition of defining terms anew has served science well. It has, however, given the verbal pres-

entation of technical terms, and their definitions, a marked prominence in science texts. Books used in secondary schools commonly contain between 300 and 2,000 such special terms, and the obligation on the learner to know the accepted statements about them is considerable. It can interfere with a fuller exploration of their meaning.

2. Suppression of Peripheral Meanings

To make clear what this involves, it is useful to distinguish between the denotative meaning of a word (how it might be defined, for example, water as a compound of hydrogen and oxygen, or as a liquid with such-and-such properties), and its connotative meaning (all the things it implies: a myriad of associations which it summons up). Some of those connotations give it added reality (for example, its fluidity and wetness). Some are emotional in character (the pleasure of cool streams, or the fear of drowning). Most of them are held to be irrelevant to how the material behaves in a test tube, so they are excluded in scientific usage. Once agreement has been achieved about what a word denotes, scientists may even come to believe that that *is* its meaning. In natural language, on the other hand, connotations are what make people choose one word rather than another in a particular context. They shape the use and understanding of it, and of course they differ from person to person, so that no *one* meaning exists. Rather, different individuals each have their own meanings, which overlap. Nor is it possible to say precisely what all the connotations are, for a particular person. All words therefore have some measure of vagueness, and some potential for change, when a speaker chooses to attend more to one group of connotations, and less to another.

A powerful way to suppress existing connotations is to avoid common words which people have heard before, and to make new ones, often from Greek or Latin. Faraday (1834), writing about electrochemical decomposition, says:

> . . . I find the greatest difficulty in stating results, as I think, correctly, whilst limited to the use of terms which are current with a certain accepted meaning.

945

He goes on to reject "pole" and to define new terms such as "electrode", which he has made. Classical scholars assured him that "anode" would suffice for "the way up" for his electric current, and "cathode" for "the way down". This device has been widely used in science, and in this way it is possible to get hydrophilic instead of "water loving", hypogeal instead of "underground", and quantum instead of "packaged amount". Hopefully, the desired meanings of such terms may be established by hearing them frequently in context in the laboratory. However, to bring the meanings of these words to life, a teacher may sometimes find it necessary to translate them back into more everyday words—making use of the ideas which led to their invention in the first place. Everyday meanings can appear as just a rather tiresome impediment, as for example in the case of the words *fruit*, *force*, *pressure*, *power*, and *work*, all of which have acquired rather precise scientific meanings, and have not been replaced by new words. Since they remain in everyday use with their older meanings, teachers may find themselves in the unfortunate position of calling upon pupils to deny what they know in that sense, and to substitute the "proper" meanings.

3. Impersonal Styles of Reporting

The importance of separating assertion from evidence, or opinion and discussion from description, has gradually brought about a stylized form of presentation in scientific reports, which excludes overt personal expression. Papers and books from the nineteenth century retain the author's expression of personal involvement in the discussion of thoughts alongside the report of observations. They are full of phrases like "The theory which I believe to be a true expression of the facts" (Faraday), or "I was much struck with certain facts" (Darwin), or "My first care was . . ." (Pasteur). Nevertheless, the depersonalized report has come to be associated with the objectivity to which scientists aspire, and it has had direct effects in education, with generations of school children drilled in a standard form of "writing up". A leading contemporary scientist (Medawar 1963) has described the standard format of scientific papers as fraudulent if it is intended to represent the process of discovery, rather than just the checking part.

4. Consequences for Teachers

Precision in language is one of the important goals of all science education. So is an understanding of the role of public, testable reporting. However, it cannot be achieved by making learners adopt the outward forms before they have explored their own understanding. Learning involves changes in the meanings that words carry for the individual, so it is important to think through what is understood by a word, and what is associated with it. By pulling out just the kernel of referential, denotative meaning, a teacher runs

the risk of letting learners isolate their knowledge of terminology from the totality of their understanding.

Scientific development also involves changes in word meanings, and despite all attempts to freeze it, the evolution of language goes on. "Planet" now does not mean what it did before Copernicus, and the changes in "element", "power", and "work" have already been mentioned.

Innovators have long recognized that making a new structure of ideas is bound up with control of the language. In the words of Lavoisier, a science cannot be improved without improving the language. Much of his nomenclature, which laid the foundations of chemistry, survives until today, but his "caloric" is no longer used, nor are the "imponderable" (unweighable) agents of his day tabulated. By such examples, teachers can show their pupils that words and concepts have a history.

Changes in conceptual structures are actually mediated through the same rhetorical devices whose excesses were rejected by scientists in the quest for a simpler, more descriptive language. Ideas captured by mere figures of speech later become core postulates of accepted theory. *Field*, *charge*, *current*, and genetic *code* are just some of the terms derived in this way, and it is no longer possible to regard scientific language as primarily descriptive. Works by Black (1962), Schon (1967), Hesse (1980), and others have established the explanatory function of metaphor at the points of innovation. Therefore exactness in scientific language remains something to aspire to, but not actually attainable (Bronowski 1966). If indeed it were attainable further invention would cease, for the source of new ideas is in the renewable ambiguity of existing terms.

Bibliography

Black M 1962 *Models and Metaphors*. Cornell University Press, Ithaca, New York

Boyle R 1662 *The Sceptical Chymist*. Dent, London

Bronowski J 1966 The logic of the mind. In: Bronowski J 1977 *A Sense of the Future*. MIT Press, Cambridge, Massachusetts

Faraday M 1834 *On Electrochemical Decomposition*. Philosophical Transactions of the Royal Society, London

Hesse M B 1980 The explanatory function of metaphor. *Revolutions and Reconstructions in the Philosophy of Science*. Harvester, Brighton

Hogben L T 1969 *The Vocabulary of Science*. Heinemann, London

Lavoisier A L 1790 *Traite elementaire de chimie*. [transl. by R Kerr] Creech, Edinburgh

Medawar P 1963 Is the scientific paper a fraud? *The Listener* British Broadcasting Corporation (BBC), London

Savory T H 1953 *The Language of Science, its Growth, Character and Usages*. Deutsch, London

Schon D A 1967 *Invention and the Evolution of Ideas*. Tavistock Social Science Publications, London

Sprat T 1667 *History of the Royal Society of London*. Routledge and Kegan Paul, London

Scientific Literacy

L. E. Klopfer

In a world where science and the applications of science play important roles in society, as they do today, it is essential that educated persons possess some basic understanding of science in order to make informed decisions in their daily lives and to function effectively as citizens. This basic understanding of science that should be possessed by everyone, not only by professionals in scientific and technical fields, is frequently referred to as "scientific literacy." The development of scientific literacy is a central concern of science education in all its ramifications, both in the formal science instruction offered to students in primary, secondary, and tertiary educational institutions, and also in the less formal teaching about science that takes place through the mass communication media, adult education programs, science museums, and science–technology centers.

1. Rationale for Scientific Literacy

For thoughtful educators throughout the world, developing their students' scientific literacy has become a central aim or purpose of science instruction at every school level. This aim partakes of the very essence of education—providing young people with opportunities to acquire the necessary skills, knowledge, understanding, and attitudes which enable them to behave as successfully functioning adults and responsible members of society. In the closing decades of the twentieth century and into the next century, virtually every nation is increasingly affected by science and its applications in technology. Though the extent and form of the scientific–technological society will differ between nations, to a greater or lesser degree adults in every country must be able to cope intelligently with two kinds of problems related to scientific literacy. The first problem is how to survive in safety, in good health, and with sanity in a physical environment pervaded by science-derived products, machines, devices, and processes whose characteristics or functions can be properly understood only with some knowledge of science. Persons lacking this knowledge are likely to behave foolishly or even make fatal mistakes. Second is the problem of participating responsibly in formulating policies and making decisions concerning public issues having technological components which involve a basic understanding of science (for example: Should a nuclear power plant be built in this valley? Should genetic engineering on human beings be regulated?). Again, persons who are ignorant about the relevant science principles, the nature of scientific evidence, and the processes of science will be unable to take responsible actions concerning certain important aspects of their lives. Added to these ideological reasons for developing students' scientific literacy through education is the pragmatic realization that desirable jobs and careers in many fields are becoming increasingly dominated by technologies which involve a basic grounding in science. The need of adults to be scientifically literate is so important today, for both ideological and practical reasons, that in countries where the formal educational system has failed to foster adequate levels of scientific literacy, massive efforts are often undertaken through retraining programs or the informal education media of publications, radio and television programs, and science–technology centers to remedy the deficiency.

2. Components of Scientific Literacy

Since the notion of scientific literacy has existed for many decades under various guises (e.g., general education in science, survival science, science for effective citizenship), it has been construed rather narrowly by some authors and very broadly by others (Pella et al. 1966). In the contemporary context, a full definition of scientific literacy is considered to be composed of these five components: (a) a knowledge of significant science facts, concepts, principles, and theories; (b) an ability to apply relevant science knowledge in situations of everyday life; (c) the ability to utilize the processes of scientific inquiry; (d) an understanding of general ideas about the characteristics of science and about the important interactions of science, technology, and society; (e) the possession of informed attitudes and interests related to science. When people's knowledge, understanding, and skills expressed in these components are fully developed, they can function successfully in a contemporary technology-based society. Without this literacy in science, people are likely to be confused by many events that happen in the world and less likely to lead healthy and secure lives.

In recent educational discourse, scientific literacy has frequently been employed as a catchphrase, though users of the term may differ widely on what they believe it includes. Their different conceptions are due to differences in their emphasis on the various kinds of knowledge and intellectual skills they believe a scientifically and technologically literate person needs to lead a successful personal and professional life, and to function effectively in the kind of society they envision for the late twentieth and early twenty-first centuries (Champagne et al. 1989). Nevertheless, despite variations in the conceptions of scientific and technological literacy, there is a general consensus that scientific literacy is essential to people's everyday lives.

The development of the knowledge, understanding, and skills encompassed by the five components of scientific literacy through school instruction requires attention over a long period of time. Moreover, at various educational levels, different components of scientific literacy may be emphasized and different levels of sophistication in the students' understanding and skills will be sought. For example, the scientific literacy component concerning the ability to utilize some processes of scientific inquiry (observing, measuring, etc.) may be emphasized at the primary level, while understanding of general ideas about the characteristics of science and about the interactions of science, technology, and society may be more appropriately emphasized at the secondary and tertiary levels. To illustrate, an emphasis on processes appears to be central in the elementary-school science programs offered in Japan and the Phillipines (Mori et al. 1980). However, understanding of the general characteristics of science and its interactions is emphasized in certain secondary and tertiary level courses for students not specializing in science, of which the "Science in Society" course in the United Kingdom (Lewis 1981) and the "Knowledge and Power" course at Deakin University in Australia are just two illustrations (Deakin University 1979). In the Soviet Union, the science courses required of all students in the ten-year general education schools place greatest emphasis on the first, second, and fourth scientific literacy components (McFadden 1982). All four scientific literacy components are well represented, though with different emphases, in recent recommendations for designing science curricula for elementary and secondary schools in Wales (Department of Education and Science and the Welsh Office 1988) and the United States (American Association for the Advancement of Science 1989).

3. Assessment of Scientific Literacy

Techniques for assessing scientific literacy are not essentially different from those employed to assess other desired educational outcomes. Paper-and-pencil objective tests, essay examinations, questionnaires, interviews or surveys, and observation instruments can be used to assess a student's or adult's status with respect to different aspects of scientific literacy. The only difficulty is obtaining sufficiently clear and usable specifications of some of the components of scientific literacy. The first two components, concerning science knowl-

edge and its application, present little difficulty, and specifications for the third component, the processes of scientific inquiry, are also readily available in the science education literature. Specifications relevant to the fourth and fifth components can be found in Klopfer (1976). Several objective-type instruments which assess understanding of certain general characteristics of science and scientists have been developed. Of these, perhaps the most widely used internationally is the *Test On Understanding Science* (Cooley and Klopfer 1961). The assessment of attitudes and interests related to science has also received considerable attention. Recent critiques of the work on assessing this component of scientific literacy are available (Gardner 1975, Haladyna and Shaughnessy 1982).

Bibliography

Champagne A B, Lovitts B E, Calinger B J (eds.) 1989 *This Year in School Science 1989: Scientific Literacy*. American Association for the Advancement of Science, Washington, DC

Cooley W W, Klopfer L E 1961 *Test on Understanding Science (TOUS)*. Educational Testing Service, Princeton, New Jersey

Daedalus 1983, Vol. 112, No. 2 (issue devoted to Scientific Literacy)

Deakin University 1979 *Knowledge and Power*. Open Campus Program, Deakin University, Waurn Ponds, Victoria

Gardner P L 1975 Attitudes to science: A review. *Stud. Sci. Educ.* 2: 1–41

Haladyna T, Shaughnessy J 1982 Attitudes toward science: A quantitative synthesis. *Sci. Educ.* 66: 547–63

Klopfer L E 1976 A structure for the affective domain in relation to science education. *Sci. Educ.* 60: 299–312

Lewis J L 1981 *Science in Society: Teacher's Guide*. Heinemann, London

McFadden C P 1982 Science education in the USSR. *Sci. Educ.* 66: 123–37

Mori I, Yano H, Lee J, Tadang N, Medel T E 1980 Comparison of elementary school science curricula in four East Asian Countries. *Sci. Educ.* 64: 405–12

Pella M O, O'Hearn G T, Gale C W 1966 Referents to scientific literacy. *J. Res. Sci. Teach.* 4: 199–208

Science for Ages 5 to 16. 1988 Department of Education and Science and the Welsh Office, London

Science for All Americans: A Project 2061 Report on Literacy Goals in Science, Mathematics, and Technology. 1989 American Association for the Advancement of Science, Washington, DC

Science, Technology and Society as a Curricular Topic

J. Solomon

Although science, technology and society (STS) has now achieved recognition and visibility as a subject in the school science curricula of several countries, it is difficult to define. The nature of STS courses varies and depends strongly on the purpose for which it is being taught. It is essentially interdisciplinary in that it aims

to explore the interactions between science knowledge, technological application, and the social context which directs the endeavours and either benefits or suffers from the results. Courses differ because the emphasis may be placed upon understanding the kinds of decisions society makes (which includes political and economic considerations), exploring particular issues for their own interest, or using topical concerns for the purposes of teaching science.

1. Early Instances of STS Courses

In earlier years the courses had a variety of names. In 1977 an international group of scholars interested in the public policy aspects of science and technology published a collection of papers under the heading *Science, Technology and Society* (Spiegel-Rosing and Price 1977). The economic and government policy dimensions of this approach were not to find their way into many high school courses but it claimed a coherent academic foundation for the subject and also coined the name. The British Science, Technology and Society Association was formed soon after, but this was directly descended from SISCON (Science in a Social Context) which had been inaugurated in 1970. The founders of this movement for fostering the teaching of various kinds of STS courses in universities and polytechnics were, in many cases, also active members of the British Society for Social Responsibility in Science, which in turn was influenced by the international Pugwash movement.

It could be argued that elements of the social history of technology were the precursors of the modern STS courses. Many school textbooks, going back to the early years of the twentieth century, were in the habit of including examples from the Industrial Revolution, or from the development of the chemical industry, to illustrate the scientific principles being taught and to emphasize their importance. Holmyard's widely used book on school chemistry, first published in 1924 which remained in use virtually unchanged until 1960, is a case in point. In university education the history of science, which rarely included technology, was often coupled with the philosophy of science, but neither subject included controversial or public decision-making aspects of technology. Nor were they common in school curricula. School science courses designed in the 1960s, like the American PSSC (Physical Science Study Committee) and BSCS (Biological Science Curriculum Study), and the British Nuffield Sciences, contained references to some of the historical figures who had originated theoretical advances but, as the courses were strongly oriented towards intellectual discovery, neither the social nor the technological elements of STS were represented (Layton 1982).

Two of the earliest courses in school STS show a very clear commitment to explaining the special nature of scientific "knowing" and relating it not so much to traditional philosophy as to the social decision making of a citizen which must take into account many other kinds of "knowing". In Britain the SCISP (Schools Council Integrated Science Project) course, which was explicitly based on the work of the US educationalist Robert Gagné, taught that seeking "patterns" was the objective of science, and brought the special patterns

of social and economic reactions to technology into the broad scheme (e.g. Hall 1973). In Canada the commitment surfaced more strongly still in the work of Aikenhead and Fleming (1975). The authors reported that they had intended teaching the interactions of science and society, but the ignorance of their high-school students forced them to teach first about the different possible kinds of knowing, and then about science and scientists. Only after this, in the third section, did they reach the ways in which science affects the community. The same general focus is to be found in the later British SISCON-in-Schools course (Solomon 1983). Despite the varied titles of the booklets, a unified perspective is presented and the citizen's knowledge quandary is addressed throughout by an analysis of ways of knowing, the historical background, and the political decision-making possibilities.

In educational terms the justification for such STS courses was very clear. Not all pupils would become scientists but, as citizens, all would be involved in democratic processes. On both sides of the Atlantic, science education policy makers began to adopt the STS cause. In Britain the influential science teachers association, the Association for Science Education (ASE), published a discussion document *Alternatives for Science Education* (1979) and followed this in 1981 with a policy document *Education through Science*. Both of these documents gave high priority to the interactions of science and society as a part of the drive for "science education for all". In the United States a similar emphasis on a curricular content in science and technology, relevant to students other than those interested in careers in science, is to be found in the National Science Foundation's report (Hufstedler and Langenberg 1980). The early years of the 1980s also saw an international stream of general theoretical papers defining the subject in different ways and urging its adoption by the world of science education (e.g. Bybee et al. 1980, Ziman 1980, McConnell 1982).

2. Varieties of STS Programmes

From the early 1980s there has been an outpouring of STS curriculum materials. Apart from the holistic kind already mentioned, these may be separated into two more general categories which have a fundamental difference in curricular intention. A few examples of each will be given.

In the most prolific group are to be found the STS modules which take one topic at a time and treat it as a particular problem area which is specific in its complexities of social and technological issues. No general lessons in either social decision making, or in science and technology, seem to be intended. One of the most comprehensive of these is the British *Science in Society* (Lewis 1980). Each topic has its own student reader, written by experts, with some practical details and arguments presented for and against particular solutions. The curricular purpose was to fill a slot in the examination-ridden British system where this kind of less specialized syllabus might be acceptable as a means of broadening education. Later a similar package *Science And Technology In Society* (Holman 1986) was produced for slightly younger pupils. Here each leaflet is designed for one or two lessons only, to be fitted into the "interstices" of the normal science curriculum.

This problem-based approach has become very popular. It enables different communities to teach about their own particular issues in compact and easily handled packages. Materials produced in Israel, for example, on drugs and on smoking, claim to be teaching about informed decision making, and yet bear a strong similarity to the kind of sound health education programmes to be found in most school systems (Zoller 1982). Israel has also developed units under the banner of STS on copper mining, the fertilizer industry, and the Mediterranean–Dead Sea Canal. In each case the choice of topic is specific—this time to national economic aspirations. In the most general sense ecology lies at the heart of these kinds of STS modules in that they focus on the relation of the organism to its total environment. Many of the earliest STS courses in North America were direct descendants of environmental studies of the life in lakes, and of acid rain. When no integrating theme is present, the geographical and cultural variation of possible units becomes quite bewildering. At the other extreme, the UNESCO–UNEP (United Nations Environmental Programme) International Environmental Education programme, set up in 1975, has developed materials to be used worldwide on such issues as the exploitation of natural resources, pollution, health, and nutrition. Although these demonstrate a way of teaching and give some examples, they can suffer from a lack of local impact.

The same motive of using a contemporary issue of special national importance can be seen in several units on wider political issues such as nuclear energy, nuclear weapons (e.g. the United Kingdom), and mineral wealth (e.g. Canada). This national selectivity is often reproduced on a smaller scale: it is not difficult to find curriculum materials developed by teachers in a particular school or area where some local development is made the focus of teaching. Some courses bring in more social decision making, some are more illustrative of the applications of technology, but none appear to see STS as more than a valuable adjunct to the normal science lessons.

This kind of study is often claimed to be strongly motivating for the students, as well as holistic and interdisciplinary in its learning method. These units certainly bring variety into the syllabus: they often lend themselves to simulations of public inquiries, to class discussion, or to some other type of "games", and so call for the use of skills not often practised in school science (e.g. Ellington and Langton 1975). It has also been claimed for STS that in so far as it allows the expression of social concern, or student self-expression,

it proves more attractive to girls than the normal ways of learning science (Harding and Sutoris 1984).

The third of the three broad categories of curriculum projects are those which aim to change the nature of the whole science curriculum. Their proponents argue that occasional snippets of STS material, with its assumptions of the negotiability of scientific and technological outcomes, will be at odds with the authoritarian face of the science knowledge being taught in the majority of the student's lessons. They may argue that the essentially consensual nature of scientific knowledge itself, or the poor image of conventional high school science, calls for a complete change of emphasis. Ambitious projects of this kind, which aim to change the whole of science learning, need generous funding and so far are only to be found in the Dutch PLON project and the American Science through STS project (S-STS) at Pennsylvania State University. Once again national variation seems inevitable because school systems and educational expectations are so different.

3. Evaluating STS Programmes

The claim that school science can be changed, and so made more effective, either from the point of view of the reception of scientific knowledge, or of holistic education, certainly requires evaluation through research. These two objectives are themselves disparate and the research methodology also presents difficulties. So far the best studies are concerned with the untutored views of students on STS issues (e.g. Fleming 1986), and here all the evidence shows that social and personal views tend to override knowledge derived from school science. Indeed the students may consider scientific knowledge to be totally irrelevant; this is sometimes referred to as the "two domain" problem. Further limited data seem to suggest, however, that fluency in crossing to and fro between the domains of social everyday knowing and that of scientific knowing, brings more reflective and durable knowledge (Solomon 1985). Far more research centred on classes of students who have learnt their science by an STS method is required if the movement's large educational claims are to be vindicated.

Bibliography

Addinell S, Solomon J 1983 *Science in a Social Context. Teachers Guide.* Association for Science Education, Hatfield
Aikenhead G S 1979 Science: A way of knowing. *Sci. Teach.* 46(6): 23–25
Aikenhead G, Fleming R 1975 *Science: A Way of Knowing.* Department of Curriculum Studies, University of Saskatchewan, Saskatoon
Association for Science Education 1979 *Alternatives for Science Education.* Association for Science Education, Hatfield
Association for Science Education 1981 *Education through Science.* Association for Science Education, Hatfield
Bybee R W, Harms N, Ward B, Yager R 1980 Science, society and science education. *Sci. Educ.* 64(3): 377–95

Ellington H I, Langton N H 1975 The power station game. *Phys. Educ.* 10: 445–47

Fleming R W 1986 Adolescent reasoning in socio-scientific issues, part 1. *J. Res. Sci. Teach.* 23(8); 677–98

Hall W 1973 *Science and Decision-Making.* Longman, London

Harding J, Sutoris M 1984 An object relations account of the differential involvement of boys and girls in science and technology. In: Lehrke M, Hoffmann I, Gardner P (eds.) 1984 *Interests in Science and Technology Education.* IPN (Institut für Pädagogik der Naturwissenschaften), Kiel, pp. 259–80

Holman 1986 *Science And Technology In Society.* Association for Science Education, Hatfield

Holmyard E J 1924 *Elementary Chemistry.* E. Arnold, London

Hufstedler S M, Langenberg D N 1980 *Science Education for the 1980s and Beyond.* National Science Foundation and the Department of Education, Washington, DC

Layton D 1982 Science education and values education—An essential tension. In: *Proc. Int. Seminar.* Chelsea College, London

Lewis J L 1980 *Science in Society. Readers and Teachers' Guide.* Heinemann, London

McConnell M C 1982 Teaching about science, technology, and society at the secondary school level in the United States: An educational dilemma for the 1980s. *Stud. Sci. Educ.* 9: 1–32

Solomon J 1983 *SISCON-in-Schools,* eight booklets and teachers' guide. Basil Blackwell, Oxford

Solomon J 1985 Learning and evaluation: A study of school children's views on the social uses of energy. *Soc. Stud. Sci.* 15: 343–71

Spiegel-Rosing I, Price D de S (eds.) 1977 *Science Technology and Society: A Cross-disciplinary Perspective.* Sage, Beverley Hills, California

Ziman J 1980 *Teaching and Learning about Science and Society.* Cambridge University Press, Cambridge

Zoller U 1982 Interdisciplinary decision-making in the science curriculum in the modern socio-economic context. In: Harrison E (ed.) 1985 *World Trends in Science and Technology Education,* Report on 2nd Int. Symp. Trent Polytechnic, Nottingham

Science Concepts and Skills

W. Harlen

This article is concerned with two issues relating to scientific concepts and process skills: first, the interrelationship of the two; second, the extent to which process skills and concepts are generalizable from one context to another. In relation to the first, research leads to the view that there is a close interdependence between concepts and process skills. Whilst it continues to be useful to define and discuss each separately, they should be thought of as facets of a whole such that one cannot exist alone. In relation to the second, work exploring generalizability has shown that concepts and process skills, once learned and demonstrated in a particular context, are not necessarily applied wherever they are relevant. In the discussion, it becomes clear that these issues are not unrelated to each other.

It should be noted that the term *process skills* is used here in order to avoid misinterpretation of skills as narrow, well-practised activities which are often associated with this word. Science process skills are mental skills which are generally taken to include observation, interpretation, formulation of hypotheses, creation of plans for systematic investigations, identification of patterns or regularities, and the drawing of conclusions.

1. The Interdependence of Process Skills and Concepts

In much of the debate about the objectives of science education in the 1960s and 1970s, science process skills and science concepts were treated as if they were separable and independent. This resulted in the creation of curriculum materials with an emphasis on one or the other, for example, Elementary Science Study (1966) (process skill based) and COPES (Conceptually Oriented Program in Elementary Science 1971). There is now convincing argument and supporting evidence that these aspects of scientific activity and of learning in science are unavoidably interdependent. This same conclusion is reached whether one begins from consideration of concepts or of process skills.

Work on science concepts and particularly that which has probed students' own ideas (Osborne and Freyberg 1985, Driver et al. 1985, Gilbert et al. 1982, Black and Lucas 1989, Russell and Watt 1989a, 1989b) has led to recognition of the important role in learning of students' existing ideas. Learning which is more than rote memorization depends on the linking of existing ideas to new experience and the modification of initial ideas to fit the evidence (Harlen 1985). In this model, learning is equated with change in ideas and process skills. However, the extent to which these changes lead to ideas which are progressively more powerful and widely applicable—more scientific in other words—depends on how the process skills involved in linking and testing are carried out. Often process skills are used in a less critical way than is required for an idea to advance: it may appear to have been considered but the evidence used may be partial and selected to confirm rather than challenge it. Thus process skills are central to concept development and need to be developed if ideas are to become progressively more scientific.

The connection does not stop there, for concepts have to be used to be seen to exist in people's minds. Concepts are accessed through the use of process skills; they also have to be assessed through application, which again involves the use of process skills such as recognition of similarities and regularities, interpretation, inference, hypothesizing.

Starting from the consideration of process skills leads to the same conclusion about the interdependence of concepts and process skills. There is considerable evidence that the use of process skills is influenced by existing concepts. For example, Finlay (1983) cites the case of the geologist viewing a thin section of rock under a microscope. The geologist will see details which are significant in indicating, perhaps, that sedimentary particles are beginning to undergo metamorphism. Someone without the knowledge of the geologist would see only a variety of shapes and colours and would be unlikely even to make the observations of the relevant details, quite apart from drawing the same interpretation from them. Despite the same images being available to their eyes, the observations made would be different.

Similarly, interpretation is influenced by preconceptions (optical illusions would not work if this were not so), and numerous examples can be found in the history of science where scientists have looked for the evidence of relationships they believe to exist, ignoring other possibilities (Gauld 1985).

Approached from these two directions, the interrelationship of process skills and concepts is seen to be very strong; indeed so much so as to cast doubt on the existence of a sharp distinction between the two. Definitions of the terms can further blur the distinction rather than sharpen it. Concepts take many different forms, causing problems of their definition in terms of what they are. Instead it is useful to define them in terms of their function, as enabling past experience to be used in going beyond the observed features of new objects or events to make inferences about them, based on common properties or on relationships. Bruner et al. (1966 p. 244) give a working definition of a concept along these lines as "the network of inferences that are or may be set into play by an act of categorization". Here concepts are given a similar role to processes. At the same time, process skills which are developed to the level of metacognition (Vygotsky 1962) become aspects of mental activity which can be reflected upon and voluntarily controlled (Kuhn et al. 1988). As objects of reflection, they become little different from concepts. Thus the stage is set for a theory of scientific development which combines the process skills and concepts into an integrated whole.

2. The Generalizability of Science Concepts and Process Skills

Turning to the second focus of this article, the connection with the foregoing is apparent. There are situations where potentially an available concept is applicable but is not used because the necessary links are not made. This may be because requisite process skills are not sufficiently developed, or for various

reasons related to context, which will also be considered.

In the formation of concepts through the learner's own mental and physical activity, there is evidence that understanding develops around isolated phenomena, rather as water accumulates in drops. An important dimension of development is to link together understanding of related phenomena to give more powerful concepts, rather as drops can be linked into larger pools of water. The evidence for this process is in the research into development of understanding, which, although better known with older pupils, through the work of Osborne (1981), Gilbert Erickson (1980) and Straus (1980), *inter alia*, is even more obvious in work with younger children. Russell and Watt (1989a) have found that some children of ages five to nine make a distinction between rain and water, whilst others up to the age of 11 have quite different explanations for the disappearance of water (due to evaporation) from a wet cloth hung on a washing line, a fish tank without a lid, and a puddle on the ground (Russell and Watt 1989b). This research identified some successful strategies for teachers to use in helping children to link the related phenomena together. However, with young children, rapid change cannot be expected because linking depends on children's ability to see similarities between different objects and events, to transfer hypotheses from one situation to another, and to interpret evidence; that is, to use process skills, which are still limited. Once more it emerges that an important strategy in developing concepts is to develop children's process skills.

In considering the influence of context, it seems hardly necessary to invoke systematic enquiry to demonstrate the variation in use of skills according to context, for it is within the everyday experience of most people. As Claxton (1984) puts it "how well a person can do sums may depend crucially on whether he is in a maths class or out with his friends ten-pin bowling or playing darts . . . The fluency of a black child's language depends on whether he is talking to his best friend or a white educational psychologist" (p. 43). However, the research shows that the context effect operates not only between school and the outside world but within the context of school. In both the learning and the assessment of concepts and process skills, there has to be a context. What that context is may be perceived differently by individuals and has many dimensions (White 1988) which influence performance in varied and unanticipated ways.

Evidence from the National Surveys carried out in England, Wales, and Northern Ireland by the Assessment of Performance Unit (APU) shows clearly the influence of the context presented within a test item. In one survey, some questions requiring planning skills were set in two forms, one as a problem encountered in an everyday context and the other as one encountered within the context of school learning activities. Differences were found which could not be explained in terms of the complexity or familiarity of the problem, and were not all in favour of one type of context (Harlen et al. 1985).

It is likely that an important factor in such cases is connected with students' views of the relevance of science learning to a particular context. For example, an investigation presented in terms of a problem of choosing a fabric for a raincoat will not necessarily lead to careful experiment and controlled testing if the student believes that other criteria (e.g. the fashion for using certain fabrics) would be taken into account in the real situation. Thus, an attempt to increase relevance by presenting real problems may deter application of skills which are not seen as relevant to such a problem.

Murphy (1989) has made a particular study of gender-related differences of context within items and other variable features of test questions using the APU item bank. Her findings indicate that girls perform less well in items which are set within a context which relates to male activities (cars, certain sport), are multiple choice in answer format, have a single correct answer, require manipulation of structural or mechanistic variables, or expect explanations in abstract terms. Boys perform less well on questions with the reverse characteristics. The same individual will succeed on one item and fail in another (or more likely fail to attempt it) where the context varies along these gender-related lines. Murphy suggests some characteristics of neutral questions: that they require the use of knowledge, are set in a practical context, are open in format, enable the pupils to determine the relevance of the question, and allow for variable responses.

There are profound implications of these findings, not only for assessment, but also for curriculum development and teaching. Contexts which do not present opportunities for pupils to apply process skills and concepts which are available to them may produce assessment results of low validity, but equally such contexts can reduce learning opportunities in classrooms and laboratories. A key aspect of these contexts is perceived relevance. The students' view of relevance may be more restricted than the teacher's and the student may indeed be applying knowledge wherever it appears to be relevant. White (1988) suggests that conscious measures need to be taken to change both the context and the students' perceptions of the context in which they work, if they are to be freed to make full use of the skills and concepts which they have.

Bibliography

Black P J, Lucas A 1989 *Children's Informal Ideas*. Croom Helm, London

Bruner J S, Goodnow J J, Austin G A 1966 *A Study of Thinking*. Science Editions, New York

Conceptually Oriented Program in Elementary Science 1971 Center for Field Research and School Sciences, University of New York, New York

Claxton G 1984 *Live and Learn*. Harper and Row, London

Driver R, Guesne E, Tiberghien A (eds.) 1985 *Children's Ideas in Science*. Open University Press, Milton Keynes

Elementary Science Study 1966 McGraw-Hill, New York

Erickson G 1980 Children's viewpoints of heat: A second look. *Sci. Educ.* 64(3): 323–36

Finlay F N 1983 Science processes. *J. Res. Sci. Teach.* 20(1): 47–54

Gauld C 1985 Empirical evidence and conceptual change. In: Osborne R J, Gilbert J (eds.) 1985 *Some Issues of Theory in Science Education*. Science Education Research Unit, University of Waikato, Hamilton, pp. 66–80

Gilbert J K, Osborne R J, Fensham P J 1982 Children's science and its consequences for teaching. *Sci. Educ.* 66(4): 623–33

Harlen W 1985 *Teaching and Learning Primary Science*. Harper and Row, London

Harlen W, Black P J, Khaligh N, Palacio D, Russell T J 1985 *Science in Schools: Age 11: Report No. 4*. Department of Education and Science, London

Kuhn D, Amsel E, O'Loughlin M 1988 *The Development of Scientific Thinking Skills*. Academic Press, San Diego, California

Murphy P 1989 Gender and Assessment in Science. In: Murphy P, Moon B (eds.) 1989 *Developments in Learning and Assessment*. Open University Press, Milton Keynes, pp. 321–36

Osborne R J 1981 Children's ideas about electric current. *New Zealand Sci. Teach.* 29: 12–19

Osborne R J, Freyberg P 1985 *Learning in Science: The Implications of "Children's Science"*. Heinemann, Auckland

Russell T J, Watt D 1989a *Everyday Chemical Changes in Non-Living Materials*. Report of the Primary Science Processes and Concept Exploration Project, Centre for Research in Primary Science and Technology, University of Liverpool, Liverpool

Russell T J, Watt D 1989b *Evaporation and Condensation*. Report of the Primary Science Processes and Concept Exploration Project, Centre for Research in Primary Science and Technology, University of Liverpool, Liverpool

Straus S 1980 *U-Shaped Behavioural Growth*. Academic Press, London

Vygotsky L 1962 *Thought and Language*. MIT Press, Cambridge, Massachusetts

White R T 1988 *Learning Science*. Blackwell, Oxford

Attitude Towards Science

W. W. Welch

An attitude is an emotional reaction toward a person or thing. It is a personal response to an object, developed through experience, which can be characterized as favorable or unfavorable. The use of science as the object or stimulus of these feelings delineates that set of attitudes known as "attitudes toward science." The scope of attitudes to be included in the definition depends on what is included in the word "science." For purposes of this article, science will be defined as the subject matter of science. The definition excludes such things as attitudes toward science teachers, scientists, or the learning of science. Similarly, studies of desired ways of thinking, for example open mindedness or honesty, which are sometimes called scientific attitudes, are excluded from this review.

Developing positive attitudes toward science has been an espoused goal of most curriculum development efforts since the late 1950s (Welch 1979). It was hoped that increasing interest in science would result in increased science enrollments, which in turn would yield a larger science work force pool and a science literate public. The increased attention to the affective outcomes of science has also resulted in a proliferation of attitude research studies (more than 30 such studies were published in 1979 in the United States), more measuring techniques (one recent review identified 50 techniques), and several attempts to measure attitudes toward science on an international scale.

Reviews of research on science attitudes also reflect the burgeoning work in this area. Aiken and Aiken (1969) reviewed 54 studies in the United States; Gardner (1975) referenced more than 200 British, Australian, and United States studies, while Ormerod and Duckworth (1975) include nearly 500 studies in their book on the subject.

Sufficient studies now exist to enable researchers to conduct quantitative syntheses of research results. These integrative studies, called meta-analyses, have been done for science attitudes (Haladyna and Shaughnessy 1982; Willson 1983) and provide additional understanding of the accomplishments and problems in this area.

1. Measuring Techniques

The most commonly used procedures to assess attitudes are summed rating scales (Likert), semantic differential scales, interest inventories, and questionnaires. In addition, projective techniques, preference rankings, anthropological observations, and enrollment data have also been used in various studies. Gardner (1975) provides an excellent review of most of these procedures.

Several concerns have been voiced over the quality of these techniques, particularly the lack of a theoretical base for development, low reliability, and a failure to demonstrate validity. The lack of a commonly accepted definition of science attitudes has resulted in an assortment of techniques, but each with the same claim, that is, to measure attitudes toward science.

Initial attempts by the International Association for the Evaluation of Educational Achievement (IEA) to assess science attitudes illustrates some of the measurement problems (Comber and Keeves 1973). In spite of much early planning, time pressures, technical shortcomings, and scoring problems made it necessary to discard much of the original material. In fact, only 4 of 12 original scales had sufficiently high reliabilities to use them in further analysis and these scales were not effective across all age levels. The Second International

Science Study also included attitude items in its 1983 and 1986 testing. However, at the time of this printing, international results on these items are not yet available.

It seems clear that although there has been some improvement in the measurement of attitudes, there is much to be done. National assessments in Canada, the United Kingdom, Israel, and the United States, and an international assessment conducted by the Educational Testing Service (NAEP 1989) provide one avenue to improve the situation. However, a report of the National Research Council (1988) concluded: "Given the importance attached by science and mathematics educators to the development of attitudes that will foster continuing engagement with science and mathematics, the committee recommends that research be conducted to establish which attitudes affect future student and adult behavior in this regard and to develop unambiguous measures for those that matter most" (p. 9).

2. Present Status of Attitudes Toward Science

There is a widespread belief among scientists and science educators that attitudes toward science are more negative than is desired. Declining enrollments, results of national polls, research reports, and personal experiences have created a generally discouraging situation. The time alloted to science in the schools has diminished and fewer students are choosing science careers. Teachers and principals report their belief that the public's image of science has declined in recent years. In the United States, national polls rank science seventh out of ten subjects in terms of usefulness in later life. Concern over the declining status of science has been voiced in the United Kingdom and Australia, as well.

Attitudes toward science are known to decrease as students progress through their schooling years. Many studies have shown a reduced interest in science as a result of studying various science subjects. A situation seems to exist where science is generally viewed as an important and critical endeavor, but one to be pursued by somebody else. It is difficult, if not impossible, for science educators to understand why others do not enjoy the challenge and excitement of the scientific pursuit, but it is increasingly obvious that the majority of people do not share this feeling. At a personal level, science is seen as difficult, often dull, and not important in one's own life. In spite of much recent attention and effort to change these perceptions, the current general status of science attitudes is viewed with disappointment by those in the profession.

3. Correlates of Science Attitudes

Considerable attention has been directed towards the identification of variables which may be related to attitudes toward science. The studies have focused on two classes of variables: (a) those under the direct influence of the schooling process, for example, teaching behavior, and (b) those located outside the influence of the institution of schooling, for example, gender of the student. The former are sometimes called endogenous or internal variables while the latter are classified as exogenous or external. Knowledge of the role of both classes of variables helps people to understand the nature of science attitudes, but it is the endogenous variables that offer most potential for improving attitudes through such things as new curricula, better teaching, and practical science experiences.

3.1 Endogenous Variables

The endogenous variable set will be examined first. In spite of the apparent logical connection between science attitudes and science achievement, the research results suggest a very modest positive relationship. For example, the median correlation between achievement and science attitude in the IEA studies was +0.20 (Comber and Keeves 1973). More recently, Willson (1983) reported a mean value of 0.17 for 48 studies of elementary children he analyzed. Similarly, a meta-analysis of 49 studies conducted by Haladyna and Shaughnessy (1982) found a median correlation of +0.15 between scores on various achievement and attitude measures. The strength of this relationship tends to increase somewhat in the higher grades (probably due to selection factors) but seldom goes above +0.40. In some studies a negative relationship between achievement and attitude has been found. Further work is needed to understand these surprising results.

A consistent positive relationship has been noted between gender and attitudes. Males take more science courses and show more interest, especially in the physical sciences. In fact, sex is probably the most consistent variable related to science attitudes even though the variance accounted for seldom exceeds 10 per cent. There has been a surge of interest in this area as investigators seek to understand the social forces and cognitive factors that may account for these differences (Gardener 1975).

Several researchers have pointed out that interest in science develops early in life (between the ages of 8 and 13) and call for increased attention to the science experiences of that age group. At that age, many children express positive attitudes toward science but this attitude decreases over time. For example, 70 percent of the 9-year-old children in the United States have positive attitudes towards their science experiences in school but this number drops to half when 13- and 17-year-olds (Welch 1986; Mullis and Jenkins 1988). Something occurs to turn children away from science. Perhaps it is the inherent difficulty of science, the way in which it is taught, the curriculum, or merely part of a maturing process among children. More likely it is a combination of these factors and others that creates this situation.

Those that do tend to choose science courses and careers appear to have certain personality traits which are related to positive science attitudes. Generally they are serious, achievement oriented, realistic, independent, and conventional (Gardner 1975). Making science appealing for other personality types still presents a formidable challenge to science educators.

One consistent set of attitude correlates to other measures of science attitudes. For example, interest in doing laboratory work is likely to be positively correlated with attitudes towards biology or towards other science careers. People who find satisfaction with one characteristic of the scientific enterprise are likely to find it with another. While it is possible that part of this relationship is due to similarities in items and item formats, it seems reasonable to conclude that attitudes toward science comprise both general and specific attributes.

Another group of endogenous variables which have been correlated with student attitudes are the home background variables. Included here are such things as geographic location, parents' education, fathers' occupation, and science materials in the home. While it is possible to conceive of modifying these variables in order to change student attitudes, it appears that the scope of such activity is beyond the reach of the educational system. However, they are included because of the understanding they provide and because of their potential influence on other variables.

Geographic location (e.g., urban, suburban, or rural), as well as native country, are related to science attitudes. In general, suburban students report more positive attitudes than do their urban or rural counterparts. The IEA study reported variations among the 19 countries it assessed but no clear-cut pattern is discernable (Comber and Keeves 1973).

Socioeconomic status and science opportunities in the home are correlated moderately with science interest and science career choice. The results are in the expected direction with upper- and middle-class families providing more science opportunities and encouragement and their children responding accordingly (Gardner 1975).

The direct influence of the home and background factors is difficult to assess because they interact with each other. Parents' attitude toward science seems important but it in turn is related to parents' education, home opportunity, college choice and so on. Although many variables have been found to be related to attitudes, the generally "weak" effect of these variables and their interaction, as yet, does not provide a clear picture of their individual and collective influence.

A series of studies using US national assessment data has examined possible correlates of attitudes toward science in the context of testing a model of educational productivity (Walberg et al. 1986). With 11 predictor variables controlled for one another, student attitude was related to student ability, motivation, class environment, attitude toward teacher, and homework (Welch et al. 1986). They found that quality of instruction, quantity of instruction, home environment, gender, and race were not related to science attitudes when the predictor variables were controlled. These studies represent an initial attempt to untangle the interactions among variables, however, more work is needed with better measures of these variables as well as replication among different populations.

3.2 Exogenous Variables

Several researchers have turned to those variables under the potential control of the schools in their attempts to discover the means by which attitudes toward science could be enhanced. Although some important relationships have been discovered, much remains to be done in this area.

In general, there are low, but positive, relationships between teaching and behavior, the science curriculum, and student attitudes. Curricula which have focused directly on the issue of student interest, for example, Science 5/13, Harvard Project Physics, have shown some successes in accomplishing these goals without the loss of science content. Similarly, some studies of smaller pieces of the curricula, for example a film, unit, or laboratory experiment, have often shown more positive attitudes when compared to control groups. Unfortunately the methodological weaknesses, for example, design errors and unreliable outcome measures of many of the smaller studies, make it hazardous to generalize the results. It seems reasonable to conclude that curriculum effects may account for perhaps 5–10 percent of student variance in attitude (and achievement) (Ormerod and Duckworth 1975, Welch 1979), but other factors, especially student and teacher variables, appear to be more influential.

The teacher is thought to play an important role in the development or hindrance of student attitudes. Although much more work has been done on student achievement than on student attitudes, attributes such as enthusiasm, respect for students, and personality traits have been shown to influence student attitudes in science as well as in other subjects. However, the strength and direction of these relationships is quite varied. Some have found very little correlation, while others have found moderate to strong relationships. It is difficult to sort out the meaning of the discrepant studies and considerably more work is needed in this area.

The influence of student peers has been the subject of some recent investigations and appears to provide some explanation of attitude development. The social learning environment, peer pressure, and nature of student interactions seems to be related to the attitudes that students have towards science and their science classes. The exact nature of these relationships is still not clear but the social experiences a student has in a class with his or her classmates, and more importantly with the teacher, are powerful influences on the attitudes a student carries away from that class.

There are marked differences in the classroom climate across subject areas, teachers, age groups, and even from year to year. Just how these factors influence the development of attitudes toward science appears to be an important area of investigation. Equally important is the role that the teacher plays in shaping the classroom climate and its influence on fostering positive attitudes.

In summary, attitude towards science is a growing area for research, but attitudes are difficult to measure effectively, are perceived as generally low, and seem to reflect a declining image of science. There is a low positive correlation between science achievement and attitudes, and in addition, males generally express more positive attitudes towards science than females. Attitudes decline across age levels and exposure to science experience often produces negative attitude changes. Small curriculum and peer effects have been noted and some potential for enhancing science attitudes seems to exist with classroom environment, motivation and teacher behavior.

Bibliography

Aiken L R, Aiken D R 1969 Recent research on attitudes concerning science. *Sci. Educ.* 53: 295–305

Comber L C, Keeves J P 1973 *Science Education in Nineteen Countries: An Empirical Study.* Wiley, New York

Gardner P L 1975 Attitudes to science: A review. *Stud. Sci. Educ.* 2: 1–41

Haladyna T, Shaughnessy J 1982 Attitudes toward science: A quantitative synthesis. *Sci. Ed.* in press

Lapointe A E, Mead N A, Phillips G W 1988 *A World of Differences: An International Assessment of Mathematics and Science.* Educational Testing Service, Princeton, New Jersey

Mullis I V S, Jenkins L B 1988 *The Science Report Card: Elements of Risk and Recovery.* Educational Testing Service, Princeton, New Jersey

Murnane R J, Raizen S A 1988 *Improving Indicators of the Quality of Science and Mathematics Education in Grades K-12.* National Academy Press, Washington, DC

National Assessment of Educational Progress 1979 *Attitudes Toward Science.* Report 08-5-02. Education Commission of the States, Denver, Colorado

Ormerod M B, Duckworth D 1975 *Pupils Attitudes to Science: A Review of Research.* National Foundation for Educational Research, Slough

Walberg H J, Fraser B J, Welch W W 1986 A test of a model of educational productivity among senior high school students. *J. Educ. Res.* 79(3): 133–39

Welch W W Twenty years of science curriculum development: A look back. In: Berliner O (ed.) 1979 *Review of Research in Education.* American Educational Research Association, Washington, DC

Welch W W 1986 Attitudes toward science in the U.S.A.—Results from the 1981–82 national assessment. In: Lehrke M, Hoffman L, Gardner P (eds.) *Interests in Science and Technology.* Schmidt and Klaunig, Kiel, West Germany

Welch W W, Walberg H J, Fraser B F 1986 Predicting elementary science learning using national assessment data. *J. Res. Sci. Teach.* 23: 699–706

Willson V L 1983 A meta-analysis of the relationship between science achievement and science attitude. *J. Res. Sci. Teach.* 20: 839–50

Section 12

Physical Education

Overview

This Section provides an overview of major developments in physical education. According to present educational philosophy, the whole child is educated. Physical education, with the many kinds of activities offered to develop the whole child, has an important place in the school program.

Haag and Nixon suggest that the theoretical framework of a physical education program is based upon the disciplines of sport sciences (such as sport medicine, biomechanics, and psychology) and educational sciences (such as curriculum and instructional theory). The article, *Physical Education Programs*, discusses phases of program development in light of factors related to them, and identifies four phases—preconditions, planning, implementing and evaluating—and six factors which comprise sociological preconditions, anthropological preconditions, aims and objectives, content, instructional methods and organization, and the media.

Physical education curriculum planning relies heavily on Robinsohn's conception of a model which includes analyzing and social context, drawing conclusions concerning curricular aims and objectives, and selecting appropriate curriculum content and experiences. The analysis of the social context refers to the social situation of the individual, the class, the school and the society. The analysis of the anthropological context refers to the philosophical and anthropological concepts which are prevalent in a particular society regarding physical activity, body image, psychological and motor behaviors. Based upon this analysis, the program is designed with consideration of the motor, cognitive, and affective domains. Input evaluation from and about the student, as well as the role of the physical educator and the interactions between them, are very important steps in the design of physical education programs, along with planning, conducting, and evaluating them. Haag and Nixon discuss these steps in detail and conclude that sport education is one of the central theory fields of sport sciences, and that the field of physical education curricula is a fundamental field within sport education.

Pieron discusses the theory and practices of *Physical Education Instruction*, as part of the study of the teaching process. He defines the physical education area of knowledge as the study of the characteristics of human movement performed by individuals and the effects of motor activity on the physiological and psychological characteristics and the social environment of the individual. Physical education uses knowledge from many other disciplines, such as physiology, anatomy, psychology, and sociology. Two viewpoints are frequently considered: the academic discipline and the profession.

The concept of academic discipline assumes that the pursuit of knowledge in this area is self-justifying, and it requires the development of academic knowledge in exercise physiology and biochemistry, biomechanics, sports philosophy, psychology, sociology and history, all of which are included in teacher preparation programs. The profession, on the other hand, is supposed to pursue varied educational objectives, according to sociopolitical conditions. Professionals use knowledge from sport sciences and educational sciences in their practice.

In discussing practices in physical education instruction, Pieron refers to two different approaches: the "education of the physical," emphasizing health and fitness goals, and "education through the physical," associated with goals similar to those of general education. The greatest part of the theory of physical education instruction is an adaptation of general theories from education psychology. However, efforts have been made to establish specific research data regarding learning theory and motor skill learning sequences in order to facilitate the learning process. In order to understand these processes, studies are being conducted in the areas of teaching process, classroom climate, teacher behavior, teacher effectiveness, and teacher preparation.

The issue of attitudes towards physical education is generally dealt with within the framework of examination of attitudes toward school activities, in which the importance attributed to, or love of, physical education is subject to comparison to other school subjects. This is also examined in sport attitude studies (willingness to voluntarily get involved and adhere to sport participation in a particular sport field, discipline, organization, etc). In school attitude studies it was found that physical education has long been one of the best-liked school subjects in many countries. However, its popularity is relatively high in the early school years and gradually diminishes in the higher grade levels. The article on this subject, by Bielefeld, also analyzes some studies related to sport attitude as a predictor variable to participation in voluntary sport activities, adherence to and success in them, and the measurement of sport-specific attitudes. It concludes that despite the fact that research in this area has been conducted for many years, it is still premature to formulate structures or a coherent theory of specific attitudes towards sports, because of a methodological restriction of data gathering and simplistic statistical analysis. The topic of *Health Education* is dealt with in an article by Loupe.

H. Ruskin

Physical Education Instruction

M. Piéron

In the 1970s research in physical education teaching developed considerably by adopting several methodologies from the classroom teaching research model. The most striking progress occurred in the study of the teaching process. This research focused particularly on the study of teacher behaviour, pupil behaviour, and teacher–pupil interactions.

The physical education area of knowledge can be defined as the study of: (a) the characteristics of human movement performed by individuals, from the physically or mentally handicapped to the highest achiever or the top-level athlete; and (b) the effects of motor activity (from innate movement to especially devised exercises in formal gymnastics or to complex sports skills) on the physiological and psychological characteristics of individuals in their social environment. In its broadest interpretation, physical education focuses on the art and science of voluntary, purposeful human movement. Physical education uses knowledge from many other disciplines, for example, physiology, anatomy, psychology, and sociology. Located at a crossroads, it represents an attractive field of investigation for other specialities. Inside this framework, two viewpoints are frequently considered in introductory textbooks on physical education: the academic discipline and the profession. The concept of academic discipline emerged in the early 1960s. As in other fields, the basic assumption was that the pursuit of knowledge is self-justifying and that no immediate application has to be foreseen before it can be started. Several subdomains more or less related to physical education were developed: these included exercise physiology (including biochemistry of exercise), biomechanics, sports psychology, sports sociology, history of sports, and the philosophy of sports. Most of these subject matters are included in teacher preparation programmes. The bulk of academic knowledge gathered through research and the multidisciplinarian approach led to dissatisfaction with the term physical education. Yet, great difficulty has been experienced in replacing it. Several other terms such as "homokinetics", and "human movement sciences" were proposed to cover the field. Some of them did not meet with any success, others were more widely used, such as "sport sciences", an expression emanating from the audience of several preolympic international conferences.

The profession is supposed to pursue educational objectives that vary according to many sociopolitical conditions. These general objectives might include the development of a communist, individual, strong defender of the country and of the ideology, to the development of an autonomous individual able to adapt him/herself in society and be able to induce some changes in that society. The profession uses means such as games, exercises, sport, and systematic training to achieve its goals. Professionals should use knowledge from sports sciences and from educational sciences in their practice.

A shift of emphasis has occurred in recent years that broadens the basis of physical education programmes from a school-centred activity to lifetime and sports for all practice.

1. Practices and Theory

1.1 Practices

Two different approaches are currently referred to when considering physical education teaching. "Education-of-the-physical" has applied primarily to programmes of physical education emphasizing health and fitness goals where it is intended to develop endurance, strength, speed, and flexibility. "Education-through-the-physical" has been associated with activities and programmes whose goals are similar to goals of general education. Practices used in the approach "education-of-the-physical" are subject to strong influences from: (a) the imitation and adaptation of top-level sports practices and (b) research data dealing with the quantitative aspect of motor performance. The effects of the programmes are measured by well devised tests. The means used to improve physical fitness are largely justified by specific research. Methods, such as interval training, power training, and isometric exercises could be applied under strict control conditions. Their effects are well known and largely foreseeable. It must be pointed out that some practical innovations have been implemented very quickly in physical education teaching. They have resulted from the success of top athletes in worldwide competitions rather than from theoretical or research breakthroughs. The most striking example is the Fosbury flop style of high jumping. It was taught just a few weeks after the victory of this athlete at the Mexico Olympic Games in 1968. Other examples are available.

In the "education-through-the-physical" approach, the achievement of educational objectives and of learning aims in complex situations is considerably more difficult to appraise than the quantitative aspects of physical fitness. Physical education is faced with the same kind of evaluation problems which are encountered in classroom teaching. Variables that could validly represent teacher effectiveness are frequently out of reach.

Although the two approaches differ largely, means used in teaching are often identical. They can be organized and classified according to many standpoints.

1.2 Theory of Physical Education Instruction

The greatest part of this theory remains still largely inferential or simply an adaptation of general theories from educational psychology. For example, in Europe, Rogers, Piaget, Wallon, and many other scientists exerted a strong influence on the theories sustaining several school physical education curricula. Nevertheless, efforts have been made to help physical education teachers found their educational actions on specific research data. Two main sources of inspiration can be identified. Learning theory and the motor skill learning sequences were the first aspects to be developed. It is assumed that once the learning of sports skills is understood, it can be inferred how teachers can facilitate the learning process. The second source is to be found in classroom research and can be organized according to the "presage–process–product" paradigm.

Gentile (1972) developed a model substantiated by research data, which illustrates the dynamics of motor skill learning. The model explaining motor skill acquisition can be summarized as follows. The learner: (a) perceives what is to be learnt and desires to try; (b) identifies the relevant stimuli in the environment; (c) formulates a motor plan; (d) emits a response; (e) evaluates the result; (f) revises the motor plan; (g) emits another response. This model was used to classify and summarize most of the research related to the motor skill acquisition that could be helpful to the teacher (Nixon and Locke 1972). It deals with relevant stimuli for the learner (research on whole and parts, level of difficulty, progression, simulation, demonstration, practice without instruction, programmed learning, principles, attention, and distraction), directions for performance (motor plans, speed, and accuracy sets), feedback (open and closed skills, knowledge of performance, knowledge of results, feedback media), guided adjustment of performance (learning strategies, incentive motivation, mental practice), and pace and sequence of practice (distribution of practice, mastery, and advanced phases of practice). It is important to know and understand the nature of a motor skill proposed to pupils. Data generated from the motor learning research have provided teachers with greater insight and information about processes involved in motor skill acquisition. Unfortunately, that type of research gives little information to teachers about how to teach or how to help pupils learn a motor skill. Moreover, tasks frequently used in motor learning research are so far removed from sports skill that they often appear to be meaningless to physical education teachers.

Physical education contributes to the general educational aims of the school. It must abide by the same laws and regulations as other subjects. Coeducation and mainstreaming in the United States are two examples. It is therefore logical to find a trend to use data, adopt ideas, or research methodologies from the field of classroom teaching research in physical education teaching research.

There are enough discrepancies between the characteristics of classroom teaching and of physical education teaching to make generalization from one context to the other a matter of substantial concern. Many classroom teaching researchers emphasized that their findings were probably highly specific. It is amazing to observe the absence of caution of physical education researchers when adopting these data. Examples of hasty generalizations are easy to find in interaction analysis, in the guided discovery approach, and in the expectancy phenomenon.

Some characteristics of physical education teaching must be emphasized before interpreting data gathered in physical education teaching research according to the classroom model. The specificity of physical education has to be pointed out in many aspects: (a) the objectives (priority is given to "doing" rather than to "knowing"), and the status (physical education is not considered as a subject to be promoted); (b) motivation must be found within pupils rather than induced extrinsically through grades; (c) the structure of performance (achievement and performance of both teacher and pupils are highly visible, weaknesses and fear of participation cannot be hidden); and (d) the organization of the class (space and more freedom to move).

As reported earlier, the research data gathered in the field of teaching physical education can be organized around the well-known "presage–process–product" paradigm. Presage studies have failed to identify the common characteristics of successful teachers. Typical variables investigated have included teachers' age, sex, teaching preparation and/or experience, attitude towards teaching, and personality traits.

Research based on the product could be tentatively entitled "In search of the perfect method of teaching". The physical education domain has been particularly receptive to this approach and prone to use it in research. In several countries and especially in Europe, teaching physical education has been characterized for many years by what could be labelled a "war of methods". Methods have been advocated by charismatic initiators who strongly supported the method A versus method B research methodology.

It is not surprising that research has failed to substantiate a superior method. Individual differences among pupils, in terms of interests, values, needs, attitudes, and abilities preclude any single system from meeting the requirements of all pupils.

In the 1970s, these studies were harshly criticized by authors taking their research models in the science of education. Several weaknesses were underscored in the product research. These were: (a) a lack of control over the content; (b) ignorance as to how this content is transmitted to pupils (what is going on in the class); and (c) use of inadequate evaluation instruments.

2. Study of the Teaching Process

Finding out what is happening in a physical education class has been considered as something like looking into a black box. There is not a clear image of the events occurring during teaching yet. In physical education, the first attempts to systematically record behaviours and teacher–pupil interactions with a minimum of observer bias occurred in the late 1960s and in the early 1970s. Limited at the beginning to a few doctoral dissertations presented in United States universities, teaching analysis spread into Canada and Europe. Later on it provoked a strong interest in Australia and in Latin America. This interest has been sustained. International meetings dealing with the subject provide a good illustration of this development. In 1974/75, a few papers appeared unnoticed in physical education congresses. Five years later, sections of important congresses or/ and complete seminars were devoted to the subject (Schilling and Baur 1980, Haag et al. 1981).

Finding a single framework within which to classify studies dealing with what is going on in a class seems to be difficult and hazardous. Classification entries are multiple according to: the communication mode (verbal–nonverbal), the categories of teachers involved (master teachers, student teachers, coaches), the class or population taught (elementary level, junior- or senior-high school, mainstreamed classes), and the educational theory sustaining the teaching strategies (direct and indirect approaches).

For the purposes of this presentation, it is necessary to distinguish between teacher behaviours, pupil behaviours, classroom climate and content of teaching. It must be kept in mind that all of these variables are strongly interrelated. Inevitably, teachers influence the development of their pupils, who in turn provoke the teachers' reactions and influence their behaviours. One is faced with a double causality phenomenon. It will be taken into account when interpreting data provided by observation. Researchers have had the choice of existing observation systems or specifically devised systems.

The use of existing systems can be viewed from the perspective that physical education is one of many educational subjects and, as such, attempts to achieve general educational objectives, as well as its specific aims. Studies are needed to answer questions such as: how well does physical education fulfil educational aims; how much does physical education differ from other subject matter? Studies using the Cheffers Adaptation of Flanders Interaction Analysis System (CAFIAS) are the best examples of this trend (Cheffers et al. 1981).

The development of original observation systems demonstrates an intention to take into account the specific aims of physical education teaching, its specific structure of performance, and its variety of teaching environments. The Video Data Bank Project from Teachers College, Columbia University, represents an example of this trend (Anderson and Barrette 1978).

In accordance with chronological development, this review will start with studies which have dealt with the emotional climate of the class, leading to those concerned with teacher and pupil behaviours.

2.1 Classroom Climate

The Flanders observation system of verbal interactions between teacher and pupils can be considered as the starting point for many studies describing the teaching of physical education. The approach relies on several assumptions. The teacher would exert two types of influence on the class, namely a dominant, authoritarian, direct influence and/or an integrative, democratic influence. Using direct influence, teachers control the decision-making process. They exert this influence by lecturing, giving directions, or justifying their authority. They are supposed to provoke submission from the pupil and realize a decrease of teaching efficiency unless continuously stimulating the pupils. In an indirect approach, teachers involve pupils in the decision-making process. Their motivations are considered to be higher than in classes directed by a dominant teacher. In this approach, teachers welcome pupils' feelings and use their ideas and suggestions. They mainly utilize psychological reinforcement through the use of praise and frequent questions are asked.

In physical education classes, direct influence has been found to prevail overwhelmingly, frequently in a ratio approximately equal to 8 to 1. The dominant direct approach has also been confirmed by other observation methods. A ratio close to 10 to 1 between teacher talk and pupil talk has frequently been reported. These ratios reflect only a global view of the interaction. It must be emphasized that the adequacy of each approach must be linked more accurately to the objectives to be fulfilled.

Correlation studies have evidenced a strong stability of the teacher–pupil interactions showing in some way a lack of flexibility in the pedagogical approach used by physical education teachers. This observation has been made of student teachers as well as experienced teachers.

In physical education, the Flanders system has been strongly criticized because it is confined to the study of verbal interactions in a domain wherein the essential pupils' participation is of a motor nature. The most interesting adaptation designed to overcome the weaknesses in physical education was made by Cheffers in a system which accounted for nonverbal behaviours, for teaching agencies other than just the teacher (such as other pupils or the environment), and which describe classes other than the "traditional classroom" (Cheffers et al. 1981). In this observation schedule, each verbal intervention is paralleled by a nonverbal category. For example, corresponding to a verbal category, "predictable students' responses that require some measure of evaluation, synthesis, and interpretation from the student" is a nonverbal category reflecting "arrangement that requires interpretative thinking", for example, works on gymnastic routine or game playing.

Studies have been conducted to verify methodologies, to determine sex differences, to describe teaching with special populations, and to estimate and predict behaviours. Comparisons between male and female teachers, and between elementary and secondary teachers have revealed minimal differences in category usage and in interaction parameters and patterns. Teachers used lecture and direction as their overwhelmingly predominant mode of teaching. Virtually no acceptance of student feelings and ideas, questioning behaviours, or genuine student-initiated activity were recorded (Cheffers et al. 1981).

Studies using a Flanders or adapted Flanders systems seem to reflect a strong commitment to the assumptions of teaching effects expected from direct and indirect approaches. The educational meaning of several variables used, for example in the Cheffers Adaptation of the Flanders Interaction Analysis System, are still unexplained. Some studies have fallen into a kind of formalism in dealing with data gathered through this observational system.

2.2 Teachers' Behaviours

Teachers are accountable for what is happening in a class and are the primary decision makers. Tasks on which pupils have to spend time are defined and identified mostly by teachers. Therefore it is understandable that many studies aimed at finding out what is occurring in the sports class have started by emphasizing teachers' behaviours. Nevertheless, it is important to remain realistic about the probable magnitude of the effects of a teachers' intervention. Educational and learning outcomes can be explained only as the result of an interplay of numerous factors.

Observation studies of teachers' behaviours can be categorized into two groups: (a) description of a comprehensive profile of teachers' interventions and behaviours (Anderson and Barrette 1978, Piéron 1982); and (b) multidimensional analysis of specific interventions supposed to be essential in the teaching process or to facilitate the motor skill development (Piéron and Delmelle 1981). Theoretically, there are three kinds of such behaviours: presentation of the task or of subject matter; feedback on the performance; and organization and management of the class. In fact, in many studies, these three sets of behaviours have accounted for the biggest part of all observed behaviours.

Affectivity has been found to represent only a small amount of observed behaviours. Teachers spent a high portion of time in silently observing pupils. It has been observed also that teachers did not spend long periods of time performing uninterrupted functions but rather continuously shifted from one behaviour to another, seemingly attempting to keep up with the needs of the students and demands of the learning environment in a reactive or reflective sense (Anderson and Barrette 1978) (see Table 1).

Functions of organization or management account frequently for more than 20 percent of the total verbal teaching events. A high level of managerial behaviour seems to characterize the teaching of physical education. These interventions are concerned with statements dealing with equipment, discipline, and conduct of the class, with the pace of exercises imposed by the teacher and commands at the start and the end of an activity. The managerial behaviours reflect a praiseworthy concern to provide pupils with the best possible conditions to

Table 1
Teaching behaviours: 20 elementary and 20 secondary physical education classes (data from Anderson and Barrette 1978)

	Mean	S.D.	Elementary	Secondary
(a) *Active instructional functions*				
Preparatory instructing	14.2	10.5	15.5	12.7
Concurrent instructing	17.2	11.9	19.0	14.8
Intervening instructing	5.7	5.1	4.7	6.6
(b) *Observation*				
Observing	20.5	13.5	19.2	22.7
(c) *Managing pupils and environment functions*				
Organizing	7.5	4.4	7.6	6.5
Providing equipment	2.1	2.1	2.0	2.2
Administering	4.7	5.1	2.5	6.8
Establishing and enforcing codes of behaviours	1.9	2.1	2.5	1.4
(d) *Instruction-related function*				
Officiating	8.0	8.9	6.5	8.5
Spotting	0.6	2.0	0.7	0.7
Leading exercises	1.2	1.2	1.2	1.1
Participating	1.1	3.3	1.7	0.3
Other interacting related to motor activities	6.7	3.6	7.1	5.7
Other noninteractive intervals	8.6		9.8	10.0

practise a skill and to repeat it as many times as possible. Effective managerial behaviours are prerequisite conditions for efficient learning. However, these behaviours do not produce a direct educational effect on the learner.

As far as teaching efficiency is concerned, there is no single particular method for organizing a class. However, it is sound organization that seems to be a characteristic of effective teachers. Several differences in the pattern of the organizational events probably could differentiate between more and less effective teachers. Compared with inexperienced teachers, master teachers have been found to use fewer organization events in managing classes. Transition time was lower in master teachers' classes. Organizing, locating, or relocating pupils, and starting an activity needed less time with master teachers. Moreover, the allocated time for practice was converted into more time-on-task (Piéron 1982).

It is amazing to observe that research has gathered very little data on how specific content information is provided to pupils in physical education classes. An alternative is generally envisioned for the teacher: (a) providing or giving the information; (b) seeking the information or helping the pupil to seek the information by a guided discovery approach or problem-solving process. Usually observation systems describe the subject matter content only through global and rather inaccurate categories such as lecturing, asking questions, or input. It arises in several studies that teachers ask few questions regarding the cognitive content of physical activities (Anderson and Barrette 1978). When used in physical education, the guided discovery approach seemed to be a formal copy of what is done in the classroom. It was frequently characterized by poorly formulated questions involving very few students in the problem-solving process. Asking questions to the whole class generally leads to high nonengaged time and to frequent off-task behaviours from pupils.

The popular concept that physical education teachers use skill demonstration or visual aids to provide pupils with a performance model is generally unsupported by observation data. In the Video Data Bank Research Project demonstrations were scarce. Sophisticated visual aids like charts, loop films, or videotape recordings were almost nonexistent (Anderson and Barrette 1978). In another study, it was observed that master teachers used more accurate models than novices (Piéron 1982).

In learning a motor skill, individuals gain information about their responses with no external help. It is feedback inherent in the task itself, namely intrinsic feedback. Informative or augmented feedback is information given to a learner, designed to help him/her repeat correct behaviours, eliminate incorrect behaviours, and achieve the desired outcome. The need for informative feedback to improve and sustain performance is an essential learning experience.

Motor performance fails to improve unless augmented feedback is provided. Furthermore, performance improves with informative feedback and will either deteriorate or show no further improvement if informative feedback is withdrawn.

Feedback can be considered to be located at a crossroads of learning and teaching. In teaching, informative feedback exceeds a mere knowledge of results or information gained about the correctness or incorrectness of one's behaviours.

Most of process occurrence studies related to augmented feedback can be distributed among three categories which attempt to answer questions related to: (a) the quantitative role played by feedback in the total teacher–pupil relationship; (b) the distribution of positive versus negative aspects of evaluation; and (c) the complex structure of feedback studied through multidimensional analysis.

Most observation schedules of teacher behaviours devote a category to feedback. Feedback occurrence has been shown to be extremely variable: from less than 10 percent to more than 25 percent of the behaviours recorded and from less than one feedback to approximately four per minute. Master teachers have been observed to give significantly more frequent feedback than student teachers (Piéron 1982).

The amount of negative feedback exceeds positive evaluations. Positive evaluations are provided without any further comment. Many teachers justify their negative feedback by giving specific information and allowing pupils to become more aware of their errors.

Multidimensional observation systems have been devised to study feedback as a central element of the analysis. These studies aim at describing mostly form, content, intent, general and specific referents, and direction of feedback.

In several studies, large differences have appeared in the structure of augmented feedback. From 25 to 50 percent of feedback took an evaluative aspect by which teachers informed learners about their performance using a positive or negative sentence. Teachers frequently neglected to provide them with specific information related to the performance. It seemed that teachers only intended to rate the performance rather than to seek for some behaviour modification by reinforcement techniques. In addition to its evaluative aspect, augmented feedback was observed to be verbal and to emphasize the cognitive aspect of performance. A prescriptive intent was predominant. It was overwhelmingly directed toward a single pupil, referring to the whole form of movement. Specific information referred to space rather than to the rate or to the force of movement (Piéron and Delmelle 1982) (see Table 2).

Two important questions about feedback need to be asked. One relates to the origin of feedback in the pupils' observation and the other to its effectiveness in changing pupils' motor behaviours. Before emitting feedback, teachers need to analyse both the skill and factors critical to proficiency as well as identify aspects of the response which are preventing the pupil from

Table 2
Distribution of types of informative feedback and
gymnastics; feedback, n = 3,341 (Piéron and Delmelle 1982)

	Gymnastics		Volleyball	
	Mean	Min–Max	Mean	Min–Max
(a) *Intent*				
Evaluative	34.7	16.1–47.8	27.3	22.0–33.6
Descriptive	23.4	16.5–29.9	25.7	17.4–34.2
Prescriptive	28.9	19.8–43.1	41.2	31.7–46.5
Affective	5.5	1.6–17.7	4.3	1.5–11.1
Interrogative	7.5	0.0–18.1	1.5	0.3– 3.7
(b) *Content*				
No content	39.6	23.4–56.3	28.3	21.4–39.1
Cognitive	52.9	35.7–65.8	63.6	49.3–72.3
Perceptive	7.5	1.1–14.6	8.0	1.5–17.4
(c) *Form*				
Auditory	85.5	72.4–92.2	83.9	71.2–92.8
Tactile	1.4	0.0– 4.8	0.3	0.0– 0.7
Visual	0.7	0.0– 1.8	1.4	0.0– 4.3
Auditory-tactile	6.3	1.1–12.7	2.8	0.0– 9.8
Auditory-visual	6.2	2.7– 9.5	11.6	3.3–18.6
(d) *Direction*				
Class	16.4	9.1–29.1	13.3	5.6–30.7
Group	7.0	1.0–13.9	12.5	2.8–28.3
Individual	76.6	65.2–89.9	74.2	61.9–91.1

attaining the skill objective. Teachers have to make decisions about the pupils' needs. Is additional practice or supplementary information needed? In the first case, encouragement and not information must be provided. Teachers can modify the task presented to meet the needs of individuals. Among the first results in detecting performance errors, novice teachers raised more false alarms, that is, they reported the presence of an error when the error was not demonstrated in the illustration, more often than experienced teachers. Longer teaching experience seemed to increase the tendency to identify performance error rather than proficiency in the sports observed.

2.3 Pupils' Behaviours

The importance of communication in the teaching process clearly justifies the analysis of verbal interactions in a class or of teachers' interventions even in physical education. Nevertheless one cannot guess pupils' learning gains by relying only on teachers' interventions. Recently researchers have moved from a primary concern with teachers' behaviours to other instructional variables and especially pupil variables. Everyone realizes that interaction is a two-way phenomenon. It is clear that the pupils' ability and behaviours influence interactions and therefore are associated with teaching behaviours. The first attempt to appraise the teaching process using the pupils as starting points pursued only descriptive purposes. The focus had been placed on a

pupil's motor activity during class time. One of the striking conclusions was that subject matter whose objective was movement was mostly characterized by nonmovement periods.

Several approaches are used to "measure" pupils' behaviours: (a) observation of a target pupil—a pupil is randomly selected and his/her behaviours are timed or recorded according to an event observation schedule; (b) spot checking or planned activity check which involves quickly scanning the behaviours of several or all pupils during a short time interval and classifying the behaviours of each student into categories; (c) recording at a given time interval the behaviours showed by the majority of pupils (Siedentop 1976).

Studies based on pupil observation gained some momentum from the trends in teacher effectiveness research. Pupils' activities are central to their learning. The total amount of active learning time on a particular motor skill seems to be the most important determinant of pupil achievement on that motor skill. Most physical educators share a concern for improving the pupils' proficiency in motor skills. Since improved achievement comes with practice most teachers are reasonably committed to providing adequate amounts of practice for their pupils.

Several variables around the concepts of time and of time-on-task according to learning opportunities have received attention. In physical education classes there is an enormous variation for different pupils in time needed to learn a task, and in the total amount of active learning time. Inspired by the Beginning Teacher Evaluation Study research programme, Siedentop adapted to physical education teaching the variable labelled academic learning time (ALT) and made it more specific with the academic learning time (physical education)-motor or ALT(PE)-M. The ALT was defined as the portion of engaged time in which the pupil is performing at a low error rate. The ALT is used with the underlying assumption that improvement in this variable is related to improved pupil achievement. From Siedentop's perspective, when achievement is difficult to measure as for some physical education learning objectives, time-on-task becomes a legitimate substitute for pupils' achievement. The constructed variable of ALT stands between measures of teaching and measures of student learning gains.

In physical education teaching, descriptive studies have stressed the point that the level of motor activity was relatively low. It was estimated to amount frequently to less than 30 percent and ALT studies confirmed this (Brunelle et al. 1981). Large and significant differences have been observed according to the subject matter taught. For example, pupil engagement time was significantly lower in gymnastics or in track and field sports, than in team sports like basketball and volleyball. To conclude that activities which enable less time-on-task are of less educational value must be resisted and discarded. The lower ALT or time-on-task stressed different teaching or management problems to keep students strongly engaged. Differences between sex or grade level were observed to be of less magnitude.

The use of time by pupils is characterized by a "funnelling" effect from an allocated time to physical education, to an individual engaged time. Comparison between master teachers and beginning or/and student teachers seemed to confirm that the magnitude of this "funnelling" effect could reflect partially teacher effectiveness. Although the relationship is probably not linear, time-on-task is expected to be a strong positive correlate of pupils' achievement. However, experimental teaching units underscored that the time-on-task variable has to be stated more precisely before gaining full predictive value to teacher effectiveness in physical education. The specificity of the tasks practised and the level of success achieved in performing the task must be taken into account. Significant sports skill learning occurs only when some prerequisite level of performance is fulfilled.

"Not engaged time", a counterpart of time-on-task, seems to be negatively related to teachers' effectiveness. Some behaviours considered as nonproductive as far as learning objectives are concerned were observed to last a large amount of class time, sometimes exceeding 35 percent. The waiting time was found to be positively related to the occurrence of off-task behaviours (see Table 3).

2.4 Some Current Perspectives in Teacher Effectiveness

Although descriptive studies have multiplied in recent years, they are still far from providing the profession with a complete image of the way the teaching–learning phenomenon occurs in physical education classes. They still remain limited in scope and extent. Up to now, descriptions of teachers' and pupils' behaviours have focused on comparisons according to sex, to grade level, and sometimes to lesson format. Differences according to these criteria were found to be slight. More striking discrepancies were evidenced when the specialities taught were considered. Teachers' and pupils' behaviours were observed to differ considerably in track and field sports, gymnastics, and dual or team sports lessons. Many observed behaviours seem to be situation specific.

Observational studies helped to point out that many teaching behaviours differed largely from those expected or advocated by methodologists or by actual theories of physical education teaching. These differences concerned the lesson content, the emotional climate of the class, the frequency and the structure of several teacher's interventions, and the time devoted to movement in physical education lessons. Many descriptive studies are still needed before gaining a clear image of what teaching physical education looks like and before there can be an identification of the significant variables in this area.

Recently, a strong interest has developed in describing teacher effectiveness. This trend followed a research methodology or research ideas emerging from the same movement in general education. The process–product approach is still limited to experimental teaching units. Teachers are presented with identical objectives and they are left free to prepare and implement the instruction. Pupils' achievement is evaluated during pre- and post-test evaluation. Throughout the teaching unit, multifaceted teacher and pupil observation data are collected. This kind of study is intended to control certain sources of variation left uncontrolled in the more complex setting of physical education teaching.

Two main questions need to be answered: (a) Is there any correlation between different types or patterns of teaching and gains in motor skill learning? (b) Are there teachers who produce greater changes than other teachers? What makes the difference between more or less effective teachers? Correlational studies showed that the pupils' initial and final level of ability were strongly related and that the teachers' behaviours could explain only a very small part of the total variance (Yerg 1981). The short duration of experimental teaching units could be held partially accountable for this lack of teacher influence. It must be remembered that in motor activity the pupil can learn quite a lot from practising alone. The teacher's role seems to be favouring the learning process and avoiding some dead ends for the learner obstructing his/her progress further. Comparison of less and more effective classes as far as learning is concerned underlined the role of the time-on-task variable in more effective classes. Specificity of the task performed by learners and the level of success of this performance account for a large part of learning opportunities.

Table 3
Distribution of pupil behaviours according to school level and to teaching experience, percentages of time spent in different behaviours

	Junior-high school	Senior-high school	Master teachers	Student teachers
Engaged time	20.9	8.4	20.8	15.2
Information receiving	45.7	33.6	34.5	14.4
Waiting	17.1	35.6	22.1	40.8
Managerial	5.8	8.4	15.2	17.9
Various	10.5	14.0	7.4	11.7

Due partly to the lack of money available to study physical education teaching, full-scale process–product studies are unlikely to be seen in the near future. A shift has been observed from the present interest in investigating pupils' outcomes (over which teachers have little control) to the use of pupils' time (over which teachers have some more control). The state of physical education teaching research is still far from knowing the right thing to do at the right time for the right student.

3. Teacher Preparation

It is impossible to provide a universal image of teacher preparation in physical education. Several international inquiries have clearly shown the diversity to be found in this area. The duration and the status of preparation range from a one-, two-, or three-year professional preparation in technical superior schools to a five-year preparation in universities. The first type of study precludes any multidisciplinary contact and any kind of research. In several universities physical education institutions have gained a full recognition and a faculty status. They are strongly involved in research.

The content of teacher preparation is extremely diversified. More than 150 course titles from the human sciences, sciences, and biomedical sciences domains were listed by Cagigal (1977) in an international inquiry involving approximately 100 institutions throughout the world. A strong emphasis is still maintained on the health and fitness aspects of physical education in the teacher preparation.

In a very well-documented review of the American literature, Locke and Dodds (1981) have allocated studies according to presage variables (trainee characteristics), programme variables (programme characteristics), content variables (what is learned), process variables (microteaching, early field experiences, student teaching), product variables (programme impact on trainee and teacher behaviours), research (methods and management of the knowledge base), and programme change. These authors reported numerous studies dealing with trainee characteristics with most of them comparing physical education majors with students from other subjects. Their results seem to have very low predictive value. In the United States, studies evaluating programmes by the application of score cards are frequently reported.

Many articles developing, describing, and comparing programmes in different countries can be found in the international literature. They could be labelled as "programme-sharing experiences". They are very limited in scope and implications.

A strong interest toward studying teaching skills and competencies, their learning, and their modification developed in the 1970s. Within the competency-based teacher education movement, teacher competencies lists were established. Usually they are devised from the professional literature and then submitted to experts

to be validated. As data consist only of opinions, conclusions deserve only the credibility awarded to opinions.

In physical education, microteaching received very limited research attention as a technique helping the trainee to learn some specific teaching skills (Graham 1973). Teaching analysis contributed to the identification of the most frequently occurring behaviours in teaching. It produced a profound reflection on the significance and value of various teacher interventions. That provoked some important changes in the content of methods courses.

Two kinds of studies are used in the framework aiming to answer two questions: (a) To what extent does training in a teaching analysis system affect teacher–pupil interactions? (b) Is it possible to change teaching behaviours through interventions like feedback, specific objectives, and so on?

Teaching analysis used as an independent variable to study the effect of training in teaching analysis produced some divergent results that could perhaps be explained by the length of implementation periods used in the studies. Nevertheless, other findings lend support to the theory that the combined use of instruction in the knowledge and practical application of interaction analysis and the review of videotapes in the supervision and preparation of teachers are beneficial (Cheffers et al. 1981).

Teachers' behaviours were shown to be changed by a behaviour modification programme including goals, explanatory materials, regular observation, feedback, and graphing. It was shown in a programmed research effort at Ohio State University that it is possible to decrease the teachers' management intervention rate, to reduce time spent in silently observing pupils, to increase positive interventions and positive feedback, and to use more frequently pupils' first names. All these modifications could be implemented without negatively affecting pupils' engagement. However, when intervention treatment is withdrawn, the teaching behaviours changed partially in the direction of the original data. This incomplete reversal would indicate some degree of permanent behaviour change (Siedentop 1981).

Student teaching is the most common means used to provide school experience. It is retained as a required final step of professional preparation. In several countries (US, USSR), the use of internship is increasing. Benefits expected from the student teaching experience include opportunities to develop teaching skills, understand children and youth, and increase knowledge about the schools.

Besides the behaviour modification studies already reported, research on student teaching has tended to focus on the university supervisor, the cooperating teacher, and the student teacher triad in describing accurately the supervision conference and in identifying the most striking problems occurring during the student teaching experience. The critical incident technique underlined a strong desire by the student teacher to be awarded complete control of the class (total responsibility for preparing lessons and for conducting instruction) and an urgent need to receive documented, nonthreatening, and frequent feedback (Brunelle et al. 1981).

As a result of their literature review, Locke and Dodds (1981) noticed that graduates generally were satisfied with their preparation and considered student teaching to be the most helpful part of their training. Graduates complained that several courses were too theoretical and that they felt unprepared to cope effectively with class discipline and coeducational classes, or to deal with individual differences among pupils.

Bibliography

Anderson W G, Barrette G T 1978 *What's Going on in Gym: Descriptive Studies of Physical Education Classes.* Motor Skills, Newton, Connecticut

Association Internationale des Ecoles Supérieures d'Education Physique 1981 *Study of Teaching Physical Education, Teacher Effectiveness, Teacher Students Interactions and Related Subjects: A Bibliography.* University of Liège, Belgium

Brunelle J, Tousignant M, Piéron M 1981 Student teachers' perceptions of cooperating teachers' effectiveness. *J. Teach. Phys. Educ.* Introductory Issue: 80–87

Cagigal J M 1977 *Las Escuelas de educación física en el mondo.* Instituto Nacional Educación Fisica, Madrid

Cheffers J T F, Amidon E J, Rodgers K D 1981 *Interaction Analysis: An Application to Nonverbal and Verbal Activity.* Association for Productive Teaching, Minneapolis, Minnesota

Gentile A M 1972 A working model of skill acquisition with application to teaching. *Quest* 17: 3–23

Graham G M 1973 The effects of a micro-teaching laboratory on the ability of teacher trainees to teach a novel motor skill to fifth and sixth grade children (Doctoral dissertation, University of Oregon)

Haag H et al. 1981 Sporterziehung und Evaluation. *Physical Education and Evaluation: Proceedings of the 17th International Council on Health, Physical Education and Recreation World Congress*, Kiel, July 23–27, 1979. Hofmann, Schorndorf

Locke L F, Dodds P 1981 *Research on Preservice Teacher Education for Physical Education.* Artus, Rio de Janeiro, pp 60–67

Nixon J E, Locke L F 1972 Research on teaching physical education. In: Travers R M W (ed.) 1972 *Second Handbook of Research on Teaching: A Project of the American Educational Research Association.* Rand McNally, Chicago, Illinois

Piéron M 1982 *Analyse de l'enseignement des activités physiques.* Ministère de l'Education Nationale et de la Culture Francaise, Brussels

Piéron M, Delmelle R 1982 *Descriptive Study of Teacher Feedback in Two Educational Situations.* Artus, Rio de Janeiro pp. 193–96

Schilling G, Baur W 1980 *Audiovisuelle Medien im Sport: Moyens Audiovisuels dans le Sport.* [*Audiovisual Means in Sports*]. Birkhauser, Basel

Siedentop D 1976 *Developing Teaching Skills in Physical Education.* Houghton Mifflin, Boston, Massachusetts

Siedentop D 1981 The Ohio State University Supervision Research Program Summary Report. *J. Teach. Phys. Educ.* Introductory Issue: 30–38

Yerg B J 1981 Reflections on the use of the RTE model in physical education. *Res. Quart. Exercise and Sport* 52: 38–47

Physical Education Programs

H. Haag and J. E. Nixon

The theoretical framework of physical education programs is anchored in the disciplines of sport sciences and educational sciences. Sport pedagogy is directly related to these two broad areas of scholarly endeavor, the development of physical education programs being a particular area of concern within the framework of sport pedagogy. Description of such programs and their analysis require reference to the theoretical construct from educational sciences (particularly from curriculum and instructional theory) and the sport sciences such as sport medicine, sport biomechanics, sport psychology, and so on (see *Curriculum Theory*).

Physical education programs and their rationale are usually described in terms of dynamic processes and static factors. The first group refers to phases in the process of program development and the second, to the preconditions and the product of the development process. This article examines the various phases of program development in the light of the factors which bear relationship to them. The four phases to be discussed are preconditions, planning, implementing, and evaluating. The six factors related to these phases are sociocultural preconditions, anthropological preconditions, aims and objectives, content, instructional methods and organization, and finally, media.

1. Preconditions of Program Planning

Sport-specific curriculum planning relies heavily on Robinsohn's (1969) conception suggesting a three-phase model which includes (a) analyzing the social context; (b) drawing conclusions concerning curricula aims and objectives; and (c) selecting appropriate curriculum contents and elements to provide effective educational experiences.

Within this widely used curriculum model, two factors are crucial for understanding the social context well, namely, the sociocultural preconditions and the anthropological preconditions of physical education instruction.

1.1 Sociocultural Preconditions of Physical Education Programs

These preconditions are very complex. They can be presented as four interacting major types of preconditions starting with the individual and continuing to expand to the global characteristics of a specific society in a given time frame.

(a) *Social situation of the individual.* According to Grupe (1969), movement has instrumental, exploratory, social, and personal meanings. The social meaning of movement is of special relevance because movement and movement actions are socially determined. Through movement, nonverbal social communication takes place. Research relating to social stratification and social mobility has indicated that members of the upper-middle classes show the highest rate of participation in sport.

It is also obvious that the type of sport involvement varies according to social class. Eggert and Schuck (1975) have shown that with preschool children there is a positive correlation between intelligence, motor behavior, and social status. It can be asserted that the social environment of the individual is largely responsible for the degree of access to sport available to him or her for the levels of motor development achieved by children in general.

(b) *Social situations in the class/group.* Research has shown that the social structure of a class or similar group is related to the kind and amount of physical activity engaged in. The physical environment, group composition, and group structure are of relevance to educational progress made by the participants (Landers et al. 1981).

(c) *Social situation in the school/club.* Social institutions are closely connected with sport. This relationship also occurs in schools (Snyder and Spreitzer 1981), in sport organizations, and in sport clubs (Lüschen 1981). This dimension of institutional organization must be considered closely in analyzing the preconditions for physical education programs.

(d) *Social situation today.* Finally, a complete time span (e.g., the 1980s) has to be taken into consideration as an important factor in determining the type of physical education activities and programs to be sanctioned by society.

1.2 Anthropological Preconditions of Physical Education Programs

These preconditions relate to the students and physical education teachers. With regard to the student, the following aspects have to be taken into consideration (Grössing 1981):

(a) The interpretation of a person's body based on philosophical and anthropological concepts (Grupe 1969) including instrumental, exploratory, social, and personal meanings.

(b) Development as a basic process of natural maturation, especially in regard to phases and signs of human growth and development related to body image, psychosocial behaviors, and to motor behaviors which are sanctioned by the parent society at a given time.

(c) The "problem" pupil and his or her causal links with hereditary defects and environment deprivation that may contribute to weak performance, fear, and unacceptable social behaviors.

In order to plan an effective physical education program it is important to consider sport-specific input data for each student which relate to:

(a) the motor domain—development of basic motor capacities, skills, and abilities to participate in a sport discipline;

(b) the cognitive domain—development of sport-specific knowledge and understanding;

(c) the affective domain—development of sport-relevant attitudes, values, and behavior patterns.

Input evaluation from and about the student is very important. If output evaluation is done carefully, the results also can be used partially as input data in order to plan appropriate physical education programs. Output evaluation refers to pupil demonstration of current skills and abilities in various sports, of knowledge and understanding about major concepts involved in the physical education curriculum, as well as of derived behavior patterns and attitudes.

In regard to the physical education teacher, the following aspects must be taken into consideration (Grössing 1981).

The role of the physical education teacher depends to a great extent on the professional training received previously. A new model, developed by the German Sport Federation (1975), which has received recent recognition, and is geared towards competency-based teacher training, proposes four competencies for physical education teacher excellence, namely sportive, scientific, instructional, and political knowledge bases.

The professional role is still misunderstood by other teachers and the general public. The feeling of being underprivileged and unrecognized still exists widely. This image can only be overcome by selecting teachers and coaches with strong, intelligent personalities into the field of physical education and sport, who can demonstrate the excellence of their instructional competencies and the mastery of the basic concepts which undergird their academic discipline, physical education, and sport.

Appropriate teaching behaviors are important preconditions for the realization of sound physical education instructional programs. Three major teaching styles are commonly recognized, namely, "laissez faire," "dominant," and "social–integrative." Recent research on this topic is beginning to provide strands of evidence about effective teacher behaviors that contribute significantly to improved student behaviors, skills, and conceptual knowledge relevant to important physical education objectives ("social–integrative" style).

Closely related to teaching behaviors are the many interactions between teacher and pupil which can be observed within physical education instructional groups.

Concerning these preconditions of physical education programs, analysis (input evaluation) is an important step along with planning, conducting, and evaluating the physical education programs.

2. Planning the Physical Education Program

The starting point in the planning and development of new physical education programs is the definition of the general aim of a particular program, followed by decisions about the objectives and content, all of which interact with each other in a close relationship.

2.1 Aims and Objectives of Physical Education Programs

Within the professional field there is a long continuing, intensive debate about the aims and objectives most appropriate for a physical education program.

If education is defined as a process which produces desired changes in student behaviors, it must also specify the nature of the changes in pupil behaviors which are intended to be attained through the physical education experience. Aims and objectives have been formulated in rather general terms over the years. For example, Grupe (1969) proposed five major objectives:

(a) to engage in primary experiences through human movement;

(b) to develop health and physical performance skills;

(c) to promote aesthetic behaviors;

(d) to develop desirable social attitudes;

(e) to engage in play as an elective life activity.

Another approach stresses the importance of learning about the concept of human movements. The purpose–process curriculum framework by Jewett (1978) includes 22 purpose elements which identify the content of physical education movement experiences within three major categories:

(a) Man, master of himself: he moves to adapt and control his physical environment. He moves to fulfill his human development potential.

(b) Man in space: he moves to adapt to and control his physical environment.

(c) Man in a social world: he moves to relate to others.

A model by Haag (1971) takes as a starting point three basic behavioral dimensions of human beings: movement, health, and recreational behaviors, in which learning takes place in motor (basic motor capacities/

skill), cognitive (sport-discipline-specific/general sport-related), and affective (individually/socially oriented) dimensions.

Annarino et al. (1980) developed a comprehensive "operational taxonomy for physical education objectives," a detailed outline of the specific objectives and content. Teachers should follow a taxonomy in order to provide the most comprehensive and quality-based experiences and to encourage changes in desired student behaviors in the physical education curriculum over extended time in school settings.

This taxonomy contains four major sections of physical education objectives:

(a) physical domain (organic development);

(b) psychomotor domain (neuromuscular development);

(c) cognitive domain (intellectual development);

(d) affective domain (social–personal–emotional development).

Under each of these major categories there is listed a large number of more specific, behaviorally stated objectives toward the attainment of which the teachers should instruct, and which the pupils should attempt to learn and achieve.

2.2 Content of Physical Education Programs

Physical education teachers can adapt the Annarino et al. curriculum model to their own classes by using the four curriculum areas as content of their physical education programs.

(a) Basic motor capacities (condition and coordination aspects).

(b) Technical and tactical skills (sport disciplines). The variety of sport disciplines can be grouped according to criteria such as:
   (i) social relationships (individual, dual, team sports);
   (ii) movement criteria (moving the body, moving an object, moving an object by a medium, moving on an apparatus, being moved by external forces);
   (iii) evaluation criteria (cm/gr/sec; measuring and estimating sport performance; estimating sport performance);
   (iv) environmental criteria (facilities, weather, space, inside, outside, medium, etc.).

(c) Sport-specific knowledge (sport discipline specific and general sport-related). Examples are:
   (i) sport-discipline-specific: historical development, social structure and function, medical-health aspects, movement theory, teaching aspects, coaching aspects;
   (ii) general sport-related: sport and movement, sport and health, sport and recreation.

Additional topics might be sport and the Olympic Games: sport and performance; sport and mass media; sport and socialization.

(d) Sport-specific attitudes, emotions, and behaviors: these attitudes can be either socially or individually oriented, or both. They can be developed through sport participation and can be evaluated in a variety of sports environments.

From these examples it is demonstrated that the range of aims and objectives, and the content of physical education programs, are wide and varied thereby requiring a balanced approach in the planning stage of physical education program development.

3. Implementing the Physical Education Program

The transition from planning to carrying out physical education programs can be described best by so-called "action forms" of sport instruction (Grössing 1981). These "forms" have a relationship to the content as well as to the elements of instruction including: learning, exercising, training (workout), playing, performing, competing, creating, testing, speaking (in order to realize cognitive and affective aims and objectives), and many forms of nonverbal expressions and communications.

Basically, there are educational principles which guide the successful conduct of physical education programs such as natural talent, learner development, individualization of participation and instruction, community involvement, totality of experiences, clearness of purposes, relationships to established norms, individual creative spontaneity, as well as standard and novel structural environments.

The second factor, called method, can be analyzed on the following levels: (a) general education; (b) general sport related; (c) methods for specific sport disciplines.

Within the hierarchy of methods available, two basic approaches, which seem to prevail today, include inductive and deductive principles and concepts to guide proper instruction.

Teaching principles are vital to effective teaching as well as coaching methods and processes. Teaching principles can be categorized into four major groups (Grössing 1981):

(a) Verbal modes (description and explanation of movements, indication of movements to be desired and associated movement tasks, acoustic help, and instructional evaluation and correction through verbal communication).

(b) Visual modes (demonstration, visual means such as charts, pictures, slow motion pictures, diagrams, television replays).

(c) Audiovisual modes (technology has become part of the instructional processes).

(d) Instrumental and tactical modes (correction by the teachers, enforcement of safety measures, and other helpful teacher behaviors).

Mosston (1966) has developed well-recognized proposals for improving the teaching of physical education. His concept of "teaching styles" is a bridge between subject matter and the structure of learning. Using these approaches, individualized learning and the cognitive processes are emphasized. Eight aspects of teaching styles are part of this approach by Mosston: teaching by command, teaching by task, reciprocal teaching, the use of a partner, the use of the small group, the individualized program, guided discovery, and problem solving. Physical education teachers should study Mosston's "teaching styles" and then evaluate themselves against these descriptions as a guide for improving their own teaching behaviors.

Anderson (1980), from his many years of pioneer research on effective teaching in physical education by means of slow-motion pictures, classifies teaching behaviors into the following categories: instructing, monitoring motor activities, officiating, regulating motor activities, class management, and behavior management.

Within this process-oriented approach for improving physical education programs and teaching effectiveness it is especially important to consider recent results of research concerning sport instruction, which can be summarized in the following way: organizational patterns for the flexible grouping of students into small, intermediate, and large groups; measurements and estimates as essential elements in sport instruction; textbooks for supplementing physical education practice and game participation; team instruction which involves teaching by two or more instructors; mental training through self-concept rehearsal; programmed instruction; and new audiovisual equipment, with emphasis on self-playback on videotape.

New approaches, when properly implemented, can assist in the extension of content areas in physical education and can become essential aspects of the physical education curriculum.

4. Evaluating the Physical Education Program

Evaluation is considered to be a procedure of valuation, judging, estimating, and deciding about different aspects of the physical education program concerning basic conditions, essential processes, and the extent of pupil learnings acquired in the program. Evaluation plays a vital role in two systems which make up the physical education program.

Curriculum development systems and processes are based on a curriculum theory of sport and physical education usually implicitly held by the teachers. Sometimes it is written in a curriculum guide. Curriculum evaluation is concerned with the collection, treatment, and interpretation of pupil-generated learning data and teacher observations for the purpose of assessing the extent to which the objectives of the program have been met by each pupil and to make decisions in regard to improving the curriculum in the future.

Instructional realization systems should be based on an instructional theory of sports. Instructional evaluation means the assessment of instructional processes, the interactions, and behaviors of teachers and pupils with the aim of providing feedback for all persons interested in the instruction.

4.1 Collection of Data and Assessment

Estimating procedures for physical education programs are needed as well as measuring procedures using clocks, measuring tape, and other mechanical measurement tools in order to collect data on the assessment level.

The collection of data (assessment) as a basis of evaluation in regard to the physical education program can be related to eight major components of the physical education program (Haag 1981).

Four clearly student-related program components to be evaluated in any physical education program are: basic motor capacities, technical and tactical skills, sport-specific knowledges, and sport-specific attitudes. Two components would relate mainly to the physical education teacher: personality traits and teaching abilities. One component concerns both: interaction between teachers and student; and one component the overall program: curriculum evaluation.

4.2 Tests as Major Tools for Evaluating a Physical Education Program

Tests are examination procedures carried out under standardized conditions which meet scientific criteria. The aim is to collect as accurately as possible quantitative data reporting the relative degree of development of individual trait characteristics of each pupil. Standardized conditions are necessary for the realization of the test as well as for the evaluation and interpretation of the test results in order to make possible inter- and intra-individual comparisons.

In addition to tests as formal procedures for evaluation (in the form of measuring and estimating), informal procedures also play an important role for the evaluation of physical education programs. Another important aspect is the fact that learning-aim-oriented tests (LOT) are gaining more and more recognition in comparison with norm-oriented tests (NOT).

4.3 Basic Considerations for the Evaluation of Physical Education Programs

Certain points have to be considered to insure a valid evaluation phase in the physical education program:

(a) Obtainment of a high degree of objectivity in the database. This is not always possible but should be a constant aim of the evaluation program (e.g., sport-specific attitudes).

(b) Unbiased assessment of data as a basis for the evaluation of the physical education program.

(c) Fulfillment of a twofold function, namely information for the participants of the physical education program (pupil/teacher) and for interested persons who are responsible for the constant improvement of educational policies concerning physical education and sport (school board members, teacher committees, parents).

Evaluation, therefore, is a fundamental segment within the action field of sport through which a favorable attitude regarding sport and physical education programs can be created, thus leading to the continuing improvement and further expansion of the physical education program in the future.

5. Conclusion

Sport pedagogy is one of the central theory fields of sport science or sport sciences. The theme, "physical education programs," is a fundamental field within sport pedagogy. A twofold approach was used to discuss and examine important concepts involved in physical education programs:

(a) The static-oriented approach was used to analyze six fundamental factors which compose the so-called learning-oriented didactic model of physical education programs.

(b) The process-oriented approach, composed of four stages (analysis, planning, realization, and evaluation), to understand the importance of carefully selected and designed processes and procedures required to properly understand and ensure the efficacy of any school physical education program.

These two major approaches have been described as highly interrelated and integrated so as to create a comprehensive mosaic depiction of how and why these two major approaches must be combined and interrelated if a viable physical education program is to be created.

Bibliography

Anderson W G 1980 *Analysis of Teaching Physical Education.* Mosby, St. Louis, Missouri

Annarino A A, Cowell C C, Hazelton H W 1980 *Curriculum Theory and Design in Physical Education,* 2nd edn. Mosby, St. Louis, Missouri

Eggert D, Schuck K D 1975 *Untersuchungen zu Zusammenhängen zwischen Intelligenz, Motorik und Sozialstatus im Vorschulalter.* Hofmann, Schorndorf, pp. 67–82

Grössing S 1981 *Handbuch zur Pädagogik und Didaktik des Sports,* Vol. 1: *Einführung in die Sportdidaktik: Lehren und Lernen im Sportunterricht,* 3rd edn. Limpert, Bad Homburg

Grupe O 1969 *Grundlagen der Sportpädagogik: Anthropologisch-Didaktische Untersuchungen.* Barth, Munich

Haag H 1971 *Die amerikanische Gesundheitserziehung.* Hofmann, Schorndorf

Haag H (ed.) 1981 *Sporterziehung und Evaluation: Bewegungs-, Gesundheits, Freizeiterziehung durch Sport, Evaluation von Lehr- und Lernprozessen im Sport.* Hofmann, Schorndorf

Jewett A E 1978 Aims and objectives of physical education: Subject matter and research methods of sport pedagogy as a behavioral science. In: Haag H (ed.) 1978 *Sport Pedagogy, Content and Methodology.* 1st Int. Symp. on Sport Pedagogy, Karlsruhe, 1975. University Park Press, Baltimore, Maryland, pp. 213–25

Landers D M et al. 1981 Group performance, interaction and leadership. In: Lüschen G R F, Sage G H (eds.) 1981 *Handbook of Social Science of Sport.* Stipes, Champaign, Illinois, pp. 297–315

Lüschen G R F 1981 The analysis of sport organizations. In: Lüschen G R F, Sage G H (eds.) 1981 *Handbook of Social Science of Sport.* Stipes, Champaign, Illinois, pp. 316–29

Mosston M 1966 *Teaching Physical Education: From Command to Discovery.* Merrill, Columbus, Ohio

Nixon J E, Jewett A E 1980 *An Introduction to Physical Education*, 9th edn. Saunders College, Philadelphia, Pennsylvania

Robinsohn S B 1969 *Bildungsreform als Revision des Curriculum*, 2nd edn. Luchterhand, Neuwied

Snyder E E, Spreitzer E 1981 Sport, education and schools. In: Lüschen G R F, Sage G H (eds.) 1981 *Handbook of Social Science of Sport.* Stipes, Champaign, Illinois, pp. 119–46

Attitude Towards Physical Education

J. Bielefeld

Attitude towards physical education is dealt with both within the framework of attitudes towards school activities and attitudes towards sport. It is an element in both of these broad fields of attitude research. In school attitude studies, the importance attributed to physical education or love for this subject in comparison to other subjects taught is examined. In sport attitude studies, researchers are concerned with the association between certain attitude patterns and the willingness to voluntarily get involved in physical activities of various types and adhere to them. A broad array of issues are examined within the framework of sport attitude studies, relating to particular sport activities (such as jogging, swimming, and climbing), to sport disciplines (such as gymnastics, track and field), to forms of organization (such as school sport, sport of the retarded and handicapped, and voluntary sports clubs), and to active participation in sport as well as an interest in competitive sport.

1. Attitude as Predictor and as Outcome of Sport Activities

The first attitude studies in this field posed the simple question whether children like the physical education lessons in their school. The researchers compared attitude to physical education with attitude to other subjects without examining whether these differences are rooted in out-of-school factors or, alternatively, are results of what is going on in the school. Studies of this type were published as early as the beginning of the century (Hoffman 1911) and this basic question has been recurrently posed (see Telema 1978). The findings have not changed since the beginning of the twentieth century. As confirmed in 1911 as well as in 1978, physical education is one of the best-liked subjects in the Federal Republic of Germany, Norway, Finland, Denmark, and many other countries. Liking of this subject is relatively high in the early school years, gradually diminishing as the higher grade levels are reached. In the 1970s,

numerous studies examined attitudinal outcomes of participating in physical activities of various types. Impetus to such studies was given by the increased interest in attitudinal or affective outcomes of schooling in general, and the development of theoretical frameworks for studying such outcomes. Affective objectives in the field of physical education were defined: for example, cooperation with others, solidarity and fairness, and also lasting interest in sport. The long-term motivation to engage in sport implies the development of a positive and stable sport-related attitude.

A series of studies treated sport attitude as a predictor variable and examined whether such attitudes can predict initial participation in voluntary sport activities of various types, adherence to such activities, and success in them. Most studies of this type deal with narrowly defined variables (a sport activity of a particular type like tennis or soft ball; a particular population like middle class female high-school juniors, etc.). Most studies of this type report positive results, but due to methodological restrictions, the results can hardly be generalized. Sonstroem and Kampper (1980) specify four factors which should be considered in any study attempting to predict sport-related behavior: interest in the particular sport branch, attitude towards performing an action of a certain type, the social context, and the time.

2. Measuring Sport-specific Attitudes

In examining measures of sport-specific attitudes, their meagerness can be observed. When examining the form of sport-specific attitudes, the researchers utilized the whole range of the scientifically legitimized repertoire (Thurstone scales, Likert scales, Semantic differential, and so on), whereas from the point of view of their content, the majority of the instruments consists of a series of items formulated on the basis of semantic considerations. Thus, for example, the Adams scale (Adams 1963) contains items such as "Physical education is my favorite subject" or "Physical education gives lasting satisfaction." Relatively few scales are rooted in some conceptual framework. For example, Kenyon (1968) a priori defined six types of interests for participating in sport activities: social experience, health and fitness, pursuit of thrill and excitement, aesthetic experience, catharsis (recreation and relaxation), and the challenge. Accordingly, he developed six scales and validated them through the technique of factor analysis. Sonstroem and Kampper (1980) distinguish between two factors which determine the willingness of a person to participate in a particular sport activity: (a) estimation towards self as possessing the needed capabilities, and (b) attraction towards an activity of a particular type. Bielefeld (1978) was interested in the long-term influence of physical education programs on the learner's sport attitude, and on the basis of congruent results obtained from cluster, factor, and scalogram analyses identified the following five factors: positive stereotype of sport activity, negative stereotype of sport activity, sport activity as individual need versus social obligation, as carefully directed activity, and as experience of frustration.

3. Conclusion

In spite of the fact that research in the field of sport-related attitudes has been conducted since the beginning of the twentieth century, its state may be summarized in the words of Becker:

At present it seems premature to formulate structures or even coherent theory of specific attitudes towards sport. The shown methodological restriction of data gathering on one side, and the relatively simple statistic processing on the other side have not allowed up to now the portrayal of attitude structures relatively differentiated and exactly descriptive. Additionally there is no considerable spatial–temporal relativation for statements by the exclusive concentration on student population. (Becker 1976)

Bibliography

Adams J L 1963 Two Scales for measuring attitude towards physical education. *Res. Q.* 34: 91–94
Becker P 1976 Sportspezifische Einstellungsdimensionen und ihre Veränderung (Doctoral dissertation, University of Frankfurt)
Bielefeld J 1978 Development and first application of an attitude scale towards physical activity. *Int. J. Phys. Educ.* 15(4): 25–35
Bielefeld J 1981 *Einstellung zum Sport: Begründung und Überprüfung eines zentralen Anliegens des Sportunterrichts.* Hofmann, Schorndorf
Hoffman P 1911 Das Interesse de Schuler and den Unterrichtsfachen. *Zeitschrift für Pädagogische Psychologie* 12: 458–69
Kenyon G S 1968 Six scales for assessing attitude towards physical activity. *Res. Q.* 39: 566–74
Sonstroem R J, Kampper K P 1980 Prediction of athletic participation in middle school males. *Res. Q.* 51: 685–94
Telema R 1978 Pupils' interest and motivation for sport in Finland. *Int. J. Phys. Educ.* 15: 14–23

Health Education

M. J. Loupe

According to the World Health Organization, the goals of health education programs are that people should learn to adopt and maintain healthy life-styles, use available health services effectively, and control individual and community decisions that affect their health or environments (World Health Organization 1974). The ultimate purpose of these goals is, of course, to improve health; however, this purpose is often difficult to achieve for at least two reasons. First, the connections between personal health and health behaviors that are influenced by educational programs are usually less than perfect. Thus, changes in behavior often are not followed by desired changes in health. Second, health behaviors have often proven to be very resistant to the influence of educational programs, possibly because of the difficulty of anticipating and dealing with the multitudinous influences on health behavior. The potential variety of influences is so broad that a recent text (Ross and Mico 1980) considers health education to be a problem of organizational behavior rather than individual behavior and, therefore, cites numerous sociological, political, and psychological theories as relevant

to its success. Because of this complexity, researchers and practitioners in health education frequently borrow theoretical constructs and research methods from one or another of these sciences with the result that there has been little theoretical coherence to health education research, and more often than not, little demonstration of effective change due to health education programs (Rothman and Byrne 1981). However, in spite of this, the literature in this interdisciplinary field does suggest a number of areas that are particularly fruitful for continued educational research.

1. Multiple Objectives of Health Education Programs

Programs that have attempted to improve health by teaching single skills have often failed, either because the behaviors proved to be too difficult to control, or because the connections between the behaviors and health proved to be less direct than originally had been anticipated. The goals of these programs have often been limited to only one of the major goals of health education, the adoption of healthy life-styles, yet the effectiveness of health education programs might be enhanced by increasing the scope of programs to include the two other major goals of health education. For example, some health educators recommend that programs consider environmental and hereditary (in addition to strictly behavioral) factors in health and disease by teaching about such topics as susceptibility, early disease detection, primary prevention, and environmental change to prevent disease (Ross and Mico 1980). Others recommend that health education should place greater emphasis on teaching information about such topics as the relative effectiveness of various private and public health preventive procedures so that students can make informed decisions about their health in the future (Frazier 1980). It still remains for researchers to determine whether such programs can affect broad patterns of attitude and habit or whether such changes will have lasting and positive effects on health.

2. Complexity of Health Behaviors

Single health behaviors may be difficult to control because they are, in fact, not isolated behaviors but instead are components of complex habit patterns that organize the daily lives of people. Improving health by changing isolated behaviors may be impractical or impossible for most people. Chambers (1975), while writing of the problems in changing dental patients' behaviors, concludes that health behavior-change programs will succeed only with people who already observe life-styles that are compatible with the behavioral regimens that are being taught. Therefore, health educators should not expect that their programs will succeed in changing specific health habits of children whose family or cultural behavior patterns do not support the new preventive behavior. Educational research is certainly warranted here, to test the conclusion that health behaviors belong to habit complexes that are relatively unaffected by traditional educational methods. Research is also appropriate to explore the educational implications of this position, for example, the implication that the effectiveness of individual health education programs might be improved by coordinating the separate program efforts in schools, thereby affecting collectively a broad segment of the students' health habits.

3. Maintenance of Healthy Behavior Patterns

School health education programs are often organized to maintain existing behaviors and to prevent anticipated changes in behavior rather than to change problematic behaviors. Antismoking programs and programs to prevent drug abuse are of this type. Green et al. (1980) offer a model that may be particularly appropriate to these kinds of problems. They recommend that health educators should attempt to "inno-culate" students against influences that may bring about future negative changes in health behavior. To do so they recommend that health education programs deal with factors that predispose students to health problems, that support unhealthy changes in their behaviors, and that reinforce unhealthy behaviors once the initial changes have occurred. This model implies that the appropriate position for health education programs in a school curriculum is at a grade level or student age *before* the problem itself actually occurs, and possibly before the predisposing factors are seen. Here, more research is needed that deals with the phenomena of social influence as they relate to the learning of health behaviors.

4. The School Environment

One of the perennial problems faced by health educators is that the environments in which children live and learn are incompatible with the health-promoting behaviors and practices that are being taught. The consequence is that there is little opportunity at home or school for practice, reinforcement, or appropriate modeling. But teachers themselves are rarely in positions to make basic changes in the school environment, beyond the classroom. Therefore, health education programs, the basic goals of which are to improve the health of students, can legitimately be extended beyond the classroom to address administrators and even health professionals who, in turn, affect the health environments and health care services of students. Research is needed to determine the extent to which the school environment actually does affect certain aspects of students' health and the extent to which changes in the school environment can affect health behaviors.

5. Evaluation of Program Effectiveness

Possibly the greatest problem that faces researchers in health education is the lack of agreement about appropriate criteria for evaluating program effectiveness. The desired outcomes of health education programs are changes in health, yet these may not be observable until years after the end of the particular educational experience. This problem is common to much of health care and so programs are often evaluated according to their organization and methods rather than their results. Some authors believe that school health education should be evaluated in the same way that other health programs and school curricula are evaluated, that is, according to the use of appropriate methods and materials, and according to short-term measures of student learning. Accurate prediction and control of future voluntary behavior patterns is beyond the scope of health education, these authors believe (Green et al. 1980). This is certainly a practical approach to evaluation since there is no solid body of longitudinal research that shows long-term changes in health as a function of health education.

Other authors argue that outcomes are the only appropriate criteria by which programs can be evaluated. Short-term outcomes include changes in students' knowledge and behavior patterns; long-term outcomes include actual changes in health (Frazier 1980). This position, that the effectiveness of health education should be evaluated in terms of ultimate changes in health, clearly has the greater heuristic potential. The purpose of health education is improvement of health and it is against this criterion that decisions about objectives, content, and methods should be made. Unfortunately, knowledge about connections between short-term indicators of program quality and long-term measures of health is lacking and it is in this area that educational research may have its greatest potential for effect.

Bibliography

Chambers D W 1975 Susceptibility to preventive dental treatment. *J. Public Health Dentistry* 33(2): 82–90

Frazier P J 1980 School-based instruction for improving oral health. *Int. Dental J.* 30: 257–68

Green L W, Kreuter M W, Deeds S G, Partridge K B 1980 *Health Education Planning: A Diagnostic Approach.* Mayfield, Palo Alto, California

Ross H S, Mico P R 1980 *Theory and Practice in Health Education.* Mayfield, Palo Alto, California

Rothman A I, Byrne N 1981 Health education for children and adolescents. *Rev. Educ. Res.* 51: 85–100

World Health Organization 1974 *Health Education: A Programme Review.* Report by the Director-General to the 53rd session of the Executive Board. Offset Publication No. 7. World Health Organization, Geneva

Section 13

International Curriculum Associations and Journals

International Curriculum Associations and Journals

Curriculum Associations and Journals

E. C. Short

International communication among curriculum officials, practitioners, and scholars, while increasing each year, continues to be fragmented in structure and uneven in effectiveness. Books, journal articles, and association meetings remain the primary means of communication. Computerized systems of interacting and publishing as well as electronic video and telecommunication systems have not yet been extensively explored for use by the world-wide curriculum community despite their increasing availability. Most of the professionals in curriculum still seem to be relatively parochial in their contacts, and the patterns that have arisen to facilitate their intercommunications are largely national or regional and are usually language-specific.

The purpose of this article is to identify some of the most important organizations and publications currently functioning to facilitate communication among curriculum professionals. Their potential for international communication will be stessed, although most of them are nationally or regionally focused. The organizations and journals in English-speaking countries will be listed, and a selected list of publications in other languages will follow.

1. Organizations and Journals in English-speaking Countries

The World Council for Curriculum and Instruction (WCCI) is the primary association dedicated to the interests of professionals in curriculum and their work on behalf of the education of children and youth throughout the world. WCCI is a truly international organization, founded in 1970, which holds triennial world conferences and other occasional meetings in six regions of the world. WCCI has approximately 500 members and publishes a directory, proceedings, and newsletters. In 1987 it also began publishing a journal. The purposes of WCCI include "cross-cultural collaboration relating curriculum to issues in the world community," "relating research to peace and stability," "cross-cultural exchange of professional knowledge, theory, practices," "opportunities for education contributing to peace and human rights," and "cooperation with other initiatives and groups with compatible purposes" (Berman et al. 1982 p. 56). Office of the WCCI executive secretary, Maxine Dunfee: School of Education, Indiana University, Bloomington, Indiana 47405 USA.

Next in importance is Division B—Curriculum Studies of the American Educational Research Association (AERA). This group of curriculum scholars, which meets annually as part of the larger association (AERA), numbers about 2,500 and in 1986 drew curriculum researchers from eight countries besides the United States. The primary activity of Division B is to read and critique reports of new research in the areas of curriculum content, theory, contexts, practice, history, comparative and international studies, and policy making. Exchange of papers is facilitated through these meetings and through a directory of program presenters included in the annual program book. Division B publishes no research journal of its own, but curriculum studies frequently appear in various AERA journals and other publications. All members of AERA's 10 divisions receive the Association's general interest journal, *Educational Researcher*. AERA also publishes eight other journals, handbooks, and annuals, including *Review of Educational Research*, *Educational Evaluation and Policy Analysis*, and *Handbook of Research on Teaching*. Several special interest groups (SIG) within AERA focus on specific subjects in the curriculum, such as mathematics and reading, and an important SIG on "Critical Issues in Curriculum" is concerned with relating curriculum research to practice. Office of AERA executive officer, William J Russell: 1230 17th Street, NW, Washington, DC 20036 USA.

The Association for Supervision and Curriculum Development (ASCD) is an organization of 100,000 professional educators, primarily in the United States and Canada, and provides professional support for the work of curriculum and supervision leaders in schools. Its purposes include the review, dissemination, and improvement of curriculum and instructional practices; the encouragement of research, evaluation, and theory development; and the demonstration of leadership in dealing with common educational issues. As many as 8,000 people attend an ASCD annual conference; the number coming from overseas increases year by year. ASCD has units in all the US states and territories and in Canada, Germany, and the United Kingdom. A very large communications network is operated by ASCD through committees, study institutes, newsletters, the publication of books, yearbooks, films, videotapes, and journals, as well as the annual conferences. *Educational Leadership* is the professional journal received by all members. The *Journal of Curriculum and Supervision* is a scholarly journal focusing on policy and professional practice research and is received by 4,500 subscribers, 300 beyond the United States. Office of ASCD executive director, Gordon Cawelti: 125 N. West Street, Alexandria, Virginia 22314 USA.

The *Journal of Curriculum Studies* is an international scholarly quarterly which began publishing in 1968. It has editors in Europe, the United States, Canada, and Australia, and attracts articles from all parts of the world. The journal publishes "reflective essays, research articles, case studies, essay reviews, short reports, and book reviews" on curriculum history and scholarship, theory, economics and management of curriculum, epistemology and curriculum, evaluation, innovation, planning, policy making, sociological research, and teaching. It is published by Taylor and Francis. Office of the executive editor, William A Reid: Institute of Education, University of London, 20 Bedford Place, London WC4 0AL, United Kingdom.

Curriculum Inquiry is an international scholarly quarterly which began publishing in 1968 as *Curriculum Theory Network*. In 1973 it became a journal of the Ontario Institute for Studies in Education (OISE); its name was changed in 1976. It publishes contributions on all matters related to curriculum development, evaluation, and theory. Critical reviews of books appear regularly, along with scholarly responses to earlier published work. It is published by John Wiley and Sons. Office of the editor of *Curriculum Inquiry*, F Michael Connelly: OISE, 252 Bloor Street West, Toronto, Ontario M5S 1V6, Canada.

The *Journal of Curriculum Theorizing* began publishing in 1979 to advance curriculum theory, teaching, and learning. It is a quarterly interdisciplinary journal of curriculum studies, with essays, political notes, reports, reviews, letters, and poetry. Some of the most innovative thinking in the field often appears first in this journal. The journal sponsors an annual conference on curriculum theory and practice which draws over 300 of the field's leading scholars, many of whom come from countries other than the United States. Office of the chief administrative office, Margaret S Zaccone: 53 Falstaff Road, Rochester, New York 14609 USA.

Curriculum Perspectives is a quarterly journal published since 1980 by the Australian Curriculum Studies Association (ACSA). It has international consulting editors and publishes theoretical and practical work related

to curriculum. Issues, case studies, and book reviews also appear. Its editor is Colin J Marsh, Murdoch University. Also published by ACSA is a newsletter for members of the Association called *Curriculum Concerns*. Office for ACSA correspondence, Russell Matthews: School of Education, Deakin University, Victoria 3217, Australia.

Curriculum is the journal of the Association for the Study of Curriculum (ASC) in the United Kingdom. It contains both professional and scholarly articles of interest to its membership. Office of the editor, Terry Brown: School of Education, University of Durham, Leazes Road, Durham DH1 3JH, United Kingdom.

Curriculum Canada is a series of proceedings of annual invitational conferences sponsored by the Canadian Association for Curriculum Studies (CACS). Volumes in this series, which began in 1979, may be obtained through the Centre for the Study of Curriculum and Instruction, Faculty of Education, University of British Columbia, Vancouver, British Columbia V6T 1Z5, Canada. CACS also publishes a newsletter. Officer of the Secretariat for the Canadian Society for the Study of Education (of which CACS is a unit): 14 Henderson Avenue, Ottawa, Ontario K1N 7P1, Canada.

The Society for the Study of Curriculum History was founded in the United States 1977 to foster historical studies in curriculum as a means of influencing curriculum practice. It maintains ties with curriculum historians in Europe, the United Kingdom, Canada, and Australia. Proceedings have been published periodically. Contact the Society's founding president, Laurel N Tanner: College of Education, Temple University, Philadelphia, Pennsylvania 19122 USA.

Professors of Curriculum is an informal association of 100 leading professors from several countries who met annually to address current curriculum problems of concern to schools. There is no continuing office for this group. Curriculum Teachers Network is an inclusive organization of all interested professors of curriculum which was established in 1986. Both of these groups may be contacted through the Office of the ASCD executive director (address given above).

The African Curriculum Organization (ACO) was formed in 1976 following a UNESCO curriculum development and evaluation training seminar. The members are national curriculum development centers from 14 anglophone African countries. The headquarters are at the University of Ibadan in Nigeria.

2. Associations and Journals in non-English-speaking Countries

In non-English-speaking countries most curriculum-related research and publications are produced by national curriculum centers.

In Spanish there is an irregularly appearing publication titled *Curriculum*, which is sponsored by the

Projecto Multinational de Desarollo Curricular y Capacitacion de Docentes para la Educacion Basica affiliated to the Ministry of Education of Venezuela.

The German-speaking countries' leading role in the area is fulfilled by the *Institut für die Pädagogik der Naturwissenschaften* (IPN) affiliated to the University of Kiel (address: Universität Kiel, Olshausenstr. 40, 2300 Kiel 1.) The institute publishes a *Handbuch der Curriculumforschung* every five years, which summarizes curriculum research and studies in German-speaking countries and in other coutries of Europe.

A comprehensive summary of curriculum research in Europe was published by the Council of Europe. This book describes curriculum-related research and studies in the following countries: Austria, Germany, France, Luxembourg, Greece, Italy, the Netherlands, Scandinavia, Spain, the United Kingdom, and Yugoslavia (Hameyer et al. 1986).

The Hungarian National Institute of Pedagogie (address: Budapest, Gorkij fasor 21) publishes a series of monographs in curriculum theory (*Tantervelméleti füzetek*) and a series of curriculum sources (*Tantervelmélet forrasai*).

A curriculum research yearbook (*Kyo ooyk Kwa Zong Yun Koo*) is published in Korean by the Korean Society for Studies in Education (address: Korean Educational Development Centre, 20-1 Umyeon-Dong, Gangnam-Gu, Seoul, Korea), and a curriculum research journal, *Halaha uMaase bTichnun Limudim* (Theory and Practice in Curriculum Planning), is published by the Israel Curriculum Center (address: Ministry of Education, Israel Curriculum Center, Jerusalem). It appears at irregular intervals.

Bibliography

Berman L M, Miel A, Overly N 1982 *The World Council for Curriculum and Instruction: The Story of the Early Years.* World Council for Curriculum and Instruction, Indiana University School of Education, Bloomington, Indiana

Hameyer U, Frey K, Haft H, Kuebart F (eds.) 1986 *Curriculum Research in Europe.* Swets and Zeitlinger, Lisse, Netherlands

Contributors Index

Contributors are listed in alphabetical order together with their affiliations. Titles of articles which they have authored follow in alphabetical order, along with the respective page numbers. Where articles are co-authored, this has been indicated by an asterisk preceding the article title.

† deceased

GAY, G. (Purdue University, Lafayette, Indiana, USA)
Curriculum Development, 293-302

GIBB, E. G. (University of Texas, Austin, Texas, USA)
Estimation in Mathematics Education, 853-54

GILLESPIE, J. A. (Boston University, Boston, Massachusetts, USA)
Social Studies: Secondary-school Programs, 731-36

GLASERSFELD, E. VON, (University of Georgia, Athens, Georgia, USA)
Constructivism in Education, 31-32

GLATTHORN, A. A. (University of Pennsylvania, Philadelphia, Pennsylvania, USA)
Integrated Curriculum, 160-62

GLUCK, P. G. (Brooklyn College, CUNY, Brooklyn, New York, USA)
Introduction: Arts Education, 673-74

GOFFREE, F. (Foundation for Curriculum Development, Enschede, The Netherlands)
Mathematics: Elementary-school Programs, 821-25

GOODLAD, J. I. (University of Washington, Seattle, Washington, USA)
Introduction: Curriculum as a Field of Study, 3-7; *Overview: Conceptual Framework*, 11-14

GOODSON, I. (University of Western Ontario, London, Ontario, Canada)
Social History of Curriculum Subjects, 58-63

GORDON, D. (Ben Gurion University, Beer Sheba, Israel)
Neo-Marxist Approach, 28-31

GREANEY, V. (St. Patrick's College, Dublin, Ireland)
Reading Interest, 541-44

GREEN, P. S. (University of York, York, UK)
Foreign Language Curricula: Secondary Schools, 575-79

GROBMAN, A. B. (University of Missouri, St. Louis, Missouri, USA)
Curriculum Adaptation, 384-86

GRUMET, M. R. (School of Education, Brooklyn College, Brooklyn, New York, USA)
Introduction: Humanities Education, 629-32

GUNSTONE, R. F. (Monash University, Clayton, Victoria, Australia)
Science Education: Secondary School, 911-16

† deceased

GURUGÉ, A. W. P. (UNESCO, Paris, France)
Buddhist Education, 255-61

HAAG, H. (University of Kiel, Kiel, Germany)
Physical Education Programs, 969-74

HAERTEL, G. D. (Stanford University, Stanford, California, USA)
Cognitive Psychology and Curriculum, 110-14

HALLER, H.-D. (Georg August Universität, Göttingen, Germany)
Curriculum Personnel, 354-57

HAMBLETON, R. K. (University of Massachusetts, Amherst, Massachusetts, USA)
Criterion-referenced Measurement, 454-59

HAMEYER, U. (University of Kiel, Kiel, Germany)
Curriculum Theory, 19-28

HANSON, D. J. (State University of New York, Potsdam, New York, USA)
Drug Education Programs, 786-88

HARLEN, W. (Scottish Council for Research in Education, Edinburgh, UK)
Science Concepts and Skills, 951-53; *Science Education: Primary School*, 906-11

HARRIMAN, L. C. (Oklahoma State University, Stillwater, Oklahoma, USA)
Family-life Education, 789-92

HATFIELD, L. L. (University of Georgia, Athens, Georgia, USA)
Computers in Mathematics Education, 883-88

HAUNER, M. (University of Wisconsin, Madison, Wisconsin, USA)
Swahili, 623-24

HAWES, H. W. R. (University of London, London, UK)
Third World Countries, 242-44

HEATER, D. (Brighton, Sussex, UK)
Area Studies, 769-70; *International Education*, 775-77

HERRING, J. E. (Robert Gordon Institute of Technology, Aberdeen, UK)
Library User Education, 812-13

HIGGINS, J. J. (The British Council, London, UK)
Language Laboratories, 598-600

HILL, W. R. (State University of New York, Buffalo, New York, USA)
Reading Methods in Secondary Schools, 511-13

LANGEVELD, W. (University of Amsterdam, Amsterdam, The Netherlands)
Political Education, 771-74

LANTZ, O. C. (University of Alberta, Edmonton, Alberta, Canada)
*Definitions of Curriculum: An Introduction, 15-18

LAUGLO, J. (University of London, London, UK)
Diversified Curriculum, 201-02

LAWTON, D. (University of London, London, UK)
United Kingdom, 244-46

LEE, S. E. (Cleveland Museum of Art, Cleveland, Ohio, USA)
*Museum Education, 686-88

LEITHWOOD, K. A. (Ontario Institute for Studies in Education, Toronto, Ontario, Canada)
Curriculum Diffusion, 373-75; *Implementation Evaluation*, 444-48

LEONTIEV, A. A. (Pushkin Institute, Moscow, USSR)
Russian, 620-21

LESH, R. (Northwestern University, Evanston, Illinois, USA)
Mathematical Applications: Primary School, 844-45; *Rational Numbers in Mathematics Education*, 857-58

LEVIN, T. (School of Education, Tel Aviv University, Tel Aviv, Israel)
Arithmetic: Educational Programs, 833-35; *Evaluating Computerized Curriculum Materials*, 474-77

LEWIS, J. (Malvern College, Malvern, Worcestershire, UK)
Energy Education, 941-42

LEWY, A. (Tel Aviv University, Tel Aviv, Israel)
*Curriculum Personnel, 354-57; *Curriculum Tryout*, 440-41; *Decisions at Educational System Level*, 349-54; *Formative and Summative Evaluation*, 406-09; **Introduction: Curriculum Processes*, 277-78; **Introduction: Three Decades of Curriculum Evaluation*, 399-400; **Overview: Conceptual Framework*, 11-14; *Overview: Curriculum Approaches and Methods*, 145-48; **Overview: Curriculum Processes*, 275; **Overview: Curriculum Evaluation*, 397-98; *Overview: Foreign Language Studies*, 549-50; *Overview: Humanities Curricula*, 627; *Overview: Arts Curricula*, 671-72; *Overview: Social Studies*, 717-19; *Overview: Mathematics Education*, 817-18

LIPMAN, M. (Montclair State College, Upper Montclair, New Jersey, USA)
Philosophy Programs: Primary Schools, 635-36

LOUCKS, S. F. (Andover, Massachusetts, USA)
Curriculum Adoption, 376-78

LOUPE, M. J. (University of Minnesota, Minneapolis, Minnesota, USA)
Health Education, 975-77

LUCAS, A. M. (University of London, London, UK)
Environmental Education, 770-71; *Environmental Education Programs*, 927-29

LUCAS, E. (Tel Aviv University, Tel Aviv, Israel)
*Foreign Language Education, 553-69

LUNDGREN, U. P. (University of Stockholm, Stockholm, Sweden)
*Curriculum Pacing, 389-91

LUNETTA, V. N. (Pennsylvania State University, Pennsylvania, USA)
Physics Programs, 930-35

MARCUCELLA, H. (Boston University, Boston, Massachusetts, USA)
*Psychology: Educational Programs, 760-61

MARKLUND, S. (University of Stockholm, Stockholm, Sweden)
Sweden, 241-42

MARSTON, E. W. (Harvard University, Cambridge, Massachusetts, USA)
*Independent Reading, 544-46

MASSIALAS, B. G. (Florida State University, Tallahassee, Florida, USA)
Discovery and Inquiry Methods, 210-13

MAXWELL, T. W. (University of New England, Armidale, New South Wales, Australia)
Curriculum Consultants, 357-59

MAY, W. T. (School of Education, Michigan State University, East Lansing, Michigan, USA)
Curriculum and Supervision, 359-61

McCLURE, R. (National Education Association, Washington DC, USA)
Curriculum Balance, 466-68

McNEIL, J. (University of California, Los Angeles, California, USA)
Teacher's Guide, 81-84

MEAD, N. A. (Education Commission of the States, Denver, Colorado, USA)
Listening Comprehension, 524-26

MEHAFFY, G. L. (Eastern New Mexico University, Portales, New Mexico, USA)
Outdoor Education, 810-12

MERRITT, J. E. (Open University, Milton Keynes, UK)
Phonics, 502-03

MEVARECH, Z. R. (Bar-Ilan University, Ramat-Gan, Israel)
Analysis in Mathematics: Educational Programs, 837-39

MIKLOS, T. (Investigación Sobre la Educación, Naucalpan de Juarez, Mexico)
Elective Subjects, 203-04

MILLER, J. L. (Hofstra University, Hempstead, New York, USA)
Gender Studies: Impact on Curriculum, 139-42

MORRIS, J. W. (Miami University, Oxford, Ohio, USA)
Attitude Towards Art, 684-85

MORRISSETT, I. (Social Science Educational Consortium, Boulder, Colorado, USA)
Key Concepts: Social Studies, 183-84; *Social Science Versus Social Studies*, 723-25

MORROW, J. K. (Institute for Multimedia Learning, Westford, Massachusetts, USA)
Media Literacy, 713-14

MORTIMER, R. (Urbana, Illinois, USA)
Safety Education, 795-96

NANAVATY, J. J. (Central and Bombay Education Service, Pune, India)
Hindu Education, 261-65

NESHER, P. (University of Haifa, Haifa, Israel)
The Language of Mathematics, 866-68

NEWMANN, F. M. (University of Wisconsin, Madison, Wisconsin, USA)
Community Education, 767-68

NIR, R. (Hebrew University, Jerusalem, Israel)
Hebrew, 616-18

NIXON, J. E. (Stanford University, Stanford, California, USA)
Physical Education Programs, 969-74

NOMOTO, K. (National Language Research Institute, Tokyo, Japan)
Japanese, 619-20

OBERG, A. A. (University of Victoria, Victoria, British Columbia, Canada)
Curriculum Decisions, 302-03

OLIVE, J. (University of Georgia, Athens, Georgia, USA)
Computers in Mathematics Education, 883-88

OLIVER, A. I. (University of Pennsylvania, Philadelphia, Pennsylvania, USA)
Honors Courses, 198-200; *Minicourses*, 170-71

OLSHTAIN, E. (Tel Aviv University, Tel Aviv, Israel)
Foreign Language Education, 553-69; *Introduction: Foreign Language Education*, 551-52; *Pedagogic Grammar*, 585-86

OREN, A. (Tel Aviv University, Tel Aviv, Israel)
Knowledge Technology and Curriculum Theory, 131-37

OTTO, G. (University of Hamburg, Hamburg, Germany)
Aesthetic Education, 675-77

PARKER, R. L. (Milperra College of Advanced Education, Milperra, New South Wales, Australia)
Critical Reading Instruction, 521-22

PARLETT, M. R. (Open University, Milton Keynes, UK)
Illuminative Evaluation, 420-24

PASSOW, A. H. (Teachers College, Columbia University, New York, USA)
Accelerated Programs, 197-98

PAULSTON, C. B. (University of Pittsburgh, Pittsburgh, Pennsylvania, USA)
English, 608-11

PELLENS, K. (Pädagogische Hochschule Weingarten, Baden-Württemberg, Germany)
History: Educational Programs, 743-46

PELLEREY, M. (University of Salesiano, Rome, Italy)
Mathematics Instruction, 870-81

PETERS, M. L. (Cambridge Institute of Education, Cambridge, UK)
Spelling Instruction, 532-35

PEZARO, P. E. (Ohio State University, Columbus, Ohio, USA)
Earth Sciences Programs, 939-40

PIÉRON, M. (University of Liège, Liège, Belgium)
Physical Education Instruction, 961-69

PINAR, W. F. (Louisiana State University, Baton Rouge, Louisiana, USA)
The Reconceptualist Approach, 35-37

SCHUBERT, A. L. (University of Illinois at Chicago, Illinois, USA)
Curriculum Inquiry: Alternative Paradigms, 51-56

SCHUBERT, W. H. (University of Illinois at Chicago, Illinois, USA)
Course Offering, 388-89; *Curriculum Inquiry: Alternative Paradigms*, 51-56; *Curriculum Validation*, 441-42; *Elective Subjects*, 203-04; *Experimental Curriculum*, 451-52; *National Curriculum Histories: An Overview*, 225-26; *Prerequisite Knowledge*, 468-71

SCHUBRING, G. (University of Bielefeld, Bielefeld, Germany)
History of Mathematics Education, 863-66

SCHUMANN, J. H. (University of California, Los Angeles, California, USA)
Interlanguage, 591

SHOHAMY, E. (Tel Aviv University, Tel Aviv, Israel)
Foreign Language Education, 553-69

SHORT, E. C. (Pennsylvania State University, University Park, Pennsylvania, USA)
Curriculum Associations and Journals, 981-83

SHUCHAT-SHAW, F. B. (New York University, New York, USA)
Film Studies, 705-08

SILBERSTEIN, M. (University of Tel Aviv, Tel Aviv, Israel)
Curriculum Studies in Teachers' Education, 392-94

SINGER, H. (University of California, Riverside, California, USA)
Comprehension Instruction, 514-21

SKILBECK, M. (University of London, London, UK)
Curriculum Organization, 342-46; *Economic, Social, and Cultural Factors*, 122-25

SMYLIE, M. A. (University of Illinois, Chicago, Illinois, USA)
Curriculum Adaptation within the Class, 386-88

SOLENDER, K. (Cleveland Museum of Art, Cleveland, Ohio, USA)
Museum Education, 686-88

SOLOMON, J. (University of Oxford, Oxford, UK)
Science, Technology, and Society as a Curricular Topic, 948-51

SOSNIAK, L. A. (University of Illinois at Chicago, Illinois, USA)
Feasibility Studies, 438-40

SPOLSKY, B. (Bar-Ilan University, Ramat-Gan, Israel)
Educational Linguistics, 581-85; *Foreign Language Education*, 553-69

STAHL, S. A. (Harvard University, Cambridge, Massachusetts, USA)
Initial Reading, 504-06

STAKE, R. E. (University of Illinois, Urbana-Champaign, Illinois, USA)
Responsive Evaluation, 418-20

STECHER, B. (University of California, Los Angeles, California, USA)
Goal-free Evaluation, 413-14

STEELE, R. (University of Sydney, Sydney, New South Wales, Australia)
Foreign Language Education, 553-69

STEFFY, B. E. (Lynbrook Public Schools, Lynbrook, New York, USA)
Community Participation, 363-65; *Involving Parents*, 361-63

STERN, H. H. (Ontario Institute for Studies in Education, Toronto, Ontario, Canada)
Foreign Language Curricula: Primary Schools, 569-75

STOWASSER, R. (Technical University, Berlin, Germany)
History of Mathematics Education, 863-66

STRAUSS, S. (Tel Aviv University, Tel Aviv, Israel)
U-shaped Behavioral Growth: Implications for Curriculum Development, 114-16

STRICKLAND, K. (University of Texas, San Antonio, Texas, USA)
Student-centered Curriculum, 192-93

SUAREZ, T. M. (University of North Carolina, Chapel Hill, North Carolina, USA)
Needs Assessment Studies, 433-35

SUTTON, C. (University of Leicester, Leicester, UK)
Language of Science, 945-46

SWAIN, M. (Ontario Institute for Studies in Education, Toronto, Ontario, Canada)
Immersion Education, 597-98

TABACHNICK, B. R. (University of Wisconsin, Madison, Wisconsin, USA)
Social Studies: Elementary-school Programs, 725-31

TAKALA, S. (University of Jyväskylä, Jyväskylä, Finland)
Foreign Language Education, 553-69

WESTBURY, I. (University of Illinois, Urbana-Champaign, Illinois, USA)
Textbooks, 74-77

WHITE, A. M. (Harvey Mudd College, Claremont, California, USA)
Mathematics as a Humanistic Discipline, 891-94

WHITE, K. M. (Boston University, Boston, Massachusetts, USA)
*Psychology: Educational Programs, 760-61

WIEMANN, J. M. (University of California, Santa Barbara, California, USA)
Communication Skills, 802-05

WILLINSKY, J. M. (University of Calgary, Calgary, Alberta, Canada)
Writing in the Humanities, 663-64

WILLIS, G. (University of Rhode Island, Rhode Island, USA)
Qualitative Evaluation, 427-29

WILSON, P. S. (University of Georgia, Athens, Georgia, USA)
Estimation in Mathematics Education, 853-54

WOLF, R. M. (Teachers College, Columbia University, New York, USA)
Tyler Evaluation Model, 411-13

WORTHEN, B. R. (Utah State University, Logan, Utah, USA)
Program Evaluation, 401-06

WULF, C. (Freie University, Berlin, Germany)
Federal Republic of Germany, 230-33; *Peace Education*, 774-75

ZAHN, L. (Pädagogische Hochschule, Schwäbisch Gmund, Germany)
Philosophy Programs, 637-38

ZHANG LIZHONG Huazhong University of Science and Technology, Wuhan, People's Republic of China)
*People's Republic of China, 228-30

Name Index

The Name Index has been compiled so that the reader can proceed either directly to the page where an author's work is cited, or to the reference itself in the bibliography. For each name, the page numbers for the bibliographic citation are given first, followed by the page number(s) in parentheses where that reference is cited in text. Where a name is referred to only in text, and not in the bibliography, the page number appears only in parentheses.

The accuracy of the spelling of authors' names has been affected by the use of different initials by some authors, or a different spelling of their name in different papers or review articles (sometimes this may arise from a transliteration process), and by those journals which give only one initial to each author.

Subject Index

The Subject Index has been compiled as a guide to the reader who is interested in locating all the references to a particular subject area within the Encyclopedia. Entries may have up to three levels of heading. Where the page numbers appear in bold italic type, this indicates a substantive discussion of the topic. Every effort has been made to index as comprehensively as possible and to standardize the terms used in the index. Given the diverse nature of the field and the varied use of terms throughout the international community, synonyms and foreign language terms have been included with appropriate cross-references. As a further aid to the reader, cross-references have also been given to terms of related interest.

compensatory education 927
developing nations 927
evolution of 926
nonvocational 926
trends in 926
United Kingdom 926, 927
United States 926
Alcohol abuse
See also
Drug education
Algebra *835-36*, 874
and modern mathematics 843
calculators 835
computers 835
definition of 835
equations 835
graphing software 836
historical perspective 871
New Mathematics movement 835
research on learning 836
solving of 835
symbolic 835
technology-intensive approach 836
American Association of Theatre for
Youth 709
American Educational Research
Association (AERA)
curriculum studies 981
Analysis
educational programs
learning process 837
spiral approach 837
mathematics
education implications 838
educational programs *837-38*
first course 837
teaching methods 837
objectives of educational taxonomy
318
Analytical skills
philosophy
elementary-school programs 636
social studies
secondary-school programs 734,
735
Animals
use in zoology 925
See also
zoology
Anthropology
as an elective course 765
cultural 765, 766
discipline of
concepts 184
educational programs *765-66*
curriculum development 765
curriculum rationale 766
India 765
Man: A Course of Study (MACOS)
765, 766
Mexico 765
precollege 766
research 766
student academic achievement
766

teacher feedback 766
United States 765
physical 765, 766
physical education programs 970
Anthropomorphism
life sciences
educational programs 922
Application
objectives of educational taxonomy
318
Applied linguistics 587, 614
Arabic
classical 605
difficulties of 605
educated colloquial 605
illiterate colloquial 605
modern standard 605
research needs 605, 606
standard colloquial 605
teaching as a foreign language
605-6
objectives 605
present needs 606
preuniversity programs 605
publications 606
teacher education programs 605
trained personnel 605
university-type programs 606
vocational programs 605
varieties of 605
Archeology
educational programs 766
Area studies *769-70*
Canada 769
definition 769
evolution of 769
interdisciplinary approach 769
interpretation of 769
United Kingdom 769, 770
United States 769
Arithmetic
definition of 833
educational programs *833-35*
curriculum development 834
formalized drill 834
research 834
historical view 833
meaning theory 834
meaningful 834
mental 834
place value 185
teaching methods
structural or holistic 834
teaching needs 834
Art
and lifelong education 685
attitude measures 685
attitude towards *684-85*
measurement scales 685
research 684, 685
students' 685
teachers' 684
museums 686
Art academies
dissatisfaction with 678

Art appreciation
and aesthetic education 676
Art attitudes
definition 684
use of term 684
Art education
after the Second World War 680
and free expression 679, 680
Bauhaus 679, 680
commercial art 679
cultural implications 679
developing nations 682
drawing 678
early twentieth-century development
679
foundations 678
France 678, 681
geometric methods 678
Germany, Federal Republic of 681
gewerbeschule model 678
in schools *678-83*
industrial drawing 678
instructional materials 679, 680
Japan 682
kindergarten movement 678
late nineteenth-century
developments 679
later twentieth-century
developments 680
nineteenth-century developments 678
practical studies 679
Project Zero 683
purpose of 678
research 682
secondary school 679
Soviet Union 680, 681, 683
United Kingdom 678, 681
United States 679, 680, 682, 683
use of term 678
Art history 678
Art materials
art education 679, 680
Art museums
United States 686, 687
Art schools
museum 686
Art teachers
and art education 680
Artificial intelligence
and Knowledge technology 133, 135
and resource management 889
mathematics education 887
Artificial languages 588
Artificial speech 91
Arts
interrelating 685
Arts education
categorization 674
discipline-based 673
funding 673
need for 673-74
Assertive behavior
social skills 801
Assessment
listening skills 525